THE NATIONAL ROLL OF THE GREAT WAR.

The National Roll of the Great War

One of the most sought-after sets of reference books of the First World War is the *National Roll of the Great War*. The National Publishing Company attempted, shortly after hostilities ceased, to compile a brief biography of as many participants in the War as possible. The vast majority of entries refer to combatants who survived the Great War and the *National Roll* is often the only source of information available. Fourteen volumes were completed on a regional basis; **the Naval & Military Press has compiled a fifteenth volume which contains an alphabetic index to the fourteen now republished volumes**.

The National Roll - complete 15 vol. set	ISBN: 1 847340 33 4	£285.00
Section I - London	ISBN: 1 847340 34 2	£22.00
Section II - London	ISBN: 1 847340 35 0	£22.00
Section III - London	ISBN: 1 847340 36 9	£22.00
Section IV - Southampton	ISBN: 1 847340 37 7	£22.00
Section V - Luton	ISBN: 1 847340 38 5	£22.00
Section VI - Birmingham	ISBN: 1 847340 39 3	£22.00
Section VII - London	ISBN: 1 847340 40 7	£22.00
Section VIII - Leeds	ISBN: 1 847340 41 5	£22.00
Section IX - Bradford	ISBN: 1 847340 42 3	£22.00
Section X - Portsmouth	ISBN: 1 847340 43 1	£22.00
Section XI - Manchester	ISBN: 1 847340 44 X	£22.00
Section XII - Bedford & Northampton	ISBN: 1 847340 45 8	£22.00
Section XIII - London	ISBN: 1 847340 46 6	£22.00
Section XIV - Salford	ISBN: 1 847340 47 4	£22.00
Section XV - Index to all 14 volumes	ISBN: 1 847340 48 2	£22.00

The Naval & Military Press Ltd
Unit 10, Ridgewood Industrial Park, Uckfield,
East Sussex, TN22 5QE, England
Tel: 01825 749494   Fax: 01825 765701
www.naval-military-press.com
www.military-genealogy.com

THE NATIONAL ROLL
OF THE GREAT WAR
1914-1918

CONTAINED WITHIN
THE PAGES OF THIS
VOLUME WILL BE
FOUND THE NAMES
AND RECORDS OF
SERVICE OF THOSE
WHO HELPED TO
SECURE VICTORY FOR
THE EMPIRE DURING
THE GREAT WAR OF
1914-1918.

THE
NAVAL &
MILITARY
PRESS LTD
2006

Published by

The Naval & Military Press Ltd

Unit 10, Ridgewood Industrial Park,

Uckfield, East Sussex,

TN22 5QE England

Tel: +44 (0) 1825 749494

Fax: +44 (0) 1825 765701

www.naval-military-press.com

www.military-genealogy.com

© The Naval & Military Press Ltd 2006

Alphabetical Index

A

Name	Initial	Volume	Page No.
A'COURT	GA	3	261
A'COURT	WC	3	261
AARON	JJ	4	1
ABBATT	E	4	1
ABBETT	H	7	1
ABBETT	W	7	1
ABBEY	A	9	379
ABBEY	A	10	1
ABBEY	CS	1	1
ABBEY	E	8	1
ABBEY	E	12	251
ABBEY	H	9	219
ABBEY	J	12	251
ABBEY	JW	8	1
ABBEY	W	1	1
ABBISS	AD	5	1
ABBISS	B	5	1
ABBISS	F	5	1
ABBISS	FE	5	1
ABBISS	R	5	1
ABBOTT	A	1	1
ABBOTT	A	11	1
ABBOTT	AE	1	1
ABBOTT	AE	4	1
ABBOTT	AE	5	1
ABBOTT	AE	12	1
ABBOTT	AE	13	1
ABBOTT	AH	1	1
ABBOTT	AJ	12	1
ABBOTT	AO	10	1
ABBOTT	BT	3	261
ABBOTT	C	1	1
ABBOTT	C	2	1
ABBOTT	C	8	1
ABBOTT	C	9	1
ABBOTT	C	12	251
ABBOTT	CG	1	1
ABBOTT	E	1	1
ABBOTT	E	1	1
ABBOTT	E	3	261
ABBOTT	E	4	1
ABBOTT	E	5	1
ABBOTT	E	9	219
ABBOTT	E	10	259
ABBOTT	E	12	421
ABBOTT	EA	5	1
ABBOTT	EA	7	1
ABBOTT	EV	12	1
ABBOTT	F	2	1
ABBOTT	F	5	1
ABBOTT	F	7	1
ABBOTT	F	8	1
ABBOTT	F	9	1
ABBOTT	G	13	1
ABBOTT	GC	12	1
ABBOTT	GE	10	1
ABBOTT	GJ	1	1
ABBOTT	GJ	5	1
ABBOTT	H	5	1
ABBOTT	H	5	1
ABBOTT	H	5	1
ABBOTT	H	5	1
ABBOTT	H	5	1
ABBOTT	H	7	1
ABBOTT	H	12	1
ABBOTT	H	13	1
ABBOTT	H	14	1
ABBOTT	HB	4	1
ABBOTT	HV	4	1
ABBOTT	J	1	1
ABBOTT	J	2	1
ABBOTT	J	8	1
ABBOTT	J	9	219
ABBOTT	J	10	1
ABBOTT	J	11	1
ABBOTT	JH	1	1
ABBOTT	JH	6	1
ABBOTT	JWC	12	1
ABBOTT	LA	1	1
ABBOTT	OC	1	1
ABBOTT	P	4	1
ABBOTT	PE	13	1
ABBOTT	R	11	1
ABBOTT	SC	3	9
ABBOTT	T	12	251
ABBOTT	W	9	219
ABBOTT	W	11	1
ABBOTT	W	12	1
ABBOTT	W	12	1
ABBOTT	WC	5	1
ABBOTT	WJ	12	1
ABBOTTS	J	6	1
ABBOTTS	T	6	1
ABBOTTS	W	6	1
ABBOTTS	WE	6	1
ABBS	AH	3	261
ABBS	FH	2	1
ABBS	WJ	13	1
ABEL	B	8	1
ABEL	HS	1	1
ABEL	J	7	1
ABEL	JE	12	1
ABEL	LA	6	1
ABEL	R	7	1
ABEL	RJ	1	1
ABEL	W	11	1
ABEL	WH	6	1
ABELL	F	6	1
ABELL	RN	9	1
ABELL	TCW	3	9
ABELL	TE	3	9
ABERCROMBIE	EA	4	1
ABERCROMBIE	TH	3	9
ABERDEEN	G	7	1
ABERDEIN	CE	1	1
ABERDEIN	EA	1	1
ABERNETHY	J	11	1
ABERY	E	3	9
ABERY	FH	7	1
ABERY	T	10	1
ABERY	WW	1	1
ABIGAIL	SH	1	2
ABLARD	A	9	1
ABLETT	CP	3	261
ABLETT	JW	3	261
ABLEY	W	3	261
ABLITT	W	1	2
ABRAHAM	A	12	1
ABRAHAM	AJ	12	1
ABRAHAM	C	8	1
ABRAHAM	CE	4	1
ABRAHAM	EA	12	1
ABRAHAM	EP	12	1
ABRAHAM	F	4	1
ABRAHAM	F	12	1
ABRAHAM	G	4	1
ABRAHAM	HW	12	1
ABRAHAM	J	1	2
ABRAHAM	J	13	1
ABRAHAM	R	11	1
ABRAHAM	W	12	2
ABRAHAM	WL	4	1
ABRAHAMS	A	4	1
ABRAHAMS	A	14	1
ABRAHAMS	B	4	1
ABRAHAMS	E	12	2
ABRAHAMS	EJ	4	1
ABRAHAMS	ERG	12	2
ABRAHAMS	F	4	2
ABRAHAMS	FC	13	1
ABRAHAMS	H	4	2
ABRAHAMS	H	5	1
ABRAHAMS	I	6	1
ABRAHAMS	I	14	1
ABRAHAMS	J	4	2
ABRAHAMS	J	11	1
ABRAHAMS	J	12	2
ABRAHAMS	L	14	1
ABRAHAMS	P	2	1
ABRAHAMS	PE	3	9
ABRAHAMS	SH	3	9
ABRAHAMS	WE	5	2
ABRAHAMS	WG	12	2
ABRAHAMSON	H	14	1
ABRAHART	WG	1	2
ABRAM	EM	13	1
ABRAMS	A	3	261
ABRAMS	AE	5	2
ABRAMS	ATH	10	259
ABRAMS	E	14	1
ABRAMS	F	2	1
ABRAMS	T	2	1
ABRAMS	W	9	1
ABRAMS	W	9	379
ABRAMSON	D	8	1
ABSOLOM	AJ	7	1
ABURROW	G	4	2
ABURROW	JC	4	2
ACASON	FC	1	2
ACCA	AJ	13	1
ACHESON	JE	11	1
ACKERLEY	RH	11	1
ACKERLEY	W	14	1
ACKERMAN	AJ	13	1
ACKERMAN	C	3	261
ACKERMAN	EJ	10	1
ACKERMAN	FC	13	1
ACKERMAN	J	3	261
ACKERMAN	R	3	261
ACKERMAN	R	3	261
ACKERS	J	11	1
ACKERY	AA	13	1
ACKFORD	RH	13	1
ACKFORD	WT	13	1
ACKLAND	FJ	13	1
ACKLAND	W	13	1
ACKREL	WF	9	1
ACKRILL	FW	6	1
ACKROID	J	9	1

ACKROYD	A	8	1
ACKROYD	A	11	1
ACKROYD	C	9	219
ACKROYD	CH	9	1
ACKROYD	E	3	261
ACKROYD	E	9	219
ACKROYD	F	8	1
ACKROYD	F	8	1
ACKROYD	F	13	2
ACKROYD	FC	9	1
ACKROYD	G	9	219
ACKROYD	GE	12	2
ACKROYD	H	3	261
ACKROYD	H	8	1
ACKROYD	H	9	219
ACKROYD	J	9	1
ACKROYD	J	9	1
ACKROYD	J	9	1
ACKROYD	J	9	379
ACKROYD	M	8	1
ACKROYD	M	9	219
ACKROYD	R	9	379
ACKROYD	S	9	1
ACKROYD	W	8	1
ACKROYD	WH	9	1
ACOTT	J	13	2
ACRES	E	9	2
ACTON	AE	3	9
ACTON	E	11	1
ACTON	H	14	1
ACTON	J	6	1
ACTON	J	14	1
ACTON	J	14	1
ACTON	JA	6	1
ACTON	L	14	1
ACTON	N	6	1
ACTON	W	13	2
ACUTT	AG	1	2
ACUTT	JE	1	2
ADAIR	JK	12	421
ADAIR	WR	8	415
ADAM	AJ	3	261
ADAMES	AE	4	2
ADAMS	A	1	3
ADAMS	A	2	1
ADAMS	A	2	1
ADAMS	A	3	262
ADAMS	A	6	1
ADAMS	A	6	2
ADAMS	A	6	2
ADAMS	A	8	1
ADAMS	A	8	1
ADAMS	A	12	2
ADAMS	A	12	251
ADAMS	A	12	251
ADAMS	A	12	251
ADAMS	A	13	2
ADAMS	A	13	2
ADAMS	A	13	2
ADAMS	AC	4	2
ADAMS	AE	6	2
ADAMS	AE	12	251
ADAMS	AE	12	251
ADAMS	AF	1	3
ADAMS	AF	13	2
ADAMS	AG	2	1
ADAMS	AG	10	1
ADAMS	AH	1	3
ADAMS	AH	3	9
ADAMS	AH	7	1
ADAMS	AJ	4	2
ADAMS	AM	2	1
ADAMS	AW	12	251
ADAMS	B	6	2
ADAMS	B	7	1
ADAMS	BF	12	251
ADAMS	BJ	5	2
ADAMS	BW	1	2
ADAMS	C	1	2
ADAMS	C	3	262
ADAMS	C	6	2
ADAMS	C	6	2
ADAMS	C	6	2
ADAMS	C	7	1
ADAMS	C	8	1
ADAMS	C	10	1
ADAMS	C	11	1
ADAMS	C	13	2
ADAMS	CE	1	2
ADAMS	CE	12	251
ADAMS	CH	6	2
ADAMS	CH	13	2
ADAMS	CJ	1	2
ADAMS	CM	6	2
ADAMS	CR	1	2
ADAMS	D	5	2
ADAMS	D	8	1
ADAMS	D	12	2
ADAMS	DH	12	2
ADAMS	DJ	1	3
ADAMS	E	1	2
ADAMS	E	1	3
ADAMS	E	1	3
ADAMS	E	4	2
ADAMS	E	6	2
ADAMS	E	7	1
ADAMS	E	13	2
ADAMS	EA	1	3
ADAMS	EC	13	2
ADAMS	EF	1	2
ADAMS	EG	1	3
ADAMS	EG	1	3
ADAMS	EG	3	262
ADAMS	EG	4	2
ADAMS	EH	11	421
ADAMS	EJ	12	2
ADAMS	ET	1	3
ADAMS	ET	12	2
ADAMS	EV	8	1
ADAMS	EW	5	2
ADAMS	EZ	13	2
ADAMS	F	1	2
ADAMS	F	5	2
ADAMS	F	6	2
ADAMS	F	6	2
ADAMS	F	10	1
ADAMS	F	12	2
ADAMS	F	12	251
ADAMS	F	13	2
ADAMS	FA	2	1
ADAMS	FE	5	2
ADAMS	FG	5	2
ADAMS	FG	12	251
ADAMS	FH	1	2
ADAMS	FJ	1	3
ADAMS	FJ	3	262
ADAMS	FJ	6	2
ADAMS	FS	10	259
ADAMS	FT	6	2
ADAMS	FW	3	262
ADAMS	G	4	2
ADAMS	G	4	2
ADAMS	G	10	1
ADAMS	G	13	2
ADAMS	GA	1	3
ADAMS	GD	13	2
ADAMS	GH	7	1
ADAMS	GW	1	3
ADAMS	GW	5	2
ADAMS	GW	14	1
ADAMS	H	6	2
ADAMS	H	11	2
ADAMS	H	12	2
ADAMS	H	13	2
ADAMS	HG	13	2
ADAMS	HH	7	2
ADAMS	HJ	1	3
ADAMS	HJL	1	2
ADAMS	HR	5	2
ADAMS	HW	12	2
ADAMS	J	1	2
ADAMS	J	1	3
ADAMS	J	3	9
ADAMS	J	4	2
ADAMS	J	5	2
ADAMS	J	5	2
ADAMS	J	6	2
ADAMS	J	6	2
ADAMS	J	8	1
ADAMS	J	8	2
ADAMS	J	8	2
ADAMS	J	8	2
ADAMS	J	8	415
ADAMS	J	11	2
ADAMS	J	11	2
ADAMS	J	13	3
ADAMS	J	13	3
ADAMS	JA	1	2
ADAMS	JCW	12	251
ADAMS	JD	4	2
ADAMS	JE	1	2
ADAMS	JE	3	262
ADAMS	JE	7	2
ADAMS	JG	4	2
ADAMS	JG	12	2
ADAMS	JH	6	2
ADAMS	JH	9	2
ADAMS	JH	12	2
ADAMS	JL	7	2
ADAMS	JT	1	3
ADAMS	JT	1	3
ADAMS	JT	7	2
ADAMS	JW	1	3
ADAMS	JW	2	1
ADAMS	JW	8	2
ADAMS	JW	12	251
ADAMS	JW	13	2
ADAMS	L	4	2
ADAMS	LH	13	3
ADAMS	LJ	11	2
ADAMS	M	1	3
ADAMS	M	4	2
ADAMS	NG	2	1
ADAMS	O	12	252
ADAMS	OG	12	2
ADAMS	P	5	2
ADAMS	R	1	3
ADAMS	R	3	9
ADAMS	RJ	7	2
ADAMS	RS	10	1
ADAMS	S	11	2
ADAMS	S	12	252
ADAMS	SH	1	3
ADAMS	SJ	10	1
ADAMS	SJ	10	1
ADAMS	SW	5	2
ADAMS	T	1	2
ADAMS	T	2	1
ADAMS	T	6	3
ADAMS	T	11	2

Surname	Init.			Surname	Init.			Surname	Init.			Surname	Init.		
ADAMS	T	12	2	ADCOCK	W	9	2	ADKINS	GW	12	252	AINGE	JW	6	4
ADAMS	T	13	3	ADDE	JW	10	2	ADKINS	JF	13	3	AINLEY	G	8	2
ADAMS	TH	3	262	ADDENBROOKE	H	6	3	ADKINS	P	13	4	AINSCOW	J	14	2
ADAMS	TH	6	3	ADDERLEY	AH	6	3	ADKINS	R	5	2	AINSCOW	W	14	2
ADAMS	TJ	4	2	ADDERLEY	E	6	3	ADLAM	A	2	1	AINSLEY	E	8	2
ADAMS	TJ	13	3	ADDERLEY	EF	4	3	ADLAM	E	2	2	AINSLEY	J	14	2
ADAMS	TJ	13	3	ADDERLEY	H	6	3	ADLAM	J	1	4	AINSWORTH	A	8	2
ADAMS	TR	10	1	ADDERLEY	J	6	3	ADLAM	W	2	2	AINSWORTH	C	7	2
ADAMS	W	1	3	ADDERLEY	L	6	3	ADLEMAN	S	8	415	AINSWORTH	EW	1	4
ADAMS	W	1	3	ADDERLEY	WH	4	3	ADMANS	FT	4	3	AINSWORTH	G	2	2
ADAMS	W	1	3	ADDERLEY	WH	11	2	ADOLPH	C	5	3	AINSWORTH	GE	2	2
ADAMS	W	3	262	ADDICOTT	A	12	2	ADSHEAD	CC	10	259	AINSWORTH	H	11	3
ADAMS	W	3	262	ADDICOTT	F	12	252	ADSHEAD	CW	11	2	AINSWORTH	HW	10	259
ADAMS	W	4	2	ADDICOTT	FH	6	3	ADSHEAD	J	11	2	AINSWORTH	PA	1	4
ADAMS	W	4	2	ADDINELL	JR	9	219	ADSHEAD	J	14	2	AINSWORTH	R	14	2
ADAMS	W	6	3	ADDINGTON	C	12	252	ADSHEAD	W	6	4	AINSWORTH	T	4	3
ADAMS	W	7	2	ADDINGTON	ER	5	2	AFFECTION	WH	3	262	AINSWORTH	T	11	3
ADAMS	W	8	2	ADDINGTON	GL	13	3	AFFLECK	C	11	2	AINSWORTH	W	4	3
ADAMS	W	10	1	ADDINGTON	H	3	262	AFFLECK	W	1	4	AINSWORTH	W	8	415
ADAMS	W	11	2	ADDINSON	JW	9	219	AFFORD	A	5	3	AINSWORTH	W	11	3
ADAMS	W	12	2	ADDIS	E	3	262	AFFORD	D	5	3	AINSWORTH	WE	6	4
ADAMS	W	12	2	ADDIS	F	13	3	AFFORD	SA	12	252	AINSWORTH	WH	1	4
ADAMS	W	13	3	ADDIS	FH	14	1	AFFRON	TH	6	4	AIRD	AA	1	4
ADAMS	W	14	1	ADDIS	H	13	3	AFFRON	WR	6	4	AIRD	CJ	12	2
ADAMS	WA	7	2	ADDIS	RG	13	3	AGAR	S	13	4	AIRD	HD	14	2
ADAMS	WC	1	3	ADDIS	S	14	2	AGAR	W	8	2	AIRD	HW	1	4
ADAMS	WC	3	262	ADDISON	C	1	4	AGATE	GT	1	4	AIRD	WJ	1	4
ADAMS	WD	10	1	ADDISON	C	14	2	AGATE	PJ	1	4	AIREY	FR	8	2
ADAMS	WE	6	3	ADDISON	G	11	2	AGATE	SW	1	4	AIREY	G	9	2
ADAMS	WG	14	1	ADDISON	PA	13	3	AGATE	W	1	4	AIREY	G	9	2
ADAMS	WH	5	2	ADDRISON	FA	7	2	AGER	H	13	4	AIREY	G	9	220
ADAMS	WH	6	3	ADDY	AG	8	2	AGER	J	12	252	AIREY	J	8	2
ADAMS	WH	7	2	ADDY	H	11	2	AGER	WG	12	252	AIREY	J	8	2
ADAMS	WJ	1	2	ADDY	T	14	2	AGERS	T	9	219	AIREY	J	14	2
ADAMS	WJ	3	262	ADDYMAN	C	8	2	AGGAS	W	8	2	AIRS	AJ	1	4
ADAMS	WJ	13	3	ADEY	A	6	3	AGGER	H	11	2	AIRTON	A	9	2
ADAMS	WR	4	3	ADEY	AE	6	3	AGGER	RM	4	3	AISH	W	1	5
ADAMS	WR	7	2	ADEY	C	6	3	AGGETT	CB	10	259	AITCHISON	F	5	3
ADAMS	WT	1	4	ADEY	F	6	3	AGGUS	A	1	4	AITCHISON	F	14	2
ADAMS	WW	10	2	ADEY	J	6	3	AGLEY	F	9	2	AITKEN	AWE	10	2
ADAMSON	ET	1	4	ADEY	J	6	3	AGLEY	F	9	219	AITKEN	J	8	2
ADAMSON	F	5	2	ADEY	JW	11	2	AGLEY	GT	13	4	AITKEN	M	14	2
ADAMSON	J	11	2	ADEY	T	1	4	AGONBAR	FG	1	4	AITKEN	R	13	4
ADAMSON	J	14	1	ADGIE	C	8	2	AGUS	F	9	219	AITKIN	F	3	9
ADAMSON	K	1	4	ADKIN	FE	12	252	AHEARN	T	10	259	AKAM	SH	1	5
ADAMSON	R	8	2	ADKIN	G	8	2	AHERN	M	10	2	AKEHURST	HW	4	3
ADAMSON	S	1	4	ADKIN	J	9	219	AHERN	MHY	10	2	AKEHURST	JA	2	2
ADAMSON	W	5	2	ADKIN	J	13	3	AHIER	H	2	2	AKERMAN	VA	1	5
ADAMSON	W	8	2	ADKIN	LG	13	3	AHRENS	CW	3	9	AKERMAN	W	1	5
ADCOCK	A	9	2	ADKIN	ME	13	3	AIERS	M	1	4	AKERMAN	WJ	3	262
ADCOCK	BJ	1	4	ADKINS	AD	13	3	AIKMAN	W	9	2	AKEROYD	W	9	2
ADCOCK	CP	13	3	ADKINS	AV	1	4	AIMSON	F	11	2	AKERS	AC	3	9
ADCOCK	SJ	6	3	ADKINS	BT	13	3	AIMSON	W	11	2	AKERS	AM	13	4
ADCOCK	T	6	3	ADKINS	ER	1	4	AINGE	AA	12	252	AKERS	FJ	13	4
ADCOCK	W	6	3	ADKINS	FV	13	3	AINGE	CH	6	4	AKHURST	AJ	4	3

AKHURST	CS	3	9	ALDEN	WA	1	6	ALDOUS	S	5	3	ALEXANDER	A	7	3
AKID	A	11	3	ALDER	F	1	6	ALDOUS	W	6	4	ALEXANDER	A	10	2
AKITT	B	8	2	ALDER	FH	1	6	ALDRED	A	14	2	ALEXANDER	A	13	4
ALABASTER	J	1	5	ALDER	J	1	6	ALDRED	HW	5	3	ALEXANDER	AA	10	259
ALABASTER	JL	13	4	ALDER	JE	6	4	ALDRED	J	11	3	ALEXANDER	AJ	2	2
ALABASTER	WH	1	5	ALDER	JH	3	262	ALDRED	TH	10	2	ALEXANDER	B	11	3
ALABASTER	WP	1	5	ALDER	JJ	1	6	ALDRED	W	3	262	ALEXANDER	C	1	7
ALAND	AW	1	5	ALDER	W	1	6	ALDREN	WT	13	4	ALEXANDER	EA	2	2
ALAND	JD	1	5	ALDERMAN	C	5	3	ALDRICH	FA	3	10	ALEXANDER	EA	4	4
ALAND	SJ	1	5	ALDERMAN	E	1	6	ALDRICH	N	13	4	ALEXANDER	F	7	3
ALAWAY	CE	1	5	ALDERMAN	F	4	3	ALDRIDGE	A	13	4	ALEXANDER	FC	1	7
ALAWAY	CF	1	5	ALDERMAN	FC	3	262	ALDRIDGE	ACS	4	3	ALEXANDER	FH	7	3
ALAWAY	RA	1	5	ALDERMAN	FW	7	2	ALDRIDGE	AE	1	6	ALEXANDER	FT	10	2
ALBAN	FV	12	2	ALDERMAN	FW	12	252	ALDRIDGE	AG	4	3	ALEXANDER	G	1	7
ALBANS	W	8	2	ALDERMAN	H	1	6	ALDRIDGE	B	5	3	ALEXANDER	G	8	3
ALBERT	A	2	2	ALDERMAN	H	3	10	ALDRIDGE	CW	13	4	ALEXANDER	GE	6	5
ALBERT	AH	1	5	ALDERMAN	HT	1	6	ALDRIDGE	D	1	6	ALEXANDER	GW	2	2
ALBERT	AH	1	5	ALDERMAN	HT	5	3	ALDRIDGE	EH	2	2	ALEXANDER	H	1	7
ALBERT	AJ	2	2	ALDERMAN	P	8	3	ALDRIDGE	F	14	2	ALEXANDER	H	4	4
ALBERT	AT	7	2	ALDERMAN	PRH	3	10	ALDRIDGE	FC	10	2	ALEXANDER	H	9	2
ALBERT	JA	1	5	ALDERMAN	W	7	2	ALDRIDGE	FW	5	3	ALEXANDER	H	9	220
ALBERT	WF	1	5	ALDERMAN	W	12	3	ALDRIDGE	GH	5	3	ALEXANDER	H	10	2
ALBERY	A	4	3	ALDERMAN	WH	3	262	ALDRIDGE	H	12	252	ALEXANDER	H	13	4
ALBERY	RT	1	5	ALDERMAN	WTG	1	6	ALDRIDGE	HE	4	3	ALEXANDER	I	4	4
ALBON	E	1	5	ALDERSLEY	CH	7	2	ALDRIDGE	HJ	10	2	ALEXANDER	J	4	4
ALBON	H	5	3	ALDERSON	G	11	3	ALDRIDGE	HW	10	2	ALEXANDER	J	6	5
ALBONE	C	5	3	ALDERSON	G	11	3	ALDRIDGE	J	6	4	ALEXANDER	J	6	5
ALBONE	HG	5	3	ALDERSON	GAS	13	4	ALDRIDGE	J	14	2	ALEXANDER	J	8	3
ALBOROUGH	AA	1	5	ALDERSON	R	8	3	ALDRIDGE	JA	1	6	ALEXANDER	J	13	4
ALBOROUGH	AC	1	5	ALDERSON	S	8	3	ALDRIDGE	JW	1	6	ALEXANDER	JL	1	7
ALBOROUGH	FO	1	5	ALDERSON	W	2	2	ALDRIDGE	KM	1	6	ALEXANDER	M	1	7
ALBOROUGH	HW	1	5	ALDERSON	WB	11	3	ALDRIDGE	M	1	6	ALEXANDER	P	4	4
ALBURY	AW	5	3	ALDERTON	C	1	6	ALDRIDGE	N	4	3	ALEXANDER	P	9	2
ALBUTT	F	6	4	ALDERTON	C	7	2	ALDRIDGE	NA	3	10	ALEXANDER	P	13	4
ALBUTT	WH	6	4	ALDERTON	E	1	6	ALDRIDGE	R	1	6	ALEXANDER	PF	1	7
ALCOCK	B	14	2	ALDERTON	E	1	6	ALDRIDGE	T	7	3	ALEXANDER	PJ	4	4
ALCOCK	EG	5	3	ALDERTON	F	7	2	ALDRIDGE	T	13	4	ALEXANDER	R	3	263
ALCOCK	FF	3	9	ALDERTON	FW	2	2	ALDRIDGE	T	14	2	ALEXANDER	R	13	5
ALCOCK	J	4	3	ALDERTON	W	2	2	ALDRIDGE	W	6	5	ALEXANDER	RW	4	4
ALCOCK	J	14	2	ALDERTON	WG	2	2	ALDRIDGE	W	7	3	ALEXANDER	S	4	4
ALCOCK	JW	12	252	ALDGATE	B	11	3	ALDRIDGE	W	12	3	ALEXANDER	SMS	2	2
ALCOCK	W	4	3	ALDHAM	AJ	3	10	ALDRIDGE	W	13	4	ALEXANDER	SWG	13	5
ALCOCK	WR	13	4	ALDHOUSE	A	6	4	ALDRIDGE	W	14	3	ALEXANDER	T	14	3
ALCORN	WJ	1	5	ALDHOUSE	B	6	4	ALDRIDGE	WAJ	10	259	ALEXANDER	W	1	7
ALDCROFT	F	11	3	ALDHOUSE	R	6	4	ALDRIDGE	WC	4	4	ALEXANDER	W	4	4
ALDCROFT	H	11	3	ALDINGTON	HS	4	3	ALDRIDGE	WE	4	4	ALEXANDER	W	10	2
ALDCROFT	J	11	3	ALDIS	H	4	3	ALDRIDGE	WE	14	3	ALEXANDER	W	13	5
ALDCROFT	P	14	2	ALDIS	JH	13	4	ALDRIDGE	WF	1	6	ALEXANDER	WT	2	2
ALDEN	HG	1	5	ALDIS	OB	4	3	ALDWORTH	J	4	4	ALEXANDRA	CJ	3	263
ALDEN	J	6	4	ALDOAS	W	8	3	ALEFOUNDER	JW	1	6	ALEXANDRA	W	6	5
ALDEN	J	6	4	ALDOUS	A	7	3	ALEXANDER	A	1	7	ALEXANDRIA	H	9	2
ALDEN	J	9	2	ALDOUS	AF	5	3	ALEXANDER	A	4	4	ALEY	WA	1	7
ALDEN	M	10	259	ALDOUS	EF	5	3	ALEXANDER	A	4	4	ALFORD	AO	1	7
ALDEN	SF	6	4	ALDOUS	HH	1	6	ALEXANDER	A	6	5	ALFORD	HJ	3	10
ALDEN	SF	6	4	ALDOUS	JW	6	4	ALEXANDER	A	6	5	ALFORD	HW	4	4

ALFORD	J	7	3	ALLBUTT	F	6	5	ALLEN	AE	1	8	ALLEN	EJ	1	8				
ALFORD	JE	8	3	ALLBUTT	J	6	5	ALLEN	AE	2	3	ALLEN	EJ	1	8				
ALFORD	L	4	4	ALLBUTT	JE	1	7	ALLEN	AE	2	3	ALLEN	ES	10	259				
ALFORD	SW	3	263	ALLBUTT	T	6	5	ALLEN	AE	7	3	ALLEN	EV	2	3				
ALFRED	GW	14	3	ALLCHIN	CD	7	3	ALLEN	AE	13	5	ALLEN	F	1	8				
ALFRED	J	14	3	ALLCHIN	J	13	5	ALLEN	AF	2	3	ALLEN	F	2	3				
ALGAR	H	10	2	ALLCHURCH	HFW	7	3	ALLEN	AF	12	3	ALLEN	F	3	10				
ALGAR	HA	3	263	ALLCHURCH	HS	7	3	ALLEN	AG	4	5	ALLEN	F	3	263				
ALGATE	WC	7	3	ALLCOCK	G	4	4	ALLEN	AG	10	2	ALLEN	F	4	5				
ALGER	AJ	13	5	ALLCOCK	J	8	3	ALLEN	AG	10	259	ALLEN	F	4	5				
ALGER	CF	4	4	ALLCOCK	J	11	3	ALLEN	AG	12	3	ALLEN	F	4	5				
ALGER	E	2	3	ALLCOCK	JA	8	3	ALLEN	AH	7	3	ALLEN	F	6	6				
ALIBONE	AV	12	252	ALLCOCK	JH	6	5	ALLEN	AH	12	3	ALLEN	F	6	6				
ALISS	B	6	5	ALLCOCK	L	14	3	ALLEN	AJ	3	10	ALLEN	F	7	4				
ALISS	T	6	5	ALLCOCK	S	14	3	ALLEN	AJ	5	4	ALLEN	F	9	2				
ALKER	A	11	3	ALLCOCK	W	8	3	ALLEN	AJ	10	2	ALLEN	F	11	4				
ALLAM	CG	2	3	ALLCOCK	W	14	3	ALLEN	AJ	13	5	ALLEN	FA	2	4				
ALLAM	J	5	3	ALLCOTT	A	6	5	ALLEN	AP	3	10	ALLEN	FA	5	4				
ALLAM	R	3	263	ALLCROFT	WA	11	4	ALLEN	AW	3	10	ALLEN	FC	7	4				
ALLAN	D	1	7	ALLDAY	AE	9	220	ALLEN	AW	10	3	ALLEN	FE	6	6				
ALLAN	DC	2	3	ALLDAY	L	9	220	ALLEN	B	7	3	ALLEN	FE	12	3				
ALLAN	FW	4	4	ALLDEN	B	7	3	ALLEN	B	12	3	ALLEN	FF	13	5				
ALLAN	G	9	220	ALLDEN	EJ	6	6	ALLEN	B	13	5	ALLEN	FH	4	5				
ALLAN	GA	1	7	ALLDEN	HJ	6	6	ALLEN	C	1	8	ALLEN	FH	10	3				
ALLAN	GA	11	3	ALLDEN	WB	7	3	ALLEN	C	5	4	ALLEN	FH	11	4				
ALLAN	J	6	5	ALLDER	GL	6	6	ALLEN	C	10	259	ALLEN	FH	12	3				
ALLAN	J	11	3	ALLDER	L	2	3	ALLEN	CA	1	8	ALLEN	FJ	1	8				
ALLAN	J	11	3	ALLDIS	A	13	5	ALLEN	CC	12	3	ALLEN	FJ	2	4				
ALLAN	JH	9	220	ALLDIS	G	13	5	ALLEN	CE	2	3	ALLEN	FJ	5	4				
ALLAN	R	10	2	ALLDIS	H	3	263	ALLEN	CE	3	263	ALLEN	FJ	7	4				
ALLAN	SW	2	3	ALLDREAD	WT	2	3	ALLEN	CE	3	263	ALLEN	FJD	13	5				
ALLAN	W	1	7	ALLDRED	CJ	4	5	ALLEN	CH	8	3	ALLEN	FO	3	10				
ALLANBY	G	8	3	ALLDRICK	E	6	6	ALLEN	CJ	7	4	ALLEN	FS	1	8				
ALLANSON	V	8	3	ALLDRICK	JT	6	6	ALLEN	CJ	11	4	ALLEN	FW	1	8				
ALLARD	H	6	5	ALLDRICK	WH	6	6	ALLEN	CP	13	5	ALLEN	G	3	10				
ALLARD	JW	12	252	ALLEESON	AE	13	6	ALLEN	CS	1	7	ALLEN	G	3	263				
ALLARD	MT	2	3	ALLEESON	W	2	3	ALLEN	CW	6	6	ALLEN	G	3	263				
ALLARD	T	12	252	ALLEN	A	2	3	ALLEN	D	2	3	ALLEN	G	3	263				
ALLATT	H	11	3	ALLEN	A	4	5	ALLEN	D	6	6	ALLEN	G	4	5				
ALLATT	TH	11	3	ALLEN	A	5	3	ALLEN	DE	6	6	ALLEN	G	5	4				
ALLAWAY	AR	1	7	ALLEN	A	5	3	ALLEN	DH	3	10	ALLEN	G	6	6				
ALLAWAY	AR	6	5	ALLEN	A	5	4	ALLEN	E	1	7	ALLEN	G	6	6				
ALLAWAY	CA	2	3	ALLEN	A	6	6	ALLEN	E	3	10	ALLEN	G	8	3				
ALLAWAY	WH	1	7	ALLEN	A	6	6	ALLEN	E	3	263	ALLEN	G	12	253				
ALLAWAY	WH	2	3	ALLEN	A	10	2	ALLEN	E	5	4	ALLEN	G	13	5				
ALLAWAY	WJ	2	3	ALLEN	A	10	2	ALLEN	E	5	4	ALLEN	G	13	5				
ALLBERREY	W	13	5	ALLEN	A	11	4	ALLEN	E	6	6	ALLEN	G	13	5				
ALLBRIGHT	AG	12	252	ALLEN	A	12	252	ALLEN	E	8	3	ALLEN	GA	4	5				
ALLBRIGHT	J	12	252	ALLEN	A	12	253	ALLEN	E	10	3	ALLEN	GA	13	5				
ALLBRIGHT	V	7	3	ALLEN	A	13	5	ALLEN	E	10	3	ALLEN	GA	13	6				
ALLBRIGHT	WA	1	7	ALLEN	A	14	3	ALLEN	E	11	4	ALLEN	GE	10	3				
ALLBUT	GT	6	5	ALLEN	AA	14	3	ALLEN	E	12	3	ALLEN	GG	4	5				
ALLBUTT	CH	6	5	ALLEN	AB	7	3	ALLEN	EA	6	6	ALLEN	GH	3	263				
ALLBUTT	CW	2	3	ALLEN	AC	5	4	ALLEN	EG	5	4	ALLEN	GH	10	3				
ALLBUTT	E	6	5	ALLEN	AC	10	259	ALLEN	EH	4	5	ALLEN	GL	12	3				

ALLEN	GS	13	6
ALLEN	H	1	7
ALLEN	H	1	8
ALLEN	H	3	10
ALLEN	H	4	5
ALLEN	H	4	5
ALLEN	H	5	4
ALLEN	H	5	4
ALLEN	H	6	6
ALLEN	H	7	4
ALLEN	H	8	3
ALLEN	H	10	3
ALLEN	H	10	259
ALLEN	H	11	4
ALLEN	H	11	4
ALLEN	H	12	3
ALLEN	H	12	3
ALLEN	H	12	3
ALLEN	H	12	253
ALLEN	H	13	6
ALLEN	H	14	3
ALLEN	HA	3	263
ALLEN	HDB	10	3
ALLEN	HFE	13	6
ALLEN	HG	2	4
ALLEN	HG	7	4
ALLEN	HGF	10	260
ALLEN	HJ	11	4
ALLEN	HJ	12	3
ALLEN	HJ	12	253
ALLEN	HM	2	4
ALLEN	HO	5	4
ALLEN	HR	12	3
ALLEN	HS	1	7
ALLEN	HT	3	10
ALLEN	HW	13	6
ALLEN	IH	12	253
ALLEN	J	2	4
ALLEN	J	2	4
ALLEN	J	2	4
ALLEN	J	3	10
ALLEN	J	4	5
ALLEN	J	5	4
ALLEN	J	5	4
ALLEN	J	6	6
ALLEN	J	6	7
ALLEN	J	7	4
ALLEN	J	8	3
ALLEN	J	9	220
ALLEN	J	10	260
ALLEN	J	11	4
ALLEN	J	11	4
ALLEN	J	12	3
ALLEN	J	12	253
ALLEN	J	12	253
ALLEN	J	12	253
ALLEN	J	12	253
ALLEN	J	13	6
ALLEN	J	13	6
ALLEN	J	14	3
ALLEN	J	14	3
ALLEN	J	14	3
ALLEN	JA	6	7
ALLEN	JB	4	5
ALLEN	JB	6	7
ALLEN	JC	4	5
ALLEN	JE	2	4
ALLEN	JE	4	5
ALLEN	JE	14	3
ALLEN	JEC	3	263
ALLEN	JG	2	4
ALLEN	JH	11	4
ALLEN	JH	13	6
ALLEN	JJ	3	263
ALLEN	JK	7	4
ALLEN	JL	2	4
ALLEN	JM	10	3
ALLEN	JR	13	6
ALLEN	JT	5	4
ALLEN	JT	11	421
ALLEN	JT	14	3
ALLEN	JW	2	4
ALLEN	JW	2	4
ALLEN	JW	3	10
ALLEN	JW	5	4
ALLEN	JW	9	379
ALLEN	JW	11	4
ALLEN	JW	12	3
ALLEN	JW	14	3
ALLEN	L	5	4
ALLEN	L	10	260
ALLEN	LG	12	253
ALLEN	LS	12	3
ALLEN	LW	1	7
ALLEN	M	5	4
ALLEN	M	10	3
ALLEN	M	11	4
ALLEN	P	9	2
ALLEN	R	5	4
ALLEN	R	5	4
ALLEN	R	11	4
ALLEN	R	14	3
ALLEN	RA	1	8
ALLEN	RA	7	4
ALLEN	RE	6	7
ALLEN	RH	6	7
ALLEN	RS	5	5
ALLEN	RW	5	5
ALLEN	S	4	5
ALLEN	S	4	5
ALLEN	S	6	7
ALLEN	S	9	220
ALLEN	SA	7	4
ALLEN	SG	1	8
ALLEN	SGJ	13	6
ALLEN	SH	7	4
ALLEN	SR	5	5
ALLEN	SW	2	4
ALLEN	T	3	10
ALLEN	T	3	263
ALLEN	T	4	5
ALLEN	T	4	6
ALLEN	T	5	5
ALLEN	T	12	3
ALLEN	T	12	253
ALLEN	T	12	253
ALLEN	TE	2	4
ALLEN	TE	6	7
ALLEN	TH	2	4
ALLEN	TH	3	11
ALLEN	TH	5	5
ALLEN	TH	6	7
ALLEN	TH	6	7
ALLEN	TP	1	8
ALLEN	TR	7	4
ALLEN	TW	4	5
ALLEN	TW	10	260
ALLEN	V	1	7
ALLEN	VE	2	4
ALLEN	VF	13	6
ALLEN	VZ	5	5
ALLEN	W	2	4
ALLEN	W	3	11
ALLEN	W	3	11
ALLEN	W	4	6
ALLEN	W	5	5
ALLEN	W	6	7
ALLEN	W	6	7
ALLEN	W	9	2
ALLEN	W	9	220
ALLEN	W	11	4
ALLEN	W	12	3
ALLEN	W	12	3
ALLEN	W	14	4
ALLEN	W	14	4
ALLEN	WA	12	4
ALLEN	WAF	10	3
ALLEN	WC	7	4
ALLEN	WC	12	4
ALLEN	WC	13	6
ALLEN	WE	6	7
ALLEN	WE	6	7
ALLEN	WE	12	4
ALLEN	WG	4	6
ALLEN	WG	5	5
ALLEN	WG	7	4
ALLEN	WG	12	253
ALLEN	WH	2	4
ALLEN	WH	7	4
ALLEN	WH	13	6
ALLEN	WH	13	6
ALLEN	WH	13	6
ALLEN	WHA	4	6
ALLEN	WHJ	2	4
ALLEN	WJ	1	8
ALLEN	WJ	2	5
ALLEN	WJ	4	6
ALLEN	WJ	4	6
ALLEN	WJ	6	7
ALLEN	WJ	10	260
ALLEN	WJ	12	4
ALLEN	WM	6	7
ALLEN	WS	12	4
ALLEN	WW	6	7
ALLEN-STIMPSON	G	3	11
ALLENBY	JE	8	3
ALLERTON	B	11	4
ALLERTON	J	1	8
ALLERTON	JA	1	8
ALLEWAY	A	13	6
ALLEWAY	FC	1	8
ALLEY	F	1	8
ALLEY	J	3	11
ALLEY	TJ	3	11
ALLEY	WJ	6	7
ALLFORD	C	13	6
ALLFORD	J	13	7
ALLFORD	TH	13	7
ALLFORD	W	13	7
ALLFORD	WE	13	7
ALLIBONE	A	12	253
ALLIBONE	HE	6	7
ALLIBONE	WGH	12	253
ALLIN	G	12	4
ALLIN	R	3	264
ALLINGHAM	A	2	5
ALLINGHAM	AH	2	5
ALLINGTON	C	7	4
ALLINGTON	W	13	7
ALLINSON	GF	1	8
ALLINSON	HW	1	8
ALLINSON	J	8	3
ALLINSON	R	9	2
ALLINSON	RH	8	3
ALLINSON	W	8	4
ALLISON	A	8	4
ALLISON	AG	9	379
ALLISON	DWS	4	6
ALLISON	E	1	8
ALLISON	E	5	5

ALLISON	E	8	4
ALLISON	EW	8	4
ALLISON	H	5	5
ALLISON	H	5	5
ALLISON	HC	10	260
ALLISON	J	9	2
ALLISON	J	11	4
ALLISON	J	14	4
ALLISON	SF	12	253
ALLISON	TJ	1	8
ALLISON	WG	2	5
ALLISON	WJ	13	7
ALLISTONE	S	2	5
ALLITT	CF	11	4
ALLMAN	A	2	5
ALLMAN	G	11	5
ALLMAN	GR	3	11
ALLMARK	F	11	5
ALLMEN	J	3	11
ALLMEN	P	3	11
ALLNUT	T	3	11
ALLNUTT	A	2	5
ALLNUTT	CF	2	5
ALLNUTT	TH	2	5
ALLOM	J	5	5
ALLOWAY	E	2	5
ALLPORT	E	2	5
ALLPORT	J	3	11
ALLPORT	LG	6	7
ALLPORT	TJ	6	8
ALLRED	J	14	4
ALLSO	J	7	4
ALLSOP	B	2	5
ALLSOP	C	3	264
ALLSOP	E	6	8
ALLSOP	F	3	264
ALLSOP	HG	2	5
ALLSOP	J	6	8
ALLSOP	J	6	8
ALLSOP	J	6	8
ALLSOP	JG	1	9
ALLSOP	RG	3	264
ALLSOP	RH	2	5
ALLSOP	S	6	8
ALLSOP	TW	3	264
ALLSOP	W	1	9
ALLSOPP	AP	1	9
ALLSOPP	C	12	4
ALLSOPP	CWJ	7	4
ALLSOPP	J	3	11
ALLSOPP	M	3	11
ALLSUP	JA	2	5
ALLTREE	H	9	379
ALLTREE	JE	11	5
ALLUM	FAV	13	7
ALLUM	G	2	5
ALLUM	J	1	9
ALLUM	RJ	2	5
ALLWOOD	C	11	5
ALLWOOD	CA	2	5
ALLWOOD	JP	6	8
ALLWRIGHT	CL	2	5
ALLWRIGHT	FE	2	6
ALLWRIGHT	S	2	6
ALMAND	E	1	8
ALMGILL	NF	8	4
ALMOND	AW	2	6
ALMOND	EW	8	4
ALMOND	H	8	4
ALMOND	J	11	5
ALMOND	JR	7	4
ALMOND	JW	5	5
ALMOND	P	5	5
ALMOND	S	5	5
ALMOND	W	11	5
ALPE	FC	13	7
ALRED	E	9	220
ALSEPT	AG	7	5
ALSFORD	AE	1	8
ALSFORD	F	1	8
ALSFORD	HS	3	11
ALSFORD	JF	3	11
ALSOP	FW	7	5
ALSOP	J	12	4
ALSOP	WCP	3	11
ALSOPP	J	6	8
ALSTON	A	14	4
ALTUCCINI	A	1	9
ALTY	D	11	5
ALVEY	AE	3	264
ALVEY	EW	3	264
ALVEY	J	6	8
ALVIN	D	9	3
ALVIN	DG	9	3
ALVIS	ES	4	6
ALWAY	AE	10	260
ALWAY	J	2	6
ALWAY	ZW	2	6
AMBLE	A	9	220
AMBLER	BR	13	7
AMBLER	E	9	3
AMBLER	E	9	3
AMBLER	E	9	220
AMBLER	ERE	2	6
AMBLER	F	8	4
AMBLER	GH	5	5
AMBLER	H	9	220
AMBLER	JW	9	3
AMBLER	LG	9	220
AMBLER	R	9	3
AMBLER	S	9	220
AMBLER	T	8	4
AMBLER	W	2	6
AMBLER	W	8	4
AMBLER	W	9	3
AMBLER	W	9	3
AMBLER	WA	8	4
AMBRIDGE	AJ	1	9
AMBRIDGE	AJ	5	5
AMBRIDGE	AW	5	5
AMBRIDGE	CT	5	5
AMBRIDGE	E	5	6
AMBRIDGE	JE	2	6
AMBRIDGE	WJ	5	6
AMBROSE	A	12	4
AMBROSE	A	12	4
AMBROSE	AA	13	7
AMBROSE	AE	1	9
AMBROSE	AE	2	6
AMBROSE	AP	3	11
AMBROSE	E	8	4
AMBROSE	F	5	6
AMBROSE	F	5	6
AMBROSE	GT	3	11
AMBROSE	J	11	5
AMBROSE	M	8	4
AMBROSE	MA	3	264
AMBROSE	MJ	11	5
AMBROSE	T	14	4
AMBROSE	V	4	6
AMBROSE	W	2	6
AMBROSE	W	3	264
AMENT	HC	7	5
AMER	R	13	7
AMES	A	1	9
AMES	AE	4	6
AMES	AJ	12	4
AMES	C	9	3
AMES	CA	3	264
AMES	CE	2	6
AMES	CJA	12	4
AMES	CT	12	4
AMES	CW	8	4
AMES	EM	2	6
AMES	ES	3	264
AMES	F	2	6
AMES	F	4	6
AMES	FC	12	4
AMES	G	2	6
AMES	H	8	4
AMES	HC	7	5
AMES	J	5	6
AMES	J	9	3
AMES	JH	2	6
AMES	JH	4	6
AMES	MH	2	6
AMES	MJ	3	264
AMES	O	7	5
AMES	PA	2	6
AMES	RE	4	6
AMES	RS	12	4
AMES	WAJ	12	4
AMES	WH	12	4
AMES	WJ	2	6
AMES	WJ	5	6
AMESS	HL	3	12
AMESS	JF	3	12
AMEY	A	10	3
AMEY	AE	7	5
AMEY	AG	7	5
AMEY	F	1	9
AMEY	F	4	6
AMEY	W	2	6
AMEY	W	7	5
AMEY	WT	10	3
AMOR	F	3	264
AMOR	FT	7	5
AMOR	W	2	6
AMOS	AC	1	9
AMOS	CJ	12	253
AMOS	CTB	12	4
AMOS	CW	8	4
AMOS	E	14	4
AMOS	EF	9	3
AMOS	F	8	4
AMOS	H	13	7
AMOS	HL	13	7
AMOS	J	6	8
AMOS	JR	1	9
AMOS	RS	6	8
AMOS	S	6	8
AMOS	S	6	8
AMOS	SA	13	7
AMOS	SG	12	253
AMOS	WRE	1	9
AMOS	WT	9	3
AMOSS	J	8	4
AMPLEFORD	AH	1	9
AMPLEFORD	G	1	9
AMPLEFORD	WT	2	7
AMPSTEAD	JE	2	7
AMSDEN	J	1	9
AMY	L	4	6
AMY	PA	4	6
AMY	W	4	6
AMYS	A	8	4
AMYS	J	9	3
ANCELL	H	10	3
ANCHORS	CJ	13	7
ANCOATS	C	11	5

ANCSELL	ED	10	3	ANDERSON	G	3	264	ANDERSON	TA	2	7	ANDREWS	A	3	12
ANDERS	TJ	10	3	ANDERSON	G	5	6	ANDERSON	TH	13	8	ANDREWS	A	5	7
ANDERSEN	SA	5	6	ANDERSON	G	13	8	ANDERSON	W	1	9	ANDREWS	A	6	9
ANDERSON	A	2	7	ANDERSON	G	13	8	ANDERSON	W	3	264	ANDREWS	A	10	4
ANDERSON	A	4	6	ANDERSON	GA	11	5	ANDERSON	W	5	7	ANDREWS	A	12	254
ANDERSON	A	5	6	ANDERSON	GE	1	9	ANDERSON	W	7	5	ANDREWS	A	13	8
ANDERSON	A	5	6	ANDERSON	GJ	4	7	ANDERSON	W	8	5	ANDREWS	AC	13	8
ANDERSON	A	6	8	ANDERSON	GW	13	8	ANDERSON	W	8	5	ANDREWS	AE	6	9
ANDERSON	A	6	8	ANDERSON	H	5	6	ANDERSON	W	9	3	ANDREWS	AG	2	7
ANDERSON	A	7	5	ANDERSON	H	5	6	ANDERSON	W	11	6	ANDREWS	AG	4	7
ANDERSON	A	13	7	ANDERSON	H	5	6	ANDERSON	W	12	253	ANDREWS	AG	5	7
ANDERSON	AC	2	7	ANDERSON	HH	5	6	ANDERSON	W	13	8	ANDREWS	AH	4	7
ANDERSON	AC	13	7	ANDERSON	HJ	3	12	ANDERSON	WC	2	7	ANDREWS	AH	7	5
ANDERSON	AE	4	6	ANDERSON	HW	3	264	ANDERSON	WH	12	5	ANDREWS	AH	10	260
ANDERSON	AJ	2	7	ANDERSON	HW	4	7	ANDERSON	WJ	2	7	ANDREWS	AJ	4	7
ANDERSON	AJ	7	5	ANDERSON	HW	5	7	ANDERSON	WJ	10	4	ANDREWS	AV	4	7
ANDERSON	AM	4	7	ANDERSON	IWG	13	8	ANDERSON	WJ	10	260	ANDREWS	AW	4	7
ANDERSON	AV	3	12	ANDERSON	J	1	9	ANDERSON	WJ	13	8	ANDREWS	AW	13	8
ANDERSON	B	5	6	ANDERSON	J	5	7	ANDERSON	WR	3	12	ANDREWS	B	4	7
ANDERSON	C	1	9	ANDERSON	J	8	5	ANDERTON	A	3	12	ANDREWS	B	12	5
ANDERSON	C	2	7	ANDERSON	J	8	5	ANDERTON	A	11	6	ANDREWS	C	1	9
ANDERSON	C	4	7	ANDERSON	J	8	5	ANDERTON	AA	3	265	ANDREWS	C	4	7
ANDERSON	C	5	6	ANDERSON	J	8	5	ANDERTON	F	14	4	ANDREWS	C	5	7
ANDERSON	C	11	5	ANDERSON	J	8	5	ANDERTON	G	11	6	ANDREWS	C	6	9
ANDERSON	C	14	4	ANDERSON	J	10	3	ANDERTON	J	9	379	ANDREWS	C	7	6
ANDERSON	CB	6	8	ANDERSON	J	10	3	ANDERTON	JE	11	6	ANDREWS	C	12	5
ANDERSON	CC	13	7	ANDERSON	J	10	4	ANDERTON	S	12	5	ANDREWS	C	12	254
ANDERSON	CE	13	7	ANDERSON	J	11	5	ANDERTON	T	11	6	ANDREWS	CA	9	3
ANDERSON	CJ	3	12	ANDERSON	J	11	5	ANDERTON	TB	6	8	ANDREWS	CG	4	7
ANDERSON	CJ	10	3	ANDERSON	J	11	5	ANDERTON	W	3	12	ANDREWS	CG	7	6
ANDERSON	CWC	3	12	ANDERSON	J	13	8	ANDERTON	W	14	4	ANDREWS	CH	7	6
ANDERSON	D	3	12	ANDERSON	J	14	4	ANDERTON	WE	6	8	ANDREWS	CH	10	4
ANDERSON	DGG	13	8	ANDERSON	JA	2	7	ANDERTON	WE	6	8	ANDREWS	CH	13	8
ANDERSON	E	5	6	ANDERSON	JD	9	3	ANDRE	FW	3	12	ANDREWS	CHW	6	9
ANDERSON	E	5	6	ANDERSON	JF	1	9	ANDRE	LW	3	12	ANDREWS	CJ	10	4
ANDERSON	E	8	4	ANDERSON	JS	3	12	ANDRE	RO	3	12	ANDREWS	CJ	13	8
ANDERSON	E	8	4	ANDERSON	JT	11	5	ANDREASSON	W	2	7	ANDREWS	CR	2	7
ANDERSON	E	11	5	ANDERSON	JT	12	4	ANDREW	AC	10	4	ANDREWS	CT	13	8
ANDERSON	E	13	8	ANDERSON	JW	3	264	ANDREW	CA	11	6	ANDREWS	CW	3	12
ANDERSON	E	14	4	ANDERSON	JW	5	7	ANDREW	CH	11	6	ANDREWS	D	4	7
ANDERSON	E	14	4	ANDERSON	JW	8	5	ANDREW	FW	7	5	ANDREWS	D	6	9
ANDERSON	EJ	13	8	ANDERSON	M	3	12	ANDREW	H	10	4	ANDREWS	DW	7	6
ANDERSON	ES	4	7	ANDERSON	P	5	7	ANDREW	HG	5	7	ANDREWS	E	1	10
ANDERSON	ES	12	4	ANDERSON	P	8	5	ANDREW	J	11	6	ANDREWS	E	8	5
ANDERSON	EV	3	12	ANDERSON	P	11	5	ANDREW	J	14	4	ANDREWS	EA	3	12
ANDERSON	EW	1	9	ANDERSON	R	2	7	ANDREW	JD	14	4	ANDREWS	EE	4	7
ANDERSON	F	1	9	ANDERSON	R	7	5	ANDREW	SJ	12	253	ANDREWS	EJ	1	10
ANDERSON	F	3	264	ANDERSON	RHT	7	5	ANDREW	T	10	4	ANDREWS	ESW	10	4
ANDERSON	F	5	6	ANDERSON	RJ	7	5	ANDREW	T	11	6	ANDREWS	F	3	265
ANDERSON	FC	10	3	ANDERSON	S	8	5	ANDREW	TAG	10	4	ANDREWS	F	4	7
ANDERSON	FH	14	4	ANDERSON	SW	2	7	ANDREW	TP	14	4	ANDREWS	F	4	7
ANDERSON	FJA	9	3	ANDERSON	T	9	220	ANDREW	WE	2	7	ANDREWS	F	5	7
ANDERSON	FT	12	4	ANDERSON	T	11	5	ANDREW	WJ	7	5	ANDREWS	F	12	5
ANDERSON	G	2	7	ANDERSON	T	13	8	ANDREWARTHA	A	10	4	ANDREWS	F	12	5
ANDERSON	G	2	7	ANDERSON	T	13	8	ANDREWARTHA	P	10	4	ANDREWS	FCM	12	5

Surname	Init			Surname	Init			Surname	Init			Surname	Init		
ANDREWS	FE	4	7	ANDREWS	J	10	4	ANDREWS	WH	3	265	ANNESS	A	9	220
ANDREWS	FG	5	7	ANDREWS	JA	2	8	ANDREWS	WH	5	7	ANNETT	EE	4	9
ANDREWS	FG	5	7	ANDREWS	JB	2	8	ANDREWS	WH	13	9	ANNETT	H	14	5
ANDREWS	FJ	7	6	ANDREWS	JB	4	8	ANDREWS	WJ	4	8	ANNETT	P	4	9
ANDREWS	FR	13	9	ANDREWS	JC	12	5	ANDREWS	WJ	7	6	ANNETT	VR	4	9
ANDREWS	FS	13	9	ANDREWS	JH	3	13	ANDREWS	WJ	13	9	ANNING	AG	5	8
ANDREWS	FW	10	4	ANDREWS	JH	11	6	ANDREWS	WL	4	8	ANNING	E	5	8
ANDREWS	FW	13	9	ANDREWS	JJ	1	10	ANDREWS	WW	4	8	ANNING	PJ	13	10
ANDREWS	G	1	9	ANDREWS	JJ	3	265	ANDRUS	FA	13	9	ANNING	W	5	8
ANDREWS	G	1	10	ANDREWS	JW	6	9	ANGEL	EW	3	13	ANNIS	A	6	9
ANDREWS	G	1	10	ANDREWS	JW	8	5	ANGEL	FW	4	8	ANNIS	BR	6	9
ANDREWS	G	3	12	ANDREWS	L	4	8	ANGEL	G	3	13	ANNIS	E	12	6
ANDREWS	G	4	7	ANDREWS	L	5	7	ANGEL	RJ	3	13	ANNIS	F	6	9
ANDREWS	G	4	8	ANDREWS	L	5	7	ANGEL	RT	3	13	ANNIS	J	11	7
ANDREWS	G	7	6	ANDREWS	M	11	6	ANGEL	T	13	9	ANNIS	V	6	9
ANDREWS	G	12	5	ANDREWS	MM	4	8	ANGEL	WT	3	13	ANNIS	WG	12	6
ANDREWS	GA	4	8	ANDREWS	O	4	8	ANGEL	WT	3	13	ANNISON	J	11	7
ANDREWS	GCA	13	9	ANDREWS	O	6	9	ANGELL	AE	7	6	ANNISON	JT	11	7
ANDREWS	GE	2	7	ANDREWS	OG	4	8	ANGELL	AW	13	9	ANNISON	W	11	7
ANDREWS	GE	4	8	ANDREWS	P	3	265	ANGELL	CHC	4	8	ANSCOMB	CH	2	8
ANDREWS	GE	7	6	ANDREWS	P	6	9	ANGELL	GE	5	7	ANSDELL	E	7	6
ANDREWS	GH	4	8	ANDREWS	R	2	8	ANGELL	H	4	8	ANSELL	A	13	10
ANDREWS	GH	13	9	ANDREWS	R	10	4	ANGELL	H	5	7	ANSELL	AR	13	10
ANDREWS	GP	10	4	ANDREWS	R	10	260	ANGELL	J	2	8	ANSELL	BG	5	8
ANDREWS	GP	11	6	ANDREWS	RC	13	9	ANGELL	R	2	8	ANSELL	C	5	8
ANDREWS	GS	10	4	ANDREWS	RT	13	9	ANGELL	SH	2	8	ANSELL	C	13	10
ANDREWS	GW	1	10	ANDREWS	S	3	13	ANGELL	W	5	8	ANSELL	CG	5	8
ANDREWS	GW	1	10	ANDREWS	S	4	8	ANGIER	GT	12	6	ANSELL	E	10	4
ANDREWS	GW	6	9	ANDREWS	SC	12	254	ANGLE	T	9	4	ANSELL	G	3	265
ANDREWS	H	1	10	ANDREWS	SW	7	6	ANGLEY	R	4	9	ANSELL	G	5	8
ANDREWS	H	4	8	ANDREWS	T	12	5	ANGLIN	AV	1	10	ANSELL	G	5	8
ANDREWS	H	6	9	ANDREWS	T	14	4	ANGLIS	A	2	8	ANSELL	GA	1	10
ANDREWS	H	11	6	ANDREWS	TG	12	5	ANGLISS	GJW	1	10	ANSELL	GH	3	13
ANDREWS	H	12	5	ANDREWS	TH	12	254	ANGOLD	HW	11	6	ANSELL	GH	13	10
ANDREWS	H	12	5	ANDREWS	TH	13	9	ANGUS	A	11	6	ANSELL	GW	10	260
ANDREWS	H	13	9	ANDREWS	TR	7	6	ANGUS	F	9	4	ANSELL	H	4	9
ANDREWS	HD	2	7	ANDREWS	TW	11	6	ANGUS	J	14	5	ANSELL	H	5	8
ANDREWS	HE	4	8	ANDREWS	TW	12	5	ANGUS	O	9	4	ANSELL	H	5	8
ANDREWS	HG	7	6	ANDREWS	W	1	10	ANKERS	T	11	6	ANSELL	H	13	10
ANDREWS	HH	4	8	ANDREWS	W	2	8	ANKERS	W	11	6	ANSELL	HV	5	8
ANDREWS	HJ	1	10	ANDREWS	W	3	265	ANKERS	W	11	7	ANSELL	J	5	8
ANDREWS	HJ	2	7	ANDREWS	W	4	8	ANKERS	WR	11	7	ANSELL	J	7	6
ANDREWS	HJ	10	4	ANDREWS	W	6	9	ANNABLE	R	11	7	ANSELL	JE	13	10
ANDREWS	HJ	12	5	ANDREWS	W	12	5	ANNABLE	TH	11	7	ANSELL	JH	10	4
ANDREWS	HJ	13	9	ANDREWS	W	12	5	ANNAKIN	A	8	5	ANSELL	S	5	8
ANDREWS	HT	12	5	ANDREWS	W	12	5	ANNAKIN	W	1	10	ANSELL	SW	5	8
ANDREWS	HW	5	7	ANDREWS	W	13	9	ANNAL	WE	8	5	ANSELL	TA	6	9
ANDREWS	J	1	10	ANDREWS	WA	13	9	ANNALLS	AG	13	9	ANSELL	VA	5	8
ANDREWS	J	2	8	ANDREWS	WC	3	13	ANNALLS	FC	4	8	ANSELL	W	1	10
ANDREWS	J	2	8	ANDREWS	WF	1	10	ANNAND	JW	13	9	ANSELL	W	2	8
ANDREWS	J	3	13	ANDREWS	WF	6	9	ANNELEY-LAMB	R	13	10	ANSELL	W	5	8
ANDREWS	J	3	13	ANDREWS	WG	2	8	ANNELLS	AJ	7	6	ANSELL	WJ	3	265
ANDREWS	J	5	7	ANDREWS	WG	12	6	ANNELLS	FA	3	13	ANSELL	WT	13	10
ANDREWS	J	7	6	ANDREWS	WG	13	9	ANNELLS	RC	3	13	ANSET	WH	7	6
ANDREWS	J	8	5	ANDREWS	WH	3	13	ANNESLEY	J	14	5	ANSLEY	FL	14	5

ANSLEY	JEA	7	6
ANSLOW	AW	6	9
ANSLOW	J	11	7
ANSON	A	6	9
ANSON	JF	13	10
ANSTEAD	J	1	10
ANSTEE	A	7	7
ANSTEE	AE	5	8
ANSTEE	CG	3	265
ANSTEE	E	5	8
ANSTEE	FC	5	8
ANSTEY	A	7	7
ANSTEY	CJ	12	6
ANSTEY	P	13	10
ANSTISS	FW	3	13
ANSTISS	HA	3	13
ANSTISS	HA	13	10
ANSTY	GH	7	7
ANSWORTH	C	9	220
ANTENEY	A	4	9
ANTHONY	AJ	7	7
ANTHONY	G	2	8
ANTHONY	G	7	7
ANTHONY	GW	13	10
ANTHONY	HJ	5	8
ANTHONY	JH	5	9
ANTHONY	JR	6	9
ANTHONY	P	4	9
ANTHONY	S	2	8
ANTHONY	WCG	11	7
ANTILL	H	13	10
ANTLEY	R	11	7
ANTLEY	R	11	7
ANTONIO	M	13	10
ANTRAM	AG	10	260
ANTRAM	AG	10	260
ANTRAM	F	10	260
ANWELL	PW	7	7
ANWELL	RW	7	7
ANZALUCCA	D	10	5
ANZALUCCA	M	10	5
APARK	EW	7	7
APICELLA	F	2	8
APLIN	E	7	7
APLIN	JW	7	7
APLIN	S	2	8
APLIN	VJ	7	7
APLIN	WE	4	9
APPELMAN	FH	3	265
APPELMAN	GA	7	7
APPERLEY	FV	2	8
APPLEBAUM	L	14	5
APPLEBEE	HJ	7	7
APPLEBY	AJ	7	7
APPLEBY	AR	12	6
APPLEBY	G	8	5
APPLEBY	G	11	7
APPLEBY	GH	6	10
APPLEBY	H	5	9
APPLEBY	J	9	220
APPLEBY	J	9	220
APPLEBY	JC	8	5
APPLEBY	JE	12	6
APPLEBY	P	5	9
APPLEBY	SR	8	5
APPLEBY	TH	1	10
APPLEBY	W	14	5
APPLEFORD	G	13	10
APPLEGATE	G	7	7
APPLETON	A	8	5
APPLETON	A	8	5
APPLETON	C	12	254
APPLETON	CH	4	9
APPLETON	E	11	7
APPLETON	F	12	254
APPLETON	GV	8	5
APPLETON	HC	10	5
APPLETON	LW	13	10
APPLETON	RW	4	9
APPLETON	T	11	7
APPLETON	W	8	6
APPLETON	W	14	5
APPLETON	WG	10	5
APPLETON	WJ	11	7
APPLETON	WJ	13	10
APPLEYARD	A	8	6
APPLEYARD	AE	8	6
APPLEYARD	E	8	6
APPLEYARD	E	8	6
APPLEYARD	E	11	421
APPLEYARD	G	8	6
APPLEYARD	H	8	6
APPLEYARD	J	8	6
APPLEYARD	J	8	6
APPLEYARD	JA	8	6
APPLEYARD	JE	8	6
APPLEYARD	JW	8	6
APPLEYARD	T	8	6
APPLIN	F	7	7
APPLIN	HW	9	4
APPLIN	W	3	13
APPLIN	W	11	7
APPS	AE	4	9
APPS	GWP	13	10
APPS	HB	4	9
APPS	HW	4	9
APPS	JH	4	9
APPS	JH	7	7
APPS	RF	4	9
APPS	S	13	11
APSEY	AJ	4	9
APSEY	TJ	4	9
APSEY	WG	4	9
ARBER	W	10	260
ARBON	SA	4	9
ARBON	WW	RF4	9
ARBUCKLE	M	3	13
ARCH	FW	12	254
ARCHARD	FJ	6	10
ARCHBALD	E	14	5
ARCHDEACON	J	4	9
ARCHELL	E	13	11
ARCHELL	JE	13	11
ARCHELL	TE	2	8
ARCHENOUL	TB	13	11
ARCHER	A	3	265
ARCHER	A	5	9
ARCHER	A	12	254
ARCHER	A	14	5
ARCHER	AC	13	11
ARCHER	AF	3	13
ARCHER	AG	13	11
ARCHER	AJ	5	9
ARCHER	BW	7	7
ARCHER	C	5	9
ARCHER	C	8	6
ARCHER	CD	9	4
ARCHER	CE	7	7
ARCHER	DJ	14	5
ARCHER	E	3	14
ARCHER	E	5	9
ARCHER	EC	4	10
ARCHER	F	13	11
ARCHER	FG	6	10
ARCHER	FH	3	14
ARCHER	FT	13	11
ARCHER	FWA	5	9
ARCHER	G	14	5
ARCHER	H	12	254
ARCHER	HE	4	10
ARCHER	HW	1	10
ARCHER	HW	4	10
ARCHER	J	3	14
ARCHER	J	9	4
ARCHER	J	11	7
ARCHER	J	14	5
ARCHER	JA	4	10
ARCHER	JA	7	7
ARCHER	JH	6	10
ARCHER	JW	4	10
ARCHER	JW	14	5
ARCHER	L	3	14
ARCHER	LC	7	8
ARCHER	LC	7	8
ARCHER	PB	1	10
ARCHER	PF	13	11
ARCHER	R	13	11
ARCHER	RG	7	8
ARCHER	SW	13	11
ARCHER	T	5	9
ARCHER	T	6	10
ARCHER	T	11	7
ARCHER	TB	8	6
ARCHER	TH	7	8
ARCHER	TJ	4	10
ARCHER	TP	3	14
ARCHER	W	11	7
ARCHER	WA	12	254
ARCHER	WJ	7	8
ARCHER	WJ	12	6
ARCHER	WP	13	11
ARCHER	WT	3	265
ARCHER	WT	3	265
ARCHIBALD	AM	2	8
ARDELL	J	14	5
ARDELL	W	14	5
ARDEN	H	3	14
ARDEN	RW	3	14
ARDERN	W	14	5
ARDING	MH	4	10
ARDREY	C	3	14
ARDREY	GU	3	14
ARDREY	J	14	5
ARDRON	F	11	8
ARDRON	R	11	8
ARDRON	T	14	5
ARDRON	W	11	8
AREY	L	8	6
ARGENT	CE	5	9
ARGENT	CF	3	265
ARGENT	EA	3	14
ARGENT	F	7	8
ARGENT	HF	5	9
ARGENT	HG	10	260
ARGENT	HV	9	221
ARGENT	J	1	10
ARGENT	WE	10	5
ARGENT	WG	3	265
ARGENT	WS	3	14
ARGENT	WT	2	8
ARGER	H	5	9
ARGER	TL	5	9
ARGYLE	AH	2	9
ARGYLE	RCB	2	9
ARIENT	H	1	10
ARIS	EG	7	8
ARIS	F	7	8
ARIS	S	2	9
ARIS	W	5	9
ARISNISKY	I	14	5

ARISS	AMH	6	10	ARMITAGE	T	11	8	ARMSTRONG	JC	3	14	ARNOLD	CV	6	10				
ARISS	CT	6	10	ARMITAGE	TW	3	265	ARMSTRONG	JC	9	4	ARNOLD	CW	7	8				
ARISS	D	6	10	ARMITAGE	W	1	10	ARMSTRONG	JC	11	8	ARNOLD	CW	11	9				
ARKELL	EE	6	10	ARMITAGE	W	3	266	ARMSTRONG	JE	11	8	ARNOLD	DHC	13	12				
ARKELL	H	3	265	ARMITAGE	W	9	4	ARMSTRONG	JH	11	8	ARNOLD	E	2	9				
ARKELL	H	6	10	ARMITAGE	WG	5	9	ARMSTRONG	JW	7	8	ARNOLD	E	3	15				
ARKELL	SJ	7	8	ARMITAGE	WT	2	9	ARMSTRONG	P	7	8	ARNOLD	E	9	5				
ARKWELL	G	6	10	ARMITT	A	1	11	ARMSTRONG	RG	3	14	ARNOLD	E	10	5				
ARKWRIGHT	H	11	8	ARMITT	C	1	11	ARMSTRONG	RJ	3	15	ARNOLD	EA	4	10				
ARKWRIGHT	W	11	8	ARMITT	G	14	6	ARMSTRONG	T	8	7	ARNOLD	EF	4	10				
ARLETT	PL	13	11	ARMITT	W	1	11	ARMSTRONG	T	9	4	ARNOLD	EF	4	10				
ARLETT	W	4	10	ARMOND	F	5	10	ARMSTRONG	T	12	6	ARNOLD	EM	3	15				
ARLISS	BA	10	260	ARMOUR	AW	1	11	ARMSTRONG	W	2	9	ARNOLD	EW	7	8				
ARM	AW	4	10	ARMOUR	EH	13	11	ARMSTRONG	W	3	15	ARNOLD	F	8	7				
ARMAND	M	3	14	ARMOUR	J	12	6	ARMSTRONG	W	6	10	ARNOLD	F	13	12				
ARMAND	VA	3	14	ARMOUR	T	9	4	ARMSTRONG	W	9	221	ARNOLD	FA	12	254				
ARMES	HA	12	6	ARMSBY	TE	7	8	ARMSTRONG	W	11	9	ARNOLD	FC	1	11				
ARMES	I	14	5	ARMSDEN	C	5	10	ARMSTRONG	W	12	6	ARNOLD	FF	10	5				
ARMETT	W	14	6	ARMSDEN	R	11	8	ARMSTRONG	W	12	6	ARNOLD	FH	8	7				
ARMIGER	C	5	9	ARMSTEAD	A	9	379	ARMSTRONG	W	14	6	ARNOLD	FS	4	10				
ARMIGER	H	5	9	ARMSTEAD	H	9	4	ARMSTRONG	W	14	6	ARNOLD	G	12	254				
ARMIN	C	11	8	ARMSTON	S	14	6	ARMSTRONG	WA	9	4	ARNOLD	G	13	12				
ARMIN	JC	11	8	ARMSTON	WE	11	8	ARMSTRONG	WF	11	9	ARNOLD	G	13	12				
ARMISTEAD	J	8	6	ARMSTRONG	A	4	10	ARMSTRONG	WG	8	7	ARNOLD	G	13	12				
ARMISTEAD	R	8	6	ARMSTRONG	A	5	10	ARMSTRONG	WH	9	221	ARNOLD	GH	13	12				
ARMISTEAD	W	9	4	ARMSTRONG	A	6	10	ARMSTRONG	WP	7	8	ARNOLD	GJ	12	6				
ARMITAGE	A	5	9	ARMSTRONG	A	8	7	ARMSTRONG	WT	10	5	ARNOLD	GW	13	12				
ARMITAGE	A	8	6	ARMSTRONG	A	14	6	ARNALD	E	9	5	ARNOLD	H	1	11				
ARMITAGE	A	8	7	ARMSTRONG	AC	5	10	ARNALL	GO	6	10	ARNOLD	H	4	11				
ARMITAGE	A	9	4	ARMSTRONG	AW	3	14	ARNELL	F	4	10	ARNOLD	H	4	11				
ARMITAGE	AW	9	4	ARMSTRONG	C	13	11	ARNELL	JE	13	11	ARNOLD	H	9	379				
ARMITAGE	C	2	9	ARMSTRONG	C	14	6	ARNETT	FA	6	10	ARNOLD	HC	1	11				
ARMITAGE	D	11	8	ARMSTRONG	E	3	14	ARNEY	F	4	10	ARNOLD	HE	10	5				
ARMITAGE	E	8	7	ARMSTRONG	F	3	14	ARNEY	RC	4	10	ARNOLD	HM	12	254				
ARMITAGE	EC	2	9	ARMSTRONG	F	3	266	ARNEY	WH	4	10	ARNOLD	HTG	12	7				
ARMITAGE	EGT	7	8	ARMSTRONG	F	8	7	ARNILL	HJ	7	8	ARNOLD	HW	1	11				
ARMITAGE	F	11	8	ARMSTRONG	F	12	6	ARNOLD	A	2	9	ARNOLD	HW	2	9				
ARMITAGE	G	8	7	ARMSTRONG	FW	5	10.	ARNOLD	A	4	10	ARNOLD	HW	10	5				
ARMITAGE	G	8	7	ARMSTRONG	FW	7	8	ARNOLD	A	11	9	ARNOLD	J	6	11				
ARMITAGE	GS	8	7	ARMSTRONG	G	1	11	ARNOLD	A	11	9	ARNOLD	JC	3	15				
ARMITAGE	GW	2	9	ARMSTRONG	G	2	9	ARNOLD	A	12	6	ARNOLD	JG	1	11				
ARMITAGE	H	5	9	ARMSTRONG	G	4	10	ARNOLD	A	12	6	ARNOLD	JH	6	10				
ARMITAGE	H	8	7	ARMSTRONG	G	11	8	ARNOLD	AG	13	11	ARNOLD	JW	4	11				
ARMITAGE	H	9	379	ARMSTRONG	G	14	6	ARNOLD	AJ	6	10	ARNOLD	LR	3	266				
ARMITAGE	HG	5	9	ARMSTRONG	GA	4	10	ARNOLD	AJ	12	6	ARNOLD	NG	4	11				
ARMITAGE	J	8	7	ARMSTRONG	GC	3	14	ARNOLD	AOC	2	9	ARNOLD	O	5	10				
ARMITAGE	J	8	7	ARMSTRONG	H	13	11	ARNOLD	AS	13	12	ARNOLD	PJ	3	15				
ARMITAGE	J	8	7	ARMSTRONG	HJ	5	10	ARNOLD	AV	10	261	ARNOLD	R	4	11				
ARMITAGE	J	9	4	ARMSTRONG	HW	10	260	ARNOLD	AV	13	12	ARNOLD	R	6	11				
ARMITAGE	RE	11	8	ARMSTRONG	ID	13	11	ARNOLD	AV	13	12	ARNOLD	R	12	7				
ARMITAGE	RM	8	7	ARMSTRONG	J	5	10	ARNOLD	AW	12	254	ARNOLD	R	12	7				
ARMITAGE	T	8	7	ARMSTRONG	J	8	7	ARNOLD	B	13	12	ARNOLD	RC	12	7				
ARMITAGE	T	8	7	ARMSTRONG	J	9	379	ARNOLD	CE	13	12	ARNOLD	RW	2	9				
ARMITAGE	T	8	7	ARMSTRONG	J	11	8	ARNOLD	CL	10	261	ARNOLD	S	2	9				
ARMITAGE	T	9	4	ARMSTRONG	J	14	6	ARNOLD	CR	1	11	ARNOLD	S	3	15				

ARNOLD	S	5	10
ARNOLD	SG	12	7
ARNOLD	SJF	1	11
ARNOLD	SR	2	9
ARNOLD	SW	5	10
ARNOLD	T	1	11
ARNOLD	TA	12	7
ARNOLD	TF	3	15
ARNOLD	W	1	11
ARNOLD	W	5	10
ARNOLD	W	5	10
ARNOLD	W	14	6
ARNOLD	WA	10	5
ARNOLD	WA	13	12
ARNOLD	WG	13	12
ARNOLD	WH	3	15
ARNOLD	WH	10	261
ARNOLD	WJ	1	11
ARNOLD	WJ	1	11
ARNOLD	WJ	13	12
ARNOLD	WT	12	7
ARNOTT	G	11	9
ARNOTT	GW	2	9
ARNOTT	JR	9	5
ARNOTT	W	14	6
ARNOULD	JW	3	266
ARNOULD	RH	7	8
ARNSBY	FW	12	254
ARNUP	VF	13	12
ARPINO	A	12	7
ARRAND	GG	9	379
ARRAND	S	9	5
ARRANDALE	J	11	9
ARRANDALE	J	11	9
ARRIS	TB	6	11
ARRONSON	LWS	14	6
ARROWSMITH	AE	6	11
ARROWSMITH	ATF	6	11
ARROWSMITH	FL	6	11
ARROWSMITH	G	11	9
ARROWSMITH	H	6	11
ARSCOTT	C	4	11
ARTER	C	13	12
ARTHINGTON	H	11	9
ARTHUR	AH	4	11
ARTHUR	CG	4	11
ARTHUR	F	9	221
ARTHUR	FW	12	7
ARTHUR	G	11	9
ARTHUR	GF	3	266
ARTHUR	H	4	11
ARTHUR	J	3	266
ARTHUR	JG	14	6
ARTHUR	WG	13	12
ARTHURS	J	5	10
ARTIS	HJ	7	8
ARTIST	TE	9	221
ARTLETT	R	10	5
ARY	RW	7	9
ARYLE	JG	9	5
ASBURY	A	13	12
ASBURY	AJ	5	10
ASBURY	C	5	10
ASBURY	J	3	266
ASBURY	J	3	266
ASBURY	J	3	266
ASBURY	W	5	10
ASCHERI	FA	3	266
ASCOTT	D	1	11
ASCOTT	EF	2	9
ASCOTT	T	6	11
ASCROFT	J	11	9
ASH	A	1	11
ASH	A	2	10
ASH	AG	7	9
ASH	C	13	13
ASH	CA	2	10
ASH	CE	13	13
ASH	EGW	13	13
ASH	F	13	13
ASH	FT	7	9
ASH	GE	6	11
ASH	GE	7	9
ASH	GR	10	261
ASH	HJG	13	13
ASH	J	1	11
ASH	J	6	11
ASH	J	13	13
ASH	J	13	13
ASH	JR	3	15
ASH	JR	13	13
ASH	LM	10	5
ASH	PW	13	13
ASH	R	13	13
ASH	RA	8	8
ASH	RW	13	13
ASH	S	13	13
ASH	TJB	1	11
ASH	WG	3	266
ASH	WJ	3	15
ASHARD	CA	2	10
ASHBERY	HD	6	11
ASHBOURNE	T	3	15
ASHBROOK	HO	14	6
ASHBY	A	5	10
ASHBY	A	5	10
ASHBY	A	7	9
ASHBY	AA	5	10
ASHBY	AE	12	254
ASHBY	AJ	12	254
ASHBY	AV	1	11
ASHBY	CE	5	10
ASHBY	EO	5	11
ASHBY	F	8	8
ASHBY	F	12	254
ASHBY	F	12	254
ASHBY	F	12	254
ASHBY	G	7	9
ASHBY	G	12	255
ASHBY	G	12	255
ASHBY	H	5	11
ASHBY	H	5	11
ASHBY	H	12	255
ASHBY	HA	3	15
ASHBY	HG	12	255
ASHBY	J	5	11
ASHBY	J	12	255
ASHBY	JT	13	13
ASHBY	JW	12	255
ASHBY	L	5	11
ASHBY	W	2	10
ASHBY	W	5	11
ASHBY	WG	2	10
ASHBY	WG	13	13
ASHBY	WH	12	255
ASHBY	WJ	5	11
ASHBY	WJF	3	15
ASHBY	WJJ	5	11
ASHBY	WR	2	10
ASHCROFT	E	8	8
ASHCROFT	E	10	5
ASHCROFT	F	10	5
ASHCROFT	J	14	6
ASHCROFT	J	14	6
ASHCROFT	P	12	7
ASHCROFT	R	11	9
ASHCROFT	R	11	9
ASHCROFT	R	14	6
ASHCROFT	TH	11	9
ASHDOWN	A	1	11
ASHDOWN	AD	4	11
ASHDOWN	AE	7	9
ASHDOWN	E	6	11
ASHDOWN	JG	7	9
ASHDOWN	LC	1	12
ASHDOWN	W	1	11
ASHDOWN	W	3	15
ASHELFORD	E	13	13
ASHELFORD	HG	13	13
ASHELFORD	TC	3	266
ASHENDEN	G	3	266
ASHENDEN	W	3	266
ASHER	CGR	5	11
ASHER	F	4	11
ASHFIELD	AG	6	11
ASHFIELD	H	6	11
ASHFIELD	MW	6	11
ASHFIELD	TC	13	13
ASHFIELD	WR	13	13
ASHFORD	AA	6	11
ASHFORD	AH	2	10
ASHFORD	AW	6	11
ASHFORD	AW	6	11
ASHFORD	C	14	6
ASHFORD	F	3	266
ASHFORD	G	6	12
ASHFORD	GH	6	12
ASHFORD	H	6	12
ASHFORD	JP	1	12
ASHFORD	JW	11	9
ASHFORD	PS	14	6
ASHFORD	R	6	12
ASHFORD	RHS	7	9
ASHFORD	TG	13	13
ASHFORD	WE	13	14
ASHFORTH	J	6	12
ASHFORTH	J	9	221
ASHLEY	A	2	10
ASHLEY	A	11	9
ASHLEY	A	12	7
ASHLEY	AW	3	266
ASHLEY	C	1	12
ASHLEY	C	7	9
ASHLEY	CH	12	7
ASHLEY	D	14	7
ASHLEY	FT	4	11
ASHLEY	GA	4	11
ASHLEY	GE	12	7
ASHLEY	GH	12	7
ASHLEY	H	11	9
ASHLEY	H	12	7
ASHLEY	H	13	14
ASHLEY	HG	4	11
ASHLEY	J	1	12
ASHLEY	J	1	12
ASHLEY	J	3	15
ASHLEY	JH	14	7
ASHLEY	JJ	2	10
ASHLEY	JW	7	9
ASHLEY	SH	12	7
ASHLEY	T	14	7
ASHLEY	W	7	9
ASHLEY	W	7	9
ASHLEY	WG	11	10
ASHLING	HJ	13	14
ASHMAN	A	8	8
ASHMAN	AH	13	14
ASHMAN	C	7	9
ASHMAN	EJ	2	10
ASHMAN	GH	14	7

ASHMAN	HEV	1	12
ASHMAN	TC	1	12
ASHMAN	WA	5	11
ASHMELL	AE	8	8
ASHMELL	JF	8	8
ASHMORE	A	5	11
ASHMORE	BEA	6	12
ASHMORE	CE	6	12
ASHMORE	E	6	12
ASHMORE	E	6	12
ASHMORE	F	11	10
ASHMORE	FE	6	12
ASHMORE	FW	6	12
ASHMORE	G	11	10
ASHMORE	H	6	12
ASHMORE	S	8	415
ASHMORE	WA	6	12
ASHPLANT	JH	2	10
ASHPOLE	B	12	7
ASHPOLE	E	12	7
ASHPOLE	F	12	8
ASHPOLE	FJ	12	8
ASHPOLE	G	12	8
ASHPOLE	GW	12	8
ASHPOLE	RT	12	8
ASHPOLE	WE	12	8
ASHPOOL	F	5	11
ASHTON	A	2	10
ASHTON	A	7	9
ASHTON	A	7	9
ASHTON	A	11	10
ASHTON	CH	11	10
ASHTON	CR	3	15
ASHTON	CS	5	11
ASHTON	D	12	8
ASHTON	E	3	15
ASHTON	E	11	10
ASHTON	EE	3	15
ASHTON	EM	3	16
ASHTON	F	2	10
ASHTON	F	3	16
ASHTON	F	3	266
ASHTON	FDH	9	5
ASHTON	G	9	5
ASHTON	G	11	10
ASHTON	G	12	255
ASHTON	G	14	7
ASHTON	G	14	7
ASHTON	H	5	11
ASHTON	H	11	10
ASHTON	H	11	10
ASHTON	H	11	10
ASHTON	J	8	8
ASHTON	J	11	10
ASHTON	J	11	10
ASHTON	JR	14	7
ASHTON	JW	11	10
ASHTON	M	11	10
ASHTON	N	9	5
ASHTON	N	9	5
ASHTON	OWH	2	10
ASHTON	PR	12	255
ASHTON	PW	2	10
ASHTON	R	6	12
ASHTON	R	9	221
ASHTON	R	10	5
ASHTON	RA	9	5
ASHTON	RF	10	5
ASHTON	T	9	5
ASHTON	T	11	10
ASHTON	T	11	10
ASHTON	T	12	255
ASHTON	W	1	12
ASHTON	W	9	5
ASHTON	WC	12	255
ASHTON	WH	11	10
ASHTON	WW	11	10
ASHURST	E	14	7
ASHURST	T	14	7
ASHWELL	AE	7	9
ASHWELL	AE	9	5
ASHWELL	C	12	8
ASHWELL	C	13	14
ASHWELL	CW	12	8
ASHWELL	E	9	5
ASHWELL	WH	13	14
ASHWELL	WJ	5	11
ASHWOOD	F	1	12
ASHWOOD	W	13	14
ASHWORTH	A	9	221
ASHWORTH	A	14	7
ASHWORTH	A	14	7
ASHWORTH	CE	7	9
ASHWORTH	CH	14	7
ASHWORTH	CH	14	7
ASHWORTH	CW	9	379
ASHWORTH	E	2	10
ASHWORTH	E	14	7
ASHWORTH	F	7	9
ASHWORTH	F	9	221
ASHWORTH	G	4	11
ASHWORTH	GT	13	14
ASHWORTH	H	4	11
ASHWORTH	H	14	7
ASHWORTH	J	9	5
ASHWORTH	J	9	379
ASHWORTH	J	11	10
ASHWORTH	J	14	7
ASHWORTH	JH	14	7
ASHWORTH	NB	11	11
ASHWORTH	P	9	5
ASHWORTH	R	11	11
ASHWORTH	S	9	221
ASHWORTH	S	11	11
ASHWORTH	TB	9	379
ASHWORTH	W	11	11
ASHWORTH	W	14	7
ASHWORTH	W	14	8
ASHWORTH	WH	11	11
ASKAM	WS	3	266
ASKER	F	5	11
ASKEW	CC	12	8
ASKEW	CTE	2	10
ASKEW	GV	12	8
ASKEW	J	12	8
ASKEW	JH	3	266
ASKEW	W	13	14
ASKEY	AE	7	10
ASKEY	AJ	1	12
ASKEY	C	1	12
ASKEY	F	2	10
ASKEY	HG	7	10
ASKEY	J	6	12
ASKEY	M	1	12
ASKEY	R	6	12
ASKEY	TP	1	12
ASKEY	WJ	6	12
ASKHAM	CF	2	10
ASKHAM	J	9	5
ASKIN	A	8	8
ASKIN	A	8	8
ASKIN	A	8	8
ASKIN	C	8	8
ASLET	W	7	10
ASLET	WE	4	11
ASLETT	A	7	10
ASLETT	CJ	4	11
ASLETT	G	4	11
ASLETT	JJ	10	5
ASPA	J	14	8
ASPEY	E	10	261
ASPIN	J	8	8
ASPIN	J	8	8
ASPIN	J	14	8
ASPIN	W	8	8
ASPINALL	FW	6	12
ASPINALL	G	14	8
ASPINALL	J	8	8
ASPINALL	J	14	8
ASPINALL	S	13	14
ASPINALL	T	11	11
ASPINALL	WH	6	12
ASPITAL	AW	3	267
ASPLAND	A	6	12
ASPLAND	WJ	2	10
ASPLEN	C	3	267
ASPLET	SJ	10	5
ASPLEY	AE	12	8
ASPLEY	HG	12	8
ASPLIN	HF	12	8
ASPLIN	HJ	12	8
ASQUITH	A	8	8
ASQUITH	G	8	8
ASQUITH	H	8	8
ASQUITH	S	8	8
ASQUITH	T	9	5
ASQUITH	WC	8	8
ASSER	DG	1	12
ASSER	DW	1	12
ASSER	GA	1	12
ASSETER	E	13	14
ASTBURY	A	14	8
ASTBURY	CE	6	12
ASTBURY	W	11	11
ASTELL	AE	7	10
ASTELL	AF	13	14
ASTILL	H	13	14
ASTILL	M	2	10
ASTILL	R	2	11
ASTIN	H	11	11
ASTLE	J	14	8
ASTLETT	W	6	13
ASTLEY	F	5	11
ASTLEY	F	11	11
ASTLEY	GJ	6	13
ASTLEY	T	6	13
ASTLING	FS	5	11
ASTLING	HJ	5	11
ASTON	A	2	11
ASTON	A	6	13
ASTON	AJ	6	13
ASTON	CV	2	11
ASTON	FT	13	14
ASTON	GW	3	267
ASTON	H	6	13
ASTON	H	6	13
ASTON	J	6	13
ASTON	J	6	13
ASTON	JT	3	16
ASTON	JW	6	13
ASTON	T	14	8
ASTON	T	14	8
ASTON	W	6	13
ASTON	WJ	13	14
ASTON	WT	5	12
ATACK	GIK	8	8
ATACK	GW	8	9
ATACK	J	9	6
ATACK	T	9	221
ATCHELER	WS	13	14

ATHA	A	8	9
ATHA	V	8	9
ATHA	W	8	9
ATHA	WA	8	9
ATHERLEY	ES	10	5
ATHERTON	F	9	221
ATHERTON	F	11	11
ATHERTON	J	11	11
ATHERTON	PP	2	11
ATHERTON	WB	14	8
ATHERTON	WH	11	11
ATHERTON	WJ	4	11
ATHOL	J	2	11
ATHORN	J	8	9
ATHOW	FHJ	12	8
ATHY	T	14	8
ATKIN	F	2	11
ATKIN	GW	11	11
ATKIN	K	6	13
ATKIN	TE	2	11
ATKINS	A	1	12
ATKINS	A	2	11
ATKINS	A	2	11
ATKINS	A	3	267
ATKINS	AC	12	8
ATKINS	AG	5	12
ATKINS	AH	7	10
ATKINS	AR	7	10
ATKINS	ARC	13	14
ATKINS	B	6	13
ATKINS	B	12	255
ATKINS	C	1	12
ATKINS	C	5	12
ATKINS	C	13	14
ATKINS	CRW	13	15
ATKINS	DD	2	11
ATKINS	E	1	12
ATKINS	E	2	11
ATKINS	E	2	11
ATKINS	E	2	11
ATKINS	E	5	12
ATKINS	E	5	12
ATKINS	E	6	13
ATKINS	E	10	261
ATKINS	EA	5	12
ATKINS	EW	5	12
ATKINS	F	1	12
ATKINS	F	4	11
ATKINS	FB	2	11
ATKINS	FC	3	267
ATKINS	FJ	12	9
ATKINS	FMV	4	12
ATKINS	FT	1	12
ATKINS	G	5	12
ATKINS	G	9	6
ATKINS	G	10	6
ATKINS	GB	12	9
ATKINS	GE	10	6
ATKINS	GT	2	11
ATKINS	GW	12	255
ATKINS	H	5	12
ATKINS	H	6	13
ATKINS	H	11	11
ATKINS	HA	7	10
ATKINS	HB	5	12
ATKINS	HE	11	11
ATKINS	J	5	12
ATKINS	J	5	12
ATKINS	J	6	13
ATKINS	J	6	13
ATKINS	JH	8	9
ATKINS	JT	1	12
ATKINS	JW	2	11
ATKINS	L	5	12
ATKINS	LG	12	421
ATKINS	LH	3	267
ATKINS	MJ	1	12
ATKINS	PA	2	11
ATKINS	R	1	13
ATKINS	R	3	267
ATKINS	RJ	1	12
ATKINS	S	9	6
ATKINS	S	11	11
ATKINS	SA	2	11
ATKINS	SV	2	11
ATKINS	T	5	12
ATKINS	T	5	12
ATKINS	TG	7	10
ATKINS	TW	12	9
ATKINS	W	3	267
ATKINS	W	6	13
ATKINS	W	6	13
ATKINS	W	6	13
ATKINS	W	7	10
ATKINS	W	10	6
ATKINS	WA	5	12
ATKINS	WA	6	13
ATKINS	WA	10	6
ATKINSON	A	1	13
ATKINSON	A	1	13
ATKINSON	A	8	9
ATKINSON	A	9	6
ATKINSON	A	9	6
ATKINSON	A	9	6
ATKINSON	A	9	221
ATKINSON	A	9	221
ATKINSON	A	11	11
ATKINSON	A	14	8
ATKINSON	AE	7	10
ATKINSON	AE	11	11
ATKINSON	AP	9	6
ATKINSON	AP	9	379
ATKINSON	BJ	13	15
ATKINSON	CH	7	10
ATKINSON	CW	9	221
ATKINSON	D	11	11
ATKINSON	D	11	12
ATKINSON	E	8	9
ATKINSON	E	9	6
ATKINSON	E	9	221
ATKINSON	E	11	12
ATKINSON	F	8	9
ATKINSON	F	8	9
ATKINSON	F	8	9
ATKINSON	F	9	6
ATKINSON	F	9	6
ATKINSON	F	12	9
ATKINSON	F	13	15
ATKINSON	F	14	8
ATKINSON	F	14	8
ATKINSON	F	14	8
ATKINSON	FG	7	10
ATKINSON	FG	7	10
ATKINSON	FJ	12	255
ATKINSON	G	11	12
ATKINSON	G	14	8
ATKINSON	GC	13	15
ATKINSON	GE	8	9
ATKINSON	H	2	11
ATKINSON	H	8	9
ATKINSON	H	8	9
ATKINSON	H	8	9
ATKINSON	H	9	6
ATKINSON	H	9	221
ATKINSON	H	11	12
ATKINSON	H	12	255
ATKINSON	HA	9	221
ATKINSON	HC	9	6
ATKINSON	HG	12	9
ATKINSON	HR	2	12
ATKINSON	J	7	10
ATKINSON	J	8	9
ATKINSON	J	8	9
ATKINSON	J	8	9
ATKINSON	J	9	6
ATKINSON	J	9	221
ATKINSON	J	9	221
ATKINSON	J	11	12
ATKINSON	J	11	12
ATKINSON	J	12	9
ATKINSON	J	12	9
ATKINSON	J	14	8
ATKINSON	J	14	8
ATKINSON	JC	2	12
ATKINSON	JE	9	6
ATKINSON	JS	2	12
ATKINSON	JW	5	12
ATKINSON	JW	10	261
ATKINSON	JW	14	9
ATKINSON	L	9	380
ATKINSON	MC	13	15
ATKINSON	P	8	9
ATKINSON	P	8	9
ATKINSON	P	12	255
ATKINSON	R	1	13
ATKINSON	R	8	10
ATKINSON	R	9	222
ATKINSON	S	8	10
ATKINSON	S	8	10
ATKINSON	S	8	10
ATKINSON	S	9	6
ATKINSON	SM	8	10
ATKINSON	T	8	10
ATKINSON	T	8	10
ATKINSON	T	8	10
ATKINSON	T	9	6
ATKINSON	T	9	380
ATKINSON	T	14	9
ATKINSON	TE	11	12
ATKINSON	TW	10	261
ATKINSON	V	14	9
ATKINSON	W	3	267
ATKINSON	W	8	10
ATKINSON	W	9	6
ATKINSON	W	9	6
ATKINSON	W	9	222
ATKINSON	W	9	222
ATKINSON	W	11	12
ATKINSON	W	12	9
ATKINSON	W	14	9
ATKINSON	WA	8	10
ATKINSON	WGG	14	9
ATKINSON	WH	11	12
ATKINSON	WM	8	10
ATKINSON	WT	11	12
ATKISS	M	6	14
ATRILL	GW	10	6
ATTACK	C	8	10
ATTACK	H	8	10
ATTACK	TD	8	10
ATTENBOROUGH	E	11	12
ATTER	WG	3	267
ATTERBURY	AE	2	12
ATTFIELD	H	3	267
ATTFIELD	LG	3	267
ATTFIELD	R	10	6
ATTHIS	CR	2	12
ATTREE	AE	4	12
ATTREE	EC	2	12
ATTREE	G	3	267

ATTREE	WJ	3	267	AUGER	J	1	13	AUSTIN	J	2	13	AVERY	A	14	9
ATTRIDGE	AW	13	15	AUGER	JLJ	3	267	AUSTIN	J	6	14	AVERY	AG	6	14
ATTRIDGE	F	7	10	AUKER	F	9	7	AUSTIN	J	9	7	AVERY	AW	4	12
ATTRIDGE	WA	13	15	AULT	F	6	14	AUSTIN	J	10	6	AVERY	AW	4	12
ATTRILL	FA	6	14	AULT	HR	14	9	AUSTIN	JA	1	13	AVERY	B	4	12
ATTRILL	TA	10	6	AULT	JJ	13	15	AUSTIN	JA	12	255	AVERY	C	1	13
ATTWELL	AH	3	16	AUST	T	11	12	AUSTIN	JH	2	13	AVERY	C	4	12
ATTWELL	HR	2	12	AUSTEN	RP	4	12	AUSTIN	JW	2	13	AVERY	E	13	16
ATTWELL	J	2	12	AUSTEN	VG	2	12	AUSTIN	M	10	6	AVERY	FH	6	14
ATTWELL	RS	5	12	AUSTERBEERY	A	11	12	AUSTIN	R	3	268	AVERY	G	2	13
ATTWOOD	A	12	255	AUSTICK	J	9	7	AUSTIN	R	4	12	AVERY	G	3	268
ATTWOOD	AC	5	12	AUSTIN	A	1	13	AUSTIN	R	4	12	AVERY	GA	12	9
ATTWOOD	AEG	1	13	AUSTIN	A	9	7	AUSTIN	R	11	12	AVERY	H	1	13
ATTWOOD	AH	3	267	AUSTIN	A	10	6	AUSTIN	RG	6	14	AVERY	JW	12	9
ATTWOOD	AJ	13	15	AUSTIN	A	12	255	AUSTIN	RH	4	12	AVERY	PJ	2	13
ATTWOOD	C	6	14	AUSTIN	A	13	15	AUSTIN	SG	1	13	AVERY	R	4	12
ATTWOOD	DC	13	15	AUSTIN	A	13	15	AUSTIN	T	12	256	AVERY	RA	1	13
ATTWOOD	FE	13	15	AUSTIN	AA	13	16	AUSTIN	TEA	13	16	AVERY	S	6	15
ATTWOOD	FJ	4	12	AUSTIN	AE	2	12	AUSTIN	W	1	13	AVERY	TE	4	13
ATTWOOD	G	4	12	AUSTIN	AE	6	14	AUSTIN	W	2	13	AVERY	W	4	12
ATTWOOD	GH	4	12	AUSTIN	AG	10	6	AUSTIN	W	4	12	AVERY	W	5	13
ATTWOOD	HHV	4	12	AUSTIN	AW	4	12	AUSTIN	W	6	14	AVERY	WA	12	9
ATTWOOD	HS	6	14	AUSTIN	AW	13	16	AUSTIN	W	9	222	AVERY	WE	1	13
ATTWOOD	J	1	13	AUSTIN	B	10	6	AUSTIN	W	11	12	AVERY	WR	7	11
ATTWOOD	J	2	12	AUSTIN	C	1	13	AUSTIN	W	12	9	AVES	G	3	268
ATTWOOD	J	6	14	AUSTIN	CA	10	6	AUSTIN	W	12	256	AVESON	C	4	13
ATTWOOD	T	6	14	AUSTIN	CJ	5	13	AUSTIN	W	12	256	AVEY	F	13	16
ATTWOOD	W	1	13	AUSTIN	E	3	267	AUSTIN	W	13	16	AVEY	WG	10	6
ATTWOOD	WA	2	12	AUSTIN	E	10	6	AUSTIN	WA	3	268	AVEYARD	A	9	7
ATTWOOD	WD	6	14	AUSTIN	E	13	16	AUSTIN	WA	12	256	AVEYARD	A	9	7
ATTWOOD	WH	2	12	AUSTIN	E	13	16	AUSTIN	WE	3	16	AVEYARD	MV	9	222
ATTWOOD	WP	13	15	AUSTIN	EC	2	12	AUSTIN	WH	3	268	AVIS	A	10	261
ATWATER	AR	13	15	AUSTIN	EC	4	12	AUSTIN	WH	10	6	AVIS	F	3	268
ATWELL	A	9	7	AUSTIN	EH	2	12	AUSTIN	WH	12	256	AVIS	F	13	16
ATWELL	FF	9	7	AUSTIN	EJ	7	10	AUSTIN	WHR	3	16	AVIS	JH	1	13
ATWOOD	FW	5	13	AUSTIN	EW	10	261	AUSTIN	WJ	5	13	AVIS	JR	10	261
AUBEN	F	5	13	AUSTIN	F	2	13	AUSTIN	WJ	7	11	AVIS	JS	10	261
AUBREY	A	13	15	AUSTIN	F	4	12	AUSTIN	WJT	2	13	AVIS	W	3	268
AUBREY	F	1	13	AUSTIN	F	12	255	AUSTINS	J	6	14	AVIS	W	10	261
AUBREY	W	2	12	AUSTIN	F	13	16	AUTON	G	5	13	AVIS	WJ	10	6
AUBURN	E	5	13	AUSTIN	FA	5	13	AUTON	W	5	13	AVISON	A	9	222
AUBURN	WC	5	13	AUSTIN	FAA	5	13	AUTY	H	8	10	AVORY	WE	3	268
AUBUSSON	FW	2	12	AUSTIN	G	4	12	AUTY	W	8	10	AWCOCK	GJ	10	6
AUCKLAND	C	9	7	AUSTIN	G	11	12	AVANT	BF	3	268	AWCOCK	JTW	13	16
AUCKLAND	F	1	13	AUSTIN	G	12	9	AVELINE	A	6	14	AWDE	R	9	7
AUCKLAND	J	8	10	AUSTIN	GBP	13	16	AVENELL	D	13	16	AXBEY	WT	2	13
AUCKLAND	S	8	10	AUSTIN	GD	7	10	AVERIES	H	12	9	AXE	FC	2	13
AUCKLAND	W	1	13	AUSTIN	GE	4	12	AVERILL	C	6	14	AXELSON	CE	3	16
AUCOCK	GH	2	12	AUSTIN	GH	7	11	AVERILL	J	11	12	AXFORD	J	3	268
AUDEMARD	EJ	1	13	AUSTIN	GR	5	13	AVERILL	WT	11	12	AXFORD	W	12	256
AUDLEY	PW	12	9	AUSTIN	GT	3	268	AVERN	SH	7	11	AXON	CE	14	9
AUDLEY	TF	6	14	AUSTIN	GW	13	16	AVERS	W	13	16	AXON	JC	14	9
AUDLEY	W	6	14	AUSTIN	H	2	13	AVERTS	H	6	14	AXTELL	A	12	9
AUFFORTH	AGA	2	12	AUSTIN	H	7	11	AVERY	A	1	13	AXTELL	FH	5	13
AUGER	C	13	15	AUSTIN	HM	5	13	AVERY	A	3	268	AXTELL	H	5	13

AXTELL	NJ	3	268	AYLOTT	J	12	10	BABBAGE	E	3	269	BACON	AE	11	13
AXTEN	HJ	2	13	AYLWARD	AE	13	17	BABBAGE	H	3	269	BACON	AV	7	12
AXTEN	NCL	2	13	AYLWARD	CJ	13	17	BABBAGE	W	3	269	BACON	C	3	16
AXWORTHY	AF	7	11	AYLWARD	H	1	14	BABBEGE	SJ	13	17	BACON	DJ	13	18
AXWORTHY	AJ	4	13	AYLWARD	HS	13	17	BABBINGTON	J	12	256	BACON	H	3	269
AXWORTHY	C	4	13	AYLWARD	JW	7	11	BABBS	HC	7	11	BACON	H	5	14
AXWORTHY	C	10	261	AYLWARD	W	13	17	BABBS	JF	7	11	BACON	JS	9	7
AXWORTHY	J	10	6	AYLWARD	WG	7	11	BABBS	JW	9	222	BACON	R	5	14
AYERS	A	7	11	AYLWARD	WG	13	17	BABER	B	10	261	BACON	RJF	3	16
AYERS	A	11	12	AYRE	E	8	10	BABER	HA	10	7	BACON	T	12	10
AYERS	LH	2	13	AYRE	HB	5	13	BABINGTON	E	8	11	BACON	WG	7	12
AYLAND	TH	10	6	AYRE	J	3	268	BABINGTON	E	13	17	BACON	WH	3	269
AYLEN	FTJ	10	7	AYRE	J	8	10	BABINGTON	EA	6	15	BACON	WJ	13	18
AYLEN	JJ	13	16	AYRE	JM	5	13	BABINGTON	HA	13	17	BADAMS	J	6	15
AYLEN	RAA	10	7	AYRES	A	3	16	BABINGTON	WH	6	15	BADBY	TF	3	17
AYLEN	WD	13	16	AYRES	A	12	10	BACCIOCHI	G	6	15	BADCOCK	AJ	4	13
AYLES	DE	3	268	AYRES	AJ	13	17	BACH	AR	6	15	BADCOCK	EC	7	12
AYLES	GT	7	11	AYRES	C	3	16	BACH	SF	6	15	BADDELEY	HF	3	269
AYLES	HG	10	7	AYRES	EA	13	17	BACH	W	6	15	BADELOW	CW	13	18
AYLES	JA	7	11	AYRES	G	3	16	BACHCINI	C	5	13	BADELOW	S	13	18
AYLES	JA	7	11	AYRES	GF	2	14	BACHE	E	6	15	BADELOW	S	13	18
AYLES	V	4	13	AYRES	H	12	256	BACHE	JK	6	15	BADENOCH	GC	1	14
AYLESBURY	A	7	11	AYRES	HJ	3	268	BACIGALUPO	J	9	7	BADENOCK	H	8	11
AYLESBURY	C	13	16	AYRES	HJ	10	261	BACK	A	1	14	BADGER	AC	7	12
AYLESBURY	WC	7	11	AYRES	J	4	13	BACK	A	1	14	BADGER	B	3	17
AYLETT	C	3	16	AYRES	J	10	7	BACK	AE	3	16	BADGER	E	14	9
AYLETT	CE	1	13	AYRES	JA	6	15	BACK	M	3	16	BADGER	EA	1	14
AYLETT	R	1	14	AYRES	JC	12	10	BACKHOUSE	A	9	7	BADGER	F	7	12
AYLETT	RA	1	14	AYRES	JJ	12	256	BACKHOUSE	A	9	222	BADGER	GW	3	17
AYLETT	VW	1	14	AYRES	S	3	16	BACKHOUSE	A	9	222	BADGER	HW	11	13
AYLETT	W	13	16	AYRES	TP	12	256	BACKHOUSE	CA	9	7	BADGER	L	6	15
AYLETT	WA	1	14	AYRES	W	6	15	BACKHOUSE	E	8	11	BADGER	T	7	12
AYLIFFE	FCJ	3	268	AYRES	W	12	10	BACKHOUSE	EC	1	14	BADGER	W	7	12
AYLING	A	2	13	AYRES	W	12	256	BACKHOUSE	EV	4	13	BADGER	WR	6	15
AYLING	A	4	13	AYRES	W	12	256	BACKHOUSE	FW	12	10	BADHAM	E	2	14
AYLING	A	10	7	AYRES	W	14	9	BACKHOUSE	G	1	14	BADHAM	JR	2	14
AYLING	AH	4	13	AYRES	WJ	13	17	BACKHOUSE	GS	9	7	BADHAM	W	6	15
AYLING	CHJ	13	17	AYRES	WJP	10	7	BACKHOUSE	H	13	17	BADHAM	W	12	10
AYLING	D	2	13	AYRES	WT	2	14	BACKHOUSE	H	14	9	BADKIN	R	8	11
AYLING	E	10	7	AYRTEN	EW	9	7	BACKHOUSE	HF	13	18	BADLAND	EH	6	15
AYLING	F	10	7	AYRTON	A	9	222	BACKHOUSE	J	1	14	BADLAND	J	9	222
AYLING	F	13	17	AYTON	A	10	261	BACKHOUSE	J	8	11	BADLAND	SH	9	222
AYLING	FA	13	17	AYTON	AE	3	268	BACKHOUSE	J	9	222	BADMAN	LB	3	269
AYLING	FH	2	13	AYTON	EA	3	16	BACKHOUSE	J	13	18	BADMAN	RJ	3	269
AYLING	JG	2	13	AYTON	FG	3	16	BACKHOUSE	RJ	4	13	BADNELL	W	4	13
AYLING	WA	2	13	AYTON	G	1	14	BACKHOUSE	W	1	14	BADRICK	C	3	269
AYLING	WT	10	261	AYTON	RG	13	17	BACKHOUSE	W	8	11	BADRICK	C	5	14
AYLMER	E	10	7	AYTON	W	13	17	BACKHOUSE	W	14	9	BADRICK	HG	5	14
AYLMER	E	10	7	AYTON	WC	1	14	BACKLER	R	5	14	BADRICK	T	12	10
AYLMER	H	10	7	AYTON	WJ	3	16	BACKSHALL	WH	10	262	BADRICK	W	5	14
AYLOTT	AJ	2	13					BACON	A	1	14	BADSTEVENER	JW	7	12
AYLOTT	CG	5	13					BACON	A	3	269	BADSWORTH	WP	5	14
AYLOTT	CH	5	13					BACON	A	5	14	BADWELL	FJ	5	14
AYLOTT	E	1	14	BABBAGE	AJ	7	11	BACON	A	12	10	BAGELEY	J	11	13
AYLOTT	G	12	9	BABBAGE	CV	7	11	BACON	AA	3	269	BAGG	FW	4	13

B

BAGGETT	WH	3	17
BAGGIN	RW	8	11
BAGGOLEY	R	11	13
BAGGOLEY	RH	11	13
BAGGOTT	J	8	11
BAGGOTT	W	8	11
BAGGS	GW	10	7
BAGGS	TW	6	15
BAGGS	W	10	7
BAGLEY	E	4	13
BAGLEY	H	7	12
BAGLEY	JH	7	12
BAGLEY	W	4	13
BAGLEY	WCH	1	14
BAGLIN	EA	7	12
BAGLIN	G	7	12
BAGLIN	W	14	9
BAGNALL	A	6	15
BAGNALL	A	6	16
BAGNALL	A	6	16
BAGNALL	A	12	10
BAGNALL	D	6	16
BAGNALL	E	11	13
BAGNALL	FW	6	16
BAGNALL	J	8	11
BAGNALL	J	11	13
BAGNALL	J	14	9
BAGNALL	JE	6	16
BAGNALL	S	14	9
BAGOT	R	11	13
BAGOT	R	11	13
BAGRIDGE	WH	14	9
BAGSHAW	AE	13	18
BAGSHAW	G	8	11
BAGSHAW	G	14	9
BAGSHAW	J	14	9
BAGSHAW	RL	7	12
BAGSTAFF	BB	12	10
BAGULY	H	11	13
BAGWELL	A	7	12
BAGWELL	AE	4	13
BAHAIRE	F	10	7
BAILDON	J	8	11
BAILES	H	8	11
BAILES	H	8	11
BAILEY	A	3	269
BAILEY	A	4	13
BAILEY	A	4	13
BAILEY	A	6	16
BAILEY	A	7	12
BAILEY	A	9	222
BAILEY	A	10	7
BAILEY	A	13	18
BAILEY	A	14	10
BAILEY	AC	12	10
BAILEY	AE	4	13
BAILEY	AE	11	13
BAILEY	AE	12	256
BAILEY	AG	3	269
BAILEY	AG	4	13
BAILEY	AG	12	256
BAILEY	AH	2	14
BAILEY	AH	10	7
BAILEY	AH	12	10
BAILEY	AJ	1	14
BAILEY	AJ	13	18
BAILEY	AL	12	10
BAILEY	AO	6	16
BAILEY	ATC	4	14
BAILEY	AW	2	14
BAILEY	AWJ	10	7
BAILEY	B	10	8
BAILEY	B	13	18
BAILEY	C	7	12
BAILEY	C	10	8
BAILEY	C	12	256
BAILEY	C	13	18
BAILEY	CG	12	256
BAILEY	CH	1	14
BAILEY	CH	4	14
BAILEY	CO	10	8
BAILEY	CP	13	18
BAILEY	CTJ	2	14
BAILEY	CW	4	14
BAILEY	D	11	13
BAILEY	E	4	14
BAILEY	E	6	16
BAILEY	E	6	16
BAILEY	E	10	8
BAILEY	E	11	13
BAILEY	E	12	10
BAILEY	E	13	18
BAILEY	E	13	18
BAILEY	E	14	10
BAILEY	E	14	10
BAILEY	EA	1	14
BAILEY	EA	5	14
BAILEY	EDW	14	10
BAILEY	EM	4	14
BAILEY	ER	13	18
BAILEY	ET	6	16
BAILEY	F	1	15
BAILEY	F	4	14
BAILEY	F	8	11
BAILEY	F	11	13
BAILEY	F	12	256
BAILEY	F	13	18
BAILEY	F	14	10
BAILEY	FA	10	8
BAILEY	FB	12	10
BAILEY	FC	13	18
BAILEY	FF	3	269
BAILEY	FG	12	10
BAILEY	FJ	4	14
BAILEY	FR	4	14
BAILEY	FS	3	17
BAILEY	FS	13	19
BAILEY	FW	1	14
BAILEY	FW	10	8
BAILEY	FW	13	18
BAILEY	G	3	269
BAILEY	G	4	14
BAILEY	G	6	16
BAILEY	G	7	12
BAILEY	G	10	8
BAILEY	G	10	8
BAILEY	G	11	13
BAILEY	G	12	11
BAILEY	G	13	18
BAILEY	G	13	19
BAILEY	GF	2	14
BAILEY	GR	7	12
BAILEY	GW	3	17
BAILEY	GW	8	11
BAILEY	GW	10	8
BAILEY	GW	11	13
BAILEY	H	1	15
BAILEY	H	1	15
BAILEY	H	2	14
BAILEY	H	4	14
BAILEY	H	5	14
BAILEY	H	7	13
BAILEY	H	8	11
BAILEY	H	9	7
BAILEY	H	10	8
BAILEY	H	11	13
BAILEY	H	13	19
BAILEY	H	14	10
BAILEY	H	14	10
BAILEY	H	14	10
BAILEY	HA	3	269
BAILEY	HA	7	13
BAILEY	HC	5	14
BAILEY	HD	12	256
BAILEY	HG	4	14
BAILEY	HH	7	13
BAILEY	HH	10	8
BAILEY	HJ	7	13
BAILEY	HJ	7	13
BAILEY	HP	5	14
BAILEY	HR	3	270
BAILEY	HT	14	10
BAILEY	J	5	14
BAILEY	J	6	16
BAILEY	J	6	16
BAILEY	J	7	13
BAILEY	J	8	11
BAILEY	J	10	8
BAILEY	J	11	13
BAILEY	J	11	14
BAILEY	J	11	14
BAILEY	J	11	14
BAILEY	J	11	14
BAILEY	J	14	10
BAILEY	JE	4	14
BAILEY	JE	10	8
BAILEY	JH	5	14
BAILEY	JH	14	10
BAILEY	JHJ	10	8
BAILEY	JJ	4	14
BAILEY	JP	10	8
BAILEY	JR	13	19
BAILEY	JW	1	15
BAILEY	JW	3	270
BAILEY	JW	7	13
BAILEY	JW	11	14
BAILEY	LT	5	14
BAILEY	M	10	8
BAILEY	M	12	11
BAILEY	N	11	14
BAILEY	NA	1	15
BAILEY	P	7	13
BAILEY	PH	4	14
BAILEY	PH	10	8
BAILEY	PJ	12	11
BAILEY	PRA	10	8
BAILEY	PW	13	19
BAILEY	R	1	15
BAILEY	R	12	11
BAILEY	RC	12	11
BAILEY	RW	6	16
BAILEY	S	4	14
BAILEY	S	8	11
BAILEY	S	12	11
BAILEY	S	14	10
BAILEY	SJ	12	256
BAILEY	SW	3	270
BAILEY	T	6	16
BAILEY	T	8	11
BAILEY	T	11	14
BAILEY	T	14	10
BAILEY	TA	6	16
BAILEY	TC	4	14
BAILEY	TE	2	14
BAILEY	TE	8	12
BAILEY	TF	10	9
BAILEY	V	10	9
BAILEY	VC	7	13
BAILEY	W	4	14
BAILEY	W	4	14

BAILEY	W	6	16	BAINES	A	11	14	BAKER	AA	7	14	BAKER	DF	13	19				
BAILEY	W	6	16	BAINES	A	12	257	BAKER	AC	3	270	BAKER	DJ	13	19				
BAILEY	W	7	13	BAINES	AS	1	15	BAKER	AC	7	14	BAKER	E	3	270				
BAILEY	W	7	13	BAINES	AT	1	15	BAKER	AC	13	19	BAKER	E	5	15				
BAILEY	W	8	12	BAINES	CW	2	14	BAKER	AE	3	270	BAKER	E	5	15				
BAILEY	W	9	7	BAINES	F	9	8	BAKER	AE	4	15	BAKER	E	7	14				
BAILEY	W	11	14	BAINES	H	8	12	BAKER	AE	4	15	BAKER	E	9	8				
BAILEY	W	11	14	BAINES	HC	6	17	BAKER	AE	7	14	BAKER	E	12	257				
BAILEY	W	11	14	BAINES	J	5	14	BAKER	AE	7	14	BAKER	E	12	257				
BAILEY	W	12	256	BAINES	J	14	11	BAKER	AE	10	9	BAKER	EAH	6	17				
BAILEY	W	12	256	BAINES	J	14	11	BAKER	AE	10	262	BAKER	EC	10	9				
BAILEY	W	13	19	BAINES	J	14	11	BAKER	AE	13	19	BAKER	EE	1	15				
BAILEY	W	14	10	BAINES	JTA	12	257	BAKER	AF	4	15	BAKER	EG	1	15				
BAILEY	W	14	10	BAINES	JW	14	11	BAKER	AF	4	15	BAKER	EJ	12	11				
BAILEY	W	14	10	BAINES	L	4	15	BAKER	AF	10	262	BAKER	EL	4	15				
BAILEY	WC	4	14	BAINES	M	8	12	BAKER	AG	4	15	BAKER	ET	3	270				
BAILEY	WF	4	15	BAINES	R	6	17	BAKER	AG	5	15	BAKER	ET	10	9				
BAILEY	WG	4	15	BAINES	R	9	222	BAKER	AG	6	17	BAKER	EW	4	15				
BAILEY	WG	7	13	BAINES	T	8	12	BAKER	AG	7	14	BAKER	F	1	15				
BAILEY	WH	10	9	BAINES	T	11	14	BAKER	AJ	4	15	BAKER	F	1	15				
BAILEY	WHJ	4	15	BAINES	W	5	14	BAKER	AJ	10	262	BAKER	F	4	16				
BAILEY	WJ	1	15	BAINES	W	8	12	BAKER	AJ	12	11	BAKER	F	4	16				
BAILEY	WJ	4	14	BAINES	W	8	12	BAKER	AJ	13	19	BAKER	F	6	17				
BAILEY	WJ	7	13	BAINES	WC	12	257	BAKER	AM	10	9	BAKER	F	7	14				
BAILEY	WJ	10	9	BAINES	WJ	5	14	BAKER	AR	3	270	BAKER	F	7	14				
BAILEY	WJ	10	9	BAIRD	E	11	14	BAKER	AR	4	15	BAKER	F	8	12				
BAILEY	WJ	14	10	BAIRD	J	11	14	BAKER	ATC	4	15	BAKER	F	8	12				
BAILEY	WJH	3	270	BAIRD	J	11	14	BAKER	AV	1	15	BAKER	F	12	257				
BAILEY	WJP	4	15	BAIRNSTONE	W	9	8	BAKER	AW	10	9	BAKER	F	13	19				
BAILEY	WN	1	15	BAIRSTON	W	9	222	BAKER	B	4	15	BAKER	FA	1	15				
BAILEY	WR	7	13	BAIRSTOW	A	9	380	BAKER	B	7	14	BAKER	FF	10	9				
BAILEY	WR	7	13	BAIRSTOW	A	9	380	BAKER	B	7	14	BAKER	FG	2	14				
BAILEY	WS	6	16	BAIRSTOW	E	8	12	BAKER	B	8	12	BAKER	FJ	1	16				
BAILEY	WT	4	15	BAIRSTOW	H	9	8	BAKER	BF	4	15	BAKER	FJ	3	17				
BAILEY	WT	7	13	BAIRSTOW	J	9	8	BAKER	BG	10	262	BAKER	FJ	10	262				
BAILEY	WT	11	14	BAIRSTOW	J	9	8	BAKER	BJ	6	17	BAKER	FR	1	16				
BAILEY	WV	14	10	BAIRSTOW	JB	9	380	BAKER	BT	7	14	BAKER	FW	6	17				
BAILIFF	W	11	14	BAIRSTOW	JW	9	8	BAKER	C	2	14	BAKER	FW	6	17				
BAILY	BW	13	19	BAIRSTOW	W	9	8	BAKER	C	9	8	BAKER	FW	7	14				
BAIN	G	7	13	BAISLEY	C	12	11	BAKER	C	9	8	BAKER	FW	7	14				
BAIN	RG	1	15	BAITES	H	9	380	BAKER	C	10	9	BAKER	G	1	16				
BAIN	W	2	14	BAKER	A	1	15	BAKER	C	11	14	BAKER	G	4	16				
BAINBOROUGH	EJ	1	15	BAKER	A	1	15	BAKER	C	12	11	BAKER	G	5	15				
BAINBRIDGE	A	11	14	BAKER	A	3	270	BAKER	C	12	257	BAKER	G	5	15				
BAINBRIDGE	A	11	14	BAKER	A	4	15	BAKER	CC	12	257	BAKER	G	8	12				
BAINBRIDGE	A	14	10	BAKER	A	4	15	BAKER	CE	13	19	BAKER	G	9	8				
BAINBRIDGE	E	8	12	BAKER	A	6	17	BAKER	CF	7	14	BAKER	G	10	9				
BAINBRIDGE	FG	7	13	BAKER	A	6	17	BAKER	CFJ	3	270	BAKER	G	10	9				
BAINBRIDGE	HE	9	8	BAKER	A	6	17	BAKER	CH	3	270	BAKER	G	10	262				
BAINBRIDGE	HG	7	14	BAKER	A	6	17	BAKER	CH	4	15	BAKER	G	13	19				
BAINBRIDGE	HJ	7	14	BAKER	A	6	17	BAKER	CH	10	9	BAKER	GC	13	19				
BAINBRIDGE	WR	7	14	BAKER	A	8	12	BAKER	CR	1	15	BAKER	GE	1	16				
BAINES	A	9	8	BAKER	A	10	9	BAKER	CW	10	262	BAKER	GE	4	16				
BAINES	A	9	8	BAKER	A	10	9	BAKER	CWR	11	15	BAKER	GE	4	16				
BAINES	A	9	222	BAKER	A	10	262	BAKER	D	2	14	BAKER	GE	12	11				

BAKER	GE	13	19	BAKER	J	11	15	BAKER	T	2	15	BAKER	WW	13	20
BAKER	GE	13	19	BAKER	J	12	11	BAKER	T	3	270	BAKERSON	L	14	11
BAKER	GF	6	17	BAKER	J	13	20	BAKER	T	4	17	BAKES	J	9	9
BAKER	GF	6	17	BAKER	JA	9	9	BAKER	T	5	15	BAKEWELL	H	7	15
BAKER	GR	10	9	BAKER	JA	13	20	BAKER	T	7	15	BAKEWELL	LM	11	15
BAKER	GT	10	262	BAKER	JAL	4	16	BAKER	T	7	15	BAKEWELL	WH	6	18
BAKER	GW	2	14	BAKER	JCS	7	15	BAKER	T	12	11	BALCH	A	3	271
BAKER	GW	5	15	BAKER	JE	2	15	BAKER	T	13	20	BALCH	FS	4	17
BAKER	GW	12	11	BAKER	JE	2	15	BAKER	T	14	11	BALCH	HG	4	17
BAKER	GW	12	257	BAKER	JE	10	10	BAKER	T	14	11	BALCHEN	AT	13	20
BAKER	GW	13	19	BAKER	JG	13	20	BAKER	TC	4	17	BALCOM	H	10	10
BAKER	H	2	14	BAKER	JH	4	16	BAKER	TH	13	20	BALCOM	JE	6	18
BAKER	H	2	14	BAKER	JH	4	16	BAKER	TW	6	18	BALCOMBE	A	3	271
BAKER	H	3	270	BAKER	JH	4	16	BAKER	W	1	16	BALCOMBE	J	13	20
BAKER	H	4	16	BAKER	JJ	4	16	BAKER	W	1	16	BALCOMBE	JJ	13	21
BAKER	H	4	16	BAKER	JR	1	15	BAKER	W	2	15	BALDERSON	A	12	257
BAKER	H	5	15	BAKER	JRC	13	20	BAKER	W	2	15	BALDERSON	BH	12	257
BAKER	H	5	15	BAKER	JT	6	18	BAKER	W	3	17	BALDERSON	FC	12	257
BAKER	H	6	17	BAKER	JW	1	16	BAKER	W	3	270	BALDING	H	14	11
BAKER	H	7	14	BAKER	JW	1	16	BAKER	W	4	17	BALDING	RH	6	18
BAKER	H	7	14	BAKER	JW	6	18	BAKER	W	5	15	BALDOCK	AG	5	15
BAKER	H	9	8	BAKER	JW	6	18	BAKER	W	5	15	BALDOCK	AW	10	10
BAKER	HC	1	16	BAKER	JW	7	15	BAKER	W	6	18	BALDOCK	DL	12	11
BAKER	HC	4	16	BAKER	JW	13	20	BAKER	W	7	15	BALDOCK	EA	12	11
BAKER	HC	10	9	BAKER	K	13	20	BAKER	W	8	12	BALDOCK	F	8	12
BAKER	HE	4	16	BAKER	L	3	270	BAKER	W	8	12	BALDOCK	F	13	21
BAKER	HG	5	15	BAKER	L	5	15	BAKER	W	9	9	BALDOCK	H	6	18
BAKER	HG	7	14	BAKER	LA	5	15	BAKER	W	10	10	BALDOCK	JF	4	17
BAKER	HH	7	15	BAKER	LA	10	10	BAKER	W	12	257	BALDOCK	JW	12	12
BAKER	HJ	3	270	BAKER	LRJ	4	16	BAKER	W	13	20	BALDOCK	T	12	12
BAKER	HJ	10	10	BAKER	LT	13	20	BAKER	W	14	11	BALDOCK	W	6	18
BAKER	HJ	10	262	BAKER	M	14	11	BAKER	WA	5	15	BALDOCK	WF	3	17
BAKER	HJ	13	20	BAKER	M	14	11	BAKER	WA	6	18	BALDOCK	WG	3	17
BAKER	HJW	7	15	BAKER	ML	14	11	BAKER	WA	13	20	BALDOCK	WG	10	10
BAKER	HJW	7	15	BAKER	P	4	16	BAKER	WB	1	16	BALDOCK	WT	6	18
BAKER	HL	1	16	BAKER	PC	7	15	BAKER	WC	10	262	BALDREY	FG	12	12
BAKER	HT	2	14	BAKER	PE	7	15	BAKER	WCE	4	17	BALDRICK	JL	2	15
BAKER	I	4	16	BAKER	PW	2	15	BAKER	WD	3	17	BALDRY	AJ	3	17
BAKER	I	10	262	BAKER	R	3	270	BAKER	WEJ	13	20	BALDRY	EE	7	15
BAKER	J	1	15	BAKER	R	4	16	BAKER	WG	4	17	BALDRY	J	3	271
BAKER	J	2	15	BAKER	R	4	17	BAKER	WH	1	16	BALDRY	JW	3	271
BAKER	J	3	17	BAKER	R	6	18	BAKER	WH	4	17	BALDRY	W	7	15
BAKER	J	3	17	BAKER	R	11	15	BAKER	WH	4	17	BALDWIN	A	1	16
BAKER	J	4	16	BAKER	R	13	20	BAKER	WH	4	17	BALDWIN	A	5	15
BAKER	J	5	15	BAKER	R	13	20	BAKER	WH	6	18	BALDWIN	A	9	222
BAKER	J	5	15	BAKER	RA	12	11	BAKER	WH	7	15	BALDWIN	AC	1	16
BAKER	J	6	17	BAKER	RJ	4	17	BAKER	WH	12	11	BALDWIN	AC	12	257
BAKER	J	6	17	BAKER	RV	12	257	BAKER	WJ	3	271	BALDWIN	AE	5	16
BAKER	J	6	17	BAKER	S	8	415	BAKER	WJ	4	17	BALDWIN	AV	3	17
BAKER	J	6	18	BAKER	S	10	10	BAKER	WJ	4	17	BALDWIN	BH	13	21
BAKER	J	7	15	BAKER	S	12	11	BAKER	WJ	12	257	BALDWIN	C	5	16
BAKER	J	9	8	BAKER	SH	6	18	BAKER	WJH	6	18	BALDWIN	C	8	12
BAKER	J	9	9	BAKER	SHJ	4	17	BAKER	WS	13	20	BALDWIN	CA	13	21
BAKER	J	10	262	BAKER	SO	10	262	BAKER	WT	6	18	BALDWIN	CHR	12	12
BAKER	J	11	15	BAKER	T	1	16	BAKER	WW	6	18	BALDWIN	E	2	15

Surname	Initials	No.	No.
BALDWIN	E	2	15
BALDWIN	E	8	12
BALDWIN	E	9	9
BALDWIN	F	2	15
BALDWIN	F	11	15
BALDWIN	F	13	21
BALDWIN	FG	5	16
BALDWIN	FW	10	262
BALDWIN	G	12	257
BALDWIN	GL	14	11
BALDWIN	GL	14	11
BALDWIN	H	1	16
BALDWIN	H	5	16
BALDWIN	H	5	16
BALDWIN	H	8	12
BALDWIN	H	10	10
BALDWIN	H	13	21
BALDWIN	J	2	15
BALDWIN	J	6	19
BALDWIN	J	11	15
BALDWIN	JE	5	16
BALDWIN	JF	13	21
BALDWIN	JH	7	15
BALDWIN	JH	13	21
BALDWIN	JHJ	4	17
BALDWIN	JT	12	257
BALDWIN	JW	3	271
BALDWIN	JW	3	271
BALDWIN	JW	5	16
BALDWIN	JW	5	16
BALDWIN	L	1	16
BALDWIN	L	6	18
BALDWIN	L	9	9
BALDWIN	L	9	222
BALDWIN	P	9	9
BALDWIN	R	3	271
BALDWIN	W	1	16
BALDWIN	W	5	16
BALDWIN	W	11	15
BALDWIN	WE	1	16
BALDWIN	WF	12	12
BALDWIN	WG	5	16
BALDWIN	WH	1	16
BALDWIN	WH	5	16
BALDWIN	WJ	12	12
BALDWIN	WJ	12	257
BALES	JH	3	271
BALES	NAF	3	17
BALESTERI	E	8	13
BALFE	J	14	11
BALFOUR	A	3	17
BALFOUR	HE	5	16
BALK	J	8	415
BALKWILL-LACY	H	2	15
BALL	A	1	16
BALL	A	3	271
BALL	A	10	262
BALL	A	11	15
BALL	A	13	21
BALL	A	14	11
BALL	AE	3	271
BALL	AE	3	271
BALL	AH	11	15
BALL	AJ	6	19
BALL	AJ	7	15
BALL	AR	13	21
BALL	AT	3	271
BALL	AW	3	271
BALL	AW	4	17
BALL	AW	12	257
BALL	B	6	19
BALL	BAJ	10	10
BALL	BJ	2	15
BALL	CA	2	15
BALL	CE	1	16
BALL	CJ	6	19
BALL	CS	4	17
BALL	CW	13	21
BALL	D	1	16
BALL	DW	10	10
BALL	E	4	17
BALL	E	6	19
BALL	E	8	13
BALL	EC	7	15
BALL	EM	4	18
BALL	F	4	18
BALL	F	6	19
BALL	F	12	12
BALL	FA	10	10
BALL	FC	5	16
BALL	FE	6	19
BALL	FL	6	19
BALL	G	6	19
BALL	G	6	19
BALL	G	7	16
BALL	G	8	13
BALL	GA	6	19
BALL	GE	1	17
BALL	GR	10	10
BALL	GW	6	19
BALL	H	1	17
BALL	H	2	15
BALL	H	5	16
BALL	H	6	19
BALL	H	9	9
BALL	H	13	21
BALL	H	13	21
BALL	HG	7	16
BALL	HG	13	21
BALL	HH	5	16
BALL	HW	7	16
BALL	HW	7	16
BALL	J	3	18
BALL	J	6	19
BALL	J	7	16
BALL	J	11	15
BALL	J	11	15
BALL	J	12	12
BALL	J	14	11
BALL	JD	13	21
BALL	JF	1	17
BALL	JH	3	271
BALL	JJ	6	19
BALL	JR	14	11
BALL	JW	6	19
BALL	JW	7	16
BALL	JW	8	13
BALL	JW	14	12
BALL	L	10	262
BALL	LCR	6	19
BALL	P	9	223
BALL	PH	7	16
BALL	R	4	18
BALL	R	6	19
BALL	R	11	15
BALL	R	14	12
BALL	RR	4	18
BALL	RS	12	12
BALL	RW	3	271
BALL	S	6	19
BALL	S	12	12
BALL	SJ	7	16
BALL	W	4	18
BALL	W	4	18
BALL	W	6	19
BALL	W	6	20
BALL	W	9	9
BALL	W	9	223
BALL	W	9	223
BALL	W	14	12
BALL	WC	4	18
BALL	WD	1	16
BALL	WE	6	20
BALL	WE	7	16
BALL	WG	3	271
BALL	WH	4	18
BALL	WH	5	16
BALL	WH	6	20
BALL	WH	7	16
BALL	WJ	10	263
BALL	WJ	12	258
BALL	WM	11	15
BALLAM	A	14	12
BALLAM	AE	5	16
BALLAM	AJ	5	16
BALLAM	J	13	21
BALLANCE	A	1	17
BALLANCE	CH	8	13
BALLANCE	T	1	17
BALLANTINE	A	5	17
BALLANTYNE	E	8	13
BALLANTYNE	GHP	2	15
BALLANTYNE	GW	9	223
BALLARD	A	1	17
BALLARD	A	3	271
BALLARD	A	6	20
BALLARD	A	7	16
BALLARD	AC	5	17
BALLARD	AH	13	21
BALLARD	AS	1	17
BALLARD	CH	12	12
BALLARD	EJ	5	17
BALLARD	F	2	15
BALLARD	G	1	17
BALLARD	G	5	17
BALLARD	H	5	17
BALLARD	J	1	17
BALLARD	J	1	17
BALLARD	JT	4	18
BALLARD	JT	7	16
BALLARD	L	5	17
BALLARD	RG	10	10
BALLARD	SR	10	10
BALLARD	T	1	17
BALLARD	TW	13	21
BALLARD	W	2	16
BALLARD	W	7	16
BALLARD	WJ	6	20
BALLENNIE	GW	10	10
BALLER	GF	7	16
BALLINGALL	W	11	15
BALLM	CL	12	12
BALM	HH	2	16
BALM	HP	2	16
BALMAN	A	13	21
BALMER	GT	10	10
BALMFORTH	A	8	13
BALMFORTH	A	8	13
BALMFORTH	E	9	223
BALMFORTH	GH	8	13
BALMFORTH	JE	7	16
BALMOND	WA	10	10
BALMONEN	I	4	18
BALSON	FT	4	18
BALSON	R	4	18
BALSTON	H	4	18
BAMBER	G	11	15
BAMBER	H	8	415
BAMBER	T	11	15
BAMBERGER	ES	10	10

BAMBERGER	FLJ	13	22
BAMBERY	J	7	16
BAMBRIDGE	FC	1	17
BAMBRIDGE	FC	3	272
BAMBRIDGE	M	1	17
BAMBRIDGE	M	3	271
BAMBRIDGE	SH	7	16
BAMBRIDGE	WT	12	12
BAMBRIDGE	WT	12	12
BAMBROOK	A	5	17
BAMBROUGH	HH	4	18
BAMBROUGH	SC	4	18
BAMBURY	B	4	18
BAMFIELD	F	8	13
BAMFORD	AC	12	258
BAMFORD	E	6	20
BAMFORD	E	8	13
BAMFORD	FH	6	20
BAMFORD	G	11	15
BAMFORD	H	11	16
BAMFORD	J	11	16
BAMFORD	JW	14	12
BAMFORD	R	14	12
BAMFORD	S	6	20
BAMFORD	S	6	20
BAMFORD	W	6	20
BAMFORD	WH	8	13
BAMPING	A	14	12
BAMPTON	AV	10	11
BAMPTON	HG	4	18
BAMPTON	J	4	18
BAMPTON	L	6	20
BAMPTON	WD	10	11
BAMPTON	WH	10	11
BAMRBOUGH	W	4	18
BANBURY	CW	13	22
BANBURY	JE	13	22
BANBURY	WT	13	22
BANCE	H	13	22
BANCROFT	E	8	13
BANCROFT	JW	11	16
BANCROFT	P	11	16
BANCROFT	RI	10	11
BANCROFT	T	2	16
BANCROFT	TH	14	12
BANCROFT	TO	2	16
BAND	H	13	22
BANDEY	A	3	272
BANDY	A	5	17
BANDY	AE	5	17
BANDY	AFW	5	17
BANDY	CJ	12	12
BANDY	EL	5	17
BANDY	EW	5	17
BANDY	JA	5	17
BANDY	JD	7	16
BANDY	JF	12	258
BANDY	LJ	12	12
BANDY	R	5	17
BANDY	WG	5	17
BANDY	WJ	5	17
BANE	S	1	17
BANES	FJ	12	12
BANFIELD	A	3	18
BANFIELD	A	7	16
BANFIELD	B	5	17
BANFIELD	CJ	12	12
BANFIELD	EJ	10	11
BANFIELD	FJ	3	272
BANFIELD	G	4	18
BANFIELD	H	7	16
BANFIELD	JG	7	17
BANFIELD	PA	7	17
BANFIELD	VE	4	19
BANFIELD	W	13	22
BANFORD	A	6	20
BANFORD	A	6	20
BANFORD	H	3	272
BANFORD	J	6	20
BANFORD	J	6	20
BANFORD	W	6	20
BANGAY	FWA	3	272
BANGAY	H	3	272
BANGER	HW	4	19
BANGERT	FG	1	17
BANGERT	L	3	18
BANGLE	A	5	17
BANGS	EJ	7	17
BANGS	G	5	17
BANGS	GW	1	17
BANGS	H	5	17
BANGS	J	3	272
BANGS	W	1	17
BANHAM	A	13	22
BANHAM	E	13	22
BANHAM	HA	7	17
BANHAM	T	14	12
BANHAM	T	14	12
BANKOFSKY	A	14	12
BANKS	A	4	19
BANKS	A	4	19
BANKS	A	5	18
BANKS	A	8	13
BANKS	A	13	22
BANKS	AD	10	263
BANKS	AE	9	9
BANKS	AH	13	22
BANKS	AS	13	22
BANKS	B	4	19
BANKS	BA	7	17
BANKS	C	1	17
BANKS	C	5	18
BANKS	C	6	20
BANKS	C	12	13
BANKS	CA	1	17
BANKS	D	4	19
BANKS	E	4	19
BANKS	E	8	13
BANKS	E	10	11
BANKS	E	11	16
BANKS	EJ	1	17
BANKS	F	7	17
BANKS	F	7	17
BANKS	F	7	17
BANKS	F	9	9
BANKS	F	13	22
BANKS	FH	9	9
BANKS	FW	13	22
BANKS	G	4	19
BANKS	G	4	19
BANKS	G	5	18
BANKS	G	10	263
BANKS	GE	13	22
BANKS	GJ	13	22
BANKS	H	4	19
BANKS	H	4	19
BANKS	H	6	20
BANKS	HE	10	11
BANKS	HP	1	17
BANKS	J	1	17
BANKS	J	5	18
BANKS	J	11	16
BANKS	J	11	16
BANKS	J	11	16
BANKS	JE	13	22
BANKS	JH	7	17
BANKS	JO	10	263
BANKS	JW	9	9
BANKS	L	2	16
BANKS	L	14	12
BANKS	LA	1	17
BANKS	LH	10	263
BANKS	LW	6	20
BANKS	O	4	19
BANKS	P	4	19
BANKS	P	5	18
BANKS	S	2	16
BANKS	T	6	21
BANKS	V	7	17
BANKS	W	4	19
BANKS	W	6	21
BANKS	W	9	9
BANKS	W	9	223
BANKS	WC	13	22
BANKS	WF	12	258
BANKS	WG	7	17
BANKS	WH	10	263
BANKS	WJ	11	16
BANN	E	14	12
BANN	S	14	12
BANNELL	C	4	19
BANNELL	J	4	19
BANNER	AE	14	12
BANNER	B	6	21
BANNER	J	8	13
BANNER	S	14	12
BANNER	W	8	13
BANNER	WJ	6	21
BANNING	A	7	17
BANNING	AE	7	17
BANNING	AW	1	18
BANNISTER	A	6	21
BANNISTER	A	8	13
BANNISTER	A	13	23
BANNISTER	AE	11	16
BANNISTER	AG	10	11
BANNISTER	E	9	9
BANNISTER	GAL	1	18
BANNISTER	GE	6	21
BANNISTER	H	8	13
BANNISTER	H	9	9
BANNISTER	J	8	13
BANNISTER	J	8	14
BANNISTER	JW	10	11
BANNISTER	RC	14	12
BANNISTER	W	8	14
BANNISTER	WA	6	21
BANNISTER	WH	9	223
BANNISTER	WJ	6	21
BANNON	E	11	16
BANNON	P	14	13
BANTICK	FW	8	14
BANTICK	JW	8	14
BANTIN	HP	2	16
BANTING	E	7	17
BANTOCK	R	14	13
BANTON	J	11	16
BANYARD	GH	9	9
BANYARD	RJ	10	11
BAPTISTE	HC	4	19
BAPTY	A	8	14
BAPTY	H	8	14
BAPTY	L	8	14
BAPTY	W	8	14
BARB	F	1	18
BARB	G	2	16
BARBARA	A	10	11
BARBARY	WJ	7	17
BARBEARY	AE	10	11
BARBER	A	3	18

BARBER	A	4	19	BARBER	T	8	14	BARDSLEY	H	11	17	BARKER	A	11	17		
BARBER	A	6	21	BARBER	TH	7	18	BARDSLEY	HJ	8	14	BARKER	A	11	17		
BARBER	A	9	223	BARBER	TH	13	23	BARDSLEY	J	11	17	BARKER	A	14	13		
BARBER	A	13	23	BARBER	TJ	7	18	BARDSLEY	JN	10	263	BARKER	AC	13	24		
BARBER	AE	13	23	BARBER	TW	12	258	BARDSLEY	R	11	17	BARKER	AE	5	18		
BARBER	AG	7	17	BARBER	W	7	18	BARDSLEY	TA	14	13	BARKER	AG	1	18		
BARBER	AJ	13	23	BARBER	W	8	14	BARDWELL	RJ	10	11	BARKER	AG	12	13		
BARBER	AW	8	14	BARBER	W	12	258	BAREFOOT	TJ	13	23	BARKER	AJ	12	258		
BARBER	BA	7	17	BARBER	W	14	13	BARFE	L	5	18	BARKER	AV	13	24		
BARBER	C	8	14	BARBER	W	14	13	BARFOOT	AL	12	13	BARKER	AW	7	18		
BARBER	C	13	23	BARBER	WA	6	21	BARFOOT	CE	4	20	BARKER	BMJ	1	18		
BARBER	CB	13	23	BARBER	WB	5	18	BARFOOT	CW	4	20	BARKER	C	5	18		
BARBER	CH	3	18	BARBER	WC	2	16	BARFOOT	E	4	20	BARKER	C	5	19		
BARBER	CWS	4	19	BARBER	WG	5	18	BARFOOT	EG	10	11	BARKER	C	5	19		
BARBER	D	13	23	BARBER	WJ	12	258	BARFOOT	EG	12	13	BARKER	C	7	18		
BARBER	E	6	21	BARBER	WP	7	18	BARFOOT	F	5	18	BARKER	C	7	18		
BARBER	E	10	11	BARBER	WS	7	18	BARFOOT	G	4	20	BARKER	C	9	10		
BARBER	E	13	23	BARBER	WT	8	14	BARFOOT	GW	10	11	BARKER	C	11	17		
BARBER	E	14	13	BARBER	WW	7	18	BARFOOT	HG	13	23	BARKER	C	13	24		
BARBER	EFR	13	23	BARBET	WG	7	18	BARFOOT	HS	12	13	BARKER	C	14	13		
BARBER	EW	1	18	BARBET	WJ	7	18	BARFOOT	I	5	18	BARKER	CA	12	258		
BARBER	F	9	223	BARBIER	A	4	20	BARFOOT	LC	4	20	BARKER	CH	2	16		
BARBER	F	12	13	BARBIER	A	4	20	BARFOOT	LG	4	20	BARKER	CW	13	24		
BARBER	FA	12	258	BARBOUR	JR	5	18	BARFOOT	R	4	20	BARKER	DG	8	15		
BARBER	FC	5	18	BARBOUR	W	5	18	BARFOOT	RF	4	20	BARKER	DS	13	24		
BARBER	FC	10	11	BARBURY	FA	7	18	BARFORD	E	5	18	BARKER	E	1	18		
BARBER	FM	6	21	BARCLAY	AE	8	14	BARFORD	J	12	258	BARKER	E	2	16		
BARBER	FT	4	19	BARCLAY	AS	13	23	BARFORD	PR	5	18	BARKER	E	5	19		
BARBER	FW	4	20	BARCLAY	H	8	14	BARFORD	SGW	13	24	BARKER	E	8	15		
BARBER	G	3	18	BARCLAY	JF	7	18	BARFORD	W	12	258	BARKER	E	9	10		
BARBER	G	4	20	BARCLAY	T	11	16	BARGATE	J	8	14	BARKER	E	9	223		
BARBER	G	6	21	BARCLAY	VAW	3	272	BARGE	AA	4	20	BARKER	E	11	17		
BARBER	GH	11	16	BARCOCK	AG	12	13	BARGE	HE	4	20	BARKER	EC	12	13		
BARBER	H	9	9	BARCOCK	HW	12	13	BARGENT	WR	10	12	BARKER	EC	12	258		
BARBER	H	12	258	BARDELL	A	7	18	BARGER	W	10	11	BARKER	EE	7	19		
BARBER	HE	7	17	BARDELL	C	13	23	BARGETON	CJ	2	16	BARKER	EL	8	15		
BARBER	HG	13	23	BARDELL	H	6	21	BARGETON	JJ	1	18	BARKER	ER	6	22		
BARBER	HJ	13	23	BARDELL	W	7	18	BARGETON	PB	1	18	BARKER	ES	1	18		
BARBER	J	4	20	BARDELL	W	12	13	BARGETON	SM	1	18	BARKER	EW	1	18		
BARBER	J	6	21	BARDEN	B	1	18	BARGH	L	14	13	BARKER	EW	7	19		
BARBER	J	8	14	BARDEN	E	13	23	BARHAM	A	7	18	BARKER	F	1	18		
BARBER	J	11	16	BARDEN	FH	12	13	BARHAM	CL	5	18	BARKER	F	1	18		
BARBER	J	12	258	BARDEN	FH	12	13	BARHAM	F	7	18	BARKER	F	9	10		
BARBER	JH	10	263	BARDEN	HG	12	13	BARHAM	RS	7	18	BARKER	F	9	10		
BARBER	JH	11	16	BARDEN	RF	13	23	BARHAM	WH	4	20	BARKER	F	9	223		
BARBER	JR	7	18	BARDEN	W	12	258	BARK	S	9	10	BARKER	F	11	17		
BARBER	N	12	258	BARDEN	WG	3	18	BARKER	A	5	18	BARKER	F	12	13		
BARBER	OJ	7	17	BARDEN	WG	12	13	BARKER	A	5	18	BARKER	FE	4	20		
BARBER	P	7	17	BARDILL	H	1	18	BARKER	A	6	21	BARKER	FG	10	263		
BARBER	P	12	13	BARDRICK	AE	13	23	BARKER	A	6	21	BARKER	FJ	4	20		
BARBER	S	10	11	BARDRICK	GT	13	23	BARKER	A	6	22	BARKER	G	1	19		
BARBER	S	12	13	BARDSLEY	D	11	16	BARKER	A	8	14	BARKER	G	5	19		
BARBER	S	14	13	BARDSLEY	G	11	16	BARKER	A	8	15	BARKER	G	5	19		
BARBER	SJ	6	21	BARDSLEY	G	11	17	BARKER	A	9	10	BARKER	G	8	15		
BARBER	T	6	21	BARDSLEY	G	14	13	BARKER	A	9	223	BARKER	G	8	15		

BARKER	G	9	10	BARKER	S	11	17	BARLOW	AJ	11	17	BARLOW	T	8	16
BARKER	G	9	10	BARKER	SB	8	15	BARLOW	AJ	13	24	BARLOW	T	14	14
BARKER	GA	14	13	BARKER	ST	1	18	BARLOW	AR	14	13	BARLOW	T	14	14
BARKER	GE	7	19	BARKER	T	6	22	BARLOW	B	14	13	BARLOW	T	14	14
BARKER	GE	10	12	BARKER	T	8	15	BARLOW	BW	14	14	BARLOW	TE	11	19
BARKER	GE	11	17	BARKER	T	8	15	BARLOW	C	9	10	BARLOW	TH	13	24
BARKER	GF	2	16	BARKER	T	8	15	BARLOW	C	11	18	BARLOW	TW	11	19
BARKER	GF	8	15	BARKER	T	9	380	BARLOW	C	14	14	BARLOW	W	11	19
BARKER	GH	5	19	BARKER	T	11	17	BARLOW	C	14	14	BARLOW	W	11	19
BARKER	GH	13	24	BARKER	TE	8	15	BARLOW	CF	11	18	BARLOW	W	11	19
BARKER	GN	13	24	BARKER	TG	12	258	BARLOW	CWJ	12	14	BARLOW	W	14	14
BARKER	GW	6	22	BARKER	TH	10	12	BARLOW	E	6	22	BARLOW	W	14	14
BARKER	H	1	18	BARKER	W	1	18	BARLOW	E	6	22	BARLOW	WS	4	21
BARKER	H	6	22	BARKER	W	1	18	BARLOW	E	9	10	BARLTROP	EJ	4	21
BARKER	H	7	19	BARKER	W	1	19	BARLOW	E	11	18	BARMFORTH	H	8	16
BARKER	H	8	15	BARKER	W	4	21	BARLOW	E	11	18	BARNABY	FE	13	25
BARKER	H	8	15	BARKER	W	5	19	BARLOW	FA	11	18	BARNABY	J	4	21
BARKER	H	11	17	BARKER	W	5	19	BARLOW	FJ	6	22	BARNACLE	CW	6	22
BARKER	H	12	13	BARKER	W	8	15	BARLOW	FW	2	16	BARNARD	AG	3	18
BARKER	H	13	24	BARKER	W	8	15	BARLOW	G	6	22	BARNARD	AH	13	25
BARKER	HD	2	16	BARKER	W	8	16	BARLOW	G	12	14	BARNARD	C	13	25
BARKER	J	1	18	BARKER	W	8	16	BARLOW	G	14	14	BARNARD	E	13	25
BARKER	J	3	272	BARKER	W	9	223	BARLOW	GE	11	18	BARNARD	EF	10	12
BARKER	J	7	19	BARKER	W	10	12	BARLOW	GE	14	14	BARNARD	EJ	13	25
BARKER	J	8	15	BARKER	W	12	14	BARLOW	H	5	19	BARNARD	ER	13	25
BARKER	J	8	15	BARKER	W	12	258	BARLOW	H	9	10	BARNARD	F	6	22
BARKER	J	12	13	BARKER	W	12	259	BARLOW	H	11	18	BARNARD	FM	2	17
BARKER	J	13	24	BARKER	W	14	13	BARLOW	H	11	18	BARNARD	G	10	12
BARKER	JA	12	13	BARKER	WA	12	14	BARLOW	H	11	18	BARNARD	G	10	12
BARKER	JC	4	20	BARKER	WA	12	14	BARLOW	H	14	14	BARNARD	G	12	259
BARKER	JC	7	19	BARKER	WC	12	14	BARLOW	HJ	7	19	BARNARD	H	1	19
BARKER	JH	8	15	BARKER	WJ	12	259	BARLOW	J	6	22	BARNARD	H	3	18
BARKER	JR	7	19	BARKWOOD	WC	12	259	BARLOW	J	7	19	BARNARD	HR	2	17
BARKER	JR	13	24	BARLEY	A	12	14	BARLOW	J	11	18	BARNARD	J	12	259
BARKER	JS	11	17	BARLEY	B	12	14	BARLOW	J	11	18	BARNARD	JET	10	263
BARKER	JW	1	19	BARLEY	E	6	22	BARLOW	J	11	18	BARNARD	JT	12	259
BARKER	JW	11	17	BARLEY	F	12	14	BARLOW	J	11	18	BARNARD	JW	3	18
BARKER	JW	13	24	BARLEY	GW	6	22	BARLOW	J	11	18	BARNARD	W	2	17
BARKER	JW	13	24	BARLEY	J	3	272	BARLOW	J	13	24	BARNARD	WA	3	18
BARKER	L	1	19	BARLEY	J	12	14	BARLOW	J	14	14	BARNARD	WC	1	19
BARKER	ME	4	21	BARLEY	JW	6	22	BARLOW	JA	11	18	BARNBROOK	E	11	19
BARKER	N	9	380	BARLEY	TL	12	14	BARLOW	JA	14	14	BARNBROOK	J	10	263
BARKER	P	1	19	BARLEY	W	1	19	BARLOW	JH	2	16	BARNBY	NE	9	10
BARKER	P	12	14	BARLING	E	4	21	BARLOW	JH	11	18	BARNELL	HC	13	25
BARKER	P	12	14	BARLING	J	3	272	BARLOW	JH	11	18	BARNELL	PH	5	19
BARKER	PW	12	258	BARLOW	A	3	272	BARLOW	JW	11	18	BARNELL	RG	5	19
BARKER	R	8	15	BARLOW	A	7	19	BARLOW	LT	6	22	BARNES	A	1	19
BARKER	R	9	10	BARLOW	A	7	19	BARLOW	M	9	380	BARNES	A	4	21
BARKER	R	14	13	BARLOW	A	11	17	BARLOW	R	2	16	BARNES	A	4	21
BARKER	RH	5	19	BARLOW	A	11	17	BARLOW	R	11	18	BARNES	A	5	19
BARKER	RH	13	24	BARLOW	A	14	13	BARLOW	R	11	19	BARNES	A	11	19
BARKER	RO	13	24	BARLOW	A	14	13	BARLOW	R	14	14	BARNES	A	14	14
BARKER	RW	6	22	BARLOW	AE	6	22	BARLOW	RA	11	19	BARNES	AE	3	18
BARKER	S	8	15	BARLOW	AE	10	12	BARLOW	SD	14	14	BARNES	AE	10	12
BARKER	S	11	17	BARLOW	AH	2	16	BARLOW	T	6	22	BARNES	AE	13	25

BARNES	AH	1	19	BARNES	G	13	25	BARNES	JE	1	19	BARNES	WHP	4	22
BARNES	AH	3	272	BARNES	G	14	15	BARNES	JE	5	19	BARNES	WJ	4	22
BARNES	AH	11	19	BARNES	GA	4	21	BARNES	JE	12	259	BARNES	WJ	7	19
BARNES	AHJ	13	25	BARNES	GA	11	19	BARNES	JE	14	15	BARNES	WJ	14	15
BARNES	AJ	3	272	BARNES	GA	13	25	BARNES	JF	8	16	BARNES	WP	7	19
BARNES	AJ	3	272	BARNES	GE	1	19	BARNES	JG	9	10	BARNES	WR	13	26
BARNES	AK	1	19	BARNES	GE	3	272	BARNES	JGM	5	19	BARNETT	A	1	20
BARNES	AV	12	14	BARNES	GF	2	17	BARNES	JJ	10	12	BARNETT	A	14	15
BARNES	AW	5	19	BARNES	GJ	2	17	BARNES	JRH	14	15	BARNETT	AE	9	10
BARNES	AW	13	25	BARNES	GJ	2	17	BARNES	JW	1	19	BARNETT	AJ	7	19
BARNES	B	1	19	BARNES	GR	5	19	BARNES	JW	3	273	BARNETT	ASH	1	20
BARNES	B	5	19	BARNES	GW	1	19	BARNES	JW	4	22	BARNETT	AT	1	20
BARNES	C	4	21	BARNES	GWH	3	272	BARNES	JW	9	223	BARNETT	AW	6	23
BARNES	CA	1	19	BARNES	H	1	20	BARNES	JW	10	12	BARNETT	BJ	7	20
BARNES	CA	2	17	BARNES	H	4	21	BARNES	JW	14	15	BARNETT	C	14	15
BARNES	CE	13	25	BARNES	H	6	23	BARNES	M	7	19	BARNETT	CW	1	20
BARNES	CP	4	21	BARNES	H	7	19	BARNES	M	9	223	BARNETT	CW	2	17
BARNES	CR	6	22	BARNES	H	8	16	BARNES	N	13	26	BARNETT	DLW	11	20
BARNES	CW	4	21	BARNES	H	8	16	BARNES	P	1	19	BARNETT	E	1	20
BARNES	D	2	17	BARNES	H	8	16	BARNES	PE	11	19	BARNETT	E	14	15
BARNES	DER	6	23	BARNES	H	9	10	BARNES	R	3	18	BARNETT	EE	12	15
BARNES	E	1	19	BARNES	H	10	12	BARNES	R	11	19	BARNETT	EG	3	273
BARNES	E	1	19	BARNES	H	11	19	BARNES	R	14	15	BARNETT	EJ	6	23
BARNES	E	1	19	BARNES	H	12	14	BARNES	RE	14	15	BARNETT	F	6	23
BARNES	E	4	21	BARNES	H	13	25	BARNES	RW	12	259	BARNETT	F	14	15
BARNES	E	7	19	BARNES	H	13	25	BARNES	S	11	19	BARNETT	F	14	15
BARNES	E	13	25	BARNES	H	14	15	BARNES	S	11	19	BARNETT	FD	4	22
BARNES	E	14	14	BARNES	HA	1	20	BARNES	S	11	20	BARNETT	FJ	7	20
BARNES	EG	13	25	BARNES	HA	10	263	BARNES	S	13	26	BARNETT	GE	10	13
BARNES	EJ	10	12	BARNES	HC	4	21	BARNES	SG	2	17	BARNETT	H	5	20
BARNES	EJ	13	25	BARNES	HC	7	19	BARNES	SH	4	22	BARNETT	H	11	20
BARNES	EJ	13	25	BARNES	HFC	10	12	BARNES	SI	5	19	BARNETT	H	14	15
BARNES	EM	4	21	BARNES	HG	12	14	BARNES	SS	4	22	BARNETT	H	14	15
BARNES	ER	4	21	BARNES	HJ	10	263	BARNES	SW	14	15	BARNETT	HE	6	23
BARNES	ES	14	14	BARNES	HJ	12	259	BARNES	T	4	22	BARNETT	HE	9	10
BARNES	EW	12	259	BARNES	HN	2	17	BARNES	T	4	22	BARNETT	HJ	6	23
BARNES	F	10	12	BARNES	HN	3	18	BARNES	T	12	15	BARNETT	J	1	20
BARNES	F	12	14	BARNES	HV	11	19	BARNES	T	13	26	BARNETT	J	4	22
BARNES	F	13	25	BARNES	HW	10	12	BARNES	TA	6	23	BARNETT	J	7	20
BARNES	F	14	14	BARNES	J	1	20	BARNES	VW	1	19	BARNETT	J	10	13
BARNES	FE	2	17	BARNES	J	1	20	BARNES	W	3	273	BARNETT	J	11	20
BARNES	FE	12	259	BARNES	J	2	17	BARNES	W	4	22	BARNETT	JH	1	20
BARNES	FG	2	17	BARNES	J	4	22	BARNES	W	5	20	BARNETT	MK	11	20
BARNES	FW	4	21	BARNES	J	4	22	BARNES	W	5	20	BARNETT	P	13	26
BARNES	FW	4	21	BARNES	J	4	22	BARNES	W	7	19	BARNETT	PJ	11	20
BARNES	FW	5	19	BARNES	J	5	19	BARNES	W	8	16	BARNETT	PJT	12	15
BARNES	FW	10	263	BARNES	J	6	23	BARNES	W	9	223	BARNETT	R	10	13
BARNES	G	1	19	BARNES	J	9	10	BARNES	W	12	259	BARNETT	S	7	20
BARNES	G	3	18	BARNES	J	10	12	BARNES	WD	10	13	BARNETT	T	8	16
BARNES	G	3	18	BARNES	J	11	19	BARNES	WE	4	22	BARNETT	TN	10	13
BARNES	G	4	21	BARNES	J	11	19	BARNES	WE	6	23	BARNETT	W	6	23
BARNES	G	5	19	BARNES	J	13	25	BARNES	WE	8	16	BARNETT	W	8	16
BARNES	G	6	23	BARNES	J	13	26	BARNES	WF	3	273	BARNETT	W	9	223
BARNES	G	6	23	BARNES	J	13	26	BARNES	WH	7	19	BARNETT	W	9	223
BARNES	G	10	12	BARNES	J	14	15	BARNES	WH	13	26	BARNETT	W	9	380

BARNETT	W	11	20	BARR	TA	6	23	BARRATT	J	14	16	BARRETT	G	8	17
BARNETT	W	14	15	BARR	TR	6	24	BARRATT	JH	8	17	BARRETT	G	8	17
BARNETT	WE	7	20	BARR	W	1	20	BARRATT	JT	12	259	BARRETT	G	9	11
BARNETT	WF	1	20	BARRACLOUGH	A	9	223	BARRATT	JW	1	20	BARRETT	GS	13	26
BARNETT	WG	1	20	BARRACLOUGH	AE	9	11	BARRATT	P	11	21	BARRETT	H	3	273
BARNETT	WJ	3	18	BARRACLOUGH	BF	8	16	BARRATT	P	14	16	BARRETT	H	4	23
BARNEVELD	AO	13	26	BARRACLOUGH	C	9	11	BARRATT	R	12	15	BARRETT	H	4	23
BARNFIELD	J	7	20	BARRACLOUGH	D	9	11	BARRATT	RE	14	16	BARRETT	H	7	21
BARNFIELD	T	14	16	BARRACLOUGH	D	9	11	BARRATT	RR	10	13	BARRETT	HC	7	21
BARNFIELD	T	14	16	BARRACLOUGH	E	8	16	BARRATT	W	12	15	BARRETT	HG	6	24
BARNICKLE	J	6	23	BARRACLOUGH	F	9	11	BARRATT	W	14	16	BARRETT	HH	3	19
BARNINGHAN	GH	8	16	BARRACLOUGH	H	8	16	BARRATT	WG	12	259	BARRETT	HH	13	26
BARNS	E	10	13	BARRACLOUGH	H	9	11	BARRELL	A	7	20	BARRETT	HJ	11	21
BARNS	JS	1	20	BARRACLOUGH	H	11	20	BARRELL	G	3	273	BARRETT	HT	6	24
BARNSHAW	JJ	11	20	BARRACLOUGH	I	9	223	BARRELL	R	10	263	BARRETT	HW	10	13
BARNSLEY	F	6	23	BARRACLOUGH	J	9	224	BARRELL	W	7	20	BARRETT	J	3	273
BARNSLEY	F	11	20	BARRACLOUGH	J	9	224	BARRETT	A	3	19	BARRETT	J	6	24
BARNSLEY	H	6	23	BARRACLOUGH	JA	8	16	BARRETT	A	4	22	BARRETT	J	8	17
BARNSLEY	H	11	20	BARRACLOUGH	JH	9	11	BARRETT	A	7	20	BARRETT	J	9	11
BARNSLEY	HS	3	18	BARRACLOUGH	JP	7	20	BARRETT	A	8	17	BARRETT	J	9	224
BARNSLEY	JF	3	273	BARRACLOUGH	L	9	11	BARRETT	A	9	11	BARRETT	J	13	26
BARNSLEY	W	11	20	BARRACLOUGH	LS	8	16	BARRETT	A	9	224	BARRETT	J	13	27
BARNSLEY	W	11	20	BARRACLOUGH	M	9	11	BARRETT	A	10	263	BARRETT	J	14	16
BARNSLEY	WC	3	273	BARRACLOUGH	W	9	224	BARRETT	AH	9	11	BARRETT	JA	4	23
BARNSLEY	WC	7	20	BARRALET		5	20	BARRETT	AH	10	13	BARRETT	JE	10	13
BARNWELL	CJ	5	20	BARRALET	JJ	5	20	BARRETT	AH	13	26	BARRETT	JH	13	27
BARNWELL	CT	12	15	BARRAN	P	8	16	BARRETT	AJ	6	24	BARRETT	JJ	3	19
BARNWELL	DJ	12	15	BARRAND	F	6	24	BARRETT	AJ	7	20	BARRETT	JR	13	27
BARNWELL	EJ	2	17	BARRAS	JW	8	16	BARRETT	AV	10	263	BARRETT	JW	4	23
BARNWELL	GW	3	19	BARRASS	A	8	16	BARRETT	AW	6	24	BARRETT	JW	13	27
BARNWELL	WC	12	15	BARRASS	J	8	17	BARRETT	B	4	23	BARRETT	L	10	13
BARNWELL	WG	12	15	BARRASS	JT	8	17	BARRETT	B	11	21	BARRETT	LM	4	23
BARON	AE	7	20	BARRATT	A	3	19	BARRETT	B	14	16	BARRETT	M	8	17
BARON	C	4	22	BARRATT	A	12	15	BARRETT	C	8	17	BARRETT	M	8	17
BARON	EC	1	20	BARRATT	A	14	16	BARRETT	C	13	26	BARRETT	M	11	21
BARON	EC	4	22	BARRATT	A	14	16	BARRETT	CT	7	20	BARRETT	M	13	27
BARON	G	9	11	BARRATT	AB	6	24	BARRETT	E	3	273	BARRETT	O	3	273
BARON	HK	11	20	BARRATT	AB	7	20	BARRETT	E	5	20	BARRETT	P	11	21
BARON	J	11	20	BARRATT	AE	1	20	BARRETT	E	6	24	BARRETT	PJ	6	24
BARON	W	8	16	BARRATT	AW	12	15	BARRETT	E	14	16	BARRETT	R	14	16
BARON	WH	4	22	BARRATT	C	11	21	BARRETT	EC	4	23	BARRETT	S	9	11
BARR	A	2	17	BARRATT	CT	13	26	BARRETT	EH	5	20	BARRETT	SD	5	20
BARR	AG	4	22	BARRATT	EDW	14	16	BARRETT	EH	11	21	BARRETT	T	6	24
BARR	AS	6	23	BARRATT	F	11	21	BARRETT	EJ	4	23	BARRETT	T	7	21
BARR	C	13	26	BARRATT	F	12	15	BARRETT	EW	10	13	BARRETT	T	11	21
BARR	CE	13	26	BARRATT	F	12	259	BARRETT	F	3	19	BARRETT	T	14	16
BARR	E	12	259	BARRATT	FE	13	26	BARRETT	F	6	24	BARRETT	TJ	1	20
BARR	F	11	20	BARRATT	FJ	13	26	BARRETT	F	7	20	BARRETT	TW	4	23
BARR	GS	6	23	BARRATT	G	7	20	BARRETT	F	7	21	BARRETT	VA	4	23
BARR	H	5	20	BARRATT	H	1	20	BARRETT	F	7	21	BARRETT	W	1	20
BARR	HG	1	20	BARRATT	H	10	13	BARRETT	FC	10	13	BARRETT	W	3	273
BARR	J	1	20	BARRATT	H	14	16	BARRETT	FH	3	273	BARRETT	W	4	23
BARR	J	4	22	BARRATT	HJT	13	26	BARRETT	FT	5	20	BARRETT	W	6	24
BARR	PJ	11	20	BARRATT	HT	7	20	BARRETT	FW	2	17	BARRETT	W	8	17
BARR	S	11	20	BARRATT	I	14	16	BARRETT	FW	10	13	BARRETT	W	9	224

BARRETT	W	10	13	BARROW	S	8	17	BARTER	G	4	24	BARTLETT	FT	4	25
BARRETT	W	10	13	BARROW	S	10	263	BARTER	H	4	24	BARTLETT	FW	4	25
BARRETT	W	11	21	BARROW	T	14	17	BARTER	HF	1	21	BARTLETT	G	4	25
BARRETT	W	13	27	BARROW	W	11	21	BARTER	J	4	24	BARTLETT	G	4	25
BARRETT	WA	3	19	BARROW	WE	4	24	BARTER	J	7	21	BARTLETT	GC	1	21
BARRETT	WC	4	23	BARROW	WH	13	27	BARTER	JS	4	24	BARTLETT	GJ	13	28
BARRETT	WC	4	23	BARROWCLIFT	B	6	24	BARTER	PJ	4	24	BARTLETT	GW	4	25
BARRETT	WC	6	24	BARROWCLIFT	F	6	24	BARTER	R	4	24	BARTLETT	GW	4	25
BARRETT	WG	4	23	BARROWMAN	JB	4	24	BARTER	RH	10	14	BARTLETT	H	7	21
BARRETT	WH	1	20	BARRS	AL	1	21	BARTER	S	2	17	BARTLETT	H	8	18
BARRETT	WH	3	273	BARRS	JA	1	21	BARTER	SJ	10	264	BARTLETT	HJ	10	14
BARRETT	WH	6	24	BARRS	RA	1	21	BARTER	W	4	24	BARTLETT	HJ	10	14
BARRETT	WH	8	17	BARRS	WA	3	273	BARTER	WJH	7	21	BARTLETT	HR	3	273
BARRETT	WH	14	16	BARRY	A	7	21	BARTHOLEMEW	C	6	25	BARTLETT	HWA	10	264
BARRETT	WJR	13	27	BARRY	D	4	24	BARTHOLMEW	T	12	16	BARTLETT	J	4	25
BARRIER	HG	13	27	BARRY	E	11	21	BARTHOLOMEW	AW	10	14	BARTLETT	J	10	14
BARRINGER	AB	12	15	BARRY	H	13	27	BARTHOLOMEW	C	6	24	BARTLETT	JC	13	28
BARRINGER	AG	12	15	BARRY	IW	1	21	BARTHOLOMEW	EC	4	24	BARTLETT	JR	4	25
BARRINGER	GT	12	15	BARRY	J	3	273	BARTHOLOMEW	G	13	28	BARTLETT	JR	7	21
BARRINGER	HJ	12	15	BARRY	J	7	21	BARTHOLOMEW	GF	13	28	BARTLETT	JR	10	14
BARRINGER	JT	12	15	BARRY	J	8	17	BARTHOLOMEW	H	10	14	BARTLETT	R	4	25
BARRINGER	T	12	259	BARRY	J	11	21	BARTHOLOMEW	H	13	28	BARTLETT	R	4	25
BARRINGER	W	12	15	BARRY	J	13	27	BARTHOLOMEW	HS	10	14	BARTLETT	R	10	14
BARRINGTON	H	13	27	BARRY	L	8	17	BARTHOLOMEW	JE	14	17	BARTLETT	S	10	14
BARRINGTON	J	13	27	BARRY	PJ	4	24	BARTHOLOMEW	WA	10	14	BARTLETT	T	4	25
BARRINGTON	JT	13	27	BARRY	T	11	21	BARTLAM	AH	6	25	BARTLETT	T	4	25
BARRINGTON	W	13	27	BARRY	W	8	18	BARTLAM	F	8	18	BARTLETT	T	4	25
BARRINGTON	WH	10	13	BARRY	W	9	11	BARTLAM	JE	8	18	BARTLETT	TF	10	15
BARRITT	E	12	259	BARRY	W	13	28	BARTLAM	T	8	18	BARTLETT	TH	13	28
BARRITT	R	10	13	BARRY	W	14	17	BARTLE	A	9	224	BARTLETT	V	10	15
BARRITT	TG	13	27	BARRY	WG	10	13	BARTLE	E	9	224	BARTLETT	W	3	19
BARRON	A	8	17	BARSBY	G	5	20	BARTLE	JS	5	20	BARTLETT	WE	6	25
BARRON	A	8	17	BARSBY	RS	13	28	BARTLE	JW	9	11	BARTLETT	WE	6	25
BARRON	AF	7	21	BARSLEY	R	5	20	BARTLE	WH	9	224	BARTLETT	WE	6	25
BARRON	C	8	17	BARSON	W	9	224	BARTLE	WR	5	20	BARTLETT	WG	4	25
BARRON	D	8	17	BARSTOW	C	8	18	BARTLEMAN	PA	13	28	BARTLETT	WJ	1	21
BARRON	G	6	24	BARSTOW	EF	4	24	BARTLETT	A	3	19	BARTLETT	WT	8	18
BARRON	L	12	259	BARSTOW	GP	8	18	BARTLETT	A	6	25	BARTLEY	D	8	18
BARROW	A	14	16	BARSTOW	H	4	24	BARTLETT	A	9	224	BARTLEY	E	9	12
BARROW	AE	13	27	BARSTOW	M	4	24	BARTLETT	AE	1	21	BARTLEY	WE	11	21
BARROW	AW	13	27	BARTER	A	3	19	BARTLETT	AE	8	18	BARTON	A	2	17
BARROW	CW	4	23	BARTER	AEA	10	14	BARTLETT	AF	4	25	BARTON	A	4	25
BARROW	EJ	4	23	BARTER	ASJ	4	24	BARTLETT	AG	3	273	BARTON	A	5	20
BARROW	F	4	23	BARTER	AW	1	21	BARTLETT	AJT	3	19	BARTON	AC	3	19
BARROW	FAJ	4	23	BARTER	C	4	24	BARTLETT	AT	10	264	BARTON	AE	5	20
BARROW	GS	4	23	BARTER	CH	10	14	BARTLETT	AV	1	21	BARTON	AE	5	20
BARROW	H	4	23	BARTER	E	10	14	BARTLETT	C	9	12	BARTON	AE	11	22
BARROW	HJ	11	21	BARTER	E	10	14	BARTLETT	CA	13	28	BARTON	AG	3	19
BARROW	HW	4	24	BARTER	EW	4	24	BARTLETT	E	1	21	BARTON	AJ	5	20
BARROW	J	8	17	BARTER	F	4	24	BARTLETT	E	13	28	BARTON	AL	13	28
BARROW	J	11	21	BARTER	F	10	264	BARTLETT	EE	4	25	BARTON	AW	12	260
BARROW	J	11	21	BARTER	FC	10	14	BARTLETT	EGH	4	25	BARTON	C	4	25
BARROW	JH	11	21	BARTER	G	1	21	BARTLETT	EW	10	14	BARTON	C	4	26
BARROW	JH	14	17	BARTER	G	3	273	BARTLETT	F	4	25	BARTON	C	13	28
BARROW	JH	14	17	BARTER	G	4	24	BARTLETT	FA	10	14	BARTON	CB	5	20

BARTON	CN	1	21
BARTON	CW	5	21
BARTON	EJ	1	21
BARTON	ET	12	260
BARTON	F	1	21
BARTON	F	5	21
BARTON	FA	5	21
BARTON	FG	10	15
BARTON	FW	6	25
BARTON	G	1	21
BARTON	G	4	26
BARTON	G	4	26
BARTON	G	13	28
BARTON	GA	12	16
BARTON	GR	2	17
BARTON	GW	1	21
BARTON	GW	1	21
BARTON	H	2	18
BARTON	H	6	25
BARTON	HJ	1	21
BARTON	J	1	21
BARTON	J	3	19
BARTON	J	5	21
BARTON	J	9	380
BARTON	J	11	22
BARTON	J	14	17
BARTON	J	14	17
BARTON	JF	6	25
BARTON	JW	3	19
BARTON	JW	5	21
BARTON	L	3	19
BARTON	M	6	25
BARTON	MF	4	26
BARTON	R	2	18
BARTON	R	5	21
BARTON	R	11	22
BARTON	RH	7	21
BARTON	RH	12	16
BARTON	RJ	12	260
BARTON	S	11	22
BARTON	SF	6	25
BARTON	SH	8	18
BARTON	T	1	21
BARTON	T	2	18
BARTON	T	3	274
BARTON	T	12	16
BARTON	TH	1	21
BARTON	TW	14	17
BARTON	W	3	274
BARTON	W	11	22
BARTON	WH	7	21
BARTON	WH	7	21
BARTON	WH	13	28
BARTON	WJ	1	21
BARTON	WR	1	21
BARTRAM	AT	12	16
BARTRAM	E	12	16
BARTRAM	EE	5	21
BARTRAM	FW	12	16
BARTRAM	J	6	25
BARTRAM	JT	7	21
BARTRAM	P	8	18
BARTRAM	RJ	12	16
BARTRAM	S	13	28
BARTRAM	W	13	28
BARTRAM	WE	5	21
BARTRAM	WF	13	28
BARTROP	H	9	224
BARTY	JW	3	19
BARUDI	EP	13	29
BARWELL	C	1	22
BARWELL	F	14	17
BARWELL	GW	13	29
BARWELL	H	6	25
BARWELL	V	13	29
BARWELL	W	13	29
BARWICK	E	8	18
BARWICK	FGE	1	22
BARWICK	GW	8	18
BARWICK	J	14	17
BASELEY	CA	10	15
BASELEY	CF	12	260
BASELEY	FC	12	260
BASEY	AC	5	21
BASFORD	A	12	16
BASFORD	F	14	17
BASFORD	J	11	22
BASFORD	JB	4	26
BASGALLOP	WE	13	29
BASH	AJ	6	25
BASHAM	FJ	1	22
BASHAM	GW	11	22
BASHFORD	HE	6	25
BASHFORD	JE	13	29
BASING	WH	1	22
BASKERVILLE	F	8	18
BASKERVILLE	H	13	29
BASKETFIELD	JW	3	274
BASKETT	AC	13	29
BASKETT	G	6	25
BASKETT	GO	13	29
BASKETTER	FA	14	17
BASKEWILL	E	9	12
BASKWELL	W	13	29
BASLEY	A	7	21
BASLEY	JJ	7	21
BASLEY	RH	7	21
BASON	A	12	260
BASON	W	7	21
BASS	A	12	16
BASS	A	12	16
BASS	AE	12	16
BASS	AH	5	21
BASS	AH	5	21
BASS	ASJ	12	260
BASS	B	9	12
BASS	C	5	21
BASS	CF	12	16
BASS	CW	5	21
BASS	DJ	12	16
BASS	E	13	29
BASS	FW	12	16
BASS	GC	3	274
BASS	GH	2	18
BASS	GW	12	260
BASS	GW	13	29
BASS	JA	12	16
BASS	JH	13	29
BASS	JHD	12	260
BASS	JW	3	19
BASS	ME	5	21
BASS	O	12	16
BASS	T	5	21
BASS	T	5	21
BASS	W	5	21
BASS	W	5	21
BASS	W	5	21
BASS	WA	10	15
BASS	WC	5	21
BASS	WH	3	274
BASS	WJ	5	21
BASS	WJ	5	22
BASS	WJ	12	16
BASSAM	A	5	22
BASSAM	FG	7	22
BASSELL	G	5	22
BASSETT	AA	13	29
BASSETT	C	5	22
BASSETT	CW	1	22
BASSETT	D	5	22
BASSETT	EA	1	22
BASSETT	FR	13	29
BASSETT	G	6	25
BASSETT	GE	6	25
BASSETT	GE	13	29
BASSETT	GS	5	22
BASSETT	J	3	274
BASSETT	JA	4	26
BASSETT	JA	13	29
BASSETT	LA	6	26
BASSETT	P	1	22
BASSETT	R	6	25
BASSETT	WE	1	22
BASSETT	WH	1	22
BASSETT	WH	12	260
BASSEY	CA	7	22
BASSILL	AWG	5	22
BASSILL	JW	5	22
BASSNETT	T	11	22
BASSOM	A	13	30
BASSON	EJ	12	16
BASSON	F	14	17
BASSON	GA	12	17
BASTABLE	JCH	6	26
BASTABLE	JE	6	26
BASTABLE	JW	10	264
BASTED	I	13	29
BASTER	H	4	26
BASTEY	W	9	224
BASTIN	A	1	22
BASTIN	AT	7	22
BASTIN	B	6	26
BASTIN	F	6	26
BASTIN	J	5	22
BASTIN	W	6	26
BASTONE	F	4	26
BASTOW	E	9	12
BASTOW	G	8	18
BASTOW	JT	9	12
BASTOW	W	9	12
BASTOW	W	9	12
BASTOW	WH	9	12
BATCHELOR	A	3	274
BATCHELOR	A	4	26
BATCHELOR	AH	5	22
BATCHELOR	AJ	3	274
BATCHELOR	AJ	3	274
BATCHELOR	AT	5	22
BATCHELOR	B	10	15
BATCHELOR	CL	12	260
BATCHELOR	CR	7	22
BATCHELOR	CWF	1	22
BATCHELOR	E	5	22
BATCHELOR	E	6	26
BATCHELOR	EC	5	22
BATCHELOR	EG	5	22
BATCHELOR	ET	5	22
BATCHELOR	EW	1	22
BATCHELOR	F	5	22
BATCHELOR	F	12	17
BATCHELOR	FF	5	22
BATCHELOR	FF	5	22
BATCHELOR	FW	3	274
BATCHELOR	G	3	20
BATCHELOR	G	7	22
BATCHELOR	GH	5	22
BATCHELOR	GH	12	260
BATCHELOR	GWJ	3	274
BATCHELOR	H	5	22
BATCHELOR	H	5	23
BATCHELOR	HL	5	23

BATCHELOR	J	5	23
BATCHELOR	J	10	15
BATCHELOR	JA	10	264
BATCHELOR	JA	12	17
BATCHELOR	JP	5	23
BATCHELOR	MD	4	26
BATCHELOR	P	5	23
BATCHELOR	P	10	15
BATCHELOR	PG	10	15
BATCHELOR	PS	5	23
BATCHELOR	RC	10	15
BATCHELOR	S	4	26
BATCHELOR	SG	3	274
BATCHELOR	SH	13	30
BATCHELOR	SRN	1	22
BATCHELOR	W	3	20
BATCHELOR	W	12	17
BATCHELOR	WA	10	264
BATCHELOR	WH	10	15
BATCHELOR	WS	7	22
BATCHELTOR	C	6	26
BATE	DH	11	22
BATE	FW	2	18
BATE	H	9	12
BATE	H	14	17
BATE	HA	7	22
BATE	HE	13	30
BATE	J	14	17
BATE	O	5	23
BATE	S	14	17
BATE	S	14	17
BATE	WA	6	26
BATE	WC	13	30
BATEMAN	A	5	23
BATEMAN	A	5	23
BATEMAN	A	8	18
BATEMAN	A	13	30
BATEMAN	AE	9	224
BATEMAN	AH	6	26
BATEMAN	DF	1	22
BATEMAN	E	9	12
BATEMAN	EJ	13	30
BATEMAN	EJ	13	30
BATEMAN	F	1	22
BATEMAN	F	9	380
BATEMAN	F	10	15
BATEMAN	G	11	22
BATEMAN	G	13	30
BATEMAN	J	5	23
BATEMAN	JH	13	30
BATEMAN	O	10	264
BATEMAN	R	11	22
BATEMAN	SJ	13	30
BATEMAN	TJ	13	30
BATEMAN	W	1	22
BATEMAN	W	1	22
BATEMAN	W	5	23
BATEMAN	W	7	22
BATEMAN	W	10	15
BATEMAN	WA	13	30
BATES	A	5	23
BATES	A	5	23
BATES	A	6	26
BATES	A	6	26
BATES	A	8	18
BATES	A	8	18
BATES	A	9	12
BATES	A	9	224
BATES	A	10	264
BATES	A	11	22
BATES	A	11	22
BATES	A	11	22
BATES	A	12	260
BATES	A	12	260
BATES	A	12	260
BATES	A	13	30
BATES	AA	6	26
BATES	AB	5	23
BATES	AC	13	30
BATES	AG	13	30
BATES	AH	4	26
BATES	AH	5	23
BATES	AJ	1	22
BATES	AJ	3	274
BATES	AR	1	22
BATES	AS	1	22
BATES	AW	13	30
BATES	B	14	17
BATES	C	5	23
BATES	CG	5	23
BATES	CVH	11	22
BATES	E	1	22
BATES	E	5	23
BATES	E	13	30
BATES	E	14	18
BATES	EJ	1	22
BATES	F	5	23
BATES	F	5	24
BATES	F	5	24
BATES	G	5	24
BATES	G	6	26
BATES	G	12	260
BATES	GA	7	22
BATES	GH	8	18
BATES	H	5	24
BATES	H	7	22
BATES	H	9	12
BATES	H	9	12
BATES	H	9	224
BATES	HC	7	22
BATES	HE	5	24
BATES	HJ	6	26
BATES	HJR	7	22
BATES	HW	13	30
BATES	HW	13	31
BATES	HW	13	31
BATES	HW	14	18
BATES	J	1	22
BATES	J	1	22
BATES	J	6	26
BATES	J	11	22
BATES	J	11	22
BATES	J	12	17
BATES	J	12	260
BATES	J	13	31
BATES	J	14	18
BATES	J	14	18
BATES	JE	13	30
BATES	JG	14	18
BATES	JH	1	22
BATES	JH	6	26
BATES	JH	13	31
BATES	JH	14	18
BATES	JJG	13	31
BATES	JT	13	31
BATES	JV	7	22
BATES	JW	4	26
BATES	JW	12	17
BATES	L	5	24
BATES	L	11	22
BATES	LF	5	24
BATES	P	11	23
BATES	P	11	23
BATES	PE	6	26
BATES	R	11	23
BATES	R	11	23
BATES	S	8	18
BATES	S	13	31
BATES	SE	4	26
BATES	SG	4	26
BATES	SH	7	22
BATES	T	6	27
BATES	T	11	23
BATES	T	13	31
BATES	T	14	18
BATES	TA	13	31
BATES	TH	13	31
BATES	V	11	23
BATES	W	5	24
BATES	W	6	27
BATES	W	7	22
BATES	W	9	224
BATES	W	11	23
BATES	W	11	23
BATES	W	11	23
BATES	W	11	23
BATES	W	13	31
BATES	W	14	18
BATES	W	14	18
BATES	W	14	18
BATES	WA	6	27
BATES	WC	6	27
BATES	WG	12	17
BATES	WH	11	23
BATES	WJ	12	260
BATES	WS	7	22
BATESON	C	8	19
BATESON	CH	8	19
BATESON	E	8	19
BATESON	E	8	19
BATESON	G	8	19
BATESON	J	9	224
BATESON	JW	9	12
BATESON	L	8	19
BATESON	T	7	22
BATESON	W	9	12
BATEY	AT	6	27
BATH	AJ	10	15
BATH	CE	4	26
BATH	G	1	23
BATH	G	2	18
BATH	G	7	22
BATH	GH	10	264
BATH	H	5	24
BATH	HG	10	264
BATH	HW	10	15
BATH	J	1	23
BATH	J	1	23
BATH	LA	10	264
BATH	LH	4	26
BATH	P	1	23
BATH	R	10	264
BATH	T	1	23
BATH	W	4	26
BATH	W	5	24
BATHAM	A	1	23
BATHAM	GE	1	23
BATHAM	SG	3	274
BATHE	D	1	23
BATHURST	AE	3	274
BATHURST	FH	7	23
BATHURST	WT	7	22
BATKIN	EJ	13	31
BATLEY	A	8	19
BATLEY	H	9	12
BATLEY	JW	8	19
BATLEY	S	8	19
BATLEY	WB	11	23
BATLEY	WH	11	23
BATMAN	A	9	12

BATRAM	H	3	274	BATTERICK	AV	4	27	BAUCHOP	AL	8	20	BAX	WJ	13	32
BATSFORD	AW	6	27	BATTERS	A	6	27	BAUCUTT	D	12	261	BAXENDALE	E	11	23
BATSFORD	FC	6	27	BATTERS	H	6	27	BAUCUTT	J	12	261	BAXENDALE	GE	11	24
BATSFORD	HG	6	27	BATTERS	HW	6	27	BAUCUTT	WJ	12	261	BAXTER	A	8	20
BATSFORD	JE	6	27	BATTERS	WG	4	27	BAUDONCQ	F	3	275	BAXTER	A	8	20
BATSON	AE	7	23	BATTERSBY	C	8	19	BAUDONCQ	M	3	275	BAXTER	A	9	13
BATSON	ET	3	274	BATTERSBY	CE	8	19	BAUGH	BC	3	275	BAXTER	A	9	13
BATSTONE	H	3	20	BATTERSBY	H	7	23	BAUGH	CJ	13	31	BAXTER	A	9	225
BATSTONE	WJ	1	23	BATTERSBY	W	8	19	BAUGH	EE	7	23	BAXTER	A	9	225
BATT	A	3	274	BATTERSHILL	GW	12	260	BAUGH	JG	6	27	BAXTER	AE	8	20
BATT	C	3	274	BATTERSON	JWC	4	27	BAUGHAN	RH	1	23	BAXTER	AF	13	32
BATT	F	3	275	BATTISON	AV	12	261	BAUGHEN	GR	7	23	BAXTER	AG	1	23
BATT	F	10	15	BATTISON	CT	12	261	BAUGHEN	H	6	27	BAXTER	AL	5	25
BATT	G	1	23	BATTISON	T	12	261	BAUGHEN	P	6	27	BAXTER	AM	6	27
BATT	GSW	11	23	BATTISSON	A	12	261	BAUGHN	J	13	31	BAXTER	B	12	17
BATT	RM	11	23	BATTISSON	J	12	261	BAULCH	WE	7	23	BAXTER	B	12	17
BATT	W	10	15	BATTISTA	DA	6	27	BAULCH	WH	2	18	BAXTER	CE	13	32
BATT	W	13	31	BATTLE	A	14	18	BAULCH	WH	13	31	BAXTER	E	2	18
BATT	WA	10	15	BATTLE	FW	12	17	BAULF	AE	10	16	BAXTER	E	8	20
BATT	WJ	4	26	BATTLE	M	9	224	BAULF	F	10	16	BAXTER	E	13	32
BATT	WJ	7	23	BATTLE	PS	12	17	BAULF	G	10	16	BAXTER	EC	6	28
BATTAM	WG	4	26	BATTLEY	AE	7	23	BAULK	GW	5	25	BAXTER	EJ	6	28
BATTAMS	AT	5	24	BATTMAN	AN	11	23	BAULSON	F	13	31	BAXTER	EW	6	28
BATTAMS	CE	5	24	BATTMAN	WH	13	31	BAUMAN	C	1	23	BAXTER	EWD	13	32
BATTAMS	EC	12	17	BATTRICK	AV	5	24	BAUMAN	G	1	23	BAXTER	F	3	20
BATTAMS	GW	1	23	BATTRICK	B	5	24	BAUMGARD	S	14	18	BAXTER	F	6	28
BATTAMS	HV	5	24	BATTRICK	G	5	24	BAURMEISTER	EW	3	275	BAXTER	F	8	20
BATTAMS	JH	5	24	BATTS	A	7	23	BAVERSTOCK	AD	10	16	BAXTER	F	8	20
BATTAMS	JH	12	17	BATTY	A	8	19	BAVERSTOCK	AJ	4	27	BAXTER	F	9	13
BATTAMS	JT	1	23	BATTY	A	8	19	BAVERSTOCK	C	2	18	BAXTER	F	10	16
BATTAMS	P	12	260	BATTY	A	9	224	BAVERSTOCK	CJ	1	23	BAXTER	FH	13	32
BATTAMS	RE	7	23	BATTY	CHW	1	23	BAVERSTOCK	EF	10	16	BAXTER	FJ	13	32
BATTAMS	T	5	24	BATTY	E	8	19	BAVERSTOCK	F	4	27	BAXTER	FS	13	32
BATTAMS	W	5	24	BATTY	F	8	19	BAVERSTOCK	G	3	275	BAXTER	G	12	17
BATTAMS	WJ	12	17	BATTY	F	8	19	BAVERSTOCK	H	3	275	BAXTER	G	13	32
BATTELL	JT	14	18	BATTY	F	9	13	BAVERSTOCK	H	3	275	BAXTER	GA	12	17
BATTEN	A	4	27	BATTY	G	8	19	BAVERSTOCK	J	3	275	BAXTER	H	12	17
BATTEN	AH	5	24	BATTY	G	8	19	BAVERSTOCK	T	7	23	BAXTER	HC	2	18
BATTEN	E	4	27	BATTY	G	14	18	BAVERSTOCK	WA	4	27	BAXTER	HJ	13	32
BATTEN	EWC	4	27	BATTY	GGA	7	23	BAVIN	A	14	18	BAXTER	HW	7	23
BATTEN	FC	4	27	BATTY	H	8	19	BAVIN	F	7	23	BAXTER	HWA	13	32
BATTEN	FW	4	27	BATTY	H	8	20	BAVINGTON	FH	3	275	BAXTER	J	1	23
BATTEN	GA	4	27	BATTY	H	9	13	BAVINGTON	RJ	3	275	BAXTER	J	7	23
BATTEN	GL	10	264	BATTY	J	8	20	BAVISTER	HE	5	25	BAXTER	J	9	225
BATTEN	J	6	27	BATTY	J	14	18	BAVISTER	W	5	25	BAXTER	J	11	24
BATTEN	J	11	23	BATTY	J	14	18	BAWCUTT	H	12	261	BAXTER	J	11	24
BATTEN	L	10	16	BATTY	JE	8	20	BAWDEN	A	7	23	BAXTER	J	12	17
BATTEN	RA	4	27	BATTY	JW	11	23	BAWDEN	F	7	23	BAXTER	JW	9	13
BATTEN	ST	4	27	BATTY	R	8	20	BAWN	JA	3	275	BAXTER	JW	12	17
BATTEN	WJ	4	27	BATTY	T	2	18	BAWN	JF	3	275	BAXTER	LN	13	32
BATTEN	WJ	7	23	BATTY	WE	14	18	BAWN	T	8	20	BAXTER	PH	13	32
BATTENSBY	JW	8	19	BATTYE	J	8	20	BAX	AF	13	32	BAXTER	RE	10	16
BATTER	CJ	1	23	BATTYE	JW	9	13	BAX	HE	4	27	BAXTER	T	8	20
BATTERHAM	C	10	16	BATTYE	R	9	13	BAX	HS	13	31	BAXTER	T	13	32
BATTERHAM	G	10	16	BATUTE	GJ	1	23	BAX	HS	13	32	BAXTER	TR	5	25

BAXTER	V	10	16	BAYLISS	W	6	28	BEAL	D	5	25	BEAN	W	9	13
BAXTER	W	6	28	BAYLISS	WF	12	261	BEAL	F	3	20	BEAN	WE	1	24
BAXTER	W	6	28	BAYLISS	WF	12	261	BEAL	F	8	20	BEAN	WF	12	262
BAXTER	W	8	20	BAYLISS	WJ	6	29	BEAL	H	5	25	BEAN	WJ	5	26
BAXTER	W	8	20	BAYLY	E	10	264	BEAL	HOA	10	16	BEANES	EJ	1	24
BAXTER	W	8	20	BAYMAN	WH	13	33	BEAL	HW	5	25	BEANEY	FE	5	26
BAXTER	W	9	225	BAYNES	E	7	24	BEAL	J	5	25	BEANEY	H	7	24
BAXTER	W	10	16	BAYNES	G	5	25	BEAL	J	12	262	BEANEY	J	13	33
BAXTER	W	14	19	BAYNES	GE	13	33	BEAL	S	12	421	BEANEY	JRS	7	24
BAXTER	W	14	19	BAYNES	JE	3	20	BEAL	W	12	18	BEANLAND	DH	8	21
BAXTER	WA	5	25	BAYNHAM	D	6	29	BEAL	W	12	421	BEANLAND	F	9	13
BAXTER	WB	13	32	BAYNHAM	H	6	29	BEALE	A	5	25	BEANLAND	H	8	21
BAXTER	WG	1	23	BAYNTON	A	10	264	BEALE	A	13	33	BEANLAND	H	9	13
BAXTER	WW	12	18	BAYS	J	3	275	BEALE	AE	4	28	BEANLAND	J	9	225
BAYES	CW	12	261	BAYSTON	G	7	24	BEALE	AW	3	20	BEANLAND	L	8	21
BAYES	F	12	261	BAYSTON	JW	7	24	BEALE	CW	3	20	BEANLAND	W	8	21
BAYES	GH	12	261	BAZELEY	A	12	261	BEALE	F	4	28	BEANLAND	W	9	14
BAYES	JW	5	25	BAZELEY	AE	12	261	BEALE	F	6	29	BEANLAND	W	9	225
BAYES	WH	12	261	BAZELEY	F	12	261	BEALE	FJ	5	26	BEAR	E	1	24
BAYFIELD	F	13	32	BAZELEY	H	6	29	BEALE	G	6	29	BEAR	WA	1	24
BAYFIELD	H	9	13	BAZELEY	JA	1	24	BEALE	G	10	16	BEARCHELL	GH	13	33
BAYFORD	A	1	23	BAZZI	JH	7	24	BEALE	GJ	7	24	BEARD	A	5	26
BAYFORD	A	1	24	BEACH	C	5	25	BEALE	H	3	276	BEARD	A	7	24
BAYFORD	AH	3	275	BEACH	E	9	380	BEALE	H	5	26	BEARD	B	12	18
BAYFORD	T	2	18	BEACH	F	6	29	BEALE	H	7	24	BEARD	C	12	18
BAYLEY	A	11	24	BEACH	JW	1	24	BEALE	HE	6	29	BEARD	EC	1	24
BAYLEY	AE	4	27	BEACH	S	14	19	BEALE	JH	4	28	BEARD	EJ	12	18
BAYLEY	AW	7	23	BEACH	W	10	264	BEALE	PD	5	26	BEARD	EJ	14	19
BAYLEY	E	14	19	BEACH	WA	7	24	BEALE	SH	5	26	BEARD	F	7	24
BAYLEY	FTJ	4	27	BEACHAM	FD	3	276	BEALE	WE	6	29	BEARD	GW	9	14
BAYLEY	J	1	24	BEACHAM	FH	4	27	BEALE	WF	4	28	BEARD	GW	9	14
BAYLEY	V	5	25	BEACHER	CA	10	16	BEALE	WJ	2	18	BEARD	H	1	24
BAYLEY	WBB	4	27	BEACHER	FG	10	16	BEALE	WP	9	225	BEARD	H	6	29
BAYLEY	WJ	3	275	BEACHER	J	5	25	BEALES	JS	7	24	BEARD	H	10	16
BAYLIS	CA	11	24	BEACON	C	2	18	BEALL	W	9	225	BEARD	H	12	18
BAYLIS	IJ	3	275	BEADEL	F	13	33	BEAMAN	F	6	29	BEARD	H	12	262
BAYLIS	J	3	275	BEADELL	AE	13	33	BEAMAN	JJ	7	24	BEARD	HR	12	18
BAYLIS	W	7	24	BEADLE	A	3	276	BEAMAN	JW	6	29	BEARD	J	14	19
BAYLISS	A	13	33	BEADLE	GE	7	24	BEAMAN	T	6	29	BEARD	M	6	29
BAYLISS	AE	6	28	BEADLE	GF	3	276	BEAMENT	A	4	28	BEARD	P	6	29
BAYLISS	BC	6	28	BEADLE	GF	3	276	BEAMES	FEJ	10	265	BEARD	PC	2	18
BAYLISS	CE	12	261	BEADLE	J	3	276	BEAMISH	HG	13	33	BEARD	R	6	29
BAYLISS	DI	3	20	BEADLE	LG	1	24	BEAMISH	WH	9	13	BEARD	S	7	24
BAYLISS	EH	6	28	BEADLE	W	7	24	BEAN	A	8	20	BEARD	SA	7	25
BAYLISS	F	5	25	BEADLE	WH	5	25	BEAN	AA	12	262	BEARD	T	6	29
BAYLISS	G	6	28	BEAGLE	SM	13	33	BEAN	C	8	20	BEARD	W	7	25
BAYLISS	H	6	28	BEAGLES	EG	13	33	BEAN	G	10	16	BEARD	W	7	25
BAYLISS	H	6	28	BEAGLEY	GH	13	33	BEAN	GA	9	225	BEARDALL	H	9	14
BAYLISS	J	6	28	BEAHAN	JD	14	19	BEAN	H	9	13	BEARDALL	J	14	19
BAYLISS	J	9	13	BEAK-ROBERTS	CL	3	20	BEAN	H	9	380	BEARDMORE	RH	6	29
BAYLISS	M	6	28	BEAKE	C	10	264	BEAN	J	9	13	BEARDOW	JWE	8	21
BAYLISS	MP	6	28	BEAKE	J	10	265	BEAN	R	9	13	BEARDSALL	A	11	24
BAYLISS	S	6	28	BEAKEN	RP	12	262	BEAN	R	9	13	BEARDSHAM	W	6	30
BAYLISS	SJ	6	28	BEAL	A	5	25	BEAN	R	9	380	BEARDSLEY	J	10	17
BAYLISS	T	3	20	BEAL	C	7	24	BEAN	W	7	24	BEARE	AC	4	28

BEARE	EJH	4	28
BEARE	IB	10	265
BEARE	J	4	28
BEARE	MF	10	265
BEARE	W	10	265
BEARE	WV	10	265
BEARLEY	AE	6	30
BEARMAN	F	7	25
BEARPARK	H	11	24
BEARSBY	EJ	13	33
BEARSLY	SP	13	33
BEART	WE	3	276
BEASLEY	A	12	262
BEASLEY	E	4	28
BEASLEY	EH	12	262
BEASLEY	F	12	262
BEASLEY	F	13	33
BEASLEY	FA	12	262
BEASLEY	FG	6	30
BEASLEY	G	12	262
BEASLEY	H	12	18
BEASLEY	HC	5	26
BEASLEY	J	7	25
BEASLEY	JC	12	262
BEASLEY	W	6	30
BEASON	A	6	30
BEATON	FC	4	28
BEATON	HC	4	28
BEATON	WH	4	28
BEATTIE	A	6	30
BEATTIE	A	10	17
BEATTIE	A	12	18
BEATTIE	CJ	1	24
BEATTIE	G	10	17
BEATTIE	J	11	24
BEATTIE	M	10	17
BEATY	WJ	14	19
BEAUCHAMP		1	24
BEAUCHAMP	AJ	7	25
BEAUCHAMP	AJ	12	18
BEAUCHAMP	F	10	17
BEAUCHAMP	W	10	17
BEAUMONT	A	7	25
BEAUMONT	A	8	21
BEAUMONT	A	9	14
BEAUMONT	A	10	17
BEAUMONT	C	5	26
BEAUMONT	C	5	26
BEAUMONT	DH	8	21
BEAUMONT	E	9	225
BEAUMONT	E	11	24
BEAUMONT	EG	4	28
BEAUMONT	F	5	26
BEAUMONT	G	5	26
BEAUMONT	G	8	21
BEAUMONT	G	9	14
BEAUMONT	GA	8	21
BEAUMONT	GA	13	33
BEAUMONT	GF	8	21
BEAUMONT	H	5	26
BEAUMONT	H	5	26
BEAUMONT	J	8	21
BEAUMONT	J	9	14
BEAUMONT	J	14	19
BEAUMONT	J	14	19
BEAUMONT	JA	8	21
BEAUMONT	JE	8	21
BEAUMONT	JH	14	19
BEAUMONT	P	11	24
BEAUMONT	PV	12	18
BEAUMONT	R	5	26
BEAUMONT	RA	12	18
BEAUMONT	RE	13	33
BEAUMONT	RE	13	33
BEAUMONT	S	8	21
BEAUMONT	T	9	14
BEAUMONT	T	9	14
BEAUMONT	TCH	4	28
BEAUMONT	TW	8	21
BEAUMONT	W	7	25
BEAUMONT	W	8	21
BEAUMONT	W	11	24
BEAUMONT	WF	5	26
BEAUTIMAN	A	8	21
BEAVEN	C	3	276
BEAVEN	CT	2	18
BEAVEN	EV	7	25
BEAVEN	GJ	7	25
BEAVEN	HA	2	18
BEAVEN	J	2	18
BEAVEN	ME	7	25
BEAVEN	R	2	19
BEAVER	F	14	19
BEAVER	GH	13	33
BEAVER	SG	7	25
BEAVERSTOCK	HW	1	24
BEAVINGTON	CH	13	33
BEAVINGTON	WF	13	34
BEAVIS	AMD	7	25
BEAVIS	E	4	28
BEAVIS	EL	3	20
BEAVIS	FG	4	28
BEAVIS	HT	3	20
BEAVIS	W	7	25
BEAZLEY	A	4	28
BEAZLEY	BCS	4	28
BEAZLEY	CT	4	28
BEAZLEY	DH	3	20
BEAZLEY	E	13	34
BEAZLEY	F	10	17
BEAZLEY	GW	4	28
BEAZLEY	H	3	276
BEAZLEY	TC	5	26
BEBB	H	9	14
BEBBINGTON	F	11	24
BEBBINGTON	S	14	19
BEBINGTON	S	14	19
BECK	AE	6	30
BECK	AE	7	25
BECK	AL	10	265
BECK	C	8	21
BECK	E	9	14
BECK	EC	10	17
BECK	FC	7	25
BECK	FF	10	265
BECK	FJ	7	25
BECK	FT	6	30
BECK	GS	8	21
BECK	H	8	21
BECK	HG	4	29
BECK	HG	10	265
BECK	HW	5	26
BECK	J	8	21
BECK	JF	13	34
BECK	RC	10	265
BECK	SJ	7	25
BECK	T	11	24
BECK	WJ	1	24
BECKER	GC	1	24
BECKER	H	7	26
BECKER	J	7	26
BECKET	E	7	26
BECKETT	A	8	22
BECKETT	AB	2	19
BECKETT	AG	10	265
BECKETT	AHC	2	19
BECKETT	AJ	6	30
BECKETT	AR	2	19
BECKETT	C	7	26
BECKETT	E	2	19
BECKETT	F	5	26
BECKETT	FE	7	26
BECKETT	FL	5	27
BECKETT	G	7	26
BECKETT	GH	6	30
BECKETT	GW	3	276
BECKETT	H	6	30
BECKETT	H	6	30
BECKETT	H	13	34
BECKETT	HD	7	26
BECKETT	HJ	13	34
BECKETT	HJT	3	20
BECKETT	HW	2	19
BECKETT	J	8	22
BECKETT	J	8	22
BECKETT	J	9	14
BECKETT	J	9	225
BECKETT	J	14	19
BECKETT	JDR	3	20
BECKETT	JE	4	29
BECKETT	JH	2	19
BECKETT	JT	6	30
BECKETT	RV	6	30
BECKETT	TH	6	30
BECKETT	TIJ	4	29
BECKETT	W	2	19
BECKETT	W	13	34
BECKETT	WG	2	19
BECKETT	WH	4	29
BECKETT	WJ	6	30
BECKFORD	F	13	34
BECKHAM	A	7	26
BECKHAM	C	13	34
BECKHAM	WH	2	19
BECKINGHAM	H	10	265
BECKINSALE	G	5	27
BECKLEY	A	6	30
BECKLEY	HJ	1	24
BECKLEY	J	2	19
BECKMAN	W	3	20
BECKWITH	AW	13	34
BECKWITH	CA	1	24
BECKWITH	EW	9	225
BECKWITH	F	8	22
BECKWITH	H	8	22
BECKWITH	H	8	22
BECKWITH	H	14	19
BECKWITH	J	8	22
BECKWITH	J	8	22
BECKWITH	JH	9	225
BECKWITH	JL	8	22
BECKWITH	JW	11	24
BECKWITH	RC	1	24
BECKWITH	SC	5	27
BECKWITH	T	8	22
BECKWORTH	JA	8	22
BEDBOROUGH	F	1	24
BEDBROOK	KWH	4	29
BEDDALL	MT	6	30
BEDDARD	ED	6	31
BEDDINGTON	CE	6	31
BEDDINGTON	S	6	31
BEDDOE	AJ	6	31
BEDDOE	G	2	19
BEDDOE	SH	10	265
BEDDOE	WJ	10	17
BEDDOES	E	11	24
BEDDOES	L	6	31
BEDDOES	W	6	31
BEDDOES	WG	6	31

BEDDOWES	A	6	31	BEE	W	8	22	BEER	TH	7	27	BEGRAVE	AC	12	18
BEDDOWES	A	6	31	BEEBY	A	12	262	BEER	W	8	22	BEHAGG	FH	12	18
BEDDOWS	A	6	31	BEEBY	GR	12	262	BEER	W	10	17	BEHAN	GW	11	25
BEDDOWS	D	6	31	BEEBY	JW	5	27	BEER	W	11	24	BEHENNA	G	11	25
BEDDOWS	H	6	31	BEECH	A	14	19	BEER	W	11	24	BEHR	C	7	27
BEDDOWS	H	11	24	BEECH	C	13	34	BEES	WG	5	27	BEHR	CT	7	27
BEDDOWS	JH	6	31	BEECH	F	6	32	BEESLEY	AW	9	14	BEHR	LG	13	35
BEDDOWS	L	11	24	BEECH	FW	6	32	BEESLEY	AW	9	225	BEIRNE	MJ	14	20
BEDFORD	AJ	10	17	BEECH	H	9	14	BEESLEY	CH	3	276	BELAND	AW	13	35
BEDFORD	AR	7	26	BEECH	H	14	20	BEESLEY	HC	13	35	BELAND	GW	13	35
BEDFORD	B	4	29	BEECH	J	6	32	BEESLEY	J	9	380	BELANT	J	3	21
BEDFORD	B	6	31	BEECH	J	14	20	BEESLEY	L	2	19	BELBEN	T	7	27
BEDFORD	BJ	10	17	BEECH	JH	6	32	BEESLEY	M	4	29	BELBIN	EP	4	29
BEDFORD	CA	7	26	BEECH	LG	6	32	BEESON	A	6	32	BELBIN	GT	4	29
BEDFORD	CL	12	262	BEECH	W	9	225	BEESON	CJE	7	27	BELBIN	HC	4	29
BEDFORD	EA	12	262	BEECHAM	A	6	32	BEESON	EW	5	27	BELBIN	RR	4	29
BEDFORD	EW	3	276	BEECHAM	E	2	19	BEESON	J	6	32	BELCHAMBER	CJ	4	29
BEDFORD	F	6	31	BEECHAM	E	2	19	BEESON	S	5	27	BELCHER	A	13	35
BEDFORD	F	7	26	BEECHES	J	2	19	BEESON	S	13	35	BELCHER	AH	4	29
BEDFORD	G	5	27	BEECHES	JW	2	19	BEESTON	A	6	32	BELCHER	E	5	27
BEDFORD	GFE	7	26	BEECHEY	A	2	19	BEESTON	EL	10	17	BELCHER	F	13	35
BEDFORD	H	8	22	BEECHEY	A	4	29	BEESTON	H	10	17	BELCHER	H	5	27
BEDFORD	HW	12	262	BEECHEY	A	4	29	BEESTON	HL	6	32	BELCHER	HF	3	276
BEDFORD	J	6	31	BEECHEY	CFE	14	20	BEESTON	WH	6	32	BELCHER	JC	7	27
BEDFORD	J	10	17	BEECHEY	F	6	32	BEET	HD	6	32	BELCHER	JM	3	276
BEDFORD	JA	8	22	BEECHEY	FE	7	26	BEET	WE	6	32	BELCHER	LP	13	35
BEDFORD	JW	10	265	BEECHEY	HW	13	34	BEETHAM	BPA	12	18	BELCHER	SJ	5	27
BEDFORD	M	4	29	BEECHING	EL	13	34	BEETHAM	C	9	14	BELDHAM	T	13	35
BEDFORD	P	5	27	BEECHING	STN	7	27	BEETHAM	J	9	14	BELDON	F	8	22
BEDFORD	P	12	18	BEECHING	W	13	34	BEETHAM	J	9	225	BELFIELD	O	9	225
BEDFORD	RT	12	262	BEECHING	WG	10	17	BEETHAM	JW	9	225	BELHAM	WJ	13	35
BEDFORD	S	12	18	BEECROFT	F	9	380	BEETHAM	RA	12	18	BELITHER	A	13	35
BEDFORD	ST	3	20	BEECROFT	GW	13	34	BEETHOLME	C	13	35	BELITHER	HJ	13	35
BEDFORD	T	8	22	BEECROFT	H	3	21	BEETISON	WT	6	32	BELITHER	R	13	35
BEDFORD	TE	12	262	BEECROFT	H	9	14	BEETLES	L	9	15	BELK	SH	9	226
BEDFORD	W	7	26	BEEDELL	T	3	276	BEETLESTONE	W	6	32	BELL	A	8	23
BEDFORD	W	8	22	BEEDHAM	GE	9	14	BEETLESTONE	WE	6	32	BELL	A	11	25
BEDFORD	W	8	22	BEEDHAM	J	3	276	BEETON	CH	9	225	BELL	A	11	25
BEDFORD	W	10	17	BEEDIE	D	10	265	BEETON	R	5	27	BELL	A	14	20
BEDINGFIELD	A	12	262	BEEDLE	FGH	13	34	BEETON	WJ	5	27	BELL	A	14	20
BEDINGHAM	FJ	7	26	BEEDON	EG	6	32	BEEVERS	A	9	15	BELL	A	14	20
BEDLOW	AP	6	31	BEELEY	R	6	32	BEEVERS	S	9	15	BELL	AA	3	21
BEDMAN	W	4	29	BEEMAN	JH	6	32	BEEVERS	T	9	15	BELL	AE	13	35
BEDMAN	WJ	7	26	BEENHAM	JE	13	34	BEEVERS	W	9	15	BELL	AJ	4	30
BEDSON	HG	6	31	BEENHAM	TC	13	34	BEEZER	WJ	13	35	BELL	AT	4	30
BEDSON	J	3	276	BEENY	EE	13	34	BEEZLEY	F	4	29	BELL	B	6	33
BEDWELL	AE	7	26	BEENY	WEA	13	35	BEEZLEY	J	4	29	BELL	C	11	25
BEDWELL	CWG	1	24	BEER	D	6	32	BEEZLEY	J	4	29	BELL	C	11	25
BEDWELL	G	7	26	BEER	F	7	27	BEGBIE	WDA	13	35	BELL	CF	6	33
BEDWIN	H	7	26	BEER	G	1	24	BEGENT	A	7	27	BELL	CG	4	30
BEE	C	8	22	BEER	J	1	24	BEGENT	AE	7	27	BELL	CL	4	30
BEE	E	2	19	BEER	JR	3	21	BEGG	A	10	18	BELL	CS	9	15
BEE	H	8	22	BEER	M	7	27	BEGLEY	FA	12	18	BELL	D	9	15
BEE	J	10	17	BEER	PS	1	24	BEGLEY	S	3	21	BELL	D	11	25
BEE	OR	8	22	BEER	SE	4	29	BEGLEY	WJ	12	18	BELL	DF	4	30

BELL	E	2	19	BELL	JP	4	30	BELLAMY	C	12	262	BELLIS	HH	5	28
BELL	E	5	27	BELL	JR	8	23	BELLAMY	CC	8	23	BELLIS	JW	5	28
BELL	E	8	23	BELL	JR	11	25	BELLAMY	CW	4	30	BELLIS	L	8	24
BELL	E	8	23	BELL	JS	7	27	BELLAMY	D	6	33	BELLISIE	F	2	20
BELL	EA	5	27	BELL	JW	8	23	BELLAMY	E	12	263	BELLMAIN	HR	10	18
BELL	EO	14	20	BELL	JW	9	15	BELLAMY	EA	12	19	BELLMAN	WJ	9	226
BELL	F	8	23	BELL	L	4	30	BELLAMY	EC	12	263	BELLOWS	H	4	30
BELL	F	10	18	BELL	L	8	23	BELLAMY	F	12	19	BELLOWS	H	4	31
BELL	F	13	35	BELL	LJ	5	28	BELLAMY	FH	12	19	BELLOWS	T	4	31
BELL	FA	5	27	BELL	N	10	18	BELLAMY	FJ	12	263	BELLWOOD	E	8	24
BELL	FH	7	27	BELL	P	10	265	BELLAMY	G	1	25	BELLWOOD	HR	8	24
BELL	FV	13	36	BELL	P	11	25	BELLAMY	HR	6	33	BELLWOOD	JW	8	24
BELL	FW	8	23	BELL	PG	5	28	BELLAMY	J	7	27	BELLWOOD	T	8	24
BELL	FW	10	265	BELL	R	11	26	BELLAMY	J	11	26	BELLWORTHY	AWH	1	25
BELL	G	11	25	BELL	R	11	26	BELLAMY	P	13	36	BELLWORTHY	EL	1	25
BELL	GD	13	36	BELL	R	14	20	BELLAMY	RW	1	25	BELSEY	JH	7	27
BELL	GE	11	25	BELL	RE	9	226	BELLAMY	S	12	263	BELSHAM	AE	3	277
BELL	GF	2	20	BELL	RJ	13	36	BELLAMY	T	14	20	BELSHAW	RI	11	421
BELL	GH	10	18	BELL	RT	13	36	BELLAMY	VS	8	23	BELSHAW	W	11	421
BELL	GH	14	20	BELL	S	4	30	BELLAMY	WG	3	277	BELSTEN	EJ	14	21
BELL	GV	13	36	BELL	T	4	30	BELLAMY	WH	12	263	BELT	H	9	226
BELL	GW	11	25	BELL	T	6	33	BELLARD	W	14	20	BELT	TA	6	33
BELL	H	1	25	BELL	T	8	23	BELLARS	FC	13	36	BELTON	A	7	27
BELL	H	4	30	BELL	T	8	23	BELLCHAMBERS	F	3	277	BELTON	E	6	33
BELL	H	6	33	BELL	T	11	25	BELLCHAMBERS	WH	3	277	BELTON	F	8	24
BELL	H	8	23	BELL	T	14	20	BELLEM	GF	4	30	BELTON	GH	7	27
BELL	H	8	23	BELL	TR	13	36	BELLENGER	G	3	277	BELTON	JE	8	24
BELL	H	9	15	BELL	V	13	36	BELLER	R	3	277	BELTON	WF	1	25
BELL	H	9	226	BELL	VT	4	30	BELLER	RG	3	277	BELTON	WH	1	25
BELL	H	9	226	BELL	W	5	28	BELLERBY	EE	2	20	BELVERSTON	E	1	25
BELL	H	11	25	BELL	W	5	28	BELLERBY	R	14	20	BEMAN	P	8	24
BELL	H	11	25	BELL	W	8	23	BELLERBY	T	9	15	BEN	BW	9	15
BELL	H	14	20	BELL	W	10	18	BELLERBY	T	9	226	BENBOW	CJ	12	19
BELL	HC	3	277	BELL	W	11	26	BELLEVUE DE SYLVA AA		1	25	BENBOW	HR	3	277
BELL	HE	5	27	BELL	W	11	26					BENBOW	WG	2	20
BELL	HE	10	18	BELL	W	11	26	BELLEVUE DE SYLVA PG		1	25	BENCH	SJ	3	21
BELL	HR	10	18	BELL	W	11	26					BENDALL	G	2	20
BELL	HWT	3	277	BELL	W	11	26	BELLEW	H	13	36	BENDELL	WA	10	18
BELL	J	3	277	BELL	W	12	19	BELLEW	J	4	30	BENDELL	WD	4	31
BELL	J	4	30	BELL	W	14	20	BELLFIELD	W	11	26	BENDER	ARE	4	31
BELL	J	4	30	BELL	WA	11	26	BELLHAM	A	12	263	BENDER	D	14	21
BELL	J	8	23	BELL	WG	11	26	BELLHAM	AE	12	263	BENDER	EG	1	25
BELL	J	8	23	BELL	WH	11	26	BELLHOUSE	JW	8	23	BENDLE	AG	1	25
BELL	J	8	23	BELL	WL	4	30	BELLHOUSE	L	8	23	BENEST	W	7	27
BELL	J	10	265	BELL	WRW	5	28	BELLIHOMJEE	CC	3	277	BENEY	WJG	10	18
BELL	J	11	25	BELL-RENNIE	W	14	21	BELLINGER	CA	4	30	BENFIELD	AW	7	28
BELL	J	11	25	BELLAIRS	A	7	27	BELLINGER	HT	3	277	BENFIELD	CA	10	18
BELL	J	11	25	BELLAIRS	SH	14	20	BELLINGER	JW	4	30	BENFIELD	CTE	10	18
BELL	J	12	19	BELLAMY	A	12	19	BELLINGER	WCJ	13	36	BENFIELD	F	6	33
BELL	J	13	36	BELLAMY	A	12	19	BELLINGHAM	F	11	26	BENFIELD	HJ	7	28
BELL	JA	11	25	BELLAMY	AE	6	33	BELLINGHAM	H	8	24	BENFIELD	SC	13	36
BELL	JG	10	265	BELLAMY	B	12	19	BELLINGHAM	J	5	28	BENFIELD	TG	3	277
BELL	JH	2	20	BELLAMY	C	6	33	BELLINGHAM	W	8	24	BENFORD	HE	1	25
BELL	JH	14	20	BELLAMY	C	8	23	BELLIS	A	7	27	BENFORD	JML	7	28
				BELLAMY	C	12	19	BELLIS	A	14	21	BENFORD	SW	1	25
								BELLIS	FT	5	28				

BENGALL	T	4	31	BENNETT	C	11	26	BENNETT	H	8	24	BENNETT	O	10	19				
BENHAM	D	10	18	BENNETT	CA	12	19	BENNETT	H	9	15	BENNETT	P	5	29				
BENHAM	FE	4	31	BENNETT	CD	5	28	BENNETT	H	9	15	BENNETT	P	12	20				
BENHAM	FG	4	31	BENNETT	CE	10	266	BENNETT	H	9	226	BENNETT	PG	6	34				
BENHAM	HV	4	31	BENNETT	CE	13	36	BENNETT	H	10	19	BENNETT	PJ	1	25				
BENHAM	W	10	18	BENNETT	CH	6	33	BENNETT	H	11	27	BENNETT	PJ	12	20				
BENIAMS	BA	4	31	BENNETT	CH	7	28	BENNETT	H	12	19	BENNETT	R	2	20				
BENIFER	E	7	28	BENNETT	CL	12	19	BENNETT	H	14	21	BENNETT	R	4	32				
BENINGFIELD	AT	13	36	BENNETT	CW	1	25	BENNETT	HAW	4	31	BENNETT	RE	2	20				
BENIT	SJ	7	28	BENNETT	DHW	4	31	BENNETT	HE	10	19	BENNETT	RE	5	29				
BENJAMAN	J	14	21	BENNETT	DS	2	20	BENNETT	HH	1	25	BENNETT	RF	5	29				
BENJAMAN	W	14	21	BENNETT	E	2	20	BENNETT	HH	4	31	BENNETT	RG	7	28				
BENJAMIN	P	14	21	BENNETT	E	4	31	BENNETT	HJ	5	28	BENNETT	RJ	7	28				
BENN	F	9	15	BENNETT	E	6	33	BENNETT	HJ	11	27	BENNETT	RS	1	25				
BENN	G	9	226	BENNETT	E	13	37	BENNETT	HJ	12	19	BENNETT	S	11	27				
BENN	H	8	24	BENNETT	EJ	10	18	BENNETT	HJ	12	19	BENNETT	SAG	10	19				
BENN	H	9	226	BENNETT	EJ	13	36	BENNETT	HL	13	37	BENNETT	SG	13	37				
BENN	JC	8	24	BENNETT	ERE	10	18	BENNETT	HM	13	37	BENNETT	T	8	24				
BENN	T	9	15	BENNETT	EW	5	28	BENNETT	HR	3	21	BENNETT	TC	3	21				
BENN	WH	8	24	BENNETT	F	5	28	BENNETT	HT	10	19	BENNETT	TE	4	32				
BENNELL	EE	12	19	BENNETT	F	10	19	BENNETT	I	12	263	BENNETT	VB	12	20				
BENNELL	JA	5	28	BENNETT	F	12	19	BENNETT	J	2	20	BENNETT	W	1	25				
BENNELL	W	11	26	BENNETT	F	12	263	BENNETT	J	5	29	BENNETT	W	2	20				
BENNELL	W	11	26	BENNETT	FA	1	25	BENNETT	J	6	34	BENNETT	W	5	29				
BENNET	C	9	15	BENNETT	FA	12	19	BENNETT	J	8	24	BENNETT	W	6	34				
BENNET	WG	3	277	BENNETT	FCPB	4	31	BENNETT	J	9	15	BENNETT	W	6	34				
BENNETT	A	2	20	BENNETT	FG	13	36	BENNETT	J	9	226	BENNETT	W	7	28				
BENNETT	A	3	277	BENNETT	FH	10	19	BENNETT	J	11	27	BENNETT	W	7	28				
BENNETT	A	5	28	BENNETT	FHGG	2	20	BENNETT	J	11	27	BENNETT	W	8	24				
BENNETT	A	5	28	BENNETT	FJ	1	25	BENNETT	J	11	27	BENNETT	W	11	27				
BENNETT	A	6	33	BENNETT	G	2	20	BENNETT	J	11	27	BENNETT	W	13	37				
BENNETT	A	6	33	BENNETT	G	3	21	BENNETT	J	11	27	BENNETT	W	13	37				
BENNETT	A	6	33	BENNETT	G	3	277	BENNETT	J	11	27	BENNETT	W	13	37				
BENNETT	A	7	28	BENNETT	G	3	277	BENNETT	J	14	21	BENNETT	WA	10	19				
BENNETT	A	9	226	BENNETT	G	4	31	BENNETT	J	14	21	BENNETT	WA	11	27				
BENNETT	A	9	226	BENNETT	G	6	33	BENNETT	J	14	21	BENNETT	WC	5	29				
BENNETT	A	10	18	BENNETT	G	11	26	BENNETT	JA	6	34	BENNETT	WC	6	34				
BENNETT	A	10	266	BENNETT	G	11	27	BENNETT	JC	1	25	BENNETT	WC	12	20				
BENNETT	A	11	26	BENNETT	G	12	19	BENNETT	JH	4	31	BENNETT	WDF	1	25				
BENNETT	A	11	26	BENNETT	GA	2	20	BENNETT	JJG	5	29	BENNETT	WE	1	26				
BENNETT	A	13	36	BENNETT	GD	10	266	BENNETT	JT	6	34	BENNETT	WE	2	21				
BENNETT	AE	5	28	BENNETT	GE	4	31	BENNETT	JT	9	16	BENNETT	WE	13	37				
BENNETT	AE	5	28	BENNETT	GF	2	20	BENNETT	JW	8	24	BENNETT	WF	1	26				
BENNETT	AE	14	21	BENNETT	GF	2	20	BENNETT	JW	12	19	BENNETT	WF	10	19				
BENNETT	AF	10	266	BENNETT	GF	6	33	BENNETT	K	10	19	BENNETT	WF	11	27				
BENNETT	AH	10	18	BENNETT	GF	13	36	BENNETT	L	4	31	BENNETT	WG	5	29				
BENNETT	AH	13	36	BENNETT	GH	6	33	BENNETT	L	10	19	BENNETT	WG	7	28				
BENNETT	AJ	12	421	BENNETT	GH	7	28	BENNETT	L	11	27	BENNETT	WG	10	19				
BENNETT	AWR	10	18	BENNETT	GH	9	15	BENNETT	LA	2	20	BENNETT	WH	3	278				
BENNETT	B	4	31	BENNETT	GH	13	37	BENNETT	LA	10	19	BENNETT	WH	7	28				
BENNETT	B	7	28	BENNETT	GR	13	37	BENNETT	LF	2	20	BENNETT	WH	8	24				
BENNETT	C	5	28	BENNETT	H	2	20	BENNETT	LJ	4	31	BENNETT	WH	9	226				
BENNETT	C	7	28	BENNETT	H	3	21	BENNETT	LS	7	28	BENNETT	WH	12	20				
BENNETT	C	8	24	BENNETT	H	3	277	BENNETT	M	12	20	BENNETT	WH	14	21				
BENNETT	C	10	18	BENNETT	H	6	33	BENNETT	MF	12	20	BENNETT	WJ	1	26				

BENNETT	WJ	3	278	BENSON	J	14	21	BENTLEY	J	11	28	BERRILL	G	1	26
BENNETT	WJ	6	34	BENSON	JS	11	27	BENTLEY	J	12	263	BERRILL	G	12	20
BENNETT	WJ	12	20	BENSON	L	2	21	BENTLEY	J	13	38	BERRIMAN	F	8	25
BENNETT	WJJ	13	37	BENSON	R	11	27	BENTLEY	L	9	16	BERRINGER	AH	12	20
BENNETT	WJS	12	20	BENSON	R	14	21	BENTLEY	RGD	8	25	BERRINGER	AR	12	20
BENNETT	WP	1	25	BENSON	T	8	25	BENTLEY	S	11	28	BERRINGTON	AG	12	20
BENNETT	WP	8	24	BENSON	T	12	263	BENTLEY	S	12	263	BERRINGTON	H	5	29
BENNETT	WR	3	278	BENSON	T	12	263	BENTLEY	S	14	22	BERRINGTON	HJ	5	30
BENNETT	WR	4	32	BENSON	WG	13	37	BENTLEY	SA	1	26	BERRINGTON	RR	12	20
BENNEY	E	7	28	BENT	A	5	29	BENTLEY	TH	3	278	BERRINGTON	WH	6	35
BENNEY	G	7	28	BENT	C	10	19	BENTLEY	WH	6	34	BERRISFORD	J	11	28
BENNEYWORTH	M	10	19	BENT	C	11	28	BENTON	A	7	29	BERROW	T	6	35
BENNIE	G	2	21	BENT	C	12	263	BENTON	CE	12	263	BERRY	A	1	26
BENNIE	J	7	29	BENT	C	14	21	BENTON	G	3	278	BERRY	A	9	227
BENNIFER	CH	5	29	BENT	E	2	21	BENTON	JW	12	20	BERRY	A	10	19
BENNIFER	TW	5	29	BENT	H	5	29	BENTON	M	9	226	BERRY	A	11	28
BENNING	H	2	21	BENT	H	5	29	BENTON	T	12	263	BERRY	A	13	38
BENNINGTON	EE	13	37	BENT	H	14	22	BENTON	W	7	29	BERRY	AF	3	278
BENNINGTON	F	13	37	BENT	J	14	22	BENTZ	JC	7	29	BERRY	AH	3	21
BENNINGTON	L	14	21	BENT	JGT	14	22	BENZEVAL	EG	10	19	BERRY	AL	5	30
BENNINGTON	WJ	13	37	BENT	M	14	22	BERAET	C	1	26	BERRY	AT	6	35
BENNION	A	10	266	BENT	S	12	263	BERENBAUM	J	14	22	BERRY	C	1	26
BENNION	C	11	27	BENT	SC	5	29	BERENBAUM	L	14	22	BERRY	C	3	21
BENNION	CT	14	21	BENT	W	11	28	BERESFORD	AJ	6	34	BERRY	CE	9	227
BENNION	HW	3	278	BENTHAM	C	3	278	BERESFORD	F	6	34	BERRY	CH	6	35
BENNISON	W	2	21	BENTHAM	T	14	22	BERESFORD	FG	1	26	BERRY	CRR	2	21
BENNY	GA	10	266	BENTHAM	W	14	22	BERESFORD	HF	6	34	BERRY	D	1	26
BENSON	A	8	25	BENTICK	H	11	28	BERESFORD	JT	11	28	BERRY	E	3	21
BENSON	A	11	27	BENTLEY	A	6	34	BERESFORD	R	11	28	BERRY	E	3	278
BENSON	A	13	37	BENTLEY	AJ	1	26	BERESFORD	R	11	28	BERRY	E	13	38
BENSON	AE	4	32	BENTLEY	C	4	32	BERESFORD	TE	6	35	BERRY	E	13	38
BENSON	BT	1	26	BENTLEY	C	5	29	BERESFORD	WA	2	21	BERRY	E	14	22
BENSON	CJ	3	21	BENTLEY	D	9	16	BERESFORD	WE	1	26	BERRY	EG	3	278
BENSON	CJ	6	34	BENTLEY	E	11	28	BERESFORD	WJ	13	38	BERRY	F	1	26
BENSON	E	8	25	BENTLEY	EE	13	37	BERGAN	H	9	226	BERRY	F	2	21
BENSON	E	9	16	BENTLEY	EM	5	29	BERGAN	H	9	227	BERRY	F	7	29
BENSON	E	9	16	BENTLEY	F	1	26	BERGER	HFC	10	266	BERRY	F	9	16
BENSON	EE	6	34	BENTLEY	F	5	29	BERGIN	E	11	28	BERRY	FC	9	16
BENSON	EK	1	26	BENTLEY	F	9	16	BERGIN	T	14	22	BERRY	FG	3	21
BENSON	ET	13	37	BENTLEY	F	14	22	BERKELEY	FW	6	35	BERRY	FW	4	32
BENSON	F	4	32	BENTLEY	G	6	34	BERKMAN	J	14	22	BERRY	FW	6	35
BENSON	FE	9	16	BENTLEY	G	9	16	BERNARD	HV	7	29	BERRY	G	2	21
BENSON	FG	4	32	BENTLEY	G	10	266	BERNER	M	14	22	BERRY	G	3	21
BENSON	FG	6	34	BENTLEY	GA	13	38	BERNHARDT	A	8	25	BERRY	G	4	32
BENSON	FR	11	421	BENTLEY	GF	3	21	BERNSTEIN	D	14	22	BERRY	G	9	16
BENSON	FW	12	20	BENTLEY	H	9	16	BERNSTEIN	J	10	19	BERRY	G	9	17
BENSON	G	8	25	BENTLEY	H	9	16	BERRA	A	11	28	BERRY	G	13	38
BENSON	G	12	20	BENTLEY	H	9	226	BERRESFORD	E	9	16	BERRY	GC	14	22
BENSON	GE	13	37	BENTLEY	H	10	266	BERRESFORD	S	9	16	BERRY	GD	12	20
BENSON	H	8	25	BENTLEY	HE	6	34	BERRETT	SJC	13	38	BERRY	GH	5	30
BENSON	H	9	226	BENTLEY	HF	2	21	BERRIDGE	A	2	21	BERRY	GH	6	35
BENSON	H	11	27	BENTLEY	HJ	5	29	BERRIDGE	A	5	29	BERRY	GH	10	19
BENSON	J	7	29	BENTLEY	J	8	25	BERRIDGE	HE	9	16	BERRY	GT	2	21
BENSON	J	8	25	BENTLEY	J	8	25	BERRIL	W	9	16	BERRY	GW	5	30
BENSON	J	13	37	BENTLEY	J	9	16	BERRILL	A	12	20	BERRY	GW	5	30

BERRY	H	1	26	BERRYMAN	JA	3	22	BEST	BM	7	29	BESWICK	H	11	29
BERRY	H	4	32	BERRYMAN	JJ	3	22	BEST	BR	2	22	BESWICK	H	11	29
BERRY	H	9	227	BERRYMAN	TH	7	29	BEST	C	1	27	BESWICK	J	11	29
BERRY	H	11	28	BERSON	D	8	25	BEST	CF	6	35	BESWICK	J	11	29
BERRY	H	14	22	BERSON	J	8	25	BEST	E	10	266	BESWICK	JC	1	27
BERRY	HE	12	21	BERSON	M	8	25	BEST	EA	4	33	BESWICK	P	14	23
BERRY	HG	1	26	BERTENSHAW	J	11	29	BEST	EA	7	29	BESWICK	R	11	29
BERRY	HJ	2	21	BERTINAT	WP	3	22	BEST	EW	8	25	BESWICK	RA	1	27
BERRY	HR	1	26	BERTRAM	E	4	32	BEST	F	9	17	BESWICK	S	6	36
BERRY	HR	2	21	BERTRAM	H	14	23	BEST	FV	1	27	BESWICK	T	14	23
BERRY	HT	3	278	BERTRAM	HE	4	32	BEST	G	1	27	BESWICK	W	11	29
BERRY	HW	3	278	BERTRAM	J	14	23	BEST	GE	7	29	BESWICK	W	14	23
BERRY	J	2	21	BERTRAM	LH	4	32	BEST	GW	8	25	BESZANT	F	13	38
BERRY	J	3	21	BERVIN	EF	10	266	BEST	H	7	29	BETHEL	A	6	36
BERRY	J	6	35	BERWICK	A	2	21	BEST	HC	7	29	BETHEL	A	14	24
BERRY	J	10	20	BERWICK	A	12	263	BEST	HG	6	35	BETHEL	AA	14	24
BERRY	J	11	28	BERWICK	AJ	12	21	BEST	HM	2	22	BETHEL	H	14	24
BERRY	J	11	28	BERWICK	W	3	278	BEST	HT	7	29	BETHEL	W	14	24
BERRY	J	13	38	BERYL	A	9	227	BEST	HW	13	38	BETHELL	F	7	30
BERRY	J	14	22	BERYL	O	9	17	BEST	J	1	27	BETHELL	FT	3	22
BERRY	J	14	23	BESANT	WE	4	32	BEST	J	3	278	BETHELL	HJ	5	30
BERRY	J	14	23	BESFOR	J	2	21	BEST	J	4	33	BETHELL	J	14	24
BERRY	JA	7	29	BESFOR	M	2	21	BEST	J	6	35	BETHELL	RJ	14	24
BERRY	JA	14	23	BESFORD	E	7	29	BEST	J	9	227	BETHELL	T	6	36
BERRY	JE	11	28	BESLINGTON	M	8	25	BEST	J	11	29	BETHELL	WP	5	30
BERRY	JG	12	21	BESLINGTON	S	8	25	BEST	LG	4	33	BETSWORTH	GS	10	266
BERRY	JH	9	17	BESSANT	A	4	32	BEST	ME	9	17	BETSWORTH	WJ	10	20
BERRY	JR	13	38	BESSANT	A	5	30	BEST	S	9	227	BETT	GJ	2	22
BERRY	JT	6	35	BESSANT	AA	4	32	BEST	ST	7	29	BETTAM	AA	3	22
BERRY	JT	14	23	BESSANT	AR	7	29	BEST	T	1	27	BETTERIDGE	AEF	4	33
BERRY	JW	9	227	BESSANT	BV	6	35	BEST	TL	13	38	BETTERIDGE	AG	4	33
BERRY	JW	10	20	BESSANT	E	4	32	BEST	TV	7	30	BETTERIDGE	D	4	33
BERRY	MA	1	26	BESSANT	EC	4	32	BEST	TW	13	38	BETTERIDGE	EM	2	22
BERRY	O	9	17	BESSANT	FA	4	32	BEST	W	5	30	BETTERIDGE	H	4	33
BERRY	OW	1	26	BESSANT	GE	10	266	BEST	W	5	30	BETTERIDGE	J	10	20
BERRY	R	3	278	BESSANT	H	4	33	BEST	W	7	30	BETTERIDGE	JT	8	26
BERRY	R	10	266	BESSANT	RAJ	4	33	BEST	WL	2	22	BETTERIDGE	R	6	36
BERRY	RA	11	28	BESSANT	RV	4	33	BEST	WR	7	30	BETTERIDGE	RA	4	33
BERRY	T	6	35	BESSANT	S	4	33	BESTE	HP	13	38	BETTERIDGE	RF	4	33
BERRY	T	9	380	BESSANT	TJ	4	33	BESTER	G	2	22	BETTERIDGE	SWG	4	33
BERRY	T	14	23	BESSANT	W	4	33	BESTER	HA	12	21	BETTERIDGE	W	4	33
BERRY	T	14	23	BESSANT	WF	4	33	BESTER	JTH	2	22	BETTERIDGE	W	8	26
BERRY	T	14	23	BESSANT	WH	4	33	BESTER	S	13	38	BETTERIDGE	WE	4	34
BERRY	TH	11	28	BESSELL	FJ	1	27	BESTIER	WH	1	27	BETTERTON	G	6	36
BERRY	TW	11	29	BESSELL	HG	1	26	BESTLEY	AJ	14	23	BETTIS	HJ	7	30
BERRY	VW	5	30	BESSELL	HT	2	21	BESTLEY	F	7	30	BETTIS	R	3	278
BERRY	W	6	35	BESSELL	W	14	23	BESWICK	A	11	29	BETTIS	WG	1	27
BERRY	W	6	35	BESSENT	A	10	20	BESWICK	C	11	29	BETTISON	C	8	26
BERRY	W	8	25	BEST	A	2	22	BESWICK	C	11	29	BETTISON	H	13	38
BERRY	W	9	17	BEST	A	7	29	BESWICK	F	11	29	BETTISON	J	3	278
BERRY	W	14	23	BEST	A	8	25	BESWICK	G	11	29	BETTLE	AS	5	30
BERRY	WH	5	30	BEST	AE	1	27	BESWICK	G	14	23	BETTLE	G	5	30
BERRY	WH	13	38	BEST	AE	5	30	BESWICK	G	14	23	BETTLE	J	12	21
BERRY	WR	10	20	BEST	AE	6	35	BESWICK	G	14	23	BETTLE	JS	5	30
BERRYMAN	FC	4	32	BEST	B	4	33	BESWICK	GE	6	36	BETTLE	JW	12	21

BETTLE	W	12	21	BEVER	JT	10	20	BEYNON	TE	2	22	BICKLEY	WL	6	37
BETTLES	A	11	29	BEVER	SM	10	20	BEYNON	W	10	21	BICKNELL	AM	6	37
BETTLES	A	12	21	BEVERIDGE	DT	1	27	BEYNON	W	10	266	BICKNELL	FT	7	30
BETTLES	CJ	13	39	BEVERLEY	A	8	26	BEZANT	JW	13	38	BICKNELL	J	4	34
BETTLEY	WH	4	34	BEVERLEY	AE	14	24	BEZZANT	H	10	21	BICKNELL	M	1	27
BETTRIDGE	A	4	34	BEVERLEY	C	9	17	BEZZANT	JA	10	266	BICKNELL	M	4	34
BETTS	A	6	36	BEVERLEY	E	8	26	BIANCHI	M	4	34	BICKNELL	RC	2	23
BETTS	A	6	36	BEVERLEY	G	8	26	BIBB	AG	6	37	BICKNELL	TW	1	27
BETTS	AO	1	27	BEVERLEY	G	8	26	BIBB	G	6	37	BICKNELL	W	4	34
BETTS	C	10	20	BEVERLEY	H	8	26	BIBB	HH	6	37	BICKNELL	W	6	37
BETTS	E	2	22	BEVERLEY	JB	14	24	BIBBS	CS	7	30	BIDDIS		3	279
BETTS	E	6	36	BEVINGTON	A	6	36	BIBBY	H	14	24	BIDDIS	J	3	279
BETTS	EJ	2	22	BEVINGTON	H	6	36	BIBBY	J	14	24	BIDDIS	J	3	279
BETTS	F	1	27	BEVINGTON	JE	6	37	BIBBY	JT	14	24	BIDDISS	J	13	39
BETTS	F	6	36	BEVINGTON	S	6	37	BIBBY	W	13	39	BIDDISS	T	13	39
BETTS	F	13	39	BEVINGTON	WR	6	37	BICE	FG	4	34	BIDDLE	A	10	21
BETTS	G	6	36	BEVINS	A	11	29	BICHENER	E	12	21	BIDDLE	EC	6	37
BETTS	GD	2	22	BEVINS	J	11	29	BICHENER	FH	12	21	BIDDLE	J	6	37
BETTS	GW	7	30	BEVINS	W	11	30	BICHENER	HF	12	21	BIDDLE	LJ	2	23
BETTS	H	6	36	BEVIS	A	10	20	BICHENER	JL	12	21	BIDDLE	WJ	6	37
BETTS	J	6	36	BEVIS	AH	10	20	BICHENO	A	10	21	BIDDLECOMBE	AE	4	35
BETTS	J	6	36	BEVIS	AJ	10	20	BICHENO	C	10	21	BIDDLECOMBE	AS	4	34
BETTS	J	13	39	BEVIS	FE	2	22	BICHENO	W	10	21	BIDDLECOMBE	C	4	34
BETTS	JA	8	26	BEVIS	FN	4	34	BICK	AE	2	22	BIDDLECOMBE	E	4	34
BETTS	LE	13	39	BEVIS	FW	10	20	BICK	AJ	2	23	BIDDLECOMBE	EJ	1	27
BETTS	SB	10	20	BEVIS	H	10	20	BICK	GV	13	39	BIDDLECOMBE	ET	4	34
BETTS	W	8	26	BEVIS	H	10	21	BICK	JA	13	39	BIDDLECOMBE	F	4	34
BETTS	W	10	20	BEVIS	J	4	34	BICK	LE	12	21	BIDDLECOMBE	FS	4	34
BETTS	WC	2	22	BEVIS	JH	3	278	BICK	T	6	37	BIDDLECOMBE	FT	4	35
BETTS	WH	8	26	BEVIS	PAE	4	34	BICK	WF	2	23	BIDDLECOMBE	GE	4	35
BETTS	WJ	12	263	BEVIS	W	4	34	BICK	WR	12	21	BIDDLECOMBE	GT	4	35
BETTS	WT	5	30	BEVIS	W	10	21	BICKEL	HE	13	39	BIDDLECOMBE	HG	4	35
BEVAN	EE	7	30	BEVIS	W	13	39	BICKERDIKE	CE	8	26	BIDDLECOMBE	I	10	21
BEVAN	FH	13	39	BEVIS	WF	10	21	BICKERDIKE	JJ	8	26	BIDDLECOMBE	TE	4	35
BEVAN	FW	6	36	BEW	AE	7	30	BICKERDIKE	JL	8	26	BIDDLECOMBE	W	4	35
BEVAN	G	1	27	BEW	F	1	27	BICKERDIKE	S	8	26	BIDDLECOMBE	W	4	35
BEVAN	G	6	36	BEW	PA	1	27	BICKERDIKE	T	8	26	BIDDLECOMBE	W	4	35
BEVAN	G	13	39	BEW	W	7	30	BICKERDYKE	J	11	30	BIDDLECOMBE	WWB	4	35
BEVAN	I	11	29	BEW	WF	7	30	BICKERDYKE	W	11	30	BIDDLES	E	1	27
BEVAN	J	2	22	BEWELL	JR	12	21	BICKERS	EA	10	21	BIDDLES	G	1	28
BEVAN	JD	6	36	BEWLEY	J	3	22	BICKERS	JR	11	30	BIDDLESTON	R	6	37
BEVAN	JO	3	22	BEWLEY	JFB	2	22	BICKERSTAFF	F	12	264	BIDDLESTONE	A	6	37
BEVAN	JW	14	24	BEWLEY	WC	4	34	BICKERSTAFF	T	11	30	BIDDULPH	W	6	38
BEVAN	N	2	22	BEWS	FW	7	30	BICKERSTAFF	WH	10	267	BIDEN	EL	7	30
BEVAN	T	14	24	BEWS	J	13	39	BICKERTON	AE	13	39	BIDEWELL	H	5	30
BEVAN	TH	13	39	BEWSEY	FV	13	39	BICKERTON	H	11	30	BIDGOOD	JM	2	23
BEVAN	TH	14	24	BEWSEY	WS	7	30	BICKERTON	TA	5	30	BIDGWAY	HJJ	3	22
BEVAN	TW	1	27	BEX	JR	12	263	BICKFORD	T	2	23	BIDWELL	AS	3	279
BEVAN	W	1	27	BEX	P	8	26	BICKLE	HM	4	34	BIDWELL	F	13	39
BEVAN	W	2	22	BEXHELL	G	1	27	BICKLEY	B	6	37	BIDWELL	JR	10	267
BEVAN	WG	13	39	BEXLEY	EE	8	26	BICKLEY	GH	6	37	BIDWELL	T	1	28
BEVANS	AJ	9	17	BEXLEY	FA	5	30	BICKLEY	N	14	24	BIELBY	CJ	4	35
BEVANS	E	2	22	BEYER	C	3	278	BICKLEY	R	13	39	BIERMAN	J	14	24
BEVER	J	10	20	BEYER	GH	3	279	BICKLEY	S	6	37	BIERTON	AR	5	31
BEVER	J	10	20	BEYNON	FC	10	21	BICKLEY	TW	6	37	BIERTON	D	5	31

BIERTON	J	5	31
BIFFIN	A	4	35
BIFFIN	E	3	22
BIFFIN	EC	4	35
BIFFIN	EC	4	35
BIFFIN	HJ	3	22
BIFFIN	J	4	35
BIFFIN	WE	13	40
BIFIELD	WJ	1	28
BIGENT	HGC	7	30
BIGG	AV	1	28
BIGG	F	12	21
BIGGADI	BJ	5	31
BIGGERSTAFF	G	1	28
BIGGERSTAFF	H	13	40
BIGGERSTAFF	L	5	31
BIGGS	A	3	279
BIGGS	A	10	267
BIGGS	A	13	40
BIGGS	AL	7	30
BIGGS	AW	1	28
BIGGS	AW	4	35
BIGGS	BJ	3	279
BIGGS	C	5	31
BIGGS	CT	11	30
BIGGS	E	12	264
BIGGS	EH	4	35
BIGGS	F	1	28
BIGGS	F	2	23
BIGGS	FA	5	31
BIGGS	FE	12	21
BIGGS	FJS	12	21
BIGGS	G	5	31
BIGGS	G	6	38
BIGGS	GH	2	23
BIGGS	GH	6	38
BIGGS	H	12	264
BIGGS	HC	1	28
BIGGS	J	3	279
BIGGS	J	3	279
BIGGS	J	6	38
BIGGS	JH	2	23
BIGGS	JJ	6	38
BIGGS	JM	7	30
BIGGS	JT	12	21
BIGGS	LE	6	38
BIGGS	PE	4	35
BIGGS	PE	4	35
BIGGS	R	3	279
BIGGS	SH	7	31
BIGGS	T	4	35
BIGGS	W	4	36
BIGGS	W	12	264
BIGGS	WC	2	23
BIGGS	WE	1	28
BIGGS	WG	4	36
BIGGS	WH	13	40
BIGGS	WW	4	36
BIGINTON	HE	13	40
BIGINTON	J	13	40
BIGINTON	JH	13	40
BIGLEY	TF	7	31
BIGMORE	HJ	5	31
BIGNALL	A	1	28
BIGNELL	AJ	12	22
BIGNELL	AR	12	264
BIGNELL	AW	12	264
BIGNELL	CJ	2	23
BIGNELL	CT	2	23
BIGNELL	FG	5	31
BIGNELL	FJ	1	28
BIGNELL	G	4	36
BIGNELL	GJ	4	36
BIGNELL	GW	12	22
BIGNELL	H	12	22
BIGNELL	H	12	264
BIGNELL	HA	5	31
BIGNELL	J	4	36
BIGNELL	J	6	38
BIGNELL	J	12	264
BIGNELL	JH	12	22
BIGNELL	JW	6	38
BIGNELL	O	6	38
BIGNELL	S	2	23
BIGNELL	SJ	12	22
BIGNELL	TH	2	23
BIGNELL	TH	3	279
BIGNELL	W	4	36
BIGNELL	W	6	38
BIGNELL	WC	4	36
BIGNOLD	A	7	31
BIGSBY	WB	2	23
BIGWELL	EP	1	28
BIGWOOD	A	10	267
BIGWOOD	CW	2	23
BIGWOOD	EG	13	40
BIGWOOD	H	13	40
BIGWOOD	J	13	40
BILBEE	H	1	28
BILBEE	HG	2	23
BILBY	F	13	40
BILCOCK	E	5	31
BILDING	H	13	40
BILES	EJ	4	36
BILES	J	4	36
BILES	JM	4	36
BILEY	WH	5	31
BILHAM	G	7	31
BILL	J	9	17
BILL	W	10	267
BILLBROUGH	F	8	26
BILLBROUGH	J	8	26
BILLEN	P	2	23
BILLERS	J	1	28
BILLERS	J	7	31
BILLERS	WG	7	31
BILLETT	C	12	264
BILLETT	LJ	1	28
BILLHAM	J	2	24
BILLIARDS	E	8	26
BILLING	AE	1	28
BILLING	AF	5	31
BILLING	EW	12	22
BILLING	F	1	28
BILLING	F	9	227
BILLING	FH	5	31
BILLING	J	12	264
BILLING	JG	9	227
BILLING	JJ	10	21
BILLING	T	12	22
BILLING	TH	12	264
BILLINGHAM	A	12	264
BILLINGHAM	A	12	264
BILLINGHAM	A	12	264
BILLINGHAM	AH	12	264
BILLINGHAM	AR	12	264
BILLINGHAM	C	12	264
BILLINGHAM	E	12	264
BILLINGHAM	EA	12	22
BILLINGHAM	F	12	264
BILLINGHAM	F	12	264
BILLINGHAM	H	12	264
BILLINGHAM	HF	12	265
BILLINGHAM	JC	12	265
BILLINGHAM	JG	12	265
BILLINGHAM	OG	12	265
BILLINGHAM	R	11	30
BILLINGHAM	R	12	265
BILLINGHAM	T	5	31
BILLINGHAM	T	12	265
BILLINGHAM	TW	12	22
BILLINGHAM	W	12	265
BILLINGHAM	W	12	265
BILLINGHAM	W	12	265
BILLINGHAM	W	12	265
BILLINGHAM	WP	12	265
BILLINGHAM	WR	12	265
BILLINGHURST	AH	4	36
BILLINGHURST	AW	4	36
BILLINGS	H	11	30
BILLINGS	J	11	30
BILLINGS	J	14	24
BILLINGS	T	12	22
BILLINGS	WF	6	38
BILLINGS	WN	6	38
BILLINGSLEY	A	6	38
BILLINGSLEY	CH	6	38
BILLINGSLEY	JM	6	38
BILLINGSLEY	TR	6	38
BILLINGTON	A	5	31
BILLINGTON	C	5	31
BILLINGTON	E	12	22
BILLINGTON	E	14	24
BILLINGTON	F	2	24
BILLINGTON	F	5	31
BILLINGTON	F	6	38
BILLINGTON	F	8	27
BILLINGTON	F	12	22
BILLINGTON	FE	12	22
BILLINGTON	FR	5	31
BILLINGTON	G	2	24
BILLINGTON	GE	2	24
BILLINGTON	H	5	31
BILLINGTON	H	5	32
BILLINGTON	HF	5	32
BILLINGTON	J	5	32
BILLINGTON	J	11	30
BILLINGTON	J	14	25
BILLINGTON	J	14	25
BILLINGTON	JT	6	39
BILLINGTON	L	5	32
BILLINGTON	O	5	32
BILLINGTON	S	12	22
BILLINGTON	T	12	265
BILLINGTON	V	5	32
BILLINGTON	W	5	32
BILLINGTON	W	5	32
BILLINGTON	W	8	27
BILLINGTON	W	11	30
BILLINGTON	W	14	25
BILLINGTON	WC	5	32
BILLINNESS	BC	4	36
BILLINNESS	GT	4	36
BILLOT	PH	4	36
BILLOWS	AG	4	36
BILLOWS	T	4	36
BILLSBERRY	M	8	27
BILLSBURY	JW	8	27
BILLSON	AC	12	265
BILLSON	FC	2	24
BILLSON	G	7	31
BILLSON	GA	1	28
BILLSON	MA	1	28
BILLSON	W	12	265
BILSDON	E	3	279
BILTON	G	8	27
BILTON	P	8	27
BILTON	W	9	17
BILTON	W	9	227
BILYARD	CH	3	279

BINDER	ER	2	24	BINNS	W	9	227	BIRCH	JJ	4	37	BIRD	A	8	28
BINDOFF	EJJ	13	40	BINNS	W	9	227	BIRCH	JW	3	279	BIRD	A	9	228
BINDON	HC	2	24	BINSLEY	J	8	27	BIRCH	JW	6	39	BIRD	AE	6	39
BING	GF	13	40	BINSTEAD	WJ	10	21	BIRCH	L	5	32	BIRD	AE	12	22
BING	N	13	40	BINSTEAD	WT	4	37	BIRCH	L	5	32	BIRD	AF	6	39
BING	NEL	13	40	BINT	FGW	12	22	BIRCH	L	14	25	BIRD	AG	5	33
BING	WH	13	40	BINT	WH	12	22	BIRCH	P	6	39	BIRD	AJ	6	39
BINGE	F	4	36	BINTCLIFFE	F	4	37	BIRCH	R	2	24	BIRD	AJ	12	23
BINGHAM	A	5	32	BINTCLIFFE	FN	4	37	BIRCH	R	3	280	BIRD	AJ	12	266
BINGHAM	A	11	30	BINYON	M	2	24	BIRCH	R	8	28	BIRD	B	5	33
BINGHAM	AF	1	28	BINYON	O	14	25	BIRCH	R	12	265	BIRD	B	6	40
BINGHAM	AJ	2	24	BINYON	TF	13	41	BIRCH	RH	7	31	BIRD	BJ	12	23
BINGHAM	F	11	30	BINYON	WF	13	41	BIRCH	S	12	23	BIRD	BR	12	23
BINGHAM	GW	11	30	BIOLETTI	CW	3	279	BIRCH	SW	2	24	BIRD	C	5	33
BINGHAM	HE	1	28	BIRBECK	HF	6	39	BIRCH	T	14	25	BIRD	C	7	31
BINGHAM	J	10	21	BIRCH	A	2	24	BIRCH	TFC	10	21	BIRD	C	8	28
BINGHAM	J	14	25	BIRCH	A	4	37	BIRCH	W	1	29	BIRD	C	12	23
BINGHAM	J	14	25	BIRCH	A	5	32	BIRCH	W	3	22	BIRD	CH	11	31
BINGHAM	WJ	10	21	BIRCH	A	7	31	BIRCH	W	3	280	BIRD	CH	14	26
BINGHAM	WJ	11	30	BIRCH	A	8	27	BIRCH	W	5	32	BIRD	CJ	7	31
BINGLEY	A	8	27	BIRCH	A	12	22	BIRCH	W	5	32	BIRD	CR	13	41
BINGLEY	WC	9	17	BIRCH	A	14	25	BIRCH	W	8	28	BIRD	DS	10	267
BINKS	CW	8	27	BIRCH	AG	12	22	BIRCH	W	11	31	BIRD	E	12	266
BINKS	D	9	380	BIRCH	AJ	14	25	BIRCH	W	12	265	BIRD	EG	7	31
BINKS	W	8	27	BIRCH	AL	3	279	BIRCH	WA	5	32	BIRD	EI	10	21
BINNELL	SJ	6	38	BIRCH	AT	4	37	BIRCH	WG	5	32	BIRD	EW	1	29
BINNEY	AE	4	36	BIRCH	AW	8	28	BIRCH	WH	11	31	BIRD	F	6	39
BINNING	CC	13	40	BIRCH	CF	3	279	BIRCH	WH	12	265	BIRD	F	12	23
BINNING	WJ	1	28	BIRCH	CJ	11	30	BIRCH	WJ	1	28	BIRD	F	12	266
BINNINGTON	G	2	24	BIRCH	D	6	39	BIRCH	WJ	1	29	BIRD	FC	12	266
BINNION	A	6	39	BIRCH	DG	6	39	BIRCH	WJ	2	24	BIRD	FE	13	41
BINNION	F	6	39	BIRCH	E	7	31	BIRCH	WJ	2	24	BIRD	FGN	1	29
BINNS	A	8	27	BIRCH	E	12	265	BIRCH	WJ	12	23	BIRD	FJ	13	41
BINNS	A	9	17	BIRCH	EG	3	279	BIRCH	WJ	13	41	BIRD	FS	6	40
BINNS	A	9	17	BIRCH	F	6	39	BIRCH	WS	7	31	BIRD	FW	11	31
BINNS	A	9	17	BIRCH	F	6	39	BIRCHALL	A	14	25	BIRD	G	3	22
BINNS	A	9	227	BIRCH	F	11	30	BIRCHALL	CJ	13	41	BIRD	G	5	33
BINNS	B	9	227	BIRCH	F	13	41	BIRCHALL	H	14	25	BIRD	G	8	28
BINNS	D	8	27	BIRCH	G	12	265	BIRCHALL	J	14	25	BIRD	G	10	22
BINNS	F	9	227	BIRCH	GW	5	32	BIRCHALL	J	14	25	BIRD	G	12	23
BINNS	GA	9	17	BIRCH	H	2	24	BIRCHALL	J	14	25	BIRD	G	12	266
BINNS	GW	8	27	BIRCH	H	4	37	BIRCHALL	P	11	31	BIRD	G	13	41
BINNS	J	6	39	BIRCH	H	8	28	BIRCHALL	TW	14	25	BIRD	GH	2	25
BINNS	J	8	27	BIRCH	H	12	265	BIRCHELL	H	13	41	BIRD	GH	6	40
BINNS	J	8	27	BIRCH	H	13	41	BIRCHELL	JR	13	41	BIRD	GR	12	266
BINNS	J	9	227	BIRCH	HA	2	24	BIRCHENOUGH	D	14	25	BIRD	GS	7	31
BINNS	J	9	227	BIRCH	HR	14	25	BIRCHENOUGH	F	11	31	BIRD	GW	5	33
BINNS	JT	2	24	BIRCH	HS	13	41	BIRCHENOUGH	G	13	41	BIRD	H	5	33
BINNS	R	8	27	BIRCH	J	2	24	BIRCHENOUGH	J	14	25	BIRD	H	6	40
BINNS	R	8	27	BIRCH	J	6	39	BIRCHLEY	WW	3	22	BIRD	H	8	28
BINNS	TH	8	27	BIRCH	J	6	39	BIRCHMORE	AJ	3	22	BIRD	H	8	28
BINNS	W	6	39	BIRCH	J	9	18	BIRD		2	25	BIRD	H	8	28
BINNS	W	8	27	BIRCH	J	11	31	BIRD	A	5	32	BIRD	H	11	31
BINNS	W	9	17	BIRCH	JA	8	28	BIRD	A	5	33	BIRD	H	13	41
BINNS	W	9	17	BIRCH	JF	1	29	BIRD	A	6	39	BIRD	HC	3	280

BIRD	HC	6	40	BIRD	WER	3	280	BIRT	FG	10	22	BISHOP	F	7	32
BIRD	HE	3	280	BIRD	WF	6	40	BIRT	HE	3	23	BISHOP	FA	13	42
BIRD	HG	5	33	BIRD	WH	3	280	BIRT	HE	6	40	BISHOP	FH	2	25
BIRD	HR	12	23	BIRD	WS	2	25	BIRT	SF	3	23	BISHOP	FH	10	22
BIRD	HT	12	266	BIRDS	H	11	31	BIRT	TH	4	37	BISHOP	FJ	2	25
BIRD	HW	5	33	BIRDSELL	F	8	28	BIRT	W	8	28	BISHOP	FW	3	280
BIRD	J	1	29	BIRDSEY	HF	5	33	BIRTLES	H	11	31	BISHOP	G	10	267
BIRD	J	2	25	BIRDSEY	JC	5	33	BIRTLES	H	14	26	BISHOP	G	13	42
BIRD	J	5	33	BIRDSEY	WT	5	34	BIRTSALL	C	9	18	BISHOP	GA	6	41
BIRD	J	6	40	BIRDSEYE	J	7	32	BIRTWHISTLE	F	8	29	BISHOP	GA	13	42
BIRD	J	6	40	BIRDSEYE	M	7	32	BIRTWISTLE	A	14	26	BISHOP	GD	7	32
BIRD	J	6	40	BIRDSEYE	TH	3	280	BIRTWISTLE	E	14	26	BISHOP	GH	10	267
BIRD	J	7	31	BIRDSWORTH	WE	14	26	BIRTWISTLE	H	14	26	BISHOP	GW	12	23
BIRD	J	11	31	BIRKATT	GW	5	34	BIRTWISTLE	J	14	26	BISHOP	H	6	41
BIRD	J	11	31	BIRKBECK	A	9	18	BISCARDINE	H	13	42	BISHOP	H	12	23
BIRD	J	12	23	BIRKBECK	E	14	26	BISCARDINE	I	13	42	BISHOP	H	13	42
BIRD	J	13	41	BIRKBY	AA	13	42	BISCARDINE	V	13	42	BISHOP	H	13	43
BIRD	JE	10	267	BIRKBY	AA	13	42	BISCOE	V	10	267	BISHOP	H	13	43
BIRD	JS	5	33	BIRKBY	GH	13	42	BISCOMBE	F	8	29	BISHOP	H	13	43
BIRD	JT	9	18	BIRKENSHAW	G	8	28	BISEKER	CW	12	266	BISHOP	HG	1	29
BIRD	JW	6	40	BIRKENSHAW	H	8	28	BISH	AJ	2	25	BISHOP	HH	2	25
BIRD	JW	12	23	BIRKETT	A	14	26	BISHOP	A	3	23	BISHOP	J	3	23
BIRD	L	3	22	BIRKETT	CA	7	32	BISHOP	A	6	40	BISHOP	JH	3	280
BIRD	L	5	33	BIRKETT	E	8	28	BISHOP	A	7	32	BISHOP	JJ	7	32
BIRD	L	5	33	BIRKETT	H	9	18	BISHOP	A	10	267	BISHOP	JW	5	34
BIRD	LA	2	25	BIRKETT	HE	13	42	BISHOP	AC	6	40	BISHOP	L	2	25
BIRD	LM	2	25	BIRKETT	N	9	18	BISHOP	AE	4	37	BISHOP	LGW	2	25
BIRD	LS	6	40	BIRKETT	R	9	18	BISHOP	AG	4	37	BISHOP	NJ	1	29
BIRD	M	3	280	BIRKETT	RD	1	29	BISHOP	AH	5	34	BISHOP	O	6	41
BIRD	P	5	33	BIRKETT	W	8	28	BISHOP	AHT	13	42	BISHOP	R	2	25
BIRD	P	11	31	BIRKHEAD	D	9	228	BISHOP	AJ	4	37	BISHOP	R	7	32
BIRD	PA	5	33	BIRKIN	J	8	28	BISHOP	AJ	5	34	BISHOP	R	13	43
BIRD	R	13	41	BIRKINHEAD	HA	6	40	BISHOP	AS	1	29	BISHOP	R	13	43
BIRD	R	13	42	BIRKS	C	14	26	BISHOP	AT	6	40	BISHOP	RJ	4	37
BIRD	R	14	26	BIRKS	E	3	280	BISHOP	AW	7	32	BISHOP	RJ	13	43
BIRD	RA	8	28	BIRKS	F	1	29	BISHOP	B	6	41	BISHOP	SA	7	32
BIRD	S	5	33	BIRKS	FA	13	42	BISHOP	BW	6	41	BISHOP	SF	7	32
BIRD	S	5	33	BIRKS	FE	3	280	BISHOP	C	5	34	BISHOP	SG	2	25
BIRD	S	6	40	BIRKS	JE	7	32	BISHOP	CH	2	25	BISHOP	SGC	7	32
BIRD	S	12	23	BIRKS	N	8	28	BISHOP	CH	6	41	BISHOP	T	4	37
BIRD	SJ	12	23	BIRKS	RF	2	25	BISHOP	CJ	13	42	BISHOP	T	13	43
BIRD	T	6	40	BIRLEY	SH	14	26	BISHOP	CV	1	29	BISHOP	TA	6	41
BIRD	T	14	26	BIRMINGHAM	F	14	26	BISHOP	CW	2	25	BISHOP	TE	6	41
BIRD	TJ	7	31	BIRMINGHAM	T	1	29	BISHOP	D	1	29	BISHOP	TR	7	32
BIRD	W	6	40	BIRMINGHAM	W	13	42	BISHOP	E	8	29	BISHOP	W	1	29
BIRD	W	7	31	BIRRELL	A	3	22	BISHOP	EA	1	29	BISHOP	W	2	26
BIRD	W	7	32	BIRRELL	D	7	32	BISHOP	EA	3	23	BISHOP	W	2	26
BIRD	W	7	32	BIRRELL	L	3	22	BISHOP	EB	1	29	BISHOP	W	3	23
BIRD	W	8	28	BIRRELL	WE	3	22	BISHOP	EC	2	25	BISHOP	W	6	41
BIRD	W	12	266	BIRSDALL	JT	9	228	BISHOP	EC	13	42	BISHOP	WA	10	22
BIRD	W	12	266	BIRT	A	4	37	BISHOP	EH	7	32	BISHOP	WC	4	37
BIRD	W	12	266	BIRT	A	10	22	BISHOP	EM	4	37	BISHOP	WF	13	43
BIRD	W	12	266	BIRT	AH	6	40	BISHOP	F	3	280	BISHOP	WH	2	26
BIRD	WA	10	21	BIRT	CA	2	25	BISHOP	F	5	34	BISHOP	WH	2	26
BIRD	WA	14	26	BIRT	F	3	22	BISHOP	F	5	34	BISHOP	WH	6	41

Name	In.			Name	In.			Name	In.			Name	In.		
BISHOP	WH	7	32	BLACK	HE	12	23	BLACKBURN	S	9	18	BLACKMORE	W	4	38
BISHOP	WH	7	33	BLACK	HS	13	43	BLACKBURN	T	9	18	BLACKMORE	WJ	4	38
BISHOP	WH	13	43	BLACK	J	11	31	BLACKBURN	T	9	381	BLACKNELL	JW	2	27
BISHOP-BENNIE	J	2	26	BLACK	J	14	26	BLACKBURN	T	14	27	BLACKSHAW	A	14	27
BISHOPP	MC	3	280	BLACK	JF	4	38	BLACKBURN	T	14	27	BLACKSHAW	JW	11	31
BISNELL	W	7	33	BLACK	JRC	4	38	BLACKBURN	W	3	23	BLACKSHAW	TH	7	33
BISNEY	E	5	34	BLACK	L	14	27	BLACKBURN	W	8	29	BLACKSHAW	TWA	1	30
BISNEY	H	5	34	BLACK	LC	4	38	BLACKBURN	W	8	29	BLACKWELL	A	5	34
BISNEY	P	5	34	BLACK	LH	1	29	BLACKBURN	W	8	29	BLACKWELL	A	5	34
BISNEY	WJ	5	34	BLACK	M	11	31	BLACKBURN	W	9	228	BLACKWELL	AA	6	41
BISPHAM	HM	10	267	BLACK	R	4	38	BLACKBURN	W	9	228	BLACKWELL	AC	13	43
BISPHAN	WJ	4	37	BLACK	R	10	22	BLACKBURN	WA	8	29	BLACKWELL	AF	5	34
BISS	C	10	22	BLACK	RA	14	27	BLACKBURN	WF	1	30	BLACKWELL	C	7	33
BISS	F	10	22	BLACK	RF	14	27	BLACKETT	WF	9	18	BLACKWELL	E	5	34
BISS	FE	1	29	BLACK	S	14	27	BLACKFORD	JH	7	33	BLACKWELL	E	12	23
BISS	G	1	29	BLACK	T	1	29	BLACKFORD	W	3	280	BLACKWELL	EN	9	18
BISS	J	10	22	BLACK	TH	6	41	BLACKHAM	F	1	30	BLACKWELL	F	3	281
BISS	WJ	2	26	BLACK	W	3	280	BLACKHAM	F	6	41	BLACKWELL	G	12	24
BISSEKER	WH	6	41	BLACK	W	14	27	BLACKHAM	FC	1	30	BLACKWELL	GT	5	34
BISSELL	FC	1	29	BLACK	WE	12	23	BLACKHAM	H	6	41	BLACKWELL	H	9	19
BISSITT	JW	8	29	BLACKAH	HE	10	267	BLACKHAM	J	3	23	BLACKWELL	HC	5	34
BISSITT	W	8	29	BLACKAH	W	9	228	BLACKHAM	TH	2	26	BLACKWELL	J	7	33
BISTWISTLE	JE	9	18	BLACKALL	G	13	43	BLACKHURST	SC	14	27	BLACKWELL	J	8	29
BITCHERS	HW	9	18	BLACKALLER	J	2	26	BLACKLEY	J	11	31	BLACKWELL	JE	6	41
BITHELL	GW	6	41	BLACKARY	AW	3	280	BLACKMAN	AE	3	281	BLACKWELL	JE	11	31
BITHELL	L	6	41	BLACKBAND	JH	11	31	BLACKMAN	AE	10	22	BLACKWELL	JH	13	44
BITMEAD	C	2	26	BLACKBAND	JJ	8	29	BLACKMAN	AJ	3	281	BLACKWELL	JJ	2	27
BITMEAD	GS	2	26	BLACKBOROUGH	A	2	26	BLACKMAN	E	10	22	BLACKWELL	JS	12	24
BITTEN	J	7	33	BLACKBURN	A	2	26	BLACKMAN	EG	7	33	BLACKWELL	JS	14	27
BIXBY	C	3	280	BLACKBURN	A	2	26	BLACKMAN	ER	4	38	BLACKWELL	JW	5	34
BIZZELL	FA	12	23	BLACKBURN	A	8	29	BLACKMAN	ER	7	33	BLACKWELL	LF	12	24
BLABER	G	3	23	BLACKBURN	A	9	18	BLACKMAN	F	2	26	BLACKWELL	LH	2	27
BLABER	J	2	26	BLACKBURN	BM	8	29	BLACKMAN	FT	10	267	BLACKWELL	PB	13	44
BLABER	J	7	33	BLACKBURN	CN	3	23	BLACKMAN	G	2	27	BLACKWELL	R	5	35
BLABER	SJ	2	26	BLACKBURN	E	8	29	BLACKMAN	G	3	281	BLACKWELL	TH	12	266
BLACHER	GE	2	26	BLACKBURN	E	8	29	BLACKMAN	J	10	22	BLACKWELL	WJ	13	44
BLACHFORD	A	4	37	BLACKBURN	E	14	27	BLACKMAN	J	13	43	BLACKWELL	WJ	13	44
BLACHFORD	AC	4	37	BLACKBURN	EA	7	33	BLACKMAN	JO	3	281	BLADEN	B	9	228
BLACHFORD	ES	4	37	BLACKBURN	F	8	29	BLACKMAN	R	4	38	BLADEN	G	6	41
BLACHFORD	F	4	38	BLACKBURN	F	9	18	BLACKMAN	R	10	22	BLADEN	W	6	41
BLACK	A	4	38	BLACKBURN	F	9	18	BLACKMAN	R	10	22	BLADES	G	10	22
BLACK	A	10	22	BLACKBURN	FG	1	29	BLACKMAN	T	1	30	BLADON	EJ	5	35
BLACK	AC	10	22	BLACKBURN	FJ	1	30	BLACKMAN	TA	4	38	BLADON	FC	5	35
BLACK	AS	14	26	BLACKBURN	G	8	29	BLACKMAN	TW	13	43	BLADON	TH	6	42
BLACK	AT	7	33	BLACKBURN	H	2	26	BLACKMAN	WHE	4	38	BLAGBROUGH	WJ	11	32
BLACK	C	1	29	BLACKBURN	HW	9	228	BLACKMORE	A	1	30	BLAGDEN	FJ	10	267
BLACK	CF	1	29	BLACKBURN	J	8	29	BLACKMORE	A	2	27	BLAGDON	AJ	13	44
BLACK	CJ	13	43	BLACKBURN	J	9	18	BLACKMORE	AH	4	38	BLAGDON	WC	13	44
BLACK	E	8	29	BLACKBURN	J	14	27	BLACKMORE	CH	4	38	BLAGG	A	11	32
BLACK	F	3	280	BLACKBURN	J	14	27	BLACKMORE	HJ	13	43	BLAGG	EJ	2	27
BLACK	F	14	26	BLACKBURN	JT	8	29	BLACKMORE	JA	2	27	BLAGG	JW	11	32
BLACK	GH	8	29	BLACKBURN	JV	5	34	BLACKMORE	JH	2	27	BLAGROVE	WR	2	27
BLACK	GS	11	31	BLACKBURN	L	9	18	BLACKMORE	M	10	22	BLAIN	A	12	24
BLACK	GW	13	43	BLACKBURN	R	9	228	BLACKMORE	RH	13	44	BLAIN	D	6	42
BLACK	H	13	43	BLACKBURN	RW	8	29	BLACKMORE	TR	2	27	BLAIN	F	11	32

BLAIN	PW	12	24	BLAKE	GEW	7	33	BLAKE	WJ	1	30	BLAKIE	A	5	35
BLAINE	A	14	27	BLAKE	GH	4	39	BLAKE	WJ	4	40	BLAKISTON	LV	2	27
BLAIR	FH	11	32	BLAKE	GJ	3	281	BLAKE	WJ	5	35	BLAMIRE	G	13	44
BLAIR	JJ	14	27	BLAKE	GJ	3	281	BLAKE	WJC	7	34	BLAMIRE	HC	8	31
BLAIR	S	11	32	BLAKE	GJ	7	33	BLAKE	WL	6	42	BLAMIRE	R	13	44
BLAIR	T	8	30	BLAKE	GT	4	39	BLAKEBOROUGH	CE	8	30	BLAMIRES	H	9	228
BLAIR	W	11	32	BLAKE	H	5	35	BLAKEBOROUGH	CE	8	30	BLAMIRES	JE	9	19
BLAIR	W	11	32	BLAKE	H	7	33	BLAKEBOROUGH	G	8	30	BLAMIRES	JE	9	228
BLAKE	A	1	30	BLAKE	H	9	19	BLAKEBOROUGH	GE	8	30	BLAMPIED	P	4	40
BLAKE	A	3	281	BLAKE	HE	4	39	BLAKEBOROUGH	H	8	30	BLANCH	F	3	281
BLAKE	A	4	38	BLAKE	HE	14	27	BLAKEBOROUGH	H	8	30	BLANCH	JA	7	34
BLAKE	A	5	35	BLAKE	HG	10	268	BLAKEBOROUGH	J	8	30	BLANCH	JR	7	34
BLAKE	A	7	33	BLAKE	I	1	30	BLAKEBOROUGH	WA	8	30	BLANCH	SF	7	34
BLAKE	AA	1	30	BLAKE	J	4	39	BLAKEBOROUGH	WH	8	30	BLANCHARD	E	14	28
BLAKE	AE	3	281	BLAKE	J	4	39	BLAKELEY	A	8	30	BLANCHARD	F	4	40
BLAKE	AE	4	38	BLAKE	J	7	33	BLAKELEY	A	11	32	BLANCHARD	F	4	40
BLAKE	AE	4	38	BLAKE	J	10	268	BLAKELEY	B	11	32	BLANCHARD	FW	5	35
BLAKE	AE	13	44	BLAKE	JH	6	42	BLAKELEY	BH	13	44	BLANCHARD	G	3	23
BLAKE	AG	1	30	BLAKE	JR	11	32	BLAKELEY	C	8	30	BLANCHARD	G	11	33
BLAKE	AH	4	38	BLAKE	JS	7	33	BLAKELEY	C	8	30	BLANCHARD	G	13	44
BLAKE	AH	7	33	BLAKE	JT	6	42	BLAKELEY	C	14	27	BLANCHARD	GH	10	268
BLAKE	AJ	4	38	BLAKE	JT	10	23	BLAKELEY	E	8	30	BLANCHARD	GW	4	40
BLAKE	AW	6	42	BLAKE	JW	7	33	BLAKELEY	G	14	27	BLANCHARD	R	3	281
BLAKE	B	12	266	BLAKE	JW	7	34	BLAKELEY	H	8	30	BLANCHARD	RJ	12	24
BLAKE	BC	10	267	BLAKE	JW	11	32	BLAKELEY	H	8	30	BLANCHARD	SA	11	33
BLAKE	BR	1	30	BLAKE	JW	13	44	BLAKELEY	W	8	30	BLANCHETTE	G	13	44
BLAKE	C	5	35	BLAKE	L	5	35	BLAKELEY	W	11	32	BLANCHFLOWER	W	13	45
BLAKE	CH	10	267	BLAKE	LC	9	19	BLAKELEY	WM	14	27	BLAND	AE	12	24
BLAKE	CH	10	268	BLAKE	LH	4	39	BLAKEMAN	H	12	266	BLAND	AE	12	266
BLAKE	CJ	13	44	BLAKE	M	13	44	BLAKEMAN	S	6	42	BLAND	BW	5	35
BLAKE	CN	1	30	BLAKE	MA	3	23	BLAKEMAN	W	12	266	BLAND	CA	12	24
BLAKE	CP	13	44	BLAKE	MJ	8	30	BLAKEMORE	E	6	42	BLAND	E	9	19
BLAKE	CW	2	27	BLAKE	P	4	39	BLAKEMORE	H	14	28	BLAND	EH	5	35
BLAKE	CWE	4	38	BLAKE	PL	4	39	BLAKEMORE	RGR	13	44	BLAND	FJ	5	35
BLAKE	E	3	281	BLAKE	PW	4	39	BLAKEMORE	SCB	13	44	BLAND	FM	1	30
BLAKE	E	4	39	BLAKE	R	2	27	BLAKER	C	4	40	BLAND	G	8	31
BLAKE	E	5	35	BLAKE	R	4	39	BLAKEWAY	F	11	32	BLAND	H	8	31
BLAKE	E	5	35	BLAKE	R	10	23	BLAKEWAY	JA	11	32	BLAND	H	9	19
BLAKE	E	9	228	BLAKE	RC	4	39	BLAKEWAY	R	11	32	BLAND	H	12	24
BLAKE	E	13	44	BLAKE	S	4	40	BLAKEWAY	S	11	32	BLAND	HBS	12	266
BLAKE	EE	4	39	BLAKE	S	4	40	BLAKEWAY	WH	11	33	BLAND	J	9	228
BLAKE	EF	4	39	BLAKE	SG	4	40	BLAKEY	AB	10	23	BLAND	JW	9	228
BLAKE	F	4	39	BLAKE	SH	4	40	BLAKEY	BT	9	19	BLAND	L	9	19
BLAKE	F	4	39	BLAKE	T	3	23	BLAKEY	CE	4	40	BLAND	LV	5	35
BLAKE	F	4	39	BLAKE	TH	11	32	BLAKEY	GS	9	19	BLAND	OW	8	31
BLAKE	F	5	35	BLAKE	TM	2	27	BLAKEY	GW	8	30	BLAND	P	1	30
BLAKE	FC	4	39	BLAKE	W	4	40	BLAKEY	H	8	31	BLAND	S	5	35
BLAKE	FE	10	268	BLAKE	W	8	30	BLAKEY	J	8	31	BLAND	W	3	23
BLAKE	FJ	1	30	BLAKE	WA	4	40	BLAKEY	J	8	31	BLAND	W	8	31
BLAKE	FWG	4	39	BLAKE	WA	10	268	BLAKEY	J	9	19	BLAND	WC	10	23
BLAKE	G	1	30	BLAKE	WAE	3	23	BLAKEY	JC	10	23	BLAND	WG	12	24
BLAKE	G	4	39	BLAKE	WB	7	34	BLAKEY	JW	9	228	BLAND	WH	5	35
BLAKE	G	7	33	BLAKE	WG	4	40	BLAKEY	R	4	40	BLAND	WH	6	42
BLAKE	G	8	30	BLAKE	WH	4	40	BLAKEY	W	8	31	BLAND	WW	12	266
BLAKE	G	10	22	BLAKE	WH	4	40	BLAKEY	WH	8	31	BLANDFORD	E	1	30

BLANDFORD	GW	6	42	BLENCOWE	JH	12	24	BLOOM	AP	12	24	BLOXHAM	W	2	27
BLANDFORD	W	8	31	BLENCOWE	W	12	24	BLOOM	FH	1	31	BLOXIDGE	GW	6	43
BLANDFORD	WH	10	268	BLENCOWE	W	12	267	BLOOM	J	3	24	BLUCK	H	6	43
BLANEY	G	1	30	BLENKIRON	WA	6	42	BLOOM	S	14	28	BLUCK	T	6	43
BLANEY	H	11	33	BLESSINGTON	E	9	19	BLOOMER	AE	6	43	BLUETT	F	1	31
BLANEY	J	9	228	BLESSINGTON	E	9	381	BLOOMER	E	8	31	BLUETT	F	8	31
BLANEY	R	6	42	BLESSINGTON	H	9	19	BLOOMFIELD	A	7	34	BLUMBERG	IR	8	31
BLANEY	W	9	228	BLESSINGTON	J	9	19	BLOOMFIELD	AA	7	34	BLUMENTHAL	M	2	27
BLANKS	B	13	45	BLETSO	F	1	31	BLOOMFIELD	AE	4	41	BLUMSUM	JC	7	34
BLANN	HL	13	45	BLETSO	H	1	31	BLOOMFIELD	AW	3	24	BLUNDELL	C	1	31
BLANTERN	WH	11	33	BLETSO	J	1	31	BLOOMFIELD	CE	10	23	BLUNDELL	EE	6	43
BLANTHORN	EH	6	42	BLEW	H	5	36	BLOOMFIELD	CE	10	23	BLUNDELL	G	10	268
BLASHKEY	A	8	31	BLEW	WJ	5	36	BLOOMFIELD	FR	13	45	BLUNDELL	GE	10	268
BLASHKEY	M	8	31	BLEWER	JA	6	42	BLOOMFIELD	G	7	34	BLUNDELL	GW	14	28
BLASHKEY	M	8	31	BLEWER	WG	6	42	BLOOMFIELD	H	3	24	BLUNDELL	H	13	45
BLASON	AH	12	267	BLEWETT	E	4	41	BLOOMFIELD	JJ	3	24	BLUNDELL	JW	14	28
BLASON	FE	12	267	BLEWETT	HW	2	27	BLOOMFIELD	JS	14	28	BLUNDELL	S	3	24
BLATCH	AJ	3	23	BLEWITT	A	14	28	BLOOMFIELD	L	7	34	BLUNDELL	WH	6	43
BLATCH	C	4	40	BLEWITT	AE	6	42	BLOOMFIELD	M	7	34	BLUNDEN	AG	5	36
BLATCH	WE	3	281	BLEWITT	G	6	42	BLOOMFIELD	S	7	34	BLUNDEN	AJ	3	282
BLATCHFORD	JA	11	33	BLICK	CH	6	43	BLOOMFIELD	WJ	5	36	BLUNDEN	DP	4	41
BLATHERWICK	G	11	33	BLICK	R	11	33	BLOOR	E	11	33	BLUNDEN	FJ	1	31
BLATHERWICK	GE	11	33	BLIGH	A	5	36	BLOOR	JA	5	36	BLUNDEN	WG	4	41
BLAVER	A	1	30	BLIGH	B	10	268	BLOOR	PJ	7	34	BLUNN	AF	6	43
BLAVER	AG	1	30	BLIGH	E	3	281	BLOSS	AE	1	31	BLUNN	LG	6	43
BLAVER	S	1	30	BLIGH	EE	1	31	BLOSSE	AE	13	45	BLUNSON	C	3	282
BLAY	AC	4	40	BLIGH	F	4	41	BLOUNT	A	8	31	BLUNT	A	12	267
BLAYDEN	A	9	228	BLIGH	GH	4	41	BLOW	AA	1	31	BLUNT	AJ	12	24
BLAYDEN	FW	2	27	BLIGH	R	4	41	BLOW	AH	4	41	BLUNT	F	12	24
BLAYDEN	J	9	229	BLIGH	RG	1	31	BLOW	AJH	4	41	BLUNT	G	12	267
BLAYDON	J	14	28	BLIGH	TW	4	41	BLOW	AW	1	31	BLUNT	H	12	24
BLAYMIRES	F	9	229	BLIGHT	R	1	31	BLOW	AW	4	41	BLUNT	J	6	43
BLAYNEY	JH	1	31	BLINCO	E	5	36	BLOW	AWF	4	41	BLUNT	M	12	267
BLAYNEY	LJH	13	45	BLINCOW	A	12	267	BLOW	B	4	41	BLUNT	VER	8	32
BLAZEY	AG	1	31	BLINDELL	W	5	36	BLOW	EL	4	41	BLUNT	W	11	33
BLAZEY	AL	7	34	BLINKHORN	J	14	28	BLOW	R	11	33	BLUNTACH	A	7	34
BLEACH	A	10	23	BLISS	BB	12	24	BLOW	WR	7	34	BLUNTACH	A	7	34
BLEACH	AW	10	23	BLISS	F	5	36	BLOWER	G	10	23	BLUNTACH	E	7	34
BLEACH	SG	10	23	BLISS	FG	3	23	BLOWER	SG	4	41	BLUNTACH	WB	7	34
BLEALE	WL	10	16	BLISS	G	3	23	BLOWER	SH	4	41	BLUTE	F	13	45
BLEANEY	B	5	36	BLISS	G	3	281	BLOWERS	C	9	229	BLUTE	R	13	45
BLEANEY	C	5	36	BLISS	O	3	23	BLOWERS	HP	4	41	BLYTH	G	2	28
BLEANEY	W	5	36	BLISS	TW	5	36	BLOWES	A	4	41	BLYTH	GA	13	45
BLEASBY	R	8	31	BLISS	WO	3	24	BLOWES	EW	1	31	BLYTH	HE	13	45
BLEASBY	R	8	31	BLISS	WS	5	36	BLOWFIELD	WB	3	281	BLYTH	JA	13	45
BLEASDALE	FC	11	33	BLISSET	JT	3	281	BLOWS	A	1	31	BLYTH	JH	9	20
BLEASDALE	J	11	33	BLISSETT	F	3	281	BLOWS	HA	1	31	BLYTH	TFW	1	31
BLEASDALE	S	9	19	BLIZZARD	W	1	31	BLOWS	HJ	13	45	BLYTH	TJ	13	45
BLEAZARD	A	8	31	BLOCKLEY	W	11	33	BLOWS	JH	7	34	BLYTH	W	2	28
BLEAZARD	F	9	19	BLOCKRIDGE	I	8	31	BLOXAM	FB	13	45	BLYTH	W	2	28
BLEAZARD	F	9	229	BLOMFIELD	AE	3	24	BLOXAM	H	5	36	BLYTH	WW	13	45
BLEAZARD	S	9	19	BLOOD	A	14	28	BLOXHAM	H	12	267	BLYTHE	AA	2	28
BLEIVERS	A	9	19	BLOOD	E	9	229	BLOXHAM	J	5	36	BLYTHE	AW	6	43
BLEIVERS	CJ	9	19	BLOOD	EJ	14	28	BLOXHAM	JG	6	43	BLYTHE	CH	2	28
BLENCOWE	F	12	24	BLOOD	S	9	229	BLOXHAM	LJ	10	23	BLYTHE	W	2	28

Surname	Initials	No.	No.
BLYTHE	W	10	23
BLYTHIN	T	10	23
BLYTHING	G	14	28
BLYTON	J	11	33
BOAM	S	11	33
BOARD	D	1	31
BOARD	H	5	36
BOARD	HW	13	45
BOARD	PC	2	28
BOARD	RF	4	41
BOARDER	J	7	35
BOARDMAN		4	41
BOARDMAN	GL	11	33
BOARDMAN	H	14	28
BOARDMAN	J	11	33
BOARDMAN	J	11	34
BOARDMAN	JH	11	34
BOARDMAN	R	14	28
BOARDMAN	S	14	28
BOARDMAN	T	4	42
BOARDMAN	T	14	28
BOARDMAN	T	14	28
BOARDMAN	W	14	28
BOARDMAN	WH	14	29
BOAS	D	7	35
BOAST	CH	8	32
BOAST	E	14	29
BOAST	JR	4	42
BOATMAN	FC	5	36
BOATMAN	NM	1	31
BOATMAN	WJ	1	31
BOATWRIGHT	GA	7	35
BOATWRIGHT	WH	4	42
BOAZMAN	A	6	43
BOAZMAN	W	6	43
BOBB	L	9	20
BOBBINS	H	1	31
BOBEY	GW	13	45
BOBEY	S	13	46
BOCCIUS		1	32
BOCCIUS	F	1	32
BOCCIUS	FC	1	32
BODDEN	EG	3	24
BODDILL	H	8	32
BODDILL	HE	8	32
BODDINGTON	AJT	3	24
BODDINGTON	CH	6	43
BODDINGTON	EEE	12	267
BODDINGTON	F	13	46
BODDINGTON	HM	7	35
BODDINGTON	T	12	267
BODDINGTON	W	6	43
BODDY	A	8	32
BODDY	C	5	37
BODDY	G	9	20
BODDY	J	3	282
BODDY	PR	2	28
BODDY	W	4	42
BODEL	AB	10	23
BODELL	P	2	28
BODEN	C	6	43
BODEN	CH	11	34
BODEN	F	6	43
BODEN	F	6	44
BODEN	F	13	46
BODEN	H	6	44
BODEN	H	14	29
BODEN	SW	2	28
BODEN	T	11	34
BODEN	TH	6	44
BODEN	WW	2	28
BODENHAM	AE	6	44
BODENHAM	WCH	6	44
BODENHAN	J	10	23
BODFIELD	T	13	46
BODGERS	HT	11	34
BODILY	A	12	267
BODILY	F	12	267
BODILY	J	12	267
BODIMEADE	EE	1	32
BODIMEADE	W	3	24
BODLE	C	12	24
BODLE	RA	12	25
BODLEY	JA	2	28
BODLEY	VC	2	28
BODMAN	W	6	44
BODNER	M	14	29
BODSWORTH	E	5	37
BODSWORTH	FC	5	37
BODSWORTH	FC	12	267
BODSWORTH	FP	5	37
BODSWORTH	J	12	267
BODSWORTH	JW	5	37
BODSWORTH	LB	12	25
BODY	E	3	24
BODY	W	11	34
BODYCOTE	IE	6	44
BOFF	C	11	34
BOFFIN	H	6	44
BOFFIN	J	6	44
BOGEN	J	11	34
BOGG	F	11	34
BOGG	H	8	32
BOGG	M	8	32
BOGG	W	11	34
BOGGIANI	P	4	42
BOGGISS	OJ	13	46
BOGGITT	G	10	23
BOGGUST	AH	4	42
BOGGUST	C	4	42
BOGGUST	EH	4	42
BOGIE	D	2	28
BOHAM	J	4	42
BOHRINGER	AJ	3	282
BOILING	HC	13	46
BOLAND	A	13	46
BOLAND	E	3	24
BOLAND	F	3	24
BOLAND	H	14	29
BOLAND	J	3	24
BOLAND	J	14	29
BOLAND	JW	9	229
BOLAND	WH	10	268
BOLAS	C	11	34
BOLAS	G	11	34
BOLAS	G	14	29
BOLCH	HS	2	28
BOLD	AP	11	34
BOLD	HV	6	44
BOLD	JR	6	44
BOLDEN	BA	2	28
BOLDISON	G	8	32
BOLDY	H	9	229
BOLDY	L	9	20
BOLEY	FW	2	28
BOLGER	J	12	267
BOLINGBROKE	GW	8	32
BOLLAND	A	14	29
BOLLAND	AE	9	20
BOLLAND	H	4	42
BOLLAND	H	13	46
BOLLARD	E	14	29
BOLLARD	J	11	34
BOLLEN	TG	13	46
BOLLINGTON	JH	2	28
BOLMER	H	4	42
BOLSOVER	C	11	34
BOLSTER	A	7	35
BOLSTER	E	7	35
BOLSTER	P	7	35
BOLT	DV	5	37
BOLT	G	12	267
BOLT	J	1	32
BOLTER	A	2	28
BOLTER	P	13	46
BOLTON	A	3	282
BOLTON	A	5	37
BOLTON	ACW	10	23
BOLTON	AJ	1	32
BOLTON	AR	14	29
BOLTON	AV	4	42
BOLTON	AW	5	37
BOLTON	AW	5	37
BOLTON	B	5	37
BOLTON	BC	1	32
BOLTON	C	6	44
BOLTON	C	6	44
BOLTON	C	13	46
BOLTON	CA	2	29
BOLTON	CAR	8	32
BOLTON	CH	7	35
BOLTON	CJ	2	29
BOLTON	CJ	14	29
BOLTON	CR	11	34
BOLTON	D	12	25
BOLTON	E	2	29
BOLTON	EE	1	32
BOLTON	ES	14	29
BOLTON	EW	13	46
BOLTON	F	3	282
BOLTON	F	10	23
BOLTON	F	13	46
BOLTON	FC	7	35
BOLTON	FJ	11	35
BOLTON	G	7	35
BOLTON	G	9	229
BOLTON	G	13	46
BOLTON	GE	9	20
BOLTON	GR	2	29
BOLTON	H	6	44
BOLTON	H	9	20
BOLTON	H	11	35
BOLTON	H	12	25
BOLTON	HL	13	46
BOLTON	J	5	37
BOLTON	J	5	37
BOLTON	J	9	20
BOLTON	J	14	29
BOLTON	JE	8	32
BOLTON	JG	1	32
BOLTON	JH	2	29
BOLTON	JH	13	46
BOLTON	JJ	3	282
BOLTON	JJ	14	29
BOLTON	JM	6	44
BOLTON	JR	1	32
BOLTON	LL	4	42
BOLTON	LR	3	282
BOLTON	S	9	229
BOLTON	S	9	229
BOLTON	SA	6	44
BOLTON	T	11	34
BOLTON	TE	7	35
BOLTON	TW	10	23
BOLTON	W	2	29
BOLTON	W	6	44
BOLTON	WH	13	46
BOLTON	WJ	10	24
BOLTON	WR	2	29
BOLUS	E	8	32

BOLWELL	JH	1	32	BOND	JH	4	42	BONE	WW	4	43	BONNER	SM	5	38
BONAR	WY	5	37	BOND	JH	12	267	BONEFIELD	J	5	37	BONNER	TH	5	38
BONAS	H	6	44	BOND	JJ	10	24	BONEHILL	CJ	3	282	BONNER	W	5	38
BOND	A	11	35	BOND	JW	1	32	BONEHILL	D	6	45	BONNER	WG	13	47
BOND	A	11	35	BOND	JW	13	47	BONEHILL	JT	6	45	BONNER	WT	2	29
BOND	AB	7	35	BOND	JW	14	29	BONEHILL	T	6	45	BONNETT	WH	12	25
BOND	AW	2	29	BOND	PG	13	47	BONELL	C	6	45	BONNEY	F	2	29
BOND	AW	6	44	BOND	R	11	35	BONESS	F	12	25	BONNEY	W	3	25
BOND	AW	13	46	BOND	RJ	4	42	BONESS	GH	5	37	BONNICK	AH	7	36
BOND	BE	8	32	BOND	SH	2	29	BONESS	HW	12	25	BONNIE	H	2	29
BOND	BF	2	29	BOND	T	2	29	BONESS	PJ	12	25	BONSALL	EJ	14	30
BOND	BG	1	32	BOND	T	13	47	BONFIELD	CH	10	24	BONSALL	T	14	30
BOND	C	9	20	BOND	TD	1	32	BONFIELD	J	13	47	BONSELS	PJH	3	25
BOND	C	9	229	BOND	TJ	7	35	BONFIELD	W	1	33	BONTOFT	G	9	229
BOND	C	14	29	BOND	W	2	29	BONHAM	A	5	38	BOOCOCK	C	8	32
BOND	CA	13	47	BOND	W	7	35	BONHAM	AG	12	25	BOOCOCK	G	8	32
BOND	CE	1	32	BOND	W	9	20	BONHAM	C	12	268	BOOCOCK	H	9	20
BOND	CE	7	35	BOND	W	14	30	BONHAM	E	11	35	BOOCOCK	H	9	229
BOND	D	13	46	BOND	WCR	4	42	BONHAM	G	12	268	BOOCOCK	H	14	30
BOND	DG	2	29	BOND	WE	11	35	BONHAM	H	5	38	BOOCOCK	J	8	32
BOND	E	11	35	BOND	WF	11	35	BONHAM	H	6	45	BOOCOCK	J	9	20
BOND	E	14	29	BOND	WG	3	24	BONHAM	H	12	268	BOOCOCK	J	9	20
BOND	EC	3	24	BOND	WG	13	47	BONHAM	J	11	35	BOOCOCK	J	9	229
BOND	EK	2	29	BOND	WW	4	42	BONHAM	J	12	25	BOOCOCK	JW	8	32
BOND	EW	2	29	BONDFIELD	R	1	32	BONHAM	M	12	268	BOOCOCK	O	9	20
BOND	F	11	35	BONDFIELD	RJ	1	32	BONHAM	WJ	3	282	BOOCOCK	R	9	20
BOND	F	11	35	BONDSFIELD	HW	4	42	BONHAM	WJI	12	268	BOOCOCK	U	9	20
BOND	FA	3	282	BONE	A	4	42	BONHAM	WW	12	25	BOOCOCK	W	9	229
BOND	FE	9	20	BONE	A	4	42	BONIFACE	A	3	282	BOOCOCK	WJ	9	20
BOND	FH	13	47	BONE	AE	12	25	BONIFACE	F	9	229	BOOKER	A	6	45
BOND	FJ	10	24	BONE	AE	12	267	BONIFACE	J	11	35	BOOKER	AE	3	25
BOND	G	3	24	BONE	AH	10	268	BONKEN	AW	7	36	BOOKER	AW	13	47
BOND	G	10	24	BONE	AS	1	32	BONNAMY	AV	3	25	BOOKER	E	10	24
BOND	G	13	47	BONE	CE	4	42	BONNAMY	ES	3	25	BOOKER	FE	12	268
BOND	GF	2	29	BONE	CG	5	37	BONNER	A	1	33	BOOKER	G	7	36
BOND	GH	10	24	BONE	CS	13	47	BONNER	AE	4	43	BOOKER	H	2	30
BOND	GR	1	32	BONE	EJ	1	32	BONNER	AH	13	47	BOOKER	J	9	21
BOND	GW	7	35	BONE	EJ	5	37	BONNER	CF	1	33	BOOKER	L	8	32
BOND	H	1	32	BONE	F	4	43	BONNER	E	5	38	BOOKER	ME	9	381
BOND	H	6	45	BONE	F	5	37	BONNER	EJ	13	47	BOOKER	S	13	47
BOND	H	7	35	BONE	FW	1	32	BONNER	F	1	33	BOOKER	T	10	24
BOND	H	9	229	BONE	G	4	43	BONNER	F	10	24	BOOKER	WH	1	33
BOND	H	11	35	BONE	G	10	24	BONNER	FJ	7	36	BOOKHAM	WG	10	24
BOND	HJ	6	45	BONE	HJ	1	33	BONNER	G	1	33	BOOM	EE	8	32
BOND	HS	6	45	BONE	HJ	5	37	BONNER	H	7	36	BOOM	MD	7	36
BOND	IW	14	29	BONE	HJ	10	268	BONNER	H	8	32	BOOM	PW	8	33
BOND	J	6	45	BONE	JE	7	35	BONNER	HJ	5	38	BOOMER	G	11	35
BOND	J	8	32	BONE	JJ	13	47	BONNER	J	2	29	BOON	AE	12	25
BOND	J	11	35	BONE	JW	10	268	BONNER	J	5	38	BOON	BJ	12	25
BOND	J	13	47	BONE	LE	1	32	BONNER	J	7	36	BOON	C	2	30
BOND	J	14	29	BONE	N	5	37	BONNER	J	13	47	BOON	F	5	38
BOND	JA	13	47	BONE	TW	3	24	BONNER	JE	5	38	BOON	F	12	25
BOND	JF	1	32	BONE	W	4	43	BONNER	LG	2	29	BOON	G	11	35
BOND	JF	7	35	BONE	WH	10	268	BONNER	R	6	45	BOON	H	3	282
BOND	JG	13	47	BONE	WJ	10	24	BONNER	S	7	36	BOON	HF	3	282

BOON	LC	13	48	BOOTH	FR	2	30	BOOTH	WH	14	30	BOSANKO	WH	11	37
BOON	LE	7	36	BOOTH	G	6	45	BOOTH	WH	14	31	BOSDET	VJH	2	30
BOON	OJ	12	25	BOOTH	G	11	36	BOOTH	WJ	11	37	BOSHELL	FJ	8	33
BOON	SP	7	36	BOOTH	G	14	30	BOOTHMAN	H	14	31	BOSHER	AG	7	36
BOON	TF	5	38	BOOTH	H	3	25	BOOTHMAN	JW	10	24	BOSHER	JF	3	283
BOON	W	14	30	BOOTH	H	8	33	BOOTHROYD	JH	9	230	BOSIER	A	4	43
BOON	WE	5	38	BOOTH	H	8	33	BOOTHROYD	W	9	230	BOSLEY	B	2	30
BOON	WH	13	48	BOOTH	H	10	268	BOOTMAN	AE	1	33	BOSLEY	E	5	38
BOON	WJ	5	38	BOOTH	H	14	30	BOOTMAN	M	2	30	BOSLEY	H	5	38
BOONE	J	5	38	BOOTH	HG	11	36	BOOTS	H	6	45	BOSLEY	S	5	38
BOONE	WJ	5	38	BOOTH	J	2	30	BORAGE	WC	9	21	BOSLEY	SJ	3	25
BOORER	H	10	24	BOOTH	J	7	36	BORASTON	W	6	45	BOSLEY	WC	10	24
BOORER	WC	2	30	BOOTH	J	8	33	BORDMAN	JW	6	45	BOSOMWORTH	AM	8	34
BOORMAN	J	13	48	BOOTH	J	9	230	BORE	ER	13	48	BOSS	A	7	36
BOORMAN	S	1	33	BOOTH	J	11	36	BOREHAM	GM	4	43	BOSS	CT	6	46
BOORMAN	WS	13	48	BOOTH	J	11	36	BOREHAM	H	1	33	BOSSON	AW	2	30
BOOT	EG	7	36	BOOTH	J	14	30	BOREHAM	HH	2	30	BOSSON	HW	2	30
BOOT	F	8	33	BOOTH	J	14	30	BOREHAM	HJ	1	33	BOSTOCK	CL	14	31
BOOTH	A	1	33	BOOTH	J	14	30	BOREHAM	J	7	36	BOSTOCK	E	11	37
BOOTH	A	4	43	BOOTH	JA	11	36	BOREHAM	M	7	36	BOSTOCK	F	11	37
BOOTH	A	7	36	BOOTH	JH	9	230	BOREHAM	T	7	36	BOSTOCK	H	7	37
BOOTH	A	8	33	BOOTH	JW	3	282	BOREHAM	W	2	30	BOSTOCK	J	11	37
BOOTH	A	8	33	BOOTH	JW	8	33	BOREHAM	WC	2	30	BOSTON	AF	12	25
BOOTH	A	8	33	BOOTH	JW	11	36	BOREHAM	WF	3	25	BOSTON	C	1	33
BOOTH	A	8	33	BOOTH	L	14	30	BORHAM	F	12	25	BOSTON	C	8	34
BOOTH	A	9	21	BOOTH	M	8	33	BORKETT	C	3	282	BOSTON	CH	5	38
BOOTH	A	9	229	BOOTH	M	11	36	BORKETT	TJ	13	48	BOSTON	E	12	26
BOOTH	A	11	35	BOOTH	P	6	45	BORLAND	J	11	37	BOSTON	F	14	31
BOOTH	A	11	36	BOOTH	P	8	33	BORLE	JC	14	31	BOSTON	P	12	26
BOOTH	A	14	30	BOOTH	PH	9	21	BORLE	L	14	31	BOSTON	W	1	33
BOOTH	A	14	30	BOOTH	R	11	36	BORLEY	C	5	38	BOSTON	WS	12	26
BOOTH	A	14	30	BOOTH	R	11	36	BORLEY	E	13	48	BOSTRIDGE	FJ	13	48
BOOTH	AE	9	21	BOOTH	RA	11	36	BORLEY	FA	2	30	BOSTWICK	TJ	7	37
BOOTH	AJ	11	36	BOOTH	RA	13	48	BORLEY	JE	1	33	BOSWARD	HB	14	31
BOOTH	AW	2	30	BOOTH	RL	11	37	BORLEY	RS	1	33	BOSWARD	W	14	31
BOOTH	AW	2	30	BOOTH	RW	12	25	BORMAN	H	1	33	BOSWELL	A	6	45
BOOTH	C	9	21	BOOTH	S	8	33	BORNER	AH	13	48	BOSWELL	A	6	45
BOOTH	C	11	36	BOOTH	S	9	230	BORNER	W	3	282	BOSWELL	D	11	37
BOOTH	C	14	30	BOOTH	S	14	30	BOROWS	JR	9	21	BOSWELL	E	11	37
BOOTH	E	1	33	BOOTH	SD	11	36	BORRETT	AH	7	36	BOSWELL	FJ	13	48
BOOTH	E	8	33	BOOTH	T	9	21	BORRETT	AL	1	33	BOSWELL	J	7	37
BOOTH	E	8	33	BOOTH	TI	13	48	BORRETT	GF	7	36	BOSWELL	VR	12	268
BOOTH	E	9	230	BOOTH	W	8	33	BORRETT	JV	13	48	BOSWELL	W	6	46
BOOTH	E	11	36	BOOTH	W	8	33	BORRICK	R	14	31	BOSWELL	WA	6	46
BOOTH	F	2	30	BOOTH	W	8	33	BORRICK	R	14	31	BOSWELL	WA	12	26
BOOTH	F	4	43	BOOTH	W	9	21	BORRICK	W	14	31	BOSWORTH	AC	12	268
BOOTH	F	8	33	BOOTH	W	9	230	BORROW	FL	13	48	BOSWORTH	C	6	46
BOOTH	F	9	230	BOOTH	W	11	36	BORROW	G	13	48	BOSWORTH	JW	8	34
BOOTH	F	9	230	BOOTH	W	11	37	BORROW	W	13	48	BOSWORTH	R	6	46
BOOTH	F	9	381	BOOTH	W	11	37	BORSBERRY	CH	12	268	BOSWORTH	T	12	268
BOOTH	F	11	36	BOOTH	W	14	30	BORTOFT	J	11	37	BOSWORTH	TH	12	268
BOOTH	F	11	36	BOOTH	W	14	30	BORTON	A	12	25	BOSWORTH	W	6	46
BOOTH	F	11	36	BOOTH	WA	1	33	BORTON	AW	12	25	BOSWORTHICK	F	4	43
BOOTH	F	13	48	BOOTH	WG	3	282	BORTON	FA	6	45	BOSWORTHICK	WA	4	43
BOOTH	F	13	48	BOOTH	WH	2	30	BORWELL	TFF	8	33	BOTCHETT	CA	11	37

BOTELER	JH	2	30	BOTTRELL	T	6	46	BOULTER	R	7	37	BOURNE	F	13	49
BOTELL	TA	7	37	BOTTWOOD	H	3	283	BOULTER	RT	4	43	BOURNE	FA	13	49
BOTELL	WL	7	37	BOTWOOD	G	12	268	BOULTER	W	2	31	BOURNE	FJ	4	44
BOTFIELD	FG	6	46	BOTWOOD	J	14	31	BOULTER	W	13	49	BOURNE	G	3	283
BOTHAN	E	2	30	BOTWRIGHT	AE	2	31	BOULTER	WC	12	268	BOURNE	G	5	39
BOTHERWAY	CR	2	31	BOTWRIGHT	D	2	31	BOULTER	WC	13	49	BOURNE	GW	5	39
BOTSFORD	AA	5	39	BOTWRIGHT	PG	13	49	BOULTER	WH	10	269	BOURNE	H	2	31
BOTSFORD	H	5	39	BOUCHER	J	8	34	BOULTON	A	10	24	BOURNE	H	6	47
BOTT	A	8	34	BOUCHER	LJ	7	37	BOULTON	A	11	37	BOURNE	H	6	47
BOTT	AB	12	268	BOUCHER	WF	10	24	BOULTON	BH	10	25	BOURNE	H	8	35
BOTT	AEW	2	31	BOUD	A	14	31	BOULTON	EA	13	49	BOURNE	H	8	35
BOTT	CE	8	34	BOUD	DM	7	37	BOULTON	HS	13	49	BOURNE	H	8	35
BOTT	G	6	46	BOUD	FE	7	37	BOULTON	J	11	38	BOURNE	J	8	35
BOTT	W	4	43	BOUD	H	7	37	BOULTON	JB	4	43	BOURNE	JAG	13	49
BOTTERILL	A	13	48	BOUD	HJ	12	26	BOULTON	T	8	34	BOURNE	JE	6	47
BOTTERILL	AE	13	49	BOUD	WA	7	37	BOULTON	TH	4	43	BOURNE	JF	12	269
BOTTERILL	HT	12	268	BOUD	WE	7	37	BOULTON	WH	6	46	BOURNE	JH	7	37
BOTTERILL	W	12	268	BOUDIER	J	1	33	BOULTWOOD	CH	2	31	BOURNE	LW	5	39
BOTTERILL	WT	12	268	BOUDIER	WC	1	33	BOULTWOOD	G	5	39	BOURNE	S	6	47
BOTTING	J	13	49	BOUGH	JA	2	31	BOUND	AW	4	44	BOURNE	T	5	39
BOTTJER	WJ	2	31	BOUGH	LH	6	46	BOUND	FJ	4	44	BOURNE	TH	6	47
BOTTLE	DR	2	31	BOUGHEN	FC	1	33	BOUND	HC	4	44	BOURNE	W	13	50
BOTTOM	FW	14	31	BOUGHEN	RG	1	34	BOUND	S	7	37	BOURNE	WH	6	47
BOTTOMLEY	CS	8	34	BOUGHTON	F	5	39	BOUND	W	4	44	BOURNE	WR	2	31
BOTTOMLEY	E	8	34	BOUGHTON	H	12	26	BOUND	WR	10	269	BOURNER	A	7	37
BOTTOMLEY	E	9	230	BOUGHTON	H	12	26	BOUNDS	A	12	269	BOURNER	A	7	38
BOTTOMLEY	F	9	21	BOUGHTON	HF	6	46	BOUNDS	B	12	269	BOURSNELL	H	4	44
BOTTOMLEY	F	9	230	BOUGOURD	C	4	43	BOUNDS	F	12	269	BOURSNELL	J	4	44
BOTTOMLEY	GW	8	34	BOUGOURD	FG	10	268	BOUNDS	G	12	269	BOUSEFIELD	J	8	35
BOTTOMLEY	H	9	230	BOULBY	A	8	34	BOUNDS	G	12	269	BOUSEFIELD	TE	4	44
BOTTOMLEY	H	10	24	BOULBY	G	8	34	BOUNDS	RW	12	269	BOUSFIELD	E	8	35
BOTTOMLEY	IH	11	37	BOULBY	J	8	34	BOUNDY	C	4	44	BOUSFIELD	F	6	47
BOTTOMLEY	J	8	34	BOULD	A	9	230	BOUNE	H	13	49	BOUSFIELD	FH	2	31
BOTTOMLEY	J	9	21	BOULD	ASV	1	34	BOURDON	CJ	3	25	BOUSKILL	H	8	35
BOTTOMLEY	J	11	37	BOULD	LA	1	34	BOURKE	E	8	34	BOUSKILL	J	8	35
BOTTOMLEY	J	11	37	BOULDING	GH	2	31	BOURKE	EL	8	34	BOUSTEAD	A	14	31
BOTTOMLEY	J	14	31	BOULDING	ME	2	31	BOURKE	EW	4	44	BOUSTEAD	R	11	38
BOTTOMLEY	JA	9	230	BOULT	AF	3	283	BOURKE	J	11	38	BOUSTEAD	R	11	38
BOTTOMLEY	JW	9	230	BOULT	D	3	283	BOURN	SG	2	31	BOUSTRED	CF	1	34
BOTTOMLEY	P	14	31	BOULT	HF	3	283	BOURNE	A	2	31	BOUSTRED	HW	2	31
BOTTOMLEY	R	8	34	BOULT	WP	7	37	BOURNE	A	6	46	BOVARD	J	3	283
BOTTOMLEY	S	11	37	BOULTER	A	12	268	BOURNE	A	13	49	BOVINGDON	W	1	34
BOTTOMLEY	TA	8	34	BOULTER	AJ	2	31	BOURNE	AE	6	46	BOVINGTON	J	10	269
BOTTOMLEY	W	8	34	BOULTER	B	14	31	BOURNE	AJ	4	44	BOW	A	7	38
BOTTOMLEY	W	9	230	BOULTER	CH	4	43	BOURNE	AV	2	31	BOW	AT	7	38
BOTTOMS	BJ	5	39	BOULTER	DG	7	37	BOURNE	AW	6	46	BOWATER	H	14	31
BOTTOMS	E	11	37	BOULTER	EJ	13	49	BOURNE	B	6	46	BOWATER	HW	6	47
BOTTOMS	FG	5	39	BOULTER	F	12	268	BOURNE	C	6	47	BOWATER	L	11	38
BOTTOMS	H	5	39	BOULTER	FJ	2	31	BOURNE	CT	5	39	BOWCOCK	J	11	38
BOTTOMS	WC	5	39	BOULTER	FJ	12	268	BOURNE	E	13	49	BOWCOTT	A	6	47
BOTTON	H	13	49	BOULTER	GF	4	43	BOURNE	EA	4	44	BOWD	A	12	26
BOTTRELL	A	14	31	BOULTER	H	4	43	BOURNE	EA	6	47	BOWDEN	AH	5	39
BOTTRELL	F	6	46	BOULTER	J	10	24	BOURNE	EE	6	47	BOWDEN	C	9	21
BOTTRELL	JE	6	46	BOULTER	JA	4	43	BOURNE	EG	13	49	BOWDEN	C	13	50
BOTTRELL	S	6	46	BOULTER	JJC	13	49	BOURNE	EW	13	49	BOWDEN	EA	12	26
												BOWDEN	EG	1	34

BOWDEN	EH	4	44	BOWEN	P	11	38	BOWES	A	9	231	BOWLES	F	10	25				
BOWDEN	FG	2	32	BOWEN	R	1	34	BOWES	AWC	13	50	BOWLES	G	4	45				
BOWDEN	FJ	2	32	BOWEN	R	12	26	BOWES	C	12	26	BOWLES	H	2	32				
BOWDEN	FJ	4	44	BOWEN	R	14	32	BOWES	CA	13	50	BOWLES	H	5	40				
BOWDEN	G	14	32	BOWEN	T	9	21	BOWES	H	9	22	BOWLES	H	8	35				
BOWDEN	H	3	25	BOWEN	T	9	21	BOWES	J	11	38	BOWLES	J	4	45				
BOWDEN	H	11	38	BOWEN	W	6	48	BOWES	JF	11	38	BOWLES	J	14	32				
BOWDEN	HE	5	39	BOWEN	W	11	38	BOWES	JW	9	231	BOWLES	JG	4	45				
BOWDEN	HW	2	32	BOWEN	WC	13	50	BOWES	M	13	50	BOWLES	JW	7	38				
BOWDEN	J	1	34	BOWEN	WH	6	48	BOWES	PA	11	39	BOWLES	MB	3	283				
BOWDEN	JJ	1	34	BOWEN	WJ	4	45	BOWES	S	11	39	BOWLES	S	5	40				
BOWDEN	JW	11	38	BOWEN	WJ	6	48	BOWES	WJ	13	50	BOWLES	T	3	283				
BOWDEN	L	9	21	BOWER	A	4	45	BOWFIELD	A	2	32	BOWLES	T	11	39				
BOWDEN	PB	3	283	BOWER	A	5	39	BOWHAY	WGA	10	269	BOWLES	W	11	39				
BOWDEN	RD	2	32	BOWER	A	9	21	BOWKER	A	14	32	BOWLES	WF	10	269				
BOWDEN	SA	5	39	BOWER	A	11	38	BOWKER	B	6	48	BOWLES	WH	3	283				
BOWDEN	TF	13	50	BOWER	A	14	32	BOWKER	C	14	32	BOWLES	WH	4	45				
BOWDEN	TJ	12	26	BOWER	A	14	32	BOWKER	ER	11	39	BOWLEY	AA	13	50				
BOWDEN	TW	2	32	BOWER	F	10	25	BOWKER	GW	6	48	BOWLEY	FC	7	38				
BOWDEN	W	11	38	BOWER	G	4	45	BOWKER	H	6	48	BOWLEY	FW	2	32				
BOWDEN	W	14	32	BOWER	G	9	230	BOWKER	H	14	32	BOWLEY	FW	7	38				
BOWDEN	WA	4	44	BOWER	G	9	230	BOWKER	J	11	39	BOWLEY	JA	5	40				
BOWDEN	WH	11	38	BOWER	GW	8	35	BOWKER	JA	14	32	BOWLEY	R	5	40				
BOWDEN	WM	4	44	BOWER	H	8	35	BOWKER	R	11	39	BOWLING	T	1	34				
BOWDEN	WP	9	381	BOWER	H	9	21	BOWKER	R	11	39	BOWLING	W	8	35				
BOWDERY	H	3	283	BOWER	H	10	25	BOWKER	R	14	32	BOWLTING	A	1	34				
BOWDERY	W	7	38	BOWER	HJ	5	39	BOWKER	S	11	39	BOWMAN	AJ	2	32				
BOWDERY	W	7	38	BOWER	J	9	22	BOWKER	T	11	39	BOWMAN	D	9	22				
BOWDIDGE	EE	13	50	BOWER	JJ	4	45	BOWKER	W	14	32	BOWMAN	J	8	35				
BOWDIDGE	JS	13	50	BOWER	JW	9	22	BOWKETT	W	6	48	BOWMAN	JB	14	32				
BOWDIDGE	WL	13	50	BOWER	R	9	381	BOWKETT	WGT	13	50	BOWMAN	JC	3	283				
BOWDITCH	AR	4	44	BOWER	RP	2	32	BOWLAND	GM	8	35	BOWMAN	JS	3	283				
BOWDITCH	CS	10	25	BOWER	TAN	3	283	BOWLAND	JW	9	231	BOWMAN	JW	11	39				
BOWDITCH	EJ	7	38	BOWERMAN	BH	1	34	BOWLD	E	1	34	BOWMAN	M	8	35				
BOWDITCH	F	6	47	BOWERMAN	E	2	32	BOWLER	AC	7	38	BOWMAN	R	11	39				
BOWDITCH	FC	7	38	BOWERMAN	GE	1	34	BOWLER	AW	6	48	BOWMAN	S	7	38				
BOWDITCH	RP	4	44	BOWERMAN	JL	4	45	BOWLER	EW	12	26	BOWMAN	S	7	38				
BOWDITCH	WJ	4	44	BOWERMAN	TF	1	34	BOWLER	FJ	12	26	BOWMAN	SW	13	50				
BOWDLER	H	6	47	BOWERMAN	WA	2	32	BOWLER	FR	12	26	BOWMAN	T	9	231				
BOWE	K	11	38	BOWERS	A	9	231	BOWLER	FS	5	39	BOWMAN	W	3	284				
BOWELL	H	8	35	BOWERS	AH	2	32	BOWLER	G	12	26	BOWMER	H	3	284				
BOWEN	A	6	47	BOWERS	BW	5	39	BOWLER	H	11	39	BOWN	B	7	38				
BOWEN	A	6	47	BOWERS	D	11	38	BOWLER	RW	12	26	BOWN	C	7	38				
BOWEN	A	10	25	BOWERS	E	4	45	BOWLER	W	11	39	BOWN	J	2	33				
BOWEN	CF	3	283	BOWERS	E	12	26	BOWLER	WC	12	26	BOWN	W	7	38				
BOWEN	D	14	32	BOWERS	F	4	45	BOWLES	AC	5	39	BOWN	W	9	231				
BOWEN	E	6	47	BOWERS	F	4	45	BOWLES	B	13	50	BOWNAS	RF	3	25				
BOWEN	F	1	34	BOWERS	HA	1	34	BOWLES	CR	12	27	BOWNES	WT	11	39				
BOWEN	F	11	38	BOWERS	HV	10	269	BOWLES	D	11	39	BOWNES	WT	11	39				
BOWEN	F	13	50	BOWERS	J	2	32	BOWLES	DG	2	32	BOWRING	F	7	38				
BOWEN	FE	6	47	BOWERS	J	12	269	BOWLES	DG	3	25	BOWRING	H	7	39				
BOWEN	IJ	4	44	BOWERS	JJ	12	269	BOWLES	E	2	32	BOWRON	J	6	48				
BOWEN	J	1	34	BOWERS	JW	2	32	BOWLES	E	2	32	BOWRON	JC	1	34				
BOWEN	J	11	38	BOWERS	O	2	32	BOWLES	E	13	50	BOWRY	C	2	33				
BOWEN	M	9	21	BOWERS	S	4	45	BOWLES	EA	3	283	BOWRY	F	3	25				

BOWRY	GH	2	33	BOYCE	C	2	33	BOYES	GH	12	269	BOYSON	FG	12	269
BOWSER	A	6	48	BOYCE	C	12	27	BOYES	P	9	381	BOYSON	FJ	12	269
BOWSER	E	6	48	BOYCE	CE	4	45	BOYES	PJ	12	269	BOYSON	HB	12	269
BOWSER	H	6	48	BOYCE	CJ	10	25	BOYES	RA	12	269	BOYSON	JF	12	269
BOWSHER	SF	7	38	BOYCE	EA	3	284	BOYES	W	4	46	BOYSON	R	12	270
BOWSKILL	J	6	48	BOYCE	EA	4	45	BOYES	W	8	35	BOYSON	TE	12	270
BOWSTEAD	CD	13	50	BOYCE	ET	3	284	BOYES	W	8	35	BOYTON	T	8	36
BOWTELL	E	5	40	BOYCE	F	3	284	BOYES	WH	4	46	BOZEAT	F	12	27
BOWTELL	EW	11	39	BOYCE	GE	4	45	BOYETT	AE	10	269	BOZIER	AGW	5	40
BOWYER	A	12	27	BOYCE	HJ	3	284	BOYETT	GV	10	25	BOZIER	PC	5	40
BOWYER	AF	5	40	BOYCE	HJ	4	45	BOYETT	HJ	10	269	BOZIER	V	5	40
BOWYER	AG	12	27	BOYCE	J	1	34	BOYLAND	EE	10	269	BRABBS	TA	8	36
BOWYER	AH	12	27	BOYCE	JF	6	48	BOYLE	B	6	49	BRABIN	J	11	40
BOWYER	FT	12	27	BOYCE	LH	10	25	BOYLE	D	9	231	BRABIN	L	14	33
BOWYER	H	12	27	BOYCE	RL	4	45	BOYLE	E	9	231	BRABROOK	GE	1	35
BOWYER	HF	12	27	BOYCE	W	3	25	BOYLE	GW	7	39	BRACE	AF	12	27
BOWYER	J	10	269	BOYCE	WH	2	33	BOYLE	J	8	35	BRACE	F	12	27
BOWYER	JRJ	10	25	BOYCE	WJ	3	284	BOYLE	J	9	22	BRACE	G	1	35
BOWYER	SJ	12	27	BOYCE	WJ	5	40	BOYLE	J	9	22	BRACE	G	12	27
BOWYER	ST	7	39	BOYD	A	13	51	BOYLE	J	11	40	BRACE	JF	1	35
BOWYER	W	1	34	BOYD	A	14	32	BOYLE	J	11	40	BRACE	PG	1	35
BOWYER	W	1	34	BOYD	CF	6	49	BOYLE	J	13	51	BRACE	ST	1	35
BOWYER	W	6	48	BOYD	CF	11	40	BOYLE	J	13	51	BRACE	WJ	12	27
BOWYER	W	12	27	BOYD	E	11	40	BOYLE	J	14	33	BRACEGIRDLE	A	14	33
BOWYER	WH	12	27	BOYD	EA	6	49	BOYLE	JA	13	51	BRACEGIRDLE	F	14	33
BOWYER	WRC	10	269	BOYD	EG	12	27	BOYLE	JW	9	231	BRACEGIRDLE	J	11	40
BOX	A	6	48	BOYD	FH	9	22	BOYLE	P	9	22	BRACEGIRDLE	R	11	40
BOX	AF	6	48	BOYD	FH	9	22	BOYLE	R	8	35	BRACEGIRDLE	T	14	33
BOX	AJ	14	32	BOYD	H	14	32	BOYLE	T	9	22	BRACEGIRDLE	W	11	40
BOX	CH	11	40	BOYD	HG	6	49	BOYLE	W	9	231	BRACEGIRDLE	W	14	33
BOX	WE	11	39	BOYD	HWS	6	49	BOYLE	W	9	231	BRACEWELL	A	8	36
BOXALL	A	2	33	BOYD	J	11	40	BOYLE	W	11	40	BRACEWELL	J	8	36
BOXALL	A	13	50	BOYD	J	11	40	BOYLE	WN	2	33	BRACEY	AW	5	40
BOXALL	AA	2	33	BOYD	J	14	32	BOYLES	B	8	36	BRACEY	F	5	40
BOXALL	FC	2	33	BOYD	JW	14	32	BOYLES	HA	6	49	BRACEY	R	5	40
BOXALL	G	2	33	BOYD	LJ	6	49	BOYLES	WH	10	25	BRACHER	AC	4	46
BOXALL	GA	10	25	BOYD	R	11	40	BOYLES	WJ	12	27	BRACHER	RH	4	46
BOXALL	GC	3	284	BOYD	R	14	32	BOYLING	A	2	33	BRACK	O	8	36
BOXALL	HR	10	25	BOYD	R	14	33	BOYLING	JH	6	49	BRACK	W	3	25
BOXALL	JR	2	33	BOYD	RK	4	45	BOYNE	C	7	39	BRACKEN	J	14	33
BOXALL	W	2	33	BOYD	S	14	33	BOYNE	T	11	40	BRACKENBURY	GT	9	22
BOXALL	W	10	25	BOYD	T	14	33	BOYNS	EB	10	25	BRACKENRIDGE	JT	11	40
BOXALL	WC	2	33	BOYD	WT	9	22	BOYNS	WH	13	51	BRACKIN	F	8	36
BOXALL	WG	3	25	BOYD	WT	9	231	BOYNTON	E	9	22	BRACKIN	TW	11	40
BOXALL	WJ	4	45	BOYDEN	GW	3	25	BOYNTON	H	9	381	BRACKLEY	A	2	33
BOXELL	H	1	34	BOYDEN	L	9	22	BOYNTON	J	8	36	BRACKLEY	G	2	34
BOXER	A	13	51	BOYES	A	3	284	BOYNTON	JE	9	22	BRACKLEY	H	5	40
BOXER	ARJ	2	33	BOYES	A	4	46	BOYNTON	JL	8	36	BRACKLEY	I	7	39
BOXER	JH	13	51	BOYES	AE	4	46	BOYNTON	V	1	35	BRACKLEY	J	1	35
BOXFORD	WS	5	40	BOYES	CH	8	35	BOYS	CA	2	33	BRACKLEY	M	2	34
BOXHALL	H	7	39	BOYES	E	12	269	BOYS	J	2	33	BRACKSTON	FH	4	46
BOYALL	H	1	34	BOYES	EA	4	46	BOYS	T	13	51	BRACKSTONE	CA	7	39
BOYCE	A	2	33	BOYES	F	9	381	BOYSON	A	12	269	BRACKSTONE	WA	4	46
BOYCE	AE	13	51	BOYES	FA	4	46	BOYSON	ET	12	269	BRACKWELL	W	7	39
BOYCE	AL	10	25	BOYES	G	8	35	BOYSON	F	12	269	BRADBEAR	PT	10	269

BRADBERRY	ET	7	39	BRADFORD	GJ	11	41	BRADLEY	J	9	23	BRADSHAW	G	14	34				
BRADBERRY	H	13	51	BRADFORD	J	3	284	BRADLEY	J	9	23	BRADSHAW	GE	6	50				
BRADBROOK	J	2	34	BRADFORD	J	8	36	BRADLEY	J	9	231	BRADSHAW	GT	13	52				
BRADBROOK	RG	13	51	BRADFORD	J	14	33	BRADLEY	J	14	34	BRADSHAW	H	3	284				
BRADBURN	A	14	33	BRADFORD	JA	6	49	BRADLEY	JW	2	34	BRADSHAW	H	6	50				
BRADBURN	AE	3	284	BRADFORD	JH	6	49	BRADLEY	LA	6	49	BRADSHAW	H	11	41				
BRADBURY	A	12	27	BRADFORD	JW	2	34	BRADLEY	PJ	2	34	BRADSHAW	HJ	11	41				
BRADBURY	A	12	270	BRADFORD	PJ	5	40	BRADLEY	R	3	284	BRADSHAW	HJ	13	52				
BRADBURY	AM	6	49	BRADFORD	TC	2	34	BRADLEY	R	6	50	BRADSHAW	J	3	284				
BRADBURY	D	11	40	BRADFORD	TE	2	34	BRADLEY	R	9	23	BRADSHAW	J	11	42				
BRADBURY	ES	14	33	BRADFORD	TH	13	51	BRADLEY	R	14	34	BRADSHAW	J	14	34				
BRADBURY	FH	6	49	BRADFORD	WE	7	39	BRADLEY	S	11	41	BRADSHAW	JE	6	50				
BRADBURY	G	8	36	BRADFORD	WH	7	39	BRADLEY	SJL	3	284	BRADSHAW	JH	11	42				
BRADBURY	G	11	40	BRADFORD	WJ	13	52	BRADLEY	T	9	23	BRADSHAW	JH	12	28				
BRADBURY	H	2	34	BRADFORD	WT	2	34	BRADLEY	T	9	23	BRADSHAW	L	9	23				
BRADBURY	H	11	40	BRADING	E	4	46	BRADLEY	T	9	23	BRADSHAW	R	14	34				
BRADBURY	H	12	28	BRADING	G	4	46	BRADLEY	T	11	41	BRADSHAW	RA	12	270				
BRADBURY	HG	1	35	BRADISH	OA	13	51	BRADLEY	T	14	34	BRADSHAW	SR	1	35				
BRADBURY	J	6	49	BRADLEY	A	6	49	BRADLEY	TF	2	34	BRADSHAW	T	11	42				
BRADBURY	J	8	36	BRADLEY	A	9	22	BRADLEY	TS	6	50	BRADSHAW	T	12	270				
BRADBURY	J	11	41	BRADLEY	A	11	41	BRADLEY	VA	9	381	BRADSHAW	T	14	34				
BRADBURY	JE	5	40	BRADLEY	AM	3	284	BRADLEY	W	3	284	BRADSHAW	TD	12	270				
BRADBURY	JE	7	39	BRADLEY	C	1	35	BRADLEY	W	8	36	BRADSHAW	TE	14	34				
BRADBURY	P	3	284	BRADLEY	C	8	36	BRADLEY	W	9	23	BRADSHAW	V	1	35				
BRADBURY	R	6	49	BRADLEY	C	9	23	BRADLEY	W	9	231	BRADSHAW	W	7	39				
BRADBURY	T	8	36	BRADLEY	C	9	23	BRADLEY	W	9	231	BRADSHAW	W	8	36				
BRADBURY	TH	5	40	BRADLEY	C	11	41	BRADLEY	W	11	41	BRADSHAW	W	8	36				
BRADBURY	TJ	4	46	BRADLEY	CF	12	28	BRADLEY	WH	9	23	BRADSHAW	W	9	231				
BRADBURY	W	4	46	BRADLEY	D	11	41	BRADLEY	WH	14	34	BRADSHAW	W	11	42				
BRADBURY	W	11	41	BRADLEY	D	11	41	BRADLEY	WJ	10	26	BRADSHAW	W	11	42				
BRADBURY	W	11	41	BRADLEY	E	9	231	BRADLEY	WL	7	39	BRADSHAW	W	11	42				
BRADBURY	WH	14	33	BRADLEY	EAW	13	51	BRADLEY	WL	14	34	BRADSHAW	W	11	42				
BRADBY	RJ	1	35	BRADLEY	EG	10	25	BRADNOCK	FE	6	50	BRADSHAW	W	12	28				
BRADD	JF	8	36	BRADLEY	EH	1	35	BRADSHAW	A	1	35	BRADSHAW	WA	1	35				
BRADD	WE	8	36	BRADLEY	EH	14	33	BRADSHAW	A	2	34	BRADSHAW	WB	6	50				
BRADDISH	J	2	34	BRADLEY	EW	13	51	BRADSHAW	A	6	50	BRADSHAW	WE	3	26				
BRADDOCK	FS	11	41	BRADLEY	F	1	35	BRADSHAW	A	11	41	BRADSHAW	WG	12	28				
BRADE	AE	1	35	BRADLEY	F	9	23	BRADSHAW	A	11	42	BRADSHAW	WT	14	34				
BRADEN	AE	11	41	BRADLEY	F	9	231	BRADSHAW	A	12	28	BRADSTREET	J	3	26				
BRADEN	J	7	39	BRADLEY	F	14	33	BRADSHAW	AE	5	41	BRADWELL	CS	11	42				
BRADER	H	11	41	BRADLEY	F	14	33	BRADSHAW	BW	10	26	BRADY	C	9	23				
BRADER	JT	13	51	BRADLEY	FW	13	51	BRADSHAW	C	6	50	BRADY	C	9	231				
BRADER	P	5	40	BRADLEY	G	8	36	BRADSHAW	C	14	34	BRADY	C	10	26				
BRADEY	H	14	33	BRADLEY	GL	9	23	BRADSHAW	CE	6	50	BRADY	CW	13	52				
BRADFIELD	CW	13	51	BRADLEY	H	6	49	BRADSHAW	CJ	1	35	BRADY	D	11	42				
BRADFORD	AE	3	25	BRADLEY	H	8	36	BRADSHAW	E	9	231	BRADY	E	2	34				
BRADFORD	AJ	3	26	BRADLEY	H	11	41	BRADSHAW	E	11	42	BRADY	F	1	36				
BRADFORD	AJ	3	26	BRADLEY	H	11	41	BRADSHAW	E	14	34	BRADY	GC	2	34				
BRADFORD	E	8	36	BRADLEY	H	11	41	BRADSHAW	EB	1	35	BRADY	J	1	36				
BRADFORD	E	9	22	BRADLEY	HB	1	35	BRADSHAW	EE	13	51	BRADY	J	8	37				
BRADFORD	EV	2	34	BRADLEY	HR	10	25	BRADSHAW	ET	1	35	BRADY	J	8	37				
BRADFORD	F	6	49	BRADLEY	HR	10	269	BRADSHAW	F	5	41	BRADY	J	11	42				
BRADFORD	FW	5	40	BRADLEY	J	1	35	BRADSHAW	FA	14	34	BRADY	J	11	42				
BRADFORD	G	13	51	BRADLEY	J	7	39	BRADSHAW	FW	12	270	BRADY	J	14	34				
BRADFORD	GE	6	49	BRADLEY	J	9	23	BRADSHAW	G	1	35	BRADY	JH	8	37				

BRADY	JS	10	26	BRAITHWAITE	T	14	35	BRANCH	FA	1	36	BRANNAN	B	9	24
BRADY	N	14	34	BRAITHWAITE	W	8	37	BRANCH	FG	1	36	BRANNAN	D	9	24
BRADY	P	9	23	BRAITHWAITE	W	8	37	BRANCH	G	13	52	BRANNAN	F	11	43
BRADY	P	11	42	BRAITHWAITE	WA	8	37	BRANCH	TC	2	35	BRANNAN	H	9	24
BRADY	PW	4	46	BRAKESPEAR	J	2	35	BRANCHER	JJ	7	40	BRANNAN	H	14	35
BRADY	RB	14	34	BRAMALL	JA	3	26	BRANCHER	PE	7	40	BRANNAN	J	9	24
BRADY	S	8	37	BRAMAN	J	9	232	BRANCHETT	A	7	40	BRANNAN	J	9	24
BRADY	T	8	37	BRAMBLE	A	10	26	BRAND	C	4	47	BRANNAN	J	14	35
BRADY	T	9	23	BRAMBLE	A	13	52	BRAND	H	2	35	BRANNAN	J	14	35
BRADY	T	14	34	BRAMBLE	EJ	10	26	BRAND	JW	3	285	BRANNAN	JJ	14	35
BRADY	W	7	39	BRAMBLE	FT	10	26	BRAND	M	3	26	BRANNAN	JW	8	37
BRADY	W	13	52	BRAMBLE	J	10	269	BRAND	M	4	47	BRANNAN	P	14	35
BRADY	WA	7	39	BRAMBLE	J	14	35	BRAND	R	3	285	BRANNAN	R	14	35
BRAGG	C	6	50	BRAMBLE	RS	13	52	BRAND	R	4	47	BRANNAN	T	8	37
BRAGG	FC	10	26	BRAMBLEBY	FJ	5	41	BRAND	R	4	47	BRANNAN	W	2	35
BRAGG	GJH	1	36	BRAMBLEY	W	7	40	BRAND	SE	4	47	BRANNAN	W	8	37
BRAGG	H	6	50	BRAMBLEY	W	10	26	BRAND	VT	3	26	BRANNEN	M	9	381
BRAGG	J	6	50	BRAME	CE	9	23	BRAND	WG	2	35	BRANNICK	W	11	43
BRAGG	JN	6	50	BRAMFITT	A	12	270	BRANDEN	B	6	51	BRANNIGAN	A	11	43
BRAGG	JSH	7	40	BRAMFITT	WH	9	24	BRANDOM	C	5	41	BRANNON	JW	11	43
BRAGG	SC	12	270	BRAMFORD	W	5	41	BRANDOM	E	5	41	BRANSBURY	HE	13	52
BRAGG	W	6	50	BRAMHALL	JW	11	42	BRANDOM	GA	5	41	BRANSBURY	W	13	52
BRAGG	WJ	13	52	BRAMHALL	W	11	42	BRANDOM	L	1	36	BRANSBY	A	13	52
BRAGGER	SE	1	36	BRAMHALL	WH	14	35	BRANDOM	SC	5	41	BRANSCOMBE	EG	2	35
BRAGGER	WE	1	36	BRAMLEY	A	10	26	BRANDOM	W	5	41	BRANSGROVE	HS	7	40
BRAGGINS	G	4	46	BRAMLEY	C	9	24	BRANDOM	W	5	41	BRANSGROVE	JA	13	52
BRAGGINS	J	4	46	BRAMLEY	G	10	26	BRANDOM	WJ	5	41	BRANSOM	LW	8	38
BRAGGS	W	2	34	BRAMLEY	J	11	42	BRANDON	A	3	285	BRANSON	AG	12	270
BRAHAM	F	2	34	BRAMLEY	P	6	51	BRANDON	A	5	41	BRANSON	CJ	5	41
BRAHAM	F	7	40	BRAMLEY	W	12	270	BRANDON	AE	5	41	BRANSON	E	12	28
BRAHANY	JE	1	36	BRAMMER	A	8	37	BRANDON	AE	13	52	BRANSON	E	12	270
BRAIDMAN	A	7	40	BRAMMER	A	14	35	BRANDON	B	5	41	BRANSON	ED	5	41
BRAIDMAN	J	7	40	BRAMMER	AA	8	37	BRANDON	C	5	41	BRANSON	G	1	36
BRAIDWOOD	AJ	7	40	BRAMMER	J	11	42	BRANDON	C	7	40	BRANSON	MI	12	270
BRAILEY	GAB	10	269	BRAMMER	T	8	37	BRANDON	E	1	36	BRANSON	W	6	51
BRAILSFORD	RF	4	46	BRAMPTON	A	2	35	BRANDON	EG	12	28	BRANSON	W	12	28
BRAIN	ES	13	52	BRAMPTON	AE	2	35	BRANDON	F	12	28	BRANSON	WE	1	36
BRAIN	F	6	50	BRAMPTON	J	6	51	BRANDON	HE	1	36	BRANSON	WE	12	270
BRAIN	FF	6	50	BRAMPTON	J	6	51	BRANDON	J	7	40	BRANT	E	4	47
BRAIN	GF	10	26	BRAMPTON	PL	6	51	BRANDON	W	1	36	BRANT	JR	9	232
BRAIN	H	6	50	BRAMPTON	WA	5	41	BRANDON	W	3	285	BRANT	W	13	52
BRAIN	J	6	50	BRAMWELL	D	6	51	BRANDON	W	5	41	BRANTOM	HM	1	36
BRAIN	W	3	26	BRAMWELL	WE	11	42	BRANDON	W	5	41	BRASH	AC	3	285
BRAIN	WH	6	50	BRAMWORTH	T	14	35	BRANDON	WG	12	28	BRASH	JG	10	26
BRAINT	HS	7	40	BRAN	JL	4	46	BRANDRETH	T	14	35	BRASHIER	JJ	12	28
BRAITHWAITE	E	8	37	BRAN	L	4	46	BRANDRICK	J	14	35	BRASHIER	SM	12	28
BRAITHWAITE	GA	6	51	BRAN	WR	4	47	BRANFIELD	CA	3	26	BRASIER	S	5	42
BRAITHWAITE	H	8	37	BRANAGAN	C	11	43	BRANFIELD	CE	3	26	BRASIER	W	5	42
BRAITHWAITE	HG	7	40	BRANAGAN	CW	11	43	BRANFOOT	T	8	37	BRASON	AJ	12	28
BRAITHWAITE	J	9	232	BRANAGH	T	7	40	BRANFORD	J	7	40	BRASSELL	D	13	52
BRAITHWAITE	JS	8	37	BRANCH	AH	1	36	BRANIGAN	C	9	24	BRASSINGTON	B	11	43
BRAITHWAITE	L	9	232	BRANCH	AW	2	35	BRANN	WH	2	35	BRASSINGTON	G	14	35
BRAITHWAITE	S	8	37	BRANCH	CW	1	36	BRANNAN	A	9	24	BRATBY	EW	11	43
BRAITHWAITE	S	8	37	BRANCH	EC	1	36	BRANNAN	A	9	232	BRATBY	WD	3	26
BRAITHWAITE	T	11	42	BRANCH	F	3	285	BRANNAN	AE	2	35	BRATCHER	FC	10	26

BRATCHER	G	10	26	BRAYBROOK	F	5	42	BREAKSPEAR	F	6	51	BREEZE	JH	11	43
BRATCHER	H	10	26	BRAYBROOK	F	12	28	BREAKWELL	F	6	51	BREEZE	SE	3	285
BRATT	G	11	43	BRAYBROOK	FL	5	42	BREAKWELL	JA	6	51	BREEZE	W	1	37
BRATT	W	9	24	BRAYBROOK	WEC	2	35	BREAKWELL	P	6	52	BREHAUT	J	10	270
BRATTON	R	2	35	BRAYBROOKE	JE	2	35	BREAM	JH	7	41	BREHAUT	TJ	4	47
BRATTON	T	1	36	BRAYBROOKS	B	12	28	BREAR	F	9	24	BREHME	AF	7	41
BRAUND	H	6	51	BRAYBROOKS	CW	12	28	BREAR	J	9	25	BREMNER	EA	11	43
BRAUNSTON	O	12	270	BRAYBROOKS	E	12	29	BREAR	W	9	25	BREMNER	J	14	36
BRAUNTON	WJH	5	42	BRAYBROOKS	FJ	5	42	BREARLEY	A	8	38	BRENCHLEY	J	13	53
BRAUTIGAM	D	7	40	BRAYBROOKS	FJ	12	29	BREARLEY	A	9	232	BRENCHLEY	R	3	285
BRAVERY	W	13	52	BRAYBROOKS	G	12	29	BREARLEY	A	14	35	BRENNAN	A	9	381
BRAVINGTON	H	10	26	BRAYBROOKS	H	12	29	BREARLEY	J	8	38	BRENNAN	C	14	36
BRAVO	DB	14	35	BRAYBROOKS	S	12	29	BREARLEY	J	14	35	BRENNAN	CH	11	43
BRAWN	TE	13	53	BRAYFORD	ES	6	51	BREARLEY	P	9	232	BRENNAN	G	4	48
BRAWN	WE	5	42	BRAYFORD	F	10	27	BREARLEY	S	8	38	BRENNAN	J	8	38
BRAXTON	F	4	47	BRAYFORD	T	11	43	BREARTON	H	9	25	BRENNAN	J	9	25
BRAY	A	8	38	BRAYSHAW	F	9	24	BREARTON	J	9	25	BRENNAN	J	9	232
BRAY	A	9	24	BRAYSHAW	H	9	24	BREAVINGTON	GC	12	271	BRENNAN	J	11	43
BRAY	AE	12	270	BRAYSHAW	T	9	24	BRECKELL	JH	11	43	BRENNAN	J	11	43
BRAY	AJ	3	285	BRAYSHAW	W	8	38	BRECKIN	T	14	36	BRENNAN	J	14	36
BRAY	B	9	24	BRAYSHAW	WM	8	38	BRECKLEY	HG	1	37	BRENNAN	JE	8	38
BRAY	CD	12	270	BRAYSHER	O	2	35	BREDGER	NE	12	29	BRENNAN	JW	11	43
BRAY	CH	12	270	BRAZIER	A	7	40	BREE	A	4	47	BRENNAN	JW	14	36
BRAY	CJ	3	26	BRAZIER	AG	2	35	BREE	GW	12	271	BRENNAN	M	14	36
BRAY	CT	13	53	BRAZIER	AT	3	26	BREE	H	12	271	BRENNAN	P	2	36
BRAY	ES	4	47	BRAZIER	CP	7	40	BREED	A	5	42	BRENNAN	P	8	38
BRAY	F	1	36	BRAZIER	E	5	42	BREED	AC	5	42	BRENNAN	P	11	43
BRAY	F	4	47	BRAZIER	EM	2	35	BREED	AW	12	29	BRENNAN	P	11	44
BRAY	F	11	43	BRAZIER	ES	2	36	BREED	B	5	42	BRENNAN	T	11	44
BRAY	F	12	270	BRAZIER	H	5	42	BREED	E	1	37	BRENNAN	T	11	44
BRAY	H	8	38	BRAZIER	HA	7	41	BREED	EG	12	29	BRENNAN	W	8	38
BRAY	H	9	24	BRAZIER	HJ	2	36	BREED	F	5	42	BRENNAN	W	11	44
BRAY	HS	13	53	BRAZIER	HN	1	36	BREED	F	5	43	BRENNAN	WJ	13	53
BRAY	HW	5	42	BRAZIER	J	5	42	BREED	G	12	29	BRENT	B	4	48
BRAY	J	13	53	BRAZIER	JH	7	41	BREED	GE	12	29	BRENT	ED	3	285
BRAY	JA	10	27	BRAZIER	JH	8	38	BREED	GH	13	53	BRENT	EP	3	285
BRAY	JA	12	28	BRAZIER	JW	1	36	BREED	JH	13	53	BRENT	PJ	3	285
BRAY	JE	12	270	BRAZIER	SA	6	51	BREED	OA	12	29	BRENT	T	5	43
BRAY	JF	6	51	BRAZIER	TH	1	37	BREED	W	5	43	BRENT	THV	7	41
BRAY	LE	7	40	BRAZIER	W	5	42	BREEDEN	B	6	52	BRENTLEY	R	9	25
BRAY	P	5	42	BRAZIER	W	5	42	BREEDEN	HW	7	41	BRENTON	F	4	48
BRAY	PC	2	35	BRAZIER	WL	7	41	BREEDS	B	10	269	BRENTON	TR	3	285
BRAY	R	13	53	BRAZIL	EF	3	26	BREEN	M	12	29	BRENTON	WH	3	285
BRAY	RA	5	42	BRAZNELL	AE	6	51	BREEN	T	4	47	BRERETON	E	7	41
BRAY	RF	6	51	BRAZNELL	C	6	51	BREESE	BS	6	52	BRERETON	G	11	44
BRAY	RH	2	35	BRAZNELL	H	6	51	BREESE	H	6	52	BRERETON	J	11	44
BRAY	S	4	47	BRAZNELL	J	6	51	BREESE	HJ	10	27	BRERETON	RF	14	36
BRAY	S	4	47	BRCE	A	2	44	BREESE	W	6	52	BRERTON	E	11	44
BRAY	T	8	38	BREACH	HG	7	41	BREESE	WJ	2	36	BRESNAHAN	D	13	53
BRAY	TF	2	35	BREACH	J	10	269	BREEZE	E	10	27	BRESNAHAN	E	13	53
BRAY	W	8	38	BREADMORE	TH	4	47	BREEZE	G	6	52	BRESNAHAN	P	13	53
BRAY	W	10	26	BREAKER	AE	4	47	BREEZE	G	14	36	BRETHERICK	J	9	25
BRAY	W	13	53	BREAKER	FC	4	47	BREEZE	GM	14	36	BRETHERTON	CH	6	52
BRAY	WH	1	36	BREAKER	JFC	4	47	BREEZE	HT	6	52	BRETON	TJ	13	53
BRAY	WH	4	47	BREAKS	H	9	24	BREEZE	JF	2	36	BRETT	AC	4	48

BRETT	AH	2	36	BREWER	GE	13	54	BRIANT	AM	13	54	BRIDGE	M	13	54
BRETT	AL	1	37	BREWER	GT	2	36	BRIANT	CW	1	37	BRIDGE	PA	7	42
BRETT	B	5	43	BREWER	GW	10	27	BRIANT	CW	1	37	BRIDGE	S	6	52
BRETT	C	1	37	BREWER	H	1	37	BRIANT	EH	13	54	BRIDGE	TH	6	52
BRETT	CJ	13	53	BREWER	H	7	41	BRIANT	FL	7	41	BRIDGE	W	14	36
BRETT	CL	4	48	BREWER	HB	8	38	BRIANT	SG	13	54	BRIDGE	WA	5	43
BRETT	EC	7	41	BREWER	HJ	13	54	BRIANT	TA	2	36	BRIDGE	WA	7	42
BRETT	F	6	52	BREWER	HR	3	285	BRIANT	WJ	13	54	BRIDGEMAN	J	1	37
BRETT	G	4	48	BREWER	J	4	48	BRIARIS	A	13	54	BRIDGEMAN	J	11	45
BRETT	GJ	13	53	BREWER	JB	10	27	BRIARIS	H	13	54	BRIDGEMAN	JE	11	45
BRETT	GW	3	26	BREWER	JE	5	43	BRIARS	C	5	43	BRIDGEMAN	WTH	7	42
BRETT	H	1	37	BREWER	JG	13	54	BRIARS	H	12	29	BRIDGEN	G	13	54
BRETT	H	11	44	BREWER	JR	10	27	BRIARS	R	12	29	BRIDGENS	EC	6	52
BRETT	HJ	6	52	BREWER	JR	10	27	BRIARS	W	12	29	BRIDGENS	P	4	48
BRETT	HT	13	53	BREWER	JT	1	37	BRICE	A	4	48	BRIDGER	AC	13	54
BRETT	HW	7	41	BREWER	JTG	5	43	BRICE	AB	12	29	BRIDGER	CA	4	48
BRETT	J	8	38	BREWER	JW	5	43	BRICE	AJ	5	43	BRIDGER	FB	4	48
BRETT	J	9	25	BREWER	M	4	48	BRICE	CW	12	29	BRIDGER	H	3	286
BRETT	J	9	25	BREWER	NW	10	27	BRICE	FJ	10	27	BRIDGER	HC	8	38
BRETT	J	9	232	BREWER	PE	10	270	BRICE	H	4	48	BRIDGER	J	7	42
BRETT	J	14	36	BREWER	R	11	44	BRICE	H	5	43	BRIDGER	PV	10	27
BRETT	JD	11	44	BREWER	RG	2	36	BRICE	H	13	54	BRIDGER	RC	2	36
BRETT	JH	5	43	BREWER	RW	13	54	BRICE	HA	5	43	BRIDGER	T	10	27
BRETT	KA	1	37	BREWER	S	8	38	BRICE	HJ	2	36	BRIDGER	WA	10	27
BRETT	M	9	232	BREWER	T	1	37	BRICE	J	12	29	BRIDGER	WA	10	27
BRETT	R	1	37	BREWER	T	6	52	BRICE	JT	12	271	BRIDGES	A	1	37
BRETT	R	4	48	BREWER	T	6	52	BRICE	P	12	29	BRIDGES	A	3	286
BRETT	RS	13	53	BREWER	W	2	36	BRICE	RJ	12	271	BRIDGES	A	5	43
BRETT	S	11	44	BREWER	W	2	36	BRICE	VA	5	43	BRIDGES	A	6	52
BRETT	SG	1	37	BREWER	W	8	38	BRICKELL	T	6	52	BRIDGES	AE	12	30
BRETT	T	9	232	BREWER	WC	10	270	BRICKELL	TR	6	52	BRIDGES	AV	1	37
BRETT	W	1	37	BREWER	WE	13	54	BRICKNELL	CA	2	36	BRIDGES	E	1	38
BRETT	WG	1	37	BREWER	WG	7	41	BRICKNELL	E	1	37	BRIDGES	EE	1	38
BRETT	WJ	1	37	BREWER	WJ	7	41	BRICKNELL	LG	4	48	BRIDGES	EW	2	36
BRETTELL	L	6	52	BREWER	WT	2	36	BRICKNELL	RW	4	48	BRIDGES	FG	7	42
BRETTELL	L	6	52	BREWERTON	AE	3	285	BRICKNELL	W	1	37	BRIDGES	FWJ	5	43
BREW	CAM	13	54	BREWERTON	H	11	44	BRICKWOOD	A	12	271	BRIDGES	G	12	30
BREW	CW	1	37	BREWERTON	JF	3	285	BRIDCUTT	CA	5	43	BRIDGES	GJ	5	44
BREWER	A	7	41	BREWIN	HE	10	27	BRIDDOCK	W	11	44	BRIDGES	JM	1	38
BREWER	AE	7	41	BREWOOD	SF	3	285	BRIDDON	G	11	45	BRIDGES	JM	2	36
BREWER	AFJ	3	26	BREWSTER	A	3	26	BRIDDON	JJ	11	45	BRIDGES	JT	2	37
BREWER	AG	13	54	BREWSTER	A	11	44	BRIDDON	L	11	45	BRIDGES	JT	6	53
BREWER	B	4	48	BREWSTER	A	11	44	BRIDEWELL	AJ	2	36	BRIDGES	NS	1	38
BREWER	CA	5	43	BREWSTER	A	11	44	BRIDGE	AE	1	37	BRIDGES	RG	1	38
BREWER	DM	3	285	BREWSTER	FH	12	271	BRIDGE	AE	3	286	BRIDGES	RJ	2	37
BREWER	E	10	27	BREWSTER	FW	5	43	BRIDGE	AE	13	54	BRIDGES	W	7	42
BREWER	E	11	44	BREWSTER	GA	2	36	BRIDGE	CJJ	12	30	BRIDGES	W	14	36
BREWER	EE	5	43	BREWSTER	H	8	38	BRIDGE	F	14	36	BRIDGES	WJ	1	38
BREWER	F	2	36	BREWSTER	JWH	3	285	BRIDGE	GF	12	30	BRIDGES	WJ	13	55
BREWER	F	4	48	BREWSTER	R	3	27	BRIDGE	HC	12	30	BRIDGES	WK	7	42
BREWER	F	13	54	BREWSTER	S	11	44	BRIDGE	J	3	286	BRIDGES	WS	7	42
BREWER	FJ	4	48	BREWSTER	WE	7	41	BRIDGE	J	11	45	BRIDGES	WS	7	42
BREWER	FW	4	48	BREWSTER	WJ	7	41	BRIDGE	J	14	36	BRIDGES	WW	1	38
BREWER	G	14	36	BREWSTER	WR	2	36	BRIDGE	JW	2	36	BRIDGEWOOD	T	11	45
BREWER	GA	3	26	BRIAN	M	9	25	BRIDGE	M	6	52	BRIDGLAND	G	1	38

BRIDGMAN	AH	1	38	BRIGGS	A	9	232	BRIGGS	W	9	26	BRIGHTWELL	R	13	55
BRIDGMAN	J	2	37	BRIGGS	A	10	270	BRIGGS	W	9	233	BRIGHTWELL	W	12	271
BRIDGNES	WH	2	37	BRIGGS	A	14	37	BRIGGS	W	9	233	BRIGHTY	F	14	37
BRIDGWATER	A	6	53	BRIGGS	A	14	37	BRIGGS	W	9	381	BRIGINSHAW	W	5	44
BRIDGWATER	DA	6	53	BRIGGS	C	7	42	BRIGGS	W	12	271	BRIGLAND	HJ	13	55
BRIDGWATER	E	9	25	BRIGGS	C	9	25	BRIGGS	WG	9	233	BRILEY	HRC	3	286
BRIDGWATER	F	6	53	BRIGGS	E	9	232	BRIGGS	WH	8	40	BRILL	A	2	37
BRIDGWATER	WA	9	25	BRIGGS	E	9	232	BRIGHAM	C	9	26	BRILL	HJ	3	286
BRIDGWATER	WRC	6	53	BRIGGS	EW	6	53	BRIGHAM	D	8	40	BRILL	MJ	2	37
BRIDLE	AC	4	49	BRIGGS	F	7	42	BRIGHAM	JW	8	40	BRILL	WJE	2	37
BRIDLE	AWH	1	38	BRIGGS	F	8	39	BRIGHAM	P	8	40	BRIM	EE	5	44
BRIDLE	E	1	38	BRIGGS	F	9	25	BRIGHAM	RJ	3	27	BRIMACOMBE	CE	3	286
BRIDLE	E	10	27	BRIGGS	F	9	25	BRIGHAM	W	9	381	BRIMBLE	FW	6	53
BRIDLE	G	10	28	BRIGGS	F	9	232	BRIGHAN	H	9	26	BRIMBLE	G	6	53
BRIDLE	G	10	28	BRIGGS	FC	2	37	BRIGHT	A	4	49	BRIMBLE	WH	6	53
BRIDLE	H	2	37	BRIGGS	GF	2	37	BRIGHT	A	5	44	BRIMECOME	GH	10	28
BRIDLE	HG	14	36	BRIGGS	GN	9	25	BRIGHT	A	6	53	BRIMELOW	W	14	37
BRIDLE	SJ	10	28	BRIGGS	GW	14	37	BRIGHT	A	6	53	BRIMER	FWG	10	270
BRIDLE	T	10	28	BRIGGS	H	8	39	BRIGHT	AA	6	53	BRIMER	PA	10	270
BRIDLE	TH	14	36	BRIGGS	H	8	39	BRIGHT	D	7	42	BRIMFIELD	E	2	38
BRIDLE	W	10	28	BRIGGS	H	8	39	BRIGHT	FH	12	30	BRIMFIELD	F	1	38
BRIDLE	WG	4	49	BRIGGS	H	8	39	BRIGHT	FW	2	37	BRIMICOMBE	W	2	38
BRIDSON	W	8	39	BRIGGS	H	8	39	BRIGHT	G	9	26	BRIMICOMBE	WJ	3	27
BRIEN	GA	1	38	BRIGGS	H	9	25	BRIGHT	H	4	49	BRIMLEY	F	5	44
BRIEN	HJ	3	27	BRIGGS	H	9	26	BRIGHT	HC	4	49	BRIMLEY	FC	12	30
BRIEN	HJF	12	30	BRIGGS	H	11	45	BRIGHT	I	4	49	BRIMMELL	G	3	286
BRIEN	J	2	37	BRIGGS	H	13	55	BRIGHT	J	6	53	BRIMMER	TA	7	42
BRIENT	A	2	37	BRIGGS	J	8	39	BRIGHT	J	7	42	BRIMMICOMBE	C	1	38
BRIER	T	8	39	BRIGGS	J	8	39	BRIGHT	JA	7	42	BRIMSON	WA	13	55
BRIERLEY	A	8	39	BRIGGS	J	9	26	BRIGHT	LC	5	44	BRINAN	CH	13	55
BRIERLEY	C	11	45	BRIGGS	J	9	26	BRIGHT	S	5	44	BRINAN	E	13	55
BRIERLEY	C	14	36	BRIGGS	J	9	232	BRIGHT	T	6	53	BRINDLE	F	3	286
BRIERLEY	E	14	37	BRIGGS	J	9	232	BRIGHT	T	7	42	BRINDLE	F	11	45
BRIERLEY	E	14	37	BRIGGS	J	11	45	BRIGHT	W	3	286	BRINDLE	WT	6	54
BRIERLEY	G	11	45	BRIGGS	JH	6	53	BRIGHT	W	4	49	BRINDLEY	A	14	37
BRIERLEY	H	8	39	BRIGGS	JH	9	26	BRIGHT	W	11	45	BRINDLEY	H	6	54
BRIERLEY	J	11	45	BRIGGS	JH	9	233	BRIGHT	W	13	55	BRINDLEY	J	11	45
BRIERLEY	J	11	45	BRIGGS	JT	13	55	BRIGHT	WH	3	27	BRINDLEY	JT	11	45
BRIERLEY	RT	2	37	BRIGGS	JW	9	233	BRIGHT	WL	6	53	BRINDLEY	T	14	37
BRIERLEY	S	14	37	BRIGGS	JW	12	30	BRIGHT	WW	2	37	BRINE	D	11	46
BRIERLEY	T	14	37	BRIGGS	L	9	233	BRIGHTMAN	A	5	44	BRINE	EC	10	28
BRIERLEY	W	8	39	BRIGGS	OT	8	39	BRIGHTMAN	A	12	271	BRINE	FH	4	49
BRIERS	A	11	45	BRIGGS	RG	7	42	BRIGHTMAN	FG	12	30	BRINE	GE	4	49
BRIERS	F	11	45	BRIGGS	S	9	26	BRIGHTMAN	FT	12	30	BRINE	WC	4	49
BRIERS	J	10	270	BRIGGS	S	9	233	BRIGHTMAN	K	5	44	BRINING	E	8	40
BRIFFITT	J	13	55	BRIGGS	T	2	37	BRIGHTMORE	EH	2	37	BRINKLER	JA	7	42
BRIGDEN	GE	13	55	BRIGGS	T	8	39	BRIGHTMORE	EJH	2	37	BRINKLER	JJ	7	42
BRIGDEN	H	6	53	BRIGGS	T	8	39	BRIGHTMORE	FL	2	37	BRINKLEY	CT	3	27
BRIGDEN	J	7	42	BRIGGS	TH	8	39	BRIGHTMORE	G	2	37	BRINKLEY	E	3	27
BRIGDEN	R	6	53	BRIGGS	V	9	233	BRIGHTMORE	R	14	37	BRINKLEY	GW	1	38
BRIGDEN	RJ	13	55	BRIGGS	W	8	39	BRIGHTMORE	RD	2	37	BRINKLEY	JW	2	38
BRIGDEN	W	6	53	BRIGGS	W	8	39	BRIGHTON	HJ	2	37	BRINKLEY	R	3	27
BRIGDEN	WO	13	55	BRIGGS	W	8	40	BRIGHTWELL	D	3	286	BRINKLEY	RG	2	38
BRIGGS	A	9	232	BRIGGS	W	9	26	BRIGHTWELL	F	1	38	BRINKLEY	RL	7	43
BRIGGS	A	9	232	BRIGGS	W	9	26	BRIGHTWELL	JHF	13	55	BRINKLOW	A	5	44

Surname	Initials	Col A	Col B
BRINKLOW	D	5	44
BRINKLOW	E	12	271
BRINKLOW	F	5	44
BRINKLOW	G	12	30
BRINKLOW	H	5	44
BRINKLOW	H	12	271
BRINKLOW	JC	5	44
BRINKLOW	L	5	44
BRINKLOW	SC	5	44
BRINKLOW	W	12	30
BRINKMAN	G	1	38
BRINN	FWF	1	38
BRINN	J	3	286
BRINN	J	8	40
BRINNAND	TT	12	30
BRINSLEY	G	13	55
BRINSON	H	1	38
BRINT	FJ	10	28
BRINTON	GW	2	38
BRIODY	TC	12	271
BRISCOE	E	1	38
BRISCOE	G	6	54
BRISCOE	GJ	1	38
BRISCOE	HA	2	38
BRISCOE	HB	8	40
BRISCOE	HC	10	28
BRISCOE	JI	6	54
BRISCOE	M	8	40
BRISCOE	T	1	38
BRISCOE	W	1	38
BRISKE	F	11	46
BRISKHAM	JG	3	286
BRISLAND	CJ	4	49
BRISTEIR	GE	2	38
BRISTER	JF	3	27
BRISTIER	G	2	38
BRISTOW	AW	2	38
BRISTOW	B	9	233
BRISTOW	EJT	3	286
BRISTOW	F	3	27
BRISTOW	F	6	54
BRISTOW	G	1	38
BRISTOW	GH	2	38
BRISTOW	J	6	54
BRISTOW	JO	2	38
BRISTOW	SJ	4	49
BRISTOW	W	2	38
BRISTOW	W	6	54
BRISTOW	W	6	54
BRISTOW	WG	14	37
BRISTOWE	GJ	3	27
BRISTOWE	H	3	27
BRISTOWE	T	3	27
BRITCHER	RA	3	286
BRITCHFORD	AJ	13	55
BRITCHFORD	CC	5	44
BRITLAND	J	3	27
BRITNELL	PW	5	44
BRITON	F	9	26
BRITT	S	10	270
BRITTAIN	A	12	30
BRITTAIN	BE	12	30
BRITTAIN	FW	2	38
BRITTAIN	G	12	30
BRITTAIN	H	8	40
BRITTAIN	J	11	46
BRITTAIN	JW	2	38
BRITTAIN	W	12	30
BRITTAIN	W	12	271
BRITTAN	AE	13	55
BRITTAN	WA	13	55
BRITTANY	G	5	44
BRITTANY	T	5	44
BRITTEN	CA	2	38
BRITTEN	CR	12	271
BRITTEN	E	12	271
BRITTEN	JW	12	271
BRITTEN	R	12	271
BRITTEN	RG	2	38
BRITTEN	RG	12	31
BRITTEN	WC	4	49
BRITTEN	WJ	12	271
BRITTLE	F	6	54
BRITTLE	L	6	54
BRITTON	AG	6	54
BRITTON	AH	7	43
BRITTON	CE	6	54
BRITTON	CJ	2	38
BRITTON	D	13	56
BRITTON	F	12	31
BRITTON	FH	9	26
BRITTON	G	14	37
BRITTON	H	8	40
BRITTON	HA	4	49
BRITTON	HV	8	40
BRITTON	J	6	54
BRITTON	J	7	43
BRITTON	J	8	40
BRITTON	J	9	233
BRITTON	J	9	233
BRITTON	J	14	37
BRITTON	JJ	7	43
BRITTON	JR	7	43
BRITTON	LY	6	54
BRITTON	P	9	233
BRITTON	T	9	26
BRITTON	W	8	40
BRITTON	W	8	40
BRITTON	WC	7	43
BRITTON	WEH	4	49
BRIXTON	FH	3	27
BROAD	C	3	286
BROAD	CJ	3	286
BROAD	CJ	13	56
BROAD	E	3	286
BROAD	EG	13	56
BROAD	G	13	56
BROAD	H	11	46
BROAD	HA	13	56
BROAD	J	10	28
BROAD	JA	3	27
BROAD	RA	2	38
BROAD	W	2	38
BROADBELT	C	8	40
BROADBENT	A	11	46
BROADBENT	BM	9	26
BROADBENT	C	9	233
BROADBENT	CR	9	26
BROADBENT	E	9	26
BROADBENT	E	11	46
BROADBENT	F	9	26
BROADBENT	F	9	233
BROADBENT	H	8	40
BROADBENT	H	8	40
BROADBENT	H	9	26
BROADBENT	H	9	233
BROADBENT	H	9	233
BROADBENT	H	11	46
BROADBENT	J	8	40
BROADBENT	J	8	40
BROADBENT	J	9	27
BROADBENT	J	9	27
BROADBENT	J	9	233
BROADBENT	JE	9	27
BROADBENT	JR	9	27
BROADBENT	M	9	27
BROADBENT	S	8	40
BROADBELT	T	6	54
BROADBENT	T	9	233
BROADBENT	T	11	46
BROADBENT	W	1	39
BROADBENT	WE	9	27
BROADBENT	WJ	14	37
BROADBRIDGE	H	1	39
BROADBRIDGE	J	13	56
BROADBRIDGE	W	1	39
BROADEY	CR	13	56
BROADEY	W	13	56
BROADFIELD	F	4	49
BROADFIELD	FG	6	54
BROADFIELD	W	6	54
BROADFIELD	WL	3	287
BROADHEAD	A	8	41
BROADHEAD	A	11	46
BROADHEAD	E	14	37
BROADHEAD	H	8	41
BROADHEAD	J	14	37
BROADHEAD	J	14	38
BROADHEAD	L	8	41
BROADHEAD	M	9	27
BROADHEAD	O	8	41
BROADHEAD	T	8	41
BROADHEAD	W	8	41
BROADHEAD	W	8	41
BROADHEAD	W	8	41
BROADHEAD	W	11	46
BROADHIRST	T	8	41
BROADHURST	A	6	55
BROADHURST	AC	7	43
BROADHURST	AJ	7	43
BROADHURST	G	6	54
BROADHURST	G	11	46
BROADHURST	H	11	46
BROADHURST	J	1	39
BROADHURST	J	13	56
BROADHURST	J	14	38
BROADHURST	S	14	38
BROADHURST	SJ	6	55
BROADHURST	V	11	46
BROADHURST	W	9	27
BROADHURST	W	11	46
BROADHURST	WH	11	46
BROADLEY	AC	1	39
BROADLEY	AJ	6	55
BROADLEY	F	9	27
BROADLEY	G	9	27
BROADLEY	H	14	38
BROADLEY	J	9	233
BROADLEY	J	9	381
BROADLEY	LA	2	38
BROADLEY	RE	2	39
BROADMORE	EA	6	55
BROADRIBB	J	7	43
BROADRIBB	W	4	49
BROADWAY	A	12	31
BROADWAY	BJ	10	28
BROADWAY	CV	2	39
BROADWAY	HC	13	56
BROADWAY	HF	6	55
BROADWAY	JG	6	55
BROADWAY	JH	12	31
BROADWAY	PG	10	28
BROADWAY	S	12	31
BROADWAY	SJ	6	55
BROADWAY	W	6	55
BROADWAY	W	12	31
BROADWAY	WE	6	55
BROADY	J	11	46
BROBBIN	J	11	46
BROBSON	C	10	28

BROCK	A	5	45
BROCK	F	4	49
BROCK	JH	13	56
BROCK	L	5	45
BROCK	RF	3	287
BROCK	TA	2	39
BROCK	WG	13	56
BROCK	WJ	12	272
BROCK	WJW	13	56
BROCKBANK	A	11	46
BROCKBANK	GE	14	38
BROCKBANK	HH	11	47
BROCKETT	AAV	12	31
BROCKETT	FC	13	56
BROCKETT	JT	7	43
BROCKETT	JW	12	31
BROCKETT	WJ	12	31
BROCKLEHURST	G	14	38
BROCKLEHURST	H	14	38
BROCKLEHURST	WE	1	39
BROCKS	WJ	10	28
BROCKWAY	AS	4	49
BROCKWAY	FJ	4	49
BROCKWAY	WA	4	50
BROCKWELL	EG	13	56
BROCKWELL	GA	13	56
BROCKWELL	J	3	287
BROCKWELL	J	13	56
BROCKWELL	JH	2	39
BROCKWELL	W	11	47
BROCKWELL	WJ	7	43
BRODERICK	J	11	47
BRODERICK	J	11	47
BRODERICK	W	11	47
BRODERICK	WC	4	50
BRODIE	A	6	55
BRODIE	A	8	41
BRODIE	G	6	55
BRODIE	G	8	41
BRODIE	GH	1	39
BRODIE	H	14	38
BRODIE	RP	4	50
BRODIE	TP	3	27
BRODKIN	JW	6	57
BRODY	TG	13	57
BROE	A	2	39
BROGAN	E	11	47
BROGAN	J	11	47
BROGAN	JH	11	47
BROGAN	W	8	41
BROGAN	W	11	47
BROGDEN	H	11	47
BROGDEN	HP	9	27
BROGDEN	J	8	41
BROGDEN	J	8	41

BROGDEN	J	9	27
BROGDEN	JW	8	41
BROGDEN	N	11	47
BROGDEN	W	8	41
BROGDON	J	8	41
BROMAGE	H	12	272
BROMAGE	JA	3	27
BROMBY	AJ	4	50
BROMBY	RW	4	50
BROMBY	WJ	4	50
BROMFIELD	A	10	28
BROMHAM	S	2	39
BROMHEAD	R	7	43
BROMILEY	T	14	38
BROMLEY	A	9	234
BROMLEY	A	14	38
BROMLEY	AJ	7	43
BROMLEY	F	8	41
BROMLEY	F	10	28
BROMLEY	G	4	50
BROMLEY	H	14	38
BROMLEY	J	8	41
BROMLEY	J	9	27
BROMLEY	JT	2	39
BROMLEY	JW	14	38
BROMLEY	R	11	47
BROMLEY	W	10	28
BROMLEY	W	13	57
BROMPTON	J	2	39
BROMWELL	JH	6	55
BROMWELL	RC	6	55
BROMWELL	WG	6	55
BROMWICH	A	12	272
BROMWICH	AJ	6	55
BROMWICH	B	6	55
BROMWICH	HM	2	39
BROMWICH	HW	6	55
BRONGER	AW	2	39
BRONS	C	7	43
BRONSELL	AH	5	45
BROOK	A	8	41
BROOK	A	8	42
BROOK	A	9	27
BROOK	A	9	234
BROOK	A	9	234
BROOK	AB	13	57
BROOK	AE	2	39
BROOK	AE	13	57
BROOK	AH	9	234
BROOK	AJ	8	42
BROOK	B	8	42
BROOK	C	8	42
BROOK	C	9	27
BROOK	E	8	42
BROOK	E	8	42

BROOK	E	9	234
BROOK	F	9	27
BROOK	F	9	27
BROOK	F	9	234
BROOK	F	9	381
BROOK	GD	8	42
BROOK	GE	8	42
BROOK	GL	8	42
BROOK	H	8	42
BROOK	H	8	42
BROOK	H	9	27
BROOK	H	9	28
BROOK	H	9	28
BROOK	H	9	28
BROOK	H	9	28
BROOK	HM	2	39
BROOK	J	8	42
BROOK	J	8	42
BROOK	J	9	28
BROOK	J	9	28
BROOK	JA	8	42
BROOK	JJ	5	45
BROOK	JJ	8	42
BROOK	JW	8	42
BROOK	L	9	28
BROOK	L	9	234
BROOK	M	8	42
BROOK	M	8	42
BROOK	R	8	42
BROOK	S	8	42
BROOK	S	8	42
BROOK	S	8	42
BROOK	S	9	28
BROOK	SH	4	50
BROOK	T	8	43
BROOK	T	9	28
BROOK	W	8	43
BROOK	W	9	28
BROOK	W	9	234
BROOK	WH	8	43
BROOK	WM	9	28
BROOKBANK	A	11	47
BROOKBANK	W	9	234
BROOKE	A	7	43
BROOKE	A	8	43
BROOKE	AE	6	56
BROOKE	AE	6	56
BROOKE	E	8	43
BROOKE	F	8	43
BROOKE	FC	8	43
BROOKE	G	6	56
BROOKE	GF	6	56
BROOKE	H	9	28
BROOKE	I	9	28
BROOKE	JW	2	39

BROOKE	RJ	3	28
BROOKE	RW	3	28
BROOKE	W	8	43
BROOKE	WV	7	43
BROOKER	AJC	13	57
BROOKER	B	2	39
BROOKER	BW	13	57
BROOKER	E	7	43
BROOKER	F	1	39
BROOKER	F	13	57
BROOKER	FC	13	57
BROOKER	FW	2	39
BROOKER	G	7	43
BROOKER	GW	3	287
BROOKER	H	1	39
BROOKER	H	2	39
BROOKER	H	12	31
BROOKER	J	12	31
BROOKER	J	12	31
BROOKER	J	13	57
BROOKER	JG	5	45
BROOKER	JLR	13	57
BROOKER	LGA	13	57
BROOKER	R	12	31
BROOKER	R	13	57
BROOKER	TE	13	57
BROOKER	W	2	39
BROOKER	W	13	57
BROOKER	WJ	7	43
BROOKES	A	6	56
BROOKES	A	6	56
BROOKES	A	8	43
BROOKES	A	11	47
BROOKES	A	11	47
BROOKES	AE	2	39
BROOKES	AJ	6	56
BROOKES	AS	12	31
BROOKES	AW	6	56
BROOKES	B	5	45
BROOKES	E	8	43
BROOKES	E	11	47
BROOKES	FTG	7	44
BROOKES	GA	2	39
BROOKES	GJ	6	56
BROOKES	H	5	45
BROOKES	H	6	56
BROOKES	H	11	47
BROOKES	HT	6	56
BROOKES	J	5	45
BROOKES	J	6	56
BROOKES	J	6	56
BROOKES	J	6	56
BROOKES	J	6	56
BROOKES	J	6	56
BROOKES	J	14	38

BROOKES	JC	2	39	BROOKS	F	9	28	BROOKS	S	9	234	BROOME	HJ	5	45
BROOKES	JE	6	56	BROOKS	F	12	31	BROOKS	S	11	48	BROOME	J	6	57
BROOKES	JHW	2	40	BROOKS	F	13	58	BROOKS	SH	7	44	BROOME	J	6	57
BROOKES	JJ	14	38	BROOKS	FE	1	39	BROOKS	SW	7	44	BROOME	J	6	57
BROOKES	R	11	47	BROOKS	FH	7	44	BROOKS	SW	10	29	BROOME	J	14	39
BROOKES	S	6	56	BROOKS	FJ	3	28	BROOKS	T	2	40	BROOME	JH	11	48
BROOKES	S	14	38	BROOKS	FJ	7	44	BROOKS	TA	14	39	BROOME	JW	1	40
BROOKES	W	11	48	BROOKS	FM	6	57	BROOKS	TE	12	32	BROOME	TS	14	39
BROOKES	W	14	38	BROOKS	G	1	39	BROOKS	TH	11	48	BROOME	W	11	48
BROOKFIELD	RH	13	57	BROOKS	G	2	40	BROOKS	TW	1	39	BROOME	WE	12	272
BROOKLEY	W	6	57	BROOKS	G	2	40	BROOKS	VJ	2	40	BROOME	WEF	3	28
BROOKMAN	EJ	13	57	BROOKS	G	5	45	BROOKS	W	1	39	BROOME	WW	2	40
BROOKMAN	KG	10	28	BROOKS	G	6	57	BROOKS	W	4	50	BROOMER	C	11	48
BROOKMAN	R	7	44	BROOKS	G	9	234	BROOKS	W	5	45	BROOMFIELD	A	4	50
BROOKS	A	2	40	BROOKS	G	13	58	BROOKS	W	8	43	BROOMFIELD	AHS	4	51
BROOKS	A	4	50	BROOKS	G	14	39	BROOKS	W	11	48	BROOMFIELD	AJ	4	51
BROOKS	A	4	50	BROOKS	GA	4	50	BROOKS	W	13	58	BROOMFIELD	AJ	4	51
BROOKS	A	7	44	BROOKS	GC	10	29	BROOKS	W	14	39	BROOMFIELD	ANR	4	51
BROOKS	A	14	38	BROOKS	GE	14	39	BROOKS	W	14	39	BROOMFIELD	AV	10	29
BROOKS	A	14	38	BROOKS	GH	4	50	BROOKS	WA	2	40	BROOMFIELD	B	4	51
BROOKS	AC	5	45	BROOKS	GW	3	287	BROOKS	WC	12	32	BROOMFIELD	C	4	51
BROOKS	AE	1	39	BROOKS	H	5	45	BROOKS	WE	4	50	BROOMFIELD	E	4	51
BROOKS	AE	1	39	BROOKS	H	6	57	BROOKS	WH	12	32	BROOMFIELD	EJ	4	51
BROOKS	AE	2	40	BROOKS	HA	1	39	BROOKS	WH	13	58	BROOMFIELD	F	4	51
BROOKS	AE	5	45	BROOKS	HC	12	31	BROOKS	WJ	3	287	BROOMFIELD	G	4	51
BROOKS	AE	14	38	BROOKS	HE	12	32	BROOKS	WJ	7	44	BROOMFIELD	GH	4	51
BROOKS	AE	14	38	BROOKS	HG	10	270	BROOKS	WT	1	39	BROOMFIELD	H	4	51
BROOKS	AJ	12	31	BROOKS	HH	2	40	BROOKSBANK	A	9	234	BROOMFIELD	HS	4	51
BROOKS	AL	13	57	BROOKS	HJ	2	40	BROOKSBANK	C	14	39	BROOMFIELD	JTWH	10	29
BROOKS	AS	7	44	BROOKS	IJ	7	44	BROOKSBANK	E	8	43	BROOMFIELD	M	4	51
BROOKS	AS	13	57	BROOKS	J	2	40	BROOKSBANK	F	8	43	BROOMFIELD	P	4	51
BROOKS	AW	7	44	BROOKS	J	4	50	BROOKSBANK	J	8	43	BROOMFIELD	W	10	29
BROOKS	B	7	44	BROOKS	J	6	57	BROOKSBANK	S	8	43	BROOMFIELD	WB	4	51
BROOKS	BJ	10	28	BROOKS	J	8	43	BROOKSON	A	13	58	BROOMFIELD	WJ	10	29
BROOKS	C	5	45	BROOKS	J	8	43	BROOKSON	AW	7	44	BROOMFIELD	WR	7	45
BROOKS	C	9	28	BROOKS	J	10	29	BROOM	AW	2	40	BROOMFIELD	WRJ	7	45
BROOKS	C	10	29	BROOKS	J	12	272	BROOM	B	7	44	BROOMHALL	AJ	6	57
BROOKS	C	14	39	BROOKS	J	13	58	BROOM	CG	3	287	BROOMHALL	TH	6	57
BROOKS	CE	2	40	BROOKS	JA	2	40	BROOM	F	2	40	BROOMHEAD	J	8	43
BROOKS	CV	2	40	BROOKS	JE	2	40	BROOM	H	5	45	BROOMHEAD	R	11	48
BROOKS	DH	1	39	BROOKS	JE	7	44	BROOM	H	6	57	BROOMHEAD	T	11	48
BROOKS	E	1	39	BROOKS	JH	7	44	BROOM	H	7	45	BROOMING	CH	10	29
BROOKS	E	1	39	BROOKS	JJ	1	39	BROOM	HJ	4	50	BROSCOMBE	C	9	28
BROOKS	E	7	44	BROOKS	JK	13	58	BROOM	JH	1	39	BROSNAHAN	R	13	58
BROOKS	E	8	43	BROOKS	JW	3	287	BROOM	L	7	45	BROSNAN	P	13	58
BROOKS	E	12	31	BROOKS	L	1	39	BROOM	MA	2	40	BROSTER	J	14	39
BROOKS	E	12	272	BROOKS	LG	6	57	BROOM	PS	1	40	BROSTER	P	14	39
BROOKS	EAB	4	50	BROOKS	LH	6	57	BROOM	S	7	45	BROSTER	V	14	39
BROOKS	EC	2	40	BROOKS	N	6	57	BROOM	T	11	48	BROSTER	W	13	58
BROOKS	EG	10	29	BROOKS	R	2	40	BROOM	T	14	39	BROTHERDALE	J	11	48
BROOKS	EJ	1	39	BROOKS	R	6	57	BROOM	W	7	45	BROTHERS	JF	2	41
BROOKS	ES	6	57	BROOKS	R	9	28	BROOM	WJ	4	50	BROTHERS	S	2	41
BROOKS	EW	5	45	BROOKS	R	14	39	BROOME	A	4	50	BROTHERSTON	AW	1	40
BROOKS	F	5	45	BROOKS	RM	7	44	BROOME	G	11	48	BROTHERSTON	E	1	40
BROOKS	F	7	44	BROOKS	RT	13	58	BROOME	H	9	28	BROTHERSTON	HV	2	41

BROTHERSTON	JEM	2	41
BROTHERSTON	W	2	41
BROTHERTON	J	11	48
BROTHERTON	JW	1	40
BROTHERTON	TJ	11	48
BROTHERTON	W	11	48
BROTHERTON	WW	6	57
BROUGH	AH	6	57
BROUGH	C	6	57
BROUGH	W	6	58
BROUGHALL	W	5	45
BROUGHAM	E	11	48
BROUGHAM	EVA	11	48
BROUGHAM	W	11	48
BROUGHTON	A	12	272
BROUGHTON	AE	6	58
BROUGHTON	AE	12	32
BROUGHTON	AE	13	58
BROUGHTON	AT	9	28
BROUGHTON	BJ	9	28
BROUGHTON	CHL	3	287
BROUGHTON	E	2	41
BROUGHTON	F	2	41
BROUGHTON	F	2	41
BROUGHTON	F	10	270
BROUGHTON	G	8	43
BROUGHTON	H	2	41
BROUGHTON	J	9	29
BROUGHTON	J	11	48
BROUGHTON	J	13	58
BROUGHTON	L	9	234
BROUGHTON	S	2	41
BROUGHTON	TJ	2	41
BROUGHTON	TJ	13	58
BROUGHTON	W	4	51
BROUGHTON	W	8	43
BROUGHTON	W	12	272
BROUGHTON	WA	10	270
BROUGHTON	WC	12	32
BROUGHTON	WM	12	32
BROWELL	R	1	40
BROWETT		2	41
BROWETT	A	13	58
BROWETT	J	12	272
BROWN	A	1	40
BROWN	A	1	40
BROWN	A	2	41
BROWN	A	2	41
BROWN	A	2	41
BROWN	A	3	287
BROWN	A	3	287
BROWN	A	4	51
BROWN	A	4	51
BROWN	A	4	51
BROWN	A	5	45
BROWN	A	5	46
BROWN	A	7	45
BROWN	A	7	45
BROWN	A	7	45
BROWN	A	8	43
BROWN	A	8	44
BROWN	A	8	44
BROWN	A	11	49
BROWN	A	11	49
BROWN	A	11	49
BROWN	A	12	32
BROWN	A	12	32
BROWN	A	12	272
BROWN	A	13	58
BROWN	A	13	58
BROWN	A	14	39
BROWN	AA	4	52
BROWN	AA	7	45
BROWN	AA	8	44
BROWN	AA	13	58
BROWN	AC	4	52
BROWN	AC	6	58
BROWN	AC	7	45
BROWN	AC	10	29
BROWN	AC	12	32
BROWN	AE	1	40
BROWN	AE	1	40
BROWN	AE	1	40
BROWN	AE	2	41
BROWN	AE	2	41
BROWN	AE	3	287
BROWN	AE	4	52
BROWN	AE	6	58
BROWN	AE	6	58
BROWN	AE	7	45
BROWN	AE	7	45
BROWN	AE	7	45
BROWN	AE	10	29
BROWN	AE	14	39
BROWN	AF	2	41
BROWN	AF	4	52
BROWN	AFW	11	49
BROWN	AG	1	40
BROWN	AG	1	40
BROWN	AG	1	40
BROWN	AG	7	45
BROWN	AG	13	59
BROWN	AH	3	287
BROWN	AH	4	52
BROWN	AH	13	59
BROWN	AI	8	44
BROWN	AJ	1	40
BROWN	AJ	2	41
BROWN	AJ	3	287
BROWN	AJ	3	287
BROWN	AJ	5	46
BROWN	AJ	7	45
BROWN	AJ	11	49
BROWN	AJ	12	272
BROWN	AJ	14	39
BROWN	AP	5	46
BROWN	AR	2	41
BROWN	AR	2	42
BROWN	AR	13	59
BROWN	AS	12	32
BROWN	AT	7	45
BROWN	AT	12	32
BROWN	AW	2	42
BROWN	AW	5	46
BROWN	AW	6	58
BROWN	AW	7	45
BROWN	AW	10	29
BROWN	AW	10	29
BROWN	B	6	58
BROWN	B	11	49
BROWN	C	1	40
BROWN	C	2	42
BROWN	C	2	42
BROWN	C	3	287
BROWN	C	4	52
BROWN	C	4	52
BROWN	C	4	52
BROWN	C	4	52
BROWN	C	4	52
BROWN	C	5	46
BROWN	C	5	46
BROWN	C	8	44
BROWN	C	9	29
BROWN	C	9	29
BROWN	C	9	234
BROWN	C	9	234
BROWN	C	10	29
BROWN	C	11	49
BROWN	C	12	32
BROWN	C	12	32
BROWN	C	12	32
BROWN	C	14	39
BROWN	C	14	39
BROWN	CA	10	29
BROWN	CA	10	29
BROWN	CC	10	270
BROWN	CE	1	40
BROWN	CE	12	32
BROWN	CE	12	272
BROWN	CG	7	46
BROWN	CH	1	40
BROWN	CH	2	42
BROWN	CH	5	46
BROWN	CH	7	45
BROWN	CH	12	32
BROWN	CJ	2	42
BROWN	CJ	5	46
BROWN	CL	5	46
BROWN	CR	4	52
BROWN	CR	10	270
BROWN	CR	13	59
BROWN	CS	2	42
BROWN	CT	5	46
BROWN	CW	2	42
BROWN	CW	3	287
BROWN	CW	7	46
BROWN	CW	7	46
BROWN	CW	13	59
BROWN	D	2	42
BROWN	D	4	52
BROWN	D	4	52
BROWN	D	5	46
BROWN	D	6	58
BROWN	D	6	58
BROWN	D	14	40
BROWN	DT	5	46
BROWN	E	1	40
BROWN	E	3	28
BROWN	E	3	287
BROWN	E	5	46
BROWN	E	5	46
BROWN	E	6	58
BROWN	E	8	44
BROWN	E	8	44
BROWN	E	8	44
BROWN	E	9	29
BROWN	E	9	381
BROWN	E	10	270
BROWN	E	11	49
BROWN	E	12	32
BROWN	E	12	32
BROWN	E	12	272
BROWN	E	14	40
BROWN	EA	7	46
BROWN	EA	11	49
BROWN	EAJ	13	59
BROWN	EC	13	59
BROWN	EE	1	40
BROWN	EE	3	287
BROWN	EE	7	46
BROWN	EE	12	32
BROWN	EE	13	59
BROWN	EG	2	42
BROWN	EG	12	272
BROWN	EH	10	30
BROWN	EH	13	59
BROWN	EJ	2	42
BROWN	EJ	5	46
BROWN	EJ	5	46

Name	In.			Name	In.			Name	In.			Name	In.		
BROWN	EJ	10	270	BROWN	FJ	3	28	BROWN	GA	4	53	BROWN	H	8	45
BROWN	EL	13	59	BROWN	FJ	3	288	BROWN	GC	10	30	BROWN	H	10	30
BROWN	EL	13	59	BROWN	FJ	3	288	BROWN	GE	5	47	BROWN	H	11	50
BROWN	EM	7	46	BROWN	FJ	3	288	BROWN	GE	6	58	BROWN	H	12	33
BROWN	EO	12	272	BROWN	FJ	4	52	BROWN	GE	8	44	BROWN	H	12	33
BROWN	ER	1	40	BROWN	FJ	4	52	BROWN	GE	10	30	BROWN	H	12	33
BROWN	ER	10	29	BROWN	FJ	5	47	BROWN	GE	12	33	BROWN	H	12	272
BROWN	ER	10	270	BROWN	FJH	2	42	BROWN	GE	12	33	BROWN	H	12	272
BROWN	ET	1	40	BROWN	FO	1	41	BROWN	GE	13	59	BROWN	H	12	272
BROWN	ET	2	42	BROWN	FR	8	44	BROWN	GE	13	59	BROWN	H	12	273
BROWN	EW	2	42	BROWN	FS	9	234	BROWN	GF	2	43	BROWN	H	13	60
BROWN	EW	4	52	BROWN	FT	1	41	BROWN	GF	4	53	BROWN	H	13	60
BROWN	EW	13	59	BROWN	FT	6	58	BROWN	GF	12	33	BROWN	H	13	60
BROWN	F	1	40	BROWN	FW	2	42	BROWN	GF	13	59	BROWN	H	14	40
BROWN	F	1	41	BROWN	FW	4	53	BROWN	GH	2	43	BROWN	H	14	40
BROWN	F	2	42	BROWN	FW	10	30	BROWN	GH	2	43	BROWN	HA	1	41
BROWN	F	2	42	BROWN	FW	11	49	BROWN	GH	4	53	BROWN	HA	4	53
BROWN	F	4	52	BROWN	FW	11	49	BROWN	GH	6	58	BROWN	HA	10	30
BROWN	F	4	52	BROWN	FW	13	59	BROWN	GH	7	46	BROWN	HA	12	33
BROWN	F	5	46	BROWN	FWH	4	53	BROWN	GH	9	235	BROWN	HA	12	273
BROWN	F	5	46	BROWN	G	1	41	BROWN	GH	10	30	BROWN	HC	12	273
BROWN	F	6	58	BROWN	G	2	42	BROWN	GH	11	49	BROWN	HE	6	58
BROWN	F	6	58	BROWN	G	3	28	BROWN	GH	11	49	BROWN	HE	6	58
BROWN	F	7	46	BROWN	G	4	53	BROWN	GH	14	40	BROWN	HE	6	59
BROWN	F	7	46	BROWN	G	4	53	BROWN	GJ	7	46	BROWN	HE	12	33
BROWN	F	7	46	BROWN	G	4	53	BROWN	GJH	7	46	BROWN	HE	13	60
BROWN	F	8	44	BROWN	G	4	53	BROWN	GM	8	44	BROWN	HE	13	60
BROWN	F	8	44	BROWN	G	4	53	BROWN	GS	7	46	BROWN	HG	3	28
BROWN	F	8	44	BROWN	G	5	47	BROWN	GT	2	43	BROWN	HG	3	288
BROWN	F	9	29	BROWN	G	6	58	BROWN	GT	7	46	BROWN	HG	7	46
BROWN	F	9	234	BROWN	G	6	58	BROWN	GV	10	270	BROWN	HG	7	46
BROWN	F	11	49	BROWN	G	7	46	BROWN	GW	4	53	BROWN	HH	12	33
BROWN	F	11	49	BROWN	G	7	46	BROWN	GW	10	30	BROWN	HJ	2	43
BROWN	F	12	33	BROWN	G	8	44	BROWN	H	1	41	BROWN	HJ	13	60
BROWN	F	12	33	BROWN	G	8	44	BROWN	H	1	41	BROWN	HP	2	43
BROWN	F	12	33	BROWN	G	8	44	BROWN	H	1	41	BROWN	HR	13	60
BROWN	F	14	40	BROWN	G	9	29	BROWN	H	1	41	BROWN	HR	13	60
BROWN	F	14	40	BROWN	G	9	29	BROWN	H	2	43	BROWN	HS	5	47
BROWN	FA	10	30	BROWN	G	9	234	BROWN	H	2	43	BROWN	HS	12	33
BROWN	FB	3	28	BROWN	G	9	234	BROWN	H	3	288	BROWN	HT	2	43
BROWN	FC	5	47	BROWN	G	9	234	BROWN	H	4	53	BROWN	HT	13	60
BROWN	FC	5	47	BROWN	G	10	30	BROWN	H	4	53	BROWN	HV	7	47
BROWN	FC	5	47	BROWN	G	10	270	BROWN	H	4	53	BROWN	HW	1	41
BROWN	FC	12	33	BROWN	G	11	49	BROWN	H	5	47	BROWN	HW	5	47
BROWN	FC	12	33	BROWN	G	11	49	BROWN	H	5	47	BROWN	HW	5	47
BROWN	FC	13	59	BROWN	G	12	33	BROWN	H	5	47	BROWN	HW	13	60
BROWN	FF	5	47	BROWN	G	12	33	BROWN	H	6	58	BROWN	IW	7	47
BROWN	FG	3	288	BROWN	G	12	33	BROWN	H	8	44	BROWN	J	1	41
BROWN	FG	3	288	BROWN	G	12	272	BROWN	H	8	44	BROWN	J	1	41
BROWN	FG	13	59	BROWN	G	13	59	BROWN	H	8	44	BROWN	J	2	43
BROWN	FH	4	52	BROWN	G	13	60	BROWN	H	8	44	BROWN	J	2	43
BROWN	FH	7	46	BROWN	G	14	40	BROWN	H	8	45	BROWN	J	3	28
BROWN	FH	12	33	BROWN	G	14	40	BROWN	H	8	45	BROWN	J	3	28
BROWN	FJ	1	41	BROWN	G	14	40	BROWN	H	8	45	BROWN	J	3	288
BROWN	FJ	1	41	BROWN	GA	1	41	BROWN	H	8	45	BROWN	J	4	53

BROWN	J	5	47
BROWN	J	5	47
BROWN	J	5	47
BROWN	J	6	59
BROWN	J	6	59
BROWN	J	6	59
BROWN	J	6	59
BROWN	J	7	47
BROWN	J	7	47
BROWN	J	7	47
BROWN	J	8	45
BROWN	J	8	45
BROWN	J	9	29
BROWN	J	9	29
BROWN	J	9	29
BROWN	J	10	271
BROWN	J	11	49
BROWN	J	11	50
BROWN	J	11	50
BROWN	J	11	50
BROWN	J	11	50
BROWN	J	11	50
BROWN	J	11	50
BROWN	J	11	50
BROWN	J	12	33
BROWN	J	12	273
BROWN	J	12	273
BROWN	J	12	273
BROWN	J	13	60
BROWN	J	13	60
BROWN	J	13	60
BROWN	J	13	60
BROWN	J	14	40
BROWN	J	14	40
BROWN	J	14	40
BROWN	J	14	40
BROWN	J	14	40
BROWN	JA	2	43
BROWN	JA	8	45
BROWN	JA	13	60
BROWN	JB	1	41
BROWN	JD	5	47
BROWN	JE	3	288
BROWN	JE	4	53
BROWN	JE	4	53
BROWN	JE	4	53
BROWN	JE	5	47
BROWN	JE	7	47
BROWN	JE	9	29
BROWN	JE	11	50
BROWN	JE	11	50
BROWN	JFL	13	60
BROWN	JG	12	34
BROWN	JH	1	41
BROWN	JH	14	40
BROWN	JHG	4	53
BROWN	JJ	6	59
BROWN	JJ	7	47
BROWN	JJ	10	30
BROWN	JJ	12	34
BROWN	JJ	12	34
BROWN	JJF	10	30
BROWN	JM	13	60
BROWN	JO	4	54
BROWN	JP	8	45
BROWN	JR	7	47
BROWN	JR	9	235
BROWN	JR	11	50
BROWN	JS	9	235
BROWN	JS	10	271
BROWN	JS	12	34
BROWN	JT	4	54
BROWN	JT	9	235
BROWN	JTJ	7	47
BROWN	JW	6	59
BROWN	JW	7	47
BROWN	JW	7	47
BROWN	JW	8	45
BROWN	JW	9	29
BROWN	JW	9	29
BROWN	JW	10	271
BROWN	JW	11	50
BROWN	JW	12	34
BROWN	JWT	13	60
BROWN	L	5	47
BROWN	L	6	59
BROWN	L	8	45
BROWN	L	8	45
BROWN	L	9	29
BROWN	L	11	50
BROWN	L	12	34
BROWN	L	13	61
BROWN	LC	5	48
BROWN	LC	10	30
BROWN	LCF	4	54
BROWN	LR	3	288
BROWN	LW	5	48
BROWN	M	7	47
BROWN	M	8	45
BROWN	M	10	271
BROWN	M	13	61
BROWN	MJ	14	40
BROWN	N	2	43
BROWN	N	4	54
BROWN	N	7	47
BROWN	N	14	40
BROWN	NE	1	41
BROWN	P	1	41
BROWN	P	2	43
BROWN	P	2	43
BROWN	P	4	54
BROWN	P	8	45
BROWN	P	9	29
BROWN	P	11	50
BROWN	P	11	50
BROWN	P	12	34
BROWN	P	14	41
BROWN	PE	7	47
BROWN	PF	13	61
BROWN	PG	1	41
BROWN	PH	12	273
BROWN	PJ	2	43
BROWN	PW	3	28
BROWN	PW	3	288
BROWN	R	1	41
BROWN	R	4	54
BROWN	R	4	54
BROWN	R	4	54
BROWN	R	7	47
BROWN	R	8	45
BROWN	R	9	29
BROWN	R	9	29
BROWN	R	10	30
BROWN	R	10	271
BROWN	R	11	50
BROWN	R	12	34
BROWN	R T	14	41
BROWN	RAJ	4	54
BROWN	RC	3	288
BROWN	RC	7	47
BROWN	RC	13	61
BROWN	RD	6	59
BROWN	RE	4	54
BROWN	RE	4	54
BROWN	RE	13	61
BROWN	RH	4	54
BROWN	RH	13	61
BROWN	RH	14	41
BROWN	RJ	8	45
BROWN	RJ	14	41
BROWN	RP	12	273
BROWN	RRT	3	288
BROWN	RS	4	54
BROWN	RW	5	48
BROWN	S	1	41
BROWN	S	1	41
BROWN	S	2	43
BROWN	S	2	43
BROWN	S	3	288
BROWN	S	5	48
BROWN	S	7	47
BROWN	S	8	45
BROWN	S	8	45
BROWN	S	8	45
BROWN	S	9	29
BROWN	S	13	61
BROWN	S	14	41
BROWN	S	14	41
BROWN	S	14	41
BROWN	SA	4	54
BROWN	SA	12	273
BROWN	SB	1	42
BROWN	SF	13	61
BROWN	SG	3	288
BROWN	SG	7	47
BROWN	SH	6	59
BROWN	SJ	5	48
BROWN	SJ	11	50
BROWN	SV	13	61
BROWN	SW	12	34
BROWN	T	3	28
BROWN	T	3	28
BROWN	T	3	288
BROWN	T	6	59
BROWN	T	7	47
BROWN	T	7	48
BROWN	T	9	30
BROWN	T	12	273
BROWN	T	14	41
BROWN	TA	2	43
BROWN	TA	8	45
BROWN	TB	6	59
BROWN	TE	4	54
BROWN	TE	11	51
BROWN	TF	12	273
BROWN	TH	6	59
BROWN	TH	7	48
BROWN	TH	8	45
BROWN	TH	9	235
BROWN	TH	10	271
BROWN	TJ	4	54
BROWN	TJ	13	61
BROWN	TM	12	34
BROWN	TW	5	48
BROWN	TW	6	59
BROWN	TW	7	48
BROWN	TW	8	46
BROWN	TW	10	30
BROWN	TW	12	273
BROWN	VH	12	34
BROWN	W	1	42
BROWN	W	1	42
BROWN	W	2	43
BROWN	W	2	44
BROWN	W	2	44
BROWN	W	3	28

BROWN	W	3	288	BROWN	WC	14	41	BROWNE	JH	3	289	BRUCE	A	10	31
BROWN	W	3	288	BROWN	WE	2	44	BROWNE	R	13	62	BRUCE	A	12	35
BROWN	W	3	288	BROWN	WE	4	55	BROWNE	S	11	51	BRUCE	A	14	41
BROWN	W	4	54	BROWN	WEA	7	48	BROWNE	SE	2	44	BRUCE	AWG	10	271
BROWN	W	4	54	BROWN	WG	1	42	BROWNE	T	11	51	BRUCE	CW	6	60
BROWN	W	4	54	BROWN	WG	5	48	BROWNE	W	9	30	BRUCE	E	3	289
BROWN	W	4	55	BROWN	WG	7	48	BROWNETT	J	3	28	BRUCE	F	12	35
BROWN	W	5	48	BROWN	WG	13	62	BROWNETT	T	3	28	BRUCE	G	4	55
BROWN	W	6	59	BROWN	WH	2	44	BROWNFIELD	H	13	62	BRUCE	H	1	42
BROWN	W	6	59	BROWN	WH	2	44	BROWNHILL	A	11	46	BRUCE	H	11	51
BROWN	W	6	59	BROWN	WH	6	60	BROWNHILL	E	8	46	BRUCE	HE	12	273
BROWN	W	6	59	BROWN	WH	6	60	BROWNHILL	EB	8	46	BRUCE	HT	7	48
BROWN	W	6	59	BROWN	WH	6	60	BROWNHILL	T	11	51	BRUCE	J	11	51
BROWN	W	6	60	BROWN	WH	7	48	BROWNHILL	W	8	46	BRUCE	J	11	51
BROWN	W	7	48	BROWN	WH	13	62	BROWNING	A	3	289	BRUCE	J	14	41
BROWN	W	7	48	BROWN	WJ	1	42	BROWNING	AG	7	48	BRUCE	JP	4	55
BROWN	W	8	46	BROWN	WJ	1	42	BROWNING	AT	4	55	BRUCE	T	2	44
BROWN	W	8	46	BROWN	WJ	3	289	BROWNING	CP	2	44	BRUCE	T	12	35
BROWN	W	8	46	BROWN	WJ	3	289	BROWNING	CW	13	62	BRUCE	TO	14	41
BROWN	W	8	46	BROWN	WJ	4	55	BROWNING	E	1	42	BRUCE	W	3	289
BROWN	W	8	46	BROWN	WJ	10	30	BROWNING	E	2	44	BRUCE	W	8	46
BROWN	W	9	30	BROWN	WJ	10	30	BROWNING	E	9	30	BRUCE	W	11	51
BROWN	W	10	30	BROWN	WJ	10	31	BROWNING	ED	14	41	BRUCE	W	14	41
BROWN	W	10	30	BROWN	WJ	11	51	BROWNING	EH	3	289	BRUCE	WE	14	41
BROWN	W	10	30	BROWN	WJ	12	34	BROWNING	F	4	55	BRUDENELL	HC	10	271
BROWN	W	11	51	BROWN	WJ	12	34	BROWNING	FH	13	62	BRUDENELL	J	10	31
BROWN	W	11	51	BROWN	WJ	12	34	BROWNING	FW	4	55	BRUDENELL	ME	12	273
BROWN	W	11	51	BROWN	WJ	12	273	BROWNING	GA	6	60	BRUDENELL	WP	5	48
BROWN	W	11	51	BROWN	WJ	13	62	BROWNING	HJ	3	289	BRUFORD	FAG	10	31
BROWN	W	12	34	BROWN	WJ	13	62	BROWNING	HW	13	62	BRUM	F	2	44
BROWN	W	12	34	BROWN	WJ	13	62	BROWNING	J	4	55	BRUM	FA	2	44
BROWN	W	12	34	BROWN	WJJ	13	62	BROWNING	J	10	271	BRUMAGE	R	2	44
BROWN	W	12	34	BROWN	WL	13	61	BROWNING	JP	3	289	BRUMBILL	H	11	51
BROWN	W	12	34	BROWN	WM	3	289	BROWNING	P	3	29	BRUMBY	DA	10	31
BROWN	W	12	273	BROWN	WR	5	48	BROWNING	TE	2	44	BRUMFITT	H	11	51
BROWN	W	12	273	BROWN	WR	7	48	BROWNING	TW	10	271	BRUMHILL	A	12	273
BROWN	W	13	61	BROWN	WR	10	271	BROWNING	W	4	55	BRUMHILL	SC	12	273
BROWN	W	13	61	BROWN	WR	11	51	BROWNING	WA	13	62	BRUMHILL	WJ	12	273
BROWN	W	13	61	BROWN	WT	4	55	BROWNING	WJ	1	42	BRUMMELL	H	12	35
BROWN	W	13	61	BROWN	WT	4	55	BROWNING	WJ	6	60	BRUMMELL	WH	12	35
BROWN	W	13	61	BROWN	WT	6	60	BROWNLEY	S	6	60	BRUMPTON	EW	10	31
BROWN	W	13	61	BROWN	WT	9	30	BROWNLIE	AJ	7	48	BRUN	ED	2	44
BROWN	WA	1	42	BROWN	WT	10	31	BROWNLOW	TE	13	62	BRUNDELL	T	10	271
BROWN	WA	9	30	BROWN	WW	1	42	BROWNOFFSKY	JM	8	46	BRUNDISH	ER	13	62
BROWN	WA	11	51	BROWNBILL	A	14	41	BROWNRIDGE	FW	8	46	BRUNDLE	FW	3	289
BROWN	WA	13	61	BROWNBILL	JH	14	41	BROWNSWORD	A	14	41	BRUNDLE	HG	2	44
BROWN	WA	13	61	BROWNE	AE	10	31	BROWSE	P	2	44	BRUNDLE	S	12	35
BROWN	WA	13	62	BROWNE	AW	7	48	BROXHOMB	A	9	235	BRUNDRED	JS	8	46
BROWN	WA	13	62	BROWNE	B	14	41	BROXHOMB	A	9	235	BRUNDRED	W	8	46
BROWN	WC	1	42	BROWNE	CH	5	48	BROXTON	C	6	60	BRUNDRETT	G	10	31
BROWN	WC	2	44	BROWNE	FJ	13	62	BROXUP	W	9	30	BRUNDRITT	S	4	55
BROWN	WC	3	289	BROWNE	GH	6	60	BROYD	A	3	289	BRUNSDON	GA	4	55
BROWN	WC	3	289	BROWNE	HH	3	289	BROYD	EA	3	289	BRUNET	ES	13	63
BROWN	WC	7	48	BROWNE	J	13	62	BRUCASS	J	3	29	BRUNGER	T	2	44
BROWN	WC	13	62	BROWNE	JC	2	44	BRUCE	A	7	48	BRUNIGES	GW	7	48

BRUNNEN	C	10	31	BRYAN	J	6	61	BRYANT	J	7	49	BUCHANAN	BHC	10	32
BRUNNING	EF	13	63	BRYAN	JT	11	52	BRYANT	J	12	35	BUCHANAN	GG	1	43
BRUNNING	EJ	13	63	BRYAN	LW	1	42	BRYANT	JB	2	45	BUCHANAN	GL	14	42
BRUNNING	G	13	63	BRYAN	P	9	30	BRYANT	JCT	13	63	BUCHANAN	H	2	45
BRUNNING	JH	13	63	BRYAN	PJ	1	42	BRYANT	JE	2	45	BUCHANAN	J	10	32
BRUNNING	ST	2	44	BRYAN	R	10	31	BRYANT	JO	2	45	BUCHANAN	MA	1	43
BRUNSDON	AFE	3	29	BRYAN	T	11	52	BRYANT	JT	6	61	BUCHANAN	N	3	290
BRUNSKILL	H	8	46	BRYAN	TE	3	29	BRYANT	L	3	290	BUCHANAN	P	14	42
BRUNSKILL	J	8	46	BRYAN	W	6	61	BRYANT	L	11	52	BUCHANAN	R	3	290
BRUNSKILL	J	8	46	BRYAN	W	6	61	BRYANT	LL	3	290	BUCHANAN	R	14	42
BRUNT	A	4	55	BRYAN	WF	6	61	BRYANT	N	3	290	BUCHANAN	W	3	290
BRUNT	C	5	48	BRYAN	WG	6	61	BRYANT	NW	10	31	BUCK	A	1	43
BRUNT	D	6	60	BRYAN	WH	6	61	BRYANT	P	7	49	BUCK	A	1	43
BRUNT	ET	6	60	BRYANS	W	14	42	BRYANT	R	3	290	BUCK	A	12	421
BRUNT	H	6	60	BRYANT	A	3	290	BRYANT	RC	10	31	BUCK	A	13	64
BRUNT	JR	5	48	BRYANT	A	6	61	BRYANT	TE	13	63	BUCK	AV	3	290
BRUNT	R	11	51	BRYANT	A	8	46	BRYANT	TW	1	42	BUCK	C	1	43
BRUNTON	G	3	29	BRYANT	A	13	63	BRYANT	W	2	45	BUCK	C	1	43
BRUNTON	GF	11	51	BRYANT	AA	10	31	BRYANT	W	7	49	BUCK	C	3	290
BRUNTON	H	3	289	BRYANT	AC	7	49	BRYANT	W	10	32	BUCK	C	4	55
BRUNTON	H	14	41	BRYANT	AE	13	63	BRYANT	W	11	52	BUCK	C	12	421
BRUNTON	J	9	235	BRYANT	AH	1	42	BRYANT	WC	6	61	BUCK	C	14	42
BRUNTON	JG	5	48	BRYANT	AV	7	49	BRYANT	WE	10	32	BUCK	CH	3	290
BRUSH	EC	6	60	BRYANT	AW	1	42	BRYANT	WG	13	63	BUCK	E	12	35
BRUSH	EE	7	48	BRYANT	AWK	7	49	BRYANT	WH	2	45	BUCK	EJ	5	49
BRUSH	TC	2	45	BRYANT	BT	13	63	BRYANT	WJ	2	45	BUCK	EV	5	49
BRUSHETT	SG	4	55	BRYANT	C	1	42	BRYANT	WJ	10	32	BUCK	F	11	52
BRUSHWOOD	HE	10	31	BRYANT	CF	2	45	BRYANT	WJ	13	63	BUCK	G	9	30
BRUSHWOOD	HTR	10	31	BRYANT	CW	6	61	BRYANT	WT	7	49	BUCK	H	12	35
BRUSHWOOD	JH	13	63	BRYANT	D	5	48	BRYAR	H	9	30	BUCK	J	2	45
BRUSHWOOD	TW	10	31	BRYANT	E	8	46	BRYAR	TJ	9	30	BUCK	J	8	47
BRUTON	AC	5	48	BRYANT	E	10	31	BRYCE	AT	4	55	BUCK	J	13	64
BRUTON	EW	5	48	BRYANT	EJ	1	42	BRYCE	G	11	52	BUCK	J	13	64
BRUTON	FW	12	35	BRYANT	EJ	2	45	BRYCE	H	11	52	BUCK	JT	4	55
BRUTON	HB	10	31	BRYANT	EM	2	45	BRYCE	J	11	52	BUCK	JW	7	49
BRUTON	J	1	42	BRYANT	F	7	49	BRYCE	J	14	42	BUCK	M	8	47
BRUTON	RB	5	48	BRYANT	F	10	271	BRYDEN	SA	3	290	BUCK	RJ	4	55
BRUTON	W	6	60	BRYANT	FA	1	42	BRYDON	WJ	10	32	BUCK	S	10	32
BRUTY	AH	13	63	BRYANT	FE	13	63	BRYEN	J	9	30	BUCK	SC	13	64
BRUTY	C	5	48	BRYANT	FG	13	63	BRYEN	T	9	30	BUCK	TA	3	291
BRYAN	A	8	46	BRYANT	G	2	45	BRYER	A	13	63	BUCK	W	6	61
BRYAN	AC	13	63	BRYANT	G	7	49	BRYER	FJ	2	45	BUCKBY	RHH	12	274
BRYAN	BJ	6	60	BRYANT	GAS	7	49	BRYNE	GW	3	290	BUCKELL	AE	4	55
BRYAN	C	12	35	BRYANT	GR	6	61	BRYNING	TH	11	52	BUCKELL	E	7	49
BRYAN	CE	6	60	BRYANT	GW	5	49	BRYON	S	1	42	BUCKELL	H	7	49
BRYAN	E	7	48	BRYANT	H	1	42	BRYSON	H	1	43	BUCKERIDGE	G	1	43
BRYAN	F	2	45	BRYANT	H	3	290	BRYSON	WR	7	49	BUCKERIDGE	H	1	43
BRYAN	FH	3	290	BRYANT	H	6	61	BRYSON	WS	2	45	BUCKETT	FE	10	32
BRYAN	FW	10	271	BRYANT	H	13	63	BUBB	C	12	274	BUCKETT	FG	13	64
BRYAN	G	2	45	BRYANT	H	13	63	BUBB	E	12	274	BUCKEY	W	7	49
BRYAN	G	8	46	BRYANT	HA	3	290	BUBB	H	12	274	BUCKINGHAM	A	5	49
BRYAN	H	11	52	BRYANT	HJ	10	31	BUBEAR	H	9	30	BUCKINGHAM	A	5	49
BRYAN	H	12	35	BRYANT	HL	5	49	BUBEAR	SH	13	64	BUCKINGHAM	AF	5	49
BRYAN	HC	13	63	BRYANT	J	1	42	BUCHAN	PJ	13	64	BUCKINGHAM	BW	5	49
BRYAN	HJ	12	274	BRYANT	J	3	290	BUCHANAN	A	8	46	BUCKINGHAM	D	12	35

BUCKINGHAM	E	4	56	BUCKLE	A	9	30	BUCKLEY	TE	14	42	BUDDEN	L	10	32
BUCKINGHAM	E	5	49	BUCKLE	A	10	271	BUCKLEY	W	1	43	BUDDEN	LE	4	57
BUCKINGHAM	E	5	49	BUCKLE	F	12	35	BUCKLEY	W	11	52	BUDDEN	LE	10	32
BUCKINGHAM	F	3	29	BUCKLE	F	12	35	BUCKLEY	W	11	52	BUDDEN	RT	4	57
BUCKINGHAM	F	3	29	BUCKLE	FT	3	291	BUCKLEY	WH	8	47	BUDDEN	WH	5	50
BUCKINGHAM	G	4	56	BUCKLE	GH	2	46	BUCKLEY	WH	9	235	BUDDEN	WN	4	57
BUCKINGHAM	G	5	49	BUCKLE	GW	2	46	BUCKLEY	WH	14	42	BUDDIN	AV	13	64
BUCKINGHAM	G	5	49	BUCKLE	J	12	36	BUCKLEY	WJ	6	61	BUDDIN	CV	13	64
BUCKINGHAM	G	5	49	BUCKLE	SG	6	61	BUCKLEY	WJ	13	64	BUDDIN	F	13	64
BUCKINGHAM	G	12	35	BUCKLE	WA	8	47	BUCKMAN	AE	2	46	BUDDLE	TJ	7	49
BUCKINGHAM	GEW	5	49	BUCKLE	WE	8	47	BUCKMAN	WHJ	2	46	BUDGE	FC	1	43
BUCKINGHAM	GR	1	43	BUCKLE	WJF	3	291	BUCKMASTER	TW	3	291	BUDGE	HJW	4	57
BUCKINGHAM	H	5	49	BUCKLE	WML	1	43	BUCKNALL	FG	8	47	BUDGE	S	10	33
BUCKINGHAM	H	10	32	BUCKLER	EW	2	46	BUCKNALL	H	6	62	BUDGELL	AW	2	46
BUCKINGHAM	HC	5	49	BUCKLER	RF	10	32	BUCKNELL	JH	7	49	BUDGEN	CS	3	291
BUCKINGHAM	HG	5	49	BUCKLER	TH	6	61	BUCKNELL	ME	3	291	BUDGEN	HW	3	291
BUCKINGHAM	J	3	29	BUCKLEY	A	8	47	BUCKNELL	RO	4	56	BUDGEN	TL	2	46
BUCKINGHAM	J	5	49	BUCKLEY	A	9	235	BUCKNER	WC	3	29	BUDSWORTH	TE	11	53
BUCKINGHAM	JA	8	47	BUCKLEY	A	11	52	BUCKOKE	W	5	50	BUER	GH	2	46
BUCKINGHAM	JE	5	50	BUCKLEY	AE	1	43	BUCKRIDGE	C	13	64	BUET	T	6	62
BUCKINGHAM	LM	5	50	BUCKLEY	AH	14	42	BUCKROYD	H	9	30	BUFFERY	FS	3	291
BUCKINGHAM	P	5	50	BUCKLEY	CR	2	46	BUCKROYD	J	8	47	BUFFHAM	JW	12	274
BUCKINGHAM	R	5	50	BUCKLEY	D	3	29	BUCKTON	T	8	47	BUFFIN	CJ	4	57
BUCKINGHAM	R	8	47	BUCKLEY	E	1	43	BUCKWELL	HW	2	46	BUFFIN	PC	13	65
BUCKINGHAM	RJ	1	43	BUCKLEY	E	8	47	BUCKWELL	LM	2	46	BUFTON	E	12	36
BUCKINGHAM	RS	5	50	BUCKLEY	E	9	30	BUDD	AE	4	56	BUFTON	W	10	33
BUCKINGHAM	RS	12	35	BUCKLEY	FE	3	291	BUDD	E	1	43	BUFTON	WH	12	36
BUCKINGHAM	S	5	50	BUCKLEY	G	14	42	BUDD	EE	4	56	BUFTON	WJ	10	272
BUCKINGHAM	SG	5	50	BUCKLEY	GE	14	42	BUDD	F	4	56	BUGDEN	CT	10	33
BUCKINGHAM	SH	2	45	BUCKLEY	H	9	235	BUDD	F	5	50	BUGDEN	GE	4	57
BUCKINGHAM	T	1	43	BUCKLEY	H	14	42	BUDD	FL	4	56	BUGDEN	GG	12	36
BUCKINGHAM	T	3	291	BUCKLEY	HE	9	235	BUDD	GE	4	56	BUGDEN	OWH	10	272
BUCKINGHAM	W	5	50	BUCKLEY	HH	10	271	BUDD	GE	4	56	BUGDEN	SC	10	33
BUCKINGHAM	W	5	50	BUCKLEY	J	1	43	BUDD	J	4	56	BUGG	EE	5	50
BUCKINGHAM	W	12	35	BUCKLEY	J	2	46	BUDD	J	7	49	BUGG	PO	7	50
BUCKINGHAM	WC	5	50	BUCKLEY	J	3	291	BUDD	LM	2	46	BUGG	RE	1	43
BUCKINGHAM	WJ	13	64	BUCKLEY	J	3	291	BUDD	M	1	43	BUGGINS	DE	12	36
BUCKLAND	AB	6	61	BUCKLEY	J	5	50	BUDD	RG	4	56	BUGGY	F	13	65
BUCKLAND	AB	10	32	BUCKLEY	J	7	49	BUDD	S	3	291	BUGGY	JW	13	65
BUCKLAND	CR	11	52	BUCKLEY	J	10	32	BUDD	S	13	64	BUGLEY	DB	3	291
BUCKLAND	EA	3	291	BUCKLEY	J	11	52	BUDD	T	4	56	BUIST	A	10	272
BUCKLAND	EA	4	56	BUCKLEY	J	14	42	BUDD	TJ	1	43	BUIST	RH	7	50
BUCKLAND	F	2	45	BUCKLEY	J	14	42	BUDD	VG	4	56	BULBECK	A	10	33
BUCKLAND	FE	6	61	BUCKLEY	J	14	42	BUDD	W	13	64	BULBECK	T	10	33
BUCKLAND	FJ	2	45	BUCKLEY	JH	2	46	BUDD	WG	4	56	BULBROOKE	F	4	57
BUCKLAND	FW	3	291	BUCKLEY	JH	14	42	BUDD	WJR	2	46	BULL	A	4	57
BUCKLAND	J	1	43	BUCKLEY	JP	2	46	BUDDEN	A	7	49	BULL	AA	1	43
BUCKLAND	J	2	46	BUCKLEY	JT	11	52	BUDDEN	A	10	32	BULL	AA	12	36
BUCKLAND	J	13	64	BUCKLEY	JW	8	47	BUDDEN	AE	10	32	BULL	AE	3	29
BUCKLAND	JE	10	32	BUCKLEY	RP	2	46	BUDDEN	E	10	32	BULL	AE	10	33
BUCKLAND	JG	13	64	BUCKLEY	RW	11	52	BUDDEN	FG	4	56	BULL	AH	13	65
BUCKLAND	NH	13	64	BUCKLEY	S	14	42	BUDDEN	FJ	4	56	BULL	AJ	12	36
BUCKLAND	SG	13	64	BUCKLEY	T	9	235	BUDDEN	G	2	46	BULL	AJ	12	274
BUCKLAND	W	4	56	BUCKLEY	T	10	271	BUDDEN	J	4	56	BULL	AV	13	65
BUCKLAND	W	4	56	BUCKLEY	T	11	52	BUDDEN	JTWF	4	57	BULL	AW	13	65

BULL	AW	13	65	BULL	VW	13	65	BULLIVANT	A	6	62	BULPITT	S	4	58				
BULL	B	8	47	BULL	WF	12	274	BULLIVANT	H	6	62	BULPITT	W	4	58				
BULL	BJ	12	36	BULL	WG	1	44	BULLIVANT	W	6	62	BULSTRODE	G	4	58				
BULL	C	1	43	BULL	WG	4	57	BULLIVENT	SC	4	57	BULWER	FW	5	50				
BULL	C	4	57	BULL	WH	3	292	BULLIVENT	WE	4	57	BULWER	MH	5	51				
BULL	CD	12	36	BULL	WH	3	292	BULLIVENT	WH	4	57	BULWICH	J	11	53				
BULL	CL	2	47	BULL	WJ	12	37	BULLOCK	A	3	29	BUMAN	DE	4	58				
BULL	DA	3	291	BULL	WJ	13	65	BULLOCK	AA	6	62	BUMAN	FEJ	4	58				
BULL	E	1	44	BULL	WJR	12	37	BULLOCK	AAJ	4	58	BUMAN	FJ	4	58				
BULL	E	3	291	BULL	WS	2	47	BULLOCK	AE	1	44	BUMAN	GL	4	58				
BULL	EA	4	57	BULLARD	A	3	292	BULLOCK	AE	4	58	BUMBY	W	14	43				
BULL	EA	7	50	BULLARD	AHE	12	37	BULLOCK	EW	7	50	BUMPUS	AE	3	29				
BULL	EG	2	47	BULLARD	G	13	65	BULLOCK	F	8	47	BUMPUS	J	13	66				
BULL	EG	4	57	BULLARD	H	10	33	BULLOCK	FHT	8	47	BUMSTEAD	WR	7	50				
BULL	EJ	12	274	BULLARD	H	13	65	BULLOCK	GE	1	44	BUMSTED	JJW	3	29				
BULL	F	3	29	BULLARD	J	7	50	BULLOCK	GFT	4	58	BUNCE	AE	4	58				
BULL	F	3	291	BULLARD	JH	2	47	BULLOCK	GH	2	47	BUNCE	CE	5	51				
BULL	F	6	62	BULLARD	JL	3	29	BULLOCK	GL	6	62	BUNCE	E	8	48				
BULL	FC	4	57	BULLARD	S	13	65	BULLOCK	HA	6	62	BUNCE	F	5	51				
BULL	FG	3	292	BULLEN	A	13	65	BULLOCK	JA	7	50	BUNCE	F	5	51				
BULL	FJ	12	36	BULLEN	AE	7	50	BULLOCK	JR	7	50	BUNCE	FH	7	50				
BULL	FP	12	36	BULLEN	C	2	47	BULLOCK	JR	11	53	BUNCE	FW	5	51				
BULL	FR	4	57	BULLEN	C	14	42	BULLOCK	LS	13	66	BUNCE	GH	7	50				
BULL	FW	1	44	BULLEN	CH	14	42	BULLOCK	M	4	58	BUNCE	HA	2	47				
BULL	FW	12	36	BULLEN	CW	7	50	BULLOCK	N	9	235	BUNCE	HJ	13	66				
BULL	G	12	36	BULLEN	FL	6	62	BULLOCK	P	6	62	BUNCE	J	3	292				
BULL	GH	12	36	BULLEN	GW	11	53	BULLOCK	R	6	62	BUNCE	JR	3	29				
BULL	GR	2	47	BULLEN	H	8	47	BULLOCK	RL	1	44	BUNCE	R	14	43				
BULL	GR	13	65	BULLEN	J	1	44	BULLOCK	RT	7	50	BUNCE	TH	13	66				
BULL	GS	13	65	BULLEN	J	14	43	BULLOCK	S	14	43	BUNCE	W	6	62				
BULL	GW	2	47	BULLEN	JD	2	47	BULLOCK	SL	7	50	BUNCE	WR	2	47				
BULL	GW	10	33	BULLEN	JH	1	44	BULLOCK	T	14	43	BUNCE	WS	13	66				
BULL	H	3	292	BULLEN	M	1	44	BULLOCK	W	6	62	BUNCH	J	13	66				
BULL	H	7	50	BULLEN	ML	1	44	BULLOCK	W	6	62	BUNCLARK	CG	2	47				
BULL	HE	4	57	BULLEN	RB	7	50	BULLOCK	WC	3	292	BUNCLARK	JR	3	292				
BULL	HV	12	274	BULLEN	WA	5	50	BULLOCK	WJ	2	47	BUNCOMBE	B	4	58				
BULL	J	13	65	BULLER	AF	6	62	BULLOUGH	F	11	53	BUND	FA	2	47				
BULL	JA	12	36	BULLER	BP	3	292	BULLOWS	CH	6	62	BUND	HF	12	37				
BULL	JC	12	274	BULLER	H	3	292	BULMAN	WE	10	33	BUNDAY	E	4	58				
BULL	JH	10	33	BULLER	P	3	292	BULMER	AW	8	47	BUNDAY	EE	4	58				
BULL	JL	8	47	BULLER	R	9	235	BULMER	D	8	47	BUNDAY	HJ	10	33				
BULL	L	2	47	BULLER	RH	3	292	BULMER	E	7	50	BUNDAY	WA	4	59				
BULL	OC	3	292	BULLER	TH	1	44	BULMER	G	8	48	BUNDELL	WLJ	10	33				
BULL	RJ	3	292	BULLER	WJ	6	62	BULMER	J	14	43	BUNDOCK	G	10	33				
BULL	RJ	12	36	BULLERS	JA	8	47	BULMER	W	8	48	BUNDY	A	4	59				
BULL	RJ	12	274	BULLEY	A	2	47	BULMER	W	8	48	BUNDY	A	12	37				
BULL	RM	2	47	BULLEY	CS	2	47	BULPETT	E	4	58	BUNDY	AW	4	59				
BULL	S	5	50	BULLEY	CT	1	44	BULPETT	GP	4	58	BUNDY	J	12	37				
BULL	S	10	272	BULLEY	G	1	44	BULPETT	PE	4	58	BUNDY	JHA	4	59				
BULL	SE	13	65	BULLEY	W	2	47	BULPIN	FA	1	44	BUNDY	JR	4	59				
BULL	SJ	13	65	BULLIMORE	AW	12	274	BULPIT	C	1	44	BUNDY	WL	4	59				
BULL	T	12	36	BULLIN	T	13	66	BULPIT	J	1	44	BUNFORD	J	9	31				
BULL	T	12	36	BULLIONS	FW	13	66	BULPITT	FC	4	58	BUNGARD	SG	12	274				
BULL	TA	3	292	BULLIONS	J	13	66	BULPITT	GH	4	58	BUNGAY	AF	4	59				
BULL	VS	5	50	BULLIONS	LA	6	62	BULPITT	HW	4	58	BUNGAY	CT	2	48				

BUNGAY	F	4	59	BUNYAN	A	5	51	BURCKETT	J	6	63	BURGAR	JW	2	48
BUNGAY	G	4	59	BUNYAN	AE	5	51	BURCKETT	W	6	63	BURGAR	ML	3	30
BUNGAY	JHT	4	59	BUNYAN	C	12	37	BURCOMBE	AW	3	30	BURGE	A	3	293
BUNGAY	P	4	59	BUNYAN	E	5	51	BURD	AH	13	66	BURGE	EE	2	48
BUNGEY	H	4	59	BUNYAN	F	5	51	BURDEN	A	3	30	BURGE	EE	3	293
BUNKER	A	1	44	BUNYAN	F	5	52	BURDEN	A	7	51	BURGE	EP	5	52
BUNKER	A	4	59	BUNYAN	FJ	5	52	BURDEN	A	10	272	BURGE	F	8	48
BUNKER	A	5	51	BUNYAN	G	2	48	BURDEN	AE	10	272	BURGE	G	12	274
BUNKER	A	5	51	BUNYAN	H	5	52	BURDEN	CE	4	59	BURGE	WJ	4	59
BUNKER	AE	5	51	BUNYAN	H	5	52	BURDEN	CJ	4	59	BURGEN	A	3	293
BUNKER	FG	5	51	BUNYAN	HG	12	37	BURDEN	D	13	66	BURGER	AE	3	30
BUNKER	FJ	1	44	BUNYAN	HR	5	52	BURDEN	E	8	48	BURGER	AW	3	30
BUNKER	FJ	5	51	BUNYAN	JCJ	13	66	BURDEN	F	10	272	BURGES	WG	2	48
BUNKER	H	1	44	BUNYAN	S	5	52	BURDEN	FW	2	48	BURGESS	A	3	30
BUNKER	H	5	51	BUNYAN	T	5	52	BURDEN	G	12	37	BURGESS	A	5	52
BUNKER	HCE	5	51	BUNYAN	WA	12	37	BURDEN	J	10	272	BURGESS	A	5	52
BUNKER	HS	5	51	BUNYAN	WC	5	52	BURDEN	JA	10	33	BURGESS	A	5	52
BUNKER	J	12	37	BUNYAN	WG	5	52	BURDEN	JJ	13	66	BURGESS	A	6	64
BUNKER	RH	5	51	BUNYARD	HJ	3	292	BURDEN	RH	10	34	BURGESS	A	6	64
BUNKER	WE	1	44	BURBAGE	AG	1	44	BURDEN	W	2	48	BURGESS	A	10	272
BUNKHOLE	J	9	31	BURBAGE	B	7	51	BURDEN	W	14	43	BURGESS	A	11	53
BUNN	AS	10	272	BURBAGE	FJ	7	51	BURDEN	WJ	2	48	BURGESS	A	13	67
BUNN	CF	6	63	BURBAGE	WH	7	51	BURDETT		4	59	BURGESS	A	14	43
BUNN	FC	6	63	BURBANK	H	6	63	BURDETT	A	7	51	BURGESS	A	14	43
BUNN	GW	2	48	BURBERRY	ARC	10	33	BURDETT	AE	7	51	BURGESS	AC	10	34
BUNN	GW	8	48	BURBIDGE	CE	11	53	BURDETT	G	6	63	BURGESS	AD	7	51
BUNN	H	6	63	BURBIDGE	E	11	53	BURDETT	GST	11	53	BURGESS	AE	2	49
BUNN	J	6	63	BURBIDGE	H	1	44	BURDETT	R	11	53	BURGESS	AE	2	49
BUNN	JJ	2	48	BURBIDGE	HE	12	37	BURDETT	RA	1	45	BURGESS	AE	13	67
BUNN	JT	6	63	BURBIDGE	WJ	3	30	BURDETT	T	7	51	BURGESS	AG	5	52
BUNN	M	14	43	BURBRIDGE	E	1	44	BURDETT	TR	3	293	BURGESS	AG	10	34
BUNN	RF	2	48	BURBRIDGE	JH	6	63	BURDETT	TR	7	51	BURGESS	AH	5	52
BUNN	S	11	53	BURBRIDGE	JW	12	37	BURDON	AF	2	48	BURGESS	AJ	3	293
BUNN	W	6	63	BURBRIDGE	RC	6	63	BURFIELD	DA	13	67	BURGESS	AS	1	45
BUNN	WG	3	29	BURBRIDGE	WJ	1	45	BURFIELD	H	13	67	BURGESS	C	5	52
BUNNAGE	AW	12	37	BURCH	A	3	30	BURFIELD	JH	3	293	BURGESS	C	13	67
BUNNELL	FB	10	33	BURCH	E	2	48	BURFITT	AE	4	59	BURGESS	CD	2	49
BUNNELL	FJ	10	33	BURCH	FG	5	52	BURFITT	TF	10	272	BURGESS	CE	7	51
BUNNER	TF	11	53	BURCH	H	13	66	BURFOOT	DW	13	67	BURGESS	CP	13	67
BUNNEY	P	4	59	BURCH	HE	14	43	BURFORD	A	6	63	BURGESS	CS	10	34
BUNNEY	WE	9	31	BURCH	HW	13	66	BURFORD	A	6	63	BURGESS	E	1	45
BUNNING	W	8	48	BURCH	K	3	292	BURFORD	ET	6	63	BURGESS	E	5	52
BUNSTEAD	PS	7	50	BURCH	T	2	48	BURFORD	GJ	6	63	BURGESS	E	5	53
BUNTING	BCT	10	33	BURCH	W	1	45	BURFORD	GW	6	63	BURGESS	E	6	64
BUNTING	EG	12	37	BURCH	W	5	52	BURFORD	J	6	63	BURGESS	E	6	64
BUNTING	JA	12	37	BURCHAEL	J	14	43	BURFORD	J	6	64	BURGESS	EA	5	53
BUNTING	JE	11	53	BURCHALL	H	2	48	BURFORD	JR	6	64	BURGESS	EF	1	45
BUNTING	JS	5	51	BURCHAM	AR	3	293	BURFORD	R	6	64	BURGESS	EJF	7	51
BUNTING	RJ	10	33	BURCHELL	H	13	66	BURFORD	SJ	6	64	BURGESS	F	9	235
BUNTING	WT	4	59	BURCHELL	W	5	52	BURFUTT	LR	13	67	BURGESS	F	11	53
BUNTON	A	1	44	BURCHETT	G	13	66	BURGAR	AW	2	48	BURGESS	F	13	67
BUNTON	AA	7	50	BURCHETT	HR	4	59	BURGAR	EP	3	30	BURGESS	FC	10	34
BUNTON	HJ	3	292	BURCHETT	JE	13	66	BURGAR	ES	2	48	BURGESS	FC	13	67
BUNTON	WJ	7	51	BURCHETT	SJ	13	66	BURGAR	JE	3	30	BURGESS	FG	3	293
BUNYAN	A	5	51	BURCKETT	A	6	63	BURGAR	JF	2	48	BURGESS	FG	5	53

BURGESS	FH	4	60	BURGESS	S	14	44	BURKE	EA	3	293	BURKETT	CE	5	53
BURGESS	FJ	3	293	BURGESS	ST	1	45	BURKE	EF	4	60	BURKETT	GH	10	272
BURGESS	G	2	49	BURGESS	ST	10	272	BURKE	F	2	49	BURKETT	JT	12	37
BURGESS	G	3	293	BURGESS	SW	1	45	BURKE	F	2	49	BURKHILL	W	14	44
BURGESS	G	7	51	BURGESS	T	1	45	BURKE	F	8	48	BURKITT	A	12	38
BURGESS	G	13	67	BURGESS	T	14	44	BURKE	F	8	48	BURKITT	LF	12	38
BURGESS	G	13	67	BURGESS	T	14	44	BURKE	GHF	10	34	BURKMAR	JF	13	68
BURGESS	GJ	7	51	BURGESS	TB	14	44	BURKE	J	3	294	BURLACE	CJ	3	294
BURGESS	GJ	7	51	BURGESS	TH	10	34	BURKE	J	8	48	BURLEFINGER	CM	4	60
BURGESS	GP	10	34	BURGESS	W	2	49	BURKE	J	8	48	BURLES	A	2	50
BURGESS	GT	13	67	BURGESS	W	2	49	BURKE	J	8	48	BURLES	AR	7	51
BURGESS	H	1	45	BURGESS	W	3	293	BURKE	J	8	48	BURLES	J	13	68
BURGESS	H	2	49	BURGESS	W	6	64	BURKE	J	8	48	BURLEY	C	2	50
BURGESS	H	4	60	BURGESS	W	14	44	BURKE	J	8	48	BURLEY	C	12	38
BURGESS	H	5	53	BURGESS	WA	3	293	BURKE	J	9	31	BURLEY	CF	10	34
BURGESS	H	6	64	BURGESS	WB	11	53	BURKE	J	9	31	BURLEY	EJ	2	50
BURGESS	H	10	272	BURGESS	WC	2	49	BURKE	J	11	54	BURLEY	F	5	54
BURGESS	H	11	53	BURGESS	WE	5	53	BURKE	J	11	54	BURLEY	FP	5	54
BURGESS	HA	13	67	BURGESS	WE	5	53	BURKE	J	11	54	BURLEY	FR	5	54
BURGESS	HAG	7	51	BURGESS	WE	13	67	BURKE	J	11	54	BURLEY	FS	12	38
BURGESS	HH	5	53	BURGESS	WJ	1	45	BURKE	J	14	44	BURLEY	G	11	54
BURGESS	HL	13	67	BURGESS	WJ	3	293	BURKE	JC	3	294	BURLEY	GW	12	38
BURGESS	HR	1	45	BURGESS	WJ	3	293	BURKE	JE	8	49	BURLEY	J	5	54
BURGESS	HTC	2	49	BURGESS	WJ	6	64	BURKE	JF	11	54	BURLEY	JH	5	54
BURGESS	IJ	2	49	BURGESS	WW	6	64	BURKE	JG	13	68	BURLEY	R	5	54
BURGESS	J	3	293	BURGG	A	12	37	BURKE	JM	11	54	BURLEY	R	7	52
BURGESS	J	10	34	BURGH	AM	3	30	BURKE	JT	9	235	BURLEY	WE	6	64
BURGESS	J	11	53	BURGH	JG	3	30	BURKE	JW	6	64	BURLEY	WH	13	68
BURGESS	J	11	53	BURGH	WH	3	30	BURKE	JW	8	49	BURLINGHAM	GH	4	60
BURGESS	J	14	43	BURGHAM	R	6	64	BURKE	JW	8	49	BURLISON	C	10	272
BURGESS	JA	14	43	BURGHART	JE	2	49	BURKE	JW	11	54	BURLISON	F	13	68
BURGESS	JCD	2	49	BURGIE	C	1	45	BURKE	JW	14	44	BURLISON	W	9	31
BURGESS	JG	11	53	BURGIN	A	5	53	BURKE	L	2	49	BURLS	FA	7	52
BURGESS	JH	1	45	BURGIN	JH	8	48	BURKE	L	14	44	BURLS	HG	7	52
BURGESS	JH	7	51	BURGIN	W	5	53	BURKE	M	8	49	BURLS	JAE	5	54
BURGESS	JH	14	43	BURGOINE	HJ	5	53	BURKE	M	8	49	BURLS	WA	7	52
BURGESS	JJ	5	53	BURGON	C	4	60	BURKE	MP	2	49	BURMAN	AE	2	50
BURGESS	JJ	12	37	BURGON	J	9	31	BURKE	P	8	49	BURMAN	S	14	44
BURGESS	JR	14	43	BURGOYNE	C	5	53	BURKE	P	14	44	BURN	A	8	49
BURGESS	L	5	53	BURGOYNE	CE	13	67	BURKE	R	3	294	BURN	AS	1	45
BURGESS	LG	13	67	BURGOYNE	GF	12	37	BURKE	R	6	64	BURN	E	8	49
BURGESS	P	11	53	BURGOYNE	H	5	53	BURKE	S	6	64	BURN	F	2	50
BURGESS	P	14	43	BURGOYNE	J	5	53	BURKE	T	8	49	BURN	JL	6	65
BURGESS	PF	13	67	BURGOYNE	J	11	54	BURKE	T	8	49	BURN	RW	13	68
BURGESS	PJ	5	53	BURGOYNE	OP	5	53	BURKE	T	8	49	BURNAGE	A	12	38
BURGESS	PT	1	45	BURGOYNE	P	11	54	BURKE	T	9	31	BURNAGE	AG	5	54
BURGESS	PW	14	43	BURGUM	EW	13	67	BURKE	T	9	235	BURNAGE	AJ	5	54
BURGESS	R	6	64	BURGUM	G	2	49	BURKE	T	11	54	BURNAGE	F	5	54
BURGESS	RW	7	51	BURHOUSE	F	8	48	BURKE	W	8	49	BURNAGE	F	12	38
BURGESS	S	2	49	BURKE	A	14	44	BURKE	W	8	49	BURNAGE	FE	5	54
BURGESS	S	3	30	BURKE	C	3	293	BURKE	W	8	49	BURNAGE	G	12	38
BURGESS	S	5	53	BURKE	E	6	64	BURKE	W	11	54	BURNAGE	GH	12	38
BURGESS	S	5	53	BURKE	E	8	48	BURKE	W	14	44	BURNAGE	H	12	38
BURGESS	S	5	53	BURKE	E	14	44	BURKE	W	14	44	BURNAGE	H	12	421
BURGESS	S	14	43	BURKE	E	14	44	BURKE				BURNAGE	TC	12	421

BURNAGE	W	12	38
BURNAND	T	2	50
BURNAPP	CWH	12	38
BURNE	CC	13	68
BURNE	WA	2	50
BURNELL	CE	7	52
BURNELL	CH	9	31
BURNELL	F	9	31
BURNELL	G	12	274
BURNELL	HM	12	274
BURNELL	J	9	31
BURNELL	JW	4	60
BURNELL	R	13	68
BURNELL	W	7	52
BURNELL	W	12	274
BURNELL	WH	2	50
BURNELL	WJ	13	68
BURNESS	T	13	68
BURNET	F	4	60
BURNET	J	4	60
BURNET	J	4	60
BURNET	W	4	60
BURNETT	A	8	49
BURNETT	AE	3	294
BURNETT	AE	6	65
BURNETT	AG	13	68
BURNETT	AW	4	60
BURNETT	B	14	44
BURNETT	B	14	44
BURNETT	C	8	49
BURNETT	E	10	272
BURNETT	E	14	45
BURNETT	EA	4	60
BURNETT	EB	4	60
BURNETT	EH	3	294
BURNETT	F	9	235
BURNETT	FO	13	68
BURNETT	FW	10	34
BURNETT	G	9	235
BURNETT	G	14	45
BURNETT	GE	8	49
BURNETT	H	8	49
BURNETT	HA	8	49
BURNETT	HG	10	273
BURNETT	HJ	3	294
BURNETT	HW	1	45
BURNETT	JD	4	60
BURNETT	JE	3	294
BURNETT	JG	1	45
BURNETT	JH	3	294
BURNETT	JW	10	34
BURNETT	JW	14	45
BURNETT	LE	4	60
BURNETT	RH	2	50
BURNETT	T	6	65
BURNETT	WE	13	68
BURNETT	WHG	10	34
BURNETT	WJ	10	273
BURNEY	J	11	54
BURNHAM	AE	5	54
BURNHAM	AE	12	38
BURNHAM	C	5	54
BURNHAM	E	5	54
BURNHAM	E	5	54
BURNHAM	EB	12	38
BURNHAM	EC	14	45
BURNHAM	F	9	31
BURNHAM	HT	5	54
BURNHAM	JS	11	54
BURNHAM	T	9	31
BURNHAM	T	9	235
BURNHAM	T	13	68
BURNHAM	WJ	2	50
BURNIDGE	J	5	54
BURNISTON	GE	8	49
BURNLEY	A	8	49
BURNLEY	A	9	31
BURNLEY	B	8	50
BURNLEY	H	9	31
BURNLEY	H	9	236
BURNS	A	6	65
BURNS	A	8	50
BURNS	A	8	50
BURNS	A	11	54
BURNS	A	12	274
BURNS	AE	10	34
BURNS	B	8	50
BURNS	D	11	421
BURNS	DFW	1	45
BURNS	E	7	52
BURNS	E	11	54
BURNS	E	14	45
BURNS	EH	1	45
BURNS	F	9	31
BURNS	F	11	54
BURNS	F	11	54
BURNS	F	14	45
BURNS	FG	12	275
BURNS	G	7	52
BURNS	G	11	55
BURNS	GP	11	421
BURNS	H	9	31
BURNS	HB	9	31
BURNS	HP	1	45
BURNS	HW	12	275
BURNS	J	3	294
BURNS	J	6	65
BURNS	J	8	50
BURNS	J	8	50
BURNS	J	9	32
BURNS	J	9	32
BURNS	J	9	32
BURNS	J	9	236
BURNS	J	11	55
BURNS	J	11	55
BURNS	J	11	55
BURNS	J	11	55
BURNS	J	11	55
BURNS	J	11	55
BURNS	J	11	55
BURNS	J	11	55
BURNS	J	11	55
BURNS	J	12	38
BURNS	J	14	45
BURNS	J	14	45
BURNS	J	14	45
BURNS	J	14	45
BURNS	J	14	45
BURNS	J	14	45
BURNS	J	14	45
BURNS	J	14	45
BURNS	JA	11	55
BURNS	JF	10	34
BURNS	JT	6	65
BURNS	L	11	55
BURNS	L	14	45
BURNS	M	8	50
BURNS	M	8	50
BURNS	M	9	32
BURNS	M	9	32
BURNS	M	11	55
BURNS	PC	1	45
BURNS	PT	9	32
BURNS	PW	13	68
BURNS	R	1	46
BURNS	R	6	65
BURNS	R	6	65
BURNS	R	11	55
BURNS	R	11	56
BURNS	T	6	65
BURNS	T	10	34
BURNS	T	11	56
BURNS	T	11	56
BURNS	T	11	56
BURNS	T	12	275
BURNS	T	14	45
BURNS	T	14	45
BURNS	TA	11	56
BURNS	TH	11	56
BURNS	W	6	65
BURNS	W	6	65
BURNS	W	8	50
BURNS	W	8	50
BURNS	W	9	236
BURNS	W	9	236
BURNS	W	10	34
BURNS	W	11	421
BURNS	W	14	46
BURNS	WE	3	294
BURNS	WJ	12	275
BURNS	WP	6	65
BURNS	WP	14	46
BURNS	WT	7	52
BURNSIDE	W	8	50
BURNSIDE	WB	10	35
BURNSIDE	WHS	10	35
BURR	AE	1	46
BURR	AE	1	46
BURR	CR	12	38
BURR	EG	5	54
BURR	F	12	38
BURR	G	12	38
BURR	MA	1	46
BURR	SR	5	54
BURR	WH	2	50
BURR	WT	2	50
BURRAGE	CG	6	65
BURRAGE	D	5	54
BURRAGE	GE	7	52
BURRAGE	GJ	14	46
BURRAGE	GW	14	46
BURRAGE	J	2	50
BURRAGE	JB	14	46
BURRAGE	RA	7	52
BURRAGE	V	7	52
BURRAGE	WC	7	52
BURRAS	A	8	50
BURRAS	G	8	50
BURRAWAY	A	12	38
BURREE	E	7	52
BURREE	G	7	52
BURREE	TH	7	52
BURRELL	A	9	236
BURRELL	AE	13	68
BURRELL	AF	7	52
BURRELL	AH	13	68
BURRELL	B	3	30
BURRELL	CD	3	294
BURRELL	E	13	68
BURRELL	F	1	46
BURRELL	F	9	32
BURRELL	F	9	236
BURRELL	FG	8	50
BURRELL	H	8	50
BURRELL	H	8	50
BURRELL	JH	2	50
BURRELL	P	5	54

BURRELL	RG	2	50	BURROWS	GW	1	46	BURT	G	4	61	BURTON	EA	4	61
BURRELL	RN	10	35	BURROWS	GW	13	69	BURT	GA	10	35	BURTON	EA	12	39
BURRELL	WH	13	69	BURROWS	H	4	60	BURT	H	4	61	BURTON	EC	4	61
BURRELLS	AA	1	46	BURROWS	H	12	275	BURT	HE	2	51	BURTON	EG	10	36
BURRELLS	CS	1	46	BURROWS	HC	2	51	BURT	HF	2	51	BURTON	EJ	3	295
BURRIDGE	AT	10	35	BURROWS	HJ	2	51	BURT	HG	10	35	BURTON	F	2	51
BURRIDGE	CE	5	55	BURROWS	I	11	56	BURT	HJ	13	69	BURTON	F	2	51
BURRIDGE	CW	2	50	BURROWS	IB	1	46	BURT	HLS	4	61	BURTON	F	6	66
BURRIDGE	F	13	69	BURROWS	J	5	55	BURT	HT	1	46	BURTON	F	13	69
BURRIDGE	GW	1	46	BURROWS	J	9	32	BURT	J	13	69	BURTON	FE	10	273
BURRIDGE	J	10	35	BURROWS	J	10	35	BURT	LG	13	69	BURTON	G	3	31
BURRIDGE	J	12	39	BURROWS	JC	7	53	BURT	LR	4	61	BURTON	G	3	295
BURRIDGE	JJ	1	46	BURROWS	JE	2	51	BURT	SR	3	30	BURTON	G	6	66
BURRIDGE	JM	13	69	BURROWS	JR	11	56	BURT	TW	10	35	BURTON	G	14	46
BURRIDGE	MJ	13	69	BURROWS	JV	5	55	BURT	W	4	61	BURTON	GH	14	46
BURRIDGE	W	2	50	BURROWS	L	5	55	BURT	W	12	275	BURTON	GR	12	39
BURRIDGE	WE	7	52	BURROWS	M	1	46	BURT	WG	12	39	BURTON	H	1	46
BURRIDGE	WG	2	50	BURROWS	MA	7	53	BURT	WH	7	53	BURTON	H	3	31
BURRON	H	9	32	BURROWS	PC	5	55	BURT	WK	8	51	BURTON	H	4	61
BURROUGH	SJ	1	46	BURROWS	PJ	5	55	BURT	WM	11	56	BURTON	H	6	66
BURROUGHS	FWA	2	50	BURROWS	PL	4	60	BURT	WP	2	51	BURTON	H	7	53
BURROUGHS	J	13	69	BURROWS	R	14	46	BURTENSHAW	AJ	10	35	BURTON	H	8	51
BURROUGHS	JT	10	35	BURROWS	RA	7	53	BURTENSHAW	FH	7	53	BURTON	H	8	51
BURROUGHS	R	10	35	BURROWS	S	14	46	BURTENSHAW	W	10	35	BURTON	H	8	51
BURROUGHS	WG	10	35	BURROWS	T	8	50	BURTLE	VV	8	51	BURTON	H	10	273
BURROW	B	8	50	BURROWS	T	9	32	BURTON	A	8	51	BURTON	H	13	70
BURROW	E	4	60	BURROWS	T	12	275	BURTON	A	8	51	BURTON	H	13	70
BURROW	JW	8	50	BURROWS	T	12	275	BURTON	A	10	273	BURTON	HC	7	53
BURROWS	A	3	294	BURROWS	W	6	65	BURTON	A	12	39	BURTON	HGJ	13	70
BURROWS	A	4	60	BURROWS	W	11	56	BURTON	AC	10	35	BURTON	HH	6	66
BURROWS	A	8	50	BURROWS	W	12	39	BURTON	AC	13	69	BURTON	HS	14	46
BURROWS	A	10	35	BURROWS	WA	13	69	BURTON	ACE	13	69	BURTON	J	3	31
BURROWS	A	11	56	BURROWS	WC	10	35	BURTON	AE	4	61	BURTON	J	6	66
BURROWS	A	12	275	BURROWS	WE	14	46	BURTON	AE	4	61	BURTON	J	8	51
BURROWS	A	14	46	BURROWS	WJ	1	46	BURTON	AE	7	53	BURTON	J	10	36
BURROWS	AE	7	53	BURROWS	WJ	2	51	BURTON	AE	11	56	BURTON	J	11	56
BURROWS	AF	4	60	BURROWS	WT	6	65	BURTON	AE	13	69	BURTON	J	11	56
BURROWS	AH	2	51	BURRUP	FG	6	65	BURTON	AF	1	46	BURTON	JE	4	61
BURROWS	AS	11	56	BURRUP	W	6	65	BURTON	AF	4	61	BURTON	JH	2	51
BURROWS	AT	6	65	BURRY	ELE	3	294	BURTON	AH	12	39	BURTON	JH	13	70
BURROWS	AT	7	53	BURRY	EW	3	294	BURTON	AJ	6	66	BURTON	JJ	7	53
BURROWS	AW	3	30	BURRY	LG	13	69	BURTON	AJC	13	69	BURTON	JJ	14	46
BURROWS	AW	7	53	BURSEY	E	3	294	BURTON	AWJ	4	61	BURTON	JL	5	55
BURROWS	CM	3	294	BURSNELL	CJ	3	294	BURTON	B	3	30	BURTON	JR	6	66
BURROWS	D	10	35	BURSON	AG	6	66	BURTON	C	1	46	BURTON	JW	12	39
BURROWS	E	11	56	BURSTOW	WJ	2	51	BURTON	C	3	30	BURTON	L	9	381
BURROWS	EW	5	55	BURT	A	12	275	BURTON	C	3	295	BURTON	LC	7	53
BURROWS	EW	12	275	BURT	AE	12	275	BURTON	C	4	61	BURTON	LJ	3	31
BURROWS	F	10	35	BURT	AJ	4	61	BURTON	C	9	236	BURTON	P	8	51
BURROWS	FA	13	69	BURT	AJ	13	69	BURTON	CF	1	46	BURTON	R	4	61
BURROWS	FC	12	275	BURT	CG	4	61	BURTON	CW	2	51	BURTON	R	8	51
BURROWS	FG	6	65	BURT	EJ	2	51	BURTON	DJ	13	69	BURTON	RC	11	56
BURROWS	G	7	53	BURT	ER	8	50	BURTON	E	4	61	BURTON	RJ	4	61
BURROWS	G	14	46	BURT	F	6	66	BURTON	E	9	32	BURTON	RLD	12	275
BURROWS	GT	10	273	BURT	FC	4	61	BURTON	E	11	56	BURTON	RR	4	61

BURTON	SE	13	70	BUSBY	H	2	52	BUSHELL	G	14	46	BUTCHER	EC	5	56
BURTON	T	3	295	BUSBY	H	2	52	BUSHELL	H	4	62	BUTCHER	EJ	7	54
BURTON	T	4	62	BUSBY	HG	12	275	BUSHELL	H	4	62	BUTCHER	EW	4	63
BURTON	T	5	55	BUSBY	HW	13	70	BUSHELL	H	6	67	BUTCHER	F	4	63
BURTON	T	8	51	BUSBY	J	10	36	BUSHELL	HG	6	67	BUTCHER	F	12	39
BURTON	T	12	39	BUSBY	W	2	52	BUSHELL	HN	4	62	BUTCHER	FJ	3	295
BURTON	T	14	46	BUSBY	W	2	52	BUSHELL	J	4	62	BUTCHER	FT	5	56
BURTON	TP	12	39	BUSBY	W	6	66	BUSHELL	S	12	275	BUTCHER	G	1	47
BURTON	W	1	46	BUSBY	WC	1	47	BUSHELL	SP	12	275	BUTCHER	G	5	56
BURTON	W	1	46	BUSBY	WG	1	47	BUSHELL	TB	4	62	BUTCHER	G	13	70
BURTON	W	1	46	BUSBY	WS	10	36	BUSHELL	W	4	62	BUTCHER	GA	3	295
BURTON	W	3	295	BUSE	C	5	55	BUSHELL	W	6	67	BUTCHER	GW	10	36
BURTON	W	4	62	BUSFIELD	H	9	236	BUSHELL	W	11	57	BUTCHER	H	1	47
BURTON	W	5	55	BUSH	AA	1	47	BUSHELL	WG	4	62	BUTCHER	H	3	295
BURTON	W	6	66	BUSH	AA	1	47	BUSHER	AJ	3	295	BUTCHER	H	14	47
BURTON	W	6	66	BUSH	AB	4	62	BUSHER	GR	3	295	BUTCHER	HE	1	47
BURTON	W	9	236	BUSH	AG	2	52	BUSHER	JW	3	295	BUTCHER	HG	13	70
BURTON	W	10	36	BUSH	CH	7	54	BUSHNELL	F	1	47	BUTCHER	J	7	54
BURTON	W	12	39	BUSH	CM	1	47	BUSHNELL	T	2	52	BUTCHER	J	9	32
BURTON	WB	7	53	BUSH	CW	2	52	BUSHNELL	WW	10	36	BUTCHER	JH	5	56
BURTON	WF	1	46	BUSH	E	7	54	BUSLEY	S	9	32	BUTCHER	JH	5	56
BURTON	WG	4	62	BUSH	HC	2	52	BUSNELL	W	10	273	BUTCHER	LGE	4	63
BURTON	WH	8	51	BUSH	HJ	4	62	BUSS	EA	13	70	BUTCHER	P	12	39
BURTON	WH	10	36	BUSH	J	1	47	BUSS	FC	12	275	BUTCHER	R	12	276
BURTON	WJG	1	46	BUSH	JC	2	52	BUSS	HC	2	52	BUTCHER	S	12	39
BURTON	WR	1	46	BUSH	JH	9	236	BUSS	RE	1	47	BUTCHER	SW	13	70
BURTON	WT	2	51	BUSH	JT	2	52	BUSSEY	F	3	31	BUTCHER	W	1	47
BURTON	WTN	13	70	BUSH	PW	2	52	BUSSEY	H	6	67	BUTCHER	W	1	47
BURTROP	H	9	236	BUSH	TH	1	47	BUSSEY	J	9	32	BUTCHER	W	4	63
BURVILL	AE	13	70	BUSH	TR	7	54	BUSSEY	RC	7	54	BUTCHER	W	5	56
BURVILL	C	7	53	BUSH	TW	14	46	BUSSY	AL	1	47	BUTCHER	W	6	67
BURVILL	HR	7	53	BUSH	W	1	47	BUSSY	GH	1	47	BUTCHER	W	7	54
BURVILL	SJ	13	70	BUSH	W	2	52	BUSTIN	OF	2	52	BUTCHER	W	8	51
BURWELL	GF	13	70	BUSH	W	7	54	BUSTIN	WH	12	276	BUTCHER	W	13	70
BURWOOD	A	2	51	BUSH	W	13	70	BUSWELL	GC	12	276	BUTCHER	W	13	71
BURWOOD	AR	4	62	BUSH	WH	1	47	BUSWELL	J	12	39	BUTCHER	WC	13	71
BURWOOD	TF	4	62	BUSHBY	EJ	5	55	BUSWELL	W	12	276	BUTCHER	WH	2	53
BURY	E	8	51	BUSHBY	FH	11	56	BUSWELL	W	12	276	BUTCHER	WJ	12	39
BUSANSKI	D	14	46	BUSHBY	GF	5	55	BUTCHARD	HN	4	62	BUTCHERS	WH	3	295
BUSBY	AE	10	36	BUSHBY	TW	7	54	BUTCHER	A	2	52	BUTERFIELD	AT	8	51
BUSBY	AGE	7	54	BUSHBY	W	5	55	BUTCHER	A	5	55	BUTEUX	AR	7	54
BUSBY	CW	12	275	BUSHBY	W	9	236	BUTCHER	AB	5	55	BUTEUX	WS	7	54
BUSBY	CWL	2	51	BUSHBY	WA	7	54	BUTCHER	AE	2	52	BUTFOY	R	2	53
BUSBY	E	2	51	BUSHBY	WG	5	55	BUTCHER	AJ	4	62	BUTFOY	W	2	53
BUSBY	EL	2	52	BUSHE	W	11	57	BUTCHER	AL	5	55	BUTLAND	B	2	53
BUSBY	F	6	66	BUSHEL	HJ	7	54	BUTCHER	AP	2	52	BUTLER	A	6	67
BUSBY	FE	13	70	BUSHELL	A	6	66	BUTCHER	AP	5	56	BUTLER	A	6	67
BUSBY	FG	1	47	BUSHELL	A	6	66	BUTCHER	AW	13	70	BUTLER	A	6	67
BUSBY	FT	2	52	BUSHELL	AW	6	66	BUTCHER	B	12	39	BUTLER	A	7	54
BUSBY	FWS	2	52	BUSHELL	D	11	57	BUTCHER	C	4	62	BUTLER	A	9	32
BUSBY	G	6	66	BUSHELL	E	3	295	BUTCHER	C	4	62	BUTLER	A	10	36
BUSBY	GC	5	55	BUSHELL	EL	4	62	BUTCHER	C	4	62	BUTLER	A	12	39
BUSBY	GE	12	275	BUSHELL	F	6	67	BUTCHER	C	5	56	BUTLER	A	12	276
BUSBY	GH	6	66	BUSHELL	FG	4	62	BUTCHER	CM	4	63	BUTLER	AE	7	55
BUSBY	GW	6	66	BUSHELL	FR	6	67	BUTCHER	CW	13	70	BUTLER	AG	8	51

BUTLER	AH	13	71
BUTLER	AJ	10	273
BUTLER	AS	10	36
BUTLER	B	7	55
BUTLER	C	1	47
BUTLER	C	8	51
BUTLER	C	8	51
BUTLER	C	12	40
BUTLER	C	13	71
BUTLER	CE	7	55
BUTLER	CF	1	47
BUTLER	CH	1	47
BUTLER	DW	9	32
BUTLER	E	2	53
BUTLER	E	3	31
BUTLER	E	6	67
BUTLER	E	6	67
BUTLER	E	7	55
BUTLER	E	11	57
BUTLER	E	11	57
BUTLER	E	12	40
BUTLER	E	13	71
BUTLER	E	14	47
BUTLER	EG	1	47
BUTLER	EG	13	71
BUTLER	EJ	7	55
BUTLER	EJ	10	36
BUTLER	F	6	67
BUTLER	F	6	67
BUTLER	F	6	67
BUTLER	F	6	67
BUTLER	FA	13	71
BUTLER	FG	6	67
BUTLER	FG	6	67
BUTLER	FM	1	48
BUTLER	FW	10	36
BUTLER	FW	13	71
BUTLER	G	6	67
BUTLER	G	6	68
BUTLER	G	10	273
BUTLER	GH	7	55
BUTLER	GS	4	63
BUTLER	GW	4	63
BUTLER	GW	8	51
BUTLER	H	2	53
BUTLER	H	2	53
BUTLER	H	6	68
BUTLER	H	9	236
BUTLER	H	10	36
BUTLER	H	10	273
BUTLER	H	12	40
BUTLER	H	13	71
BUTLER	H	13	71
BUTLER	HC	7	55
BUTLER	HF	7	55
BUTLER	HH	14	47
BUTLER	HJ	1	48
BUTLER	HP	6	68
BUTLER	I	8	51
BUTLER	J	2	53
BUTLER	J	2	53
BUTLER	J	4	63
BUTLER	J	6	68
BUTLER	J	6	68
BUTLER	J	6	68
BUTLER	J	6	68
BUTLER	J	8	51
BUTLER	J	8	52
BUTLER	J	8	52
BUTLER	J	9	32
BUTLER	J	9	236
BUTLER	J	11	57
BUTLER	J	11	57
BUTLER	J	12	40
BUTLER	J	14	47
BUTLER	J	14	47
BUTLER	JC	6	68
BUTLER	JC	10	36
BUTLER	JE	10	36
BUTLER	JF	3	295
BUTLER	JH	6	68
BUTLER	JH	6	68
BUTLER	JH	10	273
BUTLER	JP	14	47
BUTLER	JW	1	48
BUTLER	JW	6	68
BUTLER	LW	4	63
BUTLER	MJ	10	36
BUTLER	P	2	53
BUTLER	R	4	63
BUTLER	R	8	52
BUTLER	R	9	236
BUTLER	RA	13	71
BUTLER	RG	5	56
BUTLER	ROD	10	273
BUTLER	RP	3	31
BUTLER	RW	6	68
BUTLER	RW	13	71
BUTLER	S	6	68
BUTLER	S	9	236
BUTLER	S	9	236
BUTLER	SC	4	63
BUTLER	T	3	31
BUTLER	T	8	52
BUTLER	T	13	71
BUTLER	T	13	71
BUTLER	TG	6	68
BUTLER	TH	8	52
BUTLER	TH	13	71
BUTLER	TI	6	68
BUTLER	TJ	12	40
BUTLER	TJ	13	71
BUTLER	TL	14	47
BUTLER	TW	3	31
BUTLER	TWR	12	421
BUTLER	W	3	31
BUTLER	W	6	68
BUTLER	W	7	54
BUTLER	W	8	52
BUTLER	W	11	57
BUTLER	W	13	71
BUTLER	W	14	47
BUTLER	WA	13	71
BUTLER	WC	4	63
BUTLER	WE	2	53
BUTLER	WE	9	32
BUTLER	WG	12	40
BUTLER	WG	12	276
BUTLER	WH	1	48
BUTLER	WH	9	32
BUTLER	WJ	1	48
BUTLER	WJ	10	36
BUTLER	WL	12	40
BUTLER	WP	5	56
BUTLER	WW	2	53
BUTLIN	E	2	53
BUTLIN	GJ	12	276
BUTLIN	HE	12	276
BUTLIN	JH	12	276
BUTSON	W	9	33
BUTT	A	4	63
BUTT	AE	7	55
BUTT	AG	4	63
BUTT	C	1	48
BUTT	C	12	276
BUTT	EC	4	63
BUTT	EL	10	273
BUTT	EW	4	63
BUTT	F	4	63
BUTT	F	4	63
BUTT	FET	4	63
BUTT	G	12	276
BUTT	HF	5	56
BUTT	HV	2	53
BUTT	JG	7	55
BUTT	N	4	63
BUTT	SG	12	276
BUTT	W	4	63
BUTT	WA	10	36
BUTT	WJ	9	236
BUTTELL	EB	5	56
BUTTELL	EO	5	56
BUTTEN	W	7	54
BUTTERFIELD	A	5	56
BUTTERFIELD	A	5	56
BUTTERFIELD	A	5	56
BUTTERFIELD	A	8	52
BUTTERFIELD	A	8	52
BUTTERFIELD	A	8	52
BUTTERFIELD	A	9	33
BUTTERFIELD	AE	2	53
BUTTERFIELD	AG	5	56
BUTTERFIELD	C	8	52
BUTTERFIELD	C	8	52
BUTTERFIELD	C	8	52
BUTTERFIELD	CH	9	33
BUTTERFIELD	CJ	3	295
BUTTERFIELD	E	5	56
BUTTERFIELD	E	8	52
BUTTERFIELD	F	9	236
BUTTERFIELD	G	5	56
BUTTERFIELD	G	5	57
BUTTERFIELD	G	5	57
BUTTERFIELD	H	5	57
BUTTERFIELD	H	5	57
BUTTERFIELD	H	8	52
BUTTERFIELD	H	8	52
BUTTERFIELD	H	9	33
BUTTERFIELD	H	9	237
BUTTERFIELD	J	5	57
BUTTERFIELD	J	5	57
BUTTERFIELD	J	8	52
BUTTERFIELD	J	11	57
BUTTERFIELD	JA	9	237
BUTTERFIELD	JH	5	57
BUTTERFIELD	L	8	52
BUTTERFIELD	O	5	57
BUTTERFIELD	P	5	57
BUTTERFIELD	W	8	52
BUTTERFIELD	WL	10	273
BUTTERHILL	W	8	52
BUTTERILL	A	8	52
BUTTERILL	JW	8	52
BUTTERS	E	3	31
BUTTERS	H	9	237
BUTTERS	HF	11	57
BUTTERS	JT	13	71
BUTTERS	M	9	237
BUTTERS	R	8	53
BUTTERTON	G	5	57
BUTTERWOOD	A	8	53
BUTTERWORTH	A	14	47
BUTTERWORTH	E	8	53
BUTTERWORTH	E	11	57
BUTTERWORTH	E	14	47
BUTTERWORTH	F	11	57
BUTTERWORTH	G	8	53
BUTTERWORTH	G	8	53
BUTTERWORTH	G	11	57

BUTTERWORTH	H	11	57
BUTTERWORTH	H	11	57
BUTTERWORTH	J	9	33
BUTTERWORTH	J	11	57
BUTTERWORTH	J	11	57
BUTTERWORTH	JE	14	47
BUTTERWORTH	JW	8	53
BUTTERWORTH	W	14	47
BUTTERWORTH	WS	11	57
BUTTERY	A	8	53
BUTTERY	AE	13	72
BUTTERY	CW	12	276
BUTTERY	GW	13	72
BUTTIGIEG	J	10	273
BUTTIVANT	HW	7	55
BUTTOLPH	GE	13	72
BUTTON	G	13	72
BUTTON	H	2	53
BUTTON	HJ	5	57
BUTTON	J	13	72
BUTTON	JE	3	295
BUTTON	L	2	53
BUTTON	P	1	48
BUTTON	SG	5	57
BUTTON	T	13	72
BUTTON	WA	5	57
BUTTON	WJ	13	72
BUTTONSHAW	J	10	273
BUTTRUM	AH	12	40
BUTTS	F	5	57
BUTTS	S	6	68
BUTTS	W	5	57
BUTTS	W	5	57
BUTZBACK	AC	13	72
BUTZBACK	AS	13	72
BUTZBACK	AW	13	72
BUXEY	AR	10	36
BUXEY	FW	4	64
BUXEY	RC	4	64
BUXTON	H	10	37
BUXTON	L	1	48
BUXTON	R	9	33
BUXTON	RGM	7	55
BUXTON	T	11	58
BUXTON	VE	1	48
BUXTON	WJ	4	64
BUY	PW	1	48
BUZZA	A	11	58
BUZZA	H	11	58
BUZZA	J	11	58
BUZZA	J	14	47
BUZZA	JH	14	47
BUZZA	RJ	14	47
BUZZARD	H	10	273
BYARD	HG	2	53
BYATT	AW	1	48
BYATT	AW	7	55
BYATT	F	2	53
BYATT	GT	1	48
BYATT	P	12	40
BYATT	PC	4	64
BYATT	PE	12	40
BYATT	R	1	48
BYE	GF	12	40
BYE	HG	2	53
BYE	JA	2	54
BYE	L	4	64
BYE	RH	5	57
BYERS	GFH	2	54
BYERS	GH	7	55
BYERS	SW	2	54
BYFIELD	AC	1	48
BYFIELD	FT	5	57
BYFIELD	WJ	6	68
BYFORD	AH	2	54
BYFORD	F	2	54
BYFORD	F	13	72
BYFORD	HA	2	54
BYGRAVE	EH	12	40
BYGRAVE	GA	13	72
BYGRAVE	J	13	72
BYGRAVE	LJ	5	57
BYGRAVE	P	5	57
BYGRAVES	F	5	57
BYGRAVES	H	3	295
BYGRAVES	JC	12	40
BYGRAVES	S	5	58
BYHAM	AG	7	55
BYHAM	HW	7	55
BYHAM	VM	7	55
BYHAM	WH	13	72
BYLETT	HC	2	54
BYNG	C	10	37
BYNG	I	10	37
BYNG	JW	6	68
BYOTT	GV	3	296
BYRAM	RA	5	58
BYRAM	W	11	58
BYRCH	AW	4	64
BYRES	R	4	64
BYRNE	AE	3	296
BYRNE	AH	12	276
BYRNE	F	10	37
BYRNE	H	10	37
BYRNE	J	11	58
BYRNE	J	11	58
BYRNE	J	11	58
BYRNE	J	13	72
BYRNE	JE	11	58
BYRNE	JF	4	64
BYRNE	JH	3	296
BYRNE	JH	14	47
BYRNE	JT	12	276
BYRNE	JT	14	47
BYRNE	M	11	58
BYRNE	M	14	47
BYRNE	M	14	47
BYRNE	P	3	296
BYRNE	PG	4	64
BYRNE	R	13	72
BYRNE	RT	7	55
BYRNE	T	11	58
BYRNE	T	11	58
BYRNE	T	14	48
BYRNE	TH	11	58
BYRNE	TJ	2	54
BYRNE	TW	8	53
BYRNE	WE	4	64
BYROM	G	11	58
BYROM	H	3	296
BYROM	W	3	296
BYRON	CF	11	58
BYRON	J	7	56
BYRON	J	8	53
BYRON	J	8	53
BYRON	W	2	54
BYRON	W	2	54
BYRON	W	13	72
BYSOUTH	S	5	58
BYTHEWAY	P	6	68
BYWATER	A	9	33
BYWATER	A	9	237
BYWATER	AG	6	69
BYWATER	E	6	69
BYWATER	H	8	53
BYWATER	H	8	53
BYWATER	J	9	237
BYWATER	JW	6	69
BYWATER	WS	8	53
BYWATERS	HE	7	56
BYWATERS	T	2	54
BYWOOD	H	8	53

C

CABELL	G	2	54
CABELL	H	2	54
CABELL	WS	13	72
CABLE	C	4	64
CABLE	G	7	56
CABLE	J	6	69
CABLE	J	10	37
CABLE	W	4	64
CABLE	WJ	7	56
CABNAGH	J	9	33
CABOT	AJ	4	64
CABOT	P	4	64
CABOT	PHJ	4	64
CACKETT	F	7	56
CACKETT	WG	7	56
CADBY	E	3	296
CADBY	F	3	296
CADBY	PH	6	69
CADBY	R	3	296
CADD	EA	12	276
CADD	J	12	40
CADDEN	HG	3	31
CADDEY	J	5	58
CADDICK	A	6	69
CADDICK	A	10	37
CADDICK	J	13	72
CADDY	AW	10	37
CADDY	WJ	6	69
CADDYE	WJ	10	274
CADE	A	2	54
CADE	FH	12	40
CADE	H	12	40
CADE	L	12	40
CADEN	W	6	69
CADGE	F	3	296
CADMAN	AT	5	58
CADMAN	E	11	58
CADMAN	FT	13	72
CADMAN	G	5	58
CADMAN	H	1	48
CADMAN	H	6	69
CADMAN	J	11	58
CADMAN	J	11	59
CADMAN	J	12	40
CADMAN	S	2	54
CADMAN	TH	6	69
CADWALLADER	A	14	48
CADWALLADER	R	14	48
CADWALLADER	W	14	48
CADYWOULD	GH	11	59
CAEN	G	3	296
CAESAR	C	14	48
CAFE	JP	4	64
CAFE	W	4	64
CAFERTY	PA	8	53
CAFFERTY	J	9	33
CAFFERTY	M	9	33
CAFFERTY	P	9	33
CAFFEY	C	14	48
CAFFREY	DJ	11	59
CAFFREY	J	11	59
CAFFREY	J	14	48
CAFFREY	P	14	48
CAHALAN	J	9	33
CAHALANE	J	10	37

CAHALARNE	H	1	48	CAINE	G	4	64	CALLAGHAN	E	8	54	CALLOWAY	H	7	57
CAHALARNE	J	1	48	CAINE	J	9	237	CALLAGHAN	F	14	48	CALLOWAY	H	9	33
CAHALARNE	J	1	48	CAINE	J	9	237	CALLAGHAN	G	1	49	CALLOWAY	H	9	237
CAHALARNE	JT	1	48	CAINE	J	11	59	CALLAGHAN	GH	10	37	CALLOWAY	R	4	65
CAHILL	A	7	56	CAINE	JB	6	69	CALLAGHAN	H	5	59	CALLOWAY	S	6	70
CAHILL	B	12	41	CAINE	JP	6	69	CALLAGHAN	J	3	296	CALNAN	H	7	57
CAHILL	H	1	48	CAINE	NT	6	69	CALLAGHAN	J	8	54	CALNAN	HJ	7	57
CAHILL	H	11	59	CAINE	T	7	56	CALLAGHAN	M	8	54	CALOW	GF	11	60
CAHILL	J	4	64	CAIRNCROSS	S	4	65	CALLAGHAN	P	10	37	CALOW	J	14	48
CAHILL	J	4	64	CAIRNS	E	8	53	CALLAGHAN	P	11	60	CALROW	J	13	73
CAHILL	J	4	64	CAIRNS	GH	1	49	CALLAGHAN	T	8	54	CALT	J	6	70
CAHILL	J	10	274	CAIRNS	GJ	12	276	CALLAGHAN	T	11	60	CALVER	A	9	33
CAHILL	J	13	73	CAIRNS	H	7	56	CALLAGHAN	T	11	60	CALVER	E	9	33
CAHILL	P	14	48	CAIRNS	J	10	37	CALLAGHAN	T	11	60	CALVER	H	5	59
CAHILL	T	1	49	CAIRNS	J	11	59	CALLAGHAN	W	3	296	CALVER	JEM	10	37
CAHILL	VJ	7	56	CAIRNS	JA	1	49	CALLAGHAN	W	8	54	CALVER	RE	1	49
CAHILL	W	9	237	CAIRNS	JV	13	73	CALLAN	AC	3	296	CALVER	W	10	274
CAHILL	W	11	59	CAIRNS	WD	6	69	CALLAN	BA	5	59	CALVER	WH	2	55
CAIGER	EC	12	276	CAISLEY	H	8	53	CALLAN	W	11	60	CALVERLEY	C	8	54
CAIGER	W	2	54	CAKE	AE	10	37	CALLAN	WJ	11	60	CALVERLEY	F	8	54
CAIN	AA	5	58	CAKE	D	10	37	CALLARD	A	13	73	CALVERLEY	T	8	54
CAIN	AC	5	58	CAKEBREAD	AEW	7	56	CALLARD	WC	10	37	CALVERT	A	8	54
CAIN	AM	2	54	CAKEBREAD	R	1	49	CALLARD	WG	8	54	CALVERT	A	9	33
CAIN	AT	2	54	CAKEBREAD	W	7	56	CALLAWAY	A	10	274	CALVERT	A	11	60
CAIN	E	11	59	CAKEBREAD	WE	7	56	CALLAWAY	AH	4	65	CALVERT	AJ	13	73
CAIN	F	2	55	CALCOTT	BF	5	58	CALLAWAY	AW	4	65	CALVERT	C	8	54
CAIN	F	5	58	CALCRAFT	WE	5	59	CALLAWAY	F	4	65	CALVERT	CA	4	65
CAIN	G	3	296	CALCUTT	AJ	7	56	CALLAWAY	SJ	10	274	CALVERT	E	8	54
CAIN	G	5	58	CALCUTT	WG	2	55	CALLAWAY	W	10	37	CALVERT	F	8	54
CAIN	H	5	58	CALDER	A	8	53	CALLAWAY	WJ	7	56	CALVERT	F	9	237
CAIN	H	11	59	CALDER	D	11	59	CALLCUTT	FH	2	55	CALVERT	F	9	237
CAIN	HE	5	58	CALDER	HW	13	73	CALLEN	A	4	65	CALVERT	G	9	34
CAIN	HW	5	58	CALDER	R	6	69	CALLEN	F	4	65	CALVERT	G	9	237
CAIN	J	5	58	CALDERWOOD	J	2	55	CALLEN	WT	4	65	CALVERT	GH	9	34
CAIN	J	6	69	CALDICOTT	C	6	69	CALLENNE	AE	13	73	CALVERT	H	8	54
CAIN	J	11	59	CALDICOTT	G	6	69	CALLENNE	CE	13	73	CALVERT	H	11	60
CAIN	J	11	59	CALDICOTT	J	6	70	CALLENNE	TJ	13	73	CALVERT	J	8	54
CAIN	J	14	48	CALDICOTT	T	9	33	CALLF	J	7	56	CALVERT	J	13	73
CAIN	JC	3	296	CALDWELL	D	11	60	CALLIGAN	J	8	54	CALVERT	J	14	48
CAIN	JE	13	73	CALDWELL	H	7	56	CALLIGAN	W	8	54	CALVERT	L	9	34
CAIN	JM	11	59	CALDWELL	J	11	60	CALLIGHAN	J	9	33	CALVERT	S	14	48
CAIN	JT	11	59	CALDWELL	J	11	60	CALLINGHAM	AG	13	73	CALVERT	TA	11	60
CAIN	M	11	59	CALDWELL	J	14	48	CALLINGHAM	AV	1	49	CALVERT	W	8	54
CAIN	MJ	11	59	CALDWELL	JL	14	48	CALLINGHAM	WE	7	56	CALVERT	W	9	237
CAIN	O	8	53	CALDWELL	T	14	48	CALLIS	T	7	57	CALVERT	W	11	60
CAIN	PH	5	58	CALDWELL	W	12	41	CALLOW	A	2	55	CALVERT	WH	9	381
CAIN	S	5	58	CALE	A	11	60	CALLOW	C	6	70	CALVEY	JB	6	70
CAIN	S	8	53	CALE	C	2	55	CALLOW	H	6	70	CALVEY	MT	6	70
CAIN	T	5	58	CALE	F	9	237	CALLOW	H	6	70	CALVEY	MT	6	70
CAIN	T	13	73	CALE	J	8	54	CALLOW	HG	6	70	CAMBERS	AC	12	41
CAIN	TG	6	69	CALENO	A	3	296	CALLOW	SJ	1	49	CAMBERS	CW	2	55
CAIN	W	2	55	CALEY	J	2	55	CALLOW	TS	1	49	CAMBERS	E	12	41
CAIN	W	5	58	CALEY	T	8	54	CALLOW	W	6	70	CAMBERS	FJ	12	41
CAIN	W	5	58	CALLABY	EAG	13	73	CALLOW	WH	1	49	CAMBERS	FW	12	41
CAIN	WT	11	59	CALLABY	P	12	41	CALLOWAY	F	10	37	CAMBERS	H	12	41

Name	In.			Name	In.			Name	In.			Name	In.		
CAMBERS	JW	12	41	CAMP	WH	3	297	CAMPBELL	TJ	11	61	CANE	FE	10	274
CAMBERS	PC	12	41	CAMPAIN	J	9	34	CAMPBELL	TW	13	74	CANE	JFW	7	57
CAMBERS	W	12	41	CAMPBELL		4	65	CAMPBELL	V	14	49	CANE	M	2	56
CAMBERS	WJ	12	41	CAMPBELL	A	2	55	CAMPBELL	W	8	55	CANE	W	4	66
CAMBRIDGE	J	7	57	CAMPBELL	A	4	65	CAMPBELL	W	9	237	CANEY	AG	13	74
CAMBRIDGE	N	8	54	CAMPBELL	A	9	34	CAMPBELL	W	11	61	CANFIELD	Q	7	57
CAMBRIDGE	N	8	55	CAMPBELL	A	11	60	CAMPBELL	W	12	41	CANFIELD	W	7	57
CAMBRIDGE	TB	2	55	CAMPBELL	A	14	49	CAMPBELL	W	14	49	CANHAM	AC	5	59
CAMBURS	AT	12	41	CAMPBELL	AJ	4	65	CAMPBELL	WA	3	31	CANHAM	AH	7	57
CAME	AA	6	70	CAMPBELL	C	8	55	CAMPBELL	WC	13	74	CANHAM	CH	12	277
CAME	E	1	49	CAMPBELL	CE	10	38	CAMPBELL	WH	13	74	CANHAM	FW	2	56
CAME	EJ	6	70	CAMPBELL	CW	3	297	CAMPBELL	WS	1	49	CANHAM	G	2	56
CAME	H	1	49	CAMPBELL	E	1	49	CAMPEY	J	8	55	CANHAM	G	2	56
CAME	W	1	49	CAMPBELL	F	11	60	CAMPEY	W	8	55	CANHAM	GH	7	57
CAMERFORD	J	6	89	CAMPBELL	FD	13	74	CAMPION	C	1	50	CANHAM	WH	2	56
CAMERON	A	8	55	CAMPBELL	FG	14	49	CAMPION	CH	13	74	CANHAM	WJ	7	57
CAMERON	B	11	60	CAMPBELL	G	10	38	CAMPION	E	1	50	CANHAN	D	1	50
CAMERON	D	1	49	CAMPBELL	GA	13	74	CAMPION	EL	7	57	CANHAN	H	1	50
CAMERON	GP	1	49	CAMPBELL	GE	4	65	CAMPION	EP	11	61	CANHAN	T	1	50
CAMERON	HJ	3	296	CAMPBELL	GL	8	55	CAMPION	JW	13	74	CANING	W	11	61
CAMERON	J	1	49	CAMPBELL	GW	11	61	CAMPION	R	2	56	CANKER	E	8	55
CAMERON	J	8	55	CAMPBELL	GW	13	74	CAMPION	W	12	41	CANN	A	3	297
CAMERON	JJ	2	55	CAMPBELL	H	8	55	CAMPION	WT	3	297	CANN	A	4	66
CAMERON	NB	7	57	CAMPBELL	H	8	55	CAMPKIN	EJ	13	74	CANN	GH	9	34
CAMERON	RA	3	296	CAMPBELL	H	11	61	CAMPLEMAN	CR	8	55	CANN	GR	1	50
CAMERON	RF	1	49	CAMPBELL	H	11	61	CAMPLIN	JFJ	10	274	CANN	H	1	50
CAMERON	W	3	31	CAMPBELL	HA	10	38	CAMPS	AE	8	55	CANN	H	3	297
CAMERON	W	10	38	CAMPBELL	HS	2	56	CAMPS	SG	2	56	CANN	H	10	274
CAMERON	W	13	73	CAMPBELL	HW	7	57	CAMPSON	WH	6	89	CANN	HWA	3	297
CAMERON	WEG	2	55	CAMPBELL	HW	7	57	CAMWELL		6	70	CANN	JP	1	50
CAMFIELD	H	4	65	CAMPBELL	J	2	55	CANAVAN	F	14	49	CANNAFORD	AS	1	50
CAMFIELD	W	4	65	CAMPBELL	J	9	34	CANDELENT	HJ	6	70	CANNAN	A	14	49
CAMFIELD	W	4	65	CAMPBELL	J	9	381	CANDERTON	AN	2	56	CANNAN	MJ	9	34
CAMIDGE	P	8	55	CAMPBELL	J	11	61	CANDERTON	JT	5	59	CANNAN	T	14	49
CAMILLERI	A	10	274	CAMPBELL	J	14	49	CANDERTON	WEE	5	59	CANNELL	S	1	50
CAMM	A	1	49	CAMPBELL	JC	14	49	CANDEY	A	10	274	CANNING	AW	1	50
CAMM	GE	2	55	CAMPBELL	JE	1	49	CANDEY	M	10	274	CANNING	C	13	74
CAMM	J	1	49	CAMPBELL	JJ	10	38	CANDLAND	J	14	49	CANNING	G	6	70
CAMM	J	14	48	CAMPBELL	JV	11	61	CANDLER	C	13	74	CANNINGS	J	13	74
CAMM	W	8	55	CAMPBELL	JW	8	55	CANDLER	HC	1	50	CANNINGS	PG	4	66
CAMMERER	FP	4	65	CAMPBELL	M	3	31	CANDLER	J	1	50	CANNINGS	W	4	66
CAMP	A	3	297	CAMPBELL	P	11	61	CANDLIN	R	6	70	CANNINGS	W	4	66
CAMP	AC	3	31	CAMPBELL	P	11	61	CANDY	AH	4	65	CANNOCK	W	4	66
CAMP	CT	2	55	CAMPBELL	R	1	49	CANDY	AJ	4	65	CANNON	A	6	70
CAMP	E	5	59	CAMPBELL	R	4	65	CANDY	AJ	13	74	CANNON	A	7	58
CAMP	EH	7	57	CAMPBELL	R	7	57	CANDY	CE	4	66	CANNON	A	8	55
CAMP	H	2	55	CAMPBELL	R	7	57	CANDY	EV	4	66	CANNON	AE	2	56
CAMP	HH	5	59	CAMPBELL	R	8	55	CANDY	FG	4	66	CANNON	AE	5	59
CAMP	HW	13	73	CAMPBELL	R	8	55	CANDY	H	10	274	CANNON	AJW	1	50
CAMP	J	1	49	CAMPBELL	R	8	55	CANDY	J	10	274	CANNON	AV	6	70
CAMP	PF	13	73	CAMPBELL	R	11	61	CANDY	WA	4	66	CANNON	C	8	55
CAMP	R	10	274	CAMPBELL	SG	13	74	CANDY	WD	13	74	CANNON	DF	9	34
CAMP	RW	3	31	CAMPBELL	SJ	7	57	CANDY	WH	10	274	CANNON	E	5	59
CAMP	SH	13	73	CAMPBELL	T	2	55	CANDY	WHN	4	66	CANNON	E	11	61
CAMP	W	3	31	CAMPBELL	T	14	49	CANDY	WV	4	66	CANNON	EC	5	59

CANNON	EG	5	59	CAPELL	O	1	50	CARDALL	A	6	71	CAREY	GH	6	71				
CANNON	EW	13	74	CAPELL	R	1	50	CARDEN	A	4	67	CAREY	H	7	58				
CANNON	F	1	50	CAPELL	T	5	60	CARDEN	W	11	62	CAREY	HA	13	75				
CANNON	FC	8	55	CAPELLA	A	11	61	CARDER	G	12	41	CAREY	J	11	62				
CANNON	FE	7	58	CAPES	HC	1	50	CARDEW	A	2	56	CAREY	L	3	297				
CANNON	FJ	5	59	CAPLAN	B	8	415	CARDEW	C	2	56	CAREY	R	1	51				
CANNON	G	5	59	CAPLAN	M	14	49	CARDEW	ES	1	51	CAREY	R	11	62				
CANNON	GS	1	50	CAPLAN	WJ	3	297	CARDEW	FT	1	51	CAREY	S	11	62				
CANNON	HH	7	58	CAPLE	A	10	38	CARDEW	S	1	51	CAREY	TG	13	75				
CANNON	HJ	5	59	CAPLE	E	10	275	CARDIN	JF	11	62	CAREY	W	3	297				
CANNON	HJ	7	58	CAPLE	WC	10	275	CARDIN	W	11	62	CAREY	W	7	59				
CANNON	J	7	58	CAPLEN	EJ	4	66	CARDUS	F	8	56	CAREY	W	10	38				
CANNON	J	7	58	CAPLEN	PC	4	66	CARDUS	J	8	56	CAREY	WA	13	75				
CANNON	J	7	58	CAPLEN	R	4	66	CARDUS	W	8	56	CAREY	WH	11	62				
CANNON	J	9	237	CAPLIN	E	8	56	CARDWELL	T	12	277	CAREY	WJ	7	59				
CANNON	MT	5	59	CAPLIN	EA	3	297	CARDY	EC	4	67	CAREY	WJ	13	75				
CANNON	P	11	61	CAPLIN	EA	3	297	CARDY	FR	7	58	CARFRAE	F	10	275				
CANNON	R	5	59	CAPNERHURST	J	6	71	CARDY	HJ	4	67	CARINS	J	13	75				
CANNON	SH	1	50	CAPON	A	1	50	CARDY	TG	4	67	CARIVEN	FB	13	75				
CANNON	SW	7	58	CAPON	A	2	56	CARDY	WH	4	67	CARIVEN	GV	13	75				
CANNON	T	1	50	CAPON	CG	13	75	CARDY	WJ	4	67	CARLE	C	13	76				
CANNON	T	13	74	CAPON	E	7	58	CARE	A	12	277	CARLESS	R	7	59				
CANNON	TA	6	70	CAPON	F	3	297	CARE	G	13	75	CARLILE	AG	3	297				
CANNON	TE	7	58	CAPON	G	1	51	CARE	JS	2	56	CARLIN	J	8	56				
CANNON	VS	13	75	CAPON	H	1	51	CARE	W	6	71	CARLIN	J	11	62				
CANNON	WJ	7	58	CAPON	HG	1	51	CARE	WA	6	71	CARLIN	T	8	56				
CANSFIELD	J	9	34	CAPON	HT	1	51	CARE	WG	12	277	CARLIN	TG	6	71				
CANSFIELD	R	9	237	CAPON	R	1	51	CAREFULL	H	14	49	CARLINE	F	14	49				
CANSFIELD	S	9	34	CAPON	W	13	75	CARELESS	AFW	5	60	CARLINE	S	14	49				
CANT	SH	13	75	CAPON	WRH	4	66	CARELESS	GH	6	71	CARLING	H	8	56				
CANTELL	F	7	58	CAPP	F	5	60	CARELESS	J	6	71	CARLING	JW	14	49				
CANTELLO	A	3	32	CAPP	W	5	60	CARESS	A	12	41	CARLISLE	S	11	62				
CANTELLOW	EJ	3	297	CAPP	W	7	58	CARESS	F	12	41	CARLISLE	W	11	62				
CANTERBURY	H	10	274	CAPPELL	EM	8	56	CARESS	GC	12	41	CARLOSS	FA	7	59				
CANTLE	F	4	66	CAPPER	A	11	61	CARESS	R	12	41	CARLOSS	J	2	56				
CANTLOW	PE	10	275	CAPPER	A	11	61	CARESS	S	12	42	CARLSON	C	1	51				
CANTOR	L	14	49	CAPPER	CS	5	60	CARESWELL	EF	1	51	CARLTON	CA	10	275				
CANTRELL	J	9	34	CAPPER	G	10	38	CARESWELL	FJ	1	51	CARLTON	F	1	51				
CANTRILL	F	9	34	CAPPER	GH	6	71	CARESWELL	GW	1	51	CARLTON	JE	8	56				
CANTWELL	J	11	61	CAPPER	WF	11	61	CARESWELL	H	1	51	CARLYSLE	W	13	76				
CANTY	A	9	237	CAPSEY	G	7	58	CARESWELL	RW	1	51	CARMALT	E	13	76				
CANTY	T	7	58	CAPSEY	GE	7	58	CAREY	A	11	62	CARMAN	A	9	34				
CANTY	WA	13	75	CAPSEY	WE	2	56	CAREY	AH	3	297	CARMAN	DAA	1	51				
CANWELL	J	5	59	CAPSTICK	FHA	9	238	CAREY	AR	3	297	CARMAN	EG	3	298				
CANWELL	S	8	55	CAPSTICK	W	9	34	CAREY	C	2	56	CARMAN	EH	3	298				
CANYIN	AWG	5	59	CAPTAIN	TD	8	56	CAREY	C	13	75	CARMAN	H	9	34				
CAPATOFSKY	A	14	49	CARBERY	J	9	34	CAREY	CA	7	58	CARMAN	H	9	238				
CAPE	JT	8	56	CARCAUD	JJ	4	66	CAREY	D	3	297	CARMAN	WA	3	298				
CAPEL	CP	10	275	CARD	AT	4	66	CAREY	ES	3	297	CARMAN	WJ	3	298				
CAPEL	SE	12	41	CARD	F	4	66	CAREY	ES	13	75	CARMEN	ES	13	76				
CAPEL	WH	3	297	CARD	FL	5	60	CAREY	EW	1	51	CARMEN	FC	13	76				
CAPELIN	CC	13	75	CARD	H	2	56	CAREY	EW	2	56	CARMEN	W	13	76				
CAPELL	A	1	50	CARD	H	13	75	CAREY	F	6	71	CARMER	WA	13	113				
CAPELL	G	5	60	CARD	JL	13	75	CAREY	G	6	71	CARMICHAEL	F	7	59				
CAPELL	G	12	277	CARD	WF	4	67	CAREY	GB	13	75	CARMICHAEL	FE	14	50				

CARMICHAEL	J	7	59
CARMICHAEL	JA	11	62
CARMICHAEL	T	1	51
CARMICHAEL	W	11	62
CARMICHAEL	W	14	50
CARMICHEL	F	4	67
CARMOODY	TH	7	59
CARNALL	GH	14	50
CARNALL	JA	14	50
CARNE	GW	13	76
CARNE	JG	14	50
CARNE	TJ	14	50
CARNE	WC	13	76
CARNELL	JR	3	298
CARNELL	R	10	275
CARNELL	S	10	38
CARNELL	TW	10	38
CARNEY	C	9	238
CARNEY	C	14	50
CARNEY	CJ	4	67
CARNEY	J	3	298
CARNEY	J	6	71
CARNEY	J	8	56
CARNEY	J	10	38
CARNEY	J	11	62
CARNEY	JP	7	59
CARNEY	T	8	56
CARNEY	T	9	34
CARNEY	T	11	62
CARNEY	TJ	13	76
CARNEY	WP	4	67
CARNLEY	W	8	56
CAROLINE	H	4	67
CARP	S	14	50
CARPENTER	A	2	56
CARPENTER	A	3	298
CARPENTER	A	13	76
CARPENTER	A	13	76
CARPENTER	AA	2	57
CARPENTER	AB	2	57
CARPENTER	AE	12	42
CARPENTER	AE	13	76
CARPENTER	AF	5	60
CARPENTER	AH	10	275
CARPENTER	AJ	7	59
CARPENTER	AWH	3	298
CARPENTER	B	5	60
CARPENTER	C	5	60
CARPENTER	C	7	59
CARPENTER	C	13	76
CARPENTER	E	5	60
CARPENTER	EE	4	67
CARPENTER	EL	10	38
CARPENTER	FJ	13	76
CARPENTER	GE	4	67
CARPENTER	GH	3	32
CARPENTER	GH	4	67
CARPENTER	HE	1	51
CARPENTER	HG	5	60
CARPENTER	HG	7	59
CARPENTER	J	5	60
CARPENTER	J	5	60
CARPENTER	J	5	60
CARPENTER	J	5	60
CARPENTER	J	12	277
CARPENTER	JA	3	298
CARPENTER	JH	3	298
CARPENTER	JH	4	67
CARPENTER	JH	10	38
CARPENTER	JJJ	13	76
CARPENTER	JW	10	275
CARPENTER	P	13	76
CARPENTER	PF	13	76
CARPENTER	SW	13	76
CARPENTER	TC	7	59
CARPENTER	TG	3	298
CARPENTER	TM	4	67
CARPENTER	W	5	60
CARPENTER	W	6	71
CARPENTER	W	14	50
CARPENTER	WE	4	67
CARPENTER	WH	2	57
CARPENTER	WH	12	42
CARPENTER	WHT	1	51
CARPENTER	WJ	1	51
CARPENTER	WM	7	59
CARPENTIER	FA	4	67
CARR	A	1	51
CARR	A	6	71
CARR	A	8	56
CARR	A	12	42
CARR	A	14	50
CARR	A	14	50
CARR	AE	4	67
CARR	AE	8	56
CARR	AEJ	7	59
CARR	AG	3	298
CARR	B	9	35
CARR	C	8	56
CARR	C	12	42
CARR	C	14	50
CARR	CC	1	51
CARR	CJ	2	57
CARR	CW	12	277
CARR	D	1	52
CARR	D	9	35
CARR	D	14	50
CARR	EW	1	52
CARR	F	7	59
CARR	F	8	56
CARR	F	14	50
CARR	G	8	56
CARR	GF	13	76
CARR	GS	4	68
CARR	H	8	56
CARR	H	9	238
CARR	H	14	50
CARR	HA	1	52
CARR	HH	3	298
CARR	J	1	52
CARR	J	6	71
CARR	J	8	56
CARR	J	8	57
CARR	J	8	57
CARR	J	8	57
CARR	J	9	35
CARR	J	10	38
CARR	J	11	62
CARR	J	11	62
CARR	J	11	63
CARR	J	13	77
CARR	J	14	50
CARR	J	14	50
CARR	J	14	50
CARR	JC	6	71
CARR	JC	13	77
CARR	JH	12	277
CARR	JJ	6	71
CARR	JT	9	238
CARR	L	14	50
CARR	M	5	60
CARR	N	14	51
CARR	NA	4	68
CARR	R	12	277
CARR	T	8	57
CARR	T	12	42
CARR	T	14	51
CARR	TJ	6	71
CARR	W	4	68
CARR	W	8	57
CARR	W	11	63
CARR	W	11	63
CARR	W	12	277
CARR	W	13	77
CARR	W	14	51
CARR	WB	9	35
CARR	WF	3	298
CARR	WG	4	68
CARR	WH	7	59
CARR	WH	13	77
CARR	WJ	8	57
CARR	WS	1	52
CARRABY	W	8	57
CARRACK	A	8	57
CARRACK	JF	8	57
CARRELL	AE	2	57
CARRELL	E	10	38
CARRELL	H	10	38
CARRICK	A	6	72
CARRICK	G	8	57
CARRICK	R	8	57
CARRICK	W	5	60
CARRINGTON	A	5	60
CARRINGTON	A	5	60
CARRINGTON	A	5	61
CARRINGTON	C	9	238
CARRINGTON	E	5	61
CARRINGTON	E	9	238
CARRINGTON	EJ	1	52
CARRINGTON	H	5	61
CARRINGTON	H	13	77
CARRINGTON	J	5	61
CARRINGTON	JT	13	77
CARRINGTON	R	11	63
CARRINGTON	R	13	77
CARRINGTON	RS	2	57
CARRINGTON	S	11	63
CARRINGTON	W	13	77
CARRINGTON	WE	5	61
CARRITT	HN	5	61
CARRITT	TW	8	57
CARROD	A	8	57
CARROL	LH	10	275
CARROL	R	9	35
CARROLE	L	11	63
CARROLL	A	11	63
CARROLL	A	11	63
CARROLL	A	14	51
CARROLL	AE	4	68
CARROLL	AE	9	238
CARROLL	CE	4	68
CARROLL	E	2	57
CARROLL	E	3	298
CARROLL	E	9	35
CARROLL	E	11	63
CARROLL	E	11	63
CARROLL	F	4	68
CARROLL	F	6	72
CARROLL	F	11	63
CARROLL	F	11	63
CARROLL	FC	4	68
CARROLL	G	3	32
CARROLL	H	9	35
CARROLL	J	3	32
CARROLL	J	7	59
CARROLL	J	8	57
CARROLL	J	8	57
CARROLL	J	9	35
CARROLL	J	9	35
CARROLL	J	9	35

Surname	Initials	Col	Page
CARROLL	J	11	63
CARROLL	J	11	63
CARROLL	J	11	63
CARROLL	J	11	63
CARROLL	J	11	63
CARROLL	J	11	63
CARROLL	J	14	51
CARROLL	J	14	51
CARROLL	J	14	51
CARROLL	JB	13	77
CARROLL	JD	7	59
CARROLL	JJ	11	64
CARROLL	JW	9	35
CARROLL	JW	11	64
CARROLL	M	8	57
CARROLL	M	11	64
CARROLL	M	14	51
CARROLL	P	3	298
CARROLL	P	8	57
CARROLL	P	8	57
CARROLL	P	11	64
CARROLL	R	9	35
CARROLL	R	11	64
CARROLL	R	13	77
CARROLL	T	6	72
CARROLL	T	9	35
CARROLL	T	14	51
CARROLL	V	13	77
CARROLL	W	8	57
CARROLL	W	11	64
CARROLL	W	14	51
CARROLL	WH	7	59
CARROLL	WJ	14	51
CARRUTHERS	AM	2	57
CARSON	AM	11	64
CARSON	D	11	64
CARSON	G	11	64
CARSON	H	14	51
CARSTON	E	4	68
CARSWELL	CG	1	52
CARSWELL	D	2	57
CARSWELL	WJD	1	52
CARTER	A	2	57
CARTER	A	4	68
CARTER	A	4	68
CARTER	A	5	61
CARTER	A	5	61
CARTER	A	5	61
CARTER	A	5	61
CARTER	A	7	60
CARTER	A	9	35
CARTER	A	9	238
CARTER	A	10	38
CARTER	A	10	38
CARTER	A	11	64
CARTER	A	12	42
CARTER	A	13	77
CARTER	A	13	77
CARTER	A	13	77
CARTER	A	14	51
CARTER	A	14	51
CARTER	AA	4	68
CARTER	AA	10	38
CARTER	AC	2	57
CARTER	AC	4	68
CARTER	AC	12	42
CARTER	AE	2	57
CARTER	AE	2	57
CARTER	AE	4	68
CARTER	AE	4	68
CARTER	AE	7	60
CARTER	AE	12	42
CARTER	AE	12	42
CARTER	AF	13	77
CARTER	AG	12	42
CARTER	AJ	1	52
CARTER	AJ	3	298
CARTER	AJ	5	61
CARTER	AJ	5	61
CARTER	AJ	7	60
CARTER	AL	7	60
CARTER	AL	12	277
CARTER	AN	8	58
CARTER	AR	1	52
CARTER	AR	3	298
CARTER	AR	5	61
CARTER	ART	1	52
CARTER	AS	4	68
CARTER	AT	3	298
CARTER	AT	12	42
CARTER	AW	4	68
CARTER	AW	12	42
CARTER	B	14	51
CARTER	BF	3	32
CARTER	BH	5	61
CARTER	BL	12	42
CARTER	C	2	57
CARTER	C	2	57
CARTER	C	3	299
CARTER	C	5	61
CARTER	C	10	38
CARTER	C	11	64
CARTER	CA	7	60
CARTER	CD	12	42
CARTER	CE	6	72
CARTER	CJ	7	60
CARTER	CL	2	57
CARTER	CL	10	275
CARTER	CP	13	77
CARTER	CR	12	277
CARTER	CW	5	61
CARTER	D	3	299
CARTER	DJ	1	52
CARTER	DT	3	299
CARTER	E	1	52
CARTER	E	1	52
CARTER	E	5	61
CARTER	E	6	72
CARTER	E	7	60
CARTER	E	7	60
CARTER	E	8	58
CARTER	E	10	39
CARTER	E	10	39
CARTER	E	11	64
CARTER	E	12	277
CARTER	EC	6	72
CARTER	EC	13	77
CARTER	EE	3	32
CARTER	EE	12	42
CARTER	EF	13	77
CARTER	EH	6	72
CARTER	EH	10	39
CARTER	EHA	1	52
CARTER	EJ	7	60
CARTER	F	1	52
CARTER	F	2	57
CARTER	F	5	61
CARTER	F	5	62
CARTER	F	7	60
CARTER	F	9	238
CARTER	F	11	64
CARTER	FC	5	62
CARTER	FC	6	72
CARTER	FE	10	39
CARTER	FG	3	299
CARTER	FG	3	299
CARTER	FH	8	58
CARTER	FH	10	39
CARTER	FJ	3	32
CARTER	FJ	4	68
CARTER	FJ	5	62
CARTER	FT	2	57
CARTER	FW	1	52
CARTER	FW	2	57
CARTER	FW	3	32
CARTER	FW	3	299
CARTER	G	1	52
CARTER	G	5	62
CARTER	G	5	62
CARTER	G	10	39
CARTER	G	12	42
CARTER	G	13	78
CARTER	G	13	78
CARTER	GA	13	78
CARTER	GAT	10	39
CARTER	GC	1	52
CARTER	GC	9	238
CARTER	GD	3	32
CARTER	GE	1	52
CARTER	GE	6	72
CARTER	GE	9	35
CARTER	GE	10	39
CARTER	GE	12	42
CARTER	GH	4	68
CARTER	GH	5	62
CARTER	GR	13	78
CARTER	GS	4	68
CARTER	GW	1	52
CARTER	GW	7	60
CARTER	GW	11	64
CARTER	GW	12	43
CARTER	GW	13	78
CARTER	H	1	52
CARTER	H	2	58
CARTER	H	5	62
CARTER	H	5	62
CARTER	H	5	62
CARTER	H	9	35
CARTER	H	12	43
CARTER	H	13	78
CARTER	H	13	78
CARTER	H	14	51
CARTER	HC	2	58
CARTER	HE	2	58
CARTER	HFB	10	39
CARTER	HG	5	62
CARTER	HH	13	78
CARTER	HJ	5	62
CARTER	HJ	10	39
CARTER	HJ	13	78
CARTER	HO	13	78
CARTER	HS	12	43
CARTER	HT	13	78
CARTER	HW	4	69
CARTER	HW	10	39
CARTER	HW	13	78
CARTER	J	1	52
CARTER	J	2	58
CARTER	J	2	58
CARTER	J	3	299
CARTER	J	3	299
CARTER	J	4	69
CARTER	J	4	69
CARTER	J	5	62
CARTER	J	6	72
CARTER	J	6	72
CARTER	J	10	39
CARTER	J	10	39
CARTER	J	10	39

CARTER	J	10	39
CARTER	J	10	275
CARTER	J	11	64
CARTER	J	12	43
CARTER	J	13	78
CARTER	J	13	78
CARTER	J	13	78
CARTER	J	13	78
CARTER	J	14	51
CARTER	JE	4	69
CARTER	JF	12	43
CARTER	JG	13	78
CARTER	JH	8	58
CARTER	JH	9	35
CARTER	JH	10	275
CARTER	JH	12	43
CARTER	JJ	1	52
CARTER	JL	13	78
CARTER	JP	11	64
CARTER	JS	1	53
CARTER	JS	4	69
CARTER	JSB	14	51
CARTER	JT	2	58
CARTER	JT	13	78
CARTER	JW	8	58
CARTER	JW	8	58
CARTER	JW	11	64
CARTER	JW	11	64
CARTER	JW	11	65
CARTER	JW	12	43
CARTER	JW	13	78
CARTER	L	10	39
CARTER	LG	10	275
CARTER	LG	13	79
CARTER	LJ	3	299
CARTER	M	10	39
CARTER	O	5	62
CARTER	OE	7	60
CARTER	OG	4	69
CARTER	P	11	65
CARTER	P	12	43
CARTER	R	8	58
CARTER	R	10	39
CARTER	R	11	65
CARTER	R	13	79
CARTER	RF	3	299
CARTER	RH	10	39
CARTER	RJ	10	275
CARTER	RW	12	43
CARTER	S	4	69
CARTER	S	7	60
CARTER	S	8	58
CARTER	S	12	277
CARTER	SC	6	72
CARTER	SR	12	43
CARTER	ST	4	69
CARTER	T	6	72
CARTER	T	6	72
CARTER	T	8	58
CARTER	T	10	40
CARTER	T	13	79
CARTER	T	14	51
CARTER	TG	1	53
CARTER	TH	5	62
CARTER	TJ	10	40
CARTER	TS	10	275
CARTER	TW	5	62
CARTER	TWC	13	79
CARTER	V	2	58
CARTER	VR	5	62
CARTER	W	2	58
CARTER	W	6	72
CARTER	W	6	72
CARTER	W	8	58
CARTER	W	8	58
CARTER	W	8	58
CARTER	W	8	58
CARTER	W	9	35
CARTER	W	9	238
CARTER	W	10	40
CARTER	W	11	65
CARTER	W	12	43
CARTER	W	12	43
CARTER	W	12	277
CARTER	W	13	79
CARTER	W	14	52
CARTER	WA	9	35
CARTER	WA	10	40
CARTER	WA	12	277
CARTER	WAH	10	40
CARTER	WC	1	53
CARTER	WC	5	62
CARTER	WE	1	53
CARTER	WE	2	58
CARTER	WE	4	69
CARTER	WF	10	40
CARTER	WG	4	69
CARTER	WG	10	40
CARTER	WG	12	277
CARTER	WH	3	299
CARTER	WH	4	69
CARTER	WH	5	62
CARTER	WJ	3	32
CARTER	WJ	4	69
CARTER	WJ	4	69
CARTER	WJ	7	60
CARTER	WJ	12	277
CARTER	WP	13	79
CARTER	WR	3	32
CARTER	WW	1	53
CARTER	WW	4	69
CARTEY	F	2	58
CARTEY	R	11	65
CARTHEW	OWH	2	58
CARTHY	AJ	6	72
CARTHY	F	11	65
CARTHY	J	14	52
CARTLEDGE	A	9	36
CARTLEDGE	G	11	65
CARTLEDGE	H	14	52
CARTLEDGE	J	9	36
CARTLEDGE	J	9	36
CARTMELL	HJ	6	72
CARTWRIGHT	A	6	73
CARTWRIGHT	A	14	52
CARTWRIGHT	AH	6	73
CARTWRIGHT	B	2	58
CARTWRIGHT	C	7	60
CARTWRIGHT	C	14	52
CARTWRIGHT	CE	6	73
CARTWRIGHT	E	2	58
CARTWRIGHT	E	7	60
CARTWRIGHT	E	11	65
CARTWRIGHT	E	11	65
CARTWRIGHT	EL	6	73
CARTWRIGHT	EL	6	73
CARTWRIGHT	F	6	73
CARTWRIGHT	F	14	52
CARTWRIGHT	F	14	52
CARTWRIGHT	FE	13	79
CARTWRIGHT	G	7	60
CARTWRIGHT	GF	3	299
CARTWRIGHT	GH	8	58
CARTWRIGHT	H	6	73
CARTWRIGHT	H	13	79
CARTWRIGHT	H	14	52
CARTWRIGHT	H	14	52
CARTWRIGHT	HL	10	40
CARTWRIGHT	HT	12	277
CARTWRIGHT	HW	10	40
CARTWRIGHT	J	6	73
CARTWRIGHT	J	6	73
CARTWRIGHT	J	6	73
CARTWRIGHT	J	6	73
CARTWRIGHT	J	6	73
CARTWRIGHT	J	8	58
CARTWRIGHT	JA	6	73
CARTWRIGHT	JC	8	58
CARTWRIGHT	JH	6	73
CARTWRIGHT	JW	14	52
CARTWRIGHT	P	6	73
CARTWRIGHT	RC	4	69
CARTWRIGHT	S	2	58
CARTWRIGHT	T	11	65
CARTWRIGHT	T	14	52
CARTWRIGHT	W	8	58
CARTWRIGHT	W	13	79
CARTY	FJ	2	58
CARTY	J	11	65
CARTY	J	11	65
CARVEL	T	11	65
CARVELL	J	5	62
CARVELL	WA	7	60
CARVER	E	9	36
CARVER	F	8	58
CARVER	HJ	13	79
CARVER	W	10	40
CARWELL	WG	12	277
CARY	J	2	58
CARY	SC	1	53
CASASOLA	RW	14	52
CASBARD	S	2	58
CASBOLT	AR	3	299
CASBURN	SEV	12	43
CASBY	CD	12	43
CASBY	WCF	10	40
CASE	A	1	53
CASE	ACE	13	79
CASE	CA	13	79
CASE	CR	4	69
CASE	FW	13	79
CASE	J	2	58
CASELY	W	1	53
CASEMORE	GF	2	58
CASEY	AE	4	69
CASEY	C	2	58
CASEY	E	14	52
CASEY	F	8	58
CASEY	GR	14	52
CASEY	H	2	59
CASEY	J	2	59
CASEY	J	2	59
CASEY	J	8	58
CASEY	J	8	59
CASEY	J	8	59
CASEY	J	8	59
CASEY	J	8	59
CASEY	J	8	59
CASEY	J	11	65
CASEY	J	11	65
CASEY	J	12	43
CASEY	J	13	79
CASEY	J	14	52
CASEY	J	14	52
CASEY	J	14	52
CASEY	JJ	14	53
CASEY	JM	14	53
CASEY	M	11	65
CASEY	M	11	65
CASEY	M	14	53

CASEY	PF	11	65	CASSERLEY	J	11	66	CASTLEMAN	W	4	70	CATLING	EJ	5	63
CASEY	R	11	65	CASSERLEY	JB	14	53	CASTLES	RA	13	80	CATLING	J	11	66
CASEY	R	14	53	CASSFORD	WE	10	40	CASTLETON	B	10	40	CATLING	S	9	36
CASEY	T	5	63	CASSIDY	CS	10	276	CASTLETON	FA	3	299	CATLOW	F	8	59
CASEY	T	12	43	CASSIDY	EL	10	40	CASTLETON	HW	7	61	CATLOW	G	6	74
CASEY	TF	3	299	CASSIDY	H	13	80	CASTLING	HA	7	61	CATLOW	HW	11	66
CASEY	W	7	61	CASSIDY	HJ	10	40	CASTON	H	9	238	CATLOW	J	14	53
CASEY	W	11	66	CASSIDY	J	11	66	CASWELL	A	6	74	CATLOW	R	11	66
CASEY	W	14	53	CASSIDY	J	14	53	CASWELL	AE	6	74	CATLOW	WL	11	66
CASEY	W	14	53	CASSIDY	L	13	80	CASWELL	FW	6	74	CATMULL	CW	12	44
CASEY	WEJ	2	59	CASSIDY	LC	11	66	CASWELL	G	4	70	CATMULL	H	7	61
CASEY	WM	8	59	CASSIDY	M	14	53	CASWELL	GW	10	40	CATO	B	5	63
CASH	D	11	66	CASSIDY	P	2	59	CASWELL	H	1	53	CATO	W	2	59
CASH	E	6	73	CASSIDY	P	11	66	CASWELL	J	6	74	CATON	DW	8	59
CASH	EH	6	73	CASSIDY	R	14	53	CASWELL	WG	1	53	CATON	J	11	66
CASH	F	1	53	CASSIDY	VS	10	40	CATCHESIDES	AE	13	80	CATON	J	14	53
CASH	J	4	69	CASSIDY	W	14	53	CATCHESIDES	SG	13	80	CATT	JG	10	276
CASH	J	14	53	CASSIDY	WB	13	80	CATCHPOLE	C	13	80	CATT	WH	10	41
CASH	T	6	73	CASSIDY	WJ	10	40	CATCHPOLE	PE	3	299	CATT CAMFIELD	EC	2	59
CASH	W	6	74	CASSIDY	WS	3	299	CATCHPOLE	TI	3	32	CATTELL	A	6	74
CASH	W	6	74	CASSON	A	14	53	CATCHPOLE	WH	3	32	CATTELL	A	8	59
CASHIAN	J	11	66	CASSON	EM	10	276	CATCHPOLE	WH	7	61	CATTELL	A	12	278
CASHION	J	11	66	CASSON	GH	14	53	CATCHPOWLE	A	6	74	CATTELL	A	12	278
CASHMAN	E	13	79	CASSON	H	13	80	CATCHPOWLE	W	6	74	CATTELL	E	3	32
CASHMAN	W	13	79	CASSON	L	12	277	CATER	AG	13	81	CATTELL	EG	12	278
CASHMERE	M	13	79	CASSON	T	6	74	CATER	JW	1	53	CATTELL	GW	13	81
CASHMORE	CH	6	74	CASSWILL	LV	4	70	CATER	W	1	53	CATTELL	IW	6	74
CASHMORE	G	6	74	CASTELOW	A	8	59	CATER	W	3	299	CATTELL	M	3	32
CASHMORE	JE	6	74	CASTLE	A	5	63	CATERER	A	2	59	CATTELL	TW	12	278
CASHMORE	T	6	74	CASTLE	A	13	80	CATES	A	9	36	CATTELL	W	12	278
CASPARD	S	7	61	CASTLE	AE	7	61	CATES	H	9	36	CATTERALL	J	14	53
CASPER	J	11	66	CASTLE	AHC	7	61	CATES	WS	1	53	CATTERALL	J	14	54
CASS	AE	4	69	CASTLE	E	1	53	CATH	WG	13	81	CATTERICK	RE	8	60
CASS	F	8	59	CASTLE	E	6	74	CATHERALL	G	8	59	CATTERMOLE	AFG	10	41
CASS	F	8	59	CASTLE	EA	10	40	CATHERALL	H	8	59	CATTERMOLE	FC	7	61
CASS	G	8	59	CASTLE	EA	13	80	CATHERALL	W	8	59	CATTERMOLE	WG	1	53
CASS	HB	8	59	CASTLE	F	5	63	CATHERSIDES	EJ	13	81	CATTERMOLE	WT	1	53
CASS	JE	13	79	CASTLE	FG	5	63	CATHERSIDES	GW	13	81	CATTERMORE	CE	6	74
CASS	JP	8	59	CASTLE	FW	2	59	CATHERSIDES	JA	13	81	CATTLE	AB	13	81
CASS	SW	13	80	CASTLE	G	1	53	CATLEY	A	8	59	CATTLE	AC	6	75
CASS	W	10	40	CASTLE	G	7	61	CATLEY	HC	13	81	CATTLE	CH	8	60
CASS	WF	3	32	CASTLE	GE	1	53	CATLIN	A	5	63	CATTLEY	E	3	300
CASS	WG	7	61	CASTLE	GH	10	276	CATLIN	A	13	81	CATTLEY	T	8	60
CASS	WH	3	32	CASTLE	HF	13	80	CATLIN	AS	1	53	CATTLEY	W	8	60
CASSEDY	AJ	4	70	CASTLE	J	11	66	CATLIN	ES	7	61	CATTON	FJ	3	300
CASSEL-CLEMMET	W	10	275	CASTLE	JE	1	53	CATLIN	F	5	63	CATTON	W	8	60
CASSELDEN	F	1	53	CASTLE	S	3	299	CATLIN	FJ	5	63	CATTON	W	8	60
CASSELL	A	13	80	CASTLE	TA	13	80	CATLIN	G	5	63	CATTON	W	8	60
CASSELL	EH	10	276	CASTLE	TJ	1	53	CATLIN	HW	13	81	CATTON	WA	7	61
CASSELL	H	1	53	CASTLE	W	5	63	CATLIN	J	11	66	CATTON	WJ	5	63
CASSELL	J	6	74	CASTLE	W	13	80	CATLIN	J	11	66	CATTON	WJ	6	75
CASSELL	J	13	80	CASTLE	WG	13	80	CATLIN	J	12	43	CATTRALL	RG	4	70
CASSELL	J	14	53	CASTLE	WJ	13	80	CATLIN	V	12	44	CAUDELL	SL	6	75
CASSELL	T	12	43	CASTLEMAN	F	4	70	CATLIN	W	5	63	CAUDERY	GH	1	54
CASSERLEY	AH	6	74	CASTLEMAN	F	12	43	CATLING	CR	5	63	CAUDERY	N	1	54

CAUDLE	C	1	54	CAVE	E	12	278	CAWS	CW	4	70	CHADWICK	GA	14	54
CAUDWELL	J	11	66	CAVE	EH	10	276	CAWS	JN	4	70	CHADWICK	H	8	61
CAUDWELL	O	12	278	CAVE	EM	2	59	CAWS	W	4	70	CHADWICK	H	8	61
CAULDERWOOD	H	9	238	CAVE	F	12	278	CAWS	WE	4	70	CHADWICK	H	14	54
CAULDWELL	F	1	54	CAVE	GH	12	278	CAWSON	RJ	7	61	CHADWICK	HA	4	71
CAULDWELL	F	14	54	CAVE	GH	13	81	CAWTE	B	4	70	CHADWICK	I	8	61
CAULEY	J	8	60	CAVE	H	2	59	CAWTE	CS	10	276	CHADWICK	J	11	68
CAULEY	W	8	60	CAVE	H	13	81	CAWTE	EA	4	70	CHADWICK	J	11	68
CAULTER	E	8	60	CAVE	H	13	81	CAWTE	H	10	41	CHADWICK	J	11	68
CAUNCE	G	11	67	CAVE	HC	7	61	CAWTE	J	10	41	CHADWICK	J	14	55
CAUNCE	R	14	54	CAVE	HF	4	70	CAWTE	J	10	41	CHADWICK	J	14	55
CAUNT	HP	4	70	CAVE	JT	12	278	CAWTE	WG	4	71	CHADWICK	JJ	7	62
CAUSER	C	14	54	CAVE	LP	6	75	CAWTHERAY	H	8	60	CHADWICK	JJ	11	68
CAUSER	J	11	67	CAVE	MW	12	278	CAWTHORNE	J	2	60	CHADWICK	JT	14	55
CAUSER	T	6	75	CAVE	S	14	54	CAWTHRA	A	9	238	CHADWICK	JW	8	61
CAUSER	T	14	54	CAVE	TW	5	63	CAWTHRA	H	9	36	CHADWICK	LV	13	82
CAUSER	TG	3	300	CAVE	W	9	36	CAWTHRA	H	9	382	CHADWICK	R	14	55
CAUSFIELD	W	9	36	CAVE	W	12	278	CAWTHRA	TH	9	238	CHADWICK	RK	7	62
CAUSON	FA	3	300	CAVE	WH	8	60	CAWTHRAY	C	8	60	CHADWICK	T	8	61
CAUSON	J	6	75	CAVE	WJ	13	81	CAWTHRAY	W	8	60	CHADWICK	T	10	41
CAUSON	WE	6	75	CAVELL	CB	1	54	CAYTON	W	11	67	CHADWICK	T	14	55
CAUSSIDIERE	FA	11	67	CAVELL	FJ	4	70	CAYWOOD	G	8	61	CHADWICK	TW	11	68
CAUSTIN	J	2	59	CAVELL	JB	6	75	CAZZAMALI	C	2	60	CHADWICK	W	8	61
CAUSTIN	L	2	59	CAVELL	SH	1	54	CECIL	A	3	300	CHADWICK	W	9	239
CAUSTIN	WL	13	81	CAVENDISH	H	13	82	CECIL	F	9	36	CHADWICK	W	11	68
CAUSTON	C	9	36	CAVENEY	ED	11	67	CECIL	W	3	33	CHADWICK	W	11	68
CAVALIER	A	2	59	CAVENEY	R	4	70	CECIL	W	10	41	CHADWICK	W	14	55
CAVALIER	V	2	59	CAVENEY	W	11	67	CENGI	N	2	60	CHADWICK	WJ	14	55
CAVANAGH	CH	11	67	CAVENEY	WE	6	75	CERVI	B	11	67	CHAFE	TW	4	71
CAVANAGH	E	11	67	CAVES	CW	12	44	CESSARE	A	1	54	CHAFE	WH	4	71
CAVANAGH	E	12	44	CAVES	H	12	44	CESSARE	J	1	54	CHAFEN	AM	4	71
CAVANAGH	F	11	67	CAVES	HC	5	63	CESSARE	W	1	54	CHAFEN	M	4	71
CAVANAGH	J	2	59	CAVILL	CB	1	54	CHABLE	R	13	82	CHAFER	G	2	60
CAVANAGH	J	5	63	CAVILLA	RJ	7	61	CHAD	W	3	33	CHAFEY	AW	3	300
CAVANAGH	J	11	67	CAWDELL	H	5	63	CHADAWAY	E	6	75	CHAFFE	GF	7	62
CAVANAGH	J	14	54	CAWDELL	S	5	64	CHADBURN	W	9	238	CHAFFE	WH	7	62
CAVANAGH	JJ	4	70	CAWDRON	RH	2	59	CHADD	B	7	61	CHAFFER	G	9	239
CAVANAGH	M	4	70	CAWDRY	E	9	382	CHADD	F	10	41	CHAFFERS	WH	3	33
CAVANAGH	M	9	381	CAWKWELL	JC	9	36	CHADD	F	11	67	CHAINEY	C	7	62
CAVANAGH	MP	2	59	CAWLEY	A	11	67	CHADD	TH	14	54	CHAINEY	F	4	71
CAVANAGH	P	8	60	CAWLEY	B	11	67	CHADDICK	MA	6	75	CHAINEY	F	7	62
CAVANAGH	P	11	67	CAWLEY	F	11	67	CHADWICK	A	8	61	CHAINEY	G	7	62
CAVANAGH	T	11	67	CAWLEY	F	14	54	CHADWICK	A	8	61	CHAINEY	H	4	71
CAVANAGH	T	14	54	CAWLEY	FW	3	33	CHADWICK	A	9	238	CHAISTY	R	10	41
CAVANAGH	TM	4	70	CAWLEY	H	11	67	CHADWICK	A	14	54	CHALCROFT	WH	3	300
CAVANAGH	W	6	75	CAWLEY	H	14	54	CHADWICK	A	14	54	CHALDERLEY	E	12	44
CAVANAGH	W	11	67	CAWOOD	A	8	60	CHADWICK	AJ	12	278	CHALDERLEY	J	12	44
CAVANAGH	WJ	4	70	CAWOOD	A	8	60	CHADWICK	B	3	300	CHALDERLEY	J	12	44
CAVANAH	F	14	54	CAWOOD	E	9	382	CHADWICK	DR	14	54	CHALK	A	1	54
CAVE	AGH	13	81	CAWOOD	F	8	60	CHADWICK	F	6	75	CHALK	AJ	4	71
CAVE	AJ	13	81	CAWOOD	F	8	60	CHADWICK	F	11	68	CHALK	D	4	71
CAVE	AJ	13	81	CAWOOD	F	9	238	CHADWICK	F	14	54	CHALK	DE	4	71
CAVE	BG	12	278	CAWOOD	H	8	60	CHADWICK	FW	8	61	CHALK	ET	1	54
CAVE	C	9	36	CAWOOD	SB	8	60	CHADWICK	G	7	61	CHALK	EV	1	54
CAVE	CW	12	278	CAWOOD	W	9	238	CHADWICK	G	11	68	CHALK	F	5	64

CHALK	FE	1	54	CHALMERS	AH	10	276	CHAMBERLAIN	W	8	61	CHAMBERS	RA	2	60
CHALK	FL	4	71	CHALMERS	AJ	10	41	CHAMBERLAIN	W	11	68	CHAMBERS	RE	13	82
CHALK	GA	1	54	CHALMERS	E	10	41	CHAMBERLAIN	W	12	44	CHAMBERS	S	1	55
CHALK	GH	1	54	CHALMERS	FA	10	41	CHAMBERLAIN	WF	5	64	CHAMBERS	S	8	62
CHALK	HW	1	54	CHALMERS	FAB	10	41	CHAMBERLAIN	WJ	10	42	CHAMBERS	S	12	279
CHALK	JA	1	54	CHALMERS	GE	13	82	CHAMBERLAIN	WR	10	42	CHAMBERS	SC	12	45
CHALK	JK	7	62	CHALMERS	GF	4	72	CHAMBERLIN	JE	7	62	CHAMBERS	SG	3	300
CHALK	JW	4	71	CHALMERS	H	10	41	CHAMBERLIN	TA	1	55	CHAMBERS	SG	13	82
CHALK	LC	10	276	CHALMERS	JC	13	82	CHAMBERS	A	2	60	CHAMBERS	T	3	33
CHALK	N	1	54	CHALMERS	JE	10	41	CHAMBERS	A	4	72	CHAMBERS	T	6	76
CHALK	R	2	60	CHALMERS	O	14	55	CHAMBERS	A	6	75	CHAMBERS	T	7	62
CHALK	R	4	71	CHALMERS	RO	13	82	CHAMBERS	A	11	68	CHAMBERS	TA	10	42
CHALK	SW	4	71	CHALMERS	TD	10	276	CHAMBERS	A	12	44	CHAMBERS	TH	8	62
CHALK	T	4	71	CHALMERS	V	9	239	CHAMBERS	A	12	278	CHAMBERS	TW	1	55
CHALK	TA	1	54	CHALMERS	W	10	41	CHAMBERS	AE	13	82	CHAMBERS	VS	1	55
CHALK	W	1	54	CHALONER	E	11	68	CHAMBERS	AV	12	44	CHAMBERS	W	8	62
CHALK	W	4	71	CHALONER	H	11	68	CHAMBERS	AWR	12	44	CHAMBERS	W	9	36
CHALK	W	13	82	CHALONER	R	11	68	CHAMBERS	E	7	62	CHAMBERS	W	12	45
CHALK	WG	1	54	CHAMBERLAIN	A	1	54	CHAMBERS	EA	1	55	CHAMBERS	W	14	55
CHALK	WG	4	71	CHAMBERLAIN	A	13	82	CHAMBERS	EE	12	44	CHAMBERS	WA	1	55
CHALK	WJ	4	71	CHAMBERLAIN	AJ	2	60	CHAMBERS	EE	12	44	CHAMBERS	WC	4	72
CHALKE	GF	4	72	CHAMBERLAIN	AJ	12	278	CHAMBERS	ET	12	45	CHAMBERS	WC	12	279
CHALKER	A	7	62	CHAMBERLAIN	B	10	276	CHAMBERS	F	6	76	CHAMBERS	WG	10	276
CHALKLEY	A	5	64	CHAMBERLAIN	C	1	54	CHAMBERS	FH	4	72	CHAMBERS	WJ	5	65
CHALKLEY	H	5	64	CHAMBERLAIN	C	3	33	CHAMBERS	FH	13	82	CHAMBERS	WJE	14	55
CHALKLEY	H	5	64	CHAMBERLAIN	C	7	62	CHAMBERS	FW	2	60	CHAMLEY	M	14	55
CHALKLEY	H	5	64	CHAMBERLAIN	C	12	44	CHAMBERS	FW	2	60	CHAMMINGS	HF	7	62
CHALKLEY	P	5	64	CHAMBERLAIN	E	12	44	CHAMBERS	G	2	60	CHAMP	A	13	83
CHALKLEY	PG	1	54	CHAMBERLAIN	F	3	300	CHAMBERS	G	2	60	CHAMP	AHW	1	55
CHALKLEY	S	5	64	CHAMBERLAIN	F	3	300	CHAMBERS	G	8	61	CHAMP	G	13	82
CHALKLEY	S	5	64	CHAMBERLAIN	F	3	300	CHAMBERS	G	13	82	CHAMP	WH	7	62
CHALKLEY	W	5	64	CHAMBERLAIN	G	4	72	CHAMBERS	GE	3	300	CHAMPION		7	62
CHALLEN	H	3	300	CHAMBERLAIN	G	12	44	CHAMBERS	GH	5	64	CHAMPION	A	3	300
CHALLENDER	W	14	55	CHAMBERLAIN	H	1	54	CHAMBERS	GH	8	61	CHAMPION	AD	1	55
CHALLENER	H	6	75	CHAMBERLAIN	H	3	33	CHAMBERS	GV	1	55	CHAMPION	AG	3	300
CHALLINGSWORTH	SG	6	75	CHAMBERLAIN	H	5	64	CHAMBERS	GW	3	300	CHAMPION	F	3	301
CHALLINOR	A	11	68	CHAMBERLAIN	H	5	64	CHAMBERS	GW	10	276	CHAMPION	F	3	301
CHALLINOR	J	14	55	CHAMBERLAIN	H	5	64	CHAMBERS	H	5	64	CHAMPION	GF	7	63
CHALLINOR	JJ	7	62	CHAMBERLAIN	HJ	5	64	CHAMBERS	H	5	64	CHAMPION	H	3	33
CHALLIS	E	5	64	CHAMBERLAIN	J	5	64	CHAMBERS	H	5	65	CHAMPION	H	7	63
CHALLIS	E	13	82	CHAMBERLAIN	J	8	61	CHAMBERS	H	5	65	CHAMPION	J	2	60
CHALLIS	H	8	61	CHAMBERLAIN	J	10	41	CHAMBERS	HN	5	65	CHAMPION	JE	7	63
CHALLIS	H	10	41	CHAMBERLAIN	JG	6	75	CHAMBERS	J	2	60	CHAMPION	JW	7	63
CHALLIS	J	8	61	CHAMBERLAIN	JH	6	75	CHAMBERS	J	5	65	CHAMPION	L	3	301
CHALLIS	K	8	61	CHAMBERLAIN	JW	10	41	CHAMBERS	J	6	76	CHAMPION	WG	1	55
CHALLIS	M	8	61	CHAMBERLAIN	JW	12	44	CHAMBERS	J	11	68	CHAMPKIN	E	13	83
CHALLIS	R	3	33	CHAMBERLAIN	L	11	68	CHAMBERS	JA	1	55	CHAMPKIN	F	5	65
CHALLIS	SE	13	82	CHAMBERLAIN	M	2	60	CHAMBERS	JE	6	76	CHAMPKIN	J	13	83
CHALLIS	TG	13	82	CHAMBERLAIN	M	4	72	CHAMBERS	JE	6	76	CHAMPKINS	A	5	65
CHALLIS	W	2	60	CHAMBERLAIN	MM	10	41	CHAMBERS	JTT	12	278	CHAMPKINS	EM	7	63
CHALLONER	FG	13	82	CHAMBERLAIN	NS	14	55	CHAMBERS	L	12	45	CHAMPLIN	R	8	62
CHALLONER	T	12	278	CHAMBERLAIN	R	3	33	CHAMBERS	O	8	61	CHAMPNEY	GE	1	55
CHALLONER	W	11	68	CHAMBERLAIN	SF	2	60	CHAMBERS	P	3	300	CHAMPNEY	RW	1	55
CHALLONER	W	14	55	CHAMBERLAIN	T	12	278	CHAMBERS	PH	13	82	CHAMPNEY	RW	1	55
CHALMERS	A	10	41	CHAMBERLAIN	TH	7	62	CHAMBERS	R	12	279	CHAMPNISS	EE	13	83

CHANCE	A	5	65	CHANDLER	JEJ	7	63	CHANTER	R	9	239	CHAPMAN	C	5	66
CHANCE	AW	2	60	CHANDLER	JG	1	55	CHANTRELL	B	11	69	CHAPMAN	C	6	76
CHANCE	E	5	65	CHANDLER	JJ	1	55	CHANTRY	B	7	63	CHAPMAN	CB	13	83
CHANCE	FG	5	65	CHANDLER	JT	12	45	CHAPELL	A	11	69	CHAPMAN	CF	13	83
CHANCE	G	5	65	CHANDLER	JT	12	45	CHAPERLIN	WH	3	301	CHAPMAN	CH	13	83
CHANCE	GH	5	65	CHANDLER	KA	10	276	CHAPLAIN	E	6	76	CHAPMAN	CH	13	83
CHANCE	H	5	65	CHANDLER	L	10	42	CHAPLAIN	F	12	45	CHAPMAN	CR	10	276
CHANCE	H	5	65	CHANDLER	L	12	45	CHAPLAIN	W	12	45	CHAPMAN	CW	1	56
CHANCE	H	6	76	CHANDLER	M	8	62	CHAPLIN	A	12	279	CHAPMAN	CW	13	83
CHANCE	H	6	76	CHANDLER	ML	8	62	CHAPLIN	AM	3	301	CHAPMAN	D	3	33
CHANCE	LHP	6	76	CHANDLER	PH	5	65	CHAPLIN	AW	3	301	CHAPMAN	DHC	2	61
CHANCE	P	5	65	CHANDLER	R	10	42	CHAPLIN	C	4	73	CHAPMAN	E	1	56
CHANCE	P	6	76	CHANDLER	R	13	83	CHAPLIN	C	12	279	CHAPMAN	E	13	84
CHANCE	R	2	60	CHANDLER	RA	14	55	CHAPLIN	CR	2	61	CHAPMAN	EG	12	279
CHANCE	SH	2	61	CHANDLER	RH	11	69	CHAPLIN	F	3	33	CHAPMAN	EG	13	83
CHANCE	SJ	7	63	CHANDLER	RJ	10	42	CHAPLIN	F	12	279	CHAPMAN	EGT	13	84
CHANDLER	A	8	62	CHANDLER	RJ	12	279	CHAPLIN	G	2	61	CHAPMAN	EH	2	61
CHANDLER	A	12	45	CHANDLER	S	5	66	CHAPLIN	G	2	61	CHAPMAN	EL	6	76
CHANDLER	AB	1	55	CHANDLER	S	12	45	CHAPLIN	H	12	279	CHAPMAN	F	1	56
CHANDLER	ACH	3	33	CHANDLER	S	13	83	CHAPLIN	HOA	13	83	CHAPMAN	F	5	66
CHANDLER	AE	5	65	CHANDLER	SA	14	55	CHAPLIN	J	1	56	CHAPMAN	F	7	63
CHANDLER	AG	10	42	CHANDLER	SF	7	63	CHAPLIN	JT	6	76	CHAPMAN	F	8	62
CHANDLER	AH	4	72	CHANDLER	SH	5	66	CHAPLIN	P	12	279	CHAPMAN	F	8	62
CHANDLER	AR	3	301	CHANDLER	SS	12	45	CHAPLIN	R	1	56	CHAPMAN	F	9	36
CHANDLER	AT	2	61	CHANDLER	T	1	55	CHAPLIN	RH	6	76	CHAPMAN	F	9	36
CHANDLER	C	10	42	CHANDLER	T	1	56	CHAPLIN	T	12	279	CHAPMAN	F	12	279
CHANDLER	CE	12	45	CHANDLER	T	4	72	CHAPLIN	WJ	1	56	CHAPMAN	F	13	84
CHANDLER	CH	4	72	CHANDLER	TJ	12	45	CHAPLIN	WS	6	76	CHAPMAN	FC	13	83
CHANDLER	CW	3	301	CHANDLER	W	5	66	CHAPMAN	A	3	301	CHAPMAN	FE	1	56
CHANDLER	CW	4	72	CHANDLER	W	10	42	CHAPMAN	A	5	66	CHAPMAN	FE	12	279
CHANDLER	E	5	65	CHANDLER	WA	1	56	CHAPMAN	A	9	36	CHAPMAN	FG	10	42
CHANDLER	ET	2	61	CHANDLER	WA	14	55	CHAPMAN	A	9	239	CHAPMAN	FJ	3	33
CHANDLER	F	3	301	CHANDLER	WF	7	63	CHAPMAN	A	12	45	CHAPMAN	FW	12	279
CHANDLER	F	4	72	CHANDLER	WH	5	66	CHAPMAN	A	12	279	CHAPMAN	G	1	56
CHANDLER	F	5	65	CHANDLER	WH	12	45	CHAPMAN	A	13	83	CHAPMAN	G	3	301
CHANDLER	F	13	83	CHANDLER	WHJ	12	45	CHAPMAN	A	14	55	CHAPMAN	G	5	66
CHANDLER	FA	1	55	CHANDLER	WL	1	56	CHAPMAN	A	14	56	CHAPMAN	G	6	76
CHANDLER	FE	4	72	CHANDLER	WL	3	33	CHAPMAN	AE	12	45	CHAPMAN	G	8	62
CHANDLER	FJ	1	55	CHANDLER	WT	3	301	CHAPMAN	AG	2	61	CHAPMAN	G	9	37
CHANDLER	FJ	7	63	CHANDLER	WT	4	72	CHAPMAN	AG	7	63	CHAPMAN	G	13	84
CHANDLER	FR	4	72	CHANDLER	WT	5	66	CHAPMAN	AG	12	279	CHAPMAN	G	13	84
CHANDLER	GA	1	55	CHANDLER	WT	5	66	CHAPMAN	AH	1	56	CHAPMAN	G	13	84
CHANDLER	GA	1	55	CHANEY	T	3	33	CHAPMAN	AH	3	33	CHAPMAN	G	14	56
CHANDLER	GA	2	61	CHANEY	TC	3	33	CHAPMAN	AH	3	301	CHAPMAN	G	14	56
CHANDLER	GA	7	63	CHANNELL	J	4	72	CHAPMAN	AJ	7	63	CHAPMAN	GA	10	276
CHANDLER	H	10	42	CHANNELL	T	4	73	CHAPMAN	AJ	13	83	CHAPMAN	GA	12	279
CHANDLER	H	13	83	CHANNELL	WH	1	56	CHAPMAN	AJ	14	56	CHAPMAN	GE	1	56
CHANDLER	H	13	83	CHANNER	E	1	56	CHAPMAN	AJS	2	61	CHAPMAN	GE	13	84
CHANDLER	HA	4	72	CHANNER	H	1	56	CHAPMAN	AW	5	66	CHAPMAN	GF	1	56
CHANDLER	HL	12	279	CHANNER	H	1	56	CHAPMAN	B	5	66	CHAPMAN	GH	1	56
CHANDLER	HW	1	55	CHANNER	JA	7	63	CHAPMAN	B	12	279	CHAPMAN	GW	4	73
CHANDLER	J	3	301	CHANNING	HC	1	56	CHAPMAN	C	1	56	CHAPMAN	GW	6	76
CHANDLER	J	4	72	CHANNING	HC	5	66	CHAPMAN	C	3	301	CHAPMAN	GW	9	37
CHANDLER	J	4	72	CHANNON	AC	10	42	CHAPMAN	C	5	66	CHAPMAN	H	1	56
CHANDLER	JC	5	65	CHANT	WC	4	73	CHAPMAN	C	5	66	CHAPMAN	H	4	73

CHAPMAN	H	6	77
CHAPMAN	H	9	37
CHAPMAN	H	9	239
CHAPMAN	H	13	84
CHAPMAN	H	14	56
CHAPMAN	HB	2	61
CHAPMAN	HCP	10	276
CHAPMAN	HF	12	45
CHAPMAN	HJ	2	61
CHAPMAN	HJ	4	73
CHAPMAN	HO	3	301
CHAPMAN	HW	6	77
CHAPMAN	I	14	56
CHAPMAN	J	1	56
CHAPMAN	J	1	57
CHAPMAN	J	3	301
CHAPMAN	J	5	66
CHAPMAN	J	6	77
CHAPMAN	J	6	77
CHAPMAN	J	7	63
CHAPMAN	J	8	62
CHAPMAN	J	8	62
CHAPMAN	J	8	62
CHAPMAN	J	8	62
CHAPMAN	J	11	69
CHAPMAN	J	12	46
CHAPMAN	J	12	46
CHAPMAN	J	12	46
CHAPMAN	J	12	279
CHAPMAN	J	13	84
CHAPMAN	J	13	84
CHAPMAN	J	13	84
CHAPMAN	J	13	84
CHAPMAN	J	14	56
CHAPMAN	J	14	56
CHAPMAN	JA	13	84
CHAPMAN	JH	7	63
CHAPMAN	JH	13	84
CHAPMAN	JR	14	56
CHAPMAN	JS	13	84
CHAPMAN	JT	8	62
CHAPMAN	JW	3	34
CHAPMAN	JW	8	62
CHAPMAN	JW	11	69
CHAPMAN	JW	12	46
CHAPMAN	JW	14	56
CHAPMAN	L	8	62
CHAPMAN	L	11	69
CHAPMAN	L	12	280
CHAPMAN	L	12	280
CHAPMAN	LJ	7	63
CHAPMAN	NG	4	73
CHAPMAN	NG	4	73
CHAPMAN	P	8	62
CHAPMAN	P	12	280
CHAPMAN	P	14	56
CHAPMAN	PP	12	280
CHAPMAN	R	2	61
CHAPMAN	R	13	84
CHAPMAN	RE	1	57
CHAPMAN	RJ	9	239
CHAPMAN	S	2	61
CHAPMAN	S	9	239
CHAPMAN	S	12	280
CHAPMAN	S	14	56
CHAPMAN	SB	11	69
CHAPMAN	SC	10	42
CHAPMAN	SJ	1	57
CHAPMAN	SJ	1	57
CHAPMAN	SJ	5	66
CHAPMAN	T	2	61
CHAPMAN	T	4	73
CHAPMAN	T	8	62
CHAPMAN	T	8	62
CHAPMAN	T	9	239
CHAPMAN	T	10	42
CHAPMAN	T	12	280
CHAPMAN	TE	8	62
CHAPMAN	TW	10	276
CHAPMAN	V	5	66
CHAPMAN	W	2	61
CHAPMAN	W	3	302
CHAPMAN	W	5	66
CHAPMAN	W	7	64
CHAPMAN	W	8	63
CHAPMAN	W	12	280
CHAPMAN	W	13	84
CHAPMAN	W	14	56
CHAPMAN	WAA	10	42
CHAPMAN	WC	10	42
CHAPMAN	WC	14	56
CHAPMAN	WF	1	57
CHAPMAN	WF	12	280
CHAPMAN	WG	1	57
CHAPMAN	WH	4	73
CHAPMAN	WH	9	239
CHAPMAN	WH	14	56
CHAPMAN	WJ	7	64
CHAPMAN	WT	13	84
CHAPPEL	A	8	63
CHAPPEL	H	5	67
CHAPPEL	H	8	63
CHAPPELL	A	9	37
CHAPPELL	AE	5	67
CHAPPELL	AH	2	61
CHAPPELL	ASS	5	67
CHAPPELL	AW	7	64
CHAPPELL	C	5	67
CHAPPELL	C	13	85
CHAPPELL	C	14	56
CHAPPELL	EG	1	57
CHAPPELL	EG	5	67
CHAPPELL	FA	13	85
CHAPPELL	GL	5	67
CHAPPELL	J	2	62
CHAPPELL	J	9	239
CHAPPELL	J	12	280
CHAPPELL	JE	7	64
CHAPPELL	JE	7	64
CHAPPELL	JG	7	64
CHAPPELL	JH	7	64
CHAPPELL	PJ	10	42
CHAPPELL	R	3	302
CHAPPELL	SE	3	34
CHAPPELL	W	2	62
CHAPPELL	WE	1	57
CHAPPELOW	H	8	63
CHAPPLE	AE	1	57
CHAPPLE	CJ	2	61
CHAPPLE	H	7	64
CHAPPLE	H	7	64
CHAPPLE	JS	4	73
CHAPPLES	W	11	69
CHARD	EG	12	46
CHARD	JR	7	64
CHARD	WE	7	64
CHARGE	J	5	67
CHARGE	R	5	67
CHARIE	H	3	302
CHARKER	T	1	57
CHARKER	T	7	64
CHARLAND	W	2	62
CHARLES	A	2	62
CHARLES	AGC	5	67
CHARLES	ED	2	62
CHARLES	F	8	63
CHARLES	FT	2	62
CHARLES	G	7	64
CHARLES	GW	9	37
CHARLES	H	2	62
CHARLES	H	2	62
CHARLES	H	5	67
CHARLES	H	7	64
CHARLES	M	7	64
CHARLES	R	8	63
CHARLES	R	8	63
CHARLES	W	2	62
CHARLES	W	7	64
CHARLES	W	11	69
CHARLESON	A	14	56
CHARLESON	A	14	56
CHARLESON	F	14	57
CHARLESON	T	14	57
CHARLESWORTH	AJ	3	302
CHARLESWORTH	B	13	85
CHARLESWORTH	E	8	63
CHARLESWORTH	EV	3	34
CHARLESWORTH	G	11	69
CHARLESWORTH	GH	13	85
CHARLESWORTH	S	9	239
CHARLESWORTH	SJ	10	277
CHARLESWORTH	T	8	63
CHARLETT	JT	1	57
CHARLTON	A	11	69
CHARLTON	AJ	1	57
CHARLTON	F	6	77
CHARLTON	F	9	37
CHARLTON	HA	3	302
CHARLTON	J	9	382
CHARLTON	R	14	57
CHARLTON	S	6	77
CHARLTON	T	9	37
CHARLTON	T	13	85
CHARLTON	T	14	57
CHARLTON	WG	2	62
CHARLTON	WG	4	73
CHARLTON	WT	4	73
CHARLWOOD	H	3	34
CHARMAN	A	2	62
CHARMAN	A	13	85
CHARMAN	AGH	10	277
CHARMAN	AR	7	64
CHARMAN	E	9	37
CHARMAN	EW	10	277
CHARMAN	FE	7	64
CHARMAN	FG	2	62
CHARMAN	H	7	64
CHARMAN	J	7	65
CHARMAN	JH	13	85
CHARMAN	W	13	85
CHARNLEY	RR	13	85
CHARNOCK	G	5	67
CHARNOCK	J	14	57
CHARNOCK	JS	9	239
CHARNOCK	L	11	69
CHARNOCK	R	11	69
CHARNOCK	S	8	63
CHARRETT	GJH	4	73
CHARRETT	W	4	73
CHARRINGTON	P	13	85
CHART	AE	7	65
CHART	GJS	13	85
CHART	HJ	7	65
CHART	HR	7	65
CHARTER	AR	5	67
CHARTER	HJ	1	57
CHARTER	TJ	5	67
CHARTERS	SH	2	62
CHARTERS	W	11	69
CHARVILL	EG	12	280

CHARVILL	HG	12	280	CHEATER	HW	4	74	CHENERY	W	4	74	CHESHIRE	FW	5	68
CHASE	A	1	57	CHECKETTS	A	6	77	CHENERY	WE	13	86	CHESHIRE	HJ	5	68
CHASE	A	10	277	CHECKETTS	EG	6	77	CHENEY	E	13	86	CHESHIRE	JJ	2	63
CHASE	AE	10	42	CHECKETTS	FR	6	77	CHENEY	FW	10	277	CHESHIRE	LW	5	68
CHASE	F	5	67	CHECKLEY	F	6	77	CHENEY	GW	10	277	CHESHIRE	R	5	68
CHASE	FW	10	277	CHECKLEY	J	6	77	CHENEY	J	10	277	CHESHIRE	R	6	78
CHASE	G	3	34	CHECKLEY	W	9	382	CHENEY	J	12	46	CHESHIRE	RG	5	68
CHASE	G	10	42	CHECKLEY	WD	12	280	CHENEY	JW	12	280	CHESHIRE	TJ	6	78
CHASE	HJ	10	43	CHECKLING	S	6	78	CHENEY	TJS	10	277	CHESHIRE	TJ	13	86
CHASE	P	11	69	CHEDZEY	A	3	302	CHENEY	WHH	10	277	CHESHIRE	W	6	78
CHASE	WA	5	67	CHEEK	LW	2	62	CHENEY	WJ	2	62	CHESHIRE	WC	7	65
CHASE	WT	5	67	CHEESE	AA	7	65	CHERER	HA	13	86	CHESHIRE	WH	6	78
CHASMAR	FA	3	302	CHEESE	R	6	78	CHERRETT	CF	4	74	CHESHIRE	WH	6	78
CHASMAR	FA	7	65	CHEESEMAN	C	3	302	CHERRETT	E	4	74	CHESHIRE	WV	2	63
CHASTON	G	7	65	CHEESEMAN	CJ	13	85	CHERRETT	GA	4	74	CHESHIRE	WWW	5	68
CHASTY	J	14	57	CHEESEMAN	F	13	85	CHERRETT	HJ	4	74	CHESLEY	CA	2	63
CHATER	D	7	65	CHEESEMAN	G	13	85	CHERRETT	J	4	74	CHESLIN	R	6	78
CHATER	GS	6	77	CHEESEMAN	H	13	85	CHERRETT	J	10	43	CHESNEY	J	11	70
CHATER	HW	12	280	CHEESEMAN	H	13	85	CHERRETT	JC	4	74	CHESNEY	V	8	63
CHATER	JH	12	46	CHEESEMAN	H	13	85	CHERRETT	S	4	74	CHESSBROUGH	J	11	70
CHATER	R	1	57	CHEESEMAN	HW	3	302	CHERRIE	J	3	302	CHESSELL	HS	3	302
CHATER	TL	12	280	CHEESEMAN	J	12	46	CHERRILL	A	6	78	CHESSHIRE	JA	6	78
CHATFIELD	H	6	77	CHEESMAN	A	10	43	CHERRILL	H	2	63	CHESSHYRE	F	11	70
CHATFIELD	PC	4	73	CHEESMAN	AC	10	277	CHERRILL	J	7	65	CHESSUM	E	5	68
CHATFIELD	WH	2	62	CHEESMAN	AT	4	74	CHERRILL	RE	7	65	CHESSUM	W	2	63
CHATHAM	G	1	57	CHEESMAN	B	10	43	CHERRINGTON	AT	6	78	CHESSUN	CJ	7	65
CHATTAWAY	R	9	382	CHEESMAN	G	10	43	CHERRINGTON	AT	6	78	CHESSUN	G	3	302
CHATTELL	H	12	46	CHEESMAN	RAR	10	43	CHERRINGTON	B	6	78	CHESTER	A	4	74
CHATTEN	EM	5	67	CHEESMAN	RS	4	74	CHERRINGTON	HI	6	78	CHESTER	C	12	46
CHATTERLEY	JW	6	77	CHEESMAN	W	5	67	CHERRITT	FH	4	74	CHESTER	CJ	13	86
CHATTERS	PJ	12	280	CHEESMAN	W	7	65	CHERRITT	WC	4	74	CHESTER	F	5	68
CHATTERTON	HF	1	57	CHEESMAN	W	10	277	CHERRY	A	5	68	CHESTER	F	5	69
CHATTERTON	J	7	65	CHEESMORE	F	10	277	CHERRY	A	9	37	CHESTER	HT	13	86
CHATTERTON	J	14	57	CHEETHAM	A	13	85	CHERRY	A	12	46	CHESTER	M	3	302
CHATTERTON	JC	11	69	CHEETHAM	CH	14	57	CHERRY	AJ	6	78	CHESTER	RW	10	277
CHATTERTON	L	11	69	CHEETHAM	CJ	12	280	CHERRY	CE	9	37	CHESTERMAN	DJ	3	302
CHATTERTON	P	14	57	CHEETHAM	E	8	63	CHERRY	CF	7	65	CHESTERS	E	14	57
CHATTERTON	RJ	11	69	CHEETHAM	G	8	63	CHERRY	F	6	78	CHESTERS	W	11	70
CHATTERTON	T	14	57	CHEETHAM	H	11	69	CHERRY	JA	2	63	CHESTERTON	AE	2	63
CHATTERTON	W	1	57	CHEETHAM	H	11	70	CHERRY	JH	5	68	CHESTERTON	J	2	63
CHATWIN	A	6	77	CHEETHAM	JH	8	63	CHERRY	LC	6	78	CHESWORTH	A	10	43
CHATWIN	J	13	85	CHEETHAM	JJ	14	57	CHERRY	RH	5	68	CHESWORTH	AC	3	302
CHATWIN	WJ	6	77	CHEETHAM	JL	14	57	CHERRY	W	6	78	CHESWORTH	F	11	70
CHAVE	B	4	73	CHEETHAM	T	8	63	CHERRY	W	10	277	CHETTER	H	13	86
CHAVE	CH	7	65	CHEETHAM	W	8	63	CHERRY	WH	1	57	CHETTLEBURGH	AT	4	74
CHAWNER	A	6	77	CHEETHAM	W	11	70	CHERRY	WH	5	68	CHETWOOD	J	11	70
CHEADLE	A	14	57	CHELL	G	6	78	CHERRY	WL	5	68	CHEVAL	W	7	65
CHEADLE	ET	7	65	CHELSOM	JR	1	57	CHESHER	F	12	46	CHEVERTON	H	7	66
CHEADLE	J	14	57	CHELSOM	WJ	12	46	CHESHER	S	5	68	CHEVERTON	MA	12	280
CHEADLE	W	6	77	CHELTON	T	13	85	CHESHIRE	A	5	68	CHEW	R	8	63
CHEAL	F	10	43	CHENERY	FC	13	86	CHESHIRE	AA	5	68	CHEWTER	JW	13	86
CHEAL	JLV	4	73	CHENERY	HJ	7	65	CHESHIRE	B	12	46	CHEWTER	WE	13	86
CHEAL	WH	13	85	CHENERY	J	2	62	CHESHIRE	C	5	68	CHICK	AJ	1	57
CHEATER	AAC	1	57	CHENERY	M	1	57	CHESHIRE	E	5	68	CHICK	AT	2	63
CHEATER	HR	4	73	CHENERY	T	5	67	CHESHIRE	F	5	68	CHICK	BC	13	86

CHICK	E	4	74	CHILDE	R	8	64	CHILLERY	CW	12	47	CHISWELL	JR	7	66
CHICK	H	14	57	CHILDES	W	8	64	CHILLERY	F	12	47	CHISWELL	VD	7	66
CHICK	HJ	13	86	CHILDS	A	3	302	CHILLERY	HK	12	47	CHITHAM	FJ	13	87
CHICK	HW	4	74	CHILDS	A	3	303	CHILLERY	HK	12	421	CHITTENDEN	AF	13	87
CHICK	JBL	2	63	CHILDS	A	4	74	CHILLERY	JJ	12	47	CHITTENDEN	HE	2	64
CHICK	JW	2	63	CHILDS	AE	4	75	CHILLERY	RF	12	47	CHITTICK	AW	13	87
CHICK	P	14	57	CHILDS	AE	12	46	CHILLINGWORTH	CH	1	58	CHITTICK	GA	13	87
CHICK	R	10	277	CHILDS	AW	12	46	CHILLINGWORTH	G	13	87	CHITTICK	SF	13	87
CHICK	TW	12	280	CHILDS	BH	1	58	CHILLMAN	A	7	66	CHITTLEBOROUGH	CR	13	87
CHICK	VJ	10	43	CHILDS	DA	5	69	CHILLMAN	GF	3	303	CHITTY	FJ	1	58
CHICK	W	5	69	CHILDS	E	5	69	CHILTERN	R	9	239	CHITTY	H	1	58
CHIDGEY	A	13	86	CHILDS	E	8	64	CHILTON	C	11	70	CHITTY	JHV	4	75
CHIDGEY	GW	7	66	CHILDS	EE	12	46	CHILTON	H	3	303	CHITTY	T	1	58
CHIDGEY	J	14	57	CHILDS	F	1	58	CHILTON	J	14	58	CHITTY	WC	1	58
CHIDGEY	W	3	302	CHILDS	F	3	303	CHILTON	R	9	37	CHIVERS	A	4	75
CHIDLOW	B	6	79	CHILDS	FH	5	69	CHILTON	S	11	70	CHIVERS	AC	7	66
CHIDWICK	JG	3	34	CHILDS	FW	1	58	CHILTON	VE	14	58	CHIVERS	AD	4	75
CHIDWICK	WA	3	34	CHILDS	G	6	79	CHILVERS	GH	13	87	CHIVERS	AE	8	64
CHIDWICK	WE	2	63	CHILDS	G	12	280	CHILVERS	SJ	8	64	CHIVERS	AR	10	278
CHIDY	S	8	63	CHILDS	GG	4	75	CHILVERS	WA	2	64	CHIVERS	CT	4	75
CHIEZA	A	5	69	CHILDS	GH	3	303	CHINERY	FW	10	43	CHIVERS	E	9	239
CHIFFINS	CH	10	43	CHILDS	GW	4	75	CHINN	E	10	278	CHIVERS	FG	3	34
CHIFFINS	J	10	277	CHILDS	H	1	58	CHINN	H	6	79	CHIVERS	H	5	69
CHILCOTT	A	2	63	CHILDS	HC	12	46	CHINN	H	6	79	CHIVERS	HL	10	278
CHILCOTT	A	4	74	CHILDS	HE	7	66	CHINN	HA	12	47	CHIVERS	J	4	75
CHILCOTT	FE	2	63	CHILDS	J	12	47	CHINN	L	2	64	CHIVERS	JFB	10	278
CHILCOTT	HG	4	74	CHILDS	J	14	58	CHINNERY	R	14	58	CHIVERS	TW	4	75
CHILCOTT	PJ	6	79	CHILDS	JC	2	63	CHINNERY	WR	1	58	CHIVERS	W	2	64
CHILCOTT	SH	6	79	CHILDS	L	2	63	CHIPCHASE	R	14	58	CHIVERTON	BC	4	75
CHILD	A	8	63	CHILDS	NG	4	75	CHIPLING	C	3	303	CHIVERTON	CL	4	75
CHILD	A	8	63	CHILDS	PE	1	57	CHIPLING	WE	7	66	CHIVERTON	D	10	278
CHILD	AC	6	79	CHILDS	RB	1	57	CHIPMAN	A	8	64	CHIVERTON	EA	10	43
CHILD	B	8	63	CHILDS	RG	4	75	CHIPPENDALE	A	9	37	CHIVERTON	EH	4	75
CHILD	C	2	63	CHILDS	RW	4	75	CHIPPENDALE	G	9	37	CHIVERTON	FC	1	58
CHILD	C	5	69	CHILDS	S	12	47	CHIPPENDALE	GH	9	37	CHIVERTON	FC	10	43
CHILD	GT	9	239	CHILDS	T	2	64	CHIPPENDALE	J	9	37	CHIVERTON	FW	10	43
CHILD	H	1	57	CHILDS	T	14	58	CHIPPENDALE	J	9	37	CHIVERTON	HGJ	4	75
CHILD	H	8	64	CHILDS	TG	2	64	CHIPPENDALE	R	9	37	CHIVERTON	JI	1	58
CHILD	HH	6	79	CHILDS	W	1	58	CHIPPENDALE	S	9	38	CHIVERTON	JW	1	58
CHILD	HW	5	69	CHILDS	W	2	64	CHIPPENDALE	T	9	38	CHIVERTON	WE	4	76
CHILD	J	8	64	CHILDS	W	5	69	CHIPPERTON	JFD	1	58	CHOAT	F	7	66
CHILD	JJ	9	37	CHILDS	W	5	69	CHIPPERTON	WJ	1	58	CHOAT	H	7	66
CHILD	JJH	7	66	CHILDS	W	7	66	CHIPPETT	CS	5	69	CHOJECKI	J	14	58
CHILD	JRW	1	58	CHILDS	W	13	86	CHIPPETT	SC	5	69	CHOLERTON	FA	14	58
CHILD	JT	13	86	CHILDS	WA	13	86	CHIPPINDALE	T	9	38	CHOLERTON	J	14	58
CHILD	L	1	58	CHILDS	WG	4	75	CHIPPINDALE	W	9	38	CHOPPIN	FR	13	87
CHILD	L	13	86	CHILDS	WH	1	58	CHIPPING	FS	3	303	CHOPPING	A	3	34
CHILD	LM	6	79	CHILDS	WHF	13	87	CHIPPING	FW	3	303	CHOPPING	CJ	7	66
CHILD	MJ	7	66	CHILDS	WT	2	64	CHIPPS	SW	10	43	CHOPPING	J	7	66
CHILD	RA	4	74	CHILDS	WW	2	64	CHIPPS	WH	7	66	CHORLEY	FW	2	64
CHILD	S	8	64	CHILDS	WW	4	75	CHISHOLM	P	13	87	CHORLEY	P	11	70
CHILD	T	9	239	CHILES	CT	13	87	CHISMAN	EJ	4	75	CHORLEY	T	9	239
CHILD	TJ	2	63	CHILES	EFW	6	79	CHISNALL	HE	1	58	CHORLTON	G	14	58
CHILD	W	6	79	CHILES	JW	13	87	CHISNELL	JW	2	64	CHORLTON	H	11	421
CHILD	W	8	64	CHILLERY	AC	12	47	CHISP	HP	12	47	CHORLTON	JL	11	70

CHORLTON	P	11	70
CHOWN	AJ	2	64
CHOWN	EM	7	66
CHOWN	JFR	4	76
CHOWN	JWH	12	281
CHOWNS	AE	2	64
CHOWNS	FW	2	64
CHOWNS	GN	1	58
CHOWNS	GW	2	64
CHOWNS	H	2	64
CHOWNS	J	2	64
CHOWNS	J	6	79
CHRISP	CJ	12	47
CHRISTER	GD	13	87
CHRISTEY	AF	13	87
CHRISTIAN	A	11	70
CHRISTIAN	E	11	70
CHRISTIAN	FW	14	58
CHRISTIAN	GE	13	87
CHRISTIAN	J	11	70
CHRISTIAN	J	11	70
CHRISTIE	CH	7	66
CHRISTIE	D	1	58
CHRISTIE	EG	1	58
CHRISTIE	J	1	58
CHRISTIE	OW	10	43
CHRISTIE	WDA	1	59
CHRISTMAS	A	5	69
CHRISTMAS	A	5	69
CHRISTMAS	AC	13	87
CHRISTOPHER	AS	13	87
CHRISTOPHER	AW	4	76
CHRISTOPHER	CV	13	87
CHRISTOPHER	E	3	34
CHRISTOPHER	E	4	76
CHRISTOPHER	FJ	12	47
CHRISTOPHER	GJ	3	303
CHRISTOPHER	J	3	34
CHRISTOPHER	J	4	76
CHRISTOPHER	TA	2	64
CHRISTY	A	1	59
CHRISTY	N	1	59
CHRYSTAL	J	11	71
CHUBB	A	9	239
CHUBB	ELW	13	87
CHUBB	HE	5	69
CHUBB	JW	8	64
CHUBB	WG	7	66
CHURCH	A	3	303
CHURCH	AB	7	66
CHURCH	AE	12	281
CHURCH	AH	7	67
CHURCH	AJ	13	88
CHURCH	AL	10	43
CHURCH	AW	12	47
CHURCH	C	5	69
CHURCH	C	13	88
CHURCH	CE	3	34
CHURCH	CF	3	303
CHURCH	CW	1	59
CHURCH	DA	7	67
CHURCH	EF	2	64
CHURCH	EJB	12	47
CHURCH	F	5	69
CHURCH	F	12	47
CHURCH	F	12	47
CHURCH	FJ	13	88
CHURCH	FR	2	64
CHURCH	FW	13	88
CHURCH	G	3	303
CHURCH	GE	7	67
CHURCH	GE	12	47
CHURCH	GH	12	47
CHURCH	H	5	69
CHURCH	H	12	47
CHURCH	H	12	47
CHURCH	H	12	48
CHURCH	H	13	88
CHURCH	H	13	88
CHURCH	HC	2	65
CHURCH	HJ	7	67
CHURCH	J	5	70
CHURCH	J	12	48
CHURCH	JT	12	281
CHURCH	JWG	7	67
CHURCH	R	12	48
CHURCH	RA	2	65
CHURCH	RF	12	48
CHURCH	RT	1	59
CHURCH	S	13	88
CHURCH	SC	13	88
CHURCH	SW	7	67
CHURCH	T	5	70
CHURCH	T	5	70
CHURCH	W	1	59
CHURCH	W	5	69
CHURCH	W	12	48
CHURCH	WC	12	48
CHURCHARD	S	3	34
CHURCHER	A	10	44
CHURCHER	AE	7	67
CHURCHER	AG	7	67
CHURCHER	E	4	76
CHURCHER	E	10	43
CHURCHER	E	10	44
CHURCHER	EA	4	76
CHURCHER	EH	7	67
CHURCHER	EJ	7	67
CHURCHER	EM	10	44
CHURCHER	FA	10	44
CHURCHER	H	4	76
CHURCHER	J	10	44
CHURCHER	JA	4	76
CHURCHER	L	4	76
CHURCHER	L	4	76
CHURCHER	LC	7	67
CHURCHER	RA	4	76
CHURCHER	TC	4	76
CHURCHER	WG	4	76
CHURCHHOUSE	CE	5	70
CHURCHILL	A	7	67
CHURCHILL	A	10	44
CHURCHILL	ACN	4	76
CHURCHILL	C	13	88
CHURCHILL	CE	10	278
CHURCHILL	CJ	12	48
CHURCHILL	EG	4	76
CHURCHILL	FA	12	48
CHURCHILL	FC	2	65
CHURCHILL	FW	2	65
CHURCHILL	GW	13	88
CHURCHILL	HJ	4	76
CHURCHILL	J	1	59
CHURCHILL	JJ	13	88
CHURCHILL	T	14	58
CHURCHILL	W	10	44
CHURCHILL	WC	13	88
CHURCHLEY		1	59
CHURCHLEY	AA	6	79
CHURCHLEY	EV	6	79
CHURCHLEY	JH	6	79
CHURCHLEY	RJ	6	79
CHURCHLEY	W	1	59
CHURCHMAN	EA	12	281
CHURCHMAN	EG	12	48
CHURCHMAN	ES	12	48
CHURCHMAN	FC	12	48
CHURCHMAN	JW	1	59
CHURCHMAN	LE	10	44
CHURCHMAN	W	12	281
CHURCHMAN	WO	12	281
CHURCHMAN	WW	12	48
CHURCHYARD	WM	1	59
CHURM	JW	11	71
CHURM	L	14	58
CHURM	SF	14	58
CHUSSUM	RC	3	303
CHUTE	GJ	3	303
CHUTER	AO	12	48
CHUTER	CW	13	88
CIRCUIT	F	5	70
CIRCUIT	F	5	70
CIRCUIT	G	12	48
CIRCUIT	LF	11	71
CIRCUIT	P	12	48
CIRCUIT	SJ	5	70
CIRCUS	AG	2	65
CIVIL	J	12	281
CIVIL	W	12	281
CLACK	A	7	67
CLACK	C	2	65
CLACK	CF	2	65
CLACK	GH	2	65
CLACK	GL	7	67
CLACK	H	2	65
CLACK	HJ	2	65
CLACK	ITH	7	67
CLACK	WG	10	44
CLACK	WS	2	65
CLACKETT	RW	3	303
CLAGGETT	AG	7	67
CLAGUE	N	14	58
CLAGUE	WE	12	281
CLAMP	H	5	70
CLAMP	HE	6	79
CLAMP	RE	6	79
CLAMP	T	6	80
CLANCY	D	14	58
CLANCY	F	14	58
CLANCY	HJ	2	65
CLANCY	J	11	71
CLANCY	J	11	71
CLANCY	J	11	71
CLANCY	T	11	71
CLANCY	WJ	10	44
CLAPHAM	A	8	64
CLAPHAM	AB	2	65
CLAPHAM	F	5	70
CLAPHAM	H	9	38
CLAPHAM	H	9	239
CLAPHAM	HE	11	71
CLAPHAM	J	6	80
CLAPHAM	J	13	88
CLAPHAM	JD	2	65
CLAPHAM	L	9	38
CLAPHAM	RS	9	38
CLAPHAM	RS	9	240
CLAPHAM	T	11	71
CLAPHAM	W	9	240
CLAPPINSON	JG	3	303
CLAPSON	JH	3	34
CLAR	W	3	34
CLARE	A	11	71
CLARE	A	11	71
CLARE	AE	13	88
CLARE	AW	12	48
CLARE	C	3	303
CLARE	C	5	70
CLARE	C	12	281
CLARE	E	12	48

CLARE	FSW	2	65	CLARK	AE	10	44	CLARK	E	8	64	CLARK	G	10	278
CLARE	GJ	3	303	CLARK	AE	10	278	CLARK	E	8	64	CLARK	G	10	278
CLARE	H	14	58	CLARK	AF	3	34	CLARK	E	12	49	CLARK	G	12	49
CLARE	HM	12	48	CLARK	AF	13	88	CLARK	E	13	89	CLARK	G	12	281
CLARE	HW	10	44	CLARK	AG	1	59	CLARK	E	13	89	CLARK	G	13	89
CLARE	JE	2	65	CLARK	AG	5	70	CLARK	EC	3	304	CLARK	G	14	59
CLARE	JH	11	71	CLARK	AH	10	44	CLARK	EC	7	68	CLARK	GA	3	35
CLARE	JH	12	48	CLARK	AJ	5	70	CLARK	EC	8	64	CLARK	GA	7	68
CLARE	JR	11	71	CLARK	AN	2	66	CLARK	EE	10	45	CLARK	GA	12	49
CLARE	W	3	303	CLARK	AT	1	59	CLARK	EE	13	89	CLARK	GB	2	66
CLARE	W	13	88	CLARK	AV	10	44	CLARK	EH	1	59	CLARK	GC	1	60
CLARENCE	A	6	80	CLARK	AW	3	34	CLARK	EH	3	304	CLARK	GE	1	60
CLARENCE	J	6	80	CLARK	B	5	70	CLARK	EH	7	68	CLARK	GE	7	68
CLAREY	W	9	240	CLARK	B	8	64	CLARK	EJ	2	66	CLARK	GE	12	49
CLARIDGE	AJ	12	48	CLARK	B	12	49	CLARK	EM	10	45	CLARK	GF	13	89
CLARIDGE	CF	7	67	CLARK	B	12	49	CLARK	ET	7	68	CLARK	GH	10	45
CLARIDGE	EM	3	304	CLARK	BA	5	70	CLARK	EW	7	68	CLARK	GH	12	281
CLARIDGE	F	7	67	CLARK	BA	10	44	CLARK	F	3	35	CLARK	GH	13	89
CLARIDGE	HV	7	68	CLARK	BE	5	70	CLARK	F	4	77	CLARK	GH	13	89
CLARIDGE	NF	5	70	CLARK	BE	13	88	CLARK	F	5	71	CLARK	GJ	7	68
CLARIDGE	RD	3	304	CLARK	BW	3	304	CLARK	F	5	71	CLARK	GJF	10	278
CLARIDGE	RJ	3	304	CLARK	C	1	59	CLARK	F	8	65	CLARK	GW	1	60
CLARIDGE	SC	5	70	CLARK	C	2	66	CLARK	F	9	38	CLARK	GW	2	66
CLARIDGE	SP	3	304	CLARK	C	3	304	CLARK	F	9	240	CLARK	GW	2	66
CLARIDGE	T	1	59	CLARK	C	4	77	CLARK	F	9	240	CLARK	GW	10	45
CLARIDGE	W	3	304	CLARK	C	7	68	CLARK	F	10	45	CLARK	GW	10	45
CLARK	A	1	59	CLARK	C	8	64	CLARK	F	10	45	CLARK	H	1	60
CLARK	A	1	59	CLARK	C	9	240	CLARK	F	12	49	CLARK	H	1	60
CLARK	A	1	59	CLARK	C	10	44	CLARK	F	13	89	CLARK	H	2	66
CLARK	A	1	59	CLARK	C	12	49	CLARK	F	13	89	CLARK	H	4	77
CLARK	A	2	65	CLARK	C	12	49	CLARK	F	13	89	CLARK	H	5	71
CLARK	A	2	65	CLARK	C	12	49	CLARK	F	13	89	CLARK	H	5	71
CLARK	A	3	34	CLARK	CA	2	66	CLARK	FA	5	71	CLARK	H	5	71
CLARK	A	3	34	CLARK	CC	1	59	CLARK	FA	7	68	CLARK	H	5	71
CLARK	A	3	304	CLARK	CE	10	44	CLARK	FA	7	68	CLARK	H	5	71
CLARK	A	4	76	CLARK	CF	12	49	CLARK	FA	10	45	CLARK	H	6	80
CLARK	A	4	76	CLARK	CF	13	89	CLARK	FA	13	89	CLARK	H	7	68
CLARK	A	4	76	CLARK	CG	3	304	CLARK	FB	1	59	CLARK	H	8	65
CLARK	A	4	77	CLARK	CG	5	70	CLARK	FE	1	60	CLARK	H	9	38
CLARK	A	5	70	CLARK	CG	12	281	CLARK	FE	3	304	CLARK	HA	3	35
CLARK	A	7	69	CLARK	CH	2	66	CLARK	FG	1	60	CLARK	HA	4	77
CLARK	A	8	64	CLARK	CJ	2	66	CLARK	FG	5	71	CLARK	HA	7	68
CLARK	A	8	64	CLARK	CR	3	35	CLARK	FG	13	89	CLARK	HD	10	45
CLARK	A	9	38	CLARK	CT	13	89	CLARK	FH	2	66	CLARK	HE	4	77
CLARK	A	11	71	CLARK	CW	2	66	CLARK	FS	5	71	CLARK	HG	2	66
CLARK	A	12	48	CLARK	CW	13	89	CLARK	FT	3	304	CLARK	HG	10	278
CLARK	A	12	49	CLARK	D	4	76	CLARK	FW	3	304	CLARK	HG	13	89
CLARK	A	12	49	CLARK	DT	2	66	CLARK	FW	5	71	CLARK	HGJ	1	60
CLARK	A	13	88	CLARK	DW	8	64	CLARK	FW	12	281	CLARK	HJ	3	304
CLARK	AA	7	68	CLARK	E	2	66	CLARK	G	6	80	CLARK	HM	10	45
CLARK	AB	8	64	CLARK	E	2	66	CLARK	G	7	68	CLARK	HR	3	35
CLARK	AE	1	59	CLARK	E	5	70	CLARK	G	8	65	CLARK	HR	7	68
CLARK	AE	2	65	CLARK	E	5	71	CLARK	G	8	65	CLARK	HR	13	89
CLARK	AE	9	240	CLARK	E	6	80	CLARK	G	10	45	CLARK	HS	2	66

CLARK	HT	2	66	CLARK	JW	11	71	CLARK	TH	6	80	CLARK	WH	2	67
CLARK	HT	7	68	CLARK	JW	14	59	CLARK	TH	6	80	CLARK	WH	2	68
CLARK	HT	9	38	CLARK	JWE	4	77	CLARK	TH	8	66	CLARK	WH	7	69
CLARK	HW	3	304	CLARK	L	3	305	CLARK	TH	11	72	CLARK	WH	8	66
CLARK	HW	4	77	CLARK	L	5	71	CLARK	TJ	3	35	CLARK	WH	9	38
CLARK	HW	11	71	CLARK	L	8	65	CLARK	TM	7	69	CLARK	WH	10	45
CLARK	IJ	13	89	CLARK	LA	10	278	CLARK	TR	13	90	CLARK	WH	10	278
CLARK	IWH	8	65	CLARK	LM	7	68	CLARK	TV	7	69	CLARK	WH	10	278
CLARK	J	1	60	CLARK	M	1	60	CLARK	TW	10	45	CLARK	WH	11	72
CLARK	J	1	60	CLARK	M	4	77	CLARK	V	9	38	CLARK	WH	11	72
CLARK	J	1	60	CLARK	M	9	38	CLARK	VR	13	90	CLARK	WJ	1	60
CLARK	J	2	66	CLARK	M	12	49	CLARK	W	1	60	CLARK	WJ	3	305
CLARK	J	2	66	CLARK	NS	2	67	CLARK	W	1	60	CLARK	WJ	5	72
CLARK	J	3	305	CLARK	P	9	240	CLARK	W	1	60	CLARK	WJ	13	90
CLARK	J	4	77	CLARK	PEV	5	72	CLARK	W	2	67	CLARK	WJ	13	90
CLARK	J	5	71	CLARK	PJ	13	90	CLARK	W	2	67	CLARK	WJ	13	90
CLARK	J	5	71	CLARK	R	1	60	CLARK	W	2	67	CLARK	WJG	2	68
CLARK	J	5	71	CLARK	R	1	60	CLARK	W	2	67	CLARK	WT	3	305
CLARK	J	5	71	CLARK	R	2	67	CLARK	W	4	77	CLARK	WT	12	50
CLARK	J	8	65	CLARK	R	3	305	CLARK	W	4	77	CLARK	WT	13	90
CLARK	J	8	65	CLARK	R	6	80	CLARK	W	5	72	CLARK	WW	13	90
CLARK	J	8	65	CLARK	R	7	69	CLARK	W	6	80	CLARK	WW	13	90
CLARK	J	8	65	CLARK	R	7	69	CLARK	W	7	69	CLARKE	A	2	68
CLARK	J	8	65	CLARK	R	7	69	CLARK	W	8	66	CLARKE	A	3	35
CLARK	J	8	65	CLARK	R	8	65	CLARK	W	10	45	CLARKE	A	6	80
CLARK	J	8	65	CLARK	R	8	66	CLARK	W	12	50	CLARKE	A	6	80
CLARK	J	8	65	CLARK	R	11	72	CLARK	W	12	50	CLARKE	A	6	80
CLARK	J	10	278	CLARK	R	12	49	CLARK	W	12	50	CLARKE	A	10	45
CLARK	J	11	71	CLARK	RH	2	67	CLARK	W	13	90	CLARKE	A	11	72
CLARK	J	11	71	CLARK	RHG	3	35	CLARK	W	13	90	CLARKE	A	12	50
CLARK	J	12	49	CLARK	RJ	2	67	CLARK	W	13	90	CLARKE	A	12	50
CLARK	J	14	59	CLARK	RL	5	72	CLARK	W	14	59	CLARKE	A	12	281
CLARK	J	14	59	CLARK	S	6	80	CLARK	WA	1	60	CLARKE	A	12	281
CLARK	J	14	59	CLARK	S	7	69	CLARK	WA	9	38	CLARKE	AA	11	72
CLARK	J	14	59	CLARK	S	10	45	CLARK	WA	12	281	CLARKE	AB	3	35
CLARK	JA	1	60	CLARK	S	12	49	CLARK	WAC	13	90	CLARKE	AC	3	35
CLARK	JA	1	60	CLARK	S	12	281	CLARK	WC	3	35	CLARKE	AC	5	72
CLARK	JA	2	67	CLARK	S	13	90	CLARK	WC	5	72	CLARKE	AC	12	50
CLARK	JA	3	305	CLARK	SA	13	90	CLARK	WD	2	67	CLARKE	AD	6	80
CLARK	JA	14	59	CLARK	SC	4	77	CLARK	WE	2	67	CLARKE	AD	10	278
CLARK	JC	10	45	CLARK	SC	7	69	CLARK	WE	3	305	CLARKE	AE	4	77
CLARK	JD	8	65	CLARK	SC	12	49	CLARK	WE	7	69	CLARKE	AE	12	281
CLARK	JE	9	240	CLARK	SCJ	2	67	CLARK	WE	7	69	CLARKE	AG	5	72
CLARK	JG	12	49	CLARK	SG	7	69	CLARK	WEC	3	305	CLARKE	AH	4	77
CLARK	JH	2	67	CLARK	SJ	2	67	CLARK	WF	1	60	CLARKE	AH	6	80
CLARK	JH	8	65	CLARK	T	2	67	CLARK	WF	2	67	CLARKE	AH	13	91
CLARK	JJ	3	35	CLARK	T	2	67	CLARK	WF	2	67	CLARKE	AJ	2	68
CLARK	JJ	13	89	CLARK	T	7	69	CLARK	WF	13	90	CLARKE	AJ	6	80
CLARK	JR	8	65	CLARK	T	8	66	CLARK	WF	13	90	CLARKE	AJ	7	69
CLARK	JW	3	35	CLARK	T	8	66	CLARK	WFE	7	69	CLARKE	AJ	12	50
CLARK	JW	5	71	CLARK	T	9	38	CLARK	WG	2	67	CLARKE	AR	13	91
CLARK	JW	8	65	CLARK	T	9	382	CLARK	WG	12	50	CLARKE	AT	1	60
CLARK	JW	8	65	CLARK	T	13	90	CLARK	WG	12	50	CLARKE	AT	2	68
CLARK	JW	10	45	CLARK	TD	2	67	CLARK	WG	13	90	CLARKE	AT	3	305
CLARK				CLARK	TH	6	80	CLARK	WH	1	60	CLARKE	AT	13	91

Name	Init	Bn	Regt	Name	Init	Bn	Regt	Name	Init	Bn	Regt	Name	Init	Bn	Regt	Name	Init	Bn	Regt
CLARKE	AV	6	80	CLARKE	E	14	59	CLARKE	G	3	305	CLARKE	J	5	73	CLARKE	J	5	73
CLARKE	AW	3	35	CLARKE	EC	2	68	CLARKE	G	5	73	CLARKE	J	5	73	CLARKE	J	5	73
CLARKE	AW	12	50	CLARKE	EC	7	70	CLARKE	G	6	81	CLARKE	J	5	73	CLARKE	J	6	81
CLARKE	AW	12	50	CLARKE	EC	10	46	CLARKE	G	7	70	CLARKE	J	6	81	CLARKE	J	6	81
CLARKE	AW	12	50	CLARKE	ED	5	72	CLARKE	G	11	72	CLARKE	J	6	81	CLARKE	J	6	81
CLARKE	B	4	77	CLARKE	EE	3	35	CLARKE	G	12	51	CLARKE	J	6	81	CLARKE	J	7	70
CLARKE	B	7	69	CLARKE	EE	12	282	CLARKE	G	12	51	CLARKE	J	6	81	CLARKE	J	8	66
CLARKE	B	8	66	CLARKE	EH	4	77	CLARKE	G	12	282	CLARKE	J	6	81	CLARKE	J	11	73
CLARKE	B	10	46	CLARKE	EH	7	70	CLARKE	G	12	282	CLARKE	J	7	70	CLARKE	J	11	73
CLARKE	B	12	281	CLARKE	EHR	5	72	CLARKE	G	12	282	CLARKE	J	8	66	CLARKE	J	11	73
CLARKE	BJ	12	50	CLARKE	EJ	11	72	CLARKE	G	14	59	CLARKE	J	11	73	CLARKE	J	11	73
CLARKE	C	2	68	CLARKE	EJ	13	91	CLARKE	GA	12	282	CLARKE	J	11	73	CLARKE	J	11	73
CLARKE	C	5	72	CLARKE	EJE	2	68	CLARKE	GA	14	59	CLARKE	J	11	73	CLARKE	J	11	73
CLARKE	C	5	72	CLARKE	EM	12	282	CLARKE	GE	1	61	CLARKE	J	11	73	CLARKE	J	12	282
CLARKE	C	5	72	CLARKE	ER	1	61	CLARKE	GE	2	68	CLARKE	J	11	73	CLARKE	J	13	91
CLARKE	C	5	72	CLARKE	ER	5	72	CLARKE	GE	2	68	CLARKE	J	11	73	CLARKE	J	14	59
CLARKE	C	10	46	CLARKE	EV	11	72	CLARKE	GE	6	81	CLARKE	J	12	282	CLARKE	J	14	59
CLARKE	C	12	50	CLARKE	F	2	68	CLARKE	GE	13	91	CLARKE	J	13	91	CLARKE	J	14	59
CLARKE	CE	1	60	CLARKE	F	5	72	CLARKE	GH	1	61	CLARKE	J	14	59	CLARKE	JA	5	73
CLARKE	CE	2	68	CLARKE	F	5	72	CLARKE	GH	3	35	CLARKE	J	14	59	CLARKE	JA	13	91
CLARKE	CE	11	72	CLARKE	F	5	73	CLARKE	GH	13	91	CLARKE	J	14	59	CLARKE	JAG	2	68
CLARKE	CE	12	50	CLARKE	F	5	73	CLARKE	GJ	2	68	CLARKE	J	5	73	CLARKE	JD	12	282
CLARKE	CF	1	61	CLARKE	F	6	81	CLARKE	GR	2	68	CLARKE	J	5	73	CLARKE	JH	3	305
CLARKE	CG	6	81	CLARKE	F	7	70	CLARKE	GT	13	91	CLARKE	J	6	81	CLARKE	JH	3	305
CLARKE	CG	7	70	CLARKE	F	10	46	CLARKE	GW	1	61	CLARKE	J	6	81	CLARKE	JH	6	81
CLARKE	CGT	1	61	CLARKE	F	11	72	CLARKE	GW	3	305	CLARKE	J	7	70	CLARKE	JH	10	46
CLARKE	CH	1	61	CLARKE	F	11	72	CLARKE	H	1	61	CLARKE	J	8	66	CLARKE	JJ	12	282
CLARKE	CH	2	68	CLARKE	F	11	72	CLARKE	H	2	68	CLARKE	J	11	73	CLARKE	JOR	7	70
CLARKE	CH	12	50	CLARKE	F	11	421	CLARKE	H	6	81	CLARKE	J	11	73	CLARKE	JP	6	81
CLARKE	CH	12	50	CLARKE	F	12	51	CLARKE	H	6	81	CLARKE	J	12	282	CLARKE	JR	6	82
CLARKE	CH	12	282	CLARKE	F	12	282	CLARKE	H	6	81	CLARKE	J	13	91	CLARKE	JS	6	82
CLARKE	CH	13	91	CLARKE	F	12	282	CLARKE	H	8	66	CLARKE	J	14	59	CLARKE	JS	9	38
CLARKE	CH	13	91	CLARKE	F	12	282	CLARKE	H	8	66	CLARKE	J	14	59	CLARKE	JT	1	61
CLARKE	CJ	3	305	CLARKE	F	13	91	CLARKE	H	11	73	CLARKE	J	5	73	CLARKE	JT	4	77
CLARKE	CM	3	305	CLARKE	F	13	91	CLARKE	H	11	73	CLARKE	J	6	81	CLARKE	JT	11	73
CLARKE	CM	6	81	CLARKE	F	14	59	CLARKE	H	11	73	CLARKE	J	7	70	CLARKE	JT	11	73
CLARKE	CS	13	91	CLARKE	FC	5	73	CLARKE	H	11	73	CLARKE	J	8	66	CLARKE	JT	12	283
CLARKE	CT	6	81	CLARKE	FC	6	81	CLARKE	H	12	51	CLARKE	J	11	73	CLARKE	JW	5	73
CLARKE	CT	10	46	CLARKE	FC	10	46	CLARKE	H	12	51	CLARKE	J	11	73	CLARKE	JW	6	82
CLARKE	CT	12	50	CLARKE	FE	4	77	CLARKE	H	12	282	CLARKE	J	12	282	CLARKE	JW	11	73
CLARKE	CW	12	282	CLARKE	FE	6	81	CLARKE	H	13	91	CLARKE	J	14	59	CLARKE	JW	12	283
CLARKE	D	13	91	CLARKE	FE	7	70	CLARKE	H	14	59	CLARKE	J	5	73	CLARKE	JW	14	59
CLARKE	E	1	61	CLARKE	FH	10	46	CLARKE	HC	7	70	CLARKE	J	6	81	CLARKE	KLD	13	91
CLARKE	E	1	61	CLARKE	FJ	7	70	CLARKE	HE	1	61	CLARKE	J	7	70	CLARKE	L	6	82
CLARKE	E	3	35	CLARKE	FJH	4	77	CLARKE	HE	12	282	CLARKE	J	11	73	CLARKE	L	8	66
CLARKE	E	5	72	CLARKE	FL	12	282	CLARKE	HF	3	35	CLARKE	J	12	282	CLARKE	L	12	283
CLARKE	E	5	72	CLARKE	FP	11	72	CLARKE	HF	5	73	CLARKE	J	13	91	CLARKE	L	12	283
CLARKE	E	7	70	CLARKE	FT	11	72	CLARKE	HF	6	81	CLARKE	J	14	59	CLARKE	LE	1	61
CLARKE	E	8	66	CLARKE	FW	5	73	CLARKE	HGC	12	51	CLARKE	J	5	73	CLARKE	LH	6	82
CLARKE	E	11	72	CLARKE	FW	11	73	CLARKE	HH	12	51	CLARKE	J	6	81	CLARKE	LJ	2	68
CLARKE	E	11	72	CLARKE	FW	12	51	CLARKE	HJ	3	305	CLARKE	J	7	70	CLARKE	LJ	12	283
CLARKE	E	11	72	CLARKE	FW	12	51	CLARKE	HJ	12	51	CLARKE	J	11	73	CLARKE	LL	1	61
CLARKE	E	12	50	CLARKE	FW	12	282	CLARKE	HS	12	282	CLARKE	J	12	282	CLARKE	LS	1	61
CLARKE	E	12	282	CLARKE	G	1	61	CLARKE	J	5	73	CLARKE	J	5	73				
				CLARKE	G	2	68	CLARKE	J	5	73								

CLARKE	M	11	73	CLARKE	VG	5	74	CLARKE	WR	6	82	CLAVIN	C	9	39
CLARKE	M	11	74	CLARKE	W	1	61	CLARKE	WRS	6	82	CLAXTON	ABC	7	71
CLARKE	MA	12	51	CLARKE	W	2	69	CLARKE	WT	4	78	CLAXTON	AW	7	71
CLARKE	MM	10	279	CLARKE	W	2	69	CLARKE	WT	12	52	CLAXTON	CT	13	92
CLARKE	MW	12	283	CLARKE	W	2	69	CLARKE	WT	12	283	CLAXTON	DC	7	71
CLARKE	OG	12	51	CLARKE	W	3	306	CLARKE	WW	13	92	CLAXTON	E	10	46
CLARKE	P	1	61	CLARKE	W	3	306	CLARKE	WW	13	92	CLAXTON	H	2	69
CLARKE	P	2	69	CLARKE	W	4	78	CLARKSON	A	6	82	CLAXTON	JC	2	70
CLARKE	P	13	91	CLARKE	W	5	74	CLARKSON	ACV	2	69	CLAXTON	R	13	92
CLARKE	PJ	5	73	CLARKE	W	5	74	CLARKSON	AF	3	306	CLAXTON	W	7	71
CLARKE	R	1	61	CLARKE	W	5	74	CLARKSON	AL	3	306	CLAXTON	WA	13	92
CLARKE	R	6	82	CLARKE	W	6	82	CLARKSON	C	14	60	CLAY	C	13	92
CLARKE	R	7	70	CLARKE	W	6	82	CLARKSON	CE	1	62	CLAY	CT	3	306
CLARKE	R	10	46	CLARKE	W	7	70	CLARKSON	EF	7	71	CLAY	E	13	92
CLARKE	RH	1	61	CLARKE	W	7	70	CLARKSON	F	8	66	CLAY	F	2	70
CLARKE	RH	12	283	CLARKE	W	10	46	CLARKSON	F	8	66	CLAY	F	10	46
CLARKE	RJ	4	78	CLARKE	W	11	74	CLARKSON	F	9	39	CLAY	FC	10	47
CLARKE	RJ	12	51	CLARKE	W	11	74	CLARKSON	FR	1	62	CLAY	FC	13	93
CLARKE	RP	4	78	CLARKE	W	11	74	CLARKSON	G	8	66	CLAY	FW	6	83
CLARKE	RW	5	73	CLARKE	W	12	51	CLARKSON	H	8	66	CLAY	G	8	67
CLARKE	RW	11	73	CLARKE	W	12	283	CLARKSON	H	10	46	CLAY	GJ	10	46
CLARKE	RW	11	73	CLARKE	W	12	283	CLARKSON	H	13	92	CLAY	H	8	67
CLARKE	RWT	12	283	CLARKE	W	13	91	CLARKSON	HL	2	69	CLAY	H	8	67
CLARKE	S	3	35	CLARKE	W	13	92	CLARKSON	HV	8	66	CLAY	H	9	39
CLARKE	S	12	51	CLARKE	WA	4	78	CLARKSON	J	2	69	CLAY	H	10	46
CLARKE	SA	12	283	CLARKE	WC	5	74	CLARKSON	J	6	82	CLAY	J	5	74
CLARKE	SF	4	78	CLARKE	WC	6	82	CLARKSON	J	8	66	CLAY	J	13	93
CLARKE	SJ	1	61	CLARKE	WD	2	69	CLARKSON	JC	8	66	CLAY	JW	10	46
CLARKE	SJ	12	51	CLARKE	WD	5	74	CLARKSON	JW	8	66	CLAY	L	6	83
CLARKE	SN	6	82	CLARKE	WE	1	62	CLARKSON	JW	8	66	CLAY	W	5	74
CLARKE	SS	7	70	CLARKE	WE	2	69	CLARKSON	M	3	306	CLAY	WH	9	240
CLARKE	SW	12	283	CLARKE	WE	4	78	CLARKSON	T	7	71	CLAYBROUGH	H	8	67
CLARKE	T	1	61	CLARKE	WF	12	51	CLARKSON	TV	11	74	CLAYBROUGH	H	8	67
CLARKE	T	1	61	CLARKE	WF	13	92	CLARKSON	W	7	71	CLAYBURN	R	9	39
CLARKE	T	2	69	CLARKE	WF	13	92	CLARKSON	W	8	67	CLAYDEN	FR	5	74
CLARKE	T	4	78	CLARKE	WF	13	92	CLARKSON	W	9	39	CLAYDEN	S	2	70
CLARKE	T	5	73	CLARKE	WG	7	70	CLARKSON	WH	8	67	CLAYDEN	W	1	62
CLARKE	T	5	73	CLARKE	WG	8	66	CLARSON	T	6	82	CLAYDEN	WG	2	70
CLARKE	T	6	82	CLARKE	WG	12	52	CLARY	SA	2	69	CLAYDEN	WR	2	70
CLARKE	T	7	70	CLARKE	WH	1	62	CLARY	W	13	92	CLAYDEN	WR	5	74
CLARKE	T	11	73	CLARKE	WH	2	69	CLASBY	FS	10	46	CLAYDON	AT	12	283
CLARKE	T	12	283	CLARKE	WH	2	69	CLASBY	SC	4	78	CLAYDON	EJ	12	52
CLARKE	T	14	59	CLARKE	WH	5	74	CLASPER	JP	13	92	CLAYDON	F	12	283
CLARKE	TA	10	278	CLARKE	WH	6	82	CLASPER	WH	13	92	CLAYDON	F	13	93
CLARKE	TF	10	46	CLARKE	WH	7	70	CLASSEY	AJ	2	69	CLAYDON	G	13	93
CLARKE	TH	3	306	CLARKE	WH	12	283	CLASSEY	RO	2	69	CLAYDON	H	3	36
CLARKE	TH	4	78	CLARKE	WHG	3	36	CLATWORTHY	G	5	74	CLAYDON	H	12	283
CLARKE	TH	5	73	CLARKE	WJ	4	78	CLAUD	HF	8	67	CLAYDON	JE	12	283
CLARKE	TH	6	82	CLARKE	WJ	4	78	CLAUDE	O	4	78	CLAYDON	W	5	74
CLARKE	TH	14	60	CLARKE	WJ	6	82	CLAUGHTON	A	9	240	CLAYDON	W	12	284
CLARKE	TJ	5	73	CLARKE	WJ	12	52	CLAUS	AC	13	92	CLAYDON	WW	1	62
CLARKE	TS	10	279	CLARKE	WJ	12	52	CLAUS	EG	13	92	CLAYFIELD	A	13	93
CLARKE	TS	12	51	CLARKE	WJ	12	283	CLAUS	J	13	92	CLAYFIELD	EH	3	306
CLARKE	TW	5	73	CLARKE	WJ	14	60	CLAVEN	H	9	39	CLAYFORTH	HW	8	67
CLARKE	TWG	10	279	CLARKE	WR	2	69	CLAVEY	FC	3	36	CLAYPOLE	T	11	74

CLAYSMITH	GE	13	93	CLAYTON	J	11	74	CLEAVE	S	13	93	CLEMAS	E	1	62
CLAYSON	A	12	284	CLAYTON	J	14	60	CLEAVER	A	6	83	CLEMENS	JP	3	36
CLAYSON	A	12	284	CLAYTON	J	14	60	CLEAVER	AFC	5	75	CLEMENT	AC	6	83
CLAYSON	AVG	7	71	CLAYTON	JA	7	71	CLEAVER	AJ	5	75	CLEMENT	FG	4	78
CLAYSON	B	12	52	CLAYTON	JA	7	71	CLEAVER	BG	5	75	CLEMENT	GH	1	62
CLAYSON	H	12	284	CLAYTON	JA	14	60	CLEAVER	BG	6	83	CLEMENTS	A	2	70
CLAYSON	HL	2	70	CLAYTON	JH	8	67	CLEAVER	CAH	6	83	CLEMENTS	A	3	306
CLAYSON	J	12	284	CLAYTON	JH	13	93	CLEAVER	EF	6	83	CLEMENTS	A	4	78
CLAYSON	W	12	284	CLAYTON	JW	6	83	CLEAVER	J	12	284	CLEMENTS	A	5	75
CLAYSON	WC	12	284	CLAYTON	JW	8	67	CLEAVER	JS	5	75	CLEMENTS	AA	2	70
CLAYTON	A	6	83	CLAYTON	L	5	74	CLEAVER	JT	1	62	CLEMENTS	AA	12	52
CLAYTON	A	8	67	CLAYTON	O	8	67	CLEAVER	L	1	62	CLEMENTS	AD	4	79
CLAYTON	A	14	60	CLAYTON	PS	6	83	CLEAVER	RD	6	83	CLEMENTS	AE	7	71
CLAYTON	A	14	60	CLAYTON	PS	7	71	CLEAVER	RH	6	83	CLEMENTS	AH	6	83
CLAYTON	AE	9	240	CLAYTON	R	2	70	CLEAVER	SC	5	75	CLEMENTS	AJ	1	62
CLAYTON	AE	10	47	CLAYTON	R	8	67	CLEAVER	WH	1	62	CLEMENTS	ATE	13	93
CLAYTON	AN	9	240	CLAYTON	RA	13	93	CLEAVER	WJ	5	75	CLEMENTS	C	5	75
CLAYTON	AP	11	74	CLAYTON	S	5	74	CLEAVER	WT	10	279	CLEMENTS	C	8	68
CLAYTON	B	8	67	CLAYTON	T	9	240	CLEEVE	AJ	10	47	CLEMENTS	CA	13	93
CLAYTON	B	9	39	CLAYTON	T	11	74	CLEGG	A	9	39	CLEMENTS	CE	4	79
CLAYTON	C	2	70	CLAYTON	TS	1	62	CLEGG	CB	9	240	CLEMENTS	E	1	62
CLAYTON	C	3	306	CLAYTON	W	6	83	CLEGG	E	9	240	CLEMENTS	E	4	79
CLAYTON	C	5	74	CLAYTON	W	11	74	CLEGG	G	11	75	CLEMENTS	E	13	94
CLAYTON	C	8	67	CLAYTON	W	14	60	CLEGG	GE	11	75	CLEMENTS	EA	12	52
CLAYTON	C	14	60	CLAYTON	W	14	60	CLEGG	H	9	241	CLEMENTS	EJ	7	71
CLAYTON	CH	6	83	CLAYTON	WE	7	71	CLEGG	H	11	75	CLEMENTS	EK	4	79
CLAYTON	E	8	67	CLAYTON	WE	7	71	CLEGG	H	11	75	CLEMENTS	EWF	5	75
CLAYTON	E	8	67	CLAYTON	WG	13	93	CLEGG	J	8	67	CLEMENTS	F	1	62
CLAYTON	E	11	74	CLAYTON	WH	9	39	CLEGG	J	9	241	CLEMENTS	F	4	79
CLAYTON	EA	3	306	CLAYTON	WN	11	74	CLEGG	J	10	47	CLEMENTS	FC	4	79
CLAYTON	F	6	83	CLEAK	AE	13	93	CLEGG	J	11	75	CLEMENTS	FP	4	79
CLAYTON	F	12	52	CLEAK	CE	13	93	CLEGG	J	11	75	CLEMENTS	FW	1	62
CLAYTON	FWA	1	62	CLEAK	CH	13	93	CLEGG	J	11	75	CLEMENTS	G	1	62
CLAYTON	G	5	74	CLEAK	FCC	13	93	CLEGG	JE	11	75	CLEMENTS	GH	1	62
CLAYTON	G	9	240	CLEAK	TW	13	93	CLEGG	JE	14	60	CLEMENTS	H	2	70
CLAYTON	G	11	74	CLEAK	WGE	13	93	CLEGG	JS	8	68	CLEMENTS	H	3	306
CLAYTON	GA	2	70	CLEAL	AE	10	47	CLEGG	JW	9	39	CLEMENTS	H	5	75
CLAYTON	GA	10	279	CLEAL	AE	10	47	CLEGG	RT	11	75	CLEMENTS	H	9	39
CLAYTON	GE	7	71	CLEAR	G	4	78	CLEGG	T	8	68	CLEMENTS	HA	1	62
CLAYTON	GT	12	52	CLEARY	B	14	60	CLEGG	VW	3	36	CLEMENTS	HE	10	47
CLAYTON	H	9	39	CLEARY	J	9	39	CLEGG	W	9	39	CLEMENTS	HG	5	75
CLAYTON	H	9	39	CLEARY	J	9	240	CLEGG	W	9	39	CLEMENTS	HH	1	62
CLAYTON	H	9	39	CLEARY	J	11	74	CLEGG	W	9	241	CLEMENTS	HJ	13	94
CLAYTON	H	9	240	CLEARY	JE	11	74	CLEGG	W	9	241	CLEMENTS	HR	12	52
CLAYTON	H	11	74	CLEARY	JE	11	74	CLEGG	W	9	382	CLEMENTS	HW	2	71
CLAYTON	HB	2	70	CLEARY	JP	2	70	CLEGG	W	11	75	CLEMENTS	IC	4	79
CLAYTON	HE	7	71	CLEARY	JW	3	306	CLEGG	WH	11	75	CLEMENTS	J	1	62
CLAYTON	HG	5	74	CLEARY	P	2	70	CLEGHORN	E	8	68	CLEMENTS	J	7	71
CLAYTON	HM	5	74	CLEARY	R	14	60	CLEGHORN	J	8	68	CLEMENTS	JH	2	71
CLAYTON	HT	4	78	CLEARY	W	10	47	CLEGHORN	T	2	70	CLEMENTS	JH	2	71
CLAYTON	J	2	70	CLEARY	W	13	93	CLEIFE	HW	4	78	CLEMENTS	JR	5	75
CLAYTON	J	4	78	CLEARY	WJ	3	36	CLEIFE	HW	4	78	CLEMENTS	JT	3	306
CLAYTON	J	7	71	CLEASBY	RB	11	75	CLEIFE	RC	10	47	CLEMENTS	JT	4	79
CLAYTON	J	8	67	CLEAVE	CS	3	306	CLELAND	EJ	2	70	CLEMENTS	NHR	1	62
CLAYTON	J	9	240	CLEAVE	JB	4	78	CLELFORD	WH	4	78	CLEMENTS	PW	5	75

CLEMENTS	R	3	36	CLIFF	L	8	68	CLIFTON	E	12	52	CLODE	FA	5	76
CLEMENTS	R	4	79	CLIFF	R	9	40	CLIFTON	EK	10	279	CLODE	FM	13	94
CLEMENTS	R	9	39	CLIFF	R	11	76	CLIFTON	F	10	47	CLODE	J	7	72
CLEMENTS	R	13	93	CLIFF	S	8	68	CLIFTON	FC	10	279	CLODE	SI	5	76
CLEMENTS	SG	2	71	CLIFF	T	7	72	CLIFTON	FG	12	52	CLOHOSY	WJ	2	71
CLEMENTS	SG	13	94	CLIFF	T	14	60	CLIFTON	FS	3	307	CLOKE	E	7	72
CLEMENTS	W	5	75	CLIFF	W	8	68	CLIFTON	FW	12	52	CLOKE	RA	2	72
CLEMENTS	WA	5	75	CLIFF	W	11	76	CLIFTON	G	6	84	CLOONEY	JJ	10	47
CLEMENTS	WC	2	71	CLIFFE	A	9	40	CLIFTON	H	6	84	CLOONEY	RM	10	47
CLEMENTS	WG	12	52	CLIFFE	F	14	60	CLIFTON	H	12	284	CLORAN	P	11	76
CLEMENTS	WH	3	306	CLIFFE	GH	14	61	CLIFTON	HG	6	84	CLORLEY	D	11	76
CLEMENTS	WJ	4	79	CLIFFE	H	8	68	CLIFTON	J	2	71	CLOSE	CR	8	68
CLEMIE	E	2	71	CLIFFE	H	14	61	CLIFTON	J	4	79	CLOSE	GW	13	94
CLEMIE	EB	2	71	CLIFFE	SO	1	62	CLIFTON	JH	6	84	CLOSE	H	8	68
CLEMIE	H	9	39	CLIFFE	W	11	76	CLIFTON	P	12	52	CLOSE	JH	9	241
CLEMIE	J	2	71	CLIFFE	WH	14	61	CLIFTON	SC	13	94	CLOSE	JW	9	241
CLEMINSON	J	14	60	CLIFFORD	A	8	68	CLIFTON	SEW	5	76	CLOSE	S	9	241
CLEMSON	EC	2	71	CLIFFORD	A	11	76	CLIFTON	T	12	53	CLOSE	TW	13	94
CLEMSON	W	6	83	CLIFFORD	C	10	47	CLIFTON	T	12	53	CLOTHIER	LV	3	307
CLETON	J	6	83	CLIFFORD	CJ	13	94	CLIFTON	WF	12	53	CLOUD	SF	2	72
CLEVEIL	H	9	40	CLIFFORD	E	9	40	CLIFTON	WG	7	72	CLOUD	W	2	72
CLEVELAND	G	3	306	CLIFFORD	ER	9	40	CLIGGETT	D	1	63	CLOUDSDALE	HL	11	76
CLEVELAND	HD	13	94	CLIFFORD	GF	3	306	CLIGGETT	N	1	63	CLOUGH	A	9	40
CLEVERLEY	RF	13	94	CLIFFORD	GH	9	40	CLIMO	JB	1	63	CLOUGH	A	9	241
CLEVERLY	FE	7	72	CLIFFORD	H	8	68	CLIMO	JH	11	76	CLOUGH	A	9	382
CLEVERLY	SG	10	47	CLIFFORD	H	14	61	CLIMPSON	TF	2	71	CLOUGH	AH	9	241
CLEVERSLEY	TC	13	94	CLIFFORD	HE	9	40	CLINCH	CH	2	71	CLOUGH	E	9	40
CLEWER	HS	7	72	CLIFFORD	HF	6	84	CLINCH	GE	12	53	CLOUGH	E	14	61
CLEWER	WE	4	79	CLIFFORD	J	2	71	CLINCH	JM	4	79	CLOUGH	E	14	61
CLEWES	J	11	75	CLIFFORD	J	6	84	CLINCH	JMC	4	79	CLOUGH	F	9	40
CLEWLEY	FWJ	1	62	CLIFFORD	J	7	72	CLINE	C	11	76	CLOUGH	F	9	241
CLEWLEY	J	6	84	CLIFFORD	JA	6	84	CLINE	G	6	84	CLOUGH	G	8	68
CLEWORTH	TH	14	60	CLIFFORD	JE	9	40	CLINE	HI	8	68	CLOUGH	G	8	68
CLEWS	A	5	75	CLIFFORD	JWH	14	61	CLINE	J	6	84	CLOUGH	GH	9	382
CLEWS	AE	6	84	CLIFFORD	OVO	1	63	CLINE	W	11	76	CLOUGH	H	9	382
CLEWS	AV	11	75	CLIFFORD	P	11	76	CLINES	W	8	68	CLOUGH	H	14	61
CLEWS	D	11	75	CLIFFORD	S	9	40	CLINKER	AC	13	94	CLOUGH	HG	1	63
CLEWS	E	11	75	CLIFFORD	T	7	72	CLINTON	AS	3	307	CLOUGH	J	8	69
CLEWS	F	5	75	CLIFFORD	TE	1	63	CLINTON	JF	7	72	CLOUGH	J	9	241
CLEWS	FH	6	84	CLIFFORD	W	2	71	CLINTON	S	4	79	CLOUGH	J	9	241
CLEWS	FR	11	75	CLIFFORD	W	4	79	CLINTON	T	4	79	CLOUGH	JA	9	241
CLEWS	J	11	75	CLIFFORD	W	6	84	CLINTON	W	4	79	CLOUGH	JB	1	63
CLEWS	JW	5	75	CLIFFORD	WG	13	94	CLIPSHAM	A	10	279	CLOUGH	JH	8	69
CLIBBON	W	5	75	CLIFFORD	WH	6	84	CLIPSTON	AJ	12	284	CLOUGH	JH	9	241
CLIBBON	W	5	75	CLIFT	AE	7	72	CLISBY	W	8	68	CLOUGH	O	9	40
CLIFF	A	11	76	CLIFT	CB	13	94	CLISSOLD	F	2	71	CLOUGH	O	9	40
CLIFF	AC	14	60	CLIFT	GW	1	63	CLISSOLD	SH	6	84	CLOUGH	S	11	76
CLIFF	CW	6	84	CLIFT	R	13	94	CLITHEROE	FA	4	79	CLOUGH	T	9	40
CLIFF	E	2	71	CLIFT	WH	2	71	CLITHEROE	J	4	79	CLOUGH	W	14	61
CLIFF	F	8	68	CLIFTON	AJ	3	36	CLIVE	A	13	94	CLOUGH	WE	9	241
CLIFF	H	9	40	CLIFTON	AJ	12	52	CLIVE	H	4	79	CLOUGH	WK	9	241
CLIFF	H	11	76	CLIFTON	C	12	52	CLOAD	L	11	76	CLOUT	AW	12	284
CLIFF	HS	13	94	CLIFTON	C	12	284	CLOAD	W	2	71	CLOUT	DT	5	76
CLIFF	J	7	72	CLIFTON	CA	10	47	CLODD	GA	13	94	CLOUT	ED	5	76
CLIFF	J	8	68	CLIFTON	D	6	84	CLODE	AB	7	72	CLOUT	WR	5	76

CLOUT	WT	5	76	COAKLEY	JC	13	95	COATES	W	9	242	COBBING	A	13	95
CLOUTT	H	8	69	COAKLEY	TR	13	95	COATES	W	9	382	COBBING	PA	13	95
CLOUTT	HA	8	69	COALBRAN	FC	10	279	COATES	W	10	279	COBBINGS	TAE	3	307
CLOVER	F	7	72	COALES	LD	7	73	COATES	WA	9	41	COBBOLD	A	4	80
CLOVER	IW	1	63	COALES	N	7	73	COATES	WH	6	85	COBBOLD	AW	1	63
CLOVES	H	6	84	COAN	C	8	69	COATES	WH	7	73	COBBOLD	H	7	73
CLOW	B	9	241	COAN	PO	1	63	COATES	WJ	6	85	COBBOLD	H	10	48
CLOW	C	1	63	COATES	A	2	72	COATH	R	3	36	COBBOLD	HWC	7	73
CLOW	C	14	61	COATES	A	5	76	COATH	SRG	7	73	COBDEN	S	13	95
CLOW	EH	7	72	COATES	A	9	40	COATS	A	9	41	COBERN	PH	4	80
CLOW	J	9	241	COATES	A	11	77	COATS	A	9	41	COBERN	WW	4	80
CLOW	JT	9	40	COATES	A	11	77	COATS	AT	2	72	COBLE	E	10	48
CLOW	JT	14	61	COATES	A	14	61	COATS	E	9	41	COBLES	W	5	76
CLOWES	A	1	63	COATES	AC	1	63	COATS	E	9	41	COBLEY	J	8	69
CLOWES	A	12	284	COATES	AE	8	69	COATS	H	9	41	COBLEY	W	6	85
CLOWES	J	11	76	COATES	AJ	10	48	COATS	JW	9	41	COBLEY	WJ	13	95
CLOWES	J	12	284	COATES	AW	6	85	COATS	P	9	41	COBOURNE	GE	6	85
CLOWES	JF	14	61	COATES	C	8	69	COATS	W	9	41	COBURN	A	14	62
CLOWES	W	14	61	COATES	C	8	69	COBAIN	W	11	77	COBURN	F	13	95
CLOWREY	F	11	76	COATES	C	11	77	COBB	A	2	72	COBURN	HC	2	72
CLOWSLEY	A	7	72	COATES	CG	14	61	COBB	A	13	95	COBURN	J	11	78
CLOY	H	11	76	COATES	DF	3	307	COBB	AE	10	48	COBURN	JG	13	95
CLOY	H	11	77	COATES	E	8	69	COBB	AG	6	85	COBURN	WH	14	62
CLUBB	RE	5	76	COATES	E	9	41	COBB	B	13	95	COCHRANE	A	5	76
CLUBLEY	E	9	40	COATES	F	6	85	COBB	C	3	36	COCHRANE	C	14	62
CLUCAS	H	11	77	COATES	F	9	41	COBB	C	11	77	COCHRANE	HT	2	72
CLUDERAY	G	9	241	COATES	F	9	242	COBB	CH	11	77	COCHRANE	J	14	62
CLUDERAY	T	8	69	COATES	F	9	242	COBB	F	2	72	COCHRANE	PE	14	62
CLUDERAY	T	8	69	COATES	FJ	2	72	COBB	F	5	76	COCHRANE	WJ	11	78
CLUE	S	10	47	COATES	FW	6	85	COBB	F	10	48	COCK	D	1	63
CLUEARD	GL	11	77	COATES	G	8	69	COBB	F	13	95	COCK	E	1	63
CLUEIT	N	6	84	COATES	G	8	69	COBB	FE	1	63	COCK	G	1	64
CLUER	M	13	94	COATES	GE	8	69	COBB	FT	10	279	COCK	H	1	64
CLUES	G	12	284	COATES	GH	8	69	COBB	G	10	48	COCK	P	1	64
CLUETT	ML	10	47	COATES	GR	11	77	COBB	H	13	95	COCKAYNE	J	8	70
CLUETT	RH	10	47	COATES	H	6	85	COBB	HA	10	279	COCKBILL	F	6	85
CLUETT	WW	10	48	COATES	H	8	69	COBB	HG	10	48	COCKBILL	J	13	95
CLULOW	E	11	77	COATES	H	9	41	COBB	HG	12	284	COCKBURN	AA	2	72
CLULOW	H	11	77	COATES	HR	10	279	COBB	HM	13	95	COCKCROFT	CH	9	242
CLULOW	W	11	77	COATES	J	8	69	COBB	J	11	77	COCKCROFT	FO	9	41
CLUNN	A	7	72	COATES	J	9	41	COBB	ML	1	63	COCKCROFT	W	11	78
CLUTTEN	AV	5	76	COATES	J	9	41	COBB	R	7	73	COCKER	H	8	70
CLUTTEN	ET	2	72	COATES	J	9	242	COBB	W	1	63	COCKERELL	H	12	284
CLUTTEN	HW	5	76	COATES	J	10	48	COBB	W	8	69	COCKERELL	JT	12	284
CLUTTERBUCK	AH	2	72	COATES	J	13	95	COBB	W	10	48	COCKERHAM	A	8	70
CLUTTERBUCK	WC	14	61	COATES	JC	8	69	COBB	WE	1	63	COCKERHAM	GW	8	70
CLUTTERBUCK	WH	6	84	COATES	JW	1	63	COBB	WT	4	80	COCKERHAM	S	8	70
CLYNES	S	14	61	COATES	JW	11	77	COBBETT	AG	4	80	COCKERHAM	S	11	78
COACKLEY	F	14	61	COATES	LA	1	63	COBBETT	C	4	80	COCKERILL	AA	12	284
COAD	EA	7	72	COATES	RE	11	77	COBBETT	CT	2	72	COCKERILL	DA	12	284
COAD	GW	2	72	COATES	S	8	69	COBBETT	F	13	95	COCKERILL	W	6	85
COAK	AE	4	80	COATES	S	9	242	COBBETT	F	13	95	COCKERTON	HC	7	73
COAK	HW	4	80	COATES	S	11	77	COBBETT	GH	10	48	COCKETT	AW	13	95
COAKER	W	1	63	COATES	W	8	69	COBBETT	J	10	279	COCKETT	J	13	96
COAKLEY	C	13	95	COATES	W	9	41	COBBETT	J	13	95	COCKFIELD	CJ	13	96

COCKIN	H	9	41	COE	GH	7	73	COHEN	H	14	62	COLBURT	C	12	53
COCKIN	T	9	41	COE	J	9	42	COHEN	H	14	62	COLCLOUGH	C	6	85
COCKING	JW	12	284	COE	J	9	242	COHEN	H	14	62	COLDBECK	AG	8	70
COCKING	W	11	78	COE	J	11	78	COHEN	I	14	62	COLDER	FA	6	86
COCKINGS	GH	12	53	COE	J	14	62	COHEN	J	2	73	COLDHAM	B	11	78
COCKLE	JA	13	96	COE	R	3	307	COHEN	J	8	70	COLDRICK	A	6	86
COCKLE	SWG	4	80	COE	RW	1	64	COHEN	L	14	62	COLDRICK	A	6	86
COCKLIN	J	3	307	COE	RWM	1	64	COHEN	M	6	85	COLDWELL	E	9	242
COCKMAN	J	7	73	COEN	CL	3	36	COHEN	M	14	62	COLDWELL	GA	9	242
COCKMAN	M	7	73	COFFEE	R	13	96	COHEN	M	14	62	COLDWELL	H	8	70
COCKMAN	OL	7	73	COFFEY	C	2	72	COHEN	M	14	62	COLDWELL	J	14	63
COCKRAM	G	4	80	COFFEY	J	3	307	COHEN	N	2	73	COLDWELL	JA	3	36
COCKRAM	P	10	48	COFFIELD	G	7	73	COHEN	N	14	63	COLDWELL	T	14	63
COCKRAM	WJ	6	85	COFFIELD	H	13	96	COHEN	P	2	73	COLE	A	1	64
COCKRAN	AJ	10	48	COFFILL	DH	3	36	COHEN	S	14	63	COLE	A	1	64
COCKRANE	R	10	48	COFFILL	SA	3	36	COHEN	S	14	63	COLE	A	1	64
COCKRELL	J	13	96	COFFIN	A	7	73	COHEN	S	14	63	COLE	A	2	73
COCKRILL	CFP	2	72	COFFIN	C	10	48	COHEN	S	14	63	COLE	A	2	73
COCKROFT	F	9	41	COFFIN	CJ	4	80	COHEN	T	6	85	COLE	A	4	81
COCKROFT	G	10	48	COFFIN	FW	1	64	COHEN	T	14	62	COLE	A	4	81
COCKROFT	H	8	70	COFFIN	G	6	85	COHEN	W	14	63	COLE	A	4	81
COCKROFT	J	9	42	COFFIN	HJ	6	85	COILE	EJ	10	48	COLE	A	8	70
COCKROFT	T	9	42	COFFIN	J	7	73	COIT	G	4	80	COLE	A	13	97
COCKS	AJC	1	64	COFFIN	JL	10	280	COIT	WJ	4	80	COLE	AA	11	78
COCKS	GF	7	73	COFFIN	LJ	4	80	COKER	A	13	97	COLE	AD	4	81
COCKS	H	8	70	COFFIN	WH	6	85	COKER	AE	5	76	COLE	AE	4	81
COCKS	J	13	96	COGAN	E	1	64	COKER	C	3	36	COLE	AE	4	81
COCKS	JH	13	96	COGAN	F	9	42	COKER	E	13	97	COLE	AE	9	242
COCKS	WT	1	64	COGAN	FT	1	64	COKER	F	4	80	COLE	AF	10	48
COCKSEDGE	A	9	242	COGAN	H	1	64	COKER	FW	4	80	COLE	AG	10	280
COCKSHOTT	F	9	42	COGAN	T	13	96	COKER	G	2	73	COLE	AH	7	73
COCKSHOTT	H	9	42	COGDELL	EC	2	72	COKER	H	13	97	COLE	AJ	2	73
COCKSON	T	9	42	COGGAN	H	2	73	COKER	H	13	97	COLE	AJ	5	76
COCKWILL	F	9	42	COGGER	O	13	96	COKER	P	1	64	COLE	AJ	12	53
COCKWILL	J	9	42	COGGILL	F	8	70	COKER	PJ	1	64	COLE	AJ	13	97
COCUP	C	1	64	COGGINS	AH	3	36	COKER	WA	13	97	COLE	B	12	421
CODD	F	3	307	COGGINS	G	6	85	COKER	WJ	2	73	COLE	B	13	97
CODD	J	4	80	COGGINS	H	1	64	COLBECK	W	8	70	COLE	BG	4	81
CODDINGTON	WJ	13	96	COGGINS	H	2	73	COLBECK	W	8	70	COLE	C	3	36
CODLING	A	1	64	COGGINS	WT	13	96	COLBERN	FH	4	80	COLE	C	4	81
CODLING	A	1	64	COGGLES	AG	5	76	COLBERN	HG	4	80	COLE	C	4	81
CODLING	A	13	96	COGGS	E	9	42	COLBERT	EJ	12	53	COLE	C	7	73
CODLING	E	10	279	COGHILL	AS	1	64	COLBERT	GH	12	53	COLE	C	10	49
CODLING	E	10	279	COGHLAN	A	11	78	COLBERT	H	12	53	COLE	CD	7	74
CODLING	G	1	64	COGILL	WH	8	70	COLBETT	M	1	64	COLE	CF	2	73
CODLING	HC	2	72	COGLAN	E	11	78	COLBON	CB	12	53	COLE	CH	3	36
CODLING	JT	12	53	COGLAN	T	11	78	COLBORNE	BW	4	80	COLE	CH	4	81
CODLING	RJ	3	36	COGMAN	WS	4	80	COLBORNE	FS	4	80	COLE	CJ	4	81
CODY	HJ	13	96	COGSWELL	EA	13	96	COLBORNE	V	4	81	COLE	CR	10	280
CODY	WJ	13	96	COHEN	A	8	70	COLBOURN	AP	12	53	COLE	CT	4	81
COE	A	3	36	COHEN	B	14	62	COLBOURNE	A	10	48	COLE	CWJ	4	81
COE	BMO	12	53	COHEN	BT	14	62	COLBOURNE	EB	4	81	COLE	DA	3	307
COE	CT	12	285	COHEN	H	8	70	COLBOURNE	G	7	73	COLE	E	4	81
COE	F	9	42	COHEN	H	14	62	COLBOURNE	JA	10	48	COLE	E	6	86
COE	G	11	78	COHEN	H	14	62	COLBOURNE	JH	10	280	COLE	EA	4	81
								COLBRIDGE	J	11	78				

COLE	EE	10	49	COLE	J	7	74	COLEBOURN	J	11	78	COLEMAN	J	1	65
COLE	EG	4	81	COLE	J	8	70	COLEBOURN	W	11	78	COLEMAN	J	1	65
COLE	EJ	2	73	COLE	J	10	49	COLECLIFFE	J	11	78	COLEMAN	J	3	307
COLE	ER	1	64	COLE	J	14	63	COLEGATE	W	13	98	COLEMAN	J	6	86
COLE	ET	1	65	COLE	JA	7	74	COLEMAN	A	1	65	COLEMAN	J	8	71
COLE	F	1	65	COLE	JA	12	53	COLEMAN	A	1	65	COLEMAN	J	9	42
COLE	F	2	73	COLE	JH	11	78	COLEMAN	A	3	37	COLEMAN	J	14	63
COLE	F	3	37	COLE	JH	13	97	COLEMAN	A	5	77	COLEMAN	M	1	66
COLE	F	5	76	COLE	JJ	8	70	COLEMAN	A	9	42	COLEMAN	O	6	86
COLE	F	6	86	COLE	JT	13	97	COLEMAN	A	10	49	COLEMAN	PC	2	74
COLE	F	12	53	COLE	JW	4	82	COLEMAN	AE	1	65	COLEMAN	PW	5	77
COLE	FA	3	307	COLE	L	4	82	COLEMAN	AE	7	74	COLEMAN	R	2	74
COLE	FC	6	86	COLE	M	12	421	COLEMAN	AJ	2	73	COLEMAN	S	2	74
COLE	FG	1	65	COLE	M	14	63	COLEMAN	AJ	12	285	COLEMAN	S	12	54
COLE	FH	5	76	COLE	PE	4	82	COLEMAN	AL	1	65	COLEMAN	S	13	98
COLE	FJ	1	65	COLE	R	1	65	COLEMAN	AW	1	65	COLEMAN	SE	12	54
COLE	FJ	10	280	COLE	RC	4	82	COLEMAN	AW	7	74	COLEMAN	SJ	6	86
COLE	FL	3	37	COLE	RH	5	77	COLEMAN	AW	12	285	COLEMAN	ST	1	66
COLE	FT	4	81	COLE	RJ	10	49	COLEMAN	C	2	73	COLEMAN	T	8	71
COLE	FW	10	280	COLE	RJ	10	280	COLEMAN	C	3	307	COLEMAN	TB	5	77
COLE	G	4	81	COLE	RM	12	421	COLEMAN	C	3	307	COLEMAN	VW	13	98
COLE	G	5	76	COLE	RS	1	65	COLEMAN	C	6	86	COLEMAN	W	3	307
COLE	G	5	77	COLE	SF	4	82	COLEMAN	C	7	74	COLEMAN	W	7	74
COLE	G	7	74	COLE	SM	7	74	COLEMAN	CG	12	285	COLEMAN	W	12	285
COLE	G	10	49	COLE	SW	4	82	COLEMAN	CJ	12	53	COLEMAN	W	14	63
COLE	GE	4	82	COLE	T	4	82	COLEMAN	CS	2	73	COLEMAN	W	14	63
COLE	GE	4	82	COLE	T	4	82	COLEMAN	CT	1	65	COLEMAN	WA	2	74
COLE	GH	4	82	COLE	T	13	97	COLEMAN	D	12	53	COLEMAN	WC	6	86
COLE	GL	4	82	COLE	TH	3	307	COLEMAN	E	1	65	COLEMAN	WC	12	54
COLE	GP	13	97	COLE	TJ	2	73	COLEMAN	E	8	70	COLEMAN	WG	2	74
COLE	GW	4	82	COLE	TL	4	82	COLEMAN	E	12	54	COLEMAN	WG	5	77
COLE	H	4	82	COLE	V	12	421	COLEMAN	E	12	54	COLEMAN	WH	1	66
COLE	H	4	82	COLE	W	2	73	COLEMAN	E	12	54	COLEMAN	WH	3	307
COLE	H	6	86	COLE	W	4	82	COLEMAN	E	14	65	COLEMAN	WJ	2	74
COLE	H	8	70	COLE	W	10	280	COLEMAN	EH	13	98	COLEMAN	WJ	5	77
COLE	H	9	242	COLE	W	13	97	COLEMAN	EL	13	98	COLEMAN	WL	5	77
COLE	H	12	53	COLE	W	14	63	COLEMAN	F	5	77	COLEMAN	WR	2	74
COLE	H	13	97	COLE	WA	13	97	COLEMAN	FC	10	49	COLEMAN	WR	3	308
COLE	H	14	63	COLE	WC	2	73	COLEMAN	FP	6	86	COLERIDGE	ERC	7	74
COLE	HA	3	307	COLE	WE	6	86	COLEMAN	FW	13	98	COLES	A	5	77
COLE	HAG	13	97	COLE	WE	14	63	COLEMAN	FWG	3	37	COLES	A	12	54
COLE	HC	4	82	COLE	WF	1	65	COLEMAN	G	2	74	COLES	A	13	98
COLE	HC	7	74	COLE	WFW	10	49	COLEMAN	G	10	49	COLES	AB	7	74
COLE	HC	10	280	COLE	WH	1	65	COLEMAN	G	12	54	COLES	AW	7	74
COLE	HE	2	73	COLE	WH	4	82	COLEMAN	GF	3	37	COLES	B	12	54
COLE	HG	10	49	COLE	WH	13	97	COLEMAN	GR	10	280	COLES	C	12	54
COLE	HJ	12	421	COLE	WH	13	98	COLEMAN	GT	10	49	COLES	CH	10	280
COLE	HR	1	65	COLE	WJ	1	65	COLEMAN	H	4	82	COLES	E	12	54
COLE	HW	6	86	COLE	WJ	3	307	COLEMAN	H	7	74	COLES	EF	12	285
COLE	HW	10	49	COLE	WJ	13	97	COLEMAN	H	7	74	COLES	FA	4	83
COLE	HW	13	97	COLE	WNE	6	86	COLEMAN	H	12	54	COLES	FA	4	83
COLE	J	1	65	COLE	WR	7	74	COLEMAN	HA	7	74	COLES	FL	7	74
COLE	J	1	65	COLE	WS	1	65	COLEMAN	HA	13	98	COLES	FL	12	285
COLE	J	3	307	COLE	WW	13	98	COLEMAN	HB	1	65	COLES	FR	5	77
COLE	J	4	82	COLEBOURN	J	11	78	COLEMAN	HG	1	65	COLES	FW	4	83

COLES	G	10	49	COLEY	WF	6	86	COLLIER	BC	11	79	COLLINGE	J	4	83
COLES	G	12	54	COLGAN	E	14	63	COLLIER	C	1	66	COLLINGE	J	11	79
COLES	G	14	63	COLGATE	HC	2	74	COLLIER	C	12	285	COLLINGRIDGE	W	7	75
COLES	GBH	12	285	COLIN	W	13	98	COLLIER	EA	7	75	COLLINGS	A	4	83
COLES	GD	5	77	COLL	J	11	79	COLLIER	F	4	83	COLLINGS	AJ	2	75
COLES	GF	10	49	COLLAR	DA	12	285	COLLIER	FG	4	83	COLLINGS	GW	4	83
COLES	GH	5	77	COLLAR	F	12	285	COLLIER	FJ	11	79	COLLINGS	H	4	83
COLES	GH	10	49	COLLAR	JW	12	285	COLLIER	FR	12	285	COLLINGS	J	2	75
COLES	GL	1	66	COLLAR	TH	12	285	COLLIER	G	3	37	COLLINGS	P	7	75
COLES	GW	5	77	COLLARBONE	AE	5	78	COLLIER	G	5	78	COLLINGS	SB	7	75
COLES	H	12	54	COLLARBONE	HH	5	78	COLLIER	G	9	242	COLLINGS	SH	2	75
COLES	HC	5	77	COLLARBONE	W	5	78	COLLIER	G	14	64	COLLINGS	WJ	7	75
COLES	HE	4	83	COLLARD	AJ	2	74	COLLIER	GH	1	66	COLLINGS	WJ	13	99
COLES	HE	6	86	COLLARD	EG	2	74	COLLIER	GW	7	75	COLLINGWOOD	ARC	1	66
COLES	HJ	5	77	COLLARD	FE	1	66	COLLIER	H	8	71	COLLINGWOOD	CC	10	280
COLES	HJ	13	98	COLLARD	FG	10	49	COLLIER	H	11	79	COLLINGWOOD	F	10	50
COLES	HW	12	54	COLLARD	FWJ	1	66	COLLIER	H	14	64	COLLINGWOOD	H	12	55
COLES	J	5	77	COLLARD	HJ	3	308	COLLIER	HJ	5	78	COLLINGWOOD	S	4	83
COLES	J	12	285	COLLARD	W	10	49	COLLIER	HW	5	78	COLLINS	A	1	66
COLES	JC	13	98	COLLARD	W	13	98	COLLIER	J	3	37	COLLINS	A	2	75
COLES	JJ	7	74	COLLEDGE	H	8	71	COLLIER	J	11	79	COLLINS	A	2	75
COLES	JW	13	98	COLLEDGE	WH	6	87	COLLIER	J	11	79	COLLINS	A	4	83
COLES	M	12	54	COLLEPY	H	8	71	COLLIER	J	13	99	COLLINS	A	4	83
COLES	P	12	54	COLLER	FA	2	74	COLLIER	J	13	99	COLLINS	A	4	83
COLES	PG	12	54	COLLER	W	5	78	COLLIER	J	14	64	COLLINS	A	4	83
COLES	PR	5	77	COLLETT	AG	5	78	COLLIER	J	14	64	COLLINS	A	5	78
COLES	R	12	54	COLLETT	C	2	74	COLLIER	J	14	64	COLLINS	A	6	87
COLES	R	12	285	COLLETT	EB	13	99	COLLIER	J	14	64	COLLINS	A	6	87
COLES	RT	5	77	COLLETT	F	9	242	COLLIER	J	14	64	COLLINS	A	6	87
COLES	S	5	78	COLLETT	HJ	10	49	COLLIER	JD	14	64	COLLINS	A	6	87
COLES	S	13	98	COLLETT	HJ	13	99	COLLIER	JH	2	75	COLLINS	A	6	87
COLES	S	14	63	COLLETT	JW	10	49	COLLIER	JH	11	79	COLLINS	A	11	79
COLES	SG	5	78	COLLETT	NH	10	49	COLLIER	JH	12	285	COLLINS	AC	12	286
COLES	SJ	7	74	COLLETT	R	2	74	COLLIER	JT	13	99	COLLINS	AE	6	87
COLES	T	1	66	COLLETT	R	5	78	COLLIER	JT	14	64	COLLINS	AG	4	83
COLES	T	12	54	COLLETT	W	2	74	COLLIER	JW	11	79	COLLINS	AH	3	308
COLES	TE	2	74	COLLETT	W	4	83	COLLIER	N	14	64	COLLINS	AH	9	242
COLES	TE	12	285	COLLETT	WR	7	75	COLLIER	PW	7	75	COLLINS	AH	9	382
COLES	TW	4	83	COLLEY	A	5	78	COLLIER	S	11	79	COLLINS	AJ	1	66
COLES	W	13	98	COLLEY	AJ	5	78	COLLIER	T	5	78	COLLINS	AJ	3	37
COLES	WG	12	55	COLLEY	J	7	75	COLLIER	TR	14	64	COLLINS	AJ	4	84
COLESBY	F	11	78	COLLEY	J	8	71	COLLIER	TS	12	285	COLLINS	AJ	6	87
COLESHILL	J	1	66	COLLEY	JH	6	87	COLLIER	W	11	79	COLLINS	AT	4	84
COLESHILL	R	1	66	COLLEY	RT	8	71	COLLIER	W	11	79	COLLINS	AT	13	99
COLESHILL	R	1	66	COLLEY	TG	3	308	COLLIER	WD	12	285	COLLINS	AW	6	87
COLESHILL	W	2	74	COLLEY	W	13	99	COLLIER	WFD	12	286	COLLINS	B	1	66
COLESHILL	WE	1	66	COLLEY	WH	4	83	COLLIER	WP	12	286	COLLINS	B	9	382
COLEWELL	PJ	5	78	COLLEY	WJ	11	79	COLLIHOLE	VWA	3	308	COLLINS	B	13	99
COLEY	A	8	71	COLLIE	C	13	99	COLLIMORE	WJ	4	83	COLLINS	C	3	308
COLEY	A	11	79	COLLIE	F	12	55	COLLING	B	13	99	COLLINS	C	3	308
COLEY	BJ	6	86	COLLIE	RW	2	74	COLLING	EJ	13	99	COLLINS	C	6	87
COLEY	FC	13	98	COLLIER	A	13	99	COLLING	H	13	99	COLLINS	C	10	280
COLEY	JR	12	55	COLLIER	AE	1	66	COLLING	WBC	12	55	COLLINS	C	12	286
COLEY	PA	4	83	COLLIER	AE	14	63	COLLINGBOURNE	HA	3	37	COLLINS	C	14	64
COLEY	SW	12	55	COLLIER	AF	2	74	COLLINGE	A	14	64	COLLINS	CA	3	309
								COLLINGE	HW	14	64	COLLINS	CA	12	55

COLLINS	CC	5	78	COLLINS	GR	2	75	COLLINS	JH	13	100	COLLINS	VC	13	100
COLLINS	CE	1	66	COLLINS	GR	10	280	COLLINS	JJ	7	75	COLLINS	W	1	67
COLLINS	CH	4	84	COLLINS	GW	3	308	COLLINS	JJ	11	80	COLLINS	W	1	67
COLLINS	CT	3	37	COLLINS	H	2	75	COLLINS	JT	6	88	COLLINS	W	3	308
COLLINS	CT	4	84	COLLINS	H	2	75	COLLINS	JT	6	88	COLLINS	W	4	84
COLLINS	CW	10	50	COLLINS	H	3	308	COLLINS	JW	5	79	COLLINS	W	6	88
COLLINS	D	3	308	COLLINS	H	3	308	COLLINS	JW	7	75	COLLINS	W	6	88
COLLINS	DC	13	99	COLLINS	H	4	84	COLLINS	JW	13	100	COLLINS	W	7	76
COLLINS	E	3	37	COLLINS	H	6	87	COLLINS	L	6	88	COLLINS	W	7	76
COLLINS	E	6	87	COLLINS	H	6	88	COLLINS	M	1	67	COLLINS	W	7	76
COLLINS	E	7	75	COLLINS	H	6	88	COLLINS	M	6	88	COLLINS	W	8	71
COLLINS	E	7	75	COLLINS	H	6	88	COLLINS	M	13	100	COLLINS	W	10	50
COLLINS	E	8	71	COLLINS	H	6	88	COLLINS	N	3	37	COLLINS	W	11	80
COLLINS	E	9	42	COLLINS	H	7	75	COLLINS	O	14	65	COLLINS	W	12	55
COLLINS	E	9	42	COLLINS	H	8	71	COLLINS	P	6	88	COLLINS	W	12	286
COLLINS	E	11	79	COLLINS	H	11	79	COLLINS	P	9	242	COLLINS	W	12	286
COLLINS	EA	4	84	COLLINS	H	12	286	COLLINS	P	10	50	COLLINS	W	13	100
COLLINS	EA	6	87	COLLINS	H	12	286	COLLINS	P	12	286	COLLINS	W	13	100
COLLINS	EA	9	42	COLLINS	H	13	100	COLLINS	PC	9	382	COLLINS	W	13	100
COLLINS	EH	3	308	COLLINS	H	14	64	COLLINS	PF	14	65	COLLINS	W	14	65
COLLINS	EJ	12	55	COLLINS	HA	5	79	COLLINS	R	3	308	COLLINS	WA	3	309
COLLINS	EL	4	84	COLLINS	HE	3	308	COLLINS	R	7	76	COLLINS	WB	6	88
COLLINS	ET	4	84	COLLINS	HE	4	84	COLLINS	R	7	76	COLLINS	WC	12	286
COLLINS	EV	13	99	COLLINS	HJ	6	88	COLLINS	R	13	100	COLLINS	WE	6	88
COLLINS	F	1	66	COLLINS	HJ	7	75	COLLINS	RC	10	50	COLLINS	WE	6	88
COLLINS	F	1	66	COLLINS	HJ	7	75	COLLINS	RF	3	37	COLLINS	WE	10	280
COLLINS	F	2	75	COLLINS	HJ	13	99	COLLINS	RF	4	84	COLLINS	WE	11	80
COLLINS	F	4	84	COLLINS	HW	13	100	COLLINS	RH	3	37	COLLINS	WE	12	286
COLLINS	F	5	78	COLLINS	J	2	75	COLLINS	RJ	10	280	COLLINS	WE	13	100
COLLINS	F	5	78	COLLINS	J	2	75	COLLINS	RL	7	76	COLLINS	WF	3	309
COLLINS	F	6	87	COLLINS	J	3	37	COLLINS	RL	11	80	COLLINS	WG	6	89
COLLINS	F	7	75	COLLINS	J	3	37	COLLINS	S	6	88	COLLINS	WH	2	75
COLLINS	F	7	75	COLLINS	J	3	308	COLLINS	S	7	76	COLLINS	WH	10	50
COLLINS	F	8	71	COLLINS	J	8	71	COLLINS	S	9	42	COLLINS	WH	11	80
COLLINS	F	9	242	COLLINS	J	8	71	COLLINS	S	10	50	COLLINS	WH	14	65
COLLINS	F	14	64	COLLINS	J	8	71	COLLINS	S	11	80	COLLINS	WJ	1	67
COLLINS	F	14	64	COLLINS	J	8	71	COLLINS	SA	6	88	COLLINS	WJ	7	76
COLLINS	F	14	64	COLLINS	J	8	71	COLLINS	SF	4	84	COLLINS	WJ	12	286
COLLINS	FE	3	37	COLLINS	J	10	280	COLLINS	SH	7	76	COLLINS	WP	3	38
COLLINS	FG	6	87	COLLINS	J	11	80	COLLINS	SJ	4	84	COLLINS	WP	6	89
COLLINS	FJ	3	37	COLLINS	J	11	80	COLLINS	SJ	12	286	COLLINS	WT	4	84
COLLINS	FJW	10	50	COLLINS	J	11	80	COLLINS	SP	11	80	COLLINS	WW	10	280
COLLINS	FW	3	37	COLLINS	J	11	80	COLLINS	SW	7	76	COLLINSON	A	14	65
COLLINS	FW	4	84	COLLINS	J	13	100	COLLINS	T	1	67	COLLINSON	CV	10	50
COLLINS	G	2	75	COLLINS	J	13	100	COLLINS	T	1	67	COLLINSON	D	14	65
COLLINS	G	6	87	COLLINS	J	13	100	COLLINS	T	3	308	COLLINSON	GH	10	50
COLLINS	G	9	42	COLLINS	J	13	100	COLLINS	T	5	79	COLLINSON	H	8	71
COLLINS	G	11	79	COLLINS	J	14	64	COLLINS	T	11	80	COLLINSON	HR	10	50
COLLINS	GA	6	87	COLLINS	J	14	64	COLLINS	TA	3	37	COLLINSON	HW	8	71
COLLINS	GA	9	42	COLLINS	J	14	65	COLLINS	TB	7	76	COLLINSON	J	8	71
COLLINS	GE	4	84	COLLINS	JD	2	75	COLLINS	TE	13	100	COLLINSON	J	8	72
COLLINS	GEC	1	66	COLLINS	JE	1	67	COLLINS	TG	13	100	COLLINSON	J	8	72
COLLINS	GFH	5	79	COLLINS	JH	1	67	COLLINS	TP	2	75	COLLINSON	JE	9	43
COLLINS	GJ	13	99	COLLINS	JH	6	88	COLLINS	TW	1	67	COLLINSON	M	9	43
COLLINS	GJR	2	75	COLLINS	JH	7	75	COLLINS	TW	7	76	COLLINSON	S	9	43

COLLINSON	S	9	242	COLSTON	CF	2	76	COMPTON	CH	10	281	CONKLING	WG	2	76
COLLINSON	W	8	72	COLSTON	ES	3	309	COMPTON	EC	10	50	CONLEY	CJ	2	76
COLLINSON	W	8	72	COLTON	AW	2	76	COMPTON	ES	7	77	CONLEY	E	2	76
COLLINSON	WH	1	67	COLTON	PE	3	309	COMPTON	FJ	5	79	CONLEY	F	11	81
COLLINTON	HW	12	286	COLTON	T	12	287	COMPTON	FW	7	77	CONLEY	G	6	89
COLLIS	A	2	75	COLUMBINE	GW	3	309	COMPTON	GH	10	281	CONLEY	J	2	77
COLLIS	C	4	84	COLUMBINE	HJ	14	65	COMPTON	H	11	80	CONLEY	J	11	81
COLLIS	CH	2	75	COLUMBINE	JP	14	65	COMPTON	J	12	286	CONLEY	JT	11	81
COLLIS	CJ	4	84	COLUMBINE	RJ	14	65	COMPTON	JW	4	86	CONLEY	W	6	89
COLLIS	GW	12	286	COLVERSON	F	4	85	COMPTON	PC	4	86	CONLIN	W	14	66
COLLIS	H	6	89	COLVERSON	WJ	4	85	COMPTON	PR	4	86	CONLON	A	14	66
COLLIS	HG	10	280	COLVIL	GL	2	76	COMPTON	R	13	101	CONLON	H	8	72
COLLIS	J	14	65	COLVIL	J	2	76	COMPTON	RL	2	76	CONLON	J	9	43
COLLIS	ME	4	84	COLVILLE	E	4	85	COMPTON	RW	4	86	CONN	D	8	72
COLLIS	T	14	65	COLVIN	F	2	76	COMPTON	T	12	55	CONN	GR	6	89
COLLIS	WH	6	89	COLWELL	D	1	67	COMPTON	W	7	77	CONNELL	DO	3	38
COLLIS	WT	10	281	COLWELL	D	1	67	COMPTON	WE	10	50	CONNELL	E	9	243
COLLISON	GW	3	309	COLWELL	F	1	67	COMPTON	WJ	2	76	CONNELL	E	11	81
COLLISON	H	3	309	COLWELL	FJ	10	50	COMSTIVE	H	8	72	CONNELL	EJ	13	101
COLLISON	H	9	43	COLWELL	H	10	50	CONAN-DOYLE	E	10	281	CONNELL	F	9	43
COLLISON	JE	1	67	COLWELL	J	1	67	CONAWAY	A	13	101	CONNELL	F	11	81
COLLISS	W	4	85	COLWELL	J	13	101	CONCANNON	W	14	65	CONNELL	G	2	77
COLLMAN	PE	2	75	COLWELL	JHT	14	65	CONDICK	JJ	2	76	CONNELL	GE	1	67
COLLMAN	WHA	7	76	COLWELL	T	9	43	CONDICK	JJ	2	76	CONNELL	HP	1	68
COLLOM	WT	7	76	COLWELL	W	2	76	CONDLIFFE	E	10	50	CONNELL	J	1	68
COLLORAN	HW	4	85	COLWELL	W	11	80	CONDON	AJ	3	309	CONNELL	J	7	77
COLLS	CC	1	67	COLWELL	WC	1	67	CONDON	D	11	80	CONNELL	J	9	382
COLLYER	AT	13	100	COLWELL	WG	13	101	CONDON	DH	3	309	CONNELL	JJ	6	89
COLLYER	FB	4	85	COLWICK	W	11	80	CONDON	J	14	66	CONNELL	JM	1	68
COLLYER	GW	7	76	COLYER	GL	4	85	CONDON	P	3	309	CONNELL	JW	7	77
COLLYER	LW	5	79	COLYER	GL	4	85	CONDON	R	1	67	CONNELL	JW	8	72
COLLYER	TJ	13	101	COLYER	W	13	101	CONDON	S	3	309	CONNELL	L	3	38
COLLYER	W	2	76	COMAN	CH	7	76	CONDON	W	1	67	CONNELL	RH	3	309
COLLYER	WH	4	85	COMAR	W	11	80	CONDON	W	4	86	CONNELL	W	14	66
COLLYER	WJ	4	85	COMB	TJ	7	77	CONDREN	CR	6	89	CONNELL	WP	14	66
COLLYER	WJ	12	286	COMBE	W	9	242	CONDRON	J	11	80	CONNELLY	H	4	86
COLLYER	WJ	13	101	COMBEN	HE	3	309	CONDRON	WH	14	66	CONNELLY	MC	1	68
COLMAN	EC	5	79	COMBEN	RG	10	50	CONDUC	WG	4	86	CONNELLY	T	9	43
COLMAN	GJW	4	85	COMBER	A	3	309	CONDUIT	G	11	80	CONNELLY	T	9	243
COLMAN	HW	10	50	COMBER	J	1	67	CONEY	A	3	38	CONNELLY	T	14	66
COLMAN	JF	4	85	COMBEY	W	14	65	CONEY	AF	13	101	CONNELLY	WH	3	310
COLMAN	JF	4	85	COMELANSKY	S	14	65	CONEY	AJ	14	66	CONNER	A	4	86
COLMAN	JM	4	85	COMER	SW	13	101	CONEY	ER	6	89	CONNER	CH	6	89
COLMAN	JW	2	76	COMERFORD	F	14	65	CONEY	G	6	89	CONNER	F	11	81
COLMAN	TW	4	85	COMFORT	H	2	76	CONEY	I	2	76	CONNER	J	11	81
COLMAN	W	3	38	COMLAY	AG	10	50	CONEY	J	4	86	CONNETT	AE	3	310
COLMER	A	4	85	COMLAY	WJ	10	50	CONFREY	J	8	72	CONNETT	EE	3	310
COLMER	F	4	85	COMLEY	MJ	13	101	CONFREY	W	8	72	CONNETT	H	2	77
COLMER	GR	4	85	COMMESKY	JW	14	65	CONGDON	W	6	89	CONNETT	W	7	77
COLMER	P	4	85	COMMONS	J	8	72	CONGERTON	AE	2	76	CONNIRE	M	1	68
COLMER	S	4	85	COMMONS	W	13	101	CONGLETON	JW	14	66	CONNOCK	J	13	101
COLMER	WR	13	101	COMPTON	AA	10	50	CONGREVE	C	5	79	CONNOCK	JAE	4	86
COLQUHOUN	GW	3	309	COMPTON	BW	4	85	CONGREVE	J	6	89	CONNOCK	OM	13	101
COLQUHOUN	J	7	76	COMPTON	C	4	86	CONIE	A	12	286	CONNOCK	TJ	3	310
COLRILL	J	3	309	COMPTON	CE	10	281	CONJUITE	AG	13	101	CONNOLL	E	2	77

CONNOLLY	C	8	72	CONNOR	T	14	67	CONSTERDINE	F	11	82	COOK	AG	12	56
CONNOLLY	F	7	77	CONNOR	TJ	13	102	CONVOY	GJ	3	310	COOK	AH	3	38
CONNOLLY	GA	13	101	CONNOR	W	6	90	CONVY	F	8	72	COOK	AH	4	86
CONNOLLY	J	2	77	CONNOR	W	11	82	CONWAY	C	8	72	COOK	AH	5	79
CONNOLLY	J	14	66	CONNOR	W	13	102	CONWAY	C	11	82	COOK	AJ	2	77
CONNOLLY	JE	2	77	CONNOR	WE	14	67	CONWAY	CE	10	281	COOK	AJ	4	86
CONNOLLY	M	11	81	CONNORTON	H	3	38	CONWAY	CW	1	68	COOK	AJ	5	79
CONNOLLY	M	14	66	CONOLLY	CH	7	77	CONWAY	F	13	102	COOK	AJ	5	79
CONNOLLY	M	14	66	CONOLLY	F	4	86	CONWAY	G	8	72	COOK	AJ	10	51
CONNOLLY	P	6	89	CONOLLY	SE	7	77	CONWAY	H	9	243	COOK	AL	6	90
CONNOLLY	P	13	102	CONQUEST	A	5	79	CONWAY	J	3	310	COOK	AR	5	80
CONNOLLY	T	11	81	CONQUEST	C	3	310	CONWAY	J	3	310	COOK	AT	1	68
CONNOLLY	T	14	66	CONQUEST	HE	14	67	CONWAY	J	8	72	COOK	AT	1	68
CONNOLLY	W	3	310	CONQUEST	HJ	5	79	CONWAY	J	13	102	COOK	ATW	7	78
CONNOLLY	W	11	81	CONRAN	A	3	310	CONWAY	JW	13	102	COOK	AV	10	281
CONNOLLY	WJ	9	243	CONROY	AD	9	43	CONWAY	KL	11	82	COOK	AW	5	80
CONNOLLY	WT	11	81	CONROY	E	11	82	CONWAY	SE	5	79	COOK	AW	7	78
CONNON	WB	1	68	CONROY	EA	1	68	CONWAY	W	14	67	COOK	AW	13	103
CONNOR	A	10	51	CONROY	EW	1	68	CONWAY	WB	7	77	COOK	AW	13	103
CONNOR	A	12	55	CONROY	H	9	43	CONWELL	TH	11	82	COOK	B	4	86
CONNOR	B	13	102	CONROY	J	11	82	CONWELL	W	9	43	COOK	BR	2	77
CONNOR	C	11	81	CONROY	J	11	82	CONYERS	J	6	90	COOK	BW	5	80
CONNOR	CA	2	77	CONROY	J	14	67	CONYERS	JA	8	73	COOK	C	1	68
CONNOR	D	6	89	CONROY	JW	4	86	COOGAN	J	14	67	COOK	C	1	68
CONNOR	D	11	81	CONROY	P	9	382	COOGAN	PG	10	51	COOK	C	2	77
CONNOR	E	3	310	CONROY	W	11	82	COOK	A	4	86	COOK	C	2	77
CONNOR	E	7	77	CONS	A	7	77	COOK	A	5	79	COOK	C	4	86
CONNOR	E	11	81	CONS	S	7	77	COOK	A	5	79	COOK	C	5	80
CONNOR	E	11	81	CONS	WR	7	77	COOK	A	7	77	COOK	C	5	80
CONNOR	F	11	81	CONSTABLE	AA	3	38	COOK	A	7	78	COOK	C	7	78
CONNOR	F	14	66	CONSTABLE	C	1	68	COOK	A	8	73	COOK	C	12	56
CONNOR	G	11	81	CONSTABLE	E	2	77	COOK	A	10	51	COOK	C	12	287
CONNOR	GW	11	81	CONSTABLE	EA	5	79	COOK	A	11	82	COOK	C	13	103
CONNOR	H	3	38	CONSTABLE	EV	2	77	COOK	A	12	55	COOK	C	13	103
CONNOR	H	3	310	CONSTABLE	FW	12	286	COOK	A	12	55	COOK	C	13	103
CONNOR	H	11	82	CONSTABLE	G	12	286	COOK	A	12	55	COOK	CA	4	86
CONNOR	H	14	66	CONSTABLE	G	13	102	COOK	A	12	55	COOK	CA	6	90
CONNOR	I	7	77	CONSTABLE	GT	7	77	COOK	A	13	102	COOK	CA	7	78
CONNOR	J	1	68	CONSTABLE	JE	7	77	COOK	A	13	103	COOK	CAJ	13	103
CONNOR	J	8	72	CONSTABLE	JG	13	102	COOK	AA	1	68	COOK	CE	3	38
CONNOR	J	11	82	CONSTABLE	P	5	79	COOK	AA	1	68	COOK	CF	2	77
CONNOR	J	11	82	CONSTABLE	R	3	310	COOK	AAN	12	55	COOK	CF	3	38
CONNOR	J	14	66	CONSTABLE	RJ	11	82	COOK	AB	2	77	COOK	CF	12	56
CONNOR	J	14	66	CONSTABLE	SH	13	102	COOK	AC	10	281	COOK	CFR	2	77
CONNOR	J	14	66	CONSTABLE	T	13	102	COOK	AC	12	55	COOK	CFR	2	77
CONNOR	JE	3	310	CONSTABLE	WH	1	68	COOK	AE	1	68	COOK	CG	1	68
CONNOR	JH	14	67	CONSTABLE	WJ	12	287	COOK	AE	1	68	COOK	CH	2	77
CONNOR	M	3	310	CONSTANT	D	12	55	COOK	AE	1	68	COOK	CH	7	78
CONNOR	M	11	82	CONSTANT	J	12	55	COOK	AE	5	79	COOK	CH	12	56
CONNOR	M	13	102	CONSTANTINE	AJ	13	102	COOK	AE	12	287	COOK	CJ	5	80
CONNOR	M	14	67	CONSTANTINE	B	9	243	COOK	AE	13	103	COOK	CR	3	310
CONNOR	P	13	102	CONSTANTINE	JW	14	67	COOK	AF	7	78	COOK	CW	1	68
CONNOR	PW	8	72	CONSTANTINE	R	13	102	COOK	AG	3	310	COOK	CW	10	281
CONNOR	R	6	90	CONSTANTINE	T	9	43	COOK	AG	5	79	COOK	CW	12	287
CONNOR	T	8	72	CONSTANTINE	WG	13	102	COOK	AG	12	56	COOK	CWG	1	69

COOK	D	5	80	COOK	GE	3	38	COOK	J	13	104	COOK	T	4	87								
COOK	E	1	69	COOK	GE	5	80	COOK	J	14	67	COOK	T	5	81								
COOK	E	4	86	COOK	GF	13	103	COOK	JA	13	104	COOK	T	5	81								
COOK	E	4	87	COOK	GH	1	69	COOK	JH	8	73	COOK	T	12	56								
COOK	E	5	80	COOK	GH	5	80	COOK	JH	12	287	COOK	T	13	104								
COOK	E	5	80	COOK	GH	13	103	COOK	JH	12	287	COOK	T	13	104								
COOK	E	5	80	COOK	GH	14	67	COOK	JH	13	104	COOK	TA	2	78								
COOK	E	9	243	COOK	GK	2	78	COOK	JH	14	67	COOK	TA	5	81								
COOK	E	9	382	COOK	GS	5	80	COOK	JR	2	78	COOK	TA	12	287								
COOK	E	11	82	COOK	GT	10	51	COOK	JT	13	104	COOK	TFW	7	79								
COOK	E	13	103	COOK	GW	12	287	COOK	JW	5	81	COOK	TG	5	81								
COOK	E	13	103	COOK	H	5	80	COOK	JW	7	78	COOK	TH	9	243								
COOK	E	13	103	COOK	H	5	80	COOK	JW	7	78	COOK	TJ	4	87								
COOK	E	13	103	COOK	H	5	80	COOK	JW	7	78	COOK	TJ	4	87								
COOK	EA	10	51	COOK	H	6	90	COOK	JW	8	73	COOK	TW	2	78								
COOK	EB	3	38	COOK	H	6	90	COOK	JW	8	73	COOK	VG	1	69								
COOK	EC	3	311	COOK	H	11	82	COOK	JW	9	43	COOK	VG	10	281								
COOK	EE	5	80	COOK	H	12	56	COOK	JW	14	67	COOK	VJ	1	69								
COOK	EE	7	78	COOK	H	13	103	COOK	L	5	81	COOK	W	2	78								
COOK	EF	1	69	COOK	H	13	103	COOK	LA	6	90	COOK	W	3	311								
COOK	EF	4	87	COOK	H	13	103	COOK	LF	2	78	COOK	W	5	81								
COOK	EH	5	80	COOK	HA	12	287	COOK	LG	13	104	COOK	W	5	81								
COOK	EK	4	87	COOK	HAH	13	103	COOK	LW	1	69	COOK	W	6	90								
COOK	EN	1	69	COOK	HC	10	281	COOK	M	3	311	COOK	W	9	43								
COOK	ER	1	69	COOK	HC	12	56	COOK	M	8	73	COOK	W	9	243								
COOK	ER	1	69	COOK	HE	5	81	COOK	ME	5	81	COOK	W	10	51								
COOK	ER	5	80	COOK	HG	13	104	COOK	MF	7	78	COOK	W	12	287								
COOK	ER	7	78	COOK	HJ	3	38	COOK	N	13	104	COOK	W	13	104								
COOK	ET	2	77	COOK	HJ	13	104	COOK	P	1	69	COOK	W	13	104								
COOK	EW	4	87	COOK	HT	2	78	COOK	P	13	104	COOK	WA	7	79								
COOK	F	1	69	COOK	HT	2	78	COOK	PH	6	90	COOK	WA	12	56								
COOK	F	5	80	COOK	HT	12	56	COOK	PH	7	78	COOK	WA	12	56								
COOK	F	7	78	COOK	HT	13	104	COOK	PMA	7	78	COOK	WB	2	78								
COOK	FA	1	69	COOK	HW	5	81	COOK	R	3	38	COOK	WDG	10	51								
COOK	FA	4	87	COOK	HW	5	81	COOK	R	5	81	COOK	WE	2	78								
COOK	FC	3	38	COOK	I	1	69	COOK	R	6	90	COOK	WE	3	311								
COOK	FC	12	56	COOK	J	2	78	COOK	R	7	79	COOK	WE	3	311								
COOK	FG	2	77	COOK	J	2	78	COOK	RC	5	81	COOK	WE	5	81								
COOK	FG	10	51	COOK	J	3	38	COOK	RG	12	56	COOK	WF	4	87								
COOK	FG	10	281	COOK	J	3	311	COOK	RG	13	104	COOK	WF	12	56								
COOK	FG	12	56	COOK	J	4	87	COOK	RJ	5	81	COOK	WG	1	69								
COOK	FJ	1	69	COOK	J	4	87	COOK	RS	2	78	COOK	WG	2	78								
COOK	FJ	5	80	COOK	J	6	90	COOK	RW	7	79	COOK	WG	2	78								
COOK	FJ	10	51	COOK	J	6	90	COOK	S	4	87	COOK	WG	7	79								
COOK	FW	2	78	COOK	J	7	78	COOK	S	4	87	COOK	WH	6	90								
COOK	FW	2	78	COOK	J	7	78	COOK	S	5	81	COOK	WH	10	51								
COOK	FW	7	78	COOK	J	8	73	COOK	SA	3	39	COOK	WH	10	281								
COOK	FW	12	287	COOK	J	8	73	COOK	SF	5	81	COOK	WHE	3	39								
COOK	G	4	87	COOK	J	8	73	COOK	SG	8	73	COOK	WJ	1	69								
COOK	G	4	87	COOK	J	8	73	COOK	SH	4	87	COOK	WJ	5	82								
COOK	G	8	73	COOK	J	9	243	COOK	SR	12	56	COOK	WJ	5	82								
COOK	G	10	51	COOK	J	10	281	COOK	ST	5	81	COOK	WJ	7	79								
COOK	G	11	82	COOK	J	11	82	COOK	SW	7	79	COOK	WJ	12	56								
COOK	G	13	103	COOK	J	11	83	COOK	T	1	69	COOK	WJ	13	104								
COOK	GC	1	69	COOK	J	12	56	COOK	T	1	69	COOK	WL	5	82								

COOK	WN	2	78
COOK	WT	5	82
COOK	WW	1	69
COOKE	A	7	79
COOKE	A	11	83
COOKE	A	12	287
COOKE	A	14	67
COOKE	AE	2	78
COOKE	AE	12	56
COOKE	AF	12	287
COOKE	AM	3	311
COOKE	AS	7	79
COOKE	BE	12	57
COOKE	C	3	311
COOKE	C	5	82
COOKE	C	6	90
COOKE	CG	8	73
COOKE	CH	3	311
COOKE	D	9	243
COOKE	E	4	87
COOKE	E	11	83
COOKE	EG	5	82
COOKE	F	7	79
COOKE	F	14	67
COOKE	FR	14	67
COOKE	FV	14	67
COOKE	G	2	78
COOKE	G	7	79
COOKE	G	10	51
COOKE	G	12	57
COOKE	G	12	287
COOKE	H	12	57
COOKE	H	14	67
COOKE	HE	4	87
COOKE	HJ	4	87
COOKE	HW	4	88
COOKE	J	5	82
COOKE	J	6	90
COOKE	J	6	90
COOKE	J	11	83
COOKE	J	12	287
COOKE	J	13	104
COOKE	JE	2	79
COOKE	JH	11	83
COOKE	JO	12	287
COOKE	JT	12	57
COOKE	JW	8	73
COOKE	JW	14	68
COOKE	P	6	90
COOKE	P	7	79
COOKE	PA	4	88
COOKE	PG	5	82
COOKE	PW	3	311
COOKE	R	11	83
COOKE	RC	4	88
COOKE	T	11	83
COOKE	T	14	68
COOKE	TH	4	88
COOKE	TS	3	39
COOKE	W	12	57
COOKE	WE	4	88
COOKE	WG	4	88
COOKE	WH	1	69
COOKE	WH	12	287
COOKLAND	A	9	43
COOKLAND	J	9	43
COOKLAND	J	9	43
COOKLAND	L	9	43
COOKSEY	AE	7	79
COOKSEY	AV	3	39
COOKSEY	EC	3	39
COOKSEY	H	6	90
COOKSEY	JM	4	88
COOKSEY	JRH	4	88
COOKSEY	S	4	88
COOKSEY	SP	5	82
COOKSEY	TG	2	79
COOKSON	A	8	73
COOKSON	E	11	83
COOKSON	F	11	83
COOKSON	J	14	68
COOKSON	JH	12	288
COOKSON	L	14	68
COOKSON	W	6	90
COOL	EG	4	88
COOL	WH	4	88
COOLE	L	1	69
COOLEY	H	2	79
COOLEY	HJ	10	51
COOLEY	W	5	82
COOLING	J	2	79
COOM	MA	13	104
COOM	P	4	88
COOMBER	A	1	69
COOMBER	A	2	79
COOMBER	AA	3	39
COOMBER	AG	10	51
COOMBER	AJ	7	79
COOMBER	F	13	104
COOMBER	J	13	104
COOMBER	W	2	79
COOMBES	A	13	105
COOMBES	A	13	105
COOMBES	AJ	1	70
COOMBES	B	7	79
COOMBES	CA	1	70
COOMBES	CS	4	88
COOMBES	F	10	51
COOMBES	FE	7	79
COOMBES	G	7	79
COOMBES	G	7	79
COOMBES	GA	7	79
COOMBES	J	11	83
COOMBES	J	11	83
COOMBES	JW	12	288
COOMBES	P	2	79
COOMBES	RJ	7	80
COOMBES	WB	12	288
COOMBES	WE	7	79
COOMBES	WH	11	83
COOMBS	AE	4	88
COOMBS	CE	4	88
COOMBS	CH	13	105
COOMBS	CW	2	79
COOMBS	FG	7	80
COOMBS	FG	13	105
COOMBS	FS	7	80
COOMBS	GD	1	70
COOMBS	HV	13	105
COOMBS	J	2	79
COOMBS	J	3	311
COOMBS	J	4	88
COOMBS	J	14	68
COOMBS	R	7	80
COOMBS	R	10	281
COOMBS	RAHS	10	281
COOMBS	SM	3	311
COOMBS	TPG	10	281
COOMBS	W	3	311
COOMBS	W	3	311
COOMBS	WC	4	88
COOMBS	WF	13	105
COOMBS	WJ	4	88
COOMBS	WJ	4	89
COOMBS	WJ	7	80
COOMBS	WJ	13	105
COOMES	EW	13	105
COOMES	HT	10	281
COOMS	WJ	4	88
COONAN	J	9	43
COONEY	AW	3	39
COONEY	J	9	243
COONEY	J	11	83
COONEY	J	11	83
COONEY	J	14	68
COONEY	JMF	5	82
COONEY	S	8	73
COONEY	W	11	83
COONEY	W	11	83
COOP	A	6	91
COOP	H	11	83
COOP	HH	8	73
COOP	V	11	83
COOP	W	11	84
COOPE	CS	9	44
COOPE	E	9	44
COOPE	G	9	243
COOPE	G	14	68
COOPE	H	8	73
COOPE	H	9	44
COOPE	H	14	68
COOPE	S	14	68
COOPE	T	6	91
COOPE	W	14	68
COOPER	A	1	70
COOPER	A	2	79
COOPER	A	2	79
COOPER	A	3	39
COOPER	A	3	311
COOPER	A	5	82
COOPER	A	5	82
COOPER	A	5	82
COOPER	A	6	91
COOPER	A	6	91
COOPER	A	6	91
COOPER	A	8	73
COOPER	A	8	74
COOPER	A	8	74
COOPER	A	8	74
COOPER	A	9	44
COOPER	A	9	44
COOPER	A	9	44
COOPER	A	9	243
COOPER	A	10	51
COOPER	A	11	84
COOPER	A	11	84
COOPER	A	12	57
COOPER	A	13	105
COOPER	A	14	68
COOPER	AB	4	89
COOPER	AE	1	70
COOPER	AE	2	79
COOPER	AE	2	79
COOPER	AE	4	89
COOPER	AE	6	91
COOPER	AE	10	51
COOPER	AE	10	281
COOPER	AF	3	311
COOPER	AF	9	243
COOPER	AG	4	89
COOPER	AG	5	82
COOPER	AG	13	105
COOPER	AH	6	91
COOPER	AH	7	80
COOPER	AH	14	68
COOPER	AJ	2	79
COOPER	AJ	4	89
COOPER	AJ	10	52
COOPER	AJ	10	281
COOPER	AJ	12	57

COOPER	AM	1	70	COOPER	E	9	382	COOPER	G	9	44	COOPER	J	9	44
COOPER	ARJ	2	79	COOPER	E	13	105	COOPER	G	10	52	COOPER	J	10	52
COOPER	AS	3	39	COOPER	E	13	105	COOPER	G	11	84	COOPER	J	10	52
COOPER	AT	11	84	COOPER	E	13	105	COOPER	G	12	57	COOPER	J	11	84
COOPER	AV	1	70	COOPER	E	14	68	COOPER	G	12	288	COOPER	J	11	84
COOPER	AW	2	79	COOPER	EC	13	105	COOPER	G	13	105	COOPER	J	11	84
COOPER	AW	2	79	COOPER	EE	7	80	COOPER	G	13	105	COOPER	J	12	57
COOPER	AW	4	89	COOPER	EG	2	80	COOPER	GA	8	74	COOPER	J	12	58
COOPER	AW	9	243	COOPER	EG	7	80	COOPER	GA	12	57	COOPER	J	12	58
COOPER	AW	12	57	COOPER	EH	1	70	COOPER	GC	2	80	COOPER	J	13	106
COOPER	B	5	82	COOPER	EJ	3	39	COOPER	GE	3	312	COOPER	J	13	106
COOPER	BS	5	82	COOPER	EJ	3	39	COOPER	GE	4	89	COOPER	J	13	106
COOPER	C	1	70	COOPER	EJ	12	57	COOPER	GE	7	80	COOPER	J	13	106
COOPER	C	3	312	COOPER	EJW	3	312	COOPER	GE	10	282	COOPER	J	13	106
COOPER	C	3	312	COOPER	ES	7	80	COOPER	GEB	13	105	COOPER	J	14	69
COOPER	C	3	312	COOPER	ES	10	282	COOPER	GP	7	80	COOPER	J	14	69
COOPER	C	3	312	COOPER	ET	1	70	COOPER	GW	1	70	COOPER	J	14	69
COOPER	C	5	82	COOPER	ET	4	89	COOPER	GW	2	80	COOPER	J	14	69
COOPER	C	5	82	COOPER	EW	2	80	COOPER	GW	3	312	COOPER	J	14	69
COOPER	C	6	91	COOPER	F	3	312	COOPER	GW	9	243	COOPER	J	14	69
COOPER	C	10	52	COOPER	F	4	89	COOPER	GW	12	57	COOPER	J	14	69
COOPER	C	12	57	COOPER	F	5	83	COOPER	GW	14	68	COOPER	JA	7	80
COOPER	C	12	57	COOPER	F	5	83	COOPER	H	1	70	COOPER	JAC	12	58
COOPER	C	14	68	COOPER	F	5	83	COOPER	H	3	39	COOPER	JB	11	84
COOPER	CA	1	70	COOPER	F	6	91	COOPER	H	6	91	COOPER	JC	7	81
COOPER	CA	1	70	COOPER	F	8	74	COOPER	H	6	91	COOPER	JE	2	80
COOPER	CA	2	79	COOPER	F	9	243	COOPER	H	6	91	COOPER	JE	4	90
COOPER	CAJ	9	44	COOPER	F	10	52	COOPER	H	6	91	COOPER	JE	4	90
COOPER	CF	7	80	COOPER	F	11	84	COOPER	H	8	74	COOPER	JE	14	69
COOPER	CF	10	52	COOPER	F	12	57	COOPER	H	8	74	COOPER	JF	6	91
COOPER	CF	10	282	COOPER	F	12	57	COOPER	H	8	74	COOPER	JF	12	287
COOPER	CFJ	2	79	COOPER	F	12	57	COOPER	H	9	44	COOPER	JH	4	90
COOPER	CH	1	70	COOPER	F	12	287	COOPER	H	9	383	COOPER	JH	5	83
COOPER	CH	4	89	COOPER	F	12	288	COOPER	H	12	57	COOPER	JH	6	92
COOPER	CJ	3	312	COOPER	F	14	68	COOPER	HA	4	90	COOPER	JH	6	92
COOPER	CJ	4	89	COOPER	F	14	68	COOPER	HA	7	80	COOPER	JH	6	92
COOPER	CJ	10	52	COOPER	F	14	68	COOPER	HAG	10	52	COOPER	JH	10	282
COOPER	CL	10	52	COOPER	FA	14	68	COOPER	HE	7	80	COOPER	JS	10	52
COOPER	CR	7	80	COOPER	FE	10	282	COOPER	HF	1	70	COOPER	JT	7	80
COOPER	CS	3	312	COOPER	FF	4	89	COOPER	HG	4	90	COOPER	JW	2	80
COOPER	CW	2	80	COOPER	FG	4	89	COOPER	HJ	2	80	COOPER	JW	5	83
COOPER	CW	4	89	COOPER	FJ	5	83	COOPER	HJ	5	83	COOPER	JW	12	58
COOPER	CW	13	105	COOPER	FM	1	70	COOPER	HJ	6	91	COOPER	JW	12	288
COOPER	D	2	80	COOPER	FS	2	80	COOPER	HJ	13	106	COOPER	JW	14	69
COOPER	D	10	52	COOPER	FW	4	89	COOPER	HT	4	90	COOPER	JW	14	69
COOPER	DR	1	70	COOPER	G	1	70	COOPER	HW	3	312	COOPER	JWT	2	80
COOPER	DV	1	70	COOPER	G	3	312	COOPER	J	2	80	COOPER	LJ	1	70
COOPER	E	1	70	COOPER	G	4	89	COOPER	J	2	80	COOPER	LW	13	106
COOPER	E	3	312	COOPER	G	4	89	COOPER	J	4	90	COOPER	M	9	44
COOPER	E	4	89	COOPER	G	4	89	COOPER	J	6	91	COOPER	M	9	243
COOPER	E	5	82	COOPER	G	5	83	COOPER	J	7	80	COOPER	ME	3	39
COOPER	E	8	74	COOPER	G	6	91	COOPER	J	7	80	COOPER	N	13	106
COOPER	E	8	74	COOPER	G	6	91	COOPER	J	8	74	COOPER	P	6	92
COOPER	E	8	74	COOPER	G	6	91	COOPER	J	8	74	COOPER	P	12	58
COOPER	E	8	74	COOPER	G	9	44	COOPER	J	9	44	COOPER	PA	3	312

COOPER	PJ	4	90	COOPER	W	8	74	COPE	AE	13	106	COPLEY	J		9	45
COOPER	PW	4	90	COOPER	W	9	243	COPE	AL	1	71	COPLEY	JW		8	75
COOPER	R	2	80	COOPER	W	10	282	COPE	B	6	92	COPLEY	T		9	244
COOPER	R	3	312	COOPER	W	11	84	COPE	C	6	92	COPLEY	TE		10	282
COOPER	R	6	92	COOPER	W	11	84	COPE	C	9	44	COPLEY	W		9	45
COOPER	R	8	74	COOPER	W	12	58	COPE	C	9	383	COPLEY	WH		9	244
COOPER	R	9	44	COOPER	W	12	58	COPE	C	11	84	COPP	A		2	81
COOPER	R	14	69	COOPER	W	12	288	COPE	CW	1	71	COPP	AE		12	288
COOPER	RC	5	83	COOPER	W	13	106	COPE	CW	14	70	COPP	AS		12	288
COOPER	RF	1	70	COOPER	W	13	106	COPE	EAG	12	58	COPP	JE		2	81
COOPER	RF	4	90	COOPER	W	14	69	COPE	FW	1	71	COPP	SJ		3	313
COOPER	RG	12	58	COOPER	W	14	69	COPE	G	9	44	COPP	WL		13	106
COOPER	RH	10	52	COOPER	W	14	69	COPE	G	12	58	COPPARD	CR		7	81
COOPER	RJ	4	90	COOPER	WC	4	90	COPE	H	8	75	COPPARD	EE		7	81
COOPER	RT	14	69	COOPER	WC	12	58	COPE	H	9	45	COPPARD	EG		7	81
COOPER	RW	2	80	COOPER	WC	12	58	COPE	H	9	45	COPPARD	FS		7	81
COOPER	RW	11	84	COOPER	WE	2	80	COPE	H	9	244	COPPARD	W		9	45
COOPER	S	6	92	COOPER	WF	6	92	COPE	H	9	383	COPPELLA	A		11	85
COOPER	S	7	81	COOPER	WG	1	71	COPE	H	10	52	COPPEN	TJ		13	107
COOPER	S	7	81	COOPER	WG	4	90	COPE	HA	1	71	COPPENS	F		3	39
COOPER	S	8	74	COOPER	WG	12	288	COPE	J	9	244	COPPER	CT		7	81
COOPER	S	8	74	COOPER	WH	4	90	COPE	J	12	58	COPPERTHWAITE	AJ		4	90
COOPER	S	8	74	COOPER	WH	5	83	COPE	JT	11	84	COPPERTHWAITE	F		4	90
COOPER	S	9	243	COOPER	WH	6	92	COPE	T	2	81	COPPERWAITE	A		5	83
COOPER	S	14	69	COOPER	WH	6	92	COPE	T	2	81	COPPERWAITE	AW		5	84
COOPER	S	14	69	COOPER	WH	14	69	COPE	TD	6	92	COPPERWAITE	WG		5	84
COOPER	SA	2	80	COOPER	WJ	3	312	COPE	TD	6	92	COPPERWHEAT	C		12	58
COOPER	SC	9	44	COOPER	WJ	6	92	COPE	W	3	313	COPPERWHEAT	G		12	58
COOPER	SG	13	106	COOPER	WJ	13	106	COPE	W	6	93	COPPERWHEAT	WG		1	71
COOPER	ST	5	83	COOPER	WM	11	84	COPE	WG	13	106	COPPIN	BJH		12	288
COOPER	T	3	39	COOPER	WR	7	81	COPE	WJ	6	92	COPPIN	CE		4	90
COOPER	T	4	90	COOPER	WTF	1	71	COPELAND	A	8	75	COPPIN	FEH		4	91
COOPER	T	6	92	COOPIN	AH	7	81	COPELAND	AE	5	83	COPPIN	H		2	81
COOPER	T	8	74	COOTE	A	8	74	COPELAND	E	11	84	COPPIN	H		3	313
COOPER	T	9	44	COOTE	AC	1	71	COPELAND	EV	13	106	COPPIN	JA		5	84
COOPER	T	11	84	COOTE	B	8	75	COPELAND	F	11	84	COPPIN	ND		4	91
COOPER	T	12	58	COOTE	CJ	1	71	COPELAND	FE	13	106	COPPIN	S		11	85
COOPER	TA	4	90	COOTE	CJ	7	81	COPELAND	FG	3	313	COPPIN	WR		7	81
COOPER	TG	13	106	COOTE	CS	1	71	COPELAND	J	14	70	COPPING	AE		10	52
COOPER	TJ	6	92	COOTE	F	5	83	COPELAND	M	14	70	COPPING	H		7	81
COOPER	V	4	90	COOTE	GH	10	52	COPELAND	N	11	85	COPPING	T		10	282
COOPER	VJ	3	312	COOTE	H	5	83	COPELAND	R	11	85	COPPINGS	H		2	81
COOPER	W	1	71	COOTE	TW	7	81	COPELAND	W	11	85	COPPLE	E		14	70
COOPER	W	1	71	COOTE	W	9	44	COPELAND	W	11	85	COPPLE	G		14	70
COOPER	W	1	71	COOTE	WS	7	81	COPEMAN	CG	6	93	COPPLE	H		14	70
COOPER	W	1	71	COOTES	A	2	81	COPESTAKE	WJ	10	282	COPPLE	W		14	70
COOPER	W	2	80	COOTES	JT	2	81	COPLAND	LG	10	52	COPPLESTONE	H		10	282
COOPER	W	3	39	COPAS	AW	3	312	COPLEY	A	8	75	COPPLESTONE	HB		9	45
COOPER	W	3	39	COPAS	CE	3	39	COPLEY	A	8	75	COPPLESTONE	HB		9	383
COOPER	W	4	90	COPAS	CJ	3	313	COPLEY	AE	11	85	COPPLESTONE	JA		10	282
COOPER	W	5	83	COPAS	CJ	3	313	COPLEY	D	8	75	COPPOCK	F		14	70
COOPER	W	5	83	COPE	A	6	92	COPLEY	GC	5	83	COPPOCK	FC		7	81
COOPER	W	6	92	COPE	AE	1	71	COPLEY	GE	9	45	COPPOCK	J		12	58
COOPER	W	7	81	COPE	AE	6	92	COPLEY	H	5	83	COPPOCK	W		12	58
COOPER	W	7	81	COPE	AE	6	92	COPLEY	J	5	83	COPPS	W		4	91

Surname	Init	A	B	Surname	Init	A	B	Surname	Init	A	B	Surname	Init	A	B
COPSEY	AW	2	81	CORBY	RH	12	59	COREY	JW	6	93	CORNELL	H	8	75
COPSEY	CG	7	81	CORBY	RT	7	82	CORFE	J	10	53	CORNELL	HE	7	82
COPSEY	F	3	39	CORBY	S	1	71	CORFIELD	A	3	40	CORNELL	HF	1	72
COPSEY	HS	7	81	CORBYN	AA	10	282	CORFIELD	A	3	313	CORNELL	J	3	313
COPSEY	RJ	10	52	CORBYN	GV	2	81	CORFIELD	EJ	13	107	CORNELL	JH	1	72
COPSON	A	5	84	CORBYN	RE	2	81	CORFIELD	J	5	84	CORNELL	SF	2	82
COPSON	A	6	93	CORCORAN	C	11	85	CORFIELD	J	14	70	CORNELL	WJ	3	313
COPSON	GW	6	93	CORCORAN	J	11	85	CORFIELD	R	11	85	CORNELY	H	4	91
COPSON	HO	12	288	CORCORAN	J	11	85	CORFIELD	W	10	53	CORNELY	M	4	91
COPSON	J	6	93	CORCORAN	L	8	75	CORIO	PW	1	72	CORNELY	W	4	91
COPUS	SJ	13	107	CORCORAN	L	8	75	CORK	CH	2	81	CORNER	A	11	86
CORBEN	A	3	313	CORCORAN	R	12	288	CORK	EP	2	81	CORNER	A	11	86
CORBEN	A	13	107	CORCORAN	SF	13	107	CORK	GWA	13	107	CORNER	H	8	75
CORBEN	AH	10	282	CORDEAUX	L	8	75	CORK	LA	13	107	CORNER	J	9	45
CORBEN	AJ	13	107	CORDEAUX	W	8	75	CORK	W	2	81	CORNER	J	11	86
CORBEN	AS	7	82	CORDEAUX	W	8	75	CORK	WHE	3	40	CORNER	T	8	75
CORBET	GJ	7	82	CORDELL	WFE	7	82	CORK	WT	11	86	CORNER	T	9	45
CORBETT	A	3	313	CORDEN	A	6	93	CORKE	HH	2	82	CORNER	TG	4	91
CORBETT	AH	13	107	CORDEN	J	10	53	CORKE	ST	4	91	CORNES	R	14	70
CORBETT	BL	1	71	CORDEN	RW	14	70	CORKER	LE	3	313	CORNEY	AG	2	82
CORBETT	C	7	82	CORDEROY	G	3	40	CORKER	WG	13	107	CORNEY	E	2	82
CORBETT	C	12	58	CORDEROY	JJ	3	313	CORKERY	J	3	40	CORNEY	RW	12	59
CORBETT	C	14	70	CORDEROY	R	3	40	CORKETT	E	5	84	CORNEY	T	13	108
CORBETT	CT	2	81	CORDEROY	R	3	313	CORKETT	FA	5	84	CORNFIELD	GW	13	108
CORBETT	E	10	53	CORDEROY	W	3	313	CORKIN	H	11	86	CORNFORTH	AG	4	91
CORBETT	EJ	7	82	CORDERY	A	4	91	CORLESS	F	11	86	CORNFORTH	J	9	45
CORBETT	F	6	93	CORDERY	CH	3	40	CORLESS	G	10	53	CORNFORTH	JW	9	45
CORBETT	F	6	93	CORDEY	GH	13	107	CORLESS	H	11	86	CORNFORTH	S	9	45
CORBETT	G	5	84	CORDIER	E	13	107	CORLESS	T	11	86	CORNFORTH	T	8	75
CORBETT	HG	6	93	CORDINER	A	2	81	CORLEY	C	3	313	CORNHILL	R	10	53
CORBETT	HV	2	81	CORDING	A	1	71	CORLEY	H	5	84	CORNHILL	W	3	313
CORBETT	J	6	93	CORDING	GJ	2	81	CORLEY	J	9	45	CORNICK	EA	10	53
CORBETT	J	6	93	CORDING	J	11	85	CORLEY	LJ	5	84	CORNICK	G	4	91
CORBETT	J	12	421	CORDING	T	11	85	CORMACK	H	13	107	CORNICK	HC	4	91
CORBETT	J	13	107	CORDINGLEY	A	9	45	CORMACK	TE	2	82	CORNICK	J	4	91
CORBETT	JC	6	93	CORDINGLEY	A	9	244	CORMER	E	8	75	CORNILLY	C	13	108
CORBETT	JJ	1	71	CORDINGLEY	G	11	85	CORN	H	14	70	CORNISH	AC	2	82
CORBETT	RA	7	82	CORDINGLEY	G	13	107	CORN	RR	10	53	CORNISH	C	13	108
CORBETT	SA	3	39	CORDINGLEY	H	9	383	CORNACHIA	CJ	7	82	CORNISH	DCR	2	82
CORBETT	SWH	4	91	CORDINGLEY	J	9	45	CORNELIUS	A	13	107	CORNISH	E	7	82
CORBETT	T	14	70	CORDINGLEY	J	9	244	CORNELIUS	C	13	108	CORNISH	H	7	82
CORBETT	TC	6	93	CORDINGLEY	J	9	383	CORNELIUS	CH	10	53	CORNISH	J	4	91
CORBETT	TL	7	82	CORDINGLEY	T	14	70	CORNELIUS	J	6	93	CORNISH	JA	6	94
CORBETT	W	3	40	CORDNER	J	14	70	CORNELIUS	J	6	93	CORNISH	JA	6	94
CORBETT	WA	6	93	CORDON	GR	1	72	CORNELIUS	J	6	93	CORNISH	M	4	91
CORBEY	TH	7	82	CORDREY	HW	13	107	CORNELIUS	J	6	93	CORNISH	M	4	91
CORBIN	AW	4	91	CORDREY	S	3	40	CORNELIUS	JE	12	288	CORNISH	NW	2	82
CORBIN	F	10	53	CORDWELL	ET	2	81	CORNELIUS	R	4	91	CORNISH	PE	2	82
CORBISHLEY	F	11	85	CORDWELL	JL	2	81	CORNELIUS	RC	4	91	CORNISH	R	3	314
CORBLE	TC	9	45	CORDWENT	GA	1	72	CORNELIUS	T	13	107	CORNISH	TH	6	94
CORBOULD	A	1	71	CORE	H	11	85	CORNELL	C	3	313	CORNISH	WH	13	108
CORBR	HE	7	82	CORE	J	9	244	CORNELL	E	3	313	CORNISH	WW	1	72
CORBY	FG	12	59	CORE	T	11	85	CORNELL	E	10	53	CORNOCK	J	6	94
CORBY	H	1	71	COREFIELD	J	8	75	CORNELL	G	1	72	CORNS	J	11	86
CORBY	H	12	288	CORESMITH	J	11	85	CORNELL	H	1	72	CORNS	S	11	86

Name	Init			Name	Init			Name	Init			Name	Init		
CORNWALL	TT	6	94	COSGROVE	C	11	86	COTCHIN	J	5	84	COTTON	E	13	109
CORNWELL	A	8	75	COSGROVE	F	11	86	COTCHIN	J	5	84	COTTON	EJ	7	83
CORNWELL	A	8	75	COSGROVE	G	11	86	COTCHING	H	1	72	COTTON	F	12	59
CORNWELL	CG	1	72	COSGROVE	H	13	108	COTGROVE	JR	10	53	COTTON	FC	7	83
CORNWELL	E	2	82	COSGROVE	J	14	71	COTON	GHC	6	94	COTTON	FJ	1	72
CORNWELL	E	2	82	COSGROVE	J	14	71	COTON	J	6	94	COTTON	FJ	4	92
CORNWELL	G	8	75	COSGROVE	LW	11	86	COTSFORD	A	3	314	COTTON	G	13	109
CORNWELL	J	1	72	COSGROVE	P	2	82	COTSON	J	8	76	COTTON	GA	14	71
CORNWELL	JE	3	314	COSGROVE	P	4	92	COTT	J	11	86	COTTON	GT	12	59
CORNWELL	L	14	70	COSGROVE	W	11	86	COTTAM	C	1	72	COTTON	H	10	54
CORPE	FT	13	108	COSIER	B	6	94	COTTAM	JJ	5	84	COTTON	H	13	109
CORPE	JW	13	108	COSIER	CM	2	82	COTTAM	W	14	71	COTTON	HL	7	83
CORPE	THE	13	108	COSIER	E	7	83	COTTELL	GH	10	53	COTTON	HT	10	54
CORPE	W	2	82	COSIER	E	7	83	COTTEN	AH	10	53	COTTON	I	14	71
CORPS	AJ	13	108	COSIER	P	7	83	COTTEN	AH	10	54	COTTON	J	13	109
CORPSE	AE	2	82	COSS	J	9	45	COTTEN	FC	13	108	COTTON	J	13	109
CORRAN	J	14	70	COSSER	W	2	82	COTTER	A	6	94	COTTON	J	14	71
CORRIE	FJ	3	40	COSSEY	B	9	383	COTTER	CJ	2	83	COTTON	JA	2	83
CORRIE	HG	3	314	COSSINS	FJ	8	76	COTTER	GA	10	54	COTTON	L	6	95
CORRIE	RA	3	314	COSSOM	LA	7	83	COTTER	J	7	83	COTTON	L	14	71
CORRIE	SJ	13	108	COSSTICK	W	10	282	COTTER	J	9	46	COTTON	LM	12	59
CORRIE	WR	1	72	COSSTICK	WG	10	282	COTTER	JC	4	92	COTTON	LT	6	95
CORRIE	WR	1	72	COSTA	H	2	82	COTTER	W	6	94	COTTON	PH	3	40
CORRIGAN	H	10	53	COSTA	W	11	86	COTTER	W	9	46	COTTON	RH	4	92
CORRIGAN	P	14	71	COSTALL	S	6	94	COTTER	WJ	7	83	COTTON	RL	7	83
CORRIS	H	14	71	COSTELLA	T	7	83	COTTER	WM	7	83	COTTON	T	3	314
CORRIS	WH	10	282	COSTELLO	A	8	76	COTTERELL	GW	5	84	COTTON	T	7	83
CORRISTINE	JB	14	71	COSTELLO	H	6	94	COTTERELL	W	5	84	COTTON	T	12	59
CORRY	F	11	86	COSTELLO	J	8	76	COTTERELL	WH	6	94	COTTON	W	7	83
CORRY	H	9	383	COSTELLO	J	14	71	COTTERILL	CA	13	108	COTTON	W	12	289
CORRY	HE	8	76	COSTELLO	J	14	71	COTTERILL	E	6	94	COTTON	W	13	109
CORSBY	HG	12	288	COSTELLO	J	14	71	COTTERILL	EH	6	95	COTTON	W	14	71
CORSBY	JC	12	288	COSTELLO	J	14	71	COTTERILL	FA	6	95	COTTON	WE	12	59
CORSER	GA	8	76	COSTELLO	JHC	13	108	COTTERILL	HC	6	95	COTTON	WH	12	289
CORSTON	WNE	7	82	COSTELLO	P	9	46	COTTERILL	MW	6	95	COTTON	WHG	10	54
CORT	F	6	94	COSTELLO	T	6	94	COTTERILL	R	6	95	COTTON	WJ	3	314
CORTIS	WA	10	53	COSTELLO	W	6	94	COTTERILL	WH	6	95	COTTRELL	A	10	54
CORWOOD	J	12	59	COSTELLO	W	9	46	COTTERILL	WJ	13	109	COTTRELL	AE	1	72
CORY	WS	12	288	COSTELLO	W	14	71	COTTERRELL	LR	12	59	COTTRELL	B	3	40
COSBY	H	5	84	COSTELLO	WC	11	86	COTTERS	J	2	83	COTTRELL	E	6	95
COSBY	HD	7	82	COSTEN	JE	1	72	COTTEY	ET	13	109	COTTRELL	EJ	2	83
COSBY	HW	7	82	COSTER	A	13	108	COTTINGHAM	G	5	84	COTTRELL	F	3	40
COSENS	W	4	91	COSTER	BC	10	53	COTTINGHAM	H	1	72	COTTRELL	FJ	6	95
COSENS	WH	4	91	COSTER	CJ	2	83	COTTINGHAM	J	7	83	COTTRELL	H	3	40
COSFORD	A	12	288	COSTER	GA	10	53	COTTINGHAM	T	7	83	COTTRELL	HW	13	109
COSFORD	F	12	288	COSTER	HG	5	84	COTTIS	E	9	46	COTTRELL	R	6	95
COSFORD	G	3	314	COSTER	WH	4	92	COTTLE	AH	13	109	COTTRELL	SM	1	72
COSFORD	J	12	288	COSTICK	W	10	53	COTTLE	CT	13	109	COTTRELL	SR	3	40
COSFORD	JH	2	82	COSTIGAN	D	9	46	COTTON	A	5	84	COTTRELL	WV	6	95
COSFORD	W	13	108	COSTIGAN	J	9	46	COTTON	A	14	71	COTTRILL	H	9	46
COSFORD	WB	12	289	COSTIN	D	13	108	COTTON	A	14	71	COTTRILL	H	14	72
COSFORD	WC	2	82	COSTIN	HR	3	40	COTTON	AG	2	83	COUCH	A	3	314
COSGRAVE	G	7	82	COSTIN	HV	3	40	COTTON	AG	7	83	COUCH	J	1	72
COSGRAVE	P	14	71	COSTON	TW	1	72	COTTON	AJ	10	282	COUCH	R	3	40
COSGROVE	A	3	40	COTCHIN	H	12	289	COTTON	DH	7	83	COUCHMAN	A	4	92

COUCHMAN	AR	2	83	COULTON	FW	12	289	COUSENS	W	4	92	COVENTRY	HA	2	84
COUCHMAN	FW	4	92	COULTON	H	9	46	COUSENS	WH	4	92	COVENTRY	JA	6	96
COUCHMAN	G	2	83	COULTON	J	1	73	COUSINS	A	9	46	COVENTRY	RM	1	73
COUCHMAN	H	4	92	COUNSELL	W	11	87	COUSINS	A	9	244	COVENTRY	WC	1	73
COUCHMAN	T	1	72	COUNTER	JH	1	73	COUSINS	AE	1	73	COVER	RP	11	87
COUCHMAN	W	4	92	COUNTER	S	13	109	COUSINS	AH	2	83	COVERDALE	AE	10	54
COUGHLAN	E	13	109	COUPE	E	14	72	COUSINS	B	5	85	COVERDALE	C	11	87
COUGHLAN	JW	13	109	COUPE	J	11	87	COUSINS	CH	3	314	COVERLEY	AJ	12	59
COUGHLAN	PF	13	109	COUPER	L	4	92	COUSINS	D	9	46	COVERLEY	F	12	59
COUGILL	GH	10	54	COUPER	NGA	10	283	COUSINS	EH	1	73	COVERLEY	P	3	314
COULBERT	CO	10	282	COUPLAND	A	9	46	COUSINS	F	5	85	COVEY	E	4	93
COULBORN	W	14	72	COUPLAND	GE	13	110	COUSINS	F	8	76	COVEY	RW	4	93
COULBY	W	9	46	COUPLAND	H	8	76	COUSINS	FJ	4	93	COVEY	WA	4	93
COULDRY	WF	13	109	COUPLAND	J	8	76	COUSINS	GF	3	314	COVIL	W	3	41
COULDWELL	WM	5	85	COUPLAND	W	9	244	COUSINS	H	5	85	COVINGTON	A	10	54
COULING	C	6	95	COURAGE	HJ	4	92	COUSINS	H	8	76	COVINGTON	H	12	59
COULLING	H	13	109	COURCEY	J	10	54	COUSINS	H	12	289	COVINGTON	J	13	110
COULLING	JH	2	83	COURSE	AC	12	59	COUSINS	HA	1	73	COVINGTON	JH	13	110
COULMAN	J	7	84	COURSE	P	12	59	COUSINS	HE	1	73	COVINGTON	RW	2	84
COULSON	A	2	83	COURSE	P	12	59	COUSINS	HG	1	73	COWAN	CE	11	87
COULSON	AH	7	84	COURSE	R	12	59	COUSINS	HG	3	314	COWAN	J	11	87
COULSON	AJ	9	46	COURSE	VJ	10	54	COUSINS	HW	7	84	COWAN	J	14	72
COULSON	AL	7	84	COURT	F	1	73	COUSINS	J	5	85	COWAN	JW	11	87
COULSON	E	8	76	COURT	JR	13	110	COUSINS	JGF	13	110	COWAN	P	2	84
COULSON	EJ	2	83	COURT	S	6	95	COUSINS	MH	1	73	COWAN	VJ	10	283
COULSON	EJ	12	289	COURT	SJ	13	110	COUSINS	P	5	85	COWAN	W	2	84
COULSON	ES	6	95	COURT	WH	6	95	COUSINS	PJ	4	93	COWAP	O	14	72
COULSON	F	12	289	COURT	WH	10	54	COUSINS	SA	3	314	COWAP	W	14	72
COULSON	F	12	289	COURTENEY	T	11	87	COUSINS	T	8	76	COWARD	AS	1	73
COULSON	F	12	289	COURTIER	GH	4	92	COUSINS	W	3	41	COWARD	C	4	93
COULSON	GH	12	289	COURTIER	RF	4	92	COUSINS	WC	4	93	COWARD	C	8	76
COULSON	GH	13	109	COURTNALL	AF	3	41	COUSINS	WE	10	283	COWARD	CE	13	110
COULSON	GV	10	283	COURTNALL	EM	3	41	COUSINS	WW	13	110	COWARD	EG	10	54
COULSON	H	2	83	COURTNEIDGE	AJ	7	84	COUSLAND	H	2	83	COWARD	FC	10	54
COULSON	H	12	289	COURTNELL	AW	6	95	COUSNER	AR	12	289	COWARD	FW	4	93
COULSON	J	9	46	COURTNELL	JH	6	95	COUZENS	BGM	10	283	COWARD	G	8	76
COULSON	R	7	84	COURTNEY	A	8	76	COUZENS	CC	10	283	COWARD	HG	1	73
COULSON	T	9	46	COURTNEY	AG	2	83	COUZENS	HJ	10	54	COWARD	HH	10	283
COULSON	T	10	283	COURTNEY	F	13	110	COVE	D	7	84	COWARD	J	8	77
COULSON	W	8	76	COURTNEY	HG	4	92	COVE	E	10	283	COWARD	J	9	244
COULSON	WT	3	41	COURTNEY	J	8	76	COVE	EG	5	85	COWARD	LV	10	54
COULSTON	J	7	84	COURTNEY	J	11	87	COVE	H	13	110	COWARD	ME	5	85
COULT	J	9	46	COURTNEY	J	11	87	COVE	J	3	314	COWARD	R	10	54
COULTAS	A	9	46	COURTNEY	J	14	72	COVE	JF	5	85	COWARD	RT	10	54
COULTAS	M	8	76	COURTNEY	JHJ	2	83	COVE	JW	13	110	COWARD	S	13	110
COULTATE	T	8	76	COURTNEY	L	11	87	COVE	P	2	83	COWARD	TH	4	93
COULTATE	T	8	76	COURTNEY	PGW	2	83	COVE	PW	13	110	COWARD	WH	4	93
COULTER	AM	1	72	COURTNEY	WG	3	41	COVE	T	2	83	COWARD	WN	1	73
COULTER	CA	14	72	COURTNEY	WG	7	84	COVE	WG	5	85	COWBURN	A	8	77
COULTER	E	8	76	COURTNEY	WH	4	92	COVELL	A	13	110	COWBURN	AG	11	87
COULTER	E	13	109	COURTNEY	WJC	4	92	COVELL	G	13	110	COWBURN	F	14	72
COULTER	N	9	46	COURTS	H	6	95	COVELL	J	8	76	COWBURN	W	8	77
COULTER	S	2	83	COUSENS	A	10	54	COVELL	W	9	47	COWCHER	GT	10	283
COULTHARD	GW	11	86	COUSENS	LB	4	92	COVELL	WE	10	283	COWDEN	A	14	72
COULTHARD	T	11	87	COUSENS	RC	4	92	COVENEY	J	13	110	COWDEROY	C	7	84

COWDEROY	WA	7	84	COWLEY	JW	4	93	COX	AC	13	111	COX	EG	13	111
COWDERY	C	7	84	COWLEY	JW	8	77	COX	AE	1	73	COX	EJ	12	60
COWDERY	F	7	84	COWLEY	OS	12	60	COX	AE	2	84	COX	EW	12	60
COWDERY	H	7	84	COWLEY	T	11	87	COX	AE	6	96	COX	F	1	74
COWDERY	LJ	4	93	COWLIN	EM	7	84	COX	AE	10	55	COX	F	1	74
COWDERY	WH	3	41	COWLIN	FA	7	84	COX	AE	12	60	COX	F	1	74
COWDREY	B	10	54	COWLIN	W	3	41	COX	AF	5	85	COX	F	5	86
COWDREY	F	10	55	COWLING	AA	13	111	COX	AG	5	85	COX	F	5	86
COWDREY	MA	2	84	COWLING	AE	13	111	COX	AG	13	111	COX	F	5	86
COWDREY	TW	1	73	COWLING	AG	12	289	COX	AH	4	93	COX	F	5	86
COWDROY-GADNEY				COWLING	EH	8	77	COX	AH	6	96	COX	F	6	96
	JS	13	110	COWLING	JA	13	111	COX	AH	13	111	COX	F	6	96
COWDRY	AE	2	84	COWLING	JW	8	77	COX	AJ	1	73	COX	F	8	77
COWELL	A	1	73	COWLING	W	8	77	COX	AJ	6	96	COX	F	12	290
COWELL	A	6	96	COWLISHAW	C	14	72	COX	AJ	12	60	COX	F	14	72
COWELL	E	7	84	COWLISHAW	J	14	72	COX	AJ	12	289	COX	FA	2	84
COWELL	FW	1	73	COWLISHAW	WE	11	87	COX	AL	3	315	COX	FC	6	96
COWELL	HJ	12	289	COWMAN	R	9	244	COX	AS	2	84	COX	FC	6	96
COWELL	R	8	77	COWNE	A	1	73	COX	AT	6	96	COX	FC	6	96
COWELL	RC	3	314	COWPE	B	8	77	COX	AW	5	85	COX	FG	1	74
COWELL	T	9	47	COWPER	ET	13	111	COX	AW	6	96	COX	FH	6	97
COWELL	W	7	84	COWPER	WA	13	111	COX	AWT	5	85	COX	FJ	1	74
COWELL	W	8	77	COWPER	WH	1	73	COX	B	5	85	COX	FJ	2	84
COWELL	W	8	77	COWTON	WT	9	244	COX	B	12	289	COX	FJ	4	93
COWELL	W	9	244	COX	A	1	73	COX	BS	5	85	COX	FJ	10	55
COWELL	WR	3	314	COX	A	2	84	COX	C	1	74	COX	FJ	12	60
COWEN	FA	13	110	COX	A	3	41	COX	C	2	84	COX	FR	6	97
COWEN	H	13	111	COX	A	3	41	COX	C	5	86	COX	FR	13	111
COWEN	T	11	87	COX	A	3	41	COX	C	5	86	COX	FS	2	84
COWGILL	JA	9	47	COX	A	3	314	COX	C	8	77	COX	FT	1	74
COWIE	BG	13	111	COX	A	4	93	COX	C	9	244	COX	FT	3	315
COWIE	JL	6	96	COX	A	4	93	COX	C	10	55	COX	FW	4	94
COWIE	JL	14	72	COX	A	4	93	COX	C	12	60	COX	FW	7	85
COWIN	A	4	93	COX	A	5	85	COX	CA	3	315	COX	FW	12	60
COWIN	CA	6	96	COX	A	5	85	COX	CA	7	85	COX	FW	12	60
COWIN	J	11	87	COX	A	5	85	COX	CC	3	41	COX	G	1	74
COWL	G	8	77	COX	A	6	96	COX	CE	5	86	COX	G	2	84
COWL	J	8	77	COX	A	6	96	COX	CF	1	74	COX	G	5	86
COWLAND	AE	13	111	COX	A	6	96	COX	CG	5	86	COX	G	6	97
COWLAND	C	13	111	COX	A	8	77	COX	CG	7	85	COX	G	11	88
COWLAND	S	1	73	COX	A	12	60	COX	CH	2	84	COX	GB	1	74
COWLAND	WG	2	84	COX	A	12	60	COX	CH	10	283	COX	GB	10	55
COWLARD	E	13	111	COX	A	12	60	COX	DR	7	85	COX	GC	13	112
COWLARD	H	13	111	COX	A	12	289	COX	E	5	86	COX	GE	12	60
COWLARD	P	13	111	COX	A	12	289	COX	E	5	86	COX	GH	11	87
COWLER	W	2	84	COX	A	12	289	COX	E	8	77	COX	GHS	1	74
COWLES	E	2	84	COX	A	13	111	COX	E	10	55	COX	GR	2	85
COWLES	G	2	84	COX	A	13	111	COX	E	11	87	COX	GT	6	97
COWLES	JG	6	96	COX	A	14	72	COX	E	12	60	COX	GT	12	60
COWLEY	CA	12	59	COX	AA	12	60	COX	E	12	290	COX	GW	3	315
COWLEY	G	11	87	COX	AA	12	60	COX	EA	10	55	COX	GW	3	315
COWLEY	GH	12	59	COX	AC	3	41	COX	EC	5	86	COX	H	1	74
COWLEY	HC	12	60	COX	AC	3	41	COX	EC	7	85	COX	H	5	86
COWLEY	HW	12	60	COX	AC	4	93	COX	EE	1	75	COX	H	5	86
COWLEY	J	3	314	COX	AC	5	85	COX	EFJ	7	85	COX	H	6	97
COWLEY	JJ	4	93												

COX	H	6	97	COX	JL	6	97	COX	W	6	97	COY	W	14	73
COX	H	6	97	COX	JM	5	86	COX	W	6	98	COY	WH	5	87
COX	H	6	97	COX	JM	14	72	COX	W	9	244	COYLE	AF	8	78
COX	H	6	97	COX	JP	8	78	COX	W	12	61	COYLE	E	9	47
COX	H	8	77	COX	JR	13	112	COX	W	12	61	COYLE	F	9	47
COX	H	8	77	COX	JS	5	87	COX	W	12	61	COYLE	J	8	78
COX	H	8	77	COX	JT	10	283	COX	W	12	61	COYLE	J	11	88
COX	H	8	77	COX	JW	5	87	COX	W	12	61	COYLE	J	14	73
COX	H	12	290	COX	L	5	87	COX	W	12	61	COYLE	PT	13	112
COX	H	12	290	COX	LS	3	315	COX	W	12	290	COYNE	A	11	88
COX	HC	3	315	COX	LW	8	78	COX	WA	3	41	COYNE	CA	10	55
COX	HD	4	94	COX	N	1	74	COX	WA	6	98	COYNE	JP	8	78
COX	HE	10	283	COX	P	7	85	COX	WB	10	55	COYNE	MJ	11	88
COX	HF	7	85	COX	PH	3	41	COX	WD	12	290	COZENER	W	12	290
COX	HG	10	283	COX	PH	5	87	COX	WEH	2	85	COZENS	BC	3	315
COX	HJ	5	86	COX	PW	5	87	COX	WF	2	85	COZENS	F	4	94
COX	HJ	10	55	COX	R	9	244	COX	WG	1	74	COZENS	FC	2	85
COX	HJG	1	74	COX	R	10	55	COX	WG	7	85	COZENS	FC	3	41
COX	HJG	10	55	COX	R	12	61	COX	WG	13	112	COZENS	N	3	42
COX	HW	7	85	COX	RA	2	85	COX	WH	1	75	COZENS	PA	4	94
COX	J	1	74	COX	RC	7	85	COX	WH	1	75	COZENS	PW	4	94
COX	J	1	74	COX	RG	12	61	COX	WH	4	94	COZENS	TH	13	112
COX	J	1	74	COX	RH	12	61	COX	WH	4	94	COZENS	W	4	94
COX	J	2	85	COX	RW	1	74	COX	WH	12	61	COZENS	WG	1	75
COX	J	2	85	COX	S	1	74	COX	WH	12	290	CRABB	A	10	55
COX	J	3	315	COX	S	1	74	COX	WH	13	112	CRABB	B	4	94
COX	J	4	94	COX	S	6	97	COX	WJ	2	85	CRABB	FJ	1	75
COX	J	4	94	COX	S	8	78	COX	WJ	5	87	CRABB	HA	4	94
COX	J	5	86	COX	SE	3	315	COX	WJ	10	55	CRABB	J	13	112
COX	J	5	86	COX	SE	7	85	COX	WJ	12	61	CRABB	P	8	78
COX	J	6	97	COX	SH	4	94	COX	WJ	12	290	CRABB	SJ	4	94
COX	J	6	97	COX	SH	12	61	COX	WO	6	98	CRABB	W	7	85
COX	J	6	97	COX	SW	2	85	COX	WS	3	315	CRABBE	W	6	98
COX	J	7	85	COX	T	2	85	COX	WT	12	61	CRABBE	WW	2	85
COX	J	8	77	COX	T	2	85	COX	WW	5	87	CRABTREE	A	9	47
COX	J	8	78	COX	T	3	41	COXAN	CA	12	61	CRABTREE	A	9	47
COX	J	12	61	COX	T	5	87	COXAN	JH	12	61	CRABTREE	E	3	42
COX	JA	4	94	COX	T	6	97	COXEN	FJ	3	315	CRABTREE	E	9	47
COX	JA	13	112	COX	T	6	97	COXEN	FTC	12	61	CRABTREE	F	9	244
COX	JA	13	112	COX	T	6	98	COXEN	RH	12	61	CRABTREE	F	11	88
COX	JC	4	94	COX	T	8	78	COXFORD	J	12	290	CRABTREE	H	1	75
COX	JC	5	86	COX	T	8	78	COXFORD	W	12	290	CRABTREE	J	14	73
COX	JC	10	55	COX	T	8	78	COXHEAD	E	7	85	CRABTREE	JE	5	87
COX	JE	2	85	COX	T	11	88	COXHEAD	G	7	85	CRABTREE	S	14	73
COX	JE	4	94	COX	T	12	61	COXHILL	EF	3	41	CRACK	TG	2	85
COX	JE	6	97	COX	T	12	290	COXON		14	72	CRACK	W	10	283
COX	JE	11	88	COX	T	13	112	COXON	B	14	72	CRACKER	HE	7	86
COX	JE	12	61	COX	T	13	112	COXON	J	9	47	CRACKLE	W	9	383
COX	JG	1	74	COX	TH	8	78	COXON	JM	10	283	CRACKNELL	A	8	78
COX	JH	2	85	COX	TH	11	88	COXSON	CE	6	98	CRACKNELL	AA	1	75
COX	JH	6	97	COX	TJ	7	85	COXWELL	AF	7	85	CRACKNELL	AH	7	86
COX	JH	6	97	COX	TW	11	88	COXWELL	W	4	94	CRACKNELL	C	8	78
COX	JH	10	55	COX	VC	5	87	COY	A	6	98	CRACKNELL	CA	2	85
COX	JH	13	112	COX	W	2	85	COY	E	2	85	CRACKNELL	CE	2	85
COX	JJ	1	74	COX	W	4	94	COY	F	6	98	CRACKNELL	E	7	85

CRACKNELL	E	8	78
CRACKNELL	F	13	112
CRACKNELL	FP	3	42
CRACKNELL	GE	2	85
CRACKNELL	GF	3	42
CRACKNELL	H	7	86
CRACKNELL	H	13	112
CRACKNELL	H	13	112
CRACKNELL	J	7	85
CRACKNELL	L	8	78
CRACKNELL	PW	3	42
CRACKNELL	R	7	86
CRACKNELL	RJ	2	85
CRACKNELL	T	7	86
CRACKNELL	TR	7	86
CRADDOCK	CF	6	98
CRADDOCK	E	6	98
CRADDOCK	HL	12	62
CRADDOCK	J	6	98
CRADDOCK	JJ	1	75
CRADDOCK	T	6	98
CRADDOCK	TH	1	75
CRADDOCK	W	6	98
CRADDOCK	WE	2	86
CRADDOCK	WT	4	95
CRADOCK	CE	1	75
CRADOCK	J	9	244
CRAFT	C	7	86
CRAFT	C	7	86
CRAFT	G	3	42
CRAFT	J	4	95
CRAFTER	HP	7	86
CRAGAN	J	10	55
CRAGEN	JE	9	47
CRAGG	H	14	73
CRAGG	JS	9	47
CRAGG	TJ	9	244
CRAGGS	AB	3	42
CRAGGS	J	14	73
CRAGGS	O	9	47
CRAGGS	R	10	55
CRAGGS	T	14	73
CRAGGS	W	8	78
CRAGGS	W	14	73
CRAGGS	W	14	73
CRAIG	A	1	75
CRAIG	A	9	244
CRAIG	AE	1	75
CRAIG	EG	2	86
CRAIG	FAM	1	75
CRAIG	G	8	78
CRAIG	GA	10	283
CRAIG	H	9	47
CRAIG	HB	11	88
CRAIG	HG	10	55
CRAIG	J	7	86
CRAIG	JV	11	88
CRAIG	R	11	88
CRAIG	RC	7	86
CRAIG	W	8	78
CRAIG	W	14	73
CRAINE	T	11	88
CRAKANTHORP	R	1	75
CRAKER	EA	12	62
CRAKER	J	1	75
CRAMB	C	1	75
CRAMB	GW	1	75
CRAMB	J	1	75
CRAMBAC	H	2	86
CRAMER	AG	13	112
CRAMER	AH	13	112
CRAMER	GR	13	112
CRAMER	JW	10	55
CRAMER	M	4	95
CRAMER	P	13	112
CRAMMOND	A	2	86
CRAMMOND	SC	13	113
CRAMMOND	TC	1	75
CRAMOND	WD	1	75
CRAMP	FE	2	86
CRAMP	HG	10	284
CRAMP	LP	3	42
CRAMPHORN	SA	13	113
CRAMPHORN	W	5	87
CRAMPHORN	WA	5	87
CRAMPTON	CT	13	113
CRAMPTON	DLT	6	98
CRAMPTON	J	13	113
CRANBROOK	W	2	86
CRANCH	H	3	315
CRANE	AP	10	56
CRANE	AS	12	62
CRANE	C	7	86
CRANE	CH	13	113
CRANE	CW	1	75
CRANE	E	1	75
CRANE	E	3	42
CRANE	F	11	88
CRANE	FC	7	86
CRANE	GT	2	86
CRANE	H	11	88
CRANE	J	1	75
CRANE	J	7	86
CRANE	J	9	47
CRANE	J	9	245
CRANE	JH	2	86
CRANE	JJ	11	88
CRANE	T	11	88
CRANE	T	14	73
CRANE	TA	11	88
CRANE	THJ	13	113
CRANE	W	11	89
CRANE	WA	12	290
CRANEFIELD	LH	13	113
CRANFIELD	GW	5	87
CRANFIELD	H	5	87
CRANFIELD	J	12	62
CRANFIELD	JW	13	113
CRANFIELD	W	3	42
CRANHAM	GD	3	315
CRANK	T	11	89
CRANMER	A	2	86
CRANMER	AV	1	75
CRANMER	J	8	78
CRANMER	JW	9	47
CRANMER	WR	13	113
CRANN	JA	1	76
CRANSAZ	WA	6	98
CRANSHAW	FA	1	76
CRANSTON	AF	13	113
CRANSTON	AG	4	95
CRANSTON	BM	3	42
CRANSTON	E	3	42
CRANSTON	GA	1	76
CRANSTON	GWO	4	95
CRANSTON	JA	7	86
CRANSTON	W	11	89
CRANSTONE	TF	2	86
CRANSTOUN	WH	13	113
CRANTON	JH	4	95
CRANWELL	EP	12	62
CRAPPER	AT	12	290
CRAPPER	C	14	73
CRAPPER	EA	3	42
CRARGEN	E	11	88
CRASHILL	JW	12	62
CRASHLEY	H	8	79
CRASHLEY	J	8	78
CRASKE	A	2	86
CRASKE	EW	7	86
CRASKE	H	7	86
CRASKE	SW	7	86
CRASKE	WE	2	86
CRASTER	J	2	86
CRAVEN	A	8	79
CRAVEN	A	8	79
CRAVEN	A	9	47
CRAVEN	A	9	245
CRAVEN	A	11	89
CRAVEN	A	11	89
CRAVEN	AE	9	47
CRAVEN	AW	8	79
CRAVEN	B	8	79
CRAVEN	D	10	56
CRAVEN	E	8	79
CRAVEN	E	9	47
CRAVEN	F	9	47
CRAVEN	F	9	245
CRAVEN	G	8	79
CRAVEN	GE	8	79
CRAVEN	GH	8	79
CRAVEN	H	8	79
CRAVEN	H	9	48
CRAVEN	J	8	79
CRAVEN	J	9	48
CRAVEN	J	9	245
CRAVEN	J	11	89
CRAVEN	J	13	113
CRAVEN	JE	9	48
CRAVEN	JW	8	79
CRAVEN	L	9	48
CRAVEN	O	9	48
CRAVEN	P	6	98
CRAVEN	S	8	79
CRAVEN	S	10	56
CRAVEN	T	8	79
CRAVEN	T	9	48
CRAVEN	T	9	48
CRAVEN	T	9	48
CRAVEN	T	10	56
CRAVEN	T	14	73
CRAVEN	TR	14	73
CRAVEN	W	8	79
CRAVEN	WJ	10	56
CRAWFORD	A	6	98
CRAWFORD	A	6	98
CRAWFORD	A	11	89
CRAWFORD	AH	13	113
CRAWFORD	C	7	86
CRAWFORD	CA	5	87
CRAWFORD	CJ	2	86
CRAWFORD	D	13	113
CRAWFORD	E	4	95
CRAWFORD	F	12	290
CRAWFORD	FTE	3	315
CRAWFORD	G	8	79
CRAWFORD	GF	9	48
CRAWFORD	GH	10	56
CRAWFORD	GJ	10	56
CRAWFORD	GJ	10	56
CRAWFORD	GW	9	48
CRAWFORD	H	8	79
CRAWFORD	H	10	56
CRAWFORD	H	13	113
CRAWFORD	J	1	76
CRAWFORD	J	2	86
CRAWFORD	J	8	79
CRAWFORD	J	11	89
CRAWFORD	J	14	73
CRAWFORD	JB	11	89

CRAWFORD	JH	10	56	CRAYDEN	AE	10	56	CRESPIN	EM	4	95	CRIGHTON	W	11	90
CRAWFORD	JJ	2	86	CRAYMER	FG	1	76	CRESPIN	FC	4	95	CRIMES	WR	11	90
CRAWFORD	M	1	76	CRAYTHORNE	AL	6	98	CRESPIN	HF	4	95	CRIMMINGS	M	2	87
CRAWFORD	R	11	89	CRAYTHORNE	CC	10	56	CRESSEY	WE	1	76	CRIMMINS	A	9	48
CRAWFORD	RA	14	73	CREAK	WF	7	87	CRESSWELL	A	11	89	CRIMMINS	P	11	90
CRAWFORD	S	11	89	CREAK	WF	7	87	CRESSWELL	C	11	89	CRIMMINS	W	10	57
CRAWFORD	T	4	95	CREAL	AW	4	95	CRESSWELL	G	9	48	CRINION	WM	3	42
CRAWFORD	TA	8	79	CREAM	J	3	42	CRESSWELL	H	7	87	CRIPP	B	3	43
CRAWFORD	W	9	48	CREAMER	A	5	88	CRESSWELL	JH	9	48	CRIPPS	AE	2	87
CRAWFORD	WH	7	87	CREAMER	CE	10	56	CRESSWELL	NS	2	87	CRIPPS	AG	10	284
CRAWLEY	A	1	76	CREAMER	JW	13	113	CRESSWELL	P	14	74	CRIPPS	AH	10	57
CRAWLEY	A	3	42	CREAMER	RW	5	88	CRESSWELL	R	1	76	CRIPPS	AR	1	76
CRAWLEY	A	8	79	CREANEY	MO	13	113	CRESSWELL	R	4	95	CRIPPS	CH	10	57
CRAWLEY	AA	1	76	CREASE	CJ	4	95	CRESSWELL	R	11	90	CRIPPS	CJ	2	87
CRAWLEY	AF	5	87	CREASE	DP	4	95	CRESSWELL	WEJ	10	57	CRIPPS	CT	10	57
CRAWLEY	AJ	1	76	CREASE	TMCB	4	95	CRESSWELL	WG	2	87	CRIPPS	EG	7	87
CRAWLEY	AJ	2	86	CREASEY	C	7	87	CRESSWELL	WH	6	99	CRIPPS	FAV	5	89
CRAWLEY	AR	5	87	CREASEY	C	7	87	CRESSY	F	4	95	CRIPPS	FH	7	87
CRAWLEY	AW	3	42	CREASEY	H	7	87	CRESWELL	E	6	99	CRIPPS	G	5	89
CRAWLEY	BJ	5	87	CREASEY	S	10	56	CRESWELL	G	11	90	CRIPPS	G	10	57
CRAWLEY	CF	5	88	CREASEY	WA	7	87	CRESWELL	H	3	42	CRIPPS	GE	13	114
CRAWLEY	CW	5	88	CREASK	W	2	87	CRESWELL	J	6	99	CRIPPS	GH	12	62
CRAWLEY	D	5	88	CREASSER	FM	8	80	CRESWELL	J	6	99	CRIPPS	H	5	89
CRAWLEY	D	7	87	CREASY	CG	3	315	CRESWELL	J	6	99	CRIPPS	HG	13	114
CRAWLEY	DT	5	88	CREASY	DMR	1	76	CRESWELL	W	6	99	CRIPPS	J	10	57
CRAWLEY	EG	5	88	CREASY	FW	3	42	CRESWICK	A	2	87	CRIPPS	JA	7	88
CRAWLEY	EJ	2	86	CREASY	S	5	88	CREW	AE	5	89	CRIPPS	JT	1	76
CRAWLEY	EJ	2	86	CREATES	EJ	7	87	CREW	AJ	13	114	CRIPPS	JW	10	57
CRAWLEY	F	12	62	CREBER	F	13	113	CREW	BW	5	89	CRIPPS	T	1	76
CRAWLEY	FJ	2	87	CREE	F	14	74	CREW	F	5	89	CRIPPS	T	2	87
CRAWLEY	FJ	12	62	CREE	H	14	74	CREW	FJ	10	284	CRIPPS	T	5	89
CRAWLEY	FWP	5	88	CREED	AG	5	89	CREW	HE	13	114	CRIPPS	TW	10	57
CRAWLEY	G	12	62	CREED	H	8	80	CREW	HR	13	114	CRIPPS	W	5	89
CRAWLEY	GW	5	88	CREED	JGA	3	315	CREW	W	7	87	CRIPPS	W	10	57
CRAWLEY	GW	10	56	CREED	KJ	2	87	CREWE	EJ	11	90	CRISELL	A	2	87
CRAWLEY	H	5	88	CREED	S	7	87	CREWE	FD	2	87	CRISELL	PH	1	76
CRAWLEY	H	5	88	CREED	W	13	114	CRIBB	T	7	87	CRISP	A	6	99
CRAWLEY	H	5	88	CREEDEN	J	10	56	CRIBBIN	H	11	90	CRISP	A	10	57
CRAWLEY	J	10	56	CREEK	C	8	80	CRICHTON	WJ	13	114	CRISP	A	12	62
CRAWLEY	JH	10	56	CREEK	C	8	80	CRICK	A	3	42	CRISP	A	12	290
CRAWLEY	JJ	2	87	CREEK	W	12	62	CRICK	BF	5	89	CRISP	AG	7	88
CRAWLEY	P	4	95	CREER	P	7	87	CRICK	EM	1	76	CRISP	CB	2	87
CRAWLEY	R	5	88	CREES	AC	5	89	CRICK	FA	12	290	CRISP	CE	12	62
CRAWLEY	SP	5	88	CREES	EG	2	87	CRICK	H	1	76	CRISP	CH	6	99
CRAWLEY	W	5	88	CREESE	EJ	13	114	CRICK	JW	12	62	CRISP	CJ	5	89
CRAWLEY	WJ	5	88	CREGAN	T	11	89	CRICKMAY	S	7	87	CRISP	E	6	99
CRAWSHAW	AE	8	79	CREIGHTON	F	7	87	CRICKMORE	J	9	48	CRISP	G	2	87
CRAWSHAW	ET	1	76	CREIGHTON	FA	11	89	CRICKMORE	SG	13	114	CRISP	GH	13	114
CRAWSHAW	H	14	73	CREIGHTON	J	11	89	CRICKMORE	W	4	95	CRISP	H	2	87
CRAWSHAW	R	8	80	CREIGHTON	T	14	74	CRIDDLE	A	9	245	CRISP	H	13	114
CRAWSHAW	T	14	73	CREIGHTON	TH	11	89	CRIDDLE	J	1	76	CRISP	JH	4	96
CRAWSHAW	W	8	80	CREMER	W	5	89	CRIGHTON	D	1	76	CRISP	JH	6	99
CRAY	AH	5	88	CRESDEE	A	13	114	CRIGHTON	ET	11	90	CRISP	JW	6	99
CRAY	H	7	87	CRESDEE	CSD	6	98	CRIGHTON	G	1	76	CRISP	L	8	80
CRAY	TE	5	88	CRESPIN	AE	4	95	CRIGHTON	J	14	74	CRISP	PG	7	88

CRISP	RJW	12	62	CROFT	AE	14	74	CROMBIE	A	7	88	CROOK	CJ	7	88
CRISP	S	6	99	CROFT	AF	2	88	CROMBIE	C	4	96	CROOK	E	1	77
CRISP	W	12	62	CROFT	AW	1	77	CROMBIE	SJ	4	96	CROOK	EC	10	284
CRISP	WC	12	62	CROFT	E	2	88	CROMBIE	WG	2	88	CROOK	EE	4	96
CRISP	WR	2	87	CROFT	F	2	88	CROMEY	R	2	88	CROOK	EL	7	88
CRISPIN	R	9	245	CROFT	F	5	89	CROMPTON	EW	14	74	CROOK	F	6	100
CRISPIN	RJC	2	88	CROFT	F	10	57	CROMPTON	G	11	90	CROOK	FC	7	88
CRITCH	H	14	74	CROFT	FC	5	89	CROMPTON	H	9	48	CROOK	FE	2	88
CRITCHELL	WF	10	57	CROFT	FG	7	88	CROMPTON	HA	9	245	CROOK	GF	13	115
CRITCHER	EC	5	89	CROFT	H	6	99	CROMPTON	J	11	90	CROOK	GW	7	88
CRITCHETT	HE	10	284	CROFT	H	7	88	CROMPTON	J	11	90	CROOK	H	3	316
CRITCHLEY	AW	3	43	CROFT	H	8	80	CROMPTON	L	14	74	CROOK	HR	5	90
CRITCHLEY	EP	6	99	CROFT	H	13	114	CROMPTON	WJ	12	62	CROOK	J	4	96
CRITCHLEY	GP	6	99	CROFT	H	13	114	CROMWELL	M	14	74	CROOK	J	14	74
CRITCHLEY	J	4	96	CROFT	J	8	80	CRONAN	D	10	57	CROOK	J	14	74
CRITCHLEY	JW	9	383	CROFT	J	9	48	CRONAN	WT	4	96	CROOK	JAS	14	75
CRITOPH	P	2	88	CROFT	J	9	383	CRONE	A	1	77	CROOK	JC	10	284
CRIVI	A	9	48	CROFT	J	11	90	CRONE	J	11	91	CROOK	JS	10	284
CROAD	CF	4	96	CROFT	JR	8	80	CRONE	JB	5	90	CROOK	JW	2	88
CROAD	FW	7	88	CROFT	JW	5	89	CRONIN	FA	3	43	CROOK	L	4	96
CROAD	GC	10	284	CROFT	JW	13	114	CRONIN	FC	13	115	CROOK	PJ	2	88
CROAD	I	10	284	CROFT	L	8	80	CRONIN	HE	7	88	CROOK	R	4	96
CROAN	T	9	245	CROFT	PC	6	99	CRONIN	HW	7	88	CROOK	RA	14	75
CROASDALE	W	11	90	CROFT	R	11	90	CRONIN	J	13	115	CROOK	RDL	13	115
CROCKER	AC	2	88	CROFT	R	14	74	CRONIN	M	8	80	CROOK	T	8	80
CROCKER	E	7	88	CROFT	T	8	80	CRONIN	R	10	57	CROOK	T	13	115
CROCKER	EG	13	114	CROFT	TA	2	88	CRONIN	WD	14	74	CROOK	T	14	75
CROCKER	HCG	10	57	CROFT	V	13	114	CRONK	B	1	77	CROOK	W	4	96
CROCKER	HW	1	77	CROFT	W	1	77	CRONK	F	10	58	CROOK	W	5	90
CROCKER	HW	13	114	CROFT	W	5	90	CRONK	G	1	77	CROOK	W	6	100
CROCKER	J	4	96	CROFT	W	8	80	CRONK	GO	13	115	CROOK	W	6	100
CROCKER	JC	10	57	CROFT	WG	13	115	CRONK	HJ	13	115	CROOK	W	7	88
CROCKER	PW	2	88	CROFTON	W	11	90	CRONK	J	1	77	CROOK	WF	4	96
CROCKER	WH	1	77	CROFTS	A	11	90	CRONK	JC	13	115	CROOK	WJ	5	90
CROCKER	WH	2	88	CROFTS	C	13	115	CRONK	MC	13	115	CROOK	WR	2	88
CROCKETT	C	1	77	CROFTS	ER	12	290	CRONK	W	1	77	CROOKES	CH	3	316
CROCKETT	C	1	77	CROFTS	J	12	290	CRONK	W	13	115	CROOME	J	4	96
CROCKETT	CH	6	99	CROFTS	T	14	74	CRONSHAW	AE	11	91	CROOME	JC	2	88
CROCKETT	CW	6	99	CROKE	E	14	74	CRONSHAW	D	11	91	CROOT	HJ	5	90
CROCKETT	GA	6	99	CROKER	CG	1	77	CRONSHAW	J	11	91	CROPLEY	AL	5	90
CROCKETT	JW	6	99	CROKER	E	8	80	CRONSHAW	J	11	91	CROPLEY	AW	3	316
CROCKFORD	A	2	88	CROKER	HF	1	77	CRONSHAW	R	11	91	CROPLEY	JH	1	77
CROCKFORD	A	7	88	CROKER	HP	3	315	CRONSHAW	T	14	74	CROPLEY	P	5	90
CROCKFORD	CH	10	57	CROKER	JW	1	77	CROOK	A	1	77	CROPLEY	RJ	2	88
CROCKFORD	CH	10	57	CROKER	R	1	77	CROOK	A	4	96	CROPP	C	4	96
CROCKFORD	EM	10	57	CROKER	SW	7	88	CROOK	A	6	100	CROPP	CT	1	77
CROCKFORD	WB	1	77	CROKER	T	3	315	CROOK	A	7	88	CROPPER	D	14	75
CROCOME	W	7	88	CROLEY	HC	1	77	CROOK	A	9	49	CROPPER	F	14	75
CRODEN	JE	14	74	CROLLA	H	11	90	CROOK	AE	5	90	CROPPER	F	14	75
CRODEN	L	14	74	CROLY	CP	13	115	CROOK	AE	5	90	CROPPER	H	11	91
CROFT	A	3	43	CROLY	FD	13	115	CROOK	AG	10	58	CROPPER	J	3	43
CROFT	A	5	89	CROLY	J	13	115	CROOK	AT	13	115	CROPPER	J	11	91
CROFT	A	8	80	CROLY	W	13	115	CROOK	AW	4	96	CROPPRO	J	14	75
CROFT	A	8	80	CROMAC	AE	9	245	CROOK	C	4	96	CROSBIE	A	8	80
CROFT	A	12	62	CROMBELHOLME	D	11	90	CROOK	C	4	96	CROSBIE	FF	10	58

CROSBY	A	8	80
CROSBY	FW	2	88
CROSBY	H	8	81
CROSBY	H	9	245
CROSBY	H	11	91
CROSBY	J	9	49
CROSBY	JE	2	89
CROSBY	JE	10	58
CROSBY	JE	12	63
CROSBY	S	11	91
CROSBY	T	2	89
CROSBY	W	11	91
CROSBY	WE	10	58
CROSBY	WJ	1	78
CROSDALE	JD	9	245
CROSHAW	HA	12	63
CROSHAW	SR	12	63
CROSS	A	1	78
CROSS	A	4	96
CROSS	A	5	90
CROSS	A	6	100
CROSS	A	10	58
CROSS	AC	3	43
CROSS	AE	7	89
CROSS	AE	10	58
CROSS	AH	4	96
CROSS	AH	10	58
CROSS	AH	10	284
CROSS	AS	7	89
CROSS	B	6	100
CROSS	C	3	316
CROSS	C	4	96
CROSS	C	12	63
CROSS	CE	4	97
CROSS	CJ	1	78
CROSS	E	2	89
CROSS	E	10	58
CROSS	EP	12	63
CROSS	ET	1	78
CROSS	ET	1	78
CROSS	F	2	89
CROSS	FEA	3	43
CROSS	FW	5	90
CROSS	FW	12	63
CROSS	G	2	89
CROSS	G	6	100
CROSS	GD	12	63
CROSS	GJ	1	78
CROSS	H	3	316
CROSS	H	7	89
CROSS	H	11	91
CROSS	H	12	63
CROSS	H	12	63
CROSS	H	14	75
CROSS	HA	4	97
CROSS	HA	4	97
CROSS	HC	2	89
CROSS	HG	10	58
CROSS	J	3	43
CROSS	J	10	58
CROSS	J	12	290
CROSS	J	13	115
CROSS	J	14	75
CROSS	JA	7	89
CROSS	JE	4	97
CROSS	JH	14	75
CROSS	JJ	5	90
CROSS	JJ	6	100
CROSS	JS	5	90
CROSS	KE	12	63
CROSS	LE	10	58
CROSS	LG	10	58
CROSS	OF	12	290
CROSS	PA	2	89
CROSS	R	4	97
CROSS	RH	2	89
CROSS	RH	12	291
CROSS	S	1	78
CROSS	S	1	78
CROSS	S	2	89
CROSS	S	2	89
CROSS	S	14	75
CROSS	SA	6	100
CROSS	T	4	97
CROSS	T	12	63
CROSS	V	4	97
CROSS	W	3	43
CROSS	W	4	97
CROSS	W	9	383
CROSS	W	11	91
CROSS	W	12	63
CROSS	W	12	291
CROSS	WC	12	63
CROSS	WC	13	116
CROSS	WE	1	78
CROSS	WE	10	58
CROSS	WG	7	89
CROSS	WGF	2	89
CROSS	WJ	1	78
CROSS	WJ	12	291
CROSS	WM	3	43
CROSSDALE	JD	9	49
CROSSE	EJ	13	116
CROSSFIELD	C	8	81
CROSSFIELD	J	8	81
CROSSFIELD	JW	8	81
CROSSFIELD	T	11	91
CROSSHAW	FR	14	75
CROSSKEY	E	13	116
CROSSLAND	F	9	245
CROSSLAND	H	9	245
CROSSLAND	J	8	81
CROSSLAND	J	9	245
CROSSLAND	J	14	75
CROSSLAND	S	9	49
CROSSLEY		4	97
CROSSLEY	A	13	116
CROSSLEY	AJ	2	89
CROSSLEY	C	13	116
CROSSLEY	CJ	12	63
CROSSLEY	F	11	91
CROSSLEY	F	14	75
CROSSLEY	G	11	91
CROSSLEY	J	11	91
CROSSLEY	JH	11	91
CROSSLEY	JHW	14	75
CROSSLEY	JT	9	49
CROSSLEY	JT	14	75
CROSSLEY	JW	11	91
CROSSLEY	O	9	49
CROSSLEY	R	11	91
CROSSLEY	SM	11	92
CROSSLEY	WA	10	284
CROSSLEY	WH	11	92
CROSSMAN	A	12	291
CROSSMAN	G	12	291
CROSSMAN	GH	4	97
CROSSMAN	GJ	10	58
CROSSMAN	H	12	291
CROSSMAN	HW	12	291
CROSSMAN	KLM	4	97
CROSSMAN	S	12	291
CROSSMAN	WF	1	78
CROSSWAITE	J	8	81
CROSSWAITE	JH	11	92
CROSSWELL	FG	7	89
CROSSWELL	W	14	75
CROSTON	J	14	75
CROSTON	J	14	75
CROSWELLER	F	13	116
CROSWELLER	VE	13	116
CROSWELLER	WJ	13	116
CROTCH	A	9	245
CROTON	G	1	78
CROTON	G	1	78
CROTON	J	1	78
CROTTERILL	JG	14	76
CROTTY	J	2	89
CROTTY	T	9	49
CROUCH	A	5	90
CROUCH	A	7	89
CROUCH	A	12	63
CROUCH	A	13	116
CROUCH	AE	13	116
CROUCH	AR	7	89
CROUCH	AW	13	116
CROUCH	AW	13	116
CROUCH	CE	7	89
CROUCH	EG	2	89
CROUCH	EJ	4	97
CROUCH	G	2	89
CROUCH	G	13	116
CROUCH	GH	2	89
CROUCH	H	2	89
CROUCH	J	5	90
CROUCH	JW	9	49
CROUCH	ML	4	97
CROUCH	NM	4	97
CROUCH	PH	10	58
CROUCH	RAG	12	63
CROUCH	WF	10	284
CROUCH	WJ	12	422
CROUCH	WJ	13	116
CROUCHER	A	4	97
CROUCHER	AHC	2	89
CROUCHER	C	1	80
CROUCHER	C	4	97
CROUCHER	F	3	43
CROUCHER	G	2	89
CROUCHER	H	4	97
CROUCHER	HJ	10	58
CROUCHER	S	4	97
CROUCHER	W	3	316
CROUCHER	WH	11	92
CROUCHER	WR	5	90
CROUCHER	WT	2	89
CROUCHMAN	AJ	2	90
CROUGHAN	FS	10	284
CROUT	TW	7	89
CROW	AA	10	58
CROW	AT	10	284
CROW	E	7	89
CROW	E	8	81
CROW	G	5	91
CROW	H	8	81
CROW	HA	8	81
CROW	HC	7	89
CROW	JE	7	89
CROW	JG	7	89
CROW	PG	5	91
CROW	PJ	10	58
CROW	TF	7	89
CROW	TH	10	284
CROW	W	2	90
CROW	W	6	100
CROW	WA	6	100
CROWCHER	G	5	91
CROWDER	FW	6	100
CROWDER	H	13	116
CROWDER	W	3	316

CROWDER	W	6	100	CROWTHER	D	9	245	CROZIER	WS	13	117	CRYER	JHG	9	49
CROWDY	CG	1	78	CROWTHER	E	9	49	CRUCEFIX	RJ	1	78	CRYER	JW	8	82
CROWE	A	14	76	CROWTHER	F	9	49	CRUICKSHANK	AR	10	59	CRYER	R	8	82
CROWE	AH	1	78	CROWTHER	F	9	245	CRUICKSHANKS	G	1	78	CUBBAGE	W	13	117
CROWE	F	3	316	CROWTHER	F	9	383	CRUISE	T	11	92	CUBIN	H	14	76
CROWE	F	7	89	CROWTHER	G	8	81	CRUMFORD	W	6	101	CUBITT	J	2	90
CROWE	FW	5	90	CROWTHER	GW	11	92	CRUMLEY	H	11	92	CUCKSON	HW	2	90
CROWE	H	7	89	CROWTHER	H	2	90	CRUMP	A	3	43	CUDD	F	7	90
CROWE	H	12	63	CROWTHER	H	8	81	CRUMP	A	10	59	CUDD	FD	3	316
CROWE	J	8	81	CROWTHER	H	14	76	CRUMP	C	12	291	CUDD	H	3	316
CROWE	R	3	316	CROWTHER	HA	9	245	CRUMP	E	6	101	CUDD	HR	2	90
CROWE	RA	12	63	CROWTHER	J	8	81	CRUMP	F	3	316	CUDD	J	3	316
CROWE	S	3	316	CROWTHER	J	14	76	CRUMP	JFA	3	43	CUDD	WG	3	316
CROWE	S	8	81	CROWTHER	JA	6	100	CRUMP	L	6	101	CUDD	WG	3	317
CROWE	S	14	76	CROWTHER	JH	14	76	CRUMP	R	6	101	CUDD	WG	13	117
CROWE	W	6	100	CROWTHER	JJ	14	76	CRUMP	R	7	90	CUDDINGTON	W	13	117
CROWFOOT	A	2	90	CROWTHER	ME	3	316	CRUMP	RW	6	101	CUDDY	H	9	50
CROWHURST	CA	9	49	CROWTHER	ME	8	81	CRUMP	S	7	90	CUDDY	H	11	92
CROWHURST	GH	7	89	CROWTHER	P	8	81	CRUMP	T	6	101	CUDDY	JW	8	82
CROWHURST	H	2	90	CROWTHER	R	9	245	CRUMP	T	6	101	CUDE	WJ	4	98
CROWHURST	HW	13	116	CROWTHER	R	11	92	CRUMP	W	6	101	CUDLIPP	R	13	117
CROWHURST	J	1	78	CROWTHER	S	9	246	CRUMP	W	13	117	CUDLIPP	W	2	90
CROWHURST	JH	13	116	CROWTHER	T	8	82	CRUMP	WGA	3	43	CUDLIPP	WM	13	117
CROWHURST	W	13	116	CROWTHER	TH	8	82	CRUMPLIN	B	4	97	CUDWORTH	H	8	82
CROWLE	RH	4	97	CROWTHER	W	8	82	CRUMPLIN	CH	5	91	CUDWORTH	R	8	82
CROWLE	TJ	4	97	CROWTHER	W	8	82	CRUMPLIN	F	5	91	CUDWORTH	V	8	82
CROWLEY	C	3	316	CROWTHER	W	11	421	CRUMPLIN	PC	4	98	CUE	A	13	117
CROWLEY	C	13	116	CROWTHER	WH	9	49	CRUMPTON	JA	6	101	CUELL	JA	10	59
CROWLEY	E	11	92	CROWTHER	WW	9	49	CRUMPTON	TH	6	101	CUELL	JH	4	98
CROWLEY	H	12	291	CROWTHER	WW	9	49	CRUMPTON	W	6	101	CUFAUDE	EH	12	291
CROWLEY	HL	9	49	CROWTON	FJ	6	100	CRUNDEN	JA	1	78	CUFF	CH	10	59
CROWLEY	J	9	383	CROXALL	GT	3	43	CRUSE	AC	7	90	CUFF	CR	10	59
CROWLEY	J	13	116	CROXFORD	AF	3	43	CRUSE	HE	3	316	CUFF	EJ	11	92
CROWLEY	M	10	284	CROXFORD	C	1	78	CRUSE	J	13	117	CUFF	HJ	7	90
CROWLEY	P	2	90	CROXFORD	CT	2	90	CRUSE	JF	2	90	CUFF	PG	2	90
CROWLEY	S	11	92	CROXFORD	GEH	2	90	CRUSE	JW	14	76	CUFFE	JJ	12	64
CROWLEY	T	2	90	CROXFORD	T	5	91	CRUSE	SA	6	101	CUFFIN	GA	10	284
CROWLEY	T	6	100	CROXFORD	WG	5	91	CRUST	C	1	78	CUFFLEY	JR	7	90
CROWLEY	W	6	100	CROXFORD	WJ	12	291	CRUST	EH	1	78	CULHAM	JW	7	90
CROWLEY	W	13	117	CROXON	EF	2	90	CRUTCH	H	6	101	CULL	EA	10	284
CROWLEY	W	13	117	CROXSON	E	7	90	CRUTCHFIELD	WJ	1	79	CULL	F	4	98
CROWLEY	W	13	117	CROXSON	FS	10	58	CRUTCHLEY	AB	12	291	CULL	H	6	101
CROWNE	H	3	316	CROXSON	FS	10	58	CRUTCHLEY	AE	12	291	CULL	S	8	82
CROWSLEY	A	5	91	CROYDEN	AW	3	43	CRUTCHLEY	WG	12	291	CULLABINE	C	12	64
CROWSLEY	A	12	63	CROYDON	EA	2	90	CRUTCHLOW	T	7	90	CULLEARN	C	9	246
CROWSLEY	AS	12	63	CROYDON	R	2	90	CRUTCHLOW	W	7	90	CULLEN	A	14	78
CROWSLEY	GW	12	64	CROYDON	S	7	90	CRUTTWELL	CR	13	117	CULLEN	C	11	92
CROWSON	JW	8	81	CROZIER	FJ	8	82	CRUTTWELL	RH	13	117	CULLEN	EA	1	79
CROWTHER	A	1	78	CROZIER	J	6	100	CRYER	A	9	49	CULLEN	F	11	92
CROWTHER	A	8	81	CROZIER	J	11	92	CRYER	A	9	246	CULLEN	HR	10	284
CROWTHER	A	11	92	CROZIER	J	11	92	CRYER	E	8	82	CULLEN	J	4	98
CROWTHER	AC	11	92	CROZIER	J	11	92	CRYER	EL	3	44	CULLEN	J	9	246
CROWTHER	C	8	81	CROZIER	JW	13	117	CRYER	H	13	117	CULLEN	J	10	59
CROWTHER	C	8	81	CROZIER	L	11	92	CRYER	J	8	82	CULLEN	J	14	76
CROWTHER	CA	8	81	CROZIER	WH	6	101	CRYER	JE	9	246	CULLEN	JF	2	91

Name	Init	Col	Pg	Name	Init	Col	Pg	Name	Init	Col	Pg	Name	Init	Col	Pg
CULLEN	JF	3	317	CULVERHOUSE	WC	5	91	CUNDALL	W	11	93	CUNNINGHAM	W	13	118
CULLEN	JW	10	285	CULVERWELL	GC	10	59	CUNLIFFE	A	9	246	CUNNINGHAM	WT	7	90
CULLEN	R	3	44	CULWICK	WJ	7	90	CUNLIFFE	D	13	118	CUNNINGTON	DA	12	64
CULLEN	R	11	93	CUMBER	HT	2	91	CUNLIFFE	D	14	76	CUNNINGTON	JW	8	82
CULLEN	SA	3	317	CUMBERBIRCH	E	11	93	CUNLIFFE	E	9	50	CUNNINGTON	O	6	102
CULLEN	T	11	93	CUMBERLAND	G	5	91	CUNLIFFE	E	9	50	CUPIT	WA	13	118
CULLEN	TF	9	50	CUMBERLAND	H	5	92	CUNLIFFE	EC	14	77	CURCARAN	J	8	82
CULLEN	TJB	4	98	CUMBERLAND	H	5	92	CUNLIFFE	H	11	94	CURCHIN	EA	5	92
CULLEY	AE	4	98	CUMBERLAND	JE	5	92	CUNLIFFE	J	11	94	CURD	A	7	90
CULLEY	CH	11	93	CUMBERLAND	JG	6	102	CUNLIFFE	J	14	77	CURD	J	7	90
CULLEY	H	11	93	CUMBERLAND	PF	5	92	CUNLIFFE	J	14	77	CURE	A	6	102
CULLEY	HP	1	79	CUMBERLAND	RT	12	64	CUNLIFFE	J	14	77	CURE	GA	10	59
CULLEY	JH	11	93	CUMBERLAND	S	5	92	CUNLIFFE	T	14	77	CURGENVEN	AE	4	98
CULLEY	JW	11	93	CUMBERLAND	S	5	92	CUNLIFFE	TE	11	94	CURL	AT	5	92
CULLIGAN	C	9	246	CUMBERLAND	TS	5	92	CUNLIFFE	W	11	94	CURL	E	2	91
CULLING	A	5	91	CUMBERLAND	V	5	92	CUNLIFFE	WB	14	77	CURL	E	10	59
CULLING	A	9	50	CUMBERLAND	WJ	12	64	CUNNAH	AV	9	50	CURL	ED	5	92
CULLING	C	10	59	CUMBERPATCH	F	12	291	CUNNAH	W	9	50	CURL	F	2	91
CULLING	C	13	117	CUMBERPATCH	HJ	12	291	CUNNINGHAM	A	3	44	CURL	FC	2	91
CULLING	E	13	117	CUMBERPATCH	HJ	12	291	CUNNINGHAM	A	10	285	CURL	J	1	79
CULLING	E	13	117	CUMBERPATCH	JH	12	292	CUNNINGHAM	A	14	77	CURL	J	2	91
CULLING	G	13	118	CUMERFORD	T	11	93	CUNNINGHAM	C	10	59	CURL	TH	1	79
CULLING	HH	5	91	CUMMING	A	11	93	CUNNINGHAM	CA	5	92	CURL	W	5	92
CULLING	L	5	91	CUMMING	F	11	93	CUNNINGHAM	E	9	50	CURLEY	GW	11	94
CULLING	W	9	50	CUMMING	JH	2	91	CUNNINGHAM	EH	2	91	CURLEY	J	14	77
CULLINGFORD	JW	9	50	CUMMING	WH	14	76	CUNNINGHAM	F	3	44	CURLEY	J	14	77
CULLINGS	A	9	50	CUMMING	WH	14	76	CUNNINGHAM	F	9	50	CURLEY	JT	11	94
CULLINGS	JW	9	50	CUMMINGS	AH	3	44	CUNNINGHAM	F	14	77	CURLEY	M	11	94
CULLIS	GJ	5	91	CUMMINGS	AJ	3	317	CUNNINGHAM	FG	4	98	CURLEY	T	11	94
CULLIS	H	10	285	CUMMINGS	AT	13	118	CUNNINGHAM	FJ	14	77	CURLEY	T	11	94
CULLIS	JR	5	91	CUMMINGS	C	11	93	CUNNINGHAM	G	13	118	CURLEY	T	14	77
CULLIS	TW	6	101	CUMMINGS	EG	4	98	CUNNINGHAM	G	14	77	CURLEY	TB	6	102
CULLOCH	M	5	91	CUMMINGS	G	1	79	CUNNINGHAM	GAF	14	77	CURLING	C	13	118
CULLOP	W	12	64	CUMMINGS	HW	13	118	CUNNINGHAM	H	8	82	CURLING	GA	3	317
CULLUM	D	7	90	CUMMINGS	J	3	317	CUNNINGHAM	H	14	77	CURME	R	5	92
CULLUM	FC	7	90	CUMMINGS	J	10	59	CUNNINGHAM	J	4	98	CURNICK	AE	7	91
CULLY	E	14	76	CUMMINGS	J	14	76	CUNNINGHAM	J	6	102	CURNOW	C	13	118
CULLY	HP	6	101	CUMMINGS	L	11	93	CUNNINGHAM	J	6	102	CURNOW	E	2	91
CULLY	WF	6	101	CUMMINGS	M	2	91	CUNNINGHAM	J	14	77	CURNOW	HG	1	79
CULM	F	6	102	CUMMINGS	R	11	93	CUNNINGHAM	JF	1	79	CURNOW	WA	2	91
CULMER	G	13	118	CUMMINGS	S	6	102	CUNNINGHAM	JW	8	82	CURPHEY	A	8	415
CULMER	RA	13	118	CUMMINGS	T	8	82	CUNNINGHAM	L	7	90	CURPHEY	A	9	246
CULMER	WD	13	118	CUMMINGS	W	11	93	CUNNINGHAM	M	4	98	CURPHEY	WH	14	78
CULPAN	J	9	50	CUMMINS	AC	4	98	CUNNINGHAM	M	10	59	CURR	HEA	7	91
CULSHAW	J	14	76	CUMMINS	E	14	76	CUNNINGHAM	M	10	285	CURR	LE	7	91
CULVER	FC	3	317	CUMMINS	J	11	93	CUNNINGHAM	M	11	94	CURRALL	F	6	102
CULVER	SJ	3	317	CUMMINS	L	10	59	CUNNINGHAM	ME	6	102	CURRAN	C	4	98
CULVER	WH	2	91	CUMMINS	RJ	4	98	CUNNINGHAM	R	8	82	CURRAN	F	11	94
CULVERHOUSE	AJ	5	91	CUMMINS	T	10	59	CUNNINGHAM	T	3	44	CURRAN	F	11	94
CULVERHOUSE	B	5	91	CUMMINS	WH	3	44	CUNNINGHAM	T	11	94	CURRAN	H	11	94
CULVERHOUSE	EAG	3	44	CUMNER	FC	5	92	CUNNINGHAM	T	14	77	CURRAN	J	4	98
CULVERHOUSE	HH	5	91	CUMPSTY	G	14	76	CUNNINGHAM	T	14	77	CURRAN	J	11	94
CULVERHOUSE	J	2	91	CUNDALL	J	11	93	CUNNINGHAM	TH	14	77	CURRAN	J	14	78
CULVERHOUSE	S	10	59	CUNDALL	J	11	93	CUNNINGHAM	W	2	91	CURRAN	J	14	78
CULVERHOUSE	TH	12	291	CUNDALL	LR	11	93	CUNNINGHAM	W	7	90	CURRAN	JA	14	78

CURRAN	R	11	94
CURRAN	T	11	94
CURRAN	T	11	94
CURRAN	W	11	94
CURRANT	D	5	92
CURRANT	F	5	92
CURRANT	GH	5	92
CURREY	EG	2	91
CURREY	F	13	118
CURREY	H	12	292
CURREY	HJ	13	118
CURREY	JW	13	118
CURRIE	E	6	102
CURRIE	G	2	91
CURRIE	J	1	79
CURRIE	J	6	102
CURRIE	JD	9	50
CURRIE	JJ	2	91
CURRIE	P	11	95
CURRIE	PB	14	78
CURRIE	RG	11	95
CURRIE	S	2	91
CURRIE	W	3	317
CURRIE	W	4	98
CURRIE	WA	3	44
CURRIER	J	2	91
CURRIN	M	1	79
CURRIN	T	12	292
CURRINGTON	AE	5	92
CURRINGTON	E	12	64
CURRINGTON	JZ	12	64
CURRINGTON	S	12	64
CURRINGTON	W	5	92
CURRINGTON	W	12	64
CURRINGTON	W	12	64
CURRY	A	12	64
CURRY	DP	13	118
CURRY	E	14	78
CURRY	H	11	95
CURRY	M	11	95
CURRY	S	13	118
CURRY	W	5	93
CURRY	WJ	5	93
CURRY	WP	2	91
CURSON	JW	6	102
CURSONS	AM	7	91
CURSONS	C	10	59
CURSONS	HL	10	60
CURSONS	JT	7	91
CURTAIN	JA	13	118
CURTAIN	LA	13	118
CURTIN	JF	8	83
CURTIS	A	4	98
CURTIS	AA	4	98
CURTIS	AA	10	285
CURTIS	AAH	12	64
CURTIS	AD	4	98
CURTIS	AE	9	246
CURTIS	AF	4	98
CURTIS	AT	1	79
CURTIS	B	1	79
CURTIS	BF	4	99
CURTIS	BJ	5	93
CURTIS	C	4	99
CURTIS	C	7	91
CURTIS	C	10	60
CURTIS	C	12	64
CURTIS	CF	4	99
CURTIS	CR	3	317
CURTIS	E	2	92
CURTIS	F	12	64
CURTIS	FF	12	64
CURTIS	FJ	4	99
CURTIS	FW	3	44
CURTIS	FW	12	64
CURTIS	G	7	91
CURTIS	G	11	95
CURTIS	GA	12	292
CURTIS	GB	1	79
CURTIS	GE	1	79
CURTIS	GF	12	292
CURTIS	GH	4	99
CURTIS	GJ	7	91
CURTIS	GTA	1	79
CURTIS	H	9	246
CURTIS	H	13	119
CURTIS	H	13	119
CURTIS	HA	1	79
CURTIS	HC	1	79
CURTIS	HC	3	317
CURTIS	HT	8	83
CURTIS	HT	12	292
CURTIS	J	1	79
CURTIS	J	4	99
CURTIS	J	7	91
CURTIS	J	8	83
CURTIS	J	10	60
CURTIS	JH	13	119
CURTIS	JJ	6	102
CURTIS	JM	1	79
CURTIS	JR	12	292
CURTIS	JW	4	99
CURTIS	L	4	99
CURTIS	LA	2	92
CURTIS	MH	12	292
CURTIS	N	4	99
CURTIS	PJ	4	99
CURTIS	R	6	102
CURTIS	R	8	83
CURTIS	S	5	93
CURTIS	S	6	102
CURTIS	SA	2	92
CURTIS	T	12	292
CURTIS	TH	5	93
CURTIS	TW	4	99
CURTIS	TW	12	64
CURTIS	TW	12	292
CURTIS	W	1	79
CURTIS	W	7	91
CURTIS	W	10	60
CURTIS	W	11	95
CURTIS	W	12	292
CURTIS	WC	3	44
CURTIS	WE	1	79
CURTIS	WE	12	292
CURTIS	WH	4	99
CURTIS	WH	4	99
CURTIS	WH	4	99
CURTIS	WJ	13	119
CURTIS	WW	3	317
CURTIS	WW	3	317
CURTISS	SC	13	119
CURWOOD	HR	13	119
CURZON	S	14	78
CUSHELSON	J	14	78
CUSHEN	EE	10	285
CUSHION	A	11	95
CUSHION	C	11	95
CUSHION	J	3	44
CUSHION	J	11	95
CUSHION	T	11	95
CUSICK	CW	2	92
CUSICK	CW	2	92
CUSICK	FA	1	79
CUSICK	J	1	79
CUSICK	JAT	1	80
CUSICK	T	11	95
CUSNORTH	W	6	102
CUSSANS	R	8	83
CUSSANS	WA	2	92
CUSSENS	TE	7	91
CUST	CW	8	83
CUSTANCE	V	5	93
CUSWORTH	F	11	95
CUSWORTH	H	8	83
CUSWORTH	H	8	83
CUSWORTH	RH	8	83
CUTBILL	A	2	92
CUTBUSH	FE	12	64
CUTBUSH	WF	4	99
CUTCHE	W	2	92
CUTHBERT	AG	2	92
CUTHBERT	FL	11	95
CUTHBERT	H	7	91
CUTHBERT	JH	9	50
CUTHBERT	W	7	91
CUTHBERT	WHG	2	92
CUTHBERTSON	AA	7	91
CUTHBERTSON	FW	7	91
CUTHBERTSON	W	4	99
CUTLER		2	92
CUTLER	A	11	95
CUTLER	A	14	78
CUTLER	AE	5	93
CUTLER	CB	2	92
CUTLER	EW	4	99
CUTLER	F	5	93
CUTLER	F	12	292
CUTLER	FJ	2	92
CUTLER	G	4	99
CUTLER	HW	5	93
CUTLER	HW	5	93
CUTLER	J	6	102
CUTLER	JS	6	103
CUTLER	L	4	99
CUTLER	RH	9	246
CUTLER	SA	13	119
CUTLER	T	4	99
CUTLER	T	6	103
CUTLER	W	4	100
CUTLER	WJ	4	100
CUTMORE	R	6	103
CUTMORE	RE	6	103
CUTNER	EW	11	95
CUTRESS	CG	3	317
CUTRESS	HW	3	317
CUTTEN	H	1	80
CUTTER	WA	1	80
CUTTING	AE	11	95
CUTTING	BE	2	92
CUTTING	CF	1	80
CUTTING	CHW	2	92
CUTTING	E	2	92
CUTTING	EJ	7	91
CUTTING	F	7	91
CUTTING	HA	7	91
CUTTING	HS	11	95
CUTTING	J	7	91
CUTTING	JW	13	119
CUTTS	AE	3	317
CUTTS	AJ	3	317
CUTTS	CF	6	103
CUTTS	CR	3	317
CUTTS	E	7	91
CUTTS	EG	1	80
CUTTS	EG	13	119
CUTTS	FG	7	92
CUTTS	FJ	1	80
CUTTS	GW	13	119
CUTTS	JA	13	119

CUTTS	JF	1	80
CUTTS	L	8	83
CUZICK	AE	6	103
CYSTER	AE	1	80

D

D'ALBERT	G	2	92
D'ARCY	A	6	104
D'ARCY	A	6	105
D'ARCY	E	8	85
D'ARCY	FB	4	102
D'ARCY	GA	8	85
D'ARCY	GM	4	102
D'ARCY	H	6	105
D'ARCY	H	8	85
D'ARCY	RW	4	102
D'EATH	JH	11	102
DA COSTA	A	3	318
DABBS	J	6	103
DABIN	IG	13	119
DABIN	T	13	119
DABLE	F	9	50
DABLE	G	9	246
DABLE	H	9	51
DABLE	H	9	246
DABLEY	E	3	47
DACCUS	B	8	83
DACEY	MA	6	103
DACHTLER	FW	7	92
DACHTLER	RJ	7	92
DACK	A	4	100
DACK	AR	4	100
DACK	GS	4	100
DACK	HG	3	44
DACK	HJ	13	119
DACK	RP	7	92
DACK	WH	4	100
DACK	ZG	4	100
DACKOMBE	CW	3	318
DACKOMBE	J	7	92
DACOMBE	AL	4	100
DACOMBE	R	4	100
DACRE	CJ	4	100
DACRE	GW	4	100
DACRE	W	8	83
DADD	W	4	100
DADDS	GW	3	318
DADDS	TE	7	92
DADLEY	W	12	292
DADSWELL	HC	12	292
DAFFEY	WA	7	92
DAFYDD	RE	14	78
DAGG	CF	10	60
DAGG	MA	4	100
DAGLAN	W	9	246
DAGLESS	JW	8	83
DAGLEY	A	3	318
DAGLEY	E	3	44
DAGLEY	HH	3	318
DAGLEY	HJW	3	44
DAGLISH	TR	10	285
DAGNALL	F	14	78
DAGNELL	CE	4	100
DAGNELL	FT	4	100
DAGNELL	J	10	60
DAGNELL	WJ	4	100
DAGOSTINO	A	11	95
DAGOSTINO	C	11	95
DAGOSTINO	D	11	96
DAGWELL	CJ	7	92
DAGWELL	MR	7	92
DAGWELL	WC	10	60
DAHMEN	A	13	119
DAILY	TS	13	119
DAILY	W	13	119
DAINS	EE	7	92
DAINS	J	8	83
DAINTER	W	6	103
DAINTER	W	6	103
DAINTON	WJ	7	92
DAINTREE	JH	2	92
DAINTREE	W	7	92
DAINTY	A	7	92
DAISEY	T	9	383
DAISH	BJ	4	100
DAISH	WJ	4	100
DAISH	WJ	4	100
DAKER	AS	1	80
DAKER	S	9	383
DAKIN	A	14	78
DAKIN	E	3	44
DAKIN	H	14	78
DAKIN	JC	3	44
DAKIN	S	8	83
DAKIN	W	3	318
DAKIN	WH	2	92
DALBY	A	8	83
DALBY	E	9	246
DALBY	F	9	246
DALBY	G	9	51
DALBY	GH	9	51
DALBY	J	8	83
DALBY	JA	9	246
DALBY	JWC	13	119
DALBY	S	9	51
DALBY	TA	14	78
DALBY	W	8	83
DALBY	W	10	60
DALDY	A	3	44
DALE	A	6	103
DALE	A	7	92
DALE	A	11	96
DALE	A	11	96
DALE	AG	11	96
DALE	AG	11	96
DALE	AV	8	83
DALE	AW	11	96
DALE	C	6	103
DALE	CF	1	80
DALE	EE	1	80
DALE	EP	8	83
DALE	F	11	96
DALE	FW	3	45
DALE	G	1	80
DALE	GA	1	80
DALE	GH	7	92
DALE	HJ	13	119
DALE	J	6	103
DALE	J	7	92
DALE	J	11	96
DALE	J	11	96
DALE	JE	11	96
DALE	JMC	11	96
DALE	JT	14	78
DALE	JW	8	83
DALE	JW	11	96
DALE	P	13	120
DALE	RA	13	120
DALE	S	7	92
DALE	W	3	318
DALE	W	11	96
DALE	WG	1	80
DALE	WW	2	93
DALES	H	10	285
DALEY	B	8	84
DALEY	C	3	318
DALEY	E	6	103
DALEY	E	8	84
DALEY	FC	1	80
DALEY	GF	2	93
DALEY	H	2	93
DALEY	H	3	45
DALEY	J	2	93
DALEY	J	14	78
DALEY	J	14	78
DALEY	J	14	78
DALEY	JE	14	79
DALEY	L	3	318
DALEY	MC	3	318
DALEY	P	11	96
DALEY	PD	3	318
DALEY	R	8	84
DALEY	S	14	79
DALEY	T	6	103
DALEY	T	6	103
DALEY	WH	1	80
DALGETTY	H	6	103
DALGLIESH	HB	9	246
DALLADAY	WJ	13	120
DALLADAY	WM	13	120
DALLAS	AE	10	60
DALLEN	H	7	92
DALLEY	AE	12	65
DALLEY	C	13	120
DALLEY	CAJ	10	285
DALLEY	H	4	101
DALLEY	H	4	101
DALLEY	HD	12	292
DALLEY	HT	12	292
DALLEY	J	3	45
DALLEY	RS	4	101
DALLEY	WO	13	120
DALLIGAN	L	3	318
DALLIMER	FW	1	80
DALLIMORE	AEJ	10	285
DALLIMORE	WJ	13	120
DALLINGER	JR	7	92
DALLISON	AH	4	101
DALLISON	T	7	93
DALLOW	FB	3	318
DALLOW	R	13	120
DALOTTO	F	1	80
DALRYMPLE	J	4	101
DALRYMPLE	J	12	422
DALRYMPLE	JA	4	101
DALSKI	J	8	84
DALTON	A	6	103
DALTON	A	7	93
DALTON	A	14	79
DALTON	C	6	103
DALTON	C	7	93
DALTON	F	4	101
DALTON	FCJ	4	101
DALTON	GS	10	60
DALTON	GW	8	84
DALTON	H	9	246
DALTON	H	14	79
DALTON	H	14	79
DALTON	HG	7	93
DALTON	HGW	7	93
DALTON	HH	5	93
DALTON	J	8	84
DALTON	JC	7	93
DALTON	JH	14	79
DALTON	M	8	84
DALTON	O	6	103
DALTON	PE	7	93
DALTON	R	7	93
DALTON	R	9	246

DALTON	RC	1	80	DANGERFIELD	FG	10	60	DANIELS	GH	7	93	DARBY	CWW	8	84
DALTON	RH	11	96	DANGERFIELD	JH	10	60	DANIELS	H	1	81	DARBY	D	8	85
DALTON	T	6	104	DANGERFIELD	WE	13	120	DANIELS	H	8	84	DARBY	G	6	104
DALTON	WG	10	285	DANIEL	AWG	12	65	DANIELS	H	12	65	DARBY	G	14	79
DALWOOD	C	1	80	DANIEL	B	13	120	DANIELS	H	12	292	DARBY	GW	6	104
DALY	AE	10	60	DANIEL	CW	11	96	DANIELS	HE	13	121	DARBY	H	5	93
DALY	D	8	84	DANIEL	G	8	84	DANIELS	HG	12	65	DARBY	J	6	104
DALY	D	8	84	DANIEL	G	11	96	DANIELS	HG	13	121	DARBY	J	6	104
DALY	G	13	120	DANIEL	G	13	120	DANIELS	HJ	10	60	DARBY	JW	11	97
DALY	HW	4	101	DANIEL	GL	7	93	DANIELS	HJ	12	65	DARBY	R	14	79
DALY	J	3	45	DANIEL	J	11	97	DANIELS	J	3	318	DARBY	W	7	93
DALY	J	11	96	DANIEL	J	11	97	DANIELS	J	8	84	DARBY	WJ	5	94
DALY	JA	10	60	DANIEL	L	9	51	DANIELS	J	14	79	DARBY	WJ	6	104
DALY	R	6	104	DANIEL	T	8	84	DANIELS	JF	13	121	DARBYSHIRE	WR	14	79
DALY	T	9	51	DANIEL	W	9	51	DANIELS	O	5	93	DARCH	TE	3	45
DALZIEL	C	10	60	DANIEL	WW	9	383	DANIELS	RJ	1	81	DARCY	J	10	61
DAMARY	CA	2	93	DANIELL	EE	3	45	DANIELS	S	5	93	DARCY	P	10	61
DAMER	FA	4	101	DANIELL	GW	3	45	DANIELS	TG	1	81	DARDIS	T	13	121
DAMER	RG	4	101	DANIELL	NJ	3	45	DANIELS	W	4	102	DARDY	PR	5	94
DAMER	SG	4	101	DANIELL	RA	3	45	DANIELS	W	13	121	DARE	F	7	93
DAMERELL	G	1	80	DANIELL	W	3	45	DANIELS	WA	6	104	DARE	G	3	318
DAMERELL	H	1	81	DANIELLS	CH	12	65	DANIELS	WA	12	65	DARE	JJ	1	81
DAMERELL	J	1	81	DANIELLS	F	4	102	DANIELS	WE	13	121	DARE	W	3	318
DAMERELL	R	1	81	DANIELLS	G	1	81	DANIELS	WF	4	102	DAREY	HG	10	285
DAMPIER	GC	4	101	DANIELLS	J	13	121	DANIELS	WG	1	81	DARGIE	HJL	3	319
DAMPIER	TE	4	101	DANIELLS	JC	12	65	DANIELS	WH	10	60	DARK	FW	3	319
DAMPIER	WF	6	104	DANIELLS	JJ	13	120	DANIELS	WTG	7	93	DARK	HJ	7	93
DAMSELL	JWC	1	81	DANIELLS	R	13	121	DANKS	A	6	104	DARK	J	3	319
DANAFORD	H	4	101	DANIELLS	WE	12	65	DANKS	C	6	104	DARK	ME	3	319
DANBY	H	8	84	DANIELLS	WJ	12	65	DANKS	E	6	104	DARKE	FE	7	93
DANBY	J	13	120	DANIELS	A	1	81	DANKS	FJ	6	104	DARKE	GF	6	105
DANBY	JW	8	84	DANIELS	A	10	285	DANKS	GW	6	104	DARKE	GH	4	102
DANCE	AT	7	93	DANIELS	A	13	121	DANKS	WR	10	60	DARKE	HWL	7	94
DANCE	EG	13	120	DANIELS	AH	13	121	DANKS	WTE	6	104	DARKES	F	6	105
DANCE	H	11	96	DANIELS	AW	8	84	DANN	AP	4	102	DARKES	H	6	105
DANCE	J	6	104	DANIELS	AW	12	65	DANN	EE	13	121	DARKIN	J	9	247
DANCE	SA	4	101	DANIELS	C	4	102	DANN	F	4	102	DARLEY	HL	7	94
DANCE	T	7	93	DANIELS	C	7	93	DANN	FJ	4	102	DARLING	GR	5	94
DANCE	T	11	96	DANIELS	CH	6	104	DANN	PH	4	102	DARLING	H	3	45
DANCE	TF	4	101	DANIELS	D	14	79	DANN	WG	1	81	DARLING	HP	9	383
DANCE	WH	6	104	DANIELS	E	1	81	DANNATT	JW	10	61	DARLING	J	7	94
DANCER	JE	8	84	DANIELS	E	4	102	DANNATT	TL	11	97	DARLING	JW	9	383
DANCER	JR	13	120	DANIELS	E	5	93	DANSEY	LJ	5	93	DARLING	T	13	121
DANCEY	RW	4	101	DANIELS	EC	12	65	DANSEY	S	13	121	DARLING	W	1	81
DANCEY	W	3	318	DANIELS	F	1	81	DANSEY	WG	5	93	DARLING	WH	3	319
DANCY	JH	4	101	DANIELS	F	12	65	DANSON	R	11	97	DARLINGTON	H	11	97
DANCY	WH	10	285	DANIELS	F	14	79	DANSON	S	11	97	DARLINGTON	HE	8	85
DANDO	AW	13	120	DANIELS	FA	1	81	DANSON	W	14	79	DARLOW	A	5	94
DANDRIDGE	R	13	120	DANIELS	FG	7	93	DANTON	J	6	104	DARLOW	AE	12	65
DANE	GF	13	120	DANIELS	FJ	6	104	DAPP	ET	3	318	DARLOW	AE	12	65
DANES	DVB	13	120	DANIELS	FJ	13	121	DAPP	HI	3	318	DARLOW	AJ	12	65
DANES	FD	5	93	DANIELS	FSC	5	93	DAPP	OM	3	318	DARLOW	B	12	422
DANES	WC	4	101	DANIELS	G	13	121	DARBY	ARW	2	93	DARLOW	CJ	12	65
DANGERFIELD	AB	8	84	DANIELS	GA	9	51	DARBY	C	10	285	DARLOW	EW	12	65
DANGERFIELD	E	8	84	DANIELS	GA	13	121	DARBY	CJ	13	121	DARLOW	FJ	12	65

DARLOW	G	8	85
DARLOW	GL	12	66
DARLOW	OT	12	66
DARLOW	S	12	66
DARLOW	SW	12	66
DARLOW	W	12	66
DARLOW	WH	12	66
DARLOW	WL	12	292
DARNBROOK	WT	9	247
DARNBROUGH	SW	11	97
DARNE	P	4	102
DARNELL	AP	3	319
DARNELL	C	5	94
DARNELL	FA	3	45
DARNELL	FP	12	66
DARNELL	G	12	66
DARNELL	GH	12	66
DARNELL	HJ	12	66
DARNELL	HW	1	81
DARNELL	HW	12	66
DARNELL	J	12	66
DARNELL	J	12	293
DARNELL	R	5	94
DARNELL	R	12	66
DARNELL	S	5	94
DARNELL	W	12	293
DARNELL	WG	12	66
DARRALL	B	6	105
DARRINGTON	A	12	66
DARRINGTON	A	12	66
DARRINGTON	J	12	66
DARRINGTON	JS	12	66
DARRINGTON	P	12	66
DARSLEY	WR	5	94
DART	FG	10	285
DART	JH	7	94
DART	WJ	4	102
DARTER	WJ	3	319
DARTNALL	CJ	4	102
DARTNELL	AA	13	121
DARTNELL	E	7	94
DARTNELL	GW	12	293
DARTNELL	PW	13	121
DARTON	HA	1	81
DARTON	JW	5	94
DARTON	WJ	5	94
DARTS	A	12	66
DARTS	F	12	67
DARTS	J	12	67
DARTY	E	2	93
DARVELL	TE	3	319
DARVILL	A	3	319
DARVILL	G	3	319
DARVILL	G	7	94
DARVILL	GF	7	94
DARVILL	H	7	94
DARVILL	J	5	94
DARVILL	W	5	94
DARVILLE	B	3	319
DASH	AC	13	122
DASH	AES	3	319
DASH	S	10	61
DASH	WG	13	122
DASHEFSKOY	L	14	79
DASHEY	F	6	105
DASHEY	G	6	105
DASHWOOD	CH	4	102
DASHWOOD	RE	13	122
DASLEY	F	13	122
DASTON	W	13	122
DATSON	CR	4	102
DATSON	CR	4	102
DAUBNEY	EF	4	102
DAUGHTERS	R	13	122
DAUGHTREY	J	10	61
DAUGHTREY	W	10	61
DAULTRY	E	3	319
DAURIS	C	3	45
DAURIS	J	2	93
DAVAGE	A	4	103
DAVAGE	A	4	103
DAVAGE	C	4	103
DAVAGE	EJ	4	103
DAVAGE	G	4	103
DAVAGE	J	4	103
DAVALL	AF	7	94
DAVENPORT	A	11	97
DAVENPORT	A	14	79
DAVENPORT	BA	11	97
DAVENPORT	C	11	97
DAVENPORT	C	11	97
DAVENPORT	CS	11	97
DAVENPORT	E	4	103
DAVENPORT	G	5	94
DAVENPORT	G	8	85
DAVENPORT	J	11	97
DAVENPORT	J	11	97
DAVENPORT	J	11	97
DAVENPORT	J	14	79
DAVENPORT	JA	11	97
DAVENPORT	JH	6	105
DAVENPORT	O	14	79
DAVENPORT	PW	5	94
DAVENPORT	S	11	97
DAVENPORT	W	11	97
DAVENPORT	W	14	79
DAVENPORT	WH	14	79
DAVERSON	HG	12	293
DAVEY	A	7	94
DAVEY	A	10	61
DAVEY	AE	3	319
DAVEY	AG	7	94
DAVEY	C	2	93
DAVEY	C	3	319
DAVEY	C	7	94
DAVEY	C	10	61
DAVEY	E	1	81
DAVEY	E	7	94
DAVEY	E	9	51
DAVEY	F	6	105
DAVEY	FE	10	61
DAVEY	FE	13	122
DAVEY	FJ	3	45
DAVEY	FO	13	122
DAVEY	FR	7	94
DAVEY	HE	3	45
DAVEY	J	13	122
DAVEY	J	13	122
DAVEY	JA	3	45
DAVEY	JH	10	285
DAVEY	JJ	13	122
DAVEY	JR	9	247
DAVEY	JT	7	94
DAVEY	JW	12	67
DAVEY	SE	11	98
DAVEY	T	7	94
DAVEY	T	10	61
DAVEY	T	13	122
DAVEY	TW	13	122
DAVEY	W	1	81
DAVEY	W	2	93
DAVEY	W	3	45
DAVEY	W	5	94
DAVEY	W	7	94
DAVEY	W	9	247
DAVEY	WA	2	93
DAVEY	WA	8	85
DAVEY	WC	3	46
DAVEY	WS	3	319
DAVID	C	10	61
DAVIDGE	AH	4	103
DAVIDGE	AWR	2	93
DAVIDGE	CJE	2	93
DAVIDGE	HF	2	93
DAVIDSON	A	1	81
DAVIDSON	A	3	319
DAVIDSON	A	8	85
DAVIDSON	AJ	1	81
DAVIDSON	AL	13	122
DAVIDSON	AR	13	122
DAVIDSON	C	8	85
DAVIDSON	CV	4	103
DAVIDSON	E	7	94
DAVIDSON	E	7	95
DAVIDSON	E	7	95
DAVIDSON	E	11	98
DAVIDSON	EI	7	95
DAVIDSON	EP	13	122
DAVIDSON	F	6	105
DAVIDSON	H	8	85
DAVIDSON	J	3	319
DAVIDSON	J	14	79
DAVIDSON	J	14	80
DAVIDSON	JH	9	51
DAVIDSON	JR	9	51
DAVIDSON	JS	11	98
DAVIDSON	MP	8	85
DAVIDSON	P	14	80
DAVIDSON	R	14	80
DAVIDSON	RA	7	95
DAVIDSON	S	14	80
DAVIDSON	T	14	80
DAVIDSON	W	2	93
DAVIDSON	W	11	98
DAVIDSON	W	11	98
DAVIDSON	WJ	7	95
DAVIE	GB	4	103
DAVIE	JE	1	81
DAVIES	A	1	82
DAVIES	A	2	93
DAVIES	A	6	105
DAVIES	A	6	105
DAVIES	A	7	95
DAVIES	A	8	85
DAVIES	A	11	98
DAVIES	A	11	98
DAVIES	A	11	98
DAVIES	A	11	98
DAVIES	A	11	98
DAVIES	A	14	80
DAVIES	A	14	80
DAVIES	AA	10	285
DAVIES	AB	14	80
DAVIES	AC	2	93
DAVIES	AC	6	105
DAVIES	ADA	1	81
DAVIES	AE	6	105
DAVIES	AE	6	105
DAVIES	AE	11	98
DAVIES	AG	10	61
DAVIES	AJ	6	105
DAVIES	AL	4	103
DAVIES	AS	1	82
DAVIES	B	5	94
DAVIES	B	6	105
DAVIES	BG	4	103
DAVIES	C	5	94
DAVIES	C	7	95
DAVIES	CA	14	80
DAVIES	CF	7	95

DAVIES	CF	13	122	DAVIES	HJ	6	106	DAVIES	PS	1	82	DAVIES	WJ	1	82
DAVIES	CH	11	98	DAVIES	HJ	13	123	DAVIES	R	1	82	DAVIES	WJ	6	107
DAVIES	CJ	8	85	DAVIES	HT	4	103	DAVIES	R	13	123	DAVIES	WP	14	81
DAVIES	CW	11	98	DAVIES	HW	7	95	DAVIES	RR	6	106	DAVIES	WT	4	103
DAVIES	D	11	98	DAVIES	HW	14	80	DAVIES	RV	11	99	DAVIES	WT	13	123
DAVIES	D	11	98	DAVIES	I	7	95	DAVIES	RWN	1	82	DAVIES	WW	5	95
DAVIES	D	12	293	DAVIES	J	3	46	DAVIES	S	7	95	DAVIS	A	1	82
DAVIES	D	13	122	DAVIES	J	3	320	DAVIES	S	11	99	DAVIS	A	3	320
DAVIES	D	13	123	DAVIES	J	6	106	DAVIES	SA	1	82	DAVIS	A	4	103
DAVIES	DE	3	320	DAVIES	J	8	85	DAVIES	SF	7	95	DAVIS	A	4	103
DAVIES	DG	10	61	DAVIES	J	8	85	DAVIES	T	2	94	DAVIS	A	4	104
DAVIES	DT	6	105	DAVIES	J	11	99	DAVIES	T	6	106	DAVIS	A	6	107
DAVIES	E	7	95	DAVIES	J	11	99	DAVIES	T	8	86	DAVIS	A	7	96
DAVIES	E	8	85	DAVIES	J	11	99	DAVIES	T	11	99	DAVIS	A	8	86
DAVIES	E	11	98	DAVIES	J	11	99	DAVIES	T	12	67	DAVIS	A	8	86
DAVIES	E	11	98	DAVIES	J	14	81	DAVIES	T	14	81	DAVIS	A	10	62
DAVIES	E	14	80	DAVIES	J	14	81	DAVIES	T	14	81	DAVIS	A	12	67
DAVIES	E	14	80	DAVIES	J	14	81	DAVIES	TH	10	61	DAVIS	A	13	123
DAVIES	EA	7	95	DAVIES	J	14	81	DAVIES	TJ	11	99	DAVIS	A	13	123
DAVIES	EL	5	94	DAVIES	JA	3	320	DAVIES	TJ	14	81	DAVIS	A	13	123
DAVIES	ET	1	82	DAVIES	JA	14	81	DAVIES	V	10	62	DAVIS	AB	2	94
DAVIES	ET	11	99	DAVIES	JB	13	123	DAVIES	W	1	82	DAVIS	AC	2	94
DAVIES	EW	6	105	DAVIES	JC	3	46	DAVIES	W	2	94	DAVIS	AC	2	94
DAVIES	F	2	93	DAVIES	JC	7	95	DAVIES	W	3	320	DAVIS	AC	13	123
DAVIES	F	5	94	DAVIES	JE	7	95	DAVIES	W	5	95	DAVIS	AD	2	94
DAVIES	F	6	105	DAVIES	JE	7	95	DAVIES	W	6	106	DAVIS	AE	1	82
DAVIES	F	10	61	DAVIES	JE	14	81	DAVIES	W	6	106	DAVIS	AE	6	107
DAVIES	F	11	98	DAVIES	JF	14	81	DAVIES	W	7	96	DAVIS	AF	3	320
DAVIES	F	11	99	DAVIES	JH	6	106	DAVIES	W	7	96	DAVIS	AF	4	104
DAVIES	F	14	80	DAVIES	JH	8	85	DAVIES	W	9	51	DAVIS	AG	10	286
DAVIES	F	14	80	DAVIES	JH	11	99	DAVIES	W	11	99	DAVIS	AH	7	96
DAVIES	FC	9	51	DAVIES	JI	14	81	DAVIES	W	11	99	DAVIS	AH	10	62
DAVIES	FH	4	103	DAVIES	JJ	11	99	DAVIES	W	11	99	DAVIS	AO	12	293
DAVIES	FJ	1	82	DAVIES	JL	1	82	DAVIES	W	11	100	DAVIS	AR	13	123
DAVIES	G	4	103	DAVIES	JM	1	82	DAVIES	W	11	100	DAVIS	AT	1	82
DAVIES	G	6	106	DAVIES	JT	14	81	DAVIES	W	11	100	DAVIS	AW	2	94
DAVIES	G	7	95	DAVIES	JW	6	106	DAVIES	W	13	123	DAVIS	AW	10	62
DAVIES	G	11	99	DAVIES	JW	6	106	DAVIES	W	14	81	DAVIS	B	4	104
DAVIES	G	11	99	DAVIES	JW	8	85	DAVIES	W	14	81	DAVIS	B	8	86
DAVIES	GA	14	80	DAVIES	JW	9	247	DAVIES	WA	6	106	DAVIS	B	11	100
DAVIES	GH	10	286	DAVIES	JWC	14	81	DAVIES	WA	7	96	DAVIS	C	1	82
DAVIES	GT	11	99	DAVIES	KH	7	95	DAVIES	WA	7	96	DAVIS	C	2	94
DAVIES	GW	10	61	DAVIES	L	6	106	DAVIES	WA	9	247	DAVIS	C	2	94
DAVIES	H	2	93	DAVIES	L	8	85	DAVIES	WA	14	81	DAVIS	C	3	320
DAVIES	H	3	320	DAVIES	LER	6	106	DAVIES	WB	6	106	DAVIS	C	3	320
DAVIES	H	5	95	DAVIES	LJ	12	293	DAVIES	WC	3	320	DAVIS	C	6	107
DAVIES	H	8	85	DAVIES	LL	1	82	DAVIES	WD	3	320	DAVIS	C	6	107
DAVIES	H	10	61	DAVIES	LS	1	82	DAVIES	WE	6	106	DAVIS	C	13	123
DAVIES	H	13	123	DAVIES	MG	11	99	DAVIES	WE	13	123	DAVIS	C	13	123
DAVIES	H	13	123	DAVIES	MS	6	106	DAVIES	WE	14	81	DAVIS	CC	4	104
DAVIES	H	14	80	DAVIES	OE	6	106	DAVIES	WH	3	320	DAVIS	CE	4	104
DAVIES	H	14	80	DAVIES	P	6	106	DAVIES	WH	6	107	DAVIS	CE	6	107
DAVIES	H	14	80	DAVIES	P	10	61	DAVIES	WH	6	107	DAVIS	CF	4	104
DAVIES	HE	4	103	DAVIES	PH	5	95	DAVIES	WH	7	96	DAVIS	CF	4	104
DAVIES	HEG	10	61	DAVIES	PJ	6	106	DAVIES	WH	10	62	DAVIS	CF	6	107

DAVIS	CF	13	123	DAVIS	FML	13	124	DAVIS	HF	6	108	DAVIS	P	12	67
DAVIS	CG	3	320	DAVIS	FS	2	94	DAVIS	HG	6	108	DAVIS	PC	13	124
DAVIS	CG	7	96	DAVIS	FS	10	286	DAVIS	HGE	4	104	DAVIS	PF	11	100
DAVIS	CH	3	320	DAVIS	FV	7	96	DAVIS	HH	6	108	DAVIS	R	3	321
DAVIS	CH	6	107	DAVIS	FW	3	46	DAVIS	HJ	4	104	DAVIS	R	6	109
DAVIS	CH	9	51	DAVIS	FW	3	46	DAVIS	HM	13	124	DAVIS	R	6	109
DAVIS	CH	12	293	DAVIS	FW	13	124	DAVIS	HT	7	97	DAVIS	R	7	97
DAVIS	CJ	6	107	DAVIS	G	1	82	DAVIS	HV	10	62	DAVIS	R	9	51
DAVIS	CR	13	124	DAVIS	G	4	104	DAVIS	IB	6	108	DAVIS	R	10	62
DAVIS	CT	1	82	DAVIS	G	4	104	DAVIS	J	1	83	DAVIS	R	13	124
DAVIS	CTW	7	96	DAVIS	G	5	95	DAVIS	J	4	104	DAVIS	RA	6	109
DAVIS	CW	1	82	DAVIS	G	5	95	DAVIS	J	5	95	DAVIS	RA	6	109
DAVIS	CW	10	62	DAVIS	G	6	107	DAVIS	J	6	108	DAVIS	RAC	2	94
DAVIS	D	2	94	DAVIS	G	6	107	DAVIS	J	6	108	DAVIS	RD	9	51
DAVIS	D	6	107	DAVIS	G	6	108	DAVIS	J	6	108	DAVIS	RE	4	105
DAVIS	D	7	96	DAVIS	G	6	108	DAVIS	J	6	108	DAVIS	RF	2	94
DAVIS	D	12	293	DAVIS	G	9	51	DAVIS	J	6	108	DAVIS	S	6	109
DAVIS	DR	11	100	DAVIS	G	9	384	DAVIS	J	6	108	DAVIS	S	6	109
DAVIS	DW	6	107	DAVIS	G	12	67	DAVIS	J	7	97	DAVIS	S	8	86
DAVIS	E	3	320	DAVIS	GA	6	108	DAVIS	J	7	97	DAVIS	S	13	124
DAVIS	E	3	320	DAVIS	GA	7	96	DAVIS	J	9	51	DAVIS	S	14	82
DAVIS	E	3	320	DAVIS	GA	13	124	DAVIS	J	12	67	DAVIS	SC	7	97
DAVIS	E	5	95	DAVIS	GD	7	96	DAVIS	J	12	67	DAVIS	SF	12	67
DAVIS	E	6	107	DAVIS	GE	3	46	DAVIS	J	12	293	DAVIS	T	1	83
DAVIS	E	6	107	DAVIS	GE	4	104	DAVIS	J	13	124	DAVIS	T	4	105
DAVIS	EC	12	293	DAVIS	GE	10	62	DAVIS	J	14	81	DAVIS	T	13	124
DAVIS	ECN	7	96	DAVIS	GF	2	94	DAVIS	JA	3	320	DAVIS	TA	10	62
DAVIS	EG	4	104	DAVIS	GF	5	95	DAVIS	JA	7	97	DAVIS	TF	7	97
DAVIS	EG	5	95	DAVIS	GH	6	108	DAVIS	JA	13	124	DAVIS	TG	1	83
DAVIS	EG	10	286	DAVIS	GH	10	286	DAVIS	JC	3	321	DAVIS	TH	14	82
DAVIS	EH	4	104	DAVIS	GJ	1	83	DAVIS	JD	4	105	DAVIS	TJ	12	67
DAVIS	EH	11	100	DAVIS	GS	7	96	DAVIS	JD	13	124	DAVIS	TW	10	62
DAVIS	EH	13	124	DAVIS	H	2	94	DAVIS	JE	7	97	DAVIS	V	10	286
DAVIS	EM	1	82	DAVIS	H	2	94	DAVIS	JF	4	105	DAVIS	W	2	95
DAVIS	EN	10	286	DAVIS	H	3	46	DAVIS	JH	6	109	DAVIS	W	3	46
DAVIS	ER	4	104	DAVIS	H	3	320	DAVIS	JH	7	97	DAVIS	W	3	321
DAVIS	ER	7	96	DAVIS	H	4	104	DAVIS	JH	14	81	DAVIS	W	6	109
DAVIS	EW	6	107	DAVIS	H	5	95	DAVIS	JS	7	97	DAVIS	W	6	109
DAVIS	EW	12	67	DAVIS	H	5	95	DAVIS	JT	13	124	DAVIS	W	6	109
DAVIS	F	1	82	DAVIS	H	6	108	DAVIS	JW	10	62	DAVIS	W	6	109
DAVIS	F	2	94	DAVIS	H	6	108	DAVIS	JW	13	124	DAVIS	W	9	51
DAVIS	F	4	104	DAVIS	H	6	108	DAVIS	JWR	6	109	DAVIS	W	10	286
DAVIS	F	7	96	DAVIS	H	6	108	DAVIS	LA	6	109	DAVIS	W	12	67
DAVIS	F	8	86	DAVIS	H	6	108	DAVIS	LJ	7	97	DAVIS	W	12	67
DAVIS	F	8	86	DAVIS	H	7	96	DAVIS	LV	13	124	DAVIS	W	13	124
DAVIS	F	10	62	DAVIS	H	7	96	DAVIS	M	1	83	DAVIS	W	13	125
DAVIS	F	12	293	DAVIS	H	7	96	DAVIS	M	2	94	DAVIS	W	14	82
DAVIS	F	13	124	DAVIS	H	7	97	DAVIS	M	10	286	DAVIS	WA	7	97
DAVIS	FA	3	46	DAVIS	H	8	86	DAVIS	M	14	82	DAVIS	WA	7	97
DAVIS	FAC	3	46	DAVIS	H	13	124	DAVIS	M	14	82	DAVIS	WA	12	293
DAVIS	FAW	3	46	DAVIS	HB	4	104	DAVIS	MD	2	94	DAVIS	WB	4	105
DAVIS	FG	6	107	DAVIS	HC	2	94	DAVIS	MRS	11	100	DAVIS	WC	7	97
DAVIS	FH	4	104	DAVIS	HE	1	83	DAVIS	O	7	97	DAVIS	WD	3	321
DAVIS	FH	6	107	DAVIS	HE	4	104	DAVIS	OE	12	67	DAVIS	WD	10	62
DAVIS	FL	10	286	DAVIS	HE	13	124	DAVIS	P	8	86	DAVIS	WG	13	125

Surname	Initials	Vol	Page
DAVIS	WH	2	95
DAVIS	WH	3	321
DAVIS	WH	6	109
DAVIS	WH	6	109
DAVIS	WH	7	97
DAVIS	WH	10	62
DAVIS	WJ	4	105
DAVIS	WJ	6	109
DAVIS	WJ	9	52
DAVIS	WJ	9	247
DAVIS	WJ	12	293
DAVIS	WJ	13	125
DAVIS	WJ	13	125
DAVIS	WL	1	83
DAVIS	WL	12	293
DAVIS	WM	12	67
DAVIS	WM	13	125
DAVIS	WT	6	109
DAVIS	WW	6	110
DAVISON	AJ	2	95
DAVISON	EG	1	83
DAVISON	G	1	83
DAVISON	GE	9	247
DAVISON	H	14	82
DAVISON	HB	12	67
DAVISON	J	8	86
DAVISON	J	9	384
DAVISON	JE	9	247
DAVISON	JE	9	384
DAVISON	JJ	13	125
DAVISON	JR	7	97
DAVISON	JT	9	247
DAVISON	S	13	125
DAVISON	T	8	86
DAVISON	W	9	247
DAVISON	W	9	247
DAVISON	WH	9	52
DAVITT	J	9	52
DAVY	A	8	86
DAVY	C	8	86
DAVY	E	8	86
DAVY	E	13	125
DAVY	T	9	247
DAW	AA	7	98
DAW	GH	13	125
DAW	J	6	110
DAW	R	2	95
DAW	SH	1	83
DAW	WH	3	321
DAWBORN	AJ	3	46
DAWBORN	H	5	95
DAWBORN	W	5	95
DAWBORN	W	12	67
DAWE	E	1	83
DAWE	F	12	293
DAWES	A	8	86
DAWES	AE	2	95
DAWES	AH	13	125
DAWES	BC	10	286
DAWES	C	5	95
DAWES	C	6	110
DAWES	CJ	2	95
DAWES	CW	7	98
DAWES	EL	13	125
DAWES	FA	13	125
DAWES	FJ	11	100
DAWES	G	7	98
DAWES	G	10	62
DAWES	G	12	293
DAWES	GH	1	83
DAWES	GHU	2	95
DAWES	HW	13	125
DAWES	J	8	86
DAWES	SH	5	95
DAWES	W	3	46
DAWES	WF	7	98
DAWES	WJ	2	95
DAWES	WJA	7	98
DAWKES	A	11	100
DAWKES	SG	2	95
DAWKINS	A	7	98
DAWKINS	AW	2	95
DAWKINS	C	4	105
DAWKINS	C	10	286
DAWKINS	CG	4	105
DAWKINS	D	4	105
DAWKINS	G	7	98
DAWKINS	GJ	7	98
DAWKINS	H	4	105
DAWKINS	H	4	105
DAWKINS	H	12	293
DAWKINS	HWC	1	83
DAWKINS	J	4	105
DAWKINS	LF	4	105
DAWKINS	SF	4	105
DAWKINS	TJ	4	105
DAWKINS	W	4	105
DAWKINS	W	4	105
DAWKINS	W	4	105
DAWKINS	W	4	105
DAWKINS	W	10	286
DAWKS	HN	5	95
DAWS	DHA	7	98
DAWS	H	7	98
DAWS	JR	8	86
DAWSON	A	1	83
DAWSON	A	2	95
DAWSON	A	5	95
DAWSON	A	9	52
DAWSON	A	9	247
DAWSON	A	10	286
DAWSON	A	14	82
DAWSON	AB	14	82
DAWSON	AC	4	105
DAWSON	AE	3	321
DAWSON	AJ	6	110
DAWSON	AT	3	321
DAWSON	C	9	52
DAWSON	C	9	52
DAWSON	C	12	67
DAWSON	CB	3	321
DAWSON	CH	13	125
DAWSON	CJ	3	46
DAWSON	CJ	11	100
DAWSON	CW	10	286
DAWSON	CW	12	68
DAWSON	D	8	86
DAWSON	DW	3	321
DAWSON	E	14	82
DAWSON	EI	12	68
DAWSON	EJ	10	286
DAWSON	F	3	46
DAWSON	F	6	110
DAWSON	F	8	86
DAWSON	F	8	86
DAWSON	F	8	86
DAWSON	F	8	87
DAWSON	F	8	87
DAWSON	F	9	247
DAWSON	F	11	100
DAWSON	F	14	82
DAWSON	FA	12	68
DAWSON	FB	11	100
DAWSON	FH	13	125
DAWSON	FM	7	98
DAWSON	G	6	110
DAWSON	G	9	52
DAWSON	G	11	100
DAWSON	G	11	100
DAWSON	G	12	293
DAWSON	GAR	8	87
DAWSON	GE	8	87
DAWSON	GE	13	125
DAWSON	GF	10	286
DAWSON	GG	6	110
DAWSON	GTC	12	68
DAWSON	H	2	95
DAWSON	H	3	46
DAWSON	H	7	98
DAWSON	H	8	87
DAWSON	H	9	52
DAWSON	H	9	247
DAWSON	HA	9	52
DAWSON	HG	7	98
DAWSON	HV	8	87
DAWSON	J	1	83
DAWSON	J	7	98
DAWSON	J	8	87
DAWSON	J	8	87
DAWSON	J	8	87
DAWSON	J	8	87
DAWSON	J	9	52
DAWSON	J	9	247
DAWSON	J	10	287
DAWSON	J	11	100
DAWSON	J	14	82
DAWSON	JA	2	95
DAWSON	JA	11	100
DAWSON	JH	1	83
DAWSON	JW	13	125
DAWSON	M	3	321
DAWSON	M	8	87
DAWSON	M	8	415
DAWSON	MA	11	100
DAWSON	P	2	95
DAWSON	P	8	87
DAWSON	P	8	87
DAWSON	P	11	101
DAWSON	P	12	68
DAWSON	P	13	125
DAWSON	PSG	14	82
DAWSON	R	3	321
DAWSON	R	5	95
DAWSON	R	13	125
DAWSON	RS	13	125
DAWSON	S	8	87
DAWSON	SC	5	96
DAWSON	SG	13	126
DAWSON	T	6	110
DAWSON	T	9	247
DAWSON	T	11	100
DAWSON	T	14	82
DAWSON	TH	9	52
DAWSON	TJ	2	95
DAWSON	TW	3	321
DAWSON	W	2	95
DAWSON	W	5	96
DAWSON	W	8	87
DAWSON	W	9	52
DAWSON	W	13	126
DAWSON	W	14	82
DAWSON	WD	12	293
DAWSON	WH	1	83
DAWSON	WH	12	68
DAWSON	WJ	1	83
DAWSON	WJ	7	98
DAWSON	WM	3	321
DAY	A	1	83
DAY	A	1	83
DAY	A	2	95
DAY	A	3	321

DAY	A	5	96
DAY	A	5	96
DAY	A	5	96
DAY	A	5	96
DAY	A	5	96
DAY	A	7	98
DAY	A	7	98
DAY	A	8	87
DAY	A	8	87
DAY	A	8	87
DAY	A	10	62
DAY	A	11	101
DAY	A	13	126
DAY	AA	3	321
DAY	AE	2	95
DAY	AE	2	95
DAY	AE	5	96
DAY	AH	12	68
DAY	AJ	6	110
DAY	AJ	7	98
DAY	AR	12	68
DAY	AT	5	96
DAY	AT	10	62
DAY	AV	12	294
DAY	AVG	5	96
DAY	AW	5	96
DAY	AW	5	96
DAY	AW	7	98
DAY	B	5	96
DAY	BD	5	96
DAY	C	1	83
DAY	C	2	96
DAY	C	7	98
DAY	C	10	62
DAY	C	12	68
DAY	C	13	126
DAY	CE	13	126
DAY	CF	1	83
DAY	CG	3	46
DAY	CH	2	96
DAY	CH	6	110
DAY	CH	10	62
DAY	CR	10	287
DAY	CRG	5	96
DAY	CT	6	110
DAY	CW	8	87
DAY	D	3	322
DAY	E	1	83
DAY	E	1	84
DAY	E	2	96
DAY	E	5	96
DAY	E	5	96
DAY	E	7	99
DAY	E	8	87
DAY	E	9	384
DAY	E	12	68
DAY	EA	12	294
DAY	EH	6	110
DAY	EH	8	88
DAY	EJ	6	110
DAY	F	2	96
DAY	F	2	96
DAY	F	3	46
DAY	F	5	96
DAY	F	5	96
DAY	F	9	52
DAY	F	12	68
DAY	F	13	126
DAY	FA	2	96
DAY	FA	5	96
DAY	FG	5	97
DAY	FHL	6	110
DAY	FJ	3	322
DAY	FS	13	126
DAY	FW	6	110
DAY	G	12	68
DAY	GE	2	96
DAY	GF	1	84
DAY	GH	10	63
DAY	GH	10	63
DAY	GH	13	126
DAY	GR	13	126
DAY	GT	7	99
DAY	GT	12	68
DAY	H	1	84
DAY	H	2	96
DAY	H	4	106
DAY	H	5	97
DAY	H	5	97
DAY	H	5	97
DAY	H	8	88
DAY	H	10	63
DAY	H	12	68
DAY	H	12	68
DAY	H	12	68
DAY	HE	2	96
DAY	HE	3	322
DAY	HJ	1	84
DAY	HW	2	96
DAY	HW	13	126
DAY	HW	13	126
DAY	J	2	96
DAY	J	2	96
DAY	J	2	96
DAY	J	5	97
DAY	J	5	97
DAY	J	6	110
DAY	J	6	110
DAY	J	7	99
DAY	J	7	99
DAY	J	7	99
DAY	J	10	63
DAY	J	12	68
DAY	J	13	126
DAY	JF	10	63
DAY	JW	2	96
DAY	JW	5	97
DAY	JWF	7	99
DAY	L	14	82
DAY	LB	10	63
DAY	M	9	247
DAY	P	5	97
DAY	P	5	97
DAY	PB	5	97
DAY	PG	5	97
DAY	R	1	84
DAY	R	2	96
DAY	R	2	96
DAY	R	8	88
DAY	R	11	101
DAY	R	12	68
DAY	RA	13	126
DAY	RE	4	106
DAY	S	5	97
DAY	S	7	99
DAY	SEW	2	96
DAY	SG	3	322
DAY	SH	2	96
DAY	SH	4	106
DAY	SJS	12	294
DAY	ST	13	126
DAY	SW	12	68
DAY	T	3	322
DAY	T	9	52
DAY	T	9	384
DAY	T	10	63
DAY	TG	13	126
DAY	W	2	96
DAY	W	5	97
DAY	W	5	97
DAY	W	7	99
DAY	W	10	63
DAY	W	12	294
DAY	WA	2	96
DAY	WA	11	101
DAY	WC	13	126
DAY	WEC	1	84
DAY	WG	4	106
DAY	WG	4	106
DAY	WG	10	63
DAY	WH	12	294
DAY	WJ	10	63
DAY	WJ	10	63
DAY	WJ	13	126
DAYKIN	AR	1	84
DAYKIN	FC	1	84
DAYKIN	H	9	247
DAYKIN	HJ	1	84
DAYKIN	HJ	1	84
DAYLESS	JA	8	88
DAYMAN	E	4	106
DAYSH	G	2	97
DAYSH	J	10	287
DAYTON	SG	5	97
DAZELEY	F	12	294
DAZELEY	H	12	294
DAZELEY	H	12	294
DAZELEY	J	12	294
DAZLEY	A	12	69
DE BANK	WL	1	84
DE BAUGHN	GH	9	248
DE BOTTE	LM	11	102
DE BUSSEY	W	8	88
DE FEW	W	13	129
DE FRATES	TC	13	129
DE LA PORTE	LW	4	106
DE MATOSE	JW	10	63
DE ORFE	F	4	107
DE ORFE	F	4	107
DE ROSA	A	1	84
DE STE CROIX	GP	4	107
DE VIELL	A	13	130
DE-GRUSSA	AW	1	84
DE-LA-HAYE	HW	12	70
DE-STE-CROIX	G	10	64
DE-STE-CROIX	JA	10	64
DE-VILLE	HW	2	100
DE-VILLE	R	2	100
DEACON	A	1	84
DEACON	AE	12	294
DEACON	AR	1	84
DEACON	ER	1	84
DEACON	F	5	97
DEACON	FG	13	126
DEACON	FH	13	126
DEACON	G	4	106
DEACON	G	13	126
DEACON	G	13	127
DEACON	GA	13	127
DEACON	H	5	97
DEACON	HE	10	287
DEACON	J	5	97
DEACON	JW	8	88
DEACON	JW	9	52
DEACON	T	13	127
DEACON	TJE	1	84
DEACON	W	5	97
DEACON	WJ	12	69
DEACON	WO	1	84
DEADMAN	G	3	322
DEADMAN	H	13	127

DEADMAN	JW	1	84
DEADMAN	T	10	63
DEAKIN	A	11	101
DEAKIN	AL	6	110
DEAKIN	C	6	110
DEAKIN	G	11	101
DEAKIN	GE	6	111
DEAKIN	H	11	101
DEAKIN	J	11	101
DEAKIN	J	14	82
DEAKIN	J	14	82
DEAKIN	JE	13	127
DEAKIN	M	6	111
DEAKIN	R	6	111
DEAKIN	R	11	101
DEAKIN	W	11	101
DEAKINS	A	1	84
DEAL	J	13	127
DEAL	W	13	127
DEALEY	A	5	98
DEALEY	AT	5	98
DEALEY	E	5	98
DEALL	ST	2	97
DEAMER	E	5	98
DEAMER	G	5	98
DEAMER	J	12	69
DEAMER	S	5	98
DEAMER	WHJ	13	127
DEAMER	WL	5	98
DEAMON	HW	6	111
DEAN	A	1	84
DEAN	A	5	98
DEAN	A	5	98
DEAN	A	9	52
DEAN	A	14	82
DEAN	A	14	83
DEAN	A	14	83
DEAN	AC	6	111
DEAN	AE	5	98
DEAN	AE	5	98
DEAN	AE	12	69
DEAN	AH	7	99
DEAN	AJ	2	97
DEAN	AP	11	101
DEAN	AW	1	84
DEAN	B	3	46
DEAN	B	8	415
DEAN	C	1	84
DEAN	C	11	101
DEAN	C	11	101
DEAN	C	12	69
DEAN	CA	10	287
DEAN	CJ	7	99
DEAN	CW	13	127
DEAN	DG	4	106
DEAN	E	8	88
DEAN	E	8	88
DEAN	E	12	69
DEAN	E	13	127
DEAN	E	13	127
DEAN	EA	13	127
DEAN	EH	13	127
DEAN	F	2	97
DEAN	F	2	97
DEAN	F	7	99
DEAN	F	7	99
DEAN	F	9	52
DEAN	F	11	101
DEAN	F	13	127
DEAN	FA	1	85
DEAN	FC	2	97
DEAN	FC	6	111
DEAN	FJ	12	69
DEAN	FW	13	127
DEAN	G	1	85
DEAN	G	8	88
DEAN	G	11	101
DEAN	G	14	83
DEAN	GAM	2	97
DEAN	GT	13	127
DEAN	H	9	248
DEAN	H	12	69
DEAN	HD	1	85
DEAN	HE	13	127
DEAN	HE	14	83
DEAN	HJ	1	85
DEAN	HJ	1	85
DEAN	HJ	12	69
DEAN	J	4	106
DEAN	J	6	111
DEAN	J	8	88
DEAN	J	8	88
DEAN	J	10	63
DEAN	J	11	101
DEAN	J	11	101
DEAN	J	11	101
DEAN	J	11	101
DEAN	J	13	127
DEAN	JC	12	294
DEAN	JE	11	102
DEAN	JE	13	128
DEAN	JH	5	98
DEAN	JJ	12	69
DEAN	JM	5	98
DEAN	JR	14	83
DEAN	JW	1	85
DEAN	JW	5	98
DEAN	JW	9	52
DEAN	JW	9	248
DEAN	M	6	111
DEAN	M	13	128
DEAN	P	8	88
DEAN	PT	13	128
DEAN	R	11	102
DEAN	R	14	83
DEAN	RJ	1	85
DEAN	S	9	248
DEAN	T	1	85
DEAN	T	8	88
DEAN	T	12	69
DEAN	T	12	69
DEAN	T	14	83
DEAN	TC	8	88
DEAN	TH	9	52
DEAN	TN	2	97
DEAN	V	14	83
DEAN	VF	12	69
DEAN	VJ	1	85
DEAN	VW	8	88
DEAN	W	1	85
DEAN	W	7	99
DEAN	W	12	69
DEAN	W	12	69
DEAN	W	14	83
DEAN	WC	6	111
DEAN	WC	12	69
DEAN	WF	12	69
DEAN	WG	2	97
DEAN	WH	3	322
DEAN	WH	13	128
DEAN	WM	14	83
DEAN	WT	13	128
DEANE	A	8	88
DEANE	AO	3	322
DEANE	C	2	97
DEANE	D	12	69
DEANE	GF	13	128
DEANE	HB	3	46
DEANE	J	8	88
DEANE	S	14	83
DEANE	WN	11	102
DEANS	H	2	97
DEANUS	W	1	85
DEANUS	W	3	322
DEAR	A	2	97
DEAR	A	5	98
DEAR	A	12	70
DEAR	A	12	70
DEAR	AA	4	106
DEAR	AE	7	99
DEAR	AJ	5	98
DEAR	AW	13	128
DEAR	B	12	70
DEAR	C	5	98
DEAR	C	10	63
DEAR	CH	12	70
DEAR	CJ	5	98
DEAR	EH	1	85
DEAR	F	5	98
DEAR	F	5	98
DEAR	FG	7	99
DEAR	FW	12	70
DEAR	G	4	106
DEAR	G	5	99
DEAR	H	5	99
DEAR	H	12	70
DEAR	J	7	99
DEAR	J	12	70
DEAR	LA	8	88
DEAR	PW	5	99
DEAR	R	4	106
DEAR	R	5	99
DEAR	RF	5	99
DEAR	W	2	97
DEAR	W	12	70
DEAR	WA	2	97
DEAR	WC	1	85
DEAR	WT	4	106
DEARDEN	E	11	102
DEARDEN	F	11	102
DEARDEN	JW	11	102
DEARDS	R	12	70
DEARIE	CS	2	97
DEARING	A	13	128
DEARING	A	13	128
DEARING	CA	1	85
DEARING	G	1	85
DEARING	JA	1	85
DEARING	T	1	85
DEARING	WE	5	99
DEARLOVE	AEJ	1	85
DEARMAN	CW	1	85
DEARMAN	EF	1	85
DEARMAN	HM	10	63
DEARMAN	WC	13	128
DEARMAN	WE	2	97
DEARN	J	6	111
DEARN	JT	6	111
DEARN	W	6	111
DEARNE	K	6	111
DEARTH	AE	2	97
DEARTH	ME	2	97
DEAS	WAF	12	70
DEATH	E	1	85
DEATH	W	1	85
DEATHE	B	4	106
DEATHE	RJ	7	99
DEATHE	SC	7	99
DEATHE	WD	7	100
DEATHRIDGE	W	6	111

DEAVES	AC	13	128	DEIGHTON	A	9	384	DELLAR	A	7	100	DENDLE	S	6	112
DEAVES	F	13	128	DEIGHTON	AH	1	86	DELLAR	AJ	1	86	DENDY	J	3	322
DEAVIN	JW	13	128	DEIGHTON	C	9	53	DELLAR	AS	7	100	DENGEL	HFJ	1	86
DEAVIN	W	7	100	DEIGHTON	E	8	89	DELLAR	R	12	70	DENGEL	J	1	86
DEBANK	HW	13	128	DEIGHTON	F	14	83	DELLAR	SF	5	99	DENHAM	AS	10	287
DEBENHAM	FC	3	322	DEIGHTON	S	9	248	DELLAR	TC	5	99	DENHAM	CH	3	47
DEBIO	A	11	102	DEIGHTON	W	8	89	DELLBRIDGE	EJ	13	129	DENHAM	CH	3	47
DEBLEY	AE	1	85	DEIGNAN	R	8	89	DELLER	AW	5	99	DENHAM	E	6	112
DEBLEY	RJ	1	86	DELACOUR	C	4	106	DELLER	B	7	100	DENHAM	EC	3	322
DEBNAM	GW	13	128	DELACOUR	JG	4	106	DELLER	F	12	70	DENHAM	ET	3	322
DEBNAM	WJ	13	128	DELACOUR	RJ	4	106	DELLER	FB	7	100	DENHAM	F	8	89
DECAEN	W	10	287	DELAHIDE	J	14	83	DELLER	G	5	99	DENHAM	H	7	100
DECAEN	WT	10	287	DELAHUNT	JC	7	100	DELLER	J	2	98	DENHAM	HE	10	287
DECOURCY	H	9	53	DELAHUNTY	J	9	53	DELLER	J	2	98	DENHAM	JT	10	63
DEDDEN	WE	2	97	DELAMAIN	SJ	13	129	DELLER	JC	7	100	DENHAM	NF	9	248
DEDMAN	HG	13	128	DELAMORE	A	10	287	DELLER	SJT	7	100	DENHAM	R	8	89
DEDMAN	PG	10	287	DELANEY	A	1	86	DELLER	WJ	3	322	DENHAM	W	3	323
DEE	C	2	98	DELANEY	A	6	112	DELLOW	AJ	1	86	DENHAM	WJ	5	99
DEE	J	3	47	DELANEY	AA	1	86	DELLOW	FM	1	86	DENIS	GA	12	294
DEE	JW	3	47	DELANEY	BE	1	86	DELLOW	H	2	98	DENISON	A	9	53
DEEBLE	H	5	99	DELANEY	CR	6	112	DELLOW	H	2	98	DENISON	C	9	248
DEEGAN	J	9	53	DELANEY	G	9	53	DELLOW	JA	1	86	DENISON	G	9	53
DEEHEN	W	14	83	DELANEY	H	11	102	DELLOW	SG	2	98	DENISON	GF	1	87
DEEKS	EW	3	322	DELANEY	J	6	112	DELLOW	SP	1	86	DENISON	M	9	248
DEEKS	H	13	128	DELANEY	J	8	89	DELLOW	T	2	98	DENISON	W	8	89
DEEKS	JR	9	53	DELANEY	J	14	83	DELLOW	WT	1	86	DENISON	WRW	2	98
DEEKS	WJD	13	128	DELANEY	R	14	83	DELO	CW	2	98	DENLEY	AW	8	89
DEELEY	A	6	111	DELANEY	WH	11	102	DELO	EM	2	98	DENLEY	GA	7	100
DEELEY	EW	5	99	DELANTY	WM	14	83	DELOCHE	TF	7	100	DENLEY	W	4	107
DEELEY	GW	6	111	DELANY	F	8	89	DELUCHI	JJ	10	63	DENMAN	AP	2	98
DEELEY	JA	6	111	DELANY	JE	3	47	DELVE	LCA	14	84	DENMAN	FA	7	101
DEELEY	JP	5	99	DELASALLE	AE	1	86	DELVE	W	10	63	DENMAN	FE	1	86
DEELEY	JS	6	111	DELASALLE	HF	1	86	DELVES	BT	4	107	DENMAN	H	11	102
DEEM	W	4	106	DELDERFIELD	E	1	86	DELVES	CS	14	84	DENMAN	J	2	98
DEEMING	A	6	111	DELDERFIELD	LA	1	86	DELVES	E	13	129	DENMAN	W	14	84
DEEMING	CH	6	112	DELEMENT	AG	4	106	DEMAIN	WF	14	84	DENMAN	WA	13	129
DEEMING	FF	6	112	DELIEU	T	13	129	DEMAINE	JP	8	89	DENMARK	WJ	13	129
DEEMING	HA	6	112	DELL	A	2	98	DEMBOVITCH	M	14	84	DENN	HG	7	101
DEEMING	J	6	112	DELL	EM	3	322	DEMERY	E	13	129	DENNANT	ER	13	129
DEERING	D	3	322	DELL	F	2	98	DEMPSEY	AJ	7	100	DENNARD	DA	13	129
DEERING	E	1	86	DELL	F	10	287	DEMPSEY	E	9	53	DENNE	A	10	63
DEERING	N	8	88	DELL	FC	11	102	DEMPSEY	F	7	100	DENNE	VP	7	101
DEETMAN	A	1	86	DELL	FW	3	47	DEMPSEY	H	9	53	DENNELL	JW	8	89
DEETMAN	A	7	100	DELL	GG	5	99	DEMPSEY	J	4	107	DENNELL	L	8	89
DEFEW	CR	13	128	DELL	GL	3	322	DEMPSEY	J	6	112	DENNELLY	FJ	6	112
DEFFEE	ES	7	100	DELL	H	2	98	DEMPSEY	JW	8	89	DENNER	A	5	99
DEFFLEY	HJ	6	112	DELL	J	3	322	DEMPSTER	OB	6	112	DENNER	S	5	99
DEFFLEY	R	6	112	DELL	JA	7	100	DENAHY	JF	13	129	DENNER	S	5	99
DEFOE	W	5	99	DELL	JL	12	70	DENBIGH	J	8	89	DENNES	AW	2	98
DEGAVINO	PC	7	100	DELL	P	5	99	DENBOW	WR	2	98	DENNESS	F	13	129
DEGNAN	J	11	102	DELL	PW	13	129	DENBY	A	9	53	DENNESS	WA	2	99
DEGNAN	M	8	89	DELL	SA	3	322	DENBY	R	8	89	DENNETT	A	10	287
DEGNAN	M	8	89	DELL	TJ	2	98	DENBY	W	9	53	DENNETT	H	4	107
DEGNAN	W	8	89	DELLA	I	14	83	DENCH	AT	2	98	DENNETT	H	5	99
DEIGHTON	A	9	53	DELLALANDE	M	6	112	DENCHFIELD	W	1	86	DENNETT	S	4	107

DENNETT	SW	4	107	DENNISON	F	1	87	DENTON	A	12	70	DENTON	WA	2	99	DENTON	WA	2	99
DENNEY	EG	13	129	DENNISON	F	9	53	DENTON	A	12	70	DENTON	WA	12	294	DENTON	WA	12	294
DENNING	G	7	101	DENNISON	F	9	54	DENTON	AA	12	294	DENTON	WC	2	99	DENTON	WC	2	99
DENNING	W	9	248	DENNISON	F	14	84	DENTON	AP	5	100	DENTON	WJR	2	99	DENTON	WJR	2	99
DENNING	WJ	6	112	DENNISON	FW	3	323	DENTON	AW	1	87	DENTON	WS	12	295	DENTON	WS	12	295
DENNINGTON	E	7	101	DENNISON	G	8	90	DENTON	AWG	12	70	DENTRY	B	7	101	DENTRY	B	7	101
DENNINGTON	HR	2	99	DENNISON	H	9	54	DENTON	C	5	100	DENTRY	H	1	87	DENTRY	H	1	87
DENNINGTON	JP	12	294	DENNISON	H	9	248	DENTON	C	6	113	DENTTEN	FC	13	130	DENTTEN	FC	13	130
DENNIS	A	8	89	DENNISON	H	9	248	DENTON	CD	2	99	DENVANEY	F	9	54	DENVANEY	F	9	54
DENNIS	A	10	63	DENNISON	J	8	90	DENTON	CG	2	99	DENVIR	K	8	90	DENVIR	K	8	90
DENNIS	AA	3	47	DENNISON	N	9	54	DENTON	CG	2	99	DENWOOD	W	7	101	DENWOOD	W	7	101
DENNIS	AE	1	86	DENNISON	T	9	248	DENTON	CG	4	107	DENYER	AW	7	101	DENYER	AW	7	101
DENNIS	AE	4	107	DENNISON	W	7	101	DENTON	EHT	12	71	DENYER	G	1	87	DENYER	G	1	87
DENNIS	AJ	12	70	DENNISON	W	9	54	DENTON	EJ	1	87	DENYER	T	2	99	DENYER	T	2	99
DENNIS	C	2	99	DENNISON	W	9	54	DENTON	F	8	90	DEPLEDGE	G	13	130	DEPLEDGE	G	13	130
DENNIS	DH	4	107	DENNISON	W	9	54	DENTON	F	9	54	DEPLEDGE	JF	13	130	DEPLEDGE	JF	13	130
DENNIS	E	1	86	DENNISON	WF	3	323	DENTON	F	12	71	DEPLEDGE	JW	8	90	DEPLEDGE	JW	8	90
DENNIS	E	14	84	DENNISON	WG	9	384	DENTON	G	8	90	DEPLEDGE	JW	13	130	DEPLEDGE	JW	13	130
DENNIS	EA	4	107	DENNON	G	14	84	DENTON	G	8	90	DEPLEDGE	N	13	130	DEPLEDGE	N	13	130
DENNIS	FA	3	47	DENNON	GD	11	102	DENTON	G	12	71	DEPLEDGE	RC	5	100	DEPLEDGE	RC	5	100
DENNIS	FR	12	70	DENNON	T	11	102	DENTON	GA	8	90	DEPPER	W	6	113	DEPPER	W	6	113
DENNIS	GH	4	107	DENNY	A	6	112	DENTON	GE	8	90	DERBYSHIRE	A	14	84	DERBYSHIRE	A	14	84
DENNIS	GL	2	99	DENNY	A	13	129	DENTON	GE	13	130	DERBYSHIRE	A	14	84	DERBYSHIRE	A	14	84
DENNIS	GT	10	287	DENNY	EJ	2	99	DENTON	GF	5	100	DERBYSHIRE	C	11	103	DERBYSHIRE	C	11	103
DENNIS	H	5	100	DENNY	FG	13	130	DENTON	H	8	90	DERBYSHIRE	E	5	100	DERBYSHIRE	E	5	100
DENNIS	HS	2	99	DENNY	G	12	294	DENTON	H	9	54	DERBYSHIRE	EJ	3	47	DERBYSHIRE	EJ	3	47
DENNIS	J	1	86	DENNY	GF	2	99	DENTON	H	9	54	DERBYSHIRE	H	8	90	DERBYSHIRE	H	8	90
DENNIS	J	3	323	DENNY	JE	14	84	DENTON	H	11	103	DERBYSHIRE	J	11	103	DERBYSHIRE	J	11	103
DENNIS	J	5	100	DENNY	R	12	294	DENTON	H	12	294	DERBYSHIRE	J	14	84	DERBYSHIRE	J	14	84
DENNIS	J	10	64	DENNY	W	7	101	DENTON	HG	1	87	DERBYSHIRE	J	14	84	DERBYSHIRE	J	14	84
DENNIS	J	10	64	DENNY	W	12	294	DENTON	HJ	5	100	DERBYSHIRE	JW	11	103	DERBYSHIRE	JW	11	103
DENNIS	J	11	102	DENNY	WA	13	130	DENTON	HR	12	71	DERBYSHIRE	JW	11	103	DERBYSHIRE	JW	11	103
DENNIS	J	14	84	DENNY	WA	13	130	DENTON	J	8	90	DERBYSHIRE	R	11	103	DERBYSHIRE	R	11	103
DENNIS	PC	5	100	DENNY	WE	5	100	DENTON	J	11	103	DERBYSHIRE	R	11	103	DERBYSHIRE	R	11	103
DENNIS	PW	2	99	DENSON	J	11	102	DENTON	JF	12	71	DERBYSHIRE	T	11	103	DERBYSHIRE	T	11	103
DENNIS	T	5	100	DENSON	W	11	102	DENTON	JH	1	87	DERBYSHIRE	T	11	103	DERBYSHIRE	T	11	103
DENNIS	T	8	90	DENT	A	11	103	DENTON	JH	5	100	DERBYSHIRE	TE	11	103	DERBYSHIRE	TE	11	103
DENNIS	T	13	129	DENT	AJ	7	101	DENTON	JW	8	90	DERBYSHIRE	W	11	103	DERBYSHIRE	W	11	103
DENNIS	TH	13	129	DENT	AS	9	54	DENTON	S	12	71	DERHAM	BD	12	295	DERHAM	BD	12	295
DENNIS	VL	5	100	DENT	C	13	130	DENTON	SH	12	294	DERHAM	DV	12	295	DERHAM	DV	12	295
DENNIS	W	1	87	DENT	E	3	323	DENTON	SJ	12	71	DERHAM	F	13	130	DERHAM	F	13	130
DENNIS	W	3	47	DENT	F	9	248	DENTON	T	9	54	DERHAM	GF	8	90	DERHAM	GF	8	90
DENNIS	W	4	107	DENT	F	11	103	DENTON	TG	13	130	DERKIN	F	9	54	DERKIN	F	9	54
DENNIS	W	6	112	DENT	FW	3	323	DENTON	TH	1	87	DERKIN	J	9	54	DERKIN	J	9	54
DENNIS	W	7	101	DENT	HD	7	101	DENTON	TW	9	54	DERKIN	M	9	54	DERKIN	M	9	54
DENNIS	W	10	64	DENT	HG	7	101	DENTON	V	11	103	DERRICK	B	9	54	DERRICK	B	9	54
DENNIS	W	12	70	DENT	J	2	99	DENTON	W	2	99	DERRICK	JE	6	113	DERRICK	JE	6	113
DENNIS	WA	5	100	DENT	W	5	100	DENTON	W	5	100	DERRICK	JH	3	47	DERRICK	JH	3	47
DENNIS	WP	13	129	DENT	W	6	113	DENTON	W	5	100	DERRICK	S	14	84	DERRICK	S	14	84
DENNIS	WW	5	100	DENT	WJ	10	287	DENTON	W	5	100	DERRICK	SEJ	10	287	DERRICK	SEJ	10	287
DENNISON	AW	9	53	DENTITH	A	11	103	DENTON	W	5	100	DERRICK	TL	10	64	DERRICK	TL	10	64
DENNISON	C	9	53	DENTITH	AW	14	84	DENTON	W	11	103	DERRICK	W	11	103	DERRICK	W	11	103
DENNISON	E	8	90	DENTITH	J	14	84	DENTON	W	12	71	DERRIMAN	J	13	130	DERRIMAN	J	13	130
DENNISON	E	9	53	DENTON	A	5	100	DENTON	W	12	71	DERRINGTON	WG	6	113	DERRINGTON	WG	6	113
DENNISON	EA	9	53	DENTON	A	8	90	DENTON	W	12	71	DERRY	E	8	90	DERRY	E	8	90

DERRY	ER	1	87	DEVERILL	E	12	71	DEWEY	EM	4	108	DIAMOND	G	6	113				
DERRY	JT	6	113	DEVERSON	JS	13	130	DEWEY	F	3	323	DIAMOND	I	14	85				
DERRY	S	11	104	DEVEY	CH	10	64	DEWEY	FH	4	108	DIAMOND	RR	10	64				
DERRY	W	6	113	DEVEY	F	2	99	DEWEY	FHW	10	288	DIAPER	A	4	108				
DERVIN	A	14	84	DEVEY	G	6	113	DEWEY	GE	2	100	DIAPER	A	10	64				
DERVIN	J	11	104	DEVILLE	CH	8	90	DEWEY	GWA	1	87	DIAPER	EC	4	108				
DERVIN	J	11	421	DEVILLE	G	1	87	DEWEY	HJ	4	108	DIAPER	FC	4	108				
DERVIN	J	14	84	DEVILLE	JG	1	87	DEWEY	HW	4	108	DIAPER	GC	4	108				
DESALEUX	A	7	101	DEVILLE	M	7	101	DEWEY	HW	4	108	DIAPER	HJ	4	108				
DESBOROUGH	AG	5	101	DEVILLE	S	7	102	DEWEY	L	4	108	DIAPER	HM	4	108				
DESBOROUGH	G	5	101	DEVINE	C	3	323	DEWEY	LO	4	108	DIAPER	J	4	108				
DESBOROUGH	GW	5	101	DEVINE	C	9	248	DEWEY	W	12	71	DIAPER	WC	4	108				
DESBOROUGH	J	14	85	DEVINE	D	8	90	DEWEY	WA	4	108	DIAPER	WM	4	108				
DESBOROUGH	W	1	87	DEVINE	J	1	87	DEWEY	WC	7	102	DIBB	CF	8	415				
DESBROW	PD	10	287	DEVINE	J	1	87	DEWHIRST	B	9	55	DIBB	F	14	85				
DESBURGH	F	12	295	DEVINE	J	2	100	DEWHIRST	H	9	55	DIBB	F	14	85				
DESMOND	FP	3	47	DEVINE	J	9	384	DEWHIRST	H	11	104	DIBB	JG	14	86				
DESMOND	J	3	47	DEVINE	J	11	104	DEWHIRST	O	9	55	DIBB	JW	8	91				
DESMOND	WL	3	323	DEVINE	P	4	107	DEWHIRST	O	9	248	DIBBEN	AH	4	108				
DESORMEAUX	V	5	101	DEVINE	TJ	13	131	DEWHIRST	T	8	91	DIBBEN	FT	10	64				
DESSER	I	14	85	DEVINE	W	3	323	DEWHIRST	T	9	384	DIBBEN	H	13	131				
DESSON	AE	13	130	DEVINE	W	11	421	DEWHURST	A	14	85	DIBBENS	CW	3	47				
DETHERIDGE	T	6	113	DEVITT	E	14	85	DEWHURST	F	11	104	DIBBENS	E	7	102				
DETHERIDGE	W	6	113	DEVITT	HE	13	131	DEWHURST	TL	14	85	DIBBENS	EJ	3	47				
DETHRIDGE	GW	3	47	DEVITT	J	7	102	DEWHURST	W	11	104	DIBBINS	R	3	325				
DETHRIDGE	W	3	323	DEVITT	JE	14	85	DEWHURST	W	14	85	DIBBLE	HJ	14	86				
DETTMER	GA	1	87	DEVITT	P	8	90	DEWITT	S	14	85	DIBBLE	SA	1	88				
DETTMER	HG	3	323	DEVLIN	R	10	288	DEWITT	W	14	85	DIBBLIN	SA	7	102				
DEUBERT	SC	2	99	DEVLIN	W	11	104	DEWLEY	SW	10	64	DIBDEN	G	10	64				
DEVAL	WH	14	85	DEVLIN	W	14	85	DEWS	D	6	113	DIBDEN	WE	4	108				
DEVANE	E	7	101	DEVONALD	E	2	100	DEWS	H	6	113	DIBLEY	AE	14	86				
DEVANE	J	7	101	DEVONPORT	F	6	113	DEWSALL	W	1	87	DIBLEY	HW	7	102				
DEVANEY	S	11	104	DEVONPORT	F	10	288	DEWSE	W	9	55	DIBLEY	J	7	102				
DEVANNY	E	9	54	DEVONPORT	G	14	85	DEWSNAP	SE	7	102	DIBLEY	J	13	131				
DEVAUX	E	13	130	DEVONPORT	J	8	91	DEWSNUP	E	11	104	DIBLIN	T	3	47				
DEVEAUX	GV	4	107	DEVONPORT	WH	14	85	DEWSNUP	F	11	104	DIBSDALE	CNG	7	102				
DEVENISH	CN	10	288	DEVONSHIRE	AE	1	87	DEWSNUP	J	11	104	DIBSDALE	F	5	101				
DEVENISH	FE	10	288	DEVONSHIRE	EG	1	87	DEWSNUP	N	11	104	DIBSDALL	H	4	109				
DEVENISH	HG	13	130	DEVONSHIRE	EV	1	87	DEWSON	GE	2	100	DICK	J	7	102				
DEVENISH	PG	4	107	DEVOY	PL	4	107	DEXTER	A	2	100	DICK	W	10	64				
DEVENISH	TW	3	323	DEW	EW	2	100	DEXTER	AH	6	113	DICK	WJ	2	100				
DEVENISH	WE	3	323	DEW	G	2	100	DEXTER	E	7	102	DICKASON	W	3	47				
DEVERE	F	6	113	DEW	H	2	100	DEXTER	GH	13	131	DICKEN	AH	10	64				
DEVERELL	SG	5	101	DEW	H	4	108	DEXTER	HD	12	295	DICKEN	EW	7	102				
DEVEREUX	A	12	71	DEW	S	5	101	DEXTER	J	2	100	DICKENS	A	5	101				
DEVEREUX	AE	5	101	DEWAN	T	14	85	DEXTER	WH	11	104	DICKENS	A	5	101				
DEVEREUX	E	5	101	DEWAR	CD	5	101	DEY	C	9	55	DICKENS	A	12	71				
DEVEREUX	H	5	101	DEWAR	WR	3	323	DEY	W	11	104	DICKENS	C	12	71				
DEVEREUX	J	9	55	DEWARS	AK	8	91	DIAMOND	A	11	104	DICKENS	C	14	86				
DEVEREUX	P	12	71	DEWBREY	HB	9	55	DIAMOND	AFT	1	87	DICKENS	E	2	100				
DEVEREUX	T	6	113	DEWDNEY	G	10	64	DIAMOND	AT	1	88	DICKENS	EJ	12	71				
DEVEREUX	W	13	130	DEWES	L	8	91	DIAMOND	B	14	85	DICKENS	EW	12	72				
DEVEREUX	WF	12	71	DEWES	W	8	91	DIAMOND	BW	10	64	DICKENS	F	5	101				
DEVERICK	F	12	71	DEWETT	P	14	85	DIAMOND	FE	13	131	DICKENS	F	12	72				
DEVERICK	WG	12	71	DEWEY	EC	10	64	DIAMOND	FE	13	131	DICKENS	F	12	72				

DICKENS	FC	12	295	DICKINSON	C	8	91	DICKS	J	2	101	DIGHTON	EW	12	72				
DICKENS	G	5	101	DICKINSON	C	8	91	DICKS	PG	4	109	DIGHTON	GH	12	72				
DICKENS	GE	14	86	DICKINSON	CH	10	65	DICKS	S	12	295	DIGHTON	JH	12	72				
DICKENS	H	5	101	DICKINSON	E	8	91	DICKS	T	6	114	DIGHTON	R	12	72				
DICKENS	HS	2	100	DICKINSON	E	8	91	DICKS	TG	12	72	DIGHTON	WT	12	72				
DICKENS	R	2	100	DICKINSON	E	14	86	DICKS	TH	13	131	DIGNAM	M	9	248				
DICKENS	S	12	72	DICKINSON	EWS	3	48	DICKS	WA	12	295	DIGNUM	JW	7	103				
DICKENS	T	11	104	DICKINSON	F	3	48	DICKSON	A	7	103	DIGNUM	RR	7	103				
DICKENS	T	12	72	DICKINSON	F	8	91	DICKSON	A	14	86	DIGNUM	WG	7	104				
DICKENS	WA	5	101	DICKINSON	FC	14	86	DICKSON	E	8	415	DIGNY	F	9	55				
DICKENS	WF	2	100	DICKINSON	GR	14	86	DICKSON	FE	7	103	DIGWEED	B	4	109				
DICKENS	WH	12	72	DICKINSON	GT	11	104	DICKSON	G	7	103	DIGWEED	F	3	48				
DICKENS	WJ	12	72	DICKINSON	H	8	91	DICKSON	GL	5	102	DIGWEED	FW	4	109				
DICKENS	WT	12	72	DICKINSON	H	9	248	DICKSON	H	7	103	DIGWEED	MA	3	48				
DICKENSON	A	8	91	DICKINSON	HG	14	86	DICKSON	H	7	103	DILBECK	AHV	1	88				
DICKENSON	AG	7	102	DICKINSON	J	3	324	DICKSON	HJ	3	324	DILGER	JE	9	55				
DICKENSON	DJ	12	295	DICKINSON	J	8	91	DICKSON	T	7	103	DILKS	JA	5	102				
DICKENSON	F	4	109	DICKINSON	J	8	91	DICKSON	W	7	103	DILLEY	A	5	102				
DICKENSON	G	2	100	DICKINSON	J	11	105	DICKSON	WJ	13	131	DILLEY	A	12	72				
DICKENSON	H	11	104	DICKINSON	J	11	105	DIDCOCK	AG	2	101	DILLEY	AJ	5	102				
DICKENSON	HH	7	102	DICKINSON	J	11	105	DIDCOCK	DJ	7	103	DILLEY	C	5	102				
DICKENSON	J	14	86	DICKINSON	J	11	105	DIDCOCK	EJ	7	103	DILLEY	D	5	102				
DICKENSON	JR	11	104	DICKINSON	JA	11	105	DIDCOCK	FJ	7	103	DILLEY	E	5	102				
DICKER	AC	7	102	DICKINSON	JA	14	86	DIDCOCK	FR	3	48	DILLEY	EG	5	102				
DICKER	AE	7	102	DICKINSON	JC	14	86	DIDCOCK	PE	7	103	DILLEY	HH	2	101				
DICKER	E	3	323	DICKINSON	JT	7	103	DIDCOTT	GA	6	114	DILLEY	SA	1	88				
DICKER	F	4	109	DICKINSON	JW	8	91	DIDDAMS	T	2	101	DILLEY	W	5	102				
DICKER	FJ	7	102	DICKINSON	JW	8	91	DIDYMUS	WJ	10	65	DILLEY	WF	2	101				
DICKER	H	13	131	DICKINSON	L	8	91	DIEMER	C	12	72	DILLEY	WJ	12	295				
DICKER	HW	13	131	DICKINSON	L	8	92	DIEMER	W	12	72	DILLEYSTON	JM	2	101				
DICKER	R	3	323	DICKINSON	N	8	92	DIETT	JT	13	131	DILLING	E	13	132				
DICKER	RJ	7	102	DICKINSON	N	11	105	DIETT	TW	13	131	DILLING	HC	13	132				
DICKER	S	13	131	DICKINSON	P	8	92	DIFFEY	CJ	4	109	DILLINGHAM	GW	5	102				
DICKER	WG	3	323	DICKINSON	R	11	105	DIGBY	AC	12	295	DILLINGHAM	GW	12	72				
DICKERSON	F	5	101	DICKINSON	S	5	102	DIGBY	FJ	2	101	DILLINGHAM	JT	5	102				
DICKERSON	FA	12	295	DICKINSON	S	8	92	DIGBY	H	2	101	DILLINGHAM	P	5	102				
DICKERSON	H	5	101	DICKINSON	T	2	100	DIGBY	J	3	324	DILLINGHAM	SA	5	103				
DICKERSON	N	2	100	DICKINSON	T	8	92	DIGBY	LW	13	131	DILLINGHAM	W	5	103				
DICKERSON	T	12	295	DICKINSON	TW	11	105	DIGBY	SJ	3	48	DILLINGHAM	W	12	73				
DICKERSON	W	5	102	DICKINSON	W	6	113	DIGDALE	D	4	109	DILLINGHAM	WD	5	103				
DICKESON	AE	2	100	DICKINSON	W	9	248	DIGGENS	J	7	103	DILLON	AC	7	104				
DICKESON	C	3	323	DICKINSON	W	11	105	DIGGER	CA	6	114	DILLON	D	9	248				
DICKESON	R	2	101	DICKINSON	W	11	105	DIGGERSON	GW	13	131	DILLON	E	11	105				
DICKETTS	TC	2	101	DICKINSON	W	14	86	DIGGERSON	J	13	131	DILLON	GF	14	86				
DICKIE	AT	13	131	DICKINSON	WCJ	6	114	DIGGINS	EG	5	102	DILLON	H	3	324				
DICKIE	G	10	288	DICKINSON	WE	11	105	DIGGINS	F	1	88	DILLON	HJ	11	105				
DICKINS	CH	2	101	DICKINSON	WP	3	324	DIGGINS	GL	3	48	DILLON	J	2	101				
DICKINSON	A	5	102	DICKINSON	WP	7	103	DIGGINS	HT	5	102	DILLON	J	4	109				
DICKINSON	A	7	102	DICKINSON	WP	13	131	DIGGINS	OA	5	102	DILLON	J	4	109				
DICKINSON	A	7	103	DICKMAN	CE	2	101	DIGGLE	F	14	86	DILLON	J	8	92				
DICKINSON	A	8	91	DICKMAN	HAH	2	101	DIGGLE	J	9	55	DILLON	J	10	65				
DICKINSON	AG	3	324	DICKMAN	J	3	324	DIGGLE	W	14	86	DILLON	J	11	105				
DICKINSON	AG	7	103	DICKOX	F	10	65	DIGHT	B	6	114	DILLON	J	13	132				
DICKINSON	AJ	10	64	DICKS	H	3	324	DIGHTON	AV	12	72	DILLON	JH	11	105				
DICKINSON	AM	5	102	DICKS	HC	12	295	DIGHTON	EA	13	131	DILLON	L	8	92				

DILLON	MD	13	132	DINE	GR	10	65	DISMORE	FE	4	109	DIXON	E	11	106
DILLON	P	11	105	DINE	HW	10	65	DISNEY	AH	8	92	DIXON	E	11	106
DILLON	P	11	105	DINES	AT	1	88	DISS	W	3	324	DIXON	EC	7	104
DILLON	R	6	114	DINES	F	1	88	DITCH	C	1	88	DIXON	EJ	14	87
DILLON	R	11	105	DINES	WE	2	101	DITCH	F	1	88	DIXON	F	9	249
DILLON	T	11	105	DINES	WH	1	88	DITCHFIELD	E	14	87	DIXON	F	13	133
DILLON	TC	13	132	DINGLE	C	3	48	DITCHFIELD	GW	11	106	DIXON	FW	13	133
DILLON	TW	2	101	DINGLE	JH	6	114	DITCHFIELD	T	11	106	DIXON	G	3	324
DILLON	W	6	114	DINGLE	LAC	10	65	DITE	H	3	324	DIXON	G	4	109
DILLON	W STJ	13	132	DINGLEY	AB	3	48	DITTON	A	13	132	DIXON	G	8	92
DILLON	WA	8	92	DINGLEY	G	5	103	DITTON	JT	13	132	DIXON	G	11	106
DILLOW	E	1	88	DINGLEY	H	5	104	DITTON	WH	2	102	DIXON	GP	8	93
DILLOW	G	1	88	DINHAM	C	3	324	DIVER	AG	10	65	DIXON	GR	1	88
DILLOW	N	1	88	DINHAM	WA	5	104	DIVERS	FG	7	104	DIXON	H	7	104
DILLOWAY	JG	10	288	DINMORE	JA	7	104	DIVES	P	13	132	DIXON	H	8	93
DILREW	S	4	109	DINNAGE	VJ	10	65	DIVIANI	PW	10	288	DIXON	H	8	93
DILTHEY	C	1	88	DINNES	RJ	3	48	DIVINE	J	8	92	DIXON	H	9	249
DILWORTH	C	8	92	DINNEWELL	F	8	92	DIVINE	J	12	295	DIXON	H	14	87
DIMBLEBY	GA	1	88	DINNEWELL	W	8	92	DIX	A	12	295	DIXON	H	14	87
DIMELOE	J	11	106	DINSDALE	A	8	92	DIX	EF	5	104	DIXON	HJ	6	115
DIMLOW	J	14	86	DINSDALE	A	8	92	DIX	F	5	104	DIXON	HL	6	115
DIMMER	FE	4	109	DINSDALE	F	4	109	DIX	G	10	65	DIXON	J	2	102
DIMMICK	J	6	114	DINSDALE	FJ	3	324	DIX	GR	5	104	DIXON	J	3	48
DIMMOCK	A	6	114	DINSDALE	G	11	106	DIX	H	3	324	DIXON	J	5	104
DIMMOCK	AG	5	103	DINSDALE	G	13	132	DIX	HW	5	104	DIXON	J	8	93
DIMMOCK	AJ	5	103	DINSDALE	H	11	106	DIX	M	6	115	DIXON	J	8	93
DIMMOCK	AS	12	295	DINSDALE	H	11	106	DIX	S	3	324	DIXON	J	8	93
DIMMOCK	AW	5	103	DINSDALE	JE	2	101	DIX	T	10	65	DIXON	J	9	249
DIMMOCK	BA	3	324	DINSDALE	R	9	55	DIX	W	12	295	DIXON	J	11	106
DIMMOCK	C	5	103	DINSDALE	R	11	106	DIXEY	R	13	132	DIXON	J	11	106
DIMMOCK	CE	12	73	DINSDALE	W	13	132	DIXEY	S	10	288	DIXON	J	11	106
DIMMOCK	EW	7	104	DINSEY	WJ	5	104	DIXON	A	6	115	DIXON	J	11	106
DIMMOCK	EW	10	288	DINTINGER	C	5	104	DIXON	A	8	92	DIXON	J	11	106
DIMMOCK	F	2	101	DIPPER	H	6	114	DIXON	A	10	65	DIXON	JA	8	93
DIMMOCK	F	5	103	DIPPER	JG	12	295	DIXON	AC	12	73	DIXON	JA	11	106
DIMMOCK	F	13	132	DIPPER	T	6	114	DIXON	AE	14	87	DIXON	JA	14	87
DIMMOCK	FJ	12	73	DIPPIE	K	13	132	DIXON	AE	14	87	DIXON	JC	7	104
DIMMOCK	H	5	103	DIPPIE	R	13	132	DIXON	AG	4	109	DIXON	JE	9	55
DIMMOCK	H	5	103	DIPPIE	R	13	132	DIXON	AH	6	115	DIXON	JE	11	106
DIMMOCK	H	5	103	DIPPLE	ER	2	101	DIXON	AM	10	288	DIXON	JH	2	102
DIMMOCK	J	3	48	DIPPLE	GW	6	114	DIXON	B	8	92	DIXON	JH	10	65
DIMMOCK	J	3	48	DIPPLE	TH	6	114	DIXON	B	8	92	DIXON	JH	11	106
DIMMOCK	J	5	103	DIPPLE	W	6	114	DIXON	BR	10	288	DIXON	JH	12	73
DIMMOCK	JW	1	88	DIPPLE	W	6	114	DIXON	C	3	324	DIXON	JH	13	133
DIMMOCK	L	5	103	DIPPLE	WJ	13	132	DIXON	C	5	104	DIXON	JJ	6	115
DIMMOCK	M	12	73	DIPROSE	W	3	48	DIXON	C	7	104	DIXON	JL	11	106
DIMMOCK	P	5	103	DISBREY	W	8	92	DIXON	C	8	92	DIXON	JW	6	115
DIMMOCK	RG	13	132	DISDALE	FC	3	48	DIXON	C	9	55	DIXON	L	7	104
DIMMOCK	RJ	3	48	DISDALE	RW	1	88	DIXON	C	13	133	DIXON	L	8	93
DIMMOCK	W	5	103	DISHART	ET	13	132	DIXON	CBD	2	102	DIXON	R	7	104
DIMMOCK	WA	5	103	DISHER	G	2	101	DIXON	CE	9	55	DIXON	R	11	107
DIMMOCK	WH	13	132	DISLEY	C	14	86	DIXON	CH	14	87	DIXON	RE	9	55
DIMMOCK	WM	5	103	DISLEY	TJ	14	87	DIXON	DW	13	133	DIXON	RHG	1	88
DIMSFORD	R	5	103	DISLEY	WE	6	114	DIXON	E	2	102	DIXON	S	13	133
DINE	CA	13	132	DISMORE	EG	2	102	DIXON	E	7	104	DIXON	SG	5	104

DIXON	SG	10	288	DOBSON	C	8	93	DOCKER	G	6	115	DODD	WEL	4	109
DIXON	SS	9	249	DOBSON	C	8	93	DOCKER	S	6	115	DODD	WG	4	109
DIXON	ST	7	104	DOBSON	CA	12	73	DOCKER	TE	2	102	DODD	WH	10	65
DIXON	T	7	104	DOBSON	CH	7	104	DOCKERILL	FS	5	104	DODDINGTON	JR	7	105
DIXON	TF	9	249	DOBSON	DJH	13	133	DOCKERTY	E	8	94	DODDS	AJ	14	88
DIXON	TG	12	73	DOBSON	DS	14	87	DOCKERTY	J	8	94	DODDS	E	5	104
DIXON	W	8	93	DOBSON	E	2	102	DOCKERTY	J	8	94	DODDS	H	13	133
DIXON	W	8	93	DOBSON	E	8	93	DOCKERTY	T	8	94	DODDS	LH	11	107
DIXON	W	10	65	DOBSON	E	14	87	DOCKERY	AM	13	133	DODDS	R	1	89
DIXON	W	11	107	DOBSON	ED	9	55	DOCKERY	J	6	115	DODDS	TG	5	104
DIXON	W	11	107	DOBSON	EG	12	73	DOCKERY	W	6	115	DODDS	W	13	134
DIXON	W	14	87	DOBSON	F	8	93	DOCKRAY	JS	8	94	DODGE	LE	13	134
DIXON	WA	12	73	DOBSON	F	8	93	DOCKRELL	GD	1	89	DODGON	T	9	56
DIXON	WA	13	133	DOBSON	F	9	55	DOCKREY	A	8	94	DODGSON	F	8	94
DIXON	WE	1	88	DOBSON	F	9	55	DOCWRA	SJ	1	89	DODGSON	JH	8	94
DIXON	WG	5	104	DOBSON	F	11	107	DOD	CF	12	422	DODKIN	H	5	104
DIXON	WG	7	104	DOBSON	FJ	1	89	DODBELL	A	9	56	DODMAN	CE	12	296
DIXON	WH	3	48	DOBSON	FW	13	133	DODBELL	TH	9	56	DODMAN	J	4	110
DIXON	WH	6	115	DOBSON	GE	7	104	DODD	AM	7	105	DODMAN	SH	13	134
DIXON	WJ	2	102	DOBSON	H	8	93	DODD	C	6	115	DODSON	A	11	107
DIXON	WT	2	102	DOBSON	H	8	93	DODD	C	14	87	DODSON	AJ	5	105
DIXSON	T	13	133	DOBSON	H	8	94	DODD	CV	14	87	DODSON	RJ	5	105
DIXSON	TH	13	133	DOBSON	H	8	94	DODD	EFS	7	105	DODSON	W	2	103
DIXSON	WJ	13	133	DOBSON	H	9	56	DODD	EG	7	105	DODSWORTH	A	9	249
DIYMENT	F	12	295	DOBSON	H	10	65	DODD	F	3	48	DODSWORTH	JW	9	56
DOAK	JJ	4	109	DOBSON	H	14	87	DODD	FM	10	288	DODSWORTH	P	8	94
DOBBIN	D	10	65	DOBSON	HEV	1	89	DODD	FW	7	105	DODWELL	JF	2	103
DOBBINS	CJ	13	133	DOBSON	HW	2	102	DODD	G	6	115	DOE	A	4	110
DOBBINS	W	3	325	DOBSON	I	8	94	DODD	GF	14	87	DOE	A	6	116
DOBBS	A	6	115	DOBSON	J	8	94	DODD	GH	6	115	DOE	A	6	116
DOBBS	EC	5	104	DOBSON	J	9	56	DODD	GJH	10	65	DOE	CH	10	66
DOBBS	GA	2	102	DOBSON	J	9	56	DODD	GW	11	107	DOE	D	4	110
DOBBS	GL	5	104	DOBSON	J	9	384	DODD	H	2	102	DOE	E	10	288
DOBBS	M	5	104	DOBSON	JF	2	102	DODD	H	5	104	DOE	ES	4	110
DOBBY	F	9	249	DOBSON	JR	8	94	DODD	H	6	115	DOE	FH	4	110
DOBBY	WH	13	133	DOBSON	JW	9	249	DODD	H	6	115	DOE	H	13	134
DOBELL	W	2	102	DOBSON	ME	8	94	DODD	H	11	107	DOE	J	13	134
DOBIE	AE	7	104	DOBSON	R	8	94	DODD	J	6	115	DOE	LT	10	65
DOBIE	SS	7	104	DOBSON	R	11	107	DODD	J	9	56	DOE	MC	13	134
DOBIE	WW	11	107	DOBSON	S	8	94	DODD	J	11	107	DOE	RA	10	288
DOBINSON	HE	1	88	DOBSON	TA	3	48	DODD	J	11	107	DOE	RH	1	89
DOBINSON	J	4	109	DOBSON	TA	3	325	DODD	J	12	296	DOE	SF	13	134
DOBINSON	JR	1	88	DOBSON	W	8	94	DODD	J	14	87	DOE	W	4	110
DOBLE	AJ	2	102	DOBSON	W	8	94	DODD	J	14	87	DOE	WA	7	105
DOBLE	HG	2	102	DOBSON	W	8	94	DODD	JA	1	89	DOE	WT	2	103
DOBNEY	AF	12	73	DOBSON	W	8	94	DODD	JA	2	102	DOEL	HT	4	110
DOBNEY	G	12	73	DOBSON	W	8	94	DODD	JR	14	87	DOEL	R	4	110
DOBNEY	H	8	93	DOBSON	W	9	56	DODD	LS	14	88	DOETZEL	F	14	88
DOBRISKEY	GH	2	102	DOBSON	W	13	133	DODD	R	11	107	DOGGETT	EC	5	105
DOBSON	A	8	93	DOBSON	WH	3	325	DODD	R	14	88	DOGGETT	GW	12	73
DOBSON	A	8	93	DOBSON	WL	13	133	DODD	T	2	103	DOGGETT	J	5	105
DOBSON	A	12	296	DOBY	HA	12	73	DODD	T	11	107	DOGGETT	J	5	105
DOBSON	AE	1	89	DOCK	JJ	13	133	DODD	W	11	107	DOGGETT	T	5	105
DOBSON	AW	13	133	DOCKER	A	2	102	DODD	WE	11	107	DOGGETT	WA	1	89
DOBSON	B	8	93	DOCKER	C	1	89	DODD	WE	14	88	DOGGETT	WJ	5	105

DOHERTY	C	9	384	DOLEY	F	6	116	DONALD	BT	10	66	DONNELLY	TH	11	109
DOHERTY	E	5	105	DOLEY	SW	6	116	DONALD	FA	7	105	DONNELLY	W	11	109
DOHERTY	E	9	249	DOLING	CW	4	110	DONALD	GS	11	108	DONNELLY	W	13	135
DOHERTY	E	14	88	DOLING	GA	4	110	DONALD	LJ	1	89	DONNELLY	W	14	89
DOHERTY	H	3	325	DOLING	M	4	110	DONALD	WA	9	56	DONNOLLY	AE	3	325
DOHERTY	H	9	249	DOLING	ML	4	110	DONALDSON	C	4	111	DONOGHUE	E	9	57
DOHERTY	J	8	95	DOLING	P	4	110	DONALDSON	D	4	111	DONOGHUE	E	13	135
DOHERTY	J	8	95	DOLING	RG	4	110	DONALDSON	DA	4	111	DONOGHUE	F	8	95
DOHERTY	J	9	56	DOLING	WH	13	134	DONALDSON	GH	3	325	DONOGHUE	H	3	325
DOHERTY	J	14	88	DOLLERY	EH	10	288	DONALDSON	GW	3	325	DONOGHUE	H	9	57
DOHERTY	M	11	107	DOLLERY	H	10	288	DONALDSON	JF	11	108	DONOGHUE	J	3	325
DOHERTY	P	9	249	DOLLERY	WH	10	289	DONALDSON	JW	14	88	DONOGHUE	J	13	135
DOHERTY	T	11	107	DOLLIMORE	CT	5	105	DONALDSON	R	3	325	DONOGHUE	O	4	111
DOHERTY	T	14	88	DOLLIMORE	EG	5	105	DONALDSON	R	6	116	DONOGHUE	TP	13	135
DOHERTY	W	1	89	DOLLIMORE	EJ	5	105	DONALDSON	S	6	116	DONOGHUE	W	3	325
DOIDGE	GC	6	116	DOLLIMORE	EJ	5	105	DONALDSON	SH	12	296	DONOGHUE	W	7	105
DOIDGE	J	6	116	DOLLIMORE	FG	5	105	DONALDSON	TC	3	325	DONOHOA	G	9	57
DOIDGE	WH	7	105	DOLLIN	AE	4	110	DONALDSON	W	10	66	DONOHUE	E	11	109
DOIG	P	1	89	DOLLIN	J	4	110	DONALDSON	W	13	134	DONOHUE	H	14	89
DOIGE	JE	10	66	DOLLIN	J	4	110	DONBAVAND	SW	11	108	DONOHUE	J	4	111
DOIGNIE	TJ	13	134	DOLLIN	T	4	110	DONCOM	EJ	4	111	DONOHUE	J	11	109
DOLAMORE	G	5	105	DOLLIN	WG	4	110	DONCOM	W	4	111	DONOHUE	T	11	109
DOLAMORE	WF	5	105	DOLLING	FE	7	105	DONE	C	9	56	DONOVAN	AE	10	289
DOLAN	A	8	95	DOLLING	JWJ	7	105	DONE	J	14	88	DONOVAN	AG	1	90
DOLAN	A	14	88	DOLLING	SG	2	103	DONE	J	14	88	DONOVAN	AJ	1	90
DOLAN	E	14	88	DOLLING	SH	3	325	DONE	JW	9	57	DONOVAN	D	3	49
DOLAN	J	8	95	DOLLINGS	E	13	134	DONE	S	14	88	DONOVAN	DT	3	49
DOLAN	J	8	95	DOLLMAN	TE	2	103	DONE	WT	6	116	DONOVAN	F	2	103
DOLAN	J	9	56	DOLLY	JP	10	289	DONEGAN	AJ	12	73	DONOVAN	G	3	49
DOLAN	J	9	56	DOLLYMORE	HM	2	103	DONIGAN	W	11	108	DONOVAN	G	13	135
DOLAN	J	11	108	DOLPHIN	A	1	89	DONKIN	A	4	111	DONOVAN	H	1	90
DOLAN	J	11	108	DOLPHIN	F	1	89	DONKIN	W	1	89	DONOVAN	J	4	111
DOLAN	J	11	108	DOLPHIN	G	6	116	DONLAN	J	14	88	DONOVAN	J	7	105
DOLAN	J	11	108	DOLPHIN	GR	6	116	DONLAN	J	14	88	DONOVAN	J	13	135
DOLAN	J	14	88	DOLPHIN	HT	13	134	DONLAN	M	14	88	DONOVAN	JM	3	325
DOLAN	JH	9	56	DOLPHIN	J	6	116	DONLAN	T	14	89	DONOVAN	W	13	135
DOLAN	JW	8	95	DOLTON	AC	1	89	DONLEVY	GT	7	105	DONOWA	JT	4	111
DOLAN	JW	14	88	DOLTON	ATC	3	49	DONLON	J	9	57	DONOWHO	J	14	89
DOLAN	N	11	108	DOLTON	EA	12	73	DONLY	J	11	108	DONSON	W	8	95
DOLAN	P	9	56	DOLTON	EF	1	89	DONMALL	HR	1	89	DOODSON	E	11	109
DOLAN	SH	11	108	DOLTON	GH	5	105	DONN	WH	10	66	DOODSON	R	11	109
DOLAND	FM	4	110	DOLTON	H	1	89	DONNE	C	1	89	DOODSON	T	11	109
DOLBY	L	9	56	DOLTON	WG	5	105	DONNE	V	1	90	DOODSON	T	11	109
DOLBY	P	5	105	DOMING	A	2	103	DONNE	WE	1	90	DOODY	AW	4	111
DOLDEN	ED	2	103	DOMINY	AE	10	66	DONNELL	O	8	95	DOOLAN	J	11	109
DOLDING	A	13	134	DOMINY	JC	10	66	DONNELLY	A	11	108	DOOLE	HS	13	135
DOLDING	A	13	134	DOMINY	WJ	4	111	DONNELLY	D	3	325	DOOLE	WA	13	135
DOLDING	AJ	7	105	DOMMETT	AJ	10	289	DONNELLY	E	11	108	DOOLER	RJ	11	109
DOLDING	F	13	134	DOMMETT	HF	3	49	DONNELLY	GW	2	103	DOOLEY	A	11	109
DOLDING	G	13	134	DOMMETT	J	3	49	DONNELLY	J	4	111	DOOLEY	A	14	89
DOLDING	J	13	134	DOMMETT	RP	10	289	DONNELLY	J	11	108	DOOLEY	AE	2	103
DOLEMAN	A	11	108	DOMNINNY	S	13	134	DONNELLY	J	14	89	DOOLEY	CH	11	109
DOLEMAN	JE	11	108	DOMNINNY	WL	13	134	DONNELLY	J	14	89	DOOLEY	EA	14	89
DOLEMAN	R	11	108	DOMONEY	W	1	89	DONNELLY	J	14	89	DOOLEY	HW	9	249
DOLEMORE	FD	5	105	DONAGHER	F	9	56	DONNELLY	T	14	89	DOOLEY	J	3	325

DOOLEY	J	9	249
DOOLEY	M	11	109
DOOLEY	N	14	89
DOOLEY	SB	4	111
DOOLEY	T	8	95
DOPSON	J	10	289
DOPSON	W	10	66
DORAN	AC	3	326
DORAN	C	13	135
DORAN	D	2	103
DORAN	E	11	109
DORAN	E	13	135
DORAN	E	14	89
DORAN	FW	6	116
DORAN	H	8	95
DORAN	JF	11	109
DORAN	T	9	57
DORAN	T	11	109
DORBER	F	11	109
DORE	A	1	90
DORE	A	10	66
DORE	AJ	4	111
DORE	AR	4	111
DORE	AW	10	66
DORE	F	10	66
DORE	F	10	289
DORE	FW	4	111
DORE	H	4	111
DORE	S	10	66
DORE	W	10	66
DORE	W	10	66
DORE	WH	4	112
DORE	WJ	3	326
DOREY	CR	4	112
DOREY	JS	1	90
DOREY	L	4	112
DOREY	M	7	105
DOREY	PE	7	105
DOREY	RA	7	105
DORKINS	CR	1	90
DORLING	A	5	106
DORLING	AE	13	135
DORLING	E	13	135
DORLING	F	5	106
DORMAN	H	4	112
DORMAN	R	1	90
DORMER	A	12	73
DORMER	AF	4	112
DORMER	AW	3	326
DORMER	CA	1	90
DORMER	CA	3	49
DORMER	EA	13	135
DORMER	EC	1	90
DORMER	EJ	2	103
DORMER	HH	1	90
DORMER	R	1	90
DORMER	WH	2	103
DORMON	A	2	103
DORMON	MA	10	66
DORMON	P	2	103
DORNEY	J	14	89
DORNHORST	FS	5	106
DORNING	A	14	89
DORNING	H	14	89
DORR	G	12	296
DORRELL	AE	1	90
DORRELL	FR	3	49
DORRELL	GT	1	90
DORRELL	GT	3	49
DORRELL	H	3	326
DORRELL	HE	7	105
DORRELL	ME	1	90
DORRICOTT	P	6	116
DORRICOTT	T	11	110
DORRILL	AR	12	73
DORRILL	W	12	73
DORRINGTON	A	2	103
DORRINGTON	CJ	3	326
DORRINGTON	E	2	103
DORRINGTON	EH	5	106
DORRINGTON	GF	2	104
DORRINGTON	H	2	104
DORRINGTON	HG	5	106
DORRINGTON	HT	13	135
DORRINGTON	HT	13	135
DORRINGTON	JA	4	112
DORRINGTON	RS	4	112
DORRINGTON	W	12	74
DORSETT	FJ	7	106
DORSETT	G	11	110
DORSETT	JA	1	90
DORSETT	JT	7	105
DORSETT	R	3	326
DORSETT	T	3	49
DORSETT	WH	6	116
DORSETT	WJ	7	106
DORTON	AG	13	135
DORTON	WE	13	135
DORWARD	W	11	110
DOSQUET	H	14	89
DOSS	WG	7	106
DOSSET	CA	10	66
DOSSETT	F	4	112
DOSSETT	FW	7	106
DOSSETT	H	10	66
DOSSETT	WH	6	116
DOSWELL	E	3	326
DOSWELL	W	4	112
DOTTIE	A	14	89
DOTTIE	JR	14	89
DOUBLE	A	13	135
DOUBLE	AG	3	326
DOUBLE	BE	13	136
DOUBLE	C	7	106
DOUBLE	G	2	104
DOUBLE	H	1	90
DOUBLE	RM	7	106
DOUBTFIRE	AH	2	104
DOUBTFIRE	HE	13	136
DOUBTFIRE	J	13	136
DOUCE	A	12	296
DOUCETTE	WJ	6	116
DOUCH	WE	13	136
DOUGGEN	G	9	249
DOUGGEN	JA	9	249
DOUGHERTY	A	8	95
DOUGHERTY	CJ	3	326
DOUGHERTY	RH	3	326
DOUGHERTY	T	9	57
DOUGHERTY	T	9	249
DOUGHTY	AC	10	66
DOUGHTY	F	6	116
DOUGHTY	FE	10	289
DOUGHTY	FH	6	117
DOUGHTY	FL	7	106
DOUGHTY	G	6	117
DOUGHTY	HT	3	326
DOUGHTY	HT	6	117
DOUGHTY	J	10	289
DOUGHTY	JL	10	289
DOUGHTY	TH	5	106
DOUGHTY	W	12	74
DOUGHTY	WG	7	106
DOUGILL	A	8	95
DOUGLAS	A	6	117
DOUGLAS	A	8	95
DOUGLAS	A	11	110
DOUGLAS	A	13	136
DOUGLAS	AO	13	136
DOUGLAS	AW	8	95
DOUGLAS	C	12	296
DOUGLAS	CT	7	106
DOUGLAS	CW	7	106
DOUGLAS	CW	13	136
DOUGLAS	ER	2	104
DOUGLAS	F	9	57
DOUGLAS	FA	7	106
DOUGLAS	GH	1	90
DOUGLAS	GW	7	106
DOUGLAS	J	8	95
DOUGLAS	J	9	57
DOUGLAS	M	1	90
DOUGLAS	M	5	106
DOUGLAS	PW	7	106
DOUGLAS	R	9	57
DOUGLAS	R	11	110
DOUGLAS	R	12	296
DOUGLAS	R	13	136
DOUGLAS	RC	13	136
DOUGLAS	SAH	12	296
DOUGLAS	SW	12	296
DOUGLAS	TJ	3	326
DOUGLAS	W	2	104
DOUGLAS	W	7	106
DOUGLAS	W	8	95
DOUGLAS	W	9	249
DOUGLAS	W	11	110
DOUGLAS	WD	5	106
DOUGLAS	WE	5	106
DOUGLASS	A	10	289
DOUGLASS	H	10	289
DOUGLASS	WJ	13	136
DOUGLASS	WR	13	136
DOULT	G	3	326
DOULT	WH	3	326
DOUNING	C	7	106
DOUSE	FW	10	66
DOUSETT	WJ	13	136
DOUST	AW	1	90
DOUST	JH	13	136
DOUTHWAITE	A	7	106
DOUTHWAITE	AG	7	106
DOUTHWAITE	AH	13	136
DOUTHWAITE	CE	7	106
DOUTHWAITE	H	11	110
DOVASTON	T	5	106
DOVASTON	W	5	106
DOVE	A	11	110
DOVE	AW	13	136
DOVE	B	1	91
DOVE	C	12	296
DOVE	CW	6	117
DOVE	DE	4	112
DOVE	FR	7	107
DOVE	N	12	74
DOVE	R	6	117
DOVE	T	9	57
DOVE	TG	12	296
DOVE	W	12	74
DOVE	WF	1	91
DOVE	WH	1	91
DOVENER	A	9	57
DOVENER	P	9	249
DOVER	A	9	57
DOVER	CW	2	104
DOVER	DM	11	110
DOVER	E	9	57
DOVER	H	1	91
DOVER	HA	1	91
DOVER	HR	5	106

DOVER	R	11	110	DOWLING	HT	13	137	DOWNING	CE	10	67	DOWSE	EF	13	137
DOVEY	AE	6	117	DOWLING	J	3	49	DOWNING	D	6	117	DOWSE	FG	5	106
DOVEY	AE	6	117	DOWLING	JE	7	107	DOWNING	EJ	6	117	DOWSE	G	5	106
DOVEY	AJ	6	117	DOWLING	JT	10	290	DOWNING	F	12	296	DOWSE	J	2	105
DOVEY	EE	3	49	DOWLING	L	11	110	DOWNING	FM	7	107	DOWSE	JH	4	113
DOVEY	F	6	117	DOWLING	M	2	104	DOWNING	H	5	106	DOWSE	MA	4	113
DOVEY	FH	12	296	DOWLING	S	3	326	DOWNING	J	6	117	DOWSE	SH	2	105
DOVEY	H	11	110	DOWLING	WJ	10	289	DOWNING	J	11	110	DOWSE	W	13	137
DOVEY	ST	1	91	DOWLINGS	W	6	117	DOWNING	JE	11	110	DOWSE	WF	4	113
DOVEY	WH	1	91	DOWMAN	AH	5	106	DOWNING	JW	3	49	DOWSETT	AN	10	67
DOVEY	WJ	3	49	DOWN	AW	2	104	DOWNING	JWS	3	49	DOWSETT	G	2	105
DOWAS	A	8	95	DOWN	EW	3	49	DOWNING	M	10	67	DOWSETT	GAT	13	137
DOWDALL	G	11	110	DOWN	F	12	74	DOWNING	P	10	67	DOWSETT	HH	7	107
DOWDELL	H	10	289	DOWN	FG	13	137	DOWNING	T	6	117	DOWSETT	HR	10	67
DOWDEN	FJW	12	296	DOWN	H	12	74	DOWNING	T	12	296	DOWSETT	JF	13	137
DOWDEN	W	13	136	DOWN	ST	13	137	DOWNING	TG	6	117	DOWSETT	P	10	67
DOWDESWELL	J	3	326	DOWN	WF	4	112	DOWNING	TM	11	111	DOWSETT	WH	1	91
DOWDESWELL	WC	7	107	DOWNE	HH	3	49	DOWNING	W	5	106	DOWSING	HS	3	327
DOWDESWELL	WG	7	107	DOWNER	AW	10	290	DOWNING	W	6	117	DOWSON	A	12	296
DOWDING	A	7	107	DOWNER	DE	10	290	DOWNING	WD	6	118	DOWSON	CSS	4	113
DOWDING	AE	4	112	DOWNER	EC	10	290	DOWNING	WH	11	111	DOWSON	J	9	250
DOWDING	CS	11	110	DOWNER	FC	4	112	DOWNS	A	11	111	DOWSON	JA	2	105
DOWDING	HC	3	49	DOWNER	FL	10	290	DOWNS	A	13	137	DOWSON	S	1	91
DOWDING	HCJ	4	112	DOWNER	JH	10	290	DOWNS	AJ	2	104	DOWTON	ER	13	137
DOWDING	JH	4	112	DOWNER	JW	3	326	DOWNS	AJ	13	137	DOWZALL	AE	1	91
DOWDING	LG	7	107	DOWNER	LT	4	112	DOWNS	CH	1	91	DOWZALL	HF	2	105
DOWDY	A	12	296	DOWNER	PB	13	137	DOWNS	CW	1	91	DOXEY	F	10	67
DOWE	T	8	95	DOWNER	RE	10	290	DOWNS	E	1	91	DOXEY	N	9	250
DOWELL	HCF	2	104	DOWNER	RJ	4	113	DOWNS	F	1	91	DOYLE	A	3	327
DOWELL	LE	13	136	DOWNER	WA	4	113	DOWNS	FW	2	104	DOYLE	A	11	111
DOWELL	W	3	49	DOWNER	WC	4	113	DOWNS	G	1	91	DOYLE	A	11	111
DOWER	J	2	104	DOWNER	WF	3	326	DOWNS	H	14	90	DOYLE	AJ	1	91
DOWIE	EC	13	136	DOWNER	WG	4	113	DOWNS	J	8	96	DOYLE	CG	8	96
DOWIE	HJ	13	136	DOWNER	WG	10	290	DOWNS	J	11	111	DOYLE	F	8	96
DOWIE	RW	13	136	DOWNES	CJ	4	113	DOWNS	J	11	111	DOYLE	F	8	96
DOWLE	AG	4	112	DOWNES	CW	4	113	DOWNS	JGA	2	104	DOYLE	F	11	111
DOWLE	RHD	1	91	DOWNES	F	3	326	DOWNS	N	14	90	DOYLE	H	7	107
DOWLE	W	10	66	DOWNES	F	6	117	DOWNS	P	8	96	DOYLE	H	14	90
DOWLE	W	10	67	DOWNES	F	11	110	DOWNS	RK	2	105	DOYLE	HP	11	111
DOWLER	E	12	74	DOWNES	FW	13	137	DOWNS	S	10	67	DOYLE	I	8	96
DOWLER	RW	12	74	DOWNES	J	6	117	DOWNS	W	1	91	DOYLE	J	1	91
DOWLEY	AS	11	110	DOWNES	JT	2	104	DOWNS	WH	14	90	DOYLE	J	3	50
DOWLEY	EN	10	289	DOWNES	R	2	104	DOWNSBOROUGH	E	8	96	DOYLE	J	7	107
DOWLEY	NW	11	110	DOWNES	W	14	90	DOWNSON	FH	14	90	DOYLE	J	9	57
DOWLING	A	2	104	DOWNEY	A	11	110	DOWNTON	FW	3	50	DOYLE	J	9	250
DOWLING	BF	4	112	DOWNEY	A	14	90	DOWNTON	J	3	50	DOYLE	J	9	384
DOWLING	CF	1	91	DOWNEY	C	4	113	DOWRICK	RC	4	113	DOYLE	J	11	111
DOWLING	E	1	91	DOWNEY	F	13	137	DOWRICK	TL	4	113	DOYLE	J	14	90
DOWLING	GHW	13	137	DOWNEY	FF	13	137	DOWRY	HT	3	327	DOYLE	J	14	90
DOWLING	H	1	91	DOWNEY	H	13	137	DOWSE	A	9	249	DOYLE	JG	11	111
DOWLING	H	4	112	DOWNEY	JJ	4	113	DOWSE	AW	13	137	DOYLE	JJ	11	111
DOWLING	H	10	289	DOWNEY	T	4	113	DOWSE	CP	3	327	DOYLE	JW	8	96
DOWLING	H	14	89	DOWNEY	T	8	95	DOWSE	DA	2	105	DOYLE	L	7	107
DOWLING	HH	10	289	DOWNHAM	WF	2	104	DOWSE	DF	13	137	DOYLE	RV	13	137
DOWLING	HL	7	107	DOWNING	AJ	1	91	DOWSE	EA	2	105	DOYLE	W	3	327

DOYLE	W	11	111	DRAKE	FC	7	107	DRAPER	AC	5	107	DRAY	JF	13	138
DOYLE	W	14	90	DRAKE	FE	1	92	DRAPER	AC	10	68	DRAY	P	13	138
DOYLE	W	14	90	DRAKE	FE	5	107	DRAPER	AE	4	114	DRAY	SJ	13	138
DOYLE	WH	4	113	DRAKE	FS	4	114	DRAPER	AL	7	108	DRAYCOTT	B	8	96
DRABBLE	J	8	96	DRAKE	G	14	90	DRAPER	AW	5	107	DRAYCOTT	E	8	96
DRACKETT	AE	10	67	DRAKE	GF	9	250	DRAPER	C	1	92	DRAYCOTT	M	5	108
DRACKLEY	TG	5	106	DRAKE	GL	4	114	DRAPER	C	12	297	DRAYCOTT	WH	5	108
DRACUP	AF	12	74	DRAKE	GM	5	107	DRAPER	CG	7	108	DRAYSON	AA	13	138
DRACUP	B	9	250	DRAKE	GR	13	138	DRAPER	D	5	107	DRAYTON	AH	10	68
DRACUP	F	9	250	DRAKE	GWE	7	107	DRAPER	E	6	118	DRAYTON	G	1	92
DRAGE	A	12	296	DRAKE	H	1	92	DRAPER	E	11	111	DRAYTON	HS	1	92
DRAGE	A	12	297	DRAKE	H	4	114	DRAPER	EA	5	107	DRAYTON	RC	4	114
DRAGE	AE	10	67	DRAKE	H	5	107	DRAPER	F	1	92	DRAYTON	WG	4	114
DRAGE	CE	12	297	DRAKE	H	5	107	DRAPER	F	3	327	DREDGE	HA	1	92
DRAGE	ES	12	297	DRAKE	H	7	107	DRAPER	F	12	74	DREELING	MF	2	105
DRAGE	F	12	297	DRAKE	H	8	96	DRAPER	FA	5	107	DREIER	LJ	10	68
DRAGE	G	12	74	DRAKE	H	13	138	DRAPER	FC	5	107	DRENNAN	C	10	68
DRAGE	H	12	74	DRAKE	HE	7	107	DRAPER	FT	5	107	DRESCH	WV	7	108
DRAGE	J	12	297	DRAKE	HG	13	138	DRAPER	FW	4	114	DREW	A	3	327
DRAGE	P	12	297	DRAKE	HJ	7	107	DRAPER	G	6	118	DREW	A	6	118
DRAGE	TW	12	74	DRAKE	IF	9	250	DRAPER	GA	5	107	DREW	AC	5	108
DRAGE	W	12	297	DRAKE	INF	9	250	DRAPER	GF	4	114	DREW	AR	13	138
DRAGON	A	4	113	DRAKE	J	1	92	DRAPER	GS	3	50	DREW	AV	10	68
DRAGON	G	4	113	DRAKE	J	1	92	DRAPER	GV	3	50	DREW	BF	3	327
DRAGON	J	4	113	DRAKE	J	9	57	DRAPER	GW	5	107	DREW	ET	13	139
DRAIN	A	10	67	DRAKE	J	13	138	DRAPER	GW	7	108	DREW	H	1	92
DRAIN	A	13	138	DRAKE	J	13	138	DRAPER	H	1	92	DREW	H	1	92
DRAIN	AH	10	67	DRAKE	JE	10	67	DRAPER	H	1	92	DREW	J	6	118
DRAIN	F	10	67	DRAKE	JE	13	138	DRAPER	H	2	105	DREW	MC	3	327
DRAIN	GA	10	67	DRAKE	P	1	92	DRAPER	H	5	107	DREW	PW	7	108
DRAIN	JR	13	138	DRAKE	P	13	138	DRAPER	H	6	118	DREW	R	11	111
DRAIN	R	10	67	DRAKE	R	14	90	DRAPER	H	7	108	DREW	S	14	90
DRAIN	WJ	10	67	DRAKE	RG	10	67	DRAPER	H	13	138	DREW	SE	11	111
DRAKE	A	3	50	DRAKE	RO	2	105	DRAPER	HC	12	74	DREW	W	8	96
DRAKE	A	5	106	DRAKE	SC	4	114	DRAPER	HH	3	327	DREW	WH	4	114
DRAKE	A	7	107	DRAKE	SH	10	290	DRAPER	J	5	107	DREWELL	EM	2	105
DRAKE	AS	3	327	DRAKE	T	4	114	DRAPER	J	6	118	DREWELL	SW	2	105
DRAKE	AT	4	114	DRAKE	TE	4	114	DRAPER	L	4	114	DREWETT	FF	13	139
DRAKE	B	4	114	DRAKE	TE	4	114	DRAPER	LA	3	327	DREWETT	HW	13	139
DRAKE	C	2	105	DRAKE	TG	1	92	DRAPER	LW	5	107	DREWITT	W	5	108
DRAKE	C	8	96	DRAKE	W	3	327	DRAPER	P	5	107	DREWREY	TW	1	92
DRAKE	CH	9	250	DRAKE	W	3	327	DRAPER	RJ	12	74	DRING	G	8	96
DRAKE	CW	8	96	DRAKE	W	8	96	DRAPER	S	5	107	DRING	H	12	74
DRAKE	D	2	105	DRAKE	W	8	96	DRAPER	SEC	2	105	DRING	J	12	74
DRAKE	D	5	106	DRAKE	W	9	57	DRAPER	TW	14	90	DRING	WH	3	50
DRAKE	D	8	96	DRAKE	WG	13	138	DRAPER	W	2	105	DRINKALL	CA	9	57
DRAKE	E	13	138	DRAKE	WH	3	327	DRAPER	W	4	114	DRINKALL	H	9	250
DRAKE	EG	2	105	DRAKE	WJ	2	105	DRAPER	W	5	108	DRINKROW	JW	11	111
DRAKE	EJ	3	50	DRAKE	WS	7	108	DRAPER	W	5	108	DRINKWATER	AT	7	108
DRAKE	EW	10	67	DRAKE	WH	8	96	DRAPER	W	11	111	DRINKWATER	E	11	112
DRAKE	F	4	114	DRAKEFORD	WH	8	96	DRAPER	WH	5	108	DRINKWATER	F	6	118
DRAKE	F	13	138	DRANE	CH	13	138	DRAPER	WH	7	108	DRINKWATER	F	6	118
DRAKE	F	14	90	DRANE	J	11	111	DRAWATER	FH	1	92	DRINKWATER	GA	1	92
DRAKE	FA	1	92	DRANSFIELD	CR	9	57	DRAWWATER	W	3	327	DRINKWATER	H	14	90
DRAKE	FC	4	114	DRANSFIELD	JR	5	107	DRAPER	A	6	118	DRAY	ETE	1	92	DRINKWATER	J	1	92

DRINKWATER	J	12	297	DRURY	E	9	58	DUCKWORTH	E	9	384	DUDLEY	W	4	115	DUDLEY	W	4	115
DRINKWATER	JJ	14	91	DRURY	GH	5	108	DUCKWORTH	H	9	58	DUDLEY	W	5	109	DUDLEY	W	5	109
DRINKWATER	JW	1	92	DRURY	H	8	97	DUCKWORTH	J	6	118	DUDLEY	WA	5	109	DUDLEY	WA	5	109
DRINKWATER	PM	13	139	DRURY	J	8	97	DUCKWORTH	J	9	250	DUDLEY	WG	7	109	DUDLEY	WG	7	109
DRINKWATER	T	2	105	DRURY	RG	5	108	DUCKWORTH	J	11	112	DUDLEY	WJ	1	93	DUDLEY	WJ	1	93
DRINKWATER	TW	14	91	DRURY	S	3	328	DUCKWORTH	J	14	91	DUDMAN	AV	1	93	DUDMAN	AV	1	93
DRINKWATER	W	1	92	DRURY	W	2	106	DUCKWORTH	JH	6	118	DUDMAN	CE	13	139	DUDMAN	CE	13	139
DRINKWATER	W	6	118	DRY	W	8	97	DUCKWORTH	L	9	58	DUDMAN	F	10	290	DUDMAN	F	10	290
DRINKWATER	W	11	112	DRY	WN	2	106	DUCKWORTH	R	9	58	DUDMAN	FJ	13	139	DUDMAN	FJ	13	139
DRISCOLL	A	4	115	DRYDEN	AH	3	328	DUCKWORTH	R	9	250	DUDSON	A	11	112	DUDSON	A	11	112
DRISCOLL	A	8	97	DRYDEN	C	10	290	DUCKWORTH	T	9	250	DUELL	EC	4	115	DUELL	EC	4	115
DRISCOLL	A	14	91	DRYDEN	J	3	328	DUCKWORTH	W	14	91	DUER	ETG	2	106	DUER	ETG	2	106
DRISCOLL	AH	3	327	DRYE	FG	7	109	DUCKWORTH	WE	8	97	DUFALL	GH	10	290	DUFALL	GH	10	290
DRISCOLL	C	7	108	DRYE	J	8	97	DUDDEN	JF	2	106	DUFALL	T	10	290	DUFALL	T	10	290
DRISCOLL	D	3	50	DRYERRE	HE	5	108	DUDDERIDGE	C	7	109	DUFF	AJ	10	68	DUFF	AJ	10	68
DRISCOLL	D	3	327	DRYHURST	J	6	118	DUDDERIDGE	H	7	109	DUFF	H	14	91	DUFF	H	14	91
DRISCOLL	DJ	7	108	DRYSDALE	H	14	91	DUDDERIDGE	J	7	109	DUFF	W	2	106	DUFF	W	2	106
DRISCOLL	G	1	93	DRYWOOD	FH	7	109	DUDDING	FWG	4	115	DUFFELL	AJ	7	109	DUFFELL	AJ	7	109
DRISCOLL	J	3	327	DUARTE	W	4	115	DUDDLE	A	11	112	DUFFELL	GE	6	119	DUFFELL	GE	6	119
DRISCOLL	JM	13	139	DUBBER	AE	10	290	DUDDRIDGE	E	2	106	DUFFELL	J	2	106	DUFFELL	J	2	106
DRISCOLL	JR	3	328	DUBBER	FJ	10	68	DUDDRIDGE	GH	5	108	DUFFELL	SE	3	328	DUFFELL	SE	3	328
DRISCOLL	M	3	328	DUBBER	G	10	68	DUDEY	F	5	108	DUFFETT	W	10	291	DUFFETT	W	10	291
DRISCOLL	P	7	108	DUBBER	R	7	109	DUDFIELD	WG	6	118	DUFFEY	JW	14	91	DUFFEY	JW	14	91
DRISCOLL	T	13	139	DUBERY	AV	1	93	DUDLEY	A	10	290	DUFFEY	T	11	112	DUFFEY	T	11	112
DRISCOLL	TE	7	108	DUBERY	GA	2	106	DUDLEY	A	12	74	DUFFIELD	A	8	97	DUFFIELD	A	8	97
DRISCOLL	W	7	108	DUBERY	RG	2	106	DUDLEY	A	12	74	DUFFIELD	AF	11	112	DUFFIELD	AF	11	112
DRIVER	CE	12	297	DUBERY	RJ	1	93	DUDLEY	AC	13	139	DUFFIELD	F	8	97	DUFFIELD	F	8	97
DRIVER	H	7	108	DUCE	H	9	58	DUDLEY	AJ	6	118	DUFFIELD	J	2	106	DUFFIELD	J	2	106
DRIVER	H	9	58	DUCE	J	8	97	DUDLEY	BT	2	106	DUFFIELD	JW	7	109	DUFFIELD	JW	7	109
DRIVER	H	9	58	DUCE	W	8	97	DUDLEY	BW	12	297	DUFFIELD	LV	6	119	DUFFIELD	LV	6	119
DRIVER	H	14	91	DUCK	A	4	115	DUDLEY	D	13	139	DUFFIELD	RG	2	106	DUFFIELD	RG	2	106
DRIVER	H	14	91	DUCK	A	7	109	DUDLEY	E	10	68	DUFFIELD	SN	1	93	DUFFIELD	SN	1	93
DRIVER	HC	5	108	DUCK	AE	10	290	DUDLEY	E	12	297	DUFFIELD	T	8	97	DUFFIELD	T	8	97
DRIVER	R	11	112	DUCK	CL	4	115	DUDLEY	ED	5	108	DUFFILL	E	6	119	DUFFILL	E	6	119
DRIVER	R	11	112	DUCK	EH	4	115	DUDLEY	EM	1	93	DUFFILL	GA	10	291	DUFFILL	GA	10	291
DRIVER	W	10	68	DUCK	G	7	109	DUDLEY	F	1	93	DUFFIN	AJ	4	115	DUFFIN	AJ	4	115
DRIVETT	FC	2	105	DUCK	H	7	109	DUDLEY	F	14	91	DUFFIN	CW	4	115	DUFFIN	CW	4	115
DRUCE	JH	2	106	DUCK	SV	10	68	DUDLEY	FW	12	74	DUFFIN	E	4	115	DUFFIN	E	4	115
DRUCE	JS	7	108	DUCK	TH	5	108	DUDLEY	G	5	108	DUFFIN	G	10	291	DUFFIN	G	10	291
DRUCE	L	14	91	DUCK	WC	1	93	DUDLEY	H	6	118	DUFFIN	GH	4	115	DUFFIN	GH	4	115
DRUCE	SH	2	106	DUCK	WG	3	50	DUDLEY	H	10	68	DUFFIN	H	4	115	DUFFIN	H	4	115
DRUCE	W	2	106	DUCKENFIELD	FH	6	118	DUDLEY	HEY	12	297	DUFFIN	J	5	109	DUFFIN	J	5	109
DRUCE	WJ	7	108	DUCKER	J	10	68	DUDLEY	HJ	12	75	DUFFIN	TC	4	115	DUFFIN	TC	4	115
DRUMEY	TA	2	106	DUCKER	J	14	91	DUDLEY	J	6	118	DUFFIN	W	10	68	DUFFIN	W	10	68
DRUMMOND	HC	7	108	DUCKER	W	14	91	DUDLEY	J	14	91	DUFFING	BA	10	68	DUFFING	BA	10	68
DRUMMOND	J	10	68	DUCKETT	F	6	118	DUDLEY	JW	10	68	DUFFING	FA	10	68	DUFFING	FA	10	68
DRUMMOND	JF	7	108	DUCKETT	H	8	97	DUDLEY	JW	13	139	DUFFY	AB	3	328	DUFFY	AB	3	328
DRUMMOND	M	11	112	DUCKETT	H	9	58	DUDLEY	LW	10	290	DUFFY	B	9	58	DUFFY	B	9	58
DRUMMOND	P	14	91	DUCKETT	HE	7	109	DUDLEY	OF	4	115	DUFFY	C	4	115	DUFFY	C	4	115
DRUMMOND	RC	3	328	DUCKETT	JE	7	109	DUDLEY	P	5	108	DUFFY	CG	11	112	DUFFY	CG	11	112
DRUMMOND	SB	7	109	DUCKETT	W	9	58	DUDLEY	R	12	297	DUFFY	D	8	97	DUFFY	D	8	97
DRUMMOND	SF	3	328	DUCKETT	WT	2	106	DUDLEY	T	5	108	DUFFY	DE	11	112	DUFFY	DE	11	112
DRUMMOND	W	3	328	DUCKHAM	S	8	97	DUDLEY	T	5	108	DUFFY	E	6	119	DUFFY	E	6	119
DRUMMY	P	7	109	DUCKWORTH	A	8	97	DUDLEY	T	14	91	DUFFY	E	8	97	DUFFY	E	8	97
DRURY	E	8	97	DUCKWORTH	AH	8	97	DUDLEY	W	1	93	DUFFY	E	9	58	DUFFY	E	9	58

DUFFY	EH	13	139	DUGDALE	F	11	112	DULSON	T	6	119	DUNCAN	W	4	116
DUFFY	F	9	384	DUGDALE	J	11	113	DUMARESQ	AJ	4	116	DUNCAN	WF	3	50
DUFFY	F	13	139	DUGDALE	J	11	113	DUMAYNE	GH	12	297	DUNCOMBE	FJ	12	75
DUFFY	F	14	91	DUGDALE	S	4	115	DUMBELTON	GJ	5	109	DUNCOMBE	H	7	110
DUFFY	H	8	97	DUGDALE	V	4	115	DUMBELTON	HW	5	109	DUNCOMBE	LD	3	50
DUFFY	H	11	112	DUGDALE	W	4	116	DUMBLETON	JH	11	113	DUNDAS	G	4	116
DUFFY	J	3	328	DUGGAN	AM	13	139	DUMBLETON	JJ	13	140	DUNDEE	H	4	116
DUFFY	J	8	97	DUGGAN	AW	10	69	DUMBRELL	A	10	69	DUNDEE	W	4	116
DUFFY	J	8	98	DUGGAN	F	13	139	DUMBRELL	GE	13	140	DUNDERDALE	E	8	98
DUFFY	J	8	98	DUGGAN	J	1	93	DUMBRELL	H	10	69	DUNDERDALE	JM	8	98
DUFFY	J	8	98	DUGGAN	J	3	328	DUMMER	A	1	93	DUNEASE	T	11	113
DUFFY	J	9	58	DUGGAN	J	6	119	DUMMER	AGW	1	93	DUNFORD	A	4	116
DUFFY	J	9	58	DUGGAN	J	7	109	DUMMER	JP	2	107	DUNFORD	B	13	140
DUFFY	J	9	250	DUGGAN	JM	13	139	DUMMER	WC	4	116	DUNFORD	F	4	116
DUFFY	J	14	91	DUGGAN	P	11	113	DUMPER	EJ	10	291	DUNFORD	FG	10	69
DUFFY	J	14	92	DUGGAN	R	9	59	DUMPER	GE	10	69	DUNFORD	G	2	107
DUFFY	JE	1	93	DUGGAN	W	9	250	DUMPER	GV	10	69	DUNFORD	GA	11	113
DUFFY	JF	9	58	DUGGAN	W	13	139	DUMPER	W	4	116	DUNFORD	HA	4	117
DUFFY	JF	11	112	DUGGATT	W	11	113	DUMPHREY	J	11	113	DUNFORD	HE	5	109
DUFFY	JH	8	98	DUGGIN	WH	8	98	DUMPLETON	P	5	109	DUNFORD	J	5	109
DUFFY	JT	4	115	DUGMORE	E	6	119	DUMVILLE	N	11	113	DUNFORD	J	13	140
DUFFY	JT	14	92	DUGMORE	F	6	119	DUNBAR	ET	3	328	DUNFORD	JW	13	140
DUFFY	JW	11	112	DUGMORE	FR	6	119	DUNBAR	FW	4	116	DUNFORD	R	6	119
DUFFY	JW	14	92	DUGMORE	H	10	69	DUNBAR	H	14	92	DUNFORD	RJ	6	119
DUFFY	L	14	92	DUGMORE	JE	6	119	DUNBAR	J	14	92	DUNFORD	S	4	116
DUFFY	M	8	98	DUIGMAN	JJ	6	119	DUNBAR	J	14	92	DUNFORD	SL	4	116
DUFFY	R	8	98	DUKE	AJE	13	139	DUNBAR	JW	9	59	DUNFORD	TJ	13	140
DUFFY	S	9	58	DUKE	CT	2	106	DUNBAR	N	2	107	DUNFORD	W	13	140
DUFFY	T	9	250	DUKE	FC	7	110	DUNBAR	RJ	12	75	DUNGAY	H	9	250
DUFFY	T	11	112	DUKE	FW	1	93	DUNBAR	S	14	92	DUNHAM	AC	1	94
DUFFY	T	11	112	DUKE	FW	2	106	DUNBAR	T	11	113	DUNHAM	AJ	12	75
DUFFY	T	14	92	DUKE	G	7	110	DUNBAR	WH	11	113	DUNHAM	CS	1	94
DUFFY	T	14	92	DUKE	GA	10	69	DUNCAN	AE	14	92	DUNHAM	D	12	75
DUFFY	TC	14	92	DUKE	HJ	2	106	DUNCAN	AT	1	93	DUNHAM	DA	1	94
DUFFY	TL	2	106	DUKE	J	10	69	DUNCAN	D	3	50	DUNHAM	MCW	12	75
DUFFY	W	9	58	DUKE	JJW	10	69	DUNCAN	D	8	98	DUNHAM	SA	14	92
DUFFY	W	9	58	DUKE	RL	14	92	DUNCAN	E	1	94	DUNHAM	WAJ	2	107
DUFFY	W	9	250	DUKE	RM	10	69	DUNCAN	E	11	113	DUNHAM	WC	12	75
DUFFY	WP	1	93	DUKE	TG	13	140	DUNCAN	EEE	7	110	DUNHILL	A	8	98
DUFFY	WP	14	92	DUKE	WG	7	110	DUNCAN	H	6	119	DUNICLIFF	FG	3	50
DUFOUR	AH	1	93	DUKE	WH	13	140	DUNCAN	HA	2	107	DUNING	WR	13	140
DUFOUR	SL	1	93	DUKES	AC	2	107	DUNCAN	J	1	94	DUNK	B	1	94
DUFTON	H	8	98	DUKES	AL	1	93	DUNCAN	J	8	98	DUNK	E	7	110
DUFTON	H	9	58	DUKES	AW	13	140	DUNCAN	J	8	98	DUNK	HW	7	110
DUFTON	H	9	58	DUKES	CE	5	109	DUNCAN	J	13	140	DUNK	WH	2	107
DUFTON	H	9	250	DUKES	E	2	107	DUNCAN	JP	3	50	DUNKASON	A	4	116
DUFTON	J	8	98	DUKES	H	6	119	DUNCAN	JT	1	94	DUNKASON	E	4	116
DUFTON	J	9	59	DUKES	HH	5	109	DUNCAN	K	14	92	DUNKASON	FR	4	116
DUFTON	W	8	98	DUKES	TJ	3	328	DUNCAN	P	1	94	DUNKASON	HA	4	116
DUFTY	E	4	115	DUKES	W	10	291	DUNCAN	RF	2	107	DUNKASON	W	4	116
DUGAN	B	10	68	DULAKE	SH	7	110	DUNCAN	RG	6	119	DUNKERLEY	C	11	113
DUGAN	H	10	68	DULEY	R	1	93	DUNCAN	RG	9	59	DUNKERLEY	D	11	113
DUGAN	PJ	12	297	DULLEY	E	13	140	DUNCAN	RHH	1	94	DUNKERLEY	GH	11	113
DUGDALE	AR	7	109	DULSON	A	14	92	DUNCAN	RJ	7	110	DUNKERLEY	W	11	113
DUGDALE	C	11	112	DULSON	T	1	93	DUNCAN	T	9	59	DUNKERTON	FJ	2	107

DUNKIN	AG	13	140	DUNLOP	WJ	4	116	DUNN	JR	11	113	DUNNING	SC	5	109
DUNKLEY	A	5	109	DUNLOP	WW	4	117	DUNN	L	9	59	DUNNING	W	14	93
DUNKLEY	A	7	110	DUNMORE	FC	13	140	DUNN	L	11	114	DUNNINGS	A	4	117
DUNKLEY	A	12	297	DUNMORE	G	12	298	DUNN	LA	5	109	DUNNINGS	A	4	117
DUNKLEY	A	12	297	DUNMORE	HJ	12	298	DUNN	M	14	93	DUNNINGS	H	4	117
DUNKLEY	A	12	297	DUNMOW	J	1	94	DUNN	N	8	99	DUNNINGS	H	4	117
DUNKLEY	A	12	298	DUNN	A	2	107	DUNN	OJ	13	141	DUNNINGTON	A	8	99
DUNKLEY	A	13	140	DUNN	A	6	119	DUNN	P	8	99	DUNSDON	E	1	94
DUNKLEY	A	14	92	DUNN	A	6	120	DUNN	PE	5	109	DUNSFORD	GT	2	108
DUNKLEY	AA	12	298	DUNN	A	9	59	DUNN	R	11	114	DUNSHEE	ER	6	120
DUNKLEY	AE	12	75	DUNN	AC	2	107	DUNN	S	8	99	DUNSHEE	H	6	120
DUNKLEY	AJ	10	69	DUNN	AE	2	107	DUNN	S	9	59	DUNSHEE	JLR	6	120
DUNKLEY	AT	12	298	DUNN	AE	9	250	DUNN	S	14	93	DUNSMUIR	F	4	117
DUNKLEY	CE	12	75	DUNN	AG	2	107	DUNN	SC	6	120	DUNSTAN	F	11	114
DUNKLEY	E	12	75	DUNN	AV	8	98	DUNN	SD	6	120	DUNSTAN	G	10	69
DUNKLEY	E	13	140	DUNN	B	6	120	DUNN	T	4	117	DUNSTAN	GAF	2	108
DUNKLEY	F	12	298	DUNN	B	8	98	DUNN	T	8	99	DUNSTAN	HJ	4	117
DUNKLEY	FC	12	75	DUNN	B	10	69	DUNN	T	8	99	DUNSTER	A	13	141
DUNKLEY	FG	12	298	DUNN	B	13	140	DUNN	T	11	114	DUNSTER	EC	13	141
DUNKLEY	G	12	75	DUNN	BE	14	93	DUNN	TC	6	120	DUNSTER	HJ	13	141
DUNKLEY	G	12	75	DUNN	C	6	120	DUNN	TJ	9	59	DUNSTER	TW	13	141
DUNKLEY	G	12	75	DUNN	C	7	110	DUNN	TJ	14	93	DUNSTONE	WJ	10	69
DUNKLEY	G	12	298	DUNN	C	8	98	DUNN	W	1	94	DUNTON	EI	3	329
DUNKLEY	H	12	298	DUNN	C	9	59	DUNN	W	6	120	DUNTON	J	1	94
DUNKLEY	HTW	12	75	DUNN	CE	9	250	DUNN	W	7	110	DUNTON	JC	2	108
DUNKLEY	J	10	69	DUNN	CJ	10	291	DUNN	W	7	110	DUNTON	JE	5	109
DUNKLEY	J	12	75	DUNN	D	7	110	DUNN	W	8	99	DUNTON	SW	13	141
DUNKLEY	J	12	298	DUNN	D	13	140	DUNN	W	11	114	DUNTON	TA	3	329
DUNKLEY	J	12	298	DUNN	E	9	59	DUNN	WA	10	69	DUNWELL	A	9	251
DUNKLEY	JC	7	110	DUNN	EM	3	328	DUNN	WA	12	298	DUNWELL	A	9	251
DUNKLEY	JE	6	119	DUNN	F	2	107	DUNN	WJ	1	94	DUNWELL	GS	8	99
DUNKLEY	JG	12	75	DUNN	F	9	59	DUNN	WJ	3	328	DUNWELL	J	8	99
DUNKLEY	JH	12	298	DUNN	G	8	98	DUNN	WJ	13	141	DUNWELL	JW	8	99
DUNKLEY	JR	10	69	DUNN	G	8	99	DUNN	WP	10	291	DUNWELL	JW	9	251
DUNKLEY	JW	12	75	DUNN	G	8	99	DUNN	WS	3	328	DUNWELL	M	9	59
DUNKLEY	L	12	75	DUNN	GA	6	120	DUNN	WS	3	329	DUNWOODIE	D	9	59
DUNKLEY	L	12	75	DUNN	GF	2	107	DUNNAGE	WJ	13	141	DUNWOODY	J	6	120
DUNKLEY	RW	12	298	DUNN	GH	6	120	DUNNE	A	3	50	DUNWOODY	SC	13	141
DUNKLEY	S	12	76	DUNN	H	2	107	DUNNE	J	11	114	DUNWORTH	E	3	329
DUNKLEY	S	12	298	DUNN	HR	12	298	DUNNE	J	14	93	DUPONTET	SFW	2	108
DUNKLEY	S	12	298	DUNN	HS	7	110	DUNNE	R	13	141	DUPOY	C	13	141
DUNKLEY	WEJ	12	298	DUNN	HT	13	141	DUNNE	R	14	93	DUPOY	FC	13	141
DUNKLEY	WR	12	298	DUNN	IT	2	107	DUNNE	T	14	93	DUPREE	W	2	108
DUNKLEY	WT	12	76	DUNN	J	6	120	DUNNE	TJ	9	251	DURACK	A	3	50
DUNKLEY	WT	12	76	DUNN	J	7	110	DUNNELL	W	8	99	DURACK	FC	1	94
DUNKLIN	P	2	107	DUNN	J	9	59	DUNNETT	HJS	1	94	DURAND	CV	13	141
DUNKLING	A	12	76	DUNN	J	9	59	DUNNETT	WJ	5	109	DURANT	DJ	10	291
DUNKLING	A	12	76	DUNN	J	9	59	DUNNING	A	2	107	DURANT	E	13	141
DUNKLING	FA	12	76	DUNN	J	9	251	DUNNING	CJH	13	141	DURANT	FWC	10	69
DUNLAVEY	JW	8	98	DUNN	J	11	113	DUNNING	E	8	99	DURANT	R	3	329
DUNLEAVY	F	6	119	DUNN	J	14	93	DUNNING	F	2	107	DURBIN	F	3	329
DUNLOP	D	11	113	DUNN	J	14	93	DUNNING	F	4	117	DURBIN	IF	3	329
DUNLOP	J	4	116	DUNN	J	14	93	DUNNING	FH	4	117	DURBIN	LA	1	94
DUNLOP	RM	1	94	DUNN	JH	1	94	DUNNING	HJ	4	117	DURBRIDGE	M	7	110
DUNLOP	WH	12	298	DUNN	JL	9	251	DUNNING	S	1	94	DURDEN	RC	12	299

DURDIN	A	6	120	DURRANT	FA	2	108	DUTTON	J	14	93	DYER	AE	2	108
DURDIN	WG	6	120	DURRANT	FA	13	142	DUTTON	J	14	93	DYER	AG	1	95
DURE	W	3	329	DURRANT	GT	1	95	DUTTON	J	14	93	DYER	AW	3	50
DUREE	A	9	60	DURRANT	H	13	142	DUTTON	J	14	93	DYER	AW	8	100
DURELL	G	2	108	DURRANT	JT	10	70	DUTTON	JA	8	100	DYER	B	6	122
DURGAN	GC	7	110	DURRANT	M	5	110	DUTTON	JD	8	100	DYER	B	6	122
DURHAM	A	12	76	DURRANT	MW	5	110	DUTTON	JR	13	142	DYER	CJ	10	70
DURHAM	AE	10	291	DURRANT	R	1	95	DUTTON	JW	13	143	DYER	CR	10	70
DURHAM	CB	8	99	DURRANT	R	2	108	DUTTON	L	11	114	DYER	D	11	114
DURHAM	CW	5	109	DURRANT	R	5	110	DUTTON	L	14	93	DYER	E	3	51
DURHAM	FW	3	329	DURRANT	S	1	95	DUTTON	RA	9	60	DYER	E	6	121
DURHAM	G	8	99	DURRANT	SE	5	110	DUTTON	S	6	121	DYER	E	8	100
DURHAM	HA	7	111	DURRANT	SH	5	110	DUTTON	S	6	121	DYER	EJ	5	110
DURHAM	HA	12	76	DURRANT	WG	10	70	DUTTON	T	11	114	DYER	ER	2	108
DURHAM	HC	5	109	DURRANT	WJ	7	111	DUTTON	TH	8	100	DYER	F	5	110
DURHAM	J	2	108	DURRELL	JR	10	70	DUTTON	TJ	11	114	DYER	FH	3	329
DURHAM	J	5	109	DURTNALL	RF	10	70	DUTTON	TS	11	114	DYER	FJ	4	118
DURHAM	J	8	99	DUTFIELD	A	13	142	DUTTON	W	11	114	DYER	FW	2	108
DURHAM	WF	12	76	DUTFIELD	A	13	142	DUTTON	W	11	114	DYER	FW	10	291
DURKIN	F	9	384	DUTFIELD	C	13	142	DUTTON	W	14	93	DYER	G	6	122
DURKIN	J	8	99	DUTFIELD	ED	7	111	DUTTON	W	14	94	DYER	H	2	108
DURKIN	J	8	99	DUTFIELD	G	13	142	DUVALL	V	5	110	DYER	H	6	122
DURKIN	J	9	60	DUTFIELD	G	13	142	DUVALL	WG	5	110	DYER	HA	3	51
DURKIN	J	9	60	DUTFIELD	H	13	142	DUVALL	WT	5	110	DYER	HA	3	329
DURKIN	J	9	60	DUTFIELD	S	13	142	DUXBERRY	HH	3	50	DYER	J	1	95
DURKIN	J	9	251	DUTFIELD	SJ	7	111	DUXBURY	HH	8	100	DYER	J	8	100
DURKIN	J	9	384	DUTFIELD	T	13	142	DUXBURY	T	8	100	DYER	J	11	114
DURKIN	P	9	60	DUTFIELD	T	13	142	DWAN	G	13	143	DYER	J	14	94
DURKIN	TE	9	60	DUTSON	P	6	121	DWAN	R	8	100	DYER	JA	9	60
DURLING	AJ	13	141	DUTSON	P	8	99	DWANE	JH	6	121	DYER	JE	8	100
DURLING	TR	13	141	DUTSON	WL	6	121	DWANE	JW	6	121	DYER	JF	12	299
DURNELL	C	10	291	DUTTON	A	2	108	DWIAR	HC	3	329	DYER	JR	3	51
DURNFORD	AA	4	117	DUTTON	A	6	121	DWYER	A	14	94	DYER	R	3	51
DURNFORD	FW	4	117	DUTTON	A	7	111	DWYER	E	7	111	DYER	RA	3	51
DURNFORD	RG	4	117	DUTTON	A	11	114	DWYER	E	7	111	DYER	RG	10	70
DUROW	B	6	120	DUTTON	A	11	114	DWYER	HW	10	291	DYER	SJ	5	110
DUROW	CR	4	117	DUTTON	A	13	142	DWYER	JP	13	143	DYER	T	9	60
DUROW	F	4	117	DUTTON	AW	6	121	DWYER	P	9	60	DYER	T	10	291
DUROW	W	6	120	DUTTON	AW	6	121	DWYER	T	3	329	DYER	TC	13	143
DURR	J	14	93	DUTTON	DE	6	121	DWYER	W	10	70	DYER	VW	10	291
DURRANCE	A	9	60	DUTTON	E	8	100	DWYER	WP	2	108	DYER	W	2	108
DURRANS	H	8	99	DUTTON	EFH	2	108	DYALL	TH	1	95	DYER	W	9	60
DURRANS	H	9	60	DUTTON	F	6	121	DYAS	H	6	121	DYER	W	9	60
DURRANS	H	9	384	DUTTON	F	6	121	DYAS	JE	6	121	DYER	W	10	70
DURRANS	JG	4	117	DUTTON	F	11	114	DYBLE	JJ	4	117	DYER	W	10	291
DURRANT	A	5	110	DUTTON	F	11	114	DYDE	J	5	110	DYER	WE	6	122
DURRANT	A	13	142	DUTTON	F	13	142	DYE	A	7	111	DYER	WE	10	292
DURRANT	AH	6	120	DUTTON	F	14	93	DYE	AE	7	111	DYER	WE	13	143
DURRANT	C	1	94	DUTTON	G	6	121	DYE	DT	7	111	DYER	WG	10	70
DURRANT	CA	1	95	DUTTON	GE	13	142	DYE	EJ	7	111	DYER	WR	10	291
DURRANT	E	1	95	DUTTON	H	13	142	DYE	RJ	13	143	DYER	WR	13	143
DURRANT	E	2	108	DUTTON	HG	13	142	DYE	W	2	108	DYETT	C	13	143
DURRANT	EE	10	69	DUTTON	J	3	329	DYER	A	3	329	DYETT	J	13	143
DURRANT	EF	10	291	DUTTON	J	6	121	DYER	A	5	110	DYETT	WD	13	143
DURRANT	EG	13	142	DUTTON	J	9	251	DYER	A	13	143	DYETT	WT	13	143

DYHOUSE	FE	6	122
DYHOUSE	W	6	122
DYKE	CA	6	122
DYKE	CH	6	122
DYKE	EH	10	292
DYKE	FA	10	70
DYKE	FR	4	118
DYKE	GE	4	118
DYKE	GW	4	118
DYKE	H	3	51
DYKE	J	6	122
DYKE	MV	10	292
DYKE	PL	4	118
DYKE	R	10	292
DYKE	W	13	143
DYKE	WE	6	122
DYKE	WF	10	70
DYKES	CEL	4	118
DYKES	EJ	2	109
DYKES	RJ	9	60
DYKES	W	10	70
DYMOCK	ATJ	1	95
DYMOCK	GT	2	109
DYMOND	C	4	118
DYMOND	CH	13	143
DYMOND	HE	7	111
DYMOND	J	4	118
DYMOND	JD	3	329
DYMOTT	CW	4	118
DYMOTT	HE	4	118
DYMOTT	HS	4	118
DYMOTT	RF	4	118
DYMOTT	WE	4	118
DYMOTT	WJ	7	111
DYNE	FG	7	111
DYNE	L	7	111
DYNES	WJ	12	76
DYSON	B	9	251
DYSON	D	9	60
DYSON	E	5	110
DYSON	E	6	122
DYSON	E	9	60
DYSON	G	6	122
DYSON	GW	14	94
DYSON	H	6	122
DYSON	H	9	60
DYSON	HF	8	100
DYSON	J	9	251
DYSON	J	9	251
DYSON	J	14	94
DYSON	JA	14	94
DYSON	M	9	251
DYSON	P	11	114
DYSON	PS	8	100
DYSON	RJ	6	122
DYSON	S	6	122
DYSON	T	6	122
DYSON	T	8	100
DYSON	T	9	60
DYSON	W	9	251
DYSON	WG	11	114
DYTCH	S	14	94
DYTHAM	LT	12	76

E

EACOTT	T	8	100
EADDIE	A	8	100
EADE	A	1	95
EADE	AG	7	111
EADE	EA	7	111
EADE	J	1	95
EADE	M	1	95
EADES	A	7	112
EADES	A	13	143
EADES	A	13	143
EADES	C	4	118
EADES	FJ	4	118
EADES	G	4	118
EADES	G	4	118
EADES	GF	2	109
EADES	HJ	13	143
EADES	R	13	143
EADLE	HH	6	122
EADLE	J	5	110
EADS	HE	6	123
EADSFORTH	G	11	115
EADY	F	2	109
EAGAN	C	7	112
EAGER	E	2	109
EAGER	FE	5	110
EAGER	GF	10	292
EAGER	WF	5	110
EAGERS	EA	14	94
EAGERS	J	8	100
EAGLAN	F	8	100
EAGLAND	HJ	14	94
EAGLE	A	2	109
EAGLE	AG	12	299
EAGLE	CAG	13	143
EAGLE	CL	4	118
EAGLE	HC	2	109
EAGLE	J	3	329
EAGLE	J	7	112
EAGLE	J	7	112
EAGLE	JT	2	109
EAGLE	TCW	10	70
EAGLE	W	12	299
EAGLE	W	13	144
EAGLEN	AH	13	144
EAGLEN	J	8	100
EAGLEN	LE	7	112
EAGLES	AA	6	123
EAGLES	CH	6	123
EAGLES	E	2	109
EAGLES	GH	10	292
EAGLES	J	14	94
EAGLES	L	5	110
EAGLES	RE	12	76
EAGLES	SA	5	111
EAGLESTONE	EG	13	144
EAGLESTONE	WF	13	144
EAKINS	ES	12	299
EAKINS	JE	11	115
EALAND	JB	8	100
EALES	AA	12	299
EALES	AE	12	299
EALES	C	12	76
EALES	GT	2	109
EALES	GW	12	299
EALES	H	10	292
EALES	H	12	299
EALES	R	12	299
EALES	RB	12	299
EALES	SA	2	109
EALES	SA	2	109
EALES	WT	12	299
EALEY	J	1	95
EALING	FH	5	111
EAMES	AJ	5	111
EAMES	E	1	95
EAMES	FC	12	76
EAMES	G	1	95
EAMES	GW	5	111
EAMES	H	12	76
EAMES	HC	4	118
EAMES	J	1	95
EAMES	J	5	111
EAMES	JA	2	109
EAMES	JW	5	111
EAMES	LH	10	70
EAMES	RJ	12	76
EAMES	T	5	111
EAMES	W	5	111
EAMES	WG	10	70
EAMES	WH	7	112
EARDLEY	A	11	115
EARDLEY	A	14	94
EARDLEY	AWE	13	144
EARDLEY	J	11	115
EARDLEY	JA	14	94
EARDLEY	JL	13	144
EARDLEY	WJW	13	144
EARL	AJ	7	112
EARL	AW	12	76
EARL	DJ	12	76
EARL	EE	10	292
EARL	ELV	10	292
EARL	F	2	109
EARL	FA	6	123
EARL	FG	7	112
EARL	G	3	51
EARL	GL	5	111
EARL	GT	10	292
EARL	H	10	70
EARL	HS	5	111
EARL	JT	3	51
EARL	PA	10	71
EARL	R	5	111
EARL	R	6	123
EARL	S	10	71
EARL	SJS	13	144
EARL	T	7	112
EARL	TF	12	76
EARL	W	2	109
EARL	W	12	77
EARL	W	12	299
EARL	WC	13	144
EARL	WJ	7	112
EARL	WT	6	123
EARLE	AB	10	292
EARLE	E	7	112
EARLE	HCF	10	292
EARLE	JT	12	77
EARLE	MJ	4	119
EARLE	TH	10	292
EARLE	W	8	101
EARLEY	AJ	10	71
EARLEY	C	4	119
EARLEY	DJ	5	111
EARLEY	FC	4	119
EARLEY	FG	4	119
EARLEY	FTL	4	119
EARLEY	GT	13	144
EARLEY	HE	4	119
EARLEY	HE	11	115
EARLEY	R	13	144
EARLEY	T	13	144
EARLS	W	12	299
EARLY	GW	4	119
EARLY	HC	10	71
EARLY	HH	4	119
EARLY	J	9	384
EARNEY	AGA	4	119
EARNEY	J	7	112
EARNSHAW	E	14	94
EARNSHAW	FE	14	94
EARNSHAW	G	8	101
EARNSHAW	GH	11	115
EARNSHAW	J	8	101

EARNSHAW	J	11	115	EASTER	JR	3	51	EASTWELL	J	1	96	EATON	J	14	95
EARNSHAW	JW	11	115	EASTER	RJ	7	112	EASTWELL	WE	2	110	EATON	JAT	13	145
EARNSHAW	LW	9	251	EASTER	SA	1	96	EASTWICK	GT	2	110	EATON	JE	3	330
EARNSHAW	RA	11	115	EASTER	WE	3	51	EASTWOOD	A	8	101	EATON	JR	14	95
EARNSHAW	W	14	94	EASTER	WG	7	112	EASTWOOD	A	8	101	EATON	JT	11	116
EARP	AW	8	101	EASTERBY	H	9	251	EASTWOOD	A	11	115	EATON	JW	4	120
EARP	C	6	123	EASTERBY	W	4	119	EASTWOOD	A	11	115	EATON	O	5	112
EARP	E	6	123	EASTGATE	EJ	2	109	EASTWOOD	B	11	115	EATON	O	12	77
EARP	F	6	123	EASTGATE	J	13	144	EASTWOOD	E	9	251	EATON	RT	1	96
EARP	F	6	123	EASTHAM	GH	4	119	EASTWOOD	F	11	115	EATON	SJ	14	95
EARP	GH	6	123	EASTHAM	R	14	94	EASTWOOD	GF	8	101	EATON	T	2	110
EARP	W	11	115	EASTHAM	TE	11	115	EASTWOOD	H	11	115	EATON	T	11	116
EARTHEY	HR	5	111	EASTHAM	W	9	61	EASTWOOD	J	1	96	EATON	W	2	110
EARTHY	CA	7	112	EASTHER	H	7	112	EASTWOOD	J	8	101	EATON	W	11	116
EARTHY	WT	3	329	EASTHOPE	A	11	115	EASTWOOD	W	1	96	EATON	W	12	77
EARWAKER	CJ	4	119	EASTHOPE	W	6	123	EASY	S	8	101	EATON	W	13	145
EARWAKER	WH	4	119	EASTLAND	AW	10	71	EATCH	T	9	61	EATON	WF	12	77
EASEN	W	10	71	EASTLAND	CW	10	71	EATHERLEY	GE	4	120	EATON	WG	2	110
EASEN	W	10	71	EASTLAND	P	10	71	EATLY	FW	3	51	EATON	WS	7	113
EASMAN	FJ	13	144	EASTLAND	W	7	112	EATON	A	3	51	EATS	T	12	77
EASMAN	T	13	144	EASTLEIGH	AE	12	299	EATON	A	5	112	EATWELL	GH	6	123
EASON	A	12	299	EASTMAN	A	4	119	EATON	A	6	123	EAVES	AC	2	110
EASON	CW	3	51	EASTMAN	A	8	101	EATON	A	12	77	EAVES	CH	2	110
EASON	F	11	115	EASTMAN	AV	4	119	EATON	A	13	145	EAVES	R	6	123
EAST	A	5	111	EASTMAN	CW	4	119	EATON	AA	3	51	EAYKROYD	AE	9	251
EAST	AF	5	111	EASTMAN	FW	4	119	EATON	AE	3	330	EBBORN	C	4	120
EAST	CW	5	111	EASTMAN	G	8	101	EATON	AH	12	300	EBBS	G	11	116
EAST	CW	5	111	EASTMAN	OW	4	119	EATON	AJ	11	116	EBBS	HWJ	2	110
EAST	D	5	111	EASTMAN	W	7	113	EATON	C	12	77	EBBS	L	5	112
EAST	EW	12	299	EASTMAN	W	13	144	EATON	CE	1	96	EBBS	R	1	96
EAST	F	12	77	EASTMAN	WH	4	119	EATON	CJ	3	330	EBBS	W	1	96
EAST	FG	13	144	EASTMAN	WS	4	119	EATON	CL	3	330	EBDON	G	3	330
EAST	G	5	111	EASTMEAD	WE	10	292	EATON	D	13	145	EBERS	GJ	2	110
EAST	GW	3	51	EASTMENT	M	2	109	EATON	E	11	116	EBNER	AE	3	330
EAST	J	5	111	EASTMENT	W	12	299	EATON	F	3	330	ECCLES	AH	11	116
EAST	J	12	299	EASTOE	D	2	109	EATON	F	5	112	ECCLES	CH	3	330
EAST	J	13	144	EASTON	A	13	145	EATON	F	5	112	ECCLES	E	14	95
EAST	JC	1	95	EASTON	CJ	5	112	EATON	FH	2	110	ECCLES	H	9	61
EAST	JW	1	95	EASTON	CW	5	112	EATON	FW	12	77	ECCLES	H	11	116
EAST	N	1	95	EASTON	DJE	10	292	EATON	G	3	51	ECCLES	H	14	95
EAST	PA	5	112	EASTON	E	10	292	EATON	G	13	145	ECCLES	H	14	95
EAST	T	3	329	EASTON	F	13	145	EATON	G	13	145	ECCLES	H	14	95
EAST	TR	1	95	EASTON	G	4	120	EATON	G	14	94	ECCLES	P	9	61
EAST	W	3	329	EASTON	H	10	71	EATON	GF	3	330	ECCLES	P	9	251
EAST	WG	1	95	EASTON	HC	7	113	EATON	GF	13	145	ECCLES	R	14	95
EAST	WG	5	112	EASTON	R	3	330	EATON	GT	10	292	ECCLES	S	14	95
EAST	WJ	5	112	EASTON	R	8	101	EATON	H	3	51	ECCLES	W	9	61
EASTAFF	T	1	95	EASTON	R	13	145	EATON	H	12	77	ECCLES	W	13	145
EASTBURN	F	8	101	EASTON	S	2	110	EATON	HJ	12	77	ECCLESTON	B	14	95
EASTBURN	JA	8	101	EASTON	TC	7	113	EATON	J	6	123	ECCLESTON	BB	6	123
EASTER	AG	13	144	EASTON	W	4	120	EATON	J	11	116	ECCLESTON	CSP	6	123
EASTER	AH	1	96	EASTOUGH	FW	2	110	EATON	J	12	77	ECCLESTON	J	14	95
EASTER	FS	2	109	EASTWELL	AF	12	77	EATON	J	12	77	ECCLESTON	W	6	123
EASTER	GH	7	112	EASTWELL	F	1	96	EATON	J	14	94	ECKEL	AH	6	123
EASTER	HP	10	71	EASTWELL	FC	2	110	EATON	J	14	95	ECKERSALL	A	14	95

ECKERSLEY	C	11	116
ECKERSLEY	J	11	116
ECKERSLEY	R	14	95
ECKERSLEY	R	14	95
ECKERSLEY	WT	14	95
ECKETT	WC	1	96
ECKFORD	JW	11	116
ECKFORD	PGP	4	120
ECKFORD	W	11	116
ECKHOFF	RE	13	145
ECKTON	AW	4	120
ECKTON	SV	4	120
ECOTT	B	5	112
ECOTT	FG	5	112
ECTCHELLS	J	11	116
ECUYER	A	1	96
EDDELS	J	7	113
EDDELS	JJ	7	113
EDDEN	JH	1	96
EDDEN	JV	1	96
EDDIE	JAR	4	120
EDDINGTON	E	1	96
EDDINS	GH	6	124
EDDISON	A	8	415
EDDISON	C	8	101
EDDISON	C	8	101
EDDLES	H	10	292
EDDLESTON	D	11	116
EDDLESTON	F	11	116
EDDLESTON	W	11	116
EDDOWES	GW	10	71
EDDY	AM	10	292
EDE	ET	4	120
EDE	GF	1	96
EDE	HA	1	96
EDE	HG	4	120
EDE	HJ	2	110
EDE	JA	7	113
EDEMANIGER	J	3	330
EDEN	F	6	124
EDEN	G	6	124
EDEN	GH	1	96
EDEN	GH	6	124
EDEN	H	5	112
EDEN	J	1	96
EDEN	J	2	110
EDEN	J	6	124
EDEN	J	11	116
EDEN	JW	7	113
EDEN	P	6	124
EDEN	PL	1	96
EDEN	SW	1	96
EDEN	T	6	124
EDEN	WB	7	113
EDEN	WJ	4	120
EDENBOROUGH	WJ	13	145
EDENS	J	5	112
EDEY	J	1	97
EDGAR	A	11	116
EDGAR	CB	6	124
EDGAR	E	7	113
EDGAR	EM	13	145
EDGAR	H	3	51
EDGAR	JT	14	95
EDGE	AJ	6	124
EDGE	BG	1	97
EDGE	C	1	97
EDGE	C	3	330
EDGE	E	2	110
EDGE	GH	2	110
EDGE	H	14	95
EDGE	J	8	101
EDGE	J	14	96
EDGE	J	14	96
EDGE	JH	1	97
EDGE	JH	11	117
EDGE	JH	14	96
EDGE	JPM	7	113
EDGE	N	14	96
EDGE	PO	6	124
EDGE	RW	13	145
EDGE	T	1	97
EDGE	W	6	124
EDGE	W	11	117
EDGE	W	14	96
EDGELEY	J	12	77
EDGELL	A	8	101
EDGELL	F	8	101
EDGERTON	F	6	124
EDGES	L	6	124
EDGHILL	JW	13	145
EDGINGTON	AW	6	124
EDGINGTON	G	6	124
EDGINGTON	HJ	6	124
EDGLEY	GW	9	61
EDGLEY	H	12	300
EDGLEY	JW	8	101
EDGLEY	L	9	61
EDGLEY	P	9	61
EDINBOROUGH	E	1	97
EDIS	EC	7	113
EDISBURY	A	11	117
EDISS	A	11	117
EDISS	AC	13	145
EDISS	E	11	117
EDISS	E	11	117
EDKINS	A	6	124
EDKINS	A	6	124
EDKINS	F	1	97
EDKINS	G	6	124
EDKINS	H	6	125
EDKINS	JH	2	110
EDMANSON	A	9	61
EDMEADES	D	1	97
EDMEADES	J	1	97
EDMEADES	WT	1	97
EDMED	WF	2	110
EDMETT	B	7	113
EDMONDS	A	11	117
EDMONDS	ACE	2	111
EDMONDS	ACE	2	111
EDMONDS	AE	3	51
EDMONDS	AJ	1	97
EDMONDS	AS	3	330
EDMONDS	CA	1	97
EDMONDS	CHE	4	120
EDMONDS	CW	2	111
EDMONDS	EJK	10	293
EDMONDS	EWC	2	111
EDMONDS	F	1	97
EDMONDS	F	3	52
EDMONDS	F	7	113
EDMONDS	G	2	111
EDMONDS	G	3	330
EDMONDS	G	5	112
EDMONDS	G	6	125
EDMONDS	G	7	113
EDMONDS	GE	1	97
EDMONDS	GE	10	292
EDMONDS	H	1	97
EDMONDS	H	4	120
EDMONDS	H	6	125
EDMONDS	HF	4	120
EDMONDS	HG	10	293
EDMONDS	I	2	111
EDMONDS	J	2	111
EDMONDS	J	3	330
EDMONDS	J	6	125
EDMONDS	J	6	125
EDMONDS	J	7	113
EDMONDS	J	13	145
EDMONDS	JR	3	52
EDMONDS	RA	10	71
EDMONDS	RA	13	145
EDMONDS	S	6	125
EDMONDS	S	11	117
EDMONDS	SJ	7	113
EDMONDS	TJ	1	97
EDMONDS	W	3	330
EDMONDS	WA	13	146
EDMONDS	WJ	1	97
EDMONDS	WJ	2	111
EDMONDSON	AE	8	102
EDMONDSON	BA	8	102
EDMONDSON	BJ	10	71
EDMONDSON	D	9	61
EDMONDSON	F	9	61
EDMONDSON	H	4	120
EDMONDSON	J	9	61
EDMONDSON	J	9	61
EDMONDSON	J	9	252
EDMONDSON	JW	9	385
EDMONDSON	M	9	252
EDMONDSON	P	9	61
EDMONDSON	P	9	252
EDMONDSON	R	14	96
EDMONDSON	W	4	120
EDMONDSON	W	9	61
EDMONDSON	W	14	96
EDMONDSON	WH	14	96
EDMONSTONE	WJ	2	111
EDMUND	AS	3	330
EDMUND	J	11	117
EDMUNDS	A	6	125
EDMUNDS	A	10	71
EDMUNDS	A	12	77
EDMUNDS	A	12	77
EDMUNDS	AJ	13	146
EDMUNDS	BG	4	120
EDMUNDS	J	12	77
EDMUNDS	JS	4	120
EDMUNDS	M	12	77
EDMUNDS	RG	10	71
EDMUNDS	T	8	102
EDMUNDS	W	10	71
EDMUNDS	W	12	78
EDMUNDS	W	14	96
EDMUNDS	WH	10	71
EDNEY	A	10	293
EDNEY	F	10	293
EDNEY	F	10	293
EDNEY	GW	10	293
EDNEY	H	12	78
EDNEY	HJ	13	146
EDNEY	JA	7	113
EDNEY	JE	7	114
EDNEY	JH	7	114
EDNEY	R	3	330
EDNEY	RT	13	146
EDNEY	W	10	71
EDRIDGE	HJ	7	114
EDROP	GT	6	125
EDSON	W	8	102
EDWARD	C	9	61
EDWARD	F	7	114
EDWARD	H	7	114
EDWARD	H	9	61
EDWARD	H	9	61
EDWARD	J	9	61
EDWARD	J	11	117

EDWARD	P	4	121
EDWARD	W	7	114
EDWARD	WE	8	102
EDWARDES	GH	3	52
EDWARDS	A	4	120
EDWARDS	A	6	125
EDWARDS	A	6	125
EDWARDS	A	6	125
EDWARDS	A	11	117
EDWARDS	A	12	300
EDWARDS	A	13	146
EDWARDS	A	13	146
EDWARDS	A	14	96
EDWARDS	A	14	96
EDWARDS	A	14	96
EDWARDS	AA	10	72
EDWARDS	AA	13	146
EDWARDS	AB	5	112
EDWARDS	AE	13	146
EDWARDS	AG	1	97
EDWARDS	AG	14	96
EDWARDS	AH	2	111
EDWARDS	AH	3	52
EDWARDS	AJ	3	52
EDWARDS	AJ	6	125
EDWARDS	AP	4	121
EDWARDS	AS	12	78
EDWARDS	AT	6	125
EDWARDS	AV	7	114
EDWARDS	AW	13	146
EDWARDS	B	2	111
EDWARDS	B	7	114
EDWARDS	B	10	72
EDWARDS	C	2	111
EDWARDS	C	3	52
EDWARDS	C	3	331
EDWARDS	C	5	112
EDWARDS	C	7	114
EDWARDS	C	8	102
EDWARDS	C	10	293
EDWARDS	C	14	96
EDWARDS	C	14	96
EDWARDS	CF	3	331
EDWARDS	CH	7	114
EDWARDS	CO	12	78
EDWARDS	CW	1	97
EDWARDS	D	5	112
EDWARDS	D	12	300
EDWARDS	E	3	52
EDWARDS	E	3	331
EDWARDS	E	6	125
EDWARDS	E	6	125
EDWARDS	E	7	114
EDWARDS	E	11	117
EDWARDS	E	11	117
EDWARDS	E	11	117
EDWARDS	E	12	300
EDWARDS	E	13	146
EDWARDS	E	13	146
EDWARDS	E	14	96
EDWARDS	E	14	96
EDWARDS	EE	1	97
EDWARDS	EG	13	146
EDWARDS	EW	6	125
EDWARDS	EW	12	78
EDWARDS	EW	13	146
EDWARDS	F	2	111
EDWARDS	F	2	111
EDWARDS	F	6	125
EDWARDS	F	6	125
EDWARDS	F	7	114
EDWARDS	F	10	72
EDWARDS	F	11	117
EDWARDS	F	14	97
EDWARDS	FA	2	111
EDWARDS	FG	13	146
EDWARDS	FH	14	97
EDWARDS	FJ	12	300
EDWARDS	FT	13	146
EDWARDS	FW	1	98
EDWARDS	FW	3	52
EDWARDS	G	1	97
EDWARDS	G	1	97
EDWARDS	G	1	98
EDWARDS	G	2	111
EDWARDS	G	2	111
EDWARDS	G	2	111
EDWARDS	G	4	121
EDWARDS	G	6	125
EDWARDS	G	6	125
EDWARDS	G	6	125
EDWARDS	G	8	102
EDWARDS	G	11	117
EDWARDS	G	12	78
EDWARDS	G	13	146
EDWARDS	G	13	146
EDWARDS	GA	6	125
EDWARDS	GB	10	72
EDWARDS	GC	2	111
EDWARDS	GE	3	331
EDWARDS	GH	1	98
EDWARDS	GH	13	146
EDWARDS	GJ	6	126
EDWARDS	GW	2	112
EDWARDS	GW	2	112
EDWARDS	H	2	112
EDWARDS	H	3	52
EDWARDS	H	3	331
EDWARDS	H	4	121
EDWARDS	H	4	121
EDWARDS	H	5	113
EDWARDS	H	6	126
EDWARDS	H	6	126
EDWARDS	H	6	126
EDWARDS	H	6	126
EDWARDS	H	8	102
EDWARDS	H	9	61
EDWARDS	H	11	117
EDWARDS	H	11	117
EDWARDS	H	12	78
EDWARDS	H	13	147
EDWARDS	H	14	97
EDWARDS	H	14	97
EDWARDS	H	14	97
EDWARDS	HA	3	331
EDWARDS	HE	6	126
EDWARDS	HE	13	146
EDWARDS	HF	12	78
EDWARDS	HF	13	147
EDWARDS	HG	13	147
EDWARDS	HJ	13	147
EDWARDS	HS	3	52
EDWARDS	IH	13	147
EDWARDS	J	2	112
EDWARDS	J	2	112
EDWARDS	J	2	112
EDWARDS	J	2	112
EDWARDS	J	4	121
EDWARDS	J	4	121
EDWARDS	J	5	113
EDWARDS	J	6	126
EDWARDS	J	7	114
EDWARDS	J	11	117
EDWARDS	J	11	118
EDWARDS	J	11	118
EDWARDS	J	11	118
EDWARDS	J	11	118
EDWARDS	J	13	147
EDWARDS	J	14	97
EDWARDS	J	14	97
EDWARDS	J	14	97
EDWARDS	JC	7	114
EDWARDS	JD	2	112
EDWARDS	JE	2	112
EDWARDS	JE	8	102
EDWARDS	JFG	1	98
EDWARDS	JGB	6	126
EDWARDS	JH	2	112
EDWARDS	JH	3	52
EDWARDS	JH	6	126
EDWARDS	JH	6	126
EDWARDS	JH	13	147
EDWARDS	JR	4	121
EDWARDS	JT	11	118
EDWARDS	JT	12	78
EDWARDS	JW	1	98
EDWARDS	JW	7	114
EDWARDS	JW	7	114
EDWARDS	JW	9	252
EDWARDS	L	4	121
EDWARDS	L	6	126
EDWARDS	L	6	126
EDWARDS	L	14	97
EDWARDS	LC	2	112
EDWARDS	LC	10	293
EDWARDS	LR	2	112
EDWARDS	LWJ	13	147
EDWARDS	M	1	98
EDWARDS	M	12	78
EDWARDS	O	2	112
EDWARDS	O	12	300
EDWARDS	P	7	114
EDWARDS	P	13	147
EDWARDS	PJ	1	98
EDWARDS	R	1	98
EDWARDS	R	2	112
EDWARDS	R	4	121
EDWARDS	R	11	118
EDWARDS	R	14	97
EDWARDS	RA	6	126
EDWARDS	RG	6	126
EDWARDS	RG	7	114
EDWARDS	RG	13	147
EDWARDS	RS	11	118
EDWARDS	S	14	97
EDWARDS	SC	5	113
EDWARDS	SJ	12	78
EDWARDS	SW	5	113
EDWARDS	T	6	126
EDWARDS	T	6	126
EDWARDS	T	6	126
EDWARDS	T	6	126
EDWARDS	T	11	118
EDWARDS	T	11	118
EDWARDS	T	11	118
EDWARDS	T	12	78
EDWARDS	T	13	147
EDWARDS	T	14	97
EDWARDS	T	14	97
EDWARDS	T	14	97
EDWARDS	TH	5	113
EDWARDS	TH	6	126
EDWARDS	TWA	3	331
EDWARDS	V	14	97
EDWARDS	W	1	98
EDWARDS	W	2	112
EDWARDS	W	3	331
EDWARDS	W	5	113
EDWARDS	W	5	113

EDWARDS	W	6	126	EGAN	J	5	113	ELBOURN	H	5	113	ELEY	AT	10	72
EDWARDS	W	8	102	EGAN	J	8	102	ELBOURN	RP	5	113	ELEY	E	7	115
EDWARDS	W	8	102	EGAN	J	8	102	ELBRA	JJ	1	98	ELEY	FG	10	72
EDWARDS	W	11	118	EGAN	J	11	118	ELBROW	JF	1	98	ELEY	H	1	99
EDWARDS	W	11	118	EGAN	J	11	118	ELBROW	WT	1	98	ELEY	HJ	2	113
EDWARDS	W	12	300	EGAN	J	14	98	ELCOCK	A	14	98	ELEY	HW	13	148
EDWARDS	W	12	300	EGAN	JP	14	98	ELCOCK	J	4	121	ELEY	J	14	98
EDWARDS	W	13	147	EGAN	M	8	102	ELCOCK	WJ	1	99	ELEY	S	9	252
EDWARDS	WA	13	147	EGAN	N	9	385	ELCOMBE	JH	4	121	ELEY	W	12	300
EDWARDS	WC	4	121	EGAN	P	3	331	ELCOMBE-BREACH	CB	7	115	ELFORD	BC	4	122
EDWARDS	WC	13	147	EGAN	P	11	118	ELCOME	R	5	113	ELFORD	EL	4	122
EDWARDS	WD	14	97	EGAN	W	9	385	ELDERFIELD	S	4	122	ELFORD	J	11	119
EDWARDS	WFL	13	147	EGERTON	A	11	118	ELDERFIELD	TD	1	99	ELFORD	W	11	119
EDWARDS	WG	4	121	EGERTON	GF	10	72	ELDERFIELD	WF	1	99	ELFORD	W	12	78
EDWARDS	WG	10	72	EGERTON	H	4	121	ELDERFIELD	WR	7	115	ELGAR	AW	8	102
EDWARDS	WH	1	98	EGERTON	H	7	115	ELDERGILL	R	13	148	ELGER	A	11	119
EDWARDS	WH	2	112	EGERTON	HA	4	121	ELDIM	JA	8	102	ELGOOD	CF	7	115
EDWARDS	WH	6	127	EGERTON	HG	4	121	ELDRED	AJ	13	148	ELGOOD	L	1	99
EDWARDS	WH	6	127	EGERTON	IM	10	293	ELDRED	E	5	113	ELIAS	WJ	13	148
EDWARDS	WH	11	118	EGERTON	J	14	98	ELDRED	H	1	99	ELING	E	6	127
EDWARDS	WH	13	147	EGERTON	J	14	98	ELDRED	LC	13	148	ELING	W	6	127
EDWARDS	WJ	1	98	EGERTON	RC	10	293	ELDRET	E	1	99	ELITSKY	J	14	98
EDWARDS	WJ	3	52	EGERTON	W	4	121	ELDRETT	WJ	2	113	ELKERTON	J	5	114
EDWARDS	WJ	6	127	EGG	F	4	121	ELDRIDGE	A	1	99	ELKES	J	11	119
EDWARDS	WJ	10	72	EGGAR	WG	3	331	ELDRIDGE	AE	4	122	ELKIN	G	6	127
EDWARDS	WJ	13	147	EGGERTON	HA	6	127	ELDRIDGE	B	4	122	ELKIN	GF	1	99
EDWARDS	WL	1	98	EGGETT	J	3	52	ELDRIDGE	CA	13	148	ELKIN	P	11	119
EDWARDS	WL	6	127	EGGETT	LG	13	147	ELDRIDGE	CC	3	52	ELKIN	W	6	127
EDWARDS	WR	10	72	EGGETT	R	9	62	ELDRIDGE	CH	4	122	ELKINGTON	E	6	127
EDWARDS	WS	5	113	EGGINGTON	AS	6	127	ELDRIDGE	CJ	1	99	ELKINGTON	JT	8	102
EDWARDS	WST	1	98	EGGINGTON	C	6	127	ELDRIDGE	EM	4	122	ELKINS	AC	2	113
EDWICK	J	9	252	EGGINGTON	GS	6	127	ELDRIDGE	EW	4	122	ELKINS	AG	2	113
EDWICKER	JW	4	121	EGGLESTON	GT	10	72	ELDRIDGE	F	8	102	ELKINS	AG	13	148
EDWIN	H	6	127	EGGLESTON	JA	2	112	ELDRIDGE	G	7	115	ELKINS	CA	2	113
EDY	C	7	114	EGGLESTON	T	10	72	ELDRIDGE	H	2	113	ELKINS	FAH	4	122
EDY	FA	7	115	EGGLETON	FT	1	98	ELDRIDGE	HJ	13	148	ELKINS	G	4	122
EDY	JC	7	115	EGGLETON	H	1	98	ELDRIDGE	J	4	122	ELKINS	JC	5	114
EDY	WA	7	115	EGGLETON	HC	2	113	ELDRIDGE	J	13	148	ELKINS	L	4	122
EELE	BW	2	112	EGGLETON	TW	10	72	ELDRIDGE	J	13	148	ELKINS	RJ	5	114
EELE	HF	2	112	EGGLETON	W	13	147	ELDRIDGE	JP	2	113	ELKINS	RW	4	122
EELES	A	7	115	EGGLETON	WA	1	98	ELDRIDGE	JR	3	52	ELKINS	RW	4	122
EELES	BJ	7	115	EGGLETON	WC	7	115	ELDRIDGE	JW	4	122	ELKINS	SM	4	122
EELES	W	10	293	EGLESE	J	13	148	ELDRIDGE	PAC	1	99	ELKINS	W	13	148
EELES	W	14	97	EGLINGTON	HJ	7	115	ELDRIDGE	S	13	148	ELKINS	WE	7	115
EELES	WJ	1	98	EGNAR	S	3	52	ELDRIDGE	TCH	4	122	ELLABY	F	14	98
EELES	WJ	6	127	EICKHOFF	HJ	2	113	ELDRIDGE	TE	4	122	ELLAM	H	14	98
EFFORD	FE	5	113	EKE	A	1	98	ELDRIDGE	W	4	122	ELLAMS	A	14	98
EFFORD	W	10	72	EKE	P	13	148	ELDRIDGE	WH	2	113	ELLARD	H	6	127
EGAN	AJR	10	293	EKE	W	1	98	ELDRIDGE	WH	10	72	ELLARD	J	6	128
EGAN	ASTS	12	300	EKINS	FH	12	78	ELEMENT	A	5	113	ELLARD	J	12	300
EGAN	D	14	97	EKINS	L	5	113	ELEMENT	G	5	113	ELLARD	W	6	127
EGAN	F	14	98	ELAM	SS	7	115	ELEMENT	J	5	114	ELLARY	WE	13	148
EGAN	GWE	8	102	ELAM	W	8	102	ELEMENT	JW	5	114	ELLAWAY	F	4	122
EGAN	H	11	118	ELBOURN	G	5	113	ELEMENT	JW	5	114	ELLEDGE	NH	1	99
EGAN	J	2	112	ELBOURN	H	5	113	ELEMENT	R	6	127	ELLEMENT	SE	6	128

ELLEMENT	W	5	114
ELLEN	AW	7	115
ELLENBAUM	S	14	98
ELLENS	CL	3	331
ELLENS	JH	7	115
ELLER	FA	7	115
ELLERAY	B	14	98
ELLERAY	C	11	119
ELLERINGTON	H	7	115
ELLERINGTON	RH	3	331
ELLERSHAW	TW	14	98
ELLERY	AW	3	331
ELLERY	G	4	123
ELLERY	J	7	116
ELLERY	JJ	11	119
ELLERY	SG	3	331
ELLICOTT	SA	7	116
ELLICOTT	W	14	98
ELLIFF	AW	1	99
ELLIFF	FG	1	99
ELLIFF	JE	1	99
ELLIKER	F	8	102
ELLIKER	M	8	103
ELLIMAN	J	6	128
ELLIMAN	L	6	128
ELLINER	W	8	103
ELLINGHAM	CJ	7	116
ELLINGHAM	E	5	114
ELLINGHAM	EH	5	114
ELLINGHAM	HA	5	114
ELLINGHAM	S	5	114
ELLINS	R	10	72
ELLIOT	A	5	114
ELLIOT	AE	1	99
ELLIOT	CJ	7	116
ELLIOT	EJ	7	116
ELLIOT	EP	7	116
ELLIOT	G	12	78
ELLIOT	GG	14	98
ELLIOT	NG	4	123
ELLIOTT	A	2	113
ELLIOTT	A	2	113
ELLIOTT	A	4	123
ELLIOTT	A	4	123
ELLIOTT	A	6	128
ELLIOTT	A	9	252
ELLIOTT	A	11	119
ELLIOTT	A	12	300
ELLIOTT	A	13	148
ELLIOTT	A	14	98
ELLIOTT	AAJ	1	99
ELLIOTT	AAJ	2	113
ELLIOTT	AC	2	113
ELLIOTT	AC	2	113
ELLIOTT	AC	2	113
ELLIOTT	AC	3	331
ELLIOTT	AE	4	123
ELLIOTT	AG	2	113
ELLIOTT	AG	12	300
ELLIOTT	AH	4	123
ELLIOTT	AJ	2	113
ELLIOTT	AJ	12	78
ELLIOTT	BG	6	128
ELLIOTT	BSJ	12	78
ELLIOTT	C	3	331
ELLIOTT	C	4	123
ELLIOTT	C	13	148
ELLIOTT	C	14	98
ELLIOTT	CA	2	113
ELLIOTT	CH	6	128
ELLIOTT	CH	13	148
ELLIOTT	CW	14	99
ELLIOTT	DA	10	293
ELLIOTT	DA	10	293
ELLIOTT	E	1	99
ELLIOTT	E	4	123
ELLIOTT	E	13	148
ELLIOTT	EWS	2	113
ELLIOTT	F	1	99
ELLIOTT	F	7	116
ELLIOTT	F	10	72
ELLIOTT	F	14	99
ELLIOTT	F	14	99
ELLIOTT	FB	10	293
ELLIOTT	FC	7	116
ELLIOTT	FG	1	99
ELLIOTT	FG	1	99
ELLIOTT	FG	2	114
ELLIOTT	FH	6	128
ELLIOTT	FJ	1	99
ELLIOTT	G	4	123
ELLIOTT	G	4	123
ELLIOTT	G	10	72
ELLIOTT	G	12	300
ELLIOTT	GH	10	73
ELLIOTT	GHL	12	300
ELLIOTT	GV	4	123
ELLIOTT	GW	7	116
ELLIOTT	H	2	114
ELLIOTT	H	13	149
ELLIOTT	H	14	99
ELLIOTT	HB	10	73
ELLIOTT	HE	3	52
ELLIOTT	HM	1	100
ELLIOTT	HS	10	293
ELLIOTT	J	7	116
ELLIOTT	J	8	103
ELLIOTT	J	8	103
ELLIOTT	J	9	62
ELLIOTT	J	9	252
ELLIOTT	JBG	7	116
ELLIOTT	JE	8	103
ELLIOTT	JH	7	116
ELLIOTT	JH	11	119
ELLIOTT	JH	13	149
ELLIOTT	JW	9	62
ELLIOTT	M	1	100
ELLIOTT	M	3	331
ELLIOTT	PR	1	100
ELLIOTT	R	7	116
ELLIOTT	R	8	103
ELLIOTT	R	10	73
ELLIOTT	R	13	149
ELLIOTT	RG	4	123
ELLIOTT	SH	1	100
ELLIOTT	SJ	4	123
ELLIOTT	SJ	6	128
ELLIOTT	SJ	6	128
ELLIOTT	T	6	128
ELLIOTT	T	14	99
ELLIOTT	TB	9	62
ELLIOTT	TWR	10	293
ELLIOTT	W	2	114
ELLIOTT	W	4	123
ELLIOTT	W	6	128
ELLIOTT	W	6	128
ELLIOTT	W	6	128
ELLIOTT	WG	10	73
ELLIOTT	WH	11	119
ELLIOTT	WHE	4	123
ELLIOTT	WR	13	149
ELLIS	A	6	128
ELLIS	A	8	103
ELLIS	A	8	103
ELLIS	A	9	252
ELLIS	A	12	300
ELLIS	A	12	300
ELLIS	A	13	149
ELLIS	AAC	12	78
ELLIS	AB	10	73
ELLIS	AC	5	114
ELLIS	AE	2	114
ELLIS	AE	5	114
ELLIS	AE	11	119
ELLIS	AH	2	114
ELLIS	AH	6	128
ELLIS	AH	7	116
ELLIS	AH	10	73
ELLIS	AJ	1	100
ELLIS	AJ	2	114
ELLIS	AJ	3	331
ELLIS	B	8	103
ELLIS	BB	13	149
ELLIS	BE	9	62
ELLIS	BW	11	119
ELLIS	C	6	128
ELLIS	C	7	116
ELLIS	C	9	62
ELLIS	CA	10	294
ELLIS	CH	10	294
ELLIS	CJ	7	116
ELLIS	CRJ	7	116
ELLIS	CW	5	114
ELLIS	CW	8	103
ELLIS	D	4	123
ELLIS	E	4	123
ELLIS	E	4	123
ELLIS	E	6	128
ELLIS	E	8	103
ELLIS	E	9	62
ELLIS	E	9	252
ELLIS	E	11	119
ELLIS	E	14	99
ELLIS	EA	1	100
ELLIS	ES	4	123
ELLIS	EW	2	114
ELLIS	EW	4	123
ELLIS	F	5	114
ELLIS	F	5	114
ELLIS	F	8	103
ELLIS	F	12	78
ELLIS	FC	2	114
ELLIS	FGH	2	114
ELLIS	FH	5	114
ELLIS	FJ	6	128
ELLIS	FL	5	114
ELLIS	FR	3	52
ELLIS	G	1	100
ELLIS	G	7	117
ELLIS	G	8	103
ELLIS	G	8	103
ELLIS	G	8	103
ELLIS	G	8	103
ELLIS	G	10	73
ELLIS	G	12	78
ELLIS	G	12	300
ELLIS	GA	11	119
ELLIS	GE	3	331
ELLIS	GH	12	79
ELLIS	GH	13	149
ELLIS	GT	2	114
ELLIS	GW	12	79
ELLIS	H	2	114
ELLIS	H	3	52
ELLIS	H	3	332
ELLIS	H	6	128
ELLIS	H	6	128
ELLIS	H	7	117
ELLIS	H	8	103
ELLIS	H	8	103

ELLIS	H	9	62	ELLIS	SD	10	73	ELLISON	GE	8	104	ELSE	B	5	115
ELLIS	H	11	119	ELLIS	SJ	6	129	ELLISON	J	3	332	ELSE	CF	5	115
ELLIS	H	12	79	ELLIS	T	1	100	ELLISON	J	8	104	ELSE	E	11	120
ELLIS	H	12	79	ELLIS	T	2	114	ELLISON	J	11	120	ELSE	G	11	120
ELLIS	H	13	149	ELLIS	T	12	79	ELLISON	J	11	120	ELSE	J	6	129
ELLIS	H	13	149	ELLIS	TA	4	124	ELLISON	J	14	99	ELSEGOOD	AE	10	73
ELLIS	H	14	99	ELLIS	TH	3	53	ELLISON	R	8	104	ELSEY	A	1	100
ELLIS	HA	2	114	ELLIS	TH	3	53	ELLISON	TH	7	117	ELSEY	AP	13	149
ELLIS	HJ	6	129	ELLIS	TM	8	104	ELLISON	WA	8	104	ELSEY	BJ	2	115
ELLIS	HW	4	123	ELLIS	TS	4	124	ELLISON	WH	8	104	ELSEY	CR	13	149
ELLIS	I	9	62	ELLIS	TW	8	104	ELLISS	J	8	104	ELSEY	F	7	117
ELLIS	J	6	129	ELLIS	TW	12	79	ELLISTON	JF	13	149	ELSEY	FE	13	149
ELLIS	J	8	103	ELLIS	W	1	100	ELLISTON	JO	2	115	ELSEY	G	3	332
ELLIS	J	8	103	ELLIS	W	1	100	ELLMAN	CH	10	73	ELSEY	G	4	124
ELLIS	J	8	103	ELLIS	W	2	114	ELLNER	PG	1	100	ELSEY	H	9	62
ELLIS	J	11	119	ELLIS	W	3	332	ELLOWAY	C	3	332	ELSEY	J	7	117
ELLIS	J	11	119	ELLIS	W	4	124	ELLOWAY	W	3	332	ELSEY	J	13	150
ELLIS	J	11	119	ELLIS	W	6	129	ELLOWAY	W	10	294	ELSEY	MWF	5	115
ELLIS	J	11	119	ELLIS	W	6	129	ELLS	LF	13	149	ELSEY	S	13	150
ELLIS	J	11	120	ELLIS	W	6	129	ELLS	T	7	117	ELSEY	TR	3	332
ELLIS	J	11	120	ELLIS	W	8	104	ELLSMORE	R	1	100	ELSEY	WH	10	73
ELLIS	J	12	79	ELLIS	W	8	104	ELLSON	E	3	53	ELSIP	A	1	100
ELLIS	J	12	79	ELLIS	W	8	104	ELLSON	J	7	117	ELSMERE	AC	2	115
ELLIS	J	14	99	ELLIS	W	8	104	ELLSON	J	13	149	ELSMERE	FW	2	115
ELLIS	JC	3	53	ELLIS	W	8	104	ELLSON	JG	3	53	ELSMERE	GE	2	115
ELLIS	JE	12	79	ELLIS	W	8	104	ELLSON	T	3	53	ELSMERE	GF	2	115
ELLIS	JH	6	129	ELLIS	W	9	252	ELLSON	W	3	53	ELSOM	C	7	117
ELLIS	JH	8	104	ELLIS	W	9	252	ELLUM	A	8	104	ELSOM	W	7	117
ELLIS	JH	14	99	ELLIS	W	9	252	ELLWOOD	R	11	120	ELSON	A	5	115
ELLIS	JR	2	114	ELLIS	W	10	73	ELMA	HT	11	120	ELSON	R	7	117
ELLIS	JW	8	104	ELLIS	W	11	120	ELMER	EA	2	115	ELSON	WTD	3	332
ELLIS	JW	8	104	ELLIS	W	11	120	ELMER	W	13	149	ELSTER	WEJ	2	115
ELLIS	JW	9	252	ELLIS	W	11	120	ELMER	WS	7	117	ELSTON	AW	1	100
ELLIS	JWF	12	300	ELLIS	W	11	120	ELMORE	H	1	100	ELSTON	E	5	115
ELLIS	LM	3	53	ELLIS	WA	5	115	ELMORE	HE	1	100	ELSTON	EG	1	100
ELLIS	LT	6	129	ELLIS	WC	2	114	ELMORE	RH	3	332	ELSTON	FK	12	301
ELLIS	NG	10	73	ELLIS	WC	3	332	ELMS	A	12	301	ELSTON	R	9	252
ELLIS	O	6	129	ELLIS	WE	2	114	ELMS	AC	2	115	ELSTON	T	12	301
ELLIS	PJ	1	100	ELLIS	WE	2	114	ELMS	AH	13	149	ELSTON	T	12	301
ELLIS	R	7	117	ELLIS	WG	5	115	ELMS	F	2	115	ELSTON	TG	5	115
ELLIS	R	11	120	ELLIS	WG	6	129	ELMS	FC	10	73	ELSTON	W	5	115
ELLIS	R	11	120	ELLIS	WG	6	129	ELMS	WJ	4	124	ELSTOW	T	12	79
ELLIS	RH	6	129	ELLIS	WH	13	149	ELMSLIE	G	1	100	ELSTUB	G	9	385
ELLIS	RH	11	120	ELLIS	WJ	6	129	ELMSLIE	L	1	100	ELSTUB	R	9	385
ELLIS	RH	12	301	ELLIS	WJ	10	73	ELMWOOD	C	8	104	ELSWOOD	F	14	99
ELLIS	RJ	7	117	ELLIS	WJ	12	79	ELPHICK	A	8	104	ELSWORTH	AG	8	104
ELLIS	RP	1	100	ELLIS	WL	2	114	ELPHICK	AH	10	73	ELSWORTH	C	8	105
ELLIS	RP	4	124	ELLIS	WR	6	129	ELPHICK	G	11	120	ELSWORTH	RJ	8	105
ELLIS	RP	5	114	ELLIS	WS	12	79	ELRIDGE	A	8	104	ELSWORTH	W	8	105
ELLIS	RT	4	124	ELLIS	WW	2	114	ELRIDGE	A	8	104	ELSWORTHY	J	2	115
ELLIS	S	5	115	ELLISON	A	6	129	ELSDEN	A	9	252	ELTHAM	JH	6	130
ELLIS	S	6	129	ELLISON	A	9	62	ELSDON	EJ	5	115	ELTON	AE	4	124
ELLIS	S	13	149	ELLISON	AG	9	62	ELSDON	F	7	117	ELTON	T	1	100
ELLIS	S	14	99	ELLISON	E	8	104	ELSDON	PH	5	115	ELVEN	FH	13	150
ELLIS	SC	13	149	ELLISON	G	9	252	ELSE	A	6	130	ELVERSON	BF	3	332

ELVERSON	D	10	73	EMERTON	M	5	115	EMLER	JW	2	116	EMPLETON	GH	3	53
ELVERSON	JF	3	332	EMERTON	P	5	115	EMLY	HE	2	116	EMPRINGHAM	WJ	10	294
ELVES	HJ	13	150	EMERTON	RN	12	301	EMMANS	TCP	2	116	EMSDEN	LH	5	116
ELVEY	RM	5	115	EMERTON	S	2	115	EMMERSON	GW	8	105	EMSLEY	A	8	105
ELVEY	WJ	1	101	EMERTON	WP	5	115	EMMERSON	J	8	105	EMSLEY	G	14	100
ELVIN	A	2	115	EMERTON	WT	12	301	EMMERSON	J	8	105	EMSLEY	JW	9	62
ELVIN	AE	1	101	EMERY	A	2	115	EMMERSON	S	8	105	EMSLEY	JW	9	253
ELVIN	EJ	1	101	EMERY	A	4	124	EMMETT	A	4	124	EMSLEY	W	9	253
ELVIN	H	1	101	EMERY	AJ	5	115	EMMETT	A	9	62	EMSLEY	W	14	100
ELVIN	J	2	115	EMERY	AJ	5	116	EMMETT	A	9	252	EMSLIE	G	11	121
ELVINS	WJ	3	332	EMERY	AL	2	115	EMMETT	A	9	253	EMSLIE	J	6	130
ELVIS	A	6	130	EMERY	C	3	332	EMMETT	AG	4	124	EMSLIE	M	10	74
ELVIS	B	6	130	EMERY	CR	10	74	EMMETT	AH	4	124	EMSLIE	WD	10	74
ELVIS	S	6	130	EMERY	DH	5	116	EMMETT	AS	2	116	EMSLIE	WG	10	74
ELWELL	A	6	130	EMERY	DL	12	79	EMMETT	CH	3	53	EMSON	FJ	6	130
ELWELL	EG	10	73	EMERY	E	1	101	EMMETT	CH	4	124	EMUSS	H	6	130
ELWELL	ET	6	130	EMERY	E	2	116	EMMETT	EA	4	124	END	F	13	150
ELWELL	W	6	130	EMERY	E	14	99	EMMETT	F	9	253	ENDACOTT	F	1	101
ELWORTHY	RF	7	117	EMERY	EA	2	116	EMMETT	G	8	105	ENDEACOTT	G	8	105
ELY	H	4	124	EMERY	EJ	1	101	EMMETT	HL	4	124	ENDEAN	A	10	74
ELY	J	7	117	EMERY	F	12	79	EMMETT	J	4	125	ENDEAN	A	10	74
ELY	J	7	117	EMERY	FE	1	101	EMMETT	J	8	105	ENDEAN	A	10	294
ELY	SC	2	115	EMERY	FJ	4	124	EMMETT	J	11	121	ENDEAN	AN	10	74
EMANUEL	CA	7	118	EMERY	G	4	124	EMMETT	JT	7	118	ENDEAN	AW	10	294
EMANUEL	H	14	99	EMERY	G	12	79	EMMETT	M	8	105	ENDERSBY	EA	12	80
EMBER	CH	4	124	EMERY	GACJ	4	124	EMMETT	M	9	62	ENDERSBY	EJ	12	80
EMBERSON	CG	3	53	EMERY	GW	13	150	EMMETT	R	13	150	ENDERSBY	FJ	12	80
EMBERSON	F	13	150	EMERY	H	1	101	EMMETT	S	9	62	ENDERSBY	FW	5	116
EMBERSON	RG	3	53	EMERY	H	6	130	EMMETT	W	7	118	ENDERSBY	HW	12	80
EMBERSON	WE	3	53	EMERY	HB	4	124	EMMETT	W	10	74	ENDERSBY	W	7	118
EMBERTON	W	11	120	EMERY	J	3	53	EMMETT	W	14	99	ENDERSBY	WC	5	116
EMBERY	AW	13	150	EMERY	J	5	116	EMMETT	WC	13	150	ENDRICKS	F	2	116
EMBLEN	W	7	118	EMERY	J	10	294	EMMETT	WH	8	105	ENEAS	CG	10	74
EMBLETON	E	3	53	EMERY	J	12	79	EMMETT	WR	4	125	ENEAS	FR	10	74
EMBLETON	FO	1	101	EMERY	JF	1	101	EMMETT	WW	13	150	ENEVER	J	3	53
EMBLETON	FW	1	101	EMERY	JG	12	301	EMMINS	P	2	116	ENFIELD	A	12	80
EMBLETON	GAV	3	332	EMERY	JH	14	99	EMMINS	WA	2	116	ENFIELD	GJ	10	294
EMBLETON	JW	7	118	EMERY	O	12	79	EMMITT	J	8	105	ENFIELD	I	12	301
EMBLEY	W	6	130	EMERY	R	14	99	EMMONDS	A	8	105	ENFIELD	S	12	80
EMBLOW	J	11	120	EMERY	S	5	116	EMMOTT	A	9	62	ENFIELD	S	12	301
EMBRAY	H	2	115	EMERY	T	12	79	EMMOTT	A	9	62	ENGLAND	A	12	301
EMBUREY	FG	7	118	EMERY	W	1	101	EMMOTT	H	8	105	ENGLAND	A	12	301
EMBURY	A	1	101	EMERY	W	5	116	EMMOTT	J	4	125	ENGLAND	AF	4	125
EMBURY	E	11	120	EMERY	W	7	118	EMMS	AE	2	116	ENGLAND	AT	9	253
EMBURY	SG	1	101	EMERY	W	12	80	EMMS	AV	1	101	ENGLAND	B	9	62
EMBURY	SW	1	101	EMERY	WC	5	116	EMMS	AV	10	74	ENGLAND	E	5	116
EMBURY	TW	1	101	EMERY	WC	12	301	EMMS	AW	1	101	ENGLAND	E	14	100
EMENS	BE	12	79	EMERY	WH	1	101	EMMS	FA	14	100	ENGLAND	F	11	121
EMENS	H	12	79	EMERY	WP	12	301	EMMS	HT	14	100	ENGLAND	FEE	5	116
EMERSON	C	13	150	EMES	WG	5	116	EMMS	JW	1	101	ENGLAND	FG	2	116
EMERSON	H	2	115	EMETT	E	11	121	EMMS	R	8	105	ENGLAND	G	9	253
EMERSON	T	14	99	EMIS	EV	10	294	EMMS	T	1	101	ENGLAND	GC	4	125
EMERTON	H	5	115	EMIS	G	10	294	EMMS	WA	2	116	ENGLAND	GM	4	125
EMERTON	HJ	5	115	EMIS	TH	10	294	EMONSON	CG	7	118	ENGLAND	GW	5	116
EMERTON	JC	2	115	EMIS	WJ	10	294	EMONSON	H	7	118	ENGLAND	GW	8	105

ENGLAND	H	14	100	ENTWISTLE	JR	11	121	ESSAM	R	12	301	ETHERINGTON	LJ	10	294
ENGLAND	HD	5	116	ENTWISTLE	JW	5	117	ESSAM	W	12	302	ETHERINGTON	MA	10	294
ENGLAND	HJ	4	125	ENTWISTLE	P	11	121	ESSERY	F	10	74	ETHERINGTON	OG	10	74
ENGLAND	J	3	332	ENTWISTLE	R	11	121	ESSERY	G	7	118	ETHERINGTON	OG	10	294
ENGLAND	J	6	130	ENTWISTLE	S	11	121	ESSERY	SA	10	294	ETHERINGTON	TS	9	63
ENGLAND	JH	2	116	ENTWISTLE	S	14	100	ESSEX	C	6	131	ETHERINGTON	W	8	106
ENGLAND	JJ	5	116	ENTWISTLE	T	8	106	ESSEX	DL	6	131	ETHERINGTON	W	8	106
ENGLAND	JW	8	416	ENTWISTLE	W	8	106	ESSEX	H	1	102	ETHRIDGE	J	1	102
ENGLAND	OC	12	301	ENTWISTLE	W	8	106	ESSEX	H	5	117	ETOE	GW	1	102
ENGLAND	P	8	105	ENTWISTLE	WE	8	106	ESSEX	HA	13	151	ETTE	A	12	302
ENGLAND	R	10	74	EPHGRAVE	HA	2	116	ESSEX	J	1	102	ETTERINGTON	J	9	253
ENGLAND	T	5	116	EPHRAIM	C	1	102	ESSEX	JE	1	102	ETTERSHANK	C	8	106
ENGLAND	T	11	121	EPPS	L	4	125	ESSEX	W	5	117	ETTERSHANK	T	8	106
ENGLAND	W	1	102	EPPS	RH	2	116	ESTCOURT	RES	2	117	ETTERY	T	11	122
ENGLAND	W	14	100	EPSTEIN	I	14	100	ESTILL	A	8	106	EUEN	E	8	106
ENGLAND	WJ	13	150	EPSTEIN	L	14	100	ESTILL	AA	8	106	EUGENE	T	2	117
ENGLAND	WT	1	102	EPTHORP	A	13	150	ESTILL	TW	8	106	EUINTON	DL	5	117
ENGLEBACK	J	2	116	EREAUX	A	4	125	ESTOLL	CM	7	118	EUINTON	EA	5	117
ENGLEFIELD	CE	4	125	ERIKSEN	A	13	150	ESTWICK	S	5	117	EVANS	A	2	117
ENGLEFIELD	CG	4	125	ERINGTON	WH	2	116	ESWORTHY	GW	1	102	EVANS	A	5	117
ENGLEFIELD	J	4	125	ERLAM	J	14	100	ETCHELLS	EG	11	121	EVANS	A	6	131
ENGLEFIELD	WD	4	125	ERNEST	A	13	150	ETCHELLS	J	11	121	EVANS	A	6	131
ENGLEMAN	W	1	102	ERNEST	CH	2	116	ETCHELLS	J	11	122	EVANS	A	6	131
ENGLISH	AA	2	116	ERNSTONE	AM	4	125	ETCHELLS	J	11	122	EVANS	A	6	131
ENGLISH	G	1	102	ERRATT	AG	3	53	ETCHELLS	JW	11	122	EVANS	A	6	131
ENGLISH	HS	2	116	ERRETT	F	3	53	ETCHES	F	5	117	EVANS	A	6	131
ENGLISH	M	1	102	ERRIDGE	AW	4	125	ETESON	CH	1	102	EVANS	A	6	131
ENGLISH	R	4	125	ERRIDGE	FG	4	125	ETESON	J	1	102	EVANS	A	6	131
ENGLISH	W	1	102	ERRIDGE	FW	10	74	ETESON	JW	1	102	EVANS	A	8	106
ENGLISH	W	8	105	ERRILL	JA	13	150	ETHERAGE	G	9	253	EVANS	A	8	106
ENGLISH	WD	9	63	ERRINGTON	C	3	332	ETHERALL	CH	11	122	EVANS	A	10	74
ENGWELL	CH	1	102	ERRINGTON	CH	4	125	ETHERALL	D	11	122	EVANS	A	11	122
ENNIS	A	11	121	ERRINGTON	JG	13	150	ETHEREDGE	GW	4	126	EVANS	A	11	122
ENNIS	F	14	100	ERSKINE	RD	4	125	ETHEREDGE	SL	4	125	EVANS	A	13	151
ENNIS	T	11	121	ERSSER	A	3	332	ETHERIDGE	AE	7	118	EVANS	A	14	100
ENNIS	W	6	130	ERSSER	WG	13	151	ETHERIDGE	AE	13	151	EVANS	A	14	100
ENNIS	WH	6	130	ERSSER	WT	7	118	ETHERIDGE	AJ	13	151	EVANS	AA	2	117
ENO	AG	12	80	ERWOOD	ACH	13	151	ETHERIDGE	BB	14	100	EVANS	AE	2	117
ENO	F	12	80	ERWOOD	AGV	13	151	ETHERIDGE	C	4	126	EVANS	AE	6	131
ENRIGHT	J	8	105	ERWOOD	EJ	1	102	ETHERIDGE	F	4	126	EVANS	AE	7	118
ENRIGHT	P	3	53	ERWOOD	H	13	151	ETHERIDGE	HC	4	126	EVANS	AE	10	294
ENRIGHT	TF	6	130	ESCOTT	FS	6	130	ETHERIDGE	JR	13	151	EVANS	AF	4	126
ENRIGHT	TM	2	116	ESCOTT	WC	13	151	ETHERIDGE	L	4	126	EVANS	AF	13	151
ENRIGHT	WR	3	53	ESCRITT	A	8	106	ETHERIDGE	SA	4	126	EVANS	AG	2	117
ENSOR	EE	6	130	ESCRITT	G	8	106	ETHERIDGE	TE	13	151	EVANS	AG	4	126
ENSTEN	AJ	5	116	ESCUDIER	W	7	118	ETHERIDGE	WG	13	151	EVANS	AG	7	119
ENSTONE	F	1	102	ESKEY	G	11	121	ETHERINGTON	EC	7	118	EVANS	AG	13	151
ENSTONE	WC	5	117	ESLAND	H	13	151	ETHERINGTON	EG	10	74	EVANS	AH	1	102
ENTWISTLE	A	11	121	ESPIN	J	8	416	ETHERINGTON	H	8	106	EVANS	AJ	13	151
ENTWISTLE	C	14	100	ESPINER	F	12	301	ETHERINGTON	H	8	106	EVANS	AL	1	102
ENTWISTLE	E	12	301	ESPINER	J	8	106	ETHERINGTON	H	9	63	EVANS	AM	6	131
ENTWISTLE	G	11	121	ESPLEY	FW	6	131	ETHERINGTON	HG	2	117	EVANS	AO	6	131
ENTWISTLE	J	11	121	ESSAM	AH	12	301	ETHERINGTON	J	8	106	EVANS	AP	4	126
ENTWISTLE	J	11	121	ESSAM	B	12	301	ETHERINGTON	J	8	106	EVANS	AR	6	131
ENTWISTLE	J	14	100	ESSAM	G	12	301	ETHERINGTON	JA	9	63	EVANS	AS	1	102

EVANS	AW	2	117	EVANS	F	7	119	EVANS	H	14	101	EVANS	MP	5	118
EVANS	B	3	54	EVANS	F	9	253	EVANS	HA	1	103	EVANS	MP	7	119
EVANS	B	8	107	EVANS	F	11	122	EVANS	HA	6	133	EVANS	N	8	107
EVANS	B	12	80	EVANS	F	13	152	EVANS	HJ	3	54	EVANS	O	5	118
EVANS	BC	13	151	EVANS	FA	2	117	EVANS	HW	7	119	EVANS	O	14	102
EVANS	BE	13	151	EVANS	FA	3	54	EVANS	HW	14	101	EVANS	OC	6	133
EVANS	BWG	5	117	EVANS	FA	12	302	EVANS	J	2	117	EVANS	P	6	133
EVANS	C	1	103	EVANS	FB	6	132	EVANS	J	2	117	EVANS	P	7	119
EVANS	C	5	117	EVANS	FG	6	132	EVANS	J	3	333	EVANS	P	11	122
EVANS	C	6	131	EVANS	FH	11	122	EVANS	J	4	126	EVANS	PE	1	103
EVANS	C	7	119	EVANS	FJ	5	117	EVANS	J	5	118	EVANS	PW	12	80
EVANS	C	12	80	EVANS	FJ	12	80	EVANS	J	6	133	EVANS	R	6	133
EVANS	C	14	100	EVANS	FW	10	74	EVANS	J	6	133	EVANS	R	7	119
EVANS	CE	2	117	EVANS	FW	11	122	EVANS	J	7	119	EVANS	R	7	120
EVANS	CH	11	122	EVANS	G	1	103	EVANS	J	8	107	EVANS	R	12	80
EVANS	CH	12	302	EVANS	G	2	117	EVANS	J	11	122	EVANS	R	14	102
EVANS	CH	13	152	EVANS	G	3	333	EVANS	J	12	80	EVANS	RH	7	120
EVANS	CHJ	7	119	EVANS	G	5	117	EVANS	J	12	80	EVANS	RH	11	123
EVANS	CR	1	103	EVANS	G	5	117	EVANS	J	13	152	EVANS	RJ	4	126
EVANS	CS	3	333	EVANS	G	6	132	EVANS	J	14	101	EVANS	RS	14	102
EVANS	CT	1	103	EVANS	G	6	132	EVANS	J	14	101	EVANS	RW	1	103
EVANS	CT	6	131	EVANS	G	7	119	EVANS	J	14	101	EVANS	RW	6	133
EVANS	CV	6	132	EVANS	G	7	119	EVANS	J	14	101	EVANS	RW	12	81
EVANS	CW	2	117	EVANS	G	10	74	EVANS	J	14	101	EVANS	S	6	133
EVANS	D	6	132	EVANS	G	10	295	EVANS	JC	4	126	EVANS	S	6	133
EVANS	DCB	6	132	EVANS	G	12	80	EVANS	JC	10	295	EVANS	S	13	152
EVANS	DH	2	117	EVANS	G	14	101	EVANS	JCJ	7	119	EVANS	SR	11	123
EVANS	E	3	54	EVANS	G	14	101	EVANS	JE	14	101	EVANS	ST	1	103
EVANS	E	6	132	EVANS	G	14	101	EVANS	JF	11	122	EVANS	SWN	3	54
EVANS	E	6	132	EVANS	G	14	101	EVANS	JH	1	103	EVANS	T	2	118
EVANS	E	6	132	EVANS	GA	8	107	EVANS	JH	2	117	EVANS	T	4	126
EVANS	E	6	132	EVANS	GA	9	253	EVANS	JH	6	133	EVANS	T	6	133
EVANS	E	7	119	EVANS	GE	1	103	EVANS	JH	11	122	EVANS	T	6	133
EVANS	E	8	107	EVANS	GE	5	117	EVANS	JH	14	101	EVANS	T	6	134
EVANS	E	9	253	EVANS	GF	12	80	EVANS	JJ	4	126	EVANS	T	11	123
EVANS	E	10	294	EVANS	GH	2	117	EVANS	JJ	5	118	EVANS	T	11	123
EVANS	E	13	152	EVANS	GH	2	117	EVANS	JJ	6	133	EVANS	T	11	123
EVANS	E	14	100	EVANS	GH	5	118	EVANS	JL	3	333	EVANS	T	13	152
EVANS	EA	5	117	EVANS	GH	6	132	EVANS	JS	11	123	EVANS	T	14	102
EVANS	EA	6	132	EVANS	GP	6	132	EVANS	JT	9	63	EVANS	TB	13	152
EVANS	EA	6	132	EVANS	GW	2	117	EVANS	JT	13	152	EVANS	TC	12	81
EVANS	EA	6	132	EVANS	H	2	117	EVANS	JW	10	74	EVANS	TD	13	152
EVANS	EA	11	122	EVANS	H	4	126	EVANS	JW	14	102	EVANS	TE	12	81
EVANS	EBJ	1	103	EVANS	H	5	118	EVANS	K	1	103	EVANS	TH	6	134
EVANS	EC	2	117	EVANS	H	6	133	EVANS	KG	12	80	EVANS	TH	8	107
EVANS	EC	7	119	EVANS	H	6	133	EVANS	L	1	103	EVANS	THL	6	134
EVANS	EJ	1	103	EVANS	H	7	119	EVANS	L	6	133	EVANS	TW	9	253
EVANS	EJ	5	117	EVANS	H	7	119	EVANS	L	14	102	EVANS	V	14	102
EVANS	ET	13	152	EVANS	H	9	253	EVANS	LF	5	118	EVANS	VA	13	152
EVANS	F	3	333	EVANS	H	10	295	EVANS	LJ	4	126	EVANS	VF	7	120
EVANS	F	5	117	EVANS	H	11	122	EVANS	M	1	103	EVANS	W	1	103
EVANS	F	5	117	EVANS	H	12	302	EVANS	M	6	133	EVANS	W	2	118
EVANS	F	6	132	EVANS	H	14	101	EVANS	M	7	119	EVANS	W	3	54
EVANS	F	6	132	EVANS	H	14	101	EVANS	MH	6	133	EVANS	W	4	126
EVANS	F	6	132	EVANS	H	14	101	EVANS	MM	3	54	EVANS	W	5	118

EVANS	W	5	118	EVENETT	W	1	103	EVERITT	JW	2	118
EVANS	W	5	118	EVENETT	WH	1	103	EVERITT	M	1	104
EVANS	W	6	134	EVERALL	A	11	123	EVERITT	R	1	104
EVANS	W	6	134	EVERALL	S	11	123	EVERITT	T	7	120
EVANS	W	6	134	EVERARD	C	1	103	EVERITT	W	7	120
EVANS	W	7	120	EVERARD	H	1	103	EVERITT	WS	5	118
EVANS	W	8	107	EVERARD	JW	1	103	EVERNDON	E	12	81
EVANS	W	10	74	EVERARD	T	1	104	EVERS	JW	8	107
EVANS	W	10	75	EVERARD	WG	13	152	EVERSDEN	CW	2	118
EVANS	W	10	295	EVERDEN	AW	13	152	EVERSFIELD	MD	13	153
EVANS	W	11	123	EVEREST	H	1	104	EVERSON	F	9	63
EVANS	W	11	123	EVEREST	HC	7	120	EVERSON	HT	2	118
EVANS	W	11	123	EVEREST	R	3	333	EVERSON	T	1	104
EVANS	W	12	81	EVEREST	RC	1	104	EVERTON	TW	6	134
EVANS	W	13	152	EVEREST	TF	7	120	EVERY	TA	3	54
EVANS	W	13	152	EVEREST	WG	10	75	EVERY	WH	10	295
EVANS	W	14	102	EVERETT	A	6	134	EVES	A	10	295
EVANS	W	14	102	EVERETT	A	13	153	EVES	A	14	102
EVANS	W	14	102	EVERETT	AE	1	104	EVES	AG	7	120
EVANS	WA	7	120	EVERETT	AE	5	118	EVES	AW	7	120
EVANS	WA	12	81	EVERETT	AES	3	54	EVES	E	1	104
EVANS	WB	14	102	EVERETT	AH	3	333	EVES	E	10	295
EVANS	WC	12	81	EVERETT	AT	13	153	EVES	EJN	10	295
EVANS	WC	12	302	EVERETT	CF	2	118	EVES	J	1	104
EVANS	WC	13	152	EVERETT	CJ	3	54	EVES	WH	10	295
EVANS	WE	6	134	EVERETT	CJW	2	118	EVES	WH	14	102
EVANS	WE	13	152	EVERETT	DR	13	153	EVESON	J	3	333
EVANS	WE	14	102	EVERETT	EJ	1	104	EVESON	J	3	333
EVANS	WF	6	134	EVERETT	F	5	118	EVETTS	JH	5	118
EVANS	WG	12	81	EVERETT	FH	13	153	EVETTS	WA	5	118
EVANS	WG	12	302	EVERETT	HG	13	153	EVINTON	AE	5	118
EVANS	WH	2	118	EVERETT	J	4	126	EVISON	A	14	102
EVANS	WH	6	134	EVERETT	JG	13	153	EVISON	M	14	102
EVANS	WH	12	81	EVERETT	JGH	13	153	EWART	TC	3	333
EVANS	WH	13	152	EVERETT	L	1	104	EWART	W	3	333
EVANS	WJ	2	118	EVERETT	RE	1	104	EWBANK	T	14	103
EVANS	WJ	3	333	EVERETT	RE	12	81	EWELL	F	6	362
EVANS	WJ	5	118	EVERETT	RH	7	120	EWENS	A	10	295
EVANS	WJ	6	134	EVERETT	T	9	253	EWENS	AH	2	118
EVANS	WJ	6	134	EVERETT	T	13	153	EWENS	SF	10	295
EVANS	WJ	7	120	EVERETT	TE	6	134	EWER	AJ	1	104
EVANS	WJT	13	152	EVERETT	TH	10	75	EWER	CA	10	75
EVANS	WL	2	118	EVERETT	W	1	104	EWER	CW	5	119
EVANS	WS	7	120	EVERETT	W	13	153	EWER	FS	1	104
EVANS	WSC	6	134	EVERETT	WA	12	81	EWER	H	1	104
EVANS	WT	14	102	EVERETT	WG	4	126	EWER	JW	10	75
EVANS	WV	2	118	EVERETT	WG	13	153	EWER	W	5	119
EVATT	R	8	107	EVEREX	SJ	6	134	EWERS	A	6	134
EVE	J	2	118	EVERITE	SH	12	302	EWERS	EG	13	153
EVE	W	7	120	EVERITT	A	6	134	EWERT	F	8	107
EVE	WF	3	333	EVERITT	AT	5	118	EWING	J	9	253
EVELING	RE	7	120	EVERITT	B	5	118	EWINGS	ME	1	104
EVENDEN	H	13	152	EVERITT	CF	2	118	EWINGS	WH	1	104
EVENDEN	WH	3	333	EVERITT	H	1	104	EWINGTON	HJ	5	119
EVENETT	A	1	103	EVERITT	H	1	104	EWINS	B	6	134

EWINS	EW	2	118
EWINS	HC	2	118
EXALL	AH	10	75
EXCELL	CW	1	104
EXELL	E	9	253
EXELL	J	9	253
EXLEY	A	11	123
EXLEY	E	9	63
EXLEY	J	8	107
EXLEY	JW	9	63
EXLEY	S	8	107
EXNER	RE	2	118
EXTANCE	AJ	4	126
EXTANCE	K	4	127
EXTON	JW	11	123
EXTON	W	14	103
EXWORTH	H	1	104
EYCOTT	FC	13	153
EYCOTT	JJ	11	123
EYDEN	FC	6	134
EYDMANN	SC	1	105
EYERS	F	2	118
EYERS	FVA	13	153
EYERS	GH	6	135
EYERS	RC	13	153
EYERS	W	12	302
EYLES	C	12	302
EYLES	JH	1	105
EYLES	O	12	302
EYLES	R	1	105
EYLES	S	14	103
EYRE	C	11	123
EYRE	CW	3	333
EYRE	E	7	120
EYRE	E	14	103
EYRE	F	11	123
EYRE	H	8	107
EYRE	HE	14	103
EYRE	J	14	103
EYRE	JT	12	302
EYRE	RG	13	153
EYRE	S	9	253
EYRE	W	14	103
EYRES	C	11	123
EYRES	F	10	295
EYRES	F	10	295
EYRES	F	14	103
EYRES	FH	4	127
EYRES	J	14	103
EYRES	W	3	333
EYRES	W	4	127
EYRES	W	11	123
EZARD	E	14	103
EZARD	J	14	103
EZARD	T	14	103

F

Name	Init.	Col.	Page
EZRA	G	5	119
FABER	C	14	103
FABER	MF	14	103
FABIAN	F	7	120
FABIAN	J	7	121
FABIAN	JC	10	295
FABIAN	PR	10	75
FABLE	WH	12	81
FACER	AW	10	75
FACER	C	5	119
FACER	CW	12	302
FACER	E	4	127
FACER	EC	12	302
FACER	FW	4	127
FACER	H	5	119
FACER	PW	12	302
FACER	W	3	333
FACER	W	6	135
FACEY	AT	12	81
FACEY	CE	12	81
FACEY	EH	1	105
FACEY	GH	12	81
FACEY	JA	3	54
FACEY	SW	12	81
FACON	A	3	334
FADE	HJ	3	334
FAEIBET	J	9	385
FAGAN	HE	4	127
FAGAN	J	14	103
FAGAN	JH	11	124
FAGAN	JW	8	107
FAGAN	M	7	121
FAGENCE	TH	10	295
FAGG	A	1	105
FAGG	CH	3	54
FAGG	GW	7	121
FAGG	W	1	105
FAGG	WC	13	153
FAGON	JW	8	107
FAGOT	AE	10	295
FAHY	P	6	135
FAIERS	AE	13	153
FAIERS	AJG	13	153
FAIERS	JW	5	119
FAILES	H	9	254
FAILES	HY	3	54
FAIR	BA	13	153
FAIR	GH	13	154
FAIR	JE	3	334
FAIRBAIRN	AH	4	127
FAIRBAIRN	HG	13	154
FAIRBAIRN	SJ	3	54
FAIRBANK	A	11	124
FAIRBANK	AE	7	121
FAIRBANK	GA	8	107
FAIRBANK	WR	1	105
FAIRBANKS	AJT	3	54
FAIRBANKS	J	8	107
FAIRBRASS	JW	1	105
FAIRBROTHER	A	8	107
FAIRBROTHER	AV	7	121
FAIRBROTHER	HE	12	302
FAIRBROTHER	J	14	103
FAIRBROTHER	JF	12	302
FAIRBROTHER	LW	8	107
FAIRBURN	G	8	107
FAIRBURN	J	8	107
FAIRCHIELD	GR	4	127
FAIRCHILD	GH	4	127
FAIRCHILD	PH	2	118
FAIRCLOUGH	C	7	121
FAIRCLOUGH	F	7	121
FAIRCLOUGH	GE	11	124
FAIRCLOUGH	H	7	121
FAIRCLOUGH	JA	2	119
FAIRCLOUGH	JA	8	108
FAIRCLOUGH	JE	9	254
FAIRCLOUGH	R	11	124
FAIRCLOUGH	WR	7	121
FAIREY	A	5	119
FAIREY	AC	12	81
FAIREY	CH	12	302
FAIREY	W	12	81
FAIRFAX	TH	7	121
FAIRFIELD	H	11	124
FAIRHALL	F	7	121
FAIRHALL	FC	7	121
FAIRHALL	HJ	7	121
FAIRHEAD	EF	13	154
FAIRHURST	AW	1	105
FAIRHURST	E	10	296
FAIRHURST	H	14	103
FAIRHURST	HG	1	105
FAIRHURST	W	11	124
FAIRINGSIDE	TH	10	75
FAIRINGSIDE	WG	10	75
FAIRMAN	G	13	154
FAIRMAN	J	13	154
FAIRMAN	JA	7	121
FAIRMAN	JD	7	121
FAIRMAN	W	13	154
FAIRMAN	WF	1	105
FAIRMANER	T	3	54
FAIRS	EE	3	54
FAIRS	GR	3	55
FAIRWEATHER	WJ	1	105
FAIRWEATHER	WS	7	121
FAIRY	JW	12	302
FAITH	AT	3	55
FAITH	CFW	7	121
FAITH	WH	7	122
FAITHFUL	HB	13	154
FAITHFUL	JW	7	122
FAITHFULL	ET	12	81
FAITHFULL	G	7	122
FAITHFULL	JW	4	127
FAITHFULL	WJ	4	127
FAKE	AC	2	119
FAKE	H	8	108
FAKE	W	8	108
FAKES	WG	3	334
FALCONER	GF	1	105
FALCONER	J	6	135
FALCONER	R	1	105
FALEY	T	11	124
FALK	F	2	119
FALK	S	14	104
FALKINER	B	6	135
FALKINGHAM	C	8	108
FALKINGHAM	H	9	254
FALKNER	PJ	12	303
FALL	A	8	108
FALL	A	8	108
FALL	H	4	127
FALL	H	9	254
FALLA	FJ	4	127
FALLON	A	9	63
FALLON	CH	9	63
FALLON	E	9	63
FALLON	ET	6	135
FALLON	F	9	63
FALLON	F	9	63
FALLON	H	6	135
FALLON	J	8	108
FALLON	J	9	63
FALLON	J	14	104
FALLON	JE	8	108
FALLON	JF	6	135
FALLON	JF	11	124
FALLON	L	14	104
FALLON	P	9	63
FALLON	P	9	63
FALLON	T	6	135
FALLOWFIELD	G	5	119
FALLOWS	G	3	55
FALLOWS	GJ	2	119
FALLOWS	S	14	104
FALLOWS	T	14	104
FAMBELY	L	14	104
FANCEY	AH	10	296
FANCUTT	C	12	81
FANCY	AH	4	127
FANCY	AR	4	127
FANCY	FG	10	75
FANCY	FT	4	127
FANE	AJ	1	105
FANNING	A	11	124
FANNING	C	13	154
FANNING	E	3	55
FANNING	JE	3	55
FANSTONE	A	4	127
FANSTONE	B	4	127
FANSTONE	SH	4	127
FANSTONE	TS	4	127
FANTHAM	T	6	135
FARACY	BW	10	75
FARADAY	G	11	124
FARAGHER	F	6	135
FARAGHER	T	6	135
FAREY	E	5	119
FAREY	M	5	119
FAREY	M	8	108
FARLANDER	FT	2	119
FARLEY	AA	13	154
FARLEY	AE	2	119
FARLEY	DF	7	122
FARLEY	E	13	154
FARLEY	E	13	154
FARLEY	EE	3	55
FARLEY	EJ	13	154
FARLEY	FV	2	119
FARLEY	G	4	128
FARLEY	G	9	385
FARLEY	H	3	334
FARLEY	J	7	122
FARLEY	J	11	124
FARLEY	J	14	104
FARLEY	L	7	122
FARLEY	RH	2	119
FARLEY	S	11	124
FARLEY	W	1	105
FARLEY	W	11	124
FARLEY	W	14	104
FARMAN	H	8	108
FARMAR	WA	13	154
FARMER	A	2	119
FARMER	AC	7	122
FARMER	AE	5	119
FARMER	AJ	4	128
FARMER	AJ	12	82
FARMER	AL	4	128
FARMER	AS	12	303
FARMER	AW	4	128
FARMER	CW	10	75
FARMER	EA	13	154
FARMER	EJ	1	105
FARMER	EN	4	128

FARMER	EW	12	303	FARNHAM	H	10	296	FARRAND	JW	8	108	FARRELL	J	7	123
FARMER	F	12	82	FARNHAM	J	5	119	FARRANT	A	10	75	FARRELL	J	8	109
FARMER	F	13	154	FARNHAM	LF	5	120	FARRANT	AA	3	55	FARRELL	J	8	109
FARMER	FG	13	154	FARNSWORTH	B	3	334	FARRANT	AJ	3	334	FARRELL	J	11	124
FARMER	FW	7	122	FARNSWORTH	GA	1	105	FARRANT	FHG	10	296	FARRELL	J	14	104
FARMER	FW	12	303	FARNSWORTH	JT	6	135	FARRANT	FW	7	122	FARRELL	J	14	105
FARMER	GA	6	135	FARNSWORTH	S	6	135	FARRANT	HJ	7	122	FARRELL	JF	14	105
FARMER	H	4	128	FARNSWORTH	W	1	105	FARRANT	HJJ	2	119	FARRELL	JJ	2	119
FARMER	H	5	119	FARNSWORTH	W	6	135	FARRANT	JE	7	122	FARRELL	JJ	3	55
FARMER	HC	12	303	FARNSWORTH	W	6	135	FARRANT	JF	2	119	FARRELL	JJ	8	109
FARMER	HC	13	154	FARNWORTH	A	11	124	FARRANT	JG	3	55	FARRELL	JW	3	55
FARMER	HE	10	75	FARNWORTH	J	14	104	FARRANT	RJ	7	123	FARRELL	L	7	123
FARMER	HF	12	303	FARNWORTH	T	11	124	FARRANT	TWG	7	123	FARRELL	L	11	124
FARMER	HR	5	119	FARNWORTH	T	14	104	FARRANT	WJC	7	123	FARRELL	M	14	105
FARMER	J	4	128	FARQUHARSON	W	14	104	FARRAR	B	8	108	FARRELL	R	11	125
FARMER	J	5	119	FARR	A	4	128	FARRAR	D	9	254	FARRELL	T	14	105
FARMER	J	5	119	FARR	A	7	122	FARRAR	DC	8	108	FARRELL	T	14	105
FARMER	J	12	303	FARR	AC	6	136	FARRAR	F	12	82	FARRELL	T	14	105
FARMER	JF	14	104	FARR	AJ	7	122	FARRAR	F	14	104	FARRELL	W	1	106
FARMER	JFC	2	119	FARR	AL	6	136	FARRAR	FS	10	76	FARRELL	W	6	136
FARMER	JR	7	122	FARR	C	4	128	FARRAR	FT	12	82	FARRELL	WE	10	296
FARMER	JW	9	254	FARR	CW	5	120	FARRAR	GW	9	64	FARRELLY	JJ	11	125
FARMER	L	5	119	FARR	EC	2	119	FARRAR	H	8	108	FARRELLY	JV	11	125
FARMER	M	1	105	FARR	F	4	128	FARRAR	H	8	108	FARREN	FG	3	334
FARMER	R	5	119	FARR	F	5	120	FARRAR	H	9	64	FARRER	A	2	119
FARMER	RLN	1	105	FARR	F	10	75	FARRAR	H	9	64	FARRER	AB	1	106
FARMER	RS	6	135	FARR	F	12	82	FARRAR	HA	8	108	FARRER	AH	12	82
FARMER	T	12	82	FARR	FWJ	10	75	FARRAR	J	8	108	FARRER	CH	8	109
FARMER	TH	12	82	FARR	H	4	128	FARRAR	J	9	64	FARRER	E	2	120
FARMER	W	5	120	FARR	H	5	120	FARRAR	J	9	254	FARRER	H	14	105
FARMER	W	10	296	FARR	H	8	108	FARRAR	JA	8	109	FARRER	J	3	55
FARMER	W	12	303	FARR	HO	6	136	FARRAR	JA	8	109	FARRER	R	9	254
FARMER	WE	13	154	FARR	HO	6	136	FARRAR	JF	12	82	FARRER	RS	8	109
FARMER	WF	13	154	FARR	J	10	296	FARRAR	JW	12	82	FARRER	RW	12	82
FARMER	WG	4	128	FARR	JW	8	108	FARRAR	M	8	109	FARRER	S	8	109
FARMER	WG	5	120	FARR	L	4	128	FARRAR	P	8	109	FARRICKER	FW	11	125
FARMER	WHJ	13	154	FARR	L	9	63	FARRAR	S	8	109	FARRICKER	J	11	125
FARMINER	A	10	75	FARR	R	7	122	FARRAR	S	8	109	FARRILLY	W	4	129
FARMINER	HR	4	128	FARR	RJ	2	119	FARRAR	S	8	109	FARRINGTON	A	8	109
FARMINER	SG	10	296	FARR	S	4	128	FARRAR	S	8	109	FARRINGTON	A	11	125
FARNAN	AG	4	128	FARR	TJ	1	106	FARRAR	W	8	109	FARRINGTON	AW	3	334
FARNAN	CE	4	128	FARR	TW	6	136	FARRAR	W	14	104	FARRINGTON	C	10	76
FARNDON	TE	3	334	FARR	W	2	119	FARRAR	W	14	104	FARRINGTON	D	6	136
FARNELL	C	8	108	FARR	W	10	75	FARRELL	AE	6	136	FARRINGTON	D	7	123
FARNELL	E	6	135	FARR	WH	4	128	FARRELL	B	6	136	FARRINGTON	EH	3	334
FARNELL	H	9	63	FARR	WJ	2	119	FARRELL	C	11	124	FARRINGTON	F	3	334
FARNELL	H	14	104	FARRAH	J	8	108	FARRELL	CB	7	123	FARRINGTON	GH	12	82
FARNELL	VB	4	128	FARRAH	JW	9	64	FARRELL	CP	10	296	FARRINGTON	J	11	125
FARNES	A	4	128	FARRAN	P	14	104	FARRELL	F	6	136	FARRINGTON	J	11	125
FARNFIELD	AE	2	119	FARRAN	TH	13	154	FARRELL	F	7	123	FARRINGTON	L	11	125
FARNFIELD	J	7	122	FARRANCE	CE	1	106	FARRELL	F	13	155	FARRINGTON	W	1	106
FARNFIELD	L	7	122	FARRAND	A	9	64	FARRELL	FJ	7	123	FARRINGTON	W	11	125
FARNHAM	A	5	120	FARRAND	A	9	254	FARRELL	GW	14	104	FARROW	C	4	128
FARNHAM	A	7	122	FARRAND	B	11	124	FARRELL	H	6	136	FARROW	CG	5	120
FARNHAM	H	5	120	FARRAND	F	9	64	FARRELL	H	6	136	FARROW	E	6	136
												FARRELL	J	7	123				

FARROW	E	12	82	FAULKNER	GF	4	129	FAVELL	O	12	422	FEAR	AE	1	106
FARROW	G	11	125	FAULKNER	GF	7	123	FAVELL	W	3	334	FEAREY	GH	1	106
FARROW	H	7	123	FAULKNER	GH	14	105	FAVILL	W	8	109	FEAREY	JL	11	126
FARROW	HA	7	123	FAULKNER	GS	12	82	FAWCETT	A	8	109	FEAREY	PE	12	304
FARROW	HS	12	303	FAULKNER	H	12	82	FAWCETT	A	8	109	FEARN	A	6	137
FARROW	J	13	155	FAULKNER	H	12	303	FAWCETT	A	8	109	FEARN	AE	5	121
FARROW	JA	3	334	FAULKNER	HE	12	82	FAWCETT	AL	8	110	FEARN	CE	5	121
FARROW	JA	6	136	FAULKNER	HG	13	155	FAWCETT	E	11	126	FEARN	W	5	121
FARROW	JE	11	125	FAULKNER	J	6	136	FAWCETT	E	13	155	FEARN	WT	6	137
FARROW	JR	4	129	FAULKNER	J	7	123	FAWCETT	EW	1	106	FEARNCLOUGH	S	11	126
FARROW	PJ	4	129	FAULKNER	J	11	125	FAWCETT	F	9	64	FEARNELEY	HC	14	106
FARROW	R	12	303	FAULKNER	J	11	125	FAWCETT	G	9	254	FEARNHEAD	RV	10	76
FARROW	RJ	13	155	FAULKNER	J	11	125	FAWCETT	GM	9	64	FEARNLEY	A	9	64
FARTHING	CH	1	106	FAULKNER	J	12	303	FAWCETT	H	8	110	FEARNLEY	C	8	110
FARTHING	J	14	105	FAULKNER	JG	12	303	FAWCETT	J	8	110	FEARNLEY	E	9	65
FARTHING	J	14	105	FAULKNER	JH	1	106	FAWCETT	J	8	110	FEARNLEY	G	9	65
FARTHING	J	14	105	FAULKNER	JW	13	155	FAWCETT	J	9	64	FEARNLEY	G	9	65
FARTHING	R	13	155	FAULKNER	JW	14	105	FAWCETT	JA	7	124	FEARNLEY	J	8	110
FARWIG	HF	7	123	FAULKNER	L	5	120	FAWCETT	JD	8	110	FEARNLEY	J	9	65
FATHERS	AW	6	136	FAULKNER	L	10	76	FAWCETT	JH	8	110	FEARNLEY	J	14	106
FATHERS	EG	5	120	FAULKNER	RH	3	334	FAWCETT	JH	9	385	FEARNLEY	JA	8	110
FATHERS	F	1	106	FAULKNER	S	12	82	FAWCETT	JM	9	254	FEARNLEY	JW	9	65
FATHERS	JA	1	106	FAULKNER	SJT	1	106	FAWCETT	JP	9	64	FEARNLEY	R	8	110
FATHERS	JT	4	129	FAULKNER	SOR	12	303	FAWCETT	JW	3	334	FEARNLEY	R	9	65
FATHERS	T	6	136	FAULKNER	T	4	129	FAWCETT	JW	11	126	FEARNLEY	WF	9	65
FAULCONBRIDGE	W	9	64	FAULKNER	T	6	137	FAWCETT	LH	7	124	FEARNSIDE	E	9	65
FAULDER	PG	5	120	FAULKNER	T	11	125	FAWCETT	RC	9	64	FEARNSIDE	H	9	254
FAULDER	RA	1	106	FAULKNER	T	12	303	FAWCETT	S	8	110	FEARNSIDE	W	8	110
FAULKES	B	13	155	FAULKNER	TG	5	120	FAWCETT	TW	8	110	FEARY	E	12	83
FAULKES	H	14	105	FAULKNER	TJ	7	124	FAWCETT	W	8	110	FEARY	JW	12	83
FAULKNER	A	5	120	FAULKNER	W	5	120	FAWCETT	W	8	110	FEARY	WJ	10	76
FAULKNER	A	6	136	FAULKNER	W	6	137	FAWCETT	W	8	110	FEASEY	D	6	137
FAULKNER	A	10	296	FAULKNER	W	12	82	FAWCETT	W	8	110	FEASEY	HA	12	83
FAULKNER	A	11	125	FAULKNER	W	12	83	FAWCETT	W	8	110	FEASEY	JH	12	83
FAULKNER	A	11	125	FAULKNER	W	14	105	FAWCETT	W	9	254	FEASEY	VD	6	137
FAULKNER	A	14	105	FAULKNER	W	14	105	FAWCETT	WAV	6	137	FEAST	G	1	106
FAULKNER	AE	12	82	FAULKNER	WA	7	124	FAWCETT	WF	9	64	FEATHER	A	8	110
FAULKNER	AG	5	120	FAULKNER	WA	8	109	FAWDRY	JH	6	137	FEATHER	JW	9	385
FAULKNER	AG	13	155	FAULKNER	WH	7	124	FAWLEY	J	8	110	FEATHER	W	8	110
FAULKNER	AJ	7	123	FAULKNER	WJ	6	137	FAWLEY	T	11	126	FEATHERS	WN	1	106
FAULKNER	B	12	82	FAULKNER	WS	12	303	FAWLEY	W	8	110	FEATHERSTONE	CJ	4	129
FAULKNER	B	12	303	FAULKNER	WW	13	155	FAWTHORP	J	9	64	FEATHERSTONE	G	13	155
FAULKNER	C	5	120	FAULTLESS	H	6	137	FAWTHROP	A	9	64	FEAVER	E	1	106
FAULKNER	C	6	136	FAUNCH	J	5	120	FAWTHROP	A	9	254	FEAY	J	14	106
FAULKNER	CA	5	120	FAUNTHORPE	B	9	64	FAWTHROP	W	9	64	FEAZEY	WE	5	121
FAULKNER	D	11	125	FAUTLEY	H	13	155	FAWTHROP	W	9	254	FEE	EN	4	129
FAULKNER	D	11	125	FAUX	AH	7	124	FAY	AA	4	129	FEE	SE	4	129
FAULKNER	E	12	303	FAUX	CH	7	124	FAY	J	7	124	FEE	W	4	129
FAULKNER	F	10	296	FAVELL	E	5	121	FAY	P	14	106	FEEHAN	J	11	126
FAULKNER	F	14	105	FAVELL	E	12	83	FAY	W	11	126	FEELEY	AG	13	155
FAULKNER	FH	4	129	FAVELL	FW	12	83	FAY	WH	14	106	FEELEY	WJ	4	129
FAULKNER	G	12	303	FAVELL	G	5	121	FAZACKARLEY	T	10	76	FEELY	J	9	65
FAULKNER	G	12	303	FAVELL	G	12	83	FAZACKERLEY	R	7	124	FEENEY	L	6	137
FAULKNER	G	13	155	FAVELL	H	12	83	FAZAKERLEY	A	14	106	FEENEY	T	14	106
FAULKNER	G	14	105	FAVELL	HG	12	304	FEAKINS	PJ	1	106	FEENY	J	4	129
								FEAKS	FA	10	296				

FEGAN	J	4	129	FELTHAM	M	4	129	FENSOM	L	5	121	FENTON	W	3	55
FELCE	F	12	83	FELTHAM	W	10	76	FENSOM	WC	12	83	FENTON	W	13	156
FELCE	RE	12	304	FELTON	F	6	137	FENSOM	WW	5	121	FENTON	W	14	106
FELDMAN	D	14	106	FELTON	FJ	2	120	FENSOME	A	5	121	FENTON	WSCH	10	76
FELDON	DC	3	334	FELTON	G	6	137	FENSOME	AH	5	122	FENTON-YORKE	HW	10	297
FELDWICK	EF	2	120	FELTON	HW	2	120	FENSOME	AJ	5	122	FENTUM	HE	2	120
FELGATE	E	9	254	FELTON	SG	4	129	FENSOME	B	5	122	FENWICK	AG	3	55
FELIX	HA	13	155	FELTON	TJ	4	130	FENSOME	CF	5	122	FENWICK	GW	8	111
FELIX	WA	1	106	FELTON	TW	4	130	FENSOME	CH	5	122	FERBRACHE	A	4	130
FELIX	WA	1	106	FELTS	CE	1	106	FENSOME	CR	5	122	FEREADY	CV	1	107
FELKS	A	5	121	FELTS	CE	2	120	FENSOME	EA	5	122	FEREBEE	AE	3	55
FELKS	H	5	121	FENABLES	F	12	83	FENSOME	EW	5	122	FEREDAY	FG	6	138
FELKS	T	5	121	FENBY	WM	14	106	FENSOME	F	5	122	FERGOOD	EW	7	124
FELKS	TS	5	121	FENDLEY	AF	13	155	FENSOME	G	5	122	FERGUSON	A	13	156
FELL	FH	1	106	FENELEY	DJ	12	83	FENSOME	G	5	122	FERGUSON	B	8	111
FELL	HF	9	65	FENEMORE	LT	5	121	FENSOME	GA	5	122	FERGUSON	D	8	111
FELL	J	9	65	FENGE	A	2	120	FENSOME	H	5	122	FERGUSON	DC	3	55
FELL	J	9	254	FENLEY	J	5	121	FENSOME	HC	5	122	FERGUSON	E	8	111
FELL	MF	12	304	FENLON	JH	14	106	FENSOME	J	12	83	FERGUSON	EJ	13	156
FELL	N	5	121	FENLON	SW	13	155	FENSOME	J	13	156	FERGUSON	G	1	107
FELL	S	13	155	FENLON	WA	13	156	FENSOME	L	5	122	FERGUSON	G	1	107
FELL	T	9	65	FENN	AG	10	296	FENSOME	MC	13	156	FERGUSON	GA	9	65
FELL	W	9	65	FENN	AW	12	83	FENSOME	P	5	122	FERGUSON	GB	14	106
FELLOWES	SG	4	129	FENN	JA	12	304	FENSOME	PE	5	122	FERGUSON	GW	10	76
FELLOWES	W	11	126	FENN	LW	12	304	FENSOME	S	5	122	FERGUSON	HC	8	111
FELLOWES	WJ	13	155	FENN	RA	12	304	FENSOME	S	8	111	FERGUSON	J	8	111
FELLOWS	A	9	254	FENN	S	2	120	FENSOME	SC	5	123	FERGUSON	J	8	111
FELLOWS	AE	10	76	FENN	T	13	156	FENSOME	T	5	123	FERGUSON	J	8	111
FELLOWS	AT	6	137	FENN	TJ	2	120	FENSOME	W	5	123	FERGUSON	J	11	126
FELLOWS	E	14	106	FENNALL	CE	13	156	FENSOME	W	5	123	FERGUSON	J	11	126
FELLOWS	G	10	296	FENNELL	CW	2	120	FENSOME	WE	12	83	FERGUSON	J	11	126
FELLOWS	GF	6	137	FENNELL	FG	10	76	FENTIMAN	R	2	120	FERGUSON	J	14	106
FELLOWS	GW	2	120	FENNELL	FG	10	297	FENTON	A	9	65	FERGUSON	M	9	66
FELLOWS	H	6	137	FENNELL	HJ	7	124	FENTON	AE	10	297	FERGUSON	S	11	126
FELLOWS	H	6	137	FENNELL	JH	13	156	FENTON	CD	3	335	FERGUSON	S	14	106
FELLOWS	H	6	137	FENNELL	JW	1	107	FENTON	E	8	111	FERGUSON	TA	12	84
FELLOWS	H	10	296	FENNELL	RJ	1	107	FENTON	E	8	111	FERGUSON	W	4	130
FELLOWS	JW	6	137	FENNELL	SA	2	120	FENTON	E	9	65	FERGUSON	W	14	106
FELLOWS	PA	6	137	FENNELL	SW	1	107	FENTON	E	14	106	FERGUSON	WA	14	107
FELLOWS	S	5	121	FENNELL	TE	2	120	FENTON	G	9	65	FERGUSON	WJ	13	156
FELLOWS	TH	3	55	FENNELL	W	1	107	FENTON	G	9	254	FERGUSON	WP	2	120
FELLOWS	TH	10	296	FENNELL	WC	13	156	FENTON	H	8	111	FERIN	CS	13	156
FELLS	B	12	83	FENNEMORE	AE	1	107	FENTON	H	8	111	FERMALON	EH	6	138
FELLS	BN	12	304	FENNEMORE	AL	1	107	FENTON	IT	14	106	FERN	FJ	2	120
FELLS	FRG	7	124	FENNEMORE	H	1	107	FENTON	J	3	55	FERN	ST	1	107
FELLS	H	5	121	FENNEMORE	R	1	107	FENTON	J	8	111	FERNANDEZ	RW	10	297
FELLS	HJ	12	304	FENNEMORE	WJ	1	107	FENTON	J	8	111	FERNELEY	J	11	126
FELLS	WJF	12	304	FENNER	F	3	55	FENTON	J	11	126	FERNEYHOUGH	TH	13	156
FELSTEAD	CR	11	126	FENNER	G	2	120	FENTON	J	11	126	FERNIE	D	14	107
FELSTEAD	F	1	106	FENNER	H	3	335	FENTON	J	11	126	FERNIE	J	14	107
FELSTEAD	FW	7	124	FENNINGS	FC	7	124	FENTON	JL	8	111	FERNLEY	C	2	120
FELSTEAD	HC	7	124	FENNYMORE	GT	3	55	FENTON	M	9	65	FERNLEY	W	14	107
FELSTEAD	HE	7	124	FENSOM	CW	12	83	FENTON	M	14	106	FERNOT	A	13	156
FELTHAM	C	4	129	FENSOM	J	12	83	FENTON	N	8	111	FERNS	HJ	10	297
FELTHAM	G	13	155	FENSOM	J	12	83	FENTON	RT	8	111	FERNS	M	11	126
								FENTON	T	13	156				

FERNSIDE	JW	9	385
FERRE	H	10	76
FERRE	W	10	76
FERRER	H	2	120
FERRETT	BP	10	76
FERRIMAN	H	6	138
FERRIMAN	PG	2	121
FERRIS	CW	11	421
FERRIS	E	13	156
FERRIS	JS	10	76
FERRIS	P	13	156
FERRIS	T	8	111
FERRIS	WJ	10	76
FERRISS	GR	11	126
FERRY	E	9	255
FERRY	G	4	130
FERRY	GH	4	130
FERRY	GH	4	130
FERRY	HH	13	156
FERRY	JE	4	130
FERRY	JH	4	130
FESSEY	GF	12	84
FESSEY	J	12	84
FESSEY	WF	12	84
FETHERSTON	T	11	126
FETT	LC	8	111
FEVER	H	1	107
FEVER	J	1	107
FEVER	W	1	107
FEW	G	6	138
FEW	LC	3	56
FEWINGS	GD	10	76
FEWINS	GH	13	156
FEWINS	H	13	156
FEWSTER	BV	8	111
FEWSTER	CR	1	107
FEWTRELL	A	6	138
FEWTRELL	AE	3	335
FEWTRELL	EG	6	138
FEWTRELL	GS	7	124
FEWTRELL	KF	6	138
FEWTRELL	R	11	127
FEWTRELL	RG	3	335
FEWTRELL	W	6	138
FEY	AA	3	335
FIANDER	EG	4	130
FICE	PA	1	107
FICE	ST	1	107
FICKEN	JH	10	76
FICKLING	E	5	123
FIDDES	F	3	56
FIDDES	W	2	121
FIDDIS	RF	10	297
FIDDLER	EHS	6	138
FIDDLER	ES	6	138
FIDDLER	G	11	127
FIDDLER	J	11	127
FIDDY	AE	12	304
FIDLER	F	13	157
FIDLER	FC	2	121
FIDLER	FG	3	335
FIDLER	JH	14	107
FIDLER	L	5	123
FIDLER	R	10	77
FIDLER	TH	11	127
FIDO	WC	13	157
FIELD	A	1	107
FIELD	A	3	335
FIELD	A	4	130
FIELD	A	5	123
FIELD	A	6	138
FIELD	A	9	255
FIELD	A	12	84
FIELD	A	13	157
FIELD	A	13	157
FIELD	AC	5	123
FIELD	AE	3	56
FIELD	AJ	12	84
FIELD	AW	3	335
FIELD	B	1	107
FIELD	B	6	138
FIELD	BA	2	121
FIELD	C	6	138
FIELD	C	12	84
FIELD	CE	6	138
FIELD	CF	5	123
FIELD	COW	13	157
FIELD	CW	9	66
FIELD	DAR	4	130
FIELD	E	5	123
FIELD	E	6	138
FIELD	EJ	5	123
FIELD	ES	2	121
FIELD	F	1	107
FIELD	F	3	335
FIELD	F	5	123
FIELD	F	5	123
FIELD	F	5	123
FIELD	F	12	84
FIELD	FC	13	157
FIELD	FF	5	123
FIELD	FG	6	138
FIELD	FJ	10	77
FIELD	FW	6	138
FIELD	G	5	123
FIELD	G	6	138
FIELD	G	6	138
FIELD	GE	5	123
FIELD	GE	5	123
FIELD	GF	6	138
FIELD	GH	2	121
FIELD	GH	10	77
FIELD	GL	12	304
FIELD	H	5	124
FIELD	H	6	138
FIELD	H	8	112
FIELD	H	9	66
FIELD	H	9	66
FIELD	H	9	255
FIELD	H	11	127
FIELD	H	12	84
FIELD	H	13	157
FIELD	H	13	157
FIELD	H	13	157
FIELD	HE	12	84
FIELD	HP	1	108
FIELD	HR	13	157
FIELD	J	1	108
FIELD	J	2	121
FIELD	J	2	121
FIELD	J	4	130
FIELD	J	5	124
FIELD	J	5	124
FIELD	JA	6	139
FIELD	JB	8	112
FIELD	JG	2	121
FIELD	JG	5	124
FIELD	JG	12	304
FIELD	JH	2	121
FIELD	JT	4	130
FIELD	JW	2	121
FIELD	JW	3	335
FIELD	JW	3	335
FIELD	JW	8	112
FIELD	K	2	121
FIELD	L	5	124
FIELD	P	5	124
FIELD	PR	7	124
FIELD	R	5	124
FIELD	RW	1	108
FIELD	S	5	124
FIELD	SH	13	157
FIELD	T	5	124
FIELD	T	9	66
FIELD	T	11	127
FIELD	T	12	304
FIELD	W	5	124
FIELD	W	6	139
FIELD	W	6	139
FIELD	W	8	112
FIELD	W	8	112
FIELD	W	12	84
FIELD	W	13	157
FIELD	W	13	157
FIELD	W	13	157
FIELD	WA	5	124
FIELD	WA	5	124
FIELD	WD	6	139
FIELD	WE	2	121
FIELD	WH	2	121
FIELD	WJ	7	125
FIELD	WR	13	157
FIELD	WT	5	124
FIELDEN	A	9	255
FIELDEN	W	11	127
FIELDEOVITCH	H	2	121
FIELDER	AE	10	77
FIELDER	AH	1	108
FIELDER	AJ	2	121
FIELDER	AW	4	130
FIELDER	BE	7	125
FIELDER	E	2	121
FIELDER	EC	4	130
FIELDER	EW	2	121
FIELDER	FD	4	130
FIELDER	H	4	130
FIELDER	JA	10	77
FIELDER	JS	10	77
FIELDER	R	9	66
FIELDER	W	4	130
FIELDHOUSE	AE	9	255
FIELDHOUSE	C	8	112
FIELDHOUSE	E	9	255
FIELDHOUSE	G	6	139
FIELDHOUSE	GJ	6	139
FIELDHOUSE	H	9	255
FIELDHOUSE	H	9	255
FIELDHOUSE	J	8	112
FIELDHOUSE	J	9	66
FIELDHOUSE	J	9	385
FIELDHOUSE	JW	9	66
FIELDHOUSE	JW	9	255
FIELDHOUSE	JW	11	127
FIELDHOUSE	JWH	9	255
FIELDHOUSE	L	8	112
FIELDHOUSE	R	9	66
FIELDHOUSE	S	8	112
FIELDHOUSE	S	11	127
FIELDHOUSE	W	8	112
FIELDING	A	7	125
FIELDING	AW	1	108
FIELDING	C	9	255
FIELDING	C	11	127
FIELDING	CF	11	127
FIELDING	E	8	112
FIELDING	E	11	127
FIELDING	E	14	107
FIELDING	F	8	112
FIELDING	F	8	112
FIELDING	F	11	127

FIELDING	FA	9	255	FILKIN	A	4	131	FINCH	HT	7	125	FINLEY	F	6	139
FIELDING	G	11	127	FILKINS	J	3	335	FINCH	J	11	128	FINLEY	HW	11	128
FIELDING	G	14	107	FILKINS	JW	13	158	FINCH	J	14	107	FINLEY	W	14	107
FIELDING	HA	6	139	FILLER	CD	5	124	FINCH	JA	2	122	FINLEY	WH	11	128
FIELDING	J	8	112	FILLERY	AC	3	335	FINCH	JF	12	304	FINN	A	14	107
FIELDING	J	9	255	FILLERY	AE	3	335	FINCH	JW	4	131	FINN	B	8	113
FIELDING	J	9	255	FILLERY	AJ	13	158	FINCH	NC	10	297	FINN	E	13	159
FIELDING	J	11	127	FILLERY	CW	13	158	FINCH	NH	10	297	FINN	FC	6	139
FIELDING	J	12	304	FILLERY	WE	3	335	FINCH	NL	2	122	FINN	FT	1	108
FIELDING	J	14	107	FILLINGHAM	WH	2	122	FINCH	R	7	125	FINN	FT	1	108
FIELDING	JE	8	112	FILLIS	C	7	125	FINCH	RF	1	108	FINN	J	6	139
FIELDING	LF	6	139	FILLIS	H	13	158	FINCH	RT	1	108	FINN	J	7	125
FIELDING	N	8	112	FILLIS	J	7	125	FINCH	SF	12	84	FINN	J	8	113
FIELDING	NT	6	139	FILMER	AJ	2	122	FINCH	T	4	131	FINN	J	10	77
FIELDING	R	11	127	FILMER	CA	13	158	FINCH	T	7	125	FINN	J	13	159
FIELDING	S	8	112	FILMER	ES	2	122	FINCH	TB	4	131	FINN	JG	6	139
FIELDING	W	8	112	FILMER	OW	3	335	FINCH	TJ	2	122	FINN	R	8	113
FIELDING	W	11	127	FILMORE	E	13	158	FINCH	TW	13	158	FINN	RH	2	122
FIELDING	WH	7	125	FINAL	G	5	124	FINCH	VE	3	335	FINN	S	2	122
FIELDING	WH	13	157	FINALL	E	2	122	FINCH	W	3	56	FINN	T	8	113
FIELDS	E	8	112	FINAN	E	9	66	FINCH	W	3	335	FINN	WJ	13	159
FIELDS	J	9	66	FINAN	E	9	385	FINCH	W	3	336	FINNEGAN	LW	2	122
FIELDS	WG	8	112	FINAN	W	9	255	FINCH	W	8	113	FINNERAN	H	14	107
FIENBURGH	M	9	66	FINAR	GW	5	124	FINCH	W	11	128	FINNERTY	LF	1	108
FIFIELD	F	10	77	FINBOW	AE	1	108	FINCH	W	13	158	FINNERTY	MJ	11	128
FIFIELD	F	10	77	FINBOW	F	7	125	FINCH	WJ	11	128	FINNERTY	T	13	159
FIFIELD	FH	13	157	FINBOW	FG	3	56	FINCH	WT	12	84	FINNERTY	WA	1	108
FIFIELD	H	10	77	FINBOW	HG	1	108	FINCHAM	S	2	122	FINNEY	A	11	128
FIFIELD	W	10	77	FINCH	A	13	158	FINCHER	H	3	56	FINNEY	C	11	421
FIFIELD	W	10	77	FINCH	AE	2	122	FINCHER	JG	12	84	FINNEY	GH	10	297
FIFIELD	WE	10	77	FINCH	AG	13	158	FINCHETT	J	11	128	FINNEY	R	11	128
FIFORD	RJ	10	297	FINCH	AH	4	131	FINCK	CB	6	139	FINNEY	W	11	128
FIGG	A	5	124	FINCH	AS	2	122	FINDEN	H	2	122	FINNEY	W	14	107
FIGG	E	10	77	FINCH	B	2	122	FINDING	C	12	84	FINNIGAN	A	6	139
FIGG	H	5	124	FINCH	BA	12	84	FINDING	R	13	158	FINNIGAN	E	11	128
FIGG	LC	13	157	FINCH	C	1	108	FINDLAW	F	11	128	FINNIGAN	JC	2	122
FIGG	TH	13	157	FINCH	C	4	131	FINDLAY	JL	13	158	FINNIS	HJ	2	123
FIGG	WG	5	124	FINCH	C	10	77	FINDLAY	PJ	13	158	FINNY	H	6	139
FIGG	WR	13	158	FINCH	CA	13	158	FINDLAY	RE	13	159	FINTER	EF	9	66
FIGGINS	AE	10	77	FINCH	CE	10	297	FINDLEY	W	4	131	FINUCANE	HT	1	108
FIGGINS	JA	4	131	FINCH	D	9	66	FINDLOW	JH	11	128	FIRBANK	E	8	113
FILBEY	T	2	122	FINCH	E	3	56	FINDON	AB	6	139	FIRBANK	MH	8	113
FILBURN	J	8	113	FINCH	E	4	131	FINDON	T	1	108	FIRBANK	W	8	113
FILBURN	R	8	113	FINCH	EW	1	108	FINDON	WH	7	125	FIRBY	AM	11	128
FILBY	C	13	158	FINCH	EW	13	158	FINEDON	JW	12	304	FIRKIN	W	6	139
FILBY	GW	2	122	FINCH	F	1	108	FINEL	L	5	124	FIRKINS	GJ	6	140
FILBY	TC	2	122	FINCH	F	7	125	FINEMORE	WGJ	7	125	FIRKINS	W	6	140
FILBY	WH	12	84	FINCH	F	8	113	FINK	N	14	107	FIRKINS	W	6	140
FILCE	GH	13	158	FINCH	F	12	84	FINLAY	FW	10	77	FIRMAN	B	13	159
FILDES	J	11	127	FINCH	FB	7	125	FINLAY	G	11	128	FIRMAN	CG	2	123
FILDES	J	14	107	FINCH	FJ	7	125	FINLAY	J	10	77	FIRMAN	FL	10	297
FILDES	JH	14	107	FINCH	FR	3	56	FINLAY	JR	13	159	FIRMAN	SH	1	108
FILDES	JJ	11	127	FINCH	GF	3	56	FINLAY	KL	13	159	FIRMIN	G	13	159
FILDES	JT	11	128	FINCH	HGS	2	122	FINLAYSON	A	2	122	FIRMIN	HA	10	77
FILES	R	14	107	FINCH	HR	4	131	FINLEY	E	6	139	FIRMINGER	E	3	56

FIRMINGER	J	3	56	FIRTH	W	9	67	FISHER	E	12	84	FISHER	JE	4	131
FIRMSTON	HJ	13	159	FIRTH	W	9	67	FISHER	E	13	159	FISHER	JE	13	159
FIRN	G	8	113	FIRTH	W	9	256	FISHER	EE	3	56	FISHER	JH	1	109
FIRN	J	8	113	FIRTH	W	11	128	FISHER	EG	12	305	FISHER	JW	8	114
FIRSTBROOK	J	11	128	FIRTH	WH	8	114	FISHER	EM	1	109	FISHER	JW	11	129
FIRTH	A	9	66	FIRTH	WT	14	108	FISHER	EW	10	78	FISHER	L	8	114
FIRTH	A	9	66	FISCHER	A	9	256	FISHER	F	1	109	FISHER	L	10	297
FIRTH	A	9	255	FISH	AR	1	108	FISHER	F	3	336	FISHER	L	13	160
FIRTH	A	14	107	FISH	AW	2	123	FISHER	F	5	125	FISHER	L	13	160
FIRTH	AE	8	113	FISH	C	7	125	FISHER	F	6	140	FISHER	LP	3	56
FIRTH	AR	8	113	FISH	CG	2	123	FISHER	F	7	126	FISHER	M	8	114
FIRTH	B	9	255	FISH	GE	8	114	FISHER	F	12	85	FISHER	M	8	114
FIRTH	C	9	66	FISH	H	14	108	FISHER	F	12	85	FISHER	M	10	78
FIRTH	C	9	66	FISH	J	1	108	FISHER	F	13	159	FISHER	M	12	305
FIRTH	C	9	67	FISH	J	8	114	FISHER	F	14	108	FISHER	R	8	115
FIRTH	CH	14	108	FISH	N	10	297	FISHER	FH	9	385	FISHER	R	8	115
FIRTH	E	8	113	FISH	S	7	125	FISHER	FJ	10	78	FISHER	R	11	129
FIRTH	E	9	67	FISH	T	11	129	FISHER	FS	4	131	FISHER	R	12	85
FIRTH	E	9	67	FISH	T	14	108	FISHER	FW	2	123	FISHER	RE	10	78
FIRTH	E	9	255	FISH	TF	7	126	FISHER	G	2	123	FISHER	RH	4	131
FIRTH	E	9	255	FISH	TF	7	126	FISHER	G	4	131	FISHER	RM	9	67
FIRTH	E	9	256	FISH	TL	2	123	FISHER	G	9	256	FISHER	RT	7	126
FIRTH	F	9	256	FISH	W	1	108	FISHER	G	10	78	FISHER	RW	6	140
FIRTH	F	9	256	FISH	W	14	108	FISHER	G	12	85	FISHER	S	6	140
FIRTH	F	9	256	FISH	W	14	108	FISHER	G	13	159	FISHER	S	8	115
FIRTH	F	9	256	FISH	W	14	108	FISHER	GA	11	129	FISHER	S	14	108
FIRTH	F	14	108	FISH	WT	3	56	FISHER	GF	5	125	FISHER	SW	5	125
FIRTH	G	14	108	FISHBURN	A	8	114	FISHER	GH	7	126	FISHER	T	4	131
FIRTH	H	8	113	FISHBURN	T	11	129	FISHER	GHA	1	109	FISHER	T	10	78
FIRTH	H	8	113	FISHER	A	3	56	FISHER	GR	2	123	FISHER	TB	3	56
FIRTH	H	8	113	FISHER	A	5	124	FISHER	GW	5	125	FISHER	TD	12	85
FIRTH	H	8	113	FISHER	A	7	126	FISHER	H	1	109	FISHER	W	1	109
FIRTH	H	8	113	FISHER	A	8	114	FISHER	H	8	114	FISHER	W	1	109
FIRTH	H	9	256	FISHER	A	8	114	FISHER	H	8	114	FISHER	W	1	109
FIRTH	H	13	159	FISHER	A	12	84	FISHER	H	11	129	FISHER	W	2	123
FIRTH	HS	9	256	FISHER	AE	14	108	FISHER	H	14	108	FISHER	W	5	125
FIRTH	J	8	113	FISHER	AG	3	56	FISHER	HE	6	140	FISHER	W	8	115
FIRTH	J	8	113	FISHER	AH	10	78	FISHER	HE	8	114	FISHER	W	9	67
FIRTH	J	8	114	FISHER	AH	12	304	FISHER	HJ	5	125	FISHER	W	11	129
FIRTH	J	9	256	FISHER	AT	12	304	FISHER	HL	7	126	FISHER	W	12	305
FIRTH	J	14	108	FISHER	AW	13	159	FISHER	HS	6	140	FISHER	W	14	108
FIRTH	JH	8	114	FISHER	B	6	140	FISHER	IG	2	123	FISHER	W	14	109
FIRTH	JK	9	67	FISHER	C	8	114	FISHER	J	1	109	FISHER	W	14	109
FIRTH	JT	9	67	FISHER	C	10	297	FISHER	J	5	125	FISHER	W	14	109
FIRTH	JW	8	114	FISHER	C	13	159	FISHER	J	6	140	FISHER	WB	10	78
FIRTH	JW	9	67	FISHER	C	14	108	FISHER	J	6	140	FISHER	WE	7	126
FIRTH	JW	9	67	FISHER	CF	6	140	FISHER	J	8	114	FISHER	WE	10	78
FIRTH	L	9	67	FISHER	CH	2	123	FISHER	J	8	114	FISHER	WE	12	305
FIRTH	M	9	256	FISHER	CH	3	336	FISHER	J	11	129	FISHER	WF	1	109
FIRTH	R	9	67	FISHER	CH	4	131	FISHER	J	11	129	FISHER	WF	13	160
FIRTH	R	11	128	FISHER	CJ	12	305	FISHER	J	13	159	FISHER	WG	9	67
FIRTH	T	8	114	FISHER	CW	4	131	FISHER	J	13	159	FISHER	WH	9	67
FIRTH	T	9	67	FISHER	D	1	109	FISHER	J	14	108	FISHER	WJ	5	125
FIRTH	T	9	256	FISHER	E	6	140	FISHER	J	14	108	FISHER	WJ	7	126
				FISHER	E	9	256	FISHER	JA	6	140	FISHER	WJ	13	160

FISHER	WMG	4	131	FITZGERALD	J	14	109	FITZSIMMONS	P	4	132	FLATMAN	GWH	13	160
FISHER	WMJ	5	125	FITZGERALD	JH	3	336	FITZSIMMONS	R	11	130	FLATT	CH	7	127
FISHER	WR	13	160	FITZGERALD	JP	1	109	FITZSIMMONS	W	11	130	FLATT	G	1	109
FISHER	WT	2	123	FITZGERALD	MAJ	4	132	FITZSIMMONS	WH	8	115	FLATT	GH	1	110
FISHLOCK	JA	3	336	FITZGERALD	RW	3	336	FITZWATER	W	11	130	FLATT	GH	3	56
FISHLOCK	WR	1	109	FITZGERALD	T	11	129	FITZWILLIAM	C	2	123	FLATT	HJ	1	110
FISHWHICK	C	11	129	FITZGERALD	TG	10	78	FIVEASH	AS	13	160	FLATT	HJ	1	110
FISHWICK	J	14	109	FITZGERALD	TJ	11	129	FIVEASH	GT	7	126	FLATT	TF	1	110
FISHWICK	R	14	109	FITZGERALD	TM	11	129	FIVEASH	JA	13	160	FLATT	WW	7	127
FISHWICK	S	14	109	FITZGERALD	W	2	123	FLACK	AE	2	123	FLAVELL	CF	12	305
FISHWICK	W	14	109	FITZGERALD	W	13	160	FLACK	AG	5	125	FLAVILL	AEJ	2	124
FISK	FW	6	140	FITZGERALD	WA	4	132	FLACK	AWA	4	132	FLAVILL	H	1	110
FISK	JT	4	131	FITZGERALD	WK	3	336	FLACK	EJ	7	126	FLAVILL	W	2	124
FISK	W	11	129	FITZGIBBON	J	1	109	FLACK	H	7	127	FLAWN	A	11	130
FITCH	AG	7	126	FITZGIBBONS	G	4	132	FLACK	LW	7	127	FLAXINGTON	A	9	257
FITCH	AJ	1	109	FITZGIBBONS	H	4	132	FLACK	R	10	78	FLAXINGTON	A	9	257
FITCH	B	2	123	FITZGIBBONS	W	4	132	FLACK	W	7	127	FLAXINGTON	W	8	115
FITCH	EW	1	109	FITZHUGH	A	1	109	FLACK	WJ	3	336	FLAXINGTON	W	9	68
FITCH	H	2	123	FITZHUGH	E	12	305	FLAGG	H	10	78	FLAXMAN	WH	3	336
FITCH	SA	2	123	FITZHUGH	GT	12	305	FLAHERTY	B	9	68	FLEAR	GJ	6	141
FITCH	SJ	13	160	FITZHUGH	GW	12	305	FLAHERTY	F	6	141	FLEAT	WS	4	132
FITCH	WJ	1	109	FITZJOHN	A	7	126	FLAHERTY	J	9	256	FLECKNEY	C	5	125
FITCHEN	H	6	140	FITZJOHN	AV	5	125	FLAHERTY	M	11	130	FLECKNEY	CW	5	125
FITCHES	FG	2	123	FITZJOHN	F	4	132	FLAHERTY	T	14	109	FLECKNEY	S	5	125
FITCHETT	HS	12	305	FITZJOHN	S	2	123	FLAIN	R	7	127	FLECKNEY	T	5	125
FITCHETT	J	12	305	FITZJOHN	WJ	7	126	FLAKE	FG	10	78	FLECKNOE	EW	5	125
FITCHETT	JW	12	305	FITZMAURICE	B	6	141	FLAMENI	E	8	115	FLECKNOE	WT	5	125
FITCHETT	PG	6	140	FITZMAURICE	H	6	141	FLANAGAN	A	9	68	FLEET	A	5	125
FITHIE	H	4	132	FITZMAURICE	JE	6	141	FLANAGAN	D	11	130	FLEET	AF	12	85
FITTER	C	6	141	FITZMAURICE	JE	6	141	FLANAGAN	D	14	109	FLEET	AH	6	141
FITTER	H	6	140	FITZMAURICE	RM	7	126	FLANAGAN	GJ	8	115	FLEET	C	11	130
FITTON	B	9	67	FITZMAURICE	TB	6	141	FLANAGAN	H	1	109	FLEET	E	11	422
FITTON	C	8	115	FITZMAURICE	TF	7	126	FLANAGAN	J	8	115	FLEET	F	4	132
FITTON	G	9	67	FITZPATRICK	AT	7	126	FLANAGAN	J	9	68	FLEET	HJ	10	78
FITTON	J	11	129	FITZPATRICK	C	9	256	FLANAGAN	J	11	130	FLEET	JP	6	141
FITTON	J	14	109	FITZPATRICK	E	14	109	FLANAGAN	J	14	109	FLEET	S	11	422
FITTON	T	11	129	FITZPATRICK	F	11	129	FLANAGAN	T	8	115	FLEET	W	2	124
FITTON	TA	14	109	FITZPATRICK	J	2	123	FLANAGAN	T	11	422	FLEETWOOD	FP	6	141
FITZ-JOHN	BF	12	85	FITZPATRICK	J	8	115	FLANAGAN	TC	13	160	FLEETWOOD	J	6	141
FITZER	JT	6	141	FITZPATRICK	J	8	115	FLANAGAN	TH	14	109	FLEETWOOD	JE	14	109
FITZGERALD	A	1	109	FITZPATRICK	J	11	129	FLANAGAN	W	11	130	FLEGG	GW	2	124
FITZGERALD	AD	10	78	FITZPATRICK	J	11	129	FLANAGAN	W	12	305	FLEMING	A	1	110
FITZGERALD	AG	12	85	FITZPATRICK	J	11	421	FLANAGAN	WJ	13	160	FLEMING	A	1	110
FITZGERALD	AJ	13	160	FITZPATRICK	JH	6	141	FLANNAGAN	T	11	130	FLEMING	AEV	1	110
FITZGERALD	C	13	160	FITZPATRICK	JM	11	130	FLANNERY	T	11	130	FLEMING	B	3	56
FITZGERALD	C	14	109	FITZPATRICK	JT	6	141	FLANNIGAN	J	14	109	FLEMING	DG	5	125
FITZGERALD	E	3	336	FITZPATRICK	M	9	68	FLANNIGAN	TM	7	127	FLEMING	F	10	297
FITZGERALD	F	4	132	FITZPATRICK	T	7	126	FLASKETT	FE	13	160	FLEMING	F	13	160
FITZGERALD	GA	11	129	FITZPATRICK	W	14	109	FLAT	CH	9	68	FLEMING	G	10	78
FITZGERALD	H	3	336	FITZPATRICK	WT	13	160	FLATERY	W	9	256	FLEMING	GE	10	78
FITZGERALD	J	1	109	FITZSIMMONS	A	3	336	FLATHER	E	9	68	FLEMING	GH	8	115
FITZGERALD	J	3	336	FITZSIMMONS	A	11	130	FLATHER	E	9	68	FLEMING	GJ	13	160
FITZGERALD	J	3	336	FITZSIMMONS	H	4	132	FLATHER	TW	9	68	FLEMING	GS	7	127
FITZGERALD	J	9	67	FITZSIMMONS	H	14	109	FLATLEY	P	8	115	FLEMING	HW	10	297
FITZGERALD	J	13	160	FITZSIMMONS	J	10	78	FLATMAN	FA	12	85	FLEMING	J	8	115

FLEMING	J	9	68	FLETCHER	E	7	127	FLETCHER	J	11	422	FLEXMAN	AJ	7	128
FLEMING	J	11	130	FLETCHER	E	8	116	FLETCHER	J	11	422	FLEXMAN	EL	7	128
FLEMING	J	11	130	FLETCHER	E	13	161	FLETCHER	J	14	110	FLEXON	S	7	128
FLEMING	J	13	161	FLETCHER	EA	10	79	FLETCHER	J	14	110	FLIGG	A	9	69
FLEMING	JF	12	305	FLETCHER	EC	10	79	FLETCHER	J	14	110	FLIGG	WE	8	116
FLEMING	JG	7	127	FLETCHER	EG	10	79	FLETCHER	JE	8	116	FLINN	B	4	132
FLEMING	L	6	141	FLETCHER	EK	1	110	FLETCHER	JH	1	110	FLINT	A	12	85
FLEMING	M	2	124	FLETCHER	F	5	126	FLETCHER	JH	10	79	FLINT	C	4	132
FLEMING	M	8	115	FLETCHER	F	6	142	FLETCHER	JHC	10	79	FLINT	C	11	131
FLEMING	MH	4	132	FLETCHER	F	7	127	FLETCHER	JT	7	127	FLINT	E	6	142
FLEMING	P	8	115	FLETCHER	F	8	116	FLETCHER	JW	1	110	FLINT	E	8	117
FLEMING	R	1	110	FLETCHER	F	9	68	FLETCHER	JW	6	142	FLINT	F	11	131
FLEMING	R	1	110	FLETCHER	F	11	130	FLETCHER	JW	8	116	FLINT	F	12	85
FLEMING	S	8	115	FLETCHER	F	14	110	FLETCHER	KI	13	161	FLINT	FH	7	128
FLEMING	S	11	130	FLETCHER	FAG	13	161	FLETCHER	LW	11	131	FLINT	FJ	5	126
FLEMING	T	13	160	FLETCHER	FC	7	128	FLETCHER	R	2	124	FLINT	G	6	142
FLEMING	TC	8	115	FLETCHER	FE	6	142	FLETCHER	R	14	110	FLINT	G	6	142
FLEMING	TF	1	110	FLETCHER	FG	5	126	FLETCHER	R	14	110	FLINT	G	8	117
FLEMING	W	8	116	FLETCHER	G	1	110	FLETCHER	REE	1	110	FLINT	GA	7	128
FLEMMING	B	7	127	FLETCHER	G	4	132	FLETCHER	S	1	110	FLINT	HAC	5	126
FLEMMING	HW	7	127	FLETCHER	G	5	126	FLETCHER	S	9	68	FLINT	HC	13	161
FLEMMING	W	11	130	FLETCHER	G	8	116	FLETCHER	SC	3	56	FLINT	J	8	117
FLEMONS	PEF	12	85	FLETCHER	G	8	116	FLETCHER	SJ	11	131	FLINT	JO	5	126
FLESHER	E	9	68	FLETCHER	G	8	116	FLETCHER	SM	1	110	FLINT	JR	11	131
FLESHER	R	8	116	FLETCHER	G	9	257	FLETCHER	T	9	257	FLINT	JT	12	85
FLETCHER	A	2	124	FLETCHER	G	11	130	FLETCHER	T	10	79	FLINT	JW	9	257
FLETCHER	A	5	125	FLETCHER	G	12	85	FLETCHER	T	11	131	FLINT	M	5	126
FLETCHER	A	6	141	FLETCHER	GH	1	110	FLETCHER	T	14	110	FLINT	P	7	128
FLETCHER	A	6	141	FLETCHER	GH	8	116	FLETCHER	TH	14	110	FLINT	R	2	124
FLETCHER	A	6	141	FLETCHER	GM	9	385	FLETCHER	TW	3	336	FLINT	R	5	126
FLETCHER	A	6	142	FLETCHER	GR	7	127	FLETCHER	TW	7	128	FLINT	R	11	131
FLETCHER	A	9	68	FLETCHER	H	6	142	FLETCHER	W	1	110	FLINT	TH	5	126
FLETCHER	A	14	110	FLETCHER	H	6	142	FLETCHER	W	1	111	FLINT	W	8	117
FLETCHER	A	14	110	FLETCHER	H	9	68	FLETCHER	W	8	116	FLINT	W	11	131
FLETCHER	AC	1	110	FLETCHER	H	11	130	FLETCHER	W	8	116	FLINT	W	12	85
FLETCHER	AE	6	142	FLETCHER	H	11	131	FLETCHER	W	8	116	FLINT	W	14	110
FLETCHER	AS	2	124	FLETCHER	H	11	131	FLETCHER	W	11	131	FLINT	WA	1	111
FLETCHER	AT	1	110	FLETCHER	H	12	305	FLETCHER	W	11	131	FLINTHAM	CA	4	133
FLETCHER	AT	13	161	FLETCHER	H	14	110	FLETCHER	W	11	131	FLINTHAM	J	7	128
FLETCHER	AW	3	56	FLETCHER	H	14	110	FLETCHER	W	13	161	FLIPPANCE	G	12	305
FLETCHER	B	8	116	FLETCHER	HE	14	110	FLETCHER	WA	9	385	FLITCROFT	H	11	131
FLETCHER	C	6	142	FLETCHER	HF	5	126	FLETCHER	WC	2	124	FLITCROFT	W	11	131
FLETCHER	C	7	127	FLETCHER	HG	3	336	FLETCHER	WF	1	111	FLITCROFT	W	14	110
FLETCHER	C	8	116	FLETCHER	HJ	2	124	FLETCHER	WG	10	297	FLITTON	B	5	126
FLETCHER	C	8	116	FLETCHER	HJ	13	161	FLETCHER	WH	6	142	FLITTON	CG	5	126
FLETCHER	C	14	110	FLETCHER	HL	6	142	FLETCHER	WH	7	127	FLITTON	H	5	126
FLETCHER	CF	13	161	FLETCHER	J	5	126	FLETCHER	WJ	3	57	FLITTON	H	5	126
FLETCHER	CGH	10	79	FLETCHER	J	6	142	FLETCHER	WS	6	142	FLITTON	H	5	126
FLETCHER	CH	4	132	FLETCHER	J	8	116	FLETCHER	WT	6	142	FLITTON	WG	5	126
FLETCHER	CP	12	305	FLETCHER	J	8	116	FLETTON	A	5	126	FLOCKHART	A	11	131
FLETCHER	CV	5	125	FLETCHER	J	8	116	FLETTON	W	5	126	FLOCKHART	R	13	161
FLETCHER	CW	13	161	FLETCHER	J	9	68	FLEWIN	J	10	79	FLOCKTON	H	8	117
FLETCHER	D	6	142	FLETCHER	J	9	68	FLEXEN	HS	13	161	FLOCKTON	JW	8	117
FLETCHER	E	1	110	FLETCHER	J	10	79	FLEXMAN	AC	13	161	FLOOD	BA	7	128
FLETCHER	E	6	142	FLETCHER	J	11	131	FLEXMAN	AE	7	128	FLOOD	EH	3	336

FLOOD	EJ	14	110	FLUX	WH	4	133	FOGERTY	AL	4	133	FOLKERD	FW	7	129
FLOOD	G	4	133	FLYNN	A	8	117	FOGERTY	EW	7	128	FOLKES	C	1	111
FLOOD	J	3	336	FLYNN	D	9	69	FOGERTY	HE	7	128	FOLKES	FJ	12	85
FLOOD	J	14	110	FLYNN	D	9	257	FOGERTY	LAG	4	133	FOLKES	J	12	86
FLOOD	W	10	297	FLYNN	E	9	69	FOGG	H	11	132	FOLKS	JO	5	127
FLOOD	W	14	111	FLYNN	EC	5	127	FOGG	JE	11	132	FOLLAND	A	4	134
FLOOK	E	13	161	FLYNN	EW	2	124	FOGG	RJ	1	111	FOLLAND	SJ	10	297
FLOOK	JT	13	161	FLYNN	H	1	111	FOGG	W	5	127	FOLLAND	TJ	7	129
FLOOK	WJ	10	79	FLYNN	HC	13	162	FOGG	W	11	132	FOLLETT	B	4	134
FLOOKS	H	4	133	FLYNN	HJ	2	124	FOGGERTY	D	8	117	FOLLETT	HJ	4	134
FLORENCE	E	6	142	FLYNN	HP	12	305	FOGGERTY	P	9	385	FOLLETT	J	4	134
FLORENCE	HB	13	161	FLYNN	J	4	133	FOGGERTY	S	9	69	FOLLETT	JP	7	129
FLORENCE	WJH	13	161	FLYNN	J	6	143	FOGWILL	AE	10	79	FOLLIS	PA	6	143
FLOREY	RJ	7	128	FLYNN	J	6	143	FOGWILL	JV	10	79	FOLLON	P	8	117
FLOWER	AE	1	111	FLYNN	J	7	128	FOLDS	EC	5	127	FOLLOWS	A	3	337
FLOWER	AJ	13	161	FLYNN	J	8	117	FOLDS	WC	5	127	FOLLOWS	FH	13	162
FLOWER	FJ	7	128	FLYNN	J	9	69	FOLEY	A	4	134	FOLLOWS	JF	13	162
FLOWER	G	4	133	FLYNN	J	11	131	FOLEY	AJ	7	129	FOLWELL	A	12	306
FLOWER	JP	4	133	FLYNN	J	13	162	FOLEY	AJ	10	79	FOLWELL	FG	12	306
FLOWER	VC	3	57	FLYNN	J	14	111	FOLEY	CA	6	143	FONE	F	4	134
FLOWER	W	4	133	FLYNN	J	14	111	FOLEY	CA	6	143	FONE	T	11	132
FLOWER	W	12	305	FLYNN	J	14	111	FOLEY	D	7	129	FONTANA	A	1	111
FLOWER	WH	4	133	FLYNN	JA	6	143	FOLEY	E	8	117	FOOD	A	14	111
FLOWERDAY	C	13	161	FLYNN	JE	9	69	FOLEY	E	11	132	FOOKES	AW	13	162
FLOWERS	AT	13	161	FLYNN	JJ	11	131	FOLEY	E	13	162	FOOKES	F	12	86
FLOWERS	EH	1	111	FLYNN	JJ	14	111	FOLEY	EJ	2	124	FOOKS	C	1	111
FLOWERS	GA	1	111	FLYNN	JT	14	111	FOLEY	EW	13	162	FOOLKES	F	12	86
FLOWERS	HH	13	162	FLYNN	M	9	69	FOLEY	F	8	117	FOOLKES	J	12	86
FLOWERS	JE	1	111	FLYNN	MEA	3	337	FOLEY	FWG	7	129	FOOLKES	TG	12	86
FLOYD	A	4	133	FLYNN	MT	3	337	FOLEY	J	8	117	FOORD	AE	10	79
FLOYD	A	4	133	FLYNN	P	2	124	FOLEY	J	10	79	FOORD	BJ	3	337
FLOYD	A	13	162	FLYNN	P	9	69	FOLEY	J	11	132	FOORD	EW	3	337
FLOYD	AT	1	111	FLYNN	P	9	257	FOLEY	J	11	132	FOORD	FS	13	163
FLOYD	BW	6	143	FLYNN	P	11	131	FOLEY	J	13	162	FOORD	FVV	4	134
FLOYD	CE	1	111	FLYNN	R	14	111	FOLEY	J	13	162	FOORD	GE	13	163
FLOYD	CJ	1	111	FLYNN	T	8	117	FOLEY	JP	2	124	FOORD	HWW	4	134
FLOYD	EW	13	162	FLYNN	T	8	117	FOLEY	JR	13	162	FOORD	RK	13	163
FLOYD	F	13	162	FLYNN	T	9	69	FOLEY	M	1	111	FOORD	RT	3	337
FLOYD	H	6	143	FLYNN	T	9	257	FOLEY	M	4	134	FOORD	WG	13	163
FLOYD	JA	14	111	FLYNN	T	11	132	FOLEY	M	8	117	FOOT	A	8	117
FLOYD	JH	6	143	FLYNN	T	11	132	FOLEY	MA	8	117	FOOT	AS	1	111
FLOYD	T	5	126	FLYNN	T	14	111	FOLEY	MR	13	162	FOOT	C	8	118
FLOYD	TF	4	133	FLYNN	TP	6	143	FOLEY	MR	13	162	FOOT	CH	10	79
FLOYD	WG	7	128	FLYNN	W	11	132	FOLEY	P	8	117	FOOT	F	4	134
FLOYD	WJ	4	133	FLYNN	W	13	162	FOLEY	PS	2	124	FOOT	GF	10	298
FLUELLEN	HG	10	79	FLYNN	WJ	7	128	FOLEY	RF	1	111	FOOT	GT	13	163
FLUELLEN	HW	4	133	FOALE	WH	2	124	FOLEY	RW	11	132	FOOT	JA	4	134
FLUKE	GH	3	57	FODEN	E	3	57	FOLEY	SJ	6	143	FOOT	JA	13	163
FLUKE	HC	3	337	FODEN	W	11	132	FOLEY	W	6	143	FOOT	JJ	13	163
FLUKE	SG	3	337	FODEN	W	11	132	FOLEY	WH	13	162	FOOT	K	1	111
FLUTE	FE	12	85	FOES	F	2	124	FOLGER	EG	4	134	FOOT	PE	4	134
FLUTE	W	12	85	FOGARTY	D	11	132	FOLGER	HC	4	134	FOOT	PEL	4	134
FLUX	EA	4	133	FOGARTY	R	11	132	FOLKARD	C	8	117	FOOT	RFG	7	129
FLUX	GE	4	133	FOGDEN	H	9	69	FOLKARD	HMR	13	162	FOOT	WAC	4	134
FLUX	H	4	133	FOGELL	D	11	132	FOLKARD	J	3	337	FOOT	WH	4	134

FOOTE	C	4	134	FORD	F	11	133	FORD	RE	4	136	FOREMAN	CE	2	125
FOOTE	EC	3	57	FORD	FB	4	135	FORD	RH	5	127	FOREMAN	CR	13	164
FOOTE	EJ	1	111	FORD	FC	13	163	FORD	RP	1	112	FOREMAN	ET	13	164
FOOTE	HW	3	57	FORD	FF	4	135	FORD	RW	3	337	FOREMAN	F	2	125
FOOTE	L	3	57	FORD	FG	7	129	FORD	S	1	112	FOREMAN	FW	7	129
FOOTE	T	12	86	FORD	FJ	2	125	FORD	S	1	112	FOREMAN	FW	7	130
FOOTE	WH	12	86	FORD	FJ	4	135	FORD	S	4	136	FOREMAN	HF	13	164
FOOTITT	WS	11	132	FORD	FW	1	112	FORD	S	11	133	FOREMAN	HW	3	57
FORAN	W	11	132	FORD	FW	1	112	FORD	SC	4	136	FOREMAN	S	10	298
FORBES	A	8	118	FORD	G	1	112	FORD	T	1	112	FOREMAN	TA	13	164
FORBES	A	14	111	FORD	G	4	135	FORD	T	7	129	FOREMAN	W	9	257
FORBES	AE	12	306	FORD	G	4	135	FORD	TG	10	80	FOREMAN	WG	9	385
FORBES	JH	1	111	FORD	G	7	129	FORD	TJ	4	136	FOREMAN	WJ	13	164
FORBES	JH	3	57	FORD	G	10	80	FORD	W	4	136	FOREST	A	8	118
FORBES	JW	8	118	FORD	G	12	86	FORD	W	5	127	FOREST	E	11	133
FORD	A	3	337	FORD	GA	2	125	FORD	WA	1	112	FOREST	S	8	118
FORD	A	4	135	FORD	GF	1	112	FORD	WJ	11	133	FORESTER	E	6	144
FORD	A	4	135	FORD	GH	6	143	FORD	WJ	13	163	FORESTER	F	2	125
FORD	A	6	143	FORD	GH	6	143	FORD	WJE	6	144	FORFAR	JV	10	80
FORD	A	7	129	FORD	GH	13	163	FORD	WL	7	129	FORFITT	EA	4	136
FORD	A	10	298	FORD	GR	4	135	FORD	WR	1	112	FORFITT	JH	4	136
FORD	A	10	298	FORD	GW	5	127	FORD	WT	3	337	FORKERT	WF	11	133
FORD	A	11	133	FORD	H	1	112	FORD	WT	12	306	FORMAN	J	8	118
FORD	A	13	163	FORD	H	4	135	FORDEN	T	11	133	FORMAN	TG	2	125
FORD	AA	13	163	FORD	H	4	135	FORDER	F	4	136	FORMHALS	B	4	136
FORD	AE	2	124	FORD	H	4	135	FORDER	GA	1	112	FORMSTONE	H	12	86
FORD	AE	7	129	FORD	H	8	118	FORDER	R	3	337	FORREST	A	2	125
FORD	AF	4	135	FORD	H	13	163	FORDER	W	4	136	FORREST	A	3	337
FORD	AH	1	112	FORD	HE	12	86	FORDHAM	AJ	1	112	FORREST	AA	13	164
FORD	AR	7	129	FORD	HJ	3	57	FORDHAM	C	13	163	FORREST	B	3	57
FORD	AW	1	112	FORD	HR	5	127	FORDHAM	CW	1	112	FORREST	E	3	57
FORD	AW	4	135	FORD	HS	2	125	FORDHAM	CW	1	113	FORREST	E	3	337
FORD	AW	10	298	FORD	J	1	112	FORDHAM	G	13	163	FORREST	F	1	113
FORD	B	1	112	FORD	J	4	136	FORDHAM	H	1	113	FORREST	FC	11	133
FORD	C	4	135	FORD	J	5	127	FORDHAM	H	1	113	FORREST	GH	1	113
FORD	C	4	135	FORD	J	6	143	FORDHAM	H	5	127	FORREST	GW	9	69
FORD	C	4	135	FORD	J	6	143	FORDHAM	H	13	163	FORREST	H	3	57
FORD	CE	13	163	FORD	J	8	118	FORDHAM	HJ	2	125	FORREST	HV	7	130
FORD	CH	4	135	FORD	J	8	118	FORDHAM	J	13	163	FORREST	J	7	130
FORD	CH	10	79	FORD	J	11	133	FORDHAM	JH	3	337	FORREST	J	11	133
FORD	CJ	1	112	FORD	JE	6	143	FORDHAM	JW	1	113	FORREST	J	11	133
FORD	CT	4	135	FORD	JH	10	80	FORDHAM	R	5	127	FORREST	L	6	144
FORD	CW	8	118	FORD	JSW	7	129	FORDHAM	RH	13	164	FORREST	M	3	57
FORD	D	3	337	FORD	JW	12	86	FORDHAM	S	13	164	FORREST	M	7	130
FORD	DJ	1	112	FORD	K	1	112	FORDHAM	T	3	57	FORREST	RA	6	144
FORD	E	2	125	FORD	KL	10	80	FORDHAM	W	1	113	FORREST	RG	12	306
FORD	E	6	143	FORD	L	4	135	FORDHAM	W	10	80	FORREST	S	7	130
FORD	E	7	129	FORD	L	10	80	FORDHAM	WA	3	337	FORREST	SH	7	130
FORD	E	8	118	FORD	LC	7	129	FORDHAM	WC	1	113	FORREST	W	3	57
FORD	E	11	133	FORD	LG	4	136	FORDHAM	WJ	1	113	FORREST	WA	14	111
FORD	EG	10	79	FORD	LG	4	136	FORDYCE	T	13	164	FORREST	WD	8	118
FORD	EGA	10	298	FORD	O	10	298	FOREMAN	A	2	125	FORRESTER	A	3	338
FORD	EH	13	163	FORD	P	8	118	FOREMAN	AA	3	57	FORRESTER	AW	1	113
FORD	EJ	1	112	FORD	PL	13	163	FOREMAN	C	3	57	FORRESTER	D	6	144
FORD	F	7	129	FORD	R	6	144	FOREMAN	C	13	164	FORRESTER	H	14	111

FORRESTER	J	14	111	FOSKETT	A	3	57	FOSTER	E	2	126	FOSTER	J	12	306
FORRESTER	R	14	111	FOSKETT	AH	7	130	FOSTER	E	5	128	FOSTER	J	13	165
FORRESTER	T	13	164	FOSKETT	AW	7	130	FOSTER	E	9	385	FOSTER	J	13	165
FORRESTER	W	14	111	FOSKETT	E	13	165	FOSTER	E	13	165	FOSTER	J	14	112
FORRESTER	W	14	111	FOSKETT	FG	5	127	FOSTER	EF	5	128	FOSTER	JA	6	144
FORSCUTT	HM	2	125	FOSKETT	G	5	127	FOSTER	EM	1	113	FOSTER	JC	5	128
FORSDICK	A	13	164	FOSKETT	H	4	136	FOSTER	EW	1	113	FOSTER	JG	1	113
FORSDICK	AE	10	80	FOSKETT	HJ	13	165	FOSTER	EW	2	126	FOSTER	JGP	10	80
FORSDICK	JF	5	127	FOSKETT	L	13	165	FOSTER	EW	5	128	FOSTER	JH	1	113
FORSDYKE	CE	7	130	FOSKETT	S	13	165	FOSTER	F	4	136	FOSTER	JH	1	113
FORSDYKE	J	7	130	FOSKEY	F	2	125	FOSTER	F	4	136	FOSTER	JH	6	144
FORSE	TW	6	144	FOSS	AW	5	127	FOSTER	F	8	119	FOSTER	JH	10	80
FORSELL	F	8	118	FOSSEY	AG	5	127	FOSTER	F	8	119	FOSTER	JJ	10	80
FORSHAW	B	6	144	FOSSEY	E	5	127	FOSTER	F	9	69	FOSTER	JL	9	257
FORSHAW	EH	13	164	FOSSEY	H	5	127	FOSTER	F	9	385	FOSTER	JR	12	86
FORSHAW	GW	11	133	FOSSEY	HFJ	5	128	FOSTER	F	10	80	FOSTER	JS	4	136
FORSHAW	J	14	111	FOSSEY	HG	5	128	FOSTER	F	12	86	FOSTER	JT	6	145
FORSHAW	JH	11	133	FOSSEY	WC	5	128	FOSTER	FC	2	126	FOSTER	JW	5	128
FORSHAW	R	6	144	FOSTER	A	4	136	FOSTER	G	2	126	FOSTER	JW	8	119
FORSHAW	R	13	164	FOSTER	A	5	128	FOSTER	G	2	126	FOSTER	JW	9	69
FORSHAW	R	14	111	FOSTER	A	5	128	FOSTER	G	5	128	FOSTER	JW	14	112
FORSHAW	W	14	111	FOSTER	A	6	144	FOSTER	G	7	131	FOSTER	KG	7	131
FORSHAW	W	14	112	FOSTER	A	8	118	FOSTER	G	8	119	FOSTER	L	4	137
FORSKITT	H	12	306	FOSTER	A	8	118	FOSTER	G	12	86	FOSTER	L	11	134
FORSTER	B	7	130	FOSTER	A	9	385	FOSTER	GE	9	69	FOSTER	LH	1	113
FORSTER	CB	4	136	FOSTER	A	12	86	FOSTER	GH	1	113	FOSTER	LO	1	113
FORSTER	E	4	136	FOSTER	A	12	306	FOSTER	GH	10	298	FOSTER	M	9	69
FORSTER	GF	13	164	FOSTER	A	14	112	FOSTER	GHP	12	306	FOSTER	MH	13	165
FORSTER	J	11	133	FOSTER	AC	10	80	FOSTER	GW	6	144	FOSTER	MR	12	87
FORSTER	R	11	133	FOSTER	AE	2	125	FOSTER	GW	7	131	FOSTER	MW	9	69
FORSTER	RS	2	125	FOSTER	AE	2	125	FOSTER	GW	10	80	FOSTER	P	11	134
FORSTER	WG	7	130	FOSTER	AE	7	130	FOSTER	H	2	126	FOSTER	PC	5	128
FORSYTH	A	10	80	FOSTER	AE	10	298	FOSTER	H	6	144	FOSTER	PJ	6	145
FORSYTH	AE	10	80	FOSTER	AE	12	306	FOSTER	H	8	119	FOSTER	R	8	119
FORSYTH	G	7	130	FOSTER	AH	5	128	FOSTER	H	9	257	FOSTER	R	14	112
FORSYTH	G	14	112	FOSTER	AH	5	128	FOSTER	H	10	298	FOSTER	RC	10	80
FORSYTH	GJ	3	338	FOSTER	AH	12	86	FOSTER	H	11	133	FOSTER	RD	5	128
FORSYTH	JH	14	112	FOSTER	AJ	10	80	FOSTER	H	14	112	FOSTER	RG	12	87
FORSYTH	WF	6	144	FOSTER	AJ	10	298	FOSTER	H	14	112	FOSTER	RH	7	131
FORT	J	13	164	FOSTER	AJ	12	86	FOSTER	HA	12	86	FOSTER	RN	10	81
FORT	WS	7	130	FOSTER	AS	12	86	FOSTER	HC	2	126	FOSTER	RR	5	128
FORTH	G	11	133	FOSTER	AT	7	131	FOSTER	HF	7	131	FOSTER	RS	1	114
FORTH	W	11	133	FOSTER	AT	13	165	FOSTER	HJ	4	136	FOSTER	RW	11	134
FORTIN	EA	2	125	FOSTER	AV	8	118	FOSTER	HL	1	113	FOSTER	S	9	69
FORTNAM	GW	6	144	FOSTER	B	8	118	FOSTER	HW	7	131	FOSTER	SF	13	165
FORTNUM	H	13	164	FOSTER	C	1	113	FOSTER	J	2	126	FOSTER	SJ	1	114
FORTNUM	W	10	80	FOSTER	C	8	118	FOSTER	J	5	128	FOSTER	ST	2	126
FORTUNE	CG	2	125	FOSTER	C	9	257	FOSTER	J	5	128	FOSTER	ST	13	165
FORTUNE	D	9	257	FOSTER	C	12	306	FOSTER	J	6	144	FOSTER	T	6	145
FORWARD	ER	7	130	FOSTER	CC	1	113	FOSTER	J	6	144	FOSTER	T	9	257
FORWARD	WG	2	125	FOSTER	CH	7	131	FOSTER	J	6	144	FOSTER	T	9	257
FORWOOD	GA	13	164	FOSTER	CWE	5	128	FOSTER	J	7	131	FOSTER	T	12	87
FOSBROOK	F	11	133	FOSTER	D	8	118	FOSTER	J	8	119	FOSTER	T	12	87
FOSBURY	G	13	164	FOSTER	D	8	119	FOSTER	J	8	119	FOSTER	TD	8	119
FOSDIKE	AG	13	164	FOSTER	E	2	125	FOSTER	J	10	80	FOSTER	TH	13	165

FOSTER	TJ	2	126	FOUNTAIN	CE	1	114	FOWLER	AW	5	130	FOWLER	WD	7	132
FOSTER	TJ	3	338	FOUNTAIN	CJ	1	114	FOWLER	B	5	130	FOWLER	WE	7	132
FOSTER	V	4	137	FOUNTAIN	CJ	12	306	FOWLER	C	2	126	FOWLER	WE	7	132
FOSTER	V	10	81	FOUNTAIN	CT	7	131	FOWLER	C	6	145	FOWLER	WG	3	338
FOSTER	W	2	126	FOUNTAIN	E	5	129	FOWLER	C	7	132	FOWLER	WG	12	87
FOSTER	W	3	57	FOUNTAIN	E	5	129	FOWLER	CCW	9	70	FOWLER	WJ	5	130
FOSTER	W	6	145	FOUNTAIN	E	9	70	FOWLER	CF	12	87	FOWLER	WS	4	137
FOSTER	W	9	69	FOUNTAIN	EAG	5	129	FOWLER	CH	6	145	FOWLES	AJ	13	166
FOSTER	W	12	306	FOUNTAIN	GW	4	137	FOWLER	D	13	166	FOWLES	F	13	166
FOSTER	W	13	165	FOUNTAIN	GW	8	119	FOWLER	E	9	70	FOWLES	FA	10	81
FOSTER	W	13	165	FOUNTAIN	H	5	129	FOWLER	E	10	81	FOWLES	FE	13	166
FOSTER	WA	5	129	FOUNTAIN	H	5	129	FOWLER	EG	7	132	FOWLES	J	13	166
FOSTER	WC	5	129	FOUNTAIN	H	12	87	FOWLER	ET	7	132	FOWLES	RJ	10	81
FOSTER	WC	12	306	FOUNTAIN	HW	5	129	FOWLER	EW	3	338	FOWLES	T	4	137
FOSTER	WE	1	114	FOUNTAIN	J	5	129	FOWLER	F	3	338	FOWLES	WE	10	81
FOSTER	WG	2	126	FOUNTAIN	J	5	129	FOWLER	F	4	137	FOX	A	1	114
FOSTER	WH	1	114	FOUNTAIN	J	7	131	FOWLER	FB	7	132	FOX	A	5	130
FOSTER	WH	14	112	FOUNTAIN	JW	7	131	FOWLER	FJ	7	132	FOX	A	8	120
FOSTER	WJ	12	87	FOUNTAIN	JW	12	422	FOWLER	G	5	130	FOX	A	9	70
FOSTER	WS	5	129	FOUNTAIN	MG	5	129	FOWLER	G	5	130	FOX	A	11	134
FOSTER	WS	12	87	FOUNTAIN	MR	13	165	FOWLER	G	11	134	FOX	A	11	134
FOSTER	WT	7	131	FOUNTAIN	S	5	129	FOWLER	G	14	112	FOX	AG	1	114
FOTHERBY	F	8	119	FOUNTAIN	SG	5	129	FOWLER	GA	12	87	FOX	AG	5	130
FOTHERBY	H	8	119	FOUNTAIN	T	5	129	FOWLER	GR	13	166	FOX	AL	1	114
FOTHERBY	WN	8	119	FOUNTAIN	V	5	130	FOWLER	GW	8	119	FOX	AL	13	166
FOTHERGILL	F	8	119	FOUNTAIN	W	1	114	FOWLER	H	5	130	FOX	AV	4	137
FOTHERGILL	J	9	257	FOUNTAIN	W	13	165	FOWLER	H	11	134	FOX	B	5	130
FOULDS	AV	7	131	FOUNTAIN	WE	13	165	FOWLER	H	12	87	FOX	B	7	132
FOULDS	E	9	69	FOUNTAIN	WH	1	114	FOWLER	HG	2	126	FOX	C	6	145
FOULDS	H	9	257	FOUNTAIN	WJ	1	114	FOWLER	HG	5	130	FOX	E	1	114
FOULDS	JJ	9	70	FOUNTAIN	WJ	13	165	FOWLER	HH	13	166	FOX	E	11	134
FOULDS	R	11	134	FOURACRE	C	2	126	FOWLER	HT	12	87	FOX	EJ	2	127
FOULDS	WA	9	70	FOURACRE	H	14	112	FOWLER	J	3	58	FOX	EJ	10	298
FOULGER	RA	1	114	FOURNESS	F	8	119	FOWLER	J	8	119	FOX	EM	9	386
FOULGER	W	9	257	FOURNISS	EJ	2	126	FOWLER	J	11	134	FOX	F	13	166
FOULKES	F	11	134	FOURNISS	GH	2	126	FOWLER	J	13	166	FOX	FJ	4	137
FOULKES	J	11	134	FOWELL	A	8	119	FOWLER	JE	7	132	FOX	FR	10	298
FOULKES	J	14	112	FOWELL	T	8	119	FOWLER	JF	9	70	FOX	FT	10	298
FOULKES	J	14	112	FOWKES	E	6	145	FOWLER	JF	9	70	FOX	FW	5	130
FOULKES	W	11	134	FOWKES	G	6	145	FOWLER	JR	14	112	FOX	G	1	114
FOULKES	W	14	112	FOWKES	G	12	87	FOWLER	JT	7	132	FOX	G	1	114
FOULSER	W	13	165	FOWKES	HA	14	112	FOWLER	LJ	6	145	FOX	G	2	127
FOULSHAM	FA	7	131	FOWLE	AJ	7	132	FOWLER	NJ	5	130	FOX	GE	8	120
FOULSHAM	HAK	7	131	FOWLE	H	7	132	FOWLER	R	2	126	FOX	GF	11	134
FOULSHAM	LF	10	81	FOWLER	A	1	114	FOWLER	R	6	145	FOX	GG	13	166
FOUND	A	11	134	FOWLER	A	6	145	FOWLER	R	13	166	FOX	GH	1	114
FOUNTAIN	A	5	129	FOWLER	A	7	132	FOWLER	RC	1	114	FOX	H	6	145
FOUNTAIN	AH	7	131	FOWLER	A	8	119	FOWLER	RG	2	127	FOX	H	6	145
FOUNTAIN	AR	7	131	FOWLER	A	9	70	FOWLER	S	5	130	FOX	H	7	132
FOUNTAIN	AW	5	129	FOWLER	A	13	166	FOWLER	T	5	130	FOX	H	8	120
FOUNTAIN	B	5	129	FOWLER	AE	13	166	FOWLER	T	10	81	FOX	H	9	70
FOUNTAIN	BC	5	129	FOWLER	AG	1	114	FOWLER	TE	8	120	FOX	H	9	257
FOUNTAIN	C	1	114	FOWLER	AJ	2	126	FOWLER	W	6	145	FOX	HA	3	338
FOUNTAIN	C	5	129	FOWLER	AJ	7	132	FOWLER	W	10	81	FOX	HE	9	70
FOUNTAIN	C	13	165	FOWLER	AJ	7	132	FOWLER	W	13	166	FOX	HJ	4	137

FOX	HR	4	137	FOX	WH	10	81	FRAIN	P	8	120	FRANCIS	C	9	71
FOX	I	9	70	FOXALL	A	6	146	FRAIN	W	10	81	FRANCIS	EF	12	87
FOX	J	1	115	FOXALL	F	6	146	FRAIN	W	11	135	FRANCIS	ER	13	167
FOX	J	1	115	FOXALL	H	6	146	FRAME	AE	7	133	FRANCIS	F	1	115
FOX	J	2	127	FOXALL	H	6	146	FRAME	F	6	146	FRANCIS	F	4	138
FOX	J	5	130	FOXALL	JP	6	146	FRAME	H	3	58	FRANCIS	F	4	138
FOX	J	6	145	FOXCROFT	H	2	127	FRAME	HW	3	58	FRANCIS	F	8	120
FOX	J	7	133	FOXCROFT	W	9	70	FRAME	WE	6	146	FRANCIS	F	12	87
FOX	J	8	120	FOXEN	JW	5	131	FRAME	WJ	3	58	FRANCIS	F	13	167
FOX	J	11	134	FOXHALL	F	13	166	FRAMPTON	A	3	338	FRANCIS	FH	1	115
FOX	J	14	112	FOXLEE	AJ	4	137	FRAMPTON	A	4	137	FRANCIS	FV	13	167
FOX	J	14	112	FOXLEY	JR	11	135	FRAMPTON	AW	4	137	FRANCIS	G	1	115
FOX	JA	5	130	FOXTON	J	13	167	FRAMPTON	AWE	4	137	FRANCIS	GA	7	133
FOX	JAJ	6	145	FOXTON	JT	14	113	FRAMPTON	BG	4	137	FRANCIS	GE	3	338
FOX	JE	9	258	FOXTON	S	11	135	FRAMPTON	C	7	133	FRANCIS	GF	1	115
FOX	JEW	7	132	FOXWELL	CE	3	338	FRAMPTON	CCG	4	137	FRANCIS	GF	1	115
FOX	JP	13	166	FOXWELL	FW	2	127	FRAMPTON	CW	4	137	FRANCIS	GH	13	167
FOX	JR	8	120	FOY	E	11	135	FRAMPTON	E	4	137	FRANCIS	GV	13	167
FOX	JW	9	70	FOY	E	11	135	FRAMPTON	E	6	146	FRANCIS	H	6	146
FOX	JW	9	70	FOY	G	14	113	FRAMPTON	EM	4	137	FRANCIS	H	6	147
FOX	JW	9	386	FOY	GJ	3	338	FRAMPTON	J	4	138	FRANCIS	H	10	81
FOX	L	5	130	FOY	J	6	146	FRAMPTON	J	4	138	FRANCIS	H	11	135
FOX	L	9	70	FOY	J	11	135	FRAMPTON	JS	4	138	FRANCIS	HC	1	115
FOX	LA	3	58	FOY	J	11	135	FRAMPTON	LJ	7	133	FRANCIS	HE	1	115
FOX	LH	5	130	FOY	JH	11	135	FRAMPTON	T	6	146	FRANCIS	HJ	1	115
FOX	M	13	166	FOY	RJ	13	167	FRAMPTON	TH	4	138	FRANCIS	HJ	10	298
FOX	P	5	131	FOY	T	6	146	FRAMPTON	W	2	127	FRANCIS	HVG	2	127
FOX	PW	10	81	FOY	T	8	120	FRAMPTON	W	4	138	FRANCIS	J	1	115
FOX	R	3	58	FOY	W	1	115	FRAMPTON	WE	7	133	FRANCIS	J	1	115
FOX	R	10	81	FOY	W	11	135	FRAMPTON	WF	4	138	FRANCIS	J	6	146
FOX	RA	5	131	FOY	W	13	167	FRAMPTON	WG	4	138	FRANCIS	J	7	133
FOX	RH	11	134	FOY	WG	13	167	FRANCE	A	7	133	FRANCIS	J	10	82
FOX	RH	11	134	FOYLE	A	10	81	FRANCE	C	11	135	FRANCIS	JA	2	127
FOX	RT	1	115	FOYLE	DC	3	338	FRANCE	E	4	138	FRANCIS	JA	14	113
FOX	S	6	145	FOYLE	G	6	146	FRANCE	J	4	138	FRANCIS	JE	3	338
FOX	S	8	120	FOYLE	GW	1	115	FRANCE	J	14	113	FRANCIS	JE	8	120
FOX	T	8	120	FOYLE	GW	6	146	FRANCE	J	14	113	FRANCIS	JH	2	127
FOX	T	9	70	FOYLE	LJ	3	338	FRANCE	JA	11	422	FRANCIS	JH	6	147
FOX	T	11	135	FOYLE	PE	10	81	FRANCE	JO	14	113	FRANCIS	JJ	6	147
FOX	TF	3	58	FOYLE	S	10	81	FRANCE	R	9	70	FRANCIS	JP	1	115
FOX	TJ	13	166	FOYLE	T	1	115	FRANCE	W	4	138	FRANCIS	JT	2	127
FOX	W	1	115	FOYLE	TC	13	167	FRANCE	W	6	146	FRANCIS	JT	9	386
FOX	W	2	127	FOYSTER	T	11	135	FRANCE	W	6	146	FRANCIS	JT	10	298
FOX	W	8	120	FOZARD	A	8	120	FRANCES	SA	7	133	FRANCIS	JW	10	299
FOX	W	8	120	FOZARD	JW	9	258	FRANCIS	A	6	146	FRANCIS	LF	13	167
FOX	W	9	70	FOZZARD	G	8	120	FRANCIS	A	7	133	FRANCIS	M	9	386
FOX	W	11	135	FOZZARD	J	8	416	FRANCIS	A	8	120	FRANCIS	MJ	6	147
FOX	W	11	135	FOZZARD	JE	8	120	FRANCIS	A	12	87	FRANCIS	OJ	6	147
FOX	W	14	113	FOZZARD	M	11	135	FRANCIS	A	13	167	FRANCIS	PE	4	138
FOX	WC	5	131	FOZZARD	R	8	120	FRANCIS	AC	4	138	FRANCIS	R	7	133
FOX	WD	1	115	FRADGLEY	GH	10	81	FRANCIS	AE	1	115	FRANCIS	R	14	113
FOX	WE	5	131	FRADGLEY	GH	10	81	FRANCIS	AJ	7	133	FRANCIS	RA	11	135
FOX	WF	4	137	FRADLEY	J	11	135	FRANCIS	AJ	13	167	FRANCIS	RH	7	133
FOX	WG	6	146	FRADLEY	WH	12	306	FRANCIS	AW	3	58	FRANCIS	S	1	115
FOX	WG	10	298	FRAIN	J	14	113	FRANCIS	C	6	146	FRANCIS	S	3	58

FRANCIS	S	5	131
FRANCIS	SW	4	138
FRANCIS	T	1	115
FRANCIS	TA	5	131
FRANCIS	W	2	127
FRANCIS	W	5	131
FRANCIS	W	7	133
FRANCIS	W	8	120
FRANCIS	W	8	120
FRANCIS	W	9	71
FRANCIS	W	9	258
FRANCIS	W	11	135
FRANCIS	W	11	135
FRANCIS	W	13	167
FRANCIS	W	13	167
FRANCIS	WC	1	116
FRANCIS	WP	3	338
FRANCKE	FW	1	116
FRANK	A	8	121
FRANK	E	8	121
FRANK	GF	9	71
FRANK	J	8	121
FRANK	J	11	136
FRANKCOM	CV	1	116
FRANKEL	A	6	147
FRANKHAM	F	10	299
FRANKIS	A	10	299
FRANKIS	G	13	167
FRANKISH	H	11	136
FRANKLAND	A	8	121
FRANKLAND	EA	9	71
FRANKLAND	T	9	386
FRANKLAND	T	9	386
FRANKLIN	A	1	116
FRANKLIN	A	3	58
FRANKLIN	A	5	131
FRANKLIN	A	5	131
FRANKLIN	A	5	131
FRANKLIN	A	7	133
FRANKLIN	A	8	121
FRANKLIN	A	11	136
FRANKLIN	A	12	306
FRANKLIN	A	13	167
FRANKLIN	AC	7	133
FRANKLIN	AE	7	133
FRANKLIN	AJ	1	116
FRANKLIN	AJF	1	116
FRANKLIN	AL	5	131
FRANKLIN	AR	10	82
FRANKLIN	AV	4	138
FRANKLIN	AW	6	147
FRANKLIN	AWD	3	338
FRANKLIN	B	11	136
FRANKLIN	C	6	147
FRANKLIN	C	6	147
FRANKLIN	C	8	121
FRANKLIN	C	12	87
FRANKLIN	CG	3	58
FRANKLIN	CT	12	87
FRANKLIN	E	6	147
FRANKLIN	E	8	121
FRANKLIN	F	5	131
FRANKLIN	F	6	147
FRANKLIN	FE	1	116
FRANKLIN	G	1	116
FRANKLIN	G	2	127
FRANKLIN	GE	6	147
FRANKLIN	GJ	7	134
FRANKLIN	GJW	7	134
FRANKLIN	GW	12	87
FRANKLIN	H	5	131
FRANKLIN	H	5	131
FRANKLIN	H	5	131
FRANKLIN	H	7	134
FRANKLIN	H	8	121
FRANKLIN	H	12	87
FRANKLIN	HB	12	88
FRANKLIN	HJ	4	138
FRANKLIN	HJ	12	88
FRANKLIN	HL	13	167
FRANKLIN	HRA	5	131
FRANKLIN	J	1	116
FRANKLIN	J	6	147
FRANKLIN	J	6	147
FRANKLIN	J	7	134
FRANKLIN	J	11	136
FRANKLIN	J	11	136
FRANKLIN	J	12	88
FRANKLIN	J	14	113
FRANKLIN	JC	11	136
FRANKLIN	JE	3	338
FRANKLIN	JO	6	147
FRANKLIN	PJ	6	147
FRANKLIN	R	10	82
FRANKLIN	RA	5	131
FRANKLIN	S	1	116
FRANKLIN	S	5	131
FRANKLIN	S	8	121
FRANKLIN	SG	12	88
FRANKLIN	SJ	1	116
FRANKLIN	SWW	3	339
FRANKLIN	T	1	116
FRANKLIN	T	11	136
FRANKLIN	T	12	88
FRANKLIN	T	12	88
FRANKLIN	W	2	127
FRANKLIN	W	2	127
FRANKLIN	W	8	121
FRANKLIN	WF	6	147
FRANKLIN	WG	4	138
FRANKLIN	WG	5	131
FRANKLIN	WGH	13	167
FRANKLIN	WJ	5	132
FRANKPITT	A	12	306
FRANKS	A	6	147
FRANKS	AG	4	138
FRANKS	AH	13	167
FRANKS	B	6	148
FRANKS	B	6	148
FRANKS	C	12	88
FRANKS	CH	4	138
FRANKS	D	8	121
FRANKS	E	12	88
FRANKS	EJ	13	168
FRANKS	EW	4	138
FRANKS	F	6	147
FRANKS	F	13	168
FRANKS	G	7	134
FRANKS	H	7	134
FRANKS	H	8	121
FRANKS	H	13	168
FRANKS	HF	13	168
FRANKS	HJ	3	339
FRANKS	J	6	148
FRANKS	J	9	258
FRANKS	J	11	136
FRANKS	JE	3	58
FRANKS	JL	8	121
FRANKS	L	7	134
FRANKS	S	12	88
FRANKS	WC	12	88
FRANKS	WG	12	88
FRANKUM	CJ	1	116
FRANKUM	P	10	82
FRANSHAM	AM	4	138
FRANSHAM	AM	4	139
FRANSHAM	LG	4	139
FRANTER	W	11	136
FRANZ	P	9	71
FRASER	A	14	113
FRASER	AJ	13	168
FRASER	CJ	4	139
FRASER	EH	3	339
FRASER	ER	13	168
FRASER	G	8	121
FRASER	G	11	136
FRASER	H	8	121
FRASER	H	8	121
FRASER	HJ	7	134
FRASER	HJ	7	134
FRASER	J	8	121
FRASER	J	8	121
FRASER	J	10	82
FRASER	J	10	82
FRASER	J	14	113
FRASER	JC	7	134
FRASER	JD	14	113
FRASER	JE	13	168
FRASER	R	14	113
FRASER	S	7	134
FRASER	T	5	132
FRASER	T	8	121
FRASER	V	14	113
FRASER	W	7	134
FRASER	W	14	113
FRASER	W	14	113
FRASER	WA	7	134
FRASER	WJ	1	116
FRATER	CA	1	116
FRAWLEY	FTC	3	339
FRAY	A	4	139
FRAY	AJ	4	139
FRAY	BA	4	139
FRAY	E	4	139
FRAY	M	4	139
FRAY	R	6	148
FRAY	RF	4	139
FRAY	W	4	139
FRAY	W	6	148
FRAY	WJ	4	139
FRAYNE	W	3	339
FRAZER	CR	3	58
FRAZER	EM	12	88
FRAZER	FC	12	88
FRAZER	M	8	121
FRAZIER	H	6	148
FRAZINSKY	H	14	113
FREAK	EG	13	168
FREAK	EM	13	168
FREAK	M	4	139
FREAK	WA	13	168
FREAKE	G	10	82
FREAKES	A	11	136
FREAKLEY	AE	6	148
FREAME	AG	12	88
FREAME	CP	12	88
FREAME	EA	12	88
FREAR	J	9	258
FRECKLETON	F	6	148
FRECKLETON	JA	6	148
FRECKNALL	T	6	148
FREDERICK	A	11	136
FREDERICK	C	9	258
FREDERICK	FW	4	139
FREDERICK	G	6	148
FREDERICK	G	8	122
FREDERICK	P	14	114
FREDERICK	W	4	139
FREDERICK	WH	11	136
FREDERICKS	C	4	139

FREDERICKS	E	2	127	FREEMAN	EJ	13	168	FREEMAN	SR	3	339	FRENCH	A	5	133
FREE	CT	1	116	FREEMAN	EL	13	168	FREEMAN	T	6	148	FRENCH	A	13	169
FREE	H	1	116	FREEMAN	EL	13	168	FREEMAN	T	12	307	FRENCH	A	13	169
FREEAR	CH	9	71	FREEMAN	F	5	132	FREEMAN	TA	7	135	FRENCH	AC	5	133
FREEAR	JW	9	71	FREEMAN	F	12	307	FREEMAN	TR	5	132	FRENCH	AE	2	128
FREEAR	TW	9	71	FREEMAN	F	12	307	FREEMAN	TW	13	169	FRENCH	AE	6	149
FREEBAIRN	A	1	116	FREEMAN	F	13	168	FREEMAN	W	2	128	FRENCH	AE	7	135
FREEBODY	SH	4	139	FREEMAN	FC	5	132	FREEMAN	W	4	140	FRENCH	AEM	12	89
FREEBORN	F	1	116	FREEMAN	FE	13	168	FREEMAN	W	5	132	FRENCH	AF	6	149
FREEBORN	F	4	139	FREEMAN	FGW	10	299	FREEMAN	W	6	148	FRENCH	AG	12	89
FREEBORN	FG	4	139	FREEMAN	FH	6	148	FREEMAN	W	7	135	FRENCH	AP	10	82
FREEBORN	WF	4	139	FREEMAN	FM	13	169	FREEMAN	W	12	89	FRENCH	AR	2	128
FREEBORN	WT	4	139	FREEMAN	FR	7	134	FREEMAN	W	12	89	FRENCH	AR	7	135
FREEBURY	HC	10	82	FREEMAN	G	5	132	FREEMAN	W	13	169	FRENCH	AR	7	135
FREEBURY	J	13	168	FREEMAN	G	7	134	FREEMAN	W	13	169	FRENCH	AW	2	128
FREEDMAN	H	8	122	FREEMAN	G	7	135	FREEMAN	W	14	114	FRENCH	AW	3	58
FREEL	T	11	136	FREEMAN	G	11	136	FREEMAN	WC	12	89	FRENCH	BG	5	133
FREELAND	A	7	134	FREEMAN	G	12	307	FREEMAN	WH	14	114	FRENCH	BJ	10	299
FREELAND	HT	13	168	FREEMAN	GH	1	117	FREEMAN	WJ	12	89	FRENCH	C	5	133
FREELAND	JH	10	299	FREEMAN	GH	13	169	FREEMAN	WT	7	135	FRENCH	C	5	133
FREELAND	JH	13	168	FREEMAN	GHS	13	169	FREEMAN	WV	13	169	FRENCH	C	13	169
FREELEY	F	6	148	FREEMAN	GR	13	169	FREEMANTLE	A	4	140	FRENCH	C	13	169
FREEMAN	A	1	116	FREEMAN	GWV	7	135	FREEMANTLE	AE	4	140	FRENCH	CE	12	89
FREEMAN	A	1	116	FREEMAN	H	6	148	FREEMANTLE	AW	10	299	FRENCH	CFG	2	128
FREEMAN	A	1	116	FREEMAN	H	13	169	FREEMANTLE	CW	10	82	FRENCH	CS	5	133
FREEMAN	A	4	140	FREEMAN	H	13	169	FREEMANTLE	F	4	140	FRENCH	E	7	135
FREEMAN	A	8	122	FREEMAN	HA	5	132	FREEMANTLE	G	4	140	FRENCH	E	9	258
FREEMAN	A	12	88	FREEMAN	HE	13	169	FREEMANTLE	PJ	4	140	FRENCH	EJ	2	128
FREEMAN	A	12	306	FREEMAN	HF	7	135	FREEMANTLE	WE	4	140	FRENCH	EW	2	128
FREEMAN	AC	12	306	FREEMAN	HH	12	89	FREER	A	2	128	FRENCH	F	8	122
FREEMAN	AE	2	127	FREEMAN	HJG	12	307	FREER	A	6	149	FRENCH	F	9	71
FREEMAN	AE	5	132	FREEMAN	HW	12	89	FREER	AD	13	169	FRENCH	F	12	89
FREEMAN	AE	12	88	FREEMAN	J	1	117	FREER	AW	12	307	FRENCH	FA	5	133
FREEMAN	AH	12	88	FREEMAN	J	1	117	FREER	FW	6	149	FRENCH	FJ	2	128
FREEMAN	BA	4	140	FREEMAN	J	1	117	FREER	FW	6	149	FRENCH	FW	6	149
FREEMAN	BT	5	132	FREEMAN	J	2	127	FREER	H	10	299	FRENCH	G	4	140
FREEMAN	C	6	148	FREEMAN	J	4	140	FREER	MS	10	299	FRENCH	G	4	140
FREEMAN	C	12	88	FREEMAN	J	14	114	FREER	SE	7	135	FRENCH	G	7	135
FREEMAN	C	13	168	FREEMAN	JA	8	122	FREER	T	14	114	FRENCH	G	13	169
FREEMAN	C	14	114	FREEMAN	JE	12	307	FREER	W	6	149	FRENCH	GC	4	140
FREEMAN	CC	5	132	FREEMAN	JH	2	128	FREER	WG	7	135	FRENCH	GC	4	140
FREEMAN	CE	12	306	FREEMAN	JK	5	132	FREESTONE	AE	12	307	FRENCH	GH	5	133
FREEMAN	CH	2	127	FREEMAN	JT	14	114	FREESTONE	AW	7	135	FRENCH	GH	10	82
FREEMAN	CJ	7	134	FREEMAN	JW	8	122	FREESTONE	F	6	149	FRENCH	H	3	339
FREEMAN	D	5	132	FREEMAN	JW	12	89	FREESTONE	HF	5	132	FRENCH	H	5	133
FREEMAN	D	13	168	FREEMAN	L	4	140	FREESTONE	HM	5	132	FRENCH	H	5	133
FREEMAN	D	14	114	FREEMAN	L	5	132	FREESTONE	R	2	128	FRENCH	H	5	133
FREEMAN	DL	10	82	FREEMAN	L	8	122	FREESTONE	T	5	132	FRENCH	H	5	133
FREEMAN	E	1	117	FREEMAN	P	2	128	FREESTONE	T	12	307	FRENCH	H	7	135
FREEMAN	E	6	148	FREEMAN	P	12	89	FREETH	TW	6	149	FRENCH	H	10	82
FREEMAN	E	12	88	FREEMAN	P	12	307	FREMAN	CR	2	128	FRENCH	H	13	169
FREEMAN	E	14	114	FREEMAN	PJ	6	148	FREMONT	LG	1	117	FRENCH	H	13	169
FREEMAN	EE	5	132	FREEMAN	R	3	339	FRENCH	A	1	117	FRENCH	HG	12	89
FREEMAN	EH	12	307	FREEMAN	R	12	307	FRENCH	A	5	132	FRENCH	HJ	4	140
FREEMAN	EJ	5	132	FREEMAN	S	13	169	FRENCH	A	5	132	FRENCH	J	5	133

FRENCH	J	5	133	FREY	WG	2	129	FRITH	F	7	136	FROST	FD	9	71
FRENCH	J	5	133	FRIAR	J	13	170	FRITH	GH	11	137	FROST	FG	10	299
FRENCH	J	7	135	FRIAR	RW	3	58	FRITH	J	11	137	FROST	FH	5	134
FRENCH	J	7	135	FRIARY	H	14	114	FRITH	W	1	117	FROST	FJ	1	118
FRENCH	J	7	135	FRIARY	J	14	114	FRITH	W	1	117	FROST	FT	9	71
FRENCH	J	11	136	FRIBBENS	HW	13	170	FRITH	W	9	71	FROST	FW	13	170
FRENCH	J	11	136	FRIBBINS	AW	1	117	FRITH	WJ	11	137	FROST	G	5	134
FRENCH	J	12	89	FRIBBINS	TN	1	117	FROBISHER	J	11	137	FROST	G	12	90
FRENCH	J	13	170	FRICKER	CF	4	140	FROBISHER	W	11	137	FROST	G	13	170
FRENCH	J	13	170	FRICKER	EA	9	258	FRODSHAM	G	11	137	FROST	GB	2	129
FRENCH	J	13	170	FRICKER	F	9	258	FROGGART	J	11	137	FROST	GR	13	170
FRENCH	JC	3	58	FRICKER	G	9	258	FROGGATT	BG	11	137	FROST	H	6	149
FRENCH	JE	5	133	FRICKER	GE	9	258	FROGGATT	EB	14	114	FROST	H	6	149
FRENCH	JJ	2	128	FRICKER	S	9	258	FROGGATT	F	14	115	FROST	H	7	137
FRENCH	JW	10	82	FRIDAY	HJ	2	129	FROGGATT	G	6	149	FROST	H	7	137
FRENCH	LC	2	128	FRIDAY	HW	13	170	FROGGATT	H	11	137	FROST	H	12	90
FRENCH	LG	4	140	FRIDAY	JT	2	129	FROGGATT	S	11	137	FROST	H	13	170
FRENCH	R	5	133	FRIDAY	TC	1	117	FROGGATT	S	11	137	FROST	HC	1	118
FRENCH	R	7	136	FRIDAY	TC	7	136	FROGGETT	C	14	115	FROST	HG	10	83
FRENCH	R	7	136	FRIEDLANDER	H	14	114	FROGGETT	R	9	258	FROST	HH	9	71
FRENCH	R	13	170	FRIEDLANDER	J	14	114	FROGLEY	E	2	129	FROST	J	5	134
FRENCH	SGB	13	170	FRIEND	A	6	149	FROGLEY	J	2	129	FROST	JA	13	171
FRENCH	SH	2	128	FRIEND	A	8	122	FROGLEY	T	7	136	FROST	JE	6	149
FRENCH	SH	7	136	FRIEND	AC	1	117	FROGLEY	W	2	129	FROST	JH	12	307
FRENCH	TH	13	170	FRIEND	AR	1	117	FROMANT	SA	2	129	FROST	JH	13	171
FRENCH	TJ	3	339	FRIEND	AR	1	117	FROMBERG	L	1	117	FROST	JS	5	134
FRENCH	W	5	133	FRIEND	FC	1	117	FROOME	F	2	129	FROST	LF	7	137
FRENCH	W	5	133	FRIEND	FJ	10	82	FROOME	T	7	136	FROST	PH	13	171
FRENCH	W	12	89	FRIEND	H	8	122	FROST	A	1	118	FROST	RAW	2	129
FRENCH	WH	1	117	FRIEND	H	13	170	FROST	A	7	136	FROST	TJ	13	171
FRENCH	WH	1	117	FRIEND	HE	13	170	FROST	A	11	137	FROST	W	1	118
FRENCH	WE	10	82	FRIEND	HL	13	170	FROST	A	11	137	FROST	W	11	137
FRENCH	WH	7	136	FRIEND	J	13	170	FROST	A	11	137	FROST	WE	8	122
FRENCH	WH	13	170	FRIEND	LW	10	82	FROST	A	11	137	FROST	WH	1	118
FRENCH	WJ	2	128	FRIEND	MG	4	141	FROST	AA	5	134	FROST	WH	7	137
FRENCH	WJ	7	136	FRIEND	O	8	122	FROST	AE	12	307	FROST	WJ	4	141
FRENCH	WT	12	89	FRIEND	RE	4	141	FROST	AH	12	90	FROST	WJ	12	307
FRESHWATER	C	3	339	FRIEND	T	14	114	FROST	AT	10	82	FROST	WJ	13	171
FRESHWATER	C	5	133	FRIEND	TH	7	136	FROST	AV	10	83	FROSTICK	J	1	118
FRESHWATER	F	12	89	FRIEND	W	10	82	FROST	B	5	134	FROUD	EA	13	171
FRESHWATER	G	12	89	FRIER	J	14	114	FROST	B	6	149	FROUD	F	13	171
FRETTINGHAM	WS	4	140	FRIER	JW	9	258	FROST	BJ	12	307	FROUD	G	7	137
FRETTON	EA	7	136	FRIES	M	8	122	FROST	C	3	58	FROUD	GH	4	141
FRETWELL	A	7	136	FRIEZE	S	8	122	FROST	C	6	149	FROUD	GW	13	171
FRETWELL	AW	9	71	FRINDLE	A	1	117	FROST	C	8	122	FROUD	WA	4	141
FRETWELL	R	7	136	FRIPP	W	5	134	FROST	C	10	83	FROW	G	6	150
FREW	EH	12	89	FRISBY	E	9	71	FROST	C	12	90	FROW	GR	8	122
FREWER	GF	2	128	FRISBY	PF	7	136	FROST	C	13	170	FROWD	FC	13	171
FREWER	H	2	128	FRISBY	T	8	122	FROST	C	13	170	FROWD	G	13	171
FREWER	HV	7	136	FRISTON	RT	2	129	FROST	DA	10	299	FROWD	GH	13	171
FREWIN	JS	1	117	FRISWELL	TW	7	136	FROST	E	9	71	FROY	E	5	134
FREWIN	WC	2	129	FRISWELL	W	6	149	FROST	E	11	137	FROY	F	5	134
FREWING	F	1	117	FRISWELL	WH	6	149	FROST	E	11	137	FROY	J	5	134
FREY	JA	2	129	FRITH	E	2	129	FROST	E	12	307	FRUDD	C	9	71
FREY	L	3	58	FRITH	E	9	71	FROST	E	14	115	FRUDD	E	9	72

FRUEN	A	3	339	FRYER	CW	7	137	FUGLER	WRJ	10	299	FULLER	HA	1	118
FRUEN	AW	4	141	FRYER	EH	4	142	FULCHER	A	7	137	FULLER	HT	1	119
FRUEN	WA	3	339	FRYER	ES	13	172	FULCHER	AC	13	172	FULLER	HT	13	172
FRUIN	JW	2	129	FRYER	F	4	142	FULCHER	AV	5	134	FULLER	J	12	90
FRY	A	4	141	FRYER	F	5	134	FULCHER	HW	7	137	FULLER	J	13	173
FRY	A	13	171	FRYER	F	11	137	FULCHER	J	5	134	FULLER	JH	13	173
FRY	A	13	171	FRYER	FA	4	142	FULCHER	TH	10	83	FULLER	JJ	1	119
FRY	A	13	171	FRYER	FC	3	59	FULCHER	WJ	5	134	FULLER	JR	14	115
FRY	A	14	115	FRYER	FL	6	150	FULFORD	A	4	142	FULLER	L	1	119
FRY	AE	1	118	FRYER	FW	13	172	FULFORD	EG	6	150	FULLER	LA	1	119
FRY	AF	2	129	FRYER	G	8	122	FULFORD	EH	7	137	FULLER	P	2	130
FRY	AG	3	58	FRYER	H	4	142	FULFORD	HG	4	142	FULLER	PE	3	59
FRY	AH	6	150	FRYER	H	13	172	FULFORD	HJS	2	130	FULLER	R	12	90
FRY	AO	1	118	FRYER	HA	14	115	FULFORD	HTG	2	130	FULLER	R	13	173
FRY	BR	1	118	FRYER	HJ	5	134	FULFORD	HW	6	150	FULLER	RH	2	130
FRY	CH	4	141	FRYER	HT	2	129	FULFORD	J	4	142	FULLER	S	12	90
FRY	E	4	141	FRYER	J	1	118	FULFORD	JW	13	172	FULLER	SC	3	59
FRY	EA	10	83	FRYER	J	8	122	FULFORD	T	4	142	FULLER	SG	1	119
FRY	F	4	141	FRYER	J	12	307	FULFORD	W	4	142	FULLER	SJ	5	134
FRY	F	4	141	FRYER	JR	8	122	FULKER	EC	3	59	FULLER	T	2	130
FRY	G	13	171	FRYER	JW	8	122	FULL	SS	2	130	FULLER	T	10	83
FRY	GC	1	118	FRYER	JW	14	115	FULLAGAR	EA	2	130	FULLER	T	11	138
FRY	GE	14	115	FRYER	LH	10	83	FULLAM	G	11	138	FULLER	TC	3	59
FRY	GH	2	129	FRYER	N	9	258	FULLARTON	G	5	134	FULLER	W	7	137
FRY	GH	4	141	FRYER	PE	7	137	FULLBROOK	A	2	130	FULLER	W	12	90
FRY	H	10	83	FRYER	R	2	130	FULLBROOK	FS	1	118	FULLER	WA	3	339
FRY	H	13	171	FRYER	R	13	172	FULLBROOK	JT	7	137	FULLER	WF	7	137
FRY	H	13	171	FRYER	RB	10	299	FULLER	A	8	123	FULLER	WG	2	130
FRY	HD	10	83	FRYER	RB	10	299	FULLER	A	13	172	FULLER	WH	7	137
FRY	HJ	13	171	FRYER	RD	13	172	FULLER	AA	13	172	FULLER	WJ	5	134
FRY	J	1	118	FRYER	RW	4	142	FULLER	AE	11	138	FULLER	WT	1	119
FRY	J	6	150	FRYER	S	10	299	FULLER	AF	7	137	FULLERTON	C	13	173
FRY	JEA	4	141	FRYER	W	3	59	FULLER	AH	12	90	FULLERTON	CM	13	173
FRY	L	4	141	FRYER	W	10	83	FULLER	AH	13	172	FULLERTON	HA	4	142
FRY	LG	10	83	FRYER	WC	13	172	FULLER	AV	1	118	FULLERTON	ID	4	142
FRY	LM	4	141	FRYER	WEA	10	83	FULLER	B	7	137	FULLICK	ET	1	119
FRY	LW	13	171	FRYER	WH	2	130	FULLER	B	12	90	FULLICK	J	1	119
FRY	PG	1	118	FRYER	WH	4	142	FULLER	C	1	118	FULLILOVE	AJ	3	339
FRY	PJ	10	83	FRYER	WM	4	142	FULLER	D	13	172	FULLILOVE	E	4	142
FRY	SW	13	172	FRYER	WW	3	339	FULLER	E	13	172	FULLILOVE	TE	3	339
FRY	TC	13	172	FRYERS	J	11	137	FULLER	EG	5	134	FULLJAMES	HG	7	137
FRY	W	4	141	FRYETT	JW	1	118	FULLER	EJ	1	118	FULLJAMES	HJ	13	173
FRY	W	4	141	FRYTH	EJ	10	299	FULLER	F	9	258	FULLJAMES	LJ	7	138
FRY	W	4	141	FUDGE	A	13	172	FULLER	FH	7	137	FULLON	M	12	307
FRY	WJ	2	129	FUDGE	E	2	130	FULLER	G	3	339	FULLWELL	G	6	150
FRY	WS	4	141	FUDGE	FW	10	83	FULLER	G	9	258	FULTHORP	H	8	123
FRYATT	AHD	3	58	FUDGE	TA	6	150	FULLER	GA	1	118	FULTON	E	2	130
FRYATT	AJ	10	299	FUDGE	WG	4	142	FULLER	GA	2	130	FULTON	E	2	130
FRYATT	D	14	115	FUDGE	WH	4	142	FULLER	GE	8	123	FULTON	REC	12	308
FRYATT	F	10	83	FUDGE	WH	13	172	FULLER	GG	1	118	FULTON	WJH	2	130
FRYATT	J	2	129	FUDGE	WJ	4	142	FULLER	GH	13	172	FULWELL	W	6	150
FRYATT	SH	3	59	FUELLING	GW	1	118	FULLER	GR	13	172	FUNCK	G	8	123
FRYER	A	8	122	FUFF	E	5	134	FULLER	H	3	59	FUNGE	E	5	135
FRYER	AE	4	141	FUGGLE	H	1	118	FULLER	H	12	90	FUNGE	T	13	173
FRYER	BC	4	142	FUGLER	CJ	2	130	FULLER	H	12	90	FUNGE	W	5	135

FUNNELL	A	1	119	FURNISS	J	8	123	GADSBY	HP	3	340	GAINS	GR	3	340
FUNNELL	AV	13	173	FURNISS	J	14	115	GADSBY	J	12	90	GAINS	H	7	138
FUNNELL	HE	10	83	FURNISS	JHT	2	131	GADSBY	W	12	308	GAINS	J	7	138
FUNNELL	HJ	4	143	FURNIVALL	HW	10	83	GADSBY	WA	12	308	GAINSBURY	C	1	120
FUNNELL	TR	10	83	FURPHEY	J	14	115	GADSBY	WE	5	135	GAINSBURY	V	1	120
FUNNELL	WA	2	130	FURR	A	5	135	GADSBY	WJ	12	308	GAIR	HE	6	150
FUNNELL	WJ	14	115	FURR	C	5	135	GADSDEN	G	3	340	GAIR	TH	6	150
FURBER	A	11	138	FURR	EW	5	135	GADSDEN	H	5	135	GALASZIA	F	6	150
FURBER	AW	7	138	FURR	W	12	90	GADSDEN	J	2	131	GALASZIA	UG	6	151
FURBER	J	4	143	FURSEY	E	7	138	GADSDEN	J	5	135	GALAUD	CH	3	59
FURBER	JK	11	138	FURZER	W	7	138	GADSDEN	JF	12	90	GALBRAITH	AA	5	135
FURBER	WA	11	138	FUSCO	F	8	123	GADSDEN	JHH	2	131	GALBRAITH	FAG	7	138
FURBY	WR	2	130	FUSSEL	WA	1	119	GADSDEN	W	5	135	GALBRAITH	RJ	14	116
FUREY	JJ	9	386	FUSSEY	F	2	131	GADSDEN	W	5	135	GALE	A	1	120
FUREY	RH	8	123	FUSSEY	F	2	131	GADSDEN	W	5	135	GALE	A	12	91
FURGUSON	JJ	7	138	FUSSEY	S	7	138	GADSDEN	WJ	5	135	GALE	AR	7	138
FURLONG	B	13	173	FUTCHER	A	4	143	GADSDON	F	10	84	GALE	AV	1	120
FURLONGER	GE	13	173	FUTCHER	BA	4	143	GADSDON	H	3	340	GALE	AW	4	143
FURLONGER	JEJ	3	339	FUTCHER	CF	10	84	GAFFEE	E	7	138	GALE	C	8	123
FURMAGE	AW	4	143	FUTCHER	FA	10	84	GAFFEY	T	6	150	GALE	DW	4	143
FURMAGE	NJ	4	143	FUTCHER	FG	4	143	GAFFIN	W	11	138	GALE	E	10	84
FURMAN	BG	2	130	FUTCHER	FG	4	143	GAFFNEY	J	14	115	GALE	EEG	4	144
FURMEDGE	AJW	1	119	FUTCHER	HP	10	84	GAFNEY	J	14	115	GALE	EH	3	59
FURNELL	H	1	119	FUTERILL	JW	6	150	GAGE	B	12	90	GALE	F	2	131
FURNELL	H	4	143	FUTTER	E	8	123	GAGE	FE	10	299	GALE	F	3	340
FURNELL	HS	2	130	FUTTER	EF	13	173	GAGE	G	1	119	GALE	F	3	340
FURNELL	HT	1	119	FUTTER	G	13	173	GAGE	HJ	13	173	GALE	FC	2	131
FURNELL	L	1	119	FUTTER	H	3	340	GAGE	HJ	13	173	GALE	FG	3	340
FURNELL	WC	4	143	FUTYMED	S	2	131	GAGE	J	8	123	GALE	FG	4	144
FURNER	FJ	13	173	FYFE	H	4	143	GAGE	SA	12	90	GALE	FW	4	144
FURNER	WJ	13	173	FYLES	FW	2	131	GAGE	W	8	123	GALE	G	4	144
FURNESS	AA	2	131	FYNES	H	11	138	GAGER	CJ	13	173	GALE	GF	10	300
FURNESS	E	5	135	FYNN	RB	8	123	GAHAGAN	GE	2	131	GALE	H	2	131
FURNESS	GW	5	135	FYSH	WG	10	299	GAHAN	H	14	115	GALE	H	4	144
FURNESS	H	1	119					GAHAN	J	14	116	GALE	H	8	123
FURNESS	H	6	150					GAHAN	W	14	116	GALE	H	9	72
FURNESS	H	6	150	**G**				GAIGER	EEK	4	143	GALE	HB	11	138
FURNESS	H	6	150					GAIGER	RA	10	300	GALE	J	2	131
FURNESS	H	8	123	GABBITAS	E	3	59	GAIGER	WGA	7	138	GALE	J	3	340
FURNESS	J	1	119	GABBOTT	H	8	123	GAILER	AJ	12	91	GALE	J	8	123
FURNESS	J	1	119	GABLE	AET	7	138	GAILER	BS	4	143	GALE	J	9	72
FURNESS	J	8	123	GABLE	AM	13	173	GAILER	WJ	4	143	GALE	JF	4	144
FURNESS	JA	11	138	GABLE	IGH	12	90	GAILEY	CT	6	150	GALE	JH	1	120
FURNESS	JS	9	259	GABRILOVITCH	L	8	123	GAIN	DV	13	174	GALE	JH	11	138
FURNESS	W	8	123	GADD	AA	10	84	GAIN	GA	13	174	GALE	JR	10	300
FURNICE	JF	10	83	GADD	E	10	84	GAIN	GWE	13	174	GALE	JT	12	91
FURNIFER	J	11	138	GADD	F	7	138	GAIN	GWE	13	174	GALE	JW	1	120
FURNIFER	W	11	138	GADD	J	1	119	GAINES	EH	4	143	GALE	JW	7	138
FURNISH	HF	9	72	GADD	J	2	131	GAINES	H	9	259	GALE	MF	4	144
FURNISH	WH	1	119	GADD	JJ	13	173	GAINES	HG	4	143	GALE	R	7	139
FURNISS	AJ	14	115	GADD	SW	7	138	GAINES	S	8	123	GALE	S	8	124
FURNISS	E	9	72	GADD	W	3	340	GAINES	WP	2	131	GALE	SR	11	138
FURNISS	F	9	72	GADDES	T	7	138	GAINEY	RA	1	120	GALE	W	1	120
FURNISS	F	14	115	GADSBY	AE	4	143	GAINNAN	F	14	116	GALE	W	1	120
FURNISS	H	9	72	GADSBY	CG	3	340	GAINON	GA	14	116	GALE	W	5	135
				GADSBY	F	12	90								

GALE	W	9	259	GALLON	WM	6	151	GAMBLIN	AJ	10	300	GANT	T	2	132
GALE	WA	4	144	GALLOP	HJ	3	59	GAMBLIN	E	10	300	GARBER	I	14	116
GALE	WB	8	124	GALLOP	W	12	91	GAMBLIN	EA	10	84	GARBETT	CA	3	340
GALE	WC	13	174	GALLOPE	H	4	144	GAMBLIN	FW	10	84	GARBETT	G	6	151
GALE	WJ	3	340	GALLOWAY	AV	9	72	GAMBLIN	H	10	300	GARBETT	J	13	174
GALE	WJ	10	300	GALLOWAY	J	7	139	GAMBLIN	J	10	300	GARBITT	W	6	151
GALE	WS	2	131	GALLOWAY	J	14	116	GAMBLING	AA	13	174	GARBITT	WH	6	151
GALER	AJ	5	135	GALLOWAY	W	11	139	GAMBLING	WS	4	145	GARBUTT	CW	10	300
GALIGER	SR	9	72	GALLOWAY	W	11	139	GAMBRILL	SAA	7	139	GARBUTT	GH	14	116
GALL	J	1	120	GALLUP	L	13	174	GAME	AG	1	120	GARBUTT	J	8	124
GALLAGER	CH	9	259	GALOIS	FE	3	340	GAME	G	8	124	GARBUTT	JA	7	139
GALLAGHAN	MG	10	300	GALOIS	FH	3	340	GAME	LC	5	136	GARBUTT	JW	9	72
GALLAGHAR	B	9	72	GALPIN	B	6	151	GAME	WG	5	136	GARBUTT	R	8	124
GALLAGHAR	F	9	72	GALPIN	J	4	144	GAMESTER	S	1	120	GARD	A	13	174
GALLAGHAR	R	11	138	GALPIN	J	4	144	GAMMAGE	EA	12	308	GARD	AJ	10	300
GALLAGHER	B	1	120	GALPIN	R	4	144	GAMMAGE	FH	5	136	GARD	W	13	174
GALLAGHER	E	10	300	GALPIN	W	13	174	GAMMAGE	J	12	308	GARDEN	JC	1	121
GALLAGHER	EA	10	84	GALTHEN	RW	9	72	GAMMAGE	S	12	308	GARDEN	LE	1	121
GALLAGHER	EJ	10	300	GALTON	HV	1	120	GAMMAGE	TF	12	308	GARDENER	AE	7	139
GALLAGHER	H	9	72	GALTON	WL	4	144	GAMMELL	J	2	131	GARDENER	AT	7	140
GALLAGHER	J	1	120	GALTRESS	F	12	91	GAMMELL	J	2	131	GARDENER	CW	2	132
GALLAGHER	J	4	144	GALTRESS	G	12	91	GAMMOND	R	1	120	GARDENER	JAA	1	121
GALLAGHER	J	11	138	GALTRESS	H	11	91	GAMMONS	FC	12	91	GARDENER	PT	7	140
GALLAGHER	J	14	116	GALVIN	A	1	120	GAMMONS	GM	12	91	GARDENER	WA	2	132
GALLAGHER	J	14	116	GALVIN	A	1	120	GAMMONS	HJ	5	136	GARDENER	WH	7	140
GALLAGHER	JC	5	135	GALVIN	C	13	174	GAMMONS	LG	12	91	GARDINER	A	6	151
GALLAGHER	JF	10	84	GALVIN	CW	11	139	GAMMONS	M	12	91	GARDINER	AH	8	124
GALLAGHER	JJ	11	138	GALVIN	DF	9	259	GAMMONS	S	5	136	GARDINER	B	1	121
GALLAGHER	P	4	144	GALVIN	E	1	120	GAMMONS	W	12	308	GARDINER	B	4	145
GALLAGHER	R	9	72	GALVIN	H	11	139	GANDER	AJ	5	136	GARDINER	B	4	145
GALLAGHER	R	9	386	GALVIN	J	1	120	GANDER	C	7	139	GARDINER	BF	4	145
GALLAHER	W	4	144	GALVIN	J	14	116	GANDER	C	10	84	GARDINER	C	13	174
GALLANT	AC	7	139	GALVIN	JC	2	131	GANDER	D	7	139	GARDINER	CH	2	132
GALLANT	WJ	7	139	GALVIN	JW	1	120	GANDER	FE	3	59	GARDINER	E	1	121
GALLANTRY	AJ	4	144	GALWAY	HL	4	144	GANDER	R	1	121	GARDINER	EM	7	140
GALLARD	PT	7	139	GAMAGE	AE	12	91	GANDER	T	5	136	GARDINER	F	6	151
GALLEARS	EJ	6	151	GAMAGE	AP	12	91	GANDY	C	4	145	GARDINER	FA	2	132
GALLER	D	13	174	GAMAGE	HH	12	91	GANDY	GW	2	132	GARDINER	FC	10	84
GALLERY	A	7	139	GAMAGE	WR	12	91	GANDY	J	11	139	GARDINER	FJ	1	121
GALLETT	AG	6	151	GAMBIE	AJ	7	139	GANGE	EW	10	84	GARDINER	FJ	3	340
GALLETT	AJ	6	151	GAMBIER	F	3	59	GANLEY	C	6	151	GARDINER	FR	1	121
GALLETT	K	6	151	GAMBLE	A	6	151	GANLEY	CT	6	151	GARDINER	FR	3	341
GALLEY	CA	7	139	GAMBLE	B	5	135	GANN	JA	7	139	GARDINER	G	4	145
GALLEY	RT	14	116	GAMBLE	E	14	116	GANNAWAY	AE	4	145	GARDINER	G	6	152
GALLIERS	H	1	120	GAMBLE	F	6	151	GANNON	AE	1	121	GARDINER	GA	13	174
GALLIERS	MJ	1	120	GAMBLE	FW	12	91	GANNON	HG	7	139	GARDINER	GH	7	140
GALLIMORE	G	11	138	GAMBLE	J	12	308	GANNON	J	8	124	GARDINER	GT	12	91
GALLIMORE	JG	14	116	GAMBLE	JF	13	174	GANNON	JP	6	151	GARDINER	H	3	59
GALLIMORE	R	14	116	GAMBLE	JW	13	174	GANNON	L	14	116	GARDINER	H	4	145
GALLIMORE	S	11	139	GAMBLE	R	7	139	GANNON	ME	7	139	GARDINER	H	9	259
GALLIN	A	7	139	GAMBLE	S	13	174	GANT	E	10	84	GARDINER	H	14	116
GALLON	EH	4	144	GAMBLE	TA	8	124	GANT	E	10	300	GARDINER	HE	1	121
GALLON	GB	9	72	GAMBLE	V	9	72	GANT	EJ	10	300	GARDINER	HE	7	140
GALLON	J	4	144	GAMBLE	W	14	116	GANT	G	10	300	GARDINER	HWH	7	140
GALLON	SA	4	144	GAMBLE	WE	6	151	GANT	M	10	300	GARDINER	J	6	152

GARDINER	J	7	140
GARDINER	J	13	174
GARDINER	JJH	13	174
GARDINER	JR	3	341
GARDINER	L	7	140
GARDINER	LC	1	121
GARDINER	MJ	7	140
GARDINER	R	6	152
GARDINER	RA	1	121
GARDINER	RJ	2	132
GARDINER	RW	7	140
GARDINER	TB	12	308
GARDINER	W	1	121
GARDINER	WA	10	84
GARDINER	WE	4	145
GARDINER	WGJP	12	91
GARDINER	WH	3	59
GARDINER	WH	6	152
GARDINER	WJ	4	145
GARDINER	WJ	13	175
GARDINER	WS	2	132
GARDNER	A	1	121
GARDNER	A	6	152
GARDNER	A	9	72
GARDNER	A	10	84
GARDNER	A	11	139
GARDNER	A	12	91
GARDNER	AG	2	132
GARDNER	AP	6	152
GARDNER	AR	1	121
GARDNER	B	4	145
GARDNER	C	1	121
GARDNER	C	11	139
GARDNER	CR	6	152
GARDNER	CW	2	132
GARDNER	D	3	59
GARDNER	E	4	145
GARDNER	E	6	152
GARDNER	E	6	152
GARDNER	EC	2	132
GARDNER	ED	12	308
GARDNER	EH	11	139
GARDNER	ER	6	152
GARDNER	F	4	145
GARDNER	F	6	152
GARDNER	F	12	308
GARDNER	F	12	308
GARDNER	F	14	116
GARDNER	FE	2	132
GARDNER	FH	13	175
GARDNER	FJ	1	121
GARDNER	FJ	1	121
GARDNER	FM	7	140
GARDNER	G	1	121
GARDNER	G	4	145
GARDNER	G	6	152
GARDNER	GE	14	117
GARDNER	GF	2	132
GARDNER	GH	2	132
GARDNER	GH	13	175
GARDNER	GT	2	132
GARDNER	H	1	121
GARDNER	H	9	73
GARDNER	H	9	259
GARDNER	H	12	308
GARDNER	HP	10	300
GARDNER	HW	1	121
GARDNER	I	1	121
GARDNER	I	6	152
GARDNER	J	1	121
GARDNER	J	2	132
GARDNER	J	9	73
GARDNER	J	12	91
GARDNER	J	12	92
GARDNER	J	12	308
GARDNER	J	14	117
GARDNER	JA	9	73
GARDNER	JH	14	117
GARDNER	JR	14	117
GARDNER	JT	2	132
GARDNER	M	8	124
GARDNER	PGT	12	308
GARDNER	R	6	152
GARDNER	RGH	4	145
GARDNER	RH	13	175
GARDNER	RJ	12	308
GARDNER	RR	11	139
GARDNER	RW	3	341
GARDNER	S	3	341
GARDNER	S	3	341
GARDNER	S	7	140
GARDNER	S	10	84
GARDNER	S	13	175
GARDNER	SA	12	308
GARDNER	SG	2	132
GARDNER	ST	12	92
GARDNER	SW	1	122
GARDNER	T	1	122
GARDNER	TA	12	308
GARDNER	TAO	10	84
GARDNER	TW	1	122
GARDNER	V	6	152
GARDNER	W	6	152
GARDNER	W	11	139
GARDNER	W	11	139
GARDNER	W	12	308
GARDNER	W	12	309
GARDNER	W	12	309
GARDNER	WA	10	301
GARDNER	WA	13	175
GARDNER	WC	12	92
GARDNER	WE	11	139
GARDNER	WG	2	132
GARDNER	WH	12	309
GARDNER	WH	13	175
GARDNER	WH	13	175
GARDNER	WJ	5	136
GARDNER	WJ	12	309
GARDNER	WRJL	10	301
GARDOM	JW	11	139
GARE	AE	4	145
GARE	F	7	140
GARE	J	9	259
GARE	TW	7	140
GAREHAN	D	14	117
GAREY	AJ	12	92
GAREY	D	2	132
GAREY	R	12	92
GAREY	W	2	132
GARFIELD	AJB	6	152
GARFORD	HE	2	133
GARFORD	J	11	139
GARFORD	T	1	122
GARGAN	G	9	259
GARGAN	J	9	259
GARGAN	M	9	259
GARGINI	J	7	140
GARGRAVE	GW	10	85
GARLAND	FF	4	145
GARLAND	FJ	13	175
GARLAND	G	13	175
GARLAND	H	11	139
GARLAND	HN	10	85
GARLAND	JG	9	73
GARLAND	JM	4	145
GARLAND	M	4	145
GARLAND	R	6	152
GARLAND	RM	7	140
GARLETT	CA	7	140
GARLIC	F	10	85
GARLICK	AE	2	133
GARLICK	C	14	117
GARLICK	DJ	2	133
GARLICK	E	1	122
GARLICK	FM	1	122
GARLICK	FZ	2	133
GARLICK	GW	8	124
GARLICK	JG	12	309
GARLICK	SH	12	309
GARLICK	V	8	124
GARLICK	W	8	124
GARLINGE	WG	11	139
GARLOCK	G	13	175
GARMAN	BC	1	122
GARMANT	FW	4	145
GARMENT	CH	5	136
GARMENT	LC	5	136
GARMEY	FG	7	140
GARMORY	D	11	139
GARMSTON	AS	7	141
GARMSTON	GS	7	141
GARMSTON	H	7	141
GARNER	A	1	122
GARNER	A	9	73
GARNER	A	12	92
GARNER	A	12	309
GARNER	AE	5	136
GARNER	AG	4	146
GARNER	BS	5	136
GARNER	C	14	117
GARNER	CEJ	12	309
GARNER	CJ	6	152
GARNER	CR	4	146
GARNER	CV	11	140
GARNER	D	14	117
GARNER	E	5	136
GARNER	E	12	92
GARNER	EWF	12	92
GARNER	F	5	136
GARNER	F	9	259
GARNER	F	14	117
GARNER	FC	1	122
GARNER	FC	5	136
GARNER	FJ	5	136
GARNER	G	1	122
GARNER	G	5	136
GARNER	G	5	136
GARNER	G	13	175
GARNER	GT	12	92
GARNER	H	6	153
GARNER	H	12	92
GARNER	H	12	92
GARNER	H	12	309
GARNER	HR	5	137
GARNER	J	3	341
GARNER	J	9	73
GARNER	J	10	301
GARNER	J	11	139
GARNER	J	14	117
GARNER	M	9	73
GARNER	P	4	146
GARNER	R	14	117
GARNER	S	2	133
GARNER	S	5	137
GARNER	S	7	141
GARNER	S	12	309
GARNER	T	9	73
GARNER	T	14	117
GARNER	W	11	140
GARNER	W	12	309

GARNER	WA	1	122	GARRATT	T	6	153	GARRUD	G	1	122	GASCOYNE	F	5	137
GARNER	WA	11	140	GARRATT	TW	9	73	GARRY	J	11	140	GASCOYNE	J	12	92
GARNER	WG	5	137	GARRATT	W	8	125	GARRY	J	14	117	GASCOYNE	PWG	12	92
GARNET	JT	8	124	GARRATY	H	14	117	GARRY	J	14	117	GASCOYNE	SA	12	310
GARNET	JW	4	146	GARRAWAY	AH	13	175	GARRY	T	14	118	GASCOYNE	TJ	12	92
GARNETT	A	8	124	GARRETT	A	1	122	GARSIDE	C	9	73	GASH	AC	5	137
GARNETT	AG	10	301	GARRETT	A	12	309	GARSIDE	E	8	125	GASH	RW	5	137
GARNETT	C	8	124	GARRETT	AG	1	122	GARSIDE	G	10	85	GASH	TE	6	153
GARNETT	E	8	124	GARRETT	AJ	4	146	GARSIDE	J	10	301	GASIE	M	8	125
GARNETT	E	8	124	GARRETT	BE	12	92	GARSIDE	JE	8	125	GASKELL	AE	11	141
GARNETT	E	11	140	GARRETT	CE	4	146	GARSIDE	L	9	259	GASKELL	H	11	141
GARNETT	FG	10	301	GARRETT	CR	4	146	GARSIDE	R	11	140	GASKELL	JR	11	141
GARNETT	G	8	124	GARRETT	EE	6	153	GARSIDE	R	11	140	GASKELL	W	14	118
GARNETT	H	8	124	GARRETT	EH	3	341	GARSIDE	S	14	118	GASKILL	W	14	118
GARNETT	H	14	117	GARRETT	EW	13	175	GARSIDE	W	8	125	GASKIN	A	7	141
GARNETT	J	8	124	GARRETT	F	1	122	GARSIDE	W	9	259	GASKIN	AT	7	141
GARNETT	JH	11	140	GARRETT	F	5	137	GARSIDE	W	14	118	GASKIN	O	12	92
GARNETT	S	8	125	GARRETT	FCH	12	309	GARSTANG	G	11	140	GASKIN	PA	12	92
GARNETT	T	9	73	GARRETT	FE	5	137	GARTELL	W	13	176	GASSER	AE	10	85
GARNETT	W	5	137	GARRETT	FE	13	175	GARTHWAITE	G	9	259	GASSER	G	10	85
GARNETT	W	5	137	GARRETT	FG	2	133	GARTLAND	J	14	118	GASSON	E	12	310
GARNETT	W	8	125	GARRETT	GW	8	125	GARTLEY	M	11	140	GASSON	TW	12	310
GARNETT	W	9	73	GARRETT	H	1	122	GARTNER	JCW	2	133	GAST	GC	10	301
GARNETT	WJ	2	133	GARRETT	HE	13	175	GARTON	F	14	118	GAST	WT	10	85
GARNHAM	A	2	133	GARRETT	HW	12	309	GARTON	F	14	118	GASTALDO	HF	3	60
GARNHAM	AJ	13	175	GARRETT	J	1	122	GARTON	J	14	118	GASTALDO	JA	3	60
GARNHAM	G	1	122	GARRETT	J	11	140	GARTON	JHC	13	176	GASTIN	A	6	153
GARNHAM	J	3	59	GARRETT	JA	10	301	GARTON	TF	3	341	GASTON	FF	4	146
GARNHAM	JW	13	175	GARRETT	JC	12	309	GARTON	W	13	176	GASTON	H	4	146
GARNHAM	R	4	146	GARRETT	JW	13	175	GARTSIDE	JW	11	140	GASTON	HT	10	85
GARNHAM	R	5	137	GARRETT	L	2	133	GARTSIDE	OS	11	422	GASWORTHY	E	7	141
GARNSEY	FC	2	133	GARRETT	RC	12	309	GARVAN	C	11	140	GASWORTHY	JW	7	141
GARNSEY	WG	7	141	GARRETT	SS	5	137	GARVAN	EC	11	140	GATE	AE	11	141
GAROGHAN	T	3	341	GARRETT	TW	12	309	GARVEY	A	11	140	GATE	W	4	146
GARRAD	AN	2	133	GARRETT	W	1	122	GARVEY	C	6	153	GATE	WR	1	123
GARRAD	HH	2	133	GARRETT	WG	13	176	GARVEY	EE	1	123	GATEHOUSE	A	8	125
GARRAD	RW	7	141	GARRETT	WS	5	137	GARVEY	MJW	1	123	GATEHOUSE	A	8	125
GARRARD	FG	1	122	GARRETT	WS	7	141	GARVEY	T	9	73	GATEHOUSE	A	9	259
GARRARD	G	10	301	GARRINGTON	AT	12	422	GARVEY	W	14	118	GATEHOUSE	A	9	386
GARRARD	HJ	9	259	GARRINGTON	E	6	153	GARVICAN	J	6	153	GATEHOUSE	E	4	146
GARRARD	JR	2	133	GARRINGTON	G	12	422	GARVIE	O	8	125	GATEHOUSE	HE	12	310
GARRATT	A	8	125	GARRINGTON	JA	6	153	GARVIN	A	14	118	GATEHOUSE	RJ	4	146
GARRATT	E	14	117	GARRINGTON	JH	12	422	GARWELL	D	14	118	GATEHOUSE	W	11	141
GARRATT	FA	3	341	GARRINGTON	W	6	153	GARWOOD	AJ	7	141	GATEHOUSE	WG	2	133
GARRATT	FO	12	309	GARRISON	TH	6	153	GARWOOD	EJ	12	310	GATEHOUSE	WS	5	137
GARRATT	GH	8	125	GARRISON	WE	6	153	GARWOOD	TH	3	341	GATENBY	JA	13	176
GARRATT	H	8	125	GARRITTLEY	J	6	153	GARY	G	6	153	GATENBY	JW	3	60
GARRATT	H	11	140	GARRITY	J	9	73	GARY	W	6	153	GATENBY	N	9	73
GARRATT	HS	2	133	GARRITY	J	11	140	GASBY	H	6	153	GATER	BJ	2	134
GARRATT	J	9	73	GARROD	AC	2	133	GASCOIGNE	HRB	3	341	GATES	AR	12	310
GARRATT	J	11	140	GARROD	EE	13	176	GASCOIN	F	12	92	GATES	AT	1	123
GARRATT	J	14	117	GARROD	JA	2	133	GASCOINE	AE	2	133	GATES	C	8	125
GARRATT	R	12	309	GARROD	W	1	122	GASCOINE	WA	2	133	GATES	CW	3	341
GARRATT	RD	12	309	GARROD	WA	7	141	GASCOYNE	ACJ	12	92	GATES	E	5	137
GARRATT	S	6	153	GARRUD	A	1	122	GASCOYNE	EM	12	310	GATES	E	9	386

GATES	EE	5	137	GAUL	TE	6	154	GAY	NC	10	301	GEAR	SRN	4	147
GATES	EJ	5	137	GAUNT	A	8	125	GAY	RE	1	123	GEAR	TW	13	177
GATES	F	5	137	GAUNT	FL	3	341	GAY	SN	13	176	GEAR	W	7	142
GATES	FW	5	138	GAUNT	H	3	60	GAY	T	4	147	GEARD	ECS	7	142
GATES	G	2	134	GAUNT	H	8	125	GAY	T	4	147	GEARD	SA	1	123
GATES	G	10	301	GAUNT	H	9	259	GAYLER	FC	3	60	GEARD	ST	7	142
GATES	GHT	10	301	GAUNT	I	8	125	GAYLER	HCW	3	60	GEARING	A	7	142
GATES	GJ	2	134	GAUNT	J	9	260	GAYLOR	F	12	93	GEARING	A	7	142
GATES	H	3	341	GAUNT	JW	9	73	GAYLOR	H	12	93	GEARING	AM	1	123
GATES	H	10	301	GAUNT	L	9	73	GAYNOR	FH	3	342	GEARING	MP	1	123
GATES	HE	12	92	GAUNT	M	8	125	GAYTON	A	12	310	GEARING	SC	2	134
GATES	HJ	5	138	GAUNT	P	12	93	GAYTON	G	2	134	GEARING	W	1	123
GATES	HW	1	123	GAUNT	R	11	141	GAYWOOD	AG	3	342	GEARY	AE	4	147
GATES	HW	4	146	GAUNT	TA	11	141	GAYWOOD	CH	13	176	GEARY	AS	13	177
GATES	J	5	138	GAUNT	TW	3	341	GAYWOOD	F	3	342	GEARY	CC	13	177
GATES	J	13	176	GAUNT	W	8	125	GAYWOOD	GH	13	176	GEARY	J	5	139
GATES	JE	10	85	GAUNT	W	11	141	GAYWOOD	P	13	176	GEARY	O	6	154
GATES	S	5	138	GAUNT	W	12	93	GAYWOOD	WE	13	176	GEARY	RS	12	93
GATES	S	5	138	GAUNT	W	14	118	GAYWOOD	WJ	4	147	GEAVES	J	7	142
GATES	S	10	85	GAUNT	WJ	12	93	GAZARD	AG	4	147	GEDDES	R	14	118
GATES	T	4	146	GAUNT	WT	12	93	GAZE	GF	3	60	GEDDIS	F	4	147
GATES	W	4	146	GAUNTLETT	WJJ	10	85	GAZELEY	E	5	138	GEDDIS	H	4	148
GATES	W	4	146	GAUTON	A	14	118	GAZELEY	F	12	93	GEDGE	AC	2	134
GATES	W	5	138	GAVARON	C	1	123	GAZELEY	G	5	138	GEDGE	CF	1	123
GATES	WC	7	141	GAVARON	J	1	123	GAZELEY	G	5	138	GEDGE	RG	1	123
GATES	WG	10	85	GAVARON	W	1	123	GAZELEY	H	5	138	GEDYE	JB	4	148
GATES	WH	5	138	GAVEN	JF	11	141	GAZELEY	H	12	93	GEE	A	6	154
GATES	WJ	12	310	GAVIN	DH	6	154	GAZELEY	HG	5	138	GEE	A	6	154
GATES	WL	14	118	GAVIN	EH	2	134	GAZELEY	J	5	138	GEE	B	11	141
GATES	WR	3	341	GAVIN	JGE	2	134	GAZELEY	J	12	93	GEE	C	6	154
GATESHILL	F	14	118	GAVIN	NJ	14	118	GAZELEY	L	5	139	GEE	E	14	119
GATFIELD	ALF	10	85	GAVIN	T	3	60	GAZELEY	R	5	139	GEE	FG	10	85
GATFIELD	JW	13	176	GAVIN	T	3	342	GAZELEY	T	5	139	GEE	G	10	85
GATH	R	9	259	GAVIN	W	7	141	GAZELEY	W	5	139	GEE	I	8	126
GATHARD	A	5	138	GAVIN	WC	10	85	GAZELEY	WW	5	139	GEE	IJ	12	310
GATHARD	GW	13	176	GAVINS	J	8	126	GAZEY	G	6	154	GEE	J	3	342
GATHERCOLE	HF	7	141	GAVIS	A	7	141	GAZEY	J	6	154	GEE	J	11	141
GATHERGOOD	AH	12	93	GAW	CA	4	147	GAZEY	TH	6	154	GEE	J	14	119
GATLEY	W	11	141	GAWES	G	2	134	GAZLEY	T	5	139	GEE	R	11	141
GATLING	H	13	176	GAWN	AC	10	85	GEAKE	FC	7	142	GEE	R	11	141
GATNELL	JT	3	341	GAWN	CH	4	147	GEAKE	WS	7	142	GEE	S	2	134
GATRELL	E	4	146	GAWN	S	10	301	GEAL	E	7	142	GEE	S	14	119
GATRELL	F	4	146	GAWN	WE	13	176	GEALL	A	1	123	GEE	W	14	119
GATTER	FC	3	341	GAWTHROPE	JT	13	176	GEALL	F	1	123	GEE	W	14	119
GATTRELL	G	4	147	GAY	A	4	147	GEALL	W	1	123	GEE	WH	5	139
GATTY	T	1	123	GAY	AG	2	134	GEAPIN	WF	4	147	GEE	WH	12	93
GATWARD	E	5	138	GAY	E	2	134	GEAR	A	7	142	GEE	WH	14	119
GATWARD	F	5	138	GAY	FA	1	123	GEAR	BH	4	147	GEER	E	6	154
GATWARD	H	5	138	GAY	FA	7	141	GEAR	CD	4	147	GEER	PJ	7	142
GATWARD	S	5	138	GAY	G	6	154	GEAR	EAC	13	177	GEERING	A	1	123
GATWOOD	HC	5	138	GAY	GA	13	176	GEAR	EG	4	147	GEERING	HGW	1	124
GAUL	BW	6	153	GAY	H	4	147	GEAR	EJ	4	147	GEES	J	10	86
GAUL	C	2	134	GAY	J	1	123	GEAR	HS	3	342	GEESON	EJ	5	139
GAUL	J	10	85	GAY	J	4	147	GEAR	JC	13	177	GEEVES	C	1	124
GAUL	L	6	154	GAY	L	10	301	GEAR	O	4	147	GEEVES	E	7	142

GEEVES	FC	1	124	GEORGE	E	3	60	GERMAN	FC	4	148	GIBBINS	RH	3	60
GEEVES	JH	1	124	GEORGE	E	6	154	GERONTO	N	6	154	GIBBINS	SH	13	177
GEFCOCK	S	8	126	GEORGE	EF	11	141	GERRARD	E	11	141	GIBBINS	TH	12	311
GEFFNEY	CJ	4	148	GEORGE	F	2	134	GERRARD	F	7	143	GIBBINS	W	12	311
GEIGHAN	G	9	386	GEORGE	F	5	139	GERRARD	GF	11	142	GIBBINS	WE	12	311
GELDARD	A	8	126	GEORGE	F	7	142	GERRARD	H	14	119	GIBBINS	WR	7	143
GELDARD	AE	8	126	GEORGE	FC	7	142	GERRARD	T	11	142	GIBBON	AJ	6	155
GELDARD	F	8	126	GEORGE	FH	13	177	GERRARD	W	4	148	GIBBON	CJ	6	155
GELDARD	RW	8	126	GEORGE	FJ	5	139	GERRELLI	J	1	124	GIBBON	CM	6	155
GELDART	A	8	126	GEORGE	FV	2	134	GERRELLI	M	2	135	GIBBON	JA	8	126
GELDER	GLA	13	177	GEORGE	G	1	124	GERRES	JB	7	143	GIBBON	WJ	6	155
GELL	J	8	126	GEORGE	G	12	310	GERRETTY	JT	8	126	GIBBONS	A	12	94
GELLARD	FC	13	177	GEORGE	GE	1	124	GERRISH	GM	13	177	GIBBONS	B	1	124
GELLARD	WE	13	177	GEORGE	H	2	134	GERRISH	H	2	135	GIBBONS	B	6	155
GELLENDER	AG	10	86	GEORGE	H	5	139	GERRISH	MC	13	177	GIBBONS	C	8	126
GENEVER	H	2	134	GEORGE	H	6	154	GERRITY	J	11	142	GIBBONS	CB	5	140
GENGELL	H	3	342	GEORGE	H	7	142	GERRITY	J	11	142	GIBBONS	CH	1	124
GENIN	AE	3	342	GEORGE	H	8	126	GERROD	W	10	86	GIBBONS	D	5	140
GENIN	L	3	342	GEORGE	HR	10	301	GETHING	C	5	140	GIBBONS	E	2	135
GENNOE	J	14	119	GEORGE	J	6	154	GETHING	G	11	142	GIBBONS	E	5	140
GENSON	P	14	119	GEORGE	JH	7	142	GETHING	W	5	140	GIBBONS	E	14	119
GENTLE	A	8	126	GEORGE	L	1	124	GETHINS	J	12	93	GIBBONS	E	14	119
GENTLE	E	5	139	GEORGE	L	4	148	GETTENS	WA	5	140	GIBBONS	EE	7	143
GENTLE	H	5	139	GEORGE	OJ	12	93	GETTINS	GE	6	154	GIBBONS	EJ	2	135
GENTLE	JW	8	126	GEORGE	P	2	134	GEVAUX	JW	9	74	GIBBONS	F	2	135
GENTLE	T	5	139	GEORGE	R	10	301	GEVAUX	JW	9	74	GIBBONS	F	5	140
GENTLE	TM	13	177	GEORGE	S	5	139	GEWITZKE	FP	13	177	GIBBONS	F	14	119
GENTLE	W	5	139	GEORGE	S	12	310	GEYVE	C	7	143	GIBBONS	FS	10	86
GENTLES	TJ	4	148	GEORGE	SD	12	93	GEYVE	RJG	7	143	GIBBONS	FW	10	86
GENTRY	CW	3	342	GEORGE	SG	5	139	GHENT	EJ	7	143	GIBBONS	FW	13	178
GENTRY	GF	1	124	GEORGE	SW	5	140	GIALLONARDI	A	3	60	GIBBONS	G	4	148
GENTRY	S	3	342	GEORGE	T	11	141	GIBB	AE	2	135	GIBBONS	GA	2	135
GENTRY	W	3	342	GEORGE	T	13	177	GIBB	J	8	126	GIBBONS	GH	12	311
GENTY	JW	14	119	GEORGE	W	7	142	GIBB	JA	3	60	GIBBONS	H	3	60
GEOGHEGAN	TH	9	74	GEORGE	W	13	177	GIBBARD	G	12	310	GIBBONS	H	3	342
GEORGE	A	1	124	GEORGE	WA	5	140	GIBBARD	JT	2	135	GIBBONS	H	6	155
GEORGE	A	4	148	GEORGE	WH	2	134	GIBBARD	RE	5	140	GIBBONS	H	11	142
GEORGE	A	6	154	GEORGE	WH	12	310	GIBBARD	W	1	124	GIBBONS	H	14	120
GEORGE	A	9	260	GEORGE	WJ	2	135	GIBBENS	S	1	124	GIBBONS	HT	10	86
GEORGE	A	12	93	GEORGE	WJ	14	119	GIBBINS	A	12	310	GIBBONS	J	1	124
GEORGE	A	14	119	GERAGHTY	A	6	154	GIBBINS	AJ	4	148	GIBBONS	J	1	125
GEORGE	AA	7	142	GERAGHTY	L	2	135	GIBBINS	AWH	3	60	GIBBONS	J	4	148
GEORGE	AFA	1	124	GERAHTY	P	1	124	GIBBINS	B	3	60	GIBBONS	J	6	155
GEORGE	AM	11	141	GERARD	RT	8	126	GIBBINS	C	2	135	GIBBONS	J	8	126
GEORGE	AP	1	124	GERAUGHTY	J	9	260	GIBBINS	C	2	135	GIBBONS	J	11	142
GEORGE	AS	13	177	GERAUSKY	J	14	119	GIBBINS	C	6	155	GIBBONS	JA	4	148
GEORGE	AW	5	139	GERBER	E	14	119	GIBBINS	EE	2	135	GIBBONS	M	11	142
GEORGE	AW	12	93	GERBER	J	14	119	GIBBINS	ER	12	310	GIBBONS	N	3	60
GEORGE	B	11	141	GERCKEN	CEW	1	124	GIBBINS	F	3	60	GIBBONS	P	6	155
GEORGE	C	13	177	GERKEN	JE	2	135	GIBBINS	FA	12	310	GIBBONS	P	11	142
GEORGE	CE	14	119	GERLIS	H	2	135	GIBBINS	J	1	124	GIBBONS	P	13	178
GEORGE	CH	2	134	GERMAIN	GW	13	177	GIBBINS	JC	3	60	GIBBONS	R	3	342
GEORGE	CS	12	93	GERMAIN	T	3	342	GIBBINS	JW	3	60	GIBBONS	R	6	155
GEORGE	CT	3	60	GERMAINE	E	5	140	GIBBINS	JW	12	310	GIBBONS	T	6	155
GEORGE	E	1	124	GERMAINE	W	7	143	GIBBINS	RC	12	310	GIBBONS	T	11	142

GIBBONS	T	14	120	GIBBS	JA	1	125	GIBSON	EF	12	311
GIBBONS	TF	10	86	GIBBS	JF	7	143	GIBSON	ER	1	125
GIBBONS	TM	5	140	GIBBS	JF	7	143	GIBSON	ER	1	125
GIBBONS	W	5	140	GIBBS	JT	3	61	GIBSON	F	6	156
GIBBONS	WE	3	61	GIBBS	JW	3	61	GIBSON	F	8	127
GIBBONS	WT	13	178	GIBBS	L	6	156	GIBSON	FC	14	120
GIBBONS	WW	2	135	GIBBS	M	8	126	GIBSON	FW	2	136
GIBBS	A	1	125	GIBBS	R	3	343	GIBSON	G	8	127
GIBBS	A	2	135	GIBBS	RFJ	7	144	GIBSON	G	13	178
GIBBS	A	3	342	GIBBS	RJ	13	178	GIBSON	GE	9	74
GIBBS	A	6	155	GIBBS	RS	13	178	GIBSON	GE	9	386
GIBBS	A	6	155	GIBBS	SJ	7	144	GIBSON	GF	11	142
GIBBS	A	10	86	GIBBS	T	6	155	GIBSON	GT	1	125
GIBBS	A	10	301	GIBBS	T	7	144	GIBSON	GV	4	148
GIBBS	AE	6	155	GIBBS	W	7	144	GIBSON	H	1	125
GIBBS	AE	7	143	GIBBS	WA	13	178	GIBSON	H	2	136
GIBBS	AE	7	143	GIBBS	WC	2	136	GIBSON	H	6	156
GIBBS	AJ	12	311	GIBBS	WC	4	148	GIBSON	H	8	127
GIBBS	AV	12	94	GIBBS	WE	5	140	GIBSON	H	10	86
GIBBS	AW	2	135	GIBBS	WF	2	136	GIBSON	H	11	142
GIBBS	BE	10	86	GIBBS	WG	5	140	GIBSON	H	11	142
GIBBS	C	9	74	GIBBS	WH	1	125	GIBSON	HH	6	156
GIBBS	C	13	178	GIBBS	WH	2	136	GIBSON	HW	9	74
GIBBS	CH	2	135	GIBBS	WH	6	156	GIBSON	J	3	343
GIBBS	CH	3	343	GIBBS	WHS	7	144	GIBSON	J	4	148
GIBBS	CH	12	94	GIBBS	WJ	3	343	GIBSON	J	8	127
GIBBS	CW	5	140	GIBBS	WJ	7	144	GIBSON	J	9	74
GIBBS	E	6	155	GIBBS	WJ	7	144	GIBSON	J	11	142
GIBBS	EJ	1	125	GIBBS	WJ	10	86	GIBSON	J	11	142
GIBBS	F	7	143	GIBBS	WJ	14	120	GIBSON	J	11	142
GIBBS	F	12	311	GIBBS	WP	12	94	GIBSON	J	13	178
GIBBS	FA	7	143	GIBLEN	TH	6	156	GIBSON	JA	13	178
GIBBS	FE	5	140	GIBLETT	JW	12	94	GIBSON	JF	10	86
GIBBS	FJ	2	135	GIBLIN	J	11	142	GIBSON	JG	3	61
GIBBS	FJ	4	148	GIBLIN	L	14	120	GIBSON	JG	3	61
GIBBS	FT	7	143	GIBLIN	M	6	156	GIBSON	JW	7	144
GIBBS	G	6	155	GIBLING	G	7	144	GIBSON	L	3	61
GIBBS	G	10	86	GIBLING	W	2	136	GIBSON	LF	13	178
GIBBS	G	12	311	GIBSON	A	1	125	GIBSON	M	8	127
GIBBS	G	12	311	GIBSON	A	9	260	GIBSON	P	11	142
GIBBS	G	13	178	GIBSON	AA	2	136	GIBSON	R	2	136
GIBBS	GT	1	125	GIBSON	AA	12	311	GIBSON	R	8	127
GIBBS	GW	1	125	GIBSON	AE	8	126	GIBSON	R	9	74
GIBBS	H	1	125	GIBSON	AG	1	125	GIBSON	SP	12	311
GIBBS	H	6	155	GIBSON	AH	13	178	GIBSON	T	8	127
GIBBS	H	12	94	GIBSON	AV	12	311	GIBSON	T	9	74
GIBBS	H	13	178	GIBSON	B	12	311	GIBSON	T	9	74
GIBBS	HA	2	136	GIBSON	CE	1	125	GIBSON	T	9	260
GIBBS	HJ	2	136	GIBSON	CE	2	136	GIBSON	T	9	260
GIBBS	HJ	10	86	GIBSON	D	3	61	GIBSON	TH	8	127
GIBBS	HP	12	94	GIBSON	DJ	1	125	GIBSON	TW	6	156
GIBBS	J	2	136	GIBSON	E	9	74	GIBSON	W	8	127
GIBBS	J	6	155	GIBSON	E	9	74	GIBSON	W	8	127
GIBBS	J	7	143	GIBSON	E	14	120	GIBSON	W	8	127
GIBBS	J	8	126	GIBSON	EE	12	311	GIBSON	W	11	142

GIBSON	W	11	142	GIDDINGS	JH	13	178
GIBSON	WC	4	148	GIDDINGS	L	2	136
GIBSON	WE	3	343	GIDDINGS	RH	5	141
GIDDENS	JG	2	136	GIDDINGS	T	13	178
GIDDENS	WJ	5	140	GIDDINGS	TC	8	127
GIDDINGS	A	2	136	GIDDINS	C	5	141
GIDDINGS	C	5	140	GIDDINS	H	5	141
GIDDINGS	EH	5	141	GIDDINS	W	5	141
GIDDINGS	F	5	141	GIDDLEY	J	6	156
GIDDINGS	FE	2	136	GIDEON	L	10	86
GIDDINGS	H	12	94	GIDLEY	C	11	143
GIDDINGS	HC	2	136	GIDLEY	F	7	144
GIDDINGS	J	5	141	GIDLEY	HG	2	136
				GIDLEY	L	7	144
				GIDLEY	RA	13	178
				GIDLOW	FA	8	127
				GIFFEN	EF	1	125
				GIFFORD	A	6	156
				GIFFORD	BJ	3	61
				GIFFORD	E	4	148
				GIFFORD	FW	4	148
				GIFFORD	HE	4	148
				GIFFORD	W	4	149
				GIGG	AF	1	125
				GIGG	GW	2	136
				GIGG	JF	2	136
				GIGG	RH	2	137
				GIGGINS	G	3	343
				GIGGINS	GJ	3	343
				GIGGS	C	2	137
				GILBERT	A	5	141
				GILBERT	A	5	141
				GILBERT	A	6	156
				GILBERT	A	12	94
				GILBERT	A	13	178
				GILBERT	AE	5	141
				GILBERT	AE	6	156
				GILBERT	AE	7	144
				GILBERT	AJ	1	125
				GILBERT	AR	5	141
				GILBERT	AT	5	141
				GILBERT	AV	6	156

GILBERT	BW	3	343	GILBERT	S	5	141	GILES	AE	4	149	GILHAM	AH	13	179
GILBERT	C	7	144	GILBERT	SA	12	94	GILES	AE	6	156	GILHAM	FC	4	149
GILBERT	C	13	178	GILBERT	ST	12	94	GILES	AE	14	120	GILHAM	HA	4	149
GILBERT	CB	7	144	GILBERT	T	11	143	GILES	AE	14	120	GILHAM	HC	13	179
GILBERT	CF	4	149	GILBERT	W	2	137	GILES	AJ	6	156	GILHAM	PG	4	149
GILBERT	CG	5	141	GILBERT	W	4	149	GILES	BW	1	126	GILHAM	WH	13	179
GILBERT	CJ	5	141	GILBERT	W	5	142	GILES	C	2	137	GILKERSON	EA	10	87
GILBERT	CJ	10	86	GILBERT	W	5	142	GILES	C	2	137	GILKES	FA	3	344
GILBERT	F	1	125	GILBERT	W	10	86	GILES	CA	6	157	GILKES	JHK	2	138
GILBERT	F	5	141	GILBERT	W	13	179	GILES	CH	4	149	GILKS	CE	5	142
GILBERT	F	9	74	GILBERT	WH	10	86	GILES	CH	10	87	GILKS	FC	5	142
GILBERT	FJ	12	94	GILBERT	WH	11	143	GILES	DWP	3	343	GILKS	GW	5	142
GILBERT	FM	13	178	GILBERT	WH	13	179	GILES	E	11	143	GILKS	JF	5	142
GILBERT	FT	13	179	GILBERT	WR	2	137	GILES	EE	1	126	GILKS	JW	5	142
GILBERT	GH	1	125	GILBERT	WT	12	94	GILES	EM	1	126	GILKS	TE	5	142
GILBERT	GW	12	94	GILBERTSON	F	8	127	GILES	F	1	126	GILKS	WH	5	142
GILBERT	H	1	125	GILBERTSON	F	8	127	GILES	F	2	137	GILKS	WR	6	157
GILBERT	H	2	137	GILBERTSON	L	8	127	GILES	F	13	179	GILL	A	8	128
GILBERT	H	2	137	GILBEY	A	2	137	GILES	FH	4	149	GILL	A	9	260
GILBERT	H	3	343	GILBEY	C	2	137	GILES	FW	4	149	GILL	AH	1	126
GILBERT	H	5	141	GILBEY	F	9	74	GILES	G	6	157	GILL	AH	6	157
GILBERT	H	6	156	GILBEY	F	9	260	GILES	G	6	157	GILL	AJ	4	149
GILBERT	H	9	74	GILBEY	GE	7	144	GILES	GHH	2	137	GILL	AJ	6	157
GILBERT	H	9	74	GILBEY	HS	2	137	GILES	GW	4	149	GILL	AT	11	143
GILBERT	H	11	143	GILBEY	J	3	61	GILES	H	4	149	GILL	AW	5	142
GILBERT	H	12	311	GILBEY	J	6	156	GILES	H	7	145	GILL	AW	6	157
GILBERT	H	12	311	GILBEY	VG	5	142	GILES	H	14	120	GILL	B	9	75
GILBERT	H	14	120	GILBODY	JA	11	143	GILES	HC	3	343	GILL	C	5	142
GILBERT	HC	3	61	GILBODY	JH	14	121	GILES	HG	13	179	GILL	C	14	120
GILBERT	HC	4	149	GILBOY	J	8	127	GILES	J	3	343	GILL	CE	13	180
GILBERT	HE	7	144	GILBOY	J	14	120	GILES	J	11	143	GILL	CH	10	87
GILBERT	HG	12	94	GILBRIDE	A	8	127	GILES	J	14	120	GILL	CJ	13	180
GILBERT	HJ	12	94	GILBRIDE	AP	8	127	GILES	JG	10	87	GILL	E	2	138
GILBERT	HJ	13	179	GILBY	GW	2	137	GILES	JH	11	143	GILL	E	6	157
GILBERT	J	2	137	GILBY	R	2	137	GILES	JHA	3	61	GILL	E	9	75
GILBERT	J	2	137	GILCHRIST	W	11	143	GILES	LB	3	344	GILL	E	9	75
GILBERT	J	5	141	GILDEA	E	11	143	GILES	M	1	126	GILL	E	13	180
GILBERT	J	6	156	GILDEA	F	11	143	GILES	RG	8	127	GILL	EG	13	180
GILBERT	J	7	144	GILDEA	W	11	143	GILES	RL	13	179	GILL	EH	6	157
GILBERT	J	10	302	GILDEN	HF	3	343	GILES	RW	13	179	GILL	F	1	126
GILBERT	J	12	311	GILDER	AE	13	179	GILES	S	13	179	GILL	F	4	149
GILBERT	J	13	179	GILDER	AE	13	179	GILES	SR	12	94	GILL	F	9	75
GILBERT	J	14	120	GILDER	EWH	13	179	GILES	T	2	138	GILL	F	9	260
GILBERT	JA	5	141	GILDER	JE	3	343	GILES	T	7	145	GILL	F	9	260
GILBERT	JB	3	61	GILDER	SL	13	179	GILES	T	8	127	GILL	F	12	94
GILBERT	JH	7	144	GILDER	WF	3	343	GILES	W	1	126	GILL	FF	6	157
GILBERT	JJ	3	343	GILDER	WJ	2	137	GILES	W	13	179	GILL	FJ	6	157
GILBERT	JR	12	94	GILDERDALE	D	9	74	GILES	WA	7	144	GILL	G	1	126
GILBERT	JW	4	149	GILDERSON	WC	1	126	GILES	WH	4	149	GILL	GW	8	128
GILBERT	JW	12	311	GILDING	E	10	86	GILES	WP	4	149	GILL	H	6	157
GILBERT	M	14	120	GILDON	SH	1	126	GILFOYLE	P	9	74	GILL	H	8	128
GILBERT	OW	5	141	GILES	A	4	149	GILFOYLE	R	8	128	GILL	H	8	128
GILBERT	RH	6	156	GILES	A	6	156	GILFOYLE	W	11	143	GILL	H	8	128
GILBERT	RJJ	4	149	GILES	AE	2	137	GILFRIN	J	13	179	GILL	H	9	75
GILBERT	RW	1	125	GILES	AE	2	137	GILHAM	AH	12	311	GILL	H	9	75

Name	I	C	P	Name	I	C	P	Name	I	C	P	Name	I	C	P
GILL	H	9	260	GILLAM	HGW	13	180	GILLETT	M	12	95	GILLIVER	WE	14	121
GILL	H	14	120	GILLAM	P	1	126	GILLETT	W	7	145	GILLIVER	WH	14	121
GILL	H	14	120	GILLAM	W	13	180	GILLETT	WG	6	158	GILLMAN	AW	10	302
GILL	HE	6	157	GILLAM	WG	1	126	GILLETT	WH	6	158	GILLMAN	F	6	158
GILL	HHW	13	180	GILLAM	WH	1	126	GILLHAM	A	14	121	GILLMAN	JE	10	302
GILL	HJ	13	180	GILLAN	EJ	1	126	GILLHAM	C	7	145	GILLMAN	JW	1	127
GILL	J	8	128	GILLAN	RJ	13	180	GILLHAM	FC	13	180	GILLMAN	W	6	158
GILL	J	9	75	GILLAND	E	11	144	GILLHAM	FW	13	180	GILLMORE	E	2	138
GILL	J	9	75	GILLAND	JT	11	144	GILLHAM	GEC	1	127	GILLON	JA	1	127
GILL	J	9	260	GILLAND	W	11	144	GILLHAM	GW	3	344	GILLOTT	F	13	181
GILL	J	9	386	GILLARD	A	12	95	GILLHAM	H	7	145	GILLOTT	JAC	13	181
GILL	J	12	94	GILLARD	AF	4	149	GILLHAM	H	12	311	GILLOTT	T	14	121
GILL	J	12	95	GILLARD	AF	4	150	GILLHAM	H	13	181	GILMAN	F	4	150
GILL	JD	11	143	GILLARD	AJ	3	344	GILLHAM	HJ	4	150	GILMAN	GA	13	181
GILL	JE	7	145	GILLARD	F	13	180	GILLHAM	JA	1	127	GILMAN	J	11	144
GILL	JH	8	128	GILLARD	G	4	150	GILLHESPIE	CJ	4	150	GILMAN	T	11	144
GILL	JH	11	143	GILLARD	G	13	180	GILLHESPIE	WH	4	150	GILMARTIN	J	9	261
GILL	JH	14	120	GILLARD	ME	4	150	GILLIBRAND	DJ	11	144	GILMARTIN	J	11	144
GILL	JVH	1	126	GILLARD	R	4	150	GILLIBRAND	J	11	144	GILMARTIN	J	14	121
GILL	JW	8	128	GILLARD	R	13	180	GILLIBRAND	R	11	144	GILMARTIN	T	14	121
GILL	JW	13	180	GILLARD	RW	4	150	GILLIES	WE	10	87	GILMER	C	3	61
GILL	L	8	128	GILLARD	SV	1	126	GILLIGAN	C	11	144	GILMORE	AAJ	7	145
GILL	L	9	75	GILLARD	W	2	138	GILLIGAN	F	14	121	GILMORE	CJW	6	158
GILL	L	9	260	GILLARD	W	9	75	GILLIGAN	J	8	128	GILMORE	F	14	121
GILL	M	11	143	GILLARD	W	12	95	GILLIGAN	J	11	144	GILMORE	FG	14	121
GILL	N	9	260	GILLARD	WAA	3	344	GILLIGAN	J	14	121	GILMORE	G	14	122
GILL	O	1	126	GILLARD	WG	2	138	GILLIGAN	L	11	144	GILMORE	H	8	128
GILL	PC	6	157	GILLARD	WG	4	150	GILLIGAN	P	14	121	GILMORE	J	14	122
GILL	R	1	126	GILLARD	WJ	12	95	GILLIGAN	T	11	144	GILMORE	J	14	122
GILL	R	9	75	GILLARD	WR	13	180	GILLILAND	W	5	142	GILMORE	T	6	158
GILL	R	11	143	GILLASPY	A	14	121	GILLIN	P	11	144	GILMORE	TW	10	87
GILL	S	6	157	GILLASPY	A	14	121	GILLING	EW	1	127	GILPIN	WA	2	138
GILL	S	7	145	GILLASPY	CH	14	121	GILLINGHAM	A	10	87	GILPIN	WJ	2	138
GILL	S	9	260	GILLASPY	RL	14	121	GILLINGHAM	A	13	181	GILROY	B	4	150
GILL	S	14	120	GILLEN	J	4	150	GILLINGHAM	CW	7	145	GILROY	GF	1	127
GILL	SR	2	138	GILLEN	J	8	128	GILLINGHAM	F	5	142	GILROY	J	8	128
GILL	T	14	121	GILLEN	M	8	128	GILLINGHAM	F	10	87	GILSON	JT	11	144
GILL	V	1	126	GILLENEY	JF	11	144	GILLINGHAM	FC	7	145	GILSON	R	11	144
GILL	W	6	157	GILLESPIE	A	7	145	GILLINGHAM	J	4	150	GILTROW	AE	1	127
GILL	W	8	128	GILLESPIE	EJ	13	180	GILLINGHAM	J	5	142	GILTROW	CA	1	127
GILL	W	9	75	GILLESPIE	H	6	157	GILLINGHAM	RE	4	150	GILTROW	D	5	142
GILL	W	9	75	GILLESPIE	MW	3	344	GILLINGHAM	WA	10	87	GILTROW	E	5	142
GILL	W	9	260	GILLETT	A	1	126	GILLINGS	AE	1	127	GILTROW	GJ	5	143
GILL	W	11	143	GILLETT	AG	12	95	GILLINGS	AE	1	127	GILTROW	P	5	143
GILL	W	11	144	GILLETT	AJ	12	95	GILLINGS	RJ	1	127	GILTROW	WA	1	127
GILL	W	11	422	GILLETT	E	6	158	GILLINGS	WH	2	138	GILTROW	WR	12	312
GILL	WF	12	95	GILLETT	E	9	260	GILLINGWATER	A	1	127	GILYARD	TA	8	128
GILL	WH	2	138	GILLETT	FR	13	180	GILLINGWATER	AJ	1	127	GILYEAT	E	8	128
GILL	WH	6	157	GILLETT	FW	12	95	GILLINGWATER	EA	1	127	GIMBER	W	13	181
GILL	WH	6	157	GILLETT	H	2	138	GILLINGWATER	EHR	5	142	GIMSON	JE	14	122
GILL	WH	6	157	GILLETT	HA	7	145	GILLINGWATER	HW	1	127	GIMSON	SG	2	138
GILL	WJ	13	180	GILLETT	HC	1	126	GILLINGWATER	SL	1	127	GINGELL	C	13	181
GILL	WL	6	157	GILLETT	IF	12	95	GILLION	HJB	13	181	GINGELL	S	13	181
GILLAM	AJ	10	87	GILLETT	LA	6	158	GILLIS	G	5	142	GINGELL	TE	1	127
GILLAM	F	9	260	GILLETT	LCH	7	145	GILLIS	H	14	121	GINGER	A	3	61

GINGER	A	5	143	GITTINS	E	11	144	GLASSBOROW	AW	13	182	GLEDHILL	N	8	129
GINGER	A	13	181	GITTINS	J	6	158	GLASSBOROW	FJ	13	182	GLEDHILL	TW	4	151
GINGER	F	5	143	GITTINS	R	13	181	GLASSBOROW	TG	13	182	GLEDHILL	W	8	129
GINGER	FW	2	138	GITTINS	W	10	87	GLASSER	FH	11	145	GLEDHILL	W	9	261
GINGER	G	5	143	GIVENS	J	5	143	GLASSFORD	D	8	128	GLEDHILL	W	14	122
GINGER	J	5	143	GLACCUM	W	6	158	GLASSON	EJ	3	344	GLEED	AA	12	312
GINGER	JW	5	143	GLADDIS	AO	10	87	GLASSON	H	10	302	GLEED	HT	12	312
GINGER	RW	5	143	GLADDISH	E	10	302	GLASSON	WB	6	158	GLEESON	J	14	122
GINGER	S	3	61	GLADDON	AW	3	61	GLASSPOOL	AF	4	151	GLEESON	L	9	76
GINGER	W	2	138	GLADDON	CG	2	138	GLASSPOOL	CEF	4	151	GLEESON	T	14	122
GINGLE	JF	4	150	GLADMAN	AF	7	146	GLASSPOOL	FT	4	151	GLEGG	PG	14	122
GINIFER	G	6	158	GLADMAN	B	3	61	GLASSPOOL	GHC	4	151	GLEN	EW	13	182
GINLECK	EW	13	181	GLADMAN	EJ	3	344	GLASSPOOL	PJS	10	87	GLEN	H	13	182
GINLEY	M	8	128	GLADMAN	F	1	127	GLASSPOOL	RG	4	151	GLENDENEN	RD	1	128
GINN	A	7	145	GLADMAN	W	3	344	GLASSPOOL	WD	10	87	GLENDENING	FF	8	129
GINN	AC	12	95	GLADMAN	W	7	146	GLASSPOOL	WHJ	4	151	GLENDENNING	WC	1	128
GINN	EA	13	181	GLADSTONE	GM	10	302	GLASSPOOL	WJ	4	151	GLENDINING	CJ	13	182
GINN	EJ	13	181	GLADSTONE	J	14	122	GLASSPOOLE	DR	2	139	GLENDINNING	AJ	3	62
GINN	F	7	145	GLADSTONE	TJ	10	302	GLASTONBURY	AJ	7	146	GLENDINNING	GJ	3	62
GINN	FW	5	143	GLADWELL	FJ	5	143	GLAXTON	ABC	3	344	GLENDINNING	JE	3	62
GINN	HJ	4	150	GLADWELL	H	2	138	GLAYSHER	H	7	146	GLENDINNING	WD	14	122
GINN	J	2	138	GLADWELL	T	11	145	GLAZBROOK	H	7	146	GLENISTER	A	5	143
GINN	J	7	145	GLADWIN	FT	2	139	GLAZEBROOK	B	12	312	GLENISTER	AT	1	128
GINN	JH	5	143	GLADWIN	J	2	139	GLAZEBROOK	G	1	128	GLENISTER	E	5	143
GINN	LHO	13	181	GLADWIN	WR	2	139	GLAZEBROOK	JW	13	182	GLENISTER	EE	1	128
GINN	WC	12	95	GLAFIELD	A	1	128	GLAZEBROOK	R	1	128	GLENISTER	FA	5	143
GINNS	H	12	312	GLANFIELD	W	5	143	GLAZEBROOK	W	1	128	GLENISTER	G	5	143
GINSBERG	H	14	122	GLANFIELD	WJ	1	128	GLAZIER	JA	13	182	GLENISTER	HW	5	144
GIORGI	EG	7	145	GLANISTER	EA	12	312	GLAZIER	JW	13	182	GLENISTER	J	5	144
GIORGI	WM	7	145	GLANISTER	EA	12	312	GLAZIER	PE	6	158	GLENISTER	JC	7	146
GIPP	HA	2	138	GLANISTER	EJ	12	312	GLEADALL	AE	4	151	GLENISTER	W	5	144
GIPSON	AC	4	150	GLANISTER	RHP	12	312	GLEADOW	F	9	261	GLENISTER	W	5	144
GIRDLER	AW	3	344	GLANVILLE	G	10	87	GLEASON	AJG	7	146	GLENN	A	14	122
GIRDLER	GS	7	146	GLANVILLE	G	10	87	GLEAVE	G	11	145	GLENN	C	1	128
GIRDLESTON	E	1	127	GLANVILLE	H	5	143	GLEAVE	J	11	145	GLENN	F	12	312
GIRLING	A	4	150	GLANVILLE	H	10	302	GLEAVE	JW	11	145	GLENN	WC	12	312
GIRLING	G	13	181	GLANVILLE	HJ	10	302	GLEAVE	PG	12	312	GLENNON	F	14	122
GIRLING	H	2	138	GLANVILLE	J	1	128	GLEAVE	T	11	145	GLENNON	GA	13	182
GIRLING	J	5	143	GLANVILLE	J	4	151	GLEAVES	A	9	75	GLENNON	J	14	122
GIRLING	JF	3	61	GLASBY	AG	6	158	GLEDHALL	GW	8	128	GLENNON	M	9	76
GIRLING	LT	2	138	GLASBY	H	9	75	GLEDHILL	A	9	75	GLENNON	P	11	145
GIRLING	T	13	181	GLASGOW	AG	2	139	GLEDHILL	B	8	129	GLENNON	T	11	145
GIRLING	W	10	87	GLASGOW	C	13	182	GLEDHILL	CF	4	151	GLEW	F	10	87
GIRLING	WH	4	151	GLASGOW	G	11	145	GLEDHILL	E	9	75	GLEW	J	6	159
GISBORNE	W	10	302	GLASGOW	S	11	145	GLEDHILL	E	9	75	GLEW	T	8	129
GISBOURNE	EF	6	158	GLASGOW	W	11	145	GLEDHILL	E	9	261	GLEW	W	11	145
GISBOURNE	JT	9	75	GLASPELL	AE	12	312	GLEDHILL	F	9	75	GLIBBERY	A	1	128
GISLINGHAM	AGK	7	146	GLASPOLL	AT	12	312	GLEDHILL	GH	4	151	GLICK	J	14	122
GISSING	A	9	261	GLASS	B	7	146	GLEDHILL	GH	11	145	GLIDDEWELL	J	12	95
GITTENS	CW	6	158	GLASS	EE	2	139	GLEDHILL	H	1	128	GLIDEWELL	WJ	12	95
GITTENS	G	13	181	GLASS	ET	1	128	GLEDHILL	H	9	75	GLINWOOD	JW	2	139
GITTENS	W	6	158	GLASS	RJ	13	182	GLEDHILL	H	9	386	GLITHERO	CW	2	139
GITTINGS	WJ	7	146	GLASS	SJ	13	182	GLEDHILL	J	8	129	GLOAG	J	11	145
GITTINS	AL	13	181	GLASS	W	14	122	GLEDHILL	J	9	76	GLOAG	L	11	145
GITTINS	CH	6	158	GLASS	WT	13	182	GLEDHILL	N	8	129	GLOCK	AEA	13	182

GLOCKLING	G	7	146	GLYDE	J	8	129	GODDARD	F	7	147	GODDIN	WJ	1	128
GLOSTER	HW	6	159	GLYN	H	13	183	GODDARD	F	10	88	GODDING	A	4	153
GLOVER	A	4	151	GLYNN	J	11	146	GODDARD	F	13	184	GODDING	A	10	303
GLOVER	A	6	159	GLYNN	JA	11	145	GODDARD	FJ	4	152	GODDING	C	4	153
GLOVER	A	9	76	GLYNN	T	14	123	GODDARD	G	4	152	GODDING	EH	10	88
GLOVER	A	9	386	GLYNN	W	14	123	GODDARD	G	14	123	GODDING	F	4	153
GLOVER	AG	4	151	GOAD	WA	13	183	GODDARD	GE	4	152	GODDING	HA	10	88
GLOVER	AS	5	144	GOANES	JA	4	151	GODDARD	GH	10	88	GODDING	JH	9	76
GLOVER	BA	6	159	GOATER	FC	4	151	GODDARD	H	2	139	GODDON	J	4	153
GLOVER	C	7	146	GOATER	HW	13	183	GODDARD	H	7	147	GODFREY	A	5	144
GLOVER	C	13	182	GOATER	L	4	151	GODDARD	H	7	147	GODFREY	A	13	184
GLOVER	CW	4	151	GOATER	M	4	151	GODDARD	HC	7	147	GODFREY	AC	6	159
GLOVER	EW	13	182	GOATER	RG	13	183	GODDARD	J	1	128	GODFREY	AT	12	95
GLOVER	F	13	182	GOATER	W	4	152	GODDARD	J	2	139	GODFREY	C	2	140
GLOVER	F	13	183	GOATER	WE	13	183	GODDARD	J	2	139	GODFREY	C	5	144
GLOVER	FJ	5	144	GOATES	SE	12	95	GODDARD	J	6	159	GODFREY	E	1	129
GLOVER	FJ	13	183	GOATLEY	AE	12	95	GODDARD	J	11	146	GODFREY	EA	5	144
GLOVER	G	6	159	GOATLEY	AE	12	95	GODDARD	J	11	146	GODFREY	EC	5	144
GLOVER	G	6	159	GOATLY	H	2	139	GODDARD	JA	2	139	GODFREY	F	4	153
GLOVER	G	8	129	GOATMAN	AJ	7	146	GODDARD	JE	4	152	GODFREY	F	11	146
GLOVER	G	9	261	GOBBETT	F	13	183	GODDARD	JM	10	302	GODFREY	FW	5	145
GLOVER	GA	1	128	GOBBY	FA	5	144	GODDARD	LG	4	152	GODFREY	G	2	140
GLOVER	GH	3	344	GOBBY	T	5	144	GODDARD	ME	13	184	GODFREY	G	5	145
GLOVER	GH	6	159	GOBEY	G	5	144	GODDARD	R	13	184	GODFREY	G	5	145
GLOVER	H	8	129	GOBLE	A	10	302	GODDARD	RR	7	147	GODFREY	G	12	95
GLOVER	H	9	261	GOBLE	A	10	302	GODDARD	S	6	159	GODFREY	GA	13	184
GLOVER	H	13	183	GOBLE	C	10	302	GODDARD	SL	2	140	GODFREY	GS	5	145
GLOVER	HH	2	139	GOBLE	HT	4	152	GODDARD	W	1	128	GODFREY	GV	6	159
GLOVER	HJ	13	183	GOBLE	J	2	139	GODDARD	W	4	152	GODFREY	H	5	145
GLOVER	J	2	139	GOBLE	J	2	139	GODDARD	W	4	152	GODFREY	H	7	147
GLOVER	J	8	129	GOBLE	JC	10	87	GODDARD	W	10	88	GODFREY	H	7	147
GLOVER	J	14	122	GOBLE	LJ	10	87	GODDARD	W	10	88	GODFREY	H	9	261
GLOVER	JF	7	146	GOBLE	T	4	152	GODDARD	WA	10	302	GODFREY	H	10	88
GLOVER	JF	7	146	GOBLE	WA	10	88	GODDARD	WG	4	152	GODFREY	HT	2	140
GLOVER	JH	7	146	GOCHER	HHP	13	183	GODDARD	WJ	13	184	GODFREY	J	4	153
GLOVER	JH	13	183	GODBEHERE	EL	5	144	GODDARD	WL	11	146	GODFREY	J	6	159
GLOVER	JS	11	145	GODBEHERE	W	5	144	GODDEN	AE	3	344	GODFREY	J	7	147
GLOVER	JS	13	183	GODBER	TW	13	183	GODDEN	CJ	7	147	GODFREY	J	8	129
GLOVER	JW	9	261	GODDARD	A	2	139	GODDEN	D	3	344	GODFREY	J	10	303
GLOVER	JW	9	261	GODDARD	A	2	139	GODDEN	E	13	184	GODFREY	JE	1	129
GLOVER	OO	2	139	GODDARD	A	3	62	GODDEN	EE	10	302	GODFREY	JE	7	147
GLOVER	R	8	129	GODDARD	AE	13	183	GODDEN	ES	2	140	GODFREY	JS	3	62
GLOVER	R	8	129	GODDARD	AH	13	183	GODDEN	F	10	88	GODFREY	JS	5	145
GLOVER	R	9	261	GODDARD	AM	7	147	GODDEN	F	10	302	GODFREY	JW	13	184
GLOVER	RF	2	139	GODDARD	B	3	62	GODDEN	FE	7	147	GODFREY	L	11	146
GLOVER	RW	8	129	GODDARD	C	3	344	GODDEN	FG	2	140	GODFREY	RC	2	140
GLOVER	V	14	122	GODDARD	C	4	152	GODDEN	J	4	152	GODFREY	RM	5	145
GLOVER	VB	4	151	GODDARD	CA	4	152	GODDEN	JA	10	302	GODFREY	SF	2	140
GLOVER	W	13	183	GODDARD	CF	4	152	GODDEN	L	4	152	GODFREY	SS	7	147
GLOVER	WE	13	183	GODDARD	CH	4	152	GODDEN	PW	7	147	GODFREY	TA	11	146
GLOVER	WG	5	144	GODDARD	CW	4	152	GODDEN	RH	1	128	GODFREY	WE	4	153
GLOVER	WJ	11	145	GODDARD	E	4	152	GODDEN	T	4	152	GODFREY	WJ	4	153
GLOYNE	FG	3	62	GODDARD	EE	3	344	GODDEN	W	4	153	GODFREY	WJ	8	129
GLOYNES	WT	5	144	GODDARD	EL	13	183	GODDEN	W	4	153	GODFREY	WO	2	140
GLYDE	A	8	129	GODDARD	F	1	128	GODDEN	W	7	147	GODFREY	WP	1	129

GODFREY	WS	9	76	GODWIN	PR	10	88	GOLDIE	AC	6	160	GOLDSBOROUGH	A	9	261
GODGEMAN	WG	12	422	GODWIN	S	6	159	GOLDIE	C	4	154	GOLDSBOROUGH	A	9	261
GODIER	C	1	129	GODWIN	S	8	130	GOLDIE	J	4	154	GOLDSBOROUGH	S	9	261
GODING	JJ	13	184	GODWIN	TE	11	146	GOLDING	A	3	62	GOLDSBY	A	6	160
GODLEMAN	CR	3	62	GODWIN	W	4	153	GOLDING	A	4	154	GOLDSMITH	AE	3	345
GODLEMAN	J	3	62	GODWIN	W	7	147	GOLDING	A	12	96	GOLDSMITH	AL	1	129
GODLEMAN	S	3	62	GODWIN	WA	4	153	GOLDING	A	12	96	GOLDSMITH	C	1	129
GODLEMAN	SG	3	62	GODWIN	WF	14	123	GOLDING	A	13	184	GOLDSMITH	CJ	12	96
GODLEMAN	WJ	5	145	GODWIN	WJ	10	88	GOLDING	C	6	160	GOLDSMITH	EW	13	185
GODLEY	AE	8	129	GODWYN	A	13	184	GOLDING	E	4	154	GOLDSMITH	F	10	89
GODLEY	C	4	153	GOEBECK	E	1	129	GOLDING	E	7	148	GOLDSMITH	F	12	96
GODLEY	D	10	303	GOFF	A	12	312	GOLDING	E	10	303	GOLDSMITH	F	13	185
GODLEY	G	13	184	GOFF	AH	13	184	GOLDING	FG	12	96	GOLDSMITH	FG	10	89
GODLEY	J	13	184	GOFF	AT	6	159	GOLDING	FW	12	96	GOLDSMITH	FW	4	154
GODLEY	R	14	123	GOFF	C	12	95	GOLDING	G	3	62	GOLDSMITH	G	13	185
GODLEY	WR	7	147	GOFF	E	4	153	GOLDING	G	3	345	GOLDSMITH	GA	13	185
GODLIMAN	AH	2	140	GOFF	EH	12	96	GOLDING	G	5	145	GOLDSMITH	H	10	89
GODLIMAN	F	5	145	GOFF	F	12	312	GOLDING	GWP	1	129	GOLDSMITH	H	10	89
GODLIMAN	W	3	62	GOFF	FJ	4	153	GOLDING	H	4	154	GOLDSMITH	HA	2	140
GODMAN	A	3	344	GOFF	FJ	12	96	GOLDING	HJ	13	184	GOLDSMITH	HJ	10	89
GODMAN	A	3	345	GOFF	G	8	130	GOLDING	HS	3	62	GOLDSMITH	HO	10	89
GODMAN	F	7	147	GOFF	GW	13	184	GOLDING	J	4	154	GOLDSMITH	HT	13	185
GODMAN	FC	5	145	GOFF	J	12	96	GOLDING	J	10	88	GOLDSMITH	JH	7	148
GODMAN	H	5	145	GOFF	L	4	153	GOLDING	JH	10	88	GOLDSMITH	JW	13	185
GODMAN	HAW	2	140	GOFF	M	4	153	GOLDING	JP	6	160	GOLDSMITH	L	3	62
GODMAN	J	5	145	GOFF	PC	7	147	GOLDING	JT	1	129	GOLDSMITH	O	4	154
GODMAN	TA	5	145	GOFF	T	6	159	GOLDING	JT	1	129	GOLDSMITH	O	5	145
GODMAN	W	1	129	GOFF	WG	12	96	GOLDING	L	13	184	GOLDSMITH	T	13	185
GODMAN	WA	5	145	GOFF	WH	12	312	GOLDING	M	10	88	GOLDSMITH	TJ	2	140
GODOLPHIN	JR	3	62	GOFFE	JG	4	153	GOLDING	PV	13	184	GOLDSMITH	W	13	185
GODRELL	H	14	123	GOFFE	W	12	96	GOLDING	R	1	129	GOLDSMITH	WA	13	185
GODRICH	J	8	129	GOGGIN	JE	1	129	GOLDING	R	1	129	GOLDSMITH	WE	4	154
GODRICH	S	8	129	GOGGIN	JM	1	129	GOLDING	R	10	88	GOLDSMITH	WE	12	312
GODSALL	AE	10	88	GOGGIN	M	1	129	GOLDING	RA	4	154	GOLDSPINK	J	6	160
GODSALL	E	3	345	GOGUEL	GS	2	140	GOLDING	RE	12	96	GOLDSPINK	T	2	140
GODSALL	H	3	345	GOLBEY	J	10	303	GOLDING	RH	13	185	GOLDSTEIN	J	2	140
GODSELL	EA	10	88	GOLD	AJ	1	129	GOLDING	RW	4	154	GOLDSTEIN	S	14	123
GODSELL	HJ	10	303	GOLD	C	1	129	GOLDING	T	4	154	GOLDSTONE	A	13	185
GODSON	CA	6	159	GOLD	GF	13	184	GOLDING	T	6	160	GOLDSTONE	A	14	123
GODWARD	H	9	261	GOLD	GR	6	160	GOLDING	W	5	145	GOLDSTONE	AJ	7	148
GODWIN	A	4	153	GOLD	H	6	160	GOLDING	WC	13	185	GOLDSTONE	G	14	123
GODWIN	A	5	145	GOLD	J	6	160	GOLDING	WH	12	96	GOLDSTONE	J	14	123
GODWIN	AH	3	345	GOLD	ME	1	129	GOLDING	WJ	1	129	GOLDSTONE	L	13	185
GODWIN	AJ	6	159	GOLDBERG	B	14	123	GOLDINGAY	G	6	160	GOLDSTONE	M	13	185
GODWIN	AR	2	140	GOLDBERG	HL	14	123	GOLDINGAY	J	6	160	GOLDSTONE	M	14	123
GODWIN	AR	3	345	GOLDEN	A	6	160	GOLDINGAY	JR	13	185	GOLDSTONE	W	12	96
GODWIN	B	6	159	GOLDEN	CE	2	140	GOLDMAN	B	9	76	GOLDSTONE	WJ	13	185
GODWIN	E	2	140	GOLDEN	F	4	154	GOLDMAN	C	14	123	GOLDSTRAW	A	14	123
GODWIN	FP	4	153	GOLDEN	HS	9	261	GOLDMAN	H	8	130	GOLDSWAIN	J	13	185
GODWIN	G	11	146	GOLDER	W	3	345	GOLDMAN	J	14	123	GOLDSWAIN	JT	13	185
GODWIN	H	1	129	GOLDFINCH	EW	10	303	GOLDRING	C	10	88	GOLDSWORTHY	A	13	185
GODWIN	H	13	184	GOLDFINCH	J	3	345	GOLDRING	SJ	10	303	GOLDSWORTHY	CT	14	123
GODWIN	HW	12	95	GOLDFINCH	RL	10	303	GOLDS	C	13	185	GOLDSWORTHY	RM	13	186
GODWIN	JF	3	345	GOLDFINCH	WL	10	303	GOLDSACK	AJ	10	88	GOLDTHORP	W	8	130
GODWIN	P	6	159	GOLDIE	A	4	154	GOLDSACK	CP	7	148	GOLDTHORP	W	9	261

GOLDTHORPE	F	8	130
GOLDTHORPE	H	8	130
GOLDTHORPE	JA	8	130
GOLDTHORPE	SC	1	129
GOLDWICK	H	11	146
GOLDWIN	FW	2	140
GOLEBY	A	9	76
GOLEBY	A	9	262
GOLEBY	H	9	262
GOLLAR	JW	8	130
GOLLEDGE	AA	7	148
GOLLEDGE	FE	7	148
GOLLINS	S	14	123
GOLLOP	CH	2	141
GOLLOP	E	13	186
GOLLOP	F	7	148
GOLLOP	P	4	154
GOLLOP	SE	7	148
GOLLOP	WH	7	148
GOLTON	FE	11	146
GOLTON	IH	11	146
GOLTON	JH	11	146
GOMER	GA	10	303
GOMER	GH	10	89
GOMERSALL	A	8	130
GOMERSALL	AGW	7	148
GOMERSALL	FL	8	130
GOMERSHALL	H	11	146
GOMM	J	3	345
GOMM	W	3	345
GOMME	W	5	145
GOMMON	G	1	130
GONDOLPHIN	F	14	124
GONDOUIN	CF	1	130
GONLEN	J	8	130
GONSALVES	HLT	3	345
GOOCH	ACM	1	130
GOOCH	AE	2	141
GOOCH	C	5	145
GOOCH	CE	2	141
GOOCH	CN	10	89
GOOCH	E	2	141
GOOCH	ET	5	145
GOOCH	GW	3	62
GOOCH	H	14	124
GOOCH	HM	1	130
GOOCH	HW	7	148
GOOCH	JHJ	1	130
GOOCH	LM	1	130
GOOCH	R	5	146
GOOCH	TFA	1	130
GOOCH	V	3	345
GOOCH	WH	13	186
GOOD	A	7	148
GOOD	AE	4	154
GOOD	AH	13	186
GOOD	E	14	124
GOOD	EG	13	186
GOOD	EWE	4	154
GOOD	FM	13	186
GOOD	H	7	148
GOOD	J	5	146
GOOD	RE	4	154
GOOD	SH	4	155
GOOD	WC	2	141
GOODACRE	AF	1	130
GOODACRE	E	1	130
GOODACRE	E	1	130
GOODAIR	C	5	146
GOODAIR	H	5	146
GOODAIR	H	5	146
GOODALE	AG	13	186
GOODALL	A	9	76
GOODALL	A	9	76
GOODALL	AG	4	155
GOODALL	AJ	4	155
GOODALL	AJCR	13	186
GOODALL	B	1	130
GOODALL	B	4	155
GOODALL	CD	1	131
GOODALL	F	8	130
GOODALL	FJ	10	303
GOODALL	FW	2	141
GOODALL	GH	13	186
GOODALL	GJ	10	89
GOODALL	H	4	155
GOODALL	HWG	10	89
GOODALL	J	2	141
GOODALL	J	7	148
GOODALL	J	8	130
GOODALL	JA	1	130
GOODALL	JG	13	186
GOODALL	JT	1	130
GOODALL	JT	1	130
GOODALL	JT	8	130
GOODALL	JT	8	130
GOODALL	JW	8	130
GOODALL	NH	13	186
GOODALL	S	4	155
GOODALL	T	2	141
GOODALL	TH	13	186
GOODALL	W	2	141
GOODALL	W	8	130
GOODALL	W	8	130
GOODALL	WG	13	186
GOODALL	WH	4	155
GOODALL	WT	4	155
GOODAY	E	3	345
GOODAY	GP	3	345
GOODBODY	T	9	76
GOODBODY	WJ	2	141
GOODCHILD	A	7	148
GOODCHILD	AE	2	141
GOODCHILD	AJ	1	130
GOODCHILD	AL	1	130
GOODCHILD	FR	3	345
GOODCHILD	GW	2	141
GOODCHILD	J	1	130
GOODCHILD	J	4	155
GOODCHILD	JF	3	62
GOODCHILD	JI	1	130
GOODCHILD	M	3	345
GOODCHILD	OE	1	130
GOODCHILD	PF	2	141
GOODCHILD	PJ	2	141
GOODCHILD	R	1	130
GOODCHILD	SC	5	146
GOODCHILD	T	4	155
GOODCHILD	TW	2	141
GOODE	AE	5	146
GOODE	AE	12	312
GOODE	AE	12	312
GOODE	AG	9	262
GOODE	BJ	12	313
GOODE	DS	6	160
GOODE	H	3	346
GOODE	HJ	13	186
GOODE	J	6	160
GOODE	J	6	160
GOODE	J	8	130
GOODE	J	12	313
GOODE	JH	5	146
GOODE	LT	9	76
GOODE	PA	12	313
GOODE	T	12	313
GOODE	TA	5	146
GOODE	W	7	148
GOODE	W	12	313
GOODE	WA	8	130
GOODE	WJ	12	313
GOODEN	EJ	7	148
GOODEN	F	12	96
GOODEN	HW	3	62
GOODENOUGH	A	3	63
GOODENOUGH	C	3	63
GOODENOUGH	FW	7	148
GOODENOUGH	H	3	63
GOODENOUGH	J	5	146
GOODENOUGH	JE	8	131
GOODENOUGH	W	3	63
GOODER	W	8	131
GOODERHAM	A	3	346
GOODERHAM	AE	3	346
GOODERHAM	C	3	346
GOODERHAM	E	5	146
GOODERHAM	H	9	76
GOODERHAM	H	9	76
GOODERHAM	H	9	262
GOODERHAM	JB	3	63
GOODERHAM	RR	9	262
GOODERHAM	SH	3	346
GOODERHAM	W	3	63
GOODERSON	AE	13	186
GOODERSON	L	13	186
GOODES	A	1	130
GOODES	CA	12	96
GOODES	G	1	130
GOODES	H	12	96
GOODES	HE	1	131
GOODES	JE	12	96
GOODEVE	R	10	89
GOODEY	C	12	96
GOODFELLOW	A	2	141
GOODFELLOW	ATD	3	63
GOODFELLOW	BG	4	155
GOODFELLOW	FG	10	89
GOODFELLOW	HG	1	131
GOODFELLOW	RA	11	146
GOODFELLOW	W	4	155
GOODFELLOW	W	11	146
GOODGE	CW	5	146
GOODGE	EW	13	186
GOODGER	CH	12	97
GOODGER	GH	12	97
GOODGER	GW	2	141
GOODGER	RH	12	422
GOODHALL	JH	5	146
GOODHAND	F	6	160
GOODHEW	FI	3	346
GOODING	A	4	155
GOODING	AG	12	97
GOODING	AJ	4	155
GOODING	EJ	13	186
GOODING	FJ	3	63
GOODING	G	4	155
GOODING	GH	13	186
GOODING	HA	2	141
GOODING	J	3	63
GOODLAD	JP	2	141
GOODLEY	T	8	131
GOODLEY	W	8	131
GOODLIFF	AB	3	63
GOODLIFF	CH	14	124
GOODLIFFE	A	9	262
GOODLIFFE	H	9	262
GOODLIFFE	JC	7	149
GOODLIFFE	W	11	146
GOODMAN	A	1	131
GOODMAN	A	12	97
GOODMAN	A	12	313

GOODMAN	A	14	124	GOODMAN	T	10	89	GOODWIN	CL	3	346	GOODYER	GE	10	303
GOODMAN	AA	13	186	GOODMAN	TE	12	313	GOODWIN	EJ	12	313	GOODYER	W	5	147
GOODMAN	AR	5	146	GOODMAN	W	2	142	GOODWIN	F	14	124	GOOKEY	AE	4	156
GOODMAN	AR	13	186	GOODMAN	WA	12	313	GOODWIN	FH	2	142	GOOKEY	GV	4	156
GOODMAN	B	12	97	GOODMAN	WJ	4	155	GOODWIN	G	7	149	GOOM	J	8	131
GOODMAN	C	3	63	GOODMAN	WJ	5	147	GOODWIN	G	13	187	GOOM	J	8	131
GOODMAN	C	5	146	GOODMAN	WL	12	97	GOODWIN	G	14	124	GOOM	TR	12	313
GOODMAN	CJ	6	160	GOODRICH	A	12	313	GOODWIN	GF	1	131	GOOSE	C	5	147
GOODMAN	D	2	142	GOODRICH	F	13	186	GOODWIN	GH	3	346	GOOSE	EW	8	131
GOODMAN	E	14	124	GOODRICH	J	13	187	GOODWIN	GW	11	147	GOOSE	SR	5	147
GOODMAN	EC	7	149	GOODRICH	TW	8	131	GOODWIN	H	14	124	GOOSEY	G	12	313
GOODMAN	ER	12	97	GOODRICH	WJ	13	187	GOODWIN	H	14	124	GOOZEE	FC	7	149
GOODMAN	F	1	131	GOODRICK	JJ	8	131	GOODWIN	HC	5	147	GOOZEE	HR	7	149
GOODMAN	F	12	313	GOODRIDGE	AE	4	155	GOODWIN	HE	1	131	GORBELL	EN	4	156
GOODMAN	F	14	124	GOODRIDGE	CS	4	156	GOODWIN	HJ	12	97	GORD	TW	3	346
GOODMAN	FW	7	149	GOODRIDGE	D	12	97	GOODWIN	HW	1	131	GORDAN	H	8	131
GOODMAN	FW	12	97	GOODRIDGE	FT	4	155	GOODWIN	J	2	142	GORDGE	WA	2	142
GOODMAN	G	7	149	GOODRIDGE	J	12	97	GOODWIN	J	6	161	GORDING	RE	2	142
GOODMAN	G	7	149	GOODRIDGE	JW	1	131	GOODWIN	J	9	76	GORDON	A	8	132
GOODMAN	G	14	124	GOODRIDGE	RA	4	156	GOODWIN	J	11	147	GORDON	AC	2	142
GOODMAN	G	14	124	GOODRIDGE	TW	2	142	GOODWIN	J	11	147	GORDON	AC	10	89
GOODMAN	GA	8	131	GOODRIDGE	WE	12	313	GOODWIN	J	14	124	GORDON	B	13	187
GOODMAN	GA	12	313	GOODRUM	FT	7	149	GOODWIN	J	14	125	GORDON	CH	11	147
GOODMAN	H	1	131	GOODSELL	CE	9	262	GOODWIN	JA	1	131	GORDON	CR	3	63
GOODMAN	H	1	131	GOODSHIP	B	12	97	GOODWIN	JA	9	76	GORDON	CW	3	63
GOODMAN	H	2	141	GOODSHIP	F	9	76	GOODWIN	M	1	131	GORDON	D	4	156
GOODMAN	H	5	146	GOODSHIP	FA	12	97	GOODWIN	MW	12	98	GORDON	E	3	346
GOODMAN	H	5	146	GOODSHIP	FH	5	147	GOODWIN	R	5	147	GORDON	E	14	125
GOODMAN	H	11	147	GOODSHIP	H	5	147	GOODWIN	R	6	161	GORDON	EA	12	313
GOODMAN	I	14	124	GOODSHIP	H	12	97	GOODWIN	R	14	125	GORDON	ED	2	142
GOODMAN	J	5	146	GOODSHIP	WJ	5	147	GOODWIN	RR	8	131	GORDON	FE	3	63
GOODMAN	J	5	146	GOODSON	A	3	346	GOODWIN	RT	5	147	GORDON	GH	3	346
GOODMAN	J	5	146	GOODSON	A	8	131	GOODWIN	S	5	147	GORDON	HG	13	187
GOODMAN	J	12	97	GOODSON	A	9	262	GOODWIN	S	8	131	GORDON	J	7	149
GOODMAN	JA	8	131	GOODSON	HA	5	147	GOODWIN	S	13	187	GORDON	J	11	147
GOODMAN	JA	12	97	GOODSON	HA	12	313	GOODWIN	S	14	125	GORDON	J	14	125
GOODMAN	JA	12	313	GOODSON	HJ	5	147	GOODWIN	SA	4	156	GORDON	J	14	125
GOODMAN	JJ	7	149	GOODSON	JJ	3	346	GOODWIN	SW	5	147	GORDON	JA	3	63
GOODMAN	JT	3	63	GOODSON	W	2	142	GOODWIN	T	6	161	GORDON	M	2	142
GOODMAN	JT	3	63	GOODSPEED	A	7	149	GOODWIN	T	11	147	GORDON	SM	4	156
GOODMAN	JT	12	97	GOODSPEED	B	7	149	GOODWIN	T	11	147	GORDON	SW	4	156
GOODMAN	JW	12	97	GOODSPEED	E	7	149	GOODWIN	V	3	346	GORDON	W	11	147
GOODMAN	M	5	147	GOODSPEED	H	7	149	GOODWIN	W	10	89	GORDON	W	12	313
GOODMAN	M	11	147	GOODSWEN	AG	7	149	GOODWIN	W	11	147	GORDON	WC	7	149
GOODMAN	M	14	124	GOODWARD	AAN	9	76	GOODYEAR	CE	9	262	GORDON	WJ	11	147
GOODMAN	M	14	124	GOODWAY	BR	3	63	GOODYEAR	EP	5	147	GORE	E	11	147
GOODMAN	PJ	4	155	GOODWAY	D	1	131	GOODYEAR	F	8	131	GORE	EH	10	89
GOODMAN	R	9	262	GOODWAY	E	6	160	GOODYEAR	FC	2	142	GORE	EJ	3	63
GOODMAN	S	6	160	GOODWAY	R	10	303	GOODYEAR	G	10	89	GORE	F	9	77
GOODMAN	SA	4	155	GOODWAY	W	6	160	GOODYEAR	G	12	98	GORE	GT	13	187
GOODMAN	SC	12	97	GOODWAY	WJE	1	131	GOODYEAR	H	8	131	GORE	H	2	142
GOODMAN	SC	12	97	GOODWILL	E	8	131	GOODYEAR	P	1	131	GORE	HA	2	142
GOODMAN	SJ	5	147	GOODWILL	S	9	76	GOODYEAR	VG	6	161	GORE	RR	12	314
GOODMAN	SJ	10	89	GOODWILLIE	W	10	303	GOODYEAR	W	8	131	GORE	T	2	142
GOODMAN	T	9	76	GOODWIN	AH	4	156	GOODYER	AJ	10	303	GORE	T	5	147

GORE	W	5	147	GOSDEN	JW	1	131	GOST	EJ	5	148	GOUGH	W	11	148
GORE	WF	9	77	GOSDEN	WG	2	142	GOSTICK	JA	12	98	GOUGH	W	12	98
GORE	WGH	7	149	GOSDIN	E	13	187	GOSTLING	WA	1	132	GOUGH	WC	3	346
GORE	WMB	2	142	GOSHAM	HC	4	156	GOSTRIDGE	G	14	126	GOUGH	WJ	7	150
GOREHAM	J	13	187	GOSHAM	S	4	156	GOSTRIDGE	J	14	126	GOUGH	WL	10	90
GOREHAM	R	13	187	GOSLEY	G	8	132	GOTCH	FG	2	143	GOUGH	WM	10	90
GORELL	A	9	262	GOSLIN	E	4	156	GOTT	A	9	77	GOUGH	WTJ	1	132
GORELL	J	9	262	GOSLING	A	3	64	GOTT	A	9	262	GOULBOURN	G	14	126
GORHAM	GW	2	142	GOSLING	A	4	156	GOTT	J	11	148	GOULBOURN	T	14	126
GORING	G	5	147	GOSLING	A	13	187	GOTT	RE	11	148	GOULD	A	5	148
GORING	G	7	150	GOSLING	AE	4	156	GOTT	T	9	262	GOULD	A	7	150
GORING	J	14	125	GOSLING	AE	4	156	GOTT	W	8	132	GOULD	AC	7	150
GORING	JM	2	142	GOSLING	AH	3	64	GOTTLIER	H	14	126	GOULD	AH	6	162
GORING	T	13	187	GOSLING	AH	6	161	GOTTLIER	M	14	126	GOULD	AJ	1	132
GORLE	JJ	6	161	GOSLING	BAJ	12	98	GOTZ	J	1	132	GOULD	AJ	4	157
GORMAN	C	13	187	GOSLING	C	11	148	GOUCHER	JW	8	132	GOULD	AW	2	143
GORMAN	D	9	77	GOSLING	EA	2	143	GOUDE	WW	12	314	GOULD	C	13	188
GORMAN	D	9	262	GOSLING	F	13	187	GOUDIE	CH	1	132	GOULD	CH	13	188
GORMAN	E	1	131	GOSLING	FA	4	157	GOUDY	A	8	132	GOULD	F	8	132
GORMAN	H	9	77	GOSLING	G	13	187	GOUGE	CH	4	157	GOULD	FA	7	150
GORMAN	H	11	147	GOSLING	HEJ	4	157	GOUGH	A	6	161	GOULD	FW	13	188
GORMAN	J	9	77	GOSLING	J	11	148	GOUGH	A	6	161	GOULD	G	7	150
GORMAN	J	9	262	GOSLING	JC	13	187	GOUGH	A	10	90	GOULD	GA	14	126
GORMAN	J	9	262	GOSLING	L	11	148	GOUGH	AE	6	161	GOULD	GH	4	157
GORMAN	J	11	147	GOSLING	M	9	77	GOUGH	AG	1	132	GOULD	GW	6	162
GORMAN	J	14	125	GOSLING	R	13	187	GOUGH	AV	6	161	GOULD	H	3	347
GORMAN	J	14	125	GOSLING	S	2	143	GOUGH	B	6	161	GOULD	H	4	157
GORMAN	J	14	125	GOSLING	T	7	150	GOUGH	C	6	161	GOULD	H	6	162
GORMAN	J	14	125	GOSLING	W	12	314	GOUGH	C	12	98	GOULD	H	7	150
GORMAN	L	9	386	GOSLING	W	13	187	GOUGH	CB	10	90	GOULD	H	13	188
GORMAN	W	6	161	GOSLING	WA	13	188	GOUGH	CJ	12	314	GOULD	HJ	4	157
GORMLEY	TB	11	147	GOSLING	WC	4	157	GOUGH	E	6	161	GOULD	HJ	6	162
GORMLY	W	14	125	GOSNELL	AJ	7	150	GOUGH	EG	10	90	GOULD	JA	7	150
GORMON	P	9	262	GOSNEY	AG	10	89	GOUGH	FG	12	98	GOULD	JHW	4	157
GORNALL	J	11	147	GOSNEY	D	4	157	GOUGH	G	1	132	GOULD	JJ	13	188
GORNELL	JH	9	77	GOSNEY	J	8	132	GOUGH	GE	3	346	GOULD	JS	2	143
GORRELL	R	4	156	GOSNEY	T	8	132	GOUGH	GH	12	98	GOULD	LN	4	157
GORRINGE	EH	14	125	GOSNEY	TH	4	157	GOUGH	GW	6	161	GOULD	MJ	2	143
GORRINGE	R	13	187	GOSNEY	WJ	10	90	GOUGH	H	6	161	GOULD	ML	7	150
GORRINGE	WT	1	131	GOSS	A	8	132	GOUGH	J	6	161	GOULD	P	4	157
GORSDEN	H	8	132	GOSS	AG	13	188	GOUGH	J	11	148	GOULD	P	13	188
GORST	CF	14	125	GOSS	AW	5	148	GOUGH	JA	6	161	GOULD	PE	13	188
GORST	J	11	148	GOSS	B	7	150	GOUGH	JB	6	161	GOULD	RC	4	157
GORSUCH	HE	10	303	GOSS	H	2	143	GOUGH	JE	4	157	GOULD	RS	13	188
GORTON	CW	14	125	GOSS	M	9	77	GOUGH	L	1	132	GOULD	SA	13	188
GORTON	E	4	156	GOSS	R	5	148	GOUGH	P	6	161	GOULD	T	13	188
GORTON	J	3	63	GOSS	S	5	148	GOUGH	R	5	148	GOULD	W	2	143
GORTON	J	4	156	GOSS	S	14	125	GOUGH	RH	2	143	GOULD	W	5	148
GORTON	R	14	125	GOSS	TE	8	132	GOUGH	RH	6	162	GOULD	WC	3	64
GORTON	W	14	125	GOSS	W	12	98	GOUGH	T	11	148	GOULD	WH	6	162
GORVIN	AG	2	142	GOSS	WA	13	188	GOUGH	TL	12	98	GOULDBOURN	R	11	148
GOSCHEN	S	3	346	GOSS	WC	12	98	GOUGH	W	2	143	GOULDEN	A	14	126
GOSDEN	A	2	142	GOSSAGE	G	10	303	GOUGH	W	3	64	GOULDEN	C	8	132
GOSDEN	AC	2	142	GOSSON	OG	1	131	GOUGH	W	11	148	GOULDEN	E	11	148
GOSDEN	GA	4	156	GOSSON	WF	1	131	GOUGH	W	11	148	GOULDEN	E	14	126

GOULDEN	EC	4	157	GOVER	WA	2	143	GRACE	AF	12	98	GRAHAM	GH	3	347
GOULDEN	F	11	148	GOVER	WA	10	90	GRACE	AW	3	347	GRAHAM	H	8	133
GOULDEN	HC	4	157	GOVIER	GF	3	347	GRACE	B	11	149	GRAHAM	H	8	133
GOULDEN	J	8	132	GOVIER	GJ	10	304	GRACE	BF	6	162	GRAHAM	H	14	126
GOULDEN	J	11	148	GOVIER	HT	1	132	GRACE	C	3	347	GRAHAM	HA	7	151
GOULDEN	S	6	162	GOVIER	VS	3	64	GRACE	CH	4	158	GRAHAM	HJ	13	189
GOULDEN	W	8	132	GOW	A	7	151	GRACE	CH	4	158	GRAHAM	J	6	162
GOULDEN	W	8	132	GOW	TAO	7	151	GRACE	CH	5	148	GRAHAM	J	9	77
GOULDER	LJE	7	150	GOWAN	A	2	143	GRACE	E	4	158	GRAHAM	J	9	263
GOULDER	T	7	150	GOWAN	AJ	2	143	GRACE	E	13	189	GRAHAM	J	9	263
GOULDING	AC	13	188	GOWAN	GH	2	143	GRACE	ES	5	148	GRAHAM	JA	6	162
GOULDING	AE	3	64	GOWAN	M	8	132	GRACE	F	9	77	GRAHAM	JA	13	189
GOULDING	B	1	132	GOWAN	PL	2	143	GRACE	F	9	263	GRAHAM	JE	11	149
GOULDING	BA	4	157	GOWAR	E	2	144	GRACE	FF	10	90	GRAHAM	JH	11	149
GOULDING	FG	3	64	GOWARD	A	8	132	GRACE	FJ	3	347	GRAHAM	JP	11	149
GOULDING	H	11	148	GOWEN	A	12	314	GRACE	FW	1	132	GRAHAM	JW	8	133
GOULDING	J	6	162	GOWEN	H	12	314	GRACE	FWG	4	158	GRAHAM	JW	11	149
GOULDING	J	9	77	GOWEN	JT	12	314	GRACE	H	5	148	GRAHAM	JW	12	98
GOULDING	J	9	263	GOWER	C	7	151	GRACE	HD	12	98	GRAHAM	M	9	263
GOULDING	M	4	157	GOWER	E	5	148	GRACE	J	5	148	GRAHAM	P	8	133
GOULDING	T	9	386	GOWER	E	13	189	GRACE	J	11	149	GRAHAM	PJ	8	133
GOULDING	TJ	12	98	GOWER	EE	7	151	GRACE	J	11	149	GRAHAM	R	1	133
GOULDING	W	8	132	GOWER	EW	1	132	GRACE	J	14	126	GRAHAM	R	11	149
GOULDS	S	13	188	GOWER	FW	5	148	GRACE	JE	6	162	GRAHAM	RE	3	347
GOULDSBOROUGH	TW	9	77	GOWER	G	3	64	GRACE	JW	3	64	GRAHAM	RG	14	126
GOULDSTONE	W	6	162	GOWER	G	10	90	GRACE	S	3	347	GRAHAM	RS	7	151
GOULDSWORTHY	F	6	162	GOWER	H	5	148	GRACE	SFJ	5	148	GRAHAM	S	14	126
GOULSON	F	11	148	GOWER	HT	10	90	GRACE	T	3	347	GRAHAM	T	8	133
GOULSTONE	GF	7	150	GOWER	RJ	3	64	GRACE	W	1	132	GRAHAM	T	14	126
GOULSTONE	WG	7	150	GOWER	V	11	148	GRACE	W	5	148	GRAHAM	TW	14	126
GOULT	EA	2	143	GOWER	WEP	7	151	GRACE	W	13	189	GRAHAM	W	8	133
GOULTER	JW	10	303	GOWERS	A	3	347	GRACE	WF	9	77	GRAHAM	W	12	314
GOULTON	FW	2	143	GOWERS	EH	3	347	GRACE	WF	9	263	GRAHAM	WE	8	133
GOULY	SE	2	143	GOWERS	W	7	151	GRACE	WT	4	158	GRAHAM	WH	14	126
GOURLAY	DJ	5	148	GOWERS	WG	5	148	GRACO	AG	1	132	GRAHAM	WM	13	189
GOURLEY	AG	13	188	GOWIN	E	3	64	GRACO	HA	1	133	GRAHAM	WP	13	189
GOURLEY	W	13	188	GOWIN	JW	7	151	GRACO	WT	1	133	GRAHAM	WS	4	158
GOURRIET	LE	7	150	GOWIN	WC	7	151	GRADIDGE	FH	4	158	GRAHAM	WV	11	149
GOVAN	WB	10	90	GOWING	EW	2	144	GRADWELL	H	9	77	GRAHAME-PARKER	J	3	64
GOVE	JC	13	188	GOWING	GW	10	304	GRADY	J	14	126	GRAINGER	A	9	77
GOVE	JS	7	150	GOWING	SG	12	314	GRADY	JT	7	151	GRAINGER	AJ	6	162
GOVEN	WA	1	132	GOWING	TA	2	144	GRADY	R	11	149	GRAINGER	CH	7	151
GOVER	A	10	304	GOWING	WG	10	90	GRADY	S	7	151	GRAINGER	CW	10	304
GOVER	AE	4	157	GOWING	WJ	10	90	GRADY	WR	14	126	GRAINGER	E	7	151
GOVER	EM	4	158	GOWLER	EJ	12	98	GRAFHAM	VH	13	189	GRAINGER	FC	6	162
GOVER	HE	2	143	GOWLER	T	12	98	GRAFTON	J	9	77	GRAINGER	FW	3	347
GOVER	J	1	132	GOWLER	T	12	98	GRAFTON	R	7	151	GRAINGER	G	7	151
GOVER	J	1	132	GOWLETT	H	13	189	GRAHAM	A	11	149	GRAINGER	G	11	149
GOVER	J	1	132	GOWN	E	3	347	GRAHAM	C	8	132	GRAINGER	G	13	189
GOVER	JW	1	132	GOWN	E	3	347	GRAHAM	C	12	98	GRAINGER	GA	13	189
GOVER	JW	3	347	GOWNEY	G	10	90	GRAHAM	F	1	133	GRAINGER	GL	13	189
GOVER	R	4	158	GRABURN	W	11	148	GRAHAM	F	1	133	GRAINGER	J	1	133
GOVER	TG	1	132	GRACE	A	4	158	GRAHAM	F	8	132	GRAINGER	J	6	162
GOVER	W	1	132	GRACE	A	5	148	GRAHAM	FW	10	90	GRAINGER	JE	7	151
GOVER	WA	1	132	GRACE	A	13	189	GRAHAM	G	8	133	GRAINGER	PT	13	189

GRAINGER	T	9	77
GRAINGER	W	7	152
GRAINGER	W	8	133
GRAINGER	W	9	77
GRAINGER	W	13	189
GRAMSON	HJ	13	189
GRAMSON	RE	13	189
GRANAGE	A	14	126
GRANBY	C	12	98
GRANBY	FJ	12	99
GRANDIDGE	TH	8	133
GRANDSOME	W	14	127
GRANDY	FD	4	158
GRANDY	HJ	4	158
GRANDY	V	3	64
GRANGE	A	5	149
GRANGE	C	1	133
GRANGE	E	1	133
GRANGE	E	9	78
GRANGE	F	2	144
GRANGE	M	14	127
GRANGE	W	9	78
GRANGE	WG	6	162
GRANGER	A	7	152
GRANGER	A	8	133
GRANGER	AJ	13	189
GRANGER	EI	12	99
GRANGER	ES	11	149
GRANGER	HH	8	133
GRANGER	JW	12	99
GRANGER	L	8	133
GRANGER	SJ	4	158
GRANGER	W	13	189
GRANNER	J	6	162
GRANT	A	3	347
GRANT	A	8	133
GRANT	AC	4	158
GRANT	AC	4	158
GRANT	AF	4	158
GRANT	AJ	4	158
GRANT	AJ	7	152
GRANT	AL	4	158
GRANT	AW	6	163
GRANT	AW	13	190
GRANT	CH	10	90
GRANT	D	7	152
GRANT	D	7	152
GRANT	D	14	127
GRANT	EF	4	158
GRANT	F	1	133
GRANT	F	4	158
GRANT	F	10	304
GRANT	FA	2	144
GRANT	FA	4	159
GRANT	FE	10	90
GRANT	FH	4	159
GRANT	FS	1	133
GRANT	G	4	159
GRANT	GJ	3	347
GRANT	GW	10	91
GRANT	GWD	3	64
GRANT	H	7	152
GRANT	H	8	133
GRANT	H	10	91
GRANT	HE	7	152
GRANT	HF	13	190
GRANT	HM	5	149
GRANT	HR	1	133
GRANT	HS	14	127
GRANT	HW	12	99
GRANT	J	3	347
GRANT	J	11	149
GRANT	JC	7	152
GRANT	JC	7	152
GRANT	JE	4	159
GRANT	JE	4	159
GRANT	JE	4	159
GRANT	JH	10	91
GRANT	JPD	12	99
GRANT	JRJ	12	314
GRANT	JW	4	159
GRANT	JW	7	152
GRANT	JW	7	152
GRANT	L	1	133
GRANT	L	2	144
GRANT	M	1	133
GRANT	M	3	348
GRANT	M	7	152
GRANT	M	10	304
GRANT	ME	1	133
GRANT	PE	10	91
GRANT	PH	1	133
GRANT	R	4	159
GRANT	R	11	149
GRANT	SE	7	152
GRANT	TW	7	152
GRANT	W	4	159
GRANT	W	7	152
GRANT	W	10	304
GRANT	W	14	127
GRANT	WC	4	159
GRANT	WF	1	133
GRANT	WJ	1	133
GRANT	WJ	10	91
GRANT	WJ	13	190
GRANTHAM	AE	2	144
GRANTHAM	EH	6	163
GRANTHAM	G	1	133
GRANTHAM	G	11	149
GRANTHAM	H	11	149
GRANTHAM	J	11	149
GRANTHAM	J	11	150
GRANTHAM	S	11	149
GRANTHAM	T	11	150
GRANTHAM	WA	5	149
GRANTHAM	WH	7	152
GRANTHAM	WH	11	150
GRANVILLE	A	3	64
GRANVILLE	C	3	64
GRANVILLE	F	3	64
GRAPES	H	8	133
GRASS	J	13	190
GRASSBY	H	9	78
GRASSO	A	7	153
GRASTON	GW	3	65
GRATER	GJ	7	153
GRATION	H	9	263
GRATION	JM	9	263
GRATION	JW	8	133
GRATION	T	9	78
GRATION	TJ	9	78
GRATREX	WJC	7	153
GRATRIX	EJ	14	127
GRATRIX	J	14	127
GRATRIX	T	14	127
GRATRIX	W	14	127
GRATTIDGE	CH	6	163
GRATTON	E	9	263
GRATTON	H	9	78
GRATTON	J	14	127
GRATTON	T	11	150
GRATTON	WH	11	150
GRAVELING	JVH	9	263
GRAVELING	W	9	78
GRAVENOR	J	3	65
GRAVENOR	S	3	348
GRAVER	WJ	2	144
GRAVES	A	1	133
GRAVES	A	9	263
GRAVES	AF	1	133
GRAVES	AGP	13	190
GRAVES	CE	13	190
GRAVES	E	5	149
GRAVES	E	8	133
GRAVES	G	4	159
GRAVES	GC	4	159
GRAVES	GH	12	99
GRAVES	GW	13	190
GRAVES	H	5	149
GRAVES	H	9	78
GRAVES	JC	3	65
GRAVES	JN	3	348
GRAVES	L	9	78
GRAVES	N	8	133
GRAVES	R	8	133
GRAVES	RP	2	144
GRAVES	W	8	133
GRAVES	WT	7	153
GRAVESTOCK	A	2	144
GRAVESTOCK	GH	3	65
GRAVESTOCK	H	7	153
GRAVESTOCK	HW	5	149
GRAVESTOCK	J	1	133
GRAVESTOCK	J	5	149
GRAVESTOCK	JH	1	133
GRAVESTOCK	RH	5	149
GRAVESTOCK	SA	5	149
GRAVESTOCK	W	5	149
GRAVETT	SW	13	190
GRAVIL	JW	8	134
GRAY	A	1	134
GRAY	A	2	144
GRAY	A	4	159
GRAY	A	5	149
GRAY	A	5	149
GRAY	A	6	163
GRAY	A	12	99
GRAY	AC	3	348
GRAY	AC	4	159
GRAY	AE	12	314
GRAY	AG	4	159
GRAY	AJ	5	149
GRAY	AL	10	91
GRAY	AR	9	78
GRAY	AS	2	144
GRAY	C	1	134
GRAY	C	7	153
GRAY	C	12	314
GRAY	C	14	127
GRAY	CE	12	99
GRAY	CF	4	159
GRAY	CF	5	149
GRAY	CG	2	144
GRAY	CH	12	99
GRAY	CJ	4	159
GRAY	CO	5	149
GRAY	CT	6	163
GRAY	CW	1	134
GRAY	CW	3	65
GRAY	CW	3	65
GRAY	CW	3	348
GRAY	DC	1	134
GRAY	E	1	134
GRAY	E	5	149
GRAY	E	8	134
GRAY	E	9	78
GRAY	E	11	150
GRAY	E	14	127
GRAY	EC	13	190
GRAY	ED	5	149

GRAY	EH	7	153	GRAY	N	11	150	GREASLEY	HW	3	65	GREAVES	W	6	164
GRAY	EJ	5	149	GRAY	N	12	99	GREATBANKS	EH	14	127	GREAVES	W	6	164
GRAY	EJ	5	149	GRAY	P	5	150	GREATHEAD	H	6	163	GREAVES	W	8	135
GRAY	EM	4	159	GRAY	P	8	134	GREATOREX	F	14	127	GREAVES	W	9	79
GRAY	ES	5	149	GRAY	R	2	144	GREATOREX	J	11	150	GREAVES	W	9	79
GRAY	EV	3	65	GRAY	R	3	65	GREATOREX	W	14	128	GREAVES	WJ	6	164
GRAY	F	4	159	GRAY	R	11	150	GREATOREX	WJ	13	190	GREAVES	WR	12	99
GRAY	F	5	150	GRAY	R	11	150	GREATREX	GE	6	163	GREED	J	9	386
GRAY	F	8	134	GRAY	S	1	134	GREATREX	H	6	163	GREEN	A	1	134
GRAY	FE	13	190	GRAY	S	6	163	GREATREX	P	6	163	GREEN	A	1	134
GRAY	FJ	4	160	GRAY	SF	12	99	GREATREX	SJ	6	163	GREEN	A	2	145
GRAY	FR	7	153	GRAY	SG	7	153	GREAVES	A	8	134	GREEN	A	3	65
GRAY	G	2	144	GRAY	SHH	12	99	GREAVES	A	12	314	GREEN	A	4	160
GRAY	G	3	348	GRAY	SM	5	150	GREAVES	A	14	128	GREEN	A	4	160
GRAY	G	9	78	GRAY	T	3	348	GREAVES	AE	12	314	GREEN	A	4	160
GRAY	G	10	304	GRAY	TC	13	190	GREAVES	AJ	12	99	GREEN	A	4	160
GRAY	GE	12	99	GRAY	TH	10	91	GREAVES	AV	13	190	GREEN	A	6	164
GRAY	GF	1	134	GRAY	TJ	3	65	GREAVES	B	9	78	GREEN	A	6	164
GRAY	GH	4	160	GRAY	W	2	144	GREAVES	E	8	134	GREEN	A	7	153
GRAY	GT	6	163	GRAY	W	2	144	GREAVES	F	6	163	GREEN	A	8	135
GRAY	H	3	348	GRAY	W	4	160	GREAVES	F	6	163	GREEN	A	8	135
GRAY	H	4	160	GRAY	W	4	160	GREAVES	F	9	263	GREEN	A	8	135
GRAY	H	4	160	GRAY	W	5	150	GREAVES	G	8	134	GREEN	A	9	263
GRAY	H	5	150	GRAY	W	5	150	GREAVES	GB	8	134	GREEN	A	10	304
GRAY	H	12	99	GRAY	W	5	150	GREAVES	GB	9	78	GREEN	A	11	150
GRAY	H	13	190	GRAY	W	5	150	GREAVES	GT	12	314	GREEN	A	12	99
GRAY	H	14	127	GRAY	W	8	134	GREAVES	H	3	348	GREEN	A	12	99
GRAY	HC	5	150	GRAY	W	8	134	GREAVES	H	6	163	GREEN	A	12	100
GRAY	HG	4	160	GRAY	W	9	78	GREAVES	H	8	134	GREEN	A	12	100
GRAY	HG	10	304	GRAY	W	14	127	GREAVES	H	9	78	GREEN	A	12	314
GRAY	HW	6	163	GRAY	WAV	12	314	GREAVES	H	9	78	GREEN	A	13	191
GRAY	J	1	134	GRAY	WE	2	144	GREAVES	H	9	263	GREEN	A	14	128
GRAY	J	2	144	GRAY	WE	4	160	GREAVES	H	14	128	GREEN	A	14	128
GRAY	J	3	348	GRAY	WJ	12	314	GREAVES	HMF	12	99	GREEN	AE	6	164
GRAY	J	3	348	GRAY	WM	2	144	GREAVES	J	6	163	GREEN	AE	7	153
GRAY	J	5	150	GRAY	WR	1	134	GREAVES	J	6	163	GREEN	AG	2	145
GRAY	J	8	134	GRAY	WR	13	190	GREAVES	J	8	134	GREEN	AG	2	145
GRAY	J	8	134	GRAY	WS	5	150	GREAVES	J	9	78	GREEN	AG	5	150
GRAY	J	10	304	GRAY	XW	7	153	GREAVES	J	9	78	GREEN	AG	10	91
GRAY	J	11	150	GRAYER	A	4	160	GREAVES	JH	4	160	GREEN	AG	13	191
GRAY	J	12	314	GRAYER	AW	4	160	GREAVES	JH	9	78	GREEN	AH	10	91
GRAY	J	13	190	GRAYER	BJ	4	160	GREAVES	JR	8	134	GREEN	AJ	1	134
GRAY	JA	4	160	GRAYER	H	4	160	GREAVES	JT	6	163	GREEN	AJ	1	134
GRAY	JA	4	160	GRAYER	TC	4	160	GREAVES	L	6	164	GREEN	AJ	4	161
GRAY	JE	13	190	GRAYSON	B	11	150	GREAVES	M	8	134	GREEN	AJ	5	150
GRAY	JG	13	190	GRAYSON	J	8	134	GREAVES	P	8	134	GREEN	AM	12	314
GRAY	JGA	4	160	GRAYSON	J	14	127	GREAVES	R	8	134	GREEN	AT	1	134
GRAY	JH	5	150	GRAYSON	JW	9	263	GREAVES	R	14	128	GREEN	AT	1	134
GRAY	JH	9	78	GRAYSON	T	8	134	GREAVES	S	9	79	GREEN	AT	1	134
GRAY	JP	12	99	GRAYSON	T	14	127	GREAVES	S	9	386	GREEN	AT	6	164
GRAY	JT	13	190	GRAYSON	TR	2	144	GREAVES	T	8	135	GREEN	AT	10	304
GRAY	L	9	263	GRAYSON	W	11	150	GREAVES	T	11	150	GREEN	AT	12	100
GRAY	L	11	150	GREADY	WG	4	160	GREAVES	T	14	128	GREEN	AT	12	315
GRAY	LRR	7	153	GREAR	A	9	263	GREAVES	TH	5	150	GREEN	AW	8	135
GRAY	LS	5	150	GREASLEY	CE	8	134	GREAVES	TWF	6	164	GREEN	B	12	315

GREEN	BF	13	191	GREEN	F	6	164	GREEN	GP	7	153	GREEN	J	11	151
GREEN	BG	6	164	GREEN	F	6	164	GREEN	GT	2	145	GREEN	J	12	100
GREEN	BW	13	191	GREEN	F	6	164	GREEN	GW	2	145	GREEN	J	12	100
GREEN	C	2	145	GREEN	F	11	151	GREEN	GW	5	151	GREEN	J	14	128
GREEN	C	3	65	GREEN	F	11	151	GREEN	H	1	135	GREEN	J	14	128
GREEN	C	4	161	GREEN	F	12	100	GREEN	H	1	135	GREEN	J	14	128
GREEN	C	4	161	GREEN	F	12	315	GREEN	H	4	161	GREEN	J	14	128
GREEN	C	6	164	GREEN	F	14	128	GREEN	H	6	165	GREEN	J	14	129
GREEN	C	7	153	GREEN	F	14	128	GREEN	H	6	165	GREEN	JA	2	145
GREEN	C	8	135	GREEN	FC	1	134	GREEN	H	7	153	GREEN	JA	3	348
GREEN	C	9	79	GREEN	FC	4	161	GREEN	H	8	135	GREEN	JA	7	154
GREEN	C	11	150	GREEN	FC	4	161	GREEN	H	10	91	GREEN	JB	12	315
GREEN	C	11	150	GREEN	FE	2	145	GREEN	H	11	151	GREEN	JC	10	91
GREEN	C	11	150	GREEN	FE	6	164	GREEN	H	11	151	GREEN	JD	1	135
GREEN	C	12	100	GREEN	FF	12	100	GREEN	H	11	151	GREEN	JE	8	135
GREEN	C	12	100	GREEN	FG	4	161	GREEN	H	11	151	GREEN	JH	4	161
GREEN	C	12	315	GREEN	FG	14	128	GREEN	H	11	151	GREEN	JH	7	154
GREEN	C	12	315	GREEN	FH	2	145	GREEN	H	11	151	GREEN	JH	11	151
GREEN	CC	3	65	GREEN	FH	6	164	GREEN	H	12	100	GREEN	JJ	8	135
GREEN	CE	2	145	GREEN	FJ	5	150	GREEN	H	13	191	GREEN	JJ	12	100
GREEN	CE	3	65	GREEN	FJ	5	150	GREEN	HA	5	151	GREEN	JR	10	304
GREEN	CE	13	191	GREEN	FREJ	13	191	GREEN	HC	2	145	GREEN	JR	11	151
GREEN	CF	11	150	GREEN	FT	5	150	GREEN	HC	3	65	GREEN	JT	2	145
GREEN	CG	2	145	GREEN	FT	5	150	GREEN	HG	6	165	GREEN	JT	3	66
GREEN	CH	3	348	GREEN	FT	6	164	GREEN	HH	2	145	GREEN	JW	2	145
GREEN	CH	13	191	GREEN	FV	13	191	GREEN	HH	7	153	GREEN	JW	3	348
GREEN	CH	13	191	GREEN	G	1	134	GREEN	HJ	3	348	GREEN	JW	9	79
GREEN	CJ	12	315	GREEN	G	1	134	GREEN	HJ	5	151	GREEN	JW	11	152
GREEN	CT	4	161	GREEN	G	1	135	GREEN	HP	1	135	GREEN	JW	12	315
GREEN	CW	2	145	GREEN	G	1	135	GREEN	HP	13	191	GREEN	JW	13	191
GREEN	CW	3	65	GREEN	G	3	348	GREEN	HT	1	135	GREEN	JWE	3	66
GREEN	CW	14	128	GREEN	G	5	151	GREEN	HT	13	191	GREEN	L	2	145
GREEN	D	4	161	GREEN	G	5	151	GREEN	HT	13	191	GREEN	L	4	161
GREEN	D	8	135	GREEN	G	6	164	GREEN	HW	7	153	GREEN	L	6	165
GREEN	D	10	304	GREEN	G	6	165	GREEN	J	1	135	GREEN	L	13	192
GREEN	E	1	134	GREEN	G	6	165	GREEN	J	1	135	GREEN	LH	8	135
GREEN	E	8	135	GREEN	G	8	135	GREEN	J	1	135	GREEN	M	2	145
GREEN	E	9	263	GREEN	G	8	135	GREEN	J	2	145	GREEN	M	6	165
GREEN	E	11	151	GREEN	G	8	135	GREEN	J	3	66	GREEN	M	9	263
GREEN	E	13	191	GREEN	G	9	79	GREEN	J	3	66	GREEN	M	11	152
GREEN	E	14	128	GREEN	G	10	304	GREEN	J	3	348	GREEN	M	14	129
GREEN	EA	13	191	GREEN	G	11	151	GREEN	J	4	161	GREEN	O	4	161
GREEN	EB	3	65	GREEN	G	13	191	GREEN	J	5	151	GREEN	O	4	161
GREEN	EB	12	315	GREEN	G	14	128	GREEN	J	5	151	GREEN	O	4	161
GREEN	EC	10	91	GREEN	G	14	128	GREEN	J	5	151	GREEN	O	6	165
GREEN	EE	2	145	GREEN	G	14	128	GREEN	J	6	165	GREEN	OG	1	135
GREEN	EE	5	150	GREEN	GA	6	165	GREEN	J	7	154	GREEN	P	1	135
GREEN	EE	6	164	GREEN	GA	9	79	GREEN	J	8	135	GREEN	P	8	135
GREEN	EJ	4	161	GREEN	GB	8	135	GREEN	J	10	91	GREEN	P	9	79
GREEN	EM	12	100	GREEN	GE	3	65	GREEN	J	10	91	GREEN	PA	1	135
GREEN	ET	4	161	GREEN	GF	1	135	GREEN	J	10	91	GREEN	PC	10	91
GREEN	EW	12	315	GREEN	GF	10	91	GREEN	J	11	151	GREEN	PG	10	91
GREEN	EW	13	191	GREEN	GH	9	79	GREEN	J	11	151	GREEN	R	1	135
GREEN	F	1	134	GREEN	GI	10	304	GREEN	J	11	151	GREEN	R	3	66
GREEN	F	1	134	GREEN	GN	6	165	GREEN	J	11	151	GREEN	R	8	136

GREEN	R	8	136	GREEN	W	13	192	GREENFIELD	EJ	7	154	GREENING	GS	5	151
GREEN	R	8	136	GREEN	W	14	129	GREENFIELD	F	8	136	GREENING	J	11	152
GREEN	R	12	100	GREEN	WA	2	146	GREENFIELD	F	9	264	GREENING	JW	1	136
GREEN	RA	2	146	GREEN	WC	1	135	GREENFIELD	G	3	66	GREENING	P	2	147
GREEN	RC	2	146	GREEN	WC	4	162	GREENFIELD	G	8	136	GREENLAND	H	1	136
GREEN	RCE	13	192	GREEN	WC	6	165	GREENFIELD	GT	13	192	GREENLAND	L	13	192
GREEN	RF	6	165	GREEN	WE	1	135	GREENFIELD	JA	7	154	GREENLAND	V	13	192
GREEN	RH	3	348	GREEN	WE	6	166	GREENFIELD	JR	8	136	GREENLAND	W	3	349
GREEN	RJ	11	152	GREEN	WE	9	386	GREENFIELD	L	1	136	GREENLEES	H	11	152
GREEN	RV	5	151	GREEN	WF	5	151	GREENFIELD	S	2	146	GREENLEY	D	13	193
GREEN	RW	3	66	GREEN	WF	10	91	GREENFIELD	S	13	192	GREENMAN	JW	9	79
GREEN	S	2	146	GREEN	WFR	3	348	GREENFIELD	TG	7	154	GREENO	WR	2	147
GREEN	S	4	161	GREEN	WG	13	192	GREENFIELD	W	1	136	GREENOUGH	J	9	264
GREEN	S	7	154	GREEN	WGA	4	162	GREENFIELD	W	8	136	GREENOVITCH	A	14	129
GREEN	S	8	136	GREEN	WH	1	135	GREENFIELD	WE	11	152	GREENOVITCH	I	14	129
GREEN	S	8	136	GREEN	WH	2	146	GREENFIELD	WJ	1	136	GREENROD	TE	1	136
GREEN	S	12	100	GREEN	WH	2	146	GREENHALF	H	8	136	GREENSALL	G	6	166
GREEN	S	12	100	GREEN	WH	6	166	GREENHALGH	A	14	129	GREENSHIELDS	JT	3	349
GREEN	SA	2	146	GREEN	WH	11	152	GREENHALGH	F	14	129	GREENSHIELDS	TG	1	136
GREEN	SH	2	146	GREEN	WH	11	152	GREENHALGH	H	8	136	GREENSLADE	A	13	193
GREEN	T	2	146	GREEN	WH	12	315	GREENHALGH	J	11	152	GREENSLADE	AA	13	193
GREEN	T	3	66	GREEN	WJ	1	135	GREENHALGH	J	11	152	GREENSLADE	CE	3	349
GREEN	T	6	165	GREEN	WJ	2	146	GREENHALGH	J	14	129	GREENSLADE	F	10	305
GREEN	T	8	136	GREEN	WJ	6	166	GREENHALGH	JT	14	129	GREENSLADE	FG	13	193
GREEN	T	11	152	GREEN	WJ	6	166	GREENHALGH	R	14	129	GREENSLADE	J	2	147
GREEN	TE	2	146	GREEN	WJ	7	154	GREENHALGH	T	8	136	GREENSLADE	J	2	147
GREEN	TF	6	165	GREEN	WJ	7	154	GREENHALGH	T	14	129	GREENSLADE	JA	3	66
GREEN	TH	6	165	GREEN	WJ	8	136	GREENHALGH	WJ	14	129	GREENSLADE	W	10	305
GREEN	TH	13	192	GREEN	WJ	13	192	GREENHAM	AH	10	304	GREENSMITH	A	3	349
GREEN	TH	13	192	GREEN	WJ	13	192	GREENHAM	AH	10	304	GREENSTREET	FJ	10	92
GREEN	TM	13	192	GREEN	WP	11	152	GREENHAM	AL	10	305	GREENTREE	CW	10	92
GREEN	TO	3	66	GREEN	WR	6	166	GREENHAM	C	12	100	GREENTREE	GR	10	305
GREEN	TW	1	135	GREEN	WR	13	192	GREENHAM	FHJ	5	151	GREENWAY	A	6	166
GREEN	TW	4	161	GREEN	WR	13	192	GREENHEAD	AJ	3	349	GREENWAY	G	10	92
GREEN	V	4	161	GREEN	WRJ	12	100	GREENHEAD	FT	13	192	GREENWAY	HW	7	154
GREEN	V	12	100	GREEN	WS	1	135	GREENHILL	A	2	146	GREENWAY	W	6	166
GREEN	V	12	100	GREEN	WW	12	100	GREENHILL	AM	6	166	GREENWAY	W	8	136
GREEN	VW	1	135	GREENAWAY	A	7	154	GREENHILL	FC	10	91	GREENWAY	WA	1	136
GREEN	W	2	146	GREENAWAY	CF	1	136	GREENHILL	GH	8	136	GREENWAY	WT	13	193
GREEN	W	2	146	GREENAWAY	F	2	146	GREENHILL	J	1	136	GREENWELL	W	7	154
GREEN	W	3	66	GREENAWAY	FC	4	162	GREENHILL	OC	2	147	GREENWOOD	A	8	137
GREEN	W	4	161	GREENAWAY	FG	7	154	GREENHILL	W	6	166	GREENWOOD	A	8	137
GREEN	W	6	165	GREENAWAY	GA	1	136	GREENHOOD	C	5	151	GREENWOOD	A	8	137
GREEN	W	6	165	GREENAWAY	GE	7	154	GREENHOOD	HEG	5	151	GREENWOOD	A	8	137
GREEN	W	6	165	GREENAWAY	GW	2	146	GREENHOOD	WJ	5	151	GREENWOOD	A	9	79
GREEN	W	6	165	GREENAWAY	HT	2	146	GREENHOUGH	D	8	136	GREENWOOD	A	9	79
GREEN	W	7	154	GREENAWAY	J	7	154	GREENHOUGH	F	9	264	GREENWOOD	AA	13	193
GREEN	W	7	154	GREENAWAY	JH	1	136	GREENHOUGH	G	9	79	GREENWOOD	AS	7	155
GREEN	W	8	136	GREENAWAY	R	1	136	GREENHOUGH	GH	11	152	GREENWOOD	C	2	147
GREEN	W	8	136	GREENAWAY	S	5	151	GREENHOUGH	H	8	136	GREENWOOD	C	8	137
GREEN	W	9	79	GREENAWAY	TE	7	154	GREENHOUGH	R	8	136	GREENWOOD	CR	12	100
GREEN	W	9	79	GREENE	JS	13	192	GREENHOUGH	S	8	136	GREENWOOD	D	9	79
GREEN	W	9	264	GREENE	R	2	146	GREENHOUGH	T	11	152	GREENWOOD	D	9	79
GREEN	W	9	264	GREENE	W	9	79	GREENHOUSE	J	6	166	GREENWOOD	E	2	147
GREEN	W	13	192	GREENFIELD	AJ	3	348	GREENING	CW	5	151	GREENWOOD	E	9	79

Surname	In.			Surname	In.			Surname	In.			Surname	In.		
GREENWOOD	F	7	155	GREENWOOD	WF	1	136	GREGORY	FR	13	193	GREGORY	WG	2	148
GREENWOOD	F	8	137	GREENWOOD	WH	10	92	GREGORY	FT	7	155	GREGORY	WG	4	162
GREENWOOD	F	9	79	GREENWOOD	WM	9	80	GREGORY	G	1	137	GREGORY	WH	11	153
GREENWOOD	F	9	79	GREER	AJ	1	136	GREGORY	G	1	137	GREGORY	WJ	4	162
GREENWOOD	F	14	129	GREER	CW	10	92	GREGORY	G	3	349	GREGORY	WS	2	148
GREENWOOD	F	14	129	GREER	RW	7	155	GREGORY	G	3	349	GREGORY	WS	7	155
GREENWOOD	FL	9	80	GREER	S	10	305	GREGORY	G	6	166	GREGSON	AJ	6	167
GREENWOOD	FP	2	147	GREER	TC	10	305	GREGORY	G	9	80	GREGSON	H	14	130
GREENWOOD	G	10	92	GREER	TRG	4	162	GREGORY	G	13	193	GREGSON	HG	14	130
GREENWOOD	G	11	152	GREER	W	14	130	GREGORY	G	14	130	GREGSON	JA	8	137
GREENWOOD	G	11	152	GREETHAM	R	4	162	GREGORY	GB	6	166	GREGSON	JJ	11	153
GREENWOOD	G	11	152	GREGG	B	8	137	GREGORY	H	1	137	GREGSON	JWE	11	153
GREENWOOD	GA	9	80	GREGG	CH	11	153	GREGORY	H	2	147	GREGSON	RW	14	130
GREENWOOD	GG	1	136	GREGG	H	14	130	GREGORY	H	6	166	GREGSON	T	11	153
GREENWOOD	GH	10	92	GREGG	J	8	137	GREGORY	H	6	166	GREGSON	W	9	387
GREENWOOD	GH	13	193	GREGG	J	14	130	GREGORY	H	8	137	GREIG	DL	7	155
GREENWOOD	H	8	137	GREGG	R	9	80	GREGORY	H	8	137	GREIG	J	8	137
GREENWOOD	H	8	137	GREGG	T	2	147	GREGORY	H	11	153	GRENDER	G	10	305
GREENWOOD	H	9	80	GREGORY	A	2	147	GREGORY	H	12	315	GRENESKI	G	1	137
GREENWOOD	H	9	80	GREGORY	A	2	147	GREGORY	HC	2	147	GRESHAM	CP	12	315
GREENWOOD	H	9	80	GREGORY	A	14	130	GREGORY	HC	5	152	GRESSWELL	S	9	264
GREENWOOD	H	9	80	GREGORY	A	14	130	GREGORY	HE	4	162	GRESTY	A	11	153
GREENWOOD	H	9	80	GREGORY	AE	6	166	GREGORY	J	3	349	GRESTY	H	11	153
GREENWOOD	HD	2	147	GREGORY	AF	6	166	GREGORY	J	5	152	GRESTY	J	11	153
GREENWOOD	J	1	136	GREGORY	AG	12	101	GREGORY	J	6	167	GRESTY	S	11	153
GREENWOOD	J	2	147	GREGORY	AH	4	162	GREGORY	J	10	92	GRESTY	T	11	153
GREENWOOD	J	9	264	GREGORY	AJ	5	151	GREGORY	J	11	153	GRETTON	FM	1	137
GREENWOOD	J	11	152	GREGORY	AV	7	155	GREGORY	JF	5	152	GRETTON	JH	1	137
GREENWOOD	J	14	129	GREGORY	AV	10	305	GREGORY	JR	8	137	GREVATT	GW	3	349
GREENWOOD	J	14	129	GREGORY	AW	13	193	GREGORY	P	2	147	GREVIER	FG	2	148
GREENWOOD	J	14	129	GREGORY	B	11	153	GREGORY	PB	7	155	GREW	FW	7	155
GREENWOOD	JA	9	80	GREGORY	C	3	66	GREGORY	PJ	6	166	GREY	ARE	13	193
GREENWOOD	JOE	14	129	GREGORY	C	3	349	GREGORY	R	9	80	GREY	B	14	130
GREENWOOD	JW	3	349	GREGORY	C	4	162	GREGORY	R	13	193	GREY	EC	13	193
GREENWOOD	JW	8	137	GREGORY	C	9	80	GREGORY	RW	5	152	GREY	F	3	349
GREENWOOD	JW	9	80	GREGORY	C	14	130	GREGORY	S	3	349	GREY	H	9	80
GREENWOOD	JW	14	129	GREGORY	CA	4	162	GREGORY	S	6	167	GREY	H	9	264
GREENWOOD	M	9	80	GREGORY	CA	13	193	GREGORY	S	14	130	GREY	H	11	153
GREENWOOD	M	9	264	GREGORY	CB	2	147	GREGORY	SG	10	305	GREY	I	10	305
GREENWOOD	P	9	264	GREGORY	CM	2	147	GREGORY	SJ	13	193	GREY	JW	12	315
GREENWOOD	R	8	137	GREGORY	CR	13	193	GREGORY	T	5	152	GREY	L	8	137
GREENWOOD	RH	11	153	GREGORY	CT	6	166	GREGORY	T	14	130	GREY	R	1	137
GREENWOOD	T	7	155	GREGORY	CW	4	162	GREGORY	T	14	130	GREY	S	7	155
GREENWOOD	T	7	155	GREGORY	D	1	136	GREGORY	TC	10	92	GREY	W	10	305
GREENWOOD	T	9	80	GREGORY	D	2	147	GREGORY	TJ	4	162	GREY	W	14	130
GREENWOOD	T	9	264	GREGORY	E	1	136	GREGORY	W	1	137	GREYGOOSE	A	1	137
GREENWOOD	TA	10	92	GREGORY	E	1	136	GREGORY	W	2	148	GRIBBIN	E	14	130
GREENWOOD	W	7	155	GREGORY	E	2	147	GREGORY	W	2	148	GRIBBIN	J	11	153
GREENWOOD	W	8	137	GREGORY	E	3	66	GREGORY	W	8	137	GRIBBIN	L	9	80
GREENWOOD	W	9	80	GREGORY	E	8	137	GREGORY	W	9	386	GRIBBLE	A	12	101
GREENWOOD	W	9	264	GREGORY	EE	10	305	GREGORY	W	10	305	GRIBBLE	CHT	2	148
GREENWOOD	W	9	264	GREGORY	F	10	92	GREGORY	WA	4	162	GRIBBLE	GF	12	101
GREENWOOD	W	14	130	GREGORY	FF	5	151	GREGORY	WA	7	155	GRIBBLE	H	12	315
GREENWOOD	WA	14	130	GREGORY	FJ	7	155	GREGORY	WC	13	193	GRIBBLE	H	12	315
GREENWOOD	WE	10	305	GREGORY	FM	5	152	GREGORY	WD	6	167	GRICE	CE	6	167

GRICE	H	8	138	GRIFFIN	D	14	131	GRIFFIN	T	8	138	GRIFFITHS	FW	2	148
GRICE	H	11	153	GRIFFIN	E	1	137	GRIFFIN	T	12	316	GRIFFITHS	G	7	156
GRICE	J	14	131	GRIFFIN	E	3	349	GRIFFIN	TH	6	168	GRIFFITHS	GA	10	306
GRICE	JA	6	167	GRIFFIN	E	5	152	GRIFFIN	TJ	7	156	GRIFFITHS	GE	8	138
GRICE	JA	9	80	GRIFFIN	E	12	315	GRIFFIN	TP	3	66	GRIFFITHS	GH	14	131
GRICE	JT	6	167	GRIFFIN	EA	4	162	GRIFFIN	VJW	10	306	GRIFFITHS	H	2	148
GRICE	LV	14	131	GRIFFIN	EA	10	92	GRIFFIN	W	3	66	GRIFFITHS	H	6	168
GRICKS	T	10	92	GRIFFIN	EB	3	66	GRIFFIN	W	5	153	GRIFFITHS	H	8	138
GRIDLEY	C	7	155	GRIFFIN	ET	3	66	GRIFFIN	W	6	168	GRIFFITHS	H	10	92
GRIDLEY	FA	1	137	GRIFFIN	FC	1	137	GRIFFIN	W	11	153	GRIFFITHS	H	11	154
GRIDLEY	FD	5	152	GRIFFIN	FJ	4	163	GRIFFIN	W	12	316	GRIFFITHS	H	11	154
GRIDLEY	H	7	155	GRIFFIN	G	1	137	GRIFFIN	WA	3	66	GRIFFITHS	H	11	422
GRIDLEY	H	7	155	GRIFFIN	G	10	92	GRIFFIN	WG	10	92	GRIFFITHS	H	12	316
GRIDLEY	H	7	155	GRIFFIN	G	10	305	GRIFFIN	WH	6	168	GRIFFITHS	HT	5	153
GRIER	AS	13	193	GRIFFIN	GE	5	152	GRIFFIN	WH	6	168	GRIFFITHS	J	1	138
GRIER	JG	4	162	GRIFFIN	GE	10	306	GRIFFIN	WJ	5	153	GRIFFITHS	J	2	148
GRIER	W	13	194	GRIFFIN	GH	6	167	GRIFFIN	WJ	10	92	GRIFFITHS	J	3	67
GRIERSON	F	13	194	GRIFFIN	GH	7	156	GRIFFIN	WJ	12	101	GRIFFITHS	J	6	168
GRIERSON	GJ	13	194	GRIFFIN	GR	6	167	GRIFFINS	J	8	138	GRIFFITHS	J	6	168
GRIERSON	JH	14	131	GRIFFIN	GT	1	137	GRIFFITH	A	1	138	GRIFFITHS	J	6	168
GRIERSON	WF	2	148	GRIFFIN	GT	3	66	GRIFFITH	AC	12	101	GRIFFITHS	J	7	156
GRIEVE	B	1	137	GRIFFIN	GT	7	156	GRIFFITH	EG	3	349	GRIFFITHS	J	7	156
GRIEVE	GW	9	81	GRIFFIN	GW	5	152	GRIFFITH	FH	12	316	GRIFFITHS	J	11	154
GRIEVE	JD	14	131	GRIFFIN	GW	7	156	GRIFFITH	HT	6	168	GRIFFITHS	J	11	154
GRIEVE	JF	7	156	GRIFFIN	H	1	137	GRIFFITH	JH	12	101	GRIFFITHS	J	12	101
GRIEVE	M	1	137	GRIFFIN	H	6	167	GRIFFITH	RO	4	163	GRIFFITHS	J	12	101
GRIEVES	EA	6	167	GRIFFIN	H	12	101	GRIFFITH	RS	7	156	GRIFFITHS	J	13	194
GRIEVES	JC	6	167	GRIFFIN	HJ	4	163	GRIFFITH	S	6	168	GRIFFITHS	J	14	131
GRIEVESON	H	14	131	GRIFFIN	J	5	152	GRIFFITHS	A	1	138	GRIFFITHS	J	14	131
GRIEVSON	SJ	1	137	GRIFFIN	J	5	152	GRIFFITHS	A	1	138	GRIFFITHS	J	14	131
GRIFFEN	A	2	148	GRIFFIN	J	6	167	GRIFFITHS	A	6	168	GRIFFITHS	JE	9	264
GRIFFEN	E	2	148	GRIFFIN	J	6	167	GRIFFITHS	A	7	156	GRIFFITHS	JG	14	131
GRIFFEN	H	2	148	GRIFFIN	J	9	81	GRIFFITHS	A	11	154	GRIFFITHS	JH	11	154
GRIFFEN	SH	2	148	GRIFFIN	J	13	194	GRIFFITHS	A	13	194	GRIFFITHS	JP	10	92
GRIFFIN	A	5	152	GRIFFIN	J	14	131	GRIFFITHS	A	13	194	GRIFFITHS	JR	2	148
GRIFFIN	A	6	167	GRIFFIN	JA	12	315	GRIFFITHS	A	14	131	GRIFFITHS	JW	14	131
GRIFFIN	A	6	167	GRIFFIN	JD	13	194	GRIFFITHS	AE	14	131	GRIFFITHS	LD	5	153
GRIFFIN	A	10	305	GRIFFIN	JF	6	167	GRIFFITHS	AJ	2	148	GRIFFITHS	M	7	156
GRIFFIN	A	12	315	GRIFFIN	JH	4	163	GRIFFITHS	AL	12	101	GRIFFITHS	M	11	154
GRIFFIN	A	13	194	GRIFFIN	JW	1	137	GRIFFITHS	AV	6	168	GRIFFITHS	O	12	316
GRIFFIN	A	13	194	GRIFFIN	JW	7	156	GRIFFITHS	AW	14	131	GRIFFITHS	PJ	5	153
GRIFFIN	AE	10	305	GRIFFIN	JW	12	315	GRIFFITHS	CD	5	153	GRIFFITHS	PR	11	154
GRIFFIN	AG	1	137	GRIFFIN	L	5	152	GRIFFITHS	CS	14	131	GRIFFITHS	R	3	67
GRIFFIN	AG	3	349	GRIFFIN	M	8	138	GRIFFITHS	DH	2	148	GRIFFITHS	R	6	168
GRIFFIN	AG	6	167	GRIFFIN	MJ	6	167	GRIFFITHS	DJ	6	168	GRIFFITHS	R	6	168
GRIFFIN	AL	5	152	GRIFFIN	ML	7	156	GRIFFITHS	DW	9	264	GRIFFITHS	R	11	154
GRIFFIN	AP	5	152	GRIFFIN	N	5	152	GRIFFITHS	E	9	81	GRIFFITHS	R	14	131
GRIFFIN	BA	13	194	GRIFFIN	N	8	138	GRIFFITHS	E	12	101	GRIFFITHS	RL	10	93
GRIFFIN	C	10	305	GRIFFIN	R	4	163	GRIFFITHS	EJ	7	156	GRIFFITHS	S	4	163
GRIFFIN	CE	12	315	GRIFFIN	R	4	163	GRIFFITHS	EW	7	156	GRIFFITHS	S	6	168
GRIFFIN	CGP	4	162	GRIFFIN	RJ	5	153	GRIFFITHS	FC	2	148	GRIFFITHS	S	6	168
GRIFFIN	CT	4	162	GRIFFIN	S	13	194	GRIFFITHS	FC	10	92	GRIFFITHS	S	7	156
GRIFFIN	CW	1	137	GRIFFIN	SG	4	163	GRIFFITHS	FE	4	163	GRIFFITHS	S	14	132
GRIFFIN	D	5	152	GRIFFIN	SG	10	306	GRIFFITHS	FE	5	153	GRIFFITHS	SA	12	101
GRIFFIN	D	10	305	GRIFFIN	ST	13	194	GRIFFITHS	FS	7	156	GRIFFITHS	T	2	148

GRIFFITHS	T	6	168	GRIMES	P	11	154	GRIMSHAW	TH	14	132	GRITT	AC	2	149
GRIFFITHS	T	6	169	GRIMES	R	8	138	GRIMSHAW	W	7	157	GRITT	B	10	93
GRIFFITHS	T	6	169	GRIMES	SR	4	163	GRIMSHAW	W	11	155	GRITT	F	4	164
GRIFFITHS	T	9	264	GRIMES	W	3	349	GRIMSHAW	W	11	155	GRITT	F	4	164
GRIFFITHS	T	10	93	GRIMES	W	3	350	GRIMSHAW	W	11	155	GRITT	L	4	164
GRIFFITHS	T	11	154	GRIMES	W	8	138	GRIMSHAW	W	14	132	GRITT	W	4	164
GRIFFITHS	T	14	132	GRIMES	WE	2	149	GRIMSHAW	W	14	132	GRITTEN	A	4	164
GRIFFITHS	TA	5	153	GRIMLEY	H	6	169	GRIMSHAW	W	14	132	GRITZMAN	S	7	157
GRIFFITHS	TE	11	154	GRIMLEY	J	9	81	GRIMSON	TH	1	138	GRIVES	AW	5	153
GRIFFITHS	TG	11	154	GRIMLEY	W	13	194	GRIMSTER	JH	7	157	GRIVES	WS	5	153
GRIFFITHS	W	3	67	GRIMMER	DH	3	67	GRIMWADE	NVE	1	138	GRIVVELL	A	2	149
GRIFFITHS	W	6	169	GRIMMER	GS	3	67	GRIMWARD	EW	2	149	GRIVVELL	FO	3	67
GRIFFITHS	W	6	169	GRIMMER	RJ	3	67	GRIMWOOD	AE	7	157	GROCOCK	AE	11	155
GRIFFITHS	W	6	169	GRIMMETT	A	1	138	GRIMWOOD	AJ	13	194	GROCOTT	T	14	132
GRIFFITHS	W	6	169	GRIMMETT	A	1	138	GRIMWOOD	E	13	194	GROEGER	W	13	195
GRIFFITHS	W	11	154	GRIMMETT	A	6	169	GRIMWOOD	EH	13	195	GROGAN	A	9	265
GRIFFITHS	W	11	154	GRIMMETT	F	7	157	GRIMWOOD	F	13	195	GROGAN	F	6	170
GRIFFITHS	W	14	132	GRIMMETT	GH	9	81	GRIMWOOD	G	12	101	GROGAN	FF	13	195
GRIFFITHS	W	14	132	GRIMMETT	T	6	169	GRIMWOOD	H	8	138	GROGAN	H	9	81
GRIFFITHS	W	14	132	GRIMMITT	H	6	169	GRINDLE	CH	9	265	GROGAN	MM	13	195
GRIFFITHS	WA	5	153	GRIMMO	AEP	4	163	GRINDLEY	D	11	155	GROGAN	W	6	170
GRIFFITHS	WB	7	157	GRIMMO	WR	4	163	GRINDLEY	W	3	67	GROGAN	W	8	138
GRIFFITHS	WC	12	316	GRIMMOND	JE	7	157	GRINDLEY	W	14	132	GROGAN	W	9	265
GRIFFITHS	WE	6	169	GRIMSDALE	GB	5	153	GRINDROD	E	11	155	GROGAN	WH	9	265
GRIFFITHS	WF	7	157	GRIMSDALE	H	1	138	GRINDROD	W	5	153	GROGAN	WL	13	195
GRIFFITHS	WH	6	169	GRIMSDALE	SG	5	153	GRINGER	B	10	93	GROOBY	S	9	81
GRIFFITHS	WH	6	169	GRIMSEY	G	10	93	GRINNELL	FW	6	169	GROOCOCK	A	11	155
GRIFFITHS	WJ	10	306	GRIMSHAW	B	9	264	GRINNETT	JH	9	387	GROOM	A	5	153
GRIFFITHS	WJ	11	154	GRIMSHAW	B	14	132	GRINSELL	JT	6	170	GROOM	B	12	316
GRIFITH	RB	9	264	GRIMSHAW	BN	3	67	GRINSELL	JTA	6	170	GROOM	E	11	155
GRIGG	APG	12	316	GRIMSHAW	C	8	138	GRINT	W	4	163	GROOM	EWT	5	153
GRIGG	ER	13	194	GRIMSHAW	C	9	81	GRINYER	AC	13	195	GROOM	F	5	153
GRIGG	FW	7	157	GRIMSHAW	D	9	81	GRINYER	AF	1	138	GROOM	F	5	154
GRIGG	L	7	157	GRIMSHAW	E	8	138	GRINYER	CL	4	163	GROOM	FS	5	154
GRIGG	LB	5	153	GRIMSHAW	EI	4	163	GRINYER	EM	1	138	GROOM	G	5	154
GRIGG	LGA	12	316	GRIMSHAW	F	3	67	GRINYER	HP	4	164	GROOM	H	12	316
GRIGG	S	4	163	GRIMSHAW	GH	3	350	GRINYER	SR	4	164	GROOM	HH	13	195
GRIGG	S	6	169	GRIMSHAW	H	3	67	GRIPTON	WH	12	316	GROOM	HL	13	195
GRIGG	T	7	157	GRIMSHAW	H	11	154	GRIST	A	2	149	GROOM	HS	3	350
GRIGG	TGW	7	157	GRIMSHAW	J	8	138	GRIST	A	10	93	GROOM	J	5	154
GRIGG	W	6	169	GRIMSHAW	J	11	155	GRIST	AA	10	93	GROOM	JA	5	154
GRIGG	W	10	93	GRIMSHAW	J	14	132	GRIST	CH	13	195	GROOM	JR	11	155
GRIGGS	E	2	148	GRIMSHAW	J	14	132	GRIST	F	2	149	GROOM	S	2	149
GRIGGS	EJ	2	149	GRIMSHAW	J	14	132	GRIST	J	3	67	GROOM	SW	5	154
GRIGGS	H	2	149	GRIMSHAW	JE	3	350	GRIST	J	7	157	GROOM	T	5	154
GRIGGS	W	8	138	GRIMSHAW	JH	11	155	GRIST	J	10	93	GROOM	T	6	170
GRIGSON	WE	13	194	GRIMSHAW	JW	9	81	GRIST	JA	7	157	GROOM	TA	5	154
GRIMES	CL	6	169	GRIMSHAW	L	9	81	GRIST	JL	2	149	GROOM	V	5	154
GRIMES	GH	6	169	GRIMSHAW	L	9	264	GRIST	RG	13	195	GROOM	W	5	154
GRIMES	H	4	163	GRIMSHAW	N	8	138	GRISTEY	A	3	350	GROOM	W	12	316
GRIMES	JE	4	163	GRIMSHAW	P	9	81	GRISTWOOD	J	5	153	GROOM	WG	5	154
GRIMES	JF	3	349	GRIMSHAW	R	14	132	GRISTWOOD	JW	7	157	GROOM	WH	5	154
GRIMES	JW	7	157	GRIMSHAW	RE	4	163	GRISWOOD	JA	13	195	GROOMBRIDGE	A	13	195
GRIMES	L	14	132	GRIMSHAW	S	11	155	GRISWOOD	JW	1	138	GROOMBRIDGE	AE	2	149
GRIMES	P	3	349	GRIMSHAW	TH	11	422	GRISWOOD	JW	1	138	GROOMBRIDGE	C	13	195

GROOTHUIS	JA	4	164	GROVES	HW	10	93	GUBBINS	EV	4	164	GUILMANT	M	4	165
GROSE	A	13	195	GROVES	J	4	164	GUBBINS	GEN	4	165	GUINN	A	14	133
GROSE	HC	13	195	GROVES	J	6	170	GUBBY	GW	1	139	GUINN	TA	14	133
GROSE	IW	10	93	GROVES	JH	8	138	GUDDE	H	2	149	GUINN	W	14	133
GROSE	V	10	93	GROVES	JR	14	133	GUDGEON	A	8	139	GUINNEY	R	14	133
GROSSE	F	8	138	GROVES	JW	6	170	GUDGEON	AC	12	101	GUINNEY	S	14	133
GROSSE	JW	13	195	GROVES	JW	7	158	GUDGEON	AE	1	139	GUISE	AB	6	171
GROSVENOR	E	6	170	GROVES	JW	10	93	GUDGEON	AE	1	139	GUIVER	R	5	155
GROSVENOR	TH	10	306	GROVES	L	14	133	GUDGEON	CW	1	139	GULLETT	WJ	7	158
GROSVENOR	WA	7	157	GROVES	OG	12	101	GUDGEON	E	5	155	GULLEY	S	8	139
GROUKE	M	9	265	GROVES	R	10	93	GUDGEON	E	9	81	GULLEY	W	4	165
GROUNDS	J	14	132	GROVES	RJ	5	154	GUDGEON	G	14	133	GULLICK	A	6	171
GROUNDSELL	W	4	164	GROVES	SC	10	93	GUDGEON	H	5	155	GULLICK	WT	6	171
GROUNSELL	EH	7	157	GROVES	WE	10	93	GUDGEON	R	8	139	GULLIVER	A	4	165
GROUNSELL	WL	2	149	GROVES	WE	10	306	GUDGEON	T	1	139	GULLIVER	A	12	102
GROUSE	FT	7	158	GROWNS	AW	1	138	GUDGIN	AE	5	155	GULLIVER	C	10	94
GROUT	AE	10	93	GROWNS	C	1	139	GUDGIN	B	12	101	GULLIVER	CO	1	139
GROUT	G	6	170	GROWNS	FT	1	139	GUDGIN	G	5	155	GULLIVER	EG	10	306
GROVE	AH	1	138	GRUBB	AJ	10	93	GUDGIN	HG	5	155	GULLIVER	RS	1	139
GROVE	GJH	1	138	GRUBB	E	2	149	GUDGIN	PH	5	155	GULLIVER	W	4	165
GROVE	HG	7	158	GRUBB	EA	4	164	GUDYER	J	2	149	GULVIN	EA	1	139
GROVE	TH	12	316	GRUBB	FJ	7	158	GUESS	AG	5	155	GULVIN	FW	1	139
GROVE	WH	1	138	GRUBB	H	5	154	GUESS	G	5	155	GUMBLE	L	2	150
GROVENOR	A	6	170	GRUBB	JT	13	196	GUESS	GA	5	155	GUMBLETON	LG	10	94
GROVER	AGF	7	158	GRUBB	W	10	94	GUESS	T	5	155	GUMBLEY	AE	6	171
GROVER	AH	13	195	GRUBER	AS	2	149	GUESS	T	5	155	GUMBLEY	C	6	171
GROVER	BJ	1	138	GRUBER	ASG	3	67	GUESS	W	5	155	GUMBLEY	J	12	102
GROVER	E	3	67	GRUMLEY		6	170	GUEST	A	6	170	GUMBLEY	W	6	171
GROVER	E	3	67	GRUMLEY	J	6	170	GUEST	A	6	170	GUMERY	E	3	67
GROVER	F	1	138	GRUMMITT	AE	5	154	GUEST	A	9	265	GUMERY	E	6	171
GROVER	F	5	154	GRUMMITT	FC	5	154	GUEST	A	12	101	GUMERY	J	6	171
GROVER	GE	13	195	GRUMMITT	H	5	155	GUEST	AE	6	170	GUMM	FW	1	139
GROVER	GEV	5	154	GRUMMITT	M	5	155	GUEST	AJ	10	94	GUMMER	WE	2	150
GROVER	GJ	4	164	GRUMMITT	R	5	155	GUEST	B	6	171	GUMMERY	J	9	265
GROVER	HF	1	138	GRUMMITT	R	5	155	GUEST	C	12	101	GUMMERY	JW	9	265
GROVER	W	4	164	GRUNDON	CM	2	149	GUEST	G	6	171	GUNBY	E	8	139
GROVER	W	13	195	GRUNDON	F	1	139	GUEST	H	6	171	GUNBY	T	11	155
GROVES	A	5	154	GRUNDON	G	1	139	GUEST	H	6	171	GUNDER	H	14	133
GROVES	A	10	306	GRUNDON	G	1	139	GUEST	H	6	171	GUNDRY	A	13	196
GROVES	AC	13	196	GRUNDON	T	1	139	GUEST	H	9	265	GUNDRY	F	4	165
GROVES	AE	4	164	GRUNDON	W	1	139	GUEST	HJ	6	171	GUNDRY	FA	1	139
GROVES	AW	4	164	GRUNDY	AR	14	133	GUEST	J	6	171	GUNDRY	HC	5	155
GROVES	C	7	158	GRUNDY	F	10	94	GUEST	J	9	265	GUNDRY	WC	4	165
GROVES	C	10	93	GRUNDY	G	11	155	GUEST	JE	6	171	GUNDRY	WE	3	350
GROVES	CH	4	164	GRUNDY	H	10	94	GUEST	L	6	171	GUNN	A	1	139
GROVES	E	2	149	GRUNDY	HS	14	133	GUEST	L	6	171	GUNN	AF	7	158
GROVES	E	10	93	GRUNDY	S	8	138	GUEST	TE	10	94	GUNN	AJ	7	158
GROVES	EP	10	93	GRUNDY	T	8	138	GUEST	W	12	101	GUNN	CF	11	155
GROVES	F	5	154	GRUNDY	T	14	133	GUFFICK	JH	9	265	GUNN	EF	7	158
GROVES	F	12	316	GRUNDY	WH	14	133	GUILBERT	TM	10	306	GUNN	F	2	150
GROVES	GH	12	316	GUARD	CA	4	164	GUILDFORD	HP	3	67	GUNN	G	6	171
GROVES	GT	6	170	GUARD	FG	4	164	GUILDFORD	SC	3	67	GUNN	H	1	140
GROVES	H	1	138	GUARD	GE	4	164	GUILFORD	A	11	155	GUNN	H	5	155
GROVES	H	14	132	GUARE	WC	12	316	GUILLE	WE	13	196	GUNN	HC	7	158
GROVES	HW	2	149	GUBB	E	1	139	GUILMANT	D	4	165	GUNN	J	5	156

GUNN	J	7	158
GUNN	JW	2	150
GUNN	JW	13	196
GUNN	L	9	265
GUNN	N	4	165
GUNN	RS	5	156
GUNN	T	13	196
GUNN	W	6	171
GUNNELL	W	2	150
GUNNER	AW	4	165
GUNNER	F	6	172
GUNNER	H	3	68
GUNNER	JJ	4	165
GUNNER	R	3	68
GUNNING	ST	5	156
GUNNING	WW	2	150
GUNSON	B	9	265
GUNTER	J	4	165
GUNTHER	SE	2	150
GUNTHORPE	RRG	12	102
GUNTRIP	AG	1	140
GUNTRIP	J	12	102
GUNTRIP	J	12	102
GUNTRIP	JJ	12	102
GUPWELL	J	6	172
GURD	AG	4	165
GURD	CWH	10	94
GURD	H	2	150
GURD	PE	4	165
GURD	PJ	4	165
GURD	TG	4	165
GURD	W	4	165
GURD	WE	4	165
GURDEN	EH	1	140
GURDEN	TWE	1	140
GURDEN	W	6	172
GURDLER	A	5	156
GURDLER	H	5	156
GURDLER	W	5	156
GURLEY	AJ	6	172
GURLING	FJ	1	140
GURNETT	AJ	2	150
GURNETT	FC	4	165
GURNETT	LJ	4	165
GURNEY	A	5	156
GURNEY	A	5	156
GURNEY	A	5	156
GURNEY	AA	10	94
GURNEY	AF	5	156
GURNEY	AGV	1	140
GURNEY	AH	1	140
GURNEY	AH	5	156
GURNEY	AR	5	156
GURNEY	BJ	5	156
GURNEY	CW	1	140
GURNEY	E	5	156
GURNEY	E	5	156
GURNEY	E	6	172
GURNEY	EC	5	156
GURNEY	F	5	156
GURNEY	F	5	156
GURNEY	FG	5	156
GURNEY	FW	12	102
GURNEY	G	5	156
GURNEY	G	5	157
GURNEY	GA	3	350
GURNEY	J	5	157
GURNEY	JE	3	68
GURNEY	JT	5	157
GURNEY	LS	13	196
GURNEY	PJ	5	157
GURNEY	PW	1	140
GURNEY	SJ	5	157
GURNEY	T	12	102
GURNEY	TJ	3	350
GURNEY	WH	1	140
GURNEY	WS	10	306
GURR	C	3	350
GURR	FW	7	158
GURR	TH	10	94
GURREY	C	6	172
GUSCOTT	E	7	158
GUSH	LJ	13	196
GUTHRIE	AR	13	196
GUTHRIE	H	8	139
GUTHRIE	J	11	156
GUTHRIE	PJ	11	155
GUTSELL	MJ	4	165
GUTTERIDGE	A	9	265
GUTTERIDGE	C	5	157
GUTTERIDGE	CJ	11	156
GUTTERIDGE	F	5	157
GUTTERIDGE	FJ	5	157
GUTTERIDGE	H	5	157
GUTTERIDGE	HC	2	150
GUTTERIDGE	HD	5	157
GUTTERIDGE	HW	2	150
GUTTERIDGE	MH	3	350
GUTTERIDGE	W	5	157
GUTTERIDGE	W	13	196
GUTTERIDGE	WT	12	316
GUTTRIDGE	RE	6	172
GUY	A	14	133
GUY	AG	6	172
GUY	AG	10	306
GUY	AW	1	140
GUY	CE	4	165
GUY	EG	7	158
GUY	FS	10	306
GUY	G	10	306
GUY	GA	1	140
GUY	GP	13	196
GUY	H	3	68
GUY	H	13	196
GUY	HA	4	166
GUY	HW	6	172
GUY	J	10	94
GUY	PN	13	196
GUY	R	8	139
GUY	R	9	387
GUY	R	14	133
GUY	S	1	140
GUY	T	1	140
GUY	T	6	172
GUY	TE	13	196
GUY	WH	1	140
GUY	WJ	10	94
GUY	WT	6	172
GUYATT	A	13	196
GUYATT	EEH	1	140
GUYATT	F	13	196
GUYATT	FC	2	150
GUYATT	J	4	166
GUYATT	J	13	196
GUYATT	JB	10	94
GUYATT	JC	13	196
GUYATT	LA	4	166
GUYATT	LGJO	4	166
GUYATT	LM	13	196
GUYATT	S	4	166
GUYATT	T	2	150
GUYATT	WJ	1	140
GUYMER	E	4	166
GUYTON	B	10	94
GUYVER	PG	1	140
GUYVER	SG	1	140
GWENWILL	LF	14	133
GWILLIAM	S	2	150
GWYN	C	9	81
GWYNNE	E	6	172
GWYNNE	HE	6	172
GYDE	WJB	7	158
GYER	F	1	140
GYLES	AH	13	196
GYPPS	F	1	140
GYTE	H	13	197

H

HABBERLEY	T	4	166
HABEN	A	13	197
HABEN	W	13	197
HABERGHAM	E	9	81
HACK	A	5	157
HACK	C	4	166
HACK	CF	6	172
HACK	FW	6	172
HACK	HA	6	172
HACKER	CS	14	133
HACKER	FG	7	158
HACKER	H	3	350
HACKER	JW	9	81
HACKER	WE	14	133
HACKER	WT	7	159
HACKERMAN	G	5	157
HACKETT	A	6	172
HACKETT	A	12	102
HACKETT	C	7	159
HACKETT	CW	12	102
HACKETT	D	12	316
HACKETT	E	9	387
HACKETT	E	12	102
HACKETT	F	14	133
HACKETT	G	12	102
HACKETT	H	10	94
HACKETT	HC	13	197
HACKETT	J	11	156
HACKETT	J	13	197
HACKETT	J	13	197
HACKETT	JF	11	156
HACKETT	JT	12	102
HACKETT	T	6	172
HACKETT	TE	12	316
HACKETT	TJ	1	141
HACKETT	TW	10	306
HACKETT	W	1	141
HACKETT	WJ	14	134
HACKING	CH	4	166
HACKING	H	11	156
HACKMAN	EF	5	157
HACKNEY	HK	11	156
HACKNEY	M	11	156
HACKNEY	W	6	172
HACKWORTHY	H	10	94
HADDEN	WR	6	173
HADDICAN	E	4	166
HADDOCK	C	2	150
HADDOCK	CA	8	139
HADDOCK	E	6	173
HADDOCK	GA	8	139
HADDOCK	HJ	13	197
HADDOCK	N	9	81
HADDOCK	WH	6	173
HADDOCK	WR	7	159
HADDON	A	12	102
HADDON	C	1	141
HADDON	C	7	159
HADDON	CA	12	316
HADDON	E	6	173
HADDON	E	12	102

HADDON	FW	12	317	HADLEY	JA	6	174	HAGUE	SJ	6	175	HAINES	AJ	7	159
HADDON	G	11	156	HADLEY	JJ	6	174	HAGUE	W	6	175	HAINES	AJ	10	94
HADDON	HJ	12	102	HADLEY	JN	6	174	HAGUE	WJ	14	134	HAINES	AW	4	166
HADDON	HV	12	102	HADLEY	JT	6	174	HAHNER	E	1	141	HAINES	DG	4	167
HADDON	JE	3	350	HADLEY	K	6	174	HAHNER	H	1	141	HAINES	DG	4	167
HADDON	LJ	6	173	HADLEY	RC	12	317	HAIG	G	9	387	HAINES	DP	4	167
HADDON	TT	12	317	HADLEY	S	6	174	HAIG	H	1	141	HAINES	E	7	159
HADDON	W	6	173	HADLEY	W	6	174	HAIGH	A	8	139	HAINES	F	10	94
HADDON	W	12	102	HADLEY	WB	6	174	HAIGH	AE	9	81	HAINES	FJ	7	159
HADDON	WJ	5	157	HADLEY	WJ	6	174	HAIGH	B	9	265	HAINES	GE	13	197
HADDOW	A	4	166	HADLEY	WJ	6	174	HAIGH	C	9	265	HAINES	GR	3	350
HADDOW	AG	5	157	HADLINGTON	E	6	174	HAIGH	C	14	134	HAINES	H	10	94
HADDOW	AG	12	102	HADLINGTON	JT	6	174	HAIGH	D	4	166	HAINES	H	10	95
HADDOW	BBA	5	157	HADON	S	13	197	HAIGH	D	9	387	HAINES	HS	2	151
HADDOW	ER	5	157	HADRILL	AJ	2	150	HAIGH	E	8	139	HAINES	J	4	167
HADDOW	PJ	5	157	HADRILL	VCT	13	197	HAIGH	E	9	266	HAINES	MH	1	141
HADDOW	S	5	158	HADRILL	WHG	7	159	HAIGH	F	8	139	HAINES	PE	12	103
HADDRICK	O	2	150	HADWELL	TF	1	141	HAIGH	F	8	139	HAINES	PG	4	167
HADEN	F	6	173	HADWIN	G	11	156	HAIGH	GE	4	166	HAINES	R	5	158
HADEN	W	6	173	HAFFORD	AC	12	317	HAIGH	H	8	139	HAINES	R	6	175
HADFIELD	A	11	156	HAGAN	F	11	156	HAIGH	H	9	82	HAINES	R	8	140
HADFIELD	CF	11	156	HAGAN	TJ	6	175	HAIGH	H	9	82	HAINES	RJ	4	167
HADFIELD	CF	11	156	HAGEMAN	FW	2	150	HAIGH	H	9	82	HAINES	SW	4	167
HADFIELD	E	5	158	HAGEN	T	8	139	HAIGH	H	11	157	HAINES	TW	6	175
HADFIELD	FC	4	166	HAGER	AG	2	150	HAIGH	HH	8	139	HAINES	W	3	350
HADFIELD	FW	11	156	HAGER	EM	2	151	HAIGH	J	8	139	HAINES	W	7	159
HADFIELD	HG	4	166	HAGERTY	C	9	265	HAIGH	J	8	139	HAINES	W	7	159
HADFIELD	J	11	156	HAGGAN	J	14	134	HAIGH	J	9	82	HAINES	WA	13	197
HADFIELD	J	11	156	HAGGAR	EW	4	166	HAIGH	J	9	266	HAINES	WA	13	197
HADFIELD	LW	4	166	HAGGAR	M	4	166	HAIGH	J	9	266	HAINES	WE	4	167
HADFIELD	W	7	159	HAGGAS	C	9	81	HAIGH	JW	8	139	HAINESWORTH	WL	13	197
HADFIELD	W	11	156	HAGGAS	EH	11	157	HAIGH	L	8	139	HAINSBY	F	3	68
HADFIELD	W	14	134	HAGGAS	TW	9	265	HAIGH	S	9	82	HAINSTOCK	H	8	140
HADFIELD	WT	11	156	HAGGATA	HJ	13	197	HAIGH	T	9	82	HAINSWORTH	A	8	416
HADGKISS	J	6	173	HAGGER	BJ	3	68	HAIGH	W	8	139	HAINSWORTH	A	9	82
HADINGUE	AE	13	197	HAGGER	EA	12	103	HAIGH	W	8	140	HAINSWORTH	A	9	266
HADLAND	NG	2	150	HAGGER	GD	5	158	HAIGH	W	9	82	HAINSWORTH	E	8	140
HADLEY	A	6	173	HAGGER	HC	5	158	HAIGH	W	9	266	HAINSWORTH	I	8	140
HADLEY	AJ	6	173	HAGGER	TE	6	175	HAIGH	W	9	266	HAINSWORTH	I	9	82
HADLEY	AW	6	173	HAGGER	WJ	1	141	HAIGH	WH	9	266	HAINSWORTH	J	8	140
HADLEY	B	6	173	HAGGERTY	E	1	141	HAIGHWAY	W	6	175	HAINSWORTH	J	8	140
HADLEY	E	6	173	HAGGERTY	JP	3	68	HAILE	F	6	175	HAINSWORTH	J	9	82
HADLEY	E	6	173	HAGGERTY	W	1	141	HAILES	J	2	151	HAINSWORTH	J	9	266
HADLEY	F	6	173	HAGGERWOOD	J	12	103	HAILEY	C	5	158	HAINSWORTH	J	9	266
HADLEY	F	6	173	HAGGIE	GG	5	158	HAILEY	E	8	140	HAINSWORTH	JW	8	140
HADLEY	FE	6	173	HAGGIS	HW	14	134	HAILEY	HJ	5	158	HAINSWORTH	S	8	140
HADLEY	FJ	4	166	HAGGIS	RF	2	151	HAILEY	J	1	141	HAINSWORTH	SW	4	167
HADLEY	GW	7	159	HAGGIT	R	8	139	HAILSTON	FWC	7	159	HAINSWORTH	T	8	140
HADLEY	H	6	173	HAGON	E	11	157	HAILSTONE	F	7	159	HAINSWORTH	W	8	140
HADLEY	HJ	6	174	HAGON	WR	13	197	HAINE	BL	13	197	HAINSWORTH	WA	9	266
HADLEY	HR	6	174	HAGREEN	F	1	141	HAINES	A	7	159	HAIR	JE	9	82
HADLEY	IH	6	174	HAGREEN	WC	1	141	HAINES	AE	6	175	HAIST	A	8	140
HADLEY	J	6	174	HAGUE	E	9	81	HAINES	AE	7	159	HAIST	H	8	140
HADLEY	J	6	174	HAGUE	J	8	139	HAINES	AEEM	4	166	HAITHWAITE	H	9	82
HADLEY	JA	6	174	HAGUE	J	11	157	HAINES	AG	6	175	HAKE	H	8	140

HAKE	S	13	198	HALES	C	3	350	HALFORD	TM	4	168	HALL	B	8	141
HAKE	W	13	197	HALES	CSS	7	160	HALFORD	W	4	168	HALL	BJ	4	168
HAKES	J	12	317	HALES	E	5	158	HALFORD	W	6	176	HALL	BW	3	68
HALCROW	B	3	68	HALES	F	12	103	HALFORD	W	14	134	HALL	C	1	142
HALDANE	J	2	151	HALES	FH	5	158	HALFORD	WH	7	160	HALL	C	2	151
HALDEN	JPH	2	151	HALES	G	14	134	HALFORD	WS	2	151	HALL	C	5	159
HALDEN	RJ	14	134	HALES	H	1	141	HALFPENNY	A	5	158	HALL	C	7	160
HALDEN	T	14	134	HALES	H	3	350	HALFPENNY	AC	5	158	HALL	C	11	157
HALE	A	6	175	HALES	HA	1	141	HALFPENNY	C	5	159	HALL	C	11	157
HALE	A	13	198	HALES	HE	2	151	HALFPENNY	CH	13	198	HALL	C	11	157
HALE	AE	1	141	HALES	HJ	7	160	HALFPENNY	G	5	159	HALL	CA	3	68
HALE	AH	4	167	HALES	HP	3	68	HALFPENNY	GE	13	198	HALL	CC	5	159
HALE	BW	1	141	HALES	IL	2	151	HALFPENNY	HC	5	159	HALL	CD	2	151
HALE	E	7	159	HALES	J	5	158	HALFPENNY	J	9	83	HALL	CE	6	176
HALE	E	7	159	HALES	J	11	157	HALFPENNY	P	5	159	HALL	CG	4	168
HALE	EA	13	198	HALES	JG	4	167	HALFPENNY	W	13	198	HALL	CH	4	168
HALE	EC	7	159	HALES	JW	4	167	HALIDAY	J	9	266	HALL	CH	6	176
HALE	ET	2	151	HALES	R	7	160	HALL	A	1	142	HALL	CL	3	68
HALE	F	6	175	HALES	W	5	158	HALL	A	3	68	HALL	CM	14	134
HALE	FA	6	175	HALES	W	5	158	HALL	A	3	351	HALL	CP	7	160
HALE	FH	2	151	HALES	WF	2	151	HALL	A	4	168	HALL	CP	7	160
HALE	FRB	1	141	HALES	WJ	6	175	HALL	A	4	168	HALL	CW	4	168
HALE	FT	10	95	HALEY	B	8	140	HALL	A	5	159	HALL	CW	5	159
HALE	G	2	151	HALEY	B	9	82	HALL	A	6	176	HALL	CW	10	95
HALE	G	4	167	HALEY	C	9	82	HALL	A	6	176	HALL	CW	12	317
HALE	GA	13	198	HALEY	CH	9	266	HALL	A	6	176	HALL	D	1	142
HALE	GG	5	158	HALEY	D	8	140	HALL	A	6	176	HALL	D	7	160
HALE	GT	10	95	HALEY	D	10	95	HALL	A	8	141	HALL	DCW	7	160
HALE	HG	1	141	HALEY	E	8	140	HALL	A	8	141	HALL	DJ	6	176
HALE	HH	6	175	HALEY	E	9	82	HALL	A	8	141	HALL	E	2	151
HALE	J	7	160	HALEY	E	9	266	HALL	A	8	141	HALL	E	4	168
HALE	J	13	198	HALEY	E	13	198	HALL	A	9	266	HALL	E	6	176
HALE	JG	5	158	HALEY	G	9	82	HALL	A	10	95	HALL	E	9	83
HALE	JH	12	103	HALEY	H	8	140	HALL	A	11	157	HALL	E	9	267
HALE	JH	14	134	HALEY	J	4	167	HALL	A	13	198	HALL	E	11	157
HALE	JT	6	175	HALEY	J	8	140	HALL	A	14	134	HALL	E	11	157
HALE	JT	10	95	HALEY	J	8	140	HALL	A	14	134	HALL	EA	4	168
HALE	JW	7	160	HALEY	J	9	266	HALL	AC	3	68	HALL	EA	12	103
HALE	JW	10	95	HALEY	J	11	157	HALL	AC	5	159	HALL	EA	12	103
HALE	LE	4	167	HALEY	J	12	317	HALL	AC	13	198	HALL	EE	7	160
HALE	O	5	158	HALEY	JL	9	82	HALL	AE	3	68	HALL	EG	5	159
HALE	P	5	158	HALEY	JW	8	141	HALL	AE	5	159	HALL	EH	5	159
HALE	RJ	3	350	HALEY	M	9	266	HALL	AE	6	176	HALL	EJ	4	168
HALE	S	6	175	HALEY	MW	8	141	HALL	AH	4	168	HALL	EJ	7	160
HALE	SA	6	175	HALEY	N	9	266	HALL	AH	4	168	HALL	ER	3	351
HALE	SH	13	198	HALEY	N	9	266	HALL	AH	4	168	HALL	ER	7	160
HALE	VP	4	167	HALEY	P	9	266	HALL	AH	14	134	HALL	ETL	1	142
HALE	W	4	167	HALEY	T	7	160	HALL	AJ	3	351	HALL	EW	7	160
HALE	W	4	167	HALEY	W	9	82	HALL	AJS	2	151	HALL	F	4	168
HALE	W	6	175	HALEY	W	9	82	HALL	AT	2	151	HALL	F	4	168
HALE	W	14	134	HALFACRE	FW	7	160	HALL	AT	6	176	HALL	F	5	159
HALE	WA	13	198	HALFORD	AE	4	167	HALL	AT	13	198	HALL	F	5	159
HALE	WE	7	160	HALFORD	J	1	142	HALL	AW	2	151	HALL	F	7	161
HALES	A	11	157	HALFORD	J	5	158	HALL	AW	12	103	HALL	F	8	141
HALES	A	14	134	HALFORD	PS	6	176	HALL	B	2	151	HALL	F	8	141

HALL	F	9	83	HALL	H	8	141	HALL	JJ	6	177	HALL	W	4	169
HALL	F	11	157	HALL	H	9	83	HALL	JS	11	158	HALL	W	4	169
HALL	F	12	103	HALL	H	9	83	HALL	JT	12	103	HALL	W	5	160
HALL	F	13	198	HALL	H	9	83	HALL	JV	3	68	HALL	W	5	160
HALL	F	13	198	HALL	H	10	95	HALL	JW	6	177	HALL	W	5	160
HALL	F	13	198	HALL	H	12	103	HALL	JW	6	177	HALL	W	5	160
HALL	F	13	198	HALL	H	14	135	HALL	JW	8	141	HALL	W	6	177
HALL	F	14	134	HALL	H	14	135	HALL	JW	8	141	HALL	W	6	177
HALL	F	14	134	HALL	H	14	135	HALL	JW	10	95	HALL	W	8	141
HALL	FC	4	168	HALL	HA	4	169	HALL	JW	11	158	HALL	W	8	141
HALL	FG	6	176	HALL	HA	5	160	HALL	JW	11	158	HALL	W	8	141
HALL	FG	13	198	HALL	HA	7	161	HALL	LA	9	83	HALL	W	8	141
HALL	FJ	3	351	HALL	HA	14	135	HALL	LW	5	160	HALL	W	9	83
HALL	FJ	5	159	HALL	HE	2	152	HALL	M	9	83	HALL	W	10	95
HALL	FM	1	142	HALL	HG	14	135	HALL	MA	3	351	HALL	W	11	158
HALL	FN	7	161	HALL	HH	1	142	HALL	N	14	135	HALL	W	11	158
HALL	FR	13	199	HALL	HJ	3	68	HALL	NA	5	160	HALL	W	11	158
HALL	FS	9	267	HALL	HJ	5	160	HALL	P	4	169	HALL	WA	4	169
HALL	FT	7	161	HALL	HJ	12	103	HALL	P	5	160	HALL	WA	8	142
HALL	FV	3	351	HALL	HJ	13	199	HALL	R	1	142	HALL	WA	10	307
HALL	FW	1	142	HALL	HS	2	152	HALL	R	7	161	HALL	WC	4	169
HALL	FW	4	168	HALL	HS	10	95	HALL	R	10	95	HALL	WE	14	135
HALL	FW	11	157	HALL	I	6	176	HALL	R	12	103	HALL	WF	4	169
HALL	G	1	142	HALL	IR	1	142	HALL	R	12	103	HALL	WF	9	83
HALL	G	2	152	HALL	J	1	142	HALL	R	13	199	HALL	WF	12	317
HALL	G	5	159	HALL	J	1	142	HALL	RD	9	83	HALL	WG	1	142
HALL	G	5	159	HALL	J	2	152	HALL	RG	7	161	HALL	WG	7	161
HALL	G	5	159	HALL	J	6	176	HALL	RGB	10	95	HALL	WG	14	135
HALL	G	5	160	HALL	J	6	177	HALL	RH	13	199	HALL	WH	1	143
HALL	G	7	161	HALL	J	7	161	HALL	RRP	7	161	HALL	WH	6	177
HALL	G	8	141	HALL	J	7	161	HALL	RS	7	161	HALL	WH	8	142
HALL	G	8	141	HALL	J	8	141	HALL	S	4	169	HALL	WH	10	306
HALL	G	11	157	HALL	J	9	83	HALL	S	9	267	HALL	WH	13	199
HALL	G	12	103	HALL	J	11	157	HALL	S	14	135	HALL	WH	14	135
HALL	G	13	199	HALL	J	11	157	HALL	SJ	2	152	HALL	WJ	1	143
HALL	G	14	134	HALL	J	11	157	HALL	SL	5	160	HALL	WJ	5	160
HALL	G	14	135	HALL	J	11	158	HALL	T	3	351	HALL	WJ	6	177
HALL	GA	14	135	HALL	J	12	103	HALL	T	6	177	HALL	WJ	12	103
HALL	GE	9	267	HALL	J	13	199	HALL	T	7	161	HALL	WJ	13	199
HALL	GH	1	142	HALL	J	13	199	HALL	T	8	141	HALL	WL	5	160
HALL	GO	2	152	HALL	J	13	199	HALL	T	9	83	HALL	WT	1	143
HALL	GW	6	176	HALL	J	13	199	HALL	T	9	267	HALL	WT	11	158
HALL	GW	13	199	HALL	J	13	199	HALL	T	11	158	HALL	WT	11	158
HALL	H	1	142	HALL	J	14	135	HALL	T	12	103	HALL	WW	7	161
HALL	H	1	142	HALL	J	14	135	HALL	T	13	199	HALL-CATHERALL	R	10	307
HALL	H	1	142	HALL	JA	6	177	HALL	T	14	135	HALLADAY	LA	6	177
HALL	H	4	168	HALL	JB	10	95	HALL	TE	9	267	HALLADAY	S	4	169
HALL	H	4	168	HALL	JC	11	158	HALL	TE	13	199	HALLAM	EJ	2	152
HALL	H	5	160	HALL	JE	4	169	HALL	TFC	9	83	HALLAM	GL	14	135
HALL	H	5	160	HALL	JF	7	161	HALL	TJ	14	135	HALLAM	GT	11	158
HALL	H	6	176	HALL	JH	1	142	HALL	TR	14	135	HALLAM	H	11	158
HALL	H	6	176	HALL	JH	4	169	HALL	TRW	8	141	HALLAM	IE	4	169
HALL	H	6	176	HALL	JH	6	177	HALL	TW	5	160	HALLAM	J	4	169
HALL	H	8	141	HALL	JH	6	177	HALL	TW	14	135	HALLAM	JE	11	158
HALL	H	8	141	HALL	JI	6	177	HALL	W	2	152	HALLAM	JJ	6	177

Name	Init.	Vol	Pg	Name	Init.	Vol	Pg	Name	Init.	Vol	Pg	Name	Init.	Vol	Pg
HALLAM	JM	2	152	HALLIWELL	A	11	159	HALSEY	T	3	69	HAMES	G	2	152
HALLAM	S	8	142	HALLIWELL	C	14	136	HALSTEAD	AH	2	152	HAMES	W	6	178
HALLAM	TF	3	351	HALLIWELL	F	13	200	HALSTON	HA	2	152	HAMID	F	13	200
HALLAM	W	8	142	HALLIWELL	HED	3	69	HALTON	CE	8	142	HAMILTON	A	8	142
HALLAM	W	9	267	HALLIWELL	J	11	159	HALVORSEN	E	6	177	HAMILTON	A	9	83
HALLAM	W	11	158	HALLIWELL	TE	8	142	HALY	EN	4	170	HAMILTON	A	14	137
HALLARD	JF	6	177	HALLIWELL	W	9	83	HAM	A	6	178	HAMILTON	C	13	200
HALLARD	P	12	103	HALLMAN	A	4	169	HAM	E	8	142	HAMILTON	EM	3	69
HALLAS	JH	8	142	HALLORAN	FW	10	96	HAM	E	13	200	HAMILTON	ES	3	69
HALLAS	S	14	135	HALLOWAY	C	8	142	HAM	FR	3	351	HAMILTON	EV	13	200
HALLE	CRF	1	143	HALLOWAY	H	8	142	HAM	WT	6	177	HAMILTON	F	4	170
HALLEN	JV	13	199	HALLS	EA	7	161	HAMBELTON	HS	2	152	HAMILTON	F	14	137
HALLETT	AW	1	143	HALLS	F	3	351	HAMBIDGE	D	4	170	HAMILTON	F	14	137
HALLETT	C	4	169	HALLS	F	14	136	HAMBIDGE	H	4	170	HAMILTON	FT	1	143
HALLETT	CA	3	68	HALLS	G	3	351	HAMBIDGE	I	1	143	HAMILTON	G	11	159
HALLETT	E	11	158	HALLS	H	1	143	HAMBIDGE	JL	1	143	HAMILTON	G	14	137
HALLETT	F	4	169	HALLS	J	7	161	HAMBIDGE	W	2	152	HAMILTON	H	3	351
HALLETT	FT	4	169	HALLS	M	7	161	HAMBIDGE	W	12	317	HAMILTON	HK	11	159
HALLETT	FW	13	199	HALLS	OG	3	69	HAMBLETON	B	6	178	HAMILTON	HW	13	200
HALLETT	GH	13	199	HALLSEY	TG	5	160	HAMBLETON	ED	7	162	HAMILTON	J	1	143
HALLETT	H	10	95	HALLSOR	A	11	159	HAMBLETON	F	2	152	HAMILTON	J	3	69
HALLETT	HE	3	68	HALLSTEAD	T	9	83	HAMBLETON	G	6	178	HAMILTON	J	8	142
HALLETT	J	4	169	HALLUM	CW	10	96	HAMBLETT	AE	14	136	HAMILTON	J	10	96
HALLETT	RE	3	69	HALLUM	HJ	10	96	HAMBLETT	CW	14	136	HAMILTON	J	11	159
HALLETT	WH	3	69	HALLUM	W	4	169	HAMBLETT	I	14	136	HAMILTON	J	11	159
HALLETT	WJP	1	143	HALLUM	W	4	170	HAMBLETT	J	14	136	HAMILTON	J	14	137
HALLFORD	WF	3	69	HALLWOOD	J	14	136	HAMBLETT	J	14	136	HAMILTON	J	14	137
HALLIDAY	A	8	142	HALLWORTH	WR	5	161	HAMBLETT	W	14	136	HAMILTON	J	14	137
HALLIDAY	B	14	136	HALLYBONE	A	5	160	HAMBLIN	CR	7	162	HAMILTON	J	14	137
HALLIDAY	D	9	267	HALMSHAW	H	9	387	HAMBLIN	GA	4	170	HAMILTON	JA	9	83
HALLIDAY	E	8	142	HALPERN	J	14	136	HAMBLING	A	10	307	HAMILTON	JA	13	200
HALLIDAY	F	9	83	HALPIN	JP	3	351	HAMBLING	J	10	307	HAMILTON	JA	13	200
HALLIDAY	F	9	267	HALSALL	J	14	136	HAMBLYN	JH	3	69	HAMILTON	JC	2	152
HALLIDAY	F	10	95	HALSEY	A	1	143	HAMBRIDGE	H	2	152	HAMILTON	JH	10	96
HALLIDAY	G	9	267	HALSEY	A	5	161	HAMBROOK	G	10	307	HAMILTON	JW	3	351
HALLIDAY	G	10	95	HALSEY	AJ	1	143	HAMBROOK	H	13	200	HAMILTON	P	3	69
HALLIDAY	HV	8	142	HALSEY	C	5	161	HAMBROOK	WHR	1	143	HAMILTON	RG	7	162
HALLIDAY	J	8	142	HALSEY	CR	5	161	HAMER	F	12	317	HAMILTON	RG	8	142
HALLIDAY	J	9	267	HALSEY	E	3	69	HAMER	FJ	1	143	HAMILTON	T	3	69
HALLIDAY	J	9	267	HALSEY	EC	5	161	HAMER	GE	2	152	HAMILTON	T	3	69
HALLIDAY	J	11	158	HALSEY	EJ	5	161	HAMER	J	11	159	HAMILTON	T	11	159
HALLIDAY	J	11	158	HALSEY	EL	7	161	HAMER	J	11	422	HAMILTON	TR	9	84
HALLIDAY	J	13	200	HALSEY	F	12	104	HAMER	J	14	136	HAMILTON	V	7	162
HALLIDAY	JW	14	136	HALSEY	FH	7	162	HAMER	J	14	136	HAMILTON	W	7	162
HALLIDAY	LA	13	200	HALSEY	G	3	69	HAMER	J	14	136	HAMILTON	W	14	137
HALLIDAY	RS	9	267	HALSEY	G	5	161	HAMER	NW	6	178	HAMILTON	WA	11	159
HALLIDAY	S	9	267	HALSEY	GF	3	69	HAMER	W	14	136	HAMILTON	WB	8	142
HALLIDAY	S	9	267	HALSEY	GFW	7	162	HAMER	W	14	136	HAMILTON	WH	13	200
HALLIDAY	TW	9	267	HALSEY	GH	7	162	HAMERTON	EH	4	170	HAMLET	C	1	143
HALLIDAY	W	8	142	HALSEY	GT	5	161	HAMERTON	ES	4	170	HAMLET	C	11	159
HALLIDAY	W	9	267	HALSEY	H	14	136	HAMERTON	GA	14	137	HAMLET	J	1	143
HALLIN	A	10	95	HALSEY	HJ	7	162	HAMERTON	R	11	159	HAMLET	JA	1	143
HALLIN	EA	10	96	HALSEY	J	5	161	HAMERTON	TS	4	170	HAMLET	T	14	137
HALLIN	FGE	10	95	HALSEY	JTW	5	161	HAMES	AEW	12	317	HAMLETT	A	11	159
HALLINGDRAKE	J	9	267	HALSEY	R	5	161	HAMES	CWR	7	162	HAMLETT	A	11	159

HAMLETT	C	7	162	HAMMOND	F	4	170	HAMOND	EF	4	170	HANBY	F	11	160
HAMLETT	T	11	159	HAMMOND	F	6	178	HAMPSHIRE	JW	8	143	HANBY	T	8	143
HAMLETT	WH	11	422	HAMMOND	G	5	161	HAMPSHIRE	WT	5	161	HANCE	C	5	161
HAMLEY	C	10	307	HAMMOND	G	8	142	HAMPSON	A	14	137	HANCE	EE	7	163
HAMLIN	FH	13	200	HAMMOND	G	10	96	HAMPSON	AE	11	160	HANCHER	H	6	178
HAMLIN	W	14	137	HAMMOND	GW	12	104	HAMPSON	CH	11	160	HANCOCH	HA	6	178
HAMLYN	WP	1	143	HAMMOND	H	4	170	HAMPSON	E	11	160	HANCOCK	A	8	143
HAMM	ECW	1	144	HAMMOND	H	6	178	HAMPSON	F	3	70	HANCOCK	A	9	267
HAMMANT	JC	13	200	HAMMOND	H	7	163	HAMPSON	H	11	160	HANCOCK	A	13	201
HAMMENSON	ALH	1	144	HAMMOND	H	9	84	HAMPSON	H	11	160	HANCOCK	A	14	138
HAMMERSLEY	A	3	351	HAMMOND	H	9	387	HAMPSON	J	11	160	HANCOCK	AE	1	144
HAMMERSLEY	R	14	137	HAMMOND	H	13	201	HAMPSON	J	14	137	HANCOCK	AE	7	163
HAMMERTON	A	6	178	HAMMOND	HT	12	104	HAMPSON	JH	11	160	HANCOCK	AE	12	104
HAMMERTON	S	5	161	HAMMOND	IT	4	170	HAMPSON	S	11	160	HANCOCK	AJ	2	153
HAMMERTON	W	7	162	HAMMOND	J	8	142	HAMPSON	T	11	160	HANCOCK	AS	10	96
HAMMETT	G	12	317	HAMMOND	J	11	159	HAMPSON	W	14	137	HANCOCK	AT	12	317
HAMMETT	J	3	69	HAMMOND	JH	2	153	HAMPTON	AE	10	307	HANCOCK	C	2	153
HAMMETT	JG	10	307	HAMMOND	JW	9	84	HAMPTON	AJ	13	201	HANCOCK	CE	10	96
HAMMETT	WW	1	144	HAMMOND	JW	12	104	HAMPTON	AJ	13	201	HANCOCK	EN	2	153
HAMMOCK	R	13	200	HAMMOND	LB	12	104	HAMPTON	ATE	4	171	HANCOCK	ET	1	144
HAMMOCKS	H	2	152	HAMMOND	PJ	1	144	HAMPTON	B	4	171	HANCOCK	EW	2	153
HAMMON	MF	3	69	HAMMOND	R	6	178	HAMPTON	C	4	171	HANCOCK	EW	4	171
HAMMOND	A	4	170	HAMMOND	RG	1	144	HAMPTON	C	10	96	HANCOCK	FM	4	171
HAMMOND	A	4	170	HAMMOND	RWJ	1	144	HAMPTON	CJ	4	171	HANCOCK	G	1	144
HAMMOND	A	6	178	HAMMOND	S	2	153	HAMPTON	F	6	178	HANCOCK	G	12	317
HAMMOND	A	7	162	HAMMOND	T	5	161	HAMPTON	F	13	201	HANCOCK	GR	4	171
HAMMOND	A	11	159	HAMMOND	T	12	104	HAMPTON	FW	4	171	HANCOCK	H	14	138
HAMMOND	AA	10	307	HAMMOND	TD	6	178	HAMPTON	G	10	307	HANCOCK	HE	4	171
HAMMOND	AE	7	162	HAMMOND	TJ	12	104	HAMPTON	GH	6	178	HANCOCK	HG	4	171
HAMMOND	AE	10	96	HAMMOND	TP	4	170	HAMPTON	H	4	171	HANCOCK	HR	12	104
HAMMOND	AG	7	162	HAMMOND	TW	7	162	HAMPTON	H	7	163	HANCOCK	JA	11	160
HAMMOND	AH	3	351	HAMMOND	W	3	70	HAMPTON	H	11	160	HANCOCK	JH	11	160
HAMMOND	AJ	1	144	HAMMOND	W	7	163	HAMPTON	HJH	2	153	HANCOCK	JJ	2	153
HAMMOND	AJ	1	144	HAMMOND	W	7	163	HAMPTON	HW	1	144	HANCOCK	MA	2	153
HAMMOND	AJ	10	96	HAMMOND	W	7	163	HAMPTON	JK	4	171	HANCOCK	PT	14	138
HAMMOND	AT	13	200	HAMMOND	W	9	84	HAMPTON	L	10	307	HANCOCK	REG	1	144
HAMMOND	AW	1	144	HAMMOND	W	9	84	HAMPTON	R	13	201	HANCOCK	RW	2	153
HAMMOND	AW	7	162	HAMMOND	W	10	96	HAMPTON	R	14	137	HANCOCK	S	11	160
HAMMOND	AW	13	200	HAMMOND	W	12	104	HAMPTON	SH	4	171	HANCOCK	SC	13	201
HAMMOND	C	3	70	HAMMOND	W	13	201	HAMPTON	W	4	171	HANCOCK	SH	13	201
HAMMOND	CE	10	96	HAMMOND	W	14	137	HAMPTON	WA	4	171	HANCOCK	T	8	143
HAMMOND	CE	13	200	HAMMOND	WE	12	104	HAMPTON	WJ	13	201	HANCOCK	TH	3	352
HAMMOND	CFJ	7	162	HAMMOND	WG	13	201	HAMSHAW	AH	7	163	HANCOCK	TJ	7	163
HAMMOND	CH	12	104	HAMMOND	WJ	3	351	HAMSON	AJ	12	317	HANCOCK	TR	12	317
HAMMOND	CJ	2	152	HAMMOND	WJ	7	163	HAMSON	FA	12	317	HANCOCK	W	4	171
HAMMOND	CW	12	104	HAMMOND	WJ	7	163	HAMSON	H	11	160	HANCOCK	WC	4	171
HAMMOND	DC	1	144	HAMMOND	WJ	13	201	HAMSON	HA	12	317	HANCOCK	WE	2	153
HAMMOND	E	3	351	HAMMOND	WL	13	201	HAMSON	T	11	160	HANCOCK	WJ	5	161
HAMMOND	E	7	163	HAMMOND	WT	4	170	HAMSTEAD	J	2	153	HANCOCK	WR	5	161
HAMMOND	E	9	84	HAMMONDS	A	12	317	HAMSTEAD	JH	2	153	HANCOCKS	W	6	178
HAMMOND	EC	1	144	HAMNETT	J	11	159	HANAHOE	M	14	138	HANCOX	A	6	178
HAMMOND	EE	12	104	HAMNETT	J	11	422	HANAKIN	T	8	143	HANCOX	C	6	178
HAMMOND	EJ	13	201	HAMNETT	R	11	160	HANBRIDGE	A	14	138	HANCOX	T	6	178
HAMMOND	EW	10	96	HAMON	GE	4	170	HANBRIDGE	W	14	138	HANCOX	W	6	178
HAMMOND	F	1	144	HAMON	JW	4	170	HANBURY	W	7	163	HAND	A	4	171

HAND	F	2	153	HANDYSIDE	J	3	70	HANNA	H	13	202	HANSLIP	F	4	172
HAND	F	3	352	HANGER	H	3	352	HANNABUSS	FC	1	145	HANSLIP	N	4	172
HAND	F	12	104	HANGLE	G	14	138	HANNAFORD	AE	1	145	HANSLIP	S	9	268
HAND	G	10	96	HANKIN	L	7	163	HANNAFORD	JF	1	145	HANSON	A	1	145
HAND	J	4	171	HANKIN	T	7	163	HANNAFORD	LJ	7	164	HANSON	A	4	172
HAND	J	9	84	HANKIN	WF	7	163	HANNAFORD	WH	12	318	HANSON	A	8	143
HAND	JH	9	267	HANKIN	WJ	7	163	HANNAH	A	8	143	HANSON	A	9	268
HAND	JJ	11	160	HANKINS	A	5	162	HANNAH	F	11	161	HANSON	A	9	268
HAND	JW	7	163	HANKINS	FW	6	179	HANNAH	J	11	161	HANSON	A	13	202
HAND	RC	6	179	HANKINS	R	5	162	HANNAH	JC	5	162	HANSON	AE	10	307
HAND	S	6	179	HANKINS	WE	2	153	HANNAH	JW	11	161	HANSON	AJ	7	164
HAND	T	11	160	HANKINSON	G	14	138	HANNAH	WJ	1	145	HANSON	B	6	180
HAND	TH	11	160	HANKINSON	JB	14	138	HANNAM	AT	3	70	HANSON	BE	6	180
HAND	W	12	318	HANKS	G	6	179	HANNAM	FG	3	70	HANSON	C	4	172
HAND	W	14	138	HANKS	J	7	163	HANNAM	GW	8	416	HANSON	DJ	7	164
HAND	WT	12	318	HANKS	JCEG	1	145	HANNAM	HJ	3	352	HANSON	E	9	84
HANDCOCK	HG	4	171	HANKS	JJ	6	179	HANNAM	JJ	3	70	HANSON	E	9	84
HANDFORD	EJ	1	144	HANKS	JP	10	307	HANNAM	SF	3	70	HANSON	EB	6	180
HANDFORD	H	3	70	HANKS	TH	1	145	HANNAM	TW	3	70	HANSON	F	8	144
HANDFORD	JA	8	143	HANKS	WF	6	179	HANNAN	J	9	268	HANSON	G	9	84
HANDLEY	C	1	144	HANLAN	W	1	145	HANNAN	W	6	180	HANSON	G	9	268
HANDLEY	E	8	143	HANLEY	A	11	161	HANNAN	W	6	180	HANSON	GE	13	202
HANDLEY	F	8	143	HANLEY	AH	8	143	HANNAN	W	9	84	HANSON	H	6	180
HANDLEY	F	11	161	HANLEY	FJ	6	179	HANNAN	W	9	268	HANSON	H	6	180
HANDLEY	G	2	153	HANLEY	FJ	6	179	HANNANT	D	10	96	HANSON	H	8	144
HANDLEY	G	8	143	HANLEY	FP	6	179	HANNAY	HT	1	145	HANSON	H	9	84
HANDLEY	G	9	387	HANLEY	GE	11	161	HANNELL	H	1	145	HANSON	H	9	84
HANDLEY	GE	8	143	HANLEY	H	4	172	HANNEN	D	14	138	HANSON	H	9	268
HANDLEY	J	5	161	HANLEY	J	4	172	HANNEN	J	13	202	HANSON	H	9	268
HANDLEY	J	11	161	HANLEY	J	11	161	HANNESS	J	3	70	HANSON	H	11	161
HANDLEY	RG	4	172	HANLEY	JJ	4	172	HANNEY	G	6	180	HANSON	JH	9	268
HANDLEY	T	6	179	HANLEY	JN	14	138	HANNINGTON	G	7	164	HANSON	JL	8	144
HANDLEY	T	14	138	HANLEY	M	7	164	HANNINGTON	GP	7	164	HANSON	JO	11	161
HANDLEY	W	8	143	HANLEY	M	14	138	HANNON	J	10	96	HANSON	JW	8	144
HANDS	A	1	144	HANLEY	P	6	179	HANNON	M	11	161	HANSON	L	8	144
HANDS	A	6	179	HANLON	A	14	138	HANNON	RB	6	180	HANSON	M	13	202
HANDS	A	8	143	HANLON	AJ	4	172	HANNON	T	11	161	HANSON	RJ	6	180
HANDS	E	8	143	HANLON	F	4	172	HANRAHAN	J	3	70	HANSON	S	9	84
HANDS	F	6	179	HANLON	H	8	143	HANRAHAN	J	14	138	HANSON	S	14	138
HANDS	GB	6	179	HANLON	J	7	164	HANSBRO	J	8	143	HANSON	T	8	144
HANDS	GM	12	104	HANLON	J	11	161	HANSBRO	T	8	143	HANSON	T	8	144
HANDS	H	12	104	HANLON	JJ	6	179	HANSCOMBE	FJ	13	202	HANSON	T	9	268
HANDS	JE	6	179	HANLON	R	9	268	HANSCOMBE	HAW	1	145	HANSON	T	11	161
HANDS	LC	3	70	HANLON	T	3	70	HANSELL	A	8	143	HANSON	W	6	180
HANDS	WG	13	201	HANLON	W	4	172	HANSELL	GF	10	96	HANSON	W	6	180
HANDS	WJ	2	153	HANMER	EA	6	179	HANSELL	HW	2	154	HANSON	W	6	180
HANDS	WJ	6	179	HANMER	J	14	138	HANSELL	WC	4	172	HANSON	W	8	144
HANDS	WT	1	145	HANMER	SA	6	180	HANSELL	WJ	1	145	HANSON	W	9	268
HANDSCOMB	CW	2	153	HANMER	WA	6	180	HANSEN	E	1	145	HANSON	W	9	268
HANDSCOMB	HG	13	201	HANMORE	AE	10	96	HANSFORD	E	4	172	HANSON	WA	8	144
HANDSCOMB	JJ	13	201	HANN	AT	2	154	HANSFORD	EJ	2	154	HANSON	WG	10	97
HANDSCOMBE	J	5	162	HANN	AT	2	154	HANSFORD	GF	9	268	HANSON	WR	1	145
HANDY	EW	6	179	HANN	J	13	201	HANSGATE	J	8	143	HANTON	S	13	202
HANDY	GF	13	201	HANN	R	2	154	HANSHAW	W	11	161	HANVEY	HP	7	164
HANDY	R	1	145	HANN	W	4	172	HANSLIP	F	4	172	HANVEY	J	9	268

HANVEY	JR	7	164	HARDEN	GW	8	144	HARDING	EJ	1	146	HARDING	LP	4	173	HARDING	LP	4	173
HANWELL	AG	7	164	HARDEN	J	8	144	HARDING	F	4	173	HARDING	LR	12	105				
HARAGAN	JW	13	202	HARDEN	J	14	138	HARDING	F	4	173	HARDING	P	10	97				
HARBAGE	GF	12	318	HARDEN	JA	8	144	HARDING	F	10	97	HARDING	PA	5	162				
HARBEN	W	11	161	HARDEN	OG	5	162	HARDING	F	12	105	HARDING	RD	11	162				
HARBER	A	5	162	HARDEN	W	7	164	HARDING	F	12	105	HARDING	RJ	4	173				
HARBER	T	4	172	HARDER	E	4	172	HARDING	FA	4	173	HARDING	RJ	10	97				
HARBERD	SC	13	202	HARDER	H	4	172	HARDING	FA	5	162	HARDING	S	11	162				
HARBERT	HF	7	164	HARDESTY	RW	1	146	HARDING	FH	3	352	HARDING	S	12	105				
HARBERT	SW	10	97	HARDGRAVE	E	8	145	HARDING	FJ	5	162	HARDING	T	3	352				
HARBIDGE	GW	6	180	HARDGRAVE	E	8	145	HARDING	FS	5	162	HARDING	T	6	181				
HARBIN	EL	10	307	HARDGRAVE	F	8	145	HARDING	FW	4	173	HARDING	TG	13	202				
HARBIN	FFO	10	307	HARDGRAVE	H	8	145	HARDING	FW	10	97	HARDING	TJ	12	105				
HARBORNE	AT	6	180	HARDHAM	A	10	97	HARDING	G	2	154	HARDING	TW	1	146				
HARBORNE	W	6	180	HARDHAM	E	10	97	HARDING	G	6	181	HARDING	V	10	308				
HARBOROW	EA	3	70	HARDHAM	H	10	97	HARDING	G	7	165	HARDING	W	1	146				
HARBOTTLE	JT	10	97	HARDIE	A	7	164	HARDING	G	12	105	HARDING	W	4	173				
HARBOUR	A	10	307	HARDIE	HG	4	172	HARDING	G	14	139	HARDING	W	7	165				
HARBOUR	JW	10	307	HARDIE	PA	7	164	HARDING	GE	7	165	HARDING	W	8	145				
HARBOUR	WD	1	145	HARDIMAN	EM	7	164	HARDING	GF	1	146	HARDING	WA	1	146				
HARBRIDGE	G	11	161	HARDIMAN	WG	7	164	HARDING	GFE	5	162	HARDING	WHR	12	105				
HARBRIDGE	RC	1	145	HARDIMAN	WJ	7	165	HARDING	GW	8	145	HARDING	WJ	2	154				
HARBRIDGE	T	11	161	HARDIMAN	WT	7	165	HARDING	H	2	154	HARDINGHAM	V	8	145				
HARBRON	E	9	84	HARDIMENT	AB	1	146	HARDING	H	2	154	HARDISTY	E	8	145				
HARBRON	W	9	84	HARDING	A	1	146	HARDING	H	2	154	HARDISTY	J	9	85				
HARBUT	AGR	4	172	HARDING	A	3	70	HARDING	H	4	173	HARDISTY	WH	8	145				
HARBUTT	L	1	146	HARDING	A	4	172	HARDING	H	5	162	HARDLEY	BF	13	202				
HARBUTT	WE	7	164	HARDING	A	6	181	HARDING	H	7	165	HARDMAN	A	14	139				
HARCKHAM	C	10	97	HARDING	A	6	181	HARDING	H	13	202	HARDMAN	G	11	162				
HARCOMBE	FD	13	202	HARDING	A	7	165	HARDING	HA	13	202	HARDMAN	GF	6	181				
HARCOMBE	FW	13	202	HARDING	A	11	162	HARDING	HJ	2	154	HARDMAN	GR	14	139				
HARCOURT	JC	10	307	HARDING	A	12	105	HARDING	HJ	4	173	HARDMAN	GW	14	139				
HARCOURT	W	12	104	HARDING	A	12	105	HARDING	HJ	12	105	HARDMAN	H	9	85				
HARCOURT	WR	12	104	HARDING	AE	10	97	HARDING	HV	4	173	HARDMAN	J	14	139				
HARDAKER	A	9	84	HARDING	AG	4	173	HARDING	HW	7	165	HARDMAN	J	14	139				
HARDAKER	H	9	84	HARDING	AGL	2	154	HARDING	J	1	146	HARDMAN	J	14	139				
HARDAKER	H	9	268	HARDING	AJ	2	154	HARDING	J	2	154	HARDMAN	JH	11	162				
HARDAKER	JH	9	85	HARDING	AJ	7	165	HARDING	J	2	154	HARDMAN	JJ	11	162				
HARDAKER	P	8	144	HARDING	AJ	12	105	HARDING	J	4	173	HARDMAN	JM	9	268				
HARDCASTLE	D	8	144	HARDING	AP	2	154	HARDING	J	6	181	HARDMAN	RJ	11	162				
HARDCASTLE	E	8	144	HARDING	B	12	105	HARDING	J	7	165	HARDMAN	T	11	162				
HARDCASTLE	G	8	144	HARDING	C	6	181	HARDING	J	8	145	HARDMAN	W	10	308				
HARDCASTLE	GL	1	146	HARDING	C	11	161	HARDING	J	10	97	HARDMAN	W	11	162				
HARDCASTLE	GW	8	144	HARDING	CE	5	162	HARDING	J	10	97	HARDMAN	W	14	139				
HARDCASTLE	H	7	164	HARDING	CF	6	181	HARDING	J	13	202	HARDMAN	W	14	139				
HARDCASTLE	H	8	144	HARDING	CH	4	173	HARDING	JB	12	105	HARDS	AN	6	181				
HARDCASTLE	J	9	268	HARDING	CJ	10	97	HARDING	JC	2	154	HARDS	CA	13	203				
HARDCASTLE	JF	1	146	HARDING	D	11	161	HARDING	JE	7	165	HARDS	F	4	173				
HARDCASTLE	M	7	164	HARDING	E	2	154	HARDING	JH	10	307	HARDS	J	13	203				
HARDCASTLE	S	8	144	HARDING	E	13	202	HARDING	JT	10	97	HARDS	W	6	181				
HARDCASTLE	T	8	144	HARDING	E	13	202	HARDING	JW	6	181	HARDWARE	AI	6	181				
HARDCASTLE	W	8	144	HARDING	EA	4	173	HARDING	JW	12	318	HARDWARE	T	6	181				
HARDCASTLE	W	8	144	HARDING	EE	4	173	HARDING	L	2	154	HARDWARE	VI	6	181				
HARDEE	H	1	146	HARDING	EG	6	181	HARDING	L	4	173	HARDWICK	A	12	105				
HARDEN	AL	5	162	HARDING	EH	13	202	HARDING	L	13	202	HARDWICK	ES	9	85				

HARDWICK	F	14	139	HARDY	HR	4	174	HARFIELD	GH	10	308	HARKNESS	D	5	163
HARDWICK	FG	12	105	HARDY	HW	3	352	HARFIELD	J	7	165	HARKNESS	W	9	269
HARDWICK	FT	5	162	HARDY	J	2	155	HARFIELD	JF	10	308	HARKNETT	GM	4	174
HARDWICK	H	5	162	HARDY	J	9	269	HARFIELD	JG	4	174	HARLAND	AJ	3	352
HARDWICK	H	9	85	HARDY	J	9	269	HARFIELD	S	4	174	HARLAND	C	13	203
HARDWICK	HL	12	105	HARDY	J	9	269	HARFORD	F	10	308	HARLAND	EG	13	203
HARDWICK	HS	5	162	HARDY	J	14	139	HARFORD	H	10	308	HARLAND	G	8	146
HARDWICK	J	9	85	HARDY	J	14	139	HARFORD	JH	6	182	HARLAND	GJ	4	174
HARDWICK	JA	9	268	HARDY	JA	11	162	HARFORD	R	10	308	HARLAND	PC	3	352
HARDWICK	JH	12	318	HARDY	JE	11	162	HARFORD	T	9	85	HARLAND	T	8	146
HARDWICK	P	6	181	HARDY	JT	11	162	HARFORD	W	13	203	HARLE	G	7	166
HARDWICK	RG	12	105	HARDY	JT	11	162	HARFORD	W	14	139	HARLE	SC	10	98
HARDWICK	S	9	85	HARDY	L	8	145	HARGRAVE	A	8	145	HARLEY	A	7	166
HARDWICK	T	3	352	HARDY	N	9	387	HARGRAVE	C	9	85	HARLEY	AG	2	155
HARDWICK	T	9	269	HARDY	R	2	155	HARGRAVE	J	8	145	HARLEY	AJ	10	98
HARDWICK	W	6	181	HARDY	S	6	181	HARGRAVES	J	8	145	HARLEY	E	7	166
HARDY	A	3	352	HARDY	T	11	162	HARGREAVES	A	8	145	HARLEY	E	13	203
HARDY	A	4	173	HARDY	T	14	139	HARGREAVES	A	9	269	HARLEY	EA	4	174
HARDY	A	4	173	HARDY	TC	1	146	HARGREAVES	A	11	163	HARLEY	F	4	174
HARDY	A	6	181	HARDY	W	1	146	HARGREAVES	A	14	139	HARLEY	G	12	318
HARDY	A	7	165	HARDY	W	8	145	HARGREAVES	A	14	139	HARLEY	GA	5	163
HARDY	A	11	162	HARDY	W	8	145	HARGREAVES	ARW	7	166	HARLEY	GE	2	155
HARDY	A	13	203	HARDY	W	11	162	HARGREAVES	B	8	145	HARLEY	GT	6	182
HARDY	AC	2	154	HARDY	WA	8	145	HARGREAVES	C	11	163	HARLEY	H	6	182
HARDY	AHJ	13	203	HARDY	WH	6	182	HARGREAVES	CH	11	163	HARLEY	J	13	203
HARDY	AW	7	165	HARDY	WH	11	162	HARGREAVES	E	11	163	HARLEY	JH	2	155
HARDY	B	3	70	HARDY	WJ	13	203	HARGREAVES	E	11	163	HARLEY	JW	9	269
HARDY	B	4	173	HARE	A	10	97	HARGREAVES	F	14	140	HARLEY	LC	7	166
HARDY	B	8	145	HARE	A	12	106	HARGREAVES	G	8	146	HARLEY	MJ	13	203
HARDY	C	5	162	HARE	AH	1	146	HARGREAVES	H	8	146	HARLEY	RA	2	155
HARDY	CE	12	105	HARE	AM	2	155	HARGREAVES	H	9	269	HARLEY	RG	3	352
HARDY	CE	12	105	HARE	BA	13	203	HARGREAVES	HJ	2	155	HARLEY	SR	2	155
HARDY	CJ	10	97	HARE	CW	7	165	HARGREAVES	J	11	163	HARLEY	TP	12	318
HARDY	CJ	13	203	HARE	EJ	10	308	HARGREAVES	JJ	8	146	HARLEY	W	12	318
HARDY	CT	11	162	HARE	G	11	162	HARGREAVES	JR	8	146	HARLEY	WG	13	204
HARDY	CW	13	203	HARE	GA	10	308	HARGREAVES	L	9	269	HARLOTT	AC	12	106
HARDY	E	11	162	HARE	J	7	165	HARGREAVES	W	8	146	HARLOW	A	5	163
HARDY	E	14	139	HARE	JT	10	98	HARGREAVES	W	8	146	HARLOW	A	12	106
HARDY	E	14	139	HARE	JW	3	70	HARGREAVES	W	9	85	HARLOW	A	12	106
HARDY	F	12	318	HARE	OG	2	155	HARGREAVES	W	9	85	HARLOW	C	12	106
HARDY	G	7	165	HARE	PA	10	308	HARGREAVES	W	9	269	HARLOW	E	12	106
HARDY	G	13	203	HARE	R	1	146	HARGREAVES	W	11	163	HARLOW	GH	11	163
HARDY	G	14	139	HARE	R	7	165	HARGREAVES	WE	11	163	HARLOW	HA	12	106
HARDY	GF	13	203	HARE	RE	5	162	HARGREAVES	WH	9	85	HARLOW	HJ	12	106
HARDY	GM	13	203	HARE	T	1	146	HARGREAVES	WH	9	269	HARLOW	HJ	13	204
HARDY	GW	10	97	HARE	T	11	163	HARGREAVES	WH	14	140	HARLOW	HL	12	106
HARDY	GW	12	105	HARE	W	5	162	HARKER	A	8	146	HARLOW	LG	12	106
HARDY	H	2	155	HARE	W	13	203	HARKER	A	9	85	HARLOW	S	12	106
HARDY	H	8	145	HARE	WE	7	165	HARKER	A	14	140	HARLOW	SG	12	106
HARDY	H	8	145	HARE	WJ	13	203	HARKER	H	8	146	HARLOW	V	12	318
HARDY	H	9	269	HARE	WW	2	155	HARKER	HJ	8	146	HARLOW	WAG	13	204
HARDY	H	9	269	HARFFY	T	7	165	HARKER	J	9	269	HARLOW	WH	7	166
HARDY	HA	9	387	HARFIELD	A	2	155	HARKER	R	14	140	HARMAN	A	7	166
HARDY	HD	8	145	HARFIELD	E	4	174	HARKIN	JE	10	98	HARMAN	A	7	166
HARDY	HF	13	203	HARFIELD	F	10	308	HARKIN	R	10	308	HARMAN	A	13	204

HARMAN	AD	10	98	HARNETTY	TC	1	147	HARPER	J	4	174	HARRAWAY	S	7	167
HARMAN	AE	10	98	HARNEY	G	11	163	HARPER	J	6	182	HARRE	W	13	204
HARMAN	AH	4	174	HARNEY	J	3	352	HARPER	J	12	106	HARRIET	SH	14	140
HARMAN	AM	4	174	HARNEY	J	9	85	HARPER	J	14	140	HARRIGAN	G	13	204
HARMAN	AR	7	166	HARNEY	J	9	387	HARPER	JA	1	147	HARRIGAN	J	3	71
HARMAN	CB	10	98	HARNEY	JC	9	85	HARPER	JJ	6	182	HARRIGAN	T	3	71
HARMAN	E	1	146	HARNEY	T	9	85	HARPER	JL	6	182	HARRIGAN	W	13	204
HARMAN	E	3	70	HARNEY	W	9	387	HARPER	JR	11	163	HARRINGTON	A	4	175
HARMAN	E	13	204	HARNWELL	EA	12	318	HARPER	JT	6	182	HARRINGTON	A	4	175
HARMAN	G	5	163	HAROLD	AGR	13	204	HARPER	JT	11	163	HARRINGTON	AF	1	148
HARMAN	H	3	71	HAROLD	CE	1	147	HARPER	ME	1	147	HARRINGTON	AR	3	71
HARMAN	L	5	163	HAROLD	JR	8	146	HARPER	R	12	107	HARRINGTON	AW	3	71
HARMAN	SJ	3	352	HAROLD	T	9	86	HARPER	RB	10	98	HARRINGTON	B	8	146
HARMAN	V	1	147	HAROLD	W	4	175	HARPER	RC	5	163	HARRINGTON	C	1	148
HARMAN	W	10	98	HARPER	A	8	146	HARPER	RS	6	182	HARRINGTON	C	10	308
HARMAN	WH	1	147	HARPER	A	12	106	HARPER	RW	12	107	HARRINGTON	CH	11	163
HARMAN	WH	3	71	HARPER	AH	3	71	HARPER	RW	13	204	HARRINGTON	D	11	164
HARMAN	WJ	13	204	HARPER	AV	1	147	HARPER	S	10	98	HARRINGTON	EV	2	155
HARMAN	WT	1	147	HARPER	B	13	204	HARPER	S	13	204	HARRINGTON	F	4	175
HARMER	A	7	166	HARPER	C	12	106	HARPER	T	6	182	HARRINGTON	FH	3	71
HARMER	AW	7	166	HARPER	C	13	204	HARPER	T	11	163	HARRINGTON	FJ	3	71
HARMER	C	7	166	HARPER	CE	14	140	HARPER	T	11	163	HARRINGTON	G	2	155
HARMER	FA	7	166	HARPER	D	1	147	HARPER	T	14	140	HARRINGTON	HJ	13	205
HARMER	HT	7	166	HARPER	E	1	147	HARPER	TE	9	86	HARRINGTON	HS	7	167
HARMER	R	9	269	HARPER	E	1	147	HARPER	TE	10	98	HARRINGTON	J	14	140
HARMER	T	4	174	HARPER	E	1	147	HARPER	TWJ	7	167	HARRINGTON	JH	4	175
HARMER	TH	1	147	HARPER	E	14	140	HARPER	V	11	163	HARRINGTON	JRW	10	308
HARMER	TJ	1	147	HARPER	EA	12	106	HARPER	W	1	147	HARRINGTON	JS	4	175
HARMER	W	1	147	HARPER	EB	10	98	HARPER	W	2	155	HARRINGTON	JT	1	148
HARMON	LH	3	352	HARPER	EL	6	182	HARPER	W	2	155	HARRINGTON	LE	10	99
HARMS	C	4	174	HARPER	F	6	182	HARPER	W	4	175	HARRINGTON	P	3	352
HARMS	SA	7	166	HARPER	F	8	146	HARPER	W	5	163	HARRINGTON	R	3	71
HARMS	ST	7	166	HARPER	FG	7	166	HARPER	W	6	182	HARRINGTON	RA	4	175
HARMS	WD	10	98	HARPER	FJ	4	174	HARPER	W	14	140	HARRINGTON	SA	13	205
HARMSTON	W	9	269	HARPER	G	4	174	HARPER	W	14	140	HARRINGTON	SW	13	205
HARMSWORTH	FW	5	163	HARPER	G	6	182	HARPER	W	14	140	HARRINGTON	T	13	205
HARMSWORTH	L	9	85	HARPER	G	11	163	HARPER	WC	5	163	HARRINGTON	WJ	10	99
HARMSWORTH	WJ	13	204	HARPER	G	12	106	HARPER	WE	1	148	HARRINGTON	WR	6	183
HARNDEN	AA	10	98	HARPER	GH	6	182	HARPER	WG	1	148	HARRIOTT	HR	3	353
HARNDEN	AA	10	98	HARPER	GH	12	106	HARPER	WH	12	107	HARRIS	A	2	155
HARNDEN	H	10	98	HARPER	GW	12	106	HARPER	WJ	6	183	HARRIS	A	2	155
HARNDEN	HH	10	308	HARPER	H	4	174	HARPER	WS	1	148	HARRIS	A	3	71
HARNDEN	HWJ	10	98	HARPER	H	6	182	HARPER	WT	13	204	HARRIS	A	5	163
HARNDEN	JL	7	166	HARPER	H	6	182	HARPHAM	G	11	163	HARRIS	A	5	163
HARNDEN	WG	7	166	HARPER	H	6	182	HARPIN	AP	12	107	HARRIS	A	5	163
HARNESS	F	10	98	HARPER	H	7	167	HARPIN	CE	12	107	HARRIS	A	5	163
HARNETT	CJ	4	174	HARPER	H	8	146	HARPIN	RE	12	107	HARRIS	A	6	183
HARNETT	G	3	71	HARPER	H	10	308	HARPIN	W	12	107	HARRIS	A	6	183
HARNETT	GJ	4	174	HARPER	H	12	106	HARPUR	W	12	107	HARRIS	A	7	167
HARNETT	HH	10	308	HARPER	H	14	140	HARRADINE	A	12	107	HARRIS	A	7	167
HARNETT	JL	4	174	HARPER	HJ	5	163	HARRALD	FC	12	107	HARRIS	A	7	167
HARNETT	JP	3	71	HARPER	HJ	6	182	HARRALD	GW	12	107	HARRIS	A	9	86
HARNETTY	EE	1	147	HARPER	HR	1	147	HARRALD	KM	13	204	HARRIS	A	12	318
HARNETTY	EJ	1	147	HARPER	HR	13	204	HARRALD	WJ	13	204	HARRIS	A	13	205
HARNETTY	J	1	147	HARPER	HS	13	204	HARRAP	W	9	86	HARRIS	A	13	205

HARRIS	AA	4	175	HARRIS	CH	13	205	HARRIS	FC	13	205	HARRIS	H	7	168				
HARRIS	AB	9	387	HARRIS	CJ	1	148	HARRIS	FE	4	176	HARRIS	H	7	168				
HARRIS	AB	13	205	HARRIS	CJ	7	167	HARRIS	FG	2	156	HARRIS	H	7	168				
HARRIS	AE	5	163	HARRIS	CL	12	318	HARRIS	FG	3	71	HARRIS	H	7	168				
HARRIS	AF	1	148	HARRIS	CS	7	167	HARRIS	FG	4	176	HARRIS	H	8	146				
HARRIS	AF	6	183	HARRIS	CW	1	148	HARRIS	FH	4	176	HARRIS	H	8	146				
HARRIS	AG	4	175	HARRIS	CW	2	156	HARRIS	FJ	1	149	HARRIS	H	10	309				
HARRIS	AG	4	175	HARRIS	CW	4	175	HARRIS	FJ	3	353	HARRIS	H	11	164				
HARRIS	AG	7	167	HARRIS	D	1	148	HARRIS	FJ	13	205	HARRIS	H	11	164				
HARRIS	AG	12	318	HARRIS	D	8	146	HARRIS	FJG	7	168	HARRIS	H	12	107				
HARRIS	AG	13	205	HARRIS	D	13	205	HARRIS	FN	13	206	HARRIS	H	12	319				
HARRIS	AH	2	156	HARRIS	E	5	163	HARRIS	FT	10	308	HARRIS	H	13	206				
HARRIS	AH	4	175	HARRIS	E	5	163	HARRIS	FW	5	164	HARRIS	HA	4	176				
HARRIS	AH	4	175	HARRIS	E	5	163	HARRIS	FW	7	168	HARRIS	HA	7	168				
HARRIS	AH	6	183	HARRIS	E	7	167	HARRIS	FW	9	86	HARRIS	HB	10	99				
HARRIS	AH	6	183	HARRIS	E	9	86	HARRIS	FW	9	269	HARRIS	HE	10	99				
HARRIS	AJ	3	353	HARRIS	E	10	309	HARRIS	FW	9	387	HARRIS	HG	1	149				
HARRIS	AJ	6	183	HARRIS	E	11	164	HARRIS	G	1	149	HARRIS	HJ	7	168				
HARRIS	AJ	6	183	HARRIS	E	13	205	HARRIS	G	1	149	HARRIS	HN	11	164				
HARRIS	AJ	6	183	HARRIS	EA	1	148	HARRIS	G	3	71	HARRIS	HR	11	164				
HARRIS	AJ	12	107	HARRIS	EA	2	156	HARRIS	G	3	353	HARRIS	HW	3	71				
HARRIS	AL	3	71	HARRIS	EA	3	353	HARRIS	G	5	164	HARRIS	J	1	149				
HARRIS	AL	4	175	HARRIS	ED	13	205	HARRIS	G	6	183	HARRIS	J	1	149				
HARRIS	AL	7	167	HARRIS	EE	1	148	HARRIS	G	11	164	HARRIS	J	2	156				
HARRIS	AL	12	107	HARRIS	EE	4	176	HARRIS	G	12	107	HARRIS	J	2	156				
HARRIS	AN	2	156	HARRIS	EE	12	107	HARRIS	G	12	318	HARRIS	J	2	156				
HARRIS	AR	10	308	HARRIS	EF	5	163	HARRIS	G	12	422	HARRIS	J	3	71				
HARRIS	AT	1	148	HARRIS	EG	6	183	HARRIS	G	14	140	HARRIS	J	4	176				
HARRIS	AW	1	148	HARRIS	EJ	5	163	HARRIS	GA	14	140	HARRIS	J	4	176				
HARRIS	AW	1	148	HARRIS	EJ	7	167	HARRIS	GB	6	183	HARRIS	J	5	164				
HARRIS	AW	1	148	HARRIS	EK	12	318	HARRIS	GF	2	156	HARRIS	J	5	164				
HARRIS	AW	4	175	HARRIS	EO	7	167	HARRIS	GF	6	183	HARRIS	J	5	164				
HARRIS	AW	14	140	HARRIS	EW	1	149	HARRIS	GFW	12	318	HARRIS	J	5	164				
HARRIS	B	2	156	HARRIS	EWS	2	156	HARRIS	GH	3	353	HARRIS	J	6	184				
HARRIS	B	13	205	HARRIS	F	1	149	HARRIS	GH	3	353	HARRIS	J	6	184				
HARRIS	BD	13	205	HARRIS	F	2	156	HARRIS	GH	6	184	HARRIS	J	6	184				
HARRIS	BG	4	175	HARRIS	F	3	353	HARRIS	GH	7	168	HARRIS	J	6	184				
HARRIS	C	1	148	HARRIS	F	4	176	HARRIS	GH	10	99	HARRIS	J	7	168				
HARRIS	C	2	156	HARRIS	F	4	176	HARRIS	GH	12	107	HARRIS	J	8	146				
HARRIS	C	4	175	HARRIS	F	4	176	HARRIS	GH	14	140	HARRIS	J	9	86				
HARRIS	C	4	175	HARRIS	F	5	164	HARRIS	GJ	2	156	HARRIS	J	9	269				
HARRIS	C	6	183	HARRIS	F	5	164	HARRIS	GL	3	353	HARRIS	J	9	269				
HARRIS	C	10	99	HARRIS	F	5	164	HARRIS	GR	1	149	HARRIS	J	10	99				
HARRIS	C	13	205	HARRIS	F	6	183	HARRIS	GT	1	149	HARRIS	J	11	164				
HARRIS	CD	3	353	HARRIS	F	7	167	HARRIS	GT	7	168	HARRIS	J	12	107				
HARRIS	CE	7	167	HARRIS	F	7	167	HARRIS	GW	1	149	HARRIS	J	12	107				
HARRIS	CE	13	205	HARRIS	F	7	168	HARRIS	GW	4	176	HARRIS	J	13	206				
HARRIS	CH	1	148	HARRIS	F	11	164	HARRIS	GW	5	164	HARRIS	J	13	206				
HARRIS	CH	1	148	HARRIS	F	12	107	HARRIS	GWH	3	71	HARRIS	J	14	140				
HARRIS	CH	3	71	HARRIS	F	12	318	HARRIS	H	4	176	HARRIS	JA	4	176				
HARRIS	CH	4	175	HARRIS	F	12	318	HARRIS	H	4	176	HARRIS	JC	6	184				
HARRIS	CH	5	163	HARRIS	F	13	205	HARRIS	H	5	164	HARRIS	JCR	4	176				
HARRIS	CH	10	99	HARRIS	F	13	205	HARRIS	H	6	183	HARRIS	JD	5	164				
HARRIS	CH	10	99	HARRIS	FAJ	12	318	HARRIS	H	6	184	HARRIS	JD	6	184				
HARRIS	CH	11	164	HARRIS	FC	6	183	HARRIS	H	6	184	HARRIS	JE	3	72				

HARRIS	JF	12	319	HARRIS	ST	6	184	HARRIS	WH	7	169	HARRISON	C	6	185
HARRIS	JG	12	319	HARRIS	STG	4	177	HARRIS	WH	10	99	HARRISON	C	6	185
HARRIS	JG	13	206	HARRIS	SV	2	156	HARRIS	WH	10	309	HARRISON	C	8	147
HARRIS	JH	4	176	HARRIS	T	5	164	HARRIS	WH	10	309	HARRISON	C	9	86
HARRIS	JL	4	176	HARRIS	T	6	184	HARRIS	WH	10	309	HARRISON	C	11	164
HARRIS	JS	12	319	HARRIS	T	7	169	HARRIS	WH	13	206	HARRISON	CA	6	185
HARRIS	JT	6	184	HARRIS	T	8	146	HARRIS	WHG	7	169	HARRISON	CA	10	99
HARRIS	JT	6	184	HARRIS	T	8	146	HARRIS	WJ	1	149	HARRISON	CA	11	164
HARRIS	JT	7	168	HARRIS	T	8	146	HARRIS	WJ	3	353	HARRISON	CE	9	86
HARRIS	JW	11	164	HARRIS	T	10	99	HARRIS	WJ	4	177	HARRISON	CE	11	164
HARRIS	L	2	156	HARRIS	T	12	319	HARRIS	WJ	5	165	HARRISON	CE	13	206
HARRIS	L	3	72	HARRIS	TE	6	184	HARRIS	WJ	7	169	HARRISON	CW	4	177
HARRIS	L	4	176	HARRIS	TF	12	319	HARRIS	WJ	10	99	HARRISON	D	9	86
HARRIS	L	5	164	HARRIS	TH	7	169	HARRIS	WJ	13	206	HARRISON	D	10	99
HARRIS	L	5	164	HARRIS	TL	12	107	HARRIS	WL	10	99	HARRISON	D	11	164
HARRIS	L	6	184	HARRIS	TW	1	149	HARRIS	WS	4	177	HARRISON	DJ	9	270
HARRIS	L	10	309	HARRIS	TW	14	141	HARRIS	WT	7	169	HARRISON	E	7	169
HARRIS	LF	4	176	HARRIS	VC	9	86	HARRIS	WT	13	206	HARRISON	E	9	86
HARRIS	LJ	10	99	HARRIS	W	2	156	HARRIS	WW	6	185	HARRISON	E	9	86
HARRIS	M	1	149	HARRIS	W	2	157	HARRISON		6	185	HARRISON	E	9	86
HARRIS	M	6	184	HARRIS	W	2	157	HARRISON	A	6	185	HARRISON	E	9	387
HARRIS	MA	1	149	HARRIS	W	2	157	HARRISON	A	6	185	HARRISON	E	10	100
HARRIS	ME	12	319	HARRIS	W	3	72	HARRISON	A	6	185	HARRISON	E	14	141
HARRIS	MT	13	206	HARRIS	W	3	353	HARRISON	A	7	169	HARRISON	EE	4	177
HARRIS	P	13	206	HARRIS	W	4	177	HARRISON	A	7	169	HARRISON	EGH	2	157
HARRIS	PA	7	168	HARRIS	W	4	177	HARRISON	A	7	169	HARRISON	EH	12	108
HARRIS	PC	4	176	HARRIS	W	4	177	HARRISON	A	7	170	HARRISON	EJ	6	185
HARRIS	PEH	10	99	HARRIS	W	5	164	HARRISON	A	8	147	HARRISON	EW	2	157
HARRIS	PJ	5	164	HARRIS	W	5	164	HARRISON	A	8	147	HARRISON	F	4	177
HARRIS	R	3	353	HARRIS	W	5	164	HARRISON	A	8	147	HARRISON	F	6	185
HARRIS	R	7	168	HARRIS	W	5	164	HARRISON	A	9	86	HARRISON	F	8	147
HARRIS	R	11	164	HARRIS	W	5	165	HARRISON	A	9	86	HARRISON	F	9	387
HARRIS	RA	4	176	HARRIS	W	6	185	HARRISON	A	9	270	HARRISON	F	10	309
HARRIS	RA	4	177	HARRIS	W	6	185	HARRISON	A	11	164	HARRISON	F	11	164
HARRIS	RB	4	177	HARRIS	W	6	185	HARRISON	A	11	422	HARRISON	F	12	108
HARRIS	RC	2	156	HARRIS	W	6	185	HARRISON	A	12	319	HARRISON	F	13	206
HARRIS	RC	4	177	HARRIS	W	7	169	HARRISON	A	14	141	HARRISON	F	14	141
HARRIS	RG	10	99	HARRIS	W	7	169	HARRISON	AB	4	177	HARRISON	FA	6	185
HARRIS	RH	3	353	HARRIS	W	7	169	HARRISON	AC	8	147	HARRISON	FA	13	207
HARRIS	RH	4	177	HARRIS	W	7	169	HARRISON	AD	6	185	HARRISON	FC	12	319
HARRIS	RS	7	168	HARRIS	W	9	269	HARRISON	AE	1	149	HARRISON	FE	6	186
HARRIS	RT	7	168	HARRIS	W	13	206	HARRISON	AE	3	353	HARRISON	FH	11	165
HARRIS	RW	6	184	HARRIS	W	14	141	HARRISON	AE	12	319	HARRISON	FW	3	353
HARRIS	RW	7	168	HARRIS	WA	13	206	HARRISON	AG	7	169	HARRISON	G	4	177
HARRIS	S	3	72	HARRIS	WC	1	149	HARRISON	AG	10	309	HARRISON	G	6	186
HARRIS	S	3	353	HARRIS	WC	7	169	HARRISON	AG	12	319	HARRISON	G	6	186
HARRIS	S	6	184	HARRIS	WE	10	99	HARRISON	AJ	4	177	HARRISON	G	8	147
HARRIS	S	6	184	HARRIS	WE	13	206	HARRISON	AT	6	185	HARRISON	G	8	147
HARRIS	S	7	169	HARRIS	WF	10	99	HARRISON	B	8	147	HARRISON	G	9	86
HARRIS	S	12	319	HARRIS	WG	6	185	HARRISON	B	9	86	HARRISON	G	9	86
HARRIS	SA	2	156	HARRIS	WG	6	185	HARRISON	B	12	108	HARRISON	G	9	87
HARRIS	SA	7	168	HARRIS	WG	13	206	HARRISON	B	13	206	HARRISON	G	14	141
HARRIS	SF	1	149	HARRIS	WH	3	353	HARRISON	BA	5	165	HARRISON	G	14	141
HARRIS	SF	13	206	HARRIS	WH	6	185	HARRISON	C	1	150	HARRISON	G	14	141
HARRIS	SH	4	177	HARRIS	WH	7	169	HARRISON	C	3	72	HARRISON	GA	9	270

HARRISON	GE	8	147	HARRISON	J	14	141	HARRISON	TS	12	319	HARROW	F	7	170
HARRISON	GG	8	147	HARRISON	J	14	141	HARRISON	W	1	150	HARROW	JE	7	170
HARRISON	GJ	6	186	HARRISON	J	14	141	HARRISON	W	4	178	HARROWELL	HE	1	150
HARRISON	GR	4	177	HARRISON	J	14	141	HARRISON	W	5	165	HARROWELL	LJ	3	72
HARRISON	GR	6	186	HARRISON	JA	1	150	HARRISON	W	5	165	HARROWELL	LS	3	72
HARRISON	GR	8	147	HARRISON	JA	4	178	HARRISON	W	6	186	HARROWELL	M	1	150
HARRISON	GR	13	207	HARRISON	JA	6	186	HARRISON	W	8	148	HARROWELL	WJ	1	150
HARRISON	GT	9	87	HARRISON	JB	2	157	HARRISON	W	8	148	HARROWSMITH	G	14	142
HARRISON	GW	6	186	HARRISON	JE	6	186	HARRISON	W	8	148	HARRUP	F	5	165
HARRISON	GW	8	147	HARRISON	JH	1	150	HARRISON	W	8	148	HARRY	DE	10	100
HARRISON	GW	8	147	HARRISON	JH	9	87	HARRISON	W	9	87	HARRY	ES	10	100
HARRISON	GW	9	87	HARRISON	JH	14	141	HARRISON	W	9	270	HARRY	JM	10	100
HARRISON	H	1	150	HARRISON	JJ	6	186	HARRISON	W	12	319	HARRY	WG	2	157
HARRISON	H	2	157	HARRISON	JJ	9	270	HARRISON	W	14	142	HARRYMAN	F	13	207
HARRISON	H	6	186	HARRISON	JL	10	100	HARRISON	W	14	142	HARRYMAN	S	13	207
HARRISON	H	6	186	HARRISON	JT	4	178	HARRISON	WE	8	148	HARSANT	A	7	170
HARRISON	H	6	186	HARRISON	JW	5	165	HARRISON	WF	4	178	HARSLETT	F	2	157
HARRISON	H	7	170	HARRISON	JW	9	87	HARRISON	WG	1	150	HARSTON	CA	1	150
HARRISON	H	8	147	HARRISON	JW	9	270	HARRISON	WG	4	178	HART	A	2	157
HARRISON	H	8	147	HARRISON	JW	9	270	HARRISON	WG	6	186	HART	A	5	165
HARRISON	H	9	87	HARRISON	JW	9	387	HARRISON	WG	8	148	HART	AA	2	157
HARRISON	H	9	87	HARRISON	JWG	2	157	HARRISON	WG	13	207	HART	AC	10	100
HARRISON	H	9	87	HARRISON	L	12	108	HARRISON	WH	4	178	HART	AG	7	170
HARRISON	H	9	270	HARRISON	LJ	2	157	HARRISON	WH	11	165	HART	AG	10	309
HARRISON	H	10	100	HARRISON	LJ	11	165	HARRISON	WH	13	207	HART	AH	1	150
HARRISON	H	11	165	HARRISON	LJ	12	319	HARRISON	WJ	1	150	HART	AJ	5	165
HARRISON	H	11	165	HARRISON	M	1	150	HARRISON	WJ	4	178	HART	AJ	12	108
HARRISON	H	12	319	HARRISON	NA	11	165	HARRISON	WJ	10	100	HART	AJ	12	319
HARRISON	H	14	141	HARRISON	O	8	147	HARRISS	FG	5	165	HART	C	5	165
HARRISON	HE	11	165	HARRISON	P	2	157	HARRISS	J	9	270	HART	C	11	166
HARRISON	HE	13	207	HARRISON	P	6	186	HARRISS	TH	5	165	HART	C	12	108
HARRISON	HJ	6	186	HARRISON	P	9	87	HARROD	J	9	87	HART	CA	13	207
HARRISON	HW	2	157	HARRISON	P	9	87	HARROLD	AH	5	165	HART	CJ	7	170
HARRISON	J	1	150	HARRISON	P	12	319	HARROLD	C	7	170	HART	CS	12	319
HARRISON	J	1	150	HARRISON	R	6	187	HARROLD	H	6	187	HART	CS	12	320
HARRISON	J	3	354	HARRISON	R	7	170	HARROLD	HW	6	187	HART	CW	3	72
HARRISON	J	4	177	HARRISON	R	11	165	HARROLD	RC	2	157	HART	CW	4	178
HARRISON	J	6	186	HARRISON	R	14	141	HARROLD	RE	2	157	HART	CW	5	165
HARRISON	J	7	170	HARRISON	R	14	141	HARROLD	TJH	9	270	HART	E	4	178
HARRISON	J	8	147	HARRISON	RA	14	142	HARROLD	W	8	148	HART	E	8	148
HARRISON	J	8	147	HARRISON	RC	2	157	HARROLD	WJ	3	72	HART	E	10	100
HARRISON	J	8	147	HARRISON	RH	7	170	HARROP	A	11	165	HART	EF	3	72
HARRISON	J	9	87	HARRISON	RJ	7	170	HARROP	CH	11	165	HART	EH	8	148
HARRISON	J	9	87	HARRISON	RS	13	207	HARROP	CH	14	142	HART	ES	3	72
HARRISON	J	9	270	HARRISON	S	4	178	HARROP	F	11	165	HART	F	5	165
HARRISON	J	9	270	HARRISON	S	8	148	HARROP	H	11	165	HART	F	11	166
HARRISON	J	9	270	HARRISON	S	12	108	HARROP	HR	11	166	HART	F	11	166
HARRISON	J	10	100	HARRISON	S	12	319	HARROP	J	11	165	HART	F	12	320
HARRISON	J	11	165	HARRISON	SH	11	165	HARROP	JA	11	166	HART	F	13	207
HARRISON	J	11	165	HARRISON	SW	14	142	HARROP	JE	11	166	HART	FG	3	72
HARRISON	J	11	165	HARRISON	T	11	165	HARROP	JH	14	142	HART	FG	10	100
HARRISON	J	12	319	HARRISON	T	14	142	HARROP	S	11	166	HART	FH	7	170
HARRISON	J	14	141	HARRISON	TA	4	178	HARROP	T	11	166	HART	FJ	3	72
HARRISON	J	14	141	HARRISON	TH	9	87	HARROP	WA	11	166	HART	FN	13	207
HARRISON	J	14	141	HARRISON	TH	10	100	HARROP	WH	11	166	HART	FRA	12	108

HART	FT	7	170	HART	T	11	166	HARTLEY	H	14	142	HARVEY	A	4	178
HART	FW	1	150	HART	T	14	142	HARTLEY	J	4	178	HARVEY	A	5	166
HART	FW	7	170	HART	T	14	142	HARTLEY	J	9	88	HARVEY	A	6	187
HART	FW	12	320	HART	TB	5	166	HARTLEY	J	11	166	HARVEY	A	13	208
HART	G	5	165	HART	TF	5	166	HARTLEY	J	11	166	HARVEY	AA	4	178
HART	GA	7	170	HART	TG	5	166	HARTLEY	JA	8	149	HARVEY	AE	4	178
HART	GD	10	100	HART	W	5	166	HARTLEY	JP	14	142	HARVEY	AJ	4	179
HART	GF	13	207	HART	W	5	166	HARTLEY	JW	9	88	HARVEY	AJ	4	179
HART	GH	1	150	HART	W	6	187	HARTLEY	L	14	142	HARVEY	AJ	7	171
HART	GH	8	148	HART	W	6	187	HARTLEY	N	14	142	HARVEY	AWH	10	309
HART	GW	3	354	HART	W	8	148	HARTLEY	O	13	208	HARVEY	B	3	72
HART	GW	7	170	HART	W	8	148	HARTLEY	R	11	166	HARVEY	B	3	72
HART	H	1	150	HART	W	9	270	HARTLEY	R	14	142	HARVEY	B	4	179
HART	H	7	170	HART	W	10	309	HARTLEY	S	11	166	HARVEY	C	2	158
HART	H	8	148	HART	W	12	108	HARTLEY	T	8	149	HARVEY	C	2	158
HART	H	8	148	HART	WA	3	354	HARTLEY	T	8	149	HARVEY	E	14	143
HART	H	12	320	HART	WB	5	166	HARTLEY	TW	8	149	HARVEY	E	14	143
HART	H	13	207	HART	WG	1	151	HARTLEY	V	8	149	HARVEY	EF	1	151
HART	H	14	142	HART	WG	5	166	HARTLEY	W	9	88	HARVEY	EG	5	166
HART	HC	4	178	HART	WH	6	187	HARTNELL	AJ	10	100	HARVEY	EJ	4	179
HART	HE	13	207	HART	WH	13	207	HARTNELL	FC	10	100	HARVEY	F	1	151
HART	HG	10	100	HART	WJ	5	166	HARTNELL	G	10	100	HARVEY	F	1	151
HART	HG	13	207	HART	WP	13	207	HARTNELL	RG	6	187	HARVEY	F	13	208
HART	HGH	5	165	HARTBURY	J	10	100	HARTNELL	RW	10	101	HARVEY	FC	4	179
HART	HH	12	108	HARTFORD	WLH	1	151	HARTNEY	FW	11	166	HARVEY	FDV	3	72
HART	HJ	2	157	HARTGILL	B	10	100	HARTON	G	8	149	HARVEY	FJ	7	171
HART	HJ	12	108	HARTIGAN	JS	7	171	HARTOP	F	9	88	HARVEY	FM	10	309
HART	J	1	151	HARTILL	JL	12	108	HARTOPP	E	3	72	HARVEY	G	10	101
HART	J	8	148	HARTILL	WJ	1	151	HARTRUPP	W	12	108	HARVEY	G	11	167
HART	J	9	87	HARTLAND	AB	6	187	HARTSHORN	FH	7	171	HARVEY	GE	3	72
HART	J	10	100	HARTLAND	E	6	187	HARTSHORN	JS	8	149	HARVEY	GF	1	151
HART	J	12	108	HARTLAND	E	6	187	HARTT	PW	5	166	HARVEY	GH	12	320
HART	JA	2	158	HARTLAND	G	6	187	HARTUP	EA	12	108	HARVEY	GW	1	151
HART	JE	1	151	HARTLAND	H	6	187	HARTUP	H	12	108	HARVEY	GW	3	72
HART	JE	7	171	HARTLAND	T	6	187	HARTUP	HH	12	108	HARVEY	H	2	158
HART	JF	5	165	HARTLE	B	6	187	HARTUP	RF	12	108	HARVEY	H	7	171
HART	JL	10	309	HARTLEY	A	8	148	HARTWELL	AH	14	142	HARVEY	H	7	171
HART	JL	11	166	HARTLEY	A	11	166	HARTWELL	AMC	12	109	HARVEY	H	10	101
HART	JT	9	270	HARTLEY	AC	13	207	HARTWELL	AW	6	187	HARVEY	H	11	167
HART	JW	1	151	HARTLEY	C	8	148	HARTWELL	CA	1	151	HARVEY	H	12	109
HART	L	7	171	HARTLEY	CJ	5	166	HARTWELL	F	1	151	HARVEY	H	12	109
HART	LS	5	165	HARTLEY	DR	8	148	HARTWELL	F	12	109	HARVEY	H	13	208
HART	M	2	158	HARTLEY	E	8	148	HARTWELL	G	12	109	HARVEY	HD	3	73
HART	R	3	72	HARTLEY	E	9	87	HARTWELL	GSB	12	320	HARVEY	HD	13	208
HART	RD	5	165	HARTLEY	E	9	270	HARTWELL	GWJ	12	109	HARVEY	HE	6	187
HART	RJ	5	165	HARTLEY	E	13	207	HARTWELL	JT	6	187	HARVEY	HF	12	109
HART	RV	13	207	HARTLEY	EE	12	108	HARTWELL	SF	6	187	HARVEY	HH	1	151
HART	S	7	171	HARTLEY	F	8	148	HARTWELL	SJ	1	151	HARVEY	HJ	7	171
HART	SA	7	171	HARTLEY	F	9	87	HARTY	LD	13	208	HARVEY	HS	13	208
HART	SA	12	108	HARTLEY	G	8	148	HARTZIG	ER	9	88	HARVEY	HV	7	171
HART	SG	1	151	HARTLEY	G	12	320	HARVELL	FW	4	178	HARVEY	HWH	1	151
HART	SH	7	171	HARTLEY	G	14	142	HARVELL	J	4	178	HARVEY	J	1	151
HART	T	8	148	HARTLEY	H	8	148	HARVELL	WGC	4	178	HARVEY	J	4	179
HART	T	9	87	HARTLEY	H	9	87	HARVERSON	SM	2	158	HARVEY	J	7	171
HART	T	9	270	HARTLEY	H	11	166	HARVEY	A	1	151	HARVEY	J	10	309

Surname	Initials	No.	Page
HARVEY	J	11	167
HARVEY	J	12	320
HARVEY	J	14	143
HARVEY	JA	11	167
HARVEY	JDV	2	158
HARVEY	JH	6	188
HARVEY	JH	11	167
HARVEY	JH	13	208
HARVEY	JJ	2	158
HARVEY	JL	11	167
HARVEY	JM	7	171
HARVEY	JS	6	188
HARVEY	JW	3	73
HARVEY	L	2	158
HARVEY	L	4	179
HARVEY	LA	12	109
HARVEY	O	12	109
HARVEY	P	3	73
HARVEY	P	4	179
HARVEY	PJ	2	158
HARVEY	R	10	309
HARVEY	R	13	208
HARVEY	R	14	143
HARVEY	S	6	188
HARVEY	S	7	171
HARVEY	S	7	172
HARVEY	S	10	101
HARVEY	S	10	101
HARVEY	S	12	109
HARVEY	SD	1	152
HARVEY	SH	4	179
HARVEY	SJ	1	152
HARVEY	T	11	167
HARVEY	T	11	167
HARVEY	T	12	109
HARVEY	TH	7	172
HARVEY	W	2	158
HARVEY	W	4	179
HARVEY	W	5	166
HARVEY	W	6	188
HARVEY	W	7	172
HARVEY	W	7	172
HARVEY	W	9	270
HARVEY	W	10	101
HARVEY	W	11	167
HARVEY	WE	4	179
HARVEY	WFG	13	208
HARVEY	WGA	2	158
HARVEY	WH	3	73
HARVEY	WH	5	166
HARVEY	WJ	6	188
HARVEY	WJ	7	172
HARVEY	WT	3	73
HARVEY	WW	2	158
HARVEY	WW	3	73
HARWARD	FCS	2	158
HARWARD	FJ	2	158
HARWARD	TWF	2	158
HARWOOD	A	2	158
HARWOOD	A	9	88
HARWOOD	A	11	167
HARWOOD	A	14	143
HARWOOD	AE	13	208
HARWOOD	AG	5	166
HARWOOD	AJ	6	188
HARWOOD	AW	7	172
HARWOOD	CR	7	172
HARWOOD	DW	6	188
HARWOOD	E	4	179
HARWOOD	E	6	188
HARWOOD	ET	6	188
HARWOOD	F	1	152
HARWOOD	F	4	179
HARWOOD	FA	1	152
HARWOOD	FC	1	152
HARWOOD	G	10	101
HARWOOD	G	14	143
HARWOOD	GJ	3	354
HARWOOD	GW	10	101
HARWOOD	J	7	172
HARWOOD	J	13	208
HARWOOD	JB	7	172
HARWOOD	JD	4	179
HARWOOD	JT	7	172
HARWOOD	RC	10	309
HARWOOD	RI	1	152
HARWOOD	RW	13	208
HARWOOD	T	2	158
HARWOOD	W	7	172
HARWOOD	WJ	4	179
HARWOOD	WT	10	101
HASDELL	EW	12	320
HASE	BC	4	179
HASE	GR	11	167
HASE	R	11	167
HASELDEN	GH	11	167
HASELDEN	T	13	208
HASELDINE	A	11	167
HASELDINE	JH	12	109
HASELL	WJ	3	354
HASEY	F	11	167
HASKELL	E	3	354
HASKELL	EWW	4	179
HASKELL	F	4	179
HASKELL	FG	4	179
HASKELL	FH	12	109
HASKELL	JJ	13	208
HASKELL	WF	4	179
HASKELL	WF	4	180
HASKER	A	12	320
HASKETT	AE	10	101
HASKETT	AG	10	101
HASKETT	EB	10	101
HASKETT	GT	10	101
HASKEY	GF	2	158
HASKEY	WC	2	158
HASKINS	WH	4	180
HASLAM	H	14	143
HASLAM	J	11	167
HASLAM	J	11	167
HASLAM	P	7	172
HASLAM	RP	2	159
HASLAM	S	11	167
HASLAM	W	11	167
HASLEHURST	J	13	208
HASLER	FJ	13	208
HASLER	GL	4	180
HASLER	JJ	4	180
HASLER	TJ	1	152
HASLER	WA	12	320
HASLER	WH	4	180
HASLER	WM	13	208
HASLETT	AJ	2	159
HASLETT	H	1	152
HASLETT	T	1	152
HASLETT	W	13	208
HASLOP	W	12	320
HASS	F	7	172
HASSACK	J	14	143
HASSALL	A	11	168
HASSALL	F	11	168
HASSALL	G	11	168
HASSALL	JH	11	168
HASSALL	W	4	180
HASSALL	WH	11	168
HASSELL	GA	10	309
HASSELL	JA	3	73
HASSELL	TH	4	180
HASSETT	J	13	209
HASSIN	U	12	109
HASSON	C	6	188
HASTE	C	2	159
HASTE	G	13	209
HASTING	A	7	172
HASTINGS	A	9	88
HASTINGS	A	12	320
HASTINGS	AG	3	73
HASTINGS	AH	3	73
HASTINGS	F	4	180
HASTINGS	G	14	143
HASTINGS	H	9	88
HASTINGS	H	10	309
HASTINGS	J	7	172
HASTINGS	J	13	209
HASTINGS	JG	7	172
HASTINGS	S	6	188
HASTINGS	W	6	188
HASTINGS	W	14	143
HASTINGS	WF	6	188
HASTLE	WK	7	172
HASTWELL	TE	7	172
HASTY	JT	6	188
HATCH	AG	4	180
HATCH	C	4	180
HATCH	E	10	101
HATCH	F	4	180
HATCH	FC	4	180
HATCH	FT	2	159
HATCH	JF	10	309
HATCH	T	10	101
HATCH	TGE	10	101
HATCH	WA	4	180
HATCHARD	A	10	101
HATCHARD	F	10	101
HATCHARD	JF	10	101
HATCHELL	C	11	168
HATCHELL	JE	11	168
HATCHER	A	4	180
HATCHER	AE	4	180
HATCHER	AF	4	180
HATCHER	AG	7	172
HATCHER	AG	13	209
HATCHER	AW	13	209
HATCHER	GJ	13	209
HATCHER	JG	6	188
HATCHER	W	4	180
HATCHER	W	10	101
HATCHER	WM	10	310
HATCHETT	JW	10	102
HATCHMAN	PJ	13	209
HATCHMAN	WC	13	209
HATELY	S	6	188
HATFIELD	CG	7	173
HATFIELD	DR	13	209
HATFIELD	J	3	73
HATFIELD	N	9	88
HATFIELD	TH	6	188
HATFIELD	W	7	172
HATFULL	FG	13	209
HATFULL	WE	13	209
HATHAWAY	AE	11	168
HATHAWAY	CE	3	354
HATHAWAY	FG	1	152
HATHAWAY	FW	6	188
HATHAWAY	H	5	166
HATHAWAY	H	6	188
HATHAWAY	J	5	166
HATHAWAY	J	5	166
HATHAWAY	J	6	188
HATHAWAY	J	7	173

HATHAWAY	JG	1	152	HAUGHTON	M	11	168	HAWKER	S	6	189	HAWKINS	AE	10	102
HATHAWAY	T	6	189	HAUGHTON	MA	11	168	HAWKER	T	6	189	HAWKINS	AE	13	210
HATHAWAY	VC	6	189	HAUGHTON	WR	8	149	HAWKER	TH	6	189	HAWKINS	AE	13	210
HATHAWAY	W	6	189	HAULT	J	6	189	HAWKER	TP	12	320	HAWKINS	AH	4	181
HATHERLEY	AW	10	102	HAUPT	H	1	152	HAWKER	W	6	189	HAWKINS	AJ	3	73
HATHERLY	FAJ	10	310	HAUSWIRT	D	9	88	HAWKER	WG	7	173	HAWKINS	AJ	7	173
HATHERLY	HA	10	102	HAUTOT	G	7	173	HAWKES	AA	5	167	HAWKINS	AT	1	152
HATHERLY	J	10	102	HAUTOT	JF	7	173	HAWKES	AE	3	354	HAWKINS	B	5	167
HATHRILL	R	5	166	HAVELL	WS	5	167	HAWKES	AF	5	167	HAWKINS	C	4	181
HATLEY	A	6	189	HAVER	R	3	354	HAWKES	AF	5	167	HAWKINS	C	7	174
HATLEY	FL	7	173	HAVER	WF	3	354	HAWKES	AF	13	210	HAWKINS	C	12	320
HATSWELL	J	2	159	HAVERS	W	7	173	HAWKES	AS	5	167	HAWKINS	CA	1	152
HATT	CH	13	209	HAVEY	EJ	4	180	HAWKES	C	13	210	HAWKINS	CH	10	102
HATT	EF	10	102	HAVILL	M	1	152	HAWKES	E	6	189	HAWKINS	CHG	5	167
HATTEMORE	F	13	209	HAVINDEN	GS	13	209	HAWKES	E	14	143	HAWKINS	CJ	10	102
HATTER	J	10	102	HAW	F	8	149	HAWKES	F	5	167	HAWKINS	CJR	4	181
HATTERSLEY	J	9	271	HAW	R	12	109	HAWKES	F	14	143	HAWKINS	D	1	153
HATTERSLEY	J	9	271	HAWCOCK	J	9	88	HAWKES	FA	2	159	HAWKINS	E	1	153
HATTERSLEY	J	9	271	HAWCROFT	J	11	168	HAWKES	G	6	189	HAWKINS	E	4	181
HATTERSLEY	T	14	143	HAWCROFT	J	11	169	HAWKES	H	6	189	HAWKINS	E	6	190
HATTERSLEY	W	9	271	HAWE	G	8	149	HAWKES	H	13	210	HAWKINS	E	10	102
HATTERSLEY	WO	9	271	HAWES	A	5	167	HAWKES	HC	5	167	HAWKINS	E	10	102
HATTERSTONE	J	14	143	HAWES	A	13	209	HAWKES	J	5	167	HAWKINS	EA	6	190
HATTLE	H	7	173	HAWES	AE	13	210	HAWKES	J	14	143	HAWKINS	EA	10	310
HATTO	C	14	143	HAWES	AJ	1	152	HAWKES	JJ	2	159	HAWKINS	EG	7	174
HATTON	A	5	166	HAWES	BWE	1	152	HAWKES	JL	5	167	HAWKINS	EL	3	73
HATTON	A	14	143	HAWES	C	1	152	HAWKES	RH	2	159	HAWKINS	ET	6	190
HATTON	AA	6	189	HAWES	CW	5	167	HAWKES	SR	5	167	HAWKINS	F	5	168
HATTON	C	3	73	HAWES	F	4	180	HAWKES	SW	5	167	HAWKINS	F	5	168
HATTON	C	5	166	HAWES	FC	5	167	HAWKES	W	14	143	HAWKINS	F	5	168
HATTON	E	11	168	HAWES	FR	7	173	HAWKES	WH	1	152	HAWKINS	F	5	168
HATTON	E	13	209	HAWES	GA	2	159	HAWKES	WH	7	173	HAWKINS	F	6	190
HATTON	FH	5	166	HAWES	JF	7	173	HAWKES	WJ	6	189	HAWKINS	F	6	190
HATTON	GWT	7	173	HAWES	JJ	5	167	HAWKES	WS	3	73	HAWKINS	F	7	174
HATTON	H	11	168	HAWES	JS	1	152	HAWKESLEY	F	9	88	HAWKINS	F	14	144
HATTON	H	11	168	HAWES	NF	2	159	HAWKESWOOD	C	6	190	HAWKINS	FA	1	153
HATTON	J	11	168	HAWES	OB	5	167	HAWKESWOOD	D	6	190	HAWKINS	FA	3	73
HATTON	J	11	168	HAWES	S	12	109	HAWKESWOOD	E	6	190	HAWKINS	FA	3	73
HATTON	PF	12	320	HAWES	SS	7	173	HAWKESWOOD	H	6	190	HAWKINS	FA	4	181
HATTON	RG	2	159	HAWES	W	5	167	HAWKESWOOD	H	6	190	HAWKINS	FC	10	102
HATTON	RJ	13	209	HAWES	W	7	173	HAWKESWOOD	JD	6	190	HAWKINS	FE	5	168
HATTON	RT	10	310	HAWES	WE	2	159	HAWKHEAD	WA	8	149	HAWKINS	FG	1	153
HATTON	S	5	167	HAWES	WW	4	181	HAWKIN	H	7	173	HAWKINS	FH	13	210
HATTON	S	6	189	HAWGOOD	WG	3	73	HAWKINS	A	3	354	HAWKINS	FJ	5	168
HATTON	SC	13	209	HAWKE	C	8	149	HAWKINS	A	3	354	HAWKINS	FL	1	153
HATTON	TJ	13	209	HAWKE	H	8	149	HAWKINS	A	6	190	HAWKINS	FP	12	320
HATTON	W	11	168	HAWKER	A	7	173	HAWKINS	A	6	190	HAWKINS	FW	3	74
HATTON	WD	12	320	HAWKER	A	13	210	HAWKINS	A	10	102	HAWKINS	G	5	168
HATTON	WH	13	209	HAWKER	AJ	13	210	HAWKINS	A	10	102	HAWKINS	G	6	190
HATWELL	JW	6	189	HAWKER	B	6	189	HAWKINS	A	10	310	HAWKINS	G	9	88
HAUGHTON	A	11	168	HAWKER	C	7	173	HAWKINS	A	13	210	HAWKINS	G	10	102
HAUGHTON	A	11	168	HAWKER	F	3	73	HAWKINS	A	13	210	HAWKINS	G	10	102
HAUGHTON	F	8	149	HAWKER	FW	13	210	HAWKINS	A	14	143	HAWKINS	GC	3	354
HAUGHTON	H	3	73	HAWKER	J	6	189	HAWKINS	AA	10	310	HAWKINS	GD	7	174
HAUGHTON	JR	11	168	HAWKER	JH	2	159	HAWKINS	AE	10	102	HAWKINS	GD	7	174

Surname	Initials	Vol	Page
HAWKINS	GFW	7	174
HAWKINS	GH	3	354
HAWKINS	H	3	354
HAWKINS	H	5	168
HAWKINS	H	5	168
HAWKINS	H	6	190
HAWKINS	H	6	190
HAWKINS	H	7	174
HAWKINS	H	10	310
HAWKINS	HA	2	159
HAWKINS	HF	10	310
HAWKINS	HG	6	190
HAWKINS	HJ	6	190
HAWKINS	HJ	13	210
HAWKINS	HP	2	159
HAWKINS	HT	1	153
HAWKINS	HW	1	153
HAWKINS	HWS	1	153
HAWKINS	J	1	153
HAWKINS	J	1	153
HAWKINS	J	2	159
HAWKINS	J	6	190
HAWKINS	J	6	191
HAWKINS	J	6	191
HAWKINS	J	12	320
HAWKINS	JA	5	168
HAWKINS	JF	6	191
HAWKINS	JH	2	159
HAWKINS	JR	4	181
HAWKINS	JW	9	88
HAWKINS	LC	10	310
HAWKINS	LD	10	310
HAWKINS	LM	1	153
HAWKINS	MG	1	153
HAWKINS	RA	5	168
HAWKINS	S	10	310
HAWKINS	S	14	144
HAWKINS	SAV	12	321
HAWKINS	SW	1	153
HAWKINS	T	6	191
HAWKINS	TC	7	174
HAWKINS	TE	7	174
HAWKINS	TE	13	210
HAWKINS	TF	7	174
HAWKINS	TG	10	102
HAWKINS	TH	6	191
HAWKINS	TJ	6	191
HAWKINS	TJ	8	149
HAWKINS	W	1	153
HAWKINS	W	4	181
HAWKINS	W	4	181
HAWKINS	W	6	191
HAWKINS	W	6	191
HAWKINS	W	7	174
HAWKINS	W	10	103
HAWKINS	W	10	103
HAWKINS	W	12	321
HAWKINS	WE	5	168
HAWKINS	WE	5	168
HAWKINS	WF	5	168
HAWKINS	WF	5	168
HAWKINS	WH	1	153
HAWKINS	WH	6	191
HAWKINS	WH	6	191
HAWKINS	WH	10	103
HAWKINS	WJ	3	354
HAWKINS	WJ	10	103
HAWKLEY	W	6	191
HAWKRIDGE	T	9	271
HAWKSHAW	A	8	149
HAWKSHAW	C	8	149
HAWKSHAW	C	9	88
HAWKSHAW	GE	8	149
HAWKSHAW	H	8	149
HAWKSHAW	H	8	149
HAWKSHAW	JH	8	149
HAWKSLEY	R	8	149
HAWKSWOOD	RH	6	191
HAWKSWOOD	TJ	6	191
HAWKSWORTH	A	9	88
HAWKSWORTH	A	9	271
HAWKSWORTH	CP	5	168
HAWKSWORTH	PC	5	168
HAWKSWORTH	R	11	169
HAWKSWORTH	S	14	144
HAWLEY	A	9	88
HAWLEY	AJ	8	149
HAWLEY	AW	2	159
HAWLEY	E	3	74
HAWLEY	E	11	169
HAWLEY	EI	8	149
HAWLEY	H	3	74
HAWLEY	H	5	168
HAWLEY	J	3	74
HAWLEY	J	6	191
HAWLEY	JA	11	169
HAWLEY	JF	8	150
HAWLEY	L	9	88
HAWLEY	P	3	74
HAWORTH	A	11	169
HAWORTH	J	14	144
HAWTHORN	CH	6	191
HAWTHORN	FT	1	153
HAWTHORN	G	5	168
HAWTHORN	H	6	191
HAWTHORN	H	13	210
HAWTHORN	JW	6	191
HAWTHORN	RG	9	271
HAWTHORN	WT	1	153
HAWTHORNE	F	10	103
HAWTHORNE	J	6	191
HAWTHORNE	TH	6	191
HAWTHORNTHWAITE	F	11	169
HAWTIN	AE	3	74
HAWTIN	HE	6	192
HAWTIN	R	14	144
HAWTIN	TS	7	174
HAWTIN	V	6	192
HAWTREE	FJ	4	181
HAXTON	W	4	181
HAY	G	14	144
HAY	W	14	144
HAYBALL	AE	4	181
HAYBALL	P	4	181
HAYBALL	V	4	181
HAYBITTLE	AG	3	354
HAYCOCK	CR	12	109
HAYCOCK	FT	6	192
HAYCOCK	G	6	192
HAYCOCK	GH	1	153
HAYCOCK	W	14	144
HAYCOX	J	6	192
HAYDAY	CLW	1	153
HAYDEN	AE	4	181
HAYDEN	C	1	153
HAYDEN	CH	3	354
HAYDEN	CH	6	192
HAYDEN	D	2	160
HAYDEN	E	1	154
HAYDEN	EJ	2	160
HAYDEN	ET	13	210
HAYDEN	FH	1	154
HAYDEN	G	6	192
HAYDEN	G	13	210
HAYDEN	GA	6	192
HAYDEN	GW	13	210
HAYDEN	J	14	144
HAYDEN	JE	5	168
HAYDEN	JH	10	310
HAYDEN	LH	6	192
HAYDEN	T	6	192
HAYDEN	W	13	210
HAYDEN	WE	6	192
HAYDEN	WH	6	192
HAYDON	BL	1	154
HAYDON	EE	1	154
HAYDON	GW	1	154
HAYDON	J	10	103
HAYDON	JC	7	174
HAYDON	P	14	144
HAYDON	SS	13	211
HAYEMES	A	13	211
HAYEMES	WJ	13	211
HAYER	E	6	192
HAYER	G	6	192
HAYER	T	6	192
HAYES	A	4	181
HAYES	A	7	174
HAYES	A	8	150
HAYES	A	9	271
HAYES	A	10	103
HAYES	A	14	144
HAYES	A	14	144
HAYES	A	14	144
HAYES	AE	10	310
HAYES	AF	1	154
HAYES	AG	4	181
HAYES	AJ	5	168
HAYES	AT	4	181
HAYES	C	8	150
HAYES	C	9	271
HAYES	C	9	271
HAYES	C	13	211
HAYES	CF	7	174
HAYES	CJ	4	182
HAYES	CT	3	354
HAYES	D	10	310
HAYES	EJ	4	182
HAYES	EW	13	211
HAYES	F	1	154
HAYES	F	7	174
HAYES	FW	6	192
HAYES	G	1	154
HAYES	G	2	160
HAYES	G	4	182
HAYES	G	4	182
HAYES	G	9	88
HAYES	G	11	169
HAYES	G	14	144
HAYES	GH	6	192
HAYES	GW	1	154
HAYES	H	3	354
HAYES	H	9	271
HAYES	H	11	169
HAYES	H	11	169
HAYES	H	13	211
HAYES	HC	2	160
HAYES	HS	4	182
HAYES	J	1	154
HAYES	J	3	355
HAYES	J	3	355
HAYES	J	4	182
HAYES	J	8	150
HAYES	J	8	150
HAYES	J	8	150
HAYES	J	11	169
HAYES	J	13	211
HAYES	J	14	144
HAYES	JA	11	169
HAYES	JF	4	182

HAYES	JJ	10	103	HAYLEY	WA	5	169	HAYNES	FJ	11	169	HAYTER	HJ	4	183
HAYES	JR	11	169	HAYLINGS	W	6	193	HAYNES	FW	5	169	HAYTER	JB	4	183
HAYES	JW	2	160	HAYLLAR	A	12	109	HAYNES	G	2	160	HAYTER	RJ	4	183
HAYES	JW	11	169	HAYLLAR	W	12	109	HAYNES	G	4	182	HAYTER	SE	13	211
HAYES	L	4	182	HAYLLAR	WB	12	110	HAYNES	G	4	183	HAYTER	W	7	175
HAYES	M	4	182	HAYLOCK	A	10	310	HAYNES	G	6	193	HAYTER	WH	2	161
HAYES	M	9	88	HAYLOCK	E	9	89	HAYNES	GH	2	160	HAYTER	WH	4	183
HAYES	N	14	144	HAYLOCK	G	1	154	HAYNES	GJ	7	175	HAYTER	WH	10	104
HAYES	R	2	160	HAYLOCK	G	9	89	HAYNES	GJ	12	321	HAYTHORNE	F	13	211
HAYES	R	14	144	HAYLOCK	GA	12	110	HAYNES	H	8	150	HAYTON	A	14	145
HAYES	RE	2	160	HAYLOCK	H	9	271	HAYNES	H	12	110	HAYTON	H	14	145
HAYES	RG	4	182	HAYLOCK	H	12	110	HAYNES	H	12	110	HAYWARD	AE	2	161
HAYES	RS	10	310	HAYLOCK	HJ	9	89	HAYNES	H	12	321	HAYWARD	AE	3	74
HAYES	RV	4	182	HAYLOCK	JH	12	110	HAYNES	HA	5	169	HAYWARD	AE	11	170
HAYES	RV	10	310	HAYLOCK	R	2	160	HAYNES	HC	12	110	HAYWARD	AET	10	311
HAYES	S	2	160	HAYLOR	G	6	193	HAYNES	HE	6	193	HAYWARD	AT	2	161
HAYES	S	6	192	HAYLOR	R	4	182	HAYNES	HEM	12	110	HAYWARD	BB	2	161
HAYES	SE	4	182	HAYMAN	A	8	150	HAYNES	HG	12	110	HAYWARD	CA	3	74
HAYES	SP	7	174	HAYMAN	HJ	13	211	HAYNES	HJ	1	155	HAYWARD	CH	3	74
HAYES	TH	13	211	HAYMAN	J	10	311	HAYNES	J	1	155	HAYWARD	E	11	170
HAYES	TW	13	211	HAYMAN	WJ	12	321	HAYNES	J	8	150	HAYWARD	EG	4	183
HAYES	W	1	154	HAYMAN	WL	7	175	HAYNES	JE	6	193	HAYWARD	EG	10	104
HAYES	W	1	154	HAYMAN	WSJ	13	211	HAYNES	JE	6	193	HAYWARD	EJ	1	155
HAYES	W	2	160	HAYMER	F	4	182	HAYNES	JH	6	193	HAYWARD	F	1	155
HAYES	W	6	192	HAYMER	WE	4	182	HAYNES	JJ	3	355	HAYWARD	F	4	183
HAYES	W	6	193	HAYMES	AV	3	355	HAYNES	L	1	155	HAYWARD	F	6	193
HAYES	W	8	150	HAYMES	F	11	169	HAYNES	N	6	193	HAYWARD	F	7	175
HAYES	W	11	169	HAYMON	JS	10	103	HAYNES	PG	2	160	HAYWARD	FC	12	110
HAYES	W	14	144	HAYNES	A	1	154	HAYNES	R	4	183	HAYWARD	FG	13	211
HAYES	WF	7	174	HAYNES	A	2	160	HAYNES	RA	12	110	HAYWARD	FJ	5	169
HAYES	WG	7	174	HAYNES	A	4	182	HAYNES	S	6	193	HAYWARD	FM	6	193
HAYES	WH	11	169	HAYNES	A	6	193	HAYNES	S	12	110	HAYWARD	FT	13	211
HAYES	WTE	6	193	HAYNES	A	8	150	HAYNES	T	2	160	HAYWARD	FW	1	155
HAYFIELD	C	5	169	HAYNES	A	12	110	HAYNES	W	7	175	HAYWARD	G	3	74
HAYFIELD	WJ	6	193	HAYNES	A	12	110	HAYNES	W	12	321	HAYWARD	G	5	169
HAYHOE	E	1	154	HAYNES	A	13	211	HAYNES	WCH	1	155	HAYWARD	G	11	170
HAYHOE	JC	3	355	HAYNES	AC	7	175	HAYNES	WG	3	355	HAYWARD	GH	4	183
HAYHOE	RG	10	103	HAYNES	AE	6	193	HAYNES	WH	3	355	HAYWARD	GW	10	311
HAYHOE	WTJ	3	74	HAYNES	AF	4	182	HAYNES	WH	6	193	HAYWARD	H	4	183
HAYHURST	J	11	169	HAYNES	AH	4	182	HAYSELDEN	F	3	74	HAYWARD	H	10	104
HAYHURST	S	14	144	HAYNES	BE	12	110	HAYSEY	HW	7	175	HAYWARD	J	3	74
HAYHURST	W	11	169	HAYNES	C	1	154	HAYSEY	RAH	7	175	HAYWARD	J	10	104
HAYLER	WH	10	103	HAYNES	C	1	154	HAYSMAN	S	1	155	HAYWARD	JC	13	211
HAYLES	E	10	103	HAYNES	CAE	1	154	HAYSOM	AR	7	175	HAYWARD	JE	6	193
HAYLES	FG	4	182	HAYNES	CH	12	110	HAYSOM	T	10	103	HAYWARD	JE	10	311
HAYLES	G	10	103	HAYNES	CM	12	321	HAYTER	CG	10	103	HAYWARD	L	6	193
HAYLES	G	13	211	HAYNES	E	1	154	HAYTER	EC	4	183	HAYWARD	LC	5	169
HAYLES	GS	10	103	HAYNES	E	1	155	HAYTER	EMM	7	175	HAYWARD	M	2	161
HAYLES	HE	10	103	HAYNES	EG	13	211	HAYTER	F	4	183	HAYWARD	M	4	183
HAYLES	J	2	160	HAYNES	F	6	193	HAYTER	FL	12	321	HAYWARD	P	5	169
HAYLES	W	10	103	HAYNES	F	7	175	HAYTER	G	10	103	HAYWARD	PA	10	311
HAYLES	W	11	169	HAYNES	F	10	311	HAYTER	GE	2	160	HAYWARD	PJ	1	155
HAYLES	WJH	10	103	HAYNES	FC	12	321	HAYTER	GW	2	160	HAYWARD	RB	13	212
HAYLEY	A	9	88	HAYNES	FF	7	175	HAYTER	H	4	183	HAYWARD	S	6	194
HAYLEY	EA	3	355	HAYNES	FH	2	160	HAYTER	H	4	183	HAYWARD	S	11	170

HAYWARD	S	14	145	HAZELWOOD	A	1	155	HEADLAND	WC	4	184	HEALING	WR	2	161
HAYWARD	SW	11	170	HAZELWOOD	EV	1	155	HEADLEY	GH	9	271	HEALY	G	1	156
HAYWARD	TA	9	89	HAZELWOOD	W	1	155	HEADLEY	H	9	271	HEALY	J	13	212
HAYWARD	TE	6	194	HAZELWOOD	WV	1	155	HEAFORD	HJ	1	155	HEALY	S	3	75
HAYWARD	W	3	74	HAZLE	JW	13	212	HEAFORD	JT	14	145	HEANEY	B	14	145
HAYWARD	W	6	194	HAZLEHURST	CH	14	145	HEAFORD	W	14	145	HEANEY	J	11	171
HAYWARD	W	10	104	HAZLETON	AR	6	194	HEAL	CJ	2	161	HEANEY	J	14	145
HAYWARD	W	13	212	HAZLETON	E	6	194	HEAL	WH	10	311	HEAP	A	10	104
HAYWARD	WJ	2	161	HAZLEWOOD	HJ	4	183	HEALD	B	11	170	HEAP	AE	3	355
HAYWARD	WJ	13	212	HAZLEWOOD	J	12	321	HEALD	E	11	170	HEAP	GC	14	145
HAYWARD	WR	3	74	HAZZARD	CJ	7	175	HEALD	JF	11	170	HEAP	H	11	171
HAYWOOD	C	3	355	HAZZARD	ET	7	175	HEALD	JW	11	170	HEAP	JOP	11	171
HAYWOOD	CH	12	321	HAZZARD	GH	10	311	HEALD	TG	11	170	HEAP	RE	6	194
HAYWOOD	E	6	194	HEAD	A	3	355	HEALD	TH	9	271	HEAP	T	11	171
HAYWOOD	F	6	194	HEAD	AA	1	155	HEALD	W	11	170	HEAP	WA	14	145
HAYWOOD	F	6	194	HEAD	AW	7	175	HEALEY	AH	5	169	HEAPS	A	11	171
HAYWOOD	F	9	89	HEAD	ED	6	194	HEALEY	AR	7	176	HEAPS	F	9	271
HAYWOOD	G	6	194	HEAD	F	3	75	HEALEY	B	14	145	HEAPS	H	9	271
HAYWOOD	GS	6	194	HEAD	F	13	212	HEALEY	C	7	176	HEAPS	J	11	171
HAYWOOD	H	13	212	HEAD	F	13	212	HEALEY	CG	7	176	HEAPS	TW	3	355
HAYWOOD	JA	3	74	HEAD	FG	13	212	HEALEY	D	11	170	HEAPY	G	11	171
HAYWOOD	JM	8	150	HEAD	FT	4	183	HEALEY	E	2	161	HEARD	A	1	156
HAYWOOD	P	8	150	HEAD	FW	5	169	HEALEY	EG	7	176	HEARD	AR	4	184
HAYWOOD	W	6	194	HEAD	FW	12	110	HEALEY	EWA	12	321	HEARD	B	7	176
HAYWOOD	W	6	194	HEAD	G	7	176	HEALEY	F	8	150	HEARD	C	6	194
HAYWOOD	WH	8	150	HEAD	H	6	194	HEALEY	F	9	271	HEARD	E	13	212
HAYWOOD	WW	6	194	HEAD	HJ	4	183	HEALEY	F	11	170	HEARD	EDT	12	321
HAZARD	GW	3	74	HEAD	J	1	155	HEALEY	FR	9	89	HEARD	EJ	1	156
HAZARD	W	10	104	HEAD	J	6	194	HEALEY	G	9	387	HEARD	F	2	161
HAZEL	FD	6	194	HEAD	JA	9	89	HEALEY	GE	1	156	HEARD	F	7	176
HAZEL	HG	7	175	HEAD	L	4	183	HEALEY	H	1	156	HEARD	ME	10	104
HAZEL	JE	13	212	HEAD	M	3	75	HEALEY	H	1	156	HEARD	MV	10	104
HAZEL	L	6	194	HEAD	R	2	161	HEALEY	H	11	170	HEARD	T	8	150
HAZEL	WJ	5	169	HEAD	R	11	170	HEALEY	H	14	145	HEARD	V	11	171
HAZELDEN	WC	13	212	HEAD	S	3	355	HEALEY	J	8	150	HEARD	W	13	212
HAZELDINE	AF	13	212	HEAD	TG	13	212	HEALEY	J	11	170	HEARD	WV	2	161
HAZELDINE	HH	7	175	HEAD	TJ	2	161	HEALEY	J	11	170	HEARD	WW	13	212
HAZELDINE	J	13	212	HEAD	W	3	75	HEALEY	J	11	170	HEARL	W	10	311
HAZELGRAVE	C	8	150	HEAD	W	4	184	HEALEY	J	11	422	HEARLE	CL	13	212
HAZELL	AW	10	104	HEAD	WH	1	155	HEALEY	JE	9	89	HEARN	A	1	156
HAZELL	CJ	2	161	HEAD	WM	7	176	HEALEY	JN	7	176	HEARN	A	11	171
HAZELL	EW	3	74	HEADDEN	EJ	10	104	HEALEY	MJ	14	145	HEARN	AE	7	176
HAZELL	F	2	161	HEADDEN	HC	10	104	HEALEY	O	14	145	HEARN	AW	12	110
HAZELL	F	2	161	HEADDEN	JA	10	104	HEALEY	P	4	184	HEARN	C	7	176
HAZELL	FF	2	161	HEADDEN	SJR	10	104	HEALEY	R	9	271	HEARN	CH	7	176
HAZELL	JH	3	355	HEADDEN	WC	10	104	HEALEY	S	13	212	HEARN	F	5	169
HAZELL	JW	3	74	HEADFORD	A	3	75	HEALEY	SCG	7	176	HEARN	F	7	176
HAZELL	M	11	170	HEADFORD	G	3	75	HEALEY	T	4	184	HEARN	F	10	104
HAZELL	T	14	145	HEADFORD	JH	14	145	HEALEY	T	5	169	HEARN	FC	13	213
HAZELL	WG	3	355	HEADING	A	1	155	HEALEY	T	14	145	HEARN	G	5	169
HAZELL	WJ	4	183	HEADING	AE	5	169	HEALEY	WG	7	176	HEARN	H	3	75
HAZELS	G	13	212	HEADING	L	5	169	HEALEY	WJ	7	176	HEARN	H	5	169
HAZELTING	G	7	175	HEADINGTON	A	4	184	HEALING	CD	6	194	HEARN	H	13	213
HAZELTING	JH	7	175	HEADINGTON	J	3	75	HEALING	PE	10	311	HEARN	HA	7	176
HAZELTON	E	10	104	HEADLAND	W	12	321	HEALING	WJ	10	311	HEARN	J	7	176

HEARN	J	7	176	HEATH	H	3	355	HEATHFIELD	A	3	356	HEBEL	P	11	172
HEARN	J	11	171	HEATH	H	6	195	HEATHFIELD	F	3	356	HEBINGTON	E	10	105
HEARN	JH	13	213	HEATH	H	7	177	HEATHFIELD	FC	5	170	HECKFORD	P	3	75
HEARN	L	7	177	HEATH	HA	7	177	HEATHFIELD	G	5	170	HECTOR	AE	8	151
HEARN	R	13	213	HEATH	HC	13	213	HEATHFIELD	JC	7	177	HECTOR	G	8	151
HEARN	RH	1	156	HEATH	HJ	1	156	HEATHFIELD	W	1	156	HECTOR	GW	7	178
HEARN	RJ	13	213	HEATH	HR	10	105	HEATHWHITE	C	7	177	HECTOR	H	2	162
HEARN	S	7	177	HEATH	HS	7	177	HEATLEY	J	13	213	HECTOR	H	8	151
HEARN	SJ	13	213	HEATH	J	6	195	HEATLEY	JA	4	184	HECTOR	J	2	162
HEARN	W	13	213	HEATH	J	6	195	HEATON	A	3	75	HECTOR	WCH	7	178
HEARN	WE	2	161	HEATH	J	6	195	HEATON	A	8	151	HEDEN	W	8	151
HEARN	WG	5	169	HEATH	J	8	151	HEATON	A	9	272	HEDGE	A	12	110
HEARNDEN	AC	4	184	HEATH	J	9	272	HEATON	E	9	272	HEDGE	A	12	110
HEARNDEN	AJ	4	184	HEATH	JH	5	170	HEATON	E	11	171	HEDGE	A	12	111
HEARNE	F	7	177	HEATH	JHE	4	184	HEATON	EJ	8	151	HEDGE	C	5	170
HEARNE	F	11	171	HEATH	JR	7	177	HEATON	F	9	89	HEDGE	CJ	5	170
HEARNE	GL	7	177	HEATH	JT	6	195	HEATON	F	9	89	HEDGE	E	12	111
HEASMAN	A	5	169	HEATH	JT	10	105	HEATON	FA	8	151	HEDGE	F	12	321
HEASMAN	GH	7	177	HEATH	ME	3	75	HEATON	H	7	177	HEDGE	F	12	321
HEASMAN	H	3	75	HEATH	P	2	161	HEATON	H	9	272	HEDGE	FW	12	321
HEASMAN	W	3	75	HEATH	P	13	213	HEATON	J	14	146	HEDGE	J	9	272
HEASMAN	W	13	213	HEATH	R	9	89	HEATON	J	14	146	HEDGE	M	2	162
HEASMAN	WJ	1	156	HEATH	RH	4	184	HEATON	LA	14	146	HEDGE	M	12	111
HEASON	H	14	145	HEATH	RH	10	311	HEATON	R	9	89	HEDGE	S	5	170
HEATH	A	8	150	HEATH	RJ	2	161	HEATON	R	11	172	HEDGE	S	12	111
HEATH	AE	6	195	HEATH	RJ	10	105	HEATON	RM	13	213	HEDGE	TJ	12	111
HEATH	AE	6	195	HEATH	S	10	105	HEATON	S	8	151	HEDGE	W	12	111
HEATH	AG	10	104	HEATH	SE	6	195	HEATON	S	11	172	HEDGECOCK	C	2	162
HEATH	AH	10	104	HEATH	SG	13	213	HEATON	T	11	172	HEDGECOCK	C	5	170
HEATH	AR	3	355	HEATH	T	8	151	HEATON	T	11	172	HEDGECOCK	CR	2	162
HEATH	AR	10	105	HEATH	T	9	272	HEATON	T	14	146	HEDGECOCK	EA	2	162
HEATH	AV	10	105	HEATH	TH	11	171	HEATON	TE	14	146	HEDGECOCK	EJ	2	162
HEATH	AW	7	177	HEATH	TS	7	177	HEATON	TM	9	272	HEDGECOCK	H	4	184
HEATH	C	8	150	HEATH	W	3	355	HEATON	W	9	89	HEDGECOCK	OA	10	311
HEATH	C	11	171	HEATH	W	3	355	HEATON	W	14	146	HEDGECOTT	EE	4	184
HEATH	E	11	171	HEATH	W	4	184	HEAVENS	E	7	178	HEDGECOTT	W	4	184
HEATH	EA	7	177	HEATH	W	13	213	HEAVENS	GW	1	156	HEDGER	HW	13	213
HEATH	EE	1	156	HEATH	W	14	145	HEAVENS	J	7	178	HEDGES	A	4	184
HEATH	EG	3	75	HEATH	WE	10	105	HEAVENS	OJ	7	178	HEDGES	A	5	170
HEATH	EM	7	177	HEATH	WG	7	177	HEAVEY	P	14	146	HEDGES	AE	5	170
HEATH	EN	13	213	HEATH	WH	7	177	HEAVISIDES	JP	9	89	HEDGES	C	2	162
HEATH	F	10	311	HEATH	WJ	1	156	HEAVISIDES	JP	9	388	HEDGES	CE	5	170
HEATH	FA	4	184	HEATHCOTE	CF	10	105	HEAVISIDES	W	9	89	HEDGES	E	3	356
HEATH	FG	5	169	HEATHCOTE	EA	12	110	HEAVISIDES	W	9	388	HEDGES	EA	1	156
HEATH	G	1	156	HEATHCOTE	FW	10	311	HEAYES	A	7	178	HEDGES	EL	3	356
HEATH	G	11	171	HEATHCOTE	JW	11	171	HEAYES	W	7	178	HEDGES	F	5	170
HEATH	G	11	171	HEATHER	AD	1	156	HEBBLETHWAITE	AW	3	75	HEDGES	F	5	170
HEATH	G	13	213	HEATHER	AP	3	75	HEBBLETWAITE	A	9	89	HEDGES	FA	1	157
HEATH	GA	6	195	HEATHER	CA	10	105	HEBBS	M	1	156	HEDGES	G	4	184
HEATH	GF	1	156	HEATHER	G	10	311	HEBBURN	HJ	4	184	HEDGES	G	11	172
HEATH	GF	6	195	HEATHER	J	2	161	HEBBURN	J	2	162	HEDGES	H	11	172
HEATH	GH	2	161	HEATHER	J	13	213	HEBDEN	J	9	89	HEDGES	J	2	162
HEATH	GH	7	177	HEATHER	JR	13	213	HEBDEN	J	9	272	HEDGES	J	5	170
HEATH	GS	10	311	HEATHER	JS	1	156	HEBDITCH	ST	13	213	HEDGES	J	11	172
HEATH	GW	11	171	HEATHER	JW	3	355	HEBDON	SH	10	105	HEDGES	JB	1	157

Name	Init.	Vol	Pg	Name	Init.	Vol	Pg	Name	Init.	Vol	Pg	Name	Init.	Vol	Pg
HEDGES	JE	10	105	HELLAS	A	9	89	HEMINGWAY	J	9	388	HEMSLEY	R	8	152
HEDGES	JW	1	157	HELLER	EE	4	185	HEMINGWAY	R	9	272	HEMSLEY	S	2	162
HEDGES	W	2	162	HELLER	EJ	4	185	HEMINGWAY	T	8	151	HEMSLEY	WR	2	162
HEDICKER	E	10	311	HELLER	HG	4	185	HEMINGWAY	T	8	151	HEMSLEY	WR	2	163
HEDICKER	R	4	185	HELLEWELL	E	9	272	HEMINGWAY	W	14	146	HEMSLEY	WT	13	214
HEDLEY	J	11	172	HELLEWELL	G	8	151	HEMINWAY	E	9	388	HEMSWORTH	E	8	152
HEDWORTH	A	9	272	HELLEWELL	L	8	151	HEMLEY	FG	5	170	HEMSWORTH	W	8	152
HEED	GW	7	178	HELLEWELL	R	9	272	HEMLEY	HW	5	170	HENBERY	A	1	157
HEED	JD	7	178	HELLEY	F	11	172	HEMLEY	JE	13	214	HENBEST	G	4	185
HEED	JH	7	178	HELLIAR	AW	2	162	HEMLEY	W	5	170	HENBEST	H	4	185
HEEL	H	12	321	HELLIER	GW	4	185	HEMMENS	JH	6	195	HENDER	FW	2	163
HEELEY	A	9	272	HELLIER	H	11	172	HEMMENS	TG	4	185	HENDER	JE	2	163
HEELEY	F	6	195	HELLIWELL	A	9	272	HEMMING	A	6	195	HENDERSON	A	11	173
HEELEY	G	9	89	HELLIWELL	A	9	272	HEMMING	AG	1	157	HENDERSON	AC	13	214
HEELEY	J	6	195	HELLIWELL	A	9	388	HEMMING	AL	5	171	HENDERSON	AJ	2	163
HEELEY	JT	6	195	HELLIWELL	G	9	90	HEMMING	B	6	195	HENDERSON	AJ	11	173
HEELEY	R	9	89	HELLIWELL	GH	9	90	HEMMING	F	6	195	HENDERSON	AM	8	152
HEFFER	FW	6	195	HELLIWELL	H	9	90	HEMMING	FW	6	195	HENDERSON	AV	5	171
HEFFER	J	2	162	HELLIWELL	S	9	90	HEMMING	H	6	195	HENDERSON	B	9	90
HEFFER	J	5	170	HELLIWELL	S	9	90	HEMMING	J	6	195	HENDERSON	C	7	178
HEFFERAN	D	11	172	HELLIWELL	WH	11	172	HEMMING	M	6	196	HENDERSON	CW	2	163
HEFFERMAN	E	13	214	HELLOWELL	OG	8	151	HEMMING	R	6	196	HENDERSON	E	4	185
HEFFORD	A	12	321	HELLOWELL	W	8	151	HEMMING	SE	4	185	HENDERSON	E	8	152
HEFFORD	AH	12	322	HELLYAR	A	4	185	HEMMING	V	5	171	HENDERSON	EA	1	157
HEFFORD	F	12	322	HELLYAR	C	4	185	HEMMING	WH	6	196	HENDERSON	ET	4	185
HEFFORD	TH	2	162	HELLYAR	F	4	185	HEMMING	WJ	6	196	HENDERSON	F	7	178
HEFFRAN	J	11	172	HELLYER	FJ	4	185	HEMMING	WT	6	196	HENDERSON	GW	13	214
HEGAN	H	11	172	HELLYER	FW	10	105	HEMMINGS	A	1	157	HENDERSON	H	6	196
HEGENBARTH	AH	6	195	HELLYER	M	4	185	HEMMINGS	A	6	196	HENDERSON	H	8	152
HEGGS	H	14	146	HELM	E	3	76	HEMMINGS	CJ	1	157	HENDERSON	H	13	214
HEGTER	BJ	3	75	HELM	FP	3	76	HEMMINGS	CWJ	13	214	HENDERSON	HJ	13	214
HEIB	A	7	178	HELM	FW	3	76	HEMMINGS	E	2	162	HENDERSON	J	3	356
HEIB	CW	7	178	HELM	ST	2	162	HEMMINGS	FJ	12	111	HENDERSON	J	8	152
HEIB	D	7	178	HELM	TH	3	76	HEMMINGS	H	6	196	HENDERSON	J	11	173
HEIER	JF	1	157	HELM	W	13	214	HEMMINGS	HW	1	157	HENDERSON	J	14	146
HEIGHINGTON	GF	3	75	HELME	RR	14	146	HEMMINGS	J	6	196	HENDERSON	J	14	146
HEIGHT	J	11	172	HELMS	CW	12	322	HEMMINGS	JG	1	157	HENDERSON	JH	9	272
HEIGHTON	AG	5	170	HELPS	E	14	146	HEMMINGS	W	3	356	HENDERSON	JJ	10	311
HEIGHTON	E	13	214	HELPS	WFH	13	214	HEMMINGS	WH	6	196	HENDERSON	JT	9	90
HEIGHTON	GE	5	170	HELPS	WT	14	146	HEMMINGS	WJ	12	111	HENDERSON	JW	8	152
HEIGHTON	H	13	214	HELSBY	J	9	90	HEMMINGTON	J	3	356	HENDERSON	NE	13	214
HEIGHTON	WG	1	157	HELSDEN	C	13	214	HEMMINGTON	R	13	214	HENDERSON	OW	4	185
HEIMERS	E	3	356	HELSDEN	J	13	214	HEMMONS	A	3	76	HENDERSON	P	11	173
HEIMERS	R	7	178	HELYAR	GW	3	76	HEMMONS	A	3	76	HENDERSON	T	14	146
HEIRONS	AC	2	162	HEMBREY	H	1	157	HEMPSALL	J	11	172	HENDERSON	T	14	146
HEIRONS	WT	2	162	HEMBREY	JW	2	162	HEMPSTEAD	FW	13	214	HENDERSON	W	8	152
HEITMAN	C	1	157	HEMBROUGH	FW	11	172	HEMPSTEAD	G	13	214	HENDERSON	W	11	173
HEITMAN	HCW	1	157	HEMBROUGH	H	1	157	HEMPSTEAD	HG	3	76	HENDERSON	W	11	173
HELBREN	LT	10	105	HEMBURY	HJ	5	170	HEMPSTOCK	SW	11	172	HENDERSON	WH	4	185
HELBROUGH	G	3	75	HEMING	EA	13	214	HEMPSTON	FW	7	178	HENDERSON	WJ	5	171
HELICON	J	11	172	HEMINGTON	AE	3	356	HEMPSTON	GF	7	178	HENDEY	FJ	2	163
HELL	JW	12	322	HEMINGTON	H	7	178	HEMS	W	6	196	HENDIN	C	5	171
HELLARD	E	13	214	HEMINGWAY	C	8	151	HEMSLEY	CG	8	151	HENDLEY	AC	4	185
HELLAS	A	8	151	HEMINGWAY	E	8	151	HEMSLEY	G	8	152	HENDON	W	6	196
HELLAS	A	9	89	HEMINGWAY	G	8	151	HEMSLEY	PA	13	214	HENDRA	WC	13	215

HENDRY	AC	7	179	HENNESSEY	J	8	152	HENSHALL	T	11	173	HEPPLESTON	H	9	273
HENDRY	AJ	7	179	HENNESSEY	SJC	1	157	HENSHAW	A	7	179	HEPPLESTON	H	9	388
HENDRY	CW	7	179	HENNESSEY	W	11	173	HENSHAW	AH	10	105	HEPPLESTON	W	9	273
HENDRY	H	2	163	HENNESSY	FH	3	76	HENSHAW	D	14	147	HEPTON	TA	8	152
HENDRY	J	4	186	HENNESSY	J	2	163	HENSHAW	F	11	173	HEPTONSTALL	J	8	153
HENDRY	P	4	186	HENNESSY	JMS	2	163	HENSHAW	F	14	147	HEPWORTH	A	8	153
HENDRY	SG	7	179	HENNESSY	L	2	163	HENSHAW	FW	12	322	HEPWORTH	AH	11	173
HENDRY	WH	4	186	HENNESSY	RA	7	179	HENSHAW	J	10	105	HEPWORTH	C	8	153
HENDY	FJ	1	157	HENNIKER	J	11	173	HENSHAW	JH	11	173	HEPWORTH	E	11	173
HENDY	OF	4	186	HENNING	A	13	215	HENSHAW	JW	14	147	HEPWORTH	F	13	215
HENDY	WJ	2	163	HENNING	C	1	158	HENSHAW	T	14	147	HEPWORTH	H	8	153
HENEBURY	A	14	146	HENNING	GA	10	105	HENSHAW	WH	14	147	HEPWORTH	HJ	3	356
HENEGAN	A	9	272	HENNING	GRF	13	215	HENSHILWOOD	GM	2	163	HEPWORTH	JW	8	153
HENEGAN	J	9	272	HENNING	JC	13	215	HENSLY	J	9	273	HEPWORTH	JW	11	173
HENEGAN	J	9	272	HENNING	RHE	10	105	HENSON	AG	1	158	HEPWORTH	S	8	153
HENEGAN	R	9	272	HENNING	W	13	215	HENSON	C	1	158	HEPWORTH	W	9	90
HENEGHAN	P	14	146	HENNING	WJ	4	186	HENSON	E	1	158	HEPWORTH	W	9	90
HENFIELD	J	6	196	HENNIS	T	14	147	HENSON	E	14	147	HEPWORTH	W	9	273
HENFREY	C	9	90	HENNRY	JW	6	197	HENSON	EF	5	171	HEPWORTH	WR	11	173
HENICK	C	14	146	HENRICK	AES	12	111	HENSON	FV	12	111	HERAPATH	AE	4	186
HENICK	H	14	146	HENRICK	C	12	111	HENSON	HH	14	147	HERAUD	CP	1	158
HENLEY	AE	2	163	HENRY	A	2	163	HENSON	HT	7	179	HERAUD	JA	1	158
HENLEY	CT	3	356	HENRY	AJ	3	76	HENSON	HW	1	158	HERBERT	A	8	153
HENLEY	E	5	171	HENRY	C	14	147	HENSON	J	8	152	HERBERT	AE	4	186
HENLEY	ET	13	215	HENRY	C	14	147	HENSON	PE	5	171	HERBERT	AG	7	179
HENLEY	G	7	179	HENRY	DJ	4	186	HENSON	RK	6	197	HERBERT	AH	13	215
HENLEY	GJ	3	356	HENRY	E	6	197	HENSON	S	3	76	HERBERT	CC	13	215
HENLEY	H	5	171	HENRY	E	8	152	HENSON	SC	7	179	HERBERT	CF	7	179
HENLEY	H	10	105	HENRY	ES	13	215	HENSON	W	2	163	HERBERT	CH	7	179
HENLEY	J	6	196	HENRY	F	2	163	HENSON	W	9	90	HERBERT	E	1	158
HENLEY	OJ	12	111	HENRY	H	13	215	HENSON	W	12	111	HERBERT	EA	5	171
HENLEY	RA	4	186	HENRY	HM	3	76	HENSON	W	13	215	HERBERT	ER	1	158
HENLEY	T	12	111	HENRY	J	4	186	HENSON	WA	4	186	HERBERT	F	2	163
HENLEY	VHH	10	105	HENRY	J	4	186	HENSON	WT	4	186	HERBERT	F	3	77
HENLEY	W	4	186	HENRY	J	8	152	HENTY	CE	8	152	HERBERT	F	10	106
HENLEY	W	4	186	HENRY	J	9	90	HENTY	CJ	10	106	HERBERT	GA	1	158
HENLEY	W	7	179	HENRY	J	9	273	HENTY	SC	10	106	HERBERT	GF	10	106
HENLY	HC	3	76	HENRY	LB	3	76	HENTY	WG	10	106	HERBERT	GW	3	77
HENLY	SF	10	312	HENRY	M	12	322	HENVEST	EJ	4	186	HERBERT	H	6	197
HENLY	W	3	76	HENRY	RW	6	197	HENVEST	S	4	186	HERBERT	H	6	197
HENMAN	A	5	171	HENRY	T	9	90	HENWOOD	F	2	163	HERBERT	H	7	179
HENMAN	A	5	171	HENRY	T	9	90	HENWOOD	HJ	3	76	HERBERT	HF	8	153
HENMAN	E	5	171	HENRY	T	14	147	HENWOOD	RJ	10	106	HERBERT	HH	7	179
HENMAN	F	5	171	HENRY	TW	4	186	HENWOOD	S	2	163	HERBERT	HJ	3	77
HENMAN	FG	12	322	HENRY	W	8	152	HENZEL	J	10	312	HERBERT	J	14	147
HENMAN	W	12	322	HENRY	W	9	90	HEPBURN	R	14	147	HERBERT	JE	1	158
HENN	A	6	196	HENRY	W	9	90	HEPBURN	W	3	76	HERBERT	JG	13	215
HENNEGAN	T	11	173	HENRY	WR	6	197	HEPPEL	WJB	12	322	HERBERT	JH	13	215
HENNELL	F	13	215	HENSBY	G	9	90	HEPPER	E	8	152	HERBERT	JW	4	187
HENNELL	SA	7	179	HENSBY	H	9	90	HEPPER	L	8	152	HERBERT	O	3	77
HENNELL	WT	3	76	HENSEY	E	6	197	HEPPER	R	8	152	HERBERT	PEH	3	77
HENNERY	AW	6	196	HENSFORD	R	4	186	HEPPER	TH	8	152	HERBERT	R	3	77
HENNESSEY	AJ	1	157	HENSHALL	D	14	147	HEPPINSTALL	F	9	273	HERBERT	RG	5	171
HENNESSEY	C	8	152	HENSHALL	G	14	147	HEPPINSTALL	J	11	173	HERBERT	RHT	2	164
HENNESSEY	J	1	157	HENSHALL	JH	11	173	HEPPLE	A	11	173	HERBERT	RN	2	164

HERBERT	RT	6	197	HERON	WP	3	356	HESKETT	J	13	216	HEWETT	WB	3	356
HERBERT	S	7	179	HERR	AVM	10	312	HESLING	F	8	153	HEWETT	WEO	7	180
HERBERT	SG	5	171	HERRERD	JH	10	312	HESLING	G	8	154	HEWETT	WG	13	216
HERBERT	SW	10	106	HERRICK	CH	6	197	HESLING	H	8	154	HEWETT	WH	3	77
HERBERT	T	7	179	HERRICK	H	13	216	HESLING	T	8	154	HEWIN	AE	6	197
HERBERT	T	11	173	HERRIDGE	EE	4	187	HESLING	W	8	154	HEWING	H	3	357
HERBERT	TJ	3	77	HERRIDGE	WH	5	171	HESLOP	E	2	164	HEWING	W	3	357
HERBERT	W	3	77	HERRIDGE	WT	5	171	HESLOP	F	14	148	HEWISON	A	8	154
HERBERT	W	7	180	HERRIES	H	4	187	HESLOP	G	11	174	HEWISON	GH	8	154
HERBERT	W	12	322	HERRING	A	7	180	HESLOP	J	2	164	HEWISON	H	8	154
HERBERT	W	13	215	HERRING	AE	13	216	HESLOP	W	11	174	HEWITSON	CE	8	154
HERBERT	WA	13	215	HERRING	EWG	4	187	HESLOP	WWA	2	164	HEWITSON	G	13	216
HERBERT	WA	13	215	HERRING	L	11	174	HESMAN	S	13	216	HEWITSON	J	13	216
HERBERT	WC	12	322	HERRING	L	13	216	HESP	W	8	154	HEWITSON	J	13	216
HERBERT	WG	4	186	HERRING	L	13	216	HESSE	A	9	91	HEWITSON	W	7	180
HERBERT	WH	3	77	HERRING	RJ	8	153	HESSE	J	13	216	HEWITT	A	3	357
HERBERT	WH	11	173	HERRING	W	3	77	HESSE	WH	9	91	HEWITT	A	5	172
HERBERT	WHJ	4	187	HERRINGTON	A	3	77	HESSELWORTH	F	7	180	HEWITT	A	6	197
HERBERT	WJ	2	164	HERRINGTON	B	4	187	HESSEY	AV	7	180	HEWITT	A	8	154
HERBERT	WJ	13	215	HERRINGTON	EW	1	158	HESSEY	G	7	180	HEWITT	A	8	154
HERBERT	WM	14	147	HERRINGTON	F	9	273	HESSING	RH	1	159	HEWITT	A	14	148
HERBERT	WS	3	77	HERRINGTON	WA	1	158	HESSION	A	11	174	HEWITT	AE	6	198
HERBERT	WW	13	215	HERRIOTT	J	11	174	HESSION	J	14	148	HEWITT	AH	3	357
HERBERTS	J	11	174	HERRIOTT	TA	10	106	HESSION	M	14	148	HEWITT	AL	3	357
HERD	C	7	180	HERRITY	A	14	148	HESTER	A	2	164	HEWITT	AT	3	78
HERD	CF	7	180	HERRITY	F	8	153	HESTER	AG	5	171	HEWITT	AV	1	159
HERD	E	7	180	HERROD	GW	7	180	HESTER	EG	2	164	HEWITT	B	12	111
HERD	EF	11	174	HERRON	GA	3	356	HESTER	GE	5	172	HEWITT	BH	11	174
HERD	L	11	174	HERRON	W	3	356	HESTER	H	5	172	HEWITT	C	1	159
HERD	TH	11	174	HERSEY	C	1	158	HESTER	RH	10	106	HEWITT	C	8	154
HERDSMAN	AE	1	158	HERSEY	M	1	158	HESTER	SG	5	172	HEWITT	DG	3	357
HERETY	J	11	174	HERSEY	W	1	159	HETERINGTON	FC	2	164	HEWITT	E	3	357
HERFIELD	F	9	90	HERSON	G	4	187	HETERINGTON	W	2	164	HEWITT	E	6	198
HERIOT	J	9	90	HERSON	W	8	153	HETHERINGTON	H	9	273	HEWITT	E	10	106
HERITAGE	AE	6	197	HESELGRAVE		8	153	HETHERINGTON	J	3	77	HEWITT	E	14	148
HERITAGE	CF	10	106	HESELGRAVE	A	8	153	HETHERINGTON	J	8	154	HEWITT	EC	7	180
HERITAGE	CJ	6	197	HESELGRAVE	AS	13	216	HETHERINGTON	L	14	148	HEWITT	EH	8	154
HERITAGE	CWA	12	322	HESELGRAVE	F	8	153	HETHERINGTON	W	3	77	HEWITT	EJ	10	106
HERITAGE	R	6	197	HESELGRAVE	F	8	153	HETHERSAY	W	7	180	HEWITT	F	6	198
HERLEY	DJ	13	215	HESELGRAVE	FW	13	216	HEVICON	W	4	187	HEWITT	F	8	154
HERLEY	RJ	10	116	HESELGRAVE	H	8	153	HEWERS	J	6	197	HEWITT	F	11	174
HERLEY	W	13	216	HESELGRAVE	HC	13	216	HEWERS	WH	6	197	HEWITT	FH	11	174
HERMAN	H	1	158	HESELGRAVE	M	8	153	HEWERTSON	E	14	148	HEWITT	FJ	12	111
HERMAN	P	1	158	HESELGRAVE	T	8	153	HEWETT	A	10	106	HEWITT	G	1	159
HERMAN	S	7	180	HESELGRAVE	T	8	153	HEWETT	AE	7	180	HEWITT	G	3	78
HERMAN	WE	1	158	HESELTINE	A	9	273	HEWETT	DE	10	106	HEWITT	G	6	198
HERMAN	WH	11	174	HESELTINE	F	8	153	HEWETT	FW	4	187	HEWITT	G	7	181
HERMES	W	14	147	HESELTINE	L	14	148	HEWETT	G	1	159	HEWITT	G	9	388
HERMITAGE	A	7	180	HESELTINE	R	14	148	HEWETT	G	3	356	HEWITT	G	12	322
HERNING	AV	1	158	HESFORD	J	11	174	HEWETT	GJ	3	77	HEWITT	G	14	148
HERNING	J	1	158	HESHON	B	8	153	HEWETT	HG	3	77	HEWITT	GS	7	181
HERNON	J	14	147	HESHON	CF	8	153	HEWETT	J	4	187	HEWITT	GW	8	154
HERON	AE	7	180	HESKETH	E	14	148	HEWETT	JW	10	106	HEWITT	H	11	174
HERON	JH	8	153	HESKETH	R	13	216	HEWETT	TC	3	77	HEWITT	H	13	216
HERON	M	11	174	HESKETH	T	11	174	HEWETT	W	3	356	HEWITT	HB	9	91

HEWITT	HE	3	78	HEWSON	A	5	172	HEYWOOD	W	8	155	HIBBLE	GJ	7	181			
HEWITT	HG	5	172	HEWSON	A	5	172	HEYWOOD	W	11	175	HIBBLE	WC	7	181			
HEWITT	HW	6	198	HEWSON	AF	5	172	HEYWOOD	W	11	176	HIBBS	A	4	188			
HEWITT	J	1	159	HEWSON	F	9	91	HEYWOOD	W	11	176	HIBON	J	2	164			
HEWITT	J	6	198	HEWSON	HF	7	181	HEYWOOD	W	13	216	HICK	GC	9	91			
HEWITT	J	7	181	HEWSON	J	14	148	HEYWOOD	W	14	149	HICK	H	6	199			
HEWITT	J	8	154	HEWSON	TE	6	198	HEYWOOD	W	14	149	HICK	J	11	176			
HEWITT	J	9	273	HEWSON	TH	6	198	HEYWOOD	WJ	14	149	HICK	JA	8	155			
HEWITT	J	10	106	HEWSON	TH	8	154	HEYWORTH	AG	11	176	HICK	W	8	155			
HEWITT	J	11	175	HEWSON	W	11	175	HEYWORTH	J	9	91	HICKEN	GT	6	199			
HEWITT	JE	9	273	HEWSTON	G	6	198	HEZELGRAVE	GW	8	155	HICKERTON	J	6	199			
HEWITT	JW	1	159	HEWTSON	W	9	91	HEZELGRAVE	M	8	155	HICKES	WH	14	149			
HEWITT	M	9	91	HEWTSON	W	9	273	HEZELGRAVE	S	8	155	HICKEY	AW	7	181			
HEWITT	MC	13	216	HEXLEY	W	6	198	HEZELWOOD	W	8	155	HICKEY	AW	13	217			
HEWITT	P	3	357	HEXTALL	J	9	91	HIAMS	C	12	322	HICKEY	D	9	91			
HEWITT	R	7	181	HEXTELL	G	6	198	HIATT	JL	6	198	HICKEY	D	9	388			
HEWITT	RG	7	181	HEY	G	9	91	HIBBARD	AE	6	198	HICKEY	E	7	181			
HEWITT	RW	9	273	HEY	H	8	155	HIBBARD	ARV	6	199	HICKEY	JA	9	91			
HEWITT	S	6	198	HEY	R	9	91	HIBBARD	FG	7	181	HICKEY	JW	14	149			
HEWITT	S	9	91	HEY	TW	8	155	HIBBARD	W	3	78	HICKEY	TE	3	78			
HEWITT	S	14	148	HEYBURN	WE	7	181	HIBBERD	AG	10	312	HICKEY	W	9	91			
HEWITT	ST	10	106	HEYDINRYCH	WA	2	164	HIBBERD	B	4	187	HICKEY	WE	7	181			
HEWITT	W	2	164	HEYDON	EH	3	78	HIBBERD	EE	4	187	HICKEY	WP	10	312			
HEWITT	W	5	172	HEYDON	WC	1	159	HIBBERD	ET	3	78	HICKFORD	CH	1	159			
HEWITT	W	6	198	HEYES	F	11	175	HIBBERD	GA	3	78	HICKFORD	ET	1	159			
HEWITT	W	8	154	HEYES	G	14	148	HIBBERD	H	4	187	HICKFORD	F	12	111			
HEWITT	W	8	154	HEYES	R	14	148	HIBBERD	H	10	106	HICKFORD	T	14	149			
HEWITT	W	11	175	HEYMER	WA	3	357	HIBBERD	HA	6	199	HICKIN	CH	10	106			
HEWITT	WF	5	172	HEYWARD	AB	7	181	HIBBERD	JB	4	187	HICKIN	R	10	107			
HEWITT	WH	6	198	HEYWARD	WT	3	357	HIBBERD	JJ	3	357	HICKIN	W	2	164			
HEWITT	WJ	5	172	HEYWOOD	A	14	148	HIBBERD	LS	4	187	HICKIN	WJ	10	107			
HEWKIN	ET	1	159	HEYWOOD	AW	2	164	HIBBERD	T	6	199	HICKINBOTHAM	C	14	149			
HEWLETT	A	10	312	HEYWOOD	E	14	148	HIBBERD	W	4	187	HICKINGBOTTOM	CG	5	172			
HEWLETT	C	2	164	HEYWOOD	F	11	175	HIBBERD	W	4	187	HICKINSON	F	8	155			
HEWLETT	E	3	78	HEYWOOD	G	11	175	HIBBERD	WG	4	187	HICKLEY	W	10	107			
HEWLETT	EG	7	181	HEYWOOD	GE	11	175	HIBBERT	A	11	176	HICKLIN	F	5	173			
HEWLETT	F	3	78	HEYWOOD	H	9	273	HIBBERT	CA	11	176	HICKLIN	J	11	176			
HEWLETT	FE	2	164	HEYWOOD	H	11	175	HIBBERT	F	5	172	HICKLING	CF	4	188			
HEWLETT	FH	6	198	HEYWOOD	H	11	175	HIBBERT	GW	5	172	HICKLING	DJ	4	188			
HEWLETT	G	1	159	HEYWOOD	J	11	175	HIBBERT	H	5	172	HICKLING	GH	4	188			
HEWLETT	GW	5	172	HEYWOOD	J	14	149	HIBBERT	H	11	176	HICKMAN	AL	6	199			
HEWLETT	H	1	159	HEYWOOD	J	14	149	HIBBERT	J	11	176	HICKMAN	AS	1	159			
HEWLETT	H	3	357	HEYWOOD	J	14	149	HIBBERT	J	14	149	HICKMAN	AW	3	78			
HEWLETT	HG	1	159	HEYWOOD	JA	13	216	HIBBERT	JT	11	176	HICKMAN	AW	4	188			
HEWLETT	HW	5	172	HEYWOOD	JE	11	175	HIBBERT	JW	11	176	HICKMAN	C	10	107			
HEWLETT	J	1	159	HEYWOOD	JE	14	149	HIBBERT	MFR	5	172	HICKMAN	CW	3	357			
HEWLETT	M	1	159	HEYWOOD	JT	11	175	HIBBERT	S	7	181	HICKMAN	E	7	181			
HEWLETT	RJ	4	187	HEYWOOD	JW	14	149	HIBBERT	S	7	181	HICKMAN	EA	7	182			
HEWLETT	SA	2	164	HEYWOOD	R	11	175	HIBBERT	TH	14	149	HICKMAN	EH	1	159			
HEWLETT	TW	3	78	HEYWOOD	S	10	106	HIBBERT	W	3	357	HICKMAN	FE	6	199			
HEWLETT	W	4	187	HEYWOOD	S	11	175	HIBBERTS	W	6	199	HICKMAN	FE	12	322			
HEWLETT	W	11	175	HEYWOOD	S	11	175	HIBBINS	FW	13	217	HICKMAN	FH	4	188			
HEWLETT	WE	11	175	HEYWOOD	S	11	175	HIBBINS	T	13	217	HICKMAN	H	5	173			
HEWLETT	WJ	4	187	HEYWOOD	T	10	106	HIBBITT	AE	5	172	HICKMAN	H	6	199			
HEWORTH	EB	8	154	HEYWOOD	TH	14	149	HIBBITTS	H	11	176	HICKMAN	HJ	7	182			

Surname	Init	Vol	Pg	Surname	Init	Vol	Pg	Surname	Init	Vol	Pg	Surname	Init	Vol	Pg
HICKMAN	HL	12	322	HIERONS	AR	3	357	HIGGINS	JH	12	112	HIGGS	JW	1	160
HICKMAN	J	6	199	HIETT	HD	6	199	HIGGINS	JJ	9	91	HIGGS	JWS	12	323
HICKMAN	JJ	7	182	HIGBEE	AHJ	13	217	HIGGINS	JW	9	91	HIGGS	LM	10	107
HICKMAN	JJ	7	182	HIGERTY	HSL	13	217	HIGGINS	L	8	155	HIGGS	M	11	177
HICKMAN	JW	12	322	HIGERTY	K	13	217	HIGGINS	M	9	273	HIGGS	R	2	165
HICKMAN	R	12	111	HIGGIN	J	14	150	HIGGINS	M	9	388	HIGGS	R	5	173
HICKMAN	S	4	188	HIGGINBOTHAM	C	14	150	HIGGINS	R	2	165	HIGGS	RC	5	173
HICKMAN	S	6	199	HIGGINBOTHAM	E	14	150	HIGGINS	SC	2	165	HIGGS	S	5	174
HICKMAN	W	4	188	HIGGINBOTHAM	HG	3	78	HIGGINS	SG	5	173	HIGGS	SJ	5	174
HICKMAN	W	6	199	HIGGINBOTHAM	R	14	150	HIGGINS	T	4	188	HIGGS	SW	5	174
HICKMAN	W	13	217	HIGGINBOTHAM	W	14	150	HIGGINS	T	11	176	HIGGS	TE	2	165
HICKMAN	WA	6	199	HIGGINBOTTOM	G	4	188	HIGGINS	T	12	112	HIGGS	W	2	165
HICKMAN	WA	7	182	HIGGINBOTTOM	JT	12	322	HIGGINS	T	14	150	HIGGS	W	6	200
HICKS	A	1	160	HIGGINBOTTOM	T	4	188	HIGGINS	TD	12	323	HIGGS	WJ	2	165
HICKS	A	10	107	HIGGINBOTTOM	T	8	155	HIGGINS	TH	3	79	HIGGS	WJ	6	200
HICKS	AJ	10	107	HIGGINBOTTOM	W	2	164	HIGGINS	W	1	160	HIGGS	WR	7	182
HICKS	C	6	199	HIGGINBOTTOM	W	11	176	HIGGINS	W	7	182	HIGGS	WT	5	174
HICKS	C	7	182	HIGGINS	A	3	78	HIGGINS	W	14	150	HIGH	A	11	177
HICKS	E	10	107	HIGGINS	A	5	173	HIGGINS	WF	5	173	HIGH	FH	6	200
HICKS	EL	10	312	HIGGINS	A	11	176	HIGGINS	WG	3	79	HIGH	HW	10	312
HICKS	F	1	160	HIGGINS	C	3	78	HIGGINS	WH	2	165	HIGH	J	7	182
HICKS	F	3	78	HIGGINS	C	12	322	HIGGINS	WH	12	112	HIGH	T	8	155
HICKS	F	5	173	HIGGINS	E	8	155	HIGGINS	WM	12	112	HIGH	TW	7	182
HICKS	F	7	182	HIGGINS	E	11	176	HIGGINSON	C	8	155	HIGHAM	A	14	150
HICKS	F	9	91	HIGGINS	EC	13	217	HIGGINSON	C	14	150	HIGHAM	H	14	150
HICKS	F	10	107	HIGGINS	EJ	12	111	HIGGINSON	E	8	155	HIGHAM	J	14	150
HICKS	FC	1	160	HIGGINS	F	4	188	HIGGINSON	HT	11	176	HIGHAM	W	14	150
HICKS	FG	7	182	HIGGINS	F	14	150	HIGGINSON	J	11	177	HIGHFIELD	FL	6	200
HICKS	FJ	4	188	HIGGINS	FJ	12	111	HIGGINSON	SG	14	150	HIGHLAND	WG	13	217
HICKS	FT	13	217	HIGGINS	FR	7	182	HIGGINSON	WH	11	177	HIGHLEY	A	9	91
HICKS	FW	3	78	HIGGINS	FW	12	112	HIGGS	A	5	173	HIGHLEY	P	3	79
HICKS	G	3	78	HIGGINS	G	3	79	HIGGS	A	6	200	HIGHO	E	10	312
HICKS	GG	6	199	HIGGINS	G	6	199	HIGGS	A	6	200	HIGHO	H	10	312
HICKS	H	11	176	HIGGINS	GA	1	160	HIGGS	A	7	182	HIGHO	T	10	312
HICKS	H	13	217	HIGGINS	GP	6	199	HIGGS	AT	10	107	HIGINBOTTOM	AG	1	160
HICKS	HG	13	217	HIGGINS	H	5	173	HIGGS	AW	6	200	HIGINBOTTOM	G	1	160
HICKS	J	12	322	HIGGINS	H	9	91	HIGGS	BJ	6	200	HIGINBOTTOM	JC	1	160
HICKS	J	14	149	HIGGINS	H	11	176	HIGGS	C	2	165	HIGINBOTTOM	WJ	1	160
HICKS	JAJ	10	312	HIGGINS	H	13	217	HIGGS	CB	10	312	HIGMAN	CA	4	188
HICKS	JW	14	149	HIGGINS	HC	12	112	HIGGS	CE	5	173	HIGMAN	H	12	112
HICKS	L	7	182	HIGGINS	HF	1	160	HIGGS	CE	5	173	HIGNELL	AS	7	182
HICKS	LL	7	182	HIGGINS	HH	6	200	HIGGS	CR	5	173	HIGNETT	GH	14	150
HICKS	LV	1	160	HIGGINS	HJ	1	160	HIGGS	D	2	165	HIGO	J	8	155
HICKS	RH	7	182	HIGGINS	HT	2	165	HIGGS	DC	1	160	HIGSON	T	14	150
HICKS	TW	10	312	HIGGINS	HT	5	173	HIGGS	E	5	173	HILAND	M	9	91
HICKS	W	9	273	HIGGINS	HW	6	200	HIGGS	FR	5	173	HILBERT	AH	6	200
HICKS	WB	3	78	HIGGINS	HW	7	182	HIGGS	G	6	200	HILDER	AT	7	182
HICKS	WJ	5	173	HIGGINS	J	2	165	HIGGS	GW	6	200	HILDER	EM	2	165
HICKS	WJ	5	173	HIGGINS	J	2	165	HIGGS	GW	10	312	HILDER	RE	7	183
HICKSON	E	14	150	HIGGINS	J	2	165	HIGGS	H	5	173	HILDER	W	2	165
HICKSON	H	13	217	HIGGINS	J	6	200	HIGGS	H	5	173	HILDICK	W	6	200
HICKSON	JR	13	217	HIGGINS	J	8	155	HIGGS	HA	1	160	HILDRED	T	9	92
HICKSON	L	8	155	HIGGINS	J	8	155	HIGGS	J	6	200	HILDREW	S	13	217
HICKSON	W	14	150	HIGGINS	J	9	273	HIGGS	J	6	200	HILES	A	9	273
HIDER	FH	13	217	HIGGINS	J	11	176	HIGGS	JT	1	160	HILES	H	9	273

HILES	J	1	160	HILL	B	14	151	HILL	F	6	201	HILL	H	10	108
HILES	JH	9	274	HILL	BT	12	323	HILL	F	6	201	HILL	H	10	313
HILEY	A	9	92	HILL	C	2	165	HILL	F	6	201	HILL	H	11	177
HILEY	F	9	92	HILL	C	4	188	HILL	F	9	92	HILL	H	13	218
HILEY	JJ	7	183	HILL	C	9	92	HILL	F	9	274	HILL	H	13	218
HILKIN	C	7	183	HILL	C	10	312	HILL	F	11	177	HILL	H	14	151
HILL	A	1	160	HILL	C	12	112	HILL	FA	10	107	HILL	HA	5	175
HILL	A	4	188	HILL	CA	7	183	HILL	FA	12	112	HILL	HA	7	183
HILL	A	5	174	HILL	CA	10	107	HILL	FAP	4	189	HILL	HG	8	156
HILL	A	5	174	HILL	CA	12	323	HILL	FE	13	218	HILL	HH	10	108
HILL	A	5	174	HILL	CF	6	201	HILL	FH	6	201	HILL	HH	12	323
HILL	A	6	200	HILL	CG	6	201	HILL	FJ	12	112	HILL	HJ	12	112
HILL	A	6	200	HILL	CH	4	188	HILL	FJ	13	218	HILL	HN	9	92
HILL	A	7	183	HILL	CH	4	188	HILL	FM	6	201	HILL	HR	1	161
HILL	A	7	183	HILL	CH	13	218	HILL	FW	1	161	HILL	HS	5	175
HILL	A	8	156	HILL	CJ	13	218	HILL	FW	12	323	HILL	HS	6	202
HILL	A	8	156	HILL	CL	7	183	HILL	G	3	357	HILL	HS	7	183
HILL	A	8	156	HILL	CV	2	165	HILL	G	5	174	HILL	HT	1	161
HILL	A	8	156	HILL	D	1	161	HILL	G	5	174	HILL	HW	10	108
HILL	A	9	92	HILL	D	5	174	HILL	G	6	201	HILL	J	1	161
HILL	A	9	92	HILL	D	6	201	HILL	G	6	201	HILL	J	5	175
HILL	A	9	274	HILL	D	6	201	HILL	G	6	201	HILL	J	6	202
HILL	A	9	274	HILL	DC	4	188	HILL	G	10	107	HILL	J	6	202
HILL	A	10	107	HILL	DG	6	201	HILL	G	13	218	HILL	J	6	202
HILL	A	11	177	HILL	E	1	161	HILL	GA	7	183	HILL	J	8	156
HILL	A	12	112	HILL	E	1	161	HILL	GE	10	313	HILL	J	9	92
HILL	A	13	217	HILL	E	3	79	HILL	GE	13	218	HILL	J	9	92
HILL	AA	1	160	HILL	E	5	174	HILL	GF	6	201	HILL	J	9	92
HILL	AA	7	183	HILL	E	5	174	HILL	GH	1	161	HILL	J	9	92
HILL	AA	10	107	HILL	E	6	201	HILL	GH	2	166	HILL	J	9	274
HILL	AA	10	107	HILL	E	6	201	HILL	GH	3	358	HILL	J	10	108
HILL	AC	1	161	HILL	E	7	183	HILL	GH	4	189	HILL	J	10	108
HILL	AC	13	217	HILL	E	9	92	HILL	GH	4	189	HILL	J	11	177
HILL	AE	1	161	HILL	E	12	112	HILL	GH	9	92	HILL	J	11	177
HILL	AE	2	165	HILL	E	14	151	HILL	GH	12	112	HILL	J	13	218
HILL	AE	2	165	HILL	E	14	151	HILL	GH	12	323	HILL	J	13	218
HILL	AE	3	357	HILL	EA	5	174	HILL	GR	1	161	HILL	J	14	151
HILL	AE	5	174	HILL	EA	10	312	HILL	GT	8	156	HILL	JA	2	166
HILL	AE	5	174	HILL	EA	12	323	HILL	GW	2	166	HILL	JA	10	108
HILL	AE	6	200	HILL	EC	1	161	HILL	GW	6	201	HILL	JC	8	156
HILL	AE	6	201	HILL	EC	10	107	HILL	GW	11	177	HILL	JE	2	166
HILL	AF	4	188	HILL	EC	13	218	HILL	GW	12	112	HILL	JE	6	202
HILL	AF	13	217	HILL	EH	13	218	HILL	GW	12	112	HILL	JE	6	202
HILL	AH	5	174	HILL	EJ	5	174	HILL	GW	13	218	HILL	JF	1	161
HILL	AH	13	218	HILL	EJ	5	174	HILL	GWT	4	189	HILL	JF	11	177
HILL	AJ	12	112	HILL	EM	10	107	HILL	H	1	161	HILL	JG	7	183
HILL	AJL	10	107	HILL	EM	10	313	HILL	H	2	166	HILL	JH	6	202
HILL	AJW	1	161	HILL	F	1	161	HILL	H	2	166	HILL	JH	10	313
HILL	AP	5	174	HILL	F	1	161	HILL	H	5	175	HILL	JT	6	202
HILL	AR	12	323	HILL	F	2	166	HILL	H	6	201	HILL	JT	7	183
HILL	AS	3	357	HILL	F	2	166	HILL	H	6	201	HILL	JT	11	177
HILL	AW	1	161	HILL	F	2	166	HILL	H	6	202	HILL	JW	7	183
HILL	AW	4	188	HILL	F	3	79	HILL	H	8	156	HILL	JW	8	156
HILL	AW	7	183	HILL	F	4	188	HILL	H	8	156	HILL	JW	9	92
HILL	AW	14	150	HILL	F	5	174	HILL	H	9	92	HILL	JW	14	151

HILL	JW	14	151	HILL	W	5	175	HILLIER	AS	7	184	HILLS	E	12	112				
HILL	JWJ	5	175	HILL	W	6	202	HILLIER	B	4	189	HILLS	E	13	219				
HILL	K	1	161	HILL	W	6	202	HILLIER	C	1	162	HILLS	F	2	166				
HILL	L	1	161	HILL	W	6	203	HILLIER	CJ	1	162	HILLS	F	2	167				
HILL	LM	13	218	HILL	W	7	184	HILLIER	D	2	166	HILLS	F	12	113				
HILL	LR	4	189	HILL	W	8	156	HILLIER	EG	10	313	HILLS	FG	13	219				
HILL	MA	1	162	HILL	W	8	156	HILLIER	EJ	4	189	HILLS	GW	1	162				
HILL	N	12	112	HILL	W	8	156	HILLIER	F	7	184	HILLS	H	1	162				
HILL	NF	7	183	HILL	W	8	156	HILLIER	GW	1	162	HILLS	H	3	79				
HILL	NN	13	218	HILL	W	9	92	HILLIER	GW	13	219	HILLS	H	12	113				
HILL	P	1	162	HILL	W	9	274	HILLIER	H	3	79	HILLS	HW	7	185				
HILL	P	5	175	HILL	W	11	177	HILLIER	H	11	177	HILLS	I	13	219				
HILL	P	6	202	HILL	W	11	177	HILLIER	JE	7	184	HILLS	J	13	220				
HILL	PJ	13	218	HILL	W	11	177	HILLIER	JF	13	219	HILLS	JA	7	185				
HILL	R	2	166	HILL	W	12	323	HILLIER	LC	13	219	HILLS	JB	1	162				
HILL	R	5	175	HILL	W	12	323	HILLIER	R	1	162	HILLS	JJ	7	185				
HILL	R	6	202	HILL	WA	5	175	HILLIER	R	3	79	HILLS	JT	7	185				
HILL	R	11	177	HILL	WC	7	184	HILLIER	R	4	189	HILLS	OOO	5	175				
HILL	R	14	151	HILL	WE	12	323	HILLIER	RJ	10	313	HILLS	PS	7	185				
HILL	RCI	7	183	HILL	WF	1	162	HILLIER	RWJ	4	189	HILLS	R	5	176				
HILL	RH	6	202	HILL	WG	4	189	HILLIER	SL	13	219	HILLS	RA	2	167				
HILL	RH	13	218	HILL	WG	11	177	HILLIER	W	13	219	HILLS	SG	13	220				
HILL	RH	13	218	HILL	WG	12	323	HILLIER	WC	10	313	HILLS	TE	7	185				
HILL	RJ	6	202	HILL	WH	5	175	HILLIER	WF	7	184	HILLS	TW	10	313				
HILL	RJ	7	184	HILL	WH	6	203	HILLIER	WH	1	162	HILLS	W	2	167				
HILL	RO	6	202	HILL	WH	6	203	HILLIER	WH	6	203	HILLS	W	2	167				
HILL	RS	6	202	HILL	WH	12	112	HILLIER	WH	7	184	HILLS	W	11	178				
HILL	RV	1	162	HILL	WH	13	219	HILLIGER	AW	3	79	HILLS	WJ	12	113				
HILL	RV	12	323	HILL	WHG	1	162	HILLING	A	7	184	HILLS	WO	5	176				
HILL	S	2	166	HILL	WJ	1	162	HILLING	HG	2	166	HILLS	WR	1	162				
HILL	S	3	358	HILL	WJ	3	79	HILLINGWORTH	E	9	93	HILLSDON	J	5	176				
HILL	SA	10	313	HILL	WJ	3	358	HILLINGWORTH	J	9	274	HILLSON	AE	12	323				
HILL	SE	8	156	HILL	WJ	7	184	HILLMAN	A	1	162	HILLSON	TJ	3	79				
HILL	SR	4	189	HILL	WL	2	166	HILLMAN	A	6	203	HILLSON	WG	3	79				
HILL	SS	13	219	HILL	WT	1	162	HILLMAN	A	6	203	HILLYARD	F	12	113				
HILL	SW	7	184	HILLAM	A	9	388	HILLMAN	AE	7	184	HILLYARD	HG	12	323				
HILL	SW	10	313	HILLARY	C	9	274	HILLMAN	AT	13	219	HILLYARD	J	5	176				
HILL	T	1	162	HILLARY	J	11	177	HILLMAN	C	6	203	HILLYARD	JW	12	113				
HILL	T	2	166	HILLARY	JH	14	151	HILLMAN	E	13	219	HILLYARD	R	12	323				
HILL	T	2	166	HILLARY	R	9	388	HILLMAN	G	6	203	HILLYARD	T	12	113				
HILL	T	4	189	HILLAS	J	9	92	HILLMAN	GE	10	313	HILLYARD	TJ	5	176				
HILL	T	9	92	HILLEARD	A	7	184	HILLMAN	J	13	219	HILLYEAR	H	4	189				
HILL	T	9	92	HILLEARD	AE	13	219	HILLMAN	L	6	203	HILLYER	AE	2	167				
HILL	T	10	108	HILLEARD	R	7	184	HILLMAN	W	10	313	HILLYER	FA	12	113				
HILL	T	13	219	HILLERY	R	12	323	HILLMAN	WJ	4	189	HILLYER	G	13	220				
HILL	TC	7	184	HILLIAR	RJ	2	166	HILLMAN	WT	7	184	HILLYER	GL	12	113				
HILL	TF	6	202	HILLIAR	WH	13	219	HILLS	A	2	166	HILLYER	H	7	185				
HILL	TH	1	162	HILLIARD	C	5	175	HILLS	A	10	108	HILLYER	J	12	323				
HILL	TH	13	219	HILLIARD	E	6	203	HILLS	B	4	189	HILLYER	JF	7	185				
HILL	TS	12	323	HILLIARD	EA	13	219	HILLS	B	13	219	HILLYER	LA	12	113				
HILL	VN	7	184	HILLIARD	P	5	175	HILLS	BJ	10	313	HILLYER	LE	2	167				
HILL	W	1	162	HILLIARD	R	5	175	HILLS	C	5	175	HILLYER	T	12	323				
HILL	W	1	162	HILLIARD	W	5	175	HILLS	C	10	108	HILLYER	WG	12	324				
HILL	W	2	166	HILLIARD	WH	5	175	HILLS	C	13	219	HILSDEN	AC	5	176				
HILL	W	5	175	HILLIER	AE	4	189	HILLS	E	7	184	HILSDON	WH	6	203				

HILSON	CT	2	167
HILTON	A	14	151
HILTON	AP	4	189
HILTON	CW	3	79
HILTON	E	8	156
HILTON	F	3	358
HILTON	F	5	176
HILTON	F	9	93
HILTON	F	12	324
HILTON	FE	7	185
HILTON	FJ	1	163
HILTON	FW	5	176
HILTON	G	11	178
HILTON	G	11	178
HILTON	G	14	151
HILTON	GHJ	14	151
HILTON	GT	3	79
HILTON	HT	7	185
HILTON	J	11	178
HILTON	L	9	93
HILTON	RJ	12	113
HILTON	SG	3	358
HILTON	W	9	93
HILTON	W	11	178
HILTON	WA	5	176
HILTON	WH	5	176
HILTON	WJ	4	189
HILTON	WJ	5	176
HIMMERFIELD	B	14	151
HIMSWORTH	W	7	185
HINCE	AS	1	163
HINCE	EM	1	163
HINCH	J	12	113
HINCHCLIFF	H	9	274
HINCHCLIFFE	H	9	93
HINCHCLIFFE	J	9	274
HINCHCLIFFE	P	9	93
HINCHCLIFFE	W	9	274
HINCHLEY	JT	6	203
HINCHLEY	NH	6	203
HINCHLIFF	AE	8	156
HINCHLIFF	JE	8	156
HINCHLIFF	T	8	156
HINCKLEY	HF	1	163
HIND	A	7	185
HIND	B	13	220
HIND	FE	4	189
HIND	FG	7	185
HIND	H	7	185
HIND	HV	7	185
HIND	N	7	185
HIND	SJ	7	185
HIND	WH	7	185
HINDE	C	12	113
HINDE	E	12	113
HINDE	F	12	113
HINDE	GT	12	113
HINDE	HJ	6	203
HINDE	J	12	113
HINDE	JW	12	113
HINDE	R	5	176
HINDE	R	12	113
HINDE	W	8	156
HINDE	WE	12	113
HINDE	WE	12	114
HINDE	WH	9	274
HINDLE	A	8	157
HINDLE	A	9	274
HINDLE	E	8	157
HINDLE	E	14	151
HINDLE	G	14	151
HINDLE	T	4	189
HINDLE	T	14	151
HINDLE	W	4	189
HINDLE	W	9	93
HINDLEY	E	11	178
HINDLEY	E	11	178
HINDLEY	H	14	151
HINDLEY	J	11	178
HINDLEY	J	11	178
HINDLEY	JP	5	176
HINDLEY	L	11	178
HINDMARSH	AG	1	163
HINDMARSH	AG	3	79
HINDS	EJ	7	186
HINDS	G	14	151
HINDS	J	11	178
HINDS	J	11	178
HINDS	J	13	220
HINDS	J	13	220
HINDS	T	5	176
HINDS	T	8	157
HINDS	T	11	178
HINDS	W	11	178
HINDS	WH	11	178
HINDSON	F	2	167
HINDSON	T	11	178
HINDSON	W	11	178
HINE	A	7	186
HINE	F	6	203
HINE	FW	4	190
HINE	J	7	186
HINE	JFC	1	163
HINE	R	14	152
HINES	A	6	203
HINES	AC	7	186
HINES	AHC	4	190
HINES	GHW	7	186
HINES	J	2	167
HINES	JC	12	114
HINES	JF	13	220
HINES	P	11	178
HINES	PL	10	108
HINES	SC	7	186
HINES	TW	13	220
HINES	W	7	186
HINES	W	11	178
HINES	WG	12	114
HINETT	T	11	179
HINGE	WJ	5	176
HINGLE	CE	2	167
HINGLE	FL	2	167
HINGLE	M	2	167
HINGLE	W	2	167
HINGSTON	W	3	79
HININGS	FO	2	167
HINITT	A	6	203
HINKINS	AJ	1	163
HINKLEY	F	7	186
HINKLEY	TC	6	203
HINKLEY	W	2	167
HINKLY	GR	7	186
HINKS	AE	6	203
HINKS	GR	6	204
HINKS	H	6	204
HINKS	H	6	204
HINKS	HJ	2	167
HINKS	J	5	176
HINKS	JW	6	204
HINKS	T	10	108
HINLEY	B	6	204
HINLEY	WH	6	204
HINNELL	A	9	93
HINNEM	WA	13	220
HINRICH	A	7	186
HINRICH	FJ	7	186
HINRICH	WA	2	167
HINSLEY	A	3	79
HINSLEY	AE	3	79
HINSLEY	E	8	157
HINSLEY	EW	6	204
HINSLEY	HB	13	220
HINSON	A	6	204
HINSON	AE	7	186
HINSON	AW	13	220
HINSON	CR	11	179
HINSON	H	2	167
HINSON	HA	13	220
HINSON	J	6	204
HINSON	J	14	152
HINSON	PR	7	186
HINSON	W	6	204
HINTON	A	6	204
HINTON	A	6	204
HINTON	AJ	4	190
HINTON	AWG	13	220
HINTON	F	2	167
HINTON	F	7	186
HINTON	FP	4	190
HINTON	HB	4	190
HINTON	HGD	10	108
HINTON	HJ	6	204
HINTON	J	1	163
HINTON	J	2	167
HINTON	JN	2	168
HINTON	TW	6	204
HINTON	WG	4	190
HINTON	WG	7	186
HINTON	WJ	4	190
HINTON	WT	2	168
HINVES	CJB	4	190
HINVEST	JP	4	190
HINXMAN	AW	7	186
HINXMAN	AW	7	186
HIPKISS	A	6	204
HIPKISS	G	6	204
HIPKISS	GM	6	204
HIPKISS	J	6	204
HIPKISS	J	6	204
HIPKISS	JJ	6	204
HIPPERSON	CF	5	176
HIPPISLEY	A	4	190
HIPWELL	AC	3	80
HIPWELL	JJ	13	220
HIPWELL	JJ	13	220
HIPWELL	W	3	80
HIRD	A	8	157
HIRD	CW	9	274
HIRD	E	9	274
HIRD	F	9	93
HIRD	F	9	388
HIRD	G	8	157
HIRD	J	8	157
HIRD	JE	9	93
HIRD	JE	9	388
HIRD	JW	9	274
HIRDLE	W	5	176
HIRON	A	7	186
HIRON	F	7	187
HIRON	S	7	187
HIRONS	A	6	205
HIRONS	CA	5	176
HIRONS	RK	6	205
HIRONS	S	12	324
HIRST	A	8	157
HIRST	A	8	157
HIRST	AT	7	187
HIRST	C	8	157
HIRST	C	8	157
HIRST	C	8	157

HIRST	C	8	157	HISCOCK	WC	13	220	HITCHINS	F	7	187	HOARE	H	5	177
HIRST	C	8	157	HISCOCK	WH	4	191	HITCHINS	JH	7	187	HOARE	H	5	177
HIRST	CRJ	2	168	HISCOCK	WS	4	191	HITCHINS	M	7	187	HOARE	H	6	205
HIRST	E	8	157	HISCOCKS	EW	4	191	HITCHMAN	GL	1	163	HOARE	H	7	187
HIRST	E	9	93	HISCOCKS	HA	2	168	HITCHMAN	GVE	1	163	HOARE	H	10	313
HIRST	E	9	274	HISCOE	GS	8	158	HITCHMAN	H	6	205	HOARE	HW	10	109
HIRST	FJ	12	114	HISCOE	H	8	158	HITCHMAN	H	7	187	HOARE	J	6	205
HIRST	G	8	157	HISCOE	WF	8	158	HITCHMAN	LH	6	205	HOARE	J	8	158
HIRST	GM	9	274	HISCUTT	HG	10	108	HITCHMAN	R	6	205	HOARE	L	1	164
HIRST	H	8	157	HISEMAN	H	5	177	HITCHMAN	T	6	205	HOARE	S	7	188
HIRST	H	9	274	HISHMURGH	S	14	152	HITCHMAN	W	1	163	HOARE	S	13	221
HIRST	H	9	275	HISKETT	AW	5	177	HITCHMAN	WJ	6	205	HOARE	SA	13	221
HIRST	H	13	220	HISKETT	F	5	177	HITE	CJ	5	177	HOARE	W	2	168
HIRST	J	8	157	HISKETT	FJ	5	177	HITE	WJ	5	177	HOARE	W	5	177
HIRST	J	8	157	HISKETT	G	2	168	HITT	CE	1	163	HOARE	WA	3	80
HIRST	J	8	157	HISKETT	H	5	177	HIVES	E	12	114	HOARE	WE	7	188
HIRST	J	11	179	HISLOP	A	7	187	HIXON	AA	12	114	HOARE	WJ	2	168
HIRST	J	11	179	HISLOP	CE	4	191	HIXSON	A	1	163	HOARE	WT	3	80
HIRST	J	14	152	HISLOP	DD	7	187	HOAD	RS	3	358	HOARE	WW	4	191
HIRST	JF	9	275	HISLOP	TWP	4	191	HOADLEY	AE	2	168	HOARE	WW	10	314
HIRST	N	11	179	HISSEY	R	3	80	HOADLEY	GHJ	4	191	HOBAN	A	8	158
HIRST	O	8	157	HISTED	G	13	220	HOAR	E	7	187	HOBAN	D	6	205
HIRST	R	8	158	HISTON	J	4	191	HOAR	F	5	177	HOBAN	J	8	158
HIRST	RD	8	158	HITCH	A	12	114	HOAR	F	10	313	HOBAN	JF	8	159
HIRST	RH	8	158	HITCHCOCK	C	10	108	HOAR	LEG	10	109	HOBAN	M	8	159
HIRST	RR	8	158	HITCHCOCK	CJ	5	177	HOAR	M	5	177	HOBAN	P	8	159
HIRST	S	9	275	HITCHCOCK	E	10	108	HOAR	S	5	177	HOBAN	T	8	159
HIRST	T	8	158	HITCHCOCK	FW	5	177	HOAR	SA	1	163	HOBBINS	FAS	6	205
HIRST	T	8	158	HITCHCOCK	H	4	191	HOAR	WJC	10	313	HOBBINS	JH	6	205
HIRST	T	9	93	HITCHCOCK	HA	10	108	HOARE	A	7	187	HOBBINS	R	6	206
HIRST	T	11	179	HITCHCOCK	HS	7	187	HOARE	A	10	109	HOBBINS	S	10	109
HIRST	W	8	158	HITCHCOCK	SL	10	108	HOARE	A	10	313	HOBBINS	SA	10	109
HIRST	W	13	220	HITCHCOCK	W	1	163	HOARE	AC	2	168	HOBBINS	T	6	205
HIRST-GEE	J	9	93	HITCHCOCK	W	14	152	HOARE	AC	7	187	HOBBIS	C	1	164
HIRST-GEE	W	9	93	HITCHCOX	AE	1	163	HOARE	AJ	7	187	HOBBIS	C	1	164
HISCOCK	A	13	220	HITCHEN	AB	8	158	HOARE	AM	1	163	HOBBIS	HH	6	206
HISCOCK	AE	4	190	HITCHEN	C	11	179	HOARE	AR	3	80	HOBBS	A	3	80
HISCOCK	AG	4	190	HITCHEN	CR	8	158	HOARE	B	8	158	HOBBS	A	6	206
HISCOCK	CH	4	190	HITCHEN	GH	8	158	HOARE	CE	13	221	HOBBS	A	10	109
HISCOCK	CW	4	190	HITCHEN	H	8	158	HOARE	CF	6	205	HOBBS	A	12	114
HISCOCK	CW	4	190	HITCHEN	JW	11	179	HOARE	CJ	7	187	HOBBS	AE	2	168
HISCOCK	EH	4	190	HITCHEN	W	8	158	HOARE	E	4	191	HOBBS	AE	3	80
HISCOCK	F	10	108	HITCHENS	AW	3	358	HOARE	E	7	187	HOBBS	AE	12	324
HISCOCK	FC	4	190	HITCHENS	EJ	6	205	HOARE	E	7	187	HOBBS	AE	13	221
HISCOCK	GN	4	190	HITCHENS	ER	2	168	HOARE	EW	7	187	HOBBS	AJ	3	80
HISCOCK	HG	4	190	HITCHENS	WA	6	205	HOARE	F	1	164	HOBBS	AW	4	191
HISCOCK	JC	4	190	HITCHIN	AW	8	158	HOARE	F	10	109	HOBBS	B	3	80
HISCOCK	JG	4	190	HITCHIN	B	8	158	HOARE	FK	10	313	HOBBS	BA	3	80
HISCOCK	RG	2	168	HITCHIN	LF	3	80	HOARE	G	1	164	HOBBS	C	5	177
HISCOCK	SJ	4	190	HITCHIN	R	8	158	HOARE	G	10	109	HOBBS	CA	10	109
HISCOCK	TG	5	177	HITCHINER	HW	1	163	HOARE	GE	7	188	HOBBS	CP	5	177
HISCOCK	W	5	177	HITCHING	AC	1	163	HOARE	GF	6	205	HOBBS	CT	10	109
HISCOCK	W	10	108	HITCHING	J	1	163	HOARE	GW	10	109	HOBBS	CW	13	221
HISCOCK	WAG	4	191	HITCHINGS	W	2	168	HOARE	H	2	168	HOBBS	E	3	358
HISCOCK	WAG	4	191	HITCHINS	AJ	7	187	HOARE	H	4	191	HOBBS	EJ	7	188

Name	Init.	Pt	Pg	Name	Init.	Pt	Pg	Name	Init.	Pt	Pg	Name	Init.	Pt	Pg
HOBBS	F	3	80	HOBDEN	AA	7	188	HOCKLEY	S	5	178	HODGES	C	7	189
HOBBS	F	13	221	HOBEN	J	11	179	HOCKLEY	TE	2	169	HODGES	CFU	8	159
HOBBS	FB	5	178	HOBIN	E	14	152	HOCKLEY	WC	10	109	HODGES	CJ	6	207
HOBBS	FC	5	178	HOBIN	F	11	179	HOCKLEY	WH	7	188	HODGES	CW	1	164
HOBBS	FJ	5	178	HOBLEY	W	6	206	HOCKNEY	A	9	93	HODGES	F	13	221
HOBBS	FJ	12	324	HOBLYN	FJ	2	169	HOCKRIDGE	AJ	1	164	HODGES	FR	5	179
HOBBS	FW	5	178	HOBOROUGH	J	7	188	HOCKRIDGE	J	1	164	HODGES	H	6	207
HOBBS	G	4	191	HOBROW	H	6	206	HOCKRIDGE	W	1	164	HODGES	H	9	93
HOBBS	G	5	178	HOBSON	A	8	159	HODBY	W	5	178	HODGES	HF	4	192
HOBBS	G	10	109	HOBSON	A	8	159	HODBY	W	12	324	HODGES	JR	1	164
HOBBS	G	10	109	HOBSON	A	8	159	HODD	FW	13	221	HODGES	JS	7	189
HOBBS	G	13	221	HOBSON	A	11	179	HODDER	AE	1	164	HODGES	JT	13	221
HOBBS	GB	10	109	HOBSON	A	14	152	HODDER	AE	2	169	HODGES	LS	3	358
HOBBS	GF	2	168	HOBSON	AR	9	275	HODDER	B	4	191	HODGES	N	4	192
HOBBS	GG	5	178	HOBSON	B	9	275	HODDER	CA	13	221	HODGES	RR	12	324
HOBBS	GL	6	206	HOBSON	C	8	159	HODDER	F	10	314	HODGES	S	4	192
HOBBS	GW	10	109	HOBSON	E	6	206	HODDER	FC	4	191	HODGES	SJ	13	222
HOBBS	GWA	5	178	HOBSON	F	8	159	HODDER	J	2	169	HODGES	T	2	169
HOBBS	H	2	168	HOBSON	G	9	93	HODDER	PR	6	206	HODGES	WH	10	110
HOBBS	H	2	168	HOBSON	H	8	159	HODDER	R	1	164	HODGES	WT	6	207
HOBBS	HF	5	178	HOBSON	H	8	159	HODDER	TG	4	191	HODGETTS	A	6	207
HOBBS	HJ	7	188	HOBSON	HJ	10	109	HODDER	W	4	192	HODGETTS	E	6	207
HOBBS	HL	4	191	HOBSON	HW	2	169	HODDINOTT	RB	3	358	HODGETTS	G	9	275
HOBBS	HW	2	168	HOBSON	J	8	159	HODDLE	RJ	1	164	HODGETTS	HAT	6	207
HOBBS	HW	7	188	HOBSON	J	11	179	HODDLE	W	12	114	HODGETTS	JE	1	165
HOBBS	J	4	191	HOBSON	J	14	152	HODDY	PJ	13	221	HODGETTS	M	6	207
HOBBS	J	5	178	HOBSON	L	8	159	HODGE	CF	10	314	HODGETTS	W	6	207
HOBBS	J	6	206	HOBSON	L	11	179	HODGE	F	2	169	HODGETTS	W	6	207
HOBBS	J	7	188	HOBSON	R	2	169	HODGE	G	5	178	HODGETTS	W	6	207
HOBBS	J	12	324	HOBSON	RWT	6	206	HODGE	H	5	178	HODGETTS	WF	6	207
HOBBS	JA	14	152	HOBSON	S	8	159	HODGE	HW	2	169	HODGETTS	WJ	4	192
HOBBS	JH	6	206	HOBSON	T	3	358	HODGE	J	7	188	HODGINS	WJ	13	222
HOBBS	LH	1	164	HOBSON	W	14	152	HODGE	J	10	109	HODGKIN	CTM	12	114
HOBBS	N	1	164	HOBSON	WH	9	93	HODGE	JC	3	80	HODGKINS	A	6	207
HOBBS	RJ	2	168	HOCKENHULL	GT	11	179	HODGE	JC	7	189	HODGKINSON	A	11	179
HOBBS	RV	5	178	HOCKENHULL	J	12	324	HODGE	T	13	221	HODGKINSON	A	14	152
HOBBS	S	7	188	HOCKENHULL	T	11	179	HODGE	TP	8	159	HODGKINSON	C	3	358
HOBBS	S	10	109	HOCKENHULL	T	12	324	HODGE	W	6	206	HODGKINSON	E	2	169
HOBBS	S	12	324	HOCKENHULL	W	12	324	HODGE	W	13	221	HODGKINSON	GW	8	159
HOBBS	SR	5	178	HOCKEY	AG	7	188	HODGE	WG	10	110	HODGKINSON	H	14	152
HOBBS	TE	5	178	HOCKEY	FC	13	221	HODGE	WRG	10	110	HODGKINSON	J	11	179
HOBBS	TJ	6	206	HOCKEY	WG	7	188	HODGEMAN	WG	12	114	HODGKINSON	J	14	152
HOBBS	W	6	206	HOCKIN	S	1	164	HODGEN	F	9	275	HODGKINSON	JE	14	152
HOBBS	W	6	206	HOCKING	HC	13	221	HODGEN	J	9	275	HODGKINSON	SC	1	165
HOBBS	W	12	114	HOCKING	J	4	191	HODGEN	W	14	152	HODGKINSON	T	11	180
HOBBS	WE	2	169	HOCKING	S	7	188	HODGES	A	3	358	HODGKINSON	W	3	358
HOBBS	WE	5	178	HOCKINS	GH	10	109	HODGES	A	12	324	HODGKISS	A	14	152
HOBBS	WG	5	178	HOCKLEY	AJ	1	164	HODGES	A	13	221	HODGKISS	EG	6	207
HOBBS	WH	5	178	HOCKLEY	EJ	2	169	HODGES	AJ	1	164	HODGKISS	EJ	5	179
HOBBS	WH	13	221	HOCKLEY	G	1	164	HODGES	AJ	6	206	HODGKISSON	H	6	207
HOBBY	AH	7	188	HOCKLEY	G	3	80	HODGES	AJ	7	189	HODGMAN	H	6	207
HOBBY	FJ	7	188	HOCKLEY	H	7	188	HODGES	AP	10	110	HODGSKIN	W	6	207
HOBDAY	F	6	206	HOCKLEY	HC	2	169	HODGES	AT	2	169	HODGSON	A	8	159
HOBDAY	F	11	179	HOCKLEY	J	7	188	HODGES	AW	13	221	HODGSON	A	8	159
HOBDAY	F	11	179	HOCKLEY	LH	4	191	HODGES	C	6	207	HODGSON	A	8	159

HODGSON	A	9	93	HODGSON	W	14	152	HOGG	ED	4	192	HOLDCROFT	J	11	180
HODGSON	A	9	93	HODGSON	WB	2	169	HOGG	G	8	160	HOLDEN	A	9	276
HODGSON	A	9	275	HODKIN	A	14	153	HOGG	H	9	276	HOLDEN	A	14	153
HODGSON	A	9	275	HODKINS	F	9	94	HOGG	HJ	2	170	HOLDEN	AW	7	189
HODGSON	AE	9	275	HODKINSON	A	11	180	HOGG	HM	7	189	HOLDEN	C	8	160
HODGSON	AJ	13	222	HODKINSON	E	11	180	HOGG	JC	7	189	HOLDEN	C	11	180
HODGSON	AP	14	152	HODKINSON	WR	14	153	HOGG	JH	8	160	HOLDEN	CG	6	208
HODGSON	B	8	160	HODNETT	J	6	208	HOGG	L	8	160	HOLDEN	CH	14	153
HODGSON	B	9	93	HODRIEN	J	6	208	HOGG	LW	10	314	HOLDEN	CL	12	324
HODGSON	C	6	207	HODSALL	F	1	165	HOGG	W	3	358	HOLDEN	ET	14	153
HODGSON	C	9	275	HODSDEN	WE	5	179	HOGG	W	14	153	HOLDEN	F	11	180
HODGSON	D	9	94	HODSON	A	11	180	HOGG	WF	7	189	HOLDEN	F	14	153
HODGSON	E	9	94	HODSON	BH	8	160	HOGGAR	AW	1	165	HOLDEN	FA	11	180
HODGSON	EC	5	179	HODSON	D	4	192	HOGGAR	SE	2	170	HOLDEN	H	8	161
HODGSON	EE	12	324	HODSON	F	6	208	HOGGARD	TM	8	160	HOLDEN	H	9	94
HODGSON	EJ	11	180	HODSON	F	6	208	HOGGART	G	8	160	HOLDEN	HW	1	165
HODGSON	EW	8	160	HODSON	H	8	160	HOGGER	AVJ	7	189	HOLDEN	J	7	189
HODGSON	FC	11	180	HODSON	J	1	165	HOGSTON	GS	7	189	HOLDEN	J	9	276
HODGSON	G	8	160	HODSON	JB	8	160	HOGWOOD	C	3	359	HOLDEN	JA	12	324
HODGSON	G	8	160	HODSON	JF	1	165	HOGWOOD	F	9	276	HOLDEN	JD	13	223
HODGSON	GL	8	160	HODSON	JW	12	324	HOIGAN	E	13	222	HOLDEN	JJ	13	223
HODGSON	H	9	94	HODSON	RW	1	165	HOIGAN	J	13	222	HOLDEN	JT	6	208
HODGSON	H	9	94	HODSON	T	8	160	HOIGAN	J	13	222	HOLDEN	JT	8	161
HODGSON	H	9	94	HODSON	W	12	114	HOIGAN	J	13	222	HOLDEN	JW	12	114
HODGSON	H	9	94	HODSON	WE	5	179	HOIGAN	JM	13	222	HOLDEN	M	2	170
HODGSON	H	13	222	HODSON	WG	11	422	HOIGAN	M	13	222	HOLDEN	N	9	276
HODGSON	HC	6	207	HODSON	WR	14	153	HOILE	WD	3	80	HOLDEN	P	9	95
HODGSON	HJ	13	222	HOENES	AE	2	169	HOIT	AA	10	110	HOLDEN	P	9	276
HODGSON	HW	2	169	HOEY	T	6	208	HOIT	F	10	110	HOLDEN	W	6	208
HODGSON	J	3	80	HOFF	RA	10	110	HOKER	F	13	222	HOLDEN	W	8	161
HODGSON	J	6	208	HOFFMAN	AC	3	80	HOLBECHE	WT	2	170	HOLDEN	W	9	276
HODGSON	J	8	160	HOFFMAN	AE	5	179	HOLBIRD	CE	13	222	HOLDEN	W	12	114
HODGSON	J	9	94	HOFFMAN	P	5	179	HOLBORN	J	9	94	HOLDEN	WJ	14	153
HODGSON	J	9	275	HOFFORD	WJ	3	358	HOLBORN	TG	3	359	HOLDER	AA	3	81
HODGSON	J	9	275	HOGAN	DA	1	165	HOLBOURN	FW	13	222	HOLDER	CH	13	223
HODGSON	JE	1	165	HOGAN	E	7	189	HOLBREY	J	9	94	HOLDER	F	1	165
HODGSON	JE	2	169	HOGAN	J	9	275	HOLBROOK	A	13	222	HOLDER	G	4	192
HODGSON	JF	6	208	HOGAN	J	9	275	HOLBROOK	AE	4	192	HOLDER	GM	3	359
HODGSON	JF	9	94	HOGAN	JP	7	189	HOLBROOK	F	7	189	HOLDER	H	2	170
HODGSON	JS	13	222	HOGAN	MJ	13	222	HOLBROOK	F	13	223	HOLDER	HC	7	189
HODGSON	JW	7	189	HOGAN	P	4	192	HOLBROOK	HJ	3	81	HOLDER	HW	12	324
HODGSON	JW	8	160	HOGAN	WC	7	189	HOLBROOK	J	11	180	HOLDER	J	1	165
HODGSON	JW	9	94	HOGARTH	GD	4	192	HOLBROOK	JH	14	153	HOLDER	J	11	180
HODGSON	L	9	94	HOGARTH	HS	9	94	HOLBROOK	JJ	11	180	HOLDER	JAE	3	81
HODGSON	M	9	94	HOGBEN	C	13	222	HOLBROOK	RD	3	80	HOLDER	JT	6	208
HODGSON	M	9	275	HOGBEN	FJ	7	189	HOLBROOK	T	2	170	HOLDER	LJ	1	165
HODGSON	N	9	94	HOGBEN	GA	2	169	HOLBROOK	TF	13	223	HOLDER	R	5	179
HODGSON	R	9	94	HOGBEN	HG	2	170	HOLCROFT	CA	9	388	HOLDER	RW	13	223
HODGSON	RC	8	160	HOGBEN	OJ	13	222	HOLCROFT	F	11	180	HOLDER	TH	6	208
HODGSON	S	8	160	HOGBIN	LP	2	170	HOLD	AE	3	359	HOLDER	WH	8	161
HODGSON	S	9	94	HOGG	AE	3	358	HOLDAWAY	G	10	314	HOLDER	WR	3	81
HODGSON	S	9	275	HOGG	B	8	160	HOLDAWAY	LH	4	192	HOLDFORD	T	1	165
HODGSON	S	11	180	HOGG	C	8	160	HOLDAWAY	PJ	4	192	HOLDGATE	W	7	189
HODGSON	W	8	160	HOGG	D	9	276	HOLDAWAY	PJ	4	192	HOLDICH	G	12	114
HODGSON	W	9	94	HOGG	E	14	153	HOLDBROOK	AE	2	170	HOLDING	AJ	13	223

HOLDING	D	11	180	HOLDSWORTH	M	9	95	HOLLADAY	A	13	223	HOLLAND	J	6	209
HOLDING	ER	7	190	HOLDSWORTH	M	9	277	HOLLAND	A	1	165	HOLLAND	J	7	190
HOLDING	F	12	324	HOLDSWORTH	P	9	277	HOLLAND	A	5	179	HOLLAND	J	11	181
HOLDING	F	13	223	HOLDSWORTH	P	9	388	HOLLAND	A	13	223	HOLLAND	J	12	325
HOLDING	FE	7	189	HOLDSWORTH	RW	3	359	HOLLAND	A	13	223	HOLLAND	J	13	224
HOLDING	GB	12	325	HOLDSWORTH	RW	8	161	HOLLAND	AE	12	114	HOLLAND	J	14	154
HOLDING	HC	2	170	HOLDSWORTH	S	13	223	HOLLAND	AE	12	325	HOLLAND	JCB	1	166
HOLDING	HW	13	223	HOLDSWORTH	T	9	95	HOLLAND	AE	13	223	HOLLAND	JG	14	154
HOLDING	J	8	161	HOLDSWORTH	T	9	277	HOLLAND	AH	13	224	HOLLAND	JJ	11	181
HOLDING	JT	14	153	HOLDSWORTH	T	12	325	HOLLAND	AH	13	224	HOLLAND	JT	1	166
HOLDING	JWT	7	190	HOLDSWORTH	TE	11	180	HOLLAND	AJ	6	208	HOLLAND	JW	1	166
HOLDING	R	14	153	HOLDSWORTH	W	8	161	HOLLAND	B	14	154	HOLLAND	L	6	209
HOLDING	W	3	359	HOLDSWORTH	W	9	277	HOLLAND	C	7	190	HOLLAND	L	13	224
HOLDING	W	13	223	HOLDSWORTH	W	9	277	HOLLAND	C	7	190	HOLLAND	MT	13	224
HOLDING	W	13	223	HOLDSWORTH	W	11	180	HOLLAND	C	9	95	HOLLAND	P	12	325
HOLDSHIP	BC	10	110	HOLDSWORTH	WH	11	180	HOLLAND	C	12	114	HOLLAND	P	13	224
HOLDSTOCK	C	5	179	HOLDWAY	H	1	165	HOLLAND	C	12	325	HOLLAND	R	11	181
HOLDSTOCK	EA	5	179	HOLDWORTH	L	8	161	HOLLAND	C	14	154	HOLLAND	S	1	166
HOLDSTOCK	FJ	5	179	HOLDWORTH	T	8	161	HOLLAND	CG	6	208	HOLLAND	SF	10	110
HOLDSTOCK	J	10	110	HOLDWORTH	W	8	161	HOLLAND	CJ	12	422	HOLLAND	T	9	95
HOLDSTOCK	J	14	153	HOLE	AR	13	223	HOLLAND	CJ	12	422	HOLLAND	T	9	277
HOLDSTOCK	OS	5	179	HOLE	AW	2	170	HOLLAND	D	10	110	HOLLAND	T	11	181
HOLDSTOCK	T	14	153	HOLE	G	4	192	HOLLAND	EG	4	192	HOLLAND	T	12	325
HOLDSTOCK	WJ	5	179	HOLE	G	13	223	HOLLAND	EG	7	190	HOLLAND	T	14	154
HOLDSWORTH	A	9	276	HOLE	GR	2	170	HOLLAND	EP	11	181	HOLLAND	TD	14	154
HOLDSWORTH	A	14	153	HOLE	H	1	165	HOLLAND	F	6	208	HOLLAND	V	1	166
HOLDSWORTH	AE	8	161	HOLE	H	4	192	HOLLAND	F	9	277	HOLLAND	W	2	170
HOLDSWORTH	B	7	190	HOLE	J	7	190	HOLLAND	F	12	325	HOLLAND	W	6	209
HOLDSWORTH	B	8	161	HOLE	JAC	13	223	HOLLAND	F	13	224	HOLLAND	W	8	161
HOLDSWORTH	B	9	276	HOLE	SJ	4	192	HOLLAND	FH	7	190	HOLLAND	W	11	181
HOLDSWORTH	E	9	95	HOLE	W	14	153	HOLLAND	FJ	3	81	HOLLAND	W	12	115
HOLDSWORTH	E	9	95	HOLE	WJ	14	153	HOLLAND	FW	6	208	HOLLAND	WA	1	166
HOLDSWORTH	E	9	95	HOLES	A	4	192	HOLLAND	G	5	179	HOLLAND	WC	10	110
HOLDSWORTH	E	9	276	HOLES	L	4	192	HOLLAND	G	6	208	HOLLAND	WG	1	166
HOLDSWORTH	E	9	276	HOLFORD	F	13	223	HOLLAND	G	11	181	HOLLAND	WH	1	166
HOLDSWORTH	E	9	276	HOLFORD	H	8	161	HOLLAND	GE	12	114	HOLLAND	WR	2	170
HOLDSWORTH	E	9	276	HOLFORD	S	10	110	HOLLAND	GF	3	81	HOLLANDS	AC	5	179
HOLDSWORTH	E	9	276	HOLGATE	A	14	154	HOLLAND	GF	6	208	HOLLANDS	EJK	3	359
HOLDSWORTH	E	9	388	HOLGATE	CH	11	181	HOLLAND	GL	12	325	HOLLANDS	HA	3	359
HOLDSWORTH	ER	8	161	HOLGATE	D	9	277	HOLLAND	GR	13	224	HOLLANDS	JG	2	170
HOLDSWORTH	F	9	95	HOLGATE	E	11	181	HOLLAND	GW	1	165	HOLLEDGE	HG	13	224
HOLDSWORTH	F	9	276	HOLGATE	F	2	170	HOLLAND	H	4	193	HOLLELY	EW	1	166
HOLDSWORTH	F	9	276	HOLGATE	H	9	277	HOLLAND	H	5	179	HOLLERTON	A	11	181
HOLDSWORTH	F	9	276	HOLGATE	H	11	181	HOLLAND	H	6	208	HOLLERWAY	A	3	81
HOLDSWORTH	H	9	276	HOLGATE	HJ	7	190	HOLLAND	H	9	95	HOLLETT	AW	2	171
HOLDSWORTH	H	9	277	HOLGATE	HJ	7	190	HOLLAND	H	9	388	HOLLETT	G	2	171
HOLDSWORTH	H	9	277	HOLGATE	HW	2	170	HOLLAND	H	10	110	HOLLEY	A	4	193
HOLDSWORTH	H	9	277	HOLGATE	J	9	277	HOLLAND	H	14	154	HOLLEY	EJ	12	115
HOLDSWORTH	H	9	277	HOLGATE	JE	11	181	HOLLAND	HG	2	170	HOLLEY	G	2	171
HOLDSWORTH	HB	9	277	HOLGATE	P	9	277	HOLLAND	HH	6	208	HOLLEY	J	1	166
HOLDSWORTH	J	9	95	HOLGATE	SH	9	95	HOLLAND	HJ	1	165	HOLLEY	JS	4	193
HOLDSWORTH	J	9	95	HOLGATE	T	11	181	HOLLAND	HV	5	179	HOLLICK	AW	10	314
HOLDSWORTH	JH	9	95	HOLGATE	W	8	161	HOLLAND	HV	6	208	HOLLICK	E	10	314
HOLDSWORTH	L	8	161	HOLIDAY	S	3	81	HOLLAND	J	1	166	HOLLICK	HL	10	314
HOLDSWORTH	LB	8	161	HOLIDAY	WJ	10	314	HOLLAND	J	3	359	HOLLICK	HW	2	171

HOLLICK	J	5	179	HOLLINS	W	11	181	HOLLOWAY	F	12	115	HOLMAN	AC	13	224
HOLLICK	LA	10	314	HOLLINS	WA	6	209	HOLLOWAY	F	12	325	HOLMAN	B	3	81
HOLLICK	WT	6	209	HOLLINS	WG	4	193	HOLLOWAY	FB	6	210	HOLMAN	CW	13	224
HOLLIDAY	A	6	209	HOLLINWORTH	J	11	182	HOLLOWAY	FS	1	166	HOLMAN	J	2	171
HOLLIDAY	A	8	161	HOLLIS	A	2	171	HOLLOWAY	FW	1	166	HOLMAN	JO	12	115
HOLLIDAY	AA	2	171	HOLLIS	A	3	359	HOLLOWAY	GA	3	359	HOLMAN	JT	13	224
HOLLIDAY	CD	4	193	HOLLIS	A	12	325	HOLLOWAY	GW	2	171	HOLMAN	JW	1	167
HOLLIDAY	F	4	193	HOLLIS	C	10	110	HOLLOWAY	H	12	115	HOLMAN	JW	3	81
HOLLIDAY	G	8	161	HOLLIS	CE	10	110	HOLLOWAY	H	13	224	HOLMAN	R	8	162
HOLLIDAY	GF	11	181	HOLLIS	E	3	81	HOLLOWAY	HG	4	193	HOLMAN	T	3	81
HOLLIDAY	GS	2	171	HOLLIS	EH	5	180	HOLLOWAY	HM	3	81	HOLMAN	TW	8	162
HOLLIDAY	H	8	161	HOLLIS	EO	6	209	HOLLOWAY	HR	6	210	HOLMAN	W	7	190
HOLLIDAY	H	12	325	HOLLIS	F	12	325	HOLLOWAY	HV	4	193	HOLMAN	WJ	7	190
HOLLIDAY	J	8	161	HOLLIS	GA	6	209	HOLLOWAY	J	2	171	HOLME	G	12	325
HOLLIDAY	J	8	162	HOLLIS	GA	10	110	HOLLOWAY	J	3	359	HOLME	SE	7	190
HOLLIDAY	J	8	162	HOLLIS	HC	5	180	HOLLOWAY	J	8	162	HOLMES	A	2	172
HOLLIDAY	J	8	162	HOLLIS	J	2	171	HOLLOWAY	JE	1	167	HOLMES	A	3	81
HOLLIDAY	J	14	154	HOLLIS	J	7	190	HOLLOWAY	JF	4	193	HOLMES	A	3	359
HOLLIDAY	JT	6	209	HOLLIS	JW	9	277	HOLLOWAY	JH	4	193	HOLMES	A	6	210
HOLLIDAY	JW	8	162	HOLLIS	RJ	13	224	HOLLOWAY	LW	4	193	HOLMES	A	7	190
HOLLIDAY	S	6	209	HOLLIS	T	8	162	HOLLOWAY	N	10	110	HOLMES	A	8	162
HOLLIDAY	SV	13	224	HOLLIS	TW	1	166	HOLLOWAY	P	10	111	HOLMES	A	9	95
HOLLIDAY	T	8	162	HOLLIS	W	7	190	HOLLOWAY	R	5	180	HOLMES	A	9	95
HOLLIDAY	W	6	209	HOLLIS	WA	10	314	HOLLOWAY	R	10	111	HOLMES	A	9	278
HOLLIDAY	W	8	162	HOLLIS	WC	10	110	HOLLOWAY	R	12	115	HOLMES	A	11	182
HOLLIDAY	W	9	95	HOLLIS	WJ	10	314	HOLLOWAY	S	4	193	HOLMES	AC	1	167
HOLLIDAY	W	9	277	HOLLISS	FC	2	171	HOLLOWAY	SJ	9	95	HOLMES	AC	13	224
HOLLIDGE	W	3	81	HOLLISS	JH	1	166	HOLLOWAY	SL	3	81	HOLMES	AE	13	224
HOLLIER	FP	6	209	HOLLISTER	CE	1	166	HOLLOWAY	T	1	167	HOLMES	AE	14	154
HOLLIER	HW	10	314	HOLLISTER	J	3	81	HOLLOWAY	T	7	190	HOLMES	AE	14	154
HOLLIER	JW	13	224	HOLLMAN	FW	5	180	HOLLOWAY	W	4	193	HOLMES	AH	12	115
HOLLIER	W	6	209	HOLLMAN	J	5	180	HOLLOWAY	W	6	210	HOLMES	AH	13	225
HOLLIMAN	HH	2	171	HOLLMAN	P	5	180	HOLLOWAY	WE	3	359	HOLMES	AJ	12	115
HOLLIMAN	J	5	179	HOLLOBON	G	2	171	HOLLOWAY	WF	4	193	HOLMES	AM	4	194
HOLLINGS	E	8	162	HOLLORAN	P	8	162	HOLLOWAY	WH	4	194	HOLMES	AS	14	154
HOLLINGS	J	8	162	HOLLORAN	W	8	162	HOLLOWELL	E	12	325	HOLMES	AW	2	172
HOLLINGS	JS	8	162	HOLLOWAY	A	6	209	HOLLOWELL	E	12	325	HOLMES	AW	4	194
HOLLINGS	S	9	277	HOLLOWAY	A	12	115	HOLLOWELL	JT	12	325	HOLMES	BW	3	359
HOLLINGSHEAD	AE	2	171	HOLLOWAY	A	13	224	HOLLOX	R	8	162	HOLMES	C	2	172
HOLLINGSHEAD	B	3	81	HOLLOWAY	A	14	154	HOLLY	G	10	111	HOLMES	C	3	81
HOLLINGSHEAD	HE	2	171	HOLLOWAY	AJ	6	209	HOLLY	H	4	193	HOLMES	C	5	180
HOLLINGSWORTH	AW	1	166	HOLLOWAY	AW	2	171	HOLLYER	HE	2	171	HOLMES	C	8	162
HOLLINGSWORTH	J	11	181	HOLLOWAY	AW	11	182	HOLLYHOMES	J	6	210	HOLMES	C	10	111
HOLLINGSWORTH	J	14	154	HOLLOWAY	B	1	166	HOLLYLEE	F	13	224	HOLMES	CA	1	167
HOLLINGSWORTH	JJ	11	181	HOLLOWAY	B	4	193	HOLLYOAK	A	2	171	HOLMES	CG	7	190
HOLLINGSWORTH	JT	11	181	HOLLOWAY	BJ	2	171	HOLLYOAK	WA	6	210	HOLMES	CH	9	388
HOLLINGSWORTH	S	6	209	HOLLOWAY	CE	3	359	HOLLYOAK	WH	6	210	HOLMES	CH	14	154
HOLLINGSWORTH	T	14	154	HOLLOWAY	CH	4	193	HOLLYOAK	WJ	6	210	HOLMES	CP	5	180
HOLLINGSWORTH	W	5	180	HOLLOWAY	CT	14	154	HOLLYOAKE	AE	12	115	HOLMES	CR	8	163
HOLLINGWORTH	A	14	154	HOLLOWAY	EC	6	209	HOLLYOAKE	AG	12	115	HOLMES	CW	1	167
HOLLINGWORTH	A	14	154	HOLLOWAY	ET	6	209	HOLLYOAKE	FH	12	115	HOLMES	CW	9	278
HOLLINGWORTH	J	8	162	HOLLOWAY	EW	1	166	HOLLYWOOD	AE	11	182	HOLMES	D	1	167
HOLLINRAKE	H	12	115	HOLLOWAY	F	4	193	HOLLYWOOD	JV	8	162	HOLMES	D	4	194
HOLLINS	A	4	193	HOLLOWAY	F	6	209	HOLLYWOOD	W	11	182	HOLMES	E	2	172
HOLLINS	HJ	10	110	HOLLOWAY	F	11	182	HOLMAN	A	10	111	HOLMES	E	8	163

HOLMES	E	8	163	HOLMES	J	9	388	HOLMES	W	9	278
HOLMES	E	8	163	HOLMES	J	14	155	HOLMES	W	10	111
HOLMES	E	9	95	HOLMES	JA	11	182	HOLMES	W	11	182
HOLMES	E	9	95	HOLMES	JB	9	278	HOLMES	W	11	182
HOLMES	E	9	278	HOLMES	JC	13	225	HOLMES	WA	5	180
HOLMES	E	11	182	HOLMES	JE	9	96	HOLMES	WE	7	191
HOLMES	E	13	225	HOLMES	JF	4	194	HOLMES	WJ	5	180
HOLMES	EE	2	172	HOLMES	JG	13	225	HOLMES	WJ	10	111
HOLMES	EG	7	191	HOLMES	JS	1	167	HOLMSHAW	WH	4	194
HOLMES	EJ	4	194	HOLMES	JT	3	360	HOLMWOOD	W	13	225
HOLMES	ES	6	210	HOLMES	JW	7	191	HOLMYARD	E	11	182
HOLMES	ES	13	225	HOLMES	JW	9	96	HOLNESS	A	13	225
HOLMES	ET	13	225	HOLMES	JW	9	278	HOLNESS	D	10	111
HOLMES	EW	2	172	HOLMES	L	6	210	HOLNESS	EJ	13	225
HOLMES	EW	3	360	HOLMES	L	7	191	HOLNESS	H	13	225
HOLMES	F	8	163	HOLMES	L	8	163	HOLNESS	RJ	3	360
HOLMES	F	9	96	HOLMES	L	8	163	HOLNESS	WH	10	111
HOLMES	F	12	115	HOLMES	L	14	155	HOLNIN	JH	2	172
HOLMES	FE	4	194	HOLMES	MB	4	194	HOLROYD	E	14	155
HOLMES	FG	1	167	HOLMES	N	6	210	HOLROYD	F	4	194
HOLMES	FW	4	194	HOLMES	O	6	210	HOLROYD	F	9	96
HOLMES	G	4	194	HOLMES	P	8	163	HOLROYD	G	14	155
HOLMES	G	8	163	HOLMES	P	8	163	HOLROYD	H	14	155
HOLMES	G	8	163	HOLMES	P	8	163	HOLROYD	N	9	389
HOLMES	G	9	96	HOLMES	P	12	115	HOLROYD	RW	9	96
HOLMES	G	9	278	HOLMES	PJ	2	172	HOLROYD	W	9	278
HOLMES	G	9	278	HOLMES	PJ	6	210	HOLROYD	W	14	155
HOLMES	GE	8	163	HOLMES	PW	5	180	HOLROYD	WHM	9	278
HOLMES	GEO	4	194	HOLMES	R	9	96	HOLSTEAD	B	9	96
HOLMES	GH	11	182	HOLMES	R	12	115	HOLSTEAD	M	8	164
HOLMES	GT	3	82	HOLMES	RH	13	225	HOLSTEIN	M	14	155
HOLMES	GW	9	278	HOLMES	RR	13	225	HOLT	A	7	191
HOLMES	GW	9	278	HOLMES	RW	10	314	HOLT	A	11	182
HOLMES	H	2	172	HOLMES	S	12	115	HOLT	A	11	182
HOLMES	H	5	180	HOLMES	SC	3	82	HOLT	A	11	182
HOLMES	H	8	163	HOLMES	SC	3	360	HOLT	AJ	7	191
HOLMES	H	8	163	HOLMES	T	3	360	HOLT	B	9	389
HOLMES	H	8	163	HOLMES	T	8	164	HOLT	BJ	5	180
HOLMES	H	8	163	HOLMES	T	8	164	HOLT	CH	6	210
HOLMES	H	8	163	HOLMES	T	9	96	HOLT	CH	6	210
HOLMES	H	9	278	HOLMES	T	9	96	HOLT	D	9	278
HOLMES	H	13	225	HOLMES	T	9	278	HOLT	E	6	210
HOLMES	H	14	155	HOLMES	TG	3	82	HOLT	E	9	279
HOLMES	HC	2	172	HOLMES	VT	4	194	HOLT	E	9	279
HOLMES	HE	14	155	HOLMES	W	2	172	HOLT	E	11	182
HOLMES	HF	12	115	HOLMES	W	3	360	HOLT	F	8	164
HOLMES	HH	8	163	HOLMES	W	4	194	HOLT	F	11	182
HOLMES	HRB	12	325	HOLMES	W	5	180	HOLT	F	11	182
HOLMES	HW	13	225	HOLMES	W	6	210	HOLT	FO	9	279
HOLMES	J	4	194	HOLMES	W	6	210	HOLT	FW	6	210
HOLMES	J	8	163	HOLMES	W	8	164	HOLT	G	11	182
HOLMES	J	9	96	HOLMES	W	8	164	HOLT	G	14	155
HOLMES	J	9	278	HOLMES	W	8	164	HOLT	GA	11	183
HOLMES	J	9	278	HOLMES	W	8	164	HOLT	H	1	167
				HOLMES	W	9	278	HOLT	H	5	180

HOLT	H	5	180
HOLT	H	5	180
HOLT	H	8	164
HOLT	H	9	96
HOLT	J	1	167
HOLT	J	5	180
HOLT	J	9	96
HOLT	J	9	279
HOLT	J	11	183
HOLT	J	11	183
HOLT	J	11	183
HOLT	J	11	183
HOLT	J	12	116
HOLT	J	14	155
HOLT	JA	11	183
HOLT	JA	14	155
HOLT	JB	11	183
HOLT	JHT	12	422
HOLT	JW	3	360
HOLT	JW	9	96
HOLT	JW	9	279
HOLT	M	1	167
HOLT	S	14	155
HOLT	T	3	82
HOLT	T	6	210
HOLT	T	9	279
HOLT	TJ	11	183
HOLT	TW	12	422
HOLT	W	5	180
HOLT	W	5	181
HOLT	W	5	181
HOLT	W	8	164
HOLT	W	13	225
HOLT	WC	12	422
HOLT	WF	14	155
HOLTER	AW	13	225
HOLTHAM	AJ	3	82
HOLTOM	F	12	116
HOLTOM	JG	3	82
HOLTOM	WH	12	116
HOLTON	A	2	172
HOLTON	D	12	116
HOLTON	E	3	82
HOLTON	E	6	210
HOLTON	EL	3	360
HOLTON	G	12	116
HOLTON	GF	1	167
HOLTON	RC	1	167
HOLTON	S	12	116
HOLTON	SA	3	360
HOLTON	SJ	1	167
HOLTON	T	12	325
HOLTON	WW	1	167
HOLWAY	WJ	3	82
HOLWILL	EC	13	225

HOLYDAY	WA	2	172	HONEYBOURNE	ST	4	195	HOOKER	FC	2	172	HOOPER	JJ	3	83
HOLYER	CJ	13	225	HONEYBUN	A	1	168	HOOKER	G	13	226	HOOPER	JJ	13	226
HOLYHEAD	WR	3	360	HONEYBUN	G	10	314	HOOKER	HS	13	226	HOOPER	JP	7	192
HOLYLAND	S	3	82	HONEYSETT	AH	7	191	HOOKER	RE	7	191	HOOPER	JW	6	211
HOLYMAN	AFG	1	167	HONEYSETT	H	13	226	HOOKER	W	5	181	HOOPER	L	4	195
HOLZMAN	C	3	82	HONEYWOOD	HA	3	360	HOOKER	WA	1	168	HOOPER	M	4	195
HOLZMEYER	JJ	5	181	HONIBROW	R	7	191	HOOKER	WC	5	181	HOOPER	S	10	111
HOMAN	F	11	183	HONIBROW	S	7	191	HOOKER	WG	4	195	HOOPER	SG	10	111
HOMANS	AG	5	181	HONLEY	A	5	181	HOOKEY	GA	4	195	HOOPER	T	3	360
HOMANS	EJ	12	116	HONLEY	S	5	181	HOOKEY	HG	3	83	HOOPER	T	6	211
HOME	J	11	183	HONNOR	AT	1	168	HOOKEY	RGF	4	195	HOOPER	W	6	211
HOMER	A	6	210	HONNOR	CH	1	168	HOOKHAM	A	12	116	HOOPER	WA	4	195
HOMER	A	6	211	HONOR	AT	13	226	HOOKHAM	FA	5	181	HOOPER	WGA	7	192
HOMER	AE	6	211	HONOR	J	3	82	HOOKHAM	GH	5	181	HOOPER	WH	3	83
HOMER	AJ	6	211	HOOD	AC	4	195	HOOKHAM	HC	1	168	HOOPER	WH	4	195
HOMER	C	14	155	HOOD	AN	3	82	HOOKHAM	I	12	116	HOOPER	WJ	4	195
HOMER	CH	10	314	HOOD	AR	8	164	HOOKHAM	RA	12	116	HOOTON	AE	13	226
HOMER	F	6	211	HOOD	AWS	4	195	HOOKHAM	RJ	12	116	HOOTON	H	4	196
HOMER	HHW	6	211	HOOD	CW	14	155	HOOKHAM	TB	5	181	HOOTON	H	11	183
HOMER	JL	11	183	HOOD	DV	12	116	HOOKHAM	TH	12	116	HOOTON	H	12	116
HOMER	KA	11	183	HOOD	E	6	211	HOOKHAM	W	1	168	HOOTON	J	11	184
HOMER	M	3	82	HOOD	GW	4	195	HOOKHAM	WGR	1	168	HOOTON	LA	13	226
HOMER	TA	6	211	HOOD	HCB	2	172	HOOKINS	AE	7	191	HOOTON	RG	13	226
HOMER	W	10	314	HOOD	J	13	226	HOOKWAY	E	6	211	HOPCRAFT	S	12	116
HOMEWOOD	A	1	167	HOOD	J	14	155	HOOKWAY	JW	14	155	HOPCRAFT	TJ	2	172
HOMEWOOD	EE	3	82	HOOD	JHT	6	211	HOOLAHAN	J	14	156	HOPCRAFT	W	6	211
HOMEWOOD	JJ	13	225	HOOD	ND	3	82	HOOLE	A	3	83	HOPE	A	13	227
HOMEWOOD	L	1	167	HOOD	SF	3	82	HOOLEY	A	14	156	HOPE	AE	4	196
HOMEWOOD	R	13	226	HOOK	A	6	211	HOOLEY	J	14	156	HOPE	AG	7	192
HOMS	A	11	183	HOOK	A	12	116	HOOLEY	JW	14	156	HOPE	AT	10	111
HONE	CT	1	167	HOOK	AJ	13	226	HOOLEY	WG	12	325	HOPE	AV	7	192
HONE	CW	1	167	HOOK	C	7	191	HOOPER	A	3	83	HOPE	B	5	181
HONE	F	9	96	HOOK	CT	13	226	HOOPER	A	4	195	HOPE	C	10	314
HONE	FA	1	168	HOOK	EA	7	191	HOOPER	A	6	211	HOPE	E	14	156
HONE	G	5	181	HOOK	EV	3	360	HOOPER	AC	4	195	HOPE	F	12	326
HONE	H	1	168	HOOK	FF	3	360	HOOPER	AE	7	191	HOPE	FJ	6	211
HONE	J	5	181	HOOK	GW	13	226	HOOPER	AG	3	83	HOPE	G	12	326
HONESS	E	13	226	HOOK	HT	3	83	HOOPER	AT	4	195	HOPE	GW	6	211
HONESS	FT	3	360	HOOK	J	8	164	HOOPER	BA	9	96	HOPE	H	3	83
HONESS	H	13	226	HOOK	J	11	183	HOOPER	BL	7	191	HOPE	H	8	164
HONESS	J	13	226	HOOK	J	11	183	HOOPER	CG	10	111	HOPE	H	12	326
HONESS	WA	13	226	HOOK	PG	3	83	HOOPER	EA	2	172	HOPE	HE	1	168
HONEY	A	1	168	HOOK	S	9	96	HOOPER	EJ	3	83	HOPE	HV	14	156
HONEY	A	11	183	HOOK	W	1	168	HOOPER	EW	5	181	HOPE	J	5	181
HONEY	G	5	181	HOOK	W	3	360	HOOPER	F	7	192	HOPE	J	6	211
HONEY	G	10	111	HOOK	W	7	191	HOOPER	FG	4	195	HOPE	J	12	326
HONEY	H	11	183	HOOKE	R	13	226	HOOPER	G	4	195	HOPE	JD	7	192
HONEY	PR	3	82	HOOKER	A	5	181	HOOPER	GH	2	172	HOPE	JG	7	192
HONEY	R	3	82	HOOKER	AH	1	168	HOOPER	GT	6	211	HOPE	PJ	3	83
HONEY	RK	4	194	HOOKER	AHW	13	226	HOOPER	H	1	168	HOPE	R	7	192
HONEY	S	2	172	HOOKER	AJ	1	168	HOOPER	H	6	211	HOPE	RA	9	96
HONEYANDS	F	3	360	HOOKER	AL	13	226	HOOPER	HA	3	83	HOPE	TG	3	83
HONEYBALL	E	7	191	HOOKER	B	5	181	HOOPER	J	7	192	HOPE	W	3	361
HONEYBALL	E	7	191	HOOKER	E	5	181	HOOPER	JA	7	192	HOPE	W	6	212
HONEYBOURNE	LL	4	194	HOOKER	EA	4	195	HOOPER	JG	4	195	HOPE	W	6	212

HOPE	W	14	156	HOPKINS	J	13	227	HOPPER	G	3	84	HORD	H	3	358
HOPES	LB	7	192	HOPKINS	J	14	156	HOPPER	H	1	169	HORDER	FA	10	111
HOPEWELL	T	8	164	HOPKINS	J	14	156	HOPPER	H	8	164	HORDER	GH	10	315
HOPGOOD	AJ	6	212	HOPKINS	JH	6	212	HOPPER	JH	3	360	HORE	GJ	3	84
HOPGOOD	C	10	314	HOPKINS	JO	6	212	HOPPER	M	6	212	HORE	W	8	165
HOPGOOD	E	1	168	HOPKINS	JT	10	111	HOPPER	RF	13	227	HORGAN	J	3	361
HOPGOOD	EC	10	315	HOPKINS	JT	12	116	HOPPER	SG	13	227	HORGAN	M	3	361
HOPGOOD	GH	10	111	HOPKINS	JW	7	192	HOPPER	T	11	184	HORGAN	N	3	361
HOPGOOD	JA	4	196	HOPKINS	M	9	96	HOPPER	WF	3	84	HORLEY	E	4	196
HOPGOOD	RJ	10	315	HOPKINS	M	9	279	HOPPEY	G	3	84	HORLEY	FW	5	182
HOPGOOD	WH	4	196	HOPKINS	O	14	156	HOPPING	A	1	169	HORLEY	HW	5	182
HOPKIN	E	3	83	HOPKINS	OH	7	192	HOPPING	AA	1	169	HORLEY	LI	5	182
HOPKINES	G	8	164	HOPKINS	P	7	192	HOPPING	EA	1	169	HORLEY	THW	5	182
HOPKINS	A	4	196	HOPKINS	R	5	182	HOPPING	J	1	169	HORLEY	WE	4	196
HOPKINS	A	5	182	HOPKINS	RC	7	192	HOPPING	J	8	164	HORLOCK	AE	1	169
HOPKINS	A	6	212	HOPKINS	RD	1	169	HOPPLEY	C	14	156	HORLOCK	C	13	227
HOPKINS	A	8	164	HOPKINS	RF	2	173	HOPPS	GF	8	165	HORLOCK	CD	2	173
HOPKINS	AE	5	182	HOPKINS	RG	5	182	HOPSON	CF	3	84	HORLOCK	HT	7	193
HOPKINS	AG	13	227	HOPKINS	SG	7	192	HOPSON	CH	3	84	HORLOCK	JE	13	227
HOPKINS	AJ	5	182	HOPKINS	T	10	111	HOPSON	EA	13	227	HORLOCK	WH	2	173
HOPKINS	AS	9	96	HOPKINS	T	14	156	HOPSON	G	13	227	HORMAN	JW	8	165
HOPKINS	AW	1	168	HOPKINS	TH	6	212	HOPSON	H	3	84	HORN	A	4	196
HOPKINS	AW	4	196	HOPKINS	TL	5	182	HOPSON	HL	7	193	HORN	A	9	97
HOPKINS	AW	13	227	HOPKINS	TM	6	212	HOPSON	J	11	184	HORN	A	13	227
HOPKINS	B	14	156	HOPKINS	TWE	6	212	HOPSON	J	14	156	HORN	A	13	227
HOPKINS	BF	3	83	HOPKINS	W	2	173	HOPSON	R	10	315	HORN	AC	3	84
HOPKINS	C	3	361	HOPKINS	W	3	361	HOPSON	W	13	227	HORN	AC	10	315
HOPKINS	C	7	192	HOPKINS	W	8	164	HOPSON	W	14	156	HORN	AJ	7	193
HOPKINS	C	10	315	HOPKINS	W	10	315	HOPTON	HCA	7	193	HORN	C	10	112
HOPKINS	CE	10	315	HOPKINS	W	12	116	HOPTON	HW	7	193	HORN	C	13	227
HOPKINS	CJ	13	227	HOPKINS	WF	3	84	HOPTON	JA	9	279	HORN	E	10	112
HOPKINS	D	6	212	HOPKINS	WG	3	84	HOPTON	T	14	157	HORN	EJ	4	196
HOPKINS	DJ	11	184	HOPKINS	WG	12	117	HOPTON	TW	11	184	HORN	F	4	196
HOPKINS	E	1	168	HOPKINS	WH	1	169	HOPTON	WT	7	193	HORN	F	8	165
HOPKINS	E	1	169	HOPKINS	WJ	6	212	HOPTROUGH	H	10	315	HORN	FW	10	112
HOPKINS	E	7	192	HOPKINS	WJ	6	212	HOPWOOD	B	8	165	HORN	G	9	279
HOPKINS	E	9	279	HOPKINSON	E	9	279	HOPWOOD	F	2	173	HORN	HEH	7	193
HOPKINS	EH	10	315	HOPKINSON	EW	10	315	HOPWOOD	FS	10	111	HORN	HR	8	165
HOPKINS	F	3	83	HOPKINSON	GG	14	156	HOPWOOD	G	11	184	HORN	J	5	182
HOPKINS	F	4	196	HOPKINSON	H	9	96	HOPWOOD	H	9	279	HORN	O	9	279
HOPKINS	F	4	196	HOPKINSON	H	13	227	HOPWOOD	I	14	157	HORN	RJ	7	193
HOPKINS	FC	3	83	HOPKINSON	HS	11	184	HOPWOOD	J	6	212	HORN	V	5	182
HOPKINS	FJ	1	169	HOPKINSON	I	14	156	HOPWOOD	J	14	157	HORN	W	13	227
HOPKINS	G	3	83	HOPKINSON	J	9	97	HOPWOOD	JE	8	165	HORN	W	14	157
HOPKINS	G	5	182	HOPKINSON	J	9	97	HOPWOOD	JR	14	157	HORN	WF	13	227
HOPKINS	G	13	227	HOPKINSON	R	11	184	HOPWOOD	S	14	157	HORN	WJ	12	326
HOPKINS	GCR	10	111	HOPKINSON	RH	11	184	HOPWOOD	T	11	184	HORNBY	A	3	84
HOPKINS	GR	5	182	HOPKINSON	S	8	164	HOPWOOD	W	14	157	HORNBY	A	7	193
HOPKINS	H	4	196	HOPKINSON	W	8	164	HOPWOOD	W	14	157	HORNBY	C	11	184
HOPKINS	H	5	182	HOPLEY	CL	14	156	HORAM	W	11	184	HORNBY	E	9	279
HOPKINS	H	6	212	HOPLEY	T	14	156	HORAN	JH	11	184	HORNBY	E	9	279
HOPKINS	HG	3	83	HOPLEY	W	3	361	HORAN	JW	11	184	HORNBY	F	11	184
HOPKINS	HG	5	182	HOPPE	H	7	193	HORAN	P	8	165	HORNBY	J	14	157
HOPKINS	J	6	212	HOPPER	AB	3	84	HORAN	T	8	165	HORNBY	M	8	165
HOPKINS	J	8	164	HOPPER	DW	1	169	HORAN	T	14	157	HORNBY	MP	14	157

Surname	In.			Surname	In.			Surname	In.			Surname	In.		
HORNBY	R	3	84	HORNER	RE	4	196	HORSACE	C	13	228	HORTON	A	1	169
HORNBY	R	14	157	HORNER	SR	13	228	HORSBURGH	G	12	117	HORTON	A	3	84
HORNBY	W	14	157	HORNER	W	8	165	HORSCROFT	ACM	10	112	HORTON	A	4	197
HORNCASTLE	FH	8	165	HORNER	W	8	165	HORSEFIELD	C	3	84	HORTON	A	6	213
HORNCASTLE	JH	8	165	HORNER	W	11	184	HORSEFIELD	J	11	185	HORTON	A	6	213
HORNE	A	5	182	HORNER	WE	14	157	HORSEFIELD	W	9	97	HORTON	A	10	315
HORNE	A	5	182	HORNER	WH	9	97	HORSEY	AR	13	228	HORTON	AB	5	183
HORNE	A	5	182	HORNER	WJ	4	196	HORSEY	GW	10	315	HORTON	AE	6	213
HORNE	A	12	117	HORNETT	H	7	193	HORSEY	LP	10	315	HORTON	AF	4	197
HORNE	AC	12	326	HORNEY	AC	13	228	HORSEY	TH	1	169	HORTON	BA	12	117
HORNE	AG	4	196	HORNEY	C	13	228	HORSFALL	A	5	183	HORTON	CA	6	213
HORNE	AJ	12	326	HORNEY	W	5	183	HORSFALL	A	8	166	HORTON	CE	7	193
HORNE	C	3	84	HORNIBROOK	A	1	169	HORSFALL	B	8	166	HORTON	CG	6	213
HORNE	E	12	117	HORNIBROOK	TA	1	169	HORSFALL	C	8	166	HORTON	E	6	213
HORNE	FW	13	227	HORNSBY	G	11	184	HORSFALL	CG	8	166	HORTON	F	5	183
HORNE	G	12	117	HORNSBY	J	7	193	HORSFALL	CH	8	166	HORTON	F	6	213
HORNE	G	13	228	HORNSBY	JH	11	184	HORSFALL	E	8	166	HORTON	FF	6	213
HORNE	GT	5	182	HORNSBY	W	8	165	HORSFALL	E	9	279	HORTON	FP	6	213
HORNE	H	5	182	HORNSBY	WE	11	184	HORSFALL	F	9	279	HORTON	G	8	166
HORNE	H	13	227	HORNSBY	WH	8	165	HORSFALL	G	10	315	HORTON	GF	6	213
HORNE	HA	13	228	HORNSEY	F	13	228	HORSFALL	J	8	166	HORTON	H	1	170
HORNE	HR	1	169	HORNSEY	H	3	84	HORSFALL	J	9	279	HORTON	H	6	213
HORNE	J	5	182	HORNSHAW	AA	8	165	HORSFALL	J	11	185	HORTON	H	6	214
HORNE	J	6	212	HORNSHAW	TL	8	166	HORSFALL	JW	9	97	HORTON	H	6	214
HORNE	J	9	97	HOROBIN	AG	7	193	HORSFALL	S	8	166	HORTON	H	6	214
HORNE	JS	7	193	HOROBIN	HJ	1	169	HORSFALL	W	14	158	HORTON	H	14	158
HORNE	JW	5	183	HOROHAN	J	13	228	HORSFALL	WH	9	280	HORTON	HG	1	170
HORNE	L	9	279	HORRABIN	C	14	157	HORSFIELD	E	9	97	HORTON	I	6	214
HORNE	L	12	326	HORRELL	TJ	3	84	HORSFIELD	J	9	280	HORTON	J	4	197
HORNE	PJ	13	228	HORRELL	WJ	2	173	HORSFIELD	J	11	185	HORTON	J	4	197
HORNE	RH	8	165	HORREX	GG	2	173	HORSLER	GS	5	183	HORTON	J	5	183
HORNE	RJ	7	193	HORRIGAN	E	13	228	HORSLER	RRG	5	183	HORTON	J	6	214
HORNE	RT	6	212	HORRIGAN	F	13	228	HORSLEY	C	1	169	HORTON	J	6	214
HORNE	S	5	183	HORRIGAN	J	8	166	HORSLEY	C	7	193	HORTON	J	6	214
HORNE	T	12	117	HORRILL	F	4	197	HORSLEY	CJ	12	326	HORTON	J	6	214
HORNE	T	12	326	HORRILL	J	4	197	HORSLEY	E	9	97	HORTON	J	6	214
HORNE	TJ	4	196	HORRILL	RJ	4	197	HORSLEY	G	8	166	HORTON	J	6	214
HORNE	W	4	196	HORRILL	W	4	197	HORSLEY	G	11	185	HORTON	JT	1	170
HORNE	W	4	196	HORRILL	W	4	197	HORSLEY	J	9	280	HORTON	L	6	214
HORNE	W	6	213	HORROBIN	W	6	213	HORSLEY	J	9	389	HORTON	M	6	214
HORNE	W	12	117	HORROCKS	AE	6	213	HORSLEY	W	6	213	HORTON	P	5	183
HORNE	WF	3	361	HORROCKS	AE	11	185	HORSMAN	E	9	97	HORTON	S	6	214
HORNE	WG	12	117	HORROCKS	C	6	213	HORSMAN	F	3	84	HORTON	S	8	166
HORNE	WJ	8	165	HORROCKS	E	6	213	HORSMAN	G	9	280	HORTON	T	6	214
HORNER	AE	12	117	HORROCKS	F	6	213	HORSMAN	H	8	166	HORTON	TG	1	170
HORNER	AW	10	112	HORROCKS	H	14	157	HORSMAN	J	9	280	HORTON	TH	6	214
HORNER	C	3	361	HORROCKS	H	14	157	HORSMAN	J	12	117	HORTON	VT	3	84
HORNER	CT	10	112	HORROCKS	J	11	185	HORSMAN	JH	8	166	HORTON	W	3	85
HORNER	EC	4	196	HORROCKS	JW	9	279	HORSMAN	RS	9	280	HORTON	W	6	214
HORNER	F	13	228	HORROCKS	T	11	185	HORSTEAD	J	13	228	HORTON	W	6	214
HORNER	G	9	97	HORROCKS	T	14	157	HORSTEAD	L	10	112	HORTON	W	8	166
HORNER	GH	13	228	HORROCKS	W	14	157	HORSTEAD	R	4	197	HORTON	W	8	166
HORNER	J	8	165	HORROD	E	13	228	HORSWELL	FE	4	197	HORTON	WH	6	214
HORNER	J	8	165	HORROD	WT	3	84	HORT	EC	1	169	HORTON	WHA	4	197
HORNER	L	8	165	HORROX	G	8	166	HORTEN	A	10	112	HORTON	WJ	2	173

HORTON	WJ	6	214	HOSTLER	A	2	173	HOUGHTON	JA	14	158	HOUSE	EC	3	85
HORWITZ	D	1	170	HOTCHKIN	JW	2	173	HOUGHTON	JJ	3	85	HOUSE	F	13	229
HORWOOD	AE	1	170	HOTHAM	TG	7	194	HOUGHTON	JV	9	97	HOUSE	FC	10	316
HORWOOD	AE	7	194	HOTHAM	TWG	7	194	HOUGHTON	JW	3	85	HOUSE	GE	4	199
HORWOOD	HA	1	170	HOTHERSALL	CH	9	97	HOUGHTON	JW	8	167	HOUSE	H	4	199
HORWOOD	HA	13	228	HOTHERSALL	RH	9	97	HOUGHTON	L	11	185	HOUSE	H	5	183
HORWOOD	HE	7	194	HOTSON	JR	12	117	HOUGHTON	PG	10	112	HOUSE	HA	12	117
HORWOOD	HG	5	183	HOTSTON	AG	3	85	HOUGHTON	RW	11	185	HOUSE	HJ	4	199
HORWOOD	JW	3	361	HOTSTON	HG	10	315	HOUGHTON	S	4	198	HOUSE	HJ	4	199
HORWOOD	T	13	228	HOUCHIN	R	13	229	HOUGHTON	SA	4	198	HOUSE	HJ	4	199
HORWOOD	V	5	183	HOUCHIN	W	7	194	HOUGHTON	T	4	198	HOUSE	I	4	199
HOSE	W	7	194	HOUGH	A	13	229	HOUGHTON	T	14	158	HOUSE	J	3	85
HOSEY	C	4	197	HOUGH	CJ	14	158	HOUGHTON	W	5	184	HOUSE	J	4	199
HOSEY	HG	4	197	HOUGH	F	10	315	HOUGHTON	W	10	112	HOUSE	J	4	199
HOSEY	L	4	197	HOUGH	H	14	158	HOUGHTON	W	11	185	HOUSE	JG	4	199
HOSEY	P	4	197	HOUGH	J	14	158	HOUGHTON	W	14	158	HOUSE	JH	7	194
HOSEY	WH	4	197	HOUGH	JT	14	158	HOUGHTON	WE	8	167	HOUSE	RAH	3	85
HOSFOLD	WH	9	97	HOUGH	NV	14	158	HOUGHTON	WE	8	167	HOUSE	RG	7	194
HOSIER	B	5	183	HOUGH	T	11	185	HOUGHTON	WL	4	198	HOUSE	RL	4	199
HOSIER	G	5	183	HOUGH	T	14	158	HOUGHTON	WR	12	326	HOUSE	S	4	199
HOSIER	H	3	85	HOUGH	TE	5	184	HOULBROOK	GA	9	280	HOUSE	T	5	184
HOSIER	J	7	194	HOUGH	W	9	280	HOULDEN	WJ	3	85	HOUSE	W	9	280
HOSIER	P	5	183	HOUGH	W	14	158	HOULDEY	JW	10	316	HOUSE	WE	4	199
HOSIER	WG	5	183	HOUGH	W	14	158	HOULGATE	JW	8	167	HOUSE	WH	4	199
HOSKEN	LC	1	170	HOUGH	W	14	158	HOULKER	A	11	185	HOUSE	WJ	3	85
HOSKIN	A	7	194	HOUGH	WG	13	229	HOULSTON	GW	1	170	HOUSE	WS	13	229
HOSKIN	J	2	173	HOUGHLAND	W	11	185	HOULSTON	HE	1	170	HOUSEGO	AJ	3	85
HOSKIN	JA	10	112	HOUGHTON	AE	10	112	HOULSTON	JA	1	170	HOUSEGO	ER	2	173
HOSKIN	WC	10	112	HOUGHTON	AE	10	112	HOULTON	S	6	215	HOUSEGO	F	3	85
HOSKINS	AD	3	85	HOUGHTON	AH	4	198	HOUNSELL	E	7	194	HOUSEGO	H	3	86
HOSKINS	AW	4	197	HOUGHTON	B	11	185	HOUNSELL	FJ	1	170	HOUSEMAN	B	8	167
HOSKINS	BG	4	197	HOUGHTON	CAG	2	173	HOUNSELL	JR	4	198	HOUSEMAN	W	8	167
HOSKINS	CF	4	197	HOUGHTON	CD	12	117	HOUNSELL	TG	4	198	HOUSENCROFT	J	9	97
HOSKINS	CG	3	85	HOUGHTON	DT	10	316	HOUNSLOW	A	1	170	HOUSLEY	H	9	97
HOSKINS	CH	10	112	HOUGHTON	E	4	198	HOUNSLOW	G	1	170	HOUSLEY	H	14	158
HOSKINS	EF	4	198	HOUGHTON	EA	4	198	HOUNSOM	AW	2	173	HOUSMAN	JC	8	167
HOSKINS	F	7	194	HOUGHTON	F	10	316	HOUNSOM	GW	2	173	HOUSON	C	9	97
HOSKINS	H	7	194	HOUGHTON	FJ	4	198	HOUNSOME	C	4	198	HOUSON	J	9	97
HOSKINS	J	3	85	HOUGHTON	FS	13	229	HOUNSOME	F	4	198	HOUSON	WT	9	97
HOSKINS	J	13	228	HOUGHTON	FT	3	85	HOUNSOME	J	10	112	HOUSTON	D	4	199
HOSKINS	JA	10	315	HOUGHTON	FT	10	112	HOUNSOME	M	4	198	HOUSTON	JS	10	113
HOSKINS	P	7	194	HOUGHTON	G	12	117	HOUNSOME	W	4	198	HOUSTON	V	11	185
HOSKINS	SH	4	198	HOUGHTON	G	12	117	HOURIGAN	E	3	85	HOUSTON	WJ	7	194
HOSKINS	WAJ	2	173	HOUGHTON	G	14	158	HOURIGAN	J	3	85	HOVELL	H	3	86
HOSKINS	WC	10	315	HOUGHTON	GH	14	158	HOUSBY	E	9	280	HOW	AR	2	174
HOSKYNS	WH	7	194	HOUGHTON	GM	12	117	HOUSDEN	A	7	194	HOW	CW	2	174
HOSLEY	JW	8	166	HOUGHTON	GW	6	214	HOUSDEN	GRT	5	183	HOW	CW	3	86
HOSSACK	EG	7	194	HOUGHTON	H	10	112	HOUSE	A	4	198	HOW	CW	3	86
HOSSACK	FG	3	85	HOUGHTON	H	10	112	HOUSE	AE	4	198	HOW	F	2	174
HOSSACK	GG	13	228	HOUGHTON	H	11	185	HOUSE	AE	4	198	HOW	F	5	184
HOSSACK	GT	13	229	HOUGHTON	HE	2	173	HOUSE	AJ	5	183	HOW	FW	1	170
HOSSACK	JP	3	85	HOUGHTON	HW	12	326	HOUSE	AR	2	173	HOW	G	5	184
HOSSLEN	G	3	361	HOUGHTON	J	11	185	HOUSE	CE	5	183	HOW	HG	5	184
HOSSLEN	J	2	173	HOUGHTON	J	11	422	HOUSE	CJ	4	198	HOW	HG	5	184
HOSTEY	D	11	185	HOUGHTON	J	12	326	HOUSE	E	4	199	HOW	W	5	184

HOW	WB	5	184
HOW	WJ	5	184
HOWARD	A	3	86
HOWARD	A	5	184
HOWARD	A	5	184
HOWARD	A	6	215
HOWARD	A	8	167
HOWARD	A	14	158
HOWARD	A	14	158
HOWARD	AC	13	229
HOWARD	AD	1	170
HOWARD	AE	1	170
HOWARD	AJ	2	174
HOWARD	AL	3	86
HOWARD	AR	1	170
HOWARD	AV	10	113
HOWARD	B	11	185
HOWARD	B	14	159
HOWARD	BP	13	229
HOWARD	C	3	86
HOWARD	C	5	184
HOWARD	C	6	215
HOWARD	C	7	195
HOWARD	C	9	98
HOWARD	C	9	98
HOWARD	C	13	229
HOWARD	C	14	159
HOWARD	CE	13	229
HOWARD	CH	2	174
HOWARD	CH	7	195
HOWARD	CH	7	195
HOWARD	CJ	2	174
HOWARD	CT	11	186
HOWARD	CWJ	7	195
HOWARD	D	9	98
HOWARD	E	1	170
HOWARD	E	2	174
HOWARD	E	9	98
HOWARD	E	11	186
HOWARD	E	12	326
HOWARD	EH	7	195
HOWARD	EJ	11	186
HOWARD	ET	10	113
HOWARD	F	4	199
HOWARD	F	8	167
HOWARD	F	14	159
HOWARD	F	14	159
HOWARD	FG	5	184
HOWARD	FJ	3	361
HOWARD	FW	7	195
HOWARD	FW	12	326
HOWARD	FWJ	3	86
HOWARD	G	2	174
HOWARD	G	5	184
HOWARD	G	8	167
HOWARD	G	12	326
HOWARD	G	14	159
HOWARD	G	14	159
HOWARD	GH	14	159
HOWARD	GN	3	86
HOWARD	GP	1	171
HOWARD	GT	7	195
HOWARD	GW	3	86
HOWARD	GW	11	185
HOWARD	H	1	171
HOWARD	H	1	171
HOWARD	H	3	86
HOWARD	H	3	361
HOWARD	H	5	184
HOWARD	H	6	215
HOWARD	H	6	215
HOWARD	H	8	167
HOWARD	H	13	229
HOWARD	H	14	159
HOWARD	H	14	159
HOWARD	HJ	1	171
HOWARD	HJ	3	86
HOWARD	HJ	6	215
HOWARD	HJ	13	229
HOWARD	HL	14	159
HOWARD	J	6	215
HOWARD	J	10	113
HOWARD	J	11	186
HOWARD	J	11	186
HOWARD	J	11	186
HOWARD	J	13	229
HOWARD	J	13	229
HOWARD	J	14	159
HOWARD	J	14	159
HOWARD	J	14	159
HOWARD	J	14	159
HOWARD	J	14	159
HOWARD	J	14	159
HOWARD	JA	6	215
HOWARD	JE	11	186
HOWARD	JE	11	186
HOWARD	L	7	195
HOWARD	M	11	186
HOWARD	MB	10	113
HOWARD	PAJ	3	361
HOWARD	PG	10	316
HOWARD	PG	12	326
HOWARD	PN	14	159
HOWARD	R	9	280
HOWARD	R	11	186
HOWARD	R	13	229
HOWARD	RH	2	174
HOWARD	S	2	174
HOWARD	S	3	86
HOWARD	S	5	184
HOWARD	S	6	215
HOWARD	S	14	159
HOWARD	SR	7	195
HOWARD	SW	13	229
HOWARD	T	1	171
HOWARD	T	3	86
HOWARD	T	9	98
HOWARD	TM	14	159
HOWARD	TW	7	195
HOWARD	VFJ	10	113
HOWARD	W	1	171
HOWARD	W	3	361
HOWARD	W	6	215
HOWARD	W	7	195
HOWARD	W	7	195
HOWARD	W	7	195
HOWARD	W	9	98
HOWARD	W	11	186
HOWARD	W	12	326
HOWARD	W	14	160
HOWARD	WE	7	195
HOWARD	WE	10	113
HOWARD	WH	5	184
HOWARD	WH	6	215
HOWARD	WJ	2	174
HOWARD	WJ	7	195
HOWARD-SPINK	B	1	171
HOWARTH	A	11	186
HOWARTH	A	11	186
HOWARTH	A	11	186
HOWARTH	A	14	160
HOWARTH	A	14	160
HOWARTH	AW	14	160
HOWARTH	BF	9	280
HOWARTH	C	11	186
HOWARTH	E	11	186
HOWARTH	E	14	160
HOWARTH	GAJ	10	113
HOWARTH	H	7	195
HOWARTH	H	9	98
HOWARTH	H	11	186
HOWARTH	H	11	186
HOWARTH	H	11	186
HOWARTH	H	11	187
HOWARTH	H	14	160
HOWARTH	HE	1	171
HOWARTH	J	11	187
HOWARTH	J	11	187
HOWARTH	J	11	187
HOWARTH	J	14	160
HOWARTH	JH	6	215
HOWARTH	JH	14	160
HOWARTH	JW	11	187
HOWARTH	R	11	187
HOWARTH	R	14	160
HOWARTH	R	14	160
HOWARTH	S	14	160
HOWARTH	S	14	160
HOWARTH	T	9	280
HOWARTH	W	8	167
HOWARTH	W	11	187
HOWARTH	W	11	187
HOWARTH	W	11	187
HOWARTH	W	14	160
HOWARTH	W	14	160
HOWARTH	WJ	1	171
HOWARTH	WT	11	187
HOWATT	A	7	195
HOWDEN	H	9	98
HOWE	A	2	174
HOWE	A	2	174
HOWE	A	3	361
HOWE	A	5	184
HOWE	A	10	113
HOWE	AG	13	229
HOWE	AH	11	187
HOWE	AJ	1	171
HOWE	AV	5	184
HOWE	AW	12	117
HOWE	C	13	230
HOWE	CE	12	117
HOWE	EA	13	230
HOWE	F	6	215
HOWE	FG	1	171
HOWE	FJ	12	118
HOWE	FJ	12	118
HOWE	FW	5	185
HOWE	FW	5	185
HOWE	FW	12	118
HOWE	G	2	174
HOWE	G	3	86
HOWE	G	5	185
HOWE	G	9	98
HOWE	GA	12	118
HOWE	GE	12	118
HOWE	GF	12	118
HOWE	GH	1	171
HOWE	GH	5	185
HOWE	GR	13	230
HOWE	H	3	86
HOWE	H	13	230
HOWE	HC	5	185
HOWE	HC	12	118
HOWE	HE	13	230
HOWE	HT	12	118
HOWE	HW	7	195
HOWE	HW	13	230
HOWE	J	1	171
HOWE	J	5	185
HOWE	J	12	118

HOWE	JC	12	118	HOWELLS	CD	3	87	HOWICK	AF	10	113	HOWSE	A	6	216
HOWE	JW	5	185	HOWELLS	FW	6	216	HOWICK	GT	3	362	HOWSE	A	13	231
HOWE	PL	12	118	HOWELLS	H	7	196	HOWICK	HG	3	362	HOWSE	AG	10	113
HOWE	S	2	174	HOWELLS	J	14	160	HOWICK	PV	10	113	HOWSE	C	13	231
HOWE	SE	5	185	HOWELLS	R	3	87	HOWIE	W	8	167	HOWSE	R	3	87
HOWE	SG	5	185	HOWELLS	RSJ	3	87	HOWITT	J	10	113	HOWSEGO	AE	4	200
HOWE	SJ	12	118	HOWELLS	W	2	174	HOWITT	T	8	167	HOWSON	A	8	168
HOWE	SW	13	230	HOWELLS	W	13	230	HOWKER	A	9	280	HOWSON	C	8	168
HOWE	T	11	187	HOWELLS	W	14	160	HOWKINS	AE	12	119	HOWSON	FE	12	119
HOWE	TG	1	171	HOWELS	F	8	167	HOWKINS	J	14	160	HOWSON	G	8	168
HOWE	W	5	185	HOWES	A	2	174	HOWLAND	A	8	168	HOWSON	H	13	231
HOWE	W	5	185	HOWES	A	12	118	HOWLAND	G	9	98	HOWSON	J	11	187
HOWE	W	7	195	HOWES	A	12	118	HOWLAND	H	7	196	HOWSON	S	9	98
HOWE	W	12	118	HOWES	A	12	326	HOWLAND	S	5	185	HOWSON	S	9	280
HOWE	W	13	230	HOWES	A	13	230	HOWLAND	W	8	168	HOWSON	W	9	280
HOWE	W	13	230	HOWES	AH	13	230	HOWLAND	WH	9	98	HOY	A	3	87
HOWE	WH	12	118	HOWES	B	1	171	HOWLE	W	6	216	HOY	A	11	187
HOWE	WS	6	215	HOWES	BFL	3	87	HOWLES	A	6	216	HOY	A	13	231
HOWE	WTJ	8	167	HOWES	C	7	196	HOWLETT	AG	1	171	HOY	AG	5	186
HOWELL	A	6	215	HOWES	C	12	118	HOWLETT	AJ	4	200	HOY	AW	11	187
HOWELL	A	9	98	HOWES	CB	12	119	HOWLETT	AT	1	171	HOY	FJ	3	87
HOWELL	CE	13	230	HOWES	CJ	6	216	HOWLETT	FJA	1	172	HOY	H	13	231
HOWELL	CF	3	86	HOWES	CT	3	361	HOWLETT	FT	5	185	HOY	J	13	231
HOWELL	E	13	230	HOWES	CW	12	119	HOWLETT	FW	3	87	HOY	JA	12	119
HOWELL	EJ	6	215	HOWES	E	6	216	HOWLETT	FW	5	185	HOY	RC	13	231
HOWELL	F	6	215	HOWES	E	12	119	HOWLETT	G	3	362	HOY	RH	5	186
HOWELL	FA	14	160	HOWES	EW	10	113	HOWLETT	G	5	185	HOY	S	2	175
HOWELL	FW	7	196	HOWES	F	12	119	HOWLETT	H	10	113	HOY	WR	5	186
HOWELL	GJ	12	118	HOWES	F	12	119	HOWLETT	HJ	12	327	HOYE	W	3	87
HOWELL	H	7	196	HOWES	F	12	326	HOWLETT	J	2	175	HOYES	J	11	187
HOWELL	H	10	316	HOWES	FH	3	87	HOWLETT	M	1	172	HOYLAND	HJ	5	186
HOWELL	H	13	230	HOWES	FR	7	196	HOWLETT	P	12	327	HOYLAND	J	5	186
HOWELL	HA	13	230	HOWES	G	13	231	HOWLETT	PJ	5	185	HOYLE	A	4	200
HOWELL	HE	3	86	HOWES	GW	3	361	HOWLETT	R	3	87	HOYLE	AE	9	98
HOWELL	HJ	3	87	HOWES	H	13	231	HOWLETT	RH	13	231	HOYLE	AE	9	389
HOWELL	J	8	167	HOWES	HJ	7	196	HOWLETT	RT	13	231	HOYLE	AH	9	98
HOWELL	J	12	118	HOWES	HJ	7	196	HOWLETT	RW	1	172	HOYLE	AH	9	280
HOWELL	JOG	4	199	HOWES	HP	13	231	HOWLETT	RW	13	231	HOYLE	F	9	98
HOWELL	JT	3	87	HOWES	HV	12	119	HOWLETT	SG	4	200	HOYLE	F	9	280
HOWELL	JT	6	215	HOWES	J	13	231	HOWLETT	W	1	172	HOYLE	H	9	98
HOWELL	JW	8	167	HOWES	JH	13	231	HOWLETT	W	3	87	HOYLE	H	9	98
HOWELL	L	7	196	HOWES	JW	3	361	HOWLETT	W	5	185	HOYLE	H	14	160
HOWELL	OA	6	215	HOWES	JW	12	119	HOWLETT	W	12	327	HOYLE	J	9	99
HOWELL	R	6	216	HOWES	PA	7	196	HOWLETT	WA	5	185	HOYLE	J	11	188
HOWELL	R	14	160	HOWES	PG	13	231	HOWLETT	WJ	1	172	HOYLE	J	11	188
HOWELL	S	6	216	HOWES	RF	13	231	HOWLETT	WM	12	327	HOYLE	JW	14	161
HOWELL	S	13	230	HOWES	RV	12	119	HOWLLET	T	11	187	HOYLE	MA	4	200
HOWELL	W	4	199	HOWES	WH	1	171	HOWORTH	EW	9	98	HOYLE	R	11	187
HOWELL	W	6	216	HOWES	WH	6	216	HOWORTH	FH	1	172	HOYLE	W	11	188
HOWELL	W	6	216	HOWES	WR	2	174	HOWORTH	G	9	98	HOYLES	A	14	161
HOWELL	W	7	196	HOWES	WT	3	361	HOWS	FG	3	87	HOYLES	J	14	161
HOWELL	W	11	187	HOWGATE	W	8	167	HOWS	HWA	7	196	HOYNE	W	11	188
HOWELL	WA	5	185	HOWGEGO	JW	4	199	HOWS	JJ	10	113	HUBAND	GR	6	216
HOWELL	WG	13	230	HOWICK	A	2	175	HOWS	S	12	327	HUBBALL	F	6	216
HOWELL	WJN	1	171	HOWICK	A	3	362	HOWSDEN	T	5	186	HUBBALL	S	6	216

HUBBARD	A	6	216	HUCKLE	HC	5	186	HUDSON	E	9	281	HUDSON	J	14	161
HUBBARD	C	13	231	HUCKLE	PW	12	120	HUDSON	E	9	281	HUDSON	J	14	161
HUBBARD	C	13	231	HUCKLE	SC	12	120	HUDSON	E	9	281	HUDSON	JA	8	168
HUBBARD	CS	13	232	HUCKLE	W	5	186	HUDSON	E	9	281	HUDSON	JA	8	168
HUBBARD	D	12	119	HUCKLE	W	12	422	HUDSON	EJ	6	216	HUDSON	JD	9	281
HUBBARD	F	6	216	HUCKLESBY	A	5	186	HUDSON	EL	1	172	HUDSON	JE	4	200
HUBBARD	GH	5	186	HUCKLESBY	AL	5	186	HUDSON	F	2	175	HUDSON	JR	9	100
HUBBARD	GW	3	87	HUCKLESBY	J	5	186	HUDSON	F	8	168	HUDSON	JT	6	217
HUBBARD	H	2	175	HUCKLESBY	LW	8	168	HUDSON	F	9	99	HUDSON	JW	7	197
HUBBARD	H	3	87	HUCKLESBY	S	5	186	HUDSON	F	9	99	HUDSON	K	1	172
HUBBARD	H	5	186	HUCKLESBY	W	5	186	HUDSON	F	9	99	HUDSON	L	11	188
HUBBARD	H	12	119	HUCKS	H	3	362	HUDSON	F	9	99	HUDSON	P	9	100
HUBBARD	JE	4	200	HUCKSTEPP	AR	7	196	HUDSON	FS	7	197	HUDSON	PA	1	172
HUBBARD	JR	9	99	HUCKSTEPP	C	7	197	HUDSON	FW	9	99	HUDSON	R	6	217
HUBBARD	JW	6	216	HUCKSTEPP	C	13	232	HUDSON	FW	14	161	HUDSON	R	8	168
HUBBARD	R	7	196	HUCKSTEPP	F	13	232	HUDSON	G	13	232	HUDSON	RAJ	2	175
HUBBARD	RW	3	87	HUCKSTEPP	HJ	7	196	HUDSON	G	13	232	HUDSON	RH	9	281
HUBBARD	TE	3	87	HUCKSTEPP	W	13	232	HUDSON	GE	9	99	HUDSON	RS	6	217
HUBBARD	WF	3	87	HUDD	A	3	362	HUDSON	GE	9	281	HUDSON	S	6	217
HUBBARD	WGT	3	88	HUDD	AF	3	362	HUDSON	GH	9	99	HUDSON	T	6	217
HUBBARD	WH	13	232	HUDD	MA	3	362	HUDSON	GW	8	168	HUDSON	T	8	169
HUBBARD	WJ	3	362	HUDD	TG	3	362	HUDSON	GW	14	161	HUDSON	T	9	281
HUBBERT	FW	10	316	HUDD	TJ	3	362	HUDSON	H	3	362	HUDSON	T	14	161
HUBBLE	AG	1	172	HUDD	WJ	3	362	HUDSON	H	7	197	HUDSON	TH	9	281
HUBBLE	AV	1	172	HUDDERT	W	14	161	HUDSON	H	8	168	HUDSON	W	3	88
HUBBLE	HE	1	172	HUDDLE	AE	13	232	HUDSON	H	8	168	HUDSON	W	3	88
HUBBLE	PF	13	232	HUDDLE	GR	5	186	HUDSON	H	8	168	HUDSON	W	5	186
HUBBLE	W	13	232	HUDDLE	JG	13	232	HUDSON	H	9	99	HUDSON	W	6	217
HUBBOCKS	T	2	175	HUDDLE	S	13	232	HUDSON	H	9	99	HUDSON	W	6	217
HUBBOLD	GA	4	200	HUDDLESTON	J	9	280	HUDSON	H	14	161	HUDSON	W	8	169
HUBBUCK	GGJ	3	88	HUDMAN	S	14	161	HUDSON	HE	9	99	HUDSON	W	8	169
HUBER	AL	12	119	HUDSMITH	S	10	316	HUDSON	HK	13	232	HUDSON	W	8	169
HUBER	JH	1	172	HUDSON	A	9	99	HUDSON	HR	7	197	HUDSON	W	9	100
HUBER	RA	1	172	HUDSON	A	9	281	HUDSON	HW	4	200	HUDSON	W	9	281
HUBERT	A	4	200	HUDSON	AE	6	216	HUDSON	J	2	175	HUDSON	W	11	188
HUBERT	AE	7	196	HUDSON	AF	5	186	HUDSON	J	3	88	HUDSON	W	12	120
HUBERT	DJ	4	200	HUDSON	AG	4	200	HUDSON	J	6	217	HUDSON	W	14	161
HUBERT	GA	7	196	HUDSON	AOF	1	172	HUDSON	J	8	168	HUDSON	W	14	161
HUBERT	H	13	232	HUDSON	AW	10	316	HUDSON	J	8	168	HUDSON	W	14	162
HUBERT	W	13	232	HUDSON	B	9	99	HUDSON	J	8	168	HUDSON	WA	14	162
HUBERT	W	13	232	HUDSON	BG	13	232	HUDSON	J	8	168	HUDSON	WE	13	232
HUBERT	W	13	232	HUDSON	BW	4	200	HUDSON	J	8	168	HUDSON	WF	6	217
HUBSDELL	AE	10	113	HUDSON	C	1	172	HUDSON	J	9	99	HUDSON	WG	11	188
HUBY	JF	14	161	HUDSON	C	2	175	HUDSON	J	9	100	HUDSON	WH	8	169
HUCKIN	FC	7	196	HUDSON	C	4	200	HUDSON	J	9	281	HUDSON	WH	9	281
HUCKLE	A	12	119	HUDSON	C	10	113	HUDSON	J	9	281	HUDSON	WH	13	232
HUCKLE	AE	12	119	HUDSON	C	11	188	HUDSON	J	11	188	HUDSON	WJ	9	281
HUCKLE	AF	12	119	HUDSON	CR	9	99	HUDSON	J	11	422	HUELIN	J	4	200
HUCKLE	B	9	99	HUDSON	CR	9	281	HUDSON	J	11	422	HUETSON	WT	3	88
HUCKLE	CS	12	119	HUDSON	D	14	161	HUDSON	J	11	423	HUFFAM	E	7	197
HUCKLE	EJ	5	186	HUDSON	E	3	88	HUDSON	J	14	161	HUFFER	P	5	187
HUCKLE	EW	12	119	HUDSON	E	6	216	HUDSON	J	14	161	HUFFER	W	5	187
HUCKLE	FC	12	120	HUDSON	E	9	99	HUDSON	J	14	161	HUFFER	W	8	169
HUCKLE	H	5	186	HUDSON	E	9	99	HUDSON	J	14	161	HUFFEY	WJ	1	172
HUCKLE	H	5	186	HUDSON	E	9	99	HUDSON	J	14	161	HUFFLETT	CO	13	233

HUFFORD	EF	3	88	HUGHES	CEW	10	114	HUGHES	HM	12	327	HUGHES	S	6	218	HUGHES	S	6	218
HUFFORD	T	12	120	HUGHES	CH	3	362	HUGHES	HR	4	201	HUGHES	S	14	162	HUGHES	S	14	162
HUGALL	FH	7	197	HUGHES	CH	13	233	HUGHES	HV	14	162	HUGHES	S	14	162	HUGHES	SE	6	219
HUGGAN	CH	9	281	HUGHES	CL	11	188	HUGHES	J	2	175	HUGHES	SE	6	219	HUGHES	SEC	4	201
HUGGAN	F	8	169	HUGHES	CRG	1	173	HUGHES	J	3	362	HUGHES	SEC	4	201	HUGHES	ST	6	219
HUGGAN	G	8	169	HUGHES	D	6	217	HUGHES	J	4	201	HUGHES	ST	6	219	HUGHES	ST	10	114
HUGGANS	W	9	100	HUGHES	D	13	233	HUGHES	J	6	218	HUGHES	ST	10	114	HUGHES	T	4	201
HUGGARD	LS	5	187	HUGHES	DH	6	217	HUGHES	J	6	218	HUGHES	T	4	201	HUGHES	T	11	189
HUGGETT	A	13	233	HUGHES	E	1	173	HUGHES	J	6	218	HUGHES	T	11	189	HUGHES	T	11	189
HUGGETT	AJ	10	113	HUGHES	E	4	200	HUGHES	J	6	218	HUGHES	T	11	189	HUGHES	T	14	163
HUGGETT	GC	10	316	HUGHES	E	7	197	HUGHES	J	6	218	HUGHES	T	14	163	HUGHES	TA	1	173
HUGGETT	HJ	5	187	HUGHES	E	9	281	HUGHES	J	6	218	HUGHES	TA	1	173	HUGHES	TE	2	175
HUGGETT	SG	13	233	HUGHES	E	9	282	HUGHES	J	7	197	HUGHES	TE	2	175	HUGHES	W	2	175
HUGGETT	TW	13	233	HUGHES	E	11	188	HUGHES	J	7	197	HUGHES	W	2	175	HUGHES	W	4	201
HUGGETT	VC	3	88	HUGHES	E	11	188	HUGHES	J	8	169	HUGHES	W	4	201	HUGHES	W	6	219
HUGGETT	W	3	88	HUGHES	E	11	188	HUGHES	J	8	169	HUGHES	W	6	219	HUGHES	W	6	219
HUGGETT	WA	7	197	HUGHES	E	11	188	HUGHES	J	9	282	HUGHES	W	6	219	HUGHES	W	6	219
HUGGINS	AE	6	217	HUGHES	EA	12	327	HUGHES	J	11	189	HUGHES	W	6	219	HUGHES	W	6	219
HUGGINS	AR	7	197	HUGHES	EC	11	188	HUGHES	J	11	423	HUGHES	W	6	219	HUGHES	W	8	170
HUGGINS	EH	1	172	HUGHES	EJ	4	200	HUGHES	J	12	327	HUGHES	W	8	170	HUGHES	W	11	189
HUGGINS	F	14	162	HUGHES	EW	13	233	HUGHES	J	12	327	HUGHES	W	11	189	HUGHES	W	11	189
HUGGINS	G	5	187	HUGHES	F	6	217	HUGHES	J	14	162	HUGHES	W	11	189	HUGHES	W	11	190
HUGGINS	H	2	175	HUGHES	F	8	169	HUGHES	J	14	162	HUGHES	W	11	190	HUGHES	W	11	190
HUGGINS	J	8	169	HUGHES	F	11	188	HUGHES	J	14	162	HUGHES	W	11	190	HUGHES	W	12	120
HUGGINS	JE	8	169	HUGHES	F	11	188	HUGHES	J	14	162	HUGHES	W	12	120	HUGHES	W	14	163
HUGGINS	JE	10	114	HUGHES	F	11	188	HUGHES	J	14	162	HUGHES	W	14	163	HUGHES	W	14	163
HUGGINS	LA	3	362	HUGHES	F	11	189	HUGHES	JD	1	173	HUGHES	W	14	163	HUGHES	W	14	163
HUGGINS	S	3	88	HUGHES	F	13	233	HUGHES	JD	4	201	HUGHES	W	14	163	HUGHES	W	14	163
HUGGON	CA	8	169	HUGHES	FA	4	200	HUGHES	JE	6	218	HUGHES	W	14	163	HUGHES	WC	14	163
HUGH	E	9	281	HUGHES	FJ	6	218	HUGHES	JE	8	169	HUGHES	W	14	163	HUGHES	WE	11	190
HUGH	W	3	88	HUGHES	FW	6	218	HUGHES	JE	11	189	HUGHES	WC	14	163	HUGHES	WH	3	88
HUGHES	A	10	316	HUGHES	G	6	218	HUGHES	JE	11	189	HUGHES	WE	11	190	HUGHES	WJ	6	219
HUGHES	A	13	233	HUGHES	G	11	189	HUGHES	JF	1	173	HUGHES	WH	3	88	HUGHES	WJ	10	114
HUGHES	A	14	162	HUGHES	GE	11	189	HUGHES	JH	6	218	HUGHES	WJ	6	219	HUGHES	WR	11	190
HUGHES	A	14	162	HUGHES	GH	3	362	HUGHES	JH	14	162	HUGHES	WJ	10	114	HUGHES	WT	3	88
HUGHES	A	14	162	HUGHES	GR	14	162	HUGHES	JM	10	114	HUGHES	WR	11	190	HUGHES	WT	3	88
HUGHES	AA	12	327	HUGHES	GW	3	88	HUGHES	JS	3	362	HUGHES	WT	3	88	HUGHESDON	H	13	233
HUGHES	AE	14	162	HUGHES	GW	6	218	HUGHES	JW	8	169	HUGHES	WT	3	88	HUGHMAN	S	5	187
HUGHES	AG	10	114	HUGHES	H	1	173	HUGHES	JW	11	189	HUGHES	L	11	189	HUGHSON	JH	11	190
HUGHES	AJ	1	172	HUGHES	H	2	175	HUGHES	JW	11	189	HUGHES	LM	4	201	HUGILL	H	9	100
HUGHES	AJ	9	100	HUGHES	H	4	201	HUGHES	L	11	189	HUGILL				HUGILL	W	8	170
HUGHES	AM	3	88	HUGHES	H	6	218	HUGHES	LM	4	201	HUGMAN				HUGMAN	GT	7	197
HUGHES	AT	4	200	HUGHES	H	6	218	HUGHES	M	3	88	HUGHES				HUGO	H	4	201
HUGHES	AT	6	217	HUGHES	H	6	218	HUGHES	M	7	197	HUGHES				HUISH	WJA	10	114
HUGHES	AT	10	114	HUGHES	H	6	218	HUGHES	M	8	169	HUGHES				HUITSON	A	14	163
HUGHES	AV	4	200	HUGHES	H	8	169	HUGHES	NW	1	173	HUGHES				HULATT	AG	12	120
HUGHES	B	6	217	HUGHES	H	8	169	HUGHES	O	6	218	HUGHES				HULATT	FW	12	120
HUGHES	B	6	217	HUGHES	H	11	189	HUGHES	O	8	169	HUGHES				HULATT	GJ	12	120
HUGHES	B	6	217	HUGHES	H	11	189	HUGHES	P	11	189	HUGHES				HULATT	H	3	89
HUGHES	B	13	233	HUGHES	H	14	162	HUGHES	P	12	120	HUGHES				HULATT	HJ	12	120
HUGHES	BG	10	114	HUGHES	HA	7	197	HUGHES	R	11	189	HUGHES				HULATT	HW	12	120
HUGHES	C	7	197	HUGHES	HE	8	169	HUGHES	R	11	189	HUGHES				HULATT	JR	12	120
HUGHES	C	11	188	HUGHES	HE	12	327	HUGHES	RJ	3	88	HUGHES							
HUGHES	CB	6	217	HUGHES	HG	7	197	HUGHES	RR	11	189	HUGHES							
HUGHES	CE	14	162	HUGHES				HUGHES	S	6	218	HUGHES							

HULATT	PCE	5	187	HULLAH	A	10	114	HUMBER	J	3	89	HUMPHREY	GW	9	100
HULATT	WA	12	120	HULLAH	AE	8	170	HUMBERTHA	J	14	163	HUMPHREY	H	1	173
HULATT	WH	12	120	HULLAH	EJ	10	114	HUMBLE	E	9	100	HUMPHREY	H	8	170
HULBERT	T	6	219	HULLAH	F	8	170	HUMBLES	FC	5	188	HUMPHREY	HL	10	114
HULCOOP	HF	2	175	HULLAH	G	8	170	HUMBLES	W	5	188	HUMPHREY	IG	1	174
HULCOOP	WS	1	173	HULLAH	J	9	100	HUMBLESTONE	WH	1	173	HUMPHREY	J	7	198
HULETT	FG	12	120	HULLAND	F	8	170	HUMBY	A	4	201	HUMPHREY	L	5	188
HULETT	W	5	187	HULLAND	GR	7	198	HUMBY	AC	4	201	HUMPHREY	L	10	114
HULFORD	L	3	89	HULLER	M	14	163	HUMBY	AG	4	201	HUMPHREY	LT	12	121
HULFORD	SA	13	233	HULLEY	G	11	190	HUMBY	AJ	4	201	HUMPHREY	M	13	233
HULFORD	WC	13	233	HULLEY	P	1	173	HUMBY	FM	4	201	HUMPHREY	O	5	188
HULKS	GA	1	173	HULLIGAN	W	9	100	HUMBY	HV	4	201	HUMPHREY	R	2	176
HULKS	JJ	1	173	HULLIGAN	W	9	282	HUMBY	J	4	201	HUMPHREY	R	5	188
HULL	A	5	187	HULLIS	AG	1	173	HUMBY	JA	4	201	HUMPHREY	R	8	170
HULL	A	5	187	HULLOCK	E	8	170	HUMBY	L	4	202	HUMPHREY	R	9	100
HULL	A	12	327	HULLOCK	E	8	170	HUMBY	PH	4	202	HUMPHREY	RC	12	327
HULL	AC	3	89	HULLOCK	T	8	170	HUMBY	WB	4	202	HUMPHREY	S	7	198
HULL	AE	12	120	HULLS	HG	7	198	HUME	E	8	170	HUMPHREY	TH	12	328
HULL	AW	1	173	HULMAN	TW	8	170	HUME	F	3	89	HUMPHREY	W	1	174
HULL	AW	13	233	HULME	A	11	190	HUME	F	4	202	HUMPHREY	W	2	176
HULL	C	14	163	HULME	A	14	163	HUME	FD	3	89	HUMPHREY	W	5	188
HULL	CE	12	120	HULME	E	11	190	HUME	GW	8	170	HUMPHREY	W	12	121
HULL	CW	3	89	HULME	ED	14	163	HUME	JA	7	198	HUMPHREY	W	13	233
HULL	DA	5	187	HULME	H	11	190	HUME	JH	13	233	HUMPHREY	WA	13	233
HULL	E	5	187	HULME	H	11	190	HUME	R	2	175	HUMPHREY	WF	13	234
HULL	EG	10	114	HULME	J	11	423	HUME	R	9	100	HUMPHREY	WG	5	189
HULL	F	5	187	HULME	J	14	163	HUME	S	9	100	HUMPHREY	WH	10	316
HULL	FW	3	89	HULME	JH	3	89	HUME	T	3	362	HUMPHREY	WJ	12	328
HULL	GH	9	100	HULME	R	14	163	HUMM	HB	3	89	HUMPHREY	WJJ	5	189
HULL	GS	5	187	HULME	W	7	198	HUMM	WGA	13	233	HUMPHREY	WL	1	174
HULL	GT	5	187	HULMES	C	11	190	HUMPHREY	A	4	202	HUMPHREY	WP	4	202
HULL	H	4	201	HULMES	J	11	190	HUMPHREY	A	5	188	HUMPHREYS	A	3	89
HULL	H	5	187	HULMES	J	14	163	HUMPHREY	A	5	188	HUMPHREYS	A	5	189
HULL	H	5	187	HULMES	JW	11	190	HUMPHREY	A	5	188	HUMPHREYS	A	7	198
HULL	HJ	5	187	HULMES	T	11	190	HUMPHREY	A	5	188	HUMPHREYS	A	9	282
HULL	J	5	187	HULMES	T	11	190	HUMPHREY	A	10	114	HUMPHREYS	A	13	234
HULL	J	5	188	HULSE	HW	13	233	HUMPHREY	A	12	327	HUMPHREYS	A	13	234
HULL	J	5	188	HULSE	J	11	191	HUMPHREY	A	12	327	HUMPHREYS	A	13	234
HULL	M	1	173	HULSE	JD	11	191	HUMPHREY	AE	3	89	HUMPHREYS	AG	13	234
HULL	R	2	175	HULSE	JW	11	191	HUMPHREY	AE	12	120	HUMPHREYS	AJ	12	328
HULL	R	3	89	HULSE	W	11	191	HUMPHREY	AH	12	327	HUMPHREYS	C	13	234
HULL	RJ	11	190	HULSE	W	11	191	HUMPHREY	AL	1	173	HUMPHREYS	CM	13	234
HULL	S	5	188	HULSTON	J	11	191	HUMPHREY	BG	2	176	HUMPHREYS	E	3	363
HULL	S	11	190	HULSTON	JM	11	191	HUMPHREY	C	1	173	HUMPHREYS	EE	13	234
HULL	V	5	188	HULSTON	JW	11	191	HUMPHREY	CA	12	121	HUMPHREYS	EN	11	191
HULL	W	1	173	HULSTON	T	11	191	HUMPHREY	CS	1	173	HUMPHREYS	FC	12	121
HULL	W	4	201	HULSTON	T	11	191	HUMPHREY	E	13	233	HUMPHREYS	FO	6	219
HULL	W	5	188	HULSTON	T	12	120	HUMPHREY	EC	5	188	HUMPHREYS	FW	12	328
HULL	WG	10	114	HULSTON	WE	11	191	HUMPHREY	EJ	10	316	HUMPHREYS	G	6	219
HULL	WJ	4	201	HULSTON	WH	11	191	HUMPHREY	F	12	327	HUMPHREYS	GF	3	89
HULL	WJ	5	188	HULTGREN	HA	12	327	HUMPHREY	FG	5	188	HUMPHREYS	GH	10	316
HULL	WR	11	190	HUM	P	5	188	HUMPHREY	FG	12	327	HUMPHREYS	GS	9	100
HULL	WT	7	198	HUMBER	AG	10	114	HUMPHREY	FV	3	362	HUMPHREYS	H	1	174
HULLAH	A	8	170	HUMBER	AH	3	89	HUMPHREY	G	2	175	HUMPHREYS	H	7	198
HULLAH	A	10	114	HUMBER	CA	10	114	HUMPHREY	GF	12	327	HUMPHREYS	H	13	234

HUMPHREYS	H	13	234	HUMPHRIES	H	6	220	HUNT	B	8	170	HUNT	G	12	121
HUMPHREYS	HC	1	174	HUMPHRIES	H	14	163	HUNT	BH	4	202	HUNT	GA	9	101
HUMPHREYS	HJ	3	363	HUMPHRIES	HC	3	363	HUNT	BJ	4	202	HUNT	GE	5	189
HUMPHREYS	HL	9	100	HUMPHRIES	HC	12	328	HUNT	BJ	13	234	HUNT	GF	6	221
HUMPHREYS	HS	1	174	HUMPHRIES	HJ	6	220	HUNT	BP	6	220	HUNT	GH	6	221
HUMPHREYS	HT	10	114	HUMPHRIES	HV	3	89	HUNT	C	4	202	HUNT	GJ	3	90
HUMPHREYS	HT	13	234	HUMPHRIES	HW	6	220	HUNT	C	6	220	HUNT	GL	6	221
HUMPHREYS	HV	11	191	HUMPHRIES	J	3	90	HUNT	C	10	115	HUNT	GR	10	115
HUMPHREYS	J	6	219	HUMPHRIES	J	11	191	HUNT	C	14	164	HUNT	GT	13	235
HUMPHREYS	J	12	328	HUMPHRIES	J	14	164	HUNT	CA	3	363	HUNT	GW	6	221
HUMPHREYS	J	14	163	HUMPHRIES	JA	7	198	HUNT	CG	4	202	HUNT	H	3	90
HUMPHREYS	JC	13	234	HUMPHRIES	JH	13	234	HUNT	CG	13	234	HUNT	H	3	90
HUMPHREYS	JE	9	100	HUMPHRIES	L	10	316	HUNT	CH	1	174	HUNT	H	3	363
HUMPHREYS	JE	10	115	HUMPHRIES	PA	12	328	HUNT	CH	5	189	HUNT	H	4	202
HUMPHREYS	JE	14	163	HUMPHRIES	RJ	3	90	HUNT	CH	7	198	HUNT	H	6	221
HUMPHREYS	JF	13	234	HUMPHRIES	RW	12	328	HUNT	CHJ	3	363	HUNT	H	7	199
HUMPHREYS	JJ	6	219	HUMPHRIES	S	6	220	HUNT	CJ	3	90	HUNT	H	8	170
HUMPHREYS	JR	3	89	HUMPHRIES	W	3	90	HUNT	CJ	3	90	HUNT	H	8	170
HUMPHREYS	L	13	234	HUMPHRIES	W	6	220	HUNT	D	6	220	HUNT	H	8	171
HUMPHREYS	LE	10	316	HUMPHRIES	W	6	220	HUNT	E	3	90	HUNT	H	9	101
HUMPHREYS	MA	12	121	HUMPHRIES	W	12	121	HUNT	E	6	221	HUNT	H	11	191
HUMPHREYS	O	5	189	HUMPHRIES	W	14	164	HUNT	E	7	199	HUNT	H	11	191
HUMPHREYS	O	5	189	HUMPHRIES	WA	6	220	HUNT	E	9	100	HUNT	H	11	192
HUMPHREYS	RA	1	174	HUMPHRIES	WE	7	198	HUNT	EA	13	234	HUNT	H	13	235
HUMPHREYS	RH	12	121	HUMPHRIES	WE	7	198	HUNT	EA	13	235	HUNT	HE	10	115
HUMPHREYS	RJ	3	89	HUMPHRIES	WG	3	90	HUNT	EC	4	202	HUNT	HG	12	121
HUMPHREYS	S	6	219	HUMPHRIES	WG	7	198	HUNT	EG	13	235	HUNT	HH	13	235
HUMPHREYS	S	9	282	HUMPHRIES	WG	12	328	HUNT	EG	13	235	HUNT	HL	10	115
HUMPHREYS	S	12	121	HUMPHRIES	WH	4	202	HUNT	EP	12	121	HUNT	HR	1	174
HUMPHREYS	SJ	7	198	HUMPHRIS	AH	7	198	HUNT	F	1	174	HUNT	HR	2	176
HUMPHREYS	TW	12	328	HUMPHRIS	P	6	220	HUNT	F	3	90	HUNT	HW	3	363
HUMPHREYS	W	5	189	HUMPHRY	BDL	10	115	HUNT	F	3	90	HUNT	J	1	174
HUMPHREYS	W	6	219	HUMPHRY	C	1	174	HUNT	F	9	282	HUNT	J	3	90
HUMPHREYS	W	11	191	HUMPHRYES	W	1	174	HUNT	F	10	115	HUNT	J	3	91
HUMPHREYS	W	13	234	HUMPHRYS	EH	3	90	HUNT	FC	4	202	HUNT	J	6	221
HUMPHREYS	WC	13	234	HUMPHRYS	GG	3	90	HUNT	FC	7	199	HUNT	J	6	221
HUMPHREYS	WE	7	198	HUMPHRYS	J	10	115	HUNT	FD	7	199	HUNT	J	9	101
HUMPHREYS	WF	4	202	HUMPHRYS	W	14	164	HUNT	FE	12	121	HUNT	J	11	191
HUMPHREYS	WG	1	174	HUMPHRYS	W	14	164	HUNT	FG	3	90	HUNT	J	13	235
HUMPHREYS	WH	1	174	HUMPHRYS	WG	10	115	HUNT	FH	3	363	HUNT	J	13	235
HUMPHREYS	WJ	3	363	HUNGERFORD	J	14	164	HUNT	FH	6	221	HUNT	J	14	164
HUMPHREYS	WJ	13	234	HUNNIBELL	FC	12	328	HUNT	FJ	5	189	HUNT	JE	3	91
HUMPHRIES	A	3	89	HUNSTON	WT	11	191	HUNT	FJ	14	164	HUNT	JG	3	363
HUMPHRIES	A	6	219	HUNT	A	3	90	HUNT	FL	3	90	HUNT	JH	3	363
HUMPHRIES	A	6	220	HUNT	A	4	202	HUNT	FT	5	189	HUNT	JH	9	101
HUMPHRIES	A	12	328	HUNT	A	6	220	HUNT	FW	4	202	HUNT	JT	6	221
HUMPHRIES	C	10	115	HUNT	A	6	220	HUNT	FW	5	189	HUNT	JW	3	91
HUMPHRIES	CC	5	189	HUNT	A	6	220	HUNT	FW	9	101	HUNT	JW	3	91
HUMPHRIES	D	6	219	HUNT	A	6	220	HUNT	G	3	90	HUNT	JW	7	199
HUMPHRIES	DA	12	328	HUNT	A	9	100	HUNT	G	3	90	HUNT	JW	13	235
HUMPHRIES	EJ	1	174	HUNT	AB	1	174	HUNT	G	6	221	HUNT	L	3	363
HUMPHRIES	F	12	121	HUNT	AJ	6	220	HUNT	G	7	199	HUNT	LJ	3	91
HUMPHRIES	FC	2	176	HUNT	AJ	10	115	HUNT	G	7	199	HUNT	MR	3	363
HUMPHRIES	FW	7	198	HUNT	AP	1	174	HUNT	G	8	170	HUNT	O	3	91
HUMPHRIES	G	10	115	HUNT	B	5	189	HUNT	G	8	170	HUNT	P	9	389

HUNT	P	12	121	HUNT	WHE	13	235	HUNTLEY	J	10	116	HURLOCK	E	1	175
HUNT	P	14	164	HUNT	WJ	1	175	HUNTLEY	J	10	116	HURLOCK	H	4	203
HUNT	PF	5	189	HUNT	WJ	3	363	HUNTLEY	PR	7	199	HURLOCK	W	1	175
HUNT	R	3	91	HUNT	WR	6	222	HUNTLEY	R	7	199	HURLOW	WH	10	317
HUNT	R	6	221	HUNT	WT	14	164	HUNTLEY	R	7	199	HURMAN	FB	3	92
HUNT	R	11	192	HUNT	WWC	10	316	HUNTLEY	T	10	116	HURN	EP	3	364
HUNT	RA	4	202	HUNTBACH	GH	14	164	HUNTLEY	W	7	199	HURN	H	9	101
HUNT	RA	5	189	HUNTER	A	3	91	HUNTON	AC	3	91	HURN	VG	3	364
HUNT	RE	4	202	HUNTER	A	3	363	HUNTON	JJ	3	92	HURRAN	GW	13	236
HUNT	RG	4	202	HUNTER	A	8	171	HUNTON	S	11	192	HURRELL	AW	4	203
HUNT	RG	13	235	HUNTER	A	8	171	HURCOMB	E	6	222	HURRELL	PW	13	236
HUNT	RJ	7	199	HUNTER	A	9	101	HURCOMB	F	6	222	HURRELL	W	3	92
HUNT	RW	10	115	HUNTER	AD	2	176	HURCOMBE	E	4	203	HURREN	C	12	121
HUNT	RW	10	115	HUNTER	CA	1	175	HURCOMBE	WH	7	199	HURREN	F	1	175
HUNT	S	1	174	HUNTER	CF	7	199	HURD	J	13	235	HURREN	FJ	11	192
HUNT	S	10	115	HUNTER	CHV	13	235	HURD	L	5	190	HURREN	JA	9	282
HUNT	SA	6	221	HUNTER	EE	10	115	HURD	T	11	192	HURREN	T	9	282
HUNT	SC	3	91	HUNTER	EE	10	115	HURDLE	A	13	235	HURRY	G	10	116
HUNT	SF	3	91	HUNTER	EW	8	171	HURDLE	W	10	116	HURRY	G	12	121
HUNT	SH	3	91	HUNTER	F	2	176	HURDLE	WA	10	116	HURRY	R	12	121
HUNT	SH	4	202	HUNTER	F	3	364	HURDLEY	G	2	176	HURSEY	H	3	92
HUNT	SR	4	203	HUNTER	F	6	222	HURDMAN	C	6	222	HURST	A	3	364
HUNT	SW	5	189	HUNTER	G	3	91	HURDMAN	E	6	222	HURST	A	4	203
HUNT	T	6	221	HUNTER	G	9	101	HURDMAN	H	6	222	HURST	A	7	200
HUNT	T	8	171	HUNTER	G	11	192	HURDMAN	W	6	222	HURST	AA	7	200
HUNT	T	12	328	HUNTER	H	2	176	HURDWELL	HG	3	92	HURST	AE	3	92
HUNT	TE	2	176	HUNTER	H	6	222	HURDWELL	WT	3	92	HURST	AE	6	222
HUNT	TH	3	363	HUNTER	H	8	171	HURFORD	F	9	282	HURST	B	6	222
HUNT	TJ	13	235	HUNTER	H	12	328	HURFORD	H	9	282	HURST	C	4	203
HUNT	W	3	91	HUNTER	H	13	235	HURFORD	H	9	282	HURST	C	13	236
HUNT	W	3	91	HUNTER	J	7	199	HURFORD	HC	4	203	HURST	CJ	1	175
HUNT	W	3	91	HUNTER	J	12	121	HURINE	A	14	164	HURST	CW	12	121
HUNT	W	3	363	HUNTER	JC	8	171	HURLEY	AR	14	164	HURST	E	4	203
HUNT	W	3	363	HUNTER	JT	14	164	HURLEY	AW	7	199	HURST	E	7	200
HUNT	W	4	203	HUNTER	P	1	175	HURLEY	CF	5	190	HURST	E	9	282
HUNT	W	4	203	HUNTER	R	14	164	HURLEY	D	3	92	HURST	E	11	192
HUNT	W	6	221	HUNTER	RH	10	115	HURLEY	FG	3	92	HURST	E	12	122
HUNT	W	6	221	HUNTER	TA	2	176	HURLEY	FG	3	92	HURST	E	14	164
HUNT	W	6	221	HUNTER	V	8	171	HURLEY	G	6	222	HURST	EF	4	203
HUNT	W	8	171	HUNTER	W	8	171	HURLEY	H	9	282	HURST	EJ	4	203
HUNT	W	9	101	HUNTER	W	8	171	HURLEY	H	12	328	HURST	EJ	4	203
HUNT	W	9	101	HUNTER	W	8	171	HURLEY	HF	3	92	HURST	F	3	92
HUNT	W	11	192	HUNTER	W	9	282	HURLEY	HJE	2	176	HURST	F	4	203
HUNT	WA	13	235	HUNTING	HW	13	235	HURLEY	J	2	176	HURST	F	11	192
HUNT	WA	14	164	HUNTING	JA	13	235	HURLEY	J	7	199	HURST	FA	12	122
HUNT	WB	4	203	HUNTINGFORD	CPW	7	199	HURLEY	J	9	101	HURST	FH	10	317
HUNT	WC	10	316	HUNTINGTON	A	9	101	HURLEY	JS	3	92	HURST	G	11	192
HUNT	WD	9	101	HUNTINGTON	C	11	192	HURLEY	JW	12	328	HURST	GE	4	203
HUNT	WF	3	91	HUNTINGTON	H	9	101	HURLEY	MT	2	176	HURST	H	6	222
HUNT	WG	3	91	HUNTINGTON	T	9	101	HURLEY	T	8	171	HURST	HE	4	203
HUNT	WG	3	363	HUNTLEY	C	5	189	HURLEY	T	8	171	HURST	HJ	1	175
HUNT	WH	6	221	HUNTLEY	EW	2	176	HURLEY	WF	13	235	HURST	HJ	7	200
HUNT	WH	6	222	HUNTLEY	FJ	5	189	HURLEY	WH	11	192	HURST	HJ	13	236
HUNT	WH	9	101	HUNTLEY	H	10	116	HURLEY	WS	13	235	HURST	I	14	164
HUNT	WH	10	115	HUNTLEY	HG	5	189	HURLING	C	3	92	HURST	J	6	222

HURST	J	11	192	HUTCHESON	AW	12	122	HUTCHINS	G	2	177	HUTCHISON	JG	7	200
HURST	J	11	192	HUTCHESON	P	14	165	HUTCHINS	GF	10	317	HUTHWAITE	LC	13	236
HURST	J	12	328	HUTCHIN	W	3	93	HUTCHINS	J	13	236	HUTLEY	PW	9	102
HURST	JW	9	101	HUTCHINGS	A	5	190	HUTCHINS	JH	1	175	HUTSON	AE	10	317
HURST	L	1	175	HUTCHINGS	A	5	190	HUTCHINS	L	1	175	HUTSON	FB	5	190
HURST	R	4	203	HUTCHINGS	A	6	222	HUTCHINS	NJ	3	93	HUTT	AJ	3	93
HURST	S	3	92	HUTCHINGS	AE	10	116	HUTCHINS	NJ	3	93	HUTT	AV	12	329
HURST	S	3	92	HUTCHINGS	BC	3	364	HUTCHINS	T	3	93	HUTT	AW	7	200
HURST	S	11	192	HUTCHINGS	E	4	204	HUTCHINS	TW	7	200	HUTT	WG	12	122
HURST	W	8	171	HUTCHINGS	E	4	204	HUTCHINS	W	5	190	HUTTON	AF	1	176
HURST	WA	13	236	HUTCHINGS	E	7	200	HUTCHINS	W	7	200	HUTTON	AG	1	176
HURST	WC	3	364	HUTCHINGS	E	10	116	HUTCHINS	WC	4	204	HUTTON	B	2	177
HURST	WE	3	364	HUTCHINGS	EA	12	328	HUTCHINS	WF	10	116	HUTTON	B	4	204
HURST	WG	12	328	HUTCHINGS	EJ	6	223	HUTCHINS	WG	13	236	HUTTON	B	6	223
HURST	WJ	4	203	HUTCHINGS	F	9	102	HUTCHINS	WS	10	116	HUTTON	C	9	102
HURST	WJ	12	122	HUTCHINGS	F	12	122	HUTCHINSON	A	8	171	HUTTON	C	11	193
HURST	WJK	4	204	HUTCHINGS	FE	2	176	HUTCHINSON	A	9	102	HUTTON	E	11	193
HURST	WR	4	204	HUTCHINGS	FHB	10	116	HUTCHINSON	A	9	282	HUTTON	E	13	236
HURST	WT	4	204	HUTCHINGS	FW	13	236	HUTCHINSON	A	13	236	HUTTON	FC	12	122
HURSTHOUSE	JE	11	192	HUTCHINGS	FW	13	236	HUTCHINSON	AE	14	165	HUTTON	FH	12	122
HURSTHOUSE	W	11	192	HUTCHINGS	G	4	204	HUTCHINSON	BH	6	223	HUTTON	FJ	10	317
HURT	RC	3	92	HUTCHINGS	G	12	122	HUTCHINSON	C	8	171	HUTTON	GH	5	190
HUSBAND	A	10	116	HUTCHINGS	GJ	2	176	HUTCHINSON	E	4	204	HUTTON	GW	13	236
HUSBAND	EA	10	317	HUTCHINGS	H	1	175	HUTCHINSON	F	9	282	HUTTON	HE	7	200
HUSBAND	W	8	171	HUTCHINGS	H	6	223	HUTCHINSON	FA	5	190	HUTTON	HH	4	204
HUSK	C	13	236	HUTCHINGS	H	12	122	HUTCHINSON	G	9	389	HUTTON	HS	4	204
HUSK	EW	2	176	HUTCHINGS	HJ	1	175	HUTCHINSON	G	13	236	HUTTON	J	8	172
HUSK	W	7	200	HUTCHINGS	J	4	204	HUTCHINSON	GF	8	171	HUTTON	J	14	165
HUSKER	R	9	101	HUTCHINGS	J	12	122	HUTCHINSON	GH	4	204	HUTTON	JH	13	237
HUSKER	R	9	282	HUTCHINGS	JJ	13	236	HUTCHINSON	GW	8	171	HUTTON	JT	11	193
HUSKINSON	E	14	165	HUTCHINGS	JP	10	317	HUTCHINSON	GW	8	172	HUTTON	N	8	172
HUSSELBEE	R	6	222	HUTCHINGS	JW	13	236	HUTCHINSON	GW	8	172	HUTTON	S	4	204
HUSSELBY	C	8	171	HUTCHINGS	K	12	122	HUTCHINSON	H	5	190	HUTTON	S	6	223
HUSSEY	A	6	222	HUTCHINGS	RA	1	176	HUTCHINSON	H	5	190	HUTTON	T	6	223
HUSSEY	A	7	200	HUTCHINGS	RGB	4	204	HUTCHINSON	H	9	282	HUTTON	T	8	172
HUSSEY	A	10	116	HUTCHINGS	RJW	10	116	HUTCHINSON	J	8	172	HUTTON	V	7	200
HUSSEY	A	10	317	HUTCHINGS	RM	10	317	HUTCHINSON	J	9	283	HUTTON	W	6	223
HUSSEY	CM	3	92	HUTCHINGS	RS	1	175	HUTCHINSON	J	9	283	HUXFORD	EH	10	117
HUSSEY	D	13	236	HUTCHINGS	S	10	116	HUTCHINSON	J	14	165	HUXLEY	A	14	165
HUSSEY	E	13	236	HUTCHINGS	T	10	116	HUTCHINSON	JB	9	102	HUXLEY	G	7	200
HUSSEY	HW	3	364	HUTCHINGS	TH	3	364	HUTCHINSON	JE	9	283	HUXLEY	J	11	193
HUSSEY	J	6	222	HUTCHINGS	W	10	116	HUTCHINSON	JE	9	283	HUXSTEP	AE	3	364
HUSSEY	J	13	236	HUTCHINGS	W	12	122	HUTCHINSON	JR	8	172	HUXTABLE	GR	3	93
HUSSEY	L	11	192	HUTCHINGS	W	12	122	HUTCHINSON	JW	8	172	HUXTABLE	HG	10	117
HUSSEY	QE	7	200	HUTCHINGS	WC	12	122	HUTCHINSON	JW	9	283	HUYTON	W	1	176
HUSSEY	S	13	236	HUTCHINGS	WG	1	175	HUTCHINSON	JW	11	193	HUZZEY	H	7	200
HUSSEY	W	14	165	HUTCHINS	A	1	175	HUTCHINSON	L	5	190	HYAM	CJ	13	237
HUSSEY	WH	6	222	HUTCHINS	A	1	175	HUTCHINSON	L	14	165	HYAM	J	3	364
HUSTLER	BJ	3	92	HUTCHINS	AE	3	364	HUTCHINSON	N	8	172	HYAM	J	8	172
HUSTLER	E	9	101	HUTCHINS	DW	3	93	HUTCHINSON	R	14	165	HYANS	R	3	93
HUSTLER	HE	9	101	HUTCHINS	EE	1	175	HUTCHINSON	S	8	172	HYATT	FG	2	177
HUSTLER	TF	3	92	HUTCHINS	F	12	122	HUTCHINSON	S	8	172	HYATT	FG	3	364
HUSTLER	WH	3	93	HUTCHINS	F	12	328	HUTCHINSON	WW	8	172	HYATT	HF	2	177
HUSTWIT	A	9	282	HUTCHINS	FC	3	93	HUTCHISON	AH	3	93	HYATT	HW	2	177
HUSTWITT	CI	3	93	HUTCHINS	G	1	175	HUTCHISON	J	10	116	HYATT	J	10	317

HYATT	W	3	93
HYATT	W	3	93
HYDE	A	5	190
HYDE	A	6	223
HYDE	A	6	223
HYDE	A	6	223
HYDE	A	11	193
HYDE	A	11	193
HYDE	AE	6	223
HYDE	AG	7	200
HYDE	B	5	190
HYDE	C	13	237
HYDE	CAW	13	237
HYDE	E	6	223
HYDE	E	7	200
HYDE	F	14	165
HYDE	FC	4	204
HYDE	G	3	364
HYDE	G	11	193
HYDE	G	12	122
HYDE	GR	5	190
HYDE	H	6	223
HYDE	H	6	223
HYDE	H	8	172
HYDE	H	11	193
HYDE	H	14	165
HYDE	J	6	223
HYDE	J	6	223
HYDE	J	12	122
HYDE	J	12	329
HYDE	JA	3	93
HYDE	JB	5	190
HYDE	JE	5	190
HYDE	JW	5	190
HYDE	JW	5	190
HYDE	JW	14	165
HYDE	L	6	223
HYDE	LJ	4	204
HYDE	M	3	93
HYDE	MH	4	204
HYDE	NV	5	190
HYDE	P	5	190
HYDE	P	5	191
HYDE	R	3	93
HYDE	R	3	364
HYDE	R	11	193
HYDE	R	14	165
HYDE	RBJ	4	204
HYDE	REA	3	364
HYDE	RJ	5	191
HYDE	RST	10	117
HYDE	S	6	223
HYDE	SF	4	205
HYDE	T	5	191
HYDE	TW	12	122
HYDE	W	4	205
HYDE	W	5	191
HYDE	W	6	223
HYDE	WA	3	93
HYDE	WA	10	317
HYDE	WC	4	205
HYDE	WF	12	122
HYDE	WG	5	191
HYDE	WJ	5	191
HYDE	WR	3	364
HYDES	G	9	283
HYETT	C	10	117
HYETT	EV	10	117
HYLAND	F	3	364
HYLAND	F	14	165
HYLAND	J	11	193
HYLAND	MH	3	365
HYLAND	RG	3	93
HYLTON	R	5	191
HYMAS	F	3	93
HYMAS	JG	3	94
HYMES	JH	5	191
HYNARD	AF	3	94
HYNARD	RA	3	94
HYNARD	RE	3	94
HYNARD	W	3	94
HYND	W	5	191
HYND	W	14	165
HYNDMAN	E	14	165
HYNDMAN	R	14	165
HYNE		1	176
HYNER	E	7	201
HYNES	GH	12	123
HYNES	J	11	193
HYNES	J	11	193
HYNES	P	9	102
HYNES	T	11	193
HYNETT	AJ	6	223
HYNETT	G	6	224

I

IANSON	JWH	6	224
IBBERSON	C	14	166
IBBERSON	G	11	193
IBBERSON	G	11	193
IBBETSON	A	9	283
IBBETSON	E	8	172
IBBETSON	G	8	172
IBBETSON	R	9	283
IBBETSON	W	13	237
IBBETT	A	12	123
IBBETT	AG	12	123
IBBETT	FW	12	123
IBBETT	J	12	123
IBBITSON	A	8	172
IBBITSON	J	8	172
IBBITSON	M	8	172
IBBITT	F	12	123
IBBOT	N	9	389
IBBOTSON	C	11	193
IBBOTT	AF	2	177
IBBOTT	H	1	176
IBERTSON	A	7	201
IDA	C	3	94
IDA	J	3	94
IDA	R	3	94
IDDLES	J	11	193
IDDLES	W	11	194
IDE	A	12	123
IDE	C	12	123
IDE	G	4	205
IDE	J	10	317
IDLE	G	8	172
IFE	FCR	3	94
IGHAM	J	14	166
IGO	J	11	194
ILBREY	J	2	177
ILBURY	FG	2	177
ILBURY	W	2	177
ILES	AE	3	94
ILES	E	7	201
ILES	EA	1	176
ILES	F	6	224
ILES	F	6	224
ILES	FCA	5	191
ILES	HV	1	176
ILES	J	9	283
ILES	JW	5	191
ILES	JW	9	102
ILES	P	13	237
ILES	W	13	237
ILETT	A	5	191
ILEY	NJ	14	166
ILIFF	AA	1	176
ILIFF	EG	1	176
ILIFF	FW	1	176
ILIFF	HW	1	176
ILIFF	WT	1	176
ILIFF	WT	1	176
ILIFFE	AC	12	329
ILIFFE	JH	12	329
ILIFFE	RW	6	224
ILIFFE	WH	12	170
ILLIDGE	S	14	166
ILLIDGE	W	3	94
ILLIDGE	W	3	365
ILLING	B	12	329
ILLING	BW	13	237
ILLING	J	3	365
ILLING	LT	12	123
ILLINGWORTH	A	8	173
ILLINGWORTH	A	9	102
ILLINGWORTH	A	9	283
ILLINGWORTH	A	9	283
ILLINGWORTH	C	1	176
ILLINGWORTH	C	9	283
ILLINGWORTH	E	9	283
ILLINGWORTH	F	8	173
ILLINGWORTH	F	9	283
ILLINGWORTH	F	11	194
ILLINGWORTH	FR	9	102
ILLINGWORTH	FW	8	173
ILLINGWORTH	J	9	102
ILLINGWORTH	J	9	102
ILLINGWORTH	JA	13	237
ILLINGWORTH	L	9	102
ILLINGWORTH	PW	1	176
ILLINGWORTH	R	9	283
ILLINGWORTH	S	8	173
ILLINGWORTH	W	9	102
ILLINGWORTH	W	9	283
ILLSTON	W	14	166
ILOTT	AE	5	191
ILOTT	E	10	117
ILSLEY	G	3	365
ILSLEY	J	3	365
IMBER	R	13	237
IMESON	A	3	94
IMESON	JC	9	102
IMISON	J	2	177
IMPEY	A	5	191
IMPEY	AG	2	177
IMPEY	AJ	2	177
IMPEY	C	5	191
IMPEY	H	5	191
IMPEY	J	5	191
IMPEY	STG	5	191
IMPEY	W	5	191
IMPEY	W	5	191
INCE	H	9	102
INCE	RH	14	166
INCE	WB	6	224
INCH	JL	14	166
INCHLEY	A	6	224
INCHLEY	H	6	224
IND	W	2	177
INDGE	B	5	191
INDGE	HR	5	192
INDGE	T	5	192
INES	CJ	6	225
INESON	P	8	173
INESON	W	8	173
ING	AE	1	176
ING	GE	1	176

ING	HE	2	177	INGRAM	E	1	177	INGS	FW	10	117	INWOOD	W	12	329
ING	JH	1	176	INGRAM	EF	13	237	INGS	H	4	206	INWOOD	WG	10	117
ING	JHG	2	177	INGRAM	F	2	177	INGS	HJ	4	206	INWOOD	WS	5	192
ING	JT	1	176	INGRAM	FE	4	205	INGS	HPJ	4	206	ION	J	7	201
ING	W	1	177	INGRAM	FJ	10	317	INGS	JG	10	117	IONTTON	AE	2	178
INGARFIELD	C	7	201	INGRAM	G	6	224	INGS	PJ	4	206	IRELAND	A	1	177
INGHAM	A	1	177	INGRAM	G	6	224	INGS	SH	4	206	IRELAND	AE	5	192
INGHAM	A	14	166	INGRAM	G	6	224	INGS	WP	4	206	IRELAND	AJ	4	206
INGHAM	AH	11	194	INGRAM	G	13	237	INKPEN	FJ	10	317	IRELAND	AR	1	177
INGHAM	F	9	102	INGRAM	H	6	224	INKPEN	LE	1	177	IRELAND	CG	12	124
INGHAM	F	9	102	INGRAM	H	12	329	INMAN	A	4	206	IRELAND	ER	4	206
INGHAM	F	9	283	INGRAM	J	4	205	INMAN	HS	6	224	IRELAND	F	4	206
INGHAM	F	9	283	INGRAM	J	8	173	INNES	R	2	178	IRELAND	F	11	194
INGHAM	FE	14	166	INGRAM	J	10	317	INNOCENT	W	2	178	IRELAND	FJ	7	201
INGHAM	G	7	201	INGRAM	J	12	329	INNS	EG	5	192	IRELAND	G	3	365
INGHAM	G	11	194	INGRAM	J	12	329	INNS	FJ	7	201	IRELAND	GH	4	206
INGHAM	H	9	103	INGRAM	J	14	166	INNS	GH	12	329	IRELAND	GS	6	224
INGHAM	H	9	103	INGRAM	JG	4	205	INNS	H	12	123	IRELAND	HJ	1	177
INGHAM	S	9	283	INGRAM	JJ	7	201	INNS	HJ	3	94	IRELAND	J	3	94
INGHAM	T	8	173	INGRAM	JS	4	205	INNS	L	3	94	IRELAND	J	4	206
INGHAM	W	9	103	INGRAM	M	8	173	INNS	PRH	12	329	IRELAND	J	6	224
INGHAM	W	9	103	INGRAM	P	4	205	INNS	TA	12	123	IRELAND	J	14	166
INGHAM	W	11	194	INGRAM	R	7	201	INNS	WG	12	329	IRELAND	JF	10	117
INGLE	GA	8	173	INGRAM	S	1	177	INSALL	GF	1	177	IRELAND	JH	6	224
INGLE	GJ	3	365	INGRAM	SFB	4	205	INSKIP	A	1	177	IRELAND	PR	1	177
INGLE	H	9	103	INGRAM	ST	13	237	INSKIP	A	5	192	IRELAND	R	8	173
INGLE	H	9	389	INGRAM	T	4	205	INSKIP	AE	12	123	IRELAND	S	6	224
INGLE	J	8	173	INGRAM	W	1	177	INSKIP	BW	5	192	IRELAND	T	6	224
INGLE	J	8	173	INGRAM	W	4	205	INSKIP	G	5	192	IRELAND	W	14	166
INGLE	P	8	173	INGRAM	W	8	173	INSKIP	J	5	192	IRELAND	WG	5	192
INGLE	S	8	173	INGRAM	W	10	117	INSKIP	PW	5	192	IRELAND	WH	3	94
INGLE	WR	8	173	INGRAM	W	10	117	INSKIP	PW	12	123	IREMONGER	H	4	206
INGLEBY	JW	9	284	INGRAM	W	14	166	INSKIP	V	12	123	IRESON	E	4	206
INGLEBY	T	6	224	INGRAM	WE	4	205	INSKIP	WJ	12	124	IRESON	GD	6	225
INGLEDEW	GWE	12	123	INGRAM	WG	13	237	INSLEY	E	2	178	IRESON	HJ	4	206
INGLES	CH	10	117	INGRAM	WG	13	237	INSLEY	P	6	224	IRESON	HV	2	178
INGLESBY	T	8	173	INGRAM	WH	2	177	INSTANCE	J	4	206	IRESON	TW	1	177
INGLESON	C	9	103	INGRAM	WH	4	205	INSTON	C	6	224	IRESON	V	1	177
INGLESON	EL	9	103	INGRAM	WH	5	192	INSTON	C	9	103	IRESON	WF	1	177
INGLESON	J	8	173	INGRAM	WH	10	117	INWARDS	B	5	192	IRESON	WH	1	177
INGLESON	J	9	103	INGRAM	WJ	7	201	INWOOD	A	2	178	IRESON	WJM	3	94
INGLIS	A	14	166	INGRAM	WT	4	205	INWOOD	A	12	329	IRESON	WR	13	237
INGLIS	D	11	194	INGREY	A	1	177	INWOOD	AE	7	201	IRISH	AE	13	237
INGLIS	WD	2	177	INGREY	AH	5	192	INWOOD	AF	12	124	IRISH	CF	4	206
INGOLD	AG	7	201	INGREY	CF	2	178	INWOOD	B	12	124	IRISH	ERA	2	178
INGRAM	A	1	177	INGREY	CR	12	123	INWOOD	CH	12	329	IRISH	JS	4	206
INGRAM	A	4	205	INGREY	F	12	123	INWOOD	CW	12	329	IRLAM	A	9	103
INGRAM	A	7	201	INGREY	HS	12	123	INWOOD	H	12	329	IRON	IH	7	201
INGRAM	ACM	5	192	INGREY	TH	12	123	INWOOD	HJ	2	178	IRONMONGER	A	6	225
INGRAM	AE	1	177	INGROVILLE	FA	10	117	INWOOD	HW	5	192	IRONMONGER	AE	13	238
INGRAM	AE	4	205	INGS	A	4	205	INWOOD	J	2	178	IRONMONGER	GR	11	194
INGRAM	AE	7	201	INGS	CE	4	205	INWOOD	J	13	237	IRONMONGER	H	9	103
INGRAM	AR	12	329	INGS	DR	4	206	INWOOD	R	12	329	IRONMONGER	JF	9	103
INGRAM	AW	4	205	INGS	EW	4	206	INWOOD	RE	5	192	IRONMONGER	JN	11	194
INGRAM	CV	2	177	INGS	FN	4	206	INWOOD	W	12	329	IRONS	A	5	192

IRONS	A	6	225	ISAACSON	A	14	167	IVES	SA	12	124	JACKAMAN	TW	13	239
IRONS	AA	12	124	ISABELL	GF	3	365	IVES	SD	5	193	JACKAMAN	WE	13	239
IRONS	CA	5	192	ISARD	G	13	238	IVES	SS	7	202	JACKEMAN	F	8	174
IRONS	E	1	178	ISARD	GA	1	178	IVES	T	5	193	JACKEMAN	W	8	174
IRONS	EW	13	238	ISARD	TH	1	178	IVES	T	7	202	JACKETT	WR	10	117
IRONS	F	12	329	ISERWOOD	H	8	173	IVES	W	4	207	JACKLIN	W	12	124
IRONS	FC	13	238	ISHAM	A	5	193	IVES	W	4	207	JACKLIN	WF	12	124
IRONS	HH	13	238	ISHAM	E	6	225	IVES	W	12	124	JACKMAN	AE	12	330
IRONS	I	3	365	ISHERWOOD	C	14	167	IVES	WF	12	124	JACKMAN	AW	3	95
IRONS	J	3	94	ISHERWOOD	H	11	194	IVESON	AB	3	365	JACKMAN	CS	13	239
IRONS	J	3	94	ISHERWOOD	HJ	11	194	IVESON	J	1	178	JACKMAN	EA	10	118
IRONS	JH	3	365	ISHERWOOD	NJ	11	194	IVESON	T	9	284	JACKMAN	EG	12	125
IRONS	JH	14	166	ISHERWOOD	S	14	167	IVETT	AC	12	124	JACKMAN	HJ	12	125
IRONS	RC	5	192	ISHERWOOD	W	11	194	IVETT	HJ	12	124	JACKMAN	J	9	284
IRONS	RJ	2	178	ISHERWOOD	W	11	194	IVEY	C	3	95	JACKMAN	J	13	239
IRONS	SD	13	238	ISITT	G	7	202	IVEY	RE	1	178	JACKMAN	M	13	239
IRONS	WT	3	95	ISITT	J	7	202	IVIMY	HJ	7	202	JACKMAN	PH	3	95
IRONSIDE	G	11	194	ISITT	JEH	7	202	IVORY	AW	5	193	JACKMAN	R	13	239
IRONSIDE	J	1	178	ISOM	LH	2	178	IVORY	JW	7	202	JACKMAN	W	3	95
IRONSIDE	TH	7	201	ISON	E	6	225	IVORY	LR	5	193	JACKMAN	W	5	194
IRVIN	E	9	103	ISON	WG	12	124	IVORY	SW	5	193	JACKMAN	WEB	13	239
IRVINE	F	8	173	ISRAEL	C	14	167	IVORY	WF	5	193	JACKS	GH	2	179
IRVING	D	7	202	ISRAEL	I	14	167	IVORY	WG	7	202	JACKS	WC	1	178
IRVING	G	14	166	ISSITT	T	13	238	IZOD	FW	13	238	JACKSON	A	1	178
IRVING	H	9	284	ISSOTT	JW	10	117	IZON	AW	6	225	JACKSON	A	1	178
IRVING	J	8	173	ISTED	A	1	178	IZZAR	M	10	117	JACKSON	A	2	179
IRVING	J	14	166	ISTED	AA	13	238	IZZARD	AW	5	193	JACKSON	A	5	194
IRVING	L	9	284	ISTED	FJ	13	238	IZZARD	BG	5	193	JACKSON	A	5	194
IRVING	RJ	8	173	ISTED	W	13	238	IZZARD	E	5	193	JACKSON	A	8	174
IRVING	W	14	166	ITTER	H	13	238	IZZARD	EB	5	193	JACKSON	A	8	174
IRWIN	DA	2	178	IVAMY	F	4	207	IZZARD	EL	12	124	JACKSON	A	8	174
IRWIN	H	9	103	IVANS	P	6	225	IZZARD	F	5	193	JACKSON	A	8	174
IRWIN	H	10	117	IVE	AC	1	178	IZZARD	F	5	193	JACKSON	A	8	174
IRWIN	HS	9	284	IVE	CA	13	238	IZZARD	F	12	124	JACKSON	A	8	174
IRWIN	L	13	238	IVE	HJ	2	178	IZZARD	H	5	194	JACKSON	A	8	174
IRWIN	S	14	166	IVE	J	13	238	IZZARD	H	12	329	JACKSON	A	8	175
IRWIN	W	8	173	IVERS	T	8	174	IZZARD	J	2	178	JACKSON	A	9	284
ISAAC	CC	4	207	IVERY	J	10	317	IZZARD	J	8	174	JACKSON	A	11	194
ISAAC	FJ	10	317	IVES	A	4	207	IZZARD	L	5	194	JACKSON	A	11	194
ISAAC	FW	10	317	IVES	AL	7	202	IZZARD	PG	5	194	JACKSON	A	11	195
ISAAC	GH	4	207	IVES	AV	13	238	IZZARD	R	5	194	JACKSON	A	11	195
ISAAC	H	1	178	IVES	AW	2	178	IZZARD	R	12	330	JACKSON	A	13	239
ISAAC	WA	10	117	IVES	C	1	178	IZZARD	RE	2	178	JACKSON	A	14	167
ISAAC	WE	12	329	IVES	C	12	124	IZZARD	S	12	124	JACKSON	A	14	167
ISAACKS	HW	7	202	IVES	CG	12	124	IZZARD	SB	5	194	JACKSON	A	14	167
ISAACS	CW	4	207	IVES	CH	5	193	IZZARD	W	13	239	JACKSON	AA	1	178
ISAACS	CW	5	193	IVES	CH	7	202					JACKSON	AC	1	178
ISAACS	F	4	207	IVES	EW	5	193					JACKSON	AE	3	95
ISAACS	FC	4	207	IVES	GS	13	238					JACKSON	AE	3	95
ISAACS	FE	2	178	IVES	H	5	193					JACKSON	AE	11	195
ISAACS	H	4	207	IVES	J	13	238					JACKSON	AG	3	95
ISAACS	J	4	207	IVES	J	13	238	JACK	AR	5	194	JACKSON	AG	6	225
ISAACS	L	3	365	IVES	P	5	193	JACK	D	2	178	JACKSON	AG	6	225
ISAACS	P	14	167	IVES	R	3	365	JACK	J	7	202	JACKSON	AH	3	95
ISAACS	S	14	167	IVES	R	12	124	JACK	W	1	178				
								JACKAMAN	J	13	239				
								JACKAMAN	TT	13	239				

J

JACKSON	AH	7	202	JACKSON	EJ	3	95	JACKSON	H	8	175	JACKSON	JF	13	240
JACKSON	AH	8	174	JACKSON	EJ	3	95	JACKSON	H	8	175	JACKSON	JH	6	226
JACKSON	AJ	4	207	JACKSON	EJ	7	202	JACKSON	H	8	175	JACKSON	JH	6	226
JACKSON	AM	7	202	JACKSON	ER	1	179	JACKSON	H	8	175	JACKSON	JH	8	175
JACKSON	AR	13	239	JACKSON	EW	1	179	JACKSON	H	8	175	JACKSON	JH	11	196
JACKSON	AT	2	179	JACKSON	F	2	179	JACKSON	H	9	104	JACKSON	JJ	7	203
JACKSON	AT	12	125	JACKSON	F	3	365	JACKSON	H	9	104	JACKSON	JJ	14	168
JACKSON	AT	13	239	JACKSON	F	8	174	JACKSON	H	9	104	JACKSON	JO	11	195
JACKSON	AW	3	95	JACKSON	F	8	174	JACKSON	H	9	284	JACKSON	JT	11	196
JACKSON	B	10	317	JACKSON	F	8	175	JACKSON	H	9	284	JACKSON	JW	7	203
JACKSON	B	11	195	JACKSON	F	8	175	JACKSON	H	9	389	JACKSON	JW	9	104
JACKSON	C	1	178	JACKSON	F	9	103	JACKSON	H	11	195	JACKSON	JW	9	104
JACKSON	C	8	174	JACKSON	F	9	284	JACKSON	H	11	195	JACKSON	JW	9	104
JACKSON	C	9	284	JACKSON	F	9	284	JACKSON	H	11	195	JACKSON	JW	11	196
JACKSON	C	12	125	JACKSON	F	11	195	JACKSON	H	12	125	JACKSON	L	3	96
JACKSON	C	13	239	JACKSON	F	11	195	JACKSON	H	14	167	JACKSON	L	9	104
JACKSON	C	14	167	JACKSON	F	11	195	JACKSON	H	14	167	JACKSON	L	9	284
JACKSON	C	14	167	JACKSON	F	11	195	JACKSON	H	14	167	JACKSON	L	11	196
JACKSON	C	14	167	JACKSON	FA	14	167	JACKSON	H	14	168	JACKSON	LG	13	240
JACKSON	CB	7	202	JACKSON	FC	10	318	JACKSON	HE	3	95	JACKSON	LM	13	240
JACKSON	CE	1	178	JACKSON	FG	9	103	JACKSON	HE	3	95	JACKSON	LP	7	203
JACKSON	CF	3	365	JACKSON	FH	2	179	JACKSON	HE	3	95	JACKSON	LS	2	179
JACKSON	CH	1	179	JACKSON	FJ	12	125	JACKSON	HH	6	226	JACKSON	M	1	179
JACKSON	CH	4	207	JACKSON	FS	7	203	JACKSON	HL	14	168	JACKSON	M	8	175
JACKSON	CH	4	207	JACKSON	FW	4	207	JACKSON	HR	1	179	JACKSON	M	9	284
JACKSON	CJ	7	203	JACKSON	FW	5	194	JACKSON	HT	12	125	JACKSON	MH	9	285
JACKSON	CJ	9	103	JACKSON	FW	7	203	JACKSON	HT	14	168	JACKSON	ML	1	179
JACKSON	CJ	12	125	JACKSON	FW	11	423	JACKSON	HW	3	95	JACKSON	N	7	203
JACKSON	CJ	13	239	JACKSON	G	1	179	JACKSON	HW	13	239	JACKSON	N	9	104
JACKSON	CT	8	174	JACKSON	G	1	179	JACKSON	J	1	179	JACKSON	P	5	194
JACKSON	CW	11	195	JACKSON	G	4	207	JACKSON	J	2	179	JACKSON	P	9	285
JACKSON	D	1	179	JACKSON	G	5	194	JACKSON	J	2	179	JACKSON	P	11	196
JACKSON	D	6	225	JACKSON	G	8	175	JACKSON	J	3	95	JACKSON	R	5	194
JACKSON	D	10	318	JACKSON	G	9	103	JACKSON	J	4	208	JACKSON	R	8	175
JACKSON	D	12	125	JACKSON	G	9	284	JACKSON	J	6	226	JACKSON	R	8	175
JACKSON	DA	4	207	JACKSON	G	11	195	JACKSON	J	9	104	JACKSON	R	8	175
JACKSON	DC	7	202	JACKSON	G	13	239	JACKSON	J	9	104	JACKSON	R	11	196
JACKSON	E	3	95	JACKSON	GE	13	239	JACKSON	J	9	104	JACKSON	R	11	196
JACKSON	E	3	95	JACKSON	GH	8	175	JACKSON	J	9	284	JACKSON	R	11	196
JACKSON	E	6	225	JACKSON	GP	7	203	JACKSON	J	9	284	JACKSON	R	12	330
JACKSON	E	8	174	JACKSON	H	1	179	JACKSON	J	11	195	JACKSON	R	13	240
JACKSON	E	8	174	JACKSON	H	1	179	JACKSON	J	11	195	JACKSON	R	14	168
JACKSON	E	8	174	JACKSON	H	2	179	JACKSON	J	11	195	JACKSON	RC	6	226
JACKSON	E	8	174	JACKSON	H	2	179	JACKSON	J	11	195	JACKSON	RC	13	240
JACKSON	E	11	195	JACKSON	H	4	207	JACKSON	J	11	423	JACKSON	RD	7	203
JACKSON	E	11	423	JACKSON	H	4	207	JACKSON	J	12	330	JACKSON	RJ	10	118
JACKSON	E	13	239	JACKSON	H	6	225	JACKSON	J	13	240	JACKSON	RJ	13	240
JACKSON	E	14	167	JACKSON	H	6	225	JACKSON	J	13	240	JACKSON	RT	7	203
JACKSON	EA	5	194	JACKSON	H	6	225	JACKSON	J	13	240	JACKSON	S	7	203
JACKSON	EA	9	284	JACKSON	H	6	225	JACKSON	J	14	168	JACKSON	S	7	203
JACKSON	EA	14	167	JACKSON	H	6	225	JACKSON	JA	13	240	JACKSON	S	8	175
JACKSON	EB	5	194	JACKSON	H	6	225	JACKSON	JA	14	168	JACKSON	S	8	175
JACKSON	EC	7	203	JACKSON	H	6	226	JACKSON	JB	14	168	JACKSON	S	9	285
JACKSON	EC	12	330	JACKSON	H	6	226	JACKSON	JC	3	365	JACKSON	S	11	196
JACKSON	EE	12	330	JACKSON	H	8	175	JACKSON	JE	8	175	JACKSON	S	14	168

JACKSON	S	14	168
JACKSON	S	14	168
JACKSON	S	14	168
JACKSON	SE	12	125
JACKSON	SE	12	125
JACKSON	SH	11	196
JACKSON	SJ	4	208
JACKSON	ST	7	203
JACKSON	T	4	208
JACKSON	T	6	226
JACKSON	T	11	196
JACKSON	T	11	196
JACKSON	T	11	196
JACKSON	T	11	196
JACKSON	TA	14	168
JACKSON	TF	12	330
JACKSON	TJ	13	240
JACKSON	TW	1	179
JACKSON	TW	14	168
JACKSON	W	1	179
JACKSON	W	1	179
JACKSON	W	2	179
JACKSON	W	5	194
JACKSON	W	5	194
JACKSON	W	5	194
JACKSON	W	6	226
JACKSON	W	7	203
JACKSON	W	7	203
JACKSON	W	8	175
JACKSON	W	8	175
JACKSON	W	8	176
JACKSON	W	8	176
JACKSON	W	8	176
JACKSON	W	9	285
JACKSON	W	10	118
JACKSON	W	10	318
JACKSON	W	11	196
JACKSON	W	11	196
JACKSON	W	12	330
JACKSON	W	13	240
JACKSON	W	14	168
JACKSON	W	14	168
JACKSON	WA	12	125
JACKSON	WA	14	168
JACKSON	WE	1	179
JACKSON	WE	3	96
JACKSON	WG	6	226
JACKSON	WH	1	179
JACKSON	WH	6	226
JACKSON	WH	12	125
JACKSON	WHG	4	208
JACKSON	WJ	7	203
JACKSON	WJ	11	196
JACKSON	WL	14	168
JACKSON	WT	6	226
JACKSON-SMITH	A	10	318
JACOB	A	7	204
JACOB	A	8	176
JACOB	A	10	318
JACOB	AO	12	125
JACOB	CRWO	12	125
JACOB	CS	3	96
JACOB	D	1	179
JACOB	GW	1	179
JACOB	JC	12	125
JACOB	LF	12	125
JACOB	RCR	13	240
JACOB	SF	1	180
JACOB	WT	1	180
JACOBS	A	6	226
JACOBS	AB	3	96
JACOBS	AE	3	96
JACOBS	AM	4	208
JACOBS	AT	8	176
JACOBS	AW	4	208
JACOBS	C	2	179
JACOBS	C	13	240
JACOBS	C	13	240
JACOBS	E	10	118
JACOBS	EF	2	179
JACOBS	EGH	7	204
JACOBS	EJ	2	179
JACOBS	F	2	179
JACOBS	F	2	179
JACOBS	F	4	208
JACOBS	F	13	240
JACOBS	FH	13	240
JACOBS	G	13	240
JACOBS	GH	7	204
JACOBS	GS	10	318
JACOBS	H	14	168
JACOBS	H	14	169
JACOBS	HC	10	118
JACOBS	HG	4	208
JACOBS	HI	13	240
JACOBS	HR	6	226
JACOBS	HW	4	208
JACOBS	I	14	169
JACOBS	J	8	176
JACOBS	J	13	240
JACOBS	L	7	204
JACOBS	L	8	176
JACOBS	LR	4	208
JACOBS	R	11	196
JACOBS	RC	6	226
JACOBS	S	4	208
JACOBS	SC	2	179
JACOBS	W	3	96
JACOBS	W	10	318
JACOBS	W	13	241
JACOBS	WA	2	179
JACOBS	WA	4	208
JACOBS	WA	10	118
JACOBS	WE	3	96
JACOBS	WE	4	208
JACOBS	WE	4	208
JACOBS	WH	13	241
JACOBS	WJ	10	318
JACOBS	WJH	10	318
JACOBSON	B	14	169
JACOBSON	E	1	180
JACOBSON	H	14	169
JACOBSON	LS	2	179
JACOMBS	FW	6	226
JACQUES	A	8	176
JACQUES	A	9	104
JACQUES	A	11	196
JACQUES	ER	1	180
JACQUES	F	8	176
JACQUES	F	10	118
JACQUES	FJ	6	226
JACQUES	J	9	285
JACQUES	TH	6	227
JACQUES	W	1	180
JACQUEST	BM	12	125
JACQUEST	E	12	125
JACQUEST	GF	12	125
JACQUEST	SC	12	125
JACQUEST	W	12	126
JACQUEST	WH	12	126
JAEGER	FH	4	208
JAFFE	A	14	169
JAFFE	J	14	169
JAGGARD	AE	5	194
JAGGARD	C	5	195
JAGGARD	D	5	195
JAGGARD	R	5	195
JAGGER	A	9	104
JAGGER	A	9	104
JAGGER	A	9	104
JAGGER	AB	9	104
JAGGER	C	5	195
JAGGER	C	9	104
JAGGER	E	9	104
JAGGER	F	3	96
JAGGER	GW	9	104
JAGGER	H	9	105
JAGGER	L	8	176
JAGGER	M	9	285
JAGGER	N	9	105
JAGGER	O	9	105
JAGGER	RW	8	176
JAGGER	W	9	105
JAGGER	W	9	105
JAGGER	W	9	285
JAGGER	WS	9	105
JAGGS	G	1	180
JAGO	A	10	318
JAGO	GF	13	241
JAGO	GJ	10	118
JAGO	J	4	208
JAGO	RC	2	179
JAKEMAN	CWH	6	227
JAKEMAN	EC	13	241
JAKEMAN	EF	13	241
JAKEMAN	H	13	241
JAKEMAN	V	6	227
JAKEMAN	W	3	365
JAKEMAN	WA	6	227
JAKEMAN	WHA	13	241
JAKEMAN	WT	12	126
JAKES	F	12	422
JAKEWAY	WHT	10	118
JAKINS	P	12	126
JAKINS	WE	5	195
JAMES	A	1	180
JAMES	A	1	180
JAMES	A	1	180
JAMES	A	1	180
JAMES	A	4	208
JAMES	A	9	105
JAMES	A	10	118
JAMES	A	10	118
JAMES	A	10	118
JAMES	A	10	118
JAMES	A	12	126
JAMES	A	12	330
JAMES	A	13	241
JAMES	A	13	241
JAMES	AB	1	180
JAMES	AE	5	195
JAMES	AE	7	204
JAMES	AE	7	204
JAMES	AE	7	204
JAMES	AE	10	318
JAMES	AE	13	241
JAMES	AG	6	227
JAMES	AG	13	241
JAMES	AH	2	179
JAMES	AH	12	330
JAMES	AJ	1	180
JAMES	AJ	10	319
JAMES	AR	3	96
JAMES	AT	2	180
JAMES	AT	3	96
JAMES	AT	12	330
JAMES	AW	3	366
JAMES	AW	12	330
JAMES	B	12	330
JAMES	C	2	180

JAMES	C	3	96
JAMES	C	3	96
JAMES	CC	4	208
JAMES	CE	2	180
JAMES	CE	12	126
JAMES	CF	6	227
JAMES	CH	1	180
JAMES	CH	1	180
JAMES	CH	10	118
JAMES	CHB	12	330
JAMES	CJ	13	241
JAMES	CW	5	195
JAMES	D	6	227
JAMES	D	11	196
JAMES	D	14	169
JAMES	DW	3	366
JAMES	E	1	180
JAMES	E	1	180
JAMES	E	3	96
JAMES	E	4	208
JAMES	EA	7	204
JAMES	EG	1	180
JAMES	EH	3	96
JAMES	EM	3	96
JAMES	ER	7	204
JAMES	ES	3	366
JAMES	ES	4	208
JAMES	EW	3	366
JAMES	F	2	180
JAMES	F	2	180
JAMES	F	2	180
JAMES	F	6	227
JAMES	F	7	204
JAMES	F	8	176
JAMES	F	10	318
JAMES	F	12	330
JAMES	F	13	241
JAMES	F	13	241
JAMES	FC	6	227
JAMES	FG	14	169
JAMES	FH	3	96
JAMES	FTW	12	330
JAMES	FW	1	180
JAMES	FW	7	204
JAMES	FW	10	118
JAMES	G	1	180
JAMES	G	3	96
JAMES	G	6	227
JAMES	G	7	204
JAMES	G	12	330
JAMES	G	12	330
JAMES	GA	13	241
JAMES	GH	10	118
JAMES	GH	10	118
JAMES	GH	14	169
JAMES	GO	12	126
JAMES	GS	10	118
JAMES	GS	13	241
JAMES	GT	13	241
JAMES	H	1	181
JAMES	H	3	96
JAMES	H	6	227
JAMES	H	7	204
JAMES	H	8	176
JAMES	H	10	318
JAMES	H	12	330
JAMES	H	13	241
JAMES	HE	4	208
JAMES	HF	3	366
JAMES	HG	12	126
JAMES	HGJ	13	241
JAMES	HS	1	181
JAMES	HTR	3	366
JAMES	HW	12	126
JAMES	J	2	180
JAMES	J	4	209
JAMES	J	6	227
JAMES	J	6	227
JAMES	J	7	204
JAMES	J	10	119
JAMES	J	12	330
JAMES	JB	10	318
JAMES	JE	1	181
JAMES	JE	13	242
JAMES	JF	2	180
JAMES	JG	4	209
JAMES	JH	7	204
JAMES	JJJ	7	204
JAMES	JR	10	318
JAMES	JS	7	205
JAMES	JW	1	181
JAMES	JW	10	119
JAMES	L	6	227
JAMES	L	14	169
JAMES	M	13	242
JAMES	ME	1	181
JAMES	ME	3	366
JAMES	NA	3	96
JAMES	P	6	227
JAMES	PW	10	119
JAMES	R	10	119
JAMES	R	10	119
JAMES	R	13	242
JAMES	RJ	13	242
JAMES	RJ	13	242
JAMES	RW	12	330
JAMES	S	3	96
JAMES	S	5	195
JAMES	S	6	227
JAMES	S	11	197
JAMES	SA	7	205
JAMES	SD	13	242
JAMES	SF	2	180
JAMES	SH	6	227
JAMES	SW	10	119
JAMES	T	1	181
JAMES	T	4	209
JAMES	T	7	205
JAMES	T	12	331
JAMES	TG	2	180
JAMES	TG	10	318
JAMES	THP	12	126
JAMES	W	1	181
JAMES	W	5	195
JAMES	W	5	195
JAMES	W	6	227
JAMES	W	6	228
JAMES	W	6	228
JAMES	W	6	228
JAMES	W	7	205
JAMES	W	7	205
JAMES	W	8	176
JAMES	W	8	176
JAMES	W	10	318
JAMES	W	12	331
JAMES	W	13	242
JAMES	WA	1	181
JAMES	WA	2	180
JAMES	WA	12	126
JAMES	WC	10	319
JAMES	WE	12	331
JAMES	WG	10	119
JAMES	WGH	11	197
JAMES	WH	3	96
JAMES	WH	4	209
JAMES	WH	8	176
JAMES	WH	13	242
JAMES	WJ	3	97
JAMES	WJ	6	228
JAMES	WJ	6	228
JAMES	WPS	10	319
JAMES	WR	2	180
JAMES	WY	6	228
JAMESON	A	8	176
JAMESON	A	10	119
JAMESON	E	8	176
JAMESON	F	7	205
JAMESON	H	11	197
JAMESON	R	9	285
JAMESON	WF	8	176
JAMIESON	F	11	197
JAMIESON	G	12	126
JAMIESON	HC	14	169
JAMIESON	J	11	197
JAMIESON	J	11	197
JAMIESON	J	11	197
JAMISON	W	11	197
JANAWAY	LR	4	209
JANAWAY	PE	4	209
JANAWAY	WH	13	242
JANES		3	366
JANES		3	366
JANES	AJ	5	195
JANES	C	5	195
JANES	E	5	195
JANES	E	5	195
JANES	EA	13	242
JANES	F	3	97
JANES	F	5	195
JANES	F	5	195
JANES	FG	5	195
JANES	FH	5	195
JANES	FW	5	196
JANES	FW	6	228
JANES	H	5	196
JANES	H	5	196
JANES	H	5	196
JANES	HJ	2	180
JANES	J	5	196
JANES	JW	5	196
JANES	L	5	196
JANES	L	5	196
JANES	RW	5	196
JANES	SE	5	196
JANES	TW	12	126
JANES	WB	5	196
JANES	WF	3	97
JANES	WTG	5	196
JANEWAY	E	5	196
JANEWAY	W	5	196
JANNAWAY	AJ	10	119
JANSON	R	9	285
JAPP	G	5	196
JAPP	H	14	169
JAQUES	GN	10	119
JAQUES	ST	1	181
JAQUES	T	1	181
JAQUES	T	8	176
JAQUES	TE	1	181
JAQUEST	H	1	181
JAQUIN	J	11	197
JARDINE	A	5	196
JARDINE	AH	5	196
JARDINE	ET	7	205
JARDINE	J	14	169
JARDINE	W	5	196
JARED	GJ	7	205
JARED	H	7	205
JARMAIN	GW	3	366
JARMAN	A	1	181

JARMAN	CE	1	181	JARVIS	E	8	176	JAY	HA	4	209	JEFFEREY	H	13	244
JARMAN	CV	12	331	JARVIS	E	11	197	JAY	O	1	182	JEFFERIES	A	10	119
JARMAN	F	13	242	JARVIS	ES	2	180	JAY	T	6	228	JEFFERIES	B	12	127
JARMAN	H	13	242	JARVIS	F	4	209	JAY	WC	2	181	JEFFERIES	BJ	3	366
JARMAN	HG	13	242	JARVIS	F	5	197	JAYES	H	7	206	JEFFERIES	E	1	182
JARMAN	HR	7	205	JARVIS	FJ	12	126	JAYES	WH	6	229	JEFFERIES	EA	3	97
JARMAN	HT	13	242	JARVIS	FW	5	197	JEACOCK	CFW	11	197	JEFFERIES	FJ	12	127
JARMAN	HW	1	181	JARVIS	G	6	228	JEACOCK	J	13	243	JEFFERIES	G	13	243
JARMAN	JH	1	181	JARVIS	GFJ	12	126	JEACOCK	SR	6	229	JEFFERIES	JS	3	366
JARMAN	JH	12	331	JARVIS	GH	6	228	JEAKINGS	CS	5	197	JEFFERIES	L	12	127
JARMAN	R	3	366	JARVIS	GJ	6	228	JEAKINGS	E	5	197	JEFFERIES	LW	7	206
JARMAN	SJ	6	228	JARVIS	GW	12	126	JEAKINGS	H	5	197	JEFFERIES	M	3	366
JARMAN	TA	10	319	JARVIS	GW	13	243	JEAKINGS	HJ	5	197	JEFFERIES	R	1	182
JARMUN	B	5	196	JARVIS	H	6	228	JEAKINGS	W	5	197	JEFFERIES	RA	3	97
JARMUN	P	5	196	JARVIS	H	11	197	JEAL	CE	7	206	JEFFERIES	S	7	206
JARRAD	S	10	319	JARVIS	H	12	126	JEAL	H	7	206	JEFFERIES	SC	13	243
JARRAMS	W	6	228	JARVIS	HF	3	97	JEAL	R	3	366	JEFFERIES	TA	6	229
JARRATT	JJ	2	180	JARVIS	HF	3	366	JEAL	W	3	366	JEFFERIES	TRP	13	243
JARRATT	T	9	105	JARVIS	HG	10	119	JEANES	HC	4	209	JEFFERIS	N	5	197
JARRATT	W	9	285	JARVIS	HJ	13	243	JEANES	WG	10	119	JEFFERS	E	11	197
JARRETT	CA	6	228	JARVIS	J	6	228	JEANS	A	4	209	JEFFERS	J	11	197
JARRETT	E	7	205	JARVIS	J	6	228	JEANS	CA	10	119	JEFFERSON	A	6	229
JARRETT	F	2	180	JARVIS	J	11	197	JEANS	F	4	209	JEFFERSON	AJ	10	120
JARRETT	F	6	228	JARVIS	J	14	169	JEANS	JAG	4	209	JEFFERSON	AR	5	197
JARRETT	FJ	13	242	JARVIS	JE	13	243	JEAVES	A	13	243	JEFFERSON	C	9	105
JARRETT	HG	10	119	JARVIS	JF	7	205	JEAVES	A	13	243	JEFFERSON	F	9	105
JARRETT	JH	12	331	JARVIS	JR	4	209	JEAVES	JE	13	243	JEFFERSON	F	9	285
JARRETT	RH	12	331	JARVIS	JW	2	180	JEAVONS	A	6	229	JEFFERSON	G	9	285
JARRETT	S	3	97	JARVIS	LC	13	243	JEAVONS	WG	6	229	JEFFERSON	J	5	197
JARRETT	W	14	169	JARVIS	R	7	205	JEE	RH	7	206	JEFFERSON	W	5	197
JARRETT	WC	2	180	JARVIS	R	13	243	JEEVES	AJ	2	181	JEFFERSON	W	5	197
JARRETT	WH	2	180	JARVIS	R	13	243	JEEVES	AW	13	243	JEFFERSON	W	6	229
JARRETT	WH	7	205	JARVIS	RW	7	206	JEEVES	CA	12	126	JEFFERY		13	243
JARRETT	WJ	10	319	JARVIS	SH	3	97	JEEVES	EC	12	127	JEFFERY	A	13	243
JARROLD	AE	13	242	JARVIS	T	11	197	JEEVES	EVG	3	97	JEFFERY	A	13	243
JARROLD	EW	7	205	JARVIS	TK	1	181	JEEVES	FA	12	127	JEFFERY	AH	10	120
JARROLD	RS	13	242	JARVIS	W	2	181	JEEVES	FH	5	197	JEFFERY	AJ	12	127
JARROLD	S	7	205	JARVIS	W	14	169	JEEVES	FW	12	127	JEFFERY	B	7	206
JARVIS	A	10	119	JARVIS	WA	1	182	JEEVES	G	3	97	JEFFERY	C	7	206
JARVIS	A	11	197	JARVIS	WA	14	169	JEEVES	H	12	127	JEFFERY	E	9	105
JARVIS	A	11	197	JARVIS	WG	2	181	JEEVES	HWD	3	97	JEFFERY	EA	2	181
JARVIS	A	12	126	JARVIS	WG	5	197	JEEVES	M	12	127	JEFFERY	F	12	331
JARVIS	AE	5	196	JARVIS	WR	9	105	JEEVES	SH	12	127	JEFFERY	F	13	244
JARVIS	AE	12	331	JARVIS	WS	7	206	JEEVES	WJ	5	197	JEFFERY	FE	10	120
JARVIS	AF	4	209	JARVIS	WT	8	176	JEEVES	WT	12	127	JEFFERY	FG	4	209
JARVIS	AF	7	205	JARY	A	10	119	JEFCOATE	HA	1	182	JEFFERY	FG	10	319
JARVIS	AH	3	97	JARY	W	10	119	JEFCUT	S	7	206	JEFFERY	FM	13	244
JARVIS	AL	4	209	JASPER	J	1	182	JEFCUT	WJ	7	206	JEFFERY	FW	1	182
JARVIS	B	4	209	JASPER	J	7	206	JEFFCOAT	C	5	197	JEFFERY	GA	9	285
JARVIS	B	14	169	JASPER	JA	13	243	JEFFCOATE	RE	2	181	JEFFERY	H	5	197
JARVIS	C	1	181	JASPER	JE	1	182	JEFFCOATE	W	5	197	JEFFERY	H	9	105
JARVIS	C	13	242	JASPER	S	5	197	JEFFCOATE	WT	1	182	JEFFERY	HC	12	127
JARVIS	CE	13	243	JAY	AA	8	176	JEFFCOCK	S	8	177	JEFFERY	HTW	12	331
JARVIS	CW	4	209	JAY	C	4	209	JEFFCOTT	J	3	97	JEFFERY	J	1	182
JARVIS	DG	12	126	JAY	F	1	182	JEFFCOTT	WH	12	331	JEFFERY	J	10	120

JEFFERY	J	12	127	JEFFRIES	W	5	198	JENINGS	FW	13	244	JENKINS	HP	7	207
JEFFERY	JC	4	209	JEFFRIES	W	12	127	JENKIN	EJ	10	319	JENKINS	J	1	183
JEFFERY	JC	13	244	JEFFRIES	W	14	169	JENKIN	F	13	244	JENKINS	J	3	98
JEFFERY	LJ	10	120	JEFFRIES	WC	12	127	JENKINS	A	1	182	JENKINS	J	7	207
JEFFERY	ME	7	206	JEFFRIES	WT	2	181	JENKINS	A	5	198	JENKINS	J	9	285
JEFFERY	R	9	105	JEFFS	AJ	5	198	JENKINS	A	5	198	JENKINS	J	10	120
JEFFERY	R	10	120	JEFFS	AT	8	177	JENKINS	A	6	229	JENKINS	J	10	120
JEFFERY	TK	13	244	JEFFS	AV	6	229	JENKINS	A	7	207	JENKINS	J	11	198
JEFFERY	W	6	229	JEFFS	C	12	128	JENKINS	A	14	170	JENKINS	J	11	198
JEFFERY	W	10	120	JEFFS	F	12	331	JENKINS	AD	5	198	JENKINS	J	14	170
JEFFERY	WA	13	244	JEFFS	F	12	331	JENKINS	AF	5	198	JENKINS	JA	2	181
JEFFERY	WF	7	206	JEFFS	G	9	105	JENKINS	AP	4	210	JENKINS	JCD	13	245
JEFFERY	WG	10	120	JEFFS	H	12	331	JENKINS	AV	13	244	JENKINS	JH	10	121
JEFFERY	WH	13	244	JEFFS	H	12	331	JENKINS	B	5	199	JENKINS	JJ	9	105
JEFFERY	WJ	7	206	JEFFS	HG	5	198	JENKINS	C	1	182	JENKINS	JW	1	183
JEFFORD	CJ	3	97	JEFFS	HR	3	97	JENKINS	C	8	177	JENKINS	L	4	210
JEFFORD	CV	5	197	JEFFS	J	5	198	JENKINS	CD	3	97	JENKINS	L	8	177
JEFFORD	DW	3	97	JEFFS	J	5	198	JENKINS	CE	6	229	JENKINS	M	4	210
JEFFORD	E	3	97	JEFFS	J	8	177	JENKINS	CF	6	229	JENKINS	M	4	210
JEFFORD	TW	3	97	JEFFS	J	12	331	JENKINS	CF	7	207	JENKINS	P	14	170
JEFFREE	G	10	120	JEFFS	JH	7	206	JENKINS	CT	13	244	JENKINS	PA	4	210
JEFFREE	GH	10	120	JEFFS	R	12	331	JENKINS	CW	4	210	JENKINS	PC	13	245
JEFFREY	A	5	198	JEFFS	S	12	128	JENKINS	E	2	181	JENKINS	R	8	177
JEFFREY	A	9	285	JEFFS	TR	5	198	JENKINS	E	2	181	JENKINS	R	14	170
JEFFREY	AJ	13	244	JEFFS	W	12	128	JENKINS	E	5	199	JENKINS	S	1	183
JEFFREY	ET	13	244	JEFFS	W	14	170	JENKINS	E	6	229	JENKINS	S	6	230
JEFFREY	HJ	12	127	JEFFS	WJ	12	331	JENKINS	E	7	207	JENKINS	S	11	198
JEFFREY	JHRA	1	182	JELLETT	A	4	210	JENKINS	EC	1	182	JENKINS	S	13	245
JEFFREY	P	5	198	JELLETT	EJ	7	206	JENKINS	EG	10	120	JENKINS	SJ	1	183
JEFFREY	W	5	198	JELLETT	LD	4	210	JENKINS	EJ	6	229	JENKINS	T	7	207
JEFFREY	WW	1	182	JELLETT	W	2	181	JENKINS	EJ	13	244	JENKINS	T	10	121
JEFFREYS	J	5	198	JELLETT	W	4	210	JENKINS	EL	5	199	JENKINS	TE	14	170
JEFFREYS	JW	8	177	JELLETT	W	4	210	JENKINS	F	1	182	JENKINS	W	6	230
JEFFREYS	RD	11	198	JELLEY	AE	6	229	JENKINS	F	2	181	JENKINS	W	7	207
JEFFREYS	TR	13	244	JELLEY	AJ	2	181	JENKINS	F	2	181	JENKINS	W	8	177
JEFFRIES	A	12	127	JELLEY	E	10	120	JENKINS	F	5	199	JENKINS	W	8	177
JEFFRIES	A	13	244	JELLEY	J	10	120	JENKINS	FC	6	230	JENKINS	W	10	121
JEFFRIES	AH	10	120	JELLEY	W	5	198	JENKINS	G	1	182	JENKINS	W	10	121
JEFFRIES	C	3	97	JELLICOE	EG	10	319	JENKINS	G	1	183	JENKINS	W	10	319
JEFFRIES	CA	10	120	JELLIE	P	12	128	JENKINS	G	5	199	JENKINS	W	13	245
JEFFRIES	D	6	229	JELLIS	J	5	198	JENKINS	G	7	207	JENKINS	W	14	170
JEFFRIES	E	10	120	JELLIS	J	12	331	JENKINS	G	11	198	JENKINS	W	14	170
JEFFRIES	EC	12	127	JELLIS	V	5	198	JENKINS	GA	6	230	JENKINS	WC	13	245
JEFFRIES	F	4	210	JELLISS	H	7	207	JENKINS	GH	13	244	JENKINS	WE	10	121
JEFFRIES	FW	5	198	JELLY	E	4	210	JENKINS	GO	10	120	JENKINS	WH	7	207
JEFFRIES	G	11	198	JELLY	EG	4	210	JENKINS	GS	13	244	JENKINS	WH	10	121
JEFFRIES	HR	5	198	JELLY	F	5	198	JENKINS	H	6	230	JENKINS	WH	14	170
JEFFRIES	HW	2	181	JELLY	J	7	207	JENKINS	H	6	230	JENKINS	WR	2	181
JEFFRIES	J	14	169	JELLY	J	14	170	JENKINS	H	6	230	JENKINS	WW	4	210
JEFFRIES	JH	6	229	JELLY	NE	4	210	JENKINS	H	8	177	JENKINSON	A	3	98
JEFFRIES	JW	10	120	JELLYMAN	AE	6	229	JENKINS	H	13	245	JENKINSON	A	8	177
JEFFRIES	L	5	198	JELLYMAN	OC	6	229	JENKINS	HE	2	181	JENKINSON	A	9	105
JEFFRIES	NF	4	210	JEMMETT	JH	14	170	JENKINS	HE	7	207	JENKINSON	A	9	389
JEFFRIES	R	12	127	JEMPSON	E	8	177	JENKINS	HG	1	183	JENKINSON	AF	10	319
JEFFRIES	S	12	127	JENINGS	CMV	13	244	JENKINS	HJ	4	210	JENKINSON	C	9	285

JENKINSON	E	8	177	JENNINGS	E	5	199	JENNINGS	SI	6	230	JERRARD	AE	3	367
JENKINSON	E	8	177	JENNINGS	E	7	208	JENNINGS	T	5	199	JERRARD	AE	10	121
JENKINSON	E	14	170	JENNINGS	ET	2	182	JENNINGS	T	6	230	JERRARD	G	10	121
JENKINSON	F	8	177	JENNINGS	F	3	98	JENNINGS	T	9	286	JERRARD	JW	4	211
JENKINSON	H	3	98	JENNINGS	F	3	98	JENNINGS	T	14	170	JERRIM	A	4	211
JENKINSON	J	8	177	JENNINGS	F	5	199	JENNINGS	T	14	170	JERRIM	EF	4	211
JENKINSON	J	10	121	JENNINGS	F	8	177	JENNINGS	T	14	170	JERROM	A	10	121
JENKINSON	JW	9	285	JENNINGS	F	11	198	JENNINGS	TW	1	183	JERROM	D	3	367
JENKINSON	SA	11	198	JENNINGS	F	11	198	JENNINGS	V	3	98	JERRUM	HCJ	10	121
JENKINSON	TR	13	245	JENNINGS	F	14	170	JENNINGS	W	1	183	JERVIS	AH	1	183
JENKINSON	W	9	105	JENNINGS	F	14	170	JENNINGS	W	4	210	JERVIS	FJ	10	121
JENKINSON	W	11	198	JENNINGS	FC	5	199	JENNINGS	W	8	178	JERVIS	FW	10	121
JENKINSON	WH	5	199	JENNINGS	FT	6	230	JENNINGS	W	9	286	JERVIS	GS	10	122
JENKS	BED	2	181	JENNINGS	FW	13	245	JENNINGS	W	12	332	JERVIS	HA	10	121
JENKS	E	6	230	JENNINGS	G	4	210	JENNINGS	W	14	171	JESSETT	GC	7	208
JENKS	EW	4	210	JENNINGS	G	5	199	JENNINGS	WG	3	98	JESSON	H	11	198
JENKS	GA	2	181	JENNINGS	G	8	177	JENNINGS	WH	4	211	JESSON	P	11	198
JENKS	JJ	7	207	JENNINGS	GE	3	98	JENNINGS	WJ	1	183	JESSOP	C	6	231
JENKS	W	4	210	JENNINGS	GJ	7	208	JENNINGS	WJ	10	121	JESSOP	EW	8	178
JENMAN	GR	4	210	JENNINGS	GV	3	98	JENNINGS	WS	1	183	JESSOP	G	2	182
JENN	LW	7	207	JENNINGS	H	3	98	JENNINGS	WT	3	98	JESSOP	GW	9	106
JENNENS	AH	6	230	JENNINGS	H	9	106	JENNISON	HO	9	106	JESSOP	J	9	106
JENNER		3	98	JENNINGS	H	11	198	JENNS	A	6	230	JESSOPP	E	5	199
JENNER	C	13	245	JENNINGS	HA	10	121	JENNS	WA	6	230	JESSOPP	W	5	199
JENNER	CM	13	245	JENNINGS	HH	12	332	JENRICK	GW	13	245	JESSUP	AM	13	246
JENNER	D	7	207	JENNINGS	I	3	98	JEPP	F	3	98	JESSUP	EW	7	208
JENNER	DJ	7	207	JENNINGS	J	3	98	JEPSON	A	8	178	JESSUP	FJ	13	246
JENNER	DSJ	5	199	JENNINGS	J	8	177	JEPSON	AH	13	245	JESSUP	SJ	13	246
JENNER	ES	13	245	JENNINGS	J	8	177	JEPSON	CC	11	198	JESTINS	FE	10	122
JENNER	F	1	183	JENNINGS	J	8	178	JEPSON	CJ	7	208	JESTINS	J	10	122
JENNER	GW	2	181	JENNINGS	J	8	178	JEPSON	G	14	171	JEUNE	F	13	246
JENNER	HC	7	207	JENNINGS	J	9	106	JEPSON	J	14	171	JEUNE	W	10	122
JENNER	JW	3	98	JENNINGS	J	9	285	JEPSON	J	14	171	JEVES	G	13	246
JENNER	ME	13	245	JENNINGS	J	9	389	JEPSON	J	14	171	JEVONS	A	6	231
JENNER	RW	13	245	JENNINGS	J	14	170	JEPSON	R	11	198	JEVONS	R	14	171
JENNER	WE	13	245	JENNINGS	JA	13	245	JERAM	FW	10	319	JEWELL	A	13	246
JENNER	WG	13	245	JENNINGS	JC	8	178	JERAM	G	10	121	JEWELL	AE	7	208
JENNING	GA	1	183	JENNINGS	JC	10	121	JERAM	WJF	4	211	JEWELL	AJ	2	182
JENNINGS	A	1	183	JENNINGS	JH	7	208	JEREMIAH	E	4	211	JEWELL	C	6	231
JENNINGS	A	3	98	JENNINGS	JJ	2	182	JEREMIAH	W	4	211	JEWELL	E	6	231
JENNINGS	A	6	230	JENNINGS	JW	9	285	JEREMY	DJ	6	230	JEWELL	FW	7	208
JENNINGS	A	12	331	JENNINGS	JW	9	286	JEREMY	J	2	182	JEWELL	JH	1	183
JENNINGS	AC	13	245	JENNINGS	JW	10	121	JERKINS	CA	2	182	JEWELL	JT	13	246
JENNINGS	AE	7	208	JENNINGS	L	8	178	JERMIN	W	13	245	JEWELL	JW	13	246
JENNINGS	AG	2	181	JENNINGS	LE	3	98	JEROME	CJ	3	98	JEWELL	S	1	183
JENNINGS	AH	8	177	JENNINGS	LH	3	98	JEROME	D	10	121	JEWELL	W	7	208
JENNINGS	AJ	9	285	JENNINGS	M	9	286	JEROME	J	6	230	JEWER	AG	4	211
JENNINGS	AR	2	182	JENNINGS	M	14	170	JEROME	JE	10	319	JEWETT	B	9	106
JENNINGS	AR	2	182	JENNINGS	P	5	199	JEROME	JW	3	99	JEWETT	F	9	106
JENNINGS	B	2	182	JENNINGS	P	9	106	JEROME	WH	3	99	JEWETT	H	4	211
JENNINGS	C	2	182	JENNINGS	PJ	3	98	JERRAM	FH	4	211	JEWETT	JF	4	211
JENNINGS	C	3	98	JENNINGS	R	5	199	JERRAM	JE	4	211	JEWITT	E	8	178
JENNINGS	C	5	199	JENNINGS	RT	7	207	JERRAM	R	4	211	JEWITT	FH	2	182
JENNINGS	C	9	106	JENNINGS	S	6	230	JERRAM	W	4	211	JEWITT	HT	1	184
JENNINGS	D	1	183	JENNINGS	SG	1	183	JERRAM	WJ	4	211	JEWITT	L	8	178
								JERRAM	WS	4	211				

JEWITT	R	8	178	JOHNSON	A	3	99	JOHNSON	B	14	171	JOHNSON	EL	1	185
JEX	WM	11	198	JOHNSON	A	3	99	JOHNSON	B	14	171	JOHNSON	EN	14	171
JEYES	AE	12	332	JOHNSON	A	4	211	JOHNSON	BP	3	367	JOHNSON	ES	8	179
JEYES	AT	12	332	JOHNSON	A	4	211	JOHNSON	BT	12	332	JOHNSON	ET	3	99
JEYES	J	12	332	JOHNSON	A	6	232	JOHNSON	BWA	12	332	JOHNSON	EW	13	246
JEYES	JW	12	332	JOHNSON	A	6	232	JOHNSON	C	2	182	JOHNSON	F	1	185
JEYNES	EJ	6	231	JOHNSON	A	7	208	JOHNSON	C	2	182	JOHNSON	F	2	183
JEYS	J	6	231	JOHNSON	A	7	208	JOHNSON	C	3	367	JOHNSON	F	3	99
JEYS	J	6	231	JOHNSON	A	8	178	JOHNSON	C	10	122	JOHNSON	F	3	99
JIGGINS	C	2	182	JOHNSON	A	8	178	JOHNSON	C	11	198	JOHNSON	F	4	212
JIGGINS	HA	7	208	JOHNSON	A	8	178	JOHNSON	C	11	199	JOHNSON	F	5	199
JIGGLES	J	12	128	JOHNSON	A	8	178	JOHNSON	C	12	128	JOHNSON	F	5	199
JILLARD	H	6	231	JOHNSON	A	8	178	JOHNSON	C	12	128	JOHNSON	F	6	232
JILLARD	W	6	231	JOHNSON	A	8	178	JOHNSON	C	14	171	JOHNSON	F	6	232
JILLEY	O	14	171	JOHNSON	A	8	178	JOHNSON	CA	2	182	JOHNSON	F	8	179
JILLEY	W	14	171	JOHNSON	A	8	178	JOHNSON	CE	1	184	JOHNSON	F	9	106
JINKS	A	6	231	JOHNSON	A	9	106	JOHNSON	CF	2	182	JOHNSON	F	9	106
JINKS	AW	6	231	JOHNSON	A	9	286	JOHNSON	CG	3	99	JOHNSON	F	9	286
JINKS	J	6	231	JOHNSON	A	12	128	JOHNSON	CH	2	183	JOHNSON	F	11	199
JINKS	L	6	231	JOHNSON	A	12	128	JOHNSON	CH	2	183	JOHNSON	F	12	129
JINKS	W	6	231	JOHNSON	A	12	332	JOHNSON	CH	4	212	JOHNSON	F	12	129
JINKS	W	6	231	JOHNSON	A	12	332	JOHNSON	CH	8	178	JOHNSON	FC	12	129
JINKS	W	10	122	JOHNSON	A	13	246	JOHNSON	CH	9	106	JOHNSON	FE	2	183
JIPPS	GA	1	184	JOHNSON	A	13	246	JOHNSON	CH	13	246	JOHNSON	FE	12	129
JIPPS	HC	1	184	JOHNSON	A	14	171	JOHNSON	CS	1	184	JOHNSON	FFO	13	246
JOAD	F	2	182	JOHNSON	AA	1	184	JOHNSON	CSA	12	128	JOHNSON	FH	7	209
JOB	F	14	171	JOHNSON	AA	9	106	JOHNSON	CT	4	212	JOHNSON	FJ	12	129
JOB	P	14	171	JOHNSON	AB	6	232	JOHNSON	CV	14	171	JOHNSON	FL	1	185
JOBBINS	A	1	184	JOHNSON	AC	8	178	JOHNSON	CW	2	183	JOHNSON	FM	12	332
JOBBINS	AS	6	231	JOHNSON	AE	4	211	JOHNSON	CW	7	208	JOHNSON	FOG	12	332
JOBBINS	BT	6	231	JOHNSON	AE	4	211	JOHNSON	CW	12	332	JOHNSON	FS	8	179
JOBBINS	CH	6	231	JOHNSON	AE	10	319	JOHNSON	D	1	184	JOHNSON	FS	12	332
JOBEY	TA	11	198	JOHNSON	AE	14	171	JOHNSON	D	5	199	JOHNSON	FT	3	99
JOBSON	R	7	208	JOHNSON	AH	6	232	JOHNSON	D	12	128	JOHNSON	FW	11	199
JOBSON	T	14	171	JOHNSON	AH	10	122	JOHNSON	E	1	185	JOHNSON	FW	12	129
JOBSON	WH	7	208	JOHNSON	AJ	1	184	JOHNSON	E	2	183	JOHNSON	FW	12	332
JOHANSEN	GM	4	211	JOHNSON	AJ	12	128	JOHNSON	E	3	367	JOHNSON	FW	13	247
JOHNCOCK	H	13	246	JOHNSON	AJ	12	128	JOHNSON	E	6	232	JOHNSON	G	1	185
JOHNCOCK	WH	13	246	JOHNSON	AJ	13	246	JOHNSON	E	6	232	JOHNSON	G	1	185
JOHNES	CW	7	208	JOHNSON	AL	13	246	JOHNSON	E	6	232	JOHNSON	G	2	183
JOHNES	GW	7	208	JOHNSON	AM	4	212	JOHNSON	E	7	209	JOHNSON	G	2	183
JOHNS	FT	12	128	JOHNSON	AM	7	209	JOHNSON	E	8	178	JOHNSON	G	3	99
JOHNS	FW	13	246	JOHNSON	AR	1	184	JOHNSON	E	9	286	JOHNSON	G	5	200
JOHNS	HR	6	232	JOHNSON	AR	1	184	JOHNSON	E	9	389	JOHNSON	G	5	200
JOHNS	L	1	184	JOHNSON	AS	1	184	JOHNSON	E	11	199	JOHNSON	G	6	232
JOHNS	P	12	128	JOHNSON	AS	1	184	JOHNSON	E	12	128	JOHNSON	G	6	232
JOHNS	TFW	1	184	JOHNSON	AT	4	212	JOHNSON	E	12	332	JOHNSON	G	6	232
JOHNS	W	3	367	JOHNSON	AT	10	319	JOHNSON	E	14	171	JOHNSON	G	7	209
JOHNS	WJ	10	319	JOHNSON	AT	12	332	JOHNSON	EA	13	246	JOHNSON	G	8	179
JOHNS	WS	10	319	JOHNSON	AT	12	332	JOHNSON	EB	9	286	JOHNSON	G	8	179
JOHNSON	A	1	184	JOHNSON	AW	1	184	JOHNSON	EC	6	232	JOHNSON	G	12	129
JOHNSON	A	1	184	JOHNSON	AW	9	286	JOHNSON	EE	10	122	JOHNSON	G	13	247
JOHNSON	A	2	182	JOHNSON	B	9	286	JOHNSON	EG	11	199	JOHNSON	G	13	247
JOHNSON	A	2	182	JOHNSON	B	12	128	JOHNSON	EJ	2	183	JOHNSON	G	14	172
JOHNSON	A	3	99	JOHNSON	B	12	128	JOHNSON	EJ	12	128	JOHNSON	GA	3	99

JOHNSON	GA	3	367	JOHNSON	HT	12	332	JOHNSON	JH	2	183	JOHNSON	R	2	183	JOHNSON	R	2	183
JOHNSON	GC	3	367	JOHNSON	HTC	7	209	JOHNSON	JH	3	367	JOHNSON	R	3	99	JOHNSON	R	3	99
JOHNSON	GC	10	320	JOHNSON	HW	2	183	JOHNSON	JH	7	209	JOHNSON	R	4	212	JOHNSON	R	4	212
JOHNSON	GC	12	332	JOHNSON	HW	7	209	JOHNSON	JH	8	179	JOHNSON	R	6	233	JOHNSON	R	6	233
JOHNSON	GE	1	185	JOHNSON	J	1	185	JOHNSON	JH	14	172	JOHNSON	R	6	233	JOHNSON	R	6	233
JOHNSON	GE	10	320	JOHNSON	J	2	183	JOHNSON	JJ	1	185	JOHNSON	R	9	286	JOHNSON	R	9	286
JOHNSON	GF	6	232	JOHNSON	J	2	183	JOHNSON	JJ	3	99	JOHNSON	R	10	122	JOHNSON	R	10	122
JOHNSON	GF	7	209	JOHNSON	J	2	183	JOHNSON	JJ	7	209	JOHNSON	R	12	129	JOHNSON	R	12	129
JOHNSON	GF	11	199	JOHNSON	J	3	99	JOHNSON	JJ	10	320	JOHNSON	R	14	172	JOHNSON	R	14	172
JOHNSON	GH	9	286	JOHNSON	J	3	99	JOHNSON	JR	6	233	JOHNSON	RC	4	212	JOHNSON	RC	4	212
JOHNSON	GP	5	200	JOHNSON	J	3	367	JOHNSON	JR	7	209	JOHNSON	RE	1	186	JOHNSON	RE	1	186
JOHNSON	GT	3	367	JOHNSON	J	4	212	JOHNSON	JRW	7	209	JOHNSON	RE	10	122	JOHNSON	RE	10	122
JOHNSON	GT	13	247	JOHNSON	J	5	200	JOHNSON	JS	13	247	JOHNSON	RH	6	233	JOHNSON	RH	6	233
JOHNSON	GV	12	129	JOHNSON	J	6	233	JOHNSON	JT	8	179	JOHNSON	RH	11	200	JOHNSON	RH	11	200
JOHNSON	GWH	4	212	JOHNSON	J	6	233	JOHNSON	JT	11	199	JOHNSON	RH	12	333	JOHNSON	RH	12	333
JOHNSON	H	1	185	JOHNSON	J	6	233	JOHNSON	JT	13	247	JOHNSON	RW	1	186	JOHNSON	RW	1	186
JOHNSON	H	1	185	JOHNSON	J	6	233	JOHNSON	JT	13	247	JOHNSON	S	6	233	JOHNSON	S	6	233
JOHNSON	H	1	185	JOHNSON	J	7	209	JOHNSON	JT	14	172	JOHNSON	S	6	233	JOHNSON	S	6	233
JOHNSON	H	2	183	JOHNSON	J	7	209	JOHNSON	JTH	1	185	JOHNSON	S	8	180	JOHNSON	S	8	180
JOHNSON	H	2	183	JOHNSON	J	7	209	JOHNSON	JW	3	99	JOHNSON	S	8	180	JOHNSON	S	8	180
JOHNSON	H	3	99	JOHNSON	J	8	179	JOHNSON	JW	7	209	JOHNSON	S	8	180	JOHNSON	S	8	180
JOHNSON	H	3	367	JOHNSON	J	8	179	JOHNSON	JW	8	179	JOHNSON	S	8	180	JOHNSON	S	8	180
JOHNSON	H	4	212	JOHNSON	J	8	179	JOHNSON	JW	8	179	JOHNSON	S	8	180	JOHNSON	S	8	180
JOHNSON	H	4	212	JOHNSON	J	8	179	JOHNSON	JW	11	200	JOHNSON	S	11	200	JOHNSON	S	11	200
JOHNSON	H	4	212	JOHNSON	J	8	179	JOHNSON	JW	12	129	JOHNSON	S	11	200	JOHNSON	S	11	200
JOHNSON	H	4	212	JOHNSON	J	9	106	JOHNSON	JW	12	129	JOHNSON	S	12	129	JOHNSON	S	12	129
JOHNSON	H	6	232	JOHNSON	J	9	286	JOHNSON	JW	12	333	JOHNSON	S	13	247	JOHNSON	S	13	247
JOHNSON	H	6	232	JOHNSON	J	11	199	JOHNSON	JW	14	172	JOHNSON	S	14	172	JOHNSON	S	14	172
JOHNSON	H	6	232	JOHNSON	J	11	199	JOHNSON	L	9	106	JOHNSON	S	14	172	JOHNSON	S	14	172
JOHNSON	H	8	179	JOHNSON	J	11	199	JOHNSON	L	13	247	JOHNSON	S	14	172	JOHNSON	S	14	172
JOHNSON	H	8	179	JOHNSON	J	11	199	JOHNSON	L	14	172	JOHNSON	SAG	9	389	JOHNSON	SAG	9	389
JOHNSON	H	8	179	JOHNSON	J	11	199	JOHNSON	LW	2	184	JOHNSON	SE	1	186	JOHNSON	SE	1	186
JOHNSON	H	8	179	JOHNSON	J	11	199	JOHNSON	LW	3	367	JOHNSON	SH	13	247	JOHNSON	SH	13	247
JOHNSON	H	8	179	JOHNSON	J	12	333	JOHNSON	M	12	129	JOHNSON	SJ	1	186	JOHNSON	SJ	1	186
JOHNSON	H	9	106	JOHNSON	J	14	172	JOHNSON	M	12	129	JOHNSON	SJ	12	129	JOHNSON	SJ	12	129
JOHNSON	H	9	286	JOHNSON	J	14	172	JOHNSON	M	12	333	JOHNSON	T	4	212	JOHNSON	T	4	212
JOHNSON	H	10	122	JOHNSON	J	14	172	JOHNSON	M	13	247	JOHNSON	T	4	212	JOHNSON	T	4	212
JOHNSON	H	10	320	JOHNSON	JA	6	233	JOHNSON	M	14	172	JOHNSON	T	8	180	JOHNSON	T	8	180
JOHNSON	H	11	199	JOHNSON	JA	6	233	JOHNSON	MSW	3	99	JOHNSON	T	8	180	JOHNSON	T	8	180
JOHNSON	H	11	199	JOHNSON	JA	10	320	JOHNSON	N	6	233	JOHNSON	T	8	180	JOHNSON	T	8	180
JOHNSON	H	11	199	JOHNSON	JB	2	183	JOHNSON	N	12	333	JOHNSON	T	9	106	JOHNSON	T	9	106
JOHNSON	H	12	129	JOHNSON	JC	5	200	JOHNSON	O	3	99	JOHNSON	T	11	200	JOHNSON	T	11	200
JOHNSON	H	14	172	JOHNSON	JD	6	233	JOHNSON	OW	10	320	JOHNSON	T	11	200	JOHNSON	T	11	200
JOHNSON	H	14	172	JOHNSON	JE	1	185	JOHNSON	P	1	185	JOHNSON	T	12	333	JOHNSON	T	12	333
JOHNSON	HC	6	232	JOHNSON	JE	1	185	JOHNSON	P	4	212	JOHNSON	T	14	172	JOHNSON	T	14	172
JOHNSON	HC	12	129	JOHNSON	JE	9	286	JOHNSON	P	4	212	JOHNSON	T	14	172	JOHNSON	T	14	172
JOHNSON	HF	1	185	JOHNSON	JE	11	199	JOHNSON	P	8	180	JOHNSON	TA	6	233	JOHNSON	TA	6	233
JOHNSON	HF	13	247	JOHNSON	JF	1	185	JOHNSON	P	8	180	JOHNSON	TC	9	106	JOHNSON	TC	9	106
JOHNSON	HH	9	286	JOHNSON	JF	5	200	JOHNSON	P	11	200	JOHNSON	TE	10	320	JOHNSON	TE	10	320
JOHNSON	HJ	4	212	JOHNSON	JF	6	233	JOHNSON	P	12	129	JOHNSON	TJ	2	184	JOHNSON	TJ	2	184
JOHNSON	HJ	14	172	JOHNSON	JFW	10	122	JOHNSON	PA	1	185	JOHNSON	TK	12	129	JOHNSON	TK	12	129
JOHNSON	HT	2	183	JOHNSON	JG	10	320	JOHNSON	PA	5	200	JOHNSON	TS	13	247	JOHNSON	TS	13	247
JOHNSON	HT	12	332					JOHNSON	PF	3	367	JOHNSON	TW	8	180	JOHNSON	TW	8	180
								JOHNSON	PW	2	184	JOHNSON	TW	12	130	JOHNSON	TW	12	130
								JOHNSON	R	1	185	JOHNSON	W	1	186	JOHNSON	W	1	186

JOHNSON	W	1	186
JOHNSON	W	4	212
JOHNSON	W	4	212
JOHNSON	W	4	212
JOHNSON	W	6	233
JOHNSON	W	7	209
JOHNSON	W	8	180
JOHNSON	W	8	180
JOHNSON	W	8	180
JOHNSON	W	8	180
JOHNSON	W	8	180
JOHNSON	W	8	180
JOHNSON	W	9	107
JOHNSON	W	9	107
JOHNSON	W	11	200
JOHNSON	W	11	200
JOHNSON	W	11	200
JOHNSON	W	11	200
JOHNSON	W	12	130
JOHNSON	W	12	130
JOHNSON	W	12	130
JOHNSON	W	12	333
JOHNSON	W	12	333
JOHNSON	W	13	247
JOHNSON	W	14	173
JOHNSON	W	14	173
JOHNSON	WA	6	234
JOHNSON	WA	12	130
JOHNSON	WC	1	186
JOHNSON	WC	13	247
JOHNSON	WCH	2	184
JOHNSON	WE	1	186
JOHNSON	WE	3	367
JOHNSON	WE	7	209
JOHNSON	WE	7	209
JOHNSON	WE	13	247
JOHNSON	WE	13	247
JOHNSON	WG	2	184
JOHNSON	WG	2	184
JOHNSON	WG	6	234
JOHNSON	WH	1	186
JOHNSON	WH	1	186
JOHNSON	WH	10	122
JOHNSON	WH	11	200
JOHNSON	WH	11	200
JOHNSON	WH	12	333
JOHNSON	WH	14	173
JOHNSON	WJ	10	122
JOHNSON	WJ	13	247
JOHNSON	WL	10	122
JOHNSON	WP	13	247
JOHNSON	WR	1	186
JOHNSON	WR	8	180
JOHNSON	WS	9	107
JOHNSON	WS	12	130
JOHNSON	WT	6	234
JOHNSON	WT	6	234
JOHNSON	WW	4	213
JOHNSON	WW	4	213
JOHNSTON	A	10	122
JOHNSTON	A	14	173
JOHNSTON	AT	2	184
JOHNSTON	C	1	186
JOHNSTON	D	3	100
JOHNSTON	E	2	184
JOHNSTON	F	10	122
JOHNSTON	FC	1	186
JOHNSTON	H	3	100
JOHNSTON	HE	7	210
JOHNSTON	HJ	1	186
JOHNSTON	J	3	100
JOHNSTON	J	4	213
JOHNSTON	J	11	200
JOHNSTON	J	12	333
JOHNSTON	J	14	173
JOHNSTON	JA	13	247
JOHNSTON	JH	10	122
JOHNSTON	L	8	180
JOHNSTON	LA	1	186
JOHNSTON	R	11	200
JOHNSTON	R	11	200
JOHNSTON	RS	2	184
JOHNSTON	T	14	173
JOHNSTON	W	9	389
JOHNSTON	W	11	200
JOHNSTON	W	14	173
JOHNSTON	WE	7	210
JOHNSTONE	A	4	213
JOHNSTONE	A	11	200
JOHNSTONE	AL	2	184
JOHNSTONE	CL	2	184
JOHNSTONE	H	6	234
JOHNSTONE	H	10	122
JOHNSTONE	H	11	200
JOHNSTONE	JE	2	184
JOHNSTONE	JS	11	201
JOHNSTONE	R	7	210
JOHNSTONE	R	11	201
JOHNSTONE	R	14	173
JOHNSTONE	R	14	173
JOHNSTONE	SA	7	210
JOHNSTONE	TE	14	173
JOHNSTONE	W	11	201
JOHNSTONE	WH	11	201
JOHSON	A	9	286
JOHSON	J	9	286
JOINER	HW	2	184
JOLIN	H	7	210
JOLL	ES	12	333
JOLLEY	AG	12	130
JOLLEY	C	13	248
JOLLEY	F	7	210
JOLLEY	FT	1	186
JOLLEY	GS	1	186
JOLLEY	H	8	180
JOLLEY	H	12	130
JOLLEY	H	12	130
JOLLEY	J	12	333
JOLLEY	R	14	173
JOLLEY	S	11	206
JOLLEY	TH	1	186
JOLLEY	TH	4	213
JOLLEY	TW	6	234
JOLLEY	W	1	186
JOLLEY	W	7	210
JOLLEYS	T	14	173
JOLLIFFE	CH	4	213
JOLLIFFE	DH	10	123
JOLLIFFE	ET	10	320
JOLLIFFE	HB	13	248
JOLLIFFE	WJ	5	200
JOLLY	A	8	181
JOLLY	A	14	173
JOLLY	BJ	12	333
JOLLY	EJ	9	389
JOLLY	FH	3	100
JOLLY	GT	3	100
JOLLY	H	1	187
JOLLY	H	14	173
JOLLY	J	8	181
JOLLY	J	9	286
JOLLY	J	12	333
JOLLY	L	9	287
JONAS	AE	7	210
JONAS	GE	14	173
JONES	A	1	187
JONES	A	1	187
JONES	A	1	187
JONES	A	1	187
JONES	A	1	187
JONES	A	2	184
JONES	A	2	184
JONES	A	2	184
JONES	A	3	100
JONES	A	3	100
JONES	A	4	213
JONES	A	6	234
JONES	A	6	234
JONES	A	6	234
JONES	A	6	234
JONES	A	6	234
JONES	A	6	234
JONES	A	6	234
JONES	A	6	234
JONES	A	8	181
JONES	A	8	181
JONES	A	8	181
JONES	A	9	107
JONES	A	9	107
JONES	A	9	107
JONES	A	9	107
JONES	A	9	107
JONES	A	9	107
JONES	A	9	287
JONES	A	9	287
JONES	A	10	123
JONES	A	11	201
JONES	A	11	201
JONES	A	11	201
JONES	A	11	201
JONES	A	11	201
JONES	A	11	201
JONES	A	11	201
JONES	A	11	201
JONES	A	11	201
JONES	A	12	130
JONES	A	12	333
JONES	A	13	248
JONES	A	13	248
JONES	A	13	248
JONES	A	14	173
JONES	A	14	173
JONES	A	14	173
JONES	A	14	174
JONES	A	14	174
JONES	A	14	174
JONES	A	14	174
JONES	AC	2	184
JONES	AC	5	200
JONES	AC	10	320
JONES	AE	2	184
JONES	AE	3	367
JONES	AE	4	213
JONES	AE	6	234
JONES	AE	7	210
JONES	AE	9	107
JONES	AE	9	287
JONES	AE	9	287
JONES	AE	11	201
JONES	AE	11	201
JONES	AE	12	333
JONES	AE	12	333
JONES	AE	13	248
JONES	AE	14	174
JONES	AF	6	234
JONES	AG	1	187

JONES AG 3 368	JONES CH 6 235	JONES E 11 202	JONES F 14 175
JONES AG 7 210	JONES CH 6 235	JONES E 11 202	JONES F 14 175
JONES AG 12 130	JONES CH 14 174	JONES E 11 202	JONES F 14 175
JONES AH 5 200	JONES CJ 1 187	JONES E 11 202	JONES FA 6 236
JONES AH 13 248	JONES CJ 3 368	JONES E 13 248	JONES FC 2 185
JONES AJ 10 123	JONES CJ 5 200	JONES E 14 174	JONES FC 13 248
JONES AL 5 200	JONES CJ 6 235	JONES E 14 174	JONES FE 14 175
JONES AL 5 200	JONES CK 6 235	JONES E 14 174	JONES FG 1 187
JONES AL 5 200	JONES CM 13 248	JONES E 14 175	JONES FG 2 185
JONES AL 9 287	JONES CMT 10 123	JONES E 14 175	JONES FG 10 123
JONES AL 12 130	JONES CR 10 123	JONES EA 1 187	JONES FH 6 236
JONES AM 1 187	JONES CT 14 174	JONES EA 5 200	JONES FH 6 236
JONES AO 6 234	JONES CW 11 202	JONES EA 11 202	JONES FH 7 210
JONES AP 13 248	JONES CW 13 248	JONES EE 13 248	JONES FJ 3 100
JONES AS 3 368	JONES D 1 187	JONES EJ 1 187	JONES FJ 4 213
JONES AS 11 201	JONES D 2 185	JONES EJ 4 213	JONES FJ 10 123
JONES AS 13 248	JONES D 4 213	JONES EJ 10 320	JONES FJ 11 202
JONES AT 4 213	JONES D 6 235	JONES EJ 14 175	JONES FN 11 202
JONES AV 1 187	JONES D 6 235	JONES ERT 14 175	JONES FR 6 236
JONES AW 2 185	JONES D 6 235	JONES ESD 3 100	JONES FW 14 175
JONES AW 3 100	JONES D 8 181	JONES ET 1 187	JONES G 2 185
JONES AW 7 210	JONES D 9 107	JONES ET 3 368	JONES G 3 368
JONES AW 7 210	JONES D 12 334	JONES ET 4 213	JONES G 4 213
JONES AW 7 210	JONES D 13 248	JONES ET 6 236	JONES G 6 236
JONES AW 10 123	JONES D 14 174	JONES EW 9 287	JONES G 6 236
JONES AW 11 202	JONES D 14 174	JONES EW 12 130	JONES G 6 236
JONES AW 12 130	JONES D 14 174	JONES EW 12 130	JONES G 6 236
JONES B 6 234	JONES DE 13 248	JONES F 2 185	JONES G 6 236
JONES B 6 235	JONES DH 11 202	JONES F 4 213	JONES G 7 210
JONES B 10 123	JONES DJ 6 235	JONES F 4 213	JONES G 8 181
JONES B 14 174	JONES DR 3 100	JONES F 5 200	JONES G 10 123
JONES BE 6 235	JONES DT 6 235	JONES F 5 201	JONES G 11 202
JONES BE 13 248	JONES DW 14 174	JONES F 6 236	JONES G 11 203
JONES BG 10 123	JONES E 1 187	JONES F 6 236	JONES G 12 130
JONES BH 6 235	JONES E 1 187	JONES F 6 236	JONES G 12 334
JONES BL 14 174	JONES E 3 100	JONES F 6 236	JONES G 13 248
JONES BM 5 200	JONES E 3 100	JONES F 6 236	JONES G 13 248
JONES C 1 187	JONES E 3 100	JONES F 6 236	JONES G 14 175
JONES C 2 185	JONES E 4 213	JONES F 6 236	JONES G 14 175
JONES C 4 213	JONES E 5 200	JONES F 6 236	JONES G 14 175
JONES C 5 200	JONES E 6 235	JONES F 6 236	JONES G 14 175
JONES C 6 235	JONES E 6 235	JONES F 7 210	JONES GA 2 185
JONES C 7 210	JONES E 6 235	JONES F 8 181	JONES GA 10 320
JONES C 8 181	JONES E 6 235	JONES F 8 181	JONES GA 12 334
JONES C 11 202	JONES E 6 235	JONES F 9 107	JONES GB 14 175
JONES C 12 130	JONES E 6 236	JONES F 10 123	JONES GD 11 203
JONES C 12 333	JONES E 7 210	JONES F 11 202	JONES GE 6 237
JONES C 14 174	JONES E 8 181	JONES F 12 130	JONES GE 6 237
JONES C 14 174	JONES E 8 181	JONES F 12 130	JONES GE 7 211
JONES C 14 174	JONES E 9 107	JONES F 12 334	JONES GE 11 203
JONES CE 1 187	JONES E 11 202	JONES F 12 334	JONES GE 12 131
JONES CE 12 333	JONES E 11 202	JONES F 12 334	JONES GE 13 249
JONES CF 6 235	JONES E 11 202	JONES F 12 334	JONES GF 6 237
JONES CG 5 200	JONES E 11 202	JONES F 13 248	JONES GF 6 237
JONES CH 2 185	JONES E 11 202	JONES F 13 248	JONES GF 6 237

JONES	GF	10	123	JONES	H	14	176	JONES	J	6	238	JONES	JE	10	124
JONES	GF	10	123	JONES	H	14	176	JONES	J	6	238	JONES	JE	11	204
JONES	GH	3	100	JONES	H	14	176	JONES	J	6	238	JONES	JE	11	204
JONES	GH	4	213	JONES	H	14	176	JONES	J	7	211	JONES	JE	14	177
JONES	GH	6	237	JONES	H	14	176	JONES	J	7	211	JONES	JG	2	185
JONES	GH	12	334	JONES	H	14	176	JONES	J	7	211	JONES	JH	1	188
JONES	GH	13	249	JONES	H	14	176	JONES	J	7	211	JONES	JH	6	238
JONES	GH	14	175	JONES	HA	1	187	JONES	J	7	211	JONES	JH	6	238
JONES	GJ	3	100	JONES	HA	8	181	JONES	J	8	181	JONES	JH	6	238
JONES	GJ	7	211	JONES	HA	13	249	JONES	J	8	181	JONES	JH	8	181
JONES	GJ	12	334	JONES	HC	2	185	JONES	J	8	181	JONES	JH	11	204
JONES	GJ	14	175	JONES	HC	6	237	JONES	J	9	107	JONES	JH	11	204
JONES	GL	12	334	JONES	HC	11	203	JONES	J	9	107	JONES	JH	11	204
JONES	GM	14	175	JONES	HC	11	203	JONES	J	9	287	JONES	JH	12	334
JONES	GP	12	131	JONES	HF	4	214	JONES	J	10	123	JONES	JH	13	249
JONES	GR	14	175	JONES	HG	5	201	JONES	J	10	123	JONES	JH	13	249
JONES	GS	6	237	JONES	HG	11	203	JONES	J	11	203	JONES	JH	14	177
JONES	GT	12	334	JONES	HG	13	249	JONES	J	11	203	JONES	JHC	6	238
JONES	GT	12	334	JONES	HJ	3	368	JONES	J	11	203	JONES	JHS	1	188
JONES	GV	14	175	JONES	HJ	13	249	JONES	J	11	203	JONES	JJ	11	423
JONES	GW	1	187	JONES	HJ	13	249	JONES	J	11	203	JONES	JJ	12	131
JONES	GW	3	100	JONES	HJH	6	237	JONES	J	11	203	JONES	JJ	12	131
JONES	GW	6	237	JONES	HM	1	188	JONES	J	11	203	JONES	JM	1	188
JONES	GW	6	237	JONES	HN	1	188	JONES	J	12	131	JONES	JM	1	188
JONES	GW	8	181	JONES	HP	13	249	JONES	J	12	131	JONES	JOS	3	368
JONES	GW	10	123	JONES	HS	12	334	JONES	J	12	131	JONES	JP	13	249
JONES	H	2	185	JONES	HT	6	237	JONES	J	12	131	JONES	JP	13	249
JONES	H	3	100	JONES	HT	12	131	JONES	J	13	249	JONES	JR	14	177
JONES	H	3	368	JONES	HW	7	211	JONES	J	13	249	JONES	JR	14	177
JONES	H	4	214	JONES	HW	12	131	JONES	J	13	249	JONES	JS	3	368
JONES	H	4	214	JONES	HW	13	249	JONES	J	14	176	JONES	JS	5	201
JONES	H	4	214	JONES	I	3	100	JONES	J	14	176	JONES	JS	6	239
JONES	H	4	214	JONES	I	10	123	JONES	J	14	176	JONES	JT	6	239
JONES	H	6	237	JONES	I	11	203	JONES	J	14	176	JONES	JT	8	181
JONES	H	6	237	JONES	I	11	203	JONES	J	14	176	JONES	JT	14	177
JONES	H	6	237	JONES	IJ	10	123	JONES	J	14	176	JONES	JW	3	101
JONES	H	6	237	JONES	J	1	188	JONES	J	14	176	JONES	JW	3	101
JONES	H	6	237	JONES	J	1	188	JONES	J	14	176	JONES	JW	3	368
JONES	H	7	211	JONES	J	2	185	JONES	J	14	176	JONES	JW	3	368
JONES	H	8	181	JONES	J	2	185	JONES	J	14	176	JONES	JW	3	368
JONES	H	9	107	JONES	J	2	185	JONES	JA	1	188	JONES	JW	6	239
JONES	H	9	107	JONES	J	3	101	JONES	JA	3	101	JONES	JW	6	239
JONES	H	10	320	JONES	J	3	101	JONES	JA	4	214	JONES	JW	8	182
JONES	H	10	320	JONES	J	3	101	JONES	JA	6	238	JONES	JW	9	107
JONES	H	11	203	JONES	J	3	368	JONES	JA	11	204	JONES	JW	10	124
JONES	H	11	203	JONES	J	5	201	JONES	JAE	3	368	JONES	JW	11	204
JONES	H	11	203	JONES	J	5	201	JONES	JB	13	249	JONES	JW	11	204
JONES	H	11	423	JONES	J	6	237	JONES	JC	3	101	JONES	JW	11	204
JONES	H	12	131	JONES	J	6	238	JONES	JC	3	101	JONES	JW	14	177
JONES	H	12	131	JONES	J	6	238	JONES	JC	6	238	JONES	K	2	185
JONES	H	12	334	JONES	J	6	238	JONES	JC	6	238	JONES	K	5	201
JONES	H	12	334	JONES	J	6	238	JONES	JD	3	101	JONES	L	3	101
JONES	H	14	176	JONES	J	6	238	JONES	JE	1	188	JONES	LM	4	214
JONES	H	14	176	JONES	J	6	238	JONES	JE	2	185	JONES	LM	13	249
JONES	H	14	176	JONES	J	6	238	JONES	JE	3	101	JONES	M	2	185

JONES	M	14	177	JONES	S	13	250	JONES	TE	8	182	JONES	W	9	287
JONES	M	14	177	JONES	S	14	178	JONES	TE	10	320	JONES	W	10	124
JONES	MC	6	239	JONES	S	14	178	JONES	TE	11	205	JONES	W	11	205
JONES	N	14	177	JONES	S	14	178	JONES	TF	3	101	JONES	W	11	205
JONES	O	6	239	JONES	S	14	178	JONES	TF	6	240	JONES	W	11	205
JONES	O	9	108	JONES	SA	10	124	JONES	TH	3	368	JONES	W	11	205
JONES	O	11	204	JONES	SA	11	204	JONES	TH	10	124	JONES	W	11	205
JONES	OW	12	131	JONES	SC	2	186	JONES	TJ	6	240	JONES	W	11	205
JONES	P	1	188	JONES	SC	2	186	JONES	TJ	11	205	JONES	W	11	205
JONES	P	6	239	JONES	SC	14	178	JONES	TL	1	188	JONES	W	11	205
JONES	P	6	239	JONES	SE	11	204	JONES	TO	14	178	JONES	W	11	205
JONES	P	8	182	JONES	SEA	7	211	JONES	TR	14	178	JONES	W	11	205
JONES	P	12	131	JONES	SH	6	239	JONES	TW	1	188	JONES	W	11	205
JONES	P	14	177	JONES	SH	6	239	JONES	TW	5	201	JONES	W	12	131
JONES	PG	10	124	JONES	SH	7	211	JONES	TW	6	240	JONES	W	12	131
JONES	PH	6	239	JONES	SH	12	131	JONES	VH	6	240	JONES	W	12	132
JONES	PH	11	204	JONES	SH	14	178	JONES	VHW	1	188	JONES	W	12	334
JONES	PW	5	201	JONES	SJ	5	201	JONES	VK	6	240	JONES	W	13	250
JONES	PW	7	211	JONES	SJ	6	239	JONES	W	1	188	JONES	W	13	250
JONES	PWE	10	124	JONES	SN	6	239	JONES	W	2	186	JONES	W	13	250
JONES	R	2	186	JONES	ST	1	188	JONES	W	2	186	JONES	W	14	178
JONES	R	3	368	JONES	ST	6	240	JONES	W	2	186	JONES	W	14	178
JONES	R	6	239	JONES	T	2	186	JONES	W	3	101	JONES	W	14	178
JONES	R	7	211	JONES	T	2	186	JONES	W	3	101	JONES	W	14	178
JONES	R	9	108	JONES	T	3	101	JONES	W	3	101	JONES	W	14	178
JONES	R	11	204	JONES	T	3	101	JONES	W	3	369	JONES	W	14	179
JONES	R	12	131	JONES	T	6	240	JONES	W	4	214	JONES	W	14	179
JONES	R	12	334	JONES	T	6	240	JONES	W	6	240	JONES	WA	4	214
JONES	R	14	177	JONES	T	6	240	JONES	W	6	240	JONES	WA	6	241
JONES	R	14	177	JONES	T	6	240	JONES	W	6	240	JONES	WA	6	241
JONES	R	14	177	JONES	T	6	240	JONES	W	6	241	JONES	WA	10	320
JONES	R	14	177	JONES	T	6	240	JONES	W	6	241	JONES	WA	11	205
JONES	R	14	177	JONES	T	8	182	JONES	W	6	241	JONES	WB	2	186
JONES	R	14	177	JONES	T	11	204	JONES	W	6	241	JONES	WB	12	132
JONES	R	14	177	JONES	T	11	204	JONES	W	6	241	JONES	WC	4	214
JONES	RA	3	101	JONES	T	11	204	JONES	W	6	241	JONES	WC	10	124
JONES	RC	1	188	JONES	T	11	205	JONES	W	6	241	JONES	WC	13	250
JONES	RE	2	186	JONES	T	11	205	JONES	W	6	241	JONES	WD	11	205
JONES	RE	3	101	JONES	T	11	205	JONES	W	6	241	JONES	WE	1	188
JONES	RE	14	177	JONES	T	11	205	JONES	W	6	241	JONES	WE	1	188
JONES	RG	13	249	JONES	T	11	205	JONES	W	6	241	JONES	WE	2	186
JONES	RH	13	249	JONES	T	12	131	JONES	W	6	241	JONES	WE	13	250
JONES	RJ	10	124	JONES	T	12	131	JONES	W	6	241	JONES	WE	13	250
JONES	RL	8	182	JONES	T	13	250	JONES	W	7	211	JONES	WE	14	179
JONES	RP	2	186	JONES	T	13	250	JONES	W	7	211	JONES	WE	14	179
JONES	RS	14	177	JONES	T	14	178	JONES	W	8	182	JONES	WF	7	212
JONES	RW	3	368	JONES	T	14	178	JONES	W	8	182	JONES	WG	6	241
JONES	RW	7	211	JONES	T	14	178	JONES	W	8	182	JONES	WH	1	188
JONES	RW	14	178	JONES	T	14	178	JONES	W	8	182	JONES	WH	2	186
JONES	S	6	239	JONES	T	14	178	JONES	W	8	182	JONES	WH	6	241
JONES	S	6	239	JONES	TA	6	240	JONES	W	8	182	JONES	WH	6	241
JONES	S	6	239	JONES	TA	7	211	JONES	W	8	182	JONES	WH	6	241
JONES	S	6	239	JONES	TA	10	124	JONES	W	9	108	JONES	WH	7	212
JONES	S	10	124	JONES	TAM	11	205	JONES	W	9	287	JONES	WH	7	212
JONES	S	11	204	JONES	TC	6	240	JONES	W	9	287	JONES	WH	8	182
												JONES	WH	10	320

JONES	WH	11	206
JONES	WH	12	334
JONES	WH	14	179
JONES	WHA	1	188
JONES	WHH	4	214
JONES	WHJ	4	214
JONES	WHS	6	241
JONES	WI	6	242
JONES	WI	14	179
JONES	WJ	2	186
JONES	WJ	2	186
JONES	WJ	4	214
JONES	WJ	6	242
JONES	WJ	6	242
JONES	WJ	10	124
JONES	WJ	11	206
JONES	WJ	12	132
JONES	WJ	12	335
JONES	WJ	13	250
JONES	WL	13	250
JONES	WM	1	189
JONES	WN	1	189
JONES	WO	5	201
JONES	WP	4	214
JONES	WR	3	102
JONES	WR	7	212
JONES	WR	14	179
JONES	WRE	1	189
JONES	WS	2	186
JONES	WSL	4	214
JONES	WT	3	102
JONES	WT	7	212
JONES	WT	7	212
JONES	WT	11	206
JONES	WT	12	132
JONES	WT	13	250
JONES	WT	14	179
JONES	WV	2	186
JONES	WV	3	102
JONES	WV	6	242
JONES	WV	14	179
JONES	WW	2	186
JORDAN	A	3	102
JORDAN	A	6	242
JORDAN	A	10	124
JORDAN	A	11	206
JORDAN	A	12	132
JORDAN	A	13	250
JORDAN	AE	1	189
JORDAN	AE	6	242
JORDAN	AH	13	250
JORDAN	AS	6	242
JORDAN	AS	10	320
JORDAN	AS	13	250
JORDAN	CI	6	242
JORDAN	D	1	189
JORDAN	E	3	102
JORDAN	E	13	250
JORDAN	EA	14	179
JORDAN	EG	5	201
JORDAN	EJ	6	242
JORDAN	EP	1	189
JORDAN	FA	10	124
JORDAN	FG	13	250
JORDAN	FG	13	250
JORDAN	FW	10	124
JORDAN	G	6	242
JORDAN	G	12	132
JORDAN	GT	6	242
JORDAN	H	7	212
JORDAN	H	11	206
JORDAN	HA	5	201
JORDAN	HH	13	250
JORDAN	HL	3	369
JORDAN	HS	13	251
JORDAN	HW	6	242
JORDAN	J	1	189
JORDAN	J	5	201
JORDAN	J	6	242
JORDAN	J	7	212
JORDAN	J	7	212
JORDAN	J	14	179
JORDAN	J	14	179
JORDAN	JA	5	201
JORDAN	JA	6	242
JORDAN	JDC	13	250
JORDAN	JE	6	242
JORDAN	JE	13	251
JORDAN	JH	6	242
JORDAN	JJ	2	186
JORDAN	K	1	189
JORDAN	M	11	206
JORDAN	MB	1	189
JORDAN	P	13	251
JORDAN	PJM	10	321
JORDAN	R	12	132
JORDAN	RJ	3	102
JORDAN	S	13	251
JORDAN	SW	4	214
JORDAN	SW	12	132
JORDAN	T	3	102
JORDAN	T	10	124
JORDAN	TA	3	102
JORDAN	TH	9	287
JORDAN	TW	9	287
JORDAN	V	3	369
JORDAN	VC	13	251
JORDAN	W	3	369
JORDAN	W	4	214
JORDAN	W	4	214
JORDAN	W	8	182
JORDAN	W	8	182
JORDAN	W	11	206
JORDAN	W	13	251
JORDAN	W	14	179
JORDAN	WC	6	242
JORDAN	WE	10	124
JORDAN	WH	11	206
JORDAN	WHJ	2	187
JORDON	H	4	214
JORDON	R	4	214
JORDORSON	HG	3	102
JORDORSON	RJ	3	102
JOSEPH	A	6	242
JOSEPH	C	4	215
JOSEPH	I	14	179
JOSEPH	W	3	102
JOSIAH	D	2	187
JOSIAH	W	2	187
JOSLAND	FCJ	7	212
JOSLIN	E	4	215
JOSLIN	FC	1	189
JOSLIN	J	3	102
JOSLIN	J	4	215
JOSLIN	J	4	215
JOSLIN	WD	5	201
JOSLYN	N	1	189
JOURDEN	C	1	189
JOURDEN	E	1	189
JOURDEN	G	1	189
JOURNEAUX	CW	4	215
JOURNEAUX	H	4	215
JOURNEAUX	HE	4	215
JOURNEAUX	J	4	215
JOWETT	A	8	182
JOWETT	A	9	108
JOWETT	A	9	108
JOWETT	AW	11	206
JOWETT	E	9	108
JOWETT	E	9	108
JOWETT	F	4	215
JOWETT	F	9	108
JOWETT	F	9	108
JOWETT	G	8	182
JOWETT	H	9	108
JOWETT	H	9	108
JOWETT	H	9	287
JOWETT	HG	4	215
JOWETT	J	9	108
JOWETT	J	11	206
JOWETT	JC	9	108
JOWETT	JW	9	108
JOWETT	JW	11	206
JOWETT	L	9	287
JOWETT	M	9	287
JOWETT	S	9	108
JOWETT	S	11	206
JOWETT	T	8	182
JOWETT	W	8	182
JOWETT	W	9	108
JOY	A	13	251
JOY	AE	2	187
JOY	C	3	102
JOY	EM	3	102
JOY	HJ	2	187
JOY	HJ	5	201
JOY	J	2	187
JOY	J	5	201
JOY	JE	2	187
JOY	JE	3	369
JOY	R	8	182
JOY	T	2	187
JOY	W	3	102
JOY	W	13	251
JOYCE	A	4	215
JOYCE	A	6	242
JOYCE	AE	4	215
JOYCE	BCL	10	124
JOYCE	CP	7	212
JOYCE	E	1	189
JOYCE	EM	4	215
JOYCE	ER	4	215
JOYCE	F	4	215
JOYCE	G	4	215
JOYCE	G	12	132
JOYCE	H	1	189
JOYCE	H	2	187
JOYCE	H	6	242
JOYCE	H	13	251
JOYCE	HJ	6	243
JOYCE	HW	4	215
JOYCE	J	4	215
JOYCE	J	5	201
JOYCE	JA	4	215
JOYCE	JE	13	251
JOYCE	JG	7	212
JOYCE	JR	8	182
JOYCE	JS	6	243
JOYCE	JT	6	243
JOYCE	JT	10	124
JOYCE	JW	4	215
JOYCE	JW	8	183
JOYCE	L	9	287
JOYCE	L	12	335
JOYCE	LM	2	187
JOYCE	MA	1	189
JOYCE	MH	9	287
JOYCE	P	14	179
JOYCE	R	12	335
JOYCE	RG	2	187

JOYCE	S	12	132	JUDE	WJ	9	287	JUPE	S	4	216	KAY	E	9	109
JOYCE	TG	4	215	JUDGE	AR	1	189	JUPE	ST	10	321	KAY	E	9	288
JOYCE	TJ	14	179	JUDGE	FW	5	201	JUPP	A	13	252	KAY	F	8	183
JOYCE	W	2	187	JUDGE	HA	4	216	JUPP	AJ	1	190	KAY	F	8	183
JOYCE	WG	6	243	JUDGE	M	11	207	JUPP	CT	13	252	KAY	F	9	109
JOYNER	AW	4	215	JUDGE	M	13	251	JUPP	EC	2	187	KAY	F	9	109
JOYNER	J	6	243	JUDGE	RM	1	189	JUPP	F	1	190	KAY	F	11	207
JOYNER	JW	4	216	JUDGE	V	1	190	JUPP	F	10	321	KAY	F	11	207
JOYNER	P	3	102	JUDGE	W	12	335	JUPP	T	10	321	KAY	FB	11	207
JOYNER	RB	4	216	JUDGE	WA	12	335	JURD	A	4	216	KAY	FH	13	252
JOYNER	RM	2	187	JUDGE	WJ	13	251	JURD	F	4	216	KAY	G	8	183
JOYNER	WE	6	243	JUDKINS	F	5	202	JURD	H	4	217	KAY	G	11	207
JOYNER	WE	6	243	JUDSON	CA	8	183	JURD	HW	4	217	KAY	G	14	179
JOYNES	FD	9	108	JUDSON	D	9	108	JURD	TG	4	217	KAY	H	9	288
JOYNES	J	12	335	JUDSON	EL	8	183	JURY	T	10	125	KAY	H	14	180
JOYNSON	DA	11	206	JUDSON	F	9	108	JURY	WA	10	321	KAY	HC	13	252
JOYNSON	E	11	206	JUDSON	JR	11	207	JUSTICE	HF	12	132	KAY	J	2	188
JOYNSON	JF	11	206	JUETT	GH	12	335	JUSTINS	R	2	187	KAY	J	8	183
JOYNSON	P	11	206	JUETT	JG	10	125					KAY	J	8	183
JOYNT	JA	11	206	JUFF	G	10	125					KAY	J	8	183
JUBB	C	8	183	JUFF	S	10	125	**K**				KAY	J	8	183
JUBB	G	8	183	JUFF	W	10	125					KAY	J	11	207
JUBBER	G	10	125	JUFF	WC	10	321					KAY	J	13	252
JUBBS	J	11	207	JUFFKINS	WH	12	335	KABERRY	A	8	183	KAY	JA	11	207
JUDD	A	1	189	JUFFS	AA	12	132	KAIL	RJB	13	252	KAY	JE	11	207
JUDD	AE	12	132	JUFFS	SGW	12	132	KAIN	W	6	243	KAY	JW	8	183
JUDD	C	3	102	JUFKINS	CA	12	132	KAKEL	J	13	252	KAY	M	9	109
JUDD	CJ	3	102	JUKES	A	6	243	KALAHER	D	9	109	KAY	M	11	207
JUDD	E	4	216	JUKES	F	6	243	KALAHER	J	9	109	KAY	M	14	180
JUDD	FC	13	251	JUKES	FW	2	187	KALE	EA	6	243	KAY	R	5	202
JUDD	G	3	102	JUKES	G	7	212	KALE	G	11	207	KAY	T	8	184
JUDD	G	3	103	JUKES	JTA	7	212	KALEY	H	7	212	KAY	W	8	184
JUDD	G	3	103	JUKES	TS	4	216	KALLMEIER	HCB	3	103	KAY	W	9	109
JUDD	G	4	216	JUKES	W	8	183	KALLMEIER	L	3	103	KAY	W	9	109
JUDD	H	4	216	JUKES	WE	6	243	KAMECKE	CH	2	187	KAY	W	9	109
JUDD	HM	12	132	JULIAN	F	11	207	KAMINSKY	SD	8	183	KAY	W	11	207
JUDD	J	2	187	JULIAN	JE	3	103	KANE	J	4	217	KAY	W	14	180
JUDD	J	3	103	JULIAN	W	3	103	KANE	J	14	179	KAYE	A	8	184
JUDD	J	4	216	JULIAN	W	8	183	KANE	WJ	10	321	KAYE	F	9	109
JUDD	J	4	216	JULIER	FB	1	190	KAPPAX	A	2	188	KAYE	F	9	109
JUDD	J	8	183	JULIUS	WP	13	251	KARP	S	14	179	KAYE	GA	8	184
JUDD	JAV	12	335	JULL	F	3	369	KARSLAKE	RL	4	217	KAYE	H	9	109
JUDD	JH	4	216	JULL	HC	13	251	KASPER	CA	7	212	KAYE	J	8	184
JUDD	M	4	216	JULL	HW	2	187	KASTELIAN	SG	2	188	KAYE	J	8	184
JUDD	M	4	216	JULL	PE	2	187	KATESMARK	AG	1	190	KAYE	JE	9	109
JUDD	ME	3	103	JULYAN	AC	6	243	KATON	AE	5	202	KAYE	JH	9	288
JUDD	P	12	132	JUNEMAN	J	7	212	KATON	CM	4	217	KAYE	O	9	109
JUDD	RF	3	103	JUNIPER	E	2	187	KAUFMAN	T	14	179	KAYE	R	8	184
JUDD	RH	4	216	JUNIPER	F	13	251	KAVANAGH	AJ	2	188	KAYE	R	11	207
JUDD	S	7	212	JUNIPER	FS	13	251	KAVANAGH	H	8	183	KAYE	W	8	184
JUDD	SG	4	216	JUNIPER	G	13	251	KAVANAGH	J	4	217	KAYE	W	9	109
JUDD	SM	13	251	JUNIPER	J	13	252	KAVANAGH	J	10	125	KAYE	WA	8	184
JUDD	T	3	103	JUPE	JB	10	321	KAVANAGH	M	2	188	KAYLES	H	8	184
JUDD	TB	4	216	JUPE	R	4	216	KAVANAGH	P	8	183	KAYLES	M	8	184
JUDD	WH	2	187	JUPE	RWP	4	216	KAVANAUGH	FJ	7	213	KEABLE	C	4	217
								KAY	A	9	287				
								KAY	B	8	183				

KEACH	F	6	243
KEALEY	OF	5	202
KEALEY	SJ	5	202
KEALEY	WE	3	103
KEALL	J	4	217
KEAN	A	1	190
KEAN	HT	6	243
KEAN	J	4	217
KEAN	JF	10	321
KEAN	RI	2	188
KEANE	AE	7	213
KEANE	AJ	2	188
KEANE	EJ	2	188
KEANE	F	9	288
KEANE	H	8	184
KEANE	J	11	207
KEANE	T	14	180
KEARIN	WHG	1	190
KEARLEY	L	4	217
KEARN	AT	10	125
KEARN	H	10	125
KEARNEY	A	11	207
KEARNEY	AW	10	125
KEARNEY	G	10	321
KEARNEY	J	8	184
KEARNEY	J	10	125
KEARNEY	JF	10	321
KEARNEY	W	10	125
KEARNEY	W	11	207
KEARNS	AW	7	213
KEARNS	B	11	207
KEARNS	J	14	180
KEARNS	JE	11	208
KEARNS	JH	4	217
KEARNS	O	11	208
KEARNS	S	8	184
KEARSEY	F	6	243
KEARSLAKE	AM	4	217
KEARSLEY	R	11	208
KEAST	WA	13	252
KEAT	F	1	190
KEAT	RJH	10	125
KEATES	A	14	180
KEATING	D	9	109
KEATING	D	9	109
KEATING	J	6	243
KEATING	J	9	109
KEATING	RJ	10	321
KEATING	TM	10	125
KEATING	W	2	188
KEATING	W	13	252
KEATINGE	H	11	208
KEATS	A	13	252
KEAVEY	J	8	184
KEAY	G	6	243
KEAYS	PA	13	252
KEBBELL	H	3	103
KEBBELL	K	3	103
KEDDLE	C	9	110
KEDGE	AJ	12	132
KEDGE	C	3	369
KEDGE	CW	2	188
KEDGE	EF	12	132
KEDGE	FA	12	132
KEDGE	FJW	2	188
KEDGE	WHJ	2	188
KEDIE	JA	11	208
KEDIE	JW	11	208
KEDIE	P	11	208
KEEBER	AF	12	335
KEEBER	FJ	12	335
KEEBER	H	12	335
KEEBLE	AL	7	213
KEEBLE	BE	13	252
KEEBLE	CE	1	190
KEEBLE	HC	3	103
KEEBLE	HW	12	133
KEEBLE	J	7	213
KEEBLE	JE	3	103
KEEBLE	L	11	208
KEEBLE	LP	2	188
KEEBLE	RW	7	213
KEEBLE	WA	7	213
KEEBY	G	4	217
KEECH	A	12	133
KEECH	AE	12	133
KEECH	AH	12	133
KEECH	ET	12	133
KEECH	F	12	133
KEECH	FO	12	133
KEECH	H	12	133
KEECH	J	3	369
KEECH	P	12	133
KEECH	W	12	133
KEEDLE	J	12	335
KEEFE	BJ	7	213
KEEFE	FW	2	188
KEEFE	GT	13	252
KEEFE	H	11	208
KEEFE	JJ	11	208
KEEFE	M	11	208
KEEFE	SA	3	369
KEEFE	T	11	208
KEEFE	TJ	3	369
KEEFE	TJ	6	243
KEEFFE	SW	7	213
KEEGAN	T	6	243
KEEGAN	T	8	184
KEEGAN	TW	2	188
KEEHN	E	3	103
KEEHN	E	3	103
KEEHN	EE	3	103
KEEHN	G	3	103
KEEL	T	11	208
KEELAN	J	11	208
KEELAN	J	11	208
KEELAN	J	11	208
KEELE	JJ	4	217
KEELER	A	1	190
KEELER	CF	1	190
KEELER	EA	6	244
KEELER	EC	6	244
KEELER	EJ	5	202
KEELER	H	1	190
KEELER	JR	2	188
KEELER	WF	13	252
KEELEY	CW	13	252
KEELEY	L	14	180
KEELEY	P	2	188
KEELEY	S	6	244
KEELEY	TH	3	103
KEELEY	W	11	208
KEELIGAN	J	8	184
KEELING	A	8	184
KEELING	A	14	180
KEELING	G	6	244
KEELING	GH	14	180
KEELING	H	14	180
KEELING	HJ	6	244
KEELING	JT	14	180
KEELING	JW	11	208
KEELING	P	12	133
KEELING	W	11	209
KEELING	W	14	180
KEELTY	L	9	110
KEELY	EC	2	189
KEEN	A	2	189
KEEN	A	2	189
KEEN	AJ	7	213
KEEN	C	1	190
KEEN	C	2	189
KEEN	C	5	202
KEEN	D	7	213
KEEN	DC	13	252
KEEN	E	1	190
KEEN	EL	1	190
KEEN	F	4	217
KEEN	F	14	180
KEEN	FW	10	321
KEEN	G	5	202
KEEN	GL	5	202
KEEN	H	1	190
KEEN	H	4	217
KEEN	HT	3	103
KEEN	J	6	244
KEEN	JG	1	190
KEEN	JW	7	213
KEEN	P	8	184
KEEN	R	13	252
KEEN	S	1	190
KEEN	SG	1	190
KEEN	T	12	133
KEEN	V	3	104
KEEN	W	3	104
KEEN	W	6	244
KEEN	WA	1	190
KEEN	WG	13	252
KEEN	WL	13	253
KEENA	WH	2	189
KEENAGHAN	M	8	184
KEENAN	A	7	213
KEENAN	J	9	110
KEENAN	J	9	288
KEENAN	J	11	209
KEENAN	S	13	253
KEENAN	W	11	423
KEENAN	WH	3	104
KEENAN	WT	7	213
KEENE	AE	3	104
KEENE	FH	2	189
KEENE	J	1	191
KEENE	JP	3	104
KEENE	S	2	189
KEENE	WFJ	2	189
KEENE	WH	2	189
KEENS	A	12	133
KEENS	AG	12	133
KEENS	EC	12	133
KEENS	EC	12	133
KEENS	PR	12	133
KEENS	W	5	202
KEEP	A	12	133
KEEP	AE	12	133
KEEP	F	12	133
KEEP	FC	2	189
KEEP	H	2	189
KEEP	J	12	134
KEEP	J	12	134
KEEP	JG	3	104
KEEP	PR	2	189
KEEP	SLT	1	191
KEEPENCE	EE	10	125
KEEPING	A	13	253
KEEPING	EJ	3	369
KEEPING	GS	4	217
KEETCH	H	2	189
KEETCH	J	13	253
KEEVER	J	14	180
KEEVES	AD	12	335
KEEVES	FJ	12	335

KEEVES	GH	12	335	KELLETT	JA	9	110	KELLY	FJ	11	209	KELLY	JW	9	111				
KEEVES	GH	12	335	KELLETT	JA	9	110	KELLY	G	7	214	KELLY	JW	9	389				
KEEVES	M	12	335	KELLETT	JE	9	288	KELLY	G	8	185	KELLY	L	9	111				
KEEVIL	W	1	191	KELLETT	JW	9	288	KELLY	GA	13	253	KELLY	M	2	190				
KEFFORD	F	5	202	KELLETT	M	8	185	KELLY	GW	13	253	KELLY	M	8	186				
KEFFORD	H	5	202	KELLETT	T	8	185	KELLY	H	11	209	KELLY	P	6	244				
KEFFORD	W	5	202	KELLETT	TW	9	288	KELLY	H	14	180	KELLY	P	8	186				
KEFFORD	W	9	110	KELLETT	W	9	110	KELLY	HD	13	253	KELLY	P	9	111				
KEIGHLEY	J	9	288	KELLETT	W	9	389	KELLY	J	1	191	KELLY	P	11	210				
KEIGHLEY	J	9	389	KELLEY	A	14	180	KELLY	J	1	191	KELLY	P	14	181				
KEIGHLEY	JB	8	184	KELLEY	AC	2	189	KELLY	J	6	244	KELLY	RO	10	321				
KEIGHLEY	W	8	184	KELLEY	E	9	110	KELLY	J	6	244	KELLY	S	8	186				
KEIGHTLEY	FE	11	209	KELLEY	EE	13	253	KELLY	J	7	214	KELLY	SJ	4	218				
KEIGHTLY	J	8	185	KELLEY	G	4	218	KELLY	J	7	214	KELLY	T	1	191				
KEILMAN	J	14	180	KELLEY	P	13	253	KELLY	J	8	185	KELLY	T	2	190				
KEIRLE	C	2	189	KELLEY	R	9	288	KELLY	J	8	185	KELLY	T	6	244				
KEIRNAN	RE	3	104	KELLEY	T	9	288	KELLY	J	8	185	KELLY	T	11	210				
KEIRNAN	WJ	3	104	KELLEY	W	9	110	KELLY	J	8	185	KELLY	T	11	210				
KEITCH	F	2	189	KELLEY	W	9	288	KELLY	J	8	185	KELLY	T	11	210				
KEITH	A	10	125	KELLEY	WH	2	189	KELLY	J	8	186	KELLY	T	11	210				
KEITH	F	8	185	KELLIE	A	7	213	KELLY	J	8	186	KELLY	T	11	210				
KEITH	RA	10	125	KELLIE	JM	7	213	KELLY	J	8	186	KELLY	T	11	210				
KEITH	RH	8	185	KELLIE	TA	7	214	KELLY	J	8	186	KELLY	T	13	253				
KEITHLEY	J	9	110	KELLIER	AJ	7	214	KELLY	J	8	416	KELLY	T	13	253				
KEITHLEY	J	9	110	KELLIER	J	7	214	KELLY	J	9	110	KELLY	T	14	181				
KELCHER	AW	4	217	KELLIHER	D	7	214	KELLY	J	9	110	KELLY	TD	7	214				
KELCHER	FJ	4	218	KELLING	A	2	190	KELLY	J	9	389	KELLY	TD	8	186				
KELCHER	JD	4	217	KELLOE	WA	3	369	KELLY	J	11	209	KELLY	TH	3	104				
KELHER	JW	9	288	KELLOW	FJ	7	214	KELLY	J	11	209	KELLY	TJ	3	104				
KELL	A	1	191	KELLS	S	13	253	KELLY	J	11	209	KELLY	TW	11	210				
KELL	B	1	191	KELLY	A	9	110	KELLY	J	11	209	KELLY	W	1	191				
KELL	CH	2	189	KELLY	A	11	209	KELLY	J	11	209	KELLY	W	3	369				
KELL	ER	2	189	KELLY	A	14	180	KELLY	J	11	209	KELLY	W	4	218				
KELL	F	1	191	KELLY	AE	10	321	KELLY	J	11	210	KELLY	W	9	111				
KELL	G	1	191	KELLY	AH	2	190	KELLY	J	11	210	KELLY	W	9	288				
KELL	H	10	125	KELLY	AR	2	190	KELLY	J	13	253	KELLY	W	10	126				
KELL	JW	1	191	KELLY	B	7	214	KELLY	J	13	253	KELLY	W	11	210				
KELL	T	1	191	KELLY	B	8	185	KELLY	J	14	181	KELLY	W	11	210				
KELL	WH	10	321	KELLY	C	8	185	KELLY	J	14	181	KELLY	W	13	253				
KELLAWAY	A	4	218	KELLY	CF	8	185	KELLY	J	14	181	KELLY	W	14	181				
KELLAWAY	A	4	218	KELLY	D	9	389	KELLY	J	14	181	KELSALL	F	11	210				
KELLAWAY	AE	10	126	KELLY	DW	11	209	KELLY	J	14	181	KELSALL	JH	11	210				
KELLAWAY	AVB	4	218	KELLY	E	8	185	KELLY	J	14	181	KELSALL	T	8	186				
KELLAWAY	WE	10	126	KELLY	E	8	185	KELLY	J	14	181	KELSALL	T	11	210				
KELLEHER	J	13	253	KELLY	E	9	288	KELLY	J	14	181	KELSEY	A	4	218				
KELLEHER	W	10	126	KELLY	E	11	209	KELLY	JB	1	191	KELSEY	A	7	214				
KELLER	AE	11	209	KELLY	E	11	209	KELLY	JE	8	186	KELSEY	GR	10	126				
KELLER	W	8	185	KELLY	EC	6	244	KELLY	JE	9	110	KELSEY	HJ	10	126				
KELLETT	A	8	185	KELLY	EJ	1	191	KELLY	JE	9	110	KELSEY	J	8	186				
KELLETT	ASP	9	110	KELLY	ES	6	244	KELLY	JE	11	210	KELSEY	JW	10	126				
KELLETT	B	9	288	KELLY	F	3	369	KELLY	JF	10	126	KELSEY	S	11	210				
KELLETT	E	8	185	KELLY	F	10	126	KELLY	JF	13	253	KELSEY	VL	9	111				
KELLETT	E	9	110	KELLY	F	14	180	KELLY	JW	8	186	KELSEY	WT	10	126				
KELLETT	FH	9	110	KELLY	FA	10	126	KELLY	JW	8	186	KELSHAW	E	11	211				
KELLETT	H	8	185	KELLY	FH	4	218	KELLY	JW	9	111								

Name	In.			Name	In.			Name	In.			Name	In.			Name	In.		
KELSHAW	W	11	211	KEMP	H	10	126	KEMPSTON	HR	1	192	KENDLY	EF	1	192	KENNEDY	J	11	211
KELVEY	FC	5	202	KEMP	HG	1	192	KEMPTON	CW	2	190	KENDREW	J	8	187				
KELWAY	AC	3	104	KEMP	HJ	7	214	KEMPTON	FC	7	215	KENDREW	W	8	187				
KELWAY	JH	13	253	KEMP	J	1	192	KEMPTON	HL	4	218	KENDRICK	AO	9	390				
KELWAY	L	3	104	KEMP	J	2	190	KEMPTON	J	13	255	KENDRICK	EG	11	211				
KEMBLE	B	7	214	KEMP	J	3	369	KEMSLEY	EA	1	192	KENDRICK	J	6	245				
KEMBLE	WH	1	191	KEMP	J	7	214	KEMSLEY	EL	1	192	KENDRICK	J	6	245				
KEMISH	AA	4	218	KEMP	J	10	322	KEMSLEY	FW	1	192	KENDRICK	JA	2	190				
KEMISH	B	4	218	KEMP	J	12	134	KEMSLEY	NG	5	203	KENDRICK	R	11	211				
KEMISH	GR	4	218	KEMP	JA	13	254	KEMSLEY	V	5	203	KENDRICK	W	10	126				
KEMISH	HD	2	190	KEMP	JEG	3	104	KEMSLEY	W	3	105	KENEFIC	B	3	105				
KEMISH	SW	4	218	KEMP	LE	2	190	KENCH	A	3	105	KENEFIC	E	3	105				
KEMISH	WA	2	190	KEMP	P	10	126	KENCH	A	7	215	KENEFIC	JE	3	105				
KEMMETT	F	13	254	KEMP	R	2	190	KENCH	AW	7	215	KENEFICK	J	9	111				
KEMMISH	VJ	4	218	KEMP	R	3	104	KENCH	EC	12	335	KENEFICK	TE	9	111				
KEMMISH	W	4	218	KEMP	R	8	186	KENCH	WWJ	13	255	KENINGALE	EW	2	190				
KEMMISH	WW	4	218	KEMP	RA	3	104	KENCHAT	HW	2	190	KENLOCK	AE	3	105				
KEMMITT	BA	13	254	KEMP	RA	14	181	KENDAL	H	6	245	KENNA	J	11	211				
KEMMITT	JW	13	254	KEMP	RJ	10	126	KENDAL	JW	8	186	KENNA	T	11	211				
KEMMITT	WEA	13	254	KEMP	S	3	105	KENDALL	A	4	219	KENNABY	T	3	369				
KEMP	A	9	111	KEMP	TJ	3	105	KENDALL	A	8	186	KENNADAY	J	8	187				
KEMP	A	11	423	KEMP	W	6	244	KENDALL	B	1	192	KENNADAY	R	8	187				
KEMP	A	13	254	KEMP	W	9	111	KENDALL	C	8	186	KENNADY	T	8	187				
KEMP	A	13	254	KEMP	W	10	126	KENDALL	C	8	186	KENNALLY	E	8	187				
KEMP	A	13	254	KEMP	W	13	254	KENDALL	C	9	288	KENNALLY	J	8	187				
KEMP	AE	3	104	KEMP	W	13	254	KENDALL	CW	9	288	KENNALLY	M	8	187				
KEMP	B	13	254	KEMP	WA	1	192	KENDALL	D	7	215	KENNARD	AW	13	255				
KEMP	C	2	190	KEMP	WA	13	254	KENDALL	E	1	192	KENNARD	GA	13	255				
KEMP	C	3	104	KEMP	WC	1	192	KENDALL	FE	5	203	KENNARD	M	10	127				
KEMP	C	6	244	KEMP	WC	7	214	KENDALL	FW	3	105	KENNARD	R	13	255				
KEMP	C	6	244	KEMP	WE	1	192	KENDALL	FWH	5	203	KENNARD	W	13	255				
KEMP	CF	3	104	KEMP	WG	12	134	KENDALL	G	14	181	KENNARDY	M	9	111				
KEMP	CW	12	134	KEMP	WH	7	215	KENDALL	G	14	181	KENNEALY	A	2	190				
KEMP	E	1	191	KEMP	WH	10	126	KENDALL	GJ	8	186	KENNEDY	A	14	181				
KEMP	E	1	191	KEMP-WEBB	A	6	245	KENDALL	GJ	10	126	KENNEDY	AC	3	105				
KEMP	E	3	104	KEMP-WEBB	T	6	245	KENDALL	GW	4	218	KENNEDY	AJ	3	105				
KEMP	EP	6	244	KEMPSON	B	6	245	KENDALL	H	4	219	KENNEDY	CS	7	215				
KEMP	ER	13	254	KEMPSON	C	1	192	KENDALL	H	8	186	KENNEDY	D	9	390				
KEMP	F	13	254	KEMPSON	F	5	203	KENDALL	H	14	181	KENNEDY	E	1	192				
KEMP	F	13	254	KEMPSON	G	1	192	KENDALL	J	2	190	KENNEDY	E	2	191				
KEMP	FC	12	134	KEMPSON	G	5	202	KENDALL	J	3	105	KENNEDY	F	2	190				
KEMP	FE	4	218	KEMPSON	J	1	192	KENDALL	J	9	288	KENNEDY	F	11	211				
KEMP	FEG	4	218	KEMPSON	JR	6	245	KENDALL	J	11	211	KENNEDY	FR	3	369				
KEMP	FH	2	190	KEMPSON	LW	14	181	KENDALL	JRH	8	187	KENNEDY	G	11	211				
KEMP	FJ	1	192	KEMPSTER	A	1	192	KENDALL	L	11	211	KENNEDY	HC	3	370				
KEMP	FMJ	7	214	KEMPSTER	A	12	134	KENDALL	M	14	181	KENNEDY	HW	6	245				
KEMP	FW	13	254	KEMPSTER	C	5	202	KENDALL	MCW	4	219	KENNEDY	HW	7	215				
KEMP	FW	13	254	KEMPSTER	D	5	202	KENDALL	RC	12	336	KENNEDY	J	8	187				
KEMP	G	6	244	KEMPSTER	G	5	202	KENDALL	T	14	181	KENNEDY	J	9	111				
KEMP	G	7	214	KEMPSTER	H	1	192	KENDALL	W	8	187	KENNEDY	J	11	211				
KEMP	GF	12	134	KEMPSTER	J	5	202	KENDALL	WFS	7	215	KENNEDY	J	11	211				
KEMP	GH	7	214	KEMPSTER	LH	5	202	KENDALL	WJ	5	203	KENNEDY	J	11	211				
KEMP	GO	10	321	KEMPSTER	T	5	203	KENDELL	G	9	289	KENNEDY	J	11	211				
KEMP	H	2	190	KEMPSTER	W	5	203	KENDELL	GA	10	126	KENNEDY	J	11	211				
KEMP	H	6	244	KEMPSTER	WCG	13	254	KENDLE	WCT	4	219	KENNEDY	J	11	211				

KENNEDY	J	11	211	KENNY	WH	11	212	KENTLETON	H	2	191	KERNOT	JA	2	191
KENNEDY	J	14	181	KENSELL	H	13	255	KENTON	C	14	182	KERNS	E	14	182
KENNEDY	J	14	182	KENSELL	JE	13	255	KENTON	J	14	182	KERNS	JA	14	182
KENNEDY	JF	6	245	KENSETT	FS	7	215	KENTSLEY	EV	13	255	KERR	AS	5	203
KENNEDY	JJ	11	211	KENSETT	GT	7	215	KENTSMITH	P	3	105	KERR	HT	4	219
KENNEDY	JT	14	182	KENT	A	5	203	KENWARD	H	7	216	KERR	J	11	213
KENNEDY	JW	8	187	KENT	A	6	245	KENWAY	A	4	219	KERR	JM	3	106
KENNEDY	KB	1	192	KENT	A	7	215	KENWOOD	FW	3	105	KERR	R	1	193
KENNEDY	L	8	187	KENT	A	7	215	KENWORTHY	FH	8	188	KERR	R	11	212
KENNEDY	MC	6	245	KENT	A	10	322	KENWORTHY	JW	14	182	KERR	RP	3	106
KENNEDY	P	8	187	KENT	B	6	245	KENWORTHY	RC	8	188	KERR	RW	2	191
KENNEDY	P	11	211	KENT	B	12	336	KENYON	A	6	246	KERR	T	11	213
KENNEDY	PG	6	245	KENT	C	4	219	KENYON	A	12	134	KERR	W	3	106
KENNEDY	PJ	9	390	KENT	C	10	127	KENYON	A	14	182	KERR	WA	11	212
KENNEDY	T	4	219	KENT	C	12	134	KENYON	A	14	182	KERRIDGE	AW	10	127
KENNEDY	T	11	212	KENT	CE	3	370	KENYON	CE	2	191	KERRIDGE	AWJ	7	216
KENNEDY	W	6	245	KENT	CE	10	127	KENYON	E	7	216	KERRIDGE	CE	7	216
KENNEDY	W	7	215	KENT	CL	13	255	KENYON	E	14	182	KERRIDGE	D	3	106
KENNEDY	W	9	111	KENT	E	6	245	KENYON	G	11	212	KERRIDGE	E	3	106
KENNEDY	W	11	212	KENT	EJ	1	193	KENYON	G	14	182	KERRIDGE	F	1	193
KENNEDY	W	13	255	KENT	EJ	3	370	KENYON	J	9	289	KERRIDGE	FG	5	203
KENNEDY	WJ	3	105	KENT	EW	3	105	KENYON	J	11	212	KERRIDGE	H	10	127
KENNEFORD	F	2	191	KENT	F	3	370	KENYON	J	14	182	KERRIDGE	J	1	193
KENNERSON	A	3	105	KENT	F	5	203	KENYON	JR	11	212	KERRIGAN	A	4	219
KENNERSON	W	3	105	KENT	FH	3	105	KENYON	R	11	212	KERRIGAN	M	14	183
KENNET	L	4	219	KENT	FJ	2	191	KENYON	S	11	212	KERRIGAN	PJ	2	191
KENNETT	GA	10	127	KENT	FR	3	105	KENYON	T	11	212	KERRIGAN	W	9	111
KENNETT	JL	2	191	KENT	G	2	191	KENYON	T	11	212	KERRIGAN	W	14	183
KENNETT	W	13	255	KENT	G	7	215	KENYON	T	14	182	KERRISON	G	2	191
KENNETT	WE	6	245	KENT	G	7	215	KENYON	TH	11	212	KERRISON	G	5	203
KENNETT	WJW	13	255	KENT	H	13	255	KEOGH	H	9	111	KERRISON	LW	5	203
KENNEY	CH	6	245	KENT	HJ	1	193	KEOGH	J	6	246	KERRS	J	11	213
KENNEY	CH	6	245	KENT	J	2	191	KEOHANE	D	7	216	KERRY	AR	6	246
KENNEY	F	8	187	KENT	J	13	255	KEOUGH	HW	5	203	KERRY	H	1	193
KENNEY	R	8	187	KENT	J	13	255	KEOUGH	J	2	191	KERRY	H	6	246
KENNEY	TW	8	187	KENT	JJ	6	246	KERBY	ER	10	127	KERRY	HEA	3	106
KENNEY	WH	11	212	KENT	JT	2	191	KERBY	JA	8	188	KERRY	LT	3	106
KENNING	G	6	245	KENT	JW	13	255	KERCHER	AW	10	127	KERRY	P	1	193
KENNING	S	6	245	KENT	L	6	246	KERDANSKY	I	14	182	KERRY	PR	3	106
KENNINGHAM	F	9	289	KENT	LF	3	370	KERDANSKY	M	14	182	KERRY	W	11	213
KENNINGHAM	HV	9	289	KENT	P	8	188	KERENS	H	10	322	KERRY	W	11	213
KENNISH	A	10	127	KENT	R	4	219	KERENS	JL	10	322	KERRY	WJ	2	191
KENNISTON	J	14	182	KENT	S	6	246	KERFOOT	TB	11	212	KERSH	J	14	183
KENNON	WC	13	255	KENT	SJ	7	215	KERFORD	W	11	212	KERSH	R	14	183
KENNY	CH	11	212	KENT	T	12	336	KERKHAM	AG	14	182	KERSHAW	A	8	188
KENNY	CI	3	370	KENT	TH	2	191	KERKHOFF	A	6	246	KERSHAW	A	9	111
KENNY	D	8	187	KENT	W	2	191	KERKHOFF	JD	6	246	KERSHAW	C	8	188
KENNY	EJ	11	212	KENT	W	6	246	KERNAN	HE	4	219	KERSHAW	E	9	111
KENNY	F	9	289	KENT	W	7	215	KERNAN	HV	4	219	KERSHAW	E	9	111
KENNY	HF	11	212	KENT	W	7	215	KERNAN	WA	4	219	KERSHAW	F	9	112
KENNY	J	8	187	KENT	W	12	336	KERNER	AJ	3	370	KERSHAW	F	9	289
KENNY	J	8	187	KENT	WJT	7	216	KERNER	EE	10	127	KERSHAW	F	9	289
KENNY	J	14	182	KENT-SMITH	B	7	216	KERNER	HS	3	370	KERSHAW	G	7	216
KENNY	J	14	182	KENTISH	BM	7	216	KERNER	RG	3	370	KERSHAW	G	9	112
KENNY	JF	14	182	KENTISH	HB	5	203	KERNICK	A	7	216	KERSHAW	GW	9	112

KERSHAW	H	8	188	KETTLE	TW	6	246	KIBBLE	E	1	193	KIFF	CD	5	204
KERSHAW	H	8	188	KETTLE	W	2	191	KIBBLE	G	13	256	KIFF	E	5	204
KERSHAW	H	9	112	KETTLES	P	12	134	KIBBLE	J	13	256	KIFF	FC	13	256
KERSHAW	H	9	289	KETTLES	W	12	134	KIBBLE	JW	3	106	KIFF	HS	5	204
KERSHAW	HS	6	246	KETTLEWELL	H	9	390	KIBBLE	WH	13	256	KIFF	J	2	192
KERSHAW	J	8	188	KEVAN	TJ	13	256	KIBBLER	D	6	247	KIFF	JE	13	256
KERSHAW	J	11	213	KEVILL	JW	11	213	KIBBLER	HJ	12	336	KIFF	L	13	256
KERSHAW	JA	9	112	KEVILL	T	11	213	KIBBLER	J	6	247	KIFF	P	5	204
KERSHAW	JR	9	289	KEW	C	8	188	KIBBLER	JW	12	336	KIFF	SG	13	257
KERSHAW	JW	9	289	KEW	JH	8	188	KIBBLES	R	6	247	KIFF	TW	13	257
KERSHAW	K	9	289	KEW	L	8	188	KIBLER	G	13	256	KIFF	W	13	257
KERSHAW	L	9	289	KEWLEY	TW	11	213	KICK	FH	2	192	KIFF	WT	2	192
KERSHAW	LG	8	188	KEY	A	6	246	KICK	W	3	370	KIFORT	J	11	213
KERSHAW	LR	8	188	KEY	AB	14	183	KICKS	AC	13	256	KIGHTLEY	E	12	336
KERSHAW	M	11	423	KEY	AW	6	246	KICKS	W	13	256	KIGHTLEY	FC	12	336
KERSHAW	S	8	188	KEY	B	10	127	KIDD	A	3	106	KIGHTLEY	W	12	336
KERSHAW	S	9	112	KEY	C	3	106	KIDD	A	7	216	KILBEG	J	11	213
KERSHAW	S	9	289	KEY	E	9	112	KIDD	AJ	8	188	KILBORN	JR	12	336
KERSHAW	SC	14	183	KEY	E	10	127	KIDD	CD	10	127	KILBOURN	AG	1	193
KERSHAW	W	9	112	KEY	FJ	12	134	KIDD	F	3	106	KILBOURN	AS	12	134
KERSHAW	W	9	112	KEY	H	6	246	KIDD	G	7	216	KILBOURN	ES	1	194
KERSLAKE	C	4	219	KEY	H	6	247	KIDD	GA	3	106	KILBOURN	H	12	134
KERSLAKE	F	4	219	KEY	H	7	216	KIDD	HW	7	217	KILBOURN	SF	1	194
KERSLAKE	F	4	219	KEY	H	9	112	KIDD	JC	3	106	KILBRIDE	A	8	188
KERSLEY	B	4	219	KEY	H	13	256	KIDD	R	13	256	KILBRIDE	J	9	289
KERSLEY	C	4	219	KEY	HW	7	216	KIDD	W	1	193	KILBRIDE	J	11	213
KERSLEY	GW	4	220	KEY	HW	12	134	KIDD	W	3	106	KILBRIDE	T	9	112
KERSLEY	J	4	220	KEY	J	6	247	KIDD	W	3	107	KILBURN	G	11	213
KERSWELL	G	3	106	KEY	L	3	106	KIDD	WH	1	193	KILBURN	H	9	112
KERSWELL	H	1	193	KEY	N	10	127	KIDDELL	A	3	370	KILBURN	H	9	289
KERSWELL	SC	3	106	KEY	S	2	192	KIDDLE	FG	4	220	KILBURN	H	9	289
KERTON	TJ	4	220	KEY	TN	10	127	KIDDLEY	FR	3	370	KILBURN	L	8	188
KERVELL	HG	10	127	KEY	W	6	247	KIDDLEY	WR	3	370	KILBURN	R	9	112
KERWIN	J	6	246	KEY	W	6	247	KIDDS	EH	1	193	KILBURN	SA	9	112
KERWIN	W	9	289	KEY	W	6	247	KIDDS	HS	3	370	KILBURN	TE	8	188
KERWOOD	AE	7	216	KEY	WE	1	193	KIDGELL	A	4	220	KILBURN	W	10	128
KERWOOD	ER	13	255	KEY	WG	10	127	KIDGELL	FW	7	217	KILBURN	WH	9	112
KESNER	HB	5	203	KEYLOCK	LJ	4	220	KIDGER	A	12	336	KILBY	A	1	194
KESSELL	RS	1	193	KEYLOCK	PT	4	220	KIDMAN	E	12	134	KILBY	AC	2	192
KESTERTON	J	6	246	KEYS	A	13	256	KIDNEY	A	3	370	KILBY	EG	5	204
KESTON	HE	3	370	KEYS	AJ	2	192	KIDNEY	D	10	322	KILBY	FG	6	248
KETLEY	SP	4	220	KEYS	E	5	203	KIDSLEY	EA	12	336	KILBY	FJ	5	204
KETLEY	WA	1	193	KEYS	E	13	256	KIDSLEY	HW	12	336	KILBY	HJ	5	204
KETTERINGHAM	EW	13	256	KEYS	JF	13	256	KIDSLEY	W	12	336	KILBY	HRC	12	336
KETTERINGHAM	FJ	13	256	KEYS	T	1	193	KIEFER	F	7	217	KILBY	J	3	107
KETTERINGHAM	GC	13	256	KEYSE	A	13	256	KIELLOR	H	1	193	KILBY	LS	7	217
KETTLE	AW	6	246	KEYSE	E	13	256	KIELLOR	J	1	193	KILBY	PS	5	204
KETTLE	C	2	191	KEYTE	AE	6	247	KIELLOR	L	1	193	KILBY	W	3	107
KETTLE	C	11	213	KEYTE	JG	7	216	KIELY	JE	3	371	KILBY	W	12	336
KETTLE	DW	6	246	KEYTE	JH	2	192	KIELY	T	3	107	KILBY	WS	5	204
KETTLE	FW	12	336	KEYTON	RP	4	220	KIERNAN	J	14	183	KILCOURSE	TD	11	213
KETTLE	G	2	191	KEYWOOD	A	10	127	KIERNAN	P	10	127	KILEY	E	14	183
KETTLE	G	3	370	KEYWOOD	T	10	127	KIESSLER	TJC	2	192	KILEY	T	11	213
KETTLE	G	7	216	KIBBLE	AB	3	106	KIFE	AH	3	107	KILFORD	EE	4	220
KETTLE	RS	10	322	KIBBLE	AG	3	106	KIFF	AJ	2	192	KILFORD	EV	4	220

KILFORD	H	4	220	KILPIN	S	8	189	KINCH	A	12	135	KING	AJ	5	205
KILFORD	SC	4	220	KILPIN	W	12	134	KINCH	C	2	192	KING	AJ	5	205
KILGALLON	JB	9	112	KILPIN	WJ	12	134	KINCH	CH	4	221	KING	AJ	10	128
KILGOUR	FG	14	183	KILROW	E	13	257	KINCH	EJ	12	135	KING	AM	2	193
KILGOUR	J	11	213	KILROY	A	11	214	KINCH	H	2	192	KING	AM	14	183
KILGOUR	J	11	213	KILSBY	AR	12	337	KINCH	JG	1	194	KING	AR	3	107
KILHAN	W	1	194	KILSBY	H	12	134	KINCH	K	12	135	KING	AR	4	221
KILKENNY	E	11	213	KILSBY	RJ	12	337	KINCH	W	12	337	KING	AT	1	195
KILKENNY	EP	8	188	KILVINGTON	HT	8	189	KINCHENTON	WCS	4	221	KING	AT	2	193
KILKENNY	J	9	289	KILVINGTON	T	8	189	KINCHINGTON	G	4	221	KING	AT	12	135
KILKENNY	T	6	247	KILVINGTON	T	8	189	KINCHLEA	HA	7	217	KING	AT	13	257
KILKENNY	W	6	247	KIMBER	A	4	220	KINCHLEA	WTD	7	217	KING	AV	13	257
KILL	A	10	128	KIMBER	A	13	257	KINDER	H	8	189	KING	AW	1	195
KILL	C	10	128	KIMBER	AW	4	220	KINDRED	HW	7	217	KING	AW	1	195
KILLARNEY	E	8	188	KIMBER	CH	4	220	KINDRED	W	2	192	KING	AW	5	205
KILLASPY	A	7	217	KIMBER	E	4	220	KINDRED	WA	7	217	KING	AW	12	135
KILLASPY	DW	7	217	KIMBER	EG	4	220	KINDRED	WG	7	217	KING	AW	13	257
KILLE	BH	12	336	KIMBER	F	4	220	KING	A	2	192	KING	B	3	107
KILLE	FA	10	322	KIMBER	F	9	112	KING	A	3	107	KING	B	7	217
KILLE	JO	10	322	KIMBER	FA	10	128	KING	A	3	107	KING	B	10	323
KILLEEN	CT	6	247	KIMBER	G	4	220	KING	A	3	107	KING	BG	1	195
KILLEEN	P	6	247	KIMBER	GE	10	128	KING	A	3	107	KING	BJ	2	193
KILLEN	J	9	289	KIMBER	HG	4	221	KING	A	3	371	KING	BJ	12	135
KILLENGRAY	W	2	192	KIMBER	HT	10	322	KING	A	4	221	KING	C	3	371
KILLERBY	RG	8	189	KIMBER	JA	14	183	KING	A	5	204	KING	C	7	217
KILLEY	C	1	194	KIMBER	JT	10	128	KING	A	5	204	KING	C	7	218
KILLHAM	EJ	10	322	KIMBER	JT	10	128	KING	A	5	204	KING	C	9	112
KILLHAM	F	10	322	KIMBER	JW	10	322	KING	A	5	204	KING	C	12	135
KILLHAM	GE	10	322	KIMBER	L	13	257	KING	A	5	204	KING	C	14	183
KILLHAM	GF	10	322	KIMBER	LS	4	221	KING	A	5	204	KING	CE	5	205
KILLHAM	L	10	322	KIMBER	S	4	221	KING	A	8	189	KING	CE	13	257
KILLIAN	B	8	189	KIMBER	W	7	217	KING	A	10	322	KING	CH	2	193
KILLICK	AE	13	257	KIMBER	WA	10	128	KING	A	13	257	KING	CH	6	247
KILLICK	AG	5	204	KIMBER	WE	10	128	KING	A	13	257	KING	CH	10	128
KILLICK	G	13	257	KIMBER	WH	7	217	KING	A	13	257	KING	CJ	7	218
KILLICK	TW	1	194	KIMBER	WH	10	128	KING	A	13	257	KING	CR	4	221
KILLICK	W	7	217	KIMBER	WJ	4	221	KING	AA	12	135	KING	CW	4	221
KILLINGBACK	EA	1	194	KIMBER	WJ	7	217	KING	AC	1	194	KING	CW	7	218
KILLINGBACK	GE	1	194	KIMBER	WW	10	128	KING	AC	4	221	KING	D	7	218
KILLINGBACK	JA	1	194	KIMBLE	LT	5	204	KING	AC	7	217	KING	D	12	135
KILLINGBACK	WJ	1	194	KIME	JA	1	194	KING	AC	12	135	KING	D	13	258
KILLINGBACK	WJ	1	194	KIMMENOE	EC	13	257	KING	AE	3	371	KING	DS	1	195
KILLINGBECK	A	8	189	KIMMINS	CA	3	107	KING	AE	4	221	KING	DW	10	128
KILLINGER	RP	1	194	KIMMINS	GW	3	107	KING	AE	5	204	KING	E	1	195
KILLINGER	SJ	13	257	KIMMINS	R	13	257	KING	AE	5	205	KING	E	2	193
KILLION	D	11	214	KIMPTON	AJ	1	194	KING	AE	10	322	KING	E	4	221
KILLION	T	8	189	KIMPTON	EW	2	192	KING	AE	12	135	KING	E	4	221
KILLIP	S	9	290	KIMPTON	G	5	204	KING	AE	12	337	KING	E	5	205
KILLMAN	AR	2	192	KIMPTON	HJ	1	194	KING	AE	14	183	KING	E	5	205
KILLORAN	P	11	214	KIMPTON	J	5	204	KING	AF	1	194	KING	E	7	218
KILLWORTH	H	6	247	KIMPTON	JF	2	192	KING	AH	3	107	KING	E	9	290
KILLWORTH	W	6	247	KIMPTON	JR	1	194	KING	AH	3	107	KING	E	11	214
KILMINSTER	W	6	247	KIMSEY	JA	2	192	KING	AH	3	371	KING	E	12	135
KILNER	WW	11	214	KINAHAN	J	14	183	KING	AJ	4	221	KING	E	12	135
KILPIN	G	12	336	KINCEY	WH	2	192	KING	AJ	4	221	KING	E	12	135

KING	E	13	258	KING	G	10	128	KING	J	6	248	KING	R	13	259
KING	EA	1	195	KING	G	10	323	KING	J	7	218	KING	RB	13	259
KING	EC	13	258	KING	G	11	214	KING	J	7	218	KING	RE	6	248
KING	ECO	12	135	KING	G	12	136	KING	J	9	290	KING	RH	4	222
KING	ED	3	107	KING	G	12	136	KING	J	9	290	KING	RH	5	206
KING	ED	5	205	KING	G	12	136	KING	J	9	390	KING	RJ	7	218
KING	ED	12	135	KING	G	12	136	KING	J	11	214	KING	S	6	248
KING	EF	1	195	KING	G	12	136	KING	J	11	214	KING	S	7	219
KING	EG	3	371	KING	G	12	136	KING	J	12	136	KING	SC	1	195
KING	EG	12	135	KING	G	14	183	KING	J	12	136	KING	SE	13	259
KING	EJ	13	258	KING	GA	7	218	KING	J	13	258	KING	SH	12	136
KING	ET	13	258	KING	GE	2	193	KING	J	14	183	KING	SJ	5	206
KING	EW	5	205	KING	GE	13	258	KING	J	14	183	KING	SJ	12	137
KING	EW	10	322	KING	GET	10	128	KING	J	14	183	KING	SP	13	259
KING	F	2	193	KING	GF	4	222	KING	JA	7	218	KING	T	1	195
KING	F	2	193	KING	GH	3	371	KING	JC	12	136	KING	T	1	195
KING	F	4	221	KING	GH	4	222	KING	JC	13	258	KING	T	1	195
KING	F	4	221	KING	GJR	12	337	KING	JDS	4	222	KING	T	2	194
KING	F	5	205	KING	GS	3	107	KING	JE	9	290	KING	T	3	371
KING	F	7	218	KING	GV	6	247	KING	JE	13	258	KING	T	5	206
KING	F	7	218	KING	H	2	193	KING	JEF	4	222	KING	T	7	219
KING	F	9	113	KING	H	2	193	KING	JF	7	218	KING	T	7	219
KING	F	9	290	KING	H	5	205	KING	JF	12	136	KING	T	8	189
KING	F	10	128	KING	H	5	205	KING	JG	10	323	KING	T	9	113
KING	F	10	323	KING	H	7	218	KING	JH	5	206	KING	T	10	129
KING	F	11	214	KING	H	7	218	KING	JH	5	206	KING	T	10	129
KING	F	12	135	KING	H	8	189	KING	JH	14	183	KING	T	11	214
KING	F	12	337	KING	H	9	113	KING	JJ	2	193	KING	T	13	259
KING	F	13	258	KING	H	12	136	KING	JT	5	206	KING	T	14	184
KING	FA	13	258	KING	H	12	136	KING	JV	2	194	KING	TA	2	194
KING	FC	3	107	KING	H	12	136	KING	JW	1	195	KING	TG	10	323
KING	FG	12	135	KING	H	12	337	KING	JW	9	290	KING	TH	6	248
KING	FG	12	135	KING	HA	5	205	KING	JW	12	337	KING	TJ	2	194
KING	FH	2	193	KING	HB	13	258	KING	L	4	222	KING	TR	3	107
KING	FJ	5	205	KING	HE	1	195	KING	L	7	218	KING	TS	6	248
KING	FJ	7	218	KING	HE	2	193	KING	L	12	136	KING	TW	2	194
KING	FJ	10	323	KING	HE	13	258	KING	L	12	136	KING	V	4	222
KING	FR	2	193	KING	HG	4	222	KING	L	12	136	KING	W	1	195
KING	FW	12	136	KING	HG	10	323	KING	L	13	258	KING	W	1	196
KING	FW	13	258	KING	HJ	2	193	KING	LD	2	194	KING	W	4	222
KING	FWA	10	128	KING	HJ	3	371	KING	LJW	10	128	KING	W	4	222
KING	G	1	195	KING	HJ	7	218	KING	M	1	195	KING	W	4	222
KING	G	2	193	KING	HJ	10	323	KING	M	14	184	KING	W	5	206
KING	G	2	193	KING	HJ	13	258	KING	MT	6	248	KING	W	5	206
KING	G	2	193	KING	HS	2	194	KING	N	7	218	KING	W	5	206
KING	G	2	193	KING	HS	8	189	KING	P	11	214	KING	W	6	248
KING	G	2	193	KING	HS	13	258	KING	P	12	136	KING	W	7	219
KING	G	4	221	KING	HT	5	205	KING	P	12	136	KING	W	8	189
KING	G	4	221	KING	HW	13	258	KING	PFG	2	194	KING	W	9	290
KING	G	4	221	KING	I	5	205	KING	PW	2	194	KING	W	9	290
KING	G	5	205	KING	J	4	222	KING	R	1	195	KING	W	9	290
KING	G	5	205	KING	J	4	222	KING	R	1	195	KING	W	10	129
KING	G	7	218	KING	J	5	205	KING	R	4	222	KING	W	12	137
KING	G	7	218	KING	J	5	205	KING	R	5	206	KING	WA	1	196
KING	G	9	113	KING	J	5	205	KING	R	13	259	KING	WC	1	196

Surname	Initials	Coy	Page
KING	WF	5	206
KING	WG	2	194
KING	WG	2	194
KING	WG	2	194
KING	WG	7	219
KING	WG	10	323
KING	WG	12	137
KING	WG	13	259
KING	WH	7	219
KING	WH	12	137
KING	WH	12	137
KING	WJ	1	196
KING	WJ	6	248
KING	WJ	10	129
KING	WJ	10	323
KING	WJ	11	214
KING	WJ	14	184
KING	WJA	2	194
KING	WL	12	137
KING	WM	3	107
KING	WN	10	323
KING	WS	13	259
KING	WT	2	194
KINGDOM	AFW	1	196
KINGDOM	FJ	1	196
KINGDOM	FJ	13	259
KINGDOM	JA	1	196
KINGDON	EA	10	323
KINGDON	GR	7	219
KINGDON	WJ	3	371
KINGETT	AH	7	219
KINGHAM	A	5	206
KINGHAM	A	5	206
KINGHAM	AH	5	206
KINGHAM	E	3	108
KINGHAM	E	3	108
KINGHAM	EA	3	371
KINGHAM	EE	2	194
KINGHAM	F	1	196
KINGHAM	F	3	108
KINGHAM	FJ	3	108
KINGHAM	FJ	3	371
KINGHAM	GW	5	206
KINGHAM	HJ	2	194
KINGHAM	J	5	206
KINGHAM	JC	1	196
KINGHAM	SDV	5	206
KINGHAM	SE	3	108
KINGHAM	SP	5	206
KINGHAM	T	3	108
KINGHAM	W	12	137
KINGLEY	H	3	108
KINGMAN	T	7	219
KINGSBURY	JA	3	371
KINGSFORD	AE	13	259
KINGSFORD	FEW	7	219
KINGSFORD	FR	1	196
KINGSHOTT	AH	3	108
KINGSHOTT	FC	3	108
KINGSHOTT	J	4	222
KINGSHOTT	PD	3	108
KINGSHOTT	WG	3	108
KINGSLAND	H	6	248
KINGSLAND	R	6	248
KINGSLEY	C	14	184
KINGSLEY	CE	3	371
KINGSLEY	CH	3	371
KINGSLEY	F	5	207
KINGSLEY	J	5	207
KINGSLEY	S	2	194
KINGSLEY	W	2	194
KINGSLEY	W	5	207
KINGSMILL	GF	7	219
KINGSNORTH	AW	1	196
KINGSTON	A	12	137
KINGSTON	A	12	337
KINGSTON	A	12	337
KINGSTON	AJ	3	108
KINGSTON	AW	4	222
KINGSTON	BJ	12	337
KINGSTON	CR	3	108
KINGSTON	CW	11	214
KINGSTON	FJ	12	137
KINGSTON	H	10	129
KINGSTON	H	12	137
KINGSTON	HC	10	323
KINGSTON	HJ	12	337
KINGSTON	JM	7	219
KINGSTON	JP	12	337
KINGSTON	JW	10	129
KINGSTON	K	2	195
KINGSTON	TJ	3	108
KINGSTON	TW	12	337
KINGSTON	W	3	371
KINGSTON	WC	12	337
KINGSTON	WF	4	222
KINGSTON	WJ	10	129
KINGSWELL	AH	10	129
KINGSWELL	CE	10	129
KINGSWELL	CM	4	222
KINGSWELL	D	4	222
KINGSWELL	FE	10	129
KINGSWELL	GF	4	222
KINGSWELL	HF	4	223
KINGSWELL	R	4	223
KINGSWELL	RF	10	323
KINGSWELL	WC	4	223
KINGTON	E	13	259
KINGWELL	W	3	108
KINNARD	AJ	4	223
KINNARD	ATE	4	223
KINNEAR	H	13	259
KINNEAR	R	13	259
KINNIER	TJ	1	196
KINNINMONT	J	11	214
KINNS	E	12	137
KINNUMAN	J	13	259
KINSBURY	A	7	219
KINSELLA	J	11	214
KINSELLA	JC	3	108
KINSELLA	M	2	195
KINSELLA	P	14	184
KINSEN	ES	7	219
KINSEY	AJ	8	189
KINSEY	CA	10	323
KINSEY	DH	11	214
KINSEY	JH	1	196
KINSEY	W	11	214
KINSEY	WT	14	184
KINSHOTT	AB	10	129
KINSLEY	J	9	113
KINSLEY	P	3	108
KINTON	W	4	223
KINTON	WE	4	223
KIPLIN	AW	4	223
KIPLING	A	8	189
KIPLING	EB	9	113
KIPLING	JW	8	189
KIPLING	T	8	189
KIPLING	WR	9	113
KIPPAX	J	11	214
KIPPEN	GW	6	248
KIPPENDALE	FW	4	223
KIPPS	L	7	219
KIRBR	HJ	7	219
KIRBY	A	6	248
KIRBY	A	8	189
KIRBY	A	10	129
KIRBY	A	12	137
KIRBY	AB	3	108
KIRBY	AB	3	108
KIRBY	AE	4	223
KIRBY	AE	10	129
KIRBY	AJ	3	108
KIRBY	AK	6	248
KIRBY	AW	6	248
KIRBY	B	12	137
KIRBY	BR	5	207
KIRBY	C	10	129
KIRBY	E	2	195
KIRBY	E	6	248
KIRBY	E	8	189
KIRBY	EC	6	248
KIRBY	EJ	3	109
KIRBY	EMG	3	109
KIRBY	F	10	129
KIRBY	F	11	423
KIRBY	F	12	137
KIRBY	F	12	137
KIRBY	FC	10	129
KIRBY	FN	14	184
KIRBY	G	5	207
KIRBY	G	9	113
KIRBY	GW	1	196
KIRBY	GW	3	109
KIRBY	H	8	189
KIRBY	H	10	129
KIRBY	H	12	137
KIRBY	H	12	137
KIRBY	HG	2	195
KIRBY	HW	10	129
KIRBY	J	6	249
KIRBY	JW	3	109
KIRBY	N	8	190
KIRBY	P	12	137
KIRBY	S	4	223
KIRBY	S	7	219
KIRBY	S	12	137
KIRBY	S	12	137
KIRBY	S	13	259
KIRBY	SF	7	219
KIRBY	T	8	190
KIRBY	W	1	196
KIRBY	W	10	130
KIRBY	W	13	259
KIRBY	WH	2	195
KIRBY	WW	2	195
KIRCHER	WH	10	323
KIRK	A	8	190
KIRK	A	9	290
KIRK	C	8	190
KIRK	CG	8	190
KIRK	CW	11	215
KIRK	D	13	259
KIRK	DJ	12	337
KIRK	EC	8	190
KIRK	EE	1	196
KIRK	F	7	220
KIRK	FH	8	190
KIRK	FS	7	219
KIRK	GA	13	259
KIRK	GM	8	190
KIRK	H	8	190
KIRK	H	8	190
KIRK	HG	1	196
KIRK	HJ	3	109
KIRK	J	5	207
KIRK	J	6	249
KIRK	J	7	220
KIRK	J	11	215

KIRK	J	12	337	KIRKMAN	R	14	184	KITCHIN	A	7	220	KLIEGL	EW	1	197
KIRK	J	12	337	KIRKMAN	W	14	184	KITCHIN	E	8	191	KLUTH	F	1	197
KIRK	JE	9	290	KIRKPATRICK	R	11	215	KITCHIN	GR	14	185	KNAGGS	H	8	191
KIRK	JH	8	190	KIRKWAN	J	4	223	KITCHING	AE	13	260	KNAGGS	R	8	191
KIRK	JH	13	259	KIRKWOOD	R	11	215	KITCHING	AW	13	260	KNAPE	F	14	185
KIRK	JW	1	196	KIRLEW	RL	2	195	KITCHING	F	9	390	KNAPMAN	JF	7	220
KIRK	L	8	190	KIRLY	H	4	223	KITCHING	H	8	191	KNAPMAN	TC	13	260
KIRK	PB	12	138	KIRMAN	CH	10	130	KITCHING	HW	7	220	KNAPP	AC	13	260
KIRK	RS	8	190	KIRSCH	TW	13	260	KITCHING	J	8	191	KNAPP	AJ	4	224
KIRK	S	3	371	KIRTLEY	E	6	249	KITCHING	SP	13	260	KNAPP	AT	3	372
KIRK	T	12	337	KIRTON	A	1	197	KITCHING	T	6	249	KNAPP	EC	4	224
KIRK	W	12	138	KIRTON	A	9	113	KITCHINGMAN	A	9	113	KNAPP	FW	3	109
KIRK	W	13	260	KIRTON	D	1	197	KITCHINGMAN	E	8	191	KNAPP	G	13	260
KIRK	W	14	184	KIRTON	G	9	113	KITCHINGMAN	R	9	290	KNAPP	GC	13	261
KIRK	WH	7	220	KIRTON	J	8	190	KITCHMAN	A	9	290	KNAPP	HW	4	224
KIRK	WJ	8	190	KIRTON	JH	4	223	KITE	C	6	249	KNAPP	J	13	260
KIRK	WJS	8	190	KIRTON	W	9	290	KITE	F	6	249	KNAPP	J	13	261
KIRK	WT	11	215	KIRVIN	A	14	185	KITE	G	2	195	KNAPP	WB	13	261
KIRK	WW	1	197	KIRWAN	FEC	4	223	KITE	HJJ	10	324	KNAPP	WD	13	261
KIRKALDIE	AE	13	260	KIRWAN	W	12	138	KITE	J	6	249	KNAPTON	B	1	197
KIRKBRIDE	VW	8	190	KIRWIN	J	14	185	KITE	NJ	6	249	KNAPTON	CA	8	191
KIRKBY	A	10	130	KIRWIN	S	11	215	KITE	W	6	249	KNEE	AE	5	207
KIRKBY	A	14	184	KISBY	CC	12	138	KITE	WH	7	220	KNEE	B	5	207
KIRKBY	H	10	130	KISSACK	J	14	185	KITOFSKY	W	14	185	KNEE	EH	1	197
KIRKBY-SODEN	G	1	196	KITCATT	AH	4	223	KITSON	A	9	113	KNEE	H	1	197
KIRKHAM	C	14	184	KITCATT	HW	4	223	KITSON	AL	9	390	KNEE	WH	1	197
KIRKHAM	CC	13	260	KITCATT	HW	4	223	KITSON	C	9	290	KNEESHAW	R	4	224
KIRKHAM	CC	13	260	KITCHEN	AE	1	197	KITSON	EH	9	390	KNEESHAW	T	8	191
KIRKHAM	E	14	184	KITCHEN	AJ	13	260	KITSON	GF	14	185	KNELLER	A	4	224
KIRKHAM	F	14	184	KITCHEN	E	9	113	KITSON	H	8	191	KNELLER	A	4	224
KIRKHAM	G	11	215	KITCHEN	EJ	1	197	KITSON	H	9	113	KNELLER	A	10	130
KIRKHAM	J	6	249	KITCHEN	F	13	260	KITSON	HH	9	390	KNELLER	ER	4	224
KIRKHAM	J	10	323	KITCHEN	G	8	190	KITSON	HJ	2	195	KNELLER	G	10	130
KIRKHAM	J	11	215	KITCHEN	JR	11	215	KITSON	J	9	113	KNELLER	J	10	130
KIRKHAM	J	11	215	KITCHEN	SS	3	372	KITSON	J	9	113	KNELLER	W	4	224
KIRKHAM	J	11	215	KITCHEN	W	9	113	KITSON	L	9	290	KNEVETT	A	13	261
KIRKHAM	J	14	184	KITCHEN	W	9	290	KITSON	LT	9	290	KNEVETT	G	13	261
KIRKHAM	JR	3	109	KITCHEN	W	14	185	KITSON	W	7	220	KNEVETT	JW	13	261
KIRKHAM	JR	3	371	KITCHEN	WG	1	197	KITT	A	14	185	KNEVETT	VG	1	197
KIRKHAM	JT	11	215	KITCHENER	A	12	138	KITT	FM	4	224	KNEVETT	WC	1	197
KIRKHAM	JW	14	184	KITCHENER	CJ	1	197	KITTLE	LL	3	109	KNIBB	W	12	337
KIRKHAM	M	11	215	KITCHENER	FD	1	197	KITTLE	NB	3	109	KNIBBS	A	4	224
KIRKHAM	R	11	215	KITCHENER	G	5	207	KITTLE	SR	3	109	KNIBBS	AH	12	138
KIRKHAM	W	6	249	KITCHENER	H	4	223	KITTLEY	W	13	260	KNIBBS	D	12	138
KIRKHAM	W	14	184	KITCHENER	H	9	113	KITTO	L	3	372	KNIBBS	ER	12	138
KIRKHAM	WR	13	260	KITCHENER	HC	5	207	KITTON	ES	4	224	KNIBBS	J	12	138
KIRKLAND	F	2	195	KITCHENER	J	5	207	KITTON	RG	4	224	KNIBBS	PH	12	138
KIRKLAND	J	11	215	KITCHENER	L	5	207	KIVEAL	J	11	216	KNIBBS	W	12	138
KIRKLAND	SA	11	215	KITCHENER	M	5	207	KIY	CS	3	372	KNIBBS	WA	1	197
KIRKLAND	W	8	190	KITCHENER	S	5	207	KIY	CS	3	372	KNIBBS	WG	12	138
KIRKLEY	D	14	184	KITCHENER	SL	1	197	KLAMKE	WF	13	260	KNIGHT	A	1	197
KIRKLEY	H	8	190	KITCHENER	WS	5	207	KLEIN	AL	13	260	KNIGHT	A	1	198
KIRKLEY	TH	11	215	KITCHER	J	10	130	KLEIN	AW	13	260	KNIGHT	A	4	224
KIRKMAN	A	14	184	KITCHER	TE	4	224	KLEIN	DD	3	109	KNIGHT	A	4	224
KIRKMAN	F	10	324	KITCHER	WJ	4	223	KLEIN	HC	13	260	KNIGHT	A	5	207

KNIGHT	A	5	207	KNIGHT	F	12	138	KNIGHT	J	2	196	KNIGHT	TJ	10	131
KNIGHT	A	10	130	KNIGHT	FCH	10	130	KNIGHT	J	3	109	KNIGHT	TJ	10	131
KNIGHT	A	11	216	KNIGHT	FG	10	324	KNIGHT	J	4	225	KNIGHT	TR	10	324
KNIGHT	A	12	338	KNIGHT	FG	12	338	KNIGHT	J	4	225	KNIGHT	TW	2	196
KNIGHT	A	13	261	KNIGHT	FJ	7	220	KNIGHT	J	5	208	KNIGHT	TW	4	225
KNIGHT	A	14	185	KNIGHT	FJ	9	291	KNIGHT	J	5	208	KNIGHT	VR	10	325
KNIGHT	AA	7	220	KNIGHT	FJ	10	130	KNIGHT	J	6	249	KNIGHT	VV	6	250
KNIGHT	AB	9	114	KNIGHT	FR	2	195	KNIGHT	J	6	249	KNIGHT	W	3	372
KNIGHT	AE	1	198	KNIGHT	FW	4	224	KNIGHT	J	7	221	KNIGHT	W	4	225
KNIGHT	AE	7	220	KNIGHT	FW	12	138	KNIGHT	J	8	191	KNIGHT	W	5	208
KNIGHT	AE	10	324	KNIGHT	G	2	195	KNIGHT	J	9	114	KNIGHT	W	5	208
KNIGHT	AE	12	338	KNIGHT	G	4	224	KNIGHT	J	10	131	KNIGHT	W	5	208
KNIGHT	AF	6	249	KNIGHT	G	5	208	KNIGHT	J	11	216	KNIGHT	W	6	250
KNIGHT	AH	5	207	KNIGHT	G	7	221	KNIGHT	J	11	216	KNIGHT	W	7	221
KNIGHT	AJ	10	324	KNIGHT	G	10	130	KNIGHT	J	11	216	KNIGHT	W	7	221
KNIGHT	AW	4	224	KNIGHT	G	10	131	KNIGHT	J	12	139	KNIGHT	W	8	191
KNIGHT	AW	10	324	KNIGHT	G	12	338	KNIGHT	J	12	338	KNIGHT	W	10	131
KNIGHT	B	5	207	KNIGHT	G	14	185	KNIGHT	J	13	261	KNIGHT	W	10	131
KNIGHT	B	10	324	KNIGHT	G	14	185	KNIGHT	J	13	261	KNIGHT	W	10	131
KNIGHT	BF	12	138	KNIGHT	GA	5	208	KNIGHT	J	14	185	KNIGHT	W	11	216
KNIGHT	BJ	10	130	KNIGHT	GA	12	138	KNIGHT	JE	2	196	KNIGHT	W	14	185
KNIGHT	C	1	198	KNIGHT	GB	3	372	KNIGHT	JH	3	109	KNIGHT	WA	12	139
KNIGHT	C	4	224	KNIGHT	GC	3	109	KNIGHT	JH	8	191	KNIGHT	WE	10	131
KNIGHT	C	7	220	KNIGHT	GF	4	225	KNIGHT	JM	7	221	KNIGHT	WG	2	196
KNIGHT	C	7	220	KNIGHT	GH	7	221	KNIGHT	JT	11	216	KNIGHT	WG	2	196
KNIGHT	C	10	130	KNIGHT	GHW	5	208	KNIGHT	JV	5	208	KNIGHT	WG	4	225
KNIGHT	C	12	138	KNIGHT	GJ	10	324	KNIGHT	JW	14	185	KNIGHT	WG	5	208
KNIGHT	C	13	261	KNIGHT	GM	10	324	KNIGHT	L	6	249	KNIGHT	WG	6	250
KNIGHT	C	14	185	KNIGHT	GR	12	139	KNIGHT	LS	12	338	KNIGHT	WJ	10	131
KNIGHT	CA	10	130	KNIGHT	GW	2	195	KNIGHT	M	9	291	KNIGHT	WJ	10	324
KNIGHT	CA	12	338	KNIGHT	GW	3	109	KNIGHT	M	12	338	KNIGHT	WJ	12	139
KNIGHT	CH	4	224	KNIGHT	GW	5	208	KNIGHT	N	6	249	KNIGHT	WJ	13	261
KNIGHT	CH	5	208	KNIGHT	GW	7	221	KNIGHT	P	13	261	KNIGHT	WM	13	261
KNIGHT	CH	9	290	KNIGHT	H	4	225	KNIGHT	PS	5	208	KNIGHT	WR	7	221
KNIGHT	CS	7	220	KNIGHT	H	4	225	KNIGHT	R	2	196	KNIGHTLEY	PE	5	208
KNIGHT	CW	10	130	KNIGHT	H	5	208	KNIGHT	R	5	208	KNIGHTON	EJ	8	191
KNIGHT	D	1	198	KNIGHT	H	6	249	KNIGHT	R	10	324	KNIGHTON	ER	8	191
KNIGHT	E	2	195	KNIGHT	H	8	191	KNIGHT	R	13	261	KNIGHTON	JH	12	338
KNIGHT	E	2	195	KNIGHT	H	10	131	KNIGHT	RC	4	225	KNIGHTON	T	10	131
KNIGHT	E	4	224	KNIGHT	H	11	216	KNIGHT	RD	4	225	KNIGHTON	TM	10	131
KNIGHT	E	6	249	KNIGHT	H	14	185	KNIGHT	RG	3	109	KNIGHTS	AE	4	225
KNIGHT	E	7	220	KNIGHT	HA	10	131	KNIGHT	RH	9	114	KNIGHTS	AWH	2	196
KNIGHT	E	7	220	KNIGHT	HA	10	324	KNIGHT	RH	11	216	KNIGHTS	EP	13	261
KNIGHT	E	10	324	KNIGHT	HC	4	225	KNIGHT	RR	13	261	KNIGHTS	F	4	225
KNIGHT	E	12	338	KNIGHT	HF	6	249	KNIGHT	S	1	198	KNIGHTS	GW	7	221
KNIGHT	EH	3	109	KNIGHT	HF	13	261	KNIGHT	S	2	196	KNIGHTS	GW	13	262
KNIGHT	EJ	10	324	KNIGHT	HG	5	208	KNIGHT	SC	8	191	KNIGHTS	HG	3	372
KNIGHT	EJ	13	261	KNIGHT	HH	2	195	KNIGHT	SF	4	225	KNIGHTS	J	4	225
KNIGHT	ET	12	138	KNIGHT	HH	11	216	KNIGHT	T	12	338	KNIGHTS	PCH	5	208
KNIGHT	EW	12	138	KNIGHT	HJ	10	324	KNIGHT	T	12	338	KNIGHTS	RC	7	221
KNIGHT	F	2	195	KNIGHT	HR	5	208	KNIGHT	T	14	185	KNIGHTS	RJ	2	196
KNIGHT	F	5	208	KNIGHT	HSC	5	208	KNIGHT	T	14	185	KNIGHTS	TH	7	221
KNIGHT	F	8	191	KNIGHT	HW	12	139	KNIGHT	TE	7	221	KNIGHTS	W	1	198
KNIGHT	F	9	114	KNIGHT	J	1	198	KNIGHT	TE	10	131	KNIGHTS	WG	13	262
KNIGHT	F	10	130	KNIGHT	J	2	195	KNIGHT	TH	6	250	KNIGHTSBRIDGE	A	1	198

KNIGHTSBRIDGE	W	1	198
KNILL	WG	4	225
KNIPE	A	10	131
KNIPE	P	4	225
KNIPE	P	14	186
KNISS	SA	2	196
KNIVETT	CL	2	196
KNIVETT	W	2	196
KNOCK	FJ	3	109
KNOCK	O	12	139
KNOCK	OA	10	131
KNOCK	R	3	109
KNOCKER	FC	7	221
KNOPWOOD	A	9	114
KNOTT	A	4	225
KNOTT	AE	1	198
KNOTT	C	11	216
KNOTT	CB	1	198
KNOTT	CT	7	221
KNOTT	E	2	196
KNOTT	ER	3	110
KNOTT	G	14	186
KNOTT	H	4	225
KNOTT	H	14	186
KNOTT	HP	10	131
KNOTT	HW	7	221
KNOTT	J	11	216
KNOTT	J	11	216
KNOTT	J	14	186
KNOTT	J	14	186
KNOTT	JF	2	196
KNOTT	L	3	110
KNOTT	PHT	2	196
KNOTT	R	13	262
KNOTT	RW	13	262
KNOTT	T	7	221
KNOTT	T	11	216
KNOTT	VG	4	225
KNOTT	W	4	225
KNOTT	W	14	186
KNOTT	WE	10	131
KNOULES	T	6	250
KNOWLER	HJ	2	196
KNOWLES	A	9	291
KNOWLES	A	11	216
KNOWLES	A	14	186
KNOWLES	AW	4	225
KNOWLES	B	13	262
KNOWLES	E	8	191
KNOWLES	E	9	291
KNOWLES	E	13	262
KNOWLES	F	8	191
KNOWLES	F	9	114
KNOWLES	F	9	114
KNOWLES	F	9	291
KNOWLES	FA	6	250
KNOWLES	FA	13	262
KNOWLES	FG	10	131
KNOWLES	G	9	114
KNOWLES	GR	13	262
KNOWLES	GW	13	262
KNOWLES	H	8	191
KNOWLES	H	9	114
KNOWLES	H	9	114
KNOWLES	H	14	186
KNOWLES	HF	13	262
KNOWLES	HG	13	262
KNOWLES	HJ	10	132
KNOWLES	HR	8	191
KNOWLES	J	6	250
KNOWLES	J	8	192
KNOWLES	J	9	291
KNOWLES	J	9	291
KNOWLES	J	13	262
KNOWLES	JF	13	262
KNOWLES	JL	8	192
KNOWLES	JT	9	114
KNOWLES	JW	11	216
KNOWLES	L	4	226
KNOWLES	L	6	250
KNOWLES	MEW	13	262
KNOWLES	P	9	291
KNOWLES	P	13	262
KNOWLES	PH	6	250
KNOWLES	R	9	291
KNOWLES	S	11	216
KNOWLES	SE	4	226
KNOWLES	SW	6	250
KNOWLES	T	9	114
KNOWLES	T	14	186
KNOWLES	TJ	14	186
KNOWLES	TW	2	196
KNOWLES	TW	13	262
KNOWLES	W	7	221
KNOWLES	W	8	416
KNOWLES	W	9	114
KNOWLES	WE	7	221
KNOWLES	WH	9	114
KNOWLES	WJ	13	262
KNOWLSON	AJ	10	132
KNOWLSON	W	13	262
KNOWLTON	AF	4	226
KNOWLTON	AV	4	226
KNOWLTON	E	4	226
KNOWLTON	HG	10	325
KNOWLTON	HWJ	10	132
KNOWLTON	R	4	226
KNOX	A	11	216
KNOX	FA	7	222
KNOX	GW	2	196
KNOX	JE	4	226
KNOX	JW	4	226
KNOX	W	7	222
KNOX	WG	7	222
KNUTTON	T	8	192
KOERNER	BW	10	132
KOERNER	FA	10	132
KOERNER	WB	10	132
KOLLER	EH	1	198
KOLLER	J	2	196
KOLLER	WD	1	198
KONKER	EC	13	262
KOPP	AH	3	110
KOPP	AJ	3	110
KOPP	E	3	110
KOPP	F	3	110
KOPP	WE	3	110
KOPP	WFS	3	110
KOPPENHAGEN	L	2	197
KORN	WW	7	220
KORNER	E	9	114
KORNER	FG	9	114
KRAMER	P	1	198
KRAUSHAAR	SJ	13	262
KRESS	GF	13	263
KRIMHOLTZ	R	5	208
KRONBACH	AE	13	263
KRONBACH	FW	13	263
KRONBACH	FW	13	263
KRUGE	AJ	2	197
KUBEROFSKY	I	14	186
KUHLMAN	TW	1	198
KUHLMAN	WA	1	198
KUHN	GC	1	198
KUMURZURNA	W	11	423
KUNZ	WHH	9	114
KUSHELL	A	8	192
KYBERT	AW	3	110
KYBERT	M	1	198
KYBERT	WA	1	199
KYLE	H	2	197
KYME	JT	8	192
KYNASTON	H	2	197
KYNNERSLEY	EC	10	325
KYTE	GE	4	226
KYTE	W	14	186

L

LABAN	AJG	13	263
LABAN	HC	1	199
LABAN	JG	1	199
LABAN	TH	1	199
LABBE	TG	3	110
LABBETT	A	1	199
LABBETT	SG	3	110
LABRUM	AE	12	139
LABRUM	F	12	338
LABRUM	H	12	338
LABRUM	H	12	338
LABRUM	J	12	338
LABRUM	JC	12	338
LABRUM	MR	12	338
LABRUM	SB	12	338
LACEY	A	3	110
LACEY	A	4	226
LACEY	A	4	226
LACEY	A	12	139
LACEY	A	13	263
LACEY	AE	3	372
LACEY	AH	2	197
LACEY	C	4	226
LACEY	CA	4	226
LACEY	E	3	110
LACEY	E	6	250
LACEY	E	11	217
LACEY	ER	13	263
LACEY	F	1	199
LACEY	FJ	5	209
LACEY	FT	10	325
LACEY	H	2	197
LACEY	H	2	197
LACEY	H	10	325
LACEY	J	1	199
LACEY	J	2	197
LACEY	J	4	226
LACEY	J	5	209
LACEY	J	8	192
LACEY	J	8	192
LACEY	J	14	186
LACEY	JP	11	217
LACEY	JT	12	139
LACEY	L	9	115
LACEY	LE	2	197
LACEY	LM	2	197
LACEY	RA	7	222
LACEY	S	1	199
LACEY	SA	2	197
LACEY	TH	4	226
LACEY	W	4	226
LACEY	W	13	263
LACEY	WA	2	197
LACEY	WC	7	222
LACK	ETW	12	139
LACK	EW	5	209
LACK	S	5	209
LACKEY	HC	6	250
LACKEY	HT	7	222
LACKEY	M	6	250
LACKEY	P	6	250

LACON	GF	10	325	LAKE	DJ	7	222	LAMB	F	8	192	LAMBERT	F	11	217
LACY	H	8	192	LAKE	EH	6	250	LAMB	FJ	6	251	LAMBERT	FA	2	198
LACY	JF	13	263	LAKE	F	2	198	LAMB	G	14	186	LAMBERT	FJ	1	200
LADBROOK	J	7	222	LAKE	FEM	10	132	LAMB	GF	12	139	LAMBERT	FR	2	198
LADBROOKE	RW	7	222	LAKE	FT	2	198	LAMB	GW	12	139	LAMBERT	FT	12	338
LADD	GR	2	197	LAKE	GA	8	192	LAMB	H	6	251	LAMBERT	G	3	110
LADD	W	7	222	LAKE	H	6	250	LAMB	H	8	192	LAMBERT	G	3	372
LADLE	WH	8	192	LAKE	HW	4	226	LAMB	J	5	209	LAMBERT	G	7	223
LADYMAN	GE	1	199	LAKE	JC	3	372	LAMB	J	8	193	LAMBERT	G	9	115
LADYMAN	WE	7	222	LAKE	JH	1	199	LAMB	JE	13	263	LAMBERT	GA	5	210
LAFBERY	JE	2	197	LAKE	JW	13	263	LAMB	JH	13	263	LAMBERT	GH	12	139
LAFFAN	J	7	222	LAKE	LB	6	250	LAMB	JR	2	198	LAMBERT	GS	7	223
LAFFIN	J	11	217	LAKE	R	9	390	LAMB	JW	9	291	LAMBERT	H	2	198
LAFFIN	WN	7	222	LAKE	SEC	2	198	LAMB	JW	11	217	LAMBERT	H	7	223
LAGDON	GR	4	226	LAKE	TH	5	209	LAMB	L	9	115	LAMBERT	H	8	193
LAGDON	HO	1	199	LAKE	W	4	226	LAMB	MH	2	198	LAMBERT	H	8	193
LAID	WP	2	197	LAKE	W	10	132	LAMB	OF	7	223	LAMBERT	H	9	115
LAIDLAW	D	11	217	LAKE	WJ	1	199	LAMB	P	5	209	LAMBERT	H	9	115
LAIDLAW	W	8	192	LAKE	WJ	6	251	LAMB	PW	7	223	LAMBERT	HC	8	193
LAIDLER	CW	10	132	LAKE	WJ	9	115	LAMB	R	11	217	LAMBERT	HJ	2	198
LAIDLER	F	10	132	LAKELAND	J	8	192	LAMB	RW	11	217	LAMBERT	HW	2	198
LAIDLER	H	10	132	LAKEMAN	AT	4	227	LAMB	S	5	209	LAMBERT	HW	2	198
LAIGHT	RE	6	250	LAKEMAN	FJ	4	227	LAMB	S	5	209	LAMBERT	J	8	193
LAIGHT	WH	6	250	LAKER	A	2	198	LAMB	SP	12	139	LAMBERT	J	8	193
LAILEY	C	7	222	LAKER	ABW	13	263	LAMB	T	8	193	LAMBERT	J	8	193
LAIMBEER	EA	13	263	LAKER	AEC	13	263	LAMB	T	11	217	LAMBERT	J	10	325
LAIN	AF	5	209	LAKER	H	4	227	LAMB	TC	3	110	LAMBERT	JA	4	227
LAIN	GC	1	199	LAKER	L	7	222	LAMB	TJ	11	217	LAMBERT	JA	6	251
LAINCHBURY	AL	3	110	LAKER	L	13	263	LAMB	W	9	291	LAMBERT	JC	5	210
LAINCHBURY	AW	3	110	LAKER	WA	10	132	LAMB	W	11	217	LAMBERT	JE	14	187
LAING	A	14	186	LAKIN	JF	6	251	LAMB	WF	1	200	LAMBERT	JF	1	200
LAING	AC	2	197	LAKIN	S	2	198	LAMB	WF	2	198	LAMBERT	JH	8	193
LAING	EL	8	192	LAKIN	W	11	217	LAMB	WG	3	110	LAMBERT	JH	12	140
LAING	J	7	222	LAKINS	VB	6	251	LAMBDEN	WJ	10	132	LAMBERT	JW	8	193
LAING	R	10	132	LALLY	A	9	291	LAMBELL	JW	4	227	LAMBERT	JW	11	217
LAING	VR	2	197	LALLY	AR	1	199	LAMBERT	A	9	115	LAMBERT	KHW	2	198
LAING	W	3	110	LALLY	C	2	198	LAMBERT	A	13	263	LAMBERT	L	12	140
LAING	W	8	192	LALLY	J	8	192	LAMBERT	AE	1	200	LAMBERT	L	14	187
LAING	WB	8	192	LALLY	J	11	217	LAMBERT	AE	11	217	LAMBERT	MA	3	110
LAINSON	FC	4	226	LALLY	J	14	186	LAMBERT	AP	5	209	LAMBERT	PG	4	227
LAIRD	AJ	12	139	LALLY	JW	2	198	LAMBERT	AW	9	115	LAMBERT	PG	4	227
LAIRD	EG	12	139	LALLY	R	2	198	LAMBERT	AW	10	132	LAMBERT	R	8	193
LAIRD	F	12	139	LAMACRAFT	A	1	199	LAMBERT	AW	10	325	LAMBERT	R	10	133
LAIRD	FH	5	209	LAMB	A	1	199	LAMBERT	B	6	251	LAMBERT	R	11	218
LAIRD	W	1	199	LAMB	A	11	217	LAMBERT	B	8	193	LAMBERT	S	6	251
LAIT	CE	7	222	LAMB	AE	12	139	LAMBERT	B	9	115	LAMBERT	SG	13	264
LAIT	SC	2	197	LAMB	AW	5	209	LAMBERT	B	9	291	LAMBERT	T	5	210
LAITHWAITE	W	11	217	LAMB	C	5	209	LAMBERT	C	13	263	LAMBERT	T	6	251
LAKE	A	6	250	LAMB	CE	3	110	LAMBERT	C	14	186	LAMBERT	T	9	115
LAKE	A	8	192	LAMB	CF	8	192	LAMBERT	CT	10	132	LAMBERT	T	9	115
LAKE	A	8	192	LAMB	CH	6	251	LAMBERT	CT	10	132	LAMBERT	T	10	325
LAKE	AD	1	199	LAMB	D	9	291	LAMBERT	E	9	291	LAMBERT	T	14	187
LAKE	AE	5	209	LAMB	DP	12	139	LAMBERT	E	10	132	LAMBERT	TA	7	223
LAKE	C	14	186	LAMB	E	11	217	LAMBERT	EF	13	264	LAMBERT	TE	13	264
LAKE	CB	2	198	LAMB	F	5	209	LAMBERT	F	8	193	LAMBERT	TP	5	210

LAMBERT	VH	3	111	LAMPHIER	L	3	111	LANCE	M	11	218	LANE	B	6	251
LAMBERT	W	12	140	LAMPHIER	W	3	111	LANCUM	GM	7	223	LANE	BG	2	199
LAMBERT	W	12	140	LAMPING	HW	3	111	LAND	A	3	111	LANE	C	2	199
LAMBERT	W	14	187	LAMPITT	P	8	193	LAND	E	13	264	LANE	C	6	251
LAMBERT	WA	7	223	LAMPON	AER	7	223	LAND	FW	5	210	LANE	C	6	251
LAMBERT	WG	10	133	LAMPON	AR	13	264	LAND	GE	3	111	LANE	C	7	224
LAMBERT	WGR	10	133	LAMPON	HC	13	264	LAND	H	9	115	LANE	CD	5	210
LAMBERT	WH	9	291	LAMPORT	AEJ	4	227	LAND	H	10	133	LANE	CEW	1	200
LAMBERT	WJ	10	325	LAMPORT	R	8	193	LAND	HJ	7	223	LANE	CF	1	200
LAMBERT	WS	8	193	LAMPORT	WJ	5	210	LAND	J	5	210	LANE	CH	4	227
LAMBERTH	B	3	372	LANAGHAN	BB	4	227	LAND	JT	3	111	LANE	CJ	4	228
LAMBERTON	FG	3	111	LANATA	S	14	187	LAND	JT	13	264	LANE	D	1	200
LAMBETH	A	2	199	LANBISCH	H	4	227	LAND	RS	13	264	LANE	DW	3	372
LAMBETH	JH	2	199	LANCASHIRE	AE	7	223	LAND	RW	3	111	LANE	E	1	200
LAMBETH	TH	10	133	LANCASHIRE	WF	7	223	LAND	TD	13	264	LANE	E	3	111
LAMBIRD	EH	1	200	LANCASHIRE	WR	3	372	LAND	W	9	115	LANE	E	3	372
LAMBIRTH	WH	1	200	LANCASTER	A	12	140	LAND	WH	13	264	LANE	E	3	373
LAMBLE	F	12	140	LANCASTER	AW	5	210	LAND	WH	13	264	LANE	E	13	264
LAMBLEY	AP	12	339	LANCASTER	CJ	2	199	LANDALE	G	9	115	LANE	EE	4	228
LAMBLEY	EW	12	339	LANCASTER	E	7	223	LANDALE	WB	5	210	LANE	EJ	6	252
LAMBLEY	FJ	12	339	LANCASTER	E	12	140	LANDER	A	10	325	LANE	EJ	13	265
LAMBLEY	JC	12	339	LANCASTER	EW	7	223	LANDER	C	1	200	LANE	F	4	228
LAMBOURN	A	3	111	LANCASTER	F	9	115	LANDER	F	6	251	LANE	F	6	252
LAMBOURN	WJ	3	111	LANCASTER	F	9	291	LANDER	FW	7	224	LANE	F	7	224
LAMBOURNE	FWJ	1	200	LANCASTER	F	10	133	LANDER	G	6	251	LANE	FB	6	252
LAMBOURNE	G	4	227	LANCASTER	F	11	218	LANDER	GW	11	218	LANE	FJ	12	339
LAMBOURNE	GS	7	223	LANCASTER	FR	12	422	LANDER	H	3	372	LANE	FM	3	111
LAMBOURNE	H	2	199	LANCASTER	G	12	339	LANDER	JH	4	227	LANE	FW	13	265
LAMBOURNE	HW	5	210	LANCASTER	GE	11	218	LANDER	MC	7	224	LANE	G	6	252
LAMBOURNE	JE	12	140	LANCASTER	GW	2	199	LANDER	R	2	199	LANE	GP	12	140
LAMBOURNE	W	7	223	LANCASTER	H	12	140	LANDER	S	11	218	LANE	H	1	200
LAMBOURNE	W	7	223	LANCASTER	HH	10	133	LANDER	TE	7	224	LANE	H	6	252
LAMBOURNE	WT	10	133	LANCASTER	HJ	13	264	LANDER	U	11	218	LANE	HA	3	111
LAMBSDOWN	A	6	251	LANCASTER	J	5	210	LANDERS	W	1	200	LANE	HA	3	373
LAMBSDOWN	L	6	251	LANCASTER	J	11	218	LANDERYOU	FH	12	423	LANE	HCJ	7	224
LAMBURN	TH	1	200	LANCASTER	J	14	187	LANDES	H	14	187	LANE	HE	4	228
LAMERTON	HH	3	111	LANCASTER	JG	2	199	LANDIS	M	14	187	LANE	HJF	12	140
LAMERTON	WG	3	111	LANCASTER	JH	14	187	LANDON	C	1	200	LANE	HM	4	228
LAMHAM	PW	4	227	LANCASTER	JP	3	111	LANDRAGIN	J	13	264	LANE	J	1	200
LAMIN	GS	3	372	LANCASTER	N	11	218	LANDS	WG	7	224	LANE	J	2	199
LAMING	CW	3	111	LANCASTER	N	11	218	LANE	A	4	227	LANE	J	2	199
LAMING	G	13	264	LANCASTER	S	11	218	LANE	A	6	251	LANE	J	2	199
LAMING	J	13	264	LANCASTER	SA	5	210	LANE	A	7	224	LANE	J	2	199
LAMKIN	BH	4	227	LANCASTER	SA	13	264	LANE	A	7	224	LANE	J	2	199
LAMLEY	CWM	2	199	LANCASTER	T	2	199	LANE	A	7	224	LANE	J	3	111
LAMMIN	CE	1	200	LANCASTER	T	12	140	LANE	A	7	224	LANE	J	3	373
LAMMIN	JW	8	193	LANCASTER	TW	1	200	LANE	A	10	133	LANE	J	6	252
LAMMING	GH	2	199	LANCASTER	TW	13	264	LANE	A	10	133	LANE	J	7	224
LAMONT	D	13	264	LANCASTER	W	5	210	LANE	A	12	339	LANE	J	9	115
LAMPARD	AW	4	227	LANCASTER	W	8	193	LANE	AC	4	227	LANE	J	9	115
LAMPARD	C	4	227	LANCASTER	W	11	218	LANE	AC	10	325	LANE	JA	5	210
LAMPARD	HA	10	133	LANCASTER	WH	5	210	LANE	AE	6	251	LANE	JAL	6	252
LAMPARD	P	10	325	LANCASTER	WT	10	133	LANE	AE	10	325	LANE	JE	4	228
LAMPARD	T	4	227	LANCASTER	WT	10	325	LANE	AH	13	264	LANE	JH	6	252
LAMPARD	WJT	10	133	LANCE	HP	2	199	LANE	AR	1	200	LANE	JH	13	265

Name	Init	Col	Pg	Name	Init	Col	Pg	Name	Init	Col	Pg	Name	Init	Col	Pg
LANE	JJ	6	252	LANGAN	TF	9	115	LANGLEY	JR	8	194	LANGTON	M	11	219
LANE	JM	14	187	LANGCAKE	SH	12	140	LANGLEY	JT	6	253	LANGTON	R	11	219
LANE	JW	1	201	LANGDALE	C	5	210	LANGLEY	P	12	339	LANGTON	RA	11	219
LANE	JW	3	112	LANGDON	A	11	218	LANGLEY	R	1	201	LANGTON	T	14	187
LANE	JW	13	265	LANGDON	C	4	228	LANGLEY	S	13	265	LANGTON	W	2	200
LANE	L	6	252	LANGDON	H	3	112	LANGLEY	T	2	200	LANGTON	W	8	194
LANE	LA	12	140	LANGDON	ST	1	201	LANGLEY	W	1	201	LANGTON	W	10	134
LANE	LG	1	201	LANGDON	WA	2	200	LANGLEY	W	6	253	LANGTON	W	14	187
LANE	M	3	373	LANGDON	WH	1	201	LANGLEY	W	13	265	LANHAM	A	4	228
LANE	ML	6	252	LANGDOWN	FG	4	228	LANGLEY	WA	1	202	LANHAM	DW	9	116
LANE	NA	10	133	LANGER	WG	10	133	LANGLEY	WA	13	265	LANHAM	F	4	228
LANE	P	2	200	LANGER	WH	10	134	LANGLEY	WG	13	265	LANHAM	H	4	228
LANE	PC	12	140	LANGFORD	AE	2	200	LANGLEY	WJ	12	140	LANHAM	M	4	229
LANE	R	1	201	LANGFORD	AS	4	228	LANGMEAD	LTW	10	325	LANHAM	RW	10	326
LANE	R	6	252	LANGFORD	C	8	193	LANGMEAD	LW	10	326	LANIGAN	E	11	219
LANE	RA	4	228	LANGFORD	E	6	252	LANGMEAD	W	1	202	LANIGAN	J	8	194
LANE	RJ	6	252	LANGFORD	E	6	252	LANGRIDGE	AJ	1	202	LANIGAN	J	8	194
LANE	S	4	228	LANGFORD	E	6	252	LANGRIDGE	E	10	134	LANIGAN	P	11	219
LANE	S	10	133	LANGFORD	EC	7	224	LANGRIDGE	E	13	265	LANKESTER	CE	1	202
LANE	SP	10	133	LANGFORD	EM	10	134	LANGRIDGE	FJ	3	112	LANKESTER	LJ	1	202
LANE	T	1	201	LANGFORD	GE	13	265	LANGRIDGE	G	1	202	LANKESTER	RW	1	202
LANE	T	11	218	LANGFORD	GR	5	211	LANGRIDGE	GL	10	326	LANKFORD	HJ	4	229
LANE	T	14	187	LANGFORD	H	6	253	LANGRIDGE	H	7	225	LANKIN	CA	5	211
LANE	T	14	187	LANGFORD	H	10	134	LANGRIDGE	N	12	423	LANKSHEAR	T	4	229
LANE	TB	10	133	LANGFORD	HE	2	200	LANGRIDGE	TD	4	228	LANKSHEAR	W	4	229
LANE	TH	4	228	LANGFORD	HG	1	201	LANGRIDGE	W	2	200	LANLY	G	2	200
LANE	TH	4	228	LANGFORD	HL	10	325	LANGRIDGE	W	13	265	LANNING	A	10	134
LANE	TW	6	252	LANGFORD	J	1	201	LANGRIDGE	WF	10	134	LANNING	H	10	134
LANE	W	4	228	LANGFORD	T	11	218	LANGRISH	HG	5	211	LANNING	H	10	134
LANE	W	11	218	LANGFORD	T	14	187	LANGRON	J	9	115	LANNING	H	13	266
LANE	W	12	339	LANGFORD	WET	2	200	LANGRON	M	11	219	LANNING	ST	2	200
LANE	W	13	265	LANGFORD	WJ	10	134	LANGSDALE	W	10	326	LANNON	O	6	253
LANE	WA	4	228	LANGFORD	WS	1	201	LANGSDON	DT	13	265	LANSBURY	CH	12	141
LANE	WA	6	252	LANGHAM	AC	13	265	LANGSFORD	W	2	200	LANSDALE	AP	7	225
LANE	WC	13	265	LANGHAM	F	7	224	LANGSHAW	AJ	13	265	LANSDOWN	RG	7	225
LANE	WG	1	201	LANGLEY	AJ	13	265	LANGSHAW	W	11	219	LANSHUTT	M	12	141
LANE	WG	3	112	LANGLEY	C	12	140	LANGSTAFF	A	8	194	LANSLEY	A	14	187
LANE	WH	1	201	LANGLEY	CA	2	200	LANGSTAFF	C	8	194	LANSLEY	C	1	202
LANE	WH	2	199	LANGLEY	D	11	219	LANGSTAFF	W	8	194	LANSLEY	PW	10	326
LANE	WH	3	112	LANGLEY	E	1	201	LANGSTON	AE	5	211	LANSLEY	TH	1	202
LANE	WH	7	224	LANGLEY	EA	2	200	LANGSTON	AP	6	253	LANT	A	5	211
LANE	WH	10	325	LANGLEY	EJ	1	201	LANGSTON	C	5	211	LANT	J	1	202
LANE	WJ	3	112	LANGLEY	EJ	3	112	LANGSTON	E	3	373	LANT	S	1	202
LANE	WKG	1	201	LANGLEY	F	1	201	LANGSTON	F	1	202	LANTSBERY	CJ	12	339
LANE	WR	7	224	LANGLEY	FH	7	224	LANGSTON	GF	11	219	LAPHAM	R	3	112
LANE	WT	5	210	LANGLEY	FWW	12	339	LANGSTON	GW	5	211	LAPHAM	T	3	112
LANEDUKES	GR	8	193	LANGLEY	G	11	219	LANGSTON	WG	5	211	LAPIDUS	A	14	188
LANFEAR	CS	9	115	LANGLEY	H	5	211	LANGSTONE	A	2	200	LAPISH	H	8	194
LANG	D	11	218	LANGLEY	H	12	140	LANGTHORN	AG	2	200	LAPISH	W	8	416
LANG	G	9	291	LANGLEY	HJ	2	200	LANGTON	A	8	194	LAPISH	W	9	291
LANG	H	11	218	LANGLEY	HS	7	225	LANGTON	A	11	219	LAPPER	G	2	200
LANG	H	14	187	LANGLEY	J	2	200	LANGTON	F	14	187	LAPPIN	G	2	200
LANG	M	4	228	LANGLEY	J	13	265	LANGTON	H	11	219	LAPPIN	WS	14	188
LANG	WA	1	201	LANGLEY	JA	7	225	LANGTON	J	11	219	LAPPING	GH	8	194
LANGAN	H	7	224	LANGLEY	JJ	5	211	LANGTON	JW	10	326	LAPSLEY	JH	10	134

LAPTHORN	A	3	373	LARKIN	S	12	339	LASHMAR	A	10	326	LAUER	AE	7	226
LAPTHORN	G	3	373	LARKIN	T	13	266	LASSAM	E	7	225	LAUER	L	3	373
LAPTHORN	J	3	373	LARKIN	WJ	1	202	LASSLETT	CW	5	211	LAUGHLIN	RH	1	203
LAPWOOD	W	7	225	LARKIN	WW	3	112	LASSLETT	H	5	211	LAUGHTON	EL	12	141
LAPWORTH	FJ	12	339	LARKING	AG	13	266	LAST	FC	2	201	LAUGHTON	HT	3	113
LAPWORTH	FTS	12	339	LARKING	GE	13	266	LAST	FF	1	203	LAUGHTON	JF	13	266
LAPWORTH	J	14	188	LARKING	JC	13	266	LAST	H	7	225	LAUMAN	S	2	201
LAPWORTH	J	14	188	LARKING	RF	13	266	LAST	JB	7	225	LAUNDY	C	3	373
LAPWORTH	JM	6	253	LARKING	SG	1	203	LAST	L	7	225	LAUNDY	JH	13	266
LAPWORTH	OV	12	339	LARKING	WH	13	266	LAST	PJ	5	212	LAURANCE	GW	2	201
LAPWORTH	W	14	188	LARKINS	TG	5	211	LAST	VE	11	219	LAURENCE	HE	2	201
LARBALESTIER	A	4	229	LARKMAN	AC	12	339	LAST	W	7	226	LAURENCE	J	2	201
LARBALESTIER	CP	4	229	LARKMAN	F	6	253	LAST	WA	13	266	LAURENCE	PJ	2	201
LARBALESTIER	OP	4	229	LARKMAN	F	12	339	LATCHFORD	A	5	212	LAURIE	A	6	253
LARBALESTIER	W	4	229	LARKMAN	G	6	253	LATCHFORD	E	5	212	LAURIE	J	6	253
LARCOMBE	B	5	211	LARKMAN	H	1	203	LATCHFORD	H	5	212	LAVARS	FJ	4	229
LARCOMBE	CR	10	134	LARKMAN	H	12	339	LATCHFORD	HB	5	212	LAVARS	HM	4	229
LARCOMBE	HH	2	200	LARKMAN	WA	12	339	LATCHFORD	RH	5	212	LAVARS	R	4	229
LARCOMBE	J	1	202	LARKWORTHY	FCG	3	112	LATCHFORD	W	13	266	LAVARS	VAE	4	229
LARD	H	12	141	LARMAN	AL	1	203	LATCHFORD	WA	7	226	LAVARS	WH	4	229
LARDNER	R	6	253	LARMAN	E	3	112	LATER	GN	11	219	LAVELLE	F	14	188
LARENCE	ER	2	201	LARMAN	E	5	211	LATER	S	11	220	LAVEN	I	2	201
LARGE	A	3	112	LARMAN	FG	2	201	LATHALL	JE	12	141	LAVEN	JJ	2	201
LARGE	A	5	211	LARMAN	WH	3	112	LATHAM	A	11	220	LAVENDER	CS	13	266
LARGE	AE	1	202	LARNDER	EC	7	225	LATHAM	A	14	188	LAVENDER	D	10	134
LARGE	E	8	194	LARNER	AJ	12	141	LATHAM	J	10	134	LAVENDER	E	5	212
LARGE	F	1	202	LARNER	F	3	113	LATHAM	J	11	220	LAVENDER	H	13	266
LARGE	FR	5	211	LARNER	G	8	194	LATHAM	JF	6	253	LAVENDER	LA	13	267
LARGE	G	2	201	LARNER	G	8	194	LATHAM	SC	6	253	LAVENDER	SA	13	267
LARGE	H	6	253	LARNER	G	11	219	LATHAM	SH	11	220	LAVENDER	TWC	12	141
LARGE	J	1	202	LARNER	GW	3	113	LATHAM	W	2	201	LAVENDER	W	1	203
LARGE	J	5	211	LARNER	H	3	113	LATHAM	W	3	113	LAVENDER	WHD	12	141
LARGE	J	8	194	LARNER	J	9	291	LATHERON	R	5	212	LAVER	FW	7	226
LARGE	M	2	201	LARNER	R	3	113	LATHOM	FWF	5	212	LAVER	W	10	134
LARGE	WA	2	201	LARNER	S	12	141	LATHWELL	AT	5	212	LAVERACK	A	9	390
LARGE	WF	14	188	LARNER	W	8	194	LATHWELL	AT	5	212	LAVERACK	FH	14	188
LARGE	WW	6	253	LARNER	WG	3	113	LATHWELL	F	5	212	LAVERICK	H	8	194
LARIGO	E	6	253	LAROCHE	AJ	14	188	LATHWELL	G	5	212	LAVERY	A	11	220
LARIGO	S	6	253	LAROUCHE	JH	3	113	LATHWELL	H	7	226	LAVERY	J	9	292
LARINGTON	FTG	2	201	LARRAD	T	11	219	LATHWOOD	TA	11	220	LAVERY	T	9	292
LARKE	AA	1	202	LARRETT	AW	1	203	LATIF	A	3	113	LAVEY	FT	1	203
LARKIN	C	3	112	LARTER	A	7	225	LATIMER	GE	2	201	LAVILL	T	6	254
LARKIN	DP	13	266	LARTER	AE	7	225	LATIMER	TW	13	266	LAVIN	E	9	116
LARKIN	E	3	112	LARTER	AW	7	225	LATTER	CH	13	266	LAVIN	F	14	188
LARKIN	F	3	112	LARTER	HG	7	225	LATTER	EA	13	266	LAVINGTON	ETH	10	134
LARKIN	FE	1	202	LARTER	WC	7	225	LATTER	ET	7	226	LAVINGTON	T	10	134
LARKIN	FG	3	112	LARVAN	M	8	194	LATTER	FW	2	201	LAVY	T	6	254
LARKIN	G	3	112	LARVIN	GE	9	116	LATTER	G	3	113	LAW	A	12	340
LARKIN	GF	1	202	LARVIN	T	9	116	LATTER	GHJ	14	188	LAW	A	12	340
LARKIN	HA	3	373	LARVIN	WF	6	253	LATTER	RS	3	113	LAW	A	12	340
LARKIN	J	9	291	LASCAR	H	10	134	LATTER	WT	13	266	LAW	AV	12	141
LARKIN	J	11	219	LASHAM	F	7	225	LATTO	A	8	194	LAW	C	3	113
LARKIN	M	9	116	LASHAM	S	13	266	LAUD	W	5	212	LAW	C	6	254
LARKIN	P	14	188	LASHBROOK	AJ	2	201	LAUD	W	5	212	LAW	C	7	226
LARKIN	R	6	253	LASHBROOK	EA	1	203	LAUER	AC	7	226	LAW	E	12	340

LAW	EA	4	229	LAWFORD	WJ	1	203	LAWRENCE	AW	5	213	LAWRENCE	GR	10	135
LAW	EP	13	267	LAWFORD	WT	3	373	LAWRENCE	B	4	230	LAWRENCE	GS	10	135
LAW	ER	9	292	LAWLAR	TA	3	113	LAWRENCE	B	10	135	LAWRENCE	GSV	2	202
LAW	ES	2	201	LAWLER	AJ	4	229	LAWRENCE	C	1	203	LAWRENCE	GT	1	203
LAW	ES	6	254	LAWLER	F	6	254	LAWRENCE	C	5	213	LAWRENCE	GW	7	226
LAW	F	8	195	LAWLER	J	11	220	LAWRENCE	C	13	267	LAWRENCE	GW	10	135
LAW	F	9	116	LAWLER	J	14	188	LAWRENCE	C	13	267	LAWRENCE	H	2	202
LAW	F	12	340	LAWLER	J	14	188	LAWRENCE	CE	3	113	LAWRENCE	H	4	230
LAW	H	6	254	LAWLER	JA	4	229	LAWRENCE	CH	2	202	LAWRENCE	H	4	230
LAW	H	9	116	LAWLER	T	2	202	LAWRENCE	CJ	2	202	LAWRENCE	H	5	213
LAW	H	9	292	LAWLER	T	3	113	LAWRENCE	E	2	202	LAWRENCE	H	6	255
LAW	H	14	188	LAWLER	T	11	220	LAWRENCE	E	5	213	LAWRENCE	H	8	195
LAW	H	14	188	LAWLER	TF	1	203	LAWRENCE	E	9	292	LAWRENCE	H	13	267
LAW	HW	12	340	LAWLER	TF	6	254	LAWRENCE	E	13	267	LAWRENCE	H	13	267
LAW	J	6	254	LAWLER	WJG	10	135	LAWRENCE	EA	10	326	LAWRENCE	HC	12	340
LAW	J	9	116	LAWLESS	F	7	226	LAWRENCE	EC	12	141	LAWRENCE	HF	7	226
LAW	J	9	292	LAWLESS	J	2	202	LAWRENCE	EE	3	114	LAWRENCE	HJ	13	267
LAW	J	11	220	LAWLEY	B	6	254	LAWRENCE	EE	6	254	LAWRENCE	HS	12	141
LAW	J	11	220	LAWLEY	H	9	116	LAWRENCE	EF	5	213	LAWRENCE	HW	5	214
LAW	J	12	141	LAWLEY	VW	11	220	LAWRENCE	EG	4	230	LAWRENCE	J	1	203
LAW	J	13	267	LAWLEY	W	6	254	LAWRENCE	EG	5	213	LAWRENCE	J	1	204
LAW	JJ	12	141	LAWLOR	J	3	113	LAWRENCE	EH	4	230	LAWRENCE	J	3	114
LAW	JT	8	195	LAWLOR	T	2	202	LAWRENCE	EH	4	230	LAWRENCE	J	3	114
LAW	LM	12	141	LAWLOR	T	11	220	LAWRENCE	EJM	9	116	LAWRENCE	J	5	214
LAW	M	10	134	LAWMAN	JT	9	116	LAWRENCE	EL	13	267	LAWRENCE	J	5	214
LAW	R	6	254	LAWMAN	JZW	5	212	LAWRENCE	ER	2	202	LAWRENCE	J	5	214
LAW	R	9	116	LAWMAN	RRJ	8	195	LAWRENCE	F	4	230	LAWRENCE	J	9	116
LAW	RJ	7	226	LAWMAN	S	14	189	LAWRENCE	F	7	226	LAWRENCE	J	9	116
LAW	S	3	113	LAWMAN	WG	5	212	LAWRENCE	F	9	116	LAWRENCE	J	12	340
LAW	SW	6	254	LAWRANCE	A	4	229	LAWRENCE	F	12	340	LAWRENCE	J	13	267
LAW	T	6	254	LAWRANCE	AG	1	203	LAWRENCE	F	13	267	LAWRENCE	JA	4	230
LAW	T	11	220	LAWRANCE	HW	1	203	LAWRENCE	FC	5	213	LAWRENCE	JD	1	204
LAW	W	9	292	LAWRANCE	JM	1	203	LAWRENCE	FG	2	202	LAWRENCE	JE	4	230
LAW	WC	9	116	LAWRANCE	P	9	116	LAWRENCE	FG	12	340	LAWRENCE	JE	13	267
LAW	WH	6	254	LAWRANCE	W	1	203	LAWRENCE	FJ	5	213	LAWRENCE	JG	2	202
LAW	WH	9	116	LAWRENCE	A	2	202	LAWRENCE	FJ	5	213	LAWRENCE	JS	5	214
LAW	WH	14	188	LAWRENCE	A	3	113	LAWRENCE	FJ	12	141	LAWRENCE	JS	12	340
LAW	WJ	12	340	LAWRENCE	A	5	213	LAWRENCE	FJP	5	213	LAWRENCE	JT	6	255
LAW	WT	14	188	LAWRENCE	A	5	213	LAWRENCE	FR	6	254	LAWRENCE	JW	9	292
LAWDAY	AWR	2	201	LAWRENCE	A	6	254	LAWRENCE	FW	7	226	LAWRENCE	JW	13	267
LAWDEN	J	6	254	LAWRENCE	A	10	135	LAWRENCE	G	4	230	LAWRENCE	L	3	373
LAWES	C	8	195	LAWRENCE	A	12	340	LAWRENCE	G	4	230	LAWRENCE	L	6	255
LAWES	D	8	195	LAWRENCE	A	12	340	LAWRENCE	G	5	213	LAWRENCE	L	6	255
LAWES	EE	2	202	LAWRENCE	A	13	267	LAWRENCE	G	5	213	LAWRENCE	L	9	116
LAWES	F	10	134	LAWRENCE	AC	5	213	LAWRENCE	G	8	195	LAWRENCE	M	4	230
LAWES	HJ	10	326	LAWRENCE	AE	3	373	LAWRENCE	G	8	195	LAWRENCE	M	13	267
LAWES	HL	10	135	LAWRENCE	AE	5	213	LAWRENCE	G	12	340	LAWRENCE	MA	2	203
LAWES	LA	4	229	LAWRENCE	AE	12	340	LAWRENCE	GC	12	340	LAWRENCE	MM	4	230
LAWES	PRG	10	135	LAWRENCE	AF	1	203	LAWRENCE	GE	13	267	LAWRENCE	P	3	373
LAWES	S	12	141	LAWRENCE	AG	2	202	LAWRENCE	GEC	3	114	LAWRENCE	R	2	203
LAWES	T	10	135	LAWRENCE	AG	4	229	LAWRENCE	GH	2	202	LAWRENCE	R	7	226
LAWES	VJ	2	202	LAWRENCE	AH	2	202	LAWRENCE	GH	4	230	LAWRENCE	R	8	195
LAWFORD	EH	13	267	LAWRENCE	AH	12	340	LAWRENCE	GH	12	340	LAWRENCE	RC	7	226
LAWFORD	J	9	292	LAWRENCE	AP	5	213	LAWRENCE	GJ	2	202	LAWRENCE	RH	5	214
LAWFORD	RH	1	203	LAWRENCE	AW	3	113	LAWRENCE	GJ	5	213	LAWRENCE	RJ	1	204

LAWRENCE	S	3	114	LAWSON	HW	5	214	LAWTON	W	2	203	LAYTON	H	6	255
LAWRENCE	S	6	255	LAWSON	J	5	215	LAWTON	W	8	196	LAYTON	H	9	117
LAWRENCE	S	7	226	LAWSON	J	8	195	LAWTON	W	11	221	LAYTON	J	3	114
LAWRENCE	S	8	195	LAWSON	J	8	195	LAWTON	WH	8	196	LAYTON	J	6	255
LAWRENCE	SA	3	114	LAWSON	J	8	195	LAXTON	AG	9	292	LAYTON	JH	10	135
LAWRENCE	SJ	2	203	LAWSON	J	8	195	LAXTON	CA	2	203	LAYTON	SW	3	114
LAWRENCE	T	14	189	LAWSON	J	11	220	LAXTON	FT	11	221	LAYTON	T	14	189
LAWRENCE	THG	1	204	LAWSON	J	14	189	LAXTON	JT	2	203	LAYTON	WJ	1	204
LAWRENCE	TJ	2	203	LAWSON	JE	8	195	LAXTON	RE	13	268	LAZAROVITCH	PG	14	189
LAWRENCE	TJ	5	214	LAWSON	JT	9	292	LAY	AF	2	203	LAZARUS	M	9	292
LAWRENCE	TS	3	373	LAWSON	JW	8	195	LAY	AH	7	227	LAZARUS	R	1	204
LAWRENCE	VA	5	214	LAWSON	JW	9	292	LAY	C	3	114	LAZARUS	S	14	189
LAWRENCE	W	5	214	LAWSON	L	14	189	LAY	E	6	255	LAZELL	WE	1	204
LAWRENCE	W	5	214	LAWSON	RG	12	340	LAY	F	2	203	LAZENBY	FT	7	227
LAWRENCE	W	5	214	LAWSON	S	14	189	LAY	FW	1	204	LAZENBY	GW	8	196
LAWRENCE	W	6	255	LAWSON	T	5	215	LAY	H	2	203	LAZENBY	H	3	114
LAWRENCE	W	8	195	LAWSON	W	1	204	LAY	JE	13	268	LAZENBY	H	9	117
LAWRENCE	W	13	268	LAWSON	W	3	373	LAY	W	3	114	LAZENBY	L	9	117
LAWRENCE	WA	13	267	LAWSON	W	5	215	LAY	WG	13	268	LAZENBY	T	9	117
LAWRENCE	WC	13	268	LAWSON	W	8	195	LAY	WH	7	227	LE BOUTILLIER	A	4	231
LAWRENCE	WG	6	255	LAWSON	W	8	195	LAY	WJ	2	203	LE BOUTILLIER	J	4	231
LAWRENCE	WG	13	268	LAWSON	W	9	292	LAY	WM	4	230	LE DUC	GW	3	115
LAWRENCE	WH	1	204	LAWSON	W	11	220	LAYBURN	W	9	292	LE FEVRE	G	1	206
LAWRENCE	WH	13	268	LAWSON	W	11	220	LAYCOCK	A	8	196	LE FEVRE	THW	1	206
LAWRENCE	WH	13	268	LAWSON	W	12	142	LAYCOCK	A	8	196	LE GRAND	JC	4	233
LAWRENCE	WJ	1	204	LAWSON	W	13	268	LAYCOCK	A	8	196	LE MAR	EW	1	207
LAWRENCE	WJ	1	204	LAWSON	WA	12	142	LAYCOCK	A	9	117	LE MARECHALL	W	4	233
LAWRENCE	WJ	4	230	LAWSON	WC	5	215	LAYCOCK	A	9	117	LE MARIE	JW	1	207
LAWRENCE	WM	2	203	LAWSON	WJ	4	230	LAYCOCK	A	9	117	LE MONNIER	EF	10	327
LAWRENCE	WWS	2	203	LAWSON	WJ	12	142	LAYCOCK	B	9	117	LE PAGE	JH	4	233
LAWRENSON	J	10	326	LAWTHER	PH	4	230	LAYCOCK	E	9	117	LE POIDEVIN	AA	4	233
LAWS	AH	10	135	LAWTON	AE	12	423	LAYCOCK	F	8	196	LE QUESNE	A	4	233
LAWS	CE	3	114	LAWTON	C	2	203	LAYCOCK	H	9	117	LE QUESNE	AP	4	233
LAWS	GA	3	373	LAWTON	C	6	255	LAYCOCK	H	9	117	LE RENDU	WA	4	233
LAWS	JJ	1	204	LAWTON	D	9	292	LAYCOCK	H	9	292	LE SAUTEUR	WP	10	327
LAWSON	AH	6	255	LAWTON	E	11	221	LAYCOCK	H	13	268	LE SCELLEUR	P	4	233
LAWSON	AR	5	214	LAWTON	E	14	189	LAYCOCK	J	9	117	LE SEELLEUR	GT	4	233
LAWSON	AW	5	214	LAWTON	F	9	292	LAYCOCK	JE	8	196	LE SUEUR	AH	4	234
LAWSON	AW	5	214	LAWTON	F	14	189	LAYCOCK	LS	1	204	LE SUEUR	HW	4	234
LAWSON	B	11	220	LAWTON	FW	8	196	LAYCOCK	S	8	196	LE VAILLANT	E	13	272
LAWSON	CP	3	373	LAWTON	FW	9	117	LAYCOCK	S	9	117	LE-BLOND	JA	3	374
LAWSON	E	12	141	LAWTON	G	6	255	LAYCOCK	TE	9	117	LE-GOOD	FJ	1	207
LAWSON	E	12	142	LAWTON	GH	6	255	LAYCOCK	WL	1	204	LE-GOOD	H	1	207
LAWSON	E	14	189	LAWTON	H	8	196	LAYCOCK	WL	7	227	LE-GOOD	H	1	207
LAWSON	EC	1	204	LAWTON	H	8	416	LAYEN	T	7	227	LE-GOOD	WA	1	207
LAWSON	F	9	116	LAWTON	H	12	423	LAYFIELD	CT	7	227	LE-POIDEVIN	T	3	116
LAWSON	F	11	220	LAWTON	J	5	215	LAYFIELD	F	5	215	LE-VAN	HA	2	206
LAWSON	F	13	268	LAWTON	J	9	292	LAYLAND	C	6	255	LEA	AH	12	341
LAWSON	FC	4	230	LAWTON	J	14	189	LAYLE	SF	7	227	LEA	AHE	6	255
LAWSON	FE	12	142	LAWTON	JG	6	255	LAYTON	CF	3	114	LEA	AT	3	114
LAWSON	G	8	195	LAWTON	JH	11	221	LAYTON	E	3	114	LEA	FB	6	256
LAWSON	G	12	142	LAWTON	JW	11	221	LAYTON	EJ	1	204	LEA	FK	12	423
LAWSON	GA	8	195	LAWTON	M	14	189	LAYTON	F	4	230	LEA	FT	12	423
LAWSON	HC	12	142	LAWTON	S	14	189	LAYTON	F	6	255	LEA	GA	12	341
LAWSON	HS	5	214	LAWTON	T	11	221	LAYTON	F	8	196	LEA	H	9	292

LEA	H	9	293	LEACH	P	3	374	LEAHEY	J	7	227	LEATHERDALE	LE	4	231
LEA	H	14	189	LEACH	S	5	215	LEAHEY	JJ	7	227	LEATHERDALE	O	1	205
LEA	JH	8	196	LEACH	S	9	390	LEAHY	FT	4	231	LEATHERLAND	HW	12	341
LEA	JH	14	189	LEACH	SAT	10	135	LEAHY	H	9	293	LEATHERLAND	J	12	341
LEA	JJ	3	374	LEACH	SH	5	215	LEAHY	JWJ	10	135	LEATHERLAND	W	12	341
LEA	PW	14	189	LEACH	T	14	190	LEAHY	PJ	10	135	LEATHLEY	DR	8	196
LEA	SW	12	341	LEACH	TJ	13	268	LEAHY	T	4	231	LEATHWHITE	GH	11	222
LEA	T	9	117	LEACH	W	3	374	LEAHY	T	4	231	LEATON	W	12	341
LEA	TE	9	293	LEACH	W	14	190	LEAHY	T	7	227	LEATT	B	1	205
LEA	TJ	4	232	LEACH	WG	10	135	LEAK	W	8	196	LEAVER	AWP	3	374
LEA	TRH	1	204	LEACH	WH	12	341	LEAKE	FW	7	227	LEAVER	B	14	190
LEA	W	5	215	LEACH	WJ	3	114	LEAKE	RO	7	228	LEAVER	CW	5	216
LEA	W	14	189	LEACH	WJ	4	231	LEAKEY	J	3	115	LEAVER	E	10	326
LEA	WG	7	227	LEACH	WM	12	423	LEAL	LR	7	228	LEAVER	EJ	7	228
LEA	WM	3	114	LEACH	WR	3	374	LEAMAN	CJ	1	205	LEAVER	H	6	256
LEACH	A	7	227	LEACH	WT	4	231	LEAMON	WH	4	231	LEAVER	J	1	205
LEACH	AA	7	227	LEADBEATER	E	11	221	LEAN	J	10	326	LEAVER	J	6	256
LEACH	AC	6	256	LEADBEATER	H	11	221	LEAN	JC	10	326	LEAVER	JF	2	203
LEACH	AC	12	423	LEADBEATER	HC	10	135	LEAN	WH	8	416	LEAVET	CE	2	203
LEACH	AE	6	256	LEADBEATER	R	3	374	LEANY	WG	5	215	LEAVEY	GC	4	231
LEACH	AE	11	221	LEADBEATER	W	11	221	LEAPER	A	5	216	LEAVEY	HW	4	231
LEACH	AG	1	204	LEADBEATTER	JV	7	227	LEAPER	R	5	216	LEBBY	A	7	228
LEACH	AG	4	231	LEADBEATTER	WH	3	374	LEAR	AE	2	203	LEBEAU	J	2	203
LEACH	AJ	1	205	LEADBEATTER	WH	7	227	LEAR	F	7	228	LEBOURNE	WJ	4	231
LEACH	AT	7	227	LEADBEATTER	WT	3	115	LEAR	R	7	228	LECKENBY	H	8	196
LEACH	C	14	189	LEADBETTER	AR	14	190	LEAR	T	6	256	LECLERCQ	PJ	10	136
LEACH	CA	3	114	LEADBETTER	AW	1	205	LEAR	T	7	228	LEDAMUN	SE	3	115
LEACH	CW	10	135	LEADBETTER	HJ	1	205	LEAR	T	7	228	LEDBROOK	WR	6	256
LEACH	E	9	117	LEADBETTER	HJ	6	256	LEAR	W	7	228	LEDDER	E	9	118
LEACH	E	9	293	LEADBETTER	J	6	256	LEAR	W	7	228	LEDDER	F	9	118
LEACH	E	11	221	LEADBETTER	JR	1	205	LEARDDODD	JW	14	190	LEDDER	J	9	118
LEACH	E	14	190	LEADBETTER	L	14	190	LEARH	HL	8	196	LEDDRA	G	10	136
LEACH	E	14	190	LEADBETTER	T	6	256	LEARMAN	W	8	196	LEDDRA	H	10	136
LEACH	EE	10	135	LEADBETTER	TA	6	256	LEARMOUTH	CG	10	135	LEDDRA	J	10	136
LEACH	EJ	1	205	LEADBETTER	TM	6	256	LEAROYD	AF	2	203	LEDGARD	H	9	390
LEACH	FA	5	215	LEADBITTER	J	4	231	LEARY	BJP	13	268	LEDGARD	H	14	190
LEACH	FA	5	215	LEADEN	J	12	142	LEARY	C	6	256	LEDGARD	J	9	118
LEACH	FF	12	423	LEADER	A	1	205	LEARY	CE	1	205	LEDGER	E	8	197
LEACH	G	1	205	LEADER	BV	3	374	LEARY	D	9	293	LEDGER	F	3	115
LEACH	G	9	293	LEADER	F	5	215	LEARY	D	10	136	LEDGER	G	2	204
LEACH	H	4	231	LEADER	L	3	374	LEARY	GW	10	326	LEDGER	JA	8	197
LEACH	H	11	221	LEADER	LA	5	215	LEARY	H	1	205	LEDGER	M	8	197
LEACH	HP	10	326	LEADER	ME	3	374	LEARY	J	9	118	LEDGER	P	7	228
LEACH	HW	1	205	LEADER	P	1	205	LEARY	JW	1	205	LEDGER	TJ	2	204
LEACH	J	5	215	LEADER	R	5	215	LEARY	W	1	205	LEDGERWOOD	FT	7	228
LEACH	J	9	117	LEADS	G	1	205	LEAT	FC	10	136	LEDGERWOOD	JH	7	228
LEACH	J	9	118	LEADSFORD	H	8	196	LEATHER	A	11	221	LEDIARD	P	6	256
LEACH	JA	3	114	LEADSFORD	T	8	196	LEATHERBARROW	J	3	115	LEDINGHAM	CS	3	374
LEACH	JD	4	231	LEADSOM	TS	11	221	LEATHERBARROW	JW	11	221	LEDINGHAM	HH	3	374
LEACH	JE	10	135	LEAF	GH	8	196	LEATHERBARROW	TE	14	190	LEDLARD	W	2	204
LEACH	JE	11	221	LEAH	G	11	221	LEATHERBARROW	TH	14	190	LEDWICH	B	13	268
LEACH	JF	13	268	LEAH	GE	9	118	LEATHERBARROW	W	11	222	LEE	A	2	204
LEACH	JR	10	135	LEAH	HJ	2	203	LEATHERDALE	AH	4	231	LEE	A	4	231
LEACH	JR	13	268	LEAH	J	11	221	LEATHERDALE	H	1	205	LEE	A	7	228
LEACH	JW	7	227	LEAHEY	EW	2	203	LEATHERDALE	H	3	115	LEE	A	8	197

LEE	A	8	197	LEE	F	8	197	LEE	J	8	197	LEE	SA	7	229
LEE	A	9	118	LEE	F	9	118	LEE	J	9	118	LEE	SE	8	197
LEE	A	9	118	LEE	F	9	118	LEE	J	9	293	LEE	SH	10	326
LEE	A	9	118	LEE	F	10	136	LEE	J	9	293	LEE	SJA	1	206
LEE	A	10	136	LEE	F	12	341	LEE	J	9	293	LEE	SW	1	206
LEE	A	11	222	LEE	F	13	269	LEE	J	11	222	LEE	T	6	257
LEE	A	13	268	LEE	FC	5	216	LEE	J	11	222	LEE	T	8	197
LEE	AA	7	228	LEE	FG	4	232	LEE	J	11	222	LEE	T	8	197
LEE	AC	14	190	LEE	FJ	10	136	LEE	J	11	222	LEE	T	9	119
LEE	AE	4	231	LEE	FJ	12	142	LEE	J	12	142	LEE	T	10	136
LEE	AE	4	232	LEE	FJ	12	341	LEE	J	13	269	LEE	T	11	222
LEE	AE	4	232	LEE	FR	2	204	LEE	J	14	190	LEE	T	14	191
LEE	AE	6	256	LEE	FT	7	229	LEE	JA	13	269	LEE	TF	13	269
LEE	AF	7	228	LEE	FW	1	206	LEE	JA	14	190	LEE	TG	11	223
LEE	AJ	13	268	LEE	FW	4	232	LEE	JB	6	257	LEE	TH	11	222
LEE	AL	2	204	LEE	FWR	3	115	LEE	JC	13	269	LEE	TT	2	204
LEE	AT	5	216	LEE	G	1	206	LEE	JG	13	269	LEE	TW	9	293
LEE	AW	1	206	LEE	G	7	229	LEE	JH	9	293	LEE	TW	12	341
LEE	AW	5	216	LEE	G	9	293	LEE	JM	6	257	LEE	W	2	204
LEE	AW	7	228	LEE	G	12	341	LEE	JW	8	197	LEE	W	2	204
LEE	B	2	204	LEE	G	13	269	LEE	JW	13	269	LEE	W	3	115
LEE	B	11	222	LEE	GA	8	197	LEE	K	2	204	LEE	W	4	232
LEE	BA	7	229	LEE	GA	8	197	LEE	L	4	232	LEE	W	5	216
LEE	BC	13	268	LEE	GH	4	232	LEE	L	8	197	LEE	W	6	257
LEE	BJ	1	206	LEE	GH	7	229	LEE	L	8	197	LEE	W	8	198
LEE	C	3	115	LEE	GW	13	269	LEE	LC	7	229	LEE	W	8	198
LEE	C	3	374	LEE	H	1	206	LEE	LG	6	257	LEE	W	8	198
LEE	C	14	190	LEE	H	6	256	LEE	M	8	197	LEE	W	8	198
LEE	CE	5	216	LEE	H	7	229	LEE	N	6	257	LEE	W	8	198
LEE	CE	9	293	LEE	H	8	197	LEE	P	1	206	LEE	W	9	119
LEE	CH	1	206	LEE	H	8	197	LEE	P	13	269	LEE	W	9	119
LEE	CH	7	229	LEE	H	8	197	LEE	P	14	190	LEE	W	9	119
LEE	CJ	8	197	LEE	H	8	197	LEE	PE	13	269	LEE	W	9	293
LEE	CW	6	256	LEE	H	9	118	LEE	PH	13	269	LEE	W	10	136
LEE	CW	8	197	LEE	H	9	118	LEE	PO	2	204	LEE	W	11	222
LEE	CW	14	190	LEE	H	9	118	LEE	PS	7	229	LEE	W	11	223
LEE	D	9	390	LEE	H	9	118	LEE	R	1	206	LEE	W	11	223
LEE	D	13	269	LEE	H	11	222	LEE	R	3	115	LEE	W	11	223
LEE	E	6	256	LEE	H	11	222	LEE	R	14	191	LEE	W	11	223
LEE	E	6	256	LEE	H	11	222	LEE	R	14	191	LEE	W	12	341
LEE	E	8	197	LEE	H	11	222	LEE	RB	13	269	LEE	W	14	191
LEE	E	9	118	LEE	HC	2	204	LEE	RC	6	257	LEE	W	14	191
LEE	E	9	118	LEE	HE	5	216	LEE	RG	13	269	LEE	W	14	191
LEE	E	11	222	LEE	HG	10	136	LEE	RR	7	229	LEE	W	14	191
LEE	E	11	222	LEE	HH	7	229	LEE	RW	3	374	LEE	WE	2	204
LEE	E	13	268	LEE	HH	14	190	LEE	RW	5	216	LEE	WE	4	232
LEE	EE	1	206	LEE	HJ	2	204	LEE	S	6	257	LEE	WH	5	216
LEE	EH	13	269	LEE	HL	9	118	LEE	S	6	257	LEE	WH	5	216
LEE	EJ	4	232	LEE	HS	6	257	LEE	S	6	257	LEE	WH	6	257
LEE	EJ	13	269	LEE	HT	12	142	LEE	S	9	119	LEE	WJ	4	232
LEE	ER	3	115	LEE	HT	14	190	LEE	S	9	390	LEE	WJ	4	232
LEE	ET	13	269	LEE	HW	10	326	LEE	S	10	136	LEE	WJ	5	216
LEE	F	2	204	LEE	J	4	232	LEE	S	11	222	LEE	WJ	12	341
LEE	F	3	115	LEE	J	5	216	LEE	S	11	222	LEE	WJ	13	269
LEE	F	3	374	LEE	J	6	257	LEE	SA	5	216	LEE	WJ	13	270

LEE	WJ	14	191	LEEMING	J	9	293	LEGG	DR	10	136	LEIGH	T	8	198
LEE	WN	3	115	LEEMING	JM	9	293	LEGG	FC	3	115	LEIGH	T	11	224
LEE	WR	4	232	LEEMING	L	9	293	LEGG	GHR	4	232	LEIGH	TB	11	224
LEE	WR	6	257	LEEMING	M	9	293	LEGG	HAV	4	232	LEIGH	W	2	205
LEE	WS	11	223	LEEMING	R	11	223	LEGG	HG	4	232	LEIGH	WR	14	192
LEE	WT	2	204	LEEMING	RE	11	223	LEGG	JE	9	119	LEIGHS	J	1	207
LEE	WTS	6	257	LEEMING	RH	8	198	LEGG	LJ	3	116	LEIGHTON	AF	4	233
LEEBETTER	J	14	191	LEEMING	W	9	293	LEGG	W	2	205	LEIGHTON	AJ	1	207
LEEBODY	T	14	191	LEEMING	WH	9	119	LEGGATT	AJ	13	270	LEIGHTON	B	10	327
LEECH	AJ	3	115	LEEPER	TE	2	205	LEGGATT	FJ	13	270	LEIGHTON	F	12	341
LEECH	D	11	223	LEES	A	8	198	LEGGATT	RG	2	205	LEIGHTON	G	3	375
LEECH	E	2	204	LEES	A	8	198	LEGGATT	RG	10	136	LEIGHTON	H	8	198
LEECH	EF	1	206	LEES	AE	2	205	LEGGATT	WJ	13	270	LEIGHTON	HW	7	229
LEECH	FA	3	115	LEES	AT	13	270	LEGGE	AJ	7	229	LEIGHTON	R	6	258
LEECH	FW	11	223	LEES	C	5	217	LEGGE	E	6	258	LEIGHTON	S	11	224
LEECH	G	14	191	LEES	CF	6	258	LEGGE	E	10	137	LEIGHTON	SJ	6	258
LEECH	J	6	257	LEES	D	11	223	LEGGE	E	10	326	LEIPNIK	EM	2	205
LEECH	J	6	257	LEES	F	9	119	LEGGE	WG	4	232	LEISHMAN	G	11	224
LEECH	J	11	223	LEES	F	9	119	LEGGETT	AG	4	232	LEITH	FC	1	207
LEECH	J	14	191	LEES	F	11	223	LEGGETT	B	4	233	LEMAINE	E	8	198
LEECH	JE	6	257	LEES	F	11	224	LEGGETT	CW	5	217	LEMAIRE	S	14	192
LEECH	JF	11	223	LEES	GE	6	258	LEGGETT	CW	13	270	LEMAUX	IF	10	137
LEECH	K	13	270	LEES	GT	6	258	LEGGETT	EH	2	205	LEMING	J	9	119
LEECH	P	13	270	LEES	HE	7	229	LEGGETT	FR	4	233	LEMMON	CV	13	271
LEECH	S	8	198	LEES	HJ	10	136	LEGGETT	FW	3	374	LEMMON	ET	13	271
LEECH	SL	10	326	LEES	HT	6	258	LEGGETT	G	5	217	LEMMON	WJ	10	137
LEECH	T	2	205	LEES	J	14	191	LEGGETT	G	10	137	LEMON	CE	7	230
LEECH	W	11	223	LEES	J	14	191	LEGGETT	GH	2	205	LEMON	E	2	205
LEECH	W	14	191	LEES	JE	11	224	LEGGETT	GW	1	207	LEMON	FJ	4	233
LEECH	WF	2	205	LEES	R	11	223	LEGGETT	M	5	217	LEMON	FR	3	375
LEECH	WH	3	115	LEES	S	11	224	LEGGETT	NR	2	205	LEMON	GM	7	230
LEEDER	AG	1	206	LEES	S	14	191	LEGGETT	P	5	217	LEMON	H	10	137
LEEDER	AH	1	206	LEES	T	10	136	LEGGETT	R	2	205	LEMON	HJ	3	375
LEEDER	H	1	206	LEES	T	11	224	LEGGETT	W	10	137	LEMON	HJ	3	375
LEEDER	LW	2	205	LEES	WE	6	258	LEGGETTER	ET	1	207	LEMON	S	12	341
LEEDHAM	WC	7	229	LEES	WJ	6	258	LEGON	A	13	270	LEMON	W	3	375
LEEDON	WH	12	341	LEESON	A	14	191	LEGON	L	13	270	LEMON	WG	13	271
LEEDS	A	1	206	LEESON	F	14	191	LEGON	S	13	270	LENARD	F	9	293
LEEDS	FJ	5	216	LEESON	G	14	192	LEGRICE	R	3	375	LENARD	G	9	293
LEEDS	GW	5	216	LEESON	H	7	229	LEHANE	M	12	142	LENARD	WT	4	233
LEEFE	CF	5	216	LEESON	J	13	270	LEHEMP	M	2	205	LENDON	JC	4	233
LEEFE	RA	5	217	LEESON	MG	12	341	LEHRLE	A	12	142	LENEY	EP	7	230
LEEK	AT	7	229	LEETE	ET	7	229	LEIB	HF	10	137	LENEY	HB	7	230
LEEK	D	13	270	LEETE	JC	2	205	LEIGH	CF	4	233	LENEY	JE	2	205
LEEK	DE	13	270	LEETE	M	13	270	LEIGH	E	11	224	LENG	JR	8	198
LEEK	H	6	258	LEEVES	AR	10	136	LEIGH	EH	3	375	LENGDEN	HJ	11	224
LEEK	JR	10	136	LEEVES	EH	13	270	LEIGH	H	14	192	LENIHAN	AG	1	207
LEEK	W	13	270	LEEVES	L	3	115	LEIGH	J	14	192	LENIHAN	H	2	206
LEEK	WA	6	258	LEEVES	MM	3	115	LEIGH	J	14	192	LENNARD	F	14	192
LEEMAN	A	8	198	LEFEVER	PD	1	206	LEIGH	JB	2	205	LENNARD	G	13	271
LEEMING	A	8	198	LEFEVRE	NP	13	270	LEIGH	L	14	192	LENNON	C	14	192
LEEMING	AE	11	223	LEFORT	W	2	205	LEIGH	LJ	14	192	LENNON	F	2	206
LEEMING	D	9	119	LEFTLEY	GM	1	206	LEIGH	M	14	192	LENNON	J	6	258
LEEMING	H	14	191	LEFTLEY	JW	1	207	LEIGH	R	11	224	LENNON	J	11	224
LEEMING	J	8	198	LEGG	A	14	192	LEIGH	SE	11	224	LENNON	JR	1	207

LENNON	R	14	192	LEONARD	L	5	217	LESTER	JW	6	259	LEVELL	EE	2	206
LENNON	TP	10	137	LEONARD	LM	3	116	LESTER	P	1	208	LEVELL	LH	2	206
LENNOX	WA	1	207	LEONARD	LT	4	233	LESTER	R	7	230	LEVENE	B	14	193
LENO	BM	3	116	LEONARD	P	8	199	LESTER	R	7	231	LEVENE	M	14	193
LENOIR	AD	3	116	LEONARD	R	2	206	LESTER	R	13	271	LEVENE	T	2	206
LENOIR	H	3	116	LEONARD	R	13	271	LESTER	SC	12	142	LEVER	AA	3	116
LENON	R	3	375	LEONARD	T	8	199	LESTER	ST	12	142	LEVER	AH	13	272
LENORD	A	8	198	LEONARD	T	11	225	LESTER	T	7	230	LEVER	B	11	225
LENORD	JH	14	192	LEONARD	T	11	225	LESTER	W	2	206	LEVER	E	4	234
LENT	CM	7	230	LEONARD	T	13	271	LESTER	W	7	231	LEVER	H	11	225
LENTELL	W	4	233	LEONARD	TE	11	225	LESTER	WJ	13	271	LEVER	TH	11	225
LENTON	AA	1	207	LEONARD	TW	3	116	LESTRILLE	J	1	208	LEVER	W	6	259
LENTON	CW	8	198	LEONARD	VA	11	225	LETBY	R	8	199	LEVER	WH	4	234
LENTON	EA	1	207	LEONARD	W	7	230	LETCHER	M	14	192	LEVERENTZ	E	7	231
LENTON	EA	7	230	LEONARD	W	13	271	LETCHFORD	C	13	271	LEVERETT	B	7	231
LENTON	EH	7	230	LEONARD	WAA	3	116	LETCHFORD	GA	13	271	LEVERETT	CWJ	7	231
LENTON	H	5	217	LEONARD	WE	1	207	LETCHFORD	H	13	271	LEVERETT	E	10	137
LENTON	H	5	217	LEONARD	WJ	13	271	LETCHFORD	LG	2	206	LEVERETT	EW	1	208
LENTON	J	6	258	LEOPOLD	AHH	4	233	LETCHFORD	T	2	206	LEVERETT	F	10	327
LENTON	JW	8	198	LEPKE	G	2	206	LETCHFORD	WC	13	271	LEVERETT	GH	1	208
LENTON	LJA	13	271	LEPPARD	DP	1	208	LETCHWOOD	A	13	271	LEVERETT	JH	10	137
LENTON	RA	12	341	LEPPER	WJ	10	137	LETHBRIDGE	A	13	272	LEVERETT	JWG	2	206
LENTON	S	8	198	LEPPINGTON	F	8	199	LETHBRIDGE	FS	13	271	LEVERETT	W	10	137
LENTON	SR	12	342	LEPPINGTON	G	8	199	LETHBRIDGE	SW	1	208	LEVERETT	WB	7	231
LENTON	W	12	142	LEPPINGWELL	H	9	119	LETHBRIDGE	T	11	225	LEVERETT	WJ	10	137
LENTON	WC	6	258	LESCOMBE	WJ	3	116	LETHBRIDGE	WH	13	272	LEVERICK	A	3	375
LENTON	WH	5	217	LESCOMBE	WJ	3	116	LETHERBARROW	W	6	259	LEVERICK	E	3	375
LENTON	WH	6	258	LESLEY	A	5	217	LETIN	R	7	231	LEVERICK	FE	3	375
LENTON	WW	7	230	LESLIE	B	1	208	LETLEY	CH	7	231	LEVERIDGE	E	3	116
LENTZ	WH	7	230	LESLIE	DA	7	230	LETT	AG	7	231	LEVERIDGE	E	3	116
LEON	F	3	116	LESLIE	E	1	208	LETT	FW	12	142	LEVERINGTON	AT	7	231
LEON	JD	3	116	LESLIE	F	3	375	LETT	GE	12	142	LEVERINGTON	E	6	259
LEONARD	A	11	224	LESLIE	FEH	12	342	LETT	GR	12	142	LEVERINGTON	H	6	259
LEONARD	AW	2	206	LESLIE	J	11	225	LETT	H	12	143	LEVERINGTON	PE	7	231
LEONARD	C	2	206	LESLIE	M	1	208	LETT	H	12	143	LEVERINGTON	V	6	259
LEONARD	C	6	258	LESLIE	W	7	230	LETT	H	13	272	LEVERMORE	JF	13	272
LEONARD	CH	2	206	LESLIE	W	8	199	LETT	HC	12	143	LEVERMORE	SC	7	231
LEONARD	CH	8	199	LESLIE	WM	3	116	LETT	JT	12	143	LEVERS	W	8	199
LEONARD	D	8	199	LESSER	M	14	192	LETT	W	12	143	LEVERSEDGE	G	14	193
LEONARD	E	11	224	LESSER	TB	11	225	LETT	WA	13	272	LEVETT	ED	3	117
LEONARD	EA	7	230	LESTER	AH	3	375	LETT	WN	14	192	LEVETT	F	5	217
LEONARD	EJ	7	230	LESTER	F	1	208	LETTEN	T	3	116	LEVETT	FW	10	327
LEONARD	FPA	3	116	LESTER	F	6	259	LETTINGTON	AW	13	272	LEVETT	G	3	117
LEONARD	G	12	342	LESTER	F	7	230	LETTS	EE	6	259	LEVETT	J	7	231
LEONARD	H	6	259	LESTER	FG	2	206	LETTS	FR	12	342	LEVETT	JF	13	272
LEONARD	H	8	199	LESTER	FG	7	230	LETTS	FW	12	342	LEVETT	JH	7	231
LEONARD	H	11	224	LESTER	FG	7	230	LETTS	H	12	143	LEVETT	SH	7	231
LEONARD	J	8	416	LESTER	G	11	225	LETTS	H	12	342	LEVETT	WJ	1	208
LEONARD	J	9	294	LESTER	H	1	208	LETTS	HT	6	259	LEVETT	WL	7	231
LEONARD	J	11	224	LESTER	H	12	342	LETTS	J	12	342	LEVEY	H	3	117
LEONARD	J	11	224	LESTER	I	13	271	LETTS	JJC	12	423	LEVEY	I	14	193
LEONARD	J	13	271	LESTER	J	1	208	LETTS	WJ	12	342	LEVEY	M	3	117
LEONARD	J	14	192	LESTER	J	10	137	LETTS	WT	12	342	LEVEY	M	14	193
LEONARD	JS	3	116	LESTER	J	11	225	LEUTY	CG	1	208	LEVEY	RA	4	234
LEONARD	JW	14	192	LESTER	JH	11	225	LEVAGGI	J	11	225	LEVEY	RB	10	137

LEVI	A	8	199	LEWIN	WJ	1	208	LEWIS	E	11	225	LEWIS	H	5	218	LEWIS	H	5	218
LEVI	H	8	199	LEWIN	WT	12	342	LEWIS	E	11	225	LEWIS	H	5	218	LEWIS	H	5	218
LEVI	H	14	193	LEWINGTON	AE	13	272	LEWIS	E	12	342	LEWIS	H	6	260	LEWIS	H	6	260
LEVICK	JH	1	208	LEWINGTON	AH	1	209	LEWIS	EC	1	209	LEWIS	H	6	260	LEWIS	H	6	260
LEVICK	JR	2	206	LEWINGTON	H	13	272	LEWIS	EE	3	375	LEWIS	H	6	260	LEWIS	H	6	260
LEVICK	WA	1	208	LEWINGTON	L	1	209	LEWIS	EG	2	207	LEWIS	H	6	260	LEWIS	H	6	260
LEVIEN	BM	14	193	LEWINGTON	TJ	13	272	LEWIS	EH	6	259	LEWIS	H	6	260	LEWIS	H	6	260
LEVIN	A	5	217	LEWIS	A	2	207	LEWIS	EJ	2	207	LEWIS	H	8	199	LEWIS	H	8	199
LEVIN	F	5	217	LEWIS	A	4	234	LEWIS	EJ	2	207	LEWIS	H	8	199	LEWIS	H	8	199
LEVIN	J	5	217	LEWIS	A	5	218	LEWIS	EJ	5	218	LEWIS	H	14	194	LEWIS	H	14	194
LEVIN	L	5	217	LEWIS	A	6	259	LEWIS	EL	1	209	LEWIS	HA	4	234	LEWIS	HA	4	234
LEVIN	L	14	193	LEWIS	A	6	259	LEWIS	EL	11	226	LEWIS	HA	13	272	LEWIS	HA	13	272
LEVINE	A	14	193	LEWIS	A	6	259	LEWIS	EM	10	327	LEWIS	HC	6	260	LEWIS	HC	6	260
LEVINE	I	8	199	LEWIS	A	11	225	LEWIS	ETW	3	375	LEWIS	HF	13	272	LEWIS	HF	13	272
LEVINE	L	8	199	LEWIS	A	14	194	LEWIS	F	1	209	LEWIS	HJ	5	218	LEWIS	HJ	5	218
LEVINGTON	H	7	231	LEWIS	A	14	194	LEWIS	F	1	209	LEWIS	HJ	5	218	LEWIS	HJ	5	218
LEVINGTON	M	7	232	LEWIS	AE	1	209	LEWIS	F	2	207	LEWIS	HJ	10	138	LEWIS	HJ	10	138
LEVIS	A	14	193	LEWIS	AE	3	117	LEWIS	F	2	207	LEWIS	HT	2	207	LEWIS	HT	2	207
LEVISON	R	9	294	LEWIS	AE	6	259	LEWIS	F	3	117	LEWIS	HW	2	207	LEWIS	HW	2	207
LEVISTON	J	14	193	LEWIS	AE	7	232	LEWIS	F	6	260	LEWIS	J	3	117	LEWIS	J	3	117
LEVISTON	JJ	10	137	LEWIS	AG	10	137	LEWIS	F	6	260	LEWIS	J	4	234	LEWIS	J	4	234
LEVITT	ER	13	272	LEWIS	AH	2	207	LEWIS	F	7	232	LEWIS	J	4	234	LEWIS	J	4	234
LEVITT	F	12	143	LEWIS	AH	2	207	LEWIS	F	7	232	LEWIS	J	4	234	LEWIS	J	4	234
LEVITT	FG	7	232	LEWIS	AJ	2	207	LEWIS	F	9	294	LEWIS	J	5	218	LEWIS	J	5	218
LEVITT	JW	9	119	LEWIS	AJ	10	137	LEWIS	F	10	327	LEWIS	J	6	260	LEWIS	J	6	260
LEVITT	M	9	294	LEWIS	AR	4	234	LEWIS	F	11	226	LEWIS	J	9	119	LEWIS	J	9	119
LEVY	A	14	193	LEWIS	AS	4	234	LEWIS	F	11	226	LEWIS	J	11	226	LEWIS	J	11	226
LEVY	A	14	193	LEWIS	AT	2	207	LEWIS	F	12	143	LEWIS	J	11	226	LEWIS	J	11	226
LEVY	B	14	193	LEWIS	AV	1	209	LEWIS	FAT	13	272	LEWIS	J	11	226	LEWIS	J	11	226
LEVY	BH	2	206	LEWIS	AW	6	259	LEWIS	FH	4	234	LEWIS	J	12	342	LEWIS	J	12	342
LEVY	H	14	193	LEWIS	AW	13	272	LEWIS	FJ	3	117	LEWIS	J	13	273	LEWIS	J	13	273
LEVY	H	14	193	LEWIS	B	7	232	LEWIS	FW	12	342	LEWIS	J	13	273	LEWIS	J	13	273
LEVY	J	14	193	LEWIS	B	7	232	LEWIS	FW	13	272	LEWIS	J	14	194	LEWIS	J	14	194
LEVY	J	14	193	LEWIS	B	8	199	LEWIS	G	2	207	LEWIS	J	14	194	LEWIS	J	14	194
LEVY	L	14	193	LEWIS	B	10	138	LEWIS	G	4	234	LEWIS	J	14	194	LEWIS	J	14	194
LEVY	M	14	194	LEWIS	B	12	342	LEWIS	G	6	260	LEWIS	JD	3	375	LEWIS	JD	3	375
LEVY	P	14	194	LEWIS	BM	12	342	LEWIS	G	11	226	LEWIS	JE	1	209	LEWIS	JE	1	209
LEVY	S	14	194	LEWIS	C	1	209	LEWIS	G	11	226	LEWIS	JE	3	117	LEWIS	JE	3	117
LEVY	W	14	194	LEWIS	C	6	259	LEWIS	GB	6	260	LEWIS	JE	4	234	LEWIS	JE	4	234
LEWELL	C	7	232	LEWIS	C	8	199	LEWIS	GE	3	117	LEWIS	JH	11	226	LEWIS	JH	11	226
LEWELL	FL	1	208	LEWIS	C	10	138	LEWIS	GE	6	260	LEWIS	JH	13	273	LEWIS	JH	13	273
LEWELL	J	11	225	LEWIS	C	14	194	LEWIS	GE	13	272	LEWIS	JR	11	226	LEWIS	JR	11	226
LEWENDON	PW	2	206	LEWIS	C	14	194	LEWIS	GF	1	209	LEWIS	JT	14	194	LEWIS	JT	14	194
LEWER	AJ	7	232	LEWIS	CE	1	209	LEWIS	GF	6	260	LEWIS	JW	5	218	LEWIS	JW	5	218
LEWER	FEG	3	117	LEWIS	CE	10	138	LEWIS	GH	10	138	LEWIS	JW	11	226	LEWIS	JW	11	226
LEWER	J	10	327	LEWIS	CH	4	234	LEWIS	GH	10	138	LEWIS	L	6	260	LEWIS	L	6	260
LEWEY	HE	2	207	LEWIS	CH	8	199	LEWIS	GH	10	327	LEWIS	L	7	232	LEWIS	L	7	232
LEWIN	A	5	217	LEWIS	CHW	1	209	LEWIS	GS	6	260	LEWIS	L	8	199	LEWIS	L	8	199
LEWIN	DW	5	218	LEWIS	CJ	1	209	LEWIS	GW	2	207	LEWIS	LL	11	226	LEWIS	LL	11	226
LEWIN	FG	12	143	LEWIS	CO	13	272	LEWIS	H	1	209	LEWIS	LO	14	194	LEWIS	LO	14	194
LEWIN	FH	5	218	LEWIS	E	2	207	LEWIS	H	4	234	LEWIS	M	1	209	LEWIS	M	1	209
LEWIN	FJ	2	207	LEWIS	E	2	207	LEWIS	H	4	234	LEWIS	ME	1	209	LEWIS	ME	1	209
LEWIN	FW	2	207	LEWIS	E	6	259	LEWIS	H	4	234	LEWIS	MH	3	117	LEWIS	MH	3	117
LEWIN	HV	12	143	LEWIS	E	10	138	LEWIS	H	5	218	LEWIS	MJ	3	117	LEWIS	MJ	3	117
LEWIN	JH	14	194	LEWIS	E	11	225	LEWIS	H	5	218	LEWIS	MJ	3	117	LEWIS	N	6	260

LEWIS	NL	13	273	LEWIS	WT	4	235	LIGGINS	WJ	6	261	LILES	EC	3	118
LEWIS	O	14	194	LEWIS	WW	13	273	LIGGITT	GH	1	210	LILES	GH	3	118
LEWIS	PH	6	260	LEWRY	A	10	138	LIGGITT	GJ	1	210	LILES	TG	3	118
LEWIS	PVW	4	234	LEWRY	A	10	138	LIGGITT	O	7	232	LILFORD	B	12	343
LEWIS	R	1	209	LEWRY	AW	3	118	LIGHT	A	6	261	LILFORD	FO	12	343
LEWIS	R	1	209	LEWRY	FC	10	327	LIGHT	A	8	200	LILFORD	WF	12	343
LEWIS	R	3	117	LEWSEY	JS	1	210	LIGHT	A	8	200	LILFORD	WJ	12	343
LEWIS	R	6	260	LEWTAS	A	14	195	LIGHT	AB	1	210	LILL	GA	7	232
LEWIS	R	14	194	LEWTAS	G	14	195	LIGHT	AF	4	235	LILLEY	A	10	138
LEWIS	RC	3	117	LEWTY	S	8	200	LIGHT	AR	1	210	LILLEY	AG	12	143
LEWIS	RC	13	273	LEWZEY	JH	7	232	LIGHT	CW	10	327	LILLEY	C	4	236
LEWIS	RE	3	117	LEY	AA	10	138	LIGHT	E	1	210	LILLEY	C	7	233
LEWIS	RG	2	207	LEY	BJ	14	195	LIGHT	EL	1	210	LILLEY	C	14	195
LEWIS	RG	10	327	LEY	JE	13	273	LIGHT	FF	4	235	LILLEY	CCT	4	236
LEWIS	RHS	1	209	LEY	TJ	13	273	LIGHT	FH	10	327	LILLEY	CR	12	143
LEWIS	RJ	13	273	LEY	W	13	273	LIGHT	FJ	4	235	LILLEY	E	1	210
LEWIS	RR	3	117	LEYBOURNE	L	1	210	LIGHT	GA	4	235	LILLEY	E	9	294
LEWIS	RT	14	194	LEYLAND	A	14	195	LIGHT	H	4	235	LILLEY	F	8	200
LEWIS	RW	13	273	LEYLAND	TW	14	195	LIGHT	H	6	261	LILLEY	F	10	138
LEWIS	S	2	207	LEYLAND	W	11	226	LIGHT	HR	4	235	LILLEY	GH	10	327
LEWIS	S	4	235	LEYLAND	WJ	14	195	LIGHT	HV	9	294	LILLEY	H	10	138
LEWIS	S	7	232	LIBERTY	FJ	2	208	LIGHT	J	4	235	LILLEY	H	12	143
LEWIS	SA	5	218	LICHFIELD	HW	10	138	LIGHT	R	10	327	LILLEY	J	7	233
LEWIS	STV	11	226	LICHFIELD	P	6	261	LIGHT	RF	4	235	LILLEY	J	7	233
LEWIS	T	14	194	LICHFIELD	W	6	261	LIGHT	SJ	10	327	LILLEY	J	8	200
LEWIS	TE	3	117	LICKLEY	A	8	200	LIGHT	VL	4	235	LILLEY	JH	14	195
LEWIS	TW	4	235	LICKMAN	A	4	235	LIGHT	W	4	235	LILLEY	JW	11	227
LEWIS	VT	3	117	LICKMAN	FG	4	235	LIGHT	WG	4	236	LILLEY	P	11	227
LEWIS	W	4	235	LIDBETTER	JJ	13	273	LIGHT	WH	6	261	LILLEY	P	12	143
LEWIS	W	4	235	LIDDARD	FC	1	210	LIGHT	WTL	10	327	LILLEY	R	10	138
LEWIS	W	7	232	LIDDARD	WP	2	208	LIGHT	WW	2	208	LILLEY	S	9	294
LEWIS	W	8	200	LIDDELL	AH	14	195	LIGHTFOOT	A	2	208	LILLEY	S	11	227
LEWIS	W	11	226	LIDDELL	J	7	232	LIGHTFOOT	A	9	294	LILLEY	SE	12	143
LEWIS	W	11	226	LIDDIARD	C	1	210	LIGHTFOOT	B	12	423	LILLEY	T	8	200
LEWIS	W	13	273	LIDDIARD	C	1	210	LIGHTFOOT	CT	11	227	LILLEY	T	11	227
LEWIS	W	14	194	LIDDIARD	PC	1	210	LIGHTFOOT	ER	6	261	LILLEY	WA	10	138
LEWIS	W	14	195	LIDDIARD	SAG	1	210	LIGHTFOOT	F	9	294	LILLEY	WC	12	144
LEWIS	WA	13	273	LIDDINGTON	C	6	261	LIGHTFOOT	H	6	261	LILLEYMAN	C	11	227
LEWIS	WC	6	260	LIDDINGTON	G	12	342	LIGHTFOOT	H	8	200	LILLEYMAN	T	11	227
LEWIS	WC	6	260	LIDDINGTON	JT	12	342	LIGHTFOOT	H	9	294	LILLIE	W	14	195
LEWIS	WE	1	210	LIDDINGTON	PJ	12	342	LIGHTFOOT	J	4	236	LILLIE	WLR	14	195
LEWIS	WF	2	208	LIDDINGTON	WJ	4	235	LIGHTFOOT	JW	8	200	LILLINGTON	AE	6	261
LEWIS	WG	4	235	LIDDINGTON	WJJ	12	343	LIGHTFOOT	N	4	236	LILLINGTON	E	12	144
LEWIS	WG	10	138	LIDDINGTON	WM	4	235	LIGHTFOOT	SR	5	218	LILLINGTON	LF	4	236
LEWIS	WH	3	117	LIDDLE	H	8	200	LIGHTFOOT	TH	9	119	LILLINGTON	RR	4	236
LEWIS	WH	5	218	LIEBENROOD	J	6	261	LIGHTFOOT	W	8	200	LILLIS	G	6	261
LEWIS	WH	6	261	LIEBIG	E	13	273	LIGHTFOOT	WC	12	423	LILLIS	JT	11	227
LEWIS	WH	6	261	LIFELY	R	13	273	LIGHTOWLER	E	9	294	LILLIS	WT	6	261
LEWIS	WJ	1	210	LIFELY	W	13	273	LIGHTOWLER	H	9	390	LILLY	FG	10	138
LEWIS	WJ	6	261	LIFFORD	AE	7	232	LIGHTOWLER	J	9	294	LILLY	WJ	5	218
LEWIS	WJ	12	143	LIFFORD	E	1	210	LIGHTOWLER	TJ	9	294	LILLY	WT	10	138
LEWIS	WJ	13	273	LIGGETT	H	11	226	LIGHTWOOD	FP	12	343	LILLYMAN	W	12	343
LEWIS	WJ	13	273	LIGGINS	C	12	143	LIKELY	FA	10	138	LILLYWHITE	A	8	200
LEWIS	WJ	13	273	LIGGINS	EJ	12	143	LIKEMAN	AW	2	208	LILLYWHITE	F	4	236
LEWIS	WM	4	235	LIGGINS	J	6	261	LILBURN	WT	3	118	LILLYWHITE	FL	4	236

LILLYWHITE	HT	10	139	LINDLEY	AE	14	195	LINES	G	6	262	LINGER	PF	5	219
LILLYWHITE	J	8	200	LINDLEY	F	11	423	LINES	GFV	3	118	LINGER	S	12	145
LILLYWHITE	L	8	200	LINDLEY	G	8	200	LINES	GH	9	119	LINGER	WH	9	119
LILLYWHITE	N	10	139	LINDLEY	T	7	233	LINES	H	6	262	LINGHAM	A	11	227
LILLYWHITE	W	7	233	LINDON	F	8	200	LINES	H	6	262	LINGHAM	SE	7	234
LILYWHITE	F	8	200	LINDON	R	8	201	LINES	HJ	6	262	LINGLEY	FW	3	119
LILYWHITE	H	8	200	LINDSAY	EA	12	343	LINES	J	3	118	LINGLEY	WJ	7	234
LIM	H	7	233	LINDSAY	ER	13	274	LINES	J	3	118	LINGS	AJ	7	234
LIM	H	7	233	LINDSAY	G	14	195	LINES	JH	2	208	LINGWOOD	F	1	212
LIMB	AGM	13	274	LINDSAY	GL	10	139	LINES	P	7	233	LINGWOOD	JW	7	234
LIMB	HVS	10	327	LINDSAY	J	4	236	LINES	R	5	219	LINGWOOD	PJ	13	274
LIMBACH	L	9	119	LINDSAY	JA	6	262	LINES	R	7	233	LINIHAN	JE	11	227
LIMBERT	A	9	294	LINDSAY	JC	12	343	LINES	S	6	262	LININGTON	WG	10	328
LIMBREY	AR	12	144	LINDSAY	JW	7	233	LINES	W	3	119	LINK	JE	6	262
LIMBREY	WAP	5	218	LINDSAY	W	8	201	LINES	W	5	219	LINLEY	E	8	201
LIMBRICK	F	6	261	LINDSELL	E	10	139	LINES	W	12	343	LINLEY	E	8	201
LIMBRICK	G	6	261	LINDSELL	EJ	3	118	LINES	W	12	343	LINLEY	H	2	208
LIMBRICK	HG	11	227	LINDSELL	WB	3	118	LINES	WH	2	208	LINLEY	J	8	201
LIMBRICK	J	6	261	LINDSEY	E	1	211	LINES	WH	5	219	LINLEY	JW	8	201
LIMMAGE	CS	12	144	LINDSEY	G	14	195	LINES	WH	12	144	LINLEY	L	8	201
LIMMER	AG	2	208	LINDSEY	GAT	4	236	LINES	WS	1	211	LINLEY	S	8	201
LIMMER	H	2	208	LINDSEY	P	7	233	LINES	WS	1	211	LINN	FA	10	139
LINAKER	F	12	343	LINDSEY	W	1	211	LINFELD	GE	13	274	LINNELL	AJD	12	145
LINCH	O	2	208	LINDSLEY	A	8	201	LINFIELD	TF	10	139	LINNELL	E	7	234
LINCOLN	A	13	274	LINDUP	J	14	195	LINFOOT	EV	8	201	LINNELL	F	12	343
LINCOLN	EJ	13	274	LINE	A	5	219	LINFOOT	MW	7	233	LINNELL	GH	10	328
LINCOLN	FA	1	210	LINE	A	12	343	LINFORD	A	1	211	LINNETT	HLJ	1	212
LINCOLN	FG	12	144	LINE	AE	1	211	LINFORD	A	12	145	LINNEY	A	4	236
LINCOLN	G	3	118	LINE	BC	12	144	LINFORD	GH	1	211	LINNEY	EG	5	219
LINCOLN	G	9	294	LINE	E	3	118	LINFORD	GR	7	233	LINNEY	F	5	219
LINCOLN	H	2	208	LINE	FG	12	144	LINFORD	H	12	145	LINNEY	FW	5	219
LINCOLN	H	3	118	LINE	FW	12	144	LINFORD	HG	12	145	LINNEY	FW	6	262
LINCOLN	HF	3	118	LINE	HT	3	118	LINFORD	MAE	3	119	LINNEY	GH	4	236
LINCOLN	HG	5	219	LINE	JA	1	211	LINFORD	TC	1	211	LINNEY	H	4	236
LINCOLN	HJ	5	219	LINE	R	12	144	LINFORD	W	10	139	LINNEY	HA	5	219
LINCOLN	J	5	219	LINE	SJ	4	236	LINFORD	WG	1	211	LINNEY	J	5	219
LINCOLN	JF	3	118	LINE	TC	12	144	LINFORD	WG	10	139	LINNEY	J	5	220
LINCOLN	JW	12	144	LINE	WH	4	236	LINFORD	WM	12	145	LINNEY	J	6	262
LINCOLN	LG	9	294	LINE	WH	10	139	LING	A	2	208	LINNEY	J	14	195
LINCOLN	MF	12	144	LINECOR	LL	8	201	LING	AE	1	211	LINNEY	J	14	195
LINCOLN	TW	12	144	LINEHAM	CH	4	236	LING	AE	7	234	LINNEY	J	14	196
LINCOLN	W	12	144	LINEHAM	E	3	118	LING	AJ	13	274	LINNEY	S	5	220
LINCOLN	W	12	144	LINEHAM	T	3	118	LING	AW	1	211	LINNEY	S	14	196
LINCOLN	WA	12	144	LINEHAM	T	6	262	LING	G	2	208	LINNEY	SL	5	220
LINCOLN	WJ	13	274	LINEHAN	C	13	274	LING	G	7	234	LINNEY	T	14	196
LINDELL	W	8	200	LINEHAN	WJ	7	233	LING	H	2	208	LINNINGTON	CR	3	119
LINDEN	OV	2	208	LINEKER	FG	13	274	LING	JJ	2	208	LINSDELL	A	7	234
LINDFIELD	AAE	1	210	LINES	A	1	211	LING	W	1	211	LINSELL	T	13	274
LINDFIELD	HC	7	233	LINES	AE	1	211	LING	W	2	208	LINSELL	W	9	119
LINDFIELD	JG	7	233	LINES	CP	1	211	LINGARD	A	6	262	LINSELL	WJ	7	234
LINDFIELD	WGF	1	211	LINES	F	6	262	LINGARD	CW	6	262	LINSKEY	H	9	119
LINDGREN	JT	5	219	LINES	F	12	144	LINGARD	T	14	195	LINSTEAD	AS	2	208
LINDGREN	JW	5	219	LINES	FG	12	144	LINGBOTHAM	JH	9	295	LINSTEAD	F	10	139
LINDGREN	L	7	233	LINES	FR	1	211	LINGE	HG	7	234	LINTER	F	4	236
LINDLEY	A	3	118	LINES	G	5	219	LINGER	EJ	5	219	LINTHWAITE	A	6	262

LINTHWAITE	H	6	262	LISTER	H	9	295	LITTLE	AJ	12	145	LITTLER	F	4	237
LINTON	A	2	208	LISTER	HG	10	328	LITTLE	BM	1	212	LITTLER	G	6	263
LINTON	AH	2	208	LISTER	J	1	212	LITTLE	CH	8	202	LITTLER	H	12	343
LINTORN	H	1	212	LISTER	J	8	202	LITTLE	CH	10	328	LITTLER	J	11	228
LINTURN	E	2	208	LISTER	J	9	295	LITTLE	CH	12	145	LITTLER	JE	10	328
LINWOOD	GW	1	212	LISTER	JA	8	202	LITTLE	CT	12	145	LITTLER	JH	14	196
LINWOOD	HE	1	212	LISTER	JL	9	295	LITTLE	D	11	227	LITTLER	WE	11	228
LIPMAN	M	8	201	LISTER	N	9	120	LITTLE	DW	13	275	LITTLEWOOD	A	8	202
LIPMANOVITCH	S	8	201	LISTER	R	8	202	LITTLE	E	1	212	LITTLEWOOD	A	8	202
LIPPARD	WJ	13	274	LISTER	R	9	120	LITTLE	E	3	119	LITTLEWOOD	A	11	423
LIPPIATT	FJO	1	212	LISTER	S	6	262	LITTLE	E	7	234	LITTLEWOOD	E	3	119
LIPSCOMBE	AV	2	209	LISTER	S	9	120	LITTLE	F	3	119	LITTLEWOOD	FAL	9	120
LIPSCOMBE	EA	2	209	LISTER	S	9	120	LITTLE	F	10	139	LITTLEWOOD	FHC	4	237
LIPSCOMBE	RJ	1	212	LISTER	T	8	202	LITTLE	FT	3	119	LITTLEWOOD	G	8	202
LIPSETT	R	4	236	LISTER	T	9	120	LITTLE	G	1	212	LITTLEWOOD	H	11	228
LIPSKIE	A	14	196	LISTER	T	10	139	LITTLE	G	13	274	LITTLEWOOD	J	8	202
LIPSKIE	L	14	196	LISTER	W	2	209	LITTLE	GW	8	202	LITTLEWOOD	J	9	295
LIPTON	S	8	201	LISTER	W	3	119	LITTLE	GW	10	139	LITTLEWOOD	J	13	275
LIPTROT	AP	11	227	LISTER	W	8	202	LITTLE	H	12	145	LITTLEWOOD	JE	9	120
LIPYEAT	E	2	209	LISTER	W	8	202	LITTLE	J	11	227	LITTLEWOOD	R	8	202
LISCOE	WEF	13	274	LISTER	WE	9	120	LITTLE	JA	11	228	LITTLEWOOD	R	8	202
LISLE	F	4	236	LISTER	WG	10	139	LITTLE	JMA	2	209	LITTLEWOOD	W	10	140
LISLE	F	6	262	LISTER	WH	8	202	LITTLE	JT	1	212	LITTLEWOOD	W	11	228
LISLE	FP	4	236	LISTIN	AG	4	237	LITTLE	JT	13	275	LITTMAN	S	2	209
LISLE	HP	4	237	LIT TLE	AE	3	119	LITTLE	S	1	212	LIVERMAN	G	3	119
LISLE	JM	4	237	LITCHFIELD	A	5	220	LITTLE	S	13	275	LIVERMAN	M	3	119
LISLE	JM	4	237	LITCHFIELD	AC	12	145	LITTLE	S	13	275	LIVERMORE	A	1	212
LISLES	J	5	220	LITCHFIELD	C	12	145	LITTLE	TW	11	228	LIVERMORE	E	3	119
LISNEY	JT	7	234	LITCHFIELD	CC	12	145	LITTLE	W	3	375	LIVERMORE	H	7	234
LISSAMAN	JE	10	139	LITCHFIELD	CF	12	145	LITTLE	WA	9	120	LIVERMORE	R	13	275
LISSEMORE	A	6	262	LITCHFIELD	E	12	145	LITTLE	WL	8	202	LIVERMORE	TA	2	209
LISSEMORE	S	6	262	LITCHFIELD	EP	2	209	LITTLEALES	HW	13	275	LIVERMORE	TG	13	275
LISSEMORE	TJ	6	262	LITCHFIELD	G	12	145	LITTLEBOY	HA	3	119	LIVERMORE	W	1	212
LISSIMORE	CJ	10	139	LITCHFIELD	GW	5	220	LITTLEBOY	S	3	119	LIVERMORE	W	2	209
LIST	F	14	196	LITCHFIELD	H	1	212	LITTLECHILDS	T	5	220	LIVERMORE	W	3	119
LIST	RE	7	234	LITCHFIELD	J	12	145	LITTLEFIELD	AG	10	139	LIVERMORE	WE	7	234
LISTER	A	8	201	LITCHFIELD	PW	5	220	LITTLEFIELD	AJ	10	139	LIVERSEDGE	AW	7	235
LISTER	A	8	201	LITCHFIELD	WB	12	145	LITTLEFIELD	AJ	10	139	LIVERSEDGE	F	8	203
LISTER	A	9	294	LITCHFIELD	WF	12	145	LITTLEFIELD	AS	10	140	LIVERSEDGE	H	7	235
LISTER	A	9	294	LITCHFIELD	WH	2	209	LITTLEFIELD	CC	10	140	LIVERSEDGE	J	9	295
LISTER	CH	8	201	LITHERLAND	E	14	196	LITTLEFIELD	EC	10	140	LIVERSEDGE	P	7	235
LISTER	DW	5	220	LITHERLAND	W	14	196	LITTLEFIELD	H	10	140	LIVERSIDGE	AG	10	140
LISTER	E	8	201	LITSTER	J	11	227	LITTLEFIELD	JF	10	328	LIVERSIDGE	F	8	203
LISTER	E	8	201	LITSTER	R	11	227	LITTLEFORD	EF	2	209	LIVERSIDGE	R	10	140
LISTER	FT	8	201	LITTELL	HS	13	274	LITTLEFORD	LL	2	209	LIVERTON	AE	7	235
LISTER	G	9	294	LITTELL	LH	13	274	LITTLEJOHN	AH	7	234	LIVESEY	A	14	196
LISTER	GB	9	119	LITTELL	RC	13	274	LITTLEJOHN	E	5	220	LIVESEY	A	14	196
LISTER	H	8	202	LITTELL	RG	13	274	LITTLEJOHN	SH	5	220	LIVESEY	F	11	228
LISTER	H	8	202	LITTELL	T	13	274	LITTLEJOHN	SW	7	234	LIVESEY	F	14	196
LISTER	H	8	202	LITTLE	A	8	202	LITTLEJOHN	T	12	145	LIVESEY	GA	14	196
LISTER	H	9	120	LITTLE	A	10	139	LITTLEJOHN	WC	2	209	LIVESEY	H	11	228
LISTER	H	9	120	LITTLE	A	11	227	LITTLEJOHNS	G	10	140	LIVESEY	J	5	220
LISTER	H	9	120	LITTLE	AC	12	145	LITTLEMORE	J	12	343	LIVESEY	J	14	196
LISTER	H	9	294	LITTLE	AEF	6	263	LITTLEMORE	JP	11	228	LIVESEY	JA	8	203
LISTER	H	9	295	LITTLE	AF	9	295	LITTLER	CG	6	263	LIVESEY	S	11	228

LIVESEY	T	11	228
LIVESEY	W	11	228
LIVESEY	W	14	196
LIVESLEY	EJ	13	275
LIVESLEY	J	14	196
LIVESTY	A	11	228
LIVINGSTONE	AE	6	263
LIVINGSTONE	G	6	263
LIVINGSTONE	J	7	235
LIVINGSTONE	JH	6	263
LIVINGSTONE	JW	4	237
LIVINGSTONE	L	14	196
LIVINGSTONE	W	14	196
LIVSEY	A	14	196
LIVSEY	W	14	197
LLEWELLYN	AE	13	275
LLEWELLYN	AW	13	275
LLEWELLYN	CT	8	203
LLEWELLYN	E	10	328
LLEWELLYN	E	11	228
LLEWELLYN	EE	14	197
LLEWELLYN	FJ	13	275
LLEWELLYN	H	3	375
LLEWELLYN	H	11	228
LLEWELLYN	H	14	197
LLEWELLYN	HT	6	263
LLEWELLYN	J	2	209
LLEWELLYN	M	10	328
LLEWELLYN	TH	13	275
LLOYD	A	3	119
LLOYD	A	6	263
LLOYD	A	6	263
LLOYD	A	7	235
LLOYD	A	7	235
LLOYD	A	11	228
LLOYD	A	13	275
LLOYD	A	14	197
LLOYD	A	14	197
LLOYD	AA	6	263
LLOYD	AE	7	235
LLOYD	AG	4	237
LLOYD	AH	3	119
LLOYD	AR	11	228
LLOYD	AS	7	235
LLOYD	AW	3	376
LLOYD	AW	6	263
LLOYD	B	6	263
LLOYD	C	7	235
LLOYD	CF	6	263
LLOYD	CJ	11	228
LLOYD	D	11	229
LLOYD	DG	2	209
LLOYD	E	9	295
LLOYD	E	11	229
LLOYD	EA	7	235
LLOYD	EC	4	237
LLOYD	EGV	2	209
LLOYD	EJ	3	376
LLOYD	EJ	13	275
LLOYD	F	1	212
LLOYD	F	10	140
LLOYD	F	10	140
LLOYD	F	13	275
LLOYD	FC	10	140
LLOYD	FV	1	212
LLOYD	FW	12	343
LLOYD	G	6	263
LLOYD	G	7	235
LLOYD	GH	2	209
LLOYD	GS	2	209
LLOYD	GS	11	229
LLOYD	GW	3	119
LLOYD	GW	5	220
LLOYD	H	6	263
LLOYD	H	6	263
LLOYD	H	6	263
LLOYD	H	7	235
LLOYD	H	11	229
LLOYD	H	11	229
LLOYD	H	13	275
LLOYD	HE	6	263
LLOYD	HF	3	119
LLOYD	HF	7	235
LLOYD	HG	6	263
LLOYD	HH	6	263
LLOYD	HL	1	212
LLOYD	HR	5	220
LLOYD	HT	3	120
LLOYD	HT	6	264
LLOYD	I	11	229
LLOYD	J	6	264
LLOYD	J	6	264
LLOYD	J	6	264
LLOYD	J	6	264
LLOYD	J	9	120
LLOYD	J	11	229
LLOYD	J	11	229
LLOYD	J	13	275
LLOYD	J	14	197
LLOYD	J	14	197
LLOYD	JA	2	209
LLOYD	JA	8	203
LLOYD	JD	13	275
LLOYD	JE	11	229
LLOYD	JH	10	140
LLOYD	JS	11	229
LLOYD	JT	11	229
LLOYD	JW	2	210
LLOYD	LF	5	220
LLOYD	LJ	10	140
LLOYD	OE	11	229
LLOYD	P	11	229
LLOYD	R	11	229
LLOYD	R	13	275
LLOYD	RS	5	220
LLOYD	RS	6	264
LLOYD	RW	14	197
LLOYD	S	14	197
LLOYD	T	8	203
LLOYD	TA	10	140
LLOYD	W	2	209
LLOYD	W	4	237
LLOYD	W	6	264
LLOYD	W	9	120
LLOYD	W	10	140
LLOYD	W	14	197
LLOYD	WJ	1	212
LLOYD	WD	2	210
LLOYD	WE	10	140
LLOYD	WF	2	210
LLOYD	WG	7	235
LLOYD	WH	13	276
LLOYD	WJ	7	235
LLOYD	WJ	7	235
LLOYD	WJ	10	140
LLOYD	WJ	10	140
LLOYD	WJ	10	328
LOACH	FJ	6	264
LOACH	J	6	264
LOACH	L	6	264
LOADER	EJ	4	237
LOADER	EM	1	213
LOADER	EM	4	237
LOADER	GA	9	295
LOADER	H	3	376
LOADER	JH	1	213
LOADER	PC	10	328
LOADER	PJ	3	120
LOADER	SA	3	120
LOADER	SC	10	140
LOADER	W	4	237
LOADER	WF	3	120
LOADER	WJ	1	213
LOADER	WL	1	213
LOAKES	C	12	343
LOAKES	C	12	343
LOAKES	F	12	344
LOAKES	H	12	344
LOAKES	H	12	344
LOAKES	TH	12	344
LOAKES	W	12	344
LOAN	CH	10	140
LOANEY	G	13	276
LOATS	HF	13	276
LOBB	C	6	264
LOBB	JW	10	328
LOBB	WHJ	1	213
LOBBAN	J	1	213
LOBBAN	J	6	264
LOBBETT	J	10	141
LOBLEY	C	9	120
LOBLEY	C	9	120
LOCHEAD	AG	7	235
LOCK	A	4	237
LOCK	A	13	276
LOCK	AC	4	237
LOCK	AD	13	276
LOCK	AE	13	276
LOCK	BC	3	376
LOCK	CA	7	236
LOCK	CE	7	236
LOCK	CG	4	237
LOCK	CG	4	237
LOCK	CH	9	120
LOCK	CT	13	276
LOCK	CW	3	376
LOCK	CW	4	237
LOCK	E	3	120
LOCK	E	4	237
LOCK	E	9	120
LOCK	ES	3	120
LOCK	EW	13	276
LOCK	FJ	3	376
LOCK	G	6	264
LOCK	H	9	120
LOCK	HH	10	328
LOCK	JS	4	237
LOCK	RE	4	237
LOCK	SG	4	238
LOCK	VN	1	213
LOCK	W	3	376
LOCK	W	10	141
LOCK	W	10	141
LOCK	W	13	276
LOCK	WA	2	210
LOCK	WH	4	238
LOCK	WH	13	276
LOCK	WJ	3	120
LOCK	WJ	4	238
LOCK	WL	10	141
LOCK	WV	4	238
LOCKE	C	11	229
LOCKE	C	13	276
LOCKE	GA	2	210
LOCKE	GF	2	210
LOCKE	GH	4	238
LOCKE	JA	13	276
LOCKE	JB	2	210
LOCKE	JH	13	276

LOCKE	M	6	264	LOCKWOOD	CD	13	277	LODGE	R	1	213	LOGHAN	A	14	198
LOCKE	PE	2	210	LOCKWOOD	E	9	121	LODGE	T	9	121	LOGUE	HP	1	214
LOCKE	RJ	4	238	LOCKWOOD	E	13	276	LODGE	W	5	221	LOLE	TJH	2	210
LOCKE	SH	13	276	LOCKWOOD	FH	1	213	LODGE	W	11	230	LOLLEY	AB	6	265
LOCKE	T	3	120	LOCKWOOD	G	9	121	LODGE	WH	10	141	LOLLEY	T	14	198
LOCKE	T	12	145	LOCKWOOD	GM	2	210	LODGE	WHS	10	141	LOMAS	A	9	295
LOCKE	W	4	238	LOCKWOOD	GW	7	236	LODGE	WJ	1	213	LOMAS	A	11	230
LOCKE	W	14	197	LOCKWOOD	H	4	238	LODGE	WN	9	295	LOMAS	A	11	230
LOCKE	WE	13	276	LOCKWOOD	H	8	203	LODGE	WR	2	210	LOMAS	A	11	230
LOCKE	WH	3	120	LOCKWOOD	H	9	295	LODWIDGE	CE	4	238	LOMAS	A	14	198
LOCKE	WW	1	213	LOCKWOOD	H	14	197	LODWIDGE	HW	4	238	LOMAS	E	6	265
LOCKER	F	11	229	LOCKWOOD	J	8	203	LOE	FW	12	344	LOMAS	FA	6	265
LOCKER	FJ	6	264	LOCKWOOD	JG	1	213	LOE	J	12	344	LOMAS	GA	11	230
LOCKER	W	5	220	LOCKWOOD	NL	6	265	LOE	JT	9	121	LOMAS	H	11	230
LOCKERBIE	J	8	203	LOCKWOOD	P	3	120	LOE	W	3	120	LOMAS	H	11	230
LOCKETT	E	14	197	LOCKWOOD	S	6	265	LOE	WL	3	120	LOMAS	H	14	198
LOCKETT	G	11	230	LOCKWOOD	S	9	121	LOFT	AH	3	120	LOMAS	J	8	203
LOCKETT	HW	12	344	LOCKWOOD	TE	13	277	LOFT	D	8	203	LOMAS	J	11	231
LOCKETT	J	11	229	LOCKWOOD	TH	9	121	LOFT	EP	3	120	LOMAS	J	14	198
LOCKETT	J	14	197	LOCKYEAR	FH	10	328	LOFT	F	11	230	LOMAS	J	14	198
LOCKETT	J	14	197	LOCKYER	AA	10	141	LOFT	T	13	277	LOMAS	W	6	265
LOCKETT	R	11	229	LOCKYER	AV	7	236	LOFTHOUSE	A	9	121	LOMAX	A	11	231
LOCKETT	TG	7	236	LOCKYER	C	2	210	LOFTHOUSE	E	8	203	LOMAX	D	11	231
LOCKETT	W	12	344	LOCKYER	CE	4	238	LOFTHOUSE	E	9	295	LOMAX	E	2	210
LOCKETT	W	14	197	LOCKYER	E	5	221	LOFTHOUSE	F	1	214	LOMAX	G	11	231
LOCKEY	JW	3	120	LOCKYER	E	7	236	LOFTHOUSE	F	10	141	LOMAX	J	8	204
LOCKEY	WR	5	221	LOCKYER	F	4	238	LOFTHOUSE	FW	3	120	LOMAX	J	11	231
LOCKHART	C	8	203	LOCKYER	G	4	238	LOFTHOUSE	J	8	203	LOMAX	JE	4	238
LOCKHART	C	10	141	LOCKYER	GH	10	328	LOFTHOUSE	J	9	121	LOMAX	JR	11	231
LOCKHART	C	10	328	LOCKYER	JE	13	277	LOFTHOUSE	JH	1	214	LOMAX	N	11	231
LOCKHART	GWS	10	141	LOCKYER	JJ	1	213	LOFTHOUSE	JJ	1	214	LOMAX	R	14	198
LOCKHART	JW	10	328	LOCKYER	PW	2	210	LOFTHOUSE	JT	1	214	LOMAX	T	3	376
LOCKIE	AW	3	120	LOCKYER	S	13	277	LOFTHOUSE	P	8	203	LOMAX	V	5	221
LOCKIE	C	3	120	LOCKYER	W	1	213	LOFTHOUSE	S	8	203	LOMER	AF	4	238
LOCKIE	L	3	120	LOCKYER	W	13	277	LOFTHOUSE	T	9	121	LONDON	E	7	236
LOCKIE	TG	3	120	LOCKYER	WEG	10	141	LOFTHOUSE	T	9	121	LONDON	HC	2	210
LOCKIE	TJ	3	120	LOCKYER	WR	6	265	LOFTHOUSE	TW	7	236	LONDON	JW	2	210
LOCKLEY	GC	1	213	LODDER	AE	10	141	LOFTHOUSE	W	1	214	LONDON	RM	6	265
LOCKLEY	J	6	264	LODER	HJ	7	236	LOFTIN	BR	3	376	LONDON	SG	2	210
LOCKLEY	JB	14	197	LODER	TJ	1	213	LOFTIN	HF	7	236	LONERGAN	T	1	214
LOCKLEY	R	11	230	LODGE	A	5	221	LOFTING	RV	2	210	LONEY	W	14	198
LOCKLEY	RH	6	264	LODGE	A	11	230	LOFTS	EG	3	376	LONG	A	4	238
LOCKLEY	TA	13	276	LODGE	C	4	238	LOFTUS	F	7	236	LONG	A	5	221
LOCKLEY	W	6	264	LODGE	CA	10	328	LOFTUS	J	11	230	LONG	A	9	295
LOCKLEY	W	6	265	LODGE	DA	2	210	LOGAN	C	3	376	LONG	A	11	231
LOCKLEY	WG	1	213	LODGE	DW	1	213	LOGAN	C	14	198	LONG	A	12	146
LOCKLIN	J	11	230	LODGE	H	8	203	LOGAN	D	14	198	LONG	A	13	277
LOCKREN	AJ	6	265	LODGE	H	14	197	LOGAN	F	8	203	LONG	AC	10	141
LOCKWELL	T	8	203	LODGE	HJ	10	141	LOGAN	F	11	230	LONG	AD	5	221
LOCKWOOD	A	7	236	LODGE	J	10	141	LOGAN	HJ	9	121	LONG	AE	3	121
LOCKWOOD	A	9	120	LODGE	J	11	230	LOGAN	J	8	203	LONG	AE	3	121
LOCKWOOD	A	13	276	LODGE	JH	8	203	LOGAN	J	8	203	LONG	AF	3	376
LOCKWOOD	AW	13	276	LODGE	JH	11	230	LOGAN	J	14	198	LONG	AW	13	277
LOCKWOOD	B	9	121	LODGE	JH	11	230	LOGAN	JD	13	277	LONG	AW	14	198
LOCKWOOD	B	9	295	LODGE	JJ	1	213	LOGAN	JW	11	230	LONG	BG	13	277

LONG	C	3	121	LONG	RG	2	211	LONGFORD	JC	6	265	LONGMUIR	J	4	240
LONG	CA	3	121	LONG	S	7	236	LONGFORD	WE	13	277	LONGSDALE	J	11	231
LONG	CJ	12	344	LONG	SR	7	236	LONGHORN	WH	8	204	LONGSHAW	C	14	198
LONG	CW	3	376	LONG	SS	3	121	LONGHURST	AE	6	265	LONGSHAW	EW	1	215
LONG	CW	11	231	LONG	T	5	221	LONGHURST	AE	13	277	LONGSHAW	G	11	232
LONG	D	1	214	LONG	T	9	295	LONGHURST	E	5	221	LONGSHAW	H	11	232
LONG	DF	7	236	LONG	T	10	329	LONGHURST	E	7	236	LONGSHAW	JE	11	232
LONG	E	8	204	LONG	T	12	146	LONGHURST	FJ	13	277	LONGSHAW	PW	11	232
LONG	E	10	328	LONG	T	12	423	LONGHURST	GA	7	237	LONGSTAFF	J	9	122
LONG	EW	4	238	LONG	TF	2	211	LONGHURST	H	7	237	LONGSTAFF	WH	8	205
LONG	F	2	211	LONG	TJ	6	265	LONGHURST	HJ	7	237	LONGSTAFF	WR	2	211
LONG	F	2	211	LONG	V	14	198	LONGHURST	JF	1	214	LONGTHORN	TH	8	205
LONG	F	3	376	LONG	W	1	214	LONGHURST	P	5	221	LONGTHORNE	G	9	122
LONG	F	6	265	LONG	W	2	211	LONGHURST	SA	1	214	LONGUEVILLE	C	13	278
LONG	F	14	198	LONG	W	3	121	LONGHURST	W	2	211	LONGWORTH	W	14	198
LONG	FW	10	141	LONG	W	5	221	LONGHURST	W	7	237	LONGWORTH	WM	14	199
LONG	FW	12	344	LONG	W	7	236	LONGHURST	WH	6	265	LONGYEAR	GE	10	142
LONG	G	5	221	LONG	W	9	121	LONGLAND	A	12	146	LONGYEAR	VG	10	142
LONG	G	5	221	LONG	W	10	141	LONGLAND	AE	4	239	LONNON	AC	12	146
LONG	G	13	277	LONG	W	10	329	LONGLAND	B	4	239	LONNON	AE	4	240
LONG	GA	7	236	LONG	W	11	231	LONGLAND	CA	4	239	LONNON	F	1	215
LONG	GF	11	231	LONG	W	14	198	LONGLAND	E	12	146	LONNON	GW	4	240
LONG	GJ	13	277	LONG	WBE	13	277	LONGLAND	E	12	344	LONNON	H	12	146
LONG	GWH	4	238	LONG	WD	10	329	LONGLAND	H	12	146	LONNON	HJ	4	240
LONG	H	3	121	LONG	WE	3	121	LONGLAND	J	12	146	LONNON	SV	12	146
LONG	H	4	238	LONG	WG	10	142	LONGLAND	JS	12	146	LONNON	T	4	240
LONG	H	4	238	LONG	WG	13	277	LONGLAND	WG	4	239	LONNON	TC	4	240
LONG	H	4	238	LONG	WJ	13	277	LONGLEY	A	13	277	LONNON	WG	5	221
LONG	H	4	239	LONGBOTTOM	A	9	121	LONGLEY	AE	13	278	LONSDALE	E	8	205
LONG	H	12	423	LONGBOTTOM	F	8	204	LONGLEY	FC	1	214	LONSDALE	H	9	122
LONG	H	14	198	LONGBOTTOM	G	9	121	LONGLEY	JW	2	211	LONSDALE	H	11	232
LONG	HG	5	221	LONGBOTTOM	H	8	204	LONGLEY	LA	13	277	LONSDALE	R	11	232
LONG	J	1	214	LONGBOTTOM	H	9	121	LONGLEY	WG	13	278	LOOBY	JH	9	122
LONG	J	4	239	LONGBOTTOM	HV	11	231	LONGLEY	WJ	10	142	LOOKER	B	11	232
LONG	J	6	265	LONGBOTTOM	J	8	204	LONGMAN	CE	4	239	LOOM	GA	7	237
LONG	J	7	236	LONGBOTTOM	J	8	204	LONGMAN	E	1	214	LOOM	HR	7	237
LONG	J	8	204	LONGBOTTOM	JA	9	121	LONGMAN	E	4	239	LOOMES	AJ	13	278
LONG	J	9	295	LONGBOTTOM	P	8	204	LONGMAN	F	1	214	LOOMES	E	5	222
LONG	JC	4	239	LONGBOTTOM	S	8	204	LONGMAN	GH	3	121	LOOMS	H	8	205
LONG	JE	10	141	LONGBOTTOM	T	8	204	LONGMAN	GW	4	239	LOOMS	JA	8	205
LONG	JH	6	265	LONGBOTTOM	W	8	204	LONGMAN	H	4	239	LOOMS	JW	8	205
LONG	JR	8	204	LONGBOTTOM	W	9	296	LONGMAN	H	4	239	LOONE	JA	6	266
LONG	JW	8	204	LONGDEN	A	11	231	LONGMAN	J	4	239	LOONEY	C	14	199
LONG	JW	8	204	LONGDEN	W	11	231	LONGMAN	J	4	239	LOONEY	G	1	215
LONG	M	9	295	LONGDON	E	8	204	LONGMAN	SA	1	214	LOONEY	J	13	278
LONG	ME	5	221	LONGDON	H	8	204	LONGMAN	SS	4	239	LOONEY	J	14	199
LONG	MMV	4	239	LONGDON	H	8	204	LONGMAN	W	1	214	LOONEY	WB	1	215
LONG	N	4	239	LONGDON	JH	4	239	LONGMAN	W	4	239	LOOSE	RH	13	278
LONG	NG	3	121	LONGFELLOW	A	8	204	LONGMAN	WH	4	240	LOOSLEY	A	12	146
LONG	P	1	214	LONGFELLOW	H	9	121	LONGMIRE	WH	11	231	LOOSLEY	PG	12	146
LONG	PA	4	239	LONGFELLOW	J	9	121	LONGMORE	FC	6	265	LORD	AE	12	146
LONG	PP	4	239	LONGFELLOW	S	11	231	LONGMORE	FL	6	265	LORD	AF	8	205
LONG	PR	5	221	LONGFIELD	H	11	231	LONGMORE	HJ	6	265	LORD	E	8	205
LONG	R	1	214	LONGFIELD	J	8	204	LONGMORE	JS	6	265	LORD	E	13	278
LONG	R	5	221	LONGFORD	H	9	121	LONGMORE	R	6	266	LORD	EPH	7	237

LORD	EW	13	278	LOVATT	J	14	199	LOVELESS	C	3	121	LOVELL	SHJ	7	238
LORD	F	11	232	LOVE	AF	13	278	LOVELESS	E	7	237	LOVELL	SL	10	142
LORD	G	12	146	LOVE	EF	4	240	LOVELESS	HW	3	121	LOVELL	SR	13	279
LORD	GW	8	205	LOVE	FC	12	147	LOVELL	AC	4	240	LOVELL	T	12	147
LORD	J	9	122	LOVE	FJ	4	240	LOVELL	AC	4	240	LOVELL	TA	10	329
LORD	JG	13	278	LOVE	G	8	205	LOVELL	AC	7	237	LOVELL	W	5	222
LORD	JW	11	232	LOVE	H	4	240	LOVELL	AE	10	329	LOVELL	W	12	345
LORD	R	8	205	LOVE	H	13	278	LOVELL	AH	10	142	LOVELL	W	13	279
LORD	SJ	12	146	LOVE	HE	10	142	LOVELL	AH	12	147	LOVELL	WC	12	147
LORD	VG	12	146	LOVE	JE	12	344	LOVELL	AN	12	147	LOVELL	WC	12	147
LORD	W	11	232	LOVE	LL	12	344	LOVELL	AP	13	279	LOVELL	WC	12	345
LORD	W	12	146	LOVE	P	12	344	LOVELL	AR	7	237	LOVELL	WE	12	345
LORD	WB	6	266	LOVE	PG	12	423	LOVELL	AT	12	423	LOVELL	WG	4	240
LORD	WG	12	146	LOVE	RG	10	329	LOVELL	AW	1	215	LOVELL	WG	7	238
LORD	WJ	12	146	LOVE	T	1	215	LOVELL	B	7	237	LOVELOCK	AJ	1	215
LORD	WT	7	237	LOVE	TA	2	211	LOVELL	BB	4	240	LOVELOCK	B	5	222
LORDAN	C	3	121	LOVE	W	12	423	LOVELL	BF	12	147	LOVELOCK	C	10	142
LORDAN	J	3	121	LOVE	WF	12	344	LOVELL	C	4	240	LOVELOCK	CS	5	222
LORDING	WF	3	121	LOVE	WJF	4	240	LOVELL	EA	4	240	LOVELOCK	EA	5	222
LORENZEN	P	14	199	LOVE	WT	2	211	LOVELL	EJ	12	147	LOVELOCK	EH	1	215
LOREY	GC	1	215	LOVEDALE	W	8	205	LOVELL	EW	11	232	LOVELOCK	ET	7	238
LORIMER	C	9	296	LOVEDAY	A	1	215	LOVELL	F	7	237	LOVELOCK	FG	13	279
LORIMER	G	9	296	LOVEDAY	AE	13	279	LOVELL	F	10	142	LOVELOCK	GH	7	238
LORING	A	13	278	LOVEDAY	AW	1	215	LOVELL	F	10	329	LOVELOCK	JJ	2	211
LORING	CC	13	278	LOVEDAY	FJ	13	279	LOVELL	FA	10	142	LOVELOCK	W	10	142
LORING	HE	13	278	LOVEDAY	H	10	329	LOVELL	FE	5	222	LOVER	W	4	241
LORKINS	EW	13	278	LOVEDAY	HG	2	211	LOVELL	FJ	4	240	LOVERIDGE	A	12	148
LORRAINE	C	13	278	LOVEDAY	JD	2	211	LOVELL	FW	12	147	LOVERIDGE	J	5	222
LORRIMAN	JW	8	205	LOVEDAY	MRE	10	329	LOVELL	G	12	147	LOVERIDGE	J	5	222
LORTOL	L	9	122	LOVEDAY	RC	13	279	LOVELL	GA	12	147	LOVERIDGE	L	5	222
LORTON	HES	12	146	LOVEDAY	RJ	3	121	LOVELL	GB	10	329	LOVERIDGE	LB	12	423
LORTON	RA	12	147	LOVEDAY	WJ	2	211	LOVELL	GF	12	344	LOVERIDGE	S	12	148
LORYMAN	C	8	205	LOVEGROVE	A	1	215	LOVELL	GH	12	344	LOVERIDGE	T	13	279
LOSBAN	I	14	199	LOVEGROVE	A	3	121	LOVELL	GR	10	329	LOVESEY	A	12	148
LOSEBY	T	11	232	LOVEGROVE	AE	1	215	LOVELL	H	5	222	LOVESEY	E	2	212
LOTEN	CJ	3	376	LOVEGROVE	AE	2	211	LOVELL	H	5	222	LOVESEY	E	12	148
LOTEN	R	10	142	LOVEGROVE	FC	10	329	LOVELL	H	5	222	LOVESEY	H	12	148
LOTT	J	2	211	LOVEGROVE	HW	1	215	LOVELL	H	12	147	LOVESEY	H	12	148
LOTT	WC	2	211	LOVEGROVE	J	10	142	LOVELL	HFT	12	147	LOVESEY	T	2	212
LOUCH	TW	1	215	LOVEGROVE	R	5	222	LOVELL	HG	12	147	LOVESY	WG	12	148
LOUGHLIN	J	9	122	LOVEGROVE	S	10	142	LOVELL	HJ	13	279	LOVETT	A	1	215
LOUGHNAN	E	14	199	LOVEGROVE	WA	3	121	LOVELL	J	1	215	LOVETT	A	1	215
LOUGHNAN	J	14	199	LOVEITT	TH	10	329	LOVELL	J	4	240	LOVETT	A	5	223
LOUGHTON	W	5	222	LOVEJOY	C	13	279	LOVELL	J	12	147	LOVETT	H	5	223
LOUIS	EG	13	278	LOVEJOY	CG	7	237	LOVELL	J	12	147	LOVETT	J	9	122
LOUIS	ER	13	278	LOVEJOY	CT	5	222	LOVELL	JH	9	122	LOVETT	J	9	390
LOUIS	ES	2	211	LOVEJOY	E	4	240	LOVELL	JH	13	279	LOVETT	J	12	148
LOUNT	H	9	122	LOVEJOY	RJ	5	222	LOVELL	JJ	12	147	LOVETT	J	13	279
LOUNT	W	9	122	LOVEJOY	WH	13	279	LOVELL	JW	7	237	LOVETT	JA	7	238
LOUNTAIN	AW	13	278	LOVELACE	FA	4	240	LOVELL	JW	12	147	LOVETT	JK	12	148
LOURAM	J	9	122	LOVELACE	IE	4	240	LOVELL	LC	12	344	LOVETT	JW	13	279
LOUT	WJ	13	278	LOVELACE	SW	7	237	LOVELL	ML	12	147	LOVETT	PD	1	215
LOUTH	H	13	278	LOVELACE	WG	7	237	LOVELL	P	12	345	LOVETT	R	5	223
LOVATT	AW	5	222	LOVELAND	LB	7	237	LOVELL	RS	4	241	LOVETT	TE	2	212
LOVATT	F	8	205	LOVELAND	WG	1	215	LOVELL	S	12	345	LOVETT	WJ	2	212

LOVITT	A	12	345
LOVITT	W	12	345
LOVRIDGE	W	6	266
LOW	AE	1	215
LOW	B	12	345
LOW	F	11	232
LOW	GF	1	216
LOW	GM	1	216
LOW	W	1	216
LOWDE	J	11	232
LOWDELL	AE	1	216
LOWDELL	GS	1	216
LOWDELL	H	8	205
LOWDEN	GH	7	238
LOWDEN	S	9	296
LOWE	A	6	266
LOWE	A	6	266
LOWE	A	11	232
LOWE	A	14	199
LOWE	AA	4	241
LOWE	AA	5	223
LOWE	AG	5	223
LOWE	AJ	1	216
LOWE	AJ	6	266
LOWE	AJ	6	266
LOWE	AT	5	223
LOWE	B	1	216
LOWE	B	4	241
LOWE	C	11	232
LOWE	CA	3	122
LOWE	CH	11	232
LOWE	CW	4	241
LOWE	D	3	122
LOWE	DE	2	212
LOWE	E	6	266
LOWE	E	9	122
LOWE	E	10	329
LOWE	E	10	329
LOWE	EC	6	266
LOWE	EF	6	266
LOWE	EJ	1	216
LOWE	EJ	12	148
LOWE	EJ	12	148
LOWE	F	2	212
LOWE	F	8	205
LOWE	F	10	142
LOWE	FJ	5	223
LOWE	FJ	10	142
LOWE	FW	3	122
LOWE	FW	10	329
LOWE	G	3	122
LOWE	G	5	223
LOWE	G	6	266
LOWE	G	8	205
LOWE	G	14	199
LOWE	GA	1	216
LOWE	GT	6	266
LOWE	H	2	212
LOWE	H	2	212
LOWE	H	5	223
LOWE	H	11	232
LOWE	HC	6	266
LOWE	HE	6	266
LOWE	HG	4	241
LOWE	HJ	4	241
LOWE	J	2	212
LOWE	J	4	241
LOWE	J	6	266
LOWE	J	8	205
LOWE	J	9	122
LOWE	J	11	232
LOWE	J	14	199
LOWE	JA	7	238
LOWE	JA	11	232
LOWE	JD	10	142
LOWE	JE	8	205
LOWE	JH	11	233
LOWE	JW	5	223
LOWE	L	3	376
LOWE	LC	3	122
LOWE	ME	6	266
LOWE	R	6	266
LOWE	R	8	206
LOWE	R	9	296
LOWE	RC	4	241
LOWE	RC	4	241
LOWE	S	1	216
LOWE	S	11	233
LOWE	S	11	233
LOWE	SC	7	238
LOWE	SS	3	376
LOWE	TC	10	329
LOWE	TJ	2	212
LOWE	TJ	6	266
LOWE	TW	2	212
LOWE	TW	12	345
LOWE	W	6	267
LOWE	W	6	267
LOWE	W	8	206
LOWE	W	9	122
LOWE	W	14	199
LOWE	W	14	199
LOWE	WE	6	267
LOWE	WH	13	279
LOWE	WHS	2	212
LOWE	WJ	4	241
LOWE	WW	5	223
LOWEN	AW	3	122
LOWEN	EJ	3	122
LOWEN	ES	2	212
LOWEN	G	1	216
LOWEN	P	2	212
LOWENS	RJ	11	233
LOWERS	E	3	377
LOWERS	ET	3	377
LOWERY	JAL	10	142
LOWES	J	8	206
LOWETH	C	1	216
LOWETH	H	1	216
LOWICK	SC	11	233
LOWINGS	MJ	12	148
LOWLES	FJ	7	238
LOWLES	GW	7	238
LOWLES	HT	7	238
LOWLEY	G	2	212
LOWLEY	JW	8	206
LOWMAN	A	4	241
LOWMAN	F	4	241
LOWMAN	GEO	4	241
LOWMAN	R	4	241
LOWN	TG	3	122
LOWN	V	13	279
LOWNDES	AJ	3	122
LOWNDES	C	6	267
LOWNDES	G	3	122
LOWNDES	MW	9	122
LOWNES	H	7	238
LOWNES	J	7	238
LOWNES	W	7	238
LOWRY	A	8	206
LOWRY	MJ	3	122
LOWTHER	A	11	233
LOWTHER	AH	7	238
LOWTHER	GW	8	206
LOWTHER	MA	7	238
LOWTHER	W	4	241
LOXAM	H	9	390
LOXAM	PE	9	296
LOXLEY	C	14	199
LOXLEY	C	14	199
LOXLEY	F	6	267
LOXLEY	L	14	199
LOXLEY	W	14	199
LOXTON	JA	1	216
LOYE	A	7	238
LOYE	AM	7	238
LOYN	H	8	206
LOYND	A	11	233
LOYNTON	CW	14	199
LOYNTON	WA	14	199
LUADAKA	W	2	212
LUBBOCK	JW	13	279
LUBY	J	11	233
LUBY	JT	8	206
LUBY	W	14	200
LUCAS	A	1	216
LUCAS	A	1	216
LUCAS	AE	4	241
LUCAS	AE	6	267
LUCAS	AE	9	122
LUCAS	AJ	3	122
LUCAS	AV	13	279
LUCAS	BR	4	241
LUCAS	BW	6	267
LUCAS	CA	9	122
LUCAS	CO	12	345
LUCAS	E	6	267
LUCAS	EF	2	212
LUCAS	EJ	2	212
LUCAS	EO	13	279
LUCAS	EW	12	148
LUCAS	F	3	377
LUCAS	F	7	239
LUCAS	F	7	239
LUCAS	F	9	296
LUCAS	F	11	233
LUCAS	F	11	233
LUCAS	FC	6	267
LUCAS	FT	4	241
LUCAS	FW	1	216
LUCAS	G	8	206
LUCAS	G	13	280
LUCAS	GH	8	206
LUCAS	GW	7	239
LUCAS	H	2	212
LUCAS	H	6	267
LUCAS	H	6	267
LUCAS	H	7	239
LUCAS	H	14	200
LUCAS	HC	4	241
LUCAS	HF	13	279
LUCAS	HG	4	242
LUCAS	HH	4	242
LUCAS	J	2	212
LUCAS	J	3	377
LUCAS	J	13	280
LUCAS	J	13	280
LUCAS	J	14	200
LUCAS	JA	6	267
LUCAS	JW	11	233
LUCAS	LF	1	216
LUCAS	PW	2	212
LUCAS	R	8	206
LUCAS	R	14	200
LUCAS	R	14	200
LUCAS	RB	4	242
LUCAS	RH	12	148
LUCAS	RH	12	148
LUCAS	RL	3	122
LUCAS	RM	3	122

LUCAS	R W	4	242	LUCKMAN	E	11	233	LUFF	P J	3	123	LUMLEY	H E	13	280
LUCAS	S	1	216	LUCKMAN	W M	6	267	LUFF	S C	12	149	LUMLEY	J	6	268
LUCAS	S A	10	143	LUCY	C	2	213	LUFF	S P	10	330	LUMLEY	J	8	206
LUCAS	S E	10	329	LUCY	J	11	233	LUFF	W	7	239	LUMLEY	J	10	143
LUCAS	T	4	242	LUCY	R	12	345	LUFF	W J	12	149	LUMLEY	J E	6	268
LUCAS	T	12	148	LUCY	W J	3	377	LUFFIUM	J	2	213	LUMLEY	R	13	280
LUCAS	T	13	280	LUDBROOK	G	8	206	LUFFMAN	C	3	123	LUMLEY	T	6	268
LUCAS	W	7	239	LUDDINGTON	F	12	148	LUFFMAN	C H	4	242	LUMLEY	W H	12	149
LUCAS	W A	1	216	LUDDINGTON	W	12	148	LUFFMAN	F C	10	143	LUMM	G	5	224
LUCAS	W B	6	267	LUDDINGTON	W M	12	148	LUFFMAN	H J	2	213	LUMM	J R	5	224
LUCAS	W C	11	233	LUDDITT	F	2	213	LUFFMAN	S G	13	280	LUMMAS	A	9	123
LUCAS	W T	13	280	LUDDITT	F C	2	213	LUFFMAN	W	4	242	LUND	A	8	207
LUCAS	W W	4	242	LUDERS	A	5	223	LUFFRUM	A F	3	123	LUND	A E	3	123
LUCAS	W W	5	223	LUDFORD	A	5	223	LUFFRUM	E M	3	123	LUND	A S	4	243
LUCCHESI	F	5	223	LUDFORD	G W	5	223	LUFFRUM	P C	3	123	LUND	B H	9	123
LUCK	A	5	223	LUDFORD	H	5	224	LUFKIN	F	14	200	LUND	C	8	207
LUCK	A	12	345	LUDFORD	S J	7	239	LUFKIN	J	14	200	LUND	H	9	123
LUCK	A B	12	345	LUDGATE	J	14	200	LUGG	J	2	213	LUND	H W	8	207
LUCK	A J	12	345	LUDGATE	R	14	200	LUGSDEN	E	5	224	LUND	J	9	123
LUCK	A W	5	223	LUDGROVE	J H	13	280	LUKE	E E	4	242	LUND	J	9	296
LUCK	C	1	217	LUDKIN	A H	13	280	LUKE	F	4	242	LUND	J A	9	123
LUCK	F	13	280	LUDLAM	C	14	200	LUKE	H	4	242	LUND	J W	8	207
LUCK	F C	2	213	LUDLAM	D	9	122	LUKE	H	6	267	LUND	R W	9	123
LUCK	F E	4	242	LUDLAM	H	11	233	LUKE	H T	10	143	LUND	W	1	217
LUCK	F J	6	267	LUDLAM	J	14	200	LUKE	J W	7	239	LUNDIE	A H	5	224
LUCK	F T	13	280	LUDLAM	L	9	122	LUKE	L E	4	242	LUNGLEY	R W B	13	280
LUCK	G E H	2	213	LUDLAN	P	9	296	LUKE	S	4	242	LUNN	A	6	268
LUCK	H S K	10	143	LUDLOW	E	9	122	LUKE	T	6	268	LUNN	A G	9	123
LUCK	T A	1	217	LUDLOW	F	3	377	LUKE	W	4	242	LUNN	C A	9	123
LUCK	T H	1	217	LUDLOW	F	7	239	LUKER	E R	12	345	LUNN	C W	3	377
LUCK	T V	4	242	LUDLOW	H	3	122	LUKER	G R	3	377	LUNN	E D	10	330
LUCK	W G	4	242	LUDLOW	J	3	377	LUKER	H W	4	242	LUNN	H	14	200
LUCK	W J	12	345	LUDLOW	T B	13	280	LUKES	W	11	233	LUNN	H A	11	233
LUCK	W S	4	242	LUDLOW	T J	7	239	LUKIN	A	4	243	LUNN	H J	4	243
LUCKCUCK	J A	11	233	LUDWIG	G A	10	143	LUMB	A	8	206	LUNN	J	6	268
LUCKETT	C F	2	213	LUDWIG	G C S	10	143	LUMB	A	8	206	LUNN	L	8	207
LUCKETT	C R	3	122	LUDWIG	W	14	200	LUMB	E	9	296	LUNN	R	9	123
LUCKETT	F	6	267	LUER	C F	7	239	LUMB	E	9	296	LUNN	V F A	10	330
LUCKETT	G	6	267	LUETCHFORD	W J	13	280	LUMB	F	8	206	LUNN	W G	6	268
LUCKETT	H A	7	239	LUFF	A C	12	148	LUMB	F	9	123	LUNN	W H	2	213
LUCKETT	R E	3	122	LUFF	A E	12	149	LUMB	F	9	390	LUNN	W P	4	243
LUCKETT	W J	1	217	LUFF	A F	7	239	LUMB	H	8	206	LUNNESS	H W	3	123
LUCKETT	W P	2	213	LUFF	A T	12	149	LUMB	J W	8	206	LUNNIS	R	3	123
LUCKHAM	A E	10	330	LUFF	C W	12	149	LUMB	N	8	206	LUNNON	C	5	224
LUCKHAM	G A	4	242	LUFF	E	10	143	LUMB	P	9	123	LUNNON	E	4	243
LUCKHAM	H J	10	330	LUFF	G	10	330	LUMB	R W	9	296	LUNNON	E W	5	224
LUCKHAM	J H	3	122	LUFF	H	10	330	LUMB	W	9	296	LUNNON	P	5	224
LUCKHAM	M A	3	122	LUFF	H	13	280	LUMB	W	9	296	LUNT	G	14	200
LUCKHURST	F A	1	217	LUFF	H W	13	280	LUMB	W	9	296	LUNT	J H S	13	280
LUCKHURST	W A	3	377	LUFF	J	10	330	LUMBERS	W	12	149	LUNTLEY	J	8	207
LUCKIE	W W	3	122	LUFF	J	12	149	LUMBERT	S	8	206	LUPSON	E	3	123
LUCKINS	J A	7	239	LUFF	J W	12	149	LUMBIS	R E	12	149	LUPSON	H E	3	123
LUCKMAN	A	6	267	LUFF	L J	10	330	LUMBY	G	8	206	LUPTON	C F	1	217
LUCKMAN	C	6	267	LUFF	L W	2	213	LUMER	A	3	377	LUPTON	E G	13	280
LUCKMAN	D	14	200	LUFF	P G	7	239	LUMLEY	G A	1	217	LUPTON	G H	13	280

LURWAY	G	1	217
LURY	H	1	217
LUSCOMBE	AG	1	217
LUSH	AH	4	243
LUSH	C	10	143
LUSH	EC	4	243
LUSH	EM	4	243
LUSHER	CJ	5	224
LUSHER	F	12	149
LUSHER	FS	3	377
LUSHER	SJ	12	149
LUSTED	AW	4	243
LUSTED	SCF	4	243
LUSTY	G	2	213
LUTEY	W	9	123
LUTLEY	A	14	200
LUTLEY	JR	11	234
LUTLEY	TH	11	234
LUTMAN	J	7	239
LUTON	A	14	200
LUTTMAN	AE	14	200
LUTTRELL	J	11	234
LUTY	A	8	207
LUTY	GW	8	207
LUXFORD	A	7	239
LUXFORD	GH	10	143
LUXFORD	J	7	239
LUXFORD	W	7	240
LUXFORD	W	7	240
LUXTON	AE	13	281
LUXTON	AE	13	281
LUXTON	CG	2	213
LUXTON	CJ	2	213
LUXTON	HWG	2	213
LUXTON	WJ	13	281
LUXTON	WJ	13	281
LYAL	JC	2	213
LYALL	C	6	268
LYALL	C	6	268
LYCETT	J	9	123
LYDER	R	8	207
LYDIATE	A	14	200
LYDIATE	J	14	201
LYDIATE	S	14	201
LYDON	J	8	207
LYE	E	4	243
LYE	HS	7	240
LYE	T	2	213
LYGO	AE	3	123
LYGO	CF	3	123
LYGO	FW	7	240
LYGO	H	6	268
LYLE	J	14	201
LYLE	W	7	240
LYLE	WH	11	234
LYMAN	AG	12	345
LYMAN	G	12	345
LYMAN	H	12	345
LYMAN	J	12	149
LYMAN	J	12	345
LYMAN	P	12	346
LYNAGH	J	14	201
LYNAM	J	14	201
LYNCH	A	2	213
LYNCH	A	7	240
LYNCH	AJ	2	213
LYNCH	AT	11	234
LYNCH	C	8	207
LYNCH	D	3	123
LYNCH	D	11	234
LYNCH	D	11	234
LYNCH	DW	3	123
LYNCH	E	8	207
LYNCH	EA	8	207
LYNCH	F	14	201
LYNCH	H	14	201
LYNCH	H	14	201
LYNCH	HA	13	281
LYNCH	HJ	3	377
LYNCH	J	1	217
LYNCH	J	2	213
LYNCH	J	3	377
LYNCH	J	11	234
LYNCH	J	11	234
LYNCH	J	14	201
LYNCH	J	14	201
LYNCH	J	14	201
LYNCH	JA	11	234
LYNCH	JF	11	234
LYNCH	JJ	11	234
LYNCH	JM	3	377
LYNCH	JW	13	281
LYNCH	R	14	201
LYNCH	T	1	217
LYNCH	T	11	234
LYNCH	T	14	201
LYNCH	T	14	201
LYNCH	T	14	201
LYNCH	TH	11	234
LYNCH	W	11	234
LYNCH	W	11	234
LYNCH	W	14	201
LYNCH	WE	2	214
LYNDON	W	6	268
LYNE	C	14	201
LYNE	GH	8	207
LYNE	JFC	7	240
LYNE	SE	2	214
LYNE	WG	8	207
LYNES	ER	5	224
LYNESS	GF	2	214
LYNESS	J	4	243
LYNESS	SH	3	123
LYNESS	WA	3	123
LYNHAM	AE	1	217
LYNHAM	FC	12	149
LYNHAM	T	12	149
LYNN	AE	2	214
LYNN	EW	7	240
LYNN	F	7	240
LYNN	FW	9	390
LYNN	J	2	214
LYNN	JR	2	214
LYNN	M	8	207
LYNN	RG	10	143
LYNN	WC	13	281
LYNN	WJ	4	243
LYNO	T	14	202
LYNO	WF	14	202
LYNOCK	T	6	268
LYON	A	5	224
LYON	AS	3	123
LYON	AW	12	346
LYON	C	12	346
LYON	D	8	207
LYON	E	2	214
LYON	FW	8	207
LYON	G	8	207
LYON	G	12	346
LYON	GW	4	243
LYON	H	3	123
LYON	H	5	224
LYON	H	5	224
LYON	HJ	6	268
LYON	HS	12	346
LYON	J	10	330
LYON	W	12	346
LYON	WH	3	123
LYONS	AH	14	202
LYONS	AJH	13	281
LYONS	BS	3	377
LYONS	C	7	240
LYONS	CWW	7	240
LYONS	D	14	202
LYONS	DP	3	123
LYONS	E	13	281
LYONS	F	9	296
LYONS	F	9	296
LYONS	FP	13	281
LYONS	G	1	217
LYONS	G	3	123
LYONS	G	14	202
LYONS	G	14	202
LYONS	G	14	202
LYONS	GF	3	124
LYONS	H	1	217
LYONS	H	3	124
LYONS	H	7	240
LYONS	H	7	240
LYONS	H	11	234
LYONS	J	6	268
LYONS	J	7	240
LYONS	J	7	240
LYONS	J	9	123
LYONS	J	9	296
LYONS	J	9	391
LYONS	J	11	234
LYONS	J	11	234
LYONS	JE	9	123
LYONS	JH	6	268
LYONS	JH	13	281
LYONS	M	9	296
LYONS	M	11	234
LYONS	M	13	281
LYONS	R	14	202
LYONS	S	8	207
LYONS	T	7	240
LYONS	TV	4	243
LYONS	TW	11	235
LYONS	W	1	217
LYONS	W	8	207
LYONS	W	9	296
LYONS	W	9	296
LYONS	W	13	281
LYSONS	H	14	202
LYSONS	J	14	202
LYSONS	JED	14	202
LYTH	G	8	208
LYTH	P	8	208
LYTHALL	JE	6	268
LYTHE	E	8	208
LYTHE	V	9	297
LYTHGOE	W	14	202
LYTHGOE	WE	3	124
LYTHGOW	J	9	123
LYUS	R	2	214

M

MABBITT	F	5	224
MABBITT	H	5	224
MABBITT	W	5	225
MABBOTT	AT	5	225
MABBOTT	BE	5	225
MABBOTT	C	8	208
MABBOTT	GW	5	225
MABBOTT	R	5	225
MABBOTT	W	8	208
MABE	WT	7	240
MABER	RA	13	281

MABERLY	JG	1	217	MACE	CJ	6	269	MACK	T	2	214	MACKLEY	HJ	1	218
MABEY	A	4	243	MACE	EW	1	218	MACK	W	4	244	MACKLEY	HJ	3	125
MABEY	CE	4	243	MACE	H	12	149	MACK	W	14	203	MACKLEY	JE	3	125
MABEY	CJ	4	243	MACE	H	12	149	MACK	WEJ	10	331	MACKLEY	SE	3	125
MABEY	F	13	281	MACE	SG	12	150	MACKAY	A	14	203	MACKLIN	A	9	126
MABEY	G	4	243	MACE	W	6	269	MACKAY	AH	6	269	MACKLIN	F	3	125
MABEY	GCG	10	143	MACEFIELD	ES	7	242	MACKAY	E	14	203	MACKLIN	G	3	125
MABEY	LC	4	243	MACEY	AE	4	244	MACKAY	F	7	243	MACKLIN	JJ	10	331
MABEY	VJH	10	143	MACEY	AF	10	145	MACKAY	FE	7	243	MACKLIN	W	7	243
MABEY	WJ	10	143	MACEY	AR	10	145	MACKAY	FH	12	150	MACKMIN	C	2	214
MABLE	G	6	268	MACEY	C	10	145	MACKAY	RT	12	346	MACKMIN	JJ	2	215
MABLEY	FJ	1	217	MACEY	E	1	218	MACKENDER	E	7	243	MACKNESS	P	12	150
MABLEY	W	5	225	MACEY	E	4	244	MACKENZIE	A	7	243	MACKNESS	R	2	215
MACALPINE	J	14	202	MACEY	EE	2	214	MACKENZIE	DG	7	243	MACKRELL	HG	4	244
MACALPINE	T	14	202	MACEY	FC	4	244	MACKENZIE	G	6	269	MACKRELL	T	10	331
MACAULAY	JE	7	240	MACEY	GA	10	145	MACKENZIE	H	3	125	MACKRILL	A	9	298
MACAULAY	R	11	235	MACEY	GA	10	145	MACKENZIE	H	9	126	MACKRILL	T	9	298
MACAULEY	J	9	123	MACEY	GF	10	145	MACKENZIE	JW	8	208	MACLARTY	H	4	244
MACAULEY	R	14	202	MACEY	H	1	218	MACKENZIE	JW	9	126	MACLAUGHIN	HJ	10	146
MACBETH	G	11	235	MACEY	J	2	214	MACKENZIE	MF	1	218	MACLEAN	BR	10	331
MACBETH	LA	13	281	MACEY	JA	4	244	MACKENZIE	RD	13	284	MACLEAN	C	6	269
MACBRIDE	F	11	235	MACEY	JC	7	242	MACKENZIE	SA	13	284	MACLEAN	WK	14	203
MACBRIDE	JA	11	235	MACEY	LC	10	145	MACKENZIE	W	6	269	MACLENNAN	J	6	269
MACBRIDE	W	11	235	MACEY	LC	10	145	MACKENZIE	W	14	203	MACMINN	CL	7	244
MACCABE	GM	2	214	MACEY	M	4	244	MACKENZIE	WJA	7	243	MACPHERSON	CH	2	215
MACCABEE	H	1	217	MACEY	WA	4	244	MACKERETH	JE	8	208	MACPHERSON	W	2	215
MACCABEE	S	1	218	MACEY	WE	10	145	MACKERETH	TW	8	208	MACPHERSON	W	9	126
MACCABEE	T	1	218	MACFARLANE	CS	10	145	MACKERNESS	AJ	12	150	MACREADY	G	12	346
MACCABEE	WE	10	143	MACFARLANE	H	14	203	MACKERNESS	P	12	150	MACREADY	H	12	346
MACCARTHY	D	14	202	MACGREGOR	AB	4	256	MACKERNESS	W	12	150	MACROW	G	1	218
MACCORMACK	FW	8	208	MACGREGOR	C	9	125	MACKESY	T	13	284	MACSWEENEY	J	3	378
MACDAUGALL	S	10	144	MACGREGOR	F	5	225	MACKEY	T	5	225	MADDAMS	W	5	226
MACDONALD	A	9	124	MACGREGOR	S	7	242	MACKEY	TJ	2	214	MADDEN	A	11	235
MACDONALD	AH	8	208	MACGUINNESS	A	2	214	MACKEY	W	7	243	MADDEN	CF	7	244
MACDONALD	AJ	4	243	MACGUINNESS	EJ	2	214	MACKIE	AS	1	218	MADDEN	CW	3	125
MACDONALD	D	9	297	MACGUINNESS	JH	2	214	MACKIE	J	14	203	MADDEN	D	11	235
MACDONALD	H	14	202	MACGUIRE	H	13	283	MACKIE	JA	1	218	MADDEN	F	8	208
MACDONALD	HW	4	244	MACHELL	PT	7	242	MACKIE	L	6	269	MADDEN	G	13	284
MACDONALD	J	10	144	MACHIN	AE	7	242	MACKIE	T	11	235	MADDEN	GAE	7	244
MACDONALD	J	14	202	MACHIN	G	3	124	MACKIE	U	10	331	MADDEN	HT	8	208
MACDONALD	J	14	202	MACHIN	GH	14	203	MACKIE	W	6	269	MADDEN	J	11	235
MACDONALD	JE	14	203	MACHIN	J	11	235	MACKIE	W	6	269	MADDEN	M	9	127
MACDONALD	JT	9	125	MACHIN	R	12	346	MACKIE	W	9	126	MADDEN	TW	14	203
MACDONALD	R	1	218	MACHIN	W	11	235	MACKIE	W	14	203	MADDEN	W	9	127
MACDONALD	R	9	297	MACHIN	WFC	7	242	MACKIE	WJ	1	218	MADDEN	W	9	127
MACDONALD	TO	4	244	MACINTOSH	A	9	298	MACKIN	T	11	235	MADDEN	W	14	203
MACDONALD	W	2	214	MACINTOSH	JH	8	208	MACKIN	W	8	208	MADDEN	W	14	203
MACDONALD	W	11	235	MACK	A	11	235	MACKINEM	AE	3	125	MADDEN	WF	9	127
MACDONALD	WG	10	144	MACK	C	4	244	MACKINEM	AW	3	125	MADDICK	AEW	10	332
MACDONALD	WH	4	244	MACK	FJ	13	283	MACKINTOSH	A	10	146	MADDIGAN	JJ	14	203
MACDOUGALL	F	11	248	MACK	GW	11	235	MACKINTOSH	D	9	126	MADDISON	CF	2	215
MACE	A	8	208	MACK	J	3	124	MACKINTOSH	D	9	298	MADDISON	GW	1	221
MACE	AA	3	124	MACK	J	14	203	MACKINTOSH	P	14	203	MADDISON	J	9	299
MACE	AE	1	218	MACK	M	11	235	MACKINTOSH	T	8	208	MADDISON	W	9	127
MACE	BL	10	145	MACK	R	11	235	MACKLEY	AE	12	346	MADDISON	W	9	299

Surname	Init.	No.	Pg.	Surname	Init.	No.	Pg.	Surname	Init.	No.	Pg.	Surname	Init.	No.	Pg.
MADDOCK	HJ	1	221	MAHER	H	7	244	MAILING	GW	12	150	MAKIN	TJ	14	205
MADDOCK	HW	2	215	MAHER	HG	7	244	MAILING	LA	12	150	MAKINS	AF	3	125
MADDOCK	JE	1	221	MAHER	J	8	208	MAILLARDET	AA	7	245	MAKINS	WD	3	126
MADDOCKS	AW	6	269	MAHOLLAND	G	14	204	MAIN	AW	7	245	MAKINS	WG	3	126
MADDOCKS	C	11	423	MAHON	A	13	285	MAIN	CJ	13	285	MAKINS	WH	10	332
MADDOCKS	F	6	269	MAHON	AWJ	10	332	MAIN	HBR	10	147	MAKS	C	12	150
MADDOCKS	GH	6	269	MAHON	C	8	208	MAIN	HW	10	147	MALABON	TO	12	346
MADDOCKS	J	6	269	MAHON	E	14	204	MAINDLEY	J	12	150	MALACRIDA	A	5	227
MADDOCKS	J	14	203	MAHON	GR	7	244	MAINE	FJ	4	244	MALACRIDA	P	5	227
MADDOCKS	R	14	203	MAHON	H	8	208	MAINE	FJ	4	245	MALAMED	W	14	205
MADDOCKS	S	14	203	MAHON	J	9	299	MAINE	J	14	204	MALAN	JD	2	216
MADDON	DM	7	244	MAHON	J	14	204	MAINEY	J	14	204	MALCHER	DE	12	346
MADDOX	H	5	226	MAHON	J	14	204	MAINPRIZE	H	8	209	MALCOLM	AG	6	270
MADDOX	JR	5	226	MAHON	T	14	204	MAINS	HV	12	346	MALCOLM	H	1	222
MADDY	CH	12	150	MAHON	W	14	204	MAIR	AW	5	226	MALCOLM	L	14	205
MADEN	DE	9	299	MAHONE	BD	2	215	MAIRS	J	7	245	MALCOLM	T	2	216
MADEN	E	9	299	MAHONEY	A	5	226	MAISEY	AF	2	215	MALE	AH	10	332
MADEN	JH	14	204	MAHONEY	AJ	13	285	MAISEY	CI	6	269	MALE	FC	10	147
MADERSON	W	9	299	MAHONEY	CA	10	147	MAISEY	HF	3	379	MALE	S	6	270
MADGWICK	JH	10	147	MAHONEY	D	2	215	MAISH	JH	2	215	MALES	F	5	227
MADIGAN	H	2	215	MAHONEY	FG	10	332	MAITLAND	W	13	285	MALES	H	5	227
MADKINS	W	6	269	MAHONEY	HW	7	244	MAIZEY	HG	13	285	MALES	L	5	227
MADY	A	13	285	MAHONEY	J	3	378	MAJOR	AJ	1	221	MALES	T	12	150
MAEERS	RB	10	332	MAHONEY	J	9	299	MAJOR	CS	4	245	MALES	W	13	285
MAFFEY	PJ	4	244	MAHONEY	J	10	332	MAJOR	FE	13	285	MALEY	BA	9	127
MAFFIA	C	14	204	MAHONEY	J	13	285	MAJOR	FT	2	215	MALEY	D	5	227
MAFFIA	JS	14	204	MAHONEY	J	14	204	MAJOR	G	12	346	MALEY	W	6	270
MAGEE	A	10	147	MAHONEY	JJ	7	244	MAJOR	G	13	285	MALHAM	G	9	299
MAGEE	C	10	147	MAHONEY	M	3	378	MAJOR	GJ	9	299	MALHAM	T	9	299
MAGEE	E	10	147	MAHONEY	T	7	244	MAJOR	H	5	226	MALIN	AJ	12	346
MAGEE	J	9	127	MAHONEY	T	14	204	MAJOR	H	12	346	MALIN	B	6	270
MAGEE	T	14	204	MAHONEY	TP	7	244	MAJOR	L	1	221	MALIN	FC	12	346
MAGEE	TD	13	285	MAHONEY	WG	2	215	MAJOR	L	1	222	MALIN	G	12	346
MAGEE	W	5	226	MAHONY	A	13	285	MAJOR	L	14	204	MALIN	G	13	285
MAGEE	WC	13	285	MAIDEN	CH	4	244	MAJOR	LW	5	226	MALIN	H	12	347
MAGGS	EF	2	215	MAIDEN	FHJ	3	378	MAJOR	P	4	245	MALIN	J	12	150
MAGGS	F	2	215	MAIDEN	NH	4	244	MAJOR	T	5	226	MALIN	R	12	347
MAGGS	JW	4	244	MAIDLOW	EW	1	221	MAJOR	T	5	226	MALIN	W	12	150
MAGGS	WJC	7	244	MAIDMAN	R	2	215	MAJOR	WG	13	285	MALING	FG	1	222
MAGILL	J	14	204	MAIDMENT	AC	10	147	MAJOR	WH	13	285	MALINS	WE	2	216
MAGINN	WC	12	346	MAIDMENT	AH	5	226	MAJOR	WH	14	204	MALKIN	A	14	205
MAGMUS	A	7	244	MAIDMENT	EE	7	245	MAJOR	WJ	4	245	MALKIN	H	14	205
MAGNER	H	1	221	MAIDMENT	FG	10	147	MAJOR	WJ	4	245	MALKIN	HG	14	205
MAGSON	L	9	127	MAIDMENT	J	4	244	MAKEHAM	GH	12	150	MALKIN	HJ	14	205
MAGSON	TAP	13	285	MAIDMENT	K	4	244	MAKENZIE	WT	13	284	MALL	A	6	270
MAGSON	W	9	127	MAIDMENT	TW	4	244	MAKEPEACE	A	5	227	MALL	R	6	270
MAGUIRE	BH	14	204	MAIDMENT	W	10	147	MAKEPEACE	C	5	226	MALL	W	6	270
MAGUIRE	F	2	215	MAIDMENT	WJ	10	147	MAKEPEACE	S	14	204	MALLABAND	E	6	270
MAGUIRE	J	2	215	MAIL	SJ	8	209	MAKEPEACE	TF	12	150	MALLABY	W	6	270
MAGUIRE	J	11	423	MAILE	A	12	150	MAKER	EW	2	216	MALLALIEU	W	8	209
MAGUIRE	JH	14	204	MAILE	J	12	150	MAKER	S	1	222	MALLARD	AJJ	12	347
MAGUIRE	T	1	221	MAILE	T	12	150	MAKIN	E	6	269	MALLARD	F	12	151
MAGUIRE	T	9	127	MAILES	J	5	226	MAKIN	G	6	269	MALLARD	F	12	347
MAGUIRE	WC	7	244	MAILING	A	3	125	MAKIN	IW	8	209	MALLARD	FW	2	216
MAHER	D	8	208	MAILING	AG	3	125	MAKIN	J	14	205	MALLARD	H	12	347
				MAILING	AP	5	226								

MALLARD	JE	11	238	MALONEY	JC	13	286	MANCHESTER	HJ	10	147	MANLEY	F	2	217
MALLARD	T	12	347	MALONEY	JW	8	209	MANCHESTER	J	13	286	MANLEY	F	9	128
MALLARD	W	12	347	MALONEY	L	10	332	MANCHETT	G	12	151	MANLEY	FJ	4	245
MALLARD	WH	12	347	MALONEY	L	11	238	MANDEL	FA	2	216	MANLEY	G	2	217
MALLEN	C	1	222	MALONEY	P	2	216	MANDER	AJ	1	222	MANLEY	GF	14	205
MALLEN	C	1	222	MALONEY	T	8	209	MANDER	J	6	270	MANLEY	HJ	3	126
MALLEN	GC	6	270	MALONEY	W	9	127	MANDER	J	6	271	MANLEY	HL	1	222
MALLETT	AB	1	222	MALONEY	WT	9	299	MANDER	J	14	205	MANLEY	J	11	238
MALLETT	AJ	3	126	MALOY	MG	6	270	MANDER	SJ	14	205	MANLEY	JP	8	209
MALLETT	AJ	10	147	MALPAS	CE	12	347	MANDER	W	6	271	MANLEY	JW	7	245
MALLETT	C	7	245	MALPAS	F	6	270	MANDERS	AT	3	126	MANLEY	JW	7	245
MALLETT	E	7	245	MALPAS	H	6	270	MANDERS	TG	6	271	MANLEY	L	7	246
MALLETT	FC	2	216	MALPAS	H	12	347	MANDERS	W	6	271	MANLEY	M	8	210
MALLETT	H	7	245	MALPAS	H	12	347	MANDERS	WJ	6	271	MANLEY	RC	2	217
MALLETT	J	7	245	MALPAS	HJ	12	347	MANDEVILLE	E	12	151	MANLEY	S	14	206
MALLETT	J	14	205	MALPAS	LC	12	347	MANDLEBERG	E	14	205	MANLY	F	1	223
MALLETT	RE	2	216	MALPAS	PW	6	270	MANDLEY	W	12	347	MANLY	JW	1	223
MALLETT	S	13	285	MALPAS	RG	12	347	MANDRY	J	4	245	MANLY	WG	1	223
MALLETT	TJ	2	216	MALPAS	T	13	286	MANESTER	AW	13	286	MANN	A	8	210
MALLETT	WAG	13	285	MALPAS	W	11	238	MANESTER	SH	7	245	MANN	A	8	210
MALLEY	R	10	147	MALPASS	C	6	270	MANEY	JA	7	245	MANN	A	8	210
MALLEY-MARTIN	CJ	3	126	MALPASS	H	12	347	MANEY	TR	2	216	MANN	A	8	210
MALLHAM	G	9	127	MALPASS	JB	6	270	MANFIELD	FE	13	286	MANN	A	8	210
MALLIN	A	6	270	MALPASS	W	14	205	MANFORD	J	11	238	MANN	A	9	128
MALLING	H	11	238	MALSTER	W	7	245	MANFORD	JJ	11	238	MANN	A	13	286
MALLINSON	E	9	127	MALTBY	G	11	238	MANFORD	W	11	238	MANN	AC	12	347
MALLINSON	G	9	127	MALTBY	P	8	209	MANGAM	P	9	299	MANN	AJ	2	217
MALLINSON	L	9	391	MALTBY	R	5	227	MANGAN	J	8	209	MANN	AW	1	223
MALLINSON	W	14	205	MALTER	C	3	126	MANGER	TH	5	227	MANN	B	1	223
MALLION	WD	13	286	MALTHOUSE	G	8	209	MANGHAM	D	9	127	MANN	CE	12	151
MALLISON	A	8	209	MALTHOUSE	J	8	209	MANGHAM	J	9	128	MANN	CJ	4	245
MALLISON	H	9	299	MALTHOUSE	WE	6	270	MANGHAM	T	8	209	MANN	CJH	4	245
MALLON	G	14	205	MALTON	H	2	216	MANGHAN	JH	8	209	MANN	EE	12	151
MALLOWS	AJ	12	151	MALYON	AG	13	286	MANGOLD	C	2	217	MANN	EG	13	286
MALLOWS	CD	12	151	MALYON	HF	13	286	MANGUM	AG	1	222	MANN	EJ	2	217
MALLYON	B	3	126	MALYON	JF	2	216	MANGUM	HJ	1	222	MANN	EJ	13	286
MALLYON	W	3	126	MALYON	W	13	286	MANGUM	JH	1	222	MANN	ET	2	217
MALONE	AW	2	216	MALYON	WJ	7	245	MANGUM	JH	1	222	MANN	F	6	271
MALONE	E	9	127	MANACKERMAN	M	14	205	MANGUM	JWG	1	222	MANN	FC	5	227
MALONE	E	11	238	MANAGER	G	2	216	MANGUM	WF	1	222	MANN	FH	12	347
MALONE	G	5	227	MANBY	A	4	245	MANIGER	L	7	245	MANN	FL	8	210
MALONE	J	8	209	MANBY	H	6	270	MANIGER	L	7	245	MANN	GCF	1	223
MALONE	J	14	205	MANBY	RA	8	209	MANION	E	8	209	MANN	GF	4	245
MALONE	PJ	4	245	MANCER	AJ	2	216	MANION	M	8	209	MANN	GW	6	271
MALONE	T	9	299	MANCEY	HG	3	126	MANION	N	8	209	MANN	H	5	227
MALONE	T	14	205	MANCEY	T	3	126	MANION	V	8	209	MANN	H	8	210
MALONEY	C	7	245	MANCEY	W	2	216	MANION	W	11	238	MANN	H	8	210
MALONEY	CA	5	227	MANCEY	W	3	126	MANISON	J	6	271	MANN	H	9	128
MALONEY	D	4	245	MANCEY	W	4	245	MANISON	L	6	271	MANN	H	12	347
MALONEY	D	11	238	MANCHEE	H	4	245	MANIX	J	1	222	MANN	HE	12	151
MALONEY	E	7	245	MANCHESTER	A	1	222	MANIX	JAS	1	222	MANN	HEP	2	217
MALONEY	FJ	10	332	MANCHESTER	A	13	286	MANIX	WN	1	222	MANN	J	8	210
MALONEY	G	10	332	MANCHESTER	AE	13	286	MANKIN	W	8	209	MANN	J	8	210
MALONEY	J	11	238	MANCHESTER	EM	9	127	MANKTELOW	PW	13	286	MANN	J	9	128
MALONEY	J	14	205	MANCHESTER	GT	2	216	MANLEY	E	3	126	MANN	J	13	286

MANN	J	14	206	MANNING	F	13	287	MANSBRIDGE	G	10	148	MANSOR	E	1	223
MANN	JB	8	210	MANNING	G	2	217	MANSBRIDGE	L	13	287	MANTEL	A	14	206
MANN	JT	6	271	MANNING	G	7	246	MANSBRIDGE	LF	1	223	MANTELL	GB	5	228
MANN	JW	9	128	MANNING	G	7	246	MANSBRIDGE	W	4	246	MANTLE	D	3	127
MANN	JW	9	391	MANNING	G	12	348	MANSBRIDGE	WF	13	287	MANTLE	GH	4	246
MANN	LA	8	210	MANNING	G	14	206	MANSELL	A	1	223	MANTLE	HH	3	127
MANN	LC	8	210	MANNING	GW	12	348	MANSELL	EH	4	246	MANTLE	HS	7	246
MANN	M	2	217	MANNING	H	7	246	MANSELL	G	2	217	MANTLE	JH	1	223
MANN	P	8	210	MANNING	H	12	348	MANSELL	GA	1	223	MANTLE	PH	13	287
MANN	P	12	151	MANNING	HG	5	227	MANSELL	H	7	246	MANTLE	S	4	246
MANN	PJ	4	245	MANNING	HJ	13	287	MANSELL	H	12	151	MANTLE	WJ	1	223
MANN	R	8	210	MANNING	HS	12	348	MANSELL	HA	6	271	MANTLE	WJ	3	127
MANN	R	12	347	MANNING	J	6	271	MANSELL	HG	1	223	MANTON	AL	12	151
MANN	R	12	423	MANNING	J	11	238	MANSELL	J	2	217	MANTON	EC	12	151
MANN	RC	12	348	MANNING	J	12	348	MANSELL	JA	6	272	MANTON	FG	12	151
MANN	RH	6	271	MANNING	J	13	287	MANSELL	JE	6	272	MANTON	FJ	12	151
MANN	S	8	210	MANNING	J	14	206	MANSELL	L	6	272	MANTON	H	9	391
MANN	T	8	210	MANNING	JE	11	238	MANSELL	R	1	223	MANTON	H	12	151
MANN	T	8	210	MANNING	JH	5	227	MANSELL	W	6	272	MANTON	HE	12	152
MANN	T	8	210	MANNING	JR	9	128	MANSELL	W	6	272	MANTON	S	5	228
MANN	TH	6	271	MANNING	JS	13	287	MANSELL	W	7	246	MANTON	T	14	206
MANN	TH	6	271	MANNING	L	5	227	MANSELL	WA	3	126	MANTON	WG	12	152
MANN	TH	7	246	MANNING	LJ	12	348	MANSELL	WJ	1	223	MANTON	WH	12	152
MANN	W	8	210	MANNING	R	11	238	MANSELL	WP	7	246	MANUAL	AW	8	211
MANN	W	8	211	MANNING	RF	1	223	MANSER	H	3	126	MANUEL	A	4	246
MANN	W	12	151	MANNING	RL	12	151	MANSER	J	13	287	MANUEL	C	11	239
MANN	W	12	151	MANNING	S	5	228	MANSER	J	13	287	MANUEL	H	7	246
MANN	W	12	348	MANNING	S	5	228	MANSER	JJT	7	246	MANUEL	T	7	246
MANN	WJJ	12	348	MANNING	S	12	348	MANSFIELD	A	12	348	MANVELL	EJ	10	332
MANN	WP	14	206	MANNING	T	9	128	MANSFIELD	B	3	126	MANVELL	FG	13	287
MANNAKEE	F	1	223	MANNING	T	14	206	MANSFIELD	C	3	127	MANWARING	A	7	247
MANNELL	WT	2	217	MANNING	VV	3	126	MANSFIELD	CW	12	348	MANWARING	HG	10	148
MANNERING	WJ	2	217	MANNING	W	5	228	MANSFIELD	E	2	217	MANWILL	AW	1	223
MANNERS	A	7	246	MANNING	W	5	228	MANSFIELD	ET	13	287	MANWILL	J	1	223
MANNERS	AE	4	245	MANNING	W	6	271	MANSFIELD	FF	2	217	MANYWEATHER	F	12	152
MANNERS	AF	13	286	MANNING	W	9	300	MANSFIELD	FJ	7	246	MAPE	J	11	239
MANNERS	AV	13	286	MANNING	W	12	151	MANSFIELD	GW	1	223	MAPLEY	GF	12	152
MANNERS	EC	4	245	MANNING	W	14	206	MANSFIELD	HC	3	379	MAPLEY	J	12	152
MANNERS	F	3	126	MANNING	WB	2	217	MANSFIELD	HW	10	148	MAPLEY	TH	12	152
MANNERS	FW	7	246	MANNING	WG	5	228	MANSFIELD	HW	13	287	MAPP	EG	5	228
MANNERS	PB	3	126	MANNING	WH	13	287	MANSFIELD	J	3	127	MAPPLEY	EJT	1	224
MANNERS	WE	13	286	MANNION	F	11	239	MANSFIELD	J	3	127	MAPPLEY	RB	13	287
MANNEY	HA	6	271	MANNION	J	11	423	MANSFIELD	J	7	246	MAPPLEY	W	1	224
MANNING	A	14	206	MANNION	T	11	238	MANSFIELD	J	13	287	MARA	EJ	7	247
MANNING	AE	5	227	MANNS	H	6	271	MANSFIELD	JJ	3	127	MARA	T	13	287
MANNING	AF	3	379	MANNS	JD	6	271	MANSFIELD	JW	13	287	MARC	EW	1	224
MANNING	C	5	227	MANOGUE	J	9	128	MANSFIELD	LM	5	228	MARCH	F	5	228
MANNING	C	7	246	MANOGUE	J	9	128	MANSFIELD	M	3	127	MARCH	F	5	228
MANNING	CJF	7	246	MANOGUE	T	9	128	MANSFIELD	MK	3	127	MARCH	FJ	5	228
MANNING	CR	12	151	MANS	GA	7	246	MANSFIELD	S	6	272	MARCH	JF	13	287
MANNING	D	2	217	MANSBRIDGE	A	4	246	MANSFIELD	S	11	239	MARCH	R	13	287
MANNING	D	14	206	MANSBRIDGE	A	4	246	MANSFIELD	S	11	239	MARCH	S	5	228
MANNING	E	10	147	MANSBRIDGE	A	10	147	MANSFIELD	WH	3	127	MARCH	WE	1	224
MANNING	EF	3	126	MANSBRIDGE	B	4	246	MANSHIP	C	10	148	MARCHAM	WG	7	247
MANNING	EJ	7	246	MANSBRIDGE	FS	4	246	MANSLEY	G	10	148	MARCHANT	A	1	224

Surname	Initials	No.	Page
MARCHANT	A	8	211
MARCHANT	ARF	2	218
MARCHANT	CE	11	239
MARCHANT	CF	2	218
MARCHANT	CJ	13	287
MARCHANT	E	2	218
MARCHANT	FJ	7	247
MARCHANT	G	10	148
MARCHANT	G	10	148
MARCHANT	G	10	148
MARCHANT	GR	4	246
MARCHANT	HFV	4	246
MARCHANT	HG	10	148
MARCHANT	HW	5	228
MARCHANT	J	11	239
MARCHANT	JH	13	288
MARCHANT	JW	2	218
MARCHANT	M	2	218
MARCHANT	W	13	288
MARCHANT	WA	13	288
MARCHANT	WR	4	246
MARCHANT	WW	10	148
MARCHBANK	P	8	211
MARCHBANK	S	9	300
MARCHI	AV	1	224
MARCHI	AV	2	218
MARCHI	E	1	224
MARCHI	E	2	218
MARCHMENT	G	10	332
MARCHMENT	WHJ	10	332
MARCK	AEV	4	246
MARCUS	H	14	206
MARDALL	F	1	224
MARDEL	AE	5	228
MARDELL	F	1	224
MARDELL	H	5	228
MARDELL	SL	5	228
MARDELL	W	5	228
MARDLE	AG	5	228
MARDLE	ELT	12	348
MARDLE	FJ	1	224
MARDLE	H	5	229
MARDLE	H	5	229
MARDLE	HA	12	152
MARDLE	W	5	229
MARDLIN	F	12	152
MARDLIN	F	12	152
MARDLIN	W	5	229
MARDLING	TE	5	229
MARDON	AG	12	152
MARDON	HW	12	152
MARDON	HW	12	152
MARDY	T	8	211
MARES	VW	4	246
MARETT	AJ	4	246
MAREY	JP	9	300
MARFELEET	A	7	247
MARFLEET	GA	7	247
MARFLEET	H	7	247
MARFLEET	WR	13	288
MARGERISON	L	9	128
MARGERUM	C	7	247
MARGETSON	AW	8	211
MARGETSON	C	8	211
MARGROVE	AW	3	127
MARGROVE	FG	3	127
MARGROVE	SD	3	127
MARGRUM	F	2	218
MARGRUM	FJ	2	218
MARGRUM	SG	2	218
MARIE	E	7	247
MARIE	FJ	7	247
MARIES	H	6	272
MARIES	WH	6	272
MARIS	H	12	348
MARJASON	J	3	379
MARK	A	8	211
MARK	C	13	288
MARK	E	9	300
MARK	H	2	218
MARK	JW	8	211
MARKE	AT	7	247
MARKE	RJ	2	218
MARKEE	E	2	218
MARKEY	JL	9	128
MARKEY	P	14	206
MARKHAM	A	8	211
MARKHAM	A	9	128
MARKHAM	A	9	300
MARKHAM	A	12	152
MARKHAM	AJ	2	218
MARKHAM	AJ	12	152
MARKHAM	AL	12	153
MARKHAM	AS	12	152
MARKHAM	EF	12	152
MARKHAM	EG	12	152
MARKHAM	F	12	152
MARKHAM	G	12	152
MARKHAM	GH	6	272
MARKHAM	H	11	239
MARKHAM	J	12	153
MARKHAM	JM	1	224
MARKHAM	JW	12	153
MARKHAM	JWC	1	224
MARKHAM	P	12	153
MARKHAM	ST	2	218
MARKHAM	T	9	128
MARKHAM	W	11	239
MARKHAM	WA	12	153
MARKHAM	WH	1	224
MARKIE	W	14	206
MARKILLIE	H	2	218
MARKLAND	GW	6	272
MARKLEW	F	6	272
MARKLEW	G	6	272
MARKLEY	G	6	272
MARKS	A	3	127
MARKS	A	5	229
MARKS	AF	5	229
MARKS	B	1	224
MARKS	B	2	218
MARKS	BJ	13	288
MARKS	C	2	218
MARKS	CJ	7	247
MARKS	E	8	211
MARKS	E	9	128
MARKS	FJ	3	127
MARKS	FR	3	127
MARKS	G	1	224
MARKS	G	1	224
MARKS	G	2	218
MARKS	G	3	127
MARKS	H	2	218
MARKS	H	5	229
MARKS	H	14	206
MARKS	J	14	206
MARKS	JO	2	219
MARKS	M	14	206
MARKS	N	12	348
MARKS	R	7	247
MARKS	RG	1	224
MARKS	RHJ	13	288
MARKS	S	8	211
MARKS	TR	2	219
MARKS	W	11	239
MARKS	WGJ	2	219
MARKS	WJR	1	224
MARKSON	L	14	206
MARKSON	M	14	206
MARKWELL	FJ	2	219
MARKWELL	J	2	219
MARKWELL	WA	2	219
MARKWELL	WE	12	153
MARKWELL	WH	10	148
MARKWELL	WHG	10	148
MARLAND	A	14	206
MARLAND	J	14	206
MARLAND	J	14	207
MARLE	J	7	247
MARLER	AF	7	247
MARLER	F	4	246
MARLER	H	4	246
MARLEY	GA	10	332
MARLEY	GH	7	247
MARLEY	J	14	207
MARLEY	R	7	247
MARLEY	WF	7	247
MARLOR	S	14	207
MARLOW	A	12	153
MARLOW	A	12	348
MARLOW	AB	4	246
MARLOW	AC	5	229
MARLOW	C	5	229
MARLOW	E	3	127
MARLOW	F	8	211
MARLOW	FC	3	128
MARLOW	G	5	229
MARLOW	G	8	211
MARLOW	G	12	348
MARLOW	H	4	246
MARLOW	H	5	229
MARLOW	J	5	229
MARLOW	RE	4	246
MARLOW	S	5	229
MARLOW	T	13	288
MARLOW	W	3	128
MARLOW	W	7	248
MARLOW	W	9	128
MARLOW	WC	5	229
MARLOW	WF	2	219
MARLOW	WG	5	229
MARLOW	WH	5	229
MARLTON	EE	7	248
MARMENT	AW	3	128
MARMENT	GF	3	128
MARMOY	EJ	2	219
MARNER	G	10	148
MARNER	HE	10	148
MARNEY	A	7	248
MARNEY	D	11	239
MARQUET	PEV	13	288
MARR	A	8	211
MARR	GB	1	224
MARR	GD	10	332
MARR	J	8	211
MARR	RT	13	288
MARRABLE	R	7	248
MARREN	JP	14	207
MARREN	JT	14	207
MARREN	M	9	128
MARRIAGE	FW	3	128
MARRIAGE	HJ	3	128
MARRIAGE	RA	3	128
MARRIAGE	SJ	7	248
MARRIAGE	T	1	224
MARRIAN	W	11	239
MARRINER	EG	13	288
MARRINER	FC	1	224
MARRINER	WA	13	288
MARRIOTT	A	7	248

MARRIOTT	A	8	211	MARSDEN	C	8	212	MARSH	F	8	212	MARSH	WA	13	289
MARRIOTT	A	12	348	MARSDEN	C	9	300	MARSH	F	10	332	MARSH	WH	10	149
MARRIOTT	AE	5	230	MARSDEN	C	11	239	MARSH	F	13	288	MARSH	WJ	4	247
MARRIOTT	AJ	12	348	MARSDEN	D	9	300	MARSH	F	14	207	MARSH	WJ	10	333
MARRIOTT	AM	4	246	MARSDEN	D	9	300	MARSH	FC	2	219	MARSHALL	A	1	225
MARRIOTT	AT	12	348	MARSDEN	E	8	212	MARSH	FH	10	148	MARSHALL	A	2	219
MARRIOTT	C	4	247	MARSDEN	E	9	129	MARSH	FS	13	289	MARSHALL	A	2	219
MARRIOTT	CE	6	272	MARSDEN	ED	14	207	MARSH	FW	7	248	MARSHALL	A	5	230
MARRIOTT	CG	8	211	MARSDEN	F	5	230	MARSH	G	4	247	MARSHALL	A	6	273
MARRIOTT	CT	5	229	MARSDEN	F	14	207	MARSH	G	11	240	MARSHALL	A	7	248
MARRIOTT	CW	12	349	MARSDEN	F	14	207	MARSH	G	13	289	MARSHALL	A	9	300
MARRIOTT	EF	12	349	MARSDEN	G	8	212	MARSH	GHW	13	289	MARSHALL	A	12	153
MARRIOTT	F	5	230	MARSDEN	G	11	239	MARSH	GS	7	248	MARSHALL	A	12	349
MARRIOTT	F	12	349	MARSDEN	GTWF	13	288	MARSH	GSW	4	247	MARSHALL	AC	3	128
MARRIOTT	F	12	349	MARSDEN	GW	14	207	MARSH	GW	7	248	MARSHALL	AE	6	273
MARRIOTT	FG	1	224	MARSDEN	J	8	212	MARSH	H	7	248	MARSHALL	AE	7	249
MARRIOTT	FH	8	211	MARSDEN	J	8	212	MARSH	H	13	289	MARSHALL	AE	13	289
MARRIOTT	G	3	128	MARSDEN	J	8	212	MARSH	H	13	289	MARSHALL	AF	3	128
MARRIOTT	GED	4	247	MARSDEN	J	11	239	MARSH	HE	2	219	MARSHALL	AH	7	249
MARRIOTT	GW	8	211	MARSDEN	J	11	239	MARSH	HJ	2	219	MARSHALL	AR	2	219
MARRIOTT	H	12	349	MARSDEN	J	14	207	MARSH	HW	2	219	MARSHALL	AR	7	249
MARRIOTT	H	12	349	MARSDEN	JD	11	239	MARSH	HW	10	148	MARSHALL	AR	9	300
MARRIOTT	J	6	272	MARSDEN	JE	8	212	MARSH	J	1	225	MARSHALL	ARF	2	219
MARRIOTT	J	9	300	MARSDEN	L	9	129	MARSH	J	3	128	MARSHALL	B	5	230
MARRIOTT	J	12	349	MARSDEN	S	7	248	MARSH	J	3	128	MARSHALL	B	7	249
MARRIOTT	J	12	349	MARSDEN	T	8	212	MARSH	J	8	212	MARSHALL	C	2	219
MARRIOTT	JJ	8	211	MARSDEN	W	8	212	MARSH	J	11	240	MARSHALL	C	7	249
MARRIOTT	JS	12	349	MARSDEN	W	9	300	MARSH	J	13	289	MARSHALL	CE	9	300
MARRIOTT	RL	12	349	MARSDEN	W	11	240	MARSH	J	13	289	MARSHALL	CJ	7	249
MARRIOTT	T	12	349	MARSDEN	W	11	240	MARSH	J	14	207	MARSHALL	CJ	10	149
MARRIOTT	W	9	300	MARSDEN	W	14	207	MARSH	JH	2	219	MARSHALL	CJ	13	289
MARRIOTT	W	9	300	MARSDEN	WA	11	240	MARSH	JH	7	248	MARSHALL	CW	4	247
MARRIOTT	W	12	349	MARSDEN	WA	14	207	MARSH	JH	8	212	MARSHALL	CW	8	213
MARRIOTT	W	12	349	MARSDEN	WH	9	129	MARSH	JH	13	289	MARSHALL	D	9	129
MARRIOTT	W	12	349	MARSH	A	7	248	MARSH	K	3	128	MARSHALL	D	14	207
MARRIOTT	WL	4	247	MARSH	A	13	288	MARSH	L	7	248	MARSHALL	DJ	6	273
MARRIOTT-REYNOLDS				MARSH	AG	1	225	MARSH	L	8	212	MARSHALL	E	4	247
	W	6	272	MARSH	AH	13	288	MARSH	L	10	148	MARSHALL	E	7	249
MARRIS	JP	5	230	MARSH	AS	10	148	MARSH	M	11	240	MARSHALL	E	8	213
MARRISON	G	9	129	MARSH	AT	2	219	MARSH	P	8	212	MARSHALL	E	8	213
MARRISON	GF	3	128	MARSH	AT	11	240	MARSH	R	5	230	MARSHALL	E	9	129
MARRISON	T	9	129	MARSH	AW	10	148	MARSH	RA	4	247	MARSHALL	E	13	289
MARRITT	SG	13	288	MARSH	B	8	212	MARSH	RE	7	248	MARSHALL	E	13	289
MARROTT	H	12	153	MARSH	C	4	247	MARSH	RG	10	149	MARSHALL	EA	12	153
MARRS	J	11	239	MARSH	CJ	5	230	MARSH	RH	13	289	MARSHALL	EA	12	153
MARS	WH	8	211	MARSH	CP	7	248	MARSH	SC	13	289	MARSHALL	EC	7	249
MARSBURG	RJ	13	288	MARSH	D	11	240	MARSH	T	3	128	MARSHALL	EJ	2	219
MARSDEN	A	8	212	MARSH	E	1	225	MARSH	T	8	212	MARSHALL	EW	1	225
MARSDEN	A	8	212	MARSH	E	3	128	MARSH	TH	7	248	MARSHALL	F	2	220
MARSDEN	A	9	300	MARSH	E	3	128	MARSH	W	1	225	MARSHALL	F	11	240
MARSDEN	A	9	300	MARSH	E	6	272	MARSH	W	5	230	MARSHALL	F	12	153
MARSDEN	A	11	239	MARSH	E	6	272	MARSH	W	8	213	MARSHALL	FA	4	247
MARSDEN	AH	8	212	MARSH	E	9	300	MARSH	W	10	149	MARSHALL	FCI	6	273
MARSDEN	B	8	212	MARSH	E	13	288	MARSH	W	12	349	MARSHALL	FE	11	240
MARSDEN	B	9	300	MARSH	ET	10	332	MARSH	WA	4	247	MARSHALL	FG	1	225
MARSDEN	C	8	212												

Surname	In.	A	B	Surname	In.	A	B	Surname	In.	A	B	Surname	In.	A	B
MARSHALL	FG	5	230	MARSHALL	J	11	240	MARSHALL	W	8	214	MARSON	E	6	273
MARSHALL	FH	9	129	MARSHALL	J	12	153	MARSHALL	W	8	214	MARSON	HA	7	250
MARSHALL	FJ	5	230	MARSHALL	J	14	207	MARSHALL	W	8	214	MARSON	JF	6	273
MARSHALL	FJ	6	273	MARSHALL	JD	7	249	MARSHALL	W	8	214	MARSON	R	6	273
MARSHALL	FL	10	149	MARSHALL	JD	7	249	MARSHALL	W	8	214	MARSON	WC	6	273
MARSHALL	FS	7	249	MARSHALL	JE	2	220	MARSHALL	W	8	214	MARSTEN	C	8	214
MARSHALL	G	3	128	MARSHALL	JE	11	240	MARSHALL	W	8	214	MARSTON	F	3	129
MARSHALL	G	5	230	MARSHALL	JF	12	349	MARSHALL	W	9	129	MARSTON	FGL	3	129
MARSHALL	G	5	230	MARSHALL	JH	6	273	MARSHALL	W	11	240	MARSTON	GH	2	220
MARSHALL	G	9	129	MARSHALL	JJ	4	247	MARSHALL	W	11	240	MARSTON	GH	6	273
MARSHALL	G	10	333	MARSHALL	JJE	7	249	MARSHALL	W	11	240	MARSTON	J	9	301
MARSHALL	G	12	153	MARSHALL	JM	12	153	MARSHALL	W	11	241	MARSTON	JP	12	350
MARSHALL	G	12	153	MARSHALL	JT	6	273	MARSHALL	W	12	154	MARSTON	L	6	273
MARSHALL	GF	7	249	MARSHALL	JT	10	333	MARSHALL	W	12	349	MARSTON	RF	2	220
MARSHALL	GF	10	149	MARSHALL	JW	9	301	MARSHALL	W	14	208	MARSTON	SML	3	129
MARSHALL	GH	1	225	MARSHALL	KB	12	153	MARSHALL	WA	10	149	MARSTON	WJ	8	214
MARSHALL	GH	14	207	MARSHALL	L	10	333	MARSHALL	WA	12	154	MART	AP	1	225
MARSHALL	GJ	9	300	MARSHALL	L	14	207	MARSHALL	WAJ	13	290	MART	SH	1	225
MARSHALL	GM	5	230	MARSHALL	M	9	129	MARSHALL	WC	2	220	MART	WH	1	225
MARSHALL	GM	12	153	MARSHALL	M	14	207	MARSHALL	WC	5	230	MARTELL	R	2	220
MARSHALL	GS	1	225	MARSHALL	NO	12	153	MARSHALL	WC	12	154	MARTELL	RHC	4	248
MARSHALL	GW	8	213	MARSHALL	OT	2	220	MARSHALL	WD	1	225	MARTELL	WF	2	220
MARSHALL	H	1	225	MARSHALL	OW	8	213	MARSHALL	WE	7	250	MARTEN	EC	4	248
MARSHALL	H	1	225	MARSHALL	P	8	213	MARSHALL	WE	11	240	MARTILL	GF	4	248
MARSHALL	H	1	225	MARSHALL	R	1	225	MARSHALL	WE	12	349	MARTIN	A	1	226
MARSHALL	H	4	247	MARSHALL	R	4	247	MARSHALL	WF	11	241	MARTIN	A	1	226
MARSHALL	H	5	230	MARSHALL	R	8	213	MARSHALL	WFJ	13	290	MARTIN	A	2	220
MARSHALL	H	7	249	MARSHALL	R	8	213	MARSHALL	WH	7	250	MARTIN	A	4	248
MARSHALL	H	8	213	MARSHALL	R	8	213	MARSHALL	WH	9	129	MARTIN	A	4	248
MARSHALL	H	8	213	MARSHALL	R	9	301	MARSHALL	WH	10	149	MARTIN	A	6	273
MARSHALL	H	9	301	MARSHALL	R	11	240	MARSHALL	WJ	3	128	MARTIN	A	6	274
MARSHALL	H	9	301	MARSHALL	RH	13	290	MARSHALL	WJ	14	208	MARTIN	A	8	214
MARSHALL	H	12	153	MARSHALL	RW	7	249	MARSHAM	JM	7	250	MARTIN	A	10	149
MARSHALL	H	12	349	MARSHALL	S	4	247	MARSHAM	R	7	250	MARTIN	A	11	241
MARSHALL	H	13	289	MARSHALL	S	7	249	MARSHMAN	A	10	149	MARTIN	A	11	241
MARSHALL	H	13	289	MARSHALL	S	8	213	MARSHMAN	AE	10	149	MARTIN	A	13	290
MARSHALL	HC	1	225	MARSHALL	S	8	213	MARSHMAN	EJ	10	149	MARTIN	A	13	290
MARSHALL	HF	10	333	MARSHALL	S	8	213	MARSHMAN	F	4	247	MARTIN	A	14	208
MARSHALL	HH	13	289	MARSHALL	SA	13	289	MARSHMAN	F	10	149	MARTIN	A	14	208
MARSHALL	HJ	13	289	MARSHALL	SJ	13	290	MARSHMAN	H	10	149	MARTIN	A	14	208
MARSHALL	HV	7	249	MARSHALL	SJ	13	290	MARSHMAN	J	10	333	MARTIN	AA	4	248
MARSHALL	HW	4	247	MARSHALL	ST	1	225	MARSHMAN	L	4	247	MARTIN	AA	10	149
MARSHALL	J	4	247	MARSHALL	T	2	220	MARSHMAN	P	10	333	MARTIN	AB	14	208
MARSHALL	J	5	230	MARSHALL	T	8	214	MARSHMAN	WA	10	149	MARTIN	AC	1	226
MARSHALL	J	5	230	MARSHALL	T	8	214	MARSHMAN	WH	4	247	MARTIN	AE	2	220
MARSHALL	J	6	273	MARSHALL	T	8	214	MARSHMENT	J	1	225	MARTIN	AE	2	220
MARSHALL	J	6	273	MARSHALL	T	11	240	MARSLAND	FP	6	273	MARTIN	AE	6	274
MARSHALL	J	8	213	MARSHALL	TE	3	128	MARSLAND	H	9	301	MARTIN	AE	7	250
MARSHALL	J	8	213	MARSHALL	TF	9	301	MARSLAND	H	14	208	MARTIN	AE	9	129
MARSHALL	J	8	213	MARSHALL	TJ	13	290	MARSLAND	J	11	241	MARTIN	AE	10	333
MARSHALL	J	8	213	MARSHALL	TW	6	273	MARSLAND	J	14	208	MARTIN	AE	10	333
MARSHALL	J	8	213	MARSHALL	W	1	225	MARSLAND	JH	8	214	MARTIN	AE	13	290
MARSHALL	J	9	129	MARSHALL	W	2	220	MARSOM	J	5	231	MARTIN	AG	1	226
MARSHALL	J	9	301	MARSHALL	W	4	247	MARSON	C	6	273	MARTIN	AH	4	248
MARSHALL	J	9	301	MARSHALL	W	7	249	MARSON	E	6	273	MARTIN	AH	6	274

MARTIN	AH	7	250	MARTIN	EJ	11	241	MARTIN	GH	14	208	MARTIN	J	11	241
MARTIN	AH	10	149	MARTIN	EM	13	290	MARTIN	GT	6	274	MARTIN	J	12	350
MARTIN	AH	14	208	MARTIN	EP	4	248	MARTIN	GT	10	150	MARTIN	J	13	291
MARTIN	AJ	4	248	MARTIN	ET	4	248	MARTIN	GW	1	226	MARTIN	J	13	291
MARTIN	AJ	5	231	MARTIN	EW	1	226	MARTIN	GW	7	251	MARTIN	JA	9	129
MARTIN	AJ	9	301	MARTIN	EW	10	333	MARTIN	GW	12	154	MARTIN	JC	1	226
MARTIN	AJ	13	290	MARTIN	F	1	226	MARTIN	H	2	221	MARTIN	JC	2	221
MARTIN	AJ	14	208	MARTIN	F	1	226	MARTIN	H	3	129	MARTIN	JE	1	226
MARTIN	AM	3	129	MARTIN	F	1	226	MARTIN	H	3	129	MARTIN	JF	10	150
MARTIN	AP	7	250	MARTIN	F	2	220	MARTIN	H	4	249	MARTIN	JH	5	231
MARTIN	AR	4	248	MARTIN	F	3	129	MARTIN	H	4	249	MARTIN	JH	10	333
MARTIN	AR	4	248	MARTIN	F	4	248	MARTIN	H	6	274	MARTIN	JJ	1	226
MARTIN	AS	4	248	MARTIN	F	4	248	MARTIN	H	6	274	MARTIN	JJ	6	274
MARTIN	AS	13	290	MARTIN	F	4	248	MARTIN	H	7	251	MARTIN	JP	11	241
MARTIN	AT	7	250	MARTIN	F	5	231	MARTIN	H	8	214	MARTIN	JR	9	301
MARTIN	AT	7	250	MARTIN	F	5	231	MARTIN	H	10	150	MARTIN	JT	10	150
MARTIN	AT	10	149	MARTIN	F	7	250	MARTIN	H	11	241	MARTIN	JW	9	129
MARTIN	AV	12	350	MARTIN	F	8	214	MARTIN	H	11	241	MARTIN	JW	11	241
MARTIN	AVB	3	129	MARTIN	F	12	154	MARTIN	H	11	241	MARTIN	L	12	350
MARTIN	AW	3	379	MARTIN	F	12	154	MARTIN	H	12	350	MARTIN	LA	7	251
MARTIN	AW	7	250	MARTIN	F	12	154	MARTIN	H	14	208	MARTIN	LM	7	251
MARTIN	AW	12	154	MARTIN	F	12	350	MARTIN	HA	3	379	MARTIN	LW	5	231
MARTIN	B	4	248	MARTIN	F	13	291	MARTIN	HA	4	249	MARTIN	M	1	226
MARTIN	BW	13	290	MARTIN	FB	4	248	MARTIN	HA	4	249	MARTIN	P	4	249
MARTIN	C	2	220	MARTIN	FC	12	154	MARTIN	HC	10	333	MARTIN	P	5	231
MARTIN	C	4	248	MARTIN	FE	2	220	MARTIN	HC	12	154	MARTIN	P	10	150
MARTIN	C	5	231	MARTIN	FE	7	250	MARTIN	HE	13	291	MARTIN	P	12	350
MARTIN	C	7	250	MARTIN	FF	10	150	MARTIN	HG	10	150	MARTIN	P	12	350
MARTIN	C	7	250	MARTIN	FG	4	249	MARTIN	HH	7	251	MARTIN	PA	5	231
MARTIN	C	10	150	MARTIN	FG	4	249	MARTIN	HJ	5	231	MARTIN	PA	10	333
MARTIN	C	10	150	MARTIN	FG	13	291	MARTIN	HJ	5	231	MARTIN	PC	1	226
MARTIN	C	11	241	MARTIN	FGC	1	226	MARTIN	HO	14	208	MARTIN	PS	5	231
MARTIN	C	13	290	MARTIN	FJ	4	249	MARTIN	HT	4	249	MARTIN	R	3	129
MARTIN	CE	2	220	MARTIN	FJ	10	150	MARTIN	HT	6	274	MARTIN	R	7	251
MARTIN	CH	1	226	MARTIN	FW	1	226	MARTIN	J	2	221	MARTIN	R	8	215
MARTIN	CH	4	248	MARTIN	FW	2	221	MARTIN	J	2	221	MARTIN	R	8	215
MARTIN	CH	11	241	MARTIN	FW	3	129	MARTIN	J	3	129	MARTIN	R	10	150
MARTIN	CJ	12	154	MARTIN	FW	4	249	MARTIN	J	3	129	MARTIN	R	14	208
MARTIN	CP	13	290	MARTIN	FW	5	231	MARTIN	J	3	129	MARTIN	R	14	208
MARTIN	CW	1	226	MARTIN	G	1	226	MARTIN	J	4	249	MARTIN	RC	2	221
MARTIN	CW	5	231	MARTIN	G	4	249	MARTIN	J	4	249	MARTIN	RC	3	379
MARTIN	D	9	301	MARTIN	G	4	249	MARTIN	J	4	249	MARTIN	RO	2	221
MARTIN	DW	13	290	MARTIN	G	6	274	MARTIN	J	4	249	MARTIN	S	2	221
MARTIN	E	3	129	MARTIN	G	7	250	MARTIN	J	5	231	MARTIN	S	4	249
MARTIN	E	4	248	MARTIN	G	7	251	MARTIN	J	5	231	MARTIN	S	8	215
MARTIN	E	6	274	MARTIN	G	7	251	MARTIN	J	6	274	MARTIN	S	13	291
MARTIN	E	7	250	MARTIN	G	8	214	MARTIN	J	6	274	MARTIN	SA	12	154
MARTIN	E	8	214	MARTIN	G	11	241	MARTIN	J	6	274	MARTIN	SH	10	150
MARTIN	E	11	241	MARTIN	G	11	241	MARTIN	J	6	274	MARTIN	SJ	1	227
MARTIN	E	12	154	MARTIN	G	12	154	MARTIN	J	7	251	MARTIN	SW	13	291
MARTIN	E	13	290	MARTIN	G	13	290	MARTIN	J	8	214	MARTIN	T	4	249
MARTIN	E	13	290	MARTIN	GA	3	129	MARTIN	J	8	214	MARTIN	T	8	215
MARTIN	E	13	290	MARTIN	GA	10	150	MARTIN	J	9	129	MARTIN	T	8	215
MARTIN	EB	13	290	MARTIN	GAE	12	350	MARTIN	J	9	301	MARTIN	T	10	150
MARTIN	EE	2	220	MARTIN	GE	1	226	MARTIN	J	11	241	MARTIN	T	11	241

MARTIN	T	13	291	MARTINDALE	AJ	5	232	MASKELL	RE	2	222	MASON	F	1	227
MARTIN	TB	9	129	MARTINDALE	E	5	231	MASKELL	RJ	2	222	MASON	F	4	250
MARTIN	TC	8	215	MARTINDALE	H	9	301	MASKELL	WJ	2	222	MASON	F	7	252
MARTIN	TE	1	227	MARTINDALE	HD	1	227	MASKELL	WM	5	232	MASON	FA	7	252
MARTIN	TF	11	242	MARTINDALE	T	1	227	MASKILL	A	8	215	MASON	FB	2	222
MARTIN	TH	3	129	MARTINDALE	W	5	232	MASKILL	H	8	215	MASON	FD	6	275
MARTIN	TH	10	150	MARTINDALE	W	5	232	MASKILL	JE	8	215	MASON	FG	4	250
MARTIN	TR	10	150	MARTINDALE	W	14	208	MASKILL	R	8	215	MASON	FG	10	333
MARTIN	TW	4	249	MARTINDALE	WJ	5	232	MASLEN	FG	4	250	MASON	FJ	2	222
MARTIN	TW	6	274	MARTINELLI	W	13	291	MASLEN	FJ	1	227	MASON	FJ	4	251
MARTIN	W	1	227	MARVELL	A	9	301	MASLEN	P	4	250	MASON	FJ	13	292
MARTIN	W	3	129	MARVELL	A	9	301	MASLEN	WA	4	250	MASON	FT	6	275
MARTIN	W	4	249	MARVELL	J	9	301	MASLIN	E	2	222	MASON	FW	12	154
MARTIN	W	4	249	MARVEN	C	2	221	MASLIN	EH	10	151	MASON	G	2	222
MARTIN	W	4	250	MARVEN	T	2	221	MASLIN	JC	1	227	MASON	G	4	251
MARTIN	W	5	231	MARVEN	WJ	1	227	MASLIN	SH	10	151	MASON	G	6	275
MARTIN	W	6	274	MARVIN	AA	6	275	MASLIN	W	1	227	MASON	G	8	215
MARTIN	W	6	274	MARVIN	AF	1	227	MASOM		4	250	MASON	G	11	242
MARTIN	W	7	251	MARVIN	CH	6	275	MASON	A	3	129	MASON	G	12	350
MARTIN	W	10	333	MARVIN	J	6	275	MASON	A	3	129	MASON	G	13	292
MARTIN	W	12	154	MARWOOD	A	14	208	MASON	A	4	250	MASON	GE	7	252
MARTIN	W	12	154	MARWOOD	E	8	215	MASON	A	6	275	MASON	GF	2	222
MARTIN	W	13	291	MARWOOD	EF	2	221	MASON	A	6	275	MASON	GF	6	275
MARTIN	W	13	291	MARWOOD	H	8	215	MASON	A	6	275	MASON	GF	12	350
MARTIN	W	14	208	MARWOOD	R	14	209	MASON	A	7	252	MASON	GH	11	242
MARTIN	WA	4	250	MARWOOD	SA	2	221	MASON	A	11	242	MASON	GL	3	130
MARTIN	WA	12	350	MARWOOD	WT	2	221	MASON	A	11	242	MASON	GM	10	334
MARTIN	WB	2	221	MARYAN	E	7	251	MASON	A	14	209	MASON	H	2	222
MARTIN	WB	3	129	MASCALL	FW	2	221	MASON	A	14	209	MASON	H	4	251
MARTIN	WC	6	274	MASCIA	G	13	291	MASON	A	14	209	MASON	H	6	275
MARTIN	WC	6	274	MASEFIELD	SG	6	275	MASON	A	14	209	MASON	H	6	275
MARTIN	WC	10	150	MASEY	RWJ	1	227	MASON	A	14	209	MASON	H	7	252
MARTIN	WC	10	150	MASH	A	7	251	MASON	AA	6	275	MASON	H	8	215
MARTIN	WE	7	251	MASH	AE	12	350	MASON	AE	4	250	MASON	H	8	215
MARTIN	WE	10	151	MASH	F	7	251	MASON	AG	4	250	MASON	H	9	301
MARTIN	WF	13	291	MASH	FL	13	291	MASON	AGE	13	292	MASON	HAR	4	251
MARTIN	WG	4	250	MASH	GC	13	291	MASON	AJ	3	130	MASON	HC	4	251
MARTIN	WG	7	251	MASH	NB	12	154	MASON	AJ	6	275	MASON	HC	6	275
MARTIN	WG	13	291	MASH	SH	13	291	MASON	AV	6	275	MASON	HC	10	151
MARTIN	WH	1	227	MASH	SR	12	350	MASON	AV	6	275	MASON	HF	13	292
MARTIN	WH	2	221	MASH	WJ	13	291	MASON	AW	4	250	MASON	HG	1	227
MARTIN	WH	3	129	MASHMAN	GW	13	291	MASON	AW	12	350	MASON	HG	6	276
MARTIN	WH	4	250	MASHMAN	WH	13	292	MASON	C	3	130	MASON	HH	3	379
MARTIN	WH	4	250	MASKELL	AJ	2	221	MASON	C	11	242	MASON	HH	10	333
MARTIN	WH	7	251	MASKELL	C	4	250	MASON	CA	12	350	MASON	HJ	2	222
MARTIN	WH	8	215	MASKELL	CC	2	221	MASON	CC	4	250	MASON	HJ	2	222
MARTIN	WH	10	333	MASKELL	CN	2	222	MASON	CF	6	275	MASON	HJ	3	130
MARTIN	WJ	1	227	MASKELL	D	9	391	MASON	CG	4	250	MASON	HK	2	222
MARTIN	WJ	1	227	MASKELL	EG	4	250	MASON	CH	9	130	MASON	HT	7	252
MARTIN	WJ	7	251	MASKELL	EH	7	251	MASON	CO	7	252	MASON	J	1	228
MARTIN	WJ	13	291	MASKELL	F	13	292	MASON	CS	7	252	MASON	J	3	130
MARTIN	WJ	13	291	MASKELL	HT	13	292	MASON	E	1	227	MASON	J	4	251
MARTIN	WL	1	227	MASKELL	J	14	209	MASON	E	6	275	MASON	J	6	276
MARTINA	AC	1	227	MASKELL	JA	4	250	MASON	E	9	301	MASON	J	7	252
MARTINDALE	A	5	232	MASKELL	MA	7	252	MASON	EF	8	215	MASON	J	7	252

Name	In.	V	Pg	Name	In.	V	Pg	Name	In.	V	Pg	Name	In.	V	Pg
MASON	J	8	215	MASON	WH	12	155	MASTERS	AW	4	251	MATHER	SG	11	243
MASON	J	9	130	MASON	WJ	13	292	MASTERS	C	4	251	MATHER	T	14	210
MASON	J	9	130	MASON	WM	5	232	MASTERS	CS	12	351	MATHER	W	7	253
MASON	J	10	151	MASON	WR	7	252	MASTERS	E	6	276	MATHER	WA	12	155
MASON	J	11	242	MASON	WT	4	251	MASTERS	F	1	228	MATHER	WH	8	216
MASON	J	12	154	MASON	WT	7	252	MASTERS	FHJ	1	228	MATHER	WH	14	210
MASON	J	13	292	MASON	WW	1	228	MASTERS	FJL	4	251	MATHERON	WJ	1	228
MASON	J	13	292	MASON	WW	13	292	MASTERS	G	1	228	MATHERS	A	9	302
MASON	J	13	292	MASSAM	A	11	242	MASTERS	GE	4	251	MATHERS	F	12	155
MASON	J	14	209	MASSEN	F	10	334	MASTERS	GW	12	351	MATHERS	G	12	155
MASON	JE	14	209	MASSEN	WE	9	130	MASTERS	H	1	228	MATHERS	H	8	216
MASON	JH	2	222	MASSEY	A	6	276	MASTERS	H	4	251	MATHERS	J	8	216
MASON	JH	10	151	MASSEY	A	11	242	MASTERS	HG	6	276	MATHERS	J	8	216
MASON	JW	2	222	MASSEY	A	11	242	MASTERS	J	12	155	MATHERS	J	8	216
MASON	JW	12	155	MASSEY	A	11	242	MASTERS	JA	4	251	MATHERS	JW	8	216
MASON	LE	6	276	MASSEY	AE	14	209	MASTERS	JJ	13	292	MATHERS	R	12	155
MASON	LF	7	252	MASSEY	AJ	6	276	MASTERS	JW	10	151	MATHERS	W	9	130
MASON	LR	4	251	MASSEY	C	14	209	MASTERS	LA	12	155	MATHERS	WG	12	155
MASON	P	7	252	MASSEY	C	14	209	MASTERS	ME	4	251	MATHERS	WJ	7	253
MASON	P	14	209	MASSEY	E	11	242	MASTERS	P	2	223	MATHERS	WR	13	292
MASON	R	4	251	MASSEY	E	11	243	MASTERS	PE	2	223	MATHERTON	A	2	223
MASON	R	11	242	MASSEY	E	14	209	MASTERS	PGE	1	228	MATHESON	GH	10	151
MASON	RE	2	222	MASSEY	E	14	209	MASTERS	T	4	251	MATHESON	JS	11	243
MASON	RHG	2	222	MASSEY	E	14	209	MASTERS	T	12	351	MATHEW	HH	7	253
MASON	RT	3	130	MASSEY	F	11	242	MASTERS	V	7	253	MATHEWS	A	5	232
MASON	S	4	251	MASSEY	FH	14	209	MASTERS	W	1	228	MATHEWS	F	2	223
MASON	S	8	215	MASSEY	FJ	1	228	MASTERS	W	4	251	MATHEWS	GA	5	232
MASON	S	9	301	MASSEY	FT	10	334	MASTERS	W	6	276	MATHEWS	GH	1	228
MASON	S	11	242	MASSEY	GB	10	151	MASTERS	WA	1	228	MATHEWS	GH	13	292
MASON	S	13	292	MASSEY	H	12	155	MASTERS	WEA	4	252	MATHEWS	GJ	11	243
MASON	SFG	3	130	MASSEY	J	8	216	MASTERS	WH	4	252	MATHEWS	GW	2	223
MASON	T	2	222	MASSEY	J	14	210	MASTERS	WT	12	351	MATHEWS	H	1	228
MASON	T	3	130	MASSEY	J	14	210	MASTERSON	B	12	155	MATHEWS	H	1	228
MASON	T	7	252	MASSEY	JR	11	243	MASTERSON	CH	4	252	MATHEWS	O	3	130
MASON	T	8	215	MASSEY	R	8	216	MASTERTON	C	13	292	MATHEWS	W	1	228
MASON	T	9	302	MASSEY	R	14	210	MASTERTON	F	13	292	MATHEWS	WG	2	223
MASON	T	11	242	MASSEY	S	14	210	MASTERTON	W	13	292	MATHEWSON	A	3	130
MASON	T	14	209	MASSEY	T	2	223	MASTON	HW	12	351	MATHEWSON	A	3	130
MASON	TG	13	292	MASSEY	T	8	216	MATCHAM	AW	10	151	MATHIAS	GA	2	223
MASON	TJ	3	379	MASSEY	T	11	243	MATCHAM	E	12	351	MATHIS	G	7	253
MASON	TW	12	350	MASSEY	W	14	210	MATCHAM	H	4	252	MATHIS	M	7	253
MASON	W	3	379	MASSEY	WG	13	292	MATCHAM	L	4	252	MATHISON	DG	7	253
MASON	W	5	232	MASSEY	WH	6	276	MATHER	C	14	210	MATLEY	D	11	243
MASON	W	6	276	MASSHEDAR	T	8	216	MATHER	CA	11	243	MATLEY	JA	14	210
MASON	W	7	252	MASSINGHAM	F	6	276	MATHER	F	14	210	MATON	A	4	252
MASON	W	8	215	MASSINGHAM	WG	7	253	MATHER	G	14	210	MATON	FF	4	252
MASON	W	8	216	MASSINGHAM	WJ	1	228	MATHER	H	8	216	MATON	FT	4	252
MASON	W	8	216	MASSOM	WH	4	251	MATHER	H	8	216	MATON	H	4	252
MASON	W	11	242	MASSON	GG	10	334	MATHER	H	14	210	MATON	P	4	252
MASON	W	11	242	MASSON	IL	10	334	MATHER	H	14	210	MATON	W	4	252
MASON	W	12	350	MASTERMAN	JE	11	243	MATHER	J	11	243	MATON	W	4	252
MASON	W	14	209	MASTERMAN	WW	8	216	MATHER	J	14	210	MATON	WD	4	252
MASON	WCJ	12	155	MASTERS	A	1	228	MATHER	J	14	210	MATSELL	JH	1	228
MASON	WE	10	334	MASTERS	A	4	251	MATHER	J	14	210	MATSON	AM	5	232
MASON	WF	4	251	MASTERS	AE	1	228	MATHER	NEG	1	228	MATSON	BEV	13	293

MATSON	C	5	232	MATTHEWS	C	9	130	MATTHEWS	H	2	224	MATTHEWS	R	2	224
MATSON	O	10	334	MATTHEWS	C	12	155	MATTHEWS	H	3	131	MATTHEWS	R	13	293
MATSON	R	4	252	MATTHEWS	CD	7	253	MATTHEWS	H	4	253	MATTHEWS	RM	10	334
MATSON	W	14	210	MATTHEWS	CE	3	130	MATTHEWS	H	7	253	MATTHEWS	S	7	254
MATTEN	A	3	130	MATTHEWS	CE	7	253	MATTHEWS	H	8	216	MATTHEWS	S	13	293
MATTEN	AMT	3	130	MATTHEWS	CG	5	232	MATTHEWS	H	8	216	MATTHEWS	SC	1	229
MATTEN	GM	12	155	MATTHEWS	CP	4	252	MATTHEWS	H	10	334	MATTHEWS	SC	3	131
MATTEN	W	12	155	MATTHEWS	CP	6	277	MATTHEWS	H	11	243	MATTHEWS	SE	10	334
MATTEY	J	1	229	MATTHEWS	CW	10	151	MATTHEWS	H	13	293	MATTHEWS	SF	4	253
MATTEY	P	6	276	MATTHEWS	D	1	229	MATTHEWS	H	13	293	MATTHEWS	SFP	1	229
MATTHEW	D	14	210	MATTHEWS	DH	11	243	MATTHEWS	HE	12	155	MATTHEWS	SH	13	293
MATTHEW	EM	3	130	MATTHEWS	E	1	229	MATTHEWS	HG	3	131	MATTHEWS	T	3	131
MATTHEW	G	12	155	MATTHEWS	E	2	223	MATTHEWS	HJ	2	224	MATTHEWS	T	13	293
MATTHEW	LW	3	130	MATTHEWS	E	9	130	MATTHEWS	HJ	3	379	MATTHEWS	T	14	211
MATTHEW	W	2	223	MATTHEWS	E	14	210	MATTHEWS	HJ	5	232	MATTHEWS	TAG	7	254
MATTHEWMAN	E	9	130	MATTHEWS	EA	4	253	MATTHEWS	HP	1	229	MATTHEWS	TG	7	254
MATTHEWMAN	J	9	130	MATTHEWS	EC	2	223	MATTHEWS	HS	4	253	MATTHEWS	THR	1	229
MATTHEWMAN	W	8	216	MATTHEWS	EH	6	277	MATTHEWS	HW	3	131	MATTHEWS	TJ	1	229
MATTHEWMAN	WH	6	276	MATTHEWS	EJ	13	293	MATTHEWS	HW	7	254	MATTHEWS	V	3	131
MATTHEWS	A	1	229	MATTHEWS	ER	5	232	MATTHEWS	J	2	224	MATTHEWS	W	2	224
MATTHEWS	A	4	252	MATTHEWS	EVT	2	223	MATTHEWS	J	3	379	MATTHEWS	W	5	233
MATTHEWS	A	4	252	MATTHEWS	EW	10	334	MATTHEWS	J	4	253	MATTHEWS	W	6	277
MATTHEWS	A	6	276	MATTHEWS	F	1	229	MATTHEWS	J	6	277	MATTHEWS	W	6	277
MATTHEWS	A	6	276	MATTHEWS	F	2	223	MATTHEWS	J	7	254	MATTHEWS	W	7	254
MATTHEWS	A	6	276	MATTHEWS	F	6	277	MATTHEWS	J	9	130	MATTHEWS	W	8	216
MATTHEWS	A	7	253	MATTHEWS	F	6	277	MATTHEWS	J	10	334	MATTHEWS	W	11	243
MATTHEWS	A	7	253	MATTHEWS	F	9	302	MATTHEWS	J	12	155	MATTHEWS	W	13	293
MATTHEWS	A	11	243	MATTHEWS	F	10	334	MATTHEWS	J	13	293	MATTHEWS	W	14	211
MATTHEWS	A	13	293	MATTHEWS	F	12	155	MATTHEWS	J	14	211	MATTHEWS	WA	1	229
MATTHEWS	A	13	293	MATTHEWS	F	14	211	MATTHEWS	J	14	211	MATTHEWS	WA	4	253
MATTHEWS	A	13	293	MATTHEWS	FA	6	277	MATTHEWS	J	14	211	MATTHEWS	WA	4	253
MATTHEWS	AC	7	253	MATTHEWS	FB	4	252	MATTHEWS	J	14	211	MATTHEWS	WA	9	302
MATTHEWS	AE	1	229	MATTHEWS	FB	10	334	MATTHEWS	JA	3	379	MATTHEWS	WA	10	151
MATTHEWS	AE	2	223	MATTHEWS	FG	5	232	MATTHEWS	JB	4	253	MATTHEWS	WC	5	233
MATTHEWS	AE	3	130	MATTHEWS	FH	1	229	MATTHEWS	JC	4	253	MATTHEWS	WE	4	253
MATTHEWS	AE	13	293	MATTHEWS	FH	6	277	MATTHEWS	JE	3	379	MATTHEWS	WE	10	151
MATTHEWS	AG	2	223	MATTHEWS	FH	7	253	MATTHEWS	JE	12	351	MATTHEWS	WG	1	229
MATTHEWS	AG	4	252	MATTHEWS	FJ	6	277	MATTHEWS	JF	7	254	MATTHEWS	WG	1	229
MATTHEWS	AH	7	253	MATTHEWS	FJ	7	253	MATTHEWS	JH	1	229	MATTHEWS	WH	2	224
MATTHEWS	AH	10	151	MATTHEWS	FJ	11	243	MATTHEWS	JH	8	216	MATTHEWS	WHE	1	230
MATTHEWS	AJ	6	276	MATTHEWS	FT	3	130	MATTHEWS	JR	4	253	MATTHEWS	WI	6	277
MATTHEWS	AJ	10	151	MATTHEWS	FW	1	229	MATTHEWS	JT	6	277	MATTHEWS	WI	6	277
MATTHEWS	AJ	10	334	MATTHEWS	FW	3	130	MATTHEWS	JW	7	254	MATTHEWS	WJ	4	253
MATTHEWS	B	5	232	MATTHEWS	G	2	223	MATTHEWS	JW	12	156	MATTHEWS	WS	1	230
MATTHEWS	B	6	276	MATTHEWS	G	6	277	MATTHEWS	JW	12	351	MATTHEWS	WT	3	379
MATTHEWS	B	10	334	MATTHEWS	G	7	253	MATTHEWS	JW	14	211	MATTHEWS	WT	7	254
MATTHEWS	BH	12	351	MATTHEWS	G	10	151	MATTHEWS	JW	14	211	MATTHEWS	WT	14	211
MATTHEWS	BW	2	223	MATTHEWS	G	13	293	MATTHEWS	LA	6	277	MATTHEWS	WV	11	243
MATTHEWS	C	1	229	MATTHEWS	GA	13	293	MATTHEWS	LC	1	229	MATTHIAS	AE	1	230
MATTHEWS	C	1	229	MATTHEWS	GF	6	277	MATTHEWS	LF	12	156	MATTHIAS	HE	1	230
MATTHEWS	C	2	223	MATTHEWS	GJ	1	229	MATTHEWS	LJ	2	224	MATTICK	S	3	131
MATTHEWS	C	3	130	MATTHEWS	GR	4	253	MATTHEWS	OW	2	224	MATTICK	TS	3	131
MATTHEWS	C	3	379	MATTHEWS	GW	2	223	MATTHEWS	P	8	216	MATTINGLEY	F	2	224
MATTHEWS	C	4	252	MATTHEWS	GW	2	224	MATTHEWS	P	14	211	MATTINGLEY	JW	1	230
MATTHEWS	C	6	277	MATTHEWS	GWA	10	151	MATTHEWS	PW	2	224	MATTINGLY	CA	4	253

MATTINGLY	ET	7	254	MAWBY	WE	12	351	MAY	C	3	131	MAY	LV	13	294				
MATTINGLY	H	4	253	MAWHOOD	A	3	131	MAY	C	4	254	MAY	PA	4	254				
MATTISON	C	4	253	MAWHOOD	HJ	3	131	MAY	C	10	335	MAY	PE	5	233				
MATTISON	J	8	216	MAWMAN	CR	8	217	MAY	CA	7	255	MAY	PT	2	225				
MATTISON	T	4	253	MAWN	T	8	217	MAY	CE	3	131	MAY	R	13	294				
MATTOCK	PA	12	351	MAWSON	A	9	130	MAY	CH	4	254	MAY	RD	1	230				
MATTOCK	WG	12	351	MAWSON	B	8	217	MAY	CH	5	233	MAY	RF	7	255				
MATTOCK	WW	2	224	MAWSON	E	8	217	MAY	CW	12	351	MAY	RJ	2	225				
MATTOCKS	I	6	277	MAWSON	E	8	217	MAY	D	11	244	MAY	S	9	302				
MATTOCKS	JW	2	224	MAWSON	F	11	243	MAY	E	1	230	MAY	TA	12	156				
MATTOCKS	JWH	7	254	MAWSON	H	8	217	MAY	E	2	225	MAY	TG	2	225				
MAUD	A	9	130	MAWSON	H	8	217	MAY	EG	5	233	MAY	W	6	278				
MAUD	JW	9	302	MAWSON	H	8	416	MAY	EW	1	230	MAY	W	9	130				
MAUD	S	8	217	MAWSON	HS	9	302	MAY	F	1	230	MAY	W	10	152				
MAUD	T	8	217	MAWSON	J	8	217	MAY	F	4	254	MAY	W	10	152				
MAUDE	A	8	217	MAWSON	JT	8	217	MAY	F	9	130	MAY	WC	4	254				
MAUDE	B	8	217	MAWSON	MH	9	302	MAY	FG	7	255	MAY	WC	7	255				
MAUDE	CE	8	217	MAWSON	T	8	217	MAY	FJ	7	255	MAY	WE	2	225				
MAUDE	FG	12	351	MAWSON	V	9	130	MAY	FJ	13	294	MAY	WE	4	254				
MAUDE	J	9	302	MAWSON	W	2	225	MAY	FJ	13	294	MAY	WE	4	254				
MAUDE	J	9	302	MAWSON	W	8	217	MAY	FW	9	130	MAY	WGH	10	334				
MAUDE	R	9	302	MAWSON	W	8	217	MAY	G	2	225	MAY	WJ	10	152				
MAUDE	S	9	130	MAWSON	W	8	217	MAY	G	6	278	MAY	WJ	10	152				
MAUDE	S	9	302	MAWSON	W	9	302	MAY	G	7	255	MAY	WJH	10	152				
MAUDE	TH	8	217	MAXEY	H	12	156	MAY	G	7	255	MAY	WT	2	225				
MAUGER	CRP	4	253	MAXFIELD	F	6	278	MAY	G	9	302	MAYBANK	D	7	255				
MAUGER	S	4	253	MAXFIELD	H	10	334	MAY	G	10	151	MAYBANK	E	5	233				
MAUGHAM	EC	2	224	MAXLOW	AW	3	131	MAY	GH	3	131	MAYBANK	J	13	294				
MAUL	R	2	224	MAXSTED	AG	2	225	MAY	GT	13	294	MAYBANK	JH	13	294				
MAULE	AH	12	351	MAXTED	AV	10	151	MAY	GT	13	294	MAYBANKS	C	10	152				
MAULE	E	6	278	MAXTED	E	1	230	MAY	H	2	225	MAYBOUR	M	10	152				
MAULE	E	6	278	MAXTED	GA	4	254	MAY	H	7	255	MAYCLEM	F	1	230				
MAULE	EW	12	351	MAXWELL	A	13	293	MAY	H	11	243	MAYCOCK	AE	11	244				
MAULE	HAG	7	254	MAXWELL	AE	7	254	MAY	HF	2	225	MAYCOCK	B	6	278				
MAULE	RWJ	7	254	MAXWELL	C	13	293	MAY	HF	10	152	MAYCOCK	G	12	351				
MAULE	WJ	6	278	MAXWELL	D	13	293	MAY	HG	7	255	MAYCOCK	GT	6	278				
MAUND	LJB	6	278	MAXWELL	G	5	233	MAY	HJ	4	254	MAYCOCK	GW	13	294				
MAUNDER	F	4	253	MAXWELL	H	4	254	MAY	HJ	13	294	MAYCOCK	L	6	278				
MAUNDER	FJ	2	224	MAXWELL	J	14	211	MAY	HR	4	254	MAYCOCK	PA	12	352				
MAUNDER	JW	2	224	MAXWELL	J	14	211	MAY	HT	3	379	MAYCOCK	S	12	352				
MAUNDER	TM	2	224	MAXWELL	JA	10	151	MAY	J	1	230	MAYCOCK	WG	1	230				
MAUNDERS	J	4	254	MAXWELL	JR	1	230	MAY	J	3	379	MAYCOX	A	14	211				
MAUNDERS	TH	3	131	MAY	A	1	230	MAY	J	8	217	MAYDEW	D	6	278				
MAUNDERS	W	4	254	MAY	A	1	230	MAY	J	8	217	MAYELL	J	4	254				
MAUNTON	HG	13	293	MAY	A	3	131	MAY	J	9	130	MAYELL	JWC	2	225				
MAURER	S	14	211	MAY	A	13	294	MAY	J	11	244	MAYER	A	1	230				
MAURICE	TF	7	254	MAY	AE	7	254	MAY	J	13	294	MAYER	G	11	244				
MAURIN	M	4	254	MAY	AF	2	225	MAY	J	13	294	MAYER	GA	2	225				
MAURY	F	2	225	MAY	AH	4	254	MAY	JA	13	294	MAYER	WH	5	233				
MAWBEY	W	2	225	MAY	AH	13	294	MAY	JH	3	380	MAYERS	A	14	211				
MAWBY	AV	3	131	MAY	AH	13	294	MAY	JJ	5	233	MAYES	A	5	233				
MAWBY	AW	12	351	MAY	AK	7	254	MAY	JJ	12	351	MAYES	A	9	302				
MAWBY	E	2	225	MAY	AL	10	334	MAY	JJW	5	233	MAYES	AE	12	156				
MAWBY	SC	3	131	MAY	AW	4	254	MAY	JP	7	255	MAYES	C	12	352				
MAWBY	TH	6	278	MAY	B	2	225	MAY	LJ	4	254	MAYES	CW	13	294				

MAYES	D	1	230	MAYNARD	EB	10	152	MAYSTON	A	3	131	MCBRIDE	J	7	241
MAYES	EG	9	302	MAYNARD	EC	2	226	MAYSTON	A	3	132	MCBRIDE	JD	9	297
MAYES	F	12	156	MAYNARD	ES	13	295	MAYSTON	CG	3	132	MCBRIDE	R	14	211
MAYES	GA	12	156	MAYNARD	F	5	233	MAYTUM	AE	13	295	MCBRIDE	T	7	241
MAYES	HW	12	156	MAYNARD	F	12	157	MAYTUM	B	13	295	MCBRYDE	A	7	241
MAYES	J	12	156	MAYNARD	H	12	157	MAYTUM	W	13	295	MCCABE	C	9	124
MAYES	J	12	156	MAYNARD	J	5	233	MAYWATERS	F	10	152	MCCABE	C	9	297
MAYES	JC	9	302	MAYNARD	L	6	278	MAYZES	GW	13	295	MCCABE	F	9	297
MAYES	JGL	12	156	MAYNARD	L	7	255	MAYZES	T	4	255	MCCABE	FW	11	244
MAYES	RT	9	302	MAYNARD	L	13	295	MAZZA	J	8	218	MCCABE	G	14	212
MAYES	SA	12	156	MAYNARD	SH	2	226	MCADAM	J	10	143	MCCABE	H	11	244
MAYES	SW	12	156	MAYNARD	W	2	226	MCADAM	T	1	218	MCCABE	J	14	212
MAYES	W	12	156	MAYNARD	W	12	157	MCADAM	W	3	124	MCCABE	JH	14	212
MAYES	WF	13	294	MAYNARD	WHF	2	226	MCADAM	WE	1	218	MCCABE	L	14	212
MAYHEAD	AH	11	244	MAYNE	A	7	255	MCADAM	WW	1	218	MCCABE	P	10	330
MAYHEAD	C	10	152	MAYNE	B	8	218	MCALEESE	E	4	255	MCCABE	P	11	245
MAYHEAD	F	10	152	MAYNE	HW	7	255	MCALEESE	W	4	255	MCCABE	TE	11	245
MAYHEAD	F	10	152	MAYNE	HW	10	152	MCALLEN	J	4	255	MCCADDEN	J	11	245
MAYHEAD	JH	10	152	MAYNE	J	5	234	MCALLEN	J	4	255	MCCAFFERY	D	11	245
MAYHEW	A	9	130	MAYNE	J	7	255	MCALLEN	P	4	255	MCCAFFREY	J	11	245
MAYHEW	AA	12	156	MAYNE	JD	4	254	MCALLEN	T	4	255	MCCALL	F	8	218
MAYHEW	AE	2	225	MAYNE	JT	10	335	MCALLEN	T	4	255	MCCALL	H	11	245
MAYHEW	AJ	2	225	MAYNE	RJ	5	234	MCALLISTER	G	10	330	MCCALL	J	11	245
MAYHEW	FF	13	294	MAYNE	WR	10	152	MCALLISTER	JP	11	244	MCCALL	T	11	424
MAYHEW	G	1	230	MAYNELL	A	8	218	MCALLISTER	T	8	218	MCCALLA	WF	7	241
MAYHEW	G	2	225	MAYNER	WA	6	278	MCALROY	F	11	244	MCCALLAN	J	7	241
MAYHEW	GH	12	156	MAYO	AE	14	211	MCANANEY	T	9	123	MCCALLUM	AD	10	330
MAYHEW	H	9	130	MAYO	CJ	13	295	MCANDREW	A	8	218	MCCALLUM	CA	10	330
MAYHEW	J	1	230	MAYO	EJ	7	255	MCANDREW	J	8	218	MCCALLUM	D	10	330
MAYHEW	J	2	226	MAYO	F	7	256	MCANDREW	M	8	218	MCCAMLEY	J	9	124
MAYHEW	LJ	2	226	MAYO	FW	2	226	MCANDREW	R	8	218	MCCANDIE	D	9	124
MAYHEW	RJ	2	226	MAYO	GP	10	335	MCANDREW	T	8	218	MCCANN	A	9	124
MAYHEW	S	10	152	MAYO	H	7	256	MCANDREW	W	8	218	MCCANN	A	14	212
MAYHEW	TC	1	231	MAYO	HG	6	278	MCANDRY	B	11	244	MCCANN	AJ	4	255
MAYHEW	WA	1	231	MAYO	J	10	152	MCANEARY	J	11	244	MCCANN	E	9	124
MAYHO	G	5	233	MAYO	J	11	244	MCARDELL	HV	13	281	MCCANN	FW	2	226
MAYLE	CS	7	255	MAYO	JA	6	278	MCARDLE	E	11	244	MCCANN	J	9	124
MAYLE	H	13	294	MAYO	JP	3	131	MCARDLE	J	9	123	MCCANN	J	14	212
MAYLE	J	7	255	MAYO	S	4	254	MCARDLE	J	14	211	MCCANN	J	14	212
MAYLE	L	13	295	MAYO	TGW	10	152	MCARTHUR	A	11	244	MCCANN	J	14	212
MAYLED	E	1	231	MAYO	W	4	255	MCARTHUR	N	11	244	MCCANN	JW	14	212
MAYLES	C	5	233	MAYOR	AE	2	226	MCAULEY	J	8	218	MCCANN	T	13	281
MAYLES	HC	5	233	MAYOR	F	11	244	MCAULIFFE	W	7	241	MCCANN	W	7	241
MAYLETT	H	11	244	MAYORS	A	11	244	MCAVAN	A	8	218	MCCANNON	CH	14	212
MAYLIN	CR	12	156	MAYOSS	FW	1	231	MCAVAN	H	9	123	MCCARDLE	D	9	124
MAYLIN	G	5	233	MAYS	C	7	256	MCAVOY	DE	2	226	MCCARLEY	T	14	212
MAYLING	H	5	234	MAYS	H	5	234	MCAVOY	RJ	2	226	MCCARNEY	O	13	282
MAYLING	JN	5	233	MAYS	J	7	256	MCBAIN	D	9	297	MCCARRICK	M	14	212
MAYMON	H	8	217	MAYS	S	13	295	MCBAIN	HT	13	281	MCCARTHY	A	14	212
MAYMON	WG	8	217	MAYS	W	7	256	MCBEATH	A	9	124	MCCARTHY	AJ	3	377
MAYNARD	AHG	2	226	MAYS	WS	2	226	MCBRAIN	AE	2	226	MCCARTHY	AJ	3	378
MAYNARD	CF	13	295	MAYSON	T	8	218	MCBRIDE	AJ	10	330	MCCARTHY	C	13	282
MAYNARD	CW	12	156	MAYSON	T	8	218	MCBRIDE	AM	9	124	MCCARTHY	D	3	378
MAYNARD	D	13	295	MAYSON	W	9	302	MCBRIDE	E	9	124	MCCARTHY	D	13	282
MAYNARD	E	12	156	MAYSON	WH	9	303	MCBRIDE	HJ	4	255	MCCARTHY	D	13	282

Name	In.			Name	In.			Name	In.			Name	In.		
MCCARTHY	D	14	212	MCCAULEY	A	14	213	MCCORMICK	EA	8	219	MCCUTCHEON	D	14	213
MCCARTHY	DC	2	226	MCCAWLEY	CG	3	124	MCCORMICK	H	11	246	MCCUTCHEON	E	14	213
MCCARTHY	DJ	13	282	MCCAWLEY	F	3	124	MCCORMICK	HW	8	219	MCCUTCHEON	J	4	255
MCCARTHY	E	1	218	MCCAWLEY	RF	2	227	MCCORMICK	J	11	246	MCCUTCHEON	S	4	255
MCCARTHY	E	10	330	MCCERTON	J	9	124	MCCORMICK	J	11	246	MCCUTCHEON	W	4	255
MCCARTHY	EV	2	226	MCCLAREN	TJ	10	144	MCCORMICK	J	14	213	MCCUTCHEON	WJ	14	214
MCCARTHY	F	4	255	MCCLEAN	J	11	245	MCCORMICK	JT	11	246	MCDANIEL	G	7	241
MCCARTHY	F	11	245	MCCLEAN	JF	2	227	MCCORMICK	JW	14	213	MCDANIEL	G	7	241
MCCARTHY	FW	11	245	MCCLEAN	R	11	245	MCCORMICK	MHP	10	331	MCDANIEL	J	7	241
MCCARTHY	G	2	226	MCCLEAVE	E	13	282	MCCORMICK	R	5	225	MCDERMOTT	A	11	247
MCCARTHY	GA	10	330	MCCLEAVE	J	7	241	MCCORMICK	T	14	213	MCDERMOTT	A	14	214
MCCARTHY	H	11	245	MCCLELLAN	A	1	219	MCCORMICK	W	6	278	MCDERMOTT	A	14	214
MCCARTHY	HE	3	124	MCCLELLAN	G	11	245	MCCORMICK	W	11	246	MCDERMOTT	B	10	144
MCCARTHY	HH	10	143	MCCLELLAN	SA	1	219	MCCORMICK	W	14	213	MCDERMOTT	E	10	144
MCCARTHY	J	1	218	MCCLELLAND	GT	8	218	MCCORMICK	W	14	213	MCDERMOTT	E	14	214
MCCARTHY	J	1	219	MCCLELLAND	HG	13	282	MCCORMICK	WF	14	213	MCDERMOTT	F	6	279
MCCARTHY	J	2	226	MCCLELLAND	WG	2	227	MCCORMICK	WH	11	246	MCDERMOTT	F	14	214
MCCARTHY	J	2	227	MCCLENNON	J	11	245	MCCORMICK	WH	11	246	MCDERMOTT	H	14	214
MCCARTHY	J	8	218	MCCLORY	JJ	14	213	MCCORMICK	WP	11	246	MCDERMOTT	J	7	241
MCCARTHY	J	8	218	MCCLOUD	C	10	144	MCCORRICK	J	11	246	MCDERMOTT	J	8	219
MCCARTHY	J	10	143	MCCLUMPHA	JH	7	241	MCCOWAN	A	11	246	MCDERMOTT	J	9	124
MCCARTHY	J	11	245	MCCLURE	D	13	282	MCCOY	AE	13	282	MCDERMOTT	J	10	144
MCCARTHY	J	13	282	MCCLURE	D	13	282	MCCOY	D	10	144	MCDERMOTT	J	10	331
MCCARTHY	J	13	282	MCCLURE	H	11	245	MCCOY	D	11	246	MCDERMOTT	J	11	247
MCCARTHY	J	14	212	MCCLURE	JW	11	246	MCCOY	G	14	213	MCDERMOTT	J	14	214
MCCARTHY	J	14	212	MCCLUSKIE	B	14	213	MCCOY	H	9	124	MCDERMOTT	JW	11	247
MCCARTHY	JE	7	241	MCCLUSKY	F	9	124	MCCOY	H	10	144	MCDERMOTT	L	1	219
MCCARTHY	JF	1	219	MCCOAN	WJ	13	282	MCCOY	J	13	282	MCDERMOTT	M	8	219
MCCARTHY	JJ	14	212	MCCONKEY	A	8	218	MCCOY	JT	11	246	MCDERMOTT	R	14	214
MCCARTHY	JM	7	241	MCCONNELL	J	4	255	MCCOY	W	14	213	MCDERMOTT	W	6	279
MCCARTHY	JS	3	378	MCCONNELL	J	11	246	MCCRACKEN	C	6	279	MCDERMOTT	WT	6	279
MCCARTHY	M	2	227	MCCONOCHIE	A	14	213	MCCRACKEN	F	6	279	MCDONALD	A	1	219
MCCARTHY	MH	8	416	MCCONOCHIE	W	14	213	MCCRACKEN	J	11	247	MCDONALD	A	9	391
MCCARTHY	N	8	218	MCCONVELL	A	7	241	MCCRACKEN	S	11	246	MCDONALD	AA	10	144
MCCARTHY	OL	10	143	MCCONVILL	J	8	218	MCCRACKEN	W	11	247	MCDONALD	AC	13	283
MCCARTHY	P	2	227	MCCONVILLE	J	14	213	MCCRACKEN	WS	8	219	MCDONALD	AW	10	144
MCCARTHY	P	4	255	MCCORKELL	WR	10	144	MCCRAE	GWF	2	227	MCDONALD	B	11	247
MCCARTHY	P	13	282	MCCORMACK	AR	2	227	MCCRAE	K	5	246	MCDONALD	C	6	279
MCCARTHY	P	13	282	MCCORMACK	C	8	219	MCCRAITH	W	8	219	MCDONALD	C	11	247
MCCARTHY	P	14	212	MCCORMACK	D	2	227	MCCRERIE	WW	10	144	MCDONALD	CW	14	214
MCCARTHY	T	2	227	MCCORMACK	D	13	282	MCCRUDDEN	D	8	219	MCDONALD	D	9	297
MCCARTHY	T	14	212	MCCORMACK	E	2	227	MCCUE	H	9	124	MCDONALD	D	10	331
MCCARTHY	TE	7	241	MCCORMACK	E	10	144	MCCULLA	F	6	279	MCDONALD	E	1	219
MCCARTHY	TJ	7	241	MCCORMACK	E	13	282	MCCULLAGH	C	11	247	MCDONALD	E	3	378
MCCARTHY	W	1	219	MCCORMACK	J	2	227	MCCULLAN	J	8	219	MCDONALD	E	4	255
MCCARTHY	W	10	144	MCCORMACK	J	6	278	MCCULLANE	P	8	219	MCDONALD	EH	4	256
MCCARTHY	W	11	245	MCCORMACK	J	9	297	MCCULLEY	R	9	124	MCDONALD	F	2	227
MCCARTHY	W	14	212	MCCORMACK	J	10	144	MCCULLOCH	D	8	219	MCDONALD	F	3	124
MCCARTHY	WC	10	144	MCCORMACK	J	11	246	MCCULLOCH	J	8	219	MCDONALD	F	5	225
MCCARTNEY	FA	14	213	MCCORMACK	JP	2	227	MCCULLOCH	J	11	247	MCDONALD	FC	2	227
MCCARTNEY	G	13	282	MCCORMACK	L	1	219	MCCULLOCK	FB	2	227	MCDONALD	FJ	2	227
MCCARTNEY	GA	13	282	MCCORMACK	RG	8	219	MCCULLOCK	RB	2	227	MCDONALD	FJ	4	256
MCCARTNEY	W	4	255	MCCORMACK	S	8	219	MCCULLOCK	W	8	219	MCDONALD	H	10	144
MCCARTNEY	WH	13	282	MCCORMICK	D	11	246	MCCULLOUGH	W	11	247	MCDONALD	J	2	228
MCCASLIN	JE	14	213	MCCORMICK	E	14	213	MCCURDY	S	11	247	MCDONALD	J	6	279

MCDONALD	J	6	279	MCDOWELL	EA	7	242	MCGARVEY	J	11	249	MCGOWAN	T	9	298
MCDONALD	J	8	219	MCDOWELL	G	1	219	MCGARVIE	TA	3	124	MCGOWEN	J	9	298
MCDONALD	J	9	125	MCDOWELL	J	2	228	MCGAW	RW	4	256	MCGOWEN	JW	8	220
MCDONALD	J	9	125	MCDOWELL	JA	14	214	MCGEACHY	J	4	256	MCGOWEN	JW	8	220
MCDONALD	J	11	247	MCDOWELL	JC	11	248	MCGEE	G	13	283	MCGRAIL	D	1	219
MCDONALD	J	14	214	MCDOWELL	R	9	297	MCGEE	H	8	220	MCGRAIL	J	1	219
MCDONALD	J	14	214	MCDOWELL	W	8	219	MCGEE	J	8	220	MCGRAIL	J	9	298
MCDONALD	J	14	214	MCDURMOTT	F	14	215	MCGEE	J	13	283	MCGRAIL	J	9	298
MCDONALD	J	14	214	MCELLIGOTT	A	3	378	MCGEE	J	14	215	MCGRAIL	P	2	228
MCDONALD	JJ	9	125	MCELROY	J	11	248	MCGEE	J	14	215	MCGRAIL	P	14	215
MCDONALD	JJ	11	247	MCEVAN	MP	9	297	MCGEE	WG	8	220	MCGRATH	C	8	220
MCDONALD	JM	3	124	MCEVILLEY	H	11	248	MCGEORGE	CH	7	242	MCGRATH	E	11	249
MCDONALD	JS	12	157	MCEVILLY	P	11	248	MCGEORGE	EW	7	242	MCGRATH	FN	14	215
MCDONALD	JS	13	283	MCEVOY	B	4	256	MCGEORGE	EWC	7	242	MCGRATH	H	14	215
MCDONALD	N	4	256	MCEVOY	H	8	220	MCGEORGE	S	14	215	MCGRATH	J	1	220
MCDONALD	P	9	125	MCEVOY	J	8	220	MCGIBBON	WA	12	352	MCGRATH	J	3	124
MCDONALD	P	9	297	MCEVOY	JH	11	248	MCGIFFEN	JE	10	145	MCGRATH	J	8	220
MCDONALD	PW	7	241	MCEVOY	JJ	4	256	MCGIFFEN	JV	10	145	MCGRATH	J	8	221
MCDONALD	R	11	247	MCEVOY	P	9	125	MCGILL	A	8	220	MCGRATH	J	8	221
MCDONALD	RB	4	256	MCEVOY	P	9	125	MCGILL	C	1	219	MCGRATH	J	11	249
MCDONALD	T	9	297	MCEVOY	P	9	297	MCGILL	D	7	242	MCGRATH	J	11	249
MCDONALD	T	11	247	MCEVOY	P	11	248	MCGILL	H	1	219	MCGRATH	J	14	215
MCDONALD	T	11	248	MCEVOY	R	14	215	MCGILL	H	1	219	MCGRATH	JC	5	225
MCDONALD	TS	1	219	MCEVOY	W	14	215	MCGILVRAY	D	8	220	MCGRATH	JW	11	250
MCDONALD	W	4	256	MCEWAN	J	10	145	MCGINLEY	E	9	297	MCGRATH	L	8	221
MCDONALD	W	8	219	MCEWAN	J	11	248	MCGINLEY	FJ	1	219	MCGRATH	M	9	125
MCDONALD	W	9	125	MCEWAN	RS	3	124	MCGINN	E	11	249	MCGRATH	M	11	250
MCDONALD	W	11	248	MCEWAN	RS	3	124	MCGINN	J	9	125	MCGRATH	R	14	215
MCDONALD	WO	14	214	MCFALL	W	11	249	MCGINN	J	9	125	MCGRATH	T	6	279
MCDONALD	WT	14	214	MCFARLAND	EDW	14	215	MCGINN	LHE	4	256	MCGRATH	W	11	250
MCDONALD-HAY	J	11	248	MCFARLAND	JW	14	215	MCGINN	M	11	249	MCGRATH	W	14	215
MCDONNEL	A	5	225	MCFARLANE	B	10	331	MCGINN	SH	4	256	MCGRATH	WJ	7	242
MCDONNELL	D	8	219	MCFARLANE	D	4	256	MCGLASHON	A	1	219	MCGRAW	J	10	145
MCDONNELL	E	13	283	MCFARLANE	G	14	215	MCGLONE	D	11	249	MCGREAVY	J	8	221
MCDONNELL	E	13	283	MCFARLANE	H	10	145	MCGLONE	J	14	215	MCGREAVY	JF	11	250
MCDONNELL	F	13	283	MCFARLANE	J	11	249	MCGLYNN	P	11	249	MCGREAVY	T	8	221
MCDONNELL	GJ	2	228	MCFARLANE	M	11	249	MCGLYNN	R	11	249	MCGREEVY	EH	3	378
MCDONNELL	J	11	248	MCFARLANE	T	11	249	MCGLYNN	W	11	249	MCGREEVY	GL	3	378
MCDONNELL	TF	13	283	MCFARLANE	W	1	219	MCGOUGH	C	8	220	MCGREEVY	TH	3	378
MCDONNELL	TJM	11	248	MCFARLANE	W	4	256	MCGOUGH	J	8	220	MCGREGOR	AM	14	215
MCDONOUGH	A	9	391	MCFARLANE	W	11	249	MCGOUGH	W	8	220	MCGREGOR	G	8	221
MCDONOUGH	A	11	248	MCFEAT	J	4	256	MCGOURTY	J	8	220	MCGREGOR	J	2	228
MCDONOUGH	J	11	248	MCFEE	G	2	228	MCGOURTY	J	8	220	MCGREGOR	J	2	228
MCDONOUGH	J	11	248	MCFERRAN	F	7	242	MCGOVERN	F	14	215	MCGREGOR	J	8	221
MCDONOUGH	J	11	248	MCGAHAN	JW	11	249	MCGOVERN	M	6	279	MCGREGOR	J	10	145
MCDONOUGH	M	11	248	MCGAHEY	J	6	279	MCGOWAN	B	9	125	MCGREGOR	OF	2	228
MCDOUGALL	NA	7	242	MCGAHEY	J	11	249	MCGOWAN	C	9	391	MCGREGOR	R	14	216
MCDOUGALL	O	14	214	MCGANN	E	13	283	MCGOWAN	E	8	220	MCGREGOR	RJ	8	221
MCDOUGALL	W	10	145	MCGANN	J	13	283	MCGOWAN	G	4	256	MCGUFFICK	W	13	283
MCDOWALL	A	14	214	MCGANN	T	13	283	MCGOWAN	J	8	220	MCGUINN	C	9	125
MCDOWALL	R	3	124	MCGANNAN	J	13	283	MCGOWAN	J	9	297	MCGUINN	J	13	283
MCDOWELL	A	9	297	MCGARRICK	AJ	7	242	MCGOWAN	L	13	283	MCGUINN	M	9	125
MCDOWELL	E	9	297	MCGARRY	E	8	220	MCGOWAN	M	2	228	MCGUINNESS	C	14	216
MCDOWELL	E	10	145	MCGARRY	H	8	220	MCGOWAN	T	1	219	MCGUINNESS	H	8	221
MCDOWELL	E	10	145	MCGARRY	M	11	249	MCGOWAN	T	9	125	MCGUINNESS	H	9	125

MCGUINNESS	J	8	221	MCINNES	AH	7	243	MCKEIRNON	M	11	251	MCKINNEY	J	11	252
MCGUINNESS	JP	8	221	MCINNES	D	11	250	MCKELL	B	9	126	MCKINNON	W	11	252
MCGUINNESS	JR	8	221	MCINNES	E	4	257	MCKELVEY	A	14	216	MCKITTERICK	AJ	1	220
MCGUINNESS	P	9	125	MCINNES	H	11	250	MCKENLEY	JH	9	126	MCKNIGHT	AE	13	284
MCGUINNESS	R	9	125	MCINNES	NA	9	298	MCKENNA	A	11	251	MCKNIGHT	C	8	223
MCGUINNESS	R	14	216	MCINNES	R	7	243	MCKENNA	C	8	222	MCKNIGHT	C	9	298
MCGUIRE	A	1	220	MCINTOSH	AJ	7	243	MCKENNA	CW	11	251	MCKNIGHT	J	11	252
MCGUIRE	A	11	250	MCINTOSH	AW	1	220	MCKENNA	H	8	222	MCKNIGHT	J	11	252
MCGUIRE	G	1	220	MCINTOSH	SG	2	228	MCKENNA	J	11	251	MCKNIGHT	W	11	252
MCGUIRE	G	2	228	MCINTOSH	W	1	220	MCKENNA	J	11	251	MCKNIGHT	WJ	11	252
MCGUIRE	J	6	279	MCINTRYE	GF	10	146	MCKENNA	J	11	251	MCKOEN	E	7	243
MCGUIRE	J	14	216	MCINTYRE	A	1	220	MCKENNA	J	14	216	MCLAREN	AW	2	229
MCGUIRE	JB	11	250	MCINTYRE	A	4	257	MCKENNA	J	14	216	MCLAREN	C	3	125
MCGUIRE	JE	8	221	MCINTYRE	C	8	222	MCKENNA	JH	11	251	MCLAREN	FW	3	378
MCGUIRE	S	7	242	MCINTYRE	C	8	222	MCKENNA	W	8	222	MCLAREN	H	6	280
MCGUIRE	T	1	220	MCINTYRE	CD	3	378	MCKENNELL	J	14	216	MCLAREN	J	9	298
MCGUIRE	T	8	221	MCINTYRE	CT	11	250	MCKENZIE	A	2	228	MCLAREN	J	11	252
MCGUIRE	T	8	221	MCINTYRE	F	3	378	MCKENZIE	A	9	298	MCLAREN	J	11	252
MCGUIRE	T	11	250	MCINTYRE	FS	10	146	MCKENZIE	A	14	216	MCLAREN	JA	13	284
MCGUIRE	T	11	250	MCINTYRE	HG	3	378	MCKENZIE	C	11	251	MCLAREN	JH	9	298
MCGUIRE	W	8	221	MCINTYRE	J	4	257	MCKENZIE	E	13	283	MCLAREN	JR	3	125
MCGUIRK	T	4	256	MCINTYRE	J	6	279	MCKENZIE	F	11	251	MCLAREN	S	7	243
MCGUIRK	W	4	256	MCINTYRE	J	10	146	MCKENZIE	FJ	10	331	MCLAREN	W	2	229
MCGUIRK	WM	4	256	MCINTYRE	J	11	250	MCKENZIE	J	9	298	MCLAUCHLAN	EW	12	352
MCGUNIGALL	J	11	250	MCINTYRE	R	11	251	MCKENZIE	J	13	284	MCLAUGHLIN	G	1	220
MCHALE	A	11	250	MCINTYRE	TG	4	257	MCKENZIE	JW	10	146	MCLAUGHLIN	J	11	252
MCHALE	A	11	250	MCINTYRE	VAE	10	146	MCKENZIE	M	9	298	MCLAUGHLIN	M	9	126
MCHALE	C	8	221	MCINTYRE	W	11	251	MCKENZIE	M	10	146	MCLAUGHLIN	W	4	257
MCHALE	J	8	221	MCINTYRE	WA	13	283	MCKEON	G	10	331	MCLAVERTY	J	10	146
MCHALE	J	8	221	MCIVER	J	8	222	MCKEON	JL	8	222	MCLAY	G	9	126
MCHALE	JF	11	424	MCIVOR	D	9	298	MCKEON	JT	10	146	MCLAY	H	9	298
MCHALE	P	10	146	MCIVOR	GH	8	222	MCKEOWN	A	4	257	MCLAY	J	9	298
MCHALE	R	4	256	MCIVOR	GJ	7	243	MCKEOWN	E	1	220	MCLAY	JB	13	284
MCHALE	R	8	221	MCKALE	G	6	279	MCKEOWN	EAJ	2	228	MCLEAN	AC	11	252
MCHALE	W	8	222	MCKAVE	W	2	228	MCKEOWN	F	1	220	MCLEAN	C	7	243
MCHATTIE	JW	2	228	MCKAY	AE	2	228	MCKEOWN	J	11	251	MCLEAN	CW	8	223
MCHUGH	E	8	222	MCKAY	EA	1	220	MCKEOWN	JM	13	284	MCLEAN	G	14	216
MCHUGH	F	4	256	MCKAY	J	8	222	MCKEOWN	M	1	220	MCLEAN	H	2	229
MCHUGH	F	14	216	MCKAY	JE	11	251	MCKEOWN	M	14	216	MCLEAN	H	14	216
MCHUGH	J	7	242	MCKAY	LH	11	251	MCKEOWN	P	14	216	MCLEAN	J	4	257
MCHUGH	J	7	243	MCKAY	LW	2	228	MCKEOWN	R	6	280	MCLEAN	J	11	252
MCHUGH	J	8	222	MCKAY	P	9	126	MCKEVITT	J	11	251	MCLEAN	N	4	257
MCHUGH	J	11	250	MCKAY	R	3	124	MCKEW	GE	11	251	MCLEAN	R	4	257
MCHUGH	JP	6	279	MCKAY	RJ	3	378	MCKIDDIE	E	11	251	MCLEAN	W	8	223
MCHUGH	JW	8	222	MCKAY	WD	8	222	MCKIE	A	8	222	MCLEAN	WJ	7	243
MCHUGH	M	8	222	MCKAY	WHG	2	228	MCKIE	JH	7	243	MCLEARY	W	11	252
MCHUGH	O	8	222	MCKAY	WW	1	220	MCKIERNEN	T	14	216	MCLEISH	J	11	252
MCHUGH	P	8	222	MCKEAGGAN	T	10	331	MCKILLIGAN	R	8	222	MCLELLAN	A	1	220
MCHUGH	S	8	222	MCKECHNIE		2	228	MCKIMMIE	CE	1	220	MCLELLAN	FW	8	223
MCHUGH	TE	8	222	MCKEE	AE	1	220	MCKINEM	AW	2	229	MCLENAHAN	J	11	252
MCHUGO	W	6	279	MCKEE	AE	3	124	MCKINLAY	HJ	10	146	MCLEOD	AR	7	244
MCINERNEY	F	4	257	MCKEE	JF	14	216	MCKINLEY	CJ	11	252	MCLEOD	H	14	216
MCINERNEY	TH	4	257	MCKEE	S	5	225	MCKINLEY	EH	13	284	MCLEOD	P	13	284
MCINERNEY	TH	4	257	MCKEEVER	J	11	251	MCKINNEY	D	11	252	MCLOUGHLIN	C	9	126
MCINNES	A	11	250	MCKEEVER	J	11	251	MCKINNEY	J	10	331	MCLOUGHLIN	C	9	299

MCLOUGHLIN	D	8	223	MCMANUS	M	6	280	MCNEAL	W	2	229	MCVETY	W	14	218
MCLOUGHLIN	E	7	244	MCMANUS	W	8	223	MCNEALY	J	14	217	MCVEY	A	5	226
MCLOUGHLIN	E	14	216	MCMEEKAN	H	11	253	MCNEIL	D	3	125	MCVEY	J	5	225
MCLOUGHLIN	G	7	244	MCMELLEN	A	9	299	MCNEIL	G	3	125	MCVEY	M	5	226
MCLOUGHLIN	G	11	252	MCMELLON	J	14	217	MCNEIL	H	14	217	MCVEY	TN	5	226
MCLOUGHLIN	H	8	223	MCMILLAN	A	2	229	MCNEIL	J	8	224	MCVEY	WM	5	226
MCLOUGHLIN	H	8	223	MCMILLAN	A	14	217	MCNEIL	J	9	299	MCVICAR	J	1	221
MCLOUGHLIN	J	8	223	MCMILLAN	BD	8	223	MCNEIL	J	14	217	MCWHARTER	J	11	254
MCLOUGHLIN	J	8	223	MCMILLAN	J	14	217	MCNEIL	JW	2	229	MCWILLIAM	A	14	218
MCLOUGHLIN	J	9	299	MCMILLAN	RA	2	229	MCNEIL	R	8	224	MCWILLIAM	G	11	254
MCLOUGHLIN	J	11	252	MCMILLAN	TW	1	220	MCNEILL	HB	5	225	MCWILLIAM	R	11	254
MCLOUGHLIN	J	11	253	MCMILLAN	TW	1	221	MCNEILL	WJ	5	225	MCWILLIAMS	AA	4	257
MCLOUGHLIN	J	11	253	MCMILLAN	W	1	221	MCNELLY	TW	2	229	MCWILLIAMS	J	13	284
MCLOUGHLIN	J	11	253	MCMILLAN	W	8	223	MCNESBY	VW	10	146	MCWILLIAMS	T	11	254
MCLOUGHLIN	J	11	253	MCMILLEN	R	5	225	MCNICHOL	M	8	224	MEABY	E	1	231
MCLOUGHLIN	JW	8	223	MCMINN	C	11	253	MCNICHOL	W	8	224	MEABY	JG	2	230
MCLOUGHLIN	M	9	126	MCMORINE	PA	11	253	MCNICHOLLS	W	11	254	MEABY	W	1	231
MCLOUGHLIN	M	11	253	MCMULLAN	J	8	224	MCNIEL	E	8	224	MEACE	N	12	157
MCLOUGHLIN	M	11	253	MCMULLEN	W	8	224	MCNIFF	A	8	224	MEACHAM	A	6	280
MCLOUGHLIN	P	9	126	MCMULLOCK	SG	13	284	MCNISH	J	1	221	MEACHAM	CT	2	230
MCLOUGHLIN	T	9	126	MCNAB	AS	4	257	MCNULTY	AV	7	244	MEACHAM	GL	12	352
MCLOUGHLIN	W	14	216	MCNAB	J	8	224	MCNULTY	E	11	254	MEACHAM	J	5	234
MCLOUGLIN	V	10	331	MCNAB	JE	8	224	MCNULTY	J	9	126	MEACHAM	J	12	157
MCLUCKIE	D	1	220	MCNAB	JS	11	253	MCNULTY	T	8	224	MEACHAM	WC	6	280
MCLUCKIE	HA	2	229	MCNAB	W	11	254	MCNULTY	T	10	146	MEACHAM	WJ	6	280
MCMAHON	CE	7	244	MCNAIR	G	14	217	MCPARLAND	A	11	254	MEACHAN	W	10	153
MCMAHON	E	11	253	MCNAIR	T	10	146	MCPHAIL	CS	11	254	MEACHEM	HJ	2	230
MCMAHON	J	7	244	MCNALLEY	W	6	280	MCPHAIL	D	2	229	MEACOCK	FW	7	256
MCMAHON	J	8	223	MCNALLY	BJ	2	229	MCPHAIL	JG	10	146	MEACOCK	HR	12	352
MCMAHON	J	11	253	MCNALLY	C	2	229	MCPHEAT	J	5	225	MEAD	A	5	234
MCMAHON	J	11	253	MCNALLY	G	11	253	MCPHEAT	M	5	225	MEAD	A	5	234
MCMAHON	J	14	217	MCNALLY	J	2	229	MCPHERSON	AL	13	284	MEAD	A	5	234
MCMAHON	J	14	217	MCNALLY	JC	2	229	MCPHERSON	J	1	221	MEAD	A	12	157
MCMAHON	J	14	217	MCNALLY	M	1	221	MCPHERSON	MR	8	224	MEAD	AC	5	234
MCMAHON	K	10	146	MCNALLY	M	10	146	MCQUEEN	CEE	10	146	MEAD	AH	5	234
MCMAHON	M	11	253	MCNALLY	P	11	254	MCQUEEN	D	1	221	MEAD	AH	6	280
MCMAHON	MT	10	146	MCNALLY	T	11	254	MCQUEEN	E	10	147	MEAD	AJ	5	234
MCMAHON	S	9	126	MCNALLY	W	9	126	MCQUILLAN	AW	3	125	MEAD	AJ	7	256
MCMAHON	TAJ	7	244	MCNALLY	W	11	254	MCQUINN	F	10	331	MEAD	AV	7	256
MCMAHON	W	11	253	MCNALUS	R	8	224	MCRAE	A	11	254	MEAD	AW	5	234
MCMAHON	W	11	253	MCNAMARA	J	13	284	MCRAE	EJ	14	217	MEAD	BW	6	280
MCMAHON	W	11	253	MCNAMARA	J	14	217	MCRAE	W	1	221	MEAD	C	2	230
MCMAHON	W	14	217	MCNAMARA	JH	9	299	MCRAE	WW	2	230	MEAD	C	5	234
MCMANINGWELL	C	8	223	MCNAMARA	M	2	229	MCSWAYNE	GH	10	147	MEAD	CH	6	280
MCMANUS	A	8	223	MCNAMARA	O	2	229	MCSWEENEY	D	1	221	MEAD	D	5	234
MCMANUS	D	14	217	MCNAMARA	T	11	254	MCSWEENEY	J	1	221	MEAD	E	4	257
MCMANUS	F	8	223	MCNAMARA	W	14	217	MCSWEENEY	J	11	254	MEAD	E	5	234
MCMANUS	F	8	223	MCNAMARA	WA	12	352	MCSWEENEY	J	13	284	MEAD	E	5	234
MCMANUS	GW	8	223	MCNAMARA	WE	13	284	MCSWEENY	EO	3	125	MEAD	E	5	234
MCMANUS	H	4	257	MCNANARA		8	224	MCTIGHE	A	14	218	MEAD	E	5	235
MCMANUS	J	8	223	MCNAUGHTAN	JNR	10	331	MCVALATINE	A	8	224	MEAD	EP	1	231
MCMANUS	J	14	217	MCNAUGHTON	FJ	13	284	MCVAY	M	9	127	MEAD	ET	6	280
MCMANUS	J	14	217	MCNAUGHTON	J	13	284	MCVEIGHTY	A	6	280	MEAD	F	5	235
MCMANUS	JT	14	217	MCNAY	JW	9	299	MCVETY	AE	2	230	MEAD	F	5	235
MCMANUS	LE	6	280	MCNEAL	J	2	229	MCVETY	J	11	254	MEAD	F	5	235

MEAD	F	8	224	MEADES	WC	3	132	MEALING	CB	6	281	MEDD	S	8	225
MEAD	F	12	157	MEADLEY	JH	8	224	MEALING	GE	7	256	MEDDEMEN	F	7	257
MEAD	FH	12	157	MEADOWCROFT	F	9	303	MEALING	HW	5	236	MEDDEN	WH	13	295
MEAD	G	5	235	MEADOWCROFT	J	11	255	MEALING	J	11	255	MEDDER	E	10	335
MEAD	G	5	235	MEADOWS	A	3	132	MEALING	JD	2	231	MEDDINGS	HL	6	281
MEAD	G	6	280	MEADOWS	A	6	280	MEALING	JE	5	236	MEDHURST	AA	4	258
MEAD	G	12	157	MEADOWS	A	14	218	MEALING	W	11	255	MEDHURST	ER	5	236
MEAD	G	14	218	MEADOWS	AR	8	224	MEALING	WA	2	231	MEDHURST	HE	4	258
MEAD	GE	12	157	MEADOWS	CS	10	153	MEANEY	ER	4	258	MEDHURST	WH	5	236
MEAD	H	5	235	MEADOWS	F	4	257	MEAR	AL	10	153	MEDLEY	AH	7	257
MEAD	H	5	235	MEADOWS	H	13	295	MEARE	JE	2	231	MEDLEY	H	8	225
MEAD	H	5	235	MEADOWS	J	2	230	MEARES	W	9	131	MEDLEY	S	14	218
MEAD	H	5	235	MEADOWS	L	3	132	MEARS	A	1	231	MEDLEY	W	4	258
MEAD	H	7	256	MEADOWS	SF	2	230	MEARS	A	1	231	MEDLEY	W	8	225
MEAD	HA	5	235	MEADOWS	SG	13	295	MEARS	A	3	132	MEDLICOTT	FP	2	231
MEAD	HA	12	157	MEADOWS	SW	4	258	MEARS	AV	13	295	MEDLICOTT	G	6	281
MEAD	HE	5	235	MEADOWS	W	7	256	MEARS	DW	3	132	MEDLICOTT	HR	11	255
MEAD	HJ	7	256	MEADS	A	12	157	MEARS	EA	13	295	MEDLICOTT	W	11	255
MEAD	J	1	231	MEADS	AT	12	157	MEARS	EH	10	153	MEDLOCK	J	11	255
MEAD	J	5	235	MEADS	C	2	230	MEARS	F	9	131	MEDLOCK	T	12	158
MEAD	JL	1	231	MEADS	CS	3	132	MEARS	GA	1	231	MEDLOW	CW	12	158
MEAD	L	5	235	MEADS	E	12	157	MEARS	GJ	3	132	MEDLOW	F	12	158
MEAD	LE	4	257	MEADS	FE	2	230	MEARS	H	3	132	MEDLYCOTT	EG	7	257
MEAD	M	3	132	MEADS	G	12	157	MEARS	H	9	131	MEDWAY	FC	4	258
MEAD	N	7	256	MEADS	JW	12	157	MEARS	HT	4	258	MEE	AE	1	231
MEAD	P	5	235	MEADS	MH	7	256	MEARS	IJ	1	231	MEE	BF	7	257
MEAD	P	5	235	MEADS	RS	2	230	MEARS	J	10	153	MEE	E	14	218
MEAD	S	9	131	MEADS	TR	2	230	MEARS	J	12	158	MEE	JW	14	218
MEAD	SC	12	157	MEADS	TW	2	230	MEARS	JH	7	256	MEE	O	7	257
MEAD	SS	1	231	MEADS	W	12	158	MEARS	JH	11	255	MEE	WH	7	257
MEAD	T	12	157	MEAGER	EA	10	153	MEARS	S	2	231	MEECH	A	13	295
MEAD	VJ	5	235	MEAGER	G	4	258	MEARS	WF	2	231	MEECH	FE	4	258
MEAD	W	2	230	MEAGER	GS	4	258	MEARS	WG	7	257	MEECH	G	13	295
MEAD	W	2	230	MEAGER	RCG	4	258	MEASHAM	MH	8	225	MEECH	JG	13	295
MEAD	W	5	235	MEAGER	W	4	258	MEASHAM	R	8	225	MEECH	JH	5	236
MEAD	W	5	236	MEAGER	WB	4	258	MEASURE	A	7	258	MEECH	PH	1	232
MEAD	W	11	254	MEAGER	WJ	1	231	MEASURES	J	12	352	MEECH	WS	7	257
MEAD	WA	13	295	MEAGER	WJ	10	153	MEASURES	JG	12	158	MEEDHAM	A	13	296
MEAD	WF	4	257	MEAKES	J	2	230	MEASURES	WJ	12	158	MEEGAN	J	8	225
MEAD	WH	5	236	MEAKIN	A	9	131	MEATCHER	E	4	258	MEEGAN	T	8	225
MEAD	WJ	5	236	MEAKIN	A	11	255	MEATON	AT	10	153	MEEGAN	W	8	225
MEADE	EJ	10	153	MEAKIN	G	14	218	MEATON	SL	13	295	MEEHAN	E	11	255
MEADE	HD	1	231	MEAKIN	H	6	280	MEATON	SV	4	258	MEEHAN	J	8	225
MEADE	HJ	2	230	MEAKIN	J	2	230	MECOY	W	2	231	MEEHAN	J	9	131
MEADE	J	11	254	MEAKIN	J	8	224	MEDCALF	AL	10	153	MEEHAN	J	11	255
MEADEN	FB	4	257	MEAKIN	J	8	224	MEDCALF	BW	2	231	MEEHAN	JM	9	131
MEADER	A	3	380	MEAKIN	J	11	255	MEDCALF	FA	1	231	MEEHAN	T	11	255
MEADER	GA	7	256	MEAKIN	JH	6	280	MEDCALF	GH	9	303	MEEHAN	W	14	218
MEADER	HJ	10	153	MEAKIN	JW	9	131	MEDCALF	GW	1	231	MEEK	AC	1	232
MEADER	TW	7	256	MEAKIN	R	6	280	MEDCALF	H	13	295	MEEK	AEL	2	231
MEADES	CH	3	132	MEAKIN	W	8	225	MEDCALF	HJ	5	236	MEEK	F	8	225
MEADES	ET	10	335	MEAKINS	E	4	258	MEDCALF	S	5	236	MEEK	GA	7	257
MEADES	J	2	230	MEAKINS	WE	11	255	MEDCALF	TW	5	236	MEEK	H	8	225
MEADES	JJ	2	230	MEALAND	T	7	256	MEDCROFT	W	4	258	MEEK	J	11	255
MEADES	ST	14	218	MEALE	WJ	1	231	MEDD	JT	10	153	MEEK	TH	2	231

MEEK	W	6	281
MEEK	W	11	255
MEEK	WJ	8	225
MEEKING	JAA	7	257
MEEKINGS	F	13	296
MEEKINGS	WH	2	231
MEEKINS	JA	3	132
MEEKINS	WJ	3	132
MEEKINS	WJ	3	132
MEEKS	BW	12	158
MEEKS	F	5	236
MEEKS	F	12	158
MEEKS	G	12	158
MEEKS	JA	5	236
MEEKS	O	5	236
MEEKS	P	5	236
MEEKS	PL	12	158
MEEKS	WE	8	225
MEERING	GH	4	258
MEERS	AE	1	232
MEERS	ARH	1	232
MEERS	HE	13	296
MEESOM	H	9	131
MEESON	A	6	281
MEESON	A	8	225
MEESON	J	2	231
MEGAN	J	8	225
MEGAN	J	10	153
MEGAN	P	8	225
MEGEARY	A	12	158
MEGGITT	HL	10	335
MEGSON	A	11	255
MEGSON	J	8	225
MEHEW	HF	12	158
MEHEW	WE	12	158
MEHIGAN	J	5	236
MEHRTENS	AE	2	231
MEIKLE	JA	5	236
MEILTON	TE	2	231
MELBOURNE	B	10	335
MELBOURNE	JA	10	153
MELBOURNE	WD	1	232
MELBOURNE	WJ	1	232
MELCHIOR	G	7	257
MELDRUM	AS	4	258
MELDRUM	DR	4	259
MELDRUM	FC	4	258
MELHUISH	AJ	13	296
MELHUISH	EC	2	231
MELHUISH	EG	2	231
MELHUISH	GFH	10	153
MELHUISH	H	2	231
MELIA	A	14	218
MELIA	F	11	255
MELIA	J	8	225
MELIA	J	8	226
MELIA	J	11	255
MELIA	JE	8	226
MELINSKY	S	14	218
MELION	W	8	226
MELL	R	9	303
MELLAND	S	6	281
MELLARS	GW	7	257
MELLIER	A	13	296
MELLIN	FW	2	231
MELLING	JO	8	226
MELLING	TP	7	257
MELLISH	CT	10	153
MELLISH	JJ	3	132
MELLISH	L	2	231
MELLISH	RG	2	232
MELLISH	W	2	232
MELLISH	W	13	296
MELLISH	W	14	218
MELLISON	H	9	303
MELLON	T	2	232
MELLOR	A	11	256
MELLOR	A	11	256
MELLOR	A	11	256
MELLOR	A	11	256
MELLOR	BW	6	281
MELLOR	E	9	131
MELLOR	E	11	256
MELLOR	FJ	6	281
MELLOR	G	11	256
MELLOR	GE	11	256
MELLOR	H	9	303
MELLOR	H	14	218
MELLOR	J	11	256
MELLOR	J	11	256
MELLOR	J	11	256
MELLOR	J	11	256
MELLOR	J	14	218
MELLOR	J	14	218
MELLOR	JH	1	232
MELLOR	JW	11	256
MELLOR	S	11	256
MELLOR	S	14	218
MELLOR	W	6	281
MELLOR	W	11	256
MELLOR	W	11	256
MELLOR	W	14	218
MELLOR	W	14	219
MELLORD	J	9	131
MELLOW	WG	3	132
MELLOWS	AF	10	335
MELLOWSHIP	WR	13	296
MELLOY	WH	13	296
MELLS	EA	13	296
MELLS	HH	13	296
MELLUISH	FTB	13	296
MELLUISH	SA	13	296
MELMOTH	A	4	259
MELOY	A	13	296
MELOY	AA	2	232
MELOY	ER	13	296
MELOY	G	10	335
MELOY	G	13	296
MELOY	GS	13	296
MELOY	HJ	2	232
MELOY	JJ	13	296
MELTCN	E	8	226
MELTON	GA	5	236
MELTON	R	7	257
MELTON	WE	7	257
MELTON	WH	1	232
MELVILLE	A	13	296
MELVILLE	E	14	219
MELVILLE	J	13	296
MELVIN	HW	1	232
MELVIN	J	6	281
MELVIN	J	6	281
MELVIN	J	8	226
MELVIN	J	9	131
MELVIN	J	9	303
MELVIN	JP	9	303
MELVIN	T	9	131
MELVIN	WJ	1	232
MELZER	HS	2	232
MENCE	CM	1	232
MENCE	FG	1	232
MENCE	GH	1	232
MENDHAM	E	12	158
MENDHAM	LF	7	257
MENNEIL	T	8	226
MENNELL	LJ	13	297
MENNELL	S	8	226
MENNISS	W	7	257
MENZIES	A	4	259
MENZIES	TMM	11	256
MENZIES	WH	2	232
MEPHAM	AG	13	297
MEPHAM	J	2	232
MEPHAM	WG	12	158
MEPSTED	W	2	232
MERCER	A	10	153
MERCER	AE	1	232
MERCER	AE	13	297
MERCER	B	9	131
MERCER	CH	9	303
MERCER	E	9	131
MERCER	E	11	256
MERCER	F	9	303
MERCER	F	11	257
MERCER	F	14	219
MERCER	G	14	219
MERCER	H	14	219
MERCER	J	8	226
MERCER	J	10	335
MERCER	J	10	335
MERCER	JH	1	232
MERCER	JW	9	131
MERCER	SHC	2	232
MERCER	W	13	297
MERCER	W	13	297
MERCHANT	A	6	281
MERCHANT	AE	6	281
MERCHANT	AH	6	281
MERCHANT	ES	6	281
MERCHANT	WJ	7	257
MERCY	J	14	219
MEREDITH	A	6	281
MEREDITH	C	14	219
MEREDITH	CE	10	335
MEREDITH	CT	10	335
MEREDITH	DF	6	281
MEREDITH	EJ	1	232
MEREDITH	EJ	14	219
MEREDITH	GL	14	219
MEREDITH	H	1	232
MEREDITH	H	7	258
MEREDITH	H	10	153
MEREDITH	HJ	5	236
MEREDITH	J	6	281
MEREDITH	J	6	282
MEREDITH	JH	6	281
MEREDITH	JTG	13	297
MEREDITH	RE	6	282
MEREDITH	T	11	257
MEREDITH	VC	11	257
MEREDITH	WJ	2	232
MEREWOOD	BR	10	154
MERHOFF	AJ	1	232
MERISON	J	3	132
MERISON	MJ	1	232
MERISON	MJ	3	132
MERKLE	FJ	13	297
MERNER	JP	3	132
MERRALL	A	2	232
MERRALLS	AJ	3	133
MERRELL	CW	13	297
MERRELL	EJ	13	297
MERRELL	WA	7	258
MERRETT	A	1	232
MERRETT	JA	1	232
MERRICK	E	6	282
MERRICK	F	12	352
MERRICK	FE	2	232
MERRICK	H	2	232
MERRICK	J	11	257

MERRICK	J	11	257	MERRY	JA	14	219	METCALF	F	8	227	METCRAFT	H	5	237
MERRICK	JR	8	226	MERRY	JC	3	133	METCALF	GH	10	335	METHVEN	FW	1	233
MERRICK	JS	8	226	MERRY	JJ	2	233	METCALF	GW	9	131	METSON	HW	10	335
MERRICK	RG	1	233	MERRY	JW	8	226	METCALF	H	4	259	METSON	TH	7	258
MERRICK	RJG	4	259	MERRY	JW	8	226	METCALF	H	8	227	METTERNICH	W	7	258
MERRICK	TV	6	282	MERRY	SJ	9	131	METCALF	H	8	227	MEW	FJ	3	380
MERRICK	TW	1	233	MERRY	WC	1	233	METCALF	H	9	303	MEW	J	1	233
MERRICK	WJ	12	352	MERRYFIELD	G	1	233	METCALF	J	14	219	MEW	OG	3	380
MERRICKS	H	2	232	MERRYWEATHER	H	3	133	METCALF	J	14	219	MEW	PC	4	259
MERRICKS	H	12	352	MERRYWEATHER	H	3	133	METCALF	JD	8	227	MEW	SF	4	259
MERRIFIELD	A	5	237	MERRYWEATHER	HC	7	258	METCALF	JE	8	227	MEWES	D	2	233
MERRIFIELD	A	5	237	MERRYWEATHER	SA	4	259	METCALF	JG	11	257	MEWETT	A	10	154
MERRIFIELD	G	5	237	MERSH	ABP	13	297	METCALF	S	10	154	MEWETT	CJ	10	154
MERRIFIELD	G	5	237	MERSON	H	8	226	METCALF	T	4	259	MEWETT	JG	10	154
MERRIFIELD	H	5	237	MERSON	W	2	233	METCALF	T	8	227	MEWETT	W	4	259
MERRILL	J	9	303	MERVIN	P	8	226	METCALF	TW	4	259	MEWIS	HA	8	227
MERRILL	J	13	297	MESKELL	JW	14	219	METCALF	W	2	233	MEWLYN	SG	5	250
MERRILL	T	11	257	MESSAGE	VA	10	335	METCALF	W	8	227	MEYER	JS	1	233
MERRIMAN	CH	5	237	MESSAM	AG	10	154	METCALF	W	8	227	MEYERN	J	7	258
MERRION	HA	7	258	MESSENBIRD	EA	7	258	METCALF	W	8	227	MEYERS	F	2	233
MERRIOTT	CJ	7	258	MESSENGER	A	5	237	METCALF	W	11	257	MEYERS	JH	10	335
MERRIOTT	SW	2	232	MESSENGER	A	5	237	METCALF	WE	12	352	MEYERS	W	5	238
MERRISHAW	J	14	219	MESSENGER	A	5	237	METCALF	WJ	4	259	MEYNARD	T	8	227
MERRITT	A	4	259	MESSENGER	AG	1	233	METCALF	WS	9	132	MEYRICK	R	1	233
MERRITT	AW	7	258	MESSENGER	CRJ	7	258	METCALFE	A	9	132	MIALL	AE	1	233
MERRITT	CJ	3	133	MESSENGER	E	7	258	METCALFE	A	9	303	MICALLEF	E	10	154
MERRITT	CJ	7	258	MESSENGER	EAT	10	154	METCALFE	C	9	132	MICHAEL	FA	6	282
MERRITT	E	3	133	MESSENGER	EG	2	233	METCALFE	E	9	132	MICHEAU	GS	13	297
MERRITT	E	8	226	MESSENGER	FJ	4	259	METCALFE	E	9	303	MICHEL	GF	5	238
MERRITT	HW	13	297	MESSENGER	GW	13	297	METCALFE	F	9	303	MICHELL	J	2	233
MERRITT	J	3	133	MESSENGER	H	1	233	METCALFE	FT	9	303	MICHELMORE	E	1	233
MERRITT	J	10	154	MESSENGER	H	13	297	METCALFE	G	9	304	MICHELMORE	F	1	233
MERRITT	P	4	259	MESSENGER	JG	5	237	METCALFE	GW	9	132	MICKELS	F	10	336
MERRITT	T	8	226	MESSENGER	JH	14	219	METCALFE	H	2	233	MICKLEBOROUGH	G	7	259
MERRITT	WG	5	237	MESSENGER	JH	14	219	METCALFE	H	8	227	MICKLEBURG	W	13	297
MERRITT	WJ	10	154	MESSENGER	JW	13	297	METCALFE	H	8	227	MICKLEFIELD	E	7	259
MERRITT	WT	10	154	MESSENGER	MC	2	233	METCALFE	H	9	132	MICKLEFIELD	E	7	259
MERRON	C	11	257	MESSENGER	T	11	257	METCALFE	H	9	304	MICKLETHWAITE	A	8	227
MERRON	D	11	257	MESSENGER	W	1	233	METCALFE	HJ	3	133	MICKLETHWAITE	CA	8	227
MERRY	A	5	237	MESSENGER	W	5	237	METCALFE	J	9	132	MICKLEWRIGHT	W	14	219
MERRY	A	12	158	MESSENGER	W	5	237	METCALFE	JD	9	304	MICKLEY	W	12	352
MERRY	AT	1	233	MESSENGER	W	6	282	METCALFE	JW	9	132	MIDDLEBROOK	HS	1	233
MERRY	C	5	237	MESSER	R	13	297	METCALFE	JW	9	132	MIDDLEBROOK	WG	13	297
MERRY	E	9	303	MESTON	F	8	226	METCALFE	JW	9	304	MIDDLEDITCH	E	2	233
MERRY	E	11	257	MESTON	W	8	226	METCALFE	L	9	132	MIDDLEDITCH	HC	7	259
MERRY	E	12	158	METCALF	A	8	226	METCALFE	R	7	258	MIDDLEDITCH	HJ	3	380
MERRY	EM	4	259	METCALF	A	8	227	METCALFE	R	9	132	MIDDLEDITCH	HJ	7	259
MERRY	F	7	258	METCALF	A	8	227	METCALFE	R	9	304	MIDDLEHAM	F	6	282
MERRY	FF	1	233	METCALF	A	9	131	METCALFE	S	9	304	MIDDLEHAM	JF	6	282
MERRY	FW	5	237	METCALF	A	9	303	METCALFE	SB	3	133	MIDDLEHAM	TF	6	282
MERRY	HM	2	232	METCALF	AF	4	259	METCALFE	T	8	227	MIDDLEMASS	AE	13	298
MERRY	HM	2	232	METCALF	AR	4	259	METCALFE	TA	3	133	MIDDLEMISS	A	9	132
MERRY	J	1	233	METCALF	CG	5	237	METCALFE	W	8	227	MIDDLEMISS	JS	14	219
MERRY	J	1	233	METCALF	E	8	227	METCALFE	W	9	132	MIDDLETON	A	6	282
MERRY	J	2	232	METCALF	ES	9	303	METCALFE	WC	8	227	MIDDLETON	A	6	282

MIDDLETON	A	8	227	MIDDLETON	T	8	228	MIHELL	EG	10	336	MILES	HW	4	260
MIDDLETON	A	11	257	MIDDLETON	V	10	154	MIHELL	JA	10	336	MILES	J	1	234
MIDDLETON	A	12	352	MIDDLETON	W	2	233	MIHELL	JE	7	259	MILES	J	1	234
MIDDLETON	A	13	298	MIDDLETON	W	8	228	MIHELL	WR	10	336	MILES	J	1	234
MIDDLETON	AJ	12	158	MIDDLETON	W	8	228	MILAM	EA	4	260	MILES	J	1	234
MIDDLETON	AR	2	233	MIDDLETON	WA	7	259	MILARICK	C	7	259	MILES	J	2	234
MIDDLETON	B	8	228	MIDDLETON	WC	1	233	MILBORROW	J	2	233	MILES	J	3	133
MIDDLETON	C	2	233	MIDDLETON	WH	12	352	MILBOURN	AH	1	234	MILES	J	13	298
MIDDLETON	C	5	238	MIDDLETON	WJ	6	282	MILBURN	GJ	7	259	MILES	KM	10	154
MIDDLETON	C	8	228	MIDDLETON	WJ	7	259	MILBURN	JR	8	229	MILES	M	1	234
MIDDLETON	C	12	158	MIDDLETON	WS	2	233	MILDENHALL	AE	13	298	MILES	MG	5	238
MIDDLETON	C	12	352	MIDDLETON	WS	6	282	MILDENHALL	EW	7	259	MILES	P	10	336
MIDDLETON	D	14	220	MIDDLEWICK	AH	4	259	MILDENHALL	G	13	298	MILES	PW	12	159
MIDDLETON	E	2	233	MIDDLEWICK	AJ	4	260	MILDENHALL	WC	13	298	MILES	R	5	238
MIDDLETON	E	3	133	MIDDLEWICK	NW	4	260	MILDREN	AH	10	336	MILES	RB	3	133
MIDDLETON	E	7	259	MIDDLEWICK	WT	4	260	MILEHAM	FW	7	259	MILES	RC	7	260
MIDDLETON	E	7	259	MIDDLEWOOD	A	10	154	MILEHAM	WA	2	234	MILES	RW	1	234
MIDDLETON	EW	6	282	MIDDLEWOOD	W	10	154	MILES		7	259	MILES	T	1	234
MIDDLETON	FR	3	133	MIDDOWS	A	9	132	MILES	A	10	154	MILES	T	2	234
MIDDLETON	G	5	238	MIDDOWS	GL	9	133	MILES	A	13	298	MILES	TW	1	234
MIDDLETON	G	6	282	MIDGLEY	A	2	233	MILES	AE	2	234	MILES	TW	7	260
MIDDLETON	G	6	282	MIDGLEY	A	8	228	MILES	AH	7	260	MILES	VCD	3	133
MIDDLETON	G	6	282	MIDGLEY	A	8	228	MILES	AJ	1	234	MILES	W	1	234
MIDDLETON	G	8	228	MIDGLEY	A	9	304	MILES	AJ	4	260	MILES	W	4	260
MIDDLETON	G	8	228	MIDGLEY	AE	9	133	MILES	AJ	11	257	MILES	W	5	238
MIDDLETON	G	14	220	MIDGLEY	AP	14	220	MILES	AV	7	260	MILES	W	12	159
MIDDLETON	GE	1	233	MIDGLEY	C	8	228	MILES	B	1	234	MILES	WA	1	234
MIDDLETON	GE	6	282	MIDGLEY	EW	8	228	MILES	C	4	260	MILES	WC	2	234
MIDDLETON	GW	3	133	MIDGLEY	F	9	304	MILES	CEV	13	298	MILES	WD	1	234
MIDDLETON	H	3	133	MIDGLEY	G	9	133	MILES	CJW	12	159	MILES	WFA	5	238
MIDDLETON	H	8	228	MIDGLEY	GA	8	228	MILES	E	6	282	MILES	WG	2	234
MIDDLETON	H	11	257	MIDGLEY	H	8	228	MILES	E	13	298	MILES	WJ	13	298
MIDDLETON	HJ	2	233	MIDGLEY	H	8	228	MILES	EA	4	260	MILES	WT	2	234
MIDDLETON	HJ	10	154	MIDGLEY	H	9	133	MILES	EC	13	298	MILES	WW	13	298
MIDDLETON	HM	14	220	MIDGLEY	H	14	220	MILES	EW	1	234	MILEY	H	14	220
MIDDLETON	J	9	132	MIDGLEY	J	8	228	MILES	F	2	234	MILEY	J	14	220
MIDDLETON	J	14	220	MIDGLEY	JA	8	228	MILES	FC	6	283	MILFORD	FG	2	234
MIDDLETON	JA	1	233	MIDGLEY	JT	8	228	MILES	FG	1	234	MILFORD	GW	1	234
MIDDLETON	JH	5	238	MIDGLEY	JT	8	228	MILES	FHP	2	234	MILGATE	JEG	7	260
MIDDLETON	JH	13	298	MIDGLEY	JW	9	133	MILES	FJ	2	234	MILL	A	10	154
MIDDLETON	JL	9	132	MIDGLEY	L	8	229	MILES	FT	11	257	MILL	AA	10	154
MIDDLETON	JW	8	228	MIDGLEY	P	12	352	MILES	FW	4	260	MILL	LM	2	234
MIDDLETON	JW	12	159	MIDGLEY	R	8	229	MILES	G	6	283	MILL	RJR	10	155
MIDDLETON	M	9	132	MIDGLEY	SJ	8	229	MILES	G	14	220	MILL	W	10	155
MIDDLETON	R	9	132	MIDGLEY	T	8	229	MILES	GS	4	260	MILLAR	A	7	260
MIDDLETON	R	9	304	MIDGLEY	T	9	133	MILES	H	10	154	MILLAR	CW	4	260
MIDDLETON	RA	13	298	MIDGLEY	W	4	260	MILES	H	13	298	MILLAR	CW	13	298
MIDDLETON	RC	8	228	MIDGLEY	WH	8	229	MILES	HC	2	234	MILLAR	D	8	416
MIDDLETON	RF	7	259	MIDMER	G	7	259	MILES	HJ	4	260	MILLAR	E	4	260
MIDDLETON	S	11	257	MIDSON	TW	3	133	MILES	HJ	4	260	MILLAR	E	8	229
MIDDLETON	SA	2	233	MIDWINTER	T	1	234	MILES	HJ	4	260	MILLAR	EE	13	298
MIDDLETON	SA	2	233	MIDWINTER	W	7	259	MILES	HJ	6	283	MILLAR	F	8	229
MIDDLETON	SC	12	159	MIDWOOD	J	8	229	MILES	HLW	1	234	MILLAR	G	2	234
MIDDLETON	SG	13	298	MIELL	A	4	260	MILES	HT	1	234	MILLAR	GN	8	229
MIDDLETON	SRG	7	259	MIHELL	A	10	336	MILES	HT	10	336	MILLAR	HJ	4	260

MILLAR	J	11	257	MILLER	A	8	229	MILLER	FC	4	261	MILLER	LS	1	235
MILLAR	J	13	299	MILLER	A	11	258	MILLER	FG	2	235	MILLER	MJ	1	235
MILLAR	L	14	220	MILLER	A	11	258	MILLER	FJ	3	134	MILLER	N	9	304
MILLAR	T	8	229	MILLER	A	11	258	MILLER	FJ	12	159	MILLER	PG	10	155
MILLAR	T	11	258	MILLER	A	12	352	MILLER	FW	4	261	MILLER	R	2	235
MILLAR	T	11	258	MILLER	AA	10	336	MILLER	G	7	260	MILLER	R	4	261
MILLAR	WJ	13	298	MILLER	AE	7	260	MILLER	G	10	155	MILLER	R	4	261
MILLAR	WO	4	261	MILLER	AE	12	353	MILLER	G	10	155	MILLER	R	4	261
MILLARD	A	4	260	MILLER	AE	13	299	MILLER	G	12	353	MILLER	R	6	283
MILLARD	AE	2	234	MILLER	AG	2	235	MILLER	GD	1	235	MILLER	R	7	261
MILLARD	AE	12	159	MILLER	AH	1	235	MILLER	GD	10	336	MILLER	R	8	229
MILLARD	AJ	7	260	MILLER	AH	10	155	MILLER	GE	4	261	MILLER	R	13	299
MILLARD	CE	7	260	MILLER	AH	10	155	MILLER	GH	7	260	MILLER	RC	7	261
MILLARD	CJ	12	159	MILLER	AHJ	5	238	MILLER	GT	12	353	MILLER	RE	1	235
MILLARD	D	6	283	MILLER	AJ	1	235	MILLER	GW	4	261	MILLER	RE	13	299
MILLARD	DD	5	238	MILLER	AJ	7	260	MILLER	H	2	235	MILLER	RF	4	261
MILLARD	EJ	6	283	MILLER	AM	10	336	MILLER	H	4	261	MILLER	RJ	2	235
MILLARD	F	4	260	MILLER	AR	9	304	MILLER	H	4	261	MILLER	RR	2	235
MILLARD	F	10	155	MILLER	AR	11	258	MILLER	H	8	229	MILLER	RT	3	134
MILLARD	G	3	133	MILLER	AT	5	238	MILLER	H	11	258	MILLER	RT	7	261
MILLARD	G	10	155	MILLER	AV	5	238	MILLER	H	12	353	MILLER	S	8	229
MILLARD	GH	4	260	MILLER	AW	1	235	MILLER	H	14	220	MILLER	SA	2	235
MILLARD	GW	11	258	MILLER	AWL	1	235	MILLER	HA	4	261	MILLER	SB	12	159
MILLARD	H	5	238	MILLER	B	8	229	MILLER	HE	4	261	MILLER	SE	13	299
MILLARD	H	10	155	MILLER	B	9	304	MILLER	HV	12	159	MILLER	SJ	4	261
MILLARD	HG	1	235	MILLER	BJ	13	299	MILLER	HW	3	134	MILLER	T	4	262
MILLARD	HJ	7	260	MILLER	C	2	235	MILLER	HW	6	283	MILLER	T	5	239
MILLARD	J	5	238	MILLER	C	2	235	MILLER	J	1	235	MILLER	TA	12	353
MILLARD	JT	8	229	MILLER	C	7	260	MILLER	J	2	235	MILLER	TH	11	258
MILLARD	M	4	261	MILLER	C	8	229	MILLER	J	5	239	MILLER	TS	12	353
MILLARD	R	2	234	MILLER	C	13	299	MILLER	J	7	260	MILLER	TS	13	299
MILLARD	SE	12	159	MILLER	CF	12	353	MILLER	J	8	229	MILLER	W	2	235
MILLARD	W	2	234	MILLER	CP	13	299	MILLER	J	8	229	MILLER	W	3	134
MILLARD	W	12	159	MILLER	CR	10	155	MILLER	J	8	229	MILLER	W	8	229
MILLARD	WA	4	261	MILLER	CW	4	261	MILLER	J	11	258	MILLER	W	8	229
MILLARD	WC	12	159	MILLER	D	13	299	MILLER	J	11	258	MILLER	W	8	230
MILLARD	WD	5	238	MILLER	D	14	220	MILLER	J	11	258	MILLER	W	8	230
MILLARD	WH	6	283	MILLER	DH	9	133	MILLER	J	11	258	MILLER	W	13	299
MILLBANK	AG	1	235	MILLER	E	1	235	MILLER	J	13	299	MILLER	W	13	299
MILLBANK	G	2	234	MILLER	E	11	258	MILLER	JA	10	155	MILLER	WA	10	155
MILLBANK	JC	1	235	MILLER	E	11	258	MILLER	JC	4	261	MILLER	WB	7	261
MILLBANK	W	9	133	MILLER	E	12	159	MILLER	JF	2	235	MILLER	WC	1	235
MILLBANK	WH	3	133	MILLER	E	14	220	MILLER	JG	7	261	MILLER	WE	2	235
MILLBERY	AE	2	235	MILLER	EC	13	299	MILLER	JGR	7	261	MILLER	WF	1	235
MILLEN	AD	3	134	MILLER	EV	4	261	MILLER	JH	7	261	MILLER	WG	10	155
MILLEN	C	12	159	MILLER	F	5	238	MILLER	JH	13	299	MILLER	WG	13	299
MILLEN	JF	7	260	MILLER	F	5	239	MILLER	JH	13	299	MILLER	WG	13	300
MILLEN	W	12	159	MILLER	F	9	133	MILLER	JO	4	261	MILLER	WJ	5	239
MILLER	A	2	235	MILLER	F	9	133	MILLER	JR	1	235	MILLER	WJ	7	261
MILLER	A	2	235	MILLER	F	10	336	MILLER	JS	11	258	MILLER	WJ	12	353
MILLER	A	2	235	MILLER	F	11	258	MILLER	JT	5	239	MILLER	WJ	13	300
MILLER	A	3	380	MILLER	F	11	258	MILLER	JT	13	299	MILLER	WJ	13	300
MILLER	A	6	283	MILLER	F	13	299	MILLER	JW	13	299	MILLER	WO	12	353
MILLER	A	7	260	MILLER	FA	1	235	MILLER	JW	14	220	MILLER	WR	1	235
MILLER	A	7	260	MILLER	FB	7	260	MILLER	L	9	133	MILLER	WR	7	261

MILLER	WW	11	259	MILLMAN	JH	2	236	MILLS	F	1	236	MILLS	IWA	7	262
MILLERICK	J	14	220	MILLMAN	M	2	236	MILLS	F	5	239	MILLS	J	2	236
MILLERSHIP	JJ	6	283	MILLMAN	PE	3	380	MILLS	F	8	230	MILLS	J	2	236
MILLEST	SE	2	235	MILLMAN	RH	3	380	MILLS	F	12	353	MILLS	J	5	239
MILLETT	GH	14	220	MILLS	A	4	262	MILLS	F	13	300	MILLS	J	5	239
MILLETT	H	7	261	MILLS	A	5	239	MILLS	FA	1	236	MILLS	J	7	262
MILLETT	H	10	336	MILLS	A	6	283	MILLS	FB	1	236	MILLS	J	7	262
MILLETT	J	7	261	MILLS	A	7	262	MILLS	FC	4	262	MILLS	J	8	230
MILLETT	WJ	7	261	MILLS	A	8	230	MILLS	FC	10	336	MILLS	J	8	230
MILLIARD	AT	10	155	MILLS	A	10	156	MILLS	FE	1	236	MILLS	J	11	259
MILLIARD	W	2	236	MILLS	A	12	159	MILLS	FG	12	159	MILLS	J	11	259
MILLICHAP	AG	7	261	MILLS	AA	6	283	MILLS	FJ	1	236	MILLS	J	11	259
MILLICHAP	AT	7	261	MILLS	AD	13	300	MILLS	FJ	4	262	MILLS	J	11	259
MILLICHAP	JA	7	261	MILLS	AE	1	235	MILLS	FJ	7	262	MILLS	J	11	259
MILLICHAP	JF	7	261	MILLS	AE	1	236	MILLS	FLA	3	134	MILLS	J	12	160
MILLICHAP	JT	7	261	MILLS	AE	4	262	MILLS	FP	1	236	MILLS	J	13	300
MILLICHIPP	T	9	304	MILLS	AE	7	261	MILLS	FS	2	236	MILLS	JAJ	3	134
MILLIGAN	AJ	13	300	MILLS	AE	10	156	MILLS	FT	4	262	MILLS	JC	7	262
MILLIGAN	EG	10	155	MILLS	AF	6	283	MILLS	FW	4	262	MILLS	JE	2	236
MILLIGAN	FA	13	300	MILLS	AF	10	156	MILLS	G	4	262	MILLS	JF	10	337
MILLIGAN	G	13	300	MILLS	AH	1	236	MILLS	G	4	262	MILLS	JG	10	337
MILLIGAN	HE	10	155	MILLS	AH	10	156	MILLS	G	10	156	MILLS	JH	14	221
MILLIGAN	J	11	258	MILLS	AH	11	259	MILLS	G	14	221	MILLS	JHC	12	353
MILLIGAN	J	11	259	MILLS	AHA	4	262	MILLS	GA	10	336	MILLS	JP	11	259
MILLIGAN	MC	13	300	MILLS	AJ	12	159	MILLS	GC	7	262	MILLS	JR	2	236
MILLIGAN	RT	9	304	MILLS	AJ	13	300	MILLS	GH	12	160	MILLS	JR	6	283
MILLIGAN	W	6	283	MILLS	AL	2	236	MILLS	GJ	4	262	MILLS	L	8	230
MILLIGAN	W	13	300	MILLS	AL	2	236	MILLS	GR	3	134	MILLS	M	1	236
MILLIGAN	WG	13	300	MILLS	AR	12	353	MILLS	GS	7	262	MILLS	M	1	236
MILLIGAN	WJ	13	300	MILLS	AS	5	239	MILLS	GT	10	336	MILLS	MA	12	160
MILLIKIN	R	11	259	MILLS	B	14	221	MILLS	GW	10	156	MILLS	N	11	259
MILLINGTON	A	11	259	MILLS	BCG	10	156	MILLS	GW	12	160	MILLS	OJ	6	284
MILLINGTON	AV	14	220	MILLS	BF	10	156	MILLS	H	1	236	MILLS	P	12	160
MILLINGTON	C	14	220	MILLS	C	1	236	MILLS	H	2	236	MILLS	P	12	160
MILLINGTON	CG	14	220	MILLS	C	4	262	MILLS	H	4	262	MILLS	PF	10	156
MILLINGTON	CH	1	235	MILLS	C	4	262	MILLS	H	7	262	MILLS	R	1	236
MILLINGTON	E	14	221	MILLS	C	4	262	MILLS	H	7	262	MILLS	R	5	239
MILLINGTON	EJ	6	283	MILLS	C	12	353	MILLS	H	8	230	MILLS	R	6	284
MILLINGTON	F	6	283	MILLS	C	13	300	MILLS	H	11	259	MILLS	R	11	259
MILLINGTON	G	4	262	MILLS	CE	2	236	MILLS	H	11	259	MILLS	RA	3	134
MILLINGTON	H	6	283	MILLS	CJ	10	156	MILLS	H	12	160	MILLS	RE	1	237
MILLINGTON	J	5	239	MILLS	D	1	236	MILLS	H	14	221	MILLS	RE	4	262
MILLINGTON	J	5	239	MILLS	D	1	236	MILLS	HA	6	284	MILLS	RJ	6	284
MILLINGTON	J	11	259	MILLS	D	2	236	MILLS	HA	7	262	MILLS	RW	7	262
MILLINGTON	J	14	221	MILLS	E	1	236	MILLS	HC	13	300	MILLS	S	2	236
MILLINGTON	JA	11	259	MILLS	E	1	236	MILLS	HE	7	262	MILLS	S	5	239
MILLINGTON	JH	11	424	MILLS	E	3	134	MILLS	HF	11	259	MILLS	S	7	262
MILLINGTON	P	11	259	MILLS	E	4	262	MILLS	HG	1	236	MILLS	S	7	262
MILLINGTON	S	11	424	MILLS	E	4	262	MILLS	HG	10	337	MILLS	S	10	337
MILLINGTON	W	14	221	MILLS	E	9	304	MILLS	HH	2	236	MILLS	SG	6	284
MILLIS	GE	13	300	MILLS	E	10	336	MILLS	HL	10	156	MILLS	SR	14	221
MILLIS	WE	10	155	MILLS	EA	10	336	MILLS	HM	3	134	MILLS	ST	1	237
MILLISS	JB	6	293	MILLS	EC	10	336	MILLS	HS	10	156	MILLS	T	12	160
MILLMAN	A	4	262	MILLS	EJ	1	236	MILLS	HW	1	236	MILLS	T	12	353
MILLMAN	H	2	236	MILLS	ES	7	262	MILLS	HW	3	134	MILLS	T	13	300

Surname	Init	V	P	Surname	Init	V	P	Surname	Init	V	P	Surname	Init	V	P
MILLS	TA	12	160	MILMER	F	10	156	MILTON	CA	13	301	MINNS	WJ	2	237
MILLS	TH	13	300	MILMER	JAW	10	156	MILTON	G	3	134	MINOR	H	14	221
MILLS	V	6	284	MILNE	A	7	263	MILTON	G	7	263	MINORS	JH	13	301
MILLS	VK	14	221	MILNE	A	8	230	MILTON	G	13	301	MINSHALL	J	14	221
MILLS	W	2	236	MILNE	AB	1	237	MILTON	G	14	221	MINSHALL	RM	10	157
MILLS	W	6	284	MILNE	AB	1	237	MILTON	GH	2	237	MINSHULL	A	11	260
MILLS	W	6	284	MILNE	AL	7	263	MILTON	H	12	160	MINSHULL	AE	8	230
MILLS	W	7	262	MILNE	F	7	263	MILTON	HA	5	239	MINSHULL	F	9	133
MILLS	W	7	263	MILNE	HG	6	284	MILTON	J	3	134	MINSHULL	J	11	260
MILLS	W	8	230	MILNE	J	4	263	MILTON	JS	2	237	MINSHULL	J	11	260
MILLS	W	10	156	MILNE	JH	7	263	MILTON	LF	12	160	MINSHULL	JR	14	222
MILLS	W	10	156	MILNE	JW	10	157	MILTON	P	2	237	MINSHULL	S	14	222
MILLS	W	11	260	MILNE	L	1	237	MILTON	PF	12	160	MINSHULL	T	11	260
MILLS	W	11	260	MILNE	WC	3	134	MILTON	RG	12	160	MINSTER	S	14	222
MILLS	W	12	160	MILNER	A	9	304	MILTON	SH	5	239	MINTER	AE	13	301
MILLS	W	12	160	MILNER	A	11	260	MILTON	VJ	12	160	MINTER	AS	10	157
MILLS	W	12	353	MILNER	AH	14	221	MILTON	W	3	134	MINTER	FA	13	301
MILLS	W	14	221	MILNER	C	8	230	MILTON	WJ	12	161	MINTER	JE	4	263
MILLS	W	14	221	MILNER	E	9	133	MILWARD	A	6	284	MINTER	W	4	263
MILLS	WA	7	263	MILNER	E	11	260	MILWARD	H	11	260	MINTER	WJ	1	237
MILLS	WD	10	337	MILNER	G	14	221	MILWARD	JE	6	284	MINTERN	A	2	237
MILLS	WF	12	160	MILNER	H	8	230	MIMMACK	DR	4	263	MINTO	F	10	337
MILLS	WG	7	263	MILNER	H	8	230	MIMMO	FG	9	133	MINTO	FW	10	337
MILLS	WG	12	160	MILNER	H	9	304	MIMMS	JHW	7	263	MINTO	WP	10	337
MILLS	WH	4	263	MILNER	HE	1	237	MINALL	G	5	239	MINTOFT	G	11	260
MILLS	WH	7	263	MILNER	J	8	230	MINALL	W	5	240	MINTON	A	2	237
MILLS	WH	8	230	MILNER	J	9	133	MINCHIN	C	6	284	MINTON	H	6	285
MILLS	WH	10	156	MILNER	J	9	133	MINCHIN	RG	4	263	MINTON	TW	6	285
MILLS	WH	10	337	MILNER	J	9	304	MINCHIN	TG	5	240	MINTON-TAYLOR	D	3	134
MILLS	WH	11	260	MILNER	J	11	260	MINDRY	JT	10	157	MINTON-TAYLOR	R	3	134
MILLS	WHA	7	263	MILNER	JW	9	304	MINEHAM	F	10	157	MINTRAM	AG	4	263
MILLS	WJ	3	134	MILNER	T	8	230	MINEHAN	J	7	263	MINTRIM	AE	4	263
MILLS	WJ	4	263	MILNER	T	9	304	MINEHAN	WJ	13	301	MINTRUM	AW	4	263
MILLS	WJ	5	239	MILNER	W	9	305	MINETT	GA	13	301	MIRAMS	FS	3	134
MILLS	WJ	10	337	MILNES	D	9	133	MING	WJ	5	240	MIRFIELD	S	8	230
MILLS	WS	4	263	MILNES	E	9	133	MINGAY	H	5	240	MISELBROOK	W	4	263
MILLS	WT	6	284	MILNES	E	9	305	MINGAY	H	5	240	MISKELLY	S	11	261
MILLSON	GW	8	230	MILNES	FG	8	230	MINGAY	H	12	161	MISKIN	JW	1	237
MILLSON	RV	10	156	MILNES	J	9	133	MINGAY	JT	5	240	MISON	C	3	135
MILLSON	ST	13	301	MILROY	J	14	221	MINGHAM	A	14	221	MISON	LA	1	237
MILLSON	T	13	300	MILROY	TW	10	157	MINIFIE	JW	6	285	MISSELBROOK	H	4	263
MILLSON	WG	7	263	MILSOM	CE	1	237	MINION	D	10	337	MISSELDINE	AG	3	135
MILLWARD	C	11	260	MILSOM	ER	7	263	MINISTER	G	1	237	MISSELDINE	EJ	3	135
MILLWARD	D	6	284	MILSOM	F	2	236	MINKER	CF	13	301	MISSELDINE	T	3	135
MILLWARD	H	11	260	MILSOM	F	4	263	MINNARDS	AR	12	353	MISSENDEN	F	12	161
MILLWARD	J	11	260	MILSOM	VH	10	157	MINNELL	GAW	12	161	MISSENDEN	G	12	161
MILLWARD	J	11	260	MILSON	SJ	4	263	MINNEY	C	12	353	MISSENDEN	J	12	161
MILLWARD	J	14	221	MILSTEAD	AWG	7	263	MINNEY	R	10	157	MISSETT	J	8	230
MILLWARD	R	11	260	MILTON	A	1	237	MINNEY	SJ	12	161	MISSETT	J	8	230
MILLWARD	T	6	284	MILTON	A	7	263	MINNIS	A	4	263	MISSETT	JE	8	230
MILLWARD	T	6	284	MILTON	A	10	337	MINNIS	AW	5	240	MISSETT	P	8	231
MILLWARD	TF	14	221	MILTON	AD	12	160	MINNIS	F	5	240	MISSETT	P	8	231
MILLWOOD	E	11	260	MILTON	AE	2	236	MINNIS	TE	12	161	MISSETT	T	8	231
MILLWOOD	TE	11	260	MILTON	AJ	1	237	MINNITT	JH	2	237	MISSON	W	1	237
MILLWOOD	W	6	284	MILTON	AJ	13	301	MINNS	EFC	5	240	MIST	GT	7	263

MIST	S	4	263	MITCHELL	ER	4	264	MITCHELL	J	4	264	MITCHELL	SN	8	232
MISTOFSKI	L	14	222	MITCHELL	ET	10	157	MITCHELL	J	6	285	MITCHELL	SR	4	264
MITCHAM	A	7	263	MITCHELL	ET	12	354	MITCHELL	J	7	264	MITCHELL	SWL	13	302
MITCHELL	A	3	135	MITCHELL	EW	3	135	MITCHELL	J	7	264	MITCHELL	T	2	237
MITCHELL	A	8	231	MITCHELL	F	8	231	MITCHELL	J	7	264	MITCHELL	T	7	264
MITCHELL	A	8	231	MITCHELL	F	10	157	MITCHELL	J	8	231	MITCHELL	T	8	232
MITCHELL	A	9	134	MITCHELL	F	11	261	MITCHELL	J	8	231	MITCHELL	T	11	261
MITCHELL	A	9	134	MITCHELL	F	13	301	MITCHELL	J	8	231	MITCHELL	TC	13	302
MITCHELL	A	9	134	MITCHELL	F	13	301	MITCHELL	J	8	231	MITCHELL	TH	3	135
MITCHELL	A	9	305	MITCHELL	FA	5	240	MITCHELL	J	8	232	MITCHELL	TR	8	232
MITCHELL	A	9	305	MITCHELL	FH	2	237	MITCHELL	J	9	134	MITCHELL	TW	13	302
MITCHELL	A	10	157	MITCHELL	FH	3	135	MITCHELL	J	9	134	MITCHELL	V	9	305
MITCHELL	A	11	261	MITCHELL	FJ	7	264	MITCHELL	J	9	134	MITCHELL	VL	1	238
MITCHELL	A	11	261	MITCHELL	FJ	10	157	MITCHELL	J	9	305	MITCHELL	W	2	237
MITCHELL	AB	6	285	MITCHELL	G	3	135	MITCHELL	J	11	261	MITCHELL	W	3	135
MITCHELL	AC	7	264	MITCHELL	G	3	135	MITCHELL	J	11	261	MITCHELL	W	4	264
MITCHELL	AE	5	240	MITCHELL	G	5	240	MITCHELL	J	12	354	MITCHELL	W	9	134
MITCHELL	AE	6	285	MITCHELL	G	9	134	MITCHELL	JA	10	158	MITCHELL	W	9	135
MITCHELL	AE	10	337	MITCHELL	G	10	337	MITCHELL	JCW	4	264	MITCHELL	W	9	135
MITCHELL	AE	14	222	MITCHELL	GA	3	135	MITCHELL	JED	14	222	MITCHELL	W	10	158
MITCHELL	AG	7	264	MITCHELL	GA	8	231	MITCHELL	JF	1	238	MITCHELL	W	10	158
MITCHELL	AG	13	301	MITCHELL	GF	2	237	MITCHELL	JH	9	134	MITCHELL	W	11	261
MITCHELL	AH	6	285	MITCHELL	GF	7	264	MITCHELL	JH	12	354	MITCHELL	W	14	222
MITCHELL	AH	10	157	MITCHELL	GH	8	231	MITCHELL	JJ	7	264	MITCHELL	W	14	222
MITCHELL	AH	11	261	MITCHELL	GH	12	161	MITCHELL	JR	9	134	MITCHELL	WA	1	238
MITCHELL	AH	13	301	MITCHELL	GR	11	261	MITCHELL	JW	6	285	MITCHELL	WH	4	264
MITCHELL	AJ	5	240	MITCHELL	GW	10	337	MITCHELL	JW	9	134	MITCHELL	WH	9	305
MITCHELL	AJ	6	285	MITCHELL	GW	13	301	MITCHELL	JW	9	134	MITCHELL	WH	10	337
MITCHELL	AJ	10	157	MITCHELL	H	4	263	MITCHELL	JW	9	305	MITCHELL	WJ	1	238
MITCHELL	AJ	10	157	MITCHELL	H	6	285	MITCHELL	JW	10	337	MITCHELL	WJ	2	237
MITCHELL	AL	3	135	MITCHELL	H	8	231	MITCHELL	JWT	10	158	MITCHELL	WJ	3	135
MITCHELL	AM	13	301	MITCHELL	H	8	231	MITCHELL	L	9	134	MITCHELL	WJ	3	380
MITCHELL	AT	12	353	MITCHELL	H	8	231	MITCHELL	LE	6	285	MITCHELL	WJ	4	264
MITCHELL	AW	4	263	MITCHELL	H	9	134	MITCHELL	LJ	7	264	MITCHELL	WJ	13	302
MITCHELL	B	2	237	MITCHELL	H	9	305	MITCHELL	LM	1	238	MITCHELL	WM	7	264
MITCHELL	B	9	134	MITCHELL	H	9	305	MITCHELL	M	2	237	MITCHELL	WP	1	238
MITCHELL	B	12	353	MITCHELL	H	9	305	MITCHELL	ME	4	264	MITCHELL	WR	11	261
MITCHELL	C	1	237	MITCHELL	H	11	261	MITCHELL	N	7	264	MITCHELL	WRC	2	237
MITCHELL	C	6	285	MITCHELL	H	11	261	MITCHELL	N	8	232	MITCHELLS	SB	3	135
MITCHELL	C	8	231	MITCHELL	H	11	261	MITCHELL	NJ	13	301	MITCHELMORE	B	10	338
MITCHELL	C	8	231	MITCHELL	HA	1	237	MITCHELL	P	9	134	MITCHELMORE	E	2	237
MITCHELL	C	8	231	MITCHELL	HA	12	161	MITCHELL	P	9	134	MITCHELMORE	EC	10	338
MITCHELL	C	9	134	MITCHELL	HF	10	158	MITCHELL	PJ	2	237	MITCHEM	HC	13	302
MITCHELL	C	11	261	MITCHELL	HF	12	354	MITCHELL	R	4	264	MITCHENER	AJ	1	238
MITCHELL	CW	7	264	MITCHELL	HG	2	237	MITCHELL	R	8	232	MITCHENER	C	4	264
MITCHELL	D	4	263	MITCHELL	HM	1	237	MITCHELL	R	9	134	MITCHENER	EJ	4	264
MITCHELL	D	8	231	MITCHELL	HM	12	354	MITCHELL	R	9	134	MITCHENER	G	4	264
MITCHELL	D	13	301	MITCHELL	HW	1	237	MITCHELL	R	13	302	MITCHENER	SA	1	238
MITCHELL	DG	10	157	MITCHELL	HW	1	237	MITCHELL	R	13	302	MITCHIE	A	7	264
MITCHELL	E	1	237	MITCHELL	HW	12	354	MITCHELL	RJF	4	264	MITCHINSON	CF	7	264
MITCHELL	E	3	135	MITCHELL	HWJ	13	301	MITCHELL	S	3	135	MITCHINSON	GW	1	238
MITCHELL	E	8	231	MITCHELL	IJ	13	302	MITCHELL	S	8	232	MITCHLEY	B	7	264
MITCHELL	E	13	301	MITCHELL	J	1	237	MITCHELL	SH	3	135	MITCHLEY	BAF	7	264
MITCHELL	EC	10	157	MITCHELL	J	1	238	MITCHELL	SH	7	264	MITCHLEY	HC	7	264
MITCHELL	EH	10	157	MITCHELL	J	3	135	MITCHELL	SJ	6	285	MITCHLEY	P	6	285

MITHALL	WP	3	135	MOGGRIDGE	HW	2	238	MOLLOY	T	11	262	MONK	J	7	265
MITTEN	CS	6	285	MOGGS	BW	2	238	MOLLOY	T	14	222	MONK	J	14	222
MITTEN	HE	6	285	MOGGS	EA	3	136	MOLLOY	WH	11	262	MONK	JC	7	265
MITTEN	HE	6	285	MOGGS	VJ	3	136	MOLTT	WH	13	302	MONK	JF	4	265
MITTON	A	9	135	MOGRIDGE	H	7	265	MOLYNEAUX	CE	11	262	MONK	PW	7	265
MITTON	H	9	305	MOIR	EBP	4	264	MOLYNEUX	AW	3	136	MONK	R	13	303
MIZEN	A	7	265	MOIR	GA	13	302	MOLYNEUX	CM	3	136	MONK	SE	13	303
MIZON	E	1	238	MOIR	LRR	7	265	MOLYNEUX	G	10	158	MONK	T	4	265
MOAKES	J	13	302	MOISER	CR	11	261	MOLYNEUX	MW	3	136	MONK	T	11	262
MOAKES	MJ	2	238	MOISTER	GW	9	135	MONAGHAN	C	8	232	MONK	TH	10	158
MOAKEY	AM	3	136	MOLCHER	FA	6	286	MONAGHAN	C	10	158	MONK	WGE	13	303
MOBBS	A	12	161	MOLCHER	HA	12	354	MONAGHAN	CE	2	238	MONK	WJ	1	239
MOBBS	A	12	161	MOLDEN	G	8	232	MONAGHAN	EJ	2	238	MONK	WJ	4	265
MOBBS	A	12	354	MOLE	A	6	286	MONAGHAN	H	14	222	MONKCOM	AJ	10	158
MOBBS	CW	12	161	MOLE	EM	3	136	MONAGHAN	J	8	232	MONKHOUSE	H	13	303
MOBBS	FG	12	161	MOLE	G	1	238	MONAGHAN	T	8	232	MONKHOUSE	WW	7	265
MOBBS	H	12	161	MOLE	J	6	286	MONAGHAN	T	13	302	MONKMAN	F	5	241
MOBBS	H	12	161	MOLE	JE	6	286	MONAGHAN	W	8	232	MONKMAN	FT	5	241
MOBBS	H	12	354	MOLE	L	6	286	MONAHAN	J	13	302	MONKS	A	7	265
MOBBS	HE	12	161	MOLE	SM	3	136	MONCHAR	H	14	222	MONKS	AHG	13	303
MOBBS	HS	12	161	MOLE	T	12	162	MONCKTON	SE	1	238	MONKS	E	14	222
MOBBS	J	12	161	MOLE	W	11	261	MONCY	W	8	232	MONKS	G	7	265
MOBBS	J	12	354	MOLES	A	2	238	MONDAY	CG	4	264	MONKS	G	13	303
MOBBS	JA	3	136	MOLES	E	3	136	MONDAY	WJ	4	264	MONKS	H	11	262
MOBBS	RA	12	162	MOLES	E	3	136	MONELLY	F	9	135	MONKS	J	14	223
MOBBS	W	7	265	MOLES	F	3	136	MONELLY	T	9	135	MONKS	J	14	223
MOBBS	WC	1	238	MOLES	GS	3	136	MONELLY	T	9	305	MONKS	JT	11	262
MOBLEY	A	6	285	MOLES	WH	3	136	MONEY	AJ	9	305	MONKS	W	14	223
MOBLEY	CH	6	285	MOLIN	VE	2	238	MONEY	EG	1	238	MONKS	W	14	223
MOBLEY	WG	5	240	MOLINEAUX	WH	4	264	MONEY	G	5	240	MONRO	JA	6	286
MOBSBY	J	4	264	MOLINEUX	GH	1	238	MONEY	H	8	232	MONSELL	P	2	238
MOCKETT	J	10	338	MOLINEUX	R	14	222	MONEY	HE	1	238	MONSHALL	E	13	303
MOCKFORD	AG	13	302	MOLL	A	3	136	MONEY	J	5	241	MONTAGUE	AH	5	241
MOCKFORD	FJ	10	158	MOLL	J	3	136	MONEY	JW	8	232	MONTAGUE	CR	2	238
MOCKRIDGE	F	1	238	MOLLARD	E	11	262	MONEY	RE	3	136	MONTAGUE	EJ	13	303
MOCKRIDGE	JT	5	240	MOLLETT	C	3	136	MONEY	T	5	246	MONTAGUE	FE	2	238
MODLEY	TJ	10	338	MOLLETT	C	4	264	MONGAN	TJ	8	232	MONTAGUE	HE	4	265
MOFFAT	JA	11	261	MOLLISON	A	10	338	MONGER	H	7	265	MONTAGUE	JT	7	265
MOFFATT	J	2	238	MOLLOY	A	1	238	MONGER	W	5	241	MONTAGUE	T	1	239
MOFFATT	JH	13	302	MOLLOY	A	10	158	MONGER	W	7	265	MONTAGUE	WE	4	265
MOFFATT	JW	2	238	MOLLOY	C	11	262	MONK	A	1	238	MONTGOMERY	F	12	354
MOFFATT	S	11	261	MOLLOY	CE	9	305	MONK	A	5	241	MONTGOMERY	H	11	262
MOFFATT	SA	2	238	MOLLOY	D	11	262	MONK	AG	2	238	MONTGOMERY	J	12	354
MOFFATT	W	13	302	MOLLOY	E	2	238	MONK	AJ	5	241	MONTGOMERY	MS	4	265
MOFFATT	W	14	222	MOLLOY	H	1	238	MONK	AJ	13	302	MONTGOMERY	SB	5	241
MOFFATT	W	14	222	MOLLOY	H	11	262	MONK	D	14	222	MONTGOMERY	W	12	354
MOFFIT	A	8	232	MOLLOY	J	11	262	MONK	E	13	302	MONTRIOU	E	1	239
MOFFIT	TW	8	232	MOLLOY	J	14	222	MONK	EC	4	264	MOODEY	W	8	232
MOGER	AW	3	136	MOLLOY	JE	11	262	MONK	EF	1	239	MOODIE	L	4	265
MOGER	JW	3	136	MOLLOY	M	10	158	MONK	F	13	303	MOODIE	LD	2	238
MOGER	WR	4	264	MOLLOY	M	14	222	MONK	FJ	4	265	MOODIE	W	3	136
MOGFORD	A	13	302	MOLLOY	N	10	158	MONK	FW	4	265	MOODY	A	4	265
MOGFORD	T	13	302	MOLLOY	R	11	262	MONK	H	9	135	MOODY	A	4	265
MOGG	J	7	265	MOLLOY	T	6	286	MONK	HJA	12	354	MOODY	A	10	338
MOGGRIDGE	HH	2	238	MOLLOY	T	8	232	MONK	J	5	241	MOODY	AE	13	303

MOODY	AG	4	265	MOODY	W	4	266	MOORCROFT	H	8	233	MOORE	CA	1	239
MOODY	AG	13	303	MOODY	W	7	265	MOORCROFT	SGR	13	303	MOORE	CA	4	267
MOODY	AJ	4	265	MOODY	W	8	233	MOORCROFT	TA	1	239	MOORE	CB	1	239
MOODY	AS	4	265	MOODY	W	9	305	MOORE	A	2	239	MOORE	CE	4	267
MOODY	AT	4	265	MOODY	W	13	303	MOORE	A	3	137	MOORE	CE	6	287
MOODY	BG	3	136	MOODY	WA	2	239	MOORE	A	6	286	MOORE	CF	10	159
MOODY	BS	2	238	MOODY	WH	4	266	MOORE	A	6	286	MOORE	CG	13	304
MOODY	C	4	265	MOODY	WH	4	266	MOORE	A	6	286	MOORE	CH	2	239
MOODY	CA	9	135	MOODY	WJ	10	158	MOORE	A	6	286	MOORE	CH	5	241
MOODY	CFA	2	239	MOON	A	8	233	MOORE	A	6	286	MOORE	CH	6	286
MOODY	CH	4	265	MOON	AC	1	239	MOORE	A	6	286	MOORE	CH	13	304
MOODY	E	1	239	MOON	C	4	266	MOORE	A	7	266	MOORE	CR	1	239
MOODY	E	4	265	MOON	G	9	305	MOORE	A	8	233	MOORE	CW	3	137
MOODY	E	4	265	MOON	GE	1	239	MOORE	A	9	135	MOORE	D	7	266
MOODY	E	10	158	MOON	GE	8	233	MOORE	A	9	306	MOORE	DS	3	137
MOODY	EJ	1	239	MOON	GJ	7	266	MOORE	A	10	159	MOORE	E	5	241
MOODY	EJ	10	158	MOON	H	1	239	MOORE	A	11	263	MOORE	E	6	287
MOODY	F	4	265	MOON	J	9	135	MOORE	A	13	303	MOORE	E	6	287
MOODY	F	5	241	MOON	J	11	262	MOORE	A	13	304	MOORE	E	8	233
MOODY	F	8	233	MOON	M	10	338	MOORE	A	14	223	MOORE	E	9	135
MOODY	F	9	305	MOON	SM	9	135	MOORE	AA	10	338	MOORE	E	9	306
MOODY	FG	4	265	MOON	TH	11	262	MOORE	AC	12	162	MOORE	E	10	159
MOODY	G	4	266	MOON	VJ	10	338	MOORE	AD	4	266	MOORE	E	12	354
MOODY	G	8	233	MOON	WG	2	239	MOORE	AE	3	137	MOORE	EA	8	233
MOODY	G	8	233	MOONE	JF	7	266	MOORE	AE	3	137	MOORE	EC	7	266
MOODY	G	10	158	MOONEY	A	9	305	MOORE	AE	7	266	MOORE	EC	12	354
MOODY	GC	3	137	MOONEY	AJ	4	266	MOORE	AE	7	266	MOORE	EE	13	304
MOODY	GR	4	266	MOONEY	C	3	137	MOORE	AE	10	338	MOORE	EG	5	241
MOODY	H	3	137	MOONEY	D	8	233	MOORE	AE	13	304	MOORE	EJ	1	239
MOODY	H	7	265	MOONEY	D	12	162	MOORE	AE	13	304	MOORE	EM	13	304
MOODY	HC	4	266	MOONEY	EC	5	241	MOORE	AG	3	137	MOORE	ER	10	159
MOODY	HC	4	266	MOONEY	F	8	233	MOORE	AG	4	266	MOORE	EW	12	162
MOODY	HJ	13	303	MOONEY	F	11	262	MOORE	AG	6	286	MOORE	EW	12	162
MOODY	HJ	13	303	MOONEY	F	14	223	MOORE	AH	2	239	MOORE	F	2	239
MOODY	HP	4	266	MOONEY	GHW	3	137	MOORE	AH	6	286	MOORE	F	5	242
MOODY	HW	4	266	MOONEY	J	7	266	MOORE	AH	13	304	MOORE	F	6	287
MOODY	J	4	266	MOONEY	J	9	306	MOORE	AJ	13	304	MOORE	F	7	266
MOODY	J	4	266	MOONEY	J	9	306	MOORE	AL	1	239	MOORE	F	8	233
MOODY	J	11	262	MOONEY	J	11	263	MOORE	AS	3	137	MOORE	F	8	233
MOODY	JG	1	239	MOONEY	J	11	263	MOORE	AT	3	380	MOORE	F	9	135
MOODY	JH	6	286	MOONEY	JW	11	263	MOORE	AT	4	266	MOORE	F	9	135
MOODY	MV	10	338	MOONEY	M	5	241	MOORE	AT	12	354	MOORE	F	9	306
MOODY	P	1	239	MOONEY	MA	11	262	MOORE	AW	7	266	MOORE	F	11	263
MOODY	S	8	233	MOONEY	P	14	223	MOORE	AW	10	338	MOORE	F	12	162
MOODY	S	8	233	MOONEY	RE	12	162	MOORE	AW	13	304	MOORE	F	12	162
MOODY	SA	13	303	MOONEY	RW	4	266	MOORE	B	6	286	MOORE	FC	3	137
MOODY	SG	4	266	MOONEY	T	5	241	MOORE	B	7	266	MOORE	FF	13	304
MOODY	T	4	266	MOONEY	T	11	263	MOORE	B	12	354	MOORE	FG	2	239
MOODY	T	7	265	MOONEY	W	3	137	MOORE	B	13	304	MOORE	FG	2	239
MOODY	T	9	305	MOONEY	W	5	241	MOORE	C	4	266	MOORE	FG	6	287
MOODY	T	13	303	MOOR	JE	9	306	MOORE	C	4	267	MOORE	FH	10	159
MOODY	TA	13	303	MOOR	WB	3	137	MOORE	C	12	162	MOORE	FJ	1	239
MOODY	TJ	10	158	MOORBY	FW	13	303	MOORE	C	13	304	MOORE	FJ	3	137
MOODY	W	1	239	MOORBY	V	10	158	MOORE	CA	1	239	MOORE	FJ	10	159
MOODY	W	4	266	MOORCRAFT	J	2	239	MOORE	CA	1	239	MOORE	FJ	12	162

MOORE	FJ	13	304
MOORE	FSC	13	304
MOORE	FTH	1	240
MOORE	FW	2	239
MOORE	FW	10	159
MOORE	G	6	287
MOORE	G	10	159
MOORE	G	11	263
MOORE	GA	11	263
MOORE	GE	3	137
MOORE	GE	7	266
MOORE	GH	3	137
MOORE	GH	7	266
MOORE	GH	10	159
MOORE	GR	13	304
MOORE	GW	10	159
MOORE	H	1	240
MOORE	H	3	137
MOORE	H	4	267
MOORE	H	5	242
MOORE	H	6	287
MOORE	H	6	287
MOORE	H	6	287
MOORE	H	7	266
MOORE	H	10	159
MOORE	H	13	304
MOORE	HC	10	159
MOORE	HD	1	240
MOORE	HE	7	266
MOORE	HF	4	267
MOORE	HJ	2	239
MOORE	HJ	12	355
MOORE	HT	7	266
MOORE	HW	3	137
MOORE	HW	7	266
MOORE	J	2	239
MOORE	J	5	242
MOORE	J	6	287
MOORE	J	7	266
MOORE	J	7	267
MOORE	J	8	233
MOORE	J	9	135
MOORE	J	9	306
MOORE	J	10	159
MOORE	J	11	263
MOORE	J	12	162
MOORE	J	12	162
MOORE	J	12	162
MOORE	J	12	355
MOORE	J	12	355
MOORE	J	12	355
MOORE	J	13	304
MOORE	JA	8	233
MOORE	JA	11	263
MOORE	JC	2	239
MOORE	JC	12	355
MOORE	JC	13	304
MOORE	JE	5	242
MOORE	JE	6	287
MOORE	JE	7	267
MOORE	JF	4	267
MOORE	JF	4	267
MOORE	JF	6	287
MOORE	JG	3	137
MOORE	JH	7	267
MOORE	JH	7	267
MOORE	JH	10	159
MOORE	JH	10	159
MOORE	JJ	14	223
MOORE	JL	7	267
MOORE	JW	6	287
MOORE	JW	7	267
MOORE	JW	8	233
MOORE	JW	10	159
MOORE	LCC	13	304
MOORE	LG	1	240
MOORE	LG	10	338
MOORE	LG	12	162
MOORE	LM	2	239
MOORE	M	7	267
MOORE	M	8	233
MOORE	M	10	338
MOORE	M	12	355
MOORE	MJ	10	338
MOORE	OJA	3	138
MOORE	PA	6	287
MOORE	PJ	12	355
MOORE	PL	1	240
MOORE	R	3	138
MOORE	R	3	138
MOORE	R	10	338
MOORE	R	12	355
MOORE	R	13	305
MOORE	RH	6	287
MOORE	RH	10	338
MOORE	RJ	13	305
MOORE	RR	12	355
MOORE	RV	4	267
MOORE	RW	13	305
MOORE	S	8	233
MOORE	S	8	233
MOORE	S	9	306
MOORE	S	12	162
MOORE	SA	2	239
MOORE	SE	7	267
MOORE	SG	13	305
MOORE	SJ	10	159
MOORE	SJ	11	263
MOORE	SP	10	159
MOORE	T	2	239
MOORE	T	4	267
MOORE	T	6	287
MOORE	T	6	287
MOORE	T	7	267
MOORE	T	7	267
MOORE	T	11	263
MOORE	T	11	263
MOORE	T	11	263
MOORE	T	13	305
MOORE	T	14	223
MOORE	TA	5	242
MOORE	TE	7	267
MOORE	TJ	10	159
MOORE	TW	6	287
MOORE	VL	14	223
MOORE	W	1	240
MOORE	W	4	267
MOORE	W	5	242
MOORE	W	6	287
MOORE	W	6	287
MOORE	W	6	288
MOORE	W	6	288
MOORE	W	6	288
MOORE	W	6	288
MOORE	W	6	288
MOORE	W	8	234
MOORE	W	11	263
MOORE	W	11	424
MOORE	W	13	305
MOORE	WA	6	288
MOORE	WC	3	380
MOORE	WE	3	138
MOORE	WE	8	234
MOORE	WF	6	288
MOORE	WG	3	138
MOORE	WG	4	267
MOORE	WG	10	159
MOORE	WH	3	138
MOORE	WH	4	267
MOORE	WH	5	242
MOORE	WJ	1	240
MOORE	WJ	3	138
MOORE	WS	2	239
MOORE	WT	3	138
MOORE	WW	13	305
MOORES	A	11	263
MOORES	A	11	263
MOORES	A	11	263
MOORES	AB	11	264
MOORES	AE	4	267
MOORES	E	11	264
MOORES	F	11	263
MOORES	F	14	223
MOORES	FP	10	160
MOORES	GA	14	223
MOORES	H	11	264
MOORES	H	11	264
MOORES	J	11	264
MOORES	J	14	223
MOORES	J	14	223
MOORES	JE	11	264
MOORES	JP	11	264
MOORES	P	11	264
MOORES	R	11	264
MOORES	S	14	223
MOORES	T	12	355
MOORES	T	14	223
MOORES	W	7	267
MOORES	W	11	264
MOORES	W	14	223
MOORES	W	14	223
MOORES	WA	11	264
MOOREY	J	4	267
MOOREY	JH	11	264
MOORHEAD	D	10	160
MOORHEAD	FJ	5	242
MOORHOUSE	A	9	306
MOORHOUSE	A	10	160
MOORHOUSE	AL	9	306
MOORHOUSE	F	8	234
MOORHOUSE	H	8	234
MOORHOUSE	H	9	135
MOORHOUSE	H	9	135
MOORHOUSE	J	9	306
MOORHOUSE	JA	11	264
MOORHOUSE	JH	9	135
MOORHOUSE	JJ	9	306
MOORHOUSE	R	8	234
MOORHOUSE	S	9	135
MOORHOUSE	S	11	264
MOORHOUSE	T	11	264
MOORHOUSE	TA	11	264
MOORHOUSE	TB	9	306
MOORHOUSE	W	14	224
MOORHOUSE	WH	8	234
MOORHOUSE	WH	9	136
MOORIN	RH	8	234
MOORING	AG	5	242
MOORING	E	8	234
MOORING	S	5	242
MOORING	SF	5	242
MOORING	W	8	234
MOORMAN	FW	1	240
MOORMAN	H	4	267
MOORMAN	J	6	288
MOORS	GL	10	339
MOORS	LF	10	338
MOORS	R	4	267
MOORSHEAD	A	3	138

MORAN	A	11	264	MOREMENT	RH	1	240	MORGAN	EC	13	305	MORGAN	S	4	268
MORAN	E	4	267	MORETON	E	4	268	MORGAN	EE	3	138	MORGAN	S	14	224
MORAN	E	8	234	MORETON	FA	1	240	MORGAN	EF	4	268	MORGAN	SA	13	305
MORAN	J	8	234	MORETON	G	14	224	MORGAN	EH	4	268	MORGAN	SR	13	306
MORAN	J	8	234	MORETON	J	5	242	MORGAN	EW	10	339	MORGAN	T	3	138
MORAN	J	8	234	MORETON	L	3	138	MORGAN	F	1	240	MORGAN	T	6	289
MORAN	J	9	136	MORETON	RV	7	267	MORGAN	F	3	138	MORGAN	T	9	136
MORAN	J	10	339	MORETON	T	5	242	MORGAN	F	6	288	MORGAN	T	11	265
MORAN	J	11	265	MORETON	T	11	265	MORGAN	F	8	234	MORGAN	T	12	162
MORAN	J	11	264	MORETON	TG	1	240	MORGAN	F	8	234	MORGAN	TW	2	240
MORAN	J	11	265	MORETON	W	3	138	MORGAN	F	11	265	MORGAN	W	1	240
MORAN	J	11	265	MORETON	W	10	160	MORGAN	FC	4	268	MORGAN	W	5	243
MORAN	J	14	224	MORETON	WH	14	224	MORGAN	FC	5	242	MORGAN	W	6	289
MORAN	J	14	224	MOREY	A	10	160	MORGAN	FR	2	240	MORGAN	W	9	136
MORAN	JC	2	240	MOREY	AJ	4	268	MORGAN	G	3	138	MORGAN	W	10	160
MORAN	JM	11	265	MOREY	BJ	10	160	MORGAN	G	9	136	MORGAN	W	10	160
MORAN	JP	13	305	MOREY	FH	4	268	MORGAN	G	12	355	MORGAN	W	11	265
MORAN	JW	10	160	MOREY	IWG	4	268	MORGAN	G	13	305	MORGAN	WA	11	265
MORAN	LE	13	305	MOREY	J	10	339	MORGAN	GA	9	136	MORGAN	WC	6	289
MORAN	M	11	265	MOREY	JW	7	267	MORGAN	GF	7	268	MORGAN	WE	4	268
MORAN	MJ	14	224	MOREY	T	7	267	MORGAN	GH	4	268	MORGAN	WG	11	266
MORAN	P	8	234	MOREY	TG	11	265	MORGAN	GJ	4	268	MORGAN	WH	4	268
MORAN	P	11	265	MOREY	W	11	265	MORGAN	H	4	268	MORGAN	WH	6	289
MORAN	S	14	224	MOREY	WE	10	160	MORGAN	H	5	242	MORGAN	WH	8	235
MORAN	T	8	234	MOREY	WJ	10	160	MORGAN	H	5	243	MORGAN	WH	13	306
MORAN	T	8	234	MORFETT	GC	10	160	MORGAN	H	5	243	MORGAN	WJ	6	289
MORAN	T	9	136	MORFFEN	AJ	2	240	MORGAN	H	10	160	MORGAN	WR	13	306
MORAN	T	11	265	MORFITT	N	9	306	MORGAN	H	14	224	MORGAN	WS	4	268
MORAN	W	11	265	MORFITT	W	9	306	MORGAN	HJ	5	242	MORGAN	WS	8	235
MORAN	W	11	265	MORGAN	A	5	242	MORGAN	HJ	7	267	MORGANS	A	13	306
MORAN	WH	10	160	MORGAN	A	5	242	MORGAN	HR	13	305	MORGANS	BT	14	224
MORANT	DB	4	267	MORGAN	A	7	267	MORGAN	HW	2	240	MORGANS	J	13	306
MORANT	ET	4	267	MORGAN	A	9	136	MORGAN	HW	5	243	MORI	J	10	160
MORANT	ET	4	267	MORGAN	A	10	160	MORGAN	HW	7	268	MORIARTY	J	9	136
MORANT	F	4	267	MORGAN	A	14	224	MORGAN	J	3	138	MORIARTY	M	9	136
MORANT	J	4	268	MORGAN	A	14	224	MORGAN	J	5	243	MORILL	H	7	268
MORANT	W	4	268	MORGAN	AE	7	267	MORGAN	J	6	288	MORIN	LG	4	269
MORANT	WJ	4	268	MORGAN	AJ	2	240	MORGAN	J	9	136	MORING	ST	12	355
MORBEY	H	2	240	MORGAN	AJ	3	138	MORGAN	J	11	265	MORISON	AT	7	268
MORBY	F	10	160	MORGAN	AJ	4	268	MORGAN	J	11	265	MORLAND	A	8	235
MORBY	WJ	12	162	MORGAN	AL	6	288	MORGAN	J	14	224	MORLEY	A	1	240
MORDEN	AG	2	240	MORGAN	AM	3	138	MORGAN	J	14	224	MORLEY	A	5	243
MORDEN	J	8	234	MORGAN	AT	6	288	MORGAN	J	14	224	MORLEY	A	7	268
MORDEY	GL	1	240	MORGAN	AT	12	162	MORGAN	JA	8	234	MORLEY	A	8	235
MORE	CJ	13	305	MORGAN	AW	4	268	MORGAN	JD	10	160	MORLEY	AA	10	161
MORE	EW	13	305	MORGAN	B	6	288	MORGAN	JD	10	160	MORLEY	AE	2	240
MORE	HE	13	305	MORGAN	CB	10	160	MORGAN	JH	13	306	MORLEY	AE	8	235
MOREBY	H	6	288	MORGAN	CHE	4	268	MORGAN	JH	14	224	MORLEY	AE	8	235
MORECRAFT	J	5	242	MORGAN	CW	6	288	MORGAN	JL	5	243	MORLEY	AJ	10	339
MORELAND	A	13	305	MORGAN	D	6	288	MORGAN	O	6	288	MORLEY	AW	13	306
MORELAND	D	13	305	MORGAN	D	8	234	MORGAN	P	2	240	MORLEY	BJ	11	266
MORELAND	P	11	265	MORGAN	D	9	306	MORGAN	PT	2	240	MORLEY	C	8	235
MORELAND	W	13	305	MORGAN	DJ	13	305	MORGAN	R	13	306	MORLEY	C	8	235
MOREMENT	P	3	138	MORGAN	E	6	288	MORGAN	R	13	306	MORLEY	D	7	268
MOREMENT	P	3	138	MORGAN	E	14	224	MORGAN	RG	2	240	MORLEY	DE	7	268

Surname	Init.	No.	Pg.	Surname	Init.	No.	Pg.	Surname	Init.	No.	Pg.	Surname	Init.	No.	Pg.	Surname	Init.	No.	Pg.
MORLEY	DWE	7	268	MORLEY	WJ	13	306	MORRIS	B	7	269	MORRIS	H	2	241	MORRIS	H	2	241
MORLEY	E	1	240	MORLIDGE	AH	2	240	MORRIS	B	8	236	MORRIS	H	5	243				
MORLEY	E	2	240	MORLING	A	1	240	MORRIS	C	2	241	MORRIS	H	6	289				
MORLEY	E	8	235	MORLING	EF	1	240	MORRIS	C	2	241	MORRIS	H	6	289				
MORLEY	E	8	235	MORLING	GP	1	241	MORRIS	C	5	243	MORRIS	H	6	289				
MORLEY	E	8	235	MORONEY	C	14	224	MORRIS	C	7	269	MORRIS	H	11	266				
MORLEY	EE	2	240	MORONEY	M	4	269	MORRIS	C	10	161	MORRIS	H	11	266				
MORLEY	ES	5	243	MORONEY	WT	3	380	MORRIS	C	11	266	MORRIS	H	13	307				
MORLEY	ET	13	306	MORPETH	A	9	136	MORRIS	C	14	225	MORRIS	H	14	225				
MORLEY	F	6	289	MORPHEW	JJ	7	268	MORRIS	CA	7	269	MORRIS	HA	2	241				
MORLEY	F	8	235	MORRALL	W	8	236	MORRIS	CF	3	139	MORRIS	HE	12	355				
MORLEY	F	10	161	MORRAN	JR	10	161	MORRIS	CH	6	289	MORRIS	HG	2	241				
MORLEY	FC	10	161	MORRELL	AJ	6	289	MORRIS	CH	13	306	MORRIS	HG	12	163				
MORLEY	G	7	268	MORRELL	CT	6	289	MORRIS	CJ	3	139	MORRIS	HG	13	307				
MORLEY	G	8	235	MORRELL	E	9	136	MORRIS	CR	3	139	MORRIS	HJ	1	241				
MORLEY	G	8	235	MORRELL	G	4	269	MORRIS	CS	10	339	MORRIS	HJ	2	241				
MORLEY	G	11	266	MORRELL	G	8	236	MORRIS	CW	4	269	MORRIS	HJ	6	289				
MORLEY	GHB	12	162	MORRELL	H	9	136	MORRIS	CW	5	243	MORRIS	HP	6	290				
MORLEY	GHW	3	138	MORRELL	H	9	307	MORRIS	D	11	266	MORRIS	HT	3	139				
MORLEY	H	4	269	MORRELL	HL	3	139	MORRIS	D	14	225	MORRIS	HT	3	139				
MORLEY	H	5	243	MORRELL	JH	2	240	MORRIS	D	14	225	MORRIS	HT	11	267				
MORLEY	H	6	289	MORRELL	L	4	269	MORRIS	E	3	139	MORRIS	I	6	290				
MORLEY	H	6	289	MORRELL	S	11	266	MORRIS	E	6	289	MORRIS	J	1	241				
MORLEY	H	9	306	MORRELL	W	4	269	MORRIS	E	6	289	MORRIS	J	2	241				
MORLEY	HG	13	306	MORREY	W	11	266	MORRIS	E	7	269	MORRIS	J	2	241				
MORLEY	HJ	2	240	MORRICE	AF	2	240	MORRIS	E	9	136	MORRIS	J	3	139				
MORLEY	HM	4	269	MORRIES	E	2	240	MORRIS	E	9	307	MORRIS	J	3	380				
MORLEY	HP	1	240	MORRIN	ED	14	224	MORRIS	E	10	161	MORRIS	J	5	243				
MORLEY	J	8	235	MORRIN	JH	9	307	MORRIS	E	11	266	MORRIS	J	6	290				
MORLEY	J	8	235	MORRIS	A	1	241	MORRIS	E	11	266	MORRIS	J	6	290				
MORLEY	J	8	235	MORRIS	A	1	241	MORRIS	E	11	266	MORRIS	J	6	290				
MORLEY	J	9	306	MORRIS	A	2	241	MORRIS	E	13	306	MORRIS	J	6	290				
MORLEY	J	14	224	MORRIS	A	6	289	MORRIS	E	14	225	MORRIS	J	7	269				
MORLEY	JE	1	240	MORRIS	A	7	268	MORRIS	EA	7	269	MORRIS	J	7	269				
MORLEY	JW	8	235	MORRIS	A	7	268	MORRIS	EC	13	306	MORRIS	J	8	236				
MORLEY	L	5	243	MORRIS	A	8	236	MORRIS	ES	13	306	MORRIS	J	8	236				
MORLEY	L	8	235	MORRIS	A	8	236	MORRIS	EW	7	269	MORRIS	J	8	236				
MORLEY	LG	4	269	MORRIS	A	8	236	MORRIS	F	3	139	MORRIS	J	9	307				
MORLEY	LV	7	268	MORRIS	A	10	161	MORRIS	F	3	139	MORRIS	J	10	161				
MORLEY	M E	7	268	MORRIS	A	11	266	MORRIS	F	4	269	MORRIS	J	11	266				
MORLEY	M E	7	268	MORRIS	A	11	266	MORRIS	F	11	266	MORRIS	J	13	307				
MORLEY	ME	1	240	MORRIS	A	13	306	MORRIS	F	13	306	MORRIS	J	14	225				
MORLEY	N	8	235	MORRIS	A	14	225	MORRIS	FB	1	241	MORRIS	J	14	225				
MORLEY	R	4	269	MORRIS	AE	4	269	MORRIS	FC	3	139	MORRIS	J	14	225				
MORLEY	R	7	268	MORRIS	AE	11	266	MORRIS	FH	10	339	MORRIS	JA	11	267				
MORLEY	RH	8	235	MORRIS	AGV	10	161	MORRIS	FJ	6	289	MORRIS	JE	6	290				
MORLEY	S	7	268	MORRIS	AH	1	241	MORRIS	FT	13	306	MORRIS	JE	6	290				
MORLEY	S	8	236	MORRIS	AH	1	241	MORRIS	FW	3	139	MORRIS	JE	11	267				
MORLEY	T	10	161	MORRIS	AH	3	139	MORRIS	G	2	241	MORRIS	JG	7	269				
MORLEY	TD	9	136	MORRIS	AH	11	266	MORRIS	G	4	269	MORRIS	JH	1	241				
MORLEY	TO	10	161	MORRIS	AH	13	306	MORRIS	G	8	236	MORRIS	JH	9	136				
MORLEY	VH	10	161	MORRIS	AHJ	4	269	MORRIS	G	14	225	MORRIS	JJ	12	355				
MORLEY	WG	5	243	MORRIS	AR	12	163	MORRIS	GH	14	225	MORRIS	JL	4	269				
MORLEY	WH	3	138	MORRIS	AT	5	243	MORRIS	GS	13	306	MORRIS	JR	6	290				
MORLEY	WH	10	161	MORRIS	AW	3	139	MORRIS	GW	13	307	MORRIS	JT	5	243				

MORRIS	JT	6	290
MORRIS	JT	7	269
MORRIS	JW	3	139
MORRIS	JW	8	236
MORRIS	JW	11	267
MORRIS	L	4	269
MORRIS	L	6	290
MORRIS	L	7	269
MORRIS	L	8	236
MORRIS	M	3	139
MORRIS	M	11	267
MORRIS	N	11	267
MORRIS	N	14	225
MORRIS	N	14	225
MORRIS	P	6	290
MORRIS	PC	3	139
MORRIS	R	6	290
MORRIS	R	11	267
MORRIS	R	13	307
MORRIS	R	14	225
MORRIS	RA	13	307
MORRIS	RD	3	139
MORRIS	RE	11	267
MORRIS	RJ	1	241
MORRIS	RS	11	267
MORRIS	S	1	241
MORRIS	S	6	290
MORRIS	S	6	290
MORRIS	S	11	267
MORRIS	S	13	307
MORRIS	S	14	225
MORRIS	SE	13	307
MORRIS	SG	4	269
MORRIS	SG	13	307
MORRIS	SH	7	269
MORRIS	SJ	7	269
MORRIS	SJ	13	307
MORRIS	ST	1	241
MORRIS	SW	7	269
MORRIS	T	1	241
MORRIS	T	2	241
MORRIS	T	3	139
MORRIS	T	7	269
MORRIS	T	8	236
MORRIS	T	10	161
MORRIS	T	11	267
MORRIS	T	11	267
MORRIS	T	14	225
MORRIS	TC	11	267
MORRIS	TE	11	267
MORRIS	TE	13	307
MORRIS	TH	8	236
MORRIS	TP	11	267
MORRIS	TR	10	161
MORRIS	TW	6	290
MORRIS	VJ	13	307
MORRIS	W	2	241
MORRIS	W	2	241
MORRIS	W	3	139
MORRIS	W	3	139
MORRIS	W	6	290
MORRIS	W	6	290
MORRIS	W	8	236
MORRIS	W	8	236
MORRIS	W	10	339
MORRIS	W	11	267
MORRIS	W	11	267
MORRIS	W	11	268
MORRIS	W	11	268
MORRIS	W	11	268
MORRIS	W	12	163
MORRIS	W	12	163
MORRIS	W	13	307
MORRIS	W	14	225
MORRIS	W	14	225
MORRIS	WA	1	241
MORRIS	WA	3	139
MORRIS	WA	13	307
MORRIS	WC	6	290
MORRIS	WE	7	269
MORRIS	WG	7	269
MORRIS	WG	10	339
MORRIS	WG	13	307
MORRIS	WH	7	269
MORRIS	WH	11	267
MORRIS	WJ	8	236
MORRIS	WJ	13	307
MORRIS	WJP	2	241
MORRIS	WS	12	355
MORRIS	WT	12	163
MORRIS	WT	12	355
MORRIS	WV	8	236
MORRISEY	J	14	225
MORRISEY	T	11	268
MORRISH	J	1	241
MORRISH	JM	1	241
MORRISH	TC	13	307
MORRISON	A	3	140
MORRISON	AE	2	241
MORRISON	C	3	140
MORRISON	C	3	140
MORRISON	CG	1	241
MORRISON	D	2	241
MORRISON	E	8	236
MORRISON	F	1	241
MORRISON	GW	8	236
MORRISON	H	2	241
MORRISON	H	3	140
MORRISON	HH	3	140
MORRISON	J	2	241
MORRISON	J	8	236
MORRISON	J	8	237
MORRISON	J	10	161
MORRISON	J	11	268
MORRISON	J	13	307
MORRISON	JW	14	226
MORRISON	M	8	237
MORRISON	Q	10	161
MORRISON	T	9	136
MORRISON	T	9	136
MORRISON	T	11	268
MORRISON	TD	2	242
MORRISON	W	8	237
MORRISON	W	8	237
MORRISON	W	11	268
MORRISON	W	14	226
MORRISON	WA	10	161
MORRISON	WF	3	140
MORRISON	WG	10	161
MORRISON	WJ	1	241
MORRISY	J	11	268
MORRITT	A	8	237
MORRITT	W	8	237
MORRITT	W	8	237
MORRITT	WH	2	242
MORROLL	AS	6	291
MORROW	E	11	268
MORROW	H	11	268
MORSE	C	2	242
MORSE	G	4	269
MORSE	JF	2	242
MORSE	JW	2	242
MORSE	WJ	1	241
MORSON	JW	14	226
MORT	A	14	226
MORT	C	8	237
MORT	G	11	268
MORT	JW	11	268
MORT	T	11	268
MORTBY	C	7	270
MORTEN	S	2	242
MORTIBOYS	AL	12	355
MORTIBOYS	E	6	291
MORTIBOYS	J	6	291
MORTIBOYS	J	6	291
MORTIMER	A	13	307
MORTIMER	B	9	136
MORTIMER	B	9	307
MORTIMER	C	6	291
MORTIMER	C	9	137
MORTIMER	CS	3	140
MORTIMER	E	4	270
MORTIMER	E	8	237
MORTIMER	E	9	307
MORTIMER	F	8	237
MORTIMER	F	8	237
MORTIMER	F	12	355
MORTIMER	FA	9	307
MORTIMER	H	5	243
MORTIMER	H	8	237
MORTIMER	H	9	307
MORTIMER	H	9	307
MORTIMER	H	9	307
MORTIMER	H	12	163
MORTIMER	HF	12	355
MORTIMER	J	8	237
MORTIMER	MA	8	237
MORTIMER	R	8	237
MORTIMER	S	9	307
MORTIMER	T	8	237
MORTIMER	T	12	163
MORTIMER	T	13	307
MORTIMER	TH	7	270
MORTIMER	W	8	237
MORTIMER	WA	3	140
MORTIMER	WA	9	137
MORTIMER	WH	8	237
MORTIMER	WJ	7	270
MORTIMER	WJ	12	163
MORTIMER	WS	12	163
MORTIMORE	E	6	291
MORTIQUE	J	11	268
MORTIQUE	W	11	268
MORTIQUE	W	11	268
MORTLOCK	J	13	307
MORTON	A	6	291
MORTON	A	6	291
MORTON	A	8	237
MORTON	A	8	237
MORTON	A	8	237
MORTON	A	8	238
MORTON	A	9	307
MORTON	A	14	226
MORTON	AC	6	291
MORTON	AE	6	291
MORTON	C	3	140
MORTON	C	6	291
MORTON	C	11	268
MORTON	DW	8	238
MORTON	E	1	242
MORTON	F	3	140
MORTON	F	6	291
MORTON	F	7	270
MORTON	F	9	137
MORTON	FH	14	226
MORTON	FW	12	356
MORTON	GW	5	244
MORTON	H	1	242
MORTON	H	2	242
MORTON	H	2	242

MORTON	H	7	270
MORTON	H	8	238
MORTON	H	8	238
MORTON	HG	8	238
MORTON	HJ	12	163
MORTON	J	8	238
MORTON	J	8	238
MORTON	J	8	238
MORTON	J	8	238
MORTON	J	11	269
MORTON	J	11	269
MORTON	J	11	269
MORTON	JD	9	137
MORTON	JGJ	10	162
MORTON	JT	8	238
MORTON	JW	9	307
MORTON	JW	14	226
MORTON	JWJ	13	308
MORTON	LS	8	238
MORTON	P	8	238
MORTON	PEJ	10	162
MORTON	RJ	12	356
MORTON	RS	7	270
MORTON	S	14	226
MORTON	S	14	226
MORTON	SL	9	137
MORTON	T	6	291
MORTON	T	8	238
MORTON	TG	7	270
MORTON	TH	10	162
MORTON	WB	8	238
MORTON	WG	3	140
MOS	AC	7	270
MOSBY	F	8	238
MOSBY	H	8	238
MOSEDALE	J	4	270
MOSELEY	A	6	291
MOSELEY	A	12	163
MOSELEY	A	12	356
MOSELEY	AC	13	308
MOSELEY	AE	6	291
MOSELEY	AH	6	291
MOSELEY	AL	12	163
MOSELEY	C	10	162
MOSELEY	E	6	291
MOSELEY	EB	12	163
MOSELEY	H	12	356
MOSELEY	J	6	291
MOSELEY	P	6	291
MOSELEY	PH	12	356
MOSELEY	W	12	163
MOSELEY	WE	6	292
MOSELEY	WF	12	163
MOSELEY	WT	1	242
MOSELY	A	11	269
MOSES	CEG	3	380
MOSES	EC	13	308
MOSES	EH	8	238
MOSES	EM	4	270
MOSES	H	8	238
MOSES	JT	4	270
MOSES	S	2	242
MOSLEY	A	4	270
MOSLEY	A	8	238
MOSLEY	A	8	238
MOSLEY	A	9	307
MOSLEY	AJ	2	242
MOSLEY	C	6	292
MOSLEY	GO	6	292
MOSLEY	H	8	238
MOSLEY	J	8	239
MOSLEY	R	9	137
MOSLEY	R	6	292
MOSLIN	R	6	292
MOSS	A	1	242
MOSS	A	3	140
MOSS	A	8	239
MOSS	A	8	239
MOSS	A	8	239
MOSS	A	10	339
MOSS	A	14	226
MOSS	A	14	226
MOSS	AH	7	270
MOSS	AS	10	339
MOSS	AW	5	244
MOSS	B	14	226
MOSS	CH	3	140
MOSS	CL	10	339
MOSS	CR	1	242
MOSS	D	7	270
MOSS	DE	1	242
MOSS	E	1	242
MOSS	E	1	242
MOSS	EH	10	162
MOSS	EJ	1	242
MOSS	EW	2	242
MOSS	F	10	162
MOSS	FW	11	269
MOSS	FW	13	308
MOSS	G	1	242
MOSS	G	7	270
MOSS	G	7	270
MOSS	GA	1	242
MOSS	GEA	1	242
MOSS	GH	8	239
MOSS	GW	7	270
MOSS	H	1	242
MOSS	H	1	242
MOSS	H	4	270
MOSS	H	9	307
MOSS	H	10	162
MOSS	H	11	269
MOSS	H	13	308
MOSS	HE	3	140
MOSS	HG	3	140
MOSS	HJ	1	242
MOSS	HS	12	356
MOSS	HT	2	242
MOSS	HV	3	140
MOSS	HW	8	239
MOSS	J	6	292
MOSS	J	11	269
MOSS	J	14	226
MOSS	JA	12	356
MOSS	JW	4	270
MOSS	JW	8	239
MOSS	JW	13	308
MOSS	LC	13	308
MOSS	MAS	12	356
MOSS	MT	13	308
MOSS	RJ	8	239
MOSS	RW	10	162
MOSS	S	14	226
MOSS	T	3	140
MOSS	T	8	239
MOSS	T	14	226
MOSS	TJ	5	244
MOSS	W	1	242
MOSS	W	2	242
MOSS	W	8	239
MOSS	WE	11	269
MOSS	WH	1	242
MOSS	WH	1	242
MOSS	WH	7	270
MOSS	WJ	8	239
MOSS	WN	3	140
MOSS	WR	9	307
MOSS	WW	1	242
MOSS	WW	6	292
MOSSESSON	M	14	226
MOSSMAN	A	7	270
MOSSMAN	H	11	269
MOSSMAN	TG	13	308
MOSSMAN	WC	13	308
MOSSOP	F	8	239
MOSSOP	JW	9	307
MOSSOP	W	8	239
MOSSOP	WH	1	242
MOSTON	R	4	270
MOSTON	W	9	137
MOSTYN	G	11	269
MOTE	RA	3	140
MOTH	CR	4	270
MOTH	E	1	243
MOTH	FE	4	270
MOTH	FW	4	270
MOTH	J	10	162
MOTH	WF	10	162
MOTHERS	C	3	141
MOTHERSOLE	A	7	270
MOTLEY	JW	5	244
MOTLEY	JW	13	308
MOTLEY	W	9	307
MOTLEY	WJ	5	244
MOTT	A	5	244
MOTT	A	11	269
MOTT	AE	3	141
MOTT	AF	3	141
MOTT	AS	13	308
MOTT	B	13	308
MOTT	C	14	226
MOTT	ES	13	308
MOTT	F	13	308
MOTT	FC	13	308
MOTT	FC	13	308
MOTT	J	14	226
MOTT	JL	12	356
MOTT	RP	13	308
MOTT	WH	12	356
MOTT	WHT	2	242
MOTT	WL	13	308
MOTTERSHEAD	A	11	269
MOTTERSHEAD	A	14	227
MOTTERSHEAD	F	11	269
MOTTERSHEAD	G	14	227
MOTTERSHEAD	HA	14	227
MOTTERSHEAD	J	14	227
MOTTERSHEAD	JA	11	269
MOTTERSHEAD	R	11	269
MOTTRAM	FC	1	243
MOTTRAM	J	10	162
MOTTRAM	T	1	243
MOTTRAM	WR	1	243
MOULAND	GW	10	162
MOULAND	SH	4	270
MOULD	AW	10	162
MOULD	F	4	270
MOULD	W	6	292
MOULD	WA	2	242
MOULD	WT	12	356
MOULDEN	C	1	243
MOULDEN	HC	5	244
MOULDER	CH	1	243
MOULDER	TH	5	244
MOULDER	WA	1	243
MOULDER	WH	13	308
MOULDER	WJ	5	244
MOULDING	B	14	227
MOULDING	GV	12	356
MOULDING	H	11	269
MOULDING	H	14	227

MOULDING	R	14	227	MOUNTFORD	WC	7	271	MOZR	A	11	270	MUIRHEAD	BC	2	243
MOULDING	WJ	2	242	MOUNTIER	A	2	243	MUCKETT	EW	3	141	MUIRHEAD	BG	13	309
MOULDS	H	13	309	MOUNTIER	A	3	141	MUCKETT	F	3	141	MUIRHEAD	E	11	270
MOULE	AE	4	270	MOUNTIER	AA	3	141	MUCKETT	PF	3	141	MUIRHEAD	J	8	239
MOULE	C	10	162	MOUNTIER	ER	3	141	MUCKFORD	HJ	5	244	MUIRHEAD	J	8	239
MOULE	E	10	162	MOUNTIER	SH	3	141	MUCKLE	EJ	13	309	MUIRHEAD	JH	13	310
MOULE	GAF	1	243	MOUNTIFIELD	MJ	13	309	MUCKLESTON	H	5	244	MUIRHEAD	SG	13	310
MOULE	M	4	270	MOUNTJOY	WA	10	162	MUCKLESTON	W	5	244	MUIRHEAD	W	11	270
MOULE	P	4	270	MOUNTNEY	J	11	270	MUCKLOW	J	6	292	MUIRHEAD	W	11	270
MOULE	T	12	163	MOUNTSTEPHENS	J	7	271	MUD	W	10	162	MULADY	DE	1	244
MOULES	A	5	244	MOUNTSTEPHENT	JC	7	271	MUDD	A	1	243	MULADY	JJ	1	244
MOULES	F	12	356	MOUQUE	FW	13	309	MUDD	CE	9	137	MULADY	T	1	244
MOULES	G	5	244	MOUSLEY	WF	7	271	MUDD	H	9	137	MULCANY	J	2	243
MOULES	GW	7	270	MOUZER	J	6	292	MUDD	H	9	137	MULCHAY	E	11	270
MOULES	JH	3	141	MOWATT	RJE	3	380	MUDD	HW	3	141	MULCHINOCK	H	13	310
MOULES	W	5	244	MOWBRAY	R	6	292	MUDD	J	11	270	MULCOCK	AE	10	339
MOULSDALE	RV	6	292	MOWER	FG	7	271	MUDD	JG	9	137	MULDOON	O	1	244
MOULSON	E	9	307	MOWER	J	1	243	MUDD	L	8	239	MULDOON	T	11	270
MOULSON	F	9	137	MOWER	PJ	1	243	MUDDIMAN	A	12	356	MULDOWNEY	JJ	9	137
MOULSON	HP	9	308	MOWER	TS	1	243	MUDDIMAN	FG	6	292	MULEAHY	J	6	292
MOULSON	WL	9	308	MOWFORTH	T	7	271	MUDDIMAN	W	12	356	MULFORD	GH	3	142
MOULT	G	2	242	MOWLEM	WG	2	243	MUDDIMAN	WG	12	356	MULFORD	HC	3	142
MOULT	J	1	243	MOWLEN	CF	1	243	MUDDIMAN	WJ	12	356	MULFORD	JC	1	244
MOULTON	AR	11	270	MOWTHORP	G	9	308	MUDDIMAN	WJ	12	356	MULFORD	SR	3	142
MOULTON	E	1	243	MOXEY	DL	7	271	MUDGE	EM	3	141	MULFORD	SR	3	142
MOULTON	E	2	242	MOXON	B	9	137	MUDGE	FG	1	243	MULHAIRE	F	8	240
MOULTON	H	2	243	MOXON	BJ	9	308	MUDGE	JE	3	141	MULHAIRE	T	8	240
MOULTON	S	11	270	MOXON	F	3	141	MUDGE	S	3	141	MULHALL	CH	14	227
MOULTON	W	10	339	MOXON	FW	7	271	MUDGE	W	1	243	MULHALL	M	14	227
MOULTON	W	11	270	MOXON	P	3	141	MUDGE	WR	10	162	MULHOLLAND	H	14	227
MOUNCEY	J	13	309	MOY	AJ	10	162	MUFF	AW	9	308	MULHOLLAND	J	14	227
MOUNCEY	MH	8	239	MOYCE	J	13	309	MUFF	E	9	308	MULHOLLAND	T	14	227
MOUNCHER	J	10	162	MOYCE	WJ	13	309	MUFF	H	9	308	MULHOLLAND	WA	8	240
MOUNCHER	SC	4	270	MOYE	A	13	309	MUFFETT	AG	3	141	MULLAN	B	7	271
MOUND	SJ	10	339	MOYE	AE	13	309	MUFFETT	FC	3	141	MULLAN	H	9	137
MOUNSEY	S	9	137	MOYES	E	9	308	MUFFETT	R	3	141	MULLAN	J	9	137
MOUNT	J	13	309	MOYES	E	9	308	MUFFETT	RJ	3	142	MULLANEY	A	9	138
MOUNT	JS	13	309	MOYES	GFW	9	308	MUGFORD	GRF	2	243	MULLANEY	D	11	270
MOUNTAIN	A	9	308	MOYES	GFW	9	308	MUGGLESTONE	F	11	270	MULLANEY	J	9	138
MOUNTAIN	BH	3	141	MOYES	H	9	308	MUGRIDGE	AJ	1	244	MULLANEY	JF	9	308
MOUNTAIN	CH	11	270	MOYES	SCH	7	271	MUGRIDGE	SW	2	243	MULLANEY	M	9	308
MOUNTAIN	E	8	239	MOYES	TM	7	271	MUGRIDGE	TO	1	244	MULLANEY	W	9	138
MOUNTAIN	E	14	227	MOYLAN	J	11	270	MUIR	A	1	244	MULLANNY	JA	9	138
MOUNTAIN	H	8	239	MOYLAN	W	1	243	MUIR	A	14	227	MULLARD	A	12	356
MOUNTAIN	H	8	239	MOYLIN	T	11	270	MUIR	AW	7	271	MULLARD	AB	6	292
MOUNTAIN	H	13	309	MOYNES	JW	13	309	MUIR	E	13	309	MULLARD	AG	6	292
MOUNTAIN	TE	8	239	MOYNIHAN	D	2	243	MUIR	EH	5	244	MULLARD	WE	6	292
MOUNTAIN	W	8	239	MOYNS	A	1	243	MUIR	F	13	309	MULLEN	A	8	240
MOUNTAIN	W	8	239	MOYNS	G	9	137	MUIR	FGJ	4	270	MULLEN	E	11	270
MOUNTAIN	WH	13	309	MOYNS	J	13	309	MUIR	J	3	142	MULLEN	F	11	271
MOUNTCASTLE	L	13	309	MOYNS	TA	13	309	MUIR	J	13	309	MULLEN	G	11	271
MOUNTFORD	A	9	137	MOYSES	AE	7	271	MUIR	JH	1	244	MULLEN	J	11	271
MOUNTFORD	DE	11	270	MOYSEY	PC	1	243	MUIR	JT	10	339	MULLEN	M	14	227
MOUNTFORD	EF	7	271	MOZLEY	E	9	137	MUIR	N	4	270	MULLENGER	J	1	244
MOUNTFORD	W	6	292	MOZLEY	G	14	227	MUIR	T	4	270	MULLETT	DH	4	270

MULLETT	E	4	270	MULVANEY	F	11	271	MUNDAY	J	5	245	MUNNERY	G	3	380
MULLETT	F	4	271	MULVANEY	FJ	12	356	MUNDAY	J	5	245	MUNNINGS	G	4	271
MULLETT	F	4	271	MULVANEY	H	7	272	MUNDAY	J	7	272	MUNNS	A	12	357
MULLETT	FG	5	244	MULVANEY	H	14	228	MUNDAY	J	7	272	MUNNS	AC	7	272
MULLEY	JW	12	163	MULVANEY	W	11	271	MUNDAY	J	7	272	MUNNS	AT	5	245
MULLICE	WH	10	340	MULVANY	M	11	271	MUNDAY	JA	10	163	MUNNS	EE	2	243
MULLIGAN	FJ	11	271	MULVEY	A	14	228	MUNDAY	JR	1	244	MUNNS	FH	13	310
MULLIGAN	JJ	14	227	MULVEY	C	11	271	MUNDAY	L	4	271	MUNNS	H	5	245
MULLIGAN	MW	8	240	MULVEY	C	11	271	MUNDAY	LA	7	272	MUNNS	W	12	357
MULLIGAN	T	6	293	MULVEY	HW	1	244	MUNDAY	M	5	245	MUNRO	A	8	240
MULLIGAN	W	11	271	MULVEY	J	14	228	MUNDAY	P	12	164	MUNRO	A	11	272
MULLIGAN	W	14	227	MULVEY	M	11	271	MUNDAY	RW	4	271	MUNRO	HW	3	142
MULLIN	C	11	271	MULVEY	R	14	228	MUNDAY	S	4	271	MUNRO	JH	1	245
MULLIN	C	11	271	MULVEY	W	11	271	MUNDAY	SW	12	164	MUNRO	M	8	240
MULLIN	G	14	228	MUMBY	H	9	138	MUNDAY	W	4	271	MUNRO	PE	1	245
MULLIN	G	14	228	MUMBY	HJ	8	240	MUNDAY	W	4	271	MUNRO	S	1	245
MULLIN	J	14	228	MUMBY	SA	8	240	MUNDAY	WC	7	272	MUNRO	WJ	6	293
MULLIN	JF	11	271	MUMBY	W	8	240	MUNDAY	WH	12	164	MUNRO	WJ	10	340
MULLIN	T	11	271	MUMFORD	AE	1	244	MUNDAY	WT	12	357	MUNROE	AE	12	357
MULLIN	T	14	228	MUMFORD	AT	7	272	MUNDELL	F	13	310	MUNROE	F	12	357
MULLINDER	W	11	271	MUMFORD	AW	1	244	MUNDELL	JH	11	272	MUNROE	W	12	357
MULLINER	G	1	244	MUMFORD	C	11	271	MUNDEN	F	4	271	MUNSLOW	AH	6	293
MULLINGS	A	7	271	MUMFORD	EJ	1	244	MUNDEN	H	10	163	MUNSON	AE	1	245
MULLINGS	C	7	271	MUMFORD	GW	2	243	MUNDEN	HC	13	310	MUNSON	CF	3	142
MULLINGS	R	7	271	MUMFORD	JJ	3	142	MUNDEN	WJ	13	310	MUNSON	CR	1	245
MULLINOR	G	14	228	MUMFORD	SJ	11	272	MUNDEY	C	10	163	MUNSON	D	3	143
MULLINS	A	2	243	MUMFORD	T	3	142	MUNDEY	J	10	163	MUNSON	W	1	245
MULLINS	AG	3	142	MUMFORD	W	7	272	MUNDS	E	12	164	MUNT	A	5	245
MULLINS	CV	1	244	MUMMERY	CW	4	271	MUNDY	C	4	271	MUNT	AG	5	245
MULLINS	E	8	240	MUNCEY	AH	13	310	MUNDY	F	13	310	MUNT	AJ	5	245
MULLINS	J	14	228	MUNDAY	A	4	271	MUNDY	FC	6	293	MUNT	F	12	164
MULLINS	JW	3	142	MUNDAY	A	5	245	MUNDY	G	8	240	MUNT	FC	7	272
MULLINS	L	8	240	MUNDAY	AE	7	272	MUNDY	GR	14	228	MUNT	GE	3	143
MULLINS	P	8	240	MUNDAY	AG	7	272	MUNDY	H	14	228	MUNT	H	5	245
MULLINS	SJ	3	142	MUNDAY	AH	13	310	MUNDY	HJ	6	293	MUNT	R	5	245
MULLINS	T	3	142	MUNDAY	C	5	245	MUNDY	J	2	243	MUNT	RW	12	164
MULLINS	TW	4	271	MUNDAY	C	12	163	MUNDY	W	14	228	MUNT	TR	5	245
MULLINS	V	6	293	MUNDAY	CL	12	163	MUNDY	WF	13	310	MUNT	W	7	272
MULLINS	W	3	142	MUNDAY	E	4	271	MUNDY	WG	2	243	MUNT	W	7	272
MULLINS	W	8	240	MUNDAY	E	5	245	MUNFORD	A	1	244	MUNTON	F	8	240
MULLINS	W	13	310	MUNDAY	EJ	2	243	MUNN	A	6	293	MUNTON	J	8	240
MULLINS	WE	3	142	MUNDAY	F	3	142	MUNN	AW	1	244	MUNTON	JC	12	357
MULLIS	A	5	244	MUNDAY	F	4	271	MUNN	E	13	321	MUNTZ	W	6	293
MULLIS	AE	4	271	MUNDAY	F	4	271	MUNN	F	1	245	MURAS	EE	10	340
MULLIS	F	6	293	MUNDAY	FE	12	164	MUNN	F	3	380	MURCH	MH	3	381
MULLIS	FB	6	293	MUNDAY	FG	4	271	MUNN	F	13	321	MURCOTT	EH	2	243
MULLIS	S	5	244	MUNDAY	FG	4	271	MUNN	J	6	293	MURCOTT	SW	6	293
MULLIS	WH	6	293	MUNDAY	G	1	244	MUNN	J	6	293	MURCUTT	CW	13	310
MULLOCK	TJ	9	308	MUNDAY	G	3	142	MUNN	JP	12	164	MURCUTT	H	1	245
MULLONEY	J	10	340	MUNDAY	GT	12	164	MUNN	SP	1	245	MURCUTT	WF	13	310
MULLY	JL	8	240	MUNDAY	H	1	244	MUNN	T	4	271	MURDEN	E	3	143
MULROONEY	M	14	228	MUNDAY	H	4	271	MUNN	TJ	6	293	MURDEN	EA	3	143
MULROY	G	3	142	MUNDAY	H	5	245	MUNN	WE	1	245	MURDEN	W	3	143
MULROY	J	11	271	MUNDAY	H	5	245	MUNN	WH	6	293	MURDIN	FV	12	357
MULRYAN	M	11	271	MUNDAY	HS	7	272	MUNN	WJ	13	310	MURDIN	J	12	357

MURDOCH	A	11	272	MURPHY	E	13	310	MURPHY	MJ	11	273	MURRAY	DJ	14	229
MURDOCH	G	11	272	MURPHY	E	14	228	MURPHY	P	4	272	MURRAY	DM	3	143
MURDOCH	R	11	272	MURPHY	EJ	13	310	MURPHY	P	8	241	MURRAY	E	2	243
MURDOCH	T	9	308	MURPHY	ET	12	164	MURPHY	P	10	163	MURRAY	E	8	241
MURDOCH	W	14	228	MURPHY	F	6	294	MURPHY	P	14	229	MURRAY	E	9	138
MURDOCK	D	1	245	MURPHY	F	8	241	MURPHY	P	14	229	MURRAY	E	9	309
MURDOCK	J	9	138	MURPHY	F	12	164	MURPHY	R	7	273	MURRAY	F	6	294
MURFIN	EAG	12	164	MURPHY	FJ	14	228	MURPHY	R	11	273	MURRAY	F	8	241
MURFIN	G	12	164	MURPHY	FT	3	143	MURPHY	R	11	424	MURRAY	F	14	229
MURFIN	H	12	164	MURPHY	G	9	309	MURPHY	RS	14	229	MURRAY	FC	7	273
MURFIN	W	12	164	MURPHY	G	11	272	MURPHY	RT	10	163	MURRAY	FR	7	273
MURFITT	AE	10	163	MURPHY	G	11	272	MURPHY	S	6	294	MURRAY	G	7	273
MURGATROYD	A	9	138	MURPHY	G	14	229	MURPHY	T	7	273	MURRAY	G	8	241
MURGATROYD	A	9	308	MURPHY	H	11	272	MURPHY	T	8	241	MURRAY	G	11	273
MURGATROYD	AE	9	308	MURPHY	H	11	272	MURPHY	T	9	309	MURRAY	GE	9	309
MURGATROYD	E	9	308	MURPHY	H	11	424	MURPHY	T	10	340	MURRAY	IH	8	241
MURGATROYD	F	9	309	MURPHY	HE	1	245	MURPHY	T	11	273	MURRAY	J	1	245
MURGATROYD	H	9	138	MURPHY	HWS	14	229	MURPHY	T	13	311	MURRAY	J	2	244
MURGATROYD	H	9	138	MURPHY	J	6	294	MURPHY	T	14	229	MURRAY	J	2	244
MURGATROYD	H	9	138	MURPHY	J	7	272	MURPHY	TE	5	246	MURRAY	J	6	294
MURGATROYD	H	9	309	MURPHY	J	7	272	MURPHY	TG	5	246	MURRAY	J	8	241
MURGATROYD	H	9	309	MURPHY	J	7	273	MURPHY	TH	11	273	MURRAY	J	9	138
MURGATROYD	J	9	309	MURPHY	J	8	241	MURPHY	TS	10	163	MURRAY	J	11	273
MURGATROYD	JI	9	309	MURPHY	J	8	241	MURPHY	W	1	245	MURRAY	J	11	273
MURGATROYD	R	14	228	MURPHY	J	8	241	MURPHY	W	2	243	MURRAY	J	11	273
MURGATROYD	T	9	309	MURPHY	J	8	241	MURPHY	W	3	143	MURRAY	J	11	274
MURGATROYD	W	9	138	MURPHY	J	10	340	MURPHY	W	6	294	MURRAY	J	11	274
MURGATROYD	W	9	138	MURPHY	J	10	340	MURPHY	W	8	241	MURRAY	J	13	311
MURGATROYD	W	9	309	MURPHY	J	11	272	MURPHY	W	10	340	MURRAY	J	14	230
MURGATROYD	W	9	309	MURPHY	J	11	273	MURPHY	W	11	273	MURRAY	J	14	230
MURKETT	H	12	164	MURPHY	J	11	273	MURPHY	W	13	311	MURRAY	JA	12	357
MURKETT	S	12	164	MURPHY	J	11	273	MURPHY	W	14	229	MURRAY	JA	13	311
MURLEY	H	10	340	MURPHY	J	11	273	MURPHY	WC	1	245	MURRAY	JCW	10	163
MURLEY	J	4	272	MURPHY	J	11	273	MURPHY	WE	6	294	MURRAY	JH	14	230
MURLEY	W	4	272	MURPHY	J	11	273	MURPHY	WH	3	143	MURRAY	JW	14	230
MURLEY	WG	1	245	MURPHY	J	13	310	MURPHY	WJ	3	143	MURRAY	L	7	273
MURNAGHAN	H	3	143	MURPHY	J	14	229	MURPHY	WJ	7	273	MURRAY	M	1	246
MURNEY	T	11	272	MURPHY	J	14	229	MURPHY	WJ	13	311	MURRAY	M	2	244
MURNEY	W	11	272	MURPHY	J	14	229	MURPHY	WJ	13	311	MURRAY	M	2	244
MURPHY	A	8	240	MURPHY	J	14	229	MURPHY	WT	14	229	MURRAY	M	11	274
MURPHY	A	11	272	MURPHY	J	14	229	MURR	W	3	143	MURRAY	M	14	230
MURPHY	A	14	228	MURPHY	J	14	229	MURRANT	CE	10	340	MURRAY	MT	6	294
MURPHY	AG	7	272	MURPHY	JC	13	310	MURRANT	WHE	7	273	MURRAY	O	2	244
MURPHY	AJ	11	272	MURPHY	JH	14	229	MURRAY	A	2	243	MURRAY	P	5	246
MURPHY	BT	11	272	MURPHY	JJ	11	273	MURRAY	A	7	273	MURRAY	R	4	272
MURPHY	C	11	272	MURPHY	JT	14	229	MURRAY	AE	7	273	MURRAY	RB	10	340
MURPHY	D	1	245	MURPHY	JV	9	309	MURRAY	AG	2	243	MURRAY	RES	1	246
MURPHY	D	8	240	MURPHY	JW	14	229	MURRAY	AJ	7	273	MURRAY	RW	7	273
MURPHY	D	8	241	MURPHY	L	11	273	MURRAY	AJ	14	229	MURRAY	S	1	246
MURPHY	D	11	272	MURPHY	M	1	245	MURRAY	B	3	143	MURRAY	SJ	13	311
MURPHY	DH	3	381	MURPHY	M	3	143	MURRAY	B	6	294	MURRAY	SV	7	273
MURPHY	E	1	245	MURPHY	M	3	143	MURRAY	C	10	163	MURRAY	TE	6	294
MURPHY	E	1	245	MURPHY	M	11	273	MURRAY	C	11	273	MURRAY	TG	3	143
MURPHY	E	6	293	MURPHY	M	13	311	MURRAY	CF	3	143	MURRAY	W	1	246
MURPHY	E	11	272	MURPHY	MJ	10	163	MURRAY	DF	7	273	MURRAY	W	2	244

MURRAY	W	3	143
MURRAY	W	7	273
MURRAY	W	8	241
MURRAY	WAE	13	311
MURRAY	WH	13	311
MURRAY	WJ	1	246
MURRAY	WJ	10	340
MURRELL	A	3	143
MURRELL	EG	3	143
MURRELL	H	8	241
MURRELL	HJ	3	381
MURRELL	HR	3	381
MURRELL	JW	13	311
MURRELL	MM	3	381
MURRELL	SP	2	244
MURRELL	W	8	241
MURRELL	W	8	241
MURRELL	W	13	311
MURRELL	WC	2	244
MURRELL	WL	7	273
MURRETT	FJ	12	164
MURREY	A	4	272
MURREY	P	4	272
MURREY	V	4	272
MURRILL	AN	2	244
MURRILL	SV	2	244
MURROCK	E	7	274
MURRY	J	8	241
MURSELL	JWM	10	340
MURTAGH	AC	4	272
MURTAGH	CW	3	144
MURTAGH	F	1	246
MURTAGH	H	1	246
MURTAGH	J	6	294
MURTAGH	JE	1	246
MURTHA	JH	14	230
MURTHICK	JW	9	138
MURTHWAITE	GW	11	274
MURTON	AJ	12	357
MURTS	BS	2	244
MUSCHAMP	AE	1	246
MUSCHAMP	E	8	241
MUSCHAMP	SJ	8	241
MUSCUTT	G	12	357
MUSCUTT	RG	12	357
MUSGRAVE	A	1	246
MUSGRAVE	GE	8	241
MUSGRAVE	H	3	144
MUSGRAVE	R	1	246
MUSGROVE	AE	6	294
MUSGROVE	AJ	7	274
MUSGROVE	C	3	144
MUSGROVE	EE	6	294
MUSGROVE	F	12	357
MUSGROVE	GH	7	274
MUSGROVE	H	6	294
MUSGROVE	J	12	164
MUSGROVE	S	11	274
MUSGROVE	SC	6	294
MUSGROVE	WF	12	357
MUSGROVE	WT	3	144
MUSHETT	A	13	311
MUSK	A	3	144
MUSK	A	5	246
MUSK	A	13	311
MUSK	CJ	3	144
MUSK	JH	13	311
MUSK	L	14	230
MUSK	T	2	244
MUSKETT	A	3	144
MUSKETT	F	5	246
MUSKETT	G	5	246
MUSKETT	G	5	246
MUSKETT	H	5	246
MUSKETT	P	5	246
MUSKETT	R	1	246
MUSKETT	W	5	246
MUSKETT	W	5	246
MUSKETT	WH	1	246
MUSON	G	9	138
MUSSARED	OE	7	274
MUSSELBROOK	B	7	274
MUSSELBROOK	F	7	274
MUSSELL	B	4	272
MUSSELL	SC	4	272
MUSSELWHITE	A	4	272
MUSSELWHITE	FA	4	272
MUSSELWHITE	JF	10	163
MUSSETT	F	13	311
MUSSETT	RE	13	311
MUSSINO	H	5	246
MUSSON	J	9	138
MUST	HTJ	7	274
MUSTOE	HC	6	294
MUSTON	A	10	163
MUTHAUTHK	J	9	309
MUTIMER	J	7	274
MUTTER	E	8	242
MUTTER	S	8	242
MUTTOCK	H	10	163
MUTTON	CH	1	246
MYATT	CE	9	138
MYATT	CH	6	294
MYATT	G	14	230
MYATT	R	6	294
MYATT	RS	6	294
MYATT	W	6	295
MYATT	W	14	230
MYCOCK	H	11	274
MYCOCK	JW	11	274
MYCOCK	JW	11	274
MYCOCK	JW	11	424
MYCOCK	T	14	230
MYCROFT	W	13	311
MYERS	A	9	138
MYERS	A	9	309
MYERS	A	9	309
MYERS	A	11	274
MYERS	AJ	12	164
MYERS	AL	9	309
MYERS	AR	11	274
MYERS	B	8	242
MYERS	DF	8	242
MYERS	E	8	242
MYERS	E	9	138
MYERS	E	9	138
MYERS	F	8	242
MYERS	FW	4	272
MYERS	G	8	242
MYERS	G	8	242
MYERS	GH	3	144
MYERS	GH	8	242
MYERS	H	8	242
MYERS	H	8	242
MYERS	J	2	244
MYERS	J	9	139
MYERS	J	9	309
MYERS	J	9	309
MYERS	J	9	310
MYERS	J	10	340
MYERS	J	14	230
MYERS	JE	9	310
MYERS	JP	9	310
MYERS	JT	14	230
MYERS	JW	12	165
MYERS	L	8	242
MYERS	M	8	242
MYERS	P	8	242
MYERS	P	12	165
MYERS	R	7	274
MYERS	R	11	274
MYERS	S	8	242
MYERS	SJ	12	165
MYERS	T	11	274
MYERS	T	11	274
MYERS	TE	11	274
MYERS	TH	8	242
MYERS	W	5	246
MYERS	W	8	242
MYERS	W	9	139
MYERS	W	9	310
MYERS	W	11	274
MYERS	WG	7	274
MYERSCOUGH	JE	11	274
MYERSON	A	7	274
MYFORD	G	2	244
MYFORD	W	2	244
MYHILL	B	7	274
MYHILL	EO	7	274
MYHILL	F	7	274
MYHILL	HP	7	274
MYHILL	W	7	274
MYLAND	IVY	8	242
MYLAND	M	8	242
MYLAND	M	8	242
MYLES	BS	13	311
MYLIE	A	2	244
MYLIE	C	2	244
MYNARD	AE	12	165
MYNARD	FE	5	246
MYNARD	GR	12	357
MYNARD	VS	3	144
MYNARD	WC	12	165
MYNETT	F	3	144
MYNETT	FTE	1	246
MYNETT	R	3	144
MYNOTT	M	6	295
MYOTT	J	10	340
MYTTON	A	6	295
MYTTON	FC	6	295
MYTTON	FS	6	295

N

NAAN	T	11	274
NABBS	CS	13	311
NABBS	E	6	295
NABBS	H	6	295
NABBS	WH	13	311
NADEN	T	11	274
NAGLE	HF	7	274
NAISBITT	W	14	230
NAISH	AR	4	272
NALDRETT	J	10	163
NALLEY	JW	8	242
NALLY	J	11	275
NALLY	W	9	139
NANCARROW	H	10	340
NANCE	WH	10	341
NANGLE	J	14	230
NANGLE	J	14	230
NANKIVELL	F	1	246
NANKIVELL	G	13	312
NANSON	WG	9	310
NAPIER	JJ	5	246
NAPPER	FJ	3	144
NAPPER	JW	3	144
NAPPER	TA	7	275
NAPPIN	E	10	163
NARBOROUGH	C	7	275

NARBOROUGH	H	7	275	NASH	GH	4	272	NASH	WF	6	295	NAYLOR	F	9	310
NAREY	J	9	139	NASH	GH	12	165	NASH	WG	7	275	NAYLOR	F	9	310
NAREY	JP	9	139	NASH	GH	12	423	NASH	WJ	4	273	NAYLOR	F	9	310
NAREY	M	9	310	NASH	GW	5	247	NASH	WJ	6	295	NAYLOR	FW	8	243
NARRAWAY	HE	1	246	NASH	GW	5	247	NASH	WT	13	312	NAYLOR	G	2	245
NARROWAY	FW	5	247	NASH	H	6	295	NASIER	T	2	245	NAYLOR	G	8	243
NARROWAY	WH	13	312	NASH	H	10	164	NASON	AM	2	245	NAYLOR	G	9	139
NARTY	FL	12	350	NASH	H	12	357	NASON	CW	2	245	NAYLOR	G	14	231
NARTY	RS	12	350	NASH	HA	1	246	NASON	GW	6	295	NAYLOR	G	14	231
NASEBY	R	12	357	NASH	HC	5	247	NASON	JE	6	295	NAYLOR	G	14	231
NASH	A	1	246	NASH	HD	10	164	NASON	TA	6	295	NAYLOR	GA	9	310
NASH	A	2	244	NASH	HG	2	245	NASON	W	4	273	NAYLOR	GH	2	245
NASH	A	3	144	NASH	HJ	4	272	NATHAN	SF	2	245	NAYLOR	GH	8	243
NASH	A	5	247	NASH	HW	10	164	NATION	FR	7	275	NAYLOR	H	8	243
NASH	A	12	165	NASH	J	2	245	NATION	SF	1	247	NAYLOR	H	9	139
NASH	A	12	357	NASH	J	3	144	NATT	WA	4	273	NAYLOR	H	9	139
NASH	AC	10	163	NASH	J	4	273	NAUGHTON	AE	2	245	NAYLOR	H	9	139
NASH	AE	4	272	NASH	J	5	247	NAUGHTON	J	6	296	NAYLOR	H	9	139
NASH	AE	6	295	NASH	J	7	275	NAUGHTON	JH	9	310	NAYLOR	H	9	310
NASH	AE	10	163	NASH	J	7	275	NAUGHTON	WE	6	296	NAYLOR	H	13	312
NASH	AG	4	272	NASH	J	8	243	NAULDER	FE	7	275	NAYLOR	HW	8	243
NASH	AG	5	247	NASH	JA	5	247	NAULDER	FE	13	312	NAYLOR	I	8	243
NASH	AG	5	247	NASH	JA	12	358	NAULDER	WW	7	275	NAYLOR	I	9	311
NASH	AG	7	275	NASH	JE	3	144	NAUNTON	JR	1	247	NAYLOR	J	8	243
NASH	AG	13	312	NASH	JF	12	165	NAUNTON	VA	1	247	NAYLOR	J	8	243
NASH	AH	5	247	NASH	JW	4	273	NAVEN	J	6	296	NAYLOR	J	8	243
NASH	AW	12	165	NASH	JW	13	312	NAVEN	J	11	275	NAYLOR	J	9	139
NASH	B	12	165	NASH	L	3	144	NAVEN	R	11	275	NAYLOR	J	9	139
NASH	B	13	312	NASH	LHJ	2	245	NAVIN	P	13	312	NAYLOR	J	9	140
NASH	BC	12	165	NASH	M	1	246	NAY	A	3	144	NAYLOR	J	9	311
NASH	C	7	275	NASH	N	10	164	NAY	C	14	231	NAYLOR	J	9	311
NASH	C	10	163	NASH	P	4	273	NAY	R	13	312	NAYLOR	J	9	311
NASH	C	12	357	NASH	P	7	275	NAYLER	ET	7	275	NAYLOR	J	9	311
NASH	C	13	312	NASH	R	1	247	NAYLER	W	7	275	NAYLOR	J	9	311
NASH	CB	7	275	NASH	R	9	310	NAYLOR	A	8	243	NAYLOR	J	11	275
NASH	CE	7	275	NASH	RF	9	139	NAYLOR	A	8	243	NAYLOR	J	11	275
NASH	CE	12	165	NASH	RS	2	245	NAYLOR	AL	9	310	NAYLOR	J	11	275
NASH	CJF	13	312	NASH	SA	6	295	NAYLOR	B	9	139	NAYLOR	J	14	231
NASH	DE	5	247	NASH	SGC	13	312	NAYLOR	B	9	310	NAYLOR	JL	8	243
NASH	E	1	246	NASH	SHW	7	275	NAYLOR	BF	9	310	NAYLOR	L	7	276
NASH	E	2	244	NASH	T	2	245	NAYLOR	C	8	243	NAYLOR	L	11	275
NASH	E	2	244	NASH	T	5	247	NAYLOR	C	8	243	NAYLOR	M	9	140
NASH	EW	3	144	NASH	T	5	247	NAYLOR	CD	9	310	NAYLOR	R	9	140
NASH	F	6	295	NASH	T	5	247	NAYLOR	E	8	243	NAYLOR	R	11	275
NASH	F	12	165	NASH	T	6	295	NAYLOR	E	8	243	NAYLOR	R	14	231
NASH	F	14	230	NASH	VF	10	164	NAYLOR	E	9	139	NAYLOR	S	8	243
NASH	FA	14	230	NASH	W	1	247	NAYLOR	E	11	275	NAYLOR	S	9	140
NASH	FB	6	295	NASH	W	5	247	NAYLOR	F	2	245	NAYLOR	S	9	140
NASH	FJ	4	272	NASH	W	6	295	NAYLOR	F	3	144	NAYLOR	T	9	140
NASH	G	2	245	NASH	W	7	275	NAYLOR	F	8	243	NAYLOR	TH	8	243
NASH	G	10	164	NASH	W	12	165	NAYLOR	F	9	139	NAYLOR	TS	12	358
NASH	G	10	164	NASH	W	14	230	NAYLOR	F	9	139	NAYLOR	W	2	245
NASH	G	11	275	NASH	WC	1	247	NAYLOR	F	9	139	NAYLOR	W	8	243
NASH	G	12	165	NASH	WC	4	273	NAYLOR	F	9	310	NAYLOR	W	11	275
NASH	GAI	2	245	NASH	WEL	1	247	NAYLOR	F	9	310	NAYLOR	W	14	231

Surname	Initials	Col	Page
NETTLETON	H	8	244
NETTLETON	H	8	244
NEVE	E	3	145
NEVE	EM	3	145
NEVE	GS	13	314
NEVE	JR	13	314
NEVE	RB	3	145
NEVE	RJ	7	277
NEVERCOTT	S	13	314
NEVETT	E	6	297
NEVILL	JR	3	146
NEVILLE	AW	13	314
NEVILLE	C	5	248
NEVILLE	E	10	341
NEVILLE	EE	4	273
NEVILLE	EE	7	277
NEVILLE	EJ	13	314
NEVILLE	F	13	314
NEVILLE	GH	13	314
NEVILLE	H	14	231
NEVILLE	HC	2	246
NEVILLE	J	1	247
NEVILLE	J	4	273
NEVILLE	J	8	244
NEVILLE	JB	1	248
NEVILLE	JH	13	314
NEVILLE	JJ	13	314
NEVILLE	JJ	13	314
NEVILLE	P	10	165
NEVILLE	R	2	246
NEVILLE	S	13	314
NEVILLE	T	11	276
NEVILLE	TH	3	146
NEVILLE	WG	5	248
NEVILLE	WG	12	358
NEVILLE	WG	12	358
NEVILLE	WJ	10	165
NEVILLE	WJ	13	314
NEVIN	PJ	11	276
NEVINS	D	8	245
NEVISON	GR	1	248
NEVISON	W	11	276
NEVITT	AC	6	297
NEVITT	BJ	6	297
NEVITT	T	6	297
NEVITT	T	6	297
NEW	A	1	248
NEW	AE	10	341
NEW	BR	1	248
NEW	C	2	246
NEW	E	7	277
NEW	E	13	314
NEW	EC	4	273
NEW	F	10	165
NEW	F	10	341
NEW	FC	10	341
NEW	FJ	10	341
NEW	FM	10	341
NEW	G	10	165
NEW	G	10	341
NEW	G	13	314
NEW	G	14	232
NEW	GW	7	277
NEW	H	10	341
NEW	HWC	4	274
NEW	I	10	341
NEW	J	13	314
NEW	J	13	314
NEW	JA	2	246
NEW	JE	10	341
NEW	JR	7	277
NEW	RA	10	342
NEW	RH	5	248
NEW	S	13	315
NEW	SF	13	315
NEW	T	10	165
NEW	WC	4	274
NEWALL	A	11	276
NEWALL	C	9	311
NEWALL	GH	8	245
NEWALL	HB	11	276
NEWALL	JE	9	311
NEWBERRY	JW	10	342
NEWBERT	F	2	246
NEWBERY	AW	5	248
NEWBERY	E	4	274
NEWBERY	FA	2	247
NEWBERY	W	6	297
NEWBIGGIN	J	11	276
NEWBOLD	AE	6	297
NEWBOLD	C	2	247
NEWBOLD	F	2	247
NEWBOLD	F	8	245
NEWBOLD	GW	3	146
NEWBOLD	J	6	297
NEWBOLD	R	14	232
NEWBOLT	C	4	274
NEWBOLT	GW	5	248
NEWBON	EI	7	277
NEWBOULD	JA	8	245
NEWBOULD	W	8	245
NEWBOULD	W	9	140
NEWBOUND	P	3	146
NEWBOUND	W	3	146
NEWBROOK	A	14	232
NEWBROOK	AL	12	358
NEWBROOK	CH	14	232
NEWBROOK	CH	14	232
NEWBROOK	H	12	358
NEWBROOK	JHA	12	358
NEWBROOK	RW	12	358
NEWBURN	GW	8	245
NEWBURN	JE	8	245
NEWBURY	A	5	249
NEWBURY	A	5	249
NEWBURY	AG	5	249
NEWBURY	AJ	5	249
NEWBURY	AT	10	342
NEWBURY	CV	7	277
NEWBURY	E	6	297
NEWBURY	EA	5	249
NEWBURY	EM	13	315
NEWBURY	FJ	5	249
NEWBURY	GR	2	247
NEWBURY	HJ	5	249
NEWBURY	HR	1	248
NEWBURY	JG	5	249
NEWBURY	JR	5	249
NEWBURY	W	5	249
NEWBURY	WF	5	249
NEWBURY	WG	12	358
NEWBY	E	2	247
NEWBY	EA	3	146
NEWBY	G	8	245
NEWBY	GE	8	245
NEWBY	H	3	146
NEWBY	J	13	315
NEWBY	L	8	245
NEWBY	W	7	277
NEWBY	W	8	245
NEWCOMBE	AJ	13	315
NEWCOMBE	E	7	277
NEWCOMBE	GR	13	315
NEWCOMBE	GS	13	315
NEWCOMBE	H	2	247
NEWCOMBE	H	8	245
NEWCOMBE	J	13	315
NEWCOMBE	R	7	277
NEWCOMBE	WB	13	315
NEWCOMBE	WH	7	277
NEWCOMBE	WH	11	276
NEWCOMEN	EJ	12	358
NEWDICK	AS	2	247
NEWELL	A	5	249
NEWELL	A	8	245
NEWELL	A	9	311
NEWELL	A	10	165
NEWELL	AE	9	140
NEWELL	AE	10	165
NEWELL	BJ	10	165
NEWELL	C	14	232
NEWELL	CH	5	249
NEWELL	E	4	274
NEWELL	E	8	245
NEWELL	E	10	165
NEWELL	EC	4	274
NEWELL	EF	1	248
NEWELL	EG	4	274
NEWELL	EJ	5	249
NEWELL	F	2	247
NEWELL	FW	10	165
NEWELL	G	2	247
NEWELL	G	5	249
NEWELL	G	8	245
NEWELL	H	6	297
NEWELL	H	8	245
NEWELL	HH	4	274
NEWELL	HR	7	277
NEWELL	HST	1	248
NEWELL	HW	12	358
NEWELL	J	3	146
NEWELL	J	9	311
NEWELL	LH	2	247
NEWELL	RA	3	146
NEWELL	RH	1	248
NEWELL	RS	12	359
NEWELL	SG	12	166
NEWELL	T	2	247
NEWELL	TW	8	245
NEWELL	WA	5	249
NEWELL	WH	7	277
NEWELL	WR	7	277
NEWENS	A	5	249
NEWENS	C	2	247
NEWEY	A	6	297
NEWEY	CT	6	297
NEWEY	FW	6	297
NEWEY	GE	6	297
NEWEY	GW	6	297
NEWEY	H	6	297
NEWEY	J	6	298
NEWEY	T	6	298
NEWEY	TH	6	298
NEWEY	W	6	298
NEWEY	W	6	298
NEWEY	W	6	298
NEWEY	WA	6	298
NEWEY	WE	6	298
NEWEY	WJ	6	298
NEWHALL	E	9	311
NEWHAM	P	8	245
NEWHAM	W	8	245
NEWHAM	WF	7	277
NEWHOOK	RJG	10	342
NEWICK	TE	12	359
NEWING	J	8	245
NEWING	J	8	245
NEWING	JE	3	146
NEWINGTON	GH	7	277
NEWINGTON	SE	10	342

Name	Init.	Col	Pg	Name	Init.	Col	Pg	Name	Init.	Col	Pg	Name	Init.	Col	Pg
NEWIS	CJ	6	298	NEWMAN	CA	7	278	NEWMAN	HG	1	248	NEWMAN	WG	4	274
NEWISS	F	11	276	NEWMAN	CA	10	342	NEWMAN	HH	10	342	NEWMAN	WG	4	275
NEWITT	A	12	359	NEWMAN	CF	10	165	NEWMAN	HJ	1	248	NEWMAN	WH	4	275
NEWITT	HJ	5	249	NEWMAN	CG	2	248	NEWMAN	HN	2	248	NEWMAN	WH	13	315
NEWITT	J	2	247	NEWMAN	CH	2	248	NEWMAN	HT	3	147	NEWMAN	WJ	2	248
NEWITT	RC	5	249	NEWMAN	CP	2	248	NEWMAN	HW	1	248	NEWMAN	WJ	3	147
NEWITT	TJFA	2	247	NEWMAN	D	13	315	NEWMAN	J	1	248	NEWMAN	WJ	4	275
NEWLAN	FR	3	146	NEWMAN	E	1	248	NEWMAN	J	1	248	NEWMAN	WP	3	147
NEWLAN	H	3	146	NEWMAN	E	3	146	NEWMAN	J	3	147	NEWNES	TJ	11	276
NEWLAN	TW	3	146	NEWMAN	E	3	146	NEWMAN	J	7	278	NEWNHAM	A	1	249
NEWLAND	A	4	274	NEWMAN	E	7	278	NEWMAN	J	7	279	NEWNHAM	AE	4	275
NEWLAND	AE	2	247	NEWMAN	E	7	278	NEWMAN	J	7	279	NEWNHAM	AE	10	166
NEWLAND	AE	7	277	NEWMAN	E	8	246	NEWMAN	J	8	246	NEWNHAM	AWC	4	275
NEWLAND	C	1	248	NEWMAN	EAF	4	274	NEWMAN	J	10	166	NEWNHAM	BWSN	4	275
NEWLAND	CHT	2	247	NEWMAN	EC	2	248	NEWMAN	J	10	342	NEWNHAM	CC	12	166
NEWLAND	CL	2	247	NEWMAN	EE	7	278	NEWMAN	J	11	276	NEWNHAM	EA	1	249
NEWLAND	CV	7	278	NEWMAN	EF	7	278	NEWMAN	JC	3	147	NEWNHAM	FW	10	166
NEWLAND	E	2	247	NEWMAN	EH	3	146	NEWMAN	JH	3	147	NEWNHAM	G	10	166
NEWLAND	E	7	278	NEWMAN	EJ	4	274	NEWMAN	JJ	1	249	NEWNHAM	H	12	166
NEWLAND	EJ	12	166	NEWMAN	EJ	6	298	NEWMAN	JJ	1	249	NEWNHAM	J	10	166
NEWLAND	FE	7	278	NEWMAN	EL	12	166	NEWMAN	JL	10	166	NEWNHAM	S	4	275
NEWLAND	J	7	278	NEWMAN	ET	7	278	NEWMAN	JM	13	315	NEWNHAM	SW	13	316
NEWLAND	L	10	165	NEWMAN	F	2	248	NEWMAN	JW	3	147	NEWNHAM	T	13	315
NEWLAND	PW	2	247	NEWMAN	F	3	146	NEWMAN	L	4	274	NEWNHAM	WB	10	166
NEWLAND	T	7	278	NEWMAN	F	5	250	NEWMAN	L	4	274	NEWNHAM	WJ	12	166
NEWLAND	TJF	2	248	NEWMAN	F	10	165	NEWMAN	L	10	166	NEWNS	HJ	4	275
NEWLAND	WHE	1	248	NEWMAN	F	10	165	NEWMAN	L	13	315	NEWPORT	C	10	166
NEWLAND	WHE	2	248	NEWMAN	F	12	166	NEWMAN	LF	10	166	NEWPORT	E	6	299
NEWMAN	A	3	146	NEWMAN	FC	6	298	NEWMAN	M	12	166	NEWPORT	T	2	248
NEWMAN	A	4	274	NEWMAN	FH	10	166	NEWMAN	MJ	10	166	NEWPORT	W	6	299
NEWMAN	A	6	298	NEWMAN	FJ	2	248	NEWMAN	R	5	250	NEWPORT	WD	6	299
NEWMAN	A	6	298	NEWMAN	FJ	5	250	NEWMAN	R	6	298	NEWSHAM	J	1	249
NEWMAN	A	6	298	NEWMAN	FJ	7	278	NEWMAN	R	13	315	NEWSHAM	J	14	232
NEWMAN	A	7	278	NEWMAN	FK	6	298	NEWMAN	RJ	1	249	NEWSHAM	JE	3	147
NEWMAN	A	7	278	NEWMAN	FR	3	146	NEWMAN	RJ	4	274	NEWSHOLME	A	9	140
NEWMAN	A	9	140	NEWMAN	FW	2	248	NEWMAN	RW	5	250	NEWSHOLME	A	9	311
NEWMAN	A	12	166	NEWMAN	FW	3	147	NEWMAN	S	5	250	NEWSHOLME	H	9	140
NEWMAN	A	12	359	NEWMAN	G	4	274	NEWMAN	SE	4	274	NEWSOM	A	8	246
NEWMAN	AB	2	248	NEWMAN	G	7	278	NEWMAN	SH	13	315	NEWSOM	JW	8	246
NEWMAN	AC	2	248	NEWMAN	GAH	1	248	NEWMAN	TC	7	279	NEWSOME	A	8	246
NEWMAN	AE	7	278	NEWMAN	GC	10	166	NEWMAN	TW	1	249	NEWSOME	A	8	246
NEWMAN	AE	10	165	NEWMAN	GF	12	166	NEWMAN	W	1	249	NEWSOME	A	8	246
NEWMAN	AE	13	315	NEWMAN	GT	5	250	NEWMAN	W	1	249	NEWSOME	A	8	246
NEWMAN	AG	2	248	NEWMAN	GT	10	166	NEWMAN	W	4	274	NEWSOME	AC	9	140
NEWMAN	AH	3	146	NEWMAN	GW	1	248	NEWMAN	W	6	299	NEWSOME	AL	9	141
NEWMAN	AN	4	274	NEWMAN	GW	2	248	NEWMAN	W	6	299	NEWSOME	B	8	246
NEWMAN	AV	10	165	NEWMAN	H	6	298	NEWMAN	W	6	299	NEWSOME	B	9	141
NEWMAN	BA	12	359	NEWMAN	H	7	278	NEWMAN	W	10	166	NEWSOME	E	8	246
NEWMAN	C	5	250	NEWMAN	H	10	342	NEWMAN	W	12	166	NEWSOME	F	8	246
NEWMAN	C	7	278	NEWMAN	H	12	166	NEWMAN	W	14	232	NEWSOME	H	11	276
NEWMAN	C	7	278	NEWMAN	H	12	166	NEWMAN	W	14	232	NEWSOME	J	9	141
NEWMAN	C	10	165	NEWMAN	H	13	315	NEWMAN	WC	5	250	NEWSOME	JW	8	246
NEWMAN	C	10	165	NEWMAN	HA	5	250	NEWMAN	WE	7	279	NEWSOME	R	9	311
NEWMAN	C	12	166	NEWMAN	HCF	3	147	NEWMAN	WF	7	279	NEWSOME	S	8	246
NEWMAN	CA	3	146	NEWMAN	HG	1	248	NEWMAN	WF	13	315	NEWSOME	S	9	141

NEWSOME	W	8	246	NEWTON	HT	7	279	NICHOLAS	FG	10	167	NICHOLLS	GF	9	141
NEWSOME	W	9	141	NEWTON	J	6	299	NICHOLAS	G	4	275	NICHOLLS	GH	6	299
NEWSOME	W	9	141	NEWTON	J	8	246	NICHOLAS	H	13	316	NICHOLLS	GH	6	299
NEWSOME	W	9	311	NEWTON	J	8	246	NICHOLAS	HA	2	249	NICHOLLS	GS	8	247
NEWSON	AC	7	279	NEWTON	J	10	167	NICHOLAS	HJ	4	275	NICHOLLS	H	1	250
NEWSON	AT	1	249	NEWTON	J	11	276	NICHOLAS	J	6	299	NICHOLLS	H	3	147
NEWSON	BS	13	316	NEWTON	J	11	277	NICHOLAS	JE	10	167	NICHOLLS	H	6	300
NEWSON	ES	1	249	NEWTON	J	11	277	NICHOLAS	JH	9	141	NICHOLLS	H	6	300
NEWSON	G	1	249	NEWTON	J	14	232	NICHOLAS	JJ	2	249	NICHOLLS	H	7	280
NEWSON	G	5	250	NEWTON	JA	7	279	NICHOLAS	M	14	232	NICHOLLS	H	11	277
NEWSON	HF	13	316	NEWTON	JE	7	279	NICHOLAS	S	6	299	NICHOLLS	H	11	277
NEWSON	R	5	250	NEWTON	JER	5	250	NICHOLAS	SJ	5	251	NICHOLLS	HB	13	316
NEWSON	SJ	3	147	NEWTON	P	8	246	NICHOLAS	TC	10	167	NICHOLLS	HH	12	167
NEWSON	W	7	279	NEWTON	R	8	246	NICHOLAS	TCB	14	232	NICHOLLS	HJ	12	167
NEWSTEAD	FJT	7	279	NEWTON	R	11	277	NICHOLAS	TF	14	233	NICHOLLS	HPW	13	316
NEWSTEAD	HG	13	316	NEWTON	R	11	277	NICHOLAS	W	6	299	NICHOLLS	J	3	147
NEWSTEAD	JR	7	279	NEWTON	SC	7	280	NICHOLAS	W	13	316	NICHOLLS	J	5	251
NEWSTEAD	WJ	13	316	NEWTON	T	4	275	NICHOLAS	WG	14	233	NICHOLLS	J	5	251
NEWSUM	AE	7	279	NEWTON	T	10	342	NICHOLAS	WH	4	275	NICHOLLS	J	6	300
NEWTON	A	10	166	NEWTON	T	11	277	NICHOLAS	WJ	10	167	NICHOLLS	J	6	300
NEWTON	A	11	276	NEWTON	T	14	232	NICHOLL	E	9	311	NICHOLLS	J	6	300
NEWTON	A	12	166	NEWTON	TB	10	342	NICHOLLS	A	1	250	NICHOLLS	J	11	277
NEWTON	AE	1	249	NEWTON	TI	1	249	NICHOLLS	A	4	275	NICHOLLS	J	11	277
NEWTON	AG	4	275	NEWTON	W	11	277	NICHOLLS	A	4	275	NICHOLLS	J	12	167
NEWTON	AJ	1	249	NEWTON	W	14	232	NICHOLLS	A	5	251	NICHOLLS	JB	6	300
NEWTON	AT	14	232	NEWTON	W	14	232	NICHOLLS	A	6	299	NICHOLLS	JW	3	147
NEWTON	C	12	166	NEWTON	W	14	232	NICHOLLS	A	7	280	NICHOLLS	JWH	13	316
NEWTON	CH	12	359	NEWTON	WA	3	147	NICHOLLS	A	12	166	NICHOLLS	LJ	3	147
NEWTON	CJ	11	276	NEWTON	WC	3	147	NICHOLLS	A	12	166	NICHOLLS	MJ	12	167
NEWTON	DG	5	250	NEWTON	WE	4	275	NICHOLLS	A	12	166	NICHOLLS	P	6	300
NEWTON	DH	11	276	NEWTON	WH	4	275	NICHOLLS	AE	13	316	NICHOLLS	P	11	277
NEWTON	E	10	166	NEWTON	WH	7	280	NICHOLLS	AG	5	250	NICHOLLS	P	12	167
NEWTON	E	11	276	NEWTON	WJ	1	249	NICHOLLS	AJ	6	299	NICHOLLS	R	3	148
NEWTON	EA	10	342	NEWTON	WT	4	275	NICHOLLS	AJ	13	316	NICHOLLS	R	4	276
NEWTON	EJ	6	299	NEYLON	J	9	141	NICHOLLS	BT	4	276	NICHOLLS	R	7	280
NEWTON	EJ	8	246	NIBBS	A	2	248	NICHOLLS	C	5	251	NICHOLLS	RE	14	233
NEWTON	EM	4	275	NIBBS	G	13	316	NICHOLLS	C	14	233	NICHOLLS	S	5	251
NEWTON	EW	1	249	NIBLETT	C	7	280	NICHOLLS	CH	1	250	NICHOLLS	S	11	277
NEWTON	EW	10	166	NIBLETT	F	6	299	NICHOLLS	CH	12	359	NICHOLLS	SO	8	247
NEWTON	F	3	147	NIBLETT	H	2	248	NICHOLLS	D	10	342	NICHOLLS	T	12	359
NEWTON	F	7	279	NICE	EV	13	316	NICHOLLS	E	5	251	NICHOLLS	TA	12	359
NEWTON	F	12	359	NICE	FE	13	316	NICHOLLS	E	7	280	NICHOLLS	W	2	249
NEWTON	G	3	147	NICE	WP	13	316	NICHOLLS	EC	14	233	NICHOLLS	W	2	249
NEWTON	G	7	279	NICHLES	JW	9	141	NICHOLLS	EE	1	250	NICHOLLS	W	3	148
NEWTON	G	7	279	NICHOL	J	9	141	NICHOLLS	F	1	250	NICHOLLS	W	5	251
NEWTON	G	13	316	NICHOL	J	14	232	NICHOLLS	F	9	312	NICHOLLS	W	11	277
NEWTON	GT	5	250	NICHOL	JG	8	246	NICHOLLS	F	12	167	NICHOLLS	W	11	277
NEWTON	GW	8	246	NICHOL	T	8	247	NICHOLLS	F	12	167	NICHOLLS	WA	1	250
NEWTON	H	1	249	NICHOLAS	A	5	250	NICHOLLS	F	13	316	NICHOLLS	WC	5	251
NEWTON	H	1	249	NICHOLAS	A	13	316	NICHOLLS	FW	3	147	NICHOLLS	WE	13	316
NEWTON	H	7	279	NICHOLAS	AG	2	248	NICHOLLS	G	6	299	NICHOLLS	WG	12	167
NEWTON	H	9	311	NICHOLAS	AW	7	280	NICHOLLS	G	6	299	NICHOLLS	WH	6	300
NEWTON	H	10	167	NICHOLAS	CF	3	147	NICHOLLS	G	7	280	NICHOLLS	WT	12	167
NEWTON	HC	7	279	NICHOLAS	EF	5	250	NICHOLLS	G	14	233	NICHOLS	A	9	141
NEWTON	HN	4	275	NICHOLAS	F	2	248	NICHOLLS	GC	7	280	NICHOLS	AE	3	148

NICHOLS	AE	12	167
NICHOLS	AEA	3	148
NICHOLS	AGH	12	424
NICHOLS	AHH	4	276
NICHOLS	B	1	250
NICHOLS	BF	7	280
NICHOLS	E	2	249
NICHOLS	E	9	312
NICHOLS	EJ	10	342
NICHOLS	F	8	247
NICHOLS	F	9	141
NICHOLS	FEG	13	317
NICHOLS	G	8	247
NICHOLS	GH	4	276
NICHOLS	H	2	249
NICHOLS	H	5	251
NICHOLS	H	8	247
NICHOLS	H	8	247
NICHOLS	HA	1	250
NICHOLS	HCW	1	250
NICHOLS	J	2	249
NICHOLS	J	8	247
NICHOLS	J	14	233
NICHOLS	JWE	12	167
NICHOLS	M	2	249
NICHOLS	M	12	167
NICHOLS	PJ	7	280
NICHOLS	RJ	2	249
NICHOLS	RJ	5	251
NICHOLS	RS	5	251
NICHOLS	S	12	167
NICHOLS	V	8	247
NICHOLS	W	1	250
NICHOLS	W	5	251
NICHOLS	W	8	247
NICHOLS	W	8	247
NICHOLS	W	9	312
NICHOLS	WG	12	359
NICHOLS	WM	1	250
NICHOLSON	A	8	247
NICHOLSON	A	8	247
NICHOLSON	A	8	247
NICHOLSON	A	9	141
NICHOLSON	A	10	342
NICHOLSON	A	11	277
NICHOLSON	AE	4	276
NICHOLSON	AJ	10	167
NICHOLSON	BJ	10	342
NICHOLSON	CB	8	247
NICHOLSON	CF	13	317
NICHOLSON	CJ	13	317
NICHOLSON	CL	8	247
NICHOLSON	CW	7	280
NICHOLSON	CWM	9	312
NICHOLSON	E	3	148
NICHOLSON	E	13	317
NICHOLSON	EJ	3	148
NICHOLSON	F	2	249
NICHOLSON	F	4	276
NICHOLSON	FC	2	249
NICHOLSON	G	4	276
NICHOLSON	G	7	280
NICHOLSON	G	9	141
NICHOLSON	GO	5	251
NICHOLSON	H	8	247
NICHOLSON	H	10	167
NICHOLSON	HC	1	250
NICHOLSON	HD	13	317
NICHOLSON	HG	3	148
NICHOLSON	HG	12	167
NICHOLSON	HM	3	148
NICHOLSON	HM	8	247
NICHOLSON	HT	3	148
NICHOLSON	HW	4	276
NICHOLSON	J	1	250
NICHOLSON	J	8	247
NICHOLSON	J	11	277
NICHOLSON	JW	8	247
NICHOLSON	JW	8	247
NICHOLSON	JW	8	247
NICHOLSON	JW	9	141
NICHOLSON	M	8	248
NICHOLSON	M	9	312
NICHOLSON	NR	4	276
NICHOLSON	P	11	277
NICHOLSON	R	4	276
NICHOLSON	R	8	248
NICHOLSON	RH	9	312
NICHOLSON	RW	13	317
NICHOLSON	S	8	248
NICHOLSON	TH	11	277
NICHOLSON	W	8	248
NICHOLSON	W	10	167
NICHOLSON	W	10	342
NICHOLSON	WC	13	317
NICHOLSON	WH	8	248
NICHOLSON	WJ	7	280
NICKEAS	GE	11	278
NICKEAS	T	11	277
NICKELLS	P	9	312
NICKELS	GJ	3	148
NICKELS	GW	3	148
NICKERSON	CJ	1	250
NICKERSON	J	12	359
NICKERSON	JA	9	312
NICKERSON	LA	11	278
NICKLEN	F	4	276
NICKLEN	HO	4	276
NICKLEN	R	4	276
NICKLEN	SA	4	276
NICKLEN	TG	4	276
NICKLES	F	9	141
NICKLESS	A	6	300
NICKLESS	W	11	278
NICKLIN	A	6	300
NICKLIN	AV	9	141
NICKLIN	E	6	300
NICKLIN	HJ	10	342
NICKLIN	J	9	142
NICKLIN	T	8	248
NICKOLDS	HW	1	249
NICKOLDS	M	6	300
NICKOLDS	W	1	249
NICKOLLS	DF	3	148
NICKOLLS	WA	3	148
NICKOLLS	WJ	3	148
NICKOLSON	FEA	12	167
NICOL	C	2	249
NICOL	GL	3	148
NICOL	W	3	148
NICOL	W	10	342
NICOLAS	P	4	276
NICOLE	HR	3	148
NICOLL	SH	4	276
NICOLLE	AE	4	276
NIEKERK	PR	13	317
NIELD	B	8	248
NIELD	H	11	278
NIELD	J	14	233
NIELD	JG	14	233
NIELSON	CR	4	276
NIGG	FV	1	250
NIGG	FX	1	250
NIGHTINGALE	A	11	278
NIGHTINGALE	A	12	359
NIGHTINGALE	A	13	317
NIGHTINGALE	BC	7	280
NIGHTINGALE	C	13	317
NIGHTINGALE	CE	14	233
NIGHTINGALE	CR	13	317
NIGHTINGALE	EJ	2	249
NIGHTINGALE	EW	13	317
NIGHTINGALE	F	12	359
NIGHTINGALE	FL	7	281
NIGHTINGALE	J	1	250
NIGHTINGALE	JW	13	317
NIGHTINGALE	P	12	359
NIGHTINGALE	PJ	7	280
NIGHTINGALE	R	13	317
NIGHTINGALE	SA	10	167
NIGHTINGALE	TW	12	359
NIGHTINGALE	V	6	300
NIGHTINGALE	W	13	317
NIGHTINGALE	WP	12	359
NIHILL	J	13	317
NIHILL	W	11	278
NILAND	J	9	142
NILES	H	13	317
NIMMO	A	14	233
NIMMO	FG	9	142
NIMMO	WE	14	233
NIMS	FW	11	278
NIMS	HH	11	278
NIND	GC	13	317
NIND	R	12	359
NINHAM	FC	2	249
NINNEY	O	5	240
NINNEY	WT	5	240
NINNIM	L	4	276
NIPPER	J	2	249
NIPPER	WH	1	250
NIPPIERD	JW	4	277
NISBET	AJ	7	281
NISBET	CJ	7	281
NISBET	GF	7	281
NISBET	J	8	248
NISBET	T	7	281
NISBETT-GARRATT	C	7	281
NISBETT-GARRATT	S	7	281
NISBETT-GARRATT	W	7	281
NIX	AC	2	249
NIX	CHJ	13	317
NIX	HR	2	250
NIXEY	G	2	250
NIXEY	J	2	250
NIXON	A	2	250
NIXON	A	10	167
NIXON	A	11	278
NIXON	CEL	6	300
NIXON	E	8	248
NIXON	E	14	233
NIXON	F	7	281
NIXON	F	8	248
NIXON	F	9	142
NIXON	G	8	248
NIXON	H	3	148
NIXON	H	4	277
NIXON	HA	7	281
NIXON	J	11	278
NIXON	J	11	278
NIXON	JW	11	278
NIXON	R	11	278
NIXON	R	11	278
NIXON	S	10	167
NIXON	T	14	233
NIXON	W	8	248
NIXON	W	14	233
NIXON	W	14	233

NIXON	WA	1	250	NOBLE	J	9	142	NOLAN	R	9	142	NORMAN	D	5	252
NIXSON	FG	1	250	NOBLE	JF	12	167	NOLAN	T	10	167	NORMAN	E	1	251
NIXSON	GWE	2	250	NOBLE	JG	1	251	NOLAN	TH	9	142	NORMAN	E	12	167
NIXSON	WT	7	281	NOBLE	JR	13	318	NOLAN	W	13	318	NORMAN	E	12	168
NOACK	CB	2	250	NOBLE	JW	1	251	NOLAN	W	14	234	NORMAN	E	13	318
NOAD	A	1	250	NOBLE	JW	12	167	NOLAN	W	14	234	NORMAN	E	13	318
NOAD	E	2	250	NOBLE	M	9	142	NOLDE	WF	2	250	NORMAN	E	13	318
NOAD	HJ	1	251	NOBLE	P	8	248	NOLDER	A	3	149	NORMAN	E	14	234
NOAD	M	8	248	NOBLE	R	13	318	NOLDER	AP	5	252	NORMAN	E	14	234
NOADES	T	8	248	NOBLE	S	9	312	NOLDER	D	3	149	NORMAN	EJ	12	168
NOADES	WR	1	251	NOBLE	SF	6	300	NOON	CF	5	252	NORMAN	F	3	149
NOAH	A	5	251	NOBLE	SW	12	167	NOON	G	5	252	NORMAN	F	12	168
NOAKES	A	6	300	NOBLE	WA	6	300	NOON	JW	14	234	NORMAN	FJ	5	252
NOAKES	B	1	251	NOBLE	WH	8	248	NOON	W	6	301	NORMAN	FW	4	277
NOAKES	E	13	317	NOBLE	WS	1	251	NOONAN	J	4	277	NORMAN	G	1	251
NOAKES	F	3	148	NOBLETT	G	11	278	NOONAN	JG	4	277	NORMAN	G	1	251
NOAKES	FJ	3	148	NOCK	FW	6	300	NOONAN	RJ	1	251	NORMAN	GA	2	250
NOAKES	G	1	251	NOCK	J	3	149	NOONAN	WJ	3	381	NORMAN	GA	10	167
NOAKES	G	2	250	NOCK	J	6	301	NOONIN	J	4	277	NORMAN	GA	12	168
NOAKES	HC	13	318	NOCK	JBW	6	301	NORBURY	CH	14	234	NORMAN	GF	11	279
NOAKES	J	6	300	NOCK	RB	6	301	NORBURY	HJ	7	282	NORMAN	GT	5	252
NOAKES	K	3	149	NOCK	W	7	281	NORBURY	J	11	279	NORMAN	H	1	251
NOAKES	R	4	277	NOCK	WF	6	301	NORBURY	S	14	234	NORMAN	H	5	252
NOAKES	S	2	250	NOCK	WG	7	281	NORBURY	TW	1	251	NORMAN	H	8	249
NOAKES	T	7	281	NOCKTON	J	6	301	NORBURY	W	14	234	NORMAN	HA	13	318
NOAKES	WT	13	318	NOCTON	W	9	312	NORCOTT	GH	1	251	NORMAN	HC	10	167
NOBBS	E	5	251	NODDER	ES	13	318	NORCROSS	R	14	234	NORMAN	HH	14	234
NOBBS	FH	7	281	NODEN	C	11	278	NORDEN	AEV	1	251	NORMAN	HR	3	149
NOBBS	FJ	2	250	NODEN	E	14	233	NORDEN	GWC	1	251	NORMAN	HR	13	318
NOBBS	FW	13	318	NODEN	J	14	233	NORDEN	HJP	1	251	NORMAN	HS	12	168
NOBBS	G	5	251	NODEN	L	14	233	NORFIELD	J	1	251	NORMAN	HW	3	149
NOBBS	JG	12	359	NOEL	GW	7	281	NORFIELD	TH	7	282	NORMAN	J	4	277
NOBBS	JP	4	277	NOKE	JW	6	301	NORFOLK	C	8	249	NORMAN	J	6	301
NOBBS	N	13	318	NOKE	SC	4	277	NORFOLK	D	3	149	NORMAN	J	7	282
NOBBS	WH	10	343	NOKE	T	6	301	NORFOLK	FE	8	249	NORMAN	J	11	279
NOBES	FT	10	167	NOKE	THC	4	277	NORFOLK	G	8	249	NORMAN	J	12	168
NOBES	H	2	250	NOKE	W	6	301	NORFOLK	JH	8	249	NORMAN	J	12	168
NOBES	WF	10	343	NOKES	B	6	301	NORGAN	B	5	252	NORMAN	JA	14	234
NOBLE	A	4	277	NOKES	J	3	381	NORGAN	H	5	252	NORMAN	JE	11	279
NOBLE	A	8	248	NOKES	RC	1	251	NORGATE	G	4	277	NORMAN	JE	11	279
NOBLE	AA	9	312	NOLAN	A	7	281	NORGATE	RF	4	277	NORMAN	JW	11	279
NOBLE	AR	8	248	NOLAN	A	9	312	NORGATE	SV	4	277	NORMAN	JWH	2	250
NOBLE	C	9	312	NOLAN	A	14	234	NORGATE	WH	4	277	NORMAN	LHJ	10	167
NOBLE	D	3	149	NOLAN	D	11	278	NORGROVE	B	6	301	NORMAN	M	11	279
NOBLE	F	12	167	NOLAN	F	14	234	NORLEY	AE	2	250	NORMAN	P	12	168
NOBLE	FG	4	277	NOLAN	G	9	142	NORMAN	A	4	277	NORMAN	R	5	252
NOBLE	GH	5	251	NOLAN	H	9	142	NORMAN	AE	5	252	NORMAN	S	2	250
NOBLE	H	8	248	NOLAN	HJ	7	281	NORMAN	AJ	12	167	NORMAN	S	14	234
NOBLE	H	8	248	NOLAN	J	9	312	NORMAN	AJ	13	318	NORMAN	SE	1	252
NOBLE	H	9	142	NOLAN	J	9	312	NORMAN	AW	3	149	NORMAN	SG	7	282
NOBLE	H	9	142	NOLAN	J	11	278	NORMAN	AW	5	252	NORMAN	SJ	7	282
NOBLE	H	9	312	NOLAN	JH	6	301	NORMAN	BG	13	318	NORMAN	T	7	282
NOBLE	H	12	167	NOLAN	JJ	14	234	NORMAN	BL	4	277	NORMAN	W	7	282
NOBLE	J	8	248	NOLAN	M	11	279	NORMAN	CG	3	149	NORMAN	WG	4	277
NOBLE	J	9	142	NOLAN	P	8	249	NORMAN	CR	3	149	NORMAN	WH	10	343

NORMAN	WJ	12	168	NORRIS	JE	10	168	NORTH	H	7	283	NORTHOVER	FA	12	360
NORMAN	WT	2	250	NORRIS	JN	14	234	NORTH	H	8	249	NORTHOVER	FE	7	283
NORMANTON	F	9	142	NORRIS	JW	8	249	NORTH	H	9	142	NORTHOVER	H	4	278
NORMANTON	T	9	312	NORRIS	L	5	252	NORTH	H	9	142	NORTHOVER	R	4	278
NORMOYLE	W	11	279	NORRIS	M	14	234	NORTH	HG	8	249	NORTHOVER	W	4	278
NORMOYLE	W	11	279	NORRIS	MA	13	319	NORTH	HH	1	252	NORTHROP	H	9	313
NORMYLE	W	11	279	NORRIS	OS	11	279	NORTH	HJ	13	319	NORTHROP	P	9	143
NORRIE	A	13	318	NORRIS	P	14	234	NORTH	HT	7	283	NORTHROP	TF	9	143
NORRIS	A	3	381	NORRIS	PW	5	252	NORTH	HV	10	168	NORTHWOOD	FO	12	168
NORRIS	A	13	318	NORRIS	R	6	301	NORTH	HW	4	278	NORTHWOOD	G	5	253
NORRIS	AB	7	282	NORRIS	RG	10	168	NORTH	HW	12	168	NORTHWOOD	G	7	283
NORRIS	AE	12	359	NORRIS	S	3	149	NORTH	J	4	278	NORTHWOOD	H	5	253
NORRIS	AJ	3	381	NORRIS	S	3	150	NORTH	J	8	249	NORTHWOOD	JT	5	253
NORRIS	AJ	10	343	NORRIS	S	4	278	NORTH	J	8	249	NORTHWOOD	P	5	253
NORRIS	AR	13	318	NORRIS	SJ	5	252	NORTH	J	9	142	NORTHWOOD	RS	12	168
NORRIS	AW	13	318	NORRIS	TG	2	251	NORTH	J	9	142	NORTON	A	7	283
NORRIS	B	10	343	NORRIS	TJ	3	150	NORTH	J	9	313	NORTON	A	8	249
NORRIS	C	3	149	NORRIS	TR	2	251	NORTH	JES	9	143	NORTON	A	13	320
NORRIS	C	7	282	NORRIS	W	2	251	NORTH	JF	10	168	NORTON	AA	6	301
NORRIS	CA	7	282	NORRIS	W	5	252	NORTH	JW	13	319	NORTON	AA	6	301
NORRIS	CJF	1	252	NORRIS	W	6	301	NORTH	L	4	278	NORTON	AH	11	279
NORRIS	CP	10	343	NORRIS	W	7	282	NORTH	LA	5	253	NORTON	AN	11	279
NORRIS	E	2	250	NORRIS	W	7	283	NORTH	OD	9	313	NORTON	B	6	301
NORRIS	E	2	250	NORRIS	W	13	319	NORTH	P	1	252	NORTON	B	9	313
NORRIS	E	9	142	NORRIS	WC	13	319	NORTH	R	2	251	NORTON	BH	6	301
NORRIS	E	13	318	NORRIS	WH	1	252	NORTH	SE	5	253	NORTON	C	7	284
NORRIS	E	14	234	NORRIS	WH	11	279	NORTH	TC	12	360	NORTON	C	8	249
NORRIS	EJ	3	149	NORRIS	WJ	2	251	NORTH	TE	1	252	NORTON	CR	4	278
NORRIS	EJ	13	319	NORRIS	WLG	13	319	NORTH	W	1	252	NORTON	E	8	249
NORRIS	EM	13	319	NORRIS	WT	13	319	NORTH	W	2	251	NORTON	E	14	235
NORRIS	F	3	149	NORRISH	RH	4	278	NORTH	WA	7	283	NORTON	EW	6	302
NORRIS	F	4	278	NORTH	A	7	283	NORTH	WA	12	360	NORTON	G	8	249
NORRIS	F	13	319	NORTH	A	12	168	NORTH	WV	5	253	NORTON	GA	4	278
NORRIS	FE	10	343	NORTH	AH	3	150	NORTHALL	H	6	301	NORTON	H	14	235
NORRIS	G	1	252	NORTH	AM	9	312	NORTHAM	AF	13	319	NORTON	HB	13	320
NORRIS	G	4	278	NORTH	AT	10	168	NORTHAM	G	7	283	NORTON	HC	13	320
NORRIS	G	7	282	NORTH	B	9	312	NORTHAM	GH	7	283	NORTON	J	2	251
NORRIS	GA	3	149	NORTH	B	11	279	NORTHAM	JH	13	319	NORTON	J	6	302
NORRIS	GE	3	149	NORTH	BE	1	252	NORTHAM	LG	1	252	NORTON	J	8	249
NORRIS	GH	1	252	NORTH	C	8	249	NORTHAM	SR	13	319	NORTON	JB	8	249
NORRIS	GS	7	282	NORTH	CA	10	343	NORTHCOTE	H	7	283	NORTON	JE	1	252
NORRIS	H	3	149	NORTH	E	3	150	NORTHCOTT	ES	4	278	NORTON	JE	10	168
NORRIS	H	4	278	NORTH	E	5	252	NORTHCOTT	G	13	319	NORTON	JW	7	284
NORRIS	H	7	282	NORTH	ED	4	278	NORTHCOTT	J	4	278	NORTON	L	5	253
NORRIS	H	7	282	NORTH	EG	4	278	NORTHEAST	WJ	7	283	NORTON	L	9	143
NORRIS	H	10	167	NORTH	F	9	142	NORTHERN	F	2	251	NORTON	L	9	143
NORRIS	HG	7	282	NORTH	FG	5	253	NORTHERN	GA	2	251	NORTON	OG	1	252
NORRIS	HGF	1	252	NORTH	FG	7	283	NORTHERN	T	12	168	NORTON	RM	13	320
NORRIS	HR	1	252	NORTH	FG	7	283	NORTHFIELD	C	8	249	NORTON	T	14	235
NORRIS	HR	7	282	NORTH	FG	7	283	NORTHFIELD	GW	8	249	NORTON	TB	6	302
NORRIS	HW	7	282	NORTH	FW	7	283	NORTHFIELD	GW	12	168	NORTON	TC	2	251
NORRIS	J	11	279	NORTH	G	13	319	NORTHFIELD	HJ	13	319	NORTON	TJ	13	320
NORRIS	JA	10	167	NORTH	GN	13	319	NORTHFIELD	HS	13	320	NORTON	TW	8	249
NORRIS	JA	13	319	NORTH	GT	5	253	NORTHFIELD	HW	7	283	NORTON	V	7	284
NORRIS	JB	13	319	NORTH	GW	13	319	NORTHOVER	E	12	360	NORTON	W	13	320

NORTON	WA	14	235	NOXHAM	CE	10	168	NUTBEAM	B	4	279	NUTTALL	W	14	236
NORTON	WG	12	168	NOY	GH	10	343	NUTBEAM	C	4	279	NUTTALL	WA	11	280
NORTON	WH	9	143	NOY	HJ	10	343	NUTBEAM	J	4	279	NUTTER	A	8	250
NORTON	WJE	2	251	NOYCE	AD	4	278	NUTBEAM	W	4	279	NUTTER	C	1	253
NORTON	WL	8	250	NOYCE	AFR	4	279	NUTBEEM	A	3	150	NUTTER	C	11	280
NORVAL	J	1	252	NOYCE	C	4	279	NUTBEEM	CH	4	279	NUTTER	C	13	321
NORWOOD	A	3	150	NOYCE	CF	4	279	NUTBEEM	J	3	150	NUTTER	H	8	250
NORWOOD	G	1	252	NOYCE	E	4	279	NUTBEEN	G	4	279	NUTTER	H	8	250
NORWOOD	GN	14	235	NOYCE	EF	13	320	NUTBEEN	R	4	279	NUTTER	JH	8	250
NORWOOD	H	1	252	NOYCE	FA	4	279	NUTBOURNE	H	4	279	NUTTING	AE	12	169
NORWOOD	J	14	235	NOYCE	FE	4	279	NUTCHER	F	12	168	NUTTING	R	13	321
NORWOOD	RW	1	253	NOYCE	H	4	279	NUTCHER	HG	12	169	NUTTMAN	A	1	253
NORWOOD	T	14	235	NOYCE	HCC	4	279	NUTCHER	W	12	169	NUTTON	F	9	143
NORWOOD	WD	1	253	NOYCE	HE	4	279	NUTKINS	E	3	150	NUTTON	H	9	143
NOSS	H	4	278	NOYCE	L	4	279	NUTLAND	JF	1	253	NUTTON	RT	9	143
NOSWORTHY	AE	2	251	NOYCE	WD	4	279	NUTLAND	S	4	280	NYE	CR	2	252
NOSWORTHY	D	2	251	NOYCE	WH	4	279	NUTLEY	A	4	280	NYE	CS	7	284
NOTHER	GT	4	278	NOYCE	WH	13	320	NUTLEY	CE	2	251	NYE	E	1	253
NOTHER	JR	10	168	NOYCE	WJ	4	279	NUTLEY	FE	1	253	NYE	GCS	12	169
NOTHER	JS	10	343	NOYE	J	13	320	NUTLEY	G	1	253	NYE	HP	7	284
NOTLEY	CG	4	278	NUGENT	AB	13	320	NUTLEY	LR	2	252	NYE	PS	7	284
NOTLEY	JA	7	284	NUGENT	CJ	13	320	NUTLEY	W	7	284	NYE	TW	7	284
NOTT	A	6	302	NUGENT	E	13	320	NUTT	AG	1	253	NYE	WJ	3	150
NOTT	E	3	150	NUGENT	GF	13	320	NUTT	BA	5	253	NYE	WL	13	321
NOTT	E	6	302	NUGENT	H	13	320	NUTT	CG	13	321	NYLAND	T	2	252
NOTT	FA	3	150	NUGENT	HE	13	320	NUTT	CM	5	253				
NOTT	M	6	302	NUGENT	MJ	14	235	NUTT	GE	6	302				
NOTTAGE	A	13	320	NUGENT	T	14	235	NUTT	J	4	280	O			
NOTTAGE	CW	12	168	NUNAN	H	1	253	NUTT	J	12	169				
NOTTAGE	GH	13	320	NUNAN	H	3	150	NUTT	J	12	360	O'BRIAN	E	6	303
NOTTINGHAM	AN	3	150	NUNAN	TW	2	251	NUTTALL	A	14	235	O'BRIAN	J	9	143
NOTTINGHAM	B	8	250	NUNN	A	1	253	NUTTALL	A	14	235	O'BRIEN	AA	7	285
NOTTINGHAM	FM	3	150	NUNN	AE	7	284	NUTTALL	AE	14	235	O'BRIEN	C	6	303
NOTTINGHAM	HG	5	253	NUNN	AJ	1	253	NUTTALL	AH	13	321	O'BRIEN	C	10	168
NOTTINGHAM	JE	5	253	NUNN	AJPW	14	235	NUTTALL	CS	9	143	O'BRIEN	CE	3	151
NOTTINGHAM	O	12	168	NUNN	AVG	13	321	NUTTALL	D	9	313	O'BRIEN	CH	13	321
NOTTINGHAM	WH	3	150	NUNN	GH	7	284	NUTTALL	E	5	253	O'BRIEN	D	3	151
NOTTON	AT	12	360	NUNN	JW	9	143	NUTTALL	E	14	235	O'BRIEN	D	4	280
NOTTON	J	12	360	NUNN	JW	9	313	NUTTALL	F	11	279	O'BRIEN	D	14	236
NOUGHTON	T	8	250	NUNN	SR	5	253	NUTTALL	FD	4	280	O'BRIEN	E	11	280
NOULTON	G	7	284	NUNN	W	2	251	NUTTALL	H	14	235	O'BRIEN	EC	3	151
NOULTON	HC	7	284	NUNN	W	5	253	NUTTALL	H	14	235	O'BRIEN	F	5	254
NOULTON	HJ	7	284	NUNN	WC	1	253	NUTTALL	J	9	143	O'BRIEN	F	14	236
NOULTON	S	3	150	NUNN	WE	7	284	NUTTALL	J	11	280	O'BRIEN	F	14	236
NOUTCH	A	9	143	NUNN	WJH	12	168	NUTTALL	J	14	235	O'BRIEN	FJ	11	280
NOUTCH	A	9	143	NUNN	WW	12	168	NUTTALL	JR	14	235	O'BRIEN	G	2	252
NOVELL	W	5	253	NUNNELEY	HE	2	251	NUTTALL	LM	7	284	O'BRIEN	G	9	391
NOWELL	GH	7	284	NUNNEY	HC	1	253	NUTTALL	SH	4	280	O'BRIEN	G	11	280
NOWELL	P	3	150	NUNNEY	WJ	2	251	NUTTALL	SW	13	321	O'BRIEN	GJ	4	280
NOWELL	RH	6	302	NURSALL	CA	5	253	NUTTALL	T	9	313	O'BRIEN	GK	3	151
NOWELL	S	11	279	NURSALL	HJ	5	253	NUTTALL	T	11	280	O'BRIEN	H	11	281
NOWLAN	AE	13	320	NURSE	C	7	284	NUTTALL	T	14	236	O'BRIEN	J	8	250
NOWLAND	E	8	250	NURSE	EG	1	253	NUTTALL	W	11	280	O'BRIEN	J	8	250
NOWLAND	E	8	250	NURSE	R	7	284	NUTTALL	W	11	280	O'BRIEN	J	8	250
NOWLAND	L	8	250	NURTHEN	AHJ	2	251	NUTTALL	W	14	236	O'BRIEN	J	9	143
												O'BRIEN	J	9	313

O'BRIEN	J	10	169	O'CONNOR	J	8	251	O'DELL	WJ	5	255	O'HARA	R	9	314
O'BRIEN	J	11	280	O'CONNOR	J	9	144	O'DONEGAN	F	2	253	O'HARA	T	8	251
O'BRIEN	J	11	280	O'CONNOR	J	10	169	O'DONNEL	HP	3	381	O'HARA	T	9	144
O'BRIEN	J	11	281	O'CONNOR	J	11	281	O'DONNELL	AE	10	343	O'HARE	B	11	282
O'BRIEN	J	11	281	O'CONNOR	J	13	322	O'DONNELL	B	9	313	O'HARE	C	6	303
O'BRIEN	J	13	321	O'CONNOR	J	14	236	O'DONNELL	D	7	285	O'HARE	HF	7	285
O'BRIEN	J	14	236	O'CONNOR	JF	11	281	O'DONNELL	D	14	236	O'HARE	JT	11	282
O'BRIEN	J	14	236	O'CONNOR	JM	9	144	O'DONNELL	GT	13	322	O'KAVANAGH	P	3	152
O'BRIEN	J	14	236	O'CONNOR	M	11	281	O'DONNELL	H	9	313	O'KEARNEY	JJ	3	152
O'BRIEN	JE	2	252	O'CONNOR	M	13	322	O'DONNELL	J	14	236	O'KEEFE	D	1	254
O'BRIEN	JE	11	281	O'CONNOR	O	9	313	O'DONNELL	W	2	254	O'KEEFE	F	2	254
O'BRIEN	JP	2	252	O'CONNOR	P	11	281	O'DONNELL	W	8	251	O'KEEFE	HS	3	152
O'BRIEN	JW	8	250	O'CONNOR	P	14	236	O'DOWD	J	14	237	O'KEEFE	HW	7	285
O'BRIEN	M	8	250	O'CONNOR	T	8	251	O'DOWD	T	2	254	O'KEEFE	JJ	13	322
O'BRIEN	MM	2	252	O'CONNOR	T	11	281	O'DRISCOLL	TW	2	254	O'KEEFFE	F	9	314
O'BRIEN	NH	13	321	O'CONNOR	TC	10	169	O'DWYER	NJ	3	152	O'KEEFFE	L	9	144
O'BRIEN	P	6	303	O'CONNOR	TF	4	281	O'DWYER	W	3	152	O'KEEFFE	T	8	251
O'BRIEN	PJ	10	169	O'CONNOR	TJ	2	253	O'FARRELL	V	6	303	O'KEEFFE	W	9	144
O'BRIEN	R	14	236	O'CONNOR	TW	7	285	O'FLAHERTY	L	14	237	O'LEARY	E	7	286
O'BRIEN	RF	11	281	O'CONNOR	W	2	253	O'FLAHERTY	WP	7	285	O'LEARY	J	9	145
O'BRIEN	S	11	281	O'CONNOR	WP	6	303	O'FLANAGAN	T	3	152	O'LEARY	J	11	283
O'BRIEN	T	5	254	O'COY	A	6	303	O'GARA	P	11	282	O'LEARY	JP	13	322
O'BRIEN	T	8	250	O'DEA	M	2	253	O'GORMAN	M	14	237	O'LEARY	M	3	152
O'BRIEN	T	9	313	O'DELL	A	2	253	O'GORMAN	TJ	14	237	O'LEARY	M	4	282
O'BRIEN	T	11	281	O'DELL	A	4	281	O'GRADY	H	11	282	O'LEARY	T	11	284
O'BRIEN	T	11	281	O'DELL	A	5	254	O'GRADY	WA	7	285	O'LEARY	W	1	254
O'BRIEN	T	13	321	O'DELL	AW	5	254	O'HAGAN	G	11	282	O'LEARY	WA	1	254
O'BRIEN	W	4	280	O'DELL	AW	5	254	O'HAGAN	P	10	343	O'LOUGHLIN	E	6	304
O'BRIEN	W	6	303	O'DELL	B	5	254	O'HALLORAN	AE	10	343	O'LOUGHLIN	J	6	304
O'BRIEN	W	8	251	O'DELL	B	5	254	O'HALLORAN	C	10	343	O'MAHONEY	DF	2	254
O'BRIEN	W	9	143	O'DELL	C	5	254	O'HALLORAN	EC	10	343	O'MAHONEY	JJ	14	238
O'BRIEN	W	11	281	O'DELL	C	5	254	O'HALLORAN	J	13	322	O'MAILEY	H	8	252
O'BRIEN	W	14	236	O'DELL	CE	4	281	O'HALLORAN	MT	2	254	O'MALLEY	C	3	153
O'BRIEN	W	14	236	O'DELL	E	5	254	O'HANLON	J	11	282	O'MARA	R	14	238
O'BRIER	D	9	313	O'DELL	EE	5	254	O'HANLON	PH	6	303	O'NEALE	J	7	286
O'BRYAN	JT	11	281	O'DELL	EV	2	253	O'HARA	C	9	144	O'NEIL	C	9	314
O'CALLAGHAN	CJ	4	280	O'DELL	FC	5	254	O'HARA	C	9	314	O'NEIL	F	11	284
O'CALLAGHAN	CL	4	280	O'DELL	FE	5	254	O'HARA	CJ	4	281	O'NEILL	AG	7	287
O'CALLAGHAN	T	13	321	O'DELL	G	5	254	O'HARA	DC	10	169	O'NEILL	AV	11	284
O'CALLAHAN	M	8	251	O'DELL	GT	5	254	O'HARA	F	8	251	O'NEILL	C	3	153
O'CALLAHAN	T	8	251	O'DELL	GW	5	254	O'HARA	F	9	314	O'NEILL	EC	1	254
O'CONNELL	J	2	253	O'DELL	H	5	254	O'HARA	F	14	237	O'NEILL	FJ	11	284
O'CONNELL	J	7	285	O'DELL	H	5	255	O'HARA	FH	9	314	O'NEILL	FJ	14	239
O'CONNELL	JT	11	281	O'DELL	H	5	255	O'HARA	HJ	10	169	O'NEILL	FW	14	239
O'CONNELL	P	2	253	O'DELL	J	4	281	O'HARA	J	8	251	O'NEILL	G	11	284
O'CONNELL	P	9	144	O'DELL	JB	5	255	O'HARA	J	8	251	O'NEILL	HJ	6	304
O'CONNELL	PJ	7	285	O'DELL	JJ	2	253	O'HARA	J	9	144	O'NEILL	J	10	344
O'CONNOR	A	2	253	O'DELL	R	5	255	O'HARA	J	9	314	O'NEILL	J	11	284
O'CONNOR	A	11	281	O'DELL	RM	5	255	O'HARA	J	9	314	O'NEILL	J	11	284
O'CONNOR	A	13	322	O'DELL	S	2	253	O'HARA	J	10	169	O'NEILL	J	11	284
O'CONNOR	C	9	144	O'DELL	W	5	255	O'HARA	JE	9	144	O'NEILL	J	11	284
O'CONNOR	D	14	236	O'DELL	W	5	255	O'HARA	L	9	144	O'NEILL	J	11	285
O'CONNOR	E	8	251	O'DELL	W	6	303	O'HARA	L	9	314	O'NEILL	J	11	285
O'CONNOR	F	8	251	O'DELL	W	13	322	O'HARA	L	14	238	O'NEILL	J	14	239
O'CONNOR	G	7	285	O'DELL	WH	5	255	O'HARA	R	9	144	O'NEILL	JF	14	239

O'NEILL	M	3	153	OAKES	FS	11	280	OARTON	W	11	280	ODELL	A	4	281
O'NEILL	M	3	153	OAKES	GB	6	302	OATES	A	14	236	ODELL	A	12	169
O'NEILL	M	7	287	OAKES	GW	6	302	OATES	AJ	7	285	ODELL	C	3	151
O'NEILL	MC	7	287	OAKES	J	11	280	OATES	F	9	143	ODELL	C	4	281
O'NEILL	P	7	287	OAKES	JH	6	302	OATES	FE	13	321	ODELL	C	4	281
O'NEILL	P	7	287	OAKES	R	8	250	OATES	G	8	250	ODELL	D	4	281
O'NEILL	P	10	170	OAKES	TGF	3	150	OATES	J	8	250	ODELL	DW	12	169
O'NEILL	P	11	285	OAKES	TW	8	250	OATES	JW	8	250	ODELL	F	12	169
O'NEILL	P	11	285	OAKES	W	10	168	OATES	W	9	313	ODELL	FG	12	169
O'NEILL	P	14	239	OAKES	W	11	280	OATES	WW	2	252	ODELL	FW	4	281
O'NEILL	P	14	239	OAKEY	C	10	168	OBEE	A	2	252	ODELL	G	12	169
O'NEILL	R	3	153	OAKEY	FG	10	168	OBEE	F	4	280	ODELL	HA	5	255
O'NEILL	R	11	285	OAKFORD	A	2	252	OBERST	CJ	3	381	ODELL	HG	12	169
O'NEILL	T	11	285	OAKFORD	H	10	168	OBERST	GH	3	151	ODELL	HS	5	255
O'NEILL	TP	3	153	OAKFORTH	G	9	143	OBERY	CH	2	252	ODELL	J	5	255
O'NEILL	W	3	153	OAKHAM	G	2	252	OBEY	HJ	4	280	ODELL	JH	5	255
O'NEILL	W	11	285	OAKHAM	H	1	253	OBEY	W	4	280	ODELL	P	12	169
O'NEILL	WH	2	254	OAKHAM	J	3	150	OBLEIN	J	2	252	ODELL	PW	5	255
O'PREY	D	4	282	OAKLAND	C	6	302	OBORN	WH	3	151	ODELL	R	5	255
O'REILLY	JB	4	283	OAKLEY	A	3	150	OBORNE	GF	13	321	ODELL	S	12	169
O'REILLY	W	13	323	OAKLEY	A	4	280	OBORNE	HC	13	321	ODELL	SC	12	169
O'RERDIEN	JW	1	254	OAKLEY	A	6	302	OBRIEN	D	1	253	ODELL	W	5	255
O'ROARK	A	6	304	OAKLEY	A	12	169	OBRIEN	J	1	253	ODELL	WC	12	170
O'ROARK	W	6	304	OAKLEY	A	12	169	OCCOMORE	S	13	321	ODELL	WF	12	170
O'ROURKE	C	9	145	OAKLEY	AE	2	252	OCKENDEN	AG	2	252	ODELL	WJ	3	151
O'ROURKE	D	1	254	OAKLEY	AJ	6	302	OCKENDEN	F	2	252	ODELL	WJ	3	151
O'ROURKE	H	11	285	OAKLEY	C	3	151	OCKENDEN	FGW	2	253	ODELL	WJ	5	255
O'ROURKE	P	9	145	OAKLEY	C	4	280	OCKENDON	PA	3	151	ODELL	WJ	12	170
O'ROURKE	P	13	323	OAKLEY	C	12	169	OCKHAM	AE	7	285	ODELL	WR	5	255
O'SHAUGHNESSY	J	3	154	OAKLEY	CT	10	168	OCKLEFORD	FI	4	280	ODEY	G	2	253
O'SHAUGHNESSY	J	11	286	OAKLEY	FC	3	151	OCKLEFORD	JI	4	280	ODEY	J	4	281
O'SHAUGHNESSY	JR	14	239	OAKLEY	FH	3	151	OCKLEFORD	JW	4	281	ODEY	M	4	281
O'SHEA	C	3	154	OAKLEY	FJ	6	302	OCKMORE	GJ	7	285	ODIAM	G	4	281
O'SHEA	D	14	240	OAKLEY	FW	6	302	OCKWELL	C	2	253	ODIAM	S	4	281
O'SHEA	W	1	255	OAKLEY	G	6	302	OCKWELL	F	2	253	ODIAM	V	4	281
O'SULLIVAN	CP	14	240	OAKLEY	GE	10	168	OCKWELL	R	2	253	ODLING	GWP	3	151
O'SULLIVAN	JJ	13	324	OAKLEY	GR	3	151	OCLEY	J	9	144	OFFEN	JE	12	170
O'SULLIVAN	SF	14	240	OAKLEY	H	4	280	OCONNELL	E	1	253	OFFER	E	14	237
O'SULLIVAN	TJ	13	324	OAKLEY	HO	4	280	OCONNELL	TA	1	253	OFFER	FE	5	256
O'SULLIVAN	WH	13	324	OAKLEY	J	8	250	ODAM	M	3	151	OFFICER	J	9	144
O'TOOLE	J	11	286	OAKLEY	J	9	313	ODAMS	J	12	360	OFFICER	T	11	281
O'TOOLE	JH	8	253	OAKLEY	JA	3	151	ODDEY	H	8	251	OFFORD	CJG	7	285
O'TOOLE	P	2	255	OAKLEY	JF	12	169	ODDON	BP	8	251	OFFORD	CS	4	281
O'TOOLE	R	6	305	OAKLEY	R	11	280	ODDON	W	8	251	OFSEANEY	J	11	282
OAK	AJ	13	321	OAKLEY	SA	4	280	ODDY	C	2	253	OGBURN	AC	3	381
OAK	H	7	285	OAKLEY	SM	6	302	ODDY	E	8	251	OGBURN	E	3	381
OAKE	AJ	1	253	OAKLEY	TG	2	252	ODDY	ER	9	313	OGBURN	FC	10	169
OAKE	P	2	252	OAKLEY	WG	12	169	ODDY	G	8	251	OGBURN	HC	10	169
OAKELEY	J	2	252	OAKLEY	WH	4	280	ODDY	GE	3	151	OGDEN	A	11	282
OAKENFULL	S	12	360	OAKLEY	WR	5	254	ODDY	H	9	144	OGDEN	A	14	237
OAKERBEE	EHJ	3	150	OAKLWY	W	7	285	ODDY	JR	7	285	OGDEN	AC	10	169
OAKES	AT	10	168	OAKS	GL	3	151	ODDY	W	2	253	OGDEN	AE	11	282
OAKES	AW	11	280	OAKSHOTT	GW	10	168	ODDY	W	9	313	OGDEN	AG	12	360
OAKES	CC	6	302	OAKSHOTT	HG	10	168	ODDY	WL	9	144	OGDEN	CA	14	237
OAKES	CW	13	321	OARTON	H	11	280	ODEA	JJ	12	360	OGDEN	DH	14	237

OGDEN	E	9	313
OGDEN	E	11	282
OGDEN	E	14	237
OGDEN	E	14	237
OGDEN	E	14	237
OGDEN	FC	10	169
OGDEN	G	11	282
OGDEN	H	11	282
OGDEN	H	11	282
OGDEN	H	11	282
OGDEN	J	8	251
OGDEN	J	9	313
OGDEN	J	14	237
OGDEN	J	14	237
OGDEN	JH	14	237
OGDEN	L	14	237
OGDEN	LH	12	360
OGDEN	M	11	282
OGDEN	OO	11	282
OGDEN	RC	9	314
OGDEN	S	9	144
OGDEN	S	9	144
OGDEN	S	10	169
OGDEN	S	14	237
OGDEN	S	14	237
OGDEN	SH	11	282
OGDEN	T	11	282
OGDEN	T	11	282
OGDEN	T	14	237
OGDEN	W	9	314
OGDEN	W	11	282
OGDEN	W	14	237
OGIER	JH	3	381
OGIER	SG	3	381
OGIER	WJ	3	381
OGILVIE	J	10	169
OGILVIE	J	13	322
OGILVIE	SH	10	169
OGLE	H	8	251
OGLESBY	R	6	303
OGLESBY	W	8	251
OKINES	G	7	286
OKINES	R	7	286
OKLEY	EW	7	286
OLANDO	G	1	254
OLBINSON	GE	11	283
OLD	A	1	254
OLD	AE	10	169
OLD	B	4	281
OLD	FH	13	322
OLD	P	4	281
OLD	T	1	254
OLDAKER	P	6	303
OLDAKER	PM	6	303
OLDBURY	A	6	303
OLDBURY	E	4	281
OLDBURY	RH	6	303
OLDEN	G	4	281
OLDEN	G	4	281
OLDEN	RF	13	322
OLDENHALL	E	6	303
OLDER	P	10	169
OLDERSHAW	R	11	283
OLDFIELD	A	7	286
OLDFIELD	A	9	144
OLDFIELD	A	11	283
OLDFIELD	B	11	283
OLDFIELD	BL	9	314
OLDFIELD	EC	8	251
OLDFIELD	G	2	254
OLDFIELD	G	3	382
OLDFIELD	GF	1	254
OLDFIELD	J	14	238
OLDFIELD	JS	4	281
OLDFIELD	JW	8	251
OLDFIELD	JW	11	283
OLDFIELD	O	9	314
OLDFIELD	S	3	152
OLDFIELD	S	11	283
OLDFIELD	TE	9	314
OLDFIELD	TG	2	254
OLDFIELD	V	3	152
OLDFIELD	W	8	252
OLDFIELD	W	12	170
OLDHAM	A	11	283
OLDHAM	A	11	283
OLDHAM	A	14	238
OLDHAM	AJ	14	238
OLDHAM	B	6	303
OLDHAM	C	2	254
OLDHAM	C	11	283
OLDHAM	E	14	238
OLDHAM	G	11	283
OLDHAM	H	12	170
OLDHAM	I	11	283
OLDHAM	J	11	283
OLDHAM	J	11	283
OLDHAM	J	11	283
OLDHAM	JW	11	283
OLDHAM	RH	6	303
OLDHAM	W	11	283
OLDHAM	W	14	238
OLDHAM	WF	3	152
OLDHAM	WJ	6	303
OLDING	F	10	169
OLDING	JW	3	152
OLDING	RW	10	169
OLDING	T	4	282
OLDING	TWG	4	282
OLDKNOW	W	8	252
OLDLAD	J	14	238
OLDLAND	G	11	283
OLDMAN	G	3	152
OLDMAN	L	3	152
OLDMAN	N	3	152
OLDMEADOW	CJ	5	256
OLDNALL	E	6	303
OLDRICH	JA	11	283
OLDRIDGE	CR	13	322
OLDRIDGE	H	8	252
OLDRIDGE	RG	13	322
OLDROYD	A	14	238
OLDROYD	E	8	252
OLDROYD	GW	8	252
OLDROYD	H	8	252
OLDROYD	L	8	252
OLDROYD	W	9	314
OLDROYD	WA	9	314
OLFORD	V	10	170
OLIPHANT	F	11	284
OLIPHANT	R	11	284
OLIPHANT	W	4	282
OLIVE	A	13	322
OLIVE	C	4	282
OLIVE	E	14	238
OLIVE	G	4	282
OLIVE	R	14	238
OLIVE	TJ	4	282
OLIVE	WG	3	152
OLIVE	WH	14	238
OLIVER	A	3	152
OLIVER	A	14	238
OLIVER	AE	3	152
OLIVER	AE	4	282
OLIVER	AJ	13	322
OLIVER	B	12	360
OLIVER	C	7	286
OLIVER	CHG	7	286
OLIVER	CV	11	284
OLIVER	E	8	252
OLIVER	E	8	252
OLIVER	E	8	252
OLIVER	E	13	322
OLIVER	EC	4	282
OLIVER	EG	13	322
OLIVER	EJ	11	284
OLIVER	EJ	13	322
OLIVER	EL	4	282
OLIVER	F	3	152
OLIVER	F	4	282
OLIVER	F	4	282
OLIVER	FFJ	10	170
OLIVER	FW	5	256
OLIVER	FW	5	256
OLIVER	G	3	382
OLIVER	G	5	256
OLIVER	G	5	256
OLIVER	G	7	286
OLIVER	G	7	286
OLIVER	G	12	360
OLIVER	GA	1	254
OLIVER	GA	1	254
OLIVER	GE	14	238
OLIVER	GT	10	343
OLIVER	GT	12	360
OLIVER	H	1	254
OLIVER	H	5	256
OLIVER	H	11	284
OLIVER	HA	10	343
OLIVER	HJ	4	282
OLIVER	HT	8	252
OLIVER	J	1	254
OLIVER	J	11	284
OLIVER	J	11	424
OLIVER	J	14	238
OLIVER	JH	4	282
OLIVER	JT	12	360
OLIVER	JW	14	238
OLIVER	LAW	3	152
OLIVER	OJC	12	360
OLIVER	PO	12	360
OLIVER	R	14	238
OLIVER	T	4	282
OLIVER	TE	11	284
OLIVER	W	1	254
OLIVER	W	3	152
OLIVER	W	4	282
OLIVER	W	4	282
OLIVER	W	5	256
OLIVER	W	9	145
OLIVER	W	9	314
OLIVER	W	10	343
OLIVER	W	12	360
OLIVER	W	13	322
OLIVER	WC	4	282
OLIVER	WE	2	254
OLIVER	WE	12	360
OLIVER	WJ	2	254
OLIVER	WR	4	282
OLIVER	WR	7	286
OLIVEY	A	10	344
OLLERENSHAW	E	14	238
OLLERTON	H	11	284
OLLETT	E	4	282
OLLIFFE	A	12	170
OLLIFFE	M	7	286
OLLIFFE	TW	3	152
OLLIS	A	6	304
OLLIVER	CE	10	170
OLLIVER	M	7	286

OLLIVER	W	10	344	ORANGE	A	8	252	ORME	W	11	285	OSBORN	AW	13	323
OLLIVIER	J	7	286	ORANGE	H	8	252	ORMEROD	A	3	153	OSBORN	CG	5	257
OLNEY	AC	5	256	ORANGE	J	8	252	ORMEROD	F	9	314	OSBORN	CR	3	153
OLNEY	AC	5	256	ORANGE	JE	8	252	ORMEROD	JA	9	314	OSBORN	E	2	255
OLNEY	C	7	286	ORANGE	S	8	252	ORMESHER	C	14	239	OSBORN	F	6	304
OLNEY	EH	7	286	ORANGO	A	7	287	ORMESHER	T	14	239	OSBORN	F	7	288
OLNEY	F	10	170	ORCHARD	E	10	170	ORMESHER	WA	8	252	OSBORN	G	12	170
OLNEY	HP	12	170	ORCHARD	E	11	285	ORMISTON	TG	8	252	OSBORN	H	1	255
OLNEY	RG	3	152	ORCHARD	EG	7	287	ORMONDROYD	A	9	145	OSBORN	H	7	288
OLNEY	S	5	256	ORCHARD	EJ	7	287	ORMONDROYD	E	9	315	OSBORN	HG	14	239
OLNEY	ST	7	286	ORCHARD	H	3	153	ORMONDROYD	F	9	145	OSBORN	HJR	13	323
OLNEY	T	13	322	ORCHARD	H	5	256	ORMONDROYD	H	9	145	OSBORN	HS	3	153
OLNEY	W	5	256	ORCHARD	HJ	11	285	ORMONDROYD	H	9	315	OSBORN	J	2	255
OLORENSHAW	T	6	304	ORCHARD	L	5	256	ORMONDROYD	R	9	145	OSBORN	J	7	288
OLSEN	W	11	284	ORCHARD	P	5	256	ORMOROD	W	14	239	OSBORN	J	12	361
OLSZEWSKI	LM	7	287	ORCHARD	W	4	283	ORMROD	AE	11	285	OSBORN	J	12	361
OLVER	WP	11	284	ORCHARD	W	7	287	ORMROD	AE	11	285	OSBORN	J	13	324
OMAN	DJN	13	323	ORCHARD	WJ	12	170	ORMROD	F	14	239	OSBORN	PJ	5	257
OMAN	WT	3	153	ORCHARD	WT	5	256	ORMROD	JR	11	285	OSBORN	RE	5	257
OMBLER	N	8	252	ORCHIN	F	13	323	ORMROYDE	J	8	252	OSBORN	S	13	324
OMNES	JW	13	323	ORCHISON	N	7	287	ORMSTON	BC	12	170	OSBORN	SC	13	324
OMNES	L	13	323	ORDERS	A	1	254	ORPIN	FP	12	170	OSBORN	SH	5	257
ONG	AW	2	254	ORDERS	AE	2	254	ORPIN	L	12	170	OSBORN	T	12	361
ONG	B	14	239	ORDISH	H	14	239	ORPIN	W	12	170	OSBORN	W	1	255
ONG	H	14	239	ORFORD	C	10	344	ORPWOOD	J	1	254	OSBORN	W	12	361
ONG	JE	14	239	ORFORD	H	2	254	ORRIDGE	HW	3	153	OSBORN	W	12	361
ONG	WH	14	239	ORFORD	HW	3	153	ORRIN	AC	7	288	OSBORN	WA	12	361
ONION	B	13	323	ORFORD	SF	3	153	ORRISS	C	7	288	OSBORN	WW	1	255
ONIONS	AV	6	304	ORFORD	SH	14	239	ORRISS	E	13	323	OSBORNE	A	4	283
ONIONS	C	6	304	ORFORD	T	11	285	ORSMAN	AB	5	256	OSBORNE	A	5	257
ONIONS	F	6	304	ORFORD	W	13	323	ORSMAN	WS	5	257	OSBORNE	A	7	288
ONIONS	GW	2	254	ORGAN	C	4	283	ORTH	C	13	323	OSBORNE	A	7	288
ONIONS	W	9	145	ORGAN	CE	6	304	ORTON	H	3	153	OSBORNE	A	11	286
ONIONS	WS	13	323	ORGAN	TF	10	344	ORTON	J	12	361	OSBORNE	A	12	361
ONLEY	CA	13	323	ORGILL	W	8	252	ORTON	R	1	254	OSBORNE	A	13	324
ONLEY	F	12	361	ORIEL	T	7	287	ORTON	S	1	255	OSBORNE	AE	3	382
ONLEY	WH	12	361	ORIENT	F	2	254	ORTON	S	8	253	OSBORNE	AE	11	286
ONLEY	WS	7	287	ORIENT	W	2	254	ORTON	TE	6	304	OSBORNE	AGR	5	257
ONN	GF	9	314	ORMAN	JA	11	285	ORTON	W	6	304	OSBORNE	AH	12	361
ONYON	AE	8	252	ORMAN	VCM	4	283	ORUM	BV	7	288	OSBORNE	AW	7	288
OPENSHAW	B	13	323	ORMAN	W	4	283	ORVIS	J	2	255	OSBORNE	C	1	255
OPIE	AG	10	344	ORME	A	6	304	ORWIN	F	3	153	OSBORNE	C	3	153
OPIE	CT	10	170	ORME	A	6	304	ORWIN	J	8	253	OSBORNE	C	10	344
OPIE	E	10	344	ORME	A	10	170	OSBALDESTON	J	9	315	OSBORNE	E	9	315
ORAM	CG	7	287	ORME	A	11	285	OSBALDESTON	JS	11	285	OSBORNE	EC	1	255
ORAM	DD	7	287	ORME	AW	12	361	OSBALDESTON	S	7	288	OSBORNE	EH	2	255
ORAM	EF	10	170	ORME	G	11	285	OSBALDESTON	W	9	145	OSBORNE	EW	13	324
ORAM	FH	13	323	ORME	GH	13	323	OSBALDESTON	W	9	145	OSBORNE	F	3	382
ORAM	FJ	1	254	ORME	GH	13	323	OSBALDSTONE	A	4	283	OSBORNE	FC	7	288
ORAM	GL	7	287	ORME	H	5	256	OSBORN	A	5	257	OSBORNE	FJ	10	170
ORAM	HJ	13	323	ORME	J	6	304	OSBORN	AC	5	257	OSBORNE	FJ	10	344
ORAM	S	7	287	ORME	JJ	7	287	OSBORN	AJ	1	255	OSBORNE	G	3	153
ORAM	T	10	344	ORME	LH	6	304	OSBORN	AJ	13	323	OSBORNE	G	10	170
ORAM	WA	10	170	ORME	RJ	2	255	OSBORN	AK	10	170	OSBORNE	G	13	324
ORAM	WJ	7	287	ORME	TW	6	304	OSBORN	AS	7	288	OSBORNE	GA	2	255

OSBORNE	GA	6	305	OSBORNE	WT	2	255	OUGHAM	E	2	255	OVERTON	AG	3	154
OSBORNE	GC	6	305	OSBORNE	WT	13	324	OUGHTON	CL	10	344	OVERTON	AL	9	145
OSBORNE	GH	12	170	OSBOURN	K	1	255	OUGHTON	T	12	361	OVERTON	F	7	289
OSBORNE	GT	1	255	OSBOURNE	JG	9	315	OULAGHAN	A	6	305	OVERTON	F	13	325
OSBORNE	H	3	153	OSCROFT	A	4	283	OULDS	GC	10	344	OVERTON	GW	4	284
OSBORNE	H	4	283	OSCROFT	M	4	283	OULDS	SL	10	344	OVERTON	H	1	256
OSBORNE	H	4	283	OSELTON	HG	1	255	OUSBY	AW	13	325	OVERTON	H	1	256
OSBORNE	H	8	253	OSGERBY	JW	5	257	OUSLEY	A	7	288	OVERTON	J	1	256
OSBORNE	H	8	253	OSGOOD	AH	4	283	OUTEN	GJ	12	170	OVERTON	J	7	289
OSBORNE	H	12	170	OSGOOD	AJ	2	255	OUTHWAITE	A	11	286	OVERTON	J	12	171
OSBORNE	H	14	239	OSGOOD	HJ	5	257	OUTHWAITE	C	9	145	OVERTON	LM	3	154
OSBORNE	HB	6	305	OSGOOD	W	10	344	OUTHWAITE	HD	13	325	OVERTON	W	3	154
OSBORNE	HE	4	283	OSGOOD	WH	10	344	OUTHWAITE	R	8	253	OVERTON	W	13	325
OSBORNE	HG	12	361	OSLER	G	13	324	OUTHWAITE	S	9	145	OVERTON	WG	5	258
OSBORNE	HGB	2	255	OSLER	H	1	255	OUTING	E	7	289	OVERTON	WG	7	289
OSBORNE	HJ	6	305	OSMAN	AE	4	283	OUTLAW	A	3	382	OVERTON	WJ	3	154
OSBORNE	HT	5	257	OSMAN	BA	4	283	OUTLAW	PG	3	382	OVERY	AN	2	255
OSBORNE	IL	3	382	OSMAN	CH	4	283	OUTRAM	E	1	255	OVERY	GW	13	325
OSBORNE	J	3	153	OSMAN	CH	4	283	OUTRAM	VH	2	255	OVERY	JT	7	289
OSBORNE	J	5	257	OSMAN	E	4	283	OUTRAM	W	1	255	OVERY	W	6	305
OSBORNE	J	5	257	OSMAN	F	4	283	OVEN	A	11	286	OVERY	W	13	325
OSBORNE	J	6	305	OSMAN	FG	4	284	OVEN	H	11	286	OWEN	A	5	258
OSBORNE	J	8	253	OSMAN	HHG	4	284	OVEN	JS	11	286	OWEN	A	6	305
OSBORNE	J	10	170	OSMAN	HW	4	284	OVENDEN	A	3	154	OWEN	A	14	240
OSBORNE	J	13	324	OSMAN	JA	4	284	OVENDEN	GH	10	344	OWEN	AE	5	258
OSBORNE	J	14	239	OSMAN	JC	4	284	OVENDEN	N	3	154	OWEN	AE	6	305
OSBORNE	JE	3	154	OSMAN	JT	5	257	OVENDEN	S	1	256	OWEN	AH	13	325
OSBORNE	JJ	3	154	OSMAN	NM	4	284	OVENS	AW	13	325	OWEN	AJ	2	255
OSBORNE	JT	5	257	OSMAN	SA	4	284	OVENS	AWS	1	256	OWEN	AW	7	289
OSBORNE	JW	8	253	OSMOND	S	1	255	OVENS	J	1	256	OWEN	AW	12	171
OSBORNE	JW	8	253	OSMOND	WJ	4	284	OVENS	RA	1	256	OWEN	AW	12	361
OSBORNE	LJ	5	257	OSSETT	G	8	253	OVENS	W	10	170	OWEN	C	6	305
OSBORNE	LV	13	324	OST	H	12	361	OVENS	W	11	286	OWEN	C	7	289
OSBORNE	M	3	154	OSTICK	JW	14	240	OVENSTON	CH	3	154	OWEN	C	9	315
OSBORNE	PC	4	283	OSWALD	CM	4	284	OVER	AL	4	284	OWEN	C	14	240
OSBORNE	R	13	324	OSWALD	R	8	253	OVER	W	1	256	OWEN	CB	3	154
OSBORNE	RH	7	288	OSWICK	GH	2	255	OVER	WJ	1	256	OWEN	CC	7	289
OSBORNE	RV	3	154	OSWICK	HE	2	255	OVERALL	H	13	325	OWEN	E	1	256
OSBORNE	RW	10	170	OTHEN	C	4	284	OVERALL	SG	13	325	OWEN	E	12	171
OSBORNE	S	6	305	OTHEN	E	4	284	OVERELL	HA	3	154	OWEN	E	13	325
OSBORNE	S	9	315	OTHEN	WB	4	284	OVERELL	HW	3	154	OWEN	EW	13	325
OSBORNE	SG	13	324	OTHICK	H	8	253	OVEREND	A	9	315	OWEN	F	11	286
OSBORNE	T	12	170	OTHICK	W	8	253	OVEREND	A	14	240	OWEN	F	11	286
OSBORNE	TH	2	255	OTRIDGE	HJ	7	288	OVEREND	F	9	145	OWEN	F	11	286
OSBORNE	TH	5	257	OTRIDGE	HW	7	288	OVEREND	J	9	145	OWEN	F	13	325
OSBORNE	TJ	1	255	OTSON	AK	9	145	OVEREND	T	14	240	OWEN	G	2	255
OSBORNE	W	1	255	OTT	AE	13	324	OVERHEAD	HJ	3	154	OWEN	G	3	154
OSBORNE	W	1	255	OTT	BW	13	324	OVERHILL	AE	12	170	OWEN	G	7	289
OSBORNE	W	6	305	OTTARWAY	PJ	1	255	OVERHILL	GR	12	171	OWEN	G	14	240
OSBORNE	W	9	315	OTTAWAY	JC	13	325	OVERINGTON	R	13	325	OWEN	GE	11	286
OSBORNE	W	12	361	OTTEN	A	7	288	OVERKOTT	C	2	255	OWEN	GW	9	145
OSBORNE	W	13	324	OTTEN	A	7	288	OVERS	CR	6	305	OWEN	H	1	256
OSBORNE	WA	13	324	OTTEN	AE	13	325	OVERS	LA	6	305	OWEN	H	6	305
OSBORNE	WH	3	154	OTTERWELL	H	9	315	OVERTHROW	AE	5	258	OWEN	H	11	286
OSBORNE	WJ	10	170	OTTWAY	FW	13	325	OVERTHROW	B	6	305	OWEN	H	14	240

OWEN	H	14	240	OWENS	H	3	155	PACK	FH	4	285	PADDON	AE	4	285
OWEN	H	14	240	OWENS	J	2	256	PACK	FM	12	171	PADDON	F	7	290
OWEN	HA	6	305	OWENS	J	5	258	PACK	FR	12	171	PADDON	H	10	171
OWEN	HCAB	4	284	OWENS	J	11	287	PACK	J	4	285	PADDON	HC	2	256
OWEN	HH	14	240	OWENS	J	13	326	PACK	J	12	171	PADDON	JE	4	285
OWEN	HJ	6	305	OWENS	JW	14	241	PACK	JT	3	155	PADDON	T	7	290
OWEN	HL	4	284	OWENS	M	9	146	PACK	LA	4	285	PADDON	W	7	290
OWEN	HM	13	325	OWENS	P	9	315	PACK	W	3	155	PADDON	WG	7	290
OWEN	HS	6	305	OWENS	W	9	315	PACKARD	A	4	285	PADGETT	A	8	254
OWEN	HW	12	171	OWLES	W	13	326	PACKARD	G	8	254	PADGETT	A	9	315
OWEN	J	11	286	OWLES	W	13	326	PACKARD	GT	7	289	PADGETT	F	9	146
OWEN	J	11	286	OWRAM	H	8	253	PACKE	AE	12	362	PADGETT	GW	8	254
OWEN	J	12	171	OWRID	J	9	146	PACKE	SA	3	155	PADGETT	J	8	254
OWEN	J	14	240	OWSTON	CEG	3	155	PACKER	BB	1	256	PADGETT	J	9	146
OWEN	J	14	240	OXBERRY	L	8	253	PACKER	C	12	362	PADGETT	J	9	315
OWEN	JD	12	171	OXBERRY	M	8	253	PACKER	CH	1	256	PADGETT	JA	9	146
OWEN	JE	1	256	OXFORD	AE	13	326	PACKER	EJ	1	256	PADGETT	JW	8	254
OWEN	JE	3	154	OXFORD	EG	7	289	PACKER	G	3	155	PADGETT	JW	9	315
OWEN	JH	4	284	OXFORD	HJ	4	285	PACKER	H	12	362	PADGETT	P	8	254
OWEN	JJ	7	289	OXFORD	JW	13	326	PACKER	HA	13	326	PADGETT	T	9	315
OWEN	JJ	11	286	OXFORD	WC	10	170	PACKER	J	5	258	PADLEY	AG	1	256
OWEN	JJ	11	286	OXFORD	WE	6	306	PACKER	JW	13	326	PADLEY	G	9	316
OWEN	JS	7	289	OXFORD	WE	13	326	PACKER	PJ	2	256	PADLEY	GW	1	256
OWEN	JS	14	240	OXFORD	WL	4	285	PACKER	S	13	326	PADLEY	LH	1	256
OWEN	L	8	253	OXLADE	JS	1	256	PACKER	T	7	289	PADLEY	P	11	287
OWEN	L	9	145	OXLAND	JFA	4	285	PACKER	W	11	287	PADLEY	PJ	1	257
OWEN	LR	7	289	OXLEY	AE	14	241	PACKER	WC	13	326	PADLEY	RB	1	257
OWEN	P	13	325	OXLEY	B	3	155	PACKHAM	C	5	258	PADMORE	FR	13	326
OWEN	S	4	284	OXLEY	EEP	3	155	PACKHAM	EC	7	290	PADMORE	H	13	327
OWEN	S	5	258	OXLEY	FS	9	146	PACKHAM	GL	2	256	PADMORE	J	13	327
OWEN	S	7	289	OXLEY	J	8	253	PACKHAM	R	5	258	PADMORE	WA	13	327
OWEN	S	11	287	OXLEY	J	13	326	PACKHAM	R	11	287	PADWICK	AW	4	285
OWEN	SW	3	154	OXLEY	JW	9	146	PACKHAM	S	11	287	PADWICK	C	4	285
OWEN	T	4	284	OXLEY	N	8	253	PACKHAM	T	13	326	PADWICK	CH	4	285
OWEN	T	11	287	OXLEY	P	8	254	PACKMAN	F	3	155	PADWICK	F	7	290
OWEN	T	14	240	OXLEY	R	9	315	PACKMAN	GR	7	290	PADWICK	G	4	285
OWEN	TBF	14	240	OXLEY	TB	13	326	PACKMAN	J	13	326	PADWICK	V	4	286
OWEN	W	3	155	OXLEY	WE	8	254	PACKMAN	NV	13	326	PADWICK	W	1	257
OWEN	W	6	306	OXSPRING	EC	3	155	PACKWOOD	AWH	1	256	PADWICK	WC	4	286
OWEN	W	8	253	OXX	A	11	287	PACKWOOD	HL	1	256	PAERSCH	HA	11	287
OWEN	W	14	240	OYER	WT	10	170	PACKWOOD	I	10	171	PAERSCH	LF	11	287
OWEN	WA	12	361	OYSTON	C	8	254	PACKWOOD	LG	1	256	PAERSCH	O	11	287
OWEN	WE	13	325	OYSTON	J	9	146	PADBURY	EA	3	155	PAFFETT	AC	10	171
OWEN	WG	10	344	OZAREOFF	A	2	256	PADBURY	H	3	382	PAFFETT	AE	10	171
OWEN	WH	4	284					PADBURY	JH	6	306	PAFFETT	FJ	10	171
OWEN	WH	14	241					PADBURY	W	8	254	PAFFETT	H	13	327
OWEN	WJ	13	326		**P**			PADBURY	WH	3	155	PAFFETT	HJ	10	171
OWEN	WS	5	258					PADDEN	J	8	254	PAFFETT	W	10	171
OWENS	A	6	306	PACE	T	11	287	PADDEN	J	8	254	PAFFETT	WH	10	171
OWENS	A	8	253	PACEY	B	12	361	PADDINGTON	EG	4	285	PAFFORD	JH	10	171
OWENS	AE	13	326	PACEY	BL	12	361	PADDISON	C	8	254	PAGAN	J	6	306
OWENS	DP	11	286	PACEY	H	11	287	PADDOCK	AT	4	285	PAGAN	T	6	306
OWENS	E	9	146	PACEY	W	12	362	PADDOCK	GH	7	290	PAGAN	W	6	306
OWENS	G	14	241	PACK	AC	4	285	PADDOCK	RE	4	285	PAGDIN	E	10	171
OWENS	GW	4	284	PACK	ECV	4	285	PADDOCK	T	7	290	PAGE	A	1	257
				PACK	F	7	289								

Surname	Init	No	Pg	Surname	Init	No	Pg	Surname	Init	No	Pg	Surname	Init	No	Pg
PAINTIN	A	12	172	PALLISER	JA	9	146	PALMER	ED	8	255	PALMER	J	1	258
PAINTIN	WE	2	257	PALLISER	JW	9	146	PALMER	EG	2	257	PALMER	J	1	258
PAINTON	A	5	259	PALLISER	R	9	316	PALMER	EG	10	171	PALMER	J	2	257
PAINTON	W	4	287	PALLISER	W	9	316	PALMER	EJ	3	158	PALMER	J	3	158
PAISLEY	W	4	287	PALLISTER	FW	8	255	PALMER	ER	5	259	PALMER	J	4	288
PAISLEY	WC	4	287	PALLISTER	G	8	255	PALMER	EW	7	292	PALMER	J	6	307
PAKES	AF	5	259	PALLITT	AJ	1	258	PALMER	F	5	260	PALMER	J	6	307
PAKES	CG	5	259	PALLITT	CV	12	172	PALMER	F	6	307	PALMER	J	6	307
PAKES	E	5	259	PALLITT	FG	12	172	PALMER	F	7	292	PALMER	J	7	292
PALER	WCL	4	287	PALLOT	JE	4	287	PALMER	F	7	292	PALMER	J	8	256
PALES	AWG	12	172	PALLOT	JG	4	287	PALMER	F	8	255	PALMER	J	8	256
PALES	FC	12	172	PALMER	A	2	257	PALMER	F	14	242	PALMER	J	9	146
PALETHORPE	GF	14	241	PALMER	A	7	291	PALMER	FC	3	158	PALMER	J	10	172
PALETHORPE	TH	14	241	PALMER	A	9	316	PALMER	FC	3	158	PALMER	J	11	288
PALETHORPE	W	11	287	PALMER	A	13	328	PALMER	FE	6	307	PALMER	J	13	328
PALEY	F	8	255	PALMER	A	13	328	PALMER	FG	3	158	PALMER	JA	5	260
PALEY	H	8	255	PALMER	A	14	241	PALMER	FG	4	287	PALMER	JA	12	362
PALEY	H	8	255	PALMER	ACH	5	259	PALMER	FG	4	287	PALMER	JC	3	158
PALEY	J	8	255	PALMER	AE	6	306	PALMER	FG	13	328	PALMER	JC	5	260
PALEY	J	8	255	PALMER	AE	7	291	PALMER	FH	3	158	PALMER	JH	8	256
PALEY	JW	8	255	PALMER	AE	7	292	PALMER	FTJ	4	287	PALMER	JH	8	256
PALEY	R	8	255	PALMER	AE	10	345	PALMER	FW	2	257	PALMER	JH	13	328
PALEY	W	8	255	PALMER	AG	14	241	PALMER	FW	5	260	PALMER	JH	13	328
PALEY	W	8	255	PALMER	AJ	1	258	PALMER	G	3	158	PALMER	L	1	258
PALFRAMAN	G	9	146	PALMER	AJ	3	382	PALMER	G	3	158	PALMER	L	2	257
PALFRAMAN	W	9	146	PALMER	AJ	5	260	PALMER	G	4	287	PALMER	L	3	158
PALFREEMAN	CB	8	255	PALMER	AJG	5	259	PALMER	G	5	260	PALMER	L	5	260
PALFREY	A	5	259	PALMER	AV	3	157	PALMER	G	7	292	PALMER	N	10	345
PALFREY	B	1	258	PALMER	AW	2	257	PALMER	G	7	292	PALMER	PC	3	158
PALFREY	DD	5	259	PALMER	AW	12	172	PALMER	G	8	256	PALMER	R	2	258
PALFREY	HJ	2	257	PALMER	B	6	306	PALMER	G	9	316	PALMER	R	3	158
PALFREY	RE	5	259	PALMER	BEM	3	157	PALMER	GA	6	307	PALMER	R	4	288
PALFREYMAN	B	11	287	PALMER	BH	7	292	PALMER	GA	13	328	PALMER	R	6	307
PALFREYMAN	B	11	287	PALMER	C	1	258	PALMER	GF	12	172	PALMER	R	6	307
PALGRAVE	L	7	291	PALMER	C	1	258	PALMER	GH	2	257	PALMER	R	14	242
PALIN	A	3	157	PALMER	C	2	257	PALMER	GH	14	242	PALMER	RE	1	258
PALIN	F	9	316	PALMER	C	3	157	PALMER	GW	10	172	PALMER	RF	3	158
PALIN	G	11	288	PALMER	C	11	288	PALMER	GW	10	345	PALMER	RG	10	172
PALIN	R	3	157	PALMER	C	11	288	PALMER	H	1	258	PALMER	RW	12	172
PALING	FW	7	291	PALMER	C	14	242	PALMER	H	3	158	PALMER	S	4	288
PALLAGRASS	F	8	255	PALMER	CE	13	328	PALMER	H	4	287	PALMER	S	5	260
PALLANT	AH	3	157	PALMER	CF	3	157	PALMER	H	7	292	PALMER	S	5	260
PALLANT	CE	7	291	PALMER	CF	12	172	PALMER	H	10	345	PALMER	S	7	292
PALLANT	HE	3	157	PALMER	CW	13	328	PALMER	H	12	362	PALMER	T	7	292
PALLENT	FR	13	328	PALMER	CW	13	328	PALMER	H	14	242	PALMER	T	11	288
PALLETT	A	6	306	PALMER	D	3	158	PALMER	HAW	3	158	PALMER	TE	10	345
PALLETT	AI	12	362	PALMER	D	3	158	PALMER	HE	3	158	PALMER	TH	3	158
PALLETT	AS	6	306	PALMER	D	6	306	PALMER	HE	6	307	PALMER	TJ	13	328
PALLETT	C	6	306	PALMER	E	4	287	PALMER	HF	10	172	PALMER	TW	2	258
PALLETT	EW	5	259	PALMER	E	4	287	PALMER	HG	4	288	PALMER	TW	6	307
PALLETT	G	3	157	PALMER	E	6	306	PALMER	HG	13	328	PALMER	TW	12	172
PALLETT	HC	5	259	PALMER	E	6	306	PALMER	HJ	6	307	PALMER	V	3	158
PALLETT	JC	6	306	PALMER	E	6	307	PALMER	HJ	13	328	PALMER	W	3	158
PALLETT	WC	12	362	PALMER	E	8	255	PALMER	HS	13	328	PALMER	W	3	159
PALLISER	E	9	146	PALMER	E	13	328	PALMER	HV	2	257	PALMER	W	6	307

PALMER	W	6	307	PANTER	AE	12	172	PARFITT	AE	2	258	PARK	WH	11	288
PALMER	W	8	256	PANTER	AR	12	172	PARFITT	E	2	258	PARKER	A	2	259
PALMER	W	9	316	PANTER	C	12	172	PARFITT	F	1	259	PARKER	A	2	259
PALMER	W	13	328	PANTER	E	11	288	PARFITT	GR	10	345	PARKER	A	4	288
PALMER	WA	13	329	PANTER	F	12	172	PARFITT	GS	7	293	PARKER	A	5	261
PALMER	WAM	13	328	PANTER	GE	12	172	PARFITT	H	10	345	PARKER	A	5	261
PALMER	WC	4	288	PANTER	J	12	173	PARFITT	T	3	159	PARKER	A	6	308
PALMER	WC	13	329	PANTER	OJ	2	258	PARFITT	TA	13	329	PARKER	A	7	293
PALMER	WFG	4	288	PANTER	S	11	288	PARFITT	W	7	292	PARKER	A	8	256
PALMER	WG	7	292	PANTER	WJ	12	362	PARFITT	WG	7	293	PARKER	A	8	256
PALMER	WH	10	345	PANTING	T	3	159	PARFOOT	A	10	172	PARKER	A	8	256
PALMER	WJ	7	292	PANTLING	A	5	260	PARFOOT	G	4	288	PARKER	A	8	256
PALMER	WJ	10	345	PANTLING	AC	5	260	PARFREY	EH	13	329	PARKER	A	9	147
PALMER	WL	13	329	PANTLING	AP	5	260	PARFREY	GH	13	329	PARKER	A	10	172
PALMER	WM	7	292	PANTLING	B	5	260	PARGETER	FE	12	173	PARKER	A	11	288
PALMER	WR	12	172	PANTLING	F	5	260	PARGETER	GE	12	173	PARKER	A	11	288
PALOMBO	J	2	258	PANTLING	G	2	258	PARGETTER	H	6	308	PARKER	A	13	329
PALPHREYMAN	AB	1	258	PANTLING	H	5	260	PARHAM	A	10	172	PARKER	A	14	242
PALPHREYMAN	GW	1	258	PANTLING	HJ	5	261	PARHAM	TW	10	172	PARKER	AC	13	329
PALTRIDGE	AJ	6	307	PANTLING	J	12	363	PARIS	AE	10	172	PARKER	AE	1	259
PALTRIDGE	AS	4	288	PANTLING	JS	12	363	PARIS	JWS	1	259	PARKER	AE	6	308
PAMMANT	AJ	2	258	PANTLING	L	1	259	PARIS	SF	5	261	PARKER	AE	7	293
PAMMENT	AE	1	258	PANTLING	WC	5	261	PARIS	WJ	2	258	PARKER	AE	13	329
PAMMENT	AE	2	258	PANTON	AC	6	307	PARISH	AJ	12	363	PARKER	AG	7	293
PAMMENT	C	5	260	PANTON	HG	2	258	PARISH	C	8	256	PARKER	AG	8	256
PAMMENT	E	1	258	PANTON	HJ	4	288	PARISH	CA	13	329	PARKER	AJ	7	293
PAMMENT	HC	1	258	PANTON	J	8	256	PARISH	CE	7	294	PARKER	AW	1	259
PAMMENT	WO	7	292	PAOLUCCI	G	9	147	PARISH	E	7	293	PARKER	AW	1	259
PAMPALONI	WR	5	260	PAPE	A	8	256	PARISH	EG	12	363	PARKER	AW	10	172
PAMPHILET	WT	7	292	PAPE	I	13	329	PARISH	F	12	363	PARKER	B	8	256
PAMPLIN	FA	13	329	PAPE	JW	9	147	PARISH	FE	2	258	PARKER	B	9	316
PAMPLIN	RHN	4	288	PAPLES	WH	10	345	PARISH	FJ	10	345	PARKER	B	9	316
PANCOUST	A	12	362	PAPWORTH	C	9	147	PARISH	FR	2	258	PARKER	C	6	308
PANCOUST	E	12	362	PAPWORTH	JW	9	316	PARISH	FW	12	363	PARKER	C	8	256
PANCOUST	HS	12	362	PAPWORTH	RG	1	259	PARISH	G	6	308	PARKER	C	8	256
PANCOUST	J	12	362	PAPWORTH	RS	1	259	PARISH	H	2	258	PARKER	C	9	316
PANE	CH	6	307	PAPWORTH	T	1	259	PARISH	H	13	329	PARKER	C	12	173
PANE	EN	9	147	PAPWORTH	TW	1	259	PARISH	H	13	329	PARKER	C	14	242
PANGBOURNE	P	5	260	PAPWORTH	W	2	258	PARISH	JA	2	258	PARKER	CA	4	288
PANKHURST	E	13	329	PAPWORTH	WC	5	261	PARISH	JC	11	288	PARKER	CE	1	259
PANKHURST	G	13	329	PARADINE	A	1	259	PARISH	JC	14	242	PARKER	CH	5	261
PANKHURST	J	6	307	PARBERY	D	12	363	PARISH	T	10	172	PARKER	CL	2	259
PANKHURST	WW	12	362	PARBERY	E	12	363	PARISH	TW	7	293	PARKER	CR	1	259
PANKOP	W	2	258	PARBERY	HFC	2	258	PARISH	W	6	308	PARKER	D	1	259
PANNALL	C	1	258	PARBERY	J	12	363	PARISH	W	7	293	PARKER	DJ	2	259
PANNEL	WJ	1	258	PARCHARDE	JE	3	167	PARISH	WA	11	288	PARKER	E	6	308
PANNELL	GF	10	172	PARCHMENT	GW	13	329	PARISH	WR	13	329	PARKER	E	8	256
PANNELL	H	1	258	PARDEY	EJ	2	258	PARK	A	8	256	PARKER	E	9	147
PANNELL	HW	10	172	PARDINGTON	PM	1	259	PARK	A	8	256	PARKER	E	9	316
PANNELL	JER	1	259	PARDOE	G	3	159	PARK	A	11	288	PARKER	E	12	173
PANNELL	P	4	288	PARDOE	GM	6	308	PARK	J	7	293	PARKER	E	13	329
PANNETT	G	13	329	PARDOE	JT	6	308	PARK	JHH	11	288	PARKER	E	14	242
PANNETT	R	8	256	PARDY	CJ	10	172	PARK	MH	10	172	PARKER	EC	4	288
PANTER	A	12	362	PARDY	E	10	345	PARK	NJ	7	293	PARKER	EC	12	173
PANTER	A	12	424	PARFITT	A	3	159	PARK	WA	3	159	PARKER	EC	12	363

PARKER	EE	12	173
PARKER	EE	14	242
PARKER	EF	6	308
PARKER	EJ	1	259
PARKER	EJ	4	288
PARKER	ET	12	363
PARKER	F	1	259
PARKER	F	3	159
PARKER	F	4	288
PARKER	F	4	288
PARKER	F	4	288
PARKER	F	6	308
PARKER	F	10	345
PARKER	F	12	173
PARKER	F	13	330
PARKER	F	13	330
PARKER	FA	1	259
PARKER	FC	4	288
PARKER	FC	4	289
PARKER	FC	12	173
PARKER	FE	4	289
PARKER	FE	12	363
PARKER	FH	2	259
PARKER	FH	13	330
PARKER	FL	7	293
PARKER	FL	12	173
PARKER	FT	3	159
PARKER	FW	2	259
PARKER	FW	10	172
PARKER	FWH	4	289
PARKER	G	1	259
PARKER	G	4	289
PARKER	G	7	293
PARKER	G	8	257
PARKER	G	8	257
PARKER	G	8	257
PARKER	G	9	316
PARKER	G	10	345
PARKER	GA	3	159
PARKER	GD	9	316
PARKER	GE	13	330
PARKER	GH	4	289
PARKER	GH	4	289
PARKER	GJ	3	159
PARKER	GJ	13	330
PARKER	GT	11	288
PARKER	GW	8	257
PARKER	GW	9	316
PARKER	H	1	259
PARKER	H	4	289
PARKER	H	6	308
PARKER	H	6	308
PARKER	H	7	293
PARKER	H	7	293
PARKER	H	7	293
PARKER	H	8	257
PARKER	H	9	147
PARKER	H	9	147
PARKER	H	9	147
PARKER	H	9	147
PARKER	H	9	147
PARKER	H	9	147
PARKER	H	9	316
PARKER	H	9	316
PARKER	H	10	172
PARKER	H	11	288
PARKER	H	11	288
PARKER	H	12	173
PARKER	H	12	173
PARKER	H	14	242
PARKER	HB	10	172
PARKER	HC	2	259
PARKER	HC	12	363
PARKER	HE	7	293
PARKER	HG	7	293
PARKER	HJ	6	308
PARKER	HM	6	308
PARKER	HT	13	330
PARKER	HW	5	261
PARKER	J	1	259
PARKER	J	4	289
PARKER	J	4	289
PARKER	J	4	289
PARKER	J	5	261
PARKER	J	6	308
PARKER	J	7	293
PARKER	J	8	257
PARKER	J	8	257
PARKER	J	8	257
PARKER	J	8	257
PARKER	J	8	257
PARKER	J	8	257
PARKER	J	8	257
PARKER	J	10	345
PARKER	J	10	345
PARKER	J	11	288
PARKER	J	11	289
PARKER	J	14	242
PARKER	JA	5	261
PARKER	JA	8	257
PARKER	JA	9	316
PARKER	JB	1	260
PARKER	JB	9	317
PARKER	JE	1	260
PARKER	JE	4	289
PARKER	JE	6	308
PARKER	JF	4	289
PARKER	JFC	10	346
PARKER	JG	6	308
PARKER	JGH	6	309
PARKER	JH	4	289
PARKER	JH	13	330
PARKER	JH	13	330
PARKER	JHH	14	242
PARKER	JP	1	260
PARKER	JW	7	294
PARKER	JW	12	363
PARKER	L	9	147
PARKER	L	11	289
PARKER	LJ	5	261
PARKER	M	4	289
PARKER	M	9	147
PARKER	NN	1	260
PARKER	OJ	1	260
PARKER	P	1	260
PARKER	PE	2	259
PARKER	PJ	7	294
PARKER	PJ	12	173
PARKER	R	3	159
PARKER	R	7	294
PARKER	R	7	294
PARKER	R	8	257
PARKER	R	8	257
PARKER	R	9	147
PARKER	R	9	317
PARKER	R	10	346
PARKER	R	11	289
PARKER	R	13	330
PARKER	R	13	330
PARKER	R	14	242
PARKER	RB	8	257
PARKER	RG	3	159
PARKER	S	5	261
PARKER	S	11	289
PARKER	S	13	330
PARKER	SC	10	346
PARKER	SC	12	173
PARKER	SCS	4	289
PARKER	SG	7	294
PARKER	SJS	1	260
PARKER	SP	4	289
PARKER	SR	5	261
PARKER	SR	6	309
PARKER	T	3	159
PARKER	T	5	261
PARKER	T	5	261
PARKER	T	9	317
PARKER	T	11	289
PARKER	T	11	289
PARKER	T	14	242
PARKER	TA	1	260
PARKER	TA	5	261
PARKER	TA	14	242
PARKER	TC	4	289
PARKER	TE	13	330
PARKER	TH	13	330
PARKER	TJ	10	173
PARKER	TW	12	173
PARKER	W	1	260
PARKER	W	2	259
PARKER	W	3	159
PARKER	W	4	289
PARKER	W	4	289
PARKER	W	7	294
PARKER	W	8	257
PARKER	W	8	257
PARKER	W	8	257
PARKER	W	8	257
PARKER	W	11	289
PARKER	W	13	330
PARKER	W	14	242
PARKER	W	14	242
PARKER	WA	11	289
PARKER	WB	9	147
PARKER	WC	5	261
PARKER	WC	13	330
PARKER	WE	6	309
PARKER	WE	6	309
PARKER	WF	1	260
PARKER	WG	4	289
PARKER	WG	10	346
PARKER	WGM	7	294
PARKER	WH	1	260
PARKER	WH	1	260
PARKER	WH	5	261
PARKER	WH	11	289
PARKER	WH	12	173
PARKER	WJ	3	159
PARKER	WJ	4	290
PARKER	WJ	5	262
PARKER	WN	14	242
PARKES	A	6	309
PARKES	AE	6	309
PARKES	AV	6	309
PARKES	B	6	309
PARKES	E	6	309
PARKES	E	6	309
PARKES	EJ	13	330
PARKES	F	6	309
PARKES	FH	4	290
PARKES	G	14	243
PARKES	GW	4	290
PARKES	GW	6	309
PARKES	H	13	330
PARKES	HM	6	309
PARKES	J	6	309
PARKES	J	6	309
PARKES	J	6	309
PARKES	J	6	309

PARKES	J	11	289	PARKINS	J	5	262	PARKINSON	W	11	290	PARRACK	HI	10	173
PARKES	OL	1	260	PARKINS	LC	5	262	PARKINSON	W	14	244	PARRATT	A	11	291
PARKES	P	6	309	PARKINS	LG	5	262	PARKINSON	WB	9	148	PARRATT	R	9	317
PARKES	P	13	330	PARKINS	PW	5	262	PARKINSON	WH	11	290	PARRATT	T	8	258
PARKES	T	6	310	PARKINS	SG	5	262	PARKINSON	WJF	3	159	PARRETT	WH	7	294
PARKES	T	14	243	PARKINS	WG	5	262	PARKINSON	WT	14	244	PARRINGTON	JR	9	148
PARKES	W	11	289	PARKINSON	A	8	258	PARKISON	H	9	317	PARRINGTON	W	9	148
PARKES	WC	11	289	PARKINSON	A	14	243	PARKMAN	RG	7	294	PARRIS	AH	10	346
PARKES	WR	6	310	PARKINSON	C	11	290	PARKS	FJ	3	159	PARRIS	AJ	13	331
PARKIN	A	6	310	PARKINSON	C	14	243	PARKS	FJ	5	262	PARRIS	W	5	263
PARKIN	A	13	330	PARKINSON	CF	3	159	PARKS	J	1	260	PARRISH	HJ	12	363
PARKIN	AE	11	289	PARKINSON	E	3	159	PARKS	WH	9	317	PARRISH	J	6	310
PARKIN	C	5	262	PARKINSON	E	6	310	PARKYN	G	10	173	PARRISH	JW	6	310
PARKIN	C	13	330	PARKINSON	E	9	148	PARKYN	RT	13	331	PARRISH	T	13	331
PARKIN	CF	11	289	PARKINSON	E	9	317	PARLE	EW	7	294	PARRISH	W	8	258
PARKIN	E	9	147	PARKINSON	E	14	243	PARLE	LL	3	159	PARRISH	WE	7	294
PARKIN	E	11	289	PARKINSON	EF	11	290	PARLE	T	7	294	PARRISS	C	12	173
PARKIN	E	11	289	PARKINSON	F	8	258	PARLES	B	5	262	PARRITT	AA	1	260
PARKIN	EK	8	258	PARKINSON	F	14	243	PARLES	GH	5	262	PARROT	A	9	317
PARKIN	EP	1	260	PARKINSON	FG	9	317	PARMAN	E	6	310	PARROT	GH	4	290
PARKIN	G	8	258	PARKINSON	G	5	262	PARMAN	T	2	259	PARROT	S	9	317
PARKIN	GH	14	243	PARKINSON	GE	13	331	PARMENTER	A	7	294	PARROTT	A	5	263
PARKIN	H	9	147	PARKINSON	GH	11	290	PARMENTER	AJ	7	294	PARROTT	A	12	174
PARKIN	H	9	147	PARKINSON	H	2	259	PARMENTER	EA	7	294	PARROTT	CD	1	260
PARKIN	J	1	260	PARKINSON	H	9	148	PARNELL	AR	11	290	PARROTT	CE	5	263
PARKIN	J	1	260	PARKINSON	H	12	363	PARNELL	CJ	10	173	PARROTT	E	13	331
PARKIN	J	8	258	PARKINSON	H	14	243	PARNELL	EH	11	290	PARROTT	EJW	12	174
PARKIN	J	9	317	PARKINSON	J	9	148	PARNELL	H	3	159	PARROTT	F	5	263
PARKIN	JH	1	260	PARKINSON	J	11	290	PARNELL	H	5	263	PARROTT	F	12	174
PARKIN	JH	11	289	PARKINSON	J	11	290	PARNELL	J	5	263	PARROTT	GC	1	260
PARKIN	JS	11	290	PARKINSON	J	13	331	PARNELL	JP	10	173	PARROTT	GH	5	263
PARKIN	JW	9	147	PARKINSON	J	14	243	PARNELL	L	3	160	PARROTT	J	11	291
PARKIN	P	8	258	PARKINSON	JH	9	148	PARNELL	WE	7	294	PARROTT	J	11	291
PARKIN	S	14	243	PARKINSON	JH	14	243	PAROISSIEN	AFE	13	331	PARROTT	J	14	244
PARKIN	T	11	290	PARKINSON	JH	14	243	PAROISSIEN	FE	13	331	PARROTT	JA	11	291
PARKIN	W	9	148	PARKINSON	JW	9	148	PARR	CH	6	310	PARROTT	JAC	5	263
PARKIN	W	9	148	PARKINSON	JW	14	243	PARR	ET	2	259	PARROTT	JW	5	263
PARKIN	W	9	317	PARKINSON	L	8	258	PARR	G	8	258	PARROTT	RF	11	291
PARKIN	W	11	290	PARKINSON	LJ	9	317	PARR	GA	10	173	PARROTT	W	3	160
PARKIN	W	11	290	PARKINSON	M	8	258	PARR	GG	10	173	PARROTT	WJ	5	263
PARKIN	W	14	243	PARKINSON	M	14	243	PARR	GW	11	290	PARRY	A	1	261
PARKIN	W	14	243	PARKINSON	N	9	148	PARR	H	13	331	PARRY	A	6	310
PARKIN	WB	9	148	PARKINSON	R	11	290	PARR	HJ	10	173	PARRY	AE	6	310
PARKINS	AC	4	290	PARKINSON	R	11	290	PARR	J	10	173	PARRY	AH	6	310
PARKINS	AJ	5	262	PARKINSON	R	14	243	PARR	J	11	291	PARRY	AH	7	294
PARKINS	BW	5	262	PARKINSON	RE	8	258	PARR	JH	11	291	PARRY	AH	14	244
PARKINS	CF	5	262	PARKINSON	RIP	9	317	PARR	JH	13	331	PARRY	AT	4	291
PARKINS	DC	12	173	PARKINSON	SB	9	148	PARR	JH	14	244	PARRY	CJ	11	291
PARKINS	EW	5	262	PARKINSON	SP	9	317	PARR	T	6	310	PARRY	CJ	11	291
PARKINS	FG	5	262	PARKINSON	T	11	290	PARR	T	11	291	PARRY	CJT	13	331
PARKINS	FJ	5	262	PARKINSON	T	11	290	PARR	T	14	244	PARRY	E	11	291
PARKINS	FW	5	262	PARKINSON	T	12	363	PARR	WA	13	331	PARRY	ET	3	160
PARKINS	H	12	173	PARKINSON	T	14	243	PARR	WE	14	244	PARRY	F	9	317
PARKINS	HC	4	290	PARKINSON	T	14	244	PARR	WG	2	259	PARRY	F	13	331
PARKINS	J	4	290	PARKINSON	W	8	258	PARR	WW	10	173	PARRY	FH	6	310

Name	Initials	No.	Page	Name	Initials	No.	Page	Name	Initials	No.	Page	Name	Initials	No.	Page
PARRY	G	11	291	PARSONS	C	13	331	PARSONS	JT	6	311	PARTLETON	B	7	295
PARRY	H	2	259	PARSONS	C	13	331	PARSONS	JW	1	261	PARTLETON	WC	7	295
PARRY	H	3	160	PARSONS	C	13	331	PARSONS	JW	7	295	PARTON	ED	3	160
PARRY	H	13	331	PARSONS	CH	1	261	PARSONS	JW	8	258	PARTRIDGE	A	2	260
PARRY	J	1	261	PARSONS	CH	7	295	PARSONS	L	1	261	PARTRIDGE	A	8	258
PARRY	J	6	310	PARSONS	CHF	4	290	PARSONS	LV	10	173	PARTRIDGE	BC	12	363
PARRY	J	9	317	PARSONS	CJ	11	292	PARSONS	M	8	258	PARTRIDGE	BE	6	311
PARRY	J	11	291	PARSONS	E	4	290	PARSONS	NA	5	264	PARTRIDGE	CH	12	174
PARRY	JA	6	310	PARSONS	E	4	290	PARSONS	P	13	332	PARTRIDGE	D	3	160
PARRY	JF	11	291	PARSONS	EJ	7	295	PARSONS	R	2	259	PARTRIDGE	E	6	311
PARRY	JH	1	261	PARSONS	ES	1	261	PARSONS	R	7	295	PARTRIDGE	E	12	174
PARRY	JW	11	291	PARSONS	F	1	261	PARSONS	R	8	258	PARTRIDGE	EJ	12	174
PARRY	JW	13	331	PARSONS	F	1	261	PARSONS	SCP	5	264	PARTRIDGE	F	6	311
PARRY	O	6	310	PARSONS	F	5	263	PARSONS	SR	2	259	PARTRIDGE	FW	12	174
PARRY	P	1	261	PARSONS	F	5	263	PARSONS	T	7	295	PARTRIDGE	FW	12	174
PARRY	RA	3	160	PARSONS	F	12	174	PARSONS	TC	4	290	PARTRIDGE	G	6	311
PARRY	RT	6	310	PARSONS	F	13	331	PARSONS	W	1	261	PARTRIDGE	G	9	148
PARRY	S	12	363	PARSONS	FA	12	174	PARSONS	W	3	160	PARTRIDGE	G	11	292
PARRY	T	7	295	PARSONS	FF	4	290	PARSONS	W	3	382	PARTRIDGE	G	12	174
PARRY	T	14	244	PARSONS	FG	5	263	PARSONS	W	4	291	PARTRIDGE	GH	6	311
PARRY	T	14	244	PARSONS	FH	5	263	PARSONS	W	4	291	PARTRIDGE	GM	7	296
PARRY	TFE	14	244	PARSONS	FH	5	263	PARSONS	W	5	264	PARTRIDGE	H	2	260
PARRY	TM	3	160	PARSONS	FW	7	295	PARSONS	W	6	311	PARTRIDGE	H	12	364
PARRY	W	6	310	PARSONS	G	5	264	PARSONS	W	6	311	PARTRIDGE	HR	6	311
PARRY	W	14	244	PARSONS	G	7	295	PARSONS	W	6	311	PARTRIDGE	HW	1	261
PARRY	WC	3	160	PARSONS	G	10	346	PARSONS	W	7	295	PARTRIDGE	J	6	311
PARRY	WC	7	295	PARSONS	G	13	332	PARSONS	W	7	295	PARTRIDGE	J	9	148
PARRY	WF	11	291	PARSONS	GF	7	295	PARSONS	W	10	346	PARTRIDGE	JC	12	174
PARRY	WH	6	310	PARSONS	GJ	10	173	PARSONS	W	13	332	PARTRIDGE	JR	11	292
PARSELLE	DCJ	1	261	PARSONS	GR	10	346	PARSONS	WE	3	160	PARTRIDGE	T	10	173
PARSELLE	MT	1	261	PARSONS	H	1	261	PARSONS	WF	1	261	PARTRIDGE	W	6	311
PARSLOW	A	1	261	PARSONS	H	3	382	PARSONS	WG	12	174	PARTRIDGE	W	9	317
PARSLOW	A	2	259	PARSONS	H	5	263	PARSONS	WH	5	264	PARTRIDGE	W	12	174
PARSON	GD	4	290	PARSONS	H	5	264	PARSONS	WH	5	264	PARTRIDGE	W	12	364
PARSON	W	11	291	PARSONS	H	6	311	PARSONS	WJ	1	261	PARTRIDGE	WJ	12	174
PARSONAGE	E	11	291	PARSONS	H	8	258	PARSONS	WJ	4	291	PARTRIDGE	WJ	12	364
PARSONAGE	GW	6	311	PARSONS	H	13	332	PARSONS	WJ	4	291	PARTRIGE	HF	13	332
PARSONAGE	TA	6	311	PARSONS	HT	1	261	PARSONS	WJ	14	244	PARTT	A	1	262
PARSONS	A	1	261	PARSONS	HT	3	160	PARSONS	WJA	4	291	PARVIN	RD	10	346
PARSONS	A	2	259	PARSONS	HT	5	264	PARSONS	WJA	6	311	PARVIN	S	10	173
PARSONS	A	4	290	PARSONS	J	4	290	PARSONS	WT	13	332	PARVIN	SF	10	174
PARSONS	A	4	290	PARSONS	J	4	290	PARSONSON	EA	2	259	PARZET	RG	10	174
PARSONS	A	4	290	PARSONS	J	4	290	PARTINGTON	C	14	244	PASBY	A	7	296
PARSONS	A	6	311	PARSONS	J	5	264	PARTINGTON	CA	14	244	PASCALL	E	11	292
PARSONS	A	6	311	PARSONS	J	6	311	PARTINGTON	D	11	292	PASCO	W	14	244
PARSONS	A	12	174	PARSONS	J	7	295	PARTINGTON	E	11	292	PASCOE	C	4	291
PARSONS	AC	7	295	PARSONS	J	8	258	PARTINGTON	GA	14	244	PASCOE	C	4	291
PARSONS	AEW	5	263	PARSONS	J	10	173	PARTINGTON	J	11	292	PASCOE	EJ	12	364
PARSONS	AH	8	258	PARSONS	J	10	173	PARTINGTON	JE	11	292	PASCOE	FC	1	262
PARSONS	AJ	5	263	PARSONS	J	10	346	PARTINGTON	JWG	3	160	PASCOE	HE	4	291
PARSONS	AR	10	173	PARSONS	J	12	174	PARTINGTON	P	14	244	PASCOE	WH	4	291
PARSONS	C	3	160	PARSONS	J	13	332	PARTINGTON	S	11	292	PASH	R	3	160
PARSONS	C	10	173	PARSONS	J	14	244	PARTINGTON	TN	11	292	PASHLEY	F	9	317
PARSONS	C	12	174	PARSONS	JH	7	295	PARTLAN	R	11	292	PASHLEY	H	9	318
PARSONS	C	12	363	PARSONS	JL	10	173	PARTLAND	W	11	292	PASHLEY	J	9	318

PASHLEY	W	9	318	PATCHETT	W	9	149	PATON	J	10	174	PATTERSON	W	4	292
PASK	CA	2	260	PATCHETT	W	11	292	PATON	L	10	174	PATTERSON	W	11	293
PASK	WE	9	148	PATCHETT	WH	9	318	PATON	W	14	245	PATTERSON	W	11	293
PASKELL	AW	7	296	PATCHETT	WH	9	318	PATRICK	A	10	174	PATTERSON	WG	3	161
PASKELL	PW	12	174	PATCHING	AA	7	296	PATRICK	AA	4	292	PATTERSON	WH	1	262
PASLEY	G	1	262	PATCHING	BJ	7	296	PATRICK	B	14	245	PATTERSON	WHJ	7	297
PASLEY	GS	4	291	PATCHING	CE	12	175	PATRICK	E	10	174	PATTERSON	WW	3	161
PASMORE	AJ	5	264	PATCHING	F	12	364	PATRICK	FW	12	364	PATTINSON	G	8	259
PASMORE	FE	3	160	PATCHING	WE	12	175	PATRICK	GA	6	312	PATTINSON	J	6	312
PASS	H	9	318	PATCHING	WJ	7	296	PATRICK	H	9	318	PATTINSON	R	14	245
PASS	SW	9	318	PATEFIELD	F	9	149	PATRICK	J	11	292	PATTINSON	TA	6	312
PASS	WFC	3	160	PATEMAN	A	3	160	PATRICK	JA	3	161	PATTISON	DJ	2	260
PASSANT	WG	4	291	PATEMAN	AH	1	262	PATRICK	N	6	312	PATTISON	F	12	364
PASSELL	A	10	174	PATEMAN	AH	12	175	PATRICK	R	2	260	PATTISON	GIB	12	364
PASSELL	AM	4	291	PATEMAN	BI	12	364	PATRICK	RAJ	10	174	PATTISON	J	8	259
PASSELL	CEG	4	291	PATEMAN	BW	12	175	PATRICK	W	14	245	PATTISON	J	9	149
PASSELL	CHC	4	291	PATEMAN	C	5	264	PATRICK	WW	3	161	PATTISON	JW	9	149
PASSELL	EH	10	174	PATEMAN	EA	12	364	PATRICKSON	H	1	262	PATTISON	WH	8	259
PASSELL	W	4	291	PATEMAN	GS	1	262	PATTEN	C	1	262	PATTISON	WH	8	259
PASSELLS	AC	4	291	PATEMAN	LM	5	264	PATTEN	C	11	292	PATTLE	GE	2	260
PASSELLS	JL	4	291	PATEMAN	M	5	264	PATTEN	EA	7	296	PATTON	A	8	259
PASSELLS	SV	4	291	PATEMAN	RG	12	175	PATTEN	FS	7	297	PATTON	RE	8	259
PASSELOW	C	8	258	PATEMAN	T	12	175	PATTEN	H	10	346	PATTRICK	GW	10	174
PASSEY	E	9	148	PATEMAN	W	4	292	PATTEN	J	10	346	PAUL	A	7	297
PASSFIELD	GS	2	260	PATEMAN	W	5	264	PATTEN	JS	4	292	PAUL	A	14	245
PASSFIELD	JH	3	160	PATEMAN	W	5	264	PATTEN	WC	3	382	PAUL	AG	2	260
PASSFIELD	KH	3	160	PATEMAN	WS	5	264	PATTEN	WF	7	296	PAUL	AJ	7	297
PASSINGHAM	AE	4	292	PATERSON	AJ	2	260	PATTENDEN	PNF	10	346	PAUL	AW	10	346
PASSINGHAM	AES	4	292	PATERSON	D	6	312	PATTENDEN	RD	7	297	PAUL	C	4	292
PASSINGHAM	JA	10	174	PATERSON	DL	3	161	PATTENDEN	RW	13	332	PAUL	C	14	245
PASSMAN	R	11	292	PATERSON	HF	3	161	PATTENDEN	WTH	1	262	PAUL	CB	8	259
PASSMORE	CP	12	364	PATERSON	J	10	174	PATTERSON	A	4	292	PAUL	E	2	260
PASSMORE	HJ	10	174	PATERSON	JN	7	296	PATTERSON	A	4	292	PAUL	EJ	13	332
PASSMORE	J	8	259	PATERSON	R	12	175	PATTERSON	A	9	149	PAUL	EM	3	161
PASTE	WC	6	312	PATES	HC	5	264	PATTERSON	AE	4	292	PAUL	ES	4	292
PATCH	JJ	1	262	PATES	SA	5	264	PATTERSON	AS	3	161	PAUL	F	4	292
PATCH	S	3	382	PATES	W	1	262	PATTERSON	C	14	245	PAUL	GE	2	260
PATCHETT	A	9	148	PATEY	AH	7	296	PATTERSON	G	3	161	PAUL	H	1	262
PATCHETT	A	9	318	PATEY	FJ	7	296	PATTERSON	GE	3	161	PAUL	HD	2	260
PATCHETT	E	9	148	PATEY	G	10	174	PATTERSON	GT	7	297	PAUL	J	4	292
PATCHETT	E	9	318	PATEY	HT	7	296	PATTERSON	H	11	293	PAUL	JA	2	260
PATCHETT	E	9	318	PATEY	W	7	296	PATTERSON	H	11	293	PAUL	JC	8	259
PATCHETT	E	9	318	PATEY	WJ	7	296	PATTERSON	J	1	262	PAUL	JHR	13	332
PATCHETT	F	9	148	PATIENCE	G	4	292	PATTERSON	J	2	260	PAUL	LH	3	161
PATCHETT	GH	9	149	PATIENCE	GF	4	292	PATTERSON	J	3	161	PAUL	MJ	7	297
PATCHETT	H	9	149	PATIENT	F	7	296	PATTERSON	J	12	175	PAUL	R	4	292
PATCHETT	H	11	292	PATIENT	G	7	296	PATTERSON	JE	10	174	PAUL	T	4	292
PATCHETT	HY	6	312	PATIENT	TC	11	292	PATTERSON	JS	10	174	PAUL	TE	9	318
PATCHETT	J	9	318	PATMAN	J	1	262	PATTERSON	L	4	292	PAUL	W	14	245
PATCHETT	J	9	318	PATMORE	GA	2	260	PATTERSON	M	2	260	PAULEY	GEF	10	174
PATCHETT	JJ	9	149	PATMORE	GT	13	332	PATTERSON	MJ	13	332	PAULEY	SW	3	161
PATCHETT	L	6	312	PATMORE	W	1	262	PATTERSON	R	3	161	PAULING	F	13	332
PATCHETT	R	9	149	PATON	C	6	312	PATTERSON	RA	3	161	PAULING	SM	3	161
PATCHETT	RA	9	149	PATON	E	3	161	PATTERSON	T	8	259	PAULIZKY	LT	7	297
PATCHETT	W	6	312	PATON	H	7	296	PATTERSON	W	3	161	PAULL	E	4	292

PAULL	EE	2	260	PAYMAN	L	14	245	PAYNE	E	10	347	PAYNE	HW	3	162
PAULL	H	2	260	PAYN	AC	13	332	PAYNE	E	11	293	PAYNE	HW	3	162
PAULL	H	11	293	PAYN	AW	13	332	PAYNE	E	12	175	PAYNE	HW	4	293
PAULYN	BN	2	261	PAYN	WJ	13	332	PAYNE	E	12	364	PAYNE	IA	3	162
PAUSEY	JD	1	262	PAYNE	A	2	261	PAYNE	EA	3	162	PAYNE	IM	12	175
PAUSEY	WC	1	262	PAYNE	A	4	292	PAYNE	EA	10	175	PAYNE	J	1	263
PAVELEY	J	6	312	PAYNE	A	5	265	PAYNE	EC	5	265	PAYNE	J	3	162
PAVELEY	W	6	312	PAYNE	A	5	265	PAYNE	EG	3	162	PAYNE	J	5	265
PAVER	FS	13	332	PAYNE	A	6	312	PAYNE	EH	9	149	PAYNE	J	5	265
PAVETT	G	1	262	PAYNE	A	7	297	PAYNE	ER	3	162	PAYNE	J	6	312
PAVEY	AWJ	3	161	PAYNE	A	12	175	PAYNE	ER	10	347	PAYNE	J	8	259
PAVEY	B	5	265	PAYNE	A	12	175	PAYNE	ES	5	265	PAYNE	J	8	260
PAVEY	CA	10	346	PAYNE	A	14	245	PAYNE	EV	10	175	PAYNE	J	8	260
PAVEY	GW	1	262	PAYNE	A E	1	263	PAYNE	F	2	261	PAYNE	J	10	175
PAVEY	H	5	264	PAYNE	AC	1	263	PAYNE	F	3	162	PAYNE	J	10	175
PAVEY	HR	10	174	PAYNE	AC	1	263	PAYNE	F	5	265	PAYNE	J	11	293
PAVEY	L	10	174	PAYNE	AC	12	175	PAYNE	F	6	312	PAYNE	J	13	333
PAVIER	E	7	297	PAYNE	AC	12	175	PAYNE	F	12	175	PAYNE	JA	5	266
PAVIOUR	A	13	332	PAYNE	ACJ	13	333	PAYNE	F	14	245	PAYNE	JE	1	264
PAWLEY	NB	6	312	PAYNE	AE	1	263	PAYNE	FCD	1	263	PAYNE	JE	2	261
PAWLING	RW	10	175	PAYNE	AE	5	265	PAYNE	FG	12	364	PAYNE	JH	4	293
PAWSON	A	8	259	PAYNE	AE	10	175	PAYNE	FH	3	162	PAYNE	JH	10	175
PAWSON	E	14	245	PAYNE	AH	1	263	PAYNE	FH	7	297	PAYNE	JH	10	175
PAWSON	F	8	259	PAYNE	AJ	1	263	PAYNE	FJ	7	297	PAYNE	JJW	3	162
PAWSON	F	8	259	PAYNE	AJ	2	261	PAYNE	FT	7	298	PAYNE	JR	7	298
PAWSON	GH	9	149	PAYNE	AJ	3	162	PAYNE	FW	4	292	PAYNE	JW	1	264
PAWSON	H	9	149	PAYNE	AM	12	364	PAYNE	FW	5	265	PAYNE	L	8	260
PAWSON	JT	8	259	PAYNE	AP	6	312	PAYNE	FW	7	298	PAYNE	LC	2	261
PAWSON	W	8	259	PAYNE	AS	1	263	PAYNE	FW	8	259	PAYNE	LJ	3	162
PAWSON	W	9	318	PAYNE	AS	13	332	PAYNE	G	7	298	PAYNE	LT	1	264
PAWSON	W	9	318	PAYNE	AV	10	175	PAYNE	G	9	318	PAYNE	M	5	266
PAWSON	WH	14	245	PAYNE	AW	5	265	PAYNE	G	13	333	PAYNE	M	12	175
PAXMAN	FJ	2	261	PAYNE	AW	5	265	PAYNE	G	13	333	PAYNE	NF	4	293
PAXON	HJ	3	161	PAYNE	B	4	293	PAYNE	GA	1	263	PAYNE	NG	7	298
PAXTON	AG	12	364	PAYNE	B	5	265	PAYNE	GA	10	175	PAYNE	O	6	312
PAXTON	AW	5	265	PAYNE	BG	1	263	PAYNE	GB	5	265	PAYNE	PG	12	365
PAXTON	E	1	262	PAYNE	BR	13	332	PAYNE	GH	1	263	PAYNE	PJ	2	261
PAXTON	ER	1	262	PAYNE	C	5	265	PAYNE	GJ	3	162	PAYNE	PR	2	261
PAXTON	F	7	297	PAYNE	C	7	297	PAYNE	GO	12	364	PAYNE	PW	12	175
PAXTON	F	7	297	PAYNE	C	8	259	PAYNE	GO	13	333	PAYNE	RA	2	261
PAXTON	HH	1	263	PAYNE	C	12	175	PAYNE	GR	4	293	PAYNE	RF	3	162
PAXTON	J	5	265	PAYNE	C	12	364	PAYNE	GR	7	298	PAYNE	RG	4	293
PAXTON	L	1	263	PAYNE	CC	2	261	PAYNE	GT	13	333	PAYNE	RH	1	264
PAXTON	T	1	263	PAYNE	CE	5	265	PAYNE	GW	7	298	PAYNE	S	13	333
PAXTON	TE	1	263	PAYNE	CF	1	263	PAYNE	H	5	265	PAYNE	SC	5	266
PAXTON	W	1	263	PAYNE	CH	2	261	PAYNE	H	10	175	PAYNE	SG	10	175
PAXTON	W	2	261	PAYNE	CH	7	297	PAYNE	H	12	364	PAYNE	SP	2	261
PAXTON	WJ	12	364	PAYNE	CH	12	175	PAYNE	H	13	333	PAYNE	STJ	5	266
PAXTON	WS	1	263	PAYNE	CHG	2	261	PAYNE	HC	4	293	PAYNE	T	4	293
PAXTON-SMITH	AE	3	162	PAYNE	CS	10	347	PAYNE	HE	4	293	PAYNE	T	5	266
PAY	AE	10	175	PAYNE	CV	8	259	PAYNE	HFS	10	175	PAYNE	T	7	298
PAY	FT	10	346	PAYNE	E	1	263	PAYNE	HH	8	259	PAYNE	T	8	260
PAY	R	10	346	PAYNE	E	6	312	PAYNE	HJ	7	298	PAYNE	T	13	333
PAYLOR	T	8	259	PAYNE	E	7	297	PAYNE	HV	7	298	PAYNE	TA	6	312
PAYMAN	L	14	245	PAYNE	E	8	259	PAYNE	HW	1	263	PAYNE	TC	1	264

Surname	Init.	Unit	Pg	Surname	Init.	Unit	Pg	Surname	Init.	Unit	Pg	Surname	Init.	Unit	Pg
PAYNE	TC	6	313	PEACH	F	8	260	PEACOCK	L	1	264	PEARCE	BW	10	347
PAYNE	TF	3	162	PEACH	F	9	319	PEACOCK	LG	1	264	PEARCE	C	2	262
PAYNE	V	4	293	PEACH	G	10	175	PEACOCK	PF	13	333	PEARCE	C	4	294
PAYNE	V	5	266	PEACH	H	12	176	PEACOCK	R	3	163	PEARCE	C	5	267
PAYNE	W	2	261	PEACH	J	10	347	PEACOCK	R	8	260	PEARCE	C	7	299
PAYNE	W	3	162	PEACH	R	8	260	PEACOCK	RW	12	176	PEARCE	C	7	299
PAYNE	W	4	293	PEACH	R	10	347	PEACOCK	S	1	264	PEARCE	C	13	334
PAYNE	W	7	298	PEACH	S	11	293	PEACOCK	S	5	266	PEARCE	CA	13	334
PAYNE	W	11	293	PEACH	TW	6	313	PEACOCK	SCW	5	266	PEARCE	CE	2	262
PAYNE	W	12	176	PEACH	W	6	313	PEACOCK	V	2	262	PEARCE	CF	4	294
PAYNE	W	12	176	PEACH	W	10	347	PEACOCK	W	1	264	PEARCE	CH	6	313
PAYNE	WA	6	313	PEACH	WH	5	266	PEACOCK	W	1	264	PEARCE	CW	5	267
PAYNE	WA	7	298	PEACHEY	A	11	293	PEACOCK	W	1	264	PEARCE	D	3	163
PAYNE	WE	1	264	PEACHEY	EL	13	333	PEACOCK	W	3	163	PEARCE	D	10	347
PAYNE	WE	4	293	PEACHEY	F	9	149	PEACOCK	W	3	163	PEARCE	E	3	163
PAYNE	WE	4	293	PEACHEY	FJ	13	333	PEACOCK	W	5	266	PEARCE	E	4	294
PAYNE	WF	5	266	PEACHEY	H	7	298	PEACOCK	WS	12	365	PEARCE	E	5	267
PAYNE	WF	7	298	PEACHEY	H	7	298	PEAD	AWR	4	293	PEARCE	E	10	347
PAYNE	WF	8	260	PEACHEY	HA	7	299	PEAD	J	13	334	PEARCE	E	13	334
PAYNE	WF	10	175	PEACHEY	HJ	13	333	PEAD	LGR	4	293	PEARCE	E	13	334
PAYNE	WG	2	261	PEACHEY	J	13	333	PEAK	A	11	293	PEARCE	EA	2	262
PAYNE	WG	3	162	PEACHEY	JH	5	266	PEAK	R	14	246	PEARCE	EA	7	299
PAYNE	WG	4	293	PEACHEY	JH	13	333	PEAK	W	12	176	PEARCE	EB	5	267
PAYNE	WG	7	298	PEACHEY	W	7	299	PEAKE	A	11	293	PEARCE	EW	1	264
PAYNE	WH	2	261	PEACHMENT	AT	7	299	PEAKE	AR	6	313	PEARCE	EW	2	262
PAYNE	WH	3	382	PEACHY	H	2	261	PEAKE	C	9	391	PEARCE	EW	6	313
PAYNE	WH	5	266	PEACOCK	A	9	149	PEAKE	FR	4	293	PEARCE	EW	7	299
PAYNE	WH	13	333	PEACOCK	A	11	293	PEAKE	GH	1	264	PEARCE	F	1	265
PAYNE	WHJ	7	298	PEACOCK	A	12	176	PEAKE	H	6	313	PEARCE	F	3	163
PAYNE	WJ	13	333	PEACOCK	AE	5	266	PEAKE	SH	14	246	PEARCE	F	3	163
PAYNE	WT	4	293	PEACOCK	AG	12	176	PEAKE	W	11	293	PEARCE	F	4	294
PAYNTER	AJ	3	162	PEACOCK	AJ	5	266	PEAKE	WG	11	294	PEARCE	F	5	267
PAYNTER	AT	4	293	PEACOCK	AJ	13	333	PEAKER	A	8	260	PEARCE	F	6	313
PAYNTER	C	3	162	PEACOCK	AWJ	3	163	PEAKS	GC	12	176	PEARCE	F	10	175
PAYNTER	FG	4	293	PEACOCK	C	12	176	PEARCE	A	3	163	PEARCE	FC	4	294
PAYNTER	RJ	1	264	PEACOCK	CS	8	260	PEARCE	A	3	163	PEARCE	FC	4	294
PAYNTER	WC	4	293	PEACOCK	CW	12	176	PEARCE	A	4	294	PEARCE	FGJ	3	163
PAYNTON	WJ	2	261	PEACOCK	E	11	293	PEARCE	A	4	294	PEARCE	FH	1	265
PAYS	JC	7	298	PEACOCK	EC	5	266	PEARCE	A	7	299	PEARCE	FJ	5	267
PAYTON	A	14	245	PEACOCK	EG	1	264	PEARCE	A	13	334	PEARCE	FJ	5	267
PAYTON	AT	6	313	PEACOCK	EG	1	264	PEARCE	AC	13	334	PEARCE	FW	1	265
PAYTON	FF	3	163	PEACOCK	EW	3	163	PEARCE	AD	7	299	PEARCE	G	3	163
PAYTON	JF	6	313	PEACOCK	FJ	5	266	PEARCE	AE	2	262	PEARCE	G	4	294
PAYTON	T	9	318	PEACOCK	G	5	266	PEARCE	AE	3	163	PEARCE	G	10	175
PAYTON	WJ	4	293	PEACOCK	H	5	266	PEARCE	AE	5	267	PEARCE	G	10	176
PEACE	D	8	260	PEACOCK	H	8	260	PEARCE	AE	10	175	PEARCE	GH	1	265
PEACE	JR	8	260	PEACOCK	H	11	293	PEARCE	AG	1	264	PEARCE	GH	7	299
PEACE	R	9	149	PEACOCK	HJ	13	333	PEARCE	AGE	5	267	PEARCE	GH	13	334
PEACEY	C	6	313	PEACOCK	J	1	264	PEARCE	AJ	4	294	PEARCE	GR	9	319
PEACH	A	9	319	PEACOCK	J	5	266	PEARCE	AJ	4	294	PEARCE	GT	5	267
PEACH	A	11	293	PEACOCK	J	9	149	PEARCE	AJ	4	294	PEARCE	H	1	265
PEACH	A	14	245	PEACOCK	J	12	176	PEARCE	AP	13	334	PEARCE	H	3	163
PEACH	CF	1	264	PEACOCK	J	14	245	PEARCE	AT	1	264	PEARCE	HE	4	294
PEACH	CF	2	262	PEACOCK	J	14	245	PEARCE	AW	10	347	PEARCE	HE	4	294
PEACH	F	8	260	PEACOCK	JH	14	245	PEARCE	B	4	294	PEARCE	HE	5	267

Surname	Init.	Pt	Pg	Surname	Init.	Pt	Pg	Surname	Init.	Pt	Pg	Surname	Init.	Pt	Pg
PEARCE	HJ	5	267	PEARCE	S	13	334	PEARL	CE	7	299	PEARSON	C	8	261
PEARCE	HJ	10	176	PEARCE	SC	10	347	PEARL	H	7	300	PEARSON	C	11	294
PEARCE	HR	3	163	PEARCE	SE	4	295	PEARL	W	7	300	PEARSON	CB	1	266
PEARCE	HRW	4	294	PEARCE	SF	3	164	PEARL	WA	7	300	PEARSON	CE	4	295
PEARCE	HV	6	313	PEARCE	SJ	3	164	PEARL	WGE	7	300	PEARSON	CH	6	314
PEARCE	HW	1	265	PEARCE	T	1	265	PEARLMAN	J	8	260	PEARSON	CH	12	176
PEARCE	IT	6	313	PEARCE	T	2	262	PEARLMAN	J	14	246	PEARSON	CW	5	268
PEARCE	J	1	265	PEARCE	T	3	164	PEARLMAN	M	8	260	PEARSON	CW	9	319
PEARCE	J	1	265	PEARCE	T	3	164	PEARLMAN	W	14	246	PEARSON	D	3	164
PEARCE	J	1	265	PEARCE	T	5	268	PEARMAIN	A	1	265	PEARSON	E	7	300
PEARCE	J	1	265	PEARCE	T	6	313	PEARMAIN	JFG	1	265	PEARSON	E	8	261
PEARCE	J	2	262	PEARCE	T	8	260	PEARMAIN	JWG	8	260	PEARSON	E	11	294
PEARCE	J	2	262	PEARCE	T	13	334	PEARMAIN	P	7	300	PEARSON	E	12	365
PEARCE	J	3	163	PEARCE	T	13	334	PEARMAN	CP	3	164	PEARSON	E	13	335
PEARCE	J	3	163	PEARCE	TG	2	262	PEARMAN	F	12	176	PEARSON	E	14	246
PEARCE	J	4	294	PEARCE	TG	3	164	PEARMAN	J	5	268	PEARSON	E	14	246
PEARCE	J	4	294	PEARCE	TG	4	295	PEARMAN	JB	7	300	PEARSON	E	14	246
PEARCE	J	5	267	PEARCE	TH	1	265	PEARMAN	JW	4	295	PEARSON	EBA	10	347
PEARCE	J	5	267	PEARCE	TH	1	265	PEARMAN	T	13	334	PEARSON	EJ	8	261
PEARCE	J	5	267	PEARCE	TH	12	176	PEARMAN	TC	5	268	PEARSON	EJ	10	347
PEARCE	J	7	299	PEARCE	TJ	1	265	PEARMAN	W	1	265	PEARSON	EW	2	263
PEARCE	J	9	319	PEARCE	TJ	13	334	PEARMAN	WC	2	262	PEARSON	F	8	261
PEARCE	JA	6	313	PEARCE	VT	7	299	PEARN	CL	3	164	PEARSON	F	11	294
PEARCE	JE	8	260	PEARCE	W	2	262	PEARSALL	A	3	164	PEARSON	F	12	365
PEARCE	JH	5	267	PEARCE	W	3	164	PEARSALL	EW	3	164	PEARSON	FC	3	164
PEARCE	JR	5	267	PEARCE	W	4	295	PEARSALL	F	3	164	PEARSON	FC	5	268
PEARCE	JR	9	319	PEARCE	W	4	295	PEARSALL	H	6	313	PEARSON	FE	7	300
PEARCE	JV	1	265	PEARCE	W	4	295	PEARSALL	S	6	314	PEARSON	FE	13	335
PEARCE	JW	3	163	PEARCE	W	4	295	PEARSALL	W	13	335	PEARSON	FH	12	365
PEARCE	JW	3	164	PEARCE	W	5	267	PEARSALL	WM	13	334	PEARSON	FJ	7	300
PEARCE	JW	10	347	PEARCE	W	6	313	PEARSE	AE	1	266	PEARSON	FW	3	382
PEARCE	JWT	4	294	PEARCE	W	7	299	PEARSE	F	3	164	PEARSON	G	3	165
PEARCE	L	6	313	PEARCE	W	10	176	PEARSE	H	1	266	PEARSON	G	8	261
PEARCE	L	13	334	PEARCE	W	10	347	PEARSE	WH	2	262	PEARSON	GT	3	165
PEARCE	LE	5	267	PEARCE	WB	7	299	PEARSE	WJ	2	263	PEARSON	GT	8	261
PEARCE	LR	4	294	PEARCE	WE	7	299	PEARSON	A	3	164	PEARSON	GW	13	335
PEARCE	N	1	265	PEARCE	WE	12	176	PEARSON	A	3	382	PEARSON	H	8	261
PEARCE	P	13	334	PEARCE	WE	13	334	PEARSON	A	4	295	PEARSON	H	8	261
PEARCE	PLJ	10	176	PEARCE	WG	4	295	PEARSON	A	8	260	PEARSON	H	8	261
PEARCE	R	2	262	PEARCE	WH	10	347	PEARSON	A	9	149	PEARSON	H	8	261
PEARCE	R	2	262	PEARCE	WJ	1	265	PEARSON	A	9	149	PEARSON	H	8	261
PEARCE	R	3	164	PEARCE	WJ	2	262	PEARSON	A	9	319	PEARSON	H	8	261
PEARCE	R	4	294	PEARCE	WJ	3	164	PEARSON	A	9	319	PEARSON	H	8	261
PEARCE	R	14	246	PEARCE	WJ	4	295	PEARSON	A	11	294	PEARSON	H	12	176
PEARCE	RA	3	164	PEARCE	WJ	7	299	PEARSON	A	11	294	PEARSON	H	13	335
PEARCE	RA	4	294	PEARCE	WT	4	295	PEARSON	A	12	365	PEARSON	H	14	246
PEARCE	RF	5	267	PEARCE	WT	13	334	PEARSON	A	13	335	PEARSON	HL	9	149
PEARCE	RG	10	347	PEARCEY	AS	4	295	PEARSON	A	14	246	PEARSON	HM	13	335
PEARCE	RH	2	262	PEARCEY	EAE	4	295	PEARSON	AA	5	268	PEARSON	HW	2	263
PEARCE	RH	4	295	PEARCEY	FG	4	295	PEARSON	AE	2	263	PEARSON	J	9	150
PEARCE	RL	3	164	PEARCEY	JH	13	334	PEARSON	AH	7	300	PEARSON	J	9	150
PEARCE	S	2	262	PEARCEY	WJ	4	295	PEARSON	AL	1	266	PEARSON	J	9	150
PEARCE	S	3	164	PEARCY	F	11	294	PEARSON	B	8	260	PEARSON	J	9	319
PEARCE	S	7	299	PEARCY	WJ	4	295	PEARSON	B	8	260	PEARSON	J	9	319
PEARCE	S	11	294	PEARCY	WJ	4	295	PEARSON	BE	12	365				

Surname	In.			Surname	In.			Surname	In.			Surname	In.		
PEARSON	J	9	319	PEARSON	W	14	246	PECK	G	11	294	PEDDER	H	5	269
PEARSON	J	11	294	PEARSON	W	14	246	PECK	GF	7	301	PEDDER	HW	5	269
PEARSON	J	12	176	PEARSON	WC	13	335	PECK	H	3	165	PEDDER	J	9	150
PEARSON	J	12	365	PEARSON	WE	1	266	PECK	HR	5	268	PEDDER	J	9	150
PEARSON	J	12	365	PEARSON	WJJ	2	263	PECK	J	1	266	PEDDER	JH	9	319
PEARSON	JA	10	176	PEARSON	WT	1	266	PECK	J	1	266	PEDDER	JM	9	150
PEARSON	JA	11	294	PEARSON	WW	5	268	PECK	J	13	335	PEDDER	JM	9	150
PEARSON	JD	1	266	PEART	AW	7	300	PECK	JES	2	263	PEDDER	M	11	295
PEARSON	JE	3	165	PEART	PT	4	295	PECK	JW	12	365	PEDDLE	G	6	314
PEARSON	JH	3	165	PEART	WG	8	262	PECK	L	10	176	PEDDLE	W	6	314
PEARSON	JH	8	261	PEARTON	JE	11	294	PECK	RG	13	335	PEDEL	FT	7	301
PEARSON	JJ	8	261	PEARTON	TW	11	294	PECK	RJ	10	176	PEDERSEN	VM	2	263
PEARSON	JJ	14	246	PEASE	A	14	246	PECK	S	5	268	PEDERSON	JH	13	335
PEARSON	JN	14	246	PEASE	CP	8	262	PECK	SC	4	296	PEDERSON	JN	13	335
PEARSON	JT	9	319	PEASE	F	5	268	PECK	SC	5	268	PEDLEY	A	1	266
PEARSON	JT	13	335	PEASE	H	9	150	PECK	SG	2	263	PEDLEY	A	6	314
PEARSON	JW	9	319	PEASE	HV	3	165	PECK	W	5	268	PEDLEY	A	12	177
PEARSON	JW	11	294	PEASE	J	8	262	PECK	W	7	301	PEDLEY	AJ	12	177
PEARSON	L	13	335	PEASE	W	5	268	PECK	WG	1	266	PEDLEY	AW	12	177
PEARSON	M	3	165	PEASE	W	8	262	PECK	WG	5	268	PEDLEY	C	12	177
PEARSON	PG	12	365	PEASE	W	8	262	PECK	WI	3	383	PEDLEY	CW	6	314
PEARSON	R	1	266	PEASLAND	JB	12	176	PECK	WS	5	269	PEDLEY	E	6	314
PEARSON	R	3	165	PEASLEY	AJ	1	266	PECK	WT	3	165	PEDLEY	EJ	12	177
PEARSON	R	8	261	PEASNELL	FA	7	300	PECKETT	J	14	246	PEDLEY	F	9	319
PEARSON	R	8	261	PEASNELL	FG	7	300	PECKETT	S	2	263	PEDLEY	G	12	177
PEARSON	R	8	261	PEASNELL	SW	7	300	PECKHAM	AT	3	165	PEDLEY	GR	9	319
PEARSON	R	10	176	PEAT	AS	5	268	PECKHAM	B	4	296	PEDLEY	JJ	12	177
PEARSON	R	11	294	PEAT	C	14	246	PECKHAM	CE	6	314	PEDLEY	JR	11	295
PEARSON	R	12	176	PEAT	CW	5	268	PECKHAM	EG	4	296	PEDLEY	LO	5	269
PEARSON	RA	1	266	PEAT	D	5	268	PECKHAM	FD	4	296	PEDLEY	R	14	246
PEARSON	RA	3	382	PEAT	ED	10	348	PECKHAM	G	3	165	PEDLY	H	8	262
PEARSON	RC	13	335	PEAT	H	8	262	PECKHAM	G	4	296	PEDLY	S	8	262
PEARSON	RJ	1	266	PEAT	H	8	262	PECKHAM	GE	4	296	PEDRICK	HJ	5	269
PEARSON	RS	12	365	PEAT	HA	3	382	PECKHAM	HJ	2	263	PEDROZA	C	2	263
PEARSON	RT	12	365	PEAT	J	5	268	PECKHAM	HW	4	285	PEEK	G	13	335
PEARSON	S	7	300	PEAT	JA	8	262	PECKHAM	PG	13	335	PEEK	JH	10	176
PEARSON	S	8	261	PEAT	JG	3	383	PECKHAM	TJW	10	176	PEEK	R	13	335
PEARSON	S	11	294	PEAT	JT	5	268	PECKHAM	TW	2	263	PEEL	A	9	320
PEARSON	T	8	262	PEAT	N	6	314	PECKHAM	W	2	263	PEEL	C	1	266
PEARSON	T	9	150	PEAT	WF	10	348	PECKHAM	W	4	296	PEEL	C	9	320
PEARSON	T	12	176	PEATTY	TC	3	165	PECKOVER	A	6	314	PEEL	E	14	247
PEARSON	T	12	365	PEATY	FN	10	176	PECKOVER	FS	9	319	PEEL	EJ	12	424
PEARSON	TH	10	176	PEATY	T	4	296	PECKOVER	H	9	150	PEEL	G	8	262
PEARSON	TJ	14	246	PECK	A	1	266	PECKOVER	T	6	314	PEEL	G	9	320
PEARSON	TR	3	165	PECK	A	10	176	PECKS	L	5	269	PEEL	GC	8	262
PEARSON	W	1	266	PECK	AB	3	165	PEDDAR	A	12	177	PEEL	J	9	320
PEARSON	W	7	300	PECK	AE	7	300	PEDDER	A	9	150	PEEL	J	9	320
PEARSON	W	8	262	PECK	AE	12	177	PEDDER	C	5	269	PEEL	O	9	320
PEARSON	W	8	262	PECK	AH	5	268	PEDDER	CG	11	295	PEEL	R	9	320
PEARSON	W	8	262	PECK	AJ	3	165	PEDDER	DM	5	269	PEEL	RA	1	266
PEARSON	W	8	262	PECK	C	1	266	PEDDER	GE	7	301	PEEL	T	9	150
PEARSON	W	9	319	PECK	C	13	335	PEDDER	GM	5	269	PEEL	T	9	320
PEARSON	W	9	319	PECK	F	12	177	PEDDER	GW	5	269	PEEL	W	9	320
PEARSON	W	9	319	PECK	FW	10	176	PEDDER	H	5	269	PEEL	WG	14	247
PEARSON	W	11	294	PECK	G	3	165	PEDDER	H	5	269	PEER	WJ	13	336

PEERING	AC	1	268	PELLANT	WR	7	301	PENDLEBURY	D	9	320	PENNECARD	F	13	336
PEERING	J	1	268	PELLATT	A	3	166	PENDLEBURY	J	11	295	PENNELL	AE	2	264
PEERLESS	HW	13	336	PELLATT	JE	3	166	PENDREY	AL	1	267	PENNELL	AE	7	302
PEERLESS	HW	13	336	PELLATT	RE	3	166	PENDRY	FW	3	166	PENNELL	C	5	269
PEERMAN	J	13	336	PELLETT	AR	13	336	PENFOLD	A	4	296	PENNELL	E	12	366
PEERS	B	4	296	PELLETT	CJ	3	166	PENFOLD	AE	10	348	PENNELL	F	7	302
PEERS	J	9	150	PELLETT	FT	13	336	PENFOLD	AG	3	166	PENNELL	FJD	7	301
PEERS	LC	2	263	PELLETT	JE	13	336	PENFOLD	AJ	2	263	PENNELL	HTN	7	302
PEERS	RK	4	296	PELLETT	R	7	301	PENFOLD	AJ	4	296	PENNELL	W	5	269
PEERS	TE	9	150	PELLOW	AH	3	166	PENFOLD	AW	4	296	PENNELLS	H	8	263
PEERS	W	5	269	PELLOW	F	3	166	PENFOLD	D	10	176	PENNEY	A	3	167
PEERS	W	6	314	PELLOW	L	5	269	PENFOLD	EW	3	166	PENNEY	AE	11	295
PEERS	W	11	295	PELLOW	M	3	166	PENFOLD	F	2	264	PENNEY	AJ	4	296
PEET	A	11	295	PELLOWES	EA	5	269	PENFOLD	F	4	296	PENNEY	AJ	4	297
PEET	AC	4	296	PELLS	CW	7	301	PENFOLD	H	2	264	PENNEY	CE	4	297
PEET	HG	11	295	PELLS	TF	7	301	PENFOLD	H	4	296	PENNEY	CE	4	297
PEET	R	4	296	PELLUET	EA	7	301	PENFOLD	HR	2	264	PENNEY	DR	3	167
PEGG	A	14	247	PELOW	J	11	295	PENFOLD	J	14	247	PENNEY	E	3	167
PEGG	C	2	263	PEMBER	EC	3	166	PENFOLD	JG	7	301	PENNEY	EC	13	336
PEGG	CH	7	301	PEMBER	WT	3	166	PENFOLD	JW	1	267	PENNEY	EL	13	336
PEGG	EG	3	165	PEMBERTON	A	6	314	PENFOLD	WF	10	348	PENNEY	FR	4	297
PEGG	FB	3	165	PEMBERTON	AEV	13	336	PENFOLD	WG	3	166	PENNEY	HD	13	337
PEGG	GH	6	314	PEMBERTON	CW	13	336	PENFOLD	WH	13	336	PENNEY	J	9	150
PEGG	H	14	247	PEMBERTON	D	1	267	PENFOLD	WJ	3	166	PENNEY	J	11	295
PEGG	JW	8	262	PEMBERTON	G	6	315	PENFORD	RA	1	267	PENNEY	J	11	295
PEGG	JW	11	295	PEMBERTON	G	8	262	PENFOUND	WS	10	348	PENNEY	JL	13	337
PEGG	L	3	165	PEMBERTON	GA	14	247	PENGELLY	LJ	13	336	PENNEY	JW	4	297
PEGG	P	6	314	PEMBERTON	GE	10	176	PENINGTON	H	14	247	PENNEY	LA	4	297
PEGG	TG	2	263	PEMBERTON	GR	5	269	PENISTON	A	8	263	PENNEY	SC	4	297
PEGG	WG	10	348	PEMBERTON	H	6	315	PENISTON	F	8	263	PENNEY	SE	3	167
PEGLER	F	3	165	PEMBERTON	H	8	262	PENISTON	W	8	263	PENNEY	TH	11	295
PEGLER	F	13	336	PEMBERTON	HT	2	263	PENISTONE	W	8	263	PENNEY	W	9	150
PEGLER	FWC	7	301	PEMBERTON	JC	6	315	PENKETHMAN	W	14	247	PENNEY	WH	13	337
PEGLER	G	6	314	PEMBERTON	M	13	336	PENLINGTON	G	14	247	PENNEY	WS	13	337
PEGLEY	CL	7	301	PEMBERTON	RE	2	263	PENMAN	A	7	301	PENNICOTT	GW	4	297
PEGLEY	F	3	165	PEMBERTON	S	13	336	PENMAN	AH	3	166	PENNICOTT	H	4	297
PEGRAM	GW	3	166	PEMBERTON	T	6	315	PENMAN	C	1	267	PENNICOTT	WJ	4	297
PEGRAM	WR	5	269	PEMBERTON	W	8	262	PENMAN	H	1	267	PENNILL	W	11	295
PEIRCE	J	10	176	PEMBERTON	W	8	263	PENMAN	RT	7	301	PENNING	BW	13	337
PEIRSON	HA	3	383	PEMBERTON	W	11	295	PENN	A	3	166	PENNING	HA	13	337
PEIRSON	JR	9	150	PEMBERTON	W	13	336	PENN	AE	12	366	PENNING	WH	13	337
PELHAM	AA	14	247	PEMBERTON	WA	7	301	PENN	CA	12	366	PENNINGTON	A	3	167
PELHAM	WF	14	247	PEMBERTON	WR	13	336	PENN	EA	3	166	PENNINGTON	A	8	263
PELL	A	6	314	PEMBERY	AS	2	263	PENN	FG	12	366	PENNINGTON	A	14	247
PELL	CE	12	177	PEMBERY	FF	3	383	PENN	FJ	10	176	PENNINGTON	A	14	247
PELL	CJ	12	177	PEMBLE	CJ	4	296	PENN	G	12	366	PENNINGTON	B	3	167
PELL	CJ	12	365	PEMBLE	CJ	4	296	PENN	GH	12	366	PENNINGTON	EH	14	247
PELL	CW	12	177	PEMBLE	EW	1	267	PENN	H	12	366	PENNINGTON	F	4	297
PELL	F	6	314	PEMBROKE	A	3	166	PENN	J	12	366	PENNINGTON	F	11	295
PELL	F	12	177	PEMBROKE	WJ	13	336	PENN	JCW	12	366	PENNINGTON	F	11	296
PELL	H	12	365	PENDERED	TA	12	365	PENN	L	9	150	PENNINGTON	G	4	297
PELL	HA	12	365	PENDERED	W	12	366	PENN	W	12	366	PENNINGTON	G	14	247
PELL	OJ	3	166	PENDLE	AP	1	267	PENN	WF	10	176	PENNINGTON	H	7	302
PELL	OW	12	365	PENDLEBURY	A	14	247	PENN	WJ	12	366	PENNINGTON	J	14	247
PELL	WG	12	365	PENDLEBURY	A	14	247	PENN	WW	3	166	PENNINGTON	J	14	248

PENNINGTON	J	14	248	PENTON	EJ	7	302	PEPPIN	JA	1	267	PERIGO	L	8	264
PENNINGTON	JC	3	167	PENTON	J	4	297	PEPPIN	JC	3	167	PERIGO	M	8	264
PENNINGTON	JH	11	296	PENTY	W	9	320	PEPPLER	A	3	167	PERIGO	W	6	315
PENNINGTON	JW	2	264	PENWARDEN	HL	10	348	PEPPRATT	A	3	167	PERKIN	A	13	338
PENNINGTON	P	14	248	PENWRIGHT	G	12	177	PEPPRATT	HS	3	167	PERKIN	F	13	338
PENNINGTON	T	7	302	PENWRIGHT	LG	12	177	PERAVAL	P	9	320	PERKIN	F	14	248
PENNINGTON	T	9	320	PENYER	S	6	315	PERCHARDE	CJ	3	167	PERKIN	GW	8	264
PENNINGTON	T	14	248	PEPALL	E	6	315	PERCIVAL	A	14	248	PERKIN	L	8	264
PENNISTONE	JE	8	263	PEPLER	G	2	264	PERCIVAL	AH	1	267	PERKINS	A	6	315
PENNOCK	AT	8	263	PEPLOE	WG	3	167	PERCIVAL	C	5	271	PERKINS	A	12	178
PENNOCK	T	8	263	PEPLOW	AE	6	315	PERCIVAL	D	11	296	PERKINS	A	12	178
PENNY	A	5	269	PEPLOW	HT	1	267	PERCIVAL	E	14	248	PERKINS	A	12	178
PENNY	A	9	150	PEPLOW	LT	10	177	PERCIVAL	EJ	1	267	PERKINS	A	13	338
PENNY	AJ	5	270	PEPLOW	SJ	3	167	PERCIVAL	ES	10	348	PERKINS	A	14	248
PENNY	AP	2	264	PEPLOW	WA	1	267	PERCIVAL	F	8	263	PERKINS	AA	3	168
PENNY	C	5	270	PEPPER	AR	13	337	PERCIVAL	F	8	263	PERKINS	AC	2	264
PENNY	C	13	337	PEPPER	AW	12	177	PERCIVAL	F	13	337	PERKINS	AC	2	264
PENNY	CJ	6	315	PEPPER	B	5	270	PERCIVAL	G	7	302	PERKINS	AE	12	366
PENNY	DB	4	297	PEPPER	B	12	177	PERCIVAL	G	11	296	PERKINS	AG	1	268
PENNY	E	1	267	PEPPER	BE	12	177	PERCIVAL	GS	7	302	PERKINS	AG	13	338
PENNY	E	2	264	PEPPER	E	5	270	PERCIVAL	J	6	315	PERKINS	AJ	12	366
PENNY	F	5	270	PEPPER	F	5	270	PERCIVAL	J	8	263	PERKINS	AR	13	338
PENNY	G	13	337	PEPPER	F	5	270	PERCIVAL	J	11	296	PERKINS	B	5	271
PENNY	H	5	270	PEPPER	FA	13	337	PERCIVAL	J	11	296	PERKINS	B	12	178
PENNY	H	13	337	PEPPER	GW	10	348	PERCIVAL	JA	12	366	PERKINS	C	12	178
PENNY	HW	13	337	PEPPER	H	5	270	PERCIVAL	JH	14	248	PERKINS	C	13	338
PENNY	J	9	320	PEPPER	HE	12	177	PERCIVAL	JW	8	263	PERKINS	CH	12	178
PENNY	JG	1	267	PEPPER	HJ	5	270	PERCIVAL	N	8	263	PERKINS	CJ	5	271
PENNY	JT	3	167	PEPPER	JN	8	263	PERCIVAL	RW	1	267	PERKINS	CW	8	264
PENNY	P	12	366	PEPPER	MW	5	270	PERCIVAL	T	8	263	PERKINS	E	1	268
PENNY	PF	4	297	PEPPER	S	12	178	PERCIVAL	W	8	264	PERKINS	E	3	168
PENNY	S	13	337	PEPPER	SF	7	302	PERCIVAL	W	12	366	PERKINS	E	7	302
PENNY	W	4	297	PEPPER	TW	14	248	PERCIVAL	WW	1	267	PERKINS	F	2	264
PENNY	W	9	320	PEPPER	W	5	270	PERCY	A	3	167	PERKINS	F	11	296
PENNY	W	11	296	PEPPER	WC	1	267	PERCY	A	3	168	PERKINS	F	12	366
PENNY	W	13	337	PEPPER	WH	10	348	PERCY	A	4	298	PERKINS	F	13	338
PENNY	WE	13	337	PEPPER	WJ	5	270	PERCY	AG	1	268	PERKINS	FA	10	348
PENNY	WP	1	267	PEPPER	WJ	8	263	PERCY	G	11	296	PERKINS	FA	13	338
PENNY	WR	7	302	PEPPER	WT	5	270	PERCY	H	4	298	PERKINS	FC	5	271
PENO	E	13	337	PEPPER	WW	7	302	PERCY	HE	1	268	PERKINS	FC	7	302
PENROSE	A	8	263	PEPPERALL	JD	10	177	PERCY	HJA	1	268	PERKINS	FJ	6	315
PENROSE	E	8	263	PEPPERELL	A	7	302	PERCY	J	3	168	PERKINS	FJ	7	302
PENROSE	R	9	150	PEPPERELL	F	7	302	PERCY	MF	3	168	PERKINS	FJ	10	177
PENROSE	R	9	151	PEPPERELL	FC	10	177	PERCY	SC	4	298	PERKINS	FJ	12	366
PENROSE	RP	4	297	PEPPERELL	HN	10	177	PERCY	WJ	2	264	PERKINS	G	1	268
PENROSE	V	8	263	PEPPERELL	J	2	264	PERDUE	H	4	298	PERKINS	G	1	268
PENSON	JG	10	348	PEPPIATT	A	1	267	PERDUE	JE	10	177	PERKINS	G	11	296
PENSON	WF	7	302	PEPPIATT	B	3	167	PERDUE	WH	4	298	PERKINS	G	12	178
PENTECOST	JA	4	297	PEPPIATT	D	5	270	PEREN	FG	4	298	PERKINS	GH	12	366
PENTECOST	RS	13	337	PEPPIATT	EEH	3	167	PERFECT	CL	13	338	PERKINS	GM	12	366
PENTLAND	T	11	296	PEPPIATT	FC	1	267	PERFECT	ED	2	264	PERKINS	GW	12	367
PENTLING	FA	5	270	PEPPIATT	T	3	167	PERFECT	FJ	2	264	PERKINS	H	6	315
PENTLOW	AE	4	297	PEPPIATT	TW	1	267	PERFECT	FJ	3	168	PERKINS	H	12	178
PENTLOW	AV	4	297	PEPPIATT	TW	3	167	PERFECT	H	5	270	PERKINS	HG	13	338
PENTLOW	HA	4	297	PEPPIATT	V	5	270	PERHAM	C	5	271	PERKINS	HGD	12	367

Surname	Init	No	Pg	Surname	Init	No	Pg	Surname	Init	No	Pg	Surname	Init	No	Pg
PERKINS	HH	12	367	PERLLMAN	T	13	338	PERRINS	J	6	316	PERRY	G	7	304
PERKINS	HV	6	315	PERLLMAN	WGC	13	338	PERRINS	J	6	317	PERRY	G	8	264
PERKINS	J	1	268	PERMAIN	AC	4	298	PERRINS	ST	6	316	PERRY	GA	7	304
PERKINS	J	1	268	PERMAN	A	4	298	PERRINS	W	6	317	PERRY	GA	13	339
PERKINS	J	1	268	PERMAN	C	7	303	PERRINS	WH	6	317	PERRY	GH	7	304
PERKINS	J	8	264	PERMAN	CH	4	298	PERRIS	R	11	296	PERRY	GJ	7	304
PERKINS	J	9	320	PERMAN	CH	4	298	PERROT	C	8	264	PERRY	GJ	12	178
PERKINS	J	12	178	PERMAN	F	3	168	PERROTT	J	9	320	PERRY	GJ	12	178
PERKINS	J	13	338	PERMAN	GJ	2	264	PERROTT	R	7	303	PERRY	GL	3	168
PERKINS	J	14	248	PERMAN	P	8	264	PERROTT	RT	7	303	PERRY	GT	5	271
PERKINS	JA	6	315	PERREN	B	3	168	PERRY	A	2	264	PERRY	GW	1	269
PERKINS	JG	12	178	PERREN	J	13	338	PERRY	A	4	298	PERRY	H	1	269
PERKINS	JH	6	315	PERREN	WH	4	298	PERRY	A	5	271	PERRY	H	5	271
PERKINS	JJ	12	178	PERRETT	A	1	268	PERRY	A	6	317	PERRY	H	5	272
PERKINS	JJE	7	302	PERRETT	A	12	367	PERRY	A	7	303	PERRY	H	5	272
PERKINS	JL	8	264	PERRETT	ER	3	168	PERRY	A	10	177	PERRY	H	6	317
PERKINS	JP	9	151	PERRETT	FH	10	177	PERRY	A	13	339	PERRY	H	6	317
PERKINS	JW	4	298	PERRETT	JA	13	338	PERRY	AB	5	271	PERRY	H	7	304
PERKINS	JW	8	264	PERRETT	JA	13	339	PERRY	AD	7	303	PERRY	HC	3	168
PERKINS	LG	6	315	PERRETT	TH	7	303	PERRY	AE	1	268	PERRY	HE	4	298
PERKINS	OR	13	338	PERRETT	W	13	339	PERRY	AE	7	303	PERRY	HG	3	168
PERKINS	P	12	367	PERRETT	WJ	14	248	PERRY	AE	14	248	PERRY	HJ	7	304
PERKINS	PG	5	271	PERRETT	WJS	14	248	PERRY	AJ	3	168	PERRY	HL	6	317
PERKINS	R	3	168	PERRIDGE	W	13	339	PERRY	AJM	6	317	PERRY	J	1	269
PERKINS	R	7	303	PERRIGO	HW	6	316	PERRY	AR	1	268	PERRY	J	4	298
PERKINS	RA	2	264	PERRIN	A	11	296	PERRY	AW	12	178	PERRY	J	4	298
PERKINS	RH	10	177	PERRIN	AE	4	298	PERRY	B	6	317	PERRY	J	4	299
PERKINS	S	8	264	PERRIN	AH	7	303	PERRY	BE	2	265	PERRY	J	6	317
PERKINS	S	12	178	PERRIN	C	7	303	PERRY	CA	7	303	PERRY	J	6	317
PERKINS	T	3	168	PERRIN	CR	13	339	PERRY	CE	6	317	PERRY	J	10	177
PERKINS	TG	13	338	PERRIN	E	3	383	PERRY	CF	3	168	PERRY	J	10	177
PERKINS	W	5	271	PERRIN	E	11	296	PERRY	CH	5	271	PERRY	J	11	297
PERKINS	W	11	296	PERRIN	EJ	13	339	PERRY	CH	7	303	PERRY	J	12	178
PERKINS	WA	2	264	PERRIN	EJ	13	339	PERRY	CR	12	178	PERRY	JA	1	269
PERKINS	WA	3	168	PERRIN	EJH	13	339	PERRY	DV	12	178	PERRY	JA	10	348
PERKINS	WGA	6	315	PERRIN	G	7	303	PERRY	E	1	268	PERRY	JF	6	317
PERKINS	WH	12	367	PERRIN	GN	6	316	PERRY	E	7	304	PERRY	JH	10	177
PERKINS	WJ	7	303	PERRIN	H	7	303	PERRY	E	11	297	PERRY	JJ	7	304
PERKINS	WS	13	338	PERRIN	HI	6	316	PERRY	EF	1	269	PERRY	JL	4	299
PERKIS	C	4	298	PERRIN	J	6	316	PERRY	EH	4	298	PERRY	JP	1	269
PERKIS	CE	4	298	PERRIN	J	10	177	PERRY	F	1	269	PERRY	JP	6	317
PERKS	A	1	268	PERRIN	J	11	296	PERRY	F	1	269	PERRY	JR	11	296
PERKS	AE	6	316	PERRIN	JD	4	298	PERRY	F	4	298	PERRY	JW	2	265
PERKS	AJ	6	316	PERRIN	PJ	5	271	PERRY	F	5	271	PERRY	JW	2	265
PERKS	AW	6	316	PERRIN	SEH	7	303	PERRY	F	6	317	PERRY	L	11	297
PERKS	C	1	268	PERRIN	T	1	268	PERRY	F	14	248	PERRY	LC	4	299
PERKS	CH	6	316	PERRIN	T	9	320	PERRY	FE	1	269	PERRY	M	6	317
PERKS	HG	6	316	PERRIN	T	11	296	PERRY	FH	5	271	PERRY	NJ	2	265
PERKS	J	6	316	PERRIN	W	5	271	PERRY	FRW	3	168	PERRY	P	10	177
PERKS	JA	6	316	PERRIN	W	6	316	PERRY	FS	7	304	PERRY	PA	5	272
PERKS	T	13	338	PERRIN	W	12	367	PERRY	G	1	269	PERRY	PA	5	272
PERKS	WE	6	316	PERRIN	WE	6	316	PERRY	G	3	168	PERRY	PH	1	269
PERKS	WH	6	316	PERRIN	WJ	12	178	PERRY	G	5	271	PERRY	R	2	265
PERKS	WH	6	316	PERRING	H	7	303	PERRY	G	5	271	PERRY	R	6	317
PERLLMAN	FG	13	338	PERRINS	E	6	316	PERRY	G	7	304	PERRY	R	11	297

PERRY	RH	6	317	PESTELL	EW	13	339	PETERS	HJ	13	340	PETTER	GH	2	266
PERRY	S	1	269	PESTELL	FR	5	272	PETERS	J	1	270	PETTERS	J	10	178
PERRY	S	7	304	PESTELL	FR	5	272	PETERS	J	5	272	PETTET	JJ	10	178
PERRY	S	11	297	PESTELL	FR	13	339	PETERS	J	13	340	PETTETT	E	13	340
PERRY	S	13	339	PESTELL	HG	5	272	PETERS	JH	6	318	PETTIFAR	A	5	273
PERRY	SAJ	13	339	PESTELL	HJ	13	339	PETERS	JJ	2	265	PETTIFAR	F	5	273
PERRY	SF	12	178	PESTELL	SJ	13	340	PETERS	JJ	3	169	PETTIFAR	H	5	273
PERRY	SH	4	299	PESTELL	W	10	178	PETERS	K	13	340	PETTIFER	CA	3	169
PERRY	SH	6	318	PESTELL	WH	13	340	PETERS	LH	5	273	PETTIFER	G	6	318
PERRY	SH	10	177	PESTRIDGE	JA	6	318	PETERS	R	2	265	PETTIFER	JW	6	318
PERRY	T	11	297	PETCH	B	8	264	PETERS	RE	10	178	PETTIFER	S	12	179
PERRY	TJ	1	269	PETCH	H	8	264	PETERS	RW	10	178	PETTIFER	TJ	12	367
PERRY	TR	5	272	PETCH	H	8	264	PETERS	SJ	1	270	PETTIFER	W	6	318
PERRY	W	1	269	PETCH	JDJ	13	340	PETERS	TG	10	348	PETTIFOR	W	7	305
PERRY	W	2	265	PETCH	JH	8	264	PETERS	TJ	1	270	PETTIFORD	FV	2	266
PERRY	W	6	318	PETCH	JH	8	264	PETERS	W	2	265	PETTIGREW	TC	1	270
PERRY	W	6	318	PETCH	WE	2	265	PETERS	W	13	340	PETTINGER	E	8	264
PERRY	W	6	318	PETCHEY	A	1	269	PETERS	WA	2	265	PETTIS	A	4	299
PERRY	W	6	318	PETCHEY	SF	1	269	PETERS	WC	4	299	PETTIT	A	12	367
PERRY	W	6	318	PETCHEY	ST	1	269	PETERS	WC	5	273	PETTIT	AA	3	169
PERRY	W	11	297	PETERS	A	13	340	PETERS	WJ	1	270	PETTIT	AJ	5	273
PERRY	W	12	367	PETERS	A	13	340	PETERS	WT	10	178	PETTIT	C	4	299
PERRY	W	12	367	PETERS	A	14	248	PETERSEN	A	11	297	PETTIT	E	5	273
PERRY	W	13	339	PETERS	AE	7	304	PETERSEN	F	3	169	PETTIT	EG	12	367
PERRY	W	14	248	PETERS	AG	3	168	PETERSON	FC	2	265	PETTIT	ER	12	367
PERRY	WEJ	4	299	PETERS	AJ	4	299	PETERSON	GA	10	178	PETTIT	F	7	305
PERRY	WF	5	272	PETERS	C	1	270	PETERSON	JW	10	178	PETTIT	F	7	305
PERRY	WH	10	177	PETERS	C	5	272	PETERSON	P	5	273	PETTIT	FW	12	179
PERRY	WJ	4	299	PETERS	C	6	318	PETFORD	FA	6	318	PETTIT	GJ	7	305
PERRY	WJ	10	177	PETERS	CE	1	270	PETFORD	WJ	6	318	PETTIT	HA	3	169
PERRY	WL	6	318	PETERS	CF	6	318	PETHER	JE	10	178	PETTIT	HE	13	340
PERRY	WR	5	272	PETERS	CW	3	169	PETHER	T	10	178	PETTIT	HG	12	179
PERRY	WW	12	179	PETERS	D	5	272	PETHERICK	EJ	7	304	PETTIT	JE	12	367
PERRYMAN		1	269	PETERS	E	2	265	PETITE	HJ	7	305	PETTIT	JM	2	266
PERRYMAN	CH	10	177	PETERS	E	6	318	PETLEY	F	8	264	PETTIT	RH	13	341
PERRYMAN	J	10	348	PETERS	E	12	179	PETO	EF	13	340	PETTIT	SA	7	305
PERRYMAN	R	3	168	PETERS	E	13	340	PETO	J	3	169	PETTIT	TW	12	179
PERRYMAN	TI	10	177	PETERS	EJ	7	304	PETRIE	AJ	2	265	PETTIT	W	7	305
PERRYMAN	W	2	265	PETERS	EM	5	272	PETRIE	AJ	13	340	PETTIT	W	7	305
PERRYMENT	RW	10	348	PETERS	EP	7	304	PETRIE	J	13	340	PETTITT	A	14	249
PERT	CA	2	265	PETERS	F	5	272	PETRY	CH	7	305	PETTITT	AC	3	169
PERTERS	MW	14	248	PETERS	F	13	340	PETRY	GF	13	340	PETTITT	AE	12	367
PERTON	AT	5	272	PETERS	FE	3	169	PETT	AA	1	270	PETTITT	AJ	1	270
PERVIN	C	10	348	PETERS	FT	7	304	PETT	C	2	265	PETTITT	D	1	270
PESCOE	A	12	367	PETERS	FW	13	340	PETT	CJ	1	270	PETTITT	FA	12	367
PESCUD	E	13	339	PETERS	G	14	249	PETT	CS	13	340	PETTITT	HH	1	270
PESKETT	AL	10	178	PETERS	GE	1	270	PETT	EJ	3	169	PETTITT	T	1	270
PESKETT	G	13	339	PETERS	GJ	6	318	PETT	F	14	249	PETTITT	TW	10	178
PESKETT	M	13	339	PETERS	H	5	272	PETT	GA	3	169	PETTITT	W	12	367
PESKETT	T	13	339	PETERS	H	6	318	PETT	H	3	169	PETTITT	WA	1	270
PESTELL	AB	5	272	PETERS	H	14	249	PETT	JH	1	270	PETTITT	WG	11	297
PESTELL	AP	7	304	PETERS	H	14	249	PETT	SG	5	273	PETTS	A	2	266
PESTELL	C	12	179	PETERS	HG	5	272	PETT	W	2	265	PETTS	F	2	266
PESTELL	CE	5	272	PETERS	HJ	2	265	PETT	WE	13	340	PETTS	GQ	7	305
PESTELL	CG	7	304	PETERS	HJ	13	340	PETTAFOR	O	1	270	PETTY	A	10	348

PETTY	A	11	297	PHELAN	JH	9	320	PHILLIPS	AE	10	349	PHILLIPS	FW	3	170
PETTY	C	9	151	PHELAN	M	14	249	PHILLIPS	AE	13	341	PHILLIPS	G	2	266
PETTY	CF	2	266	PHELAN	R	14	249	PHILLIPS	AF	7	306	PHILLIPS	G	3	170
PETTY	F	9	320	PHELAN	T	8	265	PHILLIPS	AG	1	271	PHILLIPS	G	4	300
PETTY	G	4	299	PHELAN	W	9	151	PHILLIPS	AG	3	169	PHILLIPS	G	6	319
PETTY	H	8	265	PHELPS	A	6	319	PHILLIPS	AG	13	341	PHILLIPS	G	7	306
PETTY	HV	4	299	PHELPS	E	1	271	PHILLIPS	AHD	12	179	PHILLIPS	G	7	306
PETTY	J	5	273	PHELPS	FT	6	319	PHILLIPS	AJ	3	169	PHILLIPS	G	10	349
PETTY	J	8	265	PHELPS	H	9	320	PHILLIPS	AJ	11	298	PHILLIPS	GA	6	319
PETTY	J	9	151	PHELPS	HC	6	319	PHILLIPS	AW	1	271	PHILLIPS	GE	2	266
PETTY	J	14	249	PHELPS	RC	3	169	PHILLIPS	AW	13	341	PHILLIPS	GE	10	349
PETTY	JH	2	266	PHELPS	S	10	178	PHILLIPS	C	1	271	PHILLIPS	GF	1	272
PETTY	RCT	3	169	PHELPS	W	7	305	PHILLIPS	C	11	298	PHILLIPS	GF	10	178
PETTY	SJE	5	273	PHELPS	W	7	305	PHILLIPS	CH	4	299	PHILLIPS	GH	4	300
PETTY	TC	4	299	PHELPS	WA	7	305	PHILLIPS	CH	6	319	PHILLIPS	GJ	3	170
PETTY	TH	2	266	PHELPS	WH	6	319	PHILLIPS	CH	6	319	PHILLIPS	GJ	10	349
PETTY	V	5	273	PHELPS	WH	7	305	PHILLIPS	CH	8	265	PHILLIPS	GR	4	300
PETTY	W	8	265	PHELPS	WJ	6	319	PHILLIPS	CJ	1	271	PHILLIPS	GW	4	300
PETTY	WF	9	151	PHENNA	H	14	249	PHILLIPS	CJ	4	299	PHILLIPS	H	6	319
PETWORTH	LE	10	178	PHILBEY	G	7	305	PHILLIPS	CJ	12	368	PHILLIPS	H	6	319
PETZING	A	1	270	PHILBEY	MH	2	266	PHILLIPS	D	7	306	PHILLIPS	H	6	319
PETZING	CHJ	1	270	PHILBIN	M	11	297	PHILLIPS	DG	4	299	PHILLIPS	H	6	319
PETZING	H	1	271	PHILBRICK	AC	3	170	PHILLIPS	DM	3	169	PHILLIPS	H	8	265
PEVALIN	HW	13	341	PHILBURN	H	8	265	PHILLIPS	E	3	169	PHILLIPS	H	8	265
PEVALIN	WA	13	341	PHILCOX	F	7	305	PHILLIPS	E	7	306	PHILLIPS	H	10	349
PEVERETT	F	1	271	PHILIP	E	1	271	PHILLIPS	E	9	321	PHILLIPS	H	11	298
PEVERITT	BW	7	305	PHILIP	J	11	298	PHILLIPS	E	9	321	PHILLIPS	H	11	298
PEVITT	CH	14	249	PHILIP	R	1	271	PHILLIPS	E	10	349	PHILLIPS	H	12	368
PEVITT	H	14	249	PHILIPS	FW	5	273	PHILLIPS	EA	3	169	PHILLIPS	H	13	341
PEVITT	J	14	249	PHILIPS	WF	5	273	PHILLIPS	EA	3	170	PHILLIPS	H	14	249
PEVRELL	A	5	273	PHILIPS	WH	5	273	PHILLIPS	EA	7	306	PHILLIPS	H	14	249
PEXTON	AWG	10	349	PHILIPSON	JW	10	349	PHILLIPS	EA	13	341	PHILLIPS	HB	12	179
PEXTON	CW	10	349	PHILLIMORE	AH	7	305	PHILLIPS	EC	2	266	PHILLIPS	HC	6	319
PEYTON	F	6	319	PHILLIMORE	CH	4	299	PHILLIPS	EC	10	349	PHILLIPS	HE	4	300
PEYTON	GH	1	271	PHILLIMORE	H	4	299	PHILLIPS	EE	6	319	PHILLIPS	HG	1	272
PEYTON	J	14	249	PHILLIMORE	HD	7	306	PHILLIPS	EG	13	341	PHILLIPS	HJ	10	179
PEZET	A	1	271	PHILLINGHAM	A	11	298	PHILLIPS	EJ	13	341	PHILLIPS	HJ	13	341
PHAFF	CE	1	271	PHILLINGHAM	H	11	298	PHILLIPS	EO	3	170	PHILLIPS	HJ	13	341
PHAIR	R	11	297	PHILLINGHAM	J	11	298	PHILLIPS	ES	10	349	PHILLIPS	HW	3	170
PHAROAH	E	10	178	PHILLINGHAM	J	11	298	PHILLIPS	ET	12	179	PHILLIPS	HWJ	6	320
PHAROAH	SV	10	178	PHILLINGHAM	P	11	298	PHILLIPS	F	1	271	PHILLIPS	I	14	249
PHAUP	W	11	297	PHILLIP	A	11	298	PHILLIPS	F	2	266	PHILLIPS	IC	6	320
PHEASANT	A	5	273	PHILLIPS	A	1	271	PHILLIPS	F	6	319	PHILLIPS	IE	8	265
PHEASEY	JE	11	297	PHILLIPS	A	1	271	PHILLIPS	F	7	306	PHILLIPS	J	2	266
PHEASEY	T	11	297	PHILLIPS	A	6	319	PHILLIPS	F	11	298	PHILLIPS	J	4	300
PHEBY	JG	1	271	PHILLIPS	A	6	319	PHILLIPS	F	13	341	PHILLIPS	J	6	320
PHEBY	W	3	169	PHILLIPS	A	7	306	PHILLIPS	FC	2	266	PHILLIPS	J	6	320
PHELAN	A	8	265	PHILLIPS	A	7	306	PHILLIPS	FE	13	341	PHILLIPS	J	6	320
PHELAN	DD	11	297	PHILLIPS	A	12	367	PHILLIPS	FF	13	341	PHILLIPS	J	6	320
PHELAN	G	9	151	PHILLIPS	A	13	341	PHILLIPS	FG	1	271	PHILLIPS	J	6	320
PHELAN	GH	2	266	PHILLIPS	AA	13	341	PHILLIPS	FJ	4	299	PHILLIPS	J	7	306
PHELAN	J	11	297	PHILLIPS	AE	1	271	PHILLIPS	FL	13	341	PHILLIPS	J	7	306
PHELAN	J	14	249	PHILLIPS	AE	1	271	PHILLIPS	FS	1	271	PHILLIPS	J	9	321
PHELAN	J	14	249	PHILLIPS	AE	4	299	PHILLIPS	FT	1	272	PHILLIPS	J	11	298
PHELAN	JH	9	151	PHILLIPS	AE	10	178	PHILLIPS	FT	10	178	PHILLIPS	J	13	342

PHILLIPS	J	13	342	PHILLIPS	W	12	179	PHILPS	AC	4	300	PICKARD	G	6	321
PHILLIPS	J	13	342	PHILLIPS	W	13	342	PHILPS	CE	4	300	PICKARD	G	7	307
PHILLIPS	J	14	250	PHILLIPS	W	14	250	PHILPS	G	4	300	PICKARD	H	8	265
PHILLIPS	JA	3	170	PHILLIPS	W	14	250	PHILPS	GB	4	300	PICKARD	H	9	321
PHILLIPS	JA	8	265	PHILLIPS	W	14	250	PHILPS	JV	4	300	PICKARD	HE	3	171
PHILLIPS	JA	12	179	PHILLIPS	W	14	250	PHINBOW	FW	7	307	PICKARD	J	6	321
PHILLIPS	JE	13	342	PHILLIPS	WA	13	342	PHIPPEN	L	12	368	PICKARD	R	13	343
PHILLIPS	JG	6	320	PHILLIPS	WA	13	342	PHIPPEN	W	9	321	PICKARD	S	8	266
PHILLIPS	JH	6	320	PHILLIPS	WB	4	300	PHIPPS	A	6	321	PICKARD	VG	3	171
PHILLIPS	JH	7	306	PHILLIPS	WC	4	300	PHIPPS	A	11	298	PICKARD	W	6	321
PHILLIPS	JL	12	368	PHILLIPS	WC	10	349	PHIPPS	A	12	368	PICKARD	W	8	266
PHILLIPS	JM	2	266	PHILLIPS	WF	7	306	PHIPPS	A	12	368	PICKARD	W	9	321
PHILLIPS	JT	6	320	PHILLIPS	WG	2	267	PHIPPS	A	12	368	PICKARD	WV	3	171
PHILLIPS	JT	14	250	PHILLIPS	WH	3	170	PHIPPS	AE	13	342	PICKARD	WWO	3	171
PHILLIPS	JW	7	306	PHILLIPS	WH	4	300	PHIPPS	AG	3	170	PICKBUR	C	11	299
PHILLIPS	M	9	321	PHILLIPS	WH	7	306	PHIPPS	AJ	2	267	PICKBURN	JW	7	307
PHILLIPS	P	9	151	PHILLIPS	WH	10	349	PHIPPS	AP	3	170	PICKEN	WE	7	307
PHILLIPS	PR	10	179	PHILLIPS	WJ	2	267	PHIPPS	AT	8	265	PICKER	F	11	299
PHILLIPS	PW	8	265	PHILLIPS	WJ	13	342	PHIPPS	C	7	307	PICKER	WT	11	299
PHILLIPS	RH	14	250	PHILLIPS	WJV	7	307	PHIPPS	C	12	368	PICKERING	A	8	266
PHILLIPS	S	2	266	PHILLIPS	WP	12	179	PHIPPS	G	14	250	PICKERING	A	8	266
PHILLIPS	S	14	250	PHILLIPS	WW	2	267	PHIPPS	H	13	342	PICKERING	A	11	299
PHILLIPS	SA	13	342	PHILLIPS	WW	3	170	PHIPPS	HE	3	170	PICKERING	AE	6	321
PHILLIPS	SH	3	170	PHILLIPSON	E	11	298	PHIPPS	HE	10	349	PICKERING	C	6	321
PHILLIPS	SJ	2	267	PHILLIPSON	F	8	265	PHIPPS	HF	6	321	PICKERING	C	9	151
PHILLIPS	T	6	320	PHILLIPSON	H	11	298	PHIPPS	HR	1	272	PICKERING	C	12	179
PHILLIPS	T	6	320	PHILLIPSON	H	11	298	PHIPPS	HT	7	307	PICKERING	CF	9	321
PHILLIPS	T	6	320	PHILLIS	A	8	265	PHIPPS	J	13	342	PICKERING	DG	5	274
PHILLIPS	T	6	320	PHILLIS	H	8	265	PHIPPS	R	6	321	PICKERING	E	2	267
PHILLIPS	TC	13	342	PHILLIS	H	8	265	PHIPPS	R	13	342	PICKERING	E	6	321
PHILLIPS	TD	3	170	PHILLIS	W	8	265	PHIPPS	T	6	321	PICKERING	E	11	299
PHILLIPS	TE	13	342	PHILLPOT	C	1	272	PHIPPS	T	6	321	PICKERING	F	5	274
PHILLIPS	TH	2	266	PHILLPOTT	FA	12	368	PHIPPS	T	13	342	PICKERING	F	9	321
PHILLIPS	TH	3	170	PHILLPOTT	JE	2	267	PHIPPS	W	6	321	PICKERING	F	14	250
PHILLIPS	TH	11	298	PHILLPOTT	WG	10	179	PHIPPS	W	11	299	PICKERING	FK	12	179
PHILLIPS	TH	14	250	PHILP	FL	1	272	PHIPPS	WA	3	171	PICKERING	FL	12	368
PHILLIPS	TJ	2	267	PHILP	G	3	170	PHIPPS	WH	6	321	PICKERING	FT	12	368
PHILLIPS	TW	2	267	PHILP	GH	10	179	PHIPSON	W	11	299	PICKERING	G	9	151
PHILLIPS	VR	12	179	PHILP	H	3	170	PHOENIX	E	11	299	PICKERING	G	9	151
PHILLIPS	W	1	272	PHILP	HJ	10	179	PIBWORTH	AS	1	272	PICKERING	H	6	321
PHILLIPS	W	1	272	PHILPOT	EW	10	349	PIBWORTH	CH	13	342	PICKERING	H	8	266
PHILLIPS	W	2	267	PHILPOT	HJ	1	272	PIBWORTH	FA	10	349	PICKERING	H	9	321
PHILLIPS	W	2	267	PHILPOT	HR	12	368	PICK	GF	13	343	PICKERING	H	12	179
PHILLIPS	W	2	267	PHILPOT	RA	1	272	PICK	HC	13	343	PICKERING	HH	13	343
PHILLIPS	W	3	170	PHILPOT	WJ	13	342	PICK	JJ	8	265	PICKERING	J	4	300
PHILLIPS	W	3	170	PHILPOTT	AE	4	300	PICK	RA	13	343	PICKERING	J	4	300
PHILLIPS	W	6	320	PHILPOTT	AG	13	342	PICK	W	9	321	PICKERING	J	6	322
PHILLIPS	W	6	320	PHILPOTT	AW	5	274	PICK	WJ	6	321	PICKERING	J	14	250
PHILLIPS	W	6	321	PHILPOTT	FT	5	273	PICKARD	A	6	321	PICKERING	JE	5	274
PHILLIPS	W	6	321	PHILPOTT	GA	3	170	PICKARD	A	8	265	PICKERING	JF	5	274
PHILLIPS	W	7	306	PHILPOTT	H	7	307	PICKARD	A	14	250	PICKERING	S	11	299
PHILLIPS	W	9	151	PHILPOTT	HC	5	274	PICKARD	BR	8	265	PICKERING	T	6	322
PHILLIPS	W	10	179	PHILPOTT	J	7	307	PICKARD	D	3	171	PICKERING	T	12	179
PHILLIPS	W	11	298	PHILPOTT	SH	4	300	PICKARD	F	6	321	PICKERING	W	8	266
				PHILPOTT	SP	2	267	PICKARD	F	9	321	PICKERING	W	12	179
				PHILPOTT	WGD	4	300								

PICKERING	W	13	343	PICKLES	C	9	321	PIDGEON	W	1	272	PIKE	DV	1	272
PICKERING	WG	10	179	PICKLES	E	8	266	PIERCE	CH	3	171	PIKE	E	2	268
PICKERING	WH	1	272	PICKLES	E	14	250	PIERCE	HP	13	343	PIKE	E	7	308
PICKERING	WH	8	266	PICKLES	F	8	266	PIERCE	J	8	266	PIKE	E	13	343
PICKERNELL	H	3	171	PICKLES	F	9	321	PIERCE	JJ	3	171	PIKE	EC	7	308
PICKERSGILL	A	8	266	PICKLES	G	9	151	PIERCE	R	8	267	PIKE	F	5	275
PICKERSGILL	A	12	368	PICKLES	GH	9	321	PIERCE	T	11	299	PIKE	GG	7	308
PICKERSGILL	AE	8	266	PICKLES	GW	9	151	PIERCE	W	11	299	PIKE	GJ	13	343
PICKERSGILL	AG	6	322	PICKLES	H	9	321	PIERCE	WE	5	274	PIKE	GW	8	267
PICKERSGILL	E	8	266	PICKLES	H	9	321	PIERCE	WE	13	343	PIKE	HA	7	308
PICKERSGILL	G	6	322	PICKLES	H	9	321	PIERCY	WG	12	180	PIKE	J	6	322
PICKERSGILL	G	8	266	PICKLES	J	8	266	PIERPOINT	A	14	251	PIKE	J	6	322
PICKERSGILL	J	8	266	PICKLES	J	9	151	PIERPOINT	H	6	322	PIKE	J	7	308
PICKERSGILL	ST	6	322	PICKLES	J	9	152	PIERPOINT	JH	7	307	PIKE	JA	7	308
PICKERSGILL	W	8	266	PICKLES	J	14	251	PIERSON	C	9	322	PIKE	JT	6	322
PICKET	W	9	321	PICKLES	L	9	321	PIERSON	E	4	301	PIKE	JW	7	308
PICKETT	A	4	300	PICKLES	L	14	251	PIERSON	GH	4	301	PIKE	JWK	5	275
PICKETT	CT	4	301	PICKLES	R	8	266	PIESLEY	J	3	171	PIKE	L	7	308
PICKETT	FW	1	272	PICKLES	R	9	322	PIESLEY	M	3	171	PIKE	M	10	179
PICKETT	HH	4	301	PICKLES	R	11	299	PIESSE	ES	2	268	PIKE	NF	7	308
PICKETT	HP	4	301	PICKLES	S	9	152	PIESSE	WC	2	268	PIKE	P	10	179
PICKETT	NE	4	301	PICKLES	S	9	152	PIGDEN	R	7	307	PIKE	R	6	322
PICKETT	OR	4	301	PICKLES	T	9	322	PIGDEN	R	7	307	PIKE	RJ	7	308
PICKETT	PE	3	171	PICKLES	TA	9	152	PIGGIN	FG	10	179	PIKE	RT	7	308
PICKETTS	WJ	2	267	PICKLES	W	9	152	PIGGITT	W	3	171	PIKE	S	2	268
PICKFORD	A	12	368	PICKLES	W	9	322	PIGGOTT	A	5	274	PIKE	S	6	322
PICKFORD	C	12	368	PICKLES	W	9	322	PIGGOTT	AW	3	171	PIKE	TA	10	179
PICKFORD	CE	14	250	PICKLES	WR	8	266	PIGGOTT	AW	3	171	PIKE	TW	10	179
PICKFORD	CF	12	368	PICKNELL	J	2	268	PIGGOTT	E	5	275	PIKE	W	2	268
PICKFORD	ED	11	299	PICKRELL	EW	4	301	PIGGOTT	F	5	274	PIKE	W	14	251
PICKFORD	G	14	250	PICKRELL	WH	13	343	PIGGOTT	H	5	274	PIKE	WB	3	172
PICKFORD	J	11	299	PICKSTOCK	PG	7	307	PIGGOTT	J	3	171	PIKE	WC	4	301
PICKFORD	J	12	368	PICKSTOCK	TH	7	307	PIGGOTT	J	5	275	PIKE	WC	13	343
PICKFORD	JF	7	307	PICKSTONE	H	14	251	PIGGOTT	J	12	180	PIKE	WR	13	343
PICKFORD	L	12	368	PICKSTONE	WJ	10	179	PIGGOTT	R	3	171	PIKE	WT	1	272
PICKFORD	RJ	14	250	PICKTHALL	W	9	152	PIGGOTT	RB	5	275	PIKETT	A	1	272
PICKFORD	S	2	267	PICKUP	A	9	322	PIGGOTT	T	11	299	PIKETT	A	3	172
PICKFORD	S	14	250	PICKUP	A	14	251	PIGGOTT	TJ	2	268	PIKETT	W	3	172
PICKFORD	W	12	368	PICKUP	J	8	266	PIGGOTT	WA	3	171	PILBEAM	AE	2	268
PICKFORD	WH	12	368	PICKUP	JH	9	322	PIGHTLING	EW	1	272	PILBEAM	AE	3	172
PICKFORD	WJ	6	322	PICKUP	T	3	171	PIGNON	AE	13	343	PILBEAM	AE	13	343
PICKHAVER	HG	2	267	PICTON	A	5	274	PIGOTT	E	13	343	PILBEAM	AJ	3	172
PICKHAVER	W	2	267	PICTON	B	5	274	PIGOTT	EF	7	307	PILBEAM	FA	3	172
PICKIN	D	5	274	PICTON	C	5	274	PIGOTT	RC	6	322	PILBEAM	G	3	172
PICKIN	D	5	274	PICTON	EH	7	307	PIGRAM	C	2	268	PILBEAM	G	3	172
PICKING	HJ	7	307	PICTON	GG	5	274	PIGRUM	TA	2	268	PILBEAM	GE	3	172
PICKINS	HF	11	299	PICTON	H	5	274	PIGUET	CR	7	307	PILBEAM	JF	3	383
PICKLE	M	14	250	PICTON	H	5	274	PIGUET	F	2	268	PILBEAM	N	3	172
PICKLES	A	8	266	PICTON	S	5	274	PIKE	A	1	272	PILBEAM	SA	7	308
PICKLES	A	9	151	PICTON	W	5	274	PIKE	A	14	251	PILBEAM	TH	3	172
PICKLES	A	9	151	PIDDELL	AE	10	179	PIKE	AA	3	172	PILBEAN	CJ	2	268
PICKLES	A	9	321	PIDDINGTON	G	4	301	PIKE	AJ	4	301	PILBEAN	F	2	268
PICKLES	A	9	391	PIDDINGTON	T	4	301	PIKE	AJH	10	179	PILBEAN	J	2	268
PICKLES	AE	8	266	PIDDOCK	FD	7	307	PIKE	C	4	301	PILBOROUGH	AO	10	179
PICKLES	C	9	151	PIDGEON	T	1	272	PIKE	C	11	299	PILBRO	CF	2	268

PILBRO	HS	2	268	PIMBLETT	JE	14	251	PING	FG	5	275	PINNINGTON	G	10	180
PILBROW	F	2	268	PIMBLOTT	G	14	251	PINHORN	HJ	10	180	PINNOCK	AF	5	275
PILBROW	J	7	308	PIMLATT	W	14	251	PINHORNE	GS	10	180	PINNOCK	CS	5	275
PILCH	AE	3	172	PIMLETT	WH	11	300	PINHORNE	JH	10	180	PINNOCK	H	1	273
PILCHER	CE	4	301	PIMLEY	C	14	251	PINHORNE	SH	10	180	PINNOCK	H	3	173
PILCHER	G	10	179	PIMLOTT	H	11	300	PINHORNE	WT	10	180	PINNOCK	LD	5	276
PILCHER	HG	5	275	PIMLOTT	H	11	300	PINK	A	3	172	PINNOCK	PG	5	276
PILCHER	J	4	301	PIMLOTT	R	11	300	PINK	A	10	180	PINOCK	PJ	5	276
PILCHER	JRH	10	349	PIMLY	J	11	300	PINK	AJ	2	269	PINWILL	W	10	181
PILCHER	PA	10	179	PIMM	E	6	323	PINK	CJ	8	267	PIPE	HG	13	344
PILCHER	SA	10	179	PIMM	H	2	268	PINK	E	10	349	PIPE	HS	7	309
PILCHER	SG	7	308	PIMM	H	6	323	PINK	EG	4	302	PIPE	WL	8	267
PILCHER	SL	10	349	PIMM	H	6	323	PINK	ET	7	309	PIPER	A	4	302
PILCHER	WAS	10	180	PIMM	JJ	7	308	PINK	FC	10	180	PIPER	AF	1	273
PILE	AE	4	301	PIMM	WF	5	275	PINK	H	4	302	PIPER	AF	3	173
PILE	AE	10	180	PIMM	WJ	5	275	PINK	J	4	302	PIPER	AG	10	181
PILE	AHE	2	268	PINCHBECK	CH	12	180	PINK	JE	4	302	PIPER	AH	2	269
PILE	AW	4	301	PINCHBECK	HW	6	323	PINK	PH	2	269	PIPER	AJ	13	344
PILE	EA	2	268	PINCHBECK	J	7	308	PINK	T	3	172	PIPER	AW	4	302
PILE	ER	4	301	PINCHES	A	8	267	PINK	VH	10	180	PIPER	BFJ	1	273
PILE	GH	6	322	PINCHES	AW	6	323	PINK	W	4	302	PIPER	BFJ	3	173
PILE	HJ	4	301	PINCHES	GE	7	309	PINK	W	4	302	PIPER	EP	4	302
PILE	L	10	180	PINCHES	H	10	180	PINK	WA	4	302	PIPER	F	4	302
PILGRIM	AG	5	275	PINCHES	J	10	180	PINK	WFG	10	350	PIPER	F	6	323
PILGRIM	C	5	275	PINCHES	T	10	180	PINK	WG	2	269	PIPER	F	6	323
PILGRIM	CF	13	343	PINCHES	TR	14	251	PINKARD	A	12	369	PIPER	G	6	323
PILGRIM	CR	7	308	PINCKARD	W	12	369	PINKARD	A	12	369	PIPER	GA	2	269
PILGRIM	GO	4	301	PINCOMBE	H	4	302	PINKARD	P	12	369	PIPER	H	4	302
PILGRIM	H	5	275	PINDARD	T	13	343	PINKER	FR	10	180	PIPER	H	6	323
PILGRIM	H	12	180	PINDER	A	8	267	PINKERTON	C	2	269	PIPER	HE	7	309
PILGRIM	HW	13	343	PINDER	A	11	300	PINKNEY	D	9	322	PIPER	HF	2	269
PILGRIM	LJ	7	308	PINDER	AJ	13	344	PINKNEY	D	11	300	PIPER	HJ	1	273
PILGRIM	P	12	180	PINDER	E	9	152	PINKNEY	J	9	322	PIPER	HJ	3	173
PILGRIM	R	4	302	PINDER	EW	13	344	PINKS	JBC	13	344	PIPER	L	6	323
PILGRIM	WG	5	275	PINDER	G	9	152	PINKS	JT	13	344	PIPER	P	4	302
PILKINGTON	C	4	302	PINDER	H	8	267	PINKS	T	13	344	PIPER	PEG	1	273
PILKINGTON	E	9	391	PINDER	J	7	309	PINKSTONE	WTC	10	350	PIPER	PEG	3	173
PILKINGTON	JH	8	267	PINDER	J	14	251	PINKUS	H	2	269	PIPER	PF	2	269
PILKINGTON	JH	9	391	PINDER	JH	7	309	PINN	ZTV	7	309	PIPER	W	14	251
PILKINGTON	WT	14	251	PINDER	JT	9	152	PINNEGAR	AE	13	344	PIPER	WC	10	350
PILL	J	12	180	PINDER	R	8	267	PINNEGAR	J	13	344	PIPER	WE	12	369
PILL	W	10	180	PINDER	S	14	251	PINNEGAR	J	13	344	PIPER	WF	1	273
PILLING	JH	11	299	PINDER	SH	11	300	PINNELL	FG	1	273	PIPER	WF	3	173
PILLING	T	14	251	PINDER	TH	11	300	PINNELL	FG	3	172	PIPER	WJ	7	309
PILLING	W	11	300	PINDER	W	8	267	PINNELL	SC	1	273	PIPKIN	F	5	276
PILLINGER	F	6	322	PINDRED	GF	12	180	PINNELL	SC	1	273	PIPKIN	G	7	309
PILLINGER	H	6	322	PINE	F	3	172	PINNELL	SC	3	172	PIPKIN	J	5	276
PILLINGER	L	6	322	PINE	W	3	172	PINNELL	SC	3	172	PIPKIN	J	5	276
PILLINGER	RC	9	152	PINE	WHT	5	275	PINNER	E	3	173	PIPKIN	J	12	180
PILLINGER	WF	6	322	PINFIELD	D	6	323	PINNER	HC	2	269	PIPKIN	JH	6	323
PILNICK	H	6	322	PINFIELD	FJ	3	172	PINNER	S	6	323	PIPPARD	G	7	309
PILSBURY	AE	12	369	PINFIELD	G	6	323	PINNER	WD	3	173	PIPPEN	TF	7	309
PILSBURY	F	12	369	PINFIELD	HF	12	369	PINNEY	J	5	275	PIPPET	MA	4	302
PILSTON	H	11	300	PING	AA	12	180	PINNEY	W	5	275	PIPPETT	EW	2	269
PIMBLETT	AE	11	300	PING	ASE	12	180	PINNINGTON	EF	7	309	PIPPIN	AW	13	344

PIRAWSKY	I	14	251	PITT	AK	3	174	PITTMAN	J	13	344	PLASKETT	EF	10	350
PIRRAH	L	9	322	PITT	AW	12	369	PITTS	A	9	322	PLASKETT	GA	10	350
PITCHER	A	4	302	PITT	E	3	174	PITTS	AC	12	180	PLASKETT	HW	3	174
PITCHER	AT	3	173	PITT	E	3	174	PITTS	AE	12	180	PLASKETT	J	4	303
PITCHER	D	3	173	PITT	E	13	344	PITTS	B	12	180	PLASKETT	J	4	303
PITCHER	F	2	269	PITT	EG	6	323	PITTS	CW	3	174	PLASTOW	E	10	181
PITCHER	FJ	2	269	PITT	F	12	369	PITTS	E	1	273	PLATER	CB	5	276
PITCHER	GC	4	302	PITT	FJ	7	309	PITTS	E	13	344	PLATER	F	13	345
PITCHER	HG	3	173	PITT	FW	7	309	PITTS	EB	8	267	PLATER	WF	5	276
PITCHER	JE	7	309	PITT	G	6	323	PITTS	F	9	322	PLATFORD	AE	2	270
PITCHER	L	3	173	PITT	GE	10	181	PITTS	F	9	322	PLATFORD	C	3	174
PITCHER	M	3	173	PITT	GJ	3	174	PITTS	F	12	369	PLATT	A	8	267
PITCHER	W	5	276	PITT	HC	7	309	PITTS	G	8	267	PLATT	A	11	301
PITCHER	WA	1	273	PITT	HT	3	174	PITTS	G	8	267	PLATT	A	11	301
PITCHER	WA	3	173	PITT	HW	1	273	PITTS	G	9	152	PLATT	C	2	270
PITCHER	WA	3	173	PITT	J	6	323	PITTS	H	3	383	PLATT	C	14	252
PITCHERS	J	9	152	PITT	JA	4	303	PITTS	H	8	267	PLATT	D	11	301
PITCHFORD	H	8	267	PITT	JC	3	174	PITTS	H	12	180	PLATT	E	11	301
PITCHFORTH	H	9	322	PITT	JL	4	303	PITTS	H	13	344	PLATT	FW	3	175
PITCHLEY	H	7	309	PITT	JO	6	324	PITTS	HJ	1	273	PLATT	G	6	324
PITE	EJ	3	173	PITT	JT	6	324	PITTS	J	8	267	PLATT	HWG	13	345
PITE	GF	3	173	PITT	M	1	273	PITTS	JW	3	174	PLATT	J	5	276
PITE	RH	3	173	PITT	R	6	324	PITTS	JW	3	174	PLATT	J	6	324
PITFIELD	W	1	273	PITT	RF	3	174	PITTS	M	9	152	PLATT	J	11	301
PITHER	F	1	273	PITT	S	8	267	PITTS	O	8	267	PLATT	J	11	301
PITHER	F	3	173	PITT	SA	3	174	PITTS	SH	3	174	PLATT	J	11	301
PITHER	J	1	273	PITT	SH	3	174	PITTS	W	11	300	PLATT	J	11	301
PITHER	J	3	173	PITT	T	6	324	PITTS	W	12	180	PLATT	JJ	9	152
PITHER	SR	2	269	PITT	TA	4	303	PITTS	WC	12	180	PLATT	LT	7	310
PITHER	WJ	1	273	PITT	W	4	303	PITTS	WJ	5	276	PLATT	M	14	252
PITHER	WJ	3	174	PITT	WG	7	310	PITTS	WR	1	274	PLATT	PA	3	175
PITKIN	AG	3	174	PITT	WO	1	273	PITTUCK	AE	1	274	PLATT	R	14	252
PITKIN	E	5	276	PITTAM	B	12	369	PIVAWSKI	A	14	252	PLATT	RB	2	270
PITKIN	GC	5	276	PITTAM	E	12	369	PIXLEY	A	12	180	PLATT	T	14	252
PITKIN	HW	3	174	PITTAM	GV	12	180	PIZZEY	C	2	269	PLATT	W	11	301
PITKIN	PC	3	174	PITTAM	HJ	12	369	PIZZIE	KJ	1	274	PLATT	W	14	252
PITKIN	S	12	180	PITTAM	J	6	324	PIZZIE	P	1	274	PLATT	WG	1	274
PITMAN	A	2	269	PITTAM	T	6	324	PLACE	LH	8	267	PLATTEN	C	1	274
PITMAN	A	4	302	PITTAM	WB	12	369	PLACKETT	J	12	369	PLATTS	F	8	267
PITMAN	AW	1	273	PITTARD	J	7	310	PLAISTED	H	13	344	PLATTS	G	8	268
PITMAN	AW	3	174	PITTAWAY	A	6	324	PLAITER	HR	11	300	PLATTS	JR	9	322
PITMAN	E	4	302	PITTAWAY	A	6	324	PLAITER	J	11	300	PLATTS	T	7	310
PITMAN	EJ	4	303	PITTAWAY	D	6	324	PLANK	EJ	2	270	PLATTS	W	8	268
PITMAN	FH	2	269	PITTAWAY	FR	6	324	PLANT	AE	4	303	PLATUS	N	8	268
PITMAN	FH	4	303	PITTAWAY	H	13	344	PLANT	C	14	252	PLAW	HW	1	274
PITMAN	FJ	4	303	PITTAWAY	P	13	344	PLANT	E	6	324	PLAWRIGHT	JG	12	369
PITMAN	G	7	309	PITTAWAY	WE	6	324	PLANT	F	14	252	PLAYER	EC	1	274
PITMAN	HN	10	350	PITTERS	CH	4	303	PLANT	G	5	276	PLAYER	EW	10	181
PITMAN	RHE	10	181	PITTERS	CH	4	303	PLANT	G	14	252	PLAYER	WF	13	345
PITMAN	S	11	300	PITTERS	FG	4	303	PLANT	H	8	267	PLAYFORD	E	8	268
PITMAN	SC	4	303	PITTERS	TF	4	303	PLANT	HE	1	274	PLAYFORD	F	4	303
PITMAN	W	10	350	PITTKIN	HG	3	174	PLANT	J	6	324	PLAYFORD	G	2	270
PITMAN	WG	2	269	PITTKIN	HI	3	174	PLANT	J	11	300	PLAYFORD	J	2	270
PITT	AE	6	323	PITTMAN	AE	7	310	PLANT	J	11	301	PLAYFORD	W	2	270
PITT	AF	2	269	PITTMAN	AG	13	344	PLANT	W	4	303	PLAYLE	WH	1	274

PLAYTER	PT	13	345	PLUMB	J	3	383	POCOCK	BJJ	5	277	POLGLAZE	W	7	311
PLEACE	WS	10	181	PLUMB	J	6	324	POCOCK	C	1	274	POLHILL	T	10	350
PLEASANTS	R	5	276	PLUMB	P	13	345	POCOCK	C	13	345	POLINSKY	S	14	252
PLEDGE	BS	10	181	PLUMBLY	S	3	175	POCOCK	CD	7	311	POLL	EA	6	325
PLEDGER	CE	1	274	PLUME	A	3	175	POCOCK	DS	3	175	POLL	J	2	270
PLEDGER	FA	3	175	PLUME	GT	1	274	POCOCK	FJ	9	322	POLLARD	A	5	277
PLEDGER	HE	3	175	PLUMER	JH	2	270	POCOCK	G	3	175	POLLARD	A	7	311
PLEDGER	O	3	175	PLUMERIDGE	AM	1	274	POCOCK	G	9	322	POLLARD	A	9	322
PLESTER	JG	5	276	PLUMERIDGE	CF	1	274	POCOCK	G	9	322	POLLARD	AE	1	275
PLEVEY	J	6	324	PLUMLEY	DLVE	4	304	POCOCK	GA	13	345	POLLARD	AG	1	275
PLEWS	A	9	152	PLUMLEY	E	6	324	POCOCK	H	5	277	POLLARD	AH	4	305
PLEWS	C	9	152	PLUMLEY	EJ	2	270	POCOCK	HJ	13	345	POLLARD	AH	12	370
PLEWS	E	4	303	PLUMLEY	EJ	4	304	POCOCK	N	3	175	POLLARD	C	5	277
PLEWS	G	8	268	PLUMLEY	JO	5	277	POCOCK	T	1	275	POLLARD	C	9	323
PLEWS	P	4	303	PLUMMER	A	3	175	POCOCK	WAS	3	175	POLLARD	E	5	277
PLEWS	T	4	303	PLUMMER	CW	7	310	POCOCK	WH	5	277	POLLARD	ER	13	345
PLEWS	TA	4	303	PLUMMER	E	3	175	POCOCK	WT	1	275	POLLARD	F	8	268
PLEWS	WE	4	304	PLUMMER	E	5	277	PODESTA	A	8	268	POLLARD	F	9	152
PLIMMER	J	11	301	PLUMMER	G	13	345	PODESTA	H	4	304	POLLARD	F	9	323
PLIMMER	T	3	175	PLUMMER	H	7	310	PODESTA	J	4	304	POLLARD	FJ	2	270
PLOERIGHT	J	7	310	PLUMMER	J	3	175	PODESTA	R	8	268	POLLARD	FT	13	345
PLOMER	CT	10	350	PLUMMER	J	10	350	PODMORE	G	2	270	POLLARD	FW	1	275
PLOMER	H	4	304	PLUMMER	RH	7	310	PODMORE	JE	8	268	POLLARD	G	9	152
PLOMER	MC	4	304	PLUMMER	S	10	350	PODMORE	JE	8	268	POLLARD	H	8	268
PLONSKY	M	14	252	PLUMMER	SH	1	274	PODMORE	SP	14	252	POLLARD	H	9	152
PLOWMAN	A	12	369	PLUMMER	W	1	274	POETT	G	3	176	POLLARD	H	9	323
PLOWMAN	BH	12	369	PLUMMER	W	7	310	POFF	GG	11	301	POLLARD	J	7	311
PLOWMAN	FG	4	304	PLUMMER	W	11	301	POFFLEY	EJ	10	181	POLLARD	J	9	153
PLOWMAN	G	4	304	PLUMMER	WE	4	304	POGRAND	S	8	268	POLLARD	J	14	252
PLOWMAN	GH	4	304	PLUMPTON	CW	10	181	POGSON	CW	8	268	POLLARD	JA	2	271
PLOWMAN	HL	13	345	PLUMPTON	WE	11	301	POGSON	G	9	322	POLLARD	JS	3	176
PLOWMAN	J	12	370	PLUMRIDGE	AD	1	274	POHLER	EE	2	270	POLLARD	JW	5	277
PLOWMAN	W	10	181	PLUMRIDGE	AH	10	181	POIL	FW	4	304	POLLARD	JW	9	153
PLOWMAN	W	12	370	PLUMRIDGE	J	1	274	POINTER	CF	4	304	POLLARD	P	13	345
PLOWMAN	WT	13	345	PLUMSTEAD	HR	10	181	POINTER	H	4	304	POLLARD	R	8	268
PLOWS	C	7	310	PLUNKETT	CW	11	301	POINTER	HV	4	304	POLLARD	R	9	153
PLOWS	CD	7	310	PLUNKETT	E	12	370	POINTER	HW	4	304	POLLARD	R	10	181
PLOWS	J	7	310	PLUNKETT	EJ	3	383	POINTER	WAE	5	277	POLLARD	RH	8	268
PLOWS	W	7	310	PLUNKETT	FEG	12	370	POINTER	WH	4	304	POLLARD	S	9	153
PLUCK	T	13	345	PLUNKETT	GE	11	301	POINTER	WH	4	304	POLLARD	S	9	323
PLUCK	WJ	5	276	PLUNKETT	SR	13	345	POINTER	WT	4	304	POLLARD	S	12	370
PLUCKROSE	H	2	270	PLUNKETT	VR	12	370	POINTIN	FW	4	304	POLLARD	SH	1	275
PLUCKROSE	H	2	270	POBGEE	WG	2	270	POINTING	E	3	176	POLLARD	SJ	6	325
PLUCKROSE	HF	3	175	POCKETT	AW	1	275	POINTING	WG	3	176	POLLARD	W	5	277
PLUCKROSE	J	7	310	POCKETT	G	7	311	POINTON	F	6	325	POLLARD	W	8	268
PLUM	W	5	277	POCKLINGTON	CE	14	252	POINTON	W	11	301	POLLARD	W	8	268
PLUM	WC	3	175	POCKNEE	C	2	270	POISSON	HL	10	350	POLLARD	W	9	323
PLUMB	A	3	175	POCKNEE	F	2	270	POKE	JB	11	301	POLLARD	W	12	370
PLUMB	AG	13	345	POCKNELL	J	3	175	POLAND	CRD	10	181	POLLARD	WA	13	346
PLUMB	AR	5	276	POCKNELL	J	13	345	POLANSKI	L	14	252	POLLARD	WE	1	275
PLUMB	BM	7	310	POCKNELL	TH	13	345	POLDEN	FH	1	275	POLLARD	WGA	1	275
PLUMB	F	2	270	POCOCK	A	7	311	POLE	A	14	252	POLLARD	WJ	10	181
PLUMB	GJ	7	310	POCOCK	AW	3	175	POLE	JH	3	176	POLLECUTT	G	3	176
PLUMB	H	7	310	POCOCK	B	1	274	POLE	TH	1	275	POLLEY	AJ	7	311
PLUMB	H	13	345	POCOCK	BAF	3	175	POLGLAZE	AT	7	311	POLLEY	DG	7	311

POLLEY	FS	7	311	POOLE	A	13	346	POOLE	TJ	11	302	POPE	J	5	277
POLLEY	WJ	7	311	POOLE	AE	6	325	POOLE	W	1	276	POPE	J	7	312
POLLICK	J	14	252	POOLE	AE	10	350	POOLE	W	3	176	POPE	JC	10	182
POLLINGER	J	3	383	POOLE	AJ	12	370	POOLE	W	8	269	POPE	JJ	12	370
POLLINGTON	FG	3	176	POOLE	AS	9	153	POOLE	W	11	302	POPE	JS	7	312
POLLINGTON	J	8	268	POOLE	AT	12	370	POOLE	WA	6	325	POPE	KK	4	305
POLLINGTON	J	8	268	POOLE	AW	10	350	POOLE	WF	7	312	POPE	LA	12	181
POLLITT	A	11	302	POOLE	B	3	176	POOLE	WH	2	271	POPE	LK	4	305
POLLITT	D	14	252	POOLE	C	2	271	POOLE	WH	6	325	POPE	RG	6	325
POLLITT	I	11	302	POOLE	C	2	271	POOLE	WJ	1	276	POPE	RL	6	325
POLLITT	J	14	253	POOLE	D	11	302	POOLE	WJ	4	305	POPE	RW	7	312
POLLITT	J	14	253	POOLE	DW	12	370	POOLEY	A	1	276	POPE	S	10	350
POLLITT	J	14	253	POOLE	E	11	302	POOLEY	A	3	176	POPE	SG	1	276
POLLITT	JDF	7	311	POOLE	E	11	302	POOLEY	AE	1	276	POPE	SJ	10	182
POLLITT	JJ	14	253	POOLE	EW	12	370	POOLEY	AE	5	277	POPE	TB	4	305
POLLITT	W	14	253	POOLE	F	6	325	POOLEY	AH	10	182	POPE	TW	11	302
POLLOCK	A	7	311	POOLE	F	13	346	POOLEY	AH	13	346	POPE	W	4	305
POLLOCK	M	7	311	POOLE	F	14	253	POOLEY	G	1	276	POPE	W	10	182
POLLOCK	SL	7	311	POOLE	FC	1	275	POOLEY	H	4	305	POPE	W	12	181
POLLON	MC	4	305	POOLE	FE	7	312	POOLEY	JR	2	271	POPE	W	14	253
POLTOCK	A	2	271	POOLE	FJ	6	325	POOLEY	S	1	276	POPE	WA	10	182
POLTOCK	TC	1	275	POOLE	GR	2	271	POOLEY	WF	1	276	POPE	WGH	10	182
POLTON	O	1	275	POOLE	GWH	3	176	POOLEY	WT	7	312	POPE	WH	2	271
POLTON	P	1	275	POOLE	HB	2	271	POOLTON	JH	6	325	POPE	WHC	1	276
POMEROY	HA	4	305	POOLE	HC	3	176	POORE	EE	7	312	POPE	WJ	7	313
POMFRET	A	11	302	POOLE	HJ	2	271	POORE	F	7	312	POPE	WJ	10	350
POMFRET	A	14	253	POOLE	HJ	13	346	POORE	HJ	1	276	POPE	WS	13	346
POMFRET	C	7	311	POOLE	HR	12	370	POPAY	GH	14	253	POPEJOY	GE	3	176
POMFRET	WS	7	311	POOLE	J	2	271	POPE	A	1	276	POPLE	CW	1	276
POMFRETT	A	1	275	POOLE	J	2	271	POPE	A	4	305	POPLE	CW	1	276
POMFRETT	HA	1	275	POOLE	J	3	176	POPE	A	7	312	POPLE	HJ	1	276
POMFRETT	J	11	302	POOLE	J	3	176	POPE	A	13	346	POPLE	WA	2	272
POMPHREY	WG	13	346	POOLE	J	7	312	POPE	AE	1	276	POPLETT	AG	10	351
POMROY	G	10	181	POOLE	J	8	268	POPE	AE	8	269	POPLETT	G	2	272
POND	C	2	271	POOLE	J	11	302	POPE	AK	4	305	POPLETT	JJ	3	176
POND	CA	10	181	POOLE	J	12	181	POPE	BW	2	271	POPLETT	T	3	176
POND	EC	12	180	POOLE	JA	6	325	POPE	C	5	277	POPPE	EAF	2	272
PONDER	AE	7	311	POOLE	JE	1	275	POPE	CJ	7	312	POPPLE	H	7	313
PONDER	ECA	7	311	POOLE	JN	9	153	POPE	E	1	276	POPPLE	J	8	269
PONSFORD	BE	4	305	POOLE	JR	6	325	POPE	EC	5	277	POPPLESTONE	JA	8	269
PONSFORD	JC	10	181	POOLE	L	2	271	POPE	FG	1	276	POPPLETON	WE	6	325
PONSFORD	W	10	182	POOLE	L	8	269	POPE	FJ	11	302	POPPLEWELL	WW	6	325
PONSFORD	WH	10	182	POOLE	M	6	325	POPE	G	7	312	PORCH	RF	13	346
PONTEFRACT	R	14	253	POOLE	M	6	325	POPE	G	12	181	PORRELLI	J	9	153
PONTEFRACT	TH	7	312	POOLE	M	8	269	POPE	G	12	181	PORRETT	WEJ	1	276
PONTER	W	2	271	POOLE	M	11	302	POPE	GH	12	370	PORRITT	F	8	269
PONTING	EJ	2	271	POOLE	N	14	253	POPE	H	7	312	PORT	AE	13	346
PONTON	L	10	182	POOLE	PS	13	346	POPE	H	7	312	PORT	C	7	313
POOK	AR	13	346	POOLE	R	7	312	POPE	H	10	182	PORT	HC	13	346
POOK	J	7	312	POOLE	RC	3	176	POPE	H	10	350	PORT	HG	10	182
POOKE	T	7	312	POOLE	RH	3	176	POPE	HC	4	305	PORT	JC	10	182
POOL	FHC	10	182	POOLE	S	1	275	POPE	HC	12	181	PORT	JC	13	346
POOLE	A	1	275	POOLE	SA	1	275	POPE	HH	13	346	PORT	JW	3	176
POOLE	A	2	271	POOLE	T	11	302	POPE	HJ	6	325	PORT	S	7	313
POOLE	A	9	323	POOLE	T	14	253	POPE	HJ	10	182	PORT	T	12	181

PORT	VJ	13	346	PORTER	HH	7	313	POTTER	AW	6	326	POTTER	W	11	303
PORTCH	C	7	313	PORTER	HW	5	277	POTTER	B	8	269	POTTER	W	11	303
PORTEOUS	J	10	351	PORTER	J	1	277	POTTER	BW	6	326	POTTER	WA	4	306
PORTER	A	3	176	PORTER	J	6	326	POTTER	CA	1	277	POTTER	WA	6	326
PORTER	A	3	177	PORTER	J	11	302	POTTER	CC	3	177	POTTER	WF	7	314
PORTER	A	7	313	PORTER	J	13	347	POTTER	CW	11	303	POTTER	WH	6	327
PORTER	AE	4	305	PORTER	JB	4	306	POTTER	DW	5	278	POTTER	WJ	4	306
PORTER	AE	6	325	PORTER	JH	3	177	POTTER	E	3	177	POTTER	WJG	4	306
PORTER	AJ	4	305	PORTER	JH	3	177	POTTER	E	4	306	POTTERELL	FW	7	314
PORTER	AJ	7	313	PORTER	JH	13	346	POTTER	E	5	278	POTTERTON	AE	14	253
PORTER	B	1	276	PORTER	JR	2	272	POTTER	E	14	253	POTTERTON	S	10	351
PORTER	B	2	272	PORTER	JW	7	313	POTTER	EM	4	306	POTTERVELD	EA	7	314
PORTER	B	8	269	PORTER	R	1	277	POTTER	EW	5	278	POTTERVELD	HW	7	314
PORTER	BJ	4	305	PORTER	RC	7	313	POTTER	F	6	326	POTTINGER	WG	1	277
PORTER	C	4	305	PORTER	SJ	4	306	POTTER	F	8	269	POTTLE	A	10	183
PORTER	C	5	277	PORTER	W	3	177	POTTER	F	11	303	POTTLE	FC	4	306
PORTER	C	7	313	PORTER	W	4	306	POTTER	F	12	181	POTTLE	FH	4	306
PORTER	CA	10	182	PORTER	W	4	306	POTTER	FB	3	177	POTTLE	JJ	4	306
PORTER	CB	7	313	PORTER	W	11	302	POTTER	FW	1	277	POTTLE	JW	7	314
PORTER	CD	8	269	PORTER	WC	1	277	POTTER	G	2	272	POTTLE	SJ	4	307
PORTER	CE	8	269	PORTER	WG	3	177	POTTER	G	5	278	POTTLE	SJ	12	181
PORTER	CH	2	272	PORTER	WG	13	347	POTTER	G	8	269	POTTLE	W	4	307
PORTER	CS	2	272	PORTER	WH	3	177	POTTER	G	10	182	POTTON	A	5	278
PORTER	DT	7	313	PORTER	WH	4	306	POTTER	GA	6	326	POTTON	AJ	5	278
PORTER	E	3	177	PORTER	WJ	1	277	POTTER	GF	1	277	POTTON	R	5	278
PORTER	EA	2	272	PORTER	WT	13	347	POTTER	GH	6	326	POTTON	WA	5	278
PORTER	EE	7	313	PORTLOCK	F	6	326	POTTER	GH	7	314	POTTON	WH	5	278
PORTER	EG	2	272	PORTLOCK	T	14	253	POTTER	GH	10	183	POTTS	A	1	277
PORTER	ES	7	313	PORTLOCK	WS	6	326	POTTER	GJ	6	326	POTTS	A	6	327
PORTER	EW	1	276	PORTMAN	A	6	326	POTTER	H	2	272	POTTS	A	9	153
PORTER	F	2	272	PORTMAN	GW	6	326	POTTER	H	3	177	POTTS	AJ	5	278
PORTER	F	3	177	PORTON	H	6	326	POTTER	H	8	269	POTTS	C	14	253
PORTER	F	3	177	PORTSMOUTH	G	1	277	POTTER	H	8	269	POTTS	CT	13	347
PORTER	F	4	305	PORTSMOUTH	G	10	351	POTTER	HF	3	177	POTTS	E	14	254
PORTER	F	7	313	PORTWAIN	W	12	181	POTTER	HJ	12	181	POTTS	E	14	254
PORTER	F	9	323	POSCHA	FA	11	302	POTTER	J	2	272	POTTS	EA	7	314
PORTER	F	14	253	POSFORD	C	4	306	POTTER	J	4	306	POTTS	EW	5	278
PORTER	FC	7	313	POSSEE	AH	7	314	POTTER	J	5	278	POTTS	EW	7	314
PORTER	FE	1	276	POSSEE	EG	6	326	POTTER	J	11	303	POTTS	H	14	254
PORTER	FH	3	177	POSSEE	WC	6	326	POTTER	JA	9	323	POTTS	HW	3	177
PORTER	FW	3	177	POSSEE	WH	6	326	POTTER	JH	1	277	POTTS	J	2	272
PORTER	FW	13	346	POST	AW	3	177	POTTER	JJ	7	314	POTTS	J	11	303
PORTER	G	4	305	POSTILL	HD	11	302	POTTER	JP	11	303	POTTS	J	14	254
PORTER	G	4	305	POSTLES	W	14	253	POTTER	LWG	4	306	POTTS	J	14	254
PORTER	G	5	277	POSTON	GH	9	323	POTTER	N	3	177	POTTS	JG	6	327
PORTER	G	10	182	POTHAN	RA	6	326	POTTER	N	4	306	POTTS	LM	3	178
PORTER	G	11	302	POTHECARY	AE	4	306	POTTER	OA	11	303	POTTS	MH	11	303
PORTER	GA	10	351	POTTAGE	J	9	323	POTTER	PG	4	306	POTTS	NH	3	178
PORTER	GA	13	346	POTTAGE	W	9	153	POTTER	ST	10	183	POTTS	OJ	10	351
PORTER	GW	4	305	POTTER	A	10	182	POTTER	T	8	269	POTTS	R	9	153
PORTER	GW	6	326	POTTER	A	13	347	POTTER	T	14	253	POTTS	R	9	153
PORTER	H	3	177	POTTER	AA	6	326	POTTER	W	1	277	POTTS	R	9	323
PORTER	H	4	306	POTTER	AS	7	314	POTTER	W	3	177	POTTS	R	14	254
PORTER	H	6	326	POTTER	AV	4	306	POTTER	W	8	269	POTTS	S	11	303
PORTER	HFT	13	346	POTTER	AW	4	306	POTTER	W	11	303	POTTS	S	11	303

POTTS	SG	5	278	POULTON	WE	1	278	POWELL	C	3	178	POWELL	J	7	315
POTTS	T	14	254	POUNCEY	M	9	153	POWELL	C	4	307	POWELL	J	7	315
POTTY	EJ	7	314	POUND	A	8	269	POWELL	C	4	307	POWELL	J	8	270
POUILLON	EM	1	277	POUND	CW	13	347	POWELL	C	6	327	POWELL	J	9	323
POUILLON	WAR	1	277	POUND	HJ	3	178	POWELL	C	8	270	POWELL	J	10	183
POULDEN	A	1	277	POUND	IAL	3	178	POWELL	C	8	270	POWELL	J	11	303
POULDEN	A	1	277	POUND	JW	3	178	POWELL	C	10	351	POWELL	J	11	304
POULDEN	F	1	277	POUNDER	F	8	270	POWELL	CH	6	328	POWELL	J	11	304
POULDEN	W	1	277	POUNDER	W	8	270	POWELL	D	6	327	POWELL	J	13	347
POULSOM	EA	2	272	POUNDS	WE	13	347	POWELL	D	6	328	POWELL	JE	5	279
POULSON	AS	1	277	POUNTNEY	A	6	327	POWELL	DE	3	178	POWELL	JE	10	183
POULSON	CA	5	278	POUNTNEY	AH	6	327	POWELL	E	1	278	POWELL	JG	7	315
POULSON	JF	6	327	POUNTNEY	E	9	153	POWELL	E	2	273	POWELL	JH	7	315
POULSON	OF	1	277	POUNTNEY	H	8	270	POWELL	E	4	307	POWELL	JJ	2	273
POULSON	WA	7	314	POUNTNEY	H	9	323	POWELL	E	6	328	POWELL	JJ	13	347
POULTEN	E	4	307	POUNTNEY	W	6	327	POWELL	E	8	270	POWELL	JP	7	315
POULTEN	EE	4	307	POURALLI	J	10	183	POWELL	EA	13	347	POWELL	JR	6	328
POULTEN	SA	4	307	POUT	A	1	278	POWELL	EE	2	273	POWELL	JT	5	279
POULTER	A	3	178	POUT	JJ	1	278	POWELL	EG	5	278	POWELL	JT	5	279
POULTER	AH	7	314	POVAH	T	11	303	POWELL	EH	6	328	POWELL	JW	1	278
POULTER	AH	7	314	POVER	E	14	254	POWELL	ER	5	278	POWELL	JW	13	347
POULTER	AR	3	178	POVER	F	14	254	POWELL	EV	4	307	POWELL	L	7	315
POULTER	AR	8	269	POVEY	A	2	272	POWELL	F	4	307	POWELL	L	8	270
POULTER	C	1	278	POVEY	A	13	347	POWELL	F	4	307	POWELL	LC	11	304
POULTER	FT	7	314	POVEY	C	2	272	POWELL	F	5	279	POWELL	LCA	1	278
POULTER	G	8	269	POVEY	EG	2	272	POWELL	F	9	323	POWELL	LL	4	307
POULTER	HJ	2	272	POVEY	GH	10	183	POWELL	F	10	183	POWELL	M	4	308
POULTER	HS	3	178	POVEY	H	11	303	POWELL	FG	4	307	POWELL	P	11	304
POULTER	HW	1	278	POVEY	JH	7	315	POWELL	FW	10	351	POWELL	P	12	370
POULTER	HW	3	178	POVEY	JT	6	327	POWELL	G	1	278	POWELL	PE	10	183
POULTER	J	8	269	POVEY	L	2	272	POWELL	G	2	273	POWELL	PH	1	278
POULTER	JE	9	153	POWELL	A	6	327	POWELL	G	4	307	POWELL	PL	6	328
POULTER	JH	14	254	POWELL	A	6	327	POWELL	G	6	328	POWELL	R	7	315
POULTER	P	10	351	POWELL	A	6	327	POWELL	G	6	328	POWELL	R	8	270
POULTER	PR	5	278	POWELL	A	8	270	POWELL	G	7	315	POWELL	R	9	323
POULTER	SS	9	153	POWELL	A	11	303	POWELL	G	8	270	POWELL	RE	6	328
POULTER	W	8	269	POWELL	A	11	303	POWELL	G	10	183	POWELL	RE	7	315
POULTER	WH	1	278	POWELL	A	13	347	POWELL	G	11	303	POWELL	S	14	254
POULTER	WH	7	314	POWELL	A	14	254	POWELL	GE	11	303	POWELL	SF	5	279
POULTNEY	JG	1	278	POWELL	AC	7	315	POWELL	GH	4	307	POWELL	SJ	10	183
POULTNEY	WI	6	327	POWELL	AE	4	307	POWELL	GW	2	273	POWELL	T	2	273
POULTON	C	7	314	POWELL	AE	6	327	POWELL	H	3	178	POWELL	T	6	328
POULTON	F	5	278	POWELL	AE	12	424	POWELL	H	4	307	POWELL	TEJ	2	273
POULTON	F	14	254	POWELL	AG	4	307	POWELL	H	6	328	POWELL	TP	14	254
POULTON	G	14	254	POWELL	AH	4	307	POWELL	H	7	315	POWELL	TW	1	278
POULTON	J	8	269	POWELL	AH	6	327	POWELL	H	8	270	POWELL	TW	2	273
POULTON	J	12	370	POWELL	AR	6	327	POWELL	H	9	323	POWELL	W	1	278
POULTON	OV	10	183	POWELL	AR	10	183	POWELL	H	12	370	POWELL	W	7	315
POULTON	S	11	303	POWELL	ASW	5	279	POWELL	HC	12	370	POWELL	W	11	304
POULTON	TW	1	278	POWELL	AW	1	278	POWELL	HE	3	383	POWELL	W	11	304
POULTON	W	3	178	POWELL	AW	4	307	POWELL	HH	6	328	POWELL	W	12	370
POULTON	W	3	178	POWELL	AW	7	315	POWELL	HH	13	347	POWELL	WA	1	278
POULTON	W	3	178	POWELL	B	6	327	POWELL	HW	5	279	POWELL	WA	4	308
POULTON	W	6	327	POWELL	B	13	347	POWELL	J	2	273	POWELL	WAG	3	178
POULTON	W	14	254	POWELL	C	2	273	POWELL	J	6	328	POWELL	WC	6	328

POWELL	WE	10	351	POYSER	JG	6	329	PRATT	F	9	324	PRATT	WE	1	279
POWELL	WF	7	315	POYSER	W	14	254	PRATT	F	12	371	PRATT	WF	1	279
POWELL	WG	3	178	POYSNER	S	14	254	PRATT	FC	6	329	PRATT	WF	1	279
POWELL	WG	4	308	PRAGNELL	AF	4	308	PRATT	FC	6	329	PRATT	WG	10	184
POWELL	WG	10	351	PRAGNELL	CF	4	308	PRATT	FJ	5	279	PRATT	WHJ	4	308
POWELL	WGS	3	178	PRAGNELL	E	4	308	PRATT	FJ	12	181	PRATT	WV	6	329
POWELL	WH	7	315	PRAGNELL	F	4	308	PRATT	FM	12	181	PRATTEY	A	6	329
POWELL	WHT	2	273	PRAGNELL	G	4	308	PRATT	G	5	279	PREBBLE	E	5	280
POWELL	WJ	6	328	PRAGNELL	GF	4	308	PRATT	G	5	280	PRECIOUS	F	6	329
POWELL	WR	2	273	PRAGNELL	HA	4	308	PRATT	G	12	371	PRECIOUS	G	8	271
POWER	AE	4	308	PRAGNELL	R	7	316	PRATT	GAB	4	308	PRECIOUS	P	9	324
POWER	C	2	273	PRAGNELL	W	4	308	PRATT	GBH	12	181	PREECE	A	6	329
POWER	CP	12	371	PRAGNELL	WJ	12	371	PRATT	GC	5	280	PREECE	AC	5	280
POWER	E	7	315	PRANGELL	C	13	348	PRATT	GH	11	304	PREECE	E	14	255
POWER	F	11	304	PRANGLEY	E	7	316	PRATT	H	1	279	PREECE	EC	12	371
POWER	FC	7	315	PRANGNELL	AT	3	179	PRATT	H	2	273	PREECE	GI	1	279
POWER	G	11	304	PRANGNELL	H	7	316	PRATT	H	2	273	PREECE	H	2	273
POWER	H	9	153	PRANGNELL	M	4	308	PRATT	H	5	279	PREECE	J	6	329
POWER	J	11	304	PRANKARD	FG	7	316	PRATT	H	5	280	PREECE	M	9	324
POWER	J	13	347	PRATER	CA	2	273	PRATT	H	11	304	PREECE	SJ	5	280
POWER	JJ	13	347	PRATLEY	F	6	329	PRATT	HC	2	273	PREECE	T	4	309
POWER	P	11	304	PRATLEY	P	3	179	PRATT	HF	13	348	PREECE	WJC	12	371
POWER	W	11	304	PRATOR	C	6	329	PRATT	HGM	5	280	PREEDY	FG	1	279
POWER	WM	1	278	PRATT	A	7	316	PRATT	HJ	4	308	PREEDY	H	10	351
POWER	WM	1	279	PRATT	A	8	270	PRATT	J	5	280	PREEDY	JH	11	304
POWIS	E	9	323	PRATT	A	8	270	PRATT	J	7	316	PREEGE	A	9	324
POWIS	E	9	323	PRATT	A	9	324	PRATT	J	8	270	PREIS	AE	5	281
POWIS	FV	6	328	PRATT	AE	3	383	PRATT	J	11	304	PREIST	FCH	1	279
POWIS	HJ	1	279	PRATT	AE	6	329	PRATT	JH	6	329	PRENDEGROSS	J	11	305
POWLES	JA	3	178	PRATT	AH	12	371	PRATT	JH	7	316	PRENDERGAST	A	7	316
POWLEY	F	10	183	PRATT	AJS	10	183	PRATT	JR	9	324	PRENDERGAST	F	13	348
POWLING	WA	13	347	PRATT	AV	12	181	PRATT	JW	5	280	PRENDERGAST	J	11	304
POWNALL	J	14	254	PRATT	AW	5	279	PRATT	ME	5	280	PRENDERGAST	T	11	304
POWNEY	A	8	270	PRATT	AW	5	279	PRATT	N	12	181	PRENDERVILLE	EM	2	273
POWNEY	JW	8	270	PRATT	C	5	279	PRATT	PF	10	183	PRENTICE	AJ	3	179
POWSEY	WH	13	347	PRATT	C	7	316	PRATT	PJ	10	351	PRENTICE	AJ	6	329
POWTER	A	8	270	PRATT	C	8	270	PRATT	PR	3	179	PRENTICE	F	4	309
POWTER	HE	3	178	PRATT	C	9	324	PRATT	PT	1	279	PRENTICE	HW	6	329
POWTER	S	3	178	PRATT	C	12	371	PRATT	R	5	280	PRENTICE	J	3	179
POXTON	RT	13	348	PRATT	C	14	255	PRATT	R	5	280	PRENTICE	JJ	2	273
POXTON	VG	13	347	PRATT	CH	6	329	PRATT	R	5	280	PRENTICE	T	1	279
POYNER	G	6	328	PRATT	CH	13	348	PRATT	RH	4	308	PRENTICE	TD	4	309
POYNER	T	6	328	PRATT	CW	7	316	PRATT	S	5	280	PRENTICE	W	1	279
POYNTER	ANH	3	179	PRATT	E	5	279	PRATT	S	6	329	PRENTICE	W	7	316
POYNTER	FJC	4	308	PRATT	E	5	279	PRATT	SH	5	280	PRENTICE	WHJ	12	181
POYNTER	GW	4	308	PRATT	E	8	270	PRATT	T	6	329	PRESBURY	GT	3	179
POYNTER	J	11	304	PRATT	E	8	270	PRATT	TH	1	279	PRESBURY	HE	3	179
POYNTER	JV	4	308	PRATT	E	10	351	PRATT	VW	5	280	PRESCOTT	G	4	309
POYNTER	S	3	179	PRATT	EA	11	304	PRATT	W	5	280	PRESCOTT	GW	11	305
POYNTER	W	10	183	PRATT	EG	5	279	PRATT	W	5	280	PRESCOTT	J	3	383
POYNTER	WE	7	316	PRATT	EJ	1	279	PRATT	W	5	280	PRESCOTT	J	4	309
POYNTON	A	9	153	PRATT	EW	12	371	PRATT	W	8	270	PRESCOTT	J	14	255
POYNTZ	AW	3	179	PRATT	F	1	279	PRATT	W	10	183	PRESCOTT	SJ	11	305
POYNTZ	RW	3	179	PRATT	F	5	279	PRATT	W	13	348	PRESCOTT	W	9	324
POYSER	J	6	328	PRATT	F	6	329	PRATT	WC	7	316	PRESCOTT	W	14	255

PRESCOTT	W	14	255	PRESTON	G	14	255	PRETTY	H	10	351	PRICE	CRH	13	349
PRESCOTT	WG	13	348	PRESTON	GE	3	179	PRETTY	HG	7	317	PRICE	CS	13	349
PRESGRAVE	JE	9	324	PRESTON	GL	7	316	PRETTY	TE	7	317	PRICE	CW	14	255
PRESLAND	AE	13	348	PRESTON	H	2	274	PRETTY	W	3	179	PRICE	D	6	331
PRESLAND	AM	13	348	PRESTON	H	8	271	PRETTY	W	13	349	PRICE	D	10	184
PRESLAND	CH	2	274	PRESTON	H	8	271	PRETTY	WC	3	179	PRICE	DP	3	180
PRESLAND	FA	13	348	PRESTON	H	11	305	PRETTY	WH	13	348	PRICE	E	2	274
PRESLAND	GP	4	309	PRESTON	HA	11	305	PRETTY	WJ	13	349	PRICE	E	6	331
PRESLAND	H	13	348	PRESTON	HH	3	179	PREVAL	JT	8	271	PRICE	E	10	184
PRESLAND	JR	4	309	PRESTON	HW	13	348	PREVAL	S	8	271	PRICE	E	11	305
PRESLAND	SP	4	309	PRESTON	J	3	179	PREW	EH	3	179	PRICE	E	11	305
PRESLAND	W	2	274	PRESTON	J	6	330	PREW	GS	3	180	PRICE	E	12	181
PRESLAND	W	2	274	PRESTON	J	9	154	PREW	RG	3	180	PRICE	E	14	256
PRESLEY	EE	13	348	PRESTON	J	9	324	PREWETT	RE	4	309	PRICE	EJ	7	317
PRESS	EH	1	279	PRESTON	J	9	324	PREWITT	AF	4	309	PRICE	EJ	11	305
PRESS	WGJ	3	179	PRESTON	J	14	255	PREWITT	BSA	4	309	PRICE	EL	13	349
PRESSDEE	AH	6	329	PRESTON	JA	9	324	PREWITT	J	4	310	PRICE	F	1	280
PRESSDEE	R	6	329	PRESTON	JE	14	255	PREWITT	W	4	310	PRICE	F	7	317
PRESSLAND	AF	5	281	PRESTON	JJ	6	330	PREWITT	W	6	330	PRICE	F	7	317
PRESSLEY	PC	4	309	PRESTON	JP	1	280	PRICE	A	1	280	PRICE	F	9	324
PRESSLEY	ST	4	309	PRESTON	JT	8	271	PRICE	A	2	274	PRICE	F	10	351
PREST	E	8	271	PRESTON	JW	9	154	PRICE	A	2	274	PRICE	F	11	305
PREST	H	8	271	PRESTON	JW	9	154	PRICE	A	2	274	PRICE	FA	6	331
PRESTAGE	AJ	1	279	PRESTON	JW	14	255	PRICE	A	2	274	PRICE	FG	3	180
PRESTAGE	H	6	330	PRESTON	K	14	255	PRICE	A	6	330	PRICE	FG	13	349
PRESTAGE	JH	6	330	PRESTON	LS	6	330	PRICE	A	6	330	PRICE	FJ	4	310
PRESTNEY	EW	7	317	PRESTON	PE	13	348	PRICE	A	6	330	PRICE	FJ	7	317
PRESTNEY	JH	13	348	PRESTON	RH	9	154	PRICE	A	6	330	PRICE	FR	1	280
PRESTON	A	8	271	PRESTON	TW	6	330	PRICE	A	6	330	PRICE	FW	2	274
PRESTON	A	9	153	PRESTON	W	6	330	PRICE	A	6	330	PRICE	G	1	280
PRESTON	A	14	255	PRESTON	W	9	154	PRICE	A	6	330	PRICE	G	1	280
PRESTON	AE	2	274	PRESTON	W	9	154	PRICE	A	6	330	PRICE	G	2	274
PRESTON	AE	3	179	PRESTON	W	9	154	PRICE	A	6	331	PRICE	G	2	274
PRESTON	AG	10	351	PRESTON	W	9	324	PRICE	A	10	184	PRICE	G	6	331
PRESTON	AH	1	279	PRESTON	W	9	324	PRICE	AC	6	331	PRICE	GA	6	331
PRESTON	AS	6	330	PRESTON	W	14	255	PRICE	ACW	6	331	PRICE	GA	13	349
PRESTON	C	4	309	PRESTON	W	14	255	PRICE	AE	4	310	PRICE	GE	6	331
PRESTON	C	14	255	PRESTON	W	14	255	PRICE	AE	10	184	PRICE	GE	13	349
PRESTON	CF	2	274	PRESTON	WE	6	330	PRICE	AE	10	351	PRICE	GEV	6	331
PRESTON	CF	7	316	PRESTON	WH	9	324	PRICE	AF	7	317	PRICE	GH	6	331
PRESTON	CH	2	274	PRESTON	WH	13	348	PRICE	AG	6	331	PRICE	GH	6	331
PRESTON	D	4	309	PRESTON	WJ	3	179	PRICE	AH	9	324	PRICE	GJ	14	256
PRESTON	E	1	280	PRESTON	WW	12	371	PRICE	AJ	6	331	PRICE	GL	2	275
PRESTON	E	7	316	PRESTRIDGE	GH	2	274	PRICE	AL	1	280	PRICE	GL	13	349
PRESTON	E	9	153	PRESTWICH	AH	2	274	PRICE	AT	1	280	PRICE	GW	8	271
PRESTON	E	9	154	PRESTWICH	C	2	274	PRICE	AT	3	180	PRICE	H	1	280
PRESTON	EJ	1	280	PRESTWICH	CH	2	274	PRICE	B	13	349	PRICE	H	5	281
PRESTON	EJW	4	309	PRESTWICH	JT	14	255	PRICE	B	14	255	PRICE	H	6	331
PRESTON	F	7	316	PRETLOVER	RA	1	280	PRICE	C	7	317	PRICE	H	8	271
PRESTON	FC	2	274	PRETT	HC	4	309	PRICE	C	9	154	PRICE	H	9	154
PRESTON	FJ	1	280	PRETTY	AH	1	280	PRICE	C	9	324	PRICE	H	9	324
PRESTON	FR	3	179	PRETTY	EM	13	348	PRICE	C	11	305	PRICE	H	10	184
PRESTON	FW	13	348	PRETTY	F	4	309	PRICE	C	11	305	PRICE	H	11	305
PRESTON	G	6	330	PRETTY	F	6	330	PRICE	CA	5	281	PRICE	H	11	305
PRESTON	G	11	305	PRETTY	FH	1	280	PRICE	CH	3	180	PRICE	H	11	305

PRICE	H	13	349	PRICE	P	14	256	PRICKETT	R	5	281	PRIESTLEY	W	9	325
PRICE	H	14	256	PRICE	PT	10	352	PRICKETT	RO	12	182	PRIESTLEY	W	14	256
PRICE	HA	1	280	PRICE	R	8	271	PRICKETT	T	12	182	PRIESTLY	FC	13	350
PRICE	HD	14	256	PRICE	R	11	306	PRICKETT	W	12	371	PRIESTMAN	A	9	155
PRICE	HE	1	280	PRICE	RE	6	332	PRICKETT	WE	12	182	PRIESTNALL	TW	11	306
PRICE	HE	13	349	PRICE	RH	4	310	PRIDDEY	J	6	332	PRIGMORE	AE	3	180
PRICE	HH	3	180	PRICE	RR	7	317	PRIDDEY	W	6	332	PRIGMORE	AR	3	180
PRICE	HH	7	317	PRICE	S	4	310	PRIDDIS	WG	13	350	PRIGMORE	EW	1	281
PRICE	HJ	3	180	PRICE	S	14	256	PRIDDLE	H	13	350	PRIGMORE	H	7	318
PRICE	HJ	6	331	PRICE	SN	6	332	PRIDDLE	JA	2	275	PRIGMORE	HA	3	180
PRICE	HW	3	180	PRICE	SO	6	332	PRIDDLE	SC	1	281	PRIGMORE	NT	7	318
PRICE	HW	7	317	PRICE	SS	4	310	PRIDDY	G	10	184	PRIME	AD	6	333
PRICE	J	1	280	PRICE	T	6	332	PRIDDY	H	10	184	PRIME	EW	3	180
PRICE	J	1	280	PRICE	T	6	332	PRIDE	J	13	349	PRIME	FH	3	181
PRICE	J	5	281	PRICE	T	6	332	PRIDEAUX	E	4	310	PRIME	H	2	275
PRICE	J	6	331	PRICE	T	11	306	PRIDMAN	HJ	1	281	PRIME	HE	3	181
PRICE	J	6	331	PRICE	T	13	349	PRIDMORE	E	9	325	PRIME	S	5	281
PRICE	J	6	331	PRICE	TW	13	349	PRIDMORE	G	12	182	PRIME	WH	3	181
PRICE	J	6	332	PRICE	TW	14	256	PRIDMORE	J	9	325	PRIME	WJ	12	182
PRICE	J	6	332	PRICE	W	3	180	PRIDMORE	JW	8	271	PRIMETT	A	13	350
PRICE	J	6	332	PRICE	W	3	180	PRIDMORE	JW	9	154	PRIMETT	C	5	281
PRICE	J	6	332	PRICE	W	3	180	PRIEST	A	11	306	PRIMETT	F	5	281
PRICE	J	7	317	PRICE	W	10	184	PRIEST	AJ	4	310	PRIMETT	HT	5	281
PRICE	J	7	317	PRICE	W	10	184	PRIEST	G	4	310	PRIMMER	AJ	4	310
PRICE	J	8	271	PRICE	W	11	306	PRIEST	G	6	333	PRIMMER	JW	4	310
PRICE	J	9	154	PRICE	W	11	306	PRIEST	JM	13	350	PRIMMER	T	4	310
PRICE	J	9	325	PRICE	W	11	306	PRIEST	PH	2	275	PRIMMER	W	10	184
PRICE	J	11	305	PRICE	W	13	350	PRIEST	WF	7	318	PRIMMETT	H	5	281
PRICE	J	11	305	PRICE	W	14	256	PRIEST	WJ	11	306	PRIMMETT	S	3	181
PRICE	J	13	349	PRICE	W	14	256	PRIESTLEY	A	9	154	PRIN	W	10	184
PRICE	J	14	256	PRICE	WA	7	317	PRIESTLEY	A	9	325	PRINCE	A	2	275
PRICE	J	14	256	PRICE	WA	12	181	PRIESTLEY	CW	14	256	PRINCE	A	3	181
PRICE	JA	8	271	PRICE	WE	2	275	PRIESTLEY	E	9	154	PRINCE	A	10	184
PRICE	JA	9	154	PRICE	WE	4	310	PRIESTLEY	E	9	325	PRINCE	A	14	256
PRICE	JC	13	349	PRICE	WE	7	318	PRIESTLEY	F	9	154	PRINCE	AE	6	333
PRICE	JE	3	180	PRICE	WE	11	306	PRIESTLEY	GA	9	154	PRINCE	B	3	181
PRICE	JE	14	256	PRICE	WE	12	371	PRIESTLEY	H	9	154	PRINCE	C	4	310
PRICE	JF	7	317	PRICE	WG	1	281	PRIESTLEY	H	9	154	PRINCE	CH	3	181
PRICE	JH	9	325	PRICE	WG	10	184	PRIESTLEY	H	9	155	PRINCE	CJ	1	281
PRICE	JJ	10	184	PRICE	WG	10	184	PRIESTLEY	H	9	325	PRINCE	DJ	6	333
PRICE	JR	13	349	PRICE	WH	1	281	PRIESTLEY	H	9	325	PRINCE	F	1	281
PRICE	JT	1	281	PRICE	WH	6	332	PRIESTLEY	J	3	180	PRINCE	F	3	181
PRICE	JT	3	180	PRICE	WJ	7	318	PRIESTLEY	J	9	155	PRINCE	F	4	310
PRICE	JT	6	332	PRICE	WM	3	180	PRIESTLEY	J	9	155	PRINCE	F	8	271
PRICE	JT	9	391	PRICE	WR	6	332	PRIESTLEY	J	9	155	PRINCE	FH	2	275
PRICE	JT	11	305	PRICE	WT	7	318	PRIESTLEY	J	9	325	PRINCE	GA	13	350
PRICE	JW	1	281	PRICE	WW	10	352	PRIESTLEY	L	8	271	PRINCE	GD	3	181
PRICE	JW	6	332	PRICHARD	N	6	332	PRIESTLEY	L	9	155	PRINCE	H	1	281
PRICE	JW	14	256	PRICKETT	AC	5	281	PRIESTLEY	L	9	155	PRINCE	H	4	310
PRICE	L	6	332	PRICKETT	AH	10	352	PRIESTLEY	S	9	325	PRINCE	HJ	3	181
PRICE	LA	7	317	PRICKETT	AW	12	182	PRIESTLEY	SW	9	155	PRINCE	HL	6	333
PRICE	LP	6	332	PRICKETT	C	5	281	PRIESTLEY	T	14	256	PRINCE	J	6	333
PRICE	P	6	332	PRICKETT	E	12	182	PRIESTLEY	TM	9	155	PRINCE	J	8	271
PRICE	P	10	184	PRICKETT	HH	5	281	PRIESTLEY	TW	9	391	PRINCE	J	11	306
PRICE	P	11	305	PRICKETT	M	12	182	PRIESTLEY	W	8	271	PRINCE	J	11	306

PRINCE	J	11	306	PRIOR	GA	7	318	PRITCHARD	TW	6	333	PROCTOR	H	8	272
PRINCE	J	13	350	PRIOR	GC	2	275	PRITCHARD	VE	11	307	PROCTOR	H	8	272
PRINCE	J	14	256	PRIOR	GW	8	272	PRITCHARD	W	9	325	PROCTOR	H	8	272
PRINCE	J	14	256	PRIOR	GWC	7	318	PRITCHARD	W	11	307	PROCTOR	J	8	272
PRINCE	J	14	257	PRIOR	H	1	281	PRITCHARD	W	13	351	PROCTOR	JA	9	325
PRINCE	JH	4	310	PRIOR	H	4	311	PRITCHARD	W	14	257	PROCTOR	JM	9	325
PRINCE	JH	11	306	PRIOR	H	13	350	PRITCHARD	WJ	13	351	PROCTOR	P	5	282
PRINCE	JT	4	310	PRIOR	HF	3	181	PRITCHARD	WV	4	311	PROCTOR	R	8	272
PRINCE	JW	9	325	PRIOR	HW	13	350	PRITCHETT	E	6	333	PROCTOR	R	12	182
PRINCE	JW	13	350	PRIOR	J	3	181	PRITCHETT	E	6	333	PROCTOR	RJ	2	275
PRINCE	PW	4	310	PRIOR	J	6	333	PRITCHETT	H	6	333	PROCTOR	S	11	307
PRINCE	RA	10	184	PRIOR	J	8	272	PRITCHETT	W	14	257	PROCTOR	T	8	272
PRINCE	RC	4	310	PRIOR	JH	2	275	PRITTY	C	5	281	PROCTOR	TC	12	182
PRINCE	RW	11	306	PRIOR	M	2	275	PRIVATE	GH	13	351	PROCTOR	TG	10	185
PRINCE	SA	13	350	PRIOR	PG	12	182	PRIVATE	J	13	351	PROCTOR	TH	12	182
PRINCE	SC	13	350	PRIOR	PHA	12	182	PRIZEMAN	GA	13	351	PROCTOR	W	1	282
PRINCE	T	11	306	PRIOR	T	11	307	PROBERT	J	6	333	PROCTOR	W	8	272
PRINCE	T	11	306	PRIOR	V	10	352	PROBERT	J	14	257	PROCTOR	W	8	272
PRINCE	T	11	306	PRIOR	W	1	281	PROBERT	J	14	257	PROCTOR	W	8	272
PRINCE	TG	7	318	PRIOR	W	1	281	PROBERT	W	3	181	PROCTOR	W	8	272
PRINCE	TR	3	181	PRIOR	W	1	281	PROBETS	A	7	318	PROCTOR	W	9	155
PRINCE	V	1	281	PRIOR	W	2	275	PROBETS	E	7	318	PROCTOR	WM	12	182
PRINCE	VG	4	310	PRIOR	W	13	350	PROBETS	G	2	275	PROFFITT	H	2	275
PRINCE	W	1	281	PRIOR	WH	2	275	PROCKTER	EG	7	318	PRONG	AC	13	351
PRINCE	W	11	306	PRIOR	WH	7	318	PROCTER	C	9	325	PRONGER	FA	13	351
PRINCE	W	13	350	PRIOR	WJ	1	282	PROCTER	E	14	257	PROP	A	10	185
PRINCE	W	14	257	PRISLEY	F	9	155	PROCTER	F	9	155	PROPERT	HM	2	275
PRINCE	WCH	13	350	PRISSELL	FJ	13	350	PROCTER	F	14	257	PROPHET	GA	11	307
PRINCE	WG	5	281	PRITCHARD	A	7	318	PROCTER	G	9	325	PROPHET	JW	11	307
PRINCE	WH	10	184	PRITCHARD	A	14	257	PROCTER	H	8	272	PROPHET	R	11	307
PRINCE	WJG	4	311	PRITCHARD	AC	13	350	PROCTER	H	11	307	PROSPER	A	3	181
PRINCE-COX	CF	10	352	PRITCHARD	C	4	311	PROCTER	J	9	155	PROSSER	E	1	282
PRINCE-COX	SG	10	352	PRITCHARD	C	11	307	PROCTER	J	14	257	PROSSER	F	11	307
PRINCE-COX	WH	10	352	PRITCHARD	C	14	257	PROCTER	JA	5	281	PROSSER	FJW	3	181
PRINGLE	H	11	307	PRITCHARD	CW	10	185	PROCTER	JA	5	281	PROSSER	GWC	2	275
PRINGLE	HN	8	271	PRITCHARD	D	4	311	PROCTER	JE	8	272	PROSSER	H	1	282
PRINGLE	HSF	10	185	PRITCHARD	E	13	351	PROCTER	JE	14	257	PROSSER	R	1	282
PRINGLE	J	3	181	PRITCHARD	EC	1	282	PROCTER	L	9	155	PROSSER	W	6	333
PRINGLE	J	11	307	PRITCHARD	ER	1	282	PROCTER	N	9	155	PROTHERO	WE	13	351
PRINGLE	JE	10	352	PRITCHARD	FJ	6	333	PROCTER	N	9	325	PROTHERO	WW	7	318
PRINGLE	WC	3	181	PRITCHARD	FJ	10	185	PROCTER	S	2	275	PROTHEROE	GE	2	276
PRINT	J	6	333	PRITCHARD	H	11	307	PROCTER	TJ	14	257	PROTHEROE	SF	2	275
PRIOR	AM	1	281	PRITCHARD	H	12	371	PROCTER	W	8	272	PROUD	HRA	13	351
PRIOR	B	1	281	PRITCHARD	HC	1	282	PROCTER	WE	11	307	PROUDLEY	RC	4	311
PRIOR	B	12	182	PRITCHARD	HT	13	350	PROCTER	WT	5	281	PROUSE	F	1	282
PRIOR	D	12	182	PRITCHARD	J	4	311	PROCTOR	A	5	282	PROUT	RA	1	282
PRIOR	EE	1	281	PRITCHARD	J	6	333	PROCTOR	A	8	272	PROUTING	RE	4	311
PRIOR	EF	7	318	PRITCHARD	JE	6	333	PROCTOR	AC	5	282	PROWER	FA	2	276
PRIOR	EM	1	281	PRITCHARD	JT	7	318	PROCTOR	C	8	272	PROWER	FW	2	276
PRIOR	F	11	307	PRITCHARD	JW	6	333	PROCTOR	C	8	272	PROWER	WA	2	276
PRIOR	FJ	3	181	PRITCHARD	S	14	257	PROCTOR	F	5	282	PROWL	E	8	272
PRIOR	G	4	311	PRITCHARD	T	6	333	PROCTOR	F	8	272	PROWSE	RM	1	282
PRIOR	G	10	185	PRITCHARD	T	14	257	PROCTOR	FH	14	257	PROWSE	T	4	311
PRIOR	G	12	182	PRITCHARD	TA	10	185	PROCTOR	FJ	1	282	PROWTING	AE	10	185
PRIOR	G	12	182	PRITCHARD	TE	1	282	PROCTOR	G	12	182	PROWTING	E	4	311

Name	Initials	Vol	Page
PROWTING	G	4	311
PROWTING	L	4	311
PROWTING	PC	10	185
PROYER	WHG	2	276
PRUCE	E	7	319
PRUCE	L	7	319
PRUDAN	JW	12	371
PRUDDEN	FH	4	311
PRUDDEN	SW	5	282
PRUDDEN	TC	5	282
PRUDEN	H	3	181
PRUDEN	W	3	182
PRUDHOE	A	8	273
PRUDHOE	JE	8	273
PRUST	R	8	273
PRUTTON	WC	5	282
PRYCE	F	11	307
PRYCE	GW	6	334
PRYCE	H	14	257
PRYER	JH	10	352
PRYKE	AG	2	276
PRYKE	EA	3	182
PRYOR	AJ	1	282
PRYOR	AW	5	282
PRYOR	C	2	276
PRYOR	C	7	319
PRYOR	ET	1	282
PRYOR	HH	1	282
PRYOR	J	14	257
PRYOR	TW	1	282
PRYOR	TW	13	351
PRYOR	WG	5	282
PUCKETT	JH	3	182
PUCKETT	RH	4	311
PUCKEY	TF	10	185
PUDDEPHATT	A	7	319
PUDDEPHATT	AJ	5	282
PUDDEPHATT	EE	7	319
PUDDEPHATT	H	5	282
PUDDEPHATT	LJ	5	282
PUDDEPHATT	P	5	282
PUDDICK	AJ	7	319
PUDDICK	HA	10	352
PUDDICK	WJ	4	311
PUDDICOMBE	JW	9	391
PUDDIFOOT	FJ	9	325
PUDDY	EG	10	185
PUDNEY	W	7	319
PUFFETT	JT	6	334
PUFFITT	WH	2	276
PUGH	A	4	311
PUGH	A	13	351
PUGH	AB	13	351
PUGH	AC	3	182
PUGH	C	8	273
PUGH	CH	6	334
PUGH	CH	6	334
PUGH	CR	7	319
PUGH	E	8	273
PUGH	ED	13	351
PUGH	FT	7	319
PUGH	G	2	276
PUGH	G	6	334
PUGH	G	6	334
PUGH	GW	2	276
PUGH	H	6	334
PUGH	H	7	319
PUGH	H	10	352
PUGH	H	13	351
PUGH	HJ	5	282
PUGH	J	5	282
PUGH	J	6	334
PUGH	J	14	257
PUGH	JF	6	334
PUGH	JT	11	307
PUGH	JW	6	334
PUGH	LJ	3	182
PUGH	PT	6	334
PUGH	PW	5	282
PUGH	PW	5	282
PUGH	S	5	283
PUGH	SG	3	182
PUGH	T	7	319
PUGH	TG	7	319
PUGH	W	6	334
PUGH	WH	6	334
PUGH	WT	5	283
PUGHE	HJ	6	334
PULFER	H	3	182
PULFORD	CRH	3	182
PULFORD	HT	7	319
PULFORD	JW	8	273
PULFORD	LR	7	319
PULFORD	WA	3	182
PULHAM	EW	3	182
PULHAM	HFC	3	182
PULHAM	JH	3	182
PULL	R	13	351
PULLAN	A	8	273
PULLAN	B	8	273
PULLAN	E	8	273
PULLAN	J	8	273
PULLAN	J	8	273
PULLAN	W	8	273
PULLAN	W	9	326
PULLAN	WR	8	273
PULLEN	A	7	319
PULLEN	AG	13	351
PULLEN	AJ	7	319
PULLEN	AW	7	320
PULLEN	CH	2	276
PULLEN	DJ	1	282
PULLEN	E	3	182
PULLEN	EJ	7	319
PULLEN	EJ	10	352
PULLEN	FA	7	320
PULLEN	GJ	7	320
PULLEN	H	9	155
PULLEN	H	13	351
PULLEN	HG	7	320
PULLEN	J	3	182
PULLEN	JH	3	182
PULLEN	JP	9	155
PULLEN	LP	5	283
PULLEN	ME	3	182
PULLEN	OH	5	283
PULLEN	S	3	182
PULLEN	S	7	320
PULLEN	W	5	283
PULLEN	W	10	185
PULLER	EG	11	307
PULLEY	A	12	182
PULLEY	E	12	371
PULLEY	F	12	371
PULLEY	FH	12	371
PULLEY	G	12	183
PULLEY	JH	12	371
PULLEY	M	12	183
PULLILG	FG	7	320
PULLIN	F	13	351
PULLINGER	A	9	155
PULLINGER	G	4	311
PULLINGER	RJ	7	320
PULLINGER	W	2	276
PULLINGER	W	4	311
PULLINGER	WE	7	320
PULLINGER	WG	10	352
PULLOM	A	10	352
PULMAN	E	10	352
PULMAN	F	9	156
PUNCHARD	LA	9	326
PUNCHER	BC	10	185
PUNCHER	RW	10	185
PUNGENTI	J	2	276
PUNNETT	EG	13	352
PUNSHON	AA	3	182
PUNT	C	8	273
PUNT	E	9	156
PUNT	G	9	156
PUNT	WF	13	352
PUNTER	AH	1	282
PUNTER	CI	3	182
PUNTER	FJ	14	258
PUNTER	HR	3	182
PUNTER	J	3	183
PUNTER	W	1	283
PUNTER	WJ	1	283
PUNTIS	E	10	185
PUNTIS	EG	10	185
PUPLET	TW	13	352
PUPLETT	EC	13	352
PUPLETT	J	12	183
PUPLETT	W	12	183
PURCELL	AL	9	156
PURCELL	E	6	334
PURCELL	E	11	307
PURCELL	H	11	307
PURCELL	JH	1	283
PURCELL	WH	6	334
PURCHALL	ER	4	311
PURCHASE	H	4	312
PURCHASE	HG	4	312
PURCHASE	W	4	312
PURCHES	EA	10	185
PURCHESE	AR	13	352
PURCHESE	E	13	352
PURDON	W	8	273
PURDUE	AE	3	183
PURDUE	EE	13	352
PURDUE	FJ	13	352
PURDUE	WH	4	312
PURDY	A	1	283
PURDY	A	14	258
PURDY	D	13	352
PURDY	GE	3	183
PURDY	GS	7	320
PURDY	H	14	258
PURDY	J	3	183
PURDY	J	13	352
PURDY	R	8	273
PURDY	T	1	283
PURDY	WA	1	283
PURDY	WH	3	183
PURDY	WH	14	258
PURDY	WL	1	283
PURE	W	1	283
PURKIS	A	14	258
PURKIS	AWT	10	185
PURKIS	AWT	10	352
PURKIS	J	13	352
PURKIS	JH	14	258
PURKIS	WH	1	283
PURKIS	WJ	14	258
PURKISS	F	4	312
PURKISS	FJ	4	312
PURKISS	GW	4	312
PURKISS	HC	4	312
PURKISS	HJ	4	312
PURKISS	JH	4	312
PURKISS	TF	7	320

Surname	Initials	No.	Page
PURKISS	WAB	4	312
PURLAND	WW	7	320
PURNELL	AE	2	276
PURNELL	AE	4	312
PURNELL	AE	13	352
PURNELL	G	10	185
PURNELL	HJ	3	183
PURNELL	RA	1	283
PURNELL	WG	4	312
PURNELL	WG	4	312
PURR	E	5	283
PURRENTT	WT	5	283
PURRINGTON	EV	10	186
PURSE	AV	10	186
PURSE	GS	3	183
PURSE	SJ	10	186
PURSELL	A	6	334
PURSER	G	2	276
PURSER	H	3	183
PURSER	HJ	12	183
PURSER	J	12	371
PURSER	SJ	12	183
PURSER	W	12	183
PURSER	WH	5	283
PURSER	WSL	7	320
PURSEY	OH	10	186
PURSEY	WA	7	320
PURSLOW	G	11	308
PURSLOW	WH	11	308
PURSSEY	G	7	320
PURSSEY	JA	7	320
PURSSORD	HR	8	273
PURTELL	JF	2	276
PURTELL	WJ	2	276
PURTON	C	2	276
PURTON	CW	7	320
PURTON	GV	13	352
PURVES	JA	14	258
PURVEY	C	7	320
PURVEY	F	7	320
PURVIS	HJ	3	183
PURVIS	J	11	308
PURVIS	W	1	283
PURYER	AE	7	320
PURYER	EG	5	283
PURYER	F	12	183
PURYER	G	12	183
PUSEY	A	10	352
PUSEY	AG	13	352
PUSEY	FW	1	283
PUSEY	GA	2	276
PUSEY	HH	4	312
PUSEY	JC	1	283
PUSEY	W	6	334
PUSEY	WE	1	283
PUSILL	H	11	308
PUTLAND	E	3	183
PUTLAND	FJS	5	283
PUTLAND	P	3	183
PUTMAN	A	5	283
PUTMAN	EJ	3	183
PUTMAN	H	12	183
PUTMAN	HH	10	352
PUTMAN	R	3	183
PUTMAN	T	5	283
PUTNAM	HT	13	352
PUTNAM	JG	7	320
PUTSEY	JE	12	371
PUTT	A	10	352
PUTT	TH	5	283
PUTT	WF	13	352
PUTT	WH	2	276
PUTTERFOOT	HW	3	183
PUTTERGILL	F	6	334
PUTTERILL	RW	5	283
PUTTOCK	AAJ	1	283
PUTTOCK	F	3	383
PUTTOCK	G	2	277
PUTTOCK	H	7	321
PUTTOCK	JW	13	352
PUTTOCK	LW	7	321
PUTTOCK	TW	7	321
PUTTOCK	WA	13	352
PUTZ	HH	7	321
PUZEY	F	4	312
PYBUS	CH	14	258
PYBUS	WH	14	258
PYCROFT	CC	10	353
PYCROFT	HA	8	273
PYE	A	11	308
PYE	AJ	3	183
PYE	B	6	335
PYE	C	6	335
PYE	C	7	321
PYE	F	3	183
PYE	G	11	308
PYE	HWP	2	277
PYE	I	3	183
PYE	J	4	312
PYE	L	3	183
PYE	RE	2	277
PYE	SJ	6	335
PYE	TW	8	273
PYE	WS	3	183
PYEFINCH	HJ	13	352
PYEFINCH	SG	13	353
PYETT	C	13	353
PYGOTT	T	11	308
PYKE	A	6	335
PYKE	WH	6	335
PYLE	F	1	283
PYLE	HC	4	312
PYLE	JJ	3	183
PYLE	WC	7	321
PYLE	WG	10	353
PYM	C	3	183
PYMM	FA	1	283
PYMM	SA	1	283
PYNE	A	13	353
PYNE	AE	4	312
PYNE	HC	4	313
PYNE	JJ	3	184
PYNE	LCW	4	313
PYNE	T	3	184
PYNE	W	13	353
PYNE	WE	4	313
PYNE	WJ	4	313
PYNIGAR	AH	10	353
PYPER	FT	5	283
PYPER	JE	5	283
PYRAH	F	9	156
PYRAH	JT	8	273
PYRAH	T	8	273
PYRAH	W	9	156
PYRKES	S	8	273
PYWELL	J	8	274

Q

Surname	Initials	No.	Page
QUA	J	13	353
QUAIFE	CE	7	321
QUAIFE	E	7	321
QUAKLEY	C	7	321
QUANCE	K	6	335
QUANCE	W	6	335
QUANTRILL	C	7	321
QUANTRILL	HR	7	321
QUANTRILL	JC	7	321
QUARMAN	CE	5	283
QUARMAN	J	5	284
QUARMAN	JA	5	283
QUARMAN	LS	5	283
QUARMBY	A	8	274
QUARMBY	E	11	308
QUARMBY	H	8	274
QUARMBY	J	8	274
QUARRELL	T	2	277
QUARRENDON	JH	7	321
QUARRINGTON	AB	7	321
QUARRINGTON	AJ	7	321
QUARRINGTON	TA	7	321
QUARRY	HG	12	183
QUARTERMAIN	RHW	4	313
QUARTERMAIN	TM	10	353
QUARTERMAN	G	12	372
QUARTERMAN	H	13	353
QUARTERMAN	LC	2	277
QUARTERMAN	S	5	284
QUARTERMAN	W	7	321
QUAYLE	E	11	308
QUAYLE	F	8	274
QUAYLE	JJ	9	156
QUELCH	H	3	184
QUELCH	W	3	184
QUELCH	WL	1	284
QUENNELL	F	12	372
QUENNELL	HJ	10	186
QUERISE	A	2	277
QUERSTRET	J	10	186
QUESNEL	EA	1	284
QUESNEL	J	2	277
QUIBELL	EW	5	284
QUIBELL	EW	5	284
QUIBELL	GA	5	284
QUIBELL	SW	5	284
QUIBELL	W	6	335
QUICK	A	14	258
QUICK	AG	13	353
QUICK	AJ	5	284
QUICK	CR	1	284
QUICK	EG	5	284
QUICK	F	5	284
QUICK	FA	1	284
QUICK	FG	5	284
QUICK	FJ	5	284
QUICK	G	2	277
QUICK	H	5	284
QUICK	J	4	313
QUICK	JF	4	313
QUICK	JW	9	156
QUICK	SR	5	284
QUICK	TS	5	284
QUICK	W	7	321
QUICK	WC	7	322
QUICK	WG	5	284
QUICKENDEN	GA	13	353
QUICKFALL	GF	8	274
QUICKNUTT	T	9	156
QUIGLEY	B	14	258
QUIGLEY	C	11	308
QUIGLEY	CW	11	308
QUIGLEY	E	14	258
QUIGLEY	JH	9	156
QUIGLEY	R	9	156
QUIGLEY	T	14	258
QUIGLEY	TR	14	258
QUILTER	RC	1	284
QUILTY	J	11	308
QUIMBY	H	6	335
QUIMBY	W	8	274

QUINLAN	A	13	353	QUINTON	WC	4	313	RADFORD	AG	1	284	RAGG	A	6	336
QUINLAN	D	11	308	QUIRE	JH	3	184	RADFORD	AW	6	335	RAGGETT	F	14	259
QUINLAN	E	11	308	QUIRK	C	9	156	RADFORD	C	6	335	RAGGETT	J	14	259
QUINLAN	HJ	8	274	QUIRK	E	8	274	RADFORD	CC	1	284	RAGGETT	RH	14	259
QUINLAN	J	2	277	QUIRK	J	4	313	RADFORD	CWH	7	322	RAGLESS	WE	4	314
QUINLAN	J	8	274	QUIRK	J	8	274	RADFORD	DJ	1	284	RAGON	M	9	326
QUINLAN	J	13	353	QUIRK	JR	9	156	RADFORD	E	5	285	RAGSDALE	G	8	275
QUINLAND	EL	1	284	QUIRK	P	8	274	RADFORD	EM	5	285	RAILTON	T	9	156
QUINN	A	11	308	QUIRK	P	8	274	RADFORD	F	5	285	RAINBIRD	W	3	184
QUINN	A	11	308	QUIRK	R	9	326	RADFORD	G	6	335	RAINBOW	A	5	285
QUINN	A	14	258	QUIRK	T	9	326	RADFORD	GH	3	184	RAINBOW	AG	7	322
QUINN	CH	1	284	QUY	EG	3	184	RADFORD	H	6	336	RAINBOW	AJ	12	183
QUINN	E	8	274	QUY	GC	13	353	RADFORD	H	8	274	RAINBOW	C	5	285
QUINN	E	9	156	QUY	OD	2	277	RADFORD	HG	5	285	RAINBOW	CG	12	372
QUINN	G	11	308	QUY	WJ	2	277	RADFORD	J	14	259	RAINBOW	F	9	157
QUINN	G	14	258					RADFORD	JS	12	183	RAINBOW	F	12	183
QUINN	H	11	308					RADFORD	JW	5	285	RAINBOW	F	12	372
QUINN	H	11	309					RADFORD	S	11	309	RAINBOW	FG	12	183
QUINN	H	14	258		**R**			RADFORD	T	13	353	RAINBOW	G	5	285
QUINN	J	4	313					RADFORD	T	13	353	RAINBOW	GWJ	12	372
QUINN	J	9	156	RABBETTS	EW	10	353	RADFORD	W	1	284	RAINBOW	J	5	285
QUINN	J	9	156	RABBITT	J	12	372	RADFORD	W	2	277	RAINBOW	J	12	183
QUINN	J	11	309	RABJOHNS	JH	13	353	RADFORD	W	7	322	RAINBOW	JG	12	183
QUINN	J	11	309	RABONE	AE	6	335	RADFORD	WJ	1	284	RAINBOW	TL	6	336
QUINN	J	14	259	RABSON	AR	2	277	RADFORD	WJ	5	285	RAINBOW	WG	5	285
QUINN	JJ	8	274	RABSON	FJ	1	284	RADIN	D	14	259	RAINBOW	WG	12	184
QUINN	JM	11	309	RABSON	M	1	284	RADLEY	AW	3	184	RAINE	A	9	326
QUINN	L	14	259	RABY	AE	13	353	RADLEY	EA	13	353	RAINE	WA	13	354
QUINN	M	14	259	RABY	E	14	259	RADLEY	EK	13	353	RAINES	F	12	372
QUINN	M	14	259	RABY	F	8	274	RADLEY	I	3	184	RAINES	FW	12	372
QUINN	N	4	313	RABY	HE	3	184	RADMALL	A	7	322	RAINES	P	7	322
QUINN	R	6	335	RABY	JT	11	309	RADMALL	A	7	322	RAINEY	A	8	275
QUINN	R	8	274	RACE	CH	9	156	RADMORE	AW	4	313	RAINEY	J	6	336
QUINN	R	9	326	RACE	E	9	326	RADMORE	LB	4	314	RAINEY	T	6	336
QUINN	T	11	309	RACE	G	12	372	RADNALL	H	8	275	RAINEY	TE	10	353
QUINN	TP	8	274	RACE	J	6	335	RAE	A	6	336	RAINFORD	E	4	314
QUINN	W	11	309	RACE	J	11	309	RAE	AE	14	259	RAINFORD	T	14	259
QUINN	WHA	2	277	RACE	W	14	259	RAE	F	6	336	RAINFORD	WH	10	353
QUINN	WP	14	259	RACHEL	JS	6	335	RAE	HJ	6	336	RAINFORTH	HT	1	284
QUINNELL	AE	10	186	RACINE	J	3	184	RAE	J	6	336	RAINGER	PGJ	2	277
QUINNELL	FJ	10	186	RACINE	JT	3	184	RAE	J	8	275	RAINS	G	2	277
QUINNELL	G	7	322	RACINE	OJ	3	184	RAE	WJ	6	336	RAINSBURY	E	11	309
QUINNELL	GV	10	186	RACKETT	S	7	322	RAEBURN	AJ	7	322	RAINSBURY	ML	3	184
QUINNELL	H	10	186	RACKETT	VT	4	313	RAEBURN	G	7	322	RAINSBURY	S	3	184
QUINNELL	H	10	186	RACKETT	W	7	322	RAEBURN	TH	7	322	RAINSDEN	E	5	285
QUINNELL	W	10	353	RACKHAM	P	8	274	RAFFERTY	A	11	309	RAINSDEN	F	5	285
QUINNEY	JJ	12	372	RACKLEY	ER	5	284	RAFFERTY	J	6	336	RAINSDEN	H	5	285
QUINNY	J	6	335	RACKLEY	W	5	284	RAFFERTY	J	11	309	RAINSFORD	A	6	336
QUINT	SE	11	309	RACKLEY	WA	5	285	RAFFERTY	J	11	309	RAINSFORD	G	6	336
QUINT	SE	14	259	RACKSTRAW	J	14	259	RAFFERTY	R	6	336	RAINSFORD	W	6	336
QUINT	TW	5	284	RADBAND	A	1	284	RAFFERTY	W	13	353	RAINSLEY	GR	4	314
QUINTON	EW	4	313	RADBONE	B	4	313	RAFFETY	W	10	186	RAINSLEY	WG	4	314
QUINTON	FM	4	313	RADBONE	EE	2	277	RAGAN	J	8	275	RAISON	FS	2	278
QUINTON	PT	4	313	RADBONE	W	4	313	RAGAN	L	8	275	RAISON	HF	2	278
QUINTON	W	11	309	RADCLIFFE	CF	1	284	RAGBOURN	T	3	184	RAISTRICK	BW	8	275
				RADCLIFFE	WG	12	183								
				RADFORD	A	5	285								

RAISTRICK	C	8	275	RAMSAY	E	6	337	RAMSGILL	E	8	276	RANDALL	GF	2	278
RAISTRICK	E	9	157	RAMSAY	EE	6	337	RAMSHEAD	T	11	310	RANDALL	GJW	7	323
RAISTRICK	E	9	326	RAMSAY	G	6	337	RAMSHEW	FS	4	314	RANDALL	GT	10	187
RAISTRICK	G	9	326	RAMSAY	G	11	310	RAMWELL	W	14	260	RANDALL	H	1	285
RAISTRICK	H	9	326	RAMSAY	HD	13	354	RANCE	BC	7	323	RANDALL	H	2	278
RAISTRICK	J	9	326	RAMSAY	J	9	157	RANCE	CF	7	323	RANDALL	H	4	314
RAISTRICK	J	9	326	RAMSAY	JW	7	322	RANCE	FC	10	353	RANDALL	H	5	287
RAISTRICK	T	9	157	RAMSBOTHAM	G	9	326	RANCE	FG	5	286	RANDALL	H	6	337
RAISTRICK	W	9	157	RAMSBOTHAM	R	2	278	RANCE	FG	5	286	RANDALL	H	7	323
RAISTRICK	Z	9	157	RAMSBOTTAM	J	10	353	RANCE	H	1	285	RANDALL	H	7	323
RAKE	F	1	284	RAMSBOTTOM	M	14	260	RANCE	H	5	286	RANDALL	H	7	323
RALLEY	E	12	372	RAMSDALE	E	11	310	RANCE	HA	3	185	RANDALL	H	10	187
RALLEY	W	5	285	RAMSDALE	T	8	275	RANCE	HP	3	185	RANDALL	H	12	184
RALPH	A	10	186	RAMSDEN	A	8	275	RANCE	J	5	286	RANDALL	HE	1	285
RALPH	A	14	259	RAMSDEN	A	9	157	RANCE	JW	7	323	RANDALL	HH	10	187
RALPH	A	14	259	RAMSDEN	A	11	310	RANCE	M	10	187	RANDALL	HS	10	353
RALPH	AE	12	184	RAMSDEN	E	8	275	RANCE	R	7	323	RANDALL	HW	4	314
RALPH	AH	6	336	RAMSDEN	F	11	310	RANCE	WA	7	323	RANDALL	J	6	337
RALPH	BE	13	354	RAMSDEN	GE	8	275	RANCE	WC	3	185	RANDALL	JR	5	287
RALPH	C	10	186	RAMSDEN	H	8	275	RANCE	WG	5	286	RANDALL	JS	5	287
RALPH	C	14	260	RAMSDEN	H	9	157	RANCE	WH	5	286	RANDALL	L	13	354
RALPH	DJ	6	336	RAMSDEN	J	8	275	RANCE	WH	10	187	RANDALL	R	13	354
RALPH	E	9	326	RAMSDEN	J	9	157	RAND	G	4	314	RANDALL	S	5	287
RALPH	E	9	326	RAMSDEN	J	9	326	RAND	KM	13	354	RANDALL	SC	5	287
RALPH	E	10	186	RAMSDEN	J	11	310	RAND	WH	5	286	RANDALL	SG	5	287
RALPH	EJ	13	354	RAMSDEN	JK	8	275	RAND	WL	13	354	RANDALL	SG	13	354
RALPH	EW	7	322	RAMSDEN	JR	2	278	RANDALL	A	1	285	RANDALL	SG	13	354
RALPH	F	7	322	RAMSDEN	L	9	157	RANDALL	A	5	286	RANDALL	T	1	285
RALPH	G	9	157	RAMSDEN	R	8	275	RANDALL	A	5	286	RANDALL	T	4	314
RALPH	G	10	186	RAMSDEN	S	8	275	RANDALL	AE	4	314	RANDALL	T	5	287
RALPH	HA	4	314	RAMSDEN	S	14	260	RANDALL	AG	2	278	RANDALL	T	13	354
RALPH	HF	11	309	RAMSDEN	T	8	275	RANDALL	AG	2	278	RANDALL	TE	10	187
RALPH	HG	4	314	RAMSDON	C	8	276	RANDALL	AG	5	286	RANDALL	TJ	3	185
RALPH	HM	4	314	RAMSELL	WJ	13	354	RANDALL	B	8	276	RANDALL	V	6	337
RALPH	JJ	10	186	RAMSEY	A	8	276	RANDALL	BJ	12	184	RANDALL	V	10	187
RALPH	JS	10	186	RAMSEY	AD	3	184	RANDALL	C	3	185	RANDALL	VA	10	187
RALPH	R	5	286	RAMSEY	AJ	3	184	RANDALL	C	6	337	RANDALL	VK	10	187
RALPH	R	6	336	RAMSEY	B	10	187	RANDALL	CG	5	286	RANDALL	W	4	314
RALPH	S	9	157	RAMSEY	D	10	187	RANDALL	CJ	12	372	RANDALL	W	4	314
RALPH	T	9	326	RAMSEY	D	10	187	RANDALL	CV	3	185	RANDALL	W	5	287
RALPH	T	10	186	RAMSEY	G	1	285	RANDALL	D	5	286	RANDALL	WC	4	314
RALPH	W	5	286	RAMSEY	G	2	278	RANDALL	D	5	286	RANDALL	WC	5	287
RALPH	WE	4	314	RAMSEY	G	13	354	RANDALL	DR	6	337	RANDALL	WC	12	372
RALPH	WE	6	337	RAMSEY	H	7	323	RANDALL	E	6	337	RANDALL	WF	4	314
RALPH	WH	6	337	RAMSEY	H	10	187	RANDALL	EJ	5	286	RANDALL	WG	5	287
RALPH	WJ	4	314	RAMSEY	HE	1	285	RANDALL	F	3	185	RANDALL	WR	4	315
RALPHS	E	11	309	RAMSEY	JM	2	278	RANDALL	FH	7	323	RANDALL	WT	12	184
RALPHS	W	11	309	RAMSEY	JW	11	310	RANDALL	FJ	1	285	RANDELL	A	10	187
RAMAGE	FC	1	284	RAMSEY	LA	3	185	RANDALL	FJ	5	287	RANDELL	EG	4	315
RAMAGE	HE	7	322	RAMSEY	MW	3	185	RANDALL	FT	5	286	RANDELL	EH	5	287
RAMELL	J	11	310	RAMSEY	SW	1	285	RANDALL	G	1	285	RANDELL	FE	10	353
RAMELL	W	11	310	RAMSEY	T	13	354	RANDALL	G	5	286	RANDELL	GT	10	353
RAMPLIN	SW	13	354	RAMSEY	TW	3	185	RANDALL	G	5	287	RANDELL	H	6	337
RAMPTON	AJ	10	186	RAMSEY	W	8	276	RANDALL	GA	5	287	RANDELL	JA	10	353
RAMSAY	C	6	337	RAMSGILL	C	8	276	RANDALL	GD	5	287	RANDELL	W	10	353

RANDELS	CD	2	278	RAPLEY	WO	3	185	RATHBONE	GE	2	279	RAWLINGS	AH	7	323				
RANDERSON	TH	8	276	RAPP	H	2	278	RATHBONE	GH	4	315	RAWLINGS	CA	8	277				
RANDLE	AE	6	337	RAPPS	E	4	315	RATHBONE	H	11	310	RAWLINGS	CW	12	184				
RANDLE	AG	7	323	RAPSON	A	10	187	RATHBONE	T	11	310	RAWLINGS	D	8	277				
RANDLE	E	6	337	RAPSON	E	4	315	RATHBONE	W	11	310	RAWLINGS	E	1	286				
RANDLE	GJ	6	337	RAPSON	R	4	315	RATHBONE	WE	11	310	RAWLINGS	EA	10	354				
RANDLE	J	8	276	RASELL	EO	10	187	RATHMELL	JC	10	188	RAWLINGS	FF	2	279				
RANDLE	J	8	276	RASH	HC	2	278	RATHMILL	GB	11	310	RAWLINGS	FS	3	185				
RANDLE	JJ	6	337	RASHBROOK	G	13	355	RATHMILL	R	14	260	RAWLINGS	GM	7	323				
RANDLE	R	9	327	RASHLEIGH	CF	4	315	RATHYENS	C	4	315	RAWLINGS	H	1	286				
RANDLE	WA	6	337	RASTALL-EATON	C	3	185	RATHYENS	JJ	4	315	RAWLINGS	H	12	373				
RANDLE	WG	5	287	RASTRICK	G	9	157	RATHYENS	W	4	315	RAWLINGS	HA	7	324				
RANDOLPH	RJ	4	315	RATCHFORD	D	11	310	RATICAN	J	11	311	RAWLINGS	HR	13	355				
RANDS	C	12	372	RATCHFORD	E	8	276	RATTIGAN	M	11	311	RAWLINGS	HW	3	185				
RANDS	HG	5	287	RATCHFORD	M	8	276	RATTLE	WJ	13	355	RAWLINGS	HW	7	324				
RANFORD	GH	1	285	RATCLIFF	A	8	276	RATTLEY	LV	10	188	RAWLINGS	HW	12	184				
RANFORD	GW	6	338	RATCLIFF	F	8	276	RATTRAY	CW	2	279	RAWLINGS	J	12	184				
RANGER	C	1	285	RATCLIFF	H	8	276	RATTY	F	1	286	RAWLINGS	J	12	373				
RANGER	JW	13	354	RATCLIFF	HC	1	285	RAVEN	A	1	286	RAWLINGS	J	14	260				
RANK	J	9	157	RATCLIFF	W	1	285	RAVEN	CE	8	277	RAWLINGS	JE	1	286				
RANKIN	H	8	276	RATCLIFF	WAJ	1	285	RAVEN	CS	1	286	RAWLINGS	JH	13	355				
RANKIN	JH	9	157	RATCLIFFE	A	2	278	RAVEN	HA	1	286	RAWLINGS	JT	13	355				
RANKIN	TW	13	354	RATCLIFFE	A	6	338	RAVEN	HE	3	185	RAWLINGS	LE	1	286				
RANKS	E	13	354	RATCLIFFE	A	8	276	RAVEN	HJ	1	286	RAWLINGS	LP	3	186				
RANKS	ET	10	187	RATCLIFFE	A	12	184	RAVEN	W	4	315	RAWLINGS	M	9	391				
RANN	J	10	353	RATCLIFFE	AC	11	310	RAVENING	GC	2	279	RAWLINGS	OG	12	184				
RANN	SC	10	187	RATCLIFFE	AJ	12	184	RAVENSCROFT	BS	6	338	RAWLINGS	T	14	260				
RANN	TH	3	185	RATCLIFFE	C	11	310	RAVENSCROFT	C	4	315	RAWLINGS	WE	2	279				
RANNOW	EGV	2	278	RATCLIFFE	C	12	184	RAVENSCROFT	S	6	338	RAWLINGS	WJ	2	279				
RANNOW	EGV	2	278	RATCLIFFE	CE	7	323	RAW	C	8	277	RAWLINS	CJ	12	184				
RANSBEY	F	12	372	RATCLIFFE	F	14	260	RAW	F	9	327	RAWLINS	F	10	188				
RANSBY	JA	9	157	RATCLIFFE	F	14	260	RAW	J	9	158	RAWLINS	G	4	315				
RANSCOMBE	T	1	285	RATCLIFFE	FW	5	288	RAW	RN	9	327	RAWLINS	H	11	311				
RANSLEY	GH	2	278	RATCLIFFE	H	9	157	RAW	T	11	311	RAWLINS	J	5	288				
RANSOM	A	7	323	RATCLIFFE	H	14	260	RAW	TH	14	260	RAWLINS	JH	2	279				
RANSOM	HG	4	315	RATCLIFFE	J	2	279	RAW	W	9	158	RAWLINS	LJ	12	184				
RANSOM	HH	1	285	RATCLIFFE	J	3	185	RAWBONE	AC	3	383	RAWLINS	S	9	158				
RANSOM	R	2	278	RATCLIFFE	J	8	277	RAWCLIFFE	J	3	185	RAWLINS	SC	4	316				
RANSOM	VM	2	278	RATCLIFFE	J	11	310	RAWCLIFFE	JR	3	185	RAWLINS	T	4	316				
RANSOME	CR	8	276	RATCLIFFE	JG	12	372	RAWDEN	G	1	286	RAWLINS	WE	6	338				
RANSOME	HC	9	327	RATCLIFFE	JJ	14	260	RAWDING	HB	10	354	RAWLINSON	A	14	260				
RANSON	AE	7	323	RATCLIFFE	N	8	277	RAWDON	KA	1	286	RAWLINSON	E	1	286				
RANSON	AR	7	323	RATCLIFFE	R	9	327	RAWE	CH	4	315	RAWLINSON	H	1	286				
RANSON	JT	13	354	RATCLIFFE	R	11	310	RAWE	TW	7	323	RAWLINSON	H	14	260				
RANTELL	AT	1	285	RATCLIFFE	R	14	260	RAWES	T	6	338	RAWLINSON	JJE	1	286				
RAPER	G	9	327	RATCLIFFE	R	14	260	RAWLES	J	13	355	RAWLINSON	SM	14	260				
RAPER	H	8	276	RATCLIFFE	T	9	158	RAWLES	WC	4	315	RAWLINSON	T	14	260				
RAPER	H	9	157	RATCLIFFE	T	12	184	RAWLEY	AJ	2	279	RAWLINSON	WJ	8	277				
RAPER	S	9	327	RATCLIFFE	WA	1	285	RAWLIN	PD	8	277	RAWLINSON	WO	1	286				
RAPER	W	8	276	RATCLIFFE	WC	3	185	RAWLING	A	8	277	RAWNSLEY	AE	9	327				
RAPER	W	8	276	RATE	JA	12	372	RAWLING	JW	9	158	RAWNSLEY	B	9	158				
RAPER	WM	13	355	RATE	RA	13	355	RAWLING	T	8	277	RAWNSLEY	C	8	277				
RAPHAEL	B	14	260	RATEL	EM	10	187	RAWLINGS	AE	3	383	RAWNSLEY	FW	8	277				
RAPLEY	F	3	185	RATEL	GE	10	187	RAWLINGS	AE	3	383	RAWNSLEY	HM	8	277				
RAPLEY	JS	12	184	RATHBAND	W	6	338	RAWLINGS	AG	12	184	RAWNSLEY	J	8	277				

RAWNSLEY	T	8	277	RAY	W	7	324	RAYNER	HJ	10	188	READ	AJ	7	324
RAWNSLEY	W	8	277	RAY	W	10	188	RAYNER	HT	3	186	READ	AR	4	316
RAWSON	C	8	277	RAY	W	11	311	RAYNER	J	3	186	READ	AS	4	316
RAWSON	E	9	327	RAY	WA	10	188	RAYNER	J	5	288	READ	AS	4	316
RAWSON	JT	9	158	RAY	WF	4	316	RAYNER	JC	13	355	READ	AW	4	317
RAWSON	S	9	158	RAY	WR	5	288	RAYNER	JE	14	261	READ	B	1	287
RAWSON	S	9	158	RAYBONE	A	11	311	RAYNER	JW	8	278	READ	BT	10	188
RAWSON	T	11	311	RAYBONE	BH	6	338	RAYNER	LB	3	186	READ	C	1	287
RAWSON	W	8	277	RAYBONE	HT	6	338	RAYNER	P	7	324	READ	C	1	287
RAWSTON	WW	13	355	RAYBONE	JJ	6	338	RAYNER	PP	2	279	READ	C	3	186
RAXWORTHY	EG	1	286	RAYBOULD	GW	12	373	RAYNER	S	11	311	READ	C	5	288
RAXWORTHY	GW	1	286	RAYBOULD	J	4	316	RAYNER	SF	2	279	READ	C	8	278
RAY	A	3	186	RAYBOULD	JS	6	338	RAYNER	T	9	158	READ	C	14	261
RAY	A	5	288	RAYFIELD	EJ	7	324	RAYNER	TF	4	316	READ	CH	4	317
RAY	AE	6	338	RAYMEN	AE	2	279	RAYNER	W	1	287	READ	D	8	278
RAY	AF	13	355	RAYMEN	CW	2	279	RAYNER	W	1	287	READ	E	1	287
RAY	AJ	7	324	RAYMEN	G	2	279	RAYNER	W	5	288	READ	E	2	280
RAY	AR	9	158	RAYMENT	BE	5	288	RAYNER	W	8	278	READ	E	6	339
RAY	ARE	9	327	RAYMENT	E	2	279	RAYNER	W	9	327	READ	E	7	324
RAY	AS	10	188	RAYMENT	E	5	288	RAYNER	WP	13	355	READ	E	7	324
RAY	AW	5	288	RAYMENT	HP	2	279	RAYNES	F	11	311	READ	E	9	158
RAY	C	10	188	RAYMENT	HP	10	188	RAYNHAM	WG	4	316	READ	EH	1	287
RAY	CG	13	355	RAYMENT	SE	1	286	RAYNOR	C	9	158	READ	EH	4	317
RAY	D	6	338	RAYMOND	AE	4	316	RAYNOR	EG	3	186	READ	EJ	10	188
RAY	E	4	316	RAYMOND	B	4	316	RAYNOR	JH	11	311	READ	F	1	287
RAY	E	6	338	RAYMOND	BA	13	355	RAYNOR	WH	1	287	READ	F	4	317
RAY	E	10	188	RAYMOND	F	1	287	RAYSON	D	12	185	READ	F	5	289
RAY	E	10	188	RAYMOND	G	14	261	RAYSON	G	12	373	READ	F	9	158
RAY	EE	8	277	RAYMOND	J	3	186	RAYSON	GF	11	311	READ	F	10	188
RAY	ER	2	279	RAYMOND	JF	1	287	RAYSON	RG	13	355	READ	F	10	189
RAY	F	12	184	RAYMOND	JG	10	188	RAYSON	W	10	354	READ	FC	12	185
RAY	F	13	355	RAYMOND	TL	14	261	RAYSON	WA	10	354	READ	FH	4	317
RAY	FG	2	279	RAYMOND	WH	1	287	RAYSON	WJ	4	316	READ	FJ	1	287
RAY	FW	2	279	RAYNER	A	1	287	RAYSON	WT	12	185	READ	FM	6	339
RAY	FW	5	288	RAYNER	A	2	279	RAZEY	CJ	4	315	READ	FS	13	356
RAY	GE	13	355	RAYNER	A	4	316	RAZEY	JD	4	315	READ	G	1	287
RAY	GH	10	188	RAYNER	A	7	324	RAZEY	WJ	4	315	READ	G	1	287
RAY	GJ	4	316	RAYNER	A	7	324	RAZZALL	AP	13	356	READ	G	2	280
RAY	H	8	277	RAYNER	AJ	13	355	REA	AE	6	339	READ	G	4	317
RAY	H	12	184	RAYNER	AR	3	186	REA	AE	6	339	READ	G	4	317
RAY	JE	5	288	RAYNER	ATS	3	186	REA	AL	4	316	READ	G	6	339
RAY	JH	7	324	RAYNER	CA	3	186	REA	GC	7	324	READ	GB	10	189
RAY	JHT	10	188	RAYNER	CE	13	355	REA	J	11	311	READ	GE	6	339
RAY	JS	8	277	RAYNER	CWE	7	324	REA	SR	6	339	READ	GH	1	287
RAY	LW	5	288	RAYNER	E	11	311	READ	A	4	316	READ	GH	4	317
RAY	PE	3	186	RAYNER	EJ	10	188	READ	A	5	288	READ	GW	7	324
RAY	R	12	184	RAYNER	F	1	287	READ	A	6	339	READ	GW	8	278
RAY	S	6	338	RAYNER	F	5	288	READ	A	8	278	READ	H	1	288
RAY	SJ	10	188	RAYNER	F	8	278	READ	A	10	354	READ	H	4	317
RAY	T	1	286	RAYNER	F	8	278	READ	A	12	185	READ	H	6	339
RAY	VA	6	338	RAYNER	F	11	311	READ	AE	1	287	READ	H	10	189
RAY	VG	4	316	RAYNER	FT	3	186	READ	AG	7	324	READ	H	11	311
RAY	W	5	288	RAYNER	H	5	288	READ	AJ	2	280	READ	HB	5	289
RAY	W	6	338	RAYNER	H	8	278	READ	AJ	4	316	READ	HC	10	354
RAY	W	6	338	RAYNER	H	10	188	READ	AJ	6	339	READ	HR	4	317

READ	HW	5	289	READER	F	3	186	RECORD	W	13	356	REDGATE	WG	13	356
READ	J	4	317	READER	FJ	3	186	REDBURN	AC	2	280	REDGRAVE	JT	9	158
READ	J	4	317	READER	H	6	339	REDD	W	3	187	REDGWELL	GA	13	356
READ	J	6	339	READER	JW	9	158	REDDECLIFFE	W	7	325	REDGWELL	JW	3	187
READ	J	11	311	READER	TH	3	186	REDDELL	A	6	340	REDHEAD	C	2	280
READ	J	11	311	READEY	J	11	312	REDDELL	BA	4	318	REDHEAD	R	9	158
READ	J	12	185	READEY	J	11	312	REDDELL	FR	4	318	REDHEAD	T	2	280
READ	J	14	261	READHEAD	HS	5	289	REDDELL	HH	2	280	REDHEAD	W	5	289
READ	JCL	3	383	READING	A	6	339	REDDELL	PG	4	318	REDHEAD	WR	1	289
READ	JH	10	189	READING	A	12	185	REDDELL	WA	4	318	REDIKIN	W	11	312
READ	JH	14	261	READING	AE	5	289	REDDELL	WR	3	187	REDINGTON	LJ	12	185
READ	JM	5	289	READING	AE	6	339	REDDICEN	H	11	312	REDLEY	H	12	373
READ	JT	4	317	READING	DM	1	288	REDDICK	J	1	289	REDLEY	WM	12	373
READ	JW	2	280	READING	EJ	2	280	REDDIN	J	2	280	REDMAN	AH	13	356
READ	LA	3	186	READING	EM	2	280	REDDIN	JF	7	325	REDMAN	AJ	4	318
READ	LF	4	317	READING	G	6	339	REDDIN	WC	4	318	REDMAN	AJ	12	185
READ	M	1	288	READING	H	6	339	REDDING	AE	4	318	REDMAN	B	3	187
READ	M	4	317	READING	H	6	339	REDDING	AM	6	340	REDMAN	B	9	327
READ	MT	4	317	READING	HAJ	13	356	REDDING	C	4	318	REDMAN	B	10	189
READ	P	9	327	READING	HJ	2	280	REDDING	GH	10	189	REDMAN	CW	10	189
READ	PE	3	186	READING	J	3	186	REDDING	H	4	318	REDMAN	D	10	354
READ	PH	4	317	READING	J	6	339	REDDING	H	4	318	REDMAN	E	2	280
READ	R	10	354	READING	PA	5	289	REDDING	H	7	325	REDMAN	EG	4	318
READ	RC	3	186	READING	T	1	288	REDDING	J	2	280	REDMAN	F	2	280
READ	RG	12	185	READING	W	5	289	REDDING	J	4	318	REDMAN	F	4	318
READ	RM	3	186	READINGS	AW	2	280	REDDING	J	10	189	REDMAN	G	1	289
READ	S	1	288	READWIN	B	7	324	REDDING	J	10	189	REDMAN	GF	2	281
READ	SHJ	13	356	READY	W	5	289	REDDING	R	2	280	REDMAN	H	8	278
READ	SW	5	289	READY	WJ	1	288	REDDING	R	4	318	REDMAN	H	9	159
READ	T	1	288	REAGH	S	14	261	REDDING	T	6	340	REDMAN	HJ	12	185
READ	TV	3	186	REAGRAVES	J	13	356	REDDING	TA	6	340	REDMAN	J	2	281
READ	VA	1	288	REAK	WH	10	189	REDDING	W	1	289	REDMAN	J	12	185
READ	W	1	288	REAMAN	O	9	158	REDDING	W	3	187	REDMAN	JC	11	312
READ	W	1	288	REAMS	A	1	288	REDDING	WF	4	318	REDMAN	JE	3	187
READ	W	5	289	REANEY	AT	6	339	REDDING	WH	10	189	REDMAN	LP	3	187
READ	W	7	324	REANEY	J	8	278	REDDINGTON	T	8	278	REDMAN	LW	12	185
READ	W	8	278	REARDON	FJ	1	288	REDDINGTON	T	8	278	REDMAN	PG	12	185
READ	W	10	189	REARDON	J	8	278	REDDLE	JA	6	340	REDMAN	R	8	279
READ	W	10	189	REARDON	JH	10	189	REDDY	FG	10	354	REDMAN	R	9	327
READ	WC	10	189	REARDON	JW	8	278	REDDYHOFF	GF	8	278	REDMAN	S	3	187
READ	WD	1	288	REARDON	O	8	278	REDELSPERGER	P	1	289	REDMAN	S	11	312
READ	WD	4	317	REARDON	P	13	356	REDFERN	A	11	312	REDMAN	S	14	261
READ	WF	4	317	REARDON	P	13	356	REDFERN	A	14	261	REDMAN	TE	4	318
READ	WG	1	288	REARDON	S	13	356	REDFERN	E	6	340	REDMAN	TJ	13	356
READ	WH	2	280	REARDON	T	8	278	REDFERN	E	8	278	REDMAN	TW	5	289
READ	WH	12	185	REASON	JW	1	288	REDFERN	E	11	312	REDMAN	W	4	318
READ	WH	12	185	REASON	T	6	340	REDFERN	F	11	312	REDMAN	W	12	185
READ	WJ	7	324	REASON	W	1	288	REDFERN	HJ	12	185	REDMAN	WC	5	289
READ	WR	4	317	REAVELL	EW	7	324	REDFERN	J	11	312	REDMAN	WE	4	318
READE	AA	2	280	REAVELL	L	5	289	REDFERN	JH	11	312	REDMAN	WF	10	189
READE	H	6	339	REAVEY	F	14	261	REDFERN	T	6	340	REDMAN	WH	12	185
READE	HB	2	280	REBBECK	AJ	1	288	REDFORD	A	10	189	REDMAN	WJ	10	189
READE	LL	11	311	REBBECK	RS	1	288	REDFORD	AP	14	261	REDMAYNE	TV	14	261
READE	TJ	11	312	REBBECK	WG	1	289	REDFORD	H	11	312	REDMILE	GD	7	325
READER	AR	1	288	RECORD	CH	1	289	REDFORD	W	14	261	REDMOND	F	14	261

REDMOND	J	8	279	REED	E	13	357	REED	WJ	8	279	REEVE	G	12	373
REDMOND	M	14	261	REED	EA	4	319	REED	WR	11	313	REEVE	H	12	186
REDMOND	R	8	279	REED	EG	10	190	REED	WT	7	325	REEVE	H	12	373
REDMOND	W	8	279	REED	EGW	1	289	REEDER	G	8	279	REEVE	H	12	373
REDMOND	W	9	159	REED	F	1	289	REEDER	HJ	5	290	REEVE	HGW	10	190
REDPATH	CO	1	289	REED	F	3	187	REEDER	M	8	279	REEVE	HS	12	373
REDRUP	A	5	289	REED	FC	4	319	REEDER	SA	8	279	REEVE	J	1	290
REDSELL	AW	13	356	REED	FC	10	354	REEDMAN	AB	12	186	REEVE	J	12	186
REDSHAW	A	8	279	REED	FE	4	319	REEDMAN	HWC	2	281	REEVE	JW	1	290
REDSHAW	CS	8	279	REED	FF	4	319	REEDMAN	OV	12	186	REEVE	JW	1	290
REDSHAW	H	8	279	REED	FJ	2	281	REEDMAN	W	1	289	REEVE	JW	7	325
REDSHAW	HD	9	159	REED	FR	4	319	REEGAM	J	1	289	REEVE	R	14	261
REDSHAW	L	8	279	REED	FW	10	190	REEK	LW	8	280	REEVE	RA	4	319
REDSHAW	OEG	4	318	REED	G	3	187	REEKS	E	2	281	REEVE	RH	12	373
REDSHAW	W	8	279	REED	GA	13	356	REEKS	WJ	5	290	REEVE	RJ	3	188
REDSTON	AH	11	312	REED	GF	3	187	REELAND	GJ	3	187	REEVE	S	12	373
REDSTONE	HJ	13	356	REED	GH	4	319	REEPE	B	3	188	REEVE	SL	5	290
REDSULL	RG	5	289	REED	GR	8	279	REES	AG	10	190	REEVE	SP	12	373
REDWOOD	WG	6	340	REED	GWJ	10	354	REES	AG	10	190	REEVE	SR	2	281
REE	HS	10	190	REED	H	3	187	REES	AR	13	357	REEVE	TA	12	186
REECE	A	1	289	REED	H	3	187	REES	AV	10	190	REEVE	W	6	340
REECE	A	1	289	REED	HA	13	357	REES	BJ	10	354	REEVE	W	10	190
REECE	AH	5	289	REED	HE	12	186	REES	C	3	188	REEVE	WD	12	373
REECE	E	7	325	REED	HG	4	319	REES	CA	13	357	REEVE	WG	1	290
REECE	EA	2	281	REED	HG	9	159	REES	CE	10	190	REEVELL	E	13	357
REECE	F	3	384	REED	HW	4	319	REES	DJ	3	188	REEVES	A	2	281
REECE	G	14	261	REED	J	8	279	REES	EW	10	190	REEVES	A	8	280
REECE	HA	13	356	REED	J	10	190	REES	FC	13	357	REEVES	AA	1	290
REECE	RE	2	281	REED	J	11	312	REES	G	10	190	REEVES	AE	1	290
REECE	RH	11	312	REED	JD	8	279	REES	GA	10	190	REEVES	AE	13	357
REECE	SH	2	281	REED	JE	11	313	REES	HS	9	159	REEVES	AE	13	357
REECE	T	13	356	REED	JE	13	357	REES	HS	9	327	REEVES	AF	4	319
REECE	WH	9	327	REED	JH	12	186	REES	HS	10	190	REEVES	AG	4	319
REED	A	4	318	REED	JS	11	312	REES	IT	13	357	REEVES	AG	10	191
REED	A	8	279	REED	JT	7	325	REES	JR	14	261	REEVES	AV	7	325
REED	A	8	279	REED	JW	13	357	REES	JW	7	325	REEVES	AW	2	281
REED	A	11	312	REED	K	13	357	REES	ME	9	159	REEVES	BE	4	319
REED	AE	12	185	REED	N	3	187	REES	PE	10	190	REEVES	BH	5	290
REED	AG	13	356	REED	NE	3	187	REES	R	13	357	REEVES	BJ	3	188
REED	AH	2	281	REED	R	7	325	REES	SG	10	190	REEVES	CA	4	320
REED	AH	3	187	REED	RG	4	319	REES	WH	6	340	REEVES	CB	4	320
REED	AH	4	319	REED	RR	4	319	REESE	DR	6	340	REEVES	CH	4	320
REED	AL	5	290	REED	S	3	187	REESE	EW	1	289	REEVES	CR	5	290
REED	AV	1	289	REED	SE	4	319	REESE	WH	1	289	REEVES	D	2	281
REED	B	10	190	REED	T	8	279	REEVE	A	1	289	REEVES	DA	5	290
REED	C	1	289	REED	T	8	279	REEVE	A	5	290	REEVES	E	7	325
REED	C	2	281	REED	T	13	357	REEVE	A	12	424	REEVES	E	13	357
REED	C	3	187	REED	TC	12	186	REEVE	AE	5	290	REEVES	EA	4	320
REED	C	10	190	REED	TE	10	190	REEVE	C	12	424	REEVES	EAW	1	290
REED	CC	5	290	REED	WE	4	319	REEVE	F	1	289	REEVES	EE	5	290
REED	CHT	7	325	REED	WF	12	373	REEVE	FA	7	325	REEVES	EJ	13	357
REED	CS	5	289	REED	WG	4	319	REEVE	FJ	1	290	REEVES	EM	7	325
REED	CS	12	186	REED	WH	4	319	REEVE	FJ	12	186	REEVES	EW	10	191
REED	E	3	187	REED	WH	5	290	REEVE	FS	7	325	REEVES	F	2	281
REED	E	10	190	REED	WHL	5	290	REEVE	G	12	373	REEVES	F	4	320

REEVES	F	11	313	REEVES	WH	10	191	REID	F	7	326	REMMERS	E	1	291
REEVES	FA	5	290	REEVES	WP	4	320	REID	F	10	191	REMMERS	NA	1	291
REEVES	FJ	7	325	REEVES	WP	5	291	REID	G	14	262	REMMONDS	P	8	280
REEVES	FL	10	354	REFFELL	EE	13	358	REID	GJM	4	321	REMMOS	A	11	313
REEVES	G	4	320	REGAN	C	8	280	REID	H	12	186	REMMOS	O	11	313
REEVES	G	4	320	REGAN	CF	10	191	REID	H	14	262	REMNANT	HA	4	321
REEVES	G	4	320	REGAN	D	3	188	REID	HA	12	186	REMNANT	HJ	3	188
REEVES	G	5	290	REGAN	D	6	341	REID	HA	12	186	REMSBERY	CH	4	321
REEVES	G	6	340	REGAN	D	8	280	REID	J	11	313	RENALDS	A	9	159
REEVES	G	12	186	REGAN	E	3	188	REID	J	12	186	RENDALL	A	1	291
REEVES	GF	4	320	REGAN	EJ	10	191	REID	JH	12	186	RENDALL	L	12	373
REEVES	GT	3	188	REGAN	F	7	326	REID	JR	11	313	RENDELL	F	4	321
REEVES	GW	7	325	REGAN	FA	11	313	REID	L	2	282	RENDER	RS	7	326
REEVES	H	1	290	REGAN	FW	10	191	REID	OD	3	188	RENDLE	EH	13	358
REEVES	H	4	320	REGAN	H	7	326	REID	R	1	290	RENDLE	LS	13	358
REEVES	H	5	290	REGAN	J	8	280	REID	R	8	280	RENDLE	RC	13	358
REEVES	H	6	340	REGAN	J	13	358	REID	RA	7	326	RENDLE	RC	13	358
REEVES	HG	4	320	REGAN	J	14	262	REID	T	4	321	RENFELL	A	2	282
REEVES	HG	5	290	REGAN	JE	3	188	REID	T	8	280	RENNARD	F	8	280
REEVES	HN	10	354	REGAN	JL	6	341	REID	T	14	262	RENNARD	K	8	280
REEVES	HW	5	290	REGAN	JP	13	358	REID	T	14	262	RENNETT	GM	4	321
REEVES	HW	6	340	REGAN	L	8	280	REID	TA	8	280	RENNETT	VG	4	321
REEVES	J	3	384	REGAN	P	4	320	REID	TJ	5	291	RENNIE	E	11	313
REEVES	J	6	340	REGAN	P	4	320	REID	W	3	188	RENNIE	J	2	282
REEVES	J	10	191	REGAN	P	7	326	REID	W	7	326	RENNIE	J	8	280
REEVES	J	13	357	REGAN	P	13	358	REID	W	7	326	RENNIE	J	14	262
REEVES	J	13	357	REGAN	P	13	358	REID	W	11	313	RENNIE	J	14	262
REEVES	J	14	262	REGAN	RH	13	358	REID	W	12	186	RENNIE	TN	9	327
REEVES	J	14	262	REGAN	T	8	280	REID	WA	5	291	RENNISON	E	9	159
REEVES	JC	3	188	REGAN	T	8	280	REID	WF	7	326	RENNISON	W	8	280
REEVES	JH	13	358	REGAN	T	8	280	REID	WG	12	186	RENNLES	ELG	13	358
REEVES	JO	11	313	REGAN	T	13	358	REIDY	JJ	1	290	RENSHAW	A	14	262
REEVES	JR	11	313	REGAN	W	3	188	REILLY	F	13	358	RENSHAW	CR	1	291
REEVES	L	14	262	REGAN	WE	10	191	REILLY	F	14	262	RENSHAW	CW	14	262
REEVES	M	2	281	REGAN	WJ	2	281	REILLY	J	11	313	RENSHAW	FT	11	313
REEVES	PA	3	188	REGAN	WJ	10	191	REILLY	J	11	313	RENSHAW	H	14	262
REEVES	R	4	320	REGAZZONI	FJ	3	188	REILLY	J	13	358	RENSHAW	HJ	1	291
REEVES	R	7	326	REGAZZONI	LD	3	188	REILLY	MB	14	262	RENSHAW	J	14	262
REEVES	RJ	3	188	REGESTER	G	13	358	REILLY	P	9	327	RENSHAW	T	1	291
REEVES	SJ	6	340	REGGIE	P	5	291	REILLY	P	14	262	RENSHAW	TA	14	263
REEVES	T	5	291	REGLAR	F	4	320	REILLY	T	12	373	RENSHAW	W	6	341
REEVES	T	6	341	REGLER	W	4	320	REILLY	W	1	290	RENSHAW	W	11	313
REEVES	T	6	341	REGNIER	F	1	290	REINHARDT	H	8	280	RENSHAW	W	14	263
REEVES	TR	10	354	REGNIER	LG	1	290	REISS	I	8	280	RENSHAW	W	14	263
REEVES	VG	5	290	REGNIER	W	10	191	REITH	A	10	354	RENSHAW	WH	14	263
REEVES	W	4	320	REGNIER	WJ	1	290	REITH	FW	4	321	RENSHAW	WR	14	263
REEVES	W	6	341	REID	AC	12	186	REITZ	EJ	7	326	RENTON	A	8	280
REEVES	W	6	341	REID	AJ	3	188	RELF	E	1	291	RENTON	CS	9	159
REEVES	WA	5	291	REID	AJ	8	280	RELF	E	1	291	RENTON	EA	9	159
REEVES	WA	10	354	REID	C	14	262	RELF	H	1	290	RENTON	H	8	281
REEVES	WC	2	281	REID	CA	7	326	RELF	WT	1	291	RENTON	JA	13	358
REEVES	WC	2	281	REID	CE	1	290	RELPH	C	13	358	RENTON	M	13	359
REEVES	WG	1	290	REID	CW	4	320	RELPH	F	11	313	RENTOWL	E	10	191
REEVES	WG	13	357	REID	E	7	326	RELPH	W	6	341	RENWICK	P	10	191
REEVES	WH	4	320	REID	EJ	2	281	RELPH	WM	6	341	RENYARD	A	4	321

Surname	Initials	No.	Page	Surname	Initials	No.	Page	Surname	Initials	No.	Page	Surname	Initials	No.	Page
RENYARD	G	4	321	REYNOLDS	A	6	341	REYNOLDS	HJ	12	187	REYNOLDS	TJ	5	291
RENYARD	WW	4	321	REYNOLDS	A	7	327	REYNOLDS	HV	3	384	REYNOLDS	TW	1	291
RENZER	J	9	159	REYNOLDS	A	7	327	REYNOLDS	HW	3	384	REYNOLDS	TW	1	291
RESTALL	EH	10	354	REYNOLDS	A	12	187	REYNOLDS	HW	5	291	REYNOLDS	TWJ	10	355
RESTALL	H	10	355	REYNOLDS	A	13	359	REYNOLDS	J	3	189	REYNOLDS	W	5	292
RESTALL	HM	10	354	REYNOLDS	A	14	263	REYNOLDS	J	4	321	REYNOLDS	W	6	342
RESTRICK	AS	7	326	REYNOLDS	AG	3	189	REYNOLDS	J	4	321	REYNOLDS	W	6	342
RESTRICK	E	11	313	REYNOLDS	AH	1	291	REYNOLDS	J	8	281	REYNOLDS	W	6	342
RESUGGAN	S	6	341	REYNOLDS	AJ	3	189	REYNOLDS	J	8	281	REYNOLDS	W	9	160
REUBEN	B	14	263	REYNOLDS	B	3	384	REYNOLDS	J	9	159	REYNOLDS	W	10	191
REUBEN	S	14	263	REYNOLDS	C	3	189	REYNOLDS	J	9	328	REYNOLDS	W	10	355
REUBEN	W	12	373	REYNOLDS	C	7	327	REYNOLDS	J	10	355	REYNOLDS	W	12	374
REUBENS	SE	14	263	REYNOLDS	C	7	327	REYNOLDS	J	11	314	REYNOLDS	W	14	263
REUMEL	FA	7	326	REYNOLDS	C	9	159	REYNOLDS	J	11	314	REYNOLDS	W	14	263
REUMEL	WJ	7	326	REYNOLDS	C	14	263	REYNOLDS	J	11	314	REYNOLDS	WC	7	327
REVELL	A	8	281	REYNOLDS	CB	7	327	REYNOLDS	J	11	314	REYNOLDS	WD	12	187
REVELL	C	7	326	REYNOLDS	CG	5	291	REYNOLDS	J	11	314	REYNOLDS	WE	6	342
REVELL	F	3	188	REYNOLDS	CH	8	281	REYNOLDS	J	12	187	REYNOLDS	WG	5	292
REVELL	G	8	281	REYNOLDS	CHW	7	327	REYNOLDS	JA	2	282	REYNOLDS	WG	12	187
REVELL	H	7	326	REYNOLDS	CL	2	282	REYNOLDS	JD	6	341	REYNOLDS	WG	13	359
REVELL	R	9	159	REYNOLDS	CR	11	314	REYNOLDS	JH	12	374	REYNOLDS	WJ	1	292
REVELL	RW	3	188	REYNOLDS	CS	13	359	REYNOLDS	JM	7	327	REYNOLDS	WJ	5	291
REVELL	T	7	327	REYNOLDS	CWJ	4	321	REYNOLDS	JT	9	159	REYNOLDS	WJ	13	359
REVELL	W	6	341	REYNOLDS	DE	6	341	REYNOLDS	JW	3	189	REYNOLDS	WR	10	355
REVELL	W	10	355	REYNOLDS	E	10	191	REYNOLDS	JW	8	281	REYNOLDS	WS	3	189
REVELL	W	12	187	REYNOLDS	EO	10	355	REYNOLDS	K	3	189	REYNOLDS	WT	1	292
REVELS	H	12	187	REYNOLDS	ET	13	359	REYNOLDS	L	1	291	REYPERT	F	10	191
REVETT	J	11	314	REYNOLDS	EW	1	291	REYNOLDS	L	9	159	RHAN	J	4	321
REVETT	W	11	314	REYNOLDS	F	1	291	REYNOLDS	M	6	342	RHEAD	EA	2	282
REVILL	AE	10	191	REYNOLDS	F	3	189	REYNOLDS	M	6	342	RHEUBOTTOM	J	14	263
REVILL	TW	6	341	REYNOLDS	F	5	291	REYNOLDS	M	11	314	RHIND	A	13	359
REVITT	AG	6	341	REYNOLDS	F	9	327	REYNOLDS	P	2	282	RHODES	A	8	281
REVITT	G	9	159	REYNOLDS	F	14	263	REYNOLDS	P	5	291	RHODES	A	8	281
REVITT	H	9	159	REYNOLDS	FA	3	189	REYNOLDS	P	9	160	RHODES	A	8	281
REVITT	J	13	359	REYNOLDS	FJ	5	291	REYNOLDS	P	12	187	RHODES	A	8	281
REW	E	4	321	REYNOLDS	FW	7	327	REYNOLDS	P	12	187	RHODES	A	8	281
REW	HJ	8	281	REYNOLDS	FW	12	187	REYNOLDS	P	14	263	RHODES	A	9	160
REW	T	4	321	REYNOLDS	G	1	291	REYNOLDS	PC	1	291	RHODES	A	9	160
REW	W	4	321	REYNOLDS	G	5	291	REYNOLDS	PW	5	291	RHODES	A	9	328
REWCASTLE	GB	3	188	REYNOLDS	G	9	327	REYNOLDS	RF	2	282	RHODES	A	9	328
REX	H	10	191	REYNOLDS	G	13	359	REYNOLDS	S	8	281	RHODES	A	9	328
REX	S	13	359	REYNOLDS	G	13	359	REYNOLDS	S	13	359	RHODES	AC	3	384
REXON	WG	2	282	REYNOLDS	GA	12	187	REYNOLDS	S	13	359	RHODES	AE	6	342
REYGATE	HJ	3	189	REYNOLDS	GA	13	359	REYNOLDS	SA	6	342	RHODES	AJ	6	342
REYLAND	WT	1	291	REYNOLDS	GF	3	189	REYNOLDS	SG	7	327	RHODES	AV	5	292
REYMOND	A	8	281	REYNOLDS	GH	6	341	REYNOLDS	SL	3	189	RHODES	B	3	384
REYNARD	A	8	281	REYNOLDS	GH	6	341	REYNOLDS	T	1	291	RHODES	B	9	328
REYNARD	D	9	327	REYNOLDS	GT	3	189	REYNOLDS	T	8	281	RHODES	C	9	160
REYNARD	H	5	291	REYNOLDS	H	1	291	REYNOLDS	T	9	160	RHODES	CF	1	292
REYNARD	J	5	291	REYNOLDS	H	3	189	REYNOLDS	T	9	160	RHODES	CG	12	374
REYNARD	WM	9	159	REYNOLDS	H	5	291	REYNOLDS	T	11	314	RHODES	D	14	263
REYNER	FW	13	359	REYNOLDS	H	6	341	REYNOLDS	T	14	263	RHODES	E	8	281
REYNOLDS	A	3	189	REYNOLDS	H	7	327	REYNOLDS	TGA	4	321	RHODES	E	9	160
REYNOLDS	A	4	321	REYNOLDS	H	8	281	REYNOLDS	TH	6	342	RHODES	F	6	342
REYNOLDS	A	5	291	REYNOLDS	H	8	281	REYNOLDS				RHODES	F	8	281

Name	Init	Col	Page	Name	Init	Col	Page	Name	Init	Col	Page	Name	Init	Col	Page
RHODES	F	9	160	RICE	C	6	342	RICHARDS	A	4	322	RICHARDS	J	9	160
RHODES	F	9	160	RICE	C	14	264	RICHARDS	A	5	292	RICHARDS	J	9	328
RHODES	F	9	160	RICE	CW	4	321	RICHARDS	A	6	343	RICHARDS	J	10	356
RHODES	FH	9	160	RICE	DA	1	292	RICHARDS	A	10	355	RICHARDS	J	11	314
RHODES	FW	5	292	RICE	E	6	342	RICHARDS	A	10	355	RICHARDS	J	11	424
RHODES	G	8	281	RICE	EE	9	328	RICHARDS	A	13	360	RICHARDS	JA	1	292
RHODES	G	9	328	RICE	EH	13	359	RICHARDS	AA	6	343	RICHARDS	JA	6	343
RHODES	GB	9	328	RICE	ER	1	292	RICHARDS	AAP	4	322	RICHARDS	JC	11	315
RHODES	GH	8	282	RICE	FR	1	292	RICHARDS	AC	10	355	RICHARDS	JE	13	360
RHODES	GI	8	282	RICE	FS	10	191	RICHARDS	AC	13	360	RICHARDS	JKB	7	328
RHODES	H	8	282	RICE	G	3	190	RICHARDS	AE	3	190	RICHARDS	JM	11	315
RHODES	H	8	282	RICE	G	5	292	RICHARDS	AE	4	322	RICHARDS	JW	3	190
RHODES	H	9	328	RICE	G	7	327	RICHARDS	AJ	10	192	RICHARDS	JW	3	190
RHODES	H	11	314	RICE	G	7	327	RICHARDS	AT	6	343	RICHARDS	JW	10	355
RHODES	H	11	314	RICE	GA	10	355	RICHARDS	AW	13	360	RICHARDS	JW	13	360
RHODES	H	12	187	RICE	GB	3	190	RICHARDS	B	6	343	RICHARDS	L	3	190
RHODES	J	8	282	RICE	GE	1	292	RICHARDS	C	10	355	RICHARDS	L	6	343
RHODES	J	8	282	RICE	GH	3	190	RICHARDS	CH	7	328	RICHARDS	LF	1	292
RHODES	J	8	282	RICE	GPA	3	190	RICHARDS	E	3	190	RICHARDS	M	14	264
RHODES	J	9	160	RICE	GR	13	359	RICHARDS	E	6	343	RICHARDS	MG	6	343
RHODES	J	14	263	RICE	H	4	321	RICHARDS	E	6	343	RICHARDS	P	3	190
RHODES	J	14	263	RICE	HF	6	342	RICHARDS	E	10	192	RICHARDS	P	4	322
RHODES	JB	9	160	RICE	HJ	10	355	RICHARDS	E	10	355	RICHARDS	PA	4	322
RHODES	JE	6	342	RICE	HW	2	282	RICHARDS	E	12	374	RICHARDS	PL	1	292
RHODES	JE	8	282	RICE	J	3	190	RICHARDS	E	14	264	RICHARDS	R	4	322
RHODES	JT	14	264	RICE	J	7	327	RICHARDS	EE	1	292	RICHARDS	R	6	343
RHODES	JW	9	160	RICE	J	11	314	RICHARDS	EG	3	190	RICHARDS	RG	3	190
RHODES	L	6	342	RICE	J	11	314	RICHARDS	EH	11	315	RICHARDS	S	4	322
RHODES	L	8	282	RICE	J	12	374	RICHARDS	EL	3	190	RICHARDS	S	4	322
RHODES	R	14	264	RICE	JJ	2	282	RICHARDS	EM	5	292	RICHARDS	S	6	343
RHODES	RW	9	160	RICE	JJ	2	282	RICHARDS	EW	3	190	RICHARDS	SG	6	343
RHODES	S	8	282	RICE	OL	12	374	RICHARDS	EW	4	322	RICHARDS	SJ	13	360
RHODES	T	8	282	RICE	S	13	360	RICHARDS	F	4	322	RICHARDS	T	4	322
RHODES	T	9	160	RICE	SA	1	292	RICHARDS	F	4	322	RICHARDS	T	6	343
RHODES	TH	12	374	RICE	T	1	292	RICHARDS	F	8	282	RICHARDS	T	11	315
RHODES	W	8	282	RICE	T	13	360	RICHARDS	FS	4	322	RICHARDS	T	12	187
RHODES	W	8	282	RICE	W	11	314	RICHARDS	FS	4	322	RICHARDS	VG	3	190
RHODES	W	8	282	RICE	W	13	359	RICHARDS	G	4	322	RICHARDS	VH	6	343
RHODES	W	8	282	RICE	WCH	6	342	RICHARDS	G	7	328	RICHARDS	W	3	190
RHODES	W	9	160	RICE	WH	3	190	RICHARDS	G	10	192	RICHARDS	W	3	190
RHODES	W	9	328	RICE	WJ	6	342	RICHARDS	G	11	315	RICHARDS	W	6	343
RHODES	W	9	328	RICH	AE	13	360	RICHARDS	G	11	315	RICHARDS	W	6	343
RHYL	PH	13	359	RICH	C	2	282	RICHARDS	GT	13	360	RICHARDS	W	6	344
RIBBANDS	CJ	3	189	RICH	C	7	327	RICHARDS	GW	13	360	RICHARDS	W	7	328
RIBBONS	SH	1	292	RICH	C	12	374	RICHARDS	H	9	328	RICHARDS	W	11	315
RIBCHESTER	L	1	292	RICH	EJ	7	327	RICHARDS	HA	13	360	RICHARDS	W	12	187
RIBGY	TH	12	375	RICH	FW	3	190	RICHARDS	HB	10	355	RICHARDS	WEE	4	322
RICCI	FE	3	189	RICH	H	4	322	RICHARDS	HG	10	356	RICHARDS	WJ	13	360
RICCI	RPF	3	189	RICH	HE	10	192	RICHARDS	HJ	7	328	RICHARDS	WS	5	292
RICE	A	3	189	RICH	HF	7	327	RICHARDS	HW	4	322	RICHARDS	WW	4	322
RICE	A	7	327	RICH	WJ	4	322	RICHARDS	HW	4	322	RICHARDSON	A	7	328
RICE	AC	2	282	RICHARD	A	11	314	RICHARDS	HW	6	343	RICHARDSON	A	7	328
RICE	AG	5	292	RICHARD	ER	9	160	RICHARDS	J	6	343	RICHARDSON	A	8	282
RICE	AJ	1	292	RICHARD	J	2	282	RICHARDS	J	6	343	RICHARDSON	A	8	282
RICE	AV	3	189	RICHARDS	A	4	322	RICHARDS	J	8	282	RICHARDSON	A	9	161

RICHARDSON	A	9	328	RICHARDSON	F	8	283	RICHARDSON	J	7	328	RICHARDSON	W	10	192
RICHARDSON	A	10	192	RICHARDSON	F	11	315	RICHARDSON	J	8	283	RICHARDSON	W	11	315
RICHARDSON	A	12	187	RICHARDSON	F	12	188	RICHARDSON	J	8	283	RICHARDSON	W	13	361
RICHARDSON	A	14	264	RICHARDSON	F	12	188	RICHARDSON	J	14	264	RICHARDSON	W	13	361
RICHARDSON	AC	13	360	RICHARDSON	FA	3	191	RICHARDSON	JG	2	283	RICHARDSON	W	14	264
RICHARDSON	AE	13	360	RICHARDSON	FE	12	374	RICHARDSON	JW	2	283	RICHARDSON	W	14	264
RICHARDSON	AG	12	424	RICHARDSON	FG	14	264	RICHARDSON	JW	12	188	RICHARDSON	W	14	264
RICHARDSON	AH	3	191	RICHARDSON	FHR	5	292	RICHARDSON	KC	5	292	RICHARDSON	WC	12	374
RICHARDSON	AJ	6	344	RICHARDSON	FN	11	315	RICHARDSON	LSE	5	293	RICHARDSON	WCH	13	361
RICHARDSON	AJ	12	187	RICHARDSON	FS	1	292	RICHARDSON	NB	14	264	RICHARDSON	WF	5	293
RICHARDSON	AJ	13	360	RICHARDSON	FS	13	361	RICHARDSON	O	5	293	RICHARDSON	WH	4	323
RICHARDSON	AR	12	187	RICHARDSON	FW	2	282	RICHARDSON	P	5	293	RICHARDSON	WH	7	329
RICHARDSON	AT	12	187	RICHARDSON	FW	7	328	RICHARDSON	P	5	293	RICHARDSON	WH	8	283
RICHARDSON	AW	13	360	RICHARDSON	FW	7	328	RICHARDSON	P	7	328	RICHARDSON	WJ	12	188
RICHARDSON	B	12	374	RICHARDSON	FW	12	188	RICHARDSON	P	11	315	RICHARDSON	WT	3	191
RICHARDSON	C	4	323	RICHARDSON	FW	13	361	RICHARDSON	PG	5	293	RICHARDSON	WT	12	374
RICHARDSON	C	5	292	RICHARDSON	FWP	12	188	RICHARDSON	PJ	12	374	RICHE	GT	3	191
RICHARDSON	C	6	344	RICHARDSON	G	7	328	RICHARDSON	PR	7	329	RICHELIEU	A	8	284
RICHARDSON	C	9	161	RICHARDSON	G	8	283	RICHARDSON	R	2	283	RICHENS	J	6	344
RICHARDSON	C	11	315	RICHARDSON	G	8	283	RICHARDSON	R	7	329	RICHENS	JH	4	323
RICHARDSON	C	12	187	RICHARDSON	G	10	192	RICHARDSON	R	9	328	RICHENS	JW	7	329
RICHARDSON	C	12	374	RICHARDSON	GC	9	328	RICHARDSON	RC	12	188	RICHER	EW	8	284
RICHARDSON	C	13	360	RICHARDSON	GF	7	328	RICHARDSON	RH	13	361	RICHES	AJ	12	188
RICHARDSON	CA	2	282	RICHARDSON	GF	8	283	RICHARDSON	S	1	292	RICHES	CA	2	283
RICHARDSON	CA	5	292	RICHARDSON	GG	2	283	RICHARDSON	S	4	323	RICHES	FC	2	283
RICHARDSON	CF	2	282	RICHARDSON	GH	3	191	RICHARDSON	S	5	293	RICHES	H	1	293
RICHARDSON	CF	13	360	RICHARDSON	GH	12	188	RICHARDSON	S	6	344	RICHES	L	1	293
RICHARDSON	CF	13	361	RICHARDSON	GH	13	361	RICHARDSON	S	8	283	RICHES	MA	13	361
RICHARDSON	CH	1	292	RICHARDSON	GW	2	283	RICHARDSON	S	9	161	RICHES	R	13	361
RICHARDSON	CH	5	292	RICHARDSON	GW	3	191	RICHARDSON	S	9	161	RICHES	WA	1	293
RICHARDSON	CH	8	282	RICHARDSON	H	3	191	RICHARDSON	S	11	315	RICHFIELD	EJ	13	361
RICHARDSON	CJ	8	282	RICHARDSON	H	4	323	RICHARDSON	S	11	315	RICHFIELD	F	10	192
RICHARDSON	CW	10	356	RICHARDSON	H	8	283	RICHARDSON	S	12	374	RICHFIELD	G	13	361
RICHARDSON	D	14	264	RICHARDSON	H	8	283	RICHARDSON	SA	13	361	RICHFIELD	R	10	192
RICHARDSON	E	3	191	RICHARDSON	H	8	283	RICHARDSON	SF	13	361	RICHFIELD	RJ	13	361
RICHARDSON	E	4	323	RICHARDSON	H	8	283	RICHARDSON	T	2	283	RICHINGS	E	5	293
RICHARDSON	E	4	323	RICHARDSON	H	9	161	RICHARDSON	T	4	323	RICHMAN	S	8	284
RICHARDSON	E	6	344	RICHARDSON	H	10	356	RICHARDSON	T	6	344	RICHMAN	W	4	323
RICHARDSON	E	8	283	RICHARDSON	H	12	188	RICHARDSON	T	7	329	RICHMOND	A	10	356
RICHARDSON	E	8	283	RICHARDSON	H	12	188	RICHARDSON	T	8	283	RICHMOND	A	12	374
RICHARDSON	E	8	283	RICHARDSON	H	12	188	RICHARDSON	T	11	315	RICHMOND	AE	8	284
RICHARDSON	E	9	328	RICHARDSON	H	12	374	RICHARDSON	TA	11	315	RICHMOND	AH	3	191
RICHARDSON	E	9	328	RICHARDSON	H	13	361	RICHARDSON	TH	6	344	RICHMOND	CH	8	284
RICHARDSON	E	11	315	RICHARDSON	H	14	264	RICHARDSON	TJ	1	292	RICHMOND	F	8	284
RICHARDSON	E	11	315	RICHARDSON	H	14	264	RICHARDSON	TL	12	188	RICHMOND	F	8	284
RICHARDSON	E	12	187	RICHARDSON	HD	13	361	RICHARDSON	V	10	192	RICHMOND	H	14	264
RICHARDSON	E	14	264	RICHARDSON	HEA	4	323	RICHARDSON	W	2	283	RICHMOND	J	9	329
RICHARDSON	EA	5	292	RICHARDSON	HF	12	188	RICHARDSON	W	2	283	RICHMOND	JW	11	316
RICHARDSON	EJ	6	344	RICHARDSON	HT	12	188	RICHARDSON	W	4	323	RICHMOND	S	11	316
RICHARDSON	EO	3	191	RICHARDSON	HW	2	283	RICHARDSON	W	5	293	RICHMOND	T	14	264
RICHARDSON	EW	2	282	RICHARDSON	J	5	292	RICHARDSON	W	8	283	RICHMOND	W	3	191
RICHARDSON	EW	12	188	RICHARDSON	J	6	344	RICHARDSON	W	8	283	RICHMOND	W	5	293
RICHARDSON	F	5	292	RICHARDSON	J	7	328	RICHARDSON	W	8	283	RICHMOND	W	8	284
RICHARDSON	F	5	292	RICHARDSON	J	7	328	RICHARDSON	W	8	283	RICHMOND	W	8	284
RICHARDSON	F	7	328	RICHARDSON	J	7	328	RICHARDSON	W	10	192	RICHMOND	W	8	284

RICHMOND	W	9	329	RICKWARD	AV	13	362	RIDGE	AD	2	284	RIDLEY	HE	3	192
RICK	E	2	283	RICKWOOD	G	3	191	RIDGE	C	7	330	RIDLEY	J	2	284
RICK	J	2	283	RICKWOOD	GP	7	329	RIDGE	CW	6	345	RIDLEY	J	14	265
RICK	W	12	188	RICKWOOD	J	7	329	RIDGE	E	3	191	RIDLEY	J	14	265
RICKARD	CW	8	284	RICKWOOD	SH	7	329	RIDGE	FF	10	192	RIDLEY	JAS	4	324
RICKARD	D	12	374	RIDDELL	AE	14	265	RIDGE	FJ	10	192	RIDLEY	JH	1	293
RICKARD	E	13	361	RIDDELL	W	9	329	RIDGE	GE	3	191	RIDLEY	JW	1	293
RICKARD	EC	13	361	RIDDEN	CA	6	344	RIDGE	H	7	330	RIDLEY	S	3	192
RICKARD	HP	10	192	RIDDEOUGH	F	11	316	RIDGE	I	7	330	RIDLEY	W	7	330
RICKARD	J	7	329	RIDDEOUGH	R	11	316	RIDGE	J	2	284	RIDLEY	WE	3	192
RICKARD	JW	2	283	RIDDETT	WA	4	323	RIDGE	W	2	284	RIDOUT	AJ	4	324
RICKARD	L	5	293	RIDDETT	WG	4	323	RIDGE	WH	2	284	RIDOUT	FA	7	330
RICKARD	TAE	5	293	RIDDINGTON	D	7	329	RIDGELEY	JH	6	345	RIDOUT	JE	2	284
RICKARD	TE	5	293	RIDDIOUGH	E	9	161	RIDGEON	C	3	192	RIDOUT	TW	10	192
RICKARD	WH	12	374	RIDDLE	A	10	356	RIDGERS	JR	13	362	RIDSDALE	AJH	3	192
RICKARDS	G	6	344	RIDDLE	CW	3	191	RIDGERS	LBR	13	362	RIDSDALE	R	8	284
RICKATSON	P	8	284	RIDDLE	EC	10	192	RIDGERS	WA	10	356	RIDSDALE	W	3	192
RICKERBY	FE	7	329	RIDDLE	J	12	375	RIDGES	CF	4	323	RIDSON	D	8	285
RICKERD	GD	12	374	RIDDLE	J	14	265	RIDGES	W	4	324	RIDSON	T	8	285
RICKERS	J	8	284	RIDDLE	JW	10	356	RIDGEWELL	AA	13	362	RIDYARD	G	8	285
RICKETT	E	9	161	RIDDLE	RV	7	329	RIDGEWELL	CP	13	362	RIDYARD	P	8	285
RICKETT	I	9	161	RIDDLES	HG	7	329	RIDGEWELL	HG	7	330	RIDYARD	S	8	285
RICKETT	I	9	161	RIDDLESWORTH	T	8	284	RIDGEWELL	W	7	330	RIELEY	R	11	316
RICKETT	PG	10	356	RIDDY	AE	7	329	RIDGLEY	EC	3	192	RIGBY	A	9	161
RICKETT	SS	13	361	RIDDY	CG	7	329	RIDGLEY	LG	13	362	RIGBY	CE	12	375
RICKETT	WJ	5	293	RIDDY	FH	3	191	RIDGLEY	LM	3	192	RIGBY	F	10	192
RICKETTS	C	4	323	RIDDY	LC	12	188	RIDGWAY	BW	14	265	RIGBY	F	14	265
RICKETTS	CAF	2	283	RIDDY	W	12	188	RIDGWAY	C	12	189	RIGBY	HH	4	324
RICKETTS	EJ	6	344	RIDE	J	2	283	RIDGWAY	G	11	316	RIGBY	J	8	285
RICKETTS	FL	6	344	RIDE	LG	2	283	RIDGWAY	G	14	265	RIGBY	J	11	316
RICKETTS	G	3	191	RIDE	MH	2	283	RIDGWAY	HJ	12	189	RIGBY	J	14	265
RICKETTS	G	4	323	RIDE	ML	2	284	RIDGWAY	JG	11	316	RIGBY	J	14	265
RICKETTS	GD	10	356	RIDE	P	2	283	RIDGWAY	JS	6	345	RIGBY	JW	14	265
RICKETTS	GFM	3	191	RIDEHALGH	A	11	316	RIDGWAY	LA	14	265	RIGBY	R	14	265
RICKETTS	H	1	293	RIDEHALGH	JD	11	316	RIDGWAY	T	11	316	RIGBY	S	14	265
RICKETTS	H	6	344	RIDEOUT	JS	12	189	RIDGWAY	W	11	316	RIGBY	T	12	375
RICKETTS	SH	4	323	RIDER	A	8	284	RIDGWAY	WC	14	265	RIGBY	T	14	265
RICKETTS	T	6	344	RIDER	BH	4	323	RIDING	CW	4	324	RIGBY	W	3	192
RICKETTS	W	6	344	RIDER	BW	6	344	RIDING	H	9	329	RIGBY	W	11	316
RICKMAN	A	1	293	RIDER	FJ	3	191	RIDING	J	9	329	RIGELSFORD	E	4	324
RICKMAN	A	1	293	RIDER	FW	2	284	RIDING	T	11	316	RIGELSFORD	FW	1	293
RICKMAN	A	1	293	RIDER	GV	7	329	RIDING	WH	11	316	RIGELSFORD	G	4	324
RICKMAN	AA	10	192	RIDER	GW	5	293	RIDINGS	JE	11	316	RIGELSFORD	LWH	1	293
RICKMAN	AF	1	293	RIDER	HT	3	384	RIDINGS	JJ	7	330	RIGELSFORD	ST	1	293
RICKMAN	FRC	3	384	RIDER	J	8	284	RIDINGS	S	14	265	RIGELSFORD	W	4	324
RICKMAN	HE	4	323	RIDER	J	8	284	RIDINGTON	W	3	192	RIGELSFORD	W	4	324
RICKMAN	HJ	1	293	RIDER	J	10	356	RIDINGTON	WC	13	362	RIGG	A	9	329
RICKMAN	HN	4	323	RIDER	JP	2	284	RIDLEY	A	11	316	RIGG	C	11	316
RICKMAN	J	2	283	RIDER	R	8	284	RIDLEY	AE	6	345	RIGG	J	8	285
RICKMAN	S	1	293	RIDER	RW	2	284	RIDLEY	AJ	6	345	RIGG	JW	8	285
RICKMAN	SC	1	293	RIDER	TE	6	344	RIDLEY	AW	7	330	RIGG	T	4	324
RICKMAN	W	2	283	RIDER	W	8	284	RIDLEY	CA	5	293	RIGG	T	14	265
RICKMAN	WE	1	293	RIDEWOOD	GE	7	330	RIDLEY	CA	6	345	RIGGALL	GJ	7	330
RICKS	J	3	191	RIDEWOOD	WC	7	330	RIDLEY	EJ	3	192	RIGGALL	WT	7	330
RICKS	J	7	329	RIDGE	A	2	284	RIDLEY	F	8	284	RIGGE	MS	13	362

RIGGLESFORD	H	2	284	RILEY	H	11	317	RILEY	TGS	13	362	RIPLEY	N	5	294
RIGGS	C	5	293	RILEY	H	12	189	RILEY	W	4	324	RIPLEY	NH	8	286
RIGLIN	AJ	2	284	RILEY	H	14	266	RILEY	W	4	324	RIPLEY	TH	8	286
RIGLIN	R	1	293	RILEY	HD	7	331	RILEY	W	9	329	RIPLEY	W	10	193
RIGLIN	TE	2	284	RILEY	HH	6	345	RILEY	W	11	317	RIPPIN	A	6	345
RIGNALL	AR	3	192	RILEY	J	1	293	RILEY	W	11	317	RIPPINGHAM	J	3	193
RIGNALL	WG	7	330	RILEY	J	3	192	RILEY	W	14	266	RIPPINGHAM	P	3	193
RIGNEY	W	14	266	RILEY	J	4	324	RILEY	W	14	266	RIPPINGHAM	W	3	193
RILES	E	11	316	RILEY	J	6	345	RILEY	WH	11	317	RIPPINGHAM	W	3	193
RILES	H	9	161	RILEY	J	6	345	RILEY	WT	11	317	RIPPINGHAM	W	11	318
RILEY	A	8	285	RILEY	J	8	285	RILEY	WV	11	318	RIPTON	W	13	362
RILEY	A	8	285	RILEY	J	8	285	RILLINGS	EH	5	299	RISBEY	AE	2	285
RILEY	A	9	329	RILEY	J	8	285	RILLINGS	GR	5	299	RISBEY	FC	2	285
RILEY	A	12	375	RILEY	J	8	285	RILLINGS	H	5	299	RISBEY	S	2	285
RILEY	A	14	266	RILEY	J	9	161	RIMELL	E	1	294	RISBRIDGER	E	2	285
RILEY	A	14	266	RILEY	J	9	161	RIMELL	EG	1	294	RISBRIDGER	EJ	3	193
RILEY	AC	7	330	RILEY	J	9	161	RIMELL	HJ	3	192	RISBRIDGER	F	3	384
RILEY	AE	8	285	RILEY	J	11	317	RIMELL	SW	1	294	RISBRIDGER	M	3	384
RILEY	AG	4	324	RILEY	J	11	317	RIMINGTON	WL	2	284	RISBROOK	LW	4	324
RILEY	AG	5	293	RILEY	J	11	317	RIMMELL	HH	1	294	RISBY	AJ	1	294
RILEY	AT	7	330	RILEY	J	14	266	RIMMER	F	14	266	RISBY	G	2	285
RILEY	AW	3	192	RILEY	J	14	266	RIMMER	J	11	318	RISBY	M	11	318
RILEY	C	9	161	RILEY	J	14	266	RIMMER	J	14	266	RISBY	W	1	294
RILEY	C	11	317	RILEY	J	14	266	RIMMER	J	14	267	RISDEN	L	4	324
RILEY	CEM	3	192	RILEY	J	14	266	RIMMER	W	9	329	RISDEN	M	4	325
RILEY	E	1	293	RILEY	JB	10	192	RIMMER	W	12	375	RISDON	A	9	162
RILEY	E	8	285	RILEY	JE	10	193	RIMMER	WF	14	267	RISEAM	E	1	294
RILEY	E	11	317	RILEY	JH	7	331	RIMMINGTON	L	9	329	RISEBOROUGH	J	13	362
RILEY	E	11	317	RILEY	JHS	7	331	RIMMINGTON	N	9	329	RISEBOROUGH	WJG	13	362
RILEY	EA	2	284	RILEY	JJ	11	317	RING	CJ	1	294	RISELEY	AR	12	189
RILEY	EE	1	293	RILEY	JJ	13	362	RING	H	4	324	RISELEY	G	7	331
RILEY	EJ	6	345	RILEY	JW	11	317	RING	HE	1	294	RISELEY	H	7	331
RILEY	F	6	345	RILEY	JW	14	266	RING	W	2	285	RISELEY	S	12	189
RILEY	F	11	317	RILEY	L	9	162	RING	WA	13	362	RISELY	G	12	189
RILEY	F	12	189	RILEY	L	11	317	RING	WD	2	285	RISELY	T	12	189
RILEY	FC	7	330	RILEY	M	4	324	RINGHAM	A	5	294	RISLEY	WC	1	294
RILEY	FG	2	284	RILEY	MA	1	294	RINGHAM	E	2	285	RISTOW	GJF	13	362
RILEY	FJ	2	284	RILEY	NE	11	317	RINGROSE	G	12	375	RITCHIE	A	9	162
RILEY	FJ	5	293	RILEY	P	9	162	RINGROSE	H	12	189	RITCHIE	CF	3	193
RILEY	FR	10	356	RILEY	P	14	266	RINGROSE	T	12	189	RITCHIE	E	13	362
RILEY	FW	3	192	RILEY	PE	1	294	RINGSHALL	EH	3	192	RITCHIE	J	5	294
RILEY	G	8	285	RILEY	R	6	345	RINGSHALL	GF	3	193	RITCHIE	T	12	189
RILEY	G	9	161	RILEY	RA	9	329	RINGSHALL	H	7	331	RITCHINGS	CH	1	294
RILEY	G	11	317	RILEY	RH	14	266	RINGWOOD	B	7	331	RITSON	H	11	318
RILEY	G	11	317	RILEY	RW	2	284	RINGWOOD	C	1	294	RITSON	W	11	318
RILEY	GF	4	324	RILEY	T	3	192	RINGWOOD	F	13	362	RITSON	WH	11	318
RILEY	GH	3	192	RILEY	T	8	286	RINGWOOD	R	1	294	RITTER	JW	2	285
RILEY	GW	8	285	RILEY	T	8	286	RIO	F	4	324	RIVENELL	JJ	1	294
RILEY	GW	8	285	RILEY	T	8	286	RIORDAN	E	2	285	RIVERS	A	3	193
RILEY	H	6	345	RILEY	T	9	162	RIORDAN	H	2	285	RIVERS	AR	7	331
RILEY	H	8	285	RILEY	T	11	317	RIORDAN	J	10	193	RIVERS	E	8	286
RILEY	H	9	161	RILEY	T	14	266	RIPLEY	A	8	286	RIVERS	FE	3	193
RILEY	H	9	161	RILEY	TA	8	286	RIPLEY	C	10	356	RIVERS	G	13	362
RILEY	H	9	329	RILEY	TE	9	329	RIPLEY	E	8	286	RIVERS	HJ	1	294
RILEY	H	9	329	RILEY	TE	14	266	RIPLEY	G	8	286	RIVERS	HW	12	189

RIVERS	LD	3	193	ROACH	J	14	267	ROBERSON	JW	5	294	ROBERTS	CH	3	194
RIVERS	W	6	345	ROACH	JH	4	325	ROBERSON	T	5	294	ROBERTS	CH	4	325
RIVETT	A	5	294	ROACH	P	14	267	ROBERT	W	1	295	ROBERTS	CH	6	346
RIVETT	B	12	375	ROACH	R	12	189	ROBERT	W	2	286	ROBERTS	CJ	4	325
RIVETT	FW	13	362	ROACH	R	12	189	ROBERTON	A	11	318	ROBERTS	CJ	6	346
RIVETT	GJ	6	345	ROACH	T	14	267	ROBERTON	H	11	318	ROBERTS	CJ	10	356
RIVETT	J	11	318	ROACH	T	14	267	ROBERTS	A	1	295	ROBERTS	CJ	10	356
RIVETT	JW	3	193	ROACH	TC	10	356	ROBERTS	A	2	286	ROBERTS	CJ	13	363
RIVETT	JW	5	294	ROACH	TW	11	318	ROBERTS	A	3	194	ROBERTS	CM	1	295
RIVETT	WG	7	331	ROACH	W	1	294	ROBERTS	A	7	331	ROBERTS	CS	12	375
RIVETT	WT	13	363	ROACH	W	11	318	ROBERTS	A	7	331	ROBERTS	CW	1	295
RIX	A	2	285	ROACH	W	13	363	ROBERTS	A	7	331	ROBERTS	D	7	332
RIX	A	9	329	ROACH	W	14	267	ROBERTS	A	8	286	ROBERTS	D	11	319
RIX	AE	3	193	ROADKNIGHT	J	6	345	ROBERTS	A	8	286	ROBERTS	D	14	267
RIX	FA	1	294	ROADNIGHT	HG	5	294	ROBERTS	A	8	286	ROBERTS	DC	11	319
RIX	FWL	3	193	ROADNIGHT	JT	5	294	ROBERTS	A	8	286	ROBERTS	DT	3	194
RIX	G	2	285	ROADNIGHT	JT	12	189	ROBERTS	A	9	329	ROBERTS	E	1	295
RIX	H	14	267	ROADS	E	9	162	ROBERTS	A	10	193	ROBERTS	E	4	325
RIX	LG	5	294	ROAF	FHR	1	295	ROBERTS	A	11	318	ROBERTS	E	5	294
RIX	SE	3	193	ROALF	SC	10	193	ROBERTS	A	11	318	ROBERTS	E	5	294
RIX	SG	5	294	ROAN	HJ	12	375	ROBERTS	A	12	189	ROBERTS	E	6	346
RIX	SJ	5	294	ROAST	W	3	384	ROBERTS	A	12	189	ROBERTS	E	8	286
RIX	T	14	267	ROATH	AE	6	346	ROBERTS	A	12	189	ROBERTS	E	8	287
RIX	W	3	193	ROATH	AH	6	346	ROBERTS	A	13	363	ROBERTS	E	9	330
RIX	WH	3	193	ROBARTS	AP	7	331	ROBERTS	AB	12	375	ROBERTS	E	11	318
RIX	WJ	3	193	ROBB	D	14	267	ROBERTS	AC	1	295	ROBERTS	E	11	319
RIXOM	GW	6	345	ROBB	DA	8	286	ROBERTS	AD	6	346	ROBERTS	E	11	319
RIXON	AA	1	294	ROBBIN	JA	2	285	ROBERTS	AE	2	286	ROBERTS	E	11	319
RIXON	AJ	7	331	ROBBINGS	WC	2	285	ROBERTS	AE	11	318	ROBERTS	E	13	363
RIXON	AJ	13	363	ROBBINS	AG	12	376	ROBERTS	AE	14	267	ROBERTS	EA	7	332
RIXON	CE	2	285	ROBBINS	AN	9	162	ROBERTS	AF	6	346	ROBERTS	EA	7	332
RIXON	CW	3	384	ROBBINS	C	1	295	ROBERTS	AJ	3	194	ROBERTS	EC	12	190
RIXON	CWG	3	193	ROBBINS	F	1	295	ROBERTS	AL	11	318	ROBERTS	ED	14	267
RIXON	EC	3	193	ROBBINS	GW	7	331	ROBERTS	AP	6	346	ROBERTS	EG	13	363
RIXON	F	1	294	ROBBINS	H	3	194	ROBERTS	AS	1	295	ROBERTS	EJ	13	363
RIXON	F	7	331	ROBBINS	HJ	3	194	ROBERTS	AT	5	294	ROBERTS	EJ	13	363
RIXON	FC	13	363	ROBBINS	HL	2	285	ROBERTS	AW	6	346	ROBERTS	EJ	14	267
RIXON	JC	13	363	ROBBINS	J	2	285	ROBERTS	AW	12	375	ROBERTS	EP	12	190
RIXON	JR	3	194	ROBBINS	JF	1	295	ROBERTS	B	5	294	ROBERTS	ER	1	295
RIXON	JWH	1	294	ROBBINS	JV	2	285	ROBERTS	B	8	286	ROBERTS	ES	11	319
RIXON	PT	12	375	ROBBINS	JW	2	286	ROBERTS	B	8	286	ROBERTS	ET	3	194
RIXON	R	3	194	ROBBINS	MM	9	162	ROBERTS	B	10	193	ROBERTS	F	2	286
RIXON	RA	3	194	ROBBINS	R	6	346	ROBERTS	BW	3	194	ROBERTS	F	5	294
RIXON	RW	13	363	ROBBINS	RJ	4	325	ROBERTS	C	3	194	ROBERTS	F	7	332
RIXON	SC	13	363	ROBBINS	T	1	295	ROBERTS	C	5	294	ROBERTS	F	9	330
RIXSON	J	13	363	ROBBINS	W	1	295	ROBERTS	C	8	286	ROBERTS	F	10	357
ROACH	A	9	329	ROBBINS	W	7	331	ROBERTS	C	8	286	ROBERTS	F	12	375
ROACH	AW	12	189	ROBBINS	W	13	363	ROBERTS	C	9	162	ROBERTS	F	12	375
ROACH	C	14	267	ROBBINS	WD	14	267	ROBERTS	C	9	330	ROBERTS	F	14	268
ROACH	EV	10	356	ROBBINS	WG	6	346	ROBERTS	C	12	190	ROBERTS	F	14	268
ROACH	FG	12	189	ROBBINS	WJ	1	295	ROBERTS	C	14	267	ROBERTS	FB	10	357
ROACH	G	11	318	ROBBINS	WJ	2	286	ROBERTS	C	14	267	ROBERTS	FC	5	294
ROACH	H	4	325	ROBBINS	WT	13	363	ROBERTS	CA	12	375	ROBERTS	FG	2	286
ROACH	H	6	345	ROBERSON	F	2	286	ROBERTS	CE	1	295	ROBERTS	FG	2	286
ROACH	J	7	331	ROBERSON	F	13	363	ROBERTS	CE	3	194	ROBERTS	FG	3	194

ROBERTS	FI	11	319	ROBERTS	I	12	376	ROBERTS	L	12	190	ROBERTS	W	8	287
ROBERTS	FJ	1	295	ROBERTS	J	1	296	ROBERTS	LS	2	286	ROBERTS	W	8	287
ROBERTS	FP	2	286	ROBERTS	J	1	296	ROBERTS	M	8	287	ROBERTS	W	8	287
ROBERTS	FP	3	194	ROBERTS	J	1	296	ROBERTS	M	10	193	ROBERTS	W	8	287
ROBERTS	FT	7	332	ROBERTS	J	3	194	ROBERTS	M	10	193	ROBERTS	W	8	287
ROBERTS	FT	9	330	ROBERTS	J	3	194	ROBERTS	M	12	376	ROBERTS	W	9	162
ROBERTS	FW	13	363	ROBERTS	J	3	194	ROBERTS	O	12	376	ROBERTS	W	10	193
ROBERTS	G	2	286	ROBERTS	J	3	195	ROBERTS	P	14	268	ROBERTS	W	11	320
ROBERTS	G	4	325	ROBERTS	J	5	295	ROBERTS	PF	14	268	ROBERTS	W	11	320
ROBERTS	G	5	295	ROBERTS	J	6	347	ROBERTS	PVA	3	195	ROBERTS	W	11	320
ROBERTS	G	6	346	ROBERTS	J	7	332	ROBERTS	R	6	347	ROBERTS	W	11	320
ROBERTS	G	7	332	ROBERTS	J	7	332	ROBERTS	R	8	287	ROBERTS	W	11	320
ROBERTS	G	7	332	ROBERTS	J	7	332	ROBERTS	R	10	193	ROBERTS	W	12	376
ROBERTS	G	7	332	ROBERTS	J	8	287	ROBERTS	R	11	320	ROBERTS	W	13	364
ROBERTS	G	13	363	ROBERTS	J	8	287	ROBERTS	R	11	320	ROBERTS	W	13	364
ROBERTS	G	13	364	ROBERTS	J	8	287	ROBERTS	R	11	320	ROBERTS	W	14	268
ROBERTS	GA	6	346	ROBERTS	J	8	287	ROBERTS	R	11	320	ROBERTS	WA	2	286
ROBERTS	GA	7	332	ROBERTS	J	10	193	ROBERTS	R	11	320	ROBERTS	WA	4	325
ROBERTS	GC	6	346	ROBERTS	J	10	193	ROBERTS	R	12	190	ROBERTS	WC	1	296
ROBERTS	GC	13	364	ROBERTS	J	11	319	ROBERTS	R	13	364	ROBERTS	WCS	1	296
ROBERTS	GE	10	357	ROBERTS	J	11	319	ROBERTS	R	14	268	ROBERTS	WE	1	296
ROBERTS	GH	6	346	ROBERTS	J	13	364	ROBERTS	RF	14	268	ROBERTS	WE	13	364
ROBERTS	GH	12	190	ROBERTS	J	14	268	ROBERTS	RT	6	347	ROBERTS	WF	3	195
ROBERTS	GJ	12	375	ROBERTS	J	14	268	ROBERTS	RW	11	320	ROBERTS	WF	7	333
ROBERTS	GT	7	332	ROBERTS	JA	10	193	ROBERTS	S	5	295	ROBERTS	WG	1	296
ROBERTS	GT	10	193	ROBERTS	JA	11	319	ROBERTS	S	5	295	ROBERTS	WH	4	325
ROBERTS	GV	14	268	ROBERTS	JA	14	268	ROBERTS	S	9	162	ROBERTS	WH	6	347
ROBERTS	GW	1	295	ROBERTS	JC	7	332	ROBERTS	S	11	320	ROBERTS	WH	8	287
ROBERTS	H	1	295	ROBERTS	JE	8	287	ROBERTS	S	12	190	ROBERTS	WH	10	357
ROBERTS	H	3	194	ROBERTS	JE	14	268	ROBERTS	SJ	5	295	ROBERTS	WH	14	268
ROBERTS	H	4	325	ROBERTS	JF	5	295	ROBERTS	SS	1	296	ROBERTS	WH	14	268
ROBERTS	H	6	346	ROBERTS	JF	10	357	ROBERTS	T	8	287	ROBERTS	WJ	1	296
ROBERTS	H	6	346	ROBERTS	JF	11	319	ROBERTS	T	11	320	ROBERTS	WJ	3	195
ROBERTS	H	6	347	ROBERTS	JH	3	384	ROBERTS	TA	11	320	ROBERTS	WJ	8	287
ROBERTS	H	8	287	ROBERTS	JH	11	319	ROBERTS	TA	11	320	ROBERTS	WJ	13	364
ROBERTS	H	9	162	ROBERTS	JHF	12	376	ROBERTS	TC	1	296	ROBERTS	WR	7	333
ROBERTS	H	12	190	ROBERTS	JL	2	286	ROBERTS	TE	6	347	ROBERTS	WR	13	364
ROBERTS	H	12	375	ROBERTS	JN	4	325	ROBERTS	TG	1	296	ROBERTS	WT	6	347
ROBERTS	H	14	268	ROBERTS	JR	2	286	ROBERTS	TJ	1	296	ROBERTSHAW	A	9	330
ROBERTS	H	14	268	ROBERTS	JR	11	319	ROBERTS	TJ	13	364	ROBERTSHAW	A	9	330
ROBERTS	HC	10	193	ROBERTS	JR	11	319	ROBERTS	TW	7	332	ROBERTSHAW	A	9	330
ROBERTS	HC	12	375	ROBERTS	JR	13	364	ROBERTS	V	11	320	ROBERTSHAW	AA	9	162
ROBERTS	HC	12	376	ROBERTS	JT	11	319	ROBERTS	W	1	296	ROBERTSHAW	F	9	162
ROBERTS	HF	7	332	ROBERTS	JW	6	347	ROBERTS	W	1	296	ROBERTSHAW	F	11	320
ROBERTS	HG	1	295	ROBERTS	JW	9	162	ROBERTS	W	1	296	ROBERTSHAW	F	11	321
ROBERTS	HG	1	296	ROBERTS	JW	9	330	ROBERTS	W	1	296	ROBERTSHAW	J	8	287
ROBERTS	HG	3	194	ROBERTS	JW	11	320	ROBERTS	W	2	286	ROBERTSHAW	J	8	288
ROBERTS	HJ	7	332	ROBERTS	JW	12	190	ROBERTS	W	3	195	ROBERTSHAW	J	8	288
ROBERTS	HJ	13	364	ROBERTS	JW	13	364	ROBERTS	W	3	195	ROBERTSHAW	JA	9	162
ROBERTS	HJS	12	190	ROBERTS	JW	14	268	ROBERTS	W	6	347	ROBERTSHAW	JA	9	330
ROBERTS	HP	4	325	ROBERTS	L	6	347	ROBERTS	W	6	347	ROBERTSHAW	JH	9	330
ROBERTS	HP	5	295	ROBERTS	L	8	287	ROBERTS	W	6	347	ROBERTSHAW	JW	9	162
ROBERTS	HS	12	190	ROBERTS	L	10	193	ROBERTS	W	7	332	ROBERTSHAW	P	9	162
ROBERTS	HT	5	295	ROBERTS	L	11	319	ROBERTS	W	8	287	ROBERTSHAW	S	9	163
ROBERTS	I	11	319	ROBERTS	L	11	319	ROBERTS	W	8	287	ROBERTSHAW	T	8	288

ROBERTSHAW	T	8	288
ROBERTSON	A	8	288
ROBERTSON	AB	5	295
ROBERTSON	AM	10	193
ROBERTSON	AP	10	357
ROBERTSON	AV	12	376
ROBERTSON	BD	4	325
ROBERTSON	D	8	288
ROBERTSON	D	14	268
ROBERTSON	FW	7	333
ROBERTSON	G	3	195
ROBERTSON	GH	10	357
ROBERTSON	H	1	296
ROBERTSON	H	9	163
ROBERTSON	H	14	269
ROBERTSON	J	3	195
ROBERTSON	J	6	347
ROBERTSON	JE	10	193
ROBERTSON	JW	13	364
ROBERTSON	JWJ	12	190
ROBERTSON	L	2	286
ROBERTSON	MA	10	357
ROBERTSON	MH	8	288
ROBERTSON	R	10	357
ROBERTSON	S	7	333
ROBERTSON	TE	7	333
ROBERTSON	W	12	376
ROBERTSON	WE	10	194
ROBERTSON	WG	4	325
ROBERTSON	WG	10	194
ROBERTSON	WG	12	376
ROBERTSON	WH	12	376
ROBERTSON	WW	13	364
ROBEY	AG	10	194
ROBEY	FE	10	194
ROBEY	G	10	194
ROBEY	WC	10	194
ROBINI	W	1	296
ROBINS	A	3	195
ROBINS	A	8	288
ROBINS	A	12	190
ROBINS	A	12	190
ROBINS	AJ	1	296
ROBINS	AW	1	296
ROBINS	CA	4	325
ROBINS	D	12	376
ROBINS	DE	1	297
ROBINS	F	12	190
ROBINS	FE	12	190
ROBINS	FJ	2	287
ROBINS	FJ	5	295
ROBINS	GC	3	195
ROBINS	GM	1	297
ROBINS	HW	12	376
ROBINS	J	12	190
ROBINS	JC	6	347
ROBINS	JC	12	190
ROBINS	JH	1	297
ROBINS	LA	12	190
ROBINS	LH	12	190
ROBINS	NHJ	1	297
ROBINS	PC	5	295
ROBINS	PF	2	287
ROBINS	PJ	4	325
ROBINS	S	6	347
ROBINS	SW	1	297
ROBINS	W	6	347
ROBINS	W	7	333
ROBINS	WJ	12	376
ROBINS	WJ	12	376
ROBINSON	A	1	297
ROBINSON	A	1	297
ROBINSON	A	2	287
ROBINSON	A	2	287
ROBINSON	A	5	295
ROBINSON	A	5	295
ROBINSON	A	6	347
ROBINSON	A	7	333
ROBINSON	A	7	333
ROBINSON	A	8	288
ROBINSON	A	8	288
ROBINSON	A	8	288
ROBINSON	A	8	288
ROBINSON	A	8	288
ROBINSON	A	9	163
ROBINSON	A	9	163
ROBINSON	A	9	163
ROBINSON	A	9	330
ROBINSON	A	9	330
ROBINSON	A	9	330
ROBINSON	A	10	194
ROBINSON	A	12	190
ROBINSON	A	12	190
ROBINSON	A	12	191
ROBINSON	A	14	269
ROBINSON	A	14	269
ROBINSON	AB	5	295
ROBINSON	AC	12	376
ROBINSON	AE	2	287
ROBINSON	AE	9	330
ROBINSON	AG	1	297
ROBINSON	AG	1	297
ROBINSON	AG	3	195
ROBINSON	AG	5	295
ROBINSON	AG	10	357
ROBINSON	AG	13	364
ROBINSON	AH	3	195
ROBINSON	AH	7	333
ROBINSON	AJ	2	287
ROBINSON	AJ	2	287
ROBINSON	AJ	3	195
ROBINSON	AJ	5	295
ROBINSON	AJ	12	376
ROBINSON	AJ	12	376
ROBINSON	AR	6	347
ROBINSON	AS	13	364
ROBINSON	AT	10	194
ROBINSON	AW	5	295
ROBINSON	AW	13	364
ROBINSON	B	1	297
ROBINSON	B	5	296
ROBINSON	B	9	163
ROBINSON	B	11	321
ROBINSON	BC	2	287
ROBINSON	C	1	297
ROBINSON	C	2	287
ROBINSON	C	3	195
ROBINSON	C	5	295
ROBINSON	C	5	296
ROBINSON	C	6	347
ROBINSON	C	8	288
ROBINSON	C	8	288
ROBINSON	C	11	321
ROBINSON	C	12	376
ROBINSON	C	12	424
ROBINSON	C	14	269
ROBINSON	CC	5	296
ROBINSON	CG	1	297
ROBINSON	CH	6	348
ROBINSON	CH	11	321
ROBINSON	CH	11	321
ROBINSON	CP	7	333
ROBINSON	CT	5	296
ROBINSON	CV	1	297
ROBINSON	CW	2	287
ROBINSON	CW	5	296
ROBINSON	CW	9	163
ROBINSON	D	3	195
ROBINSON	D	8	288
ROBINSON	D	9	330
ROBINSON	D	11	321
ROBINSON	DB	8	288
ROBINSON	E	1	297
ROBINSON	E	4	325
ROBINSON	E	6	348
ROBINSON	E	8	288
ROBINSON	E	8	289
ROBINSON	E	9	163
ROBINSON	E	9	163
ROBINSON	E	9	163
ROBINSON	E	9	163
ROBINSON	E	11	321
ROBINSON	E	12	376
ROBINSON	E	14	269
ROBINSON	E	14	269
ROBINSON	EA	3	195
ROBINSON	EA	13	365
ROBINSON	EAC	7	333
ROBINSON	EC	2	287
ROBINSON	EC	8	289
ROBINSON	ED	12	377
ROBINSON	EE	8	289
ROBINSON	EF	4	325
ROBINSON	EG	6	348
ROBINSON	ES	12	377
ROBINSON	ET	13	365
ROBINSON	F	3	195
ROBINSON	F	5	296
ROBINSON	F	5	296
ROBINSON	F	5	296
ROBINSON	F	6	348
ROBINSON	F	7	333
ROBINSON	F	7	333
ROBINSON	F	8	289
ROBINSON	F	8	289
ROBINSON	F	9	163
ROBINSON	F	9	330
ROBINSON	F	11	321
ROBINSON	F	11	321
ROBINSON	F	12	191
ROBINSON	F	12	191
ROBINSON	F	12	191
ROBINSON	F	14	269
ROBINSON	FE	2	287
ROBINSON	FF	13	365
ROBINSON	FG	3	195
ROBINSON	FV	7	333
ROBINSON	FW	2	287
ROBINSON	FW	13	365
ROBINSON	G	3	195
ROBINSON	G	4	325
ROBINSON	G	7	333
ROBINSON	G	7	333
ROBINSON	G	8	289
ROBINSON	G	8	289
ROBINSON	G	8	289
ROBINSON	G	8	289
ROBINSON	G	9	330
ROBINSON	G	11	321
ROBINSON	G	11	321
ROBINSON	G	12	191
ROBINSON	G	12	377
ROBINSON	G	14	269
ROBINSON	G	14	269
ROBINSON	GA	4	326
ROBINSON	GA	9	163
ROBINSON	GA	11	321

ROBINSON	GB	11	321	ROBINSON	J	8	289	ROBINSON	NF	6	348	ROBINSON	TW	10	194
ROBINSON	GC	12	377	ROBINSON	J	8	289	ROBINSON	OW	3	196	ROBINSON	V	5	297
ROBINSON	GE	3	195	ROBINSON	J	9	163	ROBINSON	P	5	296	ROBINSON	VC	10	357
ROBINSON	GE	12	377	ROBINSON	J	9	331	ROBINSON	P	8	290	ROBINSON	W	2	288
ROBINSON	GF	11	321	ROBINSON	J	9	331	ROBINSON	P	9	331	ROBINSON	W	3	196
ROBINSON	GH	8	289	ROBINSON	J	10	194	ROBINSON	PA	12	424	ROBINSON	W	5	297
ROBINSON	GJ	1	297	ROBINSON	J	10	194	ROBINSON	PJ	2	287	ROBINSON	W	5	297
ROBINSON	GP	11	321	ROBINSON	J	11	321	ROBINSON	PJ	3	196	ROBINSON	W	5	297
ROBINSON	GW	3	195	ROBINSON	J	11	322	ROBINSON	PJ	12	377	ROBINSON	W	6	348
ROBINSON	GW	5	296	ROBINSON	J	11	322	ROBINSON	PT	5	296	ROBINSON	W	6	348
ROBINSON	H	1	297	ROBINSON	J	11	322	ROBINSON	R	4	326	ROBINSON	W	6	348
ROBINSON	H	3	196	ROBINSON	J	11	322	ROBINSON	R	6	348	ROBINSON	W	8	290
ROBINSON	H	8	289	ROBINSON	J	11	322	ROBINSON	R	8	290	ROBINSON	W	8	290
ROBINSON	H	8	289	ROBINSON	J	11	322	ROBINSON	RA	12	191	ROBINSON	W	8	290
ROBINSON	H	8	289	ROBINSON	J	12	191	ROBINSON	RF	10	194	ROBINSON	W	8	290
ROBINSON	H	8	289	ROBINSON	J	12	191	ROBINSON	RG	5	297	ROBINSON	W	8	290
ROBINSON	H	8	289	ROBINSON	J	14	269	ROBINSON	RGJ	13	365	ROBINSON	W	9	164
ROBINSON	H	8	289	ROBINSON	J	14	269	ROBINSON	RH	3	196	ROBINSON	W	9	164
ROBINSON	H	8	289	ROBINSON	J	14	269	ROBINSON	RH	7	334	ROBINSON	W	9	331
ROBINSON	H	9	163	ROBINSON	J	14	269	ROBINSON	RJ	10	194	ROBINSON	W	9	331
ROBINSON	H	9	163	ROBINSON	J	14	269	ROBINSON	RS	14	270	ROBINSON	W	9	331
ROBINSON	H	9	163	ROBINSON	J	14	269	ROBINSON	RW	11	322	ROBINSON	W	11	322
ROBINSON	H	9	163	ROBINSON	JA	6	348	ROBINSON	S	5	296	ROBINSON	W	11	322
ROBINSON	H	9	330	ROBINSON	JA	14	270	ROBINSON	S	5	297	ROBINSON	W	11	323
ROBINSON	H	9	331	ROBINSON	JE	3	196	ROBINSON	S	6	348	ROBINSON	W	12	191
ROBINSON	H	9	331	ROBINSON	JE	7	334	ROBINSON	S	9	164	ROBINSON	W	12	377
ROBINSON	H	9	331	ROBINSON	JF	5	296	ROBINSON	S	9	164	ROBINSON	W	12	377
ROBINSON	H	10	194	ROBINSON	JH	8	289	ROBINSON	S	12	191	ROBINSON	W	12	377
ROBINSON	H	11	321	ROBINSON	JH	14	270	ROBINSON	S	12	191	ROBINSON	W	14	270
ROBINSON	H	11	321	ROBINSON	JH	14	270	ROBINSON	S	14	270	ROBINSON	W	14	270
ROBINSON	H	11	321	ROBINSON	JH	14	270	ROBINSON	S	14	270	ROBINSON	WA	4	326
ROBINSON	H	12	191	ROBINSON	JM	12	377	ROBINSON	SJ	12	377	ROBINSON	WA	4	326
ROBINSON	H	12	191	ROBINSON	JR	8	290	ROBINSON	SM	11	322	ROBINSON	WA	7	334
ROBINSON	H	14	269	ROBINSON	JR	10	194	ROBINSON	SN	3	196	ROBINSON	WA	11	323
ROBINSON	H	14	269	ROBINSON	JT	6	348	ROBINSON	ST	12	191	ROBINSON	WAC	3	196
ROBINSON	H	14	269	ROBINSON	JW	5	296	ROBINSON	SW	12	191	ROBINSON	WB	12	377
ROBINSON	HA	2	287	ROBINSON	JW	5	296	ROBINSON	T	3	196	ROBINSON	WC	12	191
ROBINSON	HE	2	287	ROBINSON	JW	6	348	ROBINSON	T	8	290	ROBINSON	WE	6	348
ROBINSON	HG	1	297	ROBINSON	JW	6	348	ROBINSON	T	9	164	ROBINSON	WE	11	323
ROBINSON	HG	9	331	ROBINSON	JW	8	290	ROBINSON	T	9	331	ROBINSON	WF	10	357
ROBINSON	HR	8	289	ROBINSON	JW	9	331	ROBINSON	T	9	331	ROBINSON	WG	3	196
ROBINSON	HS	8	289	ROBINSON	JW	11	322	ROBINSON	T	10	194	ROBINSON	WG	11	323
ROBINSON	HS	13	365	ROBINSON	L	9	164	ROBINSON	T	11	322	ROBINSON	WG	13	365
ROBINSON	HT	2	287	ROBINSON	L	9	331	ROBINSON	T	11	322	ROBINSON	WH	3	196
ROBINSON	HT	7	333	ROBINSON	L	14	270	ROBINSON	T	12	191	ROBINSON	WH	6	349
ROBINSON	HV	5	296	ROBINSON	L	14	270	ROBINSON	T	14	270	ROBINSON	WH	11	323
ROBINSON	J	2	287	ROBINSON	L	14	270	ROBINSON	T	14	270	ROBINSON	WJ	1	297
ROBINSON	J	3	196	ROBINSON	LG	12	377	ROBINSON	TA	11	322	ROBINSON	WJ	2	288
ROBINSON	J	3	196	ROBINSON	LW	7	334	ROBINSON	TC	10	194	ROBINSON	WJ	4	326
ROBINSON	J	4	326	ROBINSON	M	1	297	ROBINSON	TE	2	288	ROBINSON	WJ	7	334
ROBINSON	J	6	348	ROBINSON	M	5	296	ROBINSON	TE	5	297	ROBINSON	WJ	7	334
ROBINSON	J	6	348	ROBINSON	M	11	322	ROBINSON	TE	6	348	ROBINSON	WJ	7	334
ROBINSON	J	6	348	ROBINSON				ROBINSON	TG	12	191	ROBINSON	WJ	10	194
ROBINSON	J	7	333	ROBINSON				ROBINSON	TJ	14	270	ROBINSON	WK	8	290

ROBINSON	WR	10	194	ROCHESTER	F	8	291	RODGERS	JW	3	196	ROE	JWH	4	326
ROBINSON	WS	7	334	ROCHFORD	A	14	271	RODGERS	P	13	365	ROE	W	4	326
ROBINSON	WT	6	348	ROCHFORD	D	8	291	RODGERS	PH	10	357	ROE	W	9	164
ROBINSON	WT	14	270	ROCHFORD	J	14	271	RODGERS	R	11	323	ROE	W	11	324
ROBINSON	WW	12	191	ROCHFORD	T	8	291	RODGERS	S	8	291	ROE	W	12	192
ROBINSON	WW	12	377	ROCHFORD	W	11	323	RODGERS	SD	6	349	ROEBUCK	AR	9	164
ROBLOU	AG	2	288	ROCK	CE	6	349	RODGERS	T	9	331	ROEBUCK	C	13	365
ROBOTHAM	AE	6	349	ROCK	F	6	349	RODGERS	TW	6	349	ROEBUCK	F	8	292
ROBOTHAM	J	6	349	ROCK	HT	7	334	RODGERS	WP	11	424	ROEBUCK	G	13	365
ROBOTHAM	PW	6	349	ROCK	MJ	2	288	RODHOUS	A	12	377	ROEBUCK	J	14	271
ROBOTTOM	A	6	349	ROCK	T	4	326	RODLEY	W	8	291	ROFF	AS	3	196
ROBOTTOM	HW	10	195	ROCK	W	2	288	RODMELL	GD	10	195	ROFF	D	7	335
ROBSHAW	C	8	290	ROCK	WT	4	326	RODMELL	J	10	195	ROFF	H	12	378
ROBSHAW	C	8	290	ROCK	WT	6	349	RODMORE	WC	10	357	ROFF	JE	7	335
ROBSHAW	J	8	290	ROCKALL	AF	13	365	RODNEY	AL	5	297	ROFF	WG	12	378
ROBSON	A	1	297	ROCKALL	R	5	297	RODNEY	J	14	271	ROFFE	A	5	298
ROBSON	A	8	290	ROCKELL	JD	2	288	RODNEY	S	5	297	ROFFE	A	5	298
ROBSON	AE	7	334	ROCKETT	A	14	271	RODWAY	AE	1	298	ROFFE	C	2	288
ROBSON	AE	14	270	ROCKETT	AW	3	196	RODWAY	GWF	7	334	ROFFE	F	5	298
ROBSON	AH	3	196	ROCKETT	HE	14	271	RODWAY	W	3	196	ROFFE	W	5	298
ROBSON	C	14	271	ROCKETT	W	8	291	RODWAY	WC	1	298	ROFFEY	E	2	288
ROBSON	F	3	196	ROCKETT	WJ	10	195	RODWELL	A	1	298	ROFFEY	FC	7	335
ROBSON	F	7	334	ROCKEY	F	2	288	RODWELL	A	13	365	ROFFEY	HA	7	335
ROBSON	F	8	290	ROCKINGHAM	F	12	377	RODWELL	EF	5	297	ROFFEY	S	7	335
ROBSON	FJ	7	334	ROCKINGHAM	WI	2	288	RODWELL	GS	1	298	ROFFEY	S	13	365
ROBSON	FW	7	334	ROCKLIFFE	RC	7	334	RODWELL	H	10	195	ROFFEY	W	12	192
ROBSON	GF	8	290	RODD	C	5	297	RODWELL	HT	5	297	ROFFEY	WG	12	192
ROBSON	H	7	334	RODD	J	12	192	RODWELL	PL	13	365	ROFT	GC	10	195
ROBSON	H	8	290	RODDIE	J	2	288	RODWELL	T	10	195	ROGALSKI	W	11	324
ROBSON	HC	7	334	RODDIS	A	12	377	RODWELL	TB	5	298	ROGAN	J	8	292
ROBSON	HW	12	191	RODDIS	CH	12	377	RODWELL	W	8	291	ROGAN	W	8	292
ROBSON	J	1	298	RODDIS	EC	5	297	ROE	A	6	349	ROGAN	WH	10	195
ROBSON	JW	8	290	RODDIS	OH	12	192	ROE	A	6	349	ROGER	HA	7	335
ROBSON	MJ	1	298	RODDIS	WS	12	377	ROE	A	10	357	ROGER	WA	2	288
ROBSON	S	1	298	RODDY	E	8	291	ROE	AW	5	298	ROGERS	A	3	197
ROBSON	T	8	291	RODDY	H	8	291	ROE	B	5	298	ROGERS	A	3	197
ROBSON	TH	2	288	RODELL	A	5	297	ROE	C	14	271	ROGERS	A	3	197
ROBSON	W	7	334	RODELL	E	5	297	ROE	CA	10	195	ROGERS	A	5	298
ROBSON	W	10	195	RODEN	CWS	2	288	ROE	CE	12	377	ROGERS	A	6	349
ROBSON	W	10	195	RODEN	EA	13	365	ROE	CS	12	192	ROGERS	A	7	335
ROBSON	W	10	195	RODGERS	A	8	291	ROE	E	8	291	ROGERS	A	9	331
ROBSON	W	14	271	RODGERS	AE	11	323	ROE	E	11	323	ROGERS	A	10	357
ROBSON	WB	8	291	RODGERS	BWC	8	291	ROE	EJ	2	288	ROGERS	A	11	324
ROBSON	WE	1	298	RODGERS	CC	9	331	ROE	EW	7	334	ROGERS	AE	10	195
ROCCA	F	11	323	RODGERS	F	11	323	ROE	F	14	271	ROGERS	AE	10	195
ROCHE	J	1	298	RODGERS	H	8	291	ROE	G	11	324	ROGERS	AF	4	326
ROCHE	JA	11	323	RODGERS	HJ	3	196	ROE	GE	8	291	ROGERS	AG	4	326
ROCHE	JH	1	298	RODGERS	J	8	291	ROE	H	8	291	ROGERS	AH	4	326
ROCHE	JH	8	291	RODGERS	J	11	323	ROE	H	11	323	ROGERS	AJ	10	195
ROCHE	NA	14	271	RODGERS	J	11	323	ROE	HGW	13	365	ROGERS	AJ	13	366
ROCHE	P	8	291	RODGERS	J	11	323	ROE	J	8	291	ROGERS	AJ	14	271
ROCHE	VV	13	365	RODGERS	J	11	323	ROE	J	11	324	ROGERS	AO	3	197
ROCHE	W	14	271	RODGERS	J	14	271	ROE	J	12	378	ROGERS	AV	14	271
ROCHELL	GR	6	349	RODGERS	JJ	6	349	ROE	J	13	365	ROGERS	B	3	197
ROCHESTER	C	6	349	RODGERS	JT	11	323	ROE	JW	12	378	ROGERS	B	3	197

ROGERS	B	4	326	ROGERS	GJ	4	326	ROGERS	JW	11	324	ROGERS	WJ	11	324
ROGERS	B	9	164	ROGERS	GJ	4	326	ROGERS	JW	11	324	ROGERS	WJ	13	366
ROGERS	B	13	366	ROGERS	GW	3	197	ROGERS	L	10	196	ROGERS	WJH	10	358
ROGERS	C	1	298	ROGERS	GW	3	198	ROGERS	LH	2	289	ROGERS	WM	14	272
ROGERS	C	1	298	ROGERS	GW	10	196	ROGERS	ME	4	327	ROGERS	WR	6	350
ROGERS	C	7	335	ROGERS	H	1	299	ROGERS	MJ	5	298	ROGERS	WR	10	196
ROGERS	C	8	292	ROGERS	H	1	299	ROGERS	NC	6	350	ROGERS	WS	2	289
ROGERS	C	10	195	ROGERS	H	2	289	ROGERS	NJ	10	196	ROGERSON	DG	7	335
ROGERS	C	13	366	ROGERS	H	4	326	ROGERS	P	4	327	ROGERSON	DH	14	272
ROGERS	CH	6	349	ROGERS	H	5	298	ROGERS	P	8	292	ROGERSON	F	13	366
ROGERS	CJ	4	326	ROGERS	H	6	350	ROGERS	PL	10	196	ROGERSON	GH	2	289
ROGERS	CW	3	197	ROGERS	H	8	292	ROGERS	R	1	299	ROGERSON	H	6	350
ROGERS	CW	3	197	ROGERS	H	10	357	ROGERS	R	2	288	ROGERSON	H	11	324
ROGERS	E	1	298	ROGERS	H	12	378	ROGERS	R	6	350	ROGERSON	J	14	272
ROGERS	E	1	298	ROGERS	HC	4	327	ROGERS	R	10	196	ROGERSON	J	14	272
ROGERS	E	1	298	ROGERS	HE	1	299	ROGERS	R	11	324	ROGERSON	JJ	7	335
ROGERS	E	1	298	ROGERS	HE	2	288	ROGERS	R	14	271	ROGERSON	R	4	327
ROGERS	E	2	289	ROGERS	HE	10	196	ROGERS	RA	10	196	ROGERSON	T	11	325
ROGERS	E	3	197	ROGERS	HER	10	196	ROGERS	RB	14	272	ROGERSON	W	9	164
ROGERS	E	3	197	ROGERS	HF	5	298	ROGERS	RE	6	350	ROGERSON	W	14	272
ROGERS	E	3	197	ROGERS	HG	4	327	ROGERS	RFW	2	289	ROGERSON	W	14	272
ROGERS	E	4	326	ROGERS	HJ	7	335	ROGERS	RJ	1	299	ROKE	A	1	299
ROGERS	E	6	349	ROGERS	HJ	10	196	ROGERS	RL	3	198	ROKER	AJ	3	198
ROGERS	E	6	350	ROGERS	HJ	10	196	ROGERS	RS	6	350	ROKER	L	3	198
ROGERS	E	6	350	ROGERS	HJ	10	358	ROGERS	S	6	350	ROKER	RH	3	198
ROGERS	E	10	195	ROGERS	HL	1	299	ROGERS	SG	3	198	ROKER	WG	2	289
ROGERS	E	13	366	ROGERS	HP	13	366	ROGERS	SG	13	365	ROLES	AE	10	196
ROGERS	EB	13	366	ROGERS	HP	14	271	ROGERS	SR	2	289	ROLES	C	11	325
ROGERS	EE	1	298	ROGERS	HW	13	366	ROGERS	T	3	198	ROLES	FW	10	197
ROGERS	F	3	197	ROGERS	J	1	299	ROGERS	T	6	350	ROLES	PJA	10	197
ROGERS	F	4	326	ROGERS	J	3	198	ROGERS	T	6	350	ROLF	A	13	366
ROGERS	F	8	292	ROGERS	J	4	327	ROGERS	T	10	196	ROLF	AT	13	366
ROGERS	F	10	195	ROGERS	J	4	327	ROGERS	W	1	299	ROLF	H	3	198
ROGERS	FAJ	1	298	ROGERS	J	7	335	ROGERS	W	2	289	ROLF	W	8	292
ROGERS	FC	1	298	ROGERS	J	9	331	ROGERS	W	4	327	ROLFE	A	1	299
ROGERS	FC	1	299	ROGERS	J	10	196	ROGERS	W	4	327	ROLFE	A	10	358
ROGERS	FE	3	197	ROGERS	J	11	324	ROGERS	W	5	298	ROLFE	AC	13	366
ROGERS	FE	3	197	ROGERS	J	14	271	ROGERS	W	8	292	ROLFE	AT	13	366
ROGERS	FG	3	197	ROGERS	JA	2	289	ROGERS	W	8	292	ROLFE	AW	13	366
ROGERS	FH	10	357	ROGERS	JA	3	198	ROGERS	W	10	196	ROLFE	C	7	335
ROGERS	G	2	289	ROGERS	JA	4	327	ROGERS	W	11	324	ROLFE	CH	4	327
ROGERS	G	10	195	ROGERS	JA	11	324	ROGERS	W	12	378	ROLFE	DJ	7	335
ROGERS	G	11	324	ROGERS	JC	10	196	ROGERS	WA	7	335	ROLFE	E	3	198
ROGERS	G	14	271	ROGERS	JF	4	327	ROGERS	WBJ	2	289	ROLFE	EH	3	198
ROGERS	GC	3	197	ROGERS	JH	4	327	ROGERS	WC	2	289	ROLFE	EW	2	289
ROGERS	GE	4	326	ROGERS	JH	4	327	ROGERS	WE	6	350	ROLFE	F	1	299
ROGERS	GE	4	326	ROGERS	JH	8	292	ROGERS	WF	5	298	ROLFE	FA	2	289
ROGERS	GH	3	197	ROGERS	JH	10	196	ROGERS	WG	5	298	ROLFE	FH	5	299
ROGERS	GH	3	197	ROGERS	JH	11	324	ROGERS	WG	10	196	ROLFE	G	1	299
ROGERS	GH	6	350	ROGERS	JJ	4	327	ROGERS	WH	4	327	ROLFE	G	3	198
ROGERS	GH	9	164	ROGERS	JJ	9	332	ROGERS	WH	4	327	ROLFE	GDA	2	289
ROGERS	GH	10	196	ROGERS	JL	5	298	ROGERS	WJ	4	327	ROLFE	GE	3	198
ROGERS	GH	12	378	ROGERS	JS	5	298	ROGERS	WJ	10	196	ROLFE	GH	9	164
ROGERS	GH	14	271	ROGERS	JT	1	299	ROGERS	WJ	11	324	ROLFE	HA	5	299
ROGERS	GJ	3	197	ROGERS	JT	6	350	ROGERS	WJ	11	324	ROLFE	HC	4	327

ROLFE	HJ	13	366	ROLT	E	5	299	ROOKS	A	8	293	ROPER	WJ	2	290
ROLFE	J	2	289	ROLT	F	5	300	ROOKS	WAE	13	367	ROSAM	JW	10	197
ROLFE	JE	8	292	ROLT	R	3	198	ROOKS	WJ	13	367	ROSAMOND	GM	12	192
ROLFE	JE	9	164	ROMANO	F	7	335	ROOM	PF	5	300	ROSAMOND	J	12	192
ROLFE	JE	9	164	ROMANS	B	14	272	ROOM	S	5	300	ROSAMOND	JW	8	293
ROLFE	JW	12	378	ROMANS	E	14	272	ROOME	C	12	192	ROSAMOND	W	14	273
ROLFE	LH	1	299	ROMP	EJ	13	367	ROONEY	C	14	273	ROSAN	GW	13	367
ROLFE	SJ	1	299	RONALD	JD	7	336	ROONEY	H	8	293	ROSBROOK	JA	9	332
ROLFE	VH	13	366	RONAN	J	1	299	ROONEY	HE	2	290	ROSCOE	F	14	273
ROLFE	W	10	197	RONAN	M	9	164	ROONEY	J	7	336	ROSCOE	GH	3	199
ROLFE	WJ	3	198	RONAN	W	1	299	ROONEY	J	10	197	ROSCOE	JE	4	328
ROLL	SJ	7	335	RONAN	W	11	325	ROONEY	J	11	325	ROSCOE	JH	3	199
ROLLARTH	D	5	299	RONAYNE	RJ	2	289	ROONEY	J	14	273	ROSCOE	JW	11	325
ROLLASON	FW	6	350	ROND	B	13	367	ROONEY	M	11	325	ROSCOE	W	14	273
ROLLASON	HJ	6	350	RONNEY	T	14	272	ROONEY	R	3	199	ROSE		1	300
ROLLASON	J	6	351	ROO	R	8	292	ROONEY	R	14	273	ROSE	A	3	199
ROLLASON	WP	6	351	ROOBOTTOM	S	6	351	ROONEY	W	11	325	ROSE	A	9	164
ROLLEY	J	11	325	ROOD	A	4	327	ROOPER	A	6	351	ROSE	A	10	197
ROLLEY	T	11	325	ROOD	AE	7	336	ROOSE	E	3	199	ROSE	A	12	192
ROLLINGS	C	5	299	ROOD	FJ	4	327	ROOSE	TR	3	199	ROSE	A	12	192
ROLLINGS	E	8	292	ROOD	WA	4	327	ROOT	A	13	367	ROSE	A	12	193
ROLLINGS	G	14	272	ROOD	WH	4	327	ROOT	AV	2	290	ROSE	AA	12	193
ROLLINS	C	6	351	ROOFF	A	2	290	ROOT	G	13	367	ROSE	AE	2	290
ROLLINS	H	12	192	ROOFF	VA	2	290	ROOT	JT	13	367	ROSE	AE	2	290
ROLLINSON	E	8	292	ROOK	EJ	3	198	ROOT	WF	4	328	ROSE	AE	7	336
ROLLINSON	ET	6	351	ROOK	F	5	300	ROOTHAM	HA	5	300	ROSE	AE	10	197
ROLLINSON	ET	6	351	ROOK	FC	5	300	ROOTLEY	J	6	351	ROSE	AJ	3	199
ROLLINSON	FW	14	272	ROOK	H	12	378	ROOTS	DJ	7	336	ROSE	AJ	12	193
ROLLINSON	H	8	292	ROOK	HT	12	192	ROOTS	FG	2	290	ROSE	AJH	7	336
ROLLINSON	J	6	351	ROOK	THH	14	272	ROOTS	RJ	2	290	ROSE	B	2	290
ROLLINSON	JJ	11	325	ROOK	W	12	192	ROOUM	F	9	164	ROSE	C	3	199
ROLLINSON	L	14	272	ROOK	WJ	12	192	ROPER	E	5	300	ROSE	C	6	351
ROLLINSON	R	14	272	ROOKE	A	8	292	ROPER	E	8	293	ROSE	C	8	293
ROLLINSON	T	6	351	ROOKE	AE	6	351	ROPER	E	9	332	ROSE	C	10	358
ROLLINSON	W	6	351	ROOKE	C	4	328	ROPER	E	10	197	ROSE	CA	12	193
ROLLINSON	WS	14	272	ROOKE	DS	2	290	ROPER	E	11	325	ROSE	CE	5	300
ROLLS	AE	1	299	ROOKE	E	6	351	ROPER	EA	11	325	ROSE	CH	12	193
ROLLS	CJ	5	299	ROOKE	G	3	198	ROPER	EF	5	300	ROSE	CJ	6	351
ROLLS	EG	5	299	ROOKE	G	4	328	ROPER	EJ	2	290	ROSE	CW	12	193
ROLLS	G	5	299	ROOKE	G	8	292	ROPER	F	3	199	ROSE	D	3	199
ROLLS	H	7	335	ROOKE	GF	6	351	ROPER	F	9	332	ROSE	D	6	352
ROLLS	PJ	5	299	ROOKE	H	1	300	ROPER	F	12	192	ROSE	DB	3	199
ROLLS	R	5	299	ROOKE	H	2	290	ROPER	FC	13	367	ROSE	E	3	199
ROLLS	RF	10	358	ROOKE	H	14	272	ROPER	G	9	332	ROSE	E	7	336
ROLLS	W	5	299	ROOKE	HS	3	198	ROPER	HJ	13	367	ROSE	E	8	293
ROLPH	A	5	299	ROOKE	JE	9	332	ROPER	JA	3	199	ROSE	E	13	367
ROLPH	E	5	299	ROOKE	P	8	292	ROPER	JW	9	332	ROSE	EE	12	193
ROLPH	E	7	335	ROOKE	R	3	199	ROPER	L	11	325	ROSE	EF	7	336
ROLPH	GH	13	366	ROOKE	RHJ	6	351	ROPER	R	9	332	ROSE	EJ	2	290
ROLPH	SH	5	299	ROOKE	T	6	351	ROPER	RJ	10	358	ROSE	ET	10	197
ROLPH	TW	13	366	ROOKE	W	8	292	ROPER	RJ	10	358	ROSE	F	9	165
ROLPH	WC	3	198	ROOKE	WT	6	351	ROPER	SJ	13	367	ROSE	F	12	378
ROLPH	WE	5	299	ROOKES	W	3	199	ROPER	TO	9	164	ROSE	F	14	273
ROLT	AV	12	192	ROOKLEDGE	J	8	292	ROPER	W	9	164	ROSE	FA	3	199
ROLT	CH	12	192	ROOKLEDGE	M	8	293	ROPER	W	9	332	ROSE	FF	2	290

ROSE	FS	2	290	ROSENBERG	C	14	273	ROSS	F	9	165	ROSSINGTON	JS	8	294
ROSE	G	2	290	ROSENBERG	J	14	273	ROSS	F	9	165	ROSSITER	F	14	274
ROSE	G	2	290	ROSENBERG	J	14	273	ROSS	F	9	165	ROSSITER	GJ	10	197
ROSE	G	3	199	ROSENBERG	L	14	273	ROSS	FJ	7	336	ROSSITER	HGL	13	368
ROSE	GA	1	300	ROSENBERG	M	2	291	ROSS	G	1	300	ROSSITER	W	2	291
ROSE	GA	4	328	ROSENBERG	S	8	293	ROSS	GA	13	367	ROSSON	F	5	300
ROSE	GC	2	290	ROSENBERG	S	14	273	ROSS	GF	2	291	ROSSON	H	5	300
ROSE	GF	5	300	ROSENBLOOM	L	14	273	ROSS	GH	9	165	ROSSON	PL	5	300
ROSE	GF	6	352	ROSENBLOOM	L	14	273	ROSS	GR	7	336	ROSSON	W	14	274
ROSE	GH	9	332	ROSENBURY	WP	2	291	ROSS	H	7	336	ROSSON	WG	5	300
ROSE	GH	12	193	ROSENDALE	CH	4	328	ROSS	H	9	332	ROSTEN	R	6	352
ROSE	GR	13	367	ROSENDALE	EE	3	200	ROSS	H	9	332	ROSTRON	E	14	274
ROSE	GT	3	199	ROSENDALE	WA	3	200	ROSS	H	10	197	ROSTRON	G	14	274
ROSE	GW	12	193	ROSENSTEIN	B	14	273	ROSS	H	12	193	ROSTRON	H	11	326
ROSE	H	3	199	ROSENTALL	H	14	273	ROSS	H	14	274	ROSTRON	WH	14	274
ROSE	H	6	352	ROSENTHALL	A	8	293	ROSS	HA	10	197	ROSWELL	WA	7	336
ROSE	H	6	352	ROSENTHALL	A	14	274	ROSS	J	9	332	ROTHBLATT	J	14	274
ROSE	H	8	293	ROSENTHALL	J	14	274	ROSS	J	10	197	ROTHBLATT	S	14	274
ROSE	H	8	293	ROSENTHALL	S	8	293	ROSS	J	10	197	ROTHERA	J	8	294
ROSE	H	12	193	ROSER	AHE	13	367	ROSS	J	10	358	ROTHERA	J	8	294
ROSE	HJ	13	367	ROSEWELL	A	11	325	ROSS	J	11	325	ROTHERA	W	8	294
ROSE	J	6	352	ROSHIER	WA	5	300	ROSS	J	14	274	ROTHERHAM	H	6	352
ROSE	J	6	352	ROSIER	A	9	332	ROSS	JH	3	200	ROTHERY	AR	9	332
ROSE	J	7	336	ROSIER	A	9	332	ROSS	JW	8	294	ROTHERY	JD	9	165
ROSE	J	11	325	ROSIER	AW	2	291	ROSS	JW	13	368	ROTHWELL	A	2	291
ROSE	J	12	378	ROSIER	FWC	2	291	ROSS	JW	14	274	ROTHWELL	A	2	292
ROSE	J	13	367	ROSINDALE	A	8	293	ROSS	L	8	294	ROTHWELL	A	11	326
ROSE	JA	14	273	ROSINDALE	C	8	293	ROSS	LB	3	200	ROTHWELL	F	11	326
ROSE	JF	6	352	ROSINDALE	L	9	332	ROSS	ML	3	200	ROTHWELL	F	11	326
ROSE	JF	12	193	ROSINDALE	RE	8	293	ROSS	P	10	197	ROTHWELL	J	8	294
ROSE	JH	2	290	ROSINDALE	RE	8	293	ROSS	P	14	274	ROTHWELL	J	14	274
ROSE	JT	12	193	ROSINDALE	RL	8	293	ROSS	PA	4	328	ROTHWELL	J	14	274
ROSE	MJR	8	293	ROSINDALE	W	8	293	ROSS	R	2	291	ROTHWELL	R	14	275
ROSE	O	6	352	ROSINDALE	WE	8	294	ROSS	RR	9	165	ROTHWELL	T	14	274
ROSE	PR	3	199	ROSKEY	JH	13	367	ROSS	S	9	165	ROTHWELL	W	11	326
ROSE	RG	2	291	ROSKILLY	E	2	291	ROSS	T	11	326	ROTHWELL	W	11	326
ROSE	S	11	325	ROSKILLY	SE	2	291	ROSS	T	11	326	ROTHWELL	W	11	326
ROSE	ST	7	336	ROSLING	GF	3	200	ROSS	T	11	326	ROTHWELL	W	14	275
ROSE	T	12	378	ROSS	A	3	200	ROSS	T	11	326	ROTTENBURY	L	9	332
ROSE	V	2	291	ROSS	A	6	352	ROSS	VHCF	5	300	ROUD	WG	4	328
ROSE	W	1	300	ROSS	AE	3	200	ROSS	W	1	300	ROUGH	C	8	294
ROSE	W	2	291	ROSS	BG	7	336	ROSS	W	9	165	ROUGH	D	14	275
ROSE	W	3	200	ROSS	C	9	165	ROSS	WA	5	300	ROUGH	JW	2	292
ROSE	W	3	200	ROSS	C	9	165	ROSS	WE	12	193	ROUGHLEY	L	14	275
ROSE	WA	8	293	ROSS	C	10	197	ROSS	WK	6	352	ROUGHSEDGE	H	11	326
ROSE	WB	2	291	ROSS	CF	10	197	ROSS	WM	10	197	ROUGHTON	E	12	378
ROSE	WC	10	358	ROSS	D	9	165	ROSSER	A	2	291	ROUGHTON	F	12	378
ROSE	WE	1	300	ROSS	D	11	326	ROSSER	H	4	328	ROUGHTON	W	12	378
ROSE	WE	2	291	ROSS	D	13	367	ROSSER	JW	2	291	ROUGHTON	WH	12	378
ROSE	WE	6	352	ROSS	D	14	274	ROSSER	W	10	358	ROULLIER	AW	7	337
ROSE	WT	14	273	ROSS	DG	7	336	ROSSER	WS	2	291	ROULLIER	EA	13	368
ROSEBY	WF	11	325	ROSS	E	9	165	ROSSI	F	11	326	ROULLIER	JWC	13	368
ROSEHEAD	L	8	293	ROSS	E	10	358	ROSSI	J	11	326	ROULLIER	L	13	368
ROSEMELER	W	7	336	ROSS	EC	4	328	ROSSI	J	11	326	ROULLIER	ML	13	368
ROSENBAUM	J	3	200	ROSS	F	8	294	ROSSIN	FH	2	291	ROULLIER	TE	7	336

ROUND	AH	6	352	ROUTLEY	GW	2	292	ROWE	GA	3	201	ROWELL	GJ	7	337
ROUND	AR	6	352	ROUTLEY	R	3	200	ROWE	GA	3	201	ROWELL	J	4	328
ROUND	E	6	352	ROW	TR	10	358	ROWE	GA	10	198	ROWELL	W	7	337
ROUND	E	6	352	ROW	W	6	353	ROWE	GF	5	301	ROWEN	B	11	327
ROUND	GA	6	352	ROWAN	C	8	294	ROWE	GJ	7	337	ROWEN	RJ	3	201
ROUND	H	6	352	ROWAN	E	9	333	ROWE	GS	5	301	ROWING	C	13	368
ROUND	HW	3	200	ROWAN	F	8	294	ROWE	GT	4	328	ROWLAN	W	13	368
ROUND	JC	6	352	ROWAN	J	9	333	ROWE	H	5	301	ROWLAND	AB	10	358
ROUND	LE	6	353	ROWAN	J	9	333	ROWE	H	6	353	ROWLAND	AE	10	358
ROUND	M	6	353	ROWAN	T	8	294	ROWE	H	7	337	ROWLAND	AE	14	276
ROUND	R	6	353	ROWAN	T	11	327	ROWE	H	8	294	ROWLAND	CL	7	337
ROUND	R	6	353	ROWBOTHAM	A	11	327	ROWE	HA	7	337	ROWLAND	CR	2	292
ROUND	S	6	353	ROWBOTHAM	E	9	333	ROWE	HT	3	201	ROWLAND	DW	7	337
ROUND	SH	3	200	ROWBOTHAM	J	14	275	ROWE	HW	4	328	ROWLAND	E	3	201
ROUND	W	13	368	ROWBOTHAM	L	3	200	ROWE	J	3	201	ROWLAND	E	10	198
ROUNDHILL	H	8	294	ROWBOTHAM	W	8	294	ROWE	J	3	201	ROWLAND	E	11	327
ROUNDHILL	JW	8	294	ROWBOTTOM	H	9	165	ROWE	J	8	294	ROWLAND	F	3	201
ROURKE	B	14	275	ROWBOTTOM	JA	14	275	ROWE	J	9	165	ROWLAND	FM	6	353
ROURKE	EJ	10	358	ROWBOTTOM	K	2	292	ROWE	J	9	165	ROWLAND	G	9	166
ROURKE	J	9	165	ROWCROFT	JT	11	327	ROWE	JA	12	378	ROWLAND	GDC	2	292
ROURKE	J	9	332	ROWDEN	H	11	327	ROWE	JC	10	198	ROWLAND	H	5	301
ROURKE	JE	9	332	ROWDON	HR	3	200	ROWE	JF	10	198	ROWLAND	H	8	295
ROURKE	JE	11	326	ROWE	A	1	300	ROWE	JH	14	275	ROWLAND	H	9	166
ROURKE	JF	11	326	ROWE	A	3	200	ROWE	JW	4	328	ROWLAND	H	10	359
ROURKE	T	11	326	ROWE	A	3	201	ROWE	K	5	301	ROWLAND	H	10	359
ROUS	FC	2	292	ROWE	A	4	328	ROWE	LE	3	201	ROWLAND	H	11	327
ROUS	FJ	2	292	ROWE	A	7	337	ROWE	LW	2	292	ROWLAND	HA	13	368
ROUS	H	2	292	ROWE	A	13	368	ROWE	R	3	201	ROWLAND	HG	13	368
ROUS	JW	7	337	ROWE	A	14	275	ROWE	R	13	368	ROWLAND	HJ	7	337
ROUSE	AB	6	353	ROWE	AC	10	197	ROWE	R	14	275	ROWLAND	HW	7	337
ROUSE	AH	3	200	ROWE	AE	3	201	ROWE	RS	14	275	ROWLAND	J	4	328
ROUSE	AJ	6	353	ROWE	AE	3	201	ROWE	S	11	327	ROWLAND	J	6	353
ROUSE	C	13	368	ROWE	AE	7	337	ROWE	S	14	275	ROWLAND	JE	11	327
ROUSE	CW	13	368	ROWE	AN	3	201	ROWE	T	5	301	ROWLAND	JG	10	359
ROUSE	EE	3	200	ROWE	AS	5	301	ROWE	T	6	353	ROWLAND	JS	1	300
ROUSE	F	5	301	ROWE	AV	10	197	ROWE	T	6	353	ROWLAND	JW	8	295
ROUSE	J	3	200	ROWE	B	7	337	ROWE	T	10	198	ROWLAND	JW	10	198
ROUSE	JAW	9	333	ROWE	BA	3	201	ROWE	T	14	275	ROWLAND	LH	13	368
ROUSE	JE	8	294	ROWE	BJ	3	201	ROWE	TE	6	353	ROWLAND	LH	13	368
ROUSE	RW	14	275	ROWE	C	7	337	ROWE	TE	9	333	ROWLAND	MJ	6	353
ROUSE	W	7	337	ROWE	CJ	3	384	ROWE	W	2	292	ROWLAND	O	6	353
ROUSE	W	10	358	ROWE	CJ	3	384	ROWE	W	3	201	ROWLAND	PJ	10	359
ROUSE	WG	1	300	ROWE	CJ	5	301	ROWE	W	8	295	ROWLAND	R	9	166
ROUSE	WJ	8	294	ROWE	DW	10	358	ROWE	W	10	198	ROWLAND	S	4	328
ROUSELL	EG	13	368	ROWE	EC	3	201	ROWE	W	14	276	ROWLAND	T	2	292
ROUT	CB	2	292	ROWE	ET	2	292	ROWE	WG	13	368	ROWLAND	T	6	353
ROUT	E	3	200	ROWE	F	5	301	ROWE	WH	3	201	ROWLAND	T	8	295
ROUTH	GW	8	294	ROWE	F	12	193	ROWE	WH	6	353	ROWLAND	T	11	327
ROUTH	J	9	333	ROWE	FAJ	4	328	ROWE	WH	8	295	ROWLAND	T	13	368
ROUTH	JE	9	165	ROWE	FB	12	378	ROWE	WV	5	301	ROWLAND	TS	6	354
ROUTLEDGE	HH	2	292	ROWE	FEA	7	337	ROWELL	A	4	328	ROWLAND	W	3	202
ROUTLEDGE	V	14	275	ROWE	FG	2	292	ROWELL	A	8	295	ROWLAND	W	3	202
ROUTLEDGE	WH	14	275	ROWE	FG	3	201	ROWELL	CF	12	193	ROWLAND	W	5	301
ROUTLEDGE	WH	14	275	ROWE	G	8	294	ROWELL	E	8	295	ROWLAND	W	8	295
ROUTLEDGE	WT	11	326	ROWE	G	10	198	ROWELL	ET	10	358	ROWLAND	W	9	166

ROWLAND	WD	13	369	ROWLEY	W	9	333	ROYLE	H	11	328	RUDDICK	G	8	295
ROWLANDS	A	3	202	ROWLEY	W	14	276	ROYLE	H	14	276	RUDDLE	G	11	329
ROWLANDS	A	12	193	ROWLEY	WH	11	327	ROYLE	HC	11	328	RUDDOCK	A	9	166
ROWLANDS	FW	6	354	ROWLING	A	9	166	ROYLE	JH	14	276	RUDDOCK	FE	4	329
ROWLANDS	G	14	276	ROWLING	JE	2	293	ROYLE	JW	14	276	RUDDOCK	JJ	14	277
ROWLANDS	JF	11	327	ROWLING	WA	2	293	ROYLE	L	11	328	RUDDOCK	W	8	296
ROWLANDS	JG	2	292	ROWLINSON	E	7	338	ROYLE	L	14	276	RUDDOCK	WE	8	296
ROWLANDS	JW	12	378	ROWLINSON	F	7	338	ROYLE	M	11	328	RUDDOCK	WT	4	329
ROWLANDS	SC	7	337	ROWLINSON	J	11	328	ROYLE	R	14	276	RUDDY	J	8	296
ROWLANDS	W	7	338	ROWLINSON	J	11	328	ROYLE	S	11	328	RUDDY	J	14	277
ROWLANDS	WC	2	292	ROWLINSON	JG	8	295	ROYLE	T	11	328	RUDDY	T	8	296
ROWLANDS-ARMSTRONG				ROWLINSON	T	11	328	ROYLE	W	14	276	RUDGE	A	3	202
	J	14	276	ROWLINSON	T	11	328	ROYLE	W	14	277	RUDGE	AE	6	354
ROWLES	A	12	193	ROWLINSON	W	7	338	ROYLE	W	14	277	RUDGE	CA	6	354
ROWLES	A	14	276	ROWNEY	S	13	369	ROYLE	WH	14	277	RUDGE	F	6	355
ROWLES	E	5	301	ROWNTREE	F	9	333	ROYLE	WM	14	277	RUDGE	HE	3	202
ROWLES	J	11	327	ROWNTREE	H	8	295	ROYSTON	B	8	295	RUDGE	HH	6	355
ROWLES	JG	10	359	ROWNTREE	HW	3	202	ROYSTON	FF	12	194	RUDGE	HH	6	355
ROWLES	N	11	327	ROWNTREE	JR	9	166	ROYSTON	T	6	354	RUDGE	J	6	355
ROWLES	RW	2	292	ROWNTREE	S	9	333	ROYSTON	WA	9	333	RUDGE	J	6	355
ROWLES	T	11	327	ROWNTREE	SC	9	166	ROYSTON	WA	9	333	RUDGE	JR	2	293
ROWLES	V	3	202	ROWSE	H	8	295	RPLANDS	E	14	272	RUDGE	L	2	293
ROWLETT	AJ	3	202	ROWSELL	E	10	359	RUAN	G	11	328	RUDGE	PW	1	300
ROWLETT	D	5	301	ROWSELL	F	2	293	RUANE	J	8	295	RUDGE	R	3	202
ROWLETT	F	5	301	ROWSELL	H	8	295	RUBERT	E	2	293	RUDGE	RC	3	202
ROWLETT	G	3	202	ROWSON	A	14	276	RUBERY	A	9	166	RUDGE	RF	14	277
ROWLETT	HM	5	301	ROWSON	GPH	2	293	RUBERY	JW	9	166	RUDGE	S	6	355
ROWLETT	T	5	301	ROWSON	H	11	328	RUBIDGE	D	7	338	RUDGE	W	3	202
ROWLETT	W	2	293	ROWSON	TH	10	359	RUBIE	EC	4	329	RUDGE	WF	6	355
ROWLEY	AE	11	327	ROWSON	WT	2	293	RUBINSKI	M	14	277	RUDGE	WJ	2	293
ROWLEY	AJ	5	301	ROWSWELL	FE	2	293	RUBLEY	B	2	293	RUDGE	WJ	6	355
ROWLEY	AS	2	293	ROWSWELL	FG	2	293	RUBY	WS	7	338	RUDHALL	HB	7	338
ROWLEY	C	6	354	ROWTHORN	EL	4	328	RUCK	AA	7	338	RUDINGS	C	14	277
ROWLEY	E	9	333	ROXBY	R	7	338	RUCK	GH	7	338	RUDKIN	H	14	277
ROWLEY	F	6	354	ROY	JR	4	328	RUCK	HF	7	338	RUDKINS	JJ	1	300
ROWLEY	FA	6	354	ROYAL	B	2	293	RUDD	AE	6	354	RUDLING	T	8	296
ROWLEY	FW	3	202	ROYAL	E	4	329	RUDD	AR	3	202	RUDYARD	J	11	329
ROWLEY	G	11	327	ROYAL	FA	2	293	RUDD	C	8	295	RUECROFT	G	8	296
ROWLEY	H	5	301	ROYAL	WH	7	338	RUDD	EH	5	302	RUEL	WAH	3	202
ROWLEY	H	8	295	ROYALL	W	4	329	RUDD	G	4	329	RUFF	AJ	7	338
ROWLEY	HB	11	328	ROYALS	WJ	7	338	RUDD	JE	6	354	RUFF	E	12	194
ROWLEY	HF	5	301	ROYCE	H	12	378	RUDD	LJ	5	302	RUFF	F	12	379
ROWLEY	J	6	354	ROYL	BP	4	329	RUDD	N	9	166	RUFF	GE	12	194
ROWLEY	J	6	354	ROYL	E	4	329	RUDD	PA	6	354	RUFF	GS	2	293
ROWLEY	J	6	354	ROYLANCE	F	11	328	RUDD	R	11	329	RUFF	HE	1	300
ROWLEY	J	9	166	ROYLANCE	G	2	293	RUDD	S	6	354	RUFF	HS	2	294
ROWLEY	JR	2	293	ROYLE	A	11	328	RUDD	S	6	354	RUFF	J	6	355
ROWLEY	P	6	354	ROYLE	A	14	276	RUDD	WA	13	369	RUFF	J	12	194
ROWLEY	R	7	338	ROYLE	A	14	276	RUDD	WT	2	293	RUFF	JG	2	294
ROWLEY	S	5	302	ROYLE	A	14	276	RUDDELL	J	13	369	RUFF	RF	12	379
ROWLEY	SE	13	369	ROYLE	A	14	276	RUDDEN	O	11	329	RUFF	SG	1	300
ROWLEY	SR	10	198	ROYLE	C	14	276	RUDDERHAM	CW	8	295	RUFFEL	G	10	198
ROWLEY	T	6	354	ROYLE	E	11	328	RUDDERHAM	ER	7	338	RUFFELL	E	10	198
ROWLEY	TE	10	198	ROYLE	E	14	276	RUDDERHAM	PL	10	359	RUFFELL	JV	3	202
ROWLEY	W	8	295	ROYLE	ER	11	328	RUDDERHAM	W	8	295	RUFFELL	SW	13	369
ROWLEY	W	8	295												

RUFFELLS	EW	7	338	RUMSEY	VT	2	294	RUSHTON	S	9	166	RUSSELL	B	13	369
RUFFELLS	HC	7	338	RUMSEY	W	4	329	RUSHTON	W	11	329	RUSSELL	BA	4	329
RUFFETT	CH	5	302	RUMSEY	WH	3	203	RUSHWORTH	A	9	333	RUSSELL	C	8	297
RUFFETT	D	5	302	RUNAELES	H	13	369	RUSHWORTH	AE	8	296	RUSSELL	C	9	167
RUFFETT	E	5	302	RUNDLE	FC	10	198	RUSHWORTH	CE	8	296	RUSSELL	C	9	167
RUFFETT	H	5	302	RUNDLE	PG	4	329	RUSHWORTH	E	8	296	RUSSELL	C	12	379
RUFFHEAD	AEJ	12	194	RUNDLE	S	5	302	RUSHWORTH	E	8	296	RUSSELL	C	13	370
RUFFHEAD	J	12	194	RUNECKLES	F	3	203	RUSHWORTH	E	9	334	RUSSELL	CA	1	301
RUFFHEAD	R	12	194	RUNECKLES	GH	1	301	RUSHWORTH	G	9	166	RUSSELL	CA	3	203
RUFFHEAD	VG	12	194	RUNHAM	C	5	302	RUSHWORTH	GA	8	296	RUSSELL	CA	9	334
RUFFITT	G	5	302	RUNHAM	G	2	294	RUSHWORTH	GF	9	167	RUSSELL	CAO	13	370
RUFFLE	TW	10	198	RUNHAM	JC	2	294	RUSHWORTH	H	9	167	RUSSELL	CE	13	370
RUFFLES	R	2	294	RUNHAM	S	5	302	RUSHWORTH	J	8	296	RUSSELL	CER	13	370
RUFUS	W	12	379	RUNNACLES	NG	5	302	RUSHWORTH	J	8	296	RUSSELL	CFW	2	294
RUGG	SW	2	294	RUNTON	GW	9	333	RUSHWORTH	J	9	167	RUSSELL	CG	2	295
RUGG	W	2	294	RUSBRIDGE	E	3	203	RUSHWORTH	J	9	167	RUSSELL	CG	7	339
RUGLAN	F	9	166	RUSBY	G	7	339	RUSHWORTH	JW	8	296	RUSSELL	CJ	3	203
RULE	AL	7	338	RUSCOE	A	14	277	RUSHWORTH	M	8	296	RUSSELL	CJ	4	329
RULE	BA	1	300	RUSH	AH	2	294	RUSHWORTH	T	9	167	RUSSELL	CJ	8	297
RULE	FG	1	300	RUSH	AT	5	302	RUSHWORTH	T	9	334	RUSSELL	CW	3	203
RULE	GE	2	294	RUSH	EH	5	302	RUSHWORTH	T	9	334	RUSSELL	E	3	203
RULE	HG	10	359	RUSH	J	1	301	RUSHWORTH	W	8	296	RUSSELL	E	3	203
RULE	RV	2	294	RUSH	S	4	329	RUSHWORTH	W	8	296	RUSSELL	E	5	303
RULE	S	11	329	RUSH	WF	5	302	RUSHWORTH	W	8	297	RUSSELL	E	13	370
RULE	V	10	359	RUSHBROOK	HJ	13	369	RUSKIN	BF	7	339	RUSSELL	E	13	370
RULE	W	1	300	RUSHBROOKE	GW	3	203	RUSS	H	5	303	RUSSELL	E	13	370
RULER	GJ	7	339	RUSHBROOKE	WJ	3	203	RUSS	JW	5	303	RUSSELL	EA	4	329
RUMBELL	H	10	359	RUSHBY	R	10	198	RUSS	L	6	355	RUSSELL	EM	3	203
RUMBLE	AP	4	329	RUSHBY	T	14	277	RUSS	S	6	355	RUSSELL	EM	10	199
RUMBLE	F	3	202	RUSHBY	W	8	296	RUSS	WJ	5	303	RUSSELL	EW	6	355
RUMBLE	G	4	329	RUSHEN	SJ	4	329	RUSSAM	T	9	167	RUSSELL	EW	7	339
RUMBLE	JF	2	294	RUSHEN	WJ	4	329	RUSSELL	A	1	301	RUSSELL	F	4	330
RUMBLE	JH	10	198	RUSHFIRTH	JW	9	333	RUSSELL	A	3	203	RUSSELL	F	5	303
RUMBLE	WF	10	359	RUSHFORTH	EWA	7	339	RUSSELL	A	6	355	RUSSELL	F	8	297
RUMBLE	WT	2	294	RUSHFORTH	G	8	296	RUSSELL	A	7	339	RUSSELL	F	9	167
RUMBLES	J	5	302	RUSHFORTH	H	9	166	RUSSELL	A	9	334	RUSSELL	F	9	167
RUMBOL	FJ	2	294	RUSHFORTH	HP	2	294	RUSSELL	A	10	198	RUSSELL	F	12	379
RUMBOL	FT	2	294	RUSHFORTH	J	8	296	RUSSELL	A	13	369	RUSSELL	F	13	370
RUMBOL	RW	2	294	RUSHFORTH	J	9	166	RUSSELL	A	13	369	RUSSELL	FEH	10	199
RUMBOL	W	7	339	RUSHFORTH	JH	8	296	RUSSELL	A	13	369	RUSSELL	FG	6	355
RUMBOLD	EC	10	359	RUSHFORTH	TE	8	296	RUSSELL	A	13	369	RUSSELL	FHG	10	199
RUMBOLD	GT	9	166	RUSHFORTH	W	9	333	RUSSELL	A	13	369	RUSSELL	FT	10	199
RUMER	LM	10	198	RUSHMER	GR	12	194	RUSSELL	AE	4	329	RUSSELL	FW	9	334
RUMMERY	GH	3	202	RUSHMER	GW	14	277	RUSSELL	AE	5	303	RUSSELL	FW	13	370
RUMMEY	AP	3	202	RUSHTON	A	7	339	RUSSELL	AE	13	369	RUSSELL	G	3	203
RUMNEY	AE	5	302	RUSHTON	AE	6	355	RUSSELL	AG	7	339	RUSSELL	G	4	330
RUMNEY	AJ	4	329	RUSHTON	C	9	166	RUSSELL	AG	12	424	RUSSELL	G	6	355
RUMNEY	J	5	302	RUSHTON	CF	13	369	RUSSELL	AG	13	369	RUSSELL	G	10	199
RUMNEY	JE	13	369	RUSHTON	EJ	3	203	RUSSELL	AG	13	369	RUSSELL	G	12	194
RUMNEY	TL	4	329	RUSHTON	GF	7	339	RUSSELL	AJ	7	339	RUSSELL	G	13	370
RUMSEY	AE	1	300	RUSHTON	GF	13	369	RUSSELL	AJ	12	194	RUSSELL	G	13	370
RUMSEY	CJ	1	300	RUSHTON	H	9	333	RUSSELL	AL	10	198	RUSSELL	GA	2	295
RUMSEY	FE	3	202	RUSHTON	J	9	166	RUSSELL	AR	1	301	RUSSELL	GA	5	303
RUMSEY	JA	1	300	RUSHTON	J	14	277	RUSSELL	AW	7	339	RUSSELL	GA	10	359
RUMSEY	RL	3	202	RUSHTON	RH	6	355	RUSSELL	B	9	167	RUSSELL	GAV	1	301
								RUSSELL	B	10	359				

RUSSELL	GE	6	355
RUSSELL	GJ	3	203
RUSSELL	GJ	3	203
RUSSELL	GS	2	295
RUSSELL	GSW	7	339
RUSSELL	H	1	301
RUSSELL	H	4	330
RUSSELL	H	6	355
RUSSELL	H	12	194
RUSSELL	H	12	379
RUSSELL	H	12	379
RUSSELL	H	13	370
RUSSELL	H	13	370
RUSSELL	HA	4	330
RUSSELL	HA	5	303
RUSSELL	HA	13	370
RUSSELL	HC	4	330
RUSSELL	HE	6	356
RUSSELL	HF	10	199
RUSSELL	HG	6	356
RUSSELL	HH	1	301
RUSSELL	HI	3	203
RUSSELL	HJ	5	303
RUSSELL	HJ	7	339
RUSSELL	HR	5	303
RUSSELL	HT	12	379
RUSSELL	J	2	295
RUSSELL	J	3	203
RUSSELL	J	6	356
RUSSELL	J	8	297
RUSSELL	J	8	297
RUSSELL	J	10	199
RUSSELL	J	12	194
RUSSELL	J	13	370
RUSSELL	J	13	370
RUSSELL	J	14	277
RUSSELL	J	14	277
RUSSELL	J	14	277
RUSSELL	JD	4	330
RUSSELL	JE	8	297
RUSSELL	JG	2	295
RUSSELL	JG	13	370
RUSSELL	JJ	10	199
RUSSELL	JJ	13	370
RUSSELL	JR	2	295
RUSSELL	JR	10	199
RUSSELL	JS	3	203
RUSSELL	K	4	330
RUSSELL	L	9	167
RUSSELL	M	11	329
RUSSELL	MV	1	301
RUSSELL	OHE	13	370
RUSSELL	P	11	329
RUSSELL	PCW	7	339
RUSSELL	PE	2	295
RUSSELL	R	2	295
RUSSELL	R	4	330
RUSSELL	RE	3	203
RUSSELL	RH	3	204
RUSSELL	S	4	330
RUSSELL	S	6	356
RUSSELL	S	7	339
RUSSELL	S	11	329
RUSSELL	S	13	371
RUSSELL	S	14	277
RUSSELL	SJ	3	204
RUSSELL	T	2	295
RUSSELL	T	3	204
RUSSELL	T	6	356
RUSSELL	T	6	356
RUSSELL	TA	10	199
RUSSELL	TC	10	199
RUSSELL	TE	3	204
RUSSELL	TH	2	295
RUSSELL	TJ	13	371
RUSSELL	TW	14	278
RUSSELL	W	2	295
RUSSELL	W	2	295
RUSSELL	W	3	204
RUSSELL	W	3	204
RUSSELL	W	4	330
RUSSELL	W	4	330
RUSSELL	W	5	303
RUSSELL	W	7	339
RUSSELL	W	10	199
RUSSELL	W	12	379
RUSSELL	W	13	371
RUSSELL	W	13	371
RUSSELL	W	13	371
RUSSELL	WA	13	371
RUSSELL	WB	6	356
RUSSELL	WC	2	295
RUSSELL	WE	13	371
RUSSELL	WF	4	330
RUSSELL	WF	13	371
RUSSELL	WG	12	379
RUSSELL	WGH	3	204
RUSSELL	WH	3	204
RUSSELL	WH	5	303
RUSSELL	WH	13	371
RUSSELL	WJ	1	301
RUSSELL	WJ	1	301
RUSSELL	WR	4	330
RUSSELL	WT	4	330
RUSSELL	WT	4	330
RUSSEN	AE	12	194
RUSSILL	HE	1	301
RUSSON	W	6	356
RUST	A	5	303
RUST	AJ	2	295
RUST	CM	2	295
RUST	G	12	194
RUST	GR	13	371
RUST	JE	2	295
RUST	JJ	7	340
RUST	LWC	1	301
RUST	RT	7	340
RUST	T	2	295
RUST	T	12	194
RUST	WT	6	356
RUSTAGE	W	11	329
RUSTELL	C	4	330
RUSTELL	J	4	330
RUSTELL	SH	10	199
RUSTON	CH	10	359
RUSTON	T	8	297
RUSTON	W	8	297
RUTH	JA	7	340
RUTHERFORD	F	2	295
RUTHERFORD	HG	6	356
RUTHERFORD	J	2	295
RUTHERWOOD	AJ	13	371
RUTHERWOOD	AW	13	371
RUTHVEN	C	11	329
RUTLAND	F	5	303
RUTLAND	G	11	329
RUTLAND	HG	5	303
RUTLAND	HW	2	295
RUTLAND	JF	5	303
RUTLEDGE	ET	10	199
RUTLEDGE	HG	7	340
RUTLEDGE	J	10	199
RUTLEDGE	W	14	278
RUTT	A	2	296
RUTT	AJ	2	296
RUTT	H	2	296
RUTT	H	13	371
RUTT	HE	2	296
RUTTER	EM	2	296
RUTTER	FA	14	278
RUTTER	FG	4	330
RUTTER	FH	12	194
RUTTER	G	14	278
RUTTER	H	14	278
RUTTER	HA	6	356
RUTTER	I	11	329
RUTTER	J	2	296
RUTTER	J	6	356
RUTTER	J	11	329
RUTTER	JH	2	296
RUTTER	PJ	4	330
RUTTER	S	14	278
RUTTER	TW	14	278
RUTTER	W	9	167
RUTTER	W	10	199
RUTTER	WT	6	356
RVAUX	EW	10	359
RYALL	A	10	199
RYALL	AG	1	301
RYALL	AG	1	301
RYALL	F	1	301
RYALL	F	2	296
RYALL	G	5	303
RYALL	H	1	301
RYALL	RP	11	329
RYALL	T	1	301
RYAN	A	7	340
RYAN	A	7	340
RYAN	A	9	167
RYAN	A	10	199
RYAN	D	11	329
RYAN	E	11	329
RYAN	E	14	278
RYAN	FC	2	296
RYAN	FG	1	301
RYAN	G	1	302
RYAN	G	1	302
RYAN	G	9	167
RYAN	GF	14	278
RYAN	GH	2	296
RYAN	GW	8	297
RYAN	H	1	301
RYAN	H	3	204
RYAN	H	8	297
RYAN	I	8	297
RYAN	J	2	296
RYAN	J	8	297
RYAN	J	8	297
RYAN	J	8	297
RYAN	J	9	334
RYAN	J	11	329
RYAN	J	11	329
RYAN	J	11	330
RYAN	J	11	330
RYAN	J	14	278
RYAN	J	14	278
RYAN	J	14	278
RYAN	JA	7	340
RYAN	JE	7	340
RYAN	JF	13	371
RYAN	JP	8	297
RYAN	JW	8	297
RYAN	JW	12	379
RYAN	M	8	297
RYAN	M	11	330
RYAN	M	11	330
RYAN	M	11	330
RYAN	M	14	278
RYAN	MG	3	204
RYAN	P	13	371
RYAN	P	14	278

RYAN	P	14	278	RYDER	WJ	6	356	SADDEN	WE	10	360	SAGE	P	1	302
RYAN	PJ	1	302	RYDING	FT	3	204	SADDINGTON	A	2	297	SAGE	R	1	303
RYAN	PJ	7	340	RYDING	W	3	204	SADDINGTON	CW	12	195	SAGE	T	7	341
RYAN	PS	7	340	RYDINGS	J	11	330	SADLEP	AL	7	340	SAGGERS	W	9	167
RYAN	R	14	278	RYDINGS	R	11	330	SADLER	A	2	297	SAGGERS	W	9	334
RYAN	R	14	278	RYE	GE	2	296	SADLER	A	11	331	SAGGERS	WH	9	334
RYAN	S	14	278	RYE	W	4	330	SADLER	A	14	279	SAGGS	H	13	372
RYAN	T	3	204	RYE	W	7	340	SADLER	AC	11	331	SAGGS	R	13	372
RYAN	T	9	167	RYLAND	AC	6	357	SADLER	B	12	379	SAICH	F	1	303
RYAN	T	10	199	RYLETT	G	5	304	SADLER	C	1	302	SAICH	TE	1	303
RYAN	T	11	330	RYMELL	T	1	302	SADLER	D	1	302	SAINSBURY	AF	10	200
RYAN	T	11	330	RYMER	G	8	298	SADLER	D	6	357	SAINSBURY	AJ	10	200
RYAN	W	11	330	RYMER	H	13	371	SADLER	D	11	331	SAINSBURY	ECH	4	331
RYAN	WG	3	204	RYMER	HW	13	371	SADLER	E	8	298	SAINSBURY	GA	3	205
RYAN	WH	6	356	RYNHAM	WJ	11	330	SADLER	EG	13	372	SAINSBURY	LM	3	205
RYAN	WH	7	340	RYNOR	W	3	204	SADLER	EM	13	372	SAINSBURY	TA	7	341
RYAN	WJ	2	296	RYVES	AH	4	330	SADLER	F	3	205	SAINSBURY	W	10	200
RYCROFT	FH	2	296	RYVES	CB	4	331	SADLER	FG	1	302	SAINSBURY	WG	10	200
RYCROFT	FH	2	296	RYVES	F	4	331	SADLER	FW	1	302	SAINSBURY	WJ	3	205
RYCROFT	H	9	334					SADLER	G	1	302	SAINSBURY	WT	3	205
RYCROFT	J	8	297					SADLER	G	7	340	SAINT	AC	12	195
RYCROFT	J	9	167	**S**				SADLER	GA	6	357	SAINT	AG	3	205
RYCROFT	JH	9	167					SADLER	GS	7	341	SAINT	FW	3	205
RYCROFT	R	9	334	SAAR	JH	13	371	SADLER	H	2	297	SAINT	HF	4	331
RYDE	RW	13	371	SABAN	C	2	296	SADLER	H	6	357	SAINT	RC	3	205
RYDER	A	8	297	SABBATELLA	A	12	194	SADLER	H	11	331	SAINT	SP	13	372
RYDER	A	8	297	SABELL	A	6	357	SADLER	J	2	297	SAINT	W	4	331
RYDER	A	10	199	SABELL	A	6	357	SADLER	J	6	357	SAINT	WGC	4	331
RYDER	AE	11	330	SABELL	HW	6	357	SADLER	J	7	341	SAINTY	CW	7	341
RYDER	AJ	8	297	SABELL	S	6	357	SADLER	J	12	379	SAIT	AE	2	297
RYDER	B	5	303	SABERI	J	13	372	SADLER	JA	10	360	SAIT	AE	2	297
RYDER	B	6	356	SABIN	LG	3	204	SADLER	JA	12	195	SAIT	AJ	10	360
RYDER	C	11	330	SABIN	PR	10	360	SADLER	JS	2	297	SAIT	EJ	10	360
RYDER	E	11	330	SABIN	RS	3	204	SADLER	JW	14	279	SAIT	EJ	10	360
RYDER	EJ	7	340	SABIN	WJ	12	379	SADLER	S	9	334	SAIT	F	4	331
RYDER	EJ	10	200	SABINI	H	1	302	SADLER	S	13	372	SAIT	F	10	360
RYDER	G	5	304	SABINI	V	1	302	SADLER	SG	2	297	SAIT	FJ	4	331
RYDER	G	9	334	SABLES	A	6	357	SADLER	T	1	302	SAIT	HC	2	297
RYDER	GE	10	200	SABOR	M	11	331	SADLER	T	8	298	SAIT	HC	2	297
RYDER	GT	2	296	SACH	G	7	340	SADLER	W	8	298	SAIT	S	10	360
RYDER	GW	14	278	SACH	GFW	7	340	SADLER	W	13	372	SAIT	TF	4	331
RYDER	H	14	279	SACH	WE	1	302	SADLER	WH	14	279	SAIT	W	4	331
RYDER	HE	6	356	SACK	A	8	298	SADLER	WJ	7	341	SAKER	A	8	298
RYDER	J	5	304	SACK	CE	1	302	SADOWSKI	E	13	372	SAKER	CTS	3	205
RYDER	J	11	330	SACK	G	1	302	SAFFERY	WF	4	331	SALAMAN	E	4	331
RYDER	J	11	424	SACKER	L	3	204	SAFFIN	JL	2	297	SALCOMBE	H	6	357
RYDER	JB	4	330	SACKETT	GW	13	372	SAFFREY	T	14	279	SALCOMBE	JH	6	357
RYDER	JH	11	330	SACKSEN	J	6	357	SAGAR	H	8	298	SALE	CH	12	195
RYDER	P	6	356	SACRE	LF	13	372	SAGAR	H	9	334	SALE	CW	3	205
RYDER	R	11	330	SADD	CD	3	204	SAGAR	M	8	298	SALE	E	11	331
RYDER	T	8	298	SADD	CWH	2	297	SAGE	AE	1	302	SALE	ER	2	297
RYDER	T	11	330	SADD	EM	3	204	SAGE	CG	1	302	SALE	FC	2	297
RYDER	W	2	296	SADD	GE	3	204	SAGE	FW	7	341	SALE	G	3	205
RYDER	W	5	304	SADD	GT	1	302	SAGE	HC	13	372	SALE	H	12	379
RYDER	WH	10	359	SADD	TH	12	379	SAGE	HE	13	372	SALE	J	13	372
				SADDEN	EJ	10	360								

SALEM	A	12	379	SALSBURY	WE	6	357	SALWAY	C	10	200	SAMUELS	CA	5	304
SALES	E	13	372	SALT	AE	4	331	SALWAY	EE	4	332	SAMUELS	E	5	304
SALES	H	13	372	SALT	AW	6	358	SALWAY	EG	4	332	SAMUELS	G	1	303
SALES	MC	7	341	SALT	E	12	380	SALWAY	F	10	360	SAMUELS	H	5	304
SALES	S	13	372	SALT	E	14	279	SALWAY	FC	4	332	SAMUELS	H	5	304
SALES	WF	2	297	SALT	F	3	205	SAMAUELLE	EJG	7	341	SAMUELS	HC	5	305
SALES	WF	14	279	SALT	F	14	279	SAMAUELLE	HH	7	341	SAMUELS	J	1	303
SALISBURY	AE	11	331	SALT	G	6	358	SAMBROOK	G	6	358	SAMUELS	J	14	279
SALISBURY	C	2	297	SALT	HH	4	331	SAMBROOK	J	1	303	SAMUELS	L	5	305
SALISBURY	CG	2	297	SALT	HR	7	341	SAMBROOK	W	6	358	SAMUELS	M	3	206
SALISBURY	FE	11	331	SALT	J	11	331	SAMBROOK	Z	6	358	SAMUELS	SJ	5	305
SALISBURY	FW	3	205	SALT	L	6	358	SAMM	CA	5	304	SAMUELS	T	5	305
SALISBURY	FW	3	205	SALT	MP	3	206	SAMM	EA	5	304	SAMUELS	T	10	200
SALISBURY	J	14	279	SALT	R	11	331	SAMMON	C	14	279	SAMWAY	HJ	10	200
SALISBURY	P	11	424	SALT	W	6	358	SAMMONS	T	8	298	SAMWAYS	AJ	3	206
SALISBURY	R	12	195	SALTER	A	9	334	SAMMS	H	5	304	SAMWAYS	CW	10	360
SALISBURY	TJ	1	303	SALTER	CA	13	373	SAMMS	SG	5	304	SAMWAYS	G	10	200
SALISBURY	WT	3	205	SALTER	E	1	303	SAMPHIER	WG	10	200	SAMWAYS	GA	10	360
SALLIS	SR	13	372	SALTER	E	8	298	SAMPHIRE	GAJ	10	360	SAMWELL	H	12	380
SALLIS	W	4	331	SALTER	EH	7	341	SAMPSON	A	13	373	SAMWELL	HF	12	195
SALLOWS	CP	12	379	SALTER	EW	4	331	SAMPSON	AB	13	373	SAMWELL	S	12	195
SALLOWS	E	3	384	SALTER	EW	14	279	SAMPSON	AE	13	373	SANCTO	R	7	342
SALLOWS	GE	12	195	SALTER	F	6	358	SAMPSON	F	13	373	SANDALL	AE	6	358
SALMON	A	3	205	SALTER	F	7	341	SAMPSON	HP	3	206	SANDALL	AW	6	358
SALMON	AA	8	298	SALTER	F	8	298	SAMPSON	J	14	279	SANDALL	ES	3	206
SALMON	C	14	279	SALTER	G	7	341	SAMPSON	JG	9	334	SANDALL	G	4	332
SALMON	C	14	279	SALTER	G	10	360	SAMPSON	JH	13	373	SANDALL	H	4	332
SALMON	E	8	298	SALTER	GW	3	206	SAMPSON	S	5	304	SANDALL	J	4	332
SALMON	E	8	298	SALTER	GW	13	373	SAMPSON	T	9	168	SANDALLS	S	2	298
SALMON	F	10	200	SALTER	HA	10	360	SAMPSON	W	5	304	SANDBACH	J	11	331
SALMON	F	10	200	SALTER	HA	13	373	SAMPSON	WT	4	332	SANDBROOK	H	3	206
SALMON	FEJ	4	331	SALTER	J	4	331	SAMS	AE	2	298	SANDBROOK	MJ	6	358
SALMON	FJ	10	200	SALTER	J	4	332	SAMS	AH	13	373	SANDER	C	3	206
SALMON	GA	10	200	SALTER	JR	14	279	SAMS	H	13	373	SANDERS	A	2	298
SALMON	GAC	10	200	SALTER	JW	4	332	SAMS	J	10	200	SANDERS	A	5	305
SALMON	GH	13	373	SALTER	LF	7	341	SAMS	RH	7	341	SANDERS	AC	6	358
SALMON	H	2	297	SALTER	LF	12	424	SAMS	RJ	13	373	SANDERS	AE	12	195
SALMON	H	3	205	SALTER	RW	13	373	SAMS	WA	2	298	SANDERS	AF	3	206
SALMON	HGT	4	331	SALTER	SJ	10	200	SAMSON	SH	3	206	SANDERS	AS	6	358
SALMON	HJ	2	298	SALTER	W	7	341	SAMSON	T	8	298	SANDERS	AW	3	206
SALMON	HJ	7	341	SALTER	W	8	298	SAMSON	T	10	360	SANDERS	AW	7	341
SALMON	HT	4	331	SALTER	WG	3	206	SAMUEL	A	5	304	SANDERS	AWG	13	373
SALMON	J	8	298	SALTER	WR	13	373	SAMUEL	A	11	331	SANDERS	B	13	373
SALMON	JE	12	195	SALTHOUSE	E	11	331	SAMUEL	AC	1	303	SANDERS	C	1	303
SALMON	JH	2	298	SALTHOUSE	EK	11	331	SAMUEL	AE	6	358	SANDERS	C	12	195
SALMON	LW	3	205	SALTHOUSE	WB	11	331	SAMUEL	BB	5	304	SANDERS	C	13	373
SALMON	MJ	10	360	SALTMARSH	G	2	298	SAMUEL	BH	8	299	SANDERS	CG	1	303
SALMON	P	8	298	SALTMARSH	WG	1	303	SAMUEL	J	14	279	SANDERS	CJ	2	298
SALMON	PJ	3	205	SALTMER	GC	9	334	SAMUEL	JH	8	299	SANDERS	CR	1	303
SALMON	RE	13	373	SALTMER	S	9	334	SAMUEL	RG	1	303	SANDERS	D	13	374
SALMON	SJ	3	205	SALTWELL	HA	1	303	SAMUEL	WAS	8	299	SANDERS	E	1	303
SALMON	W	6	357	SALVAGE	E	4	332	SAMUELS	A	1	303	SANDERS	E	12	195
SALMONS	WC	12	379	SALVAGE	HL	4	332	SAMUELS	A	1	303	SANDERS	E	13	373
SALSBURY	JW	11	331	SALVAGE	WA	13	373	SAMUELS	AP	5	304	SANDERS	EB	1	303
SALSBURY	W	6	357	SALVIN	H	6	358	SAMUELS	AP	5	304	SANDERS	ET	12	195

SANDERS	EW	4	332
SANDERS	F	2	298
SANDERS	F	6	358
SANDERS	FG	1	303
SANDERS	FG	12	195
SANDERS	FH	6	358
SANDERS	FJ	5	305
SANDERS	G	5	305
SANDERS	G	6	358
SANDERS	G	7	342
SANDERS	GR	4	332
SANDERS	GW	6	359
SANDERS	GW	12	195
SANDERS	H	3	206
SANDERS	H	6	359
SANDERS	H	6	359
SANDERS	H	14	279
SANDERS	HC	5	305
SANDERS	HE	10	201
SANDERS	I	4	332
SANDERS	J	4	332
SANDERS	J	9	168
SANDERS	J	10	360
SANDERS	JH	6	359
SANDERS	JH	6	359
SANDERS	JW	2	298
SANDERS	JW	7	342
SANDERS	L	11	331
SANDERS	M	3	206
SANDERS	N	6	359
SANDERS	P	12	195
SANDERS	P	13	374
SANDERS	RW	2	298
SANDERS	SE	6	359
SANDERS	SE	13	374
SANDERS	T	6	359
SANDERS	T	14	279
SANDERS	T	14	280
SANDERS	TCH	7	342
SANDERS	TO	6	359
SANDERS	TW	6	359
SANDERS	W	1	304
SANDERS	W	8	299
SANDERS	W	11	331
SANDERS	WAP	3	206
SANDERS	WH	1	304
SANDERS	WJ	1	304
SANDERS	WJ	5	305
SANDERSON	A	8	299
SANDERSON	A	14	280
SANDERSON	E	8	299
SANDERSON	E	14	280
SANDERSON	F	9	168
SANDERSON	F	14	280
SANDERSON	G	3	206
SANDERSON	G	8	299
SANDERSON	G	8	299
SANDERSON	G	9	168
SANDERSON	G	9	168
SANDERSON	HC	12	380
SANDERSON	HD	1	304
SANDERSON	HM	1	304
SANDERSON	J	3	206
SANDERSON	J	9	168
SANDERSON	J	10	201
SANDERSON	J	11	331
SANDERSON	JM	12	380
SANDERSON	NW	9	334
SANDERSON	R	9	168
SANDERSON	R	14	280
SANDERSON	RH	8	299
SANDERSON	S	8	299
SANDERSON	SG	3	206
SANDERSON	T	14	280
SANDERSON	W	2	298
SANDERSON	W	8	299
SANDERSON	W	10	201
SANDERSON	WR	3	206
SANDFORD	A	1	304
SANDFORD	C	3	206
SANDFORD	CF	3	206
SANDFORD	E	13	374
SANDFORD	G	1	304
SANDFORD	G	5	305
SANDFORD	GH	3	207
SANDFORD	JT	4	332
SANDFORD	P	8	299
SANDIFER	T	5	305
SANDILAND	H	7	342
SANDISON	JC	7	342
SANDIVER	F	12	195
SANDIVER	WT	12	195
SANDLE	W	7	342
SANDLEY	W	12	195
SANDOM	EL	3	207
SANDOM	F	4	332
SANDOM	W	2	298
SANDON	EJ	2	298
SANDS	AE	9	168
SANDS	E	9	335
SANDS	ES	5	305
SANDS	J	11	332
SANDS	S	9	335
SANDS	ST	6	359
SANDS	W	9	335
SANDWELL	C	2	298
SANDWELL	HW	1	304
SANDY	CL	10	201
SANDY	H	3	207
SANDY	SE	10	201
SANDY	T	10	360
SANDYS	AE	10	360
SANDYS	F	10	361
SANDYS	HJ	10	361
SANDYS	W	10	361
SANFORD	CA	12	195
SANFORD	RP	12	196
SANGER	F	4	332
SANGER	FW	4	332
SANGER	GH	4	332
SANGER	J	4	332
SANGER	JE	4	333
SANGER	SA	4	333
SANGSTER	FA	2	298
SANGSTER	FC	4	333
SANGSTER	GD	4	333
SANGSTER	GWJ	4	333
SANGSTER	J	14	280
SANGSTER	J	14	280
SANGSTER	JE	14	280
SANGSTER	MJ	4	333
SANKY	HJ	6	359
SANRS	J	12	196
SANS	HJ	7	342
SANSBURY	C	13	374
SANSBURY	GW	10	201
SANSBURY	WH	10	201
SANSOM	A	4	333
SANSOM	B	3	207
SANSOM	E	10	361
SANSOM	F	3	207
SANSOM	HH	1	304
SANSOM	JTB	5	305
SANSOM	RJ	5	305
SANSOM	SL	7	342
SANSOME	EJO	5	305
SANSOME	H	11	332
SANSOME	W	4	333
SANSOME	WG	10	361
SANSON	WJ	2	298
SANSUM	PC	3	207
SANSUM	WJ	3	207
SAPCOTE	A	1	304
SAPP	CA	3	207
SAPSEAD	HW	14	280
SAPSED	AJ	5	305
SAPSFORD	E	1	304
SAPSFORD	W	2	298
SAPWELL	AJ	12	196
SAPWELL	CL	12	196
SAPWELL	EB	12	196
SAPWELL	TE	12	380
SAPWELL	WC	12	196
SARCHFIELD	J	7	342
SARGANT	W	6	359
SARGEANT	CE	13	374
SARGEANT	E	3	207
SARGEANT	EI	13	374
SARGEANT	EJ	13	374
SARGEANT	F	12	196
SARGEANT	F	13	374
SARGEANT	H	12	196
SARGEANT	HN	2	298
SARGEANT	J	7	342
SARGEANT	R	11	332
SARGEANT	R	11	332
SARGEANT	S	10	361
SARGEANT	TJ	12	380
SARGEANT	W	7	342
SARGEANT	WC	3	207
SARGENT	AJ	12	196
SARGENT	AJ	12	380
SARGENT	B	12	196
SARGENT	E	4	333
SARGENT	EJT	12	380
SARGENT	FG	12	196
SARGENT	GE	7	342
SARGENT	H	3	207
SARGENT	H	4	333
SARGENT	H	11	332
SARGENT	HF	10	201
SARGENT	JW	11	332
SARGENT	R	12	380
SARGENT	RT	4	333
SARGENT	W	13	374
SARGENT	WC	12	196
SARGENT	WH	7	342
SARGENT	WH	11	332
SARGENT	WH	12	380
SARGINSON	A	3	384
SARGINSON	J	3	384
SARGISON	FW	10	201
SARNEY	HF	7	342
SARSON	G	11	332
SARSON	JE	8	299
SARSON	P	11	332
SARTORIUS	E	6	359
SARTY	A	2	299
SATCHEL	GH	3	207
SATCHELL	ER	10	201
SATCHELL	H	4	333
SATCHELL	JA	14	280
SATCHELL	S	13	374
SATCHELL	W	1	304
SATCHELL	WG	10	201
SATCHELL	WJ	6	359
SATCHWELL	H	6	359
SATCHWELL	W	6	359
SATCHWELL	WOA	6	359

Surname	Initials	Vol	Page
SATTERTHWAITE	HE	6	360
SATTERTHWAITE	WEG	6	360
SATTIN	L	11	332
SAUL	A	7	342
SAUL	D	14	280
SAUL	M	14	280
SAUL	ME	2	299
SAUL	PJ	2	299
SAUL	RM	2	299
SAUL	TH	9	335
SAULSBURY	TH	3	207
SAULT	HA	6	360
SAUNDERS	A	3	207
SAUNDERS	A	4	333
SAUNDERS	A	4	333
SAUNDERS	A	4	333
SAUNDERS	A	5	305
SAUNDERS	A	6	360
SAUNDERS	A	13	374
SAUNDERS	A	14	280
SAUNDERS	A	14	280
SAUNDERS	AC	5	305
SAUNDERS	AE	10	361
SAUNDERS	AEG	12	196
SAUNDERS	AG	3	207
SAUNDERS	AG	5	306
SAUNDERS	AH	3	207
SAUNDERS	AL	1	304
SAUNDERS	AM	10	201
SAUNDERS	AR	1	304
SAUNDERS	AS	5	306
SAUNDERS	AS	12	196
SAUNDERS	BC	5	306
SAUNDERS	C	3	207
SAUNDERS	C	7	342
SAUNDERS	C	7	342
SAUNDERS	C	10	201
SAUNDERS	C	10	201
SAUNDERS	C	10	361
SAUNDERS	C	10	361
SAUNDERS	CA	10	361
SAUNDERS	CE	5	306
SAUNDERS	CE	10	201
SAUNDERS	CE	10	361
SAUNDERS	CJ	3	207
SAUNDERS	CL	5	306
SAUNDERS	CW	12	196
SAUNDERS	D	14	280
SAUNDERS	DW	1	304
SAUNDERS	E	3	207
SAUNDERS	E	3	207
SAUNDERS	E	3	208
SAUNDERS	E	7	342
SAUNDERS	E	7	343
SAUNDERS	E	10	201
SAUNDERS	EB	13	374
SAUNDERS	EF	2	299
SAUNDERS	EF	13	374
SAUNDERS	EG	5	306
SAUNDERS	EH	4	333
SAUNDERS	EH	10	201
SAUNDERS	EJ	13	374
SAUNDERS	EM	1	304
SAUNDERS	EW	3	208
SAUNDERS	F	1	304
SAUNDERS	F	2	299
SAUNDERS	F	5	306
SAUNDERS	F	7	343
SAUNDERS	F	7	343
SAUNDERS	F	12	196
SAUNDERS	F	12	196
SAUNDERS	FB	1	304
SAUNDERS	FE	5	306
SAUNDERS	FE	5	306
SAUNDERS	FE	5	306
SAUNDERS	FJ	3	208
SAUNDERS	FJ	5	306
SAUNDERS	FL	3	208
SAUNDERS	FW	10	361
SAUNDERS	G	3	208
SAUNDERS	G	3	385
SAUNDERS	G	4	333
SAUNDERS	G	6	360
SAUNDERS	G	8	299
SAUNDERS	G	12	196
SAUNDERS	GF	7	343
SAUNDERS	GG	5	306
SAUNDERS	GH	6	360
SAUNDERS	GP	13	374
SAUNDERS	GW	2	299
SAUNDERS	GW	13	374
SAUNDERS	H	3	208
SAUNDERS	H	4	333
SAUNDERS	H	7	343
SAUNDERS	H	8	299
SAUNDERS	H	9	168
SAUNDERS	H	9	335
SAUNDERS	H	12	196
SAUNDERS	H	13	374
SAUNDERS	HE	3	208
SAUNDERS	HE	7	343
SAUNDERS	HF	5	306
SAUNDERS	HG	1	304
SAUNDERS	HG	6	360
SAUNDERS	HG	13	374
SAUNDERS	HJ	5	306
SAUNDERS	HJ	12	196
SAUNDERS	HP	2	299
SAUNDERS	HW	5	306
SAUNDERS	HW	5	306
SAUNDERS	HW	5	306
SAUNDERS	J	4	333
SAUNDERS	J	5	306
SAUNDERS	J	5	306
SAUNDERS	J	7	343
SAUNDERS	J	8	299
SAUNDERS	J	10	201
SAUNDERS	J	10	361
SAUNDERS	J	11	332
SAUNDERS	J	11	332
SAUNDERS	J	12	197
SAUNDERS	J	13	375
SAUNDERS	J	13	375
SAUNDERS	J	13	375
SAUNDERS	J	14	280
SAUNDERS	JA	7	343
SAUNDERS	JA	10	202
SAUNDERS	JC	5	307
SAUNDERS	JE	3	208
SAUNDERS	JF	13	375
SAUNDERS	JH	3	208
SAUNDERS	JJ	5	307
SAUNDERS	JJ	8	299
SAUNDERS	JJF	12	197
SAUNDERS	JP	7	343
SAUNDERS	JT	12	197
SAUNDERS	JW	1	304
SAUNDERS	JW	7	343
SAUNDERS	JW	13	375
SAUNDERS	L	4	333
SAUNDERS	LF	1	305
SAUNDERS	OG	13	375
SAUNDERS	P	7	343
SAUNDERS	PAG	5	307
SAUNDERS	PV	10	201
SAUNDERS	R	5	307
SAUNDERS	R	10	202
SAUNDERS	R	10	202
SAUNDERS	R	14	280
SAUNDERS	RA	13	375
SAUNDERS	RD	11	332
SAUNDERS	RJ	3	208
SAUNDERS	RL	2	299
SAUNDERS	S	3	208
SAUNDERS	SC	4	334
SAUNDERS	SH	6	360
SAUNDERS	SR	2	299
SAUNDERS	T	6	360
SAUNDERS	TE	14	280
SAUNDERS	TR	12	197
SAUNDERS	VG	7	343
SAUNDERS	W	2	299
SAUNDERS	W	2	299
SAUNDERS	W	3	208
SAUNDERS	W	10	361
SAUNDERS	W	12	380
SAUNDERS	W	12	380
SAUNDERS	W	13	375
SAUNDERS	WA	3	208
SAUNDERS	WA	6	360
SAUNDERS	WF	13	375
SAUNDERS	WG	4	334
SAUNDERS	WH	7	343
SAUNDERS	WH	10	202
SAUNDERS	WH	14	281
SAUNDERS	WJ	3	208
SAUNDERS	WJ	10	361
SAUNDERS	WW	3	208
SAUNDERSON	WA	13	375
SAVAGE	A	8	299
SAVAGE	A	10	361
SAVAGE	AJ	3	208
SAVAGE	AM	3	208
SAVAGE	C	1	305
SAVAGE	C	3	208
SAVAGE	C	14	281
SAVAGE	CF	3	208
SAVAGE	CF	10	202
SAVAGE	CP	2	299
SAVAGE	E	5	307
SAVAGE	EC	1	305
SAVAGE	EE	3	208
SAVAGE	EH	2	299
SAVAGE	EW	10	202
SAVAGE	F	3	208
SAVAGE	F	13	375
SAVAGE	FW	4	334
SAVAGE	G	12	197
SAVAGE	GE	1	305
SAVAGE	GF	3	208
SAVAGE	GW	7	343
SAVAGE	H	3	209
SAVAGE	HG	1	305
SAVAGE	HJ	5	307
SAVAGE	J	1	305
SAVAGE	J	2	299
SAVAGE	J	9	168
SAVAGE	J	11	332
SAVAGE	J	13	375
SAVAGE	J	14	281
SAVAGE	JA	9	335
SAVAGE	JB	12	380
SAVAGE	JH	14	281
SAVAGE	JJ	4	334
SAVAGE	JR	4	334
SAVAGE	JT	6	360
SAVAGE	JT	13	375
SAVAGE	JW	6	360
SAVAGE	LH	7	343
SAVAGE	SG	12	380

SAVAGE	SH	4	334	SAWARD	F	3	209	SAYCE	T	8	300	SCALES	T	5	308
SAVAGE	V	14	281	SAWFORD	CH	12	197	SAYELL	E	12	197	SCALES	W	8	300
SAVAGE	W	6	360	SAWFORD	E	12	197	SAYELL	G	5	307	SCAMELL	E	4	335
SAVAGE	W	10	202	SAWFORD	H	12	197	SAYELL	H	5	307	SCAMMELL	A	4	335
SAVAGE	W	11	332	SAWKINS	G	1	305	SAYELL	J	5	307	SCAMMELL	E	1	305
SAVAGE	W	14	281	SAWKINS	GJ	1	305	SAYELL	M	12	197	SCAMMELL	GE	2	300
SAVAGE	WA	10	202	SAWTELL	G	4	334	SAYELL	S	5	307	SCAMMELL	GH	2	300
SAVAGE	WF	4	334	SAWYER	A	13	375	SAYELL	W	5	308	SCAMMELL	JH	4	335
SAVAGE	WG	10	202	SAWYER	AGT	13	375	SAYELL	W	5	308	SCAMMELL	R	2	300
SAVAGE	WG	10	202	SAWYER	AH	4	334	SAYER	AH	4	334	SCAMMELL	RVL	4	335
SAVAGE	WH	14	281	SAWYER	AJ	3	385	SAYER	CT	2	300	SCANDRETT	T	13	376
SAVAGE	WJ	2	299	SAWYER	AJ	7	344	SAYER	E	12	197	SCANLAN	F	14	281
SAVAGE	WL	4	334	SAWYER	C	5	307	SAYER	F	9	168	SCANLAN	J	7	344
SAVAGE	WR	10	202	SAWYER	C	10	202	SAYER	JH	13	376	SCANLAN	PC	7	344
SAVAGE	WT	12	197	SAWYER	E	5	307	SAYER	TW	13	376	SCANLAN	R	2	300
SAVEALL	W	10	362	SAWYER	G	1	305	SAYER	W	13	376	SCANLON	B	9	168
SAVEALL	WJ	13	375	SAWYER	GE	5	307	SAYERS	A	2	300	SCANLON	FG	13	376
SAVELL	SJ	13	375	SAWYER	GE	13	376	SAYERS	AG	13	376	SCAPLEHORN	C	1	305
SAVENER	AB	5	307	SAWYER	HG	7	344	SAYERS	AW	3	209	SCAPLEHORN	H	1	305
SAVERY	GE	2	299	SAWYER	HJ	13	376	SAYERS	E	2	300	SCARBOROUGH	AC	3	209
SAVERY	T	8	299	SAWYER	HRW	5	307	SAYERS	E	4	334	SCARBOROUGH	E	7	344
SAVERY	WH	3	209	SAWYER	J	2	300	SAYERS	E	4	334	SCARBOROUGH	F	10	202
SAVIGAR	G	6	360	SAWYER	J	5	307	SAYERS	EJ	3	209	SCARBOROUGH	G	2	300
SAVILL	AB	7	343	SAWYER	J	8	300	SAYERS	EWG	10	202	SCARBROW	HJ	3	210
SAVILL	AE	3	209	SAWYER	J	10	362	SAYERS	H	2	300	SCARD	DHM	13	376
SAVILL	AE	7	343	SAWYER	J	13	376	SAYERS	J	4	334	SCARFE	RA	9	335
SAVILL	BSE	3	209	SAWYER	JH	7	344	SAYERS	J	9	335	SCARFE	WS	9	168
SAVILL	CTH	13	375	SAWYER	PAC	4	334	SAYERS	JG	7	344	SCARFF	H	1	305
SAVILL	EA	13	375	SAWYER	R	13	376	SAYERS	L	13	376	SCARFF	HG	5	308
SAVILL	FR	1	305	SAWYER	RJ	13	376	SAYERS	R	5	308	SCARFF	R	13	377
SAVILL	H	3	209	SAWYER	ST	13	376	SAYERS	S	3	209	SCARLES	FW	7	344
SAVILL	J	7	343	SAWYER	W	13	376	SAYERS	SE	4	334	SCARLET	WE	1	305
SAVILL	W	2	299	SAWYERS	H	5	307	SAYERS	T	9	168	SCARLETT	AEB	3	210
SAVILL	WG	3	209	SAX	L	14	281	SAYLES	VJ	1	305	SCARLETT	E	14	281
SAVILLE	E	9	168	SAXBY	C	3	209	SAYNOR	E	8	300	SCARLETT	JT	3	210
SAVILLE	E	14	281	SAXBY	CW	4	334	SAYNOR	W	8	300	SCARLETT	L	11	333
SAVILLE	F	5	307	SAXBY	GRB	4	334	SCADDING	AJ	4	334	SCARLETT	R	2	300
SAVILLE	F	9	335	SAXBY	H	11	332	SCADGELL	FJ	10	202	SCARLETT	WJ	13	377
SAVILLE	F	9	335	SAXBY	TF	10	362	SCADGELL	JF	10	202	SCARR	H	9	168
SAVILLE	H	8	300	SAXON	A	11	332	SCAIFE	A	8	300	SCARROTT	I	10	202
SAVILLE	J	8	300	SAXON	G	11	332	SCAIFE	H	9	168	SCARROW	JW	8	300
SAVILLE	JJ	2	299	SAXON	J	11	333	SCAIFE	T	7	344	SCARSBROOK	W	12	380
SAVILLE	JW	9	168	SAXON	R	11	333	SCALES	A	3	209	SCARSEBROOK	CV	2	300
SAVILLE	R	14	281	SAXON	T	11	333	SCALES	A	5	308	SCATES	WH	13	377
SAVILLE	W	1	305	SAXON	WJ	11	333	SCALES	FG	1	305	SCATTERGOOD	L	14	281
SAVILLE	W	8	300	SAXTON	FR	1	305	SCALES	GP	13	376	SCHAFER	FW	11	333
SAVILLE	W	9	335	SAXTON	GE	1	305	SCALES	H	3	209	SCHAFER	J	1	306
SAVILLE	WH	5	307	SAXTON	J	9	335	SCALES	H	8	300	SCHAFFER	TF	1	306
SAVILLE	WH	8	300	SAXTON	JH	8	300	SCALES	J	4	334	SCHAFINSKY	A	14	281
SAVILLE	WW	1	305	SAXTON	JW	11	333	SCALES	J	12	197	SCHALCK	HF	3	210
SAVORY	E	6	360	SAXTON	RF	3	209	SCALES	J	13	376	SCHAPER	FL	2	300
SAVORY	EJ	7	344	SAY	A	13	376	SCALES	J	13	376	SCHELDT	EG	11	333
SAVORY	LJ	13	375	SAY	AW	13	376	SCALES	PA	12	197	SCHEU	DC	3	210
SAW	FT	3	209	SAY	CR	3	209	SCALES	R	5	308	SCHLATTER	H	7	344
SAW	WJ	3	209	SAY	ER	3	209	SCALES	S	5	308	SCHLESSELMAN	B	3	210

SCHLUTER	FGH	7	344	SCHOLES	JW	11	333	SCORAH	J	8	301	SCOTT	AG	13	377				
SCHMIDT	AF	2	300	SCHOLES	K	9	169	SCORAH	WT	1	306	SCOTT	AG	13	377				
SCHNAAR	CH	13	377	SCHOLES	L	11	334	SCOREY	A	4	335	SCOTT	AJ	10	203				
SCHNEIDER	E	7	344	SCHOLES	T	11	334	SCOREY	A	4	335	SCOTT	AM	3	210				
SCHOFIELD	A	8	300	SCHOLEY	A	8	301	SCOREY	A	4	335	SCOTT	AW	1	306				
SCHOFIELD	A	8	300	SCHOLEY	A	8	301	SCOREY	A	4	335	SCOTT	AW	2	301				
SCHOFIELD	A	9	168	SCHOLEY	C	8	301	SCOREY	AT	4	335	SCOTT	AW	5	308				
SCHOFIELD	AE	7	344	SCHOLEY	F	8	301	SCOREY	AW	4	335	SCOTT	B	8	302				
SCHOFIELD	AE	11	333	SCHOLEY	F	9	336	SCOREY	B	4	335	SCOTT	BA	3	210				
SCHOFIELD	B	8	300	SCHOLEY	G	8	301	SCOREY	E	4	335	SCOTT	BR	10	203				
SCHOFIELD	B	8	300	SCHOLEY	G	8	301	SCOREY	G	4	335	SCOTT	C	5	308				
SCHOFIELD	C	8	300	SCHOLEY	J	8	301	SCOREY	G	4	335	SCOTT	CA	3	210				
SCHOFIELD	C	8	300	SCHOLEY	J	8	301	SCOREY	G	4	335	SCOTT	CA	3	210				
SCHOFIELD	C	11	333	SCHOLEY	JH	8	301	SCOREY	GA	10	203	SCOTT	CG	7	345				
SCHOFIELD	CE	14	281	SCHOLEY	OS	10	362	SCOREY	IJF	4	335	SCOTT	CH	7	345				
SCHOFIELD	E	9	168	SCHOLEY	W	8	301	SCOREY	WG	4	335	SCOTT	CJ	12	380				
SCHOFIELD	E	14	281	SCHOLL	AE	13	377	SCOREY	WJ	10	203	SCOTT	DJ	2	301				
SCHOFIELD	EH	2	300	SCHOLL	AV	7	344	SCOREY	WR	10	203	SCOTT	E	3	210				
SCHOFIELD	F	2	300	SCHOLLAR	EW	10	203	SCORFIELD	E	9	169	SCOTT	E	7	345				
SCHOFIELD	F	8	300	SCHOLLEY	JT	9	169	SCORFIELD	R	8	301	SCOTT	E	8	302				
SCHOFIELD	F	9	169	SCHOLTZ	AE	2	300	SCOT	M	3	210	SCOTT	EA	7	345				
SCHOFIELD	F	9	335	SCHOM	AC	3	210	SCOTCHER	HG	13	377	SCOTT	EJ	4	336				
SCHOFIELD	F	9	335	SCHONBERG	W	14	282	SCOTCHETT	JW	5	308	SCOTT	EJ	10	203				
SCHOFIELD	G	14	281	SCHOOL	AHV	7	344	SCOTCHETT	JW	5	308	SCOTT	EW	4	336				
SCHOFIELD	G	14	281	SCHOOLING	FH	7	345	SCOTCHFORD	E	14	282	SCOTT	F	1	306				
SCHOFIELD	GW	8	300	SCHOOLING	T	2	300	SCOTCHMER	FG	5	308	SCOTT	F	3	210				
SCHOFIELD	H	8	300	SCHREIBER	ACM	5	308	SCOTCHMER	VE	5	308	SCOTT	F	3	210				
SCHOFIELD	H	9	335	SCHULER	B	7	345	SCOTFORD	S	6	360	SCOTT	F	9	336				
SCHOFIELD	H	9	335	SCHULTZ	AE	13	377	SCOTFORD	WA	6	360	SCOTT	F	10	362				
SCHOFIELD	H	10	203	SCHULTZ	JH	13	377	SCOTMAN	W	2	301	SCOTT	F	12	380				
SCHOFIELD	H	11	333	SCHULTZE	ALF	3	210	SCOTNEY	CH	10	203	SCOTT	F	13	377				
SCHOFIELD	H	14	281	SCHULZE	W	9	169	SCOTNEY	DC	10	203	SCOTT	FE	2	301				
SCHOFIELD	J	8	300	SCHUMACHER	F	10	362	SCOTNEY	TV	10	203	SCOTT	FE	5	308				
SCHOFIELD	J	14	282	SCHUMACHER	HR	1	306	SCOTNEY	WE	10	203	SCOTT	FJ	2	301				
SCHOFIELD	J	14	282	SCHUTZ	A	4	335	SCOTT	A	2	301	SCOTT	FJ	3	210				
SCHOFIELD	JA	11	333	SCHWARTZ	F	2	300	SCOTT	A	2	301	SCOTT	FJ	6	360				
SCHOFIELD	JH	8	301	SCHWARZ	J	1	306	SCOTT	A	3	210	SCOTT	FL	10	203				
SCHOFIELD	JL	8	301	SCIARRETTA	HIR	7	345	SCOTT	A	3	210	SCOTT	FS	5	309				
SCHOFIELD	M	8	301	SCILLITOE	W	10	362	SCOTT	A	4	335	SCOTT	FS	6	361				
SCHOFIELD	S	8	301	SCIVIER	C	4	335	SCOTT	A	6	361	SCOTT	FW	7	345				
SCHOFIELD	S	9	169	SCIVIER	R	10	203	SCOTT	A	7	345	SCOTT	G	3	210				
SCHOFIELD	S	9	335	SCOATS	CC	5	308	SCOTT	A	8	301	SCOTT	G	3	211				
SCHOFIELD	T	9	335	SCOATS	HJ	5	308	SCOTT	A	8	301	SCOTT	G	8	302				
SCHOFIELD	T	11	333	SCOATS	HW	5	308	SCOTT	A	8	301	SCOTT	G	8	302				
SCHOFIELD	T	14	282	SCOBEY	FH	8	301	SCOTT	A	8	302	SCOTT	G	11	334				
SCHOFIELD	W	6	360	SCOBLE	WA	2	300	SCOTT	A	9	169	SCOTT	G	12	197				
SCHOFIELD	W	9	336	SCOFFIELD	F	8	301	SCOTT	A	9	169	SCOTT	G	13	377				
SCHOFIELD	W	11	333	SCOFIELD	AC	7	345	SCOTT	A	11	334	SCOTT	GA	5	309				
SCHOFIELD	WH	11	333	SCOFIELD	H	7	345	SCOTT	A	11	334	SCOTT	GA	8	302				
SCHOLEFIELD	S	9	336	SCOFIELD	HJ	7	345	SCOTT	A	11	334	SCOTT	GC	3	211				
SCHOLES	B	7	344	SCOFIELD	WT	7	345	SCOTT	A	11	334	SCOTT	GF	4	336				
SCHOLES	HA	14	282	SCOGGINS	W	7	345	SCOTT	A	13	377	SCOTT	GW	3	211				
SCHOLES	J	11	333	SCOGING	GE	13	377	SCOTT	AC	8	302	SCOTT	GW	4	336				
SCHOLES	J	11	333	SCOLTOCK	WJ	1	306	SCOTT	AF	3	210	SCOTT	H	2	301				
SCHOLES	JB	14	282	SCORAH	D	8	301	SCOTT	AF	7	345	SCOTT	H	5	309				

SCOTT	H	5	309	SCOTT	PA	1	306	SCOTT	WE	8	302	SCRIVENER	WG	7	346
SCOTT	H	7	345	SCOTT	PS	2	301	SCOTT	WE	12	381	SCRIVENER	WT	7	346
SCOTT	H	8	302	SCOTT	R	3	211	SCOTT	WFE	2	301	SCRIVENS	A	6	361
SCOTT	H	9	169	SCOTT	R	6	361	SCOTT	WG	3	211	SCRIVENS	CE	6	361
SCOTT	H	9	169	SCOTT	R	9	336	SCOTT	WG	13	377	SCRIVENS	F	13	378
SCOTT	H	9	336	SCOTT	R	11	334	SCOTT	WH	3	211	SCRIVENS	H	14	282
SCOTT	H	9	336	SCOTT	R	14	282	SCOTT	WH	3	211	SCRIVENS	WH	6	361
SCOTT	HC	7	345	SCOTT	RE	11	334	SCOTT	WH	4	336	SCROGG	R	2	302
SCOTT	HH	5	309	SCOTT	RH	2	301	SCOTT	WH	11	334	SCROGGINS	TA	7	346
SCOTT	HJ	1	306	SCOTT	RP	12	197	SCOTT	WH	14	282	SCROGGINS	W	3	212
SCOTT	HJ	2	301	SCOTT	RRF	5	309	SCOTT	WJ	1	307	SCRUTON	F	11	424
SCOTT	HJ	3	211	SCOTT	S	1	306	SCOTT	WJ	3	385	SCRUTON	F	11	424
SCOTT	HJ	5	309	SCOTT	S	7	346	SCOTT	WJ	7	346	SCRUTON	L	8	302
SCOTT	HJ	13	377	SCOTT	S	7	346	SCOTT	WJ	13	378	SCUDDER	A	1	307
SCOTT	HV	3	211	SCOTT	S	9	169	SCOTT	WJJ	10	362	SCUDDER	A	1	307
SCOTT	HW	7	346	SCOTT	SE	5	309	SCOTT	WR	3	212	SCUDDER	H	6	361
SCOTT	J	1	306	SCOTT	SH	7	346	SCOTT	WR	7	346	SCUDDER	H	13	378
SCOTT	J	1	306	SCOTT	SJ	7	346	SCOTT	WR	13	378	SCUDDER	W	3	212
SCOTT	J	2	301	SCOTT	SM	3	211	SCOTT	WRM	2	301	SCUDDIN	G	4	336
SCOTT	J	8	302	SCOTT	ST	3	211	SCOTT	WT	5	309	SCULLEY	J	9	336
SCOTT	J	8	302	SCOTT	T	11	424	SCOUSE	A	12	381	SCULLION	P	14	283
SCOTT	J	8	302	SCOTT	TA	4	336	SCOUSE	SA	12	381	SCULLY	E	3	212
SCOTT	J	8	302	SCOTT	TA	12	381	SCOVELL	J	12	197	SCULLY	F	9	336
SCOTT	J	9	169	SCOTT	TC	13	377	SCOVELL	LD	1	307	SCULLY	G	9	169
SCOTT	J	9	336	SCOTT	TJ	1	306	SCOVELL	W	7	345	SCULLY	HS	9	169
SCOTT	J	9	336	SCOTT	TS	2	301	SCOWCROFT	F	14	282	SCULLY	J	11	334
SCOTT	J	9	336	SCOTT	TS	3	211	SCOWEN	AE	2	301	SCULLY	JG	9	169
SCOTT	J	11	334	SCOTT	W	1	306	SCOWEN	GH	10	203	SCULLY	M	3	212
SCOTT	J	11	334	SCOTT	W	2	301	SCOWEN	JES	10	203	SCULLY	M	11	334
SCOTT	J	14	282	SCOTT	W	2	301	SCRAFTON	T	11	334	SCULLY	T	9	170
SCOTT	J	14	282	SCOTT	W	2	301	SCRAGG	E	12	197	SCURR	JW	14	283
SCOTT	JA	8	302	SCOTT	W	3	211	SCRANNAGE	T	3	212	SCURRAH	A	9	336
SCOTT	JE	3	211	SCOTT	W	3	211	SCRATCHLEY	EC	1	307	SCURRAH	W	9	336
SCOTT	JE	9	336	SCOTT	W	3	211	SCREECH	FJD	10	362	SCUTCHINGS	AH	3	212
SCOTT	JE	12	380	SCOTT	W	4	336	SCREEN	W	12	381	SCUTT	EJ	7	347
SCOTT	JG	3	211	SCOTT	W	7	346	SCREETON	JF	11	334	SCUTT	FG	10	362
SCOTT	JG	12	197	SCOTT	W	8	302	SCREETON	R	14	282	SCUTT	FW	10	362
SCOTT	JH	3	211	SCOTT	W	8	302	SCRIBENS	PG	2	301	SCUTT	P	13	378
SCOTT	JH	6	361	SCOTT	W	8	302	SCRIMINGER	A	8	302	SCUTTLE	BC	12	198
SCOTT	JO	7	346	SCOTT	W	9	169	SCRIMSHAW	F	10	203	SEABORN	A	5	310
SCOTT	JP	1	306	SCOTT	W	9	169	SCRIMSHAW	W	10	203	SEABORN	AG	13	378
SCOTT	JS	14	282	SCOTT	W	9	169	SCRIPPS	A	2	302	SEABORN	RF	3	212
SCOTT	JT	7	346	SCOTT	W	11	334	SCRIPPS	F	1	307	SEABOURNE	J	8	303
SCOTT	L	6	361	SCOTT	W	11	334	SCRIVEN	F	1	307	SEABOURNE	S	8	303
SCOTT	L	7	346	SCOTT	W	12	197	SCRIVEN	R	3	212	SEABRIDGE	A	14	283
SCOTT	L	9	169	SCOTT	W	12	197	SCRIVEN	W	10	204	SEABROOK	A	5	309
SCOTT	L	9	336	SCOTT	W	12	381	SCRIVEN	WG	4	336	SEABROOK	BH	5	309
SCOTT	LJ	9	336	SCOTT	W	13	377	SCRIVENER	AE	5	309	SEABROOK	CA	3	212
SCOTT	LK	2	301	SCOTT	W	13	377	SCRIVENER	AW	5	309	SEABROOK	CR	5	309
SCOTT	LW	12	380	SCOTT	W	14	282	SCRIVENER	C	7	346	SEABROOK	CW	5	309
SCOTT	LW	14	282	SCOTT	WA	7	346	SCRIVENER	FK	3	212	SEABROOK	EG	3	212
SCOTT	M	1	306	SCOTT	WE	1	306	SCRIVENER	JS	1	307	SEABROOK	ET	3	212
SCOTT	M	7	346	SCOTT	WE	3	211	SCRIVENER	JW	14	282	SEABROOK	F	5	309
SCOTT	O	8	302	SCOTT	WE	3	211	SCRIVENER	S	5	309	SEABROOK	FG	13	378
				SCOTT	WE	7	346	SCRIVENER	W	12	198	SEABROOK	FJ	5	309

SEABROOK	GW	5	309	SEALES	HA	1	307	SEARLE	DW	13	378	SEARSON	E	1	308
SEABROOK	H	3	212	SEALES	SF	1	307	SEARLE	E	3	213	SEARSON	J	11	335
SEABROOK	HG	3	212	SEALEY	A	5	310	SEARLE	GJ	10	362	SEARSON	K	1	308
SEABROOK	JC	1	307	SEALEY	AT	6	361	SEARLE	H	7	347	SEARSON	R	11	335
SEABROOK	NW	5	310	SEALEY	B	3	212	SEARLE	H	12	198	SEATH	FW	13	379
SEABROOK	R	5	310	SEALEY	C	5	310	SEARLE	H	13	378	SEATHARD	G	1	308
SEABROOK	RJ	5	310	SEALEY	FE	5	310	SEARLE	J	7	347	SEATON	E	11	335
SEABROOK	SH	5	310	SEALEY	G	4	336	SEARLE	J	12	198	SEATON	EE	5	312
SEABROOK	W	1	307	SEALEY	H	5	310	SEARLE	J	12	198	SEATON	FJ	5	312
SEABROOK	W	2	302	SEALEY	WG	1	307	SEARLE	J	13	378	SEATON	JW	7	347
SEABROOK	W	5	310	SEALY	AO	3	213	SEARLE	JF	7	347	SEATON	LA	7	347
SEABROOK	W	5	310	SEALY	SH	3	213	SEARLE	JH	3	213	SEATON	WG	5	312
SEABROOK	W	5	310	SEAMAN	FG	2	302	SEARLE	JH	5	311	SEATON	WH	7	347
SEABROOK	WG	5	310	SEAMAN	HR	13	378	SEARLE	JHA	1	307	SEATON	WH	7	347
SEABROOK	WJ	3	212	SEAMAN	WW	3	213	SEARLE	JJ	7	347	SEAVERS	AM	9	170
SEABROOK	WJ	5	310	SEAMARK	GF	12	198	SEARLE	P	8	303	SEAVERS	J	9	170
SEABY	G	12	381	SEAMARK	J	12	198	SEARLE	R	11	335	SEAVERS	WH	9	170
SEABY	R	2	302	SEAMARK	WJ	12	198	SEARLE	RA	1	307	SEAVIOUR	GWJ	4	336
SEADON	FH	6	361	SEAMARK	WR	12	198	SEARLE	SA	10	362	SEAWARD	BD	1	308
SEAFORD	JJW	10	362	SEAMORE	A	6	361	SEARLE	SJ	5	311	SEBBAGE	EW	1	308
SEAGE	W	2	302	SEAMORE	CJ	6	361	SEARLE	SJE	5	311	SEBERECHTS	R	3	213
SEAGER	AC	6	361	SEAMORE	GP	6	361	SEARLE	TG	5	311	SECKER	AW	7	347
SEAGER	AG	2	302	SEANOR	R	10	204	SEARLE	W	12	198	SECKER	CE	7	347
SEAGER	EL	2	302	SEANOR	W	9	170	SEARLE	WA	5	312	SECKER	G	13	379
SEAGER	FA	4	336	SEAR	A	5	310	SEARLE	WA	13	379	SECKER	R	1	308
SEAGER	G	3	212	SEAR	A	5	310	SEARLE	WH	5	311	SECRETAN	AJ	3	213
SEAGER	GF	13	378	SEAR	AG	12	198	SEARLE	WR	3	213	SEDDEN	WT	13	379
SEAGER	JR	13	378	SEAR	AJ	5	311	SEARLES	A	14	283	SEDDON	A	8	303
SEAGER	TH	4	336	SEAR	AV	5	311	SEARLES	AF	14	283	SEDDON	E	14	283
SEAGLE	WE	13	378	SEAR	C	5	311	SEARLES	S	1	307	SEDDON	F	14	283
SEAGRAVE	JR	4	336	SEAR	F	5	311	SEARLES	WH	14	283	SEDDON	H	9	337
SEAGROATT	E	6	361	SEAR	FC	12	198	SEARLEY	AH	10	362	SEDDON	H	14	283
SEAGROVE	J	13	378	SEAR	G	5	311	SEARLEY	C	10	204	SEDDON	HS	14	283
SEAL	A	6	361	SEAR	H	5	311	SEARLEY	SR	10	362	SEDDON	JH	11	335
SEAL	AG	10	204	SEAR	H	5	311	SEARLEY	WR	10	204	SEDDON	S	14	283
SEAL	GE	13	378	SEAR	H	12	198	SEARS	A	2	302	SEDDON	T	14	283
SEAL	H	6	361	SEAR	H	12	198	SEARS	A	13	379	SEDDON	T	14	283
SEAL	H	10	204	SEAR	H	12	198	SEARS	C	2	302	SEDDON	W	14	283
SEAL	J	11	334	SEAR	HW	5	311	SEARS	C	7	347	SEDDON	W	14	283
SEAL	J	13	378	SEAR	R	3	213	SEARS	E	4	336	SEDDON	WT	11	335
SEAL	J	14	283	SEAR	T	5	311	SEARS	E	7	347	SEDER	H	14	284
SEAL	PA	3	212	SEAR	T	12	198	SEARS	EW	2	302	SEDGE	AE	13	379
SEAL	RJ	14	283	SEAR	W	3	213	SEARS	F	5	312	SEDGELEY	JB	4	336
SEAL	T	12	381	SEAR	W	5	311	SEARS	GW	6	361	SEDGLEY	EF	7	347
SEAL	WG	4	336	SEAR	WJ	5	311	SEARS	H	13	379	SEDGWICK	A	8	303
SEAL	WJ	13	378	SEARCH	AS	7	347	SEARS	HG	3	213	SEDGWICK	A	12	198
SEAL	WT	11	335	SEARCH	HG	7	347	SEARS	J	2	302	SEDGWICK	AE	12	198
SEALBY	JN	4	336	SEARCH	HJ	7	347	SEARS	P	6	362	SEDGWICK	C	8	303
SEALE	AE	14	283	SEARCY	C	12	381	SEARS	RL	1	307	SEDGWICK	CW	8	303
SEALE	E	4	336	SEARLE	A	2	302	SEARS	RW	3	213	SEDGWICK	E	11	335
SEALE	E	5	310	SEARLE	A	5	311	SEARS	W	1	307	SEDGWICK	F	8	303
SEALE	E	14	283	SEARLE	AG	3	213	SEARS	W	2	302	SEDGWICK	G	9	337
SEALE	TH	5	310	SEARLE	AG	3	213	SEARS	W	5	312	SEDGWICK	H	8	303
SEALES	BT	1	307	SEARLE	AJ	7	347	SEARSON	AEJ	2	302	SEDGWICK	HE	12	198
SEALES	E	13	378	SEARLE	CE	10	362	SEARSON	AJ	1	307	SEDGWICK	J	8	303

SEDGWICK	J	10	204	SELL	A	13	379	SELVEY	WG	6	362	SENNEWALD	RV	3	385
SEDGWICK	JHP	10	204	SELL	AC	5	312	SELWAY	AE	13	379	SEPHTON	H	14	284
SEDGWICK	R	8	303	SELL	AE	3	214	SELWAY	F	1	308	SEPHTON	R	14	284
SEDGWICK	TW	8	303	SELL	C	13	379	SELWAY	HC	10	363	SEPHTON	TG	14	284
SEDGWICK	W	9	337	SELL	CB	5	312	SELWOOD	A	7	348	SERGEANT	F	13	380
SEDGWICK	W	9	337	SELL	HC	5	312	SELWOOD	J	1	308	SERGEANT	G	14	284
SEE	WJ	12	198	SELL	LB	5	312	SELWOOD	SL	3	214	SERGEANT	W	4	337
SEE	WN	2	302	SELL	RD	5	312	SEMMENS	W	11	335	SERIES	WJ	3	214
SEEAR	A	5	312	SELL	WG	2	303	SEMP	H	14	284	SERLE	CW	3	214
SEEAR	EJ	13	379	SELL	WJ	3	214	SEMPERS	FG	10	204	SERLE	JL	8	304
SEEAR	G	5	312	SELL	WJ	5	312	SEMPLE	TP	4	337	SERMON	G	11	335
SEEARS	GF	13	379	SELLAR	H	2	303	SENFT	C	7	348	SERMON	S	11	336
SEED	AG	1	308	SELLAR	WH	10	204	SENFT	FW	7	348	SERVAN	A	11	336
SEED	CG	9	337	SELLARS	A	11	335	SENFT	P	3	385	SERVANT	A	7	348
SEED	D	14	284	SELLARS	G	11	335	SENFT	W	3	214	SERVANT	HF	7	348
SEED	H	9	170	SELLARS	WJ	11	335	SENHENN	EA	1	308	SERVAT	RH	1	309
SEEDMAN	F	9	337	SELLECK	AE	13	379	SENIOR	B	4	337	SERVICE	EE	4	337
SEEGER	AJ	3	213	SELLER	GC	2	303	SENIOR	C	8	303	SERVICE	PG	14	284
SEEGER	FH	3	213	SELLERS	AC	13	379	SENIOR	C	8	303	SESSIONS	GR	10	204
SEEKINGS	RJ	10	362	SELLERS	F	9	337	SENIOR	CB	11	335	SETCHELL	H	5	313
SEELEY	AW	7	347	SELLERS	J	12	199	SENIOR	E	8	303	SETCHELL	S	5	313
SEELEY	EA	6	362	SELLERS	R	9	337	SENIOR	E	9	337	SETCHFIELD	T	1	309
SEELEY	HE	10	204	SELLERS	W	9	337	SENIOR	E	14	284	SETON	JT	13	380
SEELEY	J	6	362	SELLEX	EJ	10	363	SENIOR	EA	8	303	SETTERINGTON	R	8	304
SEELEY	S	6	362	SELLEX	FAL	10	363	SENIOR	EG	4	337	SETTERS	A	7	348
SEELEY	WJ	6	362	SELLEX	J	10	363	SENIOR	F	9	170	SETTERS	F	1	309
SEELY	W	7	348	SELLEY	ACT	3	214	SENIOR	FJ	5	313	SETTERS	M	1	309
SEENEY	E	6	362	SELLEY	AH	13	379	SENIOR	FWJ	4	337	SETTLE	E	9	170
SEENEY	H	10	363	SELLEY	EW	13	379	SENIOR	G	5	313	SETTLE	T	8	304
SEERS	E	14	284	SELLEY	WH	5	312	SENIOR	GH	8	303	SETTLE	W	9	170
SEEX	SE	1	308	SELLICK	AB	2	303	SENIOR	H	5	313	SETTREE	HW	3	214
SEGAL	E	8	303	SELLICK	J	10	363	SENIOR	H	8	303	SETTREE	JR	3	214
SEIDLER	HA	7	348	SELLICK	TH	3	214	SENIOR	H	9	170	SEVENOAKS	HE	13	380
SEIGENBERG	L	14	284	SELLICK	W	2	303	SENIOR	J	8	303	SEVERN	DC	13	380
SEIRY	E	10	204	SELLICK	WH	1	308	SENIOR	J	11	335	SEVERN	F	5	313
SELBY	AH	2	302	SELLINGS	LJ	3	214	SENIOR	JJ	8	304	SEVERS	JH	5	313
SELBY	C	9	170	SELLIS	WG	1	308	SENIOR	JK	14	284	SEVIER	AC	13	380
SELBY	C	9	170	SELLS	AJ	5	312	SENIOR	JR	5	313	SEVILLE	GE	12	381
SELBY	CW	9	170	SELLS	AW	5	312	SENIOR	R	11	335	SEVILLE	JW	11	336
SELBY	F	7	348	SELLS	H	5	313	SENIOR	RM	14	284	SEVYOUR	F	4	337
SELBY	GD	11	335	SELLS	HWG	5	312	SENIOR	SG	1	308	SEVYOUR	HE	4	337
SELBY	J	2	302	SELLS	JJT	7	348	SENIOR	T	4	337	SEWARD	A	1	309
SELBY	J	6	362	SELLS	P	5	313	SENIOR	W	5	313	SEWARD	A	8	304
SELBY	M	4	336	SELLS	WG	5	313	SENIOR	W	5	313	SEWARD	AE	3	214
SELBY	PP	2	302	SELLWOOD	A	1	308	SENIOR	W	8	304	SEWARD	AJ	1	309
SELBY	RG	6	362	SELLWOOD	AD	2	303	SENIOR	W	8	304	SEWARD	CE	1	309
SELBY	WB	13	379	SELLWOOD	HE	10	204	SENIOR	W	9	170	SEWARDS	HG	1	309
SELF	AT	3	213	SELLWOOD	WC	7	348	SENIOR	W	11	335	SEWELL	A	11	336
SELF	C	7	348	SELMAN	AEJ	1	308	SENIOR	WA	14	284	SEWELL	A	12	199
SELF	EJ	7	348	SELMAN	SJ	1	308	SENNER	GE	13	379	SEWELL	AG	12	199
SELF	G	4	337	SELMES	AJ	1	308	SENNETT	AE	4	337	SEWELL	AT	5	313
SELF	P	3	213	SELMES	HR	1	308	SENNETT	G	13	379	SEWELL	C	1	309
SELFE	AE	1	308	SELSTON	GF	10	204	SENNETT	J	13	380	SEWELL	C	5	313
SELFE	R	3	213	SELVES	JC	13	379	SENNETT	R	13	380	SEWELL	FG	3	214
SELFE	WR	3	213	SELVEY	R	6	362	SENNEWALD	GJ	3	385	SEWELL	GA	7	348

SEWELL	H	3	214	SEYMOUR	T	5	314	SHAILER	WA	1	309	SHANNON	J	10	205
SEWELL	HG	2	303	SEYMOUR	T	14	284	SHAILER	WD	2	303	SHANNON	RJ	1	310
SEWELL	JE	2	303	SEYMOUR	TS	13	380	SHAKESHAFT	N	14	284	SHANNON	SO	6	363
SEWELL	JH	5	313	SEYMOUR	W	6	362	SHAKESPEARE	G	6	362	SHANNON	WJ	13	380
SEWELL	JH	9	170	SEYMOUR	W	12	199	SHAKESPEARE	GC	6	362	SHANTON	EC	10	363
SEWELL	JH	13	380	SHACKEL	GT	7	348	SHAKESPEARE	J	6	362	SHAPCOTT	F	9	337
SEWELL	L	3	214	SHACKELL	JS	2	303	SHAKESPEARE	LN	6	362	SHAPCOTT	WA	3	215
SEWELL	R	1	309	SHACKELL	LF	3	215	SHAKESPEARE	S	6	362	SHAPER	A	9	337
SEWELL	R	13	380	SHACKELL	RR	3	215	SHAKESPEARE	T	14	284	SHAPIRO	L	14	285
SEWELL	RH	3	214	SHACKLEFORD	AH	2	303	SHAKESPEARE	W	6	362	SHAPIRO	M	14	285
SEWELL	SG	7	348	SHACKLEFORD	AV	2	303	SHAKESPEARE	WE	2	303	SHAPLAND	R	3	215
SEWELL	T	6	362	SHACKLEFORD	GA	2	303	SHALE	J	6	363	SHAPLEY	C	7	349
SEWELL	TH	1	309	SHACKLEFORD	H	12	199	SHALE	JA	6	363	SHAPLEY	J	7	349
SEWELL	TH	13	380	SHACKLEFORD	HJ	2	303	SHALER	J	6	363	SHAPLEY	J	7	349
SEWELL	WG	5	313	SHACKLETON	A	8	304	SHALLAKER	AH	14	284	SHARD	A	9	170
SEWELL	WH	3	214	SHACKLETON	A	9	337	SHALLAKER	RGT	14	285	SHARD	C	9	170
SEWELL	WSH	7	348	SHACKLETON	A	14	284	SHALLARD	B	12	381	SHARD	E	9	170
SEX	A	14	284	SHACKLETON	CH	12	199	SHALLARD	JE	12	381	SHARD	E	9	338
SEXTON	AE	3	214	SHACKLETON	D	9	337	SHALLCROSS	T	14	285	SHARD	H	9	171
SEXTON	AJ	7	348	SHACKLETON	E	3	215	SHALLIKER	R	11	336	SHARDLOW	FV	10	205
SEXTON	AR	3	214	SHACKLETON	GW	8	304	SHALLIKER	S	11	336	SHARDLOW	GM	10	205
SEXTON	BJ	3	385	SHACKLETON	HLN	8	304	SHALLIS	FE	1	310	SHARE	W	6	363
SEXTON	C	12	199	SHACKLETON	JE	9	337	SHALLIS	GE	1	310	SHARGOOL	JH	7	349
SEXTON	CH	10	363	SHACKLETON	JW	8	304	SHALLIS	J	3	215	SHARKEY	C	9	171
SEXTON	CL	10	204	SHACKLETON	JW	9	170	SHALLOW	W	11	336	SHARKEY	M	6	363
SEXTON	FG	5	314	SHACKLETON	L	8	304	SHAMBLER	H	7	349	SHARKEY	T	1	310
SEXTON	GA	10	204	SHACKLETON	R	8	304	SHAMBROOK	CD	5	314	SHARKEY	T	9	171
SEXTON	GW	1	309	SHACKLETON	U	9	170	SHAMBROOK	JA	1	310	SHARKEY	W	9	171
SEXTON	H	8	304	SHACKLETON	U	9	337	SHAMBROOK	JH	4	337	SHARKEY	W	9	338
SEXTON	TK	12	199	SHACKLEY	H	8	304	SHANAHAN	F	10	205	SHARKEY	W	11	336
SEXTON	W	13	380	SHADBOLT	E	5	314	SHANAHAN	J	14	285	SHARKY	J	11	336
SEYMORE	W	3	214	SHADBOLT	G	5	314	SHAND	HF	3	215	SHARLAND	E	2	303
SEYMOUR	A	10	204	SHADBOLT	H	5	314	SHAND	HW	13	380	SHARLAND	W	2	304
SEYMOUR	AG	10	363	SHADBOLT	HE	7	349	SHANE	CH	5	314	SHARLEY	W	4	337
SEYMOUR	B	3	215	SHADBOLT	HS	5	314	SHANE	CH	5	314	SHARMAN	A	12	199
SEYMOUR	CW	3	215	SHADBOLT	HT	5	314	SHANE	H	5	314	SHARMAN	A	12	381
SEYMOUR	E	4	337	SHADBOLT	HW	5	314	SHANE	W	5	314	SHARMAN	CP	3	216
SEYMOUR	E	13	380	SHADBOLT	PC	5	314	SHANKS	AA	10	205	SHARMAN	F	9	171
SEYMOUR	F	1	309	SHADBOLT	PJ	3	215	SHANKS	J	10	205	SHARMAN	G	5	314
SEYMOUR	F	9	337	SHADBOLT	T	5	314	SHANKS	J	10	205	SHARMAN	GH	12	381
SEYMOUR	G	1	309	SHADDICK	CR	3	215	SHANKS	JW	14	285	SHARMAN	GJ	12	199
SEYMOUR	G	9	337	SHADDICK	WT	3	215	SHANKS	RE	10	205	SHARMAN	GW	11	336
SEYMOUR	G	10	204	SHADE	GR	13	380	SHANKS	WH	10	205	SHARMAN	H	8	304
SEYMOUR	GE	10	205	SHADE	KM	13	380	SHANKS	WJ	7	349	SHARMAN	H	12	199
SEYMOUR	GR	13	380	SHADGETT	E	4	337	SHANKSTER	C	3	215	SHARMAN	H	12	199
SEYMOUR	H	1	309	SHADICK	H	4	337	SHANLEY	P	14	285	SHARMAN	HJ	12	381
SEYMOUR	H	12	199	SHADRAKE	LH	12	199	SHANLY	CF	2	303	SHARMAN	HJ	12	381
SEYMOUR	HJ	3	215	SHADRAKE	RE	12	199	SHANN	C	8	304	SHARMAN	J	5	314
SEYMOUR	J	12	199	SHAFE	E	1	309	SHANN	E	8	304	SHARMAN	JL	3	216
SEYMOUR	J	12	199	SHAFE	WE	3	215	SHANN	W	11	336	SHARMAN	P	12	381
SEYMOUR	JA	13	380	SHAFE	WG	3	215	SHANNAHAN	FH	10	205	SHARMAN	R	5	315
SEYMOUR	JSP	10	205	SHAILE	F	11	336	SHANNAN	CJ	3	215	SHARMAN	S	5	315
SEYMOUR	PJ	5	314	SHAILER	AJ	3	215	SHANNON	HJC	4	337	SHARMAN	SG	7	349
SEYMOUR	RTB	7	348	SHAILER	B	3	215	SHANNON	J	3	215	SHARMAN	TH	12	199
SEYMOUR	SH	1	309	SHAILER	GJ	2	303	SHANNON	J	10	205	SHARMAN	W	1	310

Name	In.			Name	In.			Name	In.			Name	In.			Name	In.		
SHARMAN	W	5	315	SHARP	H	9	171	SHARPE	B	5	316	SHARPLES	G	11	337	SHARPLES	G	11	337
SHARMAN	W	5	315	SHARP	H	9	338	SHARPE	B	8	305	SHARPLES	J	11	337				
SHARMAN	W	5	315	SHARP	H	9	338	SHARPE	C	5	316	SHARPLES	P	11	337				
SHARMAN	W	6	363	SHARP	HE	5	315	SHARPE	C	8	305	SHARPLES	R	14	285				
SHARMAN	W	12	200	SHARP	HGA	1	310	SHARPE	CMW	6	363	SHARPLES	W	8	305				
SHARMAN	WG	12	381	SHARP	HS	5	315	SHARPE	E	8	305	SHARPLES	W	11	337				
SHARMAN	WH	10	363	SHARP	J	4	337	SHARPE	EW	12	382	SHARPLES	W	11	337				
SHARMAN	WH	12	381	SHARP	J	5	315	SHARPE	F	7	349	SHARRARD	HH	6	363				
SHARP	A	1	310	SHARP	J	8	304	SHARPE	FW	12	200	SHARRATT	A	5	316				
SHARP	A	2	304	SHARP	J	9	171	SHARPE	G	4	338	SHARRATT	FD	5	316				
SHARP	A	9	338	SHARP	J	12	200	SHARPE	G	5	316	SHARRATT	FJ	6	363				
SHARP	A	10	205	SHARP	J	12	200	SHARPE	G	8	305	SHARRATT	G	6	363				
SHARP	A	12	200	SHARP	J	12	200	SHARPE	G	12	200	SHARRATT	PA	6	363				
SHARP	A	13	380	SHARP	JA	3	216	SHARPE	GE	5	316	SHARRATT	RE	2	304				
SHARP	AA	7	349	SHARP	JA	8	305	SHARPE	GH	5	316	SHARRATT	SA	5	316				
SHARP	AB	5	315	SHARP	JH	6	363	SHARPE	GT	5	316	SHARRATT	TH	6	363				
SHARP	AH	7	349	SHARP	JH	9	338	SHARPE	GW	7	349	SHARRATT	W	2	304				
SHARP	AP	1	310	SHARP	JJ	8	305	SHARPE	H	3	216	SHARRATT	WH	2	304				
SHARP	B	5	315	SHARP	JP	2	304	SHARPE	H	7	349	SHATLIFF	T	14	285				
SHARP	B	9	171	SHARP	JW	9	171	SHARPE	H	13	381	SHATTOCK	MH	14	285				
SHARP	C	2	304	SHARP	L	8	305	SHARPE	HV	9	171	SHAVE	CA	4	338				
SHARP	C	12	200	SHARP	L	8	305	SHARPE	HW	1	310	SHAVE	CH	4	338				
SHARP	CF	3	216	SHARP	LA	1	310	SHARPE	J	5	316	SHAVE	HH	10	205				
SHARP	CH	3	216	SHARP	NA	9	171	SHARPE	J	14	285	SHAVE	HW	4	338				
SHARP	CH	5	315	SHARP	P	4	337	SHARPE	J	14	285	SHAVE	JJD	10	205				
SHARP	E	2	304	SHARP	PE	5	315	SHARPE	JEH	3	216	SHAVE	L	3	385				
SHARP	E	3	216	SHARP	R	1	310	SHARPE	JJ	12	200	SHAVE	VS	4	338				
SHARP	E	5	315	SHARP	RH	3	216	SHARPE	R	12	200	SHAVE	W	4	338				
SHARP	E	9	338	SHARP	RW	10	205	SHARPE	R	12	200	SHAW	A	3	216				
SHARP	EJ	12	381	SHARP	SH	13	381	SHARPE	RH	7	350	SHAW	A	6	363				
SHARP	EV	13	381	SHARP	ST	1	310	SHARPE	S	13	381	SHAW	A	6	363				
SHARP	F	3	216	SHARP	T	4	338	SHARPE	SH	1	310	SHAW	A	7	350				
SHARP	F	5	315	SHARP	T	8	305	SHARPE	T	7	350	SHAW	A	9	171				
SHARP	F	6	363	SHARP	T	8	305	SHARPE	TA	7	350	SHAW	A	9	171				
SHARP	F	12	200	SHARP	T	12	200	SHARPE	W	5	316	SHAW	A	9	338				
SHARP	FE	7	349	SHARP	W	5	315	SHARPE	W	5	316	SHAW	A	11	337				
SHARP	FH	3	216	SHARP	W	7	349	SHARPE	W	7	350	SHAW	A	11	337				
SHARP	FJ	12	381	SHARP	W	9	338	SHARPE	W	8	305	SHAW	A	11	337				
SHARP	FJW	13	381	SHARP	W	9	338	SHARPE	W	8	305	SHAW	A	12	382				
SHARP	FT	5	315	SHARP	W	11	336	SHARPE	W	8	305	SHAW	A	13	381				
SHARP	FW	3	216	SHARP	W	11	336	SHARPE	W	12	200	SHAW	A	13	381				
SHARP	G	7	349	SHARP	WA	5	315	SHARPE	W	12	200	SHAW	A	14	285				
SHARP	G	8	304	SHARP	WA	12	200	SHARPE	WD	1	310	SHAW	A	14	285				
SHARP	G	12	382	SHARP	WG	4	338	SHARPE	WD	9	171	SHAW	AA	12	382				
SHARP	GH	2	304	SHARP	WG	5	315	SHARPE	WH	13	381	SHAW	AC	13	381				
SHARP	GR	11	336	SHARP	WG	13	381	SHARPE	WJ	8	305	SHAW	AE	1	311				
SHARP	H	1	310	SHARP	WH	12	382	SHARPE	WM	8	305	SHAW	AE	5	316				
SHARP	H	1	310	SHARP	WJ	4	338	SHARPE	WW	1	310	SHAW	AE	12	382				
SHARP	H	4	337	SHARP	WS	12	200	SHARPES	S	11	336	SHAW	AE	14	285				
SHARP	H	4	337	SHARP	WT	1	310	SHARPIN	HR	1	311	SHAW	AG	6	363				
SHARP	H	5	315	SHARP	WT	5	316	SHARPLES	AW	11	336	SHAW	B	12	382				
SHARP	H	8	304	SHARP	WT	5	316	SHARPLES	E	14	285	SHAW	BB	8	305				
SHARP	H	9	171	SHARP	WW	7	349	SHARPLES	EY	11	336	SHAW	C	5	316				
SHARP	H	9	171	SHARPE	A	8	305	SHARPLES	F	11	336	SHAW	C	9	338				
SHARP	H	9	171	SHARPE	AW	10	205	SHARPLES	FL	13	381	SHAW	C	11	337				

SHAW	CA	6	363
SHAW	CD	1	311
SHAW	CE	3	216
SHAW	CES	5	316
SHAW	CJ	1	311
SHAW	CM	13	381
SHAW	CW	1	311
SHAW	E	2	304
SHAW	E	6	364
SHAW	E	7	350
SHAW	E	8	305
SHAW	E	11	337
SHAW	EA	13	381
SHAW	EA	13	381
SHAW	EC	3	216
SHAW	ED	10	363
SHAW	EG	3	216
SHAW	ES	5	316
SHAW	EW	3	216
SHAW	F	3	216
SHAW	F	6	364
SHAW	F	6	364
SHAW	F	8	305
SHAW	F	8	305
SHAW	F	8	305
SHAW	F	8	306
SHAW	F	9	171
SHAW	F	9	338
SHAW	F	9	338
SHAW	F	11	337
SHAW	F	11	337
SHAW	FC	1	311
SHAW	FJ	6	364
SHAW	FK	12	382
SHAW	FS	12	382
SHAW	FT	6	364
SHAW	G	1	311
SHAW	G	3	216
SHAW	G	14	285
SHAW	GA	8	306
SHAW	GE	10	206
SHAW	GH	3	216
SHAW	GH	8	306
SHAW	GL	2	304
SHAW	GW	10	206
SHAW	GWS	10	206
SHAW	H	6	364
SHAW	H	6	364
SHAW	H	8	306
SHAW	H	8	306
SHAW	H	8	306
SHAW	H	8	306
SHAW	H	9	172
SHAW	H	9	172
SHAW	H	9	172
SHAW	H	9	172
SHAW	H	9	338
SHAW	H	9	338
SHAW	H	11	337
SHAW	H	11	337
SHAW	H	11	337
SHAW	H	11	337
SHAW	H	13	381
SHAW	H	14	285
SHAW	H	14	286
SHAW	HC	10	206
SHAW	HJ	1	311
SHAW	HJ	3	216
SHAW	I	10	363
SHAW	I	11	337
SHAW	J	1	311
SHAW	J	3	217
SHAW	J	3	217
SHAW	J	4	338
SHAW	J	4	338
SHAW	J	5	316
SHAW	J	6	364
SHAW	J	6	364
SHAW	J	8	306
SHAW	J	8	306
SHAW	J	9	338
SHAW	J	10	206
SHAW	J	11	337
SHAW	J	11	337
SHAW	J	11	338
SHAW	J	11	338
SHAW	J	12	200
SHAW	J	13	381
SHAW	J	14	286
SHAW	J	14	286
SHAW	J	14	286
SHAW	J	14	286
SHAW	J	14	286
SHAW	J	14	286
SHAW	J	14	286
SHAW	JA	8	306
SHAW	JE	3	217
SHAW	JJ	1	311
SHAW	JJ	11	338
SHAW	JO	11	338
SHAW	JR	5	317
SHAW	JV	10	363
SHAW	JW	2	304
SHAW	JW	8	306
SHAW	JW	11	338
SHAW	KH	3	217
SHAW	L	5	317
SHAW	L	11	338
SHAW	L	13	381
SHAW	LE	6	364
SHAW	MA	12	382
SHAW	P	9	172
SHAW	P	9	338
SHAW	PF	3	217
SHAW	R	3	217
SHAW	R	11	338
SHAW	R	12	200
SHAW	R	13	381
SHAW	R	14	286
SHAW	RD	3	217
SHAW	RL	12	382
SHAW	RS	13	381
SHAW	S	6	364
SHAW	S	9	172
SHAW	S	9	172
SHAW	SE	7	350
SHAW	SF	10	206
SHAW	SJ	13	382
SHAW	SVJ	3	217
SHAW	SW	3	217
SHAW	SW	5	317
SHAW	T	1	311
SHAW	T	3	217
SHAW	T	11	338
SHAW	T	14	286
SHAW	T	14	286
SHAW	T	14	286
SHAW	TF	5	317
SHAW	TH	8	306
SHAW	TR	13	382
SHAW	V	14	286
SHAW	W	1	311
SHAW	W	3	217
SHAW	W	6	364
SHAW	W	6	364
SHAW	W	6	364
SHAW	W	6	364
SHAW	W	7	350
SHAW	W	8	306
SHAW	W	8	306
SHAW	W	8	306
SHAW	W	9	172
SHAW	W	11	338
SHAW	W	11	338
SHAW	W	11	338
SHAW	W	11	338
SHAW	W	13	382
SHAW	W	14	286
SHAW	W	14	286
SHAW	W	14	286
SHAW	WD	1	311
SHAW	WD	3	217
SHAW	WE	12	382
SHAW	WF	3	217
SHAW	WH	8	306
SHAW	WH	9	338
SHAW	WH	13	382
SHAW	WW	14	286
SHAWCROSS	T	11	338
SHAWCROSS	W	14	286
SHAWYER	CG	5	317
SHAWYER	E	10	363
SHAWYER	EJ	10	363
SHAWYER	HG	10	206
SHAWYER	LA	10	206
SHAWYER	T	4	338
SHAY	M	11	338
SHAYLER	HJS	13	382
SHEA	A	3	217
SHEA	EC	4	338
SHEA	J	10	206
SHEA	WD	10	206
SHEAD	J	1	311
SHEAHAN	F	2	304
SHEAHAN	JW	1	311
SHEALS	G	3	217
SHEAN	A	7	350
SHEAN	G	7	350
SHEAN	GW	12	200
SHEARD	E	8	306
SHEARD	G	8	306
SHEARD	H	8	306
SHEARD	J	8	307
SHEARD	JD	8	307
SHEARD	L	8	307
SHEARE	H	9	339
SHEARER	G	9	172
SHEARER	G	14	287
SHEARER	H	9	172
SHEARER	H	9	172
SHEARER	H	9	172
SHEARER	J	9	172
SHEARER	S	9	172
SHEARER	W	8	307
SHEARER	W	14	287
SHEARGOLD	RH	3	217
SHEARING	EW	3	217
SHEARING	F	4	338
SHEARING	GH	3	217
SHEARING	H	4	338
SHEARING	HE	3	217
SHEARING	HJ	1	311
SHEARING	HSR	4	338
SHEARING	JS	3	217
SHEARING	L	1	311
SHEARING	W	1	311
SHEARING	W	4	338
SHEARING	WG	4	338
SHEARMAN	H	9	339
SHEARMAN	WH	4	338

SHEARMUR	FG	7	350	SHEEHAN	J	3	218	SHELDRAKE	AE	5	317	SHELTON	S	12	201
SHEARN	C	4	338	SHEEHAN	J	7	350	SHELDRAKE	AW	10	363	SHELTON	W	9	392
SHEARON	J	6	364	SHEEHAN	J	8	307	SHELDRAKE	GW	5	317	SHENNAN	A	11	339
SHEARON	JE	8	307	SHEEHAN	J	14	287	SHELDRAKE	HG	7	351	SHENNAN	D	11	339
SHEARS	B	2	304	SHEEHAN	LH	3	218	SHELDRAKE	VT	7	351	SHENTON	F	1	312
SHEARS	F	4	338	SHEEHAN	M	3	218	SHELDRICK	HG	7	351	SHENTON	G	6	365
SHEARS	G	7	350	SHEEHAN	P	3	218	SHELDRICK	WC	13	382	SHENTON	G	14	287
SHEARS	GF	1	311	SHEEHAN	R	3	218	SHELFORD	HJ	3	218	SHENTON	HL	11	339
SHEARS	J	4	338	SHEEHAN	S	3	218	SHELFORD	W	2	305	SHENTON	W	14	287
SHEARS	JH	4	339	SHEEHAN	T	2	304	SHELL	FM	13	382	SHENTON	WE	10	207
SHEARS	JH	4	339	SHEEHAN	W	13	382	SHELL	H	13	382	SHEPARD	AG	2	305
SHEARS	WG	8	307	SHEEHY	J	7	350	SHELL	T	13	382	SHEPARD	C	4	340
SHEARWOOD	H	3	217	SHEEHY	JA	7	350	SHELLARD	FW	2	305	SHEPARD	F	4	340
SHEARWOOD	J	1	311	SHEEHY	WJ	13	382	SHELLARD	H	12	382	SHEPARD	J	9	339
SHEARWOOD	W	3	217	SHEEN	F	10	206	SHELLARD	T	2	305	SHEPHARD	A	1	312
SHEASBY	A	6	364	SHEEN	FW	1	312	SHELLARD	T	12	201	SHEPHARD	A	8	307
SHEASBY	JH	8	307	SHEENHAM	TG	7	350	SHELLARD	WG	12	201	SHEPHARD	A	10	364
SHEASBY	W	6	364	SHEENHAN	JP	2	304	SHELLEY	A	4	340	SHEPHARD	A	13	382
SHEATH	A	4	339	SHEEPWASH	H	2	305	SHELLEY	A	6	365	SHEPHARD	AE	7	351
SHEATH	AE	4	339	SHEERIN	W	14	287	SHELLEY	AE	1	312	SHEPHARD	AW	7	351
SHEATH	AW	13	382	SHEERMAN	WE	2	305	SHELLEY	AF	3	218	SHEPHARD	D	7	351
SHEATH	EF	13	382	SHEFFERD	FA	4	339	SHELLEY	CE	2	305	SHEPHARD	EF	3	218
SHEATH	EJJ	4	339	SHEFFIELD	AJ	4	339	SHELLEY	J	2	305	SHEPHARD	FE	9	172
SHEATH	EL	4	339	SHEFFIELD	CH	12	382	SHELLEY	J	6	365	SHEPHARD	G	5	317
SHEATH	ER	5	317	SHEFFIELD	F	4	339	SHELLEY	J	13	382	SHEPHARD	G	5	317
SHEATH	FC	2	304	SHEFFIELD	FW	4	339	SHELLEY	JS	6	365	SHEPHARD	G	11	339
SHEATH	FR	10	206	SHEFFIELD	J	7	350	SHELLEY	L	13	382	SHEPHARD	GR	13	382
SHEATH	GH	4	339	SHEHAN	M	4	339	SHELLEY	M	2	305	SHEPHARD	HA	13	383
SHEATH	H	10	206	SHEIL	W	6	365	SHELLEY	P	2	305	SHEPHARD	HG	5	317
SHEATH	HA	10	206	SHELBOURNE	AF	11	338	SHELLEY	P	2	305	SHEPHARD	HR	4	340
SHEATH	HC	4	339	SHELDON	A	4	339	SHELLEY	R	6	365	SHEPHARD	J	14	287
SHEATH	J	4	339	SHELDON	A	6	365	SHELLEY	RH	3	218	SHEPHARD	JA	3	218
SHEATH	JG	4	339	SHELDON	A	9	172	SHELLEY	SF	4	340	SHEPHARD	LA	3	218
SHEATH	JW	10	206	SHELDON	A	11	338	SHELLEY	W	5	317	SHEPHARD	S	6	365
SHEATH	P	4	339	SHELDON	A	14	287	SHELLEY	W	13	382	SHEPHARD	S	7	351
SHEATH	TW	4	339	SHELDON	AT	2	305	SHELLEY	WB	3	218	SHEPHARD	W	9	172
SHEATH	W	4	339	SHELDON	CE	10	363	SHELLIS	R	6	365	SHEPHARD	WJ	2	305
SHEATH	WE	6	364	SHELDON	E	8	307	SHELLIS	R	6	365	SHEPHEARD	FA	4	340
SHEATH	WE	10	206	SHELDON	F	10	206	SHELLIS	W	6	365	SHEPHERD	A	2	305
SHEATH	WH	5	317	SHELDON	F	10	206	SHELLIS	WJ	6	365	SHEPHERD	A	8	307
SHEATHER	CT	10	363	SHELDON	FWJ	4	340	SHELLY	J	4	340	SHEPHERD	A	9	339
SHEATHER	E	4	339	SHELDON	GE	1	312	SHELLY	JH	8	307	SHEPHERD	A	12	201
SHEATHER	F	12	382	SHELDON	J	6	365	SHELMERDINE	E	4	340	SHEPHERD	AA	4	340
SHEATHER	G	4	339	SHELDON	J	8	307	SHELMERDINE	J	11	338	SHEPHERD	AA	10	364
SHEATHER	G	12	382	SHELDON	J	9	339	SHELMERDINE	T	14	287	SHEPHERD	AE	8	307
SHEATHER	W	2	304	SHELDON	JH	8	307	SHELMERDINE	WE	11	339	SHEPHERD	AEF	1	312
SHEDDEN	JM	12	201	SHELDON	JH	11	338	SHELTON	AE	5	317	SHEPHERD	AG	7	351
SHEED	WF	1	312	SHELDON	T	1	312	SHELTON	AE	6	365	SHEPHERD	AH	5	317
SHEEDY	JB	3	218	SHELDON	T	14	287	SHELTON	C	5	317	SHEPHERD	AH	13	383
SHEEHAN	C	1	312	SHELDON	TW	9	339	SHELTON	C	12	201	SHEPHERD	AW	12	201
SHEEHAN	C	3	218	SHELDON	W	8	307	SHELTON	GW	5	317	SHEPHERD	B	2	305
SHEEHAN	D	13	382	SHELDON	W	8	307	SHELTON	H	5	317	SHEPHERD	BF	1	312
SHEEHAN	FC	7	350	SHELDON	W	9	172	SHELTON	HFA	10	364	SHEPHERD	BH	6	365
SHEEHAN	GW	13	382	SHELDON	WH	8	307	SHELTON	J	12	201	SHEPHERD	C	7	351
SHEEHAN	H	9	172	SHELDON	WL	6	365	SHELTON	J	14	287	SHEPHERD	C	8	307

SHEPHERD	CF	7	351	SHEPHERD	R	8	308	SHEPPARD	F	13	383	SHERGOLD	J	10	207
SHEPHERD	CH	10	364	SHEPHERD	R	10	207	SHEPPARD	FC	2	306	SHERGOLD	SC	4	341
SHEPHERD	CJ	7	351	SHEPHERD	RN	3	218	SHEPPARD	FC	6	366	SHERGOLD	WE	4	341
SHEPHERD	CV	3	218	SHEPHERD	RW	4	340	SHEPPARD	FGC	1	313	SHERGOLD	WG	4	341
SHEPHERD	CW	13	383	SHEPHERD	S	9	339	SHEPPARD	G	7	352	SHERGOLD	WG	4	341
SHEPHERD	E	2	305	SHEPHERD	S	10	207	SHEPPARD	G	10	207	SHERIDAN	E	14	288
SHEPHERD	E	5	317	SHEPHERD	SA	5	318	SHEPPARD	HA	3	219	SHERIDAN	J	3	219
SHEPHERD	E	9	339	SHEPHERD	SJ	10	364	SHEPPARD	HA	3	219	SHERIDAN	J	11	339
SHEPHERD	EA	1	312	SHEPHERD	SL	6	365	SHEPPARD	J	1	313	SHERIDAN	J	11	339
SHEPHERD	EG	13	383	SHEPHERD	SR	10	364	SHEPPARD	J	1	313	SHERIDAN	J	11	339
SHEPHERD	EGI	10	364	SHEPHERD	SW	10	207	SHEPPARD	J	1	313	SHERIDAN	J	14	288
SHEPHERD	ER	1	312	SHEPHERD	T	3	218	SHEPPARD	J	10	207	SHERIDAN	M	9	173
SHEPHERD	ER	11	339	SHEPHERD	T	6	366	SHEPPARD	JH	4	340	SHERIDAN	M	14	288
SHEPHERD	EW	3	218	SHEPHERD	T	8	308	SHEPPARD	JH	11	339	SHERIDAN	RJ	14	288
SHEPHERD	F	11	339	SHEPHERD	T	8	308	SHEPPARD	JHG	13	383	SHERIDAN	T	1	313
SHEPHERD	F	14	287	SHEPHERD	T	14	287	SHEPPARD	JT	10	207	SHERIDAN	WE	14	288
SHEPHERD	FB	1	312	SHEPHERD	TG	10	207	SHEPPARD	JW	10	207	SHERIFF	A	14	288
SHEPHERD	FC	1	312	SHEPHERD	TH	6	366	SHEPPARD	K	4	341	SHERIFF	F	11	339
SHEPHERD	FE	4	340	SHEPHERD	W	1	312	SHEPPARD	L	8	308	SHERIFF	FJ	6	366
SHEPHERD	FJ	9	173	SHEPHERD	W	1	312	SHEPPARD	LW	3	219	SHERIFF	HP	4	341
SHEPHERD	FO	14	287	SHEPHERD	W	4	340	SHEPPARD	R	3	219	SHERIFF	J	14	288
SHEPHERD	FR	1	312	SHEPHERD	W	5	318	SHEPPARD	R	7	352	SHERIFF	M	4	341
SHEPHERD	FT	6	365	SHEPHERD	W	5	318	SHEPPARD	R	10	364	SHERIFF	WA	12	382
SHEPHERD	FT	7	351	SHEPHERD	W	7	351	SHEPPARD	S	7	352	SHERIN	G	4	341
SHEPHERD	FW	9	339	SHEPHERD	W	8	308	SHEPPARD	SH	4	341	SHERIN	G	4	341
SHEPHERD	G	1	312	SHEPHERD	W	10	364	SHEPPARD	T	11	339	SHERING	A	1	313
SHEPHERD	GH	4	340	SHEPHERD	W	12	382	SHEPPARD	TW	13	383	SHERING	AW	5	318
SHEPHERD	GH	7	351	SHEPHERD	W	14	287	SHEPPARD	TW	13	383	SHERING	WE	10	364
SHEPHERD	GW	7	351	SHEPHERD	WA	3	218	SHEPPARD	W	2	306	SHERLIKER	R	13	383
SHEPHERD	GW	9	173	SHEPHERD	WAG	13	383	SHEPPARD	W	2	306	SHERLOCK	AE	3	219
SHEPHERD	GW	14	287	SHEPHERD	WG	13	383	SHEPPARD	W	4	341	SHERLOCK	AH	3	219
SHEPHERD	H	2	305	SHEPHERD	WJ	3	219	SHEPPARD	W	8	308	SHERLOCK	E	6	366
SHEPHERD	H	4	340	SHEPHERD	WJ	3	219	SHEPPARD	WC	10	207	SHERLOCK	FC	2	306
SHEPHERD	H	5	318	SHEPHERD	WJ	4	340	SHEPPARD	WE	4	341	SHERLOCK	J	14	288
SHEPHERD	H	8	307	SHEPHERD	WJ	10	364	SHEPPARD	WG	2	306	SHERLOCK	JW	10	207
SHEPHERD	H	12	201	SHEPHERD	WR	10	364	SHEPPARD	WJ	13	383	SHERMAN	F	2	306
SHEPHERD	H	12	201	SHEPHERD	WRV	11	339	SHEPPARD	WW	7	352	SHERMAN	H	2	306
SHEPHERD	HG	5	318	SHEPLEY	AH	9	173	SHEPPERD	J	1	313	SHERMAN	HB	6	366
SHEPHERD	HJ	13	383	SHEPLEY	AV	11	339	SHEPPERSON	C	1	313	SHERMAN	M	1	313
SHEPHERD	HO	3	218	SHEPLEY	H	8	308	SHEPPERSON	D	1	313	SHERRARD	W	8	308
SHEPHERD	HV	12	201	SHEPLEY	J	11	339	SHERBERT	FE	14	287	SHERRAT	TW	1	313
SHEPHERD	J	2	305	SHEPPARD	A	1	313	SHERBIRD	AS	2	306	SHERRATT	A	11	339
SHEPHERD	J	4	340	SHEPPARD	A	1	313	SHERBOURNE	ED	4	341	SHERRATT	G	4	341
SHEPHERD	J	7	351	SHEPPARD	AC	10	207	SHERBOURNE	EJ	4	341	SHERRATT	H	14	288
SHEPHERD	J	10	207	SHEPPARD	AS	8	308	SHERBOURNE	WC	10	207	SHERRATT	J	1	313
SHEPHERD	J	11	339	SHEPPARD	B	3	219	SHERBURN	F	8	308	SHERRATT	W	9	173
SHEPHERD	J	14	287	SHEPPARD	C	1	313	SHERBURN	J	4	341	SHERRED	AJ	10	364
SHEPHERD	J	14	287	SHEPPARD	C	13	383	SHERDEL	GH	5	318	SHERRED	WA	10	208
SHEPHERD	JE	1	312	SHEPPARD	E	2	306	SHERGOLD	AA	3	219	SHERRELL	WJ	3	219
SHEPHERD	JL	9	173	SHEPPARD	E	4	340	SHERGOLD	AC	13	383	SHERRELL	WJ	7	352
SHEPHERD	JW	7	351	SHEPPARD	E	6	366	SHERGOLD	AE	4	341	SHERRETT	GA	2	306
SHEPHERD	JW	8	308	SHEPPARD	E	6	366	SHERGOLD	FC	4	341	SHERRIDEN	J	8	308
SHEPHERD	L	10	207	SHEPPARD	E	10	364	SHERGOLD	G	10	207	SHERRIFF	C	6	366
SHEPHERD	P	9	173	SHEPPARD	EH	10	364	SHERGOLD	G	10	364	SHERRIFF	E	6	366
SHEPHERD	R	5	318	SHEPPARD	ER	4	340	SHERGOLD	GA	10	207	SHERRIFF	FM	1	313

SHERRIFF	N	11	339	SHILL	D	10	208	SHIPWAY	WP	13	383	SHOOBERT	FH	13	384
SHERRINGTON	G	14	288	SHILLABEER	J	4	342	SHIRE	WJ	1	314	SHOOBERT	LG	13	384
SHERROTT	E	11	340	SHILLABEER	J	4	342	SHIREMAN	C	11	340	SHOPLAND	WT	3	220
SHERRY	J	9	173	SHILLABEER	WJR	4	342	SHIRES	A	8	309	SHORE	A	4	342
SHERRY	W	12	382	SHILLADAY	JC	9	339	SHIRES	A	8	309	SHORE	F	6	366
SHERVILL	G	11	340	SHILLAM	CW	9	339	SHIRES	C	9	173	SHORE	GE	3	220
SHERVILL	GW	1	313	SHILLEY	HJ	4	342	SHIRES	C	9	339	SHORE	GE	3	220
SHERWIN	E	8	308	SHILLINGFORD	W	1	314	SHIRES	F	7	352	SHORE	HG	7	352
SHERWIN	E	8	308	SHILLITO	G	8	308	SHIRES	F	8	309	SHORE	JG	10	208
SHERWIN	FH	13	383	SHILLITO	H	8	308	SHIRES	H	8	309	SHORE	W	4	342
SHERWIN	J	8	308	SHILLITO	H	8	308	SHIRES	H	8	309	SHORE	WE	1	314
SHERWIN	J	11	340	SHILLITOE	M	8	308	SHIRES	J	8	309	SHORE	WE	2	306
SHERWIN	JA	9	339	SHILLUM	JW	7	352	SHIRET	W	13	383	SHOREMAN	B	11	340
SHERWOOD	F	6	366	SHILSON	WH	7	352	SHIRLEY	A	3	220	SHOREMAN	CE	11	340
SHERWOOD	F	10	208	SHILSON	WH	7	352	SHIRLEY	C	11	340	SHOREY	FE	6	367
SHERWOOD	FW	1	313	SHILTON	G	2	306	SHIRLEY	EF	4	342	SHORLAND	W	10	208
SHERWOOD	H	7	352	SHIMELL	A	10	208	SHIRLEY	EM	2	306	SHORLEY	F	12	201
SHERWOOD	J	8	308	SHINGLER	H	6	366	SHIRLEY	FW	13	384	SHORLEY	J	12	201
SHERWOOD	JA	3	219	SHINGLES	D	13	383	SHIRLEY	G	10	365	SHORRICKS	HA	3	220
SHERWOOD	JHV	12	201	SHINGLES	J	1	314	SHIRLEY	HA	10	365	SHORROCKS	FA	14	289
SHERWOOD	JM	3	219	SHINGLES	TA	1	314	SHIRLEY	J	3	220	SHORROCKS	H	14	289
SHERWOOD	T	3	219	SHINN	FL	2	306	SHIRLEY	J	7	352	SHORROCKS	J	14	289
SHERWOOD	T	10	208	SHINN	H	9	339	SHIRLEY	J	11	340	SHORROCKS	JT	11	341
SHERWOOD	WC	10	364	SHINN	HC	4	342	SHIRLEY	J	11	340	SHORT	A	1	314
SHEW	SV	1	313	SHINN	PB	10	365	SHIRLEY	JH	12	382	SHORT	A	6	367
SHEWARD	F	7	352	SHIP	CJ	1	314	SHIRLEY	JL	6	366	SHORT	A	9	173
SHEWRY	E	1	314	SHIP	DA	3	220	SHIRLEY	R	6	366	SHORT	A	11	341
SHEWRY	GH	3	219	SHIP	EW	3	220	SHIRLEY	S	6	366	SHORT	AE	10	365
SHIEL	MJ	10	364	SHIP	HW	2	306	SHIRLEY	S	13	384	SHORT	AF	2	307
SHIELD	H	9	173	SHIPLEE	CJ	2	306	SHIRLEY	T	8	309	SHORT	AH	6	367
SHIELDS	AT	3	219	SHIPLEY	E	8	308	SHIRLEY	T	11	340	SHORT	C	6	367
SHIELDS	C	2	306	SHIPLEY	GW	6	366	SHIRLEY	W	4	342	SHORT	C	10	365
SHIELDS	CF	3	219	SHIPLEY	J	1	314	SHIRLEY	W	10	208	SHORT	E	4	342
SHIELDS	E	3	219	SHIPLEY	J	1	314	SHIRLEY	WA	2	306	SHORT	EE	13	384
SHIELDS	E	11	340	SHIPLEY	J	11	340	SHIRLEY	WH	6	366	SHORT	F	6	367
SHIELDS	HA	4	341	SHIPMAN	G	3	220	SHIRLOCK	H	8	309	SHORT	F	9	173
SHIELDS	HS	13	383	SHIPMAN	J	3	220	SHIRVILL	F	3	220	SHORT	F	9	173
SHIELDS	J	11	340	SHIPMAN	W	8	309	SHIRVILL	H	3	220	SHORT	F	13	384
SHIELDS	J	14	288	SHIPMAN	W	8	309	SHIRVILL	WJ	2	306	SHORT	FJ	13	384
SHIELDS	W	14	288	SHIPP	A	1	314	SHNYDER	J	14	289	SHORT	FS	10	208
SHIELDS	WH	4	341	SHIPP	AJ	10	208	SHOEBRIDGE	E	14	289	SHORT	G	13	384
SHIELS	C	14	288	SHIPP	C	10	208	SHOEBRIDGE	HF	7	352	SHORT	GW	6	367
SHIELS	M	14	288	SHIPP	EG	2	306	SHOEBRIDGE	W	14	289	SHORT	H	1	314
SHIELS	T	14	288	SHIPP	J	10	208	SHOEMAKE	WJ	12	201	SHORT	H	1	314
SHIELS	W	14	288	SHIPP	J	10	208	SHOESMITH	A	3	220	SHORT	H	7	352
SHIER	FM	3	219	SHIPP	JW	1	314	SHOESMITH	A	8	309	SHORT	H	10	208
SHIER	JW	3	219	SHIPP	WEH	10	365	SHOESMITH	F	11	340	SHORT	H	12	201
SHIER	TF	3	220	SHIPPAM	G	11	340	SHOESMITH	G	8	309	SHORT	HA	2	307
SHIERS	EJ	10	208	SHIPPEN	C	8	309	SHOESMITH	J	9	173	SHORT	HS	4	342
SHIERS	R	11	340	SHIPPEN	D	8	309	SHOESMITH	R	9	339	SHORT	HV	10	208
SHIERS	WR	3	220	SHIPPEN	TA	8	309	SHOESMITH	W	8	309	SHORT	J	12	383
SHILCO	A	14	288	SHIPTON	A	1	314	SHOLL	E	7	352	SHORT	JA	2	307
SHILCO	E	14	288	SHIPTON	DF	10	365	SHONE	A	3	220	SHORT	JC	13	384
SHILCO	I	14	288	SHIPTON	FW	3	220	SHONE	HA	3	220	SHORT	JD	1	314
SHILHAM	AJ	1	314	SHIPTON	G	1	314	SHONGITHARM	F	11	340	SHORT	JG	12	383

SHORT	JW	3	220	SHOWELL	BH	1	315	SHULATSKY	J	14	289	SIBLEY	TH	5	319
SHORT	M	6	367	SHOWELL	GA	3	221	SHULVER	FE	1	315	SIBLEY	W	1	315
SHORT	M	9	173	SHOWELL	SH	1	315	SHUT	T	6	368	SIBLEY	W	5	319
SHORT	M	9	173	SHOWLER	G	5	318	SHUTE	EJ	13	384	SIBLEY	W	7	353
SHORT	R	4	342	SHOWLER	WJ	2	307	SHUTE	FC	10	209	SIBLEY	WA	4	343
SHORT	R	9	339	SHOWLER	WT	5	318	SHUTE	JE	10	209	SIBLEY	WT	4	343
SHORT	RA	13	384	SHOWMAN	H	14	289	SHUTE	PF	10	209	SIBSON	G	8	310
SHORT	S	14	289	SHOWMAN	S	14	289	SHUTER	A	8	310	SIBSON	JW	8	310
SHORT	SC	6	367	SHREEVE	ETS	7	353	SHUTER	EC	10	365	SIBSON	W	9	174
SHORT	TH	6	367	SHREEVE	W	7	353	SHUTER	F	6	368	SIBUN	J	13	384
SHORT	W	4	342	SHREEVES	G	12	202	SHUTT	A	9	339	SIDAWAY	A	6	368
SHORT	W	6	367	SHREEVES	HJ	12	202	SHUTT	E	9	173	SIDAWAY	WV	6	368
SHORT	W	10	365	SHREEVES	M	12	202	SHUTT	HF	13	384	SIDDALL	E	11	341
SHORT	WC	4	342	SHREEVES	R	12	202	SHUTT	JW	6	368	SIDDALL	G	11	341
SHORT	WG	2	307	SHREEVES	T	12	202	SHUTT	RG	6	368	SIDDALL	J	11	341
SHORT	WG	3	220	SHRIMPTON	A	1	315	SHUTTLER	F	8	310	SIDDALL	JW	8	310
SHORT	WHB	3	220	SHRIMPTON	A	7	353	SHUTTLEWORTH	A	9	339	SIDDALL	L	7	354
SHORT	WR	1	314	SHRIMPTON	BA	6	367	SHUTTLEWORTH	F	6	368	SIDDALL	WC	6	368
SHORT	WR	13	384	SHRIMPTON	CA	10	208	SHUTTLEWORTH	F	9	173	SIDDAWAY	J	6	368
SHORTELL	E	8	309	SHRIMPTON	CR	1	315	SHUTTLEWORTH	F	9	340	SIDDLE	A	8	310
SHORTER	A	3	220	SHRIMPTON	F	5	318	SHUTTLEWORTH	FV	14	289	SIDDLE	F	8	310
SHORTER	AJ	7	352	SHRIMPTON	H	1	315	SHUTTLEWORTH	H	9	173	SIDDLE	GH	9	174
SHORTER	F	3	385	SHRIMPTON	HJ	7	353	SHUTTLEWORTH	H	11	341	SIDDON	RH	11	341
SHORTER	FH	4	342	SHRIMPTON	JWH	2	307	SHUTTLEWORTH	H	11	341	SIDDON	WA	11	341
SHORTER	HW	13	384	SHRIMPTON	RA	5	319	SHUTTLEWORTH	J	11	341	SIDDONS	B	8	310
SHORTER	JA	4	342	SHRIMPTON	VJ	3	221	SHUTTLEWORTH	W	9	173	SIDDONS	W	2	307
SHORTER	RJ	13	384	SHRIMPTON	W	6	367	SIBBALD	A	10	209	SIDE	ET	7	354
SHORTER	S	3	221	SHRIVES	A	12	383	SIBBIT	F	11	341	SIDEBOTHAM	NW	1	315
SHORTER	W	14	289	SHRIVES	A	13	384	SIBBLES	O	11	341	SIDEBOTTOM	CE	8	310
SHORTER	WB	4	342	SHRIVES	AE	7	353	SIBILIA	F	4	342	SIDEBOTTOM	G	8	310
SHORTHILL	F	8	309	SHRIVES	G	7	353	SIBILIA	V	4	343	SIDEBOTTOM	GW	8	310
SHORTHOUSE	T	6	367	SHRIVES	G	7	353	SIBLEY	A	4	343	SIDEBOTTOM	J	8	310
SHORTHOUSE	W	6	367	SHROEDER	H	14	289	SIBLEY	AJ	7	353	SIDEBOTTOM	S	9	340
SHORTLAND	A	5	318	SHROLL	FJ	3	221	SIBLEY	AW	2	307	SIDLEY	A	3	221
SHORTLAND	A	6	367	SHRUBSALL	FH	3	221	SIBLEY	BH	5	319	SIDLEY	TH	6	368
SHORTLAND	AE	5	318	SHRUBSALL	G	8	309	SIBLEY	C	2	307	SIDNELL	AV	2	307
SHORTLAND	AJ	5	318	SHRUBSOLE	AE	10	208	SIBLEY	C	7	353	SIDNELL	R	2	307
SHORTLAND	EA	1	314	SHRUBSOLE	AEJ	7	353	SIBLEY	CL	4	343	SIDNEY	FG	3	221
SHORTLAND	F	5	318	SHRUBSOLE	CW	3	221	SIBLEY	F	1	315	SIDNEY	JH	3	221
SHORTLAND	G	12	383	SHUBOTHAM	B	8	309	SIBLEY	FG	1	315	SIDWELL	C	11	342
SHORTLAND	J	3	221	SHUBOTHAM	JW	8	309	SIBLEY	FW	12	383	SIDWELL	CAJ	6	368
SHORTLAND	J	5	318	SHUBOTHAM	T	8	310	SIBLEY	GH	7	353	SIDWELL	EM	4	343
SHORTLAND	JR	7	353	SHUCHSMITH	I	8	310	SIBLEY	GT	4	343	SIDWELL	H	6	368
SHORTLE	W	11	341	SHUFF	AH	2	307	SIBLEY	GW	1	315	SIDWELL	J	6	368
SHORTMAN	SA	7	353	SHUFFILL	WC	5	319	SIBLEY	HJ	5	319	SIDWELL	JW	6	368
SHOTBOLT	E	5	318	SHUFFILL	WH	5	319	SIBLEY	J	4	343	SIEBERT	HG	3	221
SHOTTER	EE	12	201	SHUFFLEBOTTOM	E	11	341	SIBLEY	J	5	319	SIEGERT	G	7	354
SHOTTER	F	4	342	SHUFFLEBOTTOM	G	11	341	SIBLEY	JE	5	319	SIGGERS	GW	13	384
SHOTTER	R	4	342	SHUFFLEBOTTOM	J	11	341	SIBLEY	JJ	7	353	SIGGERS	J	3	221
SHOTTON	A	6	367	SHUFFLEBOTTOM	JW	14	289	SIBLEY	LG	5	319	SIGSTON	HH	8	310
SHOULER	FE	12	201	SHUFFLEBOTTOM	S	11	341	SIBLEY	PH	12	383	SIGSTON	L	8	310
SHOULER	T	12	201	SHUFFLEBOTTOM	S	14	289	SIBLEY	RF	12	202	SIGSWORTH	GW	8	310
SHOULER	TG	12	202	SHUFFLETON	J	11	341	SIBLEY	SE	4	343	SILCOCK	J	8	310
SHOULER	WJ	12	202	SHUKER	HA	6	367	SIBLEY	SH	12	383	SILCOCK	RH	8	310
SHOULT	BH	7	353	SHUKER	WHA	6	367	SIBLEY	SR	12	383	SILCOCK	S	14	289
								SIBLEY	T	5	319				

SILCOCK	W	8	310	SILSBY	H	5	319	SIMESTER	H	2	307	SIMMONITE	F	9	340
SILCOCK	W	14	289	SILVER	AE	2	307	SIMFIELD	DJ	7	354	SIMMONS	A	5	320
SILCOCK	WJ	14	289	SILVER	G	13	385	SIMISTER	A	8	311	SIMMONS	A	6	369
SILCOX	GBE	1	315	SILVER	H	6	368	SIMISTER	J	3	222	SIMMONS	A	14	290
SILCOX	JOG	1	315	SILVER	WD	10	209	SIMISTER	J	14	290	SIMMONS	AC	3	222
SILENCE	HR	3	221	SILVER	WE	13	385	SIMKIN	F	11	342	SIMMONS	AE	3	222
SILER		3	221	SILVER	WF	13	385	SIMKINS	AW	13	385	SIMMONS	AG	13	386
SILK	F	4	343	SILVER	WG	6	368	SIMKINS	GJ	1	316	SIMMONS	AGJ	4	344
SILK	HF	10	209	SILVERBERG	J	14	290	SIMKINS	HE	1	316	SIMMONS	AJ	6	369
SILK	HJ	13	385	SILVERLOCK	W	13	385	SIMKINS	J	6	369	SIMMONS	AJ	6	369
SILK	T	10	209	SILVERS	CJ	6	369	SIMLOW	R	14	290	SIMMONS	AP	4	344
SILK	T	12	424	SILVERS	EN	6	369	SIMLOW	S	14	290	SIMMONS	B	4	344
SILK	W	8	310	SILVERS	H	10	209	SIMM	SH	14	290	SIMMONS	BJ	4	344
SILK	W	13	385	SILVERSIDE	GE	3	221	SIMMINS	EH	2	307	SIMMONS	BW	5	320
SILKSTONE	B	8	311	SILVERSIDE	GE	13	385	SIMMISTER	S	14	290	SIMMONS	C	7	354
SILKSTONE	J	8	311	SILVERSIDE	WE	13	385	SIMMOND	G	4	344	SIMMONS	C	13	386
SILKSTONE	J	8	311	SILVERTHORN	A	4	344	SIMMONDS	A	1	316	SIMMONS	D	2	308
SILKSTONE	J	8	311	SILVERWOOD	A	8	311	SIMMONDS	A	10	365	SIMMONS	E	1	316
SILKSTONE	J	8	311	SILVERWOOD	N	9	174	SIMMONDS	A	13	385	SIMMONS	E	1	316
SILKSTONE	M	8	311	SILVESTER	A	3	385	SIMMONDS	A	13	385	SIMMONS	E	4	344
SILKSTONE	M	8	311	SILVESTER	GW	10	365	SIMMONDS	AE	4	344	SIMMONS	E	5	319
SILKSTONE	P	8	311	SILVESTER	H	5	319	SIMMONDS	AM	4	344	SIMMONS	E	10	365
SILKSTONE	W	8	311	SILVESTER	HCH	1	316	SIMMONDS	AW	13	385	SIMMONS	EE	4	344
SILLENCE	G	2	307	SILVESTER	J	4	344	SIMMONDS	C	1	316	SIMMONS	EE	6	369
SILLENCE	G	4	343	SILVESTER	J	6	369	SIMMONDS	C	2	307	SIMMONS	EH	6	369
SILLENCE	G	10	365	SILVESTER	J	7	354	SIMMONDS	D	1	316	SIMMONS	EJ	13	386
SILLENCE	H	4	343	SILVESTER	J	10	209	SIMMONDS	E	10	365	SIMMONS	F	1	316
SILLENCE	J	4	343	SILVESTER	J	14	290	SIMMONDS	EE	10	209	SIMMONS	F	3	222
SILLENCE	L	4	343	SILVESTER	JS	6	369	SIMMONDS	F	13	385	SIMMONS	F	3	222
SILLENCE	R	4	343	SILVESTER	JW	6	369	SIMMONDS	FJ	2	308	SIMMONS	FC	3	222
SILLENCE	S	4	343	SILVESTER	O	9	340	SIMMONDS	FJ	10	209	SIMMONS	FG	7	354
SILLENCE	W	4	343	SILVESTER	PJ	1	316	SIMMONDS	FT	10	209	SIMMONS	FJ	2	308
SILLENCE	WE	4	343	SILVESTER	TW	1	316	SIMMONDS	G	3	222	SIMMONS	FW	7	354
SILLENCE	WH	4	343	SILVESTER	W	1	316	SIMMONDS	G	12	383	SIMMONS	FW	9	174
SILLETT	G	2	307	SILVESTER	W	7	354	SIMMONDS	G	13	385	SIMMONS	G	1	316
SILLETT	H	3	221	SILVESTER	WE	1	316	SIMMONDS	G	13	385	SIMMONS	G	2	308
SILLEY	A	13	385	SILVEY	HE	3	221	SIMMONDS	GF	7	354	SIMMONS	G	7	354
SILLITO	RJ	13	385	SILVEY	JS	2	307	SIMMONDS	GW	13	385	SIMMONS	GA	3	222
SILLITOE	JC	6	368	SILVEY	RJ	3	221	SIMMONDS	HE	1	316	SIMMONS	H	3	222
SILLITON	FC	1	315	SIM	AJ	4	344	SIMMONDS	J	3	222	SIMMONS	H	4	344
SILLITON	W	1	315	SIM	GJ	4	344	SIMMONDS	J	10	209	SIMMONS	H	5	319
SILLMAN	FG	6	368	SIM	W	2	307	SIMMONDS	J	13	386	SIMMONS	H	6	369
SILLS	AD	1	315	SIMANTS	AS	12	202	SIMMONDS	JH	13	386	SIMMONS	H	14	290
SILLS	AW	12	202	SIMANTS	GH	12	202	SIMMONDS	JW	10	209	SIMMONS	HG	13	386
SILLS	CG	5	319	SIMARTS	J	12	202	SIMMONDS	JW	10	209	SIMMONS	HR	7	354
SILLS	G	1	315	SIMCO	JG	1	316	SIMMONDS	P	3	222	SIMMONS	HR	7	354
SILLS	G	1	315	SIMCOCK	J	11	342	SIMMONDS	RW	12	383	SIMMONS	J	8	311
SILLS	HA	14	289	SIMCOE	HJ	12	202	SIMMONDS	S	6	369	SIMMONS	J	11	342
SILLS	JB	12	202	SIMCOE	J	12	202	SIMMONDS	SY	2	308	SIMMONS	J	11	342
SILLS	JH	5	319	SIMCOX	AE	6	369	SIMMONDS	T	3	222	SIMMONS	JA	3	222
SILLS	L	13	385	SIMCOX	E	6	369	SIMMONDS	TA	2	308	SIMMONS	JHE	10	209
SILMAN	HS	5	319	SIMCOX	EJ	6	369	SIMMONDS	TG	4	344	SIMMONS	JJ	7	354
SILSBURY	CF	4	343	SIMCOX	FC	10	365	SIMMONDS	W	3	222	SIMMONS	JP	13	386
SILSBURY	P	4	344	SIMCOX	H	6	369	SIMMONDS	WE	3	222	SIMMONS	JW	1	316
SILSBY	G	9	340	SIMCOX	W	6	369	SIMMONDS	WG	4	344	SIMMONS	LA	5	320

SIMMONS	LC	7	354	SIMONDS	E	6	370	SIMPSON	AV	3	223	SIMPSON	H	9	174
SIMMONS	M	2	308	SIMONDS	J	6	370	SIMPSON	AW	3	223	SIMPSON	H	10	366
SIMMONS	O	5	320	SIMONDS	M	3	223	SIMPSON	B	6	370	SIMPSON	H	11	342
SIMMONS	PA	5	320	SIMONDS	S	7	354	SIMPSON	B	6	370	SIMPSON	H	11	342
SIMMONS	PL	1	316	SIMONS	AE	10	209	SIMPSON	B	8	312	SIMPSON	H	11	342
SIMMONS	R	6	369	SIMONS	E	4	344	SIMPSON	C	2	308	SIMPSON	H	14	290
SIMMONS	RH	5	320	SIMONS	FA	3	223	SIMPSON	C	8	312	SIMPSON	HA	1	317
SIMMONS	S	3	222	SIMONS	GF	3	223	SIMPSON	C	9	340	SIMPSON	HE	7	355
SIMMONS	S	12	202	SIMONS	H	6	370	SIMPSON	CG	9	340	SIMPSON	HJ	2	308
SIMMONS	SHL	3	222	SIMONS	HJ	12	203	SIMPSON	CJ	3	385	SIMPSON	HW	7	355
SIMMONS	T	4	344	SIMONS	HJ	12	383	SIMPSON	CR	5	320	SIMPSON	J	2	308
SIMMONS	T	4	344	SIMONS	I	14	290	SIMPSON	CR	9	340	SIMPSON	J	5	321
SIMMONS	TL	5	320	SIMONS	J	14	290	SIMPSON	CR	9	340	SIMPSON	J	6	370
SIMMONS	TM	13	386	SIMONS	LI	14	290	SIMPSON	CS	3	385	SIMPSON	J	6	370
SIMMONS	TR	2	308	SIMONS	LS	8	311	SIMPSON	D	3	223	SIMPSON	J	8	312
SIMMONS	W	1	316	SIMONS	O	11	342	SIMPSON	D	8	312	SIMPSON	J	8	312
SIMMONS	W	4	344	SIMONS	O	11	342	SIMPSON	E	8	312	SIMPSON	J	8	312
SIMMONS	W	12	202	SIMONS	R	3	223	SIMPSON	E	8	312	SIMPSON	J	8	312
SIMMONS	W	13	386	SIMONS	T	2	308	SIMPSON	E	9	174	SIMPSON	J	8	312
SIMMONS	WA	7	354	SIMONS	T	6	370	SIMPSON	E	9	174	SIMPSON	J	8	312
SIMMONS	WC	5	320	SIMONS	T	12	203	SIMPSON	E	9	340	SIMPSON	J	8	312
SIMMONS	WF	10	209	SIMONS	TW	3	223	SIMPSON	E	9	340	SIMPSON	J	8	312
SIMMONS	WG	6	369	SIMONS	W	9	174	SIMPSON	EM	9	340	SIMPSON	J	9	174
SIMMONS	WH	5	320	SIMONS	W	11	342	SIMPSON	EW	1	317	SIMPSON	J	9	340
SIMMONS	WH	11	342	SIMPER	A	4	345	SIMPSON	EW	11	342	SIMPSON	J	9	341
SIMMONS	WJ	13	386	SIMPER	AM	4	345	SIMPSON	F	7	355	SIMPSON	J	10	209
SIMMONS	WS	7	354	SIMPER	G	4	345	SIMPSON	F	8	312	SIMPSON	J	11	342
SIMMS	A	6	369	SIMPKIN	AH	13	386	SIMPSON	F	9	340	SIMPSON	J	11	342
SIMMS	AC	12	202	SIMPKIN	WS	13	386	SIMPSON	F	9	340	SIMPSON	J	12	383
SIMMS	AW	3	222	SIMPKINS	A	5	320	SIMPSON	F	11	342	SIMPSON	JA	1	317
SIMMS	CA	6	370	SIMPKINS	AH	5	320	SIMPSON	F	13	386	SIMPSON	JA	3	223
SIMMS	CA	6	370	SIMPKINS	B	5	320	SIMPSON	F	14	290	SIMPSON	JB	2	308
SIMMS	E	12	202	SIMPKINS	D	5	320	SIMPSON	FA	1	317	SIMPSON	JC	8	313
SIMMS	EJ	12	203	SIMPKINS	E	5	320	SIMPSON	FE	10	209	SIMPSON	JE	5	321
SIMMS	ER	3	222	SIMPKINS	GA	1	317	SIMPSON	FH	13	386	SIMPSON	JE	8	313
SIMMS	FA	3	222	SIMPKINS	J	14	290	SIMPSON	FJ	1	317	SIMPSON	JE	13	386
SIMMS	FC	12	203	SIMPKINS	L	5	320	SIMPSON	FS	1	317	SIMPSON	JFW	5	321
SIMMS	FW	3	223	SIMPKINS	RJ	5	320	SIMPSON	G	3	223	SIMPSON	JJ	1	317
SIMMS	G	8	311	SIMPSON	A	1	317	SIMPSON	G	8	312	SIMPSON	JR	2	308
SIMMS	GA	2	308	SIMPSON	A	3	223	SIMPSON	G	8	312	SIMPSON	JR	9	341
SIMMS	GE	6	370	SIMPSON	A	4	345	SIMPSON	G	9	340	SIMPSON	JT	6	370
SIMMS	GF	6	370	SIMPSON	A	4	345	SIMPSON	GE	8	312	SIMPSON	JT	8	313
SIMMS	GL	1	316	SIMPSON	A	6	370	SIMPSON	GH	6	370	SIMPSON	JT	12	383
SIMMS	HF	12	203	SIMPSON	A	7	355	SIMPSON	GM	9	340	SIMPSON	JW	5	321
SIMMS	HT	1	317	SIMPSON	A	8	311	SIMPSON	GT	7	355	SIMPSON	JW	9	174
SIMMS	HW	10	365	SIMPSON	A	8	311	SIMPSON	GW	6	370	SIMPSON	L	8	313
SIMMS	J	7	355	SIMPSON	A	9	340	SIMPSON	GW	6	370	SIMPSON	L	8	313
SIMMS	T	10	365	SIMPSON	A	13	386	SIMPSON	H	8	312	SIMPSON	L	8	313
SIMMS	TA	1	317	SIMPSON	A	14	290	SIMPSON	H	8	312	SIMPSON	L	11	343
SIMMS	WJ	12	203	SIMPSON	AE	12	383	SIMPSON	H	8	312	SIMPSON	M	4	345
SIMNOR	R	11	342	SIMPSON	AH	3	223	SIMPSON	H	8	312	SIMPSON	P	1	317
SIMNOR	W	11	342	SIMPSON	AHW	2	308	SIMPSON	H	8	312	SIMPSON	P	8	313
SIMON	CR	8	311	SIMPSON	AJ	3	223	SIMPSON	H	9	174	SIMPSON	P	9	174
SIMON	E	8	311	SIMPSON	AS	5	321	SIMPSON	H	9	174	SIMPSON	P	10	365
SIMON	H	8	311	SIMPSON	AS	13	386	SIMPSON	H	9	174	SIMPSON	PO	2	308

SIMPSON	R	1	317	SIMS	JW	12	203	SINFIELD	H	12	203	SISSON	A	14	291
SIMPSON	S	3	223	SIMS	L	1	317	SINFIELD	HC	5	321	SISSONS	G	13	388
SIMPSON	S	5	321	SIMS	LF	4	345	SINFIELD	HJ	1	318	SISSONS	R	8	313
SIMPSON	SC	9	174	SIMS	ME	3	223	SINFIELD	HS	12	203	SISSONS	W	10	210
SIMPSON	SG	7	355	SIMS	OA	13	387	SINFIELD	J	13	387	SISSONS	W	13	388
SIMPSON	ST	6	371	SIMS	R	4	345	SINFIELD	J	13	387	SIVELL	CF	3	385
SIMPSON	T	11	343	SIMS	RJ	1	318	SINFIELD	T	12	203	SIVELL	RH	3	385
SIMPSON	T	12	383	SIMS	RL	5	321	SINFIELD	W	7	355	SIVES	EA	9	175
SIMPSON	T	14	290	SIMS	T	3	223	SINFIELD	W	12	203	SIVES	JA	9	175
SIMPSON	TF	4	345	SIMS	T	13	387	SINFIELD	W	12	203	SIVETER	JS	7	356
SIMPSON	TJ	1	317	SIMS	W	3	223	SINFIELD	W	12	203	SIVEYER	HT	2	309
SIMPSON	TW	11	343	SIMS	W	4	345	SINFIELD	WC	13	387	SIVILL	HH	10	210
SIMPSON	V	6	371	SIMS	W	13	387	SINFIELD	WH	12	203	SIVITTER	WE	6	371
SIMPSON	W	5	321	SIMS	WE	13	387	SINGER	AA	3	224	SIVYER	CW	2	309
SIMPSON	W	6	371	SIMS	WG	13	387	SINGER	F	2	309	SIVYER	W	10	210
SIMPSON	W	7	355	SIMS	WH	4	345	SINGER	G	4	346	SIXSMITH	T	8	313
SIMPSON	W	8	313	SIMS	WH	14	290	SINGER	HH	4	346	SIZE	H	14	291
SIMPSON	W	8	313	SIMS	WT	13	387	SINGER	W	7	355	SIZER	TE	4	346
SIMPSON	W	8	313	SIMSON	CM	1	318	SINGFIELD	AJ	2	309	SIZER	WJ	3	224
SIMPSON	W	9	174	SIMSON	HC	1	318	SINGFIELD	F	7	355	SKADE	H	11	343
SIMPSON	W	9	174	SINCLAIR	C	8	313	SINGFIELD	FWH	7	355	SKAIFE	F	9	341
SIMPSON	W	9	341	SINCLAIR	E	11	343	SINGFIELD	H	7	356	SKARRATTS	G	11	343
SIMPSON	W	11	343	SINCLAIR	G	4	345	SINGFIELD	J	2	309	SKATES	F	4	346
SIMPSON	WA	4	345	SINCLAIR	H	7	355	SINGLE	E	12	203	SKATES	G	13	388
SIMPSON	WA	11	343	SINCLAIR	HL	10	210	SINGLE	EM	12	203	SKATES	GA	13	388
SIMPSON	WC	3	223	SINCLAIR	J	4	345	SINGLETON	A	8	313	SKATES	RA	13	388
SIMPSON	WC	7	355	SINCLAIR	J	9	174	SINGLETON	A	14	291	SKEATES	J	4	346
SIMPSON	WC	9	174	SINCLAIR	J	11	343	SINGLETON	AL	8	313	SKEATS	CT	4	346
SIMPSON	WD	10	366	SINCLAIR	J	14	290	SINGLETON	C	9	174	SKEATS	GA	4	346
SIMPSON	WE	3	223	SINCLAIR	JA	3	224	SINGLETON	E	3	224	SKEENS	FJ	10	210
SIMPSON	WH	9	341	SINCLAIR	JD	2	309	SINGLETON	ED	3	224	SKEENS	WD	10	366
SIMPSON	WJ	2	308	SINCLAIR	MM	13	387	SINGLETON	J	2	309	SKEET	AE	1	318
SIMPSON	WJ	13	386	SINCLAIR	T	7	355	SINGLETON	J	4	346	SKEET	WO	1	318
SIMPSON	WTL	8	313	SINCLAIR	T	14	291	SINGLETON	J	8	313	SKEGGS	A	5	321
SIMPSON	WW	11	343	SINCLAIR	W	3	224	SINGLETON	JE	3	224	SKEGGS	AE	5	321
SIMS	AE	10	210	SINCLAIR	W	7	355	SINGLETON	JJH	4	346	SKEGGS	LTS	2	309
SIMS	AW	2	308	SINCLAIR	W	9	174	SINGLETON	JW	14	291	SKEGGS	TW	2	309
SIMS	BJ	13	387	SINCLAIR	W	13	387	SINGLETON	R	11	343	SKEHAN	HF	3	385
SIMS	CE	4	345	SINCLAIR	W	14	291	SINGLETON	RH	7	356	SKEIN	I	14	291
SIMS	CW	1	317	SINCLAIR-GRIMSEY	W	13	387	SINGLETON	S	11	343	SKELCHER	H	1	318
SIMS	DH	1	317	SINDEN	C	5	321	SINGLETON	T	11	343	SKELDON	A	14	291
SIMS	E	4	345	SINDEN	R	13	387	SINGLETON	W	8	313	SKELLERN	EE	14	291
SIMS	EE	4	345	SINDEN	TH	5	321	SINGLETON	W	14	291	SKELLERN	I	14	291
SIMS	F	4	345	SINDEN	WJ	4	346	SINGLETON	WM	14	291	SKELLON	W	11	343
SIMS	F	4	345	SINDER	PA	3	224	SINKINSON	W	14	291	SKELLY	A	11	343
SIMS	F	4	345	SINDON	W	3	224	SINNBERG	FT	7	356	SKELTON	AC	12	383
SIMS	FE	1	317	SINEY	W	3	224	SINNOTT	GH	4	346	SKELTON	C	3	385
SIMS	FG	1	317	SINFELD	C	13	387	SIRETT	NGJ	4	346	SKELTON	CH	3	385
SIMS	FJ	3	223	SINFIELD	A	12	203	SIRETT	WHA	3	224	SKELTON	CW	3	224
SIMS	G	2	308	SINFIELD	AW	13	387	SIRIETT	WJ	3	224	SKELTON	D	2	309
SIMS	H	13	387	SINFIELD	CJ	12	203	SIRRELL	S	6	371	SKELTON	D	2	309
SIMS	HE	4	345	SINFIELD	D	12	203	SIRRS	T	6	371	SKELTON	E	7	356
SIMS	HF	7	355	SINFIELD	D	13	387	SISMAN	D	6	371	SKELTON	GH	3	386
SIMS	JH	12	203	SINFIELD	GA	13	387	SISMAN	GH	6	371	SKELTON	GH	7	356
SIMS	JW	3	223	SINFIELD	GE	5	321	SISSINS	FJ	8	313	SKELTON	HW	1	318

SKELTON	J	8	313	SKINKIS	F	11	344	SKINNER	WF	1	318	SLADE	AG	2	310
SKELTON	R	14	291	SKINNER	A	7	356	SKINNER	WG	3	386	SLADE	AG	4	347
SKELTON	T	3	224	SKINNER	AE	1	318	SKINNER	WH	1	318	SLADE	AJ	9	341
SKELTON	T	5	321	SKINNER	AE	4	346	SKINNER	WH	4	346	SLADE	AT	7	357
SKELTON	T	11	343	SKINNER	AF	10	210	SKINNER	WJ	1	318	SLADE	B	4	347
SKELTON	WHJ	11	343	SKINNER	AP	10	210	SKINNER	WJ	12	204	SLADE	B	4	347
SKELTON	WJ	13	388	SKINNER	B	3	386	SKINNER	WN	13	388	SLADE	E	4	347
SKENE	J	4	346	SKINNER	BS	1	318	SKINNER	WTR	10	366	SLADE	EH	12	204
SKENNERTON	T	1	318	SKINNER	CA	2	309	SKIPP	A	4	347	SLADE	ER	3	225
SKERMAN	W	12	204	SKINNER	CA	10	210	SKIPP	A	6	372	SLADE	FJ	13	389
SKERRETT	JW	11	343	SKINNER	CJ	4	346	SKIPP	WJ	13	389	SLADE	GFW	7	357
SKERRITT	H	11	344	SKINNER	CR	1	318	SKIPPER	B	6	372	SLADE	H	1	319
SKERRITT	H	14	291	SKINNER	EA	1	318	SKIPPER	G	7	356	SLADE	H	7	357
SKERRITT	I	2	309	SKINNER	EHJ	3	224	SKIPPER	L	7	357	SLADE	H	8	313
SKERRY	W	10	366	SKINNER	EJ	7	356	SKIPPER	RL	1	318	SLADE	HE	2	310
SKETCHER	F	13	388	SKINNER	EM	12	383	SKIPPER	WA	13	389	SLADE	HJ	10	210
SKETCHER	G	4	346	SKINNER	EW	12	204	SKIPPER	WE	7	357	SLADE	J	8	313
SKETCHER	HW	4	346	SKINNER	F	6	371	SKIPPER	WR	3	386	SLADE	J	10	366
SKETCHLEY	J	12	383	SKINNER	F	9	341	SKIPPERS	J	11	344	SLADE	JH	6	372
SKETT	R	6	371	SKINNER	F	13	388	SKIRROW	H	9	341	SLADE	PE	2	310
SKETT	S	6	371	SKINNER	FG	5	322	SKIRROW	JH	9	175	SLADE	PJ	12	204
SKEVINGTON	CE	12	204	SKINNER	FJ	7	356	SKITT	A	11	344	SLADE	RH	5	322
SKEVINGTON	FWJ	12	204	SKINNER	FL	3	224	SKITT	R	11	344	SLADE	RH	13	389
SKEVINGTON	PE	12	204	SKINNER	FW	5	321	SKITTLETHORPE	EAJ	4	347	SLADE	TA	7	357
SKEVY	GA	11	344	SKINNER	G	9	341	SKITTLETHORPE	JG	4	347	SLADE	TH	7	357
SKEWS	AGW	2	309	SKINNER	G	13	388	SKOTTOW	F	7	357	SLADE	W	6	372
SKIDMORE	AG	3	224	SKINNER	G	13	388	SKUDDER	ET	7	357	SLADE	W	10	210
SKIDMORE	D	6	371	SKINNER	G	14	291	SKUDDER	T	7	357	SLADE	WH	2	310
SKIDMORE	D	11	424	SKINNER	GD	10	210	SKUES	G	3	225	SLADE	WJA	5	322
SKIDMORE	E	6	371	SKINNER	GFW	5	321	SKUES	HFC	3	386	SLADE	WR	2	310
SKIDMORE	F	6	371	SKINNER	GV	7	356	SKUES	V	3	225	SLADER	WJ	10	366
SKIDMORE	FW	6	371	SKINNER	H	2	309	SKULL	GH	1	319	SLAMER	A	6	372
SKIDMORE	GF	6	371	SKINNER	HF	3	386	SKULL	JJ	1	319	SLANEY	EA	9	341
SKIDMORE	J	7	356	SKINNER	HJ	13	388	SKULL	LC	2	310	SLANEY	EJ	5	322
SKIDMORE	T	6	371	SKINNER	HV	10	210	SKUSE	GL	1	319	SLANEY	T	6	372
SKIDMORE	W	6	371	SKINNER	J	13	388	SLACK	A	11	344	SLANEY	W	7	357
SKIDMORE	W	11	344	SKINNER	JA	2	309	SLACK	C	11	344	SLANEY	WE	5	322
SKILBECK	J	9	341	SKINNER	JE	1	318	SLACK	CF	13	389	SLAPE	W	10	210
SKILBECK	T	9	341	SKINNER	JH	3	386	SLACK	E	1	319	SLATER	A	3	386
SKILLERN	C	11	344	SKINNER	JJ	2	309	SLACK	F	13	389	SLATER	A	4	347
SKILLETER	GH	2	309	SKINNER	LT	7	356	SLACK	FE	11	344	SLATER	A	6	372
SKILLMAN	E	12	383	SKINNER	M	2	310	SLACK	GH	13	389	SLATER	A	7	357
SKILLMAN	F	12	383	SKINNER	OJ	6	371	SLACK	HA	8	313	SLATER	A	8	314
SKILTON	A	7	356	SKINNER	PG	3	224	SLACK	J	11	344	SLATER	A	8	314
SKILTON	C	3	224	SKINNER	R	5	322	SLACK	J	13	389	SLATER	AE	4	347
SKILTON	CL	4	346	SKINNER	RF	5	322	SLACK	J	14	291	SLATER	AE	8	314
SKILTON	E	3	224	SKINNER	SF	13	388	SLACK	JW	14	291	SLATER	AW	7	357
SKILTON	SJ	4	346	SKINNER	SH	4	346	SLADDEN	AE	13	389	SLATER	C	8	314
SKILTON	T	10	366	SKINNER	SJ	3	386	SLADDEN	E	13	389	SLATER	C	9	175
SKINGLE	C	2	309	SKINNER	SJ	13	388	SLADDEN	W	13	389	SLATER	C	10	366
SKINGLE	E	7	356	SKINNER	TR	13	388	SLADDIN	A	9	341	SLATER	CW	2	310
SKINGLE	EG	7	356	SKINNER	W	9	341	SLADDIN	C	2	310	SLATER	D	12	384
SKINGLEY	AW	13	388	SKINNER	W	13	388	SLADE	A	1	319	SLATER	E	6	372
SKINGLEY	E	13	388	SKINNER	W	13	388	SLADE	A	5	322	SLATER	E	9	341
SKINGSLEY	GS	1	318	SKINNER	WE	12	204	SLADE	AE	3	225	SLATER	E	10	366

Surname	Initials	Col	Page
SLATER	E	12	384
SLATER	EG	12	204
SLATER	EJ	12	204
SLATER	F	8	314
SLATER	F	11	344
SLATER	F	12	204
SLATER	FF	12	204
SLATER	FJ	3	386
SLATER	G	14	291
SLATER	GA	3	386
SLATER	GH	3	225
SLATER	GH	9	175
SLATER	H	2	310
SLATER	H	5	322
SLATER	H	8	314
SLATER	H	9	341
SLATER	H	11	344
SLATER	H	14	291
SLATER	H	14	292
SLATER	HW	7	357
SLATER	J	2	310
SLATER	J	3	386
SLATER	J	7	357
SLATER	J	8	314
SLATER	J	9	341
SLATER	J	13	389
SLATER	J	14	292
SLATER	J	14	292
SLATER	JG	2	310
SLATER	JH	10	366
SLATER	L	2	310
SLATER	MG	9	175
SLATER	R	14	292
SLATER	RG	2	310
SLATER	SC	1	319
SLATER	SF	2	310
SLATER	T	6	372
SLATER	T	8	314
SLATER	T	14	292
SLATER	TB	8	314
SLATER	W	9	342
SLATER	W	9	342
SLATER	W	10	366
SLATER	W	11	344
SLATER	WA	12	204
SLATER	WE	4	347
SLATER	WG	7	357
SLATER	WJ	4	347
SLATER	WT	7	357
SLATTER	A	2	310
SLATTER	C	7	358
SLATTER	CH	1	319
SLATTER	F	8	314
SLATTER	F	13	389
SLATTER	GH	13	389
SLATTER	H	1	319
SLATTER	M	1	319
SLATTER	TA	2	310
SLATTER	W	7	358
SLATTER	WH	7	358
SLATTERY	D	14	292
SLATTERY	F	11	344
SLATTERY	JJ	9	342
SLATTERY	P	11	344
SLAUGHTER	CA	13	389
SLAUGHTER	H	1	319
SLAUGHTER	H	1	319
SLAUGHTER	H	5	322
SLAUGHTER	JF	13	389
SLAUGHTER	N	5	322
SLAUGHTER	S	10	210
SLAUGHTER	WH	12	204
SLAUGHTER	WJ	3	386
SLAYFORD	C	13	389
SLAYFORD	W	13	389
SLAYMAKER	EW	10	366
SLAYMAKER	JT	1	319
SLEAMAN	LNA	10	210
SLEAP	RH	2	310
SLEDGE	WGS	10	366
SLEDMAR	TG	7	358
SLEE	J	1	319
SLEE	WJ	2	311
SLEEMAN	AH	4	347
SLEEP	WH	9	342
SLEEP	WH	10	366
SLEET	AF	1	319
SLEET	AH	7	358
SLEET	H	12	384
SLEGG	FA	14	292
SLEGG	RC	14	292
SLEIGH	F	14	292
SLEIGH	JH	14	292
SLEIGHT	A	8	314
SLEIGHT	EG	5	322
SLEIGHTHOLME	J	8	314
SLEIGTH	H	9	342
SLEITH	W	8	314
SLEMON	WH	10	366
SLETCHER	CT	12	204
SLETCHER	GWH	12	204
SLEVIN	F	1	319
SLIDEL	CN	10	210
SLIEGHT	W	8	314
SLIGHT	S	4	347
SLIGHT	WHJ	4	347
SLIMING	F	9	342
SLIMING	G	9	342
SLINEY	WE	10	210
SLING	W	11	344
SLINGER	C	8	314
SLINGER	C	8	314
SLINGER	H	8	314
SLINGER	R	9	175
SLINGER	W	9	342
SLINGER	WJ	7	358
SLINGO	FD	10	210
SLINGSBY	H	9	342
SLINGSBY	H	9	342
SLINGSBY	JH	3	386
SLINGSBY	L	9	175
SLINGSBY	TH	9	342
SLINGSLEY	JW	9	392
SLINN	F	12	384
SLINN	FH	12	384
SLINN	G	9	342
SLINN	R	12	384
SLINN	TD	12	384
SLINN	WC	12	384
SLOAN	J	14	292
SLOAN	P	8	314
SLOAN	T	3	386
SLOAN	TD	14	292
SLOAN	VS	2	311
SLOANE	A	6	372
SLOANE	E	9	175
SLOANE	F	14	292
SLOANE	H	11	344
SLOANE	ID	9	175
SLOANE	J	11	345
SLOANE	JH	11	345
SLOANE	R	6	372
SLOANE	R	8	314
SLOANE	T	6	372
SLOCOMBE	A	3	386
SLOCOMBE	AG	4	347
SLOCOMBE	DW	4	347
SLOCOMBE	R	7	358
SLOCOMBE	W	10	210
SLOGGETT	ER	2	311
SLOGGETT	F	2	311
SLOGGETT	JW	1	319
SLOPER	CJ	5	322
SLOUGH	E	5	322
SLOUGH	EC	5	322
SLOUGH	F	7	358
SLOUGH	H	5	322
SLOUGH	HW	5	322
SLOUGH	J	5	322
SLOUGH	JA	7	358
SLOUGH	JR	7	358
SLOUGH	RW	5	323
SLOW	P	10	211
SLOWE	E	14	292
SLOWLEY	HCJ	13	389
SLUMAN	AJ	7	358
SLUMAN	GE	7	358
SLY	AE	5	323
SLY	AG	4	347
SLY	JW	4	347
SLYDEL	E	7	358
SLYNE	D	12	384
SMAILES	B	8	314
SMALE	EJ	7	358
SMALE	HG	7	358
SMALE	J	7	358
SMALE	JHH	13	389
SMALE	RWV	7	359
SMALES	J	8	314
SMALES	W	8	315
SMALES	W	8	315
SMALING	TH	8	315
SMALL	A	9	342
SMALL	AV	7	359
SMALL	B	5	323
SMALL	C	3	386
SMALL	C	9	175
SMALL	CW	10	211
SMALL	E	4	347
SMALL	F	6	372
SMALL	FE	7	359
SMALL	FH	2	311
SMALL	FW	13	390
SMALL	G	1	319
SMALL	G	3	386
SMALL	G	6	372
SMALL	G	7	359
SMALL	JA	1	319
SMALL	JJ	1	320
SMALL	JW	9	175
SMALL	L	1	320
SMALL	M	3	386
SMALL	R	3	386
SMALL	R	3	387
SMALL	T	10	211
SMALL	TW	4	348
SMALL	W	7	359
SMALL	WA	3	387
SMALL	WC	10	366
SMALL	WJ	3	387
SMALL	WP	2	311
SMALLBONE	AJ	10	367
SMALLBONE	F	4	348
SMALLBONE	H	3	387
SMALLBONE	J	10	367
SMALLBONE	NF	3	387
SMALLBONE	W	2	311
SMALLBONES	A	5	323
SMALLBONES	CA	13	390
SMALLBONES	J	5	323

Surname	Initials	Col	Pg	Surname	Initials	Col	Pg	Surname	Initials	Col	Pg	Surname	Initials	Col	Pg
SMALLEY	A	8	315	SMART	GF	12	384	SMETZER	FC	13	390	SMITH	A	8	315
SMALLEY	E	8	315	SMART	GS	5	323	SMETZER	SC	13	390	SMITH	A	8	315
SMALLEY	F	8	315	SMART	H	1	320	SMEWING	W	3	387	SMITH	A	8	316
SMALLEY	FW	9	175	SMART	H	5	323	SMICKERSGILL	JA	8	315	SMITH	A	8	316
SMALLEY	J	8	315	SMART	H	12	205	SMICKERSGILL	ME	8	315	SMITH	A	8	316
SMALLEY	L	9	175	SMART	H	12	384	SMILLIE	R	8	315	SMITH	A	8	316
SMALLEY	W	8	315	SMART	HJ	12	205	SMIRK	TGH	4	348	SMITH	A	8	316
SMALLMAN	FN	6	372	SMART	HW	13	390	SMIRTHWAITE	C	6	373	SMITH	A	8	316
SMALLSHAW	S	14	292	SMART	J	6	373	SMIRTHWAITE	E	6	373	SMITH	A	8	316
SMALLSHAW	W	11	345	SMART	J	8	315	SMIRTHWAITE	WAN	6	373	SMITH	A	8	316
SMALLSHAW	WH	14	292	SMART	J	12	205	SMITCH	J	10	211	SMITH	A	8	316
SMALLWOOD	AG	6	372	SMART	J	14	293	SMITH	A	1	320	SMITH	A	8	316
SMALLWOOD	DF	4	348	SMART	JJ	7	359	SMITH	A	1	320	SMITH	A	8	316
SMALLWOOD	E	6	372	SMART	JW	12	384	SMITH	A	1	320	SMITH	A	9	175
SMALLWOOD	F	7	359	SMART	M	7	359	SMITH	A	1	320	SMITH	A	9	175
SMALLWOOD	GE	4	348	SMART	RH	8	315	SMITH	A	2	311	SMITH	A	9	175
SMALLWOOD	H	9	342	SMART	S	7	359	SMITH	A	2	311	SMITH	A	9	175
SMALLWOOD	J	6	372	SMART	SJ	5	323	SMITH	A	2	311	SMITH	A	9	175
SMALLWOOD	J	8	315	SMART	TE	4	348	SMITH	A	2	311	SMITH	A	9	176
SMALLWOOD	J	11	345	SMART	TW	5	323	SMITH	A	2	311	SMITH	A	9	176
SMALLWOOD	R	8	315	SMART	W	2	311	SMITH	A	2	311	SMITH	A	9	342
SMALLWOOD	R	8	315	SMART	W	7	359	SMITH	A	3	225	SMITH	A	9	342
SMALLWOOD	SG	7	359	SMART	WA	6	373	SMITH	A	3	225	SMITH	A	9	342
SMALLWOOD	TA	6	372	SMART	WF	12	384	SMITH	A	3	225	SMITH	A	9	342
SMALLWOOD	W	6	372	SMART	WJ	12	205	SMITH	A	3	387	SMITH	A	9	342
SMALLWOOD	W	11	345	SMART	WS	10	211	SMITH	A	4	348	SMITH	A	9	343
SMALLWOOD	W	11	345	SMART	WS	12	384	SMITH	A	4	348	SMITH	A	9	343
SMALLY	JH	6	373	SMART	WW	4	348	SMITH	A	4	348	SMITH	A	10	211
SMARDON	AJ	6	373	SMEATH	AJ	7	359	SMITH	A	5	323	SMITH	A	11	345
SMART	A	1	320	SMEATON	E	11	345	SMITH	A	5	323	SMITH	A	11	345
SMART	A	12	384	SMEATON	G	11	345	SMITH	A	5	323	SMITH	A	11	345
SMART	AE	12	204	SMEDLEY	HV	12	384	SMITH	A	5	323	SMITH	A	11	345
SMART	AF	5	323	SMEDLEY	PW	12	384	SMITH	A	5	323	SMITH	A	11	345
SMART	C	12	204	SMEE	C	4	348	SMITH	A	5	324	SMITH	A	11	346
SMART	CJ	2	311	SMEE	EH	1	320	SMITH	A	5	324	SMITH	A	11	346
SMART	E	6	373	SMEE	HC	5	323	SMITH	A	5	324	SMITH	A	11	346
SMART	E	12	384	SMEE	W	4	348	SMITH	A	5	324	SMITH	A	11	346
SMART	EA	10	211	SMEE	WH	7	359	SMITH	A	6	373	SMITH	A	11	346
SMART	EF	5	323	SMEED	DA	9	342	SMITH	A	6	373	SMITH	A	11	346
SMART	EH	6	373	SMEES	EJ	10	211	SMITH	A	6	373	SMITH	A	12	205
SMART	EJ	12	204	SMEES	GJ	10	211	SMITH	A	6	373	SMITH	A	12	205
SMART	EP	3	387	SMEETH	FL	2	311	SMITH	A	6	373	SMITH	A	12	205
SMART	ER	5	323	SMEETH	I	4	348	SMITH	A	6	373	SMITH	A	12	384
SMART	F	3	387	SMELLIE	J	8	315	SMITH	A	6	373	SMITH	A	12	384
SMART	F	6	373	SMETHAM	RC	4	348	SMITH	A	6	373	SMITH	A	12	385
SMART	F	7	359	SMETHURST	A	11	345	SMITH	A	6	374	SMITH	A	12	385
SMART	F	12	204	SMETHURST	CR	11	345	SMITH	A	6	374	SMITH	A	12	385
SMART	F	12	205	SMETHURST	H	11	345	SMITH	A	7	359	SMITH	A	12	385
SMART	F	14	292	SMETHURST	J	14	293	SMITH	A	7	359	SMITH	A	13	390
SMART	FC	10	211	SMETHURST	RA	14	293	SMITH	A	7	359	SMITH	A	13	390
SMART	FW	10	211	SMETHURST	TJ	14	293	SMITH	A	7	359	SMITH	A	13	390
SMART	G	6	373	SMETHURST	W	11	345	SMITH	A	7	359	SMITH	A	13	390
SMART	G	13	390	SMETHURST	W	14	293	SMITH	A	7	360	SMITH	A	13	390
SMART	G	14	292	SMETHURST	WB	14	293	SMITH	A	8	315	SMITH	A	13	390
SMART	G	14	292	SMETHURST	WW	14	293	SMITH	A	8	315	SMITH	A	13	390

Name	Init.	No.	Pg.	Name	Init.	No.	Pg.	Name	Init.	No.	Pg.	Name	Init.	No.	Pg.
SMITH	A	13	390	SMITH	AE	7	360	SMITH	AJ	12	385	SMITH	B	9	343
SMITH	A	13	390	SMITH	AE	7	360	SMITH	AJ	13	391	SMITH	B	10	367
SMITH	A	14	293	SMITH	AE	8	316	SMITH	AJ	13	391	SMITH	B	12	385
SMITH	A	14	293	SMITH	AE	11	346	SMITH	AJ	14	294	SMITH	BA	5	325
SMITH	A	14	293	SMITH	AE	12	385	SMITH	AJC	2	312	SMITH	BF	12	205
SMITH	A	14	293	SMITH	AE	13	390	SMITH	AJJ	2	312	SMITH	BH	3	225
SMITH	A	14	293	SMITH	AE	13	390	SMITH	AJT	10	367	SMITH	BH	12	385
SMITH	A	14	293	SMITH	AE	13	390	SMITH	AM	2	312	SMITH	BJ	5	325
SMITH	A	14	293	SMITH	AE	14	293	SMITH	AM	5	324	SMITH	BJ	7	361
SMITH	A	14	293	SMITH	AEJ	13	390	SMITH	AO	4	349	SMITH	BJE	14	294
SMITH	A	14	293	SMITH	AF	4	348	SMITH	AP	2	312	SMITH	BW	7	360
SMITH	A	14	293	SMITH	AG	1	320	SMITH	AP	7	360	SMITH	BW	14	294
SMITH	AA	2	311	SMITH	AG	2	312	SMITH	AP	13	391	SMITH	C	1	320
SMITH	AA	4	348	SMITH	AG	3	225	SMITH	AR	3	225	SMITH	C	1	320
SMITH	AB	4	348	SMITH	AG	3	225	SMITH	AR	7	360	SMITH	C	2	312
SMITH	AC	1	320	SMITH	AG	3	225	SMITH	AR	10	367	SMITH	C	2	312
SMITH	AC	3	387	SMITH	AG	3	225	SMITH	AR	13	391	SMITH	C	2	312
SMITH	AC	5	324	SMITH	AG	4	349	SMITH	AR	14	294	SMITH	C	2	312
SMITH	AC	5	324	SMITH	AG	5	324	SMITH	AS	6	374	SMITH	C	2	312
SMITH	AC	10	211	SMITH	AG	5	324	SMITH	AS	9	176	SMITH	C	3	225
SMITH	AC	12	385	SMITH	AG	6	374	SMITH	AS	13	391	SMITH	C	3	226
SMITH	AC	12	385	SMITH	AG	10	211	SMITH	AT	4	349	SMITH	C	3	226
SMITH	AC	12	385	SMITH	AG	12	205	SMITH	AT	6	374	SMITH	C	4	349
SMITH	AC	13	390	SMITH	AG	13	390	SMITH	AT	7	360	SMITH	C	4	349
SMITH	AD	12	385	SMITH	AG	13	391	SMITH	AT	10	211	SMITH	C	4	349
SMITH	AD	14	293	SMITH	AGE	10	211	SMITH	AT	12	385	SMITH	C	4	349
SMITH	AE	1	320	SMITH	AH	3	225	SMITH	AV	4	349	SMITH	C	4	349
SMITH	AE	1	320	SMITH	AH	3	225	SMITH	AV	7	360	SMITH	C	5	325
SMITH	AE	1	320	SMITH	AH	4	348	SMITH	AV	7	360	SMITH	C	5	325
SMITH	AE	2	312	SMITH	AH	5	324	SMITH	AV	7	360	SMITH	C	5	325
SMITH	AE	2	312	SMITH	AH	6	374	SMITH	AV	12	205	SMITH	C	6	374
SMITH	AE	2	312	SMITH	AH	10	367	SMITH	AW	4	349	SMITH	C	6	374
SMITH	AE	2	312	SMITH	AH	12	205	SMITH	AW	5	324	SMITH	C	6	374
SMITH	AE	3	225	SMITH	AH	12	385	SMITH	AW	5	325	SMITH	C	7	361
SMITH	AE	3	225	SMITH	AH	12	385	SMITH	AW	5	325	SMITH	C	7	361
SMITH	AE	3	225	SMITH	AH	13	391	SMITH	AW	5	325	SMITH	C	7	361
SMITH	AE	3	387	SMITH	AJ	1	320	SMITH	AW	6	374	SMITH	C	7	361
SMITH	AE	3	387	SMITH	AJ	3	387	SMITH	AW	7	360	SMITH	C	8	316
SMITH	AE	4	348	SMITH	AJ	4	349	SMITH	AW	8	316	SMITH	C	8	316
SMITH	AE	4	348	SMITH	AJ	4	349	SMITH	AW	10	367	SMITH	C	8	316
SMITH	AE	5	324	SMITH	AJ	4	349	SMITH	AW	12	205	SMITH	C	10	211
SMITH	AE	5	324	SMITH	AJ	4	349	SMITH	AW	12	205	SMITH	C	10	367
SMITH	AE	5	324	SMITH	AJ	5	324	SMITH	AW	12	205	SMITH	C	11	346
SMITH	AE	5	324	SMITH	AJ	5	324	SMITH	AW	12	385	SMITH	C	11	346
SMITH	AE	6	374	SMITH	AJ	6	374	SMITH	AWJ	11	346	SMITH	C	12	205
SMITH	AE	6	374	SMITH	AJ	6	374	SMITH	AWJ	13	391	SMITH	C	12	385
SMITH	AE	6	374	SMITH	AJ	7	360	SMITH	AWM	4	349	SMITH	C	12	385
SMITH	AE	6	374	SMITH	AJ	7	360	SMITH	B	2	312	SMITH	C	13	391
SMITH	AE	7	360	SMITH	AJ	7	360	SMITH	B	4	349	SMITH	C	13	391
SMITH	AE	7	360	SMITH	AJ	7	360	SMITH	B	4	349	SMITH	C	14	294
SMITH	AE	7	360	SMITH	AJ	10	211	SMITH	B	6	374	SMITH	CA	1	320
SMITH	AE	7	360	SMITH	AJ	10	211	SMITH	B	7	360	SMITH	CA	5	325
SMITH	AE	7	360	SMITH	AJ	10	367	SMITH	B	8	316	SMITH	CA	10	212
SMITH	AE	7	360	SMITH	AJ	12	205	SMITH	B	9	176	SMITH	CA	12	205
SMITH				SMITH				SMITH	B	9	176	SMITH			

Name	Initials	Col	Page
SMITH	CA	12	385
SMITH	CB	7	361
SMITH	CC	1	321
SMITH	CC	3	226
SMITH	CC	11	346
SMITH	CE	1	321
SMITH	CE	1	321
SMITH	CE	6	374
SMITH	CE	8	316
SMITH	CE	8	316
SMITH	CE	10	212
SMITH	CE	12	205
SMITH	CEJ	12	385
SMITH	CEM	9	176
SMITH	CF	1	321
SMITH	CF	1	321
SMITH	CF	4	349
SMITH	CF	5	325
SMITH	CF	7	361
SMITH	CF	12	205
SMITH	CF	12	386
SMITH	CFJ	2	312
SMITH	CG	1	321
SMITH	CG	3	387
SMITH	CG	5	325
SMITH	CH	4	349
SMITH	CH	4	350
SMITH	CH	4	350
SMITH	CH	5	325
SMITH	CH	7	361
SMITH	CH	8	317
SMITH	CH	8	317
SMITH	CH	13	391
SMITH	CH	14	294
SMITH	CJ	5	325
SMITH	CJ	7	361
SMITH	CJ	7	361
SMITH	CJ	13	391
SMITH	CJS	5	325
SMITH	CN	1	321
SMITH	CS	1	321
SMITH	CS	13	391
SMITH	CS	14	294
SMITH	CSB	5	325
SMITH	CT	4	350
SMITH	CW	2	312
SMITH	CW	3	226
SMITH	CW	3	387
SMITH	CW	3	387
SMITH	CW	5	325
SMITH	CW	5	325
SMITH	CW	9	343
SMITH	CW	10	212
SMITH	CW	12	206
SMITH	CW	12	206
SMITH	CW	13	391
SMITH	CWA	12	206
SMITH	D	1	321
SMITH	D	3	226
SMITH	D	7	361
SMITH	D	9	176
SMITH	D	10	212
SMITH	D	11	346
SMITH	D	14	294
SMITH	D	14	294
SMITH	DE	5	326
SMITH	DEJ	2	313
SMITH	DH	11	346
SMITH	DJ	13	391
SMITH	DO	1	321
SMITH	DS	11	346
SMITH	DT	5	325
SMITH	E	1	321
SMITH	E	1	321
SMITH	E	1	321
SMITH	E	1	321
SMITH	E	2	313
SMITH	E	2	313
SMITH	E	2	313
SMITH	E	2	313
SMITH	E	2	313
SMITH	E	3	226
SMITH	E	3	226
SMITH	E	3	226
SMITH	E	3	226
SMITH	E	4	350
SMITH	E	4	350
SMITH	E	4	350
SMITH	E	4	350
SMITH	E	5	326
SMITH	E	5	326
SMITH	E	5	326
SMITH	E	5	326
SMITH	E	5	326
SMITH	E	5	326
SMITH	E	6	374
SMITH	E	6	375
SMITH	E	6	375
SMITH	E	6	375
SMITH	E	6	375
SMITH	E	6	375
SMITH	E	6	375
SMITH	E	7	361
SMITH	E	8	317
SMITH	E	8	317
SMITH	E	8	317
SMITH	E	8	317
SMITH	E	9	176
SMITH	E	9	176
SMITH	E	9	176
SMITH	E	9	176
SMITH	E	9	176
SMITH	E	9	176
SMITH	E	9	176
SMITH	E	9	343
SMITH	E	10	212
SMITH	E	10	212
SMITH	E	10	212
SMITH	E	10	367
SMITH	E	11	346
SMITH	E	11	346
SMITH	E	11	346
SMITH	E	11	347
SMITH	E	12	206
SMITH	E	12	206
SMITH	E	12	206
SMITH	E	12	386
SMITH	E	12	386
SMITH	E	13	391
SMITH	E	13	391
SMITH	E	14	294
SMITH	E	14	294
SMITH	E	14	294
SMITH	E	14	294
SMITH	EA	3	387
SMITH	EA	6	375
SMITH	EA	13	392
SMITH	EAC	10	367
SMITH	EB	3	387
SMITH	EB	7	361
SMITH	EC	3	387
SMITH	EC	4	350
SMITH	EC	5	326
SMITH	ED	7	361
SMITH	EE	3	226
SMITH	EF	13	391
SMITH	EG	2	313
SMITH	EG	3	387
SMITH	EG	3	388
SMITH	EG	4	350
SMITH	EG	4	350
SMITH	EG	12	206
SMITH	EH	7	361
SMITH	EJ	1	321
SMITH	EJ	2	313
SMITH	EJ	2	313
SMITH	EJ	2	313
SMITH	EJ	5	326
SMITH	EJ	5	326
SMITH	EJ	6	375
SMITH	EJ	10	212
SMITH	EJ	10	212
SMITH	EJ	13	392
SMITH	EL	3	388
SMITH	EL	12	386
SMITH	EM	2	313
SMITH	EM	6	375
SMITH	EN	13	392
SMITH	ER	2	313
SMITH	ES	6	375
SMITH	EV	6	375
SMITH	EV	10	367
SMITH	EW	2	313
SMITH	EW	4	350
SMITH	EW	7	361
SMITH	EW	10	212
SMITH	EW	10	367
SMITH	EWV	10	212
SMITH	F	1	321
SMITH	F	1	321
SMITH	F	1	321
SMITH	F	1	321
SMITH	F	2	313
SMITH	F	2	313
SMITH	F	2	313
SMITH	F	2	313
SMITH	F	2	314
SMITH	F	2	314
SMITH	F	3	226
SMITH	F	3	388
SMITH	F	4	350
SMITH	F	4	350
SMITH	F	5	326
SMITH	F	5	326
SMITH	F	5	326
SMITH	F	5	326
SMITH	F	6	375
SMITH	F	6	375
SMITH	F	6	375
SMITH	F	6	375
SMITH	F	6	375
SMITH	F	6	375
SMITH	F	6	376
SMITH	F	6	376
SMITH	F	6	376
SMITH	F	6	376
SMITH	F	7	361
SMITH	F	7	361
SMITH	F	7	362
SMITH	F	7	362
SMITH	F	7	362
SMITH	F	7	362
SMITH	F	8	317
SMITH	F	9	176
SMITH	F	9	176
SMITH	F	9	176

SMITH	F	9	176	SMITH	FG	5	326	SMITH	G	2	314	SMITH	G	14	294
SMITH	F	9	176	SMITH	FG	6	376	SMITH	G	2	314	SMITH	G	14	294
SMITH	F	9	177	SMITH	FG	6	376	SMITH	G	2	314	SMITH	G	14	294
SMITH	F	9	343	SMITH	FG	10	212	SMITH	G	2	314	SMITH	GA	1	322
SMITH	F	9	343	SMITH	FG	10	367	SMITH	G	2	314	SMITH	GA	6	376
SMITH	F	9	343	SMITH	FG	13	392	SMITH	G	3	226	SMITH	GA	7	363
SMITH	F	9	343	SMITH	FH	4	350	SMITH	G	3	388	SMITH	GA	7	363
SMITH	F	9	343	SMITH	FJ	2	314	SMITH	G	3	388	SMITH	GA	8	317
SMITH	F	10	212	SMITH	FJ	4	350	SMITH	G	4	350	SMITH	GA	8	317
SMITH	F	10	367	SMITH	FJ	4	350	SMITH	G	4	350	SMITH	GA	10	213
SMITH	F	11	346	SMITH	FJ	4	350	SMITH	G	5	327	SMITH	GA	13	392
SMITH	F	11	347	SMITH	FJ	5	326	SMITH	G	5	327	SMITH	GA	14	295
SMITH	F	11	347	SMITH	FJ	5	327	SMITH	G	5	327	SMITH	GB	4	350
SMITH	F	11	347	SMITH	FJ	7	362	SMITH	G	5	327	SMITH	GC	1	322
SMITH	F	11	347	SMITH	FJ	7	362	SMITH	G	6	376	SMITH	GC	2	314
SMITH	F	11	347	SMITH	FJ	10	212	SMITH	G	6	376	SMITH	GC	8	317
SMITH	F	11	347	SMITH	FJ	10	212	SMITH	G	6	376	SMITH	GC	8	317
SMITH	F	11	347	SMITH	FJ	10	212	SMITH	G	6	376	SMITH	GC	13	392
SMITH	F	12	206	SMITH	FJ	11	347	SMITH	G	6	376	SMITH	GE	1	322
SMITH	F	12	206	SMITH	FJ	13	392	SMITH	G	6	376	SMITH	GE	4	351
SMITH	F	12	206	SMITH	FJ	13	392	SMITH	G	7	362	SMITH	GE	5	327
SMITH	F	12	386	SMITH	FJG	1	322	SMITH	G	7	362	SMITH	GE	7	363
SMITH	F	13	392	SMITH	FJH	2	314	SMITH	G	7	362	SMITH	GE	8	318
SMITH	F	13	392	SMITH	FL	6	376	SMITH	G	7	363	SMITH	GE	11	347
SMITH	F	14	294	SMITH	FL	7	362	SMITH	G	7	363	SMITH	GE	12	206
SMITH	F	14	294	SMITH	FL	8	317	SMITH	G	8	317	SMITH	GE	12	386
SMITH	F	14	294	SMITH	FL	10	367	SMITH	G	8	317	SMITH	GE	12	386
SMITH	FA	2	314	SMITH	FO	3	226	SMITH	G	8	317	SMITH	GF	3	388
SMITH	FA	2	314	SMITH	FP	10	212	SMITH	G	8	317	SMITH	GF	4	351
SMITH	FA	7	362	SMITH	FR	3	226	SMITH	G	8	317	SMITH	GF	5	327
SMITH	FA	7	362	SMITH	FS	3	226	SMITH	G	8	317	SMITH	GFO	4	351
SMITH	FA	12	206	SMITH	FS	4	350	SMITH	G	8	317	SMITH	GG	4	351
SMITH	FA	13	392	SMITH	FT	2	314	SMITH	G	8	317	SMITH	GG	4	351
SMITH	FB	5	326	SMITH	FT	5	326	SMITH	G	8	317	SMITH	GH	1	322
SMITH	FB	7	362	SMITH	FT	12	386	SMITH	G	9	177	SMITH	GH	2	314
SMITH	FC	1	321	SMITH	FW	5	327	SMITH	G	9	177	SMITH	GH	2	314
SMITH	FC	3	226	SMITH	FW	5	327	SMITH	G	9	177	SMITH	GH	3	226
SMITH	FC	5	326	SMITH	FW	6	376	SMITH	G	9	343	SMITH	GH	3	388
SMITH	FC	6	376	SMITH	FW	6	376	SMITH	G	9	343	SMITH	GH	4	351
SMITH	FC	7	362	SMITH	FW	7	362	SMITH	G	9	343	SMITH	GH	6	377
SMITH	FC	12	206	SMITH	FW	7	362	SMITH	G	9	343	SMITH	GH	6	377
SMITH	FC	12	386	SMITH	FW	9	343	SMITH	G	9	343	SMITH	GH	8	318
SMITH	FCT	1	322	SMITH	FW	12	206	SMITH	G	10	212	SMITH	GH	9	177
SMITH	FD	2	314	SMITH	FW	12	206	SMITH	G	10	212	SMITH	GH	10	213
SMITH	FD	5	326	SMITH	FW	13	392	SMITH	G	10	212	SMITH	GH	10	213
SMITH	FD	12	386	SMITH	FW	14	294	SMITH	G	10	367	SMITH	GH	10	367
SMITH	FD	13	392	SMITH	FWJ	3	226	SMITH	G	11	347	SMITH	GH	12	386
SMITH	FE	1	322	SMITH	FWJ	5	327	SMITH	G	11	347	SMITH	GH	13	392
SMITH	FE	6	376	SMITH	G	1	322	SMITH	G	11	347	SMITH	GH	13	392
SMITH	FE	7	362	SMITH	G	1	322	SMITH	G	12	206	SMITH	GH	13	392
SMITH	FE	7	362	SMITH	G	1	322	SMITH	G	12	386	SMITH	GH	14	295
SMITH	FE	13	392	SMITH	G	1	322	SMITH	G	12	386	SMITH	GHR	8	318
SMITH	FF	7	362	SMITH	G	2	314	SMITH	G	12	386	SMITH	GI	5	327
SMITH	FG	2	314	SMITH	G	2	314	SMITH	G	12	386	SMITH	GJ	3	388
SMITH	FG	3	226	SMITH	G	2	314	SMITH	G	12	386	SMITH	GJ	4	351

SMITH	GJ	7	363	SMITH	H	6	377	SMITH	H	14	295	SMITH	HP	6	377
SMITH	GJC	2	315	SMITH	H	6	377	SMITH	H	14	295	SMITH	HP	6	377
SMITH	GK	10	213	SMITH	H	6	377	SMITH	H	14	295	SMITH	HP	7	364
SMITH	GL	10	213	SMITH	H	7	363	SMITH	HA	1	322	SMITH	HPW	1	323
SMITH	GL	13	392	SMITH	H	7	363	SMITH	HA	2	315	SMITH	HR	1	323
SMITH	GM	14	295	SMITH	H	7	363	SMITH	HA	2	315	SMITH	HR	6	377
SMITH	GP	3	388	SMITH	H	7	363	SMITH	HA	2	315	SMITH	HR	10	213
SMITH	GP	7	363	SMITH	H	7	363	SMITH	HA	3	388	SMITH	HS	2	315
SMITH	GR	9	177	SMITH	H	8	318	SMITH	HA	7	363	SMITH	HS	2	315
SMITH	GS	2	315	SMITH	H	8	318	SMITH	HA	12	206	SMITH	HS	5	328
SMITH	GS	7	363	SMITH	H	8	318	SMITH	HA	13	393	SMITH	HS	5	328
SMITH	GS	9	343	SMITH	H	8	318	SMITH	HC	1	322	SMITH	HS	7	364
SMITH	GS	12	386	SMITH	H	8	318	SMITH	HC	6	377	SMITH	HS	10	213
SMITH	GT	3	388	SMITH	H	8	318	SMITH	HC	12	386	SMITH	HS	12	387
SMITH	GT	5	327	SMITH	H	8	318	SMITH	HD	12	206	SMITH	HT	13	393
SMITH	GT	7	363	SMITH	H	8	318	SMITH	HE	1	322	SMITH	HT	13	393
SMITH	GT	10	368	SMITH	H	8	318	SMITH	HE	3	226	SMITH	HV	5	328
SMITH	GW	1	322	SMITH	H	8	318	SMITH	HE	4	351	SMITH	HV	7	364
SMITH	GW	2	315	SMITH	H	9	177	SMITH	HE	7	364	SMITH	HW	5	328
SMITH	GW	4	351	SMITH	H	9	177	SMITH	HE	7	364	SMITH	HW	7	364
SMITH	GW	5	327	SMITH	H	9	177	SMITH	HF	3	226	SMITH	HW	8	318
SMITH	GW	5	327	SMITH	H	9	177	SMITH	HF	8	318	SMITH	HW	9	344
SMITH	GW	5	327	SMITH	H	9	177	SMITH	HF	10	213	SMITH	HW	10	213
SMITH	GW	5	327	SMITH	H	9	177	SMITH	HF	10	368	SMITH	HW	10	368
SMITH	GW	7	363	SMITH	H	9	177	SMITH	HFT	13	393	SMITH	HW	10	368
SMITH	GW	7	363	SMITH	H	9	343	SMITH	HG	1	322	SMITH	HW	12	387
SMITH	GW	7	363	SMITH	H	9	344	SMITH	HG	1	323	SMITH	HW	13	393
SMITH	H	1	322	SMITH	H	9	344	SMITH	HG	1	323	SMITH	HW	13	393
SMITH	H	1	322	SMITH	H	9	344	SMITH	HG	2	315	SMITH	HWF	4	351
SMITH	H	1	322	SMITH	H	9	344	SMITH	HG	3	226	SMITH	HWF	4	351
SMITH	H	2	315	SMITH	H	10	213	SMITH	HG	5	328	SMITH	HWJ	2	315
SMITH	H	2	315	SMITH	H	10	213	SMITH	HG	7	364	SMITH	I	14	295
SMITH	H	2	315	SMITH	H	10	213	SMITH	HG	12	207	SMITH	I	14	295
SMITH	H	2	315	SMITH	H	10	213	SMITH	HG	13	393	SMITH	IN	8	318
SMITH	H	4	351	SMITH	H	10	368	SMITH	HH	2	315	SMITH	J	1	323
SMITH	H	4	351	SMITH	H	10	368	SMITH	HH	6	377	SMITH	J	1	323
SMITH	H	4	351	SMITH	H	10	368	SMITH	HH	7	364	SMITH	J	1	323
SMITH	H	5	327	SMITH	H	10	368	SMITH	HIO	2	315	SMITH	J	2	315
SMITH	H	5	327	SMITH	H	10	368	SMITH	HJ	3	227	SMITH	J	2	315
SMITH	H	5	327	SMITH	H	11	347	SMITH	HJ	4	351	SMITH	J	2	316
SMITH	H	5	328	SMITH	H	11	347	SMITH	HJ	4	351	SMITH	J	2	316
SMITH	H	5	328	SMITH	H	11	347	SMITH	HJ	5	328	SMITH	J	2	316
SMITH	H	5	328	SMITH	H	11	347	SMITH	HJ	6	377	SMITH	J	3	227
SMITH	H	5	328	SMITH	H	11	347	SMITH	HJ	7	364	SMITH	J	3	227
SMITH	H	6	377	SMITH	H	11	348	SMITH	HJ	7	364	SMITH	J	4	351
SMITH	H	6	377	SMITH	H	11	348	SMITH	HJ	10	213	SMITH	J	4	351
SMITH	H	6	377	SMITH	H	12	386	SMITH	HJ	10	213	SMITH	J	4	352
SMITH	H	6	377	SMITH	H	12	386	SMITH	HJ	12	207	SMITH	J	4	352
SMITH	H	6	377	SMITH	H	13	393	SMITH	HJ	12	207	SMITH	J	4	352
SMITH	H	6	377	SMITH	H	13	393	SMITH	HJ	14	295	SMITH	J	5	328
SMITH	H	6	377	SMITH	H	13	393	SMITH	HK	5	328	SMITH	J	5	328
SMITH	H	7	363	SMITH				SMITH	HL	7	364	SMITH	J	5	328
SMITH	H	7	363	SMITH				SMITH	HL	7	364	SMITH	J	5	328
SMITH	H	8	318	SMITH				SMITH	HM	5	328	SMITH	J	5	328
SMITH	H	8	318	SMITH				SMITH	HO	7	364	SMITH	J	5	329

SMITH	J	5	329	SMITH	J	10	368	SMITH	JD	5	329	SMITH	JJ	2	316
SMITH	J	5	329	SMITH	J	11	348	SMITH	JD	11	348	SMITH	JJ	2	316
SMITH	J	5	329	SMITH	J	11	348	SMITH	JD	13	393	SMITH	JJ	6	378
SMITH	J	5	329	SMITH	J	11	348	SMITH	JE	1	323	SMITH	JJ	9	344
SMITH	J	5	329	SMITH	J	11	348	SMITH	JE	1	323	SMITH	JJ	10	214
SMITH	J	6	378	SMITH	J	11	348	SMITH	JE	2	316	SMITH	JJ	11	349
SMITH	J	6	378	SMITH	J	11	348	SMITH	JE	4	352	SMITH	JJ	12	387
SMITH	J	6	378	SMITH	J	11	348	SMITH	JE	4	352	SMITH	JJ	13	393
SMITH	J	6	378	SMITH	J	11	348	SMITH	JE	6	378	SMITH	JJ	13	394
SMITH	J	6	378	SMITH	J	11	348	SMITH	JE	6	378	SMITH	JJ	13	394
SMITH	J	6	378	SMITH	J	11	348	SMITH	JE	6	378	SMITH	JJ	13	394
SMITH	J	6	378	SMITH	J	11	348	SMITH	JE	7	365	SMITH	JL	8	319
SMITH	J	6	378	SMITH	J	11	348	SMITH	JE	7	365	SMITH	JL	13	394
SMITH	J	6	378	SMITH	J	11	348	SMITH	JE	8	319	SMITH	JL	13	394
SMITH	J	6	378	SMITH	J	12	207	SMITH	JE	8	319	SMITH	JM	3	227
SMITH	J	6	378	SMITH	J	12	207	SMITH	JE	10	368	SMITH	JP	8	319
SMITH	J	6	378	SMITH	J	12	207	SMITH	JF	3	227	SMITH	JR	7	365
SMITH	J	6	378	SMITH	J	12	207	SMITH	JF	7	365	SMITH	JR	14	296
SMITH	J	7	364	SMITH	J	12	207	SMITH	JF	7	365	SMITH	JS	1	323
SMITH	J	7	364	SMITH	J	12	387	SMITH	JF	8	319	SMITH	JS	2	316
SMITH	J	7	364	SMITH	J	12	387	SMITH	JF	11	349	SMITH	JS	2	316
SMITH	J	7	364	SMITH	J	12	387	SMITH	JF	12	207	SMITH	JS	10	214
SMITH	J	7	364	SMITH	J	12	387	SMITH	JFS	11	348	SMITH	JS	10	214
SMITH	J	7	364	SMITH	J	12	387	SMITH	JG	2	316	SMITH	JS	10	214
SMITH	J	7	365	SMITH	J	13	393	SMITH	JG	3	227	SMITH	JS	12	387
SMITH	J	7	365	SMITH	J	13	393	SMITH	JG	4	352	SMITH	JT	2	316
SMITH	J	8	318	SMITH	J	13	393	SMITH	JG	7	365	SMITH	JT	4	352
SMITH	J	8	318	SMITH	J	13	393	SMITH	JG	12	207	SMITH	JT	5	329
SMITH	J	8	318	SMITH	J	13	393	SMITH	JG	14	296	SMITH	JT	6	379
SMITH	J	8	319	SMITH	J	14	295	SMITH	JGI	13	393	SMITH	JT	7	365
SMITH	J	8	319	SMITH	J	14	295	SMITH	JH	4	352	SMITH	JT	8	319
SMITH	J	8	319	SMITH	J	14	295	SMITH	JH	5	329	SMITH	JT	10	214
SMITH	J	9	177	SMITH	J	14	295	SMITH	JH	5	329	SMITH	JT	11	349
SMITH	J	9	177	SMITH	J	14	295	SMITH	JH	5	329	SMITH	JT	12	387
SMITH	J	9	177	SMITH	J	14	295	SMITH	JH	6	379	SMITH	JT	12	387
SMITH	J	9	177	SMITH	J	14	295	SMITH	JH	7	365	SMITH	JT	12	387
SMITH	J	9	177	SMITH	J	14	295	SMITH	JH	7	365	SMITH	JT	14	296
SMITH	J	9	178	SMITH	J	14	295	SMITH	JH	7	365	SMITH	JT	14	296
SMITH	J	9	178	SMITH	J	14	296	SMITH	JH	7	365	SMITH	JV	6	379
SMITH	J	9	178	SMITH	JA	1	323	SMITH	JH	8	319	SMITH	JV	11	349
SMITH	J	9	344	SMITH	JA	2	316	SMITH	JH	8	319	SMITH	JW	1	323
SMITH	J	9	344	SMITH	JA	6	378	SMITH	JH	8	319	SMITH	JW	1	323
SMITH	J	9	344	SMITH	JA	7	365	SMITH	JH	8	319	SMITH	JW	1	323
SMITH	J	9	344	SMITH	JA	10	214	SMITH	JH	9	344	SMITH	JW	5	329
SMITH	J	9	344	SMITH	JA	11	348	SMITH	JH	10	214	SMITH	JW	5	329
SMITH	J	10	213	SMITH	JAJ	13	393	SMITH	JH	11	348	SMITH	JW	6	379
SMITH	J	10	213	SMITH	JB	9	178	SMITH	JH	11	349	SMITH	JW	7	365
SMITH	J	10	214	SMITH	JB	10	368	SMITH	JH	12	387	SMITH	JW	8	319
SMITH	J	10	214	SMITH	JB	12	387	SMITH	JH	12	387	SMITH	JW	8	319
SMITH	J	10	214	SMITH	JC	7	365	SMITH	JH	12	387	SMITH	JW	8	319
SMITH	J	10	214	SMITH	JC	10	368	SMITH	JH	13	393	SMITH	JW	9	178
SMITH	J	10	214	SMITH	JC	12	207	SMITH	JH	13	394	SMITH	JW	9	178
SMITH	J	10	214	SMITH	JC	12	387	SMITH	JH	13	394	SMITH	JW	9	344
SMITH	J	10	368	SMITH	JC	12	387	SMITH	JHC	11	349	SMITH	JW	11	349

Name	Initials	No.	Page
SMITH	JW	11	349
SMITH	JW	11	349
SMITH	JW	11	349
SMITH	JW	12	207
SMITH	JW	12	207
SMITH	JW	12	387
SMITH	JW	12	387
SMITH	JW	12	388
SMITH	JW	12	388
SMITH	JW	13	394
SMITH	JW	13	394
SMITH	JW	14	296
SMITH	JW	14	296
SMITH	JW	14	296
SMITH	JW	14	296
SMITH	JWR	5	329
SMITH	L	1	323
SMITH	L	3	388
SMITH	L	6	379
SMITH	L	7	365
SMITH	L	8	319
SMITH	L	8	319
SMITH	L	8	319
SMITH	L	9	178
SMITH	L	9	178
SMITH	L	9	344
SMITH	L	12	207
SMITH	L	14	296
SMITH	L	14	296
SMITH	LA	3	227
SMITH	LA	14	296
SMITH	LB	5	329
SMITH	LE	2	316
SMITH	LE	7	365
SMITH	LE	7	365
SMITH	LE	13	394
SMITH	LG	4	352
SMITH	LH	3	227
SMITH	LJW	3	388
SMITH	LP	1	323
SMITH	LT	7	365
SMITH	LT	12	207
SMITH	LV	10	214
SMITH	M	1	323
SMITH	M	1	323
SMITH	M	2	316
SMITH	M	2	316
SMITH	M	4	352
SMITH	M	4	352
SMITH	M	6	379
SMITH	M	8	319
SMITH	M	9	178
SMITH	M	9	178
SMITH	M	12	388
SMITH	M	12	388
SMITH	M	12	388
SMITH	M	14	296
SMITH	M	14	296
SMITH	MA	10	214
SMITH	ME	10	214
SMITH	ME	13	394
SMITH	MJ	7	366
SMITH	MM	7	366
SMITH	MM	11	349
SMITH	MS	13	394
SMITH	MW	7	366
SMITH	N	2	316
SMITH	N	8	320
SMITH	N	9	178
SMITH	N	11	349
SMITH	N	11	349
SMITH	NH	8	320
SMITH	O	6	379
SMITH	O	9	178
SMITH	OA	7	366
SMITH	OM	3	227
SMITH	ON	10	214
SMITH	OR	5	329
SMITH	P	1	323
SMITH	P	1	323
SMITH	P	2	316
SMITH	P	5	329
SMITH	P	5	329
SMITH	P	6	379
SMITH	P	8	320
SMITH	P	8	320
SMITH	P	9	178
SMITH	P	9	344
SMITH	P	10	368
SMITH	P	11	349
SMITH	P	13	394
SMITH	PA	5	330
SMITH	PA	7	366
SMITH	PA	13	394
SMITH	PD	12	207
SMITH	PF	12	207
SMITH	PH	7	366
SMITH	PH	12	388
SMITH	PJ	8	320
SMITH	PL	5	330
SMITH	PT	3	388
SMITH	PW	13	394
SMITH	R	1	324
SMITH	R	1	324
SMITH	R	2	316
SMITH	R	2	316
SMITH	R	3	227
SMITH	R	3	227
SMITH	R	4	352
SMITH	R	5	329
SMITH	R	5	330
SMITH	R	5	330
SMITH	R	5	330
SMITH	R	5	330
SMITH	R	5	330
SMITH	R	6	379
SMITH	R	6	379
SMITH	R	7	366
SMITH	R	7	366
SMITH	R	8	320
SMITH	R	8	320
SMITH	R	8	320
SMITH	R	8	320
SMITH	R	9	178
SMITH	R	9	178
SMITH	R	9	344
SMITH	R	9	344
SMITH	R	11	349
SMITH	R	11	349
SMITH	R	12	388
SMITH	R	13	394
SMITH	R	14	296
SMITH	R	14	296
SMITH	R	14	296
SMITH	R	14	296
SMITH	RA	11	349
SMITH	RB	13	394
SMITH	RC	10	214
SMITH	RC	12	388
SMITH	RE	2	316
SMITH	RE	5	330
SMITH	RF	1	324
SMITH	RF	3	388
SMITH	RF	4	352
SMITH	RF	7	366
SMITH	RG	7	366
SMITH	RH	6	379
SMITH	RH	6	379
SMITH	RH	12	388
SMITH	RH	13	395
SMITH	RJ	9	178
SMITH	RP	6	379
SMITH	RP	12	207
SMITH	RP	12	207
SMITH	RT	2	317
SMITH	RW	1	324
SMITH	RW	3	388
SMITH	RW	4	352
SMITH	RW	12	388
SMITH	S	1	324
SMITH	S	1	324
SMITH	S	2	317
SMITH	S	2	317
SMITH	S	3	388
SMITH	S	4	352
SMITH	S	4	352
SMITH	S	4	352
SMITH	S	6	379
SMITH	S	6	379
SMITH	S	6	379
SMITH	S	6	379
SMITH	S	6	379
SMITH	S	6	379
SMITH	S	6	380
SMITH	S	6	380
SMITH	S	6	380
SMITH	S	7	366
SMITH	S	7	366
SMITH	S	7	366
SMITH	S	8	320
SMITH	S	8	320
SMITH	S	8	320
SMITH	S	8	320
SMITH	S	8	320
SMITH	S	9	178
SMITH	S	9	178
SMITH	S	9	178
SMITH	S	9	345
SMITH	S	9	345
SMITH	S	9	345
SMITH	S	11	349
SMITH	S	11	349
SMITH	S	11	350
SMITH	S	12	208
SMITH	S	12	208
SMITH	S	13	395
SMITH	S	13	395
SMITH	S	13	395
SMITH	S	13	395
SMITH	S	13	395
SMITH	S	14	296
SMITH	S	14	297
SMITH	SA	1	324
SMITH	SA	3	227
SMITH	SA	7	366
SMITH	SA	10	214
SMITH	SA	12	208
SMITH	SA	12	388
SMITH	SC	1	324
SMITH	SC	5	330
SMITH	SC	6	380
SMITH	SC	11	350
SMITH	SC	12	208
SMITH	SCA	10	368
SMITH	SD	6	380
SMITH	SD	11	350
SMITH	SE	7	366
SMITH	SF	7	366
SMITH	SG	4	352

SMITH	SG	7	366	SMITH	T	13	395	SMITH	W	3	388
SMITH	SG	7	366	SMITH	T	14	297	SMITH	W	4	353
SMITH	SG	8	320	SMITH	T	14	297	SMITH	W	4	353
SMITH	SG	10	368	SMITH	T	14	297	SMITH	W	4	353
SMITH	SGW	13	395	SMITH	T	14	297	SMITH	W	4	353
SMITH	SH	7	367	SMITH	T	14	297	SMITH	W	4	353
SMITH	SH	12	208	SMITH	TB	8	321	SMITH	W	4	353
SMITH	SH	14	297	SMITH	TBS	12	388	SMITH	W	4	353
SMITH	SJ	5	330	SMITH	TC	8	321	SMITH	W	5	330
SMITH	SJ	10	368	SMITH	TE	2	317	SMITH	W	5	330
SMITH	SJ	14	297	SMITH	TE	4	353	SMITH	W	5	330
SMITH	SL	6	380	SMITH	TE	7	367	SMITH	W	5	330
SMITH	SM	5	330	SMITH	TE	9	345	SMITH	W	5	330
SMITH	SM	12	388	SMITH	TE	9	345	SMITH	W	6	380
SMITH	SR	7	367	SMITH	TE	10	369	SMITH	W	6	380
SMITH	SR	12	208	SMITH	TF	5	330	SMITH	W	6	380
SMITH	SR	12	388	SMITH	TG	7	367	SMITH	W	6	380
SMITH	SRJ	1	324	SMITH	TH	4	353	SMITH	W	6	381
SMITH	SS	1	324	SMITH	TH	6	380	SMITH	W	6	381
SMITH	ST	6	380	SMITH	TH	6	380	SMITH	W	6	381
SMITH	ST	7	367	SMITH	TH	6	380	SMITH	W	6	381
SMITH	SW	4	352	SMITH	TH	7	367	SMITH	W	7	367
SMITH	SWH	4	353	SMITH	TH	9	179	SMITH	W	7	367
SMITH	T	1	324	SMITH	TH	10	215	SMITH	W	7	367
SMITH	T	1	324	SMITH	TH	14	297	SMITH	W	7	367
SMITH	T	2	317	SMITH	THS	13	395	SMITH	W	7	367
SMITH	T	4	353	SMITH	TJ	2	317	SMITH	W	7	367
SMITH	T	4	353	SMITH	TJ	4	353	SMITH	W	7	367
SMITH	T	5	330	SMITH	TJ	7	367	SMITH	W	7	367
SMITH	T	6	380	SMITH	TJ	12	208	SMITH	W	7	367
SMITH	T	6	380	SMITH	TL	10	215	SMITH	W	7	367
SMITH	T	6	380	SMITH	TM	8	321	SMITH	W	7	368
SMITH	T	6	380	SMITH	TW	4	353	SMITH	W	7	368
SMITH	T	7	367	SMITH	TW	6	380	SMITH	W	8	321
SMITH	T	8	320	SMITH	TW	7	367	SMITH	W	8	321
SMITH	T	8	320	SMITH	TW	12	208	SMITH	W	8	321
SMITH	T	8	320	SMITH	V	4	353	SMITH	W	8	321
SMITH	T	8	320	SMITH	V	8	321	SMITH	W	8	321
SMITH	T	8	320	SMITH	V	9	345	SMITH	W	8	321
SMITH	T	8	321	SMITH	VN	9	179	SMITH	W	8	321
SMITH	T	8	321	SMITH	W	1	324	SMITH	W	8	321
SMITH	T	9	179	SMITH	W	1	324	SMITH	W	8	321
SMITH	T	9	345	SMITH	W	1	324	SMITH	W	8	321
SMITH	T	10	215	SMITH	W	2	317	SMITH	W	8	321
SMITH	T	11	350	SMITH	W	2	317	SMITH	W	8	321
SMITH	T	11	350	SMITH	W	2	317	SMITH	W	8	322
SMITH	T	11	350	SMITH	W	2	317	SMITH	W	8	322
SMITH	T	11	350	SMITH	W	2	317	SMITH	W	8	322
SMITH	T	12	208	SMITH	W	3	227	SMITH	W	8	322
SMITH	T	12	388	SMITH	W	3	227	SMITH	W	8	322
SMITH	T	13	395	SMITH	W	3	227	SMITH	W	9	179
SMITH	T	13	395	SMITH	W	3	227	SMITH	W	9	179
SMITH	T	13	395	SMITH	W	3	227	SMITH	W	9	179

SMITH	W	9	179	SMITH	W	9	179
SMITH	W	9	179				

SMITH	W	9	179
SMITH	W	9	345
SMITH	W	9	345
SMITH	W	10	215
SMITH	W	10	215
SMITH	W	10	215
SMITH	W	10	215
SMITH	W	10	215
SMITH	W	10	215
SMITH	W	11	350
SMITH	W	11	350
SMITH	W	11	350
SMITH	W	11	350
SMITH	W	11	350
SMITH	W	11	350
SMITH	W	12	208
SMITH	W	12	208
SMITH	W	12	208
SMITH	W	12	388
SMITH	W	12	388
SMITH	W	12	388
SMITH	W	12	388
SMITH	W	12	389
SMITH	W	13	395
SMITH	W	13	395
SMITH	W	13	395
SMITH	W	13	395
SMITH	W	14	297
SMITH	W	14	297
SMITH	W	14	297
SMITH	WA	2	317
SMITH	WA	2	317
SMITH	WA	2	317
SMITH	WA	5	330
SMITH	WA	6	381
SMITH	WA	6	381
SMITH	WA	7	368
SMITH	WA	8	322
SMITH	WA	12	208
SMITH	WA	13	395
SMITH	WA	13	395
SMITH	WB	3	388
SMITH	WB	6	381
SMITH	WB	13	396
SMITH	WC	1	324
SMITH	WC	1	324

SMITH	WC	2	317	SMITH	WH	3	228	SMITH	WJ	10	215	SMITHSON	JW	8	322
SMITH	WC	3	227	SMITH	WH	4	354	SMITH	WJ	10	369	SMITHSON	T	8	322
SMITH	WC	4	353	SMITH	WH	4	354	SMITH	WJ	12	389	SMITHSON	TH	8	322
SMITH	WC	4	353	SMITH	WH	5	331	SMITH	WJ	13	396	SMITHSON	WJ	13	396
SMITH	WC	5	331	SMITH	WH	6	381	SMITH	WJ	13	396	SMITHWICK	CA	4	354
SMITH	WC	10	215	SMITH	WH	6	381	SMITH	WJ	13	396	SMITHWICK	JV	4	354
SMITH	WC	10	369	SMITH	WH	6	381	SMITH	WJ	13	396	SMITHYES	WG	3	389
SMITH	WC	12	208	SMITH	WH	6	381	SMITH	WJR	2	318	SMITTEN	G	6	381
SMITH	WC	12	389	SMITH	WH	7	368	SMITH	WL	12	208	SMITTEN	H	6	381
SMITH	WC	14	297	SMITH	WH	7	368	SMITH	WM	5	331	SMITTEN	H	6	382
SMITH	WCH	4	353	SMITH	WH	7	368	SMITH	WM	12	208	SMITTEN	J	6	382
SMITH	WD	2	317	SMITH	WH	7	368	SMITH	WP	1	325	SMOKER	H	13	396
SMITH	WD	7	368	SMITH	WH	8	322	SMITH	WPC	4	354	SMOOKER	H	10	215
SMITH	WE	1	324	SMITH	WH	9	179	SMITH	WRS	12	389	SMY	C	9	179
SMITH	WE	2	317	SMITH	WH	9	179	SMITH	WS	3	228	SMYTH	W	11	351
SMITH	WE	3	227	SMITH	WH	9	179	SMITH	WS	10	215	SMYTH	WJ	13	396
SMITH	WE	3	227	SMITH	WH	11	350	SMITH	WT	3	228	SMYTHE	FW	6	382
SMITH	WE	4	353	SMITH	WH	11	351	SMITH	WT	3	388	SNAITH	A	8	323
SMITH	WE	6	381	SMITH	WH	11	351	SMITH	WT	5	331	SNAITH	CE	8	323
SMITH	WE	6	381	SMITH	WH	11	351	SMITH	WT	13	396	SNAITH	H	11	351
SMITH	WE	11	350	SMITH	WH	12	208	SMITH	WTB	3	228	SNAITH	J	8	323
SMITH	WE	11	350	SMITH	WH	12	208	SMITH	WW	3	388	SNAITH	T	14	297
SMITH	WE	12	208	SMITH	WH	12	208	SMITH	WW	5	331	SNAITH	WA	2	318
SMITH	WE	12	389	SMITH	WH	12	389	SMITH	WW	12	389	SNAITH	WE	2	318
SMITH	WE	12	389	SMITH	WH	12	389	SMITH	WW	13	396	SNAPE	G	6	382
SMITH	WEM	5	331	SMITH	WH	13	396	SMITH	WW	13	396	SNAPE	G	11	351
SMITH	WF	6	381	SMITH	WH	13	396	SMITH-HILL	W	6	381	SNAPE	JG	10	369
SMITH	WF	7	368	SMITH	WH	13	396	SMITH-RAY	AJW	2	318	SNAPE	WH	14	297
SMITH	WF	7	368	SMITH	WH	13	396	SMITH-TOMLINSON VA		2	318	SNAPES	W	7	368
SMITH	WF	13	395	SMITH	WH	14	297	SMITH-TOMLINSON VJ		2	318	SNAPS	J	1	325
SMITH	WF	13	396	SMITH	WH	14	297	SMITHARD	HO	10	369	SNEDDEN	W	10	215
SMITH	WG	1	324	SMITH	WJ	1	325	SMITHEMAN	A	11	351	SNEDDON	J	8	323
SMITH	WG	1	324	SMITH	WJ	1	325	SMITHEN	J	10	369	SNEDDON	T	5	331
SMITH	WG	1	325	SMITH	WJ	1	325	SMITHER	A	4	354	SNEDKER	CG	12	389
SMITH	WG	1	325	SMITH	WJ	1	325	SMITHERS	HT	2	318	SNEDKER	I	12	389
SMITH	WG	2	317	SMITH	WJ	1	325	SMITHERS	J	3	389	SNEDKER	W	12	389
SMITH	WG	2	318	SMITH	WJ	1	325	SMITHERS	R	8	322	SNEDKER	WH	12	389
SMITH	WG	4	353	SMITH	WJ	2	318	SMITHERS	WA	9	345	SNEE	AL	2	318
SMITH	WG	4	354	SMITH	WJ	2	318	SMITHIES	A	8	322	SNEE	J	9	345
SMITH	WG	5	331	SMITH	WJ	3	228	SMITHIES	HD	4	354	SNEE	M	9	345
SMITH	WG	6	381	SMITH	WJ	4	354	SMITHIES	J	9	179	SNEE	W	9	345
SMITH	WG	7	368	SMITH	WJ	4	354	SMITHIES	RN	12	209	SNELGROVE	A	3	389
SMITH	WG	10	215	SMITH	WJ	4	354	SMITHIES	S	9	179	SNELGROVE	CH	7	369
SMITH	WG	12	208	SMITH	WJ	5	331	SMITHIES	SS	9	179	SNELGROVE	F	4	354
SMITH	WG	13	396	SMITH	WJ	5	331	SMITHSON	A	8	322	SNELGROVE	G	4	354
SMITH	WGF	4	354	SMITH	WJ	6	381	SMITHSON	E	2	318	SNELGROVE	G	4	354
SMITH	WGN	7	368	SMITH	WJ	6	381	SMITHSON	F	2	318	SNELGROVE	G	14	297
SMITH	WH	1	325	SMITH	WJ	6	381	SMITHSON	F	8	322	SNELGROVE	H	13	396
SMITH	WH	1	325	SMITH	WJ	7	368	SMITHSON	H	8	322	SNELGROVE	HC	4	354
SMITH	WH	2	318	SMITH	WJ	7	368	SMITHSON	H	8	322	SNELGROVE	R	4	354
SMITH	WH	2	318	SMITH	WJ	7	368	SMITHSON	H	8	322	SNELL	A	12	209
SMITH	WH	2	318	SMITH	WJ	7	368	SMITHSON	H	8	322	SNELL	AJ	7	368
SMITH	WH	2	318	SMITH	WJ	10	215	SMITHSON	J	8	322	SNELL	AR	10	216
SMITH	WH	3	228	SMITH	WJ	10	215	SMITHSON	JP	1	325	SNELL	BC	7	368
SMITH	WH	3	228	SMITH	WJ	10	215	SMITHSON	JW	1	325	SNELL	C	10	216

Surname	Init.	No.	Pg.	Surname	Init.	No.	Pg.	Surname	Init.	No.	Pg.	Surname	Init.	No.	Pg.
SNELL	ECR	13	396	SNOW	E	8	323	SOFFE	E	4	355	SONGHURST	HJ	13	397
SNELL	F	3	228	SNOW	HJ	2	319	SOFFE	EM	4	355	SONLEY	T	11	351
SNELL	F	7	369	SNOW	J	2	319	SOFFE	G	5	331	SONNET	H	10	216
SNELL	FE	2	318	SNOW	LJ	4	355	SOFFE	H	5	331	SONNEX	G	7	370
SNELL	FH	4	354	SNOW	S	4	355	SOFFE	PH	4	355	SONNEX	W	7	370
SNELL	GC	1	325	SNOW	T	9	345	SOFFE	RF	4	355	SONTAG	EA	2	320
SNELL	H	1	325	SNOW	T	12	389	SOFFE	S	4	355	SOPER	A	7	370
SNELL	J	14	297	SNOWBALL	B	8	323	SOFLEY	A	3	228	SOPER	A	7	370
SNELL	JF	13	396	SNOWBALL	HS	13	397	SOFLEY	S	3	228	SOPER	AG	2	320
SNELL	L	10	216	SNOWDEN	A	8	323	SOFTLEY	CE	10	216	SOPER	C	4	355
SNELL	R	3	228	SNOWDEN	A	9	345	SOFTLEY	GJ	10	216	SOPER	CE	2	320
SNELL	SE	7	369	SNOWDEN	CH	9	179	SOILLEUX	WH	7	369	SOPER	EF	7	370
SNELL	W	8	323	SNOWDEN	F	8	323	SOLE	AT	1	326	SOPER	FG	4	355
SNELL	WG	2	318	SNOWDEN	F	11	351	SOLE	EE	1	326	SOPER	FGR	12	209
SNELLGROVE	B	4	354	SNOWDEN	G	8	323	SOLE	SE	5	332	SOPER	G	7	370
SNELLIN	JW	2	318	SNOWDEN	J	8	323	SOLE	WH	5	331	SOPER	G	12	209
SNELLING	C	7	369	SNOWDEN	JR	10	216	SOLE	WT	1	326	SOPER	GW	5	332
SNELLING	C	7	369	SNOWDEN	R	4	355	SOLESBURY	C	12	209	SOPER	H	5	332
SNELLING	CC	7	369	SNOWDON	LL	11	351	SOLLIES	WJ	6	382	SOPER	H	13	397
SNELLING	EC	1	325	SNOWDON	S	9	345	SOLLINGER	A	14	298	SOPER	HW	13	397
SNELLING	EM	2	319	SNOWDON	TWK	10	216	SOLLIS	LH	7	369	SOPER	J	7	370
SNELLING	EW	1	325	SNOXELL	CS	5	331	SOLLY	F	2	319	SOPER	RJ	3	389
SNELLING	G	2	319	SNOXELL	H	5	331	SOLLY	FP	2	319	SOPER	W	5	332
SNELLING	G	2	319	SNOXELL	S	5	331	SOLLY	H	2	319	SOPP	AJ	2	320
SNELLING	GR	7	369	SNUDDEN	TJ	10	369	SOLMAN	HT	7	369	SORRELL	A	2	320
SNELLING	H	1	325	SOAL	AJ	5	331	SOLOMAN	M	8	323	SORRELL	EE	7	105
SNELLING	JA	4	354	SOAL	JA	10	216	SOLOMON	AR	4	355	SORRELL	RJ	6	382
SNELLING	JL	7	369	SOAMES	GW	2	319	SOLOMON	HW	7	369	SOTHCOTT	FA	4	356
SNELLING	RH	4	355	SOAMES	J	12	389	SOLOMON	I	14	298	SOTHERAN	GF	1	326
SNELLING	S	7	369	SOANES	AE	2	319	SOLOMON	IT	6	382	SOTHERON	H	14	298
SNELLING	W	1	325	SOANES	JC	2	319	SOLOMON	J	11	351	SOUDET	CL	14	298
SNELLING	W	13	397	SOANES	R	2	319	SOLOMON	L	11	351	SOULE	ES	3	389
SNELLING	WC	2	319	SOANS	AF	3	389	SOLOMON	T	14	298	SOULSBY	AE	7	370
SNELLING	WT	1	326	SOANS	EW	3	389	SOLOMON	WIT	6	382	SOUNDY	AH	3	389
SNELSON	G	14	298	SOANS	SG	3	389	SOLOVATCHICK	J	14	298	SOUSTER	G	12	389
SNEYD	J	14	298	SOAR	BM	3	228	SOMERBY	A	9	345	SOUSTER	G	12	389
SNIPE	G	6	382	SOAR	E	3	228	SOMERFORD	FH	13	397	SOUSTER	GL	12	209
SNOOK	AE	7	369	SOAR	H	13	397	SOMERFORD	H	7	369	SOUSTER	I	1	326
SNOOK	AH	12	209	SOAR	HW	3	228	SOMERFORD	S	7	369	SOUSTER	W	5	332
SNOOK	AS	7	369	SOAR	LHS	7	369	SOMERFORD	S	13	397	SOUTAR	WG	10	369
SNOOK	EP	10	369	SOAR	W	14	298	SOMERS	HG	13	397	SOUTER	AC	11	351
SNOOK	GF	4	355	SOARS	FRE	4	355	SOMERS	L	9	345	SOUTER	E	1	326
SNOOK	H	4	355	SOARS	H	2	319	SOMERS	P	14	298	SOUTER	F	2	320
SNOOK	HG	4	355	SOARS	J	4	355	SOMERS	R	6	382	SOUTER	G	2	320
SNOOK	JE	10	216	SOBEY	K	2	319	SOMERVILLE	A	8	323	SOUTER	H	1	326
SNOOK	RHD	4	355	SOBEY	SA	2	319	SOMERVILLE	AR	13	397	SOUTER	J	1	326
SNOOK	W	4	355	SOBEY	SCW	2	319	SOMERVILLE	EA	7	369	SOUTER	JC	11	351
SNOOKES	W	6	382	SOCHALL	N	8	323	SOMERVILLE	F	4	355	SOUTER	W	7	370
SNOOKS	AH	13	397	SOCKETT	AE	11	351	SOMERVILLE	J	8	323	SOUTH	A	8	323
SNOOKS	JS	13	397	SOCKETT	E	11	351	SOMERVILLE	JC	1	326	SOUTH	AJ	4	356
SNOOKS	RC	13	397	SOCKETT	RW	11	351	SOMERVILLE	TC	13	397	SOUTH	CJ	6	382
SNOW	AC	6	382	SODEN	AE	6	382	SOMMA	L	9	179	SOUTH	E	2	320
SNOW	E	1	326	SODEN	F	2	319	SOMMERVILLE	J	5	332	SOUTH	F	4	356
SNOW	E	2	319	SOER	W	13	397	SONEY	A	8	323	SOUTH	F	11	351
SNOW	E	5	331	SOFFE	B	4	355	SONGER	WA	2	320	SOUTH	FA	5	332

Name	In.			Name	In.			Name	In.			Name	In.			Name	In.		
SOUTH	G	5	332	SOUTHWARD	A	11	352	SOWERBY	R	8	324	SPARKS	HG	10	369	SPARKS	HG	10	369
SOUTH	GE	5	332	SOUTHWARD	E	8	323	SOWOOD	H	9	180	SPARKS	HJ	10	370	SPARKS	HJ	10	370
SOUTH	HC	13	397	SOUTHWARD	J	1	326	SOWRY	A	8	324	SPARKS	J	13	398	SPARKS	J	13	398
SOUTH	HG	5	332	SOUTHWARD	J	14	298	SOWRY	A	8	324	SPARKS	R	7	371	SPARKS	R	7	371
SOUTH	HJ	7	370	SOUTHWELL	A	4	356	SOWTEN	GE	7	370	SPARKS	TW	3	389	SPARKS	TW	3	389
SOUTH	J	3	389	SOUTHWELL	A	4	356	SOWTER	JW	8	324	SPARKS	W	13	398	SPARKS	W	13	398
SOUTH	JB	2	320	SOUTHWELL	A	4	356	SPACEY	A	5	332	SPARKS	WG	4	357	SPARKS	WG	4	357
SOUTH	JW	7	370	SOUTHWELL	AF	4	356	SPACEY	A	5	332	SPARKS	WPH	3	389	SPARKS	WPH	3	389
SOUTH	O	13	397	SOUTHWELL	AT	4	356	SPACEY	A	5	332	SPARKS	WT	10	370	SPARKS	WT	10	370
SOUTH	R	6	382	SOUTHWELL	C	10	216	SPACEY	HV	10	216	SPARKS	WT	10	370	SPARKS	WT	10	370
SOUTH	W	5	332	SOUTHWELL	E	4	356	SPACEY	J	11	352	SPARKSMAN	A	3	228	SPARKSMAN	A	3	228
SOUTH	W	7	370	SOUTHWELL	EE	4	356	SPACEY	P	2	320	SPARKSMAN	A	5	332	SPARKSMAN	A	5	332
SOUTH	WC	7	370	SOUTHWELL	F	10	369	SPACEY	T	5	332	SPARKSMAN	A	7	371	SPARKSMAN	A	7	371
SOUTHALL	A	6	382	SOUTHWELL	FE	11	352	SPACKMAN	AV	13	398	SPARKSMAN	AJ	5	332	SPARKSMAN	AJ	5	332
SOUTHALL	A	11	352	SOUTHWELL	FW	4	356	SPACKMAN	ES	7	370	SPARKSMAN	W	3	228	SPARKSMAN	W	3	228
SOUTHALL	FP	12	389	SOUTHWELL	G	13	398	SPACKMAN	FW	5	332	SPARLING	RF	11	352	SPARLING	RF	11	352
SOUTHALL	HH	11	351	SOUTHWELL	GA	4	356	SPACKMAN	H	7	370	SPARLING	TW	2	321	SPARLING	TW	2	321
SOUTHALL	JW	14	298	SOUTHWELL	GB	3	389	SPACKMAN	JO	7	371	SPARLING	V	11	352	SPARLING	V	11	352
SOUTHALL	R	6	382	SOUTHWELL	GC	10	216	SPACKMAN	JT	2	320	SPARROW	A	6	383	SPARROW	A	6	383
SOUTHALL	T	14	298	SOUTHWELL	H	4	356	SPACKMAN	WJ	2	320	SPARROW	CJ	3	228	SPARROW	CJ	3	228
SOUTHALL	TG	6	382	SOUTHWELL	HP	4	356	SPAIN	HE	14	299	SPARROW	EG	3	228	SPARROW	EG	3	228
SOUTHALL	WH	6	383	SOUTHWELL	HS	4	356	SPALDING	AJ	7	371	SPARROW	F	12	209	SPARROW	F	12	209
SOUTHAM	AC	12	209	SOUTHWELL	J	14	298	SPALDING	I	6	383	SPARROW	H	6	383	SPARROW	H	6	383
SOUTHAM	AE	7	370	SOUTHWELL	JC	4	356	SPALDING	W	7	371	SPARROW	H	9	346	SPARROW	H	9	346
SOUTHAM	G	6	383	SOUTHWELL	JE	4	356	SPALL	AG	13	398	SPARROW	J	10	370	SPARROW	J	10	370
SOUTHAM	H	10	369	SOUTHWELL	JE	4	356	SPALL	TG	7	371	SPARROW	J	11	352	SPARROW	J	11	352
SOUTHAM	S	6	383	SOUTHWELL	JW	3	389	SPANNER	JW	4	357	SPARROW	JE	13	398	SPARROW	JE	13	398
SOUTHAM	TO	6	383	SOUTHWELL	JWO	3	389	SPANNER	RW	4	357	SPARROW	JF	6	383	SPARROW	JF	6	383
SOUTHAM	W	6	383	SOUTHWELL	RG	4	356	SPANTON	HL	12	389	SPARROW	PG	2	321	SPARROW	PG	2	321
SOUTHAM	WE	6	383	SOUTHWELL	SE	4	357	SPANTON	RS	10	369	SPARROW	SJ	2	321	SPARROW	SJ	2	321
SOUTHAN	WA	13	397	SOUTHWELL	T	4	357	SPARK	F	9	346	SPARROW	T	5	333	SPARROW	T	5	333
SOUTHARD	L	2	320	SOUTHWELL	T	4	357	SPARK	JE	1	326	SPARROW	TG	13	398	SPARROW	TG	13	398
SOUTHBY	AE	13	397	SOUTHWELL	W	4	357	SPARK	JS	1	326	SPARROW	WA	2	321	SPARROW	WA	2	321
SOUTHBY	EH	13	398	SOUTHWELL	W	4	357	SPARKES	A	7	371	SPARROW	WE	2	321	SPARROW	WE	2	321
SOUTHCLIFFE	CW	12	389	SOUTHWELL	W	4	357	SPARKES	B	10	216	SPARROW	WH	13	398	SPARROW	WH	13	398
SOUTHERN	H	11	352	SOUTHWELL	WA	14	298	SPARKES	C	9	180	SPARSHOTT	AE	10	216	SPARSHOTT	AE	10	216
SOUTHERN	JH	2	320	SOUTHWICK	EJ	6	383	SPARKES	C	10	216	SPARSHOTT	AW	10	370	SPARSHOTT	AW	10	370
SOUTHERN	JS	14	298	SOUTHWOOD	A	14	298	SPARKES	F	6	383	SPARSHOTT	EB	10	217	SPARSHOTT	EB	10	217
SOUTHERN	M	14	298	SOUTHWOOD	AR	14	299	SPARKES	G	3	389	SPARSHOTT	HW	2	321	SPARSHOTT	HW	2	321
SOUTHERN	RA	2	320	SOUTHWOOD	FJ	14	299	SPARKES	G	12	209	SPARSHOTT	JW	4	357	SPARSHOTT	JW	4	357
SOUTHEY	JC	2	320	SOUTHWOOD	T	13	398	SPARKES	J	14	299	SPARSHOTT	SJ	10	217	SPARSHOTT	SJ	10	217
SOUTHGATE	B	12	209	SOUTHWORTH	CH	8	323	SPARKES	R	10	369	SPARSHOTT	TW	10	217	SPARSHOTT	TW	10	217
SOUTHGATE	C	1	326	SOUTHWORTH	PW	11	352	SPARKES	W	10	216	SPARSHOTT	W	2	321	SPARSHOTT	W	2	321
SOUTHGATE	C	12	209	SOUWDEN	B	9	346	SPARKES	WHJ	12	209	SPARVELL	A	5	333	SPARVELL	A	5	333
SOUTHGATE	F	7	370	SOWDEN	B	11	352	SPARKMAN	JH	10	369	SPARVELL	A	5	333	SPARVELL	A	5	333
SOUTHGATE	G	13	398	SOWDEN	CH	1	326	SPARKMAN	WG	10	369	SPARVELL	CT	5	333	SPARVELL	CT	5	333
SOUTHGATE	H	2	320	SOWDEN	H	9	180	SPARKS	A	2	320	SPARVELL	GA	5	333	SPARVELL	GA	5	333
SOUTHGATE	H	7	370	SOWDEN	H	9	346	SPARKS	AH	12	209	SPARY	AE	5	333	SPARY	AE	5	333
SOUTHGATE	J	13	398	SOWDEN	H	14	299	SPARKS	CG	4	357	SPARY	F	5	333	SPARY	F	5	333
SOUTHGATE	JT	13	398	SOWDEN	J	8	323	SPARKS	CV	7	371	SPARY	H	5	333	SPARY	H	5	333
SOUTHGATE	ST	9	346	SOWDEN	R	1	326	SPARKS	E	14	299	SPARY	T	5	333	SPARY	T	5	333
SOUTHGATE	TW	13	398	SOWDEN	W	8	324	SPARKS	F	1	326	SPARY	W	5	333	SPARY	W	5	333
SOUTHGATE	W	1	326	SOWDEN	W	9	180	SPARKS	GE	10	216	SPARY	W	5	333	SPARY	W	5	333
SOUTHGATE	WG	6	383	SOWDEN	WA	8	324	SPARKS	GR	10	369	SPATCHER	W	12	390	SPATCHER	W	12	390
SOUTHON	H	10	369	SOWDON	JH	2	320	SPARKS	HG	7	371	SPATCHER	WF	5	333	SPATCHER	WF	5	333

SPAUGHTON	AH	7	371	SPEER	FR	13	398	SPENCE	E	9	346	SPENCER	F	8	325
SPAUGHTON	CJ	3	389	SPEER	HG	7	371	SPENCE	E	9	346	SPENCER	F	10	370
SPAUL	EJ	1	327	SPEER	TG	7	371	SPENCE	EF	12	390	SPENCER	F	12	209
SPAULDING	A	2	321	SPEIGAL	C	4	357	SPENCE	F	2	321	SPENCER	FAJ	13	399
SPAULDING	W	2	321	SPEIGH	E	2	321	SPENCE	F	5	333	SPENCER	FD	7	372
SPAVEN	J	8	324	SPEIGHT	A	8	324	SPENCE	F	5	333	SPENCER	FJ	10	217
SPAVEN	JR	14	299	SPEIGHT	A	8	324	SPENCE	GH	8	325	SPENCER	FN	2	322
SPAVEN	W	8	324	SPEIGHT	A	8	324	SPENCE	H	8	325	SPENCER	FW	2	322
SPAYNE	HA	4	357	SPEIGHT	A	9	180	SPENCE	H	9	180	SPENCER	G	5	333
SPEAKE	AC	14	299	SPEIGHT	AH	8	324	SPENCE	J	2	321	SPENCER	G	6	384
SPEAKE	JE	10	217	SPEIGHT	B	8	324	SPENCE	J	8	325	SPENCER	G	6	384
SPEAKMAN	F	11	352	SPEIGHT	CH	9	346	SPENCE	J	11	352	SPENCER	G	12	390
SPEAKMAN	J	11	352	SPEIGHT	E	9	346	SPENCE	J	12	209	SPENCER	G	13	398
SPEAKMAN	J	11	352	SPEIGHT	F	9	346	SPENCE	JEK	12	390	SPENCER	GA	7	372
SPEAR	AE	5	333	SPEIGHT	F	9	346	SPENCE	L	8	325	SPENCER	GB	8	325
SPEAR	C	12	390	SPEIGHT	FC	3	389	SPENCE	MV	12	390	SPENCER	GH	5	333
SPEAR	DT	12	390	SPEIGHT	FH	9	180	SPENCE	NJ	9	180	SPENCER	GH	8	325
SPEAR	FG	5	333	SPEIGHT	FH	9	346	SPENCE	P	1	327	SPENCER	GW	2	322
SPEAR	FJ	7	371	SPEIGHT	G	8	324	SPENCE	PA	2	322	SPENCER	GW	10	370
SPEAR	N	4	357	SPEIGHT	H	9	346	SPENCE	RA	5	333	SPENCER	H	1	327
SPEAR	W	14	299	SPEIGHT	J	8	324	SPENCE	RW	3	390	SPENCER	H	3	390
SPEAR	WG	10	370	SPEIGHT	J	8	324	SPENCE	S	14	299	SPENCER	H	3	390
SPEARING	AE	2	321	SPEIGHT	J	9	346	SPENCE	W	8	325	SPENCER	H	4	357
SPEARING	B	4	357	SPEIGHT	JR	8	324	SPENCE	WH	14	299	SPENCER	H	5	334
SPEARING	C	1	327	SPEIGHT	R	8	324	SPENCE	WJ	7	372	SPENCER	H	8	325
SPEARING	F	1	327	SPEIGHT	R	8	325	SPENCE	WT	9	180	SPENCER	H	8	325
SPEARING	I	1	327	SPEIGHT	S	8	325	SPENCE	WW	10	217	SPENCER	H	9	180
SPEARING	OH	13	398	SPEIGHT	T	8	325	SPENCELEY	GA	1	327	SPENCER	H	9	346
SPEARING	RF	1	327	SPEIGHT	T	9	180	SPENCER	A	4	357	SPENCER	H	9	347
SPEARING	SC	2	321	SPEIGHT	W	8	325	SPENCER	A	6	383	SPENCER	H	9	347
SPEARING	T	7	371	SPEIGHT	W	8	325	SPENCER	A	7	372	SPENCER	H	11	352
SPEARMAN	WS	6	383	SPEIGHT	W	9	180	SPENCER	A	9	180	SPENCER	H	12	209
SPEARPOINT	EE	7	371	SPELLACY	J	11	352	SPENCER	A	9	346	SPENCER	H	12	390
SPEARS	A	14	299	SPELLER	A	1	327	SPENCER	A	9	346	SPENCER	H	13	399
SPEARS	CW	7	371	SPELLER	AE	3	389	SPENCER	A	9	346	SPENCER	H	14	299
SPEARS	F	14	299	SPELLER	EF	3	390	SPENCER	A	9	346	SPENCER	HB	14	299
SPEARS	GH	3	228	SPELLER	F	2	321	SPENCER	A	10	217	SPENCER	HJ	1	327
SPEARS	GJ	3	228	SPELLER	F	2	321	SPENCER	A	12	209	SPENCER	HJ	2	322
SPEARS	PC	2	321	SPELLER	F	13	398	SPENCER	AE	2	322	SPENCER	HJ	7	372
SPEARS	WH	4	357	SPELLER	FJ	2	321	SPENCER	AE	2	322	SPENCER	J	4	357
SPEDDING	F	10	370	SPELLER	GF	3	390	SPENCER	AE	2	322	SPENCER	J	8	325
SPEED	A	7	371	SPELLER	GHH	1	327	SPENCER	AE	7	372	SPENCER	J	8	325
SPEED	A	9	180	SPELLER	H	7	372	SPENCER	AT	12	209	SPENCER	J	8	325
SPEED	AP	1	327	SPELLER	H	7	372	SPENCER	C	8	325	SPENCER	J	9	180
SPEED	CJ	7	371	SPELLER	HA	1	327	SPENCER	CH	6	383	SPENCER	J	11	352
SPEED	CR	1	327	SPELLER	JW	3	390	SPENCER	CS	2	322	SPENCER	J	11	353
SPEED	F	14	299	SPELLER	L	3	390	SPENCER	CW	7	372	SPENCER	J	11	353
SPEED	G	6	383	SPELLER	PW	1	327	SPENCER	CWA	10	217	SPENCER	J	14	300
SPEED	HA	3	228	SPELLER	WS	3	390	SPENCER	E	7	372	SPENCER	J	14	300
SPEED	HD	7	371	SPELLMAN	J	8	325	SPENCER	E	10	217	SPENCER	J	14	300
SPEED	J	3	389	SPELLMAN	J	14	299	SPENCER	E	11	353	SPENCER	JA	10	217
SPEED	JE	3	229	SPELMAN	J	11	352	SPENCER	F	2	322	SPENCER	JH	8	326
SPEED	S	6	383	SPENCE	A	8	325	SPENCER	F	4	357	SPENCER	JH	14	300
SPEED	TW	8	324	SPENCE	AJ	2	321	SPENCER	F	4	357	SPENCER	JHP	4	358
SPEER	AE	13	398	SPENCE	E	9	180	SPENCER	F	6	384	SPENCER	R	8	326

SPENCER	R	8	326	SPICER	A	10	217	SPINDLER	WJ	12	210	SPOONER	W	5	335
SPENCER	RG	2	322	SPICER	CE	13	399	SPINK	A	8	326	SPOONER	W	6	384
SPENCER	RG	10	370	SPICER	E	3	390	SPINK	A	8	326	SPOONER	W	8	326
SPENCER	RJ	12	209	SPICER	EM	1	328	SPINK	AN	13	399	SPOONER	WC	7	372
SPENCER	S	3	390	SPICER	F	5	334	SPINK	B	8	326	SPOONER	WH	2	323
SPENCER	S	10	217	SPICER	F	5	334	SPINK	B	9	347	SPOONER	WWJ	10	218
SPENCER	S	11	352	SPICER	F	10	370	SPINK	C	2	323	SPORLE	H	3	390
SPENCER	SG	5	334	SPICER	FA	6	384	SPINK	CH	13	399	SPORLE	J	1	328
SPENCER	SH	13	399	SPICER	FJ	7	372	SPINK	F	8	326	SPORLE	W	12	210
SPENCER	SJ	10	217	SPICER	FR	10	217	SPINK	G	2	323	SPORNE	AR	13	399
SPENCER	T	4	358	SPICER	GAS	7	372	SPINK	G	8	326	SPORTON	SRL	13	400
SPENCER	T	9	180	SPICER	HJ	6	384	SPINK	H	8	326	SPOWAGE	S	8	327
SPENCER	T	11	353	SPICER	J	2	322	SPINK	H	11	353	SPRADBROW	AA	7	372
SPENCER	T	12	209	SPICER	J	5	334	SPINK	J	8	326	SPRADBROW	WE	7	373
SPENCER	TH	6	384	SPICER	J	5	334	SPINK	JE	9	347	SPRADLEY	W	2	323
SPENCER	TH	12	390	SPICER	JH	2	322	SPINK	L	8	326	SPRAGG	J	11	353
SPENCER	TW	13	399	SPICER	JJ	10	217	SPINKS	CLR	10	217	SPRAGG	SH	6	384
SPENCER	VC	6	384	SPICER	L	5	334	SPINKS	JC	7	372	SPRAGG	T	6	385
SPENCER	W	1	327	SPICER	PH	4	358	SPINKS	R	5	334	SPRAGG	W	6	385
SPENCER	W	4	358	SPICER	TC	6	384	SPINKS	W	14	300	SPRAGG	WC	6	385
SPENCER	W	8	326	SPICER	TH	13	399	SPINNER	JGP	13	399	SPRAGGON	H	2	323
SPENCER	W	8	326	SPICER	W	2	322	SPINNER	W	10	218	SPRAGUE	W	14	300
SPENCER	W	8	326	SPICER	W	5	334	SPIRES	B	13	399	SPRAGUE	WJ	4	358
SPENCER	W	8	326	SPICER	WA	12	210	SPITTEL	G	5	334	SPRANKLING	C	4	358
SPENCER	W	9	180	SPICER	WA	13	399	SPITTELS	AW	1	328	SPRATLEY	A	5	335
SPENCER	W	9	347	SPICER	WH	7	372	SPITTLE	JM	3	390	SPRATLEY	EJ	4	358
SPENCER	W	9	347	SPICER	WJ	6	384	SPITTLE	JW	1	328	SPRATLEY	FC	5	335
SPENCER	W	9	347	SPICKERNELL	PJ	10	370	SPITTLE	JWG	3	390	SPRATLING	JF	7	373
SPENCER	W	9	347	SPICKERNELL	WH	2	322	SPITTLE	S	6	384	SPRATT	AAS	4	358
SPENCER	WA	2	322	SPIERS	A	6	384	SPITTLE	WA	5	334	SPRATT	AE	3	390
SPENCER	WC	8	326	SPIERS	EA	5	334	SPITTLES	EWJ	2	323	SPRATT	AG	4	358
SPENCER	WE	8	326	SPIERS	FW	13	399	SPITTLES	F	10	218	SPRATT	E	14	300
SPENCER	WG	5	334	SPIERS	GA	5	334	SPITTLES	GC	3	229	SPRATT	EA	7	373
SPENCER	WH	1	327	SPIERS	JR	5	334	SPIVEY	C	9	347	SPRATT	EG	4	358
SPENCER	WJ	2	322	SPIERS	JR	5	334	SPIVEY	G	8	326	SPRATT	FS	3	390
SPENCER	WJ	6	384	SPIERS	SB	6	384	SPOHR	EW	2	323	SPRATT	J	11	353
SPENCER	WR	7	372	SPIERS	W	14	300	SPOHR	JW	7	372	SPRATT	P	11	353
SPENCER	WT	12	390	SPIESS	HW	7	372	SPOHR	R	2	323	SPRATT	PH	4	358
SPENDELOW	RH	12	210	SPILLANE	D	13	399	SPOKES	ET	5	334	SPRATT	S	1	328
SPENDER	TW	4	358	SPILLER	A	4	358	SPOKES	EV	5	334	SPRATT	S	4	358
SPENDER	WD	2	322	SPILLER	A	12	390	SPOKES	WJ	4	358	SPRATT	W	2	323
SPENDER	WH	4	358	SPILLER	GF	1	328	SPON	J	13	399	SPRATT	W	7	373
SPENDLEY	B	13	399	SPILLER	R	6	384	SPONDER	H	4	358	SPRATT	WA	10	218
SPENSER	JR	2	322	SPILLETT	C	10	217	SPONG	AM	2	323	SPRATT	WH	6	385
SPENSLEY	G	9	347	SPILLETT	HA	1	328	SPOONER	A	6	384	SPRATT	WT	2	323
SPERBER	JA	3	390	SPILLING	C	11	353	SPOONER	AH	13	399	SPRAWLES	G	10	218
SPERINCK	P	3	390	SPILLING	EC	12	210	SPOONER	AW	2	323	SPRAWLES	SJ	10	218
SPERRING	JA	12	210	SPILMAN	FW	4	358	SPOONER	F	1	328	SPRAY	H	10	370
SPERRING	WG	13	399	SPILSBURY	E	5	334	SPOONER	FT	2	323	SPRAYSON	C	6	385
SPETCH	H	8	326	SPILSBURY	G	10	217	SPOONER	G	2	323	SPREADBOROUGH	S	12	210
SPIBY	A	14	300	SPILSBURY	H	6	384	SPOONER	G	8	326	SPREADBURY	F	10	370
SPICE	AC	1	327	SPILSBURY	JE	9	180	SPOONER	GH	3	390	SPREADBURY	FA	7	373
SPICE	EH	2	322	SPILSTEAD	WC	13	399	SPOONER	GJ	7	372	SPREADBURY	FJ	4	358
SPICE	FG	12	390	SPINDLER	AE	10	217	SPOONER	JW	13	399	SPREADBURY	HG	4	358
SPICE	N	1	328	SPINDLER	LHH	1	328	SPOONER	W	2	323	SPREADBURY	W	4	359

SPREADBURY	WFT	10	218	SPRITTLES	FJ	12	211	SQUIRES	E	12	390	STACEY	LA	6	385
SPRECKLEY	HS	9	180	SPRITTLES	JJ	12	211	SQUIRES	EH	7	373	STACEY	LW	5	335
SPRECKLY	FG	12	210	SPRITTLES	SA	5	335	SQUIRES	EJ	7	373	STACEY	RW	1	328
SPRIGG	C	6	385	SPROATES	JT	5	335	SQUIRES	F	7	374	STACEY	S	3	229
SPRIGGINS	J	2	323	SPROGET	WJ	13	400	SQUIRES	HR	10	218	STACEY	SF	7	374
SPRIGGS	BD	8	327	SPROSTON	C	12	390	SQUIRES	HR	10	218	STACEY	SW	5	335
SPRIGGS	E	10	218	SPROSTON	FS	12	390	SQUIRES	J	2	324	STACEY	T	2	324
SPRIGGS	F	12	390	SPROSTON	WE	12	390	SQUIRES	L	13	400	STACEY	T	10	218
SPRIGGS	FG	12	210	SPROUL	T	13	400	SQUIRES	RJ	4	359	STACEY	W	3	391
SPRIGGS	G	10	218	SPROUL	WC	13	400	SQUIRES	T	8	327	STACEY	W	4	360
SPRIGGS	GH	13	400	SPROUSE	CL	7	373	SQUIRES	TRG	4	359	STACEY	W	7	374
SPRIGGS	I	8	327	SPRULES	JM	13	400	SQUIRES	WS	7	373	STACEY	W	9	347
SPRIGGS	J	12	210	SPRY	F	1	328	SQUIRRELL	AJ	3	391	STACEY	W	10	218
SPRIGGS	JA	4	359	SPRY	FJ	1	328	SQUIRRELL	AW	3	391	STACEY	WH	5	335
SPRIGGS	PA	12	210	SPRY	J	2	324	SQUIRRELL	C	7	374	STACEY	WM	12	211
SPRIGGS	RT	12	210	SPUFFORD	AG	5	335	SQUIRRELL	E	2	324	STACEY	WR	13	401
SPRIGGS	S	5	335	SPURDEN	H	7	373	SQUIRRELL	W	2	324	STACK	F	6	385
SPRIGGS	W	11	353	SPURDEN	W	7	373	SQUIRRILL	TH	14	300	STACK	J	1	329
SPRIGGS	WA	12	210	SPURDEN	W	7	373	SRAWLY	WH	6	385	STACK	P	2	324
SPRIGGS	WJ	6	385	SPURGE	FW	2	324	ST.GEORGE	H	11	331	STACK	R	8	327
SPRIGGS	WJ	12	390	SPURGEON	R	4	359	ST JOHN	E	13	372	STACK	TA	2	324
SPRING	AS	12	210	SPURLING	DJ	2	324	ST JOHN	W	4	364	STACK	TE	6	385
SPRING	E	5	335	SPURLING	WJ	10	218	STABLER	J	14	300	STADDON	EJ	2	324
SPRING	E	12	390	SPURR	F	11	353	STABLES	H	9	347	STADDON	FC	3	391
SPRING	EG	12	210	SPURR	G	5	335	STABLES	HE	9	180	STADDON	GE	3	391
SPRING	F	9	347	SPURR	G	11	353	STABLES	TH	13	400	STADDON	JJ	7	374
SPRING	F	12	210	SPURR	J	8	327	STACE	CW	4	359	STADELMAN	C	2	324
SPRING	FC	12	210	SPURR	SB	5	335	STACE	EB	4	359	STADELMAN	WW	2	324
SPRING	H	12	210	SPURR	SG	5	335	STACE	JC	4	359	STADELMAN	WW	7	374
SPRING	HS	7	373	SPURRDER	C	6	385	STACE	JC	4	359	STADLER	A	7	374
SPRING	J	7	373	SPURRIER	HG	4	359	STACE	PE	3	391	STADLER	EW	7	374
SPRING	W	12	210	SPURRIER	J	7	373	STACE	WP	3	391	STADLER	SM	7	374
SPRINGALL	CE	7	373	SPYER	H	12	211	STACEY	A	3	229	STAERCK	TJ	7	374
SPRINGALL	H	13	400	SQUELCH	H	6	385	STACEY	AE	2	324	STAFFERTON	H	12	211
SPRINGALL	PA	3	390	SQUIBB	A	13	400	STACEY	AE	12	211	STAFFERTON	W	12	211
SPRINGALL	TC	3	391	SQUIBB	AA	4	359	STACEY	AE	13	401	STAFFORD	AG	6	385
SPRINGALL	WR	13	400	SQUIBB	AS	4	359	STACEY	B	1	328	STAFFORD	AJ	7	374
SPRINGER	FC	4	359	SQUIBB	E	1	328	STACEY	BH	7	374	STAFFORD	AW	6	385
SPRINGER	FC	4	359	SQUIBB	FG	4	359	STACEY	CW	13	401	STAFFORD	C	6	385
SPRINGETT	C	7	373	SQUIBB	FH	1	328	STACEY	E	4	359	STAFFORD	CE	2	325
SPRINGETT	CH	1	328	SQUIBB	HF	1	328	STACEY	EJ	3	229	STAFFORD	DN	7	374
SPRINGETT	TJ	2	323	SQUIBB	JT	4	359	STACEY	ET	4	360	STAFFORD	DS	7	374
SPRINGGAY	M	13	400	SQUIBB	WH	4	359	STACEY	F	3	391	STAFFORD	E	14	300
SPRINGHAM	AE	13	400	SQUIBB	WJ	13	400	STACEY	F	4	360	STAFFORD	EJ	13	401
SPRINGHAM	AR	13	400	SQUIRE	AR	2	324	STACEY	FW	1	328	STAFFORD	ER	13	401
SPRINGHAM	HA	13	400	SQUIRE	FH	2	324	STACEY	G	2	324	STAFFORD	ET	4	360
SPRINGHAM	JE	13	400	SQUIRE	G	13	400	STACEY	GJ	13	401	STAFFORD	FW	1	329
SPRINGHAM	WJ	13	400	SQUIRE	TJ	5	335	STACEY	GW	3	391	STAFFORD	FW	13	401
SPRINGLE	A	3	391	SQUIRE	W	11	353	STACEY	H	9	347	STAFFORD	GH	6	385
SPRINGLE	B	2	323	SQUIRE	WC	2	324	STACEY	HJ	1	328	STAFFORD	GW	2	325
SPRINGLE	H	3	391	SQUIRE	WGG	13	400	STACEY	HS	3	229	STAFFORD	H	4	360
SPRINGWELL	T	12	390	SQUIRES	AE	12	390	STACEY	I	3	229	STAFFORD	HJ	13	401
SPRINKS	G	2	324	SQUIRES	AT	10	218	STACEY	J	1	328	STAFFORD	J	1	329
SPRITTLES	AR	12	210	SQUIRES	BJT	4	359	STACEY	J	11	353	STAFFORD	J	8	327
SPRITTLES	DH	12	211	SQUIRES	CE	10	218	STACEY	JC	7	374	STAFFORD	JD	5	335

STAFFORD	JP	14	300	STAINES	RA	3	391	STAMP	T	10	219	STANFORD	E	6	386
STAFFORD	JW	1	329	STAINES	W	5	335	STAMP	WG	1	329	STANFORD	E	6	386
STAFFORD	L	11	353	STAINFIELD	ME	14	300	STAMPE	HJ	6	386	STANFORD	EC	6	386
STAFFORD	MEA	3	391	STAINFIELD	WC	6	386	STAMPS	LJ	12	391	STANFORD	ESJ	1	330
STAFFORD	P	10	218	STAINTON	J	4	360	STAMPS	T	12	391	STANFORD	FA	5	336
STAFFORD	RCW	13	401	STAINTON	WR	13	401	STANBOROUGH	B	7	375	STANFORD	FR	6	386
STAFFORD	RW	4	360	STAIRMAID	WG	2	325	STANBOROUGH	HE	1	329	STANFORD	H	6	386
STAFFORD	SJ	13	401	STAIRS	W	10	219	STANBOROUGH	P	7	375	STANFORD	H	6	386
STAFFORD	T	9	181	STAIT	TH	11	354	STANBRIDGE	A	5	336	STANFORD	H	6	386
STAFFORD	W	11	353	STAKES	G	8	327	STANBRIDGE	E	5	336	STANFORD	JT	5	336
STAFFORD	WA	1	329	STAKES	J	14	300	STANBRIDGE	EB	1	329	STANFORD	JW	12	211
STAFFORD	WE	9	181	STALEY	JE	11	354	STANBRIDGE	FA	5	336	STANFORD	TL	13	401
STAFFORD	WM	7	374	STALEY	W	14	300	STANBRIDGE	G	5	336	STANFORD	W	5	336
STAGEMAN	JW	9	181	STALGIS	J	8	327	STANBRIDGE	G	7	375	STANFORD	WC	4	360
STAGG	AG	4	360	STALKER	A	14	300	STANBRIDGE	GT	5	336	STANFORD	WC	5	336
STAGG	AJ	3	391	STALKER	D	11	354	STANBRIDGE	HJ	12	211	STANFORD	WG	6	386
STAGG	C	4	360	STALKER	JL	14	300	STANBRIDGE	HR	5	336	STANFORD	WP	12	211
STAGG	C	7	374	STALLAN	HE	5	336	STANBRIDGE	HR	5	336	STANGER	C	2	325
STAGG	D	7	375	STALLARD	AH	3	391	STANBRIDGE	JT	12	211	STANGER	J	8	328
STAGG	E	10	370	STALLARD	C	2	325	STANBRIDGE	S	5	336	STANHOPE	GR	10	219
STAGG	E	14	300	STALLARD	CR	10	219	STANBRIDGE	SJ	2	325	STANHOPE	RA	7	376
STAGG	FC	7	375	STALLARD	CW	10	370	STANBRIDGE	TW	13	401	STANHOPE	T	13	402
STAGG	FG	10	370	STALLARD	FT	10	219	STANBURY	E	2	325	STANIER	E	6	386
STAGG	FH	4	360	STALLARD	G	7	375	STANBURY	TJ	7	375	STANIER	S	6	386
STAGG	GC	4	360	STALLARD	G	10	219	STANCLIFFE	C	8	327	STANIER	V	6	386
STAGG	GF	1	329	STALLARD	HJ	10	219	STANDAGE	A	8	327	STANIFORTH	A	8	328
STAGG	J	8	327	STALLARD	TW	10	219	STANDAGE	BR	8	327	STANIFORTH	F	12	211
STAGG	MW	7	375	STALLARD	WGP	9	181	STANDAGE	R	8	327	STANIFORTH	H	11	354
STAGG	RE	7	375	STALLARD	WJ	3	391	STANDEN	AH	10	370	STANIFORTH	H	11	354
STAGG	T	1	329	STALLEY	CE	9	181	STANDEN	C	7	375	STANIFORTH	J	8	328
STAGG	TF	10	219	STALLWOOD	AH	4	360	STANDEN	ET	7	375	STANIFORTH	TH	11	354
STAGG	WE	7	375	STALLWOOD	C	3	391	STANDEN	GS	11	354	STANILAND	G	8	328
STAGG	WG	5	335	STALLWOOD	FE	2	325	STANDFORD	H	13	401	STANING	PP	10	219
STAGG	WJ	4	360	STALLWOOD	H	7	375	STANDFORD	W	13	402	STANKER	E	11	354
STAHLER	A	11	354	STALLWOOD	TFJ	4	360	STANDIN	AG	7	376	STANLEY	A	1	330
STAIGHT	WH	6	385	STALLWOOD	WH	2	325	STANDING	A	8	328	STANLEY	A	3	229
STAINER	A	2	325	STALLWOOD	WH	2	325	STANDING	C	1	329	STANLEY	A	9	347
STAINER	E	13	401	STALLWORTHY	A	13	401	STANDING	C	8	328	STANLEY	A	11	354
STAINER	EH	13	401	STALLWORTHY	AE	13	401	STANDING	H	2	325	STANLEY	AG	2	325
STAINER	FG	7	375	STALLWORTHY	C	13	401	STANDING	R	1	329	STANLEY	AR	8	328
STAINER	H	8	327	STALLWORTHY	J	13	401	STANDING	WG	13	402	STANLEY	C	10	219
STAINER	V	4	360	STAMFORD	A	8	327	STANDING	WH	13	402	STANLEY	C	10	219
STAINER	VB	4	360	STAMFORD	H	12	211	STANDISH	CA	9	347	STANLEY	C	11	354
STAINES	A	2	325	STAMFORD	JA	8	327	STANDISH	WJ	1	329	STANLEY	CHM	7	376
STAINES	A	7	375	STAMMERS	A	8	327	STANDIVAN	F	7	376	STANLEY	E	14	301
STAINES	B	4	360	STAMMERS	AA	7	375	STANDLEY	WP	6	386	STANLEY	F	6	386
STAINES	E	10	219	STAMMERS	GW	5	336	STANDLY	T	6	386	STANLEY	F	8	328
STAINES	F	1	329	STAMMERS	H	9	347	STANDRING	T	14	301	STANLEY	FC	6	386
STAINES	F	5	335	STAMMERS	J	7	375	STANDWAN	AH	7	376	STANLEY	FCH	13	402
STAINES	FE	1	329	STAMMERS	JE	8	327	STANFIELD	FW	10	219	STANLEY	FE	10	371
STAINES	HJ	5	336	STAMMERS	JH	7	375	STANFORD	A	2	325	STANLEY	FJ	3	229
STAINES	JM	1	329	STAMP	F	1	329	STANFORD	B	6	386	STANLEY	FS	11	354
STAINES	LR	1	329	STAMP	G	6	386	STANFORD	BS	5	336	STANLEY	FT	5	336
STAINES	R	1	329	STAMP	J	6	386	STANFORD	C	2	325	STANLEY	FW	10	219
STAINES	R	1	329	STAMP	JE	12	391	STANFORD	CD	13	401	STANLEY	FW	11	354

STANLEY	FWB	13	402	STANNARD	SR	1	330	STANTON	J	12	211	STAPLETON	C	10	219
STANLEY	G	2	325	STANNARD	W	7	376	STANTON	J	12	212	STAPLETON	C	12	212
STANLEY	GA	7	376	STANNARD	WA	1	330	STANTON	J	14	301	STAPLETON	EC	12	212
STANLEY	GW	13	402	STANNARD	WE	1	330	STANTON	JE	8	328	STAPLETON	EJ	9	348
STANLEY	H	2	325	STANNERS	AE	1	330	STANTON	JT	8	328	STAPLETON	F	2	326
STANLEY	H	6	387	STANNERS	FW	1	330	STANTON	P	14	301	STAPLETON	G	5	337
STANLEY	H	6	387	STANNETT	A	7	376	STANTON	P	14	301	STAPLETON	GC	7	377
STANLEY	H	6	387	STANNEY	H	3	229	STANTON	SJH	1	330	STAPLETON	GJ	10	220
STANLEY	HF	6	387	STANNEY	HW	13	402	STANTON	T	12	212	STAPLETON	H	5	337
STANLEY	HW	4	360	STANNEY	PEV	13	402	STANTON	T	14	301	STAPLETON	H	12	212
STANLEY	J	1	330	STANNEY	RGP	3	229	STANTON	W	6	387	STAPLETON	H	12	212
STANLEY	J	1	330	STANNEY	TR	3	229	STANTON	W	7	376	STAPLETON	J	4	361
STANLEY	J	3	229	STANSBRIDGE	AR	4	361	STANTON	W	11	355	STAPLETON	J	5	337
STANLEY	J	6	387	STANSBRIDGE	ET	4	361	STANTON	W	14	301	STAPLETON	J	6	388
STANLEY	J	8	328	STANSBRIDGE	JW	4	361	STANTON	WE	1	331	STAPLETON	J	7	377
STANLEY	J	11	354	STANSBRIDGE	R	4	361	STANTON	WH	2	326	STAPLETON	PW	5	337
STANLEY	J	13	402	STANSBY	AJ	1	330	STANTON	WH	12	212	STAPLETON	R	5	337
STANLEY	JF	14	301	STANSBY	CS	1	330	STANTON	WJ	12	212	STAPLETON	S	5	337
STANLEY	JP	1	330	STANSBY	WJ	1	330	STANTON	WJ	13	402	STAPLETON	S	8	329
STANLEY	JT	4	360	STANSFIELD	A	8	328	STANTON	WT	12	212	STAPLETON	SE	7	377
STANLEY	JW	7	376	STANSFIELD	E	3	229	STANWAY	A	3	391	STAPLETON	W	4	361
STANLEY	JW	14	301	STANSFIELD	F	9	347	STANWAY	B	14	301	STAPLETON	W	12	391
STANLEY	PJ	4	361	STANSFIELD	GT	11	354	STANWAY	H	14	301	STAPLETON	WJ	10	220
STANLEY	S	4	361	STANSFIELD	IA	3	229	STANWAY	H	14	301	STAPLETON COTTON			
STANLEY	S	6	387	STANSFIELD	J	11	354	STANWAY	L	3	392		FA	3	392
STANLEY	SV	6	387	STANSFIELD	L	14	301	STANWELL	FV	3	229	STAPLEY	OJ	10	371
STANLEY	T	8	328	STANSFIELD	R	14	301	STANWELL	JE	3	229	STAPLEY	WR	5	337
STANLEY	T	11	354	STANSFIELD	S	8	328	STANYARD	J	14	301	STAPPARD	J	8	329
STANLEY	T	14	301	STANSFIELD	S	8	328	STAPENHILL	A	6	387	STAPPARD	J	9	348
STANLEY	TW	6	387	STANSFIELD	W	9	181	STAPENHILL	G	6	387	STARES	EHR	4	361
STANLEY	W	10	219	STANSMORE	A	10	219	STAPLEFORD	HH	10	371	STARES	HN	10	220
STANLEY	WE	3	229	STANSWOOD	DG	10	371	STAPLES	C	7	377	STARES	J	4	361
STANLEY	WEJ	14	301	STANTIFORD	WH	10	371	STAPLES	E	6	387	STARES	JGE	10	371
STANLEY	WH	12	391	STANTON	A	1	330	STAPLES	E	13	402	STARES	WG	10	371
STANLEY	WH	14	301	STANTON	A	6	387	STAPLES	EJT	13	402	STARING	VC	2	326
STANLEY	WJ	2	325	STANTON	A	8	328	STAPLES	ER	13	403	STARK	B	8	329
STANLEY	WJ	6	387	STANTON	AA	7	376	STAPLES	F	5	336	STARK	GT	8	329
STANLEY	WWS	9	181	STANTON	AF	13	402	STAPLES	F	13	403	STARK	HL	14	302
STANLICK	H	2	326	STANTON	CD	12	211	STAPLES	FH	9	181	STARK	J	4	361
STANMORE	F	1	330	STANTON	CG	6	387	STAPLES	FH	9	347	STARK	J	4	361
STANMORE	H	14	301	STANTON	CW	6	387	STAPLES	GA	6	387	STARK	J	7	377
STANMORE	S	1	330	STANTON	D	12	211	STAPLES	HH	1	331	STARK	J	9	348
STANMORE	W	7	376	STANTON	E	1	330	STAPLES	HT	13	403	STARK	TM	11	355
STANNARD	A	4	361	STANTON	EH	10	219	STAPLES	J	10	219	STARK	WC	3	392
STANNARD	A	6	387	STANTON	F	8	328	STAPLES	J	13	403	STARKEY	A	6	388
STANNARD	A	7	376	STANTON	FC	6	387	STAPLES	JJ	13	403	STARKEY	AE	3	229
STANNARD	A	13	402	STANTON	FP	12	211	STAPLES	L	13	403	STARKEY	C	6	388
STANNARD	AC	1	330	STANTON	G	13	402	STAPLES	S	13	403	STARKEY	CA	10	371
STANNARD	EH	7	376	STANTON	GA	2	326	STAPLES	THV	1	331	STARKEY	CW	2	326
STANNARD	F	13	402	STANTON	H	12	391	STAPLES	W	7	377	STARKEY	EA	3	229
STANNARD	HE	7	376	STANTON	HJ	12	211	STAPLES	WT	5	336	STARKEY	GF	2	326
STANNARD	HG	7	376	STANTON	J	7	376	STAPLETON	A	8	328	STARKEY	HS	6	388
STANNARD	J	2	326	STANTON	J	8	328	STAPLETON	A	13	403	STARKEY	J	4	361
STANNARD	J	13	402	STANTON	J	8	328	STAPLETON	AE	5	337	STARKEY	J	8	329
STANNARD	L	1	330	STANTON	J	11	354	STAPLETON	AG	3	392	STARKEY	JH	2	326

Surname	Initials	Vol	Page
STARKEY	JJ	6	388
STARKEY	TT	6	388
STARKINS	F	5	337
STARKINS	J	5	337
STARLING	E	2	326
STARLING	ECG	10	220
STARLING	F	2	326
STARLING	TJ	5	337
STARMER	AC	11	355
STARMER	CS	12	391
STARMER	FC	12	391
STARMER	FW	12	391
STARMER	WG	3	392
STARMER	WJ	3	392
STARMORE	AS	12	212
STARMORE	ES	12	212
STARMORE	FH	12	212
STARMORE	LS	12	212
STARNES	LL	13	403
STARNS	HA	4	361
STARNS	RR	4	361
STARR	AE	2	326
STARR	EHD	4	361
STARR	H	9	181
STARR	JH	11	355
STARR	W	8	329
STARTUP	A	10	220
STARTUP	AJ	13	403
STASS	AG	2	326
STATE	A	6	388
STATE	B	6	388
STATE	JE	6	388
STATEN	J	8	329
STATHAM	A	5	337
STATHAM	AJ	5	337
STATHAM	CH	11	355
STATHAM	FG	5	337
STATHAM	G	14	302
STATHAM	JH	14	302
STATHAM	P	3	392
STATHAM	T	14	302
STATON	JH	11	355
STAUGHTON	PH	12	391
STAUGHTON	WJ	12	212
STAUNTON	J	9	181
STAVELEY	AH	14	302
STAVES	AE	10	220
STAWELL	JS	1	331
STAY	AF	4	361
STEABBEN	JD	5	337
STEAD	A	8	329
STEAD	A	8	329
STEAD	A	9	181
STEAD	C	2	326
STEAD	C	8	329
STEAD	CH	10	371
STEAD	CR	8	329
STEAD	E	8	329
STEAD	E	9	181
STEAD	E	9	348
STEAD	EO	9	181
STEAD	F	9	348
STEAD	F	9	348
STEAD	F	9	348
STEAD	G	8	329
STEAD	G	9	181
STEAD	G	11	355
STEAD	H	8	329
STEAD	H	8	329
STEAD	H	8	329
STEAD	H	9	181
STEAD	H	9	181
STEAD	H	9	348
STEAD	H	9	348
STEAD	H	11	355
STEAD	HEW	2	326
STEAD	HK	8	329
STEAD	HW	8	329
STEAD	HW	13	403
STEAD	J	8	329
STEAD	J	9	181
STEAD	J	9	348
STEAD	JH	8	330
STEAD	JR	8	330
STEAD	JW	8	330
STEAD	MC	8	330
STEAD	(MRS)	13	403
STEAD	P	9	181
STEAD	R	8	330
STEAD	R	8	330
STEAD	R	8	330
STEAD	SRH	3	392
STEAD	T	8	330
STEAD	T	9	181
STEAD	W	8	330
STEAD	W	8	330
STEAD	W	8	330
STEAD	W	8	330
STEAD	W	8	330
STEAD	W	8	330
STEAD	W	9	348
STEAD	W	9	348
STEAD	WH	9	348
STEAD	WR	8	330
STEADMAN	A	11	355
STEADMAN	C	11	355
STEADMAN	EC	13	403
STEADMAN	F	6	388
STEADMAN	H	6	388
STEADMAN	HR	11	355
STEADMAN	JR	6	388
STEADMAN	SF	4	361
STEADMAN	TW	2	326
STEADMAN	W	11	355
STEAN	J	1	331
STEARN	F	5	337
STEARN	H	5	337
STEARN	W	2	326
STEARN	W	3	392
STEARNS	CE	11	424
STEARNS	P	10	371
STEARNS	WR	11	424
STEARS	HS	13	403
STEARS	T	11	355
STEBBENS	CR	10	220
STEBBENS	JR	9	348
STEBBENS	R	9	348
STEBBIN	FJ	7	377
STEBBING	TE	13	403
STEBBINGS	HL	1	331
STEBBINGS	R	2	326
STEDALL	JJ	10	220
STEDMAN	AC	10	371
STEDMAN	C	8	330
STEDMAN	GW	4	361
STEDMAN	HE	4	362
STEDMAN	LJ	4	362
STEDMAN	R	4	362
STEDMAN	R	13	403
STEDMAN	RW	13	403
STEDMAN	W	5	337
STEDMAN	W	6	388
STEDMAN	WE	4	362
STEED	E	1	331
STEED	EG	1	331
STEED	F	4	362
STEED	J	4	362
STEED	R	2	327
STEED	T	6	388
STEED	W	4	362
STEEDEN	P	14	302
STEEDENS	R	5	338
STEEDENS	S	5	338
STEEDMAN	W	10	220
STEEL	A	8	330
STEEL	A	8	330
STEEL	A	9	181
STEEL	A	12	391
STEEL	A	13	403
STEEL	AW	6	388
STEEL	B	9	182
STEEL	C	6	388
STEEL	CA	10	220
STEEL	CW	10	371
STEEL	E	7	377
STEEL	EJ	1	331
STEEL	EWJ	1	331
STEEL	G	11	355
STEEL	G	13	404
STEEL	GA	1	331
STEEL	GE	9	182
STEEL	J	7	377
STEEL	J	10	220
STEEL	J	13	403
STEEL	JT	11	355
STEEL	JT	12	391
STEEL	JW	4	362
STEEL	KF	1	331
STEEL	L	3	392
STEEL	W	2	327
STEEL	WA	1	331
STEEL	WH	13	404
STEEL	WS	1	331
STEELE	A	9	182
STEELE	A	10	371
STEELE	A	14	302
STEELE	AG	1	331
STEELE	AG	12	212
STEELE	AP	6	388
STEELE	AT	2	327
STEELE	AWC	12	391
STEELE	B	5	338
STEELE	C	8	330
STEELE	FC	4	362
STEELE	FG	10	371
STEELE	FJ	13	404
STEELE	G	14	302
STEELE	G	14	302
STEELE	GE	4	362
STEELE	GE	4	362
STEELE	HF	4	362
STEELE	J	10	220
STEELE	J	14	302
STEELE	JA	1	331
STEELE	JC	8	331
STEELE	JE	10	220
STEELE	S	7	377
STEELE	S	9	348
STEELE	TW	5	338
STEELE	TW	11	355
STEELE	W	6	388
STEELE	W	8	331
STEELE	W	9	182
STEELE	W	10	220
STEELE	W	10	371
STEELE	W	14	302
STEELE	WH	12	391
STEELE	WT	7	377
STEELL	GP	5	338
STEEMSON	G	7	377
STEENSON	T	14	302

STEEPLE	VA	13	404	STEPHENS	B	6	388	STEPHENSON	EE	13	404	STEVENS	A	10	221
STEER	EG	10	371	STEPHENS	B	7	378	STEPHENSON	EJ	14	303	STEVENS	A	12	212
STEER	G	7	377	STEPHENS	C	7	378	STEPHENSON	G	9	182	STEVENS	A	12	391
STEER	GS	7	377	STEPHENS	CH	13	404	STEPHENSON	G	9	348	STEVENS	AE	4	363
STEER	H	5	338	STEPHENS	CR	2	327	STEPHENSON	GE	9	349	STEVENS	AE	10	221
STEER	J	7	377	STEPHENS	ECJ	13	404	STEPHENSON	H	14	303	STEVENS	AE	10	372
STEER	TH	7	377	STEPHENS	F	6	389	STEPHENSON	HE	7	378	STEVENS	AE	11	356
STEER	W	7	377	STEPHENS	F	6	389	STEPHENSON	HER	3	230	STEVENS	AE	13	404
STEER	W	7	377	STEPHENS	FC	2	327	STEPHENSON	I	9	182	STEVENS	AG	12	213
STEERE	CE	13	404	STEPHENS	FC	13	404	STEPHENSON	J	8	331	STEVENS	AH	3	392
STEFF	HJ	5	338	STEPHENS	G	8	331	STEPHENSON	J	9	349	STEVENS	AH	12	391
STEFF	MH	5	338	STEPHENS	H	3	230	STEPHENSON	JH	13	404	STEVENS	AJ	4	363
STEFF	NP	5	338	STEPHENS	H	3	230	STEPHENSON	JS	9	182	STEVENS	AJ	10	372
STEGGLE	G	7	377	STEPHENS	H	4	362	STEPHENSON	JW	9	349	STEVENS	AJ	13	404
STEGGLES	D	13	404	STEPHENS	H	6	389	STEPHENSON	N	9	349	STEVENS	AR	6	389
STEIN	J	14	302	STEPHENS	H	8	331	STEPHENSON	NN	9	349	STEVENS	AT	1	332
STEINBERG	A	7	377	STEPHENS	H	8	331	STEPHENSON	R	9	182	STEVENS	AW	1	332
STELFOX	E	11	356	STEPHENS	H	9	348	STEPHENSON	S	7	378	STEVENS	AW	7	379
STELL	TT	9	348	STEPHENS	HJ	1	331	STEPHENSON	W	8	331	STEVENS	AW	12	213
STEMBRIDGE	T	14	302	STEPHENS	J	4	362	STEPHENSON	W	8	331	STEVENS	B	1	332
STEMBRIGE	J	8	331	STEPHENS	J	10	220	STEPHENSON	W	9	182	STEVENS	B	10	372
STEMP	F	10	220	STEPHENS	J	14	302	STEPHENSON	W	9	349	STEVENS	BR	7	378
STEMSON	W	7	378	STEPHENS	JA	13	404	STEPHENSON	W	9	349	STEVENS	BW	7	379
STENHOFF	A	13	404	STEPHENS	JR	13	404	STEPHENSON	W	11	356	STEVENS	C	3	230
STENHOUSE	A	5	338	STEPHENS	L	7	378	STEPHENSON	WA	12	212	STEVENS	C	4	363
STENHOUSE	J	5	338	STEPHENS	R	6	389	STEPHENSON	WG	3	230	STEVENS	C	6	389
STENHOUSE	W	5	338	STEPHENS	S	9	182	STEPHENSON	WG	3	230	STEVENS	CA	7	379
STENNETT	EH	4	362	STEPHENS	S	14	302	STEPHENSON	WH	7	378	STEVENS	CB	3	230
STENNETT	FG	7	378	STEPHENS	SG	10	372	STEPHENSON	WJ	9	182	STEVENS	CD	9	349
STENNETT	JG	12	391	STEPHENS	T	6	389	STEPHENSON	WJ	9	349	STEVENS	CE	7	379
STENNING	C	7	378	STEPHENS	TA	12	391	STEPNEY	EW	6	389	STEVENS	CF	3	230
STENNING	FC	12	212	STEPHENS	W	4	362	STEPNEY	JH	1	332	STEVENS	CH	3	230
STENNING	FJ	7	378	STEPHENS	W	6	389	STEPNEY	R	6	389	STEVENS	CH	12	213
STENNING	H	1	331	STEPHENS	W	10	220	STEPTO	FJ	2	327	STEVENS	CW	3	392
STENNING	HW	10	371	STEPHENS	WA	10	372	STEPTO	JR	1	332	STEVENS	CW	13	404
STENNING	SG	7	378	STEPHENS	WE	2	327	STEPTOE	C	10	221	STEVENS	E	5	338
STENNING	T	7	378	STEPHENS	WF	9	182	STEPTOE	FT	1	332	STEVENS	E	5	338
STENNING	WJ	7	378	STEPHENS	WH	9	182	STEPTOE	FW	7	378	STEVENS	E	10	372
STENNINGS	H	2	327	STEPHENS	WJ	10	372	STEPTOE	GT	2	327	STEVENS	E	10	372
STENSON	M	9	182	STEPHENS	WT	1	331	STEPTOE	JT	10	221	STEVENS	E	12	213
STENT	BG	4	362	STEPHENS	WT	4	362	STERLING	JE	14	303	STEVENS	EA	1	332
STENT	EW	10	371	STEPHENS	WT	7	378	STERLING	TH	8	331	STEVENS	EJ	3	392
STENT	H	12	391	STEPHENSON	A	3	230	STERLING	V	14	303	STEVENS	EJ	4	363
STENT	HJ	4	362	STEPHENSON	A	13	404	STERLING	W	14	303	STEVENS	ES	13	405
STENT	W	1	331	STEPHENSON	A	14	302	STERNE	D	8	331	STEVENS	ET	13	405
STENT	WD	12	391	STEPHENSON	AJ	3	230	STERRY	HR	7	378	STEVENS	ETJ	1	332
STEP	AW	3	230	STEPHENSON	ATA	3	230	STEVANS	HC	5	338	STEVENS	F	1	332
STEPHEN	D	13	404	STEPHENSON	AW	6	389	STEVANS	J	5	338	STEVENS	F	3	392
STEPHEN	JE	2	327	STEPHENSON	C	9	182	STEVENS	A	2	327	STEVENS	F	4	363
STEPHEN	M	9	182	STEPHENSON	C	9	348	STEVENS	A	3	230	STEVENS	F	5	338
STEPHENS	AE	4	362	STEPHENSON	CH	8	331	STEVENS	A	3	230	STEVENS	F	5	339
STEPHENS	AE	7	378	STEPHENSON	E	14	302	STEVENS	A	3	230	STEVENS	F	6	389
STEPHENS	AH	10	220	STEPHENSON	E	14	303	STEVENS	A	4	363	STEVENS	F	6	389
STEPHENS	AJW	10	220	STEPHENSON	E	14	303	STEVENS	A	5	338	STEVENS	F	7	379
STEPHENS	AW	2	327	STEPHENSON	EB	8	331	STEVENS	A	6	389	STEVENS	F	7	379

STEVENS	F	12	392	STEVENS	JA	3	392	STEVENS	WT	3	393	STEWARD	E	3	231
STEVENS	FA	13	405	STEVENS	JC	2	327	STEVENSON	AH	3	393	STEWARD	FA	6	390
STEVENS	FAG	12	213	STEVENS	JE	1	332	STEVENSON	AH	12	392	STEWARD	G	8	332
STEVENS	FG	7	379	STEVENS	JH	13	405	STEVENSON	AR	4	363	STEWARD	GW	3	231
STEVENS	FJ	2	327	STEVENS	JR	8	331	STEVENSON	AW	12	392	STEWARD	J	7	380
STEVENS	FW	2	327	STEVENS	JW	6	389	STEVENSON	B	8	331	STEWARD	J	9	182
STEVENS	FW	5	338	STEVENS	JW	10	221	STEVENSON	C	8	331	STEWARD	J	11	356
STEVENS	G	1	332	STEVENS	JW	11	356	STEVENSON	C	8	331	STEWARD	J	14	303
STEVENS	G	1	332	STEVENS	JW	13	405	STEVENSON	C	8	331	STEWARD	W	9	182
STEVENS	G	2	327	STEVENS	LJ	3	230	STEVENSON	C	9	182	STEWARD	W	14	303
STEVENS	G	3	230	STEVENS	LT	3	392	STEVENSON	E	1	332	STEWARD	WA	13	406
STEVENS	G	4	363	STEVENS	MA	10	372	STEVENSON	EJ	6	390	STEWARD	WJ	14	303
STEVENS	G	5	339	STEVENS	R	6	389	STEVENSON	EW	3	393	STEWARDSON	S	11	356
STEVENS	G	7	379	STEVENS	R	11	356	STEVENSON	F	9	349	STEWART	A	5	339
STEVENS	G	7	379	STEVENS	RH	7	379	STEVENSON	FW	1	333	STEWART	A	8	332
STEVENS	G	8	331	STEVENS	RL	6	389	STEVENSON	G	10	221	STEWART	A	9	183
STEVENS	G	12	213	STEVENS	RV	12	213	STEVENSON	GE	13	405	STEWART	A	12	213
STEVENS	G	12	213	STEVENS	RW	13	405	STEVENSON	GJ	12	392	STEWART	A	14	303
STEVENS	G	13	405	STEVENS	SAJ	12	213	STEVENSON	H	6	390	STEWART	AA	12	213
STEVENS	GE	7	379	STEVENS	SE	1	332	STEVENSON	H	13	406	STEWART	AG	1	333
STEVENS	GJ	3	230	STEVENS	SE	12	392	STEVENSON	HA	10	372	STEWART	C	7	380
STEVENS	GJ	10	372	STEVENS	SF	10	221	STEVENSON	HF	13	406	STEWART	C	9	183
STEVENS	GK	10	221	STEVENS	SF	13	405	STEVENSON	HG	8	332	STEWART	C	11	356
STEVENS	GS	1	332	STEVENS	SJ	12	392	STEVENSON	J	12	213	STEWART	CE	13	406
STEVENS	GT	10	221	STEVENS	T	5	339	STEVENSON	J	12	392	STEWART	D	3	231
STEVENS	GW	7	379	STEVENS	T	6	390	STEVENSON	JG	12	392	STEWART	D	8	332
STEVENS	H	1	332	STEVENS	T	13	405	STEVENSON	JL	7	380	STEWART	E	14	303
STEVENS	H	2	327	STEVENS	TH	7	379	STEVENSON	L	6	390	STEWART	EA	1	333
STEVENS	H	3	230	STEVENS	W	1	332	STEVENSON	LJ	7	380	STEWART	EF	10	372
STEVENS	H	5	339	STEVENS	W	4	363	STEVENSON	M	2	328	STEWART	EG	11	356
STEVENS	H	6	389	STEVENS	W	5	339	STEVENSON	P	1	333	STEWART	F	9	183
STEVENS	H	7	379	STEVENS	W	6	390	STEVENSON	PW	13	406	STEWART	F	12	213
STEVENS	H	11	356	STEVENS	W	6	390	STEVENSON	R	1	333	STEWART	FA	7	380
STEVENS	H	13	405	STEVENS	W	10	221	STEVENSON	RCS	12	392	STEWART	FC	11	356
STEVENS	H	13	405	STEVENS	W	10	372	STEVENSON	S	1	333	STEWART	G	3	231
STEVENS	H	13	405	STEVENS	W	12	213	STEVENSON	T	4	363	STEWART	G	4	363
STEVENS	H	13	405	STEVENS	W	12	213	STEVENSON	W	6	390	STEWART	G	4	363
STEVENS	H	13	405	STEVENS	W	12	213	STEVENSON	W	14	303	STEWART	G	13	406
STEVENS	HA	13	405	STEVENS	W	13	405	STEVENSON	WAA	12	392	STEWART	G	14	303
STEVENS	HC	7	379	STEVENS	WA	5	339	STEVENSON	WE	11	356	STEWART	GS	6	390
STEVENS	HJ	3	392	STEVENS	WC	2	328	STEVENSON	WH	14	303	STEWART	GT	1	333
STEVENS	HJ	5	339	STEVENS	WC	7	380	STEVENTON	CA	7	380	STEWART	H	3	231
STEVENS	HJ	5	339	STEVENS	WE	7	380	STEVENTON	FP	3	230	STEWART	H	8	332
STEVENS	HJ	13	405	STEVENS	WE	13	405	STEVENTON	HG	3	231	STEWART	H	11	356
STEVENS	J	2	328	STEVENS	WGR	7	380	STEVENTON	JH	6	390	STEWART	HD	10	221
STEVENS	J	3	392	STEVENS	WH	1	332	STEVENTON	V	6	390	STEWART	HD	11	356
STEVENS	J	4	363	STEVENS	WH	7	380	STEVENTON	WT	6	390	STEWART	J	4	363
STEVENS	J	5	339	STEVENS	WH	12	392	STEVES	IA	7	380	STEWART	J	7	380
STEVENS	J	5	339	STEVENS	WJ	2	328	STEVONSON	E	6	390	STEWART	J	7	380
STEVENS	J	6	389	STEVENS	WJ	4	363	STEVONSON	GH	6	390	STEWART	J	8	332
STEVENS	J	7	379	STEVENS	WJ	7	380	STEVSON	S	7	380	STEWART	J	8	332
STEVENS	J	7	379	STEVENS	WJT	12	213	STEWARD	A	5	339	STEWART	J	9	349
STEVENS	J	8	331	STEVENS	WL	13	405	STEWARD	AJ	3	231	STEWART	J	11	356
STEVENS	J	10	372	STEVENS	WM	1	332	STEWARD	C	11	356	STEWART	J	11	356
STEVENS	J	12	392	STEVENS	WM	3	393	STEWARD	D	9	182	STEWART	J	13	406

STEWART	J	13	406	STILGES	W	10	221	STIRLING	W	11	357	STOCKEY	C	9	183
STEWART	J	13	406	STILGOE	JH	6	390	STIRRUP	CW	14	303	STOCKEY	GA	9	183
STEWART	JAC	11	356	STILL	CP	1	333	STIRRUP	J	4	364	STOCKEY	W	14	304
STEWART	JE	13	406	STILL	CW	3	393	STIRRUP	J	11	357	STOCKFORD	F	12	214
STEWART	JH	4	363	STILL	EW	3	393	STIRRUP	T	14	303	STOCKFORD	JE	1	334
STEWART	JH	10	221	STILL	FW	7	381	STIRZAKER	R	14	304	STOCKFORD	JW	1	334
STEWART	JT	12	424	STILL	P	3	393	STIVEY	JC	4	364	STOCKFORD	WJ	1	334
STEWART	JT	13	406	STILL	SJ	7	381	STIVEY	JWC	4	364	STOCKHILL	JW	8	332
STEWART	JW	8	332	STILL	WT	13	406	STIVEY	WG	4	364	STOCKHILL	M	8	332
STEWART	JW	8	332	STILLION	J	9	183	STOAKES	F	14	304	STOCKING	G	13	407
STEWART	JW	12	392	STILLMAN	AG	13	406	STOAKES	WJ	10	221	STOCKING	J	13	407
STEWART	LJ	2	328	STILLMAN	CB	1	333	STOAKLEY	WA	2	328	STOCKING	J	13	407
STEWART	LJ	10	372	STILLMAN	G	2	328	STOAKLEY	WH	7	381	STOCKING	R	13	407
STEWART	MH	7	380	STILLMAN	H	1	333	STOBART	F	9	183	STOCKING	S	13	407
STEWART	R	9	183	STILLMAN	WE	2	328	STOBART	J	9	183	STOCKING	SJ	7	381
STEWART	S	1	333	STILLWELL	AJ	5	339	STOBART	JW	8	332	STOCKLEY	AH	4	364
STEWART	S	11	356	STILLWELL	BC	13	406	STOBART	T	9	183	STOCKLEY	EV	5	340
STEWART	SH	13	406	STILLWELL	EJ	2	328	STOBARTS	W	9	349	STOCKLEY	HG	10	372
STEWART	SR	13	406	STILLWELL	F	1	333	STOCK	BC	12	213	STOCKLEY	M	4	364
STEWART	V	9	183	STILLWELL	G	1	333	STOCK	ES	2	328	STOCKLEY	PC	7	381
STEWART	W	2	328	STILLWELL	H	2	328	STOCK	FL	2	329	STOCKLEY	W	10	221
STEWART	W	4	363	STILLWELL	H	5	339	STOCK	H	6	390	STOCKMAN	A	4	365
STEWART	W	4	363	STILLWELL	HS	3	393	STOCK	HG	12	214	STOCKMAN	PV	4	365
STEWART	W	11	357	STILLWELL	P	5	339	STOCK	J	12	214	STOCKS	A	8	332
STEWART	W	14	303	STILLWELL	W	2	328	STOCK	L	14	304	STOCKS	FG	5	340
STEWART	WJ	8	332	STILTON	F	13	406	STOCK	N	1	334	STOCKS	FH	5	340
STEWART	WM	3	231	STIMPSON	A	5	340	STOCK	PG	5	340	STOCKS	JE	9	349
STEWART	WR	13	406	STIMPSON	E	5	339	STOCK	WJ	13	407	STOCKS	N	11	357
STEWNSON	J	14	303	STIMPSON	EJ	4	364	STOCKDALE	A	9	183	STOCKS	RCE	4	365
STICKLAND	CE	4	363	STIMPSON	ES	2	328	STOCKDALE	AH	13	407	STOCKS	T	9	183
STICKLAND	E	4	363	STIMPSON	H	4	364	STOCKDALE	E	8	332	STOCKS	W	8	332
STICKLAND	FG	4	363	STIMPSON	J	1	333	STOCKDALE	F	9	349	STOCKTON	AL	7	381
STICKLAND	H	4	364	STIMPSON	JS	1	333	STOCKDALE	GT	13	407	STOCKTON	F	7	381
STICKLAND	W	4	364	STIMPSON	L	5	339	STOCKDALE	H	8	332	STOCKTON	F	11	357
STICKLAND	WJ	4	364	STIMPSON	SA	5	339	STOCKDALE	O	9	183	STOCKTON	H	7	381
STICKLEN	GE	4	364	STIMPSON	WS	3	231	STOCKDALE	P	11	357	STOCKTON	H	13	407
STICKLEN	WE	4	364	STIMPSON	WS	7	381	STOCKDALE	W	9	183	STOCKTON	HMS	7	381
STICKLER	CW	1	333	STIMSON	A	5	340	STOCKDALE	W	9	349	STOCKTON	J	6	390
STICKLES	FC	7	380	STIMSON	WG	5	340	STOCKELL	FW	9	183	STOCKTON	JH	6	390
STICKLEY	CF	4	364	STINGEMORE	A	3	393	STOCKER	EG	13	407	STOCKTON	JR	6	390
STICKLEY	E	4	364	STINGEMORE	F	3	393	STOCKER	EJ	12	214	STOCKTON	LJ	2	329
STICKLEY	EW	2	328	STINGEMORE	R	3	393	STOCKER	FC	1	334	STOCKTON	P	14	304
STICKLEY	FA	4	364	STINGEMORE	W	3	393	STOCKER	FJ	12	214	STOCKTON	T	11	357
STICKLEY	J	2	328	STINN	G	12	392	STOCKER	FR	3	393	STOCKTON	W	6	391
STICKLEY	W	1	333	STINN	J	12	392	STOCKER	G	1	334	STOCKTON	W	11	357
STIDWORTHY	HL	1	333	STINTON	A	2	328	STOCKER	J	3	393	STOCKWELL	C	1	334
STIFF	HG	12	213	STINTON	GC	2	328	STOCKER	J	3	393	STOCKWELL	C	12	214
STIGANT	EW	10	221	STINTON	LG	2	328	STOCKER	JP	12	214	STOCKWELL	E	8	332
STIGGINS	A	13	406	STINTON	R	11	357	STOCKER	R	3	393	STOCKWELL	F	7	381
STILES	A	3	231	STINTON	W	1	334	STOCKER	S	7	381	STOCKWELL	F	8	333
STILES	CTW	4	364	STIRK	C	9	349	STOCKER	SH	3	393	STOCKWELL	G	7	381
STILES	EA	6	390	STIRK	FC	9	349	STOCKER	W	5	340	STOCKWELL	GH	9	183
STILES	G	3	231	STIRK	H	8	332	STOCKER	WGC	4	364	STOCKWELL	HT	13	407
STILES	J	3	231	STIRK	JW	9	183	STOCKER	WH	2	329	STOCKWELL	J	7	381
STILES	O	6	390	STIRK	RH	9	183	STOCKEY	BF	14	304	STOCKWELL	J	9	184

STOCKWELL	P	12	392	STOKES	HW	5	340	STONE	CH	13	407	STONE	TE	4	366
STOCKWELL	R	12	392	STOKES	HW	12	214	STONE	CJ	1	334	STONE	TR	12	214
STOCKWELL	T	13	407	STOKES	J	4	365	STONE	CW	7	382	STONE	W	3	231
STOCKWELL	TG	13	407	STOKES	J	5	340	STONE	E	1	334	STONE	W	4	366
STOCKWELL	VG	7	381	STOKES	J	5	340	STONE	E	4	366	STONE	W	4	366
STOCKWELL	WF	6	391	STOKES	JA	7	382	STONE	E	5	341	STONE	W	5	341
STOCKWIN	A	12	392	STOKES	JF	10	372	STONE	EA	10	373	STONE	W	11	357
STOCKWIN	F	12	392	STOKES	JH	6	391	STONE	EF	10	373	STONE	WA	1	335
STODDARD	J	8	333	STOKES	JT	6	391	STONE	EF	12	214	STONE	WA	10	222
STODDART	E	1	334	STOKES	JW	13	407	STONE	EJ	10	222	STONE	WD	7	382
STOFFELL	CE	7	381	STOKES	LW	4	365	STONE	ER	1	334	STONE	WE	3	394
STOFFELL	CF	7	381	STOKES	P	5	340	STONE	EWG	10	373	STONE	WE	4	366
STOKE	W	4	365	STOKES	PJ	2	329	STONE	F	1	334	STONE	WE	11	357
STOKE	WE	4	365	STOKES	R	5	340	STONE	F	3	231	STONE	WF	5	341
STOKEHILL	G	8	333	STOKES	R	5	340	STONE	F	4	366	STONE	WHA	4	366
STOKEHILL	H	8	333	STOKES	RE	2	329	STONE	F	14	304	STONE	WHJ	7	382
STOKES	A	5	340	STOKES	RF	4	365	STONE	FC	2	329	STONE	WJ	3	394
STOKES	A	6	391	STOKES	S	5	340	STONE	FC	13	408	STONE	WJ	13	408
STOKES	A	10	221	STOKES	S	9	184	STONE	G	1	334	STONE	WS	4	366
STOKES	A	14	304	STOKES	S	9	349	STONE	G	4	366	STONE	WT	4	367
STOKES	AE	2	329	STOKES	SA	6	391	STONE	G	4	366	STONEADGE	FG	4	367
STOKES	AG	6	391	STOKES	SW	12	214	STONE	G	5	341	STONEBRIDGE	A	12	214
STOKES	AH	4	365	STOKES	T	5	341	STONE	G	13	408	STONEBRIDGE	CA	12	214
STOKES	AJ	1	334	STOKES	T	12	214	STONE	GMW	4	366	STONEBRIDGE	EA	12	215
STOKES	AJ	7	381	STOKES	TS	6	391	STONE	H	2	329	STONEBRIDGE	W	5	341
STOKES	AJ	7	382	STOKES	TWS	6	391	STONE	H	13	407	STONEBRIDGE	WE	12	215
STOKES	AR	12	214	STOKES	VM	2	329	STONE	HC	1	334	STONEHAM	AA	3	394
STOKES	B	6	391	STOKES	W	4	365	STONE	HC	5	341	STONEHAM	CJ	7	382
STOKES	BR	4	365	STOKES	W	5	341	STONE	HE	1	334	STONEHAM	EA	4	367
STOKES	C	14	304	STOKES	W	7	382	STONE	HG	4	366	STONEHAM	F	3	394
STOKES	CE	14	304	STOKES	W	12	214	STONE	HN	7	382	STONEHAM	F	4	367
STOKES	CF	4	365	STOKES	WA	7	382	STONE	J	1	335	STONEHAM	GB	4	367
STOKES	CF	4	365	STOKES	WE	12	214	STONE	J	10	373	STONEHAM	H	7	382
STOKES	E	6	391	STOKES	WF	1	334	STONE	J	12	214	STONEHAM	HG	10	222
STOKES	E	6	391	STOKES	WH	4	365	STONE	J	13	408	STONEHAM	MT	3	394
STOKES	E	7	381	STOLE	W	11	357	STONE	JA	7	382	STONEHAM	WE	13	408
STOKES	E	11	357	STOLTENHOFF	H	13	407	STONE	JD	1	335	STONEHOUSE	E	8	333
STOKES	EC	1	334	STONE	A	3	231	STONE	JD	5	341	STONEHOUSE	G	8	333
STOKES	F	1	334	STONE	A	4	365	STONE	JE	4	366	STONEHOUSE	GH	14	304
STOKES	F	3	393	STONE	A	5	341	STONE	JH	1	335	STONEHOUSE	J	8	333
STOKES	F	4	365	STONE	A	5	341	STONE	JH	6	391	STONEHOUSE	RF	4	367
STOKES	FJ	3	393	STONE	A	10	373	STONE	JT	13	408	STONELAKE	DW	11	357
STOKES	FJ	5	340	STONE	AC	13	407	STONE	L	3	231	STONELAKE	H	1	335
STOKES	FW	6	391	STONE	AE	10	222	STONE	L	5	341	STONELL	CE	7	382
STOKES	FW	12	214	STONE	AE	10	373	STONE	MF	4	366	STONELL	FH	7	382
STOKES	G	4	365	STONE	AE	13	407	STONE	PJ	1	335	STONELL	T	7	382
STOKES	G	6	391	STONE	AG	2	329	STONE	R	4	366	STONEMAN	AE	3	394
STOKES	GH	3	393	STONE	AJ	3	231	STONE	R	14	304	STONEMAN	F	1	335
STOKES	GJ	4	365	STONE	AJ	4	365	STONE	RA	4	366	STONEMAN	J	1	335
STOKES	GN	8	333	STONE	AR	5	341	STONE	RA	4	366	STONEMAN	J	4	367
STOKES	H	2	329	STONE	AV	1	334	STONE	RS	10	221	STONEMAN	L	1	335
STOKES	H	5	340	STONE	AW	2	329	STONE	S	3	394	STONEMAN	T	6	391
STOKES	H	10	221	STONE	AW	4	366	STONE	SC	4	366	STONEMAN	T	6	391
STOKES	H	11	357	STONE	B	3	231	STONE	T	4	366	STONER	A	4	367
STOKES	HC	7	382	STONE	CG	2	329	STONE	T	5	341	STONER	CR	1	335

STONER	E	4	367	STOREY	A	1	335	STOTT	H	9	184	STRADLING	W	1	336
STONER	HJ	3	231	STOREY	A	1	335	STOTT	H	9	350	STRADWICK	EE	10	373
STONER	JE	13	408	STOREY	A	8	334	STOTT	H	14	304	STRADWICK	G	10	373
STONER	JH	8	333	STOREY	A	8	334	STOTT	H	14	305	STRAFFORD	A	11	358
STONER	WF	7	382	STOREY	A	9	184	STOTT	H	14	305	STRAFFORD	FE	4	367
STONER	WJ	1	335	STOREY	AA	2	329	STOTT	J	9	184	STRAFFORD	J	13	408
STONER	WJ	4	367	STOREY	CR	2	329	STOTT	J	9	350	STRAHAND	G	11	358
STONES	A	8	333	STOREY	E	8	334	STOTT	J	14	305	STRAHAND	J	11	358
STONES	A	8	333	STOREY	F	9	184	STOTT	JG	14	304	STRAIN	E	8	334
STONES	C	2	329	STOREY	F	9	350	STOTT	JW	9	184	STRAIN	T	14	305
STONES	CJ	2	329	STOREY	F	14	304	STOTT	MC	9	184	STRAKER	BJ	8	334
STONES	F	9	350	STOREY	F	14	304	STOTT	P	9	184	STRAND	AS	2	330
STONES	H	8	333	STOREY	FJ	12	215	STOTT	P	9	184	STRAND	G	11	358
STONES	H	9	184	STOREY	H	10	222	STOTT	P	9	184	STRAND	J	11	358
STONES	JC	8	333	STOREY	H	12	215	STOTT	RA	9	184	STRAND	T	2	330
STONES	JC	8	333	STOREY	HE	1	335	STOTT	T	9	184	STRANEY	F	3	394
STONES	LE	8	333	STOREY	HJ	3	232	STOTT	T	14	305	STRANG	J	1	336
STONES	LH	8	333	STOREY	HR	3	232	STOTT	W	9	184	STRANG	JH	9	185
STONES	T	8	333	STOREY	J	8	334	STOUSE	CTE	10	222	STRANGE	A	4	367
STONES	W	7	382	STOREY	J	8	334	STOUSE	RA	10	222	STRANGE	A	5	342
STONES	W	8	333	STOREY	JA	8	334	STOUT	G	11	358	STRANGE	A	5	342
STONES	W	8	333	STOREY	JH	2	329	STOVOLD	AW	7	383	STRANGE	A	5	342
STONES	W	8	333	STOREY	JH	8	334	STOVOLD	F	2	330	STRANGE	CT	13	408
STONES	W	8	333	STOREY	JJ	2	330	STOVOLD	J	2	330	STRANGE	EA	4	367
STONESTREET	E	12	215	STOREY	L	9	184	STOVOLD	JE	2	330	STRANGE	EJ	13	408
STONESTREET	EW	12	215	STOREY	L	12	215	STOW	AAE	12	393	STRANGE	FG	6	392
STONESTREET	JH	2	329	STOREY	MA	1	335	STOW	AE	5	342	STRANGE	H	11	358
STONESTREET	P	12	215	STOREY	RL	1	335	STOW	AH	1	335	STRANGE	HH	5	342
STONEY	F	9	350	STOREY	S	14	304	STOW	FC	12	393	STRANGE	HV	3	394
STONEY	F	9	350	STOREY	T	12	215	STOW	RW	7	383	STRANGE	JF	6	392
STONEY	H	3	394	STORKEY	JH	7	383	STOW	SR	4	367	STRANGE	JW	4	367
STONEY	J	9	350	STORMAN	A	8	334	STOW	T	9	184	STRANGE	JW	10	222
STONHAM	CWJ	9	350	STORMES	AE	11	358	STOWE	C	1	335	STRANGE	RC	7	383
STONIER	J	11	357	STORRS	J	9	184	STOWE	C	8	334	STRANGE	RS	5	342
STONIER	JE	11	357	STORRY	R	8	334	STOWE	E	1	335	STRANGE	S	4	367
STONTON	E	9	184	STORTON	A	12	215	STOWE	EW	12	215	STRANGE	WF	4	367
STOPES	AF	1	335	STORTON	FH	5	341	STOWE	H	1	335	STRANGE	WJ	4	368
STOPES	G	7	382	STORTON	WS	5	341	STOWE	J	6	391	STRANGEWAY	E	8	334
STOPFORD	RH	9	350	STORY	CW	8	334	STOWE	L	3	394	STRANGEWAY	H	8	335
STOPP	AH	12	215	STORY	EF	7	383	STOWE	T	12	215	STRANGWARD	A	9	350
STOPP	AW	12	215	STORY	S	7	383	STOWE	W	12	393	STRANGWAY	AE	8	335
STOPP	F	12	215	STORY	W	8	334	STOWELL	D	9	184	STRANGWAY	W	8	335
STOPP	FC	12	215	STORY	W	12	393	STOWERS	A	3	394	STRANKS	J	3	394
STOPP	FG	7	383	STOTEN	AG	5	341	STOWERS	H	3	394	STRANKS	J	3	394
STOPP	GH	12	215	STOTEN	W	5	341	STOWERS	HH	3	394	STRAPP	JJ	5	342
STOPP	WJ	12	215	STOTEN	W	5	341	STOXLEY	H	5	342	STRAPP	P	5	342
STOPPS	AE	2	329	STOTESBURY	J	13	408	STOYLE	H	8	334	STRAPP	S	5	342
STORAH	W	11	357	STOTT	A	11	358	STOYLE	WT	3	394	STRASKIN	I	8	335
STORER	AE	7	383	STOTT	A	11	358	STOYLES	A	9	350	STRATFORD	C	7	383
STORER	CE	3	231	STOTT	C	10	222	STOYLES	H	9	350	STRATFORD	CR	13	408
STORER	CW	13	408	STOTT	D	14	304	STOYLES	J	9	350	STRATFORD	F	2	330
STORER	EW	7	383	STOTT	F	8	334	STRACHAM	WH	7	383	STRATFORD	FCJ	2	330
STORER	FR	4	367	STOTT	GH	8	334	STRACHAN	SJP	4	367	STRATFORD	J	5	342
STORER	HM	3	231	STOTT	GH	14	304	STRACHAN	W	1	336	STRATFORD	JA	12	393
STORER	J	8	334	STOTT	H	8	334	STRACHAN	WA	13	408	STRATFORD	TH	10	222
STORER	SJ	7	383												

STRATFORD	VF	3	394	STREET	ES	7	383	STRETCH	JW	14	305	STRINGER	FW	12	216
STRATFORD	W	3	394	STREET	F	2	330	STRETCH	TH	6	392	STRINGER	G	5	343
STRATFULL	FP	5	342	STREET	F	4	368	STRETTEN	T	7	383	STRINGER	G	6	392
STRATH	AH	1	336	STREET	FG	5	343	STRETTON	C	12	393	STRINGER	GE	1	336
STRATH	E	14	305	STREET	FG	10	373	STRETTON	FG	6	392	STRINGER	GR	8	335
STRATH	F	11	358	STREET	G	6	392	STRETTON	J	2	330	STRINGER	GT	12	216
STRATH	H	11	358	STREET	G	10	222	STRETTON	JH	12	216	STRINGER	H	3	395
STRATTEN	H	2	330	STREET	GFL	12	393	STRETTON	W	12	216	STRINGER	H	8	335
STRATTEN	W	2	330	STREET	GH	5	343	STRETTON	WB	13	408	STRINGER	H	13	409
STRATTON	A	4	368	STREET	H	3	395	STRETTON	WH	13	409	STRINGER	HJ	2	330
STRATTON	A	5	342	STREET	H	5	343	STREVENS	GA	1	336	STRINGER	J	6	392
STRATTON	A	12	216	STREET	H	11	358	STREVENS	TA	2	330	STRINGER	J	9	185
STRATTON	AE	4	368	STREET	HG	4	368	STREVENS	WE	10	223	STRINGER	JA	7	384
STRATTON	AF	5	342	STREET	HM	8	335	STRIBBLING	B	7	384	STRINGER	JT	7	384
STRATTON	C	13	408	STREET	HN	2	330	STRICKLAND	A	7	384	STRINGER	JW	5	343
STRATTON	D	4	368	STREET	J	2	330	STRICKLAND	FD	4	369	STRINGER	LJ	1	336
STRATTON	EG	12	216	STREET	J	4	368	STRICKLAND	G	8	335	STRINGER	R	12	216
STRATTON	FG	5	342	STREET	J	5	343	STRICKLAND	H	8	335	STRINGER	RJ	5	343
STRATTON	H	4	368	STREET	J	11	358	STRICKLAND	JD	7	384	STRINGER	ST	5	343
STRATTON	H	4	368	STREET	J	11	358	STRICKLAND	O	8	335	STRINGER	W	8	335
STRATTON	PA	4	368	STREET	JW	4	368	STRICKLAND	W	14	305	STRINGER	W	10	223
STRATTON	S	4	368	STREET	JW	4	368	STRIDE	AA	4	369	STRINGER	W	11	359
STRATTON	S	14	305	STREET	L	4	368	STRIDE	CG	4	369	STRIPE	F	2	330
STRATTON	SA	5	342	STREET	LJ	4	369	STRIDE	CN	4	369	STRIPE	WH	10	223
STRATTON	SH	13	408	STREET	P	11	358	STRIDE	DB	13	409	STRIPP	E	10	223
STRATTON	TH	4	368	STREET	RGE	10	222	STRIDE	FG	1	336	STRIPP	FW	7	384
STRATTON	WW	5	342	STREET	SF	6	392	STRIDE	FT	4	369	STRONELL	AW	5	343
STRAUSS	WE	1	336	STREET	T	6	392	STRIDE	H	4	369	STRONG	AD	7	384
STRAW	LH	1	336	STREET	TH	14	305	STRIDE	HHF	1	336	STRONG	AE	13	409
STRAWFORD	CT	6	392	STREET	V	4	368	STRIDE	JA	4	369	STRONG	B	10	223
STRAWFORD	WH	6	392	STREET	W	4	369	STRIDE	JE	4	369	STRONG	CW	7	384
STRAWN	AJ	10	222	STREET	W	5	343	STRIDE	OJ	4	369	STRONG	CW	7	384
STRAWN	FA	10	222	STREET	W	10	222	STRIDE	P	1	336	STRONG	D	6	392
STRAWSON		3	394	STREET	W	11	359	STRIDE	PW	5	343	STRONG	E	3	395
STREAMES	AH	3	395	STREET	WH	4	369	STRIDE	TW	4	369	STRONG	F	12	216
STREAMES	EM	1	336	STREETER	A	3	395	STRIDE	WH	4	369	STRONG	G	3	395
STREAMES	J	1	336	STREETER	AE	13	408	STRIDE	WH	4	369	STRONG	G	4	369
STREAMES	WN	3	395	STREETER	C	3	395	STRIDE	WJ	4	369	STRONG	H	1	336
STREET	A	4	368	STREETER	EA	1	336	STRIDE	WJ	6	392	STRONG	H	7	384
STREET	A	4	368	STREETER	FE	13	408	STRIDE	WJ	6	392	STRONG	H	11	359
STREET	A	5	342	STREETER	G	1	336	STRIDE	WJ	6	392	STRONG	HG	13	409
STREET	A	12	216	STREETER	J	6	392	STRIDE-AGER	J	1	336	STRONG	J	3	395
STREET	AE	4	368	STREETER	J	13	408	STRINGER	A	3	395	STRONG	J	10	223
STREET	AE	10	222	STREETER	P	1	336	STRINGER	A	11	359	STRONG	JS	13	409
STREET	AH	4	368	STREETLEY	A	3	395	STRINGER	C	8	335	STRONG	LC	4	369
STREET	AJ	1	336	STREETLEY	WT	3	395	STRINGER	C	12	216	STRONG	LC	4	369
STREET	AJ	7	383	STREETLY	E	7	383	STRINGER	E	3	395	STRONG	LG	7	384
STREET	AR	7	383	STREETLY	W	7	383	STRINGER	E	8	335	STRONG	S	10	223
STREET	AR	7	383	STREETON	GFS	7	383	STRINGER	E	14	305	STRONG	SJ	7	384
STREET	AV	10	222	STREETS	HJ	10	222	STRINGER	EA	6	392	STRONG	W	4	369
STREET	AW	6	392	STREETS	WA	10	222	STRINGER	EW	7	384	STRONNELL	WB	5	343
STREET	C	11	358	STRETCH	AR	10	222	STRINGER	F	12	216	STROUD	A	3	395
STREET	CJ	5	342	STRETCH	C	10	223	STRINGER	F	13	409	STROUD	AG	1	336
STREET	E	5	343	STRETCH	J	11	359	STRINGER	FC	12	216	STROUD	B	2	330
STREET	E	10	373	STRETCH	J	14	305	STRINGER	FV	12	216	STROUD	E	10	223

STROUD	EH	1	337	STUBBINGTON	L	4	370	STURGESS	A	10	224	STYLES	R	6	393
STROUD	FW	2	330	STUBBINS	AH	1	337	STURGESS	B	5	344	STYLES	SJ	13	409
STROUD	GW	1	337	STUBBINS	JA	11	359	STURGESS	B	12	393	STYLES	SW	7	385
STROUD	HR	13	409	STUBBINS	WT	1	337	STURGESS	ET	3	232	STYLES	W	7	385
STROUD	J	1	337	STUBBS	A	8	335	STURGESS	F	12	393	STYLES	WJ	7	385
STROUD	J	10	373	STUBBS	AE	14	305	STURGESS	G	5	344	STYNES	J	1	338
STROUD	RJ	13	409	STUBBS	B	4	370	STURGESS	HF	10	373	SUATT	CA	2	331
STROUD	SC	1	337	STUBBS	B	8	335	STURGESS	J	12	393	SUCH	ER	4	371
STROUD	SJ	3	395	STUBBS	C	11	359	STURGESS	JR	10	373	SUCH	HJ	6	393
STROUD	T	10	223	STUBBS	EJ	3	396	STURGESS	TD	10	224	SUCH	JB	1	338
STROUD	TE	1	337	STUBBS	FE	7	384	STURGESS	W	3	232	SUCH	R	13	409
STROUD	WC	1	337	STUBBS	G	4	370	STURGESS	WJO	12	393	SUCH	WH	6	393
STROWBRIDGE	DW	3	395	STUBBS	H	6	393	STURLEY	J	1	337	SUCHARD	S	14	305
STRUCKETT	WC	3	395	STUBBS	H	14	305	STURLEY	WM	2	331	SUCKLEY	J	9	185
STRUDWICK	A	1	337	STUBBS	J	1	337	STURMAN	AH	13	409	SUCKLEY	TJ	14	305
STRUDWICK	CJ	10	223	STUBBS	JT	8	335	STURMAN	B	13	409	SUCKLING	C	6	393
STRUDWICK	H	5	343	STUBBS	K	4	370	STURMAN	E	5	344	SUCKLING	HH	2	331
STRUDWICK	HC	1	337	STUBBS	L	4	370	STURMAN	H	1	337	SUCKLING	J	5	344
STRUGNELL	CF	4	370	STUBBS	RB	7	385	STURMAN	W	5	344	SUCKLING	W	1	338
STRUGNELL	FT	4	370	STUBBS	RG	7	385	STURMEY	CT	1	337	SUCKLOCK	A	14	306
STRUGNELL	GC	10	373	STUBBS	RH	14	305	STURMEY	F	13	409	SUCKSMITH	E	9	350
STRUGNELL	GE	4	370	STUBBS	T	3	232	STURMEY	T	1	338	SUCKSMITH	EA	2	331
STRUGNELL	GH	10	223	STUBBS	TE	4	370	STURT	AG	13	409	SUCKSMITH	R	2	331
STRUGNELL	H	10	223	STUBBS	W	8	335	STURT	E	10	373	SUDD	CF	7	385
STRUGNELL	HD	4	370	STUBBS	W	11	359	STURTIVANT	GJ	5	344	SUDLOW	SG	13	409
STRUGNELL	R	10	223	STUBBS	WH	14	305	STURTON	JR	7	385	SUFFELL	FW	8	336
STRUGNELL	RE	10	223	STUCHBURY	CA	1	337	STUTCHBURY	C	4	370	SUFFIELD	W	11	359
STRUGNELL	WE	10	223	STUCKEY	F	7	385	STUTCHBURY	RP	4	370	SUGARS	WT	12	216
STRUGNELL	WT	4	370	STUCKEY	G	1	337	STUTCHBURY	WW	4	371	SUGDEN	A	9	185
STRUTTON	G	3	395	STUCKEY	G	2	331	STUTELEY	HA	7	385	SUGDEN	A	9	350
STRUTTON	M	3	395	STUCKEY	GH	2	331	STUTTARD	G	9	185	SUGDEN	A	9	350
STUART	AF	7	384	STUDD	W	4	370	STYANTS	CW	1	338	SUGDEN	C	9	185
STUART	C	6	392	STUDD	WR	7	385	STYANTS	P	1	338	SUGDEN	C	9	185
STUART	CF	7	384	STUDMAN	AM	5	343	STYCH	S	6	393	SUGDEN	EJ	7	385
STUART	GW	8	335	STUDMAN	AV	5	344	STYGALL	GA	5	344	SUGDEN	F	9	185
STUART	P	14	305	STUDMAN	R	7	385	STYGALL	GM	5	344	SUGDEN	F	9	185
STUART	T	6	392	STUDMAN	W	5	343	STYGALL	VE	5	344	SUGDEN	G	9	185
STUART	W	5	343	STUNELL	RG	7	385	STYLER	AW	6	393	SUGDEN	H	9	185
STUART-ADAMS	PN	7	384	STUNT	RH	10	373	STYLER	F	6	393	SUGDEN	H	9	350
STUBB	H	8	335	STUPPLE	JW	10	223	STYLER	H	6	393	SUGDEN	H	9	350
STUBBERFIELD	WA	13	409	STUPPLE	WH	10	223	STYLER	O	6	393	SUGDEN	J	8	336
STUBBERFIELD	WH	1	337	STURCH	RH	6	393	STYLES	A	6	393	SUGDEN	J	9	185
STUBBING	EW	10	373	STURDY	C	6	393	STYLES	A	7	385	SUGDEN	JH	9	185
STUBBING	PW	5	343	STURDY	C	9	185	STYLES	A	7	385	SUGDEN	JW	9	185
STUBBING	RJ	5	343	STURDY	HG	6	393	STYLES	A	13	409	SUGDEN	LE	2	331
STUBBINGS	C	10	373	STURDY	J	9	185	STYLES	AC	1	338	SUGDEN	RB	9	185
STUBBINGS	SC	1	337	STURDY	JT	1	337	STYLES	AJ	1	338	SUGDEN	TH	9	350
STUBBINGS	SS	3	395	STURGEON	F	8	336	STYLES	CS	1	338	SUGDEN	W	9	185
STUBBINGS	W	3	396	STURGEON	JF	8	336	STYLES	E	7	385	SUGDEN	W	9	185
STUBBINGTON	AE	10	373	STURGEON	TW	9	350	STYLES	EA	4	371	SUGDEN	WP	8	336
STUBBINGTON	C	4	370	STURGEON	W	11	359	STYLES	F	13	409	SUGDON	J	9	351
STUBBINGTON	CE	4	370	STURGES	CE	4	370	STYLES	FJ	1	338	SUGG	JW	7	385
STUBBINGTON	EE	4	370	STURGES	WG	4	370	STYLES	FW	12	424	SUGGETT	JA	8	336
STUBBINGTON	F	4	370	STURGESS	A	5	344	STYLES	J	2	331	SUGGETT	W	8	336
STUBBINGTON	L	4	370	STURGESS	A	10	223	STYLES	J	7	385	SULCH	H	8	336

SULLIVAN	A	1	338
SULLIVAN	A	7	385
SULLIVAN	A	9	351
SULLIVAN	A	11	359
SULLIVAN	A	13	410
SULLIVAN	C	8	336
SULLIVAN	C	13	410
SULLIVAN	CDR	3	232
SULLIVAN	CF	1	338
SULLIVAN	CH	2	331
SULLIVAN	CJ	13	410
SULLIVAN	D	6	393
SULLIVAN	D	11	359
SULLIVAN	E	8	336
SULLIVAN	E	13	410
SULLIVAN	E	13	410
SULLIVAN	EA	11	359
SULLIVAN	EH	10	224
SULLIVAN	FA	11	359
SULLIVAN	FJ	11	359
SULLIVAN	FP	8	336
SULLIVAN	FT	13	410
SULLIVAN	FW	2	331
SULLIVAN	FW	14	306
SULLIVAN	G	10	224
SULLIVAN	G	13	410
SULLIVAN	GE	7	386
SULLIVAN	GW	7	386
SULLIVAN	H	9	185
SULLIVAN	J	2	331
SULLIVAN	J	5	344
SULLIVAN	J	6	393
SULLIVAN	J	7	386
SULLIVAN	J	7	386
SULLIVAN	J	7	386
SULLIVAN	J	10	374
SULLIVAN	J	11	359
SULLIVAN	J	11	359
SULLIVAN	J	11	359
SULLIVAN	J	13	410
SULLIVAN	J	14	306
SULLIVAN	JA	1	338
SULLIVAN	JE	11	360
SULLIVAN	JH	7	386
SULLIVAN	JL	10	224
SULLIVAN	JP	2	331
SULLIVAN	JP	14	306
SULLIVAN	JW	9	186
SULLIVAN	M	1	338
SULLIVAN	M	8	336
SULLIVAN	M	9	186
SULLIVAN	M	10	224
SULLIVAN	P	2	331
SULLIVAN	S	7	386
SULLIVAN	SA	3	232
SULLIVAN	T	2	331
SULLIVAN	T	2	331
SULLIVAN	T	9	186
SULLIVAN	T	10	224
SULLIVAN	T	11	360
SULLIVAN	T	11	360
SULLIVAN	T	13	410
SULLIVAN	TE	1	338
SULLIVAN	TE	2	331
SULLIVAN	W	2	331
SULLIVAN	W	12	393
SULLIVAN	WF	3	232
SULLIVAN	WJ	7	386
SULLIVAN	WJ	7	386
SULLIVAN	WJ	13	410
SULLY	J	4	371
SULLY	RC	13	410
SULLY	TH	10	224
SULLY	WE	4	371
SULLY	WJ	10	224
SUMMERBEE	J	4	371
SUMMERBEE	PFV	4	371
SUMMERELL	CH	3	232
SUMMERFIELD	A	3	232
SUMMERFIELD	AE	7	386
SUMMERFIELD	B	5	344
SUMMERFIELD	B	7	386
SUMMERFIELD	C	12	216
SUMMERFIELD	CW	8	336
SUMMERFIELD	CW	10	374
SUMMERFIELD	CW	10	374
SUMMERFIELD	E	3	232
SUMMERFIELD	E	6	393
SUMMERFIELD	EE	7	386
SUMMERFIELD	F	7	386
SUMMERFIELD	F	10	374
SUMMERFIELD	F	12	393
SUMMERFIELD	FC	1	338
SUMMERFIELD	GET	7	386
SUMMERFIELD	J	12	393
SUMMERFIELD	JG	10	224
SUMMERFIELD	M	3	232
SUMMERFIELD	T	4	371
SUMMERFIELD	T	12	216
SUMMERFIELD	TJ	12	216
SUMMERFIELD	W	5	344
SUMMERFIELD	WJ	5	344
SUMMERFIELD	WJ	5	344
SUMMERILL	CW	6	393
SUMMERLIN	A	5	344
SUMMERLIN	A	5	345
SUMMERLIN	C	5	345
SUMMERLIN	G	5	344
SUMMERS	A	7	386
SUMMERS	AE	10	224
SUMMERS	AJ	4	371
SUMMERS	AL	2	331
SUMMERS	C	4	371
SUMMERS	CA	3	232
SUMMERS	D	2	332
SUMMERS	D	10	374
SUMMERS	F	11	360
SUMMERS	F	12	216
SUMMERS	G	11	360
SUMMERS	J	11	360
SUMMERS	JG	10	224
SUMMERS	JG	13	410
SUMMERS	JP	3	396
SUMMERS	JR	7	386
SUMMERS	JW	4	371
SUMMERS	P	12	216
SUMMERS	PA	4	371
SUMMERS	PR	4	371
SUMMERS	R	9	186
SUMMERS	V	3	232
SUMMERS	W	6	393
SUMMERS	W	9	186
SUMMERS	WA	10	224
SUMMERS	WC	3	396
SUMMERS	WG	4	371
SUMMERS	WR	10	224
SUMMERSBY	WT	7	386
SUMMERSGILL	D	9	351
SUMMERSGILL	FG	9	186
SUMMERSGILL	H	8	336
SUMMERSGILL	J	8	336
SUMMERSGILL	JA	9	186
SUMMERSGILL	W	14	306
SUMMERSGILL	WF	8	336
SUMMERSON	W	9	351
SUMMERTON	H	8	336
SUMNER	A	11	360
SUMNER	F	6	393
SUMNER	F	11	360
SUMNER	FJ	13	410
SUMNER	H	13	410
SUMNER	SW	13	410
SUMNER	TG	4	371
SUMNER	W	14	306
SUMNER	WGT	3	232
SUMNER	WJ	6	394
SUMNERS	WR	4	371
SUMPNER	GE	8	336
SUMPNER	S	8	336
SUMPTER	GC	1	338
SUMPTER	HS	3	396
SUMPTION	G	1	338
SUMPTION	J	1	338
SUMPTON	GA	7	386
SUNASKY	S	2	332
SUNDERLAND	A	8	337
SUNDERLAND	AMV	14	306
SUNDERLAND	CH	4	371
SUNDERLAND	E	9	186
SUNDERLAND	E	9	186
SUNDERLAND	FR	12	216
SUNDERLAND	FV	8	337
SUNDERLAND	G	14	306
SUNDERLAND	H	8	337
SUNDERLAND	H	9	186
SUNDERLAND	H	9	186
SUNDERLAND	H	9	351
SUNDERLAND	J	9	186
SUNDERLAND	J	9	186
SUNDERLAND	J	9	351
SUNDERLAND	J	14	306
SUNDERLAND	W	8	337
SUNDERLAND	W	11	360
SUNDERLAND	WH	14	306
SUNDVIK	FJ	3	396
SUNTER	C	8	337
SUNTER	GR	8	337
SUNTER	J	8	337
SUNTER	P	9	186
SUPER	W	11	360
SUPREE	L	14	306
SURGUY	A	7	387
SURMAN	GE	2	332
SURMAN	J	6	394
SURMAN	W	4	371
SURREY	AC	2	332
SURREY	SA	10	224
SURREY	T	11	360
SURREY	TW	3	396
SURRIDGE	A	11	360
SURRIDGE	AJ	5	345
SURRIDGE	C	12	393
SURRIDGE	JW	12	217
SURRIDGE	WT	12	393
SURRY	AJ	10	224
SURTIN	W	3	396
SUSANS	AG	3	396
SUSANS	T	3	396
SUSANS	W	3	396
SUSMAN	M	14	306
SUSSAMS	JS	13	410
SUSSEMS	RC	1	339
SUSSEX	EJJ	7	387
SUSSEX	J	5	345
SUSSEX	JC	7	387
SUTCH	J	3	396
SUTCH	W	2	332
SUTCLIFF	A	8	337
SUTCLIFF	A	8	337
SUTCLIFF	H	8	337

SUTCLIFFE	A	1	339	SUTTON	A	8	337	SUTTON	SE	6	394	SWAIN	J	12	217
SUTCLIFFE	A	8	337	SUTTON	A	10	225	SUTTON	SW	3	232	SWAIN	JW	5	346
SUTCLIFFE	A	9	186	SUTTON	AC	6	394	SUTTON	T	6	394	SWAIN	N	9	352
SUTCLIFFE	A	9	186	SUTTON	AC	13	410	SUTTON	T	8	338	SWAIN	RJ	5	346
SUTCLIFFE	A	9	351	SUTTON	AG	2	332	SUTTON	T	9	351	SWAIN	T	1	339
SUTCLIFFE	A	11	360	SUTTON	AG	5	345	SUTTON	TH	1	339	SWAIN	T	6	394
SUTCLIFFE	B	9	351	SUTTON	AW	3	232	SUTTON	TH	10	225	SWAIN	TJ	5	346
SUTCLIFFE	B	9	351	SUTTON	C	6	394	SUTTON	TJ	14	307	SWAIN	W	13	411
SUTCLIFFE	C	9	351	SUTTON	C	9	187	SUTTON	W	1	339	SWAIN	WH	2	332
SUTCLIFFE	C	14	306	SUTTON	C	14	306	SUTTON	W	4	372	SWAIN	WJ	5	346
SUTCLIFFE	E	8	337	SUTTON	CEA	13	410	SUTTON	W	6	394	SWAIN	WR	5	346
SUTCLIFFE	E	9	186	SUTTON	D	3	232	SUTTON	W	14	307	SWAIN	WT	3	396
SUTCLIFFE	F	9	186	SUTTON	D	11	360	SUTTON	W	14	307	SWAIN	WW	4	372
SUTCLIFFE	F	9	186	SUTTON	DF	4	372	SUTTON	WG	1	339	SWAINBANK	J	14	307
SUTCLIFFE	FW	1	339	SUTTON	EA	14	306	SUTTON	WJ	14	307	SWAINE	A	9	352
SUTCLIFFE	G	8	337	SUTTON	EE	7	387	SUTTON	WS	5	345	SWAINE	A	9	352
SUTCLIFFE	G	9	186	SUTTON	EED	10	225	SUTTON	WSH	8	338	SWAINE	AS	9	187
SUTCLIFFE	H	9	187	SUTTON	ER	4	372	SUTTON	WT	3	396	SWAINE	CS	9	352
SUTCLIFFE	H	12	217	SUTTON	F	8	337	SUTTON	WWJ	3	232	SWAINE	R	8	338
SUTCLIFFE	J	2	332	SUTTON	F	10	374	SWABEY	CFJ	7	387	SWAINE	R	9	352
SUTCLIFFE	J	8	337	SUTTON	F	11	360	SWABEY	GH	13	411	SWAINE	T	8	338
SUTCLIFFE	J	8	337	SUTTON	FG	3	396	SWABEY	J	8	338	SWAINSBURY	LJ	1	339
SUTCLIFFE	J	9	187	SUTTON	FL	4	372	SWADKINS	H	6	394	SWAINSON	A	8	338
SUTCLIFFE	J	9	187	SUTTON	G	4	372	SWAFFER	CR	5	345	SWAINSTON	W	1	339
SUTCLIFFE	J	9	351	SUTTON	GER	13	411	SWAFFER	FW	7	387	SWAIT	GE	1	339
SUTCLIFFE	J	10	224	SUTTON	GP	2	332	SWAFFIELD	FR	7	387	SWALE	HT	7	387
SUTCLIFFE	J	11	360	SUTTON	GW	11	360	SWAFFIELD	FWT	7	387	SWALE	W	7	387
SUTCLIFFE	J	14	306	SUTTON	H	4	372	SWAFFIELD	TO	7	387	SWALES	A	8	338
SUTCLIFFE	JB	9	351	SUTTON	H	6	394	SWAILES	AE	8	338	SWALES	AC	2	332
SUTCLIFFE	JE	9	187	SUTTON	H	8	337	SWAILES	H	9	352	SWALES	CL	9	187
SUTCLIFFE	JW	9	351	SUTTON	H	9	187	SWAIN	A	5	345	SWALES	F	5	346
SUTCLIFFE	L	9	187	SUTTON	H	9	351	SWAIN	A	5	345	SWALES	F	9	352
SUTCLIFFE	L	9	187	SUTTON	H	14	307	SWAIN	A	5	345	SWALES	G	9	352
SUTCLIFFE	M	9	351	SUTTON	H	14	307	SWAIN	AG	5	345	SWALES	H	8	338
SUTCLIFFE	R	9	187	SUTTON	HJ	4	372	SWAIN	C	1	339	SWALES	H	9	187
SUTCLIFFE	R	14	306	SUTTON	HV	6	394	SWAIN	C	2	332	SWALES	H	10	374
SUTCLIFFE	T	9	351	SUTTON	HV	13	411	SWAIN	C	12	393	SWALES	J	8	338
SUTCLIFFE	W	9	187	SUTTON	J	7	387	SWAIN	CE	5	345	SWALES	J	8	338
SUTCLIFFE	WH	9	187	SUTTON	J	8	337	SWAIN	CH	5	345	SWALES	JW	8	338
SUTER	AJ	1	339	SUTTON	J	8	338	SWAIN	D	12	217	SWALES	S	12	217
SUTER	AJ	10	374	SUTTON	J	9	187	SWAIN	DO	5	345	SWALES	SG	2	332
SUTER	H	14	306	SUTTON	J	11	361	SWAIN	E	5	345	SWALES	T	8	338
SUTER	J	12	217	SUTTON	J	11	361	SWAIN	E	12	393	SWALES	T	11	361
SUTHERLAND	A	9	351	SUTTON	J	13	411	SWAIN	EJ	12	393	SWALES	TA	12	217
SUTHERLAND	BT	1	339	SUTTON	J	14	307	SWAIN	F	5	345	SWALES	WH	8	338
SUTHERLAND	CF	7	387	SUTTON	JW	1	339	SWAIN	F	5	345	SWALLOW	A	5	346
SUTHERLAND	FN	7	387	SUTTON	JW	8	338	SWAIN	F	11	361	SWALLOW	F	8	338
SUTHERLAND	FW	10	224	SUTTON	JW	14	307	SWAIN	FW	12	394	SWALLOW	G	10	374
SUTHERLAND	HW	10	224	SUTTON	L	6	394	SWAIN	GH	8	338	SWALLOW	H	7	387
SUTHERLAND	JA	13	410	SUTTON	MC	6	394	SWAIN	GW	3	396	SWALLOW	J	8	339
SUTHERLAND	W	6	394	SUTTON	P	8	338	SWAIN	GWP	1	339	SWALLOW	JB	8	339
SUTHERLAND	W	11	360	SUTTON	P	11	360	SWAIN	H	13	411	SWALLOW	JE	12	394
SUTTERBY	WF	5	345	SUTTON	RA	10	374	SWAIN	J	5	345	SWALLOW	T	1	339
SUTTON	A	6	394	SUTTON	RB	9	351	SWAIN	J	5	346	SWALLOW	T	8	339
SUTTON	A	7	387	SUTTON	S	14	307	SWAIN	J	8	338	SWALLOW	W	8	339

SWALLOW	WI	1	339	SWASH	J	4	372	SWEETMAN	T	14	307	SWITZER	WH	11	361
SWAN	AC	5	346	SWATMAN	J	8	339	SWEETMAN	WC	11	361	SWOFFER	T	2	332
SWAN	AJ	5	346	SWATMAN	W	8	339	SWEETSER	CW	11	361	SWOISH	CS	7	388
SWAN	C	2	332	SWATTON	G	13	411	SWEETSER	FC	13	411	SWORD	A	6	395
SWAN	CW	5	346	SWAYNE	AI	10	374	SWEETSER	WC	13	411	SWORDS	J	13	412
SWAN	EJ	5	346	SWAYSLAND	EGC	12	394	SWETMAN	AE	1	340	SWORDS	W	13	412
SWAN	FJ	7	387	SWAYSLAND	EJC	12	394	SWETMAN	FW	7	388	SWYER	WA	10	374
SWAN	GF	1	339	SWAYSLAND	WHC	12	394	SWETMAN	JW	3	397	SYCAMORE	A	1	340
SWAN	GT	8	339	SWEENEY	C	10	225	SWIFT	CE	1	340	SYCAMORE	JJ	7	388
SWAN	H	5	346	SWEENEY	CC	10	374	SWIFT	CW	13	411	SYCAMORE	W	1	340
SWAN	H	5	346	SWEENEY	D	1	340	SWIFT	D	8	339	SYDENHAM	AW	7	388
SWAN	L	5	346	SWEENEY	G	7	388	SWIFT	E	13	411	SYDNEY	AE	2	333
SWAN	N	10	225	SWEENEY	GP	13	411	SWIFT	F	8	339	SYGROVE	HH	5	347
SWAN	R	5	346	SWEENEY	J	3	396	SWIFT	FJ	13	411	SYGROVE	JH	5	347
SWAN	WJ	10	225	SWEENEY	J	3	396	SWIFT	FJ	13	411	SYKES	A	8	339
SWANCOTT	GA	6	394	SWEENEY	J	11	361	SWIFT	G	12	217	SYKES	A	9	187
SWANCOTT	T	6	394	SWEENEY	JA	8	339	SWIFT	GE	13	411	SYKES	A	9	352
SWANN	AR	12	394	SWEENEY	MT	14	307	SWIFT	GWH	2	332	SYKES	A	11	362
SWANN	AS	12	394	SWEENEY	P	1	340	SWIFT	H	9	352	SYKES	A	12	217
SWANN	CH	6	394	SWEENEY	P	13	411	SWIFT	HG	13	411	SYKES	AT	3	233
SWANN	CJ	3	232	SWEENEY	PJ	7	388	SWIFT	J	4	372	SYKES	C	14	308
SWANN	FM	13	411	SWEENEY	WH	7	388	SWIFT	J	6	395	SYKES	CTR	7	388
SWANN	G	13	411	SWEET	AE	4	372	SWIFT	J	8	339	SYKES	D	1	340
SWANN	H	7	387	SWEET	AE	10	225	SWIFT	J	9	187	SYKES	E	5	347
SWANN	HW	12	394	SWEET	CJ	4	372	SWIFT	JH	11	361	SYKES	E	8	339
SWANN	J	12	217	SWEET	CW	4	372	SWIFT	RC	1	340	SYKES	E	8	340
SWANN	J	14	307	SWEET	F	4	372	SWIFT	S	7	388	SYKES	E	9	352
SWANN	JC	13	411	SWEET	FH	10	225	SWIFT	W	8	339	SYKES	EC	1	340
SWANN	PA	9	352	SWEET	H	4	372	SWIFT	W	8	339	SYKES	ET	8	340
SWANN	S	1	339	SWEET	H	7	388	SWIFT	WJ	1	340	SYKES	FTW	7	388
SWANN	T	6	394	SWEET	JS	10	225	SWINBOURN	C	6	395	SYKES	G	8	340
SWANN	TE	2	332	SWEET	RH	4	372	SWINBURNE	J	11	361	SYKES	G	8	340
SWANN	TR	8	339	SWEET	S	8	339	SWINDELL	E	6	395	SYKES	G	9	352
SWANN	W	8	339	SWEET	WS	4	372	SWINDELL	JA	11	361	SYKES	G	9	352
SWANN	WF	12	394	SWEETAPPLE	A	13	411	SWINDELLS	A	9	352	SYKES	GB	9	187
SWANN	WJ	12	394	SWEETENHAM	JF	10	374	SWINDELLS	A	10	225	SYKES	GF	3	233
SWANNELL	AD	12	217	SWEETING	AW	7	388	SWINDELLS	H	14	307	SYKES	GH	4	372
SWANNELL	ER	12	217	SWEETING	E	5	347	SWINDELLS	J	14	308	SYKES	GI	9	352
SWANNELL	GH	12	217	SWEETING	H	5	346	SWINDELLS	P	9	352	SYKES	GW	1	340
SWANNELL	J	12	394	SWEETING	H	5	347	SWINDELLS	TE	11	425	SYKES	H	1	340
SWANNELL	L	5	346	SWEETING	JG	5	347	SWINDEN	TW	2	332	SYKES	H	8	340
SWANNELL	WA	12	217	SWEETLAND	CP	7	388	SWINDIN	FW	1	340	SYKES	H	9	187
SWANTON	HF	10	225	SWEETMAN	A	1	340	SWINFIELD	AE	6	395	SYKES	H	9	352
SWANTON	JJ	10	225	SWEETMAN	AHS	1	340	SWINFIELD	WC	6	395	SYKES	HC	9	352
SWANWICK	HV	11	361	SWEETMAN	AJ	2	332	SWINGELL	E	6	395	SYKES	HE	8	340
SWANWICK	T	11	361	SWEETMAN	C	14	307	SWINGELL	GE	6	395	SYKES	J	1	340
SWARBRECK	P	8	339	SWEETMAN	E	1	340	SWINGELL	H	6	395	SYKES	J	11	361
SWARBRICK	H	11	361	SWEETMAN	G	3	396	SWINGLER	CE	6	395	SYKES	JA	9	188
SWARBRICK	H	14	307	SWEETMAN	G	6	395	SWINN	TW	7	388	SYKES	JC	8	340
SWARBRICK	J	14	307	SWEETMAN	GJ	1	340	SWINNERTON	CH	6	395	SYKES	JE	8	340
SWARBRICK	R	14	307	SWEETMAN	H	7	388	SWINNERTON	F	6	395	SYKES	JE	9	353
SWARBRICK	T	14	307	SWEETMAN	HC	3	396	SWINNEY	HEA	3	397	SYKES	JE	11	362
SWASH	EAH	4	372	SWEETMAN	J	11	361	SWINNEY	WG	3	397	SYKES	JW	4	373
SWASH	EF	4	372	SWEETMAN	JA	5	347	SWINSON	BH	2	332	SYKES	JW	9	188
SWASH	J	1	340	SWEETMAN	JR	1	340	SWIRE	F	11	361	SYKES	JW	9	353

SYKES	M	8	340	SYMONDS	LL	4	373	TADMAN	W	7	389	TALBOT	JWS	3	233
SYKES	P	9	353	SYMONDS	N	14	308	TAFFT	H	6	396	TALBOT	P	1	342
SYKES	R	9	353	SYMONDS	P	5	347	TAFT	J	1	341	TALBOT	RA	5	347
SYKES	R	11	362	SYMONDS	TH	1	341	TAFT	JW	1	341	TALBOT	RS	14	308
SYKES	RJ	4	373	SYMONDS	TW	12	394	TAGG	AF	1	341	TALBOT	S	11	362
SYKES	S	8	340	SYMONDS	WH	4	373	TAGG	AG	13	413	TALBOT	SB	7	389
SYKES	S	14	308	SYMONDS	WJ	1	341	TAGG	AJ	1	341	TALBOT	SW	6	396
SYKES	T	9	353	SYMONDS	WJ	13	412	TAGG	E	4	373	TALBOT	T	11	362
SYKES	T	14	308	SYMONS	A	10	225	TAGG	F	7	389	TALBOT	TH	11	362
SYKES	T	14	308	SYMONS	E	1	341	TAGG	G	2	333	TALBOT	TJ	6	396
SYKES	W	8	340	SYMONS	HG	13	412	TAGGART	E	9	353	TALBOT	W	6	396
SYKES	W	8	340	SYMONS	J	4	373	TAGGART	RH	11	362	TALBOT	W	6	396
SYKES	W	11	362	SYMONS	JW	9	353	TAGGART	W	6	396	TALBOT	W	8	340
SYKES	WH	11	362	SYMONS	W	12	394	TAGLIONE	A	9	353	TALBOT	W	8	340
SYKES	WP	9	188	SYMS	EC	13	412	TAGLIONE	N	9	188	TALBOT	WH	10	226
SYKES	WW	9	188	SYMS	GH	13	412	TAIT	AV	10	225	TALBOT	WJ	4	373
SYLVESTER	H	6	395	SYMS	H	4	373	TAIT	D	11	362	TALBOT	WJ	6	396
SYLVESTER	JW	6	395	SYMS	HA	13	412	TAIT	DH	3	397	TALBOT	WJ	6	396
SYLVESTER	W	2	333	SYMS	JS	13	412	TAIT	E	10	225	TALBOT	WJ	10	226
SYMAN	J	9	188	SYNNUCK	AG	13	412	TAIT	EL	10	225	TALBOT	WJ	13	413
SYME	T	4	373	SYNYER	R	13	412	TAIT	FT	10	225	TALINTYRE	RW	3	397
SYMES	AC	4	373	SYRATT	HT	12	217	TAIT	G	10	225	TALL	F	4	373
SYMES	C	12	217	SYRATT	WE	12	217	TAIT	GT	7	389	TALL	H	13	413
SYMES	E	1	340	SYRETT	EG	1	341	TAIT	JJ	10	225	TALL	SC	4	373
SYMES	F	1	341	SYRETT	J	13	412	TAIT	R	9	188	TALL	WG	4	373
SYMES	F	7	388	SYRETT	R	7	389	TAIT	TE	10	226	TALL	WS	4	374
SYMES	J	1	341	SYRETT	R	13	412	TAIT	W	9	188	TALLACK	R	10	226
SYMES	JH	4	373	SYRETT	TH	7	389	TAKER	JE	11	362	TALLACK	RWC	10	226
SYMES	JH	9	188	SYSUM	A	6	395	TALBOT	A	13	413	TALLACK	WH	10	374
SYMES	JS	9	353	SZARKOW	S	14	308	TALBOT	AE	10	374	TALLANT	JW	9	188
SYMES	LE	1	341					TALBOT	AG	1	341	TALLENTS	W	8	341
SYMES	S	9	188					TALBOT	AJ	1	342	TALLERSALL	W	8	341
SYMES	TJ	13	412					TALBOT	AJ	6	396	TALLET	A	2	333
SYMES	W	3	233	**T**				TALBOT	AW	4	373	TALLETT	CFW	12	394
SYMES	WE	7	388					TALBOT	CS	2	333	TALLETT	FGC	12	394
SYMES	WJ	4	373					TALBOT	F	7	389	TALLETT	J	13	413
SYMINGTON	WH	4	373	TABANOR	J	12	394	TALBOT	F	7	389	TALLETT	JA	13	413
SYMKISS	SH	3	397	TABBERER	J	6	395	TALBOT	F	8	340	TALLEY	EF	10	226
SYMKISS	WG	3	397	TABBERNER	SE	9	188	TALBOT	FH	10	226	TALLEY	WE	7	389
SYMMONS	F	7	388	TABBITT	SA	12	218	TALBOT	FP	7	389	TALLING	WJ	4	374
SYMMONS	F	7	388	TABBRON	L	11	362	TALBOT	FS	12	394	TALLIS	JA	6	396
SYMMONS	SC	2	333	TABBRON	W	11	362	TALBOT	FW	6	396	TALLON	E	11	362
SYMONDS	A	1	341	TABER	AE	6	395	TALBOT	GW	1	342	TALMADGE	WG	7	389
SYMONDS	A	12	217	TABER	AJ	6	395	TALBOT	H	1	342	TALMAGE	JW	14	308
SYMONDS	AE	5	347	TABER	JE	13	412	TALBOT	H	6	396	TALMAGE	PA	12	394
SYMONDS	AE	13	412	TABER	JP	10	374	TALBOT	H	8	340	TALMAN	C	10	226
SYMONDS	CF	6	395	TABNER	J	11	362	TALBOT	H	14	308	TAMAN	J	6	396
SYMONDS	EG	1	341	TABNER	W	11	362	TALBOT	HE	13	413	TAME	EC	6	396
SYMONDS	FE	4	373	TABOR	F	14	308	TALBOT	HE	13	413	TAME	MJ	6	396
SYMONDS	G	1	341	TABOR	HJ	2	333	TALBOT	J	8	340	TAMPLIN	JP	6	396
SYMONDS	G	13	412	TABOR	WC	13	413	TALBOT	J	11	362	TAMS	H	1	342
SYMONDS	H	7	388	TABRAHAM	E	1	341	TALBOT	J	11	362	TANDY	CM	3	233
SYMONDS	HE	13	412	TABRAHAM	WG	3	397	TALBOT	J	13	413	TANDY	F	12	395
SYMONDS	HW	1	341	TACE	JW	8	340	TALBOT	JM	13	413	TANDY	FW	13	413
SYMONDS	JW	7	389	TACK	JW	1	341	TALBOT	JR	12	394	TANDY	G	14	308
				TACK	JWE	1	341								
				TACKLEY	GH	3	397								
				TADGELL	SW	1	341								

Surname	Initials	Unit	Page
TANDY	H	6	396
TANE	P	9	188
TANKARD	A	9	353
TANKARD	H	9	188
TANKARD	J	8	341
TANKARD	W	9	188
TANKERARD	J	11	363
TANKIN	AV	13	413
TANNAR	CR	13	413
TANNER	A	6	396
TANNER	AJ	1	342
TANNER	CG	7	389
TANNER	CH	13	413
TANNER	CW	7	389
TANNER	DS	7	389
TANNER	E	10	374
TANNER	EB	10	226
TANNER	F	1	342
TANNER	FA	6	396
TANNER	FJ	7	389
TANNER	FJ	13	413
TANNER	G	3	233
TANNER	G	4	374
TANNER	G	4	374
TANNER	G	13	413
TANNER	GA	7	389
TANNER	GF	7	390
TANNER	GN	14	308
TANNER	H	1	342
TANNER	H	12	218
TANNER	H	14	308
TANNER	J	1	342
TANNER	J	13	413
TANNER	JH	7	390
TANNER	JS	3	233
TANNER	JW	4	374
TANNER	PB	10	226
TANNER	RW	7	390
TANNER	S	1	342
TANNER	SG	4	374
TANNER	TR	7	390
TANNER	W	1	342
TANNER	WW	13	414
TANNETT	WE	13	414
TANSER	AT	12	395
TANSEY	J	8	341
TANSLEY	E	5	347
TANSLEY	G	5	347
TANSLEY	JT	13	414
TANSLEY	RF	2	333
TANSLEY	WJ	13	414
TANSOM	EJ	10	374
TANSWELL	F	14	308
TANSWELL	WJ	5	347
TANT	HA	11	363
TANT	S	2	333
TANT	WE	7	390
TANTON	HW	7	390
TAPHOUSE	F	13	414
TAPLEY	DC	11	363
TAPLEY	FJ	13	414
TAPLEY	R	11	363
TAPLIN	A	4	374
TAPLIN	CG	10	375
TAPLIN	GB	13	414
TAPNER	B	1	342
TAPP	AJ	12	395
TAPP	EC	12	395
TAPP	GH	12	395
TAPP	GJ	12	218
TAPP	HW	5	347
TAPP	J	4	374
TAPP	J	6	396
TAPP	SJM	7	390
TAPPENDEN	AP	13	414
TAPPENDEN	E	1	342
TAPPENDEN	GA	7	390
TAPPENDEN	H	13	414
TAPPENDEN	W	13	414
TAPPENDEN	WA	13	414
TAPPENDEN	WJ	13	414
TAPPER	AL	4	374
TAPPER	EW	4	374
TAPPIN	B	1	342
TAPPIN	FC	1	342
TAPPIN	H	1	342
TAPPIN	HW	1	342
TAPPING	H	13	414
TAPPING	VR	1	342
TAPSELL	FS	4	374
TAPSTER	A	3	397
TAPSTER	ES	12	218
TAPUCH	J	13	414
TARBOTTOM	H	9	188
TARBOX	AC	12	218
TARBOX	AF	5	347
TARBOX	AT	12	218
TARBOX	AT	12	218
TARBOX	G	12	218
TARBROOK	C	14	308
TARGETT	AE	3	233
TARGETT	AE	3	233
TARGETT	AJ	4	374
TARGETT	AN	5	347
TARGETT	BP	3	233
TARGETT	BR	3	233
TARGETT	CA	13	414
TARGETT	CH	4	374
TARGETT	EA	4	374
TARGETT	EA	13	414
TARGETT	EH	4	374
TARGETT	FE	13	414
TARGETT	FH	4	374
TARGETT	HC	7	390
TARGETT	JH	13	414
TARGETT	S	2	333
TARGETT	SS	13	415
TARGETT	TH	13	415
TARGETT	WH	4	374
TARGUS	G	9	353
TARLING	D	3	233
TARLING	J	6	397
TARLING	WG	3	233
TARPEY	J	11	363
TARPEY	J	14	308
TARPLEE	JW	8	341
TARPLEY	HA	2	333
TARPY	J	8	341
TARR	CW	4	374
TARR	EJ	4	374
TARR	SF	4	374
TARRAN	LW	13	415
TARRANT	A	4	374
TARRANT	A	10	226
TARRANT	AG	7	390
TARRANT	AJ	3	397
TARRANT	AJ	4	375
TARRANT	C	11	363
TARRANT	EG	3	233
TARRANT	F	2	333
TARRANT	F	4	375
TARRANT	FE	3	233
TARRANT	G	14	308
TARRANT	GW	4	375
TARRANT	GW	4	375
TARRANT	H	10	375
TARRANT	HL	7	390
TARRANT	J	3	397
TARRANT	JE	4	375
TARRANT	JE	10	226
TARRANT	JT	7	390
TARRANT	R	2	333
TARRANT	SA	4	375
TARRANT	SJ	10	226
TARRANT	WJ	4	375
TARRIER	B	5	347
TARRIER	GE	5	347
TARRIER	PC	5	348
TARRIER	SF	5	348
TARRIER	WG	5	348
TARRY	A	12	395
TARRY	E	5	348
TARRY	EA	12	395
TARRY	F	12	395
TARRY	G	12	395
TARRY	G	13	415
TARRY	WC	2	333
TARSEY	WJ	5	348
TART	CR	10	226
TARTT	E	9	353
TASCH	FG	3	397
TASCH	MA	3	397
TASKER		8	341
TASKER	A	11	363
TASKER	AE	7	390
TASKER	AJ	5	348
TASKER	CH	11	363
TASKER	FG	13	415
TASKER	G	8	341
TASKER	G	11	363
TASKER	G	13	415
TASKER	H	13	415
TASKER	HP	8	341
TASKER	J	11	363
TASKER	JH	5	348
TASKER	JH	9	188
TASKER	JH	11	363
TASKER	L	9	353
TASKER	O	11	363
TASKER	P	9	353
TASKER	R	14	309
TASKER	T	8	341
TASKER	WJ	7	390
TASKER	WP	13	415
TASSAKER	J	11	363
TASSELL	CW	12	395
TASSELL	NGW	12	218
TATAM	EE	4	375
TATE	A	8	341
TATE	EA	8	341
TATE	EC	3	397
TATE	H	8	341
TATE	H	12	395
TATE	IW	2	333
TATE	JT	9	188
TATE	JW	12	395
TATE	R	8	341
TATE	T	8	341
TATE	T	9	188
TATE	WD	8	341
TATE	WJ	9	353
TATEHAM	W	11	363
TATFORD	GEF	4	375
TATLER	E	10	226
TATLOW	MML	6	397
TATMAN	A	12	218
TATMAN	AF	12	218
TATMAN	E	13	415
TATMAN	GH	1	342
TATMAN	J	12	218

TATTAM	A	12	218	TAYLES	CF	6	397	TAYLOR	ACH	12	395	TAYLOR	C	11	364
TATTAM	CW	12	218	TAYLOR	A	1	343	TAYLOR	ACJ	1	343	TAYLOR	C	12	218
TATTAM	G	12	218	TAYLOR	A	3	233	TAYLOR	AE	1	343	TAYLOR	C	13	415
TATTAM	GW	12	218	TAYLOR	A	4	375	TAYLOR	AE	2	333	TAYLOR	CA	3	398
TATTAM	WJ	5	348	TAYLOR	A	4	375	TAYLOR	AE	3	233	TAYLOR	CA	6	398
TATTERSALL	A	10	375	TAYLOR	A	5	348	TAYLOR	AE	3	234	TAYLOR	CA	7	392
TATTERSALL	E	9	188	TAYLOR	A	6	397	TAYLOR	AE	3	234	TAYLOR	CC	3	398
TATTERSALL	E	9	189	TAYLOR	A	6	397	TAYLOR	AE	5	348	TAYLOR	CE	8	342
TATTERSALL	FB	8	341	TAYLOR	A	6	397	TAYLOR	AE	6	397	TAYLOR	CE	10	227
TATTERSALL	FS	7	390	TAYLOR	A	6	397	TAYLOR	AE	9	189	TAYLOR	CE	12	219
TATTERSALL	GF	7	390	TAYLOR	A	6	397	TAYLOR	AE	10	227	TAYLOR	CEJ	3	398
TATTERSALL	GJ	7	390	TAYLOR	A	6	397	TAYLOR	AE	11	364	TAYLOR	CF	3	398
TATTERSALL	J	10	226	TAYLOR	A	6	397	TAYLOR	AE	13	415	TAYLOR	CF	6	398
TATTERSALL	J	11	363	TAYLOR	A	6	397	TAYLOR	AE	13	415	TAYLOR	CF	11	365
TATTERSALL	JW	11	363	TAYLOR	A	6	397	TAYLOR	AE	14	309	TAYLOR	CG	12	219
TATTERSALL	RJ	7	390	TAYLOR	A	7	391	TAYLOR	AE	14	309	TAYLOR	CH	4	375
TATTERSALL	W	9	189	TAYLOR	A	7	391	TAYLOR	AF	13	415	TAYLOR	CH	5	348
TATTERSALL	W	10	226	TAYLOR	A	8	342	TAYLOR	AG	5	348	TAYLOR	CH	5	349
TATTERSALL	WA	7	391	TAYLOR	A	8	342	TAYLOR	AG	12	218	TAYLOR	CH	6	398
TATTERSFIELD	AR	13	415	TAYLOR	A	8	342	TAYLOR	AH	7	391	TAYLOR	CH	7	392
TATTERSFIELD	FA	13	415	TAYLOR	A	8	342	TAYLOR	AJ	1	343	TAYLOR	CJ	1	343
TATTERTON	H	8	341	TAYLOR	A	8	342	TAYLOR	AJ	2	334	TAYLOR	CP	7	392
TATTLE	GC	1	342	TAYLOR	A	8	342	TAYLOR	AJ	4	375	TAYLOR	CR	6	398
TATTON	A	14	309	TAYLOR	A	8	342	TAYLOR	AJ	5	348	TAYLOR	CS	3	398
TATTON	G	14	309	TAYLOR	A	9	189	TAYLOR	AJ	6	397	TAYLOR	CT	6	398
TATTON	JE	11	363	TAYLOR	A	9	353	TAYLOR	AJ	6	397	TAYLOR	CVB	14	309
TAULBUTT	M	10	375	TAYLOR	A	10	375	TAYLOR	AJ	7	391	TAYLOR	CW	3	398
TAUNTON	HJ	3	397	TAYLOR	A	11	364	TAYLOR	AJ	7	391	TAYLOR	CW	13	415
TAVENDER	CH	7	391	TAYLOR	A	11	364	TAYLOR	AR	3	398	TAYLOR	D	4	375
TAVENER	E	7	391	TAYLOR	A	11	364	TAYLOR	AR	3	398	TAYLOR	D	8	342
TAVENER	HG	10	226	TAYLOR	A	11	364	TAYLOR	AR	11	364	TAYLOR	DH	4	375
TAVENER	PA	10	227	TAYLOR	A	11	364	TAYLOR	AS	7	391	TAYLOR	DM	10	227
TAVENER	T	5	348	TAYLOR	A	11	364	TAYLOR	AS	13	415	TAYLOR	E	1	343
TAVENER	WE	7	391	TAYLOR	A	11	364	TAYLOR	AV	5	348	TAYLOR	E	1	343
TAVERNER	CS	3	397	TAYLOR	A	11	364	TAYLOR	AV	6	398	TAYLOR	E	1	343
TAVERNER	T	6	397	TAYLOR	A	11	364	TAYLOR	AW	2	334	TAYLOR	E	1	343
TAVERNOR	H	14	309	TAYLOR	A	11	364	TAYLOR	AW	7	391	TAYLOR	E	3	234
TAVERNOR	W	14	309	TAYLOR	A	11	364	TAYLOR	AWO	4	375	TAYLOR	E	3	398
TAVERNOR	W	14	309	TAYLOR	A	11	364	TAYLOR	B	5	348	TAYLOR	E	4	375
TAVNER	AE	7	391	TAYLOR	A	13	415	TAYLOR	B	11	364	TAYLOR	E	4	375
TAVNER	EJ	13	415	TAYLOR	A	14	309	TAYLOR	BH	7	392	TAYLOR	E	5	349
TAVOLIERI	P	6	397	TAYLOR	A	14	309	TAYLOR	BP	8	342	TAYLOR	E	5	349
TAW	FH	10	227	TAYLOR	A	14	309	TAYLOR	C	3	398	TAYLOR	E	6	398
TAYLER	A	10	227	TAYLOR	A	14	309	TAYLOR	C	4	375	TAYLOR	E	7	392
TAYLER	GF	12	395	TAYLOR	A	14	309	TAYLOR	C	5	348	TAYLOR	E	8	342
TAYLER	HC	7	391	TAYLOR	A	14	309	TAYLOR	C	6	398	TAYLOR	E	8	342
TAYLER	J	3	233	TAYLOR	A	14	309	TAYLOR	C	6	398	TAYLOR	E	8	342
TAYLER	MP	7	391	TAYLOR	AA	5	348	TAYLOR	C	6	398	TAYLOR	E	9	189
TAYLER	S	3	233	TAYLOR	AA	6	397	TAYLOR	C	7	392	TAYLOR	E	9	189
TAYLER	SP	7	391	TAYLOR	AA	7	391	TAYLOR	C	7	392	TAYLOR	E	9	189
TAYLER	TG	12	218	TAYLOR	AB	6	397	TAYLOR	C	8	342	TAYLOR	E	9	353
TAYLER	TL	3	397	TAYLOR	AC	2	333	TAYLOR	C	9	189	TAYLOR	E	9	353
TAYLER	W	3	397	TAYLOR	AC	3	233	TAYLOR	C	9	189	TAYLOR	E	10	227
TAYLER	WW	3	398	TAYLOR	AC	6	397	TAYLOR	C	10	227	TAYLOR	E	10	227
TAYLERSON	L	7	391	TAYLOR	AC	12	395	TAYLOR	C	10	227	TAYLOR	E	11	364

TAYLOR	E	11	365	TAYLOR	F	11	365	TAYLOR	GA	6	398	TAYLOR	H	11	365
TAYLOR	E	11	365	TAYLOR	F	11	365	TAYLOR	GA	6	399	TAYLOR	H	12	219
TAYLOR	E	13	416	TAYLOR	F	11	365	TAYLOR	GA	7	392	TAYLOR	H	12	219
TAYLOR	E	13	416	TAYLOR	F	12	219	TAYLOR	GA	10	227	TAYLOR	H	12	219
TAYLOR	E	14	309	TAYLOR	F	13	416	TAYLOR	GA	10	227	TAYLOR	H	13	416
TAYLOR	E	14	309	TAYLOR	F	14	310	TAYLOR	GE	6	399	TAYLOR	H	14	310
TAYLOR	E	14	309	TAYLOR	F	14	310	TAYLOR	GE	14	310	TAYLOR	H	14	310
TAYLOR	E	14	310	TAYLOR	FA	5	349	TAYLOR	GF	6	399	TAYLOR	H	14	310
TAYLOR	E	14	310	TAYLOR	FA	10	227	TAYLOR	GF	6	399	TAYLOR	HA	1	343
TAYLOR	E	14	310	TAYLOR	FA	13	416	TAYLOR	GF	10	227	TAYLOR	HA	3	234
TAYLOR	EA	13	416	TAYLOR	FB	14	310	TAYLOR	GF	13	416	TAYLOR	HC	10	227
TAYLOR	EAG	4	375	TAYLOR	FE	2	334	TAYLOR	GH	2	334	TAYLOR	HCH	1	343
TAYLOR	EB	2	334	TAYLOR	FE	6	398	TAYLOR	GH	5	349	TAYLOR	HG	1	343
TAYLOR	EB	3	234	TAYLOR	FG	5	349	TAYLOR	GH	7	392	TAYLOR	HG	6	399
TAYLOR	EC	4	376	TAYLOR	FH	2	334	TAYLOR	GH	11	365	TAYLOR	HG	14	310
TAYLOR	EC	5	349	TAYLOR	FH	3	398	TAYLOR	GR	11	365	TAYLOR	HH	11	365
TAYLOR	EC	5	349	TAYLOR	FH	4	376	TAYLOR	GT	6	399	TAYLOR	HJ	2	334
TAYLOR	EC	7	392	TAYLOR	FJ	3	234	TAYLOR	GV	1	343	TAYLOR	HJ	4	376
TAYLOR	EE	3	398	TAYLOR	FJ	10	375	TAYLOR	GVA	7	392	TAYLOR	HJ	7	393
TAYLOR	EE	7	392	TAYLOR	FJ	11	365	TAYLOR	GW	3	398	TAYLOR	HJ	13	416
TAYLOR	EG	10	375	TAYLOR	FS	3	234	TAYLOR	GW	6	399	TAYLOR	HJ	14	310
TAYLOR	EH	1	343	TAYLOR	FV	13	416	TAYLOR	GW	7	392	TAYLOR	HL	6	399
TAYLOR	EJ	3	234	TAYLOR	FW	2	334	TAYLOR	GW	8	343	TAYLOR	HP	4	376
TAYLOR	EJ	3	234	TAYLOR	FW	10	375	TAYLOR	GW	8	343	TAYLOR	HS	9	354
TAYLOR	EJ	3	234	TAYLOR	FW	13	416	TAYLOR	GW	14	310	TAYLOR	HS	14	310
TAYLOR	EJ	3	234	TAYLOR	G	1	343	TAYLOR	GWP	12	395	TAYLOR	HW	14	311
TAYLOR	EJ	6	398	TAYLOR	G	2	334	TAYLOR	H	1	343	TAYLOR	I	8	343
TAYLOR	EJ	13	416	TAYLOR	G	2	334	TAYLOR	H	1	343	TAYLOR	IJ	5	349
TAYLOR	EJH	4	376	TAYLOR	G	3	398	TAYLOR	H	2	334	TAYLOR	J	1	344
TAYLOR	ET	7	392	TAYLOR	G	4	376	TAYLOR	H	3	398	TAYLOR	J	2	334
TAYLOR	ET	13	416	TAYLOR	G	4	376	TAYLOR	H	3	399	TAYLOR	J	2	334
TAYLOR	EW	1	343	TAYLOR	G	6	398	TAYLOR	H	4	376	TAYLOR	J	2	334
TAYLOR	EW	3	398	TAYLOR	G	6	398	TAYLOR	H	4	376	TAYLOR	J	2	334
TAYLOR	EW	3	398	TAYLOR	G	6	398	TAYLOR	H	5	349	TAYLOR	J	4	376
TAYLOR	EW	7	392	TAYLOR	G	6	398	TAYLOR	H	5	349	TAYLOR	J	4	376
TAYLOR	EWG	13	416	TAYLOR	G	7	392	TAYLOR	H	6	399	TAYLOR	J	5	349
TAYLOR	F	1	343	TAYLOR	G	7	392	TAYLOR	H	7	393	TAYLOR	J	5	349
TAYLOR	F	2	334	TAYLOR	G	7	392	TAYLOR	H	8	343	TAYLOR	J	5	349
TAYLOR	F	2	334	TAYLOR	G	8	342	TAYLOR	H	8	343	TAYLOR	J	6	399
TAYLOR	F	3	234	TAYLOR	G	8	342	TAYLOR	H	8	343	TAYLOR	J	6	399
TAYLOR	F	3	398	TAYLOR	G	8	342	TAYLOR	H	8	343	TAYLOR	J	6	399
TAYLOR	F	4	376	TAYLOR	G	8	343	TAYLOR	H	8	343	TAYLOR	J	6	399
TAYLOR	F	4	376	TAYLOR	G	8	343	TAYLOR	H	9	189	TAYLOR	J	6	399
TAYLOR	F	4	376	TAYLOR	G	9	189	TAYLOR	H	9	354	TAYLOR	J	6	399
TAYLOR	F	5	349	TAYLOR	G	9	353	TAYLOR	H	9	354	TAYLOR	J	7	393
TAYLOR	F	5	349	TAYLOR	G	10	227	TAYLOR	H	9	354	TAYLOR	J	7	393
TAYLOR	F	5	349	TAYLOR	G	10	375	TAYLOR	H	9	354	TAYLOR	J	8	343
TAYLOR	F	6	398	TAYLOR	G	11	365	TAYLOR	H	10	227	TAYLOR	J	8	343
TAYLOR	F	6	398	TAYLOR	G	11	365	TAYLOR	H	10	375	TAYLOR	J	8	343
TAYLOR	F	8	342	TAYLOR	G	12	219	TAYLOR	H	11	365	TAYLOR	J	8	343
TAYLOR	F	8	342	TAYLOR	G	14	310	TAYLOR	H	11	365	TAYLOR	J	9	189
TAYLOR	F	9	189	TAYLOR	G	14	310	TAYLOR	H	11	365	TAYLOR	J	9	189
TAYLOR	F	9	353	TAYLOR	G	14	310	TAYLOR	H	11	365	TAYLOR	J	9	189
TAYLOR	F	10	227	TAYLOR	G	14	310	TAYLOR	H	11	365	TAYLOR	J	9	189

TAYLOR	J	9	354	TAYLOR	JH	7	393	TAYLOR	PR	3	234	TAYLOR	T	9	190
TAYLOR	J	9	354	TAYLOR	JH	9	354	TAYLOR	R	1	344	TAYLOR	T	10	228
TAYLOR	J	9	354	TAYLOR	JH	11	366	TAYLOR	R	2	335	TAYLOR	T	10	228
TAYLOR	J	11	366	TAYLOR	JH	11	366	TAYLOR	R	5	350	TAYLOR	T	10	228
TAYLOR	J	11	366	TAYLOR	JH	11	366	TAYLOR	R	6	400	TAYLOR	T	11	367
TAYLOR	J	11	366	TAYLOR	JJ	1	344	TAYLOR	R	6	400	TAYLOR	T	11	367
TAYLOR	J	11	366	TAYLOR	JJ	2	334	TAYLOR	R	7	393	TAYLOR	T	11	367
TAYLOR	J	11	366	TAYLOR	JJ	14	311	TAYLOR	R	8	344	TAYLOR	T	11	367
TAYLOR	J	11	366	TAYLOR	JJ	14	311	TAYLOR	R	11	367	TAYLOR	T	11	367
TAYLOR	J	11	366	TAYLOR	JL	13	416	TAYLOR	R	11	367	TAYLOR	T	13	417
TAYLOR	J	11	366	TAYLOR	JP	13	416	TAYLOR	R	11	367	TAYLOR	T	13	417
TAYLOR	J	11	366	TAYLOR	JR	8	344	TAYLOR	R	14	312	TAYLOR	T	13	417
TAYLOR	J	11	366	TAYLOR	JR	13	416	TAYLOR	RA	14	312	TAYLOR	T	14	312
TAYLOR	J	12	219	TAYLOR	JR	14	311	TAYLOR	RE	4	376	TAYLOR	TC	10	375
TAYLOR	J	12	219	TAYLOR	JS	3	234	TAYLOR	RE	14	312	TAYLOR	TE	5	350
TAYLOR	J	12	395	TAYLOR	JS	9	354	TAYLOR	RF	2	335	TAYLOR	TE	6	400
TAYLOR	J	12	395	TAYLOR	JT	11	367	TAYLOR	RF	13	417	TAYLOR	TF	1	344
TAYLOR	J	12	395	TAYLOR	JT	11	367	TAYLOR	RH	1	344	TAYLOR	TH	6	400
TAYLOR	J	12	395	TAYLOR	JT	12	219	TAYLOR	RH	5	350	TAYLOR	TH	6	400
TAYLOR	J	13	416	TAYLOR	JT	14	311	TAYLOR	RH	9	190	TAYLOR	TH	6	400
TAYLOR	J	14	311	TAYLOR	JW	2	334	TAYLOR	RH	9	190	TAYLOR	TH	11	367
TAYLOR	J	14	311	TAYLOR	JW	2	335	TAYLOR	RH	11	367	TAYLOR	TH	14	312
TAYLOR	J	14	311	TAYLOR	JW	4	376	TAYLOR	RJ	1	344	TAYLOR	TJ	3	234
TAYLOR	J	14	311	TAYLOR	JW	5	350	TAYLOR	RJ	10	228	TAYLOR	TT	6	401
TAYLOR	J	14	311	TAYLOR	JW	5	350	TAYLOR	RS	5	350	TAYLOR	TT	6	401
TAYLOR	J	14	311	TAYLOR	JW	6	400	TAYLOR	RW	13	417	TAYLOR	TW	10	228
TAYLOR	J	14	311	TAYLOR	JW	7	393	TAYLOR	S	2	335	TAYLOR	TW	13	417
TAYLOR	J	14	311	TAYLOR	JW	7	393	TAYLOR	S	6	400	TAYLOR	V	2	335
TAYLOR	J	14	311	TAYLOR	JW	9	189	TAYLOR	S	10	375	TAYLOR	V	8	344
TAYLOR	J	14	311	TAYLOR	JW	9	354	TAYLOR	S	11	367	TAYLOR	V	14	312
TAYLOR	JA	5	349	TAYLOR	JW	12	219	TAYLOR	S	12	219	TAYLOR	VJ	12	219
TAYLOR	JA	6	399	TAYLOR	JW	13	416	TAYLOR	S	13	417	TAYLOR	W	1	344
TAYLOR	JA	8	343	TAYLOR	JW	13	416	TAYLOR	S	14	312	TAYLOR	W	1	344
TAYLOR	JA	10	227	TAYLOR	JW	14	311	TAYLOR	S	14	312	TAYLOR	W	1	344
TAYLOR	JC	8	343	TAYLOR	JW	14	312	TAYLOR	SA	6	400	TAYLOR	W	2	335
TAYLOR	JC	14	311	TAYLOR	JW	14	312	TAYLOR	SB	1	344	TAYLOR	W	4	376
TAYLOR	JE	5	349	TAYLOR	L	4	376	TAYLOR	SC	6	400	TAYLOR	W	4	377
TAYLOR	JE	8	343	TAYLOR	L	6	400	TAYLOR	SF	7	393	TAYLOR	W	5	350
TAYLOR	JE	10	228	TAYLOR	L	12	396	TAYLOR	SH	2	335	TAYLOR	W	5	350
TAYLOR	JE	11	366	TAYLOR	LC	2	335	TAYLOR	SJ	7	393	TAYLOR	W	5	350
TAYLOR	JE	11	366	TAYLOR	LE	10	375	TAYLOR	SR	3	234	TAYLOR	W	6	401
TAYLOR	JES	5	350	TAYLOR	LH	7	393	TAYLOR	SR	13	417	TAYLOR	W	6	401
TAYLOR	JF	6	399	TAYLOR	M	6	400	TAYLOR	SW	4	376	TAYLOR	W	6	401
TAYLOR	JF	6	399	TAYLOR	M	14	312	TAYLOR	T	4	376	TAYLOR	W	6	401
TAYLOR	JF	8	343	TAYLOR	N	5	350	TAYLOR	T	5	350	TAYLOR	W	6	401
TAYLOR	JF	9	189	TAYLOR	N	9	189	TAYLOR	T	5	350	TAYLOR	W	7	393
TAYLOR	JF	13	416	TAYLOR	NE	11	366	TAYLOR	T	6	400	TAYLOR	W	8	344
TAYLOR	JG	3	234	TAYLOR	O	7	393	TAYLOR	T	6	400	TAYLOR	W	8	344
TAYLOR	JG	9	354	TAYLOR	O	8	344	TAYLOR	T	6	400	TAYLOR	W	8	344
TAYLOR	JH	3	234	TAYLOR	P	2	335	TAYLOR	T	7	393	TAYLOR	W	8	344
TAYLOR	JH	6	400	TAYLOR	P	6	400	TAYLOR	T	8	344	TAYLOR	W	9	190
TAYLOR	JH	7	393	TAYLOR	P	11	367	TAYLOR	T	8	344	TAYLOR	W	9	354
				TAYLOR	P	11	367	TAYLOR	T	8	344	TAYLOR	W	9	354
				TAYLOR	PC	6	400	TAYLOR	T	9	190	TAYLOR	W	10	375
				TAYLOR	PE	2	335	TAYLOR	T	9	190	TAYLOR	W	10	375

TAYLOR	W	11	367	TAYLOR	WJ	13	417	TEARLE	H	5	351	TELLING	WH	7	394
TAYLOR	W	11	367	TAYLOR	WL	6	401	TEARLE	HC	5	351	TELMAY	J	13	418
TAYLOR	W	11	367	TAYLOR	WM	13	417	TEARLE	J	5	351	TEMPERTON	TR	1	344
TAYLOR	W	11	367	TAYLOR	WM	14	313	TEARLE	J	5	351	TEMPEST	A	9	354
TAYLOR	W	11	368	TAYLOR	WR	5	350	TEARLE	JH	1	344	TEMPEST	A	9	354
TAYLOR	W	11	368	TAYLOR	WR	6	401	TEARLE	ST	1	344	TEMPEST	D	8	345
TAYLOR	W	12	219	TAYLOR	WR	7	393	TEARLE	W	5	351	TEMPEST	E	8	345
TAYLOR	W	12	396	TAYLOR	WR	13	417	TEARLE	W	8	345	TEMPEST	E	8	345
TAYLOR	W	12	396	TAYLOR	WS	3	399	TEARLE	WM	5	351	TEMPEST	F	8	345
TAYLOR	W	13	417	TAYLOR	WT	3	399	TEARNE	H	9	190	TEMPEST	G	8	345
TAYLOR	W	13	417	TAYLOR	WT	4	377	TEASDALE	JG	2	335	TEMPEST	H	9	190
TAYLOR	W	14	312	TAYLOR	WT	13	417	TEASDALE	W	11	368	TEMPEST	H	9	355
TAYLOR	W	14	312	TAYLOR	WW	1	344	TEAT	W	12	220	TEMPEST	J	8	345
TAYLOR	W	14	312	TAYLOR	WW	6	401	TEBAY	J	11	368	TEMPEST	JS	8	345
TAYLOR	W	14	312	TAYNTON	JH	7	394	TEBB	H	11	368	TEMPEST	R	9	355
TAYLOR	W	14	312	TAYNTON	JT	7	394	TEBBEY	WG	5	351	TEMPEST	RA	8	345
TAYLOR	W	14	312	TEAGLE	CS	12	219	TEBBOTH	HW	5	351	TEMPEST	RF	9	190
TAYLOR	W	14	312	TEAGLE	J	3	399	TEBBS	TH	3	399	TEMPEST	T	9	190
TAYLOR	WA	1	344	TEAGLE	LA	2	335	TEBBUT	W	7	394	TEMPLE	A	8	345
TAYLOR	WA	2	335	TEAGUE	GE	4	377	TEBBUTT	AF	12	396	TEMPLE	A	12	220
TAYLOR	WA	7	393	TEAGUE	GE	6	401	TEBBUTT	HH	12	396	TEMPLE	C	11	368
TAYLOR	WAJ	3	399	TEAGUE	JWH	10	375	TEBBUTT	J	12	396	TEMPLE	C	12	220
TAYLOR	WB	13	417	TEAGUE	S	6	402	TEBBUTT	T	12	396	TEMPLE	C	13	418
TAYLOR	WC	3	399	TEAKLE	WG	8	344	TEBROEKE	W	13	417	TEMPLE	CA	3	235
TAYLOR	WC	6	401	TEAL	H	11	368	TEBWORTH	TA	7	394	TEMPLE	E	2	336
TAYLOR	WC	8	344	TEAL	R	8	344	TEDMAN	CSH	13	418	TEMPLE	EC	7	394
TAYLOR	WC	12	219	TEALE	A	9	190	TEDMAN	H	1	344	TEMPLE	EG	3	235
TAYLOR	WC	13	417	TEALE	E	8	344	TEDMAN	W	13	418	TEMPLE	G	1	344
TAYLOR	WC	13	417	TEALE	E	9	190	TEE	A	4	377	TEMPLE	GA	2	336
TAYLOR	WC	13	417	TEALE	E	9	190	TEE	AE	4	377	TEMPLE	H	8	345
TAYLOR	WE	5	350	TEALE	G	12	220	TEE	G	13	418	TEMPLE	H	8	345
TAYLOR	WE	6	401	TEALE	H	9	354	TEE	GA	12	396	TEMPLE	H	8	346
TAYLOR	WE	8	344	TEALE	JT	8	345	TEE	J	10	375	TEMPLE	H	12	220
TAYLOR	WES	1	344	TEALE	JW	8	345	TEE	LGW	4	377	TEMPLE	J	8	346
TAYLOR	WG	6	401	TEALE	W	8	345	TEE	TG	10	228	TEMPLE	JW	8	346
TAYLOR	WG	12	219	TEALE	W	8	345	TEE	WA	10	376	TEMPLE	JW	12	220
TAYLOR	WH	6	401	TEALE	W	9	354	TEE	WC	2	335	TEMPLE	T	10	228
TAYLOR	WH	6	401	TEAM	JW	10	228	TEE	WH	12	396	TEMPLE	W	7	394
TAYLOR	WH	6	401	TEANBY	W	11	368	TEE	WJ	7	394	TEMPLE	W	8	346
TAYLOR	WH	6	401	TEAR	AE	12	396	TEE	WRS	2	335	TEMPLE	W	8	346
TAYLOR	WH	7	393	TEAR	AT	7	394	TEERS	J	11	368	TEMPLE	WE	8	346
TAYLOR	WH	8	344	TEAR	CL	4	377	TEERS	J	11	368	TEMPLEMAN	AS	2	336
TAYLOR	WH	8	344	TEAR	E	12	396	TEERS	J	11	368	TEMPLEMAN	CH	12	396
TAYLOR	WH	8	344	TEAR	W	12	396	TEES	A	6	402	TEMPLEMAN	FE	2	336
TAYLOR	WH	11	368	TEARALL	FG	3	399	TEESDALE	E	7	394	TEMPLEMAN	GW	7	394
TAYLOR	WH	11	368	TEARALL	W	2	335	TEGERDINE	JW	10	228	TEMPLER	AH	1	344
TAYLOR	WJ	1	344	TEARE	J	14	313	TELFER	AG	7	394	TEMPLER	H	1	345
TAYLOR	WJ	2	335	TEARLE	E	5	350	TELFER	W	8	345	TEMPLETON	G	10	376
TAYLOR	WJ	3	234	TEARLE	EG	5	350	TELFORD	G	6	402	TEMPLETON	JF	10	228
TAYLOR	WJ	3	234	TEARLE	EJ	5	350	TELFORD	J	9	354	TENCH	A	1	345
TAYLOR	WJ	6	401	TEARLE	EJ	5	350	TELFORD	TA	6	402	TENCH	H	14	313
TAYLOR	WJ	6	401	TEARLE	F	5	351	TELFORD	W	8	345	TENCH	SA	12	396
TAYLOR	WJ	12	219	TEARLE	FJ	5	351	TELFORD	W	14	313	TENNANT	DB	6	402
TAYLOR	WJ	13	417	TEARLE	G	3	399	TELLING	A	2	336	TENNANT	DH	10	376
TAYLOR	WJ	13	417	TEARLE	H	5	351	TELLING	WE	2	336	TENNANT	E	14	313

TENNANT	F	13	418	TERRY	FT	13	418	TETLOW	F	11	368	THACKRAY	W	8	347
TENNANT	F	14	313	TERRY	G	3	235	TETLOW	J	11	368	THACKRAY	W	9	355
TENNANT	G	7	394	TERRY	G	7	395	TETLOW	S	14	313	THACKWELL	GA	11	368
TENNANT	GE	13	418	TERRY	GE	5	351	TETLOW	T	14	313	THAIN	AE	1	345
TENNANT	J	8	346	TERRY	GF	8	346	TETSTALL	A	6	402	THAIN	E	8	347
TENNANT	JW	9	190	TERRY	GH	10	228	TEW	AS	12	396	THAIN	F	8	347
TENNANT	P	6	402	TERRY	H	5	351	TEW	C	10	229	THAIN	H	8	347
TENNANT	R	9	190	TERRY	H	6	402	TEW	CE	5	351	THAIN	WF	7	395
TENNANT	S	6	402	TERRY	H	13	418	TEW	D	5	351	THAIN	WJ	2	336
TENNANT	S	14	313	TERRY	HA	7	395	TEW	D	6	402	THAME	AE	1	345
TENNANT	W	8	346	TERRY	HJ	3	235	TEW	EE	3	235	THANE	JST	2	336
TENNANT	W	10	228	TERRY	HJ	5	351	TEW	H	6	402	THARBY	CW	3	235
TENNANT	WC	3	235	TERRY	HWR	4	377	TEW	H	12	396	THARME	A	13	419
TENNANT	WH	7	394	TERRY	J	8	346	TEW	JE	12	396	THATCHER	AN	10	376
TENNENT	HM	10	228	TERRY	J	9	190	TEW	L	5	352	THATCHER	CB	5	352
TENNENT	WS	10	376	TERRY	JH	7	395	TEW	P	5	352	THATCHER	E	3	235
TENNET	T	12	396	TERRY	JH	13	418	TEW	TJ	3	235	THATCHER	EJ	5	352
TENNETT	C	9	355	TERRY	JW	4	377	TEW	WA	1	345	THATCHER	FH	4	378
TENWICK	JJ	13	418	TERRY	L	10	228	TEW	WR	3	235	THATCHER	FJ	2	336
TEOBALDO	J	7	394	TERRY	M	3	235	TEWSLEY	F	10	229	THATCHER	GFC	1	345
TEPPER	RC	7	394	TERRY	PE	3	235	THACKER	AE	3	235	THATCHER	GJ	5	352
TERO	A	12	396	TERRY	R	6	402	THACKER	E	6	402	THATCHER	H	13	419
TERO	HG	12	396	TERRY	R	7	395	THACKER	F	3	235	THATCHER	HS	3	235
TERRELL	A	4	377	TERRY	R	13	418	THACKER	GR	7	395	THATCHER	W	3	235
TERRELL	C	4	377	TERRY	RS	10	376	THACKER	JH	7	395	THATCHER	WC	7	395
TERRELL	F	4	377	TERRY	S	10	228	THACKER	RW	7	395	THATCHER	WG	2	336
TERRELL	GW	13	418	TERRY	T	9	355	THACKER	T	7	395	THAYERS	S	10	229
TERRETT	AG	7	394	TERRY	TA	13	418	THACKERAY	GE	8	346	THEAKER	S	8	347
TERRETT	TC	7	394	TERRY	W	4	377	THACKERAY	R	1	345	THEAKER	TG	4	378
TERREY	EL	7	394	TERRY	W	10	376	THACKERY	J	8	346	THEARLE	CW	1	345
TERREY	HG	10	228	TERRY	W	12	220	THACKHAM	JW	7	395	THEARLE	FE	1	345
TERREY	TJ	7	394	TERRY	WE	4	377	THACKRAH	B	8	346	THEARLE	S	6	402
TERRINGTON	G	8	346	TERRY	WH	10	228	THACKRAY	A	8	346	THEED	WH	12	220
TERRY	A	1	345	TERRY	WJ	4	377	THACKRAY	A	9	191	THELEN	C	11	368
TERRY	A	3	235	TERRY	WJ	4	377	THACKRAY	A	9	355	THELWELL	F	11	368
TERRY	A	7	394	TESORIERE	M	13	418	THACKRAY	AW	9	191	THELWELL	T	11	369
TERRY	A	13	418	TESSYMAN	G	8	346	THACKRAY	B	8	346	THELWELL	W	11	368
TERRY	AE	2	336	TESTER	RG	13	418	THACKRAY	CB	8	347	THEOBALD	A	13	419
TERRY	ALW	3	235	TESTER	WA	6	402	THACKRAY	E	8	347	THEOBALD	AE	1	345
TERRY	B	6	402	TETLEY	A	9	190	THACKRAY	E	8	347	THEOBALD	AR	5	352
TERRY	C	13	418	TETLEY	E	9	190	THACKRAY	F	8	347	THEOBALD	CE	13	419
TERRY	CA	5	351	TETLEY	FG	4	377	THACKRAY	F	9	191	THEOBALD	F	4	378
TERRY	CE	3	235	TETLEY	G	8	346	THACKRAY	G	8	347	THEOBALD	FW	11	369
TERRY	CH	3	235	TETLEY	G	9	190	THACKRAY	H	8	347	THEOBALD	G	6	402
TERRY	CJ	12	220	TETLEY	H	9	190	THACKRAY	HW	4	378	THEOBALD	G	12	220
TERRY	D	5	351	TETLEY	HF	9	191	THACKRAY	J	8	347	THEOBALD	GF	13	419
TERRY	E	10	376	TETLEY	J	8	346	THACKRAY	J	8	347	THEOBALD	GW	4	378
TERRY	E	13	418	TETLEY	JW	9	191	THACKRAY	J	9	191	THEOBALD	J	3	236
TERRY	EE	4	377	TETLEY	JW	9	355	THACKRAY	JT	8	347	THEOBALD	J	12	220
TERRY	EG	5	351	TETLEY	JW	9	355	THACKRAY	JW	8	347	THEOBALD	J	13	419
TERRY	EM	9	190	TETLEY	R	9	191	THACKRAY	R	8	347	THEOBALD	JW	12	397
TERRY	EP	13	418	TETLEY	W	8	346	THACKRAY	R	8	347	THEOBALD	S	11	369
TERRY	F	3	235	TETLEY	W	9	191	THACKRAY	T	9	191	THEOBALD	SR	8	347
TERRY	F	4	377	TETLEY	WH	4	378	THACKRAY	W	8	347	THEOBALD	T	9	355
TERRY	FJ	13	418	TETLOW	A	9	191	THACKRAY	W	8	347	THEOBALD	W	6	402

THEOBALD	W	11	369	THOMAS	AJ	4	378	THOMAS	GE	1	345	THOMAS	JW	9	355
THEOBALD	WE	12	397	THOMAS	AJ	7	395	THOMAS	GE	2	337	THOMAS	JW	9	355
THEOBALD	WT	12	220	THOMAS	AJ	10	229	THOMAS	GE	14	313	THOMAS	JW	11	369
THETFORD	F	14	313	THOMAS	AJ	10	229	THOMAS	GF	6	403	THOMAS	JW	14	314
THEWLIS	J	8	347	THOMAS	AL	12	424	THOMAS	GH	7	396	THOMAS	KT	13	419
THEWLISS	A	9	355	THOMAS	AM	7	395	THOMAS	GP	11	369	THOMAS	L	4	378
THEYS	AW	3	236	THOMAS	AR	2	336	THOMAS	GS	4	378	THOMAS	L	10	229
THEYS	AWS	3	236	THOMAS	AW	6	402	THOMAS	GW	2	337	THOMAS	LJ	1	346
THEYS	E	3	236	THOMAS	B	3	399	THOMAS	GW	6	403	THOMAS	LO	14	314
THICK	A	4	378	THOMAS	B	13	419	THOMAS	H	3	236	THOMAS	LT	7	396
THICK	CW	1	345	THOMAS	C	2	336	THOMAS	H	4	378	THOMAS	M	7	396
THICK	S	4	378	THOMAS	C	6	403	THOMAS	H	6	403	THOMAS	M	13	419
THICKBROOM	CH	8	348	THOMAS	C	6	403	THOMAS	H	7	396	THOMAS	ML	4	378
THICKBROOM	EF	14	313	THOMAS	C	14	313	THOMAS	H	7	396	THOMAS	MW	3	236
THICKBROOM	WAE	8	348	THOMAS	CA	1	345	THOMAS	H	7	396	THOMAS	P	10	230
THICKETT	JH	11	369	THOMAS	CE	1	345	THOMAS	H	10	229	THOMAS	R	14	314
THILTHORPE	HJ	1	345	THOMAS	CE	2	336	THOMAS	H	10	376	THOMAS	RAT	1	346
THIRGOOD	AJ	7	395	THOMAS	CF	13	419	THOMAS	H	11	369	THOMAS	RG	10	229
THIRKELL	JW	7	395	THOMAS	CG	13	419	THOMAS	H	11	369	THOMAS	RJ	2	337
THIRKETTLE	HJ	8	348	THOMAS	CH	6	403	THOMAS	H	14	313	THOMAS	RJ	6	403
THIRKETTLE	J	11	369	THOMAS	CJ	7	396	THOMAS	H	14	314	THOMAS	S	8	348
THIRKHILL	C	9	355	THOMAS	CW	4	378	THOMAS	HAJ	1	345	THOMAS	S	14	314
THIRKHILL	R	9	191	THOMAS	CW	7	396	THOMAS	HC	7	396	THOMAS	SC	11	369
THIRKILL	E	9	355	THOMAS	D	2	336	THOMAS	HF	2	337	THOMAS	SJ	6	403
THIRKILL	H	9	355	THOMAS	D	14	313	THOMAS	HG	1	345	THOMAS	SR	11	369
THIRKILL	J	9	191	THOMAS	DC	10	229	THOMAS	HG	4	378	THOMAS	SS	2	337
THIRLWELL	W	3	236	THOMAS	DHJ	7	396	THOMAS	HI	2	337	THOMAS	SW	7	397
THIRTLE	J	3	399	THOMAS	DJ	3	236	THOMAS	HJ	6	403	THOMAS	SW	13	419
THISTLEWOOD	A	8	348	THOMAS	DM	7	396	THOMAS	HN	9	191	THOMAS	T	6	403
THISTLEWOOD	TW	14	313	THOMAS	E	3	236	THOMAS	HP	1	345	THOMAS	T	10	229
THITCHENER	CS	2	336	THOMAS	E	4	378	THOMAS	HR	3	236	THOMAS	T	14	314
THITCHENER	W	2	336	THOMAS	E	7	396	THOMAS	HV	13	419	THOMAS	TRD	2	337
THIXTON	RG	7	395	THOMAS	E	10	229	THOMAS	J	3	236	THOMAS	W	2	337
THODAY	RHW	3	399	THOMAS	E	11	369	THOMAS	J	6	403	THOMAS	W	3	399
THODY	H	5	352	THOMAS	E	11	369	THOMAS	J	7	396	THOMAS	W	3	399
THOLE	PN	7	395	THOMAS	E	12	397	THOMAS	J	9	355	THOMAS	W	4	378
THOM	G	14	313	THOMAS	EAF	1	345	THOMAS	J	9	355	THOMAS	W	4	378
THOMAS	A	1	345	THOMAS	EG	7	396	THOMAS	J	9	355	THOMAS	W	6	403
THOMAS	A	3	399	THOMAS	EG	13	419	THOMAS	J	10	229	THOMAS	W	6	404
THOMAS	A	3	399	THOMAS	EH	7	396	THOMAS	J	12	397	THOMAS	W	6	404
THOMAS	A	4	378	THOMAS	EJ	13	419	THOMAS	J	13	419	THOMAS	W	6	404
THOMAS	A	6	402	THOMAS	EM	10	376	THOMAS	J	14	314	THOMAS	W	7	397
THOMAS	A	6	402	THOMAS	EMS	7	396	THOMAS	JA	7	396	THOMAS	W	8	348
THOMAS	A	7	395	THOMAS	EW	3	236	THOMAS	JA	11	369	THOMAS	W	9	191
THOMAS	AAG	13	419	THOMAS	EW	3	236	THOMAS	JC	10	376	THOMAS	W	9	355
THOMAS	AB	3	236	THOMAS	F	4	378	THOMAS	JE	13	419	THOMAS	W	10	229
THOMAS	AC	4	378	THOMAS	F	6	403	THOMAS	JEP	12	397	THOMAS	W	12	397
THOMAS	AE	2	336	THOMAS	F	6	403	THOMAS	JF	11	369	THOMAS	WC	1	346
THOMAS	AE	3	399	THOMAS	F	6	403	THOMAS	JH	6	403	THOMAS	WC	4	379
THOMAS	AE	11	369	THOMAS	F	9	355	THOMAS	JH	6	403	THOMAS	WC	7	397
THOMAS	AE	14	313	THOMAS	FG	7	396	THOMAS	JH	14	314	THOMAS	WDT	5	352
THOMAS	AG	3	236	THOMAS	FJ	3	236	THOMAS	JJ	6	403	THOMAS	WE	4	379
THOMAS	AG	7	395	THOMAS	FJ	6	403	THOMAS	JJ	11	369	THOMAS	WE	12	397
THOMAS	AH	10	376	THOMAS	G	3	236	THOMAS	JR	2	337	THOMAS	WE	14	314
THOMAS	AJ	3	236	THOMAS	G	6	403	THOMAS	JR	7	396	THOMAS	WG	7	397

THOMAS	WG	7	397
THOMAS	WH	2	337
THOMAS	WH	6	404
THOMAS	WH	10	229
THOMAS	WH	10	229
THOMAS	WH	11	369
THOMAS	WJ	2	337
THOMAS	WJ	4	379
THOMAS	WJ	6	404
THOMAS	WJ	10	376
THOMAS	WJ	11	370
THOMAS	WS	4	379
THOMAS	WS	8	348
THOMASON	F	2	337
THOMASON	GH	11	370
THOMASON	H	2	337
THOMASON	J	12	397
THOMASON	J	14	314
THOMASON	JW	12	397
THOMASON	R	14	314
THOMASON	T	14	314
THOMASON	WT	11	370
THOMASSON	E	3	236
THOMASSON	F	3	236
THOMIS	J	9	191
THOMIS	LS	9	191
THOMKINS	W	5	352
THOMOND	T	14	314
THOMOND	T	14	314
THOMPKINS	C	5	352
THOMPKINS	JS	12	220
THOMPSETT	RF	13	420
THOMPSON	A	1	346
THOMPSON	A	2	337
THOMPSON	A	2	337
THOMPSON	A	3	237
THOMPSON	A	3	237
THOMPSON	A	3	237
THOMPSON	A	4	379
THOMPSON	A	5	352
THOMPSON	A	6	404
THOMPSON	A	6	404
THOMPSON	A	6	404
THOMPSON	A	7	397
THOMPSON	A	8	348
THOMPSON	A	8	348
THOMPSON	A	9	191
THOMPSON	A	9	356
THOMPSON	A	10	229
THOMPSON	A	11	370
THOMPSON	A	12	397
THOMPSON	A	14	314
THOMPSON	A	14	314
THOMPSON	A	14	314
THOMPSON	A	14	314
THOMPSON	A	14	315
THOMPSON	AA	2	337
THOMPSON	AC	3	237
THOMPSON	AD	13	420
THOMPSON	AE	5	352
THOMPSON	AE	8	348
THOMPSON	AE	9	191
THOMPSON	AE	9	356
THOMPSON	AE	11	370
THOMPSON	AG	2	337
THOMPSON	AG	13	420
THOMPSON	AH	4	379
THOMPSON	AR	11	370
THOMPSON	AV	6	404
THOMPSON	AW	2	337
THOMPSON	B	6	404
THOMPSON	C	2	338
THOMPSON	C	5	352
THOMPSON	C	5	352
THOMPSON	C	8	348
THOMPSON	C	8	348
THOMPSON	C	8	348
THOMPSON	C	8	348
THOMPSON	C	8	348
THOMPSON	C	8	348
THOMPSON	C	9	191
THOMPSON	C	9	356
THOMPSON	C	11	370
THOMPSON	C	12	220
THOMPSON	C	14	315
THOMPSON	C	14	315
THOMPSON	CA	3	237
THOMPSON	CA	6	404
THOMPSON	CF	11	370
THOMPSON	CF	11	370
THOMPSON	CH	8	348
THOMPSON	CH	12	397
THOMPSON	D	9	192
THOMPSON	D	9	356
THOMPSON	E	2	338
THOMPSON	E	2	338
THOMPSON	E	2	338
THOMPSON	E	3	237
THOMPSON	E	5	352
THOMPSON	E	6	404
THOMPSON	E	9	192
THOMPSON	E	9	192
THOMPSON	E	9	192
THOMPSON	E	9	192
THOMPSON	E	9	192
THOMPSON	E	14	315
THOMPSON	EF	5	352
THOMPSON	EG	5	352
THOMPSON	EGB	7	397
THOMPSON	EJ	5	352
THOMPSON	EM	2	338
THOMPSON	ET	13	420
THOMPSON	EW	1	346
THOMPSON	F	1	346
THOMPSON	F	8	348
THOMPSON	F	9	192
THOMPSON	F	9	192
THOMPSON	F	9	356
THOMPSON	F	10	229
THOMPSON	F	10	229
THOMPSON	F	11	370
THOMPSON	F	12	220
THOMPSON	F	12	397
THOMPSON	F	12	397
THOMPSON	F	14	315
THOMPSON	FG	4	379
THOMPSON	FH	13	420
THOMPSON	FJ	5	352
THOMPSON	FJ	6	404
THOMPSON	FM	13	420
THOMPSON	FW	10	229
THOMPSON	G	2	338
THOMPSON	G	3	399
THOMPSON	G	4	379
THOMPSON	G	5	353
THOMPSON	G	8	348
THOMPSON	G	8	348
THOMPSON	G	8	348
THOMPSON	G	9	192
THOMPSON	G	9	356
THOMPSON	G	9	356
THOMPSON	G	11	370
THOMPSON	G	13	420
THOMPSON	G	13	420
THOMPSON	G	14	315
THOMPSON	G	14	315
THOMPSON	GA	8	349
THOMPSON	GA	10	376
THOMPSON	GA	11	370
THOMPSON	GC	2	338
THOMPSON	GC	7	397
THOMPSON	GH	1	346
THOMPSON	GH	3	237
THOMPSON	GH	10	230
THOMPSON	GJ	3	237
THOMPSON	GM	10	376
THOMPSON	GW	3	399
THOMPSON	GW	7	397
THOMPSON	H	1	346
THOMPSON	H	1	346
THOMPSON	H	1	346
THOMPSON	H	1	346
THOMPSON	H	2	338
THOMPSON	H	6	404
THOMPSON	H	6	404
THOMPSON	H	8	349
THOMPSON	H	8	349
THOMPSON	H	8	349
THOMPSON	H	8	349
THOMPSON	H	8	349
THOMPSON	H	9	356
THOMPSON	H	10	376
THOMPSON	H	11	370
THOMPSON	H	11	370
THOMPSON	H	13	420
THOMPSON	H	14	315
THOMPSON	H	14	315
THOMPSON	HJ	2	338
THOMPSON	HLE	14	315
THOMPSON	HM	3	399
THOMPSON	HM	9	192
THOMPSON	HP	12	220
THOMPSON	HR	2	338
THOMPSON	HW	1	346
THOMPSON	HW	7	397
THOMPSON	HW	7	397
THOMPSON	I	14	315
THOMPSON	J	1	346
THOMPSON	J	1	346
THOMPSON	J	2	338
THOMPSON	J	6	404
THOMPSON	J	6	404
THOMPSON	J	6	404
THOMPSON	J	6	404
THOMPSON	J	8	349
THOMPSON	J	8	349
THOMPSON	J	8	349
THOMPSON	J	8	349
THOMPSON	J	8	349
THOMPSON	J	8	349
THOMPSON	J	8	349
THOMPSON	J	8	349
THOMPSON	J	8	349
THOMPSON	J	8	349
THOMPSON	J	8	349
THOMPSON	J	8	349
THOMPSON	J	8	349
THOMPSON	J	8	349
THOMPSON	J	8	349
THOMPSON	J	9	192
THOMPSON	J	9	192
THOMPSON	J	9	356
THOMPSON	J	9	356
THOMPSON	J	10	230
THOMPSON	J	11	370
THOMPSON	J	11	370
THOMPSON	J	11	370
THOMPSON	J	11	370
THOMPSON	J	11	370
THOMPSON	J	11	371

THOMPSON	J	11	371	THOMPSON	S	8	350	THOMPSON	WJ	13	420	THORN	JH	1	347
THOMPSON	J	12	397	THOMPSON	S	9	192	THOMPSON	WRE	3	237	THORN	L	7	398
THOMPSON	J	12	397	THOMPSON	SC	8	350	THOMPSON	WS	8	350	THORN	R	4	380
THOMPSON	J	14	315	THOMPSON	T	7	397	THOMPSON	WS	13	420	THORN	R	11	371
THOMPSON	J	14	315	THOMPSON	T	8	350	THOMPSON	WS	14	316	THORN	RV	4	380
THOMPSON	J	14	315	THOMPSON	T	11	371	THOMSON	AW	2	339	THORN	S	4	380
THOMPSON	JA	4	379	THOMPSON	T	14	315	THOMSON	CS	12	398	THORN	T	9	193
THOMPSON	JE	2	338	THOMPSON	T	14	316	THOMSON	D	9	193	THORN	W	11	371
THOMPSON	JE	4	379	THOMPSON	TA	13	420	THOMSON	DJ	7	397	THORN	WJ	4	380
THOMPSON	JF	8	349	THOMPSON	TE	10	377	THOMSON	FJ	3	237	THORN	WJ	4	380
THOMPSON	JH	1	346	THOMPSON	TH	11	371	THOMSON	HG	13	420	THORN	WJ	10	377
THOMPSON	JT	8	349	THOMPSON	TJ	2	338	THOMSON	HP	3	237	THORN	WT	5	353
THOMPSON	JT	8	350	THOMPSON	TJ	4	379	THOMSON	N	4	379	THORNBER	E	7	398
THOMPSON	JT	9	192	THOMPSON	TW	9	356	THOMSON	PC	2	339	THORNBOROUGH	B	1	347
THOMPSON	JW	3	237	THOMPSON	V	1	346	THOMSON	W	7	397	THORNBURN	W	9	356
THOMPSON	JW	3	237	THOMPSON	W	2	338	THOMSON	W	11	371	THORNBURY	D	8	350
THOMPSON	JW	7	397	THOMPSON	W	2	339	THOMSON	W	14	316	THORNCROFT	FG	7	398
THOMPSON	JW	8	350	THOMPSON	W	2	339	THOMSON	W	14	316	THORNDYKE	B	13	421
THOMPSON	JW	8	350	THOMPSON	W	4	379	THOMSON	WD	8	350	THORNDYKE	C	13	421
THOMPSON	JW	11	371	THOMPSON	W	5	353	THOMSON	WH	3	237	THORNDYKE	H	13	421
THOMPSON	JW	12	220	THOMPSON	W	5	353	THOMSON	WJ	7	397	THORNE	A	5	353
THOMPSON	JW	14	315	THOMPSON	W	6	405	THOMSON	WM	14	316	THORNE	A	10	230
THOMPSON	JW	14	315	THOMPSON	W	6	405	THOMSON	WN	11	371	THORNE	AA	4	380
THOMPSON	L	8	350	THOMPSON	W	6	405	THORBURN	AJ	10	377	THORNE	AE	13	421
THOMPSON	M	3	237	THOMPSON	W	6	405	THORBURN	G	11	371	THORNE	AF	13	421
THOMPSON	M	9	356	THOMPSON	W	8	350	THORHTON	F	8	350	THORNE	AG	4	380
THOMPSON	M	12	397	THOMPSON	W	8	350	THORHTON	J	8	350	THORNE	AJ	13	421
THOMPSON	N	11	371	THOMPSON	W	8	350	THORLEY	F	13	420	THORNE	APG	13	421
THOMPSON	OT	13	420	THOMPSON	W	8	350	THORLEY	F	14	316	THORNE	C	4	380
THOMPSON	P	8	350	THOMPSON	W	9	192	THORLEY	P	11	371	THORNE	C	7	398
THOMPSON	P	8	350	THOMPSON	W	9	192	THORLEY	WA	6	405	THORNE	CH	9	193
THOMPSON	P	9	192	THOMPSON	W	9	356	THORN	A	1	346	THORNE	CJ	5	353
THOMPSON	PA	4	379	THOMPSON	W	9	356	THORN	A	4	379	THORNE	E	2	339
THOMPSON	PN	1	346	THOMPSON	W	10	377	THORN	AE	4	379	THORNE	E	4	380
THOMPSON	R	1	346	THOMPSON	W	11	371	THORN	AE	4	379	THORNE	EJ	13	421
THOMPSON	R	2	338	THOMPSON	W	11	371	THORN	AW	5	353	THORNE	F	4	380
THOMPSON	R	3	237	THOMPSON	W	11	371	THORN	CH	4	379	THORNE	F	6	405
THOMPSON	R	6	405	THOMPSON	W	12	220	THORN	CJ	4	379	THORNE	F	10	230
THOMPSON	R	7	397	THOMPSON	W	12	397	THORN	EE	4	380	THORNE	G	4	381
THOMPSON	R	8	350	THOMPSON	W	13	420	THORN	EW	5	353	THORNE	G	4	381
THOMPSON	R	9	192	THOMPSON	W	13	420	THORN	F	4	380	THORNE	G	5	353
THOMPSON	R	10	376	THOMPSON	W	14	316	THORN	F	4	380	THORNE	GF	1	347
THOMPSON	R	10	377	THOMPSON	WC	13	420	THORN	F	5	353	THORNE	GH	4	381
THOMPSON	R	11	371	THOMPSON	WCE	13	420	THORN	F	7	397	THORNE	HC	2	339
THOMPSON	R	12	220	THOMPSON	WE	6	405	THORN	FA	5	353	THORNE	J	2	339
THOMPSON	R	12	397	THOMPSON	WF	12	397	THORN	G	4	380	THORNE	JA	4	381
THOMPSON	R	14	315	THOMPSON	WH	7	397	THORN	G	4	380	THORNE	JD	7	398
THOMPSON	RB	10	230	THOMPSON	WH	8	350	THORN	G	7	398	THORNE	JE	5	353
THOMPSON	RC	3	237	THOMPSON	WH	9	192	THORN	GH	4	380	THORNE	JE	10	230
THOMPSON	RC	3	237	THOMPSON	WH	9	192	THORN	H	4	380	THORNE	JH	4	381
THOMPSON	RE	5	353	THOMPSON	WH	11	371	THORN	H	10	377	THORNE	JJ	14	316
THOMPSON	RG	3	237	THOMPSON	WJ	2	339	THORN	HA	5	353	THORNE	JW	5	353
THOMPSON	RJ	2	338	THOMPSON	WJ	12	220	THORN	HC	4	380	THORNE	P	3	237
THOMPSON	S	2	338	THOMPSON	WJ	12	221	THORN	J	4	380	THORNE	PC	4	381
THOMPSON	S	5	353	THOMPSON	WJ	12	398	THORN	J	5	353	THORNE	R	4	381

THORNE	RA	4	381	THORNTON	FW	10	377	THOROGOOD	AJ	12	221	THORPE	S	12	221
THORNE	RJ	3	238	THORNTON	FWS	8	351	THOROGOOD	C	3	238	THORPE	S	14	317
THORNE	RJ	5	353	THORNTON	G	6	405	THOROGOOD	GJ	1	347	THORPE	VW	13	422
THORNE	SA	12	221	THORNTON	GG	1	347	THOROGOOD	GJ	3	238	THORPE	W	2	340
THORNE	TH	13	421	THORNTON	H	5	353	THOROGOOD	HA	5	354	THORPE	W	3	238
THORNE	TJ	4	381	THORNTON	H	9	193	THOROGOOD	JJ	3	238	THORPE	W	9	357
THORNE	TW	6	405	THORNTON	H	14	316	THOROGOOD	TG	5	354	THORPE	W	9	357
THORNE	VB	2	339	THORNTON	HC	3	238	THOROGOOD	W	12	221	THORPE	W	11	372
THORNE	W	7	398	THORNTON	HC	13	421	THOROGOOD	WF	7	398	THORPE	W	13	422
THORNE	WT	3	238	THORNTON	HH	12	398	THOROUGHGOOD	T	2	339	THORPE	W	14	317
THORNETT	FJ	4	381	THORNTON	HJ	13	421	THORP	CP	11	372	THORPE	WB	10	230
THORNETT	JA	3	238	THORNTON	J	2	339	THORP	EH	3	238	THORPE	WE	9	193
THORNETT	WE	6	405	THORNTON	J	3	238	THORP	F	11	372	THORPE	WE	11	372
THORNEWELL	RA	6	405	THORNTON	J	6	405	THORP	HV	3	238	THORPE	WH	9	357
THORNEY	W	6	405	THORNTON	J	8	351	THORP	J	8	351	THORROWGOOD	RWT	10	377
THORNEYCROFT	W	12	398	THORNTON	J	9	193	THORP	J	8	351	THORROWGOOD	SC	10	377
THORNHILL	A	11	372	THORNTON	J	9	357	THORP	JH	11	372	THORSTON	E	2	340
THORNHILL	A	11	372	THORNTON	J	9	357	THORP	M	8	351	THRALE	E	5	354
THORNHILL	A	13	421	THORNTON	J	11	372	THORP	T	8	351	THRALE	J	5	354
THORNHILL	A	14	316	THORNTON	J	11	372	THORP	W	8	351	THRALE	WT	5	354
THORNHILL	E	4	381	THORNTON	JA	14	316	THORP	W	13	421	THRASHER	G	10	377
THORNHILL	H	8	350	THORNTON	JR	8	351	THORP	WE	9	193	THRAVES	WH	1	347
THORNHILL	H	9	356	THORNTON	JW	3	238	THORP	WG	7	398	THREADER	AC	7	398
THORNHILL	H	11	372	THORNTON	L	9	357	THORPE	A	3	238	THREADGOLD	F	14	317
THORNHILL	S	2	339	THORNTON	L	14	316	THORPE	A	7	398	THREADGOLD	G	3	238
THORNHILL	S	11	372	THORNTON	LA	2	339	THORPE	AES	10	377	THREADGOLD	J	3	238
THORNHILL	W	8	351	THORNTON	M	8	351	THORPE	AJ	2	339	THREADGOLD	J	11	373
THORNILEY	A	14	316	THORNTON	PS	4	381	THORPE	C	9	193	THREADGOLD	W	3	239
THORNLEY	AH	12	398	THORNTON	R	14	316	THORPE	C	9	357	THREADGOULD	A	8	351
THORNLEY	R	14	316	THORNTON	RC	13	421	THORPE	CH	7	398	THREADGOULD	D	8	351
THORNLEY	T	6	405	THORNTON	RH	3	238	THORPE	CW	13	421	THREADGOULD	F	8	351
THORNTON	A	8	351	THORNTON	RH	3	238	THORPE	D	6	405	THREADINGHAM	EE	10	230
THORNTON	A	9	193	THORNTON	RH	4	381	THORPE	E	7	398	THRELFALL	H	14	317
THORNTON	A	10	230	THORNTON	RL	7	398	THORPE	F	6	405	THRELFALL	T	11	373
THORNTON	A	14	316	THORNTON	S	9	193	THORPE	F	14	317	THRELFALL	WH	14	317
THORNTON	AB	9	356	THORNTON	S	11	372	THORPE	FG	2	339	THRELFARE	W	8	351
THORNTON	AC	13	421	THORNTON	SJ	11	372	THORPE	FG	8	351	THRESH	H	9	193
THORNTON	AE	9	193	THORNTON	T	8	351	THORPE	G	8	351	THRESH	H	9	357
THORNTON	AJJ	7	398	THORNTON	T	9	193	THORPE	G	12	221	THRESH	WT	9	193
THORNTON	AJT	4	381	THORNTON	T	11	372	THORPE	GW	8	351	THRESHER	FC	4	381
THORNTON	C	1	347	THORNTON	T	14	316	THORPE	H	2	339	THRING	SD	7	398
THORNTON	C	2	339	THORNTON	TW	8	351	THORPE	H	2	339	THROP	H	9	194
THORNTON	C	9	356	THORNTON	TW	9	193	THORPE	H	9	357	THROP	LW	8	352
THORNTON	C	10	377	THORNTON	TW	14	316	THORPE	H	10	377	THROSELL	W	5	354
THORNTON	CA	9	193	THORNTON	W	8	351	THORPE	H	11	372	THROSSELL	AE	12	221
THORNTON	D	11	372	THORNTON	W	8	351	THORPE	HA	2	339	THROUP	H	9	357
THORNTON	E	9	356	THORNTON	W	9	193	THORPE	HHV	10	230	THROUP	H	11	373
THORNTON	E	11	372	THORNTON	W	9	357	THORPE	HJ	8	351	THROWER	EF	2	340
THORNTON	EEA	3	238	THORNTON	W	9	357	THORPE	HT	12	221	THROWER	FR	8	352
THORNTON	EWL	12	398	THORNTON	W	9	357	THORPE	J	9	357	THRUSSELL	C	5	354
THORNTON	F	9	193	THORNTON	W	10	230	THORPE	J	11	372	THUMBWOOD	J	7	398
THORNTON	F	9	193	THORNTON	W	12	221	THORPE	JL	9	193	THUMWOOD	C	7	398
THORNTON	F	9	357	THORNTON	W	14	317	THORPE	L	2	340	THUNDER	LC	7	399
THORNTON	F	9	357	THORNTON	WH	3	238	THORPE	M	9	193	THURGOOD	FW	7	399
THORNTON	FGS	13	421	THOROGOOD	AC	3	238	THORPE	R	13	421	THURGOOD	GJ	7	399

THURGOOD	L	5	354	TIANI	A	11	373	TIERNEY	J	14	317	TILLER	A	4	382				
THURKETTLE	GH	6	405	TIBBALS	AG	7	399	TIERNEY	J	14	317	TILLER	A	4	382				
THURLBY	E	9	357	TIBBALS	JE	7	399	TIERNEY	P	14	317	TILLER	AA	10	231				
THURLBY	F	2	340	TIBBETT	J	14	317	TIERNEY	T	14	317	TILLER	AE	3	400				
THURLEY	A	12	221	TIBBETTS	A	12	221	TIFFANY	J	8	352	TILLER	DA	2	341				
THURLEY	AJ	2	340	TIBBEY	BJ	4	381	TIFFIN	A	2	341	TILLER	FC	5	355				
THURLEY	CE	12	221	TIBBITTS	A	6	406	TIFFIN	D	13	422	TILLER	FJ	4	382				
THURLEY	CH	12	221	TIBBLE	AE	4	381	TIFT	HR	5	354	TILLER	G	10	231				
THURLEY	F	12	221	TIBBLE	AH	4	381	TIFT	T	5	354	TILLER	J	10	231				
THURLEY	FW	12	221	TIBBLE	FE	3	239	TIGHE	H	9	194	TILLER	JT	10	378				
THURLEY	GJ	7	399	TIBBLE	FW	2	340	TIGHE	J	8	352	TILLER	M	10	231				
THURLEY	HW	12	221	TIBBLE	GS	7	399	TIGHE	J	8	352	TILLER	S	10	231				
THURLEY	LA	12	221	TIBBLE	JH	3	239	TIGHE	J	8	352	TILLER	T	10	231				
THURLING	C	13	422	TIBBLES	AC	5	354	TIGHE	J	11	373	TILLETT	CH	9	194				
THURLOW	A	8	352	TIBBLES	C	10	377	TIGHE	P	14	317	TILLETT	CH	9	194				
THURLOW	A	8	352	TIBBLES	EM	2	340	TIGHE	S	8	352	TILLETT	CH	9	194				
THURLOW	AR	5	354	TIBBLES	FR	10	377	TIGHE	T	9	357	TILLETT	CH	9	358				
THURLOW	FC	2	340	TIBBLES	HD	1	347	TIGHE	W	11	373	TILLETT	E	9	194				
THURLOW	FW	5	354	TIBBLES	HH	5	354	TILBE	GWW	2	341	TILLETT	F	9	358				
THURLOW	FW	13	422	TIBBLES	M	2	340	TILBEE	F	12	221	TILLETT	HA	7	400				
THURLOW	H	2	340	TIBBLES	R	2	340	TILBERN	GH	8	352	TILLETT	J	10	231				
THURLOW	JH	3	239	TIBBLES	TW	3	239	TILBROOK	AJ	5	354	TILLETT	M	10	378				
THURLOW	P	5	354	TIBBLES	W	5	354	TILBROOK	G	5	354	TILLETT	W	9	194				
THURLOW	RA	3	239	TIBBLES	W	5	354	TILBROOK	HE	13	422	TILLETT	W	13	422				
THURLOW	W	1	347	TIBBS	A	12	398	TILBUREY	C	10	230	TILLEY	A	10	378				
THURLWELL	H	8	352	TIBBS	TC	2	340	TILBURY	AO	10	230	TILLEY	AE	1	347				
THURMAN	EJ	6	405	TIBBY	CHW	3	239	TILBURY	AV	7	400	TILLEY	AW	7	400				
THURNELL	AJ	2	340	TIBBY	FC	3	239	TILBURY	AW	4	382	TILLEY	C	3	239				
THURSBY	CA	3	239	TIBBY	SC	3	239	TILBURY	CJ	10	231	TILLEY	EJ	12	398				
THURSBY	ES	3	239	TIBBY	T	1	347	TILBURY	E	2	341	TILLEY	FJ	7	400				
THURSBY	R	3	239	TICEHURST	CH	7	399	TILBURY	EJ	5	355	TILLEY	G	3	239				
THURSH	H	5	354	TICKLE	FC	11	373	TILBURY	H	10	231	TILLEY	G	10	231				
THURSTON	AJ	7	399	TICKLE	J	11	373	TILBURY	HR	5	355	TILLEY	H	10	231				
THURSTON	AJ	7	399	TICKNER	AH	10	377	TILBURY	J	4	382	TILLEY	HF	12	398				
THURSTON	G	7	399	TICKNER	GM	10	377	TILBURY	RR	7	400	TILLEY	HJ	13	422				
THURSTON	GA	7	399	TIDBALL	G	2	340	TILBY	HF	13	422	TILLEY	J	3	240				
THURSTON	GW	11	373	TIDBALL	P	2	340	TILBY	S	2	341	TILLEY	J	10	231				
THURSTON	H	7	399	TIDD	J	8	352	TILCOCK	TJ	5	355	TILLEY	JA	7	400				
THURSTON	H	11	373	TIDESWELL	H	11	373	TILDESLEY	H	10	378	TILLEY	JE	2	341				
THURSTON	RH	3	239	TIDEY	BV	3	239	TILDSLEY	A	14	317	TILLEY	LM	4	382				
THURSTON	SGH	13	422	TIDEY	WJ	3	239	TILEY	AE	3	400	TILLEY	RE	4	382				
THURSTON	WC	7	399	TIDMAN	EW	13	422	TILEY	EA	2	341	TILLEY	SJ	4	382				
THURSTON	WJW	1	347	TIDMARSH	AA	10	230	TILEY	GE	4	382	TILLEY	T	13	422				
THUSTAIN	J	10	230	TIDMARSH	F	12	221	TILFORD	GJ	10	231	TILLEY	W	4	382				
THWAITE	D	2	340	TIDMARSH	S	2	341	TILL	AW	13	422	TILLEY	WG	3	240				
THWAITE	J	8	352	TIDRIDGE	EA	4	382	TILL	EA	10	378	TILLEY	WG	7	400				
THWAITE	J	14	317	TIDSWELL	I	9	194	TILL	G	13	422	TILLEY	WG	10	378				
THWAITES	EC	7	399	TIDSWELL	J	11	373	TILL	H	13	422	TILLEY	WG	12	398				
THWAITES	GW	9	194	TIDSWELL	W	9	194	TILL	HJ	10	378	TILLEY	WH	7	400				
THWAITES	H	4	381	TIDWELL	WJ	10	230	TILL	HV	1	347	TILLEY	WJ	3	240				
THWAITES	H	9	194	TIDY	A	2	341	TILL	WA	9	357	TILLEY	WJ	12	398				
THWAITES	J	9	357	TIDY	F	1	347	TILL	WT	3	239	TILLEY	WJ	12	398				
THWAITES	S	10	230	TIDY	TRF	4	382	TILLBROOK	T	5	355	TILLEY	WJ	13	422				
THWAITES	T	4	381	TIEMAN	C	7	399	TILLEN	AE	3	239	TILLIER	EJ	4	382				
THYNNE	LG	7	399	TIERNEY	J	11	373	TILLEN	EJ	3	239	TILLIER	FGT	4	382				

TILLIER	GF	4	382
TILLIER	SH	4	382
TILLIN	AE	13	422
TILLIN	AF	7	400
TILLING	AG	7	400
TILLING	CE	7	400
TILLING	HC	10	231
TILLING	HE	5	355
TILLING	RJ	7	400
TILLING	SJ	7	400
TILLING	TB	7	400
TILLING	VA	5	355
TILLMAN	AG	7	400
TILLMAN	HG	3	240
TILLMAN	HG	7	400
TILLMAN	WJ	3	240
TILLOTSON	A	9	358
TILLOTSON	E	9	358
TILLOTSON	TH	8	352
TILLOTT	AEH	4	382
TILLSLEY	HF	2	341
TILLSLEY	T	2	341
TILLSLEY	W	2	341
TILLY	JA	6	406
TILLY	TG	4	382
TILLYARD	E	3	400
TILLYARD	HG	3	400
TILLYER	HW	4	382
TILLYER	RJ	7	400
TILNEY	C	2	341
TILSLEY	R	6	406
TILSLEY	WH	6	406
TILSON	AE	4	382
TILSON	FH	7	400
TILSON	JE	12	398
TILSON	JR	11	373
TILSTON	S	14	317
TILT	C	7	400
TILT	E	6	406
TILTMAN	JWC	1	347
TILTMAN	P	7	401
TILY	B	7	401
TILYARD	CE	10	378
TIMBERLAKE	CG	2	341
TIMBERLAKE	FW	5	355
TIMBERLAKE	RG	5	355
TIMBERLEY	RJ	10	378
TIMBRELL	E	6	406
TIMBRELL	WS	13	422
TIMBS	J	7	401
TIMCKE	A	13	422
TIMLIN	J	8	352
TIMLIN	P	8	352
TIMLIN	T	8	352
TIMMINGS	AM	9	358
TIMMINGS	EAJ	3	240
TIMMINGS	FC	3	240
TIMMINGS	WJ	3	240
TIMMINS	C	7	401
TIMMINS	F	6	406
TIMMINS	F	6	406
TIMMINS	JH	6	406
TIMMINS	T	6	406
TIMMINS	TE	6	406
TIMMINS	TR	6	406
TIMMINS	W	6	406
TIMMIS	CE	11	373
TIMMIS	W	14	317
TIMMS	A	4	382
TIMMS	A	9	194
TIMMS	A	12	398
TIMMS	BWJ	12	222
TIMMS	EE	1	347
TIMMS	EJ	7	401
TIMMS	FH	7	401
TIMMS	FJ	5	355
TIMMS	FW	6	406
TIMMS	H	5	355
TIMMS	HEL	6	406
TIMMS	J	2	341
TIMMS	J	12	222
TIMMS	J	14	317
TIMMS	J	14	318
TIMMS	JE	6	406
TIMMS	R	6	406
TIMMS	RJ	5	355
TIMMS	S	6	407
TIMMS	T	7	401
TIMMS	TA	14	318
TIMMS	TC	5	355
TIMMS	WJ	12	222
TIMPERLEY	A	11	373
TIMPERLEY	F	14	318
TIMPERLEY	G	11	373
TIMPERLEY	J	14	318
TIMPERLEY	P	14	318
TIMPERLEY	W	11	373
TIMPERLEY	W	11	374
TIMPERLEY	W	11	374
TIMPSON	SH	12	222
TIMPSON	TR	12	222
TIMS	PW	12	222
TIMS	TR	7	401
TIMSON	A	7	401
TIMSON	B	5	355
TIMSON	F	5	355
TIMSON	G	10	231
TINCKAM	JB	3	240
TINCKAM	JW	3	240
TINCKAM	PE	3	240
TINCOMBE	DJ	13	422
TINDALE	JW	9	194
TINDALE	RC	9	194
TINDALL	AE	3	240
TINDALL	C	1	347
TINDALL	C	8	352
TINDALL	CW	1	347
TINDALL	FJ	3	240
TINDALL	FJ	5	355
TINDALL	GF	5	355
TINDALL	GF	5	355
TINDALL	HB	5	356
TINDALL	JW	8	352
TINDALL	T	7	401
TINDALL	T	7	401
TINDALL	T	9	194
TINDALL	W	7	401
TINDELL		7	401
TINDELL	A	7	401
TINDELL	A	8	352
TINDELL	V	7	401
TINEY	A	12	222
TINGEY	H	12	222
TINGEY	HS	5	356
TINGEY	JE	5	356
TINGLE	A	14	318
TINGLE	C	8	352
TINGLE	J	8	353
TINGLEY	FE	13	423
TINK	RD	1	347
TINKER	EAJ	7	401
TINKER	GT	13	423
TINKER	P	8	353
TINSDALE	J	8	353
TINSDALE	JC	8	353
TINSLEY	C	3	240
TINSLEY	CE	11	374
TINSLEY	CP	13	423
TINSLEY	CP	13	423
TINSLEY	E	13	423
TINSLEY	E	14	318
TINSLEY	EW	13	423
TINSLEY	J	3	240
TINSLEY	S	11	374
TINSLEY	S	14	318
TINSLEY	WE	13	423
TINSON	EF	7	401
TINWORTH	J	7	401
TIPLADY	W	14	318
TIPLER	AT	7	401
TIPLER	HC	13	423
TIPLER	S	12	222
TIPLER	WS	12	398
TIPLING	H	8	353
TIPPEN	JW	7	402
TIPPEN	V	3	240
TIPPER	F	8	353
TIPPER	G	2	341
TIPPER	HJ	1	348
TIPPER	J	8	353
TIPPER	JA	12	222
TIPPER	JJ	11	425
TIPPER	PS	10	231
TIPPER	S	10	231
TIPPER	WG	2	341
TIPPER	WH	10	231
TIPPER	WR	12	222
TIPPETTS	W	11	374
TIPPING	AC	12	398
TIPPING	AF	6	407
TIPPING	G	12	398
TIPPING	RH	12	398
TIPPING	WJ	12	398
TIPPINS	CH	6	407
TIPSON	WL	13	423
TIPSON	WL	13	423
TIPTON	B	4	383
TIPTON	H	4	383
TIPTON	JH	11	374
TIPTON	S	4	383
TIPTON	W	22	222
TIRRELL	HE	3	240
TISBURY	CA	1	348
TISDALE	HA	2	341
TISSON	EM	10	232
TITCHEN	H	6	407
TITCHENER	EE	1	348
TITCHENER	P	4	383
TITCHENER	R	12	222
TITCHENER	TA	2	341
TITCHIN	B	6	407
TITCHMARCH	SJ	12	222
TITCHMARSH	AH	7	402
TITCHNER	AR	3	240
TITCHNER	F	3	240
TITCOMB	AC	2	341
TITCOMB	EJ	2	342
TITCOMBE	A	13	423
TITE	A	12	399
TITE	G	12	399
TITE	WE	12	399
TITFORD	C	3	400
TITFORD	R	3	400
TITHERADGE	GA	2	342
TITHERIDGE	RF	4	383
TITLE	JB	14	318
TITLEY	P	11	374
TITLEY	S	14	318
TITMAN	JT	12	399
TITMARSH	C	3	400

TITMARSH	EA	3	400	TOBUTT	M	12	222	TOKINS	A	12	222	TOMES	L	3	400
TITMARSH	S	3	400	TOBUTT	RA	3	400	TOKINS	GF	8	353	TOMKIN	FH	11	375
TITMARSH	SR	3	400	TOBUTT	W	4	383	TOKINS	J	12	222	TOMKINS	A	2	342
TITMARSH	W	2	342	TOBUTT	WC	3	400	TOLCHER	GV	10	232	TOMKINS	A	6	407
TITMUS	A	5	356	TOBY	AE	4	383	TOLEMAN	WG	10	232	TOMKINS	A	13	424
TITMUS	A	6	407	TOBY	FA	7	402	TOLFREE	C	10	232	TOMKINS	A	13	424
TITMUS	CW	5	356	TOCOCK	J	12	399	TOLFREE	EM	10	232	TOMKINS	AE	6	407
TITMUS	F	6	407	TODD	A	9	358	TOLFREE	G	4	383	TOMKINS	AJ	6	407
TITMUS	H	5	356	TODD	A	11	374	TOLFREE	ST	10	232	TOMKINS	AN	5	356
TITMUS	TH	6	407	TODD	AF	13	423	TOLFTS	CJ	1	348	TOMKINS	B	3	240
TITMUS	W	5	356	TODD	AJ	1	348	TOLHURST	A	13	423	TOMKINS	CW	2	342
TITMUSS	AE	5	356	TODD	AJ	4	383	TOLHURST	AE	13	423	TOMKINS	E	13	424
TITMUSS	F	5	356	TODD	AL	6	407	TOLHURST	FJ	8	353	TOMKINS	F	6	408
TITMUSS	H	5	356	TODD	CE	6	407	TOLHURST	G	13	423	TOMKINS	F	13	424
TITMUSS	J	5	356	TODD	CW	1	348	TOLL	H	12	222	TOMKINS	FJ	4	383
TITMUSS	L	5	356	TODD	E	8	353	TOLL	HG	2	342	TOMKINS	H	7	402
TITMUSS	W	5	356	TODD	EE	2	342	TOLLADAY	WR	6	407	TOMKINS	J	12	399
TITMUSS	WJ	5	356	TODD	ER	7	402	TOLLEMACHE	R	8	353	TOMKINS	JT	2	343
TITT	G	4	383	TODD	F	9	358	TOLLERVEY	AG	13	423	TOMKINS	PG	5	356
TITTERINGTON	J	14	318	TODD	F	11	374	TOLLERVEY	EC	13	424	TOMKINS	R	2	342
TITTERINGTON	JW	11	374	TODD	FT	11	375	TOLLERVEY	VA	13	424	TOMKINS	S	6	407
TITTERRELL	EW	13	423	TODD	G	10	232	TOLLERVEY	WA	13	424	TOMKINS	WH	6	408
TITTERTON	H	7	402	TODD	GA	1	348	TOLLETT	WH	4	383	TOMKINSON	CE	14	319
TITTERTON	JG	7	402	TODD	H	8	353	TOLLEY	A	6	407	TOMKINSON	FT	14	319
TITTLE	H	11	374	TODD	H	11	374	TOLLEY	AW	5	356	TOMKINSON	G	8	354
TITTLE	JE	11	374	TODD	HB	11	374	TOLLEY	CL	6	407	TOMKINSON	G	11	375
TITTLE	RE	11	374	TODD	HB	11	374	TOLLEY	HA	5	356	TOMKINSON	H	11	375
TIVEY	BT	3	400	TODD	HW	10	232	TOLLIDAY	ALW	2	342	TOMKINSON	TA	11	375
TIVEY	H	3	400	TODD	J	8	353	TOLLIDAY	DJ	10	378	TOMKINSON	W	6	408
TIZARD	EA	4	383	TODD	J	11	375	TOLLITT	WH	7	402	TOMKISS	W	6	408
TIZARD	EJ	10	378	TODD	JA	10	232	TOLLOTSON	W	9	194	TOMLIENS	WH	13	424
TIZARD	ER	4	383	TODD	JW	8	353	TOLMAN	SCJ	12	222	TOMLIN	A	5	357
TIZARD	GT	10	378	TODD	R	7	402	TOLMIE	J	4	383	TOMLIN	AC	10	232
TIZARD	PT	10	378	TODD	RC	1	348	TOLPUTT	HG	10	379	TOMLIN	AD	1	348
TIZARD	WJ	10	378	TODD	RE	8	353	TOLSON	HJ	7	402	TOMLIN	AH	4	383
TIZARD	WJ	12	222	TODD	TH	1	348	TOLSON	P	9	358	TOMLIN	AJ	13	424
TIZZARD	EJ	13	423	TODD	W	5	356	TOLSON	R	7	402	TOMLIN	B	10	232
TIZZARD	GW	4	383	TODD	W	8	353	TOLSON	W	8	353	TOMLIN	BN	13	424
TIZZARD	RH	4	383	TODD	W	9	358	TOLSTER	T	10	232	TOMLIN	C	5	357
TOBAR	R	7	402	TODD	W	10	378	TOLTON	F	11	375	TOMLIN	C	11	375
TOBE	M	14	318	TODD	W	11	375	TOLTON	TB	12	223	TOMLIN	CH	2	342
TOBIAS	A	14	318	TODD	WE	8	353	TOLWORTHY	A	7	402	TOMLIN	FG	13	424
TOBIAS	J	14	318	TODD	WH	14	318	TOMALIN	AJ	12	399	TOMLIN	FP	6	408
TOBIN	CD	3	400	TODD	WR	8	353	TOMBLESON	HG	2	342	TOMLIN	G	5	357
TOBIN	DG	12	399	TODD	WT	2	342	TOMBS	AE	7	402	TOMLIN	GR	12	223
TOBIN	FJ	12	399	TODHUNTER	C	14	319	TOMBS	CE	2	342	TOMLIN	H	5	357
TOBIN	J	14	318	TODHUNTER	T	11	375	TOMBS	SF	12	223	TOMLIN	HE	3	241
TOBIN	J	14	318	TODKILL	JH	8	353	TOMBS	WA	12	223	TOMLIN	HG	2	342
TOBIN	J	14	318	TOFIELD	HW	5	356	TOMES	A	1	348	TOMLIN	J	5	357
TOBIN	JH	10	232	TOFIELD	T	2	342	TOMES	AC	1	348	TOMLIN	J	9	358
TOBIN	P	13	423	TOFIELD	TH	2	342	TOMES	CA	6	407	TOMLIN	M	6	408
TOBIN	WH	12	399	TOFT	C	11	375	TOMES	FC	10	232	TOMLIN	O	10	232
TOBIN	WJ	10	378	TOFT	J	14	319	TOMES	G	3	400	TOMLIN	R	13	424
TOBONI	F	11	374	TOFT	W	2	342	TOMES	GEJ	10	232	TOMLIN	SR	12	223
TOBONI	J	11	374	TOFT	W	11	375	TOMES	HE	6	407	TOMLIN	W	4	383

Surname	Initials	No.	Page
TOMLIN	WC	4	383
TOMLIN	WG	1	348
TOMLINS	B	7	402
TOMLINS	CS	3	400
TOMLINS	EA	3	400
TOMLINS	G	7	402
TOMLINS	GC	2	343
TOMLINS	RS	3	401
TOMLINS	SH	2	343
TOMLINS	SH	3	401
TOMLINS	WK	2	343
TOMLINSON	A	7	402
TOMLINSON	A	14	319
TOMLINSON	AH	3	401
TOMLINSON	B	6	408
TOMLINSON	C	12	223
TOMLINSON	CD	10	232
TOMLINSON	CE	6	408
TOMLINSON	CFT	7	403
TOMLINSON	D	9	194
TOMLINSON	D	9	358
TOMLINSON	E	11	375
TOMLINSON	EW	6	408
TOMLINSON	EW	7	403
TOMLINSON	F	7	403
TOMLINSON	F	7	403
TOMLINSON	F	11	375
TOMLINSON	FHE	3	401
TOMLINSON	G	3	401
TOMLINSON	G	9	358
TOMLINSON	G	12	399
TOMLINSON	G	14	319
TOMLINSON	GH	4	384
TOMLINSON	GW	3	401
TOMLINSON	GW	8	354
TOMLINSON	H	9	194
TOMLINSON	H	14	319
TOMLINSON	HJ	1	348
TOMLINSON	HR	7	403
TOMLINSON	J	6	408
TOMLINSON	J	9	358
TOMLINSON	J	9	358
TOMLINSON	J	11	375
TOMLINSON	J	11	375
TOMLINSON	JH	11	375
TOMLINSON	JH	13	424
TOMLINSON	JH	14	319
TOMLINSON	M	8	354
TOMLINSON	MA	13	424
TOMLINSON	RH	14	319
TOMLINSON	RR	7	403
TOMLINSON	RR	10	232
TOMLINSON	S	6	408
TOMLINSON	S	9	194
TOMLINSON	S	14	319
TOMLINSON	ST	6	408
TOMLINSON	T	6	408
TOMLINSON	T	6	408
TOMLINSON	TE	14	319
TOMLINSON	V	8	354
TOMLINSON	W	1	348
TOMLINSON	W	2	343
TOMLINSON	W	6	408
TOMLINSON	W	8	354
TOMLINSON	W	11	375
TOMLINSON	W	11	376
TOMLINSON	W	11	376
TOMLINSON	WA	7	403
TOMLINSON	WB	7	403
TOMMONS	A	14	319
TOMMONS	W	14	319
TOMMS	F	13	424
TOMPKINS	A	1	348
TOMPKINS	AC	1	348
TOMPKINS	AJ	5	357
TOMPKINS	AJ	10	232
TOMPKINS	BM	12	399
TOMPKINS	C	6	408
TOMPKINS	C	12	223
TOMPKINS	CE	12	223
TOMPKINS	CH	12	399
TOMPKINS	DA	12	223
TOMPKINS	ED	5	357
TOMPKINS	EG	5	357
TOMPKINS	EW	7	403
TOMPKINS	F	3	241
TOMPKINS	F	5	357
TOMPKINS	FJ	12	399
TOMPKINS	FL	12	223
TOMPKINS	G	5	357
TOMPKINS	GH	12	399
TOMPKINS	GH	14	319
TOMPKINS	GW	8	354
TOMPKINS	H	12	223
TOMPKINS	J	12	223
TOMPKINS	JR	5	357
TOMPKINS	JT	8	354
TOMPKINS	JW	5	357
TOMPKINS	L	5	357
TOMPKINS	LA	5	357
TOMPKINS	O	5	357
TOMPKINS	RA	5	357
TOMPKINS	S	5	357
TOMPKINS	SWA	5	357
TOMPKINS	T	12	223
TOMPKINS	V	12	399
TOMPKINS	W	11	376
TOMPKINS	WA	12	223
TOMPKINS	WH	5	357
TOMPKINS	WM	5	358
TOMPSETT	EGD	2	343
TOMPSON	JE	2	343
TOMS	AE	10	233
TOMS	AJE	4	384
TOMS	E	5	358
TOMS	E	7	403
TOMS	EG	12	223
TOMS	FJ	13	424
TOMS	FW	5	358
TOMS	G	5	358
TOMS	H	5	358
TOMS	J	5	358
TOMS	JC	5	358
TOMS	W	5	358
TOMSETT	A	13	424
TONER	J	2	343
TONER	O	11	376
TONERI	LW	4	384
TONEY	G	2	343
TONG	C	10	233
TONG	F	10	233
TONG	G	10	233
TONG	S	10	233
TONG	TE	10	379
TONGE	A	14	319
TONGE	AB	13	424
TONGE	C	11	376
TONGE	D	14	319
TONGE	E	13	424
TONGE	F	14	319
TONGE	GH	14	319
TONGE	J	14	320
TONGE	J	14	320
TONGE	JE	13	425
TONGE	JW	14	320
TONGE	R	11	376
TONGE	T	14	320
TONGE	TH	14	320
TONGE	WH	4	384
TONGUE	W	7	403
TONKIN	G	6	408
TONKIN	H	6	408
TONKIN	H	7	403
TONKIN	HC	1	348
TONKIN	WR	10	379
TONKINS	H	8	354
TONKINS	JH	7	403
TONKS	A	6	408
TONKS	B	6	408
TONKS	FW	6	408
TONKS	FW	6	408
TONKS	H	6	409
TONKS	S	6	409
TONKS	T	6	409
TONKS	W	6	409
TOOGOOD	C	6	409
TOOGOOD	FE	4	384
TOOGOOD	HJ	4	384
TOOGOOD	L	10	379
TOOGOOD	TCE	4	384
TOOKE	W	7	403
TOOKE	WH	5	358
TOOKEY	WH	2	343
TOOLAN	H	11	376
TOOLE	E	14	320
TOOLE	G	9	358
TOOLE	H	14	320
TOOLE	J	14	320
TOOLE	P	11	376
TOOLE	R	14	320
TOOLE	SH	4	384
TOOLE	T	14	320
TOOLE	W	11	376
TOOLE	W	11	376
TOOLEY	B	2	343
TOOLEY	EG	13	425
TOOLEY	FH	2	343
TOOLEY	H	3	401
TOOLEY	RJ	12	223
TOOLEY	WJ	12	223
TOOMBS	ET	13	425
TOOMBS	JC	13	425
TOOMBS	P	4	384
TOOMBS	WW	13	425
TOOMER	CW	10	233
TOOMER	EC	4	384
TOOMER	PG	10	379
TOOMEY	M	14	320
TOOMEY	P	11	376
TOOMEY	R	11	376
TOOMEY	S	13	425
TOOMEY	T	4	384
TOOMS	F	13	425
TOOMS	GH	13	425
TOOMS	SJ	13	425
TOOMS	W	13	425
TOON	E	6	409
TOON	WL	6	409
TOOP	A	7	403
TOOP	CA	7	403
TOOP	TW	7	403
TOOTELL	T	14	320
TOOTH	AG	12	223
TOOTH	GH	6	409
TOOTH	H	6	409
TOOTH	JE	6	409
TOOTH	JG	5	358
TOOTH	MC	7	404
TOOTH	RW	12	223
TOOTH	TC	12	223

TOOVEY	A	9	194	TOTMAN	W	7	404	TOWN	E	3	241	TOWNSEND	AG	4	385
TOOVEY	HE	2	343	TOTT	A	1	348	TOWN	F	7	404	TOWNSEND	AW	12	224
TOOVEY	J	10	233	TOTT	A	2	343	TOWN	GT	4	385	TOWNSEND	B	9	195
TOPCOTT	WJ	2	343	TOTT	F	3	241	TOWN	H	8	355	TOWNSEND	C	4	385
TOPHAM	AW	5	358	TOTT	FA	2	343	TOWN	J	13	426	TOWNSEND	C	7	404
TOPHAM	E	12	223	TOTT	G	3	241	TOWN	SA	4	385	TOWNSEND	CH	13	426
TOPHAM	JB	8	354	TOTT	GTW	12	224	TOWN	W	13	426	TOWNSEND	D	7	404
TOPHAM	P	8	354	TOTT	WH	2	343	TOWN	WH	4	385	TOWNSEND	E	14	320
TOPHAM	RT	6	409	TOTTIE	E	8	354	TOWNDROW	A	11	377	TOWNSEND	EG	1	349
TOPHAM	TH	7	404	TOTTIE	G	8	354	TOWNEND	A	8	355	TOWNSEND	EJ	4	385
TOPLEY	AH	4	384	TOTTIE	WH	8	354	TOWNEND	C	8	355	TOWNSEND	F	3	241
TOPLEY	JW	8	354	TOTTMAN	WE	2	343	TOWNEND	CR	3	401	TOWNSEND	F	12	224
TOPLEY	SC	2	343	TOTTON	J	14	320	TOWNEND	D	8	355	TOWNSEND	F	12	400
TOPP	AC	4	384	TOULMIN	A	9	195	TOWNEND	D	8	355	TOWNSEND	FA	2	344
TOPP	CA	4	384	TOULSON	E	8	354	TOWNEND	E	8	355	TOWNSEND	FC	3	241
TOPP	EJ	13	425	TOULSON	EH	8	354	TOWNEND	F	8	355	TOWNSEND	FK	4	385
TOPP	F	4	384	TOULSON	H	8	354	TOWNEND	F	9	195	TOWNSEND	FW	1	349
TOPP	FC	10	233	TOUT	AJ	10	379	TOWNEND	FB	8	355	TOWNSEND	FW	2	344
TOPP	P	4	384	TOVELL	J	13	425	TOWNEND	FT	3	401	TOWNSEND	G	1	349
TOPPING	AG	7	404	TOVEY	AH	13	426	TOWNEND	GH	9	195	TOWNSEND	G	4	385
TOPPLE	D	13	425	TOVEY	J	8	354	TOWNEND	J	9	195	TOWNSEND	G	6	409
TOPPLE	F	13	425	TOVEY	S	13	426	TOWNEND	J	9	359	TOWNSEND	G	12	224
TOPPLE	FT	13	425	TOVEY	WH	1	349	TOWNEND	JA	9	195	TOWNSEND	H	4	385
TOPPLE	GJ	13	425	TOVEY	WH	3	241	TOWNEND	JA	9	359	TOWNSEND	H	8	355
TORBETT	C	3	241	TOWELL	AJ	12	400	TOWNEND	JW	8	355	TOWNSEND	H	10	233
TORBETT	MA	3	241	TOWELL	JH	12	400	TOWNEND	P	8	355	TOWNSEND	H	11	377
TORBETT	S	3	241	TOWERS	A	8	354	TOWNEND	W	8	355	TOWNSEND	H	11	377
TORBETT	WJ	3	241	TOWERS	C	8	354	TOWNEND	W	9	195	TOWNSEND	H	14	320
TORDOFF	B	9	358	TOWERS	E	8	354	TOWNEND	W	9	195	TOWNSEND	HR	9	359
TORDOFF	J	9	358	TOWERS	E	11	376	TOWNEND	W	9	195	TOWNSEND	I	3	401
TORKINGTON	AG	10	379	TOWERS	F	8	355	TOWNEND	W	9	359	TOWNSEND	J	2	344
TORKINGTON	H	11	376	TOWERS	H	2	344	TOWNER	EC	13	426	TOWNSEND	J	4	385
TORNBERG	E	12	399	TOWERS	H	3	241	TOWNING	D	8	355	TOWNSEND	J	7	405
TORODE	A	7	404	TOWERS	H	8	355	TOWNING	F	12	400	TOWNSEND	JA	1	349
TORODE	W	7	404	TOWERS	HM	3	241	TOWNING	H	12	400	TOWNSEND	JA	2	344
TORRINGTON	PDF	10	379	TOWERS	R	11	376	TOWNING	R	12	400	TOWNSEND	JA	3	241
TOSDEVINE	D	4	384	TOWERS	SAW	12	400	TOWNING	TH	12	400	TOWNSEND	JA	9	195
TOSDEVINE	J	7	404	TOWERS	W	11	376	TOWNLEY	F	11	377	TOWNSEND	JW	2	344
TOSDEVINE	TD	4	384	TOWES	J	13	426	TOWNLEY	J	11	377	TOWNSEND	JW	7	404
TOSDEVINE	VG	4	384	TOWEY	JW	1	349	TOWNLEY	WH	14	320	TOWNSEND	LS	3	241
TOSDEVINE	VH	4	384	TOWEY	W	9	358	TOWNLEY	WJ	1	349	TOWNSEND	P	3	401
TOSDEVINE	WJ	4	385	TOWLE	A	8	355	TOWNROW	F	5	358	TOWNSEND	R	13	426
TOSDEVINE	WJ	4	385	TOWLE	F	5	358	TOWNROW	G	9	359	TOWNSEND	RH	2	344
TOSDEVINE	WR	4	385	TOWLE	GF	11	376	TOWNS	EWH	7	404	TOWNSEND	S	2	344
TOSE	A	9	194	TOWLER	A	9	195	TOWNS	H	7	404	TOWNSEND	S	12	400
TOSE	J	9	195	TOWLER	AH	11	377	TOWNS	H	9	195	TOWNSEND	SC	7	405
TOSELAND	A	12	399	TOWLER	B	7	404	TOWNS	H	9	359	TOWNSEND	SE	4	385
TOSELAND	J	12	224	TOWLER	H	4	385	TOWNS	HLA	11	377	TOWNSEND	SM	2	344
TOSELAND	W	12	399	TOWLER	J	8	355	TOWNS	S	8	355	TOWNSEND	SS	6	409
TOSELAND	W	12	399	TOWLER	JW	11	377	TOWNS	TH	12	224	TOWNSEND	TW	6	409
TOSSELL	J	7	404	TOWLER	R	9	358	TOWNSEND	A	1	349	TOWNSEND	W	4	385
TOSTEVIN	AC	13	425	TOWLER	TH	2	344	TOWNSEND	A	6	409	TOWNSEND	W	6	409
TOSTEVIN	D	10	379	TOWLER	W	9	359	TOWNSEND	A	14	320	TOWNSEND	W	8	355
TOTHAM	H	7	404	TOWLER	WH	9	359	TOWNSEND	AC	7	404	TOWNSEND	W	9	195
TOTHAM	HJ	1	348	TOWN	AW	2	344	TOWNSEND	AD	12	224	TOWNSEND	W	11	377

TOWNSEND	W	13	426	TOZER	F	3	241	TRAVERS	W	4	386	TREAGUS	F	10	233
TOWNSEND	W	14	320	TOZER	F	7	405	TRAVERS	WH	10	379	TREAGUS	HJ	1	350
TOWNSEND	WC	4	385	TOZER	FJ	2	344	TRAVES	G	10	233	TREAGUS	J	1	350
TOWNSEND	WC	4	385	TOZER	FJ	11	377	TRAVESS	DB	4	386	TREAHY	J	2	345
TOWNSEND	WF	1	349	TOZER	H	3	241	TRAVESS	FW	4	386	TREANOR	F	7	406
TOWNSEND	WH	1	349	TOZER	J	7	405	TRAVILL	W	12	400	TREASURE	E	5	359
TOWNSEND	WJ	2	344	TOZER	T	3	241	TRAVILL	WT	12	400	TREAVISH	J	7	406
TOWNSEND	WJ	7	405	TOZER	W	3	242	TRAVILL	WTE	12	400	TREAYS	E	7	406
TOWNSEND	WL	3	241	TRACEY	J	9	359	TRAVIS	A	1	349	TREBECK	EH	2	345
TOWNSEND	WR	7	405	TRACEY	M	6	409	TRAVIS	CJ	4	386	TREBLE	C	1	350
TOWNSHEND	A	13	426	TRACEY	RC	13	426	TRAVIS	F	14	321	TREBLE	WG	2	345
TOWNSHEND	HA	2	344	TRACEY	W	9	359	TRAVIS	G	11	377	TREDGER	TG	13	426
TOWNSHEND	SG	1	349	TRACEY	W	11	377	TRAVIS	J	11	377	TREDGER	TJ	13	426
TOWNSIN	JE	4	385	TRACEY	W	11	377	TRAVIS	J	14	321	TREDWELL	TW	12	400
TOWNSLEY	E	8	355	TRACEY	WE	7	405	TRAVIS	JH	14	321	TREDWIN	A	7	406
TOWNSLEY	F	9	359	TRACY	P	14	321	TRAVIS	R	11	377	TREE	A	7	406
TOWNSLEY	J	8	355	TRACY	WJ	13	426	TRAVIS	R	14	321	TREE	AE	2	345
TOWNSLEY	J	9	359	TRAER	JT	7	405	TRAVIS	WH	11	378	TREE	AE	3	242
TOWNSLEY	W	9	359	TRAFFORD	CS	5	359	TRAVIS	WP	11	378	TREE	FA	3	242
TOWNSLEY	W	9	359	TRAFFORD	F	8	356	TRAVISS	WC	10	233	TREE	JG	7	406
TOWNSON	A	1	349	TRAILE	F	9	195	TRAY	C	14	321	TREE	SW	1	350
TOWNSON	F	9	195	TRAINER	C	14	321	TRAYHORN	CF	4	386	TREE	TH	13	426
TOWNSON	F	14	321	TRAINER	C	14	321	TRAYHURN	HD	2	344	TREES	JW	9	195
TOWNSON	GN	9	195	TRAINER	E	8	356	TRAYLER	EJ	2	344	TREEVES	AR	3	242
TOWNSON	HS	1	349	TRAINER	W	8	356	TRAYNOR	A	11	378	TREEVES	E	3	242
TOWNSON	J	11	377	TRAINER	W	9	359	TRAYNOR	F	2	345	TREEVES	J	3	242
TOWNSON	L	14	321	TRAINER	W	14	321	TRAYNOR	F	14	321	TREEVES	J	3	242
TOWNSON	WF	1	349	TRAMER	W	8	356	TRAYNOR	J	9	195	TREFFRY	W	4	386
TOWNSON	WH	14	321	TRAMPLEASURE	A	13	426	TRAYNOR	JA	9	195	TREGELLIS	F	3	242
TOWTON	TF	4	385	TRANAH	C	2	344	TRAYNOR	JW	14	321	TREGELLIS	J	3	242
TOY	A	6	409	TRANAH	W	2	344	TRAYNOR	P	7	405	TREGELLIS	JD	3	242
TOY	AS	4	385	TRANGMAR	HJF	7	405	TRAYNOR	T	14	321	TREGENNA	C	10	233
TOY	C	4	386	TRANGMAR	RS	7	405	TREACHER	ALJ	3	401	TREGIDGO	WH	5	359
TOY	WA	4	386	TRANSPORT	J	8	356	TREACHER	EE	3	401	TREHANE	WC	3	242
TOYE	AC	1	349	TRANTER	AJ	7	405	TREACHER	F	3	242	TREHERNE	WC	3	401
TOYE	D	6	409	TRANTER	H	6	410	TREACHER	H	11	378	TRELEAVEN	A	1	350
TOYE	W	6	409	TRANTER	HS	6	410	TREACHER	JE	5	359	TRELFORD	J	11	378
TOYER	C	5	358	TRANTER	J	6	410	TREACHER	PG	3	401	TREMAIN	GCK	4	386
TOYER	C	5	358	TRANTER	J	10	233	TREACHER	RW	5	359	TREMAINE	E	13	426
TOYER	F	5	358	TRANTER	J	10	233	TREACY	WT	6	410	TREMAINE	RH	6	410
TOYER	GA	5	358	TRANTER	W	11	377	TREADAWAY	C	3	242	TRENAM	W	8	356
TOYER	H	5	358	TRANTER	W	14	321	TREADAWAY	G	2	345	TRENAMAN	S	13	427
TOYER	HA	5	359	TRANTER	WE	11	377	TREADAWAY	HF	2	345	TRENCHARD	CJ	5	359
TOYER	HC	5	359	TRAPP	TH	6	410	TREADAWAY	W	2	345	TRENCHARD	H	5	359
TOYER	J	5	359	TRAPP	WF	2	344	TREADGOLD	SG	12	400	TRENDLE	FW	1	350
TOYER	JH	5	359	TRASK	G	10	233	TREADGOLD	WHC	12	400	TRENDLE	G	1	350
TOYER	PW	5	359	TRASK	R	4	386	TREADWAY	P	2	345	TRENDLE	S	1	350
TOYER	SW	5	359	TRASLER	WJ	12	400	TREADWAY	R	2	345	TRENERRY	B	4	386
TOYER	W	5	359	TRATTEN	T	8	356	TREADWELL	CA	6	410	TRENFIELD	A	6	410
TOYER	WC	1	349	TRAVELL	BM	12	400	TREADWELL	E	2	345	TRENHOLME	FG	12	224
TOZE	E	7	405	TRAVELL	FE	12	400	TREADWELL	FG	7	406	TRENOR	JW	14	321
TOZEE	CG	7	405	TRAVELL	PG	12	400	TREADWELL	HJ	1	349	TRENTHAM	GG	6	410
TOZER	AG	7	405	TRAVELL	RT	12	400	TREADWELL	J	2	345	TRESSLER	FJ	12	401
TOZER	D	3	241	TRAVERS	ALR	7	405	TREADWELL	WH	2	345	TREVANION	HAE	2	345
TOZER	EA	7	405	TRAVERS	CF	7	405	TREAGUS	AJ	1	350	TREVATT	F	1	350

Name	Init			Name	Init			Name	Init			Name	Init			Name	Init		
TREVE	J	2	345	TRIGGS	EH	13	427	TROKE	RW	7	407	TRUE	L	7	407				
TREVENNA	W	7	406	TRIGGS	H	2	346	TROLLEY	F	12	224	TRUE	TW	7	407				
TREVERTON	W	1	350	TRIGGS	H	7	406	TROLLEY	R	9	195	TRUELOVE	AE	9	196				
TREVETHAN	J	9	359	TRIGGS	R	10	234	TROLLOPE	CM	1	350	TRUELOVE	RH	1	350				
TREVETHAN	JD	13	427	TRIGGS	W	10	380	TROLLOPE	J	6	410	TRUELOVE	WA	7	407				
TREVETT	LV	4	386	TRIGGS	WJ	7	406	TROMAN	AV	6	410	TRUEMAN	A	6	411				
TREVILLIAN	FW	13	427	TRIGWELL	A	10	234	TROMAN	H	1	350	TRUEMAN	A	12	224				
TREVILLION	AE	13	427	TRILL	A	13	427	TROMAN	J	9	359	TRUEMAN	CF	4	387				
TREVILLION	G	1	350	TRILL	J	2	346	TROMANS	GA	9	196	TRUEMAN	F	12	224				
TREVILLION	J	13	427	TRILLIAN	J	2	346	TROMANS	H	6	410	TRUEMAN	G	6	411				
TREVIS	EW	10	379	TRIM	AC	2	346	TROOD	CWC	7	407	TRUEMAN	H	8	356				
TREVIS	WE	10	379	TRIM	AW	4	386	TROPMAN	T	6	410	TRUEMAN	JE	6	411				
TREVORROW	J	10	379	TRIM	CE	4	386	TROSSELL	A	9	359	TRUEMAN	R	12	224				
TREVOUS	F	2	345	TRIM	CG	1	350	TROTMAN	AL	1	350	TRUEMAN	W	6	411				
TREW	A	2	345	TRIM	FC	2	346	TROTMAN	CJ	4	387	TRUIN	H	11	378				
TREW	AW	3	401	TRIM	FW	4	386	TROTMAN	CS	2	346	TRUIN	S	14	322				
TREW	EH	3	401	TRIMBLE	J	14	321	TROTMAN	H	2	346	TRUMAN	AH	14	322				
TREW	F	3	242	TRIMBLE	J	14	322	TROTMAN	H	11	378	TRUMAN	B	11	378				
TREW	HFA	2	345	TRIMBLE	JF	11	378	TROTMAN	W	13	427	TRUMAN	HB	11	378				
TREW	HP	7	406	TRIMBLE	S	14	322	TROTT	GW	7	407	TRUMAN	HW	5	359				
TREW	PC	3	242	TRIMBLE	S	14	322	TROTT	J	2	346	TRUMAN	J	6	411				
TREW	WG	3	242	TRIMBOY	WV	10	380	TROTT	S	5	359	TRUMAN	V	14	322				
TREWIN	TJ	4	386	TRIMBY	JC	2	346	TROTT	WA	13	427	TRUMAN	W	6	411				
TRIANCE	GT	7	406	TRIMLETT	HJ	7	407	TROTTER	F	4	387	TRUMAN	W	6	411				
TRIANCE	JR	7	406	TRIMMER	GA	13	427	TROTTER	J	6	410	TRUMPER	EA	3	401				
TRIANCE	WH	7	406	TRIMMER	SA	10	380	TROUGHTON	AE	7	407	TRUMPER	FL	5	359				
TRIBE	AA	13	427	TRIMMINGS	WA	7	407	TROUGHTON	GW	7	407	TRUNDLER	GD	5	359				
TRIBE	AR	10	379	TRINDER	A	6	410	TROUGHTON	HJ	7	407	TRUNDLEY	JT	12	224				
TRIBE	B	10	233	TRINDER	DF	7	407	TROUGHTON	W	6	410	TRUPP	PE	6	411				
TRIBE	F	3	242	TRINDER	EG	2	346	TROUGHTON	W	6	410	TRUSCOTT	G	2	347				
TRIBE	HJ	10	233	TRINDER	EJ	7	407	TROUSDALE	W	8	356	TRUSCOTT	JT	2	347				
TRIBE	LJ	2	346	TRIPLOW	C	13	427	TROUT	A	4	387	TRUSLER	H	12	401				
TRIBE	N	10	379	TRIPLOW	W	13	427	TROUT	A	6	411	TRUSLER	W	12	401				
TRIBE	SA	10	379	TRIPP	FR	2	346	TROUT	FJ	4	387	TRUSLOW	HGT	7	407				
TRIBE	TW	10	379	TRIPP	H	12	401	TROWBRIDGE	AT	4	387	TRUSS	JJ	5	359				
TRIBE	W	10	380	TRIPP	WE	2	346	TROWBRIDGE	BGJ	10	380	TRUSSELL	CW	5	360				
TRIBE	W	13	427	TRITTON	AT	1	350	TROWBRIDGE	F	1	350	TRUSSELL	EC	2	347				
TRIBE	WWJ	10	380	TRITTON	RH	13	427	TROWELL	A	13	427	TRUSSELL	EJ	13	427				
TRIBLE	AS	2	346	TROBRIDGE	AH	8	356	TROWER	FG	7	407	TRUSSLER	AE	7	408				
TRICE	CW	9	359	TROCCHI	P	2	346	TROWMAN	A	6	411	TRUSSLER	JC	7	408				
TRICE	P	13	427	TRODD	B	4	386	TROWMAN	H	6	411	TRUSSLER	RW	7	408				
TRICKER	FW	2	346	TRODD	C	4	386	TROY	AE	2	346	TRUSTAM	H	12	224				
TRICKETT	AC	10	380	TRODD	E	4	386	TROY	EJ	3	242	TRY	TE	7	408				
TRICKETT	W	10	233	TRODD	ER	4	386	TROY	J	9	359	TUBB	FJ	4	387				
TRICKETT	WG	10	233	TRODD	F	4	387	TROY	JJ	11	378	TUBB	G	6	411				
TRICKETT	WG	10	380	TRODD	FA	4	387	TROY	JW	10	234	TUBB	GF	6	411				
TRICKETT	WJ	10	234	TRODD	G	4	387	TROY	P	6	411	TUBB	HD	12	401				
TRICKS	FJW	2	346	TRODD	G	10	380	TROY	P	6	411	TUBB	HJ	4	387				
TRIGG	F	7	406	TRODD	GJ	7	407	TROY	W	3	242	TUBB	J	1	351				
TRIGG	W	6	410	TRODD	H	4	387	TROYANOWSKI	J	11	378	TUBB	J	10	380				
TRIGGLE	G	1	350	TRODD	JT	13	427	TRUBY	J	6	411	TUBB	JE	4	387				
TRIGGS	AA	7	406	TRODD	K	4	387	TRUCKELL	GH	4	387	TUBB	JE	10	234				
TRIGGS	AH	10	234	TRODD	W	7	407	TRUCKLE	SWA	10	380	TUBB	JG	10	234				
TRIGGS	AJ	13	427	TRODDEN	T	14	322	TRUCKLE	WJ	4	387	TUBB	S	4	387				
TRIGGS	E	10	380	TROKE	HO	7	407	TRUDGILL	L	9	360	TUBB	WH	6	411				

TUBB	WH	10	234	TUCKER	J	7	408	TUFFNELL	RL	13	428	TUOHEY	HJ	2	348
TUBBS	A	9	360	TUCKER	J	11	378	TUFFNELL	W	5	360	TUPMAN	F	6	412
TUBBS	AA	9	360	TUCKER	JRH	7	408	TUFFS	AC	2	347	TUPMAN	S	6	412
TUBBS	H	4	387	TUCKER	LM	4	388	TUFFS	E	2	347	TUPPER	AE	10	234
TUBBS	L	4	387	TUCKER	M	14	322	TUFFS	J	4	388	TUPPER	EAB	13	429
TUBBS	W	7	408	TUCKER	PA	12	224	TUFNELL	JG	13	428	TUPPER	EW	4	389
TUBBS	WHJ	4	387	TUCKER	R	2	347	TUFNELL	T	13	428	TUPPER	FE	4	389
TUBBY	AE	7	408	TUCKER	R	6	411	TUFNELL	W	13	428	TUPPER	HT	7	409
TUBBY	AH	7	408	TUCKER	S	14	322	TUGBY	A	4	388	TUPPER	JM	10	234
TUCK	A	10	234	TUCKER	SCB	4	388	TUGWELL	J	10	380	TUPPIN	J	4	389
TUCK	D	12	224	TUCKER	W	2	347	TUITT	E	2	347	TUPPIN	K	4	389
TUCK	F	5	360	TUCKER	W	4	388	TUKE	T	14	322	TUPPIN	T	4	389
TUCK	F	7	408	TUCKER	W	10	380	TULEY	I	11	378	TURBEN	AJ	7	409
TUCK	FG	10	234	TUCKER	WC	6	412	TULEY	TA	5	360	TURBERFIELD	JW	6	412
TUCK	G	4	388	TUCKER	WH	3	243	TULEY	VC	2	347	TURK	JHS	13	429
TUCK	H	4	388	TUCKER	WH	4	388	TULEY	WA	13	428	TURKIN	T	8	356
TUCK	H	10	380	TUCKER	WH	7	408	TULK	AJ	10	234	TURL	FC	1	351
TUCK	JW	12	224	TUCKER	WH	9	196	TULL	ADE	12	401	TURL	MM	1	351
TUCK	R	14	322	TUCKER	WJ	2	347	TULL	E	10	234	TURLAND	C	12	401
TUCK	W	4	388	TUCKER	WJ	5	360	TULL	H	12	401	TURLAND	EW	12	401
TUCK	W	12	224	TUCKEY	AS	12	225	TULL	HJ	2	348	TURLAND	FH	12	401
TUCK-TASKER	AW	2	347	TUCKEY	CW	12	225	TULL	JW	13	428	TURLAND	LW	12	401
TUCKER	A	13	428	TUCKEY	EH	12	225	TULLETT	J	12	225	TURLAND	P	12	401
TUCKER	AE	4	388	TUCKEY	HG	12	225	TULLETT	W	2	348	TURLAND	T	12	401
TUCKER	AG	4	388	TUCKEY	W	4	388	TULLOCK	JS	6	412	TURLAND	WJ	5	360
TUCKER	AH	1	351	TUCKWELL	AH	2	347	TULLY	A	4	388	TURLEY	A	3	243
TUCKER	AJF	13	428	TUCKWELL	JT	7	408	TULLY	A	13	428	TURLEY	E	6	412
TUCKER	ATG	5	360	TUDBALL	E	9	196	TULLY	J	4	389	TURLEY	F	6	412
TUCKER	BR	4	388	TUDBALL	G	9	196	TULLY	RF	4	389	TURLEY	F	6	412
TUCKER	CH	4	388	TUDDENHAM	FAA	13	428	TULLY	WB	12	401	TURLEY	F	6	412
TUCKER	CHG	4	388	TUDDENHAM	JB	13	428	TUMA	A	14	322	TURLEY	F	11	378
TUCKER	E	6	411	TUDDENHAM	S	13	428	TUME	E	7	408	TURLEY	F	13	429
TUCKER	E	10	380	TUDENHAM	AE	13	428	TUME	G	1	351	TURLEY	H	6	412
TUCKER	E	13	428	TUDENHAM	GF	13	428	TUMEY	EJ	12	225	TURLEY	J	6	412
TUCKER	EA	7	408	TUDENHAM	M	13	428	TUNBRIDGE	G	4	389	TURLEY	JP	6	412
TUCKER	EA	7	408	TUDGAY	A	2	347	TUNBRIDGE	H	4	389	TURLEY	W	11	378
TUCKER	EJ	2	347	TUDGE	H	6	412	TUNBRIDGE	W	2	348	TURLEY	WW	6	412
TUCKER	FJ	3	242	TUDMAN	L	10	380	TUNESI	J	7	408	TURMEAU	J	2	348
TUCKER	FP	1	351	TUDOR	A	8	356	TUNESI	R	7	408	TURN	R	14	322
TUCKER	FS	13	428	TUDOR	A	10	234	TUNGATE	W	10	234	TURNBULL	DE	7	409
TUCKER	FW	2	347	TUDOR	H	8	356	TUNKS	A	1	351	TURNBULL	GH	9	196
TUCKER	G	10	234	TUDOR	JE	14	322	TUNKS	CG	7	408	TURNBULL	H	8	356
TUCKER	GM	13	428	TUDOR	RW	6	412	TUNKS	D	1	351	TURNBULL	H	8	356
TUCKER	HE	2	347	TUDOR	T	6	412	TUNLEY	WJJ	13	428	TURNBULL	J	12	401
TUCKER	HE	10	380	TUDOR	T	14	322	TUNNACLIFFE	B	9	196	TURNBULL	JJ	11	378
TUCKER	HF	4	388	TUDOR	T	14	322	TUNNACLIFFE	J	7	409	TURNBULL	RP	8	356
TUCKER	HF	12	224	TUFF	J	8	356	TUNNELL	S	5	360	TURNBULL	W	11	379
TUCKER	HJ	2	347	TUFFIELD	A	2	347	TUNNEY	A	13	428	TURNER	A	1	351
TUCKER	HR	6	411	TUFFIELD	AA	5	360	TUNNEY	D	13	429	TURNER	A	2	348
TUCKER	HW	3	243	TUFFIELD	AW	2	347	TUNNICLIFFE	E	13	429	TURNER	A	2	348
TUCKER	HW	4	388	TUFFIN	H	5	360	TUNSTALL	GE	8	356	TURNER	A	2	348
TUCKER	HW	7	408	TUFFIN	H	14	322	TUNSTALL	R	6	412	TURNER	A	3	243
TUCKER	HW	13	428	TUFFLEY	G	6	412	TUNSTALL	R	8	356	TURNER	A	7	409
TUCKER	J	4	388	TUFFLY	TG	6	412	TUNSTALL	T	6	412	TURNER	A	7	409
TUCKER	J	4	388	TUFFNELL	BW	5	360	TUNSTELL	SI	3	243	TURNER	A	7	409

TURNER	A	7	409	TURNER	E	3	402	TURNER	GN	2	348	TURNER	JH	11	379
TURNER	A	8	356	TURNER	E	7	409	TURNER	GT	7	410	TURNER	JH	14	323
TURNER	A	8	356	TURNER	E	7	410	TURNER	GW	7	410	TURNER	JJ	4	389
TURNER	A	9	196	TURNER	E	8	357	TURNER	H	2	348	TURNER	JR	7	410
TURNER	A	9	360	TURNER	E	9	360	TURNER	H	4	389	TURNER	JW	7	410
TURNER	A	9	360	TURNER	E	10	381	TURNER	H	6	413	TURNER	JW	8	357
TURNER	A	10	234	TURNER	E	10	381	TURNER	H	6	413	TURNER	JW	8	357
TURNER	A	10	234	TURNER	E	12	401	TURNER	H	8	357	TURNER	JW	9	196
TURNER	A	11	379	TURNER	EA	5	360	TURNER	H	9	196	TURNER	JW	11	379
TURNER	A	11	379	TURNER	EEY	13	429	TURNER	H	9	360	TURNER	JW	12	225
TURNER	A	13	429	TURNER	EJ	6	413	TURNER	H	10	235	TURNER	L	7	410
TURNER	A	14	322	TURNER	EM	1	351	TURNER	H	11	379	TURNER	L	8	357
TURNER	A	14	323	TURNER	EP	11	379	TURNER	HA	3	402	TURNER	L	13	429
TURNER	AB	3	401	TURNER	EW	1	351	TURNER	HC	2	348	TURNER	LA	6	413
TURNER	AC	6	413	TURNER	F	2	348	TURNER	HD	1	351	TURNER	LH	11	379
TURNER	AC	6	413	TURNER	F	5	360	TURNER	HD	9	196	TURNER	N	11	379
TURNER	AE	6	413	TURNER	F	6	413	TURNER	HE	1	351	TURNER	PA	1	352
TURNER	AE	6	413	TURNER	F	7	409	TURNER	HF	5	360	TURNER	PJ	13	429
TURNER	AE	7	409	TURNER	F	7	410	TURNER	HG	1	351	TURNER	R	1	352
TURNER	AE	8	357	TURNER	F	7	410	TURNER	HH	7	410	TURNER	R	1	352
TURNER	AE	11	379	TURNER	F	8	357	TURNER	HH	13	429	TURNER	R	6	414
TURNER	AG	3	401	TURNER	F	8	357	TURNER	HJ	2	348	TURNER	R	8	357
TURNER	AH	10	380	TURNER	F	10	381	TURNER	HJ	5	361	TURNER	R	14	323
TURNER	AJ	1	351	TURNER	F	12	401	TURNER	HN	8	357	TURNER	R	14	323
TURNER	AJ	3	401	TURNER	F	14	323	TURNER	HR	10	235	TURNER	RA	4	389
TURNER	AJ	13	429	TURNER	FA	10	381	TURNER	HW	10	381	TURNER	RC	14	323
TURNER	AM	14	323	TURNER	FG	3	402	TURNER	J	1	351	TURNER	RE	7	410
TURNER	AV	6	413	TURNER	FG	10	381	TURNER	J	1	351	TURNER	RG	7	410
TURNER	AW	7	409	TURNER	FG	12	401	TURNER	J	1	351	TURNER	RH	5	361
TURNER	BW	3	402	TURNER	FH	7	410	TURNER	J	1	351	TURNER	RT	9	360
TURNER	C	3	402	TURNER	FH	11	379	TURNER	J	2	348	TURNER	S	3	243
TURNER	C	5	360	TURNER	FH	13	429	TURNER	J	4	389	TURNER	S	5	361
TURNER	C	6	413	TURNER	FJ	2	348	TURNER	J	5	361	TURNER	S	7	410
TURNER	C	7	409	TURNER	FJ	12	401	TURNER	J	6	413	TURNER	S	8	357
TURNER	C	9	360	TURNER	FL	6	413	TURNER	J	6	413	TURNER	S	8	357
TURNER	C	10	380	TURNER	FL	10	235	TURNER	J	8	357	TURNER	S	9	360
TURNER	C	11	379	TURNER	FW	3	402	TURNER	J	9	360	TURNER	S	11	379
TURNER	C	12	225	TURNER	G	4	389	TURNER	J	10	235	TURNER	SC	10	381
TURNER	CD	2	348	TURNER	G	6	413	TURNER	J	10	381	TURNER	SF	5	361
TURNER	CE	7	409	TURNER	G	6	413	TURNER	J	11	379	TURNER	SJ	3	243
TURNER	CF	3	243	TURNER	G	8	357	TURNER	J	11	379	TURNER	T	3	243
TURNER	CH	3	402	TURNER	G	9	360	TURNER	J	11	379	TURNER	T	6	414
TURNER	CH	5	360	TURNER	GA	5	360	TURNER	J	12	401	TURNER	T	7	410
TURNER	CH	11	379	TURNER	GA	6	413	TURNER	J	14	323	TURNER	T	8	357
TURNER	CH	13	429	TURNER	GA	7	410	TURNER	J	14	323	TURNER	T	10	381
TURNER	CJ	7	409	TURNER	GC	1	351	TURNER	JA	5	361	TURNER	T	10	381
TURNER	CJ	7	409	TURNER	GC	8	357	TURNER	JA	13	429	TURNER	T	11	379
TURNER	CJ	13	429	TURNER	GE	2	348	TURNER	JB	7	410	TURNER	T	12	225
TURNER	CW	7	409	TURNER	GE	5	360	TURNER	JE	6	413	TURNER	TA	9	196
TURNER	CW	8	357	TURNER	GE	9	360	TURNER	JE	13	429	TURNER	TFC	7	410
TURNER	CW	10	381	TURNER	GF	3	243	TURNER	JE	14	323	TURNER	TH	7	410
TURNER	D	4	389	TURNER	GH	9	196	TURNER	JH	1	352	TURNER	TH	14	323
TURNER	D	7	409	TURNER	GH	10	381	TURNER	JH	1	352	TURNER	TP	7	410
TURNER	D	13	429	TURNER	GH	12	225	TURNER	JH	4	389	TURNER	TW	8	357
TURNER	DA	13	429	TURNER	GJ	13	429	TURNER	JH	5	361	TURNER	TWF	12	402

TURNER	V	8	357	TURNOCK	HW	12	402	TURVEY	S	6	414	TWIGDEN	J	12	225
TURNER	VG	12	402	TURNOCK	JS	12	402	TURVEY	SC	5	362	TWIGDEN	PR	12	225
TURNER	W	2	348	TURNPENNY	H	6	414	TURVEY	SJ	5	362	TWIGG	CA	6	415
TURNER	W	4	389	TURP	J	13	430	TURVEY	T	5	362	TWIGG	F	11	380
TURNER	W	5	361	TURPIN	F	13	430	TURVEY	W	5	362	TWIGG	FG	12	225
TURNER	W	5	361	TURPIN	FJ	3	402	TURVEY	W	5	362	TWIGG	G	14	324
TURNER	W	6	414	TURPIN	FJ	4	389	TURVEY	W	5	362	TWIGG	H	4	390
TURNER	W	7	410	TURPIN	JH	5	362	TURVEY	W	5	362	TWIGG	H	12	402
TURNER	W	8	358	TURPIN	JL	2	349	TURVEY	WA	6	414	TWIGG	J	5	362
TURNER	W	8	358	TURPIN	JL	7	411	TURVEY	WG	6	414	TWIGG	J	8	358
TURNER	W	8	358	TURPIN	N	9	196	TUSON	D	3	402	TWIGG	J	14	324
TURNER	W	9	196	TURPIN	R	9	196	TUSON	R	3	402	TWIGG	J	14	324
TURNER	W	9	196	TURPIN	TW	3	402	TUSTAIN	AH	1	352	TWIGG	JE	11	380
TURNER	W	9	360	TURPIN	W	2	349	TUSTAIN	H	1	352	TWIGG	S	8	358
TURNER	W	9	360	TURPIN	WE	7	411	TUSTIN	G	6	414	TWIGG	SE	6	415
TURNER	W	9	360	TURRALL	TG	6	414	TUSTIN	RG	11	380	TWIGG	T	6	415
TURNER	W	10	381	TURRELL	J	11	380	TUSTIN	WH	10	235	TWIGG	T	14	324
TURNER	W	13	429	TURRELL	S	10	381	TUTING	CH	4	389	TWIGG	TW	6	415
TURNER	W	13	430	TURRINGTON	AE	2	349	TUTT	FC	1	352	TWIGG	W	14	324
TURNER	WA	10	381	TURTLE	FW	8	358	TUTT	G	7	411	TWIGGER	H	6	415
TURNER	WC	7	411	TURTLE	H	11	380	TUTT	H	4	389	TWIN	CF	13	430
TURNER	WF	3	402	TURTLEBURY	J	5	362	TUTT	HC	1	352	TWINBILL	H	6	412
TURNER	WG	2	349	TURTON	B	6	414	TUTT	J	13	430	TWINE	F	3	402
TURNER	WH	8	358	TURTON	C	11	380	TUTTE	C	10	235	TWINE	G	3	402
TURNER	WH	9	196	TURTON	F	2	349	TUTTEY	CE	5	362	TWINE	J	2	349
TURNER	WH	9	360	TURTON	FC	2	349	TUTTLEBEE	JB	2	349	TWINE	J	4	390
TURNER	WH	9	360	TURTON	FG	6	414	TUTTON	CR	4	390	TWINE	R	2	349
TURNER	WH	9	360	TURTON	H	6	414	TUTTON	E	2	349	TWINE	R	3	243
TURNER	WHF	10	381	TURTON	J	8	358	TUTTON	J	4	390	TWINING	F	1	352
TURNER	WJ	1	352	TURTON	J	14	323	TUTTON	TW	7	411	TWINING	FT	10	235
TURNER	WJ	2	349	TURTON	P	8	358	TUTTY	SR	6	415	TWINING	GT	6	415
TURNER	WJ	3	243	TURTON	TF	14	323	TUVEY	AG	3	402	TWINING	HC	6	415
TURNER	WJ	9	196	TURTON	W	8	358	TUVEY	CH	3	402	TWINING	W	1	352
TURNER	WJ	13	430	TURTON	W	8	358	TUXFORD	A	9	196	TWISELTON	A	12	402
TURNER	WK	8	358	TURTON	WG	2	349	TWAMLEY	TC	14	323	TWISELTON	G	12	402
TURNER	WL	5	361	TURVER	J	8	358	TWEDDLE	H	8	358	TWISS	JR	6	415
TURNER	WL	6	414	TURVEY	A	5	362	TWEED	C	1	352	TWISS	RT	14	324
TURNER	WN	6	414	TURVEY	A	12	402	TWEED	SJ	12	225	TWITCHETT	GA	3	402
TURNER	WP	1	352	TURVEY	AC	2	349	TWEED	WH	13	430	TWITCHETT	R	9	197
TURNER	WT	1	352	TURVEY	B	6	414	TWEEDALE	A	8	358	TWITE	ST	12	402
TURNER	WT	12	225	TURVEY	C	6	414	TWEEDALE	C	11	380	TWITTY	W	6	415
TURNER	WW	1	352	TURVEY	CW	12	225	TWEEDALE	J	14	323	TWOMEY	D	13	430
TURNEY	C	5	361	TURVEY	EH	6	414	TWEEDALE	R	14	324	TWOMLOW	CH	6	415
TURNEY	C	7	411	TURVEY	FH	7	411	TWEEDALE	S	9	196	TWOMLOW	W	6	415
TURNEY	CT	5	361	TURVEY	G	5	362	TWEEDALE	W	11	380	TWORT	R	4	390
TURNEY	E	5	361	TURVEY	G	6	414	TWEEDLE	J	9	196	TWOSE	F	2	349
TURNEY	GA	2	349	TURVEY	H	5	362	TWEEDLE	S	9	197	TWYCROSS	EC	4	390
TURNEY	T	5	361	TURVEY	H	6	414	TWEEN	AE	13	430	TWYDELL	RG	1	352
TURNEY	W	5	361	TURVEY	H	10	235	TWEEN	E	2	349	TWYDELL	THA	2	350
TURNEY	W	5	361	TURVEY	H	10	235	TWEEN	S	13	430	TWYDELL	WJ	1	352
TURNEY	WE	5	361	TURVEY	HA	6	414	TWELFTREE	TH	12	402	TWYDELL	WJ	1	352
TURNEY	WH	5	361	TURVEY	J	12	225	TWEMLO	A	11	380	TWYDLE	EA	2	350
TURNHAM	E	14	323	TURVEY	R	10	235	TWIBILL	WA	2	349	TWYFORD	CH	2	350
TURNHAM	TJ	2	349	TURVEY	RG	6	414	TWIDDY	JH	13	430	TWYFORD	HJ	2	350
TURNOCK	G	14	323	TURVEY	RH	12	225	TWIGDEN	E	12	225	TWYMAN	EA	10	235
								TWIGDEN	G	12	225				

TWYMAN	WA	10	235	TYLER	W	2	350	TYSOM	JF	5	363	UNDERHILL	E	6	416
TWYNAM	WG	6	415	TYLER	W	3	403	TYSOM	WB	5	363	UNDERHILL	F	6	416
TYACK	RG	3	243	TYLER	W	13	431	TYSOME	F	5	363	UNDERHILL	FH	6	416
TYCE	EF	2	350	TYLER	WC	4	390	TYSON	A	1	353	UNDERHILL	G	8	359
TYCE	J	11	380	TYLER	WGR	13	431	TYSON	A	11	380	UNDERHILL	H	6	416
TYDEMAN	FT	3	402	TYLER	WH	3	243	TYSON	E	1	353	UNDERHILL	H	8	359
TYE	AC	12	402	TYLER	WJ	6	415	TYSON	E	11	380	UNDERHILL	JW	6	416
TYE	AE	6	415	TYLER	WR	2	350	TYSON	GH	1	353	UNDERHILL	S	2	351
TYE	AJ	13	430	TYLER	WR	7	411	TYSON	H	8	359	UNDERWOOD	A	5	363
TYE	CGW	13	430	TYLER	WS	7	411	TYSON	H	12	402	UNDERWOOD	A	5	363
TYE	GF	13	430	TYMS	JH	14	324	TYSON	HH	8	359	UNDERWOOD	A	13	431
TYE	H	3	402	TYNAN	A	6	415	TYSON	J	7	411	UNDERWOOD	AG	12	226
TYE	J	9	197	TYNAN	J	9	197	TYSON	JH	1	353	UNDERWOOD	AJ	12	227
TYE	J	9	361	TYNAN	SP	9	197	TYSON	N	1	353	UNDERWOOD	AJ	13	431
TYE	JH	7	411	TYNE	M	2	350	TYSON	VW	10	381	UNDERWOOD	AW	12	227
TYE	JJ	3	402	TYNE	W	9	197	TYSON	WE	3	403	UNDERWOOD	CH	13	431
TYE	L	9	361	TYNE	WR	2	350	TYTE	FG	1	353	UNDERWOOD	D	7	411
TYERS	CH	7	411	TYRELL	WH	12	402	TYTLER	S	4	390	UNDERWOOD	E	5	363
TYERS	GWA	7	411	TYREMAN	T	8	358	TYZACK	A	8	359	UNDERWOOD	E	5	363
TYERS	W	11	380	TYRER	F	8	358	TYZACK	A	8	359	UNDERWOOD	E	12	227
TYLDESLEY	A	14	324	TYRER	G	8	358	TYZACK	T	14	324	UNDERWOOD	EG	13	431
TYLDSEY	J	8	358	TYRER	H	14	324					UNDERWOOD	F	2	351
TYLER	A	1	353	TYROR	WA	14	324					UNDERWOOD	F	7	412
TYLER	A	6	415	TYRRELL	A	4	390					UNDERWOOD	F	12	402
TYLER	AC	2	350	TYRRELL	A	5	362	**U**				UNDERWOOD	FT	5	363
TYLER	AE	2	350	TYRRELL	AJ	12	226					UNDERWOOD	G	12	227
TYLER	AE	13	430	TYRRELL	BS	2	350	UBSDELL	J	3	243	UNDERWOOD	G	12	402
TYLER	AH	6	415	TYRRELL	C	2	350	UDALL	AEJ	4	390	UNDERWOOD	GA	5	363
TYLER	CA	2	350	TYRRELL	E	12	402	UDALL	TH	6	415	UNDERWOOD	GD	7	412
TYLER	CS	5	362	TYRRELL	EJ	7	411	UDALL	WJ	1	353	UNDERWOOD	H	5	363
TYLER	E	2	350	TYRRELL	F	4	390	UDEN	W	13	431	UNDERWOOD	H	7	412
TYLER	EC	4	390	TYRRELL	F	5	362	UDLE	H	10	235	UNDERWOOD	J	12	402
TYLER	EE	10	235	TYRRELL	FJ	4	390	UDY	TC	10	235	UNDERWOOD	JJ	5	363
TYLER	ER	4	390	TYRRELL	FW	12	226	UGLOW	FW	14	324	UNDERWOOD	JT	12	227
TYLER	F	1	353	TYRRELL	G	14	324	UGLOW	ST	2	351	UNDERWOOD	JW	7	412
TYLER	F	3	403	TYRRELL	H	2	350	ULLMAN	L	2	351	UNDERWOOD	JW	12	403
TYLER	F	7	411	TYRRELL	H	3	243	ULRICK	G	1	353	UNDERWOOD	M	6	416
TYLER	F	13	430	TYRRELL	HE	12	402	ULRICK	H	1	353	UNDERWOOD	PA	12	227
TYLER	F	13	430	TYRRELL	J	12	226	UMNEY	A	12	226	UNDERWOOD	PS	5	363
TYLER	FA	13	430	TYRRELL	JH	11	380	UMNEY	BD	12	226	UNDERWOOD	R	12	403
TYLER	H	12	226	TYRRELL	JS	12	402	UMNEY	C	12	226	UNDERWOOD	RH	4	390
TYLER	HG	3	243	TYRRELL	P	5	362	UMNEY	FF	12	226	UNDERWOOD	S	2	351
TYLER	HJ	7	411	TYRRELL	S	5	362	UMNEY	GE	12	226	UNDERWOOD	T	5	363
TYLER	HW	5	362	TYRRELL	SR	13	431	UMNEY	GF	2	351	UNDERWOOD	TA	6	416
TYLER	J	8	358	TYRRELL	T	7	411	UMNEY	HBO	12	226	UNDERWOOD	W	3	243
TYLER	JJ	3	403	TYRRELL	WW	3	403	UMNEY	HE	12	226	UNDERWOOD	W	3	244
TYLER	JS	2	350	TYSOE	FAA	12	402	UMNEY	J	12	226	UNDERWOOD	W	8	359
TYLER	L	2	350	TYSOE	FJ	12	226	UMNEY	JW	12	226	UNDERWOOD	W	12	227
TYLER	R	3	403	TYSOE	HH	12	226	UMPLEBY	F	8	359	UNDERWOOD	WA	1	353
TYLER	R	5	362	TYSOE	JS	12	226	UMPLEBY	J	8	359	UNDERWOOD	WC	5	363
TYLER	RW	11	380	TYSOE	W	12	226	UMPLEBY	JS	8	359	UNDERWOOD	WH	6	416
TYLER	T	6	415	TYSOE	WL	12	226	UNDERDOWD	T	2	351	UNDERWOOD	WJ	1	353
TYLER	TJ	6	415	TYSOM	CJ	5	363	UNDERDOWN	C	6	416	UNDERWOOD	WT	12	227
TYLER	TJ	13	430	TYSOM	H	5	363	UNDERDOWN	E	10	381	UNITT	CW	3	244
TYLER	W	2	350	TYSOM	H	5	363	UNDERDOWN	J	10	235	UNITT	JW	3	244
								UNDERHILL	AV	4	390				
								UNDERHILL	CT	6	416				

UNITT	MJ	12	227	UPSON	WA	5	364	UWINS	CW	13	431	VAN RYNE	C	3	244
UNSTEAD	HC	2	351	UPSON	WJ	13	431	UWINS	GR	7	412	VAN RYNE	FM	3	244
UNSTEAD	L	2	351	UPSTON	H	6	416	UZZELL	WF	4	391	VAN-ORDEN	T	10	236
UNSWORTH	C	14	324	UPSTON	H	6	416					VANBRUGGEN	CH	2	352
UNSWORTH	F	14	324	UPSTON	HC	13	431	**V**				VANCE	EJ	4	391
UNSWORTH	H	4	390	UPTON	A	4	390					VANDENBOSCH	FE	7	412
UNSWORTH	J	12	227	UPTON	A	8	359					VANDEPEER	A	1	353
UNSWORTH	J	14	324	UPTON	AE	7	412	VAAL	GF	7	412	VANDEPEER	A	13	432
UNSWORTH	TH	8	359	UPTON	AFG	1	353	VAAL	HM	7	412	VANDERKISTE	F	6	417
UNSWORTH	W	14	324	UPTON	ATG	2	351	VAGG	SH	14	325	VANDERPOL	JH	13	432
UNSWORTH	WF	14	325	UPTON	B	6	416	VAHEY	T	11	381	VANDIEMAN	E	14	325
UNTHANK	FS	9	197	UPTON	CR	5	364	VAIL	C	14	325	VANDIEMAN	J	14	325
UNWIN	A	9	197	UPTON	E	6	416	VAIL	G	11	381	VANDYKE	AJ	5	364
UNWIN	A	9	197	UPTON	EP	10	382	VAIL	LAM	10	382	VANE	A	4	391
UNWIN	AW	11	380	UPTON	GHF	6	416	VAIL	WS	10	382	VANE	A	4	391
UNWIN	D	13	431	UPTON	H	5	364	VAINES	AL	7	412	VANE	B	13	432
UNWIN	E	8	359	UPTON	H	6	416	VALANTINE	S	8	359	VANE	F	13	432
UNWIN	F	9	197	UPTON	H	7	412	VALE	AE	6	417	VANE	TG	13	432
UNWIN	F	9	361	UPTON	HW	5	364	VALE	AH	10	382	VANES	A	11	381
UNWIN	FR	9	361	UPTON	J	8	359	VALE	FT	12	228	VANGO	JW	1	353
UNWIN	G	11	380	UPTON	S	13	431	VALE	J	6	417	VANGO	JW	1	353
UNWIN	H	11	381	UPTON	W	4	390	VALE	T	4	391	VANGO	TL	1	354
UNWIN	H	11	381	UPTON	W	6	417	VALE	W	6	417	VANSANTER	AC	13	432
UNWIN	HW	3	244	UPTON	W	8	359	VALE	W	9	197	VANSCHAGEN	G	5	364
UNWIN	I	11	381	UPTON	WA	10	235	VALENTINE	A	7	412	VANSTONE	A	10	236
UNWIN	J	9	197	UPTON	WO	6	416	VALENTINE	AD	1	353	VARD	WG	1	354
UNWIN	J	9	361	UPTON	WR	6	417	VALENTINE	E	3	244	VARDELL	T	7	412
UNWIN	J	9	361	UPWARD	A	10	236	VALENTINE	EA	12	403	VARDEN	TG	11	381
UNWIN	JW	9	197	UPWARD	FE	2	351	VALENTINE	EC	1	353	VARDEY	E	2	352
UNWIN	TH	14	325	URMSTON	J	14	325	VALENTINE	F	4	391	VARDON	AH	3	244
UNWIN	TJ	13	431	URQUHART	RD	4	390	VALENTINE	F	12	403	VARDON	E	3	244
UNWIN	TW	13	431	URRIDGE	G	12	39	VALENTINE	GH	12	403	VARDY	CR	4	391
UNWIN	WW	2	351	URRY	AE	10	236	VALENTINE	GH	12	403	VARE	HE	4	391
UPCHURCH	AH	12	227	URRY	EC	10	236	VALENTINE	H	11	381	VARETTO	B	14	325
UPCHURCH	C	5	363	URRY	EG	10	382	VALENTINE	J	14	325	VARETTO	J	11	381
UPCHURCH	C	11	381	URSELL	AW	1	353	VALENTINE	J	14	325	VARLEY	A	8	360
UPCHURCH	E	12	227	URSELL	JJT	10	236	VALENTINE	J	14	325	VARLEY	D	9	361
UPCHURCH	F	12	227	USHER	A	12	227	VALENTINE	RE	12	403	VARLEY	E	8	360
UPCHURCH	FG	5	363	USHER	A	12	227	VALENTINE	W	14	325	VARLEY	E	8	360
UPCHURCH	W	5	364	USHER	AH	12	227	VALIANT	SH	13	432	VARLEY	E	9	197
UPCHURCH	W	5	364	USHER	AV	12	227	VALINSKY	P	14	325	VARLEY	E	13	432
UPCHURCH	W	12	227	USHER	EG	12	227	VALLANCE	AC	13	432	VARLEY	F	2	352
UPFOLD	FA	13	431	USHER	FW	12	227	VALLANCE	AE	3	244	VARLEY	F	9	197
UPHILL	AW	13	431	USHER	HA	12	228	VALLANCE	AJ	4	391	VARLEY	G	8	360
UPHILL	FE	4	390	USHER	HJ	6	417	VALLANCE	C	7	412	VARLEY	GC	11	381
UPHILL	H	13	431	USHER	P	5	364	VALLANCE	F	7	412	VARLEY	GC	14	325
UPHOFF	A	9	361	USHER	T	8	359	VALLANCE	W	9	361	VARLEY	H	8	360
UPHOFF	C	9	197	USHER	TB	12	228	VALLANCE	WJG	13	432	VARLEY	H	8	360
UPJOHN	JI	2	351	USHER	W	1	353	VALLEDY	W	2	351	VARLEY	H	8	360
UPPERTON	TW	5	364	USHER	W	8	359	VALLER	GA	10	382	VARLEY	H	9	361
UPSON	A	2	351	USHERWOOD	S	6	417	VALLER	WF	2	351	VARLEY	H	9	361
UPSON	GHA	6	416	UTLEY	W	14	325	VALLIS	F	6	417	VARLEY	J	8	360
UPSON	LG	10	235	UTTERIDGE	WG	2	351	VALLOR	EH	10	236	VARLEY	J	8	360
UPSON	M	13	431	UTTING	G	7	412	VALLOW	W	2	351	VARLEY	J	8	360
UPSON	RJ	10	235	UTTLEY	J	9	197	VAN	SF	4	391	VARLEY	J	8	360
								VAN BARRS	F	2	351	VARLEY	JA	8	360

Surname	Initials	Vol	Page
VARLEY	JW	9	197
VARLEY	R	11	381
VARLEY	R	14	325
VARLEY	T	9	361
VARLEY	W	8	360
VARLEY	W	8	360
VARLEY	W	8	360
VARLEY	W	8	360
VARLEY	W	8	360
VARLEY	W	8	360
VARLEY	W	9	361
VARLEY	W	11	381
VARLOW	H	14	325
VARNDALL	SW	6	417
VARNDELL	B	7	412
VARNDELL	J	10	236
VARNDELL	W	4	391
VARNEY	A	9	361
VARNEY	A	13	432
VARNEY	CG	12	228
VARNEY	GF	12	228
VARNEY	GS	2	352
VARNEY	H	5	364
VARNEY	JT	12	228
VARNEY	RT	12	228
VARNEY	W	5	364
VARNEY	W	6	417
VARNEY	WJ	5	364
VARNHAM	W	12	228
VARNSVERRY	WJ	12	403
VASEY	A	8	360
VASEY	J	8	360
VASEY	J	9	197
VASEY	M	9	361
VASEY	R	8	361
VASEY	W	11	381
VASS	E	2	352
VASS	GH	4	391
VASS	JB	2	352
VASS	R	10	236
VASS	RH	13	432
VASS	W	5	364
VASS	WC	13	432
VASSALLO	A	10	236
VAUDRAY	W	14	325
VAUDREY	G	14	326
VAUGHAM	A	14	326
VAUGHAN	A	4	391
VAUGHAN	AC	3	244
VAUGHAN	AR	8	361
VAUGHAN	BC	4	391
VAUGHAN	C	10	382
VAUGHAN	CH	4	391
VAUGHAN	CHL	7	413
VAUGHAN	E	4	391
VAUGHAN	E	10	236
VAUGHAN	EH	4	391
VAUGHAN	EJR	4	391
VAUGHAN	FH	4	391
VAUGHAN	FJ	12	228
VAUGHAN	G	2	352
VAUGHAN	GL	12	403
VAUGHAN	H	2	352
VAUGHAN	H	14	326
VAUGHAN	H	14	326
VAUGHAN	HA	4	391
VAUGHAN	HT	8	361
VAUGHAN	J	2	352
VAUGHAN	J	2	352
VAUGHAN	J	6	417
VAUGHAN	J	8	361
VAUGHAN	L	6	417
VAUGHAN	LC	7	413
VAUGHAN	P	3	244
VAUGHAN	P	13	432
VAUGHAN	PHV	4	391
VAUGHAN	RB	3	244
VAUGHAN	RJ	7	413
VAUGHAN	SG	4	392
VAUGHAN	SG	12	228
VAUGHAN	VH	2	352
VAUGHAN	W	14	326
VAUGHAN	WA	2	352
VAUGHAN	WCE	4	392
VAUGHAN	WF	4	392
VAUGHAN	WGA	13	432
VAUKINS	F	10	382
VAUSE	JW	8	361
VAUTREY	H	8	361
VAUX	WJ	2	352
VAYRO	SN	11	381
VEAL	E	4	392
VEAL	E	4	392
VEAL	F	4	392
VEAL	FFA	4	392
VEAL	J	3	244
VEAL	J	4	392
VEAL	RG	4	392
VEAL	W	6	417
VEALE	A	13	432
VEALE	AH	3	244
VEALE	HE	2	352
VEALE	J	6	417
VEALE	PW	2	352
VEALE	RH	2	352
VEAR	AE	4	392
VEAR	EC	10	236
VEAR	EW	2	352
VEAR	F	14	326
VEAR	T	11	381
VEARS	W	6	417
VEASEY	AJ	6	417
VEASEY	C	6	417
VEASEY	C	7	413
VEASEY	G	2	352
VEASEY	H	7	413
VEASEY	HJ	2	353
VEASEY	JR	7	413
VEASEY	T	6	418
VEATER	EJ	10	382
VECK	A	4	392
VECK	AR	4	392
VECK	C	4	392
VECK	CE	4	392
VECK	HG	4	392
VEEVERS	E	14	326
VEITCH	G	7	413
VELDEN	W	4	392
VELLENOWETH	A	2	353
VELVIN	F	2	353
VENABLES	A	2	353
VENABLES	A	14	326
VENABLES	AA	14	326
VENABLES	CE	3	244
VENABLES	CJ	3	244
VENABLES	E	10	382
VENABLES	G	13	432
VENABLES	JB	7	413
VENABLES	SG	6	418
VENABLES	SJ	13	432
VENABLES	ST	13	432
VENABLES	T	14	326
VENES	H	7	413
VENESS	EL	13	432
VENESS	J	5	364
VENESS	R	2	353
VENESS	WC	14	326
VENMAN	W	4	392
VENN	AB	3	403
VENN	AL	2	353
VENN	B	4	392
VENN	ES	2	353
VENN	G	7	413
VENN	H	2	353
VENN	J	2	353
VENN	J	2	353
VENN	J	4	392
VENN	J	4	392
VENN	LF	7	413
VENN	RE	6	418
VENN	T	3	244
VENN	WT	3	403
VENNER	HT	7	413
VENNING	B	8	361
VENT	JR	7	413
VENTHAM	AC	10	382
VENTHAM	EG	4	393
VENTHAM	GF	4	393
VENTHAM	RG	10	382
VENTON	GA	4	393
VENTRIS	AE	11	381
VENUS	C	3	244
VENUS	G	4	393
VENUS	WA	2	353
VERCOE	T	7	413
VERDON	J	3	244
VERE	E	2	353
VERE	HW	10	236
VEREY	A	13	433
VEREY	T	13	433
VEREY	W	13	433
VERGE	AW	4	393
VERITY	AE	14	326
VERITY	C	8	361
VERITY	C	8	361
VERITY	E	8	361
VERITY	E	11	381
VERITY	G	8	361
VERITY	H	8	361
VERITY	J	8	361
VERITY	J	8	361
VERITY	J	14	326
VERITY	JH	14	326
VERITY	JR	8	361
VERITY	JW	11	382
VERLANDER	WG	2	353
VERNALS	WA	6	418
VERNON	C	6	418
VERNON	C	14	326
VERNON	CA	11	382
VERNON	CC	11	382
VERNON	FH	6	418
VERNON	H	8	361
VERNON	H	11	382
VERNON	HH	2	353
VERNON	J	11	382
VERNON	J	12	403
VERNON	J	12	403
VERNON	JF	11	382
VERNON	JM	2	353
VERNON	JW	8	361
VERNON	LB	12	403
VERNON	MA	4	393
VERNON	MV	13	433
VERNON	N	2	353
VERNON	NW	1	354
VERNON	RT	2	353
VERNON	T	14	326
VERNON	TS	11	382
VERNON	WH	6	418

VERRAEZ	WE	2	353	VICKERS	J	13	433	VINCE	J	13	433	VINE	EL	3	245
VERRALL	MA	12	403	VICKERS	J	13	433	VINCE	O	1	354	VINE	F	4	393
VERRAN	J	2	353	VICKERS	JR	13	433	VINCE	W	13	433	VINE	F	10	237
VERRAN	OV	7	413	VICKERS	JS	3	245	VINCENT	AH	2	355	VINE	FA	7	414
VERRECCHIA	D	12	403	VICKERS	JW	11	382	VINCENT	ATH	6	419	VINE	FJ	2	356
VERRECCHIA	M	12	403	VICKERS	PW	5	365	VINCENT	AW	2	355	VINE	FW	4	393
VERRELL	A	2	353	VICKERS	R	6	418	VINCENT	AW	4	393	VINE	H	4	393
VERRILLS	F	7	413	VICKERS	T	2	354	VINCENT	AW	5	365	VINE	H	8	362
VERRINDER	JE	2	354	VICKERS	TJ	7	414	VINCENT	B	2	355	VINE	HC	4	394
VERS	H	8	361	VICKERS	W	5	365	VINCENT	BR	3	245	VINE	J	4	394
VERYARD	FW	10	236	VICKERS	W	6	418	VINCENT	CP	2	355	VINE	J	4	394
VERYARD	HR	13	433	VICKERS	W	11	382	VINCENT	EC	5	365	VINE	M	4	394
VESCONTE	A	10	382	VICKERS	W	13	433	VINCENT	EH	3	245	VINE	PHR	4	394
VESEY	E	1	354	VICKERS	WG	8	362	VINCENT	EH	7	414	VINE	RJ	2	355
VESEY	WLJ	5	364	VICKERS	WH	8	362	VINCENT	F	13	433	VINE	TW	1	354
VESEY	WT	11	382	VICKERY	A	8	362	VINCENT	FC	1	354	VINE	TW	1	354
VESSEY	A	2	354	VICKERY	A	13	433	VINCENT	G	7	414	VINE	W	6	419
VESTEY	HA	7	414	VICKERY	CH	5	365	VINCENT	GAR	13	433	VINE	WJ	10	236
VESTY	J	11	382	VICKERY	E	7	414	VINCENT	GL	3	245	VINE	WR	6	419
VESTY	T	14	326	VICKERY	EE	2	354	VINCENT	GR	13	433	VINE	WT	4	394
VESTY	WM	14	326	VICKERY	G	2	354	VINCENT	GW	6	419	VINER	AVG	1	354
VEVERS	H	8	362	VICKERY	GJ	2	354	VINCENT	H	6	419	VINER	NCE	1	354
VEZEY	A	2	354	VICKERY	HG	6	418	VINCENT	H	7	414	VINES	C	10	382
VIALS	E	5	364	VICKERY	R	2	354	VINCENT	H	7	414	VINES	EH	13	434
VIAN	E	7	414	VICKERY	SB	12	228	VINCENT	H	8	362	VINEY	F	4	394
VIBERT	AG	4	393	VICKERY	SH	7	414	VINCENT	J	1	354	VINEY	FE	10	382
VIBERT	PH	4	393	VICKERY	SS	4	393	VINCENT	J	1	354	VINEY	HJ	10	382
VICARS	JW	2	354	VICKERY	W	4	393	VINCENT	J	2	355	VINEY	HS	6	419
VICARY	AWE	2	354	VICKERY	WS	4	393	VINCENT	J	6	419	VINEY	LK	10	382
VICARY	FJ	7	414	VICKNELL	E	6	418	VINCENT	J	7	414	VINEY	LM	10	382
VICARY	TP	6	418	VICKNELL	L	6	418	VINCENT	JAE	2	355	VINEY	MI	2	356
VICCARS	E	3	245	VIDLER	AE	4	393	VINCENT	JW	1	354	VINEY	T	4	394
VICCARS	G	3	245	VIDLER	AE	10	236	VINCENT	LK	2	355	VINEY	WF	2	356
VICCARS	H	2	354	VIDLER	AJ	1	354	VINCENT	M	4	393	VINGAN	M	14	327
VICK	AS	3	245	VIDLER	FJ	1	354	VINCENT	R	7	414	VINGAN	P	14	327
VICK	FG	3	245	VIDLER	WJ	4	393	VINCENT	R	7	414	VINING	TH	7	414
VICK	FWH	7	414	VIDLER	WJ	13	433	VINCENT	RB	3	245	VINNICOMBE	TH	10	383
VICK	HS	3	245	VIGOR	B	2	354	VINCENT	RC	2	355	VINSENZO	F	13	434
VICK	PW	8	362	VIGOR	F	7	414	VINCENT	RT	3	245	VINSON	A	2	356
VICK	SG	3	245	VIGOR	JG	7	414	VINCENT	SF	2	355	VINTER	JW	11	382
VICKERMAN	A	11	382	VIGORS	E	12	228	VINCENT	SF	4	393	VINTER	RE	12	228
VICKERMAN	F	11	382	VIGURS	AP	10	237	VINCENT	SGW	2	355	VINTERS	DT	8	362
VICKERS	A	2	354	VIGURS	JH	2	354	VINCENT	T	3	245	VINTINER	FW	12	228
VICKERS	A	5	364	VIGUS	G	2	354	VINCENT	W	2	355	VINTNER	A	12	228
VICKERS	A	8	362	VIGUS	M	2	354	VINCENT	WE	2	355	VINTNER	A	12	228
VICKERS	AT	13	433	VILE	EL	2	354	VINCENT	WH	4	393	VINTNER	C	5	365
VICKERS	AVF	3	245	VILES	W	13	433	VINCETT	H	2	355	VINTNER	J	12	228
VICKERS	C	8	362	VILLAGE	GH	6	418	VINCNET	EHT	5	365	VINTON	J	1	354
VICKERS	D	11	382	VILLAGE	W	6	418	VINCNET	TW	5	365	VIPOND	A	14	327
VICKERS	F	9	197	VILLENEUVE	J	2	354	VINE	A	2	355	VIPOND	E	14	327
VICKERS	FG	5	365	VILLIERS	EA	2	355	VINE	AA	6	419	VIPOND	H	2	356
VICKERS	FW	5	365	VILLIERS	G	1	354	VINE	AG	4	393	VIPOND	H	14	327
VICKERS	H	8	362	VILLIERS	JG	2	354	VINE	CF	2	355	VIPOND	J	14	327
VICKERS	H	11	382	VINALL	CA	7	414	VINE	CH	4	393	VIPOND	J	14	327
VICKERS	J	6	418	VINALL	FG	2	355	VINE	EJ	2	355	VIRGIN	G	5	365

VIRGIN	GW	12	228
VIRGIN	H	5	365
VIRGO	EA	2	356
VIRGO	H	13	434
VIRNULS	AJ	6	419
VIRR	H	9	361
VITTY	E	9	361
VITUE	A	2	356
VIVIAN	E	10	237
VIVIAN	F	10	236
VIZARD	AHT	7	415
VIZARD	EC	7	415
VOADEN	WS	10	236
VOAK	CF	1	354
VOBES	JT	2	356
VOELLNER	A	11	382
VOELLNER	W	11	382
VOELLNER	W	11	382
VOGAN	AW	7	415
VOGAN	ML	1	354
VOGEL	AEJ	3	245
VOICE	BP	6	419
VOICE	CG	7	415
VOICE	EE	10	237
VOICE	JH	6	419
VOISEY	HA	10	237
VOISEY	HAC	10	237
VOISIN	SC	4	394
VOKE	F	10	237
VOKE	J	12	403
VOKES	E	2	356
VOKES	W	7	415
VOLKERT	J	7	415
VOLLANS	H	8	362
VOLLER	A	13	434
VOLLER	E	1	354
VOLLER	H	3	403
VOLLER	J	1	355
VOLLER	W	4	394
VOOGHT	H	1	355
VOOGHT	H	1	355
VOOGHT	WC	2	356
VORLEY	B	12	403
VOSE	G	3	245
VOSE	HE	3	245
VOSE	WA	3	245
VOSPER	AG	4	394
VOSPER	CA	4	394
VOSPER	HJ	10	383
VOSS	C	3	246
VOSS	EE	3	246
VOSS	O	12	403
VOSS	R	3	403
VOSS	WW	3	246
VOST	F	1	355

VOST	W	1	355
VOUSDEN	E	4	394
VOWLES	AH	3	246
VOYCE	A	1	355
VOYCE	A	7	415
VOYCE	AJ	1	355
VOYCE	WA	1	355
VOYSEY	CE	2	356
VOYSEY	E	10	383
VOYSEY	HT	2	356
VUNSON	JH	13	434
VURLEY	JR	4	394
VYNE	A	12	228
VYNE	JS	12	424
VYSE	CE	6	419
VYSE	H	6	419

W

WABY	WA	12	228
WACKETT	W	2	356
WADDAMS	CHE	3	246
WADDAMS	JW	3	246
WADDAMS	WA	3	246
WADDELL	JA	11	383
WADDELOW	FT	12	403
WADDICOR	AN	14	327
WADDICOR	G	14	327
WADDICOR	HN	14	327
WADDINGHAM	CW	3	246
WADDINGHAM	G	4	394
WADDINGTON	A	9	198
WADDINGTON	A	9	362
WADDINGTON	C	8	362
WADDINGTON	C	9	198
WADDINGTON	FV	8	362
WADDINGTON	G	9	198
WADDINGTON	G	14	327
WADDINGTON	H	9	198
WADDINGTON	H	9	198
WADDINGTON	J	9	198
WADDINGTON	J	9	198
WADDINGTON	J	14	327
WADDINGTON	JH	11	383
WADDINGTON	JW	11	383
WADDINGTON	M	9	362
WADDINGTON	T	8	362
WADDINGTON	W	8	362
WADDINGTON	W	8	362
WADDINGTON	W	9	362
WADDINGTON	W	9	362
WADDINGTON	W	11	383
WADDLE	R	4	394
WADDUP	AE	6	419
WADDUP	G	2	356

WADE	A	7	415
WADE	A	8	363
WADE	A	9	362
WADE	AE	2	356
WADE	AG	4	394
WADE	AW	2	356
WADE	C	8	363
WADE	C	12	229
WADE	CH	2	356
WADE	EA	6	419
WADE	ER	13	434
WADE	F	8	363
WADE	F	14	327
WADE	G	8	363
WADE	G	9	198
WADE	G	12	404
WADE	GB	11	383
WADE	GH	5	365
WADE	GS	10	383
WADE	H	8	363
WADE	H	8	363
WADE	H	8	363
WADE	H	9	198
WADE	HA	2	356
WADE	HJ	2	357
WADE	J	5	365
WADE	JB	10	237
WADE	JE	13	434
WADE	JG	13	434
WADE	JJ	2	356
WADE	N	9	198
WADE	R	6	419
WADE	R	8	363
WADE	R	8	363
WADE	R	9	362
WADE	S	6	419
WADE	STW	13	434
WADE	T	5	365
WADE	T	8	363
WADE	T	9	362
WADE	T	10	383
WADE	W	8	363
WADE	W	8	363
WADE	W	8	363
WADE	W	10	237
WADE	W	13	434
WADE	WE	7	415
WADE	WJ	1	355
WADE	WJ	13	434
WADESON	E	9	362
WADESON-ECKARD			
	GF	2	357
WADEY	A	13	434
WADEY	FRP	13	434
WADEY	T	13	434
WADEY	WA	13	434

WADGE	WJ	10	383
WADHAM	E	13	434
WADHAM	GH	6	419
WADHAM	JW	13	434
WADHAM	S	13	434
WADKINS	CW	2	357
WADKINS	WF	2	357
WADLEY	FJ	2	357
WADLOW	SH	2	357
WADLOW	W	2	357
WADLOW	WH	13	434
WADMAN	W	2	357
WADMORE	WC	13	434
WADSWORTH	A	9	362
WADSWORTH	AJS	12	229
WADSWORTH	F	9	362
WADSWORTH	G	8	363
WADSWORTH	G	9	362
WADSWORTH	H	6	419
WADSWORTH	H	8	363
WADSWORTH	H	9	198
WADSWORTH	J	8	363
WADSWORTH	J	9	362
WADSWORTH	J	11	383
WADSWORTH	R	12	404
WADSWORTH	RH	12	229
WADSWORTH	TJ	14	327
WADSWORTH	TW	6	419
WADSWORTH	W	8	363
WADSWORTH	W	9	198
WADSWORTH	WE	2	357
WAFFORD	G	2	357
WAGER	AG	2	357
WAGER	DK	7	415
WAGER	EH	2	357
WAGER	FW	2	357
WAGER	HC	4	394
WAGER	JW	8	363
WAGER	S	13	434
WAGER	W	8	363
WAGER	WT	7	415
WAGG	J	6	420
WAGG	J	14	327
WAGGETT	W	11	383
WAGHORN	B	13	434
WAGHORN	CJ	13	435
WAGHORN	E	7	415
WAGHORN	EW	2	357
WAGHORN	GH	13	435
WAGHORN	GJ	13	435
WAGHORN	J	14	327
WAGHORN	JE	13	435
WAGHORN	SW	2	357
WAGHORN	WA	2	357
WAGHORNE	CN	13	435

WAGHORNE	H	2	357	WAINWRIGHT	W	9	198	WAKEFIELD	C	8	365	WALBEY	H	2	358
WAGNER	F	14	327	WAINWRIGHT	WA	14	328	WAKEFIELD	EN	1	355	WALBRIDGE	EW	7	416
WAGNER	J	14	327	WAISTNEDGE	R	8	364	WAKEFIELD	F	12	229	WALBRIDGE	F	4	395
WAGSTAFF	A	8	363	WAITE	A	4	394	WAKEFIELD	FH	6	420	WALBRIDGE	H	7	416
WAGSTAFF	A	12	229	WAITE	A	8	364	WAKEFIELD	G	11	383	WALBROOK	W	4	395
WAGSTAFF	A	12	229	WAITE	AJ	3	403	WAKEFIELD	GF	1	355	WALBY	C	5	366
WAGSTAFF	AE	2	357	WAITE	B	8	364	WAKEFIELD	J	7	416	WALBY	H	5	366
WAGSTAFF	CE	12	229	WAITE	CH	12	229	WAKEFIELD	J	11	383	WALCH	T	9	198
WAGSTAFF	FA	2	357	WAITE	D	12	229	WAKEFIELD	J	11	383	WALCOTT	ES	4	395
WAGSTAFF	FH	12	229	WAITE	E	14	328	WAKEFIELD	J	14	328	WALCOTT	RS	4	395
WAGSTAFF	H	2	357	WAITE	EG	12	404	WAKEFIELD	JA	9	198	WALCROFT	T	4	395
WAGSTAFF	H	12	229	WAITE	F	8	364	WAKEFIELD	JW	7	416	WALCROFT	W	4	395
WAGSTAFF	J	2	357	WAITE	G	6	420	WAKEFIELD	M	4	395	WALDEN	B	2	358
WAGSTAFF	J	2	358	WAITE	GF	1	355	WAKEFIELD	R	9	362	WALDEN	C	13	435
WAGSTAFF	J	12	229	WAITE	H	7	415	WAKEFIELD	W	10	237	WALDEN	EA	12	404
WAGSTAFF	J	13	435	WAITE	H	7	415	WAKEFIELD	W	14	328	WALDEN	FC	3	246
WAGSTAFF	RB	12	229	WAITE	H	8	364	WAKEFORD	EG	10	237	WALDEN	G	1	356
WAGSTAFF	RH	8	363	WAITE	H	14	328	WAKEFORD	FJ	10	383	WALDEN	H	12	404
WAGSTAFF	S	2	358	WAITE	HE	14	328	WAKEFORD	LS	1	355	WALDEN	HG	10	383
WAGSTAFF	T	2	358	WAITE	I	9	362	WAKEFORD	RH	1	355	WALDEN	J	2	358
WAGSTAFF	TP	8	364	WAITE	J	8	364	WAKEFORD	WA	1	356	WALDEN	PJ	1	356
WAGSTAFF	VH	12	229	WAITE	J	8	364	WAKEHAM	JW	1	356	WALDEN	W	2	358
WAGSTAFF	WG	12	229	WAITE	J	9	362	WAKEHAM	WP	2	358	WALDEN	W	12	404
WAGSTAFFE	J	6	420	WAITE	JR	2	358	WAKELEY	CG	5	365	WALDEN	WH	8	365
WAGSTER	J	11	383	WAITE	L	8	364	WAKELIN	E	8	365	WALDEN	WJ	1	356
WAGSTER	W	11	383	WAITE	LJ	4	394	WAKELIN	FG	5	365	WALDER	W	2	358
WAICHENESS	M	9	362	WAITE	PE	1	355	WAKELIN	G	5	365	WALDIE	WH	1	356
WAIGHT	FE	10	237	WAITE	PRR	8	364	WAKELIN	H	5	365	WALDING	A	12	404
WAIN	J	9	198	WAITE	R	12	229	WAKELIN	HJ	2	358	WALDING	AE	12	404
WAIN	J	14	328	WAITE	RJ	2	358	WAKELIN	JWH	2	358	WALDING	CH	7	416
WAIN	JM	9	362	WAITE	T	8	364	WAKELIN	WJ	2	358	WALDING	H	12	404
WAIN	TW	12	229	WAITE	TB	7	415	WAKELING	A	1	356	WALDING	P	12	404
WAIN	W	14	328	WAITE	TG	7	415	WAKELING	A	6	420	WALDING	W	12	404
WAIN	WJ	13	435	WAITE	W	1	355	WAKELING	CH	9	198	WALDMANS	S	14	328
WAINE	H	12	229	WAITE	W	8	364	WAKELING	E	4	395	WALDOCK	AM	12	230
WAINES	E	3	403	WAITE	W	8	365	WAKELING	EH	7	416	WALDOCK	AT	5	366
WAINES	PW	3	403	WAITE	WA	1	355	WAKELING	H	13	435	WALDOCK	EFG	5	366
WAINMAN	W	6	420	WAITE	WJ	1	355	WAKELING	S	1	356	WALDOCK	EJ	2	358
WAINMAN	W	8	364	WAITE	WO	8	365	WAKELING	SW	13	435	WALDOCK	F	1	356
WAINWRIGHT	B	8	364	WAITES	A	8	365	WAKELING	TR	4	395	WALDOCK	P	2	358
WAINWRIGHT	B	8	364	WAITES	G	8	365	WAKELING	W	9	198	WALDOCK	TE	5	366
WAINWRIGHT	C	3	246	WAITMAN	CE	3	246	WAKEMAN	E	5	366	WALDOCK	W	8	365
WAINWRIGHT	D	8	364	WAITMAN	CJ	2	358	WAKEMAN	F	2	358	WALDOCK	WE	12	230
WAINWRIGHT	EA	6	420	WAITSON	C	13	435	WAKEMAN	GH	2	358	WALDON	WT	13	435
WAINWRIGHT	GB	11	383	WAKE	AE	6	420	WAKEMAN	T	7	416	WALDREN	A	2	359
WAINWRIGHT	H	13	435	WAKE	CH	4	394	WAKEMAN	WJA	13	435	WALDRON	AL	2	359
WAINWRIGHT	J	8	364	WAKE	EW	4	395	WAKENELL	A	1	356	WALDRON	EC	6	420
WAINWRIGHT	J	10	237	WAKE	F	5	365	WAKENELL	AV	1	356	WALDRON	F	6	420
WAINWRIGHT	J	14	328	WAKE	H	7	415	WAKERLEY	AP	6	420	WALDRON	H	6	420
WAINWRIGHT	R	11	383	WAKE	HA	10	237	WAKERLY	GW	2	358	WALDRON	T	10	237
WAINWRIGHT	T	14	328	WAKE	SH	4	395	WAKES	F	5	366	WALDRON	WJ	6	420
WAINWRIGHT	W	6	420	WAKE	WH	10	237	WAKES	JA	11	383	WALDUCK	A	12	230
WAINWRIGHT	W	8	364	WAKEFIELD	A	7	415	WAKES	WH	11	383	WALDUCK	AW	12	230
WAINWRIGHT	W	8	364	WAKEFIELD	A	14	328	WALACE	J	14	328	WALDUCK	SA	12	230
WAINWRIGHT	W	8	364	WAKEFIELD	AW	7	416	WALBANK	F	9	362	WALE	AC	2	359

WALE	H	13	435	WALKER	A	12	404	WALKER	CW	2	359	WALKER	FF	1	356
WALE	J	13	435	WALKER	A	13	435	WALKER	CW	10	238	WALKER	FG	5	367
WALE	J	13	435	WALKER	A	14	329	WALKER	CW	13	435	WALKER	FG	5	367
WALE	JH	6	420	WALKER	A	14	329	WALKER	D	8	366	WALKER	FH	2	360
WALE	T	7	416	WALKER	A	14	329	WALKER	D	9	199	WALKER	FJ	10	383
WALE	TH	6	420	WALKER	A	14	329	WALKER	D	9	362	WALKER	FS	8	367
WALE	WJ	12	230	WALKER	AC	12	230	WALKER	D	14	329	WALKER	FW	1	356
WALES	AE	10	237	WALKER	AE	2	359	WALKER	E	1	356	WALKER	FW	8	367
WALES	GB	8	365	WALKER	AE	4	395	WALKER	E	1	356	WALKER	FW	8	367
WALES	GF	7	416	WALKER	AE	6	421	WALKER	E	2	359	WALKER	FW	12	404
WALES	GW	10	237	WALKER	AE	7	416	WALKER	E	2	359	WALKER	G	5	367
WALES	J	12	217	WALKER	AE	8	365	WALKER	E	2	359	WALKER	G	6	421
WALES	J	14	328	WALKER	AF	4	395	WALKER	E	5	366	WALKER	G	8	367
WALES	JW	9	198	WALKER	AG	10	238	WALKER	E	6	421	WALKER	G	8	367
WALFORD	E	14	328	WALKER	AH	7	416	WALKER	E	7	416	WALKER	G	8	367
WALFORD	G	14	328	WALKER	AJ	2	359	WALKER	E	7	416	WALKER	G	8	367
WALFORD	H	2	359	WALKER	AJ	4	395	WALKER	E	8	366	WALKER	G	9	363
WALFORD	S	6	420	WALKER	AJ	5	366	WALKER	E	8	366	WALKER	G	11	384
WALFORD	W	14	328	WALKER	AR	4	395	WALKER	E	8	366	WALKER	G	11	384
WALKDEN	H	14	328	WALKER	AT	2	359	WALKER	E	8	366	WALKER	G	11	384
WALKER	A	2	359	WALKER	AT	11	384	WALKER	E	8	366	WALKER	GA	6	421
WALKER	A	2	359	WALKER	AV	7	416	WALKER	E	8	366	WALKER	GA	12	230
WALKER	A	5	366	WALKER	AW	1	356	WALKER	E	8	366	WALKER	GE	1	356
WALKER	A	5	366	WALKER	AW	2	359	WALKER	E	8	366	WALKER	GF	13	436
WALKER	A	5	366	WALKER	B	2	359	WALKER	E	11	384	WALKER	GF	14	329
WALKER	A	5	366	WALKER	B	3	246	WALKER	E	12	230	WALKER	GH	14	329
WALKER	A	5	366	WALKER	B	5	366	WALKER	E	12	230	WALKER	GM	13	436
WALKER	A	6	420	WALKER	B	6	421	WALKER	E	13	435	WALKER	GR	8	367
WALKER	A	6	420	WALKER	B	6	421	WALKER	EE	1	356	WALKER	GT	7	416
WALKER	A	6	421	WALKER	B	8	366	WALKER	EEG	10	383	WALKER	H	2	360
WALKER	A	8	365	WALKER	B	8	366	WALKER	EF	2	359	WALKER	H	5	367
WALKER	A	8	365	WALKER	B	8	366	WALKER	EH	10	383	WALKER	H	5	367
WALKER	A	8	365	WALKER	B	8	366	WALKER	EJ	2	360	WALKER	H	6	421
WALKER	A	8	365	WALKER	B	8	366	WALKER	EJJ	10	383	WALKER	H	6	421
WALKER	A	8	365	WALKER	B	9	199	WALKER	EW	2	360	WALKER	H	6	421
WALKER	A	8	365	WALKER	BH	13	435	WALKER	EW	7	416	WALKER	H	7	417
WALKER	A	8	365	WALKER	C	2	359	WALKER	EW	9	199	WALKER	H	8	367
WALKER	A	8	365	WALKER	C	5	366	WALKER	F	2	360	WALKER	H	8	367
WALKER	A	9	199	WALKER	C	6	421	WALKER	F	2	360	WALKER	H	8	367
WALKER	A	9	199	WALKER	C	8	366	WALKER	F	2	360	WALKER	H	8	367
WALKER	A	9	199	WALKER	C	8	366	WALKER	F	5	366	WALKER	H	8	367
WALKER	A	9	199	WALKER	C	9	362	WALKER	F	8	367	WALKER	H	8	367
WALKER	A	9	199	WALKER	C	10	383	WALKER	F	9	363	WALKER	H	8	367
WALKER	A	11	383	WALKER	C	11	384	WALKER	F	9	363	WALKER	H	9	199
WALKER	A	11	383	WALKER	C	14	329	WALKER	F	10	383	WALKER	H	9	199
WALKER	A	11	383	WALKER	CA	2	359	WALKER	F	11	384	WALKER	H	9	199
WALKER	A	11	384	WALKER	CA	7	416	WALKER	F	11	384	WALKER	H	9	363
WALKER	A	12	230	WALKER	CA	8	366	WALKER	F	11	384	WALKER	H	9	363
WALKER	A	12	230	WALKER	CE	1	356	WALKER	F	12	230	WALKER	H	12	230
WALKER	A	12	230	WALKER	CF	2	359	WALKER	F	12	404	WALKER	H	12	230
WALKER	A	12	230	WALKER	CH	4	395	WALKER	FA	4	395	WALKER	H	13	436
WALKER	A	12	404	WALKER	CH	8	366	WALKER	FA	5	366	WALKER	H	14	329
WALKER	A	12	404	WALKER	CH	11	384	WALKER	FA	13	436				
				WALKER	CHE	1	356	WALKER	FC	5	366				

WALKER	H	14	329	WALKER	JEW	1	357	WALKER	S	9	363	WALKER	WR	13	436
WALKER	H	14	329	WALKER	JH	1	357	WALKER	SH	13	436	WALKER	WT	10	238
WALKER	HE	2	360	WALKER	JH	13	436	WALKER	SJ	10	383	WALKER	WTH	13	436
WALKER	HE	12	404	WALKER	JH	14	330	WALKER	ST	12	404	WALKERDYNE	H	2	361
WALKER	HH	2	360	WALKER	JJ	6	421	WALKER	T	3	246	WALKEY	JJ	4	396
WALKER	HH	4	395	WALKER	JN	8	368	WALKER	T	5	367	WALKEY	WD	6	422
WALKER	HH	6	421	WALKER	JR	6	421	WALKER	T	8	368	WALKINGTON	T	8	369
WALKER	HJ	12	230	WALKER	JT	8	368	WALKER	T	8	369	WALKLETT	E	11	385
WALKER	HS	5	367	WALKER	JW	1	357	WALKER	T	9	199	WALKLEY	J	4	396
WALKER	HT	6	421	WALKER	JW	1	357	WALKER	T	11	385	WALKLING	GF	13	436
WALKER	HV	14	329	WALKER	JW	2	360	WALKER	T	11	385	WALKLING	P	6	422
WALKER	HW	2	360	WALKER	JW	8	368	WALKER	T	11	385	WALL	A	1	357
WALKER	J	1	357	WALKER	JW	9	199	WALKER	T	14	330	WALL	A	6	422
WALKER	J	1	357	WALKER	JW	14	330	WALKER	TA	11	385	WALL	A	7	417
WALKER	J	2	360	WALKER	JW	14	330	WALKER	TC	1	357	WALL	A	9	199
WALKER	J	2	360	WALKER	L	5	367	WALKER	TE	4	396	WALL	AC	2	361
WALKER	J	4	395	WALKER	LV	2	360	WALKER	TE	8	369	WALL	B	7	417
WALKER	J	5	367	WALKER	M	9	199	WALKER	TM	2	360	WALL	E	6	422
WALKER	J	5	367	WALKER	M	11	384	WALKER	TR	13	436	WALL	E	14	330
WALKER	J	6	421	WALKER	M	14	330	WALKER	V	8	369	WALL	EJ	6	422
WALKER	J	6	421	WALKER	N	14	330	WALKER	W	1	357	WALL	G	7	417
WALKER	J	6	421	WALKER	NTA	5	367	WALKER	W	2	360	WALL	GJ	7	417
WALKER	J	8	368	WALKER	OD	5	367	WALKER	W	3	246	WALL	GS	3	246
WALKER	J	8	368	WALKER	P	5	367	WALKER	W	3	246	WALL	GT	11	385
WALKER	J	8	368	WALKER	P	11	384	WALKER	W	7	417	WALL	H	6	422
WALKER	J	8	368	WALKER	P	11	385	WALKER	W	8	369	WALL	H	9	363
WALKER	J	8	368	WALKER	P	12	230	WALKER	W	8	369	WALL	J	1	357
WALKER	J	8	368	WALKER	P	14	330	WALKER	W	8	369	WALL	J	4	396
WALKER	J	8	368	WALKER	PJ	2	360	WALKER	W	9	199	WALL	J	9	199
WALKER	J	9	363	WALKER	PJ	5	367	WALKER	W	9	363	WALL	J	11	385
WALKER	J	9	363	WALKER	PS	7	417	WALKER	W	11	385	WALL	JC	13	436
WALKER	J	9	363	WALKER	R	2	360	WALKER	W	11	385	WALL	JH	3	246
WALKER	J	11	384	WALKER	R	4	395	WALKER	W	11	385	WALL	JN	11	385
WALKER	J	11	384	WALKER	R	6	421	WALKER	W	11	385	WALL	JW	1	357
WALKER	J	11	384	WALKER	R	8	368	WALKER	W	11	385	WALL	JW	3	403
WALKER	J	11	384	WALKER	R	8	368	WALKER	W	12	404	WALL	L	11	385
WALKER	J	11	384	WALKER	R	9	199	WALKER	W	12	405	WALL	ME	10	238
WALKER	J	11	384	WALKER	R	9	363	WALKER	W	13	436	WALL	P	7	417
WALKER	J	11	384	WALKER	R	11	385	WALKER	W	14	330	WALL	PH	2	361
WALKER	J	12	404	WALKER	R	14	330	WALKER	W	14	330	WALL	S	9	200
WALKER	J	14	329	WALKER	RA	13	436	WALKER	W	14	330	WALL	S	9	200
WALKER	J	14	329	WALKER	RB	12	231	WALKER	WC	6	422	WALL	S	14	330
WALKER	J	14	329	WALKER	RC	2	360	WALKER	WD	7	417	WALL	SG	1	357
WALKER	J	14	329	WALKER	RH	8	368	WALKER	WG	4	396	WALL	T	7	417
WALKER	J	14	329	WALKER	RL	12	404	WALKER	WG	8	369	WALL	T	9	200
WALKER	J	14	329	WALKER	RL	13	436	WALKER	WH	2	361	WALL	T	11	385
WALKER	J	14	330	WALKER	S	1	357	WALKER	WH	8	369	WALL	TS	6	422
WALKER	JA	8	368	WALKER	S	4	395	WALKER	WH	8	369	WALL	W	4	396
WALKER	JC	9	199	WALKER	S	5	367	WALKER	WH	10	383	WALL	W	6	422
WALKER	JD	11	384	WALKER	S	5	367	WALKER	WH	11	385	WALL	W	10	384
WALKER	JE	8	368	WALKER	S	6	422	WALKER	WJ	2	361	WALL	WA	3	247
WALKER	JE	10	383	WALKER	S	7	417	WALKER	WJ	10	238	WALL	WEJ	10	383
WALKER	JE	14	330	WALKER	S	8	368	WALKER	WJ	13	436	WALL	WH	11	385
WALKER				WALKER	S	8	368	WALKER	WJ	13	436	WALLACE	A	8	369
WALKER				WALKER	S	8	368	WALKER	WL	2	361	WALLACE	A	13	436
WALKER				WALKER				WALKER	WR	3	246				

WALLACE	AA	7	417
WALLACE	AJC	4	396
WALLACE	B	8	369
WALLACE	C	2	361
WALLACE	CB	12	231
WALLACE	D	1	357
WALLACE	E	2	361
WALLACE	E	3	403
WALLACE	E	8	369
WALLACE	EA	10	384
WALLACE	FH	12	231
WALLACE	G	9	363
WALLACE	G	13	436
WALLACE	G	13	436
WALLACE	GH	4	396
WALLACE	GH	6	422
WALLACE	GS	1	357
WALLACE	H	6	422
WALLACE	HE	2	361
WALLACE	HE	10	384
WALLACE	HE	13	437
WALLACE	HJ	5	367
WALLACE	HW	6	422
WALLACE	J	2	361
WALLACE	J	6	422
WALLACE	J	10	238
WALLACE	J	11	385
WALLACE	J	13	437
WALLACE	JAP	5	367
WALLACE	JG	7	417
WALLACE	JR	4	396
WALLACE	JW	13	437
WALLACE	R	4	396
WALLACE	S	9	363
WALLACE	W	4	396
WALLACE	W	6	422
WALLACE	W	7	417
WALLACE	W	8	369
WALLACE	WA	2	361
WALLACE	WEF	2	361
WALLACE	WJ	10	238
WALLAKER	E	7	417
WALLBANK	FJ	10	384
WALLBANK	H	8	369
WALLBRIDGE	AW	4	396
WALLBRIDGE	E	4	396
WALLBRIDGE	F	4	396
WALLBRIDGE	GI	10	238
WALLBRIDGE	HJ	4	396
WALLBRIDGE	WB	4	396
WALLBRIDGE	WB	4	396
WALLBRIDGE	WJ	10	238
WALLBRIDGE	WJ	10	238
WALLDER	RT	7	417
WALLEDGE	A	5	367
WALLEN	GH	4	396
WALLEN	TA	4	396
WALLER	A	2	361
WALLER	A	2	361
WALLER	A	5	367
WALLER	A	12	231
WALLER	AE	5	368
WALLER	AF	5	368
WALLER	B	5	368
WALLER	B	7	417
WALLER	CC	3	247
WALLER	CF	7	418
WALLER	CW	2	361
WALLER	E	5	368
WALLER	E	9	363
WALLER	EF	5	368
WALLER	EJ	13	437
WALLER	FE	1	357
WALLER	FE	13	437
WALLER	FG	12	231
WALLER	FHJ	3	247
WALLER	FJ	2	361
WALLER	FJ	2	361
WALLER	FJ	5	368
WALLER	G	5	368
WALLER	H	2	361
WALLER	H	3	247
WALLER	HC	3	403
WALLER	HH	7	418
WALLER	HJ	3	247
WALLER	J	9	200
WALLER	LW	1	357
WALLER	P	5	368
WALLER	RJ	5	368
WALLER	TJ	13	437
WALLER	TWG	10	238
WALLER	W	7	418
WALLER	W	9	200
WALLER	WG	2	362
WALLER	WG	13	437
WALLER	WGH	5	368
WALLER	WJ	3	247
WALLER	WJ	7	418
WALLER	WJ	10	238
WALLER	WL	2	362
WALLEY	J	11	386
WALLEY	N	11	386
WALLEY	WA	14	330
WALLEY	WJ	5	368
WALLIKER	AP	7	418
WALLING	F	2	362
WALLING	R	14	330
WALLINGER	B	12	231
WALLINGER	GA	12	231
WALLINGER	HJ	12	231
WALLINGTON	CH	7	418
WALLINGTON	CR	2	362
WALLINGTON	E	3	247
WALLINGTON	F	3	247
WALLINGTON	G	5	368
WALLINGTON	GE	2	362
WALLINGTON	HJ	2	362
WALLINGTON	J	12	405
WALLINGTON	TE	2	362
WALLINGTON	WE	2	362
WALLINGTON	WJ	2	362
WALLIS	A	2	362
WALLIS	AE	3	247
WALLIS	AE	10	238
WALLIS	AJ	2	362
WALLIS	AP	3	403
WALLIS	C	8	369
WALLIS	CJR	2	362
WALLIS	EA	7	418
WALLIS	ET	2	362
WALLIS	EW	1	357
WALLIS	F	9	200
WALLIS	F	12	405
WALLIS	FG	7	418
WALLIS	G	3	247
WALLIS	G	7	418
WALLIS	G	10	238
WALLIS	G	13	437
WALLIS	GCV	2	362
WALLIS	GT	4	396
WALLIS	GTJ	2	362
WALLIS	H	1	357
WALLIS	H	2	362
WALLIS	H	2	362
WALLIS	H	7	418
WALLIS	H	8	369
WALLIS	H	12	405
WALLIS	HE	2	363
WALLIS	HL	6	422
WALLIS	HW	10	238
WALLIS	J	10	238
WALLIS	J	10	238
WALLIS	J	10	238
WALLIS	JFJ	7	418
WALLIS	JH	8	369
WALLIS	JT	3	247
WALLIS	JW	8	369
WALLIS	L	12	231
WALLIS	RE	1	358
WALLIS	SR	2	363
WALLIS	TG	7	418
WALLIS	TW	7	418
WALLIS	TW	13	437
WALLIS	W	2	363
WALLIS	W	8	369
WALLIS	W	9	363
WALLIS	W	10	238
WALLIS	W	12	405
WALLIS	WD	7	418
WALLIS	WG	7	418
WALLIS	WJD	2	362
WALLIS	WL	2	363
WALLIS	WS	1	358
WALLIS	WSC	2	363
WALLIS	WW	2	363
WALLIS-SMITH	EJ	2	363
WALLIS-SMITH	SM	2	363
WALLIS-SMITH	WH	2	363
WALLS	E	8	370
WALLS	G	2	363
WALLS	G	8	370
WALLS	G	8	370
WALLS	H	6	422
WALLS	J	8	370
WALLS	J	9	363
WALLS	JW	6	422
WALLS	LW	8	370
WALLS	LW	8	370
WALLS	T	8	370
WALLS	T	8	370
WALLS	WJ	6	423
WALLWORK	A	14	330
WALLWORK	H	11	386
WALLWORK	H	14	330
WALLWORK	J	14	330
WALLWORK	JW	14	331
WALLWORK	T	11	386
WALLWORK	WC	14	331
WALMESLEY	FN	10	384
WALMSLEY	A	8	370
WALMSLEY	C	14	331
WALMSLEY	F	7	418
WALMSLEY	FEM	11	386
WALMSLEY	GA	11	386
WALMSLEY	GE	8	370
WALMSLEY	H	8	370
WALMSLEY	HJ	12	405
WALMSLEY	J	8	370
WALMSLEY	JE	14	331
WALMSLEY	RE	9	363
WALMSLEY	T	14	331
WALMSLEY	W	9	363
WALMSLEY	W	14	331
WALMSLEY	WF	14	331
WALPOLE	HF	5	368
WALPOLE	J	12	405
WALPOLE	JG	11	386
WALPOLE	JH	13	437
WALPOLE	JJ	11	386
WALSH	A	3	404

Surname	In.			Surname	In.			Surname	In.			Surname	In.		
WALSH	A	8	370	WALSH	M	14	331	WALTERS	AJ	12	231	WALTERS	WE	6	423
WALSH	A	11	386	WALSH	OJ	9	200	WALTERS	AT	2	264	WALTERS	WG	13	437
WALSH	A	14	331	WALSH	P	9	200	WALTERS	AW	2	264	WALTERS	WH	2	264
WALSH	B	4	397	WALSH	R	4	397	WALTERS	AW	2	264	WALTERS	WH	12	405
WALSH	B	11	386	WALSH	R	11	387	WALTERS	AW	5	368	WALTERS	WJ	3	404
WALSH	B	14	331	WALSH	R	14	331	WALTERS	BJ	13	437	WALTHAM	JH	7	419
WALSH	BW	14	331	WALSH	S	8	371	WALTERS	C	5	368	WALTHEW	F	6	423
WALSH	C	6	423	WALSH	T	2	363	WALTERS	CE	8	371	WALTOCK	GA	11	387
WALSH	C	11	386	WALSH	T	7	419	WALTERS	E	6	423	WALTON	A	8	371
WALSH	D	8	370	WALSH	T	8	371	WALTERS	EJL	6	423	WALTON	A	11	387
WALSH	E	2	363	WALSH	T	8	371	WALTERS	EW	4	397	WALTON	AA	6	423
WALSH	E	14	331	WALSH	T	9	200	WALTERS	F	2	264	WALTON	AE	12	231
WALSH	EH	8	370	WALSH	T	14	331	WALTERS	F	3	404	WALTON	AJ	7	419
WALSH	EL	2	363	WALSH	T	14	331	WALTERS	FE	6	423	WALTON	B	8	371
WALSH	ES	7	418	WALSH	T	14	331	WALTERS	FJ	4	397	WALTON	C	5	368
WALSH	F	11	386	WALSH	T	14	331	WALTERS	FL	1	358	WALTON	C	8	371
WALSH	FC	14	331	WALSH	TH	9	200	WALTERS	FT	7	419	WALTON	C	9	201
WALSH	G	9	200	WALSH	W	4	397	WALTERS	FV	2	363	WALTON	C	9	201
WALSH	H	8	370	WALSH	W	8	371	WALTERS	FW	4	397	WALTON	CH	6	423
WALSH	HJ	11	386	WALSH	W	9	200	WALTERS	FW	6	423	WALTON	CHA	7	419
WALSH	HJ	13	437	WALSH	W	9	200	WALTERS	G	9	201	WALTON	CT	4	397
WALSH	J	1	358	WALSH	W	11	387	WALTERS	G	11	387	WALTON	E	9	201
WALSH	J	7	418	WALSH	W	11	387	WALTERS	GH	6	423	WALTON	E	12	231
WALSH	J	7	419	WALSH	W	11	387	WALTERS	GH	6	423	WALTON	EH	8	371
WALSH	J	8	370	WALSH	W	11	387	WALTERS	GJ	3	247	WALTON	EJ	13	437
WALSH	J	8	370	WALSH	W	11	387	WALTERS	GT	4	397	WALTON	EW	13	437
WALSH	J	8	371	WALSH	W	14	332	WALTERS	H	10	239	WALTON	F	9	201
WALSH	J	8	371	WALSH	WC	10	384	WALTERS	HC	12	231	WALTON	F	9	364
WALSH	J	8	371	WALSH	WG	10	239	WALTERS	HJ	6	423	WALTON	FA	2	264
WALSH	J	8	371	WALSH	WT	7	419	WALTERS	HJ	7	419	WALTON	FC	14	332
WALSH	J	9	200	WALSHAM	W	8	371	WALTERS	HJ	13	437	WALTON	FG	12	231
WALSH	J	9	200	WALSHAW	H	9	200	WALTERS	J	9	364	WALTON	FJ	13	437
WALSH	J	9	200	WALSWORTH	H	9	201	WALTERS	J	10	384	WALTON	G	8	371
WALSH	J	9	363	WALSWORTH	HSI	10	384	WALTERS	JAH	10	384	WALTON	G	8	372
WALSH	J	11	386	WALTER	A	1	358	WALTERS	JE	2	264	WALTON	G	11	387
WALSH	J	11	386	WALTER	AE	2	363	WALTERS	JF	4	397	WALTON	G	14	332
WALSH	J	11	386	WALTER	AG	1	358	WALTERS	JT	3	247	WALTON	G	14	332
WALSH	J	11	386	WALTER	C	12	405	WALTERS	JW	3	247	WALTON	GE	13	438
WALSH	J	11	386	WALTER	J	2	363	WALTERS	LH	10	384	WALTON	GH	5	368
WALSH	J	11	425	WALTER	L	2	363	WALTERS	LP	2	264	WALTON	GT	8	372
WALSH	JD	2	363	WALTER	N	6	423	WALTERS	LW	4	397	WALTON	GW	8	372
WALSH	JE	13	437	WALTER	N	9	201	WALTERS	M	2	264	WALTON	H	6	423
WALSH	JF	11	386	WALTER	P	1	358	WALTERS	PJ	12	231	WALTON	H	8	372
WALSH	JF	11	387	WALTER	T	2	363	WALTERS	S	2	264	WALTON	H	8	372
WALSH	JG	9	200	WALTER	WH	14	332	WALTERS	S	8	371	WALTON	H	9	201
WALSH	JM	4	397	WALTER	WJ	10	239	WALTERS	SJ	13	437	WALTON	H	11	387
WALSH	JO	9	364	WALTERS	A	2	264	WALTERS	SW	3	404	WALTON	H	11	387
WALSH	JR	11	387	WALTERS	A	4	397	WALTERS	TE	3	247	WALTON	H	14	332
WALSH	JT	4	397	WALTERS	A	6	423	WALTERS	TW	2	264	WALTON	HE	2	264
WALSH	JT	11	387	WALTERS	A	10	239	WALTERS	W	4	397	WALTON	HJ	1	358
WALSH	JW	11	387	WALTERS	A	12	231	WALTERS	W	4	397	WALTON	HW	2	264
WALSH	L	11	387	WALTERS	A	13	437	WALTERS	W	6	423	WALTON	J	5	368
WALSH	M	8	371	WALTERS	A	14	332	WALTERS	W	6	423	WALTON	J	8	372
WALSH	M	8	371	WALTERS	AC	6	423	WALTERS	W	14	332	WALTON	J	8	372
WALSH	M	14	331	WALTERS	AJ	10	239	WALTERS	W	14	332	WALTON	J	8	372

WALTON	J	8	372	WANT	AH	3	404	WARD	A	3	247	WARD	CE	8	373				
WALTON	J	8	372	WANT	CJC	3	247	WARD	A	3	247	WARD	CF	6	424				
WALTON	J	9	201	WANT	W	8	372	WARD	A	4	397	WARD	CF	6	424				
WALTON	J	11	387	WAPLES	JW	13	438	WARD	A	4	397	WARD	CH	11	389				
WALTON	J	11	387	WAPLES	OC	12	405	WARD	A	5	369	WARD	CJ	2	365				
WALTON	J	11	388	WARANS	EA	13	438	WARD	A	5	369	WARD	CJ	6	424				
WALTON	J	12	231	WARANS	NL	13	438	WARD	A	6	424	WARD	CJ	10	384				
WALTON	J	14	332	WARBEY	E	13	438	WARD	A	6	424	WARD	CL	4	397				
WALTON	J	14	332	WARBOYS	HW	2	264	WARD	A	6	424	WARD	CS	5	369				
WALTON	JA	11	388	WARBRICK	AS	8	372	WARD	A	6	424	WARD	CW	12	232				
WALTON	JF	11	388	WARBURTON	A	8	372	WARD	A	8	373	WARD	CW	12	232				
WALTON	JH	6	423	WARBURTON	A	11	388	WARD	A	9	201	WARD	DJ	3	404				
WALTON	JJ	14	332	WARBURTON	A	14	332	WARD	A	9	364	WARD	E	1	358				
WALTON	JT	10	384	WARBURTON	AE	8	372	WARD	A	10	239	WARD	E	2	365				
WALTON	JW	5	368	WARBURTON	C	8	373	WARD	A	13	438	WARD	E	3	248				
WALTON	JW	5	369	WARBURTON	C	11	388	WARD	AC	7	419	WARD	E	9	201				
WALTON	JW	6	424	WARBURTON	C	11	388	WARD	AE	2	365	WARD	EA	1	358				
WALTON	L	9	201	WARBURTON	CF	11	388	WARD	AE	3	404	WARD	EJ	1	358				
WALTON	LE	12	231	WARBURTON	E	9	364	WARD	AE	7	419	WARD	EJ	10	239				
WALTON	ME	8	372	WARBURTON	F	8	373	WARD	AE	8	373	WARD	EJ	13	438				
WALTON	MJ	11	388	WARBURTON	F	14	332	WARD	AE	9	201	WARD	ER	2	365				
WALTON	MW	2	264	WARBURTON	FW	10	239	WARD	AE	10	239	WARD	ET	2	365				
WALTON	P	8	372	WARBURTON	G	9	364	WARD	AF	13	438	WARD	EW	10	239				
WALTON	PF	6	424	WARBURTON	G	11	388	WARD	AG	5	369	WARD	F	1	358				
WALTON	PW	2	264	WARBURTON	J	10	239	WARD	AG	13	438	WARD	F	2	365				
WALTON	R	6	424	WARBURTON	JP	11	388	WARD	AH	1	358	WARD	F	2	365				
WALTON	R	11	388	WARBURTON	JW	14	332	WARD	AH	6	424	WARD	F	5	369				
WALTON	R	12	405	WARBURTON	JW	14	332	WARD	AH	12	232	WARD	F	6	424				
WALTON	RW	5	369	WARBURTON	R	11	388	WARD	AHG	3	247	WARD	F	6	424				
WALTON	RW	9	201	WARBURTON	R	11	388	WARD	AJ	6	424	WARD	F	7	419				
WALTON	S	2	264	WARBURTON	R	11	388	WARD	AT	12	405	WARD	F	7	419				
WALTON	T	6	424	WARBURTON	RB	11	388	WARD	AV	10	239	WARD	F	8	373				
WALTON	T	8	372	WARBURTON	S	8	373	WARD	AW	2	365	WARD	F	9	201				
WALTON	T	11	388	WARBURTON	S	14	332	WARD	AW	7	419	WARD	F	9	201				
WALTON	T	14	332	WARBURTON	T	14	333	WARD	AW	11	388	WARD	F	9	364				
WALTON	W	8	372	WARBURTON	TB	8	373	WARD	B	9	201	WARD	F	10	239				
WALTON	W	12	405	WARBURTON	TH	14	333	WARD	B	11	388	WARD	F	10	239				
WALTON	W	12	405	WARBY	A	5	369	WARD	B	12	405	WARD	F	10	384				
WALTON	W	14	332	WARBY	A	5	369	WARD	B	14	333	WARD	FA	1	358				
WALTON	WC	12	231	WARBY	ER	5	369	WARD	BC	8	373	WARD	FC	2	365				
WALTON	WH	7	419	WARBY	F	5	369	WARD	BH	12	405	WARD	FC	5	369				
WALTON	WH	9	201	WARBY	FJ	2	264	WARD	BJ	5	369	WARD	FC	10	384				
WALTON	WJ	1	358	WARBY	FW	2	264	WARD	BJ	12	232	WARD	FG	12	232				
WALTZER	T	12	232	WARBY	H	5	369	WARD	BW	12	232	WARD	FJ	1	359				
WAMLSLEY	JW	9	364	WARBY	J	5	369	WARD	C	7	419	WARD	FJ	2	365				
WANBY	S	9	364	WARBY	RG	5	369	WARD	C	7	419	WARD	FL	3	404				
WAND	W	7	419	WARBY	W	2	365	WARD	C	8	373	WARD	FO	5	370				
WANDSWORTH	GT	5	369	WARBY	W	5	369	WARD	C	8	373	WARD	FT	2	365				
WANLESS	A	13	438	WARD	A	1	358	WARD	C	10	384	WARD	FWL	1	359				
WANLESS	T	10	384	WARD	A	1	358	WARD	C	11	388	WARD	G	3	248				
WANLESS	T	13	438	WARD	A	2	365	WARD	C	12	405	WARD	G	3	248				
WANNEL	GH	7	419	WARD	A	2	365	WARD	C	12	405	WARD	G	5	370				
WANNEL	GHH	7	419	WARD	A	2	365	WARD	C	14	333	WARD	G	6	424				
WANNERTON	A	1	358	WARD	A	2	365	WARD	CB	4	397	WARD	G	7	420				
WANNERTON	M	1	358	WARD	A	2	365	WARD	CC	1	358	WARD	G	7	420				

Name	Init			Name	Init			Name	Init			Name	Init		
WARD	G	8	373	WARD	J	8	373	WARD	M	5	370	WARD	W	4	398
WARD	G	8	373	WARD	J	8	373	WARD	M	6	425	WARD	W	4	398
WARD	G	8	373	WARD	J	8	373	WARD	M	14	333	WARD	W	5	370
WARD	G	10	384	WARD	J	8	374	WARD	MH	10	239	WARD	W	6	425
WARD	G	11	389	WARD	J	8	374	WARD	OW	4	398	WARD	W	6	425
WARD	G	11	389	WARD	J	9	202	WARD	P	8	374	WARD	W	7	420
WARD	G	12	405	WARD	J	9	202	WARD	P	9	202	WARD	W	8	374
WARD	G	13	438	WARD	J	9	364	WARD	P	13	439	WARD	W	8	374
WARD	GA	4	397	WARD	J	9	364	WARD	P	14	333	WARD	W	9	202
WARD	GA	9	202	WARD	J	9	364	WARD	PE	12	406	WARD	W	9	364
WARD	GE	2	365	WARD	J	9	364	WARD	PF	13	439	WARD	W	11	389
WARD	GE	12	406	WARD	J	10	239	WARD	PG	5	370	WARD	W	11	389
WARD	GF	2	365	WARD	J	11	389	WARD	PH	10	240	WARD	W	12	232
WARD	GF	5	369	WARD	J	11	389	WARD	PTS	7	420	WARD	W	12	406
WARD	GF	6	424	WARD	J	11	389	WARD	R	10	240	WARD	W	13	439
WARD	GH	4	397	WARD	J	12	406	WARD	R	11	389	WARD	W	13	439
WARD	GH	11	389	WARD	J	13	438	WARD	R	12	406	WARD	WA	7	420
WARD	GO	12	406	WARD	J	13	438	WARD	R	14	333	WARD	WC	7	420
WARD	GT	6	424	WARD	J	13	438	WARD	RC	4	398	WARD	WD	7	421
WARD	GV	9	364	WARD	J	13	438	WARD	RJ	10	240	WARD	WE	8	374
WARD	GW	9	202	WARD	J	13	439	WARD	RJ	10	240	WARD	WG	5	370
WARD	GW	9	364	WARD	J	14	333	WARD	RJ	12	406	WARD	WG	7	421
WARD	GW	12	232	WARD	J	14	333	WARD	S	5	370	WARD	WG	12	232
WARD	H	3	248	WARD	J	14	333	WARD	S	6	425	WARD	WG	12	406
WARD	H	5	370	WARD	JA	8	374	WARD	S	6	425	WARD	WH	2	366
WARD	H	6	424	WARD	JA	8	374	WARD	S	6	425	WARD	WH	5	370
WARD	H	6	424	WARD	JA	11	389	WARD	S	8	374	WARD	WH	10	240
WARD	H	8	373	WARD	JA	13	439	WARD	S	9	364	WARD	WH	12	232
WARD	H	11	389	WARD	JE	2	366	WARD	S	9	364	WARD	WJ	2	366
WARD	H	11	389	WARD	JE	6	425	WARD	S	12	406	WARD	WJ	2	366
WARD	H	12	406	WARD	JE	7	420	WARD	S	14	333	WARD	WJ	3	248
WARD	H	13	438	WARD	JE	8	374	WARD	SA	10	240	WARD	WN	5	370
WARD	HA	7	420	WARD	JE	11	389	WARD	SE	13	439	WARD	WN	14	333
WARD	HA	10	385	WARD	JE	12	406	WARD	SF	13	439	WARD	WR	10	240
WARD	HC	13	438	WARD	JF	8	374	WARD	SG	6	425	WARD	WR	11	390
WARD	HF	4	398	WARD	JG	2	366	WARD	SH	2	366	WARD	WTS	10	240
WARD	HJ	7	420	WARD	JH	3	404	WARD	SH	10	240	WARD	WW	2	366
WARD	HJ	8	373	WARD	JH	6	425	WARD	SW	5	370	WARD	WW	9	202
WARD	HJ	11	389	WARD	JH	7	420	WARD	T	3	248	WARDALE	JE	10	240
WARD	HR	12	232	WARD	JH	9	202	WARD	T	6	425	WARDALL	A	9	202
WARD	HW	7	420	WARD	JH	10	239	WARD	T	9	202	WARDE	JE	7	421
WARD	HW	7	420	WARD	JJ	6	425	WARD	T	9	364	WARDELL	CL	2	366
WARD	HW	10	239	WARD	JJ	11	389	WARD	T	11	389	WARDELL	EN	2	366
WARD	HW	12	406	WARD	JJ	13	439	WARD	T	11	389	WARDELL	J	4	398
WARD	J	2	365	WARD	JJH	12	232	WARD	T	14	333	WARDELL	JH	4	398
WARD	J	2	366	WARD	JR	4	398	WARD	TA	2	366	WARDELL	TWC	4	398
WARD	J	2	366	WARD	JR	10	239	WARD	TH	12	406	WARDELL	W	14	333
WARD	J	2	366	WARD	JS	7	420	WARD	TJ	3	248	WARDEN	AE	12	406
WARD	J	4	398	WARD	JT	8	374	WARD	TW	6	425	WARDEN	AT	13	439
WARD	J	5	370	WARD	JT	11	389	WARD	TW	7	420	WARDEN	C	1	359
WARD	J	6	424	WARD	JW	1	359	WARD	V	4	398	WARDEN	C	3	404
WARD	J	6	424	WARD	JW	7	420	WARD	V	9	202	WARDEN	CFA	2	366
WARD	J	6	425	WARD	JW	7	420	WARD	V	12	406	WARDEN	JB	12	406
WARD	J	7	420	WARD	L	13	438	WARD	W	2	366	WARDEN	JW	7	421
WARD	J	7	420	WARD	L	14	333	WARD	W	2	366	WARDEN	N	1	359

Surname	Initials	Col	Page
WARDEN	RE	1	359
WARDEN	W	1	359
WARDEN	W	11	390
WARDEN	WH	13	439
WARDER	H	6	425
WARDLE	A	8	374
WARDLE	A	8	374
WARDLE	A	9	365
WARDLE	A	9	365
WARDLE	H	11	390
WARDLE	H	11	390
WARDLE	J	2	366
WARDLE	J	8	374
WARDLE	J	8	374
WARDLE	J	11	390
WARDLE	R	11	390
WARDLE	S	11	390
WARDLE	W	10	385
WARDLE	W	11	390
WARDLE	WH	14	333
WARDLEY	T	11	390
WARDMAN	F	9	365
WARDMAN	J	8	374
WARDMAN	N	8	374
WARDMAN	S	9	202
WARDMAN	W	9	202
WARDROP	AA	4	398
WARE	A	4	398
WARE	EF	7	421
WARE	FW	7	421
WARE	HB	3	248
WARE	HR	2	366
WARE	J	7	421
WARE	J	10	240
WARE	JS	7	421
WARE	L	13	439
WARE	MW	2	366
WARE	PJ	2	366
WARE	SH	3	248
WARE	T	7	421
WARE	TW	6	425
WARE	W	7	421
WARE	W	10	240
WAREHAM	AC	13	439
WAREHAM	AH	2	367
WAREHAM	EE	7	421
WAREHAM	FAG	4	398
WAREHAM	FAG	7	421
WAREHAM	GB	6	425
WAREHAM	GE	6	425
WAREHAM	GF	10	240
WAREHAM	H	2	367
WAREHAM	HT	10	385
WAREHAM	J	11	390
WAREHAM	JW	10	385
WAREHAM	L	7	421
WAREHAM	LW	4	398
WAREHAM	R	4	398
WAREHAM	R	10	385
WAREHAM	S	7	421
WAREHAM	SG	4	398
WAREHAM	W	4	398
WAREING	A	12	406
WAREING	W	8	375
WARFIELO	A	2	367
WARFIELO	F	2	367
WARHAM	JT	14	333
WARHURST	A	11	390
WARHURST	A	11	390
WARING	AW	1	359
WARING	ECT	7	421
WARING	FG	1	359
WARING	J	8	375
WARING	J	11	390
WARING	J	14	333
WARING	RJ	6	425
WARING	WJ	1	359
WARK	A	11	390
WARK	H	11	390
WARLAND	WG	4	398
WARLEY	JA	9	365
WARLOW	AE	10	240
WARLOW	G	10	240
WARMAN	C	2	367
WARMAN	H	2	367
WARMAN	H	13	439
WARMAN	J	1	359
WARMAN	W	2	367
WARMAN	W	5	370
WARMINGTON	AF	10	240
WARMINGTON	E	7	421
WARMINGTON	J	7	421
WARMINGTON	T	13	439
WARNE	A	2	367
WARNE	AE	3	248
WARNE	E	4	399
WARNE	EG	10	240
WARNE	EJ	4	399
WARNE	ES	7	421
WARNE	F	2	367
WARNE	FM	2	367
WARNE	GH	1	359
WARNE	GH	10	240
WARNE	GW	2	367
WARNE	H	2	367
WARNE	J	1	359
WARNE	W	4	399
WARNE	WF	4	399
WARNE	WJ	10	241
WARNEFORD	W	1	359
WARNELL	EJ	1	359
WARNER	A	4	399
WARNER	A	8	375
WARNER	A	12	406
WARNER	AA	2	367
WARNER	AE	13	439
WARNER	AJ	5	370
WARNER	AJ	10	241
WARNER	ARW	7	421
WARNER	AW	5	370
WARNER	C	2	367
WARNER	C	5	370
WARNER	C	5	370
WARNER	C	5	370
WARNER	CH	7	421
WARNER	CJ	2	367
WARNER	D	12	406
WARNER	E	4	399
WARNER	E	5	370
WARNER	E	6	425
WARNER	E	12	407
WARNER	EA	5	370
WARNER	EH	12	407
WARNER	F	3	248
WARNER	F	5	370
WARNER	F	7	421
WARNER	F	12	407
WARNER	FB	1	359
WARNER	FH	13	439
WARNER	G	13	439
WARNER	GA	12	407
WARNER	GH	6	425
WARNER	GH	14	333
WARNER	GW	2	367
WARNER	H	6	426
WARNER	H	7	421
WARNER	H	8	375
WARNER	H	11	390
WARNER	HJ	5	371
WARNER	HJ	13	439
WARNER	IH	13	440
WARNER	J	5	371
WARNER	J	7	422
WARNER	J	11	390
WARNER	JE	13	440
WARNER	JG	2	367
WARNER	JT	6	426
WARNER	JT	11	391
WARNER	JW	13	440
WARNER	K	2	367
WARNER	L	2	367
WARNER	L	12	407
WARNER	MA	12	407
WARNER	R	5	371
WARNER	S	2	367
WARNER	T	6	426
WARNER	TF	12	407
WARNER	TG	1	359
WARNER	TH	12	232
WARNER	W	8	375
WARNER	W	12	232
WARNER	WD	13	440
WARNER	WE	13	440
WARNER	WH	4	399
WARNER	WH	13	440
WARNER	WJ	3	404
WARNER	WJ	13	440
WARNES	CEA	13	440
WARNES	G	4	399
WARNES	H	12	407
WARNES	JC	3	248
WARNES	JH	10	385
WARNES	W	12	407
WARNES	W	12	407
WARNOCK	BW	7	422
WARR	AS	8	375
WARR	CH	6	426
WARR	F	8	375
WARR	GW	7	422
WARR	H	1	359
WARR	H	1	359
WARR	HA	6	426
WARR	HJ	6	426
WARR	RJ	1	359
WARR	RJ	2	368
WARR	RJ	12	232
WARR	W	7	422
WARR	WE	8	375
WARR	WT	12	232
WARRAN	TS	13	440
WARREN	A	1	360
WARREN	A	5	371
WARREN	A	5	371
WARREN	A	11	391
WARREN	A	12	232
WARREN	A	13	440
WARREN	A	14	334
WARREN	AA	7	422
WARREN	AE	10	241
WARREN	AEV	12	407
WARREN	AH	6	426
WARREN	AJ	2	368
WARREN	AJ	4	399
WARREN	AJ	7	422
WARREN	AL	10	385
WARREN	AN	13	440
WARREN	AR	5	371
WARREN	AT	10	241
WARREN	AW	12	407
WARREN	B	5	371

WARREN	C	1	360	WARREN	J	5	372	WARREN	WJ	1	360	WARWICK	SG	12	408
WARREN	C	5	371	WARREN	J	7	422	WARREN	WJ	1	360	WARWICK	THR	12	408
WARREN	CA	12	232	WARREN	J	9	365	WARREN	WJ	4	399	WARWICK	TW	1	360
WARREN	CR	1	360	WARREN	J	11	391	WARREN	WJ	5	372	WARWICK	W	4	399
WARREN	CV	5	371	WARREN	J	13	440	WARREN	WJ	10	385	WARWICK	W	5	372
WARREN	CW	10	385	WARREN	J	13	440	WARREN	WP	12	408	WARWICK	W	8	375
WARREN	E	11	391	WARREN	J	14	334	WARRENDER	E	11	391	WARWICK	WE	1	361
WARREN	E	12	232	WARREN	JE	10	385	WARRENER	E	9	365	WARWICK	WG	6	426
WARREN	E	12	407	WARREN	JF	2	368	WARRENER	GA	9	365	WARWICK	WG	12	408
WARREN	EA	6	426	WARREN	JF	13	440	WARRENER	T	9	365	WARWICK	WH	6	426
WARREN	EA	10	385	WARREN	JH	12	233	WARRENER	W	9	365	WARWICKER	W	7	422
WARREN	EC	2	368	WARREN	JH	12	233	WARRICK	GC	5	372	WARWICKER	WJ	13	441
WARREN	EC	13	440	WARREN	JH	12	233	WARRICK	HT	1	360	WARWICKS	WA	12	408
WARREN	ED	13	440	WARREN	JJ	3	248	WARRILLOW	J	6	426	WASH	AV	5	372
WARREN	EG	5	371	WARREN	JJ	5	372	WARRINER	E	11	391	WASH	S	5	372
WARREN	EKT	10	385	WARREN	JJ	7	422	WARRINER	JW	11	391	WASHBROOK	A	3	248
WARREN	ER	1	360	WARREN	JW	3	404	WARRINER	T	14	334	WASHBROOK	A	8	375
WARREN	F	1	360	WARREN	JW	6	426	WARRINGTON	A	10	241	WASHBROOK	C	6	426
WARREN	F	2	368	WARREN	JW	11	391	WARRINGTON	A	12	233	WASHBROOK	GI	8	375
WARREN	F	3	248	WARREN	LJ	2	368	WARRINGTON	A	14	334	WASHBURN	A	8	375
WARREN	F	5	371	WARREN	P	5	372	WARRINGTON	E	6	426	WASHER	AT	7	422
WARREN	F	5	371	WARREN	P	13	440	WARRINGTON	E	6	426	WASHER	WA	7	422
WARREN	F	5	371	WARREN	R	2	368	WARRINGTON	FC	9	365	WASHINGTON	A	5	372
WARREN	F	10	385	WARREN	R	2	369	WARRINGTON	GW	11	391	WASHINGTON	AC	4	399
WARREN	F	13	440	WARREN	RC	7	422	WARRINGTON	J	8	375	WASHINGTON	CG	1	361
WARREN	F	14	334	WARREN	RG	2	369	WARRINGTON	J	11	391	WASHINGTON	F	8	376
WARREN	FE	2	368	WARREN	RJ	3	248	WARRINGTON	W	11	391	WASHINGTON	G	14	334
WARREN	FE	7	422	WARREN	RJ	5	372	WARRIOR	AE	12	408	WASHINGTON	J	11	391
WARREN	FF	5	371	WARREN	S	5	372	WARRIOR	TW	8	375	WASHINGTON	JH	14	334
WARREN	FF	5	371	WARREN	S	5	372	WARRY	H	7	422	WASHINGTON	SJ	2	369
WARREN	FH	2	368	WARREN	S	12	233	WARTERS	SA	1	360	WASHINGTON	WH	2	369
WARREN	FJ	2	368	WARREN	SC	7	422	WARWICK	AH	1	360	WASLEY	FR	1	361
WARREN	FJ	3	248	WARREN	SR	12	407	WARWICK	E	12	408	WASLEY	WG	1	361
WARREN	FJ	4	399	WARREN	SW	4	399	WARWICK	EC	7	422	WASLEY	WG	2	369
WARREN	FS	2	368	WARREN	T	12	407	WARWICK	EC	12	408	WASMUTH	WJ	2	369
WARREN	G	2	368	WARREN	TD	13	440	WARWICK	EP	12	408	WASPE	W	8	376
WARREN	G	2	368	WARREN	TJ	12	407	WARWICK	EV	12	408	WASS	J	1	361
WARREN	G	5	371	WARREN	TW	12	407	WARWICK	F	13	441	WASS	J	14	334
WARREN	G	11	391	WARREN	TW	12	407	WARWICK	FJ	1	360	WASS	R	2	369
WARREN	GC	2	368	WARREN	W	1	360	WARWICK	G	8	375	WASSELL	CD	5	372
WARREN	GH	4	399	WARREN	W	2	369	WARWICK	G	12	233	WASSELL	EE	4	399
WARREN	GH	12	233	WARREN	W	4	399	WARWICK	GA	1	360	WASSELL	FC	4	400
WARREN	GJ	5	371	WARREN	W	4	399	WARWICK	H	8	375	WASSELL	JW	6	426
WARREN	GL	1	360	WARREN	W	4	399	WARWICK	HG	1	360	WASSELL	SA	5	372
WARREN	GV	1	360	WARREN	W	10	241	WARWICK	J	1	360	WASTELL	C	3	404
WARREN	GW	12	233	WARREN	W	12	408	WARWICK	J	8	375	WATERFALL	EV	11	391
WARREN	H	2	368	WARREN	W	13	440	WARWICK	JA	10	241	WATERFALL	G	11	391
WARREN	H	5	371	WARREN	W	13	440	WARWICK	JC	2	369	WATERFALL	RU	11	391
WARREN	H	5	372	WARREN	WA	4	399	WARWICK	JC	12	408	WATERFALL	S	11	391
WARREN	H	12	407	WARREN	WC	5	372	WARWICK	JE	8	375	WATERFALL	TJ	11	392
WARREN	HA	2	368	WARREN	WC	13	440	WARWICK	JW	2	369	WATERFALL	WB	11	392
WARREN	HG	2	368	WARREN	WE	7	422	WARWICK	JW	12	408	WATERFIELD	AG	6	426
WARREN	HG	3	248	WARREN	WG	10	385	WARWICK	L	12	408	WATERFIELD	C	8	376
WARREN	HS	5	372	WARREN	WH	2	369	WARWICK	M	13	441	WATERFIELD	C	8	376
WARREN	J	2	368	WARREN	WH	11	391	WARWICK	S	14	334	WATERFIELD	HG	1	361

Surname	Init	C	Pg	Surname	Init	C	Pg	Surname	Init	C	Pg	Surname	Init	C	Pg
WATERFIELD	T	8	376	WATERS	AJ	2	369	WATERWORTH	GH	8	377	WATKINS	TH	2	370
WATERFIELD	TW	12	408	WATERS	C	13	441	WATERWORTH	J	8	377	WATKINS	TJ	10	241
WATERHOUSE	A	1	361	WATERS	CB	4	400	WATERWORTH	J	14	334	WATKINS	W	1	361
WATERHOUSE	A	11	392	WATERS	CH	2	369	WATERWORTH	L	9	365	WATKINS	WA	4	400
WATERHOUSE	AD	6	426	WATERS	CT	10	241	WATERWORTH	P	9	365	WATKINS	WF	7	423
WATERHOUSE	E	8	376	WATERS	EJ	14	334	WATES	J	7	423	WATKINS	WH	6	427
WATERHOUSE	F	9	202	WATERS	F	2	369	WATFORD	F	2	370	WATKINSON	AE	13	441
WATERHOUSE	G	9	202	WATERS	F	5	372	WATHEN	RH	13	441	WATKINSON	CJ	14	334
WATERHOUSE	G	9	202	WATERS	F	5	373	WATKIN	CH	8	377	WATKINSON	H	14	335
WATERHOUSE	GW	4	400	WATERS	FR	4	400	WATKIN	CW	12	408	WATKINSON	JA	8	377
WATERHOUSE	H	8	376	WATERS	FW	5	373	WATKIN	EA	12	408	WATKINSON	P	10	241
WATERHOUSE	H	9	365	WATERS	G	2	369	WATKIN	FN	14	334	WATKINSON	T	8	377
WATERHOUSE	J	8	376	WATERS	G	6	427	WATKIN	J	8	377	WATKINSON	V	9	366
WATERHOUSE	J	11	392	WATERS	G	10	385	WATKIN	L	8	377	WATKINSON	WB	13	441
WATERHOUSE	JH	4	400	WATERS	G	11	392	WATKIN	WA	14	334	WATKINSON	WE	8	377
WATERHOUSE	JT	9	202	WATERS	GE	2	369	WATKINS	A	8	377	WATKINSON	WT	8	377
WATERHOUSE	JW	11	392	WATERS	GF	11	392	WATKINS	A	14	334	WATLER	AJ	13	441
WATERHOUSE	L	9	365	WATERS	GH	6	427	WATKINS	AE	6	427	WATLER	RW	13	441
WATERHOUSE	RE	8	376	WATERS	GR	2	369	WATKINS	AE	7	423	WATLEY	F	8	377
WATERHOUSE	T	8	376	WATERS	H	2	370	WATKINS	AEC	1	361	WATLING	AW	2	370
WATERHOUSE	T	11	392	WATERS	H	4	400	WATKINS	AF	2	370	WATLING	AW	2	370
WATERHOUSE	TI	6	426	WATERS	H	11	392	WATKINS	AF	6	427	WATLING	EA	7	423
WATERHOUSE	W	6	426	WATERS	H	14	334	WATKINS	AF	6	427	WATLING	F	1	362
WATERHOUSE	W	8	376	WATERS	HW	2	370	WATKINS	AH	2	370	WATLING	GJ	1	362
WATERHOUSE	W	8	376	WATERS	J	7	422	WATKINS	AL	7	423	WATLING	GW	9	203
WATERHOUSE	W	9	365	WATERS	J	8	376	WATKINS	B	7	423	WATLING	H	2	370
WATERHOUSE	W	11	392	WATERS	J	8	376	WATKINS	C	7	423	WATLING	H	4	400
WATERHOUSE	W	11	392	WATERS	J	9	365	WATKINS	CF	2	370	WATLING	H	8	377
WATERLAND	CW	8	376	WATERS	J	9	365	WATKINS	E	1	361	WATLING	RWC	13	441
WATERLAND	H	8	376	WATERS	JC	5	373	WATKINS	E	6	427	WATLING	WJ	1	362
WATERLOO	AH	10	385	WATERS	JC	14	334	WATKINS	E	6	427	WATMORE	A	7	423
WATERMAN	A	4	400	WATERS	JF	5	373	WATKINS	E	8	377	WATMORE	AW	7	423
WATERMAN	A	7	422	WATERS	M	6	427	WATKINS	E	13	441	WATMOUGH	F	8	377
WATERMAN	A	13	441	WATERS	S	5	373	WATKINS	EC	9	203	WATMOUGH	RW	9	366
WATERMAN	CJ	4	400	WATERS	SF	13	441	WATKINS	EG	6	427	WATMOUGH	S	9	203
WATERMAN	CW	10	241	WATERS	T	13	441	WATKINS	EG	7	423	WATMUFF	E	9	366
WATERMAN	E	2	369	WATERS	TH	2	370	WATKINS	EJ	7	423	WATSON	A	1	362
WATERMAN	F	4	400	WATERS	W	7	423	WATKINS	FW	3	249	WATSON	A	1	362
WATERMAN	G	4	400	WATERS	W	7	423	WATKINS	G	1	361	WATSON	A	2	370
WATERMAN	H	1	361	WATERS	W	8	376	WATKINS	G	2	370	WATSON	A	2	370
WATERMAN	HC	4	400	WATERS	W	14	334	WATKINS	GT	3	249	WATSON	A	3	249
WATERMAN	J	2	369	WATERS	WC	7	423	WATKINS	GWB	2	370	WATSON	A	5	373
WATERMAN	JS	3	404	WATERS	WC	13	441	WATKINS	H	6	427	WATSON	A	5	373
WATERMAN	L	10	385	WATERS	WJ	5	373	WATKINS	H	8	377	WATSON	A	6	427
WATERMAN	P	2	369	WATERSON	J	11	392	WATKINS	J	2	370	WATSON	A	8	377
WATERMAN	WF	4	400	WATERSON	T	8	376	WATKINS	J	7	423	WATSON	A	8	377
WATERRS	C	1	361	WATERSON	TS	11	392	WATKINS	JE	12	408	WATSON	A	9	203
WATERRS	DJ	1	361	WATERTON	B	8	377	WATKINS	JW	5	373	WATSON	A	9	366
WATERRS	EW	1	361	WATERTON	HVG	3	248	WATKINS	N	7	423	WATSON	A	12	233
WATERRS	WJ	1	361	WATERTON	J	3	249	WATKINS	S	1	361	WATSON	A	12	233
WATERS	A	7	422	WATERTON	JT	2	370	WATKINS	SC	1	361	WATSON	A	12	408
WATERS	A	8	376	WATERTON	LH	13	441	WATKINS	SH	13	441	WATSON	A	13	441
WATERS	A	10	385	WATERWORTH	F	4	400	WATKINS	SJ	1	361	WATSON	A	13	441
WATERS	A	13	441	WATERWORTH	G	9	202	WATKINS	T	3	249	WATSON	A	14	335
WATERS	AG	5	372	WATERWORTH	G	9	365	WATKINS	TE	6	427	WATSON	AER	2	370

WATSON	AG	1	362	WATSON	G	8	378	WATSON	JA	8	378	WATSON	T	8	379
WATSON	AG	13	442	WATSON	G	9	203	WATSON	JC	2	371	WATSON	T	8	379
WATSON	AG	13	442	WATSON	G	13	442	WATSON	JC	7	424	WATSON	T	9	203
WATSON	AJ	2	370	WATSON	G	14	335	WATSON	JE	6	428	WATSON	T	9	203
WATSON	AV	13	442	WATSON	GE	4	400	WATSON	JE	9	203	WATSON	T	10	386
WATSON	B	13	442	WATSON	GH	7	424	WATSON	JH	3	249	WATSON	T	12	233
WATSON	BC	10	241	WATSON	GH	12	233	WATSON	JH	7	424	WATSON	T	13	442
WATSON	BC	10	241	WATSON	GH	12	409	WATSON	JH	10	241	WATSON	TC	8	379
WATSON	BN	13	442	WATSON	GJ	6	427	WATSON	JH	14	335	WATSON	TF	3	249
WATSON	C	1	362	WATSON	GM	13	442	WATSON	JJ	1	362	WATSON	TH	2	371
WATSON	C	5	373	WATSON	GW	1	362	WATSON	JJ	8	378	WATSON	TM	12	409
WATSON	C	5	373	WATSON	GW	12	233	WATSON	JJ	9	203	WATSON	TO	7	424
WATSON	C	8	377	WATSON	H	1	362	WATSON	JL	7	424	WATSON	TP	2	371
WATSON	C	13	442	WATSON	H	1	362	WATSON	JR	6	428	WATSON	TW	10	241
WATSON	CD	7	423	WATSON	H	3	249	WATSON	JR	8	379	WATSON	V	13	443
WATSON	CG	13	442	WATSON	H	4	401	WATSON	JR	9	366	WATSON	W	2	371
WATSON	CJ	6	427	WATSON	H	5	373	WATSON	JS	8	379	WATSON	W	2	371
WATSON	D	4	400	WATSON	H	6	427	WATSON	JT	13	443	WATSON	W	6	428
WATSON	D	4	400	WATSON	H	6	427	WATSON	JW	2	371	WATSON	W	6	428
WATSON	D	13	442	WATSON	H	7	424	WATSON	JW	11	393	WATSON	W	6	428
WATSON	E	2	370	WATSON	H	8	378	WATSON	JW	12	409	WATSON	W	7	424
WATSON	E	2	371	WATSON	H	8	378	WATSON	L	5	373	WATSON	W	8	379
WATSON	E	4	400	WATSON	H	8	378	WATSON	L	8	379	WATSON	W	8	379
WATSON	E	7	423	WATSON	H	8	378	WATSON	L	9	366	WATSON	W	8	379
WATSON	E	8	378	WATSON	H	9	366	WATSON	LJ	14	335	WATSON	W	8	379
WATSON	E	8	378	WATSON	H	9	366	WATSON	M	1	362	WATSON	W	8	379
WATSON	E	13	442	WATSON	H	9	366	WATSON	MC	3	404	WATSON	W	8	379
WATSON	E	14	335	WATSON	H	13	442	WATSON	NHJ	4	401	WATSON	W	9	203
WATSON	EA	7	423	WATSON	H	13	442	WATSON	P	2	371	WATSON	W	12	233
WATSON	EC	5	373	WATSON	H	14	335	WATSON	P	4	401	WATSON	W	12	409
WATSON	EE	11	392	WATSON	HA	9	203	WATSON	P	12	233	WATSON	WA	7	424
WATSON	EG	13	442	WATSON	HF	3	249	WATSON	PL	12	233	WATSON	WA	8	379
WATSON	EH	10	386	WATSON	HF	5	373	WATSON	PT	2	371	WATSON	WA	13	443
WATSON	EJ	3	249	WATSON	HJ	5	373	WATSON	R	5	373	WATSON	WC	5	374
WATSON	EJ	13	442	WATSON	HJ	6	427	WATSON	R	5	373	WATSON	WE	7	425
WATSON	EP	3	404	WATSON	HJ	7	424	WATSON	R	9	366	WATSON	WE	10	241
WATSON	F	2	371	WATSON	HL	13	442	WATSON	R	9	366	WATSON	WE	12	233
WATSON	F	2	371	WATSON	HP	4	401	WATSON	R	11	392	WATSON	WF	12	233
WATSON	F	4	400	WATSON	HR	2	371	WATSON	R	13	443	WATSON	WG	5	374
WATSON	F	5	373	WATSON	HR	7	424	WATSON	RC	10	241	WATSON	WG	10	241
WATSON	F	8	378	WATSON	HW	7	424	WATSON	RH	6	428	WATSON	WH	2	371
WATSON	F	8	378	WATSON	J	2	371	WATSON	RM	7	424	WATSON	WH	5	374
WATSON	F	9	203	WATSON	J	2	371	WATSON	RW	7	424	WATSON	WH	10	386
WATSON	F	13	442	WATSON	J	3	404	WATSON	RW	11	392	WATSON	WH	12	233
WATSON	FC	1	362	WATSON	J	7	424	WATSON	S	6	428	WATSON	WJ	1	362
WATSON	FG	13	442	WATSON	J	7	424	WATSON	S	6	428	WATSON	WJ	10	241
WATSON	FH	13	442	WATSON	J	8	378	WATSON	S	7	424	WATSON	WJ	10	386
WATSON	FM	9	203	WATSON	J	8	378	WATSON	S	8	379	WATSON	WN	7	424
WATSON	G	2	371	WATSON	J	8	378	WATSON	S	9	203	WATSON	WT	5	374
WATSON	G	7	424	WATSON	J	8	378	WATSON	SA	2	371	WATT	PO	8	379
WATSON	G	7	424	WATSON	J	8	378	WATSON	SC	4	401	WATT	TG	7	425
WATSON	G	8	378	WATSON	J	11	392	WATSON	SH	5	374	WATT	W	12	409
WATSON	G	8	378	WATSON	J	11	392	WATSON	SM	14	335	WATTERS	GW	1	362
WATSON	G	8	378	WATSON	J	14	335	WATSON	ST	2	371	WATTERSON	CH	6	428
WATSON	G	8	378	WATSON	J	14	335	WATSON	T	3	249	WATTERSON	J	14	335
WATSON	G	8	378									WATTHY	H	6	428

WATTON	B	14	335	WATTS	FW	12	234	WATTS	RF	4	402	WAYMAN	C	12	234
WATTON	J	6	428	WATTS	G	2	372	WATTS	RF	9	366	WAYMAN	CE	4	402
WATTON	JH	6	428	WATTS	G	5	374	WATTS	S	3	249	WAYMAN	GW	1	363
WATTON	L	4	401	WATTS	G	6	428	WATTS	S	4	402	WAYMAN	ST	13	443
WATTON	RET	4	401	WATTS	G	11	393	WATTS	SCT	12	409	WAYMAN	WS	1	363
WATTRUS	TJF	6	428	WATTS	G	12	234	WATTS	SG	3	249	WAYWELL	WH	11	393
WATTS	A	4	401	WATTS	G	12	234	WATTS	SH	13	443	WEAIT	CRJ	2	372
WATTS	A	4	401	WATTS	G	12	409	WATTS	SJ	13	443	WEAIT	RH	1	363
WATTS	A	5	374	WATTS	GA	1	362	WATTS	T	10	242	WEAKE	GT	6	428
WATTS	A	7	425	WATTS	GH	4	401	WATTS	T	11	393	WEAKE	HC	6	428
WATTS	A	8	379	WATTS	GHJ	4	401	WATTS	V	7	425	WEAKLAND	AE	6	428
WATTS	A	12	233	WATTS	GW	5	374	WATTS	W	2	372	WEAL	H	13	443
WATTS	A	13	443	WATTS	H	2	372	WATTS	W	7	425	WEAL	JE	13	443
WATTS	AE	4	401	WATTS	H	7	425	WATTS	W	11	393	WEAL	WG	2	373
WATTS	AE	5	374	WATTS	H	10	242	WATTS	W	12	234	WEALE	GH	3	249
WATTS	AF	7	425	WATTS	H	12	234	WATTS	W	14	335	WEALE	HJO	6	428
WATTS	AG	12	409	WATTS	HC	4	401	WATTS	WC	1	362	WEALE	J	6	429
WATTS	AH	1	362	WATTS	HF	1	362	WATTS	WC	5	374	WEALLANS	RJN	10	386
WATTS	AH	2	372	WATTS	HF	4	401	WATTS	WE	3	249	WEALTHY	HP	10	386
WATTS	AJ	2	372	WATTS	HG	4	402	WATTS	WG	3	404	WEAR	C	13	443
WATTS	AJ	5	374	WATTS	HJ	7	425	WATTS	WGH	13	443	WEAR	F	3	249
WATTS	AJ	12	233	WATTS	HJ	12	234	WATTS	WH	12	234	WEAR	J	13	444
WATTS	AJ	13	443	WATTS	HO	4	401	WATTS	WJ	5	374	WEARE	LO	10	242
WATTS	AO	4	401	WATTS	HS	4	402	WATTS	WJ	7	425	WEARING	AE	11	393
WATTS	AS	7	425	WATTS	HS	12	409	WATTS	WJ	7	425	WEARN	AE	10	386
WATTS	AV	1	362	WATTS	HT	2	372	WATTS	WJ	7	425	WEARN	CH	12	409
WATTS	AV	4	401	WATTS	J	1	363	WATTS	WL	13	443	WEARN	FL	10	386
WATTS	AV	13	443	WATTS	J	2	372	WATTS	WW	5	374	WEARN	J	10	242
WATTS	AW	7	425	WATTS	J	3	249	WATTS	WY	2	372	WEARN	JGT	10	386
WATTS	B	1	362	WATTS	J	3	249	WAUD	C	8	379	WEARN	LM	10	386
WATTS	B	2	372	WATTS	J	5	374	WAUDBY	T	8	379	WEARN	RM	10	386
WATTS	C	4	401	WATTS	J	11	393	WAUGH	GEJ	7	425	WEARN	TH	10	242
WATTS	C	13	443	WATTS	J	11	393	WAUGH	GW	4	402	WEARN	TH	10	386
WATTS	CC	13	443	WATTS	J	12	234	WAUGH	RF	7	425	WEARN	WH	10	386
WATTS	CJP	12	234	WATTS	J	12	234	WAUGH	W	9	366	WEARON	J	13	444
WATTS	CW	5	374	WATTS	J	12	234	WAUGH	W	14	335	WEASER	W	12	234
WATTS	D	11	393	WATTS	JA	10	242	WAWMAN	T	13	443	WEATE	A	6	429
WATTS	E	2	372	WATTS	JC	2	372	WAY	AV	13	443	WEATHERALL	AJ	12	409
WATTS	E	10	242	WATTS	JE	4	402	WAY	C	1	363	WEATHERALL	F	14	335
WATTS	EA	4	401	WATTS	JE	5	374	WAY	C	1	363	WEATHERALL	SGW	13	444
WATTS	EA	5	374	WATTS	JH	12	234	WAY	CJ	4	402	WEATHERHEAD	FA	4	402
WATTS	EA	10	386	WATTS	JR	8	379	WAY	E	1	363	WEATHERHEAD	LM	2	373
WATTS	EL	7	425	WATTS	JW	2	372	WAY	E	10	242	WEATHERILL	A	8	380
WATTS	EW	3	249	WATTS	L	5	374	WAY	F	2	372	WEATHERILL	A	13	444
WATTS	F	1	363	WATTS	L	12	234	WAY	FC	1	363	WEATHERILL	H	9	366
WATTS	F	4	401	WATTS	LA	12	409	WAY	JBF	2	372	WEATHERILL	J	13	444
WATTS	F	12	234	WATTS	LF	12	409	WAY	JE	3	249	WEATHERILL	JA	8	380
WATTS	F	12	234	WATTS	LL	4	402	WAY	JG	10	242	WEATHERILL	P	13	444
WATTS	F	13	443	WATTS	MW	8	379	WAY	W	2	372	WEATHERILT	J	11	393
WATTS	FA	12	409	WATTS	P	4	402	WAY	WJ	10	242	WEATHERILT	JS	14	335
WATTS	FC	12	409	WATTS	P	10	242	WAY	WR	7	425	WEATHERILT	T	11	393
WATTS	FH	13	443	WATTS	PG	12	234	WAYBOURNE	JH	4	402	WEATHERLEY	B	12	234
WATTS	FHT	4	401	WATTS	PW	1	363	WAYGOOD	MFR	10	242	WEATHERLEY	W	1	363
WATTS	FT	2	372	WATTS	R	2	372	WAYLEN	FR	10	242	WEATHERLEY	W	7	425
WATTS	FW	2	372	WATTS	RD	4	402	WAYMAN	C	5	374	WEATHERLY	J	5	374

WEATHERS	JM	3	250
WEATHERSTONE	E	1	363
WEAVER	AH	4	402
WEAVER	AT	6	429
WEAVER	AW	13	444
WEAVER	CA	1	363
WEAVER	CH	14	335
WEAVER	CT	10	242
WEAVER	CWJ	7	425
WEAVER	E	13	444
WEAVER	EC	7	426
WEAVER	EJ	13	444
WEAVER	F	3	404
WEAVER	F	6	429
WEAVER	F	6	429
WEAVER	FE	4	402
WEAVER	FW	7	426
WEAVER	G	1	363
WEAVER	G	4	402
WEAVER	G	4	402
WEAVER	G	7	426
WEAVER	GC	11	393
WEAVER	GT	4	402
WEAVER	H	11	393
WEAVER	HW	1	363
WEAVER	J	4	402
WEAVER	J	6	429
WEAVER	J	13	444
WEAVER	J	14	335
WEAVER	JC	2	373
WEAVER	JH	1	363
WEAVER	JT	14	335
WEAVER	M	6	429
WEAVER	M	7	426
WEAVER	RS	4	403
WEAVER	S	14	336
WEAVER	SB	8	380
WEAVER	T	6	429
WEAVER	W	6	429
WEAVER	W	6	429
WEAVER	W	7	426
WEAVER	W	11	393
WEAVER	WA	6	429
WEAVER	WB	6	429
WEAVER	WC	6	429
WEAVER	WF	1	363
WEAVER	WG	4	402
WEAVER	WH	5	375
WEAVER	WR	13	444
WEAVIL	E	4	403
WEAVING	H	6	429
WEAVING	WA	10	386
WEAVING	WE	6	429
WEBB	A	1	363
WEBB	A	2	373
WEBB	A	2	373
WEBB	A	5	375
WEBB	A	6	429
WEBB	AAJ	4	403
WEBB	AE	1	363
WEBB	AE	4	403
WEBB	AE	4	403
WEBB	AE	7	426
WEBB	AE	7	426
WEBB	AE	7	426
WEBB	AF	7	426
WEBB	AFJ	3	250
WEBB	AG	7	426
WEBB	AG	10	242
WEBB	AG	11	393
WEBB	AH	6	429
WEBB	AH	12	409
WEBB	AJ	4	403
WEBB	AL	10	242
WEBB	AP	10	386
WEBB	AR	1	363
WEBB	AS	2	373
WEBB	AS	3	250
WEBB	AS	4	403
WEBB	ASG	7	426
WEBB	AV	2	373
WEBB	AW	2	373
WEBB	AW	5	375
WEBB	AW	12	235
WEBB	B	7	426
WEBB	BJ	5	375
WEBB	C	1	363
WEBB	C	4	403
WEBB	C	8	380
WEBB	C	11	393
WEBB	CA	3	250
WEBB	CE	7	426
WEBB	CE	12	409
WEBB	CH	2	373
WEBB	CH	3	405
WEBB	CHJ	4	403
WEBB	CT	10	386
WEBB	CV	4	403
WEBB	CW	13	444
WEBB	D	2	373
WEBB	D	4	403
WEBB	D	8	380
WEBB	DA	7	426
WEBB	DJ	1	364
WEBB	DJ	4	403
WEBB	DVM	4	403
WEBB	E	2	373
WEBB	E	5	375
WEBB	E	7	426
WEBB	E	10	242
WEBB	EE	3	250
WEBB	EE	7	426
WEBB	EG	5	375
WEBB	EG	10	242
WEBB	EJ	12	235
WEBB	F	3	405
WEBB	F	4	403
WEBB	F	4	403
WEBB	F	4	403
WEBB	F	5	375
WEBB	F	5	375
WEBB	F	10	242
WEBB	F	10	243
WEBB	F	11	394
WEBB	F	12	409
WEBB	F	14	336
WEBB	FA	1	364
WEBB	FA	12	235
WEBB	FH	4	403
WEBB	FH	6	429
WEBB	FJ	5	375
WEBB	FJ	10	243
WEBB	FJ	12	409
WEBB	FM	5	375
WEBB	FRG	7	426
WEBB	FW	5	375
WEBB	FW	5	375
WEBB	FW	6	429
WEBB	G	2	373
WEBB	G	3	250
WEBB	G	3	250
WEBB	G	4	403
WEBB	G	12	235
WEBB	G	12	235
WEBB	G	12	235
WEBB	G	12	410
WEBB	G	13	444
WEBB	G	13	444
WEBB	GE	10	243
WEBB	GH	7	426
WEBB	GR	2	373
WEBB	GS	4	403
WEBB	GT	4	403
WEBB	GT	12	410
WEBB	GW	1	364
WEBB	GW	1	364
WEBB	GW	5	375
WEBB	GW	12	410
WEBB	H	2	373
WEBB	H	3	250
WEBB	H	3	405
WEBB	H	4	404
WEBB	H	4	404
WEBB	H	5	375
WEBB	H	5	375
WEBB	H	6	429
WEBB	H	6	430
WEBB	H	13	444
WEBB	HA	7	427
WEBB	HA	10	243
WEBB	HC	2	373
WEBB	HC	3	250
WEBB	HE	2	373
WEBB	HE	4	404
WEBB	HE	12	410
WEBB	HH	14	336
WEBB	HJ	2	373
WEBB	HJ	11	393
WEBB	HJ	13	444
WEBB	HN	4	404
WEBB	HR	6	430
WEBB	HW	4	404
WEBB	HW	14	336
WEBB	I	1	364
WEBB	J	3	405
WEBB	J	4	404
WEBB	J	5	375
WEBB	J	5	375
WEBB	J	5	375
WEBB	J	6	430
WEBB	J	7	426
WEBB	J	7	427
WEBB	J	10	243
WEBB	J	11	393
WEBB	J	13	444
WEBB	JA	2	374
WEBB	JB	11	394
WEBB	JE	1	364
WEBB	JG	2	373
WEBB	JH	2	374
WEBB	JH	2	374
WEBB	JH	2	374
WEBB	JJ	3	250
WEBB	JLS	13	444
WEBB	JM	5	375
WEBB	JP	10	387
WEBB	JR	7	427
WEBB	JR	12	410
WEBB	JSH	4	404
WEBB	JT	5	375
WEBB	JT	5	376
WEBB	JW	5	376
WEBB	L	10	243
WEBB	LE	3	405
WEBB	LF	1	364
WEBB	LHC	13	444
WEBB	LJ	7	427
WEBB	LW	5	376
WEBB	MAB	10	386
WEBB	ME	3	250

WEBB	OA	13	445	WEBB	WG	13	445	WEBSTER	D	9	203	WEBSTER	JR	9	204
WEBB	P	14	336	WEBB	WH	5	376	WEBSTER	D	12	410	WEBSTER	L	6	430
WEBB	PE	2	374	WEBB	WH	7	427	WEBSTER	DCG	3	250	WEBSTER	L	8	381
WEBB	PT	10	243	WEBB	WH	12	410	WEBSTER	E	8	380	WEBSTER	L	9	366
WEBB	R	5	376	WEBB	WH	14	336	WEBSTER	E	9	203	WEBSTER	N	8	381
WEBB	R	12	235	WEBB	WHG	4	404	WEBSTER	E	9	203	WEBSTER	P	2	375
WEBB	R	12	410	WEBB	WHJ	13	445	WEBSTER	E	9	203	WEBSTER	R	9	366
WEBB	R	14	336	WEBB	WJ	1	364	WEBSTER	E	14	336	WEBSTER	RHC	2	375
WEBB	RA	7	427	WEBB	WJ	2	374	WEBSTER	ET	7	428	WEBSTER	S	7	428
WEBB	RF	4	404	WEBB	WJ	3	405	WEBSTER	F	2	374	WEBSTER	S	8	381
WEBB	RF	5	376	WEBB	WJ	4	404	WEBSTER	F	8	380	WEBSTER	SF	8	381
WEBB	RJ	7	427	WEBB	WJ	12	235	WEBSTER	F	9	366	WEBSTER	T	7	428
WEBB	RJ	7	427	WEBB	WT	4	404	WEBSTER	F	11	394	WEBSTER	V	11	394
WEBB	RR	6	430	WEBB	WWJ	4	404	WEBSTER	F	11	394	WEBSTER	W	4	405
WEBB	S	1	364	WEBBER	AE	6	430	WEBSTER	FH	6	430	WEBSTER	W	5	376
WEBB	S	4	404	WEBBER	BBF	14	336	WEBSTER	FW	1	364	WEBSTER	W	6	430
WEBB	S	5	376	WEBBER	C	4	404	WEBSTER	FW	2	374	WEBSTER	W	7	428
WEBB	SC	4	404	WEBBER	CS	6	430	WEBSTER	G	6	430	WEBSTER	W	7	428
WEBB	SJ	5	376	WEBBER	F	13	445	WEBSTER	G	6	430	WEBSTER	W	7	428
WEBB	T	7	427	WEBBER	GE	6	430	WEBSTER	G	8	380	WEBSTER	W	8	381
WEBB	T	10	386	WEBBER	H	4	404	WEBSTER	G	9	203	WEBSTER	W	8	381
WEBB	T	12	410	WEBBER	HC	10	243	WEBSTER	G	12	410	WEBSTER	W	8	381
WEBB	T	12	410	WEBBER	HF	2	374	WEBSTER	G	13	445	WEBSTER	W	8	381
WEBB	TA	3	405	WEBBER	JA	6	430	WEBSTER	GE	8	380	WEBSTER	W	12	410
WEBB	TG	7	427	WEBBER	JL	12	235	WEBSTER	GG	7	428	WEBSTER	W	13	445
WEBB	TH	2	374	WEBBER	L	2	374	WEBSTER	GJ	13	445	WEBSTER	W	14	336
WEBB	TH	7	427	WEBBER	L	7	428	WEBSTER	GT	13	445	WEBSTER	W	14	336
WEBB	TJ	7	427	WEBBER	LT	6	430	WEBSTER	H	3	250	WEBSTER	WD	13	445
WEBB	TO	6	430	WEBBER	R	4	404	WEBSTER	H	3	250	WEBSTER	WE	9	204
WEBB	TW	3	250	WEBBER	R	7	427	WEBSTER	H	4	405	WEDDERBURN	JD	2	375
WEBB	TW	7	427	WEBBER	S	2	374	WEBSTER	H	8	380	WEDGBURY	SA	6	430
WEBB	V	1	364	WEBBER	SC	4	404	WEBSTER	H	8	380	WEDGE	CH	10	243
WEBB	W	1	364	WEBBER	SG	4	405	WEBSTER	H	8	380	WEDGE	FWH	4	405
WEBB	W	2	374	WEBBER	ST	1	364	WEBSTER	H	9	203	WEDGE	G	4	405
WEBB	W	2	374	WEBBER	W	4	405	WEBSTER	H	14	336	WEDGE	G	6	431
WEBB	W	3	250	WEBBER	W	4	405	WEBSTER	HE	13	445	WEDGERFIELD	AE	5	376
WEBB	W	4	404	WEBBER	W	7	427	WEBSTER	HG	8	380	WEDGERFIELD	E	5	376
WEBB	W	5	376	WEBBER	WF	6	430	WEBSTER	HJ	14	336	WEDLOCK	J	2	375
WEBB	W	6	430	WEBBER	WJ	4	405	WEBSTER	HW	1	364	WEED	WT	12	235
WEBB	W	7	427	WEBBER	WJ	12	235	WEBSTER	HW	1	364	WEEDEN	J	11	394
WEBB	W	12	235	WEBBER	WT	4	405	WEBSTER	J	7	428	WEEDEN	SF	5	376
WEBB	W	12	410	WEBBER	WW	10	387	WEBSTER	J	7	428	WEEDON	AS	7	428
WEBB	W	13	445	WEBSPER	WCJ	13	445	WEBSTER	J	8	380	WEEDON	F	2	375
WEBB	W	14	336	WEBSTER	A	8	380	WEBSTER	J	8	380	WEEDON	F	5	376
WEBB	WA	4	404	WEBSTER	A	8	380	WEBSTER	J	8	380	WEEDON	F	5	376
WEBB	WA	5	376	WEBSTER	A	11	394	WEBSTER	J	9	204	WEEDON	H	7	428
WEBB	WA	6	430	WEBSTER	AC	6	430	WEBSTER	J	11	394	WEEDON	H	7	428
WEBB	WAG	12	235	WEBSTER	AF	3	250	WEBSTER	J	14	336	WEEDON	H	9	204
WEBB	WAJ	7	427	WEBSTER	AT	2	374	WEBSTER	J	14	336	WEEDON	J	2	375
WEBB	WC	7	427	WEBSTER	C	2	374	WEBSTER	JA	2	375	WEEDON	J	4	405
WEBB	WEL	4	404	WEBSTER	C	7	428	WEBSTER	JA	9	204	WEEDON	JE	1	364
WEBB	WG	2	374	WEBSTER	C	8	380	WEBSTER	JC	5	376	WEEDON	RJ	7	428
WEBB	WG	2	374	WEBSTER	C	12	410	WEBSTER	JD	13	445	WEEDON	W	3	405
WEBB	WG	5	376	WEBSTER	CF	8	380	WEBSTER	JF	2	374	WEEDON	WE	2	375
WEBB	WG	12	410	WEBSTER	CW	7	428	WEBSTER	JR	9	204	WEEDS	B	3	405

WEEDY	WT	4	405	WEIGHT	W	7	429	WELCH	H	4	406	WELDON	S	14	337
WEEKES	EE	2	375	WEIGHTS	H	13	445	WELCH	H	5	377	WELDON	WT	2	376
WEEKES	GF	5	376	WEILDING	T	11	394	WELCH	H	5	377	WELFARE	H	4	406
WEEKES	WR	10	243	WEINBERG	H	14	336	WELCH	H	6	431	WELFORD	A	9	204
WEEKLEY	AA	2	375	WEINBERG	N	14	337	WELCH	H	7	429	WELFORD	AE	2	376
WEEKLY	AR	2	375	WEINBERG	S	14	337	WELCH	H	9	204	WELFORD	AW	2	376
WEEKLY	C	2	375	WEINER	I	14	337	WELCH	HG	10	243	WELFORD	C	13	446
WEEKLY	JW	7	428	WEINERT	FC	2	376	WELCH	HK	14	337	WELFORD	OH	12	410
WEEKS	A	6	431	WEINGARD	J	14	337	WELCH	HL	6	431	WELFORD	PJ	2	376
WEEKS	AE	7	428	WEINGARD	N	14	337	WELCH	HW	10	243	WELFORD	W	9	367
WEEKS	AE	13	445	WEIR	AV	1	364	WELCH	HWJ	3	405	WELHAM	H	8	381
WEEKS	AF	10	387	WEIR	AV	2	376	WELCH	ID	4	406	WELHAM	T	1	365
WEEKS	AJ	6	431	WEIR	J	11	394	WELCH	J	2	376	WELHAM	W	12	235
WEEKS	AV	4	405	WEIR	JT	6	431	WELCH	J	2	376	WELLACK	G	9	367
WEEKS	B	4	405	WEIR	L	6	431	WELCH	J	5	377	WELLARD	GG	1	365
WEEKS	B	4	405	WEIR	R	11	394	WELCH	J	7	429	WELLARD	GH	3	405
WEEKS	CA	4	405	WEIR	W	14	337	WELCH	J	10	243	WELLARD	WA	10	244
WEEKS	CW	7	428	WEIR	WT	1	364	WELCH	JA	7	429	WELLER	AF	1	365
WEEKS	E	4	405	WEIR	WT	1	364	WELCH	JS	2	376	WELLER	AH	2	376
WEEKS	F	2	375	WEISS	AE	7	429	WELCH	JT	10	243	WELLER	CG	2	376
WEEKS	F	4	405	WELBORN	A	8	381	WELCH	JW	7	429	WELLER	D	13	446
WEEKS	F	10	243	WELBORN	A	9	366	WELCH	L	4	406	WELLER	EHW	13	446
WEEKS	FE	2	375	WELBORN	G	8	381	WELCH	L	5	377	WELLER	ER	1	365
WEEKS	G	10	243	WELBORN	H	8	381	WELCH	M	2	376	WELLER	EWH	13	446
WEEKS	GE	2	375	WELBOURN	R	8	381	WELCH	M	13	445	WELLER	F	6	431
WEEKS	GH	3	405	WELBOURNE	JB	8	381	WELCH	MJW	4	406	WELLER	FP	2	377
WEEKS	GH	10	387	WELCH	A	5	377	WELCH	R	1	365	WELLER	GH	7	429
WEEKS	H	1	364	WELCH	AJ	2	376	WELCH	R	10	243	WELLER	GL	13	446
WEEKS	H	4	405	WELCH	AV	2	376	WELCH	R	11	394	WELLER	HE	4	406
WEEKS	J	4	405	WELCH	AW	2	376	WELCH	R	11	394	WELLER	J	10	244
WEEKS	JH	6	431	WELCH	AW	5	377	WELCH	RH	9	367	WELLER	JA	7	429
WEEKS	LM	3	250	WELCH	AW	5	377	WELCH	RH	10	244	WELLER	K	7	429
WEEKS	P	4	405	WELCH	B	12	235	WELCH	S	1	365	WELLER	PR	7	429
WEEKS	R	4	406	WELCH	C	11	394	WELCH	S	8	381	WELLER	T	3	251
WEEKS	RC	5	376	WELCH	CA	6	431	WELCH	S	11	394	WELLER	TF	7	429
WEEKS	S	4	406	WELCH	CF	4	406	WELCH	SJ	10	244	WELLER	W	2	377
WEEKS	TJ	10	387	WELCH	CH	7	429	WELCH	T	6	431	WELLER	W	4	406
WEEKS	TR	2	375	WELCH	CH	10	387	WELCH	TE	1	365	WELLER	W	7	429
WEEKS	W	2	375	WELCH	CM	7	429	WELCH	TG	10	244	WELLER	W	13	446
WEEKS	W	14	336	WELCH	DE	10	243	WELCH	TP	13	445	WELLER	WL	2	377
WEEKS	WH	2	375	WELCH	E	10	243	WELCH	W	3	251	WELLER	WT	12	235
WEEKS	WH	4	406	WELCH	EC	4	406	WELCH	W	5	377	WELLESBY	A	8	381
WEEKS	WH	4	406	WELCH	EG	10	243	WELCH	W	5	377	WELLHAM	EE	2	377
WEEKS	WJ	3	251	WELCH	F	6	431	WELCH	W	7	429	WELLHAM	G	9	367
WEEKS	WJ	4	406	WELCH	F	8	381	WELCH	W	11	394	WELLIN	G	10	387
WEEKS	WR	2	376	WELCH	F	10	387	WELCH	W	12	410	WELLING	AT	5	377
WEETCH	AV	10	243	WELCH	FC	2	376	WELCH	W	13	446	WELLING	BA	5	377
WEETCH	FJ	4	406	WELCH	FE	2	376	WELCH	W	14	337	WELLING	BJ	7	429
WEETMAN	WW	11	394	WELCH	FH	4	406	WELCH	WG	4	406	WELLING	FA	5	377
WEETON	A	8	381	WELCH	FJ	2	376	WELCH	WG	10	244	WELLINGS	A	11	395
WEETON	W	8	381	WELCH	G	1	364	WELCH	WG	13	446	WELLINGS	AS	13	446
WEIGH	R	11	394	WELCH	G	5	377	WELCH	WG	13	446	WELLINGS	J	11	395
WEIGHELL	B	13	445	WELCH	G	10	387	WELCH	WH	7	429	WELLINGS	R	6	431
WEIGHELL	JA	9	366	WELCH	G	11	394	WELDON	GH	6	431	WELLINGS	R	11	395
WEIGHT	CA	2	376	WELCH	GH	1	365	WELDON	JW	6	431	WELLINGS	T	11	395

WELLINGS	W	11	395	WELLS	ESC	2	377	WELLS	JH	7	430	WELSH	D	13	447				
WELLINGTON	TH	2	377	WELLS	F	5	378	WELLS	JH	7	430	WELSH	ES	13	447				
WELLINGTON	W	2	377	WELLS	F	8	382	WELLS	JH	8	382	WELSH	EW	5	378				
WELLMAN	A	10	387	WELLS	F	10	244	WELLS	JT	13	447	WELSH	FW	6	432				
WELLMAN	C	10	387	WELLS	F	12	410	WELLS	JW	8	382	WELSH	H	2	378				
WELLMAN	J	4	406	WELLS	FA	7	430	WELLS	M	12	236	WELSH	H	8	382				
WELLMAN	JP	4	406	WELLS	FC	8	382	WELLS	M	13	447	WELSH	J	9	204				
WELLOCK	CS	11	395	WELLS	FG	6	431	WELLS	P	5	378	WELSH	J	9	204				
WELLOCK	H	11	395	WELLS	FS	6	432	WELLS	P	11	395	WELSH	J	10	244				
WELLOCK	J	11	395	WELLS	FW	2	377	WELLS	PH	5	378	WELSH	J	11	395				
WELLS	A	1	365	WELLS	FW	2	377	WELLS	PJ	2	378	WELSH	J	11	395				
WELLS	A	3	251	WELLS	G	1	365	WELLS	R	8	382	WELSH	J	13	447				
WELLS	A	5	377	WELLS	G	1	365	WELLS	R	8	382	WELSH	M	2	378				
WELLS	A	5	377	WELLS	G	5	378	WELLS	R	9	367	WELSH	MA	7	430				
WELLS	A	9	367	WELLS	G	12	410	WELLS	R	11	395	WELSH	P	9	204				
WELLS	A	13	446	WELLS	GA	5	378	WELLS	RJ	4	407	WELSH	P	11	395				
WELLS	A	13	446	WELLS	GB	10	244	WELLS	RR	5	378	WELSH	P	14	337				
WELLS	AAH	4	406	WELLS	GE	4	407	WELLS	S	3	405	WELSH	RH	2	378				
WELLS	AC	4	406	WELLS	GE	10	387	WELLS	S	10	244	WELSH	SW	8	382				
WELLS	AE	2	377	WELLS	GE	11	395	WELLS	T	8	382	WELSH	T	9	204				
WELLS	AE	4	407	WELLS	GF	8	382	WELLS	T	11	395	WELSH	T	11	395				
WELLS	AE	6	431	WELLS	GH	3	405	WELLS	TA	7	430	WELSH	T	11	395				
WELLS	AE	13	446	WELLS	GH	13	446	WELLS	TAW	2	378	WELSH	W	2	378				
WELLS	AG	4	407	WELLS	GK	4	407	WELLS	TB	9	367	WELSH	W	11	396				
WELLS	AGH	4	407	WELLS	GR	13	446	WELLS	TG	6	432	WELSH	W	11	396				
WELLS	AH	5	377	WELLS	GWG	6	432	WELLS	W	7	430	WELSH	WH	8	382				
WELLS	AT	1	365	WELLS	H	2	377	WELLS	W	9	204	WELSHMAN	ET	4	408				
WELLS	AT	1	365	WELLS	H	3	251	WELLS	W	10	244	WELSMAN	HA	13	447				
WELLS	AT	13	446	WELLS	H	7	429	WELLS	W	13	447	WELSTEAD	AE	13	447				
WELLS	AV	2	377	WELLS	H	9	367	WELLS	W	13	447	WELSTEAD	WW	6	432				
WELLS	AW	2	377	WELLS	H	11	395	WELLS	W	14	337	WELTCH	JA	10	244				
WELLS	B	5	377	WELLS	H	13	446	WELLS	WA	7	430	WELTMAN	W	8	382				
WELLS	C	2	377	WELLS	H	13	446	WELLS	WA	10	244	WELTON	AP	2	378				
WELLS	C	3	405	WELLS	H	13	447	WELLS	WA	10	387	WELTON	G	2	378				
WELLS	C	5	377	WELLS	HA	2	377	WELLS	WC	5	378	WELTON	TP	12	410				
WELLS	C	6	431	WELLS	HE	4	407	WELLS	WC	5	378	WEM	SA	2	378				
WELLS	C	7	429	WELLS	HF	5	378	WELLS	WC	6	432	WENBORN	CF	2	378				
WELLS	C	8	381	WELLS	HJ	5	378	WELLS	WCF	7	430	WENBOURNE	SG	13	447				
WELLS	C	9	392	WELLS	HJD	2	377	WELLS	WG	5	378	WENDEL	ET	5	378				
WELLS	C	12	235	WELLS	HM	12	235	WELLS	WH	4	407	WENDEL	LH	5	378				
WELLS	C	13	446	WELLS	HR	6	432	WELLS	WJ	2	378	WENDES	C	4	408				
WELLS	C	13	446	WELLS	HT	6	432	WELLS	WJ	4	407	WENFORD	G	11	396				
WELLS	CA	5	378	WELLS	HV	12	235	WELLS	WR	4	407	WENHAM	FC	7	430				
WELLS	CA	12	235	WELLS	HW	1	365	WELLS	WS	10	244	WENHAM	H	13	447				
WELLS	CE	2	377	WELLS	J	2	378	WELLS	WT	4	407	WENLOCK	J	1	365				
WELLS	CH	1	365	WELLS	J	2	378	WELLS	WW	4	407	WENMAN	AJ	12	236				
WELLS	CT	4	407	WELLS	J	3	251	WELLSPRING	G	4	407	WENN	BW	7	430				
WELLS	D	10	387	WELLS	J	7	430	WELLSTEAD	A	4	407	WENN	JJ	7	430				
WELLS	DC	3	251	WELLS	J	7	430	WELLSTEAD	AF	4	407	WENN	TJ	7	430				
WELLS	DE	2	377	WELLS	J	8	382	WELLSTEAD	F	4	407	WENSLEY	DK	10	244				
WELLS	E	2	377	WELLS	J	13	447	WELLSTEAD	RJ	4	408	WENSLEY	HT	10	244				
WELLS	E	4	407	WELLS	JAT	2	377	WELSBY	G	14	337	WENT	W	2	378				
WELLS	E	4	407	WELLS	JE	13	447	WELSBY	JE	11	395	WENTWORTH	E	11	396				
WELLS	E	5	378	WELLS	JF	4	407	WELSH	AE	5	378	WENTWORTH	HG	13	447				
WELLS	EG	6	431	WELLS	JG	13	447	WELSH	C	8	382	WENTZELL	H	7	430				

WERENDEL	WA	2	378
WERNER	APH	3	251
WERNER	M	14	337
WERNER	P	9	367
WERNHAM	A	3	251
WERNHAM	C	2	378
WERNHAM	R	2	378
WERNHAM	SEC	2	378
WERNHAM	T	13	447
WERNICK	E	14	337
WERRELL	AS	1	365
WERRELL	AV	1	365
WERREN	ER	7	430
WERRILL	J	14	338
WESBROOM	E	2	378
WESBURY	AE	6	432
WESCOTT	F	7	430
WESLEY	AE	12	411
WESLEY	G	12	236
WESLEY	G	12	236
WESLEY	GH	5	378
WESLEY	GT	12	411
WESLEY	H	5	378
WESLEY	J	6	432
WESLEY	J	12	236
WESLEY	W	5	378
WESLEY	W	12	236
WESLEY	WG	12	236
WESSON	A	5	378
WESSON	WH	7	430
WEST	A	1	365
WEST	A	1	366
WEST	A	2	379
WEST	A	4	408
WEST	A	5	378
WEST	A	12	236
WEST	AE	1	366
WEST	AE	1	366
WEST	AEL	10	387
WEST	AJ	12	236
WEST	AT	2	379
WEST	ATW	2	379
WEST	AW	12	236
WEST	B	2	379
WEST	BJ	2	379
WEST	C	2	379
WEST	C	2	379
WEST	C	11	396
WEST	CE	3	251
WEST	CF	3	405
WEST	CH	8	382
WEST	DR	4	408
WEST	E	2	379
WEST	E	4	408
WEST	E	4	408
WEST	EA	3	251
WEST	EC	3	251
WEST	ED	10	387
WEST	EH	2	379
WEST	EL	2	379
WEST	EM	2	379
WEST	EW	4	408
WEST	F	1	366
WEST	F	12	236
WEST	FA	2	379
WEST	FD	10	244
WEST	FD	10	244
WEST	FE	2	379
WEST	FG	2	379
WEST	FJ	3	251
WEST	FJ	3	251
WEST	FJ	5	379
WEST	FJ	6	432
WEST	FR	5	379
WEST	FW	4	408
WEST	G	8	382
WEST	G	12	236
WEST	GA	1	366
WEST	GC	2	379
WEST	GD	5	379
WEST	GE	13	447
WEST	GH	12	236
WEST	GST	7	431
WEST	GV	4	408
WEST	GWA	10	387
WEST	H	1	366
WEST	H	2	379
WEST	H	3	251
WEST	H	7	431
WEST	H	10	388
WEST	H	10	388
WEST	H	12	236
WEST	H	13	448
WEST	HC	12	236
WEST	HG	4	408
WEST	HJ	2	379
WEST	HJ	5	379
WEST	HW	3	251
WEST	HW	5	379
WEST	J	2	379
WEST	J	2	379
WEST	J	2	380
WEST	J	2	380
WEST	J	4	408
WEST	J	7	431
WEST	J	8	382
WEST	J	11	396
WEST	J	11	396
WEST	J	12	236
WEST	J	12	236
WEST	JB	12	236
WEST	JC	5	379
WEST	JF	7	431
WEST	JFG	13	448
WEST	JG	7	431
WEST	JG	10	245
WEST	JH	2	380
WEST	JH	2	380
WEST	JH	6	432
WEST	JH	12	411
WEST	JP	10	387
WEST	JR	10	388
WEST	JW	1	366
WEST	JW	12	411
WEST	JWF	3	405
WEST	LB	4	408
WEST	LP	6	432
WEST	LR	3	251
WEST	M	8	382
WEST	N	9	204
WEST	NAJ	10	388
WEST	P	1	366
WEST	P	12	236
WEST	P	12	236
WEST	P	12	237
WEST	PH	7	431
WEST	PJ	12	237
WEST	R	2	379
WEST	R	7	431
WEST	R	12	237
WEST	R	12	237
WEST	RA	4	408
WEST	RF	2	380
WEST	RG	1	366
WEST	RG	6	432
WEST	RJ	4	408
WEST	SA	12	237
WEST	SC	2	380
WEST	SF	4	408
WEST	SJ	4	408
WEST	SM	10	388
WEST	SRJ	2	380
WEST	TE	3	251
WEST	TG	12	411
WEST	TH	13	448
WEST	TW	2	380
WEST	TW	7	431
WEST	TW	10	244
WEST	W	3	251
WEST	W	4	408
WEST	W	5	379
WEST	W	5	379
WEST	W	6	432
WEST	W	7	431
WEST	W	7	431
WEST	W	9	204
WEST	W	11	396
WEST	W	12	237
WEST	W	12	411
WEST	WB	7	431
WEST	WC	2	380
WEST	WC	14	337
WEST	WE	2	380
WEST	WF	2	380
WEST	WH	2	380
WEST	WH	13	448
WEST	WJ	5	379
WEST	WL	12	237
WEST	WS	3	252
WEST	WS	5	379
WEST	WT	2	380
WEST	WW	3	405
WEST	WW	4	408
WEST	WW	5	379
WESTACOTT	AH	7	431
WESTACOTT	C	1	366
WESTALL	F	9	367
WESTALL	J	2	380
WESTALL	WA	2	380
WESTAWAY	A	13	448
WESTBROOK	AW	2	380
WESTBROOK	AW	10	388
WESTBROOK	BH	4	408
WESTBROOK	CA	7	431
WESTBROOK	EG	13	448
WESTBROOK	F	11	396
WESTBROOK	G	2	380
WESTBROOK	JP	11	396
WESTBROOK	SW	7	431
WESTBROOK	T	11	396
WESTBROOK	W	11	396
WESTBROOKE	WC	2	380
WESTBURY	F	12	411
WESTBURY	GD	2	380
WESTBURY	HJ	6	432
WESTBURY	WH	12	411
WESTBURY	WT	12	411
WESTCAR	J	3	252
WESTCOMBE	H	14	337
WESTCOTT	E	5	379
WESTCOTT	E	10	245
WESTCOTT	F	5	379
WESTCOTT	F	10	245
WESTCOTT	G	4	408
WESTCOTT	GF	3	405
WESTCOTT	H	1	366
WESTCOTT	H	10	245
WESTCOTT	HJ	13	448
WESTCOTT	J	5	379
WESTCOTT	J	13	448

WESTCOTT	K	10	245	WESTNALL	T	8	383	WESTON	WA	13	449	WHALE	R	2	382
WESTCOTT	PSC	10	388	WESTNEY	A	6	432	WESTON	WGH	7	432	WHALE	W	12	412
WESTCOTT	R	10	245	WESTNEY	GW	8	383	WESTON	WH	10	245	WHALEBONE	JR	7	432
WESTCOTT	SB	7	431	WESTNEY	H	6	432	WESTOVER	TG	13	449	WHALEN	FW	11	396
WESTERMAN	A	8	382	WESTNOP	J	8	383	WESTWICK	F	6	433	WHALEN	J	14	337
WESTERMAN	A	8	382	WESTNUTT	J	5	379	WESTWOOD	AWW	7	432	WHALEN	W	14	337
WESTERMAN	FJ	4	408	WESTOBY	R	8	383	WESTWOOD	D	2	381	WHALER	AH	1	367
WESTERMAN	H	8	383	WESTON	A	1	366	WESTWOOD	E	11	396	WHALEY	WJ	7	432
WESTERMAN	H	9	204	WESTON	A	2	381	WESTWOOD	E	13	449	WHALEY	WJ	7	432
WESTERMAN	T	8	383	WESTON	A	5	379	WESTWOOD	FEG	6	433	WHALIN	G	6	433
WESTERMAN	WH	8	383	WESTON	A	8	383	WESTWOOD	G	6	433	WHALLEY	A	2	382
WESTERN	AW	13	448	WESTON	A	12	237	WESTWOOD	GA	6	433	WHALLEY	E	11	396
WESTERN	EG	4	409	WESTON	AE	2	381	WESTWOOD	GC	2	381	WHALLEY	E	14	338
WESTERN	GH	8	383	WESTON	AE	2	381	WESTWOOD	HW	6	433	WHALLEY	F	11	397
WESTERN	H	1	366	WESTON	AE	2	381	WESTWOOD	J	6	433	WHALLEY	J	11	397
WESTERN	HA	13	448	WESTON	AEV	7	432	WESTWOOD	J	6	433	WHALLEY	J	11	397
WESTERN	R	1	366	WESTON	AG	13	448	WESTWOOD	J	6	433	WHALLEY	JD	14	338
WESTFIELD	H	10	245	WESTON	AR	3	252	WESTWOOD	J	6	433	WHALLEY	L	11	397
WESTGARTH	G	4	409	WESTON	AR	7	432	WESTWOOD	JC	5	380	WHALLEY	RE	4	409
WESTGATE	JH	13	448	WESTON	AWS	2	381	WESTWOOD	JR	8	383	WHALLEY	RS	4	409
WESTHROP	WC	7	431	WESTON	C	5	379	WESTWOOD	JW	8	383	WHALLEY	T	9	367
WESTIN	AS	12	237	WESTON	C	13	448	WESTWOOD	R	6	433	WHALLEY	TW	3	252
WESTLAKE	AC	2	381	WESTON	C	13	448	WESTWOOD	S	6	433	WHALLEY	W	14	338
WESTLAKE	AE	3	406	WESTON	CW	4	409	WESTWOOD	T	5	380	WHALLEY	WH	4	409
WESTLAKE	AM	1	366	WESTON	DG	5	379	WESTWOOD	W	2	381	WHAPPLES	W	12	412
WESTLAKE	FG	1	366	WESTON	ET	13	448	WESTWOOD	W	5	380	WHAPSHARE	WG	10	388
WESTLAKE	FL	7	431	WESTON	FC	3	252	WESTWOOD	W	11	396	WHARF	GJ	13	449
WESTLAKE	G	4	409	WESTON	FC	5	379	WETHERALL	AAD	2	381	WHARF	RA	13	449
WESTLAKE	GFC	1	366	WESTON	G	4	409	WETHERGILL	F	8	383	WHARF	S	14	338
WESTLAKE	HB	1	366	WESTON	GW	12	411	WETHERILL	A	8	383	WHARFE	JW	14	338
WESTLAKE	HG	4	409	WESTON	H	10	245	WETHERILL	C	8	383	WHARFE	WH	9	367
WESTLAKE	VJ	7	431	WESTON	HE	2	381	WETHERILL	H	7	432	WHARMBY	E	2	382
WESTLAKE	W	13	448	WESTON	HF	4	409	WETHERILL	W	8	383	WHARTON	AE	2	382
WESTLAKE	WHE	1	366	WESTON	HG	5	379	WETHERILT	A	2	381	WHARTON	AE	6	433
WESTLAKE	WR	2	381	WESTON	HG	13	448	WETTON	G	11	396	WHARTON	C	1	367
WESTLAND	A	3	406	WESTON	HR	13	448	WETTON	JC	2	381	WHARTON	F	6	433
WESTLEY	AH	12	411	WESTON	J	6	432	WEYDA	JC	2	381	WHARTON	FC	12	237
WESTLEY	E	7	431	WESTON	J	6	433	WEYMAN	AG	4	409	WHARTON	G	14	338
WESTLEY	E	12	411	WESTON	J	6	433	WEYMAN	AG	7	432	WHARTON	HE	4	409
WESTLEY	F	12	411	WESTON	J	12	411	WEYMAN	AT	7	432	WHARTON	M	11	397
WESTLEY	G	6	432	WESTON	J	14	337	WEYMAN	F	4	409	WHARTON	NL	2	382
WESTLEY	GE	2	381	WESTON	JH	12	411	WEYMAN	GE	4	409	WHARTON	RE	11	397
WESTLEY	GE	12	411	WESTON	JW	12	411	WEYMAN	J	7	432	WHARTON	T	9	205
WESTLEY	H	12	411	WESTON	PF	2	381	WEYMOUTH	AP	1	367	WHARTON	T	14	338
WESTLEY	HG	3	252	WESTON	RC	2	381	WEYMOUTH	CH	2	381	WHARTON	W	9	367
WESTLEY	W	12	411	WESTON	S	5	380	WEYMOUTH	JC	1	367	WHARTON	WE	6	433
WESTMAN	E	9	204	WESTON	SC	5	380	WHAITE	H	11	396	WHARTON	WG	2	382
WESTMAN	E	9	367	WESTON	T	13	448	WHALE	AJ	13	449	WHARVILL	H	8	383
WESTMAN	EL	9	204	WESTON	TH	1	366	WHALE	G	1	367	WHATLEY	AS	4	409
WESTMAN	H	9	204	WESTON	VR	12	412	WHALE	H	4	409	WHATLEY	CH	13	449
WESTMAN	L	9	367	WESTON	W	4	409	WHALE	H	12	412	WHATLEY	CW	7	432
WESTMORE	CE	10	245	WESTON	W	6	433	WHALE	HB	2	382	WHATLEY	FJ	2	382
WESTMORELAND	F	8	383	WESTON	W	6	433	WHALE	HC	4	409	WHATLEY	FS	4	409
WESTMORLAND	F	11	396	WESTON	W	13	449	WHALE	JH	4	409	WHATLEY	H	2	382
WESTMORLAND	V	8	383	WESTON	W	13	449	WHALE	JR	2	382	WHATLEY	H	13	449

WHATLEY	RA	7	432
WHATLEY	T	11	397
WHATLEY	WE	2	382
WHATLEY	WJ	4	409
WHATMAN	WR	13	449
WHATMORE	A	6	434
WHATMORE	AJ	6	434
WHATMORE	G	6	434
WHATMOUGH	F	11	397
WHATMOUGH	G	11	397
WHATMUFF	A	9	205
WHATNALL	WC	6	434
WHATRUP	WT	2	382
WHATTON	CD	12	237
WHEABLE	AB	10	245
WHEABLE	CH	10	245
WHEABLE	F	4	410
WHEADON	S	10	245
WHEADON	W	4	410
WHEAL	F	6	434
WHEALING	JH	14	338
WHEATCROFT	D	11	397
WHEATCROFT	E	11	397
WHEATCROFT	SE	11	397
WHEATER	T	8	383
WHEATLAND	FE	7	432
WHEATLAND	HG	7	432
WHEATLAND	RG	2	382
WHEATLAND	RW	7	432
WHEATLAND	T	4	410
WHEATLEY	A	2	382
WHEATLEY	A	5	380
WHEATLEY	A	6	434
WHEATLEY	A	8	384
WHEATLEY	AF	4	410
WHEATLEY	AJ	5	380
WHEATLEY	AR	13	449
WHEATLEY	C	7	432
WHEATLEY	C	14	338
WHEATLEY	CA	8	384
WHEATLEY	CE	5	380
WHEATLEY	G	6	434
WHEATLEY	GW	13	449
WHEATLEY	H	5	380
WHEATLEY	HS	2	382
WHEATLEY	J	5	380
WHEATLEY	J	12	237
WHEATLEY	JC	5	380
WHEATLEY	JR	12	237
WHEATLEY	R	12	237
WHEATLEY	SL	6	434
WHEATLEY	TA	2	382
WHEATLEY	WA	2	382
WHEATLEY	WG	2	382
WHEATLEY	WS	1	367
WHEATON	AI	10	388
WHEATON	AJ	2	382
WHEATON	CH	2	382
WHEATON	EN	10	388
WHEATON	PM	2	383
WHEBELL	R	2	383
WHEBLE	G	3	252
WHEDDON	AHJ	7	432
WHEDDON	CH	14	338
WHEDDOW	WE	11	397
WHEELDON	A	1	367
WHEELDON	FG	4	410
WHEELDON	J	9	205
WHEELDON	JH	6	434
WHEELDON	JH	14	338
WHEELDON	JW	14	338
WHEELDON	O	1	367
WHEELDON	T	11	397
WHEELDON	W	14	338
WHEELEN	J	9	205
WHEELER	A	2	383
WHEELER	A	4	410
WHEELER	A	13	449
WHEELER	AC	13	449
WHEELER	AD	4	410
WHEELER	AE	4	410
WHEELER	AG	4	410
WHEELER	AH	1	367
WHEELER	AH	5	380
WHEELER	AH	13	449
WHEELER	AJ	8	384
WHEELER	AJ	12	237
WHEELER	AS	13	449
WHEELER	AT	13	449
WHEELER	BR	5	380
WHEELER	BS	4	410
WHEELER	C	10	388
WHEELER	CE	6	434
WHEELER	CG	13	450
WHEELER	CH	14	338
WHEELER	CR	2	383
WHEELER	E	2	383
WHEELER	E	6	434
WHEELER	E	6	434
WHEELER	EG	6	434
WHEELER	EH	2	383
WHEELER	F	1	367
WHEELER	F	2	383
WHEELER	F	4	410
WHEELER	F	8	384
WHEELER	F	10	388
WHEELER	F	12	237
WHEELER	F	12	237
WHEELER	FC	13	450
WHEELER	FG	5	380
WHEELER	FJ	1	367
WHEELER	G	1	367
WHEELER	G	3	252
WHEELER	GA	6	434
WHEELER	GB	6	434
WHEELER	GP	4	410
WHEELER	GW	8	384
WHEELER	H	2	383
WHEELER	H	6	434
WHEELER	H	6	434
WHEELER	HE	6	435
WHEELER	HJ	10	388
WHEELER	J	1	367
WHEELER	J	2	383
WHEELER	J	4	410
WHEELER	J	7	432
WHEELER	J	7	433
WHEELER	J	10	388
WHEELER	J	13	450
WHEELER	JA	7	433
WHEELER	JA	10	245
WHEELER	JF	2	383
WHEELER	JH	4	410
WHEELER	JH	7	433
WHEELER	JW	6	434
WHEELER	JW	10	245
WHEELER	P	2	383
WHEELER	PE	12	412
WHEELER	R	3	252
WHEELER	RH	4	410
WHEELER	RL	4	410
WHEELER	S	4	410
WHEELER	SH	4	410
WHEELER	SH	4	410
WHEELER	SW	7	433
WHEELER	V	3	252
WHEELER	VA	11	397
WHEELER	VE	6	435
WHEELER	W	3	252
WHEELER	W	3	252
WHEELER	W	4	410
WHEELER	W	5	380
WHEELER	W	6	435
WHEELER	W	6	435
WHEELER	W	7	433
WHEELER	W	10	245
WHEELER	W	11	397
WHEELER	W	12	412
WHEELER	W	13	450
WHEELER	W	14	338
WHEELER	WA	1	367
WHEELER	WA	5	380
WHEELER	WD	5	380
WHEELER	WFC	2	383
WHEELER	WH	2	383
WHEELER	WJ	1	367
WHEELER	WR	4	410
WHEELER	WW	2	383
WHEELER-OSMAN	AW	4	410
WHEELER-OSMAN	CR	4	411
WHEELHOUSE	B	8	384
WHEELHOUSE	G	8	384
WHEELHOUSE	JW	9	205
WHEELHOUSE	WE	9	205
WHEELS	JG	13	450
WHEELTON	S	11	397
WHEELWRIGHT	WH	3	252
WHEEWALL	SH	5	380
WHEILDON	T	6	435
WHEILDON	WG	6	435
WHELAN	B	9	205
WHELAN	F	7	433
WHELAN	F	9	205
WHELAN	J	8	384
WHELAN	J	9	205
WHELAN	J	9	205
WHELAN	J	9	367
WHELAN	J	10	245
WHELAN	J	11	397
WHELAN	JC	11	398
WHELAN	JJ	14	338
WHELAN	L	7	433
WHELAN	L	9	205
WHELAN	L	9	367
WHELAN	P	14	338
WHELAN	T	14	338
WHELAN	W	7	433
WHELAN	W	9	205
WHELAN	W	14	339
WHELAN	WP	1	367
WHELAND	F	11	398
WHELDON	CE	6	435
WHELINGS	T	4	411
WHENT	O	2	383
WHETLOR	C	7	433
WHETREN	F	4	411
WHETSTONE	JA	7	433
WHETSTONE	W	8	384
WHETSTONE	WT	7	433
WHETTALL	L	11	398
WHETTALL	WW	11	398
WHETTINGSTEEL	FJ	4	411
WHETTINGSTEELE	CG	4	411
WHETTINGSTEELE	H	4	411
WHETTLETON	CJ	4	411
WHEWAY	CP	14	339
WHEWAY	GH	14	339
WHEWAY	JK	14	339
WHICHELD	AE	1	367
WHICHELOW	HC	4	411

WHICHER	AEP	4	411	WHITAKER	H	9	205	WHITBY	E	7	434	WHITE	AJ	2	384
WHICHER	H	7	433	WHITAKER	H	9	205	WHITBY	G	12	238	WHITE	AJ	4	411
WHIDDETT	GF	7	433	WHITAKER	H	9	368	WHITBY	GH	12	238	WHITE	AJ	4	411
WHIDDETT	MF	2	383	WHITAKER	HE	2	384	WHITBY	GJ	13	450	WHITE	AJ	5	381
WHIFFEN	GE	2	383	WHITAKER	J	8	385	WHITBY	J	14	339	WHITE	AJ	12	412
WHIFFIN	A	2	383	WHITAKER	J	8	385	WHITBY	JF	7	434	WHITE	AM	13	450
WHIFFIN	E	12	237	WHITAKER	J	8	385	WHITBY	R	1	367	WHITE	AR	7	434
WHIFFIN	S	5	380	WHITAKER	J	9	205	WHITBY	W	14	339	WHITE	AT	2	384
WHIFFING	GE	3	252	WHITAKER	J	9	368	WHITCHER	A	13	450	WHITE	AV	2	384
WHILE	H	6	435	WHITAKER	JC	8	385	WHITCHER	G	4	411	WHITE	AW	2	384
WHILE	JJ	6	435	WHITAKER	JE	8	385	WHITCHER	H	4	411	WHITE	AW	2	384
WHILES	F	11	398	WHITAKER	JH	11	398	WHITCOMB	A	7	434	WHITE	B	2	384
WHILES	TW	11	398	WHITAKER	JR	9	205	WHITCOMB	J	7	434	WHITE	B	4	411
WHILEY	F	7	433	WHITAKER	JW	8	385	WHITCOMBE	A	10	246	WHITE	B	10	388
WHILEY	FJ	7	433	WHITAKER	L	8	385	WHITCOMBE	A	10	246	WHITE	B	14	339
WHILEY	JE	7	433	WHITAKER	L	9	205	WHITCOMBE	A	10	246	WHITE	BJ	13	450
WHILEY	T	6	435	WHITAKER	L	9	368	WHITCOMBE	H	7	434	WHITE	C	4	411
WHILLOCK	D	6	435	WHITAKER	M	9	368	WHITCOMBE	J	10	246	WHITE	C	4	412
WHIMPENNY	F	11	398	WHITAKER	NH	9	205	WHITCOMBE	T	10	246	WHITE	C	4	412
WHINCOP	AH	13	450	WHITAKER	R	8	385	WHITCOMBE	TC	10	246	WHITE	C	4	412
WHINCUP	JH	9	205	WHITAKER	R	9	368	WHITE	A	1	368	WHITE	C	5	381
WHINCUP	JW	8	384	WHITAKER	R	9	368	WHITE	A	2	384	WHITE	C	10	246
WHINCUP	S	8	384	WHITAKER	S	8	385	WHITE	A	2	384	WHITE	C	10	246
WHINFIELD	JW	14	339	WHITAKER	S	8	385	WHITE	A	3	252	WHITE	C	10	246
WHINFIELD	WD	2	383	WHITAKER	S	8	385	WHITE	A	4	411	WHITE	C	11	398
WHINIKER	OW	8	384	WHITAKER	S	13	450	WHITE	A	4	411	WHITE	C	12	238
WHIPDAY	JW	14	339	WHITAKER	T	8	385	WHITE	A	4	411	WHITE	C	12	238
WHIPP	AH	9	367	WHITAKER	T	8	385	WHITE	A	4	411	WHITE	C	12	412
WHIPPS	WM	13	450	WHITAKER	T	11	398	WHITE	A	5	381	WHITE	C	13	450
WHISKER	F	13	450	WHITAKER	TC	9	368	WHITE	A	5	381	WHITE	CA	2	384
WHISKER	P	2	383	WHITAKER	W	8	385	WHITE	A	5	381	WHITE	CA	13	450
WHISTLER	A	1	367	WHITAKER	W	8	385	WHITE	A	5	381	WHITE	CA	14	339
WHISTON	A	6	435	WHITAKER	W	8	385	WHITE	A	7	434	WHITE	CC	4	412
WHISTON	AE	6	435	WHITAKER	W	9	368	WHITE	A	7	434	WHITE	CE	10	246
WHISTON	E	14	339	WHITAKER	WF	10	245	WHITE	A	7	434	WHITE	CF	2	384
WHISTON	EJ	14	339	WHITAKER	WR	8	385	WHITE	A	8	386	WHITE	CF	6	435
WHISTON	H	6	435	WHITAL	J	10	245	WHITE	A	8	386	WHITE	CF	7	434
WHISTON	PS	12	412	WHITBOURNE	G	2	384	WHITE	A	9	206	WHITE	CG	13	450
WHISTON	V	14	339	WHITBREAD	AJ	5	381	WHITE	A	12	238	WHITE	CGL	1	368
WHITAKER	A	8	384	WHITBREAD	EA	2	384	WHITE	A	12	238	WHITE	CH	2	384
WHITAKER	A	9	368	WHITBREAD	EJ	5	381	WHITE	A	12	238	WHITE	CH	5	381
WHITAKER	A	9	368	WHITBREAD	F	5	381	WHITE	A	12	238	WHITE	CH	7	434
WHITAKER	B	8	384	WHITBREAD	J	5	381	WHITE	A	12	412	WHITE	CH	10	246
WHITAKER	B	8	384	WHITBREAD	J	12	237	WHITE	A	13	450	WHITE	CJ	1	368
WHITAKER	C	7	433	WHITBREAD	P	12	412	WHITE	A	13	450	WHITE	CJ	6	435
WHITAKER	D	9	368	WHITBREAD	R	5	381	WHITE	AA	4	411	WHITE	CJ	10	388
WHITAKER	E	8	384	WHITBREAD	RE	3	252	WHITE	AC	12	412	WHITE	CR	3	252
WHITAKER	E	8	384	WHITBREAD	S	4	411	WHITE	AE	2	384	WHITE	CR	13	451
WHITAKER	F	9	205	WHITBREAD	W	2	384	WHITE	AE	5	381	WHITE	CS	13	451
WHITAKER	F	9	368	WHITBREAD	W	3	252	WHITE	AG	2	384	WHITE	CT	4	412
WHITAKER	FE	8	384	WHITBREAD	W	3	252	WHITE	AH	2	384	WHITE	CW	5	381
WHITAKER	G	6	438	WHITBREAD	WJ	7	433	WHITE	AH	2	384	WHITE	CW	7	434
WHITAKER	G	8	384	WHITBY	AJ	7	434	WHITE	AH	7	434	WHITE	CW	7	434
WHITAKER	G	8	385	WHITBY	AJ	12	238	WHITE	AJ	2	384	WHITE	CW	9	206
WHITAKER	GN	1	367	WHITBY	AJ	12	238	WHITE	AJ	2	384	WHITE	CWT	4	412

WHITE	D	4	412	WHITE	F	10	246	WHITE	H	4	413	WHITE	J	8	386
WHITE	D	6	435	WHITE	F	10	389	WHITE	H	5	381	WHITE	J	8	386
WHITE	D	7	434	WHITE	F	12	238	WHITE	H	7	435	WHITE	J	8	386
WHITE	D	9	206	WHITE	FB	7	435	WHITE	H	7	435	WHITE	J	8	386
WHITE	DEM	1	368	WHITE	FB	12	238	WHITE	H	7	435	WHITE	J	9	368
WHITE	DGJ	7	434	WHITE	FC	2	385	WHITE	H	7	435	WHITE	J	10	247
WHITE	E	1	368	WHITE	FC	4	413	WHITE	H	7	435	WHITE	J	10	247
WHITE	E	2	384	WHITE	FE	2	385	WHITE	H	8	386	WHITE	J	10	247
WHITE	E	2	385	WHITE	FE	4	413	WHITE	H	8	386	WHITE	J	10	389
WHITE	E	4	412	WHITE	FE	12	238	WHITE	H	8	386	WHITE	J	10	389
WHITE	E	4	412	WHITE	FG	4	413	WHITE	H	9	206	WHITE	J	11	398
WHITE	E	4	412	WHITE	FH	4	413	WHITE	H	9	206	WHITE	J	11	398
WHITE	E	4	412	WHITE	FM	10	389	WHITE	H	9	368	WHITE	J	12	239
WHITE	E	7	434	WHITE	FP	10	389	WHITE	H	10	247	WHITE	J	12	239
WHITE	E	7	434	WHITE	FR	4	413	WHITE	H	10	247	WHITE	J	13	451
WHITE	E	10	246	WHITE	FW	4	413	WHITE	H	10	389	WHITE	J	13	451
WHITE	E	10	246	WHITE	FW	7	435	WHITE	H	11	398	WHITE	J	13	451
WHITE	E	10	388	WHITE	FW	10	246	WHITE	H	11	398	WHITE	J	14	339
WHITE	E	10	388	WHITE	FW	12	238	WHITE	H	11	398	WHITE	J	14	339
WHITE	EA	4	412	WHITE	FW	13	451	WHITE	H	12	238	WHITE	J	14	339
WHITE	EAJ	4	412	WHITE	G	2	385	WHITE	H	12	239	WHITE	J	14	339
WHITE	EE	6	435	WHITE	G	4	413	WHITE	H	12	412	WHITE	JA	4	413
WHITE	EG	7	435	WHITE	G	4	413	WHITE	H	14	339	WHITE	JA	13	451
WHITE	EG	13	451	WHITE	G	4	413	WHITE	HA	2	385	WHITE	JE	2	386
WHITE	EH	7	434	WHITE	G	4	413	WHITE	HC	2	385	WHITE	JE	4	414
WHITE	EJ	2	385	WHITE	G	7	435	WHITE	HC	4	413	WHITE	JG	1	368
WHITE	EJ	7	435	WHITE	G	7	435	WHITE	HC	5	381	WHITE	JH	2	386
WHITE	EJ	10	389	WHITE	G	8	386	WHITE	HC	13	451	WHITE	JH	2	386
WHITE	EM	4	412	WHITE	G	10	246	WHITE	HDY	7	435	WHITE	JH	4	414
WHITE	ET	1	368	WHITE	G	10	246	WHITE	HG	10	247	WHITE	JH	6	436
WHITE	ET	4	412	WHITE	G	12	238	WHITE	HJ	2	385	WHITE	JH	6	436
WHITE	ET	12	412	WHITE	G	12	238	WHITE	HJ	4	413	WHITE	JH	7	436
WHITE	EV	2	385	WHITE	G	12	238	WHITE	HJ	13	451	WHITE	JH	9	368
WHITE	EW	2	385	WHITE	G	12	238	WHITE	HJF	13	451	WHITE	JH	10	247
WHITE	EW	2	385	WHITE	G	12	238	WHITE	HLW	10	247	WHITE	JH	11	398
WHITE	EW	5	381	WHITE	G	12	412	WHITE	HR	7	435	WHITE	JH	12	412
WHITE	EW	12	238	WHITE	G	13	450	WHITE	HS	5	381	WHITE	JH	13	451
WHITE	F	2	385	WHITE	G	13	451	WHITE	HW	2	385	WHITE	JHJ	2	386
WHITE	F	2	385	WHITE	GA	1	368	WHITE	HW	4	413	WHITE	JJ	1	368
WHITE	F	4	412	WHITE	GA	4	413	WHITE	HW	13	451	WHITE	JJ	2	386
WHITE	F	4	412	WHITE	GB	7	435	WHITE	J	1	368	WHITE	JJ	13	451
WHITE	F	4	412	WHITE	GC	2	385	WHITE	J	1	368	WHITE	JP	13	451
WHITE	F	4	412	WHITE	GE	2	385	WHITE	J	2	385	WHITE	JR	7	436
WHITE	F	5	381	WHITE	GE	13	451	WHITE	J	2	385	WHITE	JRW	3	406
WHITE	F	5	381	WHITE	GF	6	436	WHITE	J	2	385	WHITE	JW	2	386
WHITE	F	6	435	WHITE	GF	7	435	WHITE	J	3	406	WHITE	JW	4	414
WHITE	F	6	435	WHITE	GF	10	246	WHITE	J	4	413	WHITE	JW	8	386
WHITE	F	7	435	WHITE	GH	2	385	WHITE	J	4	413	WHITE	JW	10	247
WHITE	F	7	435	WHITE	GJ	8	386	WHITE	J	4	413	WHITE	JW	10	389
WHITE	F	7	435	WHITE	GJ	13	451	WHITE	J	4	414	WHITE	JW	11	398
WHITE	F	9	206	WHITE	GR	8	386	WHITE	J	5	381	WHITE	KR	2	386
WHITE	F	9	206	WHITE	GT	4	413	WHITE	J	7	435	WHITE	L	1	368
WHITE	F	9	368	WHITE	GW	10	246	WHITE	J	7	436	WHITE	L	3	252
WHITE	F	9	368	WHITE	H	1	368	WHITE	J	7	436	WHITE	L	4	414
				WHITE	H	2	385								

Name			
WHITE	L	7	436
WHITE	L	7	436
WHITE	L	13	451
WHITE	LA	5	382
WHITE	LE	4	414
WHITE	LE	7	436
WHITE	LH	7	436
WHITE	LJ	4	414
WHITE	LR	2	386
WHITE	LRV	4	414
WHITE	LS	4	414
WHITE	M	3	406
WHITE	M	7	436
WHITE	M	11	398
WHITE	M	12	239
WHITE	ME	7	436
WHITE	MO	12	412
WHITE	MR	5	382
WHITE	NL	3	253
WHITE	NT	4	414
WHITE	O	7	436
WHITE	OA	12	239
WHITE	P	8	386
WHITE	P	12	239
WHITE	P	13	452
WHITE	P	13	452
WHITE	PA	4	414
WHITE	PH	4	414
WHITE	PH	5	382
WHITE	PJ	2	386
WHITE	PJ	4	414
WHITE	PR	12	239
WHITE	PS	13	452
WHITE	PT	4	414
WHITE	PT	4	414
WHITE	PT	12	412
WHITE	PW	2	386
WHITE	R	1	368
WHITE	R	2	386
WHITE	R	2	386
WHITE	R	2	386
WHITE	R	3	253
WHITE	R	4	414
WHITE	R	7	436
WHITE	R	9	206
WHITE	R	9	368
WHITE	R	10	389
WHITE	R	12	239
WHITE	R	13	452
WHITE	RA	2	386
WHITE	RA	3	406
WHITE	RA	10	247
WHITE	RAH	2	386
WHITE	RCJ	4	414
WHITE	RE	12	239
WHITE	RE	14	339
WHITE	RG	3	253
WHITE	RH	4	414
WHITE	RH	7	436
WHITE	RH	10	389
WHITE	RH	13	452
WHITE	RJ	13	452
WHITE	RJ	13	452
WHITE	RSJ	2	386
WHITE	S	7	436
WHITE	S	7	436
WHITE	S	9	369
WHITE	S	11	399
WHITE	S	14	340
WHITE	S	14	340
WHITE	SC	5	382
WHITE	SE	7	436
WHITE	SF	10	247
WHITE	SF	13	452
WHITE	SG	7	436
WHITE	SG	13	452
WHITE	SH	10	247
WHITE	SJ	4	414
WHITE	ST	13	452
WHITE	SW	10	247
WHITE	SW	12	239
WHITE	T	1	368
WHITE	T	4	414
WHITE	T	5	382
WHITE	T	6	436
WHITE	T	7	436
WHITE	T	7	436
WHITE	T	8	386
WHITE	T	8	386
WHITE	T	9	206
WHITE	T	9	369
WHITE	T	11	399
WHITE	T	12	239
WHITE	T	14	340
WHITE	TD	9	206
WHITE	TD	10	247
WHITE	TE	4	415
WHITE	TE	9	369
WHITE	TE	10	389
WHITE	TEC	2	386
WHITE	TH	2	386
WHITE	TH	2	386
WHITE	TH	11	399
WHITE	THG	4	415
WHITE	THO	4	415
WHITE	TV	9	369
WHITE	TW	12	412
WHITE	V	3	253
WHITE	VA	10	389
WHITE	W	1	368
WHITE	W	1	368
WHITE	W	2	386
WHITE	W	2	387
WHITE	W	2	387
WHITE	W	2	387
WHITE	W	2	387
WHITE	W	2	387
WHITE	W	4	415
WHITE	W	4	415
WHITE	W	4	415
WHITE	W	5	382
WHITE	W	6	436
WHITE	W	6	436
WHITE	W	6	436
WHITE	W	7	436
WHITE	W	7	436
WHITE	W	7	437
WHITE	W	8	386
WHITE	W	8	386
WHITE	W	8	386
WHITE	W	9	369
WHITE	W	10	247
WHITE	W	10	247
WHITE	W	10	389
WHITE	W	12	239
WHITE	W	12	239
WHITE	WA	2	387
WHITE	WA	12	239
WHITE	WAC	7	437
WHITE	WC	10	247
WHITE	WD	2	387
WHITE	WE	2	387
WHITE	WE	7	437
WHITE	WE	10	248
WHITE	WE	10	248
WHITE	WE	10	248
WHITE	WE	13	452
WHITE	WF	4	415
WHITE	WF	7	437
WHITE	WG	2	387
WHITE	WG	4	415
WHITE	WG	5	382
WHITE	WG	5	382
WHITE	WG	5	382
WHITE	WG	9	206
WHITE	WH	4	415
WHITE	WH	5	382
WHITE	WH	13	452
WHITE	WJ	5	382
WHITE	WJ	7	437
WHITE	WJ	7	437
WHITE	WJ	10	248
WHITE	WJ	10	389
WHITE	WJ	10	389
WHITE	WJ	14	340
WHITE	WS	2	387
WHITE	WT	2	387
WHITE	WW	4	415
WHITEAR	AE	3	253
WHITEAWAY	A	10	389
WHITEAWAY	G	10	248
WHITEFIELD	GG	10	389
WHITEFIELD	WG	10	389
WHITEHALL	E	7	437
WHITEHALL	W	7	437
WHITEHALL	W	12	413
WHITEHEAD	A	1	368
WHITEHEAD	A	8	387
WHITEHEAD	A	9	206
WHITEHEAD	A	9	206
WHITEHEAD	A	9	206
WHITEHEAD	A	9	369
WHITEHEAD	A	9	369
WHITEHEAD	A	11	399
WHITEHEAD	A	11	399
WHITEHEAD	AE	14	340
WHITEHEAD	AR	1	368
WHITEHEAD	BC	7	437
WHITEHEAD	C	6	436
WHITEHEAD	C	8	387
WHITEHEAD	C	8	387
WHITEHEAD	C	9	206
WHITEHEAD	CF	2	387
WHITEHEAD	CH	9	206
WHITEHEAD	CH	9	206
WHITEHEAD	CW	4	415
WHITEHEAD	CW	8	387
WHITEHEAD	D	6	436
WHITEHEAD	D	9	206
WHITEHEAD	E	9	206
WHITEHEAD	E	11	399
WHITEHEAD	FB	9	207
WHITEHEAD	FJ	7	437
WHITEHEAD	FW	11	399
WHITEHEAD	G	2	387
WHITEHEAD	G	9	207
WHITEHEAD	G	9	207
WHITEHEAD	G	13	452
WHITEHEAD	GH	14	340
WHITEHEAD	H	7	437
WHITEHEAD	H	8	387
WHITEHEAD	H	9	207
WHITEHEAD	H	9	207
WHITEHEAD	H	9	207
WHITEHEAD	H	9	369
WHITEHEAD	H	11	399
WHITEHEAD	H	11	399
WHITEHEAD	H	11	399
WHITEHEAD	H	13	452
WHITEHEAD	H	13	452

WHITEHEAD	H	14	340	WHITEHOUSE	A	6	436	WHITELEY	H	9	207	WHITFIELD	J	8	388				
WHITEHEAD	H	14	340	WHITEHOUSE	A	6	436	WHITELEY	HE	9	207	WHITFIELD	JW	8	388				
WHITEHEAD	H	14	340	WHITEHOUSE	AE	3	406	WHITELEY	JA	9	369	WHITFIELD	LV	9	207				
WHITEHEAD	HE	2	387	WHITEHOUSE	C	8	387	WHITELEY	JC	9	207	WHITFIELD	TS	1	369				
WHITEHEAD	J	7	437	WHITEHOUSE	C	10	248	WHITELEY	JE	11	399	WHITFIELD	V	9	208				
WHITEHEAD	J	8	387	WHITEHOUSE	E	6	436	WHITELEY	JJ	14	340	WHITFIELD	W	5	382				
WHITEHEAD	J	9	369	WHITEHOUSE	EJ	6	436	WHITELEY	JT	8	387	WHITFIELD	WH	8	388				
WHITEHEAD	J	11	399	WHITEHOUSE	F	6	436	WHITELEY	JW	8	388	WHITFIELD	WH	10	390				
WHITEHEAD	J	12	239	WHITEHOUSE	F	13	452	WHITELEY	S	8	388	WHITFORD	CJ	13	453				
WHITEHEAD	J	14	340	WHITEHOUSE	FC	6	436	WHITELEY	S	9	369	WHITFORD	FL	13	453				
WHITEHEAD	JC	12	239	WHITEHOUSE	FC	6	436	WHITELEY	T	8	388	WHITHAM	GV	9	370				
WHITEHEAD	JH	3	253	WHITEHOUSE	G	6	436	WHITELEY	T	9	207	WHITHAM	J	8	388				
WHITEHEAD	JJ	1	368	WHITEHOUSE	GH	6	437	WHITELEY	T	9	369	WHITHAM	J	9	208				
WHITEHEAD	JJ	3	406	WHITEHOUSE	GJ	6	437	WHITELEY	W	9	369	WHITHAM	L	9	208				
WHITEHEAD	JS	7	437	WHITEHOUSE	GJ	6	437	WHITELL	E	5	382	WHITHERS	J	8	388				
WHITEHEAD	JW	8	387	WHITEHOUSE	H	8	387	WHITELOCK	P	8	388	WHITHERS	P	8	388				
WHITEHEAD	JW	9	207	WHITEHOUSE	HJ	2	388	WHITELOW	E	8	388	WHITING	A	12	240				
WHITEHEAD	JWH	2	387	WHITEHOUSE	HV	8	387	WHITELOW	E	8	388	WHITING	AA	7	438				
WHITEHEAD	L	11	399	WHITEHOUSE	J	6	437	WHITELOW	H	8	388	WHITING	AA	12	413				
WHITEHEAD	N	2	387	WHITEHOUSE	J	6	437	WHITELOW	H	8	388	WHITING	AC	13	453				
WHITEHEAD	P	9	369	WHITEHOUSE	JJ	7	437	WHITEMAN	AE	7	437	WHITING	AF	4	416				
WHITEHEAD	R	8	387	WHITEHOUSE	LS	6	437	WHITEMAN	AG	12	239	WHITING	AJ	12	240				
WHITEHEAD	R	9	207	WHITEHOUSE	RA	12	239	WHITEMAN	B	10	248	WHITING	AW	2	388				
WHITEHEAD	RF	6	436	WHITEHOUSE	RW	6	437	WHITEMAN	CC	12	239	WHITING	B	7	438				
WHITEHEAD	RR	10	248	WHITEHOUSE	S	6	437	WHITEMAN	ER	12	413	WHITING	B	12	413				
WHITEHEAD	RV	14	340	WHITEHOUSE	S	11	399	WHITEMAN	EW	4	415	WHITING	C	1	369				
WHITEHEAD	RW	12	413	WHITEHOUSE	SJ	6	437	WHITEMAN	F	10	248	WHITING	C	8	388				
WHITEHEAD	S	9	207	WHITEHOUSE	T	1	369	WHITEMAN	H	4	415	WHITING	CA	12	413				
WHITEHEAD	S	11	399	WHITEHOUSE	T	5	382	WHITEMAN	J	12	240	WHITING	E	1	369				
WHITEHEAD	T	11	399	WHITEHOUSE	V	9	369	WHITEMAN	JC	7	437	WHITING	EA	12	240				
WHITEHEAD	T	11	399	WHITEHOUSE	W	6	437	WHITEMAN	W	12	240	WHITING	EG	2	388				
WHITEHEAD	T	13	452	WHITEHOUSE	W	6	437	WHITEMAN	W	12	240	WHITING	EJ	10	390				
WHITEHEAD	TH	5	382	WHITEHOUSE	W	6	437	WHITEMAN	WH	11	399	WHITING	FJ	12	240				
WHITEHEAD	W	6	436	WHITEHOUSE	WG	3	406	WHITEMORE	FJ	4	415	WHITING	FT	12	413				
WHITEHEAD	W	6	436	WHITEHOUSE	WH	6	437	WHITEMORE	G	4	416	WHITING	FW	12	240				
WHITEHEAD	W	8	387	WHITEHURST	A	6	437	WHITEN	WR	3	406	WHITING	G	3	253				
WHITEHEAD	W	8	387	WHITEHURST	J	6	437	WHITENMAIR	G	9	207	WHITING	G	7	438				
WHITEHEAD	WF	4	415	WHITEHURST	WH	6	437	WHITER	AH	3	253	WHITING	GE	11	400				
WHITEHEAD	WG	2	387	WHITEING	N	7	437	WHITEROD	HEW	2	388	WHITING	GT	12	413				
WHITEHEAD	WH	14	340	WHITEING	WJ	7	437	WHITESIDE	A	14	340	WHITING	H	8	388				
WHITEHEAD	WN	9	369	WHITELEGG	A	11	399	WHITESIDE	JW	9	207	WHITING	H	12	413				
WHITEHILL	G	11	399	WHITELEGG	JW	11	399	WHITESIDE	WJ	13	452	WHITING	H	13	453				
WHITEHILL	GW	10	248	WHITELEGG	TA	14	340	WHITEWAY	EG	10	389	WHITING	HC	2	388				
WHITEHILL	WH	14	340	WHITELEY	A	8	387	WHITEWOOD	EG	13	452	WHITING	HE	12	413				
WHITEHORN	A	4	415	WHITELEY	A	8	387	WHITEWOOD	LS	13	453	WHITING	HL	2	388				
WHITEHORN	A	4	415	WHITELEY	A	8	387	WHITFIELD	AA	10	248	WHITING	HM	2	388				
WHITEHORN	AC	3	253	WHITELEY	F	9	207	WHITFIELD	AF	4	416	WHITING	HP	13	453				
WHITEHORN	E	3	253	WHITELEY	F	9	369	WHITFIELD	AV	11	400	WHITING	HW	12	240				
WHITEHORN	F	4	415	WHITELEY	G	9	207	WHITFIELD	B	9	369	WHITING	JA	13	453				
WHITEHORN	H	4	415	WHITELEY	G	9	369	WHITFIELD	E	6	437	WHITING	JE	2	388				
WHITEHORN	J	2	387	WHITELEY	H	8	387	WHITFIELD	EE	12	240	WHITING	JH	10	390				
WHITEHORN	JE	3	253	WHITELEY	H	8	387	WHITFIELD	F	4	416	WHITING	JW	12	240				
WHITEHORN	R	2	387	WHITELEY	H	9	207	WHITFIELD	F	9	370	WHITING	R	3	253				
WHITEHORN	W	4	415	WHITELEY	H	9	207	WHITFIELD	F	13	453	WHITING	RA	1	369				
WHITEHOUSE	A	4	415	WHITELEY	H	9	207	WHITFIELD	G	4	416	WHITING	RH	5	382				

WHITING	TG	12	240	WHITMARSH	FG	4	416	WHITTAKER	J	13	453	WHITTINGHAM	H	5	383
WHITING	TWE	12	413	WHITMARSH	FW	4	416	WHITTAKER	J	14	341	WHITTINGHAM	J	11	400
WHITING	WA	2	388	WHITMARSH	HG	13	453	WHITTAKER	J	14	341	WHITTINGHAM	JH	14	341
WHITING	WG	12	413	WHITMARSH	JHF	7	438	WHITTAKER	J	14	341	WHITTINGHAM	JT	8	389
WHITING	WJ	2	388	WHITMARSH	JT	4	416	WHITTAKER	J	14	341	WHITTINGHAM	RH	6	438
WHITING	WJ	7	438	WHITMARSH	W	6	437	WHITTAKER	JA	2	388	WHITTINGHAM	T	11	400
WHITING	WJ	12	240	WHITMEE	E	12	241	WHITTAKER	JC	7	438	WHITTINGHAM	W	11	400
WHITING	WP	12	240	WHITMEE	HR	12	241	WHITTAKER	JP	9	208	WHITTINGTON	A	1	369
WHITING	WR	4	416	WHITMORE	BS	12	241	WHITTAKER	JR	8	389	WHITTINGTON	AH	4	417
WHITING	WS	1	369	WHITMORE	C	4	417	WHITTAKER	JW	10	248	WHITTINGTON	CJ	5	383
WHITLAND	WW	2	388	WHITMORE	E	6	438	WHITTAKER	JW	11	400	WHITTINGTON	EC	3	253
WHITLEY	A	9	208	WHITMORE	FW	4	417	WHITTAKER	MA	14	341	WHITTINGTON	EJ	4	417
WHITLEY	DA	14	340	WHITMORE	G	6	437	WHITTAKER	O	9	208	WHITTINGTON	EV	3	253
WHITLEY	E	3	406	WHITMORE	H	6	438	WHITTAKER	PD	7	438	WHITTINGTON	F	14	342
WHITLEY	E	8	388	WHITMORE	J	7	438	WHITTAKER	R	1	369	WHITTINGTON	H	12	241
WHITLEY	H	8	388	WHITMORE	JH	6	438	WHITTAKER	R	8	389	WHITTINGTON	R	14	342
WHITLEY	J	9	370	WHITMORE	T	12	241	WHITTAKER	S	11	400	WHITTINGTON	SG	5	383
WHITLEY	JE	9	208	WHITMORE	WT	12	241	WHITTAKER	S	14	341	WHITTINGTON	V	10	248
WHITLEY	R	9	370	WHITNE	J	9	370	WHITTAKER	T	9	208	WHITTINGTON	WJ	13	453
WHITLEY	T	3	253	WHITNELL	AJ	2	388	WHITTAKER	T	11	400	WHITTINGTON	WR	4	417
WHITLEY	T	14	340	WHITNELL	DH	2	388	WHITTAKER	T	11	400	WHITTLE	A	4	417
WHITLEY	W	9	208	WHITNEY	A	5	382	WHITTAKER	T	14	341	WHITTLE	A	6	438
WHITLEY	W	9	208	WHITNEY	A	14	340	WHITTAKER	W	8	389	WHITTLE	AV	3	406
WHITLEY	WE	6	437	WHITNEY	AC	2	388	WHITTAKER	W	8	389	WHITTLE	C	11	401
WHITLING	H	1	369	WHITNEY	FM	11	400	WHITTAKER	W	11	400	WHITTLE	CH	2	389
WHITLOCK	A	4	416	WHITNEY	G	10	248	WHITTAKER	W	14	341	WHITTLE	E	11	400
WHITLOCK	B	4	416	WHITNEY	G	11	400	WHITTAKER	W	14	341	WHITTLE	E	14	342
WHITLOCK	C	12	240	WHITNEY	GA	7	438	WHITTAKER	WR	14	341	WHITTLE	EB	3	406
WHITLOCK	EA	7	438	WHITNEY	H	14	341	WHITTAKER	WV	2	389	WHITTLE	HG	4	417
WHITLOCK	EA	12	240	WHITNEY	HV	7	438	WHITTALL	JT	11	398	WHITTLE	J	6	438
WHITLOCK	ER	12	240	WHITNEY	W	5	382	WHITTAM	H	13	453	WHITTLE	J	11	401
WHITLOCK	F	4	416	WHITSEY	B	7	438	WHITTELL	EA	2	389	WHITTLE	R	9	208
WHITLOCK	F	4	416	WHITSEY	GR	7	438	WHITTEMORE	AV	12	241	WHITTLE	R	9	208
WHITLOCK	FB	12	240	WHITTAKER	A	2	388	WHITTEMORE	C	5	382	WHITTLE	S	14	342
WHITLOCK	G	12	413	WHITTAKER	A	6	438	WHITTEMORE	EG	5	382	WHITTLE	T	11	401
WHITLOCK	GH	12	240	WHITTAKER	A	8	388	WHITTEMORE	FA	5	382	WHITTLE	T	14	342
WHITLOCK	GL	4	416	WHITTAKER	A	8	388	WHITTEMORE	GJ	12	241	WHITTLE	W	10	248
WHITLOCK	GW	2	388	WHITTAKER	A	9	208	WHITTEMORE	H	5	383	WHITTLE	W	14	342
WHITLOCK	H	12	241	WHITTAKER	A	9	208	WHITTEMORE	R	12	241	WHITTOCK	T	2	389
WHITLOCK	H	12	413	WHITTAKER	A	11	400	WHITTER	CE	11	400	WHITTOME	AW	2	389
WHITLOCK	HE	7	438	WHITTAKER	A	14	341	WHITTERANCE	EW	11	400	WHITTON	A	9	370
WHITLOCK	HL	7	438	WHITTAKER	AWR	9	208	WHITTERANCE	W	11	400	WHITTON	A	9	370
WHITLOCK	J	4	416	WHITTAKER	D	3	406	WHITTERN	T	5	383	WHITTON	CMV	2	389
WHITLOCK	R	4	416	WHITTAKER	F	13	453	WHITTEY	G	4	417	WHITTON	F	9	208
WHITLOCK	S	2	388	WHITTAKER	FH	14	341	WHITTICK	G	2	389	WHITTON	J	8	389
WHITLOCK	S	12	413	WHITTAKER	G	14	341	WHITTICK	R	1	369	WHITTON	JH	9	370
WHITLOCK	T	12	241	WHITTAKER	G	14	341	WHITTINGHAM	A	6	438	WHITTON	R	11	401
WHITLOCK	WD	4	416	WHITTAKER	G	14	341	WHITTINGHAM	A	6	438	WHITTON	W	8	389
WHITLOCK	WG	4	416	WHITTAKER	H	11	400	WHITTINGHAM	A	6	438	WHITTRED	FE	5	383
WHITLOCK	WJ	4	416	WHITTAKER	HV	13	453	WHITTINGHAM	A	10	248	WHITTY	J	1	369
WHITLOCKE	FOI	4	416	WHITTAKER	J	2	388	WHITTINGHAM	A	11	400	WHITWORTH	A	12	413
WHITLOW	J	4	416	WHITTAKER	J	9	208	WHITTINGHAM	B	6	438	WHITWORTH	AT	4	417
WHITLUM	HF	7	438	WHITTAKER	J	9	370	WHITTINGHAM	E	14	341	WHITWORTH	E	11	401
WHITMAN	C	9	370	WHITTAKER	J	9	370	WHITTINGHAM	FP	6	438	WHITWORTH	F	12	413
WHITMARSH	CE	3	253	WHITTAKER	J	11	400	WHITTINGHAM	G	11	400	WHITWORTH	F	12	413

WHITWORTH	G	11	401	WICKEN	MO	10	390	WIDDOP	J	9	209	WIGGLESWORTH	J	8	389
WHITWORTH	GH	6	438	WICKEN	TJ	7	439	WIDDOP	J	9	370	WIGGLESWORTH	JH	9	370
WHITWORTH	HJ	12	241	WICKEN	W	7	439	WIDDOP	S	8	389	WIGGLESWORTH	JW	2	390
WHITWORTH	J	11	401	WICKEN	WJ	13	453	WIDDOWS	J	6	438	WIGGLESWORTH	WHC	8	390
WHITWORTH	J	11	401	WICKENDEN	CAJ	7	439	WIDDOWS	J	11	401	WIGGS	RJ	7	440
WHITWORTH	JC	9	370	WICKENDEN	H	4	417	WIDDOWS	W	6	439	WIGGS	SA	7	439
WHITWORTH	JT	13	453	WICKENDEN	J	7	439	WIDDOWSON	G	11	401	WIGGS	W	5	383
WHITWORTH	R	12	241	WICKENDEN	JW	7	439	WIDDOWSON	JJ	13	454	WIGGS	WH	5	383
WHITWORTH	S	11	425	WICKENDEN	RH	4	417	WIDDOWSON	W	5	383	WIGGS	WH	5	383
WHITWORTH	W	14	342	WICKENDEN	WF	13	453	WIDDUP	F	9	209	WIGGS	WJ	5	384
WHITWORTH	WA	12	413	WICKENDEN	WW	13	454	WIDDUP	G	5	383	WIGHT	GR	4	417
WHITWORTH	WE	12	414	WICKENS	A	7	439	WIDGERY	W	2	390	WIGHT	RW	4	417
WHOLLEY	J	3	406	WICKENS	AR	10	249	WIDOWS	FH	9	209	WIGHT	W	8	390
WHOMACK	AS	8	389	WICKENS	EHE	3	253	WIFFEN	WJ	7	439	WIGHTMAN	AH	4	417
WHORK	T	11	401	WICKENS	ET	5	383	WIGFALL	TB	10	390	WIGHTMAN	C	11	401
WHORLEY	HJ	4	417	WICKENS	HC	7	439	WIGG	RE	7	439	WIGHTMAN	C	11	401
WHORLEY	TW	4	417	WICKENS	RA	2	389	WIGGANS	W	14	342	WIGHTMAN	JJ	3	406
WHORNE	H	12	241	WICKENS	TJ	10	249	WIGGEN	RH	5	383	WIGHTMAN	JW	9	209
WHOWALL	AG	7	438	WICKENS	W	7	439	WIGGEN	YF	5	383	WIGHTMAN	JW	9	370
WHURR	JS	10	390	WICKER	JD	10	390	WIGGER	A	2	390	WIGHTMAN	T	11	401
WHY	A	5	383	WICKERSHAM	AJ	5	383	WIGGETT	A	2	390	WIGHTMAN	WE	4	418
WHY	F	5	383	WICKERSON	GW	10	249	WIGGETT	HL	2	390	WIGINTON	A	2	390
WHY	RA	2	389	WICKES	H	3	253	WIGGETT	W	2	390	WIGLEY	AE	2	390
WHYATT	A	2	389	WICKETTS	B	6	438	WIGGINS	A	12	414	WIGLEY	CH	6	439
WHYATT	AJ	3	253	WICKHAM	FJ	2	389	WIGGINS	AE	7	439	WIGLEY	H	7	440
WHYATT	AW	6	438	WICKHAM	G	12	414	WIGGINS	AJ	12	414	WIGLEY	J	11	401
WHYATT	E	11	401	WICKHAM	H	7	439	WIGGINS	C	8	389	WIGLEY	RH	6	439
WHYATT	E	11	401	WICKHAM	J	12	414	WIGGINS	C	12	414	WIGLEY	WG	7	440
WHYATT	H	6	438	WICKHAM	SJ	13	454	WIGGINS	E	14	342	WIGMORE	J	5	384
WHYATT	J	14	342	WICKHAM	WJW	12	241	WIGGINS	F	2	390	WIGMORE	J	6	439
WHYATT	W	2	389	WICKING	WT	13	454	WIGGINS	GH	10	249	WIGMORE	R	1	369
WHYATT	W	14	342	WICKINS	WH	7	439	WIGGINS	H	3	406	WIGMORE	RH	1	369
WHYBREW	H	10	248	WICKMAN	J	14	342	WIGGINS	HS	12	414	WIGMORE	SJ	6	439
WHYBROW	HW	13	453	WICKS	AE	10	249	WIGGINS	J	8	389	WIGNALL	A	11	402
WHYBROW	JSR	7	438	WICKS	AG	2	389	WIGGINS	J	12	414	WIGNALL	H	8	390
WHYBROW	WE	13	453	WICKS	AJ	3	253	WIGGINS	J	12	414	WIGNALL	HR	13	454
WHYLAND	MJ	7	439	WICKS	CA	4	417	WIGGINS	JW	7	439	WIGNALL	PR	11	402
WHYLER	W	13	453	WICKS	E	5	383	WIGGINS	R	12	414	WIGNALL	S	14	342
WHYLEY	G	2	389	WICKS	ES	2	389	WIGGINS	R	12	414	WIGNALL	W	9	209
WHYMAN	G	2	389	WICKS	GH	2	390	WIGGINS	R	13	454	WIKES	A	6	439
WHYMAN	WC	12	414	WICKS	GR	8	389	WIGGINS	R	14	342	WILBAR	G	2	390
WHYMARK	A	2	389	WICKS	H	1	369	WIGGINS	T	1	369	WILBER	EW	2	390
WHYMARK	AW	10	248	WICKS	H	8	389	WIGGINS	TH	7	439	WILBER	J	8	390
WHYSALL	H	6	438	WICKS	HC	5	383	WIGGINS	WC	1	369	WILBERFORCE	EW	9	209
WHYTE	D	10	248	WICKS	JW	2	390	WIGGINS	WH	2	390	WILBOURNE	HT	13	454
WHYTE	L	8	389	WICKS	P	2	390	WIGGINS	WJ	2	390	WILBRAHAM	GP	2	390
WHYTE	TA	4	417	WICKS	PF	7	439	WIGGINS	WJ	7	439	WILBRAHAM	J	6	439
WHYTON	FW	12	241	WICKS	RT	3	253	WIGGINTON	RJ	10	249	WILBY	A	8	390
WIBER	JW	4	417	WICKS	TW	2	390	WIGGITT	CT	6	439	WILBY	A	8	390
WIBLIN	FJL	2	389	WICKS	WC	9	208	WIGGITT	ST	6	439	WILBY	F	8	390
WIBREW	GW	2	389	WICKS	WJ	10	249	WIGGLESWORTH	D	8	389	WILBY	F	8	390
WIBROW	EH	3	406	WICKSON	AJ	5	383	WIGGLESWORTH	E	11	401	WILBY	JF	12	414
WICHALL	A	1	369	WIDD	E	9	208	WIGGLESWORTH	H	8	389	WILCOCK	A	11	402
WICHELON	F	2	389	WIDDESON	JH	3	254	WIGGLESWORTH	H	9	370	WILCOCK	A	14	342
WICK	A	8	389	WIDDOP	C	9	370	WIGGLESWORTH	HG	8	389	WILCOCK	E	1	369

WILCOCK	G	14	342	WILD	AE	10	249	WILDMAN	HG	12	241	WILKES	H	3	254	
WILCOCK	GH	4	418	WILD	AJ	7	440	WILDMAN	JH	12	241	WILKES	HG	2	392	
WILCOCK	H	8	390	WILD	CG	7	440	WILDMAN	JT	5	384	WILKES	HT	14	343	
WILCOCK	H	9	370	WILD	CT	2	391	WILDMAN	PE	5	384	WILKES	J	13	454	
WILCOCK	J	8	390	WILD	D	7	440	WILDMAN	PE	12	242	WILKES	JC	6	440	
WILCOCK	J	14	342	WILD	EC	5	384	WILDMAN	WE	12	242	WILKES	R	6	440	
WILCOCK	JR	9	209	WILD	EW	5	384	WILDS	A	13	454	WILKES	S	4	418	
WILCOCK	JW	2	390	WILD	F	8	390	WILDS	HT	13	454	WILKES	SRCM	4	418	
WILCOCK	L	9	209	WILD	G	14	343	WILDSMITH	HG	5	384	WILKES	T	3	254	
WILCOCK	M	9	209	WILD	J	7	440	WILDSMITH	P	6	439	WILKES	T	6	440	
WILCOCK	R	14	342	WILD	J	14	343	WILDY	DB	7	440	WILKES	T	14	343	
WILCOCK	RA	14	343	WILD	JA	2	391	WILEMAN	JR	6	439	WILKES	TH	6	440	
WILCOCK	RL	11	402	WILD	JA	3	254	WILES	A	12	242	WILKES	W	6	440	
WILCOCK	TN	2	391	WILD	R	9	209	WILES	A	12	242	WILKES	WE	6	440	
WILCOCK	W	8	390	WILD	R	11	402	WILES	CAE	13	454	WILKIE	J	4	418	
WILCOCKS	A	7	440	WILD	RW	9	209	WILES	E	2	391	WILKIN	BE	13	455	
WILCOCKS	JJ	2	391	WILD	S	4	418	WILES	EJ	12	242	WILKIN	E	5	384	
WILCOCKS	R	2	391	WILD	S	6	439	WILES	F	9	371	WILKIN	EJ	7	440	
WILCOCKS	WH	8	390	WILD	T	9	370	WILES	F	12	242	WILKIN	GA	7	441	
WILCOX	A	6	439	WILD	T	11	402	WILES	FE	5	384	WILKIN	J	7	441	
WILCOX	AE	2	391	WILD	W	9	209	WILES	FW	2	391	WILKIN	JT	13	454	
WILCOX	C	6	439	WILD	W	13	454	WILES	GW	12	242	WILKIN	TW	2	392	
WILCOX	ELL	4	419	WILD	W	14	343	WILES	H	12	242	WILKINS	A	2	392	
WILCOX	F	1	370	WILD	W	14	343	WILES	HS	8	390	WILKINS	A	6	440	
WILCOX	F	11	402	WILD	WF	10	249	WILES	L	13	454	WILKINS	A	7	441	
WILCOX	FJ	12	414	WILD	WH	2	391	WILES	RJ	2	391	WILKINS	A	8	390	
WILCOX	FM	1	370	WILDE	E	14	343	WILES	W	2	391	WILKINS	A	10	249	
WILCOX	G	6	439	WILDE	FC	10	390	WILEY	W	6	439	WILKINS	A	13	455	
WILCOX	G	11	402	WILDE	G	11	402	WILFORD	A	9	209	WILKINS	AA	10	249	
WILCOX	GE	13	454	WILDE	H	9	370	WILFORD	C	9	209	WILKINS	AE	13	455	
WILCOX	H	2	391	WILDE	H	11	402	WILFORD	G	9	371	WILKINS	AEV	7	441	
WILCOX	H	11	402	WILDE	J	11	402	WILFORD	GB	9	209	WILKINS	AM	12	414	
WILCOX	HE	9	209	WILDE	JW	8	390	WILFORD	JT	8	390	WILKINS	C	2	392	
WILCOX	HP	2	391	WILDE	JW	14	343	WILFORD	R	9	209	WILKINS	C	4	418	
WILCOX	HR	12	414	WILDE	OH	11	402	WILKEN	GF	2	391	WILKINS	C	10	249	
WILCOX	J	6	439	WILDE	R	11	402	WILKES	A	6	439	WILKINS	CA	6	440	
WILCOX	J	7	440	WILDER	C	12	241	WILKES	A	6	440	WILKINS	CC	12	242	
WILCOX	J	8	390	WILDER	JH	7	440	WILKES	A	6	440	WILKINS	CD	8	390	
WILCOX	J	12	414	WILDER	W	13	454	WILKES	A	14	343	WILKINS	DK	10	249	
WILCOX	JE	13	454	WILDERS	AH	5	384	WILKES	AA	6	440	WILKINS	E	4	418	
WILCOX	P	7	440	WILDERS	B	5	384	WILKES	AD	1	370	WILKINS	E	8	391	
WILCOX	R	2	391	WILDERS	G	5	384	WILKES	AH	6	440	WILKINS	EAG	10	249	
WILCOX	R	11	402	WILDERS	T	14	343	WILKES	C	13	454	WILKINS	F	5	384	
WILCOX	S	14	343	WILDES	H	10	249	WILKES	CHJ	2	391	WILKINS	FC	3	406	
WILCOX	SG	2	391	WILDEY	E	1	370	WILKES	CL	6	440	WILKINS	FE	2	392	
WILCOX	SH	4	418	WILDING	CF	7	440	WILKES	CW	12	414	WILKINS	FG	12	414	
WILCOX	SL	13	454	WILDING	EB	14	343	WILKES	E	9	209	WILKINS	FH	4	418	
WILCOX	TE	12	414	WILDING	J	14	343	WILKES	F	3	406	WILKINS	FH	6	440	
WILCOX	W	2	391	WILDING	J	14	343	WILKES	F	6	440	WILKINS	FH	6	440	
WILCOX	W	10	249	WILDING	W	9	371	WILKES	F	8	390	WILKINS	FJ	6	440	
WILCOX	W	12	414	WILDISH	T	3	254	WILKES	FJ	6	440	WILKINS	GH	2	392	
WILCOX	WEH	7	440	WILDMAN	A	5	384	WILKES	FP	11	402	WILKINS	GH	6	441	
WILCOXON	G	7	440	WILDMAN	B	11	402	WILKES	G	6	440	WILKINS	GJ	2	392	
WILCOXON	HC	7	440	WILDMAN	C	6	439	WILKES	GS	10	390	WILKINS	H	4	418	
WILD	A	9	209	WILDMAN	C	12	241	WILKES	H	2	391	WILKINS	H	12	415	

WILKINS	H	13	455	WILKINSON	C	8	391	WILKINSON	H	9	371	WILKINSON	PJ	2	393
WILKINS	HJ	2	392	WILKINSON	C	8	391	WILKINSON	H	9	371	WILKINSON	R	8	392
WILKINS	J	2	392	WILKINSON	C	8	391	WILKINSON	H	9	371	WILKINSON	R	8	392
WILKINS	J	2	392	WILKINSON	C	9	210	WILKINSON	H	11	403	WILKINSON	R	9	372
WILKINS	J	2	392	WILKINSON	C	9	210	WILKINSON	H	11	403	WILKINSON	R	11	403
WILKINS	J	6	441	WILKINSON	C	9	371	WILKINSON	H	11	403	WILKINSON	RJW	10	250
WILKINS	J	12	242	WILKINSON	CA	2	392	WILKINSON	H	13	455	WILKINSON	S	8	392
WILKINS	J	14	343	WILKINSON	CS	2	392	WILKINSON	H	14	344	WILKINSON	S	9	372
WILKINS	JA	6	440	WILKINSON	CW	10	250	WILKINSON	HC	6	441	WILKINSON	S	11	403
WILKINS	JC	4	418	WILKINSON	E	6	441	WILKINSON	HE	3	254	WILKINSON	S	11	403
WILKINS	JH	7	441	WILKINSON	E	8	391	WILKINSON	HE	9	371	WILKINSON	T	6	441
WILKINS	JM	12	415	WILKINSON	E	9	210	WILKINSON	HH	12	242	WILKINSON	T	6	441
WILKINS	JS	10	390	WILKINSON	E	9	371	WILKINSON	HL	3	254	WILKINSON	T	8	392
WILKINS	JW	12	415	WILKINSON	EJ	9	371	WILKINSON	HS	8	391	WILKINSON	T	9	211
WILKINS	M	4	418	WILKINSON	F	8	391	WILKINSON	HSP	5	384	WILKINSON	T	11	403
WILKINS	N	5	384	WILKINSON	F	9	210	WILKINSON	HT	10	250	WILKINSON	TW	1	370
WILKINS	P	4	418	WILKINSON	F	9	371	WILKINSON	IH	9	210	WILKINSON	W	7	441
WILKINS	PF	10	249	WILKINSON	F	11	403	WILKINSON	J	2	393	WILKINSON	W	8	392
WILKINS	R	10	249	WILKINSON	F	14	343	WILKINSON	J	3	254	WILKINSON	W	8	392
WILKINS	RH	2	392	WILKINSON	F	14	343	WILKINSON	J	6	441	WILKINSON	W	8	392
WILKINS	RH	4	418	WILKINSON	FC	6	441	WILKINSON	J	8	391	WILKINSON	W	8	392
WILKINS	RV	7	441	WILKINSON	FH	10	250	WILKINSON	J	8	392	WILKINSON	W	9	211
WILKINS	S	2	392	WILKINSON	FR	4	418	WILKINSON	J	8	392	WILKINSON	W	9	211
WILKINS	S	5	384	WILKINSON	G	1	370	WILKINSON	J	9	210	WILKINSON	W	9	211
WILKINS	S	6	441	WILKINSON	G	2	392	WILKINSON	J	9	210	WILKINSON	W	9	211
WILKINS	S	6	441	WILKINSON	G	6	441	WILKINSON	J	9	210	WILKINSON	W	9	372
WILKINS	SG	10	390	WILKINSON	G	7	441	WILKINSON	J	9	210	WILKINSON	W	9	372
WILKINS	SW	4	418	WILKINSON	G	8	391	WILKINSON	J	9	371	WILKINSON	W	10	250
WILKINS	TE	7	441	WILKINSON	G	9	210	WILKINSON	J	9	371	WILKINSON	W	11	403
WILKINS	W	5	384	WILKINSON	G	9	210	WILKINSON	J	9	371	WILKINSON	W	11	403
WILKINS	W	6	441	WILKINSON	G	9	210	WILKINSON	J	11	403	WILKINSON	W	13	455
WILKINS	W	8	391	WILKINSON	G	9	371	WILKINSON	J	11	403	WILKINSON	W	14	344
WILKINS	W	10	249	WILKINSON	G	9	371	WILKINSON	J	13	455	WILKINSON	W	14	344
WILKINS	WG	4	418	WILKINSON	G	11	403	WILKINSON	J	14	344	WILKINSON	WA	10	250
WILKINS	WJ	13	455	WILKINSON	G	12	242	WILKINSON	J	14	344	WILKINSON	WH	5	384
WILKINS	WT	12	415	WILKINSON	G	14	344	WILKINSON	J	14	344	WILKINSON	WH	11	403
WILKINSON	A	2	392	WILKINSON	G	14	344	WILKINSON	J	14	344	WILKINSON	WH	14	344
WILKINSON	A	2	392	WILKINSON	G	14	344	WILKINSON	JB	9	371	WILKS	C	2	393
WILKINSON	A	3	407	WILKINSON	GA	12	242	WILKINSON	JC	8	392	WILKS	C	2	393
WILKINSON	A	7	441	WILKINSON	GB	4	418	WILKINSON	JE	1	370	WILKS	C	3	254
WILKINSON	A	8	391	WILKINSON	GE	4	419	WILKINSON	JE	5	384	WILKS	CG	2	393
WILKINSON	A	8	391	WILKINSON	GE	8	391	WILKINSON	JE	9	371	WILKS	E	9	211
WILKINSON	A	9	209	WILKINSON	GF	7	441	WILKINSON	JH	7	441	WILKS	F	8	392
WILKINSON	A	9	210	WILKINSON	GG	7	441	WILKINSON	JH	8	392	WILKS	H	8	392
WILKINSON	A	10	250	WILKINSON	GH	9	210	WILKINSON	JH	11	403	WILKS	J	8	392
WILKINSON	A	11	402	WILKINSON	GW	8	391	WILKINSON	JT	10	250	WILKS	J	8	392
WILKINSON	AP	9	210	WILKINSON	GW	11	403	WILKINSON	JW	1	370	WILKS	L	14	344
WILKINSON	AWW	6	441	WILKINSON	H	1	370	WILKINSON	JW	9	211	WILKS	N	9	211
WILKINSON	B	7	441	WILKINSON	H	8	391	WILKINSON	L	2	393	WILKS	W	6	441
WILKINSON	B	8	391	WILKINSON	H	8	391	WILKINSON	L	8	392	WILKS	WJ	7	441
WILKINSON	B	14	343	WILKINSON	H	9	210	WILKINSON	L	14	344	WILL	E	9	211
WILKINSON	C	3	407	WILKINSON	H	9	210	WILKINSON	LM	1	370	WILLAN	JF	11	403
WILKINSON	C	6	441	WILKINSON	H	9	210	WILKINSON	LT	2	393	WILLAN	JF	11	403
WILKINSON	C	6	441	WILKINSON	H	9	210	WILKINSON	MM	2	393	WILLAN	WA	11	404
WILKINSON	C	8	391	WILKINSON	H	9	210	WILKINSON	P	9	211	WILLANS	D	3	254
								WILKINSON	P	9	372				

WILLANS	H	8	392	WILLETT	NH	13	455	WILLIAMS	AB	4	419	WILLIAMS	CF	3	254			
WILLANS	J	8	393	WILLETT	RE	12	415	WILLIAMS	ACT	10	250	WILLIAMS	CF	10	390			
WILLANS	WC	8	393	WILLETT	WG	2	394	WILLIAMS	AD	10	250	WILLIAMS	CF	13	456			
WILLARD	AS	3	407	WILLETT	WH	13	455	WILLIAMS	AD	10	250	WILLIAMS	CG	12	415			
WILLARD	BA	3	407	WILLETTS	AW	6	441	WILLIAMS	AE	2	394	WILLIAMS	CH	6	442			
WILLARD	C	7	441	WILLETTS	B	11	404	WILLIAMS	AE	6	442	WILLIAMS	CH	6	442			
WILLARS	JT	12	415	WILLETTS	GH	6	441	WILLIAMS	AE	10	250	WILLIAMS	CH	7	442			
WILLATT	SD	3	254	WILLETTS	J	6	442	WILLIAMS	AE	10	390	WILLIAMS	CH	12	415			
WILLBOURN	C	2	393	WILLETTS	JG	6	442	WILLIAMS	AG	3	254	WILLIAMS	CH	13	456			
WILLBOURN	H	2	393	WILLETTS	JH	6	442	WILLIAMS	AG	10	250	WILLIAMS	CH	14	345			
WILLBOURN	P	2	393	WILLETTS	S	14	344	WILLIAMS	AH	5	385	WILLIAMS	CJ	2	394			
WILLCOCK	HJ	4	419	WILLETTS	T	14	344	WILLIAMS	AI	12	415	WILLIAMS	CJ	10	251			
WILLCOCK	J	14	344	WILLETTS	W	11	404	WILLIAMS	AJ	1	370	WILLIAMS	CP	5	385			
WILLCOCK	J	14	344	WILLEY	A	7	442	WILLIAMS	AJ	2	394	WILLIAMS	CS	2	394			
WILLCOCK	W	14	344	WILLEY	AC	7	442	WILLIAMS	AJ	2	394	WILLIAMS	CV	4	419			
WILLCOCKS	H	2	393	WILLEY	C	7	442	WILLIAMS	AJ	4	419	WILLIAMS	CW	2	395			
WILLCOCKS	HC	2	393	WILLEY	CA	5	385	WILLIAMS	AJ	7	442	WILLIAMS	CW	3	254			
WILLCOCKS	J	4	419	WILLEY	E	5	385	WILLIAMS	AJ	10	250	WILLIAMS	D	13	456			
WILLCOCKS	T	10	390	WILLEY	GE	6	442	WILLIAMS	AJ	10	250	WILLIAMS	D	14	345			
WILLCOX	A	1	370	WILLEY	H	5	385	WILLIAMS	AJ	13	455	WILLIAMS	DH	10	391			
WILLCOX	A	7	441	WILLEY	HJ	6	442	WILLIAMS	AMM	1	370	WILLIAMS	DHA	2	395			
WILLCOX	G	7	441	WILLEY	J	11	404	WILLIAMS	AO	12	415	WILLIAMS	DW	6	443			
WILLCOX	H	2	393	WILLEY	TW	12	242	WILLIAMS	AR	8	393	WILLIAMS	E	1	370			
WILLCOX	H	7	441	WILLFORD	AE	12	415	WILLIAMS	AR	13	455	WILLIAMS	E	2	395			
WILLCOX	H	7	442	WILLFORD	G	12	415	WILLIAMS	AT	3	254	WILLIAMS	E	2	395			
WILLCOX	HA	13	455	WILLFORD	JR	12	415	WILLIAMS	AW	1	370	WILLIAMS	E	3	407			
WILLCOX	J	4	419	WILLIAMES	CF	2	394	WILLIAMS	AW	2	394	WILLIAMS	E	4	419			
WILLCOX	LA	4	419	WILLIAMS	A	2	394	WILLIAMS	B	2	394	WILLIAMS	E	6	442			
WILLCOX	SJ	10	250	WILLIAMS	A	2	394	WILLIAMS	B	4	419	WILLIAMS	E	6	443			
WILLCOX	W	2	393	WILLIAMS	A	2	394	WILLIAMS	B	6	442	WILLIAMS	E	7	442			
WILLCOX	W	4	419	WILLIAMS	A	3	254	WILLIAMS	B	6	442	WILLIAMS	E	7	442			
WILLCOX	WA	1	370	WILLIAMS	A	4	419	WILLIAMS	B	11	404	WILLIAMS	E	7	442			
WILLCOX	WT	7	442	WILLIAMS	A	4	419	WILLIAMS	BH	2	394	WILLIAMS	E	9	372			
WILLDIG	J	11	404	WILLIAMS	A	6	442	WILLIAMS	BJ	6	442	WILLIAMS	E	10	391			
WILLER	F	1	370	WILLIAMS	A	6	442	WILLIAMS	BW	11	404	WILLIAMS	E	11	404			
WILLER	SA	13	455	WILLIAMS	A	6	442	WILLIAMS	C	2	394	WILLIAMS	E	11	404			
WILLERTON	A	1	370	WILLIAMS	A	7	442	WILLIAMS	C	2	394	WILLIAMS	E	11	404			
WILLERTON	G	3	407	WILLIAMS	A	7	442	WILLIAMS	C	4	419	WILLIAMS	E	11	404			
WILLES	AH	5	384	WILLIAMS	A	7	442	WILLIAMS	C	6	442	WILLIAMS	E	13	456			
WILLES	SA	13	455	WILLIAMS	A	7	442	WILLIAMS	C	6	442	WILLIAMS	E	14	345			
WILLETT	A	12	242	WILLIAMS	A	8	393	WILLIAMS	C	6	442	WILLIAMS	E	14	345			
WILLETT	AEC	13	455	WILLIAMS	A	9	211	WILLIAMS	C	7	442	WILLIAMS	E	14	345			
WILLETT	C	2	393	WILLIAMS	A	9	392	WILLIAMS	C	8	393	WILLIAMS	EA	3	407			
WILLETT	CFG	5	385	WILLIAMS	A	10	250	WILLIAMS	C	9	211	WILLIAMS	EA	6	443			
WILLETT	EA	12	415	WILLIAMS	A	10	250	WILLIAMS	C	10	390	WILLIAMS	EA	12	415			
WILLETT	EW	2	393	WILLIAMS	A	11	404	WILLIAMS	C	11	404	WILLIAMS	EC	6	443			
WILLETT	F	13	455	WILLIAMS	A	11	404	WILLIAMS	C	11	404	WILLIAMS	EC	6	443			
WILLETT	FF	12	242	WILLIAMS	A	12	242	WILLIAMS	C	12	415	WILLIAMS	EC	10	251			
WILLETT	H	13	455	WILLIAMS	A	12	415	WILLIAMS	C	12	415	WILLIAMS	EC	10	391			
WILLETT	HG	12	242	WILLIAMS	A	13	455	WILLIAMS	CA	2	394	WILLIAMS	EE	4	419			
WILLETT	J	12	242	WILLIAMS	A	14	344	WILLIAMS	CA	2	394	WILLIAMS	EF	5	385			
WILLETT	JA	5	385	WILLIAMS	A	14	344	WILLIAMS	CA	13	455	WILLIAMS	EG	4	419			
WILLETT	JH	4	419	WILLIAMS	A	14	345	WILLIAMS	CD	13	456	WILLIAMS	EH	3	407			
WILLETT	JRF	5	385	WILLIAMS	AA	2	394	WILLIAMS	CE	10	251	WILLIAMS	EH	7	442			
WILLETT	JT	7	442	WILLIAMS	AA	7	442	WILLIAMS	CE	13	456	WILLIAMS	EJ	2	395			

WILLIAMS	EJ	7	442	WILLIAMS	G	4	420	WILLIAMS	HG	14	345	WILLIAMS	JA	9	372
WILLIAMS	EJ	14	345	WILLIAMS	G	5	385	WILLIAMS	HJ	7	443	WILLIAMS	JC	3	255
WILLIAMS	ER	4	419	WILLIAMS	G	6	443	WILLIAMS	HO	11	405	WILLIAMS	JC	4	420
WILLIAMS	ER	6	443	WILLIAMS	G	6	443	WILLIAMS	HP	4	420	WILLIAMS	JC	8	393
WILLIAMS	EW	2	395	WILLIAMS	G	6	443	WILLIAMS	HS	3	254	WILLIAMS	JC	8	393
WILLIAMS	EW	7	443	WILLIAMS	G	6	443	WILLIAMS	HS	7	443	WILLIAMS	JC	13	456
WILLIAMS	EW	7	443	WILLIAMS	G	6	443	WILLIAMS	HS	12	243	WILLIAMS	JE	1	371
WILLIAMS	F	2	395	WILLIAMS	G	10	251	WILLIAMS	HV	10	391	WILLIAMS	JE	7	443
WILLIAMS	F	2	395	WILLIAMS	G	11	404	WILLIAMS	HW	10	251	WILLIAMS	JE	11	405
WILLIAMS	F	2	395	WILLIAMS	G	11	405	WILLIAMS	I	14	345	WILLIAMS	JE	12	416
WILLIAMS	F	2	395	WILLIAMS	G	12	416	WILLIAMS	I	14	345	WILLIAMS	JF	10	391
WILLIAMS	F	5	385	WILLIAMS	G	14	345	WILLIAMS	J	2	396	WILLIAMS	JF	14	346
WILLIAMS	F	6	443	WILLIAMS	GA	2	395	WILLIAMS	J	2	396	WILLIAMS	JH	5	385
WILLIAMS	F	6	443	WILLIAMS	GA	2	395	WILLIAMS	J	2	396	WILLIAMS	JH	5	385
WILLIAMS	F	6	443	WILLIAMS	GA	2	395	WILLIAMS	J	3	254	WILLIAMS	JH	5	385
WILLIAMS	F	6	443	WILLIAMS	GA	8	393	WILLIAMS	J	3	254	WILLIAMS	JH	8	393
WILLIAMS	F	6	443	WILLIAMS	GC	7	443	WILLIAMS	J	3	255	WILLIAMS	JH	12	416
WILLIAMS	F	8	393	WILLIAMS	GE	3	254	WILLIAMS	J	4	420	WILLIAMS	JH	13	456
WILLIAMS	F	10	251	WILLIAMS	GE	6	443	WILLIAMS	J	6	444	WILLIAMS	JH	14	346
WILLIAMS	F	10	390	WILLIAMS	GH	2	395	WILLIAMS	J	6	444	WILLIAMS	JJ	6	444
WILLIAMS	F	11	404	WILLIAMS	GH	2	395	WILLIAMS	J	6	444	WILLIAMS	JR	10	251
WILLIAMS	F	12	242	WILLIAMS	GH	10	251	WILLIAMS	J	6	444	WILLIAMS	JR	10	251
WILLIAMS	F	13	456	WILLIAMS	GH	12	243	WILLIAMS	J	6	444	WILLIAMS	JR	11	405
WILLIAMS	F	13	456	WILLIAMS	GH	12	416	WILLIAMS	J	6	444	WILLIAMS	JS	8	393
WILLIAMS	F	13	456	WILLIAMS	GSF	10	251	WILLIAMS	J	6	444	WILLIAMS	JS	11	405
WILLIAMS	F	14	345	WILLIAMS	GT	10	251	WILLIAMS	J	6	444	WILLIAMS	JT	6	444
WILLIAMS	F	14	345	WILLIAMS	H	2	396	WILLIAMS	J	7	443	WILLIAMS	JT	11	405
WILLIAMS	F	14	345	WILLIAMS	H	2	396	WILLIAMS	J	7	443	WILLIAMS	JTE	3	255
WILLIAMS	FA	2	395	WILLIAMS	H	2	396	WILLIAMS	J	7	444	WILLIAMS	JW	2	396
WILLIAMS	FA	3	254	WILLIAMS	H	2	396	WILLIAMS	J	8	393	WILLIAMS	JW	4	420
WILLIAMS	FA	4	420	WILLIAMS	H	2	396	WILLIAMS	J	8	393	WILLIAMS	JW	8	393
WILLIAMS	FA	4	420	WILLIAMS	H	6	443	WILLIAMS	J	8	393	WILLIAMS	JW	11	405
WILLIAMS	FA	12	415	WILLIAMS	H	6	443	WILLIAMS	J	9	211	WILLIAMS	L	1	371
WILLIAMS	FA	13	456	WILLIAMS	H	6	443	WILLIAMS	J	9	211	WILLIAMS	L	1	371
WILLIAMS	FB	4	420	WILLIAMS	H	7	443	WILLIAMS	J	9	372	WILLIAMS	L	2	396
WILLIAMS	FC	4	420	WILLIAMS	H	7	443	WILLIAMS	J	10	251	WILLIAMS	L	8	393
WILLIAMS	FC	12	243	WILLIAMS	H	8	393	WILLIAMS	J	10	251	WILLIAMS	L	8	393
WILLIAMS	FD	2	395	WILLIAMS	H	9	211	WILLIAMS	J	10	391	WILLIAMS	L	8	393
WILLIAMS	FE	12	415	WILLIAMS	H	9	211	WILLIAMS	J	11	405	WILLIAMS	L	8	393
WILLIAMS	FE	13	456	WILLIAMS	H	10	391	WILLIAMS	J	11	405	WILLIAMS	L	11	405
WILLIAMS	FE	13	456	WILLIAMS	H	11	405	WILLIAMS	J	11	405	WILLIAMS	LAF	10	251
WILLIAMS	FES	10	251	WILLIAMS	H	11	405	WILLIAMS	J	11	405	WILLIAMS	LF	13	456
WILLIAMS	FF	11	404	WILLIAMS	H	11	405	WILLIAMS	J	13	456	WILLIAMS	LH	14	346
WILLIAMS	FG	2	395	WILLIAMS	H	12	243	WILLIAMS	J	14	346	WILLIAMS	LJ	7	443
WILLIAMS	FG	13	456	WILLIAMS	H	12	416	WILLIAMS	J	14	346	WILLIAMS	LJ	10	251
WILLIAMS	FJ	10	251	WILLIAMS	H	12	416	WILLIAMS	J	14	346	WILLIAMS	M	11	405
WILLIAMS	FM	7	443	WILLIAMS	H	13	456	WILLIAMS	J	14	346	WILLIAMS	M	14	346
WILLIAMS	FO	14	345	WILLIAMS	H	13	456	WILLIAMS	J	14	346	WILLIAMS	MH	4	420
WILLIAMS	FS	7	443	WILLIAMS	H	14	345	WILLIAMS	J	14	346	WILLIAMS	MW	7	443
WILLIAMS	FW	2	395	WILLIAMS	H	14	345	WILLIAMS	J	14	346	WILLIAMS	N	3	255
WILLIAMS	FW	13	456	WILLIAMS	H	14	345	WILLIAMS	J	14	346	WILLIAMS	O	10	391
WILLIAMS	G	1	370	WILLIAMS	HA	2	396	WILLIAMS	J	14	346	WILLIAMS	OR	12	243
WILLIAMS	G	2	395	WILLIAMS	HC	1	370	WILLIAMS	J	14	346	WILLIAMS	P	11	405
WILLIAMS	G	4	420	WILLIAMS	HCV	7	443	WILLIAMS	JA	6	444	WILLIAMS	P	11	406
WILLIAMS	G	4	420	WILLIAMS	HG	2	396	WILLIAMS	JA	7	443	WILLIAMS	P	12	243
				WILLIAMS	HG	7	443								

WILLIAMS	P	14	346	WILLIAMS	TA	14	347	WILLIAMS	WHC	3	255	WILLIAMSON	R	14	348			
WILLIAMS	R	4	420	WILLIAMS	TH	6	445	WILLIAMS	WJ	6	445	WILLIAMSON	R	14	348			
WILLIAMS	R	4	420	WILLIAMS	TH	11	406	WILLIAMS	WJ	8	394	WILLIAMSON	S	2	397			
WILLIAMS	R	8	394	WILLIAMS	TH	11	406	WILLIAMS	WJ	12	243	WILLIAMSON	SE	4	420			
WILLIAMS	R	8	394	WILLIAMS	TH	14	347	WILLIAMS	WR	10	252	WILLIAMSON	SH	12	416			
WILLIAMS	R	9	211	WILLIAMS	TH	14	347	WILLIAMS	WR	11	406	WILLIAMSON	T	7	444			
WILLIAMS	R	11	405	WILLIAMS	TJ	10	391	WILLIAMS	WT	14	347	WILLIAMSON	T	9	212			
WILLIAMS	R	12	243	WILLIAMS	V	12	416	WILLIAMSON	A	1	371	WILLIAMSON	T	9	372			
WILLIAMS	R	12	416	WILLIAMS	W	1	371	WILLIAMSON	A	8	394	WILLIAMSON	T	11	407			
WILLIAMS	R	13	456	WILLIAMS	W	2	396	WILLIAMSON	A	8	394	WILLIAMSON	T	14	348			
WILLIAMS	R	13	457	WILLIAMS	W	2	396	WILLIAMSON	A	11	406	WILLIAMSON	TE	11	407			
WILLIAMS	R	14	346	WILLIAMS	W	3	255	WILLIAMSON	B	3	255	WILLIAMSON	TF	13	457			
WILLIAMS	R	14	346	WILLIAMS	W	5	385	WILLIAMSON	B	4	420	WILLIAMSON	TH	14	348			
WILLIAMS	R	14	346	WILLIAMS	W	6	444	WILLIAMSON	B	5	385	WILLIAMSON	TJ	13	457			
WILLIAMS	RC	2	396	WILLIAMS	W	6	445	WILLIAMSON	B	11	406	WILLIAMSON	TS	2	397			
WILLIAMS	RG	6	444	WILLIAMS	W	6	445	WILLIAMSON	C	10	391	WILLIAMSON	W	6	445			
WILLIAMS	RH	5	385	WILLIAMS	W	6	445	WILLIAMSON	CC	5	385	WILLIAMSON	W	8	394			
WILLIAMS	RH	13	457	WILLIAMS	W	6	445	WILLIAMSON	CG	2	397	WILLIAMSON	W	10	252			
WILLIAMS	RT	11	406	WILLIAMS	W	6	445	WILLIAMSON	CH	14	347	WILLIAMSON	W	11	407			
WILLIAMS	S	1	371	WILLIAMS	W	6	445	WILLIAMSON	E	3	255	WILLIAMSON	W	14	348			
WILLIAMS	S	2	396	WILLIAMS	W	6	445	WILLIAMSON	E	4	420	WILLIAMSON	W	14	348			
WILLIAMS	S	3	255	WILLIAMS	W	7	444	WILLIAMSON	E	11	406	WILLIAMSON	W	14	348			
WILLIAMS	S	3	407	WILLIAMS	W	8	394	WILLIAMSON	E	14	347	WILLIAMSON	WG	2	397			
WILLIAMS	S	3	407	WILLIAMS	W	8	394	WILLIAMSON	EB	14	347	WILLIAMSON	WH	11	407			
WILLIAMS	S	6	444	WILLIAMS	W	9	211	WILLIAMSON	F	5	386	WILLICOMBE	H	7	444			
WILLIAMS	S	6	444	WILLIAMS	W	9	212	WILLIAMSON	F	12	243	WILLICOTT	C	10	252			
WILLIAMS	S	10	391	WILLIAMS	W	9	212	WILLIAMSON	FJ	10	252	WILLIMOTT	E	2	397			
WILLIAMS	S	14	346	WILLIAMS	W	10	252	WILLIAMSON	G	8	394	WILLINGALE	W	1	371			
WILLIAMS	SE	12	243	WILLIAMS	W	10	252	WILLIAMSON	G	8	394	WILLINGHAM	AL	5	386			
WILLIAMS	SG	1	370	WILLIAMS	W	10	252	WILLIAMSON	G	9	372	WILLINGHAM	G	7	444			
WILLIAMS	SJ	3	255	WILLIAMS	W	11	406	WILLIAMSON	G	12	243	WILLINGHAM	H	12	416			
WILLIAMS	SP	11	406	WILLIAMS	W	11	406	WILLIAMSON	GB	8	394	WILLIS	A	1	371			
WILLIAMS	SR	10	251	WILLIAMS	W	11	406	WILLIAMSON	GF	10	391	WILLIS	A	2	397			
WILLIAMS	SW	2	396	WILLIAMS	W	13	457	WILLIAMSON	GT	14	347	WILLIS	A	5	386			
WILLIAMS	SW	10	251	WILLIAMS	W	13	457	WILLIAMSON	GW	14	347	WILLIS	A	8	394			
WILLIAMS	SW	14	347	WILLIAMS	W	14	347	WILLIAMSON	H	11	406	WILLIS	A	10	252			
WILLIAMS	T	6	444	WILLIAMS	W	14	347	WILLIAMSON	H	11	407	WILLIS	A	11	407			
WILLIAMS	T	6	445	WILLIAMS	W	14	347	WILLIAMSON	H	14	347	WILLIS	A	14	348			
WILLIAMS	T	7	444	WILLIAMS	WAS	13	457	WILLIAMSON	H	14	348	WILLIS	AAJ	13	457			
WILLIAMS	T	8	394	WILLIAMS	WB	8	394	WILLIAMSON	J	5	386	WILLIS	AE	3	255			
WILLIAMS	T	9	211	WILLIAMS	WC	2	396	WILLIAMSON	J	5	386	WILLIS	AE	4	421			
WILLIAMS	T	10	252	WILLIAMS	WC	4	420	WILLIAMSON	J	8	394	WILLIS	AE	13	457			
WILLIAMS	T	10	252	WILLIAMS	WC	13	457	WILLIAMSON	J	8	394	WILLIS	AG	4	421			
WILLIAMS	T	11	406	WILLIAMS	WD	2	397	WILLIAMSON	J	9	212	WILLIS	AG	5	386			
WILLIAMS	T	11	406	WILLIAMS	WE	12	243	WILLIAMSON	JR	11	407	WILLIS	AL	3	255			
WILLIAMS	T	11	406	WILLIAMS	WE	14	347	WILLIAMSON	JW	11	407	WILLIS	AW	3	255			
WILLIAMS	T	11	406	WILLIAMS	WG	2	397	WILLIAMSON	L	12	416	WILLIS	B	8	394			
WILLIAMS	T	11	406	WILLIAMS	WG	2	397	WILLIAMSON	M	8	394	WILLIS	B	8	394			
WILLIAMS	T	13	457	WILLIAMS	WG	4	420	WILLIAMSON	P	8	394	WILLIS	C	3	255			
WILLIAMS	T	13	457	WILLIAMS	WH	2	397	WILLIAMSON	P	14	348	WILLIS	CA	10	391			
WILLIAMS	T	14	347	WILLIAMS	WH	3	407	WILLIAMSON	R	5	386	WILLIS	CT	7	444			
WILLIAMS	T	14	347	WILLIAMS	WH	4	420	WILLIAMSON	R	7	444	WILLIS	CV	7	444			
WILLIAMS	T	14	347	WILLIAMS	WH	6	445	WILLIAMSON	R	11	407	WILLIS	E	12	243			
WILLIAMS	T	14	347	WILLIAMS	WH	6	445	WILLIAMSON	R	11	407	WILLIS	EC	2	397			
WILLIAMS	T	14	347	WILLIAMS	WH	13	457	WILLIAMSON	R	11	407	WILLIS	F	2	397			

WILLIS	F	12	416	WILLIS	WJ	6	445	WILLS	B	4	421	WILMER	A	12	417
WILLIS	FA	1	371	WILLIS	WR	6	445	WILLS	C	7	445	WILMER	J	10	392
WILLIS	FC	4	421	WILLISON	F	5	386	WILLS	C	12	416	WILMER	WH	10	392
WILLIS	FD	8	395	WILLISON	FWT	5	386	WILLS	CA	4	421	WILMHURST	WSS	2	398
WILLIS	FE	7	444	WILLISS	J	8	395	WILLS	CS	2	398	WILMORE	AE	13	458
WILLIS	FG	4	421	WILLMER	CA	2	397	WILLS	DP	13	457	WILMORE	E	7	445
WILLIS	FJ	5	386	WILLMER	H	11	407	WILLS	E	2	398	WILMOT	AE	5	387
WILLIS	FT	12	416	WILLMER	W	11	407	WILLS	G	1	371	WILMOT	CJ	5	387
WILLIS	FW	7	444	WILLMETT	AL	4	421	WILLS	G	6	446	WILMOT	F	6	446
WILLIS	G	1	371	WILLMORE	CH	4	421	WILLS	H	9	372	WILMOT	WA	12	244
WILLIS	G	12	243	WILLMORE	CH	5	386	WILLS	HC	2	398	WILMOTT	AE	11	408
WILLIS	GA	4	421	WILLMORE	DV	12	416	WILLS	J	5	387	WILMOTT	FG	7	444
WILLIS	GH	1	371	WILLMORE	WH	5	387	WILLS	J	5	387	WILMOTT	HP	11	408
WILLIS	GH	2	397	WILLMOTT	F	13	458	WILLS	J	12	417	WILMOTT	W	11	408
WILLIS	GJH	10	391	WILLMOTT	GC	13	457	WILLS	JG	12	244	WILMSHURST	CW	13	458
WILLIS	GR	5	386	WILLMOTT	GC	14	348	WILLS	SA	1	371	WILMSHURST	FC	13	458
WILLIS	H	3	255	WILLMOTT	JW	13	457	WILLS	SA	2	398	WILMSHURST	T	2	398
WILLIS	H	4	421	WILLMOTT	T	3	407	WILLS	SF	6	446	WILMSHURST	WJ	6	446
WILLIS	HA	10	391	WILLMOTT	WJ	2	397	WILLS	T	12	417	WILMSHURST	WR	13	458
WILLIS	HE	4	421	WILLMOTT	WJ	7	444	WILLS	TA	2	398	WILSDON	JW	2	398
WILLIS	HH	5	386	WILLN	R	5	387	WILLS	TF	2	398	WILSDON	WW	2	398
WILLIS	HS	5	386	WILLOCK	E	9	212	WILLS	WH	10	391	WILSHAW	AD	11	408
WILLIS	J	2	397	WILLOCK	JB	6	446	WILLS	WT	7	445	WILSHAW	HC	6	446
WILLIS	J	2	397	WILLOTT	J	11	407	WILLSHAW	A	11	408	WILSHAW	I	9	373
WILLIS	J	12	243	WILLOUGHBY	A	9	212	WILLSHEARE	JH	2	398	WILSHER	A	5	387
WILLIS	J	13	457	WILLOUGHBY	A	14	348	WILLSHEARE	N	3	255	WILSHER	EA	2	398
WILLIS	JJ	13	457	WILLOUGHBY	AE	4	421	WILLSHER	BG	3	255	WILSHER	J	5	387
WILLIS	JN	11	407	WILLOUGHBY	AE	7	444	WILLSHER	HE	4	421	WILSHER	JH	1	371
WILLIS	JR	5	386	WILLOUGHBY	CW	11	407	WILLSHER	HL	4	421	WILSHER	W	12	244
WILLIS	JW	7	444	WILLOUGHBY	F	7	445	WILLSHIRE	AE	10	252	WILSHERE	SA	5	387
WILLIS	L	5	386	WILLOUGHBY	F	8	395	WILLSON	CR	13	457	WILSHIR	H	8	395
WILLIS	LC	5	386	WILLOUGHBY	H	9	372	WILLSON	ER	5	387	WILSHIRE	E	6	446
WILLIS	LP	7	444	WILLOUGHBY	H	9	372	WILLSON	FJ	2	398	WILSHIRE	EF	2	399
WILLIS	O	6	445	WILLOUGHBY	H	12	416	WILLSON	FW	2	398	WILSHIRE	W	6	447
WILLIS	R	5	386	WILLOUGHBY	J	9	212	WILLSON	HW	2	398	WILSON	A	1	371
WILLIS	R	14	348	WILLOUGHBY	J	14	348	WILLSON	JB	2	398	WILSON	A	2	399
WILLIS	RC	7	444	WILLOUGHBY	P	2	398	WILLSON	WJ	1	371	WILSON	A	2	399
WILLIS	RH	4	421	WILLOUGHBY	T	9	372	WILLSON	WJ	2	398	WILSON	A	2	399
WILLIS	S	3	255	WILLOUGHBY	TW	3	255	WILLSTEAD	AF	4	421	WILSON	A	5	387
WILLIS	S	4	421	WILLOUGHBY	W	11	407	WILLSTEED	JH	10	392	WILSON	A	5	387
WILLIS	SS	1	371	WILLOUGHBY	WE	2	398	WILLSTEED	W	10	391	WILSON	A	5	387
WILLIS	T	5	386	WILLOWS	A	4	421	WILLY	C	2	398	WILSON	A	6	446
WILLIS	T	6	445	WILLOWS	A	12	243	WILLY	E	4	422	WILSON	A	6	446
WILLIS	T	7	444	WILLOWS	E	12	243	WILLY	E	4	422	WILSON	A	7	445
WILLIS	T	11	407	WILLOWS	E	12	243	WILLY	H	4	422	WILSON	A	7	445
WILLIS	T	12	416	WILLOX	JA	11	408	WILLY	J	13	458	WILSON	A	7	445
WILLIS	TH	1	371	WILLS	A	1	371	WILLY	J	13	458	WILSON	A	8	395
WILLIS	TJ	7	444	WILLS	A	2	398	WILLY	T	4	422	WILSON	A	8	395
WILLIS	TW	2	397	WILLS	A	6	446	WILMAN	A	8	395	WILSON	A	8	395
WILLIS	W	6	445	WILLS	AC	12	243	WILMAN	A	9	372	WILSON	A	8	395
WILLIS	W	12	243	WILLS	AE	7	445	WILMAN	C	9	372	WILSON	A	8	395
WILLIS	W	14	348	WILLS	AE	12	416	WILMAN	E	9	372	WILSON	A	9	212
WILLIS	WA	2	397	WILLS	AH	12	416	WILMAN	H	9	372	WILSON	A	9	212
WILLIS	WCR	4	421	WILLS	AL	12	416	WILMAN	J	9	372	WILSON	A	9	373
WILLIS	WJ	5	386	WILLS	AS	3	255	WILMAN	N	9	212	WILSON	A	9	373

WILSON	A	9	373	WILSON	CF	14	349	WILSON	FH	2	399	WILSON	H	9	212
WILSON	A	10	252	WILSON	CG	10	392	WILSON	FJ	11	408	WILSON	H	9	212
WILSON	A	10	252	WILSON	CG	13	458	WILSON	FJ	13	458	WILSON	H	9	373
WILSON	A	10	252	WILSON	CH	2	399	WILSON	FL	2	399	WILSON	H	10	253
WILSON	A	10	392	WILSON	CH	2	399	WILSON	FR	7	445	WILSON	H	11	408
WILSON	A	11	408	WILSON	CH	5	387	WILSON	FW	10	252	WILSON	H	11	409
WILSON	A	11	408	WILSON	CH	14	349	WILSON	G	1	372	WILSON	H	11	409
WILSON	A	11	408	WILSON	CH	14	349	WILSON	G	2	399	WILSON	H	11	409
WILSON	A	11	408	WILSON	CJ	4	422	WILSON	G	4	422	WILSON	H	12	417
WILSON	A	11	408	WILSON	CS	13	458	WILSON	G	5	388	WILSON	H	13	458
WILSON	A	12	244	WILSON	D	5	387	WILSON	G	8	396	WILSON	H	13	459
WILSON	A	12	244	WILSON	D	11	408	WILSON	G	8	396	WILSON	H	13	459
WILSON	A	12	417	WILSON	D	11	408	WILSON	G	8	396	WILSON	H	14	349
WILSON	A	13	458	WILSON	DA	8	395	WILSON	G	8	396	WILSON	HD	2	399
WILSON	A	13	458	WILSON	DD	8	396	WILSON	G	8	396	WILSON	HF	7	445
WILSON	A	13	458	WILSON	DM	14	349	WILSON	G	8	396	WILSON	HJ	2	399
WILSON	A	14	348	WILSON	DW	9	373	WILSON	G	8	396	WILSON	HJ	5	388
WILSON	A	14	348	WILSON	E	2	399	WILSON	G	10	252	WILSON	HJ	7	445
WILSON	A	14	348	WILSON	E	3	407	WILSON	G	11	409	WILSON	HJ	11	409
WILSON	A	14	348	WILSON	E	4	422	WILSON	G	12	244	WILSON	HW	13	459
WILSON	AA	8	395	WILSON	E	5	388	WILSON	G	12	244	WILSON	J	1	372
WILSON	AC	8	395	WILSON	E	7	445	WILSON	G	14	349	WILSON	J	2	399
WILSON	AD	12	244	WILSON	E	8	396	WILSON	G	14	349	WILSON	J	2	399
WILSON	AD	13	458	WILSON	E	8	396	WILSON	GA	6	446	WILSON	J	2	400
WILSON	AE	2	399	WILSON	E	8	396	WILSON	GC	10	392	WILSON	J	2	400
WILSON	AF	2	399	WILSON	E	8	396	WILSON	GE	5	388	WILSON	J	6	446
WILSON	AG	12	244	WILSON	E	8	396	WILSON	GE	9	212	WILSON	J	6	447
WILSON	AH	6	446	WILSON	E	9	212	WILSON	GE	10	252	WILSON	J	7	446
WILSON	AJ	2	399	WILSON	E	9	373	WILSON	GF	7	445	WILSON	J	8	397
WILSON	AL	9	212	WILSON	E	11	408	WILSON	GF	13	459	WILSON	J	8	397
WILSON	AL	9	373	WILSON	EE	7	445	WILSON	GJ	7	445	WILSON	J	8	397
WILSON	AL	10	252	WILSON	EF	4	422	WILSON	GK	14	349	WILSON	J	8	397
WILSON	AL	12	244	WILSON	EG	3	256	WILSON	GMH	10	252	WILSON	J	8	397
WILSON	AN	9	212	WILSON	EG	12	417	WILSON	GT	8	396	WILSON	J	8	397
WILSON	AS	9	212	WILSON	EH	6	446	WILSON	GW	2	399	WILSON	J	8	397
WILSON	AT	13	458	WILSON	EJ	5	388	WILSON	GW	8	396	WILSON	J	8	397
WILSON	AW	5	387	WILSON	ER	2	399	WILSON	GW	10	392	WILSON	J	8	397
WILSON	AW	5	387	WILSON	ER	5	388	WILSON	H	2	399	WILSON	J	8	397
WILSON	AW	7	445	WILSON	ER	12	417	WILSON	H	4	422	WILSON	J	8	397
WILSON	AW	13	458	WILSON	ER	12	417	WILSON	H	4	422	WILSON	J	9	212
WILSON	AW	13	458	WILSON	ES	1	372	WILSON	H	5	388	WILSON	J	9	213
WILSON	B	5	387	WILSON	ET	5	388	WILSON	H	5	388	WILSON	J	9	373
WILSON	B	8	395	WILSON	ET	5	388	WILSON	H	6	446	WILSON	J	9	373
WILSON	B	8	395	WILSON	EW	3	256	WILSON	H	6	446	WILSON	J	9	373
WILSON	B	9	212	WILSON	F	4	422	WILSON	H	6	446	WILSON	J	9	373
WILSON	BH	8	395	WILSON	F	5	388	WILSON	H	8	396	WILSON	J	10	253
WILSON	BW	9	373	WILSON	F	5	388	WILSON	H	8	396	WILSON	J	10	253
WILSON	C	8	395	WILSON	F	6	446	WILSON	H	8	396	WILSON	J	11	409
WILSON	C	8	395	WILSON	F	9	212	WILSON	H	8	396	WILSON	J	11	409
WILSON	C	8	395	WILSON	F	9	373	WILSON	H	8	397	WILSON	J	11	409
WILSON	C	11	408	WILSON	F	9	392	WILSON	H	8	397	WILSON	J	11	409
WILSON	C	12	244	WILSON	F	11	408	WILSON	H	8	397	WILSON	J	11	409
WILSON	C	12	244	WILSON	F	12	244	WILSON	H	8	397	WILSON	J	11	409
WILSON	C	12	417	WILSON	F	14	349	WILSON	H	8	397	WILSON	J	11	409
WILSON	CF	5	387	WILSON	F	14	349	WILSON	H	8	397	WILSON	J	11	409

WILSON	J	11	409	WILSON	M	11	410	WILSON	VJ	3	256	WILSON	WW	1	372
WILSON	J	11	409	WILSON	M	12	244	WILSON	W	2	400	WILSTHIRE	J	6	447
WILSON	J	11	409	WILSON	ME	7	446	WILSON	W	2	400	WILTCHER	J	7	446
WILSON	J	11	409	WILSON	MM	2	400	WILSON	W	4	422	WILTCHER	J	7	446
WILSON	J	12	244	WILSON	N	9	213	WILSON	W	4	422	WILTON	A	13	459
WILSON	J	12	244	WILSON	N	11	410	WILSON	W	5	388	WILTON	AE	1	372
WILSON	J	12	417	WILSON	N	14	349	WILSON	W	5	388	WILTON	AW	7	446
WILSON	J	13	459	WILSON	NG	4	422	WILSON	W	5	389	WILTON	C	9	374
WILSON	J	14	349	WILSON	O	5	388	WILSON	W	6	447	WILTON	F	6	447
WILSON	J	14	349	WILSON	OE	5	388	WILSON	W	6	447	WILTON	FA	13	459
WILSON	J	14	349	WILSON	P	14	350	WILSON	W	6	447	WILTON	GF	2	400
WILSON	J	14	349	WILSON	PJ	11	410	WILSON	W	7	446	WILTON	W	13	459
WILSON	JA	2	400	WILSON	PM	8	398	WILSON	W	8	399	WILTON	WH	6	447
WILSON	JA	6	446	WILSON	R	7	445	WILSON	W	8	399	WILTSHER	WH	1	372
WILSON	JA	8	397	WILSON	R	8	398	WILSON	W	8	399	WILTSHIER	FC	7	446
WILSON	JA	8	397	WILSON	R	8	398	WILSON	W	8	399	WILTSHIER	FJ	7	446
WILSON	JC	4	422	WILSON	R	11	410	WILSON	W	8	399	WILTSHIRE	AC	4	422
WILSON	JD	5	388	WILSON	RB	9	373	WILSON	W	8	399	WILTSHIRE	AE	4	423
WILSON	JE	2	400	WILSON	RC	2	400	WILSON	W	8	399	WILTSHIRE	AE	4	423
WILSON	JF	11	409	WILSON	RC	12	244	WILSON	W	8	399	WILTSHIRE	AW	10	253
WILSON	JF	12	244	WILSON	RJ	5	388	WILSON	W	9	213	WILTSHIRE	C	4	423
WILSON	JH	2	400	WILSON	RR	7	446	WILSON	W	9	374	WILTSHIRE	C	10	253
WILSON	JH	2	400	WILSON	RT	8	398	WILSON	W	9	374	WILTSHIRE	CE	1	372
WILSON	JH	4	422	WILSON	RV	14	350	WILSON	W	10	253	WILTSHIRE	E	10	253
WILSON	JH	4	422	WILSON	RW	1	372	WILSON	W	10	253	WILTSHIRE	EE	2	400
WILSON	JH	8	398	WILSON	S	3	407	WILSON	W	11	410	WILTSHIRE	EJ	4	423
WILSON	JH	8	398	WILSON	S	8	398	WILSON	W	12	417	WILTSHIRE	FG	4	423
WILSON	JH	10	392	WILSON	S	8	398	WILSON	W	14	350	WILTSHIRE	G	1	372
WILSON	JH	11	409	WILSON	S	9	373	WILSON	W	14	350	WILTSHIRE	G	4	423
WILSON	JH	11	410	WILSON	S	9	373	WILSON	W	14	350	WILTSHIRE	G	4	423
WILSON	JH	14	349	WILSON	SC	13	459	WILSON	WA	2	400	WILTSHIRE	GA	7	446
WILSON	JJ	13	459	WILSON	SJ	7	446	WILSON	WA	5	389	WILTSHIRE	J	2	400
WILSON	JL	4	422	WILSON	ST	2	400	WILSON	WA	13	459	WILTSHIRE	J	6	447
WILSON	JL	8	398	WILSON	T	5	388	WILSON	WC	5	389	WILTSHIRE	JF	4	423
WILSON	JP	8	398	WILSON	T	7	446	WILSON	WC	7	446	WILTSHIRE	JH	6	447
WILSON	JR	8	398	WILSON	T	8	398	WILSON	WCS	13	459	WILTSHIRE	L	6	447
WILSON	JR	11	410	WILSON	T	8	398	WILSON	WE	5	389	WILTSHIRE	PA	4	423
WILSON	JT	8	398	WILSON	T	8	398	WILSON	WER	14	350	WILTSHIRE	R	6	447
WILSON	JT	11	410	WILSON	T	8	398	WILSON	WG	2	400	WILTSHIRE	R	6	447
WILSON	JW	2	400	WILSON	T	9	213	WILSON	WG	13	459	WILTSHIRE	SA	10	253
WILSON	JW	8	398	WILSON	T	9	373	WILSON	WH	1	372	WILTSHIRE	SV	10	253
WILSON	JW	8	398	WILSON	T	9	373	WILSON	WH	5	389	WILTSHIRE	T	6	447
WILSON	JW	10	253	WILSON	T	11	410	WILSON	WH	5	389	WILTSHIRE	V	14	350
WILSON	JW	10	253	WILSON	T	11	410	WILSON	WH	9	213	WILTSHIRE	W	7	446
WILSON	JW	10	392	WILSON	T	12	244	WILSON	WH	10	253	WILTSHIRE	WG	4	423
WILSON	JW	11	410	WILSON	T	14	350	WILSON	WH	11	410	WIMBLES	C	8	399
WILSON	JW	12	244	WILSON	TE	2	400	WILSON	WJ	1	372	WIMBLES	F	8	399
WILSON	JW	14	349	WILSON	TE	9	374	WILSON	WJ	2	400	WIMBURY	B	11	410
WILSON	JWS	6	447	WILSON	TG	5	388	WILSON	WJ	2	400	WIMHURST	A	10	253
WILSON	L	9	213	WILSON	TH	7	446	WILSON	WJ	4	422	WIMPORY	G	6	447
WILSON	L	9	373	WILSON	TH	8	398	WILSON	WJ	7	446	WIMSHURST	G	13	459
WILSON	LA	14	349	WILSON	TP	9	213	WILSON	WR	8	399	WINBOURNE	CW	4	423
WILSON	LW	5	388	WILSON	TR	10	253	WILSON	WT	10	392	WINCH	A	2	400
WILSON	M	5	388	WILSON	TW	1	372	WILSON	WTR	14	350	WINCH	A	2	401
WILSON	M	8	398	WILSON	V	9	374	WILSON	WW	1	372	WINCH	AG	5	389

WINCH	FC	5	389	WINDROSS	H	8	399	WINGFIELD	WE	2	401	WINSLETT	FG	2	402
WINCH	FE	2	401	WINDSOR	AB	2	401	WINGHAM	A	4	424	WINSLEY	W	7	447
WINCH	FR	2	401	WINDSOR	AB	2	401	WINGHAM	AE	10	254	WINSLOW	HH	7	447
WINCH	G	5	389	WINDSOR	AP	13	459	WINGHAM	EW	10	254	WINSOR	AR	10	392
WINCH	RL	5	389	WINDSOR	CL	4	424	WINGHAM	F	10	254	WINSOR	EW	12	245
WINCH	W	2	401	WINDSOR	GJW	4	424	WINGHAM	R	4	424	WINSOR	FR	4	425
WINCHESTER	HB	2	401	WINDSOR	HV	13	459	WINGHAM	WGH	10	254	WINSOR	JW	4	425
WINCHESTER	HE	10	392	WINDSOR	HW	13	460	WINGRAVE	DA	11	411	WINSPEAR	F	6	448
WINCHESTER	R	3	256	WINDSOR	JH	7	446	WINGRAVE	FC	5	390	WINSPEAR	FW	7	447
WINCOTT	A	13	459	WINDSOR	RW	4	424	WINGRAVE	JF	5	390	WINSPEAR	GW	6	448
WINDAYBANK	AE	3	256	WINDSOR	W	2	401	WINGROVE	EJ	7	447	WINSPEAR	HJ	6	448
WINDAYBANK	GA	3	256	WINDSOR	W	8	399	WINGROVE	FG	6	447	WINSPEAR	J	10	254
WINDAYBANK	WJ	3	256	WINDSOR	WH	1	372	WINGROVE	G	12	417	WINSPEAR	W	7	447
WINDEATT	G	4	423	WINDUST	EW	4	424	WINGROVE	H	2	401	WINSPEARE	R	6	448
WINDEBANK	A	4	423	WINDWOOD	J	5	389	WINGROVE	W	7	447	WINSPUR	D	6	448
WINDEBANK	AE	4	423	WINEBERG	S	8	399	WINHAM	FJ	4	424	WINSTANLEY	A	8	400
WINDEBANK	E	4	423	WINESTEIN	D	8	399	WINHAM	FJ	4	424	WINSTANLEY	A	11	411
WINDEBANK	EE	4	423	WINFIELD	A	1	372	WINKLE	A	6	448	WINSTANLEY	F	8	400
WINDEBANK	G	4	423	WINFIELD	A	5	389	WINKLER	A	2	401	WINSTANLEY	J	6	448
WINDEBANK	G	4	423	WINFIELD	C	11	411	WINKLY	CH	3	256	WINSTANLEY	J	11	411
WINDEBANK	H	4	423	WINFIELD	CHR	7	447	WINKLY	J	3	256	WINSTANLEY	RA	7	447
WINDEBANK	H	4	423	WINFIELD	FA	5	389	WINKWORTH	A	4	424	WINSTANLEY	W	3	407
WINDEBANK	J	4	424	WINFIELD	G	5	389	WINKWORTH	AC	4	424	WINSTANLEY	W	14	350
WINDEBANK	M	4	424	WINFIELD	GH	7	446	WINKWORTH	BP	4	425	WINSTONE	FJW	2	402
WINDEBANK	SJ	4	424	WINFIELD	H	2	401	WINKWORTH	G	7	447	WINSTONE	T	2	402
WINDEBANK	TG	4	424	WINFIELD	HC	5	389	WINKWORTH	JAA	7	447	WINSTONE	VS	6	448
WINDEBANK	WT	10	253	WINFIELD	HJ	5	389	WINKWORTH	PAC	4	425	WINT	J	11	411
WINDELER	JA	11	410	WINFIELD	J	6	447	WINN	EM	2	401	WINTER	AE	3	256
WINDER	C	11	410	WINFIELD	JA	12	245	WINN	FJ	2	401	WINTER	AJ	7	447
WINDER	F	8	399	WINFIELD	JJ	5	390	WINN	G	11	411	WINTER	AM	2	402
WINDER	H	9	213	WINFIELD	T	7	447	WINN	GA	9	213	WINTER	AP	3	256
WINDER	H	10	253	WINFIELD	WG	7	447	WINN	H	9	374	WINTER	AT	12	245
WINDER	H	12	245	WING	B	4	424	WINN	HF	2	401	WINTER	C	4	425
WINDER	J	9	374	WING	DW	3	256	WINN	J	8	400	WINTER	C	4	425
WINDER	J	11	410	WING	F	4	424	WINN	J	8	400	WINTER	CF	10	254
WINDER	JH	13	459	WING	FT	13	460	WINN	JE	9	213	WINTER	CH	2	402
WINDER	R	13	459	WING	G	2	401	WINN	R	14	350	WINTER	CW	2	402
WINDER	U	9	213	WING	G	3	256	WINN	SC	2	402	WINTER	E	2	402
WINDLE	B	9	213	WING	GC	5	390	WINN	W	8	400	WINTER	EC	7	447
WINDLE	C	2	401	WING	GH	4	424	WINN	WH	2	401	WINTER	EE	7	447
WINDLE	E	9	213	WING	H	4	424	WINNETT	E	6	448	WINTER	EW	3	256
WINDLE	H	8	399	WINGAR	TA	2	401	WINNICOTT	A	13	460	WINTER	EW	10	254
WINDLE	H	9	213	WINGAR	WW	2	401	WINNICOTT	JT	13	460	WINTER	F	4	425
WINDLE	H	9	374	WINGATE	H	8	400	WINNICOTT	L	3	256	WINTER	F	14	350
WINDLE	JA	9	213	WINGATE	JW	10	253	WINNICOTT	L	3	256	WINTER	GF	5	390
WINDMILL	BCT	5	389	WINGATE	R	7	447	WINNING	J	7	447	WINTER	GW	3	407
WINDMILL	C	10	392	WINGATE	T	8	400	WINNINGS	WJ	3	256	WINTER	HE	7	447
WINDMILL	G	5	389	WINGATE	T	10	253	WINNINGTON	C	11	411	WINTER	HG	4	425
WINDMILL	JA	5	389	WINGER	J	5	390	WINPENNY	CE	8	400	WINTER	HW	3	256
WINDMILL	WT	5	389	WINGFIELD	A	8	400	WINPENNY	M	8	400	WINTER	J	7	448
WINDOW	S	9	213	WINGFIELD	F	1	372	WINSCOTT	H	10	254	WINTER	J	8	400
WINDOW	W	9	213	WINGFIELD	J	13	460	WINSCOTT	HW	10	254	WINTER	JL	10	392
WINDRAM	F	11	410	WINGFIELD	J	13	460	WINSLADE	A	13	460	WINTER	JS	2	402
WINDRIDGE	T	6	447	WINGFIELD	R	3	407	WINSLADE	E	7	447	WINTER	JS	3	257
WINDROSS	A	8	399	WINGFIELD	R	5	390	WINSLADE	J	2	402	WINTER	JT	2	402

WINTER	JT	10	254	WINYARD	HG	2	402	WITCHELL	TA	7	449	WITHEY	FJ	5	390
WINTER	JW	2	402	WINYARD	RC	2	403	WITCHER	FB	4	425	WITHEY	GA	2	404
WINTER	JW	3	257	WINYARD	SH	2	403	WITCHERLEY	HL	8	400	WITHEY	H	6	449
WINTER	L	4	425	WINZOR	TH	2	403	WITCOMB	AE	13	460	WITHEY	J	13	461
WINTER	R	2	402	WISBEY	C	2	403	WITCOMB	AW	6	448	WITHEY	WF	13	461
WINTER	RW	13	460	WISBEY	TW	7	448	WITCOMB	GA	6	448	WITHINGTON	H	11	412
WINTER	T	4	425	WISBY	A	1	372	WITCOMB	H	6	448	WITHINGTON	T	11	412
WINTER	T	10	254	WISBY	E	2	403	WITCOMBE	C	3	257	WITHNALL	GS	6	449
WINTER	VJ	3	257	WISE	A	13	460	WITCOMBE	G	3	257	WITHNALL	H	6	449
WINTER	W	7	448	WISE	AE	13	460	WITCOMBE	P	2	403	WITHNALL	WW	6	449
WINTER	W	9	374	WISE	AR	2	403	WITCOMBE	T	2	403	WITMAN	C	9	374
WINTER	W	14	350	WISE	B	2	403	WITHALL	ES	7	449	WITNEY	DW	13	461
WINTER	WG	11	411	WISE	C	4	425	WITHALL	F	10	254	WITNEY	WG	7	449
WINTER	WH	7	448	WISE	C	13	460	WITHAM	A	7	449	WITNEY	WW	13	461
WINTER	WH	11	411	WISE	CH	8	400	WITHAM	EO	2	403	WITSEY	C	6	449
WINTER	WJ	2	402	WISE	E	6	448	WITHAM	W	7	449	WITSEY	HE	6	449
WINTER	WJ	2	402	WISE	F	6	448	WITHECOMB	AG	13	460	WITSEY	J	6	449
WINTERBONE	VC	12	417	WISE	FF	2	403	WITHER	G	4	426	WITT	C	2	404
WINTERBOTTOM	A	11	411	WISE	FJ	5	390	WITHERDEN	CBA	1	372	WITT	EI	4	426
WINTERBOTTOM	C	9	374	WISE	G	4	425	WITHERDEN	J	13	460	WITT	EK	4	426
WINTERBOTTOM	F	9	213	WISE	G	6	448	WITHERDEN	S	1	372	WITT	H	4	426
WINTERBOTTOM	F	9	213	WISE	GH	5	390	WITHERIDGE	A	6	448	WITT	JE	5	390
WINTERBOTTOM	G	11	411	WISE	H	5	390	WITHERS	A	4	426	WITTCOMB	CH	10	254
WINTERBOTTOM	JH	14	350	WISE	HEC	12	245	WITHERS	AE	11	411	WITTEN	R	2	404
WINTERBOURNE	C	8	400	WISE	J	7	448	WITHERS	AJM	2	403	WITTER	G	11	412
WINTERBURN	A	9	374	WISE	J	8	400	WITHERS	AV	4	426	WITTIN	GA	6	449
WINTERBURN	A	9	374	WISE	JH	2	403	WITHERS	B	4	426	WITTON	W	9	214
WINTERBURN	A	14	350	WISE	S	7	448	WITHERS	B	4	426	WITTS	CJ	2	404
WINTERBURN	C	8	400	WISE	T	13	460	WITHERS	B	10	254	WITTS	FJ	2	404
WINTERBURN	HC	3	257	WISE	W	6	448	WITHERS	CE	13	460	WITTS	G	7	449
WINTERBURN	P	9	213	WISE	W	6	448	WITHERS	E	1	372	WITTS	PA	2	404
WINTERBURN	S	9	374	WISE	W	7	448	WITHERS	E	11	411	WITTS	T	6	449
WINTERBURN	W	9	214	WISE	W	12	245	WITHERS	E	11	411	WITTS	TG	10	392
WINTERFLOOD	A	4	425	WISE	W	13	460	WITHERS	EC	7	449	WITTS	WF	7	449
WINTERFLOOD	AH	7	448	WISELEY	W	11	411	WITHERS	F	7	449	WOAKES	F	6	449
WINTERFLOOD	CE	7	448	WISEMAN	A	14	350	WITHERS	F	7	449	WODE	WT	2	406
WINTERFLOOD	WP	7	448	WISEMAN	B	12	417	WITHERS	F	11	411	WOHLGEMUTH	JF	3	257
WINTERIDGE	JH	4	425	WISEMAN	C	7	448	WITHERS	FA	6	448	WOLF	AR	11	412
WINTERS	A	7	448	WISEMAN	E	4	425	WITHERS	FR	4	426	WOLFE	BH	13	461
WINTERS	AH	2	402	WISEMAN	E	4	425	WITHERS	FW	13	460	WOLFE	E	10	254
WINTERS	F	7	448	WISEMAN	F	4	425	WITHERS	G	2	404	WOLFE	J	11	412
WINTERS	FW	5	390	WISEMAN	H	11	411	WITHERS	GH	4	426	WOLFE	SJ	8	400
WINTERS	HG	7	448	WISEMAN	TW	13	460	WITHERS	H	4	426	WOLFENDALE	C	14	350
WINTERS	S	1	372	WISEMAN	W	7	449	WITHERS	H	13	461	WOLFENDALE	WC	14	351
WINTLE	AE	2	402	WISEMAN	WE	2	403	WITHERS	IE	4	426	WOLFENDEN	F	9	214
WINTLE	G	10	392	WISEMAN	WH	4	425	WITHERS	JF	6	449	WOLFINDALE	GR	6	449
WINTLE	GI	3	257	WISEMAN	WJ	2	403	WITHERS	JW	8	400	WOLFINDALE	T	6	449
WINTLE	GS	3	257	WISHART	J	3	257	WITHERS	LL	13	461	WOLITER	G	8	401
WINUP	RH	5	390	WISHART	R	8	400	WITHERS	PV	2	403	WOLSELEY	T	2	404
WINUP	TS	7	448	WISHART	WF	4	425	WITHERS	T	7	449	WOLSTENCROFT	E	11	412
WINWARD	W	14	350	WISKER	HH	2	403	WITHERS	W	1	373	WOLSTENCROFT	GT	11	412
WINWILL	CSH	5	390	WISNOFSKY	J	8	400	WITHERS	WW	10	392	WOLSTENCROFT	J	11	412
WINWOOD	W	6	448	WISTON	R	14	350	WITHERSTONE	HO	6	449	WOLSTENCROFT	J	14	351
WINYARD	A	2	402	WISTOW	EG	7	449	WITHEY	F	2	404	WOLSTENCROFT	JT	11	412
WINYARD	F	7	448	WISTOW	FA	2	403	WITHEY	FG	2	404	WOLSTENCROFT	TH	14	351

WOLSTENCROFT	TS	11	412	WOOD	B	9	374	WOOD	EG	7	450	WOOD	GP	2	405
WOLSTENHOLME	A	14	351	WOOD	B	14	351	WOOD	EJ	5	391	WOOD	GS	13	461
WOLSTENHOLME	E	1	373	WOOD	B	14	351	WOOD	EJ	7	450	WOOD	GT	5	391
WOLSTENHOLME	E	14	351	WOOD	BG	6	449	WOOD	F	2	405	WOOD	GW	8	403
WOLSTENHOLME	EH	1	373	WOOD	C	4	426	WOOD	F	2	405	WOOD	GW	8	403
WOLSTENHOLME	J	8	401	WOOD	C	5	390	WOOD	F	6	450	WOOD	GW	12	417
WOLSTENHOLME	J	14	351	WOOD	C	7	449	WOOD	F	6	450	WOOD	H	6	450
WOLSTENHOLME	T	14	351	WOOD	C	8	401	WOOD	F	6	450	WOOD	H	6	450
WOLSTENHOLME	W	9	374	WOOD	C	8	401	WOOD	F	8	402	WOOD	H	7	450
WOLSTENHOLME	W	14	351	WOOD	C	8	401	WOOD	F	8	402	WOOD	H	8	403
WOLTON	C	8	401	WOOD	C	8	401	WOOD	F	8	402	WOOD	H	8	403
WOMACK	H	8	401	WOOD	C	8	401	WOOD	F	8	402	WOOD	H	9	214
WOMERSLEY	H	9	374	WOOD	C	8	401	WOOD	F	9	214	WOOD	H	9	214
WOMERSLEY	N	8	401	WOOD	C	8	401	WOOD	F	9	214	WOOD	H	9	375
WOMERSLEY	W	9	214	WOOD	C	11	412	WOOD	F	11	413	WOOD	H	11	413
WOND	AE	1	373	WOOD	C	11	412	WOOD	F	11	413	WOOD	H	11	413
WOND	HJ	1	373	WOOD	C	13	461	WOOD	F	13	461	WOOD	H	12	245
WOND	HJ	1	373	WOOD	C	14	351	WOOD	F	13	461	WOOD	H	14	351
WOOD	A	1	373	WOOD	C	14	351	WOOD	F	14	351	WOOD	H	14	351
WOOD	A	2	404	WOOD	CA	2	404	WOOD	FC	3	257	WOOD	H	14	351
WOOD	A	4	426	WOOD	CA	8	401	WOOD	FC	8	402	WOOD	HA	2	405
WOOD	A	4	426	WOOD	CC	8	402	WOOD	FG	10	393	WOOD	HC	5	391
WOOD	A	8	401	WOOD	CCG	13	461	WOOD	FH	8	402	WOOD	HD	8	403
WOOD	A	8	401	WOOD	CE	7	450	WOOD	FJ	5	391	WOOD	HD	10	393
WOOD	A	8	401	WOOD	CFW	2	404	WOOD	FL	6	450	WOOD	HE	6	450
WOOD	A	8	401	WOOD	CG	14	351	WOOD	FM	7	450	WOOD	HG	8	403
WOOD	A	8	401	WOOD	CH	2	404	WOOD	FM	13	461	WOOD	HJ	1	373
WOOD	A	8	401	WOOD	CH	2	404	WOOD	FMA	7	450	WOOD	HJ	7	450
WOOD	A	8	401	WOOD	CH	6	449	WOOD	FS	7	450	WOOD	HL	3	407
WOOD	A	9	214	WOOD	CH	9	375	WOOD	FT	8	402	WOOD	HL	5	391
WOOD	A	9	214	WOOD	CH	12	417	WOOD	FW	7	450	WOOD	HS	13	462
WOOD	A	9	214	WOOD	CR	5	390	WOOD	G	2	405	WOOD	HT	8	403
WOOD	A	9	374	WOOD	CR	7	450	WOOD	G	2	405	WOOD	HT	9	214
WOOD	A	11	412	WOOD	CW	1	373	WOOD	G	2	405	WOOD	HW	13	462
WOOD	A	11	412	WOOD	CW	2	405	WOOD	G	5	391	WOOD	IH	6	450
WOOD	A	11	412	WOOD	CW	7	450	WOOD	G	8	402	WOOD	J	2	405
WOOD	A	11	425	WOOD	D	6	449	WOOD	G	8	402	WOOD	J	5	391
WOOD	A	12	417	WOOD	D	11	412	WOOD	G	8	402	WOOD	J	5	391
WOOD	A	13	461	WOOD	DM	5	390	WOOD	G	8	402	WOOD	J	5	391
WOOD	A	14	351	WOOD	E	6	450	WOOD	G	8	402	WOOD	J	5	391
WOOD	A	14	351	WOOD	E	7	450	WOOD	G	8	402	WOOD	J	5	391
WOOD	AA	7	449	WOOD	E	8	402	WOOD	G	8	403	WOOD	J	6	450
WOOD	AA	7	449	WOOD	E	8	402	WOOD	G	9	214	WOOD	J	7	450
WOOD	AC	10	254	WOOD	E	8	402	WOOD	G	9	375	WOOD	J	7	450
WOOD	AE	6	449	WOOD	E	8	402	WOOD	G	11	413	WOOD	J	7	450
WOOD	AE	10	254	WOOD	E	8	402	WOOD	G	11	413	WOOD	J	8	403
WOOD	AH	6	449	WOOD	E	8	402	WOOD	G	13	461	WOOD	J	8	403
WOOD	AJ	1	373	WOOD	E	9	214	WOOD	G	13	461	WOOD	J	8	403
WOOD	AJ	6	449	WOOD	E	9	375	WOOD	GE	6	450	WOOD	J	8	403
WOOD	AJ	7	449	WOOD	E	11	412	WOOD	GER	13	461	WOOD	J	8	403
WOOD	AJ	7	449	WOOD	EA	5	391	WOOD	GG	13	461	WOOD	J	9	375
WOOD	AL	2	404	WOOD	EA	7	450	WOOD	GH	2	405	WOOD	J	11	413
WOOD	AN	11	412	WOOD	EB	13	461	WOOD	GH	8	403	WOOD	J	11	413
WOOD	AWH	10	392	WOOD	EC	2	404	WOOD	GH	8	403	WOOD	J	11	413
WOOD	B	5	390	WOOD	EC	2	404	WOOD	GH	11	413	WOOD	J	14	351

WOOD	J	14	352	WOOD	S	11	413	WOOD	WH	14	352	WOODCOCK	F	14	352
WOOD	J	14	352	WOOD	S	14	352	WOOD	WJ	6	451	WOODCOCK	H	6	451
WOOD	J	14	352	WOOD	SA	8	404	WOOD	WR	3	257	WOODCOCK	H	6	451
WOOD	J	14	352	WOOD	SF	14	352	WOOD	WT	10	255	WOODCOCK	HC	13	462
WOOD	JA	8	403	WOOD	SG	7	451	WOOD	WV	2	405	WOODCOCK	JH	8	405
WOOD	JA	11	413	WOOD	SJ	9	375	WOODAGE	C	2	405	WOODCOCK	JH	8	405
WOOD	JB	13	462	WOOD	T	6	450	WOODAKER	JT	2	406	WOODCOCK	L	6	451
WOOD	JC	6	450	WOOD	T	6	450	WOODALL	A	6	451	WOODCOCK	MA	14	353
WOOD	JE	5	391	WOOD	T	7	451	WOODALL	A	6	451	WOODCOCK	RJ	14	353
WOOD	JF	6	450	WOOD	T	8	404	WOODALL	A	8	404	WOODCOCK	S	6	451
WOOD	JH	6	450	WOOD	T	8	404	WOODALL	AE	6	451	WOODCOCK	S	6	451
WOOD	JH	7	450	WOOD	T	8	404	WOODALL	C	3	257	WOODCOCK	SW	2	406
WOOD	JH	7	450	WOOD	T	8	404	WOODALL	CH	14	352	WOODCOCK	W	11	414
WOOD	JH	11	413	WOOD	T	8	404	WOODALL	F	6	451	WOODCOCK	WC	4	426
WOOD	JI	14	352	WOOD	T	9	375	WOODALL	G	13	462	WOODCOCK	WG	2	406
WOOD	JJ	5	391	WOOD	T	11	413	WOODALL	H	14	352	WOODCROFT	A	5	392
WOOD	JL	8	403	WOOD	T	14	352	WOODALL	J	13	462	WOODCROFT	A	12	245
WOOD	JM	8	403	WOOD	T	14	352	WOODALL	SH	8	405	WOODCROFT	E	5	392
WOOD	JM	9	214	WOOD	TA	2	405	WOODALL	T	8	405	WOODCROFT	FE	5	392
WOOD	JP	5	391	WOOD	TA	6	450	WOODALL	WA	14	352	WOODCROFT	N	5	392
WOOD	JP	6	450	WOOD	TH	8	404	WOODALL	WH	5	391	WOODCROFT	PE	5	392
WOOD	JR	9	375	WOOD	TR	10	254	WOODALL	WJ	6	451	WOODCROFT	S	5	392
WOOD	JS	9	214	WOOD	TW	12	245	WOODARD	AWE	2	406	WOODCROFT	WJ	5	392
WOOD	JS	9	375	WOOD	V	5	391	WOODARD	BA	10	255	WOODCROFT	WT	5	392
WOOD	JT	9	214	WOOD	VG	12	245	WOODARD	J	2	406	WOODCROFT	WW	5	392
WOOD	JW	7	450	WOOD	VS	8	404	WOODARD	JH	2	406	WOODFIELD	AH	6	451
WOOD	JW	9	375	WOOD	W	2	405	WOODBINE	E	3	257	WOODFIELD	H	2	406
WOOD	JW	9	375	WOOD	W	5	391	WOODBINE	J	11	413	WOODFIELD	S	2	406
WOOD	JW	9	375	WOOD	W	6	451	WOODBRIDGE	A	2	406	WOODFINE	F	13	462
WOOD	JW	9	375	WOOD	W	6	451	WOODBRIDGE	A	13	462	WOODFORD	A	5	392
WOOD	JW	11	413	WOOD	W	7	451	WOODBRIDGE	AJ	2	406	WOODFORD	C	4	426
WOOD	L	9	375	WOOD	W	8	404	WOODBRIDGE	C	3	257	WOODFORD	F	12	417
WOOD	L	9	375	WOOD	W	8	404	WOODBRIDGE	EJ	7	451	WOODFORD	FC	4	426
WOOD	L	11	413	WOOD	W	8	404	WOODBRIDGE	F	1	373	WOODFORD	O	5	392
WOOD	L	13	462	WOOD	W	8	404	WOODBRIDGE	F	4	426	WOODFORD	W	5	392
WOOD	LG	13	462	WOOD	W	8	404	WOODBRIDGE	G	3	257	WOODFORTH	J	5	392
WOOD	LR	2	405	WOOD	W	9	214	WOODBRIDGE	J	5	392	WOODGAR	A	4	426
WOOD	M	6	450	WOOD	W	9	214	WOODBRIDGE	J	14	352	WOODGATE	C	13	462
WOOD	M	8	403	WOOD	W	9	375	WOODBRIDGE	JT	7	451	WOODGATE	G	3	257
WOOD	M	9	375	WOOD	W	9	375	WOODBRIDGE	S	1	373	WOODGATE	GW	7	451
WOOD	MA	8	403	WOOD	W	10	255	WOODBRIDGE	T	8	405	WOODGATE	HW	12	245
WOOD	MM	7	450	WOOD	W	10	255	WOODBRIDGE	W	1	373	WOODGATE	JH	7	451
WOOD	NA	13	462	WOOD	W	10	393	WOODBRIDGE	W	2	406	WOODGATE	LCH	7	451
WOOD	PA	5	391	WOOD	W	11	413	WOODBRIDGE	WEO	13	462	WOODGATE	P	3	257
WOOD	PH	2	405	WOOD	W	14	352	WOODBRIDGE	WJ	5	392	WOODGATE	PJ	2	406
WOOD	R	5	391	WOOD	W	14	352	WOODBURY	J	11	414	WOODGATE	WG	7	451
WOOD	R	6	450	WOOD	W	14	352	WOODBURY	JG	11	414	WOODGATES	ET	3	257
WOOD	R	8	403	WOOD	WA	2	405	WOODBURY	JG	11	414	WOODGER	ME	4	426
WOOD	R	8	404	WOOD	WA	10	255	WOODCOCK	A	6	451	WOODGER	WC	4	426
WOOD	R	13	462	WOOD	WA	11	413	WOODCOCK	A	12	245	WOODHALL	A	8	405
WOOD	RB	7	451	WOOD	WC	11	413	WOODCOCK	AFG	2	406	WOODHALL	A	9	375
WOOD	RM	8	404	WOOD	WE	8	404	WOODCOCK	AT	10	393	WOODHALL	AE	6	451
WOOD	RM	13	462	WOOD	WH	2	405	WOODCOCK	E	11	414	WOODHALL	GE	9	215
WOOD	S	2	405	WOOD	WH	8	404	WOODCOCK	F	2	406	WOODHALL	SA	6	451
WOOD	S	8	404	WOOD	WH	13	462	WOODCOCK	F	6	451	WOODHALL	T	8	405

WOODHALL	T	8	405
WOODHALL	T	11	414
WOODHAM	C	12	245
WOODHAM	F	12	245
WOODHAM	FC	13	462
WOODHAM	SF	12	245
WOODHAM	W	12	245
WOODHAM	WF	2	406
WOODHAMS	JW	12	417
WOODHAMS	S	8	405
WOODHAMS	WT	2	406
WOODHEAD	A	8	405
WOODHEAD	A	9	215
WOODHEAD	A	9	375
WOODHEAD	A	9	376
WOODHEAD	A	9	392
WOODHEAD	B	8	405
WOODHEAD	C	8	405
WOODHEAD	E	8	405
WOODHEAD	E	9	215
WOODHEAD	E	9	376
WOODHEAD	E	11	414
WOODHEAD	F	9	215
WOODHEAD	F	9	392
WOODHEAD	G	9	376
WOODHEAD	G	9	392
WOODHEAD	H	8	405
WOODHEAD	H	8	405
WOODHEAD	H	8	405
WOODHEAD	H	9	215
WOODHEAD	H	9	215
WOODHEAD	H	9	376
WOODHEAD	HC	2	406
WOODHEAD	J	9	376
WOODHEAD	J	9	376
WOODHEAD	J	9	376
WOODHEAD	J	9	376
WOODHEAD	J	14	353
WOODHEAD	JA	8	405
WOODHEAD	P	9	376
WOODHEAD	W	8	405
WOODHEAD	W	9	376
WOODHEAD	W	9	376
WOODHEAD	WW	14	353
WOODHOUSE	AR	10	255
WOODHOUSE	AW	7	451
WOODHOUSE	EI	4	427
WOODHOUSE	F	6	451
WOODHOUSE	F	9	215
WOODHOUSE	F	9	215
WOODHOUSE	FW	3	257
WOODHOUSE	G	6	451
WOODHOUSE	GH	3	258
WOODHOUSE	GW	8	405
WOODHOUSE	IE	7	451
WOODHOUSE	T	6	451
WOODHOUSE	T	9	215
WOODHOUSE	TW	13	462
WOODIN	AW	7	451
WOODING	AG	5	392
WOODING	AL	12	245
WOODING	AS	8	405
WOODING	C	5	392
WOODING	CH	12	245
WOODING	FA	8	406
WOODING	G	12	245
WOODING	H	12	417
WOODING	J	12	246
WOODING	JC	5	392
WOODING	JH	12	246
WOODING	W	12	246
WOODING	WH	12	246
WOODINGS	EJ	11	414
WOODINGS	JW	11	414
WOODINGS	TR	14	353
WOODJETTS	JF	3	258
WOODLAND	EJ	5	392
WOODLAND	FR	10	255
WOODLAND	HE	10	393
WOODLAND	R	12	246
WOODLAND	WG	10	255
WOODLEY	A	6	452
WOODLEY	CJ	10	255
WOODLEY	F	3	258
WOODLEY	F	8	406
WOODLEY	FJ	2	407
WOODLEY	H	3	258
WOODLEY	H	4	427
WOODLEY	HF	7	451
WOODLEY	J	2	407
WOODLEY	J	3	407
WOODLEY	J	11	414
WOODLEY	JA	2	407
WOODLEY	JR	10	255
WOODLEY	R	3	258
WOODLEY	T	3	258
WOODLEY	W	3	258
WOODMAN	A	5	393
WOODMAN	A	7	451
WOODMAN	AE	4	427
WOODMAN	CE	7	451
WOODMAN	CH	2	407
WOODMAN	CJ	7	451
WOODMAN	ED	7	452
WOODMAN	EF	10	255
WOODMAN	EJ	2	407
WOODMAN	F	7	451
WOODMAN	G	10	255
WOODMAN	H	2	407
WOODMAN	H	11	414
WOODMAN	HE	4	427
WOODMAN	HEL	4	427
WOODMAN	J	11	414
WOODMAN	JT	7	452
WOODMAN	JW	14	353
WOODMAN	R	14	353
WOODMAN	S	1	373
WOODMAN	T	7	452
WOODMAN	T	7	452
WOODMAN	W	4	427
WOODMAN	W	7	452
WOODMAN	WH	6	452
WOODMORE	GA	10	393
WOODRIFF	W	8	406
WOODROFF	C	1	373
WOODROFF	M	1	373
WOODROOFE	FJ	2	407
WOODROUGH	F	7	452
WOODROUGH	M	7	452
WOODROW	D	11	414
WOODROW	E	8	406
WOODROW	F	5	393
WOODROW	F	7	452
WOODROW	F	7	452
WOODROW	G	2	407
WOODROW	J	9	215
WOODROW	J	11	414
WOODROW	JJ	7	452
WOODROW	TM	7	452
WOODROW	W	9	215
WOODROW	WWA	7	452
WOODRUFF	H	9	215
WOODRUFF	JHT	12	246
WOODRUFF	S	3	258
WOODRUFF	W	7	452
WOODRUFF	WG	5	393
WOODRUFF	WM	12	246
WOODS	A	1	373
WOODS	A	5	393
WOODS	A	5	393
WOODS	A	8	406
WOODS	A	10	255
WOODS	A	11	414
WOODS	AE	11	414
WOODS	AG	1	373
WOODS	AJH	13	462
WOODS	AV	12	246
WOODS	AW	7	452
WOODS	C	4	427
WOODS	C	12	246
WOODS	C	14	353
WOODS	CF	13	463
WOODS	CH	1	373
WOODS	CH	7	452
WOODS	CJL	7	452
WOODS	CR	7	453
WOODS	CT	2	407
WOODS	CT	12	246
WOODS	E	5	393
WOODS	E	7	453
WOODS	E	8	406
WOODS	ED	12	246
WOODS	EF	12	246
WOODS	EH	12	246
WOODS	ER	12	246
WOODS	F	4	427
WOODS	F	5	393
WOODS	F	5	393
WOODS	F	11	414
WOODS	F	13	463
WOODS	FJ	12	246
WOODS	FL	7	452
WOODS	FT	7	453
WOODS	GH	10	255
WOODS	GN	4	427
WOODS	GR	11	415
WOODS	GW	5	393
WOODS	H	5	393
WOODS	H	5	393
WOODS	H	7	453
WOODS	H	11	414
WOODS	HC	13	463
WOODS	IM	12	246
WOODS	J	4	427
WOODS	J	12	246
WOODS	J	12	246
WOODS	J	14	353
WOODS	JB	5	393
WOODS	JG	5	393
WOODS	JH	11	415
WOODS	JP	13	463
WOODS	JT	7	453
WOODS	PH	6	452
WOODS	S	1	373
WOODS	S	5	393
WOODS	SV	2	407
WOODS	T	12	246
WOODS	TC	2	407
WOODS	TF	2	407
WOODS	TH	10	255
WOODS	TH	14	353
WOODS	TM	9	215
WOODS	TM	9	376
WOODS	W	2	407
WOODS	W	11	415
WOODS	W	12	246
WOODS	W	12	246
WOODS	WA	7	453
WOODS	WC	3	258
WOODS	WJ	7	453

WOODSTOCK	CE	5	393	WOODWARD	W	5	394	WOOLFOOT	E	8	406	WOOLLEY	AT	7	453
WOODSTOCK	HC	5	393	WOODWARD	W	10	393	WOOLFORD	A	5	394	WOOLLEY	CW	2	409
WOODSTOCK	T	5	393	WOODWARD	W	11	415	WOOLFORD	BJ	10	256	WOOLLEY	CW	6	452
WOODSTOCK	WH	5	393	WOODWARD	WE	14	353	WOOLFORD	ES	13	463	WOOLLEY	D	6	453
WOODTHORPE	E	9	215	WOODWARD	WH	6	452	WOOLFORD	FL	1	373	WOOLLEY	D	7	453
WOODTHORPE	H	9	215	WOODWARD	WJ	11	415	WOOLFORD	G	2	408	WOOLLEY	E	14	354
WOODWARD	A	6	452	WOODWARD	WS	2	408	WOOLFORD	HA	13	463	WOOLLEY	EA	6	453
WOODWARD	A	6	452	WOODWARDS	CH	10	256	WOOLFORD	HA	13	463	WOOLLEY	G	6	453
WOODWARD	A	11	415	WOODWARDS	CS	10	256	WOOLFORD	J	2	408	WOOLLEY	G	14	354
WOODWARD	AC	5	394	WOODWORTH	A	14	354	WOOLFORD	JH	11	415	WOOLLEY	G	14	354
WOODWARD	AJ	2	407	WOODWORTH	AH	14	353	WOOLFORD	PL	7	453	WOOLLEY	GA	10	256
WOODWARD	AJ	11	415	WOODWORTH	G	11	415	WOOLFORD	SJ	13	463	WOOLLEY	GC	10	256
WOODWARD	AT	2	407	WOODWORTH	J	14	354	WOOLFSON	N	14	354	WOOLLEY	H	4	427
WOODWARD	C	6	452	WOODWORTH	J	14	354	WOOLGAR	C	10	256	WOOLLEY	H	5	395
WOODWARD	CC	6	452	WOODWORTH	R	11	415	WOOLGAR	DO	2	408	WOOLLEY	H	6	453
WOODWARD	CS	2	407	WOODWORTH	W	11	415	WOOLGAR	WC	10	256	WOOLLEY	H	9	216
WOODWARD	E	2	407	WOOKEY	S	2	408	WOOLGAR	WG	4	427	WOOLLEY	H	14	354
WOODWARD	E	5	394	WOOLASS	AS	8	406	WOOLHEAD	A	5	394	WOOLLEY	HH	10	256
WOODWARD	EJ	2	407	WOOLBERT	FH	2	408	WOOLHEAD	C	5	394	WOOLLEY	HS	2	408
WOODWARD	EJ	5	394	WOOLCOCK	EB	4	427	WOOLHEAD	E	5	394	WOOLLEY	J	6	453
WOODWARD	EW	2	408	WOOLCOCK	WJ	4	427	WOOLHEAD	E	5	395	WOOLLEY	J	9	216
WOODWARD	F	4	427	WOOLDRIDGE	A	6	452	WOOLHEAD	EF	5	395	WOOLLEY	J	14	355
WOODWARD	F	5	394	WOOLDRIDGE	A	7	453	WOOLHEAD	F	5	395	WOOLLEY	JW	6	453
WOODWARD	F	6	452	WOOLDRIDGE	CJ	3	258	WOOLHEAD	G	5	395	WOOLLEY	JW	11	416
WOODWARD	F	6	452	WOOLDRIDGE	E	4	427	WOOLHEAD	L	5	395	WOOLLEY	L	1	374
WOODWARD	FA	5	394	WOOLDRIDGE	FW	6	452	WOOLHEAD	R	2	408	WOOLLEY	R	1	374
WOODWARD	FC	5	394	WOOLDRIDGE	GH	13	463	WOOLHEAD	S	5	395	WOOLLEY	RC	11	416
WOODWARD	FJ	10	255	WOOLDRIDGE	J	6	452	WOOLHEAD	W	5	395	WOOLLEY	S	14	355
WOODWARD	FW	5	394	WOOLDRIDGE	JA	6	452	WOOLHOUSE	WFC	10	256	WOOLLEY	SE	11	415
WOODWARD	G	5	394	WOOLDRIDGE	LC	2	408	WOOLL	CC	2	408	WOOLLEY	SJ	13	463
WOODWARD	GF	11	415	WOOLDRIDGE	W	4	427	WOOLL	W	2	408	WOOLLEY	TE	14	355
WOODWARD	GH	5	394	WOOLDRIDGE	W	6	452	WOOLLAMS	A	11	415	WOOLLEY	W	8	406
WOODWARD	GW	2	408	WOOLER	H	2	408	WOOLLAMS	AG	5	395	WOOLLEY	W	11	416
WOODWARD	H	2	408	WOOLER	HS	9	215	WOOLLAMS	J	5	395	WOOLLEY	W	14	355
WOODWARD	H	12	418	WOOLER	JW	8	406	WOOLLAMS	JF	5	395	WOOLLEY	WC	1	374
WOODWARD	HG	2	407	WOOLERSON	AE	12	247	WOOLLAMS	T	11	415	WOOLLISON	G	5	395
WOODWARD	HJ	2	408	WOOLESCROFT	LG	6	452	WOOLLARD	AJ	7	453	WOOLMAN	GE	2	409
WOODWARD	HRC	10	255	WOOLESCROFT	WH	6	452	WOOLLARD	C	8	406	WOOLMER	AA	4	427
WOODWARD	I	14	353	WOOLEY	E	10	393	WOOLLARD	ES	12	247	WOOLMER	AE	1	374
WOODWARD	J	5	394	WOOLEY	HJ	5	394	WOOLLARD	HW	7	453	WOOLMER	R	1	374
WOODWARD	J	9	215	WOOLEY	J	2	408	WOOLLARD	JH	5	395	WOOLMER	TW	6	453
WOODWARD	J	14	353	WOOLF	J	5	394	WOOLLARD	JK	5	395	WOOLNOUGH	A	4	427
WOODWARD	J	14	353	WOOLFALL	G	14	354	WOOLLEN	A	2	408	WOOLNOUGH	C	3	407
WOODWARD	JA	14	353	WOOLFE	E	13	463	WOOLLER	AW	2	408	WOOLNOUGH	CW	2	409
WOODWARD	JG	11	415	WOOLFE	F	13	463	WOOLLER	H	9	215	WOOLNOUGH	JA	5	395
WOODWARD	JL	11	415	WOOLFE	GT	11	415	WOOLLER	W	9	376	WOOLRICH	WD	6	453
WOODWARD	JP	11	415	WOOLFE	H	14	354	WOOLLETON	F	9	215	WOOLSTON	AE	10	256
WOODWARD	JT	7	453	WOOLFE	J	14	354	WOOLLETT	EJ	7	453	WOOLSTON	AS	8	406
WOODWARD	JW	14	353	WOOLFE	J	14	354	WOOLLETT	H	1	374	WOOLSTON	CM	6	453
WOODWARD	JW	14	353	WOOLFE	J	14	354	WOOLLEY	A	7	453	WOOLSTON	CWT	5	395
WOODWARD	PC	6	452	WOOLFE	L	14	354	WOOLLEY	A	11	415	WOOLSTON	HJ	6	453
WOODWARD	R	5	394	WOOLFE	P	14	354	WOOLLEY	A	14	354	WOOLSTON	WH	12	418
WOODWARD	R	6	452	WOOLFE	P	14	354	WOOLLEY	A	14	354	WOOLVEN	W	10	256
WOODWARD	RC	10	255	WOOLFE	W	13	463	WOOLLEY	AE	2	408	WOOLVETT	A	7	453
WOODWARD	S	8	406	WOOLFENDEN	R	14	354	WOOLLEY	AJ	2	408	WOOLVETT	L	7	453

WOOLVIN	S	2	409
WOOR	A	2	409
WOOSTER	HT	3	407
WOOSTER	W	2	409
WOOTLIFF	L	8	406
WOOTON	L	5	396
WOOTTEN	AB	4	427
WOOTTEN	E	2	409
WOOTTEN	E	5	395
WOOTTEN	JW	1	374
WOOTTEN	R	4	427
WOOTTON	A	12	247
WOOTTON	A	12	418
WOOTTON	AE	6	453
WOOTTON	AL	12	247
WOOTTON	B	5	395
WOOTTON	CR	1	374
WOOTTON	CW	7	453
WOOTTON	DEH	1	374
WOOTTON	F	12	247
WOOTTON	FJ	4	428
WOOTTON	G	12	247
WOOTTON	GH	2	409
WOOTTON	GW	12	418
WOOTTON	HCF	1	374
WOOTTON	L	12	247
WOOTTON	S	12	418
WOOTTON	SA	12	247
WOOTTON	T	12	418
WOOTTON	TF	12	247
WOOTTON	W	6	453
WOOTTON	W	12	247
WOOTTON	WH	12	247
WOOTTON	WH	12	247
WOOTTON	WJ	12	418
WOPLING	A	10	393
WORBEY	H	5	396
WORBEY	J	5	396
WORBEY	W	5	396
WORBEY	W	5	396
WORBOYS	AE	5	396
WORBOYS	AR	5	396
WORBOYS	C	5	396
WORBOYS	CW	5	396
WORBOYS	E	7	453
WORBOYS	EF	7	454
WORBOYS	FA	5	396
WORBOYS	FG	5	396
WORBOYS	MC	2	409
WORBOYS	WG	5	396
WORDEN	A	13	463
WORDEN	F	13	463
WORDEN	H	13	463
WORDEN	WJ	7	454
WORDLEY	H	11	416
WORDSWORTH	D	8	406
WORDSWORTH	E	14	355
WORDSWORTH	TM	7	454
WORFOLK	T	8	406
WORK	C	8	406
WORKER	C	5	396
WORKER	C	12	247
WORKER	P	12	247
WORKER	S	5	396
WORKER	SG	5	396
WORKER	T	5	396
WORKMAN	AE	6	453
WORKMAN	AJ	2	409
WORKMAN	C	6	453
WORKMAN	CWE	10	256
WORKMAN	FC	6	453
WORKMAN	G	10	393
WORKMAN	HA	13	463
WORLAND	WA	2	409
WORLAND	WC	5	396
WORLD	HA	10	256
WORLEDGE	G	12	247
WORLEY	A	2	409
WORLEY	A	13	463
WORLEY	F	10	256
WORLEY	FA	13	463
WORLEY	FG	1	374
WORLEY	H	13	463
WORLEY	HA	3	408
WORLEY	JE	10	256
WORLEY	L	8	406
WORLEY	W	2	409
WORMALD	A	8	406
WORMALD	CW	8	406
WORMALD	E	8	406
WORMALD	F	9	216
WORMALD	G	8	407
WORMALD	J	8	407
WORMALD	J	8	407
WORMALD	T	8	407
WORMALD	TH	8	407
WORMBY	GH	8	407
WORMULL	A	4	428
WORMULL	AGH	7	454
WORMULL	J	4	428
WORRALL	A	11	416
WORRALL	A	12	247
WORRALL	AJ	12	247
WORRALL	C	14	355
WORRALL	CH	6	453
WORRALL	F	8	407
WORRALL	FH	12	247
WORRALL	G	6	453
WORRALL	G	6	453
WORRALL	G	8	407
WORRALL	H	6	453
WORRALL	H	14	355
WORRALL	H	14	355
WORRALL	HT	5	396
WORRALL	J	6	453
WORRALL	J	6	454
WORRALL	J	6	454
WORRALL	J	10	393
WORRALL	J	11	416
WORRALL	JW	10	393
WORRALL	L	12	247
WORRALL	PJ	12	247
WORRALL	R	6	454
WORRALL	R	12	248
WORRALL	RA	14	355
WORRALL	RS	12	248
WORRALL	S	14	355
WORRALL	TE	8	407
WORRALL	W	8	407
WORRALL	W	12	248
WORRELL	A	2	409
WORRELL	ER	2	409
WORRELL	G	7	454
WORRELL	H	5	396
WORSFIELD	H	13	464
WORSFOLD	AW	10	256
WORSFOLD	J	3	258
WORSFOLD	J	13	464
WORSFOLD	R	13	464
WORSFOLD	RG	10	256
WORSH	WG	10	393
WORSHOP	E	14	355
WORSLEY	A	9	216
WORSLEY	AF	5	397
WORSLEY	AJE	2	409
WORSLEY	AR	12	248
WORSLEY	AR	14	355
WORSLEY	D	14	355
WORSLEY	EM	5	397
WORSLEY	FWA	12	248
WORSLEY	G	14	355
WORSLEY	G	14	355
WORSLEY	HPR	12	248
WORSLEY	J	1	374
WORSLEY	J	11	416
WORSLEY	JA	9	216
WORSLEY	LA	5	397
WORSLEY	R	14	355
WORSLEY	T	11	416
WORSLEY	T	14	355
WORSLEY	W	14	355
WORSLEY	WM	14	355
WORSMAN	E	9	216
WORSMAN	F	9	376
WORSMAN	H	9	376
WORSMAN	J	9	376
WORSMAN	T	9	216
WORSNOP	A	9	216
WORSNOP	A	9	376
WORSNOP	J	8	407
WORSNOP	S	9	377
WORSNOP	WC	8	407
WORSOP	F	5	397
WORSTENCROFT	C	11	416
WORSTENCROFT	JV	14	356
WORSWICK	A	11	416
WORSWICK	CR	11	416
WORSWICK	J	11	416
WORSWICK	J	14	356
WORT	A	4	428
WORT	AH	6	454
WORT	G	4	428
WORT	GF	6	454
WORT	HC	10	393
WORT	K	4	428
WORT	N	4	428
WORT	RJ	4	428
WORT	TG	6	454
WORTH	A	8	407
WORTH	AJ	12	418
WORTH	E	6	454
WORTH	E	9	377
WORTH	FF	12	418
WORTH	FG	6	454
WORTH	J	8	407
WORTH	JGA	12	418
WORTH	SC	7	454
WORTH	W	12	418
WORTHINGTON	E	2	409
WORTHINGTON	EA	10	256
WORTHINGTON	F	14	356
WORTHINGTON	F	14	356
WORTHINGTON	G	11	416
WORTHINGTON	G	11	416
WORTHINGTON	G	11	416
WORTHINGTON	H	3	258
WORTHINGTON	H	14	356
WORTHINGTON	J	6	454
WORTHINGTON	J	14	356
WORTHINGTON	J	14	356
WORTHINGTON	P	11	416
WORTHINGTON	T	2	409
WORTHINGTON	T	11	416
WORTHINGTON	T	14	356
WORTHINGTON	T	14	356
WORTHINGTON	W	11	416
WORTHINGTON	W	14	356
WORTHINGTON	WR	11	417
WORTHY	A	4	428
WORTHY	AJ	2	409

WORTLEY	LC	4	428	WRAY	J	9	377	WRIGGLESWORTH	W	8	408	WRIGHT	AS	12	248
WORTON	GP	2	409	WRAY	J	14	356	WRIGHT	A	1	374	WRIGHT	AV	12	248
WORTON	WH	2	410	WRAY	JL	3	258	WRIGHT	A	1	374	WRIGHT	AV	13	464
WORTON	WJ	6	454	WRAY	M	9	216	WRIGHT	A	2	410	WRIGHT	AW	7	454
WOTHERSPOON	JJ	10	257	WRAY	PA	4	428	WRIGHT	A	3	408	WRIGHT	AW	7	455
WOTTON	WJ	7	454	WRAY	R	5	397	WRIGHT	A	5	397	WRIGHT	AW	9	216
WOULFE	P	1	374	WRAY	R	8	408	WRIGHT	A	5	397	WRIGHT	AWT	13	464
WRACK	FS	13	464	WRAY	S	8	408	WRIGHT	A	5	397	WRIGHT	B	5	398
WRAGG	A	13	464	WRAY	TW	14	356	WRIGHT	A	5	397	WRIGHT	B	5	398
WRAGG	AM	13	464	WRAY	W	8	408	WRIGHT	A	6	454	WRIGHT	BA	3	408
WRAGG	G	6	454	WRAY	W	8	408	WRIGHT	A	6	454	WRIGHT	BS	9	216
WRAGG	J	6	454	WRAY	W	9	377	WRIGHT	A	7	454	WRIGHT	BV	3	259
WRAGG	S	13	464	WRAY	W	14	356	WRIGHT	A	8	408	WRIGHT	BW	13	464
WRAGGE	RH	2	410	WRAY	W	14	356	WRIGHT	A	8	408	WRIGHT	C	1	374
WRAGGE	WJF	2	410	WRAY	WR	7	454	WRIGHT	A	8	408	WRIGHT	C	3	259
WRAIGHT	GR	5	397	WRELTON	S	7	454	WRIGHT	A	8	408	WRIGHT	C	4	429
WRAITH	F	9	216	WREN	A	4	428	WRIGHT	A	9	377	WRIGHT	C	5	398
WRAITH	H	8	407	WREN	AJ	2	410	WRIGHT	A	9	377	WRIGHT	C	7	454
WRAITH	J	9	377	WREN	C	1	374	WRIGHT	A	9	377	WRIGHT	C	7	455
WRANGLES	HC	2	410	WREN	C	4	428	WRIGHT	A	11	417	WRIGHT	C	8	408
WRANN	A	4	428	WREN	CW	13	464	WRIGHT	A	11	417	WRIGHT	C	8	408
WRANN	H	4	428	WREN	F	4	428	WRIGHT	A	12	418	WRIGHT	C	9	216
WRAPSON	FW	4	428	WREN	F	4	428	WRIGHT	A	14	356	WRIGHT	C	10	257
WRAPSON	GHA	10	257	WREN	F	7	454	WRIGHT	A	14	357	WRIGHT	C	13	464
WRAPSON	HW	4	428	WREN	FC	3	258	WRIGHT	AA	10	257	WRIGHT	CA	7	455
WRAPSON	WJ	10	257	WREN	FC	3	258	WRIGHT	AC	5	397	WRIGHT	CA	7	455
WRATHALL	E	8	407	WREN	FC	4	429	WRIGHT	AC	5	397	WRIGHT	CE	3	259
WRATHALL	JE	9	216	WREN	FE	4	429	WRIGHT	AC	5	397	WRIGHT	CF	12	248
WRATHMAELL	FM	13	464	WREN	FW	4	428	WRIGHT	AC	9	377	WRIGHT	CG	2	411
WRAY	A	8	407	WREN	IT	7	454	WRIGHT	AE	2	410	WRIGHT	CH	4	429
WRAY	A	8	407	WREN	J	11	417	WRIGHT	AE	2	410	WRIGHT	CH	4	429
WRAY	AE	2	410	WREN	J	11	417	WRIGHT	AE	5	397	WRIGHT	CI	13	465
WRAY	AS	13	464	WREN	J	13	464	WRIGHT	AE	5	397	WRIGHT	CJ	9	216
WRAY	AV	3	258	WREN	J	13	464	WRIGHT	AE	6	455	WRIGHT	CJ	9	377
WRAY	CJ	3	258	WREN	JA	4	429	WRIGHT	AE	7	454	WRIGHT	CJ	13	465
WRAY	D	8	407	WREN	LG	4	429	WRIGHT	AE	12	248	WRIGHT	CP	6	454
WRAY	E	2	410	WREN	R	6	454	WRIGHT	AE	13	464	WRIGHT	CS	12	248
WRAY	E	8	407	WREN	T	2	410	WRIGHT	AE	13	464	WRIGHT	CS	13	465
WRAY	EA	7	454	WREN	TG	4	429	WRIGHT	AE	14	357	WRIGHT	CV	12	248
WRAY	EC	3	258	WREN	W	2	410	WRIGHT	AF	5	397	WRIGHT	CW	12	248
WRAY	F	2	410	WREN	W	12	248	WRIGHT	AF	6	454	WRIGHT	CW	12	248
WRAY	F	2	410	WREN	WC	4	429	WRIGHT	AG	12	418	WRIGHT	CWH	10	257
WRAY	F	5	397	WREN	WG	4	429	WRIGHT	AG	13	464	WRIGHT	CWI	8	408
WRAY	F	8	408	WREN	WJ	6	454	WRIGHT	AGD	1	374	WRIGHT	D	9	216
WRAY	FF	7	454	WRENACRE	H	3	259	WRIGHT	AH	2	410	WRIGHT	D	11	417
WRAY	FN	4	428	WRENCH	HA	12	248	WRIGHT	AH	4	429	WRIGHT	E	1	375
WRAY	G	8	408	WRENCH	T	11	417	WRIGHT	AH	6	454	WRIGHT	E	1	375
WRAY	G	14	356	WRENCH	W	2	410	WRIGHT	AJ	1	374	WRIGHT	E	2	411
WRAY	GA	8	408	WRENN	PG	2	410	WRIGHT	AJ	2	411	WRIGHT	E	3	259
WRAY	GH	2	410	WRENNALL	WH	14	356	WRIGHT	AJ	5	397	WRIGHT	E	4	429
WRAY	H	9	216	WRENSHALL	F	11	417	WRIGHT	AJ	5	397	WRIGHT	E	8	409
WRAY	H	14	356	WREST	A	8	408	WRIGHT	AJ	7	454	WRIGHT	E	8	409
WRAY	J	8	408	WREST	E	8	408	WRIGHT	AJ	10	257	WRIGHT	E	8	409
WRAY	J	8	408	WRIGGLESWORTH	A	8	408	WRIGHT	AR	2	410	WRIGHT	E	8	409
WRAY	J	9	216	WRIGGLESWORTH	JA	8	408	WRIGHT	AR	3	259	WRIGHT	E	10	257

WRIGHT	E	11	417	WRIGHT	G	9	377	WRIGHT	HTG	7	455	WRIGHT	JP	6	455
WRIGHT	E	12	418	WRIGHT	G	12	249	WRIGHT	HV	2	412	WRIGHT	JP	12	419
WRIGHT	E	12	418	WRIGHT	G	12	418	WRIGHT	HW	5	398	WRIGHT	JS	13	465
WRIGHT	EA	6	455	WRIGHT	GA	9	377	WRIGHT	HW	12	249	WRIGHT	JW	2	412
WRIGHT	EA	12	248	WRIGHT	GA	11	417	WRIGHT	HW	13	465	WRIGHT	JW	6	455
WRIGHT	EC	2	411	WRIGHT	GB	3	259	WRIGHT	IJ	5	398	WRIGHT	JW	8	410
WRIGHT	EE	4	429	WRIGHT	GE	6	455	WRIGHT	J	2	412	WRIGHT	JW	8	410
WRIGHT	EE	5	398	WRIGHT	GE	8	409	WRIGHT	J	2	412	WRIGHT	JW	9	377
WRIGHT	EF	7	455	WRIGHT	GE	8	409	WRIGHT	J	3	408	WRIGHT	JW	9	377
WRIGHT	EH	10	257	WRIGHT	GE	12	418	WRIGHT	J	5	398	WRIGHT	JW	10	257
WRIGHT	EJ	5	398	WRIGHT	GF	8	409	WRIGHT	J	5	398	WRIGHT	JW	10	257
WRIGHT	EL	2	411	WRIGHT	GH	7	455	WRIGHT	J	6	455	WRIGHT	JW	10	393
WRIGHT	ER	3	259	WRIGHT	GJ	8	409	WRIGHT	J	6	455	WRIGHT	JW	12	419
WRIGHT	ER	13	465	WRIGHT	GW	2	411	WRIGHT	J	6	455	WRIGHT	JW	12	419
WRIGHT	EW	2	411	WRIGHT	GW	7	455	WRIGHT	J	8	410	WRIGHT	L	5	399
WRIGHT	EW	6	455	WRIGHT	GW	8	409	WRIGHT	J	8	410	WRIGHT	L	8	410
WRIGHT	F	2	411	WRIGHT	GW	9	217	WRIGHT	J	8	410	WRIGHT	L	8	410
WRIGHT	F	2	411	WRIGHT	H	1	375	WRIGHT	J	9	217	WRIGHT	L	8	410
WRIGHT	F	2	411	WRIGHT	H	2	411	WRIGHT	J	9	217	WRIGHT	L	9	377
WRIGHT	F	3	259	WRIGHT	H	2	411	WRIGHT	J	9	377	WRIGHT	L	9	377
WRIGHT	F	5	398	WRIGHT	H	2	411	WRIGHT	J	10	257	WRIGHT	L	14	357
WRIGHT	F	5	398	WRIGHT	H	2	411	WRIGHT	J	10	257	WRIGHT	LG	7	455
WRIGHT	F	5	398	WRIGHT	H	2	411	WRIGHT	J	11	417	WRIGHT	LJL	12	249
WRIGHT	F	7	455	WRIGHT	H	3	259	WRIGHT	J	11	417	WRIGHT	MC	1	375
WRIGHT	F	8	409	WRIGHT	H	3	259	WRIGHT	J	11	417	WRIGHT	MR	12	249
WRIGHT	F	8	409	WRIGHT	H	4	429	WRIGHT	J	11	417	WRIGHT	N	10	257
WRIGHT	F	9	216	WRIGHT	H	5	398	WRIGHT	J	11	418	WRIGHT	N	12	249
WRIGHT	F	11	417	WRIGHT	H	6	455	WRIGHT	J	11	418	WRIGHT	OW	12	419
WRIGHT	F	12	248	WRIGHT	H	6	455	WRIGHT	J	11	418	WRIGHT	P	9	217
WRIGHT	FA	5	398	WRIGHT	H	7	455	WRIGHT	J	11	418	WRIGHT	P	11	418
WRIGHT	FA	6	455	WRIGHT	H	8	409	WRIGHT	J	12	419	WRIGHT	PA	7	455
WRIGHT	FD	2	411	WRIGHT	H	8	409	WRIGHT	J	12	419	WRIGHT	PH	12	249
WRIGHT	FE	1	375	WRIGHT	H	8	409	WRIGHT	J	13	465	WRIGHT	PP	5	399
WRIGHT	FE	10	393	WRIGHT	H	8	409	WRIGHT	J	13	465	WRIGHT	PR	5	399
WRIGHT	FE	12	248	WRIGHT	H	8	409	WRIGHT	J	13	465	WRIGHT	PW	12	249
WRIGHT	FH	2	411	WRIGHT	H	9	217	WRIGHT	J	13	465	WRIGHT	R	1	375
WRIGHT	FH	6	455	WRIGHT	H	11	417	WRIGHT	J	14	357	WRIGHT	R	11	418
WRIGHT	FJ	3	259	WRIGHT	H	11	417	WRIGHT	J	14	357	WRIGHT	R	14	357
WRIGHT	FJ	6	455	WRIGHT	H	12	418	WRIGHT	JA	8	410	WRIGHT	R	14	357
WRIGHT	FJ	7	455	WRIGHT	H	12	418	WRIGHT	JA	9	217	WRIGHT	RC	5	399
WRIGHT	FJ	12	248	WRIGHT	H	12	418	WRIGHT	JC	8	410	WRIGHT	RC	7	456
WRIGHT	FT	11	417	WRIGHT	H	12	419	WRIGHT	JE	8	410	WRIGHT	RG	4	429
WRIGHT	FW	1	375	WRIGHT	H	14	357	WRIGHT	JE	12	249	WRIGHT	RI	10	257
WRIGHT	FW	2	411	WRIGHT	H	14	357	WRIGHT	JE	12	249	WRIGHT	RL	11	418
WRIGHT	G	2	411	WRIGHT	H	14	357	WRIGHT	JF	7	455	WRIGHT	RL	12	249
WRIGHT	G	3	259	WRIGHT	HA	4	429	WRIGHT	JG	5	398	WRIGHT	RO	7	456
WRIGHT	G	5	398	WRIGHT	HC	2	411	WRIGHT	JH	4	429	WRIGHT	RP	1	375
WRIGHT	G	5	398	WRIGHT	HC	7	455	WRIGHT	JH	5	398	WRIGHT	RS	9	377
WRIGHT	G	8	409	WRIGHT	HE	7	455	WRIGHT	JH	5	398	WRIGHT	RW	2	412
WRIGHT	G	8	409	WRIGHT	HES	10	257	WRIGHT	JH	6	455	WRIGHT	RW	11	418
WRIGHT	G	8	409	WRIGHT	HGH	2	412	WRIGHT	JH	7	455	WRIGHT	S	2	412
WRIGHT	G	8	409	WRIGHT	HH	3	259	WRIGHT	JH	9	217	WRIGHT	S	3	259
WRIGHT	G	9	217	WRIGHT	HJ	6	455	WRIGHT	JH	10	394	WRIGHT	S	5	399
WRIGHT	G	9	377	WRIGHT	HP	6	455	WRIGHT	JH	14	357	WRIGHT	S	6	455
WRIGHT				WRIGHT	HT	7	455	WRIGHT	JHJ	2	412	WRIGHT	S	7	455

WRIGHT	S	8	410	WRIGHT	W	9	378	WRIGLEY	T	12	419	WYATT	TF	7	456
WRIGHT	S	8	410	WRIGHT	W	9	378	WRIGLEY	TE	12	419	WYATT	TG	2	413
WRIGHT	S	11	418	WRIGHT	W	10	257	WRIGLEY	W	2	413	WYATT	TH	7	457
WRIGHT	S	12	249	WRIGHT	W	11	418	WRIGLEY	W	8	411	WYATT	W	2	413
WRIGHT	S	12	249	WRIGHT	W	11	418	WRIGLEY	W	11	419	WYATT	W	8	411
WRIGHT	S	13	465	WRIGHT	W	11	418	WRIGLEY	WJ	11	419	WYATT	WH	14	357
WRIGHT	SE	7	456	WRIGHT	W	12	249	WRIST	E	7	456	WYATT	WHG	2	413
WRIGHT	SG	12	249	WRIGHT	W	12	249	WRIXTON	H	10	258	WYATT	WJ	2	413
WRIGHT	SJ	1	375	WRIGHT	W	12	249	WROE	G	11	419	WYATT	WJ	2	413
WRIGHT	SJ	12	419	WRIGHT	W	12	419	WROE	T	14	357	WYATT	WT	13	466
WRIGHT	ST	7	456	WRIGHT	W	12	419	WROE	TR	11	419	WYBORN	RW	2	413
WRIGHT	SW	1	375	WRIGHT	W	13	465	WROE	W	11	419	WYBOURN	A	13	466
WRIGHT	SW	2	412	WRIGHT	WA	2	412	WROOT	AG	1	375	WYBOURN	R	13	466
WRIGHT	SW	10	394	WRIGHT	WA	7	456	WROOT	CH	14	357	WYBOURN	WJ	13	466
WRIGHT	T	2	412	WRIGHT	WA	11	418	WUFFINGTON	H	8	411	WYBOURNE	FFC	1	375
WRIGHT	T	2	412	WRIGHT	WA	11	418	WUIRSTUN	L	8	411	WYBOURNE	L	2	413
WRIGHT	T	4	429	WRIGHT	WA	12	419	WYANT	F	12	419	WYBREW	FJ	2	413
WRIGHT	T	6	455	WRIGHT	WE	2	412	WYARD	FJ	4	430	WYBREW	WS	1	375
WRIGHT	T	6	456	WRIGHT	WE	2	412	WYARD	FM	4	430	WYCH	J	11	419
WRIGHT	T	6	456	WRIGHT	WE	3	260	WYARTT	A	2	413	WYCH	W	11	419
WRIGHT	T	6	456	WRIGHT	WF	3	260	WYATT	AAJ	10	258	WYCHERLEY	CF	14	358
WRIGHT	T	7	456	WRIGHT	WF	7	456	WYATT	AE	7	456	WYERS	A	13	466
WRIGHT	T	10	257	WRIGHT	WG	13	465	WYATT	AJ	2	413	WYERS	WJ	13	466
WRIGHT	T	11	418	WRIGHT	WH	2	412	WYATT	AL	5	399	WYETH	A	4	430
WRIGHT	T	12	419	WRIGHT	WH	2	413	WYATT	C	9	217	WYETH	AC	4	430
WRIGHT	T	13	465	WRIGHT	WH	5	399	WYATT	C	10	258	WYETH	DA	4	430
WRIGHT	T	14	357	WRIGHT	WH	8	410	WYATT	CH	5	399	WYETH	DA	4	430
WRIGHT	T	14	357	WRIGHT	WH	12	249	WYATT	CW	4	430	WYETH	H	2	413
WRIGHT	TD	5	399	WRIGHT	WJ	1	375	WYATT	E	4	430	WYETH	H	4	430
WRIGHT	TJ	7	456	WRIGHT	WJ	2	413	WYATT	E	9	217	WYETH	H	4	430
WRIGHT	TJ	8	410	WRIGHT	WJ	4	430	WYATT	EG	2	413	WYETH	JCJ	10	394
WRIGHT	TJ	13	465	WRIGHT	WJ	6	456	WYATT	EL	12	249	WYETH	JR	4	430
WRIGHT	TJW	2	412	WRIGHT	WJ	12	419	WYATT	EP	4	430	WYETH	WEW	7	457
WRIGHT	TJW	4	430	WRIGHT	WJ	13	465	WYATT	F	3	260	WYETT	F	9	217
WRIGHT	TW	4	430	WRIGHT	WJ	14	357	WYATT	F	7	456	WYKES	A	6	456
WRIGHT	W	1	375	WRIGHT	WM	13	465	WYATT	F	9	217	WYKES	AE	12	249
WRIGHT	W	2	412	WRIGHT	WR	2	413	WYATT	FF	4	430	WYKES	C	12	419
WRIGHT	W	2	412	WRIGHT	WT	4	430	WYATT	FG	5	399	WYKES	CH	2	414
WRIGHT	W	5	399	WRIGHT	WT	5	399	WYATT	GDE	10	258	WYKES	CH	13	466
WRIGHT	W	5	399	WRIGHT	WT	10	257	WYATT	GJ	2	413	WYKES	CJ	7	457
WRIGHT	W	5	399	WRIGHT	WW	7	456	WYATT	HH	9	217	WYKES	E	4	431
WRIGHT	W	6	456	WRIGHTON	E	8	410	WYATT	HJ	4	430	WYKES	EJ	12	419
WRIGHT	W	6	456	WRIGHTON	F	12	249	WYATT	HJ	7	456	WYKES	EP	4	431
WRIGHT	W	6	456	WRIGHTSON	C	8	411	WYATT	HW	2	413	WYKES	J	12	420
WRIGHT	W	7	456	WRIGHTSON	FV	5	399	WYATT	J	6	456	WYKES	JC	6	456
WRIGHT	W	7	456	WRIGHTSON	J	9	378	WYATT	J	13	465	WYKES	LJ	12	420
WRIGHT	W	7	456	WRIGHTSON	W	9	217	WYATT	J	13	465	WYKES	W	1	375
WRIGHT	W	8	410	WRIGLEY	A	11	418	WYATT	J	13	466	WYKES	W	6	456
WRIGHT	W	8	410	WRIGLEY	F	12	419	WYATT	JG	10	258	WYKES	W	12	420
WRIGHT	W	8	410	WRIGLEY	H	8	411	WYATT	JJ	13	466	WYLDE	E	10	394
WRIGHT	W	8	410	WRIGLEY	J	8	411	WYATT	L	4	430	WYLES	A	4	431
WRIGHT	W	8	410	WRIGLEY	JH	14	357	WYATT	L	14	357	WYLES	E	7	457
WRIGHT	W	9	217	WRIGLEY	L	8	411	WYATT	MAM	7	456	WYLIE	G	8	411
WRIGHT	W	9	217	WRIGLEY	S	11	418	WYATT	P	2	413	WYLIE	W	8	411
WRIGHT	W	9	217	WRIGLEY	T	9	217	WYATT	SHC	7	456	WYLIE	WHA	2	414

WYMAN	F	2	414
WYMAN	G	12	420
WYMAN	PG	12	420
WYMAN	W	4	431
WYNDE	C	6	456
WYNDE	F	6	456
WYNDE	G	6	456
WYNESS	W	1	375
WYNIGER	EG	7	457
WYNN	C	14	358
WYNN	G	10	394
WYNN	GA	9	217
WYNN	J	14	358
WYNN	T	13	466
WYNN	TK	14	358
WYNN	WH	14	358
WYNNE	A	10	394
WYNNE	CE	8	411
WYNNE	HR	11	419
WYNNE	J	2	414
WYNNE	J	13	466
WYNNE	JH	10	258
WYNNE	P	11	419
WYNNE	R	11	419
WYRE	HA	6	456
WYRILL	CA	7	457
WYRILL	J	9	217
WYRILL	J	9	378
WYRRILL	J	7	457
WYTON	FG	2	414

X

XERRI	G	10	394

Y

YALDEN	F	7	457
YALDREN	C	4	431
YALDREN	H	4	431
YALDREN	JHC	4	431
YALE	H	14	358
YALLAP	E	2	414
YAPP	AG	2	414
YAPP	C	6	456
YAPP	R	2	414
YAPP	RJ	11	419
YARDLEY	AG	6	456
YARDLEY	AH	13	466
YARDLEY	AVE	6	456
YARDLEY	F	6	456
YARDLEY	G	6	457
YARDLEY	G	14	358
YARDLEY	HE	6	457
YARDLEY	JH	13	466
YARDLEY	S	14	358
YARDLEY	SW	7	457
YARDLEY	WH	11	419
YARDLEY	WJ	2	414
YARDLEY	WJ	6	457
YARHAM	RJ	7	457
YARHAM	WG	7	457
YARNEY	A	4	431
YARNOLD	AW	10	258
YARRINGTON	F	6	457
YARROW	C	7	457
YARROW	CJ	5	399
YARROW	DG	13	466
YARROW	E	3	260
YARROW	F	3	260
YARROW	W	3	260
YARWOOD	E	6	457
YARWOOD	H	14	358
YARWOOD	JE	11	419
YARWOOD	JW	11	419
YARWOOD	JW	11	419
YARWOOD	S	14	358
YARWOOD	TW	11	419
YARWOOD	TW	14	358
YARWOOD	W	6	457
YARWOOD	W	14	358
YARWORTH	W	6	457
YATES	A	6	457
YATES	A	6	457
YATES	A	6	457
YATES	A	8	411
YATES	A	8	411
YATES	A	8	411
YATES	A	8	411
YATES	A	11	420
YATES	A	12	420
YATES	A	13	466
YATES	A	14	358
YATES	A	14	358
YATES	AC	6	457
YATES	AE	2	414
YATES	AH	11	419
YATES	ALH	14	358
YATES	AM	13	466
YATES	AR	6	457
YATES	B	6	457
YATES	B	8	411
YATES	C	4	431
YATES	CH	2	414
YATES	CH	6	457
YATES	CS	2	414
YATES	E	5	399
YATES	E	8	411
YATES	E	11	420
YATES	E	11	420
YATES	E	14	358
YATES	EH	5	399
YATES	ES	7	457
YATES	F	6	457
YATES	F	6	457
YATES	F	6	457
YATES	F	8	411
YATES	F	8	411
YATES	FA	5	399
YATES	FG	12	420
YATES	FL	2	414
YATES	FS	2	414
YATES	G	9	378
YATES	GE	6	457
YATES	GE	6	457
YATES	GG	11	420
YATES	GH	14	358
YATES	GW	2	414
YATES	H	2	414
YATES	H	8	411
YATES	H	14	358
YATES	H	14	359
YATES	HA	12	420
YATES	HJ	13	466
YATES	HJ	13	466
YATES	HS	8	412
YATES	J	1	375
YATES	J	6	457
YATES	J	7	457
YATES	J	8	412
YATES	J	9	378
YATES	J	11	420
YATES	J	11	420
YATES	J	11	420
YATES	J	14	359
YATES	J	14	359
YATES	JA	6	458
YATES	JH	6	458
YATES	JH	6	458
YATES	JS	2	414
YATES	JW	14	359
YATES	L	8	412
YATES	M	11	420
YATES	P	11	420
YATES	PA	2	414
YATES	PA	12	250
YATES	R	3	260
YATES	R	14	359
YATES	RC	12	420
YATES	RR	14	359
YATES	S	8	412
YATES	S	9	378
YATES	S	14	359
YATES	SG	6	458
YATES	SH	11	420
YATES	SR	14	359
YATES	T	10	394
YATES	T	14	359
YATES	TM	6	458
YATES	TW	12	420
YATES	W	1	376
YATES	W	4	431
YATES	W	8	412
YATES	W	8	412
YATES	W	8	412
YATES	W	9	378
YATES	W	10	258
YATES	W	12	250
YATES	W	13	466
YATES	W	14	359
YATES	WC	4	431
YATES	WC	9	218
YATES	WG	1	376
YATES	WG	2	414
YATES	WJ	12	420
YATES	WT	5	400
YATES	WT	8	412
YATES	WT	14	359
YAXLEY	R	8	412
YEADON	A	9	218
YEADON	A	9	378
YEADON	B	9	378
YEADON	E	8	412
YEADON	H	9	378
YEADON	J	9	218
YEADON	J	14	359
YEADON	JA	8	412
YEADON	JW	9	378
YEADON	L	9	378
YEADON	N	8	412
YEADON	R	8	412
YEADON	W	9	218
YEARBY	AE	8	412
YEARDLEY	A	14	359
YEARLING	W	7	457
YEARRELL	AW	12	424
YEARRELL	H	12	424
YEARRELL	S	12	424
YEARSLEY	AR	4	431
YEARSLEY	H	4	431
YEARSLEY	S	14	359
YEARSLEY	WA	4	431
YEATES	A	4	431
YEATES	AE	7	457
YEATES	AE	7	457
YEATES	C	10	258
YEATES	CH	4	431
YEATES	FW	10	258
YEATES	H	4	431

YEATES	PJ	4	431	YIRRELL	E	5	400	YOUNG	A	8	412	YOUNG	E	4	432
YEATMAN	HG	10	394	YIRRELL	R	5	400	YOUNG	A	8	412	YOUNG	E	6	459
YEATMAN	SA	10	258	YOCKNEY	JH	7	458	YOUNG	A	10	394	YOUNG	E	11	425
YELDHAM	EC	2	414	YONWIN	GP	13	467	YOUNG	A	10	394	YOUNG	E	12	425
YELLOLY	JH	2	414	YORK	A	12	420	YOUNG	A	10	394	YOUNG	EA	4	432
YELLOP	C	5	400	YORK	AJ	5	400	YOUNG	A	10	395	YOUNG	EA	10	395
YELLOP	J	5	400	YORK	AW	7	458	YOUNG	A	10	395	YOUNG	EE	6	458
YELLOP	JC	5	400	YORK	C	12	420	YOUNG	A	11	425	YOUNG	EH	6	459
YELLOP	W	7	458	YORK	CH	5	400	YOUNG	A	12	425	YOUNG	EJ	7	458
YENDALL	F	4	431	YORK	E	12	420	YOUNG	A	13	467	YOUNG	F	3	408
YENDELL	WJ	7	458	YORK	F	6	458	YOUNG	A	14	359	YOUNG	F	4	432
YENDELL	WW	2	415	YORK	FC	12	420	YOUNG	A	14	359	YOUNG	F	4	432
YEO	A	10	394	YORK	FW	12	420	YOUNG	A	14	359	YOUNG	F	5	401
YEO	A	10	394	YORK	G	13	467	YOUNG	AA	2	415	YOUNG	F	6	459
YEO	AH	10	258	YORK	GA	11	420	YOUNG	AA	6	458	YOUNG	F	9	392
YEO	FG	10	258	YORK	GW	12	250	YOUNG	AA	7	458	YOUNG	F	10	395
YEO	H	3	260	YORK	H	12	420	YOUNG	AE	2	415	YOUNG	F	11	425
YEO	H	10	394	YORK	HN	5	400	YOUNG	AE	2	415	YOUNG	F	13	467
YEO	I	2	415	YORK	J	7	458	YOUNG	AE	6	458	YOUNG	F	13	467
YEO	T	3	260	YORK	J	13	467	YOUNG	AE	7	458	YOUNG	F	13	467
YEO	WA	3	260	YORK	JB	12	420	YOUNG	AE	10	395	YOUNG	FA	12	250
YEOMAN	AF	12	420	YORK	JE	2	415	YOUNG	AF	4	432	YOUNG	FC	12	250
YEOMAN	H	9	218	YORK	JT	12	424	YOUNG	AH	2	415	YOUNG	FE	2	415
YEOMAN	JHC	3	260	YORK	LH	9	218	YOUNG	AJ	1	376	YOUNG	FH	1	376
YEOMAN	S	2	415	YORK	PH	10	394	YOUNG	AJ	2	415	YOUNG	FJ	4	433
YEOMANS	CS	12	250	YORK	RH	12	424	YOUNG	AJ	13	467	YOUNG	FJ	5	401
YEOMANS	E	10	394	YORK	SJ	13	467	YOUNG	AJ	14	360	YOUNG	FJ	5	401
YEOMANS	F	11	420	YORK	W	5	400	YOUNG	AL	6	458	YOUNG	FR	5	401
YEOMANS	G	6	458	YORK	W	12	425	YOUNG	AS	3	260	YOUNG	FV	10	395
YEOMANS	G	11	420	YORK	WF	12	250	YOUNG	AWF	4	432	YOUNG	FW	4	433
YEOMANS	H	7	458	YORK	WF	12	425	YOUNG	B	12	425	YOUNG	FW	4	433
YEOMANS	J	6	458	YORK	WG	12	250	YOUNG	B	13	467	YOUNG	FWG	7	458
YEOMANS	O	6	458	YORK	WH	5	400	YOUNG	BJ	4	432	YOUNG	G	2	415
YEOMANS	S	6	458	YORK	WS	12	425	YOUNG	BJ	6	458	YOUNG	G	2	416
YEOMANS	S	6	458	YORKE	A	6	458	YOUNG	C	2	415	YOUNG	G	4	433
YERBURY	EC	2	415	YORKE	A	9	378	YOUNG	C	2	415	YOUNG	G	5	401
YERBY	E	2	415	YORKE	AJ	7	458	YOUNG	C	4	432	YOUNG	G	7	458
YERBY	JJ	2	415	YORKE	H	6	458	YOUNG	C	7	458	YOUNG	G	8	412
YERRELL	S	12	250	YORKE	SC	10	394	YOUNG	C	9	392	YOUNG	G	8	412
YERRILL	J	5	400	YORKE	WJ	4	432	YOUNG	C	12	250	YOUNG	G	10	395
YERRILL	J	5	400	YOUATT	BS	4	432	YOUNG	C	13	467	YOUNG	G	11	425
YERRILL	WT	5	400	YOUD	A	14	359	YOUNG	CA	1	376	YOUNG	G	12	250
YESSON	A	8	412	YOUD	F	11	420	YOUNG	CC	4	432	YOUNG	GA	2	416
YETMAN	LA	4	432	YOUD	G	14	359	YOUNG	CE	4	432	YOUNG	GE	10	395
YETMAN	R	4	432	YOUDALE	WH	7	458	YOUNG	CE	13	467	YOUNG	GE	10	395
YETMAN	W	4	432	YOUELL	AG	7	458	YOUNG	CF	13	467	YOUNG	GF	5	401
YETTON	F	6	458	YOULE	A	2	415	YOUNG	CG	3	260	YOUNG	GF	5	401
YEWDAL	P	8	412	YOUNG	A	3	260	YOUNG	CJ	10	395	YOUNG	GF	10	395
YEWDALL	F	9	218	YOUNG	A	4	432	YOUNG	CW	2	415	YOUNG	GH	4	433
YEWDALL	L	9	218	YOUNG	A	5	400	YOUNG	D	5	400	YOUNG	GH	10	395
YEWDALL	L	9	378	YOUNG	A	5	400	YOUNG	D	11	425	YOUNG	GJ	10	395
YEXLEY	CW	1	376	YOUNG	A	5	400	YOUNG	E	2	415	YOUNG	GM	3	408
YEXLEY	EA	1	376	YOUNG	A	6	458	YOUNG	E	3	408	YOUNG	GP	4	433
YEXLEY	EFJ	2	415	YOUNG	A	7	458	YOUNG	E	4	432	YOUNG	GT	3	408
YIRRELL	B	5	400	YOUNG	A	7	458	YOUNG	E	4	432	YOUNG	GT	5	401

YOUNG	GW	1	376	YOUNG	JH	9	218	YOUNG	S	2	416	YOUNG	WH	12	425
YOUNG	GW	10	395	YOUNG	JH	11	425	YOUNG	S	8	413	YOUNG	WJ	4	434
YOUNG	GW	12	250	YOUNG	JH	12	250	YOUNG	S	10	396	YOUNG	WJ	7	459
YOUNG	GW	13	467	YOUNG	JH	14	360	YOUNG	SA	9	392	YOUNG	WJ	10	396
YOUNG	H	3	408	YOUNG	JP	4	433	YOUNG	SF	7	459	YOUNG	WJJ	4	434
YOUNG	H	4	433	YOUNG	JT	4	433	YOUNG	SG	4	434	YOUNG	WR	5	401
YOUNG	H	4	433	YOUNG	JT	7	459	YOUNG	SW	2	416	YOUNG	WT	10	396
YOUNG	H	4	433	YOUNG	JW	4	433	YOUNG	T	4	434	YOUNG	WW	3	408
YOUNG	H	5	401	YOUNG	JW	8	413	YOUNG	T	8	413	YOUNGBLUTT	A	11	426
YOUNG	H	5	401	YOUNG	JW	11	425	YOUNG	T	11	425	YOUNGBLUTT	J	11	426
YOUNG	H	8	412	YOUNG	JW	13	468	YOUNG	T	12	425	YOUNGER	J	4	434
YOUNG	H	10	395	YOUNG	L	3	408	YOUNG	TH	13	468	YOUNGER	J	8	413
YOUNG	H	10	395	YOUNG	L	4	433	YOUNG	TW	7	459	YOUNGER	N	4	434
YOUNG	H	13	467	YOUNG	L	8	413	YOUNG	TW	8	413	YOUNGER	N	8	413
YOUNG	H	14	360	YOUNG	LA	2	416	YOUNG	W	2	416	YOUNGER	SW	2	416
YOUNG	HA	3	408	YOUNG	M	5	401	YOUNG	W	2	416	YOUNGMAN	E	2	416
YOUNG	HB	3	408	YOUNG	M	10	396	YOUNG	W	3	408	YOUNGMAN	WF	2	416
YOUNG	HB	10	395	YOUNG	MAE	4	433	YOUNG	W	3	408	YOURIN	S	12	250
YOUNG	HD	5	401	YOUNG	N	10	396	YOUNG	W	4	434	YOUSTER	RS	6	459
YOUNG	HG	3	408	YOUNG	OB	13	468	YOUNG	W	5	401	YOXALL	AT	10	258
YOUNG	HJ	1	376	YOUNG	P	7	459	YOUNG	W	10	258	YOXALL	FW	14	360
YOUNG	HJ	12	250	YOUNG	PC	5	401	YOUNG	W	11	425	YOXALL	WH	10	258
YOUNG	HL	7	458	YOUNG	PG	4	433	YOUNG	W	11	425	YUILL	R	14	360
YOUNG	HP	4	433	YOUNG	PG	7	459	YOUNG	W	11	425	YUILLE	JG	14	360
YOUNG	HV	5	401	YOUNG	PH	4	433	YOUNG	W	12	250	YURVITZ	A	8	413
YOUNG	HW	13	467	YOUNG	R	4	433	YOUNG	W	12	425				
YOUNG	HWG	10	395	YOUNG	R	4	433	YOUNG	WC	10	396				
YOUNG	J	3	408	YOUNG	R	4	434	YOUNG	WC	12	250				
YOUNG	J	7	459	YOUNG	R	4	434	YOUNG	WD	8	413				
YOUNG	J	8	413	YOUNG	R	6	459	YOUNG	WF	2	416				
YOUNG	J	9	218	YOUNG	R	7	459	YOUNG	WG	2	416				
YOUNG	J	11	425	YOUNG	R	8	413	YOUNG	WG	7	459				
YOUNG	J	13	467	YOUNG	RC	6	459	YOUNG	WG	7	459				
YOUNG	J	13	467	YOUNG	RF	2	416	YOUNG	WG	10	396				
YOUNG	J	13	467	YOUNG	RF	3	408	YOUNG	WG	10	396				
YOUNG	J	13	467	YOUNG	RJ	1	376	YOUNG	WG	10	396				
YOUNG	J	14	360	YOUNG	RJ	2	416	YOUNG	WG	13	468				
YOUNG	JA	4	433	YOUNG	RW	3	408	YOUNG	WH	2	416				
YOUNG	JA	8	413	YOUNG	RW	4	434	YOUNG	WH	2	416				
YOUNG	JB	6	459	YOUNG	RW	5	401	YOUNG	WH	3	408				
YOUNG	JC	4	433	YOUNG	RW	5	401	YOUNG	WH	8	413				
YOUNG	JD	6	459	YOUNG	RW	7	459	YOUNG	WH	12	425				

Z

Surname	Init.		
ZAMBRA	J	2	416
ZAMOBSKY	M	14	360
ZANG	C	14	360
ZARI	J	8	413
ZIMMERMAN	A	8	413
ZIMMERMAN	EN	7	459
ZIMMERMAN	GR	7	459
ZIMMERMAN	M	2	416
ZINNERMAN	W	6	459
ZIRFAS	HL	11	426
ZIRKE	S	8	413
ZOLLER	FJ	7	459
ZOLLER	V	2	416

Printed in the United Kingdom
by Lightning Source UK Ltd.
127394UK00002B/1-28/A